SOCIAL WORKERS' DESK REFERENCE

SOCIAL WORKERS' DESK REFERENCE

Third Edition

Kevin Corcoran

Editor-in-Chief

Albert R. Roberts

Founding Editor-in-Chief

OXFORD

UNIVERSITY PRESS

OXFORD
UNIVERSITY PRESS

Oxford University Press is a department of the University of Oxford.
It furthers the University's objective of excellence in research, scholarship,
and education by publishing worldwide.

Oxford   New York
Auckland   Cape Town   Dar es Salaam   Hong Kong   Karachi
Kuala Lumpur   Madrid   Melbourne   Mexico City   Nairobi
New Delhi   Shanghai   Taipei   Toronto

With offices in
Argentina   Austria   Brazil   Chile   Czech Republic   France   Greece
Guatemala   Hungary   Italy   Japan   Poland   Portugal   Singapore
South Korea   Switzerland   Thailand   Turkey   Ukraine   Vietnam

Published in the United States of America by
Oxford University Press
198 Madison Avenue, New York, NY 10016

Library of Congress Cataloging-in-Publication Data
Cataloging-in-Publication data is on file at the Library of Congress
ISBN 978–0–19–932964–9

9 8 7 6 5 4 3 2 1
Printed in the United States of America
on acid-free paper

Once again, for Sug and the memory of Harley Bubba Davidson.

CONTENTS

FOREWORD

For over a century the social work profession has continued to evolve and develop new responses to the issues and challenges of the times. The first and second editions of the *Social Workers' Desk Reference* highlighted and focused attention on the changes occurring in social work practice, education, and research. This third edition continues in that tradition by continuing to identify and put forth responses to the changes occurring in society, especially those that are having an impact on social work practice, education, and research.

On a daily basis people around the world are confronted by issues such as poverty, a lack of access to quality education, unaffordable and/or inadequate housing, and a lack of necessary health and mental services. Now more than ever, we need social workers who have access to the most relevant, timely, and scholarly materials. Multiple social, psychological, and biological factors determine the level of mental health of a person at any point in time. Persistent socioeconomic pressures are recognized risks to mental health for individuals and communities. The clearest evidence is associated with indicators of poverty, including low levels of education. Poor mental health is also associated with rapid social change, stressful work conditions, gender discrimination, social exclusion, unhealthy lifestyles, risks of violence and physical ill-health, and human rights violations.

Specific psychological and personality factors also make people vulnerable to mental disorders. Lastly, there are some biological causes of mental disorders, including genetic factors and chemical imbalances in the brain. (http://www.who.int/mediacentre/factsheets/fs220/en/index.html)

The focus and depth of this third edition of the *Social Workers' Desk Reference* indeed contributes to that effort. It is a useful tool for social work practitioners, educators, and students, as well as other allied professionals who together help to create interdisciplinary, interprofessional education, practice, and research. Throughout its 160 chapters this edition responds and brings attention, in a clear, scholarly, and evidence-informed manner, to some of the most important issues and areas of concern confronting current social work practice.

It is generally known that professionally trained social workers practice and provide services in a variety of settings, including child welfare and foster care agencies, community action centers, hospitals, government offices, mental health centers, homeless shelters, and schools; we also work with persons of diverse ethnic, cultural, racial, economic, sexual orientation, and social backgrounds. As professionals we help people to overcome some of life's most difficult challenges, including poverty, discrimination, abuse, addiction, physical illness, divorce, grief and loss, unemployment, underemployment, educational problems, disability, and mental illness.

Central to social work's primary mission is that of enhancing human well-being and working to ensure that people are able to meet their basic needs, especially the most vulnerable among us. We have done this through our various roles in society and in our varied fields of practice, and now we must work to ensure that those who are the most vulnerable among us are at the front of all of our efforts as we work to put in place a more just economic system.

Paulo Freire (1960) wrote that:

> The radical, committed to human liberation, does not become the prisoner of a "circle

of certainty" within which reality is also imprisoned. On the contrary, the more radical the person is, the more fully he or she enters into reality so that, knowing it better, he or she can better transform it. This individual is not afraid to confront, to listen, and to see the world unveiled. This person is not afraid to meet the people or to enter into dialogue with them. This person does not consider himself or herself the proprietor of history or of all people, or the liberator of the oppressed; but he or she does commit himself or herself, within history, to fight at their side. (Friere, 1960)

Freire also said that "those who authentically commit themselves to the people must re-examine themselves constantly" (Freire, 1 1960, p. 60), and that is just what this new edition helps us to do. This third edition of the *Social Workers' Desk Reference* is not only a major contribution to the field, but its articles focus on the important practice issues of this period. It is an important tool that can and will provide immeasurable benefits to the social work profession. Its chapters are written by some of the field's foremost experts and bring to the reader the most recent conceptual knowledge and empirical evidence to aid in their understanding of the rapidly changing field of social work practice. It offers a guide to social work interventions in a variety of settings: from the individual clinical level to community-based empowerment and advocacy.

The world is on the move with billions of people yearning to be truly secure—to be free from fear and free from want, and able to live in peace and in dignity. This is a time when global and national issues intersect, calling for a level of coordination and leadership that is essential for all of us. We must show that these concerns really can be dealt with collectively and fairly, with equity and social justice for all. As social work professionals, we cannot do that if we are not working together, and do not have at our fingertips the most relevant and timely information to ensure that our practice is the best informed that it can be! My friends, we have much work before us!

To those who have contributed to this latest edition, thank you all for your hard work.

In solidarity,
Gary Bailey, LHD (h. c.), MSW, ACSW
President, International Federation of Social Workers
Professor of Practice, Simmons College School of Social Work
Professor of Practice, Simmons College School of Nursing and Health Studies

ACKNOWLEDGMENTS

Building on the success of the second edition of *The Social Workers' Desk Reference* and Al Roberts's efforts, we have assembled an esteemed Associate Editor Board, many of whom worked so hard on the first two editions. New Associate Editors were included, however, and here I have intentionally added young talent for the simple reason of succession and the anticipated demand for additional volumes in the future. Al is gone, and by then I will likely be, too, so it is critical to identify who will carry Al's efforts forward. The Associate Editors decided on the scope and content of the sections, with only a few added by me. I am grateful to all the Associate Editors for the seriousness with which they addressed their tasks and for their dedication to producing excellent sections and, in total, an improved third edition.

I know I speak for Al when I express my gratitude to all the staff at Oxford University Press, in particular Joan Bossert, Vice President at OUP, and Dana Bliss, Senior Editor, and the support staff, Brianna Marron, Mallory Jenson and Devi Vaidyanathan. They have been terrific and this book would be the lesser without them.

And finally, this edition would not be possible without the involvement, support, and love from Vikki Vandiver. After 32 years, she is finally getting used to me (I hope).

Kevin Corcoran
VanCor Point of View
Yachats, Oregon
March 2014

CONTRIBUTORS

COEDITORS-IN-CHIEF

KEVIN CORCORAN, PHD, JD is Professor of Social Work at the University of Alabama, and has been a college professor for over 35 years. He holds a BA in English literature from Colorado State University, an MA in counseling from the University of Colorado–Colorado Springs, an MSW and PhD from the University of Pittsburgh, and a JD from the University of Houston. He has been involved in research and practice of clinical social work since 1973, and was a commercial and community mediator from 1982 to 2012. He has published over 130 ephemeral journal articles and book chapters, has authored or edited 15 books, including *Measures for Clinical Practice and Research*, the ever-entertaining cookbook, *Food for Thought: A Two-Year Cooking Guide for Social Work Students,* and is co-editor of *Best Practices in Mental Health.* He is the founder of a dotcom called EasyRATs.com (aka Rapid Assessment Tools, RATs) that performs drug, alcohol, and mental health assessments in less than a second; the urls are Do-I-need-therapy.com and Is-therapy-effective.com. He is also the designer or inventor of the "The Electric Seating Chart," the Internet-based "Sole Mate," a shoe-powered battery for charging smartphones, and "The Electric Hamster," which is designed to teach STEM to elementary school girls, and "Little Al" the Alabama cheering glove. His hobbies including gourmet cooking, portrait painting, random study of history, bonsai gardening, creative writing, and a bad golf swing; he is also trying to learn to play the piano.

ALBERT R. ROBERTS, PHD, DACFE. The late Albert R. Roberts was Professor of Social Work and Criminal Justice, and Director of Faculty and Curriculum Development in the Faculty of Arts and Sciences at Rutgers, the State University of New Jersey in Piscataway. He was a college professor for 35 years. Dr. Roberts received an MA degree in Sociology from the Graduate Faculty of Long Island University in 1967, and a doctorate in social work from the School of Social Work and Community Planning at the University of Maryland in Baltimore in 1978. Dr. Roberts was the founding Editor-in-Chief of the Brief Treatment and Crisis Intervention journal and the Victims and Offenders journal. He was a member of The Board of Scientific and Professional Advisors and a Board-Certified Expert in Traumatic Stress for The American Academy of Experts in Traumatic Stress, and a Diplomate of the American College of Forensic Examiners. Dr. Roberts authored, co-authored, or edited approximately 250 scholarly publications, including numerous peer-reviewed journal articles and book chapters, and 38 books. Among his books were the *Handbook of Domestic Violence Intervention Strategies* (Oxford University Press, 2002), *Crisis Intervention Handbook: Assessment, Treatment and Research,* 3rd edition (Oxford University Press, 2005), *Juvenile Justice Sourcebook* (Oxford University Press, 2004), *Evidence-Based Practice Manual: Research and Outcome Measures in Health and Human Services* (coedited with Kenneth R. Yeager, Oxford University Press, 2004), and *Ending Intimate Abuse* (coauthored with Beverly Schenkman Roberts, Oxford University Press, 2005). Dr. Roberts was also the editor of three book series: the Springer Series on Social Work, the Springer Series on Family Violence, and the Greenwood/Praeger Series on Social and Psychological Issues. Dr. Roberts was the recipient of many awards for his teaching and his scholarly publications.

Prior to his death in the summer of 2008, Dr. Roberts was in the midst of many projects, including his courses on Crisis Intervention, Domestic Violence, Introduction to Criminal Justice, Research Methods, Program Evaluation, Victimology and Victim Assistance, and Juvenile Justice at Rutgers University; training crisis intervention workers, crisis counselors, and clinical supervisors in crisis assessment and crisis intervention strategies; and training police officers and administrators in domestic violence policies and crisis intervention. He was a lifetime member of the Academy of Criminal Justice Sciences (ACJS), a fellow of the American Orthopsychiatric Association, a member of the Council on Social Work Education and the National Association of Social Workers (NASW) since 1974, and was listed in Who's Who in America from 1992 forward.

SECTION EDITORS

PAULA ALLEN-MEARES, PHD, is the Chancellor of the University of Illinois at Chicago. Previously she served as the Dean, Norma Radin Collegiate Professor of Social Work, and Professor of Education at the University of Michigan. Her research interests include the tasks and functions of social workers employed in educational settings; psychopathology in children, adolescents, and families; adolescent sexuality; premature parenthood; and various aspects of social work practice.

JOSÉ B. ASHFORD, MSW, PHD, LCSW is a Professor of Social Work and a member of the Doctoral Faculty in Sociology at Arizona State University. He is also the Director of the Office of Forensic Social Work Research and Training in the School of Social Work and an Affiliate Professor in the Schools of Criminology and Criminal Justice and Justice and Social Inquiry. He is the chief research consultant for the City of Phoenix Prosecutor on matters involving the implementation of principles of community prosecution, offender diversion, and problem-solving justice. He is also involved in research with the Social Intelligence Institute on prevention of

recidivism and continues as a Senior Consultant with Mercer Government Human Services Consulting on issues involving forensic and correctional mental health. Dr. Ashford has published widely on forensic matters, including a coedited book recognized as one of the most influential books on management of violence risk in the forensic literature. His most recent book on death penalty mitigation with Oxford University Press addresses an important gap in forensic literature and is receiving high praise from sentencing advocates, mitigation specialists, and lawyers.

ROWENA FONG, MSW, EDD is the Ruby Lee Piester Centennial Professor in Services to Children and Families at The University of Texas at Austin. Her scholarship and research focus on immigrant and refugee children and families, child welfare, and culturally competent practice. She has over 100 publications, including coauthored books on *Culturally Competent Practice with Immigrant and Refugee Children and Families* and *Culturally Competent Practice: Skills, Interventions, and Evaluations*.

CYNTHIA FRANKLIN, PHD, is Assistant Dean for Doctoral Education and Stiernberg/Spencer Family Professor in Mental Health at The University of Texas at Austin School of Social Work. Dr. Franklin has published widely on topics such as dropout prevention, clinical assessment, the effectiveness of solution-focused therapy in school settings, and adolescent pregnancy prevention. She is the current Editor-in-Chief of the *Encyclopedia of Social Work*.

LAURA M. HOPSON, PHD, MSW is an Associate Professor at the University of Alabama School of Social Work. She has published articles in the areas of school social work practice, school climate, substance abuse prevention, and solution-focused brief therapy, and has coauthored the book, *Research Methods for Evidence-Based Practice*.

KATHERINE L. MONTGOMERY, PHD, MSSW is the School Director at Little Sunshine's Playhouse and Preschool in Saint Louis, Missouri. She graduated with her BSW from Missouri State University and MSSW and PhD in Social Work from The University of Texas at Austin. She has over 18 years of experience working with children and families in a variety of settings, but most of her recent work focuses on early evidence-based prevention intervention delivery in school settings. She has authored over 30 publications and presented at numerous conferences both nationally and internationally.

LISA RAPP-MCCALL, PHD, MSW is a Professor in Social Work at St. Leo's University in St. Leo, Florida. Her research interests include juvenile crime and violence, at-risk children and adolescents, and prevention.

PHYLLIS SOLOMON, PHD is a Professor in the School of Social Policy & Practice and Professor of Social Work in the School of Medicine at the University of Pennsylvania. She has conducted numerous federally funded randomized clinical trials for adults with severe mental illness and their families. She reviews research grants for U.S. federal agencies, private foundations, and Canadian organizations. She also coedited another book, *The Research Process in the Human Services: Behind the Scenes.*

BRUCE A. THYER, PHD, LCSW is Professor and former Dean with the College of Social Work at Florida State University. Dr. Thyer has authored over 250 articles in refereed journals, written over 60 book chapters, and produced over 28 books. He is the Founding and current Editor of the bimonthly peer-reviewed journal *Research on Social Work Practice,* produced by Sage Publications.

VIKKI L. VANDIVER, MSW, DRPH is Dean and Professor of Social Work at the University of Alabama School of Social Work. She is the author of three books on mental health (*Maneuvering the Maze of Managed Care,* 1996, Free Press; *Integrating Health Promotion and Mental Health,* 2009, Oxford University Press; *Best Practices in Community Mental Health,* 2013, Lyceum Books) and over three dozen chapters and articles on best practices in mental health. She is also coeditor of the peer-reviewed journal, *Best Practices in Mental Health* (Lyceum Books) She has been in the field of community mental health for over 35 years, has taught *Diagnostic and Statistical Manual of Mental Disorders (DSM)* content for the last 21 years, and has recently completed a SAMHSA grant to evaluate equine-assisted therapy with at-risk tribal and nontribal youth.

LIST OF CONTRIBUTORS

Neil Able, PhD
Professor
School of Social Work
Florida State University
Tallahassee, Florida

Paula Allen-Meares, PhD
Chancellor
University of Illinois at Chicago
Chicago, Illinois

Kathleen H. Anderson, MSW, LCSW
Private Consultant
Austin, Texas

Christina M. Andrews, PhD
Assistant Professor
College of Social Work
University of South Carolina
Columbia, South Carolina

Harry J. Aponte, MSW, PhD
Clinical Associate Professor
Programs in Couple and Family Therapy
College of Nursing and Health Professions
Drexel University
Philadelphia, Pennsylvania

José B. Ashford, MSW, PhD, LCSW
Professor and Associate Director
School of Social Work
Director of the Office of Forensic Social Work
    Research and Training
Affiliate Professor in the Schools of
    Criminology and Criminal Justice and
    Justice and Social Inquiry
Arizona State University
Phoenix, Arizona

Ron Avi Astor, PhD
Professor
Schools of Social Work and Education
University of Southern California
Los Angeles, California

Gary Bailey, PhD (h. c.), MSW, ACSW
President, International Federation of
    Social Workers
Professor of Practice, Simmons College
    School of Social Work
Professor of Practice, Simmons College
    School of Nursing and Health Studies
Boston, Massachusetts

Allan Edward Barsky, JD, MSW, PhD
Professor
School of Social Work
Florida Atlantic University
Boca Raton, Florida
Member of NASW National Ethics
Committee

Kathryn Karusaitis Basham, PhD
Professor
School for Social Work
Smith College
Northampton, Massachusetts

Katherine J. W. Baucom, PhD
Department of Psychology
University of Utah
Salt Lake City, Utah

Rami Benbenishty, PhD
Gordon Brown Professor of
    Social Work
School of Social Work and Social Welfare
Hebrew University of Jerusalem
Jerusalem, Israel

Kimberly Bender, PhD
Associate Professor
School of Social Work
University of Denver
Denver, Colorado

Kia J. Bentley, PhD
Professor
School of Social Work
Virginia Commonwealth University
Richmond, Virginia

Candyce S. Berger, PhD
Professor and Director of
    Social Work
University of Texas El Paso
El Paso, Texas

Lisa K. Berger, PhD
Associate Professor
Helen Bader School of
    Social Work
University of Wisconsin–Milwaukee
Milwaukee, Wisconsin

Betty J. Blythe
Professor
Graduate School of Social Work
Boston College
Boston, Massachusetts

Ted Bober, MSW, RSW
Program Director
Certificate Program in Crisis Management
    for Workplace Trauma and Disasters
Factor-Inwentash Faculty of
    Social Work
University of Toronto
Toronto, Ontario, Canada

Mary Boes, MSW, MPH, PhD
Professor
Department of Social Work
University of Northern Iowa
Cedar Falls, Iowa

Gary R. Bond
Chancellor's Professor
Department of Psychology
Indiana University–Purdue University
    Indianapolis
Indianapolis, Indiana

William Borden, PhD
Senior Lecturer
School of Social Administration
University of Chicago
Chicago, Illinois

Gary L. Bowen, PhD
Kenan Distinguished Professor
School of Social Work
University of North Carolina
Chapel Hill, North Carolina

Natasha K. Bowen
Associate Professor
School of Social Work
University of North Carolina
Chapel Hill, North Carolina

Nancy Boyd-Webb, DSW
Distinguished Professor of
    Social Work
James R. Dumpson Chair in
    Child Welfare Studies
Graduate School of
    Social Service
Fordham University
Tarrytown, New York

Christine E. Brady, MA
Doctoral Student
Department of Psychology
Ohio University
Athens, Ohio

Jerrold R. Brandell, PhD
Professor
School of Social Work
Wayne State University
Detroit, Michigan

Denise E. Bronson, PhD
Associate Professor and
Associate Dean of Academic Affairs
College of Social Work
Ohio State University
Columbus, Ohio

Samantha M. Brown, PhD
School of Social Work
University of Denver
Denver, Colorado

Suzanne M. Brown, PhD, LICSW
Associate Professor
School of Social Work
Wayne State University
Detroit, Michigan

Daphne S. Cain, PhD
Director, School of Social Work
University of Mississippi
University, Mississippi

Michelle Mohr Carney, PhD
Professor and Director
School of Social Work
Arizona State University
Phoenix, Arizona

Andrew Christensen, PhD
Professor
Department of Psychology
University of California
Los Angeles, California

Elizabeth Clark, PhD, ACSW, MPH
Former Executive Director, NASW
Private Consultant
Rockville, Maryland

Andrea Cole, PhD Student
Silver School of Social Work
New York University
New York, New York

Jose E. Coll, PhD
Associate Professor and
Director of Veteran Services
Social Work
St. Leo University
St. Leo, Florida

Elaine P. Congress, BA, MAT, MS, MA, DSW
Professor
Graduate School of Social Service
Fordham University
New York, New York

Jacqueline Corcoran, PhD
Professor
School of Social Work
Northern Virginia Branch
Virginia Commonwealth University
Alexandria, Virginia

Kevin Corcoran, PhD, JD
Professor
School of Social Work
University of Alabama
Tuscaloosa, Alabama

Rory Crath, PhD
Professor
School of Social Work
St. Thomas University
Fredericton, New Brunswick,
Canada

James G. Daley, PhD, MSW
Associate Professor
School of Social Work
Indiana University
Indianapolis, Indiana

Julie S. Darnell, PhD, MHSA
Assistant Professor
School of Public Health
University of Illinois
Chicago, Illinois

Tara DeBraber, MSW
Clinical Social Worker
San Diego Veterans Administration
San Diego, California

Peter De Jong, PhD
Professor of Social Work
Department of Sociology and
    Social Work
Calvin College
Grand Rapids, Michigan

Alan Dettlaff, PhD
Associate Professor
College of Social Work
University of Illinois
Chicago, Illinois

Diana M. DiNitto, PhD
Cullen Trust Centennial Professor in Alcohol
  Studies and Education
Distinguished Teaching Professor
School of Social Work
University of Texas
Austin, Texas

Martha Morrison Dore, PhD
Associate Research Professor in Psychiatry
Harvard University Medical School
Cambridge, Massachusetts

James W. Drisko, PhD
Professor
School of Social Work
Smith College
Northampton, Massachusetts

Theresa J. Early, PhD
Associate Professor
College of Social Work
Ohio State University
Columbus, Ohio

Ilze A. Earner, PhD
Associate Professor
School of Social Work
Hunter College
City University of New York
New York, New York

Yvonne Eaton-Stull, MSW
Clinical Social Worker
Director of Crisis Services
Community Mental Health Services
Erie, Pennsylvania

Tonya Edmond, PhD
Associate Professor
George Warren Brown School of Social Work
Washington University
St. Louis, Missouri

Steven W. Evans, PhD
Professor
Ohio University
Athens, Ohio

Teresa A. Evans-Campbell, PhD, MSW
Associate Professor
Director, Center for Indigenous Health and
  Child Welfare Research
University of Washington
Seattle, Washington

Rowena Fong, EdD, MSW, BA
Ruby Lee Piester Centennial Professor in
  Services to Children and Families
School of Social Work
University of Texas at Austin
Austin, Texas

Anne E. Fortune, PhD
Professor
School of Social Welfare
University at Albany
State University of New York
Albany, New York

Raymond D. Fox, PhD
Professor
Graduate School of Social Service
Fordham University
New York, New York

Cynthia Franklin, PhD
Stiernberg/Spencer Family Professor in
  Mental Health
Coordinator of the Clinical Concentration for
  the Masters Program
School of Social Work
University of Texas at Austin
Austin, Texas

Mark W. Fraser, PhD
Professor
School of Social Work
University of North Carolina
Chapel Hill, North Carolina

John M. Gallagher, MSW
Doctoral Student and Faculty Associate
Office of Forensic Social Work Research and
  Training
School of Social Work
Arizona State University
Phoenix, Arizona

Dorothy N. Gamble, MSW
Clinical Associate Professor Emeritus
School of Social Work
University of North Carolina
Chapel Hill, North Carolina

Eileen Gambrill, PhD
Professor
School of Social Welfare
University of California
Berkeley, California

Genoveva Garcia, MSW
Psychotherapist and Assistant to Clinical
    Director
Metropolitan Center for Mental Health
New York, New York

Renée Bradford Garcia
Private Practice
Pflugerville, Texas

Daniel S. Gardner
Associate Professor
Silberman School of Social Work
Hunter College
New York, New York

Charles D. Garvin, PhD
Professor Emeritus of Social Work
School of Social Work
The University of Michigan
Ann Arbor, Michigan

Ann Marie Garran, PhD, MSW
Senior Clinical Supervisor
Hunter College Employee Assistance Program
New York, New York
Adjunct Professor
School for Social Work
Smith College
Northampton, Massachusetts

Felicia de la Garza-Mercer, PhD
Psychologist
Student Health and Counseling Services
University of California San Francisco
San Francisco, California

Zvi D. Gellis, PhD
Professor and Director
Center for Mental Health & Aging
School of Social Policy & Practice
University of Pennsylvania
Philadelphia, Pennsylvania

Toorjo Ghose, PhD
Associate Professor
School of Social Policy and Practice
University of Pennsylvania
Philadelphia, Pennsylvania

Leonard Gibbs, PhD (deceased)
Professor
School of Social Work
University of Wisconsin
Eau Claire, Wisconsin

Brian Giddens, LICSW, ACSW
Associate Director of Social Work and
    Care Coordination
University of Washington
    Medical Center
Clinical Associate Professor
School of Social Work
University of Washington
Seattle, Washington

Alex Gitterman, MSW, EdD
Director of PhD Program
    and Professor
School of Social Work
University of Connecticut
West Hartford, Connecticut

Stephen Gorin
Professor
Department of Social Work
Plymouth State University
Plymouth, New Hampshire

Donald K. Granvold, PhD (deceased)
Professor
School of Social Work
University of Texas at Arlington
Arlington, Texas

Diane L. Green Sherman, PhD
Associate Professor of
    Social Work
Florida Atlantic University–Jupiter Campus
Jupiter, Florida

Samantha A. Hafner, PhD, MSW
School of Social Work
University of South Florida
Tampa, Florida

Alice Schmidt Hanbidge, PhD, RSW
Assistant Professor
Renison University College School of
    Social Work
University of Waterloo
Waterloo, Ontario
Canada

Lina Hartocollis, PhD
Associate Dean
Director, Clinical Doctorate in
    Social Work Program
School of Social Policy & Practice
University of Pennsylvania
Philadelphia, Pennsylvania

Anthony Hassan, PhD
Clinical Associate Professor
School of Social Work
University of Southern California
Los Angeles, California

Kristin Heffernan, PhD
Associate Professor
Department of Social Work
College at Brockport
State University of New York
Brockport, New York

Nina Rovinelli Heller, PhD
Associate Professor
School of Social Work
University of Connecticut
West Hartford, Connecticut

Chris Herman, MSW
Senior Practice Associate
National Association of
    Social Workers
Washington DC

Carolyn Hilarski, PhD, LCSW, ACSW
Associate Professor
Department of Social Work
Buffalo State College
State University of New York
Buffalo, New York

Michael J. Holosko, PhD
Pauline M. Berger Professor of Family and
    Child Welfare
University of Georgia School of
    Social Work
Athens, Georgia

Laura M. Hopson, PhD
Associate Professor
School of Social Work
University of Alabama
Tuscaloosa, Alabama

Nicole M. Huggett, MSW
Evaluation Associate
LeCroy and Milligan Associate
Tempe, Arizona

Grafton H. Hull, Jr., EdD
Director, BSW Program
College of Social Work
University of Utah
Salt Lake City, Utah

Altaf Husain, PhD
Assistant Professor
School of Social Work
Howard University
Washington, DC

Aidyn L. Iachini, PhD
Assistant Professor
College of Social Work
University of South Carolina
Columbia, South Carolina

Katherine Ishizuka, MSW
Doctoral Student
School of Social Work
Howard University
Washington, DC

Catheleen Jordan, PhD
The Cheryl Milkes Moore Professionship
    in Mental Health and
Professor of Social Work
School of Social Work
University of Texas at Arlington
Arlington, Texas

Shannon K. Johnson, MSW
Doctoral Student
School of Social Work
University of Texas Austin
Austin, Texas

Andrea Kampfner, PhD
Evaluation Associate
LeCroy and Milligan and Associates
Tuscan, AS

Lana Sue I. Ka'opua, PhD, DCSW, LSW
Associate Professor and Head of Health
    Concentration
School of Social Work and Cancer Research
    Center of Hawai'i
University of Hawai'i, Manoa Campus
Director, Ka Lei Mana'olana
    Breast Health Project
Honolulu, Hawai'i
Co-Editor-in-Chief, Social Work
    Journal of Indigenous Matters

Patricia Kelley, PhD
Professor Emerita
School of Social Work
The University of Iowa
Iowa City, Iowa

Michael S. Kelly, PhD, LCSW
Associate Professor
School of Social Work
Loyola University
Chicago, Illinois
Coordinator of Research and Outreach,
    Loyola Family and Schools
    Partnership Program

Stephanie Kennedy, MSW
Doctoral Student
School of Social Work
Florida State University
Tallahassee, Florida

Johnny S. Kim, PhD
Assistant Professor
School of Social Work
University of Denver
Denver, Colorado

Sara Kintzle, PhD
Research Assistant Professor
School of Social Work
University of Southern California
Los Angeles, California

Karni Kissil, PhD
Licensed Marriage and
    Family Therapist
Private Practice
Jupiter, Florida

Karen S. Knox, PhD
Associate Professor
School of Social Work
Texas State University
San Marcos, Texas

Marina Kukla, PhD
Psychologist
Richard L. Roudebush VA Medical Center
Indianapolis, Indiana

Stephen R. Lankton, MSW, DAHB
Executive Director
Phoenix Institute of Ericksonian Therapy
Phoenix, Arizona

Craig Winston LeCroy, PhD
Professor
School of Social Work
Arizona State University–
    Tucson Component
Tucson, Arizona

Mo Yee Lee, PhD
Professor
College of Social Work
The Ohio State University
Columbus, Ohio

George S. Leibowitz, PhD, LICSW
Associate Professor
Department of Social Work
University of Vermont
Burlington, Vermont

John Allen Lemmon, PhD
Professor
School of Social Work
San Francisco State University
San Francisco, California

Jilan Li, PhD
Associate Professor
North Carolina A & T
    State University
Greensboro, North Carolina

Anita Lightburn, MSS, EdD
Professor of Social Work
Graduate School of
    Social Work
Fordham University
New York, New York

Elizabeth Lightfoot, PhD
Professor and PhD Program Director
School of Social Work
University of Minnesota–
    Twin Cities
St. Paul, Minnesota

Jan Ligon, PhD
Associate Professor
School of Social Work
Georgia State University
Atlanta, Georgia

Gordon E. Limb, PhD
Professor
Brigham Young University
Salt Lake City, Utah

Julia H. Littell, PhD
Professor
Graduate School of Social Work and
    Social Research
Bryn Mawr College
Bryn Mawr, Pennsylvania

Jill L. Littrell, PhD
Associate Professor
School of Social Work
Georgia State University
Atlanta, Georgia

Sadye M. L. Logan, DSW
DeQuincey Newman Professor
Director of the Newman Institute for Peace
    and Justice
College of Social Work
University of South Carolina
Columbia, South Carolina

Jack Lu, MSW
Doctoral Candidate
School of Social Work
University of Connecticut
Stores, Connecticut

Robert Lucio, PhD, LCSW
Department of Child and Family Studies
College of Behavioral and Community
    Sciences
University of South Florida
Tampa, Florida

Brandy Macaluso, BSW
Crime Victim Practitioner
Coalition for Independent Living Options, Inc.
West Palm Beach, Florida

Mark J. Macgowan, PhD
Professor
Robert Stempel College of Public Health and
    Social Work
Florida International University
Miami, Florida

Gordon MacNeil, PhD
Associate Professor
School of Social Work
The University of Alabama
Tuscaloosa, Alabama

Kimberly H. McManama O'Brien, PhD
Assistant Professor
Simmons College
Boston, Massachusetts

Roxana Marachi, PhD
Associate Professor
Department of Elementary Education
Lurie College of Education
San José State University

San José, California

Jennifer Manuel, PhD
Assistant Professor
Silver School of Social Work
New York University
New York, New York

Andrew T. Marks, LMSW
Lecturer
School of Social Work
Texas State University–San Marcos
San Marcos, Texas

Tina Bogart Marshall, PhD
Consultant and Part-time Professor
School of Social Work
University of Maryland–Baltimore County at
    Shady Grove
Rockville, Maryland

James A. Martin, PhD, BCD
Professor
Graduate School of Social Work and Social
    Research
Bryn Mawr College
Bryn Mawr, Pennsylvania
Colonel, U.S. Army (Retired)

Jannah H. Mather, PhD
Dean and Professor
College of Social Work
University of Utah
Salt Lake City, Utah

Tina Maschi, PhD, LCSW
School of Social Work
Fordham University
New York, New York

Evan Mayo-Wilson, MGA, MSc
Department Lecturer
Centre for Evidence-Based Intervention
University of Oxford
Oxford, England, United Kingdom

Monica McGoldrick, MSW, PhD (h. c.)
Director, Family Institute of
    New Jersey
Highland Park, New Jersey
Adjunct Associate Professor of Clinical
    Psychiatry
Robert Wood Johnson Medical School
University of Medicine and Dentistry
Piscataway, New Jersey

Steven L. McMurtry, PhD
Professor
Helen Bader School of Social Welfare
University of Wisconsin
Milwaukee, Wisconsin

C. Aaron McNeece, PhD
Former Dean and Walter W. Hudson
    Professor of Social Work
College of Social Work
Florida State University
Tallahassee, Florida

Joshua Miller, PhD, MSW
Professor and Chair of Policy Sequence
School for Social Work
Smith College
Northampton, Massachusetts

Shari Miller, PhD
Associate Professor
School of Social Work
University of Georgia
Athens, Georgia

Terry Mizrahi, PhD
Professor and Chair, Community
    Organization & Planning
School of Social Work
Hunter College
City University of New York
New York, New York

Lauren Mizus, MA, PhD
Master of Social Work Program
University of Vermont
Burlington, Vermont

Katherine L. Montgomery, PhD
School Director
Little Sunshine Playhouse and PreSchool
St. Louis, Missouri

Paul Montgomery, DPhil
Reader in Psycho-Social Intervention
Centre for Evidence-Based Intervention
University of Oxford
Oxford, England, United Kingdom

David P. Moxley, PhD
Oklahoma Health Care Authority Professor
Professor of Social Work
School of Social Work
University of Oklahoma
Norman, Oklahoma

Carlton E. Munson, PhD
Professor
School of Social Work
University of Maryland
Baltimore, Maryland

Laura L. Myers, MSW, PhD
Associate Professor
Department of Social Work
Florida A & M University
Tallahassee, Florida

Jason M. Newell, PhD
Associate Professor and Director of
    Social Work
University of Montevallo
Montevallo, Alabama

Barbara Van Noppen, MSW
Clinical Social Worker
Angel Wellness Center
Providence, Rhode Island

Terry B. Northcut, PhD, LCSW
Associate Professor
Director of the Doctoral Program
School of Social Work
Loyola University of Chicago
Chicago, Illinois

Julie Sarno Owens, PhD
Associate Professor
Department of Psychology
Ohio University
Athens, Ohio

William P. Panning, MSW
Private Practice and
    Guest Lecturer
College of Social Work
The Ohio State University
Columbus, Ohio

Daniel V. Papero, PhD
Private Practice
Director of Clinical Services
Georgetown Family Center
Washington, DC

Danielle E. Parrish, PhD
Associate Professor
Graduate College of
    Social Work
University of Houston
Houston, Texas

A. Raisa Petca, MA
Ohio Education Research
Ohio University
Athens Ohio

Monica Pignotti, MSW, PhD
Assistant Professor
College of Social Work
Florida State University
Tallahassee, Florida

Cathy King Pike, PhD
Professor
School of Social Work
Indiana University
Indianapolis, Indiana

Ronald O. Pitner, PhD
Independent Research Consultant
North Brunswick, New Jersey

Elizabeth C. Pomeroy, PhD
Professor
School of Social Work
University of Texas
Austin, Texas

Dennis L. Poole, PhD
Professor
College of Social Work
University of South Carolina
Columbia, South Carolina

Miriam Potocky, PhD
Professor
School of Social Work
Florida International University
Miami, Florida

James O. Prochaska, PhD
Professor and Director
Cancer Research Center and
    Department of Psychology
University of Rhode Island
Kingston, Rhode Island

Janice M. Prochaska, PhD
CEO and Social Work Consultant
Pro-Change Behavior Systems
Kingston, Rhode Island

Judith J. Prochaska, PhD, MPH
Associate Professor of Medicine
Stanford University Prevention Research Center
Stanford University
San Francisco, California

Blanca M. Ramos, PhD
Associate Professor
School of Social Work
State University of New
    York Albany
Albany, New York

Lisa Rapp-McCall, PhD, MSW
Professor
Department of Social Work
St. Leo University
St. Leo, Florida

Frederic G. Reamer, PhD
Professor
School of Social Work
Rhode Island College
Providence, Rhode Island

William J. Reid, DSW (deceased)
Distinguished Professor and Chair, PhD
    Program
School of Social Work
State University of
    New York
Albany, New York

Michael Reisch, PhD, LMSW
Daniel Thursz Distinguished Professor of
    Social Justice
School of Social Work
University of Maryland
Baltimore, Maryland

Albert R. Roberts, PhD (deceased)
Professor of Criminal Justice and
    Social Work
School of Arts and Sciences
Rutgers University
Livingston Campus
Piscataway, New Jersey

Eden Hernandez Robles, MSW, Doctoral
    Candidate
Assistant Instructor
School of Social Work
University of Texas–Austin
Austin, Texas

Susan P. Robbins, PhD
Professor
Graduate School of
Social Work
University of Houston
Houston, Texas

Susan J. Rose, PhD
Professor
Helen Bader School of
    Social Welfare
University of Wisconsin
Milwaukee, Wisconsin

Julie M. Rosenzweig, PhD
Professor
School of Social Work
Portland State University
Portland, Oregon

Juliet Cassuto Rothman, PhD, LCSW
Lecturer in Social Welfare and
    Public Health
University of California–Berkeley
Berkeley, California

William S. Rowe, DSW
Professor and Director
School of Social Work
University of South Florida
Tampa, Florida

Allen Rubin, PhD
Kantambu Latting College Professorship for
    Leadership and Change
Graduate School of
    Social Work
University of Houston
Houston, Texas

Melanie Sage, PhD
Assistant Professor
University of North Dakota
Grand Forks, North Dakota

Michael Saini, PhD
Associate Professor
Faculty of Social Work
University of Toronto
Toronto, Ontario, Canada

Alison Salloum, PhD
Associate Professor
School of Social Work
University of South Florida
Tampa, Florida

Diane Scotland-Coogan, MSW
Instructor
Social Work
St. Leo's University
St. Leo, Florida

Michael S. Shafer, PhD
Professor
School of Social Work
Arizona State University
Phoenix, Arizona

Aron Shlonsky, PhD
Associate Professor
Faculty of Social Work
University of Toronto
Toronto, Ontario, Canada

Lawrence Shulman, EdD, MSW
Professor
School of Social Work
State University of New York at Buffalo
Buffalo, New York

Debra Siegel, PhD
Professor
School of Social Work
Rhode Island College
Providence, Rhode Island

Jonathan B. Singer, LCSW
Instructor
Social Administration
Temple University
Philadelphia, Pennsylvania
Host and Founder of The Social Work Podcast

Jeff Skinner, MSW
School of Social Work
University of Georgia
Athens, Georgia

Mark Smith, PhD
Associate Professor
School of Social Work
Barry University
Miami, Florida

Phyllis Solomon, PhD
Professor
School of Social Policy & Practice
University of Pennsylvania
Philadelphia, Pennsylvania

Karen M. Sowers, PhD
Dean and Professor
College of Social Work
The University of Tennessee
Knoxville, Tennessee
Coeditor, Best Practices in Mental Health: An
    International Journal

David W. Springer, PhD
University Distinguished Teaching Professor
School of Social Work
The University of Texas
Austin, Texas

Alicia J. Stinson, MSW
School of Social Work
University of South Florida
Tampa, Florida

Jacqueline Strait, MSW, PhD
Instructor
School of Policy and Practice
University of Pennsylvania
Philadelphia, Pennsylvania

Kimberly Strom-Gottfried, MSW, PhD
Smith P. Theimann Jr. Distinguished Professor
    of Ethics and Professional Practice
School of Social Work
University of North Carolina
Chapel Hill, North Carolina

W. Patrick Sullivan, PhD
Professor
School of Social Work
Indiana University
Indianapolis, Indiana

Stephanie A. Sundborg, MA, PhD Candidate
Director of Research
Deschutes County Health Authority
Bend, Oregon

Andrea G. Tamburro, EdD, MSW
Assistant Professor
Director of Social Work
Indiana University Northwest
Gary, Indiana

A. M. Thompson
Doctoral Student
School of Social Work
University of North Carolina
Chapel Hill, North Carolina

Bruce A. Thyer, PhD
Professor
College of Social Work
Florida State University
Tallahassee, Florida
Editor, Research on Social Work Practice

Evelyn P. Tomaszewski, MSW
Project Director and Senior Policy Advisor
Practice, Human Rights, and
    International Affairs
National Association of Social Workers
Washington, DC

Elizabeth M. Tracy, PhD
Grace Longwell Coyle Professor of
    Social Work
Mandel School of Applied Social
    Sciences
Case Western Reserve University
Cleveland, Ohio

Stephen J. Tripodi, PhD
Associate Professor
College of Social Work
Florida State University
Tallahassee, Florida

Francis J. Turner, DSW
Professor and Dean Emeritus
Wilfred Laurier University
Waterloo, Ontario, Canada

Halaevalu F. Ofahengaue Vakalahi, MSW, MEd,
    BS, PhD
Associate Dean and Associate Professor
School of Social Work
Morgan State University
Baltimore, Maryland

Vikki L. Vandiver, MSW, DrPH
Dean and Professor
School of Social Work
University of Alabama
Tuscaloosa, Alabama

Katherine van Wormer, MSW, PhD
Professor
School of Social Work
University of Northern Iowa
Cedar Falls, Iowa

Mary M. Velasquez, PhD
Professor in Leadership for Community,
    Professional, and Corporate Excellence
Director of Health Behavior Research and
    Training Institute
School of Social Work
University of Texas at Austin
Austin, Texas

M. Elizabeth Vonk, MSW, PhD
Professor
School of Social Work
University of Georgia
Athens, Georgia

Kirk von Sternberg, PhD
Associate Professor
School of Social Work
University of Texas at Austin
Austin, Texas

Froma Walsh, PhD
Mose and Sylvia Firestone Professor Emerita
School of Social Service Administration
University of Chicago
Chicago, Illinois

Joseph Walsh, PhD
Professor
School of Social Work
Virginia Commonwealth University
Richmond, Virginia

Chris Warren-Adamson, MPhil
Senior Lecturer
School of Social Sciences
University of Southampton
Southampton, England,
United Kingdom

Marie Overby Weil, DSW
Berg-Beach Distinguished Professor of
    Community Practice
School of Social Work
University of North Carolina
Chapel Hill, North Carolina

Eugenia L. Weiss, PhD
Clinical Associate Professor
School of Social Work
University of Southern California
Los Angeles, California

Traci L. Wike
Assistant Professor
School of Social Work
Virginia Commonwealth University
Richmond, Virginia

Michelle F. Wright, PhD
Faculty of Social Studies
Department of Psychology
DePaul University
Brno, Czech Republic

Kenneth R. Yeager, PhD
Associate Professor of Psychiatry
Director of Quality Assurance
Department of Psychiatry
Ohio State University
Medical School
Columbus, Ohio

Dina Zempsky, MSW, LCSW
Program Director
StoryCorps
New York, New York

Charlene Zuffante, LICSW
Director of Wraparound Services
The Guidance Center, Inc.
Somerville, Massachusetts

PART I

Overview and Introduction to Social Work

1 What Changes and What Remains in a Practice Profession

Elizabeth Clark

It has been six years since the second edition of the Desk Reference was released. Since that time, our world has changed in many large and small ways. Our political landscape has become more partisan and more entrenched. The numbers of baby boomers, veterans, prisoners, and the homeless have increased. Global warming and natural disasters are on the rise. Health care reform has moved forward; immigration reform has stalled. The list goes on and on. Against this backdrop of rapid acceleration and social complexity, editors Kevin Corcoran and Albert Roberts and their editorial board had to decide what content to leave in, what to add, and what to revise. This was a formidable task, and they collectively rose to the challenge.

It has been suggested that a profession will not seek new ways or contexts until it feels the "challenge of crisis" (Kuhn, 1970, p. 144). Today, numerous factors are driving social work practice changes. These include globalization, an unending war, an uncertain economy, a fraying of the social safety net, and the speed and impact of technology.

Social work has become a global profession. In the United States, social workers serve in the United Nations, the U.S. Department of State, USAID, the World Bank, Congress, the Peace Corps, the U.S. Department of Agriculture, and many nongovernmental organizations (NGOs) that work abroad. Many schools of social work have established, or are in the process of establishing, schools and programs in countries such as China, India, Cambodia, and Viet Nam. I would contend that the profession now has a moral mandate that crosses geographic boundaries. We must become a visible and active partner in the search for solutions to the interrelated social challenges around the globe.

Social work principles of human rights and social justice underlie the efforts of our social work colleagues in both developed and developing countries. The over 200 member countries of the International Federation of Social Workers (IFSW), in partnership with the International Association of Schools of Social Work (IASSW) and the International Council on Social Welfare (ICSW), have developed a *Global Agenda for Social Work and Social Development* (http://cdn.ifsw.org/assets/globalagenda2012.pdf). The Agenda is committed to "supporting, influencing and enabling structures and systems that allow people to have power over their own lives" (IFSW, 2012). These efforts currently are focused in four areas:

- Promoting social and economic equalities
- Promoting dignity and worth of people
- Working toward environmental sustainability
- Strengthening recognition of the importance of human relationships.

Internationally, social workers are being sought for their ability to resolve human and social problems and for the contributions they can make to the emerging global social, political, and economic landscape. More specifically, social workers can help translate policy into workable projects, help design and evaluate direct services and projects, and work toward community capacity building.

In the United States, social workers work in refugee settlements and in communities with an influx of immigrants. In clinical practices, they work with victims of torture or those who were imprisoned for their political beliefs and social activism. Social workers volunteer their services and mobilize resources when natural or man-made disasters occur around the globe. At the macro level, social workers are champions of fair immigration laws, the eradication of hunger and infectious diseases such as HIV/AIDS, and the reduction of world violence.

Jane Addams was awarded the Nobel Peace Prize in 1931. Eighty years later, social worker Leymah Gbowee was a 2011 recipient for her peace efforts in Liberia (Gbowee, 2011). Efforts on behalf of peace have always been a part of the fabric of social work practice. On September 14, 2001, Congresswoman and social worker Barbara Lee was the only negative vote for House Joint Resolution 64, the Authorization of Use of Military Force against terrorists involved in the attacks on September 11. Lee said, "We must step back for a minute … and think through the implications of our actions today so that this does not spiral out of control" (*The Guardian*, 2013).

Twelve years later, the United States seems unable to extricate itself from what has been described as an endless war. The effects of the war are significant. We now have a generation of young people who have grown up against the backdrop of war. The number of American troops who have died fighting in the wars in Iraq and Afghanistan is nearing 7,000 (U.S. Department of Defense, 2013). Depending on sources used, the number physically wounded in battle has surpassed 50,000 (U.S. Department of Defense, 2013), and there have been more than 250,000 brain injuries, the signature wound of this war (American Forces Press Service, 2013).

As a country, we have been slow to recognize the sacrifices and the incredible need for assistance and services for our nation's service members and veterans. In addition to the millions of veterans from past conflicts who still deserve the care and resources that have been promised to them, there have been 2.5 million service members involved in the wars in Iraq and Afghanistan. Many of these young men and women have struggled with mental and behavioral health challenges, unemployment, homelessness, or general difficulties re-acclimating to civilian life. Social workers have been a critical component of the interdisciplinary workforce tasked with ensuring that service members,

veterans, and their families have the support that they have earned.

The United States Department of Veterans Affairs (VA) is now the largest employer of master's level social workers in the country, with over 11,000 professional social workers employed in their many settings and programs (U.S. Department of Veterans Affairs, 2011). Because this practice area continues to grow, standards for best practices and advanced credentials need to be available.

In 2012, the National Association of Social Workers (NASW) worked in partnership with the White House Joining Forces initiative, which was led by First Lady Michelle Obama and Dr. Jill Biden (NASW News, 2012). As part of NASW's commitment to Joining Forces, expert practitioners developed the *Standards for Social Work Practice with Service Members, Veterans, and Their Families* (NASW, 2012). These standards are a resource for clinical social workers providing mental and behavioral health services, direct practitioners in social service agencies, and social work advocates. In addition, NASW created three professional credentials to demonstrate in-depth knowledge, proven work experience, leadership capacity, competence, and dedication in this field of practice at the baccalaureate, advanced, or clinical levels (http://www.socialworkers.org/military.asp).

Despite the record numbers of social workers within the VA system and the Department of Defense, veterans today constitute a vulnerable population. They also highlight the inadequacy of the nation's social safety net that generations of social workers have worked to build and maintain.

RECAPTURING THE PAST

In late 2006, I had the honor of attending a "Social Work Pioneer Listening Conference" where six Pioneers talked about the investments in the social work profession from the post–World War II era through the present day. They discussed the social context, major events, and problems social work practitioners faced during that time (Stuart, 2009). They also discussed the successes they achieved.

For example, Delwin Anderson discussed his role at the VA. He joined the VA as a field social worker in Minnesota in 1947. He became the national Director of the Social Work Service in

1964, and served in that position until he retired in 1974. He was responsible for 2,600 social workers employed in 171 hospitals. Together, they revolutionized care for our veterans. They looked at treatment and rehabilitation of the whole patient, and developed ways for patients to receive community care.

Although the clinical accomplishments of Anderson and his co-presenters at the Listening Conference were remarkable, what was most impressive was their community organizing skills and expertise. They saw the need for social work in various agencies and settings and worked from both inside and outside to bring it about.

There are many, many examples of the leadership of social workers in our history. In fact, most of the social safety net we have come to rely upon today was fashioned by social work advocates.

Frances Perkins was the first woman and social worker appointed to a cabinet position. She served as Secretary of Labor from 1933 to 1945, that is, through all of President Franklin Delano Roosevelt's terms. She began her career as a crusader for factory safety. Her agenda as Secretary of Labor included a major unemployment relief program, workers' rights protections, minimum wage, and child labor laws. She also served as Chairwoman of the commission that ultimately crafted the Social Security Act (P.L. 74–271) (Downey, 2009).

Harry Hopkins began his social work career in a New York City settlement house. He was chosen by President Roosevelt to head the first state emergency relief agency during the Great Depression, and later ran the $500 million federal program (Cohen, 2009).

CRAFTING THE FUTURE

Advocacy had its roots in social work, and advocacy for social supports and increased social services deserves our full attention. In the past decade we have experienced the worst recession since the Great Depression. Salaries have remained static and the minimum wage does not cover minimal family needs. Our schools are in disrepair and their service programs are woefully inadequate.

Despite the advocacy efforts of the 12 social workers in Congress working with tens of thousands of social work activists, recent political successes have been few and far between. The one major exception has been health care reform, namely, the passage of the Patient Protection and Affordable Care Act of 2010 (ACA) (P.L. 111–148).

The ACA contains many welcome and positive changes including expanding health care coverage to millions of uninsured individuals, eliminating preexisting condition exclusions and lifetime caps, and offering mental health parity (Patient Protection and Affordable Care Act, 2010). With an emphasis on prevention, social determinants of illness, and early intervention, the ACA also offers opportunities for health care and public health social workers.

One downside of the ACA for social workers is role blurring. Over the past few decades, the diversity of practice areas in social work has widened significantly. A consequence of this rapid growth has been an expanding overlap of professional practice fields. At the same time, we have seen a narrowing of what we traditionally have called social work.

New titles and credentials, such as peer counselors (championed by Substance Abuse Mental Health Services Administration), community health workers (Centers for Disease Control and Prevention [CDC] and the Centers for Medicare and Medicaid Services [CMS] offer training grants), and patient navigators (funded by the Patient Protection and Affordable Care Act) have emerged. In many ways, these terms address functions that need to be fulfilled rather than individual professions (SWPI, 2012), but they still present challenges. Add to these the need for service integration to ensure cost-effectiveness, as well as the use of trans-disciplinary teams, and the role blurring and professional competition increase.

Another challenge is the legal regulation of the profession. Social work efforts around licensure began in the 1940s. Now all 50 states have some level of licensure for social workers to seek legal recognition, protection, and reimbursement for services. Because licensing is determined within the states, different definitions of social work and aspects of social work practice vary from state to state. This contributes to confusion about our profession among the public, lawmakers, other providers, and insurers. This lack of clarity, as well as a lack of reciprocity state-to-state, makes it harder to define and defend what we do and are entitled to do as a profession.

In 2010, the major social work organizations came together to hold a national Social Work Congress to reaffirm, revisit, and reimagine the profession. It focused on issues internal to the profession. The result was consensus around ten "Social Work Imperatives" that needed action in the next decade. They included (NASW, 2010):

1. Business of Social Work: Infuse models of sustainable business and management practice into social work education and practice.
2. Common Objectives: Strengthen collaboration across social work organizations, their leadership, and their membership for shared advocacy goals.
3. Education: Clarify and articulate the unique skills, scope of practice, and "value added" aspects of social work to prospective social work students.
4. Influence: Build a data-driven business case that demonstrates the distinctive expertise and the impact and value of social work to industry, policy makers, and the general public.
5. Influence: Strengthen the ability of national social work organizations to identify and clearly articulate, with a unified voice, issues of importance to the profession.
6. Leadership Development: Integrate leadership training in social work curricula at all levels.
7. Recruitment: Empirically demonstrate to prospective recruits the value of the social work profession in both social and economic terms.
8. Retention: Increase the number of grants, scholarships, and debt forgiveness mechanisms for social work students and graduates.
9. Retention: Ensure the sustainability of the profession through a strong mentoring program, career ladder, and succession program.
10. Technology: Integrate technologies that serve social work practice and education in an ethical, practical, and responsible manner.

In one way or another, progress toward all of these imperatives is included in this comprehensive reference volume. The last imperative, technology, is covered extensively by several authors. This highlights both the importance and the immediacy of the topic.

We are just beginning to understand the potential impact of technology on social work practice. Despite uncertainties around policy, liability, and licensing concerns, and despite increasing privacy and ethical issues, computer-based or e-therapy is accelerating (Reamer, 2013). We no sooner develop standards and guidelines than a new type of technology enters the horizon and our efforts are outdated. Young social workers are early adapters of such technology. They grew up living online, and they are not only comfortable with it, but find it essential to their lives as well. Schools and educators have struggled to keep up by using technology in the classroom and by offering classes and entire programs online. Supervision is being done electronically, and health care reform requires electronic health records and billing for services.

Technology has contributed positively to social work practice. We can find information quickly and easily. We can keep up with the literature in our fields. This can enhance practice by ensuring that our interventions are evidence based and current. We can find models and best practices, as well as locate colleagues and experts and check resources needed by our clients, our agencies, and our communities. Technology also is an asset for our social advocacy efforts. It is now easy to send an e-mail to a legislator, compose and submit a letter or blog to a news line, or get a requisite number of signatures to make a political point or request an action.

What is needed is an increased sensitivity to the potential negatives of living online, while at the same time incorporating technology into our practices and our lives. Additionally, we need the new generation of social workers, those who are expert in these areas, to take the lead in establishing acceptable parameters and guidelines for use.

CONCLUSION

The questions that remain are (1) Is social work still relevant? (2) Do we have the necessary outcomes data to show our value? (3) Can we ensure a profession appropriate to our times and for the future?

Based on the writings and shared wisdom of the scholars and expert practitioners who have authored the *Social Workers' Desk Reference*, we can answer these questions in the affirmative. They clearly show that the profession of social work continues to grow and expand through practice. They also illustrate how practice informs both research and policy and vice versa.

Forty years ago, Khan, in his preface to the book *Shaping the New Social Work*, asserted that social work practice answers the call of its time (1973, p. vii). We agree that it does. The world is changing rapidly and some things must be surrendered to progress. Yet, there are historical tenets of social work that we deem essential, if not sacred.

The purpose of the profession remains solid and steadfast—to enhance human well-being and meet the human needs of all people; to seek social justice and positive social change; to promote peace; and to practice ethically. Advocacy is our professional cornerstone. Our core values, first adopted as a *Code of Ethics* in 1960, and only amended slightly since that time, remain our guiding principles: service, social justice, dignity and worth of the person, importance of human relationships, integrity, and competence (NASW, 2008).

We have a professional obligation to live up to our founding documents and to honor, support, and advance the teachings upon which the profession of social work has been built. We also need to claim our expertise, and to assume leadership roles in addressing the social problems and issues of today.

Whitney M. Young, Jr., the social worker who transformed the National Urban League during the Civil Rights movement and who was an advisor to three presidents, challenged social workers to be more visible. He said:

There is a lot to tell the public. The important thing is that we can begin saying something as persistently as we can. The media and the government, regardless of their reasons, cannot continue to disregard the findings of current research and the knowledge of thousands of social workers who know as much or more than the so-called experts on the social problems draining the spirit and resources of our nation (Young, 1971).

The authors in the *Social Workers' Desk Reference* have answered that call to action. The content of this third edition will be an indispensable resource for practitioners, educators, researchers, policy makers, and students everywhere.

WEBSITES

International Association of Schools of Social Work, www.cdn.ifsw.org

International Council on Social Welfare, www.icsw.org
International Federation of Social Workers, www.ifsw.org
National Association of Social Workers, www.socialworkers.org
Society for Social Work and Research, www.sswr.org

References

American Forces Press Service (2013, August 15). *National plan supports veterans' mental health, brain injury care*. Retrieved October 25 from http://www.defense.gov/news/newsarticle.aspx?id=120631

Cohen, A. (2009). *Nothing to fear: FDR's Inner circle and the hundred days that created modern America*. London: Penguin Press.

Downey, K. (2009). *The woman behind the new deal: The life of Frances Perkins, FDR's Secretary of Labor and his moral conscience*. New York, NY: Nan A. Talese.

Gbowee, L. (2011). *Mighty be our powers: A memoir*. New York, NY: Perseus Books Group.

International Federation of Social Workers. (2012). *The global agenda for social work and social development: Commitment to action*. Bern, Switzerland: Author.

Kuhn, T. (1970). *The structure of scientific revolution II* (End ed., Vol. 2). Chicago, IL: University of Chicago Press. p. 144.

NASW News. (2012, March). NASW supports joining forces [Press release]. Retrieved October 24, 2013 from https://www.socialworkers.org/pubs/news/2012/03/joining-forces.asp?back=yes

National Association of Social Workers. (2008). *Code of ethics of the National Association of Social Workers*. Washington, DC: Author.

National Association of Social Workers. (2010). *Social Work Congress—Final Report*. Washington, DC: Author.

National Association of Social Workers. (2012). *Standards for social work practice with service members, veterans, and their families*. Washington, DC: Author.

Reamer, F. (2013). *Social work values and ethics* (4th ed.). New York, NY: Columbia University Press.

Social Security Act of 1935, P.L. 74-271, 49 Stat. 620 (1935).

Social Work Policy Institute. (2012). *Critical conversation brief: Social work in health and behavioral health care: Visioning the future*. Washington, DC: NASW Foundation, p. 1.

Stuart, P. (2009). *Investment in social work after World War II: Reflections on the pioneers' listening conferences*. Washington, DC: National Association of Social Workers.

The Guardian. (2013, May 7). *Barbara Lee and Dick Durbin's "nobody-could have known" defense.* Retrieved October 24, 2013 from http://www.theguardian.com/commentisfree/2013/may/07/aumf-durbin-barbara-lee-defense

The Patient Protection and Affordable Care Act of 2010, P.L. 111-148, 124 Stat. 119 (2010).

U.S. Department of Defense. (2013, October 23). *Casualty Report* [Fact sheet]. Retrieved October 24, 2013, from http://www.defense.gov/news/casualty.pdf

U.S. Department of Veterans Affairs (Ed.). (2013, March 8). *National professional social worker month.* Retrieved October 24, 2013 from http://www.martinsburg.va.gov/features/National_Professional_Social_Worker_Month.asp

U.S. Department of Veterans Affair. (2011, Nov 23)What VA Social Workers do. www.socialwortk.v.gov/SOCIALWORK/docs/whatsocialworkersdo.docx

Young, W. (1971, March). From the President. *NASW News*, p. 7.

Professional Socialization

2   *On Becoming and Being a Social Worker*

Shari Miller

Although social work in practice is a "job" (or more accurately a vast range of jobs), and while it is also a career, it can further be understood as a professional culture unto itself, replete with defined values, attitudes, norms, and a sense of identity. Would you be willing to engage in a brief thought experiment? If you like to make things visual, feel free to grab a sheet of paper and draw a picture; if you prefer to think in terms of language use words as your symbols. Now, close your eyes and think "social worker": Who do you see? How do you see her/him? Now close your eyes again and think doctor, or attorney, or nurse, etc. (select one): Now who do you see? How do you see her/him? Were they different? How so? The drawings or narratives you might craft for these respective professionals, and the notable qualitative differences between them can be explained by the idea that professions are cultures. And the differences between the cultures help to shape those narratives.

The questions that began this chapter invite us to look inside the culture of social work.

Research in this area allows us to develop an understanding of key variables, how certain processes unfold over time in particular contexts, and how they all contribute to professional development. A solid understanding of these variables and processes affords the profession of social work a much more informed understanding of its workforce and its capacity, of its educational structures, and of its realms of service provision. And with an understanding of professional socialization, social work students and practitioners are empowered to engage in their own professional development from an informed standpoint, and with agency. This chapter, with its focus on the professional socialization of social workers, invites you to spend time reflecting on the culture of the profession—this context sheds light on the "hows" and "whys" of social work so that practitioners can be best prepared to go out and do the "whats" of practice. This chapter is designed to help you understand what professional socialization is, how it fits within the historical evolution of social work as a profession, and how it might look in an applied sense.

PROFESSIONAL SOCIALIZATION DEFINED

Socialization in general can be understood as the process through which people gain knowledge, skills, and orientations that organize their membership in a society (Brim & Wheeler, 1966). This process happens over time and contains primary facets that occur during childhood, which tend to be sturdy and hard to change; a worldview becomes situated and serves as a way of making an objective-seeming reality a subjective vehicle for understanding and guiding action (Jarvis, 1983). The secondary facets happen in adulthood as people begin to locate themselves in other spheres in their interaction with the world around them (Jarvis); their functioning in society shifts and so does the emphasis of this secondary socialization. The focus of this phase of socialization is no longer so much on values and establishing a worldview, but instead is on honing and sculpting the ways in which people behave and/or act in those different spheres. Here, in this secondary phase of socialization, professional socialization can occur. Individuals entering a profession adapt "externally, in the requirements of the specific career role, and internally, in the subjective self-conceptualization associated with that role" (McGowen & Hart, 1990, p. 118). They bring their primarily socialized selves into a new cultural space and make shifts in what they think and how they act to adapt and accommodate to the new professional cultural expectations and requirements.

Though adult socialization does not rest on the acquisition of basic values, in professional socialization there is a focus on professional values and norms, which makes it a specialized form of adult socialization that does involve some active grappling with those sturdy worldviews (Shuval, 1980). The process of professional socialization happens before, during, and after formal education (Barretti, 2004; Miller, 2010) and can be understood as linked to both "the intended and unintended consequences of an educational program" (Shuval, 1980, p. 6). Over the course of time, the person entering the culture's space shifts her/his focus from those reference groups (e.g., parents, extended family, school, community) that informed her/his worldview as s/he was socialized

as a child, to new and specific reference groups that are related to the profession (e.g., classroom instructors, field instructors, peers). These new reference groups serve as her/his "principal anchoring point for values and behavior with respect to the professional role" (Shuval, p. 6). S/he locates these reference groups and makes choices about how s/he fits as s/he enters into the profession's culture. In order to be professionally socialized there needs to be a professional culture within which to be socialized; what do we know about social work's professional culture?

THE CULTURE OF SOCIAL WORK

A professional culture is typically characterized by an explicit and/or implicit set of values, preferred attitudes, and norms of behavior; its members have clear professional role identities. In order to understand the culture of a profession and the members who are socialized into it, it is essential to consider context. In this instance, it is particularly important to consider elements of social work's history, and to clarify its mission and values.

Social Work's History: Critically Reflective Identity Struggles

The social work profession has a long and storied history of grappling with its self-definition. This history and its related dialogue can be understood as part of social work's path toward professionalization—the process via which an occupation attains professional status (Abbott, 1988), which has direct implications for professional socialization. Abraham Flexner's (1915 see Flexner, 2001) "Is Social Work a Profession?" speech is often considered a pivotal moment in social work's history, and the distinct point in time that marked the beginning of the profession's ongoing and colorful discourse about its own professionalization. Here we will discuss the history from the point of Flexner's 1915 speech forward, while all the while acknowledging that the very fact he was invited to speak on this topic suggests social work began questioning its professionalization earlier than 1915.

As the Assistant Secretary of the General Education Board, Flexner was considered eminently influential in the area of professional education, though more specifically, medical education in the United States (Austin, 1983, p. 361). Because of these credentials, he was invited to speak by the

National Conference of Charities and Corrections and to answer the question "Is social work a profession?" Flexner approached the speech with his background expertise, but also with what he said was a lack of familiarity with "social work, with the literature of social work, and with social workers" (Flexner, 2001, p. 152), and warned at the opening of his speech that he doubted his "competency to undertake the discussion" (p. 152). That he was this uninformed about social work, and was invited to speak anyway because he was well informed about medicine, provides us with a window into the social work professionalization discourse at that time. With his caveat in place, Flexner moved forward and applied his set of six criteria that define a profession. There are some who have criticized his criteria as arbitrary because they were based on a subjective set of ideas rather than on detailed comparative study (Austin, 1983). He grounded his six criteria in the example of medicine as the consummate profession and indicated that professions

(1) Involve essentially intellectual operations with large individual responsibility
(2) Derive their raw material from science and learning
(3) This material they work up to a practical and definitive end
(4) Possess an educationally communicable technique
(5) Tend to self-organization
(6) Are becoming increasingly altruistic in motivation (Flexner, 2001, p. 156).

After applying these criteria to his analysis of social work, Flexner determined that social work was not a profession. To this day, you can almost hear the audience gasp at the conclusion, but in that gasp rested confirmation of doubts and impetus for future directions.

Flexner explicated in some detail his reasons for determining social work's nonprofessional status, but a full discussion of these conclusions is beyond the scope of this chapter (see Flexner, 2001 for complete transcript of speech). It was, however, his assessment that launched social work on its quest to prove its status and define its identity as a profession. Rather than regarding the pivotal Flexner moment as a blow to social work's sense of professional identity, it is crucial to instead regard it as a moment that concretized one of social work's essential defining features. The profession itself, though not without controversy and conflict, dove into the hard work of "self"-reflection and into its intentional, creative self- organization and development.

With this critically self-reflective response to Flexner's speech, a lively dialogue emerged for social work scholars that was then, and in some ways is still now, characterized by a polarized set of views: those who strive to achieve professionalism as originally defined by Flexner and those who believe that very striving to be antithetical to social work's mission (Hugman, 1998). Some have suggested that, in fact, "the quest for status and identity has occupied center stage within social work since its inception" (Gibelman, 1999, p. 298). In 2001, a special issue of the journal *Research on Social Work Practice* was published with Flexner's analysis at its core. The purpose of the special issue was to "examine the perceptions of social workers about the position of social work as a profession at the end of the 20th century against the background of the Flexner statement [made] some 85 years ago" (Austin, 2001, p. 147). The perspectives of the contributing authors unified around the idea that there are significant changes taking place with regard to the organization of human services in our society that will likely continue to be of critical importance to social work. Some suggested that in the face of these changes the profession has stood up well and others suggested that there remain critical issues to be evaluated and challenges to be met with that were as yet not being addressed (Austin, 2001).

Over time, as the profession and its scholars and members worked diligently in these ways to self-identify, while also working to serve the needs of those who seek its services, the agility of social work has been unwavering. What appears to be a never-ending quest for professional identity (Gilbert, 1977) may, in fact, be one of the defining features of social work and its very professional identity—it shifts with the changing societal tides (Gibelman, 1999) and so by its very nature cannot be structured around one static professionalized identity. Social work can be defined as a social movement (Reynolds, 1965) that is a profession (Greenwood, 1957), and as such may have adaptively shifting faces over time. This agility, flexibility, and this orientation to action are very much a part of what defines social work's culture.

As social work positions itself in the present day to meet the ever-growing demands for social services in the face of shifts in demographics, profound economic changes, global demands, etc., it is increasingly clear that it does not have the workforce capacity to meet the predicted level of need (Whitaker, Weismiller, & Clark, 2006). How social workers make their way to the profession and why they choose to remain, or not, as members of the profession is key. In order to build and maintain a professional workforce that is well prepared to meet the profound and growing needs of local and global society, social work must lend resources to understanding its own culture, its educational structure, and its applications in practice. At present, research in the area of professional socialization is limited but growing, and there is a lot of room and opportunity to learn more.

A professional culture is replete with values, attitudes, and norms—all of which rest solidly upon or emanate directly from the profession's unifying mission. These are primarily communicated through the central organizing institution, the collection of accredited schools of social work. With a history characterized by seemingly binary and simultaneous strains of influence, and questions around professionalization, social work has often grappled with whether or not there is one clear mission, and whether or not those educated and practicing as social workers are indeed true to the profession's traditional mission (Specht & Courtney, 1994). Furthering understanding of how practitioners professionally socialize to social work, who plays what roles, how this socialization looks, and what it informs in practice, will enable social work to remain both agile and sturdy in the face of change, and enable its practitioners to be best equipped to meet the critical needs of populations at risk. So, what is the mission of social work?

The Mission and Values of Social Work

In the United States, the National Association of Social Workers (NASW) indicates that the primary mission of social work is "to enhance human wellbeing and help meet the basic human needs of all people, with particular attention to the needs and empowerment of people who are vulnerable, oppressed, and living in poverty" (http://www.naswdc.org/pubs/code/code.asp). NASW denotes social work's core values as "service, social justice, dignity and worth of the person, importance of human relationships, integrity, and competence" (http://www.naswdc.org/pubs/code/code.asp). Given that the world

and our social community is becoming increasingly globalized, and that with its characteristic agility social work's professional culture is becoming increasingly transnational, it is essential to look beyond the borders of the United States to understand whether the profession's mission is consistent worldwide. According to the International Federation of Social Workers (IFSW), social work's mission is

to enable all people to develop their full potential, enrich their lives, and prevent dysfunction. Professional social work is focused on problem solving and change. As such, social workers are change agents in society and in the lives of the individuals, families and communities they serve. Social work is an interrelated system of values, theory and practice (http://ifsw.org/policies/definition-of-social-work/)

IFSW notes that, with social work's origins in humanistic and democratic ideology, the profession's values "are based on respect for the equality, worth, and dignity of all people ... human rights and social justice serve as the motivation and justification for social work action" (http://ifsw.org/policies/definition-of-social-work/). IFSW specifies that "in solidarity with those who are dis-advantaged, the profession strives to alleviate poverty and to liberate vulnerable and oppressed people in order to promote social inclusion" (http://ifsw.org/policies/definition-of-social-work/). When taken together, it appears that both the NASW and IFSW statements reflect consistency—social work's mission and values, according to these statements, emphasize working with those at greatest risk, driven by a commitment to human rights, social justice, and change. When considering professional socialization to social work, it is the essence of this mission and associated values that define the standards.

THE PROFESSIONAL SOCIALIZATION LITERATURE

When exploring the scholarly literature related to the professional socialization of social workers, there is both an expansive variety of places to look and also, within that variety, an absence of a clear and systematic body of knowledge in this area. There are rich bodies of literature related to social work values, attitudes, professional identity, the mission of the profession, and to why people become social workers, to name a few. All of this work is of profound value to the profession and this author would encourage the reader to explore it, but extensive discussion of it here is beyond the scope of this chapter. Aspects of all of this literature are relevant to how we understand professional socialization as a comprehensive process, but because the literature focuses on one of these variables at a time, or is broken up into smaller fragments, taken as a whole what we understand in a systematic way about professional socialization is characterized by more questions than answers (Barretti, 2004; Miller, 2010; Weiss, Gal, & Cnaan, 2004). (For an extensive review of the literature, see Barretti, 2004, and for further review of the literature, see Miller, 2010.)

In the interest of defining at least one common language that would enable the profession to consider questions of professional socialization, this author offered a conceptual framework for the professional socialization of social workers and some research findings designed to provide a systematic foundation for further research in this area (Miller, 2010, 2013). The next section offers an applied synthesis of the conceptual framework (for full discussion of the framework, see Miller, 2010), and highlights elements grounded in the research findings that might be helpful launching points for unraveling the complexity of professional socialization. Aspects of theory suggest that each professional who socializes to social work is going to have a unique set of influences and experiences, although there will also be things common among them, including aspects of the educational structure via which they are formally socialized. Following the applied synthesis of the conceptual framework, a case study is provided to illustrate one hypothetical social worker's (Allison's) experience of professional socialization. The case includes elements of Allison's experience across all three stages of the framework: pre-socialization, formal socialization, and practice after formal socialization. It points to factors that had a potential influence, and also what her professional socialization outcomes look like over time.

WHAT DO YOU NEED TO KNOW ABOUT THE PROFESSIONAL SOCIALIZATION OF SOCIAL WORKERS RIGHT NOW? CONCEPTUAL FRAMEWORK SYNTHESIZED

People are born into an experience and carry with them certain demographic characteristics. Over the years, events in their childhood contribute to how they view the world, how they engage in relationships, how they see themselves, and to choices they make as they develop into adults. As young adults, they may choose or find an educational path that is meant to relate in some way or another to their entry point into the adult work world. Those people who choose to enter the social work profession do so for a whole host of possible reasons and at various points in their developmental trajectories. As they make the choice to become social workers they carry their primary socialization with them (e.g., demographics, childhood experiences), and in some cases other experiences of secondary socialization (e.g., a prior career); with and through this, they begin to make some anticipatory changes/choices as they approach their formal social work education. These changes/choices are informed by what they think are the cultural expectations of social work—how do they imagine social workers act, talk, believe, think, maybe even dress, etc.? They then begin to try on for size some of these conceptions, and carry those, along with aspects of primary socialization, with them into their social work education.

When they get to their formal social work education they enter into a higher education institution, take classes, have instructors, meet their peers, and often become part of a cohort; they function as interns in typically two different field settings, and meet their field instructors, other professionals, clients, constituents, stakeholders, etc. As they engage in this process they acquire knowledge and skills, a relationship with social work values (e.g., commitment to social justice, service), norms (e.g., social workers are change agents; social workers are overworked; social workers do a lot of self-reflection), and attitudes (e.g., social workers need to hold onto their idealism in the face of great challenges; social workers are compassionate and kind; social workers do not judge), while all the while interacting in idiosyncratic settings, with people and within structures that differ. They have agency and they make choices, they are also potentially influenced via structural mechanisms, power and hierarchy, and role models. When they finish their formal social work education and head out into practice they take all of this with them into that particular context of practice. They call themselves something (e.g., social worker). Based on their practice context and what they bring with them, they adapt situationally, and their role identity and overall professional socialization continue to evolve. They may keep calling themselves social workers. Or they may identify as something else, such as a clinical social worker, community organizer; or therapist. As this process unfolds for each individual, these individually diverse experiences collectively and reciprocally feed back into the culture of the profession—this informs change and expectations moving forward.

Case Study: Allison's Professional Socialization to Social Work

Phase I: Pre-socialization. When Allison was a child she spent almost every Saturday morning with her mother and her older brother at the local community food bank packing up bags of food for families in need. Allison remembers seeing the families come into the food bank and observing that there were "kids just like me except they don't have enough food at home, and sometimes they don't even have homes." This always seemed unfair to Allison, and she wanted to do more to make things "more fair." Allison grew up in a three-bedroom apartment in an urban environment with her older brother and her single-mother. Allison's mother worked very hard to take care of Allison and her older brother and had a "good paying job" as an account manager for a large corporation. Allison and her brother went to after-school programming and she remembered how tired her mom always was when they got home. Allison and her brother helped with food preparation and other chores at home. No matter how tired her mother was, however, Allison remembers that she always made time to go to the food bank on Saturdays; she was deeply committed to service. She always talked about how she would have loved to have a different job, a job where she could help people and make the world a better place, instead of one where she managed accounts for businesses that "have more than their fair share." But, she said, she needed to make sure she earned enough money to provide for Allison and her brother and was always grateful to be able to provide in the way that she could. Allison's father was not often present in her life and rarely, if ever, provided any child support. She and her brother got birthday and holiday cards from him, but that was about it.

When Allison was in high school, she joined a student service organization; when she was a junior, she became the chairperson of that group and remained in that position until she graduated.

She also took part in yearbook and theater activities; she loved to be involved, and she loved to be around people. She did well in her classes, but was not sure what she would major in when she got to college, or what she wanted to do for work. She thought about becoming a teacher or maybe a doctor; she wanted to help people in some way, and she wanted a job that was about "doing something," not "just sitting in an office." When she got to college she decided to major in English because she was still not sure "what in the world" she wanted to do for work, and because she liked to read and loved stories about people. When she was in college she continued her civic engagement, serving as a volunteer for a local nonprofit agency focused on providing services to homeless families. This was her first notable exposure to the idea of social work; she realized there was a job you could do that "paid you to help people, to develop relationships with people, to be kind and compassionate, and to take action." After finishing her undergraduate degree, Allison was hired by the agency to do office management work. During her first year employed there, she decided to return to school and get her Master of Social Work (MSW) degree.

Anticipatory socialization. Allison began spending a lot more time talking to her friends about what needed to change in the world, and she also began paying more attention to the way she listened and how she communicated. She asked the social workers at her agency questions about their jobs, about their social work education, about their lives. She was a little worried because it seemed like they were often really tired, and from what she could tell, it did not look like they got paid that much. They also talked a lot about how the agency just did not have enough resources. But, they also seemed to be so committed to their work, and it was "amazing" to see what they could do to "help these families get back on their feet."

Allison applied to four MSW programs in her city, two at public institutions and two at private institutions; she was accepted to all four. She was so excited and could feel her future unfolding, but she did not want to take out student loans. Growing up with her mother she had learned a whole lot about managing money and what it was like to live paycheck to paycheck. She was hoping that she might be able to get a scholarship or an assistantship. Allison was offered a scholarship for her first year by one of the smaller private programs and was guaranteed an assistantship in her second year. She decided to accept this offer, but she did feel a bit uncomfortable. Because tuition to attend this program was high, she was concerned that her classmates would all come from privileged backgrounds, and that she would be out of place. In preparation for school and for her soon-to-start field internship, and with concerns about money, Allison started thinking about how professional social workers act and even dress. She looked through her closet to see if she had anything that would work. She talked to her Mom and her colleagues at the agency and decided to go to Goodwill and buy some professional clothes for her placement. She e-mailed her professors to ask whether they could let her know what she would be reading so she could buy books online, or used books in advance, to save money. She did some reading ahead and was excited to get started—she could understand what she read, but she was ready to be told how to make it all pragmatic, that is, how to actually do it.

Phase II: Formal socialization (academic settings, role models, peers). Allison went to orientation a bit nervous, but also ready and eager to begin this program and her career. She had so many ideas about what she wanted to do when she was done, maybe even start her own community organization! At her orientation she met a whole bunch of other students and realized that she was wrong, they were not all from privileged backgrounds, and even if they were, it did not really matter so much. There were a lot of approachable, friendly, open, "awesome" people. They liked to talk a lot—she thought "it was not like when you walk into a room with a group of people for the first time and everyone's quiet and awkward; there were a few people in this group who were just so outgoing and they did this amazing job getting everyone comfortable." Allison felt as though she had found her home.

She did her first-year field placement at an agency that served a formerly homeless older adult population living in a single-room occupancy residential facility. Her supervisor was a woman who had been in the field for over 20 years—she started as a community organizer and then became a licensed clinical social worker, and she functioned in both these roles in her agency. With her broad perspective, she challenged Allison to do work across and around the practice spectrum; Allison formed a meaningful relationship with her supervisor. She also had some good relationships with the other students

placed there (from another university), as well as with one of the staff social workers, and also formed some strong relationships with clients. She enjoyed her classes but sometimes found it hard to figure out how to connect what she was doing in her classes with what she was doing in the field. Her practice teacher was pretty great, but unlike her supervisor, he sometimes seemed cynical to her. He talked a lot about how under-resourced agencies were and how hard it was to function as a social worker in a healthy way. He had been in the field for 10 years before beginning to teach, and he talked a lot about burnout. Allison respected his perspective, but she wondered if he was blowing things out of proportion.

Allison ended up developing a great relationship with the professor of her Human Behavior in the Social Environment (HBSE) course. She initially found this course to be particularly frustrating; she just wanted to know how to do things already. The readings and class content were always so abstract; she told her HBSE professor that she wished they could get past all of this idea stuff and just learn what they were supposed to do. This professor talked to Allison and the rest of the class about how their energy and motivation were wonderful, and about how ready they were to go out there and change the world. She encouraged them not to let go of that, but to take a step to the side. She also encouraged them to recognize that what they were doing in class was pragmatic. Critical thinking and reflection-in-action were essential skills for social workers, she said. If they were going to go out and apply what they learned, they first had to learn it and learn how to think about it. This professor really challenged Allison to think, challenged her to locate her clients in the theories she learned in class or vice versa. This professor was available to meet with students and always had a supportive ear. Allison felt as though this professor was someone she could call a mentor. She also talked a lot about self-care in class and helped the students figure out what it actually was and how to begin to think about it. Allison's field instructor was also interested in self-care; she helped Allison to think through her own self-care plan, but also allowed Allison to do an assessment of the agency itself and the practices that either supported or inhibited worker well-being. Allison discovered during her placement that she really enjoyed the one-on-one work with clients, as well as some of the program development work. She was not sure where to concentrate her efforts during her second year of the MSW program.

After talking with her supervisor, her HBSE professor, a social worker at her agency, and some of her MSW student friends, Allison chose a clinical track. Wanting what she thought of as a balanced experience, she advocated for a research assistantship with a faculty member whose work focused on community organizing and community-based participatory research. In this second year of her MSW program, Allison was placed in a community mental health clinic that provided clinical services to a diverse population of individuals, families, and groups; clients spanned the age spectrum and were diverse across the board. Allison was excited to begin this placement; she entered this second year "feeling like a social worker." She was not concerned as much about her clothing or her relationships; she knew what she needed to do in that sense. She was concerned about whether or not clients would take her seriously; she wanted so badly to help make their lives better, to fix what was broken for them, but was scared that she would fail. Her placement last year had been an "awesome" learning experience, but this just felt different. She remembered how her HBSE professor talked about the thinking process and how powerful and important it is. She felt as though she had learned some useful skills in her classes last year and definitely from her supervisor. She felt pretty confident that she knew how to "know what she doesn't know," as her HBSE professor had said. She felt she knew how to reflect back, how to engage empathically, how to locate strengths, but she did not know whether she felt confident in her ability to deliver the best possible services. How evidence-based was her agency's practice? What did that even mean???

Allison took a deep breath, and called upon the very close friends she had made in her MSW program last year. The group of five friends met up for dinner before the semester began and talked with one another about their fears, apprehensions, and excitement. They discussed how they were planning to manage time, what their agencies were like, and what they would be doing this coming year. They talked about feeling as though they knew they had learned "stuff" last year, and they knew they were ready for this concentration placement, but what if …? They agreed to remain a support system for one another by getting together at least once a month for this kind of dinner, but for sure more often than

that if they could. They laughed a lot together and felt like they were a wonderful resource for each other. Allison's mom let her know repeatedly how proud she was of her, the work she was doing, and that she had found her way to this meaningful type of employment. Her Mom did express concerns about Allison's postgraduation income potential, but she also said she trusted Allison and knew she would "be okay." Allison's father had been a bit more present in her life over the past year, and each time she talked with him about school or her internship he said something like, "I don't know how you spend all your time around people who are so miserable. Don't you get depressed? Are you going to make any money doing this social work thing? Are you sure you don't want to go to medical school or something instead?" Allison tolerated her father's perspective, but tried her best to educate him about what social work really is, and she also tried her best to explain all the ways in which she knew he was wrong.

Allison had a deeply meaningful experience in her second-year field placement and in her research assistantship, and she very much appreciated some of the focused and applied content of her advanced coursework. She particularly enjoyed hearing about the practice experiences of her course instructors, and she engaged in reflective clinical supervision at her placement, learning a lot about herself and her work in the process. She realized she did not do a very good job making space for herself, given that each night she went home and thought about her clients. She stopped making healthy lunches, stopped exercising, and was feeling pretty stressed out and tired. She loved her job and wanted to stay at the agency after graduation, but she knew she would need to make some changes if this work was going to be sustainable. She loved the research assistantship she had and learned a great deal about advocacy and about the community. Though her internship was clinical, she was able to begin to locate some of the research work she was doing in her agency and in the community. She knew she needed to do some more self-care and she knew she needed to keep self-reflecting, but when she graduated she felt ready to call herself a social worker.

Phase III: Practice after formal socialization. After Allison graduated, she was hired on to work for the community mental health clinic. She was very excited to get under way as a practitioner. Once she got assigned her caseload of

28 regular clients and 10 intakes per week, she remembered back to what her practice instructor in her first year said about being under-resourced and over-worked. "Maybe he was not so cynical after all," she thought. At her agency, Allison worked primarily with other clinicians—some of them called themselves clinical social workers and others called themselves therapists. Her supervisor called herself a therapist so Allison tried that out for a while, but it did not really feel like her. Then she remembered the instructor of her policy analysis class, whom she admired so much. Allison had found her inspiring and always loved to listen to what she said. She remembered that professor (a grant-funded researcher who had written books and was the Director of the MSW program) coming to class on the first day and saying, "Hi, I'm Dr. Jasper and I'm a Social Worker." When Allison thought about this, she decided that no matter where she worked, or what kind of practice she did, she would always identify herself as a social worker. Over the next five years, Allison continued to practice at this agency and she also continued to do collaborative research with her former professor—she loved how it kept her out in the community. Not only was she a social worker inside this office doing work with her clients, but she was a social worker out there knocking on doors, doing community needs assessment, organizing, and working toward social justice.

CONCLUSION

Having just read about Allison, reflect back to the thought experiment that you engaged in at the beginning of this chapter. Look back at your drawing or narrative. What do you see now that you can identify as an aspect of social work's professional culture? Who is that social worker? All of this is the stuff of professional socialization; it is powerful and complex, and informs the how, what, and why of practice. Regardless of where you are in your own professional development, theories of professional socialization would suggest that you are not done. Not only is social work about lifelong learning, it is also about career-long professional socialization. Some things will remain consistent, but others may shift to stay current with and, in turn, affect the shifting culture of social work.

WEBSITES

International Association of Schools of Social Work, www.cdn.ifsw.org

International Council on Social Welfare, www.icsw.org

International Federation of Social Workers, www.ifsw.org

National Association of Social Workers, www.socialworkers.org

Society for Social Work and Research, www.sswr.org

References

Abbott, A. A. (1988). Professional choices: Values at work. DC: NASW Press.

Austin, D. M. (1983). The Flexner myth and the history of social work. *Social Service Review, 57*(3), 357–377.

Austin, D. (2001). Guest editor's foreword. *Research on Social Work Practice, 11*(2), 147–151.

Barretti, M. (2004). What do we know about the professional socialization of our students? *Journal of Social Work Education, 40,* 255–283.

Brim, O. G., Jr., & Wheeler, S. (1966). *Socialization after childhood: Two essays.* New York: John Wiley & Sons.

Flexner, A. (2001). Is social work a profession? *Research on Social Work Practice, 11*(2), 152–165.

Gibelman, M. (1999). The search for identity: Defining social work—past, present, future. *Social Work, 44*(4), 298–310.

Gilbert, N. (1977). The search for professional identity. *Social Work, 22,* 401–406.

Greenwood, E. (1957). Attributes of a profession. *Social Work, 2*(3), 45–55.

Hugman, R. (1998). Social work and de-professionalization. In P. Abbott & L. Meerabeau (Eds.). *The sociology of the caring professions* (pp. 178–199). London: UCL.

Jarvis, P. (1983). *Professional education.* London: Croom Helm.

McGowen, K. R., & Hart, L. E. (1990). Still different after all these years: Gender differences in professional identity formation. *Professional Psychology: Research and Practice, 21*(2), 118–123.

Miller, S. E. (2010). A conceptual framework for the professional socialization of social workers. *Journal of Human Behavior in the Social Environment, 20,* 924–938.

Miller, S. E. (2013). Professional socialization: A bridge between the explicit and implicit curricula. *Journal of Social Work Education, 49,* 368–386.

Reynolds, B. C. (1965). *Learning and teaching in the practice of social work*. New York: Russell & Russell.

Shuval, J. T. (1980). *Entering medicine: The dynamics of transition. A seven year study of medical education in Israel*. Oxford, England: Pergamon.

Specht, H., & Courtney, M. E. (1994). *Unfaithful angels: How social work has abandoned its mission*. New York: The Free Press.

Weiss, I., Gal, J., & Cnaan, R. A. (2004). Social work education as professional socialization: A study of the impact of social work education upon students' professional preferences, *Journal of Social Service Research, 31*, 13–31.

Whitaker, T., Weismiller, T., & Clark, E. (2006). *Assuring the sufficiency of a frontline workforce: A national study of licensed social workers. Executive summary*. Washington, DC: National Association of Social Workers.

PART II

Roles, Functions, and Fields of Social Work Practice

3 Evidence-based Social Work Practice with Children and Adolescents

Alison Salloum & Lisa Rapp-McCall

ASSESSMENT OF CHILDREN AND ADOLESCENTS

Evidence-based Assessment

Building on the growing field of evidence-based practices (EBP), the use of evidence to guide the assessment process is currently evolving. Evidence-based assessment incorporates the use of evidence and theory to select the aspects, conditions, or domains to be assessed; uses evidence-based assessment tools; and uses the best methods for the assessment processes. An evidence-based assessment can help guide the practitioner and client to choose the best available evidence-based intervention for the assessed condition and to monitor progress throughout the intervention (Hunsley & Mash, 2007).

Accessible and practical evidence-based assessment tools and methods are becoming available for practitioners and clients. These brief and easy-to-use tools, commonly referred to as rapid assessment instruments, are available to assess a child's or family's general functioning and competence relative to specific conditions. Assessment tools and processes are being developed to address situations in various settings and contexts. For example, Counts and associates (2010) have developed and tested an easy to administer self-report measure of multiple family-level protective factors against abuse and neglect. Similarly, Edelson et al. (2007) are developing a 46-item tool to assess children's exposure to domestic violence. These types of evidence-based assessment tools and methods are readily available through various websites and books on clinical measures (e.g., Corcoran & Fischer, 2013). In addition, the *Diagnostic and Statistical Manual of Mental Disorders* (American Psychiatric Association (APA), 2014) includes parent and child and adolescent measures that assess for 12 psychiatric domains and functions. These APA measures can also be used to track clinical progress (the assessment tools for children and adolescents may also be found online at http://www.psychiatry.org/practice/dsm/dsm5/online-assessment-measures#Level1

Child-focused Developmental, Ecological, and Cultural Assessment

An evidence-based assessment with children, adolescents, and their families must include a multidimensional assessment that considers development, ecological context, and cultural influences. These three areas of assessment may be considered the foundation for child-focused assessments. With children, evidence-based assessment often includes assessing caregivers, including multiple informants (such as day care providers or teachers) and sources of data (i.e., observation, school records); understanding the variations and effects of development and culture on the situation; and including a broad-based assessment of competencies and challenges (Achenbach, 2007).

Generally, the younger the child, the more involved the parent or caregiver and significant other adults in the child's daily life will be in the assessment process. With older children, especially adolescents, it is important to engage the youth directly in the assessment process. This may be accomplished by using evidence-based self-report assessment instruments with the child and adolescent. When practitioners conduct the assessment process in a collaborative fashion with the child, the assessment tool can be used to provide education and normalization and elicit specific goals for treatment, as well as to highlight the child's strengths and treatment progress.

Developmental assessments may be used to select the best available treatments for children that take into account the child's developmental status (including emotional, cognitive, biological, social, and behavioral milestones, assets, and delays). As research on EBP continues, we will learn more about which treatments work best with which populations. More specifically, we will learn how development, neurobiology, gender, culture, and context affect treatment outcomes. Developmentally specific assessment can then be used to suggest developmentally specific treatments to the child and parent or caretaker. For example, recent advances have been made in assessment processes for the mental health needs of infants, toddlers, and young children. With this knowledge, specific prevention and treatment strategies grounded in empirical research for this young population are increasing (for more information about early childhood assessment see the Zero to Three website listed at the end of this chapter). Similar advances are being made for middle childhood, early adolescence, adolescence, and late adolescence.

The child-in-environment perspective must be considered during the assessment processes. The influence of the relational processes within the child's ecological context may have a significant impact on the child's functioning and growth. Ecological relational processes may include the child's family; school environment and peers; neighborhood and community; recreational opportunities; religious or spiritual membership or rituals; national and international situations; and systems such as foster care, child welfare, and juvenile justice. Though a beginning point for the practitioner is to assess the strengths within the child and child's family (see Simmons & Lehmann, 2013 for strengths-based assessment measures) a more multidimensional assessment is optimal. This encompasses the child's and family's protective or resilience factors within the cultural context of the child and family (e.g., Cardoso & Thompson, 2010; Jones, Hopson, & Gomes, 2012), and examines the salience of specific and cumulative risk factors, including social conditions such as poverty, discrimination, and limited opportunity. A multidimensional assessment can assist the practitioner, child, and family

in choosing the most appropriate multimodal and multicontextual interventions.

In addition to developmental and ecological assessment processes, evidence-based assessment must be culturally sensitive. Specific assessment tools are being tested with various cultural groups to establish within group norms. In addition to the use of specific culturally relevant assessment tools, an understanding of the cultural context of the child may lead the practitioner and client to decide on a more culturally congruent evidence-based treatment. A cultural assessment may help the practitioner understand the child and family better and identify cultural resources to include in treatment. Discussing culturally competent practice is beyond the scope of this chapter, and practitioners are encouraged to read the National Association of Social Workers' *NASW Standards for Indicators for Cultural Competence in Social Work Practice* that was developed in 2007 (available on the NASW website). Assessments may include areas such as communication patterns, family structure, accepted roles of children, intergenerational conflicts, assimilation of family members, adherence to traditions, spiritual beliefs, values and norms, acceptance of expression of emotions and behaviors, developmental expectations, language preference and proficiency, historical experiences, views of mental health, and help-seeking behaviors.

Client-centered Process

Evidence-based practitioners value the child and family as a collaborative partner in the assessment process and treatment. Indeed, parents' and children's beliefs, values, and preferences are key factors in successfully implementing EBP. Program developers and practitioners can ensure that the child, youth, and family members play an active role in the process of assessment, goal planning, treatment choices, and evaluation. During the assessment process, practitioners should assess the client's (child and participating family members) beliefs about credibility (i.e., believable and logical) and effectiveness of the agreed-upon intervention or treatment prior to implementation. Beliefs about credibility of treatment and expectations of improvements may be associated with motivation for and adherence to treatment, which are important factors for effective outcomes (Nock, Ferriter, & Holmberg, 2007).

A collaborative practitioner–client assessment process begins with the initial meeting and continues throughout the intervention to monitor progress and assess outcome and satisfaction. Eliciting feedback from children and families regarding treatment satisfaction and the service delivery process can be empowering for clients. Valuing systematic approaches to hearing from clients about their experiences can lead to improved treatments and delivery of care (Baker, 2007). A collaborative evidence-based assessment may lead to more objective accountability of satisfaction, effectiveness, and improved services for children and families.

Considerations for Child-focused Evidence-based Assessment

- Use evidence-based assessment tools and processes to guide client and practitioner in choosing EBP.
- Conduct a multidimensional assessment that includes sources of data, including multiple informants (i.e., parents, caretakers, teachers, and other important child–adult relationships), multiple settings (i.e., home, school, peers), and multiple methods (i.e., rapid assessment instruments, interviews, observations).
- Consider using a broad assessment tool followed by a selected specific condition assessment tool.
- Assess the child's developmental status, including emotional, cognitive, biological, social, and behavioral milestones, assets, and delays and take into account the developmental stage of the child to match appropriate intervention.
- Consider the entire ecological context of child and family.
- Use standardized assessment tools and processes to assess protective factors, competencies, and strengths.
- Use standardized assessment tools or processes to assess risks and emotional, behavioral, and social difficulties.
- Understand the cultural influences on the child, family, and situation and conduct a culturally competent assessment.
- Assess throughout practice to evaluate progress, outcomes, and client satisfaction.
- Practice from a child–family-centered collaborative perspective.
- Assess the child and family's beliefs, values, preferences, and expectations about evidence-based treatment.

Promotion and Prevention

Current models to guide practices serving children and youth suggest providing promotion programs followed by prevention, treatment, and maintenance services (Frey & Alvarez, 2011; National Center for Mental Health Promotion and Youth Violence Prevention, 2011). Promotion programs focus on improving the overall emotional and social well-being of the child such that self-esteem, coping, social integration, and healthy development are promoted. Some overlap exists between promotion and prevention because both types of efforts try to intervene before the onset of problems. Previously, youth began treatment when they had significantly serious disorders or symptoms that significantly impacted their functioning at home, at school, or in the community. However, research studies have supported what practitioners have observed all along—starting treatment earlier, at the first sign or symptom of difficulty, drastically improves the outcome. This approach is also far more cost-effective than typical interventions, which wait too long and then require more intensive intervention. Thus, promotion and prevention programs have been used to promote well-being, and when needed, intervening early can prevent the disorder completely or lessen its progression. There are many empirically based prevention interventions that are used when youth present no risk factors (universal), exhibit some risk factors (selective), and/or when they evince some symptoms of the problem (indicated). These prevention interventions are now more readily available and used more frequently (e.g., Fagan & Catalano, 2013); however, there is still much work to be done in reframing our thinking to integrate preventive interventions and programs into our current systems. For example, programs need to be sufficiently funded for delivering promotion programs and preventive interventions, not just brief interventions after the problems have grown too serious to change.

Treatment and Maintenance

Treatment and maintenance that involves long-term care to minimize relapse and reoccurrence must be available to children and youth needing this level of care. Many advances have occurred in the development of EBP for children and adolescents. Currently, many social problems and disorders of childhood and adolescence have treatments that are evidence supported (Kendall & Beidas, 2007). Emerging evidence suggests that children and youth who receive EBP are more likely to improve than when non-evidence based practices are provided (e.g., Kolko, Herschell, Costello, & Kolko, 2009). The contemporary controversy lies not in *whether* to utilize these practices but *how* to consistently facilitate the implementation of these practices with fidelity in real-world community settings.

There are many barriers to implementing EBP in agencies, including limited practitioner time, training and ongoing supervision, practitioner attitudes toward EBP, and lack of adequate resources. Current implementation science, however, has focused on contributing factors to implementing and sustaining EBP in real world settings. Some factors contributing to the successful implementation of EBP include adequate funding and support for implementation, training and ongoing supervision and consultation, treatment fidelity monitoring, and "buy-in" from agency leaders and practitioners (Swain, Whitley, McHugo, & Drake, 2010). Additionally, while earlier concerns included treatment manuals that were too rigid and difficult to apply in real world settings, current manual and treatment protocols are more flexible and are transportable to community-based settings. Another barrier to implementing EBP has been that many of these treatments do not address comorbid or complex client problems that are often presented by children, youth, and families in community settings. Newer approaches to treatment are combining core components of various EBP to address multiple issues and conditions.

Scholars are not only calling for social workers to provide up-to-date EBP that match the child's and family's needs, but also to become competent in empirically supported common elements and common factors. Common elements involve using a modular approach in which specific methods common to many EBP, such as psychoeducation, exposure, and rewards, are provided based on the results of an evidence-based assessment. Common factors consist of those ingredients critical to positive outcomes, such as a strong therapeutic alliance, client engagement, motivation, and hope. The implementation of common factors and common elements requires

systematically assessing and tracking progress (Barth et al., 2012).

Multimodal and Multicontextual Interventions

Research suggests that treatments for youth be multimodal and multicontextual, meaning that interventions should be delivered in a variety of formats for learning and change to occur, and that interventions should occur in multiple environments or milieu of the youth. In other words, individual treatment for children alone, without family, school, or community intervention is rarely effective, especially for youth who are having difficulty functioning in various contexts. Likewise, one type of intervention alone, for instance, life skills, may only have a small-to-medium effect as opposed to a multimodal approach that may result in a large effect. Take the following example: a practitioner working with a child experiencing severe difficulty with controlling anger may talk about angry outbursts and their consequences with the child, teach the child anger-control skills, role-play/practice the skills, and read a story about a character who learns to control her anger. In addition, the practitioner may use functional family therapy with the child's family to intervene with family difficulties, assist the teacher in developing a behavior modification system for the child at school, and work with the child's soccer coach to help apply the newly learned anger-control skills to replace angry outbursts during soccer practice. The comprehensive nature of these interventions is more likely to produce change than one modality in one context.

Considerations for Child-focused Evidence-based Treatment

- Intervene early with empirically supported and evidence-based prevention interventions.
- Stay abreast of EBP and use with appropriate clients.
- When no known EBP exists for disorders or problems, use common elements and factors that have been associated with treating similar conditions and monitor progress carefully.
- Intervene in multiple contexts (micro, mezzo, and macro).
- Intervene with multiple approaches, when indicated.

FUTURE DIRECTION FOR
ASSESSMENT AND INTERVENTION

Understanding the complexities and uniqueness of the child or adolescent by empathetic face-to-face interaction has always been the starting point for the practitioner. Although this will not change, advances in assessment tools and methods will help the practitioner obtain a broader contextual understanding as well as more rapidly ascertain targeted goals. Advances in evidence-based assessment will lead to more research on the influence of development, context, and culture on treatment outcomes and a broader understanding of resilience in childhood. These assessment tools and methods will become standard practices and will be integrated within systems of care for children.

Collaboration with the client will remain central to evidence-based assessment and evidence-based treatment. Once the client and practitioner have collaboratively decided on which evidence-based treatment seems most appropriate, preparation for treatment may be warranted. Treatment readiness or pretreatment sessions help prepare clients for the treatment when it is delivered. The sessions are offered prior to the formal treatment and work to engage and motivate the client. The idea began with mandated adults and has found its way into the child and adolescent arena. Treatment readiness sessions seem to be more common with difficult or mandated young clients (adolescent offenders and substance abusers) but may be promising for use with other client populations. They may also show promise for reducing resistance with other interventions and with brief treatments where change is expected to occur quickly. In addition, practitioners may consider using pretreatment sessions prior to family or group treatments.

Developing and implementing empirically supported and evidence-based social work practices for children requires integration and collaboration: the integration of evidence-based assessment and promotion, prevention, and treatment; the integration of social work research and practice; and collaboration with all concerned parties, including children and families, community residents and leaders, practitioners, researchers, child advocates, child systems (i.e., education, child welfare, juvenile justice), and policy makers. Due to the complex problems and challenges that children and youth face today, we must advance our knowledge of the programs or methods that work best for particular children. We must also determine the most effective the settings, intensity of delivery, and timing of delivery. Barriers to implementation of child-focused evidence-based assessment and practices can be overcome by such tools as web-based clearinghouses, webinars, videoconferencing to engage in collaborative learning and consultation, and podcasts and apps on implementation of EBP. Although technology and new approaches may assist with dissemination and implementation of evidence-based assessment and EBP, collaboration with all stakeholders—children, adolescents, parents, community leaders, practitioners, researchers, and policy makers—is needed to advance practices to improve the well-being of children, adolescents, and their families.

WEBSITES

American Psychiatric Association, Online Assessment Measures. http://www.psychiatry.org/practice/dsm/dsm5/online-assessment-measures
Blueprints for Violence Prevention. http://www.colorado.edu/cspv/blueprints.
Campbell Collaboration. http://www.campbell-collaboration.org
National Center for Childhood Traumatic Stress Network. http://www.nccts.org. See measures review database for assessment tools. http://www.nctsn.org/resources/online-research/measures-review
National Institutes of Health. http://www.nih.gov
North Carolina Evidence-Based Practice Center (NCEBPC). http://www.ncebpcenter.org.
Substance Abuse and Mental Health Services Administration; see National Registry of Evidence-based Programs and Practices. http://www.nrepp.samhsa.gov/
The California Evidence-Based Clearinghouse for Child Welfare. http://www.cebc4cw.org/
Zero to Three. http://www.zerotothree.org/

References

American Psychiatric Association. (2014). *Diagnostic and statistical manual of mental disorders: DSM-V.* Washington, DC: American Psychiatric Press.

Achenbach, T. M. (2007). In P.S. Jensen, P. Knapp, & D.A. Mrazek, Toward a new diagnostic system for child psychopathology: Moving beyond the DSM. *Journal of Child and Family Studies, 16*, 589–591.

Baker, A. J. L. (2007). Client feedback in child welfare programs: Current trends and future directions. *Children and Youth Services Review, 29*, 1189–1200.

Barth, R. P., Lee, B. R., Lindsey, M. A., Collins, K. S., Strieder, F., Chorpita, B. F., Kimberly D., ... Sparks, J. A. (2012). Evidence-based practice at a crossroads: The timely emergence of common elements and common factors. *Research on Social Work Practice, 22*(1), 108–119. doi: 10.1177/1049731511408440

Cardoso, J. B., & Thompson, S. J. (2010). Revising risk and resilience: Common themes of resilience among Latino immigrant families: A systematic review of the literature. *Families in Society: The Journal of Contemporary Social Services, 91*, 257–265. doi: 10.1606/1044-3894.4003

Corcoran, K., & Fischer, J. (2013). *Measures for clinical practice and research.* Volume 1: *Couples, families, and children.* 5th ed. New York, NY: Oxford University Press.

Counts, J. M., Buffington, E. S., Chang-Rios, K., Rasmussen, H. N., & Preacher, K. J. (2010). The development and validation of the protective factors survey: A self-report measure of protective factors against child maltreatment. *Child Abuse & Neglect, 34*, 762–772.

Edelson, J. L., Ellerton, A. L., Seagren, E. A., Kichberg, S. L., Schmidt, S. O., & Ambrose, A. T. (2007). Assessing child exposure to adult domestic violence. *Children & Youth Services Review, 29*(7), 961–971.

Fagan, A. A., & Catalano, R. F. (2013). What works in youth violence prevention: A review of the literature. *Research on Social Work Practice, 23*(2), 141–156. doi: 10.1177/1049731512465899

Frey, A. J., & Alvarez, M. E. (2011). Social work practitioners and researchers realize the promise. *Children and Schools, 33*, 131–134.

Hunsley, J., & Mash, E. J. (2007). Evidence-based assessment. *Annual Review of Clinical Psychology, 3*, 29–51.

Jones, L. V., Hopson, L. M., & Gomes, A. M. (2012). Intervening with African-Americans: Culturally specific practice considerations. *Journal of Ethnic & Cultural Diversity in Social Work, 21*, 37–54. doi: 10.1080/15313204.2012.647389

Kolko, D. J., Herschell, A. D., Costello, A. H., & Kolko, R. P. (2009). Child welfare recommendations to improve mental health services for children who have experienced abuse and neglect: A national perspective. *Administration, Policy, and Mental Health, 36*, 50–62. doi: 10.1007/s10488-008-0202-y

Kendall, P. C., & Beidas, R. S. (2007). Smoothing the trail for dissemination of evidence-based practices for youth: Flexibility within fidelity. *Professional Psychology: Research and Practice, 38*(1), 13–20.

Nock, M. K., Ferriter, C., & Holmberg, E. (2007). Parent's beliefs about treatment credibility and effectiveness: Assessment and relation to subsequent treatment participation. *Journal of Child and Family Studies, 16*, 27–38.

National Center for Mental Health Promotion and Youth Violence Prevention. (2011). *Realizing the promise of the whole-school approach to children's mental health: A practical guide for school.* Boston, MA: Education Development Center, Inc.

Simmons, C. A., & Lehmann, P. (2013). Tools for strengths-based assessment and evaluation. New York, NY: Springer Publishing Co.

Swain, K., Whitley, R., McHugo, G. J., & Drake, R. E. (2010). The sustainability of evidence- based practices in routine mental health agencies. *Community Mental Health Journal, 46*, 119–129. doi: 10.1007/s10597-009-9202-y

Overview of Alcohol and Drug Dependence

Identification, Assessment, and Treatment

4

Kenneth R. Yeager

Alcohol and drug abuse is ubiquitous; it is associated with 2.5 million deaths annually, representative of 4% of all deaths worldwide annually. The National Council on Alcoholism and Drug Dependence (NCADD) reports "The harmful use of alcohol (defined as excessive use to the point that it causes damage to health) has many implications on public health as demonstrated in the following key findings:

- Harmful use of alcohol results in the death of 2.5 million people annually, causes illness and injury to millions more, and increasingly affects younger generations and drinkers in developing countries.
- Nearly 4% of all deaths are related to alcohol. Most deaths caused by alcohol result from injuries, cancer, cardiovascular disease, and cirrhosis of the liver.
- Among males, 6.2% of deaths are related to alcohol, compared with 1.1% of deaths among females.
- Among young people aged 15–29 years, 320,000 die annually from alcohol-related causes, resulting in 9% of all deaths in that age group.
- Almost 50% of men and two thirds of women do not consume alcohol (NCADD, 2013).

The burden of drug and alcohol dependence in the United States is estimated to be $510 billion, up from $184.6 billion per year in 2005. The break-out of the impact on children, adults, and communities in the United States is as follows (Substance Abuse and Mental Health Services Administration (SAMHSA), 2011; Harwood, 2000; Harwood & Bouchery, 2001):

- Alcohol accounts for $191.6 billion (37.5%) of the $510.8 billion.
- Tobacco is responsible for $191.6 billion (32.9%) and drug abuse for $151.4 billion (29.6%).

The majority of the costs associated with substance abuse in the United States can be related to treatment and prevention of substance abuse, medical care, police, fire department, legal and court-related expenses, property damages, theft, crime, motor vehicle crashes, and fires involving alcohol and drug abuse (Harwood & Bouchery, 2001).

Additionally, productivity costs are closely linked to the cost to society. For example: Smoking contributed to 440,000 deaths in 1999. Alcohol abuse accounted for 42,000 (Harwood, 2000) to 76,000 deaths (Midanik et al., 2004), while drug abuse accounted for an additional 23,000 deaths (Harwood & Bouchery, 2001). This loss in productivity is calculated as estimates of individual lost work time, including impairment, sickness, unemployment, incarceration, disability, and the like.

It is important to note that a significant number of persons with substance use disorders have concurrent mental health disorders. In 2011, there were an estimated 45.6 million adults age 18 years or older in the United States with any mental illness in the past year. This represents 19.6% of all adults in this country. Of this population, SAMSHA (2012) estimates 8 million adults met the criteria for a substance use disorder (i.e., illicit drug or alcohol dependence or abuse.) Additionally, among the 11.5 million adults with severe mental illness in the past year, 22.6% experienced concurrent substance dependence or abuse. This is significantly higher than the population without a mental illness, which demonstrated only a 5.8% prevalence of substance dependence or abuse, representing 10.9 million adults (SAMHSA, 2012).

When considering risk factors among persons with concurrent mental health and substance abuse, it is important to note the increased risk of self-harm among this population. SAMSHA (2012) reports: Adults aged 18 years or older with a past-year substance use disorder were more likely than those without substance use disorders to have had serious thoughts of suicide within the past year (11.2% vs. 3.0%). Those with a substance use disorder were at greater risk for suicidal ideation, and more likely to make plans for suicide, compared with adults without dependence or abuse (3.6% vs. 0.8%). They also were more likely to attempt suicide when compared with the adult population without dependence or abuse (1.9% vs. 0.4%) (SAMSHA, 2012).

Considerable gaps in the continuum of care exist when considering the need for integrated mental health and substance dependence treatment for persons with concurrent mental illness and substance use disorders. In the population of the 2.6 million adults aged 18 years or older in 2011 with both severe mental illness and substance dependence or abuse in the past year, 65.6% received substance use treatment at a specialty facility or mental health care in that time period. Included in the 65.6% are 12.4% who received both mental health care and specialty substance use treatment, 49.5% who received mental health care only, and 3.6% who received specialty substance use treatment only. Among adults who had a past year substance use disorder, those who also had past year Serious Mentally Ill (SMI) were more likely to have received mental health care or specialty substance use treatment (65.6%), followed by those who had moderate mental illness (41.0%), then by those with low (mild) mental illness (29.7%), then by those who had no mental illness in the past year (15.1%). It is important to recognize that only 12.4% of those with concurrent mental illness and substance use disorders received treatment concurrently for both disorders. This is a fact that continues to contribute to the "revolving door" aspect of persons seeking care for their disorders. Without attention paid to both

diagnoses, the effectiveness of a single approach for mental health or substance abuse is limited in levels or degree of effectiveness.

ADDICTION TREATMENT WITHIN THE HEALTH CARE ENVIRONMENT

Alcohol can be a significant contributing factor to medical conditions such as hepatitis, hypertension, tuberculosis, pneumonia, pancreatitis, and cardiomyopathy (Project CHOICES, 2003). One half of all cases of cirrhosis in the United States are due to alcohol abuse. Excess alcohol consumption also contributes to cancers of the mouth, esophagus, pharynx, larynx, and breast (Emmen, Schippers, Wollersheim, & Bleijenberg, 2005). Alcohol abuse inflicts central nervous system disease (including dementia and stroke) and peripheral nervous system disease (neuropathy and myopathy).

Excessive alcohol consumption is the third leading preventable cause of death in the United States and was estimated to be responsible for approximately 80,000 deaths annually between 2001 and 2005 (Ballesteros, Duffy et al., 2004). This appears to be related in large part to an increased risk of accidental deaths. However, nearly 17,000 traffic fatalities in the United States in 2000 were related to alcohol use, that is, 40% of all traffic deaths. It is also noteworthy that a 3.5 times greater risk for drowning exists within age adjusted populations (Bertholet, Daeppen Wietlisbach et al., 2005).

Growing evidence in the form of systematic reviews and meta-analyses confirms the efficacy of brief intervention for unhealthy alcohol use in primary care patients identified by screening. As an example, a meta-analysis of eight trials of 2,784 patients found that brief intervention decreased the proportion of patients drinking risky amounts one year later when compared to patients who did not receive brief intervention (57% vs. 69%; absolute risk reduction of 12%) (Beich, Thorsen, & Rollnick, 2003). A meta-analysis of nine trials reported consumption outcomes for intention-to-treat participants at 6 or 12 months (Bertholet, Daeppen, & Wietlisbach, 2005). Receiving brief intervention decreased patients' drinking by an additional three standard drinks per week compared with patients not receiving brief intervention.

Studies have found brief intervention in at-risk substance abusing populations functions to reduce health care utilization, and results in cost savings (Solberg, Maciosek, & Edwards, 2008). In one trial, 774 patients with unhealthy alcohol use identified by screening for risky drinking amounts were randomized to brief intervention or usual care in 17 primary care practices with a total of 64 physicians (Fleming, Mundt, French et al., 2002). The intervention, consisting of two 10- to 15-minute physician discussions and a follow-up phone call, decreased consumption more than usual care, an effect that persisted at 36 months. Hospital use was lower over the three-year period in patients assigned to the intervention compared with patients receiving usual care (420 vs. 663 days). The intervention was estimated to have saved $546 per patient in medical costs and $7,780 per patient in total costs (primarily due to a reduction in motor vehicle crashes).

What is becoming clear is the need to demonstrate multiple levels of competence in brief intervention across populations within a variety of settings to determine potential risk of active substance abuse and dependence, in order to identify, assess, and treat substance use disorders more effectively (Yeager et al., 2013). There exist growing bodies of evidence to suggest that multidisciplinary approaches across a variety of settings (e.g., substance abuse, mental health, and health care settings), focusing on identification, brief intervention, and referral to the most appropriate level of care are both effective and efficient. The goals of a brief intervention for those demonstrating nondependent behaviors should focus on reduction of use, harm reduction, or abstinence, as well as changes in risk behaviors (e.g., avoiding bars and events centered around drinking or drug use). In the population where use has been determined to be detrimental and unhealthy, abstinence is generally the best option. Those defined as being appropriate for abstinence-based intervention include any of the following:

- A diagnosis of dependence
- Failed prior attempts to moderate/control use
- A physical or mental health condition secondary to substance use
- Taking medications that contraindicates any alcohol use
- Pregnant or planning to conceive
- Prior consequences or a family history that suggest remaining abstinent may be indicated.

DIAGNOSIS OF ALCOHOL AND DRUG DEPENDENCE

Substance dependence is defined by the *DSM-IV-TR* as a maladaptive pattern of alcohol and/or drug use, leading to clinically significant impairment or distress, as manifested by three or more of the following seven criteria, occurring at any time in the same 12-month period, characterized by:

1. Tolerance, as defined:
2. Withdrawal, as defined:
3. The substance is taken in larger amounts or over a longer period than was intended.
4. There is a persistent desire or there are unsuccessful efforts to cut down or control use.
5. A great deal of time is spent in activities necessary to obtain, use, or recover from effects of the substance abused.
6. Important social, occupational, or recreational activities are given up or reduced because of substance use.
7. Substance use is continued despite knowledge of having a persistent or recurrent physical or psychological problem that is likely to have been caused or exacerbated by said substance use.

In the DSM-5, the DSM-IV criteria for substance abuse and substance dependence have been combined into single substance use disorders specific to each substance of abuse within a new "addictions and related disorders" category. Each substance use disorder has been divided into mild, moderate, and severe subtypes. Whereas DSM-IV substance abuse diagnostic criteria required only one symptom, the DSM-5 now requires at least two. The DSM-5 revisions are intended to (1) strengthen the reliability of substance use diagnoses by increasing the number of required symptoms and (2) clarify the definition of "dependence," which is often misinterpreted as implying addiction and has at its core compulsive drug-seeking behaviors. For example, features of physical dependence, such as tolerance and withdrawal, can be normal and expected responses to prescribed medications that affect the central nervous system and that need to be differentiated from addiction. There is a converse example, that is, although marijuana abuse can be functionally very impairing, physical dependence is not part of the clinical picture, even in severe cases. In this sense, the new DSM-5 criteria are specifically designed to recognize and account for mental and behavioral aspects of substance use disorders (APA, 2013).

Although the new criteria require an increased number of symptoms to qualify for a substance-related diagnosis, critics of the revision argue that chances of meeting the new criteria are now much greater. They further worry that many individuals who qualify for a substance use disorder diagnosis by the new criteria may have only minor symptoms, making it more difficult for those with more severe symptoms and distress to access already scarce treatment.

What Is Substance Dependence?

Dependence is a chronic *progressive and potentially fatal disease*, with genetic, psychosocial, and environmental factors influencing its development and manifestations. It is characterized by continuous or periodic impaired control over drinking, preoccupation with the drug or alcohol and use of drugs or alcohol despite adverse consequences, and distortions in thinking, most notably denial.

What Does "Progressive and Fatal" Mean?

"Progressive and fatal" means that the disease persists over time and physical, emotional, and social changes are often cumulative and may progress as drinking continues. Substance dependence causes premature death through overdose; organic complications involving the brain, liver, heart, and many other organs; and contributing to suicide, homicide, motor vehicle crashes, and other traumatic events.

What Does "Primary" Mean?

"Primary" refers to the nature of substance dependence as a disease entity in addition to and separate from other pathophysiologic states that may be associated with it. The term suggests that substance dependence is not a symptom of an underlying disease state.

What Does "Disease" Mean?

A disease is an involuntary disability. It represents the sum of the abnormal phenomena displayed by a group of individuals. These phenomena are associated with a specified common set of characteristics by which these individuals differ from the norm and which places them at a disadvantage.

OVERVIEW OF TREATMENT APPROACHES

Treatment of alcohol and drug dependence includes identification of alcohol and drug abuse and dependence, initiating treatment plans, educating the individual and family about the abuse and dependence, conducting clinically based interventions within group settings, and individual approaches. The interventions include referral to Alcoholics Anonymous, Narcotics Anonymous, or Cocaine Anonymous, employee assistance programs, and couple and family counseling. Early intervention is important because it serves to minimize consequences experienced by the individual abusing illicit substances. Social consequences include legal, marital, employment, and financial problems. Additionally, early intervention minimizes the potential for long-term health and mental health consequences. Later intervention includes referral to detoxification services, health and mental health services, legal intervention, and other services necessary to stabilize the individual (Holder & Blose, 1992; Yeager & Gregoire, 2005).

ASSESSING ALCOHOL AND DRUG DEPENDENCE

There are a variety of current best practices for the diagnosis and management of alcohol and drug addiction. The following case study examines the various ways that alcohol and drug addiction can impact an individual. This case represents various symptoms of dependence as well as various treatment needs.

Working with alcohol- and drug-dependent individuals is challenging and rewarding work that requires both skill and tact. Although resistance and active defense structures are hallmarks of alcohol dependence, resistance is less than one might expect. Williams et al. (2006) reported that within a sample of 6,400 patients, a full 75% demonstrated at least minimal levels of willingness to change. When placed within a stages-of-change model, approximately 24% presented in the contemplative stage of change and 51% demonstrated characteristics of taking action to change drinking patterns.

Social workers serve a unique role in assisting persons with alcohol abuse and dependence issues. Frequently, the task of conducting a complete and thorough assessment of the dependent individual falls to the social worker. Components of a thorough alcohol assessment include, but are not limited to, the following.

Establish the Individual's Perception of the Problem

Begin with the individual's perception of his or her drinking history and the exact nature of the problem. Understanding the individual's perception informs the social worker of where he or she will begin in the treatment process. A willingness to listen openly to the individual's perception of need will also provide an opportunity to begin to gently probe into sensitive areas in a manner that is less intrusive, thus opening channels of communication.

Application of a Disease Frame of Reference

Persons seeking assistance with their drinking frequently feel trapped, guilty, helpless, or hostile. Conducting the initial interview from a disease or illness frame of reference, based in nonjudgmental language, minimizes defensiveness while establishing a working relationship. In many cases, individuals are well aware of the need to become active participants in their health care. Just as persons with diabetes or hypertension are responsible for altering their lifestyle to treat their illness, alcohol-dependent persons should be encouraged to assume a greater level of self-responsibility for their treatment.

Construct a Comprehensive Family History

Alcohol and drug dependence has long been determined to have a strong genetic link, therefore, building a family history will begin to normalize the individual's perception of how he or she came to acquire this illness. A good family history should include examination of maternal and paternal drinking patterns and potential alcohol dependence. Examination of lifestyle, community involvement, reputation, marital, legal, employment, spiritual, and educational history will provide important insight into family responses to and perceptions of alcohol and drug dependence.

Establish a Timeline of Alcohol and Drug Use and Amounts Consumed

As the family history unfolds, it provides a natural segue into the individual's experience with alcohol and drug use. Again using a nonjudgmental, inquisitive approach, begin gathering history surrounding childhood perceptions of drinking and drug use, onset of use, type of substances consumed, and under what circumstances. Make a genuine effort to understand the individual's frame of reference surrounding alcohol and drug consumption (especially over-the-counter drugs). When possible, reinforce the person's self-motivational statements and problem recognition while assessing the level of desire to make positive changes in his or her life.

As accurately as possible, begin to piece together daily, weekly, and monthly drinking or drug use patterns. How do weekdays differ from weekends? What happens on payday, holidays, and vacations? Begin to weave together behavioral and consumption patterns. Discuss the meaning of alcohol and drug withdrawal: what it is, what it looks like, and the risks associated with it. Based on the individual's pattern of use and potential for withdrawal, a determination can be made regarding the most appropriate level of care. In general, the presence of withdrawal symptoms warrants an inpatient detoxification program. This, of course, will depend on the drug of use—some drugs require inpatient detoxification and others do not. Those with lesser withdrawal risk are more appropriately treated in an outpatient program.

Always be on the lookout for red-flag responses, such as arrests, domestic disturbances, accidents, and emergency room visits. Also look for comorbidities commonly associated with alcohol and or drug dependence, such as hypertension, diabetes, liver problems, gastrointestinal problems, injuries sustained through accidents, and sleep difficulties.

Examine Social and Emotional Factors

Once the lines of communication are open, the professional can begin the process of examining sensitive areas of the individual's life. While valuing the previously shared family history and perceptions associated with alcohol and drug use, begin to examine the individual's day-to-day activities to build understanding of social, emotional, and environmental factors associated with alcohol or drug consumption. Seek to understand how the use of mood-altering substances is integrated into the individual's rituals. When and where does he or she drink or use? With whom do they drink or use? Has this changed over time? If the pattern has changed, question the reason for changes. What are the most common social activities? If there are children, to what extent is the parent involved? How are things in the home? Are family members frequently together, or are there estrangements?

Examine the person's educational, vocational, military, employment, financial, legal, spiritual, and recreational history, as well as current day-to-day activity patterns. It is important to note that many alcohol or drug abusers replace previously enjoyable activities with drinking or drug use. Question whether substance use has any impact on the social aspects of the individual's life and examine what that impact has been. The assessment process is one of exploration and education, so take time to teach and set boundaries. Avoid the tendency to overexamine areas that present with emotionally charged responses. More often than not, this will lead the assessment away from productive interaction into a dead-end of rationalization, blame, and frustration. Remain positive and avoid demoralizing statements and negative attitudes about alcohol or drug problems and treatment programs.

Summarize and Teach

Use the assessment process to reinforce and direct the individual with summary statements. Summary statements are designed to present the individual with nuggets of information you have summarized. The intent is twofold. First, you are checking to be certain you have heard and understood the person's perception. Second, summarizing statements can be used to tie pieces of information together in a way that leads the individual to insights and conclusions previously not examined. Patients need to understand the impact of substance abuse and dependence. Examination of what has worked for them in the past and what has not worked is an important part of the assessment summary. Frequently, individuals will have stopped drinking for periods of time. Examine what did and did not work during those time periods. Emphasize that resumption of drinking is not a sign of failure but part of a process.

When possible, family members should be involved in the treatment process. Assessment of potential family involvement should begin with the initial assessment and continue throughout the entire treatment process. Establishing family support is a strong positive reinforcement for adopting and maintaining new approaches to establishing and maintaining abstinence. Finally, provide information on risks. Family members and patients should understand that alcohol dependence is a chronic, progressive, and potentially fatal disease. It is important to know what they are up against, what role each person has to play, and how support, openness, and self-responsibility can lead to positive changes. Figure 4.1 describes potential approaches to care and integration of social factors to be addressed by social workers when providing comprehensive addition treatment.

THERAPEUTIC APPROACHES

Motivational Interviewing and Motivational Enhancement Therapy

Motivational interviewing (MI) is a counseling technique frequently applied in the treatment of alcohol-dependent or -abusing persons. This approach elicits changes in behavior by helping the individual explore and address ambivalence about change. Motivational enhancement therapy (MET) is a nonconfrontational approach that focuses on establishing new and different approaches toward problematic drinking behaviors. Goals of this approach are:

- Seek to understand the individual's frame of reference.
- Elicit and reinforce the individual's personal motivational statements of problem recognition, desire, intent to change, and confidence in ability to change.
- Monitor the individual's readiness to change and maintain a steady and consistent approach to problem resolution.
- Provide support and affirmation of individual choice and potential for self-regulation.

Motivational interviewing is a directive, client-centered counseling style for eliciting behavior change in which patients explore and resolve ambivalence (Miller & Rollnick, 2002).

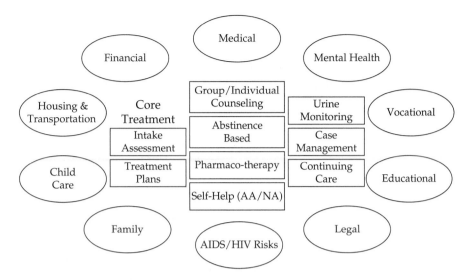

Figure 4.1 Core components of comprehensive services.

Motivational interviewing is less structured than the brief intervention described here, but effective brief interventions have been developed that are adaptations of motivational interviewing or involve similar skills. In motivational interviewing, patients are helped to recognize a discrepancy between their values and goals and their current actions, which can lead them to consider change. Motivational interviewing involves collaboration with the patient, eliciting the patient's thoughts and listening to them, and making it clear that the patient has choices and the autonomy and ability to make them (Miller & Rollnick, 2002).

The individual's perceptions of his/her readiness to change can be used to elicit change talk. For example, if the importance of change is rated as a 3 on a scale of 1 to 10, the clinician can recognize that the score was not zero and ask why. This may lead the individual in question to identify his or her concerns about their substance use. The clinician can then inquire as to what it might take for the score (or identified importance) to increase. The patient's response when examined by the individual and clinician can then be used as a starting point for discussion of how to go about initiating the process of change (Miller & Rollnick, 2002).

As this discussion continues and the individual expresses an increasing interest in change, the clinician should use reflective listening. Doing so permits the patient to hear, in their own words from the clinician, clarifying statements that help them to understand and become comfortable with motivations for change that

might not have previously been clearly understood. In motivational interviewing this concept is considered "change talk" (Miller & Rollnick, 2002).

Change talk—Miller and Rollnick suggest sessions should seek to elicit "change talk" or statements from the patient that are in the direction of change. Examples of change talk include the individual's perceptions of his or her readiness and how their current behavior relates to his or her personal goals. Elements of change talk can be abbreviated with the acronym DARN-C, that is, when the patient expresses:

- **Desire** to change
- **Ability** to change
- **Reasons** for change
- **Need** to change
- Ultimately, **Commitment** to change (Miller & Rollnick, 2002).

Carroll et al. (2006) conducted a randomized trial of MET motivational interviewing in a community-based substance abuse program setting. Findings from this study indicate that exposure to motivational interviewing demonstrated greater levels of program retention when compared to control groups. However, substance abuse outcomes at 84 days did not differ significantly from controls. Despite this disparity, MI continues to emerge as a best practice in treatment of alcohol abuse and dependence. Current literature indicates that there are more than 160 randomized trials, numerous multisite trials, and recently published meta-analyses of the effectiveness of MI. In these studies, the effectiveness of MI demonstrates wide variability within defined problem areas. In general, positive effects of MI appear early but tend to diminish over time. It is critical to remember that MI effectively captures the individual early in the treatment process, leading to increased participation and potentially increased retention in programming, both of which are key components of successful treatment outcomes.

Cognitive-Behavioral Therapy

Cognitive-behavioral therapy (CBT) is a structured, goal-directed approach designed to help patients learn how thought processes affect their behavior. The social worker helps the individual develop new ways of thinking and behaving through improved cognitive awareness. This leads to an increased ability to adapt to and alter situations within the social environment that present as potential triggers for alcohol consumption.

The evidence for CBT is favorable and indicates it is an effective treatment approach for alcohol dependence and abuse. Current evidence, however, suggests that CBT is most effective when applied as part of a comprehensive treatment plan (Cutler & Fishbain, 2005).

Solution-focused Approach

Solution-focused therapy approaches addiction issues from a prospective approach. Rather than examining problems and past behaviors, solution-focused therapy examines current reality, building on the unique strengths and abilities each individual brings to the therapy process. In the treatment of alcohol abuse and dependence, solution-focused therapy focuses on:

- Envisioning the future without alcohol and the problems that led to treatment
- Discovering effective approaches/solutions to present issues
- Encouraging the individual to build on previous successes, as well as adding new approaches to methods that have demonstrated success previously
- Directing and facilitating self discovery through self-examination

- The individual as the expert in developing effective change and solutions rather than the social worker
- The role of the social worker is to assist in the development of potential solutions.
- Emphasizing the "here and now" rather than the "then and why."

Steve de Shazer and Insoo Kim Berg of the Brief Family Therapy Center in Milwaukee are the originators of this form of therapy.

HOSPITALIZATION AND REFERRAL OPTIONS

There are times when brief intervention is not useful for patients experiencing severe alcohol abuse or alcohol dependence. If the initial assessment suggests severe alcohol dependence, and the individual indicates a willingness to stop drinking, level-of-care options should be considered. These options consist of the following:

- Inpatient detoxification
- Inpatient treatment
- Residential treatment
- Day treatment or outpatient therapy.

Patients presenting with mild-to-moderate symptoms of alcohol withdrawal have the potential to be managed within an outpatient treatment setting. Outpatient detoxification has become increasingly popular since the emergence of cost-reduction approaches to substance dependence treatment emerged in the late 1980s and early 1990s.

Patients with more severe withdrawal symptoms and susceptibility to environmental cues are better cared for in inpatient treatment environments that are free of relapse triggers. Many providers place their patients in an inpatient treatment setting to initiate detoxification and medical stabilization. This is followed by transition into residential or day-treatment programs.

The third level of step-down approaches to alcohol dependence involves transition into intensive outpatient treatment, which is comprised of education, group, and individual sessions usually three hours in duration occurring three times per week. Following completion of this level of care the individual transitions into a traditional outpatient treatment. Figure 4.2 presents options for individualized treatment

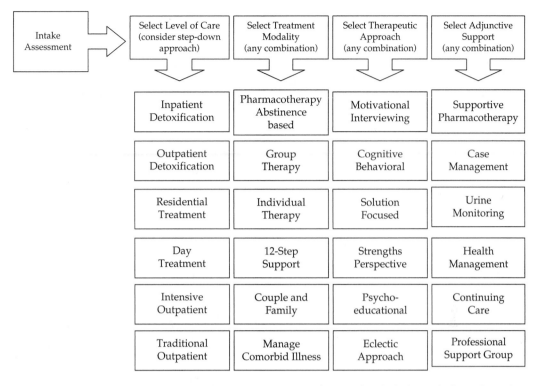

Figure 4.2 Options for individualized treatment approaches with alcohol- and drug-dependent individuals.

approaches when working with alcohol- and drug-dependent individuals.

CASE EXAMPLE

John G. is a 50-year-old self-employed civil engineer who has been extremely successful in developing his own business. John has four regional offices and travels extensively managing each of them, bidding jobs and interacting with various construction companies on business. Seven months ago, while working, John fell while jumping onto a bulldozer to speak with a friend. He injured two vertebrae (L-4 and L-5) in his lower back in this fall. This injury created severe nerve pain that radiates down his leg and causes limited mobility. John is prescribed an opiate-based pain medication. He has always been a drinker, and he enjoys drinking with business associates. His drink of choice is beer, yet there is no stated history of drug or alcohol abuse in his medical record. Initially, John used the pain meds sparingly, but as time progressed, his use increased. Soon he was taking more than the prescribed amount.

On three occasions, his physician increased the strength of his medication. John began to order prescriptions online. He doubled the prescribed dose. He began to miss business appointments and experienced increased marital stress related to his prescription medication use. Finally, John crashed his company car into a school bus when he apparently fell asleep at the wheel in the middle of the afternoon. At the point of entering treatment, John was facing legal problems related to this accident, financial problems related to lack of attention to his business, marital difficulties as a result of the prescription drug abuse, and an emerging single-episode depressive disorder.

John will benefit from a combined approach of MI and CBT. It is best to begin with motivational interviewing to ensure initial connection with treatment processes. Given John's level of cognitive functioning, CBT will be appropriate as treatment progresses. This approach can be helpful in assisting him in developing concrete plans to address issues of chronic pain, as well as establishing a plan for returning to work. An initial focus will elicit information and take advantage of change talk revealed in statements such as "I am ready to quit" or "I have to quit to get my life back in order."

Change talk is talk that recognizes a *d*esire to change, the *a*bility to change, provides *r*eason for the change, and describes a *n*eed to change. Simply remember DARN. However, change does not occur without action or positive steps in the direction of recovery. Action talk requires identification and support of *c*ommitment; a willingness, intention, determination, or readiness for treatment *a*ctivation; and the willingness and preparedness to take action and actually *t*ake positive steps toward recovery, which in John's case requires entering treatment. For action steps, simply remember CAT.

Cognitive-behavioral approaches can be used to frame very specific treatment plans to address underlying issues associated with treatment need and to facilitate continued movement toward established goals. An example of John's treatment goals might look like the following:

Goal 1: John will attend physical therapy at 10 a.m. He will work with Joan to complete 30 minutes of stretching and strengthening exercise during each session.

Goal 2: John will work with Rick (social worker) to address pending legal charges with Mr. Anderson, his attorney. John will complete necessary paperwork to document actions taken to date. This meeting will take place 9

A.M. March 9, in the fifth-floor conference room.

Goal 3: John will write a letter to each of his physicians by noon, March 12, (1) informing them of his entering treatment for substance dependence, (2) specifically describing his program of abstinence, and (3) asking for their assistance in managing his pain without the use of mood-altering substances.

Goal 4: John will continue to build his sober support network by attending three 12-step meetings of his choice on a weekly basis. He will obtain the telephone number of at least one group member per meeting and will make phone contact with at least one person whose number he has collected to discuss the progress he has made in treatment to date.

It is important that treatment goals be specific in nature, measurable, time-limited, and, most important, accomplishable. In this case, John is combining CBT with MI and health care, as well as legal and social support. In doing so, he is addressing many of the components that brought him to treatment, while establishing a firm foundation for ongoing recovery processes. Figure 4.3 outlines multiple options available to care providers when considering treatment and community based support for treatment.

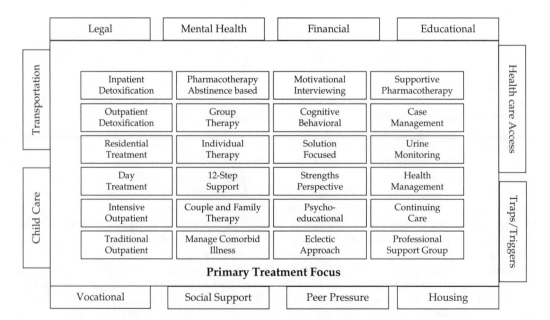

Figure 4.3 Competing social/environmental factors requiring social work intervention.

Case autopsy: John initially was treated on the inpatient unit for detoxification and stabilization. He then transitioned into intensive outpatient treatment, where he remained under the care of a social worker for a total of 16 sessions. John attended psycho-educational, group, individual, and family sessions while in treatment. He successfully resolved his pending legal issues. The DUI charge was resolved with consequences of probation, 90-day license suspension, and requirement to document ongoing treatment for a one-year period of time. John returned to his company and now has established eight years of abstinence.

CONCLUSION

Social workers have a long history of caring for persons with alcohol and drug dependence. Social workers play a key role in the management of persons with alcohol and drug abuse by facilitating acceptance into treatment programming, completing initial assessments to determine the extent and severity of alcohol consumption or substance abuse, conducting initial therapy sessions designed to optimize engagement in treatment, and establishing realistic, measurable, and specific treatment plans. The role of the social worker in addiction continues to expand and transform to meet the ever-increasing needs of those seeking treatment for substance dependence.

Increasingly, this work is being informed by evidence-based approaches to address all aspects of substance abuse and dependence. Today's social worker facilitates treatment processes not only designed to aid in patient care but to serve as an interface between the patient, a variety of caregivers, and critical community-based partners in care. Competent skill sets are required to implement complex, multifaceted approaches to care. Traditional social work skills of communication, organization and facilitation, linkage, brokering, and advocating are intertwined with newer skills of monitoring pharmacotherapy, interacting with managed care and other payer sources, performing utilization review, and dealing with an expanding array of therapeutic approaches to address this complex disease. It is our hope that this chapter serves as a foundation on which each social worker will continue to build a knowledge and skill set that reflects the needs of their individualized treatment setting.

WEBSITES

Center for Substance Abuse Treatment. http://csat.samhsa.gov.
National Association of Addiction Treatment Providers. http://www.naatp.org.
National Institute on Drug Abuse. http://www.nida.nih.gov.
Substance Abuse and Mental Health Services Administration. http://www.samhsa.gov.

References

American Psychiatric Association. (2013). *Diagnostic and statistical manual of mental disorders: DSM-5.* Washington, DC: American Psychiatric Press.

Ballesteros, J., Duffy, J. C., Querejeta, I., Ariño, J., & González-Pinto, A. (2004). Efficacy of brief interventions for hazardous drinkers in primary care: systematic review and meta-analyses. *Alcoholism, Clinical and Experimental Research, 28*(4), 608–618.

Beich, A., Thorsen, T., & Rollnick, S. (2003). Screening in brief intervention trials targeting excessive drinkers in general practice: Systematic review and meta-analysis. *BMJ: British Medical Journal, 327*(7414), 536–540.

Bertholet, N., Daeppen, J. B., Wietlisbach, V., Fleming, M., & Burnand, B. (2005). Reduction of alcohol consumption by brief alcohol intervention in primary care: systematic review and meta-analysis. *Archives of Internal Medicine, 165*(9), 986–995.

Carroll, K. M., Ball, S. A., Nich, C., et al. (2006). Motivational interviewing to improve treatment engagement and outcome in individuals seeking treatment for substance abuse: A multisite effectiveness study. *Drug and Alcohol Dependence, 81,* 301.

Cutler, R. B., & Fishbain, D. A. (2005). Are alcoholism treatments effective? The Project MATCH data. *BMC Public Health, 5,* 75.

Emmen, M. J., Schippers, G. M., Wollersheim, H., & Bleijenberg, G. (2005). Adding psychologist's intervention to physicians' advice to problem drinkers in the outpatient clinic. *Alcohol and Alcoholism (Oxford, Oxfordshire), 40*(3).

Fleming, M. F., Mundt, M. P., Frenchc, M. T., et al. (2002). Brief physician advice for problem drinkers: Longer-term efficacy and benefit-cost analysis. *Alcohol and Clinical and Experimental Research, 26,* 36–43.

Harwood, H. (2000). *Updating estimates of the economic costs of alcohol abuse in the United States: Estimates, update methods, and data.* Washington, DC: National Institute on Alcohol Abuse and Alcoholism.

Harwood, H. J., & Bouchery, E. (2001). *The economic costs of drug abuse in the United States,*

1992–1998. NCJ-190636. Washington, DC: Office of National Drug Control Policy.

Holder, H. D., & Blose, J. O. (1992). The reduction of health care costs associated with alcoholism treatment: A 14-year longitudinal study. *Journal of Studies on Alcohol, 53,* 293.

Midanik, L. T., Chaloupka, F. J., Saitz, R., et al. (2004). Alcohol-attributable deaths and years of potential life lost—United States, 2001. *Morbidity and Mortality Weekly Report, 53*(37), 866–870.

Miller W, R, & Rollnick, S., (2002). *Motivational interviewing: Preparing people for change.* New York, NY: Guilford Press.

National Council on Alcohol and Drug Addiction. (2013). In the News: 2.5 million alcohol-related deaths worldwide—annually. http://www.ncadd.org/index.php/in-the-news/155-25-million-alcohol-related-deaths-worldwide-annually. Accessed August 14, 2013.

Project CHOICES Intervention Research Group. (2003). Reducing the risk of alcohol-exposed pregnancies: A study of a motivational intervention in community settings. *Pediatrics, 111,* 1131.

Solberg, L. I., Maciosek, M. V., & Edwards, N. M. (2008). Primary care intervention to reduce alcohol misuse ranking its health impact and cost effectiveness. *American Journal of Preventive Medicine, 34,* 2, 143–152.

Substance Abuse and Mental Health Services Administration. (2011). *Leading Change: A Plan for SAMHSA's Roles and Actions 2011-2014 Executive Summary and Introduction.* HHS Publication No. (SMA) 11-4629 Summary. Rockville, MD: Author.

Substance Abuse and Mental Health Services Administration. (2012). *Results from the 2011 National Survey on Drug Use and Health: Mental Health Findings,* NSDUH Series H-45, HHS Publication No. (SMA) 12-4725. Rockville, MD: Author.

Williams, E., Kivlahan, D., Saitz, R., Merrill, J., Achtmeyer, C., McCormick, K., et al. (2006). Readiness to change in primary care patients who screened positive for alcohol misuse. *Annals of Family Medicine, 4*(3), 213–220.

Yeager, K. R., Cutler, D. L., Svendsen, D., &Sills, G. M. (2013). Introduction. In: Yeager, K. R., Cutler, D. L., Svendsen, D., & Sills, G. M. (Eds.), *Modern community mental health: An interdisciplinary approach* (pp. 3–8). New York, NY: Oxford University Press.

Yeager, K. R., & Gregoire, T. K. (2005). Crisis intervention: Application of brief solution-focused therapy in addictions. In A. R. Roberts (Ed.), *Crisis intervention handbook: Assessment, treatment and research,* 3rd ed. (pp. 566–601). New York: Oxford University Press.

5   School Social Work

Robert Lucio

While the history of school social work over the first 100 years has shown adaptability to the changing social climate, it also reveals a process of specialization (McCullah, 2004). Bartlett (1959) drew a distinction between generic social work theory and specialized social work theory. A generic social work theory was proposed for all social workers with the understanding that each field of social work also needed its own specialization-specific theory. As social workers develop specialized skills and continue working in specialized environments, there is a clear need for social workers to develop and use effective strategies in practice and research. School social workers are becoming increasingly aware of the need to be accountable for outcomes related to the services provided and are also beginning to understand the need to show decision makers the value of school social work in impacting the lives of students.

Risk and protective factor determinants can be viewed as core components of an ecologically driven approach to children's issues (Miles, Espiritu, Horen, Sebian, & Waetzig, 2010). It is the process of deciding the *if, what, where, why,* and *how* of intervening. Having a common understanding that includes assets, competence, and protective processes along with the traditional measures of risk factors, symptoms, problems, and risk-producing processes is critical for student success. As school social workers find themselves in the fight for limited resources within an educational host setting, it is vital that services and outcomes be geared toward academic achievement and success. The social work profession has the ability to influence many areas that will improve students' achievement, behaviors, and other school outcomes, but presently has few empirical ways of showing this to those who are making crucial financial decisions. School districts and school personnel need to be shown that school social workers can help impact student academic and behavioral outcomes.

Beyond understanding the current roles that school social workers play, the future of school social work is being influenced by (1) Response to Intervention (RtI); (2) data informed decisions; (3) evidence-based practices; and (4) the development of a comprehensive school social work model. In addition to these four emerging areas of school social work, the role of social workers in the future will also be discussed. These are critical areas that need to be brought to the attention of school social workers preparing for the next 100 years of practice.

SCHOOL SOCIAL WORKERS' ROLE

School social workers are already asked to do many things and wear many hats throughout the day, including clinician, case manager, advocate, and even policy maker. As the demands on social workers increase, so will the roles they are asked to fill. These range from supporting the mission of the school to serving children on multiple systemic levels in order to promote effective learning through interventions in the school and home environment. Social workers may also be called upon to select appropriate interventions for students, work in small groups or with individuals, or even provide referrals for other services.

Several recent studies of school social workers have looked at how they spend their time

(Bye, Shepard, Partridge, & Alvarez, 2009; Kelly, Berzin, Frey, Alvarez, Shaffer, & O'Brien, 2010; Whittlesey-Jerome, 2013). These researchers looked at the activities that consume their time, what services they are providing, and the broad classification of their services. It was found that almost all school social workers engage in individual counseling, group counseling, and classroom groups. In addition, a majority of school social workers perform psychosocial evaluations and case management services. In fact, school social workers reported that over 60% of their time is spent on secondary and tertiary prevention, while only 30% is spent on primary prevention. The activities are focused on school attendance, discipline problems, school climate, achievement, school violence, drop-out, and teen pregnancy (Bye et al., 2009).

When asked about things they wish they could change about their jobs, school social workers most frequently reported wanting more administrative decision-making ability and a troubling lack of understanding on the part of others regarding their roles and responsibilities (Peckover, Vasquez, Van Housen, Saunders, & Allen, 2013). When roles are not clear, there can be confusion about what school social workers actually do. This can lead to duties being assigned to them that do not fit with their skills and training.

Although school social workers have the ability to focus and direct resources where they are likely to have the greatest impact, and to where there is a high chance of sustainability, the current state of social work practice in schools points to a focus on clinical services for those students already identified as at risk. Currently, school social workers have taken limited roles as leaders in prevention, improvement of school culture, and policy change at the local, state, and national levels (Kelly et al., 2010). Despite the current roles, which often focus on direct services, with the introduction of new approaches to social work practice, namely a Response to Intervention framework, the potential exists for social workers to move beyond providing services to one student at a time. Although there is no doubt this is valuable work, a shift in focus to a prevention model in schools creates an opportunity for school social workers to be at the forefront of this movement and affect both the broader systemic influences (such as the family, teachers, school, and district) and also student level outcomes.

In an effort to expand prevention activities and impact all levels of the schools, it has been suggested that school social workers start by engaging teachers in a collaborative process by offering training and in-service opportunities to empower teachers, providing support for school personnel in dealing with academic and behavior problems, and being advocates for helping children, families, schools, and communities (Bye et al., 2009).

RESPONSE TO INTERVENTION

The *No Child Left Behind Act (NCLB) of 2001* (P.L. 107–110) and the *Individuals with Disabilities Act (IDEA)* in 2004 (P.L. 108–446) have radically changed the way in which services within education are delivered to students. These laws have introduced evidence-based practices into the realm of schools as one ingredient within the Response to Intervention (RtI) approach to services. RtI is a three-tiered framework for providing high-quality instruction and intervention matched to the student's needs. It provides intervention and educational support to all students with increasing levels of intensity based on individual student needs. The interventions can be based on academic and/or behavioral systems. The key characteristics of this approach are to identify students at risk, closely monitor behavioral or learning outcomes, provide evidence-based interventions, and adjust the intensity of the services provided depending on the student's response to the intervention.

The RtI framework is much like a public health approach to applied education in identifying students who are at risk for academic or behavioral problems and providing instruction and interventions based on the student's needs. The first tier (Tier 1) is focused on primary prevention and intervention efforts for all students at a system-wide level in order to minimize any concerns before they become a problem. For instance, a school-wide anti-bullying program could be implemented in order to reduce the risk of bullying in a specific school. For those students who do not respond to the Tier 1 interventions, small groups of students are engaged in Tier 2 secondary prevention services. These small group interventions can be specialized groups or even systems interventions for those students identified as at risk. Students who are reacting to bullying or identified as potential bullies could be offered a service if the problem persists despite the system-wide intervention program. Finally, Tier 3 tertiary interventions and services are provided at an individualized level for those students who were provided Tier 1 and Tier 2 services, but did not respond positively to the interventions. Students who continue to have concerns with bullying would be seen by school personnel on a one-to-one basis at the Tier 3 level.

RtI involves the use of data-informed decision-making to modify instruction and implement scientifically based interventions effectively, and is delivered in the following components: multiple tiers of evidence-based instructional service delivery; and problem-solving methods designed to inform decisions at each tier of service delivery. Most importantly, RtI is applicable to all general education students and exceptional student education (ESE). In fact, the nationwide *Response to Intervention* adoption survey found that 71% of school districts were in the process of implementing, piloting, or already fully using RtI district wide (Spectrum K12, 2009).

Some school social work researchers have discussed RtI specifically around the impact on school social work (Kelly et al., 2010). They note four primary principles of RtI where school social workers can have a direct impact. First is the notion that services provided by school social workers should help build the capacity of families, teachers, schools, and districts. In addition to direct services, collaborative endeavors that impact the ability of each of the systems to adopt, implement, and maintain interventions and services should be one focus of school social workers. Although this principle is one of the core building blocks of RtI and school social work, it was found that these critical activities were the least likely to be performed in the current school social worker's job activities. In order to reverse this trend, it is critical that school social workers look for opportunities to expand their role by engaging in strategies and interventions that assist each part of the system; assume leadership roles that influence the broader macro-system; support families, teachers, and administrators in making and sustaining changes; and apply the ecological model to all three tiers. This might take the form of community engagement efforts, teacher trainings, working with families, and working to change the culture of the school to support positive academic and behavioral outcomes.

The second principle relates to the provision of evidence-based practices by school social workers. Schools should use evidence-based practices based on interventions that have proven through empirical research and data to be effective in dealing with the specific academic or behavioral concern. The third principle is the application of the public health prevention framework to education, using a multi-tiered intervention approach. The fourth principle of RtI calls for data to inform decisions about the effect of interventions on student outcomes. School social workers may need to support schools in selecting and implementing interventions, or even collecting, analyzing, and interpreting data in order to ensure students are receiving appropriate services.

The adoption of this framework within the context of schools has broad implications for school social workers. This type of framework requires that school social workers be versed in more than direct clinical services or case management activities. They must also be capable of supporting each of the three tiers in order to improve student outcomes. This might involve learning new skills and taking on new roles, such as directing the implementation of evidence-based practices and assisting in helping schools collect, monitor, and interpret data that helps schools understand whether students are improving.

EVIDENCE-BASED PRACTICES

Another step impacting the future of school social work is to look at which evidence-based interventions can be applied specifically to the identified academic or behavior concerns. This gives social workers a tangible way to impact students, by referring them to or providing the appropriate services. The current research on evidence-based practice can be used as a guide in deciding which interventions to implement, thus allowing the use of best practices with students. Evidence-based practice (EBP) has had a significant impact on school social work and education.

The *No Child Left Behind Act (NCLB) of 2001* requires the use of scientifically based research in schools (Pub. L. No. 107–110). The Colorado Department of Education (2005) addresses the use of evidence-based practices within this framework by stating "evidence-based practice

is the use of practices, interventions, and treatments which have been proven, through data based research, to be effective in improving outcomes for individuals when the practice is implemented with fidelity" (p. 1). The implementation of the RtI approach is centered on evidence-based practice, and using this approach mandates that interventions "must be evidence-based" (Bureau of Exceptional Education and Student Services, 2006, p. 2). With the importance being placed on outcomes in schools, evidence-based practice is certainly moving to the forefront of school social work and has become a strong directive in school social work.

Raines (2004) provides steps in the process of implementing evidence-based practice. The list of the steps is presented as: formulating questions, investigating the evidence, appraising the evidence, applying the evidence, and evaluating progress. Under each process, an example is given so that school social workers can see how this applies to their practices. The author also notes that in order to make evidence-based practice most practical, there must be the creation of relevant knowledge and the dissemination of that knowledge. Of the seven guidelines listed for deciding which interventions to use, two refer to the interaction with theory, namely, whether there is empirical support for a theory or technique and whether the framework recognizes a person-in-the-environment perspective. The tie to theory is a vital key to integrating evidence-based practice into this new framework. Simply reading about best practices does not mean a practitioner has the ability to implement that intervention effectively.

School social workers must understand the context of the schools in which they are providing services in order to successfully implement evidence-based practices. The effective integration of these interventions and services into everyday practice requires knowledge of key organizational and political systems within schools, and knowledge of which interventions promote change, given the characteristics of the current students, teachers, school climate, and school administration (Phillippo & Stone, 2011). This also requires school social workers to have a thorough knowledge base of appropriate interventions, an understanding of how to get information on additional evidence-based practices, the ability to collect and analyze data around effectiveness of services, and an approach that encourages supporting other elements of the school system through a consultation and collaboration.

DATA INFORMED DECISIONS

The adoption of RtI as a framework for educational services has created a push toward making data-informed decisions. However, even within this new directive there are few clear guidelines as to who and how services are delivered, which adds to the confusion among student services professions regarding which roles to adopt (Weist, Ambrose, & Lewis, 2006; Weist, Lowie, Flaherty, & Pruitt, 2001). Not only do school social workers have to struggle to define their roles within the schools, but they must do so while attempting to incorporate evidence-based interventions borne from sound social work theory. Using data to inform decisions involves screening at the system and individual levels to help determine needs and the effectiveness of interventions and services in promoting or inhibiting academic and/or behavioral concerns. This might also involve identifying which children are responding to the intervention and which might require more intensive services.

In order for school social workers to engage fully in this process, they should have access to valid and reliable measures, the ability to analyze and interpret the data, and make an effort to engage key stakeholders in conversations around the meaning of the findings (Allen-Meares, Montgomery, & Kim, 2012). Having access to appropriate scales, measures, school data, and any other information will help provide an accurate and useful evaluation of student outcomes (Whittlesey-Jerome, 2013). School social workers should also develop a process to collect and organize data, especially if the data are not part of a regular school data system. Once the data are collected, analysis and interpretation of the data is another essential task that school social workers must have the ability to perform. It is not enough to provide reports if the data presented do not lead to improvements in student outcomes. Taking findings and understanding how to communicate this information to key stakeholders (e.g., community, faculty, or even schools) increases the likelihood that data will be used to inform student services and also increases the visibility of school social workers in the success of students.

SCHOOL SOCIAL WORK FRAMEWORK

The major prevailing framework in school social work is the ecological approach, which serves as a guiding framework for school social work services. This approach enables school social workers to view students, families, schools, communities, and districts within the multiple systems that interact to impact a student's academic and behavioral outcomes. Moving to a more ecological approach recognizes all of the influences on student outcomes. One of the benefits of using this systems view is the ability to be both student and system focused. The ecological model takes into account numerous factors that have an effect on an individual person, including individual, family, peer, school, and community influences. Connecting the person to the environment takes into account multiple levels of interaction and the impact of this network of social and interpersonal influences.

The ecological perspective and school social work practice go hand in hand. School social work practice has four major focus areas: (1) early intervention to reduce or eliminate stress within or between individuals or groups; (2) problem solving services to students, parents, school personnel, or community agencies; (3) early identification of students at risk; and (4) work with various groups to develop coping, social, and decision-making skills. However, because school social workers function within a larger host setting, there is a "need to develop strategies that optimize, enhance, and augment the goals of education" (Atkins, Hoagwood, Kutash, & Seidman, 2010, p. 40). As school social workers operate in a system moving toward outcomes, evidence-based practices, and accountability, it is vital to focus attention on how services ultimately impact students.

Although it is clear the ecological model takes into account numerous factors that have an effect on an individual person, a lack of uniform practice among school social workers exists due to its multiple roles and complexity. School social workers must understand all levels of the system to enact change, requiring social workers to have complete vision of the micro, meso, macro, and chrono systems. However, not having a consistent model can lead to unclear roles and misunderstanding of the capabilities of school social work by faculty and administrators (Dupper, 2003).

A new model for school social work has been called for in order to apply school social work practices consistently in a way that is useful to all parts of the "system." School social workers should be able to engage in the process of closing the "research to practice gap" and translating research into practice (Ringeisen, Henderson, & Hoagwood, 2003). Kelly and Stone (2009) looked at the contextual characteristics of school social workers and how their environment impacted which interventions were used. Looking at the characteristics of the practitioner, characteristics of the practice setting, and socio-cultural factors, they found little impact on the interventions used. This suggested the need to develop a new school social work model that includes more than individual and group counseling, although predicting the use of more systemic practice factors was more difficult.

Taking this further, Frey et al. (2013) have presented the beginning framework for a model that provides a guide for the types of services that school social workers should be expected to perform. Their goal is to present a broad model that relays school social work roles, skills, and competencies. Specifically they propose the four constructs of social justice, home-school-community linkages, ethical-legal practice, and data-informed decisions in practice as the foundation for the new model. Additionally, they see school social work practice as focused on educationally relevant mental health services, healthy school climate, healthy cultural learning environment, and utilizing access to resources. This new framework serves as a guide to where interventions can be focused to target the greatest chances of impact and success. It also gives school social workers a tool to expand their services to the system level while still embracing their clinical strengths.

CONCLUSION

Recent calls have been made in social work for more scientific and evidence-based research in social work and social work education (Corcoran, 2007; Shaw, 2003; Zlotnik & Solt, 2006). Having a solid knowledge base and clear role expectations, using data to inform student interventions, incorporating evidence-based practices, and using a clear practice model are critical components for the school social work profession to continue moving forward. Although school social workers are beginning to look at how they impact achievement, the questions about how or why this occurs still need to be examined. These processes and mechanisms for success and failure provide the key to developing and selecting useful interventions. Understanding where to put the effort is important, but it is only the first step in deciphering the complex notion of academic and behavioral success.

The ability to identify students who are at greatest risk allows for the most efficient use of time and resources by school social workers. Targeting interventions to students whose need is greatest enables school social workers to direct services where they are most vital, optimizing resources and allowing for school social workers to differentiate between individual and system concerns. This shift in thinking continues to build on the path that is being paved by evidence-based practice. Understanding which factors help make students successful allows school social workers to partner with families and other systems in addressing those areas that present as risks for academic and behavioral success.

HELPFUL WEBSITES

School Social Work Association of America (SSWAA)—http://sswaa.org/
American Council on School Social Work (ACSSW)—http://acssw.org/
National Association of Social Workers, School Social Work Practice Section—http://www.socialworkers.org/practice/school/default.asp

References

Allen-Meares, P., Montgomery, K. L., & Kim, J. S. (2012). School-based social work interventions: A cross-national systemic review. *Social Work in Education, 58*(3), 253–262.
Atkins, M., Hoagwood, K., Kutash, K., & Seidman, E. (2010). Toward the integration of education and mental health in schools. *Administration and Policy in Mental Health and Mental Health Services Research, 37,* 40–47.
Bartlett, H. (1959). The generic-specific concept in social work education and practice. In A. E. Kahn (Ed.), *Issues in American social work* (pp. 159–190). New York, NY: Columbia University Press.
Bureau of Exceptional Education and Student Services. (2006). The Response to Intervention (RtI) model: Florida Department of Education.

Bye, L., Shepard, M., Partridge, J., & Alvarez, M. (2009). School social work outcomes: Perspectives of school social workers and school administrators. *Children & Schools, 31*(2), 97–108.

Colorado Department of Education. (2005). *Fast facts: Evidence Based Practice.* Retrieved from http://www.cde.state.co.us/cdesped/download/pdf/ff-EvidenceBasedPractice_Intro.pdf.

Corcoran, K. (2007). From the scientific revolution to evidence-based practice: Teaching a short history with a long past. *Research on Social Work Practice, 17*(5), 548–552.

Dupper, D. R. (2003). *School social work: Skills and interventions for effective practice.* Hoboken, NJ: John Wiley & Sons, Inc.

Frey, A. J., Alvarez, M. E., Dupper, D. R., Sabatino, C. A., Lindsey, B. C., Raines, J. C., … Norris, M. A. (2013). School Social Work Practice Model. School Social Work Association of America. from http://sswaa.org/displaycommon.cfm?an=1&subarticlenbr=459

Kelly, M. S., Berzin, S. C., Frey, A., Alvarez, M., Shaffer, G., & O'Brien, K., U.S. Department of Veterans Affairs, 2011 (2010). The state of school social work: Findings from the national school work survey. *School Mental Health Journal, 2*(3), 132–141.

Kelly, M. S. & Stone, S. (2009). An analysis of factors shaping interventions used by school social workers. *Children & Schools, 31*(3), 163–176.

McCullah, J. G. (2004). School social work: A chronology of important events—the first 50 years. *Journal of School Social Work, 13*(2), 84–195.

Miles, J., Espiritu, R. C., Horen, N. M., Sebian, J., & Waetzig, E. (2010). *A public health approach to children's mental health: A conceptual framework.* Washington, DC: Georgetown University Center for Child and Human Development, National Technical Assistance Center for Children's Mental Health.

Peckover, C. A., Vasquez, M. L., Van Housen, S. L., Saunders, J. A., & Allen, L. (2013). Preparing school social workers for the future: An update of school social workers' tasks in Iowa. *Children & Schools, 35*(1), 9–17.

Phillippo, K., & Stone, S. (2011). Toward a broader view: A call to integrate knowledge about schools into school social work research. *Children & Schools, 33*(2), 71–82.

Raines, J. C. (2004). Evidence-based practice in school social work: A process in perspective. *Children & Schools, 26*(2), 71–85.

Ringeisen, H., Henderson, K., & Hoagwood, K. (2003). Context matters: Schools and the "research to practice gap" in children's mental health. *School Psychology Review, 32*(2), 153–168.

Shaw, I. F. (2003). Critical commentary: Cutting edge issues in social work research. *British Journal of Social Work, 33,* 107–116.

Spectrum K12. (2009). Response to intervention (RTI) adoption survey 2009. Retrieved 3/12/10, from http://www.spectrumk12.com//uploads/file/RTI_2009_Adoption_Survey_Final_Report.pdf

Weist, M., Ambrose, M., & Lewis, C. (2006). Expanded school mental health: A collaborative community/school example. *Children & Schools, 28,* 45–50.

Weist, M. D., Lowie, J. A., Flaherty, L. T., & Pruitt, M. D. (2001). Collaboration among the education, mental health, and public health systems to promote youth mental health. *Psychiatric Services, 52*(10), 1348–1351.

Whittlesey-Jerome, W. (2013). Results of the 2010 statewide New Mexico school social work survey: Implications for evaluating the effectiveness of school social work. *School Social Work Journal, 37*(2), 76–87.

Zlotnik, J. L., & Solt, B. E. (2006). The Institute for the Advancement of Social Work Research: Working to increase our practice and policy evidence base. *Research on Social Work Practice, 16*(5), 534–540.

6 Social Work Practice and Leadership

Michael J. Holosko

INTRODUCTION

Social work has a rather long and storied history of not defining core concepts that either direct and inform its practitioners or educate and train its students (Holosko, 2009). Social work leadership is an example of one such core concept. The history of North American social work is characterized by many altruistic leaders who, through their compassion for vulnerable individuals, acted humanely and made a difference in those individuals' lives. William James's (1907) classic essay on pragmatism makes the point more succinctly, as "seeking the difference that makes the difference." These early, turn-of-the-century pioneers led by advocating, reforming, transforming, reflecting, and most importantly—giving names, voice, hope, and inspiration to the clients and communities they served. They included the likes of: Jane Addams, Dorothea Dix, Josephine Shaw Lowell, Mary Richmond, Ellen Gates Starr, Frances Perkins, Florence Kelly, Ida Cannon, Grace Abbott, Lillian Wald, Paul Kellogg, Anita Rose Williams, and Sarah A. Collins—to name just a few.

Our profession's legacy of leaders is much longer than its conceptualization or research about leadership, and this reality is typical of other disciplines that similarly embrace the concept. As Graham (2002) stated:

… research into leadership is a young and still rather shapeless discipline. While leaders and leadership may provide the stuff of bar-room wisdom to glean analytical insights and perspective value at a level approaching normal academic standards. Although some literature exists offering unfalsifiable theories about leadership behavior and personality, there is a dearth of primary empirical information about leaders, the philosophical prisms through which they perceive reality and the principles by which they conduct themselves. (p. 87)

Despite the fact that leadership was a core concern of the Council of Social Work Education (CSWE) some 15 years ago, as indicated in its *Strategic Plan 1998–2000*, and the NASW, who sponsored the "Leadership Academy" from 1994 to 1997, and conducted an annual meeting on leadership development, Brilliant (1986) referred to leadership as essentially a "missing ingredient" in social work education and training. After reviewing its sporadic attention in our professional literature, she concluded it was essentially a "non-theme" in social work training and education. Later, Reamer (1993) emphatically concluded that we do little to educate for leadership in social work. Then, Stoesz (1997) lamented that social work professionals are often forced to rise to positions of leadership within the profession with little to no mentoring.

Rank and Hutchinson (2000) investigated individuals ($N = 75$) who held leadership positions within the CSWE and the NASW, and concluded that their education and training in this area fell short of both the demands for leadership in the field, and our curricula's ability to teach and educate students about the concept adequately. Their comprehensive analysis made a cogent case for the uniqueness of social work leadership, and they offered a number of constructive suggestions to direct social work in this regard into the twenty-first century. It appears that the profession has had better success in "taking the concept forward," when it responded to the leadership needs expressed by its clients and practicing professionals in its fields of practice (Holosko, 2009). For example, the National Network for Social Work Managers established in the mid-1980s developed a curriculum focused on core competencies needed to run well-functioning, high-quality health care human service agencies/organizations. Their Academy grants the Certified Social Work Manager (CSWM) credential to social work managers who meet criteria that minimally include education, training, experience, demonstrated competency in 12 core areas, and approval by the Academy (Wimpfheimer, 2004).

Similarly, the John A. Hartford Foundation (www.jhartfound.org) in conjunction with CSWE, has been integral in facilitating and elevating the profession's leadership role in gerontology in the United States. Since about 1996 to 2009, they have spent some $48 million dollars on a variety of initiatives that have promoted social work to a national leadership position through gerontological education, training, research, collations, collaborations, scholarships, and curriculum development, etc. In this burgeoning worldwide population growth area (www.jhartfound.com), the curious irony is that we routinely tout the importance of leadership within the profession. Social work's enthusiasm for the concept, however, supersedes its meaningful inclusion in education or training. For instance, in CSWE's Educational Policy and Accreditation Standards (EPAS) (2009), among 10 competency standards leadership is only mentioned once. Similarly, a word search count conducted for this chapter of the school mission statements of the top-ranked schools of social work ($N = 50$) cited in *U.S. News and World Report* (2012), and the corresponding titles of courses offered on their respective websites, revealed: (a) 51% of the schools included the word "leadership" in their mission statements; however, (b) only 27% of these same schools used the word "leadership" in any of the titles of their advertised web-listed school courses. In summary, as previously indicated, from a variety of educational perspectives, social workers seem much more enamored with the topic of leadership, and less enamored with developing its educational potential more meaningfully in their schools.

Finally here, for this chapter, a review of social work leadership literature sources only two texts, *"Facilitative Leadership in Social Work Practice"* (2013) by E. Breshars and R. Volker, and *"Social Work Management and Leadership: Managing Complexity with Creativity"* by A. Lawler and J. Bilson (2010), which used the words "social work" and "leadership" together in the same title. Similarly, in a Google search (Google Scholar) of "social work" and "leadership" of scholarly journals

in our field in the past decade, only five articles similarly linked these two terms in their titles.

Where this conceptual fuzziness has potentially a more deleterious effect is in our formal education and training (Nesoff, 2007). However one looks at the issue from this standpoint, we are professionally remiss in this regard, and it appears that we have a rather long and comfortable history of evolving without clearly defining either who we are, or how we should practice (Bartlett, 1970; Boehm, 1958; Flexner, 1915; Gitterman & Germain, 1980; Gordon, 1962; Pincus & Minahan, 1973; Reid & Epstein, 1972). Indeed, educators, accrediting bodies, and legitimizing organizations (e.g., license boards, the NSAW) should take it upon themselves to better define the very concepts we promote and use (Holosko, 2009).

ON BECOMING A SOCIAL WORK LEADER

Leadership versus Management

For a number of years in many academic fields of study, the terms "leadership" and "management" have been: (a) defined in many ways; (b) defined in various ways; (c) used as "garbage can" terms—to describe anything and everything about this content; (d) often overlapped, blurred, and not differentiated from one another; and (e) defined in rather nebulous and unclear ways. In addition: (a) more literature is published about the concept of management as opposed to the concept of leadership; (b) good leaders have a very different skill set than do good managers; (c) very few leaders are effective managers—and vice versa; (d) it appears easier to educate and train social workers and allied professionals to become managers—rather than leaders; and (e) recently, there seems to be more concern about the importance of management in nonprofit and educational settings rather than leadership (Hafford-Letchfield & Lawler, 2010; Holosko, 2009; Holosko & Skinner, 2013; Kamaria & Lewis, 2009; Paton, Mordaunt, & Cornforth, 2007).

Each of these will now be defined in consensual ways: (a) *leadership* is a process whereby an individual influences a group of persons to achieve a common goal, and b) *management* exercises executive, administrative, and supervisory direction of a group or organization. It requires goal setting, defined objectives and targets, a focus on consistently producing results through planning and budgeting, and organization and staffing, as well as coordination and problem-solving

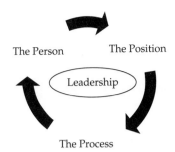

Figure 6.1 The synergistic conceptual framing components of leadership: The 3 P's of Person, Position, and Process.

(Holosko & Skinner, 2013; Kotter, 1990; Pickett & Kennedy, 2003). This chapter is about the former term, not the latter one.

Core Leadership Attributes

At a simple level, leadership is a synergistic, transformational, and interactive process anchored in the "3 P's"—the person, the position, and the process (Hartley & Allison, 2002). The "person" refers to the traits or personal characteristics of an individual; the "position" involves the use of authority, governance, and guidance to influence individuals; and the "process" involves how leaders shape events, motivate and influence people, and achieve outcomes (Taylor, 2007).

Holosko (2009) conducted one of the few empirical studies identifying core attributes of leadership in the social work literature. He content-analyzed disciplinary journals ($N = 70$) published in the social and behavioral science databases to sift out its main attributes. Ranked in descending order of importance, their frequencies were:

1. *Vision*
   a. Having one—To have a description of a desired condition at some point in the future.
   b. Implementing one—To plan and put in place strategic steps to enact the vision.
2. *Influencing others to act*—To inspire and enable others to take initiative, have a belief in a cause, and perform duties and responsibilities.
3. *Teamwork/collaboration*—To work collectively and in partnership with others toward achieving a goal.
4. *Problem-solving capacity*—To both anticipate problems and act decisively on them when they occur.
5. *Creating positive change*—Moving people in organizations to a better place than where they once were.

Having these attributes certainly is important, but being able to use them effectively in settings to influence change is the real litmus test (Holosko & Skinner, 2013).

Leaders achieve these core attributes through an ongoing interactive transformational application of (a) their personal attributes and (b) their various skill competencies, and (c) by developing a leadership intuition about the attributes indicated in Table 6.1. Thus, there is a process that defines one's leadership style and imprints one's operational footprint in moving the organization forward in overtime, by presently using any or all of these five core attributes.

As indicated in Table 6.1, effective leaders use various attributes and competencies in a variety of intuitive ways for different situations as they arise within an organization. As indicated by Snowden and Boone (2007) "truly adept leaders know not only how to identify the context they're working in, but also how to change their behavior to match" (p. 7). Given this, it becomes easier to understand how learning and imparting management skills that are fairly nonambiguous, straightforward, and less complex is simpler than learning and imparting the many interactive and interrelated social work leadership characteristics noted in Table 6.1.

Using Social Work Attributes to Analyze Leadership Effectiveness

As noted in this chapter, the author has consciously not promoted the notion that leaders are always those in an organization who hold upper level positions of power and/or authority. Although we traditionally think of most leaders as positioned atop the organizational pecking order, social work has clearly promoted the stance that all practicing Bachelor's in Social Work (BSW) and Master's in Social Work (MSW) social workers should strive to lead clients, individuals, colleagues and other stakeholders, wherever they practice in the organization's hierarchy, be it in its upper, middle, or lower ranks. This is reiterated in one of CSWE's (*EPAS*, 2009) 10 core competencies. Specifically,

TABLE 6.1 Leadership Necessities: The Synergy of Personal Attributes, Skill Competencies & Leadership Intuition

---

1. Selective Main Personal Attributes

Integrity
- Honesty
- Ethics
- Transparency

Role Modeling
- Personal
- Professional

Charisma
- Promote positive energy

Decisive
- Easy decisions
- Difficult decisions
- Be assertive

Physical Presence
Have one
"What would … do?"
Come to work

Self-Confidence
Exuding not over-bearing
Contagion effect

2. Creative Use of Main Skill Competencies

Communication
- Oral and written
- Sender and receiver
- Pleasant
- Diplomatic
- Appropriate

Knowledge Competence
- Specialized and also broad
- Develop "$ Eyes"
- Factual and researched
- "I also don't know" is OK
- Thinking smarter

Empowering
- Difference between empowering and disempowering
- Enabling
- Consciousness raising
- Believing in others

Inspiring/Influencing/Persuading
- Group vs. individual strategies
- Motivating
- Timing
- Negotiating

Managing Others
- Administering
- Collaborating
- Coordinating
- Task orientation
- Respecting governance
- Focusing on the goal
- Personal issues are not as important as organizational ones

Using Power and Authority Judiciously
- Nonauthoritative
- Tact and discretion
- Devoid of personal agenda
- Do not apologize for using power/authority
- Share power and authority

3. Developing One's Leadership Intuition

Know When To
- Pick your spots for expending resources
- Defer power and authority
- Manage conflicts
- Use your strengths
- Acknowledge your weaknesses
- Deal with troubled employees

Know How To
- Lead vs. manage
- Transform vs. transact
- Admit you were wrong
- Unlearn bad responding habits
- Make lemonade from lemons
- Provide feedback
- Provide positive reinforcement

---

in Competency 9—*Respond to Contexts That Shape Practice*, sub-section (b) states: [social workers] "provide leadership in promoting sustainable changes in service delivery and practice to improve the quality of social services" (https://www.usi.edu/libarts/socialwork/docs/Ten-Core-Competencies-current.pdf). Thus, all social workers must strive to achieve leadership in our profession, regardless of where they work in their organizational settings.

TABLE 6.2 The Leadership Attribute Grid (LAG)—Applied at All
Organization Levels

Core Leadership Attributes	Various Practice Levels		
	Front Line	Middle Managers	Upper Level Individuals

1. Vision
   a. Having one
   b. Implementing one			

2. Problem-solving capacity			
3. Team work/collaboration			
4. Creating positive change			
5. Influencing others to act			
Minor Attributes			
1. Skills 2. Personal characteristics 3. Leadership intuition			

In 2006, while teaching a graduate class at the School of Social Work, University of Windsor, in Canada, the author took this notion—"social work leaders need to lead any level in the organization" seriously, and developed a useful teaching tool interfacing the aforementioned five core social work attributes, across the three main hierarchical levels of an organization as illustrated in the Leadership Analysis Grid (LAG) presented in Table 6.2.

As displayed in Table 6.2, MSW students were asked to identify three person(s) in their places of social service employment who were in front-line, middle, or upper levels, and then identify at least three of the five core attributes (in Table 6.2), and two additional minor attributes (from Table 6.1), and provide examples of how these social workers provided leadership within their organization. Students were taught to explore and think creatively "outside of the management box" while using the LAG. In doing so, they provided rich case examples of how social work leadership is both taught and promoted in our profession.

Concluding Remarks

Although some of our professional associations and bodies, such as the Society for Social Work and Research (www.sswr.org) and the Institute for the Advancement of Social Work Research (www.iasw.soton.ac.uk), have taken proactive roles in promoting various aspects within the profession, recently the CSWE (www.cswe.org) has identified leadership as a renewed educational priority. In February 2007, CSWE sponsored a two-day conference entitled "Building Leaders in Social Work Education: Pathways to Success" in Mesa, Arizona. This entire conference was devoted to social work leadership in areas of teaching, classroom and field education, training, research, and practice. In 2009, CSWE's EPAS standard articulating the 10 core competencies that shape accreditation specifically targeted leadership (in competency #9) as an important educational area for BSW & MSW students. Given this reality, it appears that social work is slowly embracing leadership as something that holds legitimate promise for education, training, practice, and professional development. That being the case, the responsibility for defining social work leadership in ways that are simple, clear, timely, and consensually accepted and relevant is not only important, but essential. Hopefully, this chapter has assisted with this concern.

WEB RESOURCES

1. Trimberger, G. (2012). Developing leaders: Empowering human service practitioners. http://www.uwgb.edu/outreach/socialwork/assets/pdf/DevelopingLeaders%20(2).pdf

2. Social Work Leadership Institute http://www.nyam.org/social-work-leadership-institute-v2/

3. New York Academy of Medicine http://www.nyam.org/about-us/social-work-leadership/

4. Motivation and Leadership in Social Work. A Review of Theories and Related Studies. http://www.tandfonline.com/doi/abs/10.1080/03643100902769160#preview

References

Bartlett, H. M. (1970). *The common base of social work practice*. Silver Spring, MD: National Association of Social Workers.

Boehm, W. W. (1958). The nature of social work. *Social Work, 3*, 10–18.

Breshars, E., & Volker, R. (2013). *Facilitative leadership and social work practice*. New York, NY: Spring Publishing.

Brilliant, E. L. (1986). Social work leadership: A missing ingredient? *Social Work, 31*(5), 325–331.

Council on Social Work Education Strategic Plan: 1998–2000. (1998). *Social Work Education Reporter, 46*(1), 1, 15–18.

Flexner, A. (1915). Is social work a profession? Proceedings of the National Conference of Charities and Corrections. Chicago, IL: Hildmann Printing.

Gitterman A., & Germain, C. B. (1980). *The life model of social work practice. Advances in theory and practice*. New York, NY: Columbia University Press.

Gordon, W. E. (1962). A critique of the working definition. *Social Work, 7*(4), 3–13.

Graham, K. (2002). *Studies in vision and management: Interviews with UN leaders*. Unpublished paper. Amman, Jordan: UN Leadership Academy.

Hafford-Letchfield, T., & Lawler, J. (2010). Reshaping leadership and management: The emperor's new clothes? *Social Work and Social Sciences Review, 14*(1), 5–8. doi:10.1921/095352210X518153

Hartley, J., & Allison, M. (2002). The role of leadership in the modernization and improvement of public services. In J. Reynolds, J. Henderson, J. Sedan, J. Charlesworth, & A. Bullman (Eds.), *The managing care reader* (pp. 296–305). Buckingham, UK: Open University Press.

Holosko, M. J. (2009). Social work leadership: Identifying core attributes. *Journal of Human Behavior in the Social Environment, 19*, 448–459.

Holosko, M. J., & Skinner, J. (2013, in press). Leadership and management: Necessary skills for field directors. In M. Raskin, C. Hunter, & J. Moen (Eds.), *Quality Social Work Field Education: A Field Director's Guide*. Chicago, IL: Lyceum Books.

James, W. (1907). What pragmatism means. In F. Burkhardt, F. Bowers, I. Skrupskelis (Eds.), *Pragmatism and other essays* (pp. 22–28). Cambridge, MA: Harvard University Press.

Kamaria, K., & Lewis, A. (2009). The not-for-profit general management responsive capability competencies: A strategic management perspective. *Business Strategy Series, 10*(5), 296–310. doi:10.1108/17515630910989196

Kotter, J. P. (1990). *Force for change: How leadership differs from management*. New York, NY: Free Press.

Lawler, J., & Bilson, A. (2010). *Social work management and leadership: Managing complexity with creativity*. London: Routledge.

Nesoff, I. (2007). The importance of revitalizing management education for social workers. *Social Work, 52*(3), 283–285.

Paton, R. Mordaunt, J., & Cornforth, C. (2007). Beyond nonprofit management education: Leadership development in a time of blurred boundaries and distributed learning. *Nonprofit and Voluntary Sector Quarterly, 36*(4), 148S–162S.

Pickett, R. B., & Kennedy, M. M. (2003). Career development strategies: The stages of a manager's life Part II. *Clinical Leadership and Management Review, 17*(5), 283–285.

Pincus, A., & Minahan, A. (1973). *Social work practice: Model and method*. Itasca, IL: F. E. Peacock.

Rank, M. G., & Hutchinson, W. S. (2000). An analysis of leadership within the social work profession. *Journal of Social Work Education, 36*(3), 487–502.

Reamer, F. G. (1993). Cultivating leadership in social work education. *Journal of Social Work Education, 29*(2), 139–141.

Reid, W., & Epstein, L. (1972). *Task-centered casework*. New York, NY: Columbia University Press.

Snowden, D. J., & Boone, M. E. (2007). A leader's framework for discriminating. *Harvard Business Review*, 69–76.

Stoesz, D. (1997). The end of social work. In M. Reisch & E. Gambrill (Eds.), *Social work in the twenty-first century* (pp. 368–375). Thousand Oaks, CA: Pine Forge.

Taylor, V. (2007). Leadership for service improvement. *Nursing Management, 13*(9), 30–34.

Wimpfheimer, J. (2004). Leadership and management competencies defined by practice social work managers. *Administration in Social Work, 28*(1), 45–56.

7   Essentials of Private Practice

Raymond D. Fox

INTRODUCTION

Ups and downs, rewards and challenges, merits and limitations in private practice emanate from its nature—being at the same time a professional endeavor and a business venture. Private practitioners assume total responsibility for every aspect of practice. This includes such diverse constituents as observing ethical standards, setting hours and fees, obtaining insurance, assessing and, most importantly, evaluating their effectiveness. In my view, social workers are particularly well educated as practitioners, but poorly prepared as entrepreneurs. Cox (2009) emphasizes this point.

Consistent with the definition of social work from the International Federation of Social Workers, private practice "bases its methodology on a systematic body of evidence-based knowledge derived from research and practice evaluation, including local and indigenous knowledge specific to its context. It recognizes the complexity of interactions between human beings and their environment, and the capacity of people both to be affected by and to alter the multiple influences upon them including bio-psychosocial factors (2000).

A practitioner for the past 40 years and a teacher, consultant, and supervisor for 35 years, I have come to appreciate the need for a common-sense and down-to-earth approach to private practice. Theoretical frameworks and research findings provide a scientific basis for practice, but little guidance by way of its art and craft. A creative leap is required to bridge abstract theory and concrete reality. Another creative leap is required to close the gap between the professional and the business dimensions of private practice.

THE PROFESSIONAL DIMENSION

Personal Aspect

Only when you are alert to who you are and what you are doing are you sufficiently relaxed, clear, and open-minded to establish and maintain a private practice and better understand clients. It is not possible to be tuned into the feelings of others without first being attuned to your own. Your constant challenge is to understand the interplay between your personal and professional roles and responses. Your personality, values, and sensitivity are the very tools that make you an effective therapeutic instrument. Take time to inventory your unique attributes and skills. Your *personhood*, in other words, is the essential feature in the establishment and maintenance of the therapeutic alliance.

Because you can react only from what is within yourself, you must know yourself so that your capacity for being in relationship is increased, your ability to react consciously is intensified, and you are freer to make deliberate choices about how to respond to clients. Only by knowing yourself are you in a position to make active and creative use of feelings, thoughts, intentions, and motives to optimize the helping process. Only by knowing your assets and shortcomings in terms of a knowledge and skill base, professionally and entrepreneurially, are you in a reasonable position to choose to practice privately.

Awareness leads to more disciplined and clearly directed work as reported in numerous studies. In brief, do what you expect clients to do. Take a hard look at yourself. What is your motivation? Being your own boss? Status? Growing professionally? Earning more money? Minimizing bureaucracy? Maximizing autonomy and independence? Selecting your own client population? Being more creative?

Will you specialize in a method? With a population? With a symptom? Are you fully qualified? Licensed? Do you want a full- or part-time practice? How will you further hone your skills? Advance your knowledge? Do you fully appreciate the consequences in terms of the commitment of time, energy, and money involved in such an enterprise?

Creativity and Fluidity

I encourage a fluid and personal approach to respond differentially and effectively to a wide range of clients with a broad array of problems. As an autonomous practitioner you can enjoy the freedom, within the bounds of accepted ethical and empirical standards, to employ innovative methods for helping clients fathom their lives and gain deeper understanding. I utilize a variety of distinctive strategies more fully described elsewhere (Fox, 2013). One method, however, which I have found indispensable, particularly when working with trauma survivors, is journal keeping. The following sketch of Joan, who used this approach, serves as one illustration.

Joan experienced extraordinary trauma throughout her life. Abandoned by her father at three, his infrequent contact with her was sexually abusive. Her mother suffered a paralyzing automobile accident leaving her disabled and shifting excessive responsibility to Joan and her younger brother. Joan had serious knee problems, which, treated by a family physician, worsened as a result of his injecting it with an unknown substance, causing excruciating pain intended to disguise his having sodomized her at age twelve; as a result she underwent a series of major and painful surgeries for her disabled knee. During our contact she oversaw the nursing home care of her mother, who suffered from Alzheimer's disease. And Joan's mother died at a critical juncture in therapy.

Finding it almost impossible to acknowledge her multiple traumas and articulate their emotional impact, Joan painted. Her's was an art journal (Carey, Fox, & Penney, 2002). An integral facet of her treatment, it contributed significantly her progress. She attributed, as did I, her steady improvement to my serious attention to her vivid entries. In these entries she portrayed unspeakable memories and depicted their emotional residue through the medium of water color. During our face-to-face contact she struggled, and struggled successfully, to translate these artful images into words. The journal served as a source of intense catharsis for her and a source of insight for both of us.

Joan's frightening nightmares dissipated, her neck problems and migraines ceased. Her alcohol use to self medicate when feeling "on edge" desisted. This innovative method promoted her healing.

Evidence Base for Practice

Social work literature promoting evidence-based practice (Pollio, 2006; Proctor, 2003; Rosen, 2003) challenges unexamined and unsystematic clinical interventions. Practitioners are induced to employ empirically validated interventions, whenever possible, linked to clients' goals and objectives and to evaluate outcome effectiveness.

Self-reflection constitutes one form of evaluation. Almost axiomatic is supervision. Case conferences and consultation are additional types of quality control and evaluation. These approaches rely almost exclusively upon subjective assessment and should be part of every practitioner's routine. An array of other means can serve as supplements—practice logs, intensive case studies, and critical incident analysis. Process recording is yet another method for self-reflection (Fox & Gutheil, 2000). All of these enable you to conceptualize all stages of practice interaction through the exercise of reconsidering and analyzing your contact with clients. All enhance your ability to discern efficiency. Especially in urban areas, often having a glut of practitioners, augmented advanced training leading toward a specialization provides an additional welcome edge.

Qualitative methods are refined when combined with objective forms of evaluation. Just as your treatment strategies need to be tailored to meet the unique needs of individual clients, so, too, should your evaluation methods be selected with care. Observations of a client over time constitute a single-subject or single-system design for evaluation. Such a quantitative design requires that client behaviors or events be specified in measurable terms. Goals provide this reference point against which change can be compared. Also emphasized are: (1) specifying target behaviors, (2) identifying a suitable measure, (3) employing it systematically, (4) analyzing observations over time, and (5) charting change. Two discrete methods—Single Subject/System Design and Practice Outcome Inventory stress establishing a clear and quantifiable "before–after" picture of interventions.

Charts or graphs help to track client progress. These make it possible to individualize evaluation to the unique characteristics, needs, and dilemmas of your clients. They provide ready visual gauges for both you and the client to track change. Decisions can follow as to whether or not there is significant change in a desired direction meeting the expressed purpose of treatment. Corrective adjustments can then be rationally and realistically taken.

Easy-to-use prepackaged standardized scales are also available to incorporate into your practice. From analysis of the information gleaned over a series of time intervals, you can make reasonable assessments about treatment success, discuss options for continuing or discontinuing treatment based on these results, alter interventions, make a referral, or terminate. When such methods are incorporated directly into treatment, they actually propel clinical work. No attempt is made here to detail either Single Subject/System Design or Practice Outcome Inventory, which can encompass sophisticated variations or statistical procedures. Rather, the following illustration is offered, with an appeal to seriously consider incorporating some structured and standardized form of evaluation into your practice.

Cognitive therapy focuses on correcting clients' negatively distorted thoughts and helping them to think more realistically. Already in a depression, Mr. H's sudden loss of employment as a middle manager activated dysfunctional automatic thoughts such as "never being able to do anything right," accompanied by feelings of dejection and devaluation and a sense of paralysis of never being able to work again. Accepting these skewed thoughts as a foregone conclusion, his depression deepened. After I had explained the cognitive approach and we had identified goals for both of us, Mr. H agreed to utilize the Beck Depression Inventory (BDI) within sessions and as homework over a three-month period in order to meet his need for recognizing progress and my need to monitor the success of selected cognitive interventions. Originally intended to be practitioner administered, the BDI is consumer-friendly. I, therefore, encourage clients, and selected others (e.g., family, friends, other involved professionals) to complete it along with the client themselves after obtaining instruction and gaining practice in its application. Mr. H completed one copy of the inventory each day. A weekly composite score of his level of depression was calculated by averaging his daily ratings. Mr. H's wife completed the Inventory weekly for that same time period. Mr. H also kept a mood log each day, which he gave me at our scheduled session.

Perusing his journal, I arrived at a separate third score, a composite weekly score, by averaging the daily entries. Such a procedure provided three independent comparative measures of his depression level over the 12-week course of treatment. These three separate indices were graphed.

Remarkable correspondence was noted among the separate scores—his own, his wife's, and mine. For the first nine weeks of treatment Mr. H's level remained severe; nevertheless, it was steadily declining. The tenth and twelfth weeks marked a sharp decrease in the level of depression. It was evident that Mr. H was recovering and making healthier adaptations in his life. Most importantly, it vividly demonstrated to him that feelings of despair could be overcome even though he initially believed that "nothing could really help." For me it affirmed that selected cognitive interventions, journal-keeping, homework, maintaining the Beck Inventory, had a positive result.

The graph made it immediately evident by charting the three separate indices that Mr. H had made substantial headway over the 12 weeks toward overcoming his depression. Added diagnostic and clinical advantages accrue from using such a visual method for tracking progress. Beyond being a tangible sign for everyone of progress, it became a catalyst for further intensive discussion about other adjustments Mr. H needed to make in his treatment as well as in his life. These discussions, in turn, led to identifying supplementary goals for treatment, including the development of strategies for finding employment.

SIGNIFICANT ADVANCES

Neuroscience and Genetics

The advances in neuroscience (brain structure, function, and chemistry), and genetics have considerable impact on present-day practice. Understanding the brain and the influence of the genome alters the process of therapy (Ilg et al., 2008). We now know that comprehending their impact along with the therapeutic relationship actually serves to create and alter neural circuits. As a consequence, we appreciate more fully what we can and cannot deliver in terms of change (Fox, 2013). It is necessary to stress that even the most sophisticated biologically based therapies will work best when combined with helping clients explore the subjective experience of their behavior and symptoms.

Mindfulness is one powerful method given credence by extant biological research. Its incorporation into practice may alleviate emotional and/or physical suffering, improve the ability to make decisions informed by compassion and kindness, and take responsibility for choices (Sanders, 2010; Turner, 2009; Davis & Hayes, 2011; Ludwig & Kabat-Zinn, 2008; Siegel, D., 2010). The benefits of mindfulness include stress-reduction, improved self-control, affect tolerance and flexibility, enhanced concentration, and mental clarity, as well as fostering kindness, acceptance, and compassion towards others and one's self (Davis & Hayes, 2011). Bruce, Manber, Shapiro, and Constantino (2010) examine the benefits of mindfulness training for mental health clinicians themselves.

DSM 5

The DSM 5 (2014) has met with considerable controversy. Despite its shortcomings, it is central to private practice. Criticized as lacking scientific validity in terms of biological influences, it remains the best tool available to guide you on diagnosing disorders. Moreover, insurance companies, governmental agencies, and the courts rely on it for determining benefits, statistics, evidence, and testimony. Although it fails to point the way to specific effective treatment, it serves as the passport to mental health coverage, and among other things, special educational and behavioral services and disability benefits. It also provides a common language for you to employ when discussing clients with colleagues, supervisors, etc. Get to know it, and get to know it well.

Technology

I would be remiss in not referring to the pervasive and accelerating use of technology. It does not supplant, but instead supplements more conventional clinical tools. Augment your repertoire with the already available and ever evolving electronic resources. The Internet has been instrumental in creating a continually updated and livelier means of contact. It also offers databases that provide highly developed methods tools for searching and analyzing literature and research on recent diagnostic and evidence-based treatment developments. Online platforms such as Skype and texting are constructive adjuncts to real time face-to-face therapy, and promote ongoing connection, communication, and interaction. After much deliberation and encouragement

from colleagues, I have recently acceded to developing a personal website. It promises to provide a beneficial addition to clinical venture. I encourage you to do the same.

Especially because various electronic apparatus is constantly emerging (e.g., the Cloud), and you are bound to face yet unheard of more sophisticated advances, become familiar with the present array of technological enhancements even though by the time you have mastered them, they likely will have been surpassed by more novel ones. I do not advocate becoming technologically dependent. Rather, I recommend that you embark on a pursuit to integrate into your practice those strategies with which you are comfortable and which serve to enhance client interaction.

As ubiquitous, prevalent, and constructive as it might be, technology is not without limitations and reservations. There is a hazard of over-reliance on it, particularly in a practice profession such as ours. Technology is no substitute for face-to-face discourse. I prefer a blend of methods, conventional and novel, distant and proximate, computer-based and personal-based. Technology alone does not make a difference. Employed judiciously and selectively, however, in combination with direct person-to-person contact, a hybrid as it were, it has great advantages.

SELF CARE

By virtue of our being fellow human beings, but more so by virtue of our role as practitioners, we are affected deeply by others' suffering and pain. Such resonance is exacerbated by our own exposure to the same incomprehensible events that affect our clients. Take time for solitude and reflection. Periodically attend to and take care of "self." It has been my experience as a practitioner, supervisor, and consultant that private practice can often be a rather solitary and isolating pursuit. It can make you vulnerable to discouragement, even disillusionment.

Repeatedly dealing with others' stress, anguish, and unexpected crises throughout a career can lead to "compassion fatigue" (Fox, 2003), which has the potential to impact your ability to give fully in your work and extract more from you than is emotionally healthy when listening and absorbing (Figley & Bender, 2012; Newell & MacNeil, 2010). Refuel yourself in healthy ways. Be sure to involve yourself regularly with sources of professional and personal support, learn to step back and put limits on yourself, make a commitment to seek out supervision and, when needed, counseling, before depletion sets in and compromises your confidence and competence. Consciously endeavor to involve yourself in satisfying experiences outside of work. Avoid the tendency to disengage, not only from clients but from peers and from your "self" as well. Foster associations with colleagues so as to be affirmed, glean support, and create avenues to share experience. **Remember that you cannot fix everything and everyone.**

ENTREPRENEURIAL DIMENSION

General Issues

Practitioners seem ill prepared for the business side of private practice. They rarely receive relevant education in money matters. Many social workers have special difficulty reconciling their backgrounds with a profit motive and with sticking to operating procedures based on management principles. Dealing with a host of financial issues, setting fees, collecting fees, dealing with nonpayment, setting policies for missed appointments, and maintaining financial records, all add to a discomfort level. Issues abound having to do with establishing and supporting an office. Options are many—developing a home office, renting shared space in or separate from a group practice, subletting a workplace. Accompanying these concerns are those focusing on how to furnish, lay out, and keep up the office. Beyond rent, routine ordinary expenses include utilities, phone, computer, and cleaning. In addition, other, more remarkable factors need to be considered. Among them are whether to offer your services as an independent provider, as part of a group practice along with social work or interdisciplinary colleagues, or as a professional corporation. Obtaining insurance of all types—disability, accident, dwelling, and malpractice absorbs extra attention.

Valuable assistance in developing preliminary plans and preparing a prospective budget can be obtained by logging onto: www.bplans.com/dp/ and www.socialworker.com.

Especially in these times of a changing and restrictive economy, be cautioned that setting up a practice, as is already evident, is complex and multifaceted. It requires a hefty investment of time and money. Be prepared and deliberate in moving forward. Recognize that diversification of your personal practice is as critical as diversification of your personal finances.

Marketing

Marketing is a further major consideration. From my observation, social workers are uncomfortable with identity, image management, and public relations. How do you present yourself? As a therapist? A counselor? A social worker?

Exposure is central to boosting a practice and requires comfort in self-promotion and marketing. Steady and reliable referral sources are the life blood of practice. Of paramount importance is networking with colleagues, with like-minded practitioners from allied professions, and with community organizations. Networking is time consuming and costly. Some questions may guide your thinking. Do you offer presentations at a local library? Join a speaker's bureau? Submit an ad to a local newspaper or the "yellow pages"? Do you place flyers and announcements in churches or with community merchants? Do you develop a website? Affiliations of every sort are required to initiate and sustain a private practice and provide ongoing support for your own professional endeavors. Do you connect with clinics, hospitals, employee assistance programs, hotlines, mental health agencies, day care facilities? Do you offer training seminars to a range of professionals? Teaching and writing also increase your exposure. Do you offer workshops to groups such as AARP, PTA, or the Elks? Do you "make the rounds" of doctors, chiropractors, physical therapists, and attorneys to acquaint them with your services? Do you speak publicly in libraries and community meetings?

Over and above being recognized and opening a private practice, you need to build arrangements with other experts with whom to consult about the special predicaments that inevitably arise. Relationships with other experts, those not in the field, are required to assist in the day-to-day operation of your practice. These might include certified public accountants (CPAs), attorneys, and insurance agents. Will you choose to employ support personnel, such as receptionists, secretaries, and office cleaners? What will your business cards look like? What will they say? How will you cover vacations? All of these points are integral to approaching practice as a commercial operation based on business principles, with contractual operations clearly defined and in writing.

Managed Care

A further important factor entails managed care with its attendant benefits and liabilities. Although enrollment in such an organization promises a steady source of referrals, often these are promises only. Frequently, financial remuneration is reduced.

Be cautioned that, increasingly, insurance covers only a minimal number of sessions; prospective clients may not have the necessary out-of-pocket financial resources to proceed. In addition, issues of privacy, confidentiality, and freedom of choice in selecting intervention strategies accompany being on the managed care roster. All these issues can affect, possibly negatively, your client-practitioner relationship. It has been my experience that practitioners are frequently forced into a position of having to adjust client contact to suit the managed care company's conditions. Negotiating the type and extent of treatment, advocating for clients' best interests, obtaining reimbursement for your best efforts constitute major predicaments and often spark ethical dilemmas.

As you think about becoming a managed care provider, become intimately familiar with its regulations about capitation, coinsurance, and copayment. Health maintenance organizations (HMOs), created by insurance companies, provide a package of services for a premium usually paid by employers. They make serious demands on the practitioner. These mostly involve accountability.

Record keeping is fundamental in any manner of practice, but especially so in managed care. More importantly, as an autonomous practitioner you are morally answerable and legally responsible. Documentation of differential diagnosis, medical necessity, treatment plan, explanation of what occurred in contact, under what circumstances, and with what results needs to be in compliance with requirements of regulatory and fiscal bodies to assure accuracy and provision of what is defined as appropriate treatment. Be sure to include in your files referral sources, brief history, medication if indicated, dates, and outcomes. Always keep privileged communication in a completely secure area, under lock and key.

It is a mistake to believe that not keeping notes will protect client confidences and avert subpoena. Do not attempt to out-think or second-guess contractual entities or legal systems. On a different note, if legal action is brought against you, without up-to-date records it would be impossible for you to construct a case retrospectively and thereby mount a defense.

ETHICAL DIMENSION

Basics

Forcefully stated: *Vigilantly observe the Code of Ethics* www.socialworkers.org/pubs/code
Become intimately acquainted with HIPPA, the Health Insurance Portability and Accountability Act of 1996 (www.hhs.gov/ocr/privacy/).

Malpractice

It is possible, but not probable, that you will be accused of malpractice. It is prudent, however, to keep in mind, the following: To be sued for malpractice, there must first be demonstrable proof that a legal duty existed between you and the client; that you violated that duty by failing to conform to professional standards of care; that evidence exists showing you to be negligent in not conforming to an accepted standard of care, and it can be demonstrated that the client has been harmed or injured in some way and that you were the proximate cause of the injury for which damages are sought. Possible infractions include abandonment of service, mismanagement of the relationship, breach of confidentiality, failure to provide appropriate treatment, and prevention of harm to third parties. Other causes are failure to consult with a specialist, defamation, violation of civil rights, failure to be available when needed, untimely termination of treatment, and inappropriate bill collecting methods. Malpractice insurance is requisite even though being sued is extremely unlikely, especially for social work practitioners.

Fundamentals

Be clear about your specialty niches—those areas of your own expertise as well as those that require involving other experts. Honor your requirement to garner full informed consent from clients. Honor your obligation toward suicidal clients and your duty to warn potential victims of clients who make threats. Acknowledge and follow through with your duty in cases of suspected or actual child or elder abuse and neglect. Grasp requirements for court testimony and the elements of sub-poena. Present danger overrides confidentiality. Protection trumps jeopardy.

Be honest with yourself and with your clients—there are no guarantees and there are no relationships, including practitioner-client relationships, that are totally risk free for either party.

ELEMENTS OF PRIVATE PRACTICE

What works? What should you keep in mind? What are key elements gleaned from my active and deep reflection on 40 years of practice? These interwoven guideposts build upon and enhance each other:

Relating

Research into practice effectiveness across modalities and theories identifies relationship as the foremost ingredient for success and effectiveness.

Hearing Their Story

Accompany clients through their life story. It creates a structure for catharsis of disturbing affects, cleansing of disquieting memories, and discovery of new perspectives.

Naming Things for What They Are

Avoid euphemisms and name the "un-nameable"— abuse, rape, assault, victimization, and trauma because honesty grounds practice and propels the process forward.

Blending Seriousness and Fun

Neither shy away from difficult material nor be too intrusive. Spontaneity, humor, and paradox advance change and provide, simultaneously, caring and challenge.

Educating

Offer practical information, advice, alternative viewpoints. Teach self-soothing techniques. Counter distorted thinking patterns.

Setting Goals

Mutually set goals to give you and your clients impetus to carry on, direction for the future, and marks of, and satisfaction in, accomplishment as you move forward.

Being Fair

Establish reasonable fees, consider a sliding scale, accommodate to contingencies in clients' lives such as unemployment, illness, disability.

Believing

Believing in the purposefulness of practice, in yourself, and in clients' strengths leads to meaningful exploration and examination, as well as recognition of choice.

Creating "Safety"

Meet clients' basic needs for security and affirmation. This fosters their ability to master their lives, face the challenge of self-discovery and the triumph of ownership.

Taking an Active Stance

Concentrate on clients' aspirations and resiliency, engaging in active and genuine collaboration toward interrupting dysfunctional patterns and fostering empowerment.

Confrontation

Challenge any discrepancy directly. Even though it is risky, it keeps both of you on track toward advancing true insight.

Balancing

Maintain a dynamic equilibrium between the interdependent features of professional standards of care and entrepreneurial realities.

A FINAL REMARK

Finally, what brings success in private practice is integrity and reputation. Develop referral sources, confer with other professionals from a variety of related disciplines, market your professional attributes, cultivate small business skills, keep abreast of the changing care environment and trends, preserve the nature of your client relationships, obtain medical and psychiatric consultation when relevant, keep accurate records, and document, document, document. To reiterate, success in private practice arises from integrity and reputation.

WEBSITES

www.bplans.com/dp/
www.hhs.gov/ocr/privacy/
www.socialworker.com
www.socialworkers.org/pubs/code

References

Bruce, N. G., Manber, R., Shapiro, S. L., & Constantine, M. J. (2010). Psychotherapist mindfulness and the psychotherapy process. *Psychotherapy Theory, Research, Practice, Training, 47*(1), 83–97.

Carey, M., Fox, R., & Penney, J. (2002). *The artful journal: A spiritual quest.* New York, NY: Watson/ Gupthil.

Cox, K. (2009). Redefining private practice: Smart ideas for a changing economy. *Social Work Today, 9*(6), 12.

Davis, D. M., & Hayes, J. A. (2011). What are the benefits of mindfulness? A practice review of psychotherapy-related research. *Journal of Psychotherapy, 48*(2), 198–208.

American Psychiatric Association. (2014). *Diagnostic and Statistical Manual of Mental Disorders* (5th ed). Arlington, VA: American Psychiatric Association Press.

Figley, C., & Bender, J. (2012). The cost of caring requires self-care. In J. Bender (Ed.), *Advances in social work practice with the military.* New York, NY: Routledge.

Fox, R. (2013). *Elements of the helping process: A guide for clinicians* (3rd ed). New York, NY: Routledge.

_____ (2003). "Traumaphobia: Traumatized therapists working with trauma," *Psychoanalytic Social Work, 10*(2), 43–55.

Fox, R., & Gutheil, I. (2000). Process Recording: A means for conceptualizing and evaluating practice. *Journal of Teaching in Social Work, 20*(1/2), 39–56.

Ilg, R., Wohlschlager, A. M., Gaser, C., Liebau, Y., Dauner, R., Woller, A., et al. (2008). Gray matter increase induced by practice correlates with talk-specific activation: A combined functional and morphometric magnetic resonance imaging study. *Journal of Neuroscience, 28,* 4210–4215.

Ludwig, D. S., & Kabat-Zinn, J. (2008). Mindfulness in medicine. *JAMA, 300*(11), 1350–1352.

Newell, J., & MacNeil, G. (2010). Professional burnout, vicarious trauma, secondary traumatic stress, and compassion fatigue: A review of theoretical terms, risk factors, and preventive methods for clinicians and researchers. *Best Practices in Mental Health, 6*(2), 57–68.

Pollio, D. E. (2006). The art of evidence-based practice. *Research on Social Work Practice, 16,* 224–232.

Proctor, E. K. (2003). Evidence for practice: Challenges, opportunities, and access. *Social Work Research, 27*(4), 195–197.

Rosen, A. (2003). Evidence-based social work practice: Challenges and promise. *Social Work Research, 27*(4), 197–208.

Sanders, K. (2010). Mindfulness and psychotherapy. *The Journal of Lifelong Learning in Psychiatry, 8*(1), 19–24.

Siegel, D. (2010). *The mindful therapist: A clinician's guide to mindsight and neural integration.* New York, NY: W. W. Norton & Company, Inc.

Turner, K. (2009). Mindfulness: The present moment in clinical social work. *Clinical Social Work Journal, 37,* 95–103.

8

Social Work Practice and the Affordable Care Act

Stephen Gorin, Julie S. Darnell, & Christina M. Andrews

BACKGROUND

The call for national health insurance (NHI) was raised as far back as 1912, when Theodore Roosevelt, the presidential candidate of the Progressive Party, called for the introduction of "'a system of social insurance,'" including the "'protection of home life against the hazards of sickness'" (cited in Birn et al., 2003). Jane Addams, an NASW Social Work Pioneer, played a leading role in Roosevelt's unsuccessful campaign.

NHI emerged again as an issue in 1934, when President Franklin D. Roosevelt appointed a Committee on Economic Security, headed by Frances Perkins, the Secretary of Labor, and another NASW Social Work Pioneer (NASW Foundation, n.d.) to address the economic crisis. Their work culminated in the enactment of Social Security. Perkins and others, including Harry Hopkins, also an NASW Social Work Pioneer, had hoped to incorporate health insurance into the bill, but they soon discovered that this would be impossible due to strong opposition from the AMA, whose members "bombarded members of Congress with letters, postcards, and phone calls decrying compulsory health insurance" (Quadagno, 2006. Although Roosevelt "pulled the plug" on the NHI component of Social Security, the final legislation did include funds for maternal and child health, public health, and assistance to children with disabilities (Downey, 2010, p. 243).

After the failure of NHI during the 1940s and 1950s, many activists concluded that it was politically unfeasible and began focusing on expanding coverage to older adults. Wilbur Cohen played a central role in the enactment in 1965 of Medicare

and Medicaid. The "architects" of this effort viewed it as a "step toward universal national health insurance" (Ball, 1995, p. 63).

Efforts for NHI emerged again during the late 1980s and early 1990s. In 1993, Bill Clinton introduced his Health Security Act (HSA), which "sought a middle path between a Canadian-style single-payer health care system ... and the largely unregulated approaches advocated by conservatives" (Gorin & Moniz, 2014, p. 412). The HSA provoked strong opposition from both the left and right and the administration pulled it without bringing it to a vote.

During the 2008 presidential campaign, Barack Obama advocated an approach to health care that built "on the current system of mixed private and public group insurance" (Collins, Nicholson, Rustgi, & Davis, 2008). After a year of fierce debate, Congress enacted the Affordable Care Act (ACA), or "Obamacare" as it became known, in March 2010. Although many social workers were disappointed that the final version of the ACA did not include a government-run public insurance option, NASW recognized the ACA as a critical step forward in the century-long struggle for NHI and a victory for social workers (Gorin, 2011).

The ACA is too complex to summarize in a short article; however, broadly speaking, it can be viewed as "a three-legged stool" (Krugman, 2013). The first leg is community rating, which requires insurers to "issue policies without regard to an individual's medical history" (Krugman, 2013). The second leg is the individual mandate, which requires all citizens to have insurance. Although the mandate is controversial, without it, healthier and younger individuals could avoid buying coverage, "leaving a relatively bad risk pool, leading to high premiums that drive out even more healthy people" (Krugman, 2013). The third leg consists of subsidies to enable individuals with low incomes to buy coverage. These pieces are interdependent; take away one and the stool collapses.

The ACA is consistent with the "Triple Aim" of expanded coverage, cost control, and improved quality that Berwick, Nolan and Wittington (2008) identified as being critical to health care reform. In terms of coverage, the Congressional Budget Office (CBO) projected that between 2013 and 2023, the share of the nonelderly population (excluding individuals without documentation) with insurance will increase from 82% to 92%. The ACA originally required states to extend Medicaid coverage to individuals with incomes at or below 138% of the federal poverty line (FPL). States refusing to expand coverage would be denied all funding for Medicaid (Gorin & Moniz, 2012). In 2012, the Supreme Court found this section unconstitutional and left it to the states to expand Medicaid without risk of losing all Medicaid funding. This decision places individuals living below the FPL at risk of having no coverage because they are not eligible for assistance to buy insurance in the marketplace. Individuals between 100% and 133% of the FPL will be eligible for subsidies, but they still may not be able to find affordable coverage (Community Catalyst, 2012).

The ACA also addresses the difficult issue of controlling costs. Aaron (2011) noted that the legislation incorporated almost every "rational" approach "analysts have advanced for slowing growth of spending" (p. 2379). The CBO (2013b) and Congress' Joint Committee on Taxation estimated that the ACA will "reduce deficits over the next 10 years and in the subsequent decade."

Finally, the ACA addresses the issue of quality (Gorin & Moniz, 2014). Concerns about the quality of health care in the United States have been raised for more than a decade, and it remains a serious issue (Swenson et al., 2010). A central concern here is the fragmented nature of our system, which is "essentially a cottage industry of non-integrated, dedicated artisans who eschew standardization" (Swenson et al., 2010). In an effort to address this, the ACA promotes the introduction into Medicare of Accountable Care Organizations (ACOs), which provide incentives for "doctors, hospitals and other health care providers to form networks to coordinate care better" (Gold, 2013). Although some have heralded ACOs as the wave of the future, their record thus far has been mixed

(Beck, 2012). The ACA also provides incentives for hospitals to reduce readmission rates for chronically ill patients (Gorin & Moniz, 2014).

Understood in its proper context, the ACA is the outcome of a century-long effort to introduce NHI. It realizes Franklin D. Roosevelt's plan to incorporate NHI into Social Security and, in a real sense, is Social Security's missing leg.

NEW ROLES AND REALITIES UNDER THE ACA: A CLOSER LOOK

Eligibility and Enrollment

By 2018, the ACA is estimated to nearly halve the number of uninsured individuals, from 55 million to 30 million (Congressional Budget Office, 2013a). Twelve million additional adults and children are expected to obtain coverage through Medicaid and the Children's Health Insurance Program (CHIP) and 25 million through the new Health Insurance Marketplaces (also known as exchanges) where individuals and small businesses can purchase health insurance coverage from among an array of plans. States have the option to run their own state-based exchange, partner with the federal government, or default into a federally facilitated exchange. Overall, the ACA is anticipated to result in 92% of Americans having insurance coverage.

Achieving the goal of near-universal health insurance coverage will require, however, that millions of people who are eligible for coverage *actually* enroll. Enrolling newly eligible people into health insurance plans will be a difficult task. Previous research estimating the size of the Medicaid eligible-but-not-enrolled population suggests that between 17% and 68% of eligible people do not enroll (B. Sommers et al., 2012; Sommers, Tomasi, Swartz, & Epstein, 2012; U.S. Government Accountability Office, 2005). The reasons for failing to enroll are wide-ranging and include lack of awareness, stigma, and administrative complexity. Among these, the lack of awareness appears to be a particularly acute problem facing the ACA; evidence from public opinion polls, focus groups, and research studies documents that most Americans have little awareness of the ACA, and that what they have heard makes them wary of it (Altman, 2011; Kaiser Family Foundation, 2013b; Perry, Muligan, Artiga, & Stephens, 2012).

Recognizing these key challenges, the ACA contains several provisions intended to improve participation. First, the ACA mandates that almost everyone purchase insurance or pay a penalty. Second, the law has a "no wrong door" policy in which individuals will be screened jointly for Medicaid, CHIP, and private coverage offered through the marketplace using a single, streamlined application. Third, it creates or expands numerous consumer assistance programs that will help uninsured individuals enroll in new coverage options. They include: (1) navigators, (2) in-person assisters, (3) certified application counselors, and (4) consumer assistance program (CAP) workers.

The ACA requires that all marketplaces establish a navigator program to assist consumers with eligibility, plan selection, and enrollment. Navigators will help consumers determine their eligibility for subsidies or Medicaid. Navigators also will help consumers understand the differences between the platinum, gold, silver, and bronze plans. Navigators may handle grievances and complaints. States have flexibility in designing and operating their navigator programs, but they must conform to the federal minimum standards related to the scope of activities, types of entities allowed to perform navigation tasks, and the competencies and training of navigators.

In-person assisters will play roles similar to navigators. Though conceived of as "non-navigator" assistance, in reality, in-person assisters share many of the same functions as navigators and receive comparable training of about 20–30 hours. This program is state-administered and its availability depends on the type of marketplace: required in partnership exchanges that take on consumer assistance, optional in state-based exchanges, and not available in federally facilitated exchanges.

Beyond navigators and assisters, community-based organizations and providers that have experience providing social services in their communities are eligible to apply to become designated as certified application counselors (CACs). In turn, their staff and volunteers may become certified to help their clients complete applications for coverage. CACs are required to provide information on the full range of coverage options. CACs must comply with privacy and security standards, complete approximately five hours of required online training, and pass a certification exam. Though exchanges must have a CAC program, the marketplaces do not provide funding for it. In addition to the Exchange CACs, states may establish Medicaid CACs to provide

information about, and help individuals enroll in, Medicaid and CHIP.

Finally, the ACA created consumer assistance programs to help consumers enroll in plans and carry out ombudsman-related activities, such as helping consumers file grievances and appeals, tracking and resolving problems, and educating consumers about their rights and responsibilities. Many states established these programs with federal monies, though some have ceased these activities due to reductions in federal funding (Kaiser Family Foundation, 2013a).

What kind of consumer assistance is available, and how much, depends on where one lives, because the responsibilities for consumer assistance functions differ by marketplace. In state-based exchanges, the state takes responsibility for implementing the core marketplace functions. In partnership exchanges, plan management and consumer assistance functions are shared. In federally facilitated exchanges, the U.S. Department of Health and Human Services performs all marketplace functions, including consumer assistance. As of September 2013, just over half of the states ($n = 27$) have defaulted into the federal exchange, 17 states and the District of Columbia have declared a state-based exchange, and seven states have entered into a partnership exchange (see http://kff.org/health-reform/state-indicator/health-insurance-exchanges/). All states regardless of type of marketplace must operate a navigator program and a certified application counselor program in the exchange. In-person assistance is required only in partnership exchanges and is not available in federally facilitated marketplaces. Statewide consumer assistance programs and certified application counselors for the Medicaid program are optional. As a result, the amount of consumer assistance resources available to educate uninsured individuals about the new coverage options and enroll them into plans will vary greatly state by state.

Care Coordination The ACA includes two major provisions designed to enhance care coordination and improve integration of primary care and behavioral health services. First, it establishes a new Medicaid option to establish patient-centered medical homes (PCMHs) for enrollees with complex health care needs. The PCMH is an enhanced model of primary care that provides accessible, comprehensive, ongoing, and coordinated patient-centered care that addresses the needs of the whole person (Patient-Centered Primary Care Collaborative, 2013). PCHMs seek to achieve these ends by organizing physician-led, interprofessional teams that provide continuous and coordinated care, emphasize prevention and effective management of chronic illness, and strive for improved access and communication. To date, the ACA has promoted the establishment of PCMHs in several ways. First, the ACA provides state Medicaid programs with the option to allow providers to create "health homes" based upon the PCMH model for enrollees with certain chronic conditions. States that participate received up to two years of an enhanced matching rate for the services they provided through health homes (Kaiser Family Foundation, 2011). At present, 25 states have implemented health homes within their Medicaid programs. Second, through the ACA-established CMS Innovation Center, new demonstration projects aim to test the effectiveness of PCMH models.

Accountable Care Organizations (ACOs) are the second major model of care coordination promoted by the ACA. Established through the Medicare Shared Savings Program (MSSP), ACOs are defined as organizations of health care providers that are accountable for the quality, cost, and overall care of Medicare beneficiaries (Centers for Medicare and Medicaid Services, 2013c). The ACO model is less structured than the PCMH, encouraging providers to develop creative approaches to providing more cost-effective, quality care that incorporates best practices in improving health care quality and reducing costs through prevention, care coordination, and elimination of unnecessary services. ACOs that meet specified quality performance standards are eligible to receive a percentage of savings incurred if the expenses for care are sufficiently low compared with cost expectations set by MSSP. The program has established five domains in which ACOs must achieve high-quality ratings to earn bonus payments: patient and caregiver experience, care coordination, safety, preventative health, and health of at-risk populations and frail older adults.

Behavioral Health Treatment

The ACA also will expand coverage for mental health and substance abuse treatment services significantly, creating new opportunities for social workers within an expanded behavioral health services system. Insurance coverage provided through the newly established Health Insurance Exchanges (HIEs) and Medicaid benchmark plans will be subject to the Mental Health Parity and Addiction Equity Act (MHPAEA). When passed in 2008, MHPAEA requirements were restricted to health insurance plans for large employers (i.e., organizations that employed more than 50 employees) that already covered behavioral health services, defined as services to treat mental health and substance abuse disorders. The MHPAEA required that large employers ensure that their limits on behavioral health services were no more restrictive than that of other health services offered by the plan. The ACA extends the MHPAEA by requiring Medicaid benchmark plans and state HIE plans to cover behavioral health services in compliance with the parity guidelines established by the MHPAEA. Consequently, it is projected that approximately 30 million people will gain coverage for behavioral health services through the ACA (Buck, 2011). A significant proportion of these people are already insured, but are covered under programs that do not provide coverage for behavioral health services.

These coverage expansions are expected to trigger significant growth in demand for behavioral health services because the proportion of Americans with behavioral health disorders is high. At present, an estimated 20% of Americans have a mental health disorder, 5% have a serious mental illness, and 12% have a substance use disorder (Substance Abuse and Mental Health Service Administration, 2012). And, the co-occurrence of these disorders/conditions is extraordinarily high. Among adults with substance use disorder, 43%—nearly 9 million— had a co-occurring mental illness. Medicaid enrollment alone is estimated to increase by 82% among states expected to participate in the expansion (Banthin et al., 2012). This is especially important because those newly eligible for coverage through the Medicaid expansion exhibit higher rates of almost every behavioral health disorder than the general population (Garfield, Lave, & Donahue, 2012). There may also be a major spike in help seeking behavioral health disorders as these coverage expansions are implemented due to pent up demand—that is, people who may have wanted to seek out behavioral health services, but have not done so in the past due to lack of health insurance coverage for these services.

Although primary care providers will provide some treatment, the need for staff to provide specialty behavioral health services is expected to grow significantly. These new additions to the workforce will be needed in greater numbers within traditional health care settings, as they strive to provide more comprehensive care, as well as in traditional specialty settings for individuals. The Bureau of Labor Statistics (2013) projects that the health care system increasingly will rely on social workers to provide these services. Their most recent estimates suggest that demand for social workers specializing in the provision of behavioral health services will increase by 31% between 2010 and 2020, faster than psychology (22%), behavioral health paraprofessionals (27%), and even medicine (24%) and nursing (26%). The biggest increases in jobs for the social work profession are expected in health social work, gerontology, and behavioral health; in each of these areas, the Bureau of Labor Statistics is projecting growth rates above 30%.

It remains unclear how the ACA will impact social workers providing behavioral health services in private practice. On the one hand, because insurance coverage for behavioral health treatment will rise, there is expected to be increased demand for behavioral health services. This surge in demand could lead to growth in behavioral health services provided in private practice settings. On the other hand, the ACA is likely to result in a contraction in the specialty behavioral health services treatment sector over time as a result of its drive to integrate behavioral health into primary care and other medical settings. Reducing emphasis on treatment modalities that are separate from primary care settings—including private practices—is an implicit goal of the ACA.

GETTING IN THE GAME

Health Insurance Coverage

Social workers can play an important role in helping to ensure that all uninsured individuals (especially the most vulnerable) get the health insurance coverage for which they are eligible. At a minimum, social workers need to know what consumer assistance programs are available in their state and how to connect their uninsured clients to these resources. Social workers ought to consider, however, a larger and more active role: *becoming* navigators, assisters, certified application counselors, or consumer assistance program workers. Because of their specialized knowledge, training, and code of ethics, social workers are uniquely qualified to assume any of the new consumer assistance roles created by the ACA (Darnell, 2013, Andrews et al., 2013). The consumer assistance positions merit serious attention from the social work profession; at their core, these new consumer assistance jobs are about linking individuals to resources, a central activity of social work practice. Furthermore, employment opportunities related to helping uninsured people understand, apply for, and enroll in health insurance coverage should be plentiful, given that navigator programs and certified application counselors are required in all 50 states, and other kinds of consumer assistance are available in many states.

The resources targeted to consumer assistance will vary state to state, with some states operating with limited resources and in political climates that are hostile to the ACA (Goodnough, 2013). These conditions likely will have a negative impact on their state's effectiveness in enrolling the uninsured into coverage. Social workers will be needed to step in to serve as "watchdogs" to assess whether the training is adequate and whether the size, composition, and geographic distribution of the consumer assistance workforce is sufficient to serve the state's uninsured population. Social workers who are working with uninsured clients will be in favored positions to judge and report on whether the system is working.

A related watchdog role for social workers is to monitor access to care for the uninsured as well as for the newly insured. There are two reasons why the remaining uninsured may face even greater difficulties in obtaining needed services when they attempt to seek care: primary care providers are expected to be dealing with high levels of pent-up demand from the newly insured and hospitals will have fewer resources than before to serve the uninsured. A portion of the newly insured population might also be unable to get the care they need due to high deductibles or co-pays, limited drug formularies, limited provider networks, and the like.

Coordinated Care Social workers are particularly well equipped to assist in the design and implementation of coordinated care models. They receive in-depth training in identifying and addressing social determinants of health critical to achieving long-term health and well-being and to do so within the social and environmental contexts in which patients are embedded. Social workers have specialized knowledge of community and social systems and training in case management that is sensitive to cultural beliefs and health literacy (Andrews et al., 2013). Finally, social workers have training in implementing models of behavior change that can help promote effective disease management and prevent illnesses from occurring or reaching stages in which acute medical treatment is needed. Research demonstrates these areas of knowledge and training are particularly effective in meeting the needs of a population referred to as "high utilizers" of health care, which includes individuals with complex health needs, such as co-occurring physical and behavioral health disorders. Social workers have a key role to play in creating the new model of health care to which the ACA aspires, in which prevention, attention to social determinants of health, and well-coordinated care are all central aims. The ACA presents a unique opportunity for social workers to enhance collaborative activities with medicine and allied health professions to maximize the profession's role in shaping these emerging models of integrative, collaborative, and coordinated care.

Behavioral Health Social workers have a long history in behavioral health and are already the predominant professionals providing these services (U.S. Department of Labor, Bureau of Labor Statistics, 2013). Yet, to expand this role, the profession must be responsive to shifts in decision-making power resulting from ACA-driven insurance expansions. Medicaid is poised to become the primary payer of behavioral health services, and in states that take the expansion option, Medicaid agencies will become the single most powerful decision makers in behavioral health. Concomitantly, state agencies that have administered the majority of public behavioral health funding through state and federal block grants are likely to decline in importance.

These changes in the financing of behavioral health services are likely to result in major changes in the distribution of decision-making power. Although the ACA requires all states to include behavioral health services in their essential benefits packages, state Medicaid agencies and HIEs will have broad discretion in determining which behavioral health services will be covered and who can be reimbursed for providing them—at least among those providers that have

not moved to fully capitated models of financing (Buck, 2011). These decisions will greatly influence the size and scope of the behavioral health workforce expansion resulting from the ACA and the relative role of social workers. It will be critical for social worker advocates and researchers to work together to cultivate strong ties to understand the changing role of Medicaid and the new roles of the HIEs in financing behavioral health treatment, and to be aware of key policy decisions that will or can influence social workers, especially as they relate to the profession's role in newly emerging models of integrated care. These tasks will need to be carried out on a state-by-state basis.

Advocating for the Most Vulnerable Social workers have a professional responsibility to advocate for social justice. In keeping with this mandate, social workers ought to be advocating for Medicaid expansions in states that have rejected extensions as a result of a 2012 ruling by the Supreme Court on the ACA (*National Federation of Independent Business v. Sebelius and Florida v. United States Department of Health and Human Services*). By October 2013, only 24 states plus the District of Columbia had agreed to expand Medicaid. The CBO (2012) has estimated that 3 million fewer people will gain insurance coverage as a consequence of the Supreme Court decision. Moreover, the states not expanding Medicaid account for 60% of the nation's "uninsured working poor people" and "68% of poor, uninsured blacks and single mothers" (Tavernise & Gebeloff, 2013).

In addition, an estimated 11 million undocumented immigrants are excluded from the new coverage options. The 5-year ban on Medicaid and CHIP for newly arrived legal immigrants set forth by the Personal Responsibility and Work Opportunity Reconciliation Act of 1996 remains in effect. These disparities in coverage hinder immigrants' ability to obtain health care. Social workers ought to advocate for health insurance for every individual living in the United States, regardless of immigration status. They must also work to ensure that care is culturally and linguistically appropriate.

CONCLUSION

The enactment of the ACA marked a critical step forward in the century-long effort to achieve universal health care coverage in the United States. Social workers have long supported, and at times played a leading role, in this effort. The ACA includes "several provisions that will directly benefit" social workers (Malamud, 2010).

Much remains to be done, however. When fully implemented, the ACA will not achieve universal coverage, and whether it will succeed in bringing costs under control remains an open question. It is also unclear how social workers will fare in the transition from a largely fee-for-service system to one based on coordinated care. In a real sense, the ACA is a work–in-progress and is best understood from this perspective.

WEBSITES

Centers for Medicare and Medicaid Services, www.innovations-cms.gov
Health Affairs, www.content-healthaffairs.org
Health and Human Services, www.hhs.gov
New England Journal of Medicine, www.nejm.org
Centers for Substance Abuse and Mental Health Administration, www.samsha.gov

References

Aaron, H. (2011). The independent advisory board—Congress's "good deed." *New England Journal of Medicine, 364,* 2377–2379. Retrieved from http://www.nejm.org/doi/full/10.1056/NEJMp1105144.

Altman, D. (2011). August Kaiser Health Tracking Poll: The uninsured and the health reform law. Retrieved from http://kff.org/healthreform/perspective/august-kaiser-health-tracking-poll-the-uninsured-and-the-health-reform-law/.

Andrews, C. M., Darnell, J. S., McBride, T. D., & Gehlert, S. (2013). Social work and implementation of the affordable care act. *Health and Social Work, 38*(2), 67–71.

Ball, R. M. (1995). Perspectives on Medicare: What Medicare's architects had in mind. *Health Affairs, 14*(4), 62–72. Retrieved from http://content.healthaffairs.org/content/14/4/62.full.pdf+html.

Banthin, J., Harvey, H., Hearne, J., Bilheimer, L., Fontaine, P., & Anders, S. (2012). Estimates for the insurance coverage provisions of the Affordable Care Act updated for the recent Supreme Court decision. Washington, DC: Congressional Budget Office.

Beck, M. (2012, September 26). Hospitals give health law real-world test. *Wall Street Journal.* Retrieved from http://stream.wsj.com/story/campaign-2012-continuous-coverage/SS-2-9156/SS-2-339324/.

Berwick, D., Nolan, T. W., & Wittington, J. (2008). The triple aim: Care, health, and cost. *Health Affairs, 27*(3), 759–769. Retrieved from http://content.healthaffairs.org/content/27/3/759.full.

Birn, A. E., Brown, T. M., Fee, E., & Lear, W. J. (2003). Struggles for national health reform in the United States. *American Journal of Public Health, 93*(1), 86–91.

Buck, J. A. (2011). The looming expansion and transformation of public substance abuse treatment under the Affordable Care Act. *Health Affairs, 30*(8), 1402–1410.

Centers for Medicare and Medicaid Services. (2013c). *Shared savings program.* Retrieved from http://www.cms.gov/Medicare/Medicare-Fee-for-Service-Payment/sharedsavingsprogram/index.html?redirect=/sharedsavingsprogram/

Collins, S. R., Nicholson, J. L., Rustgi, S. D., & David, K. (2008, October 2). *The 2008 presidential candidates' health reform proposals: Choices for America.* The Commonwealth Fund. Retrieved from http://www.commonwealthfund.org/Publications/Fund-Reports/2008/Oct/The-2008-Presidential-Candidates-Health-Reform-Proposals—Choices-for-America.aspx.

Community Catalyst. (2012, July). Supreme Court ruling on Medicaid: Challenges and opportunities for state advocates. Retrieved from http://www.communitycatalyst.org/doc_store/publications/SupremeCourt-Ruling-on-Medicaid_MemoJuly2012.pdf.

Congressional Budget Office. 2012. Estimates for the insurance coverage provisions of the Affordable Care Act updated for the recent Supreme Court decision. Washington, DC. http://www.cbo.gov/sites/default/files/cbofiles/attachments/43472-07-24-2012-CoverageEstimates.pdf

Congressional Budget Office. (2013a, May). Table 1. CBO's May 2013 estimate of the effects of the Affordable Care Act on health insurance coverage. Retrieved from https://www.cbo.gov/sites/default/files/cbofiles/attachments/44190_EffectsAffordableCareActHealthInsuranceCoverage_2.pdf.

Congressional Budget Office. (2013b, May). CBO's estimate of the net budgetary impact of the Affordable Care Act's health insurance coverage provisions has not changed much over time. Retrieved from https://www.cbo.gov/publication/44176.

Darnell, J. S. (2013). Navigators and Assisters: Two Case Management Roles for Social Workers in the Affordable Care Act. *Health & Social Work,* hlt003.

Downey, K. (2010). *The woman behind the New Deal.* New York, NY: Random House.

Garfield, R. L., Lave, J. R., & Donohue, J. M. (2012). Health reform and the scope of benefits for mental health and substance use disorder services.

Psychiatric Services, 61(11), 1081-1086. Retrieved from http://ps.psychiatryonline.org/.

Gold, J. (2013, August 23). FAQ On ACOs: Accountable Care Organizations, explained. *Kaiser Health News*. Retrieved from http://www.kaiserhealthnews.org/stories/2011/january/13/aco-accountable-care-organization-faq.aspx.

Goodnough, A. (2013). The challenge of helping the uninsured find coverage. *The New York Times*. Retrieved from http://www.nytimes.com/2013/08/15/us/politics/the-challenge-of-helping-the-uninsured-find-coverage.html?_r=0.

Gorin, S. (2011). The Affordable Care Act: Background and analysis. *Health & Social Work*, 36(1), 83–86.

Gorin, S., & Moniz, C. (2014). Health and mental health policy. In M. Reisch (Ed.), *Social policy & social justice* (pp. 405–430). Los Angeles, CA: SAGE Publications.

Gorin, S. H., & Moniz, C. (2012). Medicaid and the Affordable Care Act after the Supreme Court decision. *Health & Social Work*, 37(4), 195–196.

Kaiser Family Foundation. (2013a). Consumer assistance in health reform. Menlo Park, CA: The Henry J. Kaiser Family Foundation. Retrieved from http://kff.org/health-reform/issue-brief/consumer-assistance-in-health-reform/.

Kaiser Family Foundation. (2013b). First wave of major new survey project on California's uninsured [Press release]. Retrieved from http://kff.org/health-reform/press-release/california-uninsured-survey-wave1/.

Krugman, P. (2013, August 18). One reform, indivisible. *The New York Times*. Retrieved from http://www.nytimes.com/2013/08/19/opinion/krugman-one-reform-indivisible.html?_r=0.

Malamud, M. (2010, May). Law recognizes social workers as leading providers of health care in the U.S. *NASW News*. Retrieved from http://www.socialworkers.org/pubs/news/2010/05/health-care-reform.asp.

National Association of Social Workers (NASW) Foundation. NASW Social Work Pioneers. Retrieved from http://www.naswfoundation.org/pioneers/default.asp.

Patient Centered Primary Care Collaborative. (2013). *Defining the medical home: A patient-centered philosophy that drives primary care excellence*. Retrieved from http://www.pcpcc.org/about/medical-home.

Perry, M., Muligan, N., Artiga, A., & Stephens, J. (2012). Faces of the Medicaid expansion: Experiences of uninsured adults who could gain coverage. Washington, DC: Kaiser Commission on Medicaid and the Uninsured. Retrieved from http://kaiserfamilyfoundation.files.wordpress.com/2013/01/8385.pdf.

Quadagno, J. S. (2006). *One nation, uninsured: Why the U.S. has no national health insurance*. New York, NY: Oxford University Press.

Sommers, B., Kronick, R., Finegold, K., Po, R., Schwartz, K., & Glied, S. (2012). *Understanding participation rates in Medicaid: Implications for the Affordable Care Act*. Washington, DC. Retrieved from http://aspe.hhs.gov/health/reports/2012/medicaidtakeup/ib.shtml.

Sommers, B. D., Tomasi, M. R., Swartz, K., & Epstein, A. M. (2012). Reasons for the wide variation in Medicaid participation rates among states hold lessons for coverage expansion in 2014. *Health Affairs*, 31(5), 909–919. Retrieved from http://content.healthaffairs.org/content/31/5/909.full?sid=a8a61870-05d9-44e9-ac95-8d625dc2c7cd.

Swenson, S. J., Meyer, G. S., Nelson, E. C., Hunt, G. C., Pryor, D. B., Weissberg, J. I., … Berwick, D. M. (2010). Cottage industry to post-industrial care—the revolution in health care delivery. *The New England Journal of Medicine*, 362, 12. Retrieved from http://www.nejm.org/doi/full/10.1056/NEJMp0911199.

Tavernise, S., & Gebeloff, R. (2013, October 2). Millions of poor are left uncovered by health law. *The New York Times*. Retrieved from http://www.nytimes.com/2013/10/03/health/millions-of-poor-are-left-uncovered-by-health-law.html?_r=0.

The Henry J. Kaiser Family Foundation. (2011). *Medicaid's new "health home" option*. Retrieved from http://kff.org/health-reform/issue-brief/medicaids-new-health-home-option/.

U.S. Department of Labor, Bureau of Labor Statistics. (2013). Social workers. *Occupational outlook handbook, 2012–2013*. Retrieved from http://www.bls.gov/ooh/Community-and-Social-Service/Social-workers.htm.

U.S. Department of Health and Human Services. (2013). "New resources available to help consumers navigate the Health Insurance Marketplace" [Press release]. Retrieved from http://www.hhs.gov/news/press/2013pres/08/20130815a.html

U.S. Government Accountability Office. (2005). *Means-Tested Programs: Information on Program Access Can Be an Important Management Tool*. Washington, DC. Retrieved from http://www.gao.gov/new.items/d05221.pdf.

9 Social Work Practice in Home-based Services

Martha Morrison Dore & Charlene Zuffante

ANOTHER DAY ON THE JOB

The following reflects a typical day in the life of a social worker delivering home-based services to families and their children.

8:30–9:30 A.M.: Arrive at office. Hunt for a parking space. Check phone messages, return calls to clients, colleagues, and community partners. Find out from a call to the middle school social worker that Robbie McDonald has skipped school for two days in a row.

9:30–9:45 A.M.: Head off to Dobson family home for treatment session with Anna Dobson, her partner, Ellie, and Anna's daughter, Carrie Dobson, 13, who has just returned home from two weeks in residential treatment for a suicide attempt.

9:45–11:30 A.M.: Home-based session with the Dobson family. The relationship between Anna and Ellie is a relatively new one and Carrie, who has been alone with her mom since her parents' divorce five years before, is having a great deal of difficulty adjusting to sharing her mom with Ellie.

Carrie is also entering into adolescence, which requires its own set of developmental adjustments. She also has a very conflicted relationship with her father who has also reacted badly to Anna's involvement with Ellie and feeds Carrie's insecurities about her changing relationship with her mom. The focus of treatment at present is on the relationship between mother and daughter, as well as negotiating the role of Ellie in the family, particularly with regard to Carrie.

11:30–12:00 NOON: Travel to ML King elementary school.

12:00–1:00 P.M.: Attend Individual Education Plan (IEP) meeting at King school for Keisha Harold, age 8, who is experiencing serious attention and behavior problems in second grade. Support Keisha's mom, who is requesting additional testing by an outside evaluator.

1:00–1:30 P.M.:   Travel back to office. Hunt for parking space.

1:30–2:00 P.M.:   Check messages, return more phone calls, set up next day's home visits.

2:00–3:00 P.M.:   Write progress notes in Dobson file documenting morning's home-based treatment session. Write up summary of IEP meeting and document next steps in Harold case file.

3:00–3:30 P.M.:   Travel to el Bassel family home.

3:30–5:00 P.M.:   Accompany Mr. and Mrs. el Bassel, recent Palestinian immigrants, to the housing office to apply for an emergency transfer because their current neighbors are verbally threatening them because they are Muslims from the Middle East. During travel and waiting time, talk with parents regarding their management of son, age 11, who is having extreme difficulty adjusting to current school placement.

5:00–5:30 P.M.:   Travel back to office. No problem finding parking.

5:30–6:00 P.M.:   Work on additional case documentation needed for reimbursement under state contract.

6:00–7:00 P.M.:   Assist colleague with a domestic violence (DV) crisis unfolding in one of her home-based cases. Her client has called her to report that her boyfriend has beaten her and is threatening to harm her child unless she agrees to move to Tennessee with him. Work phones to obtain help while colleague keeps client talking on phone.

7:00–7:30 P.M.:   Travel to the McDonald family home.

7:30–8:30 P.M.:   Treatment session with Mr. and Mrs. McDonald and their four children, including 13-year-old Robbie, who has recently been skipping school to hang out with a group of delinquent older teens. The parents suspect he is using drugs and alcohol and may be committing burglaries with the teens. The session focused on bringing Mr. McDonald back into the family system. He travels constantly in his job as a long-distance truck driver and is often gone for days at a time, leaving Mrs. McDonald to manage the household alone, an overwhelming task for a working mother. Robbie, the oldest child, has functioned as the father surrogate, managing the younger children and even disciplining them when his parents are absent. Now that Robbie is becoming a teenager, he is rebelling against these responsibilities by separating himself from the family as much as possible, leading to his involvement with antisocial peers. Reconnecting father and son, who had a very positive relationship when Robbie was younger, removing Robbie from the parenting role, and establishing Mr. and Mrs. McDonald as a couple and as heads of the family are the focus of work with this family.

8:30–9:00 P.M.:   Travel to office.

9:00–10:00 P.M.:   Check phone messages, check on colleague with DV crisis, return phone calls, write progress notes on family therapy session with McDonald family, and document next steps with Robbie.

As she thinks about her work in her clients' homes and in the community during this day, the home-based social worker realizes just how much she has learned about her families and their functioning by observing them interacting in their homes and in the school settings. Those fishing poles stacked against the wall near the McDonald's back door led to a discussion of an activity that Robbie and his dad used to enjoy together nearly every weekend and gave her some ideas about how to get them reconnected now. Seeing Carrie's clothes stacked near the pull-out couch in the living room said everything about the girl's feelings of being a third wheel in her mom's new relationship and gave the family something to talk about in terms of the current apartment's physical space and need for privacy of a teenaged girl. Tasking Anna, Ellie, and Carrie with looking together for a new apartment might be a positive experience that helps to reorganize the family system. The home-based social worker smiled to herself as she thought about how satisfying it was to work with families to help them change their dynamics and move forward in a more positive direction. Whew, what a day!

INTRODUCTION TO HOME-BASED SERVICES

Social work has a long tradition of home-based service delivery, dating back over one hundred years to the friendly visitors of the Charity Organization Society. Although much has changed since that time with regard to knowledge for practice with individuals, families, and children in their own homes, these earliest social workers, like present-day practitioners, recognized that engaging with family members in the context of their daily lives greatly enriched their understanding of the forces that influence current functioning and of the strengths and resources that may be engaged to bring about change.

In the first textbook for training aspiring social workers, *Social Diagnosis*, published in 1917, Mary Richmond presented her arguments in support of working with clients in their own homes: "(a) Its challenge to the case worker at the outset to establish a human relation ... (b) Its avoidance of the need of so many questions, some of which are answered unasked by the communicative hostess and by her surroundings. To the quiet observer, the photographs on the wall ... the household arrangements are all eloquent. And far more revealing than these material items are the apparent relations of the members of the household to one another—the whole atmosphere of the home; (c) Its provision of natural openings for a frank exchange of experiences (p. 107)."

A review of the current literature on home-based practice reveals that not much has changed since Mary Richmond wrote these words. The value of working with clients in their own homes still emphasizes the importance of establishing a working relationship or "helping alliance" and the greater ease with which the therapeutic relationship develops when the client is in familiar surroundings (Damashek, Doughty, Ware, & Silovsky, 2011; Johnson, Wright, & Ketring, 2002; Thompson, Bender, Windsor, & Flynn, 2009).

Home-based work provides a ready window into the daily lives of clients. Although it may be possible to keep up a pretense that all is well for an hour a week in an out-patient clinic, it is much more difficult to hide evidence of clinical depression or ongoing substance abuse when one's living environment is filthy and in disarray. It is possible for the home-based social worker to understand quickly why a child is failing in school when there is no time or space set aside in a cramped and noisy apartment for homework, where the television blares 18 hours a day, and where no adult takes responsibility for ensuring that homework is done correctly.

The DelBlasio family consisted of Rachel, a 33-year-old mother, and her 10 children ranging in age from 3 months to 14 years. The identified patient in the family was 9-year-old Billy, who was sexually molested by a 26-year-old cousin. Billy revealed the molestation to a school nurse and Child Protective Services (CPS) was notified. The case was referred by CPS to a home-based family treatment program in an effort to strengthen the family's functioning and prevent an out-of-home placement for Billy.

When the home-based social worker, Susan, arrived at the DelBlasio home, she found a mom, Rachel, who was reluctant to become involved in treatment and a living environment that was chaotic at best. Cockroaches scurried across the trash-strewn floor. At the first family session, it was clear that the older two children, both girls, were carrying a great deal of the responsibility for managing the home and younger children and that Rachel suffered from severe depression, unable to get out of bed to get her children off to school most days. The extreme attention seeking behavior of the younger children with Susan suggested emotional neglect.

Rachel insisted that she could handle the situation with Billy on her own by confronting the perpetrator's mother and not allowing Billy to have any further contact with his cousin. Efforts to help Rachel help Billy with the emotional effects of the abuse were met with stubborn denial. After a few home visits, Billy took matters into his own hands by requesting to meet with Susan alone. He led her into the bedroom he shared with five of his siblings. The six children all slept together on two queen-sized mattresses pushed together on the floor.

Small for his age and rail thin, Billy summoned all of his strength to push a large dresser up against the bedroom door to keep out his brothers and sisters who banged at the door repeatedly, begging to come into the room to see what was going on. Billy motioned for Susan to sit on the floor where cockroaches scurried about. Feeling her commitment to the child was being tested, she joined him in his life at that moment, and the two of them sat together, flicking the bugs away, while Billy talked of his life at home, at school, and of the sexual molestation experience. In a clinic setting, without this opportunity to enter into the child's life as he lived it on a daily basis, it is doubtful that the social worker could have gained such a full and complete understanding of the client in his situation so quickly.

As Mary Richmond noted in 1917, home-based work also provides an essential opportunity to observe the interactions of those living in the home with one another. Very often when a child is referred by a school or medical provider to a mental health center for assessment and treatment, only the mother and, occasionally, a sibling or two accompany the child to the clinic. Yet, as family social workers have noted for years, it is nearly impossible to understand the functioning of an individual family member, especially a child, without also understanding the dynamics of family interaction. What better way to observe these dynamics firsthand than by providing home-based services? What better way to find out that a family's life together is totally disrupted by the demands of caring for grandpa who is 87 years old and has advanced Alzheimer's disease? What better way to find out that mother's paramour is a violent and abusive man who has punched holes in the apartment wall and kicked the family dog when the children's noisy play awakened him? What better way to discover that the parents of a boy diagnosed with ADHD are uncertain how to manage his frequently disruptive behavior and that their inability to set appropriate limits has allowed the child to "rule the roost?" Although an outpatient clinician may learn of any of these situations in due course, the home-based practitioner witnesses the interaction immediately, and firsthand, and understands implicitly its impact on the family system and on individual family members.

Carlos, a Spanish-speaking social worker in a home-based program, was assigned to a family of Puerto Rican descent, the Rodriquez family, whose 13-year-old son, Jose, had been given the diagnosis of Bi-Polar Disorder. The parents were confused about the meaning of this diagnosis and understandably concerned about its implications for the future of their child. As Carlos met with Mr. and Mrs. Rodriquez, Jose, his older brother, 15, and younger brother, 10, in their own home, a picture began to emerge of loving, well-meaning parents who were frightened by their middle son's frequent rages, which seemed to occur primarily when Jose was asked to carry out a chore such as cleaning his room or completing his homework. During these rages, which Mr. and Mrs. Rodriquez attributed to his Bi-Polar illness, Jose would appear out-of-control, throwing things and breaking up furnishings. Once, when asked to go to his room when he became enraged, Jose refused and proceeded to kick the bedroom door in.

In discussing their parenting styles, his mother readily admitted that she was intimidated by Jose when he was enraged and would retreat to her room until the storm was over. His father, who was a very large man, saw his role as de-escalating Jose's rages through physical intimidation, although he denied ever using actual physical force with the boy. Neither parent believed in setting limits with their sons, or in having a set structure in the home, such as specific times for homework or family meals. Both felt that this more laissez-faire approach to parenting had worked well with their other two boys and did not understand why Jose could not handle it also, again attributing his behavior problems to his illness.

It was quickly apparent from observing the family in their own home that Jose had learned how to use his illness to control his parents to his own benefit. Helping Mr. and Mrs. Rodriguez examine their ineffective laissez-faire parenting style and identify alternative approaches in which they both could participate was a clear focus of the work with this family. In addition, the importance of structure to a vulnerable child like Jose was part of educating the family about Bi-Polar Disorder. Setting up a schedule for homework and mealtimes, as well as for completing chores around the house, would help Jose anticipate in advance what he needed to do rather than always feeling like "things were coming at him out of the blue" as he expressed in one family session. Trying alternative ways of doing things, while receiving the support and encouragement of their home-based worker, helped the Rodriquez family, which had many inherent strengths including their commitment to one another, make positive changes that benefited all members of the family system.

In *Social Diagnosis*, Mary Richmond also noted that home-based practice provides a multitude of opportunities for "frank exchanges." The home environment is replete with "conversation starters" for clinicians who bring aspects of the environment into the therapeutic process (Macchi & O'Connor, 2010; Reiter, 2006). A picture of mother's parents on the mantel can initiate a discussion of mother's childhood, revealing that her father was a longtime alcoholic who was emotionally unavailable and that her mother compensated for his emotional absence by becoming emotionally enmeshed with her only child. This may help the home-based clinician better understand her client's difficulties in developing healthy intimate partner relationships and her inability to set appropriate limits and expectations for her 11-year-old son. Helping a mother to relate her own childhood experiences to her current parenting practices, using elements available in the home environment such as the picture on the mantel, is a strategy available to home-based clinicians that is seldom accessible to practitioners in clinic settings.

Another important advantage of home-based practice is its ability to deliver services to clients who might otherwise be inaccessible to social work clinicians (Boyd-Franklin & Bry, 2000; Carrasco & Fox, 2012; Chaffin, Hecht, Bard, Silovsky, & Beasley, 2012). One of the first home-based programs described in the contemporary social work literature grew out of a study in the 1950s by social workers in St. Paul, Minnesota, who had observed that a small number of families created a high proportion of the demands on the child welfare system there. These families demonstrated a myriad of difficulties including domestic violence, substance abuse, mental health problems, as well as child abuse and neglect. Engaging these families in efforts to address their difficulties and make substantial changes in their often-chaotic functioning proved frustrating and futile for the St. Paul social workers until it was decided to take services to these families in their own homes rather than wait for them to seek and accept therapeutic services on their own. In this way, many of these families were engaged in treatment and changes in their overall functioning were observed.

The St. Paul Family-Centered Project, as it was called, and others like it that sprang up around the country in the ensuing years, focused on families known to the child welfare system, and worked to ensure family stability and improve family functioning in order to keep children at home and out of foster care. These early home-based programs contributed to the development of what came to be known as family preservation services. Although there were several different models of family preservation services, perhaps the most widely known and utilized was Homebuilders, developed by two psychologists in Tacoma, Washington, in the early 1970s.

The Homebuilders model is a brief, six-week intervention that works with families in crisis who are about to lose their children to foster care (Kinney, Haapala, & Booth, 1991). The work is done almost entirely in the family's home or in other community locations such as schools or work settings. Homebuilders clinicians carry very small caseloads, are available on call 24 hours a day, and spend as much time as necessary working with the family in the home, especially during the first days or weeks of treatment when the family is in a crisis state. In addition to crisis theory, the model draws heavily on social learning theory to bring about changes in families' functioning.

Evaluations of the Homebuilders model suggested that it was effective in reducing the number of out-of-home placements of children as compared with usual child welfare services. Homebuilders participation also shortened the length of foster care placement and facilitated children's return to their families (Schwartz, 1995). During the 1980s and 1990s, variations on the Homebuilders model were adopted throughout the United States by state child welfare agencies as a result of federal legislation providing funding to states to strengthen families and prevent out of home placement of children. Home-based services intended to prevent child placement, and to reunify families when placement has occurred, are currently a staple of most state child welfare systems (Macchi & O'Connor, 2010).

Home-based treatment models have been developed to serve families and children involved with the juvenile justice and mental health systems as well as with child welfare. Perhaps the best known home-based model for working with delinquent youth and their families is Multisystemic Therapy, or MST. MST was developed in the early 1990s by Scott Henggeler and his colleagues at the Medical College of the University of South Carolina to address the externalizing behaviors of conduct disordered youth (Borduin, Mann, Cone, et al., 1995). As the name of the model suggests, the focus of treatment is on the multiple systems involved in delinquent behavior: the youth, the family, peers, and community institutions such as the school. MST clinicians work primarily with youth and their families in their own homes and, as in the Homebuilders model, they carry low caseloads, are available 24 hours a day, seven days a week to their clients, and the service is time-limited (3–5 months). Unlike Homebuilders, but similar to many other home-based intervention models, MST draws heavily for its theoretical base and practice approach on family systems theory and its applications in family therapy (Borduin, Mann, Cone, et al., 1995).

The growth of the family therapy movement in the 1960s and 1970s gave social workers working with families in their own homes new tools and strategies with which to approach home-based work. Family systems theory, which underpinned the family therapy movement, guided the interpretation of family dynamics. For example, Murray Bowen, one of the preeminent early theoreticians and family therapy practitioners, gave home-based clinicians working with families an intergenerational perspective on family functioning, now captured so eloquently by the intergenerational family genogram, a staple in the armamentarium of the home-based practitioner (McGoldrick, Gerson, & Shellenberger, 1999).

From family therapist Salvador Minuchin, working at the Philadelphia Child Guidance Clinic, came the focus on family structure and its importance in understanding and treating families in which the parents had lost control of their children. Minuchin's structural family therapy approach taught home-based practitioners to observe the family's structure and seek to understand the patterns of alliances and coalitions that color a family's daily life (Lindblad-Goldberg, Dore, & Stern, 1998). For instance, in families with a delinquent son or daughter, clinicians often see adults who have given up on authoritative parenting for a variety of reasons, which might include their own substance abuse, clinical depression, marital conflict, or simply being overwhelmed by life stressors. Helping the adults in such families address their own difficulties in order to resume their role as parent is a frequent focus of structural family therapy (Lindblad-Goldberg et al., 1998).

Jay Haley, Chloe Madanes, and other strategic family therapists gave home-based clinicians useful tools such as enactments, or brief playlets, to illuminate a specific sequence of events in the family, such as having the children in the family act out what happens when father gives an order to teenage son that is ignored, or what happens when the family goes on an outing together. These dramatizations of incidents in family life highlight commonly occurring negative interactions among family members as in no other way. They also give the home-based practitioner substantive material with which to initiate an alternative behavioral sequence to bring about change. If a particular sequence of events in a family customarily ends badly for some or all of the participants, illustrating this with the family, then having the family brainstorm and act out an alternative sequence has the potential for meeting the needs of all participants. And, rehearsing the sequence in an in-home session makes it more likely that family members will remember and try it out the next time the opportunity arises.

Family therapy, no matter what the theoretical orientation or school of thought, has given home-based practitioners significant permission to use themselves creatively to bring about change in a family's problematic ways of functioning. Doing something differently, whether its interacting in a new way with a partner or child, or accessing new community resources together with a parent and observing how the parent interacts with a resource provider in a community setting, differentiates home-based from clinic-based practice. In traditional clinic-based practice, the focus of interaction between the social worker and client is limited to what the client brings into the session, which represents his construction of the reality of his life. Helping the client construct a more accurate interpretation can take many weeks or months of treatment. Home-based work speeds this process greatly by giving the clinician immediate access to alternative perspectives, which he can then use to help the client experience her situation in a different way.

In addition to home-based interventions with families in the child welfare and juvenile justice systems, this approach has been extended to families in the mental health system. Spurred in the early 1980s by the federal Child and Adolescent Service System Program (CASSP) initiative, which funded development of new models of community-based children's mental health services, the state of Pennsylvania invested in developing and implementing a model of home-based services that treated children's mental health needs in the context of their families (Lindblad-Goldberg et al., 1998). The Pennsylvania model was based on an ecological and systemic understanding of factors that contributed to serious emotional and behavioral disturbances in children and drew upon structural family therapy to inform its intervention. All of the treatment was done in the home and community and was intended to prevent psychiatric hospitalization and long-term residential care.

One of the systems concepts that the Pennsylvania home-based model emphasized is that of circular causality. This concept focuses clinicians' attention on the circular feedback loops of communication and behavior among family members. These highlight repetitive patterns of family interaction that illustrate the structural difficulties the family is experiencing. For example, a mother subtly counteracts every request her husband makes of their son by negating his authority with the child, or two siblings enter into a covert alliance to act out behaviorally to draw a response from their mother who is over-involved emotionally with the third child

in the family, who suffers from a chronic illness. This way of understanding family functioning moves away from the practice of blaming specific family members for problems in the family and provides the clinician with a point of intervention and change. Circular feedback loops become apparent very quickly when a clinician spends time with the family in the comfort zone of their own home, and opportunities to challenge these customary ways of behaving are readily available.

Other models of home-based treatment for children and families involved with the mental health system have been developed as well. Beginning in the mid-1990s, clinicians at the Yale Child Study Center have developed and tested a manualized model of in-home psychiatric services called IICAPS (Intensive In-home Child and Adolescent Psychiatric Services) (Woolston, Adnopoz, & Berkowitz, 2007). The model provides for home-based assessment and treatment planning, as well as brief family therapy, parent education in child behavior management, social skills development for children, and intervention with environmental resources to build support for the child and family in the community. Each phase of the intervention process is well-defined and is accompanied by a series of measures of its effectiveness. IICAPS is a team-delivered intervention. Clinicians are expected to spend up to five hours per week in the family home and the model calls for a six-month treatment duration. IICAPS is currently a Medicaid-approved treatment for children with DSM Axis I and Axis II diagnoses in the state of Connecticut.

Another home-based intervention designed to support children and adolescents with serious emotional disturbances in their own homes and communities is the Wrap-around model, in which social workers work intensively with families to identify and put in place all of the resources and services needed to maximize the child's psychosocial functioning. In this model, the treatment plan is developed collaboratively by a care planning team that includes social workers from the Wrap-around program, one of whom acts as the primary care coordinator; representatives of community resources such as a school social worker or therapist from the local outpatient mental health clinic; members of the child's current household and others the family may wish to include such as grandparents, close friends or neighbors; and representatives of the referring agency, frequently the juvenile court or state child welfare agency. A primary focus of the

Wrap-around approach is to end the fragmented way services are often provided to children with serious emotional and behavior disturbances and their families.

The Wrap-around model emphasizes honoring the family's voice in care planning. Part of the care coordinator's role is to ensure that team meetings are safe and blame-free for all participants. There is also an emphasis on ensuring that cultural differences are acknowledged and respected in the Wrap-around treatment process. The care planning team is charged with developing the goals and strategies necessary to achieve the outcomes the family seeks with regard to maintaining the child in the home and community. These goals often include helping parents or other family members address their own problems or issues that impact the family's ability to provide the care the child needs.

In recent years, as increased attention has been paid to preventing social and emotional difficulties in young children, particularly as they impact a child's capacity to learn in school, home-based programs for at-risk infants and toddlers have sprung up across the United States. Nationally, programs such as Early Head Start and Healthy Families focus on the functioning of the whole family and may rely on social workers specially trained in early child development to engage, assess, and treat vulnerable families in their own homes (Love, Kisker, Ross, Constantine, Boller et al., 2005; Rodriguez, Dumont, Mitchell-Herzfeld, Walden, & Greene, 2010). A recent national study of Early Head Start found that families and children treated in their own homes, either fully or in combination with center-based treatment, fared significantly better than those who received only center-based care (Love et al., 2005).

Building on growing recognition of the importance of early intervention for very young children already evidencing emotional and behavioral difficulties, home-based programs to treat these youngsters in the context of their homes and families have sprung up across the country. One example of such a program is the Parenting Young Children model, which works with parents to strengthen the child's pro-social behaviors and reduce challenging behaviors in the home through parent education, skill demonstration, and coaching by the home-based clinician (Fox, Mattek, & Gresl, 2013). Studies of this model have found that low-income parents can acquire the necessary skills to help their children

in about eight treatment sessions and that children's problem behaviors can be observed to improve dramatically as a result (Carrasco & Fox, 2012).

As Mary Richmond recognized early in the profession's development, home-based services have historically been a key component of social work practice in a variety of domains. Social workers, with their eco-systemic understanding of human functioning and their trained capacity to interpret person/situation interaction, are ideally suited to be home-based clinicians. Social workers have long appreciated the importance of observing and engaging their clients where they live, in their own homes and community settings. Contemporary home-based programs build on the unique knowledge and skills of social workers developed and refined in over one hundred years of home-based practice to help individuals, families, and children achieve their goals and improve their psychosocial functioning.

WEBSITES

www.nwi.pdx.edu—Wraparound services site
www.mstservices.com—Multisystemic Therapy site
www.institutefamily.org—Homebuilders site
www.nfpn.org—National Family Preservation Network site
www.healthyfamiliesamerica.org—Healthy Families site

References

Boyd-Franklin, N., & Bry, B. H. (2000). *Reaching out in family therapy: Home-based, school, and community interventions.* New York, NY: Guilford.

Carrasco, J. M., & Fox, R. A. (2012). Varying treatment intensity in a home-based parent and child therapy program for families living in poverty: A randomized clinic trial. *Journal of Community Psychology, 40*(5), 621–630.

Borduin, C. M., Mann, B. J., Cone, L. T., et al. (1995). Multisystemic treatment of serious juvenile offenders: Long-term prevention of criminality and violence. *Journal of Consulting and Clinical Psychology, 63,* 569–578.

Chaffin, M., Hecht, D., Bard, D., Silovsky, J. F., & Beasley, W. H. (2012). A statewide trial of the Safe Care home-based services model with parents in child protective services. *Pediatrics, 129,* 509–515.

Damashek, A., Doughty, D., Ware, L., & Silovsky, J. (2011). Predictors of client engagement and attrition in home-based child maltreatment prevention services. *Child Maltreatment, 16*, 9–20.

Fox, R., Mattek, R., & Gresl, B. L. (2013). Evaluation of a university-community partnership to provide home-based, mental health services for children from families living in poverty. *Community Mental Health Journal, 49*(5), 599–610.

Johnson, L. N., Wright, D. W., & Ketring, S. A. (2002). The therapeutic alliance in home-based family therapy: Is it predictive of outcome? *Journal of Marital and Family Therapy, 28*, 93–102.

Kinney, J., Haapala, D., & Booth, C. (1991). *Keeping families together: The Homebuilders model.* New York, NY: Aldine de Gruyter.

Lindblad-Goldberg, M., Dore, M. M., & Stern, L. (1998). *Creating competence from chaos: A comprehensive guide to home-based services.* New York, NY: Norton.

Love, J. M., Kisker, E. E., Ross, C., Constantine, J., Boller, K, Chazan-Cohen, R., ... (2005). The effectiveness of Early Head Start for 3-year-old children and their parents: Lessons for policy and programs. *Developmental Psychology, 41*(6), 885–901.

Macchi, C. R., & O'Connor, N. (2010). Common components of home-based family therapy models: The HBFT partnership in Kansas. *Contemporary Family Therapy, 32*, 444–458.

McGoldrick, M., Gerson, R., & Shellenberger, S. (1999). *Genograms: Assessment and intervention* (2nd ed.). New York, NY: Norton.

Richmond, M. E. (1917). *Social diagnosis.* New York, NY: Russell Sage Foundation.

Reiter, M. (2006). Utilizing the home environment in home-based family therapy. *Journal of Family Psychotherapy, 11*(3), 27–39.

Rodriguez, M. L., Dumont, K., Mitchell-Herzfeld, S. D., Walden, N. J., & Greene, R. (2010). Effects of Healthy Families New York on the promotion of maternal parenting competencies and the prevention of harsh parenting. *Child Abuse & Neglect, 34*(10), 711–723.

Schwartz, I. M. (1995). The systemic impact of family preservation services: A case study. In I. M. Schwartz & P. AuClaire (Eds.), *Home-based services for troubled children* (pp. 157–171). Lincoln: University of Nebraska Press.

Thompson, S. J., Bender, K., Windsor, L. C., & Flynn, P. M. (2009). Keeping families engaged: The effects of home-based family therapy enhanced with experiential activities. *Social Work Research, 33*(2), 121–126.

Woolston, J., Adnopoz, J. A., & Berkowitz, S. (2007). *IICAPS: A home-based psychiatric treatment for children and adolescents.* New Haven, CT: Yale University Press.

10 Social Work Practice in Disasters

Daphne S. Cain

SOCIAL WORK INTERVENTION IN DISASTERS

The History of Social Work Intervention in Disasters

Although interest in traumatic reactions and social support following disaster has been evident in the American literature for decades, social work practices and intervention during and subsequent to disaster did not receive much attention until the 1990s and Hurricane Andrew (August 1992) (Cherry & Cherry, 1996; Sanders, Bowie, & Bowie, 2003); The Great Flood of 1993 (Sundet & Mermelstein, 1996); and the Oklahoma City Bombing (April 1995) (Levine, 1996; North, Tivis, McMillen, Pfefferbaum et al., 2002). Over the past two decades, social work intervention in disaster has become a specialization with intense interest on best practices and evidence-informed intervention. This is evident in the considerable social work literature from the 9/11 Attacks (September 2001) (Adams, Figley, & Boscarino,

2008; Bauwens & Tosone, 2010; Henley, Marshall, & Vetter, 2010; Pulido, 2012), and Hurricane Katrina (August 2005) (Bliss & Meehan, 2008; Cain, Plummer, Fisher, & Bankston, 2010; Coker et al., 2006; Elliott & Pais, 2006; Hoffpauir & Woodruff, 2008; Legerski, Vernberg, & Noland, 2012; Plummer, Cain, Fisher, & Bankston, 2008; Pyles, 2007; Terranova, Boxer, & Morris, 2009). Additionally, there is growing interest in international social work intervention in disaster. Rapid population growth, unplanned urbanization and environmental degradation (especially in disaster-prone and impoverished areas), and climate change have impacted the frequency and severity of natural disasters globally (American Red Cross, 2013). Subsequently, social work has responded to the widespread flooding, earthquakes, tsunamis, and national conflicts and hostilities around the world (Aziz & Aslam, 2012; Bourassa, 2009; Busaspathumrong, 2006; Dominelli, 2013; Goenjian, 1993; Huang, Zhou, & Wei, 2011; Javadian, 2007; Nikku, 2012; Pockett, 2006; Takahashi, Lijima, Kuzuya, Hattori, Yokono, & Morimoto, 2011; Yanay & Benjamin, 2005).

The National Association of Social Workers (NASW) adopted a national disaster policy in 2000, which asserts that, among "all the allied health and human services professionals, social work is uniquely suited to interpret the disaster context, to advocate for effective services, and to provide leadership in essential collaborations among institutions and other organizations" (NASW Press, 2000, p. 4). The social work profession is particularly appropriate for disaster work because of our holistic epistemology at the generalist social work level, our ecological framework and emphasis on the person-in-environment, our values regarding respect for diversity and empowerment and the role of relationships in the delivery of successful interventions, and our strengths-based approach (Bliss & Meehan, 2008; Cronin, Ryan, & Brier, 2007; Rowlands, 2013). More specifically, social workers are trained to apply a community oriented strengths perspective that builds upon existing capacity in a disaster affected area (Dominelli, 2013; Mathbor, 2007; Pyles, 2007; Rowlands, 2013; Tan, 2013).

DISASTER REACTIONS

Although post-disaster reactions and behaviors may appear to be symptoms of psychopathology, in fact, many of these reactions are normal in a crisis state. These reactions may include symptoms of shock, exhaustion, disorientation, irrationality, racing thoughts, and uncontrollable emotions (Brymer, Jacobs, Layne, Pynoos, Ruzek, Steinberg, Vernberg, & Watson, 2006). Most disaster survivors recover from initial reactions and symptoms with little or no psychological intervention (Norris, Friedman, Watson, Byrne, Diaz, & Kaniasty, 2002). However, some survivors have more acute reactions that may develop into Post Traumatic Stress Disorder (PTSD) or another major psychiatric disorder, including major depressive disorder, dysthymia, agoraphobia, specific phobia, social anxiety disorder, and panic disorder (Aziz & Aslam, 2012; Carroll, Balogh, Morbey, & Araoz, 2010; Hussain, Weisaeth, & Heir, 2011). Individuals who are directly impacted by disaster—those who have lost property or a loved one, or who have been injured or dislocated—are more at risk for developing long-term psychosocial conditions such as PTSD (Kreuger & Stretch, 2003).

TYPES OF DISASTER AND BARRIERS TO DISASTER WORK

Disasters can be defined as "events that disable community social functioning" (Soliman & Rogge, 2002, p. 2). There are natural disasters (tornados, hurricanes, earthquakes, fires, and floods), human-initiated disasters (air disasters, nuclear reactor explosions), and human-initiated disasters that are intentionally caused (war, terrorism, shootings). And, while there is extensive research into natural and human-initiated disasters, there is limited research specific to social work responses to such things as terrorism (Sweifach, LaPorte, & Linzer, 2010).

At the same time, there are many barriers to social work interventions during and subsequent to disasters. These include a lack of disaster/crisis training and preparedness among workers, a lack of adequate training in cultural competence, and contextual challenges including the characteristics and location of the incident(s) and the scale of destruction (Davis, 2013; Legerski, Vernberg, & Noland, 2012).

CULTURE AND DISASTER

Being culturally sensitive is crucial in disaster work. In particular, transnational disaster social workers need to be highly sensitive to ethical cultural adaptation standards in order to avert cross-cultural errors and/or harm (Bourassa, 2009; Puig & Glynn, 2003; Rowlands, 2013; Shah, 2011; Sommers-Flanagan, 2007). And, research reveals that tailoring social work services to meet the needs of diverse populations effected by disaster is associated with a greater penetration and utilization of services (Rosen, Greene, Young, & Norris, 2010).

VULNERABLE POPULATIONS

Some populations are at greater risk for psychosocial distress following disaster, and it appears that members of vulnerable populations may be less prepared for disaster (Baker, Baker, & Flagg, 2012). Vulnerable populations include children (Brymer et al.; Hayashi & Tomita, 2012), individuals who have been injured or are medically frail, older survivors (Barusch, 2011; Torgusen & Kosberg, 2006), individuals with serious mental illness, individuals with disabilities (Evans, Patt, Giosan, Spielman, & Difede, 2009; Fox, White, Rooney, & Cahill, 2010), those with substance abuse issues, pregnant women and mothers with small children and infants, and disaster response personnel including social workers (Adams, Figley, & Boscarino, 2008; Amaratunga & O'Sullivan, 2006; Brymer et al.). Additionally, marginalized, economically disadvantaged, and minority communities tend to be at greater risk following disaster due in part to the experiences of prior traumatic events and a lack of access to disaster services (Elliott & Pais, 2006; Zakour & Harrell, 2003). Finally, a sense of mistrust, a lack of knowledge about disaster relief services, stigma, and fear may make these most vulnerable populations—these marginalized groups—the least likely to take advantage of resources (Brymer et al.; National Medical Association, 2005; Quinn, 2008).

Children and Adolescents

When working with children it is important to be developmentally appropriate, to be sensitive to cultural differences, and to engage the child's adaptive and positive coping functioning ability (Ager, Stark, Akesson, & Boothby, 2010; Plummer, Cain, Fisher, & Bankston, 2008). Providing counseling services in the school system is an excellent way to reach children and families who have been affected by disaster (Kreuger & Stretch, 2003).

Around the world, disasters have forced children into armed conflict, prostitution, and drug trafficking (Nikku, 2012; Phua, 2008). Immediately after a disaster, attend to children who have been separated from their caregivers because these children are at risk for additional exploitation and psychological harm. Reconnect children with caregivers as quickly as possible, and notify appropriate authorities if caregivers cannot be located. If possible, establish a separate, child-friendly space for unaccompanied children and assign appropriate and trained personnel to staff it. Additionally, provide caregivers with information regarding typical childhood reactions to disaster including fear and anxiety, sleep disturbances, eating problems, irritability, and sadness (Speier, 2000), and refer children and families to more intensive treatment as needed.

Some specific suggestions for working with children include:

(1) Sit or crouch at the child's eye level
(2) Help school-aged children verbalize their feelings, concerns, and questions by using simple labels (e.g., mad, sad, scared, worried), but avoid extreme words (e.g., terrified or horrified).
(3) Use reflective listening skills and check with the child to make sure you understand what they are attempting to communicate.
(4) Be aware that children may regress developmentally in behavior and/or language.
(5) Be developmentally appropriate when talking with children—use direct and simple language.
(6) Talk to adolescents "adult-to-adult" to signify that you respect their feelings, concerns, and questions.
(7) Reinforce these techniques with parents and caregivers to help them provide appropriate support to their children (Brymer et al., p. 9).

Older Adults

When working with older adults:

(1) B Respect that they have both strengths and vulnerabilities and realize that many older adults have acquired effective coping skills over their lifetimes and are capable of negotiating adversities.
(2) Especially for those with hearing difficulties, speak clearly and in a low pitch.

(3) Do not make assumptions based only on physical appearance or age because some difficulties could be attributed to disaster-related illness (e.g., confusion may be caused by disaster-related disorientation due to changes in the individual's surroundings or environment, poor vision or hearing, dehydration, sleep deprivation, a medical condition or medication effects, or social isolation).

(4) An older adult with a mental health disability may have increased needs due to confusion and should be referred for a mental health consultation or referral as soon as possible (Brymer et al., p. 9; Takahashi et al., 2011).

Survivors with Disabilities

When working with survivors with disabilities:

(1) Try to provide assistance in an area with as little distraction (noise or other stimulation) as possible.

(2) Address the survivor directly rather than the caretaker unless direct communication is too difficult.

(3) When communication is impaired (hearing, speech, memory) speak simply and slowly.

(4) If unsure of how to assist, ask, "How can I assist you?" or "What can I do to help?" and trust what the person tells you; focus on strengths and when possible, enable the person to be self-sufficient.

(5) Be mindful of visually impaired individuals and offer your arm to assist them move about in unfamiliar surroundings.

(6) Offer to write down information and make arrangements for individuals to receive information in writing.

(7) Keep essential aids (medications, oxygen tank, respiratory equipment, and wheelchair) with the person (Brymer et al., pp. 9–10).

Missing Family Members

Survivors who have a missing family member, or who have a family member or close friend who has died, may require more intensive attention. Attempt to reconnect missing family members as soon as possible. The American Red Cross can be of assistance when reconnecting family, as well as official radio and television channels and the local police. What has been learned from previous disasters such as 9/11 and Hurricane Katrina is that social media—including text messaging, Facebook, and Twitter—may be the only means of communication during disaster (Barr, 2011; Cain & Barthelemy, 2008).

When working with survivors who have experienced the death of a loved one:

(1) Reassure them that what they are experiencing is understandable and expectable.

(2) Use the deceased person's name.

(3) Let them know that they will likely continue to experience feelings of sadness, loneliness, and/or anger.

(4) Refer grieving individuals to more intensive psychological services when requested or as needed (Brymer et al., p. 36).

EVIDENCE-INFORMED DISASTER SOCIAL WORK: PSYCHOLOGICAL FIRST AID

Psychological First Aid (PFA) is an evidence-informed intervention approach designed to assist children, adolescents, adults, and families subsequent to disaster (Brymer et al.; Cain et al., 2010). PFA is supported by disaster mental health experts as the "acute intervention of choice" when responding to the psychosocial needs of children, adults, and families in post-disaster distress (Brymer et al., p. 5), and is listed among the promising practices by the National Child Traumatic Stress Network (n.d.). PFA is designed to reduce the initial distress caused by disaster and to foster both short- and long-term adaptive functioning and coping (Brymer et al.). The principles and techniques of PFA are consistent with evidence-informed research on risk and resilience following trauma, can be implemented in diverse field settings, take a lifespan perspective with regard to theory and technique, and are culturally informed (Brymer et al.). The basic objectives of PFA include:

(1) Establishing a nonintrusive and compassionate human connection with survivors

(2) Enhancing safety and providing physical and emotional comfort

(3) Calming and orienting physically and emotionally overwhelmed or distraught survivors

(4) Assessing immediate needs and concerns

(5) Offering practical assistance and information to address immediate needs and concerns

(6) Connecting survivors with social support networks such as family, friends, and community helping resources as soon as possible

(7) Supporting adaptive coping— acknowledging coping efforts and strengths, and empowering and encouraging survivors to take an active role in their recovery

(8) Providing information that can help survivors cope with the psychosocial impact of disasters (Brymer et al., pp. 6–7).

Behaviors to avoid include:

(1) Do not make assumptions about survivors or what they may be experiencing or have gone through.

(2) Do not assume that everyone exposed to a disaster will be traumatized.

(3) Do not patronize survivors or focus on their helplessness, weakness, mistakes, or disability.

(4) Do not assume that all survivors will want or need to talk; being physically available in a supportive and calm manner may be all that is needed to make survivors feel safe and enhance their abilities to cope.

(5) Do not "debrief" survivors by asking for details of what happened.

(6) Do not speculate or offer potentially inaccurate information (Brymer et al., p. 8).

Prior to engaging in PFA, social workers should be trained in disaster mental health, be knowledgeable about the nature of the disaster itself and current circumstances, including the emergency management setting they will be entering, and the types and availability of support services for survivors. Social workers should consider their level of comfort with disaster work, their current health, and their family and work circumstances, as well as be mindful to engage in appropriate self-care (Brymer et al.). Disaster social work and PFA typically take place within the confines of an emergency management setting that is overseen by such agencies as the American Red Cross or the Federal Emergency

Management Agency (FEMA). It is crucial that social workers work within the framework of the emergency management agency authorized to manage the site—all communication and the coordination of services must be coordinated with authorized personnel. This is particularly important for the dissemination of accurate information that is often critical to reducing distress and promoting adaptive coping among survivors (Brymer et al.).

When initially providing disaster assistance, focus your attention on how survivors are reacting and interacting in their environment. Individuals may need immediate assistance when they exhibit signs of acute distress—disorientation; confusion; agitation, irritability, or anger; panic; or apathy (Brymer et al.). It is important when providing assistance to survivors that you as the social worker model appropriate behavior. You should remain calm, focused, mindful, thoughtful, and hopeful. Survivors can take cues from your calm, thoughtful, future-oriented behavior. It is also critical that social workers be sensitive to cultural, ethnic, religious, racial, and language differences in disaster (Brymer et al.). Be aware of your own values and prejudices and how these may influence your ability to serve survivors. Helping to reestablish and maintain customs, traditions, rituals, family structure, gender roles, and social bonds can be very therapeutic in assisting individuals and families to cope with disaster (Brymer et al.).

PFA CORE ACTIONS

Contact and Engagement

"Goal: To respond to contacts initiated by survivors, or to initiate contacts in a non-intrusive, compassionate, and helpful manner" (Brymer et al., p. 23).

The first contact with a survivor is important; be respectful, compassionate, and culturally sensitive. Respond first to those who seek you out. Introduce yourself and describe your role. Ask permission to talk with the survivor and address adult survivors using their last names (e.g., Mr. or Ms. Smith). Try to provide the survivor with as much privacy as possible. Speak softly and calmly and provide the survivor with your undivided attention. Ask the survivor first about immediate needs or problems that need immediate attention. The survivor's immediate medical condition should take priority. Prior to communicating with a child or adolescent, seek permission first from a parent or caregiver. As with all social work, client confidentiality is crucial. Mandated reporting laws and the Health Insurance Portability and Accountability Act (HIPAA) remain in effect during disaster relief work. Additionally, there are specific disaster and terrorism provisions within HIPAA (U.S. Department of Health & Human Services Emergency Preparedness Planning and Response, n.d.) with which disaster social workers should be familiar (Brymer et al.).

Safety and Comfort

"Goal: To enhance immediate and ongoing safety, and provide physical and emotional comfort" (Brymer et al., p. 27).

Restoring a sense of safety and promoting comfort are important goals following disaster. Make sure that the physical environment is as safe as possible. When working with survivors, do things that are active (not passive waiting), practical (using available resources), and familiar (draw on the past experiences of survivors) (Brymer et al.). Provide current and accurate information and avoid hearsay information or information that could be inaccurate or excessively upsetting. Inquire about health-related issues and current medication needs, as well as any needs related to tasks of daily living. Contact relatives and caregivers to assist with the immediate needs of survivors, and be alert to signs of suicidal or homicidal ideation and seek immediate medical assistance if these concerns are present (Brymer et al.).

When survivors are ready—when they are able to comprehend what is being stated and are ready to hear the content of messages—begin to reorient them by providing **accurate** information about disaster response activities and services: what to do next; what is being done to assist them; what is currently known about the unfolding event; available services; common stress reactions; and self-care, family care, and coping (Brymer et al.).

Encourage survivors to participate in making their environment comfortable (adaptive coping), and help them to soothe and comfort themselves and those around them (active coping). Promote positive group and social engagement as much as possible (Brymer et al.). Protect survivors from

additional traumatic experiences and trauma reminders including extended media coverage of the event. This is especially true for children who are at high risk for further traumatization from prolonged media exposure (Schuster et al., 2001).

Survivors may turn to their religious beliefs when reflecting on the disaster and their disaster experiences (Cain & Barthelemy, 2008). They may use religious language to discuss what has happened to them and their family, or want to engage in religious practices to cope. Listening and attending to these needs in a nonjudgmental and supportive manner may be necessary. In addition, referring those survivors who practice a religion to clergy members of their faith can be helpful.

Stabilization

"Goal: To calm and orient emotionally overwhelmed or disoriented survivors" (Brymer et al., p. 49).

You may want to enlist the assistance of the survivor's family members or close friends in orienting them and providing emotional comfort. And, while medication is not recommended as a routine way to cope with acute traumatic stress reactions, medication may be necessary when the survivor is experiencing extreme reactions such as agitation, panic, psychosis, or is a danger to themselves or others. When these reactions are evident, consult with a physician immediately. Additionally, medication may be helpful to treat specific symptoms associated with disaster such as insomnia and panic attacks (Brymer et al.).

Information Gathering

"Goal: To identify immediate needs and concerns, gather additional information, and tailor Psychological First Aid interventions" (Brymer et al., p. 57).

Social work interventions should be adapted to meet the needs of specific survivors. In order to provide tailored intervention, specific information must be gathered. Information that needs to be collected includes:

- The nature and severity of the disaster experience
- Death of a loved one

- Concerns regarding immediate post-disaster circumstances and any ongoing threat
- Separation from or concern about the safety of loved ones
- Physical illness, mental health conditions, need for medications
- Losses (home, school, neighborhood, business, personal property, and pets)
- Extreme feelings of guilt or shame
- Thoughts about causing harm to self or others
- Availability of social support
- Prior alcohol or drug use
- Prior exposure to trauma and death of loved ones
- Specific youth, adult, and family concerns over developmental impact (Brymer et al., pp. 57–62).

This information will allow you to work with the immediate concerns of the survivor and provide you with information that can determine if immediate referral for more intensive services is warranted.

Practical Assistance

"Goal: To offer practical help to survivors in addressing immediate needs and concerns" (Brymer et al., p. 65).

Social work intervention in the immediate aftermath of major incidents is more about orienting survivors and providing practical support, rather than counseling services that may be needed for some survivors later on (Davis, 2013). Indeed, social work case management is frequently neglected while counseling services are more readily available in the immediate aftermath of disaster (Ganesan, 2006). However, immediate attention needs to be paid to the difficulties survivors experience accessing services.

Connection with Social Supports

"Goal: To help establish brief or ongoing contacts with primary support persons and other sources of support, including family members, friends, and community helping resources" (Brymer et al., p. 69).

It is important to connect survivors with primary support persons and community assistance when needed. Survivors need to feel connected to family and friends, and some may need material or physical assistance that can be found in the community. It can also be helpful for survivors to give back to others and the community so they feel valued, useful, and productive.

Information on Coping

"Goal: To provide information about stress reactions and coping to reduce distress and promote adaptive functioning" (Brymer et al., p. 77).

Many disaster survivors have physical and psychological reactions to the disaster event that cause them alarm and concern, but many of these reactions are normal in a crisis state. Survivors may have intrusive reactions including dreams and flashbacks, avoidance and withdrawal reactions (avoiding reminders of the event, talking about the event, feelings of detachment and numbness), and physical arousal reactions including irritability, angry outbursts, insomnia, and difficulty concentrating (Brymer et al.). It is important to inform survivors that these reactions are normal and that many disaster survivors experience the same things. When reactions and symptoms persist for an extended period of time, however, or begin to interfere with daily life, survivors may need to seek more intensive treatment.

Survivors need to be informed that reminders of the disaster, such as sights, sounds, smells, and specific situations may cause distress. It is also good to discuss anniversary reactions of disaster (Nemeth, Kuriansky, Reeder, Lewis, Marceaux, Whittington, Olivier, May, & Safier, 2012) and how to cope with annual reminders of the disaster event.

Some basic adaptive coping behaviors include talking to another person for support; getting adequate rest, nutrition, and exercise; engaging in positive distracting activities such as sports, hobbies, and reading; maintaining a normal schedule; keeping a journal; and using relaxation methods (Brymer et al.). More maladaptive coping strategies that should be limited include using alcohol or drugs to cope; withdrawal from family, friends, and activities; engaging in risky or dangerous behaviors; excessive working; and overeating (Brymer et al.).

It is very helpful for survivors to reestablish their normal routines as soon as possible, because this provides structure and can provide comfort, especially for children. Parents may see some regression in behavior and development among children. These regressive behaviors may be a natural reaction to the disaster and should be normalized unless they cause the child significant distress or do not improve over time. Survivors may need to be referred for more intensive treatment should they have substantial anger management issues, highly negative guilt and shame reactions, extended sleep disturbances, or alcohol or substance use issues (Brymer et al.).

Collaborative Services

"Goal: To link survivors with available services needed at the time or in the future" (Brymer et al., p. 93).

Although you may be able to provide for survivors' immediate needs, many survivors discover that they are in need of additional or more intensive services over time. It is important that survivors know what resources—medical, mental health, social, child welfare, school, drug and alcohol support, senior support, and transportation services—are available for the future.

Worker Self-Care

Secondary Traumatic Stress (STS) is the stress disaster workers may experience as a result of acting as a secondary witness to a traumatic event (Figley, 1995; Naturale, 2007). Figley (1999) defined STS as "the natural, consequent behaviors and emotions resulting from knowledge about a traumatizing event experienced by a significant other. It is the stress resulting from helping or wanting to help a traumatized or suffering person" (p. 10). Symptoms of STS include anxiety, stress, disturbed sleep, anger/rage, fear, social phobia, isolation, perceptual distortions, extreme protectiveness, feeling overwhelmed, feeling depleted, helplessness, and hopelessness, (Arvay & Uhlemann, 1995; Cornille & Myers, 1999; Crothers, 1995; Figley, 1995; Naturale, 2007; Yassen, 1995). General physical conditions associated with STS are increased arousal, sweating, rapid heart rate, breathing difficulties, somatic reactions, dizziness, and an impaired immune system (American Psychiatric Association, 2004; Yassen, 1995). Recognized as an occupational hazard, current research indicates that mental health professionals working with traumatized individuals are at risk for STS (Boscarino, Figley, & Adams, 2004; Bride, 2007).

Debriefing has been the recommended therapeutic approach to treat STS (Arvay, 2001); however, the scientific community is scrutinizing this widely used method (Naturale, 2007). Indeed, research indicates that debriefing may cause more harm than help (Phipps & Byrne, 2003; Regehr, 2001). Other recommended interventions for STS are preventative in nature, such as discussing the risks of developing STS with individuals working with trauma clients, peer support, and supervision (Naturale, 2007).

Social workers engaged in trauma work are at risk for developing secondary trauma (Adams, Figley, & Boscarino, 2008). "Social workers engaged in direct practice are highly likely to be secondarily exposed to traumatic events through their work with traumatized populations, many social workers are likely to experience at least some symptoms of STS, and a significant minority may meet the diagnostic criteria for PTSD (Bride, 2007, p. 63). Studies reveal that workers who have had previous exposure to traumatic events (such as workers who are survivors of violent crime), who have higher levels of empathy and poor perceived social support, are more susceptible to developing STS (MacRitchie & Leibowitz, 2010). Due to the high levels of susceptibility to STS, worker self-care is as crucial to disaster management as other components (Rowlands, 2013). Engaging in peer support is among the best ways to prevent and/or cope with STS (Pulido, 2012).

The idea of "shared traumatic reality" has been introduced in the literature recently. This occurs when disaster workers are themselves exposed to the same communal disaster as the care recipients. These workers are thus directly exposed to the disaster (they may live in the hurricane affected area or war zone), and then are also called upon to provide care to disaster survivors. These double-exposed workers can find themselves trapped by conflicting needs to protect themselves and their loved ones from the physical and psychological distress associated with the disaster and their professional role to provide direct services to traumatized survivors (Baum, 2011). These conflicting realities can lead to a blurring of boundaries between worker and client, and may also lead to greater emotional distress and exhaustion (Carroll, Balogh, Morbey, & Araoz, 2010; Dekel & Baum, 2010).

Some suggestions to assist double-exposed workers include: ensuring the physical safety of workers; giving priority and legitimacy to workers' personal worries and needs; setting time limits and limiting caseloads for exposed workers; improving worker preparedness; working in pairs to increase peer support; and identifying workers who may be at greater risk for developing adverse traumatic reactions due to situational vulnerability (Dekel & Baum, 2010).

Posttraumatic Growth

The majority of disaster survivors will not develop short- or long-term mental health problems, and, indeed, there is a burgeoning body of research on disaster resiliency and growth (Linley & Joseph, 2006). Evidence suggests that posttraumatic growth can occur even in the case of shared traumatic experiences where workers live and work in the disaster area. For example, Bauwens and Tosone (2010) found that 9/11 clinicians from Manhattan reported that the 9/11 experience was the impetus for improved self-care and the development of new clinical skills. Given the increasingly frequent incidence of natural and human-initiated disasters in the past few years, practitioners with training in disaster social work are and may be needed more than ever. Nevertheless, the possibility that the encounter with disaster can lead to personal and professional growth offers some hope amid often trying and tragic circumstances.

WEBSITES

Health and Human Services, www.hhs.gov
Islamic version of the Red Cross, The Red Crescent, www.redcrescent.org
National Child Traumatic Stress Network, www.nctsn.org
Psychological First Aid intervention, www.nctsy.org/content/psychological-first-aid
The Red Cross, www.redcross.org

References

Adams, R. E., Figley, C. R., & Boscarina, J. A. (2008). The compassion fatigue scale: Its use with social workers following urban disaster. *Research on Social Work Practice*, 18(3), 238–250.

Ager, A., Stark, L., Akesson, B., & Boothby, N. (2010). Defining best practice in care and protection of children in crisis-affected settings: A Delphi study. *Child Development*, 81(4), 1271–1286.

Amaratunga, C. A., & O'Sullivan, T. L. (2006). In the path of disasters: Psychosocial issues for preparedness, response, and recovery. *Prehospital and Disaster Medicine* 21(3), 149–155.

American Psychiatric Association. (2004). *Diagnostic and statistical manual of mental disorders IV*. Washington, DC: Author.

American Red Cross. (2013). *Responding to disasters overseas*. Retrieved from http://www.redcross.org/what-we-do/international-services/responding-disasters-overseas

Arvay, M. J. (2001). Secondary traumatic stress among trauma counselors: What does the research say? *International Journal for the Advancement of Counselling*, 23(4), 283–293.

Arvay, M. J., & Uhlhemann, M. R. (1995). Counsellor stress in the field of trauma: A preliminary study. *Canadian Journal of Counselling*, 30, 152–169.

Aziz, S., & Aslam, N. (2012). Psychiatric morbidity and work and social adjustment among earthquake survivors extricated from under the rubble. *Indian Journal of Psychological Medicine*, 34(4), 346–349.

Baker, M. D., Baker, L. R., & Flagg, L. A. (2012). Preparing families of children with special health care needs for disasters: An education intervention. *Social Work in Health Care*, 51, 417–429.

Barr, P. (2011). Staying connected. *Modern Healthcare* 41(36), 33.

Barusch, A. S. (2011). Disaster, vulnerability, and older adults: Toward a social work response. *Journal of Gerontological Social Work*, 54, 347–350.

Baum, N. (2011). "Emergency routine": The experience of professionals in a shared traumatic reality of war. *British Journal of Social Work*, 42, 424–442.

Bauwens, J., & Tosone, C. (2010). Professional posttraumatic growth after a shared traumatic experience: Manhattan clinicians' perspectives on post-9/11 practice. *Journal of Loss and Trauma*, 15, 498–517.

Bliss, D. L., & Meehan, J. (2008). Blueprint for creating a social work-centered disaster relief initiative. *Journal of Social Service Research*, 34(3), 73–85.

Boscarino, J. A., Figley, C. R., & Adams, R. E. (2004). Compassion fatigue following the September 11 terrorist attacks: A study of secondary trauma among New York City social workers. *International Journal of Emergency Mental Health*, 6(2), 57–66.

Bourassa, J. (2009). Psychosocial interventions and mass populations. A social work perspective. *International Social Work*, 52(6), 743–755.

Bride, B. E. (2007). Prevalence of secondary traumatic stress among social workers. *Social Work*, 52(1), 63–70.

Brymer, M., Jacobs, A., Layne, C., Pynoos, R., Ruzek, J., Steinberg, A., Vernberg, E., Watson, P. (2006). *Psychological first aid: Field operations guide*

(2nd ed.). Retrieved from http://www.nctsn.org/content/psychological-first-aid

Busaspathumrong, P. (2006). The role of social workers and social service delivery during crisis interventions for tsunami survivors: A case study of Thailand. *Journal of Social Work in Disability & Rehabilitation*, 5(3–4), 127–137.

Cain, D. S., & Barthelemy, J. (2008). Tangible and spiritual relief after the storm: The religious community responds to Katrina. *Journal of Social Service Research*, 34(3), 29–42.

Cain, D. S., Plummer, C. A., Fisher, R. M., & Bankston, T. Q. (2010). Weathering the storm: Persistent effects and psychological first aid with children displaced by Hurricane Katrina. *Journal of Child & Adolescent Trauma*, 3(4), 330–343.

Carroll, B., Balogh, R., Morbey, H., & Araoz, G. (2010). Health and social impacts of a flood disaster: responding to needs and implications for practice. *Disasters*, 34(4), 1045–1063.

Cherry, A. L., & Cherry, M. E. (1996). Research as social action in the aftermath of Hurricane Andrew. *Journal of Social Service Research*, 22(1/2), 77–87.

Coker, A. L., Hanks, J. S., Eggleston, K. S., Risser, J., Tee, P. G., Chronister, K. J., ... Franzini, L. (2006). Social and mental health needs assessment of Katrina evacuees. *Disaster Management Response*, 4, 88–94.

Cornille, T., & Myers, T. W. (1999). Secondary traumatic stress among child protective service workers: Prevalence, severity, and predictive factors. *Traumatology*, 5, 1.

Cronin, M. S., Ryan, D. M., & Brier, D. (2007). Support for staff working in disaster situations: A social work perspective. *International Social Work*, 50(3), 370–382.

Crothers, D. (1995). Vicarious traumatization in the work with survivors of childhood trauma. *Journal of Psychosocial Nursing*, 33, 4.

Davis, H. (2013). Contextual challenges for crisis support in the immediate aftermath of major incidents in the UK. *British Journal of Social Work*, 43, 504–521.

Dekel, R., & Baum, N. (2010). Intervention in a shared traumatic reality: A new challenge for social workers. *British Journal of Social Work*, 40, 1927–1944.

Dominelli, L. (2013). Empowering disaster-affected communities for long-term reconstruction: Intervening in Sri Lanka after the tsunami. *Journal of Social Work in Disability & Rehabilitation*, 12, 48–66.

Elliott, J. R., & Pais, J. (2006). Race, class, and Hurricane Katrina: Social differences in human responses to disaster. *Social Science Research*, 35, 295–321.

Evans, S., Patt, I., Giosan, C., Spielman, L., & Difede, J. (2009). Disability and posttraumatic stress disorder in disaster relief workers responding to September 11, 2001 World Trade Center disaster. *Journal of Clinical Psychology*, 65(7), 684–694.

Figley, C. R. (1995). Compassion fatigue: Coping with secondary traumatic stress disorder in those who treat the traumatized. New York, NY: Brunner/Mazel.

Figley, C. R. (1999). Compassion fatigue: Toward a new understanding of the costs of caring. In B. H. Stamm (Ed.), Secondary traumatic stress: Self-care issues for clinicians, researchers, and educators (pp. 3–28). Lutherville, MD: Sidran Press.

Fox, M. H., White, G. W., Rooney, C., & Cahill, A. (2010). The psychosocial impact of Hurricane Katrina on persons with disabilities and independent living center staff living on the American Gulf Coast. *Rehabilitation Psychology*, 55(3), 231–240.

Ganesan, M. (2006). Psychosocial response to disasters—Some concerns. *International Review of Psychiatry*, 18(3), 241–247.

Goenjian, A. (1993). A mental health relief programme in Armenia after the 1988 earthquake. Implementation and clinical observations. *British Journal of Psychiatry*, 163, 230–239.

Hayashi, K., & Tomita, N. (2012). Lessons learned from the Great East Japan Earthquake: Impact on child and adolescent health. *Asia-Pacific Journal of Public Health*, 24(4), 681–688.

Henley, R., Marshall, R., & Vetter, S. (2010). Integrating mental health services into humanitarian relief responses to social emergencies, disasters, and conflicts: A case study. *The Journal of Behavioral Health Services & Research*, 38(1), 132–141.

Hoffpauir, S. A., & Woodruff, L. A. (2008). Effective mental health response to catastrophic events: Lessons learned from Hurricane Katrina. *Family and Community Health*, 31(1), 17–22.

Huang, Y., Zhou, L., & Wei, K. (2011). 5.12 Wenchuan earthquake recovery. Government policies and non-governmental organizations' participation. *Asia Pacific Journal of Social Work and Development*, 21(2), 77–91.

Hussain, A., Weisaeth, L., & Heir, T. (2011). Psychiatric disorders and functional impairment among disaster victims after exposure to a natural disaster: A population based study. *Journal of Affective Disorders*, 128, 135–141.

Javadian, R. (2007). Social work responses to earthquake disasters: A social work intervention in Bam, Iran. *International Social Work*, 50(3), 334–346.

Kreuger, L., & Stretch, J. (2003). Identifying and helping long term child and adolescent disaster victims: Model and method. *Journal of Social Service Research*, 30(2), 93–108.

Legerski, J.-P., Vernberg, E. M., & Noland, B. J. (2012). A qualitative analysis of barriers, challenges, and successes in meeting the needs of Hurricane

Katrina evacuee families. *Community Mental Health Journal, 48,* 729–740.

Levine, J. E. (1996). Oklahoma City: The storying of a disaster. *Smith College Studies in Social Work, 67*(1), 21–38.

Linley, P. A., & Joseph, S. (2006). The positive and negative effects of disaster work: A preliminary investigation. *Journal of Loss and Trauma, 11,* 229–245.

MacRitchie, V., & Leibowitz, S. (2010). Secondary traumatic stress, level of exposure, empathy and social support in trauma workers. *South African Journal of Psychology, 40*(2), 149–158.

Mathbor, G. M. (2007). Enhancement of community preparedness for natural disasters. The role of social work in building social capital for sustainable disaster relief and management. *International Social Work, 50*(3), 357–369.

NASW Press (2000). *Social work speaks (5th ed.): NASW Policy Statements 2000–2003.* Retrieved from http://www.socialworkers.org/pressroom/events/911/disasters.asp

National Child Traumatic Stress Network—Child Trauma Home. (n.d.). *National child traumatic stress network empirically supported treatments and promising practices.* Retrieved from http://www.nctsn.org/resources/topics/treatments-that-work/promising-practices

National Medical Association (2005). NMA calls response to Hurricane Katrina a "national disgrace." *Journal of the National Medical Association, 97*(10), 1334–1335.

Naturale, A. (2007). Secondary traumatic stress in social workers responding to disasters: Reports from the field. *Clinical Social Work Journal, 35,* 173–181.

Nemeth, D. G., Kuriansky, J., Reeder, K. P., Lewis, A., Marceaux, K., Whittington, T., … Safier, J. A. (2012). Addressing anniversary reactions of trauma through group process: The Hurricane Katrina anniversary wellness workshops. *International Journal of Group Psychotherapy, 62*(1), 129–142.

Nikku, B. R. (2012). Children's rights in disasters: Concerns for social work—Insights from South Asia and possible lessons for Africa. *International Social Work, 56*(1), 51–66.

Norris, F., Friedman, M., Watson, P., Byrne, C., Diaz, E., & Kaniasty, L. (2002). 6,000 disaster victims speak: Part I. An empirical review of the empirical literature, 1981–2001. *Psychiatry, 65,* 207–239.

North, C. S., Tivis, L., McMillen, J. C., Pfefferbaum, B., Cox, J., Spitznagel, E. L., … Smith, E. M. (2002). Coping, functioning, and adjustment of rescue workers after the Oklahoma City bombing. *Journal of Traumatic Stress, 15*(3), 171–175.

Phipps, A. B., & Byrne, M. K. (2003). Brief interventions for secondary trauma: review and recommendations. *Stress and Health, 19,* 139–147.

Phua, K.-L. (2008). Post-disaster victimization: How survivors of disasters can continue to suffer after the event is over. *New Solutions: A Journal of Environmental and Occupational Health Policy, 18*(2), 221–231.

Plummer, C., Cain, D. S., Fisher, R. M., & Bankston, T. Q. (2008). Practice challenges in using psychological first aid in a group format with children: A pilot study. *Brief Treatment and Crisis Intervention, 8,* 313–326.

Pockett, R. (2006). Learning from each other: The social work role as an integrated part of the hospital disaster response. *Social Work in Health Care, 43*(2/3), 131–149.

Puig, M. E., & Glynn, J. B. (2003). Disaster responders: A cross-cultural approach to recovery and relief work. *Journal of Social Service Research, 30*(2), 55–66.

Pulido, M. L. (2012). The ripple effect: Lessons learned about secondary traumatic stress among clinicians responding to the September 11th terrorist attacks. *Clinical Social Work Journal, 40,* 307–315.

Pyles, L. (2007). Community organizing for post-disaster social development. Locating social work. *International Social Work 50*(3), 321–333.

Quinn, S. C. (2008). Crisis and emergency risk communication in a pandemic: A model for building capacity and resilience of minority communities. *Health Promotion Practice, 9*(4), 18S–25S.

Regehr, C. (2001). Crisis debriefing groups for emergency responders: Reviewing the evidence. *Brief Treatment and Crisis Intervention, 1*(2), 87–100.

Rosen, C. S., Greene, C. J., Young, H. E., & Norris, F. H. (2010). Tailoring disaster mental health services to diverse needs: An analysis of 36 crisis counseling projects. *Health & Social Work, 35*(3), 211–220.

Rowlands, A. (2013). Social work training curriculum in disaster management. *Journal of Social Work in Disability & Rehabilitation, 12,* 130–144.

Sanders, S., Bowie, S. L., & Bowie, Y. D. (2003). Lessons learned on forced relocation of older adults: The impact of Hurricane Andrew on health, mental health, and social support of public housing residents. *Journal of Gerontological Social Work, 40*(4), 23–35.

Schuster, M. A., Bradley, B. D., Jaycox, L. H., Collins, R. L., Marshall, G. N., Elliott, M. N.,. . .Berry, S. H. (2001). A national survey of stress reactions after the September 11, 2001, terrorist attacks. *New England Journal of Medicine, 345*(20), 1507–1512.

Shah, S. A. (2011). Ethical standards for transnational mental health and psychosocial support (MHPSS): Do no harm, preventing cross-cultural errors and inviting pushback. *Clinical Social Work Journal, 40,* 438–449.

Soliman, H. H., & Rogge, M. E. (2002). Ethical considerations in disaster services: A social work

perspective. *Electronic Journal of Social Work,*
1(1), 1–21.

Sommers-Flanagan, R. (2007). Ethical considerations
in crisis and humanitarian interventions. *Ethics &*
Behavior, 17(2), 187–202.

Speier, A. H. (2000). Psychosocial issues for children
and adolescents in disasters (2nd ed.). Retrieved
from   http://rems.ed.gov/docs/SAMHSA_
PsychosocialIssuesChildrenAdolescentsDisasters.
pdf

Sundet, P., & Mermelstein, J. (1996). Predictors of
rural community survival after natural disaster: Implications for social work practice. *Journal*
of Social Service Research, 22(1/2), 57–70.

Sweifach, J., LaPorte, H. H., & Linzer, N. (2010). Social
work responses to terrorism: Balancing ethics and
responsibility. *International Social Work, 53*(6),
822–835.

Takahashi, T., Lijima, K., Kuzuya, M., Hattori, H.,
Yokono, K., & Morimoto, S. (2011). Guidelines
for non-medical care providers to manage the
first steps of emergency triage of elderly evacuees. *Geriatrics & Gerontology International, 11,*
383–394.

Tan, N. T. (2013). Emergency management and social
recovery from disasters in different countries. *Journal of Social Work in Disability &*
Rehabilitation, 12, 8–18.

Terranova, A. M., Boxer, P., & Morris, A. S. (2009).
Factors influencing the course of posttraumatic
stress following a natural disaster: Children's
reactions for Hurricane Katrina. *Journal*
of Applied Developmental Psychology, 30,
344–355.

Torgusen, B., & Kosberg, J. I. (2006). Assisting older
victims of disasters: Roles and responsibilities for
social workers. *Journal of Gerontological Social*
Work, 47(1/2), 27–44.

U.S. Department of Health & Human Services (n.d.).
Health information privacy: Emergency pre-
paredness planning and response. Retrieved from
http://www.hhs.gov/ocr/privacy/hipaa/under-
standing/special/emergency/index.html

Yanay, U., & Benjamin, S. (2005). The role of social
workers in disasters. The Jerusalem experience.
International Journal of Social Work, 48(3),
263–276.

Yassen, J. (1995). Preventing secondary traumatic
stress disorder. In C. R. Figley (ed.), Compassion
fatigue. Coping with secondary traumatic stress
disorder in those who treat the traumatized (pp.
178–209). New York, NY: Brunner/Rutledge.

Zakour, M. J., & Harrell, E. B. (2003). Access to disaster
services: Social work interventions for vulnerable
populations. *Journal of Social Service Research,*
30(2), 27–54.

11   Victim Services

Karen S. Knox

INTRODUCTION

In the aftermath of a traumatic incident, crime
victims and survivors and their families receive
services from social workers and other helping
professionals across a range of settings, including advocacy organizations, law enforcement, the
court systems, corrections, and probation/parole.
As frontline responders on the scene, victim services programs and services that are housed in law
enforcement agencies provide unique opportunities
to intervene at a critical time, namely, immediately
after the offense and during the investigation.
Generally, brief, time-limited, crisis intervention
services and referrals for continued mental health,
advocacy, assistance, and legal services are provided
by victim services social workers.

Victim assistance services at the court level
are provided during the court preparation time
before hearings, and focus primarily on case notification, preparation for witness testimony, and
legal advocacy. Crisis intervention and supportive

counseling services are provided during the court proceedings because survivors, family members, and significant others typically experience a form of re-traumatization as a result of the memories, emotional reactions, and psychological disturbance triggered by their possible court testimony and having to face the offender(s) in court. Victim witness advocates assess and refer clients for Post Traumatic Stress Disorder and grief and loss issues that may indicate the need for continuing longer-term therapy.

Restorative justice programs are found at the corrections and probation/parole levels, and provide services for crime survivors and family members that include release and parole notification, victim impact panels, victim-offender mediation, and restitution programs.

HISTORY

Social workers have a long history of working in law enforcement, beginning in the early 1900s with the establishment of Women's Bureaus in police departments and friendly visitors who worked with women and children in need of protective services (Roberts, 2007). However, it was not until the 1970s, when the battered women's and rape crisis movements became active that the social work presence in law enforcement gained more momentum. Advocacy groups and organizations emerged to fight for victims' rights and compensation programs, with the realization that many crime victims were being victimized twice— once, during the actual crime, and then again by the criminal justice system, which historically had been designed to protect the rights of the criminal/ defendant rather than the victim/survivor. The crime victims' movement resulted in federal legislation and funding to establish victim assistance programs in all states through the Federal Law Enforcement Assistance Administration (LEAA) and the Victims of Crime Act (VOCA) of 1984. In 1994, both the Federal Violence Against Women Act (VAWA) and the Federal Law Enforcement and Crime Control Act allocated more funding to state and city police departments to develop crisis intervention and domestic violence counseling programs (Knox & Roberts, 2007).

CASE ILLUSTRATIONS

The victim services crisis team arrives at the scene of a domestic violence incident after being notified by the police officers that the victim is requesting services. Mary is in her living room so the crisis team leader goes to check with her, while the victim services volunteer talks to the patrol officers to get more information from them about what had happened. Mary states that her boyfriend hit her in the face and stomach while they were arguing about financial problems. She reports that he left in his car and she called 911. After talking with the crisis team leader, Mary decides she would like to be transported to the hospital to get medical treatment.

While at the hospital, the crisis team leader receives a call from dispatch that a sexual assault victim is being transported to the hospital emergency room for a rape exam and the patrol officer is requesting assistance. While Mary is being treated for her physical injuries, the crisis team leader and her volunteer collaborate on how to work both cases at the same time.

TREATMENT MODELS AND PROGRAMS

The primary theoretical models used in victims services programs are crisis intervention, grief and bereavement therapy, cognitive-behavioral approaches, reality therapy, and eye-movement desensitization and reprocessing (EMDR). These provide short-term treatment with a focus on immediate needs and short-term goals, not on past issues or problems requiring long-term treatment, unless those past issues are currently impacting on the current precipitating crisis or incident. Victim services programs in law enforcement offer crisis intervention on the scene or immediately following the crime or traumatic incident, short-term counseling, assistance and referrals for the victim's immediate needs, death notification to family members, and advocacy and assistance during the investigative process. Victim services workers use a team approach with community providers and agencies, such as domestic violence programs/ shelters, rape crisis centers, mental health providers and authorities, and other public and social service agencies that can meet the needs of crime victims and survivors.

Victim witness assistance programs in the court systems try to minimize the re-victimization that can occur through involvement with the criminal justice system, defense attorneys, and the court proceedings. Re-victimization can happen when victims, survivors, and witnesses have negative experiences with attorneys, prosecutors, and others in the legal system that can be perceived as insensitive, unfair, and traumatizing, and which can provoke feelings of being victimized all over again. Reliving the traumatic events and having to testify or confront the offender can trigger posttraumatic stress disorder symptoms that result in the need for continued psychological and supportive counseling services.

The primary roles and objectives for a victim witness advocate in the court system are to inform victims and witnesses of their legal rights, such as victims' compensation and restitution benefits to which they are entitled; to provide information and notification of the court processes; and to offer court and testimony preparation, accompaniment, and crisis intervention during the court proceedings. Victim compensation programs and services are available in all 50 states and the District of Columbia, the U.S. Virgin Islands, Puerto Rico, and Guam (Knox & Roberts, 2007). Victim compensation programs can assist financially with medical expenses, lost wages, and counseling services needed as a result of a crime. However, eligibility criteria can vary across the states and financial awards can be reduced or denied if the victim/survivor has insurance that will pay for such services, and can be dependent upon prosecution and conviction in court. Restitution and criminal fines paid by offenders on probation and parole primarily fund victim compensation programs.

Victim advocacy programs in corrections provide information on offender parole or probation status and release dates, opportunities to impact on parole board and probation hearings, and involvement with victim impact panels where survivors can confront and educate offenders on the effects and consequences of their violent crimes. Restorative justice programs focus on strategies to assist offenders in realizing and understanding the extent of the harm and damages caused by their offenses, and include mediation and restitution services through which social workers advocate for crime victims, survivors, and their families. Other national crime victim advocacy organizations, such as the National Organization for Victims Assistance (NOVA) and the National Center for Victims of Crime, provide volunteer opportunities, educational and training materials for survivors, significant others, and professionals; outreach and referral services; and opportunities for political and advocacy

initiatives that address legal and governmental gaps in policies and services.

EVIDENCED-BASED PRACTICE GUIDELINES AND SPECIAL CLINICAL ISSUES

Evidence-based research in this field guides best practices for training and education of victim services professionals (McCart, Smith, & Sawyer, 2010; Parsons & Bergin, 2010). Research studies have found that providing crisis intervention, financial assistance, referral information, support, and advocacy services have a positive correlation with victim satisfaction with the criminal justice system and increased cooperation with the legal process (Camacho & Alarid, 2008; Larsen, Tax, & Botuck, 2009; Ruback, Cares, & Hoskins, 2008). Standards of practice, national credentialing programs, and other continuing education training are offered by the National Organization of Victim Assistance and the National Victim Assistance Academy, which is sponsored by the Office for Victims of Crime (OVC).

Crisis intervention requires a high level of activity and skill on the part of the social worker, and the time frame for assessment and contracting is brief by necessity. People experiencing trauma and crisis need immediate relief and assistance, and the helping process must be adapted to meet those needs as efficiently and effectively as possible. Therefore, the assessment, contracting, and intervention stages may need to be completed and implemented on the very first client contact. Clients in an active state of crisis are more amenable to the helping process, and are more likely to accept help, so this can facilitate completion of such tasks within a rapid response time frame.

Specialized knowledge about specific types of crime victims and traumatic incidents is necessary for effective intervention planning. For example, working with victims of family violence requires education and training on the dynamics and cycle of battering and abuse, familiarity with the community agencies providing services to this client population, and knowledge about the legal options available to victims. Concrete, basic needs services such as emergency safety, medical needs, food, clothing, and shelter are the first priority in crisis intervention. Mobilizing needed resources may require more direct activity by the social worker in advocating, networking, and brokering for clients, who may not have the knowledge, skills, or capacity to follow through with referrals and collateral contacts at the time of active crisis.

STEP-BY-STEP TREATMENT MODEL AND GOALS

Roberts' Seven-Stage Crisis Intervention Model is useful in police-based social work because it adapts easily to the various types of crises and to different time frames for intervention (Knox & Roberts, 2008). All of these stages can be completed within one contact if necessary, and in many crisis situations, that may be all the time that is available:

Stage 1: Plan and conduct a psychosocial and lethality assessment: Assessment is ongoing and critical to effective intervention at all stages, but begins with an assessment of the lethality and safety issues for the client. With victims of rape, family violence, child abuse, or assault, it is important to assess whether the client is in any current danger, and to consider future safety concerns in treatment planning. With suicidal clients, it is critical to assess the risk for attempts, plans, or means to harm oneself at the current time, as well as any previous history of suicidal ideations or attempts. The goals of this stage are to obtain sufficient information to determine whether the client is in imminent danger, and to identify and assess critical areas of intervention.

At present, although there is no imminent danger or harm, it is necessary to talk with Mary about a safety plan for when she is released from the hospital. She does not feel safe returning home in case her boyfriend returns. She relates that she recently moved from another city to break off this relationship, and she has no money to relocate again so soon. The victim services volunteer talks with Mary about the local domestic violence shelter and will check on availability of emergency services.

The patrol officer briefs the crisis team leader as Amy, the sexual assault victim, is being brought into the emergency room. While the medical team prepares the room for her rape exam, the crisis team leader introduces herself and explains to Amy that the medical procedures are done by a specially trained sexual assault nurse examiner, and that the crisis team will stay with her until after the examination, if she wants. The crisis team leader also offers to contact a support person if Amy wants to have a friend or relative come to the hospital.

Stage 2: Make psychological contact and rapidly establish the relationship: The main goals of this stage are to establish rapport and a supportive relationship. Crime victims may question their own safety and vulnerability, and trust may be difficult for them to establish at this time. Therefore, active listening and empathic communication skills are essential to engaging the client. During this stage, clients need support, positive regard, concern, and genuineness.

After Mary's physical exam, she starts going over the details of the night, which is common for crime victims and helps them become more oriented to the time and sequence of events and able to process what happened. It is important to listen and take notes for the incident report, and to let Mary talk without too much questioning.

Amy has already given an initial report to the patrol officers; she will also need to give a statement to the Sex Crimes Unit as soon as possible to further the investigation and possible arrest of a suspect. Amy is concerned that the rapist may return to her apartment and does not feel safe returning home. Empathic communication skills are important at this time to help establish the relationship and encourage her to ventilate and express her emotional reactions.

Stage 3: Identify the major problems: This stage focuses on prioritizing the most important problems or impacts by identifying how each affects the client's current status. The first priority in this stage is meeting the basic needs of emotional and physical health and safety. The focus must clearly be on the present crisis, and any exploration of past problems or issues must be done rapidly and only to aid in intervention planning.

Mary has decided to go to the domestic violence shelter and requests transportation to her apartment to pack a bag and get some personal items. The victim services volunteer arranges for the patrol officer to accompany them. She explains that the shelter staff will assist her with legal and court procedures for which she can apply to help meet some of her financial, medical, and legal needs.

Amy wants to know what she needs to do to give her statement to the Sex Crimes investigator. She also wants help getting some clothes and her car and calling her employer to explain about missing work tomorrow. She says she can stay with her friend for a few days, and that she does not feel safe returning to her apartment yet.

Stage 4: Deal with feelings and provide support: The primary goal in this stage is dealing with the emotional impacts of the trauma event through ventilation, expression, and exploration of the client's emotions about the crisis event and aftermath. The primary technique used is active listening, which involves listening in an accepting and supportive way, in as private and safe a setting as possible. It is critical that the victim services social worker demonstrate empathy and support. Victims sometimes blame themselves and it is important to help the client acknowledge and accept that being a victim is not one's fault. Validation and reassurance are especially useful in this stage, because survivors may be experiencing confusing and conflicting feelings.

The crisis team leader talks with Amy about support and counseling services at the local rape crisis center. She lets Amy know that a victim services counselor will be available to answer questions or provide other assistance when she goes to the police station to give her statement. The victim services counselor will also inform her about Victim's Compensation and how to apply for benefits, and will make any other necessary community referrals.

The crisis team then calls for the patrol officers to meet Amy and her friend at her apartment so she will be able to get her clothes and car before she goes to her friend's house. The crisis team then leaves with Mary to transport her to the domestic violence shelter. While driving there, the volunteer explains that the Family Violence Unit will be contacting Mary to complete the case investigation, and that she can request further services from the victim services counselor assigned to that unit.

Stage 5: Generate and explore alternatives: The goal of this stage is to achieve a pre-crisis level of functioning through the client's coping skills and support systems. If the client has unrealistic expectations or inappropriate coping skills and strategies, the victim services social worker may need to be more active and directive in this stage. Clients are still distressed and in disequilibrium at this stage, and professional expertise and guidance could be necessary to produce positive, realistic alternatives for the client.

While at the police station the next day, Mary talks to the victim services counselor about a Protective Order against her boyfriend. She is referred to the County Attorney's Office, where their victim advocate will assist her in completing the forms and provide follow-up services on the court procedures. After Amy gives her statement to the Sex Crimes investigator, she talks to the victim services counselor and is able to ventilate her fear and anger about what happened. She wants to stay with her friend for a couple of more days, because she needs to replace her front door lock and is interested in other security options for her house. Referrals for counseling at the rape crisis center are provided to Amy, and the victim services counselor offers to follow up with her next week to check whether she has any questions about the investigation or needs further services.

Stage 6: Develop and formulate an action plan: It is important for the client to look at both the short-term and long-range impacts when planning intervention. The main goals are to help the client achieve an appropriate level of functioning and maintain adaptive coping skills and resources. It is important to have a manageable treatment plan, so the client can follow through and be successful. Do not overwhelm the client with too many tasks or strategies, which may set the client up for failure. Ongoing assessment and evaluation are essential to determine whether the intervention plan is appropriate and effective in minimizing or resolving the client's identified problems. During this stage, the client should be processing and reintegrating the crisis impacts to achieve homeostasis and equilibrium in his or her life.

Although both Mary's and Amy's immediate concerns and needs have been addressed, they will need support and advocacy services through the legal and court procedures that will be provided by the victim witness advocates at the district attorney's office. The police-based victim services counselors provide short-term crisis intervention services, and the local domestic violence and rape crisis centers offer both individual and group counseling services. The agencies also have liaisons who work with the victim witness advocates at the district attorney's office to provide assistance and support when the offender goes to trial. This can be another critical time for crime victims; it may trigger memories of and reactions from their assaults that need to be addressed.

Stage 7: Termination & follow-up measures: Termination begins when the client has achieved the goals of the action plan, or has been referred for additional services through other treatment providers. This last stage should help determine whether these desired results have been maintained or whether further work remains to be done. Typically, follow-up contacts are by phone and should be done within four to six weeks after termination.

The victim services counselors from the police department will follow up with both Mary and Amy to assess whether there are any questions or problems that need to be addressed. Given that cases going through the criminal justice and legal systems often take a very long time, this period is usually when victims may have questions about what is going on with their case or what is happening in the court system. This offers an opportunity to assist with these types of legal issues and concerns. This is also a good time to check whether the victim/survivor has followed up with counseling referrals and treatment, or is still in emotional and psychological distress, and to assist with providing other referrals or treatment options. The victim witness advocates at the courts will also provide continuing services throughout the legal proceedings. Crime victim survivors and their family members also participate in crime victims' rights and advocacy organizations as a way to recover and heal from their own victimization experiences and to help others who share similar experiences.

INTERVENTION SKILLS AND COMPETENCIES

- *Communication Skills:* Social workers in victim services programs need to be attentive to the tone and level of verbal communications to help the client calm down or de-escalate from the initial trauma reactions. Observing the client's physical and facial reactions can provide cues to the client's current emotional state and level of engagement. It is important to remember that delayed reactions or flat affect are common with crime victims, and not to assume that these types of reactions mean that the client is not in crisis. Encouraging the client to ventilate about the precipitating crisis event can assist in problem identification, and clients may have an overwhelming need to talk about the specifics of the trauma situation. Others may be in shock, denial, or unable to verbalize their needs and feelings, so information may need to be obtained from collateral sources or significant others.

- *Intervention Skills:* Intervention begins at first contact when victims and survivors may be experiencing confusing and conflicting feelings. The social worker needs to be knowledgeable about the grief process, which many victims and family survivors follow when expressing and ventilating their emotions. First, clients may be in denial about the extent of their emotional reactions and may try to avoid dealing with them in hopes that they will subside. They may be in shock and not be able to access their feelings immediately. However, significant delays in expression and ventilation of feelings can be harmful to the client in processing and resolving the trauma. Some clients will express anger and rage about the situation and its effects, which can be healthy, as long as the client does not escalate out of control. Helping the client calm down or attending to physiological reactions such as hyperventilation are important interventions in this situation. Other clients may express their grief and sadness by crying, moaning, or fainting (referred to as "falling out" in some cultures), and need time and space to express their reactions, without pressure to move along too quickly.

- *Coping Skills*: Healthy coping skills promote adaptive responses and resolution of the crisis by using support systems, such as people or resources that can be helpful to the client in meeting needs and resolving problems in living that may have resulted from the crisis. Healthy coping skills can increase positive and constructive thinking patterns that reduce the client's levels of anxiety and stress. Victim services professionals can facilitate healthy coping skills by identifying client strengths and resources. Many crisis survivors feel they do not have a lot of choices, and the crisis worker needs to be familiar with both formal and informal community services to provide referrals.

- *Termination & Follow-Up Skills*: It is important to remember that final crisis resolution may take many months or years to achieve (if ever), and that certain events, places, or dates could continue to trigger emotional and physical reactions to the previous trauma. This is a normal part of the recovery process, and clients should be prepared to have contingency plans or supportive help through these difficult periods.

- *Self-Care*: Self-care and safety concerns are critical in this setting. Self-awareness of your own emotional reactions and level of comfort when working with your clients is also critical. It is important to attend to your self-care needs to avoid burnout and emotional fatigue.

HELPFUL WEBSITES

National Center for Victims of Crime: www.victimsofcrime.org

Office for Victims of Crime: www.ojp.usdoj.gov/ovc/welcome.html

Office of Justice: www.ojp.usdoj.gov/programs/victims.htm.

National Organization for Victim Assistance: www.trynova.org

References

Camacho, C. M., & Alarid, L. F. (2008). The significance of the victim advocate for domestic violence victims in municipal court. *Violence and Victims*, 23(3), 288–300. doi: 10.1891/0886-6708.23.3.288

Knox, K. S., & Roberts, A. R. (2007). Forensic social work in law enforcement and victim service/victim assistance programs: National and local perspectives. In A. R. Roberts & D. W. Springer (Eds.), *Social work in juvenile and criminal justice settings* (pp. 113–123). Springfield, IL: Charles C. Thomas, Publisher Ltd.

Knox, K. S., & Roberts, A. F. (2008). The crisis intervention model. In P. Lehmann & N. Coady (Eds.), *Theoretical perspectives for direct social work practice: A generalist-eclectic approach* (pp. 249–274). New York, NY: Springer Publishing Co.

Larsen, M., Tax, C., & Botuck, S. (2009). Standardizing practice at a victim services organization: A case analysis illustrating the role of evaluation. *Administration in Social Work*, 33, 439–449.

McCart, M., Smith, D., & Sawyer, G. (2010). Help-seeking among victims of crime: A review of the empirical literature. *Journal of Traumatic Stress*, 23(2), 190–206.

Parsons, J., & Bergin, T. (2010). The impact of criminal justice involvement on victims' mental health. *Journal of Traumatic Stress*, 23(2), 182–188.

Roberts, A. R. (2007). The history and role of social work in law enforcement. In A. R. Roberts & D. W. Springer (Eds.), *Social work in juvenile and criminal justice settings* (pp. 106–112). Springfield, IL: Charles C. Thomas, Publisher Ltd.

Ruback, R. B., Cares, A. C., & Hoskins, S. N. (2008). Crime victims' perceptions of restitution: The importance of payment and understanding. *Violence and Victims*, 23(6), 697–710.

12 Social Work in Domestic Violence Services

Brandy Macaluso & Diane L. Green Sherman

A TYPICAL DAY ON THE JOB IN DOMESTIC VIOLENCE SERVICES

Crisis Responder

7 P.M.	Shift Begins: On-Call Phone is Turned On	2 A.M.	Crisis Call from Police to Respond On-Scene to Domestic Violence Call; Victim has Injuries
8 P.M.	Crisis Call from Police Requesting Transport for Domestic Violence Victim to Emergency Shelter	2 A.M.–3 A.M.	Crisis Intervention and Transport with Victim to Local Hospital for Injury Treatment
8:30 P.M.–9 P.M.	Transport Victim to Emergency Shelter and Await Intake with Victim	3 A.M.–6 A.M.	Provide Support to Victim in Hospital for Medical Services, Law Enforcement Reporting, and Discharge
10 P.M.–11 P.M.	Leave Shelter, Return Home, and Document Information for Follow Up by Non-Crisis Staff in the Morning	6 A.M.–7 A.M.	Document Information for Follow Up by Non-Crisis Staff in the Morning
12:30 A.M.–1 A.M.	Crisis Call from Police Requesting Referral Information, No Response Needed On-Scene, Documented Request	7 A.M.	Shift Ends, On-Call Phone is Forwarded to Regular Office Phones with Noted One-Hour Response Time Indicated

Non-Crisis Responder

8 A.M.–8:30 A.M.	Start Shift. Check Voicemail Messages	1 P.M.–3 P.M.	Court: Restraining Order (RO) Hearing
9 A.M.–11 A.M.	New Victim Intakes	3 P.M.–4 P.M.	Case Work: Follow Ups
11 A.M.–NOON	Facilitate Domestic Violence Survivors Support Group	4 P.M.–5 P.M.	Set New Intake Appointments and Make Service Referrals for New Clients
NOON–1 P.M.	Lunch	5 P.M.	End Shift

Shelter Hotline Worker

2:30 P.M.–3 P.M.	Shift Begins; Receive Report of Activity from Prior Shift Worker	9 P.M.–9:30 P.M.	Counsel Victim on the Phone about Available Resources and Shelter Services
3 P.M.–7 P.M.	Receive Calls for Domestic Violence Information and Service Referral Requests	9:30 P.M.–10 P.M.	Receive Call from Police for Phone Intake of Victim
7 P.M.	Receive call from Police for Phone Intake of Victim	10 P.M.–10:30 P.M.	Arrange Victim Pick-Up with Available Shelter Advocate
8:15 P.M.	Receive call from Crisis Advocate for Phone Intake of Victim	10:30 P.M.–11 P.M.	Report of Activity to Hotline Worker on Next Shift
8:30 P.M.–9 P.M.	Arrange Victim Pick-Up with Available Shelter Advocate	11 P.M.	Shift Ends

SERVICE NEEDS OF VICTIMS

- Crisis Intervention
- Safety Planning
- Restraining Order Assistance
- Emergency Safe Shelter/Housing
- Supportive Group Work/Peer Counseling
- Individual Counseling, Therapy, and/or Medications
- Health Care
- Transportation
- Food
- Spiritual Needs
- Legal Services for Divorce/Child Custody, Support, or Visitation
- Pet Care
- Life Skills Training
- Educational Needs
- Long-term Housing
- Vocational Services
- Child Care
- Court Accompaniment/Support for RO and Criminal Case
- Any Other Need Identified by the Victim

EMERGING CONCERNS

New Abusers with Alzheimer's. In later stages of Alzheimer's disease, anger and aggression can start to manifest in violent outbursts. These outbursts can be aimed directly at caregivers who are often family or intimate partners of the individual. Unfortunately, there is no known reason for these outbursts. Doctors indicate that they could be a reaction to stimulus in the environment or they could simply be a symptom of the Alzheimer's disease itself. The key to averting them is knowing the possible triggers: confusion, overstimulation due to the environment, or discomfort of some kind.

Once caregivers recognize these triggers, taking steps to ease the person with Alzheimer's disease could be as simple as taking them to a quiet area, minimizing stimulants in the environment, sitting and listening to them talk, asking simple questions about the memories they are recalling at that moment, and/or focusing on the distant past given that the disease affects short-term memory. It may be easier and more pleasant for them to talk about memories from childhood or early adulthood, thus diffusing the aggressive behaviors or abusive outburst.

Service providers assisting victims of abuse by individuals with Alzheimer's disease should make a referral to the local Alzheimer's disease center or to programs that provide respite care, day programs, and caregiver supports.

Domestic Homicides. There recently has been a focus on homicides stemming from domestic violence. Perpetrators murder their intimate partners and/or intervening friends, family members, new intimate partners, children, or innocent bystanders. These homicides often spring from jealousy, power, and control over the intimate partner or former intimate partner. According to the *Palm Beach Post*, which has been tracking Palm Beach County's homicide figures since 2008, there were 11 domestic homicides in the year 2012 and 14 from January 2013 to October 2013 in Palm Beach County.

According to Jane Doe Inc., the Massachusetts Coalition against Sexual Assault and Domestic Violence, these homicides can be predicted and due to their predictability, these homicides are preventable. Further, according to this coalition, three commonalities emerge during case reviews: "First, while systems and services may have failed some victims, the only person ultimately responsible for the abuse, violence and homicide is the perpetrator. Similarly, regardless of what actions these domestic violence victims may or may not have taken, they are not responsible for the abuse and are not to be blamed. Second, our law enforcement, judicial and other systems as well as services have not all adopted current best practices for holding perpetrators accountable and predicting and preventing domestic violence homicides. Third, the lack of connection between the domestic violence victim and a trained domestic violence advocate from a local community (or health-care) based domestic violence program is consistently a missing link in these cases, a practice that research tells us can make the difference between life and death."

Jane Doe Inc. suggests the first step in prevention of domestic homicides is having a victim connect with a domestic violence advocate. The perpetrator of violence relies on the lack of education about services, key resources, or emergency protections as a key to preventing the victim from leaving. Bridging a victim with an advocate to discuss available programs and resources will provide that victim with needed information, adding a safety net for the victim to be able to maneuver away safely from a toxic or abusive relationship. Secondly, use a victim-centered approach which means the victim's safety and welfare is the center of the service provision. By addressing the needs identified by the victim, the success rate increases significantly for the victim to be able to leave the abusive relationship. Third, recognize that best practices exist and establish training and research-based interventions for service providers and individuals in the criminal justice system to use when assisting victims of interpersonal violence (IPV). Fourth, recognize that prevention of domestic homicides is possible, and by following the preceding steps, these victims can remain on the road to survivorship.

Traumatic Brain Injury. In 2005, 11% of the 1,400,000 Traumatic Brain Injuries were directly caused by assault. In 1999, over 90% of all injuries secondary to domestic violence occur to the head, neck, or face region, which is likely to lead to a traumatic brain injury over time. Among battered women, 30% reported a loss of consciousness at least once, and 67% of battered women reported residual problems that were potentially head-injury related, such as seizures, headaches, and vision problems.

Numerous common physical symptoms appear after a victim acquires a brain injury through violence. Those symptoms include loss of smell or taste, hearing loss, visual difficulties, balance difficulties, problems with motor control or coordination, fatigue, seizures, decreased tolerance for drugs or alcohol, headaches, and sleep disturbances. Cognitive symptoms also can occur. They include short-term memory loss, short attention span, easy loss of concentration, inability to focus, distractibility, decreased verbal fluency or inability to find words previously known to the victim, decreased comprehension, disconnects when processing information, erratic arousal, inability to problem solve, decreased intellectual functioning, inability to conceptualize, and delayed reaction time. Extreme changes in behavior may occur, including impulsivity, emotional fluctuations, irritability, decreased frustration tolerance, impaired judgment, anxiety, depression, aggressiveness, sexual urges, and personality changes.

The above symptoms combined can make safety planning for an individual with a brain injury very difficult. Often these individuals have trouble assessing inflammatory situations or lethality levels. Memory loss precludes them from following their safety plan. Their sometimes erratic behavior can make reporting difficult and in some cases can make police view them as the aggressor in the situation. These brain injuries may also affect their ability to set and maintain goals such as vocational goals, follow shelter schedules, set and keep appointments, and live independently. When it comes to the criminal case, victims with brain injuries may have their disability used against them. For example, their memory loss or inability to recall timelines or provide information in chronological order is used as a way to disregard their allegations. If they do not present well, their credibility, capacity, or competency may be questioned and they may be subject to evaluations to determine whether they are fit to proceed in the court process. Further, if the victim is on medications to control physical symptoms, mental health diagnoses, or other medical conditions related to the abuse, defense attorneys have been known to use the effects and side effects of those medications as a way to discredit the allegations and recollection of abusive events.

VICTIM PROFILE

Physical Signs of Abuse

- Burns
- Bruises, Cuts, Scars, Abrasions, Scrapes
- Marks Around Mouth from Gagging
- Imprint Injuries
- Missing Teeth
- Spotty Balding from Hair Pulling
- Eye Injuries
- Broken Bones/Sprains
- Vaginal or Rectal Pain, Inflammation, or Infections
- Bleeding from Ears, Nose, Mouth, etc
- Incontinence of someone who was previously potty-trained
- Frequent Sore Throats
- Psychosomatic Complaints (Males–Stomach Upset; Females–Headache)
- Difficulty Walking or Sitting

Nonverbal Signs of Abuse

- Change in the Show of Affection
- Fears Being Touched
- Sudden Onset of Night Terrors
- Changes in Sleep Pattern
- Unwilling to Make Eye Contact
- Timid or Submissive
- Depression/Withdrawal/Mood Swings
- Any Other Sudden Changes in Behavior

ABUSER PROFILE

Characteristics of an Abusive Person

- Low Self-Esteem
- Need to Control
- Confrontational with Anyone Appearing Inferior
- Frustration with Authority
- History of Being Neglected or Abused Themselves
- Lack of Attachment
- Abusive toward Animals
- Lack of Accountability
- Use of Threats, Looks, or Body Language for Intimidation Purposes
- Impulsive
- Devaluing Nature
- Blatant Disregard for Others
- Overly Competitive
- Unwelcoming or Uncooperative Attitude
- Frequently Changes Service Providers, Health Care Providers, and any other "Helping" Service Worker
- Under the Influence of Drugs or Alcohol
- Destroys Others' Property

INCREASED VULNERABILITY/GAPS IN SERVICE

Elderly. The elderly tend to underreport IPV. The stigma with IPV still exists in their generation and although there are some shifts in the process to address this issue, it is still under-reported. In generations past, it was very common to keep family problems in the family. Violence and relationship issues were not openly discussed outside of the immediate family. Many of the elder generation had been victimized for years before they even realized that they were victims. Some still do not realize they were victims.

Recently, after speaking with an 87-year-old woman, she described her stepfather as a caring person until he started drinking. After drinking, he would come home and tear the house apart, smashing dishes, and hitting her mother. She indicated that unless they went outside, he would come after her and her siblings, too. She stated that they would have to wait in an alley way, sometimes in snow, until he had gone to bed, before coming back into the house to go to bed themselves. After hearing her story, she was asked if she believed she was a victim of domestic violence. Her response was no.

Men. In 2010, a study done by a Campaign group called Parity in the United Kingdom found that over 40% of reported cases of domestic violence indicated that men were victimized by their wives or girlfriends, a number much higher than initially thought. Further, the study showed that violence perpetrated against men is not taken seriously by police, is "dumbed down" in the media, and there is no real emergency placement or assistance set up for male victims. It also indicated that perpetrators are often freed or given subdued sentencing. Female on male IPV is underreported for these reasons as well as the stigma of being demasculinated by appearing weak, vulnerable, or "unmanly" by being abused by a female partner.

LBGTQ. The lesbian, bisexual, gay, transgendered, and queer (LBGTQ) community still has an emerging identity in society. Although much legislation has been passed recently regarding this population, much also has been repealed or delayed for various reasons. "Unfortunately, domestic violence victims in same-sex relationships are not receiving the help they need. This is due to the lack of legal recognition of same-sex relationships, law enforcement's failure to identity and properly handle domestic violence cases involving people of the same sex, and the shortage of resources available to victims of same-sex partner domestic abuse," according to the Center on American Progress Report on Domestic Violence in the LBGT Fact Sheet. According to this same fact sheet, the reasons for lack of reporting include fear of the violent partner "outing" their sexual orientation or gender identity to family, friends, police, coworkers, etc. It also indicated that reporting may be seen as endangering solidarity by giving the LBGTQ community a bad name. Other reasons included the fact that children can be used as leverage in cases because most states do not recognize LBGTQ couples or allow same-sex couples to adopt. Lastly, same-sex couples are more likely to fight back against their perpetrator making police believe the abusive behavior may be mutual.

Victims with Disabilities. Individuals with disabilities have historically underreported crimes perpetrated against them. There are two main reasons for this. The first is physical barriers, simply meaning that they are physically unable to report due to their disability or a lack of accommodations made by society in general. This could include lack of Text Telephones (TTY) or Video Phones at local police departments, emergency shelters, or service providers; lack of or too few accessible parking areas; steep terrain or no ramps for wheelchair users; lack of information in alternative formats, such as Braille, for individuals who are blind; and similarly lacking accommodations required by those with disabilities. The second cause for underreporting is attitudinal barriers, often unintentional, found throughout society. Some individuals are unsure how to make accommodations for people with disabilities and, therefore, simply do not make necessary accommodations, nor do they go out of their way to learn what the law requires. Common attitudinal barriers include giving the person with a disability unfair advantages instead of level standards of opportunity; denial of the disability and, therefore, not making appropriate accommodations; or portraying a person with a disability as special or a hero for overcoming disability. On the other end of the spectrum is inferiority, that is, portraying a person with a disability as helpless or useless; seeing people with disabilities as incapable of managing their own lives or tasks; and, lastly, pitying or patronizing behaviors toward those with disabilities. Often, these physical and attitudinal barriers can lead to discrimination and exclusion from service provision, the court process, and other life activities.

Another issue regarding victims of domestic violence with disabilities is that the perpetrators of violence are often the caregivers for the person with the disability. Perpetrators often cite the stress from caregiving as an excuse for their violent or demeaning behavior and blame the person with the disability for the way they, themselves, act toward them. This abuse does not have to be physical in nature. It can also take the form of threats, intimidation, emotional abuse, isolation, economic abuse, or withholding, misusing, or delaying needed supports including medication, adaptive equipment, and food.

CASE SCENARIOS

Linda Devry, Age 43

Linda contacts the shelter hotline for an intake. The shelter screens her and finds that she fits criteria to enter Domestic Violence Emergency Shelter. Linda makes arrangements to meet the shelter worker. When she shows up to enter the shelter, Linda is apparently drunk. The shelter worker can smell the overwhelming smell of alcohol on her breath. The shelter worker asks the victim if she has been drinking because she can smell alcohol. The victim appears shamed and responds that she had been drinking with her boyfriend and that is what sparked the fight. She drank the last beer in the house. When he found out, he told her to go to the store, when she refused because she felt she could not drive, he pushed her and started to throw items in the house, including a book, at her. When she pulled out her phone to call police, he grabbed her arm, took the phone, and threw it against the wall, breaking it.

The shelter worker asked Linda if she would like help with alcohol abuse. Linda agreed she wanted to speak to someone. The shelter worker made a referral to the local addictions center and set up an intake for her for the following day. Linda was assigned her sleeping arrangement for shelter and was given a schedule of group and individual sessions required. She was also provided the rules for the emergency shelter.

Linda went to her appointment the next day for the addictions center and was assigned a case manager. She scheduled a follow-up and will attend the outpatient program because she scored low on their addiction screening inventories.

Linda met with the shelter advocate assigned to her later that day. The advocate met with her to get background on her. Linda is currently working a part-time job and receives a widow benefit from her late husband who was killed on active duty. She receives a decent amount of monthly income, with which she will be able to rent a small one bedroom apartment. The advocate sits with her, showing her how to look and apply for apartments. Linda advises that she does not have much family but has a coworker whom she trusts who knows her situation with her boyfriend. The coworker has encouraged her to leave in the past, but cannot assist with housing her because the coworker is in a gated community with homeowner's association rules regarding visitors.

Linda advises that she is scared of her current boyfriend and wants to be protected when he gets out of jail. The advocate explains the restraining order process to Linda and helps her complete the application. She instructs Linda how to file the order on her own at the courthouse. The advocate also tells her about a notification program that will notify her if he is released from jail. Linda is interested in applying. They complete the application.

Linda returns from the courthouse and tells the advocate that she has a court date in two weeks. The advocate refers her to domestic violence legal services to assign her an attorney to represent her during court.

Linda locates an apartment she can afford on her monthly income. She meets the management company and completes an application. Linda is accepted approximately three days later. Linda is excited but apprehensive. She then tells her advocate that she does not have any furniture to put in her apartment. The advocate completes a referral for Linda to the local thrift store for a few items: a dinette set, bed, dresser, and couch. Linda calls a coworker to help her retrieve the furniture.

Linda is given an exit date by the advocate based on the move-in date for her apartment. Linda is also given additional resources to be able to continue counseling services at the shelter outreach department. She is also given information on other community agencies that she can call for additional assistance.

Three months later, Linda completes counseling with the outreach worker and is thriving. Linda has focused on purchasing small furnishings for her apartment. She also disclosed that she bought a kitten so she would not be so lonely.

Naomi Pike, Age 35

You receive a call from the local State Attorney's Office. They are referring a young lady to you for counseling. The victim, Naomi, is having a very difficult time with the criminal court case. Naomi was dating her boyfriend for approximately five months. He had been very controlling from the start. About two months into the relationship, he was physically violent toward her. After five months, she decided to leave despite his threats to kill her. She went back to live with her family and decided to move in with her brother temporarily to get on her feet. Naomi's ex-boyfriend found out she was living at her brother's and started driving by the house, honking the horn a few nights during the week. She contacted police but he fled each time. She applied for a restraining order. The order was granted temporarily and set for a hearing. Because Naomi was unsure of her ex-boyfriend's whereabouts, she called a week after filing to advise that a mutual friend contacted her and gave her the address where he was living. Two days later, while her father was visiting, her ex-boyfriend knocked on the door. Naomi hid in a back room and called police while her brother and father went to answer the door. When they did, her ex-boyfriend pulled out a gun and fired at them killing them instantly. He called out for Naomi but she stayed quiet. She hid in the back bedroom closet and remained on the phone with 911, silently. He jumped in his car and left. She came out when she heard the car start up to find her father and brother on the floor in front of the front door. Police came within minutes and called a crisis advocate to meet with her. Police found Naomi's ex-boyfriend and arrested him.

Naomi was having a hard time having to face him in court due to the trauma she had endured during the incident. She describes feelings of extreme guilt over the death of her family members. The outreach advocate sets up weekly therapy appointments for Naomi. The advocate also tells her about a local domestic violence support group and traumatic loss group in the community. Naomi is interested in the traumatic loss group but requests that an advocate attend with her for support during her first group meeting.

The group meets monthly and is scheduled for the following Tuesday. The advocate makes arrangements and attends the group with Naomi. The advocate makes connections with group members during the first 15 minutes that are used to network with other members. After networking, the advocate introduces Naomi to group members.

The group meeting commences and Naomi is sitting rigidly next to the advocate. As the group members share their stories, they ask for any new group members who want to share their stories, emphasizing that it was OK for them to simply introduce themselves if they did not want to share right away. Naomi introduced herself and stated that it was her first meeting. She told the group that she did not want to speak about her story but that her brother and father's killer was going to trial soon and she really needed to deal with some of the things she was feeling. The lady next to her waited until Naomi was done and then described her ordeal when her ex-boyfriend came to her house after breaking up thinking that she and her friend were seeing each other. She went on to say how her boyfriend pulled out a box cutter and killed her friend and then came after her, slitting her throat. She pulled her collar back exposing her scar. Naomi started to cry but remained quiet.

After the woman shared her story, a man shared his story about his boyfriend. His boyfriend had been the target of "gay bashing" and was violently assaulted and killed by a group of individuals after leaving work one night. The man explained how guilty he felt because his boyfriend had called him during his break to tell him that he was a little disturbed by one of the tables he waited on at the restaurant. He described how the group of men asked for another waiter after he took their drink order and continued to stare at him while he waited on other tables in his section. He had also heard the men taunting him by calling him names. His boyfriend wanted him to come down to the restaurant and just hang out to keep an eye on things. When the man explained to his boyfriend that he was too tired to get up and get dressed to go out, his boyfriend seemed annoyed. They argued for a few minutes before hanging up. The man kept describing how guilty he felt for not getting up, getting dressed, and going down there.

The meeting ended and a last call for coffee was announced. After the meeting, the woman next to Naomi leaned over and said that she had seen Naomi's reaction; she hoped Naomi would share her story sometime, and that she knows what it's like to be new. She described the group as being a safe and supportive network of people. She also offered to exchange phone numbers with Naomi. Naomi agreed.

Naomi's appointment fell on the Friday following the loss group. Upon meeting with the therapist, Naomi told her that she sent a text message to the woman who gave her the phone number. The woman texted back and she met her for coffee. Naomi told her story and the woman was really supportive of her. The woman also told Naomi about a domestic violence support group that she attended and offered to attend the group with Naomi when they meet twice a month. Naomi accepted her invitation and is scheduled to go next week. Naomi seemed more empowered with the support of this woman and the group. The therapist worked with her to identify additional supports in her life during the session. She also helped her to start thinking about the types of things she would want to include in her victim impact statement for court. The session ended and Naomi seemed to be coping better than her initial visit. Naomi is scheduled for weekly therapy over the next two months before moving to biweekly appointments, followed by two monthly appointments, and her last follow-up appointment scheduled at six months from her start date.

Over the remaining appointments, the therapist notes that Naomi seems more and more adjusted to the events. She is working through the trauma and has developed a very good support system to help her cope with the incident. She also has individuals to contact if she has a particularly emotional day. She started attending a church with one of the group participants and is starting to speak out more about her experience with newer members.

At the six-month follow-up appointment, Naomi indicates that she still thinks about the loss daily and still cannot manage to stop being emotional but that she is happy with the new friends she has made and the kindness they have shown her. She is continuing with the groups and is getting involved in some other local groups that promote antiviolence and victims' rights. She is scheduled to share her story during an upcoming event to help other families who are dealing with a loved one being murdered.

WEBSITES

National Domestic Violence Hotline, www.ncadv.org
National Network to End Domestic Violence, www.ncdv.org
Office on Violence Against Women, www.ovw.usdoj.gov/domesticviolence.htm
Victim's rights, www.htnfoundation.org

Relevant References

Campbell, D. (2010, September 4). More than 40% of domestic violence victims are male, report reveals. *The Observer.* Retrieved from http://www.theguardian.com/society/2010/sep/05/men-victims-domestic-violence

Center for American Progress. *LBGT Domestic Violence Fact Sheet.* Retrieved from http://www.americanprogress.org/issues/2011/06/pdf/lgbt_domestic_violence.pdf

Glass, J. (Reviewer). *Alzheimer's Aggression.* (2012, March). WedMD. Retrieved from http://www.webmd.com/alzheimers/alzheimers-aggression

Hoog, C. Washington State Coalition Against Domestic Violence. Model Protocol on Safety Planning for Domestic Violence Victims with Disabilities. Retrieved from www.wscadv.org/docs/protocol_disability_safety_planning.pdf

Jane Doe Inc. Massachusetts Coalition Against Sexual Assault and Domestic Violence. (2013, August). *A blue print for domestic homicide prevention.* Retrieved from http://www.janedoe.org/site/assets/docs/Learn_More/DV_Homicide/2013_JDI_Blueprint_dv_homicide_prevention.pdf

Mountain State Centers for Independent Living. *Defining attitudinal barriers.* Retrieved from http://www.mtstcil.org/skills/il-4-attitudinal.html

National Center on Domestic and Sexual Violence. *Power and control wheel for people with disabilities.* Retrieved from http://www.ncdsv.org/images/DisabledCaregiverPCwheel.pdf

The VERA Institute of Justice. Safety First Initiative. Building an accessible and safe world. Retrieved from http://www.accessingsafety.org.

Whigham II, Julius, et al. Timeline: Palm Beach County homicide victims, et al. Timeline: Palm Beach County homicide victims. (2013, November). Retrieved from http://projects.palmbeachpost.com/homicides/circumstance/1/domestic/

Wisconsin Coalition Against Domestic Violence. Safety planning for people with physical disabilities. Retrieved from http://www.vaw.umn.edu/documents/safetyplandisability/safetyplandisability.pdf

13 Traumatic Stress and Emergency Services

Ted Bober

SOCIAL WORK AT AN AIRPORT EMERGENCY: INCIDENT OVERVIEW

An Airbus aircraft is on a flight to a large urban city and scheduled to arrive at 6:00 P.M. local time. There are 280 passengers and 12 crew members on board. Among the other preflight activities, the flight crew members obtained the weather forecast for their arrival, which included the possibility of snowstorms with thunder.

The take-off and flight were uneventful. While preparing for descent, the crew realized that a landing gear was not fully engaged and locked. The airport was notified and emergency operations were initiated on the airport site. According to protocols,

an additional thirty emergency contacts were made in the surrounding city. With the conditions on the ground cold and snowy, a landing was attempted. The rear landing gear failed in the process of landing and the plane slid sideways off the runway. A wing touched ground and a fire broke out.

All passengers and crew were evacuated safely, though many people suffered minor injuries and a few experienced serious but not life-threatening injuries. The fire was extinguished by airport emergency teams. A few minutes of the landing were videoed by motorists on the surrounding highways. Within minutes, the video appeared on local news with the information that there were an unknown number of deaths.

Time	Event	Time	Event
5:30 P.M.	The determination to deploy the Airport Crisis Team (Team) will usually be made by the Airport Duty Manager, in consultation with the Administrative Director and/or Clinical Director based on the details of the incident. It is quickly decided the deployment of the Team is appropriate.		Each team member will be briefed with the available details of the incident.
		5:45 P.M.	The contacted Team members arrange to meet at a designated airport site. An initial assessment indicates that there are over 75 family members and friends awaiting the arrival of the passengers. Arrangements will be coordinated between the team and the airport emergency manager to have family members and friends taken to a large ballroom at a hotel next to the airport. The room will serve as a family support and information center.
5:35 P.M.	The clinical director (a social worker) is contacted and is briefed on the unfolding event. The clinical director contacts the on-duty (on-call) crisis team members who include Emergency Professionals and Social Workers and other mental health professionals.		
		6:15 P.M.	The plane lands as described above.

6:30 P.M.   Team members are deployed to the hotel ballroom to assist the airport and airlines in supporting family and friends. Initially, the information regarding injuries is not available; soon, however, family members begin to receive text messages and cell phone calls from friends and also see news reports indicating there were several deaths. Rumors and incomplete information heighten the tension in the room.

        The social worker and emergency team members coordinate practical assistance such as the provision of water, juice, sandwiches, and blankets. Additional cell phones are arranged with long distance calling cards so relatives may contact other family members. Team members learn there were no deaths and all non-seriously injured passengers first will be taken to a nearby airplane hangar to be assessed medically. Plans are made by the airline to inform the families of the incident, the whereabouts of passengers, and the next steps to be taken. However, details on the full extent of injuries are not available, and the information session feels incomplete for many family members.

        On-site triage results in a few passengers being taken directly to hospital. The lead social worker and the Team send two team members to the hangar to assess the practical needs of the passengers. The human resource needs of the Team are reviewed and additional standby social workers and emergency professionals are contacted and requested to assist during the phase of reconnecting families and passengers.

6:45 P.M.   The Team, in collaboration with the airline's family assistance team, continues to provide practical information and support. In cooperation with the airline, family members and friends are registered. The administrative director of the team is in the emergency operation center (EOC). The team has a direct link to EOC leadership to exchange information and coordinate resources.

7:15 P.M.   At the hangar over 250 passengers are triaged based on medical needs. Additionally, the airport and social workers collect information on contacting relatives and or making arrangements for transportation and accommodation for some passengers.

        An increasing number of passengers are contacting family members and friends by cell phone and other handheld devices. The contacted family members are relieved, though many others wait anxiously for additional information. The airlines and airport provide brief details of the incident and report that there were no deaths.

7:30 P.M.   Information is received that two airport firefighters are injured on site and taken to the hospital. According to protocol, the team would initiate steps to establish a rest area for emergency professionals during the recovery and investigation period. Given the proximity of the incident to a hangar, the rest area is established at this location.

7:45 P.M.   Social workers and emergency team members continually re-evaluate the needs of three groups: the emergency responders, the family and friends, and the passengers. Plans are being established to reunite passengers and families. Practical social-emotional support at this stage focuses on information, practical health and nutrition needs, and facilitating contact with other relatives and friends.

8:30 P.M.   Passengers and family members are reunited in a separate larger meeting room. Several other community agencies, such as the Red Cross, are also present to assist the airline and airport crisis team to support passengers requiring additional clothing, transportation, or accommodation. Arrangements have been ongoing to reunite family members with those passengers taken to the hospital. In this community, all hospitals have emergency-based crisis teams staffed by social workers.

8:30 P.M. to 1:00 A.M.   Team members are available and offer support in a nonintrusive manner. A few family members and passengers experience overt signs of distress and are supported in a manner in keeping with evidenced informed psychosocial first aid. Information on practical assistance and health tips is presented verbally, through print material, and on a website.

2:00 A.M.   All nonhospitalized passengers and family members have returned home or to suitable accommodation. The team members review the evening with a focus on current and potential psychosocial needs and the appropriate follow-up in the coming day.

The airline's family support teams will remain in contact with all passengers. Contact with standby crisis team members has been ongoing and next steps are discussed regarding follow-up. On site, team members stand down knowing which team members will rotate in to follow up. Key activities and potential needs are documented.

7:00 A.M.   New team members are rotated into the incident. They are briefed and plans are made to make courtesy support calls to the responding airport services and professionals in coordination with the airport management. Print material on the role of the crisis team, professional resilience, and incident stress is made available.

Next 48 Hours

Informal support calls are made to airport services. The Crisis Team includes firefighters from local services and they make an informal outreach to the airport fire department. In this event, no requests are made for ongoing or more intensive disaster mental health service for airport staff. The airline is supported by its own internal support services and an external health provider. A few passengers do contact the crisis team for information and receive telephone support and referral information as indicated. Subsequently, the team reviews its actions and performance, as well as the implications for training, policy, and protocol revision.

SOCIAL WORK AND EMERGENCY SERVICES

For most of our human history, small group communal efforts were the heart of rescue and protection efforts. With increasing complexity and social organization, we began to develop systems to safeguard ourselves from fires, injury, and crime, and in the last century significant developments occurred in our society to move toward professional systems of emergency personnel and management. The "24/7" media coverage often dwells on communities and emergency professionals affected by large-scale dramatic emergencies and disasters, such as the earthquake and tsunami that struck Japan; severe weather-related events such as hurricanes, floods, and tornadoes; terrorist attacks; and the occurrence or risk of pandemics, such as H1N1. These massive events may distract us from appreciating that each day emergency service professionals face "routine" emergencies with their own challenges; the motor vehicle accidents, fires, shootings, and medical emergencies. These daily challenges occur in the context of government oversight, the hassles of bureaucracy and "office politics," and the increasing scrutiny of the media and public. All of this is unfolding as new and old risks in our changing world merge to create new versions of hazards, such as increasing severe-weather emergencies, pandemics, and biological or cyber terrorism.

Globally, societies have worked to improve the response to mass emergencies and disasters by developing stronger emergency and continuity management programs, moving beyond the all-hazards approach to now include the interconnected parts of emergency management, prevention/mitigation, preparedness, response, and recovery (Gordon, 2002). The first step in an all-hazards approach is to continually identify the natural and human-made hazards that exist, or may develop, in a community. The work of emergency professionals in broad terms is preventing and preparing for emergencies and their harmful effects, responding effectively and quickly when emergencies do occur, and then helping in the recovery stage.

Canada and the United States developed comprehensive emergency and continuity standards, such as the harmonized standards from the National Fire Protection Association (NFPA-1600) and the Canadian Standards Association (CSA). In the United States, the Federal Emergency Management Agency (FEMA) has incorporated the "whole community" concept to a broadening all-hazard national response strategy. The "whole community" approach seeks to engage and strengthen communities and their partnership with emergency services. The Canadian department, Public Safety Canada (PSC), has recently reissued an updated version of a national Emergency Management Framework. Internationally, the International Standards Organization (ISO) continues to add to a developing series of new standards, under the heading of "Societal security—Guideline for incident preparedness and operational continuity management." These standards outline the incident command, control, and management of an emergency and disaster. Social Workers interested in working with emergency services need to become familiar with the basics of these emergency structures and processes.

Emergency professionals train extensively and acquire specialized knowledge to deal with a wide range of emergencies and disasters. Nevertheless, there are aspects of emergency response work that may wear down even the most resilient emergency responder or team. The research literature and the popular press have often focused on high profile emergency events and their impact on emergency professionals. Research has overfocused on mass casualty events, such as severe weather-related disasters, rail or plane disasters, and terrorist attacks. Equally significant are the findings from occupational health research showing that persistent workplace stress in an unresponsive, unsupportive organization erodes the well-being of professionals. Without preparation and support, traumatic and/or persistent stress will eventually lead to wear and tear on the emergency professional's health and disrupt family and work life—even in the most resilient person. The focus of this chapter will be a discussion of the effects of daily occupational stresses, as well

as large-scale events and disasters, on emergency services at the individual, family, and organizational level, followed by an outline of a continuum of supportive actions and interventions, as well as implications for social work practice and education. This chapter on emergency services focuses on the work of professional police, firefighters, paramedics, and/or emergency medical technicians and does not specifically address other valuable emergency responders, such as emergency medical staff in hospitals and specialized disaster responders (e.g., hazardous materials professionals) and volunteers.

A social-ecological framework suggests factors related to the individuals, their workplace, and the emergency event itself combine to affect emergency and disaster-related health outcomes and performance (e.g., situational awareness, cognitive performance, or decision making). Following adversity, the emergency professional's health outcomes may range from resiliency, as demonstrated by normal stress reactions followed by a healthy adaptation to the adversity. Some professionals may develop problems in work and living (such as family conflicts or loss of productivity or absenteeism). Persistent stress affects cognitive performance and contributes to physical health problems or psychological problems (e.g., depression and/or posttraumatic stress disorder). Individual differences in outcome are the result of life experiences, organizational factors, and event factors. Individual factors include life experiences, such as general health habits, history of trauma, and personal loss. Organizational factors include the presence of effective leadership and support for both the technological and human side of emergencies. Emergency events include adverse, potentially dangerous working conditions, and witnessing the serious injury or death of children and/or colleagues. A discussion of these factors helps further our understanding of emergency services work.

DAILY OCCUPATIONAL STRESSES

Disasters of great magnitude do not happen often in the career of emergency professionals; nevertheless, most experience many gruesome and dramatic events. Most paramedics have been assaulted (almost 70%) and feel that they have been in situations where their lives were at risk (56%). Over 40% of the firefighters in

Canada witness violence against others and multiple casualties. Approximately 30% of firefighters experience the death of a person in their care (Regehr & Bober, 2005). These exposures have the potential to cause emotional and social distress in even the most seasoned responders. Events such as violence against children, dealing with the intense emotions of families, and exposure to multiple gruesome casualties, such as in a disaster, are most likely to lead to more intense reactions or potentially traumatic symptoms. A study of police officers suggested that the death of a partner, the line-of-duty death of another officer, or the suicide of another officer were among the most stressful events on the job. Large-scale events such as disasters have additional factors that lead to stress and distress and these are outlined in Table 13.1.

TABLE 13.1 Emergency Event Conditions that May Increase the Level of Stress

- Shift work, long hours and time pressures in situations where events are uncontrolled, happening quickly, and lives are threatened.
- Making decisions in chaotic situations—at times with incomplete information.
- Emotional demands of situations where peoples' health is at stake.
- Witnessing mass casualty incidents, including exposure to grotesque situations.
- Interactions with disaster survivors and bereaved family members, particularly after the death of a child.
- Adverse work environments such as cramped or toxic environments, or exposure to adverse weather conditions (cold, rain, snow, high winds).
- Intense public scrutiny, along with pressure and high expectations to resolve the crisis.
- Heightened news and social media attention and scrutiny.
- Worry associated with exposure to chemical, biological, radiological, nuclear and unknown/invisible toxic agents, or infectious diseases.
- Worry or fear for the safety of one's family.
- Witnessing the death or serious injury of a colleague.
- Being unprepared for multi-agency, multi-jurisdictional operations.

(ATSDR, 2005; Regehr & Bober, 2005)

ADDITIONAL WORKPLACE SOURCES OF STRESS

Although critical event exposures do carry risk, the nature of the emergency service workplace contributes additional risk factors for distress. One such factor is shift work, which leads to problems of fatigue, sleep disturbances, and workplace accidents, as well as health problems, such as weight gain, cardiovascular problems, and gastrointestinal disturbances. In addition, the work environment is often unpredictable, as high-stress emergency tasks frequently occur between long periods of readiness. One police officer described his work as two hours of boredom followed by two minutes of sheer terror and three hours of report writing (Regehr & Bober, 2005). Organizational changes, along with shifting demands and expectations, are an additional source of stress. A Swedish study examined the physiological reactions of police inspectors during a time of organizational change. Survey questionnaires and blood samples began to be collected shortly after the change and continued at specified time intervals until three years after the change. Significantly, cholesterol levels, cortisol, and testosterone were highly correlated with worry and workload (Grossi, Theorell, Jusisoo, & Setterlind, 1999).

Although considerable evidence exists that these emergencies have an impact on workers, many research studies suggest that it may be the everyday hassles associated with routine administrative, bureaucratic, and organizational structures that create a layer of stress and strain, and form the foundation on which critical events are heaped (Liberman et al., 2002). Critical events encountered by those who are already experiencing stress and who perceive that they do not have support from their colleagues, managers, and/or unions are more likely to result in traumatic stress reactions than are critical events encountered by individuals at their optimal level of functioning who know they can count on others when they are facing challenges.

Emergency service organizations often have strong attitudes regarding the expression of emotion. Cynicism and pessimism are frequently identified within emergency service organizations, and these factors contribute to higher levels of stress and tension in individual workers. Support from management is one of the primary protective factors in reducing stress and posttraumatic stress reactions in emergency responders. It is gratifying to note that some workers also perceived a great deal of support from both their immediate supervisors and from management (Regehr et al., 2000). One study examining over 1,700 firefighters and 248 paramedics reported that coworker support had a profound effect on both job satisfaction and work morale, and although the influence of family support was still significant, it had a much smaller influence on these factors (Beaton, Murphy, Pike, & Corneil, 1997). A negative aspect of social support occurs when the group norms lead to a prohibition on expressed emotion and a lack of encouragement to seek help. Seeking help can incur social costs, because the seeker appears incompetent, dependent, and inferior to others.

PUBLIC INQUIRIES

When tragic events occur they rarely end with the tidying of equipment and completion of paperwork. Rather, society has increasingly moved to the process of postmortem inquiries with the goal of identifying errors and avoiding future deaths. Although the goals of public accountability and quality assurance are laudable, these inquiries do not come without cost. There is a profound effect on emergency workers who testify in inquiries. Police, firefighters, and paramedics identify experiences of feeling unprotected, attacked, and presumed guilty of incompetence or negligence when testifying at a postmortem review. Media attention intensifies these feelings, particularly when the news is often sensational and vilifying, with the subsequent public response of suspicion and blame. These feelings intensify further when workers view the organizational response to be unsupportive. As a consequence, emergency workers report symptoms of intrusion, avoidance, arousal, and self-doubt that begin with the tragic event itself and continue throughout the review process. In the end, some responders are able to identify positive outcomes from the review process, such as new learning, some positive recognition, system change, and especially vindication. Nevertheless, a dominant theme is that of betrayal, anger, and reduced commitment.

THE EFFECTS OF STRESS AND TRAUMA

Due to the nature of their work, police officers, paramedics, firefighters, and other emergency responders face an increased exposure to potentially traumatic events among the public they serve, and at times, witness or personally experience life-threatening situations. Emergency responders will naturally develop some symptoms of stress. Stress in itself can be a positive, motivating force, helping professionals to be energized and focused on a task. Occasionally, however, these symptoms may reach such a level of intensity, lasting for a month or longer, that they develop into posttraumatic stress disorder (PTSD). Although many studies have supported the view that the intensity of the trauma has a bearing on the severity and chronicity of trauma symptoms in rescue workers (Weiss, Marmar, Metzler, & Ronfeldt, 1995), it is becoming increasingly clear that trauma and distress do not have a simple cause-and-effect relationship.

A second set of factors relates to the personal life experiences of the individual responder. Recent reports have highlighted the importance of individual differences in determining the intensity and duration of trauma-related symptoms (Yehuda, 2001; Regehr, Hemsworth, & Hill, 2001). Mediating variables identified by researchers include: a history of trauma before the event, previous mental health problems, and/or a family history of mental health problems (Luce et al., 2002). A cognitive appraisal of an event as manageable and within one's coping ability reduces affective arousal, influences a person's expectations of success, and promotes more adaptive behavior (Bryant & Guthrie, 2007). Thus, a sense of optimism shapes a person's reaction to a crisis and subsequently influences the outcome. Believing in one's self efficacy during a potentially traumatic event, or maintaining a sense of control despite the reactions one feels, may help people to cope more effectively. A final individual characteristic is the individual's ability to develop and sustain interpersonal relationships or relational capacity. This capacity is useful in understanding individual differences in obtaining social support.

A third second set of factors relates to the recovery environment, specifically to social support, which has been identified as one of the more powerful factors affecting the development and course of PTSD. Studies have shown that social support from spouses, family, and friends' to be significantly associated with trauma scores (Regehr et al., 2000). Additionally, the public and media responses to the event also validate or strain professional well-being.

When individuals are exposed to events that threaten their lives or cause serious injury to themselves or others, there is a risk of developing PTSD. In the recently revised edition of the *Diagnostic and Statistical Manual of Mental Disorders (DSM-5)*, PTSD was moved into a class of trauma and stressor-related disorders. Relevant to the discussion here is the DSM's recognition that a traumatic stressor may occur in the course of professional duties, such as emergency responders who experience repeated or extreme exposure to trauma-related human suffering as well as gruesome sights and sounds. PTSD symptoms occurring in the aftermath of a traumatic stressor are grouped according to four clusters, namely, intrusion, avoidance, negative alterations in cognition and mood, and alterations in arousal and reactivity.

The criteria for a PTSD diagnosis requires the following: at least one symptom of intrusion, such as recurrent intrusive memories, traumatic nightmares, flashbacks, and marked distress or physiologic reactivity after exposure to trauma-related stimuli; at least one symptom of avoidance, for example, persistent effortful avoidance of distressing trauma-related thoughts, feelings, or external reminders (e.g., people, places, conversations, activities, objects, or situations); at least two symptoms of negative alterations in cognition and mood that include the inability to recall key features of the traumatic event or persistent (and often distorted) negative beliefs and expectations about oneself or the world (e.g., "I am useless" "The world is completely dangerous."). Negative alterations in cognition and mood can also include persistent, excessive self-blame or distorted blaming of others for causing the traumatic event or for resulting consequences; persistent negative emotions (e.g., fear, horror, anger, guilt, or shame); and diminished interest in activities or a sense of detachment or estrangement from others. A diagnosis of PTSD also requires at least two symptoms of trauma-related alterations in arousal and reactivity, such as irritable or aggressive behavior, self-destructive or reckless behavior, hypervigilance, exaggerated startle response, and sleep disturbance or problems in concentration. PTSD symptoms must be present for more than one month and there needs to be evidence of significant distress or functional impairment in domain of life (e.g., social, occupational).

The prevalence of PTSD is expected to be similar to the DSM-IV rates. There is some evidence to suggest that the prevalence and the course of PTSD for intentional trauma-related events (e.g., assault, war) is higher than for a nonintentional trauma (e.g., a natural disaster). It is best to keep in mind that the trajectory of PTSD is mediated by the severity of exposure, the characteristics of the populations exposed, and the recovery environment, most importantly social support.

Research has found rates for PTSD in emergency professionals ranging from 5% to 32% and higher in the case of police officers involved in a shooting (Kleim & Westphal, 2011). Regehr and Bober (2005) found no significant differences in the scores of police, firefighters, and paramedics; at any given time, 24.6% of emergency responders had high or severe levels of trauma symptoms. A complicating factor of PTSD is that over 80% of PTSD cases are comorbid with other mental disorders or medical illnesses, with more than 50% of those diagnosed with PTSD also having depression (Shah, Shah, & Links, 2012). Other longer-term effects may include a reduced capacity to handle stressful events, substance use, health problems, and a disruption or impairment in functioning in one's work and home life.

THE EFFECTS ON EMERGENCY FAMILIES

Families of responders are also significantly affected by these incidents. One impact is the fact that the exposed worker at times feels disengaged and emotionally distant from family members: "You almost treat your spouse like another call ... there is a [emotional] deficit there." (Regehr & Bober, 2005, p. 77). Another issue is generalized anger and irritability, often vented on family members. Further, responders describe generalized fears for the safety of family members and a tendency to become overprotective. Researchers have demonstrated how job-related stresses, experienced in a variety of working environments, can be transmitted to family members once the individual returns home. In general, findings suggest that job stress dampens the quality of marital interactions and causes the other spouse to feel more negatively toward the relationship (Larson & Almeida, 1999). Another study utilizing physiological measures discovered that on the days officers reported higher levels of stress, both the officers and their wives showed greater levels of autonomic arousal during conversations (Roberts & Levenson, 2001).

SUPPORT AND INTERVENTIONS FOR EMERGENCY RESPONDERS

To provide optimal support, the best approach is a *continuum of interventions,* that is, ongoing and uninterrupted supportive interventions, though the intensity of interventions at any one time must be linked to the health and mental health needs of the emergency responder and the members of responding organizations. Interventions, for our purposes, are planned actions to promote well-being and resilience, while preventing or reducing the harm from adversity or advancing the recovery from adversity. In our experience, no matter how attractive interventions for individuals or groups of individuals may be, they are not likely to be feasible or well-implemented unless politically supported and culturally appropriate for a given organization; all organizations have a direct influence on the health and well-being of their employees. The continuum of interventions generally can be aligned with the phases of emergencies, beginning with psychosocial prevention and preparedness training, such as health promotion programs, organizational and leadership development, family education and support, disaster stress education, and peer support programs. The immediate response and recovery phases may include programs such as emergency psychosocial first aid, consultation and liaison, crisis intervention, risk communication, and posttraumatic stress treatments.

PREVENTION AND PREPAREDNESS TRAINING

There is increasing recognition that promoting resilience to stress and increasing resistance to illness begins with a healthy lifestyle. To that end, one good example of a health promotion program is PHLAME (Promoting Healthy Lifestyles: Alternative Models' Effects). This evidence-based approach is undergoing a multiyear, multisite study with firefighters. It is a very promising approach in promoting physical activity, healthy eating habits, and weight management for firefighters.

Predisaster education and training is another excellent support program. This form of preparedness accomplishes several objectives: it provides information on stressful and potentially traumatic events, normal reactions, and the recovery process; it reviews and expands on healthy and flexible coping approaches to address stressful demands and promote recovery; it builds social support among coworkers; and it reduces barriers to seeking help, such as isolation, stigma, and embarrassment. Education, for example, on the factors that intensify or mitigate the effects of disaster, prepares people to be less vulnerable to extreme stress by reducing uncertainty and helping people to appraise a situation in a way that supports their sense of competency, confidence, and control. An important component of this education is to train those in leadership positions on how to provide health promoting support to their staff before, during, and after high-stress emergency events. Training programs are also recognizing the challenges of stress on cognitive performance, as well as on mental health. One program incorporating mindfulness as a key component in mental readiness or preparation training is Mindfulness-based Mind Fitness Training (MMFT). MMFT is a course taught over eight weeks, originally designed for the military context to enhance mindfulness skills and stress resilience skills for individuals operating in extreme stress environments. The program is being adapted and considered for use by various police organizations. Research has shown promising results in promoting cognitive resilience by protecting working memory under high-stress conditions (Jha et al., 2010). Another avenue of mental readiness training for occupations in high-stress fields is mental training skills that promote performance excellence. Though there is little research with emergency professionals on the use of mental skills training, such as, enhancing attention, focus, critical curiosity, distraction control, and managing emotions during times of stress, disappointment, or adversity, there is growing evidence of the value of these skills in medicine and with elite athletes (Moulton & Epstein, 2011; Moore, 2009; Orlick, 2007).

Another stressful situation for emergency workers is an encounter with distressed family members of a victim, who possibly has been injured or killed. New efforts are underway to train firefighters in the interpersonal and problem-solving skills needed to assist a distressed family member. An excellent online training program is sponsored by the National Fallen Firefighters Foundation, and the skills presented also may be relevant to other emergency services. The program, Curbside Manner: Stress First Aid for the Street, consists of a series of practical supportive actions to assist distressed individuals and families. The approach is consistent with the evidence-based Psychosocial First Aid principles discussed below. More information regarding online training and resources is available in the resource section.

Peer support teams have formed the core of trauma-related intervention programs for the past several years. Peer support teams have many advantages, including having indigenous knowledge of the issues faced by the individual workers, and the culture and politics of the organization. Peer support programs provide a means through which to build capacity and sustain knowledge and skills in an organization over time. The challenges in establishing these teams are developing clear roles, boundaries, and ethics, and ensuring the team member's well-being. All this requires effective team selection, training, support, and accountability. Recent international consensus guidelines on peer support team standards and training have been published and social workers can play an important role as mental health clinical resources in the training and support of the teams (Creamer et al., 2012). Social workers' expertise in crisis intervention, effective interpersonal skills, and group dynamics, from a strengths-based perspective, form an excellent foundation for working with and training peer support teams. There are good resources for the development, training, and maintenance of peer support and trauma response teams listed in the resources following this chapter.

FAMILIES OF EMERGENCY PROFESSIONALS

Families are often the forgotten victims of workplace stress and trauma. Family members deal with trauma contagion as they are confronted with attitudes and behaviors of the responder emanating from the exposures on the job, and as they fear for the safety of their loved one. Organizations need to expand their notion of membership to include families and intervention programs that do not incorporate family needs. Table 13.2 outlines several steps to promoting resiliency in the family.

PSYCHOSOCIAL FIRST AID

One of the useful services and skills offered by mental health staff or peers under the supervision of mental health professionals in

TABLE 13.2 Steps to Promote Family Resiliency

- Work out family routines systems to accommodate shift work.
- Establish decompression routines between work and home.
- Acknowledge your own reactions to events and work to separate them from responses to family situations.
- Plan responses to questions and comments from children, friends, and neighbors.
- Establish a support system in both the workplace and personal life.

(Regehr & Bober, 2005)

the field is psychosocial first aid, also referred to as Psychological First Aid (PFA), originally described by Raphael (1986) and recently updated with current evidence-based practices through efforts at the National Center for PTSD and the National Child Traumatic Stress Network (Ruzek et al., 2007; Hobfoll et al., 2007; Shultz & Forbes, 2013). The field has debated the best models of support for the emergency services and there is a consensus among researchers, clinicians, the World Health Organization, and the American Firefighter Association recommending PFA as a preferred model of support, though there are emergency services who continue to use a proprietary model of critical incident stress management. The objectives of PFA are, "To establish safety and security, promote connection to social and restorative resources and modulate stress-related reactions and reduce the initial distress caused by traumatic events and foster adaptive short and long-term coping." Three practical ways to support a professional during the rescue and recovery phases are: (1) tangible support, such as food, shelter, tools, equipment, and hands on help; (2) informational support, including regular updates on risk and safety communications; and (3) social-emotional support. Recently, PFA has been modified so that the helping language and process is more culturally relevant for hierarchal emergency service organizations. This model of stress first aid for emergency professionals uses a process of check, coordinate, cover, calm, connect, and competence and confidence. More information is available through the websites listed in the references.

An important part of psychosocial aid is the consultation and liaison function that a social worker can offer to organizational leaders, peer support teams, and at the Emergency Operation Command Center, particularly during mass emergencies and disasters. Assistance may be provided with the challenging tasks, such as managing work hours, managing rotation among intense and dangerous work, assessing fatigue factors, preparing and staffing rest stations, and assessing potential risk for occupational or traumatic stress reactions. All these involve making critical decisions regarding the safety and well-being of the emergency professionals. A part of this role may include risk communication.

Increasing attention is being paid to risk communication to inform and protect emergency professionals and their families regarding work-related hazards, largely because of high-profile events such as terrorist attacks and pandemic risks. For instance, at Ground Zero, clear evidence indicates that there were health risks at the site that continue to affect emergency responders years later. At the recovery site, some people wore full protective gear, some wore simple paper masks, and some wore no respiratory protection at all. Addressing the current and future risks is a key step to assuring well-being and reducing worry among professionals and their families. The Severe Acute Respiratory Syndrome (SARS) situation in Toronto provides another example where risk communication was vital. Concerns regarding SARS continued to evolve on an hourly basis as information was gathered regarding the nature of the illness, the mechanism for transmission, and its lethality. Many emergency professionals and family members experienced the stress of quarantine, incomplete information, worry, and social isolation.

POSTTRAUMATIC STRESS TREATMENT

As we have discussed, most people recover over time from traumatic stress and yet for a number of reasons, related to their individual characteristics and resources, the nature of the event, and the quality of the psychosocial resources following the trauma, the natural recovery process may be disrupted and some may experience posttraumatic stress disorder. Treatment, or at least a consultation, is indicated when responders experience persistent difficulties in their relationships, changes in their work performance or

productivity, withdrawal from usually pleasurable activities, continual symptoms of anxiety or depression, and/or deteriorating health as noted by fatigue, poor sleep, over- or under-eating, or persistent aches and pains. A physical health examination is a useful starting point. Further, demystifying the process of treatment can be of assistance, given that movies and television generally have not portrayed the therapy process accurately or usefully.

In the many excellent reviews and meta-analyses of research related to treatment efficacy for traumatized individuals, it is generally acknowledged that only cognitive-behavioral treatment (CBT) methods have been subject to rigorous evaluation with controlled trials (Ehlers & Clark, 2003; Solomon & Johnson, 2002). Although the use of Internet-based CBT is currently the focus of a number of research studies, it is not the only treatment that works. There is good evidence for other approaches, including Eye Movement Desensitization and Reprocessing (EMDR) and pharmacological treatment to assist with symptom management for trauma sufferers.

IMPLICATIONS

There are five potentially positive social work practice, policy, and education implications of the above discussion. Firstly, given the increasing risk of large scale emergencies and disasters, Social Work education should include enhancing the knowledge base of social workers to understand the dynamics of emergencies and disasters and how to offer the full range of preparedness and recovery interventions. The strengths of social work in crisis intervention, group work, and community development are excellent foundational building blocks for this education. At a minimum, social work educational programs should offer a primer on emergency and disaster preparedness as a foundation for promoting and modeling self and community efficacy and resilience. Secondly, the academic community can also utilize theory and research-based skills to contribute to the growing knowledge regarding trauma, emergencies, and disasters among specialized populations, such as emergency professionals. Thirdly, social workers can offer the practice skills to assess post-disaster levels of distress, the risk for PTSD, and traumatic grief at the individual, family, and emergency services organizational level. Social workers can be members of emergency and crisis peer support teams, including providing effective group training and consultation to support the development of peer teams that support emergency and disaster personnel. Social workers may also apply their group and community development skills to understand broader community needs and vulnerability as means to advocate for policy and practice change. Some disasters may have long-term and enduring effects that disrupt social, emotional, and economic well-being and erode the resiliency of the public and emergency professionals. As the population grows, and new and expected hazards and new vulnerabilities evolve, social workers can ready themselves to offer their research and practice skills to provide evidence-based, culturally relevant services to high-risk professional groups, such as emergency professionals, their families, and organizations.

References and Recommended Reading

Beaton, R., Murphy, S., Pike, K., & Corneil, W. (1997). Social support and network conflict in firefighters and paramedics. *Western Journal of Nursing Research*, 19(3), 297–313.

Bryant, R. A., & Guthrie, R. M. (2007). Maladaptive self-appraisals before trauma exposure predict posttraumatic stress disorder. *Journal of Consulting and Clinical Psychology*, 75(5), 812–815.

Creamer, M. C., Varker, T., Bisson, J., Darte, K., Greenberg, N., Lau, W., … Forbes, D. (2012). Guidelines for peer support in high-risk organizations: An international consensus study using the delphi method. *Journal of Traumatic Stress*, 25(2), 134–141.

Ehlers, A., & Clark, D. (2003). Early psychological interventions for adult survivors of trauma: a review. *Biological Psychiatry*, 53, 817–826.

Gordon, J. G. (2002). Comprehensive emergency management for local governments: Demystifying emergency planning. Brookfield, CT: Rothstein Associates, Inc.

Grossi, G., Theorell, T., Jusisoo, M., & Setterlind, S. (1999). Psychophysiological correlates of organizational change and threat of unemployment among police inspectors. *Integrative Physiological and Behavioral Science*, 34(1), 30–42.

Hobfoll, S. E., Watson, P., Bell, C. C., Bryant, R. A., Brymer, M. J., & Friedman, M. J., … (2007). Five essential elements of immediate and mid-term mass trauma intervention: Empirical evidence. *Psychiatry*, 70(4), 283–315.

Jha, A. P., Stanley, E. A., Kiyonaga, A., Wong, L., & Gelfand, L. (2010). Examining the protective effects of mindfulness training on working memory capacity and affective experience. *Emotion*, 10(1), 54–64.

Liberman, A., Best, S., Metzler, T., Fagan, J., Weiss, D., & Marmar, C. (2002). Routine occupational stress and psychological distress in police. *Policing: An International Journal of Police Strategies and Management*, 25(2), 421–439.

Luce, A., Firth-Cozens, J., Midgley, S., & Burges, C. (2002). After the Omagh bomb: Post-traumatic stress disorder in health service staff. *Journal of Traumatic Stress*, 15(1), 27–30.

Larson, R., & Almeida, D. (1999). Emotional transmission in the daily lives of families: A new paradigm for studying family process. *Journal of Marriage and Family*, 61, 5–20.

Moore, Z. E. (2009). Theoretical and empirical developments of the Mindfulness-Acceptance-Commitment (MAC) approach to performance enhancement. *Journal of Clinical Sport Psychology*, 3(4), 291–302.

Moulton, C. A., & Epstein, R. M. (2011). Self-monitoring in surgical practice: Slowing down when you should. In H. Fry and R. Kneebone (Eds.), *Surgical education: Theorising an emerging domain: Vol. 2* (pp. 169–182). Washington, DC

Orlick, T. (2007). *In Pursuit of excellence* (4th ed.). Champaign, IL: Human Kinetics.

Raphael, B. (1986). *When disaster strikes: A handbook for caring professionals*. London: Unwin Hyman.

Regehr, C., Hemsworth, D., & Hill, J. (2001). Individual predictors of traumatic response: A structural equation model. *Canadian Journal of Psychiatry*, 46, 74–79.

Regehr, C., & Bober, T. (2005). *In the line of fire: Trauma in the emergency services*. New York, NY: Oxford University Press.

Regehr, C., Hill, J., & Glancy, G. (2000). Individual predictors of traumatic reactions in firefighters. *Journal of Nervous and Mental Disorders*, 188(6), 333–339.

Roberts, N., & Levenson, R. (2001). The remains of the workday: Impact of job stress and exhaustion on marital interactions in police couples. *Journal of Marriage and Family*, 63, 1052–1067.

Ruzek, J. I., Brymer, M. J., Jacobs, A. K., Layne, C. M., Vernberg, E. M., & Watson, P. J. (2007). Psychological first aid. *Journal of Mental Health Counseling*, 29(1), 17–49.

Shah, R., Shah, A., & Link, P. (2012). Post-traumatic stress disorder comorbidity: Severity across different populations. *Neuropsychiatry*, 2, 521–529.

Shultz, J. M., & Forbes, D. (2013). Psychological First Aid Rapid proliferation and the search for evidence. *Disaster Health*, 1(2), 1–10. https://www.landesbioscience.com/journals/disasterhealth/2013DH007R.pdf

Solomon, S. & Johnson, D. (2002). Psychosocial treatment of posttraumatic stress disorder: A practice friendly review of outcome research. *Psychotherapy in Practice, 58*(8), 947–959.

Weiss, D., Marmar, C., Metzler, T., & Ronfeldt, H. (1995). Predicting symptomatic distress in emergency services personnel. *Journal of Consulting and Clinical Psychology, 63,* 361–368.

Yehuda, R. (2001). Biology of posttraumatic stress disorder. *Journal of Clinical Psychiatry, 62*(Suppl. 17), 41–46.

Recommended Websites and Online Resources

Agency for Toxic Substances and Disease Registry (ATSDR). (2005). Surviving field stress for emergency responders reference manual edition 1.0 http://www2.cdc.gov/phtn/webcast/stress-05/TrainingWorkbookstress-editp1.pdf

Disaster Responders: Annotated Bibliography (Materials for Self-Care and Stress Management | General Disaster Response | Deployment Guidance Leaders and Supervisors | Substance Use after a Disaster) http://www.samhsa.gov/dtac/dbhis/dbhis_responders_bib.asp

The Federal Emergency Management Agency (FEMA) is an agency of the U. S. Department of Homeland Security. The website offers an excellent online introductory emergency management course. https://training.fema.gov/EMIWeb/IS/courseOverview.aspx?code=IS-230.c

National Child Traumatic Stress Network, National Centre for PTSD. Psychological first aid—Field operation guide (2nd ed.). Note: Mobile App: PFA Mobile Free download available from: iTunes (iOS) http://www.ptsd.va.gov/professional/manuals/psych-first-aid.asp http://www.nctsnet.org/nccts/nav.do?pid=hom_main

Firefighter Life Safety Initiative 13 focuses on behavioral health for firefighters.http://flsi13.everyonegoeshome.com/

Also see, *Curbside manner: Stress first aid* is a learning module outlining "a set of proven principles and actions that help first responders assist civilians in crisis by ensuring their safety, understanding their individual needs, meeting those needs, and promoting the connectedness and self-efficacy necessary for recovery. http://

www.fireherolearningnetwork.com/Training_Programs/Curbside_Manner__Stress_First_Aid_for_the_Street.aspx

Also see, Helping-Heroes provides a web-based (open access) training program for counselors and psychotherapists who may serve firefighters and their families. The online program is divided into 10 training modules requiring approximately one hour each to complete, and an 11th component that serves as a session-by-session toolkit guide. https://helping-heroes.org/user/login

McCarroll, J. E., Vineburgh, N. T., & Ursano, R. J. (Eds). (2013). *Disaster, disease and distress: Resources to promote psychological health and resilience in military and civilian communities.* Bethesda, MD: Center for the Study of Traumatic Stress, Department of Psychiatry, Uniformed Services University of the Health Sciences. This book features 10 years of Center fact sheets on military and disaster health and mental health topics for health care providers, government and military leadership, service members, families and communities around the effects of traumatic exposure. http://www.cstsonline.org/wp-content/uploads/CSTS_3D_FS_Book_WEB.pdf

The Center for the Study of Traumatic Stress http://www.cstsonline.org/

PHLAME wellness program for firefighters at the Oregon Health and Science University http://www.ohsu.edu/hpsm/phlame.cfm

Posttraumatic stress, assessment, and interventions. Two excellent websites with numerous links to additional resources: www.ncptsd.va.gov and www.istss.org

U.S. Department of Health & Human Services (2009, April). *Psychological and social support for essential service workers during an influenza pandemic.* April 30, 2009. Accessed through http://www.cdc.gov/niosh/topics/H1N1flu/pdfs/workfcespptpanflu.pdf

U.S. National Response Team, U.S. Environmental Protection Agency. *Guidance for managing worker fatigue during disaster operations: Vol. I.* Technical Assistance Document. April 30, 2009. http://www.cdc.gov/niosh/topics/oilspillresponse/pdfs/NRT-Fatigue-for-Emergency-Workers.pdf

14   Military Social Work

Allen Rubin & James G. Daley

THE DIVERSE NATURE OF MILITARY SOCIAL WORK

Since 1905, social workers, uniformed or civilian, have built a long, rich history of providing services to military personnel, veterans, and their families (Daley, 1999a; Rubin, Weiss, & Coll, 2013). Uniformed social workers have been in the Army, Navy, Air Force, and Public Health Services with ranks from lieutenant to colonel. Civilian military social workers have held diverse positions, including ones in mental health, substance abuse, family advocacy, medical services, and family services, as well as with Wounded Warriors and their families. The scope of their jobs and expected competencies has been recently outlined by the Council on Social Work Education (CSWE) brochure titled *"Advanced Social Work Practice in Military Social Work"* (http://www.cswe.org/File.aspx?id=42466). Established in 1926, the social work program in the Veterans Administration has developed into the largest employer of social workers in the United States (http://www.social-work.va.gov/about.asp) and offers very diverse programs from medical social work in medical centers to outreach clinics, to residential facilities, to targeted clinics for veterans of Operation Iraqi Freedom (OIF), Operation Enduring Freedom (OEF), and Operation New Dawn (OND) (U.S. Department of Veterans Affairs, 2010).

Social work roles in helping military personnel, veterans, and their families include both micro and macro levels of practice. Social workers performing these roles can be considered to be practicing military social work regardless of whether they are in uniform as commissioned officers in the armed forces or out of uniform working for the Veterans Administration, other departments of the federal government, or in community agencies or private practice. Nonuniformed military social work can also be provided contractually at military bases.

Their roles span the gamut of social work practice, and might include such services as medical social work for veterans suffering from a traumatic brain injury (TBI) or other ailments; treatment and prevention of sexual abuse, domestic violence, or substance abuse; case management; therapy for posttraumatic stress disorder (PTSD); educating family members about the difficulties they may experience when one of them is deployed overseas; developing programs in the community to help veterans transition to civilian life and alleviate homelessness among them, helping to develop policies and procedures, and many others.

NAVIGATING THE MILITARY CULTURE

The military environment has been called the "Fortress Society," with a very closed system toward outsiders understanding how the military functions and evolves (Wertsch, 2006). A multitude of rules and regulations, a vision of invulnerability, and a determined passion for mission drive the military as a system and even as an ethnic identity (Daley, 1999b). Rank is worn overtly as a ready recognition of status. Uniforms and shoes are crisp and polished as a symbol of pristine image. Orders are to be accomplished regardless of required effort with no excuses expected or accepted. Deployability is an overarching expectation, and military personnel will minimize personal issues, injuries, or insecurities to be ready to accomplish the mission. A popular saying is, "There are no problems, just opportunities to excel." Behind the public image can be service members or families who are struggling with PTSD, depression, substance abuse, and more.

To relate to the military, a social worker must be familiar with rank, chain of command, and how to frame interventions in "military-ese." The language needs to be framed as "help to ensure the client is deployable," "helping the client build better resilience skills," and other strengths-focused framing. The social worker should also be familiar with the experiences of combat and how various wars and conflicts are similar or divergent.

THE CHANGING MILITARY CONTEXT

The military has been involved in diverse settings. World War II was the largest war, lasting from 1930 to 1945, with 16 million serving in the U.S. military and 400,000 deaths (http://www.wwiimemorial.com/). The enemy was clearly defined, front lines were declared, and the cause was survival at a global level. The U.S. troops were praised as the "greatest generation" (Brokaw, 1998) with portrayed in films such as "Band of Brothers" and "the Pacific" movies. The Korean War from 1950 to 1953 was the first "military action of the Cold War" (http://www.history.com/topics/korean-war) and ended with a stalemate that divided Korea into two sections and an ongoing volatile tension that continues today. The Vietnam War escalated slowly from 1954 to a conclusion in 1975 with a peak in 1969 of 500,000 U.S. military deployed (http://www.history.com/topics/vietnam-war). The Vietnam War was the first clear defeat of U.S. military power due to political complexities and a primarily guerilla warfare, whereas the Korean War or World War II were primarily uniformed soldiers facing established front lines.

The Vietnam War was very unpopular in the United States, with massive protests held against it. The drafting of young Americans for an unwanted war fueled America's anger. After Vietnam, there have been no further declared wars, though there have been operations including Operation Restore Hope in Somalia, Operation Noble Anvil in Kosovo, Operation Quiet Resolve in Rwanda (Exum, Coll, & Weiss, 2011). The conflict in Iraq and Afghanistan was never declared a war but rather a series of operations—Operation Iraq Freedom (OIF), Operation Enduring Freedom (OEF), and Operation New Dawn (OND). Further, the Vietnam War was a draft war, whereas the current operations are being conducted by an all-volunteer force. The most recent operations have been deeply intertwined with the "war on terror," a constantly evolving effort that blends diplomatic initiatives and military might to reduce the volatility and destructiveness of terrorist organizations. Due to the guerilla warfare dynamic of the recent operations and the consequent civilian casualties and damage to homes, military personnel often have been caught in morally anguishing situations. The complexity of the global war on terrorism defines military missions that send our troops to complex settings where the troops are morally damaged.

THE COMBAT VETERAN AND IMPACT ON FAMILY

Uniformed military social workers are deployed to combat zones as part of a combat stress team. Combat can be stressful and traumatizing, certainly confusing, and hard to contextualize. Combat vets cannot adequately describe to a civilian what they have been through. Traumatic events get submerged, and often there are aspects of the events that they are afraid to allow to emerge. Combat is confusing. Social workers try to offer aid, but combat and the deployment process take a toll on many military members and their families (Kelly, Howe-Barksdale, & Gitelson, 2011; Pryce, Pryce, & Shackelford, 2012) A growing list of books provide self-help guides to coping with the deployment cycle (DeCarvalho & Whealin, 2012; Hart, 2000; Henderson, 2006; Matsakis, 2007; Pavlicin, 2003; Slone & Friedman, 2008; Whealin, DeCarvalho, & Vega, 2008). The family has to cope with predeployment (e.g., getting power of attorney for spouse, preparing children for separation), deployment (e.g., evolving roles when apart, communication while apart via electronic choices of cell phone or video links), and postdeployment (reunion and stress of established new roles) (Franklin, 2013; Pavlicin, 2003; Ponder & Aguirre, 2012).

For military members who are struggling with PTSD or other stressors, the stigma of seeking mental health care continues to be a barrier to effective and timely use of a range of services that military social workers offer (Stotzer, Whealin, & Darden, 2012). Screenings are set up in conjunction with the Veterans Administration (VA) for service members according to a three-month postdeployment time frame to try to reduce stigma and encourage seeking services for PTSD symptoms. The Institute of Medicine has defined PTSD, traumatic brain injury (TBI), and depression as the "signature injuries" for the

OIF/OEF/OND veterans. Therefore, the screenings strive to identify this triad of injuries so treatment can be initiated.

Also, suicide among military members has increased, and efforts to reach out and educate military personnel are top priorities in all the Services. The Department of Defense Suicide Event Report (DODSER) is tracking the prevalence annually, and suicide prevention and outreach programs have ramped up in all the Services and the VA. Legislative efforts have emerged, such as the Joshua Omvig Veterans Suicide Prevention Act of 2007 (Cato, 2013; Pryce, Pryce, & Shackelford, 2012). Joshua Omvig was a military policeman deployed to Iraq who, when he came home on leave, told his family he was "dead inside" and shot himself in front of his mother (http://joshua-omvig. memory-of.com/legacy.aspx).

The number of deployments for military personnel is unprecedented, with service members completing as many as five deployments. The National Guard and Reserves have had a higher deployment and combat role than ever in the history of the Guard. Related financial stressors have strained military families. Complex ethical and moral situations in combat settings have produced PTSD symptoms that are hidden from military mental health providers due to the bravado culture of the military and fear that mental health issues might be career damaging.

Women have rapidly increasing opportunities to serve in most combat-related jobs and excel when given the job (Osborne, Gage, & Rolbiecki, 2012). There is growing pressure on the military to prevent and intervene with sexual assault better, particularly in combat settings (Weiss & DeBraber, 2013). Recent military policy changes have enabled gay and lesbian military members to serve openly, although transgender military members' needs are not currently addressed. Thus, with the military constantly evolving, military social workers need to be involved in policy and practice adaptations to assist military members as they navigate these changes.

The transition from being a military member to being a veteran can be stressful, particularly if the veteran has an identified or hidden service-connected injury. The military culture is focused on mission and deployability, whereas the Veterans Administration is focused on eligibility for service and honoring the veteran's service. Thus, military members hide their injuries, fearful that they will be nondeployable, whereas

savvy veterans are vocal about the benefits they have earned. Transition programs target military members leaving the service. For example, the Wounded Warrior Program (WW) maintains service members on active duty until they either are eligible to return to the unit or are medically discharged and routed to the VA medical care system. Regardless of the disability, transitioning veterans are eligible for the GI bill for college or technical school and can have priority for some jobs. Student veterans often may find a military and veterans service center at the university they choose (Smith-Osborne, 2013). Advocacy organizations such as the Iraq and Afghanistan Veterans of America (http://iava.org/) seek to connect and support veterans transitioning into the civilian world, where only 1% of the population has ever been deployed in OIF/OEF/OND. Because some veterans deteriorate and end up homeless (Carrillo, Costello, & Ra, 2013), funded housing programs and outreach services are targeted specifically for homeless veterans. Some veterans end up in legal conflict, sometimes due to PTSD, TBI, and volatility issues. Veterans Court programs try to route impaired veterans to services rather than prison (Holbrook, 2011).

THE TRANSITION TO A FAMILY-IN-MILITARY CONTEXT

The military population has been shifting from a primarily unmarried force who only served a required brief stay in the military to a predominantly married force with children and a longer and voluntary stay in the military. As the military force changed, the roles and size of its social work staff changed and expanded (Jenkins, 1999; Nelson, 1999; Rubin & Harvie, 2013). Thus, the family-centered programs and needs have increased (Harris, 2013). Family advocacy programs have emerged, which focus on family violence prevention, detection, and interventions; assistance with family member special needs; and educational programs for family resilience building (Wheeler, McGough, & Goldfarb, 2013). Family Support Centers, Family Service Centers, and Army Community Services have developed to offer family life education, financial counseling, relocation assistance, and deployment support groups. Family Readiness Groups have evolved for the National Guard to offer support, especially during deployments (Harnett, 2013). Programs for children (e.g., camps, support groups during deployments) have been developed (Devoe, Ross, & Paris, 2012; Leskin, Garcia, D'Amico, Mogil, & Lester, 2013). Some unique stressors challenge military families. Single parents are required to have a family care plan indicating that their children will have a caretaker if they are deployed (Blanchard, 2012). Dual-career couples may have the nonmilitary career partner struggle with relocations every three years. Dual military couples can be assigned to separate military installations during their career. Deployed National Guard members can return from deployment to find the company where they worked has gone out of business.

UNIQUE ISSUES THAT MILITARY SOCIAL WORKERS FACE

Military social workers work in many settings. Both the military culture and the VA culture are complex and rule bound. The military is a closed society, and social workers can experience difficulty trying to get access to the information or resources that can help their clients. Getting collateral information to assess a client can be frustrating as well. Uniformed social workers have no confidentiality and must navigate what and how they share client information with great social skill. There is a strong dual loyalty dynamic that creates ethical dilemmas (Daley, 2013). Likewise, the Veterans Administration begins all transactions with eligibility determination. How do we provide needed help to someone dishonorably discharged? They do not get care from the VA. For clients who are eligible, how do we find the right program or resources from the VA? It takes years of gaining knowledge to navigate the programs well. For example, a Purple Heart recipient and World War II veteran who needs to go into a domiciliary in Indiana might not get into the VA home until he has been an Indiana resident for five years. Service is less valued than eligibility. Finally, there are long delays—which are only going to grow longer as more military members transition into veteran status—in processing the disability claims for which eligibility drives all benefits (Reed, 2011).

The possibility of secondary traumatization is another challenge confronting social workers who work with combat veterans and their families. The more effective they are with the client, the more traumatic experiences they will hear about in detail. Although such openness is

an important outcome, it is important for the social worker to have a supervisor or coworker to process those memories with and to strive to prevent developing PTSD themselves (Rubin & Weiss, 2013).

A distinct issue is the social worker's access, depending on their job, to the service member, the spouse, the children, the military unit, and the community. Building resources, gaining clout, and developing holistic interventions are possible. For example, the family advocacy program is an excellent example of military social workers creating comprehensive programs to prevent or reduce family violence. Likewise, some social workers are striving to develop a comprehensive suicide prevention program in the military and in the VA.

CONCLUSION

This chapter has outlined the wide range of issues and programs in which military social workers are involved. The unique dilemmas and resilience of military members, veterans, and their families are discussed. The context of the military culture and the VA culture are highlighted. Military social workers, in uniform or civilian, serve a vital role in providing effective services to their clients. As the military mission shifts, military social workers will be poised to advocate for the best care of our military personnel and veterans, whose service should be honored.

WEBSITES

Department of Defense, www.defense.gov
Department of Veterans Affair, www.va.gov
Post 9/11 GI Bill, www.gibill.va.gov
Social workers and Veterans Affairs, www.social-worker.va.gov
Wounded Warrior Project, www.wonderwarrior-project.org

References

Blanchard, S. E. (2012). Are the needs of single parents serving in the Air Force being met? *Advances in Social Work 13*(1), 83–97.

Brokaw, T. (1998). *The greatest generation*. New York, NY: Random House.

Carrillo, E. V., Costello, J. J., & Ra, C. Y. (2013). Homelessness among veterans. In A. Rubin, E. L. Weiss & J. Coll (Eds.), *Handbook of military social work* (pp. 247–269). Hoboken NJ: Wiley.

Cato, C. (2013). Suicide in the military. In A. Rubin, E. L. Weiss, & J. E. Coll (Eds.), *Handbook of military social work* (pp. 225–244). Hoboken, NJ: John Wiley & Sons.

Daley, James G. (Ed.) (1999a). *Social work practice in the military*. New York, NY: Haworth Press.

Daley, J. G. (1999b). Understanding the military as ethnic identity. In J. G. Daley (Ed.), *Social work practice in the military* (pp. 291–306). New York, NY: Haworth Press.

Daley, J. G. (2013). Ethical decision making in military social work. In A. Rubin, E. L. Weiss, & J. E. Coll (Eds.), *Handbook of military social work* (pp. 51–66). Hoboken, NJ: John Wiley & Sons.

DeCarvalho, L. T., & Whealin, J. M. (2012). *Healing stress in military families: Eight steps to wellness*. Hoboken, NJ: John Wiley & Sons.

DeVoe, E. R., Ross, A. M., & Paris, R. (2012). Child Parent Relationship Training (CPRT): Enhancing parent-child relationships for military families. *Advances in Social Work, 13*(1), 51–66.

Exum, H. A., Coll, J. E., & Weiss, E. L. (2011). *A civilian counselors primer for counseling veterans* (2nd ed.). Deer Park, NY: Linus Publications.

Franklin, K. (2013). Cycle of deployment and family well-being. In A. Rubin, E. L. Weiss, & J. E. Coll (Eds.), *Handbook of military social work* (pp. 313–333). Hoboken, NJ: John Wiley & Sons.

Harnett, C. (2013). Supporting National Guard and reserve members and their families. In A. Rubin, E. L. Weiss, & J. E. Coll (Eds.), *Handbook of military social work* (pp. 335–358). Hoboken, NJ: John Wiley & Sons.

Harris, J. (2013). A brief history of U.S. military families and the role of social workers. In A. Rubin, E. L. Weiss, & J. E. Coll (Eds.), *Handbook of military social work* (pp. 301–312). Hoboken, NJ: John Wiley & Sons.

Hart, A. B. (2000). *An operator's manual for PTSD: Essays for coping*. New York, NY: Writer's Digest.

Henderson, K. (2006). *While they're at war: The true story of American families on the home front*. New York, NY: Houghton Mifflin Company.

Jenkins, J. L. (1999). History of Air Force social work. In J. G. Daley (Ed.), *Social work practice in the military* (pp. 27–50). New York, NY: Haworth Press.

Holbrook, J. (2011). Veterans' courts and criminal responsibility: A problem-solving history and approach to the liminality of combat trauma. In D. C. Kelly, S. Howe-Barksdale, & D. Gitelson (Eds.), *Treating young veterans: Promoting resilience through practice and advocacy* (pp. 259–300). New York, NY: Springer Publishing Company.

Kelly, D. C., Howe-Barksdale, S., & Gitelson, D. (Eds). (2011). *Treating young veterans: Promoting resilience through practice and advocacy*. New York, NY: Springer Publishing Company.

Leskin, S. A., Garcia, E., D'Amico, J., Mogil, C. E., & Lester, P. E. (2013). Family-centered programs and interventions for military children and youth. In A. Rubin, E. L. Weiss & J. Coll (Eds.), *Handbook of military social work* (pp. 427–441). Hoboken NJ: Wiley.

Matsakis, A. (2007). *Back from the front: Combat trauma, love, and the family*. Baltimore, MD: Sidran Institute Press.

Nelson, J. P. (1999). Development and evolution of the family advocacy program in the Department of Defense. In J. G. Daley (Ed.), *Social work practice in the military* (pp. 51–66). New York, NY: Haworth Press.

Osborne, V. A., Gage, L. A., & Rolbiecki, A. J. (2012). The unique mental health needs of military women: A social work call to action. *Advances in Social Work, 13*(1), 166–184.

Pavlicin, K. M. (2003). *Surviving deployment: A guide for military families*. St. Paul, MN: Elva Resa Publishing.

Ponder, W. N., & Aguirre, W. T. P. (2012). Internet-based spousal communication during deployment: Does it increase post-deployment marital satisfaction? *Advances in Social Work, 13*(1), 203–215.

Pryce, J. G., Pryce, D. H., Shackelford, K. K. (2012). *The costs of courage: Combat stress, warriors, and family survival*. Chicago, IL: Lyceum Books, Inc.

Reed, T. (2011). The 21st-century veteran and the 19th century pension code: Why the VA claims process is a steam engine in an E-universe. In D. C. Kelly, S. Howe-Barksdale, & D. Gitelson (Eds.), *Treating young veterans: Promoting resilience through practice and advocacy* (pp. 313–341). New York, NY: Springer Publishing Company.

Rubin, A., Weiss, E. L., & Coll, J. E. (Eds.). (2013). *Handbook of military social work*. Hoboken, NJ: John Wiley & Sons.

Rubin, A., & Harvie, H. (2013). A brief history of social work with the military and veterans. In A. Rubin, E. L. Weiss, & J. E. Coll (Eds.), *Handbook of military social work* (pp. 3–20). Hoboken, NJ: John Wiley & Sons.

Rubin, A., & Weiss, E. L. (2013). Secondary trauma in military social work. In A. Rubin, E. L. Weiss, & J. E. Coll (Eds.), *Handbook of military social work* (pp. 67–80). Hoboken, NJ: John Wiley & Sons.

Slone, L. B. & Friedman, M. J. (2008). *After the war zone: A practical guide for returning troops and their families*. Philadelphia, PA: Perseus Books.

Smith-Osborne, A. M. (2013). Supporting resilience in the academic setting for student soldiers and veterans as an aspect of community reintegration: The design of the student veteran project study, *Advances in Social Work, 13*(1), 34–50.

Stotzer, R. L., Whealin, J. M., & Darden, D. (2012). Social work with veterans in rural communities: Perceptions of stigma as a barrier to accessing mental health care, *Advances in Social Work, 13*(1), 1–16.

U.S. Department of Veterans Affairs (2010, March 9). VA history: A fact sheet. Retrieved from http://www4.va.gov/about_va/vahistory.asp

Weiss, E. L., & DeBraber, T. (2013). Women in the military. In A. Rubin, E. L. Weiss & J. Coll (eds.) *Handbook of military social work* (pp. 37–49). Hoboken NJ: Wiley.

Wertsch, M. E. (2006). *Military brats: legacies of childhood inside the fortress.* St. Louis, MO: Brightwell Publishing.

Whealin, J. M., DeCarvalho, L. T., & Vega, E. M. (2008). *Strategies for managing stress after war: Veteran's workbook and guide to wellness.* Hoboken, NJ: John Wiley & Sons.

Wheeler, B. Y., McGough, D., & Goldfarb, F. (2013). The exceptional family member program: Helping special needs children in military families. In A. Rubin, E. L. Weiss, & J. E. Coll (Eds.), *Handbook of military social work* (pp. 359–382). Hoboken, NJ: John Wiley & Sons.

15   Military Social Work in the Community

Anthony Hassan & Sara Kintzle

Social work with service members, veterans, and their families is more critical today than ever before in our profession's history. Since the September 11, 2001 terrorist attacks, the potential threats to national security have caused the United States to respond with increased military presence and action throughout the world. Nearly two million deployments have taken place as part of the wars in Iraq and Afghanistan, with many of these including multiple tours of duty (Belasco, 2009). Ninety-seven percent of those sent to war return home—an unprecedented figure in military history. As the frequency and length of deployments have risen, so have the personal, professional, and familial challenges associated with the conditions of deployment (Hazle, Wilcox, & Hassan, 2012). These challenges require professionals, social workers specifically trained in understanding these experiences within the context of military life (Flynn & Hassan, 2010).

Military social work is defined as "direct practice; policy and administrative activities; and advocacy including providing prevention, treatment and rehabilitative services to service members, veterans, their families, and their communities" (Council on Social Work Education [CSWE], 2010, p. 2). Military social work serves all branches of the United States Armed Forces, together with veterans of all eras and conflicts served by the Department of Veterans Affairs. The roles of military social workers are expansive and vary by organization. They include providing case management and individual, couple, family, and group therapy, as well as performing community practice and research (CSWE, 2010). Military social work is distinguished from other fields of practice because it is strongly shaped by a workplace perspective and focuses on the holistic consequences of life transitions.

The United States military and associated veterans' programs represent large organized employment structures with organizational values and hierarchies. Perhaps there is no other profession like the military, in which individuals and families are required to make such frequent changes, not only in the form of transfers to other localities, but between statuses. The specialized nature of military training has created a distinctive culture often poorly understood by civilians (Hall, 2012). Building an understanding of the culture in which military social work exists is essential to working with military populations.

MILITARY CULTURE

The development of a therapeutic alliance between a social worker and service member or veteran client is often dependent on the professional's understanding of the culture in which service members exist (Weiss, Coll, & Metal, 2011). Military culture is a shared system of values, rituals, customary patterns of social relationships, and use of symbols that guides and reinforces group behavior. As one of society's oldest institutions, the traditions and meanings associated with military culture are rich and inspiring. Core military values that honor unit cohesion, teamwork, duty, integrity, service before self, loyalty, and self-sacrifice have been deeply engrained through the generations.

The military is not a one-dimensional entity, but a collection of subcultures and subgroups. The United States Armed Forces has five branches: Army, Navy, Marines Corps, Air Force, and Coast Guard. Each branch of service proudly owns its distinctive history and conventions. Sources of internal diversity include branch of service, rank, and the occupational specialty to which an individual has been assigned. For example, one Army soldier may hold the military occupation of infantryman, while another intelligence. Both soldiers belong to the Army and live together but work apart in much different environments and workplace cultures.

Within each branch of the military are two subgroups that include an active component and a reserve component. The active component includes individuals who are active, full-time, service members stationed throughout the world at combat and noncombat bases. They are considered transient and expected to move every three to five years based on the needs of their respective service. While not in combat, active service members spend their days training to improve their military occupation and combat proficiencies, along with performing their daily duties related to administration, patient care, customer service, and the many other responsibilities of military leadership. Active duty service members and their families live on or near insular military bases with their own grocery stores, shopping centers, and other conveniences of daily living.

The reserve component includes the Reserves and National Guard. The Reserves is a force that serves part-time and typically trains with units located within its home state. Reserves can be mobilized to an active, full-time, status to meet the needs of the country in times of war or national emergency. The National Guard also serves part-time and is comprised of members who work and live within their local community. The National Guard supports both federal and state missions in times of natural and man-made disaster and is mobilized to active, full-time status when needed. Reservists and National Guard members have played an integral role in recent conflicts and have been deployed to Iraq and Afghanistan at rates not seen in military history.

The power structure within the military is also a component of its cultural identity. Military rank is the mechanism through which members are promoted and assigned responsibility. The military hierarchy is more strictly delineated than hierarchies in civilian society and impinges heavily on the way in which informal and formal communications are carried out. For example, in civilian society an employee might interrupt her boss in a moment of intense discussion; this would be much less acceptable between a military officer and an enlisted service member. To be effective, military social workers must carefully learn the power and authority structure within the military from a workplace and cultural perspective, as well as an appreciation of the impact of this structure on the lives of service members and their families (Hall, 2012; Weiss, Coll, & Metal, 2011).

Also essential to navigating social work intervention within the culture of the military is an understanding of the barriers created by the stigma of seeking mental health services. Military culture has traditionally disdained weakness, and by inference, help-seeking for emotional, marital, or other personal problems. Despite new policies and a public relations campaign aimed at normalizing these issues, a stigma remains, as do the challenges faced by service members and their families, and sometimes continues on into their civilian lives.

REINTEGRATION CHALLENGES

Postdeployment and Postdischarge

Reintegration is characterized by the re-entry into everyday life after military deployment and may include reunification with family and the return to military or civilian employment (Institute of Medicine, 2011). Although most service members demonstrate exceptional resilience during this time, the reintegration into postdeployment life can create challenges for some. This transition is often met with individual challenges, including issues of physical and emotional health; interpersonal challenges, such as maintaining and improving relationships; and often, the economic challenges that come with securing employment.

The physical impacts of war are obvious in service members returning from deployment. The number of surviving service members with permanent, disabling injuries surpasses that of any previous modern conflict. In World War II, the survival rate for those suffering physical damage was 2:2; it is now 8:1. The physical wounds of the Iraq and Afghanistan wars include loss of limbs and digits, facial wounds, hearing damage, and traumatic brain injury (TBI), principally from encounters with improvised explosive devices.

Less visible are the psychological wounds of war. These include posttraumatic stress, major depressive disorder, generalized anxiety disorder, substance misuse, and suicide risk (Kang & Bullman, 2008; Miller et al., 2009). A study of nearly 300,000 Iraq and Afghanistan veterans found that approximately 20% had been diagnosed with mental health problems, typically depression or posttraumatic stress disorder (PTSD) (Hoge et al., 2006). Service members are also at increased risk for other consequential behavioral health challenges. These include hazardous drinking, drug use, sexual assaults, and misconduct.

Moreover, Schell and Tanielian (2011) have painted a daunting picture of stumbling blocks for service members transitioning to civilian communities where access and utilization of community-based support programs is complicated and fragmented. Veterans are often unaware of available services, unsure of whether a service would be helpful for their specific problems, lack information about service locations, are uncertain of eligibility requirements, and do not know how to apply for services. Although veterans who persist in searching for help or support may find an available service, they are often confronted by well-meaning but uninformed agencies and providers who do not understand the scope of the challenges they face as military-impacted individuals. This is a significant barrier to care when we consider that many service members

and veterans harbor a stigma against seeking help of any kind, especially mental health care, and might become so frustrated by a provider's ignorance of military culture and understanding of reintegration challenges that they discontinue treatment. The lack of coordination among agencies and redundancy of services make it difficult for veterans aiming to access critical resources.

The reintegration back into life after deployment is often a time of financial instability as well. Between 20% and 40% of Iraq and Afghanistan veterans have remained without a job for more than three months postdischarge (Adler et al., 2011; Burnett-Zeigler et al., 2011; Jacobson et al., 2008). Some military specialized occupational classifications do not translate directly into civilian positions (e.g., how can the skills of a combat infantryman be utilized in a civilian career?). In other instances, service members have skills that translate to civilian service well, but they may lack necessary accreditation. For example, a service member who served as a medic within the Army has tremendous medical experience related to trauma, yet may not be qualified for employment in some health care settings due to the lack of specific certifications. These challenges to securing employment, combined with low incomes and inadequate community supports, lead to economic insecurity that has a direct impact on the overall health and well-being of veterans and their families (Little & Alenkin, 2011).

What Providers Need To Know: Diagnosis and Evidence-based Practice

Social workers must acknowledge and understand the barriers to treatment faced by service members and their families. The first is stigma. The contradiction between the culture of the military and the need for supportive mental health services creates a perceived, and sometimes real, shame related to treatment. Stigma can stem from the view of society, as well as the individual, where service members internalize stigmatizing behaviors (Greene-Shortridge et al., 2007). Social workers must acknowledge and address the stigma faced by the military population.

An additional barrier to treatment includes the expectations about treatment. Beliefs about medication and what occurs during treatment often create reluctance to accept services. Some service members also report not being ready to seek services. They do not feel emotionally prepared to discuss mental health symptoms and will tend to wait until a crisis occurs before seeking help. Concerns about confidentiality and the impact that seeking treatment may have on military career or civilian employment are additional barriers.

Diagnosis and treatment of mental health issues within the military are particularly difficult for a number of reasons. Service members have little incentive to acknowledge symptoms, given that this may mean a delay in transition home or discharge. Some veterans may not manifest the disabling effects of combat experience for a year or more after returning home.

The increased occurrence and awareness of mental health problems has created a push for evidence-based interventions; several of which have emerged as particularly helpful in addressing veterans' issues of mental health. These are identified and described in Table 15.1. Interventions with service members and their families are continually being conceptualized and tested.

Services and support aimed at aiding in the transition of veterans from military to community life, as well as issues related to the aging of service members, will be critical in the years ahead. Community-based groups will play a key role in the adjustment of service members and their families throughout the life course. Military social work has never been more important in promoting positive relationships, improved social policies, and improved well-being among those who serve our country and those impacted by military presence.

COMMUNITY ENGAGEMENT

The primary purpose of the Department of Defense (DoD) military health system is to ensure that service members are maintained or rapidly restored to readiness for active service. It increasingly has been recognized, however, that combat-related disorders are persistent, may require years of subsequent attention, and may lead to premature discharge and/or retirement for some. By contrast, the Veterans Health Administration (VHA) programs focus on restoring functions impaired by war and military service; protecting those who cannot function, through various forms treatment and community-based care; and assisting veterans with transition to civilian community life. As of July 2013, there were approximately 2.6 million veterans of Iraq, Afghanistan, and other theaters of the global war on terrorism (Carter, 2013). Historically, veterans' mental health care needs have risen sharply over time, with a peak occurring 10 to 20 years after the end of a war. This was true for the Vietnam War cohort and will likely be true for the post 9/11 combat cohort (Carter, 2013).

More veterans seek care outside the VHA, than within it. Therefore, a critical part of the total care network includes the role of civilian community

TABLE 15.1 Evidence-based Practice for Military Populations

Approach	Effective For	Brief Overview
Cognitive Behavioral Therapy (CBT)	Mood disorders, including depression, anxiety disorders including PTSD, substance abuse, sleep disorders, psychotic disorders	Examines the relationship among thoughts, feelings, and behaviors by exploring how thinking leads to self-destructive actions and beliefs.
Prolonged Exposure Therapy (PE)	PTSD, clients with trauma history	Decreases distress related to trauma through education, breathing training, and talking through the trauma. Clients expose themselves to safe situations they have been avoiding since their trauma.
Cognitive Processing Therapy (CPT)	PTSD, depression, clients with trauma history	Assists in handling distressing thoughts and gaining an understanding of traumatic events. Includes education, becoming aware of thoughts and feelings, learning skills to deal with those feelings, and ultimately changing beliefs.

mental health agencies, public and private, independent of those contracting with federal agencies as service providers. In previous and future conflicts, the local mental health clinics, school mental health programs, hospital emergency rooms, and other mental health-affiliated agencies have and will continue to constitute a pillar on which recovery and veterans' support will rest. As many as 40% to 50% of veterans from the current war either do not seek health care through the VHA or discontinue treatment shortly after their first appointment. This means that civilian agencies, especially community mental health programs and primary care clinics, are very likely to become the primary resource. All social workers, not just those in the military specialty, will require an awareness of the needs of this diverse group. Critical to improving the quality of life for veterans will be timely and early mental health intervention. Efforts must be aimed at effectively engaging veterans early in their transition process, instead of at the end of the treatment spectrum.

SUMMARY AND FUTURE CHALLENGES

Military social work involves the mastery of content, skills, and intervention specific to working with service members, veterans, and their families. Today, military social workers work at all levels of practice including direct practice, research, community practice, and policy. These professionals are tasked with not only providing services within a community of distinct culture, but addressing an array of physical, mental, economic, marital, and readjustment issues experienced by this population.

One key aspect of successful community support and engagement is the extent of widespread relatedness and interaction among its citizens. Therefore, military social workers will need to create a coordinated approach to supporting and engaging veterans and their families by bringing together diverse sets of resources and identifying new opportunities across the public and private sectors. It is unlikely that the needs of veterans and their families, as well as the quality of and access to care and qualified providers, will be adequately addressed unless the profession is effective at convincing local, state, and federal agencies to join forces.

Military social workers are uniquely qualified to bring diverse resources together, identify new opportunities across public and private sectors, and lay the foundation for a coordinated approach to supporting and engaging veterans and their families. Community-based social work initiatives can help guide community practitioners, build community networks, inform policymakers, and identify broadly applicable and scalable translational research with promising real-world prevention interventions. Therefore, the overall goal for military social workers should be to ensure cultural competence, utilization of evidence-based practice, and the building of new opportunities and policies that permit more effective and fiscally sound programs for the reintegration of veterans into our civilian communities across the United States. Ultimately, military social work is the safety net for a civil society that is necessary to support the brave men and women who have served our country (Flynn & Hassan, 2010).

WEBSITES

Center for a New American Society http://www.cnas.org/

Center for Innovation and Research on Veterans & Military Families, University of Southern California School of Social Work http://cir.usc.edu/

Iraq and Afghanistan Veterans of America http://iava.org/

U.S. Department of Veteran Affairs http://www.va.gov/

References

Adler, A. B., Bliese, P. D., & Castro, C. A. E. (2011). *Deployment psychology: Evidence-based strategies to promote mental health in the military*. Washington, DC: American Psychological Association.

Belasco, A. (2009). The cost of Iraq, Afghanistan, and other global war on terror operations since 9/11. *Congressional Research Service*. Retrieved from www.crs.gov

Burnett-Zeigler, I., Valenstein, M., Ilgen, M., Blow, A .J., Gorman, L. A., & Zivin, K. (2011). Civilian employment among recently returning Afghanistan and Iraq National Guard veterans. *Military Medicine, 176,* 639–646.

Carter, P. (2013). Expanding the net: Building mental health care capacity for veterans. The Center for a New American Society. Retrieved from http://www.cnas.org/expanding-the-net

Council on Social Work Education (CSWE). (2010). *Advanced social work practice in military social work*. Retrieved from http://www.cswe.org/File.aspx?id=42466

Flynn, M., & Hassan, A. (2010). Guest editorial: Unique challenges of war in Iraq and Afghanistan. *Journal of Social Work Education, 46*(2), 169–173. doi:http://dx.doi.org/10.5175/JSWE.2010.334800002

Greene-Shortridge, T., Britt, T. W., & Andrew, C. (2007). The stigma of mental health problems in the military. *Military Medicine, 172*(2), 157–161. Retrieved from http://search.proquest.com/docview/621647199?accountid=14749

Hall, L. K. (2012). *The importance of understanding military culture* (pp. 3–17). New York, NY: Routledge/Taylor & Francis Group. Retrieved from http://search.proquest.com/docview/1027507569?accountid=14749

Hazle, M., Wilcox, S. L., & Hassan, A. M. (2012). Helping veterans and their families fight on! *Advances in Social Work, 13*(1), 229–242.

Hoge, C. W., Auchterlonie, J. L., & Milliken, C. S. (2006).Mental health problems, use of mental health services and attrition from military service after returning from deployment to Iraq or Afghanistan. *JAMA: Journal of the American Medical Association, 295*, 1023–1032.

Institute of Medicine (IOM). (2010). *Returning home from Iraq and Afghanistan. Preliminary assessment of readjustment needs of veterans, service members, and their families.* Washington, DC: The National Academies Press.

Jacobson, I. G., Ryan, M. A., Hooper, T. I., Smith, T. C., Amoroso, P. J., Boyko, E. J., & Bell, N. S. (2008). Alcohol use and alcohol-related problems before and after military combat deployment. *JAMA: Journal of the American Medical Association, 300*, 663–675.

Kang, H. K., & Bullman, T. A. (2008). Risk of suicide among U.S. veterans after returning from the Iraq or Afghanistan war zones. *JAMA: Journal of the American Medical Association, 300*(6), 652–653. doi:http://dx.doi.org/10.1001/jama.300.6.652

Little, R., & Alenkin, N. (2011). *Overcoming barriers to employment for veterans: Current trends and practical approaches.* Los Angeles, CA: USC Center for Innovation and Research on Veterans & Military Families.

Miller, K. E., Omidian, P., Kulkarni, M., Yaqubi, A., Daudzai, H., & Rasmussen, A. (2009). The validity and clinical utility of post-traumatic stress disorder in Afghanistan. *Transcultural Psychiatry, 46*(2), 219–237. doi:http://dx.doi.org/10.1177/1363461509105813

Schell, T., & Tanielian, T. (Eds.). (2011). *A needs assessment of New York state veterans. A final report to the New York State Health Foundation.* Retrieved from http://www.rand.org/pubs/technical_reports/TR920.html

Weiss, E. L., Coll, J. E., & Metal, M. (2011). The influence of military culture and veteran worldviews on mental health treatment: Implications for veteran help seeking and wellness. *International Journal of Health, Wellness and Society, 1*(2), 75–86.

16   Social Work with Military Families

Diane Scotland-Coogan

To date, approximately 1,471,088 Americans have participated in the war on terror. As of March 2010, a reported 5,376 have died in service. There are 23,442,000 living veterans and 17,456,000 living ex-service members in the United States (Library Spot, 2013). The families of those who died in service are processing the grief of a loss that will change their lives forever. Returning veterans, especially those who have experienced combat, will not come home the same person they were before they left (Coll, Weiss, & Yarvis, 2011). This causes considerable stress on the family as they seek to welcome home their loved one. Social workers will be called upon more and more to provide professional service to assist these families in the healing process.

As social workers, we understand the importance of cultural diversity in the context of practice and military culture differs greatly from civilian culture (Hall, 2011). Culture may differ somewhat between branches; however, the basic tenets are the same. Each branch of the service has pride in who they are, thus it is important to refer to those in the Air Force as Airman, in the Army as Soldiers, in the Navy as Sailors, in the Marine Corps as Marines, and in the Coast Guard as Coast Guardsmen (recently the term Guardian has been used) (National Association of Social Workers [NASW], 2013). For the purposes of this chapter, these brave men and women will be referred to as veterans, a term that reflects all branches of the service. Further details regarding military culture will be discussed later.

It would be difficult to describe the "typical" day of a social worker working with military families. This type of practice could include home visits, in-office appointments, and support group sessions. Home-based service can be beneficial for many reasons. One consideration would be the client's ability to attend sessions outside the home; we cannot assume the client has the resources to get to your office. Clients may not have access to a car, do not have a driver's license, are currently dealing with medical issues that would make driving unsafe, do not have local social support to assist, or access to bus service. If the family is caring for a veteran or family member with disabilities, coming to the office may not be an option for them. Treatment should not result in additional stress to the family; rather, it should assist in relieving some of their stresses. For a social worker, being in the home may have some benefits.

One of the advantages of in-home sessions is getting to know the client system on a more intimate level. In the comfort of their own environment, clients may let down their defenses, providing a plethora of information that may have taken months of in-office sessions to acquire. Observing how the family interacts in their home, what their living conditions may be, and identifying possible barriers to treatment can provide significant information for determining the most appropriate treatment modality. In-home sessions may also keep treatment occurring on a more regular basis, given that clients are less apt to cancel appointments if you are coming to them. There are, however, some downsides to home visits, especially the likelihood of more distractions for the family. This would need to be addressed on the first visit, as you explain the clinical process and the expectations for sessions when working together.

Office visits have the benefit of having the family's attention in a more structured environment. They also allow you to see more clients in a day because there is no travel time to consider. As mentioned earlier, the number of missed appointments may increase as clients may not have transportation, they may forget, and obligations in the home may keep them from being able to leave.

Support groups can also be very successful in working with military spouses and their children. When facilitating support groups the social worker assists clients in connecting with others who share their experience, and this can prove very validating. Support groups can include, but not be limited to, other military spouses and children, bereavement groups, domestic violence groups, and substance abuse groups such as Al-Anon. Support groups are available for spouses and children, as well as parents and extended family members. For military families, this can provide insight about their loved one's behavior. The support of those who understand can make the family members feel less isolated in their situation. The group members will share available resources with each other, which might otherwise not have been identified. Many support groups have online chats available for those who cannot get to a meeting because of lack of resources. Identifying local and online groups to work with families is important resource information to have available, and should be updated regularly to ensure accuracy. Building rapport with a client in the beginning will assist the social worker in creating a therapeutic relationship that fosters trust along with the client's ability to be more open and honest about situations and needs. Only then can the social worker truly understand what referrals and treatment are warranted. In order to build this rapport with military families, it is essential to develop a basic understanding of military culture.

MILITARY CULTURE

Military culture differs greatly from civilian culture. The veteran is taught from the onset about honor and respect. The military has its own language, acronyms, particular ways to dress, and behave, all of which may be foreign to those in civilian life. To function at optimal level, unit cohesion is promoted over autonomy (Hall, 2011; Harrison, 2006). The military is a world driven by a rigid authoritarian structure. The family must conform to the rigidity of military regimentation, possibly leaving them feeling disconnected from civilian life. They must deal with the effects of rank on social interactions, associating with those of their own rank/status (Hall, 2011). They lack any control over pay and benefits, and must navigate the inflexible system whenever circumstances require help from the military. Spouses must have the consent and participation of their veteran spouse for eligibility of available resources. Some veterans do not want to be viewed as weak or in need, so they will not assist the spouse in obtaining access to these. This can leave families unable to receive the services they may so desperately need. The military life has clearly defined rules, such as little to no tolerance of disagreeing with or questioning authority. Family members may be discouraged from demonstrating behaviors that suggest individualism. The family may experience isolation as a result of frequent moves creating distance from family and friends. Spouses and children may, over time, make limited attempts to engage in a new community with the understanding that it will only be a matter of time until they leave again (Hall, 2011).

There is cultural, religious, and ethnic diversity within the military. This suggests social workers need to practice multicultural skills, including being aware of their own biases, values, and personal limitations, and practicing without judgment. This requires actively developing and implementing appropriate and sensitive practices for working with military families (Hall, 2011; Harrison, 2006). When working with those of a different cultural background, a social worker should ask questions about the culture of the family, engaging a curiosity that seeks not only differences, but similarities in their cultures. Showing interest and acceptance about another's culture to gain an understanding for identifying appropriate treatment also assists in building rapport.

There may be concerns for the military family in working with military mental health services, as well as uneasiness about working with civilian professionals. Veterans may be skeptical about using any mental health services tied to the military, because there is a risk that information may get back to their command, with potential long-term effects on their career. In addition, there is often a stigma associated with mental health issues, for military professionals, which may be seen as a weakness. This may cause them to seek help outside the military with civilian professionals. Other issues may arise in rapport building for the civilian professional; how can someone who has not "lived the life" possibly understand (Coll, Weiss & Yarvis, 2011)? This suggests civilian professionals should seek to understand these clients by gaining a basic knowledge of military culture and how it may affect practice. Practitioners should provide a safe and nonjudgmental atmosphere, which demonstrates respect for veterans and their families, and remain professional, responsive, affirmative, and empathetic. Utilize open-ended questions to garner an understanding about military life experience. Seek to learn about the family as individuals within their family culture and within their family system.

PSYCHOEDUCATION

Psychoeducation is an important aspect of social work with military families. Part of the initial session should include helping the family understand behavioral manifestations of a given diagnosis, as well as how to respond best to these behaviors. A reported 20% of Iraqi war veterans will be diagnosed with posttraumatic stress disorder (PTSD) (National Institutes of Health, 2009). The symptoms of this disorder include a loss of interest in previously enjoyed activities, hypervigilance, heightened startle reflex, insomnia, irritability, and aggression (American Psychiatric Association, 2013). These behaviors can be confusing and anxiety producing for everyone in the family.

Military families are forced to adjust to many separations and reunions, experiencing all the emotions related to predeployment, deployment, and postdeployment. Social workers can assist by educating them about what to expect during the various stages of deployment as far as emotional functioning (Coll, Weiss, & Yarvis, 2011). In the predeployment stage, all family members begin to experience a feeling of, or an anticipation of loss. The family may find themselves starting to distance themselves from the service member in an attempt to protect their emotions. During deployment, the family must adjust to life without their loved one; it can take months before emotional stability is achieved. Postdeployment requires yet another adjustment for the family. The social worker should psycho-educate about the homecoming process (Coll, Weiss, & Yarvis, 2011; Sneath & Rheem, 2011). Assist the family to understand what their loved one may be experiencing; why they may be distant, unable to share or demonstrate emotions; why they cannot answer certain questions or attend particular functions. Share with the family the importance of not asking for too much from a returning loved one. Suggest they stay away from questions that require the veteran to share emotions, experiences, and expectations. Prepare them for the fact that the veteran may find comfort in the company of other veterans, seemingly more at ease there than when spending time with family. Veterans may feel these are the only people who truly understand them, and share the same intrusive memories that they face constantly in their own minds. These individuals also may share the same shame and guilt for what they may have witnessed or done, which may also add comfort through their shared military experiences and trainings (Hall, 2011).

Veterans have been taught certain skills, which have kept them safe when deployed, such as secretism, relying on their own perception and knowledge for reacting to situations, and being unemotional and hypervigilant. Sadly, the skills that kept them safe overseas can be a disaster for family reconnection. The veteran may shut off psychologically, even toward their spouses and children (Hall, 2011). Encourage the family members to keep things light, wait for the veteran to tell them what they may want to tell, or what they may be able to share. Help them to understand that the loved one's responses are a result of their experiences, and assist the family in developing coping skills to use when the veteran takes some distance and disconnects personally. Set up "safe zones" in the house in which no hard conversations will take place, this could be the dining table, or the couch in the family gathering area, or both, This then becomes a place the veteran can be with the family with the understanding there will be no expectations except for spending family time together. It is important to note that eliminating stress for the military family is considered an impossible task, and while they may demonstrate resilience, they may still need assistance at times when stressors become overwhelming (Hall, 2012). This is when the social worker is most needed.

CONSIDERATIONS FOR TREATMENT

In sessions with the family, use statements acknowledging you have heard what they say. This does not mean that you necessarily agree with what they said (e.g., "You felt your husband no longer loved you."), but simply means that you are listening. Also, use affirming statements, statements validating that what they are feeling is understandable, or how they may have reacted to a certain situation is understandable. Again, you are not stating that it was appropriate, only that you can understand why. Use Socratic questioning rather than suggesting what they should do; use this form of questioning to get to the family's understanding of the situation. It is important to remember we cannot assume we know what is problematic for them, or what is right for their lives. Make sure to understand the situation from each family member's point of view, and do not allow talking over one another in sessions. Everyone must be able to tell their story. This may be the first time someone has allowed some of them to tell their full story uninterrupted and actually listened to what they had to say. Clients may not have chosen to tell their story; the emotion of what they may be dealing with is so painful they avoid even thinking it. This can include dealing with the grief and loss of the person they used to know, that is, the one who did not come home from deployment. Instead they are living with a stranger, who looks just like their loved one.

Grief and loss is experienced for many reasons. For our military families the most evident and undeniable would be the death of a loved one. Psycho-education about the stages of grief, validation for what they are going through, and a referral to a bereavement group would be the first steps to helping the family move forward (Coll, Weiss, & Yarvis, 2011). Thank them for their loved one's, and their family's, contribution in serving our country. Ask them to share with you stories of their loved one, to tell you about who their loved one was. Engage the family in reflecting on special memories, responding in an affirmative way about how special this person was.

Social workers must also realize military families experience other types of losses that can have a significant effect on their functioning. This includes the loss of loved ones as they knew them, as a result of physical and/or psychological injuries received while deployed. These losses may also include loss of community and friendships through many moves, loss of physical closeness to family, and shared holidays to name a few. They may have been unable to establish a career because of the many moves. This has financial and self-esteem implications. Seek to understand and explore the losses perceived by the family, and explore and identify possible ways in which some of these may be addressed. This may assist them in bringing a sense of reconciliation to their hopes and dreams. The first step toward building a sense of cohesion for the family adjusting post-deployment may be developing and implementing positive communication skills.

Communication skills may be modeled and demonstrated by the social worker to assist the family in having more positive interactions. Encourage the members to speak to each other (e.g., "Would you share with your mom how you feel?"). Teach "I" statements to assist in sharing emotional information in ways that will not provoke a defensive reaction (e.g., "I feel sad when you call me a name," or "It frightens me when you yell."). Explore the parenting techniques being used, identifying what may and may not be working. Model and demonstrate appropriate positive parenting skills, which may also help to create more cohesion for the family. Children need to have a positive and connected relationship with their parents, especially children in a military family.

Children may deal with the psychological effects of many moves, or with the ambiguous loss of a parent, who is physically there, but not emotionally there. They may be saddened by the military parent missing memorable events and by the constant worry for the parent's safety. Emotional protection for them can be expressed by the family forming a unit that somewhat excludes the deployed parent, making it hard for this parent to reconnect upon arrival home. The military commitment to mission over all can make a child feel insignificant in the eyes of the military parent, furthering the disconnect (Hall, 2011). This may cause children to find friends who may be seen as a negative influence (Sneath & Rheem, 2011). The social worker can address these perceptions of loss and/or abandonment by assisting the family in developing a stronger bond through improving relational skills. Psycho-educate children about any diagnosis their parent has received; understanding the behavioral manifestations may assist the child in not taking these behaviors personally.

Many of our returning veterans will return home with symptoms of PTSD, including anger, nightmares, anxiety, and hypervigilance. Some will meet the *Diagnostic and Statistical Manual of Mental Disorders* criteria for a diagnosis of PTSD (American Psychiatric Association, 2013). This has been associated with domestic violence in the home. Interpersonal violence is higher among our veterans than among the civilian population. This violence is not just directed at the family, but will be seen at the workplace and in the community (Coll, Weiss, & Yarvis, 2011). Secondary trauma can be experienced by the caregivers of a physically or emotionally disabled veteran. This is usually the direct result of the stress of caring for, and wanting to help, their traumatized loved one. The symptoms will be similar to those of PTSD, including functional impairment; emotional distress; avoidance of thoughts, feelings and/or situations that are reminders of the trauma; and recurrent and involuntary intrusive imagery (Bride & Figley, 2009).

Community-based services should be explored as possible resources for the military family. Continuous updating of available community resources is an important aspect of social work practice. When those in the community, community agencies, and leaders come together they can support the military family in managing stressful events (Hertzog, Boydston, & Whitworth, 2011). Community program funding fluctuates and community needs fluctuate, suggesting the need to identify multiple sources of assistance for clients. Mental health treatment is only a part of what the family may need to achieve optimal functioning. Given the experiences of isolation, military families will benefit from being embraced and supported by their community.

CONSIDERATIONS FOR RISK ASSESSMENT

The military culture's support of cohesion extends to the family and to the military community.

An attitude of protecting those in their unit can cause situations of domestic violence to be overlooked. The reporting spouses may be avoided and ostracized by others if they tell, including their support system of other military spouses (Harrison, 2006). For this reason, the abuse may have never been addressed, and the victims may have difficulty disclosing to the social worker. Types of abuse include physical, sexual, verbal, and emotional (economic or financial abuse is a subtle form of emotional abuse). Signs of abuse include the abuser using dominance, humiliation, isolation, threats, intimidation, denial, and blame. Abusers are able to control their behavior. They choose whom they will abuse, which is usually someone whom they claim to love. Physical abusers will choose places in which the wounds will not be readily seen, and they can stop when it benefits them. If it is clear that the family is being abused the social worker should ask if something is wrong, express concern, listen and validate, offer help, and support the victims' decisions (Smith & Segal, 2013). Help would include shelter information, abuse hotline phone numbers, and creation of a safety plan. Substance abuse has also been found to be a problem for both veterans and their families.

Substance abuse for the veteran and the family must be assessed. Substance abuse has been found to be higher among those diagnosed with PTSD (Hertzog, Boydston, & Whitworth, 2011). Alcohol is a common form of self-medicating for those in the military because it is an acceptable tradition. Such is not the case with prescription medications; the stigma placed on these causes a perception of weakness. The social worker should consider providing a referral to a twelve-step program such as Alcoholics Anonymous, as well as Al-Anon for the rest of the family. With the many reasons why a veteran may self-medicate, such as anxiety, shame, guilt, and depression to name a few, concerns about suicide must also be addressed.

Social workers must complete safety and risk assessment when working with military families. In 2008, the Medical Department of the Army reported that in 26 years of records, the suicide rate of active duty veterans was higher than it had ever been (Coll, Weiss, & Yarvis, 2011). Lower suicide rates have been shown for those Air Force communities that have shown interagency collaboration with leadership as a part of their Air Force Suicide Prevention Program (Hertzog, Boydston, & Whitworth, 2011). This supports the noted importance of community involvement in available resources for military families.

SUMMARY

Best practice for working with the military family comes from a strengths-based perspective. Using a cognitive modality and avoiding long-term approaches would be the most beneficial, concentrating on emotions and feelings experienced by the family members (Hall, 2012). Our military families would best be served by a system that steers away from a disease model, and instead embraces the concept that our returning veterans require a period of adjustment supported by the community as a whole. This would not replace mental health treatment for those in need, but would call on the community to provide employment, respite, and mentoring for those who have served our country. For every five deployed service members, three have a spouse and/or children waiting for them at home. The psychological affects for the family could be eased by the support of a caring community (Straits-Troster, Brancu, Coodale, Pacelli, Wilmer, Simmons, & Kidler, 2011). This model fits with social work because itconsiders people within their environment. A social worker working with military families would serve these families best through reaching out to the local community to find appropriate resources and support groups and to strive to achieve an appropriate therapeutic relationship built on trust.

WEBSITES

U.S. Department of Veterans Affairs

- http://www.va.gov/
- http://www.vetcenter.va.gov/

Wounded Warrior Project

- http://www.woundedwarriorproject.org/

Give an Hour

- http://www.giveanhour.org/

Al-Anon Family Groups & Al-Anon Teens

- http://www.al-anon.alateen.org/

Domestic Violence Hotline

- http://www.thehotline.org/
- 1-800-799- SAFE (7233)

National Military Family Association

- www.militaryfamily.org/our-programs/

Coaching Into Care

- www.mirecc.va.gov/coaching/index.asp

National Fatherhood Initiative

- www.fatherhood.org/Military/

Transfer of Post 9/11 G.I. Bill Benefits to Dependents

- www.gibill.va.gov/benefits/post_911_gibill/transfer_of_benefits.html

The Military Spouse Career Advancement Accounts Program (MyCAA)

- http://www.militaryonesource.mil/12038/Project%20Documents/MilitaryHOMEFRONT/MyCAA/FactSheet.pdf

Survivors and Dependents Assistance (DEA)

- http://www.gibill.va.gov/benefits/other_programs/dea.html

References

American Psychiatric Association. (2013). *Diagnostic and statistical manual of mental disorders* (5th ed.). Arlington, VA: American Psychiatric Publishing.

Bride, B. E., & Figley, C. R. (2009). Secondary trauma and military veteran caregivers. *Smith College Studies in Social Work, 79*(3), 314–329, 233.

Retrieved from http://search.proquest.com.library.capella.edu/docview/749399514?accountid=27965

Coll, J. E., Weiss, E. I., & Yarvis, J. S. (2011). No one leaves unchanged: Insights for civilian mental health care professionals into the military experience and culture. *Social Work in Health Care, 50*(7), 487–500.

Hall, L. K. (2011). The importance of understanding the military culture. *Social Work in Health Care, 50*(1), 4–18.

Harrison, D. (2006). The role of military culture in military organizations' responses to women abuse in military families. *The Sociological Review, 54*(3), 546–574.

Hertzog, J. R., Boydston, C., & Whitworth, J. D. (2011). Systems approaches with Air Force members and their families: A focus on trauma. In C. R. Figley & B. Everson (Eds.), *Families under fire* (pp. 115–126). New York, NY: Routledge.

Library Spot. (2013). America's wars and casualties. Retrieved from http://www.libraryspot.com/lists/listwars.htm

National Association of Social Workers. (2013). Military branches. Retrieved from http://www.socialworkers.org/practice/military/military-branches.asp

National Institutes of Health. (2009). PTSD: A growing epidemic. http://www.nlm.nih.gov/medlineplus/magazine/issues/winter09/articles/winter09pg10-14.html

Smith, M., & Segal, J. (2013). Domestic violence and abuse: Signs of abuse and abusive relationships. Retrieved from http://www.helpguide.org/mental/domestic_violence_abuse_types_signs_causes_effects.htm

Sneath, L., & Rheem, K. D. (2011). The use of emotionally focused couples therapy with military couples and families. In C. R. Figley & B. Everson (Ed.), *Families under fire* (pp. 127–152). New York, NY: Routledge.

Straits-Troster, K. A., Brancu, M., Coodale, B., Pacelli, S., Wilmer, C., Simmons, E. M., & Kidler, H. (2011). Developing community capacity to treat post-deployment mental health problems: A public health initiative. *Psychological Trauma, Theory, Research, Practice, and Policy, 3*(3), 283–291.

17 Social Work Practice and Personal Self-care

Jeff Skinner

THE IMPERATIVE FOR PROFESSIONAL SELF-CARE

For a profession that espouses both helping and advocating for those who are marginalized, traumatized, and without resources, one would assume that the social work profession would have given some attention to improving the well-being of the helper, for example, in offering ways to build capacity for resilience and a means to prevent professional distress. Historically, this has not been the case despite numerous studies and descriptions concerning burnout and occupational stress, which were being published in the early 1980s (Gillespie, 1987). In essence, being, and/or practicing as, a social worker does not mean we are experts in exercising self-care in spite of our empowerment strategies for clients to take better care of themselves. Our professional culture now promotes well-being for both good reasons and sometimes for frivolous self-indulgence. In short, a distressed/impaired social worker is an ineffective social worker.

Being self-sacrificial to the altruism mandate of our work is not a professional virtue signifying the utmost of dedication, professionalism, or advocacy. In fact, it often reflects a negative attribute and a symptom of diminished capacity. Listed below are some of the myths, derived from the extant literature surrounding the normal and not so normal hazards of social work practice vis à vis the imperative for professional and personal self-care.

MYTHS

Personal self-care is the same as professional self-care. Although well-being is important for anyone, the purposes of professional self-care and personal self-care differ. The former is a process of self-awareness and promotes and monitors the use of self in one's professional role. Professional self-care is always connected to the "other self" in social work, namely the client. The latter does not necessarily connect to an occupational role with standards, accountability, and transparency. Personal self-care is aimed at soothing and restoring one's self. Not all personal self-care can be linked to enhancing a benefit for professional role effectiveness.

Being altruistic with our clients will almost always offset any distress felt in the important professional role of social work. Altruism is an attitude and an attribute that serves as motivation to help others foremost, and to place the welfare of others before one's self. Altruism can remind us of our motivation to help others, but unfortunately it does not have any protective properties. Helping others will always produce some distress, simply because we care enough.

Our education and training are sufficient to protect us from distress, burnout, compassion fatigue, etc. If such were the case, then there would never have been any discussion about social work burnout and fatigue, in the first place. Although our Bachelor's in Social Work/Master's in Social Work education and training offers us knowledge, values, and skills, and promotes self-awareness for the purpose of helping others, it does not provide buffers to stress. No person, regardless of education and training, can rise above the realities of day-to-day distress endemic in the nature of social work practice.

Internalizing the causes of distress is the best strategy for self-care. It is rather tempting to internalize distress as our fault—due to our not trying hard enough, which thereby hides our distress from others. This is not, however a productive strategy; distress is a product derived from the multiple interactions of a social worker, client, and the practice environment. Internalizing distress does not allow for self-examination, and/or problem resolution.

Working in a self-care friendly and facilitative environment is an extra benefit for anyone. Professional self-care by the individual social worker must be practiced alongside of workplace structures, which may also promote professional well-being. If professional self-care is an imperative, then a similar mandate should be applied to our agencies and employers.

PROFESSIONAL AND PERSONAL SELF-CARE

The social work profession, like other helping professions, recently began to give intentional regard to professional self-care in the areas of academia, field education, supervision, direct and indirect practice, research and organizational culture (Cox & Steiner, 2013). Thus, it has taken several decades for our profession to go beyond describing the process and effects of burnout, compassion fatigue, and vicarious traumatization, to requiring the need to practice professional self-care. Discussions about professional self-care occur daily in agencies, in employment interviews, during supervision, in coursework at schools of social work, in field education internships, and in research projects (Moore, Perry, Bledsoe, & Robinson, 2011). Unlike previous generations of social workers, it is universally recognized and now accepted by contemporary social work practitioners and researchers that sometimes—helping others can hurt the helper (Beckett, 2008). Further acknowledged is that such hurting cannot be attributed exclusively to faults or deficits in the character or personality of the social worker helper, but rather to our practice settings (e.g., trauma services, forensic services, military social work).

Contemporary thinking clearly identifies occupational hazards in certain practice settings within social work (e.g., working with trauma victims) and these appear to be accepted by job seekers and employees (National Association of Social Workers [NASW], 2009). The need to practice professional self-care in order to remain effective in practice is endorsed by the NASW (2009) and is

embraced as an ethical imperative and necessary practice behavior. Professions seek to self-regulate (Reamer, 1992) and mandating professional self-care is one manifestation of such regulation. The Council on Social Work Education (CSWE) Educational Policy and Accreditation Standards (EPAS) *Competency Number 1* (CSWE, 2008) and its associated practice behaviors refer specifically to self-awareness, and to conducting one's self professionally. Within this competency, practice behavior (b) calls social workers, "to practice personal reflection and self-correction to assure continual professional development" (CSWE, 2008). Empirical evidence suggests that there is an inverse correlation between stress, burnout, compassion fatigue and professional self-care. In other words, the more a social worker increases professional self-care, the less distress will be experienced, thus decreasing the possibility of deleterious practice with clients (NASW, 2009).

There is also no consensus on the definition of what constitutes professional self-care. Some refer to it as a process (strategies and practices), or as the ability (Lee & Miller, 2013) to increase levels of subjective well-being. Others see it as an outcome that produces resiliency and empowerment, and mitigates against a decline in empathy with the client, thus elevating compassion satisfaction, as contrasted to compassion fatigue (Lee & Miller, 2013). The term "personal self-care" is sometimes used outside of the context of professional practice. Here, a social worker pays attention to stressful aspects of their life outside of work, and seeks ways to address stress when it becomes distress. Although a social worker can make efforts not to have personal distress influence his/her professional performance, it is unrealistic to expect that protracted or acute personal distress outside of work will never influence one's professional effectiveness. Because social workers make frequent "use of self" for professional purposes, the conceptual separation between professional self-care and personal self-care is not always clear and there cannot always be a demarcation line.

Because social workers profess the "use of self" for professional purposes to facilitate client engagement and change, there exists the potential to meet personal needs or to re-enact personal problems with the client. For example, countertransference in its most generic definition often represents responses from the social worker that originate not from the professional voice, but rather from unresolved personal issues that are being played out unknowingly with the client. Often, this displays itself by the social worker's savior and grandiose fantasies about the client through their sense of a unique, specialized, and exclusive understanding of the client, through contempt, avoidance, and/or an over identification with a client. Sooner or later the social worker will experience some forms of distress when countertransference dominates the working alliance with a client. Inevitably both the client and the social worker will suffer. If self-awareness and self-observation (also termed "the observing ego") are limited and broken, then social work colleagues have an ethical imperative to assist an impaired colleague.

The imperative for professional self-care is associated with the notion of "fitness for duty." The NASW Code of Ethics addresses fitness for duty in subsection 4.05, concerning impairment.

(b) Social workers whose personal problems, psychosocial distress, legal problems, substance abuse, or mental health difficulties interfere with their professional judgment and performance should immediately seek consultation and take appropriate remedial action by seeking professional help, making adjustments in workload, terminating practice, or taking any other steps necessary to protect clients and others (NASW, 2008).

Professional self-care is assumed to be the primary responsibility of the individual social worker and it is implicitly driven by an ethical imperative of fitness for service. Although no consensus exists as to the definition of professional self-care, a definition offered by Lopez, as supported by NASW (NASW, 2009), captures the multiple, inter-related dynamic dimensions of professional self-care.

Professional self-care in social work can be defined as a core essential component of social work practice and reflects a choice and commitment to become actively involved in maintaining one's effectiveness as a social worker. Furthermore, in promoting the practice of self-care, a repertoire of self-care strategies is essential to support the social worker and other mental health professionals in preventing, addressing, and coping with the natural, yet unwanted, consequences of helping (Lopez, 2007).

TYPES OF DISTRESS ASSOCIATED WITH NEGLECTED PROFESSIONAL SELF-CARE

A brief description of the types of distress will illuminate portions, large and small, of the kinds of distress most social workers will encounter during their careers. When addressing distress and professional self-care the following terms frequently appear: occupational stress and distress, burnout, vicarious trauma (VT), secondary traumatic stress (STS), compassion fatigue (CF), compassion satisfaction (CS), and resilience. Occupational stress refers to either the acute or ongoing negative physical and emotional responses an employee may have in executing job tasks, or as a response to the workplace environment, such as a hostile, racist, sexist, or toxic work environment. Within the social work profession, workplace settings such as child welfare agencies, disaster and trauma-response teams, and forensic settings have higher levels of occupational stress. Over time and when left unchecked, workplace stress can evolve into distress, which results in a decrease in compassion and empathy (Maslach, 2003).

Burnout is "a syndrome of physical and emotional exhaustion, involving the development of negative self-concept, negative job attitudes, and a loss of concern and feelings for clients" (Pines & Maslach, 1978, p. 224). In her seminal work on burnout, Maslach described three distinct areas of concern: emotional exhaustion, depersonalization, and a reduced sense of accomplishment and effectiveness (Maslach, 2003). Emotional exhaustion refers to the fatigue, loss of passion for work, and the overarching sense that the social worker has nothing left to give to clients or the organization. Depersonalization entails the increasing use of cynicism, negativity, and detachment from clients and colleagues. The reduced sense of accomplishment refers to practitioners feeling as though their work with clients is ineffective, unappreciated, and without purpose and meaning. Burning out is more of a process than an event.

Vicarious traumatization (VT) (Bride, 2007) refers to the personal transformation, cognitive changes, and alterations in beliefs and worldviews that a helper may experience when working closely with trauma victims. Often, cognitive shifts center on issues of safety, trust, control, and good versus evil, as a result of empathizing with trauma victims. VT is the result of an indirect experience of the client's trauma whereas posttraumatic stress disorder (PTSD) is a result of a direct experience of trauma. Figley (1995) proposed that symptoms of VT in a social worker can resemble those of PTSD.

Secondary traumatic stress (STS) is closely related to VT, and the two terms are often used interchangeably (Bride, 2007). STS and VT are limited to those who work with trauma victims, whereas burnout is unrestricted to client populations. In essence, STS occurs as one person experiences the traumatic event through exposure to a client who has undergone a recent traumatic event (Bride, 2007). STS symptoms are similar to those symptoms presented in PTSD. These include intrusion, such as recurrent reflections on the event, distressing dreams, and feeling as though the traumatic event is recurring; arousal, as expressed in difficulty falling asleep, irritability, hypervigilance, and increased startle responses; avoidance, as expressed in detachment, avoidance of talking about the event, avoiding locations associated with the trauma, and exhibiting a limited range of affect; and, finally, distress and impairment.

Compassion fatigue (CF) is a term first used by Figley (1995) as a nonperjorative and more acceptable term for STS. CF is often used to capture a melding of the terms burnout and secondary traumatic stress. Compassion fatigue can be used to denote a momentary state of low empathy and depletion of energy, which can develop into a more chronic persistent state for the helper. Compassion satisfaction (CS) (Stamm, 2002), on the other hand, is a term used to punctuate the preferred ideal state of the positive internal, subjective altruistic sense of helping others effectively, as contrasted with the nonpreferred state of depleted and cynical CF. High workloads, lack of self-efficacy, lack of control, poor external rewards, and toxic institutionally related stress are precipitating factors associated with burnout. Exposure to traumatic material and traumatized clients are the precipitating factors for STS and VT (Bride, 2007). CF is present with all of these conditions.

RISK FACTORS AND VULNERABILITIES

Risk factors unique to social work and its practice settings, combined with any preexisting vulnerabilities in the social worker, and finally, combined with any internal and/or external mediating factors, make up the dynamic interaction of stress evolving into degrees of distress (e.g., CF and burnout). Not all people experience a stressor in the same way or cope with distress in the same way. Identifying risk factors located internally to

the social worker, as well as those located externally to the social worker (i.e., the organization and its supportive/unsupportive culture), will provide perspective later on about strategies for not neglecting professional self-care.

Practice settings and populations served are factors external to the social worker. Social workers practicing with traumatized clients, and/or dying clients, are at higher risk to experience occupational stress, VT, STS, CF, and burnout. Child welfare social workers practicing in child protective services, child forensics, and treatment agencies for physically and sexually abused children and adolescents are also at risk for extreme stress. There is an abundance of empirical research (Siegfried, 2008) discussing the correlation between working in child welfare, and developing vicarious trauma evolving into burnout, and its residual effect on workforce turnover and organizational morale. Social workers practicing in hospices, disaster services, military settings, domestic violence settings, prisons, addiction agencies, and law enforcement settings are at similar high risk for stress. Organizational cultures that are unsupportive and delimiting of professional development and control usually provide little recognition of the stressors placed upon social workers. The most frequently cited organizational culture stressors are an overload of cases, few supportive resources, oppressive policies, and most importantly, a perceived sense that one has little control over the work environment (Lee & Miller, 2013; Loone, 2003).

Risk factors and vulnerabilities unique to social workers involve previous trauma, especially sexual and physical abuse; character disorders; anxiety and depressive disorders; addictions; poor boundary control; and years of practice. Social workers who have at least a decade of practice experience, and are more likely to practice professional self-care, are less likely to describe distress in their job performance (Loone, 2003). Conversely, social workers who are just beginning their professional careers are more likely to experience debilitating stress within their first three years of practice. Such awareness can be attributed to an imbalance between professional and personal life, inadequate support and supervision, and unrealistic expectations for the profession, leading to disillusionment and poorer preparation for practice while in graduate school.

ASSESSMENT AND EVALUATION OF DISTRESS

Most of the measures and instruments developed to assess job satisfaction, job compassion, CF, STS, and VT originated from disciplines other than social work. Social work is beginning, however, to develop its own measures as applied exclusively to the profession to assess for VT and CF (Bride, Radey, & Figley, 2007). The trend among helping professions is to develop instruments that can screen and assess for areas unique to one's profession. Therefore, cross disciplinary assessment tools and measures have limited applicability. Additional resources regarding assessment and screening are available below and on this chapter's website in the subsection, "Resources on the Internet."

The following are some assessment tools commonly used by social workers and other helping professionals. Saakvitne and Pearlman (1996) developed a widely used self-care instrument that assesses the frequency with which a helper may practice personal self-care in the domains of: self-care, psychological self-care, emotional self-care, spiritual self-care, workplace self-care, and overall balance. The Professional Quality of Life Scale, (ProQOL) (Stamm, 2009) was designed primarily to assess positive and negative aspects of helping others, and it is also widely used. It aims primarily at the affective components of working and as such examines both compassion satisfaction and compassion fatigue. It has several helpful subscales: compassion satisfaction, burnout, and STS. The Figley Compassion Fatigue Self-Test (Figley, 1995) developed mainly for those working with trauma victims, has two domains of assessment: (1) areas about the helper; and (2) areas about the working environment. Its aim is to note areas where there is satisfaction, along with areas where there is some CF. The Maslach Burnout Inventory (MBI) (Maslach, Jackson & Leiter, 1996) is the most recognized self-assessment inventory for those working in human services. Having high reliability and validity, it assesses the areas of emotional exhaustion, depersonalization, and feelings of competency across many settings.

Leiter and Maslach's Areas of Worklife Survey (Leiter & Maslach, 2005) provides another assessment of the helper's external environment and contains the following subscales: workload, control over the work, reward, community, and fairness and values. Utilizing both of the MBI and the Leiter & Maslach assessment measurements can provide a social worker with a fairly accurate picture of multiple internal and external dimensions of burnout and its preceding conditions. Using such self-assessment inventories also increases self-awareness through providing information and knowledge regarding resiliency, coping, areas for self-correction, and areas of personal and professional conflict.

SOCIAL WORK AND CARE STRATEGIES

Unfortunately, there are no magical inoculations or vaccines to prevent the very real feelings of stress, anxiety, organizational uncertainty, and distress in the day-to-day practice of social work. Our responsibilities are to be as healthy as we possibly can be, in identifying and controlling our own physical health, emotional and mental health, spiritual health, and in facilitating healthier work environments. Further, we are responsible for having at hand numerous "what works for me" strategies, techniques, coping mechanisms, and professional supports for use when our professional well-being is threatened or challenged.

Prior to discussing some offsetting strategies to deal with personal and professional stress, it is important to table two issues that are endemic in the DNA of most social work practitioners. The first is personality factors; the other is our motivational reasons for choosing this noble profession. In regard to the former, factors that can mediate between the stress and the response(s) to it have much to do with work-life balance, coping skills, core personality attributes, strength of professional identity, and responsiveness from supervisors and a supportive workplace environment. In a meta-analysis of the relationship between personality and job satisfaction, Judge, Heller, and Mount (2002) related the five-factor model of personality (neuroticism, extraversion, openness to experience, agreeableness, and conscientiousness) to job satisfaction, and maladaptive responses to job stress. These authors concluded that three of these five factors function as mediators, and represent a possible positive correlation to job satisfaction. For example, persons with a negative/cynical nature (neuroticism) who are predisposed to interpreting stressors as more of a problem than a challenge, are inclined to seek job dissatisfaction. Those who are more extroverted than introverted are more disposed to experience positive emotions and value interpersonal actions as solutions to problems. Those who have higher levels of conscientiousness, demonstrate more effective coping mechanisms. These individuals have a tendency to obtain higher levels of intrinsic rewards, and thus eventually receive equal amounts of external rewards (Judge, Heller, & Mount, 2003).

Second, it has been determined that personality types are tied intimately to one's vocational career selection. This configuration is as such, "… personal traits or personality→one's values and attitudes→his or her interests→personal strengths and skills, all collectively influence→one's motivation to select a certain career; and the cornerstone domino for this chain reaction is personality traits" (Holosko, 2006, p. 428). John Holland's extensive work in the area of occupational choice and personality characteristics describes six main personality trait characteristics: realistic, investigative, artistic, enterprising, conventional, and social—that most of us fit into (Holland, 1992). Social workers almost always fall into the social category. Here, these are individuals who:

… (a) like to do things to help people—teaching, caring, giving first aid, providing information; generally avoid using machines, tools or animals to achieve goals; (b) are good at teaching, counseling, nursing or giving information; (c) value helping people and solving problems; and (d) see themselves as helpful, friendly and trustworthy (Holosko, 2006, p. 428).

This parallels directly the work commissioned in 1957, 1963, and 1988 by the NASW and CSWE in attempting to discover "who enters social work and why?" Taken together, these studies clearly demonstrated that social workers are "social types" who are attracted to the values that the profession holds most clearly: humanitarianism, service to people, altruism and *caring for others* (Morales & Schaefor, 1989). Thus, social workers are indeed correctly and colloquially referred to as "card carrying members of the altruistic society." Interestingly, and consistent with the message reiterated in this chapter, the attribute of "caring for others," was prominently noted in these studies. However, "caring for self," the focus of this chapter was conspicuously absent.

Each of us is different, with our own unique composition of ourselves and our environment, motivation to practice social work, personality type, tolerance for frustration, affective expressions, etc. Hence, there is no "one size fits all" technique or toolbox for professional self-care that can be prescribed for all. For example, a body massage one person finds soothing another person may experience as intrusive. Care techniques, which are usually person specific, follow the establishment of general strategies. Strategies in one's care are embedded in the professional self first, and constitute one of the many foundational pillars of professional practice behavior. These should address the broader landscape of professional well-being and as such, serve as blueprints for addressing workplace and occupational stressors (Norcross, 2000).

The four domains of professional self-care presented below are physical health, emotional/mental health, spiritual health, and workplace health. Suggested strategies for addressing each of the four areas are also presented below. Figure 17.1 shows the following care strategies are not the providence of either professional

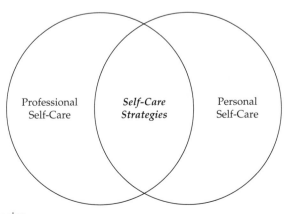

Professional Self-Care   *Self-Care Strategies*   Personal Self-Care

Figure 17.1 Care Strategies

or personal self-care, but rather appear in the eclipsed shaded areas of these overlapping circles. This describes the use of self for professional purposes.

SUGGESTED DOMAINS OF STRATEGIES

1. *Take care of your body and listen to your body's natural signals.* Our minds, hearts, and ability to empathize exist within complex interrelated molecular, neurological, and biological systems, which are vulnerable to dysfunction, but also designed to self-regulate and to self-correct. Developing personal goals to maintain healthy nutrition, adequate sleep, developing a regimen for physical exercise (or sport), scheduling regular medical check-ups, avoiding addictions, and not abusing the body are essential for optimum physical functioning (Rothschild, 2006). It is almost impossible to give ourselves to our clients when we do not have much to give, as a result of feeling acutely or chronically physically depleted. Developing strategies to stay attuned to one's physical health and knowing how your body communicates stress requires us to learn how to respond appropriately.

2. *Developing a sense of mindfulness about your thinking and feeling.* Strategies designed to address the mental and emotional aspects of stress have to do with cognitive and affective dimensions and also with professional identity, including motivation, and compassion satisfaction/dissatisfaction (Skovholt, 2001). We often fluctuate in our careers between the ends of the continuum of compassion satisfaction and compassion dissatisfaction. Our identities as social workers can be challenged based upon our experiences of being helpful; understanding the monetary dimensions of both public and private practices; aligning and realigning our expectations; retooling expectations about changes at the micro, mezzo, and macro levels; enduring early career disenchantment regarding the profession of social work; adjusting to higher case loads; inadequate salaries; and feeling unsupported (Loone, 2003). Effective self-awareness allows the social worker to determine whether any of the above are enduring and disabling enough to require examination, assessment, and change. As indicated, social workers are most vulnerable to distress during their first three years of practice, which may unfortunately encourage some to leave the profession rather early on.

Understanding the drifts in cognitions that tend toward self-deprecation, extreme negative countertransference, and negative stigmatization of clients (loss of positive regard) require attention and represent "professional acting out." Social workers must understand the basis or essence of their own negative thoughts. Some suggested strategies are to seek consultation and supervision to process their thought patterns, dissect the elements of negative countertransference, and assess the meaning of self-deprecating cognitions. The latter, as a negative thought pattern, could represent frustration with practice abilities, difficulties with a challenging client, ineffective intervention plans, etc. In all such cases, social workers need to seek consultation and learn to practice self-compassion, as a prerequisite to improving themselves as people.

One's mental health is often affected by how much input or control one may have in determining what one's work is about, and how to go about regulating and doing that work. In the professional self-care literature, a common finding noted is that social workers who feel they have some input into how their job is performed and its expectations are more likely to feel job satisfaction and less likely to feel distress, thereby preventing burnout (Newell & MacNeil, 2010). Therefore, when possible, at both the individual and organizational level, strategies should pursue increasing internal loci of control, which can be both a mediating and protective factor.

Benchmark signals of emotional exhaustion and depletion are expressed through enduring feelings of embitterment toward clients and the agency; coping by avoidance; isolation; detachment; somatization; anger; loss of empathy; and loss of passion and pride in being a social worker (Adamson, Beddoe, & Davys, 2012). These enduring affective episodes need to be examined honestly to determine how they came to be such a powerful determining presence over the social worker. Utilizing a therapist or trusted colleague will provide another set of ears and eyes for feedback. A suggested strategy here is to make an oath to yourself, namely, that you will put into words what you are feeling when distressed, and that you then will seek understanding and appropriate change. Additionally, we must recall that an overabundance of empathy in the helping relationship is not the main ingredient necessary for client change. Other factors and processes, such as strengths, assets, and client resources play a large role in producing change.

3. We all have spiritual souls: Don't be afraid to bare them. The importance of spirituality and meaning ground us existentially to our overarching motivation and to sustaining our energy in serving others. Our professional grounding here serves as a protective factor when we experience distress (McGarrigle & Walsh, 2011). We must realize that helping others can hurt, but it does not have to disable and incapacitate individuals. Accepting realistic expectations concerning yourself and your clients will potentially help guard against savior-like thinking and approaches to clients—and against the inevitable let downs in social work practice. Utilizing the strategy of engendering hope in your clients (Snyder, 2002), and practicing from a belief perspective that the human condition can always be improved, refurbishes our purpose, our altruistic drive and motivations, and our resilience in the face of adversities. This feeling of honest humanitarian giving is often our only ultimate reward.

4. Workplace Health and Stress. Working in human service organizations with marginalized clients is stressful, as we all know. Agencies push an agenda to do more with less, and to process more clients daily without offering additional resources. Now ubiquitous to all human service agencies is evaluating program outcomes with financial data (Holosko, 2006), whereby a social worker is held accountable for achieving a quota of clients served or units of services billed. This often creates a culture of "people processing" in outsourcing services or in merging agencies, which can undermine the organizational culture. Despite these realities, we must learn to persevere and endure, and not contribute to the toxicity of negative workplace environments. Here are some suggestions: parcel out the good parts of your work, reframe and redirect positive energy, not negative energy; be assertive, not aggressive when you communicate; always understand that the client is the ethical spotlight or validity check for what we do. And, finally, always "take the high ground."

Formulating clear boundaries between professional responses to clients and personal responses is a *must* for practicing professional self-care. Blurred-boundary violations often trigger the rationale for developing an initial self-care plan, and at the least serve as a wake-up call for greater self-awareness and more extensive supervision. Reviewing your work with clients each day to assess for boundary violations or boundary blurring allows for self- supervision. Seek consultation when troubled with a client, especially when you are preoccupied with the client. Inklings toward crossing boundaries must be investigated regarding their own internal motivation. Additionally, have some ready-made strategies for when to say "no," and how to say "no" to constant organizational and agency demands. These ought to be preformulated and rehearsed, because such rather difficult situations often arise unexpectedly.

The kind of pragmatic membership affiliations one has in the social work professional community, and the ways in which the workplace organization endorses and facilitates a culture of self-care will often assist in ameliorating distress. Thus, a social worker should have well-established and functional relationships with colleagues who are deemed helpful and trustworthy. This ensures that a social worker will not practice in isolation or anonymity, or avoid collegial dialogues with other social workers. In addition, talking with other colleagues can help normalize temporary distress as well as offer techniques and support, such as in peer supervision groups. Establish policies and procedures to process and debrief traumatic events. When possible, strategize to practice in a self-care friendly professional organization. If that is not possible, then strategize how to improve the self-care culture of the practice environment and organization. One frequently identified source, as evidenced in the literature, for helping with distress is the supervisory relationship (Skovholt, 2001). Thus, securing a facilitative and well-established on-site or off-site supervisor will serve as a point to address distress. Additionally, when social workers and other professionals feel they have some significant input into their work requirements and expectations, they likely will feel less isolated and estranged.

CONCLUDING REMARKS

Before developing the pragmatics of a self-care plan, which should be unique to each social worker, one must identify one's own preexisting vulnerabilities. If some are identified, then it is necessary to address those (and monitor them for toxic effects) through either supervision or personal psychotherapy. Further, one should be mindful to strive for a balance between personal and work life. After this, one should take a self-assessment for stress, distress, burnout, and compassion fatigue through using one of the measures mentioned previously and listed in the following subsection, "Resources on the Internet." Next, the real work begins— by addressing strategies used as guiding principles in the four cornerstone domains (physical health, mental/emotional health, spiritual health, and workplace health). Here is where previously mentioned techniques are developed. Each domain should also have a place for monitoring the effectiveness of the techniques, as observed. When completed, a social worker can share a plan with a colleague for critique and feedback. And, we must learn to trust and use these perspectives as valuable feedback and advice. Self-care plans are designed for long-term career use, and they should be updated annually, and revised when changing jobs or taking on additional duties. Developing a self-care plan designed to respond to urgent or emergency situations that challenge professional well-being is a wise thing. For example, having in place a network of colleagues to contact will decrease isolation.

An effective and feasible self-care plan is only as good as one is honestly aware of oneself, able to identify one's vulnerabilities and protective factors, able to assess one's work environment for professional self-care friendliness, and able and willing to use support and feedback from colleagues. We know that professional self-care plans, when implemented, help to decrease and manage job distress. Essentially, a well developed and implemented self-care plan puts the social worker in better control, rather than the other way around. This is the difference between burnout and an effective social work career and also the difference between helping and harming clients. Indeed, that is why NASW and CSWE regard professional and personal self-care as an imperative and as a required practice behavior.

RESOURCES ON THE INTERNET

The following is a first-rate, comprehensive website for students and practitioners, which contains assessment tools, self care planning, and other resources developed at the School of Social Work at the University of Buffalo. http://www.socialwork.buffalo.edu/students/self-care/

The following represents the NASW policy on self-care. http://www.naswdc.org/nasw/memberlink/2009/supportfiles/ProfessionalSelf-Care.pdf

The following contains the Maslach Burnout Inventory and the Areas of Worklife Survey. http://www.naswdc.org/nasw/memberlink/2009/supportfiles/ProfessionalSelf-Care.pdf

The following website offers a multitude of information regarding delivering trauma-informed and disaster services and standards for self-care. http://www.greencross.org/

The following resource-rich website contains these self tests: Compassion Satisfaction, Compassion Fatigue, Life Stress tests, and the Professional Quality of Life self tests. http://www.compassionfatigue.org/pages/selftest.html

The following Standards of Self Care is taken from the Green Cross organization, which serves professionals practicing with trauma and disasters. http://www.greencross.org/index.php?option=com_content&view=article&id=184&Itemi d=124

References

Adamson, C., Beddoe, L., & Davys, A. (2012). Building resilient practitioners: Definitions and practitioner understandings. *British Journal of Social Work, 32,* 1–20. doi: 10.1093/bjsw/bcs142.

Beckett, J. O. (2008). *Lifting our voices: The journeys into family caregiving of professional social workers.* New York, NY: Columbia University Press.

Bride, B. E. (2007). Prevalence of secondary traumatic stress among social workers. *Social Work, 52,* 63–70.

Bride, B., Radey, M., & Figley, C. (2007). Measuring compassion fatigue. *Clinical Social Work Journal, 35,* 155–163.

Council on Social Work Education (CSWE). (2008). Educational Policy and Accreditation Standards. Retrieved from www.cswe.org.

Cox, K., & Steiner, S. (2013). *Self-care in social work: a guide for practitioners, supervisors, and administrators.* Washington, DC: NASW Press.

Figley, C. (Ed.). (1995).*Compassion fatigue: Coping with secondary traumatic stress disorder in those who treat the traumatized.* New York, NY: Brunnel/Mazel Publishers.

Gillespie, D. F. (Ed.). (1987). *Burnout among social workers.* New York, NY: Haworth Press.

Holland, J. (1992). *Making vocational choices: A theory of vocational personalities and work environment*. Odessa, FL: Psychological Assessment Resources.

Holosko, M. (2006). Why don't social workers make better child welfare workers than non-social workers? *Research on Social Work Practice, 16*(4), 426–430.

Judge, T., Heller, D., & Mount, M. (2002). Five factor model of personality and job satisfaction: A meta-analysis. *Journal of Applied Psychology, 87*(3), 530–541.

Lee, J., & Miller, S. (2013). A self-care framework for social workers; building a strong foundation for practice. *Families in Society, 94*(2), 95–103.

Leiter, M. P., & Maslach, C. (2005). *Banishing burnout: Six strategies for improving your relationship with work*. San Francisco, CA: Jossey-Bass.

Loone, B. (2003). Social workers and human service practitioners. In M. Dollard, A. Winefield, & M. Winefield (Eds.), *Occupational stress in the service professions* (pp. 281–310). London: Taylor and Francis.

Lopez, A. (2007, July 20). *Professional self-care & social work*. Opening keynote address, NASW Texas Chapter, Leadership Institute, Austin.

McGarrigle, T & Walsh, C. (2011). Mindfulness, self-care, and wellness in social work: Effects of contemplative training. *Journal of Religion & Spirituality in Social Work: Social Thought, 30*(3), 212–233.

Maslach, C. (2003). *Burnout: The cost of caring*. Cambridge, MA: Malor Books.

Maslach, C., Jackson, S. E., & Leiter, M. P. (1996). *Maslach Burnout Inventory Manual* (3rd ed.). Palo Alto, CA: Consulting Psychologists Press, Inc.

Moore, S., Perry, A., Bledsoe, L., & Robinson, M. (2011). Social work students and self-care: a model assignment for teaching. *Journal of Social Work Teaching, 47*(3), 545–553.

Morales, A., & Schaefor, B. (1989). *Social work: A profession of many faces* (5th ed.). Boston, MA: Allyn & Bacon.

National Association of Social Workers (NASW). (2009). *Professional self-care & social work policy statement in Social Work Speaks: National Association of Social Workers Policy Statements 2009–2112* (8th ed.). Washington, DC: NASW Press.

National Association of Social Workers. (2008). NASW Code of Ethics. Retrieved from http://www.social-workers.org/pubs/code/code.asp.

Newell, J., & MacNeil, A. (2010). Professional burnout, vicarious trauma, secondary traumatic stress, and compassion fatigue: A review of theoretical terms, risk factors, and preventive methods for clinicians and researchers. *Best Practices in Mental Health, 6*(2), 57–68. Chicago, IL: Lyceum Books.

Norcross, J. C. (2000). Psychotherapist self-care: Practitioner tested, research-informed strategies. *Professional Psychology: Research and Practice, 31*, 710–713.

Pines, A., & Maslach, C. (1978). Characteristics of staff burnout in a mental health setting. *Hospital and Community Psychiatry, 29*, 233–237.

Reamer, F. (1992). The impaired social worker. *Social Work, 37*(2), 165–171.

Rothschild, B. (2006). *Help for the helper: the psychophysiology of compassion fatigue and vicarious trauma*. New York, NY: Norton.

Saakvitne, K. W., & Pearlman, L. A. (1996). *Transforming the pain: A workbook on vicarious traumatization for helping professionals who work with traumatized clients*. New York, NY: W.W. Norton and Company.

Siegfried, C. B. (2008). Child welfare and secondary traumatic stress. Retrieved from http:www.ntctsnet.org/nccts/asset.do?id=1332.

Skovholt, T. M. (2001).*The resilient practitioner: Burnout prevention and self-care strategies for counselors, therapists, teachers, and health professionals*. Boston, MA: Allyn & Bacon.

Snyder, C. (2002). Hope theory: rainbows in the mind. *Psychological Inquiry, 13*(4), 249–275.

Stamm, B. (2009). *The concise ProQOL manual*. Pocatello, ID: Retrieved from ProQOl.org at http://www.proqol.org/Home_Page.php.

Stamm, B. (2002). Measuring compassion satisfaction as well as fatigue: Developmental history of the Compassion Satisfaction and Fatigue Test. In Charles R. Figley (Ed.), *Treating compassion fatigue. Psychosocial stress series*, No. 24 (pp. 107–119). New York, NY: Brunner-Routledge.

Stamm, B. (Ed.). (1999). *Secondary traumatic stress, self-care issues for clinicians, researchers & educators*. Baltimore, MD: Sidran Press.

PART III

Social Work Values, Ethics, and Licensing Standards

18   Ethical Issues in Social Work

Frederic G. Reamer

ETHICAL DILEMMAS

Social workers encounter a wide range of ethical issues. Most such issues in the profession are routine and relatively straightforward. For example, social workers know that ordinarily they must obtain clients' consent before releasing confidential information, respect clients' right to self-determination, and obey the law. Sometimes, however, such common duties conflict with one another; when faced with these ethical dilemmas, social workers must decide which of their conflicting obligations should take precedence (Banks, 2012; Barsky, 2009; Congress, 1999; Dolgoff, Loewenberg, & Harrington, 2012; Reamer, 2013; Strom-Gottfried, 2007). For example, social workers' obligation to respect clients' right to self-determination may conflict with social workers' duty to protect third parties from harm. Social workers' duty to obey the law may conflict with their duty to challenge unjust legal policies and regulations.

Ethical dilemmas in social work take many forms. Some involve direct or clinical practice—that is, the delivery of services to individuals, families, couples, and small groups. Others involve community practice, administration, advocacy, social action, social policy, research and evaluation, relationships with colleagues, and professional education (Reamer, 2001a, 2006, 2009, 2012a). The most common involve actual or potential conflicts among social workers' duties involving the following.

Client Confidentiality and Privileged Communication

Social workers must be clear about the nature of their obligation to respect clients' right to confidentiality and exceptions to this obligation. Ethical dilemmas occur when social workers must decide whether to disclose confidential information without client consent or against a client's wishes (Dickson, 1998; Reamer, 2003, 2013). This can occur, for example, when a client threatens to seriously harm a third party, seriously injure him- or herself, or abuses or neglects a child or elderly individual. Ethical dilemmas involving privileged communication occur when social workers are asked to disclose confidential information in the context of legal proceedings (for instance, when a client's estranged spouse requests confidential clinical records as part of a child custody dispute).

The emergence of digital and other electronic technology has created new confidentiality challenges for social workers. Practitioners must ensure that their digital, online, and other electronic communications with clients (e.g., e-mail, video conferencing, text messaging communications) protect client confidentiality and adhere to strict ethical and legal standards.

Client Self-determination and Professional Paternalism

It is widely accepted among social workers that clients ordinarily have a fundamental right to self-determination. However, ethical dilemmas arise in exceptional circumstances when, in the social workers' professional judgment, clients' actions or potential actions pose a serious, foreseeable, and imminent risk to themselves or others. In these instances, social workers must decide whether to limit clients' right to self-determination.

Limiting clients' right to self-determination to protect them from harm is called *paternalism*.

Paternalism can occur in several forms, such as withholding information from clients, misleading or lying to clients, or coercing clients. Whether paternalism is morally justifiable in any given situation—for example, misleading a client about her grim medical prognosis or placing a mentally ill homeless person in a psychiatric hospital against his wishes—is often controversial.

Laws, Policies, and Regulations

Ordinarily, social workers should uphold relevant laws, policies, and regulations. Such compliance is important to the smooth functioning of human service organizations and the broader society. Circumstances may arise, however, when ethical obligations conflict with laws, policies, and regulations. In such cases, social workers must take assertive steps to resolve such conflicts, perhaps through consultation, mediation, lobbying, and other forms of advocacy and social action. On occasion, social workers may be faced with difficult decisions of conscience concerning the obligation to comply with what they believe to be unjust laws, policies, and regulations.

Conflicts of Interest and Boundary Issues

Conflicts of interest occur when a social worker's services to or relationship with a client is compromised or might be compromised because of decisions or actions in relation to another client, a colleague, him- or herself, or some other third party. Many conflicts of interest involve boundary issues or dual or multiple relationships. Boundary issues occur when social workers establish and maintain more than one relationship with clients (for example, when a social worker socializes with a client, discloses personal information to clients, or enters into a business partnership with a client). Dual or multiple relationships can occur simultaneously or consecutively (Reamer, 2006, 2012a).

Some dual and multiple relationships are patently unethical—for example, if a social worker maintains a sexual relationship with a client or borrows money from a client. Other dual and multiple relationships are more ambiguous and require careful analysis and consultation. Examples include social workers in rural communities who cannot avoid contact with clients in the supermarket or recreational settings, social workers who are invited by clients to attend an important life event, social workers' relationships with former clients, and social workers' unanticipated encounters with clients at an Alcoholics Anonymous meeting when both parties are in recovery. Social workers' and clients' use of digital social networking sites—such as Facebook and LinkedIn—has created new boundary-related challenges. Social workers must ensure that their online relationships with clients adhere to strict ethical standards with regard to unprofessional contact and practitioner self-disclosure.

Nontraditional and Unorthodox Services and Interventions

Ethical dilemmas sometimes arise when social workers consider providing nontraditional and unorthodox services and interventions that are not part of customary social work education. On the one hand, services and interventions that are not grounded in sound theory or for which there is little or no empirical evidence of effectiveness can pose significant risks to clients. On the other hand, it is important for social workers to be receptive to innovative forms of practice.

The advent of online, remote, and distance counseling has created new ethical challenges. Some social workers now provide digital and online services to clients they never meet in person. These services expand clients' opportunities to receive help, especially when clients live in remote locations or find travel to an office difficult because of a disability. At the same time, these novel services pose significant risks related to quality control, protection of client confidentiality, and informed consent (Reamer, 2012b, in press).

Professional and Personal Values

Social workers sometimes find that their personal values clash with traditional social work values or the official positions of employers or other organizations with which they are affiliated professionally. This can occur, for example, when practitioners object to their employers' political views or positions on important public policy issues, such as reproductive rights, immigration rights, or welfare reform. Social workers may also find that their personal values conflict with those of their clients. This can occur when clients engage in illegal activity or behavior that seems immoral (for example, engaging in an extramarital affair or drug dealing). Reconciling these values-related conflicts can be difficult.

Scarce and Limited Resources

Social workers often are responsible for distributing resources, such as administrative funds, shelter beds, client stipends, and mental health services. In many instances, they struggle to locate and obtain sufficient resources and must make difficult decisions about how best to allocate available resources. When making these decisions, social workers must choose which allocation criteria to use (for example, whether to distribute resources equally among eligible parties, based on first-come first-served, or based on demonstrated need or affirmative action guidelines).

Managed Care

The pervasive influence of managed care—policies designed to enhance fiscal responsibility and cost containment in health care and human services—has created many difficult ethical dilemmas for social workers (Corcoran & Vandiver, 1996). Strict funding guidelines, reimbursement policies, and utilization review have forced social workers to make difficult ethical judgments about serving clients whose insurance benefits have run out; providing inadequate services to clients with complex problems; and exposing clients to privacy and confidentiality risks as a result of sharing information with managed care staff.

Whistle-blowing

There are times when social workers may be obligated to alert people or organizations in positions of authority to colleagues' unethical behavior or impairment (Bullis, 1995; Jayaratne, Croxton, & Mattison, 1997). Decisions about whether to blow the whistle on a colleague are very difficult. Social workers generally understand that their obligation to protect clients and the public from unethical or impaired colleagues may require such action, but they also understand that whistle-blowing can have serious, harmful repercussions for colleagues whose behavior is reported to state licensing boards, the National Association of Social Workers (NASW), or employers. Whistle-blowing can also pose some risk to the individuals who report collegial

misconduct or impairment; this is also a relevant consideration. See Chapter 22 on the impaired social work professional, and Chapter 19 on whistle-blowers for more detailed information.

Evaluation and Research

Many social service agencies involve clients in evaluation or research activities (such as clinical research, needs assessments, and program evaluations). Ethical issues can arise when, for example, social work researchers decide whether to withhold potentially valuable services from clients who have been assigned to a control group as opposed to an experimental (intervention) group, whether to disclose confidential information revealed in a research interview that suggests the respondent has harmed a third party, whether to interview a respondent whose capacity to sign an informed consent form is questionable, and whether any form of deception is justifiable in social work evaluation and research (for instance, concealing the true purpose of a study to avoid influencing respondents and contaminating the results). The advent of institutional review boards (IRBs) to protect research participants has helped social workers and others address these difficult questions, although simple answers are not always possible.

ETHICAL DECISION MAKING

In the late 1970s, social workers began to explore the ways practitioners make ethical decisions and attempt to resolve ethical dilemmas. This development also occurred in many other professions during this period. Although discussions of ethics and values have taken place since the profession's formal beginning in the late 19th century, deliberate, systematic discussion of ethical decision-making strategies is more recent.

Social work, like most professions, has developed protocols to help practitioners make difficult ethical decisions when they encounter ethical dilemmas (Barsky, 2009; Congress, 1999; Dolgoff, Loewenberg, & Harrington, 2012; Reamer, 1990, 2013; Strom-Gottfried, 2007). Most of these protocols include an outline of steps that practitioners can follow to approach ethical dilemmas systematically, drawing especially on ethical theory; relevant professional literature; codes of ethics; statutes, regulations, public policies, and agency policies; and consultation. For example, one such model entails seven steps (Reamer, 2013; also see Barsky, 2009; Congress, 1999; and Dolgoff, Loewenberg, & Harrington, 2012):

1. Identify the ethical issues, including the social work values and duties that conflict.
2. Identify the individuals, groups, and organizations who are likely to be affected by the ethical decision.
3. Tentatively identify all possible courses of action and the participants involved in each, along with possible benefits and risks for each.
4. Thoroughly examine the reasons in favor of and opposed to each possible course of action, considering relevant ethical theories, principles, and guidelines; codes of ethics and legal principles; social work practice theory and principles; and personal values (including religious, cultural, and ethnic values and political ideology), particularly those that conflict with one's own.
5. Consult with colleagues and appropriate experts (such as agency staff, supervisors, agency administrators, ethics scholars, ethics committees, and, if there are pertinent legal issues, attorneys).
6. Make the decision and document the decision-making process.
7. Monitor, evaluate, and document the decision.

Some of the elements of this process require specialized knowledge and skill. For example, social workers should be familiar with ethical theories, principles, and guidelines related to professional practice. Most discussions of ethical theory in the profession's literature focus on what are commonly known as theories of normative ethics. Theories of normative ethics are typically divided into two main schools of thought: *deontological* and *teleological* (including *consequentialist* and *utilitarian* theories). Deontological theories (from the Greek *deontos*, "of the obligatory") claim that certain actions are inherently right or wrong as a matter of fundamental principle. From a strict deontological perspective, for example, social workers should always obey the law and regulations, even when they think that violating a law or regulation is in a client's best interest. From this point of view, social workers should always tell the truth and should always keep their promises to their clients, no matter how harmful the consequences may be.

In contrast, teleological (from the Greek *teleios*, "brought to its end or purpose") or consequentialist theories assert that ethical decisions should be based on social workers' assessment of which action will produce the most favorable outcome or consequences. According to the most popular teleological perspective, utilitarianism, ethical choices should be based on thorough assessments of what will produce the greatest good for the greatest number (positive utilitarianism) or the least harm (negative utilitarianism).

More recently, social workers and other professionals have broadened their application of ethical theory to include so-called virtue ethics and the ethics of care. According to virtue ethics, professionals' ethical judgments should be guided by certain core virtues, such as kindness, generosity, courage, integrity, respectfulness, justice, prudence, and compassion (MacIntyre, 2007). The ethics of care, which is related to virtue ethics, was developed mainly by feminist writers (Baier, 1995; Held, 1993, 2007). According to this view, men tend to think in masculine terms, such as justice and autonomy, whereas women think in feminine terms, such as caring. Proponents of the ethics of care argue that professionals should change how they view morality and the virtues, placing more emphasis on virtues exemplified by women, such as taking care of others, patience, the ability to nurture, and self-sacrifice.

These diverse philosophical perspectives are commonly used to analyze ethical dilemmas from different conceptual viewpoints. Thus, a deontologist might argue that social workers should always comply with child abuse and neglect reporting laws—because "the law is the law"—whereas a teleologically oriented practitioner might argue that social workers' compliance with these mandatory reporting laws should be based on their assessment of the likely consequences—that is, whether complying with the law will produce the greatest good or minimize harm to the greatest possible extent. A social worker who embraces virtue theory would be guided by his or her interpretation of the relevance of core virtues, such as autonomy, beneficence, compassion for clients, respect for human dignity, and justice (Beauchamp & Childress, 2012).

Social workers and others disagree about the strengths and limitations of these different philosophical perspectives. Nonetheless, there is general agreement that it is helpful for practitioners to examine ethical dilemmas using these different vantage points to identify, grapple with, and critically assess all pertinent dimensions of the ethical dilemmas they encounter.

Social workers also need to be familiar with updated and increasingly sophisticated professional codes of ethics, especially the current NASW *Code of Ethics* (Reamer, 2013). This is only the third code in NASW's history and reflects remarkable changes over time in social workers' understanding of and approach to ethical issues.

The first section of the code, the preamble, summarizes the mission and core values of social work. For the first time in NASW's history, the association has adopted and published in the code a formally sanctioned mission statement and an explicit summary of the profession's core values. These help distinguish social work from other helping professions, particularly with respect to social work's enduring commitment to enhancing human well-being and helping meet basic human needs, empowering clients, serving people who are vulnerable and oppressed, addressing individual well-being in a social context, promoting social justice and social change, and strengthening sensitivity to cultural and ethnic diversity.

The second section, "Purpose of the NASW Code of Ethics," provides an overview of the code's main functions, including identifying the core values, summarizing broad ethical principles that reflect these values, and specific ethical standards for the profession, helping social workers identify ethical issues and dilemmas, providing the public with ethical standards it can use to hold the profession accountable, orienting new practitioners, and articulating guidelines that the profession itself can use to enforce ethical standards among its members. This section also highlights resources social workers can use when they face ethical issues and decisions.

The third section, "Ethical Principles," presents six broad principles that inform social work practice, one for each of the six core values cited in the preamble (service, social justice, dignity and worth of the person, importance of human relationships, integrity, and competence).

The final and most detailed section, "Ethical Standards," includes 155 specific ethical standards to guide social workers' conduct and provide a basis for adjudication of ethics complaints filed against social workers. (The code, or portions of it, is also used by many state licensing boards charged with reviewing complaints filed against licensed social workers and by courts of law that oversee litigation involving alleged social worker negligence or misconduct.) The standards are grouped into six categories concerning ethical responsibilities to clients, to colleagues, in practice settings, as professionals, to the profession, and to the broader society. The code addresses many topics and issues that were not mentioned in the NASW's first two codes (1960 and 1979), including limitations of clients' right to self-determination (e.g., when clients threaten harm to themselves or others), confidentiality issues involving use of electronic media to transmit information, storage and disposal of client records, case recording and documentation, sexual contact with former clients, sexual relationships with clients' relatives and close personal acquaintances, counseling of former sexual partners, physical contact with clients, dual and multiple relationships with supervisees, sexual harassment, use of derogatory language, bartering arrangements with clients, cultural competence, labor-management disputes, and evaluation of practice. Although codes of ethics cannot provide simple, unequivocal solutions to all complex ethical dilemmas, they often provide sound conceptual guidance about important issues to consider when making difficult ethical judgments.

In addition to consulting the code, social workers can access professional ethics consultants, institutional ethics committees, and IRBs. Ethics consultation is now very common in health care settings and is increasingly available in other settings. Typically, ethics consultants are formally educated ethicists (usually moral philosophers who have experience working with professionals or professionals who have obtained formal ethics education) who provide advice on specific ethical issues that arise in practice settings. These consultants can help social workers and other staff identify pertinent ethical issues; assess ethical dilemmas; acquaint staff with relevant ethics concepts, literature, and other resources (such as codes of ethics, policies, statutes, regulations); and make difficult ethical choices.

Institutional ethics committees formally emerged in 1976, when the New Jersey Supreme Court ruled that Karen Ann Quinlan's family and physicians should consult an ethics committee in deciding whether to remove her from life-support technology (a number of hospitals have had panels resembling ethics committees since at least the 1920s). Ethics committees often include social workers as members, along with representatives from various disciplines found in health care and human service settings, such as nurses, physicians, clergy, allied health professionals, and administrators. Some committees include a lawyer, although the lawyer might not be an employee of the agency to avoid a conflict of interest (Aulisio, Arnold, & Youngner, 2003).

Most ethics committees focus on providing case consultation in the form of nonbinding advice. These committees make themselves available to agency staff, clients, and sometimes family members for consultation about challenging ethical issues. Many ethics committees also take steps to examine, draft, and critique ethics-related policies that affect agencies and their employees and clients. In addition, these committees may sponsor ethics-related educational events, such as in-service training, symposia, workshops, conferences, and what have become known as "ethics grand rounds" (Reamer, 1998, 1999, 2001b).

Social workers employed in settings that conduct research may be involved in IRBs. IRBs (sometimes known as a research ethics board or committee on the use of human participants in research) became popular in the 1970s as a result of increasing national interest in research and evaluation and concern about exploitation of research participants. All organizations and agencies that receive federal funds for research are required to have an IRB review the ethical aspects of proposals for research involving human participants.

Social workers' understanding of ethical issues has matured greatly. Literature on the subject, professional education, and in-service training have burgeoned. To practice competently, contemporary professionals must have a firm grasp of pertinent issues related to ethical dilemmas and ethical decision making. This knowledge enhances social workers' ability to protect clients and fulfill social work's critically important, values-based mission.

WEBSITES

American Board of Examiners in Clinical Social Work, Code of Ethics. http://www.abecsw.org/about-code-ethics.html

Association of Social Work Boards; approved ethics continuing education options. http://www.aswb.org/

Clinical Social Work Association, Code of Ethics. http://www.clinicalsocialworkassociation.org/about-us/ethics-code

International Federation of Social Workers: Statement of Ethical Principles. http://ifsw.org/policies/statement-of-ethical-principles/

National Association of Social Workers, Code of Ethics. http://www.socialworkers.org/pubs/code/code.asp

References

Aulisio, M., Arnold, R., & Youngner, S. (Eds.). (2003). *Ethics consultation: From theory to practice*. Baltimore, MD: Johns Hopkins University Press.

Baier, A. (1995). *Moral prejudices: Essays on ethics*. Cambridge, MA: Harvard University Press.

Banks, S. (2012). *Ethics and values in social work* (4th ed.). Basingstoke, Hampshire: Palgrave Macmillan.

Barsky, A. (2009). *Ethics and values in social work*. New York, NY: Oxford University Press.

Beauchamp, T., & Childress, J. (2012). *Principles of biomedical ethics* (7th ed.). New York, NY: Oxford University Press.

Bullis, R. K. (1995). *Clinical social worker misconduct*. Chicago, IL: Nelson-Hall.

Congress, E. (1999). *Social work values and ethics*. Belmont, CA: Wadsworth.

Corcoran, K., & Vandiver, V. (1996). *Maneuvering the maze of managed care: Skills for mental health professionals*. New York, NY: Free Press.

Dickson, D. T. (1998). *Confidentiality and privacy in social work*. New York, NY: Free Press.

Dolgoff, R., Loewenberg, F., & Harrington, D. (2012). *Ethical decisions for social work practice* (9th ed.). Belmont, CA: Brooks/Cole.

Held, V. (1993). *Feminist morality: Transforming culture, society, and politics*. Chicago, IL: University of Chicago Press.

Held, V. (2007). *The ethics of care: Personal, political, global*. New York, NY: Oxford University Press.

Jayaratne, S., Croxton, D., & Mattison, D. (1997). Social work professional standards: An exploratory study. *Social Work, 42*(2), 187–199.

MacIntyre, A. (2007). *After virtue: A study in moral theory* (3rd ed.). Notre Dame, IN: University of Notre Dame Press.

Reamer, F. G. (1990). *Ethical dilemmas in social service* (2nd ed.). New York, NY: Columbia University Press.

Reamer, F. G. (2001a). *The social work ethics audit: A risk management tool*. Washington, DC: NASW Press.

Reamer, F. G. (2001b). *Ethics education in social work*. Alexandria, VA: Council on Social Work Education.

Reamer, F. G. (2003). *Social work malpractice and liability: Strategies for prevention* (2nd ed.). New York, NY: Columbia University Press.

Reamer, F. G. (2006). *Ethical standards in social work: A review of the NASW Code of Ethics* (2nd ed.). Washington, DC: NASW Press.

Reamer, F. G. (2009). *The social work ethics casebook: Cases and commentary.* Washington, DC: NASW Press.

Reamer, F. G. (2012a). *Boundary issues and dual relationships in the human services.* New York, NY: Columbia University Press.

Reamer, F. G. (2012b). The digital and electronic revolution in social work: Rethinking the meaning of ethical practice. *Ethics and Social Welfare, 7,* 2–19 available at: http://www.tandfonline.com/doi/abs/10.1080/17496535.2012.738694

Reamer, F. G. (2013). *Social work values and ethics* (4th ed.). New York, NY: Columbia University Press.

Reamer, F. G. (in press). Social work in a digital age: Ethical and risk-management challenges. *Social Work.*

Strom-Gottfried, K. (2007). *Straight talk about professional ethics.* Chicago, IL: Lyceum.

19   Risk Management in Social Work

Frederic G. Reamer

Service delivery is also accompanied by risks and consequences, such as litigation. To protect clients and related third parties and minimize risk, social workers need to be informed about prevailing standards to prevent ethics complaints and ethics-related lawsuits. Ethics complaints—filed with social work licensing boards or with professional organizations, such as the National Association of Social Workers (NASW)—typically allege that social workers violated widely accepted ethical standards in their relationships with clients, colleagues, employers, or other parties. Ethics-related lawsuits typically claim that social workers were negligent, in the strict legal sense, by virtue of their mishandling of some ethics-related phenomenon, such as processing confidential information or informed consent, maintenance of professional boundaries, use of controversial treatment techniques, conflicts of interest, or termination of services (Reamer, 2003, 2006, 2013a).

THE NATURE OF RISK MANAGEMENT

Social workers expose themselves to risk when they practice in a manner that is inconsistent with prevailing professional standards (Houston-Vega, Nuehring, & Daguio, 1997; Reamer, 2003; Strom-Gottfried, 2000, 2003). Some ethics complaints arise out of mistakes and oversights. Examples include social workers who forget to document important clinical information in a client's case record, inadvertently disclose sensitive personal information to a client in a Facebook posting, or fail to protect confidential information transmitted via fax. Other complaints and lawsuits arise from social workers' deliberate ethical decisions—for example, when social workers attempt to manage complex boundaries in their relationships with clients in rural communities, disclose confidential information without clients' consent to law enforcement or child protective services officials, or terminate services to a noncompliant client. In addition, some complaints and lawsuits are the result of practitioners' ethical misconduct, such as sexual relationships with clients or fraudulent billing for services.

Social workers can be held accountable for negligence and ethical violations in several ways. In addition to filing lawsuits, parties can file ethics complaints with the NASW or with state licensing and regulatory boards. In some instances, social workers are also subject to review by other professional organizations to which they belong, such as the American Board of Examiners in Clinical Social Work, Clinical Social Work Association, and American Association for Marriage and Family Therapy. In exceptional circumstances, criminal charges may be filed (for example, based on allegations of sexual misconduct or fraudulent billing of an insurance company or state funding agency).

Ethics complaints filed against NASW members are processed using a peer review model that includes NASW members and, initially, the National Ethics Committee. If a request for professional review is accepted by the National Ethics Committee, a NASW Chapter Ethics Committee (or the National Ethics Committee in special circumstances) conducts a hearing during which the complainant (the person filing the complaint), the respondent (the person against whom the complaint is filed), and witnesses have an opportunity to testify. After hearing all parties and discussing the testimony, the committee presents a report to elected chapter officers that summarizes its findings and presents recommendations. Recommendations may include sanctions or various forms of corrective action, such as suspension from NASW, mandated supervision or consultation, censure in the form of a letter, or instructions to send the complainant a letter of apology. In some cases, the sanction may be publicized through local and national NASW newsletters or newspapers. NASW also offers mediation in some cases in an effort to avoid formal adjudication, particularly involving matters that do not involve allegations of extreme misconduct. If complainants and respondents agree to mediate the dispute, NASW facilitates the process.

State legislatures also empower social work licensing boards to process ethics complaints filed against social workers who hold a license (in some states the boards are interdisciplinary, including social work and allied helping professions). Ordinarily these boards appoint a panel of colleagues to review the complaint and, when warranted, conduct a formal investigation and hearing (some state boards include public members in addition to professional colleagues).

Negligence claims or lawsuits filed against social workers typically allege that they engaged in malpractice in that they failed to adhere to specific standards of care. The standard of care is based on what ordinary, reasonable, prudent practitioners with the same or similar training would have done under the same or similar circumstances (Glannon, 2010; Madden, 1998; Woody, 1996). Departures from the profession's standards of care may result from a social worker's acts of commission or acts of omission. Acts of commission can occur as a result of misfeasance (the commission of a proper act in a wrongful or injurious manner or the improper performance of an act that might have been performed lawfully) or malfeasance (the commission of a wrongful or unlawful act). An example of misfeasance is disclosing confidential information improperly; an example of malfeasance is fraudulent billing for services that the social worker did not provide. An act of omission, or nonfeasance, occurs when a social worker fails to perform certain duties that ought to have been performed. An example of nonfeasance is failure to document clinical services or inform clients of exceptions to their confidentiality rights.

Lawsuits and liability claims that allege malpractice are civil suits, in contrast to criminal proceedings. Ordinarily, civil suits are based on tort or contract law, with plaintiffs (the party bringing the lawsuit) seeking some sort of compensation for injuries they claim to have incurred as a result of the practitioner's negligence. These injuries may be economic (for example, lost wages or medical expenses), physical (for example, following a sexual relationship between a practitioner and client), or emotional (for example, depression suffered by a client who did not receive competent care from a practitioner).

As in criminal trials, defendants in civil lawsuits are presumed innocent until proven otherwise. In ordinary civil suits, defendants will be found liable for their actions based on the legal standard of preponderance of the evidence, as opposed to the stricter standard of proof beyond a reasonable doubt used in criminal trials. In some civil cases—for example, those involving contract disputes—the court may expect clear and convincing evidence, a standard of proof that is greater than preponderance of the evidence but less than proof beyond a reasonable doubt.

In general, malpractice occurs when evidence exists that (1) at the time of the alleged malpractice a legal duty existed between the social worker and the client; (2) the social worker was derelict in that duty or breached the duty, either by commission or omission; (3) the client suffered some harm or injury; and (4) the harm or injury was directly and proximately caused by the social worker's dereliction or breach of duty.

In some cases, prevailing standards of care are relatively easy to establish through citations of the profession's literature and practice standards, expert testimony, statutory or regulatory language, or relevant codes of ethics standards. Examples include standards concerning sexual relationships with current clients, disclosing confidential information to protect children who may have been abused or neglected, fraudulent billing, or falsified clinical records. In other cases, however, social workers disagree about standards of care (Austin, Moline, & Williams, 1990; Haas & Malouf, 2005). This may occur in cases involving controversial treatment methods or ambiguous clinical or administrative circumstances (Reamer, 2013a).

KEY RISKS IN SOCIAL WORK

Social workers' prevention efforts should focus on a number of risk areas (Reamer, 2001b, 2006). These include the following.

Client Rights

Especially since the 1960s, social workers have developed a keen understanding of a wide range of clients' rights, many of which were established by legislation or court ruling. These include rights related to confidentiality and privacy, release of information, informed consent, access to services, use of the least restrictive alternative, refusal of treatment, options for alternative services, access to records, termination of services, and grievance procedures.

Confidentiality, Privileged Communication, and Privacy

Social workers must understand the nature of clients' right to confidentiality and exceptions to these rights. More specifically, social workers should have sound policies and procedures in place related to:

- Solicitation of private information from clients
- Disclosure of confidential information to protect clients from self-harm and protect third parties from harm inflicted by clients

- Release of confidential information pertaining to alcohol and substance abuse assessment or treatment
- Disclosure of information about deceased clients
- Release of information to parents and guardians of minor clients
- Sharing of confidential information among participants in family, couples, and group counseling
- Disclosure of confidential information to media representatives, law enforcement officials, protective service agencies, other social service organizations, and collection agencies
- Protection of confidential written and electronic records, information transmitted to other parties through the use of computers, e-mail, fax machines, phones, and other electronic technology
- Transfer or disposal of clients' records
- Protection of client confidentiality in the event of a social worker's death, disability, or employment termination
- Precautions to prevent discussion of confidential information in public or semi-public areas, such as hallways, waiting rooms, elevators, and restaurants
- Disclosure of confidential information to third-party payers
- Disclosure of confidential information to consultants
- Disclosure of confidential information for teaching or training purposes
- Protection of confidential and privileged information during legal proceedings (e.g., divorce proceedings, custody disputes, paternity cases, criminal trials, and negligence lawsuits).

To protect clients and minimize risk, social workers should discuss with clients and other interested parties the nature of confidentiality and limitations of clients' right to confidentiality (Dickson, 1998; Fisher, 2013; Polowy & Gorenberg, 1997). Depending on the setting, these topics can include

- The importance of confidentiality in the social worker–client relationship (a brief statement of why the social worker treats the subject of confidentiality so seriously)
- Laws, ethical standards, and regulations pertaining to confidentiality (relevant federal,

state, and local laws and regulations; ethical standards in social work)

- Measures the social worker will take to protect clients' confidentiality (storing records in a secure location, limiting colleagues' and outside parties' access to records)
- Circumstances in which the social worker would be obligated to disclose confidential information (e.g., to comply with mandatory reporting laws or a court order, to protect a third party from harm or the client from self-injury)
- Procedures that will be used to obtain clients' informed consent for the release of confidential information and any exceptions to this (a summary of the purpose and importance of and the steps involved in informed consent)
- The procedures for sharing information with colleagues for consultation, supervision, and coordination of services (a summary of the roles of consultation and supervision, and coordination of services and why confidential information might be shared)
- Access that third-party payers (insurers) or employers will have to clients' records (policy for sharing information with managed care organizations, insurance companies, insurance company representatives, utilization review personnel, employers, and staff of employee assistance programs)
- Disclosure of confidential information by phone, computer, fax machine, e-mail, and the Internet
- Access to agency facilities and clients by outside parties (e.g., people who come to the agency to attend meetings or participate in a tour)
- Audiotaping and videotaping of clients.

Informed Consent

Informed consent is required in a variety of circumstances, including release of confidential information, program admission, service delivery and treatment, videotaping, and audiotaping (Berg, Appelbaum, Parker, & Lidz, 2001; Miller & Wertheimer, 2010). Although various courts, state legislatures, and agencies have somewhat different interpretations and applications of informed consent standards, there is considerable agreement about the key elements that social workers and agencies should incorporate into consent procedures (for example, that clients should be given specific details about the purposes of the consent, a verbal explanation, information about their rights to refuse consent and withdraw consent, information about alternative treatment options, and an opportunity to ask questions about the consent process).

Service Delivery

Social workers must provide services and represent themselves as competent only within the boundaries of their education, training, license, certification, consultation received, supervised experience, or other relevant professional experience. They should provide services in substantive areas and use practice approaches and techniques that are new to them only after engaging in appropriate study, training, consultation, and supervision from people who are already competent in those practice approaches, interventions, and techniques. Social workers who use practice approaches and interventions for which there are no generally recognized standards should obtain appropriate education, training, consultation, and supervision.

Digital and Online Technology

Digital, online, and other electronic technology have transformed the nature of social work practice. Contemporary social workers can provide services to clients using online counseling, telephone counseling, video counseling, cybertherapy (avatar therapy), self-guided Web-based interventions, electronic social networks, e-mail, and text messages. The introduction of diverse digital, online, and other forms of electronic social services has created a wide range of complex ethical and related risk-management issues. Compelling ethical issues pertain to practitioner competence; client privacy and confidentiality; informed consent; conflicts of interest; boundaries and dual relationships; consultation and client referral; termination and interruption of services; and documentation (Reamer, 2012, 2013a).

Boundary Issues, Dual Relationships, and Conflicts of Interest

Social workers should establish clear policies, practices, and procedures to ensure proper boundaries related to:

- Sexual relationships with current and former clients
- Counseling former sexual partners
- Sexual relationships with clients' relatives or acquaintances
- Sexual relationships with supervisees, trainees, students, and colleagues
- Physical contact with clients
- Friendships with current and former clients
- Encounters with clients in public settings
- Attending clients' social, religious, or life cycle events
- Gifts to and from clients
- Performing favors for clients
- The delivery of services in clients' homes
- Financial conflicts of interest
- Delivery of services to two or more people who have a relationship with each other (such as couples, family members)
- Bartering with clients for goods and services
- Managing relationships in small or rural communities
- Self-disclosure to clients
- Becoming colleagues with a former client (Reamer, 2001a).

Documentation

Careful documentation and comprehensive records are necessary to assess clients' circumstances; plan and deliver services appropriately; facilitate supervision; provide proper accountability to clients, other service providers, funding agencies, insurers, utilization review staff, and the courts; evaluate services provided; and ensure continuity in the delivery of future services (Kagle & Kopels, 2008; Reamer, 2005; Sidell, 2011; Wiger, 2005). Thorough documentation also helps ensure quality care if a client's primary social worker becomes unavailable because of illness, incapacitation, vacation, or employment termination. In addition, thorough documentation can help social workers who are named in ethics complaints or lawsuits (for example, when evidence is needed to demonstrate that a social worker obtained a client's informed consent before releasing confidential information, assessed for suicide risk properly, consulted with knowledgeable experts about a client's clinical issues, consulted the NASW *Code of Ethics* to make a difficult ethical decision, or referred a client to other service providers when services were terminated).

Social workers should maintain and store records for the number of years required by state statutes or relevant contracts. Practitioners should make special provisions for proper access to their records in the event of their disability, incapacitation, termination of practice, or death. This may include entering into agreements with colleagues who would be willing to assume responsibility for social workers' records if they are unavailable for any reason.

Defamation of Character

Social workers should ensure that their written and oral communications about clients are not defamatory. Libel is the written form of defamation of character; slander is the oral form. Defamation occurs when a social worker says or writes something about a client or another party that is untrue, the social worker knew or should have known that the statement was untrue, and the communication caused some injury to the client or third party (e.g., the client was terminated from a treatment program or lost custody of a child, or a colleague was disciplined by an agency administrator).

Supervision

In principle, social workers can be named in ethics complaints and lawsuits alleging ethical breaches or negligence by those under their supervision. Social work supervisors should ensure that they meet with supervisees regularly, address appropriate issues (e.g., treatment and intervention plans, case recording, correction of errors in all phases of client contact, dual relationships, protection of third parties), and document the supervision provided.

Consultation and Referral

Social workers should be clear about when consultation with colleagues is appropriate and necessary and the procedures they should use to locate competent consultants. Similarly, social workers have a responsibility to refer clients to colleagues when they do not have the expertise or time to assist clients in need. Practitioners should know when to refer clients to other professionals and how to locate competent colleagues.

Fraud

Social workers should have strict procedures in place to prevent fraud related to, for example, documentation in case records, billing, and employment applications.

Termination of Services

Social workers expose themselves to risk when they terminate services improperly—for example, when a social worker leaves an agency suddenly without adequately referring a vulnerable client to another practitioner, or terminates services to a very vulnerable client who has missed appointments or has not paid an outstanding bill. Practitioners should develop thorough and comprehensive termination protocols to prevent client abandonment.

Practitioner Impairment, Misconduct, and Incompetence

A significant percentage of ethics complaints and negligence claims are filed against social workers who meet the definition of impaired professional (impairment that may be due to factors such as substance abuse, mental illness, extraordinary personal stress, or legal difficulties). Social workers should understand the nature of professional impairment and possible causes, be alert to warning signs, and have procedures in place to prevent, identify, and respond appropriately to impairment in their own lives or colleagues' lives (Reamer, 1992; Strom-Gottfried, 2000, 2003).

In addition, social workers sometimes encounter colleagues who have engaged in ethical misconduct or are incompetent. Examples include social workers who learn that a colleague is falsifying travel expense vouchers or client records or providing services outside his or her areas of expertise.

In some instances, social workers can address these situations satisfactorily by approaching the colleague, raising the concerns, and helping the colleague devise an earnest, constructive, and comprehensive plan to stop the unethical behavior, minimize harm to affected parties, seek appropriate supervision and consultation, and develop any necessary competencies. When these measures fail or are not feasible—perhaps because of the seriousness of the ethical misconduct, impairment, or incompetence—one must consider blowing the whistle on the colleague. Whistle-blowing entails taking action through appropriate channels—such as notifying administrators, supervisors, professional organizations, and licensing and regulatory bodies—in an effort to address the problem. Before deciding to blow the whistle, social workers should carefully consider the severity of the harm and misconduct involved; the quality of the evidence of wrongdoing (one should avoid blowing the whistle without clear and convincing evidence); the effect of the decision on colleagues and one's agency; the whistle-blower's motives (that is, whether the whistle-blowing is motivated primarily by a wish for revenge); and the viability of alternative, intermediate courses of action (whether other, less drastic means might address the problem). Social work administrators need to formulate and enforce agency policies and procedures that support and protect staffers who disclose impairment, misconduct, and incompetence conscientiously and in good faith. See Chapter 22 on the impaired social work professional for more detailed information on impaired social workers and how to remedy the situation.

Management Practices

Periodically, social work administrators should assess the appropriateness or adequacy of the agency's government licenses; the agency's papers of incorporation and bylaws; the state licenses and current registrations of all professional staff; protocols for emergency action; insurance policies; staff evaluation procedures; and financial management practices (Kurzman, 1995).

IMPLEMENTING A COMPREHENSIVE RISK MANAGEMENT STRATEGY

Social workers can prevent ethics complaints and ethics-related lawsuits by conducting a comprehensive ethics audit (Reamer, 2001b, 2013a). An ethics audit entails thorough examination of major risks associated with one's practice setting (whether independent or agency-based practice). The audit involves several steps designed to identify ethics-related risks and minimize harm to clients, social workers, and social service agencies.

1. Appoint a committee or task force of concerned and informed staff or colleagues.

2. Gather the information necessary to assess the level of risk associated with each ethics-related phenomenon (i.e., clients' rights; confidentiality and privacy; informed consent; service delivery; digital and online technology; boundary issues and conflicts of interest; documentation; defamation of character; supervision; staff development and training; consultation; client referral; fraud; termination of services; practitioner impairment, misconduct, or incompetence; management practices) from such sources as agency documents, data gathered from interviews with agency staff, and national accreditation standards.
3. Review all available information.
4. Determine whether there is no risk, minimal risk, moderate risk, or high risk for each risk area.
5. Prepare an action plan to address each risk area that warrants attention, paying particular attention to the steps required to reduce risk, the resources required, the personnel who will oversee implementation of the action plan, the timetable for completion of the plan, the indicators of progress toward reducing risk, and plans to monitor implementation of the action plan.

In recent years, social workers have paid increased attention to the risk of lawsuits and ethics complaints filed against practitioners and agencies. To minimize these risks, and especially to protect clients, social workers need to understand the nature of professional standards of care, malpractice, and negligence. They also need to be familiar with major risk areas and practical steps they can take to prevent complaints.

WEBSITES

"Client Records: Keep or Toss?" NASW Assurance Services. http://www.naswassurance.org/pdf/PP_Record_Retention.pdf

NASW Code of Ethics. http://www.socialworkers.org/pubs/code/code.asp

"The Distance Counseling Cyberfrontier, Part I," NASW Assurance Services. http://www.naswassurance.org/pdf/PP_Distance_Counseling_I_Final.pdf

"The Distance Counseling Cyberfrontier, Part II," NASW Assurance Services.
http://www.naswassurance.org/pdf/PP%20_Distance_Learning_II_Final.pdf

"Facing a Malpractice Claim," NASW Assurance Services. http://www.naswassurance.org/facing_malpractice_claim.php

"Supervisor Beware: Reducing Your Exposure to Vicarious Liability," NASW Assurance Services. http://www.naswassurance.org/pdf/PP_Vicarious_Liability.pdf

References

Austin, K. M., Moline, M. E., & Williams, G. T. (1990). *Confronting malpractice: Legal and ethical dilemmas in psychotherapy.* Newbury Park, CA: Sage.

Berg, J. W., Appelbaum, P. S., Parker, L. S., & Lidz, C. W. (2001). *Informed consent: Legal theory and clinical practice* (2nd ed.). New York, NY: Oxford University Press.

Dickson, D. T. (1998). *Confidentiality and privacy in social work: A guide to the law for practitioners and students.* New York, NY: Free Press.

Fisher, M. A. (2013). *The ethics of conditional confidentiality: A practical model for mental health professionals.* New York, NY: Oxford University Press.

Glannon, J. W. (2010). *The law of torts: Examples and explanations* (4th ed.). New York, NY: Aspen.

Haas, L. J., & Malouf, J. L. (2005). *Keeping up the good work: A practitioner's guide to mental health ethics* (4th ed.). Sarasota, FL: Professional Resources Press.

Houston-Vega, M. K., Nuehring, E. M., & Daguio, E. R. (1997). *Prudent practice: A guide for managing malpractice risk.* Washington, DC: NASW Press.

Kagle, J. D., & Kopels, S. (2008). *Social work records* (3rd ed.). Long Grove, IL: Waveland Press.

Kurzman, P. (1995). Professional liability and malpractice. In R. L. Edwards (Editor-in-Chief), *Encyclopedia of social work* (19th ed.) (Vol. 3, pp. 1921–1927). Washington, DC: NASW Press.

Madden, R. (1998). *Legal issues in social work, counseling, and mental health: Guidelines for clinical practice.* Thousand Oaks, CA: Sage.

Miller, F. G., & Wertheimer, A. (Eds.). (2010). *The ethics of consent: Theory and practice.* New York, NY: Oxford University Press.

Polowy, C. I., & Gorenberg, C. (1997). *Office of General Counsel law notes: Client confidentiality and privileged communications.* Washington, DC: NASW Press.

Reamer, F. G. (1992). The impaired social worker. *Social Work, 37*(2), 165–170.

Reamer, F. G. (2001a). *Tangled relationships: Managing boundary issues in the human services.* New York, NY: Columbia University Press.

Reamer, F. G. (2001b). *The social work ethics audit: A risk management tool.* Washington, DC: NASW Press.

Reamer, F. G. (2003). *Social work malpractice and liability: Strategies for prevention* (2nd ed.). New York, NY: Columbia University Press.

Reamer, F. G. (2005). Documentation in social work: Evolving ethical and risk-management standards. *Social Work, 50*(4), 325–334.

Reamer, F. G. (2006). *Ethical standards in social work: A review of the NASW Code of Ethics* (2nd ed.). Washington, DC: NASW Press.

Reamer, F. G. (2012). The digital and electronic revolution in social work: Rethinking the meaning of ethical practice. *Ethics and Social Welfare.* Retrieved from http://www.tandfonline.com/doi/abs/10.1080/17496535.2012.738694

Reamer, F. G. (2013a). *Social work values and ethics* (4th ed.). New York, NY: Columbia University Press.

Sidell, N. L. (2011). *Social work documentation: A guide to strengthening your case recording.* Washington, DC: NASW Press.

Strom-Gottfried, K. (2000). Ensuring ethical practice: An examination of NASW code violations. *Social Work, 45*(3), 251–261.

Strom-Gottfried, K. (2003). Understanding adjudication: Origins, targets, and outcomes of ethics complaints. *Social Work, 48*(1), 85–94.

Wiger, D. (2005). *The clinical documentation sourcebook: The complete paperwork resource for your mental health practice.* Hoboken, NJ: Wiley.

Woody, R. H. (1996). *Legally safe mental health practice.* Madison, CT: Psychosocial Press.

Advocacy in Administrative Forums

20 *Guidelines for Practice in Benefit Appeals*

John M. Gallagher

This chapter examines the intersection of administrative law and social work practice. More specifically, it focuses on appeal processes available in public benefit programs and ways that social workers can help their clients utilize them. Although criminal and civil courts may come to mind more readily when considering forensic social work, these administrative forums can be used by clients and their advocates to enforce rights and meet needs. Due to the relative informality of these appeal processes, social workers can play a number of active and supportive roles. The three objectives of this chapter are (1) to explain why it is important for social workers to be aware of these forums; (2) to provide an overview of administrative appeals and hearings; and (3) to explore ways that social workers can participate in these processes. Throughout the chapter, ethical and practical issues will be raised.

WHY SHOULD SOCIAL WORKERS KNOW ABOUT ADMINISTRATIVE APPEALS?

This question must be addressed in a few different ways. First, the sheer number of individuals enrolled in programs with legally defined appeal processes is compelling. Although the specific rights and processes vary among programs and states, the material in this chapter applies to individuals receiving Medicaid, Temporary Assistance to Needy Families (TANF), Supplemental Nutrition Assistance Program (formerly called Food Stamps), Medicare, Social Security programs, Veterans Affairs disability programs, many state programs as well as students receiving special education services under the Individuals with Disabilities Education Act. Collectively, there are millions of affected individuals, a great number of whom have routine or episodic interactions with social workers.

Next, the Fifth and Fourteenth Amendments to the Constitution assert that no one shall be "deprived of life, liberty or property without due process of law." These "due process" provisions apply to both the federal and state governments and have over time been interpreted by the Supreme Court to require appeal processes to challenge denials, reductions, suspensions, and terminations of many programs that make up our social service system. Although the exact level of protection varies across programs, the classic example is *Goldberg v. Kelly* (1970), which established the right to a pre-termination hearing before an impartial decision maker for individuals receiving Aid to Families with Dependent Children (the predecessor to TANF).

Third, despite such important and powerful legal protections, anecdotal reports and the limited available research (Bell & Norvell, 1967–1968; Handler, 1969; Lens & Vorsnager, 2005) indicate that beneficiaries underutilize their appeal options. Interestingly, the same studies suggest that individuals who do file appeals experience relatively high rates of success. Lens (2007) provided further insight through interviews with TANF recipients regarding factors that affected the decision to appeal. One of the findings was that receiving information, encouragement, or support from an individual in the recipient's social network seemed to increase the utilization of appeal options. Although intended to be accessible to lay individuals, legal scholars have critiqued administrative hearings as inaccessible and intimidating to many recipients (Brodoff, 2010; Kinney, 1990–1991). The types of social, educational, and psychological issues that force many individuals to rely on such programs are often the factors that pose barriers to recognizing, understanding, and utilizing appeal options.

Finally, considering the above, the values, history, and ethical guidelines of our profession call on us to advocate for social justice in administrative as well as other contexts. As the ensuing sections will explore, many social workers are well positioned to help their clients exercise rights they would otherwise experience only in the abstract. To put a human face on this call to advocacy and to help frame the technical discussion that follows, please consider this brief scenario in thinking about the relevant practice principles described in this chapter.

Roberto is a social worker in a federally funded homeless outreach program. Although the program can provide short-term psychiatric services to individuals from its grant, Roberto is charged with helping individuals with a serious mental illness enroll in his state's mainstream service system for ongoing care. Eligibility for the state's system requires the establishment of a qualifying diagnosis and a related functional impairment. Mark, a 25-year-old man on Roberto's caseload, has been diagnosed by the program's psychiatrist as having schizophrenia. He reports episodic hospitalizations for this condition in five states over the past three years. Roberto has begun requesting records from these hospitals and they have consistent diagnoses of schizophrenia or closely related psychotic disorders. Although offered assistance to enter a shelter, Mark declined due to fear that the staff would poison him. Therefore, he remains on the streets. When referred to the state system he was denied due to a comorbid diagnosis of alcohol abuse in the outreach program's records. This denial suggests that his functional impairment is likely due to substance use. The state's program is Medicaid funded and Mark is issued a notice of action which advises him that he may appeal. He informs Roberto that he knew it would not work and mentions moving to another city.

OVERVIEW OF ADMINISTRATIVE APPEALS AND HEARINGS

Having considered why it is often appropriate for social workers to assist in such matters—and before exploring ways to do so—an overview of how these administrative forums function is in order. What follows is of necessity a broad overview. The differences between systems and jurisdictions preclude overarching specifics. However, if the issues and themes identified here are used as a starting point, program specific details can be found and addressed.

- *Notice rights:* When a government agency— or a provider working under contract— makes a decision to deny, reduce, suspend, or terminate the types of services listed above, they are generally required to provide the client or applicant with written notice. The notice should provide the agency's reason for the decision, the effective date, and what appeal or review options the individual holds.
- *Appeal initiation:* Upon learning of an adverse decision (even if the agency fails to provide appropriate notice) the client or his/ her representative generally has the right to file an appeal of the decision. There are always deadlines within which such appeals must be filed. Although some systems allow oral appeals, written appeals are best. Some agencies have specific forms and in other instances a letter will suffice. Regardless of format, it is prudent to submit the appeal in a way that provides proof of timely filing—for example, certified mail, via fax, or obtaining a signed acknowledgment from agency staff. When a service is already in place and the agency is proposing its termination or reduction, the client often has the option of requesting a service continuation during the appeal process. Although this can be a beneficial option, it is important that the client understand that the system may have the right to receive reimbursement for the service costs if he or she loses the appeal. The notice should cover these details.
- *Pre-hearing steps:* In some systems the appeal process has a level before the dispute is addressed in an administrative hearing. These pre-hearing steps can be either mandatory or an option for the client to exercise. There are two main types of preliminary steps. The first—which is common in clinically oriented systems—is a second review of existing and additional documentation by the agency making the denial. Making sure the agency reviewer has all necessary documentation is essential. For this reason, it is often helpful to request that the reviewer discuss the issue with a physician or other involved clinician who supports the service in question. The other common pre-hearing step is a meeting or conference where the hearing officer or other individual attempts to mediate the disagreement between the parties. If such preliminary steps are undertaken and prove unsuccessful, there may be a need to file an additional request for a hearing.

- *Hearing venue:* Some state agencies/ systems, as well as federal agencies, have administrative courts associated with the individual agency to hear appeals. Other states have created independent offices of administrative hearings to adjudicate disputes from a variety of state agencies. Regardless of location, the hearings are typically presided over by an administrative law judge (ALJ) or hearing's officer. Although significant variation exists among agencies and individual ALJs, these hearings are less formal than criminal or civil courts. Nonetheless, participating clients and social workers should still err on the side of formality in dress and demeanor. For individuals who would have difficulty attending the hearing in person, it is often possible to request a telephonic hearing. Such requests are made by filing a motion with the court. (This need not be a complex process and is discussed below.) Although this can be helpful for individuals who could not otherwise attend, concerns have been raised that appellants who participate by phone are less likely to introduce evidence or call witnesses (Toubman, McArdle, & Rogers-Tomer, 1995–1996).
- *Importance of policy:* Whereas criminal and civil proceedings draw upon statutes and judicial precedents, administrative hearings typically rely on administrative rules and policies issued by federal and state agencies. As these rules (also called administrative codes or regulations) and policies establish the criteria by which agencies are to make eligibility and other decisions, it is essential to consider the relevant sections before and during an appeal. Agencies often provide a citation to the rule or policy they see as supporting their position in the notice of action. In recent years, many agencies have made these guiding documents available on their websites. Legal aid agencies often publish helpful self-advocacy guides, explaining how to use specific appeal processes. It is often advantageous to prepare a short memo for the ALJ listing the policies and/or rules the appellant sees as supporting his or her position.

- *Burden of proof:* There are two issues to be aware of in all judicial hearings. The first is which party "holds the burden." Depending on a variety of factors, it can be either client or agency that has the obligation to prove the case through evidence. More consistent is the level of proof needed to prevail. Although terms like "beyond a reasonable doubt" and "clear and convincing" are commonly used to describe the level needed to render criminal or civil decisions, administrative processes typically use the lower preponderance of the evidence standard—essentially meaning the party with the burden must simply introduce more credible and relevant evidence than the opposition.

- *Types of evidence:* During hearings, both parties have the opportunity to introduce evidence. There are two basic types of evidence: testimony and documentary evidence. Testimony is provided through the calling of a witness. Although witnesses often appear in person, courts may grant permission for a witness to testify via telephone. This can be particularly helpful if trying to arrange the testimony of a clinician with limited time. As with telephonic hearings, such requests are typically made by filing a motion with the court. Depending on the nature of the appeal, documentary evidence may include clinical, financial, or other documents that demonstrate eligibility for the service or program in question. Although live testimony is generally best, a written statement from an involved clinician is often helpful if testimony is not possible.

- *Requesting a continuance:* There are times where one party needs to request a postponement of the hearing date. These requests are made through motions to the court, should be based on a legitimate reason (e.g., to secure necessary documents or a conflict in the schedule of a witness or the appellant), and the other party has the right to object. The ALJ will issue a response, granting or rejecting the request.

- *Communication during appeals:* Once an appeal has been filed—especially once a hearing has been scheduled—communication between the parties and the court becomes formal. As indicated above, requests for continuances or telephonic hearings/

testimony should be provided to the court via motions. Administrative law judges often accept relatively informal filings—especially from individuals appearing pro se or represented by a lay advocate. Some state agencies and legal aid agencies post templates on their websites. Although there is some informality in style, it is essential that any motion filed with the court is also provided to the opposing party. The failure to do so will usually result in the denial of the request because it prevents the other party from having a fair opportunity to respond. There is also likely to be a deadline by which a motion must be filed—perhaps 14 days before the scheduled hearing. If making a late filing, good cause should be noted. Extending the logic of copying the opposing party on motions, any evidence or policy memos provided to the court must also be provided to the other party.

- *Decision and further appeal:* Following the hearing, the ALJ will issue a written decision. It will generally contain a summary of the evidence introduced at the hearing, how the judge weighed the evidence, and how it related to the relevant policy and code. It often takes a month or more for the decision to be issued. An individual may have options if the decision is unfavorable. In certain instances, a review can be requested by the same administrative court and in others an appeal to a civil court is an option. These possibilities require close research and—especially the appeal to civil court—increase the importance of consulting with an attorney if available. Lay advocates cannot provide representation in civil courts.

ADVOCACY APPROACHES AND CONSIDERATIONS

As with all categories of social work intervention, advocacy with public benefit appeals can take on many forms. The scope of the assistance provided will be influenced by a variety of factors (which will be discussed in the following section).

Before reviewing forms of administrative advocacy, it is important to address a common question: how do practitioners and agencies protect themselves when using these interventions? Although manageable, there are two important issues to consider. First, the potential for providing unauthorized practice of law exists. As detailed below, when officially serving as a lay representative in a manner consistent with the rules of a system or jurisdiction, an individual is on firm legal ground to perform tasks and give advice that would otherwise constitute the practice of law. Conversely, when state law prevents lay advocacy in administrative hearings the issue is clear and the prohibition must be honored. More individual analysis is required if state direction on lay representation at administrative hearings is lacking or when providing assistance at a lower level of advocacy. There is recognition from the legal community (American Bar Association, 1995, p. 35) that "informal help with legal problems, coming from … social workers … who have had experience handling a similar legal problem or are considered to be reliable sources of information, has generally not been considered unauthorized practice." The ABA further noted that social workers often assist individuals appearing pro se in administrative hearings. Although used by the ABA in a slightly different way, the following two questions from their report are useful in evaluating when to assist. First, does the activity pose a serious risk to the client? Specific to this context, does losing an appeal carry a greater consequence than not pursuing it at all? Second, does the client have the ability to understand the social worker is not an attorney and evaluate the potential benefits of the offered assistance? Solid attention to informed consent should address this question.

The second issue is the possibility of a malpractice claim being filed against a social worker or agency due to lay representation or other administrative advocacy. Examples of such claims are not evident in the literature of social work malpractice. Nonetheless, as with any form of direct practice, there is always a possibility of a claim being filed. Although perfect protections against liability do not exist, the issues raised in this chapter and more traditional guidance on preventing social work liability (Reamer, 2003) offer sound advice.

Assisting in Self-representation

Many of the individuals served by social workers are able and willing to utilize their due process protections independently. These protections are, after all, designed to be used by service recipients. The terms pro se and pro per are often used to describe an individual who represents him or herself in a legal proceeding. When appropriate, such independent representation has the advantage of supporting client autonomy and empowerment. Nonetheless, there are often barriers to self-representation and ways that social workers can help overcome them. On the most basic level, some individuals may be unaware of the opportunity to file such appeals (despite notice obligations) or aware but skeptical that the process will work for them. Sometimes a little knowledge or encouragement goes a long way. In other instances, clients will need more concrete forms of assistance to successfully self-represent. Such assistance often includes providing computer/Internet access to research relevant law, code, or policy, or to compose and file documents; helping to obtain past treatment records for introduction as evidence; making copies of documents that will be introduced as evidence; serving as a sounding board for approaches to the appeal; or providing transportation to the hearing or related meetings. Individuals representing themselves often encounter difficulties securing witnesses to participate. When the dispute involves a clinical assessment of eligibility for a program or need for an individual service, the service system is usually at a great advantage because it employs clinicians who can testify. Licensed clinical social workers can often fill this need and other social workers can often testify to relevant facts. There are times when a social worker can help a client secure or coordinate the testimony of a psychiatrist or other clinician.

Similar to assisting with self-representation, there may be a family member or other natural support willing and able to serve as a client representative in an appeal. Types of social worker assistance for such advocates are the same as those offered to pro se representatives. Ensuring the client authorizes the sharing of information is an important additional step.

Referral to and Coordination with Attorneys

Although resources vary by community and issue type, there may be a local attorney available to represent a client in an appeal. This is most likely if a successful appeal will result in the awarding of a cash settlement for benefits not paid while the appeal was pursued—generally federal disability benefits and workers' compensation claims. In these instances, private attorneys often will provide representation in return for a percentage of the retroactive benefit payment if successful. Individual clients must decide whether they are willing to pay for such services. Legal aid and other nonprofit law firms can provide representation in limited instances. Client eligibility for these legal services is often based on being on a very low income, homeless, a domestic violence victim, or an individual with a disability.

At the most basic level, social workers can refer clients to these resources. As with other types of service referral and coordination, it is important to stay abreast of local resources and the types of cases they do and do not accept. It is often helpful to cultivate relationships with legal aid attorneys. There are times when they are seeking clients who present with a certain set of facts in order to use a small number of cases to push for larger system reform. Social workers can remain aware of such issues through both local networking and subscribing to the e-mail lists of national legally based advocacy organizations based on their area of practice.

Driven by individual client need and authorization, social workers can collaborate with attorneys representing common clients in public benefit appeals. Especially for clients whose living situations are unstable or unsafe, social workers can help with communication between attorneys and clients. For clients needing emotional support, transportation, or help understanding information, it is often beneficial to attend appointments with clients. This also helps cultivate networks with the legal services community. Social workers can again serve as witnesses or help arrange the testimony of others. This can be especially helpful with physicians— who may be inclined to assist but reluctant to spend significant time preparing.

Providing Direct Representation

There are times where it is both legally permissible and appropriate for a social worker to represent a client in a public benefits appeal. When assuming the role of a lay advocate, the social worker conducts the appeal for his or her client by filing documents with the agency or court, identifying relevant policy, introducing evidence, and examining and cross-examining witnesses at the hearing. This can be an effective form of advocacy. There are, however, several issues to consider before agreeing to represent a client in this manner.

- *Is it legally permissible?* Although the answer to this is often, "yes," it varies from program to program and state to state. It is essential to verify this before agreeing to serve as a lay representative for a client, given that some states consider it to be engaging in the unauthorized practice of law. Generally, the answer can be obtained from the involved agency, the administrative court where the hearing is held, or the state's court system. When allowed, there is often a prohibition against charging a fee for lay representation. Rules issued by the Supreme Court of the State of Arizona (Regulation of the Practice of Law, 2012) provide an example of how one state authorizes lay representation in public benefits. This rule establishes explicit exceptions to the general prohibition against unlicensed practice of law for appeals related to TANF, Medicaid, the free and appropriate public education for a child with a disability, and the public behavioral health system. In these narrow contexts, a non-attorney is allowed to prepare documents, give legal opinions, introduce evidence, and examine witnesses in administrative hearings.
- *Is legal representation available?* Although one objective of this chapter is to increase social workers' willingness and ability to provide lay representation, this is not intended to replace attorneys. Rather, it is an option that can be offered to clients when a lawyer is not available. In addition to the sources mentioned above, legal assistance may be available through Volunteer Lawyer Programs or free clinics affiliated with law schools.
- *Is your client able to self-represent?* Without pushing someone into undertaking a task for which he or she is unprepared, we must explore this option—including ways to reduce identified barriers. Doing so is consistent with social work's emphasis on strengths and autonomy. However, perception should also be considered. Although it is unfortunate, some decision makers will view an argument as more credible if it is offered by a professional as opposed to the affected individual.
- *Do you have the competence and confidence required?* Given that these appeal processes are designed to be used by service recipients, lay representation is realistic. Nonetheless,

that does not mean that every social worker will be or feel up to the task. The ethical prohibition against practicing beyond one's competence (NASW, 1996) is as relevant here as it is in more traditional practice realms.

- *How does the representation fit with the primary client relationship?* Social workers are often faced with clients whose needs stretch beyond the purview of their individual positions. Although our practice roles are diverse, an individual practitioner can never meet all needs. Without terming it inappropriate, representing a client in an administrative hearing is less likely to be a good fit for a therapist than it is for a case manager. Beyond individual role, the larger agency or program function should be considered.
- *Does the appeal have merit?* In addition to resources and agency priorities, legal aid agencies consider case merits before agreeing to provide representation. Social workers considering such representation should do the same. These decisions should not be based on what one would like to see happen, but on the likelihood of prevailing. Sometimes an individual desires a service that he or she is simply not eligible to receive. Other times the individual should be eligible but the necessary treatment records, assessment, witnesses, or other forms of evidence are not available. If taking a case would do little more than let your client know you are in his or her corner, your client would be better served by a frank conversation and the development of a realistic plan. Taking the time to develop or obtain the information required for eligibility and reapplying at a later date is often more appropriate than pursuing an appeal.
- *Is your supervisor or agency comfortable with the representation?* You should not be surprised by questions and concerns— especially the first time you propose such an intervention. Be prepared to defend the plan. Thorough internal review can strengthen the case or identify that it lacks merit. If you cannot convince your supervisor of your ability to advocate for your client effectively, perhaps you cannot effectively advocate for your client on the issue in question.
- *Is your client comfortable with you assuming this role?* This may seem obvious; the process will almost certainly require

your client to designate you as his or her representative in writing. Yet, as with other interventions, informed consent is more complicated than obtaining a signature (NASW, 1996). The questions and considerations raised in this chapter should resonate with the essential elements of informed consent: What are the advantages and disadvantages of the intervention? Are there other options available? What are the costs of doing nothing? What is the likelihood of success? How prepared are you? How well does your client understand your level of competence? It is essential to ensure that your client understands that you are not an attorney. The impact on traditional client confidentiality should be clearly discussed and appropriate authorizations obtained before testimony or records are shared with a court or attorneys.

CONCLUSION

Ours is a legally regulated society. Laws, administrative rules, and agency policy shape the rights and responsibilities we all hold. Yet, legal scholars (Felstiner, Abel & Sarat, 1980–1981; Galanter, 1974; Rhode, 2004) and legal aid organizations (Legal Services Corporation, 2009) have consistently noted that low income individuals have fewer resources to identify and enforce the rights they hold. Public benefits advocacy is an area where social workers can help our clients close this justice gap. Although there are questions to answer before providing such assistance and issues to manage while doing so, our discipline's long standing focus on social justice and advocacy suggests we should assist when we can.

WEBSITES

National Association of Secretaries of State, Web portal to state rules and regulations. http://www.administrativerules.org/
U.S. Government Printing Office, Code of Federal Regulations. http://www.gpo.gov/fdsys/browse/collectionCfr.action?collectionCode=CFR
Legal Services Corporation listing of local legal aid organizations. http://www.lsc.gov/local-programs/program-profiles

National Disability Rights Network list of state and territorial Protection & Advocacy agencies. http://www.ndrn.org/en/ndrn-member-agencies.html

References

American Bar Association. (1995). *Nonlawyer activity in law-related situations: A report with recommendations*. Chicago, IL: Author. Retrieved from: http://www.americanbar.org/groups/professional_responsibility/resources/client_protection/client.html

Bell, A. W., & Norvell, G. T. (1967–1968). Texas welfare appeals: The hidden right. *Texas Law Review, 46,* 223–253.

Brodoff, L. (2010). Lifting burdens: Proof, social justice and public assistance administrative hearings. *Journal of the National Association Administrative Law Judiciary, 30*(2), 601–680.

Felstiner, W. L. F., Abel, R. L., & Sarat, A. (1980–1981). The emergence and transformation of disputes: Naming, blaming, claiming …. *Law and Society Review, 15*(3–4), 632–654.

Galanter, M. (1974). Why the "haves" come out ahead: Speculations on the limits of legal change. *Law and Society Review, 9*(1), 95–160.

Goldberg v. Kelly, 397 U.S. 254 (1970).

Handler, J. F. (1969). Justice for the welfare recipient: Fair hearings in AFDC—The Wisconsin experience. *Social Service Review, 43*(1), 12–34.

Kinney, E. D. (1990–1991). The role of judicial review regarding Medicare and Medicaid program policy: Past experience and future expectations. *Saint Louis University Law Journal, 35,* 759–792.

Legal Services Corporation. (2009). *Documenting the justice gap in America: The current unmet civil legal needs of low-income Americans*. Washington, DC: Author. Retrieved from: http://www.lsc.gov/media/reports

Lens, V. (2007). Administrative justice in public welfare bureaucracies: When citizens (don't) complain. *Administration and Society, 39*(3), 382–408.

Lens, V., & Vorsnager, S. E. (2005). Complaining after claiming: Fair hearing after welfare reform. *Social Service Review, 79*(3), 430–453.

National Association of Social Workers. (Approved 1996, Revised 2008). *Code of ethics of the National Association of Social Workers*. Washington, DC: Author.

Reamer, F. G. (2003). *Social work malpractice and liability: Strategies for prevention* (2nd ed.). New York, NY: Columbia University Press.

Regulation of the Practice of Law, AZ Sup. Ct. R. 31(a)(1)(d) (2012).

Rhode, D. L. (2004). *Access to Justice*. New York: Oxford University Press.

Toubman, A. A., McArdle, T., & Rogers-Tomer, L. (1995–1996). Due process implications of telephone hearings: The case for an individualized approach to scheduling telephone hearings. *University of Michigan Journal of Law Reform, 29*(1&2), 407–474.

21   Social Work Regulation and Licensing

Andrew T. Marks & Karen S. Knox

Social work regulation has been a dynamic, ongoing process of debate and change since the beginnings of the profession in the early 1900s. The many influences and impacts on social work regulation range from political power through appointment to professional boards to financial impacts by third-party reimbursement. Social work regulation protects and enforces the values, ethics, and professional standards of practice and is the primary means of protecting the public and clients of social services through sanctions for professional and regulatory violations. In addition to providing a foundation for who a social worker is and what a social worker can or cannot do in a specific jurisdiction, social work regulation has both supported the acceptance of the profession and continued the quandary of what is social work and who is a social worker.

The primary focus of all regulatory bodies, whether voluntary or mandated by government legislation, is protecting the recipients of a professional's service (i.e., consumers), stated most succinctly as "protecting the public." Mandated regulatory bodies are usually created by jurisdiction governance bodies or state legislatures. Their primary goals are to set standards for professional practice, enforce the law, establish rules and regulations that determine minimum qualifications for professional practice, and establish a process to discipline those who do not maintain or continuously meet the established standards. Most regulatory bodies have authority to grant, suspend, and discipline credentials issued by the regulatory body (Biggerstaff, 1995). According to Biggerstaff (1995), social work regulation has four primary purposes:

1. Protect the service consumer
2. Protect the profession
3. Protect the individual professional
4. Aid consumers in the selection of a practitioner in the profession.

Professional regulation through licensing, certification, or registration is a result of the need for government to intervene in activities within the private sector because serious conditions exist in which unqualified practice results in serious threat of harm to public health and safety or economic welfare of the consumer (Biggerstaff, 1995). Additional reasons for social work regulation exist in that the consumer is often unable to evaluate a practitioner's qualifications correctly, and the benefits of credentialing for the consumer clearly prevail over potential harmful effects on the professional (Biggerstaff, 1995).

Another type of social work regulation is through professional organizations and associations that offer voluntary certification as a benefit of membership. Government-sanctioned social worker regulation credentials have proliferated in the United States since the 1980s, so voluntary credentials have become less utilized by practitioners because many jurisdictions have statutes protecting the practice of a profession with credentialing administered by the jurisdictional governing body. This multitude of required governmental and voluntary professional organizational

credentialing is confusing to professionals, not to mention the general public. As a result of the bifurcated credentialing processes, the public has little knowledge or understanding of the difference between mandated or voluntary credentials (Biggerstaff, 1995).

Case Illustration #1

Robert is a Licensed Master Social Worker working as a school social worker. He begins to work with a fifth grade student who is having difficulty with being bullied in class. He contacts the student's mother and explains the reason he was requested to help the student and sets an appointment time with the mother for intake paperwork. As he works with the student to successful resolution, he terminates services with the student. A few days later Robert sees the mother at school, and they strike up a conversation. A few days later the mother calls Robert to ask about a situation with one of her younger children and asks if they could meet for coffee and discuss the situation. Robert agrees and a romance develops. Soon Robert is called in to the school administrator's office because a complaint was filed. Robert reluctantly acknowledges that he is in a romantic relationship with the mother of the student, but that the relationship did not begin until after he terminated his services previously. The administrator files complaints with the School Board and Social Worker Board.

Robert appears before the social work board and explains that he considered his client to be the student and that he did not work directly with his client's mother, except for her to complete and sign the intake forms. The Social Worker Board responds that children do not have the legal right to consent to treatment, therefore, the parent is considered to be the client for minors. The Board revoked his LMSW license. Robert was fired as a result, because he no longer met the required criteria for his position. While the School Board and jurisdiction has laws against sexual activity by teachers and students, there is no school policy about parents and school personnel engaging in sexual relationships.

BRIEF HISTORY OF SOCIAL WORK REGULATION

Social work as a profession is relatively new to regulation, especially as one of the health care and helping professions. The first attempt at social work regulation dates back to the 1920s in California, and Puerto Rico passed the first credentialing statute for social workers in 1934. California was successful with implementing regulation of social workers by 1945 (Thyer & Biggerstaff, 1989). By 1993, every state and the District of Columbia had some form of social worker regulation (Biggerstaff, 1995).

The first record of a social work organization's action toward legal regulation was in 1947 by the American Association of Social Workers through their delegate assembly (Thyer & Biggerstaff, 1989). The primary purpose for this push for legal regulation was to raise the status of the profession. The National Association of Social Workers (NASW) was created in the mid-1950s with the merger of seven different social work associations and focused on seeking recognition and acceptance for the profession at a legal level in each jurisdiction. During the 1969 delegate assembly, NASW passed a resolution to pursue licensing of social workers in each state (Thyer & Biggerstaff, 1989). Today NASW continues to serve as the largest organization of social workers in the United States. Although the profession has seen a proliferation of specialty associations representing various practice aspects, NASW continues to be viewed as the primary association for the profession, producing the code of ethics which is considered a standard of conduct for social work professionals.

Social worker regulators recognized a need for a separate organization to support the burgeoning proliferation of jurisdictional regulation bodies. Although the call for regulation began within the professional associations, once implemented, the regulatory bodies and professional associations often found themselves on opposite sides of how best to regulate the social work profession. The American Association of State Social Work Boards (AASSWB) was founded in 1979 as a support mechanism for those jurisdictions with regulatory boards and to assist those considering initiating social worker regulation (ASWB, 2004). AASSWB developed the social work examination program currently in use by jurisdictions for required testing for licensure. In 1999, AASSWB was changed to the Association of Social Work Boards (ASWB) to reflect the growing number of memberships from Canadian jurisdictions (ASWB, 2004).

PROTECTING THE PRACTICE OF SOCIAL WORK

At the national level, the Association of Social Work Boards (ASWB) assists the state regulatory boards in carrying out their mandates and is responsible for the social worker licensing examination in the United States. The organization developed the Model Social Work Practice Act for state regulatory boards to use to set minimum competency and practice standards for social work practitioners and implement methods for investigating and addressing consumer complaints (ASWB, 2012). The act also includes definitions for social work practice at the bachelors, masters, and clinical levels of social work regulation. The definition of what social work is and what a social worker does is important to the protection of the profession from unqualified practitioners.

Most social worker credentialing bodies require formal education in social work with a degree from an accredited institution of higher education recognized by either the Council on Social Work Education (CSWE) or other formal accreditation body acceptable to the jurisdiction's higher education coordinating agency. Passage of the national social work licensing exam is required in almost all jurisdictions in the United States. Some have additional examination requirements, such as jurisprudence (covering jurisdictional law and rules) and cultural (covering aspects of working with specific populations). Additionally, for some levels of credentialing, qualified supervised experience may be required prior to approval to sit for the exam.

A challenge in protecting the practice of social work is found when boards grant exemptions to the required credentials for government employees or those with extensive employment experience in social services who can be "grandfathered" in, despite not meeting minimum standards. This can occur when state boards make changes or increase their standards, and it means that someone with a non–social work bachelor's degree could be licensed as a social worker solely because of previous work experience, even though the minimum educational requirement is currently a BSW. Other governmental agencies (such as child protective services and juvenile probation) have exemptions from licensing for employees, but provide services and practices typically requiring licensing in the private or nonprofit sector.

Another challenge in social work regulation is protecting the practice of social work from counseling professionals regulated by other professional boards, educational degrees, and licensing credentials, such as licensed marriage and family therapists (LMFTs), or licensed professional counselors (LPCs). Differentiating social work practice from other helping professions is paramount in defining what social workers can do and what those not regulated as social workers should not do. However, the profession has struggled with this defining activity, because social workers are educated and trained in a variety of different disciplines and therapeutic approaches, so there continues to be a murky definition of professional social work.

PROTECTING THE TITLE OF SOCIAL WORKER

Protecting the title of social worker and defining who is qualified to engage in social work service are important functions for consumer and professional protection. Defining who a social worker is appears easier than defining what a social worker does, and how that definition is displayed in credentialing can be a source of great confusion. A review of credentialing levels and acronyms for the 50 jurisdictions of the United States, 10 Canadian jurisdictions, the District of Columbia, the Virgin Islands, and Puerto Rico, reveals 42 different titles used to describe social worker credentialing (ASWB, 2013). This multilevel use of acronyms that are often interwoven with various meanings, as well as various levels of education and experience, can add a difficult dimension for both consumers and professionals in understanding the social work profession and its regulation.

The development of professional credentials begins with identifying the purpose of the enabling statute. Is the regulation intended to regulate the practice or the title of the practitioner? If the purpose of professional regulation is to ensure that only those individuals who are specifically educated, trained, and most qualified will engage in practice, then more stringent legislation is required. If the purpose is to ensure that only those meeting the highest standards of education and training are permitted to call themselves social workers but not to prevent those not specifically educated or trained in social work to engage in the practice, then legislation to protect the title is all that is required.

Social workers historically agree that those educated at a master's degree or higher and engaging in independent clinical practice need to be regulated due to the potential risk to consumers by the professional. Most jurisdictions support this philosophy by regulating the independent provision of clinical social work practice and title of clinical social worker. However, the profession remains split on the need for regulation of those at the nonclinical and bachelor's level of practice, given that much of this form of social work takes place under the auspices of an agency setting. With more individuals engaging in contract services and independent nonclinical practice, the need to monitor more individuals beyond title protection becomes important.

REGISTRATION, CERTIFICATION, AND LICENSURE

Credentialing is a part of the administrative regulatory function of government in most jurisdictions. Most licensing rules are maintained in the jurisdiction's administrative code. Regulated professionals are afforded due process, and the credential becomes a property right of the individual. The regulatory body issuing the credential may revoke it if the professional commits a violation within the jurisdiction of the regulatory body. Most professional credentialing is divided into three categories—licensing, certification, and registration. At one time, licensing and registration were considered to be government activities.

Licensing is required to participate in specific professions, whereas registration can be voluntary for those who engage in a profession whose title is protected by law. Certification can be voluntary but is not always associated with governing statutes. Certification in practice specializations, such as gerontology or chemical dependency counseling, has been established by various professional associations and organizations. Today, the terms *licensing, certification, and registration* are used almost interchangeably among jurisdictions and professions.

Licensing carries with it recognition of acceptance at the professional level and authority to practice in a profession. Licensing usually requires continuing professional education or training to maintain licensure. Certification denotes an individual who meets specific criteria to obtain recognition. In most cases, however, once certified there are no provisions that require maintaining minimum competency, such as mandatory continuing education. Registration symbolizes that one is recognized by a regulatory body as practicing but not necessarily having met specific criteria to engage in the practice of the profession.

Case Illustration #2

Susan is a Licensed Clinical Social Worker (LCSW) who has been in social work practice since 1982. She has maintained her solo private practice after opening her practice specializing in working with children in Child Protective Service (CPS) custody preparing them for return to their family or for termination of parental rights and subsequent adoption opportunities. Prior to her LCSW status, Susan was employed as a caseworker with the CPS system for 12 years, ultimately achieving the status of supervisor. Susan holds a bachelor's degree in psychology and was grandfathered in for social worker licensing based on her work experience when regulation began in her jurisdiction in 1982. She has never had a malpractice complaint or disciplinary action taken against any of her credentials during her professional career. She has successfully maintained her professional credentials through continuing education and prompt renewal of her credentials. After retirement and relocation to a new jurisdiction with a warmer climate, Susan decides she would like to maintain a small practice with geriatric clients. She applies for licensure in her new jurisdiction, but is dismayed to discover she is not eligible based on her not holding a degree in social work.

Susan appeals the board's decision, stating her extensive professional experience, successful credentialing in her previous jurisdiction, and subsequent maintenance of the credential(s) prior to relocation. Susan presents testimony, as well as testimony from her previous clients. The regulatory body upholds the denial and encourages Susan to seek appropriate education to regain her licensure status. The body also reminds her she will need to complete all requirements, which include approved supervision and experience under an approved supervisor to be eligible for the LCSW credential. Susan decides volunteering may be how she will give of her professional expertise.

ROLES AND RESPONSIBILITIES OF THE JURISDICTION REGULATORY BODY

As noted, credentialing is a local (i.e., state) jurisdictional responsibility. The right to issue or remove a credential lies within the enabling statute and structure of the oversight body responsible for implementing and monitoring the regulatory duties. A key question concerns how the regulatory body is comprised. Does it primarily comprise political appointments? Are the appointments derived from both professionals (those regulated by the enabling statue) and nonprofessionals (those having no connection to the regulated profession)? Or is the regulatory process placed within a bureaucratic agency and duties administered by agency employees with the assistance of technical advisors knowledgeable in the profession or perhaps a formal advisory board? Regardless of the regulatory body composition, the following components will need to be resolved: minimum competency and continuing competency.

Minimum Competency

1. Education: What will the minimum level of education be for credentialed individuals? This is easier to answer once the body defines whether it is a single tier (licensing at only one level) or multi-tiered system (credentialing at multiple levels). Credentialing at multiple levels lends itself to defining levels of credentialing according to levels of education. For example, those holding a bachelor's or a master's degree qualify for specific levels of credentialing. Regulatory bodies also define whether the degree must be an accredited degree by a regional or national accrediting body or university accredited by such an accreditation body.

Most schools of social work at universities and colleges in the United States are accredited by the CSWE, and many state jurisdictions specify that degrees in social work must be accredited by CSWE to be eligible for licensure. In Canada, the Canadian Association of Schools of Social Work (CASSW) is the accreditation body. This requirement assists in ensuring public protection by establishing minimum criteria for social work education and granting of social work degrees. A recent challenge in some jurisdictions concerns allowing educational institutions associated with faith-based philosophies to be exempted from

CSWE accreditation and their graduates allowed to sit for credentialing.

2. *Testing:* The profession of social work benefits by having a nationally accepted examination. Currently, California is the only statewide jurisdiction continuing to use a specific state jurisdictional exam. ASWB contracts with the ACT Center Network to administer and maintain the security of the examination process, and exams are currently offered throughout the United States, Puerto Rico, Guam, and the District of Columbia. The local jurisdiction informs candidates which level of examination they qualify to take; although there is some variation, generally the requirements are consistent with the ASWB exam levels. Currently, there are four levels of examination offered:

- Bachelors: BSW degree from a CSWE-accredited program
- Masters: MSW degree from a CSWE-accredited program
- Clinical: MSW degree from a CSWE-accredited program, plus two years postgraduate clinical experience and approved supervision
- Advanced Generalist: MSW degree from a CSWE-accredited program, plus two years postgraduate experience (ASWB, 2013).

3. *Supervision and Experience:* Some jurisdictions require a specific amount and type of work experience to be eligible for social worker credentialing. Generally, this is expected at the advanced or clinical levels of practice credentialing or to compensate for deficits in another area of minimum competency, such as formal education. Most jurisdictions define who can supervise the professional experience that is used to seek social worker credentialing. Some jurisdictions require that the supervisor be approved prior to initiating the supervised experience and many require regular updates or reports during the supervised professional experience. Jurisdictions define the amount of supervised experience and how the supervision is to occur (individual or group session). Additionally, once the professional experience is completed, supervisors must attest to the readiness of the candidate based on the supervised experience. Supervised experience is another method of ensuring the individual possesses the knowledge, skills, and abilities for social worker credentialing.

Continued Competency and Continuing Education

Once a professional has successfully achieved the social work credential, most jurisdictions require credentialed individuals to maintain minimum competency, and most hope for increased professional competency through professional experience and additional formal and informal training. Most jurisdictions require credentialed professionals to demonstrate their continued competency through completion of continuing education hours as part of their re-credentialing process. These hours may be formally acknowledged by jurisdiction rules (i.e., approved continuing education providers) or a nationally recognized accrediting body.

Traditionally, programs offered for continuing education are for skills that enhance or reaffirm a social worker's professional knowledge, not necessarily specific to those skills necessary for the professional's current employment. Therefore, many continuing education opportunities take place outside the employment setting and at a cost to the employer or professional. Many employers attempt to offer continuing education opportunities for their employees as a benefit of employment. Some offer stipends for conference or workshop attendance if it can be demonstrated that the skills garnered will benefit the credentialed person and the employing agency. Continuing education can be earned through attendance at conferences, workshops, or online completion of self-study opportunities. Obtaining continuing education credit is one way regulatory boards can verify that a professional is at least continuing to participate in professional learning and training. Whether continuing education equates continuing competency is of great debate among social work professionals, social work educators, and regulatory board members.

CURRENT ISSUES IN SOCIAL WORKER REGULATION AND LICENSING

Portability: Endorsement versus Reciprocity

Reciprocity describes the custom by which a professional licensed in one jurisdiction is automatically licensed in a separate jurisdiction based on the issuance of the original license. Because licensing is a local function, most jurisdictions do not automatically issue a license based on licensure in a different area. Most jurisdictions will provide acceptance of those activities used toward credentialing in a separate jurisdiction, as long as the criteria are as rigorous as those in the new jurisdiction. This process is known as *endorsement*. However, very few jurisdictions have exactly the same criteria for licensure.

A review of the Social Work Laws and Regulations Comparison Database shows that jurisdictions vary in the amount of supervised experience, hours of face-to-face supervision, whether the supervision can be in-group or individual sessions, the minimum frequency that supervision must occur, and the qualifications of the person providing the supervision that is acceptable for credentialing (ASWB, 2013). To this end, ASWB has created a concept for a model law and encourages all jurisdictions regulating social workers to consider adopting its criteria as a basis for licensure. ASWB has also begun a Social Work Registry to assist credentialed social workers in maintaining documentation related to their licensure, certification, or registration status. This is particularly helpful if a regulated professional has resided in multiple jurisdictions, achieved specialty recognition in one jurisdiction but not another, or has been employed by a federal institution. The goals of the registry are to make verification of information used toward credentialing easier to access, have one place to call for verification of professional credentials held, and have the criteria used to achieve the credentials in one location.

Recent events, such as the tragedy of September 11, 2001, and Hurricanes Katrina and Rita in 2005, have shown the need for greater portability of social workers to perform disaster relief efforts. Additional issues have arisen in the field of adoption or custody home studies when the guardian or adoptive family may live in one jurisdiction and the child or children live in a separate one. Whether the professional will be required to be credentialed in the jurisdiction where the matter is handled is not only in the hands of the court but in the authority of the enabling statutes for the regulatory boards. Though some areas grant permission for credentialed professionals to perform in their jurisdiction for a specified period of time without formal efforts to be recognized by the jurisdiction, others do not grant such leniency. As such, professionals who regularly work in multiple jurisdictions must achieve and maintain credentialing in each area they serve professionally. This creates greater confusion for

the consumer, especially when credential acronyms are jurisdiction-specific along with the complaint and disciplinary processes. Serving multiple masters, as it were, can also be daunting to the professional, because each jurisdiction may have specific idiosyncratic criteria to its regulatory functions.

Multiple Masters and Dual Credentialing

As market forces drive professionals to find niches to offer greater opportunity for success in providing services, many professionals look to multiple credentials or specialty credentials to boost their marketability. Specialized credentials, certifications, and licenses in play therapy, hypnosis, anger management, mediation, and sex offender therapy are a few examples. One issue is who authorizes and issues the credential. Credentials can be offered by a separate state-governing agency, or can also be sanctioned by a professional association, such as registered play therapist (RPT) and RPT-supervisor, issued by the Association for Play Therapy.

If under the regulation of two government-sanctioned regulatory boards, professionals may face multiple disciplinary processes that could run into large legal expenses. Additionally, because each process is independent of the other, the time frame for resolution will be independent as well. It is not uncommon for one regulatory body to issue a sanction and the other to issue a more severe sanction for the same complaint. Practitioners need to provide contact and complaint filing information to each regulatory body for all credentials they hold. Many jurisdictions require professionals to provide signed written statements from consumers regarding the receipt of this information. Also, some boards require their code of conduct, which contains information on initiating a disciplinary complaint against a regulated professional, to be displayed publicly in the professional's primary place of employment.

Licensing of Social Work Faculty

Thyer and Seidl (2000) debate whether the social work faculty teaching practice courses should be regulated social workers. One argument is that for social work educators to be most effective, they need to be connected to practice, and licensure is one option to ensure faculty maintain current practice knowledge and technology. However, Seidl argues that there are already adequate academic accountability measures and that requiring licensure does not ensure better teaching of practice by faculty. Marson (2006) argues that licensing of social work faculty is an ethical issue. Whether it is an ethical issue or an issue of competence, regulation of faculty is an issue of public health and safety. Social work as a profession has followed a long historical path toward establishing and maintaining its existence, status, and identity as a professional field. Though much progress has been made, there are many issues left to be resolved regarding professional regulation, including the balance of public protection, professional competence and practice, and addressing the need for consistency and continuity on a national and international scale.

WEBSITES

American Board of Examiners in Clinical Social
  Work: http://www.abecsw.org/resources.html
Association of Social Work Boards: http://
  www.aswb.org
Council on Licensure, Enforcement and
  Regulation: http://www.clearhq.org/
Council on Social Work Education: http://
  www.cswe.org

National Association of Social Work: http://
  www.socialworkers.org

References

Association of Social Work Boards. (2004). *Analysis of the practice of social work: 2003 final report.* Retrieved from: http://www.aswb.org/Practice_analysis_files/ASWBPracticeAnalysis_Final%20Report.pdf
Association of Social Works Boards. (2012). *Model social work practice act.* Retrieved from: http://www.aswb.org/pdfs/Model_law.pdf
Association of Social Work Boards. (2013). *Social work laws & regulations database.* Retrieved from: www.datapathdesign.com/ASWB/Laws/Prod/cgibin/LawWebRpts2DLL.dll/18ilt4607q92dz1e3u79i0j2sr7x/$
Biggerstaff, M. A. (1995). Licensing, regulation, and certification. In R. L. Edwards & J. G. Hopps (Eds.), *Encyclopedia of social work* (pp. 1616–1624). Washington, DC: NASW Press.
Marson, S. (2006). Editorial comment: Licensing of social work faculty. *Journal of Social Work Values and Ethics, 3*(2). Retrieved from: www.social-worker.com/jswve/content/view/42/46.
Thyer, B. A., & Biggerstaff, M. A. (1989). *Professional social work credentialing and legal regulation.* Springfield, IL: Thompson.
Thyer, B. A., & Seidl, F. (2000). Point/counterpoint: Should licensure be required for faculty who teach direct practice courses? *Journal of Social Work Education, 36*(2), 187–201.

22   The Impaired Social Work Professional

Frederic G. Reamer

All professions are paying increased attention to the problem of *impaired* practitioners. Social work's first national acknowledgment of the problem of *impaired* practitioners was in 1979, when the National Association of Social Workers (NASW) released a public policy

statement on alcoholism and alcohol-related problems (NASW, Commission on Employment and Economic Support, 1987). By 1980, a small nationwide support group for chemically dependent practitioners, Social Workers Helping Social Workers, had formed (NASW, 1987). In 1982,

NASW established the Occupational Social Work Task Force, which was charged with developing a "consistent professional approach for distressed NASW members" (NASW, 1987, p. 7). In 1984, the NASW delegate assembly issued a resolution on impairment, and in 1987, NASW published the *Impaired Social Worker Program Resource Book*, prepared by the National Commission on Employment and Economic Support, to help practitioners design a program for *impaired* social workers. In 1996, NASW completely rewrote its Code of Ethics and included several explicit standards concerning social workers' responsibility to address their own and colleagues' impairment. According to the current standards (NASW, 2008):

Social workers who have direct knowledge of a social work colleague's impairment that is due to personal problems, psychosocial distress, substance abuse, or mental health difficulties and that interferes with practice effectiveness should consult with that colleague when feasible and assist the colleague in taking remedial action. (Standard 2.09[a])

Social workers who believe that a social work colleague's impairment interferes with practice effectiveness and that the colleague has not taken adequate steps to address the impairment should take action through appropriate channels established by employers, agencies, NASW, licensing and regulatory bodies, and other professional organizations. (Standard 2.09[b])

Social workers should not allow their own personal problems, psychosocial distress, legal problems, substance abuse, or mental health difficulties to interfere with their professional judgment and performance or to jeopardize the best interests of people for whom they have a professional responsibility. (Standard 4.05[a])

Social workers whose personal problems, psychosocial distress, legal problems, substance abuse, or mental health difficulties interfere with their professional judgment and performance should immediately seek consultation and take appropriate remedial action by seeking professional help, making adjustments in workload, terminating practice, or taking any other steps necessary to protect clients and others. (Standard 4.05[b])

Organized efforts to address *impaired* workers have their historical roots in the late 1930s and early 1940s following the emergence of Alcoholics Anonymous and the need during World War II to retain a sound work force (Reamer, 1992, 2013). These early occupational alcoholism programs eventually led, in the early

1970s, to the emergence of employee assistance programs (EAPs) designed to address a broad range of problems experienced by workers. In 1972, the Council on Mental Health of the American Medical Association released a statement that physicians have an ethical responsibility to recognize and report impairment among colleagues. In 1976, a group of attorneys recovering from alcoholism started Lawyers Concerned for Lawyers to address chemical dependence in the profession, and in 1980, a group of recovering psychologists inaugurated a similar group, Psychologists Helping Psychologists (Kilburg, Nathan, & Thoreson, 1986; Knutsen, 1977; Laliotis & Grayson, 1985; McCrady, 1989). In 1981, the American Psychological Association held its first open forum on impairment at its annual meeting (Stadler, Willing, Eberhage, & Ward, 1988).

Strategies for dealing with professionals whose work is affected by problems such as substance abuse, mental illness, and emotional stress have become more prevalent and visible. Professional associations and groups of practitioners have convened to examine impairment among colleagues and organize efforts to address the problem (Bissell & Haberman, 1984; Coombs, 2000; Katsavdakis, Gabbard, & Athey, 2004; Prochaska & Norcross, 1983; Siebert, 2004, 2005). Ironically, however, in contrast to a number of other helping professions, the social work literature contains little discussion of *impaired* professionals (Bissell, Fewell, & Jones, 1980; Fausel, 1988; Reamer, 2003, 2006, 2013; Siebert, 2004, 2005).

EXTENT OF IMPAIRMENT

Both the seriousness of social workers' impairment and the forms it takes vary (Reamer, 1992, 2013; Siebert, 2004, 2005). Impairment may involve failure to provide competent care or violation of the profession's ethical standards. It may take such forms as providing flawed or inferior services to a client, sexual involvement with a client, or failure to carry out one's duties as a result of substance abuse or mental illness. Lamb et al. (1987) provided a widely cited, comprehensive definition of impairment among professionals:

Interference in professional functioning that is reflected in one or more of the following ways: (a) an inability and/or unwillingness to acquire and integrate professional standards into one's repertoire of professional behavior; (b) an inability to acquire professional skills in order to reach an acceptable level of competency; and (c) an inability to control personal stress, psychological dysfunction, and/or excessive emotional reactions that interfere with professional functioning. (p. 598)

In one of the relatively few studies of impairment among social workers, Siebert (2004) found that 19% of North Carolina social workers reported clinically significant symptoms of depression, 16% had considered suicide at some point in their lives, 20% were taking medication for depression, and 60% self-reported depression currently or at some point in the past. In a prevalence study that included social workers and other professionals, Deutsch (1985) found that more than half her sample of social workers, psychologists, and master's-level counselors reported significant problems with depression. Nearly four-fifths (82%) reported problems with relationships, approximately one-tenth (11%) reported substance abuse problems, and 2% reported past suicide attempts.

Given the distressing absence of empirical data on social workers, it is not possible to estimate the prevalence of impairment within the profession. Therefore, social workers must look primarily to what is known about impairment in professions that are allied with social work, such as psychology and psychiatry. Of course, one cannot infer prevalence rates for social workers on the basis of data from these other professions. However, despite some important differences in their mission, methods, and organizational context, practitioners in these professions offer a number of similar services and face similar forms of occupational stress and strain (Gilroy, Carroll, & Murra, 2002; Smith & Moss, 2009; Williams, et al., 2010).

Prevalence studies conducted among psychologists suggest a significant degree of distress within that profession. For example, in their study of 425 counseling psychologists, Gilroy, Carroll, and Murra (2002) found that more than three-fifths (62%) reported symptoms of depression.

In a study of 749 psychologists, Guy, Poelstra, and Stark (1989) found that 74.3% reported "personal distress" during the previous three years, and 36.7% of this group believed that their distress decreased the quality of care they provided to clients. Pope, Tabachnick, and Keith-Spiegel

(1987) reported that 62.2% of the members of division 29 (psychotherapy) of the American Psychological Association admitted to "working when too distressed to be effective" (p. 993). In their survey of 167 licensed psychologists, Wood, Klein, Cross, Lammers, and Elliott (1985) found that nearly one-third (32.3%) reported experiencing depression or burnout to an extent that interfered with their work. They also found that a significant portion of their sample reported being aware of colleagues whose work was seriously affected by drug or alcohol use, sexual overtures toward clients, or depression and burnout.

In a comprehensive review of a series of empirical studies focused specifically on sexual contact between therapists and clients, Pope (1988) concluded that the aggregate average of reported sexual contact is 8.3% by male therapists and 1.7% by female therapists. Pope reported that one study (Gechtman & Bouhoutsos, 1985) found that 3.8% of male social workers admitted to sexual contact with clients.

CAUSES OF IMPAIRMENT

Several studies report a variety of forms and sources of impairment among mental health professionals (Celenza, 2007; Gabriel, 2005; Zur, 2007). Katsavdakis, Gabbard, and Athey (2004) found that the three most commonly cited problems leading psychiatrists, other physicians, psychologists, and social workers to seek help were suicidal behavior, marital problems, and work-related problems. Guy et al. (1989) and Thoreson, Miller, and Krauskopf (1989) found diverse sources of reported stress in clinicians' lives, including their jobs, the illness or death of relatives, marital or relationship problems, financial problems, midlife crises, personal physical or mental illness, legal problems, and substance abuse.

Lamb et al. (1987) argued that professional education itself can produce unique forms of stress and impairment, primarily as a result of the close clinical supervision to which students are typically subjected, the disruption in their personal lives often caused by the demands of schoolwork and internships, and the pressures placed on them by academic programs. These authors found that the most common sources of impairment are personality disorders, depression and other emotional problems, marital problems, and physical illness.

This review of research suggests that distress among clinicians generally falls into two categories: environmental stress, which is a function of employment conditions (actual working conditions and the broader culture's lack of support of the human services mission) or professional training, and personal stress, caused by problems with one's marriage, relationships, emotional and physical health, and finances. With respect to psychotherapists in particular, Wood et al. (1985) noted that professionals encounter special problems from the extension of their therapeutic role into the nonwork aspects of their lives (such as relationships with friends and family members), the absence of reciprocity in relationships with clients (therapists are "always giving"), the frequently slow and erratic nature of the therapeutic process, and personal issues that are raised as a result of their work with clients (Kilburg, Kaslow, & VandenBos, 1988; Mahoney, 1997).

RESPONSE TO IMPAIRMENT

Little is known about the extent to which *impaired* professionals voluntarily seek help for their problems (Gutheil & Brodsky, 2008; Olsheski & Leech, 1996; Smith & Moss, 2009). In one of the few empirical studies, Guy et al. (1989) found that 70% of the distressed clinical psychologists they surveyed sought some form of therapeutic assistance. Approximately one-fourth (26.6%) entered individual psychotherapy, while 10.7% entered family therapy. A small portion of this group participated in self-help groups (3.4%) or was hospitalized (2.2%). Some were placed on medication (4.1%). Exactly 10% of this group temporarily suspended their professional practice.

These findings contrast with those of Wood et al. (1985), who found that only 55.2% of clinicians who reported problems that interfered with their work (substance abuse, sexual overtures toward clients, depression, and burnout) sought help. Approximately two-fifths (42%) of all the clinicians surveyed by Wood and colleagues, including *impaired* and nonimpaired professionals, reported having offered help to *impaired* colleagues at some time or having referred them to therapists. Only 7.9% of the sample indicated that they had reported an *impaired* colleague to a local regulatory body. Two-fifths (40.2%) were aware of instances in which they believed no action was taken to help an impaired colleague.

Several phenomena may explain *impaired* professionals' reluctance to seek help and the reluctance of their colleagues to confront them about their problems. Historically, professionals have been hesitant to acknowledge impairment within their ranks because they feared how practitioners would react to confrontation and how such confrontation might affect the future relationships of colleagues who must work together (Bernard & Jara, 1986; Coombs, 2000; McCrady, 1989; Wood et al., 1985). Thoreson, Nathan, Skorina, and Kilburg (1983) also argued that *impaired* professionals sometimes find it difficult to seek help because of their mythological belief in their nearly infinite power and invulnerability. The fact that an increasing number of psychotherapists are involved in private practice exacerbates the problem because of the reduced opportunity for colleagues to observe any unethical or inept practice.

In a valuable study by Deutsch (1985), a diverse group of therapists (including social workers) who admitted to personal problems indicated a variety of reasons for not seeking professional help, including the following: they believed that an acceptable therapist was not available, they sought help from family members or friends, they feared exposure and the disclosure of confidential information, they were concerned about the amount of effort required and the cost, they had a spouse or partner who was unwilling to participate in treatment, they failed to admit the seriousness of the problem, they believed they should be able to work their problems out themselves, and they believed that therapy would not help.

Several organized efforts have been made to identify and address the problems of *impaired* professionals. There is a growing consensus that a model strategy should include several components (Schoener & Gonsiorek, 1988; Smith & Moss, 2009; Sonnenstuhl, 1989). First, there must be adequate means for identifying *impaired* practitioners. Professionals must be willing to assume some responsibility for acknowledging impairment among colleagues. Second, a social worker's initial identification and documentation of a colleague's impairment should be followed by speculation about the possible causes and by what Sonnenstuhl (1989) described as "constructive confrontation." Third, once a social worker decides who shall carry out the confrontation, a decision must be made about whether to help the *impaired* colleague identify ways to seek help voluntarily or to refer the colleague to a supervisor, professional association, or local regulatory body (such as a NASW ethics committee or a licensing board). Assuming there are sufficient reasons to support a rehabilitation plan, the *impaired* practitioner's colleague, supervisor, or local regulatory body should make specific recommendations. The possibilities include close supervision, personal psychotherapy, and treatment for substance abuse. In some cases, it may be necessary for a licensing board or ethics committee to impose some type of sanction, such as censure, limitations on the professional's social work practice (for example, concerning clientele that can be served), termination of employment, suspension or expulsion from a professional association, or loss of license.

Unfortunately, relatively little research has been conducted on the effectiveness of efforts to rehabilitate *impaired* professionals (Fletcher & Ronis, 2005; Sonnenstuhl, 1989; Trice & Beyer, 1984). Moreover, the few published empirical evaluations—which reported mixed results for various treatment programs—focused primarily on impaired physicians (Herrington, Benzer, Jacobson, & Hawkins, 1982; Katsavdakis et al., 2004; Morse, Martin, Swenson, & Niven, 1984; Pearson, 1982; Shore, 1982).

AN AGENDA FOR SOCIAL WORK

For a profession to be truly self-regulating, it cannot rely entirely on the efforts of dissatisfied or abused clients to file complaints about *impaired* practitioners. The profession must strengthen its efforts to identify *impaired* practitioners and respond to them in a meaningful way. Social workers, like many other professionals, understandably may be reluctant to confront *impaired* colleagues. Nonetheless, it is incumbent on the profession to confront incompetence and unethical behavior and offer humane assistance. Attention should be paid to social workers in solo private practice as well as those who work in group settings, where there may be more opportunity to observe impairment.

Social workers must expand education about the problem of *impaired* practitioners. Relatively few social workers have been trained to identify and confront impairment. The profession's organizations and agencies must sponsor workshops and in-service training on the subject to acquaint social workers with information about the forms that impairment can take, the signs to look for, and ways to confront the problem.

In addition, social workers should develop collegial-assistance programs to assist *impaired* social workers. Although some cases of impairment must be dealt with through formal adjudication mechanisms (for example, conducted by NASW ethics committees or licensing boards), many cases can be handled primarily by arranging therapeutic or rehabilitative services for distressed practitioners. *Impaired* social workers should have access to competent service providers who are trained to understand professionals' special concerns and needs. For instance, state chapters of NASW can enter into agreements with local EAPs, to which *impaired* members can be referred.

Social workers have a keen understanding of human struggle and impairment. The profession has a tradition of addressing the problems of individuals, along with the environmental stresses that surround them. The same tradition must be extended to *impaired* colleagues.

WEBSITES

Journal of Social Work Values and Ethics.
  http://www.socialworker.com/jswve/
NASW Code of Ethics. http://www
  .socialworkers.org/pubs/code/code.asp
Social Work Licensing Laws and Regulations,
  including ethics guidelines. https://www
  .datapathdesign.com/ASWB/Laws/Prod/
  cgi-bin/LawWebRpts2DLL.dll/166iw4k0bdm
  ino1efrkep0cu2vy4/
Social Work Today: Eye on Ethics. http://www
  .socialworktoday.com/eye_on_ethics_index
  .shtml

References

Bernard, J., & Jara, C. (1986). The failure of clinical psychology students to apply understood ethical principles. *Professional Psychology: Research and Practice, 17*, 316–321.
Bissell, L., Fewell, L., & Jones, R. (1980). The alcoholic social worker: A survey. *Social Work in Health Care, 5*, 421–432.
Bissell, L., & Haberman, P. W. (1984). *Alcoholism in the professions.* New York, NY: Oxford University Press.
Celenza, A. (2007). *Sexual boundary violations: Therapeutic, supervisory, and academic contexts.* Lanham, MD: Aronson.

Coombs, R. H. (2000). *Drug-impaired professionals.* Cambridge, MA: Harvard University Press.

Deutsch, C. (1985). A survey of therapists' personal problems and treatment. *Professional Psychology: Research and Practice, 16,* 305–315.

Fausel, D. F. (1988). Helping the helper heal: Co-dependency in helping professionals. *Journal of Independent Social Work, 3*(2), 35–45.

Fletcher, C. E., & Ronis, D. L. (2005). Satisfaction of impaired health care professionals with mandatory treatment and monitoring. *Journal of Addictive Diseases, 24*(3), 61–75.

Gabriel, L. (2005). *Speaking the unspeakable: The ethics of dual relationships in counseling and psychotherapy.* New York, NY: Routledge.

Gechtman, L., & Bouhoutsos, J. (1985). Sexual intimacy between social workers and clients. Paper presented at the annual meeting of the Society for Clinical Social Workers, University City, California.

Gilroy, P. J., Carroll, L., & Murra, J. (2002). A preliminary survey of counseling psychologists' personal experiences with depression and treatment. *Professional Psychology, Research, and Practice, 33,* 402–407.

Gutheil, T. G., & Brodsky, A. (2008). *Preventing boundary violations in clinical practice.* New York, NY: Guilford.

Guy, J. D., Poelstra, P. L., & Stark, M. (1989). Personal distress and therapeutic effectiveness: National survey of psychologists practicing psychotherapy. *Professional Psychology: Research and Practice, 20,* 48–50.

Herrington, R. E., Benzer, D. G., Jacobson, G. R., & Hawkins, M. K. (1982). Treating substance-use disorders among physicians. *JAMA: Journal of the American Medical Association, 247,* 2253–2257.

Katsavdakis, K. A., Gabbard, G. O., & Athey, G. I. (2004). Profiles of impaired health professionals. *Bulletin of the Menninger Clinic, 68*(1), 60–72.

Kilburg, R. R., Kaslow, F. W., & VandenBos, G. R. (1988). Professionals in distress. *Hospital and Community Psychiatry, 39,* 723–725.

Kilburg, R. R., Nathan, P. E., & Thoreson, R. W. (Eds.). (1986). *Professionals in distress: Issues, syndromes, and solutions in psychology.* Washington, DC: American Psychological Association.

Knutsen, E. (1977). On the emotional well-being of psychiatrists: Overview and rationale. *American Journal of Psychoanalysis, 37,* 123–129.

Laliotis, D. A., & Grayson, J. H. (1985). Psychologist heal thyself: What is available for the impaired psychologist? *American Psychologist, 40,* 84–96.

Lamb, D. H., Presser, N. R., Pfost, K. S., Baum, M. C., Jackson, V. R., & Jarvis, P. A. (1987). Confronting professional impairment during the internship: Identification, due process, and remediation.

Professional Psychology: Research and Practice, 18, 597–603.

Mahoney, M. J. (1997). Psychotherapists' personal problems and self-care patterns. *Professional Psychology: Research and Practice, 28*(1), 14–16.

McCrady, B. S. (1989). The distressed or *impaired* professional: From retribution to rehabilitation. *Journal of Drug Issues, 19,* 337–349.

Morse, R. M., Martin, M. A., Swenson, W. M., & Niven, R. G. (1984). Prognosis for physicians treated for alcoholism and drug dependence. *JAMA: Journal of the American Medical Association, 251,* 743–746.

National Association of Social Workers, Commission on Employment and Economic Support. (1987). *Impaired* social worker program resource book. Silver Spring, MD: NASW Press.

National Association of Social Workers. (2008). *NASW code of ethics* (Rev. ed.). Washington, DC: NASW Press.

Olsheski, J., & Leech, L. L. (1996). Programmatic interventions and treatment of impaired professionals. *Journal of Humanistic Education and Development, 34*(3), 128–140.

Pearson, M. M. (1982). Psychiatric treatment of 250 physicians. *Psychiatric Annals, 12,* 194–206.

Pope, K S. (1988). How clients are harmed by sexual contact with mental health professionals: The syndrome and its prevalence. *Journal of Counseling and Development, 67,* 222–226.

Pope, K. S., Tabachnick, B. G., & Keith-Spiegel, P. (1987). Ethics of practice: The beliefs and behaviors of psychologists as therapists. *American Psychologist, 42,* 993–1006.

Prochaska, J., & Norcross, J. (1983). Psychotherapists' perspectives on treating themselves and their clients for psychic distress. *Professional Psychology: Research and Practice, 14,* 642–655.

Reamer, F. G. (1992). The impaired social worker. *Social Work, 37*(2), 165–170.

Reamer, F. G. (2003). *Social work malpractice and liability: Strategies for prevention* (2nd ed.). New York, NY: Columbia University Press.

Reamer, F. G. (2006). *Ethical standards in social work: A review of the NASW Code of Ethics* (2nd ed.). Washington, DC: NASW Press.

Reamer, F. G. (2013). *Social work values and ethics* (4th ed.). New York, NY: Columbia University Press.

Schoener, G. R., & Gonsiorek, J. (1988). Assessment and development of rehabilitation plans for counselors who have sexually exploited their clients. *Journal of Counseling and Development, 67,* 227–232.

Shore, J. H. (1982). The *impaired* physician: Four years after probation. *JAMA: Journal of the American Medical Association, 248,* 3127–3130.

Siebert, D. C. (2004). Depression in North Carolina social workers: Implications for practice and research. *Social Work Research, 28,* 30–40.

Siebert, D. C. (2005). Help seeking and AOD use among social workers: Patterns, barriers, and implications. *Social Work, 50,* 65–75.

Smith, P. L., & Moss, S. B. (2009). Psychologist impairment: What is it, how can it be prevented, and what can be done to address it? *Clinical Psychology: Science and Practice, 16,* 1–15.

Sonnenstuhl, W. J. (1989). Reaching the *impaired* professional: Applying findings from organizational and occupational research. *Journal of Drug Issues, 19,* 533–539.

Stadler, H. A., Willing, K., Eberhage, M. G., & Ward, W. H. (1988). Impairment: Implications for the counseling profession. *Journal of Counseling and Development, 66,* 258–260.

Thoreson, R. W., Miller, M., & Krauskopf, C. J. (1989). The distressed psychologist: Prevalence and treatment considerations. *Professional Psychology: Research and Practice, 20,* 153–158.

Thoreson, R. W., Nathan, P. E., Skorina, J. K., & Kilburg, R. R. (1983). The alcoholic psychologist: Issues, problems, and implications for the profession. *Professional Psychology: Research and Practice, 14,* 670–684.

Trice, H. M., & Beyer, J. M. (1984). Work related outcomes of the constructive confrontation strategy in a job-based alcoholism program. *Journal of Studies on Alcohol, 45,* 393–404.

Williams, B. E., Pomerantz, A. M., Segrist, D. J., & Pettibone, J. C. (2010). How impaired is too impaired? Ratings of psychologist impairment by psychologists in independent practice. *Ethics & Behavior, 20,* 149–160.

Wood, B. J., Klein, S., Cross, H. J., Lammers, C. J., & Elliott, J. K. (1985). *Impaired* practitioners: Psychologists' opinions about prevalence, and proposals for intervention. *Professional Psychology: Research and Practice, 16,* 843–850.

Zur, O. (2007). *Boundaries in psychotherapy: Ethical and clinical explorations.* Washington, DC: American Psychological Association.

Technology and Social Work Practice

23   *Micro, Mezzo, and Macro Applications*

Jonathan B. Singer & Melanie Sage

Social workers have an ethical responsibility to attend to the environmental forces that create, contribute to, and address problems in living (National Association of Social Workers [NASW], 1999). Developments in Internet and computer technologies (ICT) such as social networks, webcams, texting, virtual reality, and smart phone apps, have significantly changed the way we communicate with one another and interact with our environment (Mishna, Bogo, Root, Sawyer, & Khoury-Kassabri, 2012). Consider the following: Most Americans now get their health-related information from the Internet, instead of from friends, family, and health professionals as they did a decade ago (Fox & Duggan, 2013). In 2012, nearly a third of Americans reported trying to diagnose themselves or someone else using *only* information found on the Internet (Fox & Duggan, 2013). As people combine new ways of communicating with new ways of seeking health-related information, there has been a natural evolution toward new ways of providing social work services. Just as the Internet evolved from a collection of static Web pages (Web 1.0) to a virtual community called Web 2.0 (O'Reilly, 2005), the integration of social work with ICTs has created a new paradigm for social work, called *Social Work 2.0* (Singer, 2009).

The National Association of Social Workers (NASW) and the Association of Social Work Boards (ASWB) recognize technology as a significant environmental force and have published 16 standards for technology in social work, covering clinical practice, administration, advocacy and community organizing, and research (NASW, 2005). Although these standards provide a foundation for Social Work 2.0, the integration of ICTs and social work services has been limited by micro factors such as the fact that traditional consumers of social work services are the least likely to have access to ICTs (Fox & Duggan, 2013) as well as macro factors such as limited funding for current technology, and training in its possible uses (Wodarski & Frimpong, 2013). The purpose of this chapter is to review existing literature on technology and social services; identify and define key terms and concepts; and describe uses, benefits, and limitations of technology and social service delivery at the micro (clinical practice), mezzo (community practice), and macro (policy) levels. The goal is to promote dialogue and discussion about the role of current and emerging technology in social service delivery.

KEY CONCEPTS

The 15 most important Social Work 2.0 concepts are defined and illustrated in Table 23.1. Some concepts, such as online therapy, e-therapy and telehealth, have overlapping yet distinct meanings (McCarty & Clancy, 2002). For simplicity, the term "online therapy" is used when referring to any mental health service that is provided using ICTs.

USES, BENEFITS, AND LIMITATIONS OF TECHNOLOGY IN SERVICE DELIVERY

The uses, benefits, and limitations of technology in the micro, mezzo, and macro areas of clinical practice, community organizing, and policy issues have been addressed by a number of authors (Barak & Grohol, 2011; Dowling & Rickwood, 2013; Kanani & Regehr, 2003; Mishna et al., 2012; Perron, Taylor, Glass, & Margerum-Leys, 2010; Richards & Viganó, 2013; Singer, 2009; Slone, Reese, & McClellan, 2012; Wodarski & Frimpong, 2013). Whereas the clinical literature is written mostly by psychologists and counselors, with some notable contributions by social

workers (Freddolino & Blaschke, 2008; Langlois, 2011), social workers have contributed extensively to the community organizing and policy literature and have addressed issues such as how to use technology for advocacy of social action (Hick & McNutt, 2002; J. Young, 2012) and how online mental health services are regulated and reimbursed (Reamer, 2013a).

ONLINE MENTAL HEALTH

Since the publication of the previous version of this chapter (Singer, 2009), scholars have written over 500 articles about online mental health services. Meta-analyses and comprehensive reviews of those studies suggest that online mental health services are effective in reducing symptomatology and that they increase functioning for some mental health disorders (e.g., depression, anxiety, eating disorders, posttraumatic stress disorder [PTSD], and substance use disorders), but not for others, such as weight loss (Barak, Hen, Boniel-Nissim, & Shapira, 2008). This body of research has found no significant difference in outcomes between synchronous (e.g., live webcam) and asynchronous (e.g., e-mail) online therapy. While it is possible that certain online environments are better suited for certain problem areas (e.g., virtual reality for treating PTSD or phobias, and text-based reminders for medication compliance), that remains a question for empirical investigation (Pallavicini et al., 2013). Finally, and perhaps most importantly, research comparing face-to-face (F2F) therapies to online therapies has consistently found that client outcomes in online therapy are as good (Barak et al., 2008; Beatty & Lambert, 2013; Champion, Newton, Barrett, & Teesson, 2013; Dowling & Rickwood, 2013; Richards & Viganó, 2013; Slone et al., 2012), and in some cases better (Birgit, Horn, & Andreas, 2013) than F2F therapies.

Research on online and F2F therapies share many similarities: most research is on individual therapy, although interventions exist for couples (Doss, Benson, Georgia, & Christensen, 2013) and groups (van der Zanden, Kramer, Gerrits, & Cuijpers, 2012); most consumers of online mental health services are women; and most empirical studies use cognitive-behavioral and behavioral approaches (Barak et al., 2008). According to a 2008 meta-analysis, the most effective online treatment interventions were

TABLE 23.1 Definitions and Examples of Technology Terms

Term	Definition	Example of Use
Asynchronous communication	Delayed communication; does not occur in real time	Correspondence via letters or e-mail
Chat/messaging	Synchronous web-based communication	Crisis hotline provides real-time text-based services using a program that loads into a browser, allowing the worker and client to communicate instantly
E-supervision	Supervision using e-mail, chat, phone, or webcams—anything but traditional face-to-face supervision	Four clinicians from different states dial in to the same telesupervision group
Online therapy (synonymous with e-, cyber-, e-mail, or chat therapy)	Therapy using technologies, rather than traditional face-to-face services	Client and therapist conduct therapy over e-mail, chat, webcam, or a virtual-world-like Second Life
GIS (Geographical Information Systems)	Computer software that allows social workers to map services and identify where service needs exist	Crisis worker at a nationwide crisis hotline locates local referrals for a suicidal client using GIS software
mHealth	Health care delivered on mobile communication devices such as mobile phones smartphones, and tablets.	Client downloads an app that reminds her to take her medicine, prompts her to rate her mood, and uses the built-in GPS to trigger an alarm when she enters a bar.
Podcast/vodast	Subscription-based downloadable audio/video files	Client downloads and listens to an audio file created by the therapist on a clinically relevant topic (e.g., relaxation training)
Second Life	An Internet-based virtual world where people can interact with each other and communicate via chat or voice	Services, such as a rape-crisis shelter, are developed and accessed by members of the virtual community
Social Work 2.0	The integration of computer and Internet technologies with traditional social work	Service plans include relevant technology in service provision and goal attainment
Synchronous communication	Communication that occurs in real time	Traditional face-to-face social work, such as a therapy session; e-therapy using real time technology (e.g., chat)
Telehealth	The use of communication technology to provide services to remote locations	Social worker in a rural area uses the phone for assessment and diagnosis
Microblog/micropost	Short posts (usually less than 160 characters) intended to be distributed to "followers."	Stakeholders use Twitter and Facebook to disseminate information and organize "calls to action."
VoIP (voice over Internet protocol)	The routing of voice conversations over the Internet	Client uses VoIP to make free phone therapy appointments
Webinar	Internet-based seminar that allows for synchronous communication between people in remote locations and the presenter	Three social workers in different states give an interactive continuing education presentation to social workers from all over the world
Web 2.0	A conception of the Internet as an interactive medium	Consumers and staff co-create the information on an agency Web site using a wiki

cognitive behavioral therapies (CBTs), followed by psycho-educational and behavioral therapies (Barak et al., 2008). Online treatments using narrative therapy or psychodynamic approaches have received a great deal of conceptual attention because of their use of text (narrative) and self-reflection/insight (psychodynamic) (Balick, 2012; Migone, 2013), but have rarely been used in empirical studies (Andersson et al., 2012).

There are a number of notable limitations to online therapy and its existing evidence base. Although online therapies have been evaluated with people of all ages, there is some evidence to suggest that older adults and older therapists are less likely to trust online mental health services (Dowling & Rickwood, 2013; Miller & Bell, 2012). Although this might lend some support to the notion that online therapy is better suited for people who grew up with ICTs (e.g., "digital natives") than for people who did not (e.g., "digital immigrants") (Prensky, 2001), there has been no research to support the notion that online therapy is inherently more effective or feasible with younger versus older adults. There are problem areas for which no online treatments have been developed or tested (e.g., online family therapy); problem areas with only a single study (e.g., gambling addiction) (Gainsbury & Blaszczynski, 2011); and problem areas with conflicting evidence (e.g., the evidence for the efficacy of computerized CBT for depression; cf., Andrews, Cuijpers, Craske, McEvoy, & Titov, 2010; So et al., 2013). Even with problem areas for which there is evidence of efficacy, online therapies are susceptible to becoming irrelevant because of the rapid changes in technologies that are being evaluated and used in practice. Finally, in part because of the recency of online therapy, the long-term effectiveness of most online treatments has yet to be established (Dowling & Rickwood, 2013; So et al., 2013).

Types of Online Mental Health Services

Barak and Grohol suggest four distinct categories for online mental health services: (1) online counseling and psychotherapy; (2) online support groups and blogs; (3) interactive, self-guided interventions; and (4) psycho-educational websites (Barak & Grohol, 2011). These categories vary in function, evidence-base, and degree of interpersonal interaction (most = online therapy, least = psycho-educational websites).

1. *Online counseling and psychotherapy* is the provision of mental health services by a mental health professional using ICTs. Online therapy can occur in real time (synchronously) using a webcam, via virtual reality (VR) environment, chat, or other technology; or in delayed time (asynchronously) using e-mail, texting, or video responses. Providers and consumers of online therapy consistently report that one of the most important reasons to use online therapy is "convenience" (K. S. Young, 2005). For providers, it minimizes or eliminates travel time to, and overhead costs for, office space. For consumers, online therapy can reduce structural barriers to treatment, such as transportation and access to providers (McCoyd & Kerson, 2006). For example, people who travel for business, such a truck drivers, or people who stay at work sites for extended periods of time, such as oil rig crew operators or active military, can access mental health services using VoIP programs like Skype, webcams, or even texting. In theory, clients have greater choice of therapists (e.g., characteristics, education), mode of therapy (e.g., chat, webcam), length of session, and time of day. Unlike F2F therapy, clients and providers increasingly have 24/7 online access. Consequently, online therapists are encouraged to establish boundaries regarding frequency and duration of online communications (Kanani & Regehr, 2003; Kolmes, 2010).

Online mental health providers range from those who provide online therapy exclusively (e.g., http://onlinetherapyinstitute.com/) to therapists who provide mostly F2F services, but use ICTs to provide services to one or two clients. Social workers who use technology such as e-mail or texting to confirm therapy appointments are not providing online therapy (Mishna et al., 2012). Providers of online mental health services must be aware of security concerns, HIPPA regulations, and other ethical and legal issues that arise when providing therapy online (see Reamer, 2013b for a comprehensive review). Therefore, many providers pay secure, HIPPA-compliant third party online therapy sites to host their online sessions, or join a network of online therapy providers (www.telementalhealthcomparisons.com). One of the earliest selling points of online therapy was that clients could be anonymous and anywhere in the world (Schopler, Abell, & Galinsky, 1998). Today, however, nearly all professional associations (e.g., NASW, APA) recommend verification of identify and emergency contact information prior to providing services. Some third-party sites require clients to verify their identity prior to connecting them with a provider. Some therapists require at least one F2F meeting for clients who wish to meet online in order to verify the client's identify, get signatures (consent forms, treatment plan), and begin establishing a therapeutic alliance.

How Online Therapy Works: Clients register at the therapist's website with a user name and password, supply a working e-mail address, and perhaps read descriptions of participating therapists. Once the account has been verified, clients can book sessions through an online calendar and decide which type of online therapy they would like: e-mail, chat, phone (either traditional land line or Voice over Internet Protocol [VoIP]), or VR. Third-party therapy sites provide clients with verification of provider credentials, articles on treatment issues, professionally vetted links, and personalized logins where clients can access individualized content such as crisis plans and client-specific podcasts. These sites provide therapists with secure technology, HIPPA-compliant storage of documents, scheduling services, payment management, and confidential modes of communication. McCarty and Clancy (2002) suggested that the most important contribution of online therapy is in revolutionizing recordkeeping. Whereas traditional records (paper or electronic) are essentially a one-sided account of treatment, therapy conducted over e-mail, chat, and even text messaging creates a complete record of communication between client and clinician. Video therapy can be recorded and reviewed by clients either during session or in-between sessions. With either text or video, clients and clinicians can review past sessions to identify treatment progress and clinicians can use the transcripts in consultation. Currently there is no state licensing board that allows social workers to practice across state lines. As a result, clients need to be in-state in order to benefit from the protections afforded by the licensing board. Although getting licensed in all 50 states is impractical, therapists who live near state lines have the option of getting licensed in two states. Some therapists whose in-state clients are hours away develop treatment contracts and/or safety plans that include a local therapist who will be on-call for crises or any time a F2F therapy session is needed. However, given the long history of phone-based crisis intervention services, and more recently chat-based "hotlines," some argue that face-to-face services are not required, even for life and death situations (Barak, 2007).

2. Online support groups and blogs. "Online support groups" refers to peer-facilitated mutual aid groups where members meet online either using text-based ICTs such as chat, VR environments such as Second Life, or in webcam-mediated F2F settings with programs like Google Hangouts. Some research has found online support to be as effective in addressing mental health problems as psycho-educational websites and self-guided treatments (Freeman, Barker, & Pistrang, 2008; Griffiths et al., 2012). As with online therapy, the benefits of online support groups are similar to those of offline support groups. Participation leads to an increased sense of self-mastery, satisfaction, and well-being (van Uden-Kraan, Drossaert, Taal, Seydel, & van de Laar, 2009). The benefit of participation increases with interaction (Yalom, 2005). The absence of a professional means that group members can share potentially dangerous or damaging misinformation that will go unchecked. The one type of group that appears to be unique in the online environment are groups that explicitly encourage self-harm, such as "pro-suicide" and "pro-anorexia" groups.

Blogs are written by consumers or providers of mental health services. Bloggers gain social benefits through feedback from people who regularly follow the blog and provide feedback via comments. For consumers, this online community can counteract feelings of isolation, shame, or stigma associated with a mental illness. The act of writing a blog can itself be therapeutic (Pennebaker, J. W. & Chung, C. K., 2011). Therapist blogs can offer insights into the experience of providing mental health services, as well as create resources similar to psycho-education sites for consumers. Ironically, one benefit of blogging for consumers—interaction with other consumers—can become a liability for providers. For instance, if a client follows his therapist's blog or Twitter account and posts a publicly visible comment identifying himself as a client, he has breached his own confidentiality. If that client posts confidential or time-sensitive information, such as thoughts of suicide, with the intention that the provider will respond immediately, it puts the provider in a potentially liable situation if he or she does not. Online therapists are discouraged from engaging with clients in public forums like blogs, Facebook, Twitter, Pinterest, and Tumblr. Dr. Keely Kolmes, a psychotherapist in San Francisco, has developed a social media policy that clarifies her use of technology and social media and sets expectations for clients (Kolmes, 2010).

3. *Interactive, self-guided interventions.* These are typically computer-based, web or mobile app cognitive-behavioral interventions that are intended to be self-paced and self-directed. Although these programs are intended to be used without a therapist, they can be stand-alone or used as an adjunct to other mental health services including online or offline therapy (Carper, McHugh, & Barlow, 2011). They range in complexity from low (e.g., static modules that are offered to every user in the same order) to high (e.g., personalized programs that vary based on users' responses to baseline intake and are continuously modified based on user input).

The best-researched self-guided programs are computerized cognitive behavioral therapy (CCBT) programs, such as MoodGYM (Griffiths, Farrer, & Christensen, 2010; Lintvedt et al., 2013). These programs have been shown to be as effective at reducing depression and anxiety symptoms for people who complete the program as F2F therapy (Griffiths et al., 2010). Although they have been criticized for their high drop-out rates (So et al., 2013), some have argued that the completion rates for self-guided therapy are no lower than for F2F therapy (Andrews et al., 2010). Self-guided therapy programs have been consistently lauded for being cost-effective (Lintvedt et al., 2013; Powell et al., 2013); unlike F2F therapy, self-guided computer-based programs are often free to the user, cost very little to the provider (after recouping the cost of development and hosting), and are easily scaled so that one or one million people could use the program. Proponents of self-guided programs have long argued that the low cost and scalability of the programs could result in widespread adoption of psychotherapy (Bell, 2007). This proposition was recently tested by Powell et al. with the program MoodGYM (Powell et al., 2013). Although MoodGYM was developed to reduce anxiety and depression symptoms, it was hypothesized that the therapy modules would improve the mental health of those without anxiety or depression. Powell et al. recruited members of the general public to complete the modules in MoodGYM. After controlling for baseline depression and anxiety, they found that participants reported an overall improvement in well-being. This study provided the first evidence that computerized self-guided therapies could be used to improve well-being in the general population, and not just within a clinical population (Powell et al., 2013).

Interactive and self-guided interventions are increasingly being delivered over apps designed for mobile devices (e.g., mobile phones, smartphones, and tablets) (Proudfoot, 2013). The delivery of health and mental health services using mobile devices, called mHealth, has a number of advantages over other ICT-based interventions: Mobile devices travel with the client; they can be programmed to send alerts to take medication, call for an appointment, take a deep breath, or record an emotion or thought; or to deliver interventions at set times. GPS-enabled mobile devices can track exercise, or sound an alert when a person is in a pre-established "no-go-zone" such as a bar or casino. Despite their promise, apps are in their infancy, and the most capable developers (e.g., programmers) are not usually the content experts that consumers, providers, or health service organizations would be (HSOs) (Aguirre, McCoy, & Roan, 2013). Apps developed by social workers typically target other social workers, such as the ethics app, *Social Work Social Media* (Cooner, 2013).

4. *Psycho-educational websites* are online sources of information. They are analogous to offline bibliotherapy in that the purpose is to provide information, rather than contact with mental health professionals or personalized referrals. The value of websites has increased as people's access to the Internet through smartphones and tablets has increased. Examples include the *National Institute of Mental Health* (http://www.nimh.nih.gov), *Substance Abuse & Mental Health Services Administration* (http://samhsa.gov/), and *WebMD* (http://www.webmd.com/). Psycho-educational websites are only as good as the information they provide. Providers and consumers should evaluate web resources based on the *authority, accuracy,* and *objectivity* of the information (e.g., one person's opinion vs. results of a large-scale study), the comprehensiveness of the *coverage* and whether or not the site meets its stated purpose for its intended audience, how *current* the information is, and whether or not the *design* makes it easier or harder to find information on multiple platforms. Finally, consumers should know that even though they cannot find information on the Internet about a certain topic does not mean that there is no information available.

In sum, online mental health services have a growing evidence base for delivering a variety of interventions to a variety of consumers using ICTs, including those who were traditionally excluded from treatment based on geographical or other barriers. Advances in self-directed interventions and mHealth point to a future when social workers are no longer providing some mental health and linkage functions. For example, Facebook and the iPhone are programmed to recognize when users make suicidal statements and refer them to the National Suicide Prevention Lifeline or local crisis centers. There continue to be significant limitations to ICTs in social work practice. ICTs do not bridge the "digital divide" by themselves. The benefits of online therapy cannot be realized by those who lack access to technology, the technical skills to participate in therapy online, or the financial resources to pay out of pocket (unlike F2F therapy, online therapy is not covered by insurance). These barriers can be considered economic, social, and electronic justice issues. Therefore, social workers have a professional responsibility to address the mezzo- and macro-level barriers to accessing and using ICT-based services, as well as using technology in mezzo- and macro-level practice and advocacy.

COMMUNITY ORGANIZING

Social work's community organizing roots emerged in the late 19th century, in part as a response to social problems that developed out of technological advances brought on by the industrial revolution. For much of the 20th century, social workers struggled with the ways that vulnerable and marginalized groups were adversely affected by technology (Hick & McNutt, 2002). In the 21st century, some problems, such as bullying and sex trafficking, have shifted from occurring primarily on the ground to primarily online. For some, lack of access to technology has itself become a social problem. For instance, those with access to Internet-connected computers have educational advantages related to information access, can enhance their marketable computer skills, and are better able to find and apply for jobs online than people without Internet access (Araque et al., 2013). And yet, between 25% and 50% of adults without high school degrees, older adults, and those who identify as a racial/ethnic minority do not have online access (Purcell, Brenner, & Rainie, 2012). Organizing efforts that do not acknowledge or address this "digital divide" may exclude the very groups that would

most benefit from participation in advocacy efforts. And somewhat paradoxically, ICTs in the 21st century have made it possible for people who previously were marginalized because of age, geographical distance, physical or economic limitations, or social stigma, or a combination of all of these, to communicate and organize through virtual communities. Although the early days of the Internet included closed communities (e.g., CompuServ and AOL) and attempts at recreating physical communities online (e.g., Geocities.com), advances in virtual reality and 24/7 access to the Internet via smartphones and tablets has resulted in the creation of truly virtual communities with no offline counterparts. In these early days of the 21st century, social workers have to negotiate a paradox: the very technologies that marginalize and disenfranchise groups can also be used to ameliorate social problems.

In the 21st century social workers need to organize both physical and virtual communities. Technological tools that support community organizing and social work advocacy fall into two primary categories: (1) tools that mediate communication and message delivery, such as e-mail, listservs, social networks (e.g., Twitter, Facebook), and blogs; and (2) tools for data collection and visualization, such as GIS, donor management software, and automated subscription-based alert systems. Community organizers were early adopters of ICTs that mediated communication such as e-mail and listservs. These text-based technologies were inexpensive ways for organizers to communicate with and mobilize key stakeholders. The adoption of high-speed Internet and free video conferencing (via Google Hangouts or FreeVideoConference.com) simplifies and popularizes synchronous webcam-mediated F2F gatherings. Newer ICTs such as Twitter and Facebook combine text with images and videos, can be used synchronously or asynchronously, and, similar to self-guided therapy, have decreased the need for organizing efforts to be facilitated by a trained professional. The Occupy movement and the Arab Spring are examples of social movements that used Twitter and Facebook and were "marked by the absence of a clearly identified leader, a political party or figure, an association, or an organizing capacity" (Marzouki & Oullier, 2012).

Although online tools hold promise for organizing, they are often underutilized by nonprofits, especially in the realm of advocacy (Edwards & Hoefer, 2010). Despite the growing number of nonprofits that use social media sites, there continues to be a gap between available ICTs and the knowledge and skills necessary to use them to engage stakeholders effectively (J. Young, 2012). Organizers should have a clear goal in mind when adopting a new technology, and consider utilizing multiple strategies (Dunlop & Fawcett, 2008). Social workers who want to increase their proficiency for online community organizing may join online groups such as COMM-ORG (comm-org.wisc.edu/), which offers numerous links to other community organizing resources.

The following is an example of how various ICTs can be used in concert to educate and mobilize key stakeholders around the issue of housing discrimination for same-sex couples:

- A social worker in North Dakota could (1) leverage face-to-face chats in Google Hangouts to organize stakeholders across the state who are interested in housing discrimination issues that affect same-sex couples; (2) use a Facebook group to collect comments about a related nondiscrimination policy proposal and to announce a public hearing; (3) start a statewide nondiscrimination petition on causes.com; and (4) direct people to tweetcongress.org, where they can tweet messages to their elected local representatives to advocate for a policy that bans housing discrimination based on sexual orientation.

Other examples of ICTs in community organizing and advocacy include:

- Geographical Information Systems (GIS) technologies can be used to analyze information about specific geographical regions, such as neighborhoods, zip codes, cities, or counties. Advocacy groups can analyze campaign demographics to improve voter participation on key social service issues. GIS can be used by consumer rights advocates to identify areas of need to improve service delivery.
- A number of websites allow nonprofits to meet a number of community organizing needs, including fundraising, volunteer recruitment, and legislative tracking, as well as collecting signatures, and conducting outreach. For example, anyone can start a petition or fundraising campaign on the website causes.com, and the site cqrollcall.com offers a paid service by which users can add legislative tracking to their websites.
- E-mail lists and social network sites are low-cost ways of distributing action alerts (e.g., "call your representative now!"), and targeted social media campaigns can be designed specifically to recruit certain disenfranchised groups (Vyas, Landry, Schnider, Rojas, & Wood, 2012). Social media users have higher levels of political participation and civic engagement (Valenzuela, Park, & Kee, 2009); thus, social media can be an ideal facilitator of collective action, political mobilization, and community building (Obar, Zube, & Lampe, 2011). Although a primary reason nonprofits begin using social media is to engage their current audiences (J. Young, 2012), websites like Facebook, YouTube, and Twitter make it easy and economical for agencies to develop an Internet presence, facilitate communication with new and existing stakeholders, and share information about their specific causes (Edwards & Hoefer, 2010).
- Online discussion lists, websites, and blogs, as well as issues-oriented and social change websites can organize people in one neighborhood or from around the world on a specific issue. For issues such as suicide, which has a relatively low base rate (12 per 100,000) and stigma-related silence, geography and social stigma have made it difficult to organize people to promote change. However, the Internet has made it possible for the friends, family, and loved ones of the nearly 38,000 people annually who die by suicide to come together as a community (Mohatt et al., 2013). For example, in July 2013 the advocacy work of American Foundation for Suicide Prevention (AFSP) (afsp.org) provided instrumental support for expanding a bill in the Senate Labor, Health, and Human Services Committee, including a $15 million budget increase for the National Violent Death Reporting system, which will provide more timely information about national suicide statistics. AFSP used its website to send legislative alerts, raise awareness among politicians, and encourage constituents to call their representatives. They provide tips on what to say when speaking to public officials about suicide.

POLICY ISSUES

Agency Policy

Agency-level policy may inform a social worker's participation in social media and online forums. Although many agencies lack specific social media policy (J. Young, 2012), agency employees who communicate via social media from home or work should understand company policies related to social media use. Additionally, they should know how they can represent their associations with their employers, understand the relative permanence of online postings, and consider how their public online identity might influence their interactions with consumers (Kimball & Kim, 2013). Although it is illegal for employers to limit an employee's private participation in workforce organizing online, online posts that broach professional ethics are not protected (Halpern & Gardner, 2012). Social workers who are government employees should also understand that the technology used at their agency, including web-browsing and e-mail, may be monitored by the agency or subject to public disclosure through freedom of information regulations (Dawes, 2010).

Social workers may be asked to help draft their agency's e-therapy or social media policy. Policy should educate workers, be realistic about the significance of the Internet and social media in the lives of social workers, be specific with examples of justifications and prohibitions for use, include consequences of policy violation, and consider the impacts of social media use, negative and positive, on clients (Reamer, 2013).

Licensing and Regulation of Online Therapy

As with other professions such as law, medicine, and nursing, licensing and regulation of social work occurs at the state level. Online therapy has no geographic boundaries and thus creates complex regulatory issues. For example, if a client resides in Idaho and a therapist works in Georgia and they meet online for therapy, in which state are they conducting therapy? Is the therapist going to the client or is the client coming to the therapist? Which state's consumer protections apply? These questions have yet to be settled by either regulatory or legal precedent. Although groups such as the American Telemedicine Association (ATA) are working toward best practices for telemedicine delivery across professional disciplines (americantelemed. org), and some state licensing boards offer policy guidance on Internet-mediated practice (Reamer, 2013b) unless explicitly allowed by your state's licensing regulations, interstate online therapy is a violation of your licensure.

Liability and Malpractice in Online Therapy

Social workers are increasingly seen as the primary providers of mental health services and consequently are named in more malpractice lawsuits than ever before. The largest provider of malpractice insurance for social workers, NASW Assurance Services, reports that liability coverage is offered worldwide for services including online therapy unless social workers provide services for which they are not licensed (e.g., practicing social work across state lines) (naswassurance.org). They offer specific caution about the importance of protecting client confidentiality. The onus of responsibility lies with social workers to understand the limits of state licensure. Case law suggests that a professional relationship can be established by responding to an e-mail. Reamer (2013b) notes that social workers are obligated morally and ethically to be familiar with the available research regarding the efficacy of online therapy and be proficient in the use of technology needed to carry out practice; practicing outside of one's scope is an ethical and liability concern. Informed consent requires that consumers are informed of the evidence available to support a course of treatment, and of the provider's qualifications and trainings in the proposed modality. Social work programs only started offering social work and technology courses in 2013 (UB Reporter, 2013). One approach to developing competency in online therapy is for clinicians to use technology in clinical supervision to both increase their comfort level and to receive consultation on online therapy issues (Singer, 2009).

Confidentiality, Security, and Informed Consent

There is currently no case law that clarifies the confidentiality of e-mails, webcam images, or text messages. However, online therapy is bound by specific HIPAA rules that address confidentiality and the security of electronic transmissions (Eack, Singer & Greeno, 2008), and the storage of any personal health information and telehealth communications. Regulations regarding patient protection mandate the use of privacy safeguards including encryption, security passwords, and intrusion detection software (Scholl et al., 2008). Some states require specific language and signed consents for telemedicine activities (Baker & Bufka, 2011). Social workers should have clear policies related to the storage of online documentation (recordings, chats, e-mails, and records) and ensure that they are not violating any state regulations by practicing across state borders (Reamer, 2013a).

Reimbursement

Insurance reimbursement for clinical services from programs such as Medicaid, Medicare, or private insurance is organized at the state level and, therefore, varies by state. However, insurance companies typically require audio-video equipment to carry out "telemedicine" and exclude services offered via other methods such as e-mail or text (Baker & Bufka, 2011). Some insurance companies authorize e-therapy reimbursement on a case-by-case basis if a special need exists, while others, such as Magellan and Blue Shield, provide regular authorization of online therapy in California (Breakthrough Behavioral Health, n.d.). BlueCross authorizes telemedicine coverage in 21 states but can restrict the types of providers or services that are eligible, and 19 states have specific policies that mandate insurance companies pay for telemedicine services if they would be covered face-to-face (ATA, 2013; Baker & Bufka, 2011).

Online therapy groups require payment at the time of services and do not bill insurance for services. Although this arrangement is adequate for financially independent consumers, the economically disadvantaged consumers who make up social work's core service recipients will be unable to afford e-therapy. Ideally, social service organizations could develop Social Work 2.0 services, such as text-based technologies like e-mail or chat, telehealth using the phone or VoIP services, or video technologies such as webcams, to address the needs of clients for whom traditional face-to-face services are inadequate or difficult to access. However, this is unlikely until funding is available.

CONCLUSION

Advances in ICT have changed the way social workers think about and provide mental health services. Some of the advances have reduced the role of social workers in mental health treatment, community practice, and advocacy. Over the coming decades, it is likely that some social work services will be entirely computer-based, whereas others will have only minimal integration with technology. As today's youth become tomorrow's consumers, and they see fewer distinctions between their online and offline identity, social workers will have to demonstrate knowledge of and skill with ICTs to provide treatment in any environment. In an effort to address this need, social workers have taken to developing social work education apps (Cooner, 2013). But formal social work education in ICT-mediated social work is lacking; the first social work course to address the use of technology in clinical social work practice was taught as a summer elective in 2013 by Mike Langlois for the University at Buffalo School of Social Work (UB Reporter, 2013).

WEBSITES

International Society for Mental Health Online. http://www.ismho.org.

MoodGym, online cognitive behavioral therapy to prevent depression. https://moodgym.anu.edu.au/welcome.

NASW Standards for Technology and Social Work Practice. http://www.socialworkers.org/practice/standards/NASWTechnologyStandards.pdf.

References on Internet-assisted therapy and counseling. http://construct.haifa.ac.il/%7Eazy/refthrp.htm

The Social Work Podcast. http://socialworkpodcast.com.

Social Work and Technology—Google Plus Community https://plus.google.com/communities/115588985317830085141

References

Aguirre, R. T. P., McCoy, M. K., & Roan, M. (2013). Development guidelines from a study of suicide prevention mobile applications (apps). *Journal of Technology in Human Services, 31*(3), 269–293. doi:10.1080/15228835.2013.814750

Andersson, G., Paxling, B., Roch-Norlund, P., Östman, G., Norgren, A., Almlöv, J., … Silverberg, F. (2012). Internet-based psychodynamic versus cognitive behavioral guided self-help for generalized anxiety disorder: A randomized controlled trial.

Psychotherapy and Psychosomatics, 81(6), 344–355. doi:10.1159/000339371

Andrews, G., Cuijpers, P., Craske, M. G., McEvoy, P., & Titov, N. (2010). Computer therapy for the anxiety and depressive disorders is effective, acceptable and practical health care: A meta-analysis. *PLoS ONE, 5*(10), e13196. doi:10.1371/journal.pone.0013196

Araque, J. C., Maiden, R. P., Bravo, N., Estrada, I., Evans, R., Hubchik, K., … Reddy, M. (2013). Computer usage and access in low-income urban communities. *Computers in Human Behavior, 29*(4), 1393–1401. doi:10.1016/j.chb.2013.01.032

American Telemedicine Association. (2013, August 1). ATA identifies states that are leading the way in telehealth Medicaid coverage. *American Telemedicine Association.* Washington, DC. Retrieved from http://www.americantelemed.org/news-landing/2013/08/01/ata-identifies-states-that-are-leading-the-way-in-telehealth-medicaid-coverage

Baker, D. C., & Bufka, L. F. (2011). Preparing for the telehealth world: Navigating legal, regulatory, reimbursement, and ethical issues in an electronic age. *Professional Psychology: Research and Practice, 42*(6), 405–411. doi:10.1037/a0025037

Balick, A. (2012). TMI in the transference LOL: Psychoanalytic reflections on Google, social networking, and "virtual impingement." *Psychoanalysis, Culture & Society, 17*(2), 120–136. doi:10.1057/pcs.2012.19

Barak, A. (2007). Emotional support and suicide prevention through the Internet: A field project report. *Computers in Human Behavior, 23*(2), 971–984. doi:10.1016/j.chb.2005.08.001

Barak, A., & Grohol, J. M. (2011). Current and future trends in Internet-supported mental health interventions. *Journal of Technology in Human Services, 29*(3), 155–196. doi:10.1080/15228835.2011.616939

Barak, A., Hen, L., Boniel-Nissim, M., & Shapira, N. (2008). A comprehensive review and a meta-analysis of the effectiveness of Internet-based psychotherapeutic interventions. *Journal of Technology in Human Services, 26*(2–4), 109–160. doi:10.1080/15228830802094429

Beatty, L., & Lambert, S. (2013). A systematic review of Internet-based self-help therapeutic interventions to improve distress and disease-control among adults with chronic health conditions. *Clinical Psychology Review, 33*(4), 609–622.

Birgit, W., Horn, A. B., & Andreas, M. (2013). Internet-based versus face-to-face cognitive-behavioral intervention for depression: A randomized controlled non-inferiority trial. *Journal of Affective Disorders.* doi:10.1016/j.jad.2013.06.032

Breakthrough Behavioral Health. (n.d.). *Therapy from Your Own Couch.* Retrieved from https://www.breakthrough.com/

Carper, M. M., McHugh, R. K., & Barlow, D. H. (2011). The dissemination of computer-based psychological treatment: A preliminary analysis of patient and clinician perceptions. *Administration and Policy in Mental Health and Mental Health Services Research, 40*(2), 87–95. doi:10.1007/s10488-011-0377-5

Champion, K. E., Newton, N. C., Barrett, E. L., & Teesson, M. (2013). A systematic review of school-based alcohol and other drug prevention programs facilitated by computers or the Internet. *Drug and Alcohol Review, 32*(2), 115–123. doi:10.1111/j.1465-3362.2012.00517.x

Cooner, T. S. (2013). *Social Work Social Media [mobile app].* Retrieved from https://sites.google.com/site/socialworksocialmedia/

Dawes, S. S. (2010). Stewardship and usefulness: Policy principles for information-based transparency. *Government Information Quarterly, 27*(4), 377–383. doi:10.1016/j.giq.2010.07.001

Doss, B. D., Benson, L. A., Georgia, E. J., & Christensen, A. (2013). Translation of integrative behavioral couple therapy to a web-based intervention. *Family Process, 52*(1), 139–153. doi:10.1111/famp.12020

Dowling, M., & Rickwood, D. (2013). Online counseling and therapy for mental health problems: A systematic review of individual synchronous interventions using chat. *Journal of Technology in Human Services, 31*(1), 1–21. doi:10.1080/15228835.2012.728508

Dunlop, J. M., & Fawcett, G. (2008). Technology-based approaches to social work and social justice. *Journal of Policy Practice, 7*(2–3), 140–154. doi:10.1080/15588740801937961

Eack, S. M., Singer, J. B., & Greeno, C. G. (2008). Screening for anxiety and depression in community mental health: The Beck anxiety and depression inventories *Community Mental Health Journal, 44*(6), 465–474.

Edwards, H. R., & Hoefer, R. (2010). Are social work advocacy groups using Web 2.0 effectively? *Journal of Policy Practice, 9*(3–4), 220–239. doi:10.1080/15588742.2010.489037

Fox, S., & Duggan, M. (2013). *Health Online 2013.* Pew Internet & American Life Project. Retrieved from http://pewinternet.org/Reports/2013/Health-online.aspx

Freddolino, P. P., & Blaschke, C. M. (2008). Therapeutic applications of online gaming. *Journal of Technology in Human Services, 26*(2–4), 423–446. doi:10.1080/15228830802099998

Freeman, E., Barker, C., & Pistrang, N. (2008). Outcome of an online mutual support group for college students with psychological problems. *Cyberpsychology & Behavior: The Impact of the Internet, Multimedia and Virtual Reality on Behavior and Society, 11*(5), 591–593. doi:10.1089/cpb.2007.0133

Gainsbury, S., & Blaszczynski, A. (2011). A systematic review of Internet-based therapy for the treatment of addictions. *Clinical Psychology Review, 31*(3), 490–498. doi:10.1016/j.cpr.2010.11.007

Griffiths, K. M., Farrer, L., & Christensen, H. (2010). The efficacy of Internet interventions for depression and anxiety disorders: A review of randomised controlled trials. *The Medical Journal of Australia, 192*(suppl. 11), S4–S11.

Griffiths, K. M., Mackinnon, A. J., Crisp, D. A., Christensen, H., Bennett, K., & Farrer, L. (2012). The effectiveness of an online support group for members of the community with depression: a randomised controlled trial. *PloS one, 7*(12), e53244. doi:10.1371/journal.pone.0053244

Halpern, S., & Gardner, C. (2012, December 21). NLRB offers long-awaited guidance on social media policies. *Employee Benefit News.* Retrieved from http://ebn.benefitnews.com/news/nlrb-offers-long_awaited-guidance-social-media-policies-2729827-1.html

Hick, S., & McNutt, J. G. (2002). *Advocacy, activism, and the Internet: Community organization and social policy.* Chicago, IL: Lyceum Books.

Kanani, K., & Regehr, C. (2003). Clinical, ethical, and legal issues in e-therapy. *Families in Society: The Journal of Contemporary Social Services, 84*(2), 155–162. doi:10.1606/1044-3894.98

Kimball, E., & Kim, J. (2013). Virtual boundaries: Ethical considerations for use of social media in social work. *Social Work, 58*(2), 185–188.

Kolmes, K. (2010, April 26). Social Media Policy. Retrieved from http://www.drkkolmes.com/docs/socmed.pdf

Langlois, M. (2011). *Reset: Video Games & Psychotherapy.* BookBrewer. Retrieved from http://www.amazon.com/Reset-Video-Games-Psychotherapy-ebook/dp/B005KLSUPG

Lintvedt, O. K., Griffiths, K. M., Sørensen, K., Østvik, A. R., Wang, C. E. A., Eisemann, M., & Waterloo, K. (2013). Evaluating the effectiveness and efficacy of unguided Internet-based self-help intervention for the prevention of depression: A randomized controlled trial. *Clinical Psychology & Psychotherapy, 20*(1), 10–27. doi:10.1002/cpp.770

Marzouki, Y., & Oullier, O. (2012, July 17). Revolutionizing revolutions: Virtual collective consciousness and the Arab Spring. *Huffington Post.* Retrieved from http://www.huffingtonpost.com/yousri-marzouki/revolutionizing-revolutio_b_1679181.html

McCarty, D., & Clancy, C. (2002). Telehealth: Implications for social work practice. *Social Work, 47*(2), 153–161.

McCoyd, J. C., & Kerson, T. S. (2006). Conducting intensive interviews using email: A serendipitous comparative opportunity. *Qualitative Social Work, 5,* 389–406.

Migone, P. (2013). Psychoanalysis on the Internet: A discussion of its theoretical implications for both online and offline therapeutic technique. *Psychoanalytic Psychology, 30*(2), 281–299. doi:10.1037/a0031507

Miller, L. M. S., & Bell, R. A. (2012). Online health information seeking: The influence of age, information trustworthiness, and search challenges. *Journal of Aging and Health, 24*(3), 525–541. doi:10.1177/0898264311428167

Mishna, F., Bogo, M., Root, J., Sawyer, J.-L., & Khoury-Kassabri, M. (2012). "It just crept in": The digital age and implications for social work practice. *Clinical Social Work Journal, 40*(3), 277–286. doi:10.1007/s10615-012-0383-4

Mohatt, N. V., Singer, J. B., Evans, A. C., Jr, Matlin, S. L., Golden, J., Harris, C., … Tebes, J. K. (2013). A community's response to suicide through public art: Stakeholder perspectives from the Finding the Light Within Project. *American Journal of Community Psychology, 52*(1–2), 197–209. doi:10.1007/s10464-013-9581-7

National Association of Social Worker. (1999). *Code of Ethics.* Washington, DC: NASW Press.

National Association of Social Workers (NASW). (2005). *Standards for technology and social work practice.* Washington, DC: Author. Retrieved from http://www.socialworkers.org/practice/standards/NASWTechnologyStandards.pdf

O'Reilly, T. (2005, September 30). What Is Web 2.0? Design patterns and business models for the next generation of software. Retrieved from http://oreilly.com/web2/archive/what-is-web-20.html

Obar, J. A., Zube, P., & Lampe, C. (2011). Advocacy 2.0: An analysis of how advocacy groups in the United States perceive and use social media as tools for facilitating civic engagement and collective action. *SSRN Electronic Journal.* doi:10.2139/ssrn.1956352

Pallavicini, F., Cipresso, P., Raspelli, S., Grassi, A., Serino, S., Vigna, C., … Riva, G. (2013). Is virtual reality always an effective stressor for exposure treatments? Some insights from a controlled trial. *BMC Psychiatry, 13,* 52. doi:10.1186/1471-244X-13-52

Pennebaker, J. W., & Chung, C. K. (2011). Expressive writing and its links to mental and physical health. In H. S. Friedman (Ed.), *The Oxford handbook of health psychology* (pp. 417–437). Oxford; New York: Oxford University Press.

Perron, B. E., Taylor, H. O., Glass, J. E., & Margerum-Leys, J. (2010). Information and communication technologies in social work. *Advances in Social Work, 11*(2), 67–81.

Powell, J., Hamborg, T., Stallard, N., Burls, A., McSorley, J., Bennett, K., … Christensen, H. (2013). Effectiveness of a web-based cognitive-behavioral tool to improve mental well-being in the general population: Randomized controlled trial. *Journal of Medical Internet Research, 15*(1), e2. doi:10.2196/jmir.2240

Prensky, M. (2001). Digital natives, digital immigrants, Part 1. *On the Horizon, 9*(5), 1–6. doi:10.1108/10748120110424816

Proudfoot, J. (2013). The future is in our hands: The role of mobile phones in the prevention and management of mental disorders. *Australian & New Zealand Journal of Psychiatry, 47*(2), 111–113. doi:10.1177/0004867412471441

Purcell, K., Brenner, J., & Rainie, L. (2012). *Search Engine Use 2012* (p. 42). Pew Research Center. Retrieved from http://www.pewinternet.org/~/media//Files/Reports/2012/PIP_Search_Engine_Use_2012.pdf

Reamer, F. G. (2013a). The digital and electronic revolution in social work: Rethinking the meaning of ethical practice. *Ethics and Social Welfare, 7*(1), 2–19. doi:10.1080/17496535.2012.738694

Reamer, F. G. (2013b). Social work in a digital age: Ethical and risk management challenges. *Social Work, 58*(2), 163–172. doi:10.1093/sw/swt003

Richards, D., & Viganó, N. (2013). Online counseling: A narrative and critical review of the literature. *Journal of Clinical Psychology,* n/a–n/a. doi:10.1002/jclp.21974

Scholl, M., Stine, K., Bown, P., Johnson, A., Smith, C., & Steinberg, D. (2008). *An introductory resource guide for implementing the Health Insurance Portability and Accountability Act (HIPAA) security rule* (No. 800-66 R) (p. 117). Gaithersburg, MD: U.S. Department of Commerce. Retrieved from http://csrc.nist.gov/publications/nistpubs/800-66-Rev1/SP-800-66-Revision1.pdf

Schopler, J. H., Abell, M. D., & Galinsky, M. J. (1998). Technology-based groups: A review and conceptual framework for practice. *Social Work, 43,* 254–267.

Singer, J. B. (2009). The role and regulations for technology in social work practice and e-therapy: Social work 2.0. In A. R. Roberts (Ed.), *Social workers' desk reference* (2nd ed.). (pp. 186–193). Oxford; New York: Oxford University Press.

Slone, N. C., Reese, R. J., & McClellan, M. J. (2012). Telepsychology outcome research with children and adolescents: A review of the literature. *Psychological Services, 9*(3), 272–292. doi:10.1037/a0027607

So, M., Yamaguchi, S., Hashimoto, S., Sado, M., Furukawa, T. A., & McCrone, P. (2013). Is computerised CBT really helpful for adult depression? A meta-analytic re-evaluation of CCBT for adult depression in terms of clinical implementation and methodological validity. *BMC Psychiatry, 13*(1), 113. doi:10.1186/1471-244X-13-113

UB Reporter. (2013, May 2). Social Work launches part-time online MSW. *UB Reporter.* Retrieved from http://www.buffalo.edu/ubreporter/campus.host.html/content/shared/university/news/ub-reporter-articles/briefs/2013/social_work_degree.detail.html

Valenzuela, S., Park, N., & Kee, K. F. (2009). Is there social capital in a social network site? Facebook use and college students' life satisfaction, trust, and participation. *Journal of Computer-Mediated Communication, 14*(4), 875–901. doi:10.1111/j.1083-6101.2009.01474.x

Van der Zanden, R., Kramer, J., Gerrits, R., & Cuijpers, P. (2012). Effectiveness of an online group course for depression in adolescents and young adults: A randomized trial. *Journal of Medical Internet Research, 14*(3), e86. doi:10.2196/jmir.2033

Van Uden-Kraan, C. F., Drossaert, C. H. C., Taal, E., Seydel, E. R., & van de Laar, M. A. F. J. (2009). Participation in online patient support groups endorses patients' empowerment. *Patient Education and Counseling, 74*(1), 61–69. doi:10.1016/j.pec.2008.07.044

Vyas, A. N., Landry, M., Schnider, M., Rojas, A. M., & Wood, S. F. (2012). Public health interventions: Reaching Latino adolescents via short message service and social media. *Journal of Medical Internet Research, 14*(4), e99. doi:10.2196/jmir.2178

Wodarski, J., & Frimpong, J. (2013). Application of e-therapy programs to the social work practice. *Journal of Human Behavior in the Social Environment, 23*(1), 29–36. doi:10.1080/10911359.2013.737290

Yalom, I. D. (2005). *The theory and practice of group psychotherapy* (5th ed.). New York, NY: Basic Books.

Young, J. (2012, May 10). *The current status of social media use among nonprofit human service organizations: An exploratory study.* Virginia Commonwealth University. Retrieved from https://digarchive.library.vcu.edu/handle/10156/3775

Young, K. S. (2005). An empirical examination of client attitudes towards online counseling. *CyberPsychology & Behavior, 8*(2), 172–177. doi:10.1089/cpb.2005.8.172

24 Navigating Complex Boundary Challenges

Kimberly Strom-Gottfried

"Professional boundaries" typically refer to the norms that protect, ground, and guide the helping relationship. They mark a social, physical, and psychological space around the client that is protected from inappropriate intrusion by the social worker. Boundaries help assure the client that actions or expressions by the worker are made in the client's interest and for the benefit of the services being provided, not for the worker's social, financial, or sexual needs. Boundaries can be exceedingly complex, with variations in norms across cultures, geographic regions, practice settings, and populations served. Depending on their setting, clientele, and individual disposition, professionals may maintain "thick" or "thin" boundaries. In either instance, the client–worker distinction exists, but the concept acknowledges that some workers prefer to have greater privacy and distance separating their work and personal matters. Boundaries do not imply that clients are inferior to professionals; rather, they assure that the helping relationship is sacrosanct and clients' needs are accorded the utmost importance.

Boundary violations, such as dual or sexual relationships, are among the most common areas of ethical impropriety in social work and other professions (Boland-Prom, 2009; Daley & Doughty, 2006; Strom-Gottfried, 1999). Although these egregious and exploitive acts are valid areas for attention, subtle conflicts of interest are far more common and have less clear-cut solutions.

- Should a social worker on a home visit accept an offer of food, conduct the meeting with extended family nearby, or take action if illegal activity is observed?

- If a professional in the field of disabilities also has a child receiving services in that field, how should he or she relate to parents who are simultaneously peers and clients?
- A social worker activist in the lesbian, gay, bisexual, and transgender (LGBT) community is often sought for services by members of that community. When do overlapping acquaintances become dual relationships?
- A patient with a life-threatening illness asks the members of the treatment team to be her "supporters" on a Caring Bridge site. Members of the team disagree about the propriety of that role.
- Is the client who "Googles" his new worker, and discovers some unflattering findings from rating and commentary sites, a savvy consumer or a resistant trouble maker?

"Boundary crossings" indicate deviations from standard practices that are typically innocuous, done in the client's interests and without adverse effects, and are, therefore, not inherently unethical (Reamer, 2001). In the wrong context or with the wrong client, however, even simple boundary crossings may represent problematic conflicts of interest or create the first step in a "slippery slope" toward boundary violations and client exploitation (Epstein & Simon, 1990).

The National Association of Social Workers (NASW) Code of Ethics cautions practitioners to avoid or address potential conflicts of interest by taking "reasonable steps to resolve the issue in a manner that makes the clients' interests primary and protects clients' interests to the greatest extent possible" (NASW, 2008, 1.06a). Certain conflicts of interest, such as sexual relationships with clients, former clients, supervisees and others, are expressly prohibited, and social workers are further cautioned to avoid business, professional, or social relationships with clients and former clients due to the risk of harm or exploitation. Ultimately, the social worker bears the responsibility for "setting clear, appropriate and culturally sensitive boundaries" (NASW, 2008, 1.06c).

INTERSECTING ETHICAL STANDARDS

Although rural practice, in-home services, and online networking can create conflicts of interest and stretch professional boundaries, other ethical standards, including confidentiality, professionalism, and competence are also inextricably bound to these situations.

Confidentiality

Maintaining client privacy is the foundation of the helping relationship. Social workers face significant ethical and legal sanctions for the failure to protect sensitive information or for sharing information for other than professional purposes. Practitioners are expected to use informed consent at the outset of services to alert the client to the limits of privacy, typically in cases with mandatory reporting of child or elder abuse or the risk of harm to the client or someone else. Confidentiality pledges are challenged when clients share information, such as past criminal activity, that is distressing to the worker but is not reportable (Walfish, Barnett, Marlyere, & Zielke, 2010).

Confidentiality also is challenged when personal and professional relationships overlap.

- Professionals in rural areas may observe unhealthy behaviors or activities in the community that are at odds with what clients report in interviews. Should they confront the client on the disparity?
- If a clinician participates in a patient's online caring site and learns that the patient is not following discharge instructions, what is he or she to do with the information?
- During a home visit with an elderly client, the worker observes signs of drug sales out the back door by the client's grandson. Should this be ignored or reported, and if so, reported to whom?

Each of these disparate examples raises similar questions: Where and when does the professional's responsibility end?

The NASW Code of Ethics requires that social workers "... respect clients' right to privacy" and avoid soliciting "private information from clients unless it is essential to providing services or conducting social work evaluation or research" (1.07a); "protect the confidentiality of all information obtained in the course of professional service, except for compelling professional reasons" and "disclose the least amount of confidential information necessary to achieve the desired purpose ..." (1.07c); "inform clients, to the extent possible, about the disclosure of confidential information and the potential consequences, when feasible before the disclosure is made ..." (1.07d); "... protect the confidentiality of clients' written and electronic records and other sensitive information (1.07n); and "... take precautions to ensure and maintain the confidentiality of information transmitted to other parties through the use of computers, electronic mail, facsimile machines, telephones and telephone answering machines, and other electronic or computer technology" (1.07m).

Social workers should not: "... discuss confidential information in any setting unless privacy can be ensured. Social workers should not discuss confidential information in public or semipublic areas such as hallways, waiting rooms, elevators, and restaurants" (NASW, 2008, 1.07i).

Professionalism and Competence

All individuals reveal different dimensions of themselves depending on the social context and the people surrounding them at any given time (Knox & Hill, 2003). Thus, conversations and behaviors with intimate friends and family are likely more frank and unguarded than those with acquaintances or the public. In their interactions with clients and colleagues, social workers are expected to demonstrate professionalism through their integrity, appearance, conduct, and expertise.

Although professionals are urged to be "authentic," they also are cautioned to exercise restraint and be mindful of their "use of self" or the way in which aspects of the worker's own persona are employed to influence the helping relationship (Baldwin, 1987). Social workers may selectively use self-disclosure to reveal information about themselves in the course of their practice with clients and fellow professionals. Some self-disclosures occur in response to queries ("Are you married?" "How long have you worked here?"). Self-disclosures can also be voluntary and unbidden, as the professional offers information about him or herself that may be beneficial to the client. Such revelations may include coping strategies, interests, personal data, or experiences as a service recipient. The practitioner must consider how the information will be heard and used by the client, the worker's comfort should the client disclose it to others, and the availability of other techniques to assist the client that do not involve personal sharing by the worker (Farber, 2006).

Representative standards for professionalism and competence (NASW, 2008) state that social workers should:

- "… accept responsibility or employment only on the basis of existing competence or the intention to acquire the necessary competence" (4.01a)
- "… treat colleagues with respect and should represent accurately and fairly the qualifications, views, and obligations of colleagues" (2.01a)
- "… relate to both social work colleagues and colleagues from other disciplines with respect, integrity and courtesy and seek to understand differences in viewpoints and practice" (3.1)
- "… make clear distinctions between statements made and actions engaged in as a private individual and as a representative of the social work profession, a professional social work organization, or the social worker's employing agency" (4.06a).

Social workers should not:

- "… allow their own personal problems, psychosocial distress, legal problems, substance abuse, or mental health difficulties to interfere with their professional judgment and performance or to jeopardize the best interests of people for whom they have a professional responsibility" (4.05a)
- "… use derogatory language in their written or verbal communications to or about clients …" (1.12)
- "… exploit clients in disputes with colleagues or engage clients in any inappropriate discussion of conflicts between social workers and their colleagues" (2.04b)
- "… permit their private conduct to interfere with their ability to fulfill their professional responsibilities" (4.03).

Professionalism is challenged when thin boundaries reveal troubling conduct or new dimensions of the social worker.

- The professional who is bossy and defensive as a member of a peer support group may have trouble undoing that image in interactions with other members as their caseworker. Conversely, the worker may feel she cannot truly be herself in the support group because other members view her in her professional role, not as a parent with the same challenges they have.
- A social worker moonlighting as a bartender or store clerk may worry about his responsibility and legitimacy as a helping professional after encountering clients in the context of his second job.
- The home visitor may note decorations in a client's apartment that indicate common interests or religious affiliations and disclose those similarities in an effort to build rapport.
- Outraged online posts about political events may alienate the clinician's patients, supervisees, or employer. Frivolous party photos that identify or "tag" the worker may come to the attention of clients or administrators who are distressed to see this side of the professional (Decker, 2012). When medical students posed with "their cadavers," for example, or an obstetrician lamented a patient's tardiness and mused about showing up late for the delivery, the posts and derisive responses went viral (Beck, 2013; Heyboer, 2010).

COMPLEX BOUNDARY CHALLENGES

Practice in small, rural, or close-knit communities, in client's homes, and in the era of electronic communications each pose unique challenges for professionals hoping to maintain clear boundaries. They also give rise to dilemmas surrounding confidentiality, professionalism, and competence.

Rural and Close-Knit Communities

In rural and close knit communities, worker self-disclosure is rarely a concern because many people will know the worker through prominence in the community, through connected family and friends, and from activities of daily life (shopping, the faith community, schools, health care, a barbershop, or car and home repairs). This heightened visibility for the professional is true not only in small geographic communities, but in cultural communities, faith communities, and in groups defined by common interests or attributes (such as the hearing impaired community). These settings are so rife with intersecting relationships that some view dual relationships as a customary factor in service delivery, not an ethical indiscretion (Miller, 1998). The core concern in these situations is the possibility that social workers may be unable to carry out their professional responsibilities if their judgment is clouded by competing loyalties. Additionally, the visibility in these settings can create discomfort for professionals and it can constrain their own help-seeking in times of need (Beskind, Bartels, & Brooks, 1993).

Further challenges imposed by close-knit communities involve the exchange of private information; workers may observe or receive data from multiple sources but must guard against the improper disclosure of information. Worker competence can be tested in small communities when limited referral options exist or when community members prefer to seek help from someone they know instead of from a "stranger," even if the stranger possesses superior formal credentials (Pugh, 2007).

Home-based Services

Social workers in home-based care must apply recognized ethical principles to novel and, at times, unpredictable circumstances. A clear benefit of home-based care is that it allows the worker to more readily and viscerally envision the client's reality. These encounters can positively impact rapport, insight, case planning, and other features of the working relationship. Yet immersion into the client's home requires that the worker use his or her clinical and ethical acumen to decide which of the things that are observed are relevant to the helping process and which are not. For example, a worker who finds an immigrant family using a barbecue grill indoors may intervene to educate the clients about the risks of carbon monoxide poisoning and fire, irrespective of the purposes of the visit. But what if the same worker observes the misuse of disability funds or negligent treatment of a pet? Do clients, in opening their homes to professionals, open

themselves up to all manner of critiques about how they choose to live their lives? Can workers effectively carry out their responsibilities if they selectively attend to troubling data? On what basis should workers act on their observations or choose restraint? Such powerful impressions and experiences may make it difficult for the worker to maintain appropriate boundaries, to focus on professional purposes, and to avoid burnout and vicarious trauma (Naturale, 2007).

In-home work is also characterized by autonomy and isolation. Workers experience less accessible back-up and consultation, and greater risks to health and safety (Allen & Tracy, 2009). In-home employees must be trustworthy in light of their freedom from oversight and office protocols and they must manage the likelihood of role ambiguity for themselves and their clients. Is the worker a friendly visitor, a clinician, an investigator, or a friend? Clients without a history of receiving in-home services may be uncertain about the protocols for hosting such a visit. Unless they are properly informed prior to the visit, this confusion can lead to resentment, apprehension, and heightened anxiety. It can also lead to complications in the session, such as the presence of other guests in the home, offers of food, or lack of preparation for the visit, if, for example, the child client is not home. Workers who are not clear about their roles, responsibilities, and objectives for the session may have difficulty avoiding diversions, structuring the meeting, and setting appropriate boundaries.

Another defining feature of home-based care is that the environment is largely out of the worker's control. Moving the interaction from the professional's office to the client's "turf" has both perceptible and subtle implications. The client's home may be remote and isolated or teeming with activity. The time allotted to the interview may be punctuated with intrusions from neighbors, family, and pets. Clients may feel more secure in the home environment and engage in behaviors they might not otherwise do in an office setting—slapping a child, opening the door in a nightgown, using the bathroom with the door open, playing video games, preparing a snack. As with the other dynamics in home-based care, a fluid environment and client comfort can enhance the worker's capacity to understand and engage with the client system. It can also create dilemmas as workers determine where and how to draw limits on requests, behaviors, or activities.

Online Networking

The swift and pervasive rise of online networking (ON) through discussion boards, blogs, and sites such as Facebook and Caring Bridge create unique challenges in the application of familiar ethical concepts such as client privacy, professional boundaries, worker self-disclosure, conflicts of interest, and informed consent. Social workers have long used their colleagues, alumni associations, and social circles to share news and ideas, show photos of vacations and life events, organize around shared interests or causes, and seek assistance with job searches or problem-solving. Yet, ON has taken networking to a broader and potentially more complex level as personal and professional data, opinions, problems, and experiences are spread more rapidly and more widely. Once shared, such information may take on a life of its own, and be difficult if not impossible to erase, even if harmful or untrue (Boyd & Ellison, 2007).

The vastness of online networks has constructive uses for professionals seeking resources or supervision, sharing information on evidence-based practices, marketing new services, or advocating for policy changes. Conversely, ON can create risk and exposure for the professional if a query about a difficult diagnostic issue reveals too much client information or results in sarcastic, unhelpful, or even harmful suggestions.

Online interactions with clients inherently carry a risk of boundary crossings and, ultimately, harmful violations. A social worker who, through Twitter or Facebook, learns unnecessary details of a client's views or activities may have difficulty keeping those details from impinging on the helping relationship. Extraneous information revealed through ON contacts may affect the worker's objectivity, causing him or her to judge the client more favorably (or harshly) than the case, itself, suggests. Innocuous references to shared interests in online profiles may open the door to discussions and activities that are irrelevant to the helping relationship. The challenges extend beyond the client-worker dyad when professionals who serve as instructors, administrators, and supervisors allow the added dimension of ON relationships to affect their ability to carry out their professional responsibilities—the student is upset by a radical blog the professor writes, or the supervisor is disturbed by interest groups with which the employee affiliates online. The NASW Code of Ethics stipulates that supervisees should be evaluated in "a fair and considerate manner and on the basis of clearly stated criteria (NASW, 2008, 3.03). It can be difficult enough to attain objectivity in appraisals of students or staff without the issues being clouded by inapplicable information.

NAVIGATING COMPLEX BOUNDARY CHALLENGES

Professionals have an array of resources at their disposal to address complex boundary challenges. Each dilemma requires the worker to anticipate the effects of the boundary crossing, consult with ethical standards and other resources, seek supervisory guidance and demonstrate self-restraint.

Anticipation

The practice setting or community type and the information obtained at intake or during the course of treatment will allow the worker to foresee an overlapping relationship and broach the topic with the others involved. For example, "We will probably run into each other at school and other events in the community, but I won't initiate conversations with you in public and I want to assure you that I don't reveal information from work with my family." Or (to a new supervisee who previously received services at the agency) "I suspect this may be awkward at first, but I want you to know I'm glad you've been hired here and I'm confident we can work through this. If apprehensions or issues arise for either of us, I hope we'll be able to talk about them."

The prevalence of online activity demands that professionals routinely anticipate requests for electronic communications or networking. The worker's policy should be addressed in writing and verbally at the outset of service, clarifying the worker's electronic availability. ("Text and e-mail messages may be used for scheduling concerns, but we should discuss *in person*, any other information involving your case." "I do not use social networks." "It is my policy not to 'friend' or otherwise connect with clients, students, or supervisees online.")

Professionals who are active in ON venues such as Twitter, social networks, blogs, or photo sharing should be alert to the messages they are sending and the ways those messages will be received by various constituents. Tight privacy settings, discretion, and disclaimers ("This blog represents my personal views, not those of my employer or profession.") will help put the worker's posts in context and provide nominal protection, but they are far from perfect. Anticipating how clever comments, frivolous photos, complaints about work, and other posts will appear can help posters decide what to share and what to withhold.

Professionals should anticipate that signing on as a friend or supporter with clients' or former clients' networks carry a high risk for difficulties. What is expected of the worker if the client uses it as a method to extend contact with the worker or if he or she posts troubling information? ("I ought to die." "I'm not supposed to drink with this medication but one beer won't hurt.") The ambiguity of roles and responsibilities in this forum suggests that avoiding such contacts sets a proper professional boundary.

Although the social worker may routinely practice in clients' homes, the experience may be a novel one for the service recipient. Anticipation in these situations requires the worker to learn what he or she can about the client's locale and related hazards or safety concerns. If possible, the worker should also prepare the client prior to the visit with information about the purpose and length of the meeting, the family members who will be expected to attend, and any questions the client may need to have addressed.

Consultation

The NASW Code of Ethics offers guidance for practice by enumerating social work values, principles, and standards. Licensed professionals may also find guidance in the code of conduct set forth by their state or provincial regulatory board. Professional associations, certifications, and other bodies issue practice standards that may be of help in addressing complex boundaries. Organizational policies will spell out the expectations for employees. Each of these resources will provide important perspectives to the worker struggling with boundary dilemmas. Unfortunately, each may be limited by the use of contextual, vague, or unrealistic provisions. ("Set appropriate boundaries." "Disclose only in compelling circumstances." "Assure that your personal conduct does not reflect negatively on the agency." "Never accept gifts from clients.") For these reasons, professionals must participate in shaping and articulating these expectations and engage in dialogue to operationalize them in practice. Continuing education programs, news articles, and staff meetings all provide forums for interpreting standards and developing the accompanying practice norms.

Supervision

Ethical standards encourage professionals to use supervision and peer consultation when faced with ethical dilemmas (Sawyer & Prescott, 2011). Unfortunately, practitioners may be reluctant to raise issues for fear that it will reflect negatively on their competence or impinge on an already overloaded colleague's schedule (Pope & Spiegel, 2008). Nevertheless, the complexities of practice require education and conversation to assure that client needs are properly addressed.

Professionals must locate resources for ongoing conversations and make use of these resources. Reluctance to raise an issue in supervision should be examined, for it is either a red flag about the lack of trust in the supervisory relationship or the wisdom of the worker's intentions. The "principle of publicity" serves as a test of worker judgment and the advisability of certain actions (Kidder, 1995). If the worker is reluctant to share information with colleagues, to stand by an action, or even to have others know about it, it is likely that the action is unsound.

Supervisors and peers can help colleagues understand policies and standards, think through the pros and cons of various boundary crossings, prepare for difficult conversations involved in setting boundaries, and evaluate the effects of overlapping relationships on the helping process. The worker must take responsibility for cultivating and using these resources.

Self-regulation

Cautious practice and ethical standards recommend that professionals assess whether a dual relationship is avoidable (Doyle, 1997) and "if the relationship is avoidable, avoid it" (Erickson, 2001, p. 303). What is avoidable? Generally, accepting as a client those with whom the social worker has had significant past or current involvement. This includes friends, neighbors, coworkers, dates, and those with whom the social worker has had substantial business dealings or other connections that might compromise the ability to serve the client's best interests and preserve confidentiality.

Self-regulation may also include avoiding roles that lead to problematic boundary compromises—for example, declining nomination to a committee whose chair is a client, or abandoning online discussion forums frequented by past or current patients. A professional in recovery may not be able to avoid attending 12-step meetings with clients, but may forego roles (such as sponsor) that compromise his/or her needs and those of the client. Some may say, "Why should I forego this opportunity just because of the possible complications?" In fact, some opportunities may be so rare or special that they cannot be avoided. But for those that can be, or that can be deferred to another time, the advantages are numerous. First, it is the clinician's fundamental obligation "to place the interests of those who are served above his own" (Kitchener, 1988, p. 217). The inability or unwillingness to do so should be cause for some self-examination. And, on a more pragmatic level, the client and the social worker are freed from the level of vigilance required to manage boundaries in overlapping relationships; both may take more pleasure from the activity without the other's presence in it.

Professionals must exercise shrewd self-awareness to identify problematic boundary crossings. By their nature, conflicts of interest require professionals to determine what situations will compromise their objectivity and capacities with a given client. Knowledge of self, fostered by attentive supervision and ongoing education, will help identify situations where overlapping relationships can be reconciled and those where they cannot. If the client gives the in-home worker surplus vegetables from the garden, the worker must determine whether that will affect his or her objectivity in the case, create improper expectations by the client, or simply constitute a normative act of kindness for which the worker should be grateful.

If a patient assigned to the social worker bullied the worker when both were school children, the social worker must appraise his or her capacity to separate the painful past from the patient's current needs. No guideline exists to tell the worker what is right. The decision rests on his or her self-knowledge and willingness to seek the input of others.

When practicing in situations rife with boundary challenges, professionals should develop their own policies and use those to guide routine choices. Some areas for personal policy development include:

- Whether to accept invitations to client events such as graduations, quinceañeras, bar/bat mitzvahs, or birthday parties
- Whether to accept gifts, homemade objects, bartered services, or refreshments
- Setting limits on home visits around noise, smoke, interruptions, or other distractions
- Establishing understandings with family members when the worker is approached in public by clients or when the worker sets seemingly arbitrary limits on family members' actions ("We cannot hire that service for our roof repair." or "I do not want you to go there for a sleep-over.")

Weighing the Risks of Complex Boundaries

Ultimately, through anticipation, consultation, supervision and self-regulation, the worker must weigh the risks and benefits of complex boundary relationships (Erickson, 2001). One model evaluates, from the consumer's perspective where the relationship falls on the dimensions of power, duration, and clarity of termination. Thus, it asks, "How great is the power differential? How long has the relationship lasted? And has it clearly ended?" (Gottlieb, 1993, p. 45). A traditional psychotherapeutic relationship would rate high on each measure and thus would pose a higher risk if combined with another relationship. If it is not as high on these measures (for example, the social worker was responsible only for discharge planning following a brief hospital stay) then further consideration can be given to the additional relationship. The same dimensions are considered for the new relationship— "Would it involve great power over a long time with uncertain termination?" (Gottlieb, 1993, pp. 45–46). Thus, accepting a former client as an employee would rate high on these dimensions while serving together as classroom parents for the elementary school would not.

Kitchener (1988) borrows from role theory in offering three additional factors on which to evaluate the risk of harm in a dual relationship. Risk is increased when the expectations between roles are incompatible, when obligations diverge, and when there are greater differences in prestige and power. For example, serving as a client's therapist and employer reflects high risk on all variables; the demands of the roles are incompatible, the obligations of the roles may well lead to divided loyalties or decreased objectivity, and the power differential in both roles is quite vast. Contrast this with the development of a social relationship with a former student or employee where the power differential and role conflicts are minimal, in part because the dual relationships are not concurrent, but also because the differences in power, role expectations, and responsibilities are not as great.

Ebert (1997) offers another, more fully explicated model, and suggests attention to additional factors, including where the secondary role relationship occurs (i.e., how public is it?), the purpose of the activity, the extent of contact, the presence of overt or subtle coercion, the likelihood that the behavior will create confusion, how the relationship appears to others, the context in which the conduct takes place, the danger of inhibiting future therapy, threats to clinician objectivity, and the strength of the client. Each of these questions helps the worker to evaluate the potential for conflicts of interest or therapeutic complications and thus determine the relative risk of engaging in the secondary relationship. Buying groceries from a store owned by a client might be construed as lower risk than buying a car at a client's dealership, because the former is a more common, less individualized transaction and one where the prices are fixed and the threat of coercion in negotiating price is not an issue. Attending a soccer party to celebrate the youths' successful season may not raise significant, ongoing discomfort or become intrusive in the helping process, but repeatedly seeing clients at the local health club locker room might (Schank & Skovholt, 1997). A home visit with an old acquaintance is more private, and thus more hazardous than seeing the patient in an office setting.

Many situations and settings create complex boundary questions. Social workers must engage in astute self-evaluation to determine when personal and professional activities can be reconciled and the client's interests upheld. Professional standards, personal policies, and dialogue with colleagues will prepare workers to set boundaries and navigate novel challenges.

WEBSITES

Articles, Research, & Resources in Psychology (Kenneth S. Pope, PhD, ABPP). http://www.kspope.com

Clinical Social Work Association, Code of Ethics. http://www.clinicalsocialworkassociation.org/about-us/ethics-code

International Federation of Social Workers: Statement of Ethical Principles. http://ifsw.org/policies/statement-of-ethical-principles/

National Association of Social Workers Code of Ethics. http://www.socialworkers.org/pubs/code/code.asp

Virtual Mentor (American Medical Association Journal of Ethics). http://virtualmentor.amaassn.org/

References

Allen, S., & Tracy, E. (Eds.). (2009). *Delivering home-based services: A social work perspective* (pp. 14–33). New York, NY: Columbia University Press.

Baldwin, M. (1987). The use of self in therapy: An introduction. *Journal of Psychotherapy & The Family, 3*(1), 7–16.

Beck, L. (2013, February 5). Uh-oh: OB-GYN complains about patient on Facebook [Blog post]. Retrieved from http://jezebel.com/5981691/she-made-a-huge-mistake-ob+gyn-complains-about-patient-on-facebook

Beskind, H., Bartels, S. J., & Brooks, M. (1993). Practical and theoretical dilemmas of dynamic psychotherapy in a small community. In J. H. Gold & J. C. Nemiah (Eds.), *Beyond transference: When the therapist's real life intrudes* (pp. 1–19). Washington, DC: American Psychiatric Press.

Boland-Prom, K. W. (2009). Results from a national study of social workers sanctioned by state licensing boards. *Social Work, 54*(4), 351–360.

Boyd, D. M., & Ellison, N. B. (2007). Social network sites: Definition, history, and scholarship. *Journal of Computer-Mediated Communication, 13*(1), 210–230. Also available at http://jcmc.indiana.edu/vol13/issue1/boyd.ellison.html.

Daley, M. R., & Doughty, M. O. (2006). Ethics complaints in social work practice: A rural–urban comparison. *Journal of Social Work Values and Ethics, (3)*, 1. Retrieved from http://www.socialworker.com/jswve/content/view/28/44/.

Decker, J. R. (2012, February 6). 'Like'it or not, Facebook can get teachers fired [Blog post]. Retrieved from http://www.educationnation.com/index.cfm?objectid=72C543DE-4EA0-11E1-B607000C296BA163

Doyle, K. (1997). Substance abuse counselors in recovery: Implications for the ethical issue of dual relationships. *Journal of Counseling and Development, 75*, 428–432.

Ebert, B. W. (1997). Dual-relationship prohibitions: A concept whose time never should have come. *Applied and Preventative Psychology, 6*, 137–156.

Epstein, R. S., & Simon, R. I. (1990).The exploitation index: An early warning indicator of boundary violations in psychotherapy. *Bulletin of the Menninger Clinic, 54*(4), 450–465.

Erickson, S. H. (2001). Multiple relationships in rural counseling. *The Family Journal: Counseling and Therapy for Couples and Families, 9*(3), 302–304.

Farber, B. A. (2006). *Self-disclosure in psychotherapy.* New York, NY: Guilford Press.

Gottlieb, M. C. (1993). Avoiding exploitive dual relationships: A decision-making model. *Psychotherapy, 30*(1), 41–48.

Heyboer, K. (2010, March 26). Medical students' cadaver photos gets scrutiny after images show up online. *New Jersey.* Retrieved from http://www.nj.com/news/index.ssf/2010/03/medical_schools_examine_ethics.html

Kidder, R. M. (1995). *How good people make tough choices: Resolving the dilemmas of ethical living.* New York, NY: Simon and Schuster.

Kitchener, K. S. (1988). Dual relationships: What makes them so problematic? *Journal of Counseling and Development, 67,* 217–221.

Knox, S., & Hill, C. E. (2003). Therapist self-disclosure: Research-based suggestions for practitioners. *Journal of Clinical Psychology, 59*(5), 529–539.

Miller, P. J. (1998). Dual relationships in rural practice: A dilemma of ethics and culture. In L. H. Ginsberg (Ed.), *Social work in rural communities* (3rd ed., pp. 55–62). Alexandria, VA: CSWE.

National Association of Social Workers. (2008). *Code of ethics.* Washington, DC: Author.

Naturale, A. (2007). Secondary traumatic stress in social workers responding to disasters: Reports from the field. *Clinical Social Work Journal, 35*(3), 173–181.

Pope, K. S., & Keith-Spiegel, P. (2008). A practical approach to boundaries in psychotherapy: Making decisions, bypassing blunders, and mending fences. *Journal of Clinical Psychology, 64*(5), 638–652.

Pugh, R. (2007). Dual relationships: Personal and professional boundaries in rural social work. *The British Journal of Social Work, 37,* 1405–1423.

Reamer, F. G. (2001). *Tangled relationships: Managing boundary issues in the human services.* New York, NY: Columbia University Press.

Sawyer, S., & Prescott, D. (2011). Boundaries and dual relationships. *Sexual Abuse: A Journal of Research and Treatment, 23*(3), 365–380.

Schank, J. A., & Skovholt, T. M. (1997). Dual relationship dilemmas of rural and small-community psychologists. *Professional Psychology: Research and Practice, 28*(1), 44–49.

Strom-Gottfried, K. J. (1999). Professional boundaries: An analysis of violations by social workers. *Families in Society: The Journal of Contemporary Human Services, 80*(5), 439–449.

Walfish, S., Barnett, J. E., Marlyere, K., & Zielke, R. (2010). "Doc, there's something I have to tell you": Patient disclosure to their psychotherapist of unprosecuted murder and other violence. *Ethics & Behavior, 20*(5), 311–323.

25 Integrating Values into Social Work Practice

Juliet Cassuto Rothman

This article will present an overview of values in social work and their impact on our professional functioning. Methods and strategies for working with values will then assist the reader to both become aware of the importance of values and to integrate awareness of values into practice.

UNDERSTANDING VALUES

Values have always been an essential part of human life and human thought, and continue to be central today. Our personal values guide us in decision-making, in our life choices, and in our relationships. Values are subjective in the sense that each person's values are developed through personal experiences and personal thoughts. Values tend to remain stable throughout our lives, although the actions and the meanings we attach to them may change and evolve.

A part of the human endeavor is reaching out to both determine and achieve that which gives life meaning, on both a personal and a humanitarian level. Meaning is drawn from values. A person who values personal relationships may find meaning in deep friendships, in work that helps others, or in supporting human rights. A person who values nature and natural beauty may find meaning in working in the outdoors, or in becoming involved with environmental issues. A person who values freedom may find meaning in times when she or he is alone, or in working to bring political systems that value freedom to other areas of the world, or in working on equal rights legislation.

Life goals are drawn from that which gives meaning. In our profession, life goals often determine our professional choices—of contexts and fields and populations. Because of the self-awareness that is an essential part of social work practice, we may be aware of our goals, of the things that give meaning to our lives, of our values. However, it is important to recognize that values function similarly in all people, and to integrate this awareness into every aspect of our work.

Because values differ and may conflict, an exploration of values as a part of the social work process can help to increase awareness of potential conflicts, and enable these to be considered and addressed in the development of plans for services (Dolgoff, Harrington, & Loewenberg, 2012).

The theories of Kohlberg and Gilligan often have been used by social workers to understand value formation and moral development. Although their conclusions differ, both understand value development as occurring in childhood over time (Gilligan, 1982; Duska & Whelan, 1975). Values are learned from such varied sources as parents, teachers, coaches, religion, national history, culture and ethnicity, mentors, and friends, but are then filtered through each person's individual experiences.

It is also essential to recognize that the word "value" itself implies something of worth, thus, something that the holder of the value considers to be a good. In addressing behaviors that may be negative, illegal, or destructive of self and others,

it is important to seek the value that may lie hidden beneath the actions and behaviors of others. A few obvious examples:

• A gang member may value friendship, loyalty, and membership in something larger than self
• The pregnant 13-year-old may value loving another, being loved, being independent
• The seller of stolen goods may value comfort and wealth for family and friends.

Clients may be unfamiliar or uncomfortable with using the world "values," and may be able to relate more easily to a different phrasing. One possible way to initiate a discussion of values might be something like, "In order to see how we can work together to help you, we both need to understand what is *important* to you/what you *care* about/what you *want* in life."

In working with values, it is necessary to be aware of three especial challenges we face:

(1) *Abstract and concrete values:* A common difficulty is related to the terms we use in describing values. We often find agreement when we speak in abstract terms, such as "freedom," "equality," "friendship," "democracy," "God," "the natural environment," etc. This gives us a good "we-feeling" of being united and similar to others. However, it is important to be very cautious here: if we were to ask 20 people who value "freedom" to define it, we would get 20 very different definitions! When the term is abstract, it is easy to have *apparent* agreement; but when we go from this to goal setting and planning, we encounter confusion and differences. Thus, it is important to be aware that in the movement from abstract to concrete values, many differences may become visible and are essential to consider.

(2) *"Real" and "ideal" values:* In working through the values exercises that will be presented in this article, a consistent challenge is the difference between "real" and "ideal" values. This is most strongly apparent in the consideration of societal values. We value freedom, justice, democracy, religious freedom, human rights—all these lofty and wonderful concepts, which have been a part of our nation since its very formation. However, when we consider how our country operates, we often find

another set of values, such as power, wealth, material possessions, and personal gain. The former set of values encompasses those that we publicly espouse, while the latter are those that often direct actions and personal positions. We strive toward our "ideal" values, we "value" them, but many times our actions support "real" values instead!

(3) *Cultural value differences:* Our nation is a potpourri of different ethnicities, cultures, religions, and social classes. Because of the way in which values are formed, they are influenced by the context in which people have been raised and in which they live. This often creates real differences in values and priorities. Social workers are as strongly influenced by these factors as clients. Cultural competence requires an awareness of differences, including value differences.

VALUES IN SOCIAL WORK PRACTICE

Consideration of values in social work practice is complex, and often involves seven or more different value systems: (1) the worker's personal values, (2) values of supervisory and oversight personnel, (3) agency and program values, (4) social work professional values, (5) societal values, (6) client values, and (7) values of the affected system, which may not be involved in receiving direct services. Values from each of these systems have a strong impact on goal setting and achievement, and must be considered both as client services or projects are initiated and as they are evaluated. Strong value dissonances have a negative impact upon goal achievement.

(1) *Personal Values:* Social workers considering personal values often find justice, human well-being, and community among their highest-held values—after all, these values have helped to guide them toward the social work profession!

As with everyone, these and other personal values are shaped by each person's unique life experiences, and are often so well integrated that there may be little awareness of their presence or of their effect on professional service. Some of our personal values tend to be abstract: when we "fill in" the meanings with concrete terms and examples, we must be conscious of the differences among and between us. In our commitment to being nonjudgmental, and to respecting others, it is vital that we become aware of our personal values and the ways they impact our professional functioning.

(2) *Professional Values:* Social work's professional values are defined in the National Association of Social Workers (NASW, 2008) Code of Ethics. Core values of the profession include *service, human relationships, dignity and worth of person, social justice, integrity, and competence* (NASW, 2008). Professional ethical principles and standards are drawn from these values. Each value relates to a separate principle, and a series of standards for professional behavior follow. In examining the Code, the progression from abstract to more concrete values is clear in the transitions from values to principles to standards. The greater the congruence between our personal values and the profession's values, the better the "fit" between worker and profession, and the fewer value conflicts will be experienced.

Like all groupings of values applied to specific situations, social work's values may conflict with one another, and may be prioritized differently in different contexts by different practitioners. In addition, it is not possible for the Code to provide specific guidance for every situation workers encounter. To address these and other problems in applying social work values, Stewart suggests that "social justice," one of the core values, be utilized as an "organizing principle" for the profession (Stewart, 2013).

(3) *Supervisory and Oversight Values:* Because most social workers function within a system that includes supervision and oversight, the personal values of supervisors and others within the agency or program hierarchy also impact on professional services rendered.

(4) *Agency and Program Values:* Agency and program values determine process, methodology, populations, and goals of service, and are generally defined in the mission statement and goals of the organization. Many agencies have come into being through religious, cultural, or governmental organizations, and their missions and policies reflect the values of their founders. In many cases, these values continue to provide meaning and direction and guide services and programs. In others, the context and needs of the population served may have changed, subtly altering the manner in which organizational values are integrated into service. In still others, agency mission and values may

have been reconsidered and redefined to meet the changing needs of the groups and programs served.

It is important to be aware of agency and program values, and to consider these carefully both in seeking and maintaining employment. Value differences between workers and settings may affect the provision of services to clients, and can create stress and discomfort for workers as they choose between responsibility to personal values, and responsibility to those of the employing organization. Some examples of potential value conflicts include: euthanasia and end-of-life issues, abortion and birth control, incarceration and probation, children's rights and parent's rights, and marriage equality.

There may be a special challenge for social workers in a host setting where the values of another profession, or other entity, take precedence in policy, programs, and methods, potentially creating a conflict between social work's professional values and values of the employing organization.

(5) *Societal Values*: We all immediately recognize the challenges inherent in attempting to determine societal values. Who is "society"? Who defines "society"? One common response to this problem is to say that societal values are the values of the "founding fathers." What about the mothers? Slaves? Non-English speakers? More recent arrivals? Can we speak of *national* societal values, or are there many differing societal values, each defined by a community, group, or population? And, how do we resolve the difference between "real" and "ideal" values on a societal level?

Several possible avenues for arriving at an understanding of societal values include determining that (1) societal values may be defined through the Constitution; (2) societal values are embodied in our laws and can be determined by exploring law and policy; (3) because our society is so diverse, it is not possible to arrive at any agreement on what constitutes societal values; (4) our society is made up of many overlapping groups and subgroups whose values may be more or less similar, making it possible to arrive at a number of basic values that can be used to define societal values as used in the social work setting.

The challenge of determining societal values is not easily resolved. However, it is essential to be aware of these values, for social workers are, in a sense, "agents" of society. We are licensed to practice by society, given control of services and resources that society provides, and given the authority to care for vulnerable members of society. We are charged with supporting laws and policies, while at the same time advocating for changes when these are viewed as unfair.

(6) *Client Values*: Congruence between client values, goals of service, methodologies, and interventions are major factors in the achievement of service objectives. A discussion of values should be initiated early in the relationship, with service plans built upon this foundation.

Where clients appear to have limited self-insight, exploring values may be one of the first objectives to be considered. In situations where clients are unable, or unwilling, to share in a discussion of values, workers can gain insight into value systems by carefully observing clients' behaviors and choices, and/or by learning something of their histories and life experiences. As an example, in helping clients to make end-of-life decisions, Csikai and Chaitin (2006) suggest the development of a "values history" as a useful tool (Csikai & Chaitin, 2006).

It is in one-on-one values discussions with clients that we must be most careful to self-observe and to be self-aware. A word, a gesture, an expression on the part of the social worker can give the client an awareness of value differences, and of the worker's judgment of the client's values. Two other considerations are important in this regard:

(1) Where value differences are clear and easily recognized, we are most aware of the need to respect and consider the client's values. It often feels more comfortable to be working with clients whose values appear similar to our own. However, it is when values *appear* most similar that we should be most vigilant in self-monitoring! Because, as has been noted earlier, abstract words provide a sense of similarity in values, it is easy to focus on these and miss the unique experiences and shades of meaning, that makes client values different from the worker's own (Rothman, 2006).

(2) Cultural differences also affect the way in which values are integrated into the provision of services. In some cultures, the social worker is considered the "expert" whose views, ideas, and plans are easily and unquestioningly accepted by clients. Some cultures may consider objecting to the social worker's ideas and planning as a sign of disrespect for the worker. When applied to values, this may lead to a tendency to accept the worker's values and priorities, even if these differ from the client's own (Rothman, 2006).

(7) *Values of the Affected System*: In planning services and programs, and in working with individual clients, we must also consider the value systems of those who will be affected by the changes service provision will bring. Spouses and partners, children and other family members, friends, employers, community members, and neighbors may all be impacted by changes in individual clients, and client goals and objectives may conflict with their own personal values.

Beyond the individual client, values may affect program funding, service provision, policies, and populations served.

WORKING WITHIN THE VALUES CONTEXT

There are several methodologies and strategies for appropriately integrating a consideration of values into our work with clients at every level of practice from micro to macro, from young children to the elderly, from any ethnicity, religion, culture, and belief system, and in any community. These include developing and working with a values hierarchy, considering the role of real and ideal values, recognizing the importance of personal values, including our own, searching for commonalities, building on commonalities, and utilizing these to develop goals interventions, and relationships. This section will address these practical issues, and suggest methods for addressing them.

Developing a values hierarchy is the first, essential step in the process of integrating values into planning and interventions. Values hierarchies can be developed for each of the seven value systems defined in the previous section. Similar methodology can be used for each, and values hierarchies may be developed specific to different practice methodologies. As an example, in writing about spiritually oriented practice, Dezerotes suggests a practice hierarchy grounded in spiritual values. (Dezerotes, 2006) Values hierarchies can be developed by the worker, by the client, or by worker and client together.

Developing a Personal Values Hierarchy

Because the social worker's personal values hierarchy should be addressed first in order to foster self-awareness and understand the role of personal values in the worker's practice, the process will be illustrated and presented here using the worker as an example.

Step 1: Consider the things that are of value in your life. Your personal values can range from very abstract, such as "freedom," to very concrete, such as "my home," and everything in between. Do not be concerned about level of abstraction and concreteness—just consider what is important to you, and what gives life meaning. Write your values on a blank sheet of paper, leaving space between each value. Ten values are a good number to work with—but a few less or more are also workable. Writing down too few values restricts reflection and flexibility. Too many may be confusing and overwhelming.

Step 2: Examine your 10 values. You may notice that some concrete values seem to fit under the more abstract values. As an example, "my friend Sarah" and "my classmate Ethan" may both fit under the more abstract value "friendship." The value "women's rights" and "immigration reform" might both be subsumed under the value "social justice." It is your choice to either subsume concrete values under the more abstract values, or to leave them as distinct.

This step in the process will illustrate the way in which similarly stated abstract values are defined differently by different people. Many people would cite the value "social justice," but the concrete meaning of the term may vary individually to include "equal rights," "free enterprise," "quality education for all," "our country," "freedom of speech," or the "rights of the unborn." This is why it is essential for the professional to explore what others mean when they use the term "social justice"; it means very different things to different people!

Step 3: Build a hierarchy. Prioritizing your values involves making painful choices. Is "friendship" more important to you than "social justice"? Is "freedom" or "equal opportunity" more important? "The social work profession" or "my family"? When helping clients to build their own values hierarchy, it is important to remember the challenge of building one's own, and to be supportive and empathic during this process with others.

To create your values hierarchy, you may simply number each value from 1 to 10. Or, you may tear your list into strips, with one value on each strip, and place the strips into an order. The latter method may appear more cumbersome at first, but actually enables much easier movement, consideration, and changes to values in the hierarchy.

Step 4: When you have completed building your hierarchy, write it out carefully on another sheet of paper to use as a reference. Familiarity with your hierarchy increases your awareness of its impact on your work. It is not usually necessary to formally share your personal values with your clients—they will be obvious to clients from your actions in your work with them, and such sharing would deflect the focus of your work from your clients.

As noted earlier, if you are working with a client who is unable or unwilling to communicate, or with an organization or group that has not developed a formal list, it is still important to consider values. Observation and a review of history also may help you to determine values and build a values hierarchy. Try to consider values early in the professional relationship. You can help clients through this process by using empathy and support.

Values should always be expressed and discussed using the language of the person whose values are being addressed. Rather than trying to use professional, perhaps more abstract, terms for values, help the client to work within his/her own language to support empowerment and to encourage self-expression. Demonstrate acceptance of values and terms used. The process of working with values hierarchies builds trust and relationship, and can serve as an excellent tool upon which to build planning for change.

Considering "Real" and "Ideal" Values

Both "real" and "ideal" values have an important role to play in developing awareness and understanding. In the process of working with their values hierarchy, people often feel a pull between their personal ideal and real values. For example, being available to help someone in crisis is often an important value in a social worker's values hierarchy, but the social worker also values being available to her/his own children and family. "Real" values such as having a clear period of "down time" and rest may conflict with the "ideal" values of always being available to clients.

Everyone has these kinds of difficulties in trying to reconcile "real" and "ideal" values in a personal values hierarchy. "Family time" versus "career advancement"; "being there for my friends" versus "not being around people on drugs"; "being on time" versus "gathering all the information needed," are some simple examples of values conflicts. Although this can be stressful, you can learn a great deal about yourself in the process! Personal experiences and history often have great influence, and exploring these can both lead to insights and deepen a trust relationship.

Professional Values, Agency Values, and Societal Values

When you engage with a client, it is important to recognize that, for the client, you represent not only your personal values, but also the values of the social work profession, the agency, and society. This creates certain expectations of worker engagement, methodologies, and values, and is perhaps one of the most important reasons social workers must do their own values work before beginning to work with clients.

The lack of clarity in the consideration of societal values, noted earlier, may leave the worker with some sense of uncertainty. If there is a responsibility to represent society, and societal values are unclear, or conflicting, we may tend to function within the context of personal, professional, and agency values, minimizing the impact of societal values. It is generally helpful to turn for advice to a supervisor, agency director, or ethics committee to address these difficulties.

Client Values and Values of the Affected System

The NASW Code of Ethics clearly states, "Social workers' primary responsibility is to the well-being of clients" (NASW, 2008). This underscores the importance of exploring client values within the professional relationship. The method presented earlier can easily be used to consider client values, with careful clarification of abstract terms and seemingly ambiguous statements of values. A list of values can be developed, and placed within a hierarchy. Plans for services should be in agreement with client values, although consideration of client values may be more difficult in involuntary settings. Of course, clients also have "real" and "ideal" values, and these differences can offer an opportunity to explore more deeply with the client. Observing or considering behavior can also serve to illustrate some of the "real" and "ideal" value conflicts.

Clients may also find themselves with conflicting values, and find the process of exploration and the creation of a hierarchy very difficult and stressful. This conflict is most often felt between "real" and "ideal" values, but also may occur during the process of creating a hierarchy. Through careful discussion, social workers can assist their clients with this process.

Where the client is a couple, a family, a group, or other system, exploring commonly held values and value differences is an important aspect of planning. Serious differences in values can limit the success of goals and interventions. A discussion of commonly held values and goals will often reveal not only similarities and differences, but also the power structure within the client group.

If you are working with a client or a family member who is unable or unwilling to communicate, it is important to remember that values are tools for action: observation is an excellent method for determining, or confirming, client values.

You may find that you are unable to work directly to develop a values hierarchy with everyone who will be affected by your work with the client. However, it is important to have as much understanding as possible of these, for they will have an impact on the client, and on the potential achievement of goals. Clients themselves are often aware of the values of others in the client system and can assist you with understanding.

The exploration and understanding of values is often a time-consuming, though essential, process. Exploration of client, client system, and societal values may itself become a major part of the service plan, or can be limited somewhat to accommodate other needs, time constraints, and specific service methodologies.

Preparing an Overview of Values in the Wider System

Congruence between the value systems of worker, client, those potentially affected by services, the social work profession, the agency, and society will encourage and support a positive outcome. Reaching optimal congruence in values requires a clear understanding of the values hierarchy of those involved with, or affected by, the services to be provided.

In order to explore similarities and differences in values, the values hierarchies for affected parties can be prepared, always bearing in mind that the client's values are primary. A table can be constructed with all of the value hierarchies side by side. This will enable a clear assessment, and may be shared with the client if you believe it would be helpful.

Client	Client System	Agency	Community	General Society

In lieu of this formal structure, the social worker can also discuss values hierarchies and differences with clients verbally, giving opportunity for discussion and reflection.

Seeking Value Congruence, Recognizing Differences

Seeking and supporting value congruence is an essential step in planning for services and setting goals. The greater the value congruence, the greater the chance of success with services rendered to the client.

In considering the values hierarchies listed above, it is important to note

Differences in the use of language and terminology
Differences in the levels of abstraction/ concreteness
Cultural issues

Agencies and programs tend to express values using professional terminology—terminology that may be unfamiliar to the client. It is important to remain aware of a possible tendency to attribute greater importance to values stated in such terms than to the perhaps more simply expressed values of the client and the client system. Social workers should also ensure that clients understand agency and program values.

Agency and program values tend to be more abstract and focused toward their client base, community, and society at large, while client values may be focused on self and others in the client system. We can reconcile the two by considering the ways in which the agency's values can support those of the client.

human relationships // people I care about // the people in my class// my friends// my best friend Sandy

The client may identify "my best friend Sandy" as a value, while the agency's program values "human relationships." Yet, both are identifying similar things: positive, important relationships that support and sustain. Understanding that these are similar values, the social worker can help the client and/or the agency to see the connection between these two values. The movement tends to go from concrete to abstract—it is easier to find value congruence in abstract values, which have some "give" in terms of specifics than to focus on specific, concrete values.

However, the agency's value of "human relationships" may be irreconcilable with a client value of "independence and privacy." While acknowledging and respecting this difference, the social worker can continue to explore values hierarchies, seeking other values that may be more congruent.

Cultural differences may impact the congruence-seeking process as well. In some cultures, having a commitment to personal values and goals is a sign of strength, and is greatly valued, while in others, there is a tendency to defer value judgments to the professional, as the "expert" in addressing these issues.

The process of seeking value congruence and recognizing differences should be undertaken prior to any goal setting and specific service planning, as these should be grounded in value systems.

It is also important to remember that clients are very sensitive to approval, disapproval, or questioning, and it is important to carefully self-monitor through this discussion process.

Grounding Goals and Interventions on Common Goals

Once values have been clarified, workers and clients may begin the process of contracting and goal setting, being careful to consider and support client values. Goals that incorporate the client's basic values have the best chance of success. Goals that also include a consideration of the values of the client system have an even better chance of success. It is our responsibility, however, to ensure that goals and interventions also support the values of the agency and of the community.

Summary

Values are an important element in self-conception, in goal setting, and in how one understands one's place and role in society. Values are generally learned in childhood, and develop out of each person's unique life experience process. We tend to keep the same values all of our lives, though the actions that spring from them may change and evolve over time.

Clarifying and understanding values and value systems encountered in professional practice increases self-awareness, and enables a greater chance of success in service delivery. The process must begin with the worker's exploration of personal values, for these impact clients and client services as well at the relationship between worker and agency or program, the profession, and the broader society. Exploration, definition, and the development of a values hierarchy provide the personal self-awareness that is so necessary in practice.

A similar process will enhance client self-awareness, and the integration of client values into planning, goal setting, and interventions helps to ensure their success, while increasing client self-awareness and building trust in the professional relationships.

Although a consideration of client values is primary to social work practice, it is also important to consider the value systems that underlie supervisory and oversight structures, agencies and programs, the social work profession, and perhaps most challenging, broader society, over whose resources and programs our profession has been given authority. The closer the value congruence among all of the parties affected by the provision of client services, the greater the chance of success in rendering them.

WEBSITES

www.naswdc.org/pubs/code/code.asp
www.jswve.org
www.pdx.edu/ssw/values-video

References

Csikai, E., & Chaitin, E. (2006). *Ethics in end-of life decisions in social work practice*. Chicago, IL: Lyceum Books.

Dezerotes, D. (2006). *Spiritually-oriented social work practice*. Boston, MA: Pearson.

Dolgoff, R., Harrington, D., & Loewenberg, F. (2012). *Ethical decisions for social work practice*. Belmont, CA: Brooks/Cole.

Duska, R., & Whelan, M. (1975). *Moral development: A guide to Piaget and Kohlberg*. New York, NY: Paulist Press.

Gilligan, C. (1982). *In a different voice*. Cambridge, MA: Harvard University Press.

National Association of Social Workers. (2008). *Code of Ethics*. Retrieved from www.nasw.org/pubs/code

Rothman, J. (2013). *From the front lines: Student cases in social work ethics*. Boston, MA: Pearson Education.

26   Adoption Competency in Social Work Practice

Debra Siegel

Benita Sanchez, an experienced licensed clinical social worker employed at a family service agency, sits in her office with a new client, Jon, a single adoptive father, who called the agency seeking parenting guidance. Jon says, "The state child welfare agency placed my son, Mark, in foster care with me three days after he was born because both Mark and his biological mother tested positive for cocaine, alcohol, methamphetamines, and marijuana. Mark's birth mother told the delivery room staff at the hospital that she was raped and she didn't know who the baby's biological father was. His birth mother did not participate in the state child welfare agency's reunification efforts for two years, so her parental rights were involuntarily terminated and I adopted Mark when he was almost two. We've never had contact with his bio family. Mark is now eleven. He's always been a feisty, spirited youngster, and over the years he's struggled mightily with academic and social issues in school; his behavior for the past two years has become increasingly oppositional at home and school. Lately, he's been crying, kicking me, hitting me, and yelling, "I need to find my birth family NOW, not when I'm eighteen! I can't wait. I can't stand how sad I feel." I can understand Mark's strong feelings about this, and I'm also concerned for Mark's emotional and physical safety. What do I do? I realize that Mark will soon be able to use Facebook and the Internet to do the search on his own, without my involvement." Benita gulps silently, thinking to herself, "Oh dear! What do I need to know in order to be helpful here?" Like most social workers, extensive education about adoption has not been part of Benita's training. She wonders, "How many of Mark's issues are adoption related? How do I guide Mark's dad? All I know about adoption is from my sister-in-law, who adopted a girl from China."

Most social workers will encounter adoption issues in the course of their careers. Among Americans surveyed, 64% reported having a personal connection to adoption (National Adoption Attitudes Survey, 2002); an estimated one hundred million Americans are touched by adoption (Pertman, 2011); and about 2% of children in the United States under the age of 18 years, approximately 1.8 million children, are adopted (U.S. Department of Health and Human Services [HHS], 2013; U.S. Census Bureau, 2003; U.S. Children's Bureau, 2011). In addition, in 2012 approximately 115,000 U.S. children were awaiting adoption (U.S. Dept. of HHS, Adoption and Foster Care Reporting System, July 2010).

Families in which a child has been conceived by donor egg or donor sperm, gestated within a surrogate, or adopted by a biological relative or by a step-parent may encounter many of the same issues as families with children who are born to one genetic set of parents and adopted by a person with whom they have no genetic link. In short, significant numbers of people are affected in some way by adoption, perhaps as relatives or friends of adoptive or birth families. Although most people touched by adoption may not seek clinical services, studies indicate that people who have been adopted are disproportionately represented in clinical populations (Harwood & Feng, 2013; U.S. Children's Bureau, 2004; Brand & Brinich, 1999).

Given these facts, social workers engaged in child welfare, clinical practice (i.e., mental health care and individual and family therapy), policy, or administration all need adoption competency. Studies show that adoptive families often struggle to find mental health providers who have the knowledge and skills to help them (Brodzinsky, 2013; New York State Citizen's Coalition for Children, 2010; Riley, 2009; Javier, Baden, Biafora, & Camacho-Gingerich, 2007; Singer, 2004; Casey, 2003; Howard & Livingston-Smith, 1997). A 2010 survey, conducted by the North American Conference on Adoptable Children (Stevens, 2011), with one thousand adoptive parents responding, found that 39% reported having trouble finding mental health providers who understood adoption issues. The NACAC report concluded that adoption competency training for mental health providers is needed, along with greater access to mental health services, parent education and training, and educational advocacy and support.

People contemplating adoption, along with those living with adoption, must grapple with complex issues that professionals who lack adoption competency may misunderstand or leave unaddressed. Professionals' mishandling of these issues leaves clients in distress, without the help they seek and need.

Adoption competency in both child welfare practice and mental health care is not just needed; it is ethically mandated. The National Association of Social Workers (NASW) Code of Ethics (section 1.04 a, b, c; pp. 8–9, NASW, 2008) emphasizes social workers' obligation to acquire the knowledge and skills needed to provide competent services. Although "Many authors have noted the conceptual vagueness that surrounds competence as a concept" and "one true definition [of competence] does not exist" (Cooper and Menzel, 2013, p. 30), there is agreement that the competent practitioner has specific knowledge, skills, and attitudes (Cooper & Menzel, 2013).

This chapter introduces core areas of values, knowledge, and skills included in adoption competency. Many of the specific areas of knowledge and skill will vary depending upon (1) the type of adoption (e.g., via a public child welfare or private agency; domestic or inter-country; foster, guardianship, or kinship care; older child or infant; transracial or transcultural; sibling group; special educational, medical, or behavioral health needs); (2) the phase of the adoption process (e.g., pre-adoption planning and preparation or postadoption support services); and (3) the identified client (e.g., the child, biological parent, or adoptive parent). Nonetheless, there are cross-cutting issues and themes. Those are the focus of this chapter.

In addition to the above variables, drawing definitive conclusions about what adoption competency consists of remains a challenge, in part because there is no one universally accepted definition. However, the Center for Adoption Support and Education (CASE) has written a definition underpinning a post-master's degree training curriculum for mental health care providers at eight sites (in North Carolina, Minnesota, Ohio, Massachusetts, Indiana, Missouri, Nebraska, and California), with research findings indicating the training's effectiveness (CASE, 2013). Other adoption competency post-master's training programs have been implemented, for example, at Hunter College in New York, Rutgers University in New Jersey, and Portland State University in Oregon. Adoption competency curricula vary, depending on whether their focus is on training child welfare workers (e.g., National Resource Center for Adoption, 2011) or mental health clinicians with master's degrees (e.g., Riley, 2009). Nonetheless, close examination of the programs reveals at least some consensus about adoption competency.

VALUES UNDERPINNING ADOPTION COMPETENCY

Although there may always be differing views, there is widespread agreement about some guiding principles underpinning competent child welfare, clinical, and policy practices in adoption.

- The child's needs and interests are primary. The purpose of adoption is to provide the child with a family, not to provide prospective parents with a child.
- Every child needs and deserves a safe, nurturing, permanent family. Congregate care and impermanent care arrangements are not adequate substitutes for that.
- Generally, a child's interests are best served within the child's biological family, and country and culture of origin. For this reason, adequate family preservation services should be provided so that adoption is not needed. Adoptions across family, national, and ethnic boundaries should occur only when earnest efforts to find an adoptive parent within those boundaries have been unsuccessful.
- The child who is old enough to participate in the adoption decision and choice of family should be permitted to do so, as an essential component of adoption preparation.
- All people have a right to access full information about themselves. The practice of permanently sealing birth certificates should end. Secrecy, lies, and cut-offs in adoption do not serve the adopted person's best interests.
- All information known about the child should be shared with the adoptive parent(s) before they adopt.
- The child should have access to ongoing medical information that emerges in the birth family over the lifespan.
- In most cases, the child also has a right to have access to some sort of contact with the biological family. This access may range from minimal (e.g., infrequent exchange of letters via a post office box) to moderate (e.g., occasional e-mail messages or phone calls) to high (e.g., face-to-face visits in each others' homes), depending on the circumstances.
- Birth parents, including those who have had their parental rights involuntarily terminated because they abused or neglected the child, should be treated with respect.
- Deception, dishonesty, and coercion in adoption are undesirable. Client autonomy and self-determination should be supported.
- It is best to take a nonpathologizing, strengths perspective when working with people whose lives are touched by adoption. Being adopted, a birth parent, or an adoptive parent does not indicate that one is troubled or trouble. Clients should be viewed as the experts in their own lives.
- Rather than thinking in terms of an adoption triad, comprised of the child, adoptive parent, and birth parent, it is more useful to think in terms of an adoption circle composed of the many adoptive and birth family members, and other systems and players involved in forming and sustaining an adoption. The extended family formed by adoption is best understood in a societal and relational context.
- Adoption is not an event, but a process that unfolds over the lifespan. Thorough preadoption education and preparation for child, biological parents, and prospective adoptive parents is essential. After adoption, access to competent postadoption support services should also be available.

PATHWAYS TO ADOPTION

The child welfare worker or clinician who has adoption competency is able to identify and explore with clients how a child and family's route to adoption may generate issues and themes that need to be addressed both before and after an adoption is finalized. The worker or clinician recognizes that although there are cross-cutting issues that characterize all adoptions regardless of how the adoption occurs (for example, there is no adoption without loss), each adoption is as unique as the people in it, and each pathway to adoption presents different emotional and practical themes. For example, a child may enter adoption via the public child welfare agency; as an infant, older child, or adolescent; alone or as part of a sibling group; with or without special educational, physical, or mental health needs; with or without preadoption trauma. And he or she may or may not differ from the adoptive family in ethnicity, race, religion, class, sexual orientation or gender identity, and other ways. A child might enter adoption via a private agency, from another country, without licensed agency involvement, with or without preadoption counseling and education for the biological and adoptive parents, and with or without having a voice in the adoption plan. A birth parent might choose to terminate parental rights voluntarily or have parental rights involuntarily terminated by the court. An adoptive parent might pursue adoption due to infertility or myriad other reasons. Providing effective preadoption planning and education requires thorough knowledge of the issues each path to adoption presents, and skills for helping biological and adoptive parents and children plan to manage these issues across the lifespan.

For example, due to federal legislation (Adoption and Safe Families Act of 1997, P.L. 105–89) child welfare practitioners may begin "concurrent planning" for both reunification with the biological family and for adoption as soon as the state becomes involved in a biological family that has abused or neglected its children; the aim is to form a collaborative, cooperative relationship between the biological and foster parents so they can continue to form a circle of shared love around the child regardless of which permanency plan emerges. This approach seeks to build family connections and supportive relationships in the child's life rather than severing them. The approach also presents unique challenges for child welfare workers, clinicians, and clients both before and after adoption takes place.

KNOWLEDGE AND SKILLS FOR ADOPTION COMPETENT PRACTICE

The many areas of knowledge and skill comprising adoption competency can be viewed in three interwoven conceptual categories: the societal context, interpersonal relations, and intrapsychic dynamics. Although these categories are neither exhaustive nor mutually exclusive, they are useful for organizing the complex array of knowledge and skills that help define adoption competence.

Societal Context

Law. Knowledge of adoption history and law is useful, given that both shape preadoption planning and postadoption issues, not only in child welfare work but in clinical practice as well. Each of the 50 United States and the District of Columbia, and each country across the globe, has its own adoption laws, complicating adoption practice. In addition to state law, there are federal laws and international agreements with which social workers should be familiar in order to provide informed services both before and after an adoption is finalized. For example, one should be familiar with The Multiethnic Placement Act (MEPA) of 1994 as amended by the Interethnic Adoption Provisions (IEP) of 1996; Indian Child Welfare Act (ICWA) of 1978; Adoption and Safe Families Act (ASFA) of 1997; Safe and Timely Interstate Placement Act of 2006; Child and Family Services Improvement Act of 2006; Fostering Connections to Success and Increasing Adoptions Act of 2008; Hague Convention on Protection of Children in Intercountry Adoption of 1993.

Prevailing Beliefs. Adoption history and law also reflect and perpetuate myths and beliefs that may permeate unhelpful child welfare and clinical practices. Although public attitudes toward adoption have evolved away from viewing the adoptee as a "bastard" who must be protected from the truth by secrecy and total disconnection forever from the biological family (Princeton Research Associates, 1997), many social workers, along with the general public, continue to hold views and use language that unwittingly convey erroneous, pejorative misconceptions and stereotypes about adoption. For example, one hears, "I could never give up my own flesh and blood," "His real mother gave him away," or "She decided to keep the baby," phrases that imply that the adopted child was unwanted, cast away, and that birth parents are reviled. The phrase "blood is thicker than water" implies that adoptive family relationships are not as strong as biological family connections. Practitioners with adoption competency are familiar with these and other terms and phrases that may unintentionally oppress and avoid these terms in favor of "neutral language" to describe the adoption experience. For example, the phrases "The biological mother and father made an adoption plan for their child" or "The birth mother chose to parent," convey that adoption is a responsible, affirmative choice. Another example of adoption competent language is to avoid calling an expectant biological parent "birth mother" or birth father when she or he is thinking about making an adoption plan, reserving the term "birth parent" only for the biological parent who has finalized an adoption, so as to avoid exerting subtle pressure on the biological parent to choose adoption instead of choosing to parent (Smith, 2006). These and many other nuances of language exert powerful messages that shape not only adoption policy and child welfare practices, but clinical social work practice in mental health and therapy as well.

As the above suggests, adoption talk can reflect or evoke primal emotions, including within the child welfare worker or clinician, who must remain keenly aware of her or his beliefs and feelings and the ways these shape assessment and intervention. The history of adoption is fraught with examples of how well-intended, confident, but ill-informed social workers have influenced and controlled adoptees and parents, harming them in the process (Carp, 2000). For example, the birth parent who suffers from drug addiction and gives birth to a child who tests positive for cocaine, may be seen as uncaring and willfully dismissive of the child's needs, not as a person struggling with a severe medical and mental health issue; the worker's anger and pejorative judgments about addiction can interfere with effective service delivery. Similarly, the clinician might feel frustrated with the adoptive parent who continues to make condemning statements about the birth parent to a child who feels distraught by divided loyalty, or when an adoptive parent insists that the child has no questions or feelings about adoption even when the child has expressed these in family therapy sessions. Adoption competency includes awareness of and ability to effectively manage such countertransference, including one's own feelings about and experiences with adoption, and the compassion fatigue and vicarious trauma that social workers in adoption may experience.

Racism, Oppression, Discrimination. Adoption competent practitioners are cautious about "color blindness," the assumption that an adoptive family can raise a child of a different race or ethnicity as if the child comes from the adoptive family's heritage. The practitioner must know how, for example, to offer information gently to parents who adopt a child of a different race or culture, about the importance of weaving the child's racial and cultural identity into the fabric of the family's daily life, perhaps by including books, foods, music, friends, religion, schools, and other activities that reflect the child's ethnic origins. Practitioners can help parents and children anticipate the possibility of, and figure out ways one might respond to, intrusive, insensitive comments, questions, and societal racism so that the responsibility of being a transracial or transcultural family is shared, not borne by the child alone. The adoption competent practitioner is able, in a noninvasive, noncontrolling way, to explore with parents their wish that their loving and accepting the child, alone, will erase the need to do these things. Adoption competency also includes knowledge and skills for preparing and supporting adoptive families with lesbian, gay, bisexual, and transgender parents or youths.

Programs and Services. Although certainly not every adoptive family will need ongoing clinical support, the adoption competent practitioner is able to help families in need access and advocate for adequate adoption subsidy payments, special education services, residential schools and programs for significant behavioral health or learning issues, support groups, and other services (Dore, 2006). A family may benefit from access to an adoption competent clinician with whom they have a good working alliance so, if needed, they can tap into clinical services at points of discomfort for short-term help from time to time (Pavao, 2005), given that it is normal for adoption issues to re-emerge across the lifespan.

Laws, prevailing beliefs, racism, oppression and discrimination, and access, or lack thereof, to needed programs and services, highlight the need for ongoing analysis of ethical issues in adoption. Ethical dilemmas, and decision making, permeate every aspect of social work practice and policy in adoption (Siegel, 2009).

Adoption Ethics. The practitioner must be fully informed of the panoply of ethical issues, dilemmas, and choices embedded in adoption laws, policies, and clinical practices (Freundlich, 2000a, 2000b, 2000c, 2001), especially those related to issues of privacy, autonomy, paternalism and self-determination, confidentiality, informed consent, boundaries, and conflicts of interest. Adoption competency involves the ability to identify these issues, and apply ethical decision-making protocols from the professional ethics literature to address these ethical challenges in child welfare policy and clinical practice (Reamer & Siegel, 2007).

Relational Context

The relational and intrapsychic issues that may need to be addressed, and the skills involved in managing these successfully, vary depending upon the phase of the adoption process. Before a family is formed through adoption, competent preadoption education and planning are essential to enhance the participants' well-being. Once the adoption is finalized, members of the extended family formed by adoption may at times benefit from postadoption education and support.

The adoption journey entails normative, predictable developmental phases and tasks that may emerge throughout the life cycle of the family and of each individual family member. Adoption competent practitioners are aware of these likely issues. For example, often when a child in foster care is adopted by the foster family with whom he has always lived, grief over having the legal connection to the birth family severed may lead the child to misbehave, even as people are celebrating the adoption as a happy event. An adoptive parent who feels wounded by his infertility, unsure of the child's attachment to him, or not entitled to parent a child born to someone else, might hesitate to discipline the child effectively. An adopted person who moved through childhood with few adoption feelings, may experience intense adoption-related feelings for the first time upon leaving home for college or upon giving birth. A birth parent who feels guilty about terminating her parental rights might not respond to a child's or adoptive parent's request for contact. Adoption competent clinical social workers are able to identify and then address therapeutically the many different ways that living with adoption may affect the participants (Hutchison, 2007). This involves exploring for the issues without insisting on them or denying each family's uniqueness.

Family System Dynamics. All families, whether formed by birth or adoption, have internal family system dynamics; some of these dynamics reflect predictable themes in many families formed by adoption, so clinicians need specific skills to help families navigate these. For example, when a teen says, "You can't tell me what to do. You're not my real mother!" the adoptive parent may need emotional and practical support in figuring out how to assert parental authority while also responding to the teen's adoption feelings.

In some respects, the family system formed by adoption may be best understood as a complex intersecting network of biological and adoptive grandparents, aunts, uncles, cousins, siblings, friends, neighbors, teachers, clergy, physicians, lawyers, adoption professionals, and others who play a role in the adopted person's life and both affect and are affected by the adoption. The adoption competent practitioner recognizes, assesses, and intervenes with the interplay and dynamics generated by these multiple actors. For example, the practitioner anticipates how adoptions through kinship care (i.e., a member of the child's birth family becomes the adoptive parent, shifting biological family roles) present complex issues and is able to help members of the kinship system manage these.

The omnipresence of electronic communication tools and devices has introduced new issues into the child's adoptive and birth families. Where once adoptive and birth parents could reasonably expect to control the child's access to contact with biological relatives, today, social networking sites, cell phones, text and instant messaging, video conferencing, and Twitter accounts create ample opportunities for very young adoptees to communicate with birth-family members with or without a parent's knowledge. For this reason, too, families may find adoption competent guidance helpful in preadoption planning and then in living the adoption adventure that unfolds.

One size does not fit all in adoption competent practice. Hence, although it is essential to recognize that an adoptive family may encounter thematic issues, not every family experiences these issues, or does so in the same ways or at the same times, and the issues may be impossible to tease out from other challenges in the family's experiences and development (e.g., the shifting of family roles and expectations as children reach adolescence, the impact of births, unemployment, illness, divorce, or death). Family systems issues and individual psychological issues are intricately interwoven in all families; assessing for these and intervening with adoptive families requires specific, well-honed assessment and intervention skills.

Open Adoption Issues. Most adoptions in the United States today include some form of openness, in which birth family and adoptive family members, including the child, exchange identifying information and have some degree of ongoing contact with each other (Siegel & Smith, 2012). Effective clinical work with adoptive and birth families requires advanced knowledge and skill about the vast array of open adoption alternatives, the reasons for open adoption, predictable challenges that may arise during the open adoption experience, evidence-based guidelines for successful open adoptions, and skills to help biological and prospective adoptive parents negotiate and maintain workable contact agreements. Adoption competency involves knowing how to work with biological and adoptive family members, helping each clarify for themselves their hopes, needs, fears, and anxieties about contact, and then helping them communicate and negotiate with each other truthfully, respectfully, and compassionately as they develop contact agreements that shift over time as participants' needs change (Siegel, 2013; Siegel, 2012). A clinician may be helpful when families need to put contact on hold without permanently severing the relationship. In adoptions with no openness, the competent clinician knows how to identify and address the resulting issues.

Search and Reunion Issues. Each member of the extended family of adoption may face decisions about whether, when, and how to reach out to biological relatives and then how to manage the lifelong issues that reunion generates. The adoption competent practitioner is fully informed about these issues, and knows how to help participants navigate them, including how to connect participants with organizations such as the American Adoption Congress for practical and emotional supports.

Child and Family Developmental Issues. The child's biological and adoptive family units experience predictable developmental phases, as does the child and each person within the respective families. The families' and individuals' developmental phases and tasks intersect. The child's understanding of adoption changes as the brain develops. The adoption competent provider is able to identify these phases and the issues each presents, and effectively uses a variety of therapeutic methods, including psycho-education, to help participants address them. The practitioner knows how to help parents find the words to talk helpfully with the children about adoption at each stage of life, sharing difficult adoption-related information truthfully and sensitively in a timely manner. Adoption competency includes knowing how to help parent and child construct an accurate, life-affirming adoption story that acknowledges both the gains and challenges adoption brings. The adoption competent practitioner is able to help families create a birth book or life book and access support groups and Internet resources.

Intrapsychic Context

Silverstein and Roszia (1998) posit core, normative "affective responses" to adoption that birth parents, adoptive parents, and adoptees experience across the lifespan, all in their own ways. These issues include loss, rejection, guilt and shame, grief, identity, intimacy, mastery, and control. Among other core issues identified in the adoption literature are anger, fear of abandonment, trust, loyalty, and self-esteem (Javier et al., 2007). For example, the adopted person, birth parent, and adoptive parent may each fear and

avoid intimacy in different ways and for different reasons, as love and loss are closely connected in adoption. Adoption competency involves the ability to assess for these core issues without insisting on them; validate and normalize them without minimizing or exaggerating them; and use an array of therapeutic methods to support families and individuals in processing and managing them. This alleviates the client's burden of having to educate the clinician about what the issues are and what it means to live with the issues.

Trauma, Attachment, Neurobiology, and Brain Plasticity. Much has been written about the notion that even when an infant is adopted at birth there may be traumatic loss (Verrier, 1993). Certainly, children who were abused or severely neglected prior to adoption have experienced trauma. Trauma affects the child's brain development in ways that may impact attachment, social and relationship skill development, emotional self-regulation, academic performance, problem solving skills, and coping (Szalavitz & Perry, 2010; Cozolino, 2006). The adoption competent practitioner is fully informed on these issues, knows the relevant neurobiological research, and is skilled in using evidence-based methods to address the issues therapeutically with both child and family to foster secure attachments and brain plasticity.

Behavioral Health and Behavior Management. The operant conditioning methods taught in typical parenting classes may not work well with a child who has experienced traumatic loss; a particular child's brain might not be wired to learn from typical parenting tools such as logical consequences, time outs, rewards and punishments, so clinicians must know how to help parents and teachers use collaborative problem solving methods, environmental management, and other coping tools to deal with problematic behaviors, avoiding the inclination to label the child as willfully noncompliant (Greene, 2010). The child's noncompliant, inflexible, explosive, or oppositional behavior may indicate that the child is overwhelmed by internal stimuli or external situational demands. Adoptive parents, too, need strengths-based clinicians who are careful not to assume that the child is misbehaving because the parents lack basic child behavior management skills. Adoption competency involves forming collaborative, supportive alliances with parents as equal members of the treatment team, valuing their unique knowledge of the child, helping them process their frustrations and fears, and exploring with them parenting strategies that go beyond the kinds of parenting education typically offered.

Genetics. The nature versus nurture debate permeates the world of adoption. Parents who adopt tend to believe in the healing powers of love, structure, and a nurturing environment. They need social workers who both support these beliefs and help parents embrace the reality that genetics and prenatal or childhood trauma may play crucial roles in the human organism's tendency toward a particular mood, social abilities, academic, athletic, mechanical, and other proclivities. Clinicians with adoption competencies use reframing, psychodynamic, cognitive behavioral, psycho-educational, and other psychotherapeutic methods to help adoptive parents avoid blaming themselves or the child for the child's challenges. They help parents take the long view, seeing struggles as opportunities for growth, as parents strive to maintain stable, nurturing, compassionate, family relationships.

EVIDENCE BASE FOR ADOPTION COMPETENCY

It is clear that adoption competency is essential for child welfare workers, clinicians providing mental health care and therapy, administrators and policy makers. A few adoption competence training programs exist. An outcome study measuring changes in knowledge and skill of master's level mental health providers who completed the CASE curriculum demonstrates that program's effectiveness (Atkinson, Gonet, & Riley, 2013). Important next steps include (1) building into Masters of Social Work curricula the values, knowledge, and skills that underpin adoption competence; (2) offering adoption competency training for public- and private-sector child welfare workers and master's degreed clinicians in every state; and (3) completing formative and summative evaluation studies of adoption competency education efforts so that the most evidence-based protocols can be used.

WEBSITES

Center for Adoption Support and Education. http://adoptionsupport.org

Evan B. Donaldson Adoption Institute. http://adoptioninstitute.org.

Child Welfare Information Gateway. www.childwelfare.gov/adoption/

National Resource Center for Adoption. http://nrcadoption.org.

ACKNOWLEDGMENTS

The author wishes to thank the following adoption experts for reviewing drafts of this manuscript and providing feedback on it: Darlene Allen and Barbara Keefe of Adoption Rhode Island; and A. J. Atkinson, Madelyn Freundlich, Patricia Ganet, and Debbie Riley of the Center for Adoption Support and Education.

References

Atkinson, A. J., Gonet, P., & Riley, D. (2013). Adoption competent clinical practice: Defining its meaning and development. *Adoption Quarterly, 16,* 156–174.

Brand, A. E., & Brinich, P. M. (1999). Behavior problems and mental health contacts in adopted, foster, and nonadopted children. *Journal of Child Psychology and Psychiatry, 40*(8), 1221–1229.

Brodzinsky, D. M. (2013). *A need to know: Enhancing adoption competence among mental health professionals.* New York, NY: Donaldson Adoption Institute.

Carp, E. W. (2000). *Family matters: Secrecy and disclosure in the history of adoption.* Cambridge, MA: The President and Fellows of Harvard College.

Casey Family Services. (2003). *Promising practices in adoption-competent mental health services.* Washington, DC: The Casey Center for Effective Child Welfare Practice.

Center for Adoption Support and Education (CASE). (2013). *TAC evaluation highlights* [prepared by Policy Works, Ltd]. Burtonsville, MD: Author.

U.S. Department of Health and Human Services, Health Resources and Services Administration, Maternal and Child Health Bureau. (2010). *Child Health USA 2010.* Rockville, MD: Author.

Child Welfare Information Gateway. (2011). *How many children were adopted in 2007 and 2008?* Washington, DC: U.S. Department of Health and Human Services, Children's Bureau.

Cooper, T. L., & Menzel, D. C. (Eds.). (2013). *Achieving Ethical Competence for Public Service Leadership* (p. 30). Armonk, NY: M. E. Sharpe.

Cozolino, L. (2006). *The neuroscience of human relationships: Attachment and the developing social brain.* New York, NY: W. W. Norton & Co.

Dore, M. (Ed.). (2006). *The postadoption experience: Adoptive families' service needs and service outcomes*. Washington, DC: Child Welfare League of America (CWLA).

Freundlich, M. (2000a). *Adoption and ethics: The role of race, culture and national origin in adoption* (Vol. 1). Washington, DC: CWLA.

Freundlich, M. (2000b). *Adoption and ethics: Market forces* (Vol. 2). Washington, DC: CWLA.

Freundlich, M., & Lieberthal, J. K. (2000c). *Adoption and ethics: The impact of adoption on members of the triad*. Washington, DC: CWLA.

Freundlich, M. (2001). *Adoption and ethics: Adoption and assisted reproduction* (Vol. IV). Washington, DC: CWLA.

Greene, R. W. (2010). *The explosive child: A new approach for understanding and parenting easily frustrated, "chronically inflexible" children* (Rev. 4th ed.). New York, NY: HarperCollins.

Harwood, R., & Feng, X. (2013). Preadoption adversities and postadoption mediators of mental health and school outcomes among international, foster and private adoptees in the United States. *Journal of Family Psychology, 27*(3), 409–420.

Howard, J., & Livingston-Smith, S. (1997). *Strengthening adoptive families*. Normal IL: Illinois State University, Center for Adoption Studies Press.

Javier, R. A., Baden, A. L., Biafora, F. A., & Camacho-Gingerich, A. (2007). *Handbook of adoption: Implications for researchers, practitioners, and families*. Thousand Oaks, CA: Sage.

National Adoption Attitudes Survey (2002). Available at adoptioninstitute.org/old/survey/Adoption_Attitude_Survey.pdf.

National Association of Social Workers. (2008). *Code of Ethics*. Washington, DC: NASW Press.

National Resource Center for Adoption. (2011). *Adoption competency curriculum*. Southfield, MI: Michigan Federation for Children and Families. Retrieved from http://www.michfed.org/may-june_adoption_curriculum_training_free_through_national_resource_center_adoption.

New York State Citizens' Coalition for Children. (2010). *Parents and professionals identify post adoption service needs in New York state: Post-adoption services survey*. Brooklyn, NY: Author.

Pavao, J. (2005). *The family of adoption*. Boston, MA: Beacon.

Pertman, A. (2011). *Adoption nation*. Boston, MA: The Harvard Common Press.

Princeton Research Associates. (1997). *Benchmark adoption survey: Report on the findings*. Washington, DC: Princeton Survey Research Associates.

Reamer, F. G., & Siegel, D. H. (2007). Ethical issues in open adoption: Implications for practice. *Families in Society, 88*(1), 11–18.

Riley, D. (2009). *Training mental health professionals to be adoption competent*. Burtonsville, MD: Center for Adoption Support and Education (CASE).

Szalavitz, M., & Perry, B. D. (2010). *Born for love*. New York, NY: Harper Collins.

Siegel, D. (2009). Adoption. In *Encyclopedia of Applied Ethics* (2nd ed.). Oxford: Elsevier.

Siegel, D., & Smith, S. (2012). *Openness in adoption: From secrecy and stigma to knowledge and connections*. New York, NY: Evan B. Donaldson Adoption Institute.

Siegel, D. (2012). Growing up in open adoption: Young adults' perspectives. *Families in Society, 93*(2), 133–139.

Siegel, D. (2013). Open adoption: Adoptive parents' reactions two decades later. *Social Work, 58*(1), 43–51.

Silverstein, D., & Roszia, S. (1998). Adoptees and the seven core issues of adoption. *Adoptive Families Magazine*. Retrieved from http://www.adoptive-families.com/articles.php?aid=489.

Singer, Ellen. (2004). *Post adoption counseling*. Burtonsville, MD: Center for Adoption Support and Education (CASE).

Smith, S. (2006). *Safeguarding the rights and well-being of birthparents in the adoption process*. New York, NY: Evan B. Donaldson Adoption Institute.

Stevens, K. (2011). Post-adoption needs survey offers direction for continued advocacy efforts. *Adoptalk*. St. Paul, MN: North American Council on Adoptable Children (NACAC). Retrieved from http://www.nacac.org/adoptalk/postadoptionsurvey.html.

U.S. Census Bureau. (2003, October). *Census 2000 special reports: Adopted children and stepchildren: 2000*. Washington, DC: U.S. Department of Commerce, Economic and Statistics Administration, U.S. Census Bureau.

U.S. Children's Bureau. (2004). *Adoption and foster care statistics*. U.S. Department of Health and Human Services, Administration for Children and Families. AFCARS report. Retrieved from http://www.acf.hhs.gov/programs/cb/resource/afcars-report-11.

U.S. Department of Health and Human Services. (2013). *Adoption and foster care reporting system, July 2012*. Washington, DC: Author.

Verrier, N. (1993). *The primal wound: Understanding the adopted child*. Baltimore, MD: Gateway Press.

PART IV

Theoretical Foundations and Treatment Approaches in Clinical Social Work

27 Crisis Intervention with Individual and Groups

Frameworks to Guide Social Workers

Yvonne Eaton-Stull

Crises are inevitable in the social work field. No matter where practitioners work, clients will present with a variety of crises: a teenager who experiences her first breakup and is contemplating suicide, a husband who loses his job and is distraught over how he will care for his family, or a child who loses both parents in a tragic motor vehicle accident. All of these scenarios are potential situations that social workers may encounter in their work. Events known to precipitate crises often involve health/mental health issues, financial problems, legal problems, victimization, loss, or natural and other disasters (Roberts & Yeager, 2009). A crisis is individually determined—that is, the individual client lacks the resources or coping skills to handle the stressful situation with which he or she is confronted.

Several different people may experience the same traumatic event, but each responds in a unique way. A practitioner's ability to assist individuals in mobilizing their strengths, protective factors, resilience, and positive coping methods will help to resolve the crisis situation.

An understanding of crisis theory and crisis intervention is essential for competent social work practice. Social workers should be educated and skilled in handling the full range of acute crises episodes because clients frequently present with difficulties and obstacles to crisis resolution and stabilization without intervention (Knox & Roberts, 2008). Crisis intervention consists of the various techniques used to assist individuals in mobilizing resources and developing plans to overcome the temporary situation. It can provide a challenge, opportunity, and turning point (Roberts, 2005).

Unlike typical counseling interventions, crisis work requires a special set of skills and interventions to effectively assist those in need. Greenstone and Leviton (2011) refer to crisis intervention as problem management, not resolution, because it involves quick decision making and the ability to mobilize needed resources. The purpose of this chapter is to provide social workers with practical frameworks to guide individual and group intervention.

FRAMEWORKS FOR INDIVIDUAL CRISIS INTERVENTION

Although social workers have been trained in a variety of theoretical models, very little coursework has provided them with a guide to follow in dealing with crises. Roberts's (2005) seven-stage crisis intervention model and Greenstone and Leviton's (2011) crisis intervention procedures offer two useful frameworks. The subsequent sections will outline each of these models followed by a scenario to illustrate the steps involved.

Roberts Seven-stage Crisis Intervention Model

Stage 1: Plan and Conduct a Crisis Assessment The first step involves a quick assessment of risk and dangerousness, including suicide and homicide/violence risk assessment, need for medical attention, and current drug or alcohol use (Roberts, 2005). There are a variety of formal assessments for risk of suicide/homicide, but

217

these tools should always be accompanied by a thorough clinical assessment with information from the individual as well as other relevant sources of information. Key risk assessment questions are outlined in Table 27.1.

Answers to these questions will help the social worker determine the appropriate next steps. Substance use is an important factor to evaluate because it can contribute to impulsively acting on these thoughts. In addition, a substance assessment should include information about drugs used, amount used, last use, and any withdrawal symptoms the client is experiencing (Eaton & Roberts, 2002). If possible, a medical assessment should include a brief summary of the presenting problem, any medical conditions, current medications (including dosages and last dose), and allergies (Eaton & Roberts, 2002). This medical information is essential to relay to medical responders

attempting to treat problems, such as overdoses, if they are in progress.

Stage 2: Rapid Establishment of Rapport This often occurs simultaneously with stage 1. Conveying respect and acceptance are key skills in this stage. Workers must display a nonjudgmental attitude as well, ensuring that their personal opinions and values are not apparent or stated (Roberts, 2005). Roberts and Yeager (2009) also note that creativity, flexibility, and a positive attitude are additional strengths in successful crisis workers.

Stage 3: Identify the Major Problems Use of open-ended questions will offer a strategy to hear more from the client's perspective, such as asking a client what happened to bring them to this point. This provides the crisis worker with valuable insights into the nature of the presenting problem and potential precipitating events.

Stage 4: Deal with Feelings and Emotions Active listening skills are essential during this stage. Clients should be encouraged to share their story as the practitioner listens intently in order to understand their situation better (Roberts & Yeager, 2009).

Stage 5: Generate and Explore Alternatives Ideally, the ability of the worker and the client to work collaboratively during this stage should yield the widest array of potential resources and alternatives (Eaton & Roberts, 2002). According to Roberts (2005), individuals in crisis have untapped resources and coping skills, which can be utilized to help them resolve this crisis. At this point in the intervention the social worker should use solution-focused questions to explore strategies the client has used previously to help them through rough times. These may potentially be useful in formulating the action plan.

Stage 6: Develop an Action Plan The crisis worker should assist the client in the least restrictive manner, enabling them to feel empowered (Eaton & Roberts, 2002). Important steps at this stage include providing coping mechanisms and identifying persons and referral sources to be contacted (Roberts, 2005). According to Jackson-Cherry and Erford (2014), action plans should include (1) information about restricting access, such as removing guns; (2) strategies for self-care/stress management; (3) family supports;

TABLE 27.1 Questions for Assessing Risk

	Suicide & Homicide Risk Assessment
Ideation	1) Are you having thoughts to kill yourself/someone else?
Furtherance	2) Have you done anything already?
Past history	3) Have you ever tried to kill yourself/someone else in the past? If so, how?
Plan/method/ lethality	4) How might you kill yourself/someone else?
Availability of means	5) Do you have access to the methods (cited in Question 4)?
Protective factors/hope	6a) What is stopping you from acting on these thoughts? 6b) Do you feel things can get better?
Supports	7) Can you tell me who in your life might be a support to help you through this?
Substance use	8) What drugs or alcohol have you used today?

(Eaton & Roberts, 2002)

and (4) mental health resources. Writing such a plan on a carbon-copy form allows a quick way for both the social worker and client to agree and document the process.

Stage 7: Follow-up Crisis workers should follow up with the client after the initial intervention to ensure the crisis has been resolved (Roberts & Yeager, 2009). This allows an opportunity to determine whether the client has followed through with recommendations and continued care. If indicated, additional referrals can be made at this time.

Scenario 1 (Application of Roberts Seven-stage Crisis Intervention Model)

The social worker received a call from a concerned parent whose daughter posted a disturbing statement on her Facebook wall, in which she said good-bye to her friends and family because she could not take it anymore. Roberts's (2005) seven-stage crisis intervention model was initiated.

Stage 1: Assess Lethality. The mother had little information about the current mental status of the client and was fearful because she was unable to reach her by phone. The worker responded to the residence hall and found the student crying and curled up in her bed. There were bottles of over-the-counter medication on her desk. A quick assessment revealed that this female was having thoughts to kill herself by overdosing on Tylenol and ibuprofen, which were readily available to her. She had a prior overdose attempt in high school, but was physically stopped from doing so by her best friend. She did not receive any treatment at that time. She reported that the only thing stopping her now was that she hoped her ex-boyfriend, who had broken up with her earlier that day, would see the post and come over. She did not feel she would survive if he did not and was feeling more hopeless with each passing minute that he did not respond. This student had not taken any substances or any of the over-the-counter medication yet.

Stage 2: Establish Rapport. Understanding and support were two essential skills used by the crisis worker to establish a working relationship with the client. Emotional validation was especially helpful in validating how upsetting an unexpected breakup of a two-year relationship could be.

Stage 3: Identify Problems. Luckily, the client had not yet done anything to harm herself, but she was actively contemplating suicide. She had a plan to overdose, but was hoping her ex-boyfriend would see her Facebook post, and they could reconcile. The client expressed that the precipitant was the breakup with her boyfriend.

Stage 4: Deal with Feelings. The worker allowed the client to tell her story about the breakup and her relationship history. The worker was able to validate and identify the client's emotions. Based on the level of intensity of the student's emotions, it was necessary to pursue a higher level of care.

Stage 5: Explore Alternatives. Together, they began to explore more effective ways of coping with her upsetting feelings. Options were discussed, including calling her mother and giving the student the option to obtain a mental health assessment in her home city (with mother's assistance) or the nearby hospital (near the college).

Stage 6: Develop an Action Plan. The client requested that her mother be consulted to help her decide. The mother felt that being near home would allow for more family support. Luckily, the client's home was only about two hours from school, so the mother agreed to come to campus and take her daughter to a hospital near her home. A release of information was obtained for the home hospital, and a phone call was made to the crisis assessment staff to provide referral information.

Stage 7: Follow-up. A follow-up phone call was made to mother the next day. The client was admitted on an inpatient mental health unit at the hospital near her home.

Greenstone and Leviton's Crisis Intervention Procedures

Step 1: Immediacy According to Greenstone and Leviton (2011), this step is critical in assuring that clients do not harm themselves or others. Potential actions such as enlisting the assistance of emergency personnel, police, or other supports may be useful during this step.

Step 2: Control This step is a more directive process. The social worker will attempt to assess the surrounding and individuals present. The purpose of this step is to help lessen the current chaos as the practitioner maintains a calm, supportive demeanour while attempting to establish structure (Greenstone & Leviton, 2011). One key element during this step often includes separating the client from others who may be fuelling an already intense situation.

Step 3: Assessment During this step, the social worker obtains a lot of helpful information. Unlike typical social work sessions that involve a complete biopsychosocial history, a crisis assessment is more focused on the current struggle and recent precipitants. Greenstone and Leviton (2011) suggest the worker attempt to gain recent information about what happened to the client, why they are having difficulty coping, and what type of intervention is needed. This step also requires a thorough safety risk assessment as previously outlined in Table 27.1. Taking time to hear the client's stressors thoroughly helps the worker determine what areas need immediate attention and as such, what must be included in the disposition.

Step 4: Disposition Greenstone and Leviton (2011) indicate that this step includes the decision about how to handle the crisis situation. Key skills during this step include creative thinking, problem-solving, and considering various options (Greenstone & Leviton, 2011). Based on information gained in the previous step, it is hoped the social worker will have identified existing resources that may be helpful to include in the decision making process.

Step 5: Referral Almost all crises involve making referrals. Often times, this may include referrals to emergency services or hospitals with inpatient mental health care; thus, it is important to have knowledge of local resources. Greenstone and Leviton (2011) suggest that practitioners take steps to build relationships with these crisis providers before being faced with an actual crisis; for example, visiting other agencies, making a resource list, and investigating transportation options.

Step 6: Follow Up Step six is an important step many practitioners fail to complete; however, it can be potentially helpful in preventing another crisis. Greenstone and Leviton (2011) indicated it is important to determine whether the client has connected with the referrals provided or if assistance or re-referrals are needed.

Scenario 2 (Application of Greenstone and Leviton's Crisis Intervention Procedures)

A professional residence life staff member phoned the on-call worker due to a resident assistant's (RA) concern about a student who was cutting herself.

Step 1: Immediacy. In a college setting, it is not uncommon to receive a call from a concerned roommate or residence life professional. It is important to consider the safety of all involved; thus, staff members were directed to call security to assist in securing the knife and support the student until the worker could arrive. It was also suggested that the professional staff evaluate the injuries to determine whether immediate medical attention was needed, and if so, to call an ambulance.

Step 2: Control. Upon arrival, the worker determined that five individuals (security, RA, professional staff, security, and roommate) in addition to the client were present. There were approximately three scratches on the student's arm that had not required medical intervention. The student was cooperative and willing to talk. Following introductions, the student was given some control by asking which one person, if any, she would like to remain as a support. She chose her RA. Others were thanked for their help and informed that they would be contacted if further assistance was needed.

Step 3: Assessment. The student was very open and indicated that she was feeling left out by her hall mates. She admits that she took a nap after class, and therefore, her door was closed and they did not wake her up to go to dinner with them. As a freshman, she was concerned about fitting in and having friends. She denied that her cutting behavior was a suicide attempt, and in fact, denied any suicidal ideation, stating she really liked college and the freedom she had. Her cutting behavior was a past method of coping with upsetting feelings. She interpreted the event as a purposeful way of excluding her from dinner. We explored alternatives, such as the fact they may have thought she was not in her room due to the door being closed. She admitted this was possible. She acknowledged that her RA really attempts to include the floor in various events and is always available to talk to the students on her floor.

Step 4: Disposition. We talked about the need for more effective coping skills, given that her cutting behavior was concerning to others. She acknowledged this and was willing to seek assistance to manage her emotions and coping strategies better. Further, we discussed a simple strategy of writing on the dry erase board on her door that she was napping and to please wake her up for dinner; this way her friends would know she was there and was hoping to go to dinner with them.

Step 5: Referral. A referral was made to the campus counseling center for the next morning.

Step 6: Follow-up. The student kept her scheduled appointment and treatment began. A more detailed crisis plan was developed at this time to assist the student in identifying options for coping with intense emotions, which included supports and other resources.

GROUP CRISIS INTERVENTION

Individual intervention can be guided by the above frameworks, but group intervention requires a different approach. A sudden, traumatic death of a friend may impact a large group of students, or a natural disaster may impact an entire community. The scope and magnitude of a crisis may require social workers to intervene with several individuals simultaneously.

According to expert consensus, psychological first aid (PFA) is the recommended intervention (Kaul & Welzant, 2005; Watson, Brymer, & Bonanno, 2011). PFA is also endorsed by the North Atlantic Treaty Organization (NATO) as the evidence-informed approach to decreasing distress and fostering adaptive functioning and coping (NATO Joint Medical Committee, 2008). PFA includes the following actions—to be provided by the practitioner: (1) making contact and engaging with survivors, (2) enhancing safety and comfort, (3) calming and stabilizing survivors, (4) gathering information, (5) providing practical assistance, (6) connecting with social supports, (7) giving information on coping, and (8) linking with collaborative services (National Child Traumatic Stress Network [NCTSN] & National Center for PTSD [NCPTSD], 2006). Free Web-based training is available for social workers to enhance their knowledge and skills in this area.

Responders must be especially skilled in Steps 1–3 in order to facilitate the other recommended steps of PFA. For example, connecting, comforting, and calming distraught individuals leads to an increased ability to obtain critical information and facilitate appropriate connections. Properly certified crisis response dogs are a great tool to assist practitioners in accomplishing these initial steps of PFA. For more information on animal-assisted social work, readers are encouraged to read the chapter on animal-assisted social work intervention (Chapter 37). Below are three observations of PFA in action, offered by providers following traumatic crises that required group intervention. Each testimonial provides qualitative evidence of how these specially trained and certified HOPE Animal-assisted crisis response dogs engaged with, comforted, and calmed those in crisis, ultimately fostering sharing and connections to facilitate healing from traumatic events.

Example 1: Mercyhurst University, following a homicide of a student, provided intervention to a group of students/friends. Dr. Judy Smith (personal communication, August 15, 2013) offered the following observations: "The appearance of the crisis dogs provided the first felt lifting of moods that we saw in the days after the death of our student. When the teams of dogs and handlers entered the room where a large group of students were meeting, the students immediately went to the animals, petting and hugging them, and asking the handlers many questions. The sense you had as you watched this was that there was an immediate, visceral connection between canine and college student that provided students with a keen sense of comfort and reassurance. There was a clear sense of something important being exchanged as students ran their fingers thorough fur, dodged wagged tails, and buried their faces against another living creature that was willing to simply stand there in the moment with them openly offering its affection and simple presence."

Example 2: A camp director, Kerri Franks, runs an annual camp, Camp Quality, to support children with cancer, and unfortunately each year children are lost to this devastating illness. Kerri Franks (personal communication, August 13, 2013) offers this testimonial demonstrating PFA in action: "The HOPE AACR dogs have provided tremendous support to our children with cancer, especially during our Remembrance Celebration (a video slideshow/memorial of campers who have died). Not only have they helped emotionally, we also see the physical benefits of calming down, slower breathing as the children pet the dogs or talk to the dogs and the ability to sit or stay with whatever emotion they are having due to the dog laying or standing beside them. The connection the HOPE dogs make with the kids and the kids with the dogs is truly amazing. The children are captivated by each dog's personality and calmness, which in turn allows the kids to calm themselves."

Example 3: Kathleen Frisina, LPC, a grief specialist/counselor, has witnessed and utilized crisis dogs in her group work with grieving children. Kathleen Frisina (personal communication, August 12, 2013) offers the following professional insights: "When death enters a child's life, nothing is ever the same. It crashes in and changes the present and future. Someone important is missing, often on a daily basis and on those milestone events throughout their lifetime. Often there is a mix of feelings, sadness, anger, or loneliness being among them. Crisis dogs have a presence, a presence that allows the child (or adult) to feel cared for, a presence that allows petting and cuddling to bring a calming effect, and a presence that often opens conversation to a listening therapeutic animal that creates safeness."

Responding to group crises can be overwhelming, even for the experienced practitioners. The utilization of these specially trained and certified crisis response dogs can add an invaluable tool, which assists the practitioner in accomplishing the goals of crisis intervention and PFA. These specially trained animals also offer an added benefit to the practitioner personally by reducing stress caused by their work. HOPE Animal-assisted crisis response (www.hopeaacr.org) is one of two national organizations that offer certified teams to assist practitioners in responding to crises and disasters.

CONCLUSION

Social workers are increasingly being expected to provide brief interventions. Managed care restrictions and concerns of violence are placing pressure on practitioners to be skilled in effectively assessing risks and needs and in providing rapid intervention (Eaton & Roberts, 2002). Roberts's (2005) seven-stage model and Greenstone and

Leviton's (2011) crisis intervention procedures provide social workers with beneficial frameworks. Utilization of one of these models will assist practitioners in effectively resolving individual crises. Additionally, psychological first aid is the recommended strategy for group intervention. Certified crisis response dogs offer a great tool to assist practitioners in effectively meeting the PFA goals.

WEBSITES

Manuals and training www.dshs.wa.gov/manuals/socialsciences/section/crisis/crisise.cfm

Training www.childwelfare.gov/pubs/uermanual/crisis/crisis.ccfm

School based crisis intervention www.umaryland.edu/resourcepackets//file/crisisintervention.pdf

Organizations, Crisis Intervention International www.citinternational.org

References

Eaton, Y. M., & Roberts, A. R. (2002). Frontline crisis intervention: Step-by-step practice guidelines with case applications. In A. R. Roberts & G. J. Greene (Eds.), *Social workers' desk reference* (pp. 89–96). New York, NY: Oxford University Press.

Greenstone, J. L., & Leviton, S. (2011). *Elements of crisis intervention: Crises and how to respond to them*. Belmont, CA: Brooks-Cole.

Jackson-Cherry, L. R., & Erford, B. T. (2014). *Crisis assessment, intervention, and prevention* (2nd ed.). Upper Saddle River, NJ: Pearson Education, Inc.

Kaul, R. E., & Welzant, V. (2005). Disaster mental health: A discussion of best practices as applied after the Pentagon attack. In A. R. Roberts (Ed.), *Crisis intervention handbook: Assessment, treatment, and research* (pp. 200–220). New York, NY: Oxford University Press.

Knox, K. S., & Roberts, A. R. (2008). The crisis intervention model. In N. Coady & P. Lehmann (Eds.), *Theoretical perspectives for direct social work practice: A generalist-eclectic approach* (2nd ed.) (pp. 249–274). New York, NY: Springer.

National Child Traumatic Stress Network & National Center for PTSD. (2006). *Psychological First Aid: Field Operations Guide* (2nd ed.). Available at www.nctsn.org and www.ncptsd.va.gov

North Atlantic Treaty Organization (NATO) Joint Medical Committee. (2008). *Psychosocial care for people affected by disasters and major incidents*. England: Author.

Roberts, A. R. (2005). Bridging the past and present to the future of crisis intervention and crisis management. In A. R. Roberts (Ed.), *Crisis intervention handbook: Assessment, treatment, and research* (3rd ed.) (pp. 31–34). New York, NY: Oxford University Press.

Roberts, A. R., & Yeager, K. R. (2009). *Pocket guide to crisis intervention.* New York, NY: Oxford University Press.

Watson, P. J., Brymer, M. J., & Bonanno, G. A. (2011). Postdisaster psychological intervention since 9/11. *American Psychologist, 66*(6), 482–494.

28   Fundamentals of Brief Treatment

Jan Ligon

As managed care models for behavioral health and other social services have increasingly become the norm (Dziegielewski, 2004), the use of brief intervention models has continued to expand. Even before the advent of managed care, brief services were simply the nature of practice in many settings (schools, hospitals, home health services, and others). Indeed, studies cited by Miller, Hubble, and Duncan (1996) note that clients expected the duration of services to be brief, and the vast majority concluded services in four to eight sessions. Therefore, it is essential for social workers and administrators to be familiar with brief models of practice.

Following an overview of the roots and theory of brief practice, this chapter summarizes the key assumptions, practice components, and approaches to brief social work practice, along with outcome measures, evidence of effectiveness, limitations, and a case example to illustrate an application of the chapter content.

ROOTS AND THEORY

A time-limited perspective has been dated to the work of psychiatrists with World War II veterans in the mid-1940s (Budman & Gurman, 1988), although more contemporary approaches can be traced to the work of Milton Erickson in the 1950s (de Shazer et al., 1986). Many of the theoretical

approaches, assumptions, and techniques of brief work, as it is practiced today, are grounded in the endeavors of two centers—Mental Research Institute's (MRI) Brief Therapy Center in Palo Alto, California and the Brief Family Therapy Center (BFTC) in Milwaukee, Wisconsin, which provided training and resources for 25 years (1982–2007).

MRI began in 1959 and approached working with clients from a theoretical perspective that differed from the more common approaches of that time in several ways.

1. Problems were viewed as normal occurrences in life; this stance was a radical departure from theories grounded in pathology, deficits, and dysfunction.
2. The purpose of treatment was to make changes, preferably small ones. Insight and meaning, the cornerstone of some treatment, was not the goal of working with clients.
3. The role of the clinician was to be an active and engaged participant who works with what the client brings.
4. The model explicitly limited clients to a maximum of 10 sessions based on the assumption that "a time limit on treatment has some positive influence on both therapists and patients" (Weakland, Fisch, Watzlawick, & Bodin, 1974, p. 144).

Unlike MRI, the BFTC approach did not specify a number of sessions, and the focus was on developing solutions to problems (de Shazer et al., 1986). Both MRI and BFTC note the importance of how the therapist views people, their problems, and solutions.

Milton Erickson, a psychiatrist, was an important influence on those involved in the development of brief approaches to treatment. Although he claimed to not have a theoretical basis for his work (O'Hanlon & Weiner-Davis, 1989), two of his terms are fundamental to brief work. The first is *expectancy*; simply stated, this is the social worker's belief that people and situations can change and the lives of people can be better. This concept is deceptively simple; it is one thing to understand the term and another to embrace the concept to the extent that one's practice connotes this sincere belief. Clients pick up on this very quickly, and the effective social worker truly knows that things can be better; it may not happen, but it can. The object is to set the client up for a positive self-fulfilling prophecy. The second term is *utilization*; the work is conducted with what the client brings (O'Hanlon & Weiner-Davis, 1989). In fact, clients bring vast resources with them, including their past successes, survival skills, life wisdom, and stories that are used extensively in brief treatment models (Saleebey, 2012).

CORE PRACTICE SKILLS AND TECHNIQUES

Numerous authors have published detailed accounts of many techniques and strategies that can be employed in brief practice models (Budman & Gurman, 1988; de Shazer et al., 1986; de Shazer & Dolan, 2007; Dewan, Steenbarger, & Greenberg, 2004; Hudson & O'Hanlon, 1991; Miller et al., 1996; O'Hanlon & Weiner-Davis, 1989; Walter & Peller, 2000; Weakland et al., 1974). There are, however, five core areas of practice that are common to most approaches: (1) the use of time, (2) the approach to problems and solutions, (3) the use of language, (4) the development and measurement of goals, and (5) the use of a strengths perspective.

Use of Time

Obviously, time is a key concern in brief work, and given that most clients complete fewer than eight sessions, the use of time is actually a very manageable task. It is important to not view time as only that which occurs in the therapy session. Many clients arrive early, and this time can be used to complete not only initial paperwork but also tools that can be helpful in a session, such as rapid assessment instruments to measure problems (Corcoran & Fischer, 2013). Next, clients can be asked about pretreatment change; that is, what has changed since the time the client made the appointment for the first session and the occurrence of the first session? Weiner-Davis found that when asked this, "two-thirds of the clients noticed changes" (de Shazer et al., 1986, p. 215). By inquiring about what is now different and how the client was able to get those pretreatment changes to occur, the social worker can begin to hear information that will help uncover client and family strengths and form solutions for change.

Approach to Problems and Solutions

The therapist's approach to problems is critical. First, it is important to acknowledge and validate clients' problems. If the social worker moves immediately into developing goals and solutions without acknowledging and hearing the clients' problems and issues, the client may not move forward (Hudson & O'Hanlon, 1991). However, to get stuck in a repetitive cycle of only acknowledging the problems will impede forward movement. Next, it is important to ask clients whether they have had a similar problem before and to inquire about how they handled it. This information is essential for use in further identifying client strengths, developing goals, and beginning to view potential solutions. Finally, it is important to not get bogged down in the details of the problem, but rather to find out when the problem does not happen; that is, which are the times noted as the "exceptions to their problems" (de Shazer & Dolan, 2007, p. 4). This is particularly helpful when working with couples; it is easy to find that an entire session's time has been consumed with accusations about the other partner and pleas for understanding about how it really is in the relationship. The brief therapist cannot afford to lose precious time in this manner, and ultimately it is not helpful to the clients. Therefore, it is important to acknowledge, find the exceptions, and move on (Hudson & O'Hanlon, 1991).

Use of Language

The choice of words in brief treatment is critical; language needs to connote movement, openness, the future, and a feeling that is action-oriented.

For example, the early works of MRI (Weakland et al., 1974) noted the importance of discussing *what* is happening or *how* things could be changed. The choice of the word *why*, however, seeks deeper understanding or may imply the need to delve into history; this is not helpful in brief work. O'Hanlon and Weiner-Davis (1989) note that the use of *yet* is helpful; "you haven't found the right job *yet*." Similarly, *when* can keep the dialogue moving forward, which is of key importance in developing solutions; "*when* you are working again" implies hope and a future.

Development and Measurement of Goals

At the core of brief work are the development, implementation, and measurement of goals. De Jong and Miller (1995) note that a well-formed goal is one that is important to the client, framed in the client's language, small, concrete, specific, behavioral, seeks the presence rather than the absence of something, is realistic, worthy, and is a step toward an end (see case example). Clients often do not accomplish goals because they are more of a vision than a goal. For example, "to become independent" or "to live a clean and sober life" are admirable desires for a client, but both are too big. Such goals can be overwhelming and a set-up for failure; both are only attainable through steps leading toward each goal. Therefore, if goals are carefully developed with the client, the likelihood of follow-through is improved, and clients may even accomplish more than the goal once they find that they are able to experience some initial success. Once measurable goals have been developed, it is important to look at outcomes assessment.

Like all service providers, social workers and agencies are increasingly required to document the outcomes of interventions and programs. Two common methods, self-anchored scales and rapid assessment instruments (RAIs), are helpful and simple ways to quantify outcomes. A self-anchored scale is very easy to develop (see case example) by merely asking the client to rate a problem or situation, one at a time, by scoring it from low to high (1 to 5 or 1 to 10). RAIs for use in assessing a wide range of problems are available from a two-volume sourcebook (Fischer & Corcoran, 2007). Such measures can be repeated at the beginning and end of treatment to establish change from pre-test to post-test; measures may also be taken at established increments with the scores plotted to illustrate change over time. RAIs are particularly helpful during the assessment process to determine the severity of such problems as depression, anxiety, or substance use. Some instruments are also available at no cost from the Internet, including the Zung Self-Rating Depression Scale, which can be used as a screening tool for depression (see websites below for link).

Strengths Perspective

Working from a strengths perspective (Saleebey, 2012) is the antithesis of the approach used by many large human services systems that are based on pathology, dysfunction, symptoms, diseases, and the assignment of diagnoses. Inherent in these approaches, such as the medical model, is an assumption that the service provider is the expert, and the patient is advised what needs to be done by the expert. Social work practice from a strengths perspective recognizes that resources can be tapped within both the social worker and the client, as well as within the community. Therefore, the relationship is approached as collaborative and avoids hierarchy; the intent is to empower the client to collaborate actively in the change process. A strengths perspective acknowledges that the client possesses knowledge, abilities, resilience, coping, and problem-solving skills that are there to be employed. Certainly people get stuck, become overwhelmed, or experience events that render them unable to make full use of their strengths. It is important to identify and amplify strengths so that the client can go back and rediscover what has already worked for him or her in the past. Therefore, the role of the social worker is to facilitate the process, serve as a bridge to the client's own resources, move ahead, and seek solutions.

CASE EXAMPLE

This brief case example is based on an actual client and illustrates some of the fundamental techniques reviewed in this chapter. Katie, age 31, called to make an appointment with the employee assistance program (EAP) offered by her company. The service provided three free visits, although additional sessions could be added if needed. During a brief telephone screening, she stated that she had been feeling particularly down about her job and life and thought maybe it would help to talk to a professional because things were not getting better. She was seen for her first appointment three days after the initial call.

Katie completed a self-reported instrument for depression (Radloff, 1977) as well as an initial information form in the lobby prior to her appointment. After brief introductions and an overview of the EAP services, Katie discussed that she feels very stuck in her life; she has been in the same job, with a modest salary, for six years. She has a high school education and realizes that this has held her back; she wants to move on in her life but finds herself in a rut. The dialogue continues.

Client: It seems lately that I'm not only feeling stuck, but I'm cranky; I cry easier lately.

Worker: You seem to feel trapped, but you want to move on in your life. [Acknowledge] You mentioned feeling down, crying more; how would you rate just how down you've been feeling from 1 to 10 with 1 being really down and 10 feeling on top of the world? [Measurement]

Client: Oh, I think like a 4 lately.

Worker: A 4, and the rating scale you completed for me shows about the same, a moderate level of feeling down. Have you had thoughts of wanting to hurt yourself? [Acknowledgment]

Client: No, never, and I don't drink or do drugs, thank goodness. [Strength]

Worker: That's good to know. Are you taking any medications right now for any reason?

Client: No, I don't take anything, I'm lucky; I'm in good health. And it's not like I'm clueless about my situation; I know that getting a college education would help. I need to do that.

Worker: So I'm hearing that you are a determined woman; you want more. [Validate, strengths] Can you tell me *what* I would *see* you doing *when* you have the college degree? [Language]

Client: Oh that's an easy one; I'd be teaching first grade. That's exactly what I want to do.

Worker: That's great; maybe you've already thought some about the process of getting from here to there. What *will* you do first *when* you begin the process? [Validate, language, goals]

Client: Oh I've thought a lot! I guess it's pretty straightforward—enroll and start classes.

Worker: Do you know which school or program you might pursue?

Client: Oh yes, the college is near my house; I think they have a program, I need to check.

Worker: Would it be possible to pick up some information and bring it next time? [Goals]

Client: Sure, I'll do that. I can stop by after work one day this week. [Goals]

When Katie returned for the next appointment, she had not only brought the catalog but had made an appointment to meet with the admissions counselor for the elementary education program the next week. This exemplifies the importance of goals that are realistic, small, seek the presence of something (the information), and take a step toward an end (a college education).

CAVEATS AND CAUTIONS

Brief interventions have been found to be useful in working with inpatient mental health clients (Durrant, Clark, Tolland, & Wilson, 2007; Lamprecht et al., 2007), for the prevention and treatment of substance abuse (Substance Abuse and Mental Health Services Administration, 2012), with couples (Davidson & Horvath, 1997), with children and adolescents (Monroe & Kraus, 2005; Newsome, 2005; Tripodi, Springer, & Corcoran, 2007; Valdez, Cepeda, & Parrish, 2013), for gambling problems (Larimer et al., 2011), in suicide prevention (Lamprecht et al., 2007; Petrakis & Joubert, 2013), and with families who have been affected by substance abuse (Ligon, 2004; Velleman et al., 2011). Indeed, clients have been found to be satisfied with only one, two, or three sessions (Ligon, 1996).

However, no single model is universal (Stalker, Levene, & Coady, 1999), and brief therapy is not suitable to all client situations. Although brief approaches view problems in a different manner than some other methods, they do not excuse the social worker from ethical and competent practice, including the assessment of mental status, medical concerns, and risk for suicide, homicide, child abuse, intimate partner violence, or other factors.

LOOKING AHEAD

It is common in social work for terms, interventions, and techniques to evolve and change over time. When managed care quickly moved behavioral health services to a time-limited model, the interest in brief techniques escalated. Now the use of this approach is more in the mainstream of methods from which a social worker may choose, depending on the situation. Social workers are likely to continue to operate in environments that are tight on financial and human resources. Therefore, it will be important for them to continue to master the basic skills of brief practice in future years. Used appropriately by qualified and trained social workers, brief therapy models offer an approach that has been found to be helpful to a wide range of clients across many problem areas. Brief social work practice fits well with the profession's values of being with the client, self-determination, empowerment, and respect and dignity for the value and worth of each individual.

WEBSITES

Therapist's Guide to Brief Cognitive Behavioral Therapy. Published by the Department of Veterans Affairs, South Central Mental Illness Research, Education, and Clinical Center (MIRECC), 2008. http://www.mirecc.va.gov/visn16/docs/therapists_guide_to_brief_cbtmanual.pdf

SAMHSA Manual: TIP 34- Brief Interventions and Brief Therapies for Substance Abuse. http://store.samhsa.gov/product/TIP-34-Brief-Interventions-and-Brief-The rapies-for-Substance-Abuse/SMA12-3952

Zung Self-Rating Depression Scale: http://healthnet.umassmed.edu/mhealth/ZungSelfRatedDepressionScale.pdf

References

Budman, S. H., & Gurman, A. S. (1988). *Theory and practice of brief therapy.* New York, NY: Guilford.

Corcoran, K., & Fischer, J. (2013). *Measures for clinical practice and research.* NY: Oxford.

Davidson, G. N. S., & Horvath, A. O. (1997). Three sessions of brief couples therapy: A clinical trial. *Journal of Family Psychology, 11,* 422–435.

De Jong, P., & Miller, S. D. (1995). How to interview for client strengths. *Social Work, 6,* 729–736.

de Shazer, S., & Dolan, Y. (2007). *More than miracles: The state of the art of solution-focused brief therapy.* New York, NY: Haworth Press.

de Shazer, S., Berg, I. K., Lipchik, E., Nunnally, E., Molnar, A., Gingerich, W., et al. (1986). Brief therapy: Focused solution development. *Family Process, 25,* 207–221.

Dewan, M. J., Steenbarger, B. N., & Greenberg, R. P. (2004). *The art and science of brief psychotherapies.* Washington, DC: American Psychiatric Publishing.

Durrant, C., Clarke, I., Tolland, A., & Wilson, H. (2007). Designing a CBT service for an acute inpatient setting: A pilot study. *Clinical Psychology and Psychotherapy, 14,* 117–125.

Dziegielewski, S. F. (2004). *The changing face of health care social work: Professional practice in managed behavioral health care* (2nd ed.). New York, NY: Springer.

Hudson, P., & O'Hanlon, W. (1991). *Rewriting love stories: Brief marital therapy.* New York, NY: Norton.

Lamprecht, H., Laydon, C., McQuillan, C., Wiseman, S., Williams, L., Gash, A., et al. (2007). Single-session solution-focused therapy and self-harm: A pilot study. *Journal of Psychiatric & Mental Health Nursing, 14,* 601–602.

Larimer, M. E., Neighbors, C., Lostutter, T. W., Whiteside, U. (2011). Brief motivational feedback and cognitive behavioural interventions for prevention of disordered gambling: A randomized clinical trial. *Addiction, 107,* 1148–1158.

Ligon, J. (1996). Client satisfaction with brief therapy. *EAP Digest, 16*(5), 30–31.

Ligon, J. (2004). Six "Ss" for families affected by substance abuse: Family skills for survival and change. *Journal of Family Psychotherapy, 15,* 95–99.

Miller, S. D., Hubble, M. A., & Duncan, B. (Eds.). (1996). *Handbook of solution-focused brief therapy.* San Francisco, CA: Jossey-Bass.

Monroe, B., & Kraus, F. (Eds.). (2005). *Brief interventions with bereaved children.* New York, NY: Oxford University Press.

Newsome, W. S. (2005). The impact of solution-focused brief therapy with at-risk junior high students. *Children and Schools, 29,* 83–90.

O'Hanlon, W., & Weiner-Davis, M. (1989). *In search of solutions: A new direction in psychotherapy.* New York, NY: Norton.

Petrakis, M., & Joubert, L. (2013). A social work contribution to suicide prevention through assertive brief psychotherapy and community linkage: Use of the Manchester Short Assessment of Quality of Life (MANSA). *Social Work in Health Care, 52,* 239–257.

Radloff, R. S. (1977). CES-D scale: A self-report depression scale for research in the general population. *Applied Psychological Measurement, 1,* 385–401.

Saleebey, D. (2012). *The strengths perspective in social work practice* (6th ed.). New York, NY: Allyn & Bacon.

Substance Abuse and Mental Health Services Administration (SAMHSA). (2012). *Screening, brief intervention, and referral to treatment (SBIRT).* Retrieved from http://www.samhsa.gov/prevention/sbirt/.

Tripodi, S. J., Springer, D. W., & Corcoran, K. (2007). Determinants of substance abuse among incarcerated adolescents: Implications for brief treatment and crisis intervention. *Brief Treatment and Crisis Intervention, 7,* 34–39.

Valdez, A., Cepeda, A., Parrish, D. (2013). An adapted brief strategic family therapy for gang-affiliated Mexican American adolescents. *Research on Social Work Practice, 23*(4), 383–396.

Velleman, R., Orford, J., Templeton, L., Copello, A., Patel, A., Moore, L., Macleod, J., & Godfrey, C. (2011). 12-month follow-up after brief interventions in primary care for family members affected by the substance misuse problem of a close relative. *Addiction Research and Theory, 19*(4), 362–374.

Walter, J. L., & Peller, J. E. (2000). *Recreating brief therapy: Preferences and possibilities.* New York, NY: Norton.

Weakland, J. H., Fisch, R., Watzlawick, P., & Bodin, A. M. (1974). Brief therapy: Focused problem resolution. *Family Process, 13,* 141–168.

29   Common Factors in Psychotherapy

James W. Drisko

"Common factors" refers to a way of thinking about the "active ingredients" that generate change in psychotherapy and social work services. Simply put, the common factors perspective views the client–worker relationship, client factors, social environmental factors, and similarities in worldview between client and social worker as more important to creating change than any specific intervention technique. That is, rather than highlighting specific techniques, like Ellis's ABC technique for tracking irrational beliefs, the common factors approach views the larger interpersonal context, such as being able to establish a therapeutic alliance, as most important to generating change. This perspective challenges researchers and scholars to take a broader view of what makes services effective. This broader view fits well with client interests, the practice wisdom of social workers, and key social work values.

The common factors perspective also fits well with clients' own ideas about change. On a February afternoon, snow had been falling for several hours. I was unsure if I should leave my office—one client had not shown up, and another cancelled, but I had one more scheduled. Later, when Mr. B came into the office, he had a big grin on his face. He said, "I was driving over here and conditions were awful. I was sure you'd have left to go home yourself. Then I got near and even from the street I could see the lights were on. I was really sure you wouldn't be here, but you were! Now I know you care about me." As we talked about his experience, it became clear that my reliability and trustworthiness meant more to him than anything I did as a specific treatment plan. He said he had learned to doubt words spoken by people in authority, and always judged more by actions than words. A few weeks later Mr. B said his girlfriend, who had been negative on his therapy, had also changed her view because of this story. She had begun to be supportive, which made it easier for him to invest in our work together. Our work flourished.

A SCIENTIFIC UNDERSTANDING REQUIRES KNOWLEDGE OF BOTH OUTCOMES AND THEIR CAUSES

Both social work practitioners and researchers are concerned with knowing "what works" to help a given client and what aspects of intervention lead to improvement. There are two questions here. First, what is the desired outcome of intervention, and second, what caused the change? It is important to keep in mind that determining outcomes and identifying the active ingredients that lead to it are both necessary components of a full scientific understanding. Documenting outcomes alone, without knowing what caused them, is not an adequate scientific understanding of a problem (Drisko, 2000). Stated more fully, the question for clinicians and practice researchers is "*what* treatment, by *whom*, is most effective for *this* individual with *that* specific problem, under *which* set of circumstances?" (Paul, 1967, p. 111, italics in the original). Client needs, characteristics, social circumstances, and treatments are each complex and multidimensional.

Based on compilations of high-quality studies of adults with depression and anxiety problems, there is strong evidence that psychotherapy leads to improvement compared with untreated comparison groups (Lambert, 2013). How much improvement is found? Wampold (2001), synthesizing several studies using meta-analysis, provides a summary statistic called effect size from 0.75 to 0.85 for the impact of these treatments. Effect size statistics range from 0.00 to about 3.0 in value. A 0.75 to 0.85 effect size is characterized as a large impact. According to Rosenthal (1984), it means that clients who complete therapy are better off than 79% of people without treatment. Such effect sizes show that "psychotherapy is more effective than many evidence-based medical practices" across several specialities (Lambert, 2013, p. 172). This research shows that many treatments work to yield improvement on these disorders.

A great deal of recent outcome research focuses on comparing one treatment model or technique to another model on the same disorder. This is useful to determine what treatments are most effective. However, the way in which such research is done tends to emphasize only specific techniques and ignores the impact of the client–clinician relationship and other nontechnique factors that may also influence outcomes. This is because many researchers assume all providers offer sufficient warmth, empathy, and genuineness to clients (e.g., Truax & Carkhuff, 1967). If this is a core condition of psychotherapy, some say, it does not need to be specified in psychotherapy research because it is always present. On the other hand, to ignore such factors may lead to misleading or incomplete conclusions about what causes change.

As long ago as 1936, Rosenzweig stated that many different psychotherapies could lead to positive outcomes. His view was based on the idea that common factors—not specific therapeutic techniques—were indeed the most important ingredients of psychotherapeutic success. In the mid-1970s, a research method called meta-analysis was developed. Meta-analysis is a method for combining the results of many studies on the same topic to determine an overall rating of effectiveness, usually an effect size. Since then, several meta-analyses of the outcome of psychotherapy with adults who suffer from depression and anxiety have been completed. Since 1977, few enduring differences across types of psychotherapy have been demonstrated. Even as the technology of meta-analysis has been refined, a common conclusion is that there are no or minimal differences across therapies on these key adult problems (Ahn & Wampold, 2001; Grawe, Caspar, & Ambuhl, 1990; Smith & Glass, 1977; Smith, Glass, & Miller, 1980; Wampold, 2001; Wampold et al., 1997). Furthermore, researchers did not find differences in effect sizes by using a method intended to control for researcher allegiance to particular therapeutic models. Different therapies seem to produce very similar outcomes for these adult disorders.

To be thorough, some meta-analyses of psychotherapy outcomes have reported differences among treatments (see Drisko, 2004; Wampold, 2001). Systematic reviews of research, synthesizing the results of several experimental studies, may document that some psychotherapies do lead to significant outcomes while others do not. Still the question remains: If psychotherapy works, what factors within it lead to change? Given the frequent finding of no or minimal difference between therapies, perhaps technique is not the main or sole active ingredient leading to change. If so, factors other than therapeutic technique need to be more fully studied in outcome research, as well as given greater emphasis in social work education.

COMMON FACTORS IN HEALING

Psychiatrist Jerome Frank studied the characteristics of "healers" in several cultures worldwide. He identified numerous similarities in their practices despite clear diversity in their belief systems. He concluded that a number of factors might lead to change in psychotherapy, much as it did in the healing practices of other cultures (Frank, 1971). Based on Frank's work, Lambert (1992) estimated the percentage of variance attributable to each of the four common factors in psychotherapy.

In an early estimate, Lambert (1992) identified four key common factors from a synthesis of about 100 outcomes studies. These are (1) extratherapeutic factors, (2) the therapeutic relationship, (3) technical factors (specific therapeutic techniques), and (4) expectancy or placebo effects. He estimated that 40% of the variance in outcome is due to extratherapeutic factors, 30% is due to the therapeutic relationship, 15% is due to technical factors, and 15% is due to expectancy. This common factors model might explain why meta-analytic research finds no or minimal difference between therapies: extratherapeutic factors and the therapeutic relationship may outweigh the impact of technique and are rarely included in outcome research.

In an update of Lambert's original work, Norcross and Lambert (2011) revised these common factor estimates by including a large percentage of "unexplained variance." Because psychotherapy and other human endeavors are extremely complex, most statistical analyses in the social sciences "explain" only a fraction of the variance found in outcomes. This is because factors that were not specifically examined in a study may also affect its outcome. Errors in measurement and in research methods also lead to fairly large amounts of unexplained variance in outcomes.

Norcross and Lambert's (2011) current common factors model attributes 40% of the variance in psychotherapy outcomes to unexplained variance. Of the remaining 60% of explained variance in outcome, Norcross and Lambert assign 30% to the "client contribution" and another 12% to the therapeutic relationship. Another 8% of outcome variance is assigned to specific therapeutic techniques. In addition, 7% of variance is assigned to individual therapist characteristics and 3% to other factors (pp. 11–14). Norcross and Lambert also state that common factors are "spread across the therapeutic factors" (p. 14). That is, each common factor component can interact with the others to influence outcomes in combination. Common factors pertain in part to the client, some to the therapeutic relationship, some to the specific model of therapy, some to the specific practitioner, and some to interactions of these components.

It is important to note that in both these variance estimates, the client's contribution—personal capacities, the impact of social supports, motivation, and readiness—remains the largest source of variance in client outcomes. Next is the nature and quality of the therapeutic relationship. Techniques of therapy or models of therapy are the third largest influence on outcomes, but are closely followed by therapist factors. These results support the view that factors other than specific therapeutic techniques are the largest sources of variance in client outcomes.

EXPLORING THE COMMON FACTORS

The Client Contribution or "Extratherapeutic Factors"

In any client's life there are factors that will support change and others that may limit or impede change. They shape the effectiveness of psychotherapy but may not always be amenable to change using psychotherapeutic techniques. Specific to the client, Lambert and Asay (1984) list:

- Level of motivation
- Capacity to trust
- Ability to tolerate affect
- Intelligence
- Psychological mindedness
- Resilience.

These factors combine with the number and severity of challenges the client faces and the client's ability to identify and stay with a focal problem in the treatment. Outcomes will likely be better where these influences are present and positive; outcomes will probably be worse where they are absent or pose challenges. These findings suggest that pretherapeutic interventions may be helpful or even crucial for some clients to engage and make use of specific therapies.

Prochaska (1999) and others state that readiness to change is another client factor that influences capacity to change. Prochaska suggests that treatment readiness may not be a stable trait but rather a variable or cyclic phenomenon, so efforts to maximize it may enhance overall treatment effectiveness (or may undermine efforts when treatment readiness is not present). Further, recent work by Castonguay and Beutler (2006) identifying the principles of change behind empirically supported treatments suggests that very intensive, highly structured intervention from the outset is associated with positive outcomes for people with personality disorders who may prove inconsistent in motivation. To enhance motivation, pretherapeutic interventions may be useful along with attention or involvement with social supports. Motivational interviewing with the client, as well as the client's family and other supports, and working through differences early on, are all helpful approaches.

Bohart and Wade (2013) suggest two approaches to individualizing psychotherapy based on current research on the client's impact on outcomes. First, they recommend matching clients by aptitude to specific psychotherapy approaches. This recommendation links specific client factors to choice of treatment. Bohart and Wade also recommend efforts to enhance the knowledge and skill of clinicians to be responsive to different client abilities and contexts. Such knowledge and skills allows a specific clinician to work more effectively and differentially with clients who have varied needs, aptitudes, and abilities. Both client and clinician are active agents in psychotherapy and social service interventions.

Expanding The Client Contribution: The Client's Context

Social workers know that the client's context can play an important role in sustaining involvement in psychotherapy or in undermining this effort (Lambert, 1992). On the other hand, the lack of family and social support—or their absence, or active hostility—can hinder therapeutic change (Drisko, 2004). Similarly, peer and workplace supports can serves as aids, hindrances, or neutral influences to therapy. For many people, spiritual supports and support groups sharing common concerns (such as the therapeutic problem or other issues) can also influence therapy participation and outcome. All this suggests that pre-therapeutic or early therapeutic work to engage the support of key people in the client's life will be likely to reduce dropout risk, enhance motivation for change, and limit undermining influences. On a larger scale, neighborhood resources or challenges may ease involvement in therapy or increase the effort required to enter and remain in therapy. It is also clear that the meaning of engaging in psychotherapy, and its very appropriateness as a source of improvement,

differs across cultures (e.g., Sue, Zane, & Young, 1994; Zayas, Drake, & Jonson-Reid, 2010). Thus, the wisdom of seeking therapy and support for the undertaking over time may not be simple or steady for many potential clients. In this case, the following are helpful:

- Similarity of race/ethnicity between client and clinician
- Similarity of religious background
- Acceptance or openness to the client's religious/spiritual views (Castonguay & Beutler, 2006).

Extratherapeutic Factors: The Policy and Agency Context

Though he is not a social worker, Lambert (1992) concentrated on the inner world of the client and did not address the impact of policy and agency factors on the client. I argue that for a client to enter and remain in therapy, several agency factors must be present (Drisko, 2004).

- Clients need to know that services are available.
- Clients need to have trust that the services are likely to help.
- Cost of services must be reasonable in terms of the client's ability to pay.
- Services must also be accessible—within reasonable geographic proximity, accessible to transportation.
- Services should have no significant barriers for people with disabilities.
- Services also must be culturally sensitive to the potential client.
- Services should be user-friendly, even inviting, to people under stress and doubtful of being treated with respect and care.

Contacts prior to meeting the clinician (e.g., the receptionist, agency financial staff) also may aid or hinder engagement in the therapeutic work. Costs should be reasonable, and there should be no undue obstacles in referral procedures and management paperwork. In addition, reimbursement to service agencies must offset the cost of doing business and be sufficient to create supportive working conditions (pay, diversity, supervision, and site) for all staff. Sadly, reimbursement rates for many clinical services are low and may fail to fully meet the actual cost of delivering the service. In turn, insensitive events in the agency may undermine a fragile client's ability to engage with clinical services (Drisko, 2004).

Castonguay and Beutler (2006) also note that clients with a high level of impairment are less likely to benefit from therapy than those with a better level of functioning at pretreatment. In addition, clients diagnosed with a personality disorder are less likely to benefit from treatment than those without a personality disorder. Together, these extratherapeutic factors influence client engagement in services, dropout rates, and overall outcomes. They may account for more of the variance in treatment participation, completion, and outcomes than do any of the four common factors described by Lambert (1992).

The Therapeutic Relationship

The therapeutic relationship is usually what clinicians label as the *common factor* in psychotherapy (Rosenzweig, 1936). Some believe it is the single most important curative factor (Orlinsky, Grawe, & Parks, 1994). Yet the impact of the therapeutic relationship is difficult to study, because it appears to be differentially important for varied clients, with different diagnoses or problem types, and also interacts with treatment techniques (Crits-Christoph, Gibbons, & Mukherjee, 2013). Still, the psychotherapy literature since the 1950s emphasizes that the caring, warmth, empathy, and acceptance demonstrated by the clinician is vital to therapeutic result. Castonguay and Hill (2012) assert that relationship factors—as perceived by a given client—are central to a positive and productive therapeutic relationship. In addition, Lambert (1992) and Lambert and Hill (1994) note that mutual affirmation (which may include accurate and sufficient affective attunement) as well as active encouragement to support affective, cognitive, and behavioral changes, including the taking of risks by the client and clear acknowledgment of change and new mastery, are all elements of the therapeutic relationship. The importance of recovering from missteps or failures of attunement is also associated with positive outcomes in the practice literature (Tracey et al., 2003). For all clients, empathy is another vital aspect of the therapeutic relationship (Beutler et al., 2012). Bachelor (1995) found that various types of empathy (nurturant, insight-oriented, and collaborative) were more apparent and useful during different phases of treatment. Key aspects of the therapeutic relationship include:

- Affective attunement
- Mutual affirmation, including support for risks and appreciation of positive changes made
- Making efforts to discuss and resolve missteps or failures of attunement
- Goal congruence
- Use of varying types of empathy over the course of therapy.

Crits-Christoph, Gibbons, and Mukherjee (2013) argue that research seeking to identify the specific mechanisms through which the processes and outcomes of psychotherapy are linked warrants greater priority and funding. A large body of research documents that the alliance is a vital part of positive outcomes across a range of psychotherapies. Research on the therapeutic relationship has controlled for prior symptomatic improvement, the dependability of measures, and the views of both clients and clinicians. They assert that few other areas of psychotherapy research have been so fully conceptualized and so carefully examined.

Specific Techniques

Although this chapter addresses common factors rather than specific therapeutic techniques, this does not mean that knowledge of a range of intervention models and the clinical skills to implement them are unimportant. Rather than viewing common factors as a simple contrast to technique, it is optimal to think of a "both/and" relationship. Social workers do need to be knowledgeable, skilled, and well-supervised on therapeutic techniques and consistently attentive to the common factors active in intervention.

In defining principles of therapeutic change based on empirically effective treatments, Castonguay and Beutler (2006) report some technique-based findings.

- Therapy is likely enhanced if a strong working alliance is established and maintained.
- Clinicians should attempt to facilitate a high level of collaboration with client during therapy.
- The most effective treatments are those that do not induce client resistance.
- Clinicians are likely to resolve alliance ruptures when addressing such ruptures in an empathetic and flexible way.

- Clinicians should not use relational interpretations excessively.
- When relational interpretations are used, they are likely to facilitate improvement if accurate.
- Treatment benefit may be enhanced when interventions are responsive to and consistent with the client's style and level of problem assimilation.

Social workers should bear in mind that training to maximize professional use of self during interventions can be viewed as a set of techniques. Mastering such a broad set of techniques requires specific training and close supervision. Knowledge and skills in these areas can enhance the effectiveness of technical interventions.

Individual Clinician Characteristics

The characteristics of the clinician also impact on service outcomes (Blow, Sprenkle, & Davis, 2007). Castonguay and Beutler (2006) report that:

- Clinician effectiveness is increased by demonstration of open-mindedness, flexibility and creativity.
- A secure attachment pattern in the clinician appears to facilitate treatment processes.
- Positive impact is likely increased if the clinician is comfortable with emotionally intense relationships and able to tolerate his or her negative feelings toward the client.
- If clinicians are open, informed, and tolerant of various religious views, treatment effects are likely to be enhanced.
- If clients have a preference for religiously oriented therapy, benefit is enhanced if clinicians accommodate this preference.

Further, clinicians must complete thorough assessments of clients, with agency support, to fully understand and formulate client's needs and strengths (Grady & Drisko, 2014). Consistent with social work's values and ethics, the clinician's openness to differences of many kinds, including religious views and the ability to accommodate and work with religious differences, enhances therapeutic effectiveness.

Outcome research shows that clinicians vary widely in overall effectiveness. Baldwin and Imel (2013) argue for more research on individual clinician's effectiveness to identify what distinguishes more and less effective clinicians. This would allow both remedial training and improvements to the general education of clinicians across disciplines. It would also allow for the improvement of outcome research by removing an important confounding variable. That is, by removing poor outcomes due to ineffective clinicians from research studies, and focusing on demonstrated effective clinicians, research studies would yield results of greater value. Currently the effects of psychotherapy may be underdocumented in research due to the negative contributions of clinicians of limited effectiveness who yield less than optimal outcomes. Baldwin and Imel also argue for more within-clinician research. Such research would seek to identify the attributes of clients and settings that lead a specific clinician to facilitate the best outcomes. Such research could aid each clinician's professional development and point toward the types of work that produce the best outcomes they can foster.

Expectancy

Offering hope and an expectancy that change is possible can be a powerful aid to generating positive outcomes. Clients often feel stuck, bruised, or defeated by prior unsuccessful efforts to change. Clients of color or other socially marginalized groups may have suffered from insults and microaggressions from people with power over them. Thus, building a positive expectancy that change is possible may be a therapeutic gain in itself, as well as a catalyst for further progress.

Many studies show that placebos can generate useful change (Benedetti, 2008; Harrington, 1997). Placebos may involve sham medications as well as shared belief systems between client and professional and even the creation of an expectancy of change. Such studies indicate that expectancies can be very important influences on client outcomes even when known ineffective treatments are used.

Other Factors

Castonguay and Beutler (2006) found that clients with high level of impairments respond better when initially offered long-term intensive treatment than nonintensive and brief treatment, regardless of treatment model and type of treatment. This provocative finding suggests that people who do not expect to change, or who doubt that others will truly work to support their change, respond well to intensive and enduring interventions that build hope and demonstrate investment and care from others. Nelson, Beutler, and Castonguay (2012) suggest the fit of common factors and treatment selection is vital to effectively serving persons who have personality disorders. This may also be so for persons who have histories of suffering from socially structured oppression.

Insight: How the Client's Understanding of the Problem and the Therapy Influences Therapeutic Process and Outcomes

Wampold, Imel, Bhati, and Johnson-Jennings (2007) examine the idea that common factors are spread across the therapeutic processes. That is, each common factor component can interact with all the others to influence outcomes in combination. Wampold and colleagues examine how insight—which they define as a new understanding of the client's core problem and its relationship to the process of intervention—is an interaction of several common factors.

To illustrate this interaction, Wampold et al. (2007) offer four vignettes showing how four clients, each with depression, can benefit from different models of understanding their depression. The first client develops an understanding of his depression as based on distorted, overgeneralized beliefs of failure. The clinician offers cognitive behavioral therapy. Through this therapy, the client's depression improves. The second client has recurring dilemmas in interpersonal relationships with men. The clinician offers an insight-oriented therapy to explore how her early losses, including the death of her father, continue to shape her self-esteem and patterns of relationship. Through this therapy, her depression improves. The third client comes to view her depression solely as a brain disorder, rather than God's punishment for an extramarital affair. Accepting antidepressant medication after a very brief therapy, her depression improves. The fourth client, a Native American man working in a frustrating high tech job, uses therapy to reconsider his relationship with his culture of origin, from which he has become estranged. Through reconnecting with his culture of origin, and undertaking healer recommended sweats, his depression improves. Wampold et al. (2007) note that each of these very different ways of understanding depression, and the treatment each particular way of understanding indicates, are each useful and ultimately effective. The differences emerge based upon a combination of client factors (the details of each client's history, concerns, and context), therapist factors (how the clinician comes to formulate each case in context) and the therapeutic alliance

(that the client gains insight into the problem through therapeutic intervention that offers new ways of pursuing improvement).

Wampold et al. (2007) define insight as a shared way of viewing the problem developed through client–therapist interaction. Insight, defined this way, links back to the work of Rosenzweig (1936) and of Frank (1971) who believed that clinicians had to help clients develop new, acceptable, and therapeutically useful ways of understanding their problems. Wampold et al. note that such insight either can come from the client internally, or be offered by the clinician. How the insight is gained, and even its scientific truth value, are not crucial. What matters is that the new explanation makes sense to the client, fits within his or her worldview, and is fully accepted by the client. In turn, such an insight or way of viewing the problem is both adaptive and offers hope for problem resolution.

Wampold et al.'s (2007) insight model integrates the influence of several common factors. As such, it illustrates how common factors frequently act in combination. The common factors model helps clinicians and researchers conceptualize the complexity of clinical practice. It may also make some aspects of practice appear more independent or divisible than they appear at the level of intervention with a specific, unique, client. In practice, common factors are often interwoven.

COMMON FACTORS AND EVIDENCE-BASED PRACTICE

Evidence-based practice (EBP) refers to a four-part approach to practice decision making. EBP is comprised of efforts to include (a) the integration of research evidence with intervention planning that also *equally includes* (b) the client's state and circumstances, (c) the client's own values and preferences, and (d) the clinical expertise of the practitioner (Haynes, Devereaux, & Guyatt, 2002). The research evidence given the highest priority in EBP is research results based on large-scale, experimental research (Greenhalgh, 2010; Oxford University Centre for Evidence-based Medicine, 2011). Such experimental research examines the impact of one carefully defined intervention on one carefully specified disorder in order to limit the impact of unexplained factors and error terms. Most often the EBP experimental research model examines specific techniques or intervention models as though they were a single variable. This is very useful to ensure research integrity, but it means other components that may influence therapeutic change, such as the client's contribution or the quality of the therapeutic alliance, are excluded from study (Drisko & Grady, 2012). Thus the common factors model offers a way to enhance the quality of outcome research and to help identify a wider range of factors that shape client outcomes (Barth et al., 2012). Such research results could be very useful in tailoring many aspects of therapeutic interventions to specific client situations and needs (Nelson, Beutler, & Castonguay, 2012).

Joining Common Factors and Evidence-based Practice

The common factors model asserts that techniques or models alone are neither complete nor accurate descriptions of what actually happens in psychotherapy. The characteristics of specific clients, the variation in their support systems and situations, the characteristics of each specific practitioner, and the synergistic way in which client, situation, practitioner, and therapy interact, all have an impact on client outcomes. Norcross and Lambert (2011) estimate that only about 8% of variance in outcome is attributable to specific therapeutic techniques. This percentage is much lower than the 30% attributable to the client's contribution and lower than the 12% assigned to the client-therapist relationship. From a social work perspective, both Drisko (2004) and Cameron and Keenan (2010, 2012) argue that the percentage of variance assigned to specific therapeutic techniques may well be considerably lower than that resulting from social and contextual factors. This implies that the EBP focus on techniques or types of therapy alone may be too limited an evidence base for fully and successfully guiding practice. Further, it implies that research on psychotherapy and service outcomes must take a much broader view of the range of factors that influence outcomes. EBP should employ a much broader perspective on causal influences shaping treatment outcomes including client factors, clinician factors, setting, and the client-therapist alliance (Drisko & Grady, 2012).

The EBP research evidence hierarchy and the common factors approach offer quite different ways of examining client outcomes. A useful response may be the combination of attention to both common factors and specific techniques. As Cameron and Keenan (2012) point out, it is the synergy of client and clinician that combine to create a successful experience. "What works"

for a specific client in specific circumstances may vary across specific providers of several different specific interventions (Barth et al., 2012).

FUTURE PRACTICE APPLICATIONS

The common factors model encourages practitioners and researchers to take a broader, much more encompassing view of what leads to change in psychotherapy and social work interventions. Techniques are indeed important but may not be the most active ingredients in generating change in human interactions. Both meta-analyses using sophisticated statistical models and principles drawn from analyses of interventions that have been demonstrated to be effective indicate that common factors are important sources of client change. In the future, social workers may want to examine more closely how to make use of these factors in their day-to-day practices because attention to common factors will enhance therapeutic outcomes (Saggese, 2005). Practitioners are wise to take a broad view of common factors that may help their clients make and sustain change. Attention to a combination of client, extratherapeutic, relationship, and technique factors may still achieve the best overall results in psychotherapy (Barth et al., 2012; Beutler et al., 2012; Cameron & Keenan, 2012).

WEBSITES

Evidence-based Therapy Relationships. http://www.nrepp.samhsa.gov/Norcross.aspx
The Heart and Soul of Change Project. http://heartandsoulofchange.com/
Counseling resource on "What Works in Therapy." http://counsellingresource.com/books/what-works
Ingredients of Psychotherapy. http://www.psychpage.com/learning/library/counseling/ingredthx.html
Psychotherapy Integration. http://www.minddisorders.com/Ob-Ps/Psychotherapy-integration.html
Social work resources. http://www.drisko.net

References

Ahn, H., & Wampold, B. (2001). Where, oh where, are the specific ingredients? A meta-analysis of component studies in counseling and psychotherapy. *Journal of Consulting and Clinical Psychology*, 48, 251–257.

Bachelor, A. (1995). Clients' perception of the therapeutic alliance: a qualitative analysis. *Journal of Counseling Psychology, 42*(3), 323–337.

Baldwin, S., & Imel, Z. (2013). Therapist effects: Findings and methods. In M. Lambert (Ed.), *Bergin and Garfield's handbook of psychotherapy and behavior change* (6th ed., pp. 258–297). Hoboken, NJ: John Wiley.

Barth, R., Lee, B., Lindsey, M., Collins, K., Strieder, F., Chorpita, B., Becker, K., & Sparks, J. (2012). Evidence-based practice at a crossroads: The timely emergence of common elements and common factors. *Research on Social Work Practice, 22*(1), 108–119.

Benedetti, F. (2008). *Placebo effects: Understanding the mechanisms in health and disease.* NY: Oxford.

Beutler, L., Forrester, B., Gallagher-Thompson, D., Thompson, L., & Tomlins, J. (2012). Common, specific, and treatment fit variables in psychotherapy outcome. *Journal of Psychotherapy Integration, 22*(3), 255–281.

Blow, A., Sprenkle, D., & Davis, S. (2007). Is who delivers the treatment more important than the treatment itself? The role of the therapist in common factors. *Journal of Marital and Family Therapy, 33*(3), 298–317.

Bohart, A., & Wade, A. G. (2013). The client in psychotherapy. In M. Lambert (Ed.), *Bergin and Garfield's handbook of psychotherapy and behavior change* (6th ed., pp. 219–257). Hoboken, NJ: John Wiley.

Cameron, M., & Keenan, E. K. (2010). The common factors model: Implications for transtheoretical clinical social work practice. *Social Work, 55*(1), 63–73.

Cameron, M., & Keenan, E. K. (2012). *The common factors model for generalist practice.* New York, NY: Pearson.

Castonguay, L., & Beutler, L. (2006). *Principles of therapeutic change that work.* New York, NY: Oxford University Press.

Castonguay, L., & Hill, C. (2012). *Transformation in psychotherapy: corrective experiences across cognitive behavioral, humanistic, and psychodynamic approaches.* Washington, DC: American Psychological Association.

Crits-Christoph, P., Gibbons, M. B., & Mukherjee, D. (2013). Psychotherapy process-outcome research. In M. Lambert (Ed.), *Bergin and Garfield's handbook of psychotherapy and behavior change* (6th ed., pp. 298–340). Hoboken, NJ: John Wiley.

Drisko, J. (2000). Conceptualizing clinical practice evaluation: Historical trends and current issues. *Smith College Studies in Social Work, 70,* 185–205.

Drisko, J. (2004). Common factors in psychotherapy effectiveness: Meta-analytic findings and their implications for practice and research. *Families in Society 85*(1), 81–90.

Drisko, J., & Grady, M. (2012). *Evidence-based practice in clinical social work.* New York, NY: Springer-Verlag.

Frank, J. D. (1971). Therapeutic factors in psychotherapy. *American Journal of Psychotherapy, 25,* 350–361.

Grady, M., & Drisko, J. (2014). Thorough clinical assessment: The hidden foundation of evidence-based practice. *Families in Society, 95,* 5–14.

Grawe, K., Caspar, F., & Ambuhl, H. (1990). The Bernese comparative psychotherapy study. *Zeitschrift für Klinische Psychologie und Psychotherapie, 19,* 287–376.

Greenhalgh, T. (2010). *How to read a paper: The basics of evidence based medicine* (4th ed.). Hoboken, NJ: BMJ Books/Wiley–Blackwell.

Harrington, A. (Ed.) (1997). *The placebo effect: Interdisciplinary exploration.* Cambridge, MA: Harvard.

Haynes, R., Devereaux, P., & Guyatt, G. (2002). Clinical expertise in the era of evidence based medicine and patient choice. *Evidence-Based Medicine, 7,* 36–38.

Lambert, M. J. (1992). Implications of outcome research for psychotherapy integration. In J. Norcross & J. Goldstein (Eds.), *Handbook of psychotherapy integration* (pp. 94–129). New York, NY: Basic Books.

Lambert, M. (2013). The efficacy and effectiveness of psychotherapy. In M. Lambert (Ed.), *Bergin and Garfield's handbook of psychotherapy and behavior change* (6th ed., pp. 169–218). Hoboken, NJ: John Wiley.

Lambert, M. J., & Asay, T. P. (1984). Patient characteristics and their relationship to psychotherapy outcome. In M. Herson, L. Michelson, & A. Bellack (Eds.), *Issues in psychotherapy research* (pp. 313–359). New York, NY: Plenum.

Lambert, M. J., & Hill, C. E. (1994). Assessing psychotherapy outcomes and processes. In: A. E. Bergin & S. L. Garfield (Eds.), *Handbook of psychotherapy and behaviour change* (pp. 72–113). New York, NY: John Wiley & Sons.

Nelson, D., Beutler, L., & Castonguay, L. (2012). Psychotherapy integration in the treatment of personality disorders: A commentary. *Journal of Personality Disorders, 26*(1), 7–16.

Norcross, J., & Lambert, M. (2011). Evidence-based therapy relationships. In J. Norcross (Ed.), *Psychotherapy relationships that work* (pp. 3–21). New York, NY: Oxford University Press.

Orlinsky, D., Grawe, K., & Parks, B. (1994). Process and outcome in psychotherapy—Noch Einmal. In A. Bergin & S. Garfield (Eds.), *Handbook of psychotherapy and behavior change: An empirical analysis* (4th ed., pp. 152–209). New York, NY: Wiley.

Oxford University Centre for Evidence-Based Medicine. (2011). *The Oxford levels of evidence 2011.* Retrieved from http://www.cebm.net/mod_product/design/files/CEBM-Levels-of-Evidence-2.1.pdf

Paul, G. (1967). Strategy of outcome research in psychotherapy. *Journal of Consulting Psychology, 31*, 109–118.

Prochaska, J. (1999). How do people change and how can we change to help more people? In M. Hubble, B. Duncan, & S. Miller (Eds.), *The heart and soul of change: What works in therapy* (pp. 227–255). Washington, DC: American Psychological Association.

Rosenthal, R. (1984). *Meta-analytic procedures for social research.* Beverly Hills, CA: Sage.

Rosenzweig, S. (1936). Some implicit common factors in diverse methods of psychotherapy: "At last the Dodo said, 'Everybody has won and all must have prizes.'" *American Journal of Orthopsychiatry, 6*, 412–415.

Saggese, M. (2005). Maximizing treatment effectiveness in clinical practice: An outcome-informed, collaborative approach. *Families in Society, 86*(4), 558–564.

Smith, M., & Glass, G. V. (1977). Meta-analysis of psychotherapy outcome studies. *American Psychologist, 32*, 752–760.

Smith, M., Glass, G. V., & Miller, T. L. (1980). *The benefits of psychotherapy.* Baltimore, MD: John Hopkins University Press.

Sue, S., Zane, N., & Young, K. (1994). Research on psychotherapy with culturally diverse populations. In A. Bergin & S. Garfield (Eds.), *Handbook of psychotherapy and behavior change: An empirical analysis* (4th ed., pp. 783–820). New York, NY: Wiley.

Tracey, T., Lictenberg, J., Goodyear, R., Claiborn, C., & Wampold, B. (2003). Concept mapping of the therapeutic common factors. *Psychotherapy Research, 13*, 401–413.

Truax, C., & Carkhuff, R. (1967). *Toward effective counselling and psychotherapy: Training and practice.* Chicago, IL: Aldine.

Wampold, B. E. (2001). *The great psychotherapy debate: Models, methods and findings.* Mahwah, NJ: Erlbaum.

Wampold, B., Imel, Z., Bhati, K., & Johnson-Jennings, M. (2007). Insight as a common factor. In L. Castonguay & C. Hill (Eds.), *Insight in psychotherapy* (pp. 119–139). Washington, DC: American Psychiatric Association.

Wampold, B. E., Mondin, G. W., Moody, M., Stich, F., Benson, K., & Ahn, H. (1997). A meta-analysis of outcome studies comparing bona fide psychotherapies: Empirically "all must have prizes." *Psychological Bulletin, 122*(3), 203–215.

Zayas, L., Drake, B., & Jonson-Reid, M. (2010). Overrating or dismissing the value of evidence based practice: Consequences for clinical practice. *Clinical Social Work Journal, 39*(4), 400–405. doi:10.1007/s10615-010-0306-1

30 Task-centered Practice

Anne E. Fortune, Blanca M. Ramos, & William J. Reid

Task-centered practice is a short-term, problem-solving approach to social work practice (Epstein & Brown, 2001; Jagt, 2008; Marsh & Doel, 2005; Reid, 1992, 2000; Reid & Epstein, 1972). It was developed by Laura Epstein (1914–1996) and William J. Reid (1928–2003) using an empirical Research and Development (R&D) approach that tested interventions, assessed results, refined the interventions, tested them again, and so on, repeating the cycle with new clients and new problems (Reid, 1997; Fortune, 2012). It is among the few "home grown" empirical clinical practice (ECP) models in social work.

The task-centered model has been used worldwide in most types of social work settings, as a stand-alone, as part of a bundle of services, or integrated into multilevel, multisystem generalist practice (Fortune, McCallion, & Briar-Lawson,

2010; Hepworth, Rooney, Dewberry-Rooney, & Strom-Gottfried, 2013; Tolson, Reid, & Garvin, 1994). It has been used with voluntary and involuntary clients, with individuals, groups, and families, as a method of case management, as a system for agency management, as a model for clinical supervision, and as an approach to community work. Thus, it is a flexible approach to practice with many applications.

BASIC CHARACTERISTICS AND PRINCIPLES

A combination of key characteristics defines the task-centered model: a focus on client problems, problem-solving actions, integrative theoretical stance, planned brevity, a collaborative relationship, an empirical orientation, and structured interventions.

Focus on Client Problems

Task-centered practice is highly individualized in that the focus of service is on specific problems that clients explicitly acknowledge as being of concern to them. These problems-in-living usually involve personal and interpersonal difficulties, but contextual and environmental change may also be a focus.

Problem-solving Actions (Tasks)

Change in problems is brought about primarily through problem-solving actions (tasks) undertaken by clients outside of the session. The primary function of the treatment session is to lay the groundwork for such actions through systematic steps and structure. In addition, tasks by practitioner and others provide a means of effecting environmental change in the client's interest.

Integrative Theoretical Stance

The task-centered model draws selectively on theories and methods from compatible approaches—for example, problem solving, cognitive-behavioral, family structural, and interpersonal approaches. It also provides a framework and strategies that can be used with other approaches. For example, a core intervention—the task planning and implementation sequence—can be used with any intervention model. The sequence provides structured but flexible guidelines to help clients plan and carry out between-session tasks.

Planned Brevity

Service is generally planned short-term by design (6 to 12 weekly sessions within a four-month period). The short time limits capitalize on the "goal gradient effect," where individuals are motivated by deadlines and clear goals. Extensions beyond these limits are possible.

Collaborative Relationship

Relationships between clients and practitioners are both caring and collaborative. The practitioner shares assessment information and avoids hidden goals and agendas. Extensive client input while developing intervention strategies makes tasks more effective and develops the clients' problem-solving abilities.

Empirical Orientation

Within task-centered practice, methods and theories tested and supported by empirical research are preferred. Hypotheses and concepts about the client system are grounded in case data. Speculative theorizing about the client's problems and behavior is avoided. Assessment, process, and outcome data are systematically collected. Numerous studies, including eight controlled experiments, have been used to test and improve the model (Fortune, McCallion & Briar-Lawson, 2010; Reid, 1997).

Structured Intervention

Although the content of sessions (e.g., client problems, their context, task development) is individualized, task-centered sessions and intervention processes are structured. Each session in beginning, middle, and ending phases has a specific agenda that guides the client and practitioner work. In additional, some intervention processes are packaged and standardized; for example, the task implementation sequence includes steps appropriate for developing, implementing, and evaluating any client or practitioner task. Finally, because tasks are usually interim steps to a broader goal, task strategies are a series of tasks or a meta-approach to deal with specific common problems such as depression, bullying, or moving into a nursing home (Naleppa & Reid, 2003; Reid, 2000).

STRUCTURED ACTIVITIES AT THREE STAGES OF TASK-CENTERED PRACTICE WITH INDIVIDUALS AND FAMILIES

Sessions in task-centered practice are structured, although the content of sessions is individualized for clients and their problems.

I. Initial phase (Sessions 1–2). To engage clients and develop consensus on future work, the initial session(s) include:
   1. Discussion of reasons for referral, especially with nonvoluntary client(s) (see Rooney, 2009; Trotter, 2006).
   2. Exploration and assessment of client-acknowledged problems-in-living.
   3. Negotiation and agreement on a service contract, including problems and goals to be addressed, explanation of treatment methods, and agreement on durational limits.
   4. Development and implementation of initial tasks (see II.3).

II. Middle phase (each middle-phase session). Each session in the middle phase of task-centered practice includes the following activities, listed in logical order. Although task and problem review should occur early in order to focus the session, other activities are often interwoven with each other.
   1. *Problem and task review.* Problem status and accomplishment of tasks developed in previous sessions are reviewed in each session to determine progress. The task review provides a record for both the social worker and client as to how the task has gone and whether it affected the problem. This record is also useful in supervision and provides data generally about the kinds of tasks that are effective for particular clients and problems.
   2. *Identification and resolution of obstacles to task accomplishment.* If the client has experienced difficulty with the task, internal and external obstacles are reviewed and an effort is made to resolve them. If they cannot be resolved, an alternative task is developed to overcome or avoid the obstacle. For instance, a practitioner may help clients modify distorted perceptions or unrealistic expectations interfering with work on the task. Obstacles involving the external system, such as interactions between a child and school personnel or the malfunctioning of a welfare bureaucracy, may be addressed and a plan for resolving them developed.
   3. *Task planning and implementation sequence.* The task planning and implementation sequence is central to completing tasks and resolving problems (Fortune, 2012). Again, the order of activities varies for each client and situation.
      • *Task selection.* Clients will "buy in" to task actions to the extent they are involved in planning the tasks. The practitioner may ask such questions as, "What do you think you might be able to do about this problem?" Or, "Of the things you have tried, what has worked best for you?" Task selection thus begins by eliciting the client's ideas. The practitioner builds on these ideas and, if needed, suggests others. Such suggestions are intended to stimulate the client's ideas and are not "assigned" unilaterally by the practitioner. Practitioners, caregivers, and other service providers may also take on between-session tasks.
      • *Task agreement.* Explicit agreement between practitioner and client on task(s) is important. Agreement may occur after alternative possibilities have been sorted out and the best possibilities selected. Generally, agreement at this point concerns the global nature of the client's proposed action and not the detail, which is developed subsequently. If the client appears to accept the task, explicit agreement may be delayed until planning has been completed (see following item). In any case, by the end of the session, the client should agree to attempt the task.
      • *Planning specifics of implementation.* Once a task has been selected, the practitioner and client work on a plan to carry it out. Tasks suggested by practitioners should be customized and fleshed out in collaboration with clients. For example, if the practitioner suggests that a client with a drinking problem participate in a self-help program, an

implementation plan might involve determining how the program can be located, how the client can learn something about it, when he or she will attend the first meeting, what he or she might say at that meeting, and so on. Normally, the task is implemented prior to the next session.

The practitioner attempts to make sure that the task plan has a high probability of at least some success. It is better to err on the side of having the task be too easy rather than too difficult, because it is important that clients experience success in their work on their problems. Successful performance can create a sense of mastery, which can augment problem-solving efforts. For example, if it seems that the task of attending a self-help meeting has a low chance of being carried out, the task could be revised to partialize steps, for example, by first locating a group and then getting information about it.

For the task plan to work, the client must emerge with a clear notion of what he or she is to do. Generally, effort is made to spell out details of implementation that are appropriate for the task and fit the client's style and circumstances. For some tasks and some clients, a good deal of detail and structure may be required. For example, if the client is likely to procrastinate about doing the task, details like the time and place may be spelled out. For other tasks and clients, a minimum of structure and detail may make sense. For example, planning may be more general and completing the task may require a great deal of on-the-spot improvisation. In any case, the main actions of the task should be clarified, unless they are readily apparent. For example, if the task calls for a mother to show approval if her daughter cleans her room, ways of showing approval and what is meant by cleaning the room should be discussed.

- *Establishing incentives and rationale.* To help establish motivation, the practitioner and client develop a rationale for carrying out the task, if it is not already clear. "What might you gain from doing the task?" is an appropriate question. The practitioner reinforces the client's perception of realistic benefits or points out positive consequences that the client may not have perceived.

- *Identifying and resolving anticipated obstacles.* An important practitioner function in task planning is to help the client identify potential obstacles to the task and to shape plans so as to avoid or minimize these obstacles. This function is implicitly addressed when the practitioner presses for specificity in the task plan. As details of how the tasks are to be done are brought out, possible obstacles can be identified through "what if?" questions. For example, suppose the task is "Discuss with your partner ways she can help you stay sober." Among the questions the client can be asked is: "What if your partner starts to lecture you?" More generally, the practitioner can ask clients to think of ways that a task might fail. Potential obstacles and ways of resolving them can be discussed. If the obstacles appear too formidable, the task can be modified, broken down into steps, or another approach developed. Often the proposed task relates to previous efforts by the client. Consideration of these efforts and how they may have fallen short can provide another means of identifying potential obstacles. For example, a task under consideration for Mrs. S. is to reward her son with praise and approval for completing his homework. Previous discussion of the mother–son relationship revealed her difficulties in expressing positive sentiments toward the boy. Her difficulty in doing so might be identified as an obstacle.

The emphasis on identifying and avoiding obstacles—both before and after they are encountered—is an important step in task planning that is generally absent in other social work approaches (Rooney, 2010).

- *Guided practice, rehearsal.* To improve client skills or confidence, the social worker may model possible task behavior or ask clients to rehearse what they are going to say or do. For example, Mrs. S. might practice saying positive things about her son's behavior. Modeling and rehearsal may be carried out through role-playing, if appropriate. For example, if the client's problem is social phobia, the selected task might be to "speak up in a class you are attending." The practitioner might take the role of the instructor, and the client could rehearse what he or she might say. The roles could then be reversed, with the worker modeling what the client might say.

Guided practice is the performance of the actual (as opposed to simulated) task behavior by the client during the interview; thus, a child may practice reading or a couple may practice communication skills. Guided practice can also be extended to real-life situations—a practitioner might accompany a client with a fear of going to doctors to a medical clinic.

- *Summarizing and recording the task plan.* As a final step in task-planning, to clarify between-session activities, the practitioner and client go over the plan in summary fashion. For complex tasks, it is useful to elicit from the client the essentials of the plan. The client is asked to present the plan as he or she sees it. The practitioner can then underscore the essential elements of it or add parts the client has left out. Summarizing the plan gives the practitioner the opportunity to convey to the client the expectation that it will be carried out and that his or her efforts will be reviewed. "So you will try to do [thus and so] I'll do [that and this]. We'll see how it worked out next time we meet." Writing tasks down with a copy for the client and another for the practitioner is also useful, especially when tasks are complex or when several people are to perform tasks.

4. *Implementation of tasks between sessions.* Clients and (depending on the case) practitioners and others carry out tasks in the environment.

III. Terminal phase (final or last two sessions).
1. *Assessment of current status problems and overall problem situation.*
2. *Identification of successful problem-solving strategies used by client(s).* Emphasis is on establishing

client's success in problem solving and using strategies in similar situations.
3. *Discussion of other ways to maintain client gains.* Maintenance may include "fail-safe planning" (what to do if a problem crops up), self-reinforcement, practicing new behaviors in additional situations (generalization), etc.
4. *Discussion of what can be done about remaining problems,* including possible task strategies.
5. *Acknowledge reactions to ending.* Because ending is expected, reactions to termination are more likely to be ambivalent—mixed satisfaction and regret—than negative. These reactions should be acknowledged as normal and healthy but not as reasons to prolong treatment. In many circumstances, a termination ritual helps bring closure, for example, a memento of the relationship, a review of clients' accomplishments, etc.
6. *Making decisions about extensions.* Decisions are jointly made by client and practitioner. Extensions are usually time-limited and focused on particular problems or goals. In most cases, a single brief extension will suffice, but in some cases additional ones may be needed. The critical consideration is what can be accomplished by extending service. Often, cases that show little progress by the twelfth visit will show no more progress by the twentieth.

TASK-CENTERED PRACTICE IN SMALL GROUPS

The task-centered model is readily used in group treatment of individual (or family) problems (Fortune, 1985). Small groups—usually from four to eight persons—are formed around problems that are similar, such as school failure or issues in caregiving. Members specify problems and undertake tasks related to them, as in individual work. Sessions follow the same structured agenda outlined above. However, in group treatment members assist one another in formulating problems and in work on tasks, including task planning and review. Group members may act as "buddies" between meetings.

Group norms are shaped to encourage task-centered work—for example, the expectation that clients will take action and reinforce one anothers' successes. Group processes are used to enhance intervention. For example, when members have similar problems, group cohesion can occur more quickly and members have multiple role models and ideas for task strategies. Reviewing task progress in pairs makes individuals accountable for their own progress as well as aides to others' progress.

CONSIDERATIONS FOR WORK WITH ORGANIZATIONS AND OTHER CONTEXTS

The task-centered model has been adapted for use in clinical and educational supervision, case management, organizational management, and community organization. In these uses, the problems-in-living are replaced by other types of problems or goals, for example, by skills to be mastered by a supervisee, by an organization's lack of clarity about its mission, or by a community's need to develop stronger norms against violence. Once a problem/goal is negotiated among participants, the task-centered problem-solving steps are used to develop strategies and tasks to achieve the goals. Tasks are implemented, their accomplishment evaluated, and the situation reviewed systematically as in individual task-centered practice. Time limits are also used to increase motivation and participant action. The primary differences from individual practice lie in the dynamics of the unit. For example, in supervision, the employee is (we hope) motivated to improve competence, while the supervisor holds authority to enforce organizational rules to protect clients; the employee's choice of skill development may be constrained by rules about legally acceptable interventions. In interdisciplinary case management teams, disagreement about values and approaches from the different disciplines may inadvertently overshadow the client's perspective. In organizational management, problems may be readily identified, but getting the key organizational players to collaborate may require more effort than generating task strategies.

FUTURE

Task-centered practice is one of the few empirical clinical practice (ECP) models developed in social work. It has demonstrated its applicability to a wide range of problems, clients, modalities, and worldviews. It can be used as an all-purpose tool, adapted to the immediate need, or embedded in other interventions. It now appears so well-embedded in social work that one critic suggested that it is "simply good social work practice.... [whose its major contribution is] a sturdy yet flexible practice technology that contains enough rigor to be consistently effective but also enough space to be adapted creatively to an incredible number of social work practice contexts" (Kelly, 2008, p. 199).

CASE ILLUSTRATION: ANA

Ana, 66 years old, was recently diagnosed with mild depression. A year ago she emigrated from Chile where she was heavily involved in her church and had an active social life. She lives with her daughter, Liz, and a teenage granddaughter, Sofia, with whom she rarely interacts. Ana resents Liz, blaming her for "forcing" her to leave behind her family and friends whom she fears she will never see again. This has strained the relationship to the point where Ana prefers not to ask Liz for help and support when needed. Ana describes her current life as "lonely," "meaningless," and "unhappy." She longs to be back in Chile and cries "all the time."

Initial Phase

Ana and the practitioner identified two target problems: her loneliness and limited support system. They tentatively agreed on three intervention strategies: expanding her social network, increasing contact with family in Chile, and improving her relationships with Sofia and Liz. They contracted to meet weekly for three months.

The practitioner mentioned a church near Ana's house that offered Spanish Mass and educational and social activities daily for Latino seniors. For an initial task, Ana suggested with little enthusiasm she would go to the church and give it a try. With prompting, she agreed to ask Liz to help her get there on her way to work and to pick her up on her way home. Ana would go to the church at least three times a week.

Middle Phase

At the beginning of the next session, Ana reviewed her task: as agreed, she had gone to the church three times. She shared with some enthusiasm how she met other Latina immigrants to whom she could relate and found spiritual comfort attending Mass and talking to the priest. Ana was not sure she could continue working on this task because it was hard getting to the church. She struggled waking up so early and worried about making Liz late to work.

When prompted for ways to overcome this obstacle, Ana recalled befriending Tina who goes to the church daily and lives a block away. She agreed to ask Tina if she could stop by on her way over so they could go together. Ana would discuss this idea with Liz emphasizing her own concern about making her late for work.

The practitioner suggested another task: to ask Sofia to show her how to use e-mail to communicate with her loved ones in Chile. This task was also intended to facilitate closer interactions with Sofia.

During each session in the middle phase, Ana and the practitioner reviewed task progress, problem status, and obstacles to task accomplishment. Ana continues going to the church, sometimes more than three times a week, and participates actively. She walks over with Tina, and during bad weather Liz gives them both a ride. Ana was surprised when Sofia agreed to help her use e-mail. Electronic communication is challenging and frustrating, but Ana is highly motivated. Occasionally, Liz stops by the church to give Ana and Tina a ride home, and the three gossip about their days.

Terminal Phase

In the last few sessions, the practitioner reminded Ana how many sessions remained. At first, Ana wanted to continue, but she agreed that their work was almost completed and they would end when they had initially planned.

In the final session, Ana and the practitioner reviewed the status of the target problems. Ana did not feel as lonely: she talked enthusiastically about the positive changes in her life since she began attending the church. She has new friends, participates in meaningful activities, and benefits spiritually. Ana still misses her family and life in Chile and cries from time to time. She continues trying to learn how to use e-mail; it has been a long and slow process. As a result of this experience, she spends more time with Sofia, and they are successfully bonding.

Ana and Liz have grown closer. They often go grocery shopping after taking Tina home, and they prepare meals together. Ana enjoys teaching Liz the "old dishes," while Liz likes hunting ingredients in the bodega. Ana now views Liz as a supportive, caring daughter who had good intentions inviting her to live with her in this country.

The practitioner pointed out Ana's strengths including her tremendous problem solving abilities and resilience. They discussed how Ana could use these personal resources to continue working on her current and new problems. Ana plans to go to the church more often and even get there on her own when needed. She and the practitioner rehearsed what Ana would do if she found herself feeling lonely, crying when longing for her family and friends in Chile, or needing nurturing from Liz and Sofia.

Ana thanked the practitioner profusely, stating with sadness she would greatly miss their weekly sessions. The practitioner praised Ana for her accomplishments and acknowledged the sad nature of this ending and transition. Ana timidly, with teary eyes, gave the practitioner a small vase from Chile. This was graciously accepted and proudly placed on the practitioner's desk. They both contemplated it and gave each other warm smiles before Ana left the room.

References

Epstein, L., & Brown, L. B. (2001). *Brief treatment and a new look at the task-centered approach* (4th ed.). NY: Pearson.

Fortune, A. E. (Ed.). (1985). *Task-centered practice with families and groups.* New York, NY: Springer.

Fortune, A. E. (2012). Development of the task-centered model. In T. L. Rzepnicki, S. G. McCracken, & H. E. Briggs (Eds.), *From task-centered social work to evidence-based and integrative practice: Reflections on history and implementation* (pp. 15–39). Chicago, IL: Lyceum.

Fortune, A. E., McCallion, P., & Briar-Lawson, K. (Eds.). (2010). *Social work practice research for the 21st century.* Part 3, An example of empirical model development and dissemination: The task-centered model (pp. 181–249). New York, NY: Columbia University Press.

Hepworth, D. H., Rooney, R. H., Dewberry-Rooney, G., & Strom-Gottfried, K. (2013). *Direct social work practice: Theory and skills* (9th ed.). Pacific Grove, CA: Brooks/Cole.

Jagt, L. J. (2008). Van Richmond naar Reid : bronnen en ontwikkeling van taakgerichte.... Houten/ Zaventem: Bohn Stafleu van Loghum.

Kelly, M. (2008). Task-centered practice. In T. Mizrahi & L. Davis (Eds.), *Encyclopedia of social work* (20th ed.) (pp. 197–199). NY: Oxford University Press. Retrieved from doi:10.1093/acrefore/9780199975839.013.388

Marsh, P., & Doel, M. (2005). *The task-centred book.* London: Routledge with Communitycare.

Naleppa, M. J., & Reid, W. J. (2003). *Gerontological social work: A task-centered approach.* New York, NY: Columbia University Press.

Reid, W. J. (1992). *Task strategies: An empirical approach to social work practice.* New York, NY: Columbia University Press.

Reid, W. J. (1997). Research on task-centered practice. *Social Work Research, 21,* 132–137.

Reid, W. J. (2000). *The task planner.* New York, NY: Columbia University Press.

Reid, W. J., & Epstein, L. (1972). *Task-centered casework.* New York, NY: Columbia University Press.

Rooney, R. H. (2010). Task-centered practice in the United States. In A. E. Fortune, P. McCallion, & K. Briar-Lawson. (Eds.), *Social work practice research for the 21st century* (pp. 195–202). New York, NY: Columbia University Press.

Rooney, R. H. (Ed.). (2009). *Strategies for work with involuntary clients* (2nd ed.). New York, NY: Columbia University Press.

Tolson, E. R., Reid, W. J., & Garvin, C. D. (1994). *Generalist practice: A task-centered approach.* New York, NY: Columbia University Press.

Trotter, C. (2006). *Working with involuntary clients* (2nd ed.). Crows Nest, New South Wales, Australia: Allen & Unwin.

31   The Life Model of Social Work Practice

Alex Gitterman

AN OVERVIEW

In developing the Life Model, Professor Germain and I assumed that there were many common concepts and methods in working with people, no matter what the size of the system. We believed that services should be based on client needs and preferences rather than the worker's method specialization. We attempted to develop an integrated social work practice method in place of the traditional casework, group work, and community organization methods. In conceptualizing an integrated method, we recognized some distinctive knowledge and skills, such as what is required to form groups or to influence communities, organizations, and legislative processes.

Historically, the profession experienced ideological conflicts between those who emphasized bringing about social change on behalf of social justice, the "cause," as the primary characteristic of social work, and those who emphasized

"function" as the primary characteristic of social work practice, that is, the technologies used by practitioners to bring about individual change (Lee, 1929; Gitterman & Germain, 2008b). Based on our practice and teaching experiences, Professor Germain and I were committed to integrate these traditions. Hence, our second aim was to develop a model that began to build bridges between the treatment and social-reform traditions of the profession. Clearly, both cause and function must be hallmarks of practice and education for practice if social work is to be relevant in the new century. Melding cause and function is an essential part of life-modeled practice (Schwartz, 1969, 1971, 1976; Giterman & Germain, 2008b).

In building on our original ideas, we adopted a *life course* of human development and functioning. In contrast to traditional stage models of development, this formulation takes into account diversity in race, ethnicity, sex, age, socioeconomic status, sexual orientation, and physical/mental challenges, as well as environmental forces within historical, societal, and cultural contexts. We used "life course" to replace the traditional, linear "life cycle" models and their assumption that emotional and social development proceed in fixed, sequential, universal stages without reference to the diversity of life experience, culture, and environments (Gitterman & Germain, 2008a).

ECOLOGICAL PERSPECTIVE

Ecological theory is especially suited for social work because it emphasizes the interdependence of organism and environment. Given our historic commitment to the person-and-environment concept, the ecological metaphor helps the profession enact its social purpose of helping people and promoting responsive environments that support human growth, health, and satisfaction in social functioning. Ecology, a biological science that examines the relation between living organisms and all the elements of the social and physical environments, provides the theoretical perspective for an integrated practice and the theoretical foundation for the Life Model (Germain, 1981; Germain & Gitterman, 1986a, 1987, 1995, 1996; Gitterman, 1996; Gitterman & Germain, 1976, 2008a). Ecological concepts offer the theoretical lens for viewing the exchanges between people and their environments. The concepts include level of fit, transactions, adaptation, life course, and vulnerability and resilience. Principles from deep ecology further enhance our understanding that all phenomena are interconnected and interdependent as well as dependent on the cyclical processes of nature. These principles include the interdependence of networks, the self-correcting feedback loops, and the cyclical nature of ecological processes (Capra, 1996; Ungar, 2002).

Over the life course, people strive to deal with and improve the *level of fit* with their environments. When people feel positive and hopeful about their own capacities and about having their needs fulfilled, and when they view their environmental resources as responsive, they and their immediate environments are likely to achieve a reciprocally sustaining condition of *adaptedness*. Adaptive person:environment exchanges *reciprocally* support and release potential.

In contrast, when people feel negative and unhopeful about their own capacities and about having their needs fulfilled, and when they view environmental resources as unresponsive, they and their environments are likely to achieve a poor level of adaptive fit. *Stress* is the outcome of a perceived imbalance between environmental demand(s) and capability to manage it with perceived available internal and external resources. To relieve the stressful situation, the level of person:environment fit must be improved. This is accomplished by an active change in either people's perceptions and behaviors, or in environmental responses, or in the quality of their exchanges.

Poor clients live in oppressive social and physical environments. They are exposed on a daily basis to economic, social, and psychological discrimination. In *coping* with destructive environments, some people steel themselves and mobilize inner strengths and resiliencies—they become survivors rather than victims. Others internalize the oppression and turn it against themselves through such self-destructive behaviors as substance abuse and unprotected sex. Still others externalize the oppression, strike back, and vent their rage on others less powerful than they through such behaviors as violence, crime, and property destruction. Readily accessible targets often include family members, neighbors, and community residents. These *maladaptive* person:environment exchanges reciprocally frustrate and damage both human as well as environmental potentials (Gitterman, 2014).

In deep ecology, living systems are viewed as *networks* interacting with other systems of networks—"in intricate pattern of intertwined webs, networks nesting within larger networks" (Capra, 1996, p. 82). These intertwined, interdependent networks share certain common properties. Their intricate patterns are nonlinear—they go in all directions and develop feedback loops, which allow them to self-regulate by learning from and correcting mistakes. Through the process of self-regulating and self-organizing, new behaviors, patterns, and structures are spontaneously created and the networks' equilibrium constantly evolves. The interdependence of networks and the self-correcting feedback loops allow the living system to adapt to changing conditions and to survive disturbances. Thus, interdependence of networks, the self-correcting feedback loops, and the cyclical nature of ecological processes are three basic principles of deep ecology.

SOCIAL WORK PURPOSE AND FUNCTION

The Life Model conceptualizes the purpose of social work as improving the level of fit between people and their environments, especially between people's needs and their environmental resources (Gitterman, 2010). This conception of professional purpose is further specified through two inter-related professional functions: (1) to help people mobilize and draw on personal and environmental resources to eliminate, or, at least, alleviate life stressors and the associated stress; and (2) to influence social and physical environmental forces to be responsive to people's needs (Germain & Gitterman, 1979, 1980, 1986, 1996; Gitterman & Germain, 1976; 2008; Gitterman, 2010).

(1) *Helping people with life stressors*: Over the life course, people encounter life stressors. These stressors emerge in one or more aspects of living and include: *difficult life transitions and traumatic life events, environmental pressures,* and *dysfunctional transactions in collective life* (family, group, and community). In life-modeled practice, practitioners and clients assess and intervene in single and multiple life stressors.

Life transitions include stressful developmental transitions, difficult social transitions, and traumatic life events (Gitterman & Germain, 2008a). Developmental transitions, such as adolescence, impose new demands and require new adaptations and coping. While puberty is biological, adolescence is a social construction. The norms related to developmental changes vary across subcultures and dominant society. Developmental transitions are accompanied with competing expectations, changes in family, peer, and social changes in status and roles. People must also deal with the challenges of new experiences and relationships as well as leaving familiar places and relationships. Beginning a new school or job, starting a new relationship, or having a child create new demands and expectations, and therefore, are often stressful social transitions. Leaving school or a job, ending a relationship, and dealing with death and other losses are even more stressful social transitions than new experiences. Traumatic life events, often unexpected and severe, include losses such as the death of a child, loss of a home, rape, and the diagnosis of AIDS and other illnesses. Such events are perceived as overwhelming disasters and lead to intense pain.

Biological and social transitions and traumatic events require changes in ways of looking at oneself and the world, and have profound impact on interpersonal transactions.

Environmental pressures can arise from the lack of resources and social provisions on the part of some or most social and physical environments (Gitterman & Germain, 2008a). Chronic poverty is the major force responsible for both prolonged and cumulative stress. Violence, insufficient affordable housing, poor schools, inadequate heath care for children and adults, are consequences of our economic and social priorities and values. To manage environmental stressors, clients turn to institutions and organization (including social agencies) for assistance. Some provide the required resources. Others are inaccessible and inhospitable to people's needs; withhold needed resources through restrictive policies, regulations, and procedures; and exacerbate rather than ameliorate people's stress. Similarly, some social networks (kin, friends, neighbors, work mates, and acquaintances) provide essential instrumental (goods and services) and expressive (empathy, encouragement) resources. They serve as essential buffers against life stressors and the stress they generate. Others, however, are destructive, nonsupportive, or are missing altogether. Similarly, physical settings can be serious life stressors because of deteriorated dwellings, unsafe and insufficient space, and lack of required privacy.

Families, groups, and communities also experience the life transitional and environmental stressors noted above. They also experience additional stressors created by their own dysfunctional processes and exploitative and conflicted relationships (Gitterman, 2010, 2012; Gitterman & Germain, 2008a; Gitterman & Wayne, 2003; Wayne and Gitterman, 2004). Scapegoating and splintering factions are illustrative of dysfunctional processes, which simultaneously weaken individuals as well as the collective.

Life transitional, environmental, and interpersonal stressors are interrelated and, at the same time, distinct. When one is unsuccessfully managed, additional stressors often erupt in other areas of life (the "spread phenomenon"). Cumulatively, they can overwhelm individual and collective coping capacities, and the individual, group, family, or community/neighborhood may move toward disorganization.

(2) *Influencing social and physical environmental forces*: In helping people with

life stressors, social workers daily encounter the lack of environmental responsiveness. Thus, the Life Model also includes professional responsibility for influencing environmental forces and for bearing witness against social inequities and injustice. This is done by *mobilizing community resources* to improve community life, by *influencing unresponsive organizations* to develop responsive policies and services, and by *politically influencing local, state, and federal legislation and regulations* to support social justice (Gitterman & Germain, 2008b).

Intervention at the community level is essential to life-modeled practice. The social worker helps mobilize neighborhood and community residents to take action on their own behalf to secure desired formal and informal resources. Helping residents to pursue needed resources or services and to influence formal and informal structures to be receptive to their efforts are essential interventions to improving the level of fit between people and their environments. The social worker can also help neighborhood and community residents by improving the coordination of existing community resources and increasing their accessibility. When programs and services are unavailable, the social worker may engage his/her agency or a coalition of agencies to develop new programs and services.

Influencing the social worker's own organization to develop new services or improve existing ones is an essential component of the Life Model's conception of professional function (Gitterman & Miller, 1989). To be responsive to clients' needs, the social worker must have an active presence in his/her organization. An organizationally isolated worker is not in a position to influence polices, practices, and programs. Similarly, a social worker who does not question organizational structures and processes will limit his/her ability to improve agency services. The worker must move beyond prescribed organizational roles in a respectful and skillful manner. The professional task is to identify simultaneously with the organization's mission, the client's needs, and the profession's code of ethics. The Life Model proposes a professional methodology to fulfill this professional function.

The complexities of contemporary practice demand professional involvement in political activity to influence local, state, and federal legislative and regulatory processes. Political activity includes the simpler form of telephoning and writing letters to policy-makers and policy-implementers and mobilizing others to do the same. In its more complex form, political activity includes lobbying, coalition building, testifying, rallying public support, and using the press and other media to influence legislative and regulatory processes (Gitterman & Germain, 2008b).

THE HELPING PROCESS

Like life itself, this model of practice is phasic. The helping process is organized into three phases—initial, ongoing, and ending. The phases ebb and flow in response to the interplay of personal and environmental forces. Although not always distinct in actual practice, they are separated to provide practice guidelines. The initial phase presents concepts and methods on the accomplishment of two professional tasks: (1) creating a supportive environment; and (2) developing commonality of purpose. All professional helping and environmental influencing requires clarity of purpose and shared definitions of needs, concerns, goals, and respective roles. The shared understanding and initiation of problem-solving activities usher in the ongoing phase. In this phase, people are helped with their life transitional, environmental, and interpersonal stressors and the major environmental influencing activities are launched. In the ending phase, the worker deals with the feelings aroused by the termination, evaluates what has been accomplished and what remains to be achieved, and develops plans for the future. In community, organizational, and legislative activities, the worker evaluates the outcomes and, if effective, attempts to institutionalize the innovation to ensure its permanence.

In the helping process, the professional relationship is characterized by mutuality and reciprocity and conceived of as a partnership. This conception of client and worker roles requires careful attention to variations, introduced by such things as level of functioning, age, cultural expectations, and lifestyles. If strains evolve between the partners, the social worker invites open and direct communication, reaches for disappointment and anger, and strives to develop greater understanding and mutuality in the relationship.

Social workers must consistently accept and respect each client's (a) race, ethnicity, religion, and spirituality; (b) gender; (c) sexual orientation; (d) age; and (e) particular mental and physical challenges (Heller & Gitterman, 2010). Such sensitivity requires specialized knowledge about a particular population or person being served by the practitioner and a high level of self-awareness. The combination of specialized knowledge and self-awareness helps to assure a practice that is sensitive to diversity (objective) and difference (subjective) as well as sameness and is responsive to the needs and aspirations of vulnerable and oppressed populations and to the consequences of discrimination. Sensitivity to diversity also requires respect and understanding of people whose characteristics and values may differ from those of the group around them or of the worker. At times, working with people whose backgrounds are similar to ours creates its own special challenges (Lum, 2004; Swigonski, 1996).

CONCLUSION

Life model practice seeks to elevate the fit between people and their environments. In mediating the transactions between people and their environments, social workers fulfill a dual professional function: helping to eliminate, or, at least, alleviate life stressors; and influencing social and physical environmental forces to be responsive to people's needs. By integrating people's needs for individualized services (function) and for environmental reform and social action (cause), the life-modeled social worker is well positioned for the complexities of contemporary conditions and practice dilemmas. Increasingly, our profession will be called upon to bear witness against social inequalities and injustices by mobilizing community resources, influencing unresponsive organizations, and mobilizing political action, while, at the same time, providing services that build on individual and collective strengths.

WEBSITES

http://www.aaswg.org/
http://www.acosa.org/
http://www.alliance1.org/
http://www.esapubs.org/esapubs/journals/ecology.htm
http://www.ecosocialwork.org/

References and Readings

Addams, J. (1910). *Twenty years at Hull-House.* New York, NY: Macmillan.
Capra, F. (1996). *The web of life.* New York, NY: Anchor Books.
Germain, C. B. (1981). The ecological approach to people environment transactions. *Social Casework, 62*(June), 323–331.
Germain, C. B., & Gitterman, A. (1979). The Life Model of social work practice. In F. Turner (Ed.), *Social work treatment* (pp. 361–384). New York, NY: Free Press.
Germain, C. B., & Gitterman, A. (1986). Ecological social work research in the United States. *Brennpunkta sozalier arbeit* (pp. 60–76). Frankfurt: Diesterweg.
Germain, C. B., & Gitterman, A. (1986a). The Life Model of social work practice revisited. In F. Turner (Ed.), *Social work treatment* (pp. 618–644). New York, NY: Free Press.
Germain, C. B., & Gitterman, A. (1987). In A. Minahan (Ed.). Ecological perspective. *Encyclopedia of social work* (18th ed.) (pp. 488–499). Silver Spring, MD: National Association of Social Workers Press.
Germain, C. B., & Gitterman, A. (1995). Ecological perspective. In R. L. Edwards (Ed.), *Encyclopedia of social work* (19th ed.) (pp. 816–824). Silver Spring, MD: National Association of Social Workers Press.
Germain, C. B., & Gitterman, A. (1996). *The Life Model of social work practice: Advances in theory and practice* (2nd ed.). New York, NY: Columbia University Press.
Gitterman, A. (1996). Ecological perspective: Response to Professor Jerry Wakefield. *Social Service Review, 70*(2), 472–475.
Gitterman, A. (2010). Advances in the life model of social work practice. In F. Turner (Ed.), *Social work treatment: Interlocking theoretical approaches* (pp. 279–292). New York, NY: Oxford Press.
Gitterman, A. (2012). When internal processes go astray: Turning points in group. In A. M. Bergart, S. R. Simon, and M. Doel (Eds.), *Group work: Honoring our roots, nurturing our growth* (pp. 236–241). London: Whiting & Birch.
Gitterman, A. (2014). *Handbook of social work practice with vulnerable and resilient populations* (3rd ed.). New York, NY: Columbia University Press.
Gitterman, A., & Germain, C. B. (2008a). Ecological framework. In Y. Mizrahi and L. Davis (Eds.), *Encyclopedia of social work* (20th ed.) (pp. 97–102). New York, NY: Oxford University Press.
Gitterman, A., & Germain, C. B. (2008b). *The Life Model of social work practice: Advances in theory and practice* (3rd ed.). New York, NY: Columbia University Press.

Gitterman, A., & C. B. Germain. (1976). Social work practice: A Life Model. *Social Service Review, 50*(December), 601–610.

Gitterman, A., & Miller, I. (1989). The influence of the organization on clinical practice. *Clinical Social Work Journal, 17*(Summer), 151–164.

Gitterman, A., & Wayne, J. (2003). Turning points in group life: Using high tension moments to promote group purpose and mutual aid. *Families in Society, 84*(3), 433–440.

Heller, N., & Gitterman. A. (2010). *Mental health and social problems: A social work perspective.* New York, NY: Routledge.

Lee, P. R. (1929). Social work as cause and function. In *Social work cause and function: Selected papers of Porter R. Lee* (pp. 3–24). New York, NY: Columbia University Press.

Lum, D. (2004). *Social work practice and people of color: A process-stage approach* (5th ed.). Belmont, CA: Brooks/Cole.

Richmond, M. E. (1917). *Social diagnosis.* New York, NY: Russell Sage Foundation.

Schwartz, W. (1969). Private troubles and public issues: One social work job or two? *The social welfare forum* (pp. 22–43). New York, NY: Columbia University Press.

Schwartz, W. (1971). The interactionist approach. *Encyclopedia of social work* (17th ed.) (pp. 130–191). New York, NY: National Association of Social Workers Press.

Schwartz, W. (1976). Between client and system: The mediating function. In R. Roberts and H. Northen (Eds.), *Theories of social work with groups* (pp. 171–197). New York, NY: Columbia University Press.

Swigonski, M. E. (1996). Challenging privilege through Afrocentric social work practice. *Social Work, 41*(2), 153–161.

Ungar, M. (2002). A deeper, more social ecological social work practice. *Social Service Review, 76*(3), 480–497.

Wayne, J., & Gitterman, A. (2004). Offensive behaviors in groups: Challenges and opportunities. *Social Work with Groups, 26*(2), 23–34.

32   Client-centered Theory and Therapy

William S. Rowe, Samantha A. Hafner, & Alicia J. Stinson

Those who seek the help of therapists have often been badly damaged by their experience of life.

(Mearns, Lambers, Thorne, & Warner, 2000, p. 90)

INTRODUCTION

Client-centered theory was originated by Carl Rogers more than five decades ago, at a time when the humanistic approach to psychology was evolving and clearly differentiated from the more analytical styles of that period. Client-centered theory is hypothesized on the belief that all beings have innate means to grow and change beyond their perceived limitations of "self" (e.g., attitude, behavior, and self-concept) toward greater positive personal development when facilitated through consistent and reliable relationships in therapy (Cepeda & Davenport, 2006; Green, 2006; Rogers, 1957, 1961; Rowe,

2011; Snodgrass, 2007; Watchel, 2007). Although client-centered theory has recently lost focus in the United States, it has been explored by several international communities and continues to grow in popularity abroad. Along with influences on future practice, this section will discuss the foundation of client-centered theory, its relationship with social work, and its evolution within the psychotherapy community.

WHAT IS CLIENT-CENTERED THEORY AND THERAPY?

Client-centered therapy is a nondirective approach where the role of the therapist is not to offer direct advice for change or make any other type of suggestion that is usually found in the behavioral therapies but to use self-awareness in relationship to the client, focusing on the here and now of the presenting disparity, and provide a safe environment in which the client is capable of achieving self-actualization. The client-centered therapist shows respect in recognizing that the client is the expert, inherently capable of resolving his or her challenges in order to live a more complete and satisfying life (Cepeda & Davenport, 2006; Green, 2006).

Client-centered theory and therapy are not based on stages of development or steps of actions to take sequentially with the client; rather, they rely solely on the stance of the therapist to genuinely possess three key humanistic characteristics: empathy, congruency, and unconditional positive regard. Furthermore, these three attitudes are manifested by the therapist and accessed during counseling sessions with the client, who is often experiencing a sense of incongruence, vulnerability, and anxiety. In an analysis of each individual characteristic, researchers discovered several consistencies between each component. The analyses were designed to determine the effects on therapeutic outcomes when therapists incorporate a feature of client-centered therapy into their practice. It was concluded, however, that determining the effectiveness of one characteristic proved difficult, because all three often went hand-in-hand in a therapeutic environment. For example, empathy is considered to be indivisible from congruence and positive regard, and genuineness is necessary in order to portray empathy or regard adequately. Although limitations to this type of research are apparent, all three studies concluded an overall leaning toward

positive relationships between using the characteristics of client-centered therapy and therapeutic results (Elliott, Bohart, Watson, & Greenberg, 2011; Farber & Doolin, 2011; Kolden, Klein, Wang, & Austin, 2011). It is also essential to the theory of client-centered work that the client perceives and recognizes these therapeutic attitudes to some extent (Bozarth & Brodley, 1991). Table 32.1 offers a more detailed explanation of each of the three elements that are central to the therapist's behavior as client-centered.

In 1957, Carl Rogers hypothesized six conditions as "necessary and sufficient" to promote what he called "constructive personality change" in the individual (p. 241). It is also suggested that as long as the therapist is able to interrelate the three salient qualities discussed earlier (congruence, empathy, and unconditional positive regard), then at a minimum the client will experience positive growth (Snodgrass, 2007; Snyder, 2002). Table 32.2 represents the key principles of client-centered theory.

In addition to Rogers's explanation of the client-centered approach in the helping profession, there have been many others who built on his original hypothesis by expanding its application. One such contributor to this approach is Robert Carkhuff, who elaborated on the three core conditions by adding confrontation, immediacy, and concreteness, also noted as "facilitative conditions deemed essential for effective counseling" (Horan, 1977). In this realm, these qualities or conditions parallel Rogers's core conditions in the following way: concreteness in empathetic understanding is about "being specific"; immediacy with congruence refers to "what goes on between us right now"; and confrontation is seen as useful in "all three of Rogers' conditions" (Brazier, 1996) as "telling it like it is" (Carkhuff, 1971, as cited in Horan, 1977). Carkhuff's emergences in the client-centered approach are often seen as more active and direct than the original precepts and are recognized as qualities that further aid the helping process of the client.

The effectiveness of client-centered therapy is primarily dependent on the relationship between the client and therapist, whereby the therapist is completely aware of him- or herself in relationship to the client and the client is able to communicate unexpressed feelings and emotions that have caused confusion with his or her notion of self. When this ideal relationship is formed between client and therapist, even complex and deep-rooted issues can be addressed

TABLE 32.1 Characteristics of a Client-Centered Therapist

Core Attitude	Required Skill or Behavior of Therapist
Empathy	Sharing the clients' experience from their perspective and understanding it through their frame of reference. This is accomplished through verbal and nonverbal actions. This also includes seeking clarity to the client's experience, not through making an inference or assumption that is inaccurate but, rather, seeking to gain an understanding from the client when we are not certain. Requires truly being present to feeling what the client shares and also experiencing what we as therapists feel in response to the client. Empathetic understanding is not to be confused with simply mirroring or reflecting back to the client what was shared; it is more closely aligned with recognizing what the client is attempting to communicate or struggling with at a deeper level. Communicating this awareness and seeking clarity (e.g., "let me see if I have this correct") assists the client in exploring more deeply their internal process.
Unconditional positive regard (*respect*)	Communicating emotional warmth to clients' needs/issues/statements/problems and notion of self or selves while not providing recommendations, opinions, advice, or solutions. This is referred to as "prizing" the client/individual for who they are as a unique individual. It is necessary to point out that this does not mean the therapist/counselor has to agree or condone the actions/attitudes of the client; likewise, it is not for the therapist to voice personal disagreement with such experiences of the client.
Congruence (*genuineness*)	Demonstrating through (congruent) verbal and nonverbal gestures (e.g., therapist's affect and mood are the same) a deep level of understanding and ability to be honest, genuine, and "whole." This is about being real with the client, not superficial. This does not require diagnosing the client or using terms that are unknown to the client. Truly meet the client where the client is.

and understood. A case study involving a client suffering from severe childhood abuse demonstrated that client-centered therapy can be successful in cases of extreme trauma. Psychologist David Murphy utilized a strategy of empathetic response and congruent acceptance of his client that resulted in the client's personal growth and understanding (Murphy, 2009). Ultimately, clients are able to experience on their own accord that they are loved and valued, which allows them to realize their fullest potential through self-actualization.

CLIENT-CENTERED PERSPECTIVE AND SOCIAL WORK

The conditions of client-centered theory match the fundamental values and skills of social work. The two have a historically organic relationship based on the shared belief and respect for the individual's worth and dignity, autonomy, self-determination, and ability to improve whatever conditions exist through empowerment of the individual, group, or community. The core skills used by social workers in purposeful relationships include empathy, respect (unconditional positive regard), and authenticity (congruence), which are also noted as the key elements/attitudes to the client-centered approach (da Silva, 2005; Hepworth, Rooney, Dewberry Rooney, Strom-Gottfried, & Larsen, 2009; Rowe, 2011). The following case is presented to illustrate the use of the client-centered approach in social work.

Case Example

Liz, a single female, age 33, sought counseling because of conflicts between her personal needs and those of her family. Liz grew up in a lower to middle-class neighborhood outside of New York City as the older of two daughters to immigrant

TABLE 32.2 Key Principles to Client-centered Theory

Rogers's Conditions of Client-centered Theory	Underlying Assumption of Individual	Role of Therapist
Therapeutic *relationship* must exist between client and therapist/counselor	Willing to participate to some extent, capable and competent	Establishes a safe environment for cultivating the relationship; develops the conditions necessary and sufficient for constructive personality change
Client is in a state of *incongruence*	Anxious, vulnerable, distorted sense of real self vs. ideal self	Remains integrated in the relationship
Therapist/counselor is *congruent*	Will be able to recognize this through therapist's use of self and will develop trust	Genuine, sincere, authentic; demonstrates a fully integrated presence of self in relationship to client
Therapist experiences *unconditional positive regard* toward the client	Has the capacity to guide, regulate, direct, and control self providing certain conditions exist	Respect, acceptance, warmth, and a nonjudgmental attitude
Therapist is *empathetic*	Has rarely experienced this level of understanding, later begins to experience and verbalize unexpressed feelings/emotions	Feels what the client feels, active listening, verbally and nonverbally communicates back to the client in a validating (not evaluating) manner
Communication that the therapist's use of empathy and unconditional positive regard is understood	Experiences self-actualization and happiness; loved and valued by self and others	Maintains commitment to the advancement of love and peace as basic strivings; facilitates and recognizes the client's full growth and potential

parents from Europe. Her father, Edward, died suddenly from a heart attack at age 50 when Liz was 15 years old. Her remaining family includes her mother, Rose, age 65; and one younger sister, Angela, age 30. Both reside in New York. Liz lives and works in San Diego, California, where she is an executive marketing manager for a firm that she has been with for over ten years, since graduating from college. She provides financial support to her mother, who is unable to work due to poor health, and occasionally to her sister, who is unable to keep a job due to her substance use (among other problems).

Liz describes her relationship with her sister as strained. The last time they spoke it ended in a "shouting match as usual over Angela taking advantage of their mother, and her continued lack of responsibility with self-care." Liz states that she and her mother have a warm but contentious relationship. She claims that she talks with her mom every day and sends her money monthly

for medical and living expenses but is often criticized for being selfish for not doing more to help her sister. Liz says she understands her mother's concerns about Angela and sometimes feels guilty for being resentful of her mother's attitude; however, she doesn't see that it is her problem to take care of her sister any longer. She is also at a point in her life where she wants to meet someone, settle down, and hopefully start a family, but she dismisses the idea as being a "fantasy not reality." Liz describes herself as an over-achiever and the only "responsible one" in her family. She has a few close friends with whom she socializes occasionally, but she is adamantly private about her family dynamics and personal situation. Liz arrives at the social worker's office feeling depressed, withdrawn, and hopeless about her current and future situation. The following are excerpts from Liz and the social worker exploring her feelings about the people she identified as family members in her life.

Liz: [with certainty] I love my mother very much. I take care of her financially … and I don't mind. I actually feel like it's my responsibility since she's all alone … well, not really alone I suppose. My sister, I guess, lives with her, but that's a whole other story … she's such a loser. [At this point the client has become restless and is looking away and pulling nervously on her sweater.]

Social Worker: I can see you really care about your mom and her well-being. I'm also sensing that maybe you wish your sister were more responsible and involved?

Liz: Yeah … that's if she could stop using the drugs and alcohol. I get so angry when she is so neglectful of herself. It hurts my mother so much, but she just doesn't care.

Social Worker: Her lack of care upsets you the most?

Liz: Yes, care for herself and care for others. I almost don't know if I even care anymore about what she does to herself; it's just my mom that I care about. Well that's not totally true … I feel guilty saying that [pauses and starts to become tearful].

Social Worker: [leans forward and offers the client tissues and gently responds] This seems like a really sensitive place for you to be right now.

Here the social worker's use of empathetic skills encourages the client to explore more deeply her feelings of discord around family relations.

Several sessions later, Liz explores her own needs, including the desire for an intimate relationship.

Liz: [hesitantly] I've met this great guy (John) at work and we seem to have a lot in common. I really think I'm beginning to like him and I think he likes me, too.

Social Worker: Tell me more.

Liz: [enthusiastically describes some of her initial conversations with John and her attraction for him, but as she continues to offer more around her feelings she becomes sullen] Well, the truth is it probably won't work anyway. I just keep telling myself that a relationship with him is only a fantasy; it will never be a reality for me.

Social Worker: Hmmm. Let me see if I got this right. If you could, you would ideally have a relationship with John. It sounds like you have a special connection with him, and you think he feels it, too, yet you believe that this isn't a real possibility?

Liz: [tearfully] Right. I would like that, but I'm so involved with my family's problems. Why would anyone want to sign up for that? It makes me so sad I'll probably just end up alone.

Social Worker: [softly] That makes me sad, too. I wonder if you realize how others see you … how I see you. You have such a generous heart and really care deeply about relationships with people you love. These are wonderful qualities for a successful relationship. I wonder how it would feel for you to be that generous with yourself in meeting your own needs.

Again, we see the therapist is using empathetic skills, communicating her feelings of Liz's experience while remaining congruent. The social worker is able to acknowledge Liz's qualities of caring deeply for loved ones and helps her see how this does not have to mean she abandons herself or her own desires. This demonstration helps Liz accept that she is lovable, valuable, and capable of having a real relationship and not just the fantasy of one.

Liz returns for her final session after several weeks of continued therapy, where she has explored further her desire and need for a real and intimate relationship along with her feelings of responsibility to care for her mother.

Liz: [happily] John and I have been dating now for almost 8 months and it's going really well. I think he could be the one! [smiling] I feel so loved. He's a great guy. Also, I finally convinced my mom to move to California where she will be living with me until we find her a place of her own nearby. I'm so happy about this decision, especially since my sister just moved away and I was worried about [Mom] being alone. This move is really going to allow me to care for my mom in a more involved, sort of hands-on way.

Social Worker: It is such a pleasure to witness how you have grown through your process. It really gives me a great sense of hope. I can see how you have come to appreciate and accept yourself not only as a loving daughter who only wants the best for her mom, but also as a woman who is capable of having a successful relationship and meeting your own needs.

In reviewing this case, we can see that the stance of the therapist was to establish a trusting relationship with the client using the three key characteristics of a client-centered approach. Throughout this relationship the social worker shows *unconditional positive regard* for the client by being warm, accepting, and nonjudgmental of the client's presenting conflict; demonstrates *empathy* by being able to communicate an understanding through accurate reflection of the client's feelings; and remains *congruent* even with expressing her own experience of Liz as lovable. Through verbalizing unexpressed emotions, Liz succeeded in reconciling her feelings of despair over the role of caregiver versus her need to be loved and was able to fully realize her potential for happiness and achieve a greater and more fully integrated sense of self.

The Larger Perspective

Social workers can use client-centered practice in a multitude of settings, including family and couples counseling, group therapy, and the larger context of community work (see Table 32.3). In each of these settings, the therapist uses the three key skills to address each individual or family member and his or her unique needs and concerns, ultimately facilitating an ideal scene from the present scene. Also in this framework, the social worker can empower participants by teaching them how to use the client-centered principles with one another to foster the optimum development within their particular system (Barrett-Lennard, 1998; Rowe, 2011; Snyder, 2002).

BRIEF HISTORICAL MILIEU OF ROGERS AND CLIENT-CENTERED THEORY

In 1951, Carl Rogers published the text *Client-Centered Therapy,* which he frankly surmises is a book "about life, as life vividly reveals itself in the therapeutic process—with its blind power and its tremendous capacity for destruction, but with its overbalancing thrust toward growth, if the opportunity for growth is provided" (Rogers, 1951, p. 5). This last remark reflects his well-known nondirective approach and attitude toward the counseling process.

To attempt to address the complete history of who and what influenced Rogers would not be suitable for this chapter; however, suffice it to say that in his 1961 book, titled *On Becoming a Person* (which is highly recommended reading), he provides the most intimate detail of what he coins "some of the psychological highlights of my autobiography, particularly as it seems to relate to my professional life" (p. 5). Rogers was clearly influenced and inspired by a number of social-cultural-contextual factors and beliefs and has been equally reciprocal and influential on the profession of psychotherapy, including social work, over the past 50 years. For example, Hill (2007) acknowledges this influence by citing a recently published report in the *Psychotherapy Networker* (March/April 2007), which "reported that in both 1982 and 2007 Carl Rogers was nominated by a landslide as the most influential psychotherapist in the United States" (p. 260). Apparently, this was the result of a voluntary survey of 2,598 mental health professionals who claim to be "eclectic" in their

TABLE 32.3 Client-centered Principles within the Micro, Mezzo, and Macro Systems

Family (or Couple)	Group	Community
• Facilitation of children's needs to be fully functioning in the world and in the family • Recognition and encouragement of individuality • Facilitation of open and honest communication • Identification of family goals	• Facilitation of group members to take responsibility for themselves in whatever way is realistically possible • Clarification and solution of problems • Recognition of clients perceived and real self	• Facilitation of community self-perception • Recognition and encouragement of indigenous leadership • Facilitation of the communication among divergent groups • Identification of community goals

Source: Barrett-Lennard, 1988; Rowe, 2011; Snyder, 2002.

therapeutic orientations. Additionally, Goldfried (2007) reveals that Rogers's infamous 1957 article, "Necessary and Sufficient Conditions for Therapeutic Change" has been "cited in the literature over a thousand times in professional writings originating in 36 countries" (p. 249), positing that it is even "more popular now than it was 20 years ago" (p. 249).

International Advances in Client-centered Theory

Client-centered theory (more recently referred to as the person-centered approach) has continued to fluctuate in popularity in many countries throughout the world. In particular, Rogers's work and related literature have gained momentum in Australia, the United Kingdom, and Japan over the past several decades. According to Shimizu (2010), while the person-centered approach was developing in the UK, Japanese research on the topic had progressed substantially as well. One hindrance in Japan stemmed from translation barriers that prevented their literature from being published in English, and vice versa (p. 19). While professional and academic interest in Rogers's work within the United States began to trend downward, the impact on the international community picked up speed. The build-up surrounding client-centered theories in the UK also contributed to the reoccurring interest from Australia. Following Rogers's death, Australia experienced an influx of literature regarding person-centered theory. Many concepts based around client-centered theory and a humanistic approach have been utilized in a variety of training programs for counseling in Australia (Barrett-Lennard & Neville, 2010).It is also important to note that although client-centered theory is not formally used as much in the United States today, its founding principles have been incorporated into important aspects within many, if not most, counseling and interviewing practices.

CONCLUSION

If there were a code of conduct for client-centered therapy, it might read something like this. Client-centered therapy does not diagnosis, judge, assess, solve, or otherwise profess to know what is "wrong" with the individual. Client-centered therapy focuses on the uniqueness of the individual by respecting, nurturing, loving, and fostering the fragmented aspects of the client's notion of self while the therapist demonstrates and maintains an integrated sense of wholeness.

Client-centered therapy can be viewed as a significant precursor to other effective therapies that are intentionally directive, problem-solving, or behavior-changing in their focus. At a minimum, the client-centered approach is seen as significant in assisting the client to feel understood, loved, and fully integrated through establishing a safe, trusting, and reliable rapport with the therapist. Bohart and Byock (2005) recognize the uniqueness and value of the nondirective client-centered approach by asserting that "no matter how many new and effective interventions our field continues to generate, there may always be a place for providing people with a safe space where they can talk to another person who recognizes and tries to understand them primarily as persons and gives them room to think" (p. 209).

Although there are many positive attributes to traditional client-centered therapy, such as autonomy, respect, and dignity for the client, social workers need to remain culturally sensitive and aware of when this approach might not be appropriate or useful. For instance, some clients might come from a culture that highly respects the role of the authority figure and would be remarkably uncomfortable interacting in this nonauthoritative environment. Additionally, it is important to gain an understanding of the client's expectations of therapy and any desire on the part of the client for immediate and direct problem solving versus an approach that facilitates and encourages deeper exploration of the self. In these cases, the social worker/counselor is going to serve the individual better by using a different intervention or by referring to a different therapist. One other limitation to consider is that the client-centered approach assumes the client to have an intrinsic motivation to change, and there may be some instances where the individual "may lack motivation to change (e.g., substance abusers, batterers)" as cited in Goldfried (2007, p. 252), and this is obviously going to require the counselor to employ other means to assist the individual in developing this level of motivation.

The client-centered approach is often dismissed as being simple or ambivalent, when in fact it is quite the opposite—it requires the therapist to be highly skilled and evolved not only as a practitioner but also as a fully integrated, self-aware, nonjudgmental, and mature individual capable of understanding and using the core concepts of this modality effectively. Rowe (2011) defends this point well and recognizes the complexity of this approach when he offers that "it is only when (*social*) workers have had significant experience that they are in a position to rediscover person-centered theory, with its many layers of depth and meaning" (p. 73).

WEBSITES

Association for the Development of the Person-Centered Approach. http://www.adpca.org.
World Association for Person Centered & Experiential Psychotherapy & Counseling. http://pce-world.org
Classics in the History of Psychology, by Christopher D. Green. http://psychclassics.yorku.ca/Rogers/personality.htm.
Carl Rogers Biography. http://www.nrogers.com/carlrogersbio.html
Sofia University—Transpersonal Pioneers. http://www.sofia.edu/content/transpersonal-pioneers-carl-rogers
Person-Centered Counseling. http://www.person-centered-counseling.com/index.htm.
Personality Theories, by Dr. C. George Boeree. http://webspace.ship.edu/cgboer/rogers.html.

References

Barrett-Lennard, G. T. (1998).*Carl Rogers' helping system: Journey and substance*. Thousand Oaks, CA: Sage.
Barrett-Lennard, G. T., & Neville, B. (2010). The person-centered scene in Australia: Then and now. *Person-Centered and Experiential Psychotherapies, 9*(4), 265–273.
Bohart, A. C., & Byock, G. (2005). Experiencing Carl Rogers from the client's point of view: A vicarious ethnographic investigation. I. extraction and perception of meaning. *Humanistic Psychologist, 33*(3), 187–212.
Bozarth, J. D., & Brodley, B. T. (1991). Actualisation: A functional concept in client-centered therapy. *Handbook of Self-Actualisation, 6*(5), 45–60.
Brazier, D. J. (1996). The post-Rogerian therapy of Robert Carkhuff. Retrieved from http://www.amidatrust.com/article_carkhuff.html.
Carkhuff, R. R. (1971). *The development of human resources*. New York, NY: Holt, Rinehart & Winston.

Cepeda, L. M., & Davenport, D. S. (2006). Person-centered therapy and solution-focused brief therapy: an integration of present and future awareness. *Psychotherapy: Theory, Research and Practice, 43*(1), 1–12.
da Silva, R. B. (2005). Person-centered therapy with impoverished, maltreated, and neglected children and adolescents in Brazil. *Journal of Mental Health Counseling*. Retrieved from http://www.thefreelibrary.com.
Elliott, R., Bohart, A. C., Watson, J. C., & Greenberg, L. S. (2011). Empathy. *Psychotherapy, 48*(1), 43–49. doi:10.1037/a0022187
Farber, B. A., & Doolin, E. M. (2011). Positive regard. *Psychotherapy, 48*(1), 58–64. doi:10.1037/a0022141
Goldfried, M. R. (2007).What has psychotherapy inherited from Carl Rogers? *Psychotherapy: Theory, Research and Practice, 44*(3), 249–252.
Green, A. (2006). A person-centered approach to palliative care nursing. *Journal of Hospice and Palliative Nursing, 8*(5), 294–301.
Hepworth, D. H., Rooney, R. H., Dewberry Rooney, G., Strom-Gottfried, K., & Larsen, J. A. (Eds.). (2002). *Direct social work practice* (8th ed.). Pacific Grove, CA: Brooks/Cole.
Hill, C. E. (2007). My personal reactions to Rogers (1957): The facilitative but neither necessary nor sufficient conditions of therapeutic personality change. *Psychotherapy: Theory, Research and Practice, 44*(3), 260–264.
Horan, J. J. (1977). Dynamic approaches to decision-making counseling. Counseling for effective decision making. Retrieved from http://horan.asu.edu/cfedm/chapter7.php.
Kolden, G. G., Klein, M. H., Wang, C.-C., & Austin, S. B. (2011). Congruence/genuineness. *Psychotherapy, 48*(1), 65–71. doi:10.1037/a0022064
Mearns, D., Lambers, E., Thorne, B., & Warner, M. (2000). *Person-centered therapy today: New frontiers in theory and practice*. Thousand Oaks, CA: Sage.
Murphy, D. (2009). Client-centred therapy for severe childhood abuse: A case study. *Counselling & Psychotherapy Research, 9*(1), 3–10. doi:10.1080/14733140802655992
Rogers, C. (1951). Client-centered therapy. London: Constable.
Rogers, C. R. (1957). The necessary and sufficient conditions for therapeutic personality change. *Journal of Counseling Psychology, 21*, 95–103.
Rogers, C. R. (1961). *On becoming a person*. Cambridge, MA: Riverside Press.
Rowe, W. (2011). Client-centered theory: The enduring principles of a person-centered approach. In F. J. Turner (Ed.), *Social work treatment* (5th ed.). (pp. 58–76). New York, NY: Oxford University Press.
Shimizu, M. (2010). The development of the person-centered approach in Japan. *Person-Centered and Experiential Psychotherapies, 9*(1), 14–24.

Snodgrass, J. (2007). From Rogers to Clinebell: Exploring the history of pastoral psychology. *Pastoral Psychology, 55*(4), 513–525.

Snyder, M. (2002). Applications of Carl Rogers' theory and practice to couple and family therapy: A response to Harlene Anderson and David Bott. *Journal of Family Therapy, 24*(3), 317–325.

Watchel, P. L. (2007). Carl Rogers and the larger context of therapeutic thought. *Psychotherapy: Theory, Research and Practice, 44*(3), 279–284.

33   Cognitive-behavioral Therapy

M. Elizabeth Vonk & Theresa J. Early

Cognitive-behavioral therapy (CBT) is actually a number of related therapies that focus on cognition as the mediator of psychological distress and dysfunction. As the name implies, CBT draws on and combines the theoretical and practical approaches of behavior therapy, dating to the 1950s, and cognitive therapy, dating to the 1960s work of Beck and Ellis (Ledley, Marx, & Heimberg, 2010). Behavior therapy, as developed in the United States from the work of Skinner, redefined various mental illnesses as behavioral problems, hypothesized to have arisen from faulty learning. The greatest progress achieved in behavior therapy came in reducing anxiety disorders and childhood disorders, such as aggressive and oppositional behavior, and in improving the quality of life for people with mental disabilities. Whereas behavior therapy is based on various theories of learning, cognitive therapy is based on the assumption that emotional and behavioral disturbances do not arise directly in response to an experience but from the activation of maladaptive beliefs in response to an experience. Treatment from a cognitive perspective, then, is directed at identifying and changing maladaptive cognitions, attributions, and beliefs that, in turn, affect emotional, physiological, and behavioral responses (Ledley, Marx, & Heimberg, 2010).

Before moving ahead to outline the basic concepts and applications of CBT, we present a case study that will be used throughout this chapter to illustrate various aspects of CBT. John, a 38-year-old European American man, sought therapy at his wife's urging. He explained that he has worked for 15 years in the office supply business and recently received a significant promotion to a managerial position. Since receiving the promotion, he has become "extremely worried" that he will fail in his new role. His anxiety is interfering at work where he thinks that he "can't do anything right." He is particularly worried about his performance on various reports that he is responsible for completing. In spite of his efforts to get it right, minor corrections by his supervisor have been necessary on two occasions. He worries that he will lose his job and become unable to support his family if this continues.

At home, John's anxiety is interfering in his relationship with his wife, who has told him that she is irritated by his absence while he works long hours. She has also complained that when he is home, he is "off in his own world fretting." John wishes his wife would be less critical about his need to work longer hours and spend a lot of time thinking about work. He also worries, however, that he may be "a lousy husband and father"—just like he always feared. He describes a history of anxiety, particularly about work matters, with the current level of anxiety higher than at any previous time. Exploration of early history reveals that John was raised in an intact family in the rural Midwest. He describes his mother as

"loving, but always trying to please my father."
He describes his father as "mean-spirited and
never satisfied with anything, no matter how
much I tried." John would like to be less worried and feel better about his relationship with
his wife.

BASIC CONCEPTS OF
COGNITIVE-BEHAVIORAL THERAPY

Three elements of cognition are important
when assessing and treating various emotional
and behavioral disorders, the first being the
actual content of thoughts. We are most aware
of the content of automatic thoughts; these are
thoughts that come into our minds immediately
as life unfolds. More hidden from our awareness are thoughts that are referred to as rules or
assumptions; these are thoughts through which
we interpret our experiences. For example, John
may automatically think, "I can't handle this
situation" on receiving critical feedback at work.
If he were able to identify a rule related to the
situation, it might be "I must be perfect at everything I do."

Specifically, clients' perceptions of themselves,
the world, and the future are key variables among
emotional and behavioral disorders (Dienes et al.,
2011). Like John, those with anxiety may view
themselves as incapable, the world as threatening, and the future as holding great risk of
danger. Also considered important for cognitive
therapy are metacognitions, or thoughts about
cognitive processes. For example, John believes
that he has a "need to spend a lot of time thinking about work," potentially indicating a belief
that it is helpful to worry about the potential
threat of losing his job.

The second area of cognitive focus involves
core beliefs. Core beliefs are global, durable
beliefs about the self and the world that are
formed through early life experiences. They are
maintained through a process of attending to
information that supports the belief while disre-
garding information that is contrary to it (Beck,
2011). As a child, John experienced intense criticism from his father and seems to have formed a
core belief such as, "I am totally inadequate." As
an adult, he seems to ignore his history of career
successes and instead focuses on the few moments
in his day in which he has made a mistake or was
unsure of himself. At home, he focuses on his
wife's current irritation and discounts a 14-year

history of marriage that has been "mostly good
for both of us."

The third element of cognition involves maladaptive and ingrained styles of processing information, or cognitive distortions. There are many
types of distortions (Beck, 2011; Wright, Basco, &
Thase, 2006), a few of which follow, with examples that might be seen in John, who perceives
himself as inadequate.

* Catastrophizing: "If my boss criticizes a piece
  of my work, I will lose my job, be unable to
  support my family, my wife will leave me,
  and I will end up homeless."
* Emotional reasoning: "I feel horribly anxious
  about this report I just completed, so that
  proves I must have done a terrible job on it."
* Minimization: "I got the employee-of-
  the-year award purely from luck; it has
  nothing to do with how well I performed."

Many emotional and behavioral disorders
have been characterized by specific cognitive
content, schema, and information processing
styles (Dienes et al., 2011). As already mentioned, those with anxiety disorders perceive
themselves as inadequate and the world as
dangerous and threatening. Regarding information processing, those with anxiety pay
greater attention to anxiety-provoking stimuli
than they do to neutral stimuli. In panic disorder, the attentional bias is toward bodily sensation, with sufferers more acutely aware of
their heart rates than other people. People with
social phobia, on the other hand, attend to and
make negative evaluations of their own social
behavior.

Depression also has been specified in terms
of cognitive content and processing styles. Those
who are depressed have a negative view of the
self, the world, and the future (Beck, 2011). For
example, someone who is depressed may think,
"I never do anything right; people are never
there for me; and moreover, things will never
get better." Core beliefs are most often related
to perceptions of self-defect, and attention is
directed to experiences that focus on loss and
failure (Dienes et al., 2011).

Practitioners of CBT employ understanding
of the elements of cognition and their relation
to specific disorders, as described previously, in
a therapeutic relationship with well-specified
roles for both the practitioner and the client.
The hallmark of the therapeutic relationship in

CBT is collaboration, and roles of both the client and the practitioner are active. The role of the practitioner most closely resembles that of a supportive teacher or guide who holds expertise in cognitive and behavioral therapeutic methods, as well as possesses interpersonal skills (Ledley, Marx, & Heimberg, 2010). The practitioner helps the client learn to identify, examine, and alter maladaptive thoughts and beliefs and increase coping skills. Although the practitioner lends methodological expertise, the client is the source of information and expertise about his or her own idiosyncratic beliefs and assumptions. The client and practitioner thus work together to define goals, set agendas for sessions, and uncover and explore attitudes and beliefs that are significant to the client's well-being. Successful replacement of maladaptive cognitions depends on collaboration between client and practitioner, for the client can provide the most lasting and effective cognitive replacements.

APPLICATIONS OF COGNITIVE-BEHAVIORAL THERAPY

The most prominent models of CBT are Beck's cognitive therapy (Beck, 2011), Meichenbaum's cognitive behavior therapy (Meichenbaum, 1994), and Ellis's rational emotive behavior therapy (Ellis, 1996). Although there are differences among them related to, for instance, the therapist's level of direction and confrontation, all of the models share basic elements. All rely on identifying the content of cognitions, including assumptions, beliefs, expectations, self-talk, or attributions. Through various techniques, the cognitions are then examined to determine their current effects on the client's emotions and behavior. Some models also include exploration of the development of the cognitions to promote self-understanding. This is followed with use of techniques that encourage the client to adopt alternative and more adaptive cognitions. The replacement cognitions, in turn, produce positive affective and behavioral changes. Other similarities of the models include the use of behavioral techniques, the time-limited nature of the interventions, and the educative component of treatment.

It is useful to consider the application of CBT in steps. At each step, a great number of specific techniques are available. Only a few are reviewed here due to space limitations.

Assessment

As in many clinical social work assessment processes, cognitive-behavioral assessments may result in a case formulation that includes psychiatric diagnosis; definition of the client's problem in terms of duration, frequency, intensity, and situational circumstances; description of client's strengths; and treatment plan. Cognitive analysis of a client's problem, however, is unique to cognitive-behavioral assessments. Assessment and case formulation includes many of the above-mentioned items, plus a prioritized problem list and working hypothesis that provide a cognitive analysis of the problems (Ledley, Marx, & Heimberg, 2010). Problems are described very briefly and are accompanied by the client's related thoughts, emotions, and behaviors. The working hypothesis, unique to each client, proposes specific thoughts and underlying beliefs that have been precipitated by the client's current experiences. Formulations may also include an examination of the origin of the maladaptive cognitions and information processing style in the client's early life. The working hypothesis is then directly related to treatment planning. As an example, we have created a cognitive conceptualization for John, shown in Figure 33.1.

Teaching the Client the ABC Model

Concurrent with assessment, one of the first tasks of the cognitive-behavioral therapist is to educate the client about the relationship of thoughts, emotions, and behaviors. Leahy (2003) suggests contrasting the client's usual way of describing the relationship of thoughts, emotions, and behaviors with the alternative ABC model. For most people, the usual way to think about it is that an activating event (A) causes an emotional or behavioral consequence (C). For example, John states that because he received criticism on his report (A), he is feeling anxious (C). The ABC model proposes that in actuality, a thought or image representing a belief or attitude (B) intervenes between A and C. Using the same example, following the criticism (A), John may think that he will lose his job (B), resulting in anxiety (C). Clients need to become very familiar with the model through presentation of and practice with personal illustrations.

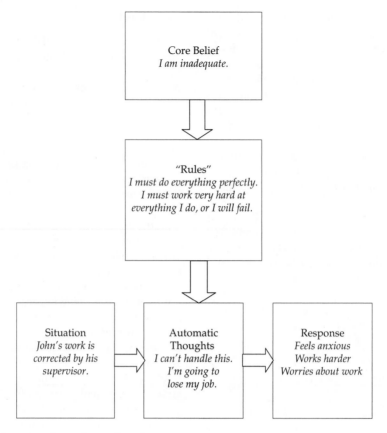

Figure 33.1 Cognitive formulation for John.

Teaching the Client to Identify Cognitions

Once the client understands the ABC model, the therapist helps him or her learn to identify thoughts and beliefs. Clients may find that many types of cognitions are relevant for analysis, including those related to expectations, self-efficacy, self-concept, attention, selective memory, attribution, evaluations, self-instruction, hidden directives, and explanatory style (McMullin, 2000). A great variety of useful techniques for the purpose of identifying cognitions are described by McMullin (2000); DeRubeis, Tang, Webb, and Beck (2010); and Leahy (2003). The daily thought record is a written method involving a form made up of columns within which clients record activating events (column A), corresponding emotional reactions (column C), and immediate thoughts related to the event (column B). In the case example, John would be taught to identify and record on the form an anxiety-provoking situation from the previous week, such as hearing from his boss that

a report needed correction. Next, he would be asked to identify his feelings when the situation occurred. Then he would be prompted to remember what went through his mind at the moment his boss spoke with him. In this instance, he would record his thought, "I can't handle this" in between the situation and the anxious feelings. Another method, the downward arrow technique, is a verbal way to discover the underlying meaning of conscious thoughts through the use of questions such as, "What would it mean to you if the [thought] were true?" Through the use of the downward arrow technique, the client may discover a core belief. John might provide an answer such as, "It would mean I'm incapable." People are generally unaware of their core beliefs that are, nonetheless, very fundamental to the way they feel and behave.

Teaching the Client to Examine and Replace the Maladaptive Cognitions

After identifying thoughts and beliefs, the client is ready to begin examining evidence for and against the cognitions. In addition, the client is encouraged to replace maladaptive cognitions with more realistic or positive ones. Replacement requires frequent repetition and rehearsal of the new cognitions. Again, McMullin (2000), DeRubeis et al. (2010), and Leahy (2003) provide a wealth of information about specific techniques, a few of which are briefly described here.

Many of the techniques are verbal, relying on shifts in language to modify cognitions. In one technique, the client is taught to identify maladaptive thoughts as one of a list of cognitive distortions. Cognitive distortions represent maladaptive thinking styles that commonly occur during highly aroused affective states, making logical thinking difficult. Identification of the use of a distortion allows for the possibility of substituting more rational thinking. Thought stopping, a behavioral means to draw attention to the need for substitution, might involve snapping an elastic band. Another technique involves the use of a variety of questions that provide opportunities to evaluate the truth, logic, or function of beliefs (Beck, 2011; Leahy, 2003). Such questions include:

- What is the evidence for and against the belief?
- What are alternative interpretations of the event or situation?
- What are the pros and cons of keeping this belief?

Imagery and visualization are also used to promote cognitive change. For example, clients may be encouraged to visualize coping effectively in difficult situations or visualize an idealized future to provide insight into current goals. McMullin (2000) suggests that imagery techniques are particularly useful to encourage perceptual shifts, whereas verbal techniques help facilitate change in more specific thoughts and beliefs. A combination of the two types of techniques is often useful.

Other Techniques

Cognitive-behavioral therapists use a wide variety of behavioral techniques, according to the needs of the client. These include relaxation training, assertion training, problem solving, activity scheduling, and desensitization

(Beck, 2011; Wright, Basco, & Thase, 2006). More recently, mindfulness has been incorporated into cognitive-behavioral therapies, such as mindfulness-based stress reduction (Stahl, Goldstein, Kabat-Zinn, & Santorelli, 2010); dialectical behavior therapy (Koerner & Linehan, 2012); and acceptance and commitment therapy (Hayes, Strosahl, & Wilson, 2012). Most likely, both relaxation and mindfulness training would be useful for John.

- Relaxation training involves teaching the client to relax muscles systematically and to slow breathing. The client learns to discriminate between tension and relaxation. Through practice, the relaxation response can be easily activated.
- Assertion training provides clients with interpersonal skills that allow for appropriate self-expression. Often these skills are taught and practiced in small groups.
- Problem solving involves teaching the client to solve personal problems through a process of specifying the problem and then devising, selecting, implementing, and evaluating a solution.
- Activity scheduling allows clients to plan for activities that will provide pleasure, socialization, or another identified need during the time between contacts with the practitioner.
- Desensitization provides clients with graduated exposure to anxiety-provoking objects or situations while engaged in behaviors that compete with anxiety, such as relaxation. The exposure may be imaginary or real.
- Mindfulness training allows clients to purposefully attend to the experience of the present moment without judging or fighting against what is occurring. Such awareness is thought to reduce emotional reactivity and suffering.

In addition, cognitive-behavioral therapists often assign homework to their clients for the purpose of extending learning beyond the therapy session. Homework assignments vary according to the idiosyncratic needs of the client and generally are designed collaboratively. One common assignment is the use of a form such as the daily thought record.

STRENGTHS OF COGNITIVE-BEHAVIORAL THERAPY

Various features of CBT fit well with social work. The collaborative nature of the therapeutic relationship is consistent with the social work value of self-determination. Additionally, the client's active involvement in the change process is consistent with an empowerment approach. CBT's use within an integrative framework that allows for specification of techniques to match individuals' needs is consistent with the ideal of individualizing treatment. More recently, those who have proposed integrative therapy models have examined the role of the client's idiosyncratic meaning in CBT, noting a close kinship with constructive models of therapy (Dienes et al., 2011).

Many characteristics of CBT lend themselves to the demands of current practice settings. The structure of CBT and the extensive description of its methods in many sources make it an accessible therapy for both novice and experienced practitioners. Because the methods of therapy require initial and ongoing recording of thoughts and behaviors, mechanisms for evaluation are built in, lending support to the use of CBT by clinicians with interest in or need to document the outcomes of their work with clients. Additionally, CBT targets specific problems, thus lending itself to a short-term approach, which is consistent with both the desires of many clients and their third-party payers. Another feature of CBT that is attractive to managed care entities is the well-supported efficacy of the approach, particularly for the treatment of depression and anxiety (Wright, Basco, & Thase, 2006).

Mounting evidence attests to the versatility of CBT. Specific cognitive-behavioral treatments have been designed for a broad variety of disorders, including some that have been considered complex or difficult to treat, such as borderline personality disorder. Depression, generalized anxiety disorder, posttraumatic stress disorder, substance misuse, eating disorders, grief and bereavement, and personality disorders are among those conditions for which CBT interventions have been developed (Wright, Basco, & Thase, 2006). (Please refer to Appendix A of Ledley, Marx, & Heimberg, 2010, pp. 259–273 for a detailed list of CBT resources related to specific psychological disorders, other problems that may be a focus of clinical attention, and populations.)

Future

As we look toward the future, CBT promises to remain vital to the treatment of emotional and behavioral disorders. In fact, it appears that the use of CBT will continue to expand as more is learned about specifying treatments and integrating additional techniques for particular problem areas and populations. At the same time, more treatment providers will apply wide-ranging techniques from CBT into integrative treatment models that include newer interventions such as mindfulness training. Moreover, the versatility of this treatment will enable its continued use in the changing environment of treatment settings. Finally, the fact that CBT has been used successfully across a variety of cultural groups from China to Sweden (Dienes et al., 2011) shows that it will be able to serve the rapidly changing needs of the increasingly diverse population of people who are served by social workers.

WEBSITES

Acceptance and Commitment Therapy. http:// contextualscience.org/act.

American Institute for Cognitive Therapy. http://www.cognitivetherapynyc.com.

Beck Institute for Cognitive Therapy and Research. http://beckinstitute.org.

Center for Mindfulness. http://www .umassmed.edu/cfm/index.aspx.

The Linehan Institute. http://marieinstitute .org/.

National Association of Cognitive Behavioral Therapists. http://www.nacbt.org.

References

Beck, J. S. (2011). *Cognitive therapy: basics and beyond* (2nd ed.). New York, NY: Guilford.

DeRubeis, R. J., Tang, T. Z., Webb, C. A., & Beck, A. T. (2010). Cognitive therapy. In K. S. Dobson (Ed.), *Handbook of cognitive-behavioral therapies* (3rd ed.) (pp. 277–316). New York, NY: Guilford.

Dienes, K. A., Torres-Harding, S., Reinecke, M. A., Freeman, A., & Sauer, A. (2011). Cognitive therapy. In S. B. Messer & A. S. Gurman (Eds.), *Essential psychotherapies* (3rd ed.) (pp. 143–183). New York, NY: Guilford.

Ellis, A. (1996). *Better, deeper, and more enduring brief therapy: The rational emotive behavior therapy approach.* New York, NY: Brunner/Mazel.

Hayes, S. C., Strosahl, K. D., & Wilson, K. G. (2012). *Acceptance and commitment therapy: The process and practice of mindful change* (2nd ed.). New York, NY: Guilford.

Koerner, K., & Linehan, M. (2012). *Doing dialectical behavior therapy: A practical guide*. New York, NY: Guilford.

Leahy, R. L. (2003). *Cognitive therapy techniques: A practitioner's guide*. New York, NY: Guilford.

Ledley, D. R., Marx, B. P., & Heimberg, R. G. (2010). *Making cognitive-behavioral therapy work* (2nd ed.). New York, NY: Guilford.

McMullin, R. E. (2000). *The new handbook of cognitive therapy techniques*. New York, NY: Norton.

Meichenbaum, D. (1994). *A clinical handbook/practical therapist manual: For assessing and treating adults with post-traumatic stress disorder*. Waterloo, Ontario: Institute Press.

Stahl, B., Goldstein, E., Kabat-Zinn, J., & Santorelli, S. (2010). *A mindfulness-based stress reduction workbook*. Oakland, CA: New Harbinger Press.

Wright, J. H., Basco, M. R., Thase, M. E. (2006). *Learning cognitive-behavioral therapy*. Arlington, VA: American Psychiatric Publishing, Inc.

34   Psychosocial Therapy

Francis J. Turner

The term *psychosocial therapy* and its identification with a specific form of therapy has held and continues to hold a long-standing illustrious place in the history of social work.

It was initially used in a generic sense to stress that an identifying feature of social work therapy consisted of a focus on the interface of person and environment.

Later, as the theoretical bases of direct practice developed with the early controversy between the Functional and Diagnostic schools very much in the foreground, the term *psychosocial* became identified with the "diagnostic school." As other theories took their place in the profession's cadre of thought systems, and as we became more comfortable with the acceptability and even importance of a diversity of theories, the psychosocial school was identified as a particular theory in its own right.

Still later, as a more holistic view of treatment attained prominence in the profession, it was recognized that all therapeutic theories, whatever their origin, were based on a person-in-situation perspective when drawn on in social work practice. To reflect this, *psychosocial* (once again) became a generic term describing the overall orientation of the clinical thrust of the profession.

More recently, this general use of the term has spread well beyond the borders of social work, and most human service professionals have moved to a broader based view of clients, their problems, their situations, and their therapeutic activities. In this way, *psychosocial* is widely used in a generic multidisciplinary, multi-theoretical manner.

Indeed, in recent years, as a part of the poly-disciplinary use of the term, there has been a growing usage, first in our profession and now in others, to add the prefix *bio-* to psychosocial. Thus, bio-psychosocial has become for many the basis on which all help is provided. Adding this further component serves to remind all social work practitioners that just as it is not possible to separate persons from their social systems, to understand the full gestalt of a client we also need to attend to our clients' physical condition and overall health.

However, even with this variation in usage and understanding, there is still extant in social work thinking a specific body of concepts, premises, values, and patterns of intervention that together constitute a unique theory of practice properly titled Psychosocial Therapy.

Historically, this theory represents the most traditional of social work theories locating its basic origins in the work of Mary Richmond and the stream of therapeutic thought and practice that emerged from her early book, *Social Diagnosis*, and the later work, *What Is Social Casework?* These two works are mentioned specifically because this theory has suffered in the sociopolitical history of the profession owing to its strong identification with tradition and the two concepts of diagnosis and casework. That is, there is a sense that, because of its origins, it is, therefore, out of date and out of fashion as a distinct theory. However these early writers have provided a foundation for growth, development, and change.

The tradition that has served as the basis of psychosocial therapy's origins with its focus principally on treatment of individuals and families and later groups was the component of social work most closely identified with psychoanalytic thinking and other dynamic theories emerging from it, such as ego psychology. However, even with psychosocial therapy's interest in these psychodynamic theories, it was far from the total identification some would hold it to be. Rather, this approach drew its unique identity from a strong identification with the implications of the "person in situation" concept while adopting and adapting from psychodynamic thinking those concepts and therapeutic strategies that best suited and fitted social work. This approach developed in its own way while being open to thinking from other sources.

The primary conceptual identification of the psychosocial school was with a method rather than a theory. The method, of course, was casework, a term long a part of the social work lexicon. Casework as it developed as an identifying term for the profession's clinical stream has become a very broad-based methodological concept, far wider than its original therapeutic orientation.

The principal flag bearer of this tradition has been Florence Hollis, whose essential text is *Social Casework: A Psychosocial Therapy* (1963). This work built strongly on the work of earlier casework writers, especially Gordon Hamilton (1951).

This seminal work originally written by Hollis, then later coauthored by Mary Woods and solely by Woods after Hollis's death, has gone through five editions, the latest one in 1999. All editions have carried the same title as the original. With the death of Mary Woods (2007) it will interesting to see whether psychosocial therapy continues in the profession with a unique identification or whether it will be viewed more as an orientation or viewpoint for the whole profession rather than as a distinct theory.

Being identified with casework, this orientation to practice viewed itself, and was viewed by others, as focusing primarily on work with individuals and secondarily with families. However, as the lines between methods began to open and blur, authors in this tradition began to speak of work with couples, groups, and social systems. Additionally, authors such as Northen (1982) and Turner (1978, 1995, 2005), persons very much in the psychosocial tradition, began to urge a broader base to the system that included work with groups and larger systems.

It would be unfair to suggest that Hollis and Woods limited their perception of practice to individuals, couples, and families. These two leaders of the theory stressed the importance of all methods, but, having been shaped by the traditions of casework as being more individually client centered, the bulk of their writings and research focused on what Hollis called direct work. In addition, because of its close relation to the casework tradition, the psychosocial school of thought is sometimes viewed as being a bit out of fashion as a free-standing theory yet very much in fashion as an important identifying concept for the profession.

A further concept that has created difficulty for the reputation of psychosocial theory among other theories has been its earlier identification with, and continued commitment to, diagnosis as an highly important component of treatment. Although once an essential component of social work practice, for a variety of reasons diagnosis has become an unpopular term in the practice and sociology of the profession for many clinicians.

Diagnosis, for those opposing it, is viewed as placing an overemphasis on pathology; the word *assessment* is preferred. Nevertheless, in practice, the term *diagnosis* does get used but in a manner that highly identifies it with the various *DSM* formulations. It is frequently used in this specific way. This, rather than viewing it as an essential component of treatment comprising a much richer and health-oriented perspective on the series of judgments or conclusions that a social work practitioner needs to reach based on the range of assessments made about the client and his or her situation, strengths and limitations, and resources.

Nevertheless, even with its collection of historical and sociocultural baggage acquired over the decades, psychosocial therapy is still an important theory in contemporary social work practice and the designated theoretical base for many North American practitioners.

A THEORETICAL OVERVIEW

Psychosocial therapy is built on the premise that ethical and effective treatment is an integrated process of assessment, diagnosis, treatment, and evaluation. These processes are not sequential in nature but are ongoing from the first instant with the client until the final closing. A component of these processes includes a formal commitment to a process of evaluation to expand our body of knowledge of evidence-based practice.

The interventive process is multifaceted and built on a paradigm that seeks to establish:

- Who is this client, historically and in the present?
- What are the current strengths and limitations?
- What does this client want?
- What does this client need?
- What can I or someone else do to assist this client in achieving the identified goals?
- What are the existing resources?

The interventive process also draws on the total range of theory and technique available from the profession or from others.

In working with clients or significant persons in their lives, there are six clusters of technique available to the therapist:

1. To utilize specific components of the relationships
2. To do specific things with the client
3. To have the client(s) do specific things within the interview
4. To have the client(s) do specific things outside of the interview
5. To do something with the client(s) outside of the interview
6. To do something for the client(s) outside of the interview

Case Summary for Psychosocial Theory

Mr. J. is a 19-year-old Latino man born in Mexico. He moved to the United States with his family when he was 10 years old. His father died in an industrial accident when he was 12. Mr. J. appears to be in good physical health and of at least normal intelligence with no evident mental health problems. He has completed high school and is currently working in the kitchen of a fast-food restaurant and living with his mother and two sisters. The family is minimally comfortable financially. He initially presents in a shy, mildly withdrawn manner and once comfortable in a relationship exhibits a quiet pleasant engaging mien.

He was referred to the family agency by his parish priest, to whom he had turned wanting help to better himself socially and economically, but he was uncertain as to how to go about this.

His male social worker used the first three interviews to help Mr. J. develop an open, trusting relationship based on his diagnosis of an early developing mildly strong positive transference, while keeping the content focused on his identified wish to "move ahead." From this basis, the social worker made use of several rapid assessment instruments that focused on identifying areas of interest and skills. From these and material shared in the interviews, it was clear that his identified area of interest was in the management side of the restaurant business, but he was uncertain how to go about it except to talk about looking for a better job.

From here, the social worker engaged Mr. J. in some simulated job interviews, at which he did reasonably well with coaching. Next, a contract was established with him that he was to formally apply for two relevant advertised positions before the next interview.

These contacts, although not leading to a job offer, helped Mr. J. clarify that a more strategic route to achieve his goals would require further education, the nature and extent of which was unclear. To assist in this and with the client's agreement, the worker arranged for an interview at the career counseling department of a local community college, and at the client's request the social worker agreed to attend with him.

This interview was very useful; however, it appeared that the client did not have the requisite courses in his high school curriculum and that some make-up work would be required.

With the client's permission, the social worker pursued this matter further and established that the client, being fluently bilingual, could substitute for the missing academic material. Mr. J. was accepted into the next class of the college's hotel management program.

Over the next three months, the case was kept open on an on-demand basis with a focus on supporting Mr. J. in his early adjustment to the program. On a 6-month routine follow-up, it was noted that the client was doing very well in the program and becoming a much more confident and outgoing person.

BASIC CONCEPTS

General

From its earliest days, psychosocial therapy has been an open searching system strongly committed to the integration of new ideas. Although its roots are originally in a psychodynamic tradition, it has integrated concepts from most other theories currently driving social work practice. Principal among these are systems theory, existential theory, crisis theory, learning theory, ego psychology, and task and problem-solving theories. This interest in other theories stems partially from an understanding of the role of values in the human condition and the awareness that various theories are built on differing value orientations and will fit some clients better than others.

Psychosocial practitioners view practice theories as tools that are differentially used to respond to where and who the client is. Thus, just as this therapy moved from a position that viewed each social worker as having competence in a single modality such as casework or group work, it now deems it essential that practitioners not only be competent in multiple methods but also multi-theoretical in their orientations. Indeed, this openness to new ideas from whatever source has been one of the areas of criticism of this theory, as well as a factor that makes it difficult for some to put firm parameters around it.

Specific

Commitment to Knowledge Building. Psychosocial therapy is very much an open, changing, dynamic theory that appreciates the expanding base of knowledge reflecting the complexities of clients' lives and the myriad influences that affect them. Thus, there is the responsibility to continually research and evaluate activities and incorporate new knowledge from whatever its source.

Positive Perception of the Human Potential. Within this system, there is a strong belief in the ability of a person to achieve high levels of satisfying functioning even with the most damaging of early histories. The therapeutic task is to build on a person's strengths and the resources of systems to foster positive growth in individuals and families.

Cognitive and Rational. Even though this system is rooted in a psychodynamic tradition, it has welcomed and adopted the insights from other therapies.

Some of the early research, as discussed by Woods, indicated that much of the verbal content of interviews consisted in reflection by the client of material that surfaced in the interviews. All of us use reflective abilities to deal with daily living. Sometimes we do this effectively, whereas at other times this leads to further problems. The opportunity to reflect with a helping understanding person, however, can lead to more effective functioning.

Power of the Helping Relationship. Much of the early writing in social work clinical practice focused on the importance and power of the helping relationship and its various characteristics. This type of relationship can and often does contain elements of significant relationships from the client's past that can affect in both positive and negative ways important relationships in the present. Thus, understanding of the reality of transference factors in relationships is still considered an important factor to be kept in mind in understanding the client, although it is much less stressed than in earlier days of this therapy.

Recognition of the Unconscious. In psychosocial therapy, the unconscious is still viewed as an important component of personality that influences but does not determine facets of present functioning. Although in day-to-day practice the major part of our work is oriented to the client's current reality, this powerful attribute of one's own personality cannot be ignored.

Importance of History. This theory recognizes that both social workers and clients bring to the present something of their respective histories. Thus, to fully understand a person we must assess to what extent their present functioning and future aspirations are influenced by their history. This does not mean that, as in earlier days, before we begin our work with a client we take a long and detailed history. It does mean, however, that we remain on the alert for significant components of earlier history, and when such components appear to be important, we pursue them or build on them as it appears necessary. This endeavor depends on diagnostic acumen, as we seek to assess all components of a client's reality and the significance of each for the present reality with which we are dealing.

Understanding of Pathology. Even though this system is optimistic and strength-oriented, it understands that pathology in all its manifestations and intensities is a reality. Thus, it is critical that when it is present we understand its nature and influence on clients, their families, and significant others. The important aspect of our responsibility to assess pathology is to view it as a continuum. It is rarely a case of yes or no but rather a question of whether there is any degree of pathology existing that may be of significance to the presenting situation. This requires, of course, a knowledge and understanding of pathology and its many forms and the many factors that go into its development, maintenance, control, and treatment.

Importance of Social Work Diagnosis. Diagnosis is a broad concept with meaning, content, and focus varying from one profession to another. It differs from assessment, which is also a part of the therapeutic process. In social work, diagnosis is much more complex than seeking to assign a mental health label. Rather, it is a multifaceted dynamic process in which the practitioner sets out in a formal manner the judgments made about clients and their situations—judgments that serve as the basis for actions to be taken in the conduct of a case, actions for which the social worker takes responsibility.

Focus on Everyday Living. Stemming from a positive view of human nature and ability to find growth-enhancing ways to address the challenges of day-to-day living, psychosocial therapy understands that many clients can benefit greatly from having these challenges addressed in a therapeutic milieu. For some, dealing with these mundane realities in clients' lives is not seen as the real essence of therapy. However, learning to deal with such life factors often brings considerable relief to clients and leads them to find ways to address other life situations.

The Importance of "Indirect Treatment." The term *indirect treatment* seeks to describe the social worker's interactions with various persons and systems in a client's life. Such interactions are intended to bring about changes that will help the client achieve his or her objective. Unfortunately, indirect treatment is often viewed as less important or less clinical than direct work with clients. Nonetheless, skill in this area can be of great assistance to clients and can help bring about important changes in their lives that would not be achieved in direct work.

Strategic Use of Time. Time is one of the important resources used in a psychosocial approach to therapy. Rather than seeing time from an administrative perspective only, time can be used therapeutically. Work with a client can be as short as a few minutes to as long as several years of weekly contact. Short-term treatment is not by definition better than long-term, nor is the reverse true. The time spent is what the client needs from our diagnostic perspective, not from some external imposition.

Practitioner Self-awareness. Not only are clients influenced by their unconscious, so, too, are therapists. Hence, it is important to ensure that responses to clients are as free as possible from distortion or misunderstanding stemming from our own histories. This, of course, is one of the important functions of our professional education.

Supervision and Consultation. Although we have moved far beyond the days when training was close to being a therapeutic experience for the student, there is still a place in our practice for a formal connection with a colleague to ensure objectivity in interactions with clients. Even though many practitioners would not see themselves as psychosocially oriented, today's pattern of student practicum and individual supervision stems from the psychosocial theorists' long-standing emphasis on the need for self-awareness as a critical component of ethical practice and for assistance in achieving it in particular situations.

Minimization of Technique. It is interesting to note that as committed as psychosocial theory is to evaluating our interventions, as with the rest of the profession to date, there has been little interest in discussing technique. That is, any ongoing effort to assess not only what is observed in treatment but how and why observed change has taken place. That is, more attention to what we have actually accomplished in our time with the client or significant others in their lives. This phenomenal also exists regarding other applications to treatment. Yet, in a profession committed to evaluating the correlations between what we do with, to, and for clients and the outcome emanating from these activities, this lacuna in evaluative activities will need to assume greater importance in the days ahead.

CONCLUSION

Psychosocial therapy is an approach to social work practice with a long tradition in the profession. It builds on a broad understanding of individuals, dyads, families, groups, systems, and other societal factors and the resources of each. Its overall goal is to assist people in achieving the highest level of psychosocial functioning through an understanding of their past, present, and future potential.

The theory reflects social work's century-old commitment. Throughout its history, social work has been committed to tested knowledge and innovations. Psychosocial therapy will continue to stay relevant and stand as the conceptual and operational basis of much of contemporary social work practice.

WEBSITES

Erik Erikson and psychosocial development. http://www.essortment.com/ psychosocialdev_rijk.htm.

GMS Psycho-Social-Medicine. http://www .egms.de/en/journals/psm/index.shtml.
International Journal of Psychosocial Rehabilitation. http://www.psychosocial .com.
Psychosocial Treatments. http://www.nami .org/Template.cfm?Section=About_ Treatments_and_Supports&Template=/ ContentManagement/ContentDisplay .cfm&ContentID=10510

References

Hamilton, G. (1951). *Theory and practice of social casework* (Rev. ed.). New York, NY: Columbia University Press.
Hollis. F. (1963). *Social casework: A psychosocial therapy* (2nd ed.). New York, NY: Random House.
Northen, H. (1982). *Clinical social work.* New York, NY: Columbia University Press.
Turner, F. J. (1978). *Psychosocial therapy.* New York, NY: Free Press.
Turner, F. J. (1995). *Differential diagnosis and treatment in social work* (4th ed.). New York, NY: Free Press.
Turner, F. J. (2005). *Social work diagnosis in contemporary practice.* New York, NY: Oxford University Press.
Woods, M. (1999). *Casework: A psychosocial therapy* (5th ed.). New York, NY: McGraw-Hill.

35   Solution-focused Therapy

Peter De Jong

The late Steve de Shazer, one of the inventors of Solution-focused Therapy (SFT), informally referred to it as a way to carry on a useful conversation with clients. The purpose of the conversation is to co-construct solutions. Practitioners ask the questions that so clearly define the approach; clients respond out of their frames of reference. The questions are not-knowing because they put clients into the position of being experts about

their own lives. Therapeutic conversations focus on what clients want to be different and how to make those things happen.

HISTORY AND DEVELOPMENT

Although rooted, in some respects, in the "uncommon" therapy of Milton Erickson and the strategic family therapy of John Weakland and his associates at the Mental Research Institute (Miller, 1997), SFT was largely developed inductively through careful observation of therapy sessions using the one-way mirror at the Brief Family Therapy Center (BFTC) in Milwaukee, Wisconsin.

In this natural inquiry, de Shazer and his colleagues attempted to set aside past assumptions about client change and pay attention to which clients seemed to be making progress and what the practitioner might be doing that was useful (de Shazer et al., 1986). During this process they made several discoveries about therapy and invented related techniques, which they continued to refine through ongoing use and observation. It soon became clear that clients who made progress had clearer visions of what they wanted to be different (goals) and could identify times in their lives when problems were not occurring or were less serious (exceptions). Consequently, more time in therapy sessions, more questioning techniques, and new assumptions about therapy and client change developed around the importance of goal formulation and exception finding.

ASSUMPTIONS

- Clients are competent to co-construct goals and strategies.
- Clients are the experts about their own lives and the meanings of their experiences. Practitioners should ask about client perceptions and accept them.
- There is not necessarily a connection between problem and solution.
- Clients must *do* something differently for change to occur.
- "Only a small change is needed." Once a small step is taken, change often snowballs beyond client and practitioner expectations.
- "If it ain't broke, don't fix it." Practitioner agendas for clients invite client resistance.
- "If it works, don't fix it." When clients can describe how exceptions occur and their contributions to them, suggest they do more of the same.
- "If it doesn't work, do something differently." Do not suggest clients do what they say is not useful. (Quoted assumptions from de Shazer, 1985; 1988).

USEFUL QUESTIONS

Goal-formulation Questions. After the client briefly describes a problem, practitioners begin the co-construction of goals by asking the following:

- When your problem becomes less of one, what will be different?
- What would have to be different by the end of our session for you to say that our time together was useful and not a waste of time?

The miracle question is the best known of SFT's goal-formulation questions. It reads:

Suppose while you are sleeping tonight a miracle happens. The miracle is that the problem that has brought you here today is solved—just like that! Only you don't know it because you're sleeping. So when you wake up tomorrow morning, what is the first thing you'll notice that will tell you: Wow! Things are really different, a miracle must have happened!

The miracle question is an opener for a series of follow-up questions formulated around the client's beginning answer to what will be different when the miracle happens. These follow-ups use who, what, when, and where questions to get details. ("Why" questions are not asked because they have not proven useful in promoting client change.) For example, to the depressed client who starts out by saying the first difference he will notice is "feeling better," the practitioner continues by asking: So, when you are feeling better, who will be the first to notice? When might (that person) notice? What will she notice? What else? What will she do when she notices you doing that? What will you do then? What will you notice that's different? And so forth.

Exception-finding Questions. Exceptions amount to client successes. Identifying them is the best route to discovering and amplifying client strengths and resources. Exceptions that are related to what clients want are the most useful for building solutions. Examples of exception-finding questions include:

- Are there times when you are even a little bit "less discouraged" (client's words)?
- Are parts of the miracle you described to me happening already?

- If your friend were here and I were to ask him about whether there are times when you are "less discouraged," what would your friend say?

Once the client identifies an exception, the interviewer follows up with several who, what, when, and where questions for details.

Scaling Questions. Scaling is a useful way to help clients express complex, intuitive observations about their past experiences and future possibilities in concrete terms. Clients are asked to scale an observation or possibility from 0 through 10 with the ends of the scale defined by the practitioner:

- On a scale from 0 through 10, where zero means there is no chance of this miracle happening and 10 means every chance, what are the chances of your miracle actually happening?
- If 0 equals where things were regarding your problems when you made the appointment to see me, and 10 equals the problem is solved, where are things today?
- Where 0 equals "no confidence at all" and 10 means "every confidence in the world," how confident are you that you will find a solution to this problem?

Once the client gives a number, the practitioner asks for details about the meaning of that number as well as what will be different when things move up one and more numbers on the scale.

Coping Questions. These are a form of exception question and used when clients seem overwhelmed and discouraged beyond the point of trying. Examples include:

- What are you doing to cope—even a little bit—with this situation?
- I'm amazed! With all that has happened to you, I don't know how you make it. How do you do it? How do you get from one minute to the next?
- Ah, so you do it by reminding yourself that "my children need me." You must love your children very much! So, how is reminding yourself that your children need you helpful to you?
- Could things be worse? How come they are not?

- Who has been most helpful to you in these struggles? What is it they do that you find helpful?

"What's Better?" Questions. Many other approaches begin second and subsequent sessions of therapy with a review of assigned suggestions or the client's estimate of progress. In SFT, practitioners simply ask another form of an exception-finding question, namely, "What's better?" This procedure is tied to the recognition that solutions are built from exceptions, and to observations at BFTC that asking this question most readily elicits mention of successes that occurred since the last session. When given time to think and answer, most clients can identify something better, which the practitioner then invites the client to amplify through additional questions.

SOLUTION-FOCUSED CO-CONSTRUCTION

The questions used in solution-focused interviews are intended to set-up a therapeutic process wherein practitioners listen for and select out the words and phrases from the client's language that are indications (initially, often only small hints) of some aspect of a solution, such as articulating what is important to the client, what he or she might want, related successes (e.g., exceptions), or client skills and resources. Once having made the selection, the therapist then composes a next question or other response (e.g., a paraphrase or summary) that connects to the language used by the client and invites the client to build toward a clearer and more detailed version of some aspect of a solution. As the client responds from his or her own frame of reference, the therapist continues to listen, select, and compose the next solution-focused (SF) question or response, one that is built on what the client has said so far in the conversation. It is through this continuing process of listening, selecting, and building on the client's language that therapists and clients together co-construct new meanings and new possibilities for solutions.

Recent and ongoing research into face-to-face therapeutic dialogues called microanalysis is adding observable detail to the understanding of how SF co-construction occurs (De Jong, Bavelas, & Korman, 2013; Froerer & Jordan, 2013; Korman, Bavelas, & De Jong, 2013; McGee, Del Vento, and

Bavelas, 2005; Jordan, Froerer, & Bavelas, 2013). (These studies indicate that therapist questions and responses (paraphrases and summaries) are not neutral or objective but contain embedded assumptions about clients and their situations. Clients, in answering the questions and accepting therapist paraphrases and summaries, are collaborating with therapists in constructing new common ground (i.e., shared understandings) about themselves and their situations. SFT, whose questions and therapist responses embed assumptions of client competence and expertise, thereby set in motion a dialogue in which clients participate in discovering and constructing themselves as persons of ability with positive qualities who are in the process of creating more satisfying lives. Here is an example of this conversational process with a client who has just answered the miracle question and is asked about exceptions related to the miracle (from De Jong & Berg, 2013, pp. 15–16):

Therapist: Rosie, I'm impressed. You have a pretty clear picture of how things will be different around your house when things are better. Are there times already, say in the last two weeks, which are like the miracle you have been describing, even a little bit?

Rosie: Well, I'm not sure. Well, about four days ago it was better.

Therapist: Tell me about four days ago. *What* was different?

Rosie: Well, I went to bed about ten the night before and had a good night of sleep. I had food in the house, because I had gone to the store and to the food pantry on Saturday. I had even set the alarm for 6:30 and got up when it rang. I made breakfast and called the kids. The boys ate and got ready for school and left on time. [remembering] One even got some homework out of his backpack and did it—real quick—before he went to school.

Therapist: [impressed] Rosie, that sounds like a big part of the miracle right there. I'm amazed. How did all that happen?

Rosie: I'm not sure. I guess one thing was I had the food in the house, and I got to bed on time.

Therapist: So, how did you make that happen?

Rosie: Ah, I decided not to see any clients that night, and I read books to my kids for an hour.

Therapist: How did you manage that, reading to four kids? That seems like it would be really tough.

Rosie: No, that doesn't work—reading to four kids at the same time. I have my oldest boy read to one baby, because that's the only way I can get him to practice his reading, and I read to my other boy and baby.

Therapist: Rosie, that seems like a great idea—having him read to the baby. It helps you, and it helps him with his reading. How do you get him to do that?

Rosie: Oh, I let him stay up a half hour later than the others because he helps me. He really likes that.

Later in the conversation, the therapist asks the client to scale how far along to a solution she is:

Therapist: I'd like you to put some things on a scale for me, on a scale from 0 to 10. First, on a scale from 0 through 10, where 0 equals the worst your problems have been and 10 means the problems we have been talking about are solved, where are you *today* on that scale?

Rosie: If you had asked me that question before we started today, I would have said about a 2. But now I think it's more like a 5.

Therapist: Great! Now let me ask you about how *confident* you are that you can have another day in the next week like the one four days ago—the one that was a lot like your miracle picture. On a scale of 0 to 10, where 0 equals no confidence and 10 means you have every confidence, how confident are you that you can make it happen again?

Rosie: Oh, about a 5.

Therapist: Suppose you were at a 6; what would be different?

Rosie: I'd have to be sure that I always had food in the house for breakfast for the kids.

BREAK AND MESSAGE

After 30 to 40 minutes of asking questions and making SF responses, the SF practitioner takes a break for 5 to 10 minutes to reflect, either individually or with a team, about how far the client has come in his or her solution building. The practitioner then formulates a message composed of compliments focusing on the client's achievements and strengths, a bridging statement reflecting the client's goals, and, in most cases, a suggestion to observe for and/or do certain things. All three components are based on the common ground the client and practitioner have co-constructed in the interview. Here is a message based on the case illustration:

Compliments: Rosie I'm impressed with how much you care about wanting to be a good mom and make a good home for you and your children. I'm also impressed with how clear your miracle picture is about what your home and life will look like after the miracle, and especially that you already are at a five on the way to that miracle.

Bridge: I agree that being a good mom and making a good home is very important right now.

Suggestions: So I suggest that between now and when we meet next, you continue to do the things that got you and your family to a 5 and pay attention for what else you might be doing to get things to a 5 that you are doing but have not noticed yet. Also, since you have an idea of what will be different when things move up to a 6, be thinking about what it will take to make that happen.

PROTOCOLS

The first session in SFT proceeds from a brief problem description to extended co-construction of goals to identification of related exceptions and scaling. Second and later sessions begin with exception finding followed by scaling to measure progress and identify next steps (ongoing goal formulation). Protocols with question prompts are given below (De Jong &Berg, 2013):

First Session
- Problem (How can I be useful? What tells you that is a problem? What have you tried so far? Was it helpful?)
- Goal Formulation (What do you want to be different as a result of coming here? Ask the miracle question.)
- Exceptions (Are there times when the problem does not happen or is less serious? When? How does that happen? Are there times a bit like your miracle picture?)
- Scaling
  - How close things are to the miracle
  - Presession change
  - Motivation to work on a solution
  - Confidence in finding a solution

- Break
- Message for Client(s)
  - Compliments
  - Bridge
  - Suggestion

Later Sessions
- What's better?
  - Elicit (What's happening that's better?)
  - Amplify (How does that happen? What do you do to make that happen? Is that new for you? Now that you are doing that, what do you notice that is different between you and [significant other]? What else is different at your house?)
  - Reinforce/Compliment (Not everyone could have said or done…. So you're the kind of person who is/does/believes….?)
  - Start Again (What else is better?)
- Doing More (What will it take to do again? To do it more often?)
- If Nothing is Better (How are you coping? How do you make it? How come things aren't even worse?)
- Scaling Progress
  - Current level
  - Next level(s) (When you move from [number for current level] to [one number up the scale], what will be different? Who will be first to notice? When s/he notices, what will s/he do differently? What would it take to pretend a [one number up the scale] has happened?)
  - Termination: (How will you know when it's time to stop seeing me? What will be different?)
- Break
- Message for Client(s)
  - Compliments
  - Bridge
  - Suggestion

Evidence Base

The main elements of SFT as we know it today began to appear during the mid-to-late 1980s (de Shazer, 1985; 1988). Consequently, outcome studies only have been added to the professional literature in the past 20 to 25 years. Despite its youth, the case for SFT's evidence-based status is persuasive (Franklin, Trepper, Gingerich, & McCollum, 2012; Gingerich & Peterson, 2013; Macdonald, 2011, 2013). Macdonald's (2013) summary of the research lists 120 studies of SFT. Twenty-three of these are randomized controlled studies, all showing benefit from SFT with twelve indicating benefit over existing treatments. Forty-five are comparison studies with thirty-six favoring SFT. Effectiveness data are available from more than 5,000 cases with a success rate exceeding 60% over an average of three to five sessions. Two meta-analyses (Kim, 2008; Stams, Dekovic, Buist, & de Vries, 2006) indicate small-to-moderate effect sizes with equivalent outcomes to other psychotherapies over a lower average number of sessions.

Gingerich and Peterson (2013) and Trepper and Franklin (2012) both document that SFT is effective across a wide variety of client groups, settings, and problems. These sources cite studies documenting SFT's effectiveness in adult mental health, child academic and behavior problems, crime and delinquency, domestic violence and abuse, health and aging, marriage and family, medication adherence, occupational rehabilitation, organizational management and coaching, and substance abuse.

SFT is now included in the U.S. federal government's Registry of Evidence-based Programs and Practices (www.nrepp.samhsa.gov), and has been approved by the State of Washington and the State of Oregon (www.oregon.gov/DHS). It is also listed in the U.S. Department of Justice's Model Programs Guide with other evidence-based programs (http://www.ojjdp.gov/mpg/mpgProgramDetails.aspx?ID=712). For those interested in conducting research on SFT, the European Brief Therapy Association (www.ebta.nu) and the Solution Focused Brief Therapy Association (www.sfbta.org) offer research manuals on SFT.

APPLICATIONS

SFT is not problem specific; instead, it is an approach to having conversations with clients about change built around their definitions of what they want different in their lives and drawing on their past successes and other relevant resources. The approach is fast being adopted in a variety of practice settings, is used the same way with voluntary and involuntary clients alike, and is practiced with individuals, couples, families, groups, organizations, and in supervisory relationships (Berg, 1994; Berg & Kelly, 2000; Berg & Miller, 1992; Berg & Shilts, 2005; Berg & Steiner, 2003; Burns, 2005; Connie, 2013; De

Jong & Berg, 2013; de Shazer & Isebaert, 2003; Fiske, 2008; Jackson & McKergow, 2007; Kelly, Kim, & Franklin, 2008; Lee, Sebold, & Uken, 2003; Nelson & Thomas, 2006; Pichot & Dolan, 2003; Sharry, 2001; Simon, 2010; Thomas, 2013; Walker & Greening, 2011; Young, 2009). The approach is now well established and continues to gather momentum.

FIT WITH SOCIAL WORK VALUES

Although SFT parts company with the profession's historic use of a problem-solving paradigm, it comports as well or better than problem-solving with core professional values such as respecting human dignity, individualizing service, fostering client vision, building on strengths, and maximizing self-determination (De Jong & Berg, 2013). It does so largely by consistently working within the client's frame of reference and asking questions in ways that always return choice to clients (De Jong & Berg, 2001; de Shazer et al., 2007).

THEORETICAL IMPLICATIONS

Although clinical observation and theory can never fully be separated, the former has played a greater role in the development of SFT than the latter. Once the techniques were refined, more writing began to appear about the approach's theoretical implications (Berg & De Jong, 1996; De Jong, Bavelas, & Korman, 2013; de Shazer, 1991, 1994; de Shazer et al., 2007; Miller, 1997). Social constructionism offers the most satisfying account of how clients change through exposure to SFT. Herein, therapeutic solutions are thought to be new or altered meanings. As explained and illustrated earlier, they are co-constructed between client and practitioner through language interaction. The key role for practitioners in this interactive process is always to struggle to formulate the next useful, solution-focused response and question from the language and meanings contained in the client's last and earlier answers.

WEBSITES

European Brief Therapy Association. www.ebta.nu
Solution Focused Brief Therapy Association. www.sfbta.org

Webpage of Dr. Alasdair Macdonald with a regularly updated summary of outcome research on SFT. www.solutionsdoc.co.uk

Website of the professional organization devoted to solution-focused practice in management and organizations. www.solworld.org

References

Berg, I. K. (1994). *Family based services: A solution-focused approach*. New York, NY: Norton.

Berg, I. K., & De Jong, P. (1996). Solution-building conversations: Co-constructing a sense of competence with clients. *Families in Society: The Journal of Contemporary Human Services, 77*, 376–391.

Berg, I. K., & Kelly, S. (2000). *Building solutions in child protective services*. New York, NY: Norton.

Berg, I. K., & Miller, S. D. (1992). *Working with the problem drinker: A solution-focused approach*. New York, NY: Norton.

Berg, I. K., & Shilts, L. (2005). Keeping the solutions within the classroom: WOWW approach. *School Counselor* (July/August), 30–35.

Berg, I. K., & Steiner, T. (2003). *Children's solution work*. New York, NY: Norton.

Burns, K. (2005). *Focus on solutions: A health professional's guide*. London: Whurr.

Connie, E. (2013). *Solution building in couples therapy*. New York, NY: Springer.

De Jong, P., Bavelas, J., & Korman, H. (2013). An introduction to using microanalysis to observe co-construction in psychotherapy. *Journal of Systemic Therapies, 32*, 18–31.

De Jong, P., & Berg, I. K. (2013). *Interviewing for solutions* (4th ed.). Belmont, CA: Brooks/Cole, Cengage Learning.

De Jong, P., & Berg, I. K. (2001). Co-constructing cooperation with mandated clients. *Social Work, 46*, 361–374.

de Shazer, S. (1985). *Keys to solution in brief therapy*. New York, NY: Norton.

de Shazer, S. (1988). *Clues: Investigating solutions in brief therapy*. New York, NY: Norton.

de Shazer, S. (1991). *Putting difference to work*. New York, NY: Norton.

de Shazer, S. (1994). *Words were originally magic*. New York, NY: Norton.

de Shazer, S., Berg, I. K., Lipchik, E., Nunnaly, E., Molnar, A., Gingerich, W., & Weiner-Davis, M. (1986). Brief therapy: Focused solution development. *Family Process, 25*, 207–221.

de Shazer, S., Dolan, Y., Korman, H., Trepper, T., McCollum, E., & Berg, I. K. (2007). *More than miracles: The state of the art of solution-focused brief therapy*. New York, NY: Haworth.

de Shazer, S., & Isebaert, L. (2003). The Bruges model: A solution-focused approach to problem drinking. *Journal of Family Psychotherapy, 14*, 43–53.

Fiske, H. (2008). Hope in action: Solution-focused conversations about suicide. New York, NY: Routledge.

Franklin, C., Trepper, T. S., Gingerich, W. J., & McCollum, E. E. (Eds.). (2012). *Solution-focused brief therapy: A handbook of evidence-based practice*. New York, NY: Oxford University Press.

Froerer, A., & Jordan, S. S. (2013). Identifying solution-building formulations through microanalysis. *Journal of Systemic Therapies, 32*, 61–75.

Gingerich, W. J., & Peterson, L. T. (2013). Effectiveness of solution-focused brief therapy: A systematic qualitative review of controlled outcome studies. *Research on Social Work Practice, 23*, 266–283.

Jackson, P. Z., & McKergow, M. (2007). *The solutions focus: Making coaching and change simple* (2nd ed.). London: Nicholas Brealey.

Jordan, S. S., Froerer, A., and Bavelas, J. (2013). Microanalysis of positive and negative content in solution-focused brief therapy and cognitive behavioral therapy expert sessions. *Journal of Systemic Therapies, 32*, 47–60.

Kelly, M., Kim, J., & Franklin, C. (2008). *Solution-focused brief therapy in schools: A 360 degree view of research and practice*. New York, NY: Oxford University Press.

Kim, J. S. (2008). Examining the effectiveness of solution-focused brief therapy: A meta-analysis using random effects modeling. *Research on Social Work Practice, 18*, 107–116.

Korman, H., Bavelas, J., & De Jong, P. (2013). Microanalysis of formulations in solution-focused brief therapy, cognitive behavioral therapy, and motivational interviewing. *Journal of Systemic Therapies, 32*, 32–46.

Lee, M. Y., Sebold, J., & Uken, A. (2003). *Solution-focused treatment of domestic violence offenders: Accountability for change*. New York, NY: Oxford University Press.

Macdonald, A. J. (2013). Solution-focused brief therapy evaluation list. Retrieved from http://www.solutionsdoc.co.uk/sft.html

Macdonald, A. J. (2011). *Solution-focused therapy: Theory, research, and practice* (2nd ed.). London: Sage.

McGee, D. R., Del Vento, A., & Bavelas, J. B. (2005). An interactional model of questions as therapeutic interventions. *Journal of Marital and Family Therapy, 31*, 371–384.

Miller, G. (1997). *Becoming miracle workers: Language and meaning in brief therapy*. New York, NY: Aldine de Gruyter.

Nelson, T. S., & Thomas, F. N. (2006). *Handbook of solution-focused brief therapy: Clinical applications*. New York, NY: Haworth.

Pichot, T., & Dolan, Y. M. (2003). *Solution-focused brief therapy: Its effective use in agency settings.* Binghamton, NY: Haworth.

Sharry, J. (2001). *Solution-focused groupwork.* London: Sage.

Simon, J. K. (2010). *Solution focused practice in end-of-life and grief counseling.* New York, NY: Springer.

Stams, G. J., Dekovic, M., Buist, K., & de Vries, L. (2006). Effectiviteit van oplossingsgerichte korte therapie: een meta-analyse (Efficacy of solution focused brief therapy: a meta-analysis). *Gedragstherapie, 39,* 81–95.

Thomas, F. N. (2013). Solution-focused supervision: A resource-oriented approach to developing clinical expertise. New York, NY: Springer.

Trepper, T. S., & Franklin, C. (2012). Epilogue: The future of research in solution-focused brief therapy. In C. Franklin, T. S. Trepper, W. J. Gingerich, & E. E. McCollum (Eds.), *Solution-focused brief therapy* (pp. 405–412). New York, NY: Oxford University Press.

Walker, L., & Greening, R. (2011). Reentry & transition planning circles for incarcerated people. Hawai'i, USA: Hawai'i Friends of Justice & Civic Education.

Young, S. (2009). *Solution-focused schools: Anti-bullying and beyond.* London: BT Press.

36 Theoretical Pluralism and Integrative Perspectives in Social Work Practice

William Borden

INTRODUCTION

Although most social workers come to characterize their clinical approach as eclectic, there is surprisingly little consideration of the ways in which practitioners engage differing theoretical perspectives, empirical findings, and technical procedures over the course of psychosocial intervention. This chapter reviews comparative approaches to clinical theory and shows how mastery of the foundational schools of thought strengthens efforts to carry out integrative forms of psychosocial intervention. The first part summarizes four lines of inquiry that have shaped integrative approaches to practice, broadly characterized as technical eclecticism, common factors perspectives, theoretical integration, and assimilative integration. The second section describes pluralist approaches to clinical theory and outlines core domains of concern in comparative analysis of explanatory systems. The third part presents a case report and shows how a pluralist

point of view informs use of differing perspectives over the course of intervention, broadening the range of theoretical concepts, empirical research, and technical procedures applied in the clinical situation.

INTEGRATIVE PERSPECTIVES IN CONTEMPORARY PRACTICE

As a starting point, it is important to acknowledge the growing emphasis on integrative approaches in contemporary psychotherapy and psychosocial intervention. Clinical scholars have increasingly realized the strengths and limits of differing theoretical perspectives, over the years, and practitioners have drawn on psychodynamic, cognitive, behavioral, humanistic, and ecological perspectives in fashioning integrative models of practice, seeking to engage a wider range of clients, broaden the scope of intervention, and improve outcomes. Borden (2010, 2013) and

Stricker (2010) review orienting perspectives and recent developments in integrative conceptions of psychosocial intervention.

Four lines of inquiry have shaped efforts to link theory, empirical data, and technical procedures in integrative conceptions of psychosocial intervention over the last quarter century, broadly characterized as technical eclecticism, common factors approaches, conceptual synthesis or theoretical integration, and assimilative integration (Goldfried & Norcross, 1995; Stricker, 2010). The perspectives emphasize differing elements and strategies in their attempts to enlarge the frame of psychosocial intervention and improve therapeutic outcomes.

TECHNICAL ECLECTICISM

According to conceptions of technical eclecticism, practitioners apply procedures pragmatically on the basis of clinical efficacy (Safran & Messer, 1997). The goal is to match specific techniques with circumscribed problems in functioning in light of empirical evidence and clinical expertise. For example, empirical findings and clinical experience support the use of cognitive and behavioral techniques for treatment of a range of problems in functioning associated with posttraumatic stress disorders and borderline personality organization. Procedures are frequently outlined in manuals that guide application in the clinical situation.

The foundation is empirical rather than theoretical, and practitioners assume that therapeutic methods can be applied independently of the theories from which they originate. Technical procedures are drawn from a variety of sources without necessarily endorsing—or even understanding—the supporting conceptual frameworks (Arkowitz, 1992; Goldfried & Norcross, 1995). In this sense, it is the most technically oriented approach to integration. The practitioner could, for example, combine procedures from cognitive, behavioral, experiential, and family systems perspectives in the course of an individual treatment. Representative examples include Arnold Lazarus' multimodal perspective (2002) and Larry Beutler's prescriptive model of intervention, specifying strategies and techniques for treatment of circumscribed problems in functioning (Beutler, 2004).

COMMON FACTORS APPROACHES

In his classic work, *Persuasion and Healing*, published in 1961, Jerome Frank explored the ways in which all forms of psychological healing share common elements, emphasizing the functions of the therapeutic relationship, the healing setting, conceptual schemes that provide plausible explanations of what is the matter and what carries the potential to help, and the core activities of psychosocial intervention that foster change and growth (Frank & Frank, 1991). More than half a century of psychotherapy research has documented the comparable effectiveness of a range of approaches, and there is growing agreement that all of the major systems of psychotherapy—psychodynamic, cognitive, behavioral, humanistic, and ecological—share common elements that account for their relative effectiveness (Wampold, 2010; Stricker, 2010).

The common factors approach is based on the assumption that all therapeutic systems exert their effects largely through the same underlying principles and processes. Clinicians reason that common factors are more important than the specific procedures that distinguish the particular schools of thought, and argue that shared elements can serve as the basis for development of more effective approaches to practice.

Accordingly, practitioners focus on the core conditions and basic elements shared by the major schools of thought encompassed in the broader field of psychotherapy. In doing so, they consider client factors, such as motivation and expectations of change; practitioner characteristics, such as warmth, empathic attunement, and authenticity; the provision of a rationale for problems in functioning and a coherent conceptual framework for interventions; and strategic processes, such as experiential learning through interpersonal interaction; interpretive procedures that enlarge understandings of self, relationships, and life experience; and the role of reinforcement, exposure, modeling, and identification in change and growth (Arkowitz, 1992; Borden, 2010; Stricker, 2010).

Practitioners attempt to identify which elements would appear to be most useful in the treatment of a particular individual on the basis of assessment data and experiential learning in the clinical situation. Some clients, for example, find it useful to explore earlier life events or process their experience of the helping relationship; others, however, make more effective use of task-centered, action-oriented, educational modes of intervention. Sol Garfield's integrative model of intervention, emphasizing experiential learning, insight, hope, and the sustaining functions of the helping relationship, exemplifies the common factors perspective (Garfield, 2000).

THEORETICAL INTEGRATION

A third approach emerged out of efforts to develop unifying frameworks that bridge theories of personality, problems in living, and methods of intervention; the aim is conceptual synthesis, beyond a blend of common factors and technical procedures (Goldfried & Norcross, 1995). Although the intervention strategies of the integrative system may encompass the procedures used in technical eclecticism, there are crucial differences in the assumptions and conceptualizations that inform decision-making and use of particular strategies (Stricker, 2010). Such frameworks broaden the range of psychological and social phenomena that potentially serve as the focus of treatment and offer varying points of entry. The enlarged conceptual perspective allows clinicians to expand the range of technical procedures used over the course of intervention (Borden, 2010).

By way of example, Paul Wachtel has developed a psychodynamic approach that encompasses behavioral, cognitive, humanistic, systemic, and ecological perspectives, extending his earlier integration of psychoanalytic theory and behavioral concepts (Wachtel, 2011). In the field of social work, Sharon Berlin has developed an integrative cognitive perspective that links neuroscience and cognitive psychology, the major schools of psychotherapy, and framing perspectives in the social work tradition (Berlin, 2010).

ASSIMILATIVE INTEGRATION

A fourth approach, conceptualized as assimilative integration, encompasses elements of technical eclecticism and theoretical integration (Messer, 2001). In working from this point of view, the clinician establishes a "home base" in a primary theoretical system and draws on ideas and techniques from other schools of thought in light of the particular needs and circumstances of the clinical situation. The concepts and techniques are blended within the conceptual framework of the central theoretical perspective. The approach potentially encompasses ideas and methods that would be viewed incompatible in purer conceptions of the helping process.

The Role of Theory in Practice

The foregoing lines of inquiry deepen our understanding of common factors that operate across the schools of thought and the range of technical strategies employed in eclectic modes of treatment, offering pragmatic frameworks for psychosocial intervention. *If clinicians are to carry out integrative forms of practice effectively, however, they must develop an understanding of the foundational theories of the field.* In the absence of theoretical knowledge, practitioners do not have conceptual frames of reference to understand the dynamics of change processes or the technical elements they are trying to integrate in eclectic, individualized approaches to intervention. Procedures are deprived of context, and clinicians run the risk of carrying out reductive, mechanized approaches to practice, lacking theoretical rationales for strategies and methods of intervention (Borden, 2010; Messer & Gurman, 2011).

Pluralism as Comparative Perspective

Clinical scholars have drawn on philosophical conceptions of pluralism in their efforts to develop frameworks for critical thinking and decision-making in comparative approaches to clinical theory (Borden, 2010, 2013). Although a review of this work is beyond the scope of the chapter, it is important to identify the defining features of pluralism and its implications for pragmatic use of theoretical concepts, empirical findings, and technical procedures in the clinical situation.

Pluralist points of view emphasize the limits of human understanding and assume that no single framework captures the variousness and complexity of actual experience in the real world. Thinkers and practitioners approach concerns from multiple, independent perspectives, realizing that there are mutually exclusive descriptions of the world and equally valid points of view that inevitably contradict one another.

In this respect pluralist perspectives challenge notions of grand theory, which presume to assert universal truths, and take the more realistic position that theoretical formulations and empirical findings *at best* provide partial, incomplete understandings of experience. William James emphasizes the importance of immediate experience, practical consequences, and implications for action in his conceptions of pluralism and pragmatism (Borden, 2013).

From a pluralist point of view, then, theories serve a range of functions, providing tools for critical thinking and decision-making as practitioners carry out their work. Every theoretical system is distinguished by its particular concerns, purposes, methods, strengths, and limits, and no single approach—however encompassing it may seem—can possibly meet all needs over the course of intervention.

In spite of the diversity of theoretical perspectives that inform psychosocial intervention, clinical scholars have identified core domains of concern that facilitate efforts to carry out comparative study, encompassing the following areas:

- Historical origins of the theoretical perspective; intellectual traditions, world views, and social, cultural, political, and economic conditions that have influenced the development of guiding assumptions and basic concepts; the types of clients, problems in living, and settings that have shaped clinical approaches;
- Conceptions of personality, self, person in context, and development across life course; empirical support for basic propositions; congruence of concepts with core social work values;
- Conceptions of resilience, health, well-being, and the common good;
- Conceptions of vulnerability, problems in living, and psychopathology; extent to which theorists encompass social, cultural, political, or economic contexts of understanding in formulations of vulnerability, need, and problems in functioning; and
- Conceptions of psychosocial intervention: core assumptions, change processes, and curative factors; structure and process of intervention; range of application; empirical support for efficacy and effectiveness of approach; implications for emerging models of evidence-based practice (see Messer & Gurman, 2011, and Wampold,

2010, for comparative review of classical and contemporary therapeutic systems).

In comparative approaches to theory, practitioners master the foundational schools of thought and engage a range of ideas as they carry out their practice, without committing themselves to any single school or tradition. Pluralist perspectives attempt to foster dialogue across the divergent perspectives that shape contemporary practice, enlarging ways of seeing, understanding, and acting as clinicians work to understand what is the matter and what carries the potential to help. The practitioner enters into different points of view and critically evaluates possible approaches, concepts, and methods in light of the particular circumstances of the clinical situation, assessing choices and potential courses of action as intervention proceeds. The validity of any theoretical concept or method is determined by its *practical outcome* in the context of the particular case (Borden, 2010, 2013).

CLINICAL APPLICATION

The following case report illustrates the ways in which a pluralist frame of reference guides use of concepts and methods from divergent perspectives over the course of intervention.

Case Report

The client, age 63, developed diffuse anxiety, signs of depression, and dissociative states eight months after he was injured in an automobile accident. He had completed a course of rehabilitation in an extended care facility, following recovery from life-threatening injuries, and had recently returned to his home. He described fluctuating periods of numbing detachment and intrusive recollections of the events surrounding the accident, and reported a growing sense of dread—the feeling that "something bad is about to happen."

The client related a range of symptoms that met diagnostic criteria for posttraumatic stress disorder. Further sources of vulnerability emerged in his developmental history. His mother had died shortly after his birth, and he described ongoing disruptions in caretaking arrangements through childhood and adolescence. He reported ongoing difficulties in establishing relationships in adulthood, and described limited contact with extended family or friends; his experience of dependency and isolation following the accident had intensified longings for closeness and connection with others.

Although the focus of intervention centered on problems in functioning precipitated by the traumatic event, the practitioner realized that the client's history of early loss, disruptions in caretaking, and subsequent modes of attachment potentially limited his capacity to establish a collaborative relationship and negotiate the interactive experience of the therapeutic process.

In light of the crucial role of the therapeutic relationship in efforts to sponsor change and growth, the practitioner attended carefully to the development of the working alliance, seeking to create conditions that would sponsor the client's engagement in the therapeutic process. The clinician's warmth, attunement, and responsiveness facilitated the client's experience of acceptance, understanding, and support. The practitioner's use of self and relational provisions were informed by person-centered conceptions of the helping relationship, psychodynamic formulations of the therapeutic alliance and the holding environment, and developmental research on the ways in which early loss and disruption in caretaking influence modes of attachment and interpersonal functioning. The clinician reviewed conceptions of posttraumatic stress syndromes with the client to help him understand the nature of his problems in functioning and the core activities of the therapeutic process.

In the first phase of treatment the client related the course of events following the accident in a detached, impersonal fashion, sometimes speaking in the third person. He showed an absence of emotional responsiveness, consistent with the denial phase of posttraumatic stress reactions, and appeared indifferent as he described events: "I don't know what good it does to talk about any of this ... we can't change what has happened ... I should be able to get beyond this and live my life." Relational concepts from self psychology and person-centered perspectives guided the clinician's reflection and validation of the client's underlying feelings of fear, helplessness, and hopelessness. The worker's attunement and empathic processing of his reactions appeared to strengthen the relationship and the holding environment, creating conditions for more active, focused exploration of traumatic events.

The client's experience of numbing detachment fluctuated with periods of diffuse anxiety as he continued to process traumatic states in the middle phase of intervention. The clinician drew on cognitive and behavioral approaches in efforts to help the client manage intrusive recollection of events and disrupt vicious circles of thought, feeling, and behavior that perpetuated problems in functioning. He had come to see the world as a "dangerous place," restricting patterns of activity, and viewed people as unsupportive and unreliable, avoiding opportunities to resume contact with extended family and friends in spite of longings for connection.

The clinician used a range of cognitive procedures in efforts to help the client challenge and revise maladaptive schemata ("The world is a dangerous place."), working assumptions ("Nobody really wants to see me."), and automatic thoughts ("I am broken"; "My life is over.") that perpetuated his experience of fear, demoralization, and disengagement from activities. The practitioner drew on behavioral methods of exposure in efforts to help the client engage feared aspects of inner experience (memories, images, and thoughts related to the accident) and feared activities in the outer world (interaction with others, activities of everyday life). The client and clinician worked collaboratively to identify tasks that provided occasions to expand patterns of activity and carry out social interaction. Such active modes of intervention provided opportunities for mastery and development of coping strategies and social skills, strengthening the client's morale, self-esteem, and sense of possibility.

He made considerable progress in efforts to recognize and accept the experience of trauma, manage fluctuations in internal states, and engage relational life. In the final phase of intervention, the clinician drew on humanistic and existential perspectives as the client explored the meaning of the accident and the implications of the event, working to clarify core values and essential concerns that would shape his life plan.

The practitioner's mastery of psychodynamic, cognitive, behavioral, humanistic, and existential perspectives provided the theoretical underpinnings for use of differing concepts, empirical findings, and technical procedures over the course of intervention. Movement from one orientation to another was guided by the nature of specific problems in functioning, the focal concerns of intervention, and the client's capacities to make use of differing strategies. The clinician emphasized the following approaches and procedures in efforts to facilitate change and growth: (1) processing of interactive experience in the therapeutic situation to deepen understanding of modes of attachment and interpersonal behavior; (2) cognitive restructuring; (3) exposure to inner and outer domains of feared experience; (4) development of behavioral skills through modeling and experiential learning, and (5) interpretive procedures to enlarge assumptive world and deepen understanding of self, others, and life experience.

Summary

In the pluralist approach to theory described here, the foundational schools of thought provide contexts of understanding for use of differing concepts, empirical findings, and technical operations over the course of intervention. The clinician

- Learns multiple theories, therapeutic languages, and modes of intervention
- Draws on concepts from a variety of perspectives in light of the specifics of the clinical situation
- Judges the validity of theoretical concepts on the basis of practical outcomes in the context of the particular case.

Comparative perspectives make the multiplicity of competing approaches a defining feature of psychosocial intervention. The practitioner aims to establish an ongoing dialogue among representatives of the major schools of thought that sponsors clarification of differing points of view and theoretically informed integration of concepts, empirical findings, and techniques in eclectic, individualized approaches to psychosocial intervention.

WEBSITES

Society for the Exploration of Psychotherapy Integration. Sepiweb.org

References

Arkowitz, H. (1992). Integrative theories of therapy. In D. K. Freedheim (Ed.), *History of psychotherapy: A century of change* (pp. 261–303). Washington, DC: American Psychological Association.

Berlin, S. (2010). Why cognitive therapy needs social work. In W. Borden (Ed.), *Reshaping theory in contemporary social work* (pp. 31–50). New York, NY: Columbia University Press.

Beutler, L. (2004). *Prescriptive psychotherapy*. London: Oxford University Press.

Borden, W. (2010). Taking multiplicity seriously: Pluralism, pragmatism, and integrative perspectives in social work practice. In W. Borden (Ed.), *Reshaping theory in contemporary social work* (pp. 3–27). New York, NY: Columbia University Press.

Borden, W. (2013). Experiments in adapting to need: Pragmatism as orienting perspective in clinical social work. *Journal of Social Work Practice, 27*(3), 259–271.

Frank, J., & Frank, J. (1991). *Persuasion and healing*. Baltimore, MD: Johns Hopkins University Press.

Garfield, S. L. (2000). Eclecticism and integration: A personal retrospective view. *Journal of Psychotherapy Integration, 10,* 341–356.

Goldfried, M., & Norcross, J. (1995). Integrative and eclectic therapies in historical perspective. In B. Bonger & L. Beutler (Eds.), *Comprehensive textbook of psychotherapy* (pp. 254–273). New York, NY: Oxford University Press.

Messer, S. (2001). Applying the visions of reality to a case of brief psychotherapy. *Journal of Psychotherapy Integration, 10,* 55–70.

Messer, S., & Gurman, A. (2011). Contemporary issues in contemporary theory, research, and practice. In S. Messer & A. Gurman (Eds.), *Essential psychotherapies* (pp. 1–33). New York, NY: Guilford.

Lazarus, A. (2002). The multimodal assessment treatment method. In J. Lebow (Ed.), *Comprehensive handbook of psychotherapy. Vol. 4: Integrative-eclectic* (pp. 241–254). New York, NY: Wiley.

Safran, J., & Messer, S. (1997). Psychotherapy integration: A postmodern critique. *Clinical Psychology: Science and Practice, 4,* 140–152.

Stricker. G. (2010). *Psychotherapy integration*. Washington, DC: American Psychological Association.

Wachtel, P. L. (2011). *Therapeutic communication*. New York, NY: Guilford.

Wampold, B. (2010). *The basics of psychotherapy*. Washington, DC: American Psychological Association.

37 Animal-assisted Interventions in Social Work Practice

Yvonne Eaton-Stull

In the era of technology, few social workers have to carry various treatment resources around in their briefcase; there is, however, a new invaluable tool they may be seen transporting today. Many have elected to integrate their best friends into their practice, and they are now armed with a leash and doggie bags. According to a recent national study, almost 25% of social work practitioners are using animals in their workplace (Risley-Curtiss, 2010). Risley-Curtiss (2010) also contends that many of these providers, however, lack essential education on this specialized topic. This chapter is written in an effort to increase knowledge and provide valuable resources to practitioners interested in utilizing animal-assisted intervention (AAI).

A "therapy dog" is a commonly used term to describe dogs that have been evaluated and registered by a professional, volunteer organization. The therapy dogs work with a handler, who is usually their owner. There are just about as many of these therapy dog organizations today as there are breeds of dogs; thus, one must carefully investigate how the handler and dog team have been evaluated. A few key questions include: Did the handler receive any special advanced training? How was the dog trained and evaluated? Is the dog re-evaluated on a regular basis to determine whether its temperament and obedience skills are still acceptable? What type of insurance accompanies this team? And are the veterinary records current and adequate? Practitioners who are using their own dogs in their employment setting should assure that their professional liability insurance covers this treatment modality because it is not covered by these volunteer organizations. Practitioners, who see the value of this intervention but do not own their own therapy

dog, can request a volunteer team to assist them from one of these organizations. Obviously, this route would also require additional permissions, consents, and agreements to bring another person into the sessions. With this latter option, it is also suggested that the practitioner meet both the handler and the dog before committing to using them so that the practitioner is comfortable with the team and believes they are well-suited to working with the intended individual or group.

Pet Partners (2012), formerly known as Delta Society, one national volunteer organization, provides a host of valuable information including research, resources, training, access to evaluators, and a registry of teams (www.petpartners.org). Pet Partners also rates a team in terms of what type of environment they are suited to work in. Dogs who are rated at a predictable environment do well with quiet environments and minimal activity; whereas dogs with complex ratings are able to handle active settings with high activity levels (Delta Society, 2000). It is essential that the dog is matched to the level of interaction and environment expected in the practitioner's setting.

These specially trained animals can fill numerous roles. Animal-assisted intervention (AAI) is an umbrella term to describe the many strategies of utilizing these animals in social work, which can include animal-assisted activities (AAA), animal-assisted therapy (AAT), and/or a highly specialized service known as animal-assisted crisis response (AACR). AAA includes activities that provide opportunity for motivational, educational, recreational, and therapeutic benefits; interactions are spontaneous and there are no required treatment goals or notes (Pet Partners, 2012). For the social work professional, AAA can be thought of as the non-client specific intervention. This can include providing professional presentations, talking with groups about services, or teaching student interns. AAT, on the other hand, is goal-directed intervention delivered by a professional within their scope of practice, which includes documentation and measurement of treatment progress (Pet Partners, 2012). Therapy dogs can be integrated into treatment plans to address a variety of issues. Finally, AACR is a very specialized service that includes the use of certified crisis dogs in providing comfort and support following crises and disasters (HOPE AACR, 2008). These dogs have extensive training and ongoing education, and they are comfortable in very chaotic, loud, crowded environments. There are many wonderful therapy dogs out there who could not handle crisis situations, thus it is important that the dogs have the proper credentials for the job. Two national AACR organizations meet the published national standards for AACR work: HOPE AACR (www.hopeaacr.org) and National AACR (www.naacr.org). Social workers can contact these organizations for voluntary assistance following crises or disasters.

It is likely that more dogs will enter social services, working alongside practitioners in a variety of settings. To prepare social workers for this inevitability, several colleges and universities throughout the United States offer specialized curriculum or certification in AAT (Chandler, 2005). In fact, the University of Denver Graduate School of Social Work houses an Institute for Human-Animal connection and offers courses in animal-assisted social work practice and integration of animals into therapeutic settings (Tedeschi, Fitchett, & Molidor, 2005). For those on the east coast, the Virginia Commonwealth University (VCU) has a Center for Human-Animal Interaction, which engages in cutting edge research, clinical work, and educational activities (VCU Medical Center, 2011). Both practitioners and educators need to consider the many benefits these dogs offer, which can help enhance and improve the lives of those we serve.

COGNITIVE BENEFITS

Case Example: A special preschool for children with autism requested a one-time visit with a therapy dog. The teacher felt it would be especially useful for a young boy who was not using language effectively and becoming increasingly *frustrated and injuring himself. She knew he loved dogs and thought a visit might provide the encouragement to talk. During the first visit, Maggie the therapy dog lied down, and this young boy came over and began to pet her. He pointed to a body part, her ear, and looked at me (the handler). I responded, "That's her ear." He quietly said "ear." We continued to play this game where he pointed to something on Maggie, I told him the word, and he repeated it. The teacher was in awe, and she consequently requested a second visit. Amazingly on this second visit, this boy ran up to greet Maggie and offered more than a single word. He asked, "Read to Maggie?" I enthusiastically responded, "Of course you can read to Maggie." He grabbed a picture book and brought it to Maggie, pointing to picture after picture telling her what she was seeing. The teacher cried as she witnessed the student's dramatic increase in verbal communication.*

Some of the cognitive benefits associated with AAI include learning and language. Bassette and Taber-Doughty (2013) conducted a small pilot study with three elementary school students who participated in an AAT intervention reading to dogs; all participants increased on-task behavior and sustained improvement over time. In a similar study targeting identified students with fluency and reading deficiencies, Newlin (2003) paired 15 students with therapy dogs. Following this AAI, most of the participants improved their reading skills by at least two grade levels (Newlin, 2003). Van Fleet (2008) concurs that these special canines can help develop language skills and facilitate communication in children. She offers examples and strategies for integrating therapy dogs into treatment plans addressing shyness, stuttering, and other communication difficulties (Van Fleet, 2008).

Various educational institutions have found that a therapy dog's presence enhances concentration, attention, and motivation (Beetz, Uvnas-Moberg, Julius, & Kotrschal, 2012). School social workers or those who are consulted to assist in developing cognitive interventions would be wise to consider this intervention.

PHYSICAL BENEFITS

Scientific evidence also supports various physical benefits of AAI. Short- and long-term health benefits, such as prevention of health issues and improved recovery are well documented (Wells, 2009), as is decreased pain (Sobo, Eng, &

Kassity-Kritch, 2006) In a literature review of health benefits, Morrison (2007) found AAI produced significant improvements in blood pressure and heart rate. A more recent review concurs and adds to these results resulting from AAI improvements in cardiovascular health and reduced cortisol (Beetz, Uvnas-Moberg, Julius, & Kotrschal, 2012). According to Sable (2013), these health-related benefits have important social work implications. For example, practitioners who are providing early intervention to those exposed to traumatic events can utilize AAI, a non-medication based solution, to prevent more serious disorders, such as posttraumatic stress disorder (PTSD). Many specific factors contribute to the development of PTSD, but one known predictor is elevated heart rate (Bryant, Creamer, O'Donnell, Silove, & McFarlane, 2008; DeYoung, Kenardy, & Spence, 2007; Kassam-Adams, Garcia-Espana, Fein, & Winston, 2005; Kuhn, Blanchard, Fuse, Hickling, & Broderick, 2006). AAI has been shown to decrease one's heart rate (Barker, Knisely, McCain, Schubert, & Pandurangi, 2010; Kaminski, Pellino, & Wish, 2002; Morrison, 2007). Perhaps physicians will see the value and write prescriptions for AAI instead of for beta blockers.

EMOTIONAL/MENTAL HEALTH BENEFITS

Testimonial: Mandy Fauble, PhD, LCSW, has utilized AAI in both individual and group therapy. She states "utilizing pet therapy helps to facilitate the alliance and rapport between clinician and client, as the dog enhances the feelings of safety, comfort, and mutuality. With children, particularly, dogs help to provide opportunities for projective identification and empathy that are unconditional and safe, allowing for practice of skills in ways that seem more like fun than therapy." (M. Fauble, personal communication, August 9, 2013).

AAI has demonstrated value in the treatment of many mental health conditions. Five randomized controlled studies, the gold standard in evidence-based practice, have contributed a wealth of valuable evidence regarding the benefit of AAT in improving symptoms of schizophrenia (Barak, Savorai, Mavashev, Beni, 2001; Berget, Ekeberg, & Braastad, 2008; Chu, Liu, Sun, & Lin, 2009; Marr et al., 2000; Nathans-Barel, Feldman, Berger, Modai, & Silver, 2005). Additional research with individuals suffering from depression has demonstrated significant benefits from

AAI (Berget et al., 2008; Marr et al., 2000; Moretti et al., 2011). Finally, in Barker and Dawson's (1998) large-scale study of 230 participants, a single AAT session resulted in significant decreases in anxiety. Similarly, decreases in anxiety have been supported in other studies as well (Hoffman et al., 2009; Lang, Jansen, Wertenauer, Gallinat, and Rapp, 2010).

SOCIAL/BEHAVIORAL BENEFITS

Testimonial: A staff member from a state correctional institution recently shared an interesting story. The prison, after experiencing significant assaults by inmates, conducted an extensive sweep of the facility to search for hidden weapons. Interestingly, home-made weapons were discovered on every unit except for the one where inmates have and train future service dogs. (Anonymous, personal communication, August 10, 2013).

The social and behavioral benefits of AAI are critical to consider if they can assist in preventing serious injury or death. Several studies in correctional settings have demonstrated increases in prosocial behavior (Cournoyer & Uttley, 2007; Fournier, Geller, & Fortney, 2007; Jasperson, 2010). In addition, Fournier et al. (2007) found decreased behavioral infractions and improved treatment progress in their prison study. Besides forensic social work, many practitioners seek to influence behavior and improve social skills. School-based AAIs have found similar results. Two studies found decreases in aggressive behavior and increased empathy (Anderson & Olson, 2006; Sprinkle, 2008). Use of an AAT anger management group was found to result in a calming effect and increase empathy (Lange, Cox, Bernert, & Jenkins, 2006). Finally, research of adults in psychiatric settings has documented significant increases in social interactions (Barak, Savorai, Mavashev, & Beni, 2001; Hall & Malpus, 2000; Marr et al., 2000).

SELF-CARE/STAFF BENEFITS

Any practitioner who owns a pet can most likely attest to the joy and benefits they bring to one's life. As we all know, having strategies for stress management is critical in this profession fraught with burnout and compassion fatigue. In an exploratory study of behavioral health staff's perceptions, treatment staff expressed a desire for more AAT groups, a positive effect on the therapeutic environment and staff morale, and enhanced communications between clients and staff (Rossetti, DeFabiis, & Belpedio, 2008). Integrating such a valuable modality in practice settings can be of great benefit to staff. Pichot and Couter (2007) indicate that the presence of a therapy dog has an incredible impact on the staff, the ability to transform the agency, and the power to facilitate positive community relations. Some case examples and practical strategies will help to illustrate the utility of this intervention in individual, group, and crisis intervention.

INDIVIDUAL INTERVENTION

Case example: A young man was mandated for counseling following an incident of fighting. He reluctantly agreed to see the counselor who had the dog. One treatment goal focused on identifying what was fueling his acting out behavior. During one session, he lowered his head and began to share a history of abuse and foster care placements. At this very moment, Maggie the therapy dog looked up from her bed, jumped onto the futon next to him, and began to kiss his face. He embraced her, and she sat beside him laying her chin on his thigh. "Why did she do that?" he asked. I replied, "Maybe she thought you needed a little comfort when discussing this hard stuff. What do you think?" He smiled and nodded his head. For the remainder of the session, Maggie remained by his side providing a consistent, comforting presence as he stroked her and talked about his past. Ultimately, we were able to identify underlying cognitive distortions that were contributing to his increased anger and acting out behavior. Was it the symbolism, a corrective emotional experience, or just a magical Maggie moment? One thing is for sure, it was a turning point. In subsequent sessions we identified times when he had received comfort and support, demonstrating that not everyone is untrustworthy. Integrating a Cognitive Behavioral Therapy (CBT) and Solution-focused Therapy (SFT) approach, we began to challenge his cognitive distortions and strengthen his supportive resources. About a year later with no further conduct violations, he graduated.

The above case example illustrates several essential elements of social work intervention: engagement, assessment, and intervention. During the first therapy session, this young man shared his love of dogs and his plan to have his own dog in the future. Wilkes (2008) indicates

that animals increase trust and act as a catalyst for sharing and healing. With Maggie's help, rapport was quickly built and an initially resistant client became engaged in treatment. Developing this therapeutic alliance was a critical first step.

The second step involved assessing the problems and underlying issues. According to Wilkes (2008), dogs enhance the environment by creating a warm, friendly, nurturing, and safe place. Maggie provided comfort and support, which made it easier for this young man to share his traumatic past.

The final step is intervention, as professionals use the dog to complement their work, as in the cognitive behavioral approach outlined above. No matter what theoretical foundation a practitioner endorses, AAT can be easily integrated. The versatility of this approach can be applied to person-centered, cognitive-behavioral, behavioral, psychoanalytic, gestalt, existential, reality, and solution-focused counseling (Chandler, Portrie-Bethke, Minton, Fernando, & O'Callaghan, 2010; Fine, O'Callaghan, Chandler, Schaffer, Pichot, & Gimeno, 2010). Grover (2010) provides many creative activities integrating the therapy dog into the treatment plan. As a result of the flexibility of this approach, an immense number of consumers stand to benefit from the implementation of AAT.

GROUP INTERVENTION

Case example: An anger management group with 10 young boys sounds like quite a challenge; however, with Maggie's assistance, it was one of the most successful groups. One particular group session focused on how to identify anger and its effects. We used Maggie to start the discussion. The boys eagerly talked about how Maggie might show her teeth, growl, bark or bite, and how those behaviors could make others scared or cause them to avoid Maggie. It provided an easy transition to what behaviors they have engaged in and how these affected others. During a subsequent session, a boy started to become upset, sighing heavily and pounding the floor. Before staff intervention was needed, another boy empathically said, "Hey, don't do that, you might scare Maggie." This boy immediately stopped his behaviors, apologizing to Maggie. Results from a pre- and post-test empathy scale demonstrated significant changes in all participants.

Integrating the dog into the group can be done in a variety of ways. One common practice that can be utilized at the beginning of group meetings is the check-in where members take turns offering an update from the past week. During this process, the therapy dog can move from member to member as they share. Another useful strategy is to include the dog in various group activities. For example, in a group on stress management, Maggie eagerly offers her belly for clients to use a handheld massager to relax her. This fun activity often lends itself to sharing of personal stress management strategies. A third strategy includes using animal-themed books, games, or music. An extensive bibliotherapy list by clinical topics is provided in Fine et al. (2010). Fourth, Maggie has an array of pre-made collages to share with clients for discussion or as an example prior to them creating their own. These include a feelings collage (with her photos and labeled feelings), a coping collage (the many ways she copes with stress), and an eco-map (with her identified supports). Finally, transitional objects can be especially useful to maintain the progress made in treatment. Maggie frequently provides trading cards or book marks with her photo that say, "Maggie says you're MAGNIFICENT." Even adults love these reminders. One adult client, who was initially very afraid of dogs, wanted a photo of Maggie to put on her refrigerator so that she could prove to her family that she overcame her fear.

CRISIS INTERVENTION

Case example: We were called to the Virginia Tech tragedy to provide support to students and faculty as they returned to campus and resumed classes after the shootings. On the drill field one day, a young girl ran up to Maggie and threw her arms around her declaring, "That's my dog." As it turned out, she had a dog at home who looked remarkably similar to Maggie. This young girl shared how she witnessed events and was thus required to remain on campus to be interviewed by law enforcement; unlike other students, she wasn't able to go home and be with her family and dog. In this example, Maggie was able to assist in reducing her stress, offer an opportunity to share her feelings, connect her with a source of support, and facilitate coping. As Watson, Brymer, and Bonanno (2011) indicate, these are the goals of providing psychological first aid following such traumatic events.

AACR offers the addition of a certified crisis response dog to practitioners as a way to help people affected by crises and disasters. Dogs help to establish rapport, build therapeutic bridges,

normalize reactions, and act as a calming agent (Greenbaum, 2006). HOPE animal-assisted crisis response (AACR), a national organization whose mission is "to provide comfort and encouragement through animal-assisted support" has about 120 certified teams across the country able to assist practitioners when needed (HOPE AACR, 2008). According to Graham (2009), these dogs offer a compassionate presence. Chandler (2008), who observed AACR during Hurricane Katrina, found these dogs were much more effective than other interventions in providing nurturance and alleviating anxiety.

CONCLUSION

It appears that dogs are quickly becoming a social worker's best friend, assisting in the provision of care to a host of individuals and groups in need. The use of properly trained, registered, and certified (in the case of crisis work) dogs offers valuable tools that can enhance the work of the practitioner. The cognitive, physical, emotional/mental health, social/behavioral, and self-care/staff benefits are well documented in the literature. Additionally, AAI is easily adaptable to a variety of settings, populations, and practitioner theoretical orientations. I hope this chapter has helped to validate AAI and convince practitioners that they should seriously consider utilizing this intervention when indicated.

WEBSITES

Center for Human-Animal Interaction, www.chai.vcu.edu
Organizations, www.petpartners.org,
Animal assisted crisis intervention, www.hopeacri.org

References

Anderson, K. L., & Olson, M. R. (2006). The value of a dog in a classroom of children with severe emotional disorders. *Anthrozoos, 19*(1), 35–49.

Barak, Y., Savorai, O., Mavashev, S., & Beni, A. (2001). Animal-assisted therapy for elderly schizophrenic patients: A one-year controlled trial. *The American Journal of Geriatric Psychiatry, 9*(4), 439–442.

Barker, S. B., & Dawson, K. S. (1998). The effects of animal-assisted therapy on anxiety ratings of hospitalized psychiatric patients. *Psychiatric Services, 49*(6), 797–801.

Barker, S. B., Knisely, J. S., McCain, N. L., Schubert, C. M., & Pandurangi, A. K. (2010). Exploratory study of stress-buffering response patterns from interaction with a therapy dog. *Anthrozoos, 23*(1), 79–91.

Bassette, L. A., & Taber-Doughty, T. (2013). The effects of a dog reading visit program on academic engagement behavior in three elementary students with emotional and behavioral disabilities: A single case design. *Child and Youth Care Forum, 42*(3), 239–256.

Beetz, A., Uvnas-Moberg, K., Julius, H., & Kotrschal, K. (2012). Psychosocial and psychophysiological effects of human-animal interactions: the possible role of oxytocin. *Frontiers in Psychology, 3*(234), 1–15.

Berget, B., Ekeberg, O., & Braastad, B. O. (2008). Animal-assisted therapy with farm animals for persons with psychiatric disorders: Effects on self-efficacy, coping ability and quality of life, a randomized controlled trial. *Clinical Practice and Epidemiology in Mental Health, 4*(9), 1–7.

Bryant, R. A., Creamer, M., O'Donnell, M., Silove, D., & McFarlane, A. C. (2008). A multisite study of initial respiration rate and heart rate as predictors of posttraumatic stress disorder. *Journal of Clinical Psychiatry, 69*(11), 1694–1701.

Chandler, C. K. (2005). *Animal assisted therapy in counseling.* New York, NY: Routledge.

Chandler, C. K. (2008, March). *Animal assisted therapy with Hurricane Katrina survivors.* Based on a program presented at the ACA Annual Conference & Exhibition, Honolulu, Hawaii. Retrieved from http://counselingoutfitters.com/vistas/vistas08/Chandler.htm

Chandler, C. K., Portrie-Bethke, T. L., Minton, C. A., Fernando, D. M., & O'Callaghan, D. (2010). Matching animal-assisted therapy techniques and intentions with counseling guiding theories. *Journal of Mental Health Counseling, 32*(4), 354–374.

Chu, C., Liu, C., Sun, C., & Lin, J. (2009). The effects of animal-assisted activity on inpatients with schizophrenia. *Journal of Psychosocial Nursing, 47*(12), 42–48.

Cournoyer, G. P., & Uttley, C. M. (2007). Cisco's kids: A pet assisted therapy behavioral intervention program. *Journal of Emotional Abuse, 7*(3), 117–126.

Delta Society. (2000). *Team training course manual.* Renton, WA: Delta Society.

DeYoung, A. C., Kenardy, J. A., & Spence, S. H. (2007). Elevated heart rate as a predictor of PTSD six months following accidental pediatric injury. *Journal of Traumatic Stress, 20*(5), 751–756.

Fine, A. H., O'Callaghan, D., Chandler, C., Schaffer, K., Pichot, T., & Gimeno, J. (2010). Application of animal-assisted interventions in counseling settings: An overview of alternatives. In A. H. Fine (Ed.), *Handbook on animal-assisted therapy: Theoretical foundations and guidelines for practice* (3rd ed.). (pp. 193–222) San Diego, CA: Academic Press.

Fournier, A. K., Geller, E. S., & Fortney, E. V. (2007). Human-animal interaction in a prison setting: Impact on criminal behavior, treatment progress, and social skills. *Behavior and Social Issues, 16*(1), 89–105.

Graham, L. B. (2009). Dogs bringing comfort in the midst of a national disaster. *Reflections, 15*(1), 76–84.

Greenbaum, S. D. (2006). Introduction to working with animal-assisted crisis response animal handler teams. *International Journal of Emergency Mental Health, 8*(1), 49–64.

Grover, S. (2010). *101 Creative ideas for animal assisted therapy: Interventions for AAT teams and working professionals.* Carlsbad, CA: Motivational Press.

Hall, P. L., & Malpus, Z. (2000). Pets as therapy: Effects on social interaction in long-stay psychiatry. *British Journal of Nursing, 9*(21), 2220–2225.

Hoffman, A., Lee, A. H., Wertenauer, F., Ricken, R., Jansen, J. J., Gallinat, J., & Lang, U. (2009). Dog-assisted intervention significantly reduces anxiety in hospitalized patients with major depression. *European Journal of Integrative Medicine, 1*, 145–148.

HOPE AACR. (2008). *Comfort in times of crisis* [Brochure]. Retrieved from http:// www.hope-aacr.org

Jasperson, R. A. (2010). Animal-assisted therapy with female inmates with mental illness: A case example from a pilot program. *Journal of Offender Rehabilitation, 49*, 417–433.

Kaminski, M., Pellino, T., & Wish, J. (2002). Play and pets: The physical and emotional impact of child-life and pet therapy on hospitalized children. *Children's Health Care, 31*(4), 321–335.

Kassam-Adams, N., Garcia-Espana, J. F., Fein, J. A., & Winston, F. K. (2005). Heart rate and posttraumatic stress in injured children. *Archives General Psychiatry, 62*, 335–340.

Kuhn, E., Blanchard, E. B., Fuse, T., Hickling, E. J., & Broderick, J. (2006). Heart rate of motor vehicle accident survivors in the emergency department, peritraumatic psychological reactions, ASD, and PTSD severity: A 6-month prospective study. *Journal of Traumatic Stress, 19*(5), 735–740.

Lang, U. E., Jansen, J. B., Wertenauer, F., Gallinat, J., & Rapp, M. A. (2010). Reduced anxiety during dog assisted interviews in acute schizophrenic patients. *European Journal of Integrative Medicine, 2*, 123–127.

Lange, A. M., Cox, J. A., Bernert, D. J., & Jenkins, C. D. (2006). Is counseling going to the dogs?

An exploratory study related to the inclusion of an animal in group counseling with adolescents. *Journal of Creativity in Mental Health, 2*(2), 17–31.

Marr, C. A., French, L., Thompson, D., Drum, L., Greening, G., Mormon, J., Henderson, I., & Hughes, C. W. (2000). Animal-assisted therapy in psychiatric rehabilitation. *Anthrozoos, 13*(1), 43–47.

Moretti, F., DeRonchi, D., Bernabei, V., Marchetti, L., Ferrari, B., Forlani, C., Negretti, F., … Atti, A. (2011). Pet therapy in elderly patients with mental illness. *Psychogeriatrics, 11*, 125–129.

Morrison, M. L. (2007). Health benefits of animal-assisted interventions. *Complementary Health Practice Review, 12*(1), 51–62.

Nathans-Barel, I., Feldman, P., Berger, B., Modai, I., & Silver, H. (2005). Animal-assisted therapy ameliorates anhedonia in schizophrenia patients. *Psychotherapy and Psychosomatics, 74*(1), 31–35.

Newlin, R. B. (2003). Paws for reading. *School Library Journal, 49*(6), 43.

Pet Partners. (2012). Pet partners: Touching lives, improving health. Retrieved from http://www.petpartners.org/

Pichot, T., & Couter, M. (2007). *Animal-assisted brief therapy: A solution-focused approach.* Binghamton, NY: Haworth Press, Inc.

Risley-Curtiss, C. (2010). Social work practitioners and the human-companion animal bond: A national study. *Social Work, 55*(1), 38–46.

Rossetti, J., DeFabiis, S., & Belpedio, C. (2008). Behavioral health staff's perceptions of pet-assisted therapy: An exploratory study. *Journal of Psychosocial Nursing, 46*(9), 28–33.

Sable, P. (2013). The pet connection: An attachment perspective. *Clinical Social Work Journal, 41*, 93–99.

Sobo, E. J., Eng, B., & Kassity-Krich, N. (2006). Canine visitation (pet) therapy. *Journal of Holistic Nursing, 24*(1), 51–57.

Sprinkle, J. E. (2008). Animals, empathy, and violence: Can animals be used to convey principles of prosocial behavior to children? *Youth Violence and Juvenile Justice, 6*(1), 47–58.

Tedeschi, P., Fitchett, J., & Molidor, C. E. (2005). The incorporation of animal-assisted interventions in social work education. *Journal of Family Social Work, 9*(4), 59–77.

Van Fleet, R. (2008). *Play therapy with kids & canines: Benefits for children's developmental and psychosocial health.* Sarasota, FL: Professional Resource Press.

VCU Medical Center. (2011). Center for Human-Animal Interaction. Retrieved from http://www.chai.vcu.edu

Watson, P. J., Brymer, M. J., & Bonanno, G. A. (2011). Postdisaster psychological intervention since 9/11. *American Psychologist, 66*(6), 482–494.

Wells, D. L. (2009). The effects of animals on human health and well-being. *Journal of Social Issues, 65*(3), 523–543.

Wilkes, J. K. (2008). *The role of companion animals in counseling and psychology: Discovering their use in the therapeutic process.* Springfield, IL: Charles C. Thomas Publisher, Ltd.

38   Narrative Therapy

Patricia Kelley & Mark Smith

This chapter is dedicated to Michael White (1948–2008)

As the 20th century drew to a close, narrative therapy (NT) became an important trend in clinical social work and family therapy and was part of the postmodern movement that crosses many disciplines, from arts and literature to the social sciences. The postmodern movement is a reaction to modernism, which holds that there are universal laws and truths that can be uncovered through scientific discovery and that all phenomena can be explained if these truths are discovered. Postmodernism challenges the idea of absolute truth and grand theories that explain human behavior.

The narrative approach was developed in the 1980s by Michael White, a social worker/family therapist from South Australia, and David Epston, a social worker/family therapist from New Zealand who also studied community organization. It has received worldwide attention since the publication of their book in North America in 1990 (White & Epston, 1990). Although NT began in the family therapy movement, it has also been applied to work at the individual, group, and community levels.

NT developed within the context of the social constructionist and second-order cybernetic movements, which have influenced the field of family therapy since the 1980s. In addition to positioning themselves within the epistemological perspective of social constructionism, White and Epston (1990) drew from the ideas of constructivism, the work of Foucault, and the field of literary criticism. Constructivism focuses on individuals' perceptions and cognitions as shaping their views of reality, whereas social constructionism focuses more on the social and cultural narratives individuals internalize, taking them for granted as constituting "reality." Both views deny objective reality, believing that one's view of reality is constructed out of language use and social interaction. White and Epston incorporate both social constructionism and constructivism in their use of a narrative metaphor in therapeutic work, believing that people create stories of their lives to make sense of all their lived experience. The stories people develop incorporate the dominant social and cultural stories of gender, ethnicity, and power, as well as personal stories co-constructed in interaction with others (family, friends, and professional helpers), and constitute the knowledge that people hold about themselves and their worlds. As in postmodern literary criticism, the narrative therapist helps clients "deconstruct" the story lines around which they have organized their lives, assessing the plot, characters, and timeline for meaning, and then look for other "truths" that also exist.

The goal of narrative therapy in social work practice is to help clients first understand the relational nature of the stories around which they have organized their lives and then challenge and broaden these, thus creating new realities that are consonant with preferred lives. These discoveries can help clients see more alternatives and ways out of an impasse. They can also help clients see more aspects of themselves, including strengths and coping skills they already have, which can be mobilized to fight the effects of the problems they are facing. Conversation is important because language creates our reality; through discourse, reality (including history) is socially constructed (created). NT is more than storytelling, it is story *changing*. The narrative therapist does not deny the harsh realities facing clients, such as poverty, racism, or illness, but rather challenges the power given to these adverse aspects of their lives and the control the problems have over their lives.

USING A NARRATIVE APPROACH

Narrative therapy takes a collaborative approach in working with clients; where clients are experts on their lives, and as the story lines unfold, the client and social worker together discover other realities and join in fighting the effects of the problem. Key concepts of NT are as follows.

- *Problem-saturated stories.* These are the one-dimensional stories clients have about themselves that they have co-constructed in interaction with others and are influenced by social-cultural forces that have restricted them. These stories are examined in session as clients are challenged to expand their views of self.
- *Double-listening.* Also referred to as attending to the *absent but implicit*, therapists listen to both the explicit expressions of client complaints/distress as well as what is absent from the expression but implicit in its meaning. This practice can help elicit a range of intentional or historical understandings for clients and set the stage for them to become more active agents in countering disabling narratives.
- *Externalizing the problem.* In conversation with clients the problem is externalized, or separated from the person, whereby the problem not the person is the target of change.
- *Mapping the problem's domain.* The effects of the problem over time (past, present, and possible future) and over many domains are examined; in so doing, the client can assess what might be done. In addition to

mapping practices, clients are often enlisted to undertake an "archeology of the present," which acknowledges influences and personal historical precursors of the client's present resolve to seek help in restoring a preferred sense of self. This reinforces client readiness and motivation to enact change behaviors.

- *Unique outcomes.* These are the times clients have not been overcome by their problems. For clients, these times may represent new truths and discoveries about themselves that are often strengths or aspects of the client's story that are not consistent with the problem-saturated dominant story. These episodes are highlighted and moved into prominence in descriptions of the client's situation.
- *Outsider witness practices.* Problems are seen as being situated relationally; therefore, clients are encouraged to call upon those who may have unique understandings that contrast, challenge, provide insight, or add perspective to the problem-saturated story. These outsider witnesses may be present in one's life, may be imaginary characters, or may even be dead, but they do provide confirmation and support for intentions and preferred actions.
- *Re-membering/Praxis.* Once clients start experiencing some positive change, they are encouraged to let others know about their successes in fighting the effects of the problems or in not giving in to the problems. This may involve celebrations, certificates, awards, letter writing, or even talking to groups of others facing similar problems. Rather than positioning the client as victim or even survivor of difficulties, client insider expertise regarding experience with this kind of problem is acknowledged, and therapists often encourage clients to join with others in forming new memberships of community engagement and advocacy.

Using this approach, the social worker does not design an intervention to do something "to" a client. Neither does the clinician assume that a problem or symptom serves a function for the individual (as in psychodynamic approaches) or the family system (as in the family systems approaches), although the problem may have influenced a family's behavior. There are no presumptions about the client.

Clients are carefully listened to so the therapist can understand their perceptions of the problem and the meanings they ascribe to it. Then, through respectful listening and deconstructive questioning, problems are externalized and the problem-saturated stories are examined through mapping and questioning. In the reconstruction stage, some truths are gently challenged through questioning, and unique outcomes are isolated. Therapy is terminated by mutual agreement with plans for spreading the news, often with celebrations or awards, and engagement in community education or advocacy. NT contains many "wondering" questions to help clients think about and reflect on their interpretations and beliefs about their lived experiences. Through such reflections, they consider other interpretations and other meanings, expanding their view of self. The concept of self is considered fluid and changing.

Even though the focus is more on meanings than specific behaviors, NT is usually short-term, with a few sessions spread over a longer period of time. The concepts and interventions of NT bear some similarity to solution-focused therapy (SFT) (de Shazer & Berg, 1993; Lee, 2011) and the strength perspective (Saleebey, 2002) in that they all are empowerment-based approaches aimed at mobilizing clients' strengths and resources. However, these approaches also have some distinct differences.

- The "Unique Outcomes" of NT are different from the SFT's "exceptions" in that they are not asked for but rather discovered through careful listening.
- In NT, the discussion of possible futures does not just focus on the hoped for (positive) future but also assesses the potential future if the problem continues to dominate clients' lives.
- Because clients come into the relationship with a problem to solve, ameliorate, or cope with, narrative therapists do not avoid discussing problems but attend to them as part of the whole story, which is then expanded.

CASE EXAMPLE

Family therapy sessions were held for a blended family comprising a mother who had married before, her 14-year-old daughter, Mary Ann, and her second husband, who had never married before. A mutual daughter, aged 7 years, was not brought to the sessions. The family was concerned that Mary Ann had become rebellious and dropped her previous friends to run with an older boyfriend and his crowd who engaged in dangerous and illegal activities and did not attend school. These activities represented a dramatic shift from her previous good behavior. Her mood had changed to surly and her grades had dropped dramatically.

In sessions, they all discussed perceptions and stories of the situation. Mary Ann discussed how she felt that she was living in a house designed for little girls, with little accommodation for her to grow up and achieve some independence. She also felt that her stepfather did not love her, was mean to her, and favored the younger daughter. The mother discussed how she lived in terror, fearing what might happen to Mary Ann if the illegal and dangerous activities continued; she mourned the loss of her close relationship with Mary Ann; and she felt torn between loyalty to husband and daughter. The stepfather discusses feeling left out of the family by the close relationship between the mother and daughter. He admitted being overly strict sometimes as he tried to join the family. After each member had heard the stories of fears and frustrations of the others, the meanings they made of events shifted. Double listening helped the family recognize that expressions such as "stepfather did not love her" and "mourning the loss of close relationships" implied that close relationships and feeling love from the stepfather were values the family shared. Control and strictness were seen as love and caring, and rebelliousness was perceived as attempts to change and grow.

After thorough discussion, adolescence was externalized as a new force entering their lives. They discussed ways to welcome the "new member," making it a positive force instead of a negative one. As the family developed more empathy and understanding for each other and began laughing as they found ways to welcome the new member, compromises were reached, where new independence could be earned by following certain rules. Better judgments equaled new freedoms. Family meetings to agree on the rules were set up and involved the father more. The biological father, 1,000 miles away, agreed to support the new rules, demonstrating that all three parents cared enough about Mary Ann to cooperate. Many old truths were deconstructed and new ways to deal with problems emerged.

NARRATIVE THERAPY AND SOCIAL WORK

Narrative therapy is compatible with the traditional social work methods and values of individualizing each client as unique, respecting each client's story, respecting cultural differences, and separating one's own beliefs and values from those of clients through self-understanding and conscious use of self. Social work values are demonstrated through the following methods.

Respectful listening. By taking a "nonexpert, not knowing" position about the clients' lives, we show respect for their knowledge, and we listen carefully to their ideas. This stance is not the same as neutrality, for some stories are clearly less useful or even harmful (e.g., violence) than others, but here the therapist assesses the outcomes and consequences with the client and may challenge the story through deconstruction and by assessing its origins.

Avoidance of labels. The use of labels and categories for totalizing clients as to who they are is questioned, and through externalization the clients are seen as afflicted with a problem but not constituted of it. For example, persons may be afflicted with a particular medical condition, such as cancer or a serious mental illness, but that affliction is just one part of who they are, not their total being. Thus, a person would not be viewed as a schizophrenic but perhaps as a person contending with the influences of schizophrenia and the effects of the diagnosis.

Fostering empowerment. The political nature of NT, wherein clients are "liberated" from dominant familial and cultural stories that have restricted them, and instead are urged to take a stand on their own behalf, makes it especially compatible with social work practice.

Emphasis on social justice. NT also takes a stand on social justice issues, as exemplified in the work of New Zealanders Waldegrave, Tamasese, Tuhaka, and Campbell (2003), who developed their own version of NT, called "just therapy" because it focuses on social justice. White worked on social justice issues and has worked with oppressed communities to challenge the dominant narratives oppressing them. Beginning in 1999, White and others at the Dulwich

Family Therapy Training Centre in Adelaide, South Australia, organized international narrative therapy conferences that focus on work with families, communities, and social justice issues.

Extensions beyond the office. The bridge between micro and macro practice is useful for social workers and fits in with newer community practice approaches. Narrative therapists work beyond office walls to foster communities of support and empower clients.

POTENTIAL CONCERNS

Although narrative therapy seems consistent with good social work practice, some problems regarding it have been raised. There is little empirical research supporting NT, partly because postmodernism denies the objectivity that is at the core of empiricism. Other research approaches, such as qualitative methods and case studies, may address this concern. In addition, family therapists might be concerned that narrative therapists have turned their backs on the defining characteristics of family therapy, not taking family dynamics into account and often not seeing the family as a unit. Kelley (1998) noted that two major trends in clinical practice, postmodernism and managed care, seem at odds with each other. Managed care demands *DSM-IV* or *DSM-5* diagnoses with preapproved treatment plans designed by the clinician and based on empirically proven methods, whereas in NT the emphasis is on the therapist and client co-constructing new realities through dialogue rather than conducting problem-solving activities designed by the therapist. Some aspects of narrative therapy, for example, its short-term nature and cognitive focus, could bridge this gap.

FUTURE PRACTICE APPLICATIONS

The questions regarding narrative therapy have not diminished its impact. As Minuchin noted (Minuchin, Nichols, and Lee, 2007), "narrative therapy … is a perfect expression of the postmodern revolution" (p.2). The approach that was once considered revolutionary has become more mainstream as evidenced by inclusion in social work (ex. Turner, 2011) and family therapy texts (Nichols, 2012), and several books and articles on the subject. A book by Freedman and Combs (1996) has long been considered a classic in the field. White and Epston continued to develop ideas and publish (Epston, 2011; White, 2007). Furthermore, changes have developed over time as NT broadened its scope to more community and group work (Kelley & Murty, 2003; Vodde & Gallant, 2003; Carey & Russell, 2011), decreasing the distinction between micro and macro practice. The movement demanding more consumer participation in decision making has called for newer methods for social work practice. NT is a product of its time.

WEBSITES

Dulwich Centre. http://www.dulwichcentre.com.au.

Planet Therapy, online mental health learning community. http://www.planet-therapy.com.

Victoria Dickerson (narrative therapy). http://www.victoriadickerson.com.

Yaletown Family Therapy. http://www.therapeuticconversations.com.

Hincks-Dellcrest Center. http://www.hincksdellcrest.org/

References

Carey, M., & Russell, S. (2011). Pedagogy shaped by culture: Teaching narrative approaches to Australian aboriginal health workers. *Journal of Systemic Therapies*, 3(3), 26–41.

de Shazer, S., & Berg, I. K. (1993). Constructing solutions. *Family Therapy Networker*, 12, 42–43.

Epston, D. (2011). More travels with Herodotus: Tripping over borders lightly or "psychiatric imperialism." *Journal of Systemic Therapies*, 30(3), 1–11.

Freedman, J., & Combs, J. (1996). *Narrative therapy: The social construction of preferred realities.* New York, NY: Norton.

Kelley, P. (1998). Narrative therapy in a managed care world. *Crisis Intervention*, 4(2/3), 113–123.

Kelley, P., & Murty, S. (2003). Teaching narrative approaches in community practice. *Social Work Review (of New Zealand)*, 15(4), 14–20.

Lee, M. Y. (2011). Solution–focused therapy. In F. J. Turner (Ed), *Social work treatment: Interlocking theoretical approaches* (5th ed.) (pp. 460–476). New York, NY: Oxford University Press.

Minuchin, S., Nichols, M., & Lee, M. Y. (2007). *Assessing families and couples: From symptom to system.* New York, NY: Allyn & Bacon.

Nichols, M. P. (2012). *Family therapy: Concepts and methods* (10th ed.). New York, NY: Pearson.

Saleebey, D. (2002). *The strengths perspective in social work practice* (3rd ed.). Boston, MA: Allyn-Bacon.

Turner, F. J. (Ed.). (2011). *Social work treatment: Interlocking theoretical approaches* (5th ed.). New York, NY: Oxford University Press.

Vodde, R., & Gallant, J. (2003). Bridging the gap between micro and macro practice: Large scale change and a unified model of narrative-deconstructive practice. *Social Work Review (of New Zealand)*, 15 (4), 4–13.

Waldegrave, C., Tamasese, K., Tuhaka, F., & Campbell, W. (2003). *Just Therapy—a Journey: A collection of papers from the just therapy team.* Adelaide, SA, Australia: Dulwich Centre Publications.

White, M. (2007). *Maps of narrative practice.* New York, NY: W. W. Norton & Co.

White, M., & Epston, D. (1990). *Narrative means to therapeutic ends.* New York, NY: Norton.

The Neurobiology of Toxic Stress

39 *Implications for Social Work Practice*

Julie M. Rosenzweig & Stephanie A. Sundborg

The past two decades have witnessed an explosion of psychological trauma-focused research, scholarship, and practice applications. Consequently, social workers are scrambling to keep up with a burgeoning amount of information and translate the knowledge into service design and delivery. Integrating this emerging stream of knowledge across a wide range of settings has included both trauma-informed approaches (see e.g., Esaki et al., 2013; Fallot & Harris, 2001; Saakvitne, Gamble, Pearlman, & Lev, 2000) and trauma-specific interventions (see e.g., Briere & Scott, 2006; Herman, 1997; Ogden, Minton, & Pain, 2006; Wilson & Tang, 2007).

Trauma-informed organizations or systems acknowledge the pervasiveness of traumatic events and adversity in the lives of service users and act accordingly by developing policies, practices, and processes that integrate knowledge about traumatic stress (Hopper, Bassuk, & Olivet, 2009). In comparison, trauma-specific interventions include therapeutic models purposefully designed to address trauma-based impairments (Cook et al., 2005) and promote healing and recovery. Trauma-specific interventions are often evidence-based models that are particular to the type of trauma exposure, the developmental stage of the individual (child, youth, or adult), co-occurring disorders, or a specific population (e.g., veterans, refugees, or survivors of interpersonal violence). They may also integrate culturally specific approaches.

Central to the development, training, and implementation of both trauma-informed approaches and trauma-specific interventions have been advancements in knowledge about the neurobiological underpinnings of psychological trauma. Following the United States Congressional designation of 1990s as The Decade of the Brain, multiple research initiatives were launched from which findings emerged that have profoundly changed how the brain is understood. Innovations in neuroimaging technology, such as functional magnetic resonance imaging (fMRI) have provided neuroscientists opportunities to learn about brain growth and development to a level of complexity unparalleled in history. New information about the brain, particularly brain plasticity, has stimulated the development of improved medical and mental health treatments.

Neurobiological research has also shed new light on the dynamics of nature–nurture, resulting in increased attention on the importance of infant and early childhood caregiver attachments, particularly to resultant lifelong physical and mental health challenges (Shonkoff, Richter, van der Gaag, & Bhutta, 2012).

Neuroscience research in general, and specific to psychological trauma, is reshaping how social workers understand typical development, the bio-psychosocial effects of traumatic events on the brain, and the resilient capacity of individuals to transform peril into wisdom. As Shonkoff (2010) asserts,

The challenge before us is to capitalize on the capacity of this scientific revolution to stimulate creative ways of thinking about how to address a much broader range of societal concerns, including education reform, workforce development, health promotion, prevention of disease and disability, protection of children from the consequences of maltreatment and exploitation, reduction in violent crime, and the alleviation of poverty (p. 357).

The purpose of this chapter is to provide social workers with neurobiological information about toxic stress that can be integrated into policy, practice, and advocacy. Information about the neurobiology of toxic stress, coupled with an understanding of affect regulation, provide an effective framework for social workers to develop and provide services to those suffering a range of sequelae from adversity. The discussion begins by defining toxic stress as an expansion of traumatic stress. An overview of key brain areas that are activated by exposure to adversity is presented, followed by a description of the mind-body stress response systems. The chapter concludes with a discussion and guiding questions to assist social workers in developing a neuro-trauma lens for their work.

WHEN STRESS BECOMES TOXIC

Potentially traumatizing events have been categorized in multiple ways: intimate partner violence, child abuse and neglect, combat, natural disasters, terrorism, and geographic displacement are only a few examples. Knowing the array of events that produce psychological trauma exposure can assist policymakers, administrators, and providers in advocating for trauma prevention, trauma-informed, and trauma-specific services in communities. Identifying and assessing the psychological effects of trauma exposure on individuals, families, and communities is more complex. The type of trauma, age at trauma exposure, duration of events, relational factors, prior trauma exposure, social ecological conditions, and cultural beliefs are only some of the variables that make differential contributions to one's individual bio-psychological experience of trauma. Importantly, in addition to understanding how trauma impairs development and functioning, researchers are learning more about resilience as it relates to trauma. Especially promising is the emerging examination of resilience as an ecological construct as well as an individual characteristic (Ungar, 2013).

Psychological trauma has been most commonly associated with the concept of traumatic stress and the diagnosis of posttraumatic stress disorder (PTSD). Once the domain of the *Diagnostic Statistical Manual (DSM)* and psychotherapy, reference to PTSD is now commonplace in the media and social conversations. However, from its inception as a diagnosis in 1980, the conceptualization of PTSD has been criticized as too restrictive in its criteria. Particularly vocal have been practitioners serving children, who have advocated for the inclusion of a developmental trauma disorder in the *DSM-5* (D'Andrea, Ford, Stolbach, Spinazzola, & van der Kolk, 2012; Ford et al., 2013).

This advocacy effort has, in part, been fueled by neuroscience research that was not available when the diagnosis of PTSD was first conceptualized. Criticism notwithstanding, increased public awareness of PTSD, largely due to media coverage of veterans returning from combat in Iraq and Afghanistan, has benefited many individuals and families. Still, defining traumatic stressors, traumatic stress responses, and recommended interventions solely by criteria within a diagnostic category used primarily by clinicians is limiting.

Toxic Stress

Bringing together neuroscience, epidemiology, developmental psychology, and ecology, The Center on the Developing Child at Harvard University proposed a bio-developmental framework that underscores the significance of the mind-body's stress response system and the concept of *toxic stress*.

Toxic stress refers to strong, frequent, and/or prolonged activation of the body's stress-response systems in the absence of buffering protection of stable adult support. Major risk factors include extreme poverty, recurrent physical and/or emotional abuse, chronic neglect, severe maternal depression, parental substance abuse, and family violence. The defining characteristic of toxic stress is that it disrupts brain architecture, adversely affects other organs, and leads to stress management systems that establish a lower threshold for responsiveness that is persistent throughout life, thereby increasing the risk of stress-related disease or disorder as well as cognitive impairment well into the adult years (Shonkoff, 2010, p. 360).

In contrast to traumatic stress, toxic stress is a more inclusive concept that comprehensively acknowledges the intricate intersection between biology (genetics) and environmental conditions, as well as the lifelong consequences of a child's stress response system being relentlessly activated (Lanius, Vermetten, & Pain, 2010). *Epigenetic adaptation,* the process by which an individual's environment shapes gene architecture and expression even influencing succeeding generations, is beginning to be better understood and will contribute significantly to understanding the complexities of toxic stress, including intergenerational transmission (Peckman, 2013). Simply stated, adversity becomes biologically embedded and creates developmental vulnerabilities that can last generations. This expanded perspective on the chronic stress of adversity is crucial for the development of trauma-informed service delivery systems, especially prevention and early intervention programs.

BRAIN STRUCTURES AND FUNCTIONS

A thorough description of all key brain structures that participate in responding to toxic stress is beyond the scope of this chapter; interested readers are encouraged to pursue the references mentioned for additional information. To facilitate understanding, a picture of the brain with key areas identified is included (See Figure 39.1). After briefly describing the fundamental features of brain regions that are most prominently involved in responding to traumatic events, the remaining portion of this section elaborates on the stress response systems. Learning more about the specialization of each area provides the practitioner with a deeper understanding of emotional

regulation strategies and meaning-making processes, both fundamental to working with individuals affected by toxic stress.

Hemispheric Specialization

The cerebral cortex has two halves, a right hemisphere (RH) and a left hemisphere (LH). Although these two halves appear identical in size and structures, there are important differences in function and processing style. The right hemisphere (RH) is dominant at birth and continues to be the primary hemisphere for the first three years of life with its functions focused on survival, attachment patterns, emotional regulation, and sensory experiences (Chiron et al., 1997; Schore, 2000). The RH is the relational hemisphere, mapping the emotional terrain of our earliest attachment experiences through cycles of dysregulation and regulation as infant and caregiver engage in reciprocity of attunement and resonance. These imprints, or internal working models of self and the world, serve as signposts for safety and promote or inhibit exploration (Beebe, Lachmann, Markese, & Bahrick, 2012).

The LH develops more slowly than the RH, not becoming fully wired-up (myelinated) until 18 to 24 months. Compared with the RH, the LH tends to be more logical, analytical, and sequential, and focuses on details in order to construct complex theories and narratives (Phelps & Gazzaniga, 1992). The *interpreter,* a name dubbed by Michael Gazzaniga (Gazzaniga et al., 1996; Gazzaniga, Holtzman, Deck, & Lee, 1985) to reflect the LH's preference for stories and understanding, "seeks explanations for internal and external events in order to produce appropriate response behaviors" (Gazzaniga, Ivry, & Mangun, 2009, p. 465).

The two hemispheres each contribute uniquely to communication. The LH is understood to be primary in producing and comprehending language, in the traditional sense; however, the RH plays an important role in understanding emotion-based nonverbal cues such as body language and facial expressions (Blonder, Bowers, & Heilman, 1991; Semrud-Clikeman, & Hynd, 1990). Both are important not only for communicating with others, but as a way of maintaining a sense of order. Meaning making is the way individuals interpret their worlds and give explanation to events that happen. Whereas the RH is dominant for emotions and relationships, the LH specializes in providing context and perspective. In other words, the LH provides

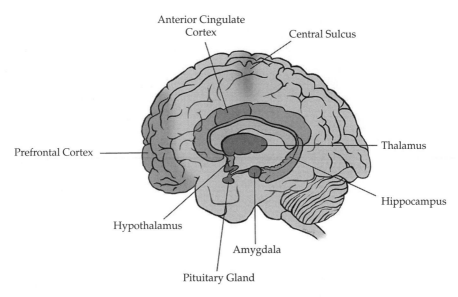

Figure 39.1 Brain structures involved in responding to traumatic events (illustration by Halorie Walker-Sands).

the narrative to emotional experiences; expanding on what is known in the present and making inferences based on past experience. This is how individuals develop a worldview, against which events are scanned to provide explanation (Roser, Fugelsang, Dunbar, Corballis, & Gazzaniga, 2005). Individuals with traumatic histories, especially early childhood experiences, are more likely to have a worldview of self-as-bad and others-dangerous and filter relationships and experiences through this lens.

The Amygdala

Responding to traumatic events and toxic stress involves many brain regions and of primary importance are the amygdales (one in each hemisphere). Acting as a first responder, this small, almond-shaped area processes input from our sensory systems, including tactile, visual, olfactory, auditory, and gustatory stimuli, determining whether the incoming information is life-sustaining or life-threatening. The amygdala automatically coordinates with brain areas involved in long-term memory (hippocampus) and inhibitory control (prefrontal cortex) through elaborate neural networks, and if warranted, participates in initiating a survival-based response.

All sensory input associated with a dangerous or threatening situation is encoded by the amygdala as a threat to survival and is formed into

memory. Before the development of language, the encoding of memories is automatic and outside of conscious awareness. These implicit-type memories do not contain autobiographical or chronological references, thus are devoid of a sense of self, time, or place and cannot be recalled voluntarily. Implicit memory encoding continues throughout the lifespan and is fundamental to encoding traumatic experiences (Amir, McNally, & Wiegartz, 1996; Elzinga & Bremner, 2002). The amygdala and the implicit memory making processes build a database of all information associated with the threat. This database is used to anticipate and respond to danger, both actual and perceived.

The Hippocampus

The hippocampi (one in each hemisphere) are also key brain areas involved in processing traumatic experiences; and are highly susceptible to the damaging effects of toxic stress. Named appropriately for its sea horse-like shape, the hippocampus is critical for learning and long-term memory processing. The explicit-type of memory, processed by the hippocampus, differs in several ways from the implicit memory formed and stored by the amygdala. First, explicit memories can be voluntarily recalled and explained using language, which is why it is often referred to as declarative memory. Second, the information encoded is factually based and represents details of people, places, and events, giving these memories a sense of self, time, and place (Kandel, 2007). Together the amygdala and hippocampus both contribute to the rich, detailed autobiographical story of our lives. "Exchange of information between the hippocampus and amygdala link the emotional and contextual aspect of events," (Joëls, Pu, Wiegert, Oitzl, & Krugers, 2006, p. 155).

The Hypothalamus and Pituitary

Located in an area between the cerebrum and the brain stem, essentially above the roof of the mouth, is the hypothalamus. This area "coordinates behavioral response to insure bodily homeostasis, the constancy of the internal environment" (Kandel, Schwartz, & Jessell, 2000, p. 960). In particular, the hypothalamus works to maintain life-essential functions, such as the regulation of blood pressure, body temperature, thirst, hunger, and reproductive behaviors (Saper, 2009). Although much of this activity engages the "rest and digest" system, under threatening conditions, the hypothalamus coordinates with the brain stem and the pituitary gland to initiate the body's stress response system, preparing for fight, flight, or freeze. The pituitary, considered to be the master gland, lies beneath the hypothalamus and acts as the "mouth piece through which the hypothalamus speaks to the body" (Bear, Connors, & Paradiso, 2007, p. 485). When activated under stress, the pituitary releases a cascade of stress hormones.

The Medial Prefrontal Cortex and Anterior Cingulate Cortex

The brain areas discussed thus far act reflexively and subconsciously, for the most part, and are involved in what can be termed *bottom-up* processing. Areas of the brain involved in *top-down* processing are located in the frontal lobe. The frontal lobe offers comparatively slower processing by filtering reactions, inhibiting responses, regulating emotions, engaging in problem solving, directing attention, making plans, and integrating information. In the case of a threatening situation, areas of the frontal lobe, specifically the medial prefrontal cortex (mPFC) and anterior cingulate cortex (ACC) help interpret threat, evaluate emotional conflict, and distract from fearful stimuli (Etkin, Egner, & Kalisch, 2011; Milad et al., 2007). Segments of these brain frontal lobe areas focus on immediate threat, while

others plan responses to anticipated threat (Etkin et al., 2011). The mPFC and ACC also monitor bodily changes, for instance, increased heart rate and breathing; insight referred to as interoceptive awareness (Critchley, Wiens, Rotshtein, Öhman, & Dolan, 2004). After interpreting the situation, these frontal lobe areas may promote a stress response, or they may quiet reactive areas such as the amygdala and hypothalamus (Schore, 2002). As discussed in the next section, when threat is consistently present or perception of danger sensitized, bottom-up processing becomes normative and the involvement of the frontal lobe in threat assessment is by-passed and thus, emotional regulation impaired.

THREAT, SURVIVAL, AND ADAPTATION

Working together through a system of complex neural networks, the brain areas described continually process physiological and affective arousal in order to maintain a state of regulation in the body and mind. When the brain interprets stimuli or experience as life-threatening, there is an automatic, subconscious activation of survival strategies, most commonly flight, fight, or freeze responses. Accompanying the physiological activation of survival responses is the affective experience of fear. The innate initiation of survival strategies to ensure safety is based both on genetically encoded ancestral memories of what was dangerous in past environments and what the individual's neurobiology has learned about threat in current environments. This on-going cataloging of threat stimuli is an example of the nature–nurture interaction, an essential part of adaptation, also known as fear conditioning (LeDoux, 2003; Perry, Pollard, Blakley, Baker, & Vigilante, 1995).

Typically, when threat has been averted, or the perception of threat by the amygdala determined to be nonthreatening by the hippocampus, the stress system response is shut off and a state of regulation is restored. However, when the threat is frequent or prolonged, the ability of the brain to bring about regulation becomes impaired. Deficits or alterations in the stress regulatory processes are the basis of many mental health impairments, including posttraumatic stress and complex trauma disorders. Recent research, most prominently the Adverse Childhood Experiences Study (Felitti et al., 1998), has established a clear link between early childhood adversity and adulthood health problems including cardiovascular and immune diseases. Practitioners working with individuals who have a history of trauma exposure, affected by adversity, are indeed working with altered stress regulatory systems. The following is a more detailed description of the stress response system and the effects of toxic stress on specific brain areas.

Stress Response Systems

When danger is detected, the hypothalamus engages two distinct stress response systems, the Sympathetic Adrenomedullary (SAM) system, and the Hypothalamic-Pituitary-Adrenal (HPA) system. Both systems respond to real or perceived threat, initiating fight, flight, or freeze behaviors. During activation, the brain prioritizes resources for activities that are essential for survival, such as heart rate, blood pressure, and muscle tension, while activities, such as digestion and higher cognitive functions are decreased (Kandel et al., 2000). The SAM system is quick acting, releasing the neurotransmitter adrenaline (Gunnar & Quevedo, 2007).

Comparatively, the HPA system is slower, exerting more prolonged effects, including toxic stress. After receiving a message of threat by the amygdala, the hypothalamus releases corticotropin-releasing hormone (CRH). This signals the pituitary gland to release adrenocorticotropic hormone (ACTH), which prompts the adrenal gland to release cortisol (Ehlert, 2013). All types and levels of stress, whether physical, psychological, or emotional, can initiate a release of cortisol (Kandel et al., 2000). Although a dysregulated cortisol level can be problematic, an adequate amount of this hormone is necessary for motivating activity as well as turning off the stress response (Gillespie & Nemeroff, 2007). When the stress system is continually activated by threat in a person's environment, the brain adapts to this environment by resetting the norm to a consistently fired-up state. This heightened, persistent level of stress-response becomes toxic to the mind and body.

Cues associated with the threat, such as visual prompts, smells, ambient sounds, time of day, etc. which ordinarily do not cause a stress response, are automatically associated with the threat itself, and the information is stored in the amygdala's implicit memory file as a warning of potential harm. As a result, negative affective states (fear, shame, rage, numbing, dissociation, etc.) and physical sensations (muscle tension, increased heart rate, rapid breathing, etc.) are easily activated to cues even in seemingly nonthreatening environments (Levine, 2010; Ogden et al., 2006; Yehuda & LeDoux, 2007).

The amygdala stores only implicit type memories and relies on the hippocampus for contextual information about its perception of threat and emotional memories (Shin, Rauch, & Pitman, 2006) to determine the "realness" of the danger. For example, an individual may initially experience a racing heart and the emotion of fear at the sound of scratching on a window in the night, because the stress response system has been activated by the amygdala's perception of threat. However, the hippocampus, based on contextual memory, sends a message that it is a tree brushing up against the house and the stress response shuts off, restoring emotional and physiological regulation. In order to not be frightened by every shadow or unknown object, this coordination between the reflexive (amygdala) and rational (frontal cortex and hippocampus) brain areas is essential (Schore, 2002). In addition to the hippocampus, the mPFC and ACC offer interpretation and regulation (Aupperle, Melrose, Stein, & Paulus, 2012; Shin & Liberzon, 2010).

Altered for Adaptation

Toxic stress profoundly impairs the HPA system and alters the structure and functioning of brain areas. A number of studies have demonstrated that the HPA system becomes highly sensitive and over-reactive when exposed to unmitigated chronic stress (Gunnar & Quevedo, 2007; Heim et al., 2000; McEwen, 2008), particularly in developing brains (Gillespie & Nemeroff, 2007; Gunnar & Loman, 2010). Closely aligned with the HPA processes, the hippocampus appears exceptionally vulnerable to the effects of stress. When there is chronic over-activation of the stress response system resulting in the brain being flooded with excess cortisol, hippocampal-dependent learning and memory processes become impaired (Joëls et al., 2006). Excessive cortisol causes a reduction in hippocampal dendrite density reducing the overall volume of the hippocampus and impacting function (Conrad, 2008). When altered by toxic stress, the hippocampus has a significantly reduced capacity to provide important contextual information to the amygdala about which conditions represent danger and which represent safety. When the hippocampus is compromised, it is not effective in sending messages to the hypothalamus to stop producing CRH and turn off the stress response (McEwen & Gianaros, 2010). Many individuals who suffer from PTSD show low baseline levels of cortisol, suggesting an exhausted HPA system, which account for the intrusive memories they experience (O'Donnell, Hegadoren, & Coupland, 2004).

The amygdala working in concert with the hippocampus and the HPA system is also changed structurally and functionally by toxic stress. The amygdala is central to relational processes and development of attachment strategies, making it extremely sensitive to excessive activation in early life. Infants, children, and youth are particularly sensitive to toxic stress and impairment in regulatory functioning in the PFC and the ACC. Again, excessive activation in the areas that respond to emotions and an underactivation in areas involved in cognitive processes of assessment and evaluation lead to developmental disruptions.

SOCIAL WORK THROUGH THE NEURO-TRAUMA LENS

Learning from research findings about the neurobiological consequences of toxic stress provides social workers with a depth of understanding about the profound effects that trauma exposure can have on individuals, families, and communities. There is still much to learn about how toxic stress affects the structures and functions of the brain, mind, and body, as well as the resultant consequences on regulating emotions, cognitions, behaviors, and sensory and somatic experiences; moreover, how the social ecology promotes, inhibits, or exacerbates these effects. Knowledge about how to infuse human service organizations with trauma-informed culture and embed trauma-specific practices across systems is only in the beginning stages. Such an expansive service transformation takes time and an investment of resources. Knowing that trauma induces alterations in the physiology of the stress response systems and brain structures will not alone shift policy and practice decisions toward those that recognize the pervasiveness of adversity among service users. This final section of the chapter presents implications for trauma-informed and trauma-specific social work, including a series of questions that practitioners can ask themselves to enhance their work through a neuro-trauma lens.

The principle and practice of universal precaution within the context of trauma-informed approaches and trauma-specific practices are based on the high prevalence of trauma-exposure, poly-traumatization, posttraumatic stress, and complex trauma among services users (Hodas, 2006). The vast majority of individuals and families who are served by social workers have significant trauma exposure; indeed, compromised neurobiological functioning due to early trauma and ongoing adversity has contributed to their need for services or involvement with mandated services.

Simply stated, implementing universal precaution means designing and delivering all aspects of services to all consumers/clients with an understanding of how trauma shapes neurobiology. The practice of universal precaution is not a model or technique; it is a frame of reference. With the understanding that service users have compromised stress regulatory systems comes the challenge to create service environments and agency-consumer interactions with the first and foremost goal of maximizing the service user's experience of physical and emotional safety. In other words, service design and delivery from the perspective of universal precaution is developed in such a manner as to minimize activating clients' trauma-based neurobiological response patterns. Service users can only establish and utilize regulatory strategies within nonthreatening environments and relationships. Brain areas necessary for cognitive processing, new learning, and meaning-making can only be accessed if emotional regulation is first established.

Both social-ecological and neuro-regulatory intervention strategies are necessary for resilience and recovery to be possible. Organizational cultures and practices that are trauma-informed create environments that are essential to initiating and maintaining neurobiological healing.

Clients' trauma-anchored neurobiologies have exquisitely perceptive threat response systems. The slightest trauma reminder—a voice tone, a question, a closed room—can set off a powerful cascade of somatic, emotional, physical responses, which are not within the service user's conscious awareness or immediate control. Agency staff and providers may misunderstand these automatic hyperarousal or hypoarousal survival oriented reactions as manipulative, oppositional, hostile, uncooperative, withdrawn, disinterested, etc. As suggested by Bloom (1999), instead of taking the position of "What's wrong with you?" to a client's behavior that is challenging or not understood, thinking or asking about "What's happened to you?" begins to shape a trauma-informed response (p. 15).

The following sample of questions is designed to assist social workers to think and act through the neuro-trauma lens.

- What changes can be made in the physical space of the service setting to increase the service user's experience of safety?
- When I apply the principle of universal precaution, how does my work change?
- When I acknowledge the service user's behavior or affect is serving a learned protective function, what changes in my response?
- How do I use knowledge about the functions of the two hemispheres to better understand the service user's state of mind and shape my response accordingly? For example, how do my verbal and nonverbal responses match with the service user's right hemisphere functioning?
- What do I know about the amygdala and hippocampus that helps me observe service users' trauma re-experiencing and intervene accordingly?
- What are some examples of service users' behaviors, emotions, and relational capacities that might represent survival responses? (Fight? Flight? Freeze?)
- What is my plan to learn more about the neurobiology of toxic stress and advocate for more trauma-informed services?

The intent of this chapter has been to focus on the neurobiology of toxic stress that is a result of psychological trauma exposure. The focus has been primarily on the individual's neurobiology and regulatory capacity because the majority of service users with whom social workers interact have pervasive trauma exposure and live in adverse circumstances. However, trauma-informed approaches must also be focused on the social ecology in which consumers live. Reduction of traumatic exposure is of equal importance. Knowledge about the enduring effects of adversity on mind and body is also the basis of addressing social policies and prevention programs.

References

Amir, N., McNally, R. J., & Wiegartz, P. S. (1996). Implicit memory bias for threat in posttraumatic stress disorder. *Cognitive Therapy and Research, 20*(6), 625–635.

Aupperle, R. L., Melrose, A. J., Stein, M. B., & Paulus, M. P. (2012). Executive function and PTSD: Disengaging from trauma. *Neuropharmacology, 62*(2), 686–694.

Bear, M. F., Connors, B. W., & Paradiso, M. A. (2007). *Neuroscience: Exploring the brain* (3rd ed.). Baltimore, MD: Lippincott Williams & Wilkins.

Beebe, B., Lachmann, F., Markese, S., & Bahrick, L. (2012). On the origins of disorganized attachment and internal working models: Paper I. A dyadic systems approach. *Psychoanalytic Dialogues: The International Journal of Relational Perspectives, 22*(2), 253–272. doi:10.1080/10481885.2012.666147.

Briere, J., & Scott, C. (2006). *Principles of trauma therapy: A guide to symptoms, evaluation and treatment.* Thousand Oaks, CA: Sage Press.

Blonder, L. X., Bowers, D., & Heilman, K. M. (1991). The role of the right hemisphere in emotional communication. *Brain, 114*(3), 1115–1127.

Bloom, S. (1999). Trauma theory abbreviated. *From the final action plan: A coordinated community response to family violence.* Harrisburg: Attorney General of Pennsylvania's Family Violence Task Force.

Chiron, C., Jambaque, I., Nabbout, R., Lounes, R., Syrota, A., & Dulac, O. (1997). The right brain hemisphere is dominant in human infants. *Brain, 120*(6), 1057–1065.

Cook, A., Spinazzola, J., Ford, J., Lanktree, C., Blaustein, M., Cloitre, M., ... van der Kolk, B. (2005). Complex trauma in children and adolescents. *Psychiatric Annals 35*(5), 390–398.

Conrad, C. (2008). Chronic stress-induced hippocampal vulnerability: The glucocorticoid vulnerability hypothesis. *Nature Review Neuroscience, 19*(6), 395–411.

Critchley, H. D., Wiens, S., Rotshtein, P., Öhman, A., & Dolan, R. J. (2004). Neural systems supporting interoceptive awareness. *Nature Neuroscience, 7*(2), 189–195.

D'Andrea, W., Ford, J., Stolbach, B., Spinazzola, J., & van der Kolk, B. A. (2012). Understanding interpersonal trauma in children: Why we need a developmentally appropriate trauma diagnosis. *American Journal of Orthopsychiatry, 82*(2), 187–200.

Ehlert, U. (2013). Enduring psychobiological effects of childhood adversity. *Psychoneuroendocrinology, 38*(9), 1850–1857.

Elzinga, B. M., & Bremner, J. D. (2002). Are the neural substrates of memory the final common pathway in posttraumatic stress disorder (PTSD)? *Journal of Affective Disorders, 70*(1), 1–17.

Esaki, N., Benamati, J., Yanosy, S., Middleton, J., Hopson, L., Hummer, V., & Bloom, S. (2013). The sanctuary model: Theoretical framework. *Families in Society: The Journal of Contemporary Social Services, 94*(2), 87–95.

Etkin, A., Egner, T., & Kalisch, R. (2011). Emotional processing in anterior cingulate and medial prefrontal cortex. *Trends in Cognitive Sciences, 15*(2), 85–93.

Fallot, R., & Harris, M. (Eds). (2001). *Using trauma theory to design service systems: New directions for mental health services.* San Francisco, CA: Jossey-Bass.

Felitti, V. J., Anda, R. F., Nordenberg, D., Williamson, D. F., Spitz, A. M., Edwards, V., ... Marks, J. S. (1998). Relationship of childhood abuse and household dysfunction to many of the leading causes of death in adults: The adverse childhood experiences (ACE) study. *American Journal of Preventive Medicine, 14*(4), 245–231.

Ford, J. D., Grasso, D., Greene, C., Levine, J., Spinazzola, J., & van der Kolk, B. (2013). Clinical significance of a proposed developmental trauma disorder diagnosis: Results of an international survey of clinicians. *Journal of Clinical Psychiatry, 74*(8), 841–849.

Gazzaniga, M. S., Eliassen, J. C., Nisenson, L., Wessinger, C. M., Fendrich, R., & Baynes, K. (1996). Collaboration between the hemispheres of a callosotomy patient—Emerging right hemisphere speech and the left hemisphere interpreter. *Brain, 119*(4), 1255–1262.

Gazzaniga, M. S., Holtzman, J. D., Deck, M. D., & Lee, B. C. (1985). MRI assessment of human callosal surgery with neuropsychological correlates. *Neurology, 35*(12), 1763–1763.

Gazzaniga, M. S., Ivry, R. B., & Mangun, G. R. (2009). *Cognitive neuroscience: The biology of the mind* (3rd ed.). New York, NY: WW Norton & Company.

Gillespie, C. F., & Nemeroff, C. B. (2007). Corticotropin-releasing factor and the psychobiology of early-life stress. *Current Directions in Psychological Science, 16*(2), 85–89.

Gunnar, M. R., & Loman, M. M. (2010). Early experience and the development of stress reactivity and regulation in children. *Neuroscience and Biobehavioral Reviews, 34*, 867–876.

Gunnar, M., & Quevedo, K. (2007). The neurobiology of stress and development. *Annual Review of Psychology, 58*, 145–173.

Heim, C., Newport, J., Heit, S., Graham, Y. P., Wilcox, M., Bonsall, R., & Nemeroff, C. (2000). Pituitary adrenal and autonomic responses to stress in women after sexual and physical abuse in childhood. *JAMA: Journal of the American Medical Association, 284*(5), 592–597.

Hodas, G. (2006). *Responding to childhood trauma: The promise and practice of trauma-informed care.* Harrisburg: Pennsylvania Office of Mental Health and Substance Abuse Services.

Herman, J. (1997). *Trauma and recovery: The aftermath of violence—from domestic abuse to political terror.* New York: NY: Basic Books.

Hopper, E. K., Bassuk, E. L., & Olivet, J. (2009). Shelter from the storm: Trauma-informed care in homelessness services settings. *Open Health Services and Policy Journal, 2*, 131–151.

Joëls, M., Pu, Z., Wiegert, O., Oitzl, M. S., & Krugers, H. J. (2006). Learning under stress: How does it work? *Trends in Cognitive Sciences, 10*(4), 152–158.

Kandel, E. R. (2007). *In search of memory: The emergence of a new science of mind.* New York, NY: WW Norton & Company.

Kandel, E. R., Schwartz, J. H., & Jessell, T. M. (2000). *Principles of neural science* (4th ed.). New York, NY: McGraw-Hill.

Lanius, R., Vermetten, E., and Pain, C. (Eds.). (2010). *The impact of early life trauma on health care and disease: The hidden epidemic.* New York, NY: Cambridge University Press.

LeDoux, J. E. (2003). The emotional brain, fear, and the amygdala. *Cellular and Molecular Neurobiology, 23*(4/5), 727–738.

Levine, P. (2010). *In an unspoken voice: How the body releases trauma and restores goodness.* Berkeley, CA: North Atlantic Books.

McEwen, B. (2008). Central effects of stress hormones in health and disease: Understanding protective and damaging effects of stress mediators. *European Journal of Pharmacology, 583*, 174–185.

McEwen, B. S., & Gianaros, P. J. (2010). Central role of the brain in stress and adaptation: Links to socioeconomic status, health, and disease. *Annals of New York Academy of Science, 1186*, 190–122.

Milad, M. R., Wright, C. I., Orr, S. P., Pitman, R. K., Quirk, G. J., & Rauch, S. L. (2007). Recall of fear extinction in humans activates the ventromedial prefrontal cortex and hippocampus in concert. *Biological Psychiatry, 62*(5), 446–454.

O'Donnell, T., Hegadoren, K. M., & Coupland, N. C. (2004). Noradrenergic mechanisms in the pathophysiology of post-traumatic stress disorder. *Neuropsychobiology, 50*(4), 273–283.

Ogden, P., Minton, K., Pain, C. (2006). *Trauma and the body: A sensorimotor approach to psychotherapy.* New York, NY: Norton & Co.

Peckman, H. (2013). Epigenetics: The dogma-defying discovery that genes learn from experience. *International Journal of Neuropsychotherapy, 1*, 9–20.

Perry, B. D., Pollard, R. A., Blakley, T. L., Baker, W. L., & Vigilante, D. (1995). Childhood trauma, the neurobiology of adaptation, and "use dependent" development of the brain: How "states" become "traits." *Infant Mental Health Journal, 16*(4), 271–291.

Phelps, E. A., & Gazzaniga, M. S. (1992). Hemispheric differences in mnemonic processing: The effects of left hemisphere interpretation. *Neuropsychologia, 30*(3), 293–297.

Roser, M. E., Fugelsang, J. A., Dunbar, K. N., Corballis, P. M., & Gazzaniga, M. S. (2005). Dissociating processes supporting causal perception and causal inference in the brain. *Neuropsychology, 19*(5), 591–602.

Saakvitne, K. W., Gamble, S., Pearlman, L., & Lev, B. (2000). *Risking connection: A training curriculum for working with survivors of childhood abuse.* Lutherville, MD: Sidran Press.

Saper, C. (2009). Hypothalamus. *Scholarpedia, 4*(1), 2791.

Schore, A. N. (2000). Attachment and the regulation of the right brain. *Attachment & Human Development, 2*(1), 23–47.

Schore, A. N. (2002). Dysregulation of the right brain: a fundamental mechanism of traumatic attachment and the psychopathogenesis of post-traumatic stress disorder. *Australian and New Zealand Journal of Psychiatry, 36*(1), 9–30.

Semrud-Clikeman, M., & Hynd, G. W. (1990). Right hemisphere dysfunction in nonverbal learning disabilities: Social, academic, and adaptive functioning in adults and children. *Psychological Bulletin, 107*(2), 196–209.

Shin, L. M., & Liberzon, I. (2010). The neurocircuitry of fear, stress, and anxiety disorders. *Neuropsychopharmacology, 35*(1), 169–191.

Shin, L. M., Rauch, S. L., & Pitman, R. K. (2006). Amygdala, medial prefrontal cortex, and hippocampal function in PTSD. *Annals of the New York Academy of Sciences, 1071*(1), 67–79.

Shonkoff, J. P. (2010). Building a new biodevelopmental framework to guide the future of early childhood policy. *Child Development, 81*(1), 357–367.

Shonkoff, J. P., Richter, L., van der Gaag, J., & Bhutta, Z. A. (2012). An integrated scientific framework for child survival and early childhood development. *Pediatrics, 129*(2), e460–e472.

Ungar, M. (2013). Resilience, trauma, context, and culture. *Trauma, Violence and Abuse, 14*(3), 255–266.

Wilson, J., & Tang, C. (Eds.). (2007). Cross-cultural assessment of psychological trauma and PTSD. New York, NY: Springer.

Yehuda, R., & LeDoux, J. (2007). Response variation following trauma: A translational neuroscience approach to understanding PTSD. *Neuron, 56*(1), 19–32.

40   Fundamental Principles of Behavioral Social Work

Denise E. Bronson

Applied behavioral methods, derived from the experimental analysis of behavior and learning in psychology, were introduced to social work in the mid-1960s when the first social work book on behavioral methods was published (Thomas, 1967). Several key texts followed (Fischer & Gochros, 1975; Schwartz & Goldiamond, 1975; Sundel & Sundel, 2005; Wodarski & Bagarozzi, 1979) and behavior therapy courses began to appear among the course offerings in many social work programs. At that time, the emphasis was clearly on the use of *behavior therapy* (also commonly referred to as *behavior modification*). But behavioral methods have continued to evolve and today include cognitive-behavioral interventions (Gonzalez-Prendes, 2012), dialectical behavioral treatment (Dimeff & Koerner, 2007), and other strategies that are based on behavioral principles. These behaviorally based methods are some of the most widely used interventions (Thyer,

2012) and share several characteristics that distinguish behavioral social work from other treatment approaches:

- Behavioral social work is based on extensive empirical work in basic and applied settings, and ongoing empirical evaluation of service is an integral part of behavioral practice.
- Behavioral interventions are highly individualized and address the unique learning history of each client. An individualized behavioral assessment (functional behavioral assessment) is, therefore, extremely important and focuses on identifying the environment in which the problem behavior occurs (antecedents), the behavior itself (response), and what happens afterwards (consequences).
- Principles of learning are applied to understand how behaviors are acquired and maintained. This occurs at all levels—individual, family, group, societal, and cultural.
- Behavioral interventions focus on the presenting problem and strive for outcomes that are clinically and socially meaningful to the client and significant others.
- Maintenance and generalization of changes are not assumed to occur automatically once the desired goals are obtained. Instead the conditions for ensuring maintenance and generalization are carefully assessed and become an important consideration in developing a successful intervention.

Contemporary behavior therapy has been used to address a variety of issues in a variety of social work settings. Systematic reviews and other outcome studies have demonstrated the effectiveness of behavioral strategies to address individual issues (e.g., anxiety disorders and phobias, anger management, depression, academic performance, employment skills, and substance abuse), family concerns (e.g., family violence, parent training, communication, and decision-making), and community/social needs (e.g., ecological behavior, seat-belt usage, littering, and recycling).

With all the developments in behaviorally based interventions it is easy to lose sight of the fundamental principles that are the foundation of all behavioral methods. This chapter will use two case examples to review these principles and illustrate the use of behavior therapy in social work. The references and additional readings at the end of the chapter provide resources for exploring these principles in much greater detail. Another chapter in this volume discusses the use of cognitive-behavioral-treatment (CBT) specifically (Vonk & Early, 2014).

CASE EXAMPLES

Case Example 1: Sally Adams developed a fear of driving over or under bridges following the collapse of an interstate highway bridge in Minneapolis. She lives in a city with many bridges and this phobia has escalated to the point that she is unable to drive without planning long, time-consuming routes to her destination. This has interfered with her ability to get to work on time and she is in danger of losing her job.

Case Example 2: John and Mary Brown's four-year-old daughter Megan has become unmanageable. Bedtime is especially problematic and it can take up to three hours to get Megan into bed. Megan pleads with her parents to stay up later then throws temper tantrums when she is told that she must go to bed. This has started to cause problems between her parents who argue over how to handle their daughter.

KEY CONCEPTS IN BEHAVIORAL SOCIAL WORK

A number of key concepts and technical terms are important in behavioral assessment and intervention (Antony & Roemer, 2011; Bailey & Burch, 2006; Cooper, Heron, & Heward, 2007; Martin & Pear, 2007; Spiegler & Guevremont, 2010). Behaviorists generally classify behavior into two broad categories—respondent behaviors and operant behaviors. *Respondent behaviors* are elicited by stimuli in the environment and involve the autonomic nervous system (i.e., blood pressure, heart rate, rapid breathing, or changes in the glandular system). For example, Sally Adams's fear of bridges in Case 1 triggers a number of physiological reactions (rapid heart rate, heightened alertness, sweating, etc.) whenever she approaches a bridge. *Operant behaviors*, on the other hand, are those which "operate" on the environment and are controlled by the environmental consequences that follow. Most overt, observable behaviors fall into this category, including language. For example in Case 2, if Megan is praised by a parent for going to bed on time, she is more likely to go to bed on time in the future and conversely, if her parents attend to her temper tantrums it is likely that the tantrums will increase in frequency or intensity. Furthermore, parents are more likely to use praise in the future if it increases the probability that their child will comply with parental requests. Historically, it was believed that respondent behaviors were controlled by antecedent stimuli and that operant behaviors were controlled by consequential stimuli. Although this distinction is still useful, recent research has demonstrated considerable overlap in the processes described by these concepts. In addition, it is clear that genetic and biological factors will set limits on the range and type of respondent and operant behaviors that are possible.

Respondent and operant behaviors are learned in two ways—respondent conditioning and operant conditioning. In *respondent conditioning*, a neutral stimulus (*conditioned stimulus—CS*) is repeatedly paired with an eliciting stimulus (*unconditioned stimulus—UCS*). Eventually the neutral stimulus will also elicit a similar response, which is now referred to as the *conditioned response (CR)*. For example, the sudden bright light of a flashbulb (UCS) elicits an eye blink (UCR). Unfortunately, the camera (CS), through its repeated pairing with the flash (UCS), can also begin to elicit an eye blink (CR), often resulting in family pictures in which the subject's eyes are closed in "anticipation" of the flash. Or in Sally Adams's case, repeatedly viewing the images of the interstate bridge collapse in Minneapolis elicited emotional reactions that were associated with a previously neutral stimulus, namely, bridges. In this way, phobias are acquired through respondent conditioning when neutral stimuli begin to elicit physiological or fear responses.

Operant conditioning refers to the process of learning in which the future likelihood of the behavior will either increase or decrease depending on the *contingencies* associated with that behavior. Contingencies refer to both the *consequences* that follow the behavior as well as the *antecedents* that precede the behavior indicating the type of consequence that is likely. For example, telling a joke at a party will probably be followed by a friend's laughter. If the same joke is told to the same friend during a lecture, however, the friend might respond with "sshhhh" rather than laughter. In this case, the antecedent conditions associated with a party signal that a positive response (a positive reinforcer) will follow telling a joke while the same behavior in class will receive a negative reaction (a punisher). Our jokester soon learns to *discriminate* the conditions under which jokes will be reinforced. Similarly, in Case 2, it is important to conduct a *functional analysis* to determine the antecedents (e.g., parental request to go to bed), the *behavior* (e.g., Megan's temper tantrums) and the *consequences* that follow Megan's outbursts, which might be increasing the future probability of those tantrums (e.g., parents acquiesce and let her stay up or parental attention).

Behaviorists refer to four types of consequences—*positive reinforcers, negative reinforcers, positive punishers,* and *negative punishers.* Any consequence that increases the future probability of the behavior it follows is a *reinforcer.* Positive reinforcers are stimuli that are presented contingent on the occurrence of the behavior (e.g., receiving an allowance for household chores). The termination or removal of an aversive stimulus (negative reinforcement) will also increase the behavior it follows (e.g., putting on a sweater when you feel cold). Conversely, any consequence that decreases the future probability of the behavior it follows is a *punisher. Positive punishment* is the presentation of an aversive stimulus contingent on a behavior (e.g., saying "no" to a child who asks for cookies before dinner) while negative punishment is the removal of a reinforcer contingent on a behavior (e.g., turning off the TV when children fight about which program to watch). What serves as reinforcers and punishers is highly individualized and varies according to one's learning history, biological and genetic characteristics, and the setting. The only way to really determine which stimuli are reinforcers and punishers is to observe the affect of those stimuli on future behavior.

The *schedule of reinforcement* is another important concept that refers to the frequency with which a behavior is reinforced. Often when new behaviors are being acquired they are reinforced after every occurrence; this is called a continuous reinforcement schedule. Usually in the natural environment, however, behaviors are reinforced only intermittently depending on the number of times the behavior is performed (ratio schedules of reinforcement), the amount of time that passes (interval schedules of reinforcement), or the rate of responding (differential reinforcement of high or low rates). Intermittent schedules of reinforcement are most resistant to periods of *extinction* when reinforcement that was previously available is withdrawn.

Finally, operant behaviors are often preceded by antecedent stimuli (*discriminative stimuli*) that cue which behavior will be reinforced in a particular setting. Through a process of discrimination training in which a behavior is consistently reinforced only in the presence of specific stimuli, individuals learn which behaviors are likely to be reinforced in each setting. To illustrate, consider Megan in Case 2. When Megan's request to stay up later is made to her mother permission is usually given; when the request is made to the father it is usually refused. Megan learns quickly to discriminate those situations (i.e., presence of mother) in which requests to stay up late (behavior) are likely to be reinforced (permission granted) from those situations in which the behavior will not be reinforced.

ENGAGING IN BEHAVIORAL SOCIAL WORK

Behavioral Assessment. Assessment in behavioral social work is an extremely important process that is closely linked to decisions about which intervention strategy to use. During assessment (also referred to as a *functional analysis*) the social worker collects information to determine the antecedents and consequences of the problem behavior, specifies the desired outcomes (the *target behavior*), and selects the most appropriate therapeutic technique. Clients and significant others are an important part of this process. A summary of the steps used by behavioral social workers during assessment is presented in Table 40.1.

Intervention Strategies. Following the assessment and collection of baseline data, behavioral social workers (1) specify the desired target behavior, antecedents, and consequences; (2) identify data

TABLE 40.1 Steps in Behavioral Assessment

Steps	Activities
1. Identify the problem areas and priorities	• Obtain a list of problem areas from the client(s) using interviews, observation, and standardized assessment questionnaires • Determine priorities for service • Select the problem(s) to be addressed and the desired outcome (target behavior)
2. Specify the target behaviors	• Describe the problem and target behaviors in observable and measurable terms • Determine whether the problem is one of behavioral excesses or behavioral deficits • Determine whether the problem is primarily operant or respondent in nature • Begin collecting pretreatment (baseline) data, if possible, using direct observation, client self-reports on internal states or emotions (using rating scales or standardized questionnaires), and physiological measures

3. Assess the controlling conditions (antecedents & consequences)	• Collect information about the environmental antecedents that precede the problem behavior
	• Collect information about the consequences that immediately follow the problem and target behavior
	• Determine whether the problem is primarily one of:
	  • Poor stimulus control (i.e., lack of cues for the appropriate behavior, poor discrimination training, or the presence of stimuli that elicit inappropriate respondent and emotional behaviors)
	  • Behavioral deficits (i.e., client lacks skills to perform the desired behavior)
	  • Inadequate or inappropriate consequences (i.e., client has the necessary skills but reinforcers for the desired behavior are missing, the reinforcers are conflicting or delayed, or the reinforcers consist of inappropriate personal reinforcers that cause harm to others or are culturally disapproved)

collection strategy for monitoring changes in the target behavior; and (3) develop an intervention plan. Maintenance and generalization of changes, once they are obtained, are not assumed to occur naturally and strategies for ensuring lasting change are included in the intervention planning.

Generally, behavioral interventions can be categorized according to whether the primary activity focuses on modifying the stimulus conditions preceding the behavior, developing the behavior itself, or altering the consequences of the behavior. In many cases, one or more strategies from these three categories are employed simultaneously to address the target problem.

Table 40.2 presents examples of commonly used intervention techniques for modifying

stimulus conditions (antecedents). These strategies are used when the assessment shows that the client is able to perform desired behavior but unable to discriminate the appropriate time/place for the behavior or that environmental stimuli elicit problematic emotional states (e.g., phobias).

In some cases the assessment indicates that the client has not learned the desired behavior and is, therefore, unable to perform it. The behavioral social worker will select an intervention designed to teach or train a new behavior. Table 40.3 presents examples of some of the commonly used strategies.

The assessment may indicate that the desired behavior does not occur because the consequences of the behavior are faulty. For example, the environment might not reinforce the desired behavior or could be reinforcing an incompatible, inappropriate behavior. Interventions to modify the consequential contingencies can be grouped into two types of strategies—those that focus on increasing the desired behavior and those that focus on decreasing an undesirable behavior. Frequently, behavioral social workers will use techniques from both groups simultaneously. Table 40.4 presents examples of both types of strategies designed to alter

TABLE 40.2 Interventions for Modifying Stimulus Conditions

Discrimination Training	Procedure in which the desired behavior is reinforced in the presence of appropriate stimuli and not reinforced in the presence of inappropriate stimuli to teach when/where to perform target behavior. Fading can be used to gradually change dimensions of the stimulus to teach difficult discrimination.
Prompting	Cues to remind or guide client to engage in the desired behavior; can be combined with *fading* to eventually remove prompt
Respondent Extinction	Process of breaking the connection between the conditioned stimulus (CS) and the unconditioned stimulus (UCS) by repeatedly presenting the CS without the UCS until it no longer elicits the conditioned response (CR)
Systematic Desensitization	Method used to treat phobias by gradually exposing client to increasingly anxiety producing stimuli while engaging in responses incompatible with the anxiety (usually relaxation)

TABLE 40.3 Interventions for Developing New Behaviors

Shaping	Teaching a new behavior through gradually reinforcing increasingly complex or precise approximations to the final desired behaviour.
Chaining	Procedure used when the final behavior consists of several steps needed to complete the action (e.g., dressing). Chaining can either begin at the beginning or end of the sequence to train each of the stimulus-response sequences needed for the desired behavior.
Modeling	Presenting a live or filmed demonstration of the desired behavior in which the client learns which behaviors are desired and the contingencies under which they occur.

TABLE 40.4 Interventions for Modifying Response Consequences

Increasing Desired Behavior	Positive & Negative Reinforcement	Presenting a reinforcing stimulus or removing an aversive stimulus, respectively, immediately following the performance of the desired behavior
	Escape & Avoidance Conditioning	Similar to negative reinforcement in that an aversive stimulus is removed (escape) or prevented (avoidance) after the occurrence of a response
Decreasing Undesired Behavior	Operant Extinction	Process in which a reinforcer is withheld following an operant response that had previously produced that reinforcer
	Positive & Negative Punishment	Presenting an aversive stimulus or removing a reinforcer immediately following the performance of the undesirable behavior
	Differential Reinforcement	Manipulating the schedule of reinforcement to decrease behavior by reinforcing low rates of responding, zero responding, or incompatible responding

the consequences following a behavior. The effectiveness of interventions to modify the consequences of a behavior will depend on a number of factors including the immediacy of the consequence, the salience of the reinforcer or punisher, and the schedule of reinforcement. The behavioral social worker will assess each of these factors and address them in deciding how to intervene.

AREAS OF APPLICATION WITH EMPIRICAL SUPPORT

Behavioral assessment and intervention techniques have been used to treat a range of problems, from individual to societal concerns, effectively. Due primarily to behaviorists' commitment to a scientific approach, a large body of empirical research exists to support the effectiveness of behavioral methods to deal with diverse problems and issues such as obsessive-compulsive disorders, parenting difficulties, treatment compliance problems, sexual dysfunction, drug and alcohol abuse, urinary incontinence, disruptive classroom behavior, attention deficit hyperactivity disorder, and juvenile offenders. Systematic reviews on the use of behavioral methods can be found on the Campbell Collaboration (http://www.campbellcollaboration.org/lib) and Cochrane

Collaboration (http://www.thecochranelibrary.com/view/0/index.html) libraries. Research articles on the clinical applications of behavioral methods are reported in journals such as Behavior Therapy, the Behavior Analyst, Journal of Applied Behavior Analysis, Journal of Positive Behavior Interventions, Journal of Behavioral Education, Behavior and Social Issues, Behavior Modification, Behaviour Research and Therapy, Behavioral Interventions, and Journal of Behavior Therapy and Experimental Psychiatry.

FUTURE DIRECTIONS

Although behavioral social work has evolved considerably since the introduction of the first textbook on behavioral social work in 1967, the paucity of articles in social work journals is problematic. Considerable misrepresentation and misunderstanding of the behavioral approach continues and those engaged in behavioral social work generally find it easier to publish their work in non-social work publications. Consequently, social workers are often not aware of recent research and developments in behavioral treatment and, unfortunately, this means that social work clients are not benefiting from intervention strategies with proven effectiveness. Greater access to systematic reviews of the research literature in electronic, online databases may make current research more accessible to practitioners in the future.

Over the years, practitioners have been reluctant to use the term *behavioral* to describe their interventions (Gambrill, 1995; Bronson & Thyer, 2001) and this situation does not seem to be changing. However, with the advent of evidence-based practice in social work the future of behavioral social work is very promising. The behavioral approach offers empirically tested, change-focused, client-centered, and environmentally based social work interventions that are highly consistent with the values and objectives of social work practice (Thyer, 2012). Increased efforts to ensure that social workers are knowledgeable and skilled in using behavioral methods will certainly enhance the effectiveness of services and the credibility of the profession.

RELATED WEBSITES

http://www.campbellcollaboration.org	The Campbell Collaboration website offers systematic reviews of research on behavioral treatment.
www.cochrane.org/	The Cochrane Collaboration website offers systematic reviews of research on behavioral treatment.
http://www.behavior.org/	The Cambridge Center for Behavioral Studies.
http://www.psychological-treatments.org/	American Psychological Association website for empirically supported treatments.

References and Additional Readings

Antony, M. M., & Roemer, L. (2011). *Behavior therapy.* Washington, DC: American Psychological Association.

Bailey, J., & Burch, M. (2006). *How to think like a behavior analyst: Understanding the science that can change your life.* New York, NY: Routledge.

Bronson, D. E., & Thyer, B. A. (2001). Behavioral social work: Where has it been and where is it going? *The Behavior Analyst, 2*(3), 192–195.

Cooper, J. O., Heron, T. E., & Heward, W. L. (2007). *Applied behavior analysis* (2nd ed.). Upper Saddle River, NJ: Pearson.

Dimeff, L. A., & Koerner, K. (Eds.). (2007). *Dialectical behavior therapy in clinical practice: Applications across disorders and settings.* New York, NY: Guilford.

Vonk, M. E., & Early, T. J. (2014). Cognitive-behavioral therapy. In K. Corcoran and A. A. Roberts (Eds.). The social worker's desk reference. New York, NY: Oxford.

Fischer, J., & Gochros, H. (1975). *Planned behavioral change in social work.* New York, NY: Prentice-Hall.

Gambrill, E. (1995). Behavioral social work: Past, present, and future. *Research on Social Work Practice, 5*(4), 460–484.

Gonzalez-Prendes, A. (2012). Cognitive Behavioral Therapy. *Oxford Bibliographies Online: Social Work.* doi:10.1093/obo/9780195389678-0149

Martin, G., & Pear, J. (2007). *Behavior modification: What it is and how to do it* (8th ed.). Upper Saddle River, NJ: Pearson Prentice Hall.

Schwartz, A., & Goldiamond, I. (1975). *Social casework: A behavioral approach.* New York, NY: Columbia University Press.

Spiegler, M. D., & Guevremont, D. C. (2010). *Contemporary behavior therapy* (5th ed.). Belmont, CA: Wadsworth.

Sundel, M., & Sundel, S. S. (2005). *Behavior change in the human services* (5th ed.). Thousand Oaks, CA: SAGE Publications.

Thomas, E. J. (1967). *The socio-behavioral approach and applications to social work.* New York, NY: Council on Social Work Education.

Thyer, B. A. (2012). Behavioral Social Work Practice. *Oxford Bibliographies Online: Social Work.* doi:10.1093/obo/9780195389678-0040

Wodarski, J. S., & Bagarozzi, D. A. (1979). *Behavioral social work.* New York, NY: Human Sciences.

41 The Miracle Question and Scaling Questions for Solution-building and Empowerment

Mo Yee Lee

The miracle question and the scaling question are an integral part of solution-focused brief therapy (SFBT), which was originally developed at the Brief Family Therapy Center at Milwaukee (Wisconsin) by Steve de Shazer, Insoo Kim Berg, and their associates. Solution-focused brief therapy begins as atheoretical, focusing instead on finding "what works in therapy" (Berg, 1994). Building on a strengths perspective and using a time-limited approach, solution-focused brief therapy postulates that positive and long-lasting change can occur in a relatively brief period of time by focusing on "solution-talk" instead of "problem talk" (de Shazer, 1985; Lee, 2013; Nelson & Thomas, 2007). One definitional characteristic of SFBT is that it equates therapeutic process with the therapeutic dialogue, with a focus on what is observable in communication and social interactions, instead of intentions, between client and therapist (Trepper et al., 2013; McKergow & Korman, 2009). Change happens through the therapeutic dialogue in which the therapist and client co-construct what is beneficial and helpful to accomplish the client's self-determined goals (Lee et al., 2003). Solution-focused brief therapy uses the language and symbols of "solution and strengths" as opposed to the language of "deficits and blame" (Lee, Sebold, & Uken, 2003). Treatment focuses on identifying exceptions and solution behaviors, which are then amplified, supported, and reinforced through a systematic solution-building process (De Jong & Berg, 2013).

Miracle question and scaling question, in many ways, synthesize the treatment orientation and practice characteristics of solution-focused brief therapy. Its conversational- and solution-based characteristics are intimately related to three definitive assumptions and practice principles of solution-focused brief therapy:

1. The power of language in creating and sustaining reality. Solution-focused therapy views language as the medium through which personal meaning and understanding are expressed and socially constructed in conversation (de Shazer, 1994). Because "what is noticed becomes reality and what is not noticed does not exist" (Lee et al., 2003, p. 32), there is a conscious effort by the therapist to help the client stay focused on envisioning a desirable future and finding small steps to actualize the solution-oriented future. Pathology or problem-talk sustains a problem reality through self-fulfilling prophecies and distracts attention from developing solutions (Miller, 1997).

2. A focus on solutions, strengths, and health. Solution-focused brief therapy assumes that clients have the resources and *have the answer*. The focus is on what clients can do versus what clients cannot do. One basic assumption of a systems perspective is that change is constant. No matter how severe the problem, there must be some "exceptions" to the problem patterns. These exceptions serve as clues to a solution and represent clients' "unnoticed" strengths and resources (de Shazer, 1985). Consequently, the task for the therapist is to assist clients

in noticing, amplifying, sustaining, and reinforcing these exceptions regardless of how small and/or infrequent they may be. Once clients are engaged in nonproblem behavior, they are on the way to a solution-building process (De Jong & Berg, 2013).

3. Solutions as clients' constructions. Solutions are not objective "realities" but are private, local, meaning-making activities by an individual (Miller, 1997). The importance of and the meaning attached to a goal or solution is individually constructed in a collaborative process. Solution-focused therapy honors clients as the "knowers" of their experiences and "creators" of solutions; they define the goals for their treatment and remain the main instigators of change (Berg, 1994).

THE USE OF QUESTIONS IN THE THERAPEUTIC PROCESS

Influenced by these assumptions and practice principles, the primary purpose of solution-focused interventions is to engage the client in a therapeutic dialogue that is conducive to a solution-building process. In this dialogue, the clinician invites the client to be the "expert" by listening and exploring the meaning of the client's perception of his or her situation. The use of solution-focused questions is instrumental in this solution-building dialogue. People need useful feedback in the process of change (Lee, 2013). The therapist can directly provide feedback via listening responses, affirming responses, restating responses, and expanding responses (Lee et al., 2003). Instead of directly providing feedback to clients, evaluative questions serve to initiate a self-feedback process within the client. Evaluative questions represent questions that ask clients to self-evaluate their situations in terms of their doing, thinking, and feeling. The therapist abstains from making any interpretation of a client's situation or suggesting any ideas; s/he just asks good questions that help clients evaluate different aspects of their unique life situation (Lee et al., 2003). Questions are perceived as better ways to create open space for clients to think about and self-evaluate their situation and solutions. Evaluative questions operate from the stance of curiosity and convey the message that we believe that clients have the answers and we do not have the answers.

The therapist utilizes solution-oriented questions, including miracle questions and scaling questions, to assist clients in constructing a reality that does not contain the problem. These questioning techniques were developed by de Shazer, Berg, and their colleagues to fully utilize the resources and potential of clients (De Jong & Berg, 2013; de Shazer, 1985).

LISTEN, SELECT, AND BUILD

The SFBT Treatment Manual endorsed by the Solution-Focused Brief Therapy Association (Bavelas et al., 2013) provides a detailed description of this co-constructive therapeutic process through the steps *listen, select, and build* (De Jong and Berg, 2013; de Shazer, 1991, 1994; de Shazer et al., 2007). In this dialogue, the therapist first listens for and selects out the words and phrases from the client's language that are indications of some aspect of a solution, including things that are important and salient to the client, past successes, exceptions to the problem pattern, resources, etc. Building on the client's descriptions and paying attention to the client's language and frame of reference, the therapist composes a next question or other responses that invites the client to further elaborate the solution picture. It is through this continuing process of listening, selecting, and building that therapists and clients together co-construct new meanings and new possibilities for solutions (Trepper et al., 2013).

MIRACLE QUESTION

The development of the miracle question was inspired by the work of Milton Erickson (the "crystal ball" technique) (de Shazer, 1985). According to Berg (1994), the miracle question invites clients to create a vision of their future without the presenting problem. A major challenge encountered by most clients in social work treatment is that they know when they have a problem but they do not know when the problem has been successfully addressed. When this happens, clients may be in treatment for a long time because there are no clear indicators of health and wellness. Helping clients to develop a clear vision of their future without the presenting problem becomes crucial in successful treatment because it establishes indicators of change and helps gauge clients' progress toward a self-defined desirable future (De Jong & Berg, 2013; Lee, 2013). When defining a future without the problem becomes a major focus of treatment, accountability for changing one's behavior can be effectively achieved. Defining a desirable future also shifts the focus of attention from what cannot be done to what can be accomplished; it moves clients away from blaming others or themselves and holds them accountable for developing a better, different future (Lee et al., 2003).

The miracle question is intended to accomplish the following therapeutic impact:

1. Allow clients to distance themselves from problem-saturated stories so that they can be more playful in creating a beneficial vision of their future.
2. Facilitate clients to develop a clear vision about a desirable future as "what is noticed becomes reality and what is not noticed does not exist" (Lee et al., 2003, p. 32).
3. Because the focus of the miracle question is for clients to identify small, observable, and concrete changes that are indicative of a desirable future without the problem, it establishes indicators of change and progress that help clients to gauge success and progress.
4. Increase clients' awareness of their choices and offer them an opportunity to play an active role in their treatment (De Jong & Berg, 2013).
5. Allow clients to be hopeful about their lives, which can be different from their current problem situation.
6. Empower clients to self-determine what constitutes a desirable future for them. "It creates a personal possible self, which is not modeled after someone else's ideas of what his life should be like" (Berg, 1994, p. 97).

A frequently used version of the miracle question is the following:

Suppose that after our meeting today, you go home, do your things, and go to bed. While you are sleeping, a miracle happens and the problem that brought you here is suddenly solved, like magic. The problem is gone. Because you were sleeping, you don't know that a miracle happened, but when you wake up tomorrow morning, you will be different. How will you know a miracle has happened? What will be the first small sign that tells you that the problem is resolved? (Berg & Miller, 1992, p. 359).

Using the process *listen, select, and build*; the therapist carefully *listens* to the client's response to the miracle question and *selects* descriptions that are indicative of the client's goal, desirable future, successes, and resources. The miracle question only initiates the process for clients to envision a desirable future. Paying particular attention and using the client's language and frame of reference, the therapist responds by developing other solution-focused questions or responses that help the client to continuously *build* and *expand* the solution picture. Note that the focus is on small signs of change. It is also important to invite the client to describe in great detail their solution picture and how that is different from their current behaviors, feelings, and thinking. The more detailed and refined the description, the clearer the indicators of change, which will increase the likelihood that the client will actualize their solution picture, because "what is noticed becomes reality" (Lee et al., 2003, p. 32).

- "Who will be the first person to notice the change? What will they be noticing about you that will tell them that you are different?"
- How will your spouse, your child (or any significant others) know that something is different? (Relationship question)
- "What are the times in your life when you have already been doing this?" (Exception question)

The essence of the miracle question is to allow clients to envision a future without problems. Given this, social work professionals can be creative in coming up with other versions of future-oriented questions. This can be helpful especially with clients from other cultures or religions, who might have their own culture-based interpretation of miracles. Some variations can be:

- If I run into you a year later and by that time you have already solved the problem that brought you in today, how will I know that you are different? How will you be like then?
- If I were to videotape you on a good day, how would you be doing/feeling/thinking differently?
- Five years down the road, what do you want yourself to be like?

Another version is the dream question that reinforces clients' sense of personal agency and, therefore, is consistent with the goal of empowering clients (Greene, Lee, Mentzer, Pinnell, & Niles, 1998).

Suppose that tonight while you are sleeping you have a dream and in this dream you discover the answers and resources you need to solve the problem that you are concerned about right now. When you wake up tomorrow you may or may not remember your dream, but you do notice you are different. As you go about starting your day, what will tell you that you discovered or developed the skills and resources necessary to solve your problem? What will be the first small sign to tell you that you solved your problem?

SCALING QUESTIONS

Scaling questions ask clients to rank their situation and/or goal on a 1-to-10 scale (Berg, 1994). Usually, 1 represents the worst scenario that could possibly be and 10 is the most desirable outcome. People need feedback on the process of change. Therefore, for change to happen, clients will need to be able to self-evaluate their progress and make adjustments accordingly. Scaling questions provide a simple tool for clients to quantify and evaluate their situation and progress so that they establish a clear indicator of progress for themselves (De Jong & Berg, 2013). More importantly, this is a self-anchored scale with no objective criteria. The constructivist characteristic of the scaling question honors clients as the "knowers" and the center of the change process. Scaling can be used to help clients rate their perception of their progress, their motivation for change, confidence to engage in solution-focused behaviors, etc. Scaling questions are also helpful in assisting clients to establish small steps and indicators of change in their solution-building process. Some common examples of scaling questions are:

1. Problem severity or progress: On a 1-to-10 scale, with 1 being the worst the problem could possibly be and 10 the most desirable outcome, where would you put yourself on the scale? What would be some small steps that you can take to move from a 4 to a 5?
2. Motivation: On a 1-to-10 scale with 1 being you have no motivation to work on the problem and 10 being you would do whatever to change the situation, where would you (or your spouse, your boss, your child, etc.) place yourself on the scale? How, on a 1-to-10 scale, would your wife (or another significant other) rank your motivation to change?

3. Confidence: "On a 1-to-10 scale, with 1 being you have no confidence that you can work on the goal and 10 being you have complete confidence that you will continue to work on the goal, where would you place yourself?" "On a scale of 1 to 10, how confident are you that you could actually do that?" "On a scale of 1 to 10, how confident are you that this will be helpful?"

Similar to using a miracle question in co-constructing change in the treatment process, the therapist carefully *listens* to a client's responses, *selects* and *focuses* on descriptions that are connected with indications and hints of solutions, and then helps the client to *build* and *expand* further on desirable change and solutions.

THE CASE OF LINDA

Linda was a 47-year-old woman who suffered chronic back pain after a car accident. The pain also affected her mobility. She was living on her own. The therapist uses the miracle question to help her envision a more hopeful future.

SWR: Suppose that after our meeting today, you go home, do your things and go to bed. While you are sleeping, a miracle happens and the problem that brought you here is suddenly solved, like magic. The problem is gone. Because you were sleeping, you don't know that a miracle happened, but when you wake up tomorrow morning, you will be different. How will you know a miracle has happened? What will be the first small sign that tells you that the problem is resolved? (*Use miracle question to engage the client in a solution-building process*)

Linda: I won't be so cranky, like an immoveable mountain.

SWR: Instead of being cranky, how do you see yourself being? (*Help client move from a negatively stated description to positively stated description*)

Linda: Be a little more upbeat, cheerful, and perky. Get my mind off of it and focus on areas not on the mountain of pain.

SWR: So you want to be more upbeat, cheerful, and perky, and distract yourself from the mountain of pain and do something different? (*Select positive description and use client's language*)

Linda: So when I am around people they are not affected by it and they aren't dragged down by it.

SWR: Let's say you woke up tomorrow after this miracle happened; what would be the first small thing you would do that you are not doing now? *(Build and expand solution-picture)*

Linda: I don't know. (Pause) Maybe instead of lying in bed staring at the wall, I would get up and open the curtain and turn on my computer, open a book, talk to the cat, anything beside lying in bed and staring at the wall.

SWR: That is what you do now, lie in bed and stare at the wall?

Linda: Yeah.

SWR: When this miracle happens, you would get out of bed, open the curtain, talk to the cat. What else would you do? *(Select and further build solution-picture)*

Linda: Turn on the computer and get out of bed and do something.

SWR: Do something? (Invite a more detailed description)

Linda: Maybe sweep, dust, or mop.

SWR: Anything else? *(Use presuppositional language that embeds an expectation of change)*

Linda: Go outside and sit in the sunshine.

SWR: Who in your home would notice the change? Is there somebody else living in your home? *(Relationship question)*

Linda: No, just my cat.

SWR: So what would your cat notice that is different about you that you are not doing now? *(Use relationship and difference question to further build the solution-picture)*

Linda: I would be up and maybe play with her.

SWR: be up and play with her? How would that make a difference in your day if you were having more fun with your cat? *(Use relationship and difference question to further build the solution-picture)*

SWR: So who else would notice the change besides your cat? (Further build and expand the solution using Relationship question)

Linda: My neighbors, friends.

SWR: What would they notice? (Invite a more detailed description)

Linda: A more positive outlook.

SWR: How would they notice? (Invite an observable description)

Linda: I would respond to them, not giving them dirty looks when it is not their fault. I would run over. I sort of give them a dirty look. It is a major hurdle for me.

SWR: Who would be most affected by this change? (Invite a description of the expected effect of change)

Linda: I suppose that it would help other people as well as me.

SWR: How so? (Invite further elaboration of the effect of change)

Linda: You know it would help me because I don't want to be a big drag and that way I won't be dragging people down and it won't be dragging me down because everyone around me is all bummed out. "Oh you poor thing," and all this and I don't want that. I want to get over it. I want to get over it; I want to get over the top of the mountain and go on from here not just hang around the base all the time.

SWR: Tomorrow, meaning the following morning or next morning, you can do this. On a 1-to-10 scale, 10 being certain that you can do this, and 1 being no chance at all, where would you think you are? *(Scaling question regarding feasibility of the change effort. Good timing to use scaling question as the client has just clearly articulated her desire and motivation for change)*

Linda: I am at a 6 right now.

SWR: So you are saying getting out of bed in the morning, opening the curtains, turning on the computer, and talking to the cat is quite doable because you are at a 6?

Linda: It is doable. I can do that.

SWR: Using the same scale, 10 being you are motivated to do this because it would improve your life, and 1 being you are wishy-washy about it, where would you put yourself on the scale? *(Scaling question regarding motivation for change)*

Linda: I would say an 8, because I don't want to be cranky anymore.

THE CASE OF ELISE

Elise was a 45-year-old Caucasian single mother with three children from 10 to 16 years of age.

Her husband passed away a year ago and she felt extremely overwhelmed trying to take care of her three children. She became depressed and attempted to commit suicide by overdosing on sleeping pills. She requested that her children be placed in foster homes while she tried to work things out for herself. She received treatment as part of her case plan to reunite with her children. While thinking what might be a helpful goal for her to work on, Elise pondered and struggled. At first, she mentioned developing a better relationship with her children as something she would like to see happen. However, she also felt overwhelmed as a single mother without the support of her husband. The therapist encouraged her to think about what will be personally meaningful and helpful to her at this time. Elise said that she would like to be more productive, although she did not have a clear idea of what a productive life would look like.

Elise: I don't know. I guess I would feel a little different. Maybe just be more productive.

SWR: In what way? (*Invite a more detailed description*)

Elise: I am not sure. … I am raising three kids and my husband passed away a year ago, and I am doing nothing myself.

SWR: So life is not cool.

Elise: Yes, not whole lot to do, so. . .

SWR: So what would you do differently to be more productive? (*Use client's language, listen and select what is important for the client*)

Elise: I don't know, but I could be more productive than I am right now. I am reading and doing the seven steps right now. That is about it.

SWR: Do you feel being more productive by reading the seven steps and maybe, as you've just said, taking walks? (*Important for the client to evaluate whether she has been more productive*)

Elise: I am thinking about when my kids come home, my relationship with them is going to be more productive. I have to feel like I've changed a little bit. (*Client is still somewhat unclear about what she can do to get herself to be more productive.*)

SWR: Let me ask you this, You wake up tomorrow morning, you do this and whatever else it is to make you more productive. At the end of the day you look at yourself and say, "Man, I am doing well. I am ready to do it now for myself." What do you think that might be? (*This is a different version of the miracle question that helps Elise to be more playful about envisioning a future when she is more productive.*)

Elise: Going through the seven steps program changes my ideas and personality more toward being a single woman.

SWR: How will people notice that you are standing as a single woman? They know that you are different. How will they know that? (*Select what is important to the client and use relationship question to invite elaboration*)

Elise: By the way I am acting.

SWR: What will tell them you have changed your attitude and you are different from before?

Elise: Oh, gosh, my weight.

SWR: So your weight will be different. I am curious, pretend for a moment that between now and next week, your weight has changed. What will be different for you in your daily life? What will you be doing that you are not doing right now? (*Invite elaboration of the expected effect of change*)

Elise: If my weight changed, I would not watch the same TV shows, I wouldn't want to read the same books, and I wouldn't eat the same junk food.

SWR: You are making big changes in your daily life.… (*Invite client to self-evaluate the feasibility of the proposed change*)

Elise: You're right, but this is something that I do want to change.

SWR: What would be the first things that you could possibly do to make this happen? (*Invite client to make a doable plan*)

Elise: I'm already walking every day. Maybe I could walk longer and not watch the eight o'clock show.

SWR: Anything else? (*Presuppositional language that embeds an expectation of change*)

Elise: Don't go to the "snack" aisle when doing my grocery shopping. That'll probably do it.

SWR: So what will you get from the store instead? (*Help client to move from a negatively stated description to a positively stated description*)

Elise: Maybe more fresh food, like veggies and fish.

SWR: What do you want to see happen when you take walks and eat more fresh food? (Build and elaborate expected effect of change efforts)

Elise: I'll feel like I'm having more control and being more productive in my life, not just lying around like a couch potato and doing nothing.

SWR: So, how confidant are you on a 1-to-10 scale that you will be able to take a longer walk and eat more fresh food between now and next time we get together? (*Scaling question regarding confidence about change*)

Elise: Well, I do want to change, but you know the temptation. (*pause*) Maybe a 3.

SWR: So, what are some small things you can do to move from a 3 to a 4? (Use scaling question to establish small steps for Elise to feel more confident)

Elise: That's not easy. Maybe talking to my sister so she can remind me once in a while.

SWR: So, maybe take it to the next step. Next week, just pretend this change is going through. Watch and see what you do differently as a result of that. I will be very interested to hear what you say next time about how just going through that next step made you do things differently and be more productive? Is that possible?

Elise: Oh, yes.

SWR: Just pay attention to, "If I would like my life to be better, what small things can I do to make it happen?"

GUIDELINES FOR USING MIRACLE QUESTION AND SCALING QUESTION IN SOCIAL WORK PRACTICE

Knowing *when* to use miracle questions and scaling questions is as important as knowing the questions. Perhaps the most important skill is to pay attention to our client's and our own moment-to-moment communication and responses in the co-constructive therapeutic process. The following are some guidelines for using

these questions, including when to use them in a beneficial way:

- Use miracle questions to assist clients develop a clear vision of a future without problems.
  - Miracle question is frequently used during the first session after the client has shared a description of the problem context and the therapist has an adequate understanding of the problem context.
  - A shift to solution-building by using miracle question is indicated when client's description of the problem context is getting repetitive and no new information is offered
- Scaling questions can be effectively used for the following purposes:
  - Evaluate confidence, ability, and motivation with respect to clients' change efforts
  - Establish small steps for further change
  - Help clients gauge their perceptions of problems and goals
- To fully utilize the constructive effect of scaling questions, use scaling questions when the client has adequately articulated his or her desire for change.
  - Avoid inviting clients to scale confidence, ability, or motivation early on in the session when there are clear indications that they are not confident or motivated to change; or, are hopeless about the problem situation.
- Be patient: Clients do not have the solution in mind when they seek treatment, and it is the responsibility of the therapist to create a safe space for them to slowly "paint" their solution picture.
- Go for details: Assist clients to move beyond vague descriptions of a desirable future, and instead describe it in terms of small, observable, specific, or behavioral steps.
- Reinforce clients' motivation: Assist clients in carefully evaluating what may be personally meaningful and useful for them.
- Respect clients' personal choice and ownership
- Compliment and acknowledge client's desire for change
- Assist clients in evaluating the feasibility of the solution picture

- Focus on small steps that can make clients' lives better
- Assist clients in developing clear indicators of change so that they can recognize successes

CONCLUSION

The purpose of the miracle and scaling questions is to assist clients in establishing indicators of wellness and gauging their progress toward a desirable future. These self-evaluative questions represent a specific type of conversation, in which the therapist talks "with" the client (instead of talking "at" the client) to co-develop new meanings and new realities through a dialogue of "solutions" (Bavelas et al., 2013; de Shazer, 1994; Lee et al., 2003). The challenge for social work practitioners is to collaboratively work with clients so that clients can find a future in which they feel comfortable as well as feel good about their choices. The therapist cautiously refrains from providing/suggesting any predetermined solutions or desirable future. Through *listen, select, and build* (Bavelas et al., 2013), the therapist creates a therapeutic dialogical context in which both clients and therapists co-construct a solution-building process, which is initiated from within and grounded in the client's personal construction of reality and cultural strengths (Lee, 2013). The therapeutic process is a collaborative and egalitarian one, in which the client's self-determination is fully respected (De Jong & Berg, 2013). The ultimate goal of miracle and scaling questions, therefore, is consistent with the goal of empowerment that focuses on increasing clients' personal and interpersonal power so that they can take relevant and culturally appropriate action to improve their situation (DuBois & Miley, 2013; Gutierrez, DeLois, & GlenMaye, 1995).

WEBSITES AND LISTSERV

http://www.brief-therapy.org/
http://www.sfbta.org/
SFT-L Solution Focused Therapy SFT-L@
    LISTSERV.ICORS.ORG

References

Berg, I. K. (1994). *Family based services: A solution-focused approach*. New York, NY: W.W. Norton.

Berg, I. K., & Miller, S. (1992). *Working with the problem drinker: A solution-focused approach*. New York, NY: W.W. Norton & Co.

De Jong, P., & Berg, I. K. (2013). *Interviewing for solutions* (4th ed.). Belmont, CA: Brooks/Cole.

DuBois, B. L., & Miley, K. K. (2013). *Social work: An empowering profession* (8th ed.). NY: Pearson.

de Shazer, S. (1994). *Words were originally magic*. New York, NY: W.W. Norton.

de Shazer, S. (1991). *Putting difference to work*. New York, NY: W.W. Norton.

de Shazer, S. (1985). *Keys to solutions in brief therapy*. New York, NY: W.W. Norton.

de Shazer, S., Dolan, Y. M., Korman, H., Trepper, T. S., McCollum, E. E., & Berg, I. K. (2007). *More than miracles: The state of the art of solution focused therapy*. New York, NY: Haworth Press.

Greene, G. J., Lee, M. Y., Mentzer, R., Pinnell, S., & Niles, D. (1998). Miracles, dreams, and empowerment: A brief practice note. *Families in Society, 79*, 395–399.

Gutierrez, L. M., DeLois, K. A., & GlenMaye, L. (1995). Understanding empowerment practice: Building on practitioner-based knowledge. *Families in Society, 76*, 534–542.

Trepper, T. S., McCollum, E. E., DeJong, P., Korman, H., Gingerich, W., & Franklin, C. (2013). *Solution focused therapy treatment manual for working with individuals* (2nd version). Milwaukee, WI: Solution Focused Brief Therapy Association.

McKergow, M., & Korman, H. (2009). Inbetween—neither inside nor outside. *Journal of Systemic Therapies, 28*(2), 34–49.

Miller, G. (1997). *Becoming miracle workers: Language and meaning in brief therapy*. New York, NY: Aldine de Gruyter.

Lee, M. Y. (2013). Solution-focused therapy. In C. Franklin (Ed.), *The 23rd Encyclopedia of Social Work*. New York, NY: Oxford University Press. http://socialwork.oxfordre.com/view/10.1093/acrefore/9780199975839.001.0001/acrefore-9780199975839-e-1039?rskey=CVCQpO&result=1

Lee, M. Y., Sebold, J., & Uken, A. (2003). *Solution-focused treatment with domestic violence offenders: Accountability for change*. New York, NY: Oxford University Press.

Nelson, T., & Thomas, F. (Eds.). (2007). *Clinical applications of Solution Focused Brief Therapy*. New York, NY: Haworth Press.

42 Gestalt Therapy

William P. Panning

INTRODUCTION

Gestalt is a German word that encompasses several concepts, including wholeness, configuration, and pattern. To those in the field of mental health, it implies a unique form of psychotherapy that holds a holistic view of human nature, focuses on the present moment-to-moment experience to develop awareness, and is more curious about *how* people have come to where they are in life than *why*. Instead of making interpretations, Gestalt therapists work to increase the client's awareness. Gestalt therapy is an existential/phenomenological, experiential approach with a holistic commitment to the intellectual, emotional, physical, and spiritual nature of the client. Therapy focuses on improving contact and awareness in the here and now. Unlike other therapeutic approaches, treatment does not specifically highlight mental illness or dysfunction, but considers the growth, enthusiasm, and liveliness of the patient. The therapist encourages patients to focus on the subtleties of how they stop themselves from being fully present and contactful. Teaching patients how to focus on being in the here and now, trust their own internal process, and welcome deep vulnerable feelings will lead to what one patient described as a "heavy, deep, and real" experience.

The main emphasis in Gestalt therapy is to not get caught up in talking about what happens in the day-to-day life of the client but to experience as fully as possible what is unfolding in the therapeutic encounter. From this here-and-now vantage point, the therapist can deal directly with what is observable in the client's style. The goals are to:

- Work through blocks to contact
- Teach awareness
- Expand contact boundaries through the help of well-crafted experiments

The therapist encourages clients to attend to themselves in the emerging process to become who they are authentically rather than trying to be something they are not. With this in mind, there is little interest in "fixing" the person. Furthermore, the therapist believes that he or she does *not* know what is best for the client *nor* how the client should think, feel, or behave. Instead, the therapist honors the client's lively process and helps clients:

- Connect their awareness with their experiences
- Develop good contact skills
- Grow through experiential learning
- Take responsibility for their thoughts, feelings, and actions

THE HISTORY OF GESTALT THERAPY

Frederick "Fritz" Perls and his wife, Laura, founded Gestalt therapy in the 1940s. Perls was trained as a psychoanalyst. In 1926, he worked under Professor Kurt Goldstein, who introduced him to the principles of Gestalt psychology and provided him with many of the organizing principles for Gestalt therapy (see Table 42.1). Perls was later influenced by the theory and practices of Wilhelm Reich, who focused on the body in therapy and introduced the concept of *character armor*. He incorporated Reich's method of present-centered examination into Gestalt by heightening awareness of the client's nonverbal communications and focusing on the client's actions and behaviors. This was practiced by paying careful attention to the stylistic ways the client communicated through gestures, body movement, breathing, musculature, speech, and posture. Thus, Gestalt therapy draws on

TABLE 42.1 Basic Principles of Gestalt Therapy

1. Careful attention to the contact experienced during the therapeutic encounter

2. The development of the experiential "present moment"—the "here and now" of experience, considered to be more reliable than interpretation

3. Field theory, which states that all phenomena are linked to a part of a larger network of interactions and can be understood only in relation to one another

4. Figure/ground formation, which states that what is most important in the moment becomes figural and invites attention, and the unimportant drifts to the background

5. Identification and exploration of resistances through awareness, exploration, and working through

6. Identification and working through of introjects, the messages internalized in childhood

7. The use of the experiment to heighten awareness and promote growth and change

---

knowledge and expertise from psychoanalysis, flavors of Zen Buddhism, Gestalt psychology, existentialism, phenomenology, field theory, psychodrama, theater, modern dance, and awareness achieved through the five senses.

THE PRACTICE OF GESTALT THERAPY

Although Gestalt therapy may be briefly introduced in graduate social work programs (Congress, 1996), most instruction is received postgraduate through an intensive three-year training program taught by seasoned therapists. Mentoring and ongoing supervision from a Gestalt practitioner round out the ideal education process. It is not uncommon for dedicated students also to engage in their own therapy to develop self-awareness and enhance their contact skills. Thus, there are as many different ways of practicing Gestalt as there are therapists. Differences arise from the fact that each therapist brings his or her own unique awareness, ability to make healthy contact, and creativity to the process of designing and implementing growth-producing experiments. In addition, "the competent practice of Gestalt Therapy requires a background in more than just Gestalt

theory. Knowledge of diagnosis, personality theory, and psychodynamic theory is also needed" (Yontef, 1993).

Rather than a strict, concrete, step-by-step series of actions, Gestalt therapy is a process that unfolds over time out of the encounter between the client and therapist. This process varies with each client depending on such factors as:

- Level of awareness of self and other
- Ability to make contact
- Personal history
- Unique resistances and introjects
- Diagnostic indicators that determine if the client is neurotic, character disordered, or psychotic

Much of the actual practice of Gestalt therapy consists of carefully examining the contact that is made in the therapeutic encounter and the resistances that emerge at the contact boundary to protect the person—in the moment—from his or her anxiety. Gestalt therapy is an exploration—a "peeling of the onion"—rather a direct modification of behavior. The intention is not to solve patients' problems directly, but rather to help them discover that through the heightening of their awareness comes choice.

The Paradoxical Theory of Change

The Paradoxical Theory of Change, which states that the more one tries to be who one is not, the more one stays the same (Beisser, 1970), is a hallmark of Gestalt therapy. Many times patients are driven by who they think they should be, instead of uncovering who they are. The more they push to be what they are not, the more resistance is set up, and little or no change occurs. Thus, the paradox: the more people attempt to be who they are not, the more they stay the same. On the other hand, when patients identify more fully with their present moment experience, growth and change are supported. Beisser (1970) says that change comes about as a result of "full acceptance of what is, rather than striving to be different." Gestalt, therefore, supports the individual in being who he or she really is as fully as possible. Thus, Gestalt Therapy is extremely useful for patients who are psychologically inclined and open to working on their own awareness. This raising of awareness will help patients understand better how they are functioning in their world—with family, friends, at work, school, and at play.

An old adage states that the gods gave people two eyes—one to view the outside world and the other to keep an eye on their internal world. From this perspective, it is not uncommon to begin a session by asking patients to slow down their thoughts, turn their attention inward, and attend to what they are aware of in the present moment. This can help them experience not only their senses, but more subtle inner awareness and bodily sensations. "Getting close to sensation is intended to enable us to just experience without the interference of thinking, accepted as it comes without judgment" (Sheldon, 2012–2013). This sets the tone for the session and emphasizes the understanding that the work will focus on the individual's process, and not exclusively on their story. Content can be seductive, but it is ultimately the villain of the creative process. The foundational questions in the following list invite patients to go deeper into their own processes.

- "What are you aware of now?"
- "What are you feeling?"
- "Can you put that thought into words?"

Dialogue between the therapist and the patient helps the individual reveal his or her "true self" with genuineness and authenticity, and communicate this experience to the therapist. Honest, direct dialogue sheds light on how the patient avoids contact with others, and highlights other important aspects of the here-and-now, such as emotions, bodily sensations, and emerging resistances. Throughout the work, the therapist evaluates the patient's contact boundaries to assess what this individual can tolerate from moment to moment. Repeated respectful contact builds trust.

CONTACT

Perls, Hefferline, and Goodman (1980) define *contact* as the experience of the individual at the boundary between *me* and *not me*. "Contact is thus interactive and emerges from the moment-to-moment experience between individuals." At any given moment, contact represents a person's best creative adjustment, the best he or she can do in the present moment. In Gestalt therapy, the contact between the therapist and the client (rather than interpretations of thoughts, feelings, or actions) forms the basis for the therapeutic encounter. Contact is the psychological process of engaging with our environment and ourselves. Good contact means to be consciously aware of the present, fully engaged in the experience, and nurtured by it. The hallmark of good contact is excitement. When you are in contact with someone, it is an energetically charged experience that you will feel as concern, interest, or curiosity. Poor contact, on the other hand, is indicated by lack of interest, boredom, or fear of being engaged by the experience. Therapeutic contact can be thought of as fully seeing and hearing the client and responding to what the individual says and does. Strengthening contact will ultimately help clients express more clearly what is on their minds, express what they feel, and take ownership of the quality of contact they are making. Ingredients of good contact include:

- Clear awareness of what am I doing in this moment
- Word choices that are clear, concise, and appropriately charged with feeling
- Responses to the here-and-now experience with an acknowledgement of each person's presence
- Integration between the body and the spoken word.

In *Gestalt Therapy Integrated*, Edwin and Sonia Nevis outlined seven contact functions/modes to be assessed: looking/seeing; listening/hearing; tasting; smelling; touching; talking; and moving. When these contact functions are weak it becomes important to teach patients how to make good contact so they will come to understand both intellectually and emotionally that good contact is vitally important to the therapeutic process, as well as for effective interpersonal relationships, closeness, and intimacy. To accomplish this, the therapist must teach clients to be present and engaged in an authentic way by focusing on the contact and resisting the temptation to get caught up in the content of the story. Although what is being said is always important, it is rarely as important as what clients do—how they are engaging as they share their story.

In the beginning stage of therapy, therapists need to ask themselves "can this patient make emotional contact?" If the answer is no, contact functions need to be addressed before the work can go any deeper. When people come into therapy they are experiencing a disturbance of some sort at the contact boundary. It is the task of the therapist to discern the type of disturbance and help the patient understand how to correct the mostly unconscious mechanisms used to diminish contact. These unconscious mechanisms are called resistances. Without first addressing disturbances in contact, the patient will not engage deeply in the therapy process; sessions risk becoming merely an exercise in questions and answers. Yet, once the disturbed contact skills are identified, the therapist can begin to point out when the contact disturbance is noticed, and provide a here-and-now experience to develop the contact skill. Examples of diminished contact include:

- An inability to listen or respond directly to what is being said
- Not acknowledging the other has spoken
- Being oblivious to another's feelings
- Not communicating in a clear direct manner that is understandable to others (i.e., being vague).

To monitor your degree of contact, ask yourself whether you are sharing your thoughts and feelings clearly and in terms the client can understand. Are you staying present with the client's process or is your mind wandering? Monitor your listening to stay focused on what the client is saying. In addition, ask yourself whether you are responding to the client directly and relevantly. In this way, you will stay aware of both the client and your own responses to the client. Awareness is for the therapist as well as the client.

Awareness

The idea of developing awareness of "what is" is originally found in Eastern philosophies, such as Taoism and Zen Buddhism. "Awareness includes knowing the environment, responsibility for choices, self-knowledge, self-acceptance, and the ability to connect" (Yontef, 1993). Perls believed awareness, or focusing attention on what is actually happening, was so important that he originally called Gestalt therapy "concentration therapy." From a Gestalt perspective, awareness is a never-ending process of self-discovery. This requires an ongoing process of "observing and attending to one's thoughts, feelings, and actions, which include somatic sensations and perceptions, language and movement" (Schilling, 1984, p. 151). This may sound like a simple task, but

to be aware moment-to-moment, and to use this awareness to be an effective therapist, is a life-long challenge.

Developing awareness in your clients involves teaching them to notice, name, and report on their internal processes. The intention of this focus is to develop insight. Fritz Perls used to encourage his patients to "lose your mind, and come to your senses." The role of the therapist is to bring into awareness that which the patients do not see. Perls used to say "a neurotic is someone who is not aware of the obvious." With increased awareness, clients discover that their sensations are saying something to them about their present experience. The therapist's task is to help clients learn to listen to what their own sensations are saying. This often begins with teaching clients to notice simple body sensations, which, if attended to, will lead to a feeling. As this process unfolds, clients learn to trust themselves and to develop valuable self-support.

Specifically, developing awareness in a session involves asking patients to take notice of any racing thoughts and slow them down; turn their attention inward; and get quiet and notice what emerges. In effect, the therapist is teaching patients to notice, label, and report their internal processes. This may include sharing thoughts, body sensations, gestures, postures, movements, facial expressions, vocal tone, breathing quality, and moment-to-moment resistances as they emerge. The therapist accomplishes this by learning to trust his or her observational skills, paying special attention to the most obvious, and giving feedback to the patient about:

- Verbal messages—noting what is said as well as how it is being said
- Content reported to you by the patient—" I feel angry," "My stomach hurts."
- Muscular constrictions—noticeable tensions and how clients are holding themselves
- Posture, gestures, and body movements
- Breathing patterns—Are clients holding their breath? Is breathing shallow or labored?
- Quality of contact and any notable resistances to contact emerging at the contact boundary
- Direct attention to internal sensations, which if followed will lead to feeling
- How you are impacted by this person—what you see, hear, and feel—Does the patient make you feel anxious, tired, bored, angry?

Although these observations may seem like obvious strategies, they will help patients to see themselves more clearly in the moment. By developing awareness, clients can expect to:

- Understand their internal process by realizing that what emerges inside them has significance
- Improve their ability to be intimate with others by valuing and reporting their moment-to-moment internal and external experiences
- Develop an increased understanding of identity by noticing, reporting, and responding to any emotional or physical sensations that lead to feelings or actions
- Develop their ability to live in the moment and to expand their contact boundaries.

THE THERAPEUTIC RELATIONSHIP

The *therapeutic relationship,* defined as the process of making contact over time, is the emotional heart and soul of Gestalt therapy. To be impactful, therapists, as well as patients, must let themselves be affected. Only then can the therapeutic relationship become the most powerful means of working through a client's problems and the medium of growth and change. Once the relationship is established, clients become more willing to explore the vulnerable areas of their lives. "The client comes into therapy expecting that their needs will meet the same traumatic fate in the hands of the therapist that they were met with in childhood" (Cole, 1994, p. 84). To alter this belief, the therapist must attend to how the client relates in the present and develop a meaningful, trusting relationship that provides nonmanipulative feedback. Therapists must practice good contact, self-awareness, and sensitivity to the emerging contact boundaries of the client. To do this effectively, the therapist must be present-centered and guided by theory that is known so well that it becomes second nature. The focus then becomes the client's humanity.

A Gestalt therapist is generally fairly active within the session, and, therefore, must possess characteristics that include sensitivity, a good sense of timing, creativity, empathy, and respect for the patient. These characteristics, along with an unshakable ethical practice, reflect the training, experience, and judgment of the therapist. The intensity of a particular therapist may not

suit every patient, so discretion must be observed and exercised. A respectful fit between the therapist's style and the needs of the specific patient is essential. To this end the therapist must keep in mind the personal boundaries of patients and support them in working at their contact boundary. The challenge is to balance being appropriately detached with being appropriately engaged—to not be too distant or removed/disengaged, and to not violate the patient's boundary, which may threaten or overwhelm the patient and cause him or her to resist or shut down.

RESISTANCES

In Gestalt therapy, resistance is accepted as *what is* for clients in their experience of the present moment. When clients are resisting, they are just being themselves. Thus, resistances are to be celebrated and encouraged. Resistances represent how clients avoid contact, block energy, and limit themselves in the present from doing things that would require them to stretch their boundaries.

Inasmuch as resistances are essential to being in the world, they are not something to be broken or beaten down. Instead, therapists work to bring them into awareness, to explore how the resistance is being expressed in the body. Supporting the resistance will help patients to feel affirmed in their character, especially before they are aware themselves of their favored or dominant means of resistance. Only with the therapist's support of the resistance will the client be able, over time, to give it up. Helping patients work through resistances will psychologically free them to deal effectively with their feelings.

Resistances are identified by observing the client's posture, body movements, expressions, breathing, speech quality, voice tones, and verbal communication. Observable indicators of resistance include:

- Body posture and movements, including legs, arms, and chest: Is there flexibility/rigidity/range of motion of body movements (e.g., clenching a fist, tightening the jaw)?
- Facial expressions: inappropriate smiling, frozen, poker-face, tightness, eye movements, quality of eye contact
- Breathing: Is it rapid and shallow or labored? Is the client holding in breath?
- Voice and speaking style: Are there noticeable changes in the voice such as the

voice cracking, jarring, harsh, or strident; changing in loudness, softness, or pitch; is the voice monotone; is there excessive wordiness or a rambling quality without silence or pause; is there frequent starting and stopping to indicate self-restraint or self-interruption?
- Verbal content: impersonal language, lack of direction or focus, frequent changes in the subject indicating deflections; use of absolutes, shoulds or ought-tos, indicating introjections, rationalizations, or intellectualizations; avoidance of specific content such as sexuality; excessive use of jargon

Once resistances are identified and named, clients are taught to report any internal cues that help them track how they experience blocking contact in the present. Growing beyond a boundary is subsequently accomplished through experimentation. The five primary resistances are briefly discussed here.

Retroflection

Retroflection is a mechanism by which people hold in what they are afraid to express to others or turn back on the self that which they would like to do to others. In both instances, they are turning back on the self what needs to be turned toward the world. The disadvantage of retroflecting is that energy is blocked and not successfully discharged. This can lead to a build-up of anxiety, constant muscle tension and pain, and physical ailments, such as ulcers, psychosomatic illnesses, and depression. Common examples of retroflection that can be witnessed in the therapeutic encounter include:

- Holding the breath
- Shallow or labored breathing
- Excessive swallowing
- Body tension
- Clenching of the jaw and/or grinding of the teeth
- Biting fingernails
- Shaky and/or monotone voice
- Stopping midsentence while speaking
- Directing anger inward toward the self instead of outward toward others.

The key to resolving unhealthy retroflection is to help clients get back into their feelings and let go of them appropriately.

Deflection

Deflection is the avoidance of contact and/or awareness by turning aside or pushing something away. The client is taking action but misses the mark by either making no contact or reducing contact. This process of distraction provides a way of avoiding contact and awareness through being vague and indirect. Deflection detracts from genuine contact and makes it difficult to maintain a sustained sense of self. Common examples of deflection include not looking at the person with whom you are attempting to make contact, using verbose/excessive language, vagueness, being abstract or indirect, over-use of humor or laughing off important things, and not receiving or taking in what someone is saying.

Projection

Projection is the confusion of self and other that results in attributing to the outside world something that truly belongs to the self. By doing so, aspects of the self are disowned and assigned to others. A part of the self or feeling about the self is experienced, but not understood or owned as self, and is attributed to another person outside the body. Projection can take the form of blaming and lack of responsibility for oneself or one's actions. Psychological growth suffers when "unacceptable" parts of the self are disowned. Proverbially, it is said that when someone points the finger at others, three fingers are pointing back at the self. Projection can take healthy forms, for example, through empathy, by which you are able to acknowledge someone else's pain by understanding and feeling your own.

Introjection

Introjection is passively and uncritically internalizing the values and norms imposed by family, religion, and society without discrimination, assimilation, or review of these beliefs and standards. As a result, foreign, undigested information is swallowed without adequate processing or ownership, and people are left not knowing what they want or need. When a client constantly takes in everything without discrimination and doesn't reject what doesn't fit, it creates an "amorphous" personality, someone who is vague, nondescript, and lacking in personality definition.

Confluence

Without well-defined boundaries, it is hard to get to know a person. *Confluence* is the fusion or merging of boundaries, the fuzzy lack of contact in which there is no clear distinction between where "I" leaves off, and "You" begins. This pseudoagreement to avoid differentiation or separation blurs and melts interpersonal boundaries and causes a loss of separate identity. When two people parallel each other without making contact, they are unable to experience each other's true feeling or opinions. No contact can develop when there is no clear distinction between where you end and another person begins.

Prolonged confluence deadens the potential for conflict to emerge. Without conflict, interactions become flat and dull. This may lead to pathological compliance, codependency, and a suppression of one's personal preferences. There is no struggle to develop one's own interests and convictions. Not surprisingly, confluent people have an extremely high need to be accepted and liked. To avoid conflict, they continuously agree with everything the other says without question or debate.

STAGES OF RESISTANCE WORK

The therapist's task is to help the client develop an understanding of the resistance process by first explaining what a resistance is, discussing how it operates, and then identifying how it surfaces in the present moment to block meaningful contact. As taught by Norman Shub, BCD, LISW, LPCC, at the Gestalt Institute of Central Ohio (Columbus, Ohio), resistance work involves the following steps:

1. Identifying and witnessing the resistance and noticing how it emerges in the client. This is accomplished through observing nonverbal behavior, attending to how it feels to sit with the client, and listening to the words in which the story is presented.
2. Sensing internal cues to assist clients in developing awareness of and connection to their internal process by noticing the unique sensations they experience.
3. Encouraging clients to begin to report their own process to the therapist (after they learn to feel/sense their resistances). This marks a shift away from the therapist doing all the work and toward clients taking responsibility for tracking their own processes.
4. Encouraging clients to move beyond their resistances by experimenting with alternatives that may stretch the contact boundary.

Playing all our hunches is an important aspect in this experiential approach. If the perception does not ring true the therapist can let it go and move on to the next emerging awareness. Yet, if the therapist observes or suspects conscious or unconscious resistance at play, it is important to circle around and attempt the intervention again, in a slightly different fashion.

THE GESTALT EXPERIMENT

"A unique quality of Gestalt therapy is its emphasis on modifying a person's behavior in the therapy situation itself. This systematic behavior modification, when it grows out of the experience of the client, is called an experiment" (Zinker, 1977a, p. 123). Gestalt experiments can take on many forms, and are the cornerstone of Gestalt therapy's experiential learning. Experiential learning transforms talking about a problem into dramatically heightening awareness through creative experimentation. With the support of the therapist, who acts as consultant and coach, clients are given the opportunity to explore their underdeveloped side, try new behaviors, and focus on verbalizations, dramatization, dialogue between self and other, fantasies, or physical functioning in the here and now to promote growth and change. Knowing when to introduce an experiment, and when to leave the patient alone is a critical step in the process. Properly preparing the client for an experiment will soften their resistance and improve the odds of a successful outcome. Once the patient engages in the creative experiment it is not uncommon to suggest that they "stay with it … lean into that … feel the feeling … put that into words" to help nurture and deepen the process.

Zinker, in *In Search of Good Form* (1977b, p. 194), states that an experiment comes out of the therapeutic encounter and generally involves the following developmental sequence:

1. Laying the groundwork
2. Negotiating consent between the therapist and client. Gaining consent is accomplished

by asking the client, "Would you like to try something?"

3. Grading the work up or down by making the experiment equal the client's readiness, need, and ability. This makes an experiment safe enough to warrant implementation, yet challenging enough to be realistic.
4. Surfacing the client's energy and motivation
5. Developing a theme
6. Generating self-support
7. Choosing an experiment, carrying it out, and debriefing the client.

SPEED, NOISE, GRAVITY

Psychotherapy is considered to be both an art and a science. Understanding Gestalt theory represents the science portion of the challenge in having a successful therapeutic encounter. The art of psychotherapy requires the therapist, as well as the patient, to be fully present in the process, with a willingness to engage emotionally and be impacted by the experience. Thus, the therapist must slow down, take notice of the present moment, tap into what is going on inside the patient, and assess what it feels like to be with them. Developing this intuitive sixth sense requires therapists to access their own internal process. "If we were to choose one key idea to stand as a symbol for the Gestalt approach, it might well be the concept of authenticity, the quest for authenticity. If we regard therapy and the therapist in the pitiless light of authenticity, it becomes apparent that the therapist cannot teach what he does not know. A therapist with some experience really knows within himself that he is communicating to his patient his own fears as well as his courage, his defensiveness as well as his openness, his confusion as well as his clarity. The therapist's awareness, acceptance, and sharing of these truths can be a highly persuasive demonstration of his own authenticity. Obviously such a position is not throughout one's career but throughout one's entire life" (Levitsky and Simkin (1972, pp. 251–252).

Dr. Joseph Zinker often said the unique challenges of the therapist can be boiled down into three basic concepts that must be assessed at all times—*speed, noise,* and *gravity. Speed* refers to the therapist's own level of nervous energy. When distracted by their own racing thoughts, agitation, or jumpiness therapists are unable to slow down and focus on the individual. *Noise* refers to the internal chatter that is going on inside the therapist's own head. Without a quieting or reduction of the internal background noise, it is nearly impossible to meet the challenge of focusing on the other person. *Gravity* refers to the ability to sit and listen while feeling supported by the present moment. This "sitting power" allows a solid touchstone from which the therapeutic experience can unfold.

Throughout the encounter the therapist is constantly monitoring and attending to various aspects of the patient to assess the patient's ability to be in good contact. Questions therapists may ask themselves are:

- How well can this patient hold a contactful gaze? What is the quality of eye contact?
- What is the patient feeling? Can clients make contact with themselves on an emotional level, or do they constantly disrupt their experience—does sadness lead to an expression of tears or are the tears retroflected?
- How is the patient responding to the therapist? Is the patient comfortable? Irritated? Agitated? What, if anything, is happening in the moment to generate these thoughts and feelings? Is something being projected onto the therapist?
- Can this patient identify and report his or her internal experience?

The Termination Process

Termination of an ongoing therapeutic encounter is generally a decision that is mutually decided and agreed upon between the therapist and patient. Changes that one can expect as a result of a successful course of treatment in Gestalt Therapy are:

- An increased awareness of a client's interior and exterior worlds
- Improved contact skills that utilize all of the five senses for awareness and decision making
- Improved identification, understanding, and management of resistances
- Heightened ability to take care of themselves, identify their needs, and search for healthy ways to get needs met
- Increased energy as a result of dealing with unfinished business of the past that had previously stolen energy and joy

- Assumption of more personal responsibility and ownership for thoughts, feelings, and actions without projecting onto others
- Improved ability to give to and receive from others in a meaningful way.

As a practicing Gestalt therapist for 30 plus years, I have witnessed the growth of managed care, a strategy by which health insurance companies provide mental health benefits in exchange for monitoring and "managing" the individual's mental health treatment. Thus, the insurance company has the power to limit or deny coverage for treatment that the patient and the therapist feel is warranted. The difficult question is whether to continue ongoing treatment if insurance benefits are discontinued. In such cases the patient is often forced to make a critical decision based on finances rather than treatment considerations. The therapeutic process may be damaged when treatment deemed necessary by the health care professional is judged unnecessary by a case manager of a managed health care organization.

What does it mean (as a patient and as a therapist) for an insurance company to become part of therapy? What happens when a direct conflict exists between the goal of helping patients with their complex mental health needs and the managed care goals of cutting costs and enhancing profits? Can business decisions impact the mental health needs of the individual?

A second dilemma centers on confidentiality. Managed care is based on a "medical model of necessity." The patient must give the therapist permission to disclose to the insurance company the intimate details of the individual's life—as a condition of receiving benefits. Disclosure includes providing an appropriately coded clinical diagnosis for the "problem" being treated, services rendered, and the duration of treatment. The insurance company may request additional information such as a detailed treatment plan with specific goals, means of achieving these benchmarks, and an acceptable "end date." Each of these is contrary to the stated process of Gestalt, which is open-ended and unfolding.

As a result of these concerns some practitioners decide not to work with managed care organizations, providing services for a stated fee; others believe that patients are entitled to use their insurance provided they understand the limitations and consequences. One advantage of a fee-for-service practice is that no private information is shared with an outside third party. The patient and the therapist together determine the length of treatment and payment plan. This tailors treatment to the patient's (rather than the insurance company's) needs.

Managed care has undoubtedly changed the practice of psychotherapy. Every social worker will face dilemmas and opportunities related to the intervention of insurance companies into their practice. Efforts are being made at many levels of government to have mental health services treated equally to any other medical illness, with the same systems of monitoring and rates of reimbursement. It will be up to future social workers to establish the validity of the Gestalt process and its relationship to a general improvement in the health, productivity, and well-being of treated clients.

Future Applications

Whether working with an individual, couple, family, or group, the practitioner provides good contact that transcends people, diversity, and cultural differences. Gestalt therapy develops a common ground for living, relating, and learning. It is more practice-driven than research-driven. As stated earlier in the chapter, there are as many different ways of practicing Gestalt therapy as there are therapists. Thus, the future of Gestalt therapy will be a holistic sum total of the practices of its therapists, guided by the basic, client-centered principles of the field.

CONCLUSION

In the early years of my practice I worked with a patient who upon termination left me a gift. She had cross-stitched the following poem that I have hanging on my office wall to this day. How often I have recognized this simple but powerful statement to be true. The poem goes like this:

> I'm OK, You're OK,
> That's only sometimes true,
> The tricky part is when we are not,
> To make that OK too.

Gestalt therapy is about humanity and human relationships. It is thus much more than a mode of treatment. It is a philosophical approach to life that recognizes the importance of awareness and genuine contact to mental health and happiness.

"To some, Gestalt is a way of life that embodies a spiritual practice, to help become more centered, more aware, more alive, more creative and present with others in a deep and meaningful way" (Sheldon, p. xi). Learning the skills of Gestalt therapy helps individuals and therapists develop the confidence to move from a self focus out into the world to get their needs met. This is accomplished by respecting the whole person as being more than the sum of independent parts and acknowledging that a trusting therapeutic relationship is indispensable in fostering growth and change. The rewards of engaging in this process will be great for you and for your clients.

WEBSITES

- Association for the Advancement of Gestalt Therapy. http://www.aagt.org.
- Gestalt Institute of Toronto. http://www.gestalt.on.ca.
- Gestalt Review. http://www.gestaltreview.com.
- Gestalt Therapy Network. http:www.gestalttherapy.net.
- Gestalt Therapy Page. http://www.gestalt.org.
- Gestalt News and Notes. http://www.gestalt.org/news.htm
- The Association for the Advancement of Gestalt Therapy. http://www.aagt.org/html/conference
- International Society for Gestalt Theory and Its Application. http://gestalttheory.net/
- Gestalt International Journal http://www.g-gei.org/
- www.gestaltcleveland.org
- www.gestalt.org/news
- Society for Gestalt Theory and Its Applications. http://www.gestalttheory.net.

VIDEO LINKS

- Fritzperls.com
- www.youtube.com/Fritzperls

References

Beisser, A. (1970). The paradoxical theory of change. In J. Fagan & I. L. Shepherd (Eds), *Gestalt therapy now: Theory, technique, applications* (pp.77–80). New York, NY: Harper & Row; Palo Alto, CA: Science and Behavior Books.

Cole, P. (1994). Resistance to awareness: A Gestalt therapy perspective. *Gestalt Journal, 17*(1), 71–94.

Congress, E. (1996). Gestalt theory and social work treatment. In F. J. Turner (Ed.), *Social work treatment: Interlocking theoretical approaches* (4th ed.) (pp. 341–361). New York, NY: Free Press.

Levitsky, A., & Simkin, J. S. (1972). Gestalt therapy. In L. N. Solomon & B. Berzon (Eds.), *New perspectives on encounter groups*. San Francisco, CA: Jossey-Bass.

Perls, F., Hefferline, R. F., & Goodman, P. (1980). *Gestalt therapy*. New York, NY: Bantam Books.

Schilling, L. E. (1984). Gestalt therapy. In *Perspectives on counseling theories* (pp. 148–165). Englewood Cliffs, NJ: Prentice Hall.

Sheldon, C. (2012–2013). *Gestalt as a way of life: Awareness practices as taught by Gestalt therapy founders and their followers*. Self-published.

Yontef, G. (1993). *Awareness, dialogue, and process: Essays on Gestalt therapy*. Highland, NY: Gestalt Journal Press, Inc.

Zinker, J. (1977a). *The Creative process in Gestalt therapy*. New York, NY: Vantage Books.

Zinker, J. (1977b). *In search of good form: Gestalt therapy with couples and families*. San Francisco, CA: Jossey-Bass.

43 Contemporary Object Relations Treatment

William Borden

INTRODUCTION

Object relations psychology has emerged as a major paradigm in contemporary psychodynamic thought. Although the perspective encompasses a variety of theoretical systems, thinkers have increasingly come to share fundamental assumptions, core concepts, and essential concerns. This overview traces the development of object relations psychology, introduces basic theoretical formulations and clinical perspectives, outlines empirical lines of inquiry, and shows how overlapping points of view deepen conceptions of personality development, psychopathology, and therapeutic action in psychosocial intervention. In doing so, it explores the ways in which relational perspectives enlarge understandings of vulnerability and interpersonal processes in emerging models of evidence-based practice.

Object relations perspectives have informed efforts to develop realistic and flexible approaches to psychosocial intervention for a range of problems in living, and relational concepts continue to shape development of empirically based methods of psychodynamic psychotherapy (see Shedler, 2010, for review of empirical evidence for the efficacy of psychodynamic treatment). Clinicians have established guidelines for treatment of maladaptive patterns of interpersonal behavior as well as problems in functioning associated with acute stress reactions, posttraumatic stress syndromes, the personality disorders, and other forms of developmental psychopathology (Roth & Fonagy, 2005). In the broader domain of social work practice, object relations perspectives deepen understanding of interactive processes and intervention approaches with couples,

families, groups, and organizations (Borden, 2009; Borden & Clark, 2012). Emerging lines of research in neuroscience and developmental psychology promise to strengthen the empirical base of object relations psychology and broaden conceptions of interpersonal behavior, experiential learning, and clinical expertise in reformulations of evidence-based practice and integrative approaches to intervention.

DEVELOPMENT OF OBJECT RELATIONS PSYCHOLOGY

Sigmund Freud first introduced the term "object" in the development of his drive psychology, but he linked the construct to notions of instinctual process rather than to concepts of relationship and social interaction; he saw the person as an "object" through which one achieves instinctual gratification. Although drive psychology served as the central paradigm in psychoanalytic understanding through the early decades of the 20th century, growing numbers of thinkers challenged Freud's vision of human nature and elaborated alternative perspectives that increasingly emphasized relational concepts and social domains of experience.

The earliest attempts to establish relational points of view encompassed the psychodynamic perspectives of Alfred Adler, C. G. Jung, Otto Rank, and Sandor Ferenczi, originally members of Freud's inner circle. They placed growing emphasis on the role of relationship and social experience in their formulations of personality development, psychopathology, and therapeutic intervention. Adler, for example, envisioned persons as "social beings" and emphasized concepts of relationship in his therapeutic approach. Jung saw persons as inherently relational and innately social. Rank based his humanistic model of personality on concepts of autonomy, dependency, and relationship, viewing psychology as the science of interpersonal relations. Ferenczi recognized the importance of the early caretaking environment in his conceptions of psychopathology, and he increasingly stressed the curative functions of the therapeutic relationship and interactive process in his reformulations of therapeutic methods. Careful readings of these revisionist thinkers, long neglected in the mainstream literature, show the extent to which they prefigure fundamental object relations concerns.

The widespread experience of separation, loss, and mourning after World War I informed further development of relational perspectives in London during the 1920s. Ian Suttie rejected Freud's drive psychology and proposed that innate needs for love and relationship are the fundamental motivational forces in personality development. He stressed the importance of the social environment in his formulations of health and psychopathology, and increasingly emphasized the curative functions of relational process in therapeutic intervention.

A second generation of British thinkers, including Melanie Klein, W. R. D. Fairbairn, Donald W. Winnicott, and John Bowlby, began to extend psychoanalytic theory in the 1930s. Working within the Freudian tradition, Klein preserved classical notions of drive and emphasized the internal realm of fantasy in her theoretical system. Over the course of her work, however, she introduced concepts of internal representation ("internal objects") and defensive process ("splitting," "projective identification") that provided crucial points of departure for Fairbairn and Winnicott in their efforts to elaborate relational and social perspectives. In this sense, Klein emerges as a key figure in the transition from drive to relational perspectives.

Fairbairn departed from the classical drive paradigm and introduced models of personality development and psychopathology that led to major reorientations of psychodynamic thought. He theorized that the core tendency in human development is to establish contact and preserve connections with others, and focused on progressive experiences of dependency in the mother-child relationship. In his model, personality is constituted and structured through ongoing internalization and representation of relational experience. Winnicott emphasized the crucial functions of caretaking figures in personality development, and

he saw relational provisions in the "holding environment" of infancy and early childhood as crucial determinants of health and psychopathology. He increasingly focused on domains of self-experience, emphasizing notions of inner coherence, agency, vitality, creativity, play, and personal meaning.

Bowlby argued that the fundamental need to establish contact and connection has adaptive roots in biological survival, and his attachment theory emerged as a major paradigm in empirical study of the mother-child relationship. He proposed that working models of self and others, established in interaction with caretaking figures, guide information processing about relational experience and shape patterns of behavior and adaptation through the life course. More than any other theorist, Bowlby attempted to bridge internal and external domains of experience and describe the processes that lead to establishment of psychic structure and modes of interpersonal functioning.

Three lines of theorizing in America have influenced the development of object relations thought, including the interpersonal tradition of Harry Stack Sullivan and Karen Horney; the self psychology of Heinz Kohut; and the overlapping contributions of Heinz Hartmann, Edith Jacobson, Margaret Mahler, and Otto Kernberg. The last group preserved Freudian concepts of drive, however, and did not embrace the interactive "two-person" psychology that has become a defining feature of contemporary object relations thought. Greenberg & Mitchell (1983) carried out the first comparative study of object relations theories; for review of subsequent accounts of relational perspectives see Borden (2009, 2012).

Theoretical Formulations and Core Concepts

Although the object relations paradigm encompasses divergent lines of inquiry, contemporary theorists increasingly share basic assumptions about the nature of personality development; notions of health, well being, and the common good; conceptions of vulnerability and psychopathology; and therapeutic elements in psychosocial intervention. The following section examines core concepts, guiding themes, and fundamental concerns in each of these areas, and considers the implications of object relations perspectives for continued development of evidence-based practice perspectives in clinical social work.

PERSONALITY DEVELOPMENT

Concepts of motivation emphasize the fundamental need for attachment and relationship through the life course. Relational experience shapes the development of mind, personality, or self. The interactive field is the central organizer of psychic structure and function; the core of the person is constituted through ongoing interaction with others in the social environment. Developmental lines of study consider the nature of early caretaking experience, social environments, and emerging capacities for relatedness. According to object relations perspectives, basic prototypes of connection, established in infancy and childhood, are preserved in the form of internalized representations of self and others. Working models of self and others influence subjective states, perceptions of persons, and modes of interpersonal behavior.

Theorists differ in their conceptions of motivational, affective, and cognitive processes believed to mediate the development of personality, but they assume that internalization of interpersonal experience shapes inner representations of self, other, and modes of relating (self in relation to others). Although core representations are derived from interaction in the social environment, they are not memories of events; rather, they are schematic structures formed from the cumulative experience of interpersonal life. Elaboration of schemas is influenced by constitution and temperament, early developmental experience, unconscious fantasy process, and life events. Presumably, ongoing experience generates multiple representation of self, others, and modes of interaction. Investigators theorize that the particular representations that guide perception and behavior at any given moment are determined largely by immediate needs, life circumstances, and social contexts.

HEALTH, WELL-BEING, AND THE COMMON GOOD

Conceptions of health center on the establishment of basic structures of mind, personality, or self and corresponding capacities for relatedness that influence overall levels of functioning. From this perspective, optimal development leads to a cohesive sense of self; affirming but realistic views and expectations of self and others (inferred self and object representations);

and stable and enduring relationships. Theorists stress the role of others in the development of the person and the sustaining functions of relationship, social interaction, and community through the life course. Most thinkers encompass concepts of mastery, coping, adaptation, and self-actualization in formulations of health and fulfillment.

VULNERABILITY AND PSYCHOPATHOLOGY

Theorists focus on the organization of the self and corresponding modes of interpersonal functioning in their conceptions of vulnerability and psychopathology. Winnicott, Fairbairn, and Kohut emphasize "arrests," "splits," and "deficits" in the organization of self structure. Bowlby describes rigid, anachronistic models of relational experience that shape problematic patterns of attachment and social interaction. Other thinkers, influenced by Klein and Kernberg, center on pathological manifestations of defensive processes, notably splitting and projective identification, associated with the personality disorders. Another group of theorists, drawing on the interpersonal theory of Sullivan and Horney, emphasize constricted patterns of interaction or "vicious circles" of behavior that perpetuate problems in functioning (Wachtel, 2008).

Thinkers distinguish predisposing, precipitating, and perpetuating factors in formulations of dysfunction. Because the relational field is the primary organizer of psychic structure and function, however, they tend to see early caretaking systems, patterns of interaction, unresponsive social environments, and traumatic events as critical determinants of vulnerability and psychopathology. Although the first generation of theorists centered largely on the nature of the maternal-child relationship and critical periods of care in infancy and early childhood, subsequent investigators have broadened perspectives to consider ways in which contemporary relational experience, life events, and social environments influence problems in living.

Object relations theorists recognize the impact of deprivation and trauma in relational and social domains of experience, just as they realize the organizing and sustaining functions of maladaptive behavior. Following contemporary relational views, most theorists assume that psychopathology is self-perpetuating because it is embedded in more general ways of being and relating that persons have established over the course of development. As Mitchell (1988) explains, there is "a pervasive tendency to preserve the continuity, connections, and familiarity of one's personal, interactional world" (1988, p. 3). Accordingly, however problematic certain behaviors may be, established modes of functioning serve to maintain cohesion and continuity in sense of self; to preserve connections with internalized representations of others; and to promote safety and security in interpersonal interaction. Clinicians assume that improved interpersonal functioning strengthens self organization and reduces problems in living associated with all forms of psychopathology.

EMPIRICAL RESEARCH

Empirical lines of study in the fields of neuroscience, cognitive psychology, developmental psychology, experimental psychology, and social psychology corroborate the basic propositions and core concepts of object relations psychology. In the domain of attachment research, findings show that infants are pre-adapted to form relationships and engage in complex forms of behavior with caretaking figures. Research on attachment and neurological development documents the crucial functions of caretaking and relational experience in personality organization, affect regulation, and patterns of interpersonal behavior over the life course (Schore, 2012). Cognitive studies of perception, learning, and memory support object relations conceptions of mental representations of self, others, and patterns of interpersonal behavior and unconscious mental processing of interpersonal functioning across the course of life (for reviews see Borden & Clark, 2012; Shedler, 2010).

In the domain of clinical practice, researchers have examined the ways in which inner models of relational experience and patterns of social cognition perpetuate problems in functioning associated with acute stress reactions, posttraumatic stress disorders, depression, personality disorders, and other types of developmental psychopathology (Luborsky & Barrett, 2006; Roth & Fonagy, 2005; Shedler, 2010; Westen & Bradley, 2005). Clinical researchers have drawn on object relations perspectives in conceptualizing patterns of interactive experience over the course of the helping process. In doing so, investigators have explored the relationship between social information processing and transference phenomena, centering on motivational, cognitive, and affective domains of experience and activation of interpersonal schemas or scripts that correspond to particular patterns of interpersonal behavior. Empirical findings in cognitive neuroscience support relational conceptions of transference, documenting the ways in which interpersonal experience activates representations of self and others; motivational, cognitive, and affective processes; and corresponding patterns of behavior in the social field (Borden, 2009; Borden & Clark, 2012; Schore, 2012; Shedler, 2010).

PSYCHOSOCIAL ASSESSMENT AND INTERVENTION

Practitioners describe guiding perspectives, core concepts, and basic principles that inform approaches to assessment and treatment. Concepts of therapeutic action emphasize the primary role of the therapeutic relationship in the process of change and the functions of *interpersonal interaction* and *experiential learning* in efforts to deepen self understanding, strengthen coping capacities, and negotiate problems in living. From this perspective, the clinician provides reparative experiences that modify maladaptive representations of self and others, reorganize patterns of defense, and facilitate more adaptive and fulfilling ways of living. The emphasis on the dynamics of the therapeutic relationship and current patterns of interaction distinguishes object relations perspectives from classical psychoanalytic approaches that focus on childhood conflict and development of insight through interpretive procedures.

Assessment. Object relations perspectives emphasize the following domains of concern in assessment of functioning:

- Subjective states, emotions, and moods
- Inner representations of self, others, and modes of relating as inferred from accounts of persons, events, and views of self
- Capacities for relatedness to others, defensive strategies, and patterns of interpersonal behavior

The following guidelines serve to focus the assessment process:

- Using a narrative perspective, the clinician encourages clients to relate problems in their own words; the practitioner explores the interpersonal contexts of symptoms or difficulties and presses for concrete detail in accounts of experience.

- The clinician explores the nature of past and current relationships as well as representative themes and concerns that emerge in discussion of self, interpersonal experience, and life events.
- The clinician observes patterns of interaction during the clinical interview, explores clients' experience of the therapeutic relationship, identifies patterns of defense, monitors evolving transference and countertransference reactions, and notes potential enactments of dysfunctional behaviors in therapeutic interaction.
- In establishing the focus, the clinician links the presenting problem to representative patterns of interaction that would appear to perpetuate difficulties.

The aims of assessment are to (1) determine general levels of personality organization and interpersonal functioning on the basis of the foregoing criteria, and (2) identify core relational themes, modes of defense, and representative patterns of interaction that precipitate problems in functioning.

Intervention. Object relations theorists recognize the potential influence of common elements believed to facilitate change across the major schools of thought (Frank & Frank, 1991), but they emphasize the role of relational provisions and experiential learning in concepts of therapeutic action. Ongoing interaction between client and clinician facilitates efforts to identify "vicious circles" of behavior and to develop more effective ways of processing information and negotiating interpersonal experience. The therapeutic relationship itself serves as a medium for change, and transference and countertransference states provide crucial sources of experiencing and understanding in efforts to revise internalized representations of self and others, reorganize patterns of defense, develop interpersonal skills, and improve social functioning. Enactments of maladaptive behavior in the therapeutic situation facilitate efforts to clarify problematic modes of interaction and to establish more effective ways of negotiating interpersonal situations and life tasks. Theorists view the clinician as a *participant-observer* and stress the reciprocal nature of therapeutic interaction.

In doing so, they deepen appreciation of subjective elements and mutuality in the helping process. Over the course of intervention the client internalizes positive aspects of the therapeutic relationship, modifying inner representations of self and others, and establishes more adaptive ways of managing vulnerability and negotiating problems in living. From the perspective of cognitive neuroscience, the core activities of the therapeutic process alter associational networks established over the course of development and facilitate formation of new, adaptive linkages and patterns of behavior (Schore, 2012).

Practitioners working from object relational perspectives emphasize the following principles of intervention:

- The clinician clarifies enactments of maladaptive behavior, exploring their defensive functions, and processes transference-countertransference reactions as they occur in order to help clients recognize and understand problems in living.
- When possible, the clinician links patterns of interpersonal functioning in the therapeutic situation to behavior in past and current relationships.
- The clinician uses descriptive, clarifying, and interpretive statements in efforts to help clients deepen awareness of their own and others' behavior, process subjective experience, better understand reactions to interpersonal events, and alter dysfunctional beliefs and maladaptive forms of behavior.
- The clinician uses problem-solving strategies, task-centered approaches, modeling, and reinforcement in efforts to help clients strengthen coping capacities and interpersonal skills.

CASE REPORT

Assessment. The client, age 28, initiated psychotherapy in a community mental health center after he was suspended from his job. He explained that his manager had placed him on leave because he was "unable to get along with people," and reported growing feelings of frustration and anger in his interaction with coworkers, characterizing them as "incompetent." Over the course of the interview the client described ongoing strain and rupture in his dealings with peers and managers, rendering relational life in absolute terms: "People are either with you or against you," he explained. He challenged the social worker's attempts to explore concerns beyond the workplace, becoming impatient and argumentative, coming to see the session as "useless." He pressured the worker to "come up with a solution" for his difficulties, showing little capacity to process his experience in the give and take of the interactive process. On the basis of his accounts of relational experience and patterns of interaction during the interview, the practitioner hypothesized that the client used splitting defenses and aggressive behavior as means of managing his experience of vulnerability. The worker realized that the client's constricted patterns of functioning would potentially limit his capacity to form a collaborative relationship and engage in the therapeutic process.

Intervention. In spite of the foregoing concerns, the client responded to the clinician's *attunement* and *empathic processing* of concerns and established a working alliance. The conditions of acceptance, understanding, and support facilitated the development of the *holding environment.* The worker attempted to validate his experience, realizing the protective functions of attitudes and behaviors. The client was increasingly able to explore the antecedents and contexts of current problems in functioning. Since childhood, he had been the object of his father's teasing, bullying, and anger. The worker hypothesized that he had internalized the experience of his father's assaults over the course of development, coming to identify with a representation of his father as hateful, relating to others as his father had interacted with him. Presumably, the representations of self and others encompassed in his working models of interactive experience shaped ways of processing information in interpersonal life and perpetuated aggressive modes of behavior, precipitating strain, rupture, and loss.

Transference and *countertransference* states provided points of entry into the dynamics of earlier family life. The client was cold, sarcastic, and bullying in his interactions with the worker. The ongoing cycle of rupture and repair in the therapeutic relationship served as a crucial source of *experiential learning,* offering opportunities to process earlier trauma, explore defensive processes, and develop skills in managing his experience of vulnerability, fear, anger, and disappointment. The clinician used *interpretive procedures* to link past experience with current patterns of behavior in the

therapeutic relationship and in the workplace, deepening his understanding of life experience, protective strategies, and ways of relating. The worker *modeled* ways of processing subjective experience and problem-solving, and used *explanation* as an educational strategy in efforts to help the client understand the nature of his reactions, defenses, and patterns of interaction, helping him to *disidentify* with aggressive aspects of his father. Over time, the client strengthened capacities to regulate emotion, disrupt "vicious circles" of interaction, limit self-defeating behavior, and negotiate the vicissitudes of interpersonal life in more adaptive and constructive ways.

RELATIONAL PERSPECTIVES AND EVIDENCE-BASED PRACTICE

Relational perspectives promise to strengthen approaches to assessment, case formulation, and treatment planning in emerging conceptions of evidence-based practice. The helping relationship serves as the facilitating medium of intervention, and object relations formulations emphasize the role of *interpersonal expertise* in efforts to establish the therapeutic alliance; address vulnerabilities and patterns of behavior that potentially compromise engagement, precipitate strain, and limit change; and make flexible use of interactive experience in light of differing capacities, problems in functioning, and the individual, social, and cultural contexts of the client. Converging lines of study document the ways in which each participant in the relationship influences the process and outcome of intervention, and relational perspectives provide nuanced ways of conceptualizing interactive experience that deepen current formulations of interpersonal behavior in models of evidence-based practice (APA Presidential Task Force on Evidence-Based Practice, 2006; Borden, 2009; Shedler, 2010; Westen & Bradley, 2005).

CONCLUSION

Overlapping domains of understanding in object relations psychology, focused on concepts of self and relationship, continue to reflect fundamental concerns in contemporary culture, social life, and psychosocial intervention. The theoretical systems encompassed in this paradigm shape ways of understanding personality development; health, well being, and common good; vulnerability and psychopathology; and modes of therapeutic action. As such they will enlarge understandings of vulnerability, problems in living, and helping processes in continued development of social work theory, research, and practice guidelines.

WEBSITES

International Association for Relational Psychoanalysis and Psychotherapy. www.iarpp.net

Psychoanalytic Electronic Publishing—Web Archives. www.pep-web.org

References

American Psychological Association Presidential Task Force on Empirical Practice. (2006). Evidence-based practice in psychology, *American Psychologist, 61*(4), 271–285.

Borden, W. (2009). *Contemporary psychodynamic theory and practice*. Chicago, IL: Lyceum Books.

Borden, W., & Clark, J. (2012). Contemporary psychodynamic theory, research, and practice: Implications for evidence-based intervention. In T. Rzepnicki, S. McCracken & H. Briggs (Eds.), *From task centered social work practice to evidence-based and integrative intervention* (pp. 65–87). Chicago, IL: Lyceum Books.

Frank, J., & Frank, J. (1991). *Persuasion and healing*. Baltimore, MD: Johns Hopkins University Press.

Greenberg, J., & Mitchell, S. (1983). *Object relations in psychoanalysis*. Cambridge, MA: Harvard University Press.

Luborsky, L., & Barrett, M. (2006). The history and empirical status of key psychoanalytic concepts, *Annual Review of Clinical Psychology, 2*, 1–19.

Mitchell, S. (1988). *Relational concepts in psychoanalysis*. Cambridge, MA: Harvard University Press.

Roth, A., & Fonagy, P. (2005). *What works for whom? A critical review of psychotherapy research* (2nd edition). New York, NY: Guilford Press.

Schore, A. (2012). *The science of the art of psychotherapy*. New York, NY: Norton.

Shedler, J. (2010). The efficacy of psychodynamic psychotherapy, *American Psychologist, 65*(2), 98–109.

Wachtel, P. (2008). *Relational theory and the practice of psychotherapy*. New York, NY: Guilford.

Westen, D., & Bradley, R. (2005). Empirically-supported complexity: Rethinking evidence-based practice in psychotherapy. *Current Directions in Psychological Science, 14*(5), 266–271.

44   Human Trafficking and Trauma-informed Care

Kristin Heffernan, Betty J. Blythe, & Andrea Cole

A young man around the age of 30 comes to the emergency room with an injured wrist. He is accompanied by another man around the same age who states that he is the patient's cousin. The social worker asks the patient what happened. The cousin says that they are both farm workers and that his cousin fell while picking apples; the patient remains quiet. The social worker makes small talk about picking apples and asks the patient the name of the farm where he works, but the cousin quickly answers the question. The patient appears nervous and uncomfortable as the cousin continues to answer most questions for him.

Are there any signs or "red flags" indicating this person could be trafficked?

Karen is a 14-year-old girl who lives in Manhattan. Her mother's boyfriend sexually abused her. When Karen told her mother what had happened, her mother threw her out of the home. Having nowhere to go, Karen went to the Port Authority where she was approached by a man in his thirties. He told Karen she was gorgeous and that he would take care of her as her boyfriend. After they had been living together for a while, he told Karen that they needed money and that prostitution was the only answer. Before she was prostituted the first time, the man gave Karen cocaine to "take the edge off." From then on, Karen was required to give all of the money she earned to this man. If she refused to be prostituted on a particular night, he would beat her and threaten to tell her family that she was a prostitute.

Although these two cases appear very different, they both are instances of human trafficking. One is no worse or better than the other, and both victims' human rights are being desecrated. Social workers and other health and mental health practitioners are in a unique position to help identify victims of human trafficking as well as assist these clients in re-establishing their rights and beginning the healing process. The following chapter will provide a brief summary of the state of human trafficking in the United States, and identify strategies that social workers and other practitioners can use to help identify victims of human trafficking, and to implement a trauma-informed lens when providing services to individuals who have been trafficked. Throughout this chapter, we will use the term "victim" to refer to persons that continue to be trafficked or have escaped or been rescued from their trafficker and "survivor" for those who are actively seeking help to escape their trafficker and/or are receiving services.

HUMAN TRAFFICKING IN THE UNITED STATES

The United States did not offer legal protection for victims of human trafficking until 2001 when the federal anti-trafficking law, the Victims of Trafficking and Violence Protection Act of 2000 (TVPA) was passed. The TVPA is one of the United States' most important tools in the fight against human trafficking. Its purpose is threefold: prevention, protection, and prosecution.

The Act established the President's Interagency Task Force to Monitor and Combat Trafficking in Persons to coordinate anti-trafficking efforts in the United States. In the TVPA, Congress defined human trafficking as:

1. "Sex trafficking in which a commercial sex act is induced by force, fraud or coercion, or in which the person induced to perform such an act has not attained 18 years of age." (Hence, all children engaged in sex exploitation are seen as victims under federal law.); or
2. "The recruitment, harboring, transportation, provision or obtaining of a person for labor or services, through the use of force, fraud, or coercion for the purpose of subjection to involuntary servitude, peonage, debt bondage, or slavery" (U.S. Department of State, 2006, p. 25).

Although most Americans think of human trafficking as an issue occurring in other countries, the United States is both a source of transit and a destination for U.S. and foreign national adults and children who are trafficked. Persons who are trafficked can be subjected to forced labor, debt bondage, involuntary servitude, and prostitution, which can occur in many licit and illicit industries or markets. These include but are not limited to brothels, massage parlors, street prostitution, hotel services, hospitality, agriculture, manufacturing, janitorial services, construction, health and elder care, and domestic service.

In recent years, many states have passed laws to address human trafficking. These statutes provide supports for victims, such as vacating prostitution convictions for individuals who were trafficked for sex, and make trafficking a criminal act. At least 32 states have passed significant legislation in this regard (http://www.polarisproject.org/storage/documents/POC/2013-State-Ratings_pamphlet-3pgr.pdf).

Human trafficking is a horrific crime against humanity, bringing both physical and emotional trauma to its victims. The very nature of human trafficking is a violation of basic human rights. In many human trafficking cases, the perpetrators induce psychological coercion by destroying the victim's sense of self in relation to others. Perpetrators frequently terrorize their victims through threats of death and/or serious harm against both the trafficked individuals as well as their families (Shigekane, 2007). They may tell victims trafficked from other countries that they will be deported if they seek help from law enforcement (Hopper, 2004), leaving their victims feeling helpless and hopeless. Hence, even if victims come into contact with law enforcement or social services, they often are hesitant to ask for help, partly as a result of psychological coercion, but also because they fear retribution from the trafficker (United States Department of Justice [US DOJ], 2006). Thus, before services can be provided to victims of human trafficking, they have to be identified and given the opportunity to leave the trafficking situation. This can be accomplished through outreach and educating others about how to identify people who have been trafficked.

Social workers need to adopt a human rights approach to dealing with this issue, especially when developing services for survivors of human trafficking. Using this perspective, social workers put the survivor's priorities and voice at the center of anti-trafficking work. Central to this approach is a model that relies on providing services in a nonjudgmental way, emphasizing client self-determination when setting both short- and long-term goals.

IDENTIFYING TRAFFICKED INDIVIDUALS

Unlike drugs and arms, human trafficking is very profitable because the victims can be sold over and over (Batstone, 2007). Trafficked victims, as well as traffickers, come in many forms. More often than not, persons are sold or recruited by someone they know; often tricked into trafficking by false promises of a better life (Sigmon, 2008). Due to the clandestine nature of trafficking, it often goes unnoticed by practitioners. Therefore, one of the key duties of the social worker is to look beneath the surface of the client's story. There are several "red flags" that social workers, doctors, nurses, practitioners, and other care workers may observe in health and social service settings. Obviously, the presence of a single red flag does not mean that a person has been trafficked, but it does mean that further exploration is indicated.

Potentially trafficked clients:

- Are accompanied by someone they refer to as their relative, friend, and/or interpreter
  - They look to this person to speak for them.

- Are not sure how long they have worked or are vague about where they work
- Do not have a sense of time (the day, month, or year)
- Are not in control of their personal schedule, money, passport, or other identity card or travel documents
- Live and work at the same address
- Have conflicting stories about why they need agency services
- Appear anxious, nervous/paranoid, submissive, or frequently shift in their seats
- Are confused and unable to answer questions
- Avoid eye contact
- Have many inconsistencies in their story or answers to questions

Specific to emergency room or visits to health care providers, another red flag is extremely poor health. If a patient is in poor health or has other physical conditions unrelated to the illness, this may indicate abuse or neglect beyond the human trafficking. An individual who has been trafficked may present with bruises, fractures, sexually transmitted diseases, or other medical conditions that have not been treated and may not be able to give a clear explanation as to why or how the injuries occurred. Malnutrition or poor personal hygiene also are commonly observed in trafficked individuals. Traffickers avoid bringing their workers in for care, and may do so only when the health condition is preventing the trafficked individual from working.

Not all victims of human trafficking recognize that they are being controlled. Some may actually identify with their trafficker and be hesitant to leave or speak against the trafficker. Social workers need to be prepared for a range of responses when assessing for trafficking in light of the trauma that has been experienced by clients. Following are some responses that individuals who have been trafficked may give to social workers and other service providers who are offering assistance. Given their circumstances, clients should not be judged or blamed if they respond in these ways:

- They state they do not want to leave the situation, and or may even say that the trafficker has treated them well.
- They do not show emotion when telling their story.

- They become angry or irritable with service providers (especially if they feel that the provider is trying to control them).
- They complain of physical symptoms, but have a clean physical examination.
- They refuse services.
- They defend their trafficker.
- They tell conflicting stories.
- They do not want to sign consent forms.
- They want to return to their trafficker.

THE PRACTITIONER'S RESPONSE

Social workers who notice any of the aforementioned red flags should ask themselves, "What has happened to this person?" as opposed to "What is wrong with this person?" If the practitioner suspects a client has been trafficked and he or she is accompanied by someone, the practitioner should attempt to separate the potential trafficking victim from the other person before asking the client any further questions. It is best to try to do this without raising the suspicions of the accompanying person. For example, the social worker might say that it is agency policy to see the client alone to ensure confidentiality. If the client has limited English skills and the worker does not speak the client's language, then a trusted interpreter who also understands the victim's cultural needs should be procured. Once these elements are in place, the worker can further question the possible victim about working conditions, asking questions such as:

- Is everything okay at your job?
- Are you able to leave your job?
- Are there any issues with your pay?
- Do you owe money to anyone?
- Have you ever experienced violence at your work?
- Does your employer control your housing, food, and/or transportation?
- Is there a lock on your door or window so you cannot get out?
- Has anyone threatened your family?
- Were you recruited for this job through false promises?

If any of the client's responses suggest a trafficking situation, the worker should make sure they feel confident to proceed and, if not, the worker should consult with a supervisor while continuing to keep the suspected trafficker separated from the suspected victim.

A priority during this interaction is to help the client feel as safe and comfortable as possible. The worker can also begin to provide information on human trafficking; indicating that the trafficked situation is not acceptable, and that the worker can help the client escape. The victim also needs to understand his or her rights, what legal options are available, and how to access an attorney. It is vital to remember, however, that a service provider cannot force intervention. In fact, the practitioner needs to build rapport with clients who have been trafficked to meet them where they are and allow them to decide if they want help. The practitioner's role at this stage is to offer information about available services that will help clients escape from their traffickers.

TRAUMA-INFORMED CARE (TIC) WITH HUMAN TRAFFICKING SURVIVORS

Trauma-informed practice suggests the service providers at an agency are aware of potential triggers and reactions to triggers for the survivors under their care and, as such, have developed methods of engaging, assessing, planning, and intervening to minimize such triggers in their practice when they are providing direct services. Such triggers may include, but are not limited to: not feeling in control of the helping interaction, being forced to stay in the confinement of a shelter, a lack of culturally sensitive foods and/or décor at the agency, asking the client to reveal more about his or her situation in order obtain services, or having a male present in a female-designated area. When working with human trafficking survivors through a trauma-informed lens, it is presupposed that the experience of trafficking in and of itself is traumatic. So while there is no single definition of what constitutes a traumatic event, it is widely accepted that a traumatic event is overwhelming and can occur either as a single catastrophic event or as a series of ordeals (Terr, 1990). Traumatic events can lead to a profound disruption or loss of one's sense of safety, predictability, and/or sense of control over one's own life, regardless of whether the threat is actual or perceived. Not surprisingly, the experience of trauma is often pervasive, encompassing all bio-psychosocial aspects of one's life.

Ideally, when engaging human trafficking victims in services, an entire agency would restructure their services to adopt a trauma-informed approach (Hummer, Dollard, Robst, & Armstrong, 2010). However, TIC also can begin with the work of a single practitioner. These principles should underpin work with any individual who experiences trauma, but more specifically here, TIC principles will be used to describe best practice when working with survivors of human trafficking. Principles of TIC include:

1. Recognize the impact of the trauma
2. Identify recovery as a primary goal
3. Employ an empowerment model
4. Maximize choice, control, and collaboration
5. Provide an atmosphere that is respectful and safe
6. Be culturally competent
7. Involve the consumer in service feedback and evaluation (Hopper, Bassuk, and Olivet, 2010)

There are a number of ways that these principles can be integrated into an individual worker's practice to help individuals who have been trafficked feel safe and comfortable.

Telling the Story

As stated earlier, the practitioner needs to move away from asking, "What is wrong with this person?" and begin asking, "What has happened to this person?" Traditional social work often requires or assumes that clients should tell the complete story of what happened to them under the pretext that this is necessary to offer the appropriate services. Some social workers also consider the sharing of information as essential to building a trusting relationship. TIC, however, recognizes that human trafficking is a traumatic event and that it may be re-traumatizing for clients to tell what has happened to them. Rather, they should be empowered to make the choice of what they want to reveal and what they want to keep to themselves.

Needless to say, the stories of trafficked persons often are devastating. Asking or demanding that clients "tell their story" as a condition of receiving services is tantamount to asking them to relive their experiences before they may be ready to do so, hence re-traumatizing them. Furthermore, due to the nature of human trafficking, many clients are referred to services via the police and already have had to tell and retell their story before even getting to see a service provider. If their experience with law enforcement officials was negative, this can cause them to view social services with suspicion or even dread.

Another concern with regard to asking clients to tell their stories relates to legal issues. If law enforcement is involved, whether it is a criminal case or civil litigation, documentation of the history can be damaging to the client's case. Agency files on clients who have been trafficked often are subpoenaed for such trials. The traffickers' attorneys are looking for inconsistencies within the trafficked persons' stories in order to discredit the trafficked individuals. The more detail within a case file, the higher the chance of discrepancies in the story.

There are other concerns with regard to obtaining a case history. Due to the extreme psychological distress that they may have experienced, clients may not be able to provide accurate or detailed information under pressure. Moreover, clients understandably may not trust a worker whom they have just met. In fact, the trafficked person may purposely give the worker incorrect information because the trafficker has told them to do so. Social workers should remember that many trafficked persons have been forced to tell lies about who they are and what they do in order to survive. So again, it is generally advised to minimize the amount of history recorded in case notes when working with human trafficking victims.

Empowerment and Offering Control

Many human trafficking victims will need immediate concrete services such as housing, food, health care, an interpreter, and legal assistance. Longer term services may include mental health, income assistance, vocational training, and further legal aid. As much as possible, the social worker needs to let the client prioritize these needs and set goals. Recovery, however, is the primary goal. Having undergone human trafficking, victims may be experiencing fear, anxiety, and lack of trust. An empowerment model will normalize their reactions to the trauma and maximize their sense of choice and control.

There are many ways a practitioner can help the client gain control. To begin, clients should be provided with the information that is necessary to help them decide whether they want to accept services. Toward this end, and following a TIC framework, the social worker should:

- Clearly state his or her role and the role of the agency
- Speak in the client's native language or provide an interpreter
- Introduce the client to other people at the agency, possibly giving the client an agency tour
- Let the client know approximately how long meetings will last
- Allow the client to control the pace of the meeting
- Make sure the client knows that they do not have to provide any information or answer any questions that they do not wish to and that they understand this will not influence the services they will receive.
- Provide a choice of beverages or refreshments (e.g., different types of tea)
- Offer choices whenever possible
- Obtain informed consent
- Actively involve clients in all steps of the process
- Make sure the client understands what they can expect from the worker and/or the agency and what is expected of them as a client.
- Allow time for questions.

TIC principles are used to help the person who has been trafficked to regain trust, a sense of safety, and self-sufficiency. The process cannot be rushed and must occur at the client's pace. The survivor is the one who chooses to accept or decline services and remains the expert with regard to his or her needs and experience. Although this mantra is often heard at every level of social work training, in practice it is still challenging for social workers to truly understand that they are not the experts on someone else's life. It can be difficult for social workers to accept clients' choices when they conflict with what the social worker thinks best for the clients.

For those who have experienced human trafficking, empowerment is a life-long process that can start with TIC. It is the practitioner's responsibility, whether offering case management, counseling, or therapy to promote client choice, self-determination, and collaboration. For example, when clients change their appointment or cancel and reschedule, especially if they have done this more than once, the worker may get irritated or may even start to believe that the clients are not serious about recovery. Some workers view such behaviors on the part of the

client as a personal affront. A related problem may occur if clients assert their own will and the practitioner describes them as "difficult." When working through a trauma-informed lens, this view of the client as "difficult" does not exist. The TIC principle of maximizing choice, control, and collaboration means that clients' ability to make decisions for themselves is celebrated insofar as they are taking back control over their lives and recovery. Does this mean that such behavior is not inconvenient to service providers? No, in fact it can be very inconvenient when clients change their minds about when they can meet with us or what services they want to receive. But, practitioners need to remember that victims of human trafficking have not had control over their lives while being trafficked. Simple decisions about when to eat, sleep, and even go to the bathroom may have been taken away from them by their traffickers.

Establishing Safety

Safety is key to the process of recovery. The practitioner needs to help the client feel grounded both physically and emotionally. There are many different ways in which social workers can create a safe environment for clients when they come for services. Some of the following suggestions have already been included in the above list for helping clients gain a sense of control over their recovery. Working from a TIC perspective, these methods serve multiple purposes. Helping clients feel physically and mentally safe may look like:

- Orienting them to the agency by giving them a tour and introducing them to the other individuals they might see at the agency
- Making sure they understand everyone's roles (case manager, director, interpreter, etc.)
- Making sure they know the location of the building exits
- Never sitting between the client and the door
- Developing a safety plan and then reviewing this plan at every meeting in case it needs updating
- Ensuring the environment is culturally inclusive (décor, sign posting, food, etc.)
- Using the same interpreter for each meeting
- Making sure the location of the meeting is easily accessible
- Establishing regular agendas and consistent timelines for meetings.

Again, the underlying principle is that clients who have been trafficked need a safe and supportive environment that offers predictability. Making sure that there is consistency throughout interactions and within the agency environment is critical to helping the client recover. Helping the client understand the boundaries and expectations of the agency, and being clear about what the agency expects from clients and what clients can expect from service providers, helps create a safe and supportive environment.

Cultural Considerations

As referred to above, via a bio-psychosocial model, culture can influence the way a person experiences trauma. Practitioners must be vigilant about adapting interventions that are culturally appropriate. This starts with making sure that the social worker has a professional interpreter with whom the client feels comfortable if the practitioner does not speak the client's native language. Furthermore, human trafficking survivors need to be active in deciding whether they are comfortable with the agency's interpreter. If the agency is located in a small town or city, the client may know the interpreter from a previous encounter with this person outside the realm of the current situation. Continuing to allow this person to act as interpreter could actually hinder the client's recovery.

Interacting with Other Systems

Trafficked persons often are arrested and treated as criminals prior to an investigation of their case. They may be handcuffed and placed in jail for lacking legal immigrant status and/or for prostitution. Upon realization that the trafficked person is a victim, law enforcement officials commonly refer them to social service agencies for help. Not every state, let alone county or city, has services that specialize in helping victims of human trafficking. Therefore, they may be referred to services for refugees, immigrants, or domestic violence victims because these may appear appropriate at first glance. Such agencies may be able to help with some of the trafficked individual's needs. Without an understanding of human trafficking and the accompanying trauma, however, these services are woefully inadequate for survivors of human trafficking and may even re-traumatize them as described above.

As an example, many domestic violence shelters have rules and regulations about receiving or making phone calls while at the shelter. This rule is intended to protect the domestic violence survivor so that his or her tormentor cannot track them during their shelter stay. Additionally, there are often specific check-in times and curfews at many of the safe homes for domestic violence survivors—again, to protect the survivors. Human trafficking victims have had little control over their own lives while being trafficked, including control over their movements. If they are allowed away from their trafficker, cell phones often are used to track and control them. They are held captive to the demands of their trafficker and, if they are placed in domestic violence shelters and made to follow the same rules and regulations as the other residents, they may inadvertently be subjected to the same barriers to freedom that they experienced at the hands of their traffickers. Such services can unintentionally re-traumatize trafficked individuals. Whenever possible, services need to be specific to the needs of survivors of human trafficking and service providers need to be aware of how services affect such clients.

Developing Trauma-informed Lenses at the Macro Level

Recognizing human trafficking as a traumatic event and having a clear understanding of what this could mean for clients is first and foremost among TIC principles. Although this recognition and understanding can begin with a single practitioner, ideally this knowledge will infiltrate the entire organization. It is beneficial to all clients and employees for all staff, including administrative, reception, and leadership staff, to become educated in the effects of traumatic experiences and the principles of TIC. This knowledge can decrease triggers that have negative effects for both clients and employees, while creating a safer and more efficient agency for clients and workers. Implementing TIC requires organizational readiness for change and evaluation of current practices (Rivard, Bloom, McCorkle, & Abramovitz, 2005). Such changes often require a freezing of what the social worker has already learned about service provision in his or her agency in order to relearn how to provide services via a TIC lens. In some cases, a social worker or other professional trained in TIC can slowly begin to educate others at the organization about the importance of understanding human trafficking as a traumatic event. Moving toward this model takes considerable time, conviction, and education and requires all staff to engage in vigilant self-care.

CONCLUSION

If practitioners can understand the ways in which their own practice, as well as their organization's policy and practices, can be re-traumatizing, we can work to change such policies and practices. Understanding and practicing a TIC model helps clients and individual social workers, as well as the agency as a whole. When social workers are affected by vicarious trauma, they cannot carry on with their work as usual.

References

Batstone, D. (2007). *Not for sale: The return of the global slave trade—and how we can fight it.* New York, NY: HarperOne.

Gajic-Veljanoski, O., & Stewart, D. E. (2007). Trafficked into prostitution: Determinants, human rights and health needs. *Transcultural Psychiatry, 44,* 338–358.

Hopper, E. K., Bassuk, E., & Olivet, J. (2010). Shelter from the storm: Trauma-informed care in homelessness services setting. *The Open Health Services and Policy Journal, 2,* 131–151.

Hopper, E. K. (2004). Under identification of human trafficking victims in the United States. *Journal of Social Work Research and Evaluation, 5*(2), 125–136.

Hummer, V. L., Dollard, N., Robst, J., & Armstrong, M. I. (2010). Innovations in implementation of trauma-informed care practices in youth residential treatment: A curriculum for organizational change. *Child Welfare 88*(2), 79–95.

Polaris Project. (2013). 2013 state ratings on human trafficking laws. http://www.polarisproject.org/storage/documents/POC/2013-State-Ratings_pamphlet-3pgr.pdf

Rivard, J. C., Bloom, S. L, McCorkle, D., & Abramovitz, R. (2005). Preliminary results of a study examining the implementation and effects of a trauma recovery framework for youths in residential treatment. *Therapeutic Community: The International Journal for Therapeutic and Supportive Organizations, 26*(1), 83–96.

Shigekane, R. (2007). Rehabilitation and community integration of trafficking survivors in the United States. *Human Rights Quarterly, 29,* 112–136.

Sigmon, J. N. (2008). Combating modern-day slavery: Issues in identifying and assisting victims of human trafficking worldwide. *Victims & Offenders: An International Journal of Evidence-based Research, Policy, and Practice, 3*(2–3), 245–257.

Terr, L. C. (1990). *Too scared to cry: Psychic trauma in childhood.* New York, NY: Harper & Row.

United States Department of Justice [US DOJ]. (2006). *Report on activities to combat human trafficking: Fiscal years 2001–2005* [Electronic version]. Washington, DC: U. S. Government Printing Office; Author.

U. S. Department of State. (2006). *Victims of trafficking and violence protection act of 2000: Trafficking in persons report.* Washington, DC: U. S. Government Printing Office; Author.

45   Using Self Psychology in Clinical Social Work

Jerrold R. Brandell & Suzanne M. Brown

The psychology of the self, which has only recently attained begrudging acceptance among psychoanalysts, has enjoyed an early and enthusiastic reception among dynamically oriented social workers since its introduction as a treatment framework in the late 1970s (e.g., Elson, 1986; Rowe & MacIsaac, 1991).

A relative newcomer among the psychoanalytic psychologies that constitute contemporary psychoanalysis (classical psychoanalysis, ego psychology, object relations theories, and relational psychoanalysis, inter alia), the psychology of the self was introduced by American psychoanalyst Heinz Kohut in a series of essays and books published between 1959 and 1984. Although Kohut originally presented the theoretical and technical innovations of his new psychology within the extant classical drive theory (Greenberg & Mitchell, 1983; Kohut, 1966, 1971), he later expanded and revised his theory (Kohut, 1977, 1984), the end result being a distinctive and fundamentally new psychoanalytic psychology (Brandell, 2004).

The development of self psychology was, in large measure, guided by Kohut's clinical experiences with analytic clients who seemed unable to benefit from his efforts to use classical formulas in his interpretive work. Despite his assiduous efforts to refine and revise interpretations or alter his timing or the breadth of his interpretive remarks, Kohut found that certain clients failed to improve. He gradually concluded that the problem lay not with technical parameters of his interpretations but with basic theoretical premises of classical psychoanalytic theory. Although these assumptions had proved quite useful in treating the classical neuroses (hysterical, phobic, or obsessive-compulsive), the modal disorders of the late 19th and early 20th centuries, Kohut reasoned that such pathology had gradually been supplanted by other disorders that proved much less amenable to such a theoretical and clinical framework.

The essence of self psychology may well be captured in its vision of the human condition. The classical or Freudian view of humankind is usually expressed in terms of disturbing wishes and conflicts, an ongoing battle between primordial desire and societal requirements and proscriptions for civilized behavior, ontogenetically recapitulated with each successive generation in an endless cycle. Within such a framework and its oedipal foundation, the development of a capacity to experience guilt, painful as it may be, assumes supreme importance as a basis for the renunciation of instinct. Freud believed that without this ability to renounce instincts, civilized behavior was not possible.

Kohut's vision of the human condition contrasts sharply with that of Freud. He focused much less on primitive desires and the intrapsychic conflicts to which they gave rise, instead focusing on the loss of meaning associated with contemporary life. The dispirited Kohutian man/woman, complaining of chronic ennui or boredom, often described the attainment of long-sought-after rewards or accomplishments as unfulfilling. Or he or she experienced life as a sort of emotional roller coaster, where "exuberant bursts of creative energy alternate with painful feelings of inadequacy," as recognition of individual failures extruded into consciousness. "Relationships, eagerly, even desperately pursued, [are] repeatedly abandoned with an increasing sense of pessimism" at the realization that the fulfillment of one's relational needs is so unlikely (Mitchell & Black, 1995, p. 149).

Kohut attempted to capture the fundamental disparity between the classical psychoanalytic view of human nature and that of self psychology in his explication of Guilty Man versus Tragic Man. "*Guilty Man* lives within the pleasure principle," attempting "to satisfy his pleasure-seeking drives to lessen the tensions that arise in his erogenous zones" (Kohut, 1977, p. 132). Kohut's archetypal Tragic Man, however—through his failures, uncompleted projects, and unrequited efforts at work and love—illuminates "the essence of fractured, enfeebled, discontinuous human existence" (p. 238). The pathological narcissist's efforts to assuage painful deficiencies, the fragmentation of the psychotic client, and the despair of parents whose children have failed to fulfill parental aspirations and ambitions may all be understood as clinical examples of this perspective, one that is considered unique to the psychology of the self.

BASIC CONCEPTS IN SELF PSYCHOLOGY

Like its psychoanalytic predecessors (classical theory, ego psychology, and object relations), self psychology encompasses not only a framework for clinical interventions but also a model for understanding certain aspects of normative human development and developmental deviations, as well as a theory of psychopathology. Though space does not allow a comprehensive examination of each of these, certain terms and concepts from self psychology are common to them all.

Selfobjects

Kohut coined the term *selfobject* to represent a specific kind of object relationship in which the object is experienced as being a part or extension of the subject's self and in which no psychological differentiation occurs. He noted that the control one expects over such selfobjects approximates "the concept of control which a grown-up expects to have over his own body and mind" in contradistinction to the "control which he expects to have over others" (Kohut, 1971, pp. 26–27). Kohut believed that human beings require three distinctly different kinds of selfobject experiences—(1) mirroring, (2) idealizing, and (3) partnering—each of which is, under optimal conditions, made available to the child in an attuned, empathetically resonant interpersonal climate. Mirroring selfobjects "respond to and confirm the child's innate sense of vigor, greatness, and perfection," whereas idealized selfobjects provide the child with the powerful and reassuring presence of caregivers "to whom the child can look up and with whom he can merge as an image of calmness, infallibility, and omnipotence" (Kohut & Wolf, 1978, p. 414). Finally, partnering selfobjects furnish the child with a range of opportunities through which a sense of belonging and of essential alikeness within a community of others may be acquired.

The Tripolar Self

The tripolar self is the name given to that intrapsychic structure associated with the three kinds of selfobject relationships just described, in effect linking each selfobject relationship to a corresponding domain of self experience. Mirroring experiences are associated with an intrapsychic structure known as the *grandiose-exhibitionistic self* and reflect the need for approval, interest, and affirmation; idealizing, with the *idealized parent imago*, reflecting the developmental need for closeness and support from an (omnipotent) idealized other; partnering, with the *alter ego*, and associated with the need for contact with others who are felt to bear an essential likeness to the self. These three poles, in effect, are structures that crystallize in consequence of the various needs of the evolving self "and the responses of those important persons in the environment who function as selfobjects" (Leider, 1996, p. 141).

These three domains are also linked to particular transference configurations that "dramatize and reflect the persistence of archaic selfobject needs" (Leider, 1996, pp. 151–154), revealing injuries to the client's self as well as particular mechanisms used to compensate, defend against, or otherwise conceal deficient self-structure. These three transference configurations (mirror, idealizing, and twinship or alter ego) may exist as pure types, though not infrequently a commingling of selfobject transferences may be observed in a particular client. Both the original, thwarted selfobject needs and the ensuing ruptures are frequently recapitulated in the transference relationship in psychotherapy.

Empathy and Transmuting Internalization

A large part of the appeal self psychology has held for social work clinicians may involve the considerable emphasis it places on the role of empathy, a concept possessing strong cachet in both the clinical social work literature and in the contemporary world of practice. Self psychology views empathetic processes as having their origin in early infancy and traversing the entire life span, imputing a special significance to traumatic breaches or disruptions in empathic attunement between self and selfobject. Defined as "vicarious introspection" or the feeling of oneself into the experience of another, the capacity of parents and others in the child's selfobject milieu for providing empathetically attuned responses is believed to be critical for healthy development of the self.

Somewhat paradoxically, Kohut also believed that comparatively minor, nontraumatic lapses in parental empathy are equally critical, constituting a sine qua non for healthy development. Such lapses, in a sense, may be thought of as optimally gratifying and optimally frustrating, serving as a catalyst for the child's development of transmuting internalizations. In other words, such breaches or lapses furnish the developing child with just the right amount of frustration to effect the development of a cohesive self-structure. Transmuting internalization is an intrapsychic process whereby a child gradually takes in or internalizes various functions associated with the selfobjects, ranging from self-calming and self-soothing to pride, humor, wisdom, and indefatigability in the pursuit of important goals. Stated somewhat differently, such functions are absorbed and metabolized in a virtually imperceptible process of incremental accretion, ultimately becoming enduring parts of the child's own self-structure, altered by his or her individual imprimatur.

Key elements identified in the sequence of transmuting internalization are, in order: (1) optimal frustration, (2) increased tension, (3) selfobject response, (4) reduced tension, (5) memory trace, and (6) development of internal regulating (self) structures. Self-psychologists view this developmental sequence as analogous, though not identical, to the therapeutic process when one approaches treatment within a self psychological framework.

The Self Types

Self-psychologists believe that the self is best understood within intersecting matrices of developmental level and structural state, and have identified four principal self types:

1. The *virtual self*, an image of the neonate's self originally existing in the parent's mind that evolves in various ways as the parental "selfobjects empathically respond to certain potentialities of the child" (Kohut, 1977, p. 100).
2. The *nuclear self*, a core self emerging in the second year of life, that serves as the basis for the "child's sense of being an independent center of initiative and perception" (Kohut, 1977, p. 177).
3. The *cohesive self*, the essential self-structure of a well-adapted, healthily functioning individual, whose self-functioning evinces the harmonious "interplay of ambitions, ideals, and talents with the opportunities of everyday reality" (Leider, 1996, p. 143).
4. The *grandiose self*, a normal self-structure during infancy and early childhood developing that comes into existence as a response to the selfobject's attunement with the child's sense of him- or herself as the center of the universe.

Psychopathology in Self Psychology: Cohesion, Fragmentation, and Disintegration Anxiety

Self-psychologists use the term *cohesion* to refer to a self state characterized by vigorous, synchronous, and integrated psychological functioning. Self-cohesion not only makes the harmonious interplay of ambitions, ideals, and talents possible in the context of everyday life; it also confers a modicum of protection from regressive fragmentation when an individual is faced with adversity or obstacles that prevent the gratification of object or selfobject needs (Leider, 1996). Those who are fragmentation-prone (who, under duress, might develop symptoms such as hypochondriasis, hypomanic excitement, or disturbances in bodily sensation or self-perception) have, by definition, failed to acquire stable, consolidated, and enduring self-structures. Such failures may arise from parental pathology, environmental uncertainties and deficiencies, or a combination of these, though invariably it is the chronic unavailability of parental selfobjects to provide needed functions that is at the root of such disturbances in self-functioning. The developmental basis for various disorders of the self (e.g., narcissistic pathology, borderline conditions, depression, and even psychosis), according to the self-psychologists, is strongly linked to chronically deficient and traumatogenic caregiving environments. Kohut believed that *disintegration anxiety*, defined as the fear of the self breaking up, was the most profound anxiety a human being is capable of experiencing; *disintegration products*, a closely related concept, refers to those symptoms generated by an enfeebled, disharmonious self. Symptoms within this system, as in other psychoanalytic theories of psychopathology, are viewed as manifestations or perhaps signifiers of important dynamic, genetic, and environmental themes. The self psychological focus on the significance of environmental deficits in shaping pathology, however, contributes to a perspective that may be somewhat unique, even when compared to other psychoanalytic perspectives on pathology.

CLINICAL CASE ILLUSTRATION

Terry is a 44-year-old unmarried white woman in a long-term heterosexual relationship with no children. She described her ethnicity as a mixture of English, Irish, and German and reports that she was raised in multiple faith traditions including Episcopalian, Quaker, and Unitarian Universalist traditions. Terry entered treatment at a local Community Mental Health Center complaining of depressed mood and episodes of angry outbursts directed at her partner and occasionally at colleagues. Terry and her partner George had been living together for 10 years. While actively involved and engaged with nieces and nephews, they eschewed parenting children of their own.

Terry was the youngest child of four, with three older brothers. Her father was an artist and a retired professor of art history who had taught at one of the city's many private universities. Her mother was deceased, having died of cancer 10 years prior to Terry seeking treatment. Terry described her father as very ambitious and self-involved throughout her life. While the children were small he had engaged in an extramarital affair with a colleague and left Terry's mother to marry the woman with whom he had been involved. Terry experienced this as a significant abandonment. She described years of having little contact with her father who, while residing in the same suburb as Terry and her brothers and mother, was preoccupied with his new family, including two children he had with his second wife. Terry also described growing up in poverty. Although they were able to continue to live in the family home in a middle class suburb of a major Northeastern city, they were frequently unable to afford basic necessities such as food and clothing, and her father offered little in the way of financial assistance, needing his money to support his second family. Terry described moments of being asked by her mother to walk to the home of her father and his new family to beg him for some money for basic necessities for herself and her brothers. The feelings of emptiness, loneliness, and sense of abandonment were palpable as Terry described these moments. She frequently expressed the wish that her father had been physically or verbally abusive to them in that he would "at least be acknowledging her existence." She described a pervasive experience of being a "nonperson" in his eyes and to "not existing" as far as he was concerned. The fact that he resided in the same town as Terry and her brothers only intensified these feelings for her.

Terry's mother had few emotional resources with which to support or enliven her children. She was a woman who struggled with depression throughout Terry's childhood, exacerbated by the divorce and its ensuing loneliness and financial stress. As her depression intensified Terry's mother attempted suicide by overdosing on prescription medications when Terry was 13 years old. Terry found her mother unconscious and was responsible for calling the ambulance and enlisting treatment for her mother.

Terry was moderately depressed at the time she sought treatment and described frequent incidents when she would become enraged and verbally abusive toward her partner, George.

These incidents were often triggered by her perception that George was criticizing or judging her negatively and harshly. Although she described herself as having been somewhat depressed throughout her adult life, her current exacerbation of symptoms appeared to have been triggered by the presence of a new boss whose feedback she also experienced as harsh and critical. Over time, as Terry's trust in the therapeutic alliance increased, she disclosed that she used marijuana and alcohol daily, sometimes to the point of passing out, and that her arguments with George were often initiated by his complaints about her substance use. In spite of these arguments, Terry refused to limit her use of alcohol or marijuana.

Discussion

Terry suffers from what has been most aptly characterized in self psychology as a depletion depression and a tendency to fragment easily when experiencing conflict or criticism in important interpersonal relationships. Depletion states and depletion depression, in contrast to the classical syndrome of guilt depression, are born neither from intrapsychic conflict nor from the problems associated with the discharge of aggression implicit in the classical model. Instead, such depression is regarded as a disintegration product, one signaling a structural deficiency that is itself a developmental sequela of early problems in the subject's self/selfobject milieu. The angry outbursts and verbal abuse that Terry described may be conceptualized as disintegration products in the self psychological model, triggered by the absence of mirroring in her environment and her own structural deficits, rather than understood as a manifestation of an inborn drive for aggression, as it would be in classical psychoanalysis. In self psychological terms, Terry failed to attain self-cohesiveness, owing to the unremitting series of traumatic losses and neglect she had suffered in her relationships with her parents. Indeed, her history was replete with such selfobject failures. Terry's mother, who was chronically overburdened, evinced a marked insensitivity and lack of attunement with her daughter's emotional needs, further compounded by her own depression. Her father, despite his many successes in the academic and artistic worlds, offered little to his daughter in the way of mirroring, leading her to experience herself as inconsequential, unimportant, and unworthy of love or attention. Lacking in self-confidence and inner vitality, Terry had come to feel an emptiness that could not be assuaged in her relationships or job. She felt devitalized and ineffectual, was subject to mercurial fluctuations of mood, and responded to narcissistic slights with heightened anger. Terry's capacity for the regulation of her self-esteem was minimal, inasmuch as she was highly reliant on the daily use of marijuana and alcohol to bolster, enliven, and soothe an empty self.

UNIQUE FEATURES OF SELF PSYCHOLOGY AS A CLINICAL SYSTEM

Although it is no longer possible to speak of self psychology as a unified theoretical system, there are two hallmarks of any clinical self-psychological approach: (1) the central importance of the therapist's sustained, empathetic immersion in the client's subjective experience; and (2) the concept of selfobjects and selfobject transferences (Mitchell & Black, 1995).

Self-psychologists believe that the therapist's basic attitude of concern and compassionate acceptance and his or her promotion of an ambience of emotional vitality and responsiveness are necessary to bring about the therapeutic remobilization of various archaic selfobject needs, considered a sine qua non for meaningful psychotherapy. This therapeutic stance has often been presented in stark contrast to the "detached, cold, abstemious, surgeonlike demeanor" attributed to Freud and to his rendering of classical psychoanalytic technique (Leider, 1996).

The interpretive process in self psychology consists of two basic phases: a phase of understanding, superceded by a phase of explanation and interpretation. Both of these phases are deemed essential to the therapeutic process (Kohut, 1984). With the unfolding of the therapeutic process and the establishment of a selfobject transference, the client unconsciously perceives the therapist as fulfilling various selfobject needs. The client's dawning perception that the therapist has somehow failed to satisfy these selfobject needs (an unavoidable eventuality) leads to fragmentation, archaic affect states, and other sequelae of misattunement. Such therapeutic breaches, however, are not just unavoidable in the view of self psychology; they are necessary for further psychological growth and structural repair (Leider, 1996).

The phase of understanding commences with the therapist's recognition of the empathetic rupture or breach, which is then conveyed to the client. Such therapeutic communications, accompanied by the therapist's attempt to reconstruct and characterize the events leading to the disruption, serve to re-establish psychological homeostasis (Kohut, 1984). This makes possible explanation, in which the significance of the therapeutic breach is recast in dynamic/genetic terms, permitting the client and therapist to reconstruct "the circumstances of the [client's] childhood in which parental selfobjects" were chronically unavailable, "analogous disruptions occurred, and the self was permanently injured" (Leider, 1996, p. 157).

FUTURE

Self psychology offers the clinician a dynamic approach to practice applicable to a wide range of presenting problems, one that may be successfully adapted to the diverse clinical populations with which social workers work. The therapeutic requirements for producing enduring structural changes in the personality cannot always be met within a framework of managed mental health services, and this may be one limitation of a self psychological approach. However, many of the insights derived from psychoanalytic self psychology can be readily applied to such modalities as crisis intervention, brief and other time-sensitive treatments, and even supportive therapy. The clinician's capacity for empathetic immersion in the client's subjective experience, a sine qua non of any self-psychological approach to treatment, may not in itself lead to a permanent restructuralization of the self, but its impact at a time of crisis should not be underestimated. Similarly, in parent guidance work, the worker may provide what has been termed "transference parenting" (Chethik, 2000) to a beleaguered parent whose own childhood consisted of an unremitting series of parental selfobject failures. This may have the effect of making the parent somewhat more attuned and responsive to his or her own child's requirements for affirmation, calming and soothing, or partnering.

In its view of normal development and developmental derailments, self psychology places considerable emphasis on the role of environment in particular, the chronic failures of the selfobject milieux within which individuals develop.

As such, it seems especially well suited as a framework for assisting social work clinicians in their continuing efforts both to understand dysfunction and pathology and to provide therapeutic responses to it.

RECENT DEVELOPMENTS IN SELF PSYCHOLOGY

Selfobject Transferences

Further elucidation of the selfobject and selfobject transferences has been the subject of more recent theorizing within the self-psychological tradition. Rowe (2005) has described the undifferentiated selfobject transference experience as a sense that there is something more, something better forthcoming in life. He identifies this as knowing or expecting that "unknown nonspecific happenings will occur throughout our lives and will be surprising, challenging, uplifting, and self-enhancing, no matter the ... nature of our current circumstances" (Rowe, 2008, p. 2). Wolf (1988) has conceptualized and described in clinical vignettes the adversarial selfobject transference. The adversarial transference is one in which the patient is frequently in opposition to the selfobject or in some way moving against the selfobject in order to grow and solidify internal structure. In this instance the client may concurrently attempt to enlist emotional support from the selfobject while also attempting to establish their autonomy; the client seeks both support and opposition from the selfobject in order to enhance self-cohesion. Not unlike those selfobject transferences discussed previously, both the undifferentiated and adversarial selfobject transferences have the potential to increase the self's cohesion and vitality.

Integration of Self Psychology with other Perspectives

Along with development in identifying and understanding selfobject transferences, theorists have also attempted to integrate a self psychological perspective with other psychoanalytic or developmental perspectives.

Motivational Factors

Lichtenberg, Lachman, and Fosshage (2011) proposed a new understanding of selfobject transference as part of an attachment motivational system with seven motivational system levels, each unfolding according to dynamic systems theory principles. These seven motivational levels include regulation of physiological demands, attachment and affiliation; exploratory-assertive, the need for antagonism or withdrawal, sensuality and sexuality, an affiliative system, and caregiving system. According to this theory, selfobject functions such as mirroring, idealization, and twinship are central to the development of attachment and to attachment motivation.

Infant Research

Infant researchers have also integrated self psychological principals with a systems perspective of dyadic relationships—specifically those between infant and primary caregiver. Daniel Stern has examined and written about the development of the infant's self and the infant's experience of that self. He delineated four senses of the infant's self. These include the *Emergent self, Core self, Subjective self*, and *Verbal self*. Each of these develops through the empathic and sensitive responses of the caregiver to the infant, optimally enabling the infant to develop the internal structures needed for a cohesive and vital self. Lachmann and Beebe (1992) have also bridged empirical infant research and self psychology in their observations of self and mutual regulation within the infant caregiver dyad and its application to the client-clinician relationship.

Interpersonal Approaches

Finally, the influence of self psychology on interpersonal psychoanalytic approaches has also been observed (Fosshage, 2003). Both perspectives recognize the importance of the clinician and of the therapeutic relationship to enhancing the client's experience of the self and self-cohesion, as well as the importance of the clinician maintaining empathic attunement and optimal empathic responsiveness.

WEBSITES

International Association for Psychoanalytic Self Psychology. http://www.psychology-oftheself.com.
New York Institute for Psychoanalytic Self Psychology. http://www.selfpsychologypsychoanalysis.org.

Self Psychology Page. http://www.selfpsychology.com.

Training and Research Institute for Self Psychology. http://www.trisp.org.

References

Brandell, J. (2004). Psychoanalytic theories of development and dysfunction: Ego psychology, object relations theories, the psychology of the self, and relational psychoanalysis. In J. Brandell (Ed.), *Psychodynamic social work* (pp. 44–69). New York, NY: Columbia University Press.

Chethik, M. (2000). *Techniques of child therapy: Psychodynamic strategies.* New York, NY: Free Press.

Elson, M. (1986). *Self psychology in clinical social work.* New York, NY: Norton.

Fosshage, J. L. (2003). Contextualizing self psychology and relational psychoanalysis: Bi-directional influence and proposed synthesis. *Contemporary Psychoanalysis 39*(3), 411–448.

Greenberg, L., & Mitchell, S. (1983). *Object relations in psychoanalytic theory.* Cambridge, MA: Harvard University Press.

Kohut, H. (1966). Forms and transformations of narcissism. *Journal of the American Psychoanalytic Association, 14*, 243–272.

Kohut, H. (1971). *Analysis of the self: A systematic approach to the treatment of narcissistic personality disorders.* New York, NY: International Universities Press.

Kohut, H. (1977). *The restoration of the self.* New York, NY: International Universities Press.

Kohut, H. (1984). *How does analysis cure?* Chicago, IL: University of Chicago Press.

Kohut, H., & Wolf, E. (1978). The disorders of the self and their treatment: An outline. *International Journal of Psychoanalysis, 59*, 413–425.

Lachmann, F., & Beebe, B. (1992). Representational and selfobject transferences: A developmental perspective. In A, Goldberg (Ed.), *New therapeutic visions: Progress in Self Psychology, 8.* Hillsdale, NJ: The Analytic Press.

Leider, R. (1996). The psychology of the self. In E. Nersessian & R. Kopff, Jr. (Eds.), *Textbook of psychoanalysis* (pp. 127–164). Washington, DC: American Psychiatric Association Press.

Lichtenberg, J. D., Lachman, F. M., & Fosshage, J. L. (2011). *Psychoanalysis and motivational systems.* Hoboken, NJ: Taylor and Francis.

Mitchell, S., & Black, M. (1995). *Freud and beyond: A history of modern psychoanalytic thought.* New York, NY: Basic Books.

Rowe, C., & MacIsaac, D. (1991). *Empathic attunement: The "technique" of psychoanalytic self psychology.* Northvale, NJ: Jason Aronson.

Rowe, C. (2005). A brief treatment of a posttraumatic stress disordered patient: A self psychological perspective. *Clinical Social Work Journal, 33*, 473–484.

Rowe, C. (2005). *Treating the basic self: Understanding addictive, suicidal, compulsive and attention-deficit hyperactivity behavior.* New York, NY: Psychoanalytic Publishers, Inc.

Rowe, C. (2008). The impact of a traumatic birth injury on the internal world of an adult patient: A self-psychological psychoanalysis. *The Psychoanalytic Review, 95*, 107–129.

Wolf, E. (1988). *Treating the self: Elements of clinical psychology.* New York, NY: Guilford Press.

PART V

Assessment in Social Work Practice: Knowledge and Skills

46

Diagnostic Formulation Using the *Diagnostic and Statistical Manual of Mental Disorders, Fifth Edition*

Carlton E. Munson

Diagnostic formulation takes on new meaning in the *Diagnostic and Statistical Manual of Mental Disorders, Fifth Edition (DSM-5)* because the multiaxial system introduced with the implementation of the *Diagnostic and Statistical Manual of Mental Disorders, Third Edition (DSM-III)* in 1980, was a major revision of the manual that introduced the modern method of diagnostic formulation. *DSM-5* remains consistent with the fundamental conceptualization of diagnosis introduced in *DSM-III*, but ties the diagnostic formulation to more recent focus on the role of clinical utility, clinical relevance, clinical significance, and clinical judgment. Although the recording and presentation of an official diagnosis has changed in *DSM-5*, some of the features of diagnostic recording introduced in *DSM-III* remain. For example, the recording of a core diagnosis, listing medical conditions, indicating level of severity, and noting principal and provisional diagnoses continue to be used with some changes. Conceptually, diagnosis is similar in *DSM-5* to earlier editions of the *DSM*, but there is no longer a sequential, numeric, formal format for recording diagnoses.

PURPOSE OF DIAGNOSIS

The American Psychological Association (APA) states the purpose of *DSM-5* is to assist mental health professionals in the diagnosis of client mental disorders as part of a "case formulation assessment that leads to a fully informed treatment plan" (APA, 2013. p. 19) for each client. The link between diagnosis and treatment has been

an evolutionary process as part of the history of the *DSM* diagnostic system. The first *Diagnostic and Statistical Manual–Mental Disorders* (APA, 1952) is referred to as *DSM-I* and its main goal was to establish a singular "nomenclature" for categorizing mental disorders due to the existing "polyglot of diagnostic labels and systems." The APA viewed the situation as one in which the "official system of nomenclature rapidly became untenable" (APA, 1952, pp. vi–vii). The aim of *DSM-I* was to bring more clarity and consistency to classification of mental disorders and focused primarily on collecting statistical information about the incidence and occurrence of mental illness (APA, 1994, p. xvii). The word treatment was mentioned in *DSM-I*, but treatment did not receive emphasis because the focus was on establishing a solely descriptive statistical classification based on a two-category system. The first category included disorders directly linked to mental disturbance resulting from brain impairment, and the second category was associated with "general difficulty in adaptation," and if brain impairment was present, it was secondary to the psychiatric disorder (APA, 1952, p. 9).

The *DSM-III* was released in 1980 and it gave rise to much controversy with some viewing it as ushering in the era of "science and objectivity" to guide the classification of mental illness (Sadler, 2005), while others saw it as a "political rather than a scientific document" (Taylor, 2013). The *DSM-III* did expand emphasis of the diagnosis and treatment connection. A subsection of the Introduction to *DSM-III* titled, "Evaluation for Treatment Planning" (APA, 1980, pp. 11–12), gives detailed instructions on how to link diagnosis to treatment using different theoretical orientations. Although some of this information is no longer relevant, much of the information continues to be useful in doing intake interviews with a focus on linking diagnosis and treatment. The *DSM-III* clearly established the diagnosis–treatment linkage with the statement, "Making a *DSM-III* diagnosis represents an initial step in a comprehensive evaluation leading to the formulation of a treatment plan" (APA, 1980, p. 11).

In *DSM-IV* the diagnosis-treatment link was continued through a statement similar to the *DSM-III* statement, and a rephrasing of the expectation that "To formulate an adequate treatment plan, the clinician will invariably require considerable additional information about the person being evaluated beyond that required to make a *DSM-IV* diagnosis" (APA, 1994, p. xxv).

The linkage of diagnosis and treatment has been refined over the last three decades stemming in part from the case of *Osheroff v. Chestnut Lodge* (1980) that had significant impact on the diagnosis and treatment planning connection (Knoll, 2013). Dr. Osheroff was a physician who was admitted to Chestnut Lodge psychiatric hospital in Maryland in January 1979. Chestnut Lodge held an important place in the history of psychiatry. It was a major source of theory development and clinical practice of psychotherapy based on psychoanalytic theory (Klerman, 1990). Psychotherapy pioneers Harry Stack Sullivan and Frieda Fromm-Reichmann practiced at Chestnut Lodge.

Dr. Osheroff was admitted to Chestnut Lodge due to anxiety and depressive symptoms with suicidal thoughts. He was diagnosed with depressive disorders and a personality disorder. The only treatment provided was psychoanalytically oriented therapy. Dr. Osheroff deteriorated significantly during his stay at Chestnut Lodge. Symptoms of a severe agitated depression developed. His family intervened and had him transferred to Silver Hill Hospital in Connecticut in September 1979. He improved quickly after treatment with medications and was discharged in November 1979. After a series of legal maneuvers, Osheroff filed a medical malpractice, inter alia, lawsuit in 1985. The lawsuit was based in part on the failure to coordinate the linkage of the diagnosis and the treatment. The case was settled in 1987 before trial under a sealed settlement. In 2001, Chestnut Lodge closed and Dr. Osheroff died in March 2012 (Hirschkop & Mook, 2012).

Given the increased emphasis placed on the diagnosis–treatment connection, it is no coincidence that the release of the *DSM-III* and Dr. Osheroff's lawsuit occurred in close proximity.

The Osheroff case has been described as "an important historical moment of transition in modern psychiatry" (Stone, 1990). The case surfaced a number of issues related to mental health intervention and highlighted the debate during the 1990s of the "decade of the brain" that symbolizes the evidence-based practice model and the role of clinical experience (Robertson, 2005). The impact of the Osheroff case has quietly shadowed and altered clinical practice standards over the last two decades with respect to the diagnosis and treatment connection. In *DSM-5* the historic diagnosis-treatment association has been reinforced and expanded in the section *Approach to Clinical Case Formulation*. The following quote from this section of *DSM-5* summarizes the expanded diagnostic formulation:

It requires clinical training to recognize when the combination of predisposing, precipitating, perpetuating, and protective factors has resulted in a psychopathological condition in which physical signs and symptoms exceed normal ranges. The ultimate goal of a clinical case formulation is to use the available contextual and diagnostic information and developing a comprehensive treatment plan that is informed by the individual's cultural and social context. (APA, 2013, p. 19)

CASE FORMULATION

The concept of case formulation emerged in the 1970s and was being described in the clinical literature by the time the Osheroff case began to have impact. Despite the growing awareness about the diagnosis–treatment linkage, educational programs and clinical supervisors have not placed much emphasis on the conceptual association of diagnosis and treatment planning. Treatment planning has most recently been articulated as "case formulation." Lazare (1976) in the early stages of modern case formulation defined the concept as "a conceptual scheme that organizes, explains, or makes sense of large amounts of data and influences treatment decisions" (p. 97). The diagnostic formulation model described in this chapter can be a standalone formulation or part of a comprehensive case formulation depending on the purpose of the diagnostic assessment. If the diagnostic formation is part of a referral for psychotherapy the diagnostic formulation should be combined with a case formulation and treatment plan. If the assessment is an evaluation in a forensic or other nontherapeutic case with no connection to intervention, the broader case formation would not be used and the diagnostic formulation would be one component of the evaluation.

A clinical case formulation used in conjunction with diagnostic formulations has not been well articulated in the past. Early studies show that training programs have placed little emphasis on the role of case formulations in mental health practice. One study (Ben-Aron & McCormick, 1980) found that 60% of psychiatry chairs and program directors believed that case formulation was important, but was inadequately stressed in training. A survey by Fleming and Patterson (1993) found that less than half of the psychiatric training programs provided guidelines for case formulation, and believed that standardized guidelines were needed. Both studies suggested that clinicians do not feel they are well trained in case formulation. Eells, Kendielic, and Lucas (1998) in a study of clinical case formulation made the finding that:

In light of the consensus that case formulation skills are important, it is striking that little research has addressed the formulation skills of clinicians. Research in this area would not only provide feedback to clinicians that could aid in training, but would also serve the goal of consumer protection by ensuring that a well-thought-out understanding of the patient has been attempted and an appropriate treatment plan developed. (p. 145)

Diagnostic formulation and case formulation as concepts are not generally used in clinical social work practice and rarely, if ever, appear in the clinical social work literature. This avoidance is not unique to the social work profession. Case formulation models have emerged and become more sophisticated over the last 30 years, but still are not widely used. This is the case because as Paris (2013) has pointed out:

All editions of the DSM have clearly stated that they are not intended to be guides to treatment. But that is not what happens in practice. Clinicians go directly from diagnosis to treatment. Moreover, they prefer diagnoses that lead to a specific treatment of some kind, even when they are wrong. (p. 13)

Clinical social workers and supervisors not familiar with clinical case formulation theory and

models should draw on the literature in this area to link their DSM-5 diagnostic formulations with a comprehensive case formulation before initiating treatment/psychotherapy. Good books to utilize in designing case formulations are: *The Case Formulation Approach to Cognitive Behavioral Therapy* by Jacqueline Persons (2008); *Clinical Case Formulations* by Barbara Ingram (2011); *Collaborative Case Conceptualization* by Christine Padesky and Robert Dudley (2008); *The Biopsychosocial Formulation Manual* by William H. Campbell and R. M. Rohrbaugh (2006); *Psychoanalytic Case Formation* (1999); and *Psychiatric Case Formulations* by Len Sperry et al. (1992).

GENERAL DIAGNOSTIC CRITERIA

Formulating a diagnosis is based on general criteria that permeate all aspects of the diagnostic formulation process. The terms used here are defined differently from the terms used in mathematical statistical research based on probability theory. Terminology used in clinical settings currently is more descriptive ranking rather than precise, quantified measures. The criteria concepts are clinical utility, clinical relevance, clinical significance, and clinical judgment. The concepts are listed in the order that they should be applied to the clinical diagnostic process. The terms are defined and explained below.

Clinical utility is a term that applies to evaluation of the validity of classification systems such as the DSM-5. Clinical utility has been defined as "the extent to which DSM assists clinical decision makers in fulfilling the various clinical functions of a psychiatric classification system" (First, Pincus, Levine, Williams, Ustun, & Peele, 2004). Clinical utility deals with the question of how useable the system is for clinicians and how much people diagnosed using the system can rely on the accuracy of the diagnosis they have received. Clinical utility comes into play when the clinician compares the person's symptoms to others who do not have the disorder. The symptoms/behaviors associated with a disorder have utility if they are observed in less than a given percentage of the nondisordered population (Angelini, 2002). Put in practical clinical terms, clinical utility is the degree of assistance a diagnostic system provides the clinician in distinguishing between illness and health in a given client (Greenberg, 2013).

The clinician should consider practical clinical utility in decision-making about the presence or absence of a disorder in a given client. The designers of the *DSM-5* have recognized that currently there is not sufficient scientific evidence to meet a high level of expectation for clinical utility and clinical significance of symptoms and behaviors because the "boundaries between disorders are more porous than originally perceived." There is evidence many mental disorders are not separate entities and many disorders are "on a spectrum" with shared symptoms, behaviors, genetics, and environmental risk factors (APA, 2013, p. 6). To aid in dealing with practical clinical utility issues, "Other specified" and "unspecified" designations are included for most disorders in *DSM-5* (APA, p. 21). These categories are in part related to the Not Otherwise Specified (NOS) classification that was used in *DSM-IV*.

Research has shown that although most diagnostic concepts have limited validity, many are good working models that show clinical utility through information about outcome, treatment response, and etiology. The research findings indicate that clinical utility is a concept that clinicians need to understand and be conscious of when doing diagnosis. Practitioner use of clinical utility can be helpful in diagnostic interviewing, considering differential diagnosis, choosing interventions to improve outcomes, and communicating clinical information to colleagues, supervisors, clients, and their family members (Kendell & Jablensky, 2003). Assessing whether a disorder has sufficient clinical utility to use it is difficult with respect to a given client and may require an informed judgment decision by the clinician. Allen Frances (2013) chair of the *DSM-IV* revisions points out that "Every disorder has its story to tell," (p. 2), and I would add every patient has a story to tell, and the clinician's job in applying clinical utility in daily practice is to determine the fit of the two stories.

Clinical relevance is not applied here from a theoretical conceptual perspective. The terminology is used as a clinician-based concept that is part of establishing whether a unit of client behavior is relevant to the diagnosis under review. In other words, does a given symptom or set of symptoms identified by a client have relevance to criteria defined for a specific *DSM-5* disorder? For example, if an adolescent being evaluated for depression is having crying spells, the crying must be differentiated by determining if the crying is typical adolescent behavior or a part of a depressive disorder. If the crying is clinically relevant (related to a disorder) the clinician moves to assessing clinical significance of the crying.

Clinical significance is identification of a set of behaviors and symptoms observed in an individual that are considered to be outside the range of normal functioning, and are the cause of distress and impaired functioning. Duration of the symptoms and behaviors can be a feature in determining significance. In *DSM-5* most disorders have a criterion of clinical significance. The expression of the criterion varies with specific disorders, but is generally indicated as impairment "in social occupational or other important areas of functioning" (APA, 2013, p. 21). Once clinical significance is determined, *DSM-5* uses specifiers to establish the level or degree of clinical significance. The most common specifier set in *DSM-5* is "mild, moderate, and severe." There are various other clinical significance models outside the *DSM-5* system that can also be used to guide the mental process of deciding level of significance. For example, a very broad classification of behavior is the "four Ds," in which a person's behavior can be judged as: "different, difficult, dysfunctional or dangerous." Another set of significance measures used in assessing potential difficulty in producing overall or specific change (treatment outcome) is: "simple, difficult, complicated, complex, and insoluble" (Munson, 2013, pp. 218–219).

Clinical judgment is the application of information based on actual observation of a patient combined with subjective and objective data that lead to a conclusion (Mosby, 2013). Clinical judgment is also referred to as critical thinking and clinical reasoning, but often these two terms are considered as working components of clinical judgment. When combining the three terms clinical judgment can be viewed as "the sum total of all the cognitive processes involved in clinical decision making" (Karthikeyan & Pais, 2010, p. 624). Dr. Allen Frances's (2013) book, *Essential of Psychiatric Diagnosis*, can be helpful in the integration and exercising of clinical utility, relevance, significance, and judgment in daily practice with respect to the controversial disorders in the *DSM-5*.

DIAGNOSTIC FORMULATION

A diagnostic formulation is the result of a process in which the clinician interviews the client with a focus of compiling the chief complaints, identifying symptoms and behaviors articulated by the client, as well as information provided by collateral sources (relatives, school officials, employers, etc.). Information is also gathered about the client's personal history and the possible prior history of diagnoses and mental health treatment and family history of mental illness. This information is assessed, integrated, and applied to the *DSM-5* criteria for various diagnostic categories. Ultimately the decision is made to assign a disorder or condition. The factual information, findings, rationale, and diagnosis are recorded through a formal written diagnostic formulation. Information in the *Introduction* and *Use of the Manual* sections of the *DSM-5* provides broad guidelines for the written diagnostic formulation. Based on the brevity of the guidelines the clinician has much flexibility in how the diagnosis is recorded. The key ethical consideration is that the written diagnostic formation must be sufficient to justify the content of the written treatment plan.

RECORDING A DIAGNOSTIC FORMULATION

The *DSM-5* expectations for recording a diagnostic formulation can be conceptualized in five categories: (1) history and background, (2) diagnoses, (3) medical conditions, (4) notations, and (5) disability severity. There is no standardized format prescribed in the *DSM-5* for recording these components of the diagnostic formulation. The diagnostic formulation becomes the guide for crafting the client's treatment plan. I recommend the diagnostic formulation be conceptualized and written before the treatment plan is established through collaboration with the client and/or family members. The *DSM-5* has a disclaimer indicating that recommendations for selection and use of treatment options for any disorder are not part of the *DSM-5* diagnostic system (APA, 2013, p. 19). The following information provides guidelines for recording a diagnostic formulation that is consistent with the *DSM-5* expectations in these five areas. A sample diagnostic formulation is illustrated for "Mr. Jones" in the descriptions of the five sections.

HISTORY AND BACKGROUND INFORMATION

The rationale for the history and background information is summarized in the *DSM-5* manual as the case formulation "must involve a careful clinical history and concise summary of the

social, psychological, and biological factors that may have contributed to developing a given mental disorder. ... it is not sufficient to simply check off for symptoms in the diagnostic criteria to make a mental disorder diagnosis" (APA, p. 19). A history and background section is important because the *DSM-5* no longer formally uses the "by prior history" or "by prior diagnosis" indicators used in *DSM-IV*. Also, the *DSM-5* "Diagnostic Features" sections for some disorders have risk and prognosis sections that describe possible genetic and physiological factors. Where heritable features of disorders are present they should be noted as part of the history and background information.

There is much flexibility in recording history and background, but the information included should be a concise summary of the key factors that are relevant to the diagnoses assigned in the diagnosis section of the diagnostic formulation. Basic demographic information should be included (age, cultural information, etc.) There should be a brief statement of the presence or absence of prior mental illness and mental health treatment episodes. Any factors that are outside the Other Conditions That May Be a Focus of Clinical Attention should be noted. An example of this first segment of the diagnostic formulation is illustrated below:

History and Background

Koma Jones, age 34, was seen today on self-referral because "I just can't shake the blues." He reports depression and anxiety symptoms for approximately two years. The depressive symptom and anxiety symptom onset occurred soon after meeting his current female companion. He and his companion have a 9-month-old son. He reports the companion has a "gambling problem" in several areas (off-track betting, casino gambling, sports gambling, and state lotteries) that preexisted their relationship. Mr. Jones reports his gambling is limited to casinos and lotteries, but he reports, "I gamble with money I can't afford to spend." Mr. Jones has been unemployed for seven months with "limited" prospects for finding employment. There is much verbal conflict between Mr. Jones and his companion. He is considering separation from the companion, but has not shared his plans with her. He reports receiving mental health diagnoses in the past during a marriage that ended in divorce six years ago. He received brief psychotherapy and medication for

Dysthymic Disorder and alcohol and substance abuse. He reports the alcohol/substance use was associated with chronic neck pain that was the result of an automobile accident. Based on Mr. Jones's self-report, screening measures, and clinical observation, he is not currently a threat to himself or others. There is a family history of bipolar disorder (paternal grandfather and maternal aunt). Based on the clinical interview, scales administered, and collateral information, the following diagnoses were made as part of this evaluation....

DIAGNOSES

Section II (Diagnostic Criteria and Codes) in *DSM-5* lists all the disorders that are cited as part of the diagnostic formulation. Section II is the core of the *DSM-5* system and combines the *DSM-IV* Axis I (Clinical Disorders), Axis II (Mental Retardation (Intellectual disability) and Personality Disorders, and Axis III (General Medical Conditions). In recording a diagnostic formulation, each disorder is listed preceded by the *International Classification Diseases* (ICD) diagnostic code. The Other Conditions That May Be a Focus of Clinical Attention listed at the end of the *DSM-5 Section II* are not diagnoses (APA, 2013, p. 715) and are recorded in a separate section of the diagnostic formulation as "Notations."

When multiple diagnoses are recorded, the previously used convention of listing the "principal diagnosis" first continues to be the recording procedure. "Principle diagnosis" is defined in *DSM-5* for inpatient settings as the condition primarily responsible for admitting the person, and in outpatient settings the "reason for the visit" is the disorder/condition that is primarily responsible for the services the person receives during the outpatient visit (APA, 2013, pp. 22–23). Other disorders diagnosed are listed in the order of how much they contribute to the treatment or service that is provided. Provisional diagnosis is also retained in *DSM-5* as a "specifier" (APA, 2013, p. 23). Provisional diagnosis is used when the information available about the client is not sufficient to determine whether the client meets the full criteria for a disorder. Provisional status of a diagnosis is indicated by entering "(Provisional)" to the right of the diagnostic entry. Generally accepted practice standards indicate that a firm diagnosis usually should be made by the third visit, but in some cases arriving at a diagnosis

may take longer. If the person ultimately meets the criteria for the disorder, the word provisional is removed or struck out in the written diagnostic entry. If the criteria for the disorder are not met, the disorder is removed or struck through on the written diagnostic entry. The following is a diagnostic formulation example of a multiple item diagnosis:

Diagnoses

F34.1[1] Persistent depressive disorder, with anxious distress, moderate, Late onset, with pure dysthymic syndrome, moderate
F63.0 Gambling disorder, episodic, moderate
F10.10 Alcohol use disorder, in early remission, mild
F12.10 Cannabis use disorder, in sustained remission, mild

MEDICAL CONDITIONS

DSM-5 indicates clinicians should continue to list the medical conditions as part of the diagnosis after listing the mental diagnoses. For nonphysicians, it is recommended that as part of nonphysician diagnostic formulation the medical conditions be listed as a separate section using the disclaimer "as reported by ..." (see Munson, 2001, p. 80). This disclaimer can prevent clinical social workers from being accused of practicing medicine by diagnosing medical conditions. Any medical conditions entered in a diagnostic formation or other assessment/evaluation should use the "as reported by ..." disclaimer listing spouse, parent, employer, primary care physician, etc., as the source of the medical information. Below is an example of recording medical conditions for Mr. Jones's diagnostic formulation:

Medical Conditions as reported by Mr. Jones (person evaluated)

Gastritis, severe
Erectile dysfunction, moderate
Asthma, chronic
Neck injury with significant pain associated with automobile accident

NOTATIONS

The *DSM-IV* Axis IV Psychosocial and Environmental Problems (PEPs) covered nine key areas through brief narrative summaries that were part of the multiaxial diagnosis. In *DSM-5*, the PEPs were eliminated and moved into the end of Section II and titled *Other Conditions That May Be a Focus of Clinical Attention*. There are nine categories of conditions. The conditions are not considered mental disorders, but the conditions may impact the individual's diagnosis, the course of disturbance, the prognosis, or the treatment (APA, 2013, p. 715). In some cases the condition can simply be listed such as "homelessness" while others, such as "low income" may need a brief supplemental statement such as: "due to being unemployed and receiving unemployment of $235 biweekly and having three children in his care with no other financial supports or resources." The details of the notations should be explained in the case formulation that should accompany the diagnostic formulation. The following illustrates the notations section for Mr. Jones:

Notations

Z63.8 High expressed emotion level within family
Z56.9 Other problems related to employment
V60.2 Insufficient social insurance or welfare support

DISABILITY SEVERITY

DSM-5 diagnostic instructions suggest that overall severity or "disability" should be recorded in the diagnostic formulation. Diagnosis is used to plan individual case and treatment plans, but it is also used to communicate diagnostic information to other clinicians who may work with the client. An overall severity indicator can be helpful in both clinical situations. No specific directions are provided in the *DSM-5* for recording this indicator as a severity specifier. There are a number of severity specifiers used within individual disorders in *DSM-5*. For example, persistent depressive disorder has five specifiers that are reviewed for the diagnosis. For clinical social workers it is recommended that clinical judgment be carefully used in determining the clinical significance of the overall clinical picture. The clinical judgment should be guided by the clinical significance criterion that is universally applied in the criteria for each disorder in the *DSM-5*. The *DSM-5* intentionally separates the concepts of mental disorder

and disability (severity of illness). Disability severity is defined as "impairment in social, academic, or other important areas of functioning" and the impairment should be assessed in the context of determining the individual's need for treatment (APA, 2013, p. 21). The overall disability severity can be presented through a brief summary statement. A sample of Mr. Jones's disability severity rating is summarized below:

Mr. Jones's overall functional severity is in the mild/moderate range. The moderate severity is present mostly in the area of personal concern about employment and his partner relationship issues. The alcohol/substance risk is in the moderate range given the early remission status, and the risk of relapse related to unemployment and personal stressors is in the moderate range. The gambling problem is at the mild level and may become nondisordered gambling if treated. The medical conditions present a moderate level of severity and if not addressed could result in alcohol/substance relapse. If Mr. Jones commits to a course of psychotherapy with a specific treatment plan the prognosis appears to be good, but the lack of insurance to cover treatment and low motivation for treatment may be barriers to a positive outcome. There is no apparent risk of harm to self and others.

ETHICS AND DIAGNOSIS

Social workers have been provided little guidance about the ethics of performing diagnosis even though the profession provides 40% to 80% of the mental health services in the United States. The National Association of Social Workers (NASW) Code of Ethics (1999) does not mention the words diagnosis, treatment, or psychotherapy. Some clinical social work organizations have adopted the NASW Code of Ethics as the guide for clinical social work practice (see for example, South Carolina Society for Clinical Social work website). The document *NASW Standards for Clinical Social Work in Social Work Practice* (NASW, 2005), which was issued in 1984 and revised in 1989 and 2005, makes one reference to the word diagnosis. Diagnosis is mentioned in the document based on Barker's (2003) definition of clinical social work as: "Clinical social work is the professional application of social work theory and methods to the diagnosis, treatment, and prevention of psychosocial dysfunction, disability, or impairment, including emotional, mental and behavioral disorders. . .." (p. 9). The NASW practice standards document indicates, "Clinical social workers shall adhere to the values and ethics of the social work profession, utilizing the NASW Code of Ethics as a guide to ethical decision making" (p. 4). As was mentioned earlier, the NASW Code of Ethics provides no ethical guidance related to diagnosis.

The Clinical Social Work Association (CSWA) (1997), formerly the Clinical Social Work Federation, does not mention the word diagnosis in the organization's 3,546 word code of ethics issued in 1997 and last reviewed in 2006 when the code was " … found to still be an accurate statement of the ethical principles governing the clinical social work profession and the professional conduct of the members of that profession (Clinical Social Work Association, p. 4). The word "diagnostic" is used once in the statement: "Diagnostic and therapeutic services for clients. … are rendered only in the context of a professional relationship" (p. 4).

The American Clinical Social Work Association (ACSWA, undated) formerly known as the American Board of Examiners in Clinical Social Work, mentions in its code of ethics the word "diagnostic" once and does not mention the word diagnosis. The ACSWA code statement on diagnosis is:

Clinical social workers observe the primacy of client need balanced with the right to self-determination. They take all reasonable steps to prevent the client from causing harm to self and others, and use their diagnostic and treatment skills to improve the mental health and social functioning of clients (American Clinical Social Work Association. (Undated)

Because professional organizations and regulatory boards provide clinical social workers little guidance about performing ethical diagnosis, providing adequate understanding of how to perform clinical diagnosis ethically is in part a responsibility of clinical supervisors through use of a mentoring and monitoring model (Munson, 2013). Supervisors need to mentor supervisees in how to develop diagnostic formulations accurately and monitor how they record diagnostic formulations, case formulations, and treatment plans. No research exists on how well clinical supervisors are prepared for this role.

Turner (2002) in his careful analysis of the history of social work diagnosis going back to the 1930s has pointed out that "unless our profession turns once again to a broad acceptance of the concept and content of diagnosis as the heart of social work practice, we deprive our clients of a powerful helping resource and thus fail in our responsibility to them" (p. 1). Ethically, any clinical social worker who provides psychotherapeutic intervention or any other treatment aimed at producing change in the client's functioning in relation to his or her mental functioning should only provide the intervention using a written treatment plan based on a case formulation that is derived from or connected to a thorough, written diagnostic formulation. The diagnostic formulation can be developed by the clinical social worker, or by an independent qualified psychiatrist, psychologist, or other qualified mental health professional within the last 30 days, and provides the treating clinical social worker with a written diagnostic formulation. In summary, Soren Kierkegaard, the famous 19th century Danish philosopher, in the broadest sense symbolically defined the bidirectional focus of diagnosis and treatment by pointing out "Life can only be understood backwards; but it must be lived forward."

WEBSITES

International Classification of Disease, ICD-9
    www.findacode.com/icp-diagnosis-codes.html
The Diagnostic and Statistical Manual, 5th edition, www.dsm5.org
American Psychiatric Association, www.apa.org

Note

1. The *ICD-10-CM* codes are used in the sample formulation. The *ICD-9-CM* codes will be used in the United States until October 1, 2014 or other date established for the official implementation of the *ICD-10-CM* codes in the United States. In the interim, United States clinicians are to use the *ICD-9-CM* codes. Both *ICD-9-CM* and *ICD-10-CM* codes are listed in the *DSM-5* (see p. 23 of the *DSM-5* for details of this requirement and the APA website: http://www.dsm5.org/Documents/FAQ).

References

American Clinical Social Work Association. (Undated). ABE Code of Ethics. Retrieved from http://www.acswa.org/
American Psychiatric Association. (2013). *Diagnostic and statistical manual of mental disorders, fifth edition*. Arlington, VA: Author. Retrieved from http://www.acswa.org/abe/code-of-ethics/

American Psychiatric Association. (1994). *Diagnostic and statistical manual of mental disorders, fourth edition*. Washington, DC: Author.

American Psychiatric Association. (1980). *Diagnostic and statistical manual of mental disorders, third edition*. Washington, DC: Author.

American Psychiatric Association. (1952). *Diagnostic and statistical manual—mental disorders*, Washington, DC: Author.

Angelini, P. (2002). Coronary artery anomalies: Current clinical issues. *Texas Heart Institute Journal, 29*(4), 271–278.

Barker, R. L. (2003). *The social work dictionary* (4th ed.). Washington, DC: NASW Press.

Ben-Aron, M., &. McCormick, W. O. (1980). The teaching of formulation: Facts and deficiencies. *Canadian Journal of Psychiatry, 25*, 163–166.

Campbell, W. H., & Rohrbaugh, R. M. (2006). *The biopsychosocial formulation manual*. London, UK: Routledge.

Clinical Social Work Association. (1997). *Clinical Social Work Association Code of Ethics*. Retrieved from http://associtioncites.comCSWA/collectionsethics/

Eells, T. D., Kendielic, E. K., & Lucas C. P. (l998). What's in a case formulation: Development and use of a content coding manual. *Journal of Psychotherapy Practice and Research, 7*(2), 144–153.

First, M. B., Pincus, H. A., Levine, J. B., Williams, J. B. W., Ustun, B., & Peele, R. (2004). Clinical utility as a criterion for revising psychiatric diagnosis. *American Journal of Psychiatry, 161*, 946–954.

Fleming J. A., & Patterson P. G. (1993). The teaching of case formulation in Canada. *Canadian Journal of Psychiatry, 38*, 345–350.

Frances, A. (2013). *Essentials of psychiatric diagnosis: Responding to the challenges of DSM-5*. New York, NY: Guilford.

Greenberg, G. (2013). *The book of woe: The DSM and the unmaking of psychiatry*. New York, NY: Penguin Group.

Hirschkop, P. J., & Mook, J. R. (2012, October). *Revisiting the lessons of Osheroff v. Chestnut Lodge*. Paper presented at 43rd Annual Meeting of the American Academy of Psychiatry and Law Montreal, Quebec, Canada.

Ingram, B. L. (2011). *Clinical case formulations: Matching the integrative treatment plan to the client* (2nd ed.). Hoboken, NJ: Wiley.

Klerman, G. L. (1990). The psychiatric patient's right to effective treatment: Implications of Osheroff v Chestnut Lodge. *American Journal of Psychiatry, 147*, 409–418.

Karthikeyan, G., & Pais, P. (2010). Clinical judgment and evidence-based medicine: Time for reconciliation. *Indian Journal of Medical Research, 132*(6), 623–628.

Kendell, R., & Jablensky, A. (2003). Distinguishing between the validity and utility of psychiatric diagnoses. *American Journal of Psychiatry, 160*, 4–12.

Knoll, J. (2013). The humanities and psychiatry: The rebirth of mind. *Psychiatric Times, 15*, 2–5.

Lazare, A. (1976). The psychiatric examination in the walk-in clinic: Hypothesis generation and hypothesis and testing. *Archives of General Psychiatry, 33*, 96–102.

McWilliams, N. (1999). *Psychoanalytic case formulation*. New York, NY: Guilford.

Mosby. (2013). *Mosby's Medical Dictionary* (9th ed.). Kidlington Oxford, UK: Elsevier.

Munson, C. E. (2001). *The mental health diagnostic desk reference* (2nd ed.). New York, NY: Haworth.

Munson, C. E. (2013). *Contemporary clinical social work supervision: A mentoring and monitoring model*. Culpeper, VA: Association of Social Work Boards.

National Association of Social Workers. (1999). *Code of ethics of the National Association of Social Workers*. Washington, DC: NASW Press.

National Association of Social Workers. (2005). *NASW standards for clinical social work in social work practice*. Washington, DC: NASW Press.

Osheroff v. Chestnut Lodge, Inc. 62 Md. App 519 (1985) 490A. 2D 720.

Padesky, C. A., & Dudley, R. (2008). *Collaborative case conceptualization: Working effectively with clients in cognitive-behavioral therapy*. New York, NY: Guilford.

Paris, J. (2013). *The intelligent clinician's guide to DSM-5*. New York, NY: Oxford.

Persons, J. B. (2008). *The case formulation approach to cognitive behavioral therapy: Guidelines to individualized evidence-based treatment*. New York, NY: Guilford.

Robertson, M. (2005). Power and knowledge in psychiatry and the troubling case of Dr. Osheroff. *Australasian Psychiatry, 13*, 343–350.

Sadler, J. Z. (2005). *Values and psychiatric diagnosis*. Oxford, UK: Oxford University Press.

Sperry, L., Gudeman, J. E., Blackwell, B., & Faulkner, L. R. (1992). *Psychiatric case formulations*. Washington, DC: American Psychiatric Publishing.

Stone, A. A. (1990). Law, science, and psychiatric malpractice: A response to Klerman's indictment of psychoanalytic psychiatry. *American Journal of Psychiatry, 147*, 419–427.

Taylor, M. A. (2013). *Hippocrates cried: The decline of American psychiatry*. New York, NY: Oxford University Press.

Turner, F. J. (2002). *Diagnosis in social work: New imperatives*. New York, NY: Haworth Press.

47

How Clinical Social Workers Can Easily Use Rapid Assessment Tools (RATs) for Mental Health Assessment and Treatment Evaluation

Kevin Corcoran

Clinical social work was once chiefly a three-party system. It was a matter between the patient and the provider, with reimbursement readily paid by insurance companies or governmental agencies. A person became a patient simply by deciding that he or she needed to see a social worker, and together they would decide what the problems and goals were, what the intervention would be, how long it should last, and the costs—although this was typically set solely by the provider. Then came managed care at both the private and public levels and everything changed; in particular, potential "clients" must be authorized for treatment based on "medical necessity." This change continues with the Affordable Care Act (see Gorin and Moniz, 2014) and state-initiated cost-cutting programs. One such program is Oregon's "Coordinated Care Organization," which is akin to an interdisciplinary team of case managers where prevention and early intervention is supposed to save billions of dollars; in this case, the team decides who will be a patient, what services are needed, and by whom.

In essence, the need for services, then, must be demonstrated before treatment, in order to get authorization and payment. This need for services may, in fact, need to be demonstrated at various points in the treatment process for the continuation of services. In both circumstances the social worker must demonstrate that clinical services are medically necessary and that there is some evidence of progress; evidence of progress from a health and mental health care administrative perspective is chiefly a reduction in symptomatology.

The critical question for the clinical social worker is how to demonstrate that the client's condition warrants treatment. There are many ways to evidence that a client's presenting problem is a mental health condition and is sufficiently distressing or disabling to require therapy. One method is a psychiatric evaluation that uses a variety of diagnostic tests. Examples of diagnostic tests include the Minnesota Multiphasic Personality Inventory and the Rorschach ink blots. These assessments have long been recognized as having a number of limitations for clinical social work (Arkava & Snow, 1978), including that they are costly, lengthy, time-consuming to administer, frequently require training to score and interpret, and some have questionable reliability and validity. Moreover, because of length, it is not practical to use them over the course of treatment and at follow-up. In contrast, there are a large number of relatively short, self-administered, and easily scored assessment tools available for use by practitioners for most clinical conditions (e.g., Corcoran & Fischer, 2013a, 2013b; Jordan & Franklin, 2011). These assessment tools are frequently called rapid assessment tools (RATs) and generally take only a few minutes to complete. RATs are useful to evidence medical necessity and when used throughout treatment to monitor symptom reduction and goal attainment.

RAPID ASSESSMENT TOOLS TO MEASURE TREATMENT NECESSITY

An additional use of RATs is to provide evidence of the need for treatment. This is based on scores obtained at the intake. Some instruments, such as Hudson's scales (Nugent, Sieppert, & Hudson, 2001), can provide this information because they have a cutting score. A cutting score is one that distinguishes those with a clinically significant problem from those without one. When using such a measure, if the score is greater or lower than the cutting score, it is persuasive evidence of a need for treatment.

Most psychological measurements do not have cutting scores. In these circumstances, an RAT score may be compared to a norm from either the general population or a clinical sample of patients in treatment. This is known as norm-referenced comparison, and it illustrates the client's problem relative to others with and without that problem. A client's score on an RAT should be different from the general population and similar to those with the same mental health condition. When these observations occur, it is reasonable to conclude that treatment is warranted.

When using RATs to illustrate the need for treatment, two assessments are recommended: a broadband measure of mental health along with a narrowband measure of the client's specific problem. Excellent broadband instruments are the various health and mental health surveys, which are all short forms (SF; Ware, Kosinski, & Keller, 1994; also see qualitymetric.com). These instruments are particularly useful because they have been evaluated in numerous countries, are inexpensive, and are accessible from the Internet (www.outcomes-trust.org; qualitymetric.com) as well as from published sources (e.g., Corcoran & Fischer, 2013b). The health and mental health survey has two composite scores, one measuring physical health and the other measuring mental health. The average score on the SF-36 and SF-12 is about 50 and 35 for the general population and a psychiatric sample, respectively; the standard deviation is 10 for both samples.

One precise way to show that a client's score is different from the general population and similar to a clinical sample is with a Z-score (Corcoran, 2008, 1997; Corcoran & Hozack, 2012; Corcoran & Vandiver, 1996; Thomlison & Corcoran, 2008). A Z-score is a standardized score that has a mean of zero, a standard deviation of 1, and generally ranges from −3 to +3.

A Z-score is easily determined by subtracting the sample mean from the client score and then dividing that difference by the standard deviation. With a Z-score, a social worker can compare a client's score with the norm by determining what percentage of the sample scored higher or lower than the client—in other words, what percentage have problems more and less severe. This is done by first finding the Z-value in Table 47.1 and then examining the percent above and below the client's score.

This information allows the social worker to interpret the client's score relative to the general population and a clinical sample. For example, if a client had a Z-score of 0.1 based on parameters from the general population, then he or she would be just about average and there would be little reason to aver treatment necessity. However, if the norm was from a clinical sample and the Z-score was 0.1 or so, it is reasonable to assert a need for treatment because the client is similar to the average person who is already in treatment. It is best to calculate a Z-score from the general population and a clinical sample, if the normative data are available. For example, a client with a Z-score of 1 from a general population would be different from 84% of the general population, and the social worker could conclude that there is likely a need for treatment. A score of −1 with a clinical sample is more severe than 16.5% of those patients in treatment, and it is still likely that treatment is necessary.

The use of Z-scores for determining treatment necessity is relatively easy after a few tries. The proportions above and below the level of the client's score enables the social worker to make rather precise statements of a client's performance compared to clinical and nonclinical samples. These data are persuasive for illustrating treatment necessity. In general, it is difficult to argue that treatment is not needed when the client is different from the general population or similar to a sample of patients already in treatment.

The above procedures allow the social worker to make comparison to a general and clinical sample for any instrument. The procedures, however, do involve some time, around 10 minutes. This time simply is not available for many clinical social workers in routine daily practice. This problem is easily solved with an Internet service (www.Do-I-need-therapy.com or www.Is-therapy-effective.com). These websites provide this

TABLE 47.1 Table of Z-Scores and Proportions

	Proportion of Score				
Z-Score	Lower Than	Higher Than	Z-Score	Lower Than	Higher Than
−3.0	0.13	99.87	0.1	53.98	46.02
−2.9	0.19	99.81	0.2	57.93	42.07
−2.8	0.26	99.74	0.3	61.79	38.21
−2.7	0.35	99.65	0.4	65.54	34.46
−2.6	0.47	99.53	0.5	69.15	30.85
−2.5	0.62	99.38	0.6	72.58	27.42
−2.4	0.82	99.18	0.7	75.80	24.20
−2.3	1.07	99.93	0.8	78.81	21.19
−2.2	1.39	98.61	0.9	81.59	18.41
−2.1	1.79	98.21	1.0	84.13	15.87
−2.0	2.29	97.73	1.1	86.43	13.57
−1.9	2.87	97.13	1.2	88.49	11.51
−1.8	3.59	96.41	1.3	90.32	9.68
−1.7	4.46	95.54	1.4	91.92	8.08
−1.6	5.48	94.52	1.5	93.32	6.68
−1.5	6.68	93.32	1.6	94.52	5.48
−1.4	8.08	91.92	1.7	95.54	4.46
−1.3	9.68	90.32	1.8	96.41	3.59
−1.2	11.51	88.49	1.9	97.13	2.87
−1.1	13.57	86.43	2.0	97.73	2.27
−1.0	15.87	84.13	2.1	98.21	1.79
−0.9	18.41	81.59	2.2	98.61	1.39
−0.8	21.19	78.81	2.3	98.93	1.07
−0.7	24.20	75.80	2.4	99.18	0.82
−0.6	27.42	72.58	2.5	99.38	0.62
−0.5	30.85	69.15	2.6	99.53	0.47
−0.4	34.46	65.54	2.7	99.65	0.35
−0.3	38.21	61.79	2.8	99.74	0.26
−0.2	42.07	57.93	2.9	99.81	0.19
−0.1	46.02	53.98	3.0	99.87	0.13

information for 10 major mental health symptoms: alcohol abuse, anger issues, anxiety, depression, drug abuse, eating problems, impulsivity, obsessions and compulsions, stress, and suicide. What would have once taken the social worker 10 or more minutes to complete is now done in .067 seconds with graphic, easy interpretation and clinically useful assessments. An illustration of the reports is displayed in Figure 47.1, which is from the following Case Study.

RAPID ASSESSMENT TOOLS AND DIFFERENTIAL DIAGNOSIS

A broadband measure, like the SF-36 or SF-12, and a narrowband measure do more than allow the social worker to determine the magnitude or severity of a presenting problem to evidence treatment necessity. RATs can also greatly facilitate the task of differential diagnosis. For example, whereas the SF-36 produces general scores

Your total score on this measure of depression is 32.0, and is shown below by the bold arrow. The area to the left of the arrow represents those with equal or less severe depression than you, and the area to the right represents those with more severe depression than you.

General

When compared to the general population of 2,293 adults, your depression score suggests that 99.99% of the typical adult has less severe depresssion than you and 0.01% have more severe depression.

Clinical

When compared to a sample of 1,340 adults who are already receiving therapy or counseling you are in the 44.31 percentile. This means that about 55.69% of patients in therapy or counseling have depression more severe than you, and you are as depressed as 44.31% of people in therapy.

Clinical Female

When compared to a sample of 373 *women* who are already in therapy or counseling you are in the 25.41 percentile. This means that about 74.59% of patients in therapy or counseling have depression more severe than you, and you are as depressed as 25.41% of women in therapy.

Compared to these groups, what is your opininon? Do you think you need therapy or counseling for depression? Does depression effect how well you function on a daily basis? If you answered "yes" to these questions, then you should obtain a referral to see a mental health professional.

If you do go for therapy or counseling, you might want to <u>print this report</u> and use it to discuss your depression with your therapist or counselor.

Figure 47.1 Easy RATs initial assessment.

on health and mental health, it also has more specific items and subscales of symptomatology, such as depression and social functioning; items and subscale scores, then, may very well point the clinician to a more specific differential diagnosis.

Differential diagnosis is essentially distinguishing one particular mental health condition from another. Although a provisional and final diagnosis are codified with the DSM-V (American Psychiatric Association, 2013), the use of rapid assessment instruments can help the social worker identify the particular pathology and concomitantly quantify this severity to observe change over the course of treatment and afterward. Moreover, a differential diagnosis is essential if the practitioner is to develop an effective treatment plan. If the client's condition is not differentiated from similar ones, a viable and effective treatment plan is impossible. When benefits of treatment are gleaned nonetheless under circumstances of misdiagnosing a mental health condition, this is likely due to nonspecific factors in treatment, such as a caring relationship, or mostly a matter of chance—dumb luck, if you will.

One of the most critical examples of this is the distinction between the bipolar affective disorders, delusional disorders, schizoaffective disorder, and the schizophrenic disorders. These mental disorders are likely to include abnormality of affect, such as an elevated, expansive, or irritable mood. All might also include disturbed cognition, such as grandiose and persecutory delusions, catatonia, or flight of ideas. Most important, all may evidence psychotic features. The distinctions are subtle but critical: the psychotic symptoms of the mood disorder do not occur in the absence of a prominent mood symptom, whereas psychotic symptoms may be manifested in the others independent of mood symptoms. Similarly, the manic or depressive symptoms may be evident in the schizophrenic disorders but are often not sufficient in duration or magnitude to warrant a diagnosis of one of the mood disorders. In spite of these differences, social workers—like other professionals—are quick to assume that if there are presenting symptoms of psychosis, it is likely a schizophrenic disorder. In fact, however, bipolar disorders are more prevalent than schizophrenia (APA, 2013), which should suggest the likelihood of a mood disorder, or possibly even a stroke, which has a defining feature of disorientation, or being out of touch with reality (i.e., a psychotic feature). As this illustration suggests, an inaccurate differential diagnosis may result in a treatment plan for schizophrenia when the focus of treatment should be for a mood disorder or the immediate admission to the emergency room in the event of a stroke.

RAPID ASSESSMENT TOOLS TO MONITOR CLIENT CHANGE AND GOAL ATTAINMENT

Another use of RATs is to monitor client change and evaluate practice (Corcoran & Fischer, 2013b). They have been used for quite some time by conscientious practitioners for these purposes. RATs are typically administered before, during, and after treatment to see whether the client's problem has changed and goal has been obtained. RATs may be used as a measurement of the treatment goal by establishing an ideal score on the instrument, one that reflects a successful outcome to be reached by the end of therapy. In the example of Olive given later, the goal of treatment was for her score to be around 6 plus or minus, which reflects depression at a nonclinical level and is about average for the general population. For a client to change from being similar to other clients to being similar to the general population would be a reasonable definition of "clinical significance."

Measurements before, during, and after treatment compose a simple AB design where scores during the treatment phase (i.e., B) are compared to the scores before treatment begins (i.e., A). This is known as self-referenced comparison. There are three essential elements in this approach to using instruments to monitor the treatment process: (1) a simple research design that reflects the treatment process, such as a treatment period (i.e., B phase) compared to a time of no treatment (i.e., A phase); (2) a systematic means to observe the client, such as an RAT or a broadband measure; and (3) the interpretation of scores by plotting them to see whether the client's behavior has changed. There are, of course, more sophisticated research designs and statistical interpretation of the data (see, e.g., Bloom, Fischer, & Orme, 2006). At minimum, however, the social worker needs to be able to see that change has occurred over the course of treatment.

For example, in the case study to follow, Olive enters therapy for depression and scored 32 on Lovibond and Lovibond's (1995) depression scale as found on Do-I-need-therapy.com and displayed in Figure 47.1. Olive completed the instrument twice to collect "retrospective baseline data" where she was instructed to answer the items she felt "at her worst," which was a score of 32 and "currently," which had a score of 32. Both are reflected under Sessions 1 and 2 in Figure 47.2. The instrument was administered weekly for seven weekly clinical sessions, which are reflected on Sessions 3 through 9. At the follow-up reported in Session 10 Olive's score was 7, which reflects the treatment goal. To compare her performance over the course of treatment, the scores are plotted on a graph for visual analysis of clinically significant change, as illustrated in the lower panel of Figure 47.2.

Visual analysis clearly requires clinical judgment, as does any statistical analysis. It must be stressed that scores on an assessment tool are simply supplemental information and not a substitute for clinical judgment. By using a simple design and RATs where scores are understood by visual interpretation, the social worker has additional information to evaluate treatment and evidence its effectiveness.

CASE ILLUSTRATION

Admittedly, the uses of RATs to evidence treatment necessity and throughout the treatment process are chores unfamiliar to many professional social workers. At first, it seems difficult to add this approach to the overburdened demands of practice. The following case illustrates how it is easy to determine treatment necessity (www.Do-I-need-therapy.com) and treatment effectiveness (www.Is-therapy-effective.com); both sites provide the same content. Olive is a college-educated woman in her late fifties who works in administration. For the past year or so, she has been feeling apathetic and is prone to crying spells. She reports she has not been able to sleep well, often waking up several times a night and early in the morning. When she is awake, she does not want to get out of bed. She avoids her family and friends. Olive was referred to a social worker after disclosing to her primary care physician that she had thoughts of suicide.

At intake, the social worker thought Olive likely had a mood disorder, and she was given the depression scale from Do-I-need-therapy.com

Your total score on this measure of depression is 7.0, and is shown below by the bold arrow. The area to the left of the arrow represents those with equal or less severe depression than you, and the area to the right represents those with more severe depression than you.

General

When compared to the general population of 2,293 adults, your depression score suggests that 65.8% of the typical adult has less severe depresssion than you and 34.2% have more severe depression.

Clinical

When compared to a sample of 1,340 adults who are already receiving therapy or counseling you are in the 1.34 percentile. This means that about 98.66% of patients in therapy or counseling have depression more severe than you, and you are as depressed as 1.34% of people in therapy.

Clinical Female

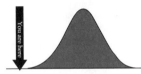

When compared to a sample of 373 *women* who are already in therapy or counseling you are in the 0.46 percentile. This means that about 99.54% of patients in therapy or counseling have depression more severe than you, and you are as depressed as 0.46% of women in therapy.

Scores Over Time

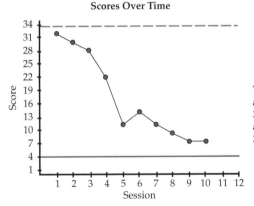

The dashed line represents the average clinical population acore, 33.73. The solid line represents the average general population score, 3.95.

Figure 47.2 Easy RATs treatment evaluation.

and the mental health survey short form (Ware, Kosinski, & Keller, 1994). Remembering that the average score is 50 and 35 for the general population and clinical samples, Olive's score at the beginning of treatment was 32, and reflects lower mental health status than about 99% of the general population while being similar to the typical psychiatric patient.

The social worker was able to reach a preliminary differential diagnosis of dysthymia because her symptoms were not due to a medical condition and were not physiological effects of substances, and there had been no evidence of an elevated or expansive mood, which would suggest one of the bipolar disorders. The differential diagnosis must be considered preliminary because at this point in the assessment it is not known whether Olive's condition has lasted at least two years, a criterion of this form of clinical depression. To help the social worker with this differential diagnosis, Olive was also asked to complete the RAT as representative of when she felt "at her worst" and how she felt "currently." Aside from showing that Olive's depression is relatively stable, these numbers do not tell the social worker much until interpreted relative to the general population or a clinical sample.

Using the website Is-therapy-effective.com, Olive was compared to a sample from the general population that had a mean depression score of about 5 with a standard deviation of 6.0. A sample of psychiatric patients had a mean of 32 and a standard deviation of 9.3. As illustrated in Figure 47.1, Olive's depression score was 32, which suggests she is more depressed than 99% of the general population and more severe than 44% of patients already receiving therapy; for women only, Olive is more depressed than 25% of the clinical sample. As for a treatment goal, Olive and her social worker decide that an appropriate goal would be to feel "as happy as the next person." This was operationalized as a score similar to the general population. Olive's progress is monitored by having her complete the scale throughout the treatment progress and at a one-month follow-up assessment. This is illustrated in the lower panel of Figure 47.2 and shows consistent decrease in depression. The case also evidences "clinical significance" in that Olive is no longer similar to patients at the end of treatment and quite similar to the typical person from the general population; this continued at the follow-up assessment.

SUMMARY

This case illustrates that RATs are useful to show the need for treatment, determine a differential diagnosis, monitor client progress over the course of clinical intervention, and set goals; that this is especially so when RATs are completed on the Internet. In summary, RATs serve three functions: (1) as evidence of treatment necessity and in determining an accurate diagnosis; (2) as a tool to monitor client progress; and (3) as an operationalization of a treatment goal. That is, they are useful almost from the beginning and throughout the course of clinical practice. When both broadband measures of mental health problems and narrowband measures of the client's particular problem are used, the social worker has additional tools to evidence that treatment is necessary and, it is hoped, effective.

WEBSITES

Health and mental health status: http://quality-metric.com; and http://www.outcome-trust.org.
Mental health assessments and treatment evaluation: www.Do-I-need-therapy.com; www.Is-therapy-effective.com
Mental health symptoms for DSM-V diagnoses: http://psychiatry.org.dsm5

References

American Psychiatric Association. (2013). *Diagnostic and statistical manual of mental disorders, fifth edition.* Washington, DC: Author.

Arkava, M. L., & Snow, M. (1978). *Psychological tests and social work.* Springfield, IL: Thomas.

Bloom, M., Fischer, J., & Orme, J. G. (2006). *Evaluating practice: Guidelines for the accountable professional.* Needham Heights, MA: Allyn & Bacon.

Corcoran, K., & Fischer, J. (2013b). *Measures for clinical practice: A sourcebook (Vol. 2: Adults).* New York, NY: Oxford.

Corcoran, K., & Fischer, J. (2013a). *Measures for clinical practice: A sourcebook (Vol. 1: Couples, families and children).* New York, NY: Oxford.

Corcoran, K. (1997).The use of rapid assessment instruments as outcomes measures. In E. Mullen & J. L. Magnabosco (Eds.), *Outcomes measurements in the human services* (pp. 137–143). Washington, DC: NASW Press.

Corcoran, K., & Hozack, N. (2012). The use of rapid assessment instruments as outcomes measures. In J. L. Magnabosco (Ed.), *Outcomes measurements in the human services* (2nd ed.) (pp. 127–143). Washington, DC: NASW Press.

Corcoran, K., & Vandiver, V. L. (1996). *Maneuvering the maze of managed care: Skills for mental health practitioners.* New York, NY: Free Press.

Gorin, S., & Moniz, C. (2014). Health and mental health policy. In M. Reisch (Ed.), *Social policy and social justice* (pp. 405–430). Thousand Oaks, CA: Sage.

Jordon, C & Franklin, C. (2011). *Clinical assessments for social workers: Qualitative and quantitative methods.* Chicago, IL: Lyceum Books.

Lovibond, S. H., & Lovibond, P. F. (1995). *Manual for the depression anxiety and stress scales.* Sydney, Australia: Psychological Foundation. www.psy.unsw.au/Groups/DASS.

Nugent, W. R., Sieppert, J., & Hudson, W. W. (2001). *Practice evaluation for the 21st century.* Pacific Grove, CA: Brooks/Cole.

Thomlison, B., & Corcoran, K. (2008). *Evidence-based internship: A field manual.* New York, NY: Oxford University Press.

Ware, J. E., Kosinski, M., & Keller, S. D. (1994). *SF-36 physical and mental health summary scales: A user's manual.* Boston, MA: Medical Outcomes Trust. Available from http://www.outcomes-trust.org.

48   Bipolar and Related Disorders

Elizabeth C. Pomeroy

The *Diagnostic and Statistical Manual of Mental Disorders, Fifth Edition* (DSM-5) has created a distinct category for Bipolar and Related Disorders (BP), separating it from Depressive Disorders (APA, 2013). The six mental disorders covered in this section are characterized as chronic, complex, disruptive, and multifactorial involving *mood lability* and extremes of behavior. The term *multifactorial disorder* refers to one caused by the interaction of genetic and environmental factors. *Mood lability* is defined as frequent or intense mood changes or shifts that are outside of normal experience. These characteristics present substantial challenges for diagnosis and treatment (APA, 2013).

Bipolar Disorders in the DSM-5 are organized around three different types of episodes that, in turn, serve as building blocks for determining specific diagnoses. An episode is a period of time during which a client evidences a particular set of symptoms and as a result, experiences a pronounced alteration in mood and/or a change in his or her social, vocational, and recreational functioning. Specifically, the three episodic states are major depressive, manic, and hypomanic. In addition, the Mixed Features Specifier replaces the Mixed Episode in the DSM IV-TR. Additionally, the DSM-5 includes developmentally appropriate symptom thresholds for children to facilitate better reliability of diagnoses and more targeted treatment for children. Furthermore, increased energy/activity has been added as a core symptom of Manic Episodes and Hypomanic Episodes (APA, 2013). The goal is to provide specific diagnostic criteria while still providing some dimensional criteria and a lifespan perspective when treating individuals with Bipolar Disorder.

Two of the diagnoses in this section are determined by the etiological factors relevant to the illness. Specifically, Bipolar Disorder Associated with Another Medical Condition is used when a bipolar episode is directly related to a diagnosable organic problem. Similarly, Substance-Induced Bipolar Disorder is used when the problematic bipolar episode is directly related to the use of a recreational drug, prescribed medication, or a toxin (e.g., lead, carbon monoxide) (APA, 2013).

The most severe disorders in this cluster include Bipolar I and Bipolar II. Assessment of these disorders is based on the number and pattern of episodes the individual has experienced in his or her lifetime. Attention is given to the severity of symptoms and specific characteristics of the most recent episode in the coding scheme (APA, 2013). Cyclothymic Disorder represents a more chronic condition that is generally less disruptive to the individual's functioning. In Cyclothymic Disorder, an alternating pattern of mood states is present but not as severe as major depressive or hypomanic episodes. For a diagnosis of Cyclothymic Disorder, the symptoms must be present for at least two years.

Finally, a broad diagnostic category of Unspecified or Other Specified Disorders is included in this chapter of the DSM-5. These diagnoses replace the earlier Not Otherwise Specified diagnostic specifier, which was overused and found lacking in terms of clinical utility. These diagnoses are used when an individual's symptoms fail to fit any of the more specific diagnoses and are not attributable to the direct physiological effects of a substance or a general medical condition. The four new diagnostic terms for Other Specified Bipolar and Related Disorders found in the DSM-5 (APA, 2013) are as follows:

1. Short Duration (2–3 days) Hypomanic Episodes and Major Depressive Episodes

2. Major Depressive Episodes and Hypomanic Episodes characterized by insufficient symptoms
3. Hypomanic Episode without Prior Major Depressive Episode
4. Short Duration (less than 2 years) Cyclothymia (APA, 2013; p. 148).

The Bipolar and Related Disorders section in the DSM-5 includes a comparatively large number of specifiers, including some that are reflected in the fourth and fifth digit of the numeric coding. A full description of the relevant specifiers is included in each disorder's diagnostic criteria. Practitioners are encouraged to take time and gather a full psychosocial history in order to ascertain the specifiers that might pertain to a particular diagnosis. It should be noted that specifiers are only used if the full criteria for a diagnosis are met (APA, 2013).

From a lifespan approach, the average age of onset for Bipolar I Disorder is 18 years; however, in rare instances it can begin in childhood. It tends to be chronic in nature, and unfortunately suicide is a common risk factor. In Bipolar II disorder, major depressive episodes alternate with hypomanic episodes. The average age of onset is in a person's mid-twenties or later. Persons with Bipolar II disorder who are experiencing hypomania are at greatest risk of suicide (MacQueen & Young, 2001). In both types of Bipolar disorders, practitioners should carefully assess clients for suicidal risk.

Advances in science and clinical research over the last quarter of a century have deepened our understanding of the diagnosis and treatment of debilitating mental conditions, including Bipolar Disorder. Individuals experiencing psychotic symptoms of either Depression or Mania, which often coexist with other conditions will likely not seek treatment independently. However, their behavior may well result in others arranging involuntary mental health treatment on their behalf. The clarification of diagnostic criteria in the DSM-5 for Bipolar Disorder is expected to help in clinical assessment and treatment.

When assessing someone suspected to have a mood disorder, particular attention should be focused on the person's emotional functioning. Although a thorough history of the presenting problem is required to make a diagnosis, it may be difficult for the client to present detailed and accurate information. People who are severely depressed can be virtually mute, and those experiencing manic mood states may be unable to express themselves coherently. Clearly, the reliability of self-report is very uncertain if someone is experiencing psychotic symptoms. Someone with a history of psychiatric treatment may fear rehospitalization and deliberately minimize symptoms. Consequently, it is often helpful to gather data from collateral sources, such as close friends or relatives, employers, or other professionals to specify both the timing and severity of symptoms.

There are many challenges and complexities to diagnosing Bipolar Disorder. Individuals assessed on the basis of current clinical features alone are often misdiagnosed because of an overlap of symptoms, especially with depression. Assessment may be further complicated by comorbid conditions (medical, psychiatric, and substance problems). Understanding age-associated variations in the presentation of Bipolar Disorder across the lifespan is critical. Being able to differentiate age-appropriate behaviors from the symptoms of bipolarity is especially important when dealing with children. The DSM-5 Task Force made a concerted effort to reduce the number of children diagnosed with Bipolar Disorder by creating a new disorder, Disruptive Mood Dysregulation Disorder, under the Depressive Disorders category of the DSM-5. Knowledge of diagnostic specifiers and their pharmacological implications is key to successful assessment and will greatly improve the treatment of this lifelong disorder.

Quite a number of rating scales and tools can be useful when assessing depressive symptoms in Bipolar Disorder. The Patient Health Questionnaire (PHQ-9) is a simple, self-administered measure of depression severity that was developed and studied in primary care settings. It generally takes under 10 minutes to complete. The PHQ-9 scores each of the nine DSM-5 "Major Depressive Episode" diagnostic criteria (APA, 2013). Individuals rate their problems/feelings over the "past 2 weeks" on a 4-point scale (from 0 = not at all to 3 = nearly every day) with total scores ranging from 0 to 27. When total score is under 5, depression severity is seen as none to minimal. Totals ranging from 5, 10, 15, and 20 represent thresholds for mild, moderate, moderately severe, and severe depression, respectively (Kroenke & Spritzer, 2002). In order to assess manic symptoms in adults, two self-report instruments have been shown to have excellent reliability and validity. The

Internal State Scale (ISS) (Bauer, Crits-Cristoph, & Ball, 1991) is a 15-item instrument in which clients indicate the intensity of their mood by marking a line denoting the level of severity of symptoms. The scale has four subscales, including well-being, perceived conflict, depression, and activation. Mania is assessed by a well-being score equal to or higher than 125 and an activation score equal to or greater than 200. Each item is "biphasic." For example, on the items indicating well-being, clients who mark the lower end of the line (scale) are assessed to have depressive symptoms, whereas clients who mark the upper end of the line are assessed to have manic symptoms.

The Mood Disorder Questionnaire is an easy to administer, 13-item questionnaire with "yes" and "no" responses. The instrument is designed to measure the presence of symptoms related to Bipolar Disorder. A total score of seven or more "yes" responses indicates that symptoms of Bipolar Disorder are present. The instrument has excellent reliability (alpha = .90). Studies have indicated excellent discriminant and concurrent validity (Corcoran & Fischer, 2013).

For bipolar clients who are unable to complete a self-report instrument, the Young Mania Rating Scale (YMRS) (Young, Biggs, & Myers, 1978) can be completed by a skilled practitioner. The scale contains 11 items measuring internal mood states and behaviors experienced by the client and reported to the practitioner. Symptoms of mania are rated on grades of severity, some items graded on a 0 to 4 scale and others are graded from 0 to 8. Higher scores indicate greater symptom severity and more psychopathology. Scores may range between 0 and 56. (Youngstrom, Danielson, Findling, Gracious, & Calabrese, 2002). (Also see Chapter 47 for discussion of free Web-based assessments, including for depression.)

EMERGENCY CONSIDERATIONS

Assessing and managing suicide risk is one of the most important components of clinical practice, especially when treating individuals for Bipolar Disorder. In some situations, people experiencing severe emotional distress may constitute a danger to themselves or others. Suicidal thinking is part of the diagnostic criteria for a major depressive and hypomanic episode of Bipolar disorders. In these situations, practitioners must attend to

issues regarding the client's safety and secure whatever level of supervision and treatment is necessary. A comprehensive suicide risk assessment will help identify the major risk factors for suicidal behavior. The risk of suicide attempts increases if clients exhibit an anxiety disorder and/or substance abuse disorder. Also, risk of death by suicide is higher in males and comorbid with anxiety disorders (Simon et al., 2007). Risk management strategies must be ongoing and should include a crisis plan that involves emergency resources such as emergency departments, telephone crisis centers, and local inpatient/outpatient mental health services. The Internet can be efficiently exploited.

Gender Differences

Gender differences in mental health utilization and symptom reporting as well as gender roles and stereotypes can affect accurate diagnosis and treatment of psychological disorders. Conformity to traditional gender roles for men, which emphasize emotional stoicism and self-reliance, may negatively impact the expression of symptoms, need for support and willingness to seek help. Women are socialized to be more emotionally expressive and are more likely to disclose symptoms and seek help. Men may be more likely to have problems with violence and/or substance abuse and women to have a history of suicide attempts (Baldassano, 2006). Female gender is a significant predictor of being diagnosed with depression; even when presentation symptoms and scores on standardized measures of depression are similar to males (World Health Organization [WHO], 2002). Gender sensitivity training and strategies aimed at decreasing biases and barriers to help seeking have important diagnostic and therapeutic implications. According to Kriegshauser, Sajatovic, & Jenkins et al. (2010) women rely on strong social supports as a coping mechanism for Bipolar Disorder, a positive factor in treatment adherence. For men, who may perceive fewer high-quality social supports, adjunctive social networks such as group therapies or advocacy initiatives (Web-based or in person) might be particularly helpful.

SOCIAL SUPPORT SYSTEMS

Bipolar disorders are serious, recurring, chronic illnesses that can overwhelm support resources and cause impairment in social, occupational, or other important areas of personal functioning. The assessment of social functioning is a significant feature of the *Diagnostic and Statistical Manual* (APA, 2013). The goals for treatment must be more than just a reduction in clinical symptoms; they must also seek to improve social functioning. Recent studies have found that social impairments in individuals with Bipolar disorders were similar in type and severity to those seen in individuals with schizophrenia (Dickerson et al., 2001). Providing support for an individual with a chronic illness is inherently stressful. Conflicts between family, friends, and the person with the disorder can arise due to disruptive thoughts and behaviors and extreme mood swings on the part of the symptomatic individual. Caregiver burden is high and largely neglected in Bipolar disorders (Ogilvie, Morant, & Goodwin, 2005). Research attests to the low rates of treatment compliance for many bipolar patients. Providing clients and caregivers with realistic expectations and practical advice on illness management along with sources of support, such as peer and psycho-educational support groups, can help mitigate the impact of the illness. Caregivers should be encouraged to meet with others to share coping strategies. Joining a group can be hard for individuals experiencing symptoms of the disease. Treatment strategies for individuals with Bipolar Disorder must consider the stigma associated with the disease, the impact of symptoms on social functioning, and the risk of not maintaining positive social networks, which is high in this population.

Differential Diagnosis

Bipolar disorders are a set of complex illnesses with many challenges and conditions involved in differential diagnosis separation. A delay in diagnosis equates to a delay in correct treatment. The first step when diagnosing Bipolar disorders is to rule out substance use or abuse (e.g., alcohol, drugs, prescription drugs) or a general medical condition as the cause of symptoms. This disorder goes primarily underdiagnosed due to misdiagnosis as major depressive disorder (MDD). Other disorders involved in differential diagnosis include other psychotic disorders, such as schizophrenia or schizoaffective disorder; anxiety disorders; and, in children, conduct disorders and Attention-Deficit/Hyperactivity Disorder (ADHD). Its developmentally distinct presentation in children makes diagnosis difficult with this population. Just as giving an antidepressant without a mood stabilizer (primary treatment for unipolar depression) may destabilize someone with Bipolar Disorder; giving a child a stimulant (primary treatment for ADHD) can lead to mood destabilization in children with Bipolar Disorder.

Furthermore, children are increasingly being diagnosed with Bipolar Disorder rather than ADHD or Conduct Disorder. In order to be diagnosed with a Bipolar I Disorder, the child must display symptoms of Mania. However, the practitioner should be careful not to make this diagnosis without a full understanding of the family situation. Some children can display manic symptoms when they are under stress. These symptoms may disappear once the stressful situation is remedied. The differential diagnosis involves the depressive episode in children with Bipolar Disorder. Children with ADHD or Conduct Disorder rarely display the depressive symptoms that are part of the criteria for Bipolar Disorder in children. In fact, Bipolar Disorder in Children should be considered a rare occurrence and a thorough psychosocial history is needed to rule out other possible disorders before a conclusive diagnosis of Bipolar Disorder is reached.

Cultural Considerations

Cultural variations impact symptom expression, and therefore, they can affect the diagnostic process. Addressing cross-cultural and gender differences is paramount when treating individuals who suffer from Bipolar Disorder. Cultural attitudes also influence whether individuals will seek help and which clinical pathways may be most effective. Multiple studies have found that individuals from Hispanic and Asian backgrounds are more likely to report physical ailments and less likely to report emotional symptoms when suffering from mental illness. In many cultures, the stigma surrounding mental illness is very strong, and the pressure "not to shame the family" often leads to underreporting symptoms. Another caution relates to the tendency for minority group members to receive more serious or more stigmatized psychiatric labels. For example, there is some evidence that Caucasians are more likely to be diagnosed with Bipolar I Disorder, while minority clients with the same symptom presentation are diagnosed with Schizophrenic Disorders (Neighbors, Trierweiler, Ford, & Muroff (2003).

These findings underscore the need to address racial and ethnocentric bias during the diagnostic process. According to the National Comorbidity Survey, Hispanic clients had surprisingly high prevalence rates of all affective disorders compared to the rates in non-Hispanic white persons and African Americans (Kessler, Chiu, Demler, & Walters, 2005. Although these higher rates may be due, in part, to the stress of acculturation and low socioeconomic status (SES), the higher reported incidence of affective disorders among Hispanic clients may be a result of communication barriers between client and practitioner. Cultural sensitivity education and training for English-speaking practitioners are important aspects of competent mental health practice.

The prevalence of mood disorders seems to be similar across subcultures, although it occurs more frequently in economically depressed areas. The practitioner should be aware of common variations in the diagnosis and presentation of mood disorders based on diversity. For example, women are roughly twice as likely as men to be diagnosed with a depressive disorder. In the United States, men have been raised to minimize emotional expression regardless of their internal state. On the other hand, women have been taught to use emotional expression as a tool for getting their needs met. Clearly, these gender differences concerning emotional expressiveness can influence the practitioner's perception and diagnosis of the client. Generally, practitioners should be careful to avoid overdiagnosing women with depression, as well as underdiagnosing men.

Social Support

Bipolar I and Bipolar II disorders are considered severe mental illnesses. Symptoms associated with these disorders cause serious impairment in the client's social and occupational functioning. Family members and close friends of a person with an affective disorder can feel confused, frustrated, fearful, or angry about the person's dramatic change in mood and inability to cope with daily life events. Families and friends may not understand the problem and why the client cannot just snap out of it.

A psycho-educational group for individuals with similar problems may be an additional source of support for the person suffering from a mood disorder. For example, there are support groups for persons suffering from Bipolar disorders as well as groups for those affected by depression.

These groups provide individuals with a sense of belonging, education concerning the illness, and mutual support. Mental health practitioners conduct some groups; others are organized and run by persons who have previous experience with the disorder (either clients themselves or their family members). With the recent increases in knowledge concerning depression and bipolar moods, there has been a corresponding increase in the numbers of organizations and agencies providing specialized support for individuals with these disorders.

For many people with affective disorders, joining a group may be problematic because of the person's symptoms or because of group availability. Similar constraints may also apply to members of the person's social support system. The Internet contains a wealth of information, including organizations specializing in the support and treatment of persons with mood disorders, online chat rooms and bulletin boards, and current reports and articles related to particular disorders. At the end of this chapter is a list of some useful Internet resources.

Following are two case examples demonstrating a strengths perspective approach.

Case Example 1

Client name: Mary Anne Philips
Age: 30 years old
Ethnicity: African American
Marital status: Married
Children: Danya, age 6

You are a caseworker in the emergency room of a large urban hospital. You work the day shift from 8 A.M. to 5 P.M. Several hours before you came to work, the police brought the client to the emergency room in restraints. The following information was gathered from the police at intake. The police state that Mary Anne Philips, a 30-year-old African American woman, was found dancing half-naked in the middle of a busy intersection in the center of the city at approximately 2 A.M. She appeared to be high on drugs when the police approached her. She told the police that she had not taken any drugs and that she was "just high on life." She said she was not doing anything wrong, just "having a party." Witnesses stated that Mary Anne had started the evening at a local restaurant and bar. She had been with a couple of gentlemen who seemed to know her. She began telling jokes and buying drinks for everyone at the bar.

At first, she seemed like a person just having fun, but she got louder and rowdier as the night progressed. The two men left, but she stayed at the restaurant, saying loudly, "I'm just getting warmed up here." She sang and danced and finally ended up shoving all the glasses onto the floor and standing on the bar, talking as fast as she could. Customers got irritated, and the bartender asked her to leave. She ignored his request and started singing at the top of her lungs. Finally, the bartender had to force her off the bar and push her out the door. At that point, she began dancing and singing in the street. The bartender told police that she had no more than two drinks throughout the evening. When the police attempted to get Mary Anne out of the road, she became belligerent and began swearing at the officers. They had to take her out of the middle of the intersection by force and handcuff her to get her into the police car. Lab tests indicated no evidence of excessive alcohol or other drugs. The physician on duty had prescribed a sedative, and Mary Anne went to sleep at approximately 5 A.M.

You go to see Mary Anne at 9:30 A.M. She is lying in bed, quietly staring at the ceiling. She seems very subdued in comparison to the description of the previous night. She glances at you as you enter the room but makes no attempt to sit up. You tell her who you are and your reasons for wanting to talk to her. Mary Anne makes no response to your introduction. You ask if she has any relatives you could call for her. She looks over at you and says, "I just want to die. If it weren't for my baby, I'd have been dead a long time ago."

"What's your baby's name?" you ask. "Danya," Mary Anne replies. "I'm such a lousy mother lying here like this. I should be home taking care of her." "Where is Danya now?" you ask.

"She's with my sister. She stayed with my sister last night," Mary Anne responds. "I knew I was racing, so I took her over to my sister's house." "You were racing?" you query.

"Yeah, you know, I start racing sometimes, feeling real good and full of energy like nothing can stop me," Mary Anne says. "But not now; I feel lousy now, like I just want to be left alone to die." "Can you tell me what happened last night?" you ask. "It's like living on a roller coaster," Mary Anne tells you. "One minute you're way up there, and the next minute you're in the blackest hole you can imagine." "And last night, you were way up there?" you query. "Yeah, I was just feeling good and having

a good time. It's like you're racing and you can't slow down. Like you're high or something, but I didn't take any drugs. I don't do drugs. This just comes over me sometimes, and I feel like I could take on the world." "Have you ever felt this way before?" you ask. "Oh yeah, up and down, that's how I am," Mary Anne says. "So, sometimes you feel really good and up, and then, sometimes you feel really down. Is that right?" you ask. "Yeah, I'm scared I'm beginning to crash now. It's bad when you come down. It feels real bad," she says. "It lasts for weeks and weeks … just down all the time." "How often does this happen, going from one extreme to another?" you ask. "Once a day or once a week or once a month?" "See, for a few weeks I feel great. I can do anything—stay up all night having a good time. I don't sleep or eat or slow down. I just keep on going for a week, maybe two. Then, I begin to crash."

"Do you hear voices or see things when you're feeling high?" you ask. "No, except for my own voice. I can't stop talking either. Gets me into trouble, sometimes," Mary Anne admits.

"What else happens when you're feeling high?" you ask. "I want to party. I can party all night when I'm high. I'm the life of the party," Mary Anne says glumly. "Have you ever gotten in trouble before, like you did last night?" you ask. "Oh yeah," Mary Anne agrees. "I've gotten thrown out of places lots of times, but I usually just move on down the street." "Are you employed?" you ask. "I've tried to keep a job. Just can't seem to stick with it," Mary Anne replies. "How are you feeling right now?" you query. "Feel like hell," she tells you. "This is a rotten way to live, I'm telling you." "How long does the crashing last?" you ask. "Sometimes a few days, sometimes a few weeks," Mary Anne says bleakly. "Describe for me what these down times are like for you," you suggest. "It's like I'm a balloon and someone stuck a needle in me. I'm so sad that nothing looks good. It's hard to get out of bed and face the world.… I sleep and sleep and sleep. When I do get up, I'm so tired that it feels like I'm carrying around invisible weights."

"What kinds of things go through your mind when you feel like this?" "I can't think of anything I want to do," Mary Anne tells you. "I can't seem to make myself think anything all the way through. Like making a decision about something no matter how trivial is just impossible. Sometimes, I just wish I were dead." "Are you wishing you would die now?" you ask. "Not yet … but it usually does get to that point when I crash." "Have you ever seen a doctor for these changes in your mood?" you ask. "One doctor told me it was just a 'female thing,'" Mary Anne states.

"Maybe it's more than a female thing," you suggest. "Maybe there's some medication that could help even out your moods. Would you be willing to talk to a doctor about how you've been feeling?" you ask. "Okay. I guess it wouldn't hurt," Mary Anne says.

The following are some questions you should consider:

- To what extent do you think Mary Anne may be a danger to herself?
- What other information would be useful in determining her risk?
- What would you like to know about Mary Anne's social support system?
- Are there any steps you would take (given the client's permission) to ensure that her support system stays intact?
- What internal and external strengths do you see in Mary Anne's case?
- What is your initial diagnosis? 296.42 Bipolar Disorder, most recent episode manic, moderate, rapid cycling.

The first three digits for bipolar I disorder are 296. The fourth digit indicates the nature of the current episode, with 4 indicating hypomania or mania (as in this case). The fifth digit would not have been used if the most recent episode were hypomania or unspecified. However, as this case indicates the most recent episode as manic, the fifth digit indicates the severity of the episode; 2 indicates a moderate severity, which is an extreme increase in activity and impairment in judgment. The specifier at the end of the diagnosis of rapid cycling is used because at least four episodes of a mood disturbance were seen in the previous 12 months.

Case Example 2

Client name: Sally Tannerg
Age: 36 years old
Ethnicity: Caucasian
Marital status: Married
Occupation: Homemaker
Children: Three children; currently pregnant with her fourth child

Little information was obtained from a phone call interview with Mrs. Tannerg by the intake worker. She stated that her psychiatrist in Massachusetts had referred her to Dr. Browning in Southfork, Oklahoma, for prescription monitoring. Dr. Browning has referred her to the Southfork Counseling Center to see a therapist. She requested an appointment with a therapist and said only that she had been hospitalized recently in Massachusetts before moving with her family to Oklahoma. She stated that it was very important that she begin therapy immediately but did not want to discuss any details of the problems she has been experiencing lately. The intake worker scheduled her for the first available appointment with you later in the week.

Sally Tannerg is an attractive, 36-year-old woman whose warm and effervescent personality is apparent from the first meeting. You notice that she is several months pregnant. She appears eager to get to your office and asks you how long you have lived in Southfork. You explain to her that you moved to Southfork after completing your master's degree two years ago. "When did you move to Southfork?" you ask. Sally wriggles in her chair and enthusiastically begins talking about her husband being relocated to Oklahoma to accept a new position with his company, which develops software for computer companies. She states that she has never lived in the Midwest, having grown up in Boston. She moved to another town in Massachusetts when she got married 10 years ago. "We've been in Southfork for three months, and I feel like a fish out of water," Sally tells you. "I've got most of the responsibility for taking care of my three children and as you can see, I'm about to have another one. Bob, my husband, travels three or four days a week with his job, so I'm stuck at home with my children most of the time … not that I'm complaining. Bob has a good job and he has to travel, but it's a lot of work for me, and I haven't made a lot of friends yet. When I lived in Revere, Massachusetts, I had a lot of neighbors who were young mothers like me with kids, and we'd get together and baby-sit for each other and take our children to different activities. It was nice until I got sick."

"What happened when you got sick?" you ask Sally. "Well, I've always been a pretty optimistic, upbeat type person with a lot of energy. Then, suddenly, I had no energy. I was drained. I was so tired I couldn't move and just got completely depressed. I was suicidal and felt hopeless about everything. I thought "here I am with three little children and I can't get off the couch to take care of them." I felt like a complete failure as a mother, just completely worthless. I didn't want to do anything except sleep and block out the entire world. I wasn't interested in sex with my husband. I didn't care if I lived or died. It just got so bad that the psychiatrist I was seeing put me in the hospital." Sally slinks down in her chair and sighed deeply.

She takes a deep breath and then begins talking again. "Everything just looked so black. I couldn't imagine feeling any worse … and my poor kids. All I could think about was that I would die and they would be motherless. And then I began to feel better. I mean like overnight I felt a whole lot better. I had plenty of energy, and thoughts and ideas just flew through my head and I was on top of the world again. I told the doctor I was just fine and he should let me go home." "How long had you been in the hospital when you began feeling so much better?" you inquire. "About four weeks," Sally says and sighs. "Then I was okay—or so I thought." "So initially, you were really depressed when you went into the hospital, and then you began to feel much better. Were you taking any medication?" you ask. "Well, that's the really scary part about this problem I have. You see, the feeling of being on top of the world didn't last very long. Pretty soon, I was in the depths of despair again, and the medicine wasn't working. So the doctor said I really needed to be on lithium. I didn't want to take anything because by then I knew I was pregnant again. But I was so depressed I didn't know what else to do. I'm so worried about the medicine affecting the baby. The doctor has put me on a low dosage until the baby is born. I'm just keeping my fingers crossed the baby will be okay. Do you think that makes me a bad mother?" "It sounds as if the psychiatrist thinks you really need to be taking lithium right now," you respond. "You're trying to take care of yourself."

"He told me it was absolutely necessary if I wanted to stay out of the hospital," Sally replies. "I never want to go through that experience again. And I'm not sure it's really helping. I have to go get my blood tested every two weeks, and I'm not sure I've got enough of the medication in me to do me any good. I have days when I feel like I can function pretty well, and then there are other days when I feel like I'm sliding into a black hole and can't get out of it. It's an awful feeling." "These feelings of depression just started about a year ago? Is that correct?" you inquire. "Yes, I never felt down in the dumps and completely hopeless like I have this year. You

know, I remember as a child, my father would have periods of deep depression. He was like Dr. Jekyll and Mr. Hyde. Some days he'd be great to be around and he'd play with us and laugh. Other times, he was really scary. He'd sit in a dark room and stare out the window for hours, and if any of us kids did anything that perturbed him, he'd get so angry that he'd take us behind the house and give us all a spanking. You could never tell what kind of mood he'd be in. I was scared of him my whole childhood. I sure hope I'm not turning into someone like him."

"Did you father ever see a doctor about his moods?" you ask. "No, he thinks only crazy people see psychiatrists. I told Bob not to tell my parents I was in the hospital. They would have disowned me. They are strict, conservative Lutherans, and believe me, they wouldn't ever understand. They'd tell me I'd be okay if I went to church."

It seems to you that Sally identifies with her father's mood swings to some degree, and you decide to get more information about her family of origin. "Tell me what it was like for you growing up in Boston," you say.

Sally sits back in her chair and looks out the window. "Well, it was your typical Lutheran family growing up in the sixties and seventies, I guess. I have five siblings—two older brothers, an older sister, and two younger sisters. My parents were strict and fairly religious. We went to church on Sundays every week without fail. My mother cared for us while my father worked. We were a middle-class family, I guess. We never had a lot of money, but we weren't starving to death either. My parents sent us all to a Lutheran school that cost more than public school but wasn't like a private school. I think I have a real problem with feeling guilty about everything. My father reinforced that feeling of guilt all the time. He was very distant and authoritarian. We got punished a lot as children, and although I don't think I really thought so at the time, it was pretty harsh punishment by today's standards. It seemed like I was always in the way when my father got mad, and I got punished more than my sisters and brothers."

"How do you feel about that time growing up?" you inquire. "I guess I consider it a pretty normal childhood," Sally suggests. "All the kids in the Lutheran school I attended grew up much the same way as I did. I think my mother saved us all from my father's wrath on many occasions. She had a way of diverting his attention away from us when we were in the line of fire." "And what is your relationship like now, with your parents?" you ask. "Since I've been in the hospital, I've discovered I have all this anger toward my father," Sally states. "I've been scared of him my whole life, and I'm tired of feeling that way and I hate how he made me feel. I've never really had any self-esteem and have always felt like I'm cowering in the corner afraid of my own shadow because of what he did to me." "And your mother? How do you get along with her?" you ask. "We get along well. We always have. I think we have a lot in common and she's had to put up with a lot, too," Sally says with a smile.

"Do you feel that the way you were raised has something to do with the depression you've been experiencing, or do you think it's unrelated to your childhood experiences?" you ask. "I don't really know," Sally states. "It's something I want to figure out. The doctor told me some of this could be a neurochemical problem. Sometimes, I feel great and full of energy. In fact, it's hard to slow down. I become really talkative and friendly. It's like everything speeds up. Thoughts run through my head really fast, and I can't even sleep when I feel that good. It's like being high." "How often does that happen?" you ask. "It seems to happen about once a month after I've been really depressed," Sally states. "But it doesn't last as long as the depressed periods." "Do you ever feel that you place yourself in high-risk or dangerous situations when you have a 'high' feeling?" you query.

"No, I don't think so," Sally reflects. "I have some pretty fantastic thoughts, but I don't actually do anything. I've got to think about my children and the one on the way." "Okay, so you feel depressed a lot of the time, and sometimes, about once a month, you feel pretty good and full of energy. How long do you usually have that 'high' feeling?" you ask. "It can last from three or four days up to a week before I begin sliding downward again," says Sally. "I always hope it will last longer, but it never does." "So, it sounds like one of your goals is to learn how to cope with some of these ups and downs you've been experiencing," you note. Sally says enthusiastically, "Yes, exactly, I need some help with the best way of coping with these moods, especially during this pregnancy." "Would it be all right with you if I talked to the psychiatrist who is prescribing the medication for you?" you inquire. "I'll need you to sign a consent form." "Absolutely. I'll give you his phone number," Sally asserts. "Would you like to make an appointment on a weekly basis?" you ask.

Sally nods her head vigorously and says, "I'm so glad I've found someone I can talk to who doesn't look at me as if I'm crazy. I definitely want to come once a week to talk to you." "Okay. We'll schedule an appointment for next week," you reply. Sally leaves your office with a little bounce in her step and talks about going to shop for the new baby as you walk her to the reception area.

From this preliminary interview, it would seem that Sally may not have much social support in Southfork.

- How would you go about exploring that issue?
- How important do you think securing local support would be?
- What is your initial diagnosis? 296.89 Bipolar II disorder, depressed, moderate, without full interepisode recovery.

A diagnosis of Bipolar II indicates recurrent major depressive episodes with hypomanic episodes. There are no additional digit specifiers because all five digits are used to indicate the diagnosis. However, you should indicate the current or most recent episode (depressed). If, and only if, the full criteria are currently met for major depressive episode, as in this case, you should specify its current clinical status or features. In this case, "moderate" is indicated. If the full criteria are not currently met for major depressive episode, you would indicate partial remission or full remission. An additional specifier of "with rapid cycling" was used to indicate that at least four episodes of a mood disturbance existed in the previous 12 months.

CONCLUSION

It is estimated that it takes an average of five years from onset of symptoms to reach the correct diagnosis of Bipolar Disorder (Evans, 2000). As such, Bipolar Disorder can be difficult to detect partly because Bipolar Disorder also shares many of the signs and symptoms associated with other psychiatric illnesses such as anxiety disorders and schizophrenia. It is important to keep in mind a common misperception that bipolar mood changes are usually quick and drastic. In reality, mood shifts are often quite gradual. An episode—whether depressive or manic—can last for weeks, months, or even years. People with Bipolar Disorder are not always depressed or manic; they can go for long stretches of time in a normal, balanced mood. The typical person with Bipolar Disorder has an average of four episodes during the first 10 years of the illness (Keck et al., 2004).

A complete medical history and physical exam should be conducted to rule out other physical conditions. A complete psychiatric history should consider the possibility of other mental disorders. Furthermore, Bipolar Disorder is characterized by mood swings that tend to cycle. In reviewing a patient's history, previous mood swings (perhaps of less severity or duration) may come to light. A family history of medical and psychiatric concerns should be taken because current research indicates a strong genetic component. Finally, a thorough evaluation of current symptoms should be examined.

WEBSITES

www.nami.org: Website of the National Alliance On Mental Illness, a grassroots advocacy, with clear and basic information on full array of mental disorders, support and awareness

www.mentalhealthamerica.net: Mental Health America's advocacy website addressing the full spectrum of mental and substance use conditions. Including information on cultural, gender and ethno-specific issues

www.dbsalliance.org: Largest national education and advocacy group on Mood Disorders

www.isbd.org: Clinical education and research resource from The International Society for Bipolar Disorders

Suicide and Emotional Crisis Hotlines:1-800-SUICIDE (1-800-784-2433) 1-800-723-TALK (1-800-723-8255)

www.Do-I-need-therapy.com www.Is-therapy-effective.com: Web-based mental health assessments and treatment evaluations.

References

American Psychiatric Association. (2013). *Diagnostic and Statistical Manual of Mental Disorders, fifth edition.* Washington, DC: Author.

Bauer, M. S., Crits-Cristoph, P., & Ball, W. A. (1991). Independent assessment of manic and depressive symptoms by self-rating. *Archives of General Psychiatry, 48,* 807–812.

Baldassano, C. F. (2006). Female gender is a significant predictor of being diagnosed with depression; even when presentation symptoms and scores on standardized measures of depression are similar to males: *Journal of Clinical Psychiatry, 67*(11), 8–11.

Corcoran, K., & Fischer, J. (2013). *Measures for clinical practice and research: A sourcebook (Vol. 2: Adults).* New York, Oxford University Press.

Dickerson, F. B., Sommerville, J., Origoni, A. E., Ringel, N. B., & Parente, F. (2001). Outpatients with schizophrenia and Bipolar I Disorder: Do they differ in their cognitive and social functioning? *Psychiatry Research, 102*(1), 21–27.

Evans, D. L. (2000). Bipolar disorder: Diagnostic challenges and treatment considerations. *Journal of Clinical Psychiatry, 61,* 26–31.

Keck, P. E., Perlis, R. H., Otto, M. W., Carpenter, D., Ross, R., & Docherty, J. P. (2004). *The expert consensus guideline series: Treatment of bipolar disorder 2004. A postgraduate medicine special report.* New York, NY: McGraw-Hill.

Kessler, R. C., Chiu, W. T., Demler, O., & Walters, E. E. (2005). Prevalence, severity, and comorbidity of twelve-month DSM-IV disorders in the National Comorbidity Survey Replication (NCS-R). *Archives of General Psychiatry, 62*(6), 617–627.

Kriegshauser, K., Sajatovic, M., Jenkins, J. H., Cassidy, K. A., Muzina, D., Fattal, O., Smith, D., & Singer, B. J. (2010). Gender differences in subjective experience and treatment of bipolar disorder. *Nervous Mental Disorders, 198*(5), 370–372. Retrieved from http://www.ncbi.nlm.nih.gov/pmc/articles/PMC3148587/

Kroenke, K., & Spritzer, R. L. (2002). The PHQ-9: A new depression and diagnostic severity measure. *Psychiatric Annals, 32,* 509–521. Retrieved from www.phqscreeners.com.

MacQueen, G. M., & Young, T. (2001). Bipolar II Disorder: Symptoms, course, and response to treatment. *Psychiatric Services, 52*(3) 358–361.

Neighbors, H. W., Trierweiler, S. J., Ford, B. C., & Muroff, J. R. (2003). Racial differences in DSM diagnosis using a semi-structured instrument: The importance of clinical judgment in the diagnosis of African Americans. *Journal of Health and Social Behavior, 44*(3), 237–256.

Ogilvie, A. D., Morant, N., & Goodwin, G. M. (2005). The burden on informal caregivers of people with bipolar disorder. *Bipolar Disorders, 7,* 25–32.

Simon, G., Hunkeler, E., Fireman, B., Lee, J. Y., Savarino, J. (2007). Risk of suicide attempt and suicide death in patients treated for bipolar disorder. *Bipolar Disorders, 9*(5), 526–530.

Young, R., Biggs, J., & Myers, D. (1978). A rating scale for mania: Reliability, validity and sensitivity. *British Journal of Psychiatry, 133,* 429–435.

Youngstrom, E. A., Danielson, C. K., Findling, R. L., Gracious, B. L., & Calabrese, J. R. (2002). Factor structure of the Young Mania Rating Scale for use with youths ages 5 to 17 years. *Journal of Clinical Child and Adolescent Psychology, 31,* 567–572.

World Health Organization (WHO). (2002). *Gender and Mental Health.* Retrieved from http://whqlibdoc.who.int/gender/2002/a85573.pdf

49 Guidelines for Selecting and Using Assessment Tools with Children

Craig Winston LeCroy, Stephanie Kennedy, & Andrea Kampfner

Assessment instruments play a vital role in both the clinical and programmatic aspects of social service delivery. Upon referral, these tools help guide effective treatment choices by providing insight into the client's presenting problem. Broadly speaking, these tools illuminate knowledge, attitudes, beliefs, behaviors, or conditions that are symptomatic and/or impede successful functioning. Instruments that track changes in these domains help establish the effectiveness of an intervention. These tools have become the central mechanism for program leadership to articulate and substantiate the positive impacts of their program to their stakeholders.

Until fairly recently the majority of high quality assessment tools were developed exclusively for adult populations. Unfortunately, the developmental differences between adults, youth, and children means that instruments designed for one group do not necessarily translate to other groups. To complicate matters further, the actual process of administering assessment instruments with children is far more nuanced than with adult populations. In addition to communication and comprehension issues, the uniquely vulnerable status of children as dependents adds new levels of complexity to assessing them. Very rarely, if ever, do children admit themselves for treatment. Consequentially, the adults in their lives—those who voiced "the complaint" or need for services—inevitably play a large role in the assessment process and often serve as a "proxy reporter" for the indicated client. The inclusion of caregivers, siblings, mentors, school personnel, or case managers can create a rich, multifaceted understanding of the presenting problem; however, it can also raise difficult questions in terms of reliability and confidentiality. There is some evidence to suggest that children's perceptions of their conditions do not correlate with those of their caregivers, particularly in social or emotional domains (LaGreca, 1990; Rutter & Taylor, 2002; Sherifali & Pinelli, 2007). As the demand for short-term and effective treatment services for children and adolescents increases (LeCroy, 2008; LeCroy, 2011), so does the need for developmentally appropriate assessment instruments. There must also be an emphasis on guiding practitioners to administer the instruments in sensitive, engaging, and ethical ways. This chapter will review the fundamentals of the construction and utility of child assessment tools, and then move to a discussion of strategies to implement them successfully in social work practice.

BASIC TYPOLOGIES

Assessment tools crystallize information into a useful summary for analysis and comparison. The client's individual scores can be contrasted to normative data sets (i.e., other children at similar developmental stages) or compared to the results before the intervention was put into place (i.e., pre/post testing). Two of the most common forms of assessment tools are behavior rating scales and standardized interviews.

Behavior rating scales are widely used with children because they are brief, they can be filled out by multiple reporters, and they generally do not require significant training to administer. Another benefit of rating scales is that they provide reporters with a more anonymous context than, for example, face-to-face interviews. This decreases the pressure on the child to report in socially desirable ways (King, 1997). Common examples of behavior rating scales include Child Behavior Checklist (CBCL), Conner's Rating Scales, and Children's Depression Inventory. Conversely, the simplicity of a rating scale can lend itself to bias, especially across ethnic groups. One example of ethnic bias is that Hispanic Americans have been found to choose the extremes ends of 5-point rating scales more than Caucasian Americans (Tyson, 2004). Optimally, a program should use measures that have been validated for their target population in terms of age, gender, ethnicity, and region.

A second typology is the standardized interview. This method refers to an in-person assessment of the child or family wherein the administrator is trained to use the same questions, procedures, and scoring of responses. In this format, clients respond to statements indicating a frequency of occurrence of a behavior, or they rate themselves on scaled items in terms of "a little" or "a lot" or "true" and "false" (see Table 49.1 for one example). The Diagnostic Interview Schedule for Children (DISC) uses software to adapt the interview as the responses are entered. The Child Assessment Schedule, while still standardized, is more qualitative. The benefit of the structured interview is increased engagement and the opportunity to include clinical observation in the process. These strategies, however, can be significantly more time intensive and complex to analyze. There is no single "best" assessment typology, but rather the aim is to find a good fit between a given instrument and the needs of the program.

ADDITIONAL USES FOR ASSESSMENT TOOLS

The main objective of assessment tools is to describe and classify a presenting problem. Additional uses for instruments include screening for early intervention, evaluation of treatment effectiveness, and diagnosis using *Diagnostic and Statistical Manual of Mental Disorders (DSM)* criteria.

TABLE 49.1 Hopelessness Scale for Children

True or false	I want to grow up because I think things will be better.
True or false	I might as well give up because I can't make things better for myself.
True or false	When things are going badly, I know they won't be as bad all the time.
True or false	I can imagine what my life will be like when I'm grown up.
True or false	I have enough time to finish the things I really want to do.
True or false	Some day I will be really good at doing the things I really care about.

Source: Kazdin, 1983.

1. Screening for Prevention/Early Intervention

Assessment tools are increasingly being used to screen children who are in the early stages of developing behavioral, social, or emotional problems (Merrell, 2007). Early screening minimizes the adverse outcomes associated with psychological disorders and "at-risk" environmental situations by initiating appropriate interventions at critical developmental stages. Screening instruments can be used to predict individuals who are at "high-risk" by offering a score that qualifies for preventive intervention. In general, there is a need for further evaluation when children score one or more standard deviations above a normative mean on an instrument.

2. Assessment of Treatment

Assessment instruments can also be useful for assessing changes over time and treatment effectiveness. Typically, these tools incorporate a Likert-scale format (e.g., "strongly disagree" to "strongly agree," "seldom" to "always") to evaluate the frequency or extent of behavioral, social, or emotional symptoms. To properly function as a gauge of an intervention, the same instrument should be administered at least twice in order to create a standard of comparison. Pre/post assessments contrast the outcome at the end of treatment against a baseline assessment before treatment began. Assessments can also be more frequently administered at various points throughout treatment in order to build a progressive picture of change. Frequent assessment throughout treatment can improve the clinical relationship and has been shown to contribute to a significant decrease in drop-out rates (Miller et al., 2006). Assessment instruments track progress while providing clients with a forum for active participation and feedback. Examples of these types of tools include the Child and Adolescent Functional Assessment Scale and the Eyberg Child Behavior Inventory.

3. Diagnosis

Assessment tools can be used to determine the presence of major categorical psychiatric disorders in children (Rutter & Taylor, 2002; Verhulst & Van der Ende, 2002). Typically, these tools are in the form of structured or semistructured interviews, where certain responses from the child, adolescent, parent, or teacher will determine the interview questions leading to a specific diagnosis. Examples of these interview schedules include the Diagnostic Interview Schedule for Children (DISC) and the Anxiety Disorders Interview Schedule for *DSM-IV* (TR): Child Version ADIS for *DSM-IV* (see Verhulst & Van der Ende, 2002, for review). A frequent challenge to consider when diagnosing children according to the *DSM* is that the time frames for establishing chronicity have not always been structured to account for the rapid nature of growth and change that occurs in children (Lollar, Simeonsson, & Nanda, 2000). Regular application of assessment tools becomes especially important to help distinguish between transient and permanent conditions.

SELECTING ASSESSMENT TOOLS

Assessment instruments are widely used with children in educational, child welfare, and juvenile justice settings. Often these assessments inform life-changing placement decisions for the child. In many cases, children have not received the appropriate care or placement as a result of clinicians using unreliable and invalid assessments (Tyson, 2004). There are numerous assessment tools available for purchase and many more that are accessible free of charge. However, not all instruments are of equivalent quality or utility, so considerable thought must be dedicated to selecting the correct measurement for a given setting. The main selection criteria are scientific acceptability, relevance, and ease of use.

The scientific acceptability of a measure is described in terms of "reliability" and established "validity." Reliability refers to the stability and consistency of the results produced by an instrument. Validity, on the other hand, refers to how well the instrument measures what it claims to measure. If a measure is not reliable or valid, the benefits of a good intervention could be masked or the harmful impacts of a poor intervention could go undetected (LeCroy, 2010). Practitioners may need to refer to a standard research text to interpret both the reliability and validity data (See Krysik & Finn, 2006). As a general rule, however, a reliability of 0.80 is considered acceptable for most purposes.

Although documented scientific credibility is beneficial, in this developing field some helpful instruments many fall short of the ideal standard of evidence. In these cases, thoughtful analysis of the individual items on an instrument can help practitioners to make a determination of the "face-validity" of a tool. Do the questions appear to be measuring the concept in a clear and logical manner? Has the measure been tested with the target demographics of a program? Does the measure test similar items in a similar way to the better known instruments for this outcome? Finally, is the instrument sensitive enough to detect meaningful changes over time?

An instrument's relevance—how well a given instrument correlates to a desired outcome—may seem like an obvious selection criteria. Yet relevance can be easily misunderstood by practitioners and administrators. The most common error is to select an instrument that is conceptually related to a desired change, but not in itself a direct indicator. For example, if a group program is designed to increase children's social skills, it could seem reasonable to track self-esteem because of an assumption that the two are linked. A clearer and more direct approach is to use a measure that has been validated for demonstrating change in social skills, such as the Matson

Evaluation of Social Skills with Youngsters. Granted, there are outcomes that do not yet have a validated measurement instrument. In these cases, it is possible to use a "proxy outcome measure," although the proxy measure should be supported by literature that draws a strong correlation between the proxy and the desired outcome. In assessing relevance, keep in mind this primary question: "Will this instrument determine whether a target is improving or deteriorating, so that any necessary modifications in the intervention plan can be undertaken?"(Bloom et al., 2005, p. 209).

Ease of use is an important criterion for real-world use of instruments. Instruments that are time intensive, costly, or require a high level of specified training to administer may not be practical in many settings. Instruments should be well designed graphically, have clear directions, and clear scoring procedures. Some instruments require software to score, which can delay results. Many rapid assessment scales—fewer than 20 questions and can be scored in minutes—are widely available. The trade off for using brief scales is that they have less specific and detailed information, which must also be weighed. High-quality assessment tools are relatively accessible in print and online resources. Some well-known resources include Corcoran and Fischer (2013); McCubbin, Thompson, and McCubbin (1996); Smith and Handler (2006); and Merrell (2007). Online resources include Measurement Instrument Database for the Social Sciences (www.midss.ie) and Ontario Centre of Excellence of Child and Youth Mental Health (http://www.excellenceforchildandyouth.ca/support-tools/measures-database).

ADMINISTERING CHILD MEASURES IN PRACTICE

One of the most important developments in the field of assessment has been the recognition that the child's voice must be central in the process (Smith & Handler, 2006). As children are more regularly included in the assessment process, new types of instruments have been adapted. Table 49.2 lists the various assessment methods that practitioners use to conduct assessments with children and youth. The techniques range from more traditional checklists to more interactive tools such as role-play interviews.

TABLE 49.2 Examples of Different Types of Assessment Measures

Type of Assessment	Example
Clinical interview	Psychosocial history
Semi-structured interview	Child Assessment Schedule
Behavioral observation	Playground observation of behavior
Role-play test	Behavioral Assertiveness Test for Children
Parent reports	Child Behavior Checklist
Teacher reports	Walker Problem Behavior Identification
Peer assessment	Peer rating of status
Self reports	Children's Depression Inventory
Client logs	Journal of critical incidents
Nonreactive measure	School records of days absent
Cognitive measure	Preschool Interpersonal Problem Solving Test
Performance measure	Matching Familiar Figures Test

In contrast to standard adult practice, with children it is critical to use multiple instruments that draw from multiple reporters (Achenbach, 2011). It is not advisable to rely solely on a parent's report of a particular behavior without eliciting information from another adult (ideally from a distinct setting, such as school) and from the child. This method is more time intensive and does demand more sophisticated practitioner discernment; there are, however, two central reasons for taking the additional steps.

First, child behaviors are often environmentally contingent. Children are under the social control of others and, as a consequence, children's behavior can be situationally specific (Achenbach, 2011). For example, hyperactive behavior in the classroom may not predict overactivity in the home. Specifying exactly when, where, and to what degree the behavior exists helps create a multidimensional understanding of the problem which, in turn, illuminates the most strategic intervention plan. Using the above example, if hyperactivity is reported only in the classroom, then the focus can shift from exploring ADHD to possible environmental factors or learning problems.

A second consideration is that administering instruments to children requires particular clinical sensitivity. Many children may lack insight into their behaviors or they may fear consequences for telling the truth. The inherent pressure of assessment can be distressing. Under duress, children are susceptible to answering according to what they believe to be socially desirable. High-quality instruments have likely been specifically designed to mitigate this effect (Achenbach, 2011), yet the onus remains on the administrator to help the child feel more comfortable. The administrator must ensure that children understand exactly why they are being asked to complete instruments, what the information will be used for, and with whom the results will be shared. Failing to do so is not only unethical, but it undermines accuracy. Simple verbal reminders throughout the process, such as "there are no right or wrong answers," can also help improve authenticity.

For certain topics—such as suicidal ideation, substance use, sexual experiences, or abuse—the administration of the measures is nearly as important as the content of the measure. In these areas, clients rarely spontaneously self-disclose (Lawrence et al., 2010). Tracking outcomes for sensitive content continues to be problematic; however, the use of touchscreen and computer-based technology has demonstrated promise as a more effective and accurate assessment format. Both adults and children are more likely to disclose sensitive information when using computer-based assessment instruments (Lawrence et al., 2010). Many children are comfortable with technology and may be more engaged in the process as a result. Opting for audio voice commands through headsets can help when literacy is a concern. Technology opens the possibility for ever more innovative and user-friendly measurement instruments. Katharina Manassis and colleagues (2009) found that traditional measures for anxiety could not be validated with children under 8 years of age because of vocabulary barriers. This is problematic because the onset of anxiety can occur as early as preschool. Nonverbal assessments, such as visual "thermometer" scales, are helpful but are also heavily contingent on cognitive ability (Shields et al., 2003). The Mood Assessment via Animated Characters (MAAC) developed by Manassis et al. uses a computer-based program with animated cartoon characters to help young children identify symptoms in a way that is developmentally adapted. Emerging measurement instruments, such as the MAAC, highlight that in clinical practice with children it is vital to select the correct instruments but also critical to implement them in engaging and thoughtful ways.

WEBSITES

Measurement Instrument Database for the Social Sciences, www.midss.ie

Ontario Centre of Excellence of Child and Youth Mental Health, www.excellenceforchildandyouth.ca/support-tools/measures-database

Health and mental health status measures, http://qualitymetric.com; and http://www.outcome-trust.org

Mental health assessments and treatment evaluation, www.Do-I-need-therapy.com and www.Is-therapy-effective.com

References and Readings

Achenbach, T. (2011). Commentary: Definitely more than measurement error: But how should we understand and deal with informant discrepancies? *Journal of Clinical Child & Adolescent Psychology, 40*(1), 80–86.

Bloom, M., Fischer, J., & Orme, J. G. (2005). *Evaluating practice: Guidelines for the accountable professional.* Boston, MA: Allyn and Bacon.

Corcoran, K., & Fischer, J. (2013). *Measures for clinical practice and research* (5th ed.) (Vols. 1–2). Oxford: Oxford University Press.

Kazdin, A. E. (1983). Hopelessness, depression, and suicidal intent among psychiatrically disturbed children. *Journal of Consulting and Clinical Psychology, 51,* 504–510.

King, R. (1997). Practice parameters for the psychiatric assessment of children and adolescents. *Journal of the American Academy of Child and Adolescent Psychiatry, 36,* 4–20.

Krysik, J., & Finn, J. (2006). *Research for effective social work practice.* New York, NY: Routledge.

LaGreca, A. (1990). *Through the eyes of the child: Obtaining self reports from children and adolescents*. Boston, MA: Allyn and Bacon.

Lawrence, S., Willig, J., Crane, H., Ye, J., Aban, I., Lober, W., Nevin, C., ... Schumacher, J. (2010). Routine, self-administered, touch screen, computer-based suicidal ideal assessment linked to automated response team notification in an HIV primary care setting. *Clinical Infectious Diseases, 50,* 1165–1173.

LeCroy, C. W. (2011). *Parenting mentally ill children: Faith, hope, support, and surviving the system*. Westport, CT: Praeger Publishing.

LeCroy, C. W. (2010). Knowledge building and social work research: A critical perspective. *Research on Social Work Practice, 20,* 321–324.

LeCroy, C. W. (2008). *Handbook of evidence-based child and adolescent treatment manuals*. New York, NY: Oxford University Press.

Lollar, D., Simeonsson, R., & Nanda, U. (2000). Measures of outcomes for children and youth. *Archives of Physical Medicine and Rehabilitation, 81*(2), S46–S52.

Manassis, K., Mendowitz, S., Kreindler, D., Lumsden, C., Sharpe, J., Simon, M., Woolridge, N., ... Adler-Nevo, G. (2009). Mood assessment via animated characters: A novel instrument to evaluate feelings in young children with anxiety disorders. *Journal of Clinical Child & Adolescent Psychology, 38*(3), 380–389.

McCubbin, H., Thompson, A., & McCubbin, M. (1996). *Family assessment: Resiliency, coping, and adaptation*. Madison, WI: University of Wisconsin Press.

Merrell, K. (2007). *Behavioral, social, and emotional assessment of children and adolescents* (3rd ed.). Mahwah, NJ: Lawrence Erlbaum.

Miller, W., Sorensen, J., Selzer, J., & Brigham, G. (2006). Disseminating evidence-based practices in substance abuse treatment: A review with suggestions. *Journal of Substance Abuse Treatment, 31,* 25–39.

Rutter, M., & Taylor, E. (2002). Clinical assessment and diagnostic formulation. In M. Rutter & E. Taylor (Eds.), *Child and adolescent psychiatry* (4th ed.) (pp. 18–32). Malden, MA: Blackwell Publishing.

Sherifali, D., & Pinelli, J. (2007) Parent as proxy reporting: Implications and recommendations for quality of life research. *Journal of Family Nursing, 13*(1), 83.

Shields, B., Palermo, T., Powers, J., Grewe, S., & Smith, G. (2003). Predictors of a child's ability to use a visual analogue scale. *Child Care, Health & Development, 29,* 281–290.

Smith, S., & Handler, L. (2006). *The clinical assessment of children and adolescents: A practitioner's handbook*. New York, NY: Routledge.

Tyson, E. (2004). Ethnic differences using behavior rating scales to assess the mental health of children: A conceptual and psychometric critique. *Child Psychiatry and Human Development, 34*(3), 167–201.

Verhulst, F., & Van der Ende, J. (2002). Rating scales. In M. Rutter & E. Taylor (Eds.), *Child and adolescent psychiatry* (4th ed.) (pp. 70–86). Malden, MA: Blackwell Publishing.

50

Assessment Protocols and Rapid Assessment Tools with Troubled Adolescents

David W. Springer, Stephen J. Tripodi, & Stephanie Kennedy

Troubled adolescents present a set of unique challenges and opportunities to social work practitioners. Though there are clearly similarities between conducting an assessment with adolescents compared with children or adults, there are also distinct differences that warrant special consideration. Adolescents are negotiating specific developmental tasks, such as transitioning from the family to the peer group, developing a sexual identity, and managing encounters with drugs and alcohol. Anyone who has worked with adolescents will certainly agree that they bring a unique (and often refreshing) perspective to the helping relationship that a competent practitioner integrates into a thorough assessment protocol.

In addition to the importance placed on recognizing the developmental tasks of adolescence during the assessment process, this chapter rests on the assumptions about assessment presented by Jordan and Franklin (1995): "(l) assessment is empirically based, (2) assessment must be made from a systems perspective, (3) measurement is essential, (4) ethical practitioners evaluate their clinical work, and (5) well qualified practitioners are knowledgeable about numerous assessment methods in developing assessments" (p. 3). These assumptions serve as a guide for social workers when determining what type of assessment protocol to implement with adolescents (and their families).

The first of these assumptions, that assessment is empirically based, was addressed in 2005 when the *Journal of Clinical Child and Adolescent Psychology* devoted a special section on developing guidelines for the evidence-based assessment of child and adolescent disorders, where evidence-based assessment (EBA) is "intended to develop, elaborate, and identify the measurement strategies and procedures that have empirical support in their behalf" (Kazdin, 2005, p. 548). In this special issue, Mash and Hunsley (2005) emphasize the great importance of assessment as part of intervention and acknowledge that the development of EBA has not kept up with the increased emphasis on evidenced-based treatment. In fact, there is a significant disconnect between EBA and evidence-based treatment. This is particularly true for youth with comorbid disorders.

COEXISTING DISORDERS

The terms comorbid disorders and coexisting disorders are frequently used interchangeably to describe adolescents who are struggling with several mental health issues, like depressive and anxiety disorders or posttraumatic stress and obsessive-compulsive disorder. The term dual diagnosis, on the other hand, refers to individuals who have both mental health diagnoses and a substance use problem. Although the newly released *Diagnostic and Statistical Manual of Mental Disorders, Fifth Edition* (DSM-5) (American Psychiatric Association, 2013) has moved away from the multiaxial system and reframes mental disorder and substance misuse categories as dimensions, the terminology above will be retained in this chapter to improve clarity. A substantial percentage of adolescents seen by social workers in the United States have coexisting disorders or a dual diagnosis. For example, findings from the National Comorbidity Study indicate that 41% to 65% of individuals with substance use disorders also meet criteria for a mental disorder, and approximately 43% to 51% of those with mental disorders are diagnosed with a substance use disorder (Kessler et al., 2005; Tripodi, Kim, & DiNitto, 2006). Roberts and Corcoran (2005) assert that dually diagnosed adolescents are, in fact, not a special subpopulation of adolescents but are instead the norm. The majority of adolescents seeking services today are thus likely to have substance use problems, mental health diagnoses, as well as myriad social, behavioral, and familial problems (Bender, Springer, & Kim, 2006).

Given the prevalence of coexisting disorders in clinical settings and the seriousness of making false-positive or false-negative diagnoses, it is critical that social work practitioners assess for the presence of coexisting disorders in a deliberate manner rather than making "on-the-spot" diagnoses. A social worker's assessment often helps guide treatment planning. Misdiagnosing an adolescent as not having (or having) a certain set of problems (e.g., mistaking acting out behaviors related to poverty as conduct disorder, confusing symptoms of ADHD with bipolar disorder) can pose serious consequences for the course of treatment (e.g., the wrong medications may be prescribed, adolescents and their families may be turned off to treatment owing to repeated treatment "failures"). Using sound assessment methods can help eliminate such pitfalls.

ASSESSMENT METHODS

There are various methods of assessment available to social work practitioners that can be used with adolescents. These include but are not limited to interviews, individualized rating scales, rapid assessment instruments, and standardized assessment tools. Though the focus of this chapter is primarily on the use of standardized assessment tools and rapid assessment instruments with adolescents, the importance and clinical utility of other available assessment methods, such as conducting a thorough interview, are also underscored.

Interviews

The assessment process typically starts with a face-to-face interview (e.g., psychosocial history) alone with the adolescent so he or she does not feel restricted disclosing information in the presence of his or her family. The family, however, should also be interviewed, both separately and with the adolescent. This allows the practitioner to hear the perspectives of, and establish rapport with, all key players in the system and gain a deeper understanding of the adolescent's life. Additionally, separate interviews enable the social worker to triangulate information, determining whether and how each version of the story differs. (It is important to note that the practitioner has to negotiate how to maintain the confidentiality of the adolescent client if also working with the family system.)

Consider the following case for illustration purposes. Robert, a 14-year-old Caucasian male, is brought to your agency by his parents because he is "failing most of his classes and is totally withdrawn." The week before, Robert's parents had discovered large quantities of marijuana and pills in his bedroom and note that he has made several recent comments about wanting to end his life. In addition to obtaining information from Robert's parents typically covered in a psychosocial history (e.g., medical, developmental, social, and family history), some areas that the social worker may cover with family members during an initial interview are as follows:

- Presenting problem and specific precipitating factor (e.g., "Tell me in your own words what prompted you to bring Robert in for help at this point in time?")
- Attempts to deal with the problem (e.g., "What has your family tried to deal with this problem(s)? What have you tried that has worked?")
- Hopes and expectations (e.g., "What do you hope to get out of coming here for services? If you could change any one thing about how things are at home, what would it be?")
- Exceptions to the problem (e.g., "When was the problem not evident in your recent past? What was different then?").

In addition to these areas of inquiry (with variations of the corresponding sample questions), consider some questions that the social worker may ask Robert individually:

- Peer relationships (e.g., "Tell me about your friends. What do you like to do together?")
- School (e.g., "What are your favorite [and least favorite] classes at school? What about those classes do you like [not like]?")
- Suicide risk (e.g., "When you feel down, do you ever have any thoughts of hurting/ killing yourself? Do you ever wish you were dead? How would you end your life?")
- Substance use (e.g., "What do you drink/ use? When was the last time you had a drink or used? How much did you have? Have you ever unsuccessfully tried to reduce your substance use?")
- Targeted behavior/goal setting (e.g., "If there was anything that you could change about yourself/your life, what would it be? What do you like most about yourself?").

Of course, the foregoing questions are meant only to illustrate the range of issues that one might address during an interview. A complete psychosocial history needs to be conducted. Information gathered from the face-to-face interview can subsequently be used to inform a more in-depth assessment in targeted areas, which, in turn, guides treatment planning. Individualized rating scales, rapid assessment instruments, and other standardized assessment protocols may prove useful for this purpose.

INDIVIDUALIZED RATING SCALES

Individualized rating scales are nonstandardized assessment tools that the client and the social work practitioner tailor to specifically meet the client's needs and measure the client's unique targeted outcomes (Bloom, Fischer, & Orme, 2009). These scales are used to measure change during the course of treatment, before, during, and after an intervention, or to track the strength or magnitude of a specific problem for one client across time.

Individualized rating scales can be an especially potent tool to show clients how they are progressing toward a goal. For example, imagine a client who comes to you for help managing severe panic attacks that occur at seemingly random intervals throughout the day. After conducting a thorough interview and obtaining a psychosocial history, you could ask the client to begin tracking the total number of panic attacks per day, the time the attacks occurred, and what

they were doing immediately preceding the attack. By the second session, you and the client would have a reference point, or baseline, of the problem (in this case, panic attacks) and a wealth of information about when and under what circumstances attacks are most likely to occur (Bloom, Fischer, & Orme, 2009). If treatment is successful, the client will be able to see the total number of panic attacks per day drop, reinforcing the good work they are doing. If, on the other hand, treatment is unsuccessful, it will be readily apparent in the client's rating scales, allowing you and your client to discuss new strategies to tackle this problem. Individualized rating scales are often used in conjunction with standardized scales as an additional, and more personal, form of assessment.

RAPID ASSESSMENT TOOLS AND STANDARDIZED ASSESSMENT TOOLS

Rapid assessment tools (RATs; Levitt & Reid, 1981) are short-form, pencil-and-paper assessment tools that are used to assess and measure change for a broad spectrum of client problems (Bloom, Fischer, & Orme, 2009; Corcoran & Fischer, 2013; Hudson, 1982). RATs are used as a method of empirical assessment, are easy to administer and score, are typically completed by the client, and can help monitor client functioning over time. Given the proliferation of RATs and standardized tools in recent years that measure various areas of adolescent functioning, it can be an overwhelming task to select a tool for use with an individual client. Thus, some guidelines are provided here.

The social work practitioner needs to take several factors into consideration when choosing an RAT or standardized protocol for use with clients, such as the tool's reliability, validity, clinical utility, directness, availability, and so on (Corcoran & Fischer, 2013). To the extent that an RAT has sound psychometric properties, it helps practitioners measure a client's problem consistently (reliability) and accurately (validity). Using reliable and valid tools becomes increasingly critical as one considers the complexities surrounding assessment with adolescents who (potentially) have comorbid disorders. A brief overview of reliability and validity is provided next; however, the reader is referred to the other sources for a more detailed exposition on these topics (Abell, Springer, & Kamata, 2009; Corcoran & Fischer,

2013; Hudson, 1982; Springer, Abell, & Hudson, 2002; Springer, Abell, & Nugent, 2002).

Reliability. A measurement instrument is reliable to the extent that it consistently yields similar results over repeated and independent administrations. There are several types of reliability, including interrater, test-retest, and internal consistency. All three types of reliability are designed to assess, and it is hoped minimize, measurement error. Interrater reliability refers to the degree of agreement between or among observers. When raters are in agreement about how they would assess a client or behavior, then the researcher can be more confident that the outcomes observed are "real" and not purely a function of measurement error. Test-retest reliability is a measure of a tool's consistency over time. Using a stable measure helps the researcher attribute changes in score to the intervention or treatment, rather than variations in measurement. Internal consistency is a measure of how strongly the items on a standardized scale correlate to one another. This information is represented through reliability coefficients, which range from 0.0 to 1.0. What constitutes a satisfactory level of reliability depends on how a measure is to be used. For use in research studies and scientific work, a reliability coefficient of 0.60 or greater is typically considered acceptable (Hudson, 1982). However, for use in guiding decision making with individual clients, a higher coefficient is needed. Springer, Abell, and Nugent (2002) provide the following guidelines for acceptability of reliability coefficients for use with individual clients:

• < 0.70 = Unacceptable
• 0.70–0.79 = Undesirable
• 0.80–0.84 = Minimally acceptable
• 0.85–0.89 = Respectable
• 0.90–0.95 = Very good
• > 0.95 = Excellent.

The greater the seriousness of the problem being measured (e.g., suicidal risk), and the graver the risk of making a wrong decision regarding a client's level of functioning, the higher the standard that should be adopted.

Validity. Where reliability represents an instrument's degree of consistency, validity represents how accurately an instrument measures what it is supposed to measure. There are various ways to determine an instrument's validity: face validity, content validity, criterion-related validity, construct validity, and factorial validity.

Face validity refers to whether the concepts in an assessment tool are in agreement with common perceptions of those concepts. For example, if we designed a depression measure, respondents should be asked about sadness and thoughts of suicide, rather than given math problems to solve. Content validity takes face validity one step further, by evaluating whether a measure covers all aspects of a concept. In our depression measure example, we would want to be sure the assessment tool did not ignore key features of what depression looks like and feels like for many people.

Criterion-related validity and construct validity, on the other hand, assess how a measure relates to some external concept. That is, individuals who score high on our depression measure should also score high on other standardized depression measures. Likewise, if our measure suggests a person might be struggling with depression, then other facets of their life should not suggest otherwise. We would not expect a person with depression to state that they feel great, have plenty of energy, and are excited for the future.

Finally, factorial validity has to do with how many concepts an assessment tool measures. For instance, if our scale measures both the physical and the emotional experience of depression, we would expect a statistical factor analysis to show two distinct factors. The items about the emotional side of depression should group together and the items assessing the physical experience of depression should group together. If they group differently than we expected them to, or if a factor analysis suggested that only one construct (or ten constructs) were actually being measured on our scale, we would have to go back to our items and consider if our content really was measuring depression in the way we intended. Additionally, the social worker must make decisions about a measure's validity in relationship to its intended use. In other words, he or she must determine if the measure is valid for that particular client in a particular setting at a given time. A measure may be valid for one client but not for another.

The number of standardized tools developed specifically for use with adolescents has grown considerably in recent years, and it is impossible to review them all here. However, selected standardized tools that may be useful in assessing for comorbid disorders in adolescents are briefly reviewed next. Each tool has sound psychometric properties and can be used to help guide treatment planning and monitor client progress over the course of treatment.

Child and Adolescent Functional Assessment Scale (CAFAS). The CAFAS (Hodges, 2000; Hodges, Xue, & Watring, 2004) is a validated standardized instrument used to measure the degree of impairment in youth ages 7 to 17 years (Bates, Furlong, & Green, 2006; Boydell, Barwick, Ferguson, & Haines, 2005). It is a clinician-rated measure, covering eight areas of functioning: school/work, home, community, behavior toward others, moods/emotions, self-harmful behavior, substance use, and thinking. In each of these domains, the practitioner chooses behavioral indicators about the youth's functioning. Some sample items are as follows:

- Frequent display of anger toward others; angry outbursts
- Talks or repeatedly thinks about harming self, killing self, or wanting to die
- Frequently intoxicated or high (e.g., more than two times a week)
- Frequently fails to comply with reasonable rules and expectations within the home.

The youth's level of functioning in each domain is then scored as severe (score of 30), moderate (score of 20), mild (score of 10), or minimal (score of 0). These scores are graphically depicted on a one-page scoring sheet that provides a profile of the youth's functioning in each area. The CAFAS also contains optional strengths-based and goal-oriented items (e.g., good behavior in classroom, obeys curfew) that are helpful in guiding treatment planning. A computerized software program is available that scores the CAFAS, generates a treatment plan, and produces outcome reports to help practitioners track client progress (Hodges, 2000).

Behavioral and Emotional Rating Scale (BERS-2). The Behavioral and Emotional Rating Scale, Second Edition (BERS-2; Epstein & Sharma, 2004) is a strengths-based battery of three instruments that measure functioning in youth across five different areas: interpersonal strength, family involvement, intrapersonal strength, school functioning, and affective strength. A key feature that distinguishes the BERS-2 from other standardized tools (e.g., Achenbach's widely used Child Behavior Checklist [CBCL]) is that it is truly based on a strengths perspective (in contrast to a deficit model), and the wording of the items reflects this outlook. The Teacher Rating Scale (TRS) has 52 items and is one of the three measures in the BERS-2 package. Some sample items from the TRS are:

- Maintains positive family relationships
- Accepts responsibility for own actions
- Pays attention in class
- Identifies own feelings.

The strengths perspective makes this tool particularly appealing to parents, adolescents, and social workers who strive for a helping relationship that centers on client strengths and empowerment. The BERS-2 has been validated with many different populations, including Hispanic and African American adolescents in the United States, and both Spanish and Arabic-language versions of the scale have been validated (Farmer et al., 2005; Gonzalez, Ryser, Esptein, & Shwery, 2006; Mooney, Epstein, Ryser, & Pierce, 2005; Mutairi & Khurinej, 2008; Sharkey, You, Morrison, & Griffiths, 2009).

Adolescent Drug Abuse Diagnosis (ADAD). The ADAD (Friedman & Utada, 1989) is a 150-item semistructured standardized assessment scale that addresses nine areas of functioning: medical, school, employment, social relations, family relations, psychological, legal, alcohol use, and drug use. Severity ratings (on a 10-point scale) are computed for each area to indicate the adolescent's need for treatment in each area. The ADAD has been validated in three recent studies—one of which compared it to another outcome scale for children and adolescents (Holzer et al., 2006) and two of which validated the scale in Swedish (Börjesson, Armelius, & Ostgård-Ybrandt, 2007; Ybrandt, 2013).

Additional Rapid Assessment Tools. In addition to the standardized tools reviewed here, there are numerous RATs that can be used with adolescents to measure functioning across various areas, such as risk of running away (e.g., Adolescent Concerns Evaluation), suicidal tendencies (e.g., Multi-Attitude Suicide Tendency Scale), posttraumatic symptoms (e.g., Child and Parent Report of Post-traumatic Symptoms), conduct-problem behaviors (e.g., Eyberg Child Behavior Checklist), family functioning (e.g., Family Assessment Device, Index of Family Relations), and peer relations (Index of Peer Relations), to name just a few (Corcoran & Fischer, 2013). There are also standardized general behavior rating scales (e.g., Louisville Behavior Checklist, Child Behavior Checklist, Conners Rating Scales) and tools that are useful for measuring the degree of functional impairment (e.g., Children's Global Assessment Scale) (Shaffer, Lucas, & Richters, 1999).

CONCLUSION

The field continues to make progress in developing user-friendly standardized assessment tools with sound psychometric properties that can be used in assessment with adolescents. Although these tools should not take the place of a face-to-face psychosocial history, they should be used to complement the assessment process and track progress in client functioning over the course of treatment. It is important to emphasize that a standardized tool does not take the place of a solid therapeutic helping relationship. Social workers should take care to build rapport with adolescent clients prior to administering standardized assessments or RATs. Establishing a relationship and explaining why and how assessments will be used can help mitigate against making treatment decisions based solely on the score of an assessment tool. After all, the goal is to help adolescents make desired changes as they move forward into adulthood.

Social workers have an ethical obligation to use empirical assessment protocols and standardized tools whenever possible, rather than relying solely on gut feelings when conducting assessments with adolescents. The importance of empirical assessments with troubled adolescents was reiterated by a Blue Ribbon Taskforce in Texas, convened after several sexual abuse scandals surfaced at the Texas Youth Commission. Professor David Springer was appointed to serve as chair of the taskforce, and asked to create a proposal to better serve the needs of Texas youth, their families, and their communities. Together with a team of juvenile justice scholars from throughout the United States, Professor Springer's taskforce made recommendations to improve prevention policies, treatment strategies, and assessment among a juvenile justice population. Regarding assessments, the Taskforce suggested that: (1) Facilities should only incarcerate high-risk, serious, and chronic juvenile offenders (determined by extensive evidence-based assessments); (2) A continuum

of care should minimize the penetration of youth into the juvenile and adult justice systems (continuum of care is determined by extensive evidence-based assessments); and (3) Referral and treatment decisions should be formed by risk assessments that are multipronged and ongoing, with services that are flexible and tailored to meet the individual needs of the client system (Springer and Colleagues, 2007).

The potential consequences of misdiagnosing a client like Robert can be severe. Thus, social work practitioners are encouraged to make use of available empirically based assessment tools within a systems framework to guide treatment planning, monitor client functioning, and evaluate the effectiveness of their interventions.

WEBSITES

Behavioral and Emotional Rating Scale: http://vinst.umdnj.edu/VAID/TestReport.asp?Code=BERS

Child and Adolescent Functional Assessment Scale: http://www.cafas.com

Institute of Behavior Research at Texas Christian University: http://www.ibr.tcu.edu

The American Academy of Child and Adolescent Psychiatry provides a comprehensive set of clinical parameters for assessing and treating children and adolescents: http://www.aacap.org/cs/root/member_information/practice_information/practice_parameters/practice_parameters

The National Institute on Alcohol Abuse and Alcoholism presents an inclusive list of validated instruments that assess adolescent alcohol abuse: http://pubs.niaaa.nih.gov/publications/Assesing%20Alcohol/behaviors.htm

The National Child Traumatic Stress Network outlines a thorough list of validated assessment tools that target trauma and substance use: http://www.nctsn.org/sites/default/files/assets/pdfs/satoolkit_4.pdf

References

Abell, N., Springer, D. W., & Kamata, A. (2009). Developing and validating rapid assessment instruments. Oxford, England: Oxford University Press.

American Psychiatric Association. (2013). *Diagnostic and statistical manual of mental disorders, fifth edition*. Arlington, VA: American Psychiatric Publishing.

Bates, M. P., Furlong, M. J., & Green, J. G. (2006). Are CAFAS subscales and item weights valid? A preliminary investigation of the child and adolescent functional assessment scale. *Administration and Policy in Mental Health and Mental Health Services Research, 33*(6), 682–695. doi:http://dx.doi.org/10.1007/s10488-006-0052-4

Bender, K., Springer, D. W., & Kim, J. S. (2006). Treatment effectiveness with dually diagnosed adolescents: A systematic review. *Brief Treatment and Crisis Intervention, 6*(3), 177–205.

Bloom, M., Fischer, J., & Orme, J. (2009). *Evaluating practice: Guidelines for the accountable professional* (6th ed.). Needham Heights, MA: Allyn & Bacon.

Boydell, K. M., Barwick, M., Ferguson, H. B., & Haines, R. (2005). A feasibility study to assess service providers' perspectives regarding the use of the child and adolescent functional assessment scale in Ontario. *The Journal of Behavioral Health Services & Research, 32*(1), 105–109.

Börjesson, J., Armelius, B., & Ostgård-Ybrandt, H. (2007). The psychometric properties of the Swedish version of the adolescent drug abuse diagnosis (ADAD). *Nordic Journal of Psychiatry, 61*(3), 225–232.

Corcoran, K., & Fischer, J. (2013). *Measures for clinical practice and research* (5th ed.) (Vols. 1–2). Oxford: Oxford University Press.

Epstein, M. H., & Sharma, J. M. (2004). *Behavioral and emotional rating scale: Examiner's manual* (2nd ed.). Austin, TX: Pro-ED Inc.

Farmer, T. W., Clemmer, J. T., Leung, M., Goforth, J. B., Thompson, J. H., Keagy, K., & Boucher, S. (2005). Strength-based assessment of rural African American early adolescents: Characteristics of students in high and low groups on the behavioral and emotional rating scale. *Journal of Child and Family Studies, 14*(1), 57–69. doi:http://dx.doi.org/10.1007/s10826-005-1113-0

Friedman, A. S., & Utada, A. A. (1989). A method for diagnosing and planning the treatment of adolescent drug abusers (the Adolescent Drug Abuse Diagnosis [ADAD] instrument). *Journal of Drug Education, 19*(4), 285–312.

Gonzalez, J. E., Ryser, G. R., Epstein, M. H., & Shwery, C. S. (2006). The behavioral and emotional rating scale-second edition: Parent rating scale (BERS-II PRS): A Hispanic cross-cultural reliability study. *Assessment for Effective Intervention, 31*(3), 33–43.

Hodges, K. (2000). *The Child and Adolescent Functional Assessment Scale: Self training manual*. Ypsilanti: Department of Psychology, Eastern Michigan University.

Hodges, K., Xue, Y., & Watring, J. (2004). Use of the CFAS to evaluate outcome for youths with severe emotional disturbance served by public mental health. *Journal of Child and Family Studies, 13*, 325–339.

Holzer, L., Tchemadjeu, I. K., Plancherel, B., Bolognini, M., Rossier, V., Chinet, L., & Halfon, O. (2006). Adolescent drug abuse diagnosis (ADAD) vs. health of nation outcome scale for children and adolescents (HoNOSCA) in clinical outcome measurement. *Journal of Evaluation in Clinical Practice, 12*(5), 482–490.

Hudson, W. W. (1982). *The clinical measurement package: field manual*. Homewood, IL: Dorsey.

Jordan, C., & Franklin, C. (1995). *Clinical assessment for social workers: Quantitative and qualitative methods*. Chicago, IL: Lyceum Books.

Kazdin, A. E. (2005). Evidence-based assessment for children and adolescents: Issues in measurement development and clinical application. *Journal of Clinical Child and Adolescent Psychology, 34*(3), 548–558.

Kessler, R. C., Berglund, P., Demler, O., Jin, R., Merikangas, K. R., & Walters, E. E. (2005). Lifetime prevalence and age-of-onset distributions of DSM-IV disorders in the National Comorbidity Survey replication. *Archives of General Psychiatry, 62*(6), 593–605.

Levitt, J., & Reid, W. (1981). Rapid-assessment instruments for practice. *Social Work Research and Abstracts, 17*(1), 13–19.

Mash, E., & Hunsley, J. (2005). Evidence-based assessment of child and adolescent disorders: Issues and challenges. *Journal of Clinical Child and Adolescent Psychology, 34*(3), 362–379.

Mooney, P., Epstein, M. H., Ryser, G., & Pierce, C. D. (2005). Reliability and validity of the behavioral and emotional rating scale-second edition: Parent rating scale. *Children & Schools, 27*(3), 147–155.

Mutairi, H. a., & Khurinej, A. a. (2008). The psychometic properties of the Arabic version of the behavioral and emotional rating scale (BERS). *DOMES: Digest of Middle East Studies, 17*(2), 54–65.

Roberts, A., & Corcoran, K. (2005). Adolescents growing up in stressful environments, dual diagnosis, and sources of success. *Brief Treatment and Crisis Intervention, 5*(1), 1–8.

Shaffer, D., Lucas, C. P., & Richters, J. E. (Eds.). (1999). *Diagnostic assessment in child and adolescent psychopathology*. New York, NY: Guilford.

Sharkey, J., You, S., Morrison, G., & Griffiths, A. (2009). Behavioral and emotional rating scale-2 parent report: Exploring a Spanish version with at-risk students. *Behavioral Disorders, 35*(1), 53–65.

Springer, D. W., Abell, N., & Hudson, W. W. (2002). Creating and validating rapid assessment instruments for practice and research: Part one. *Research on Social Work Practice, 12*, 408–439.

Springer, D. W., Abell, N., & Nugent, W. R. (2002). Creating and validating rapid assessment instruments for practice and research: Part two. *Research on Social Work Practice, 12*, 768–795.

Springer, D. W. and colleagues. (2007). *Transforming juvenile justice in Texas: A framework for action.* Blue Ribbon Task Force report. Austin, TX: The University of Texas at Austin, School of Social Work.

Tripodi, D. J., Kim, J. S., & DiNitto, D. M. (2006). Effective strategies for working with students who have co-occurring disorders. In C. Franklin, M. B. Harris, & P. Allen-Meares (Eds.), *School social work and mental health workers training and resource manual.* London: Oxford University Press.

Ybrandt, H. (2013). A normative study of the Swedish adolescent drug abuse diagnosis (ADAD). *Journal of Substance Use, 18*(2), 138–147. doi:http://dx.doi.org/10.3109/14659891.2011.632059

51   Using Standardized Tests and Instruments in Family Assessments

Jacqueline Corcoran

DEFINITIONS AND DESCRIPTIONS

A measure helps determine the existence of certain behaviors, attitudes, feelings, or qualities—and their magnitude—in clients when they come to a social work practitioner for assistance. The first rule for using measures is to employ an already established measure, one that has been standardized, rather than devising and testing a new one. An inventory (the words *measure, inventory,* and *instrument* are used interchangeably) is standardized when it has been tested (normed) on a relevant group of people, a process that results in psychometric data—specifically, information about reliability and validity—that has to meet certain acceptable standards. *Reliability* refers to the consistency and the accuracy of the measure, and *validity* involves the extent to which the instrument measures what it purports to measure. For the different methods of determining reliability and validity, please see a social work research text (e.g., Rubin & Babbie, 2010).

Standardization of an instrument also means there are certain procedures for its administration: Items are completed in the order they appear, certain items cannot be taken out at the administrator's discretion, nor can only certain items be chosen, because items are considered to be a set. A certain procedure for scoring the measure has also been developed (Corcoran & Fischer, 2013).

Standardized measures can be completed by the client (self-report); by an important collateral person who can make key observations about the client's behavior, attribute, or attitude (a parent, teacher, or spouse, for example); or by the practitioner using an observational measure. This discussion will concentrate on either client self-report measures or inventories completed by parents of children, because the emphasis here is on family assessment.

RATIONALE FOR USE OF MEASURES

Why should social workers use family assessment measures? After all, they take time away from service delivery, clients may resent filling them out and fail to see their relevance, and they require some effort for the practitioner to find and to figure out how to score. However, the use of instruments in family assessment offers several potential benefits (Corcoran & Fischer, 2013).

- They provide detailed information about feelings—attitudes and qualities, and their magnitude, information that may be difficult to observe overtly.
- They aid in the assessment process, helping the practitioner determine the specific issues to address and to select appropriate services.
- They track client progress to ascertain whether interventions proceed in the necessary direction.
- Positive changes may motivate the client to continue to participate in services and to make progress.
- If gathered in sufficient numbers, measures can provide information about the effectiveness of a particular approach or intervention with a group of individuals for an agency, funding source, or dissemination of knowledge to the field.
- They provide evidence to third-party payers for reimbursement or to establish the need for continued services.

SELECTING MEASURES

Selection of measures depends on the purpose for which measurement is targeted (screening, assessment, monitoring progress), the nature of the client's problem, practicality issues, and the psychometric capacities of the instrument (Corcoran & Fischer, 2013). In the purpose of measurement, for example, if the instrument is to assess progress, is it sensitive to clinical change (Johnson et al., 2008)? Issues of practicality include the length of the instrument and the ability of the client to complete it. Corcoran and Fischer (2013) suggest that a scale should take no longer than 10 to 15 minutes to complete. Some measures have both a longer and a shorter version. For instance, the Parenting Stress Index (Abidin, 1995) has a 120-item version and a 36-item version. Other issues of practicality specifically for supervisors and managers include the cost of purchasing measures, the resources involved in training social work staff, the length of time required to score and interpret measures (Johnson et al., 2008), and, if it is necessary to compile the results of multiple scores, the resources involved with finding a usable database system, the construction of a database, data entry, and data analysis.

Psychometric standards for selecting instruments include established validity and reliability.

Many agency personnel rely on instruments they have created to assess client functioning and to measure client change. This is ill-advised, despite the prevalence of this practice; without established reliability and validity, "various alternative explanations for the findings (e.g., examiner bias, chance, and effects of maturation) cannot be ruled out, which seriously restricts the usefulness of findings" (Johnson et al., 2008, p. 7).

Another question related to psychometrics is how similar the client population is to the characteristics of the sample on which the instrument was normed. Many psychological inventories have been normed on undergraduate samples, traditionally from white and middle- to upper-class populations, which may differ in significant ways from high school-educated, low socioeconomic status, and/or minority clients. Although a measure may not necessarily be rejected because it has been normed on a sample dissimilar from the characteristics of a particular client or client group, some care must then be taken on the interpretation of scores.

Several publications have compiled various family assessment instruments. Volume 1 of Corcoran and Fischer (2013) focuses on children, couples, and families. For child and adolescent problems, the interested reader is urged to consult Mash and Barkley (2009), which provides a comprehensive discussion of various self-report instruments, rating scales for teachers and parents, and behavioral observational measures. Corcoran (2000) compiled instruments organized by type of problems for which families may receive services. Corcoran and Walsh (2010) delineate measures that involve child and adolescent *DSM*-defined diagnoses, and Early and Newsome (2005) discuss measures that emphasize strengths for families. Finally, Johnson et al. (2008) specifically address family assessment in relation to child welfare.

The following section details information on family assessment measures, specifically family functioning, parenting practices, and marital functioning, with demonstrated validity and reliability that have been reviewed by Corcoran (2000).

FAMILY FUNCTIONING

Stemming from the field of family therapy and a family systems theoretical approach, three main self-report measures are widely used to assess the family as the unit of attention (Johnson et al., 2008): the McMaster Family Assessment Device, the Family Environment Scale, and the Family Adaptability and Cohesion Evaluation Scale. These instruments are highly correlated with one another and may be used interchangeably (Olson, 2000; Beavers & Hampson as cited in Johnson et al., 2005).

The McMaster Family Assessment Device (FAD) (Epstein, Baldwin, & Bishop, 1983) is a 60-item, Likert-type self-report measure that assesses overall health/pathology in a general score, as well as six areas of family functioning: (1) problem solving; (2) communication; (3) roles; (4) affective responsiveness; (5) affective involvement; and (6) behavior control.

The Family Environment Scale (FES) (Moos & Moos, 1981) is a 90-item, true-false questionnaire assessing ten dimensions of family life in three general areas: (1) relationship dimensions, which involve cohesion, expressiveness, and conflict; (2) personal growth dimensions, which involve independence, achievement orientation, intellectual/cultural orientation, moral-religious emphasis, and active-recreational orientation; and (3) system maintenance dimensions, which involve organization and control. There are three different forms of the FES: the real form, which assesses members' perceptions of their families; the ideal form, measuring members' preferred family environments; and the expectations form, which assesses members' expectations about family environments.

The Family Adaptability and Cohesion Evaluation Scales, version IV (FACES IV) (Olson & Gorrall, 2003). FACES-IV is a 62-item self-report measure in which members rate their families on two different dimensions: (1) adaptability (ability of a family system to alter structure, roles, and rules in response to situational and developmental stress); and (2) cohesion (emotional bonding). FACES IV also assesses family communication and satisfaction.

Parenting Assessment

Measures of parenting often stem from the field of developmental psychology with the caregiver–child dyad as the unit of analysis (Johnson et al., 2008). We focus on the Child Abuse Potential Inventory and the Parenting Stress Index as prime examples of these types of instruments.

The Child Abuse Potential Inventory (Milner, 1986), a 160-item, self-report survey, includes a 77-item physical child abuse scale with six descriptive factor scales: (1) distress, (2) rigidity, (3) unhappiness, (4) problems with child and self, (5) problems with family, and (6) problems from others. The Child Abuse Potential Inventory can be completed by those with a third-grade reading level.

The Parenting Stress Index (Abidin, 1995) is a 120-item, self-report inventory for parents of children ages 1 month to 12 years. It yields not only a total score of parenting stress but also whether sources of stress may be related to child characteristics (child's adaptability, reinforcing qualities, demandingness, activity level, mood, and acceptability to the parent) or parental functioning (the parent's sense of competence, isolation, depression, attachment to the child, parent health, perceived restrictions of role, depression, and spousal and social system support). The short form (36 items) has the following subscales: (1) total stress, (2) parental distress, (3) parent–child dysfunctional interaction, and (4) difficult child (Abidin, 1995).

Partner Relational Functioning

Several instruments are designed to assess marital functioning. The Marital Adjustment Test (Locke & Wallace, 1959) is a 15-item self-report assessing the accommodation of partners to each other. The Dyadic Adjustment Scale (Spanier, 1999) is a 32-item self-report inventory measuring marital adjustment with four subscales: (1) dyadic consensus (agreement regarding marital issues), (2) dyadic cohesion (the extent to which partners are involved in joint activities), (3) dyadic satisfaction (overall evaluation of relationship and level of commitment), and (4) affectional expression (the extent of affection and sexual involvement). To measure the frequency of various forms of overt marital hostility (e.g., quarrels, sarcasms, and physical abuse) witnessed by children, use the 20-item O'Leary-Porter Scale (Porter & O'Leary, 1980).

Intimate partner violence can be measured by the Revised Conflict Tactics Scales (Straus, Hamby, Boney-McCoy, & Sugarman, 1996). This 78-item, self-report instrument assesses psychological and physical attacks on a partner, as well as the use of negotiation, in a marital, cohabiting, or dating relationship. The following subscales are included: (1) physical assault, (2) psychological aggression, (3) negotiation, (4) injury, and (5) sexual coercion. The items are asked in the form of questions (what the participant did and what the partner did). They are written at a sixth-grade reading level.

GUIDELINES FOR USING MEASURES

The following are guidelines for the administration of measures:

When Will the Measure Be Completed?

Preferably, before services have begun (so the social worker can assess the impact of intervention), during intake, or at the first contact with the social worker.

Where Will the Measure Be Completed?

A quiet place, free of distractions, with a hard writing surface available—a desk or a clipboard—and appropriate writing utensils.

Why Should the Social Worker Be Present if All Family Members are Completing Measures?

Members might start discussing items among themselves, and the more powerful people in the family might influence others' responses. Children are particularly vulnerable because they often have difficulty reading and understanding items. If parents start reading the measure to the child, children may either respond in a way they think is desirable to the parent, or parents may more actively influence their responses ("You don't feel sad, do you?").

What Procedure Should the Worker Follow in the Administration of Measures?

- Explain the purpose of the measure (see rationale section).
- Read aloud the directions, which include how the client should respond to items.
- Check the instrument over.
- Score the instrument (in front of the client, if at all possible, so immediate feedback can be provided; Corcoran & Fischer, 2013).
- Repeat the measure at a later date (at a designated time frame, such as every month,

at the termination of services, and possibly as a follow-up to services) using similar procedures each time.
- Track scores over time and provide feedback to the client on progress.

What if Clients Seem Unable to Complete Measures?

If individuals are unsure of an answer, they should be encouraged to provide what they think is the best answer. The social worker should avoid interpreting the items or questions.

If a child seems to be struggling to complete an instrument or complains about not being able to understand the items, the practitioner can separate the child from other family members, and the measure can be read aloud to the child.

Adults will not usually volunteer that they cannot read, but if a person seems to be struggling, then the social worker may ask whether the client would prefer that items were read aloud with the worker recording responses.

For non–English-speaking clients, the best source of information on the availability of measures written in other languages is the author of the inventory or the publishing house.

If a client complains about difficulties completing a measure, perhaps he or she could agree to come earlier for subsequent sessions so that completion of an instrument can occur in the waiting area and does not interfere with session time. Other alternatives include selecting a measure with fewer items.

What Should the Practitioner Be Checking for When the Instrument Is Completed?

Items left blank, which can be pointed out to the client, so the measure is fully completed.

Bias in terms of social desirability (i.e., clients responding in a way that they think pleases the worker, or in a way to suggest that services are either not necessary or should not be terminated) or a response set bias, that is, clients answering items in a particular pattern (e.g., all 4s on a 6-point scale) (Corcoran & Fischer, 2013). Inquiring about a particular pattern may provide information about the client's level of comprehension of items or the level of cooperation.

CONCLUSION

The use of measurement instruments for assessment and evaluation will, in all likelihood, increase owing to the demands of managed care. The information provided will assist the social worker not only in choosing appropriate measures for use in family assessment but also aid in gaining familiarity with some of the practical matters involved so that the clinical utility of measurement instruments will be maximized.

WEBSITES

Assessments.com. http://www.assessments.com
American Psychological Association
    Family Assessment: http://www.
    apadivisions .org/division-54/
    evidence-based/family-assessment.aspx
UCLA Subscales of McMaster Family
    Assessment Device (FAD): http://chipts.ucla
    .edu/assessment/IB/List_Scales/McMaster_
    Family_Assessment.htm.

References

Abidin, R. R. (1995). *Parenting stress index* (3rd ed.). Professional manual. Odessa, FL: Psychological Assessment Resources.

Corcoran, J. (2000). *Evidence-based social work practice with families: A lifespan approach.* New York, NY: Springer.

Corcoran, J., & Walsh, J. (2010). *Clinical assessment and diagnosis in social work practice* (2nd ed.). New York, NY: Oxford University Press.

Early, T., & Newsome, S. (2005). Measures for assessment and accountability in practice with families from a strengths perspective. In J. Corcoran, *Building strengths and skills: A collaborative approach to working with clients* (pp. 359–393). New York, NY: Oxford University Press.

Epstein, N., Baldwin, L., & Bishop, D. (1983). The McMaster family assessment device. *Journal of Marital and Family Therapy, 9,* 171–180.

Corcoran, K., & Fischer, J. (2013). *Measures for clinical practice and research: A sourcebook, Volume 1: Couples, Families, and Children* (5th ed.). New York, NY: Oxford University Press.

Corcoran, K., & Fischer, J. (2013). *Measures for clinical practice and research: A sourcebook, Volume 2: Adults* (5th ed.). New York, NY: Oxford University Press.

Johnson, M., Stone, S., Lou, C., Vu, C., Ling, J., Mizrahi, P., Austin, M. (2008). Family assessment in child welfare services: Instrument comparisons. *Journal of Evidence Based Social Work, 5,* 57–90.

Locke, H., & Wallace, K. (1959). Short marital-adjustment and prediction tests: Their reliability and validity. *Marriage and Family Living, 21,* 251–255.

Mash, E. J., & Barkley, R. A. (2009). *Assessment of childhood disorders* (4th ed.). New York, NY: Guilford.

Milner, J. S. (1986). *The child abuse potential inventory: Manual* (2nd ed.). Webster, NC: Psytec.

Moos, R. H., & Moos, B. S. (1981). *Family environment scale manual.* Palo Alto, CA: Consulting Psychologists Press.

Olson, D. H. (2000). Circumplex model of marital and family systems. *Journal of Family Therapy, 22,* 144–167.

Olson, D., & Gorrall, D. (2003). Circumplex model of marital and family systems. In F. Walsh (Ed.), *Normal family processes: Growing diversity and complexity* (3rd ed.). (pp. 514–548). New York, NY: Guilford.

Porter, B., & O'Leary, D. (1980). Marital discord and childhood behavior problems. *Journal of Abnormal Child Psychology, 8,* 287–295.

Rubin, A., & Babbie, E. (2010). *Research methods for social work* (7th ed.). Pacific Grove, CA: Brooks/Cole.

Spanier, G. B. (1999). *Dyadic adjustment scale manual.* Toronto: Multi-Healthsystems.

Straus, M., Hamby, S., Boney-McCoy, S., & Sugarman, D. (1996). The revised Conflict Tactics Scales (CTS2). *Journal of Family Issues, 17,* 283–316.

52 Very Brief Screeners for Practice and Evaluation

Steven L. McMurtry, Susan J. Rose, & Lisa K. Berger

A child welfare worker provides in-home services to families in which allegations of abuse or neglect were substantiated, but risk levels were not great enough to warrant any child's removal for placement in out-of-home care. The worker's job is to assess the needs of the parents or adult caregivers in the home and provide services or make referrals. The problem is that in-home services last only about three months, so assessment must be done quickly to allow maximum time for service provision. Also, the worker's agency is under court supervision following a class-action lawsuit, so the worker must show that all assessments are carried out in the most valid way possible. Finally, the range of potential problems affecting caregivers is large, so the worker must be able to screen across areas that range from general mental health to substance use to domestic violence to food insecurity.

The program evaluator in a community mental health center seeks to determine the effectiveness of the center's outpatient services. These consist mostly of case management and short-term individual and group counseling for clients with concerns such as depression, alcohol and drug use, emotional and behavioral problems, and other concerns. Services are typically short-term, lasting from 10 to 90 days. The evaluator has been asked to compare clients' level of functioning on their primary presenting problem before and after intervention. However, as with the previous example, not all individuals have problems in all areas, and each assessment must be valid but brief in order to prevent the overall measurement package from becoming unmanageably lengthy.

A social worker in a Family Resource Center works to connect clients with job training or supported employment opportunities as a part of an integrated service approach in which clients receive assistance for behavioral health or other social service needs that affect their ability to find and maintain employment.

The social worker needs to determine what specific services might be helpful in the limited time available to meet with each client. Screening for potential problem substance use, domestic violence, or depression needs to be done with a measure that is valid, understandable to the client in light of their purpose for approaching the Center, and importantly, brief.

The above examples illustrate a dilemma facing many social workers in direct services and service-support roles: how to measure client problems and progress accurately but briefly. Similar to practitioners in disciplines such as psychology and psychiatry, social workers increasingly rely on *standardized scales*. These are measures composed of items and response options that are usually the same for all subjects and are scored in a specific way. The term "standardized" also implies that the measure meets certain psychometric standards and has been tested on enough subjects to provide a basis for evaluating each individual's score.

Standardized scales include broad-spectrum diagnostic tools such as the Minnesota Multiphasic Personality Inventory (MMPI). It and other early examples tended to be lengthy (100 items or more) and time-intensive (one-hour or longer to administer). Beginning about 1980, more attention was directed toward developing brief measures termed *rapid assessment instruments* (RAIs) (Fischer & Corcoran, 2007). RAIs usually have fewer than 100 items and can be administered in 15 minutes or less. These briefer measures were a better fit with the time available to social workers conducting client assessments, and RAIs such as those in Hudson's clinical measurement package (1982) became widely known. Still, the measurement task facing many social workers is neither diagnosis nor assessment but screening, which involves rapidly scanning many potential problems and identifying those that require further services. For this, the type of measure needed is what we will refer to as a *very brief screener* or VBS.

CHARACTERISTICS OF VERY BRIEF SCREENERS

VBSs are defined here as measures of known psychometric accuracy that can indicate the potential presence of clinically meaningful problems in most subjects in two minutes or less. Measures containing 200 items or more have sometimes been called "screeners," but we consider brevity to be the signal aspect of a VBS. In practice, this means a maximum of about 12 items.

Other characteristics of VBSs are that they are "first warning" rather than full diagnostic instruments, and their use assumes that further testing will occur before a more definitive decision on the presence or absence of a problem can be made. VBSs may take several forms, including that of self-administered questionnaires, interviews by clinicians or others, and observer-rating checklists. To make them acceptable to non–help-seeking respondents, VBS items tend to be worded neutrally, and they have been used for purposes as diverse as service referral, needs assessment, epidemiological studies, and measurement of key variables in surveys. Constructs measured by VBSs include both psychological states (e.g., mood, anxiety) and behaviors (substance use, eating disorders). VBSs reviewed here *do not* include mechanical or other biometric measures such as blood pressure or body chemistry. Also, due to the volume of instruments available, we will restrict our discussion to measures of adult functioning.

CHOOSING A SCREENER

The most important attribute of any assessment tool is its reliability and validity, and the best measures are those for which published results from empirical tests of these qualities are available. Of particular importance are findings regarding known-groups techniques that demonstrate each instrument's screening accuracy. The two complementary aspects of this are sensitivity and specificity. *Sensitivity* refers to the ability to assign a positive reading to all those who have the problem (i.e., minimizing false negatives). *Specificity* is a measure's ability to assign a positive reading only to those who have the problem (i.e., minimizing false positives). In a good screener both sensitivity and specificity are high, but one value can come at the expense of the other. The potential user of the measure must also consider the consequences of misidentification. The presence of false positives risks falsely stigmatizing some individuals, providing services to those who do not need them, and making the intervention appear less useful than it actually is, due to the absence of improvement among false positives. The presence of false negatives means that clients who need help will go unserved, and if the problem is a serious one, this can have dire ramifications for both the clients and others.

A technique called Receiver Operating Characteristics (ROC) curve analysis is often used to assess a measure's ability to find a balance between sensitivity and specificity (Metz, 1978). Results from the technique are usually reported as *area under the curve* (AUC). This ranges from 0 to 1 and reflects the ability of the measure to correctly classify respondents as having or not having the attribute in question (e.g., depression, alcohol dependence). Measures in which the area under the curve is large are those that accurately classify most cases, and AUC values of .80 or higher are typically seen as evidence of good measurement performance.

Another factor affecting screening accuracy is the prevalence of a problem in a population. When the target problem affects a relatively small proportion of individuals, even screeners with good specificity can produce unacceptably high ratios of false positives to true positives. For example, suppose 1,000 people are screened for a problem that affects only 2% of them, and the screener being used has a specificity of 95%. Twenty people (2%) can be expected to have the problem, and the measure will correctly identify 19 of those 20 (95%). On the other side, 980 people will not have the problem, but the screener, with its inaccuracy rate of 5%, will incorrectly identify 49 of these 980 people as having the problem. The performance of a screener in this regard is usually reported as its *positive predictive value* (PPV), which is obtained by dividing the number of true positives by the combined number of true and false positives. In the above example, this would be $19/(19 + 49) = .279$. Multiplying this result by 100 yields a figure of 27.9%, which is the fraction of all cases identified as positives that truly are positives. A related statistic called the negative predictive value (NPV) helps evaluate performance relative to sensitivity. It is computed by substituting true and false negatives for true and false positives in the above equation.

SELECTED VERY BRIEF SCREENERS

In this section we will identify VBSs that assess client functioning in six major areas within which social workers may need to screen for client problems. These include mood, anxiety, eating behaviors, alcohol use, drug use, and general mental health. Our focus is on identifying brief screeners of potential value to both practitioners and those in roles as evaluators and researchers. Most of this information is presented in tables that show the name, number of items, and source reference for each measure. If multiple screeners are available in a given category, they are listed within each table based on the frequency of citations of the measure's source article. It is important to note that some brief measures that enjoy considerable popularity in the field are not shown in the table. This is likely because, though their administration times are relatively short, they did not meet the two-minute criterion for inclusion.

In the fourth column of each table, a summary of empirical findings regarding the screening accuracy of each measure is provided. This focuses particularly on sensitivity and specificity, plus AUC, PPV, and NPV, where available. For the sake of brevity, evidence related to reliability and other types of validity is not reported, except where this is the only type of evidence available and the measure is the only VBS in that category. Prospective users of any measure should always consult its source reference(s) and familiarize themselves with results on all aspects of its validity and reliability before deciding to use it.

The final column in each table provides information such as whether the measure is copyrighted (with those that are not being identified as "public domain"), whether its items were drawn from other instruments, and general notes about its intended or most appropriate use. It also notes whether versions are available in multiple languages.

Table 52.1 identifies VBSs for screening problems related to mood. Among the most common of such problems is depression. Two options for this are the two- and nine-item versions of the Patient Health Questionnaire (PHQ), which is the self-administered form of the PRIME-MD, an interview measure created for primary-care physicians. Both the PHQ-2 and PHQ-9 have good sensitivity and, in particular, good specificity, and the PHQ-2 is exceptionally brief. Also shown in Table 52.1 is the Edinburgh Postnatal Depression Scale (EPDS), which, as its name suggests, seeks to detect postnatal depression. It is sufficiently brief to qualify as a VBS, has good measurement accuracy, and has been widely used in both practice and research. It also has been translated and validated in at least 18 different languages in addition to English, with varying recommended cut-off scores. A measure of mania, one of the defining characteristics of Bipolar disorder, is also included. The Altman Self-Rating Mania Scale is becoming widely used in research and clinical practice and compares well to other, more lengthy measures, such as the Clinician Administered Rating Scale for Mania (CARS-M). Finally, a measure of suicidal behavior intent, the Suicide Behavior Questionnaire-Revised has been added to address this serious problem. This measure in its lengthier form has enjoyed wide clinical use, and the revised measure retains good measurement accuracy.

VBSs shown in Table 52.2 address anxiety-related problems such as General Anxiety disorders, panic, dissociation, posttraumatic stress (both civilian and military), and adult Attention Deficit Hyperactivity Disorder (ADHD). Although general anxiety is a very common mental health condition, the first brief measure developed to screen for this disorder has been the GAD-7. It has good reliability and construct validity and has been shown to differentiate anxiety from symptoms of depression. With respect to panic, the Autonomic Nervous System (ANS-2) questionnaire was developed to screen patients in primary care settings, where panic symptoms can complicate medical procedures. A less-common but equally serious anxiety-related problem is dissociation, seen in traumatized persons. One available screener is the DES-T, a short version of the Dissociative Experiences Scale. Given the rarity of dissociative disorders, its ability to produce a PPV of 87% in a large general population

TABLE 52.1 Depressive and Bipolar Problems

Category/Name	Items	Key Reference(s)	Measurement Accuracy	Comments
Depression				
Patient Health Questionnaire (PHQ-9 and PHQ-2)	9	Kroenke, K., Spitzer, R. L., & Williams, J. B. W. (2001). The PHQ-9: Validity of a brief depression severity measure. *Journal of General Internal Medicine, 16*, 606–613. Kroenke, K., Spitzer, R. L., & Williams, J. B. W. (2003). The Patient Health Questionnaire-2: Validity of a two-item depression screener. *Medical Care, 41*, 1284–1292.	Validated on 6,000 patients in primary care and obstetric-gynecology clinics. Using a cutoff score of 5, sensitivity for the PHQ-9, was 88% and specificity was 88% against the 20-item General Health Survey. Using a cutoff score of 3 for the PHQ-2, sensitivity was 83% and specificity was 92% against the GHS-20.	Public domain. The PHQ-9 is the depression module of the PRIME-MD, widely used to screen for common mental disorders. The PHQ-2 reduces the length of the measure even further by using only the two necessary DSM-5 criteria for depression—the frequency of depressed mood and anhedonia
Bipolar Disorder (Mania)				
Altman Self-Rating Mania Scale (ASRM)	5	Altman, E. G., Hedeker, D. R., Peterson, J. L., & Davis, J. M. (1997). The Altman Self-Rating Mania scale. *Biological Psychiatry, 42*, 948–955.	Validated with 105 outpatients. Significant correlations with the Mania Rating Scale ($r = .718$) and the Clinician-Administered Rating Scale for Mania subscale ($r = .766$). Principal components analysis suggested three factors—mania, psychotic symptoms, and irritability. Using a cutoff score of 5, sensitivity of 85.5% and specificity of 87.3% are reported for the mania subscale.	Designed to screen for the presence and/or severity of manic symptoms in inpatient or outpatient settings, and thus the presence of hypomania as well. One of the first very brief self-report scales of mania available. Permission available from the author.

Postnatal Depression

Instrument	#	Reference	Description
Edinburgh Postnatal Depression Scale (EPDS)	10	Cox, J. L., Holden, J. M., & Sagovsky, R. (1987). Detection of postnatal depression: Development of the 10-item Edinburgh Postnatal Depression Scale. *British Journal of Psychiatry, 150,* 782–786.	Tested on 84 women who gave birth in the previous 3 months. Using a cutoff score of 12/13, sensitivity is reported as 86%, and specificity as 78%, with a PPV of 73% when tested against the Research Diagnostic Criteria of major and minor depression. Correlates well with the CPRS-Depression, the SADS, and the ICD-10 Versions with three, five, and seven items have been developed.	Public Domain. Although the EPDS can be used to detect depression in postnatal women, some studies suggest it detects symptoms of anxiety or general distress as well. In other validation studies with prenatal women in non-English speaking countries, estimates of sensitivity are reported to vary from 65% to 100%, and specificity from 49% to 100%.

Suicide

Instrument	#	Reference	Description
Suicidal Questionnaire-Revised (SBQ-R)	4	Osman, A., Bagge, C. L., Gutierrez, P. M., Konick, L. C., Kopper, B. A., & Barrios, F. X. (2001). The Suicidal Behaviors Questionnaire-Revised: validation with clinical and nonclinical samples, *Assessment, 5,* 443–453.	Tested on 120 adult inpatients, 135 young adults, 138 high school students, and 120 inpatient adolescents, a cutoff score of either 7 or 8, AUC was reported between .89 and .98, sensitivity .80 to .93, and specificity .91 to .96. PPVs ranged between .70 and .90, and NPVs reported between .86 and .99.	Public Domain. Developed to identify adults and adolescents at risk of suicidal behavior by screening for lifetime, recent past, and likelihood of future suicidal ideation and/or behavior, as well as frequency of suicidal thinking and attempts.

TABLE 52.2 Anxiety and Trauma-related Problems

Category/Name	Items	Key Reference(s)	Measurement Accuracy	Comments
General Anxiety				
Generalized Anxiety Disorder—7 (GAD-7)	7	Spitzer, R. L., Kroenke, K., Williams, J. W., & Löwe, B. (2006). A brief measure for assessing generalized anxiety disorder: The GAD-7. *Archives of Internal Medicine, 166*(10), 1092–1097.	Results are from interviews with 965 adult patients in primary care sites. Using a cutoff score of 10, sensitivity is reported as .89 and specificity as .82. Correlates well with the Beck Anxiety Inventory and the anxiety scale of the SCL-90. AUC reported as .91	Public domain. One of very few measures concordant with DSM IV (and now DSM-5) diagnostic criteria. May be used to assess symptom severity as well as change over time.
Panic				
Autonomic Nervous System Questionnaire abbreviated (ANS-2)	2	Stein, M. B., Roy-Byrne, P. P., McQuaid, J. R., Laffaye, C., Russon, J., McCahill, M. E., Katon, W., . . . Sherbourne, C. D. (1999). Development of a brief diagnostic screen for panic disorder in primary care. *Psychosomatic Medicine, 61,* 359–364.	Results are from 1,476 primary care outpatients in three primary care medical clinics. When tested against the Composite International Diagnostic Interview, sensitivity ranged from .94 to 1.00 and specificity ranged from .25 to .59 with a PPV of .18% to .4% and a NPV of .9% to 1.00.	Three- and five-item versions report only minimally improved specificity and reduced sensitivity. Responses from a subset of 511 patients were tested against the Beck Anxiety Inventory (using a cutoff of 20), resulting in sensitivity of .67.
Dissociation				
Dissociative Experiences Scale-Taxon (DES-T)	8	Waller, N. G., & Ross, C. A. (1997). The prevalence and biometric structure of pathological dissociation in the general population: taxometric and behavior genetic findings. *Journal of Abnormal Psychology, 106,* 499–510.	Results are from 1,055 adults in the general population. Using a cutoff score of 30, sensitivity of .74 and specificity of 1.00 is reported against the full DES, with a PPV of .87 and NPV of .99.	Reported to identify pathological dissociation with greater accuracy that the lengthier DES. A cutoff score of 20 is reported to identify 89% of those with dissociative identify disorder.

Posttraumatic Stress

Measure	#	Citation	Results	Notes
Primary Care PTSD Screen (PC-PTSD)	4	Prins, A., Ouimette, P., & Kimerling, R. (2003). The primary care PTSD screen (PC-PTSD): Development and operating characteristics. *Primary Care Psychiatry, 9,* 9–14.	Tested on 188 male and female primary care patients recruited at VA clinics. Using a cutoff score of 2 yields sensitivity of .91 and specificity of .72 with a PPV of .51 and a NPV of .96. Results from 97 veterans seeking treatment for substance-related disorders used a cutting score of 3 and report sensitivity of .97 and specificity of .08.	Public Domain. This is the only PTSD measure that uses a "yes/no" response format. Currently in use by the Department of Veterans Affairs to screen for PTSD among returning service persons.
Combat Exposure Scale (CES)	7	Keane, T., Fairbank, J., Caddell, J., Zimering, R., Taylor, K., & Mora, C. (1989). Clinical evaluation of a measure to assess combat exposure. *Psychological Assessment, 1,* 53–55. Lund, M., Foy, D. W., Sipprelle, R. C., & Strachan, A. (1984). The Combat Exposure Scale: A systematic assessment of trauma in the Vietnam war. *Journal of Clinical Psychology, 40,* 1323–1328.	Results are from 43 Vietnam era veterans seeking treatment at an outpatient VA facility. Sensitivity of .74 in identifying vets with PTSD.	Public Domain. Assesses severity of exposure to combat as a precursor to PTSD. Widely used as a clinical measure as well as in research studies.

Adult ADHD

Measure	#	Citation	Results	Notes
Adult ADHD Self-Report Scale (ASRS) Screener	6	Kessler, R. C., Adler, L., Ames, M., Demler, O., Faraone, S., Hiripi, E., … Walters, E. E. (2005). The World Health Organization adult ADHD self-report scale (ASRS): A short screening scale for use in the general population. *Psychological Medicine, 35*(2), 245–256.	Results are reported on 154 subjects from a large nationally representative sample of U.S. adults. PPV values are reported for different prevalence levels in the target population. Values ranged from 65.8 at 1% prevalence to 94.7 for 12% prevalence. AUC was .84.	Subset of items from full 18-item ASRS. Includes items measuring Inattention and Hyperactivity-Impulsivity. To improve classification, administration of the full version is recommended for subjects scoring positive on the screener.

sample is an indication of unusually strong measurement accuracy. Finally, measures of post-traumatic stress are being increasingly used to screen groups such as survivors of individual and large-scale trauma, as well as military personnel returning from combat areas. The Primary Care PTSD Screen has good measurement accuracy (PPV > 50%) and uses a simple "yes or no" format. It has most recently been tested with veterans who have served since September 11, 2001. The Combat Exposure Scale (CES) is now widely used among veterans to assess exposure to combat experiences, a common precursor to the development of Posttraumatic Stress Disorder (PTSD). With the increasing number of veterans of combat zones being seen by social workers in a variety of settings, these measures seem especially pertinent to include. A final anxiety-related phenomenon that social workers may need to assess is Attention-Deficit Hyperactivity Disorder, which can affect adults as well as children. The screening measure was taken from the World Health Organization (WHO) Adult ADHD Self-Report Scale (ASRS) as part of a study that revised and updated the larger WHO Composite International Diagnostic Interview.

Three VBSs designed to screen for the eating disorders and one that focuses on body dysmorphism are shown in Table 52.3. The most widely used in the first group is the SCOFF Questionnaire, named from words in its items such as whether respondents eat until they feel Sick. Though developed in Britain, and containing British terms unfamiliar to American respondents, a version using American terms has been produced and tested. Both versions appear to have good accuracy even with nonclinical populations. A second measure, the screening version of the third version of the Eating Disorder Inventory (EDI-3) showed particularly good ability to differentiate bulimia sufferers from subjects in a nonclinical population, but it is very new and has only been tested on a Danish population thus far. A third screener for eating disorders, the ESP, was developed for the purpose of screening primary-care patients. Its recommended cutoff score of 2 allows it to minimize false negatives, but the relatively low specificity this produces risks generating high ratios of false positives. Body image disorders can accompany eating disorder symptoms, and the seven-item Dysmorphic Concern Questionnaire (DCQ) has demonstrated good accuracy in discriminating between subjects in clinical and nonclinical samples. A positive

aspect of the three eating disorder screeners and the Body Concern Questionnaire BCQ are that all are in the public domain.

Table 52.4 displays six VBSs that screen for alcohol abuse, of which most are in the public domain. The CAGE is a longstanding and well-used screener for both abuse and dependence; its name is derive from four symptoms of problems with alcohol: tried Cutting down, Annoyed by criticism of drinking, feeling Guilty and needing a morning "Eye-opener". Results are available from many studies, and these suggest it is highly accurate with some populations but not with others. Users should thus familiarize themselves with this literature before choosing the CAGE. Two alternatives are the AUDIT-C and FAST, which are both subsets of the Alcohol Use Disorders Identification Test (AUDIT). Results from tests of the FAST suggest that it may have better specificity than the AUDIT-C. However, the initial validation study of the FAST was conducted among patient groups, whereas the AUDIT-C has been tested among the U.S. general population. The National Institute of Alcohol Abuse and Alcoholism (NIAAA) Single Question Screen is a newer one-item screen tested among primary care patients. The final two measures listed, the TWEAK and T-ACE, are designed to detect alcohol use during pregnancy, and both show reasonable accuracy.

Table 52.5 list three VBSs available to screen for the abuse of drugs other than alcohol. By far the most frequently cited in the research literature is the DAST-10, a short version of the Drug Abuse Screening Test. It was designed to detect substance use disorder in psychiatric patients, and both have good measurement accuracy when used for that purpose. The DrugAbuse/Dependence Screener is the only substance abuse VBS intended for use in general population samples. Results from its initial validation tests suggest it can perform well in that role. A newer one-item screener for drug use, the Single-Question Screening Test for Drug Use in Primary Care, shows promise for use in primary care settings. The final measure shown in Table 52.5 is the Substance Use Risk Profile–Pregnancy Scale for screening pregnant women for substance use, including alcohol. Sensitivity and specificity varied as expected depending on whether the population was low or high risk.

Table 52.6 offers two versatile and oft-cited screeners for general mental health—the K6 and the MHI-5. These instruments are short, accurate,

TABLE 52.3 Eating Disorders

Category/Name	Items	Key Reference(s)	Measurement Accuracy	Comments
General SCOFF Questionnaire	5	Morgan, J. F., Reid, F., & Lacey, J. H. (1999). The SCOFF questionnaire: Assessment of a new screening tool for eating disorders. *British Medical Journal, 319*, 1467–1468. Botella, J., Sepulveda, A. R., Huang, H. L., & Gambara, H. (2013). A meta-analysis of the diagnostic accuracy of the SCOFF. *Spanish Journal of Psychology, 16*, e92.	Original results were reported from studies of 214 British subjects (clinical and nonclinical) and 233 subjects (nonclinical). At cutoff of 2 or more, sensitivity ranged from 94.7% to 100%, while specificity ranged from 64% to 93%. A more recent analysis across several SCOFF studies found figures of .882 (sensitivity) and .925 (specificity).	Public domain. Results from tests of an American version in which some British vernacular was replaced completed on 305 graduate students (see Parker et al.). These show a PPV of 66.7% and NPV of 88.7%. Versions in a large variety of languages are available.
Eating Disorder Inventory (EDI-3) screening version	5	Friborg, O., Clausen, L., & Rosenvinge, J. H. (2013). A five-item screening version of the Eating Disorder Inventory (EDI-3). *Comprehensive Psychiatry, 54*, 1222–1228.	Identified items from the full 91-item EDI-3 that best discriminated between 112 patients diagnosed with anorexia or bulimia and 878 nonclinical controls. AUC, sensitivity, and specificity for the three anorexia items were .94, .91, and .86, respectively. For the two bulimia items they were .96, .94, and .94.	Public domain. The EDI is widely used in Europe and is available in multiple languages. At .70 for Cronbach's alpha, the measure's level of internal consistency compares well to other eating disorder screeners.
Eating Disorder Screen for Primary care (ESP)	5	Cotton, M. A., Ball, C., & Robinson, P. (2003). Four simple questions can help screen for eating disorders. *Journal of General Internal Medicine, 18*, 53–56.	Validated on 129 university students and 104 primary care patients in Britain. Comparing against results from the Questionnaire for Eating Disorder Diagnoses, sensitivity was 100% and specificity was 71%.	Public domain. A cutoff score of 2 questions answered "Yes" is recommended, and sensitivity and specificity values are based on this cutoff.
Body Image and Dysmorphism Dysmorphic Concern Questionnaire (DCQ)	7	Oosthuizen, P., Lambert, T., & Castle, D. J. (1998). Dysmorphic concern: Prevalence and associations with clinical variables. *Australian and New Zealand Journal of Psychiatry, 32(1)*, 129–132. Mancuso, S. G., Knoesen, N. P., & Castle, D. J. (2010). The Dysmorphic Concern Questionnaire: A screening measure for body dysmorphic disorder. *Australian and New Zealand Journal of Psychiatry, 44(6)*, 535–542.	Initial tests were conducted on small samples of psychiatric inpatients. More recent results compared the DCQ's ability to accurately differentiate clinical from nonclinical (college) samples. AUC was .98, and at the recommended clinical cutting score sensitivity was 96.4 and specificity was 90.6.	Public domain. A cutoff score of 9 is recommended. Items ask for level of concern with body appearance (e.g., whether malformed or misshapen in some way). Response options vary from "Not at all" to "Much more than most people." Most available results are from Australian samples.

TABLE 52.4 Alcohol Abuse

Category/Name	Items	Key Reference(s)	Measurement Accuracy	Comments
General Alcohol Abuse				
CAGE	4	Ewing, J. A. (1984). Detecting alcoholism: The CAGE questionnaire. *JAMA: Journal of the American Medical Association, 252,* 1905–1907. Dhalla, S., & Kopec, J. A. (2007). The CAGE questionnaire for alcohol misuse: A review of reliability and validity studies. *Clinical and Investigative Medicine, 30,* 33–41.	Tested on multiple samples. In a recent review, average sensitivity was 71%, and average specificity was 90% for alcohol abuse or dependence. The CAGE has generally not been found as effective among women, especially white women.	Public domain. Due to its brevity, the CAGE has become widely used in settings such as generalist medical care. cutoff score of 2 is recommended for alcohol abuse or dependence.
Alcohol Use Disorders Identification Test (AUDIT-C)	3	Bush, K., Kihlavan, D. R., McConell, M. B., Fihn, S. D., & Bradley, K. A. (1998). The AUDIT alcohol consumption questions (AUDIT-C): An effective brief screening test for problem drinking. *Archives of Internal Medicine, 158,* 1789–1795. de Meneses-Gaya, C., Zuardi, A. W., Loureiro, S. R., & Crippa, J. A. S. (2009). Alcohol Use Disorders Identification Test (AUDIT): An updated systematic review of psychometric properties. *Psychology & Neuroscience, 2,* 83–97.	Tested on multiple samples. In a U. S. general population survey using a risk drinking criterion, sensitivity was 91% and specificity 95% for men based on a cutoff score of 5, and sensitivity was 96% and specificity 70% for women based on a cutoff score of 3.	Public domain. Includes the first three questions of the full AUDIT, which is one of the most-used measures of hazardous/harmful drinking. The third item of the AUDIT-C, called AUDIT-3, shows some promise as a single-item screener (see FAST information below).
Fast Alcohol Screening Test (FAST)	4	Hodgson, R., Alwyn, T., John, B., Thom, B., & Smith, A. (2002). The FAST alcohol screening test. *Alcohol and Alcoholism, 37,* 61–66. Hodgson, R. J., John, B., Abbasi, T., Hodgson, R. C., Waller, S., Thom, B., & Newcombe, R. G. (2003). Fast screening for alcohol misuse. *Addictive Behaviors, 28,* 1453–1463.	Tested on patients in a variety of settings in the United Kingdom. Using the full Alcohol Use Disorders Identification Test (AUDIT) as a criterion, sensitivity ranged from 91% to 97% and specificity ranged from 86% to 95%.	Public domain. Comprises items 3, 5, 8, and 10 from the AUDIT. Item 3 can be used as a filter question. FAST scoring and item modifications, including a gender-specific asked item, can be viewed in the key reference.

Screen	Items	Validation	Notes
NIAAA Single Question Screen (NSQS)	1	Tested on primary care patients. Sensitivity was 81.8% and specificity 79.3% for unhealthy alcohol use. Sensitivity was 87.9% and specificity 66.8% for active alcohol use disorder.	Public domain. Recommended by NIAAA. The NSQS item is "How many times in the past year have you had X or more drinks in a day" where X is 5 for men and 4 for women. A drink is considered 14 g of pure alcohol. A response of 1 or more is a positive screen. It is recommended that the question "Do you sometimes drink beer, wine, or other alcoholic beverages" be asked prior to the NSQS, as some individuals do not consider beer to be alcohol. If the answer is yes, the NSQS is administered.

National Institute on Alcohol Abuse and Alcoholism (NIAAA). (2005). *Helping patients who drink too much: A clinician's guide, 2005 Edition* (NIH Publication No. 07–3769). Bethesda, MD: Reprinted 2007.

Smith, P. C., Schmidt, S. M., Allensworth-Davies, D., & Saitz, R. (2009). Primary care validation of a single-question alcohol screening test. *Journal of General Internal Medicine, 24,* 783–788. doi:10.1007/s11606-009-0928-6 Erratum (2010) in *Journal of General Internal Medicine, 25,* 375.

Risky Drinking in Pregnancy

Screen	Items	Validation	Notes
TWEAK	5	Validation sample included 4,743 African American women visiting a prenatal clinic in Detroit. Against a criterion of periconceptual risk drinking and a cut point of 2 or more "yes" answers, AUC was 0.865, sensitivity 79%, specificity 83%, and PPV 22%.	Public domain. The TWEAK is derived from the CAGE. In a recent review, the sensitivity of the TWEAK was 71%–91% and specificity 73%–83% for risk drinking.

Russell, M. (1994). New assessment tools for drinking in pregnancy: T-ACE, TWEAK, and others. *Alcohol Health and Research World, 18,* 55–61.

Chan, A. W., Pristach, E. A., Welte, J. W., & Russell, M. (1993). Use of the TWEAK test in screening for alcoholism/heavy drinking in three populations. *Alcoholism: Clinical and Experimental Research, 17,* 1188–1192.

Burns, E., Gray, R., & Smith, L. A. Brief screening questionnaires to identify problem drinking during pregnancy: A systematic review. *Addiction, 105,* 601–614.

Screen	Items	Validation	Notes
T-ACE	4	Validated on a sample of 971 pregnant African American women at an inner-city clinic. Against a criterion of periconceptual risk drinking, sensitivity was 69%, specificity 89%, and PPV 23% when using a cutoff score of 2.	Copyrighted. Contact S. Martier, Ob/Gyn, 4704 Saint Antoine, Detroit, MI 48201. In a recent review, T-ACE sensitivity was 69%–88% and specificity was 71%–89% for risk drinking.

Sokol, R. J., Martier, S. S., Ager, J. W. (1989). The T-ACE questions: Practical and prenatal detection of risk drinking, *American Journal of Obstetrics and Gynecology, 60,* 863–870.

Burns, E., Gray, R., & Smith, L. A. Brief screening questionnaires to identify problem drinking during pregnancy: A systematic review. *Addiction, 105,* 601–614.

Allen, J. P., & Columbus, M. (Eds). (1995). *Assessing alcohol problems: A guide for clinicians and researchers.* Bethesda, MD: National Institute on Alcohol Abuse and Alcoholism.

TABLE 52.5 Substance Abuse

Category/Name	Items	Key Reference(s)	Measurement Accuracy	Comments
General Drug Abuse				
Drug Abuse Screening Test (DAST-10)	10	Skinner, H. A. (1982). The Drug Abuse Screening Test. *Addictive Behaviors, 7*, 363–371. Bohn, M. J., Babor, T. F., & Kranzler, H. R. (1991). Validity of the Drug *Abuse Screening Test (DAST-10) in inpatient substance abusers: Problems of drug dependence.* Proceedings from the 53rd Annual Scientific Meeting: The Committee on Problems of Drug Dependence, Inc. Monograph 119, National Institute of Drug Abuse Research. Yudko, E., Lozhkina, O., & Fouts, A. (2007). A comprehensive review of the psychometric properties of the Drug Abuse Screening Test. *Journal of Substance Abuse Treatment, 32*, 189–198.	Tests that report screening accuracy are from samples of psychiatric patients. In a recent review, sensitivity ranged from 41% to 85% and specificity ranged from 78% to 99% against a criterion of substance use disorder or the occurrence of substance use disorder symptoms.	A cutoff score of 3 is recommended, but one study found good sensitivity and specificity with a cutoff score of 2. The measure is copyrighted, but as long as the author, Dr. Harvey Skinner, is credited, it may be reproduced for noncommercial use. A DAST-10 manual is available.
Rost Drug Dependence Screener	3	Rost, K., Burnam, M. A., & Smith, G. R. (1993). Development of screeners for depressive disorders and substance disorder history. *Medical Care, 31*, 189–200. Vernez, G., Buram, M. A., McGlynn, E. A., Trude, S., & Mittman, B. S. (1988). *Review of California's program for the homeless mentally disabled.* RAND Report #R-3631-California Department of Mental Health. Santa Monica, CA.	Against results from a standardized diagnostic instrument using DSM-III criteria, the screener showed 57%–94% sensitivity, 95%–99% specificity, PPV from 67%–88%, and NPV from 98%–99% in population-based samples. It has also been tested among homeless populations.	The Drug Abuse/Dependence Screener is three items from the Diagnostic Interview Schedule and can be viewed in the source reference. The population-based test samples involved individuals who had utilized either outpatient health services for a physical issue or outpatient health or mental health services for a mental health issue within the past 6 months.

Single-Question Screening Test for Drug Use in Primary Care	1	Smith, P. C., Schmidt, S. M., Allensworth-Davies, D., & Saitz, R. (2010). A single-question screening test for drug use in primary care. *Archives of Internal Medicine, 170,* 1155–1160.	Against several criterion measures, including current self-reported use and oral fluid testing, sensitivity ranged from 84.7% to 100% and specificity ranged from 73.5% to 96.2%. AUCs ranged from 0.89 to 0.93.	The Single-Question Screening Test for Drug Use in Primary Care is "How many times in the past year have you used an illegal drug or used a prescription medication for nonmedical reasons?" A response of 1 or more times is a positive screen test. Consult the key reference for more information.

Risky Substance Use in Pregnancy

Substance Use Risk Profile-Pregnancy Scale (SURPPS)	3	Yonkers, K. A., Gotman, N., Kershaw, T., Forray, A., Howell, H. B., & Rounsaville, B. J. (2010). Screening for prenatal substance use: Development of the Substance Use Risk Profile-Pregnancy Scale. *Obstetrics & Gynecology, 116,* 827–833.	The SURPPS items were derived from a training sample of 1,610 pregnant women from a larger cohort of 2,684. These items were tested in the validation sample of 1,074 against the criterion of self-reported substance use in the past 30 days. For low-risk populations, sensitivity was 91%, specificity 67%, and Akaike's Information Criterion 579.75.	The SURPPS instrument and scoring information can be viewed in the source reference. For high-risk populations, sensitivity was lower at 57%, but specificity was higher at 88% (Akaike's Information Criterion 616.93).

TABLE 52.6 General Mental Health and Personality Disorders

Category/Name	Items	Key Reference(s)	Measurement Accuracy	Comments
General Mental Health				
K6	6	Kessler, R. C., Andrews, G., Colpe, L. J., Hiripi, E., Mroczek, D. K., Normand, S. L. T., Walters, E. E., & Zaslavsky, A. M. (2002). Short screening scales to monitor population prevalences and trends in non-specific psychological distress. *Psychological Medicine, 32,* 959–976. Kessler, R. C., Barker, P. R., Colpe, L. J., Epstein, J. F., Gfroerer, J. C., Hiripi, E., Howes, M. J., … Zaslavsky, A. M. (2003). Screening for serious mental illness in the general population. *Archives of General Psychiatry, 60,* 184–189.	Validated on data from large mail (n > 1,000) and telephone (n > 10,000) surveys. Using Composite International Diagnostic Inventory (CIDI) results as a criterion, AUC was .875; specificity was .96; sensitivity was .36. Later studies have examined versions in other languages, typically confirming equal or better results (e. g., AUC or .92 for the Japanese version; specificity of .92 and sensitivity of .62 for French version).	Public domain. Two items address depressed mood; one item each addresses motor agitation, fatigue, worthless guilt, and anxiety. Results of follow-up studies suggest the K6 may be useful in screening for serious mental illness as well as general psychological distress. Versions in a variety of languages are available.
Mental Health Inventory (MHI-5)	5	Veit, C. T., & Ware, J. E. (1983). The structure of psychological distress and well-being in general populations. *Journal of Consulting and Clinical Psychology, 51,* 730–742. Kelly, M. J., Dunstan, F. D., Lloyd, K., & Fone, D. L. (2008). Evaluating cut points for the MHI-5 and MCS using the GHQ-12: A comparison of five different methods. *BMC Psychiatry, 8,* 1–9.	A study of 5,291 adults showed an AUC of 79.3% when compared against results from the Diagnostic Interview Schedule. Other results testing against scores from the PRIME-MD show specificity = .58 and sensitivity = .91 for major depression or panic disorder. Results from a British sample suggest an optimum cutting score of 76.	Public domain. Items are a subset of the SF-36. Focuses more than the K6 on screening for affective and anxiety-related aspects of mental health. Several studies have established accuracy levels and cutting scores by using the General Health Questionnaire (GHQ) as a criterion. Many translations available.

Personality Disorders

| McLean Screening Instrument for Borderline Personality Disorder (MSI-BPD) | 10 | Zanarini, M. C., Vujanovic, A. A., Parachini, E. A., Boulanger, J. L., Frankenburg, F. R., & Hennen, J. (2003): A screening measure for BPD: The McLean Screening Instrument for Borderline Personality Disorder (MSI-BPD). *Journal of Personality Disorders, 17*, 568–573.

Chanen, A. M., Jovev, M., Djaja, D., McDougall, M., Hok, P. Y., Rawling, D., & Jackson, H. J. (2008). Screening for borderline personality disorder in outpatient youth. *Journal of Personality Disorders, 22*(4), 353–364. | For cutoff score of 7, sensitivity = .87 and specificity = .90 for age 30 and younger; .03 points higher for each in subjects 25 and younger. In a second study of adolescents, AUC was acceptable but lower than for the longer Borderline Personality Questionnaire, so screening for BPD with a very brief scale needs further empirical support. | Based on subset of items from the DSM-IV Borderline module. In the original study, subjects were 200 community volunteers selected for some BPD characteristics and some history of psychiatric treatment. Psychiatric diagnosis was used as the comparison standard. Versions have been developed in other languages, such as Dutch. |

TABLE 52.7 Other Problems

Category/Name	Items	Key Reference(s)	Measurement Accuracy	Comments
History of Abuse				
Two-Item Screener for Detecting a History of Physical or Sexual Abuse in Childhood	2	Thombs, B. D., Bernstein, D. P., Ziegelstein, R. C., Bennett, W., & Walker, E. A. (2007). A brief two-item screener for detecting a history of physical or sexual abuse in childhood. *General Hospital Psychiatry, 29*, 8–13.	Data were gathered by surveying 1,225 women staff members of a health maintenance organization in the United States. Sensitivity was 84.8%, specificity was 88.1%, and the positive likelihood ratio was 7.1 for physical or sexual abuse in childhood, comparing against results from a semistructured interview of a subset of 216 respondents.	Public domain. The measure is intended for use by primary-care physicians and other professionals, and it is assumed that at only two items in length it is suitable for being embedded in larger interview protocols designed to gather basic information from patients.
Food Insecurity (FI) screener	2	Hager, E., Quigg, A., Black, M., Coleman, S., Heeren, T., Rose-Jacobs, R., et al. (2010). Development and validity of a two-item screen to identify families at risk for food insecurity. *Pediatrics, 126* (1), e26–e32.	Data were drawn from 30,098 hospital and emergency room interviews of mothers of children under age 3 years in six U.S. cities. Interviews included the 18-item USDA Household Food Security Survey (HFSS), from which the items were drawn. Comparing against the full version, the screener's sensitivity was 97%, and its specificity was 83%.	Public domain. Questions are: "Within the past 12 months we worried whether our food would run out before we got money to buy more" and "Within the past 12 months the food we bought just didn't last and we didn't have money to get more." Responses correlated with child health and developmental risks and lifetime hospitalizations.

well validated, easily embedded in questionnaires, and available in the public domain. The K6 has also shown some capacity to screen for serious mental illness in general population samples, and both it and the MHI-5 are frequently used in the United States and Europe. One other measure shown in Table 52.6 that is brief enough to be considered a VBS, and that continues to receive relatively frequent use, is a screener designed to detect the presence of a borderline personality disorder. None of these measures should be construed as a diagnostic tool, and all should be treated as initial indicators of the need for more comprehensive evaluation.

Two other problems for which social workers may wish to screen clients and for which two-item VBSs are available are a childhood history of abuse and food insecurity. The screener for detecting a history of physical or sexual abuse in childhood was derived from a larger measure designed to be used for clinical data-gathering by primary care physicians, but they are easily adaptable to client assessment protocols used by social workers. Similarly, the FI (food insecurity) screener comprises two items from a larger measure developed by the U. S. Department of Agriculture. Food insecurity is often a proxy for serious poverty, and it is associated with a variety of threats to children's health and well-being.

The growing availability of VBSs has the potential to improve dramatically the quality of social work assessments. We believe that accurate, versatile, easy-to-use, and no-cost measures such as the PHQ-2, CAGE, and K6 should become part of the basic measurement toolbox of all direct-service professionals in the field, and these instruments also have the potential to be similarly valuable in research and evaluation. A further rationale for their use is that they are becoming more commonplace in other disciplines, and knowing when and how to apply, score, and interpret them will allow social workers to work more closely with other professionals and to enhance the effectiveness of their own efforts.

USEFUL WEBSITES

Alcohol & Drug Abuse Institute Library, University of Washington. Substance Use Screening & Assessment Instruments Database. http://lib.adai.uw.edu/instruments/

References

Fischer, J., & Corcoran, K. (2007). *Measures for clinical practice and research: A sourcebook. Vol. 1: Couples, families, & children.* New York, NY: Oxford University Press.

Hudson, W. W. (1982). *The clinical measurement package: A field manual.* Chicago, IL: Dorsey Press.

Metz, C. E. (1978). Basic principles of ROC analysis. *Seminars in Nuclear Medicine, 8,* 283–298.

PART VI
Working with Couples and Families

53 Using Genograms to Map Family Patterns

Monica McGoldrick

Over the past several decades, genograms increasingly have been used by health care and human service professionals as a practical tool for mapping family patterns (McGoldrick, Gerson, & Petry, 2008). They are becoming a common language for tracking family history and relationships (see Figure 53.1). Genograms display family information graphically, providing a quick gestalt of complex family patterns; as such, they are a rich source of hypotheses about the evolution of both clinical problems and the family contexts within which problems develop and are generally resolved. The video, *Harnessing the Power of Genograms in Psychotherapy* (McGoldrick, 2013) demonstrates my first interview with a client. The video shows questioning around the presenting problem while gathering relevant genogram information, drawing it on the genogram, and helping the client to see its value. The video is available from www.psychotherapy.net.

Families are organized within biological, legal, cultural, and emotional structures, as well as according to generation, age, gender, and other factors. Where one fits in the family structure can influence functioning, relational patterns, and the type of family one forms in the next generation. Gender and birth order are key factors shaping sibling relationships and characteristics. When various family configurations are mapped on the genogram, the clinician can hypothesize about possible personality characteristics and relational compatibilities. Cultural issues including ethnicity, race, religion, migration, class, and other socioeconomic factors, as well as a family's time and location in history, also influence a family's structural patterns (McGoldrick, Carter, & Garcia-Preto, 2015; Congress, 1994; Hardy &

Laszloffy, 1995; McGoldrick, 2011; McGoldrick, Giordano, & Preto, 2005; Walsh, 2003). These factors, too, become part of the genogram map.

Genograms appeal to clinicians because they are tangible and graphic representations of complex family patterns. They allow the clinician to map the family structure clearly and note and update the family picture as it emerges. For a clinical record, the genogram provides an efficient summary, allowing a clinician unfamiliar with a case to quickly grasp a large amount of information about a family and have a view of potential problems. Whereas notes written in a chart or questionnaire tend to become lost in the record, genogram information is immediately recognizable and can be added to and corrected at each clinical visit as more is learned about a family.

Genograms make it easier for clinicians to keep in mind the complexity of a family's context, including family history, patterns, and events that may have ongoing significance for patient care. Just as our spoken language potentiates and organizes our thought processes, genograms, which map relationships and patterns of family functioning and cultural history, help clinicians think systemically about how events and relationships in their clients' lives are related to patterns of health, illness, and resilience.

Gathering genogram information should be an integral part of any comprehensive clinical assessment. There is no quantitative measurement scale by which the clinician can use a genogram in a cookbook fashion to make clinical predictions. Rather, it is a factual as well as interpretive tool, enabling social workers to generate tentative hypotheses for further evaluation in

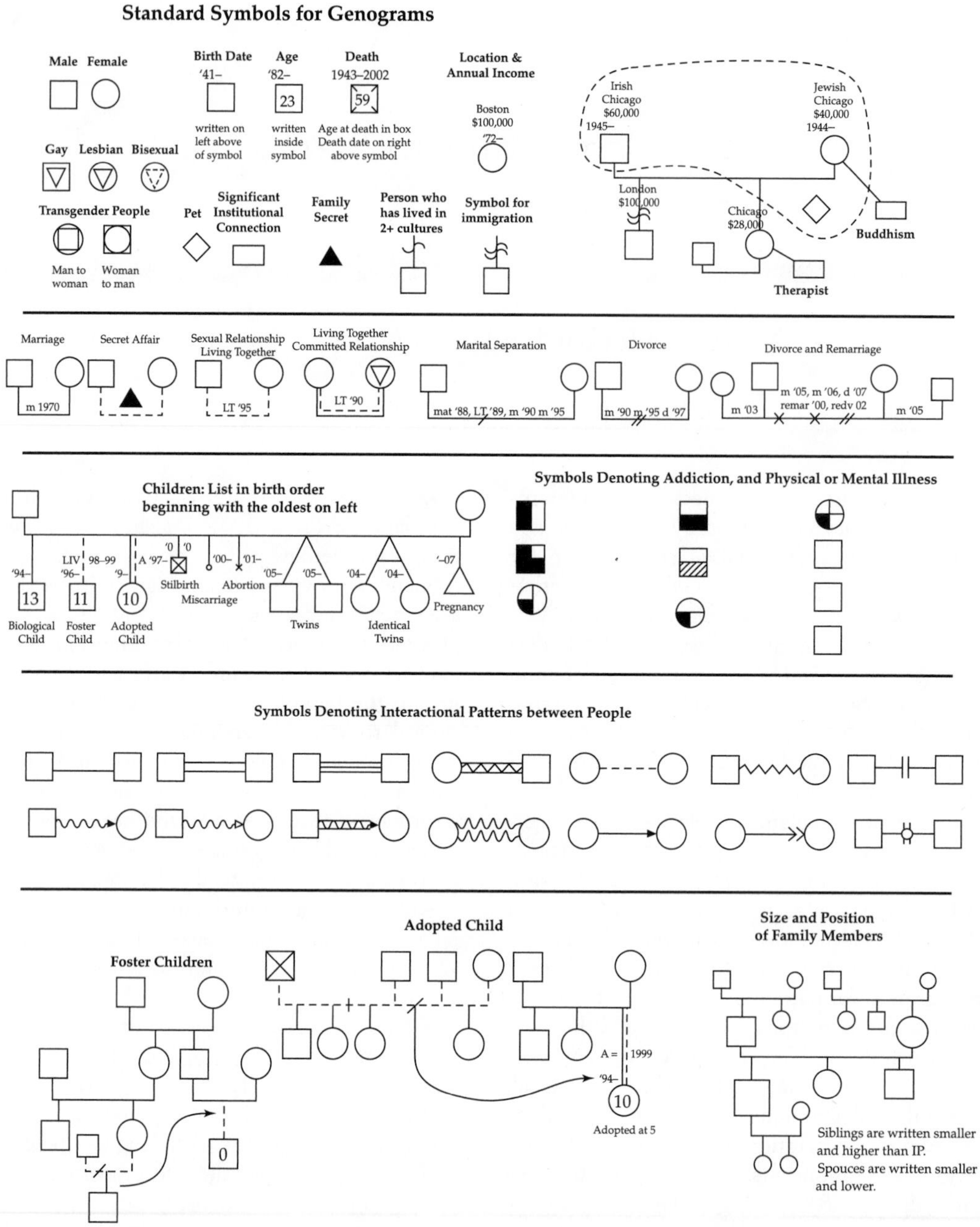

Standard Symbols for Genograms

Figure 53.1 Genogram format.

a family assessment. Typically, the genogram is constructed from information gathered during the first session and revised as new information becomes available. Thus, the initial assessment forms the basis for treatment. Of course, we cannot compartmentalize assessment and treatment. Each interaction of the social worker with the family informs the assessment and thus influences the next intervention. *Harnessing the Power of Genograms in Psychotherapy* (McGoldrick, 2013) demonstrates the back and forth necessary in learning about a client's history, while remaining relevant to his specific presenting problem.

Genograms help social workers get to know their clients; they thus become an important way of engaging with families. Creating a systemic perspective helps track family issues through space and time, and genograms enable an interviewer to reframe, detoxify, and normalize emotion-laden issues. Because the genogram interview provides a ready vehicle for systemic questioning, it begins to orient clients to a systemic perspective as well. The genogram thus helps both the social worker and the client to see the larger picture—that is, to view problems in their current and historical context. Structural, relational, and functional information about a family can be viewed on a genogram both horizontally across the family context and vertically through the generations. Scanning the breadth of the current family context allows the social worker to assess the connectedness of the immediate players in the family drama to each other, as well as to the broader system, and evaluate the family's strengths, resilience, and vulnerabilities in relation to the overall situation.

We include on the genogram the nuclear and extended family members, as well as significant non-blood kin, friends, and pets who have lived with or played a major role in the family's life. We can also note significant events and problems. Current behavior and problems of family members can be traced from multiple perspectives. The index person (IP, or person with the problem or symptom) may be viewed in the context of various subsystems, such as siblings, triangles, reciprocal relationships, multigenerational patterns, life cycle stages and transitions, as well as in relation to the broader community, social institutions (schools, courts, etc.), and sociocultural context.

By scanning the family system culturally and historically and by assessing previous life cycle transitions, the clinician can place present issues in the context of the family's evolutionary patterns. Thus, we include on a genogram cultural and demographic information about at least three generations of family members, as well as nodal and critical events in the family's history, particularly as related to family changes (migration, loss, and the life cycle). When family members are questioned about the present situation in relation to the themes, myths, rules, and emotionally charged issues of previous generations, repetitive patterns often become clear. Genograms "let the calendar speak" by suggesting possible connections between family events over time. Previous patterns of illness and earlier shifts in family relationships brought about through changes in family structure and other critical life changes can easily be noted on the genogram, providing a

framework for hypothesizing what may be influencing a current crisis. In conjunction with genograms, we also create a family chronology, which depicts the family history in a timeline; the genogram itself maps first the structure and then the chronology of generations, but may not make the timing of different events as clear as a chronology, particularly around times of individual and family stress. We also often create a sociogram or eco-map (Hartman, 1978), which shows how clients are emotionally connected to family and other resources in their lives.

THE FAMILY INFORMATION NET

The process of gathering family information can be thought of as casting out an information net in progressively larger circles to capture relevant information about the family and its broader context. The net spreads out in a number of different directions:

- From the presenting problem to the larger context of the problem;
- From the immediate household to the extended family and broader social systems;
- From the present family situation to a chronology of historical family events;
- From easy, nonthreatening queries to difficult, anxiety-provoking questions; and
- From obvious facts to judgments about functioning and relationships to hypothesized family patterns.

THE PRESENTING PROBLEM AND THE IMMEDIATE HOUSEHOLD

In health care situations, genogram information is often recorded as it emerges during medical visits. In family therapy and social service situations, specific problems may be identified, which provide the clinician's starting point. At the outset, families are told that some basic background information is needed to understand their situation fully. Such information usually grows naturally out of exploring the presenting problem and its impact on the immediate household. It makes sense to start with the immediate family and the context in which the problem occurs.

- Who lives in the household?
- How is each person related?
- Where do other family members live?

The clinician asks the name, age, gender, and occupation of each person in the household to sketch the immediate family structure. Other revealing information is elicited through inquiring about the problem.

- Which family members know about the problem?
- How does each view it? How has each of them responded?
- Has anyone in the family ever had similar problems?
- What solutions were attempted by whom in those situations?
- When did the problem begin? Who noticed it first? Who is most concerned about the problem? Who the least?
- Were family relationships different before the problem began? What other problems existed?
- Does the family see the problem as having changed? If so, in what ways? Has it changed for better or for worse?

This is also a good time to inquire about previous efforts to get help for the problem, including previous treatment, therapists, hospitalizations, and the current referring person.

The Current Situation

Next, the clinician spreads the information net into the current family situation. This line of questioning usually follows naturally from questions about the problem and who is involved.

- What has been happening recently in your family?
- Have there been any recent changes in the family (e.g., people coming or leaving, illnesses, job problems)?

It is important to inquire about recent life cycle transitions as well as anticipated changes in the family situation (especially exits and entrances of family members—births, marriages, divorces, deaths, stresses related to health, the law, behavior changes, or the departure of family members).

The Wider Family Context

The clinician looks for an opportunity to explore the wider family context by asking about the extended family and cultural background of all the adults involved. The interviewer might move into this area by saying, "I would now like to ask you something about your background to help make sense of your present problem."

The clinician inquires about each side of the family separately, beginning, for example, with the mother's side: "Let's begin with your mother's family. Your mother was which one of how many children? When and where was she born? Is she alive? If not, when did she die? What was the cause of her death? If alive, where is she now? What does she do? Is she retired? When did this happen? When and how did your mother meet your father? When did they marry? Had she been married before? If so, when? Did she have children by that relationship? Did they separate or divorce or did the spouse die? If so, when was that?" And so on. In a similar fashion, questions are asked about the father. Then the clinician might ask about each parent's family of origin— that is, father, mother, and siblings. The goal is to get information about at least three or four generations, including grandparents, parents, aunts, uncles, siblings, spouses, and children of the IP.

Dealing with a Family's Resistance to Doing a Genogram

When family members react negatively to questions about the extended family or complain that such matters are irrelevant, it often makes sense to redirect the focus to the immediate situation until the connections between the present situation and other family relationships or experiences can be established. An example of such a genogram assessment for a remarried family whose teenage daughter's behavior was the presenting problem has been produced in the videotape *The Legacy of Unresolved Loss* (McGoldrick, 2001). This video also illustrates, as does *Harnessing the Power of Genograms in Psychotherapy* (McGoldrick, 2013), how to manage a client's resistance to revealing genogram information. Gentle persistence over time will usually result in obtaining the information and demonstrating its relevance to the family.

Ethnic and Cultural History

It is essential to learn something about the family's socioeconomic, political, and cultural background to place presenting problems and current relationships in context. When the questioning expands to the extended family, it is a good point to begin exploring cultural issues, because exploring ethnicity and migration history helps establish the cultural context in which the family is operating and offers the therapist an opportunity to understand family attitudes and behaviors determined by such influences (McGoldrick et al., 2005). It is important to learn what the family's cultural traditions are for dealing with problems, health care, and healing, and where the current family members stand in relation to those traditional values. It is also important to consider the family's cultural expectations about relationships with health care professionals, given that this will set the tone for their clinical responses.

Differences in social class background among family members or between family members and the health care professional may create discomfort, which will need to be attended to in the meeting. Questions to ascertain class assumptions pertain not just to the family's current income but also to cultural background, education, and social status within their community. Once the clinician has a clear picture of the ethnic and cultural factors influencing a family (while preferably keeping his or her own biases in check), it is possible to raise delicate questions geared to helping families identify any behaviors that—even if culturally sanctioned in their original context—may be keeping them stuck (see McGoldrick, Giordano, & Garcia-Preto, 2005; McGoldrick & Hardy, 2008).

The Informal Kinship Network

The information net extends beyond the biological and legal structure of the family to encompass common-law and cohabiting relationships, miscarriages, abortions, stillbirths, foster and adopted children, and anyone else in the informal network of the family who is an important support. Inquiries are made about godparents, teachers, neighbors, friends, parents of friends, clergy, caretakers, doctors, and the like who are or have been important to the functioning of the family; this information is also included on the genogram. It is important to ask also about pets because they are often a primary source of support to family members. Pets should always be included on the genogram as a diamond (see Genogram Format) or with a small image of the pet. In exploring outside supports for the family, the clinician might ask:

- To whom could you turn for financial, emotional, physical, and spiritual help?
- What roles have outsiders played in your family?

- What is your relationship to your community?
- Who outside the family has been important in your life?
- Did you ever have a nanny, caretaker, or babysitter to whom you felt attached? What became of her or him?
- Has anyone else ever lived with your family? When? Where are they now?
- Do you have a pet, and if so, what role does s/he play in your lives?
- What has been your family's experience with doctors and other helping professionals or agencies?

For particular clients, certain additional questions are appropriate. For example, the following questions would be important in working with gay and lesbian clients (see Burke & Faber, 1997; Green, 2008).

- Who was the first person you told about your sexual orientation?
- To whom on your genogram are you out?
- To whom would you most like to come out?
- Who would be especially easy or difficult to come out to?
- Who is in your social network? (These people should always be added to the genogram.)

Tracking Family Process

Tracking shifts that occurred around births, deaths, and other transitions can lead the clinician to hypotheses about the family's adaptive style. Particularly critical are untimely or traumatic deaths and the deaths of pivotal family members (Walsh & McGoldrick, 2004). We look for specific patterns of adaptation or rigidification following such transitions. Assessment of past adaptive patterns, particularly after losses and other critical transitions, may be crucial in helping a family in the current crisis. A family's past, and the relationship family members have to it, provides important clues about family rules, expectations, patterns of organization, strengths, resources, and sources of resilience (Walsh, 2006).

The history of specific problems should also be investigated in detail. The focus should be on how family patterns have changed at different periods: before the problem began, at the time of the problem's onset, at the time of first seeking help, and presently. Specific genograms can be done for each of these time periods. Asking how family members see the future of the problem is also informative. Questions may include the following.

• What will happen in the family if the problem continues? What will happen if it goes away?
• What does the future look like?
• What changes do family members imagine are possible in the future?

Seeing the family in its historical perspective involves linking past, present, and future and noting the family's flexibility in adapting to changes.

During the mapping on the genogram of the nuclear and extended family, and the gathering of facts about various family members, the clinician also begins to make inquiries and judgments about the functioning, relationships, and roles of each person in the family. This involves going beyond the bare facts to clinical judgment and acumen. Inquiries about these issues can touch sensitive nerves in the family and should be made with care.

Difficult Questions about Individual Functioning

Family members may function well in some areas but not in others, or they may cover up their dysfunction. Often, it takes careful questioning to reveal the true level of functioning. A family member with a severe illness may show remarkable adaptive strengths, and another may show fragility in response to little apparent stress. Questions about individual functioning may be difficult or painful for family members to answer and must be approached with sensitivity and tact, such as questions about alcohol abuse, chronic unemployment, severe symptomatology, or trauma. The family members should be warned that questions may be difficult, and they should let the clinician know if there is an issue they would rather not discuss. The clinician will need to judge the degree of pressure to apply if the family resists questions that may be essential to dealing with the presenting problem.

Clinicians need to exercise extreme caution about when to ask questions that could put a family member in danger. For example, if violence toward a wife is suspected, she should never be asked about her husband's behavior in his presence, because the question assumes she is free to respond, which may not be the case. It is clinicians' responsibility to be sure their questions do not put a client in jeopardy. The following questions reflect issues of relevance, but not necessarily a format for ascertaining the information, which could require delicate and diplomatic interviewing.

Serious Problems
• Has anyone in the family had a serious medical or psychological problem? Been depressed? Had anxieties? Fears? Lost control?
• Has there been physical or sexual abuse?
• Are there any other problems that worry you? When did that problem begin? Did you seek help for it? If so, when? What happened? What is the status of that problem now?

Work
• Have there been any recent job changes?
• Has anyone been unemployed?
• Do you like your work? Do other family members like their work?

Finances
• How much income does each member generate? Does this create any imbalance in family relationships? How does the economic situation compare with that of your relatives or neighbors?
• Is there any expected inheritance? Are there family members who may need financial help or caretaking?
• Are there any extraordinary expenses? Outstanding debts? What is the level of credit card debt?
• Who controls the money? How are spending decisions made? Are these patterns different from the ways money was handled in the families of origin?

Drugs and Alcohol
• Do any family members routinely use medication? What kind and for what?
• Who prescribed it? What is the family's relationship with that physician?
• Do you think any members drink too much or have a drug problem? Has anyone else ever thought so? What drugs? When? What has the family attempted to do about it?

- How does the person's behavior change under the influence of the drug? How does the behavior of others change when a member is drug involved?

Trouble with the Law
- Have any family members ever been arrested? For what? When? What was the result? What is that person's legal status now?
- Has anyone ever lost his or her driver's license?

Physical or Sexual Abuse
- Have you ever felt intimidated in your family? Have you or others ever been hit? Has anyone in your family ever been threatened with being hit? Have you ever threatened anyone else in your family or hit them?
- Have you or any other family members ever been sexually molested or touched inappropriately by a member of your family or someone outside your family? By whom?

SETTING PRIORITIES FOR ORGANIZING GENOGRAM INFORMATION

One of the most difficult aspects of genogram assessment remains setting priorities for inclusion of family information on a genogram. Clinicians cannot follow every lead the interview suggests. Awareness of basic genogram patterns can help the clinician set such priorities. As a rule of thumb, the data are scanned for the following:

- Repetitive symptoms, relationships, or functioning patterns across the family and over the generations. Repeated cut-offs, triangles, coalitions, patterns of conflict, over- and underfunctioning.
- Coincidences of dates—for example, the death of one family member or anniversary of this death occurring at the same time as symptom onset in another, or the age at symptom onset coinciding with the age of problem development in another family member.
- The impact of change and untimely life cycle transitions, particularly changes in functioning or relationships that correspond

with critical family life events or untimely life cycle transitions—for example, births, marriages, or deaths that occur "off schedule."

Awareness of possible patterns makes the clinician more sensitive to what is missing. Missing information about important family members, events, or discrepancies in the information offered frequently reflect charged emotional issues in the family. The clinician should take careful note of the connections family members make or fail to make to various events.

A FAMILY SYSTEMS PERSPECTIVE

A family systems perspective views families as inextricably interconnected. Neither people nor their problems or solutions exist in a vacuum. Both are interwoven into broader interactional systems, the most fundamental of which is the family. The family is the primary and, except in rare instances, most powerful system to which we humans belong. In this framework, "family" consists of the entire kinship network of at least three generations, both as it currently exists and as it has evolved through time (McGoldrick, Garcia-Preto, & Carter, 2015). Family is, by our definition, those who are tied together through their common biological, legal, cultural, and emotional history and their implied future together. The physical, social, and emotional functioning of family members is profoundly interdependent, with changes in one part of the system reverberating in other parts. In addition, family interactions and relationships tend to be highly reciprocal, patterned, and repetitive. These patterns allow us to make tentative predictions from the genogram.

Coincidences of historical events or concurrent events in different parts of a family are viewed not as random happenings but as occurrences that may be interconnected systemically, though the connections may be hidden from view (McGoldrick, 2011). In addition, key family relationship changes seem more likely to occur at certain times than at others. They are especially likely at points of life cycle transition. Symptoms tend to cluster around such transitions in the family life cycle, when family members face the task of reorganizing their relations with one another to go on to the next phase (McGoldrick, Garcia-Preto & Carter, in press). The symptomatic family may become stuck in time, unable to resolve its impasse by reorganizing and moving on. The history and relationship patterns revealed in a genogram assessment provide important clues about the nature of this impasse—how a symptom may have arisen to preserve or prevent some relationship pattern or to protect some legacy of previous generations.

Families have many different types of relationship patterns. Of particular interest are patterns of relational distance. People may be very close or very distant or somewhere in between. At one extreme are family members who do not speak or are in constant conflict with each other. The family may actually be in danger of cutting off entirely. At the other extreme are families who seem almost stuck together in "emotional fusion." Family members in fused or poorly differentiated relationships are vulnerable to dysfunction, which tends to occur when the level of stress or anxiety exceeds the system's capacity to deal with it. The more closed the boundaries of a system become, the more immune it is to input from the environment, and consequently, the more rigid the family patterns become. In other words, family members in a closed, fused system react automatically to one another and may be impervious to events outside the system that require adaptation to changing conditions. Fusion may involve either positive or negative relationships—that is, family members may feel very good about each other or experience almost nothing but hostility and conflict. In either case, there is an overly dependent bond that ties the family together. With genograms, clinicians can map family boundaries and indicate which subsystems are fused and thus likely to be closed to new input about changing conditions.

As Bowen (1978) pointed out, two-person relationships seem to be unstable, under stress tending to draw in a third person. They tend to stabilize their relationship by forming a coalition of two in relation to the third. The basic unit of an emotional system thus tends to be the triangle. Genograms can help us identify key triangles in a family system, see how triangular patterns repeat from one generation to the next, and design strategies for changing them (Fogarty, 1973; Guerin, Fogarty, Fay, & Kautto, 1996).

The members of a family tend to fit together as a functional whole. That is, the behaviors of different family members tend to be complementary or reciprocal. This does not mean that family members have equal power to influence relationships, as is obvious from the power differentials between men and women, between parents and children, between the elderly and younger family members, and between family members who belong to different cultures, classes, or races (McGoldrick & Hardy, 2008). What it does mean is that belonging to a system opens people to reciprocal influences and involves them in one another's behavior in inextricable ways. This leads us to expect a certain interdependent fit or balance in families, involving give and take, action and reaction. Thus, a lack (e.g., irresponsibility) in one part of the family may be complemented by a surplus (over-responsibility) in another part. The genogram helps the clinician pinpoint the contrasts and idiosyncrasies in families that indicate this type of complementarity or reciprocal balance.

Clearly, a genogram is limited in how much information it can display at any time. Computer programs allow clinicians to examine the genogram with multiple levels of detail and explore different aspects one at a time: illness, cultural patterns, education and job history, couple relationships, and so on. Clinicians gather a great deal more important information on people's lives than can ever appear on genograms. The genogram is just one part of an ongoing clinical investigation and must be integrated into the total family assessment.

MAPPING THE GENOGRAMS OF THOSE WHO GROW UP IN MULTIPLE SETTINGS: THE MEANING OF HOME

Many children grow up in multiple settings because their parents divorce, die, remarry, migrate, or have other special circumstances that require the child to live for a while or even permanently in a different place. Yet we often fail to keep track of important information about whom children have lived with as they grow up—biological, legal, foster, adoptive, or informal kin relationships. Genograms can greatly facilitate tracking children in multiple living arrangements or foster placements, where the many different family constellations a child lives in are otherwise extremely hard to keep in mind. Indeed, genograms are an exceptionally useful tool to track children's experiences through the life cycle, taking into account the multiple family and other institutional contexts to which they have belonged (McGoldrick, Garcia-Preto, & Carter, 2015). As we all know, an individual's sense of "home" or what some have referred to as "homeplace" (Burton, Winn, Stevenson, & Clark, 2004) can be a crucial aspect of developing a healthy identity. The more clearly the clinician tracks the actuality of a person's history, however complex, the better able he or she is to validate the child's actual experience and multiple forms of belonging and to understand the child's sense of home. Such a map can begin to make order out of the sometimes chaotic or sudden placement changes a child must go through because of illness, trauma, or other loss. It can also help validate for a child the realities of his or her birth and life connections that vary from traditional norms.

More children than we realize are raised in a number of different households or shift residences many times to foster homes or to various relatives or friends. It is useful for the genogram to show as much of the information as possible on transitions and relationships in children's lives. Although many situations are very complicated, creativity and a commitment to validate

all of a child's connections facilitate the clinician's efforts to track and map the family and kin connections. Sometimes the only feasible way to clarify where children were raised is to take chronological notes on each child in a family and then transform them into a series of genograms that show family context. Especially when children have experienced many losses and changes, a complete genogram both validates the losses and offers a rich picture of all the people to whom they have belonged. It can be an important clinical tool to help put children in context.

Adoption

Couple adoption and single-parent adoption can be indicated as in Figure 53.2.

This genogram shows the family of Mia Farrow, who had biological children (including twin sons, Matthew and Sasha) and interracially adopted daughters (Soon-Yi, Lark, and Daisy) with her second husband, André Previn. She then adopted another interracial child (Moses) and one who was American born (Dylan/Eliza) during her relationship with Woody Allen, after which they had a biological child together (Satchel, now called Ronan), and finally she adopted more children

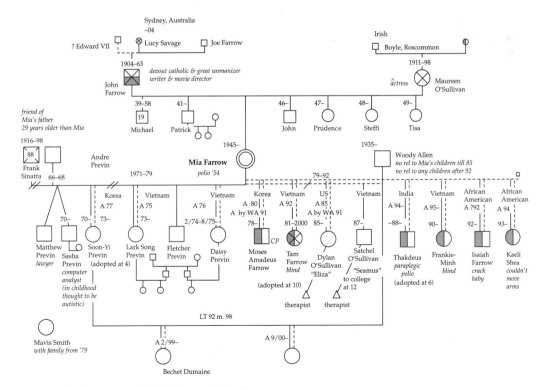

Figure 53.2 Genogram 2: Mia Farrow's Family.

on her own. If at all possible, we indicate the cultural background, because it is an important part of anyone's history. By looking at this map of the children of Mia Farrow, one may develop hypotheses about the position of different children. Soon-Yi, for example, came to the family as the oldest of three adopted Asian daughters two years after her younger Asian sister, Lark Song, and one year after her youngest Asian sister, Daisy. Not only were the two younger sisters "older" in their experience with the family, but they were both Vietnamese, whereas Soon-Yi was from Korea. So Soon-Yi's position as outsider among the three adopted Asian sisters may have been built in by the timing and her cultural difference from them. Of course, to more completely track the history of each child in this family, we would want to do genograms for each of the children, showing their biological parents and siblings and whom they lived with at every age growing up, as well as a more complete map of their caregivers and support systems. Friends and mentors, for example, may be important to show on a genogram, especially where children have experienced significant losses. Again, mapping out all these particulars is a way of assessing each family member's sense of home or homeplace and belonging, a crucial aspect of any clinical assessment.

Where living situations are complicated, a line can be drawn to encircle the households. This is especially important in multinuclear families, where children spend time in different households.

When the "functional" family is different from the biological or legal family, as when children are raised by a grandparent or in an informal adoptive family, it is useful to create a separate genogram to show the functional structure (Watts Jones, 1997). Where children have lived as part of several families—biological, foster, and adoptive—separate genograms may help depict the child's multiple families over time.

We can also indicate on a genogram (Figure 53.3) a lesbian couple with a child born to one of them and adopted by the other. The very small square indicated as the biological parent of Meg is a sperm donor. The grandparents and previous spouses of Fran and Martha are also indicated on the genogram. Burke and Faber (1997) have suggested using a "gendergrid" to help depict the liaisons, long-term bonds, communities, and social networks of lesbian couples.

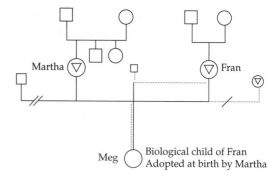

Figure 53.3 Genogram 3: Lesbian Family.

They suggest differentiating three levels of relationship: historical influences, key emotional and social relationships, and primary intimate relationships for the index individual or couple.

Foster Care

We need to acknowledge the relevance of specific foster family history for children who have lived in foster care. Psychologist Fernando Colon-Lopez grew up in several foster homes after the loss of his mother. As an adult, he has put much effort into exploring his own genogram (1973, 2006, 2008) and helping others think contextually about child placement and foster care as a valid and important aspect of a child's history, which should be attended to as any other experience (Colon, 1978). He has made it clear how important the genogram of the foster family is for the child through the life cycle. He kept ongoing connections with the biological grandchildren of his third foster mother. They shared holidays and frequent visits with their grandmother, his foster mother. They have much in common through this shared history, a history that is so often not acknowledged in our foster care system and in society at large, which underemphasizes family ties in its stress on individuality and self-determination.

Colon grew up mostly in foster homes from earliest infancy. The map of all his living situations, including three foster homes, an orphanage, his family of origin, and his family of procreation, is offered in Figure 53.4.

To understand better the sibling patterns with his brothers in the foster home where he spent most of his growing-up years, we might want to show the changing family constellations separately, as in Figure 53.5.

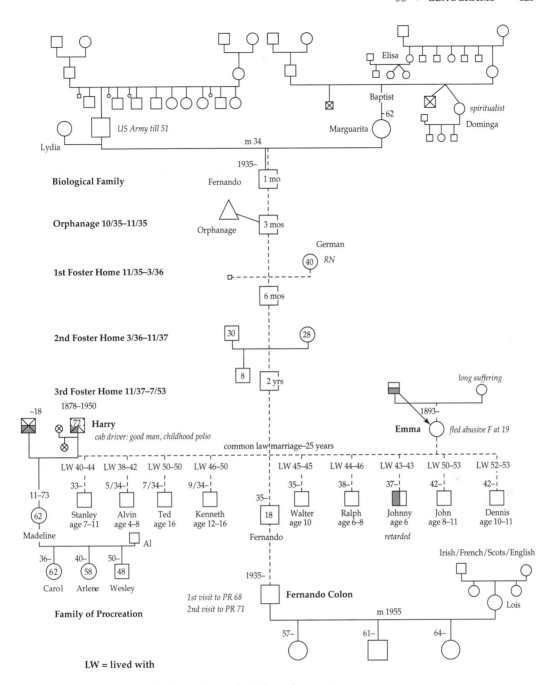

Figure 53.4 Genogram 4: Tracking Fernando Colon's living situations.

The genogram in Figure 53.5 makes evident the multiple losses that Colon and his foster family had throughout his childhood, but it also indicates their resilience and resourcefulness in being able to deal with these losses, as well as with new relationships almost each year. As is evident, Colon had experience in virtually every sibling constellation during his childhood years, a factor

that probably increased his flexibility in dealing with relationships. He was the youngest of three, the oldest of three, the middle of three, the older of two, and the younger of two, but rarely an only child, although, as the one child who remained with the family for his entire childhood, his position there was special. At the same time, the three brothers who stayed for long periods of time

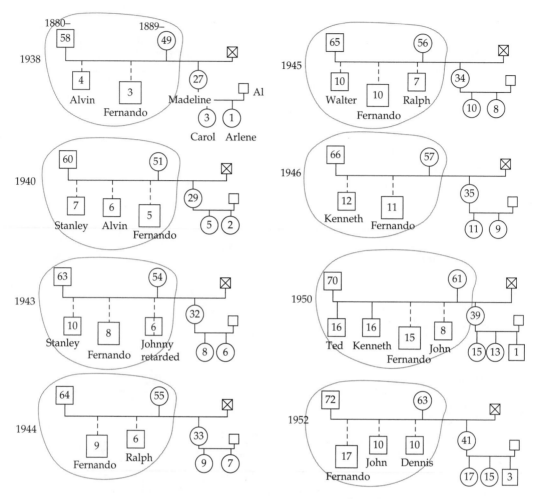

Figure 53.5 Genogram 5: Changing constellation of Colon's foster home, 1937–1953.

(4 years each) not surprisingly had more significance for him, especially because they were all close to Colon in age. Less evident from the ages alone was the extremely special relationship that Colon and his foster mother had with his brother Johnny, who lived in the family for only 4 months but to whom they became very attached. In caring for this severely retarded brother, Colon remembers clearly how hard Johnny had tried to learn to say Fernando's name and how he and his mother cried when they had to let Johnny go.

Although the foster care system at that time operated on the principle that children were never to have contact with the previous family once they moved to a new home, his foster mother did not believe in cutting off the past that way and made great efforts to reverse the process. In the early days of placement, one of Fernando Colon's foster brothers, Kenneth, was especially depressed. Kenneth was one of five brothers, and

spite of the regulations, their foster mother asked Kenneth where the brothers were and took him to see them, after which he began to adjust to his new situation. The foster mother showed great courage to challenge the cutting-off process promoted by our social service system.

Colon remains connected to his foster mother's grandchildren, in addition to his close, current connections with family members on both sides of his biological family. Whether the relationship is good or bad, beneficial or injurious, it is not to be dismissed. Organizing family data on genograms has enabled people to put the many fragments of their lives together into a meaningful whole.

Benefits of Open Adoption Policies

Genograms are equally important for children in adoptive care. Luckily, the policy of closed adoption is increasingly shifting to a policy of open adoption. After the adoption, both the biological family and the adoptive family are involved in selecting each other for placement of the child and stay connected to each other through the growing years of the child and beyond. This paradigm, which is becoming more widespread in the United States, has eliminated the harmful effects of secrecy and is a process with integrity that enables all parties to be considered in a humane way. State laws still vary widely, however, in how open or closed the adoption process may be. By using the information from genograms, child care workers can help adoptive children create scrapbooks about their lives with information, photos, and stories about both the biological and adoptive families. In this way the child is truly shared and doubly enriched by having connections with two family systems, rather than one pitted against the "failed" other.

The accepted practice of severing family ties—be they biological, adopted, foster, or blended—is, in our view, extremely detrimental and disrespectful. It has often led to clinicians being drawn into replacing other relationships in a person's natural system. Such cut-offs may leave practitioners depressed, bereft, and weakened, having a "hole" in our hearts. A cut-off of one person tends to potentiate cut-offs of other family members and the loss of other potentially enriching relationships. It weakens the entire fabric of the family. Social workers' use of genograms can help counter this tendency by making clear the enormity of the losses and validating the rich possibilities for connection and meaning.

Genograms can also be used for children who have been reared in orphanages, as the touching memoir of John Folwarski (2008) illustrates. Folwarski figures that he had approximately 3,000 siblings—that is, 3,000 other children in one generation shared the same home (St. Hedwig's Orphanage in Chicago), the same food, the same holiday rituals, and the same foster parents and grandparents, the nuns and priests who ran the home.

Figure 53.6 shows Folwarski's genogram for the family as he experienced it during the years he grew up (1937–1950). As adults, many of his "siblings" have come together to share memories, reconnecting after many years with teacher/mothers, and have strengthened their sense of family. Indeed, Folwarski describes the experience of creating and looking at his genogram, which had a powerful meaning in validating his history.

CONCLUSION

The physical genogram, which is a highly condensed map of a rich and complex family, can provide an awesome lesson for anyone unable to see beyond the cut-offs that may occur in a family (McGoldrick et al., 2008). We believe that no relationship is to be disregarded or discounted.

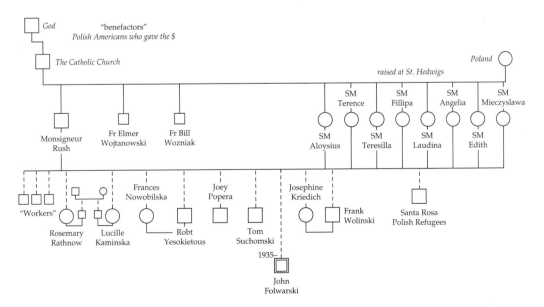

Figure 53.6 Genogram 6: St. Hedwig's orphanage family.

All our relationships inform the wholeness of who we are and where we come from and, more important, can help us make constructive, conscious choices about who we will be in the future.

One of the most powerful aspects of genograms is the way they can steer people to the rich, ongoing possibilities of complex kin relationships, which are sources of connection and life support. It is not just a shared history that matters but the spiritual power of our survival and our current connections that strengthen us and can enrich our future.

WEBSITES

GenoPro, genealogy software.
   http://www.genopro.com
Multicultural Family Institute.
   http://www.multiculturalfamily.org.

References

Bowen, M. (1978). *Family therapy in clinical practice.* New York, NY: Aronson.

Burke, J. L., & Faber, P. (1997). A genogrid for couples. *Journal of Gay and Lesbian Social Services, 7*(1), 13–22.

Burton, L. M., Winn, D. M., Stevenson, H., & Clark, S. L. (2004). Working with African American clients: Considering the "homeplace" in marriage and family therapy practices. *Journal of Marital and Family Therapy, 30*(4), 397–410.

McGoldrick, M., Carter, B., & Garcia-Preto, N. (2015). *The expanded family life cycle: Individual, family, and social perspectives* (5th ed.). Boston, MA: Allyn & Bacon.

Colon, F. (1973). In search of one's past: An identity trip. *Family Process, 12*(4), 429–438.

Colon, F. (1978). Family ties and child placement. *Family Process, 17,* 289–312.

Colon, F. (2008). The discovery of my multicultural identity. In M. McGoldrick & K. V. Hardy (Eds.), *Revisioning family therapy: Culture, race, and gender in clinical practice* (2nd ed.) (pp. 135–145). New York, NY: Guilford.

Colon-Lopez, F. (2006). *Finding my face: The memoir of a Puerto Rican American.* Victoria, BC: Trafford.

Congress, E. P. (1994, November). The use of culture-grams to assess and empower culturally diverse families. *Families in Society, 75,* 531–540.

Fogarty, T. (1973). *Triangles. The family.* New Rochelle, NY: Center for Family Learning.

Folwarski, J. (2008). No longer an orphan in history. In M. McGoldrick & K. V. Hardy (Eds.). *Revisioning family therapy: Race, culture and gender in clinical practice* (2nd ed.) (pp. 172–183). New York, NY: Guilford Press.

Green, R. (2008). Gay and lesbian couples: Successful coping with minority stress. In M. McGoldrick & K.V.Hardy (Eds.). *Revisioning family therapy: Race, culture and gender in clinical practice* (2nd ed.) (pp. 300–310). New York, NY: Guilford Press.

Guerin, P., Fogarty, T. F., Fay, L. F., & Kautto, J. G. (1996). *Working with relationship triangles.* New York, NY: Guilford.

Hardy, K. V., & Laszloffy, T. A. (1995). The cultural genogram: Key to training culturally competent family therapists. *Journal of Marital and Family Therapy, 21*(3), 227–237.

Hartman, A. (1978, October). Diagrammatic assessment of family relationships. *Social Casework, 79,* 465–476.

McGoldrick, M. (2013). *Harnessing the power of genograms in psychotherapy.* DVD available at www.psychotherapy.net.

McGoldrick, M. (2011). *The genogram journey: Reconnecting with your family.* New York, NY: Norton.

McGoldrick, M. (2001). *The legacy of unresolved loss.* DVD available at www.psychotherapy.net.

McGoldrick, M., Gerson, R., & Petry, S. (2008). *Genograms: Assessment and intervention* (3rd ed.). New York, NY: Norton.

McGoldrick, M., Giordano, J., & Garcia-Preto, N. (2005). *Ethnicity and family therapy* (3rd ed.). New York, NY: Guilford.

McGoldrick, M., & Hardy, K. V. (Eds.). (2008). *Revisioning family therapy: Culture, class, race, and gender* (2nd ed.). New York, NY: Guilford.

Walsh, F. (2003). *Spiritual resources in family therapy.* New York, NY: Guilford.

Walsh, F. (2006). *Strengthening family resilience* (2nd ed.). New York, NY: Guilford.

Walsh, F., & McGoldrick, M. (2004). *Living beyond loss: Death and the family* (2nd ed.). New York, NY: Guilford.

Watts-Jones, D. (1997). Toward an African American genogram. *Family Process, 36*(4), 373–383.

54   A Family Resilience Framework

Froma Walsh

Over recent decades, the field of family therapy has refocused attention from family deficits to family strengths. The therapeutic relationship has become more collaborative and empowering of client potential, recognizing that successful interventions depend more on tapping into family resources than on therapist techniques. Assessment and intervention are directed to how problems can be solved, identifying and amplifying existing and potential competencies. Therapist and clients work together to find new possibilities in a problem-saturated situation and overcome roadblocks to change and growth. This positive, future-oriented direction shifts the emphasis from what went wrong to what can be done for optimal functioning and well-being of families and their members.

A family resilience approach builds on these developments to strengthen family abilities to overcome adversity. A basic premise guiding this approach is that serious life crises, disruptive transitions, and persistent adversity have an impact on the whole family, and in turn, key family processes influence the recovery and resilience of all members, their relationships, and the family unit. Fostering the family's ability to master its immediate crisis situation also increases its capacity to meet future challenges. Thus, the family is strengthened as problems are resolved, and each intervention is also a preventive measure.

THE CONCEPT OF FAMILY RESILIENCE: CRISIS AND CHALLENGE

Resilience—the ability to withstand and rebound from adversity—has become an important concept in mental health theory and research. Although some are shattered by traumatic experience, others rise above it, able to live and love well. Countering the deterministic assumption that early, severe, or persistent trauma inevitably damages lives, studies have found that the same adversity may result in different outcomes. For instance, most abused children did not become abusive parents (Kaufman & Ziegler, 1987). What makes the difference?

Early studies focused on individual traits for hardiness, reflecting the dominant cultural ethos of the "rugged individual." Resilience was viewed as inborn or acquired on one's own, as "the invulnerable child" seen as impervious to stress owing to inner fortitude. An interactive perspective emerged, recognizing that the impact of initial risk conditions or traumatic events may be outweighed by mediating environmental influences that foster resilience. Major studies of resilient children and adults noted the crucial influence of significant relationships, with models and mentors—such as coaches or teachers—who supported them, believed in their potential, and encouraged them to make the best of their lives (Rutter, 1987; Werner & Smith, 2001). However, the skewed clinical focus on family pathology blinded many to the kinship resources that could be found and strengthened, even in troubled families.

A family resilience orientation fundamentally alters that traditional deficit-based lens, shifting the perspective from viewing families as *damaged* to seeing them as *challenged*. Rather than rescuing so-called survivors from dysfunctional families, this approach affirms the family's reparative potential, based on the conviction that both individual and relational healing and growth can be forged out of adversity.

The concept of family resilience has valuable potential as a framework for intervention, prevention, research, and social policy aimed at supporting and strengthening families facing adversity. Although some families are shattered by crisis or persistent stresses, others surmount their challenges and emerge stronger and more resourceful. For instance, the death of a child poses a heightened risk for parental divorce, yet couple and family bonds are strengthened when members pull together and support each other in dealing with their tragedy (Greeff & Human, 2004). The concept of resilience extends beyond coping and adaptation to recognize the enhanced strengths and growth that can be forged out of adversity. A crisis also becomes an opportunity for reappraisal of life priorities and greater investment in meaningful relationships and pursuits. Many find new purpose in efforts to prevent similar tragedies or help others who are suffering or struggling (Lietz, 2013; Walsh, 2006).

A family resilience practice approach aims to identify and build key relational processes to overcome stressful life situations, with the conviction that collaborative efforts best enable families and all members to thrive. The approach is grounded in family systems theory, combining ecological and developmental perspectives to view the family as an open system that functions in relation to its broader sociocultural context and evolves over the multigenerational life cycle.

ECOLOGICAL PERSPECTIVE

A bio-psychosocial systems orientation views problem situations and their solutions as involving multiple recursive influences of individuals, families, larger systems, and sociocultural variables. A family resilience approach recognizes that most problems involve an interaction of individual and family vulnerability with the impact of stressful life experiences and social contexts.

- Difficulties may be primarily biologically based, as in serious illness or disability, yet are largely influenced by interpersonal and sociocultural variables.
- Family distress may be fueled by external events, such as a major disaster (Walsh, 2007), or by ongoing stressors, such as persistent conditions associated with poverty,

racism, heterosexism, or other forms of discrimination (Anderson, 2012; Green, 2012; Orthner, Jones-Sanpei, & Williamson, 2004).
- Family distress may result from unsuccessful attempts to cope with an overwhelming situation or pile-up of stressors that overwhelm resources.

DEVELOPMENTAL PERSPECTIVE: FAMILY COPING, ADAPTATION, AND RESILIENCE

A family resilience approach attends to adaptational processes over time, from ongoing interactions to family life cycle passage and multigenerational influences. Life crises and persistent stresses have an impact on the functioning of a family system, with ripple effects to all members and their relationships (Patterson, 2002). Family processes in preparedness and response are crucial for coping and adaptation; one family may falter whereas with similar life challenges another rallies. How a family confronts and manages a disruptive or threatening experience, buffers stress, effectively reorganizes, and reinvests in life pursuits influences adaptation for all members.

As one example, the presumption that divorce inevitably damages children is not supported by the large body of empirical data finding that most children fare reasonably well over the long-term and nearly a third flourish. We need to take into account the multiple variables in risk and resilience over time that make a difference in children's adaptation, including the predivorce climate, postdivorce financial strains, reorganization of households, transitions with remarriage/repartnering and step-parenting, and persistent parental conflict or cutoff (Coleman, Ganong, & Russell, 2013; Greef & VanderMerwe, 2004; Greene, Anderson, Forgatch, deGarmo, & Hetherington, 2012). Research identifying family processes that distinguish those who are resilient can inform therapeutic and collaborative divorce efforts for optimal postdivorce child and family adaptation.

In resilience-oriented practice, family functioning is assessed in the context of the multigenerational system moving forward over time.

- A genogram and family time line (McGoldrick, Gerson, & Petry, 2008) are useful tools to schematize relationship information and track system patterns to guide intervention planning, noting strengths and resources—past, current, and potential—as well as problems and limitations.

- It is crucial to note linkages between the timing of symptoms and recent or impending stressful events that have disrupted or threatened the family, such as a son's drop in school grades following his father's job loss and family financial strain.
- Symptoms frequently coincide with stressful developmental transitions. Each poses particular challenges, as new developmental priorities emerge, boundaries shift, and roles and relationships are redefined. Families must deal with both predictable, normative stresses, such as becoming parents, and unpredictable, disruptive events, such as the untimely death of a young parent or birth of a child with disabilities.
- Families are more resilient when they are able to balance intergenerational continuity and change and maintain links between their past, present, and future, especially with immigration (Falicov, 2012).
- Family history, stories, and patterns of relation and functioning transmitted across the generations influence response to adversity and future expectations, hopes, dreams, and catastrophic fears.
- The convergence of developmental and multigenerational strains affects family coping ability. Strains increase exponentially when current stressors reactivate past vulnerable issues or painful losses, particularly when similar challenges are confronted, such as life-threatening illness (McGoldrick, Garcia Preto, & Carter, 2014; Rolland, 2012).
- It is crucial to inquire about models and stories of resilience and extended family, cultural, and spiritual resources in overcoming past family adversity that might be drawn on or inspire coping strategies in the current situation.

ADVANTAGES OF A FAMILY RESILIENCE FRAMEWORK

Assessment of healthy family functioning is fraught with dilemmas. Postmodern perspectives have heightened awareness that views of family normality, pathology, and health are socially constructed (Walsh, 2012b). Clinicians and researchers bring their own assumptive maps into every evaluation and intervention, embedded in cultural norms, professional orientations, and personal experience.

Moreover, the very concept of the family has been undergoing redefinition with the social and economic transformations of recent decades. Cultural diversity, varied family forms and gender roles, economic disparities, and a multiplicity of family arrangements require a broad, inclusive, and flexible view of family life (Cherlin, 2010; Walsh, 2012b). The life course is becoming more fluid, as children and their parents increasingly move in and out of varied and complex family constellations. Resilience is needed with disruptive transitions posing new adaptational challenges. Yet, a substantial body of research finds that children and families can thrive in a variety of kinship arrangements (Walsh, 2012b). What matters more than family form are the *processes* for effective family functioning and the quality of caring, committed bonds.

Systems-based research on family functioning over recent decades has offered empirical grounding to identify and facilitate key processes in intervention with distressed families (Lebow & Stroud, 2012). However, studies based on white, middle-class, intact families who are not under stress too often contribute to faulty assumptions that family distress and differences from the norm are pathological. Further, family typologies tend to be static and acontextual, not attending to a family's social or developmental influences and emerging challenges over time.

A family resilience framework offers several advantages.

- By definition, it focuses on strengths under stress.
- It is assumed that no single model fits all family situations. Functioning and resilience must be assessed in context: relative to each family's values, structure, resources, and life challenges.
- There are many, varied pathways in resilience. Processes for optimal functioning and the well-being of members will vary over time, as challenges unfold and families evolve across the life cycle.
- This approach to practice is grounded in a deep conviction in the potential for family repair, recovery, and growth out of adversity.

TABLE 54.1 Key Processes in Family Resilience

Belief Systems

Making meaning of adversity

- Relational view of resilience
- Normalize, contextualize distress; depathologize, decrease stigma, shame
- Sense of coherence: crisis as meaningful, comprehensible, manageable challenge
- Appraise adverse situation; options; future expectations

Positive outlook

- Hope, optimistic bias; confidence in overcoming barriers
- Encouragement; affirm and build strengths and potential
- Active initiative and perseverance (can-do spirit)
- Master the possible; accept what cannot be changed; tolerate uncertainty

Transcendence and spirituality

- Larger values, purpose
- Spirituality: faith, rituals and practices, congregational support
- Inspiration: new possibilities, dreams; creative expression; social action
- Transformation: learning, change, and growth from adversity

Organizational Patterns

Flexibility

- Rebound, reorganize to adapt to new challenges
- Regain stability: continuity, dependability, predictability to counter disruption
- Strong authoritative leadership: nurture, guide, protect
- Varied family forms: cooperative parenting/caregiving teams
- Couple/co-parent relationship: mutual respect; equal partners

Connectedness

- Mutual support, collaboration, and commitment
- Respect individual needs, differences, and boundaries
- Reconnection, reconciliation of wounded relationships

Social and economic resources

- Mobilize kin, social and community networks; models and mentors
- Financial security; work/family balance; institutional supports

Communication/Problem Solving

Clarity

- Clear, consistent messages (words, deeds)
- Clarify ambiguous information; truth seeking/truth speaking

Open emotional expression

- Share range of feelings with empathy; respect differences
- Pleasurable interactions, respite; humor

Collaborative problem solving

- Creative brainstorming; resourcefulness
- Shared decision making; negotiation, fairness, reciprocity
- Focus on goals, concrete steps: build on success; learn from failure
- Proactive stance: prevent crises; prepare for future challenges

KEY PROCESSES IN FAMILY RESILIENCE

The Walsh Family Resilience Framework identifies nine key processes and subcomponents for resilience, as outlined in Table 54.1. It is informed by three decades of research in the social sciences and clinical field on resilience and well-functioning family systems. The framework synthesizes major findings within three domains of family functioning: family belief systems, organizational patterns, and communication processes (Walsh, 2003, 2006).

- Family belief systems support resilience when they help members (1) make meaning of adverse experiences; (2) sustain a hopeful, positive outlook; and (3) draw on transcendent or spiritual values and purpose (Walsh, 2009).
- In family organization, resilience is fostered by (1) flexible yet stable structure, with strong leadership; (2) connectedness for mutual support; and (3) extended kin, social, and community resources.
- Communication processes facilitate resilience through (1) information clarity, (2) sharing of both painful and positive emotions, and (3) collaborative problem solving, with a proactive approach to future challenges.

APPLICATIONS OF FAMILY RESILIENCE APPROACHES

Family resilience-oriented practice shares principles and techniques common among strengths-based approaches but attends more centrally to links between presenting problems and family stressors, focusing on family coping and adaptational strategies. Interventions are directed to strengthen relational bonds and tap resources to reduce vulnerability and master family challenges. The family resilience framework is designed to guide assessment, interventions, and prevention to identify and strengthen key processes that foster recovery and growth.

A family resilience framework and supportive research find useful application in a range of adverse situations (Lietz, 2013; Rolland, 2012; Walsh, 2006; 2007; 2013):

- Healing from crisis, trauma, and loss (e.g., family bereavement, relational trauma, war-related and refugee trauma, disaster recovery)
- Navigating disruptive transitions (e.g., migration, separation/divorce, stepfamily formation, foster/kinship care)
- Mastering multi-stress challenges with chronic conditions (e.g., illness/disability, unemployment/financial strain; community violence/blight; discrimination)
- Supporting positive development of at-risk youth (family-school partnerships, gang prevention programs)

Efforts to foster family resilience benefit all family members, not only those currently presenting symptoms. A systemic assessment may lead to multilevel approaches to risk reduction, problem resolution, and individual/family well-being. Putting an ecological view into practice, interventions often involve community collaboration and change, peer groups and social networks; and workplace, school, health care, and other larger systems. Programs for youth mentoring, skill-building, parenting and caregiving and creative expression through the arts are important components of many resilience-oriented interventions (Saul, 2013).

Family resilience-oriented intervention approaches are increasingly being developed for situations of mass trauma, such as war-related trauma and major disasters (e.g., Landau, 2007; MacDermid, 2010; Saul, 2013; Walsh, 2007). In contrast to individual symptom-focused treatment programs, such multi-systemic approaches build healing networks that facilitate individual, family, and community resilience. Programs create a safe haven for family and community members to support each other in sharing both deep pain and positive strivings. They expand a shared vision of what is possible through collaboration, not only to survive trauma and loss, but also to regain their spirit to thrive.

Resilience-oriented family interventions can be adapted to a variety of formats.

- Family consultations, brief counseling, or more intensive family therapy may combine individual and conjoint sessions, including members affected by stressors and those who can contribute to resilience.
- Psycho-educational multifamily groups, workshops, and community forums provide

social support, with practical information, and concrete guidelines for stress reduction, crisis management, problem solving, and optimal functioning as families navigate through stressful periods and face future challenges.

- Brief, cost-effective periodic "modules" can be timed around critical transitions or emerging challenges in long-term adaptation, for example, a chronic illness, divorce processes, or disaster recovery.

CONCLUSION

Crisis and challenge are inherent in the human condition. In order to move beyond the rhetoric of promoting family strengths, research and practice priorities must shift focus from how families fail to how they can succeed. Conceptual and research efforts to date have laid important groundwork for understanding and facilitating family resilience in a wide range of adverse situations. Further mixed-method research is needed to advance our knowledge and practice (DeHaan, Hawley, & Deal, 2013). The field also needs to address emerging societal challenges, from workplace and health care restructuring to retirement, elder caregiving, and end-of-life dilemmas with the aging of families (Walsh, 2012a).

A research-informed family resilience framework can guide clinical and community-based practice by assessing family functioning on key system variables as they fit each family's values, structure, resources, and life challenges and then targeting interventions to strengthen family resilience as presenting problems are addressed.

WEBSITES

Building family resilience
www.resiliencei.com
www.militaryonesource.mil
www.realwarriors.net
Centers
Center for Family Resiliency Oklahoma State University at Tulsa, www.osu-tulsa.okstate.edu/cfr
National Family Resiliency Center, Inc., www.divorceabc.com
UCLA Nathanson Family Resiliency Center, www.nfrc.ucla.edu

References

Anderson, C. M. (2012). The diversity, strengths, and challenges of single-parent households. In F. Walsh (Ed.), *Normal family processes: Growing diversity and complexity* (4th ed.). (pp. 128–148). New York, NY: Guilford Press.

Cherlin, A. J. (2010). Demographic trends in the United States: A review of research in the 2000s. *Journal of Marriage and Family, 72,* 403–419.

Coleman, M., Ganong, L., & Russell, R. (2013). Resilience in stepfamilies. In D. Becvar (Ed.), *Handbook of family resilience* (pp. 85–103). New York, NY: Springer.

DeHaan, L., Hawley, D., & Deal, J. (2013). Operationalizing family resilience as a process: Proposed methodological strategies. In D. Becvar (Ed.), *Handbook of family resilience* (pp. 17–29). New York, NY: Springer.

Falicov, C. (2012). Immigrant family processes: A multi-dimensional framework (MECA). In F. Walsh (Ed.), *Normal family processes* (4th ed.) (pp. 297–323). New York, NY: Guilford Press.

Greeff, A. P., & Human, B. (2004). Resilience in families in which a parent has died. *American Journal of Family Therapy, 32*(1), 27–42.

Greeff, A. P., & Van der Merwe, S. (2004). Variables associated with resilience in divorced families. *Social Indicators Research, 68*(1), 59–75.

Green, R.-J. (2012). Gay and lesbian family life: Risk, resilience, and rising expectations. In F. Walsh (Ed.), *Normal family processes: Growing diversity and complexity* (4th ed.) (pp. 172–195). New York, NY: Guilford Press.

Greene, S., Anderson, E., Forgatch, M., deGarmo, D., & Hetherington, M. (2012). Risk and resilience after divorce. In F. Walsh (Ed.), *Normal family processes: Growing diversity and complexity* (4th ed.) (pp. 102–127). New York, NY: Guilford Press.

Kaufman, J., & Ziegler, E. (1987). Do abused children become abusive parents? *American Journal of Orthopsychiatry, 57,* 186–192.

Landau, J. (2007). Enhancing resilience: Families and communities as agents for change. *Family Process, 46*(3), 351–365.

Lebow, I., & Stroud, C. (2012). Assessment of couple and family functioning: Prevailing models and instruments. In F. Walsh (Ed.), *Normal family processes* (4th ed.). New York, NY: Guilford.

Lietz, C. (2013). Family resilience in the context of high-risk situations. In D. Becvar (Ed.), *Handbook of family resilience* (pp. 153–172). New York, NY: Springer.

MacDermid, S. M. (2010). Family risk and resilience in the context of war and terrorism. *Journal of Marriage and Family, 72,* 537–556.

McGoldrick, M., Garcia-Preto, N., & Carter, B. (Eds.). (2014). *The expanded family life cycle: Individual, family, and social perspectives* (5th ed.). Needham Hill, MA: Allyn & Bacon.

McGoldrick, M., Gerson, R., & Petry, S. (2008). *Genograms: Assessment and intervention* (3rd ed.). New York, NY: Norton.

Orthner, D. K., Jones-Sanpei, H., & Williamson, S. (2004). The resilience and strengths of low-income families. *Family Relations, 53*, 159–167.

Patterson, J. (2002). Integrating family resilience and family stress theory. *Journal of Marriage and the Family, 64*(2), 349–360.

Rolland, J. S. (2012). Mastering the challenges of illness, disability, and genetic conditions. In F. Walsh (Ed.), *Normal family processes: Growing Diversity and Complexity* (4th ed.) (pp. 452–482). New York, NY: Guilford Press.

Rutter, M. (1987). Psychosocial resilience and protective mechanisms. *American Journal of Orthopsychiatry, 57*, 316–331.

Saul, J. (2013). *Collective trauma, collective healing.* New York, NY: Springer.

Walsh, F. (2003). Family resilience: A framework for clinical practice. *Family Process, 42*(1), 1–18.

Walsh, F. (2006). *Strengthening family resilience* (2nd ed.). New York, NY: Guilford Press.

Walsh, F. (2007). Traumatic loss and major disasters: Strengthening family and community resilience. *Family Process, 46*, 207–227.

Walsh, F. (Ed.). (2009). *Spiritual resources in family therapy* (2nd ed.). New York, NY: Guilford.

Walsh, F. (2012a). Successful aging and family resilience. In B. Haslip & G. Smith (Eds.), *Emerging perspectives on resilience in adulthood and later life. Annual Review of Gerontology and Geriatrics, 32,* (pp. 153–172). New York, NY: Springer.

Walsh, F. (Ed.). (2012b). The "new normal": Diversity and complexity in 21st century families. In *Normal family processes: Growing diversity and complexity* (4th ed.) (pp. 4–27). New York, NY: Guilford Press.

Walsh, F. (2013). Community-based practice applications of a family resilience framework. In D. Becvar (Ed.), *Handbook of family resilience* (pp. 65–82). New York, NY: Springer.

Werner, E., & Smith, R. (2001). *Journeys from childhood to midlife: Risk, resiliency, and recovery.* New York, NY: McGraw-Hill.

55 Treatment Planning with Families

An Evidence-based Approach

Catheleen Jordan, Cynthia Franklin, & Shannon K. Johnson

TREATMENT PLANNING WITH FAMILIES

For the past 20 years managed behavioral health care and other accountability and cost containment approaches have encouraged the move toward formalized family treatment planning and the trend toward efficacious, brief family therapy interventions. In order to develop a formalized treatment plan social workers must be able to identify measurable goals, objectives, and outcomes as well as evidence-based treatments known to be effective with specific client problems and populations. A family treatment plan (see Figure 55.1 for an example) can be understood as a roadmap that can be used to guide a family's pursuit of its shared goals. A family treatment plan should specify the overarching treatment goal, along with objectives and interventions. It is crucial that, during the treatment planning process the social worker devise a plan for measuring and monitoring ongoing progress

---

Problem: Adolescent behavior problems

Definitions: Aggressive conduct that threatens physical harm to family members

Goals: Eliminate adolescent aggressive behavior

Objectives:	Interventions:
1. Family members learn anger management techniques	1. Teach the family the skills of recognizing one's escalating anger, taking a timeout to cool down, acknowledging one's contribution to the aggressive situation, negotiating a solution.
2. Parents and adolescent establish a behavioral contract	2. Teach the parents to negotiate a contract with the adolescent that specifies rules/expectations, consequences, and rewards

Diagnosis: 312.8 Conduct Disorder, Adolescent-Onset Type

Figure 55.1 Treatment plan example.

on each objective over the course of treatment (Hepworth et al., 2012). This means that a treatment plan is not a one-time snapshot of the family's goals but a document that guides the progress of the family over time and may also be revised over the treatment process. Treatment plan content, for example, may be modified as the family's goals are achieved or change. If a treatment team is providing services to the family, the treatment plan should specify which provider is responsible for each specified intervention.

Special challenges in treatment planning with families include selecting problems, goals, and outcomes that are meaningful to all family members. For instance, the parents may desire their child to become more compliant; the child, on the other hand, may desire an end to constant parental nagging! Also, goals and interventions should be selected with consideration for issues of diversity (Gehart, 2013). For example, the social worker should select interventions that best match the client, their culture, preferences, and circumstances. Although individual treatment planning requires careful consideration of client characteristics (e.g., ethnicity, sexual orientation, religious beliefs, physical health) and life circumstances (e.g., income, transportation, employment, and parenting demands) (Antony & Barlow, 2011), family treatment planning requires consideration of these factors

for each member of the family unit. Another challenge in family treatment planning is that problem-focused treatment planning is sometimes at odds with the systems approaches that are used in family intervention and the social work strengths-based approach, which is also used to work with families. Hepworth and colleagues (2012) advocate stating goals in positive terms. For instance, rather than stipulating than an adolescent will *reduce* noncompliance, one can indicate that the adolescent will *increase* instances of compliance with household rules.

STEPS OF TREATMENT PLANNING WITH FAMILIES

Treatment planning requires the social worker to think through the therapeutic process from assessment to intervention and evaluation. Today's focus on brief, manualized interventions is perfect for this type of planned approach, because it requires the problem to be measured. Standardized measures are instruments completed by the client and/or social worker that provide a score indicating the extent or severity of a client problem. For example, a couple may complete the Hudson Index of Marital Satisfaction; each receives a score indicating the level of satisfaction with the marriage. A score more than 25 indicates a clinically significant problem. Standardized scales should be administered repeatedly over the course of treatment so that scores can be graphed to assess, track, and evaluate client progress (Hepworth et al., 2012). Dattilio, Jongsma, and Davis (2010) identify six steps of treatment planning: (1) problem selection; (2) problem definition; (3) goal development; (4) objective construction; (5) intervention creation; (6) diagnosis determination.

Step 1: Problem Selection

Problem selection in family treatment requires the social worker to assess client problems and then prioritize them in a way meaningful to the family. Jordan and Franklin (2011) recommend a problem selection and specification process guided by a person-in-environment perspective. Problem assessment moves from a global, systems view to an operationalized view of specific problems. For example, a global assessment technique, such as an eco-map, is used to obtain a global view of the family in the context of their important environmental systems. From the map, the social worker is able to conclude that problems stem from a relationship pattern between an adolescent and parent, where the parenting and communication is not working well and the adolescent is having behavioral problems. Specific problem data specific to a particular problem or behavior (e.g., alcohol use by the adolescent) may be collected via standardized measures. In Figure 55.1, the treatment plan example, the problem is the adolescent's alcohol use. We further specify the meaning of the problem in Step 2, the problem definition.

Step 2: Problem Definition

After the problem(s) is selected, it must be defined. The *Diagnostic and Statistical Manual of Mental Disorders, Fifth Edition (DSM-5)* is the most agreed upon way of categorizing or defining problems, but is not always the most meaningful to family social workers, especially considering the controversies around its' limitations and usefulness for social work practice. As mentioned before, standardized measures have gained popularity in social work and may be used to quantify client problems. Examples of problems that may be measured in this way include family relationships and satisfaction, marital satisfaction, sexual abuse and family violence, dual career

relationship, child and parent relationships, and so forth. Individual problems such as depression, self-esteem, or anxiety, which may be a part of a family's problem, can also be easily measured using standardized instruments.

Other ways of measuring problems include counting discrete behaviors (e.g., number of family arguments or number of child tantrums) or developing goal-attainment or self-anchored scales. Goal-attainment scales, developed by the social worker, are used to identify outcomes and to operationalize categories indicating successive approximations toward 100% goal completion. Numbers are assigned to each category with minus signs indicating lack of progress or deterioration. A typical scale range is from −2 to +2. Self-anchored scales are developed by the social worker in conjunction with the family. The targeted behavior, for example family satisfaction, is rated from 1 to 5. A rating of 1 may stand for "the most satisfied" and 5 "the least satisfied" that the family can imagine. Anchors, indicating specific family behaviors, are then matched with each numerical ranking. For instance, the family may describe a category 1 ranking, the "most satisfied," as a time when they were having dinner together as a family, engaged in pleasant conversation with no fighting, and so on.

In addition to a focus on problems, the value of a strengths-based approach encourages social workers to measure and intervene by building on client strengths (e.g., number of positive family communications or family outings). These positive behavioral objectives may be incorporated into the treatment plan. In the treatment plan example, Figure 55.1, the problem is defined as underage alcohol use, truancy, breaking curfew, and disregard for household rules. We then develop a goal statement in Step 3.

Step 3: Goal Development

Dattilio, Jongsma, and Davis (2010) recommend specifying one goal statement for each problem. The goal statement is a broadly stated description of what successful outcome is expected. Goals are not necessarily operationalized in measurable terms, as are objectives. Instead, they may be broad statements of the overall anticipated positive outcome. In the sample treatment plan (Figure 55.1), the goal is to achieve abstinence from drinking and increase compliance with household rules and expectations. We could specify additional goals, such as improving parenting skills or increasing the amount of quality time the family spends together. Goals may be long-term expectations. We further operationalized the goal by specifying objectives in Step 4.

Step 4: Objective Construction

Objectives are the measurable steps that must occur for the goals to be met. Each goal should have at least two objectives that are operationalized in measurable terms and provide the short-term steps necessary to achieve the goal. In the sample plan (Figure 55.1), the social worker may measure the objective of, "adolescent to receive all services recommended by substance abuse and mental health assessors" by having the adolescent provide a copy of treatment recommendations, and then create and maintain a weekly log of participation in treatment activities. The objective is measurable. Target dates should be assigned to each objective to focus treatment sessions and to ensure brief treatment and problem resolution (Hepworth et al., 2012). As families progress through treatment, they may add additional objectives. The next step moves the treatment plan from defining and operationalizing problems to specifying the intervention.

Step 5: Intervention Creation

Interventions, the clinicians' tools for treating the problem, should be matched with each objective. Although interventions are selected according to the social worker's theoretical clinical orientation and clinical expertise, it is important to note that the trend in family social work is toward brief, evidence-based methods that have proven efficacy for specific families or family problems. When selecting interventions, social workers are advised to consider family characteristics, the target problems and diagnoses, and the evidence-base for potential interventions for those problems/diagnoses, respective to client family characteristics.

Another trend in treatment is toward manualized interventions and treatment planners that provide guidelines to the social worker as to how to proceed with specific problems. Manualized interventions involve greater operationalization of the treatment, which heightens the social worker's ability to attribute positive changes to the intervention. Meanwhile, treatment planners are designed to provide all the elements necessary to proficiently develop treatment plans that satisfy the demands of third-party payers and accrediting agencies. These elements include pre-written treatment goals, objectives, and interventions, organized around common presenting problems (Dattilio et al., 2010). In Figure 55.1, two cognitive-behavioral interventions have been specified, along with referral to individual services for the adolescent family member. Finally, the treatment concludes with a DSM diagnosis.

Step 6: Diagnosis Determination

Treatment planning assumes that an appropriate diagnosis will be determined, based on the overall client family picture. As mentioned before, the diagnostic approach has not been favored by many family social workers, due not only to its' limitations (Jongsma, 2004), but also to the value social workers place on strengths-based treatment and a systems approach to assessment (Jordan & Franklin, 2011). Nevertheless, due to the demands of third-party payers, family therapy treatment planning is primarily based on a symptom-focused medical model (Gehart, 2013). Social workers face the reality of needing to know the characteristics of DSM criteria as part of a complete assessment picture. Fortunately, as DSM has gone into its' fifth edition it has responded to some criticisms and required more of a complete assessment of a client's bio-psychosocial presentation including cultural and life span issues across specific diagnosis. In Figure 55.1, the diagnosis is 312.8 Conduct Disorder, Adolescent-Onset Type. It is possible that the adolescent may be dealing with substance use in addition to Conduct Disorder because these two diagnoses often co-occur. The social worker has made a referral to specialized outside assessment to make this determination.

TREATMENT PLANNING RESOURCES FOR FAMILY SOCIAL WORKERS

Dattilio, Jongsma, and Davis (2010) emphasize the importance of developing an individualized treatment plan for each client family, based on its own uniqueness. Following are references helpful to the social worker proceeding through each step of the treatment plan.

Problem Selection and Definition

Jordan and Franklin (2011) provide a framework for assessment that teaches the social work practitioner to move from a global, person-in-environment family picture to a more specific, measurable focus on target problems and strengths. Specific standardized instruments for measuring child and family problems are presented by Corcoran and Fischer (2013). Bloom, Fischer, and Orme (2009) discuss a variety of ways available to measure problems, including goal-attainment scaling and behavioral measurement mentioned earlier. Finally, prewritten treatment goals, objectives, and interventions and a sample treatment plan that conforms to the requirements of most third-party payers and accrediting agencies are available from Dattilio, Jongsma, and Davis (2010).

Goal and Objective Development

Jongsma (2004) discusses goal and objective setting for general practice and for family practice. Social work research-practitioners, Bloom and colleagues (2009), discuss goal and objective setting from a single subject design perspective. Their text describes not only how to measure problems but how to set up a system for tracking therapeutic progress. Finally, Gehart (2013) provides a guide to writing useful client goals that includes a goal writing worksheet that walks the practitioner through a process of identifying the linkages between the presenting problem, family dynamics, and client symptoms before identifying the most appropriate intervention, based on evidence and theory.

Intervention Construction and Differential Diagnosis

Lambert (2013) reviews the efficacy of clinical interventions, including child, family, and marital therapy. Several texts written by social workers review methods available for treating families and children (Collins, Jordan, & Coleman, 2012; Franklin, Jordan, & Hopson, 2008; Janzen, 2006). Additionally, Reid's (2000) text provides a step-by-step guide for the practitioner in intervention task planning, including tasks for family social workers. Finally, Bloom and colleagues (2009) include software called Singwin, a computerized data analysis program for the ideographic data provided by single case analysis.

Future Applications for Treatment Plans

Treatment plans help ensure a positive future for client families. They help social workers to set measurable goals and objectives for clients and offer them in a brief and timely manner. Treatment planning requires that social workers specify what we will do in our way of helping. It provides a structure for an evidence-based approach to treatment, which is strongly encouraged and in some cases mandated. Finally, treatment planning requires that social workers document what is done to ensure accountability and to monitor progress through the treatment process. Family Treatment plans further ensure that social workers offer the best possible social work treatment based on considerations of culture, socioeconomic status, family preferences, and values.

WEBSITES

NIDA/SAMHSA Blending Initiative: www.nida.nih.gov/blending/asi.html.
S.M.A.R.T. Treatment Planning: www.samhsa.gov/SAMHSA_news/VolumeXIV_5/article2.htm
Treatment Planner Software Modules: http://www.4ulr.com/products/counseling/client_groups.html
Symptom-based Treatment Planners from Dr. Arthur Jongsma: www.jongsma.com

References

Antony, M. M., & Barlow, D. H. (2011). *Handbook of assessment and treatment planning for psychological disorders* (2nd ed.). New York, NY: Guilford Press.

Bloom, M., Fischer, J., & Orme, J. G. (2009). *Evaluating practice: Guidelines for the accountable professional* (6th ed.). Boston, MA: Allyn & Bacon.

Collins, D., Jordan, C., & Coleman, H. (2012). *Brooks/Cole Empowerment Series: An Introduction to Family Social Work.* Independence, KY: Cengage Learning.

Corcoran, K., & Fischer, J. (2013). *Measures for clinical practice and research, Volume 1: Couples, families, and children.* New York, NY: Oxford University Press.

Dattilio, F. M., Jongsma, A. E., Jr, & Davis, S. D. (2010). *The family therapy treatment planner.* New York, NY: Wiley.

Franklin, C., Jordan, C., & Hopson, L. (2008). Intervention with families. In K. M. Sowers, W. Rowe, & L. A. Rapp-Paglicci (Eds.), *Comprehensive Handbook of Social Work and Social Welfare.* New York, NY: Wiley.

Gehart, D. R. (2013). *Mastering competencies in family therapy: A practical approach to theory and clinical case documentation.* Independence, KY: Cengage Learning.

Hepworth, D. H., Rooney, R. H., Rooney, G. D., Strom-Gottfried, K., & Larsen, J. A. (2012). *Direct social work practice: Theory and skills.* Belmont, CA: Brooks/Cole Publishing Company.

Janzen, C. (2006). *Family treatment: Evidence-based practice with populations at risk.* New York, NY: Thomson Brooks/Cole.

Jongsma, A. E. J. (2004). Psychotherapy treatment plan writing. In G. P. Koocher, J. C. Norcross, &

S. S. Hill, III (Eds.), *Psychologist's desk reference* (2nd ed.). New York, NY: Oxford University Press.

Jordan, C. E., & Franklin, C. (2011). *Clinical assessment for social workers: Quantitative and qualitative methods* (3rd ed.). Chicago: Lyecum Books.

Lambert, M. J. (2013). *Bergin and Garfield's handbook of psychotherapy and behavior change.* New York, NY: John Wiley & Sons.

Reid, W. J. (2000). *The task planner: An intervention resource for human service professionals.* New York, NY:Columbia University Press.

56   Effective Couple and Family Treatment

Cynthia Franklin, Catheleen Jordan, & Laura M. Hopson

INTRODUCTION

The practice and research on couple and family treatment is supported by several disciplines, including social work, psychology, family science, and marriage and family therapy. As a result of this interdisciplinary participation, a number of effective therapeutic methods have developed. This chapter offers a review of couple and family therapies for social work practitioners. The goal of the review is to help practitioners be able to select practices that have research to support their effectiveness and to be knowledgeable about which couple and family interventions may be applied with different client populations. Other chapters within this section cover in more detail different approaches to couple and family practice.

COUPLE AND FAMILY PRACTICE METHODS

The 1950s and 1960s ushered in the development of specific family therapy models grounded in systems theory that view individual problems in relationship to other family members and significant others in the social environment. One of the most influential places for early research and training on family therapy was the Mental Research Institute (MRI) in Palo Alto, California, which was founded in 1959 by psychiatrist, Don Jackson (Watzlawich, Beavin, & Jackson, 1967). The team included Gregory Bateson (1972), social worker, Virginia Satir, co-founder (Satir, 1964), John Weakland, and Paul Watzlawich (Watzlawich, Weakland, & Fisch, 1974). Many other influential family therapists were trained at the MRI such as social workers, Steve de Shazer and Insoo Kim Berg (de Shazer et al., 1986), who created the Solution-focused brief therapy and Jay Haley who founded the Strategic Family Therapy (Haley, 1976). Simultaneous to the work at the MRI, Murray Bowen developed a family systems approach in his work with families with a schizophrenic member at the Menninger Clinic, Salvador Minuchin developed structural family therapy (Minuchin, Montalvo, Guerney, Rosman, & Schumer, 1967), and Gerald

Patterson subsequently created behavioral family therapy (Patterson, 1975), an approach that is often integrated with systems approaches.

All family systems approaches have in common a focus on making changes in the family as a means of creating therapeutic change; and different approaches have increasingly been integrated in couple and family practice to develop empirically supported treatments. Family researchers, for example, are combining strategies across models to design empirically based treatments for high-risk groups, such as serious juvenile offenders and substance-abusing youths (Henggeler & Sheidow, 2012; Sells, 2000; Szapocznik, Hervis, & Schwartz, 2003). Systems approaches may also integrate diverse therapies, such as those from cognitive behavioral therapy in an attempt to create the most efficacious interventions for couple and family treatment.

Family systems models have spawned widely used couple and family practices within social work and allied disciplines as is indicated by surveys of practitioners. Results from a survey of clinicians (n = 2,281) in the *Psychotherapy Networker*, in 2007, for example, showed that couple and family systems approaches were the second most popular treatment modality (The Top 10: The Most Influential Therapists of the Past Quarter-Century. *Psychotherapy Networker*: 2007, March/April. It was also acknowledged by clinicians that client populations may be helped by the various treatment modalities differentially. Practicing therapists frequently use a combination of couple and family techniques from different models rather than adhering to one particular approach. This survey supports the trend toward integrationism, technical eclecticism, and the use of common factors as preferred ways that most practitioners work (Sprenkle, Davis, & Lebow, 2009). Multicomponent treatment programs, which emphasize the integration of more than one approach, are increasingly used with specific client populations and interventions are often purposefully designed that way as the field has moved toward evidence-based practice. Many evidence-based couple and family approaches also share common characteristics or core components. Parent management training is one of the primary components of effective treatment programs, for example (Kazdin & Whitley, 2003). Effective interventions typically include educational components and opportunities to practice new skills, such as communication and problem-solving skills. Practitioners model new behaviors and provide feedback to family members on their ability to implement the behaviors. Intervening on multiple ecological levels is also important, and many effective approaches intervene with family members, school

staff, and providers in the community (Schinke, Brounstein, & Gardner, 2002).

Couple and family approaches further may integrate feminist, postmodern, critical race, and multicultural theory into systems perspectives because these viewpoints are very significant to understanding how relationships in diverse family systems function (Boyd-Webb, 2013). Feminist theory, for example, helps practitioners be aware of the structural inequalities between men and women and the power dynamics within families that may maintain presenting problems. Multicultural perspectives help therapists to be responsive to many different kinds of families and to further be able to assess and intervene into structural inequities and issues of social justice that may be impacting on family relationships, such as issues of immigration and discrimination. A focus on couple and family treatment also calls for a broad understanding of how to define a couple or family unit. In implementing family interventions, practitioners define the couple and family system as those individuals that consider themselves a couple or family and those significant others who are involved with the presenting problem or who could be a resource in developing a solution. In addition to intervening with family members and significant people involved with the problem, therapists may intervene with an individual client, a live-in couple, a foster family, a social services agency representative, or a teacher. The phrase "problem-determined system" is sometimes used to describe this means of defining the system in which to work. Family system interventions commonly call for practitioners to intervene into whatever systems are necessary to resolve problems, whether it be, for example, an extended family, school, or peer system.

EFFECTIVENESS OF COUPLE AND FAMILY TREATMENT APPROACHES

Past meta-analyses have demonstrated that family therapy works as well as other therapies and that it can be especially efficacious for certain client groups (Shadish et al., 1993; Shadish & Baldwin, 2003). Stanton and Shadish (1997), in a meta-analysis of drug abuse outcome studies, found that family interventions are favorable to individual or peer group approaches and have higher retention rates. Among juvenile delinquents, family interventions reduce the risk of rearrest (Woolfenden, Williams, & Peat, 2005). Studies also show that family therapy reduces client utilization of the health care system (Law & Crane, 2000). Several reviews of couple and family therapy approaches have also been written for practitioners and these reviews show effective applications of the different family interventions (e.g., Carr, 2009; Corcoran, 2003; Hoagwood, 2005; Sprenkle, 2012; Thompson, Pomeroy, & Gober, 2005). Sprenkle's (2012) review suggested that the most research support for family therapies was with conduct disorder, drug abuse, psycho-education with mental illness, alcoholism, relationship distress, including relationship education, and child and adolescent disorders. Recent guidelines for classifying evidence-based treatments in couple and family therapy, developed by Sexton, Coop Gordon, Gurman, Lebow, Holtzworth-Munroe, and Johnson (2011) may be useful in selecting interventions: Category 1—some evidence for the model as compared with reasonable alternatives (i.e., treatment as usual); Category 2—promising model, has some verification; and Category 3—effective model with strong scientific evidence of effectiveness, shows change with various problems and populations. The strongest studies have relevant comparison groups, random assignment, treatment fidelity measures, and use of multiple measures to measure outcome; as mentioned, a trend in family therapy is to integrate techniques from more than one family therapy model and to operationalize these using clinical manuals and protocols.

WHAT COUPLE AND FAMILY INTERVENTION TO USE WITH YOUR CLIENTS

Across family therapy models, characteristics of the therapeutic relationship are important factors moderating the effectiveness of family interventions. One meta-analysis indicates that therapeutic relationship variables are good predictors of family therapy outcomes (Karver, Hadelsman, Fields, & Bickman, 2006) and the use of self in couple and family interventions is particularly important because these therapies are directive and rely on the person of the therapist in the change processes. It is also important to keep in mind that even though all the models of couple and family practice show potential effectiveness, certain models have better outcome research,

and evidence has accumulated suggesting that these couple and family treatments show clinical efficacy or considerable promise when applied to certain client groups (Sprenkle, 2012). At the present time, Behavioral, Cognitive-behavioral, Functional, Psycho-educational, and Ecostructural and Strategic, including Multisystemic, Emotion-focused and Solution-focused models have accumulated considerable evidence for their effectiveness with client groups. Each one of these approaches also has well-developed clinical protocols, procedures, and treatment manuals to help social workers and other therapists learn how to do the interventions.

Behavioral family therapies have shown effectiveness with child and adolescent issues and couple's distress. A number of studies support Behavioral Parent Training Intervention where studies show statistically significant findings for treating hyperactivity, parenting, behavior problems, developmental and speech disorders (Sexton, Datchi, Evans, LaFollette, & Wright, 2013; Franklin, Harris, & Allen-Meares, 2012). Functional family therapy, which integrates systems theory and behavioral methods into its own unique relationship therapy, works with juvenile offenders and their families. There is also evidence to show that functional family therapy reduces arrests in younger siblings (Sexton, 2010). Skills training approaches based on behavioral therapies also work in prevention of substance use and antisocial behaviors. Functional family therapy has also shown empirical support for treating sexual or physical or verbal abuse (Sexton, Datchi, Evans, LaFollette, & Wright, 2013). Lebensohn-Chialvo (2014) further reports that treatment programs for child maltreatment have several behavioral methods including family preservation programs and the most successful child maltreatment prevention programs are family-focused, utilize home visits and a strengths based approach, and aim to increase social supports; these were found to decrease abuse and neglect as well as to improve child adjustment and overall family functioning. Two other family interventions that are integrated programs, and which use behavioral interventions and have shown success with youth behavior problems are Incredible Years and Triple P Positive Parenting (Sexton et al., 2013).

Behavioral couple therapies are also among the most well-researched and effective treatments for distressed couples and also for the treatment of alcohol problems (Johnson & Lebow, 2000;

Lebow, Chambers, Christensen, & Johnson, 2012; O'Farrell & Clements, 2012; Perissutti & Barraca, 2013; Shadish & Baldwin, 2005). Behavioral Couple Therapy has been shown in studies to improve family relationships, decrease relationship dissatisfaction, decrease substance abuse and depression, and improve the relationship in the case of infidelity (Sexton, Datchi, Evans, LaFollette, & Wright, 2013; Lebensohn-Chialvo, 2014; O'Farrell & Clements, 2012) Another type of behavioral family therapy called, Integrated Behavioral Family Therapy, further integrates family systems theory and cognitive-behavioral therapy and demonstrates positive outcomes with substance-abusing youth (Thompson, Pomeroy, & Gober et al., 2005; Barrett Waldron, Slesnick, Brody, Turner, & Peterson, 2001).

Family Psychoeducation is also associated with Behavioral interventions and has been used in mental health and hospital settings with chronic illnesses (Lefley, 2009). It has been found to be a useful approach when families have members with mental illness such as schizophrenia or chronic health conditions such as diabetes. Psychoeducation uses multifamily group interventions and provides education and social support; it is the family treatment of choice when working with chronic health conditions. Research also demonstrates that participation in Psychoeducation is associated with increased social supports and improved ability to manage social conflicts (Magliano, Fiorillo, Malangone, De-Rosa, & Maj, 2006).

Eco-structural and Strategic interventions are successful interventions for youth with conduct disorders, eating disorders, substance abuse, and attention deficit hyperactivity disorder (ADHD). The Maudsley method for treating Anorexia and Bulimia, for example, was influenced by Minchin's Structural family therapy and added elements from Strategic interventions and created its' own unique methods for empowering parents to get adolescents to resume normal eating. Maudsley has been investigated in clinical trials research and has become an important treatment for adolescents with eating disorders (Loeb & le Grange, 2009). Brief Strategic Family Therapy (BSFT) integrates concepts from systemic, structural, and strategic models in addressing issues of delinquency, substance abuse, and family relationship problems. The BSFT model has been evaluated repeatedly over the course of 30 years and has shown effectiveness in clinical trials research treating minority and nonminority

adolescents with behavior problems including drug use (Robbins et al., 2011). Other Integrated treatments that use Eco-structural and Strategic approaches, and which show promising results, include Multisystemic Therapy (Henggeler & Sheidow, 2012) and Multidimensional Family Therapy (Henderson, Dakof, Greenbaum, & Liddle, 2010). The Multidimensional approach also integrates a developmental approach to assessment and treatment. All of these family programs have repeatedly been shown to be effective with youth with delinquent behavior and substance use.

Multisystemic therapy (MST), which uses ecological approaches, intensive family preservation, and Structural family therapy, has also demonstrated positive outcomes with hard-to-reach juvenile delinquents and substance abusers (Henggeler & Sheidow, 2012). This approach also offers sophisticated protocols for engaging hard-to-reach clients and manuals for maintaining the treatment adherence of therapists. Past controversies regarding the effectiveness of MST, however, illustrate to social workers the challenges of identifying evidence-based interventions, because researchers may not always agree what therapies have the best evidence. MST, for example, is widely accepted as evidence-based intervention by federal funding organizations and practice settings (Franklin & Hopson, 2007). Yet one systematic review conducted by the Nordic Campbell Center of the Campbell Collaboration concludes that the intervention is not consistently more effective than alternative treatments (Littell, Popa, & Forsythe, 2005). Over time, new research may call into question the effectiveness of other approaches or provide more evidence for some of the promising programs that are not currently considered to show very much empirical support. For this reason, social work practitioners must continuously stay tuned to the ongoing developments in therapy, as well as evaluate their own practices. The Sexton et al. (2011) guidelines mentioned above may be especially helpful for practitioners to consider when evaluating the efficacy of various couple and family approaches for use in their own practices. Assessment and outcome measures are especially important to use in determining the relative effectiveness of the approaches with individual cases (Jordan & Franklin, 2011).

Another efficacious intervention is the Emotion-focused therapy for couples, which emphasizes the importance of attachment and

Box 56.1 Case Study for Brief Strategic Family Therapy: The Guerrero Family

CLINICAL PRESENTATION

The Guerrero family consists of a mother, a father, and 11- and 14-year-old sons. They were referred to the clinic by the 14-year-old's school counselor after he was caught smoking marijuana in the school bathroom. The counselor visited the home and found the youngest son and the mother eating dinner. The identified patient and the father were not there. The mother immediately began to list excuses why her oldest son was not home when he should have been. She had trouble accepting what the school counselor had done and insisted that the teacher who had reported him "has it out for my son." Toward the end of the counselor's first visit, the father came home. He ignored his wife and younger son and went directly to the kitchen. On finding no food ready for him, he shouted over his shoulder at his wife, asking her why she had not made him dinner. When the father was asked to join the session, he declined, saying that his wife was in charge of discipline and that she was not doing a good job at it. The 14-year-old did not come home during the counselor's visit.

Establishing the Therapeutic System

When the counselor first arrived at the Guerrero home, he began to join with the mother. He sat at the dinner table with the mother and the younger son and validated the mother as she complained about the father's disengagement and the oldest son's out-of-control behavior. The younger son chimed in periodically about his brother's sour attitude, and the counselor empathized with his grievances. Although the counselor's initial attempts to join with the father were unsuccessful, the counselor later adopted a more focused approach. When he spoke to the father, the counselor emphasized that his participation was needed to keep his son from getting into more serious trouble. The counselor also assured the father that participating in therapy could help reduce his wife's nagging about his disengagement from the family.

Joining with the drug-abusing son was somewhat more difficult. He resisted the counselor's first few attempts to join with him over the phone and was absent from the home during the counselor's first few visits. Finally, the counselor approached the adolescent at the park after he and his father had had a major fight. The counselor assured the youth that being in BSFT could help ensure that that type of fight would not happen again.

DIAGNOSIS

When the counselor met with the whole family, the mother began to tell him about her son's problems. The counselor asked the mother to tell her son about her concerns. As the counselor encouraged the family members to speak with one another, he also observed the patterns of interaction along the following BSFT diagnostic dimensions.

Organization. A strong alliance exists between the mother and her 14-year-old (problem) son; the father is uninvolved. The children communicate with the father mostly through the mother. The mother and the father do not share much time as a couple. The mother is responsible for child-rearing nearly all the time. The mother and father ally occasionally, but only regarding unimportant issues, such as what to eat for dinner.

Resonance. The mother indicates what her 14-year-old son prefers to eat, and the mother and her 14-year-old son laugh together, both signs of enmeshment. The father is frequently "too busy" to participate in family activities, a sign of disengagement. Complaints of family members about other family members during the interview are highly specific, a sign of adaptive functioning along this dimension.

Developmental stage. The children are not allowed to play outdoors at night. The mother uses her 14-year-old son as her confidante, complaining to him that his father comes home late.

Life context. The father has a demanding job, while the mother finishes her work early and is home by 3 P.M. The family lives in a high-crime neighborhood; drug dealing gangs recruit in the area. The mother and father are not involved in arranging or supervising activities for their adolescent son and his peers. The 14-year-old son is associating with antisocial youth in the neighborhood.

Identified patient. The father comes home late and does not help with chores at home. His 14-year-old son is rebellious, refuses to do chores, and has conduct problems at home and in school. He also comes home late, often very excited and irritable. He stays up much of the night listening to music, then sleeps deep into the day. The 11-year-old son is a model child.

Conflict resolution. Conflicts are diffused through angry blaming and recriminations.

GENERAL DISCUSSION OF THE DIAGNOSIS

In the Guerrero family, the parents have assigned themselves separate role responsibilities. The mother is fully responsible for all child-rearing, and the father's responsibility in this area is very limited. Because there appears to be an unspoken agreement between the parents to be distant from each other, it can be assumed that they prefer their separate role responsibilities for their own reasons. This is maladaptive behavior in terms of child-rearing issues because the father and mother do not cooperate in parenting functions. Rather, it may appear that the mother and the troubled son are the ones allied, with the father off on the side. If one looks a little deeper, it would not be surprising to find that the same patterns of interaction occur around content areas other than child-rearing. In fact, these kinds of interactive patterns or structures are almost always found to reoccur in most aspects of family life. If they occur around one content, they are almost invariably occurring around most (if not all) contents. The lack of a strong parental alliance with regard to child-rearing issues undermines the family's ability to chart an effective and successful course of action. This is particularly troublesome when there are forces external to the family that influence the adolescent's development of behavior problems. These forces include the adolescent's peer group and the behavioral expectations that exist or to which the youth is exposed outside the home. These ecological forces provide training and opportunity for a full rebellion on the part of the adolescent.

A BSFT intervention will target changing the interactional patterns preventing the family from successfully charting the youth's path away from antisocial peer groups and externalizing behaviors. This intervention involves restoring parental leadership capabilities by first creating a parental leadership alliance. In resonance, it becomes clear that because the father is outside of the mother–child alliance, he is less concerned about what goes on within that alliance. Because he stays out, he is emotionally distant (disengaged) from both his wife and his son. In contrast to this, the mother and her 14-year-old son are much closer emotionally and psychologically; thus, they are likely to be enmeshed. Whether one defines the mother as enmeshed with the son or the mother and son as disengaged from the father, it is obvious that there is a difference in the psychological and emotional distance that exists between father and mother and father and son on the one hand and mother and son on the other.

On the dimension of developmental stage, it appears that the 14-year-old boy may be burdened with emotional responsibilities that are more appropriately assigned to a spouse, such as being the mother's confidante. The other child is not allowed out after dark. This seems appropriate given the dangerousness of the neighborhood.

In this family, the identified patient is sometimes the troubled son and sometimes the isolated father. Although the negativity the mother and the 14-year-old show toward the father functions to keep him out of the family, both the mother and father blame their current problems on their oldest son. If he were not rebellious, their separate role arrangement would work quite well for each of them. Unfortunately, conflicts between the mother and the father are not being resolved because their attempts to address their differences of opinion degenerate into blaming wars.

PLANNING TREATMENT BASED ON DIAGNOSIS

Understanding the dimensions that describe family interactions goes a long way toward helping the BSFT counselor define what he or she must do as a counselor: diagnose the problem in terms of specific dimensions of family interactions and then implement strategies to correct problems along these dimensions. Often some dimensions are more problematic than others and need to be the greater focus of the intervention. The counselor diagnosed the oldest son's drug abuse problem in terms of ineffective behavior control resulting from the following.

- Organization: absence of a parental subsystem that works together. Mother and father need to be assigned collaborative tasks that will bring them together.
- Organization: improper alliances. Boundaries must be strengthened between mother and 14-year-old son.
- Resonance: maladaptive boundaries in which one parent is too close (enmeshed) to the problem child, and a second parent is too far (disengaged) from the spouse and that same child.
- Boundaries need to be shifted so that the parents are closer to one another emotionally and interactionally, the children are more "in tune" with each other, and a healthy separation exists between the parents and the children.
- Developmental stage: developmental stage may be inappropriate in that the enmeshed child is burdened and confused by a spousal role (confidante to mom's unhappiness with dad). The counselor should encourage the mother and father to serve as each other's support system.
- Identified patient: enmeshed child is identified by the family as its major problem. The counselor needs to shift the family's attention to help family members understand that the whole system, rather than only the adolescent, is part of the problem. Also, family members need to eliminate negative attitudes and enabling behaviors they display toward the adolescent patient to "free" him to act in a socially appropriate manner.
- Life context: 14-year-old identified patient is involved with a deviant peer group. The mother, father, and patient should negotiate rules and consequences for the adolescent's misbehavior, and boundaries between the family and the outside world

need to be strengthened. Additionally, the parents may need to be more involved with the parents of their son's peers to make it easier to more effectively supervise their adolescent's activities.
- Conflict resolution: family may have certain conflicts repeatedly occur and never get resolved because each time differences emerge, they are either avoided or, more often, diffused through blaming wars. The counselor should refocus the interaction on the problem each time family members attempt to avoid the issue or change the subject so that the conflict may be negotiated and resolved.

PRODUCING CHANGE

Having diagnosed the problem in terms of these dimensions, the counselor was able to target interventions directly at the problematic interactions within these dimensions. One of the BSFT counselor's first moves was to help the disengaged father get closer to his estranged 14-year-old son. At the same time, the counselor initiated a dialogue between the parents about this youth to try to establish an alliance between the parents around the content of their mutual concern for their son. The next step was to help the parents negotiate rules for the youth that once implemented, would bring his out-of-control behavior under control. As these changes were being negotiated, the family displayed frequent conflict avoidance and diffusion. When the family attempted to diffuse or avoid the conflict, the counselor would intervene and return the topic of conversation to the original conflict. In the process, the family acquired new conflict-resolution skills. The parents were able to agree on rules and consequences for the identified patient's behavior; these were discussed and, where appropriate, negotiated between the parents and the son. Ultimately, the parents were able to set consistent limits, and the adolescent's behavior improved.

emotional processes (Basham & Miehls, 2004; Greenberg & Goldman, 2008; Johnson, 2004; Lebow, Chambers, Christensen, & Johnson, 2012). Research studies on emotion-focused therapy are rapidly progressing, and there is

evidence for its effectiveness with distressed couples, including those who experience trauma (Denton, Burleson, Clark, Rodriguez, & Hobbs, 2000; Lebow, Chambers, Christensen, & Johnson, 2012). A meta-analysis indicates that emotion-focused therapy may be more effective than behavioral models for treatment of marital distress (Wood, Crane, Schaalje, & Law, 2005). The revised behavioral couples therapy that includes components of emotion-focused interventions has also been shown to be effective with distressed couples (Lebow, Chambers, Christensen, & Johnson, 2012). Integrative couples therapy uses Acceptance strategies that reframe hard emotions, such as anger, into soft emotions, such as sadness. Discussions about attachment patterns learned in one's family of origin help couples gain insight, empathy, and acceptance of each other's behavior (Christensen, Atkins, Yi, Baucom, & George, 2006; Jacobson & Christensen, 1996).

Solution-focused brief therapy (SFBT) is a strengths-based approach that developed within brief family therapy; it can be applied to individuals or families and the research has progressed significantly on this approach over the past 15 years. Several experimental and quasiexperimental studies have accumulated on SFBT showing that it is a promising model with a wide range of problems including adult depression, and problems with child and family issues. (Franklin, Trepper, Gingerich, & McCollum, 2012; Gingerich & Peterson, 2013; Kim, 2008; Kim & Franklin, 2008; Newsome, 2004). Kim & Franklin (2008), for example, conducted a systematic review of studies of SFBT in school settings and discovered that one experimental design study, six quasiexperimental design studies, and one single-case design study on SFBT had been published since 2000. The effect sizes calculated by the authors and reported in the individual studies also show SFBT to be a promising intervention for work with children and families within school settings, with most studies having medium and some large effect sizes.

EXAMPLE OF A FAMILY INTERVENTION

Brief Strategic Family Therapy

BSFT was developed by Jose Szapocznik and colleagues at the Center for Family Studies. The model has been used in the context of prevention, early intervention, and intervention for families with children between the ages of 8 and 17 years to address issues of delinquency and substance abuse. BSFT is provided in 8 to 24 sessions, depending on the severity of the presenting problems. Sessions may be conducted in office, home, or community settings based on the needs of the family. The model aims to improve outcomes for youth by improving the family environment. Box 56.1 presents a case example from the series *Therapy Manuals for Drug Addiction*, published by the National Institute of Drug Abuse (Szapocznik, Hervis, & Schwartz et al., 2003).

SUMMARY

Family therapies based on systems theory emerged in the 1950s and 1960s and have become useful treatment approaches for many different client problems. There is consistent support for the effectiveness of couple and family therapies, although there is better research on the efficacy of specific approaches with various client populations. Behavioral, Eco-structural, and Strategic family approaches appear to have considerable experimental and clinical support for their effectiveness. They also have a long history of application within the field. Newer models, like Emotion-focused couples therapy, are also building a solid empirical base for their effectiveness. Other promising models, such as SFBT, are developing a growing experimental research base. Family therapy has come a long way in developing an understanding of the common factors shared by all effective approaches. A trend in family therapy is to integrate techniques from more than one family therapy model and to operationalize these using clinical manuals and protocols, making it possible for practitioners to apply these treatment manuals in their practices. Evidence-based approaches to family treatment share core components and are integrative by design. As we move into the future, it is important for social workers to continuously appraise the changing evidence for different approaches to couple and family treatment and to stay abreast of new developments in the field, as well as to evaluate the effectiveness of their own practices, using appropriate outcome measures.

WEBSITES

American Association for Marriage and Family Therapy. http://www.aamft.org
Mental Research Institute. http://www.mri.org

Minuchin Center for the Family.
  http://minuchincenter.org
Solution Focused Brief Therapy Association.
  http://www.sfbta.org
Family Therapy Training Institute of Miami.
http://brief-strategic-family-therapy.com/
  training/bsft-certification-program.html

References

Basham, K., & Miehls, D. (2004). *Transforming the legacy: Couple therapy with survivors of childhood trauma.* New York, NY: Columbia University Press.

Barrett Waldron, H., Slesnik, N., Brody, J. L., Tuner, C. W., & Peterson, T. R. (2001). Treatment outcomes for adolescent substance abuse at 4- and 7-month assessments. *Journal of Consulting and Clinical Psychology, 69*(5), 802–813.

Bateson, G. (1972). *Steps to an ecology of mind.* Worcester, MA: Chandler Publishing Company.

Boyd-Webb, N. (2013). *Culturally diverse parent, child and family relationships.* New York, NY: Columbia University Press.

Carr, A. (2009).The effectiveness of family therapy and systemic interventions for adult-focused problems. *Journal of Family Therapy, 31*(1), 46–74.

Christensen, A., Atkins, D. C., Yi, J., Baucom, D. H., & George, W. H. (2006). Couple and individual adjustment for two years following a randomized clinical trial comparing Traditional versus Integrative Behavioral Couple Therapy. *Journal of Consulting and Clinical Psychology, 74*(6), 1180–1191.

Corcoran, J. (2003). *Clinical applications of evidence based family interventions:* New York, NY: Oxford University Press.

de Shazer, S., Berg, I. K., Lipchik, E., Nunnally, E., Molnar, A., Gingerich, W., & Weiner-Davis, M. (1986). Brief therapy: Focused solution development. *Family Process, 25*(2), 207–221.

Denton, W. H., Burleson, B. R., Clark, T. E., Rodriguez, C. P., & Hobbs, B. V. (2000). A randomized trial of emotion-focused therapy for couples in a training clinic. *Journal of Marital and Family Therapy, 26*(1), 65–78.

Franklin, C., & Hopson L. M. (2007). Facilitating the use of evidence-based practices in community organizations. *The Journal of Social Work Education, 43*(3), 377–404.

Franklin, C., Harris, M. B., & Allen-Meares, P. (2012). *School Services Source book.* New York, NY: Oxford University Press.

Franklin, C., Trepper, T. S., Gingerich, W., & McCollum, E. (2012). *Solution-focused brief therapy: A handbook of evidence based practice.* New York, NY: Oxford University Press.

Gingerich, W. J., & Peterson, L. T. (2013). Effectiveness of solution-focused brief therapy: A systematic qualitative review of controlled outcome studies. *Research on Social Work Practice, 23*(3), 266–283.

Greenberg, L. S., & Goldman R. (2008). *Emotion-focused couples therapy: The dynamics of emotion, love, and power.* Washington, DC: American Psychological Association.

Haley, J. (1976). *Problem solving therapy.* San Francisco, CA: Jossey-Bass.

Henderson, C. E., Dakof, G. A., Greenbaum, P. E., & Liddle, H. A. (2010). Effectiveness of multidimensional family therapy with higher severity substance-abusing adolescents: Report from two randomized controlled trials. *Journal of Consulting and Clinical Psychology, 78*(6), 885–897.

Henggeler, S. W., & Sheidow, A. J. (2012). Empirically supported family-based treatments for conduct disorder and delinquency in adolescents. *Journal of Marital and Family Therapy, 38*(1), 30–58.

Hoagwood, K. E. (2005). Family-based services in children's mental health: A research review and synthesis. *Journal of Child Psychology and Psychiatry, 46*(7), 690–713.

Jacobson, N. S., & Christensen, A. (1996). *Integrative couple therapy: Promoting acceptance and change.* New York, NY: Norton.

Johnson, S. (2004). *The practice of emotionally focused marital therapy: Creating connection* (2nd ed.). New York, NY: Brunner-Routledge.

Johnson, S. M., & Lebow, J. (2000). The "coming of age" of couple therapy: A decade review. *Journal of Marital and Family Therapy, 26*(1), 23–38.

Jordan, C., & Franklin, C. (2011). *Clinical assessment for social workers: Quantitative and qualitative methods.* Chicago, IL: Lyceum Books.

Karver, M. S., Handelsman, J. B., Fields, S., & Bickman, L. (2006). Meta-analysis of therapeutic relationship variables in youth and family therapy: The evidence for different relationship variables in the child and adolescent treatment outcome literature. *Clinical Psychology Review, 26*(1), 50–65.

Kazdin, A. E., & Whitley, M. K. (2003). Treatment of parental stress to enhance therapeutic change among children referred for aggressive and antisocial behavior. *Journal of Consulting and Clinical Psychology, 71*(3), 504–515.

Kim, J. S., & Franklin, C. (2008). Solution-focused brief therapy in schools: A review of the outcome literature. *Children and Youth Services Review, 31*(4), 464–470.

Kim, J. S. (2008). Examining the effectiveness of solution-focused brief therapy: A meta-analysis. *Research on Social Work Practice, 18*(2), 107–116.

Law, D. D., & Crane, D. R. (2000). The influence of marital and family therapy on health care utilization in a health-maintenance organization. *Journal of Marital and Family Therapy, 26,* 281–291.

Lebensohn-Chialvo, F. (2014). Research on family intervention. In M. P. Nichols (Ed.), *The essentials of family therapy* (6th ed.). Boston, MA: Pearson.

Lebow, J., Chambers, A., Christensen, A., & Johnson, S. (2012). Research on the treatment of couple distress. *Journal of Marital and Family Therapy, 38*(1), 145–168.

Lefley, H. (2009). *Family psychoeducation for serious mental illness: Evidence-based practices.* New York, NY: Oxford Press.

Littell, J., Popa, J. H., & Forsythe, B. (2005). Multi-systemic therapy for social, emotional, and behavioral problems in youth aged 10–17. *Campbell Collaboration Review, 2.* Retrieved from http://www.campbellcollaboration.org/docpdf/Mst_Littell_Review.pdf.

Loeb, K. L., & le Grange, D. (2009). Family-based treatment for adolescent eating disorders: Current status, new applications and future directions. *International Journal of Child Adolescent Health, 2*(2): 243–254.

Magliano, L., Fiorillo, A., Malangone, C., De-Rosa, C., & Maj, M. (2006). Patient functioning and family burden in a controlled, real-world trial of family psychoeducation for schizophrenia. *Psychiatric Services, 57*(12), 1784–1791.

Minuchin, S., Montalvo, B., Guerney, B., Rosman, B., & Schumer, F. (1967). *Families of the slums.* NY: Basic Books.

Newsome, S. (2004). Solution-focused brief therapy (SFBT) group work with at-risk junior high school students: Enhancing the bottom-line. *Research on Social Work Practice, 14*(5), 336–343.

O'Farrell T. J., & Clements K. (2012). Review of outcome research on marital and family therapy in treatment for alcoholism. *Journal of Marital and Family Therapy, 38*(1), 122–144.

Patterson, G. R. (1975). *Families: Applications of social learning to family life.* Champaign, IL: Research Press.

Perissutti, C., & Barraca, J. (2013). Integrative Behavioral Couple Therapy vs. Traditional Behavioral Couple Therapy: A theoretical review of the differential effectiveness. *Clínica y Salud, 24,* 11–18.

Robbins, M., Feaster, D., Horigian, V., Bachrach, K., Burlew, K., Carrion, I., Schindler, E.,. . . Szapocznik, J. (2011). Brief strategic therapy versus treatment as usual: Results of a multisite randomized trial for substance using adolescents. *Journal of Consulting and Clinical Psychology, 79*(6), 713–727.

Satir, V. (1964). *Conjoint family therapy: A guide to theory and technique.* Palo Alto, CA: Science and Behavior Books.

Schinke, S., Brounstein, P., & Gardner, S. (2002). *Science-based prevention programs and principles.* Rockville, MD: U.S. Department of Health and Human Services.

Sells, S. P. (2000). *Parenting your out-of-control teenager.* New York, NY: St. Martin's.

Sexton, T. L. (2010). *Functional family therapy in clinical practice.* New York, NY: Routledge.

Sexton, T., Datchi, C., Evans, L., LaFollette, J., & Wright, L. (2013). The effectiveness of couple and family-based clinical interventions. In M. J. Lambert (Ed.), *Bergin and Garfield's handbook of psychotherapy and behavior change* (6th ed.). New York, NY: John Wiley & Sons, 587–639.

Sexton, T., Coop Gordon, K., Gurman, A., Lebow, J., Holtzworth-Munroe, A., & Johnson, S. (2011). Guidelines for classifying evidence-based treatments in couple and family therapy. *Family Process, 50*(3), 377–392.

Shadish, W. R., Montgomery, L. M., Wilson, P., Wilson, M. R., Bright, I., & Okwumabua, T. (1993). Effects of family and marital psychotherapies: A meta-analysis. *Journal of Consulting and Clinical Psychology, 61*(6), 992–1002.

Shadish, W. R., & Baldwin, S. A. (2003). Meta-analysis of MFT interventions. *Journal of Marital and Family Therapy, 29*(4), 547–570.

Shadish, W. R., & Baldwin, S. A. (2005). Effects of behavioral marital therapy: A meta-analysis of randomized controlled trials. *Journal of Consulting and Clinical Psychology, 73*(1), 6–14.

Sprenkle, D. H., Davis, S. D., & Lebow, J. L. (2009). *Common factors in couple and family therapy: The overlooked foundation for effective practice.* New York, NY: Guilford Press.

Sprenkle, D. H. (2012). Intervention research in couple and family therapy: A methodological and substantive review and an introduction to the special issue. *Journal of Marital and Family Therapy, 38*(1), 3–29.

Stanton, M. D., & Shadish, W. R. (1997). Outcome, attrition, and family-couples treatment for drug abuse: A meta-analysis and review of the controlled, comparative studies. *Psychological Bulletin, 122*(2), 170–191.

Szapocznik, J., Hervis, O., & Schwartz, S. J. (2003). *Therapy manuals for drug addiction: Brief strategic family therapy for adolescent drug abuse.* Bethesda, MD: U.S. Department of Health and Human Services, National Institutes of Health, National Institute on Drug Abuse.

The Top 10: The Most Influential Therapists of the Past Quarter-Century. (2007, March/April). *Psychotherapy Networker.*

Thompson, S. J., Pomeroy, E. C., & Gober, K. (2005). Family-based treatment models targeting substance use and high-risk behaviors among adolescents: A review. *The Journal of Evidence-Based Social Work, 2*(1–2), 207–233.

Watzlawich, P., Weakland, J. H., & Fisch, R. (1974). *Change: Principles of problem formation and problem resolution.* New York, NY: W. W. Norton and Company.

Watzlawich, P., Beavin, J., & Jackson, D. (1967). *Pragmatics of human communication.* New York, NY: W. W. Norton and Company.

Wood, N., Crane, D., Schaalje, G., & Law, D. (2005). What works for whom: A meta-analytic review of marital and couples therapy in reference to marital

distress. *American Journal of Family Therapy, 33*(4), 273–287.

Woolfenden, S. R., Williams, K., & Peat, J. K. (2005). Family and parenting interventions for conduct disorder and delinquency: A meta-analysis of randomised controlled trials. *Archives of Disease in Childhood, 86*, 251–256.

57   Structural Family Therapy

Harry J. Aponte & Karni Kissil

INTRODUCTION

Structural family therapy (SFT) addresses client objectives in the context of the current organization of client relationships vis-à-vis the issues being addressed. It is a systems-based model with one of its primary organizing principles positing that "changes in a family structure contribute to changes in the behavior and the inner psychic processes of the members of that system" (Minuchin, 1974, p. 9).

SFT has the unique legacy of having been born to meet the needs of poor inner-city youth and their families (Minuchin, Montalvo, Guerney, Rosman, & Schumer, 1967). Its approach speaks directly to how clients experience life more than to conceptual abstractions about their struggles. It aims to achieve quick, palpable results. Lessons learned from poor, underorganized families (Aponte, 1994b) who had been structurally undermined by psychological and social stressors are relevant to all families from the general population. SFT focuses on concrete issues, located in the present, mediated through the client's experience in session, based on reorganizing the structure of relationships, built on client strengths, aimed at palpable outcomes, and characterized by active therapist involvement. What follows is a brief commentary on the seven basic principles of structural family therapy.

FOCUS ON CONCRETE ISSUES

SFT looks for the urgent issue that has the family's attention and intensity of concern (Aponte, 1998b). The therapist attends to the concrete manifestation of the issue, that is, how it is being lived and experienced by the client. The underlying assumption is that the "pain" at the core of the problem-laden experience carries within it the individual, family, and social dynamics that are generating the issue. Moreover, inside the pain-filled experience of the issue lies the goad to prod the efforts needed for change. It follows that the living pain-filled experience confronts people with the challenge to make problem-solving choices. These choices carry within them the worldview, ideals, and moral imperatives that frame people's drive to change. Structural therapists are looking for what motivates clients to action because they intend to build on momentum generated by the concrete manifestation of the client's experience of the issue.

- *The therapist connects with the family around the specific issue and the urgency with which it is driving the family to seek help.*

Example: The parents come in with their adolescent son who is failing in school. Mother anxiously presents the problem. The son pouts, and the father steams silently. The therapist asks the son and father each to react to mother's concern. He wants them all to address the boy's failing, with whatever distress they are feeling around it.

LOCATED IN THE PRESENT

Structural family therapy views the past as "manifest in the present and . . . available to change by interventions that change the present" (Minuchin, 1974, p. 14). The client issue contains the focal point of today's concern, the dynamics currently generating the distress, and traces of the family's history that explain the whys and hows of the problem's genesis. By working through the present, the therapist connects with not only today's urgency for relief but also the forces concurrently precipitating the problem. The turbulence of the present provides the therapist with the most immediate and reliable access to the forces from the past being played out in today's drama. The therapist's interventions relate to the present experience of the client with the full force of its impact on the client's life today. The therapy itself is treated as another immediate context in which the issues are now alive and commanding attention.

- *The therapist relates to how the issue is affecting the family today.*

(continuing with the example above) The therapist asks specifically for details regarding the school situation right now, and where each family member stands in relation to it. The present picture is being drawn, to include the school, the mother, the father, and the boy—the facts, the thoughts, and the feelings, as they exist at this moment.

MEDIATED THROUGH THE CLIENT'S EXPERIENCE IN SESSION

The principal field of intervention for SFT is the family's enactment of their issue in the session (Aponte, 1998b; Aponte & VanDeusen, 1981; Minuchin & Fishman, 1981). The structural therapist looks beyond the verbal account of what has happened at home to how family members interact with each other now as they attempt to articulate the issue and work for a solution within the session itself (Aponte, 1990; Aponte & Hoffman, 1973). That enactment is both the immediate

material for assessment and an opportunity for intervention to change attitudes and behaviors.

The very essence of the traditional understanding of *enactment* in SFT is, "an interpersonal scenario in the session in which dysfunctional transactions among family members are played out" (Minuchin & Fishman, 1981, p. 81). The structural therapist is reading and relating to the interactions of the family members around the issue that is the source of their distress. Reliving their struggle in the presence of the therapist brings to the therapist the fullness of their experience—the words, emotions, and actions that allow the therapist to see, feel, and touch the family and its individual members so as to connect, understand, and intervene with them in the throbbing intensity of the living moment of their pain and conflict. This enactment can take place in any combination of family members or even between family members and people in their network or community who are part of their problem and/or potentially part of their solution, such as school personnel (Aponte, 1976).

- *The therapist looks to work with the family and its members in the moment in session as they interact with each other and/or with members of their community network around their focal issue.*

The therapist asks each family member to react to what she/he hears from the other about what they are presenting. The mother is anxiously protective of the son. The father is impatient with her solicitude for him, and angry with the boy about what he perceives as the boy's "laziness." The youngster appears tearful and scared. The therapist gets a glimpse of the family patterns of interaction around this issue.

BASED ON REORGANIZING THE STRUCTURE OF RELATIONSHIPS

The structural family therapist pays special attention to the structure of family relationships in relation to the focal issue. There are three basic structural dimensions to all relationships (Aponte & VanDeusen, 1981).

1. *Boundaries.* What defines who is in or out of a family's interaction vis-à-vis the focal issue, as well as what their roles are in this interaction.

2. *Alignment*. Who is with or against the other in the transactions generating the issue.
3. *Power*. What the relative influence is of the participants in the dynamics of the interaction.

A client's focal issue is connected to a characteristic pattern of family interaction that bears changing if the problem is to be solved at its source. This transactional structure is the underlying skeleton of the dynamics that generate the problem. In some circumstances, the pathological structure undergirds a conflict, whereas in others, a faulty structure is inadequate to resolve the client's issue. That is, some problems are the result of conflicting feelings and needs, and others are the consequence of weakly organized relationships, or of a combination of both conflicting and inadequate organization. Structural therapists relate to both the content and the underlying structure of issues the client presents.

Structural therapy was originally known for targeting the faulty structure of poor underorganized families (Aponte, 1994b; Aponte & DiCesare, 2000). These underorganized structures were seen as lacking the constancy, coherence, and flexibility to meet life's challenges. In working to help these families solve their problems, structural therapists deepened their appreciation of how all social functioning rests on strong and adaptable structures.

• *The therapist pays particular attention to the underlying structure of a family's relationships in terms of its boundaries, alignments, and use of power.*

The mother and son are aligned in defense against the frustrated father who is clearly on the periphery of that subsystem. However, when he intensely gives voice to the power of his anger both mother and son shrink back nervously. The therapist wants the father in the circle with his wife and son, and with the father supporting rather than attacking the boy.

BUILT ON CLIENT STRENGTHS

SFT works through a "search for strength" (Minuchin & Colapinto, 1980). The structural therapist actively engages with the family to impede old, pathological transactional patterns (Aponte & VanDeusen, 1981) while working

with the family's strengths to build new, positive patterns of interaction. The therapist aims for the family to experience these functional interactions in session as members work on the solutions to their problems. The therapist connects to aspects of the focal issue that are accessible for facilitating a positive change, however small. From an eco-systemic perspective, structural therapists build on the resources of the individual and of the family and its social context, including their psychology, personal relationships, spirituality, and community.

• *Even when the immediate objective may be to impede a dysfunctional interaction, ultimately every intervention of the therapist aims to support and mobilize the client's motivation and ability to make positive changes.*

The therapist sits next to the father, sympathizes with his worry about the boy's future, reframing the angry frustration as concern for his son. He then solicitously invites the father to ask his son whether he is afraid of him. The father is thrown off balance by the tone of the query, and tentatively asks the question. The boy so affirms, but then tearfully blurts out how he feels belittled by his father, which surprises and affects the father. The therapist will now build on how the father is moved by his son's obvious pain, a hurt inflicted by him.

AIMED AT PALPABLE OUTCOMES

In much the same way that the structural therapist looks to work through the concrete manifestation of the focal issue, the therapist looks for positive therapeutic outcomes to be represented in changes the client can experience. Because SFT builds experience upon experience, positive change builds upon positive change. The ultimate outcome of the therapy rests on positive experiences of change, session by session. These palpable goals are evident in the immediate objectives of in-session interventions with enactments and the assignment of home-based tasks. The palpable experience of change gives body to the intended goals of the intervention. The experiential emphasis is a way of looking for intensity that will mobilize motivation and energy to drive change and can reach deeply within the persons involved. The change that is actively experienced in session is more likely to be lived outside the therapy. The goal is to have clients make these changes their own as they come to know their struggles as new, hopeful levels of experience, over which they have exercised their freedom and power to choose to change.

- *The therapist looks to create an experience of change in the present so that the family can feel what it is to live whatever it has come to understand from the therapeutic process.*

The therapist, now leaning close to the father, asks the father what it is like to witness what he just saw in his son's face. He treats the father like a loving parent who is looking upon his wounded son. The father says he understands, and spontaneously recalls how hurt he felt when his father would put him down. The father accepts the therapist's recasting the boy's hurt as an expression of how much the father's opinion of him matters to him, and how this speaks to the power he has at this critical moment to be of help to his son. The therapist looks to the mother at that moment to view her husband as her partner in the work now commencing. The family leaves the session having had a new experience that portends hope.

CHARACTERIZED BY ACTIVE THERAPIST INVOLVEMENT

Structural therapists actively engage in the present with family members as clients enact their struggle in session. From outside a family enactment, they will interpret, reframe, advise, and direct the action among family members. From within an enactment, they will personally engage in family interactions to stimulate changes in the patterns of their relationships (Aponte & VanDeusen, 1981).

- The initial effort of the therapist is to strategically join (Minuchin, 1974) the family interaction "in a carefully planned way" (p. 91). The initial joining action is to gain trust. Subsequently, connecting to the family's interaction becomes a strategic intervention to alter their dysfunctional patterns of interaction.
- *Where the structures of these dysfunctional relationships are more resistant to change, therapists may intensify a conflict within a*

family by drawing attention to their areas of disagreement. Surfacing the pathological dynamics in a live enactment bares them to better assessment and more effective interventions.

- *Therapists may seek to block a pathological interaction among family members, making it difficult for them to use the old, sick pattern to deal with the current issue. Structural therapists characteristically use any of a variety of techniques (Minuchin & Fishman, 1981) to affect the family's power balance, transactional alignments, and systemic boundaries.*
- *Whether or not the therapist needs to begin by disrupting old, dysfunctional interactions, in all cases the therapist will look to support new, more functional transactional patterns. The therapist may verbally affirm the new patterns or actively engage with clients in ways that promote new behaviors and attitudes in the family's in-session enactments.*
- *In this active engagement with clients, therapists intentionally use their person (Aponte, 1992; Aponte, 1998a) to strategically affect the dynamics and structure of family interactional patterns. To achieve the therapeutic mastery of self, they must have (1) a profound knowledge and awareness of their personal selves, (2) an ability to be connected to their inner personal experience in session, and (3) the discipline to use their person as strategically intended (Aponte, 1994a).*
- *Once family members have experienced something of their ability to do things differently, structural therapists often assign home tasks meant to embody the new change. The therapy is complete when the family is able to meet its challenges without the intervention of the therapist.*

In the example above, the therapist became an actor in the play, using himself and his joining the father to reframe what was happening in the session between the father and his son. The therapist made it safe for the son to speak from his pain, and for the father to allow himself to feel for his son from his own vulnerability. The therapist blocked the escalation of anger from father to son. He spoke from his own sense of fatherhood to appeal to the father's paternal tenderness toward his son. He helped to create a new experience for all three members of the family by how he involved him-self in their interactions. The therapist actively engaged the family in a way that created a new and positive experience for them to embark on the work of therapy with him.

THE FUTURE OF STRUCTURAL FAMILY THERAPY

SFT was created to meet the needs of families whose inner structure was seriously undermined by devastating social stress. This work has con-tributed a deeper insight into the basic nature of structure in family systems and reparative structural interventions that generate organi-zational changes in families. The underlying assumption is that change in patterns of relating affect the complexion and quality of emotional interchanges among family members, which, in turn, impact the psyche of the individuals in the family system. As the social ills of American society spread beyond the inner city to the gen-eral population, the need to attend to the founda-tional structure of families in all levels of society has become apparent. Other models of therapy could well consider using the insights SFT offers to understanding and working with family structure.

New developments in SFT are the added dimension of cultural values and spirituality. The original model spoke of structure in rela-tion to function in human systems. Over time it became apparent, particularly in today's values-fragmented society that this original formulation needed to be amended to address structure in relation to function *within* the val-ues framework of the system (Aponte, 1994b). Because SFT is one of today's more active thera-pies, therapists using the model inescapably com-municate values about life philosophy, morals, and even religious practice. Now, as never before, there is a need for therapists to understand the values inherent in their therapeutic models and the values they personally bring to the work they do. Therapists' cultural, philosophical, and spiritual biases will influence what they consider healthy and pathological attitudes and behaviors. Their worldviews will affect the formulation of goals—that is, what is desirable for any particu-lar therapeutic endeavor. Their perspectives on life will help determine the interventions they believe appropriate to people's circumstances. SFT needs to incorporate into its theory and

practice greater consideration of the cultural, philosophical, and spiritual aspects of the human experience at the interface of the therapist-client relationship.

In line with the above, SFT needs to give greater consideration to the use of self within its model because of the very active personal posture of the therapist vis-à-vis the client. Minuchin's perspective has been to "expand" the "therapist's [personal] style" thereby add-ing to the clinician's "repertoire" (Minuchin, Lee, & Simon, 2006, p. X). Aponte's model for the personal aspect of training calls for enhanc-ing the therapist's ability to purposefully direct the use of self through self-knowledge and the ability to consciously access emotions, memories, and personal reactions at the moment of active engagement with clients (Aponte, 1992; Aponte & Kissil, 2012; Aponte & Winter, 2000). SFT will need to enlarge on its approaches to training in the use of self within the model if it is to include the spiritual with the emotional in a systematic person-training of therapists.

RESEARCH SUPPORTING STRUCTURAL FAMILY THERAPY

Outcome studies on SFT have been conducted since the late 1960s. The first area of SFT out-come research came out of the search for effec-tive approaches to the work with disadvantaged youth and families, with the first study conducted by Minuchin and his colleagues at the Wiltwyck School suggesting that SFT was moderately superior to conventional treatment (Minuchin, Montalvo, Guerney, Rosman, & Schumer, 1967). Another focus of early SFT outcome studies was therapy with psychosomatic families. In several studies conducted during the 1970s SFT was found effective in treating families who were dealing with diabetes (Minuchin, Baker, Rosman, Liebman, Milman, & Todd, 1975), psychogenic pain (Berger, Honig, & Liebman, 1977; Liebman, Honig, & Berger, 1976), asthma (Liebman, Minuchin, & Baker, 1974) and Anorexia Nervosa (Minuchin, Rosman, & Baker, 1978).

In the last 30 years SFT has greatly influ-enced the development of new family therapy models and has been incorporated as a core component in many integrative family ther-apy models. Family therapy with troubled youth has been the main therapy area to build on SFT. Numerous evidence-based models for treating adolescents with various problems have incorporated SFT into their models. For example, Multidimensional Family Therapy (MDFT; Liddle, 2010) is a family-based treatment model for adolescents' substance abuse. Effectiveness studies with MDFT in the United States and in various countries in Europe found MDFT effective in reducing substance abuse and related problems such as juvenile delinquency (Liddle, 2010; Liddle, Rowe, Dakof, Henderson, & Greenbaum, 2009; Rigter et al., 2012).

Two additional well-established models for treating adolescents with various problems are MST (Multisystemic Family Therapy; Henggeler & Borduin, 1990; Henggeler, Schoenwald, Borduin, Rowland, & Cunningham, 1998) and ABFT (Attachment Based Family Therapy; Diamond & Lebow, 2005; Diamond, Siqueland, & Diamond, 2003). Both models incorporate SFT and have been studied extensively and found effective in reducing adolescents' antisocial behaviors and juvenile recidivism (Henggeler, 2011), depression (Diamond, Reis, Diamond, Siqueland, & Isaacs, 2002), anxiety (Siqueland, Rynn, & Diamond, 2005) and suicidality (Diamond et al., 2010).

Szapocznik and his colleagues have studied the effectiveness of Brief Strategic Family Therapy (BSFT) with high-risk Hispanic and African American adolescents and their families since the late 1980s (Szapocznik & Williams, 2000). Their approach, founded on SFT, was found effective in reducing behavior problems, including drug abuse (Santisteban, Coatsworth, Perez-Vidal, Jean-Gilles, & Szapocznik, 1997; Santisteban, Szapocznik, Perez-Vidal, Kurtines, Murray, & LaPerriere, 1996; Szapocznik et al., 1988; Szapocznik et al., 1989; Szapocznik & Williams, 2000).

More recently, Santisteban and his colleagues (2011; 2013) studied the effectiveness of a new therapy model, CIFFTA (Culturally Informed and Flexible Family-Based Treatment for Adolescents), which evolved out of Brief Strategic Family Therapy and has SFT as its foundation. The results suggest that CIFFTA was better than traditional family therapy in reducing Hispanic adolescents' reported drug use and improving parenting practices as reported by the adolescents (Santisteban, Mena, & McCabe, 2011; 2013).

Family-Directed Structural Therapy (FDST: McLendon, McLendon, & Petr, 2005) is another family-based treatment approach, designed to be utilized with a variety of family and relationship issues, and not necessarily with problem specific populations like the models mentioned above. It is also founded on SFT. A recent study comparing the use of this model in a therapeutic wilderness family camp to community mental health services found this model to be superior in increasing family cohesiveness and reducing child internalizing and externalizing problems. Treatment gains were maintained at 6 months follow-up (McLendon, McLendon, Petr, Kapp, & Mooradian, 2009).

Another area highly influenced by SFT is treatment for eating disorders. Some of the most well-studied models in the field for treating eating disorders have evolved from SFT, especially from Minuchin's seminal work with anorexic families (Minuchin, Rosman, & Baker, 1978). For example, the evidence-based and widely studied Maudsley approach for treating anorexia nervosa, which is based on SFT principles (Lock & Le Grange, 2012) was found to be superior to individual therapy in adolescents (Eisler, Dare, Russell, Szmukler, Le Grange, & Dodge, 1997), and to both individual supportive therapy and individual psychodynamic therapy in adults with Anorexia Nervosa (Russell, Dare, Eisler, & Le-Grange, 1992). The effectiveness of SFT based models in treating Anorexia Nervosa has been described in numerous articles (e.g., Raymond, Friedlander, Heatherington, Ellis, & Sargent, 1993; Stein, Mozdzierz, & Mozdzierz, 1998; Vetere, 2001) and has been supported enough to make family therapy the treatment of choice for Anorexia Nervosa (Fishman, 2006).

Although SFT and its derivatives were mainly utilized in treating adolescents, other models were developed that focused on non-adolescent populations. For example, Structural Ecosystems Therapy, a family-based ecological approach that was developed from Brief Structural Family Therapy (Mitrani, Szapocznik, & Robinson-Batista, 2000; Szapocznik et al., 2004), was found to be effective not only with drug-abusing Hispanic and African American adolescents (Robbins, Szapocznik, Dillon, Turner, Mitrani, & Feaster, 2008), but also in increasing adherence to medication and reducing psychological distress in HIV-seropositive African American women (Feaster, Brinks, Mitrani, Prado, Schwartz, & Szapocznik, 2010; Szapocznik et al., 2004).

In summary, SFT has been extensively researched for over 50 years. Even though it appears that SFT has not been studied as a stand-alone approach in the last 30 years, and the integrative models incorporating SFT have not studied its specific contribution to their success, the fact that SFT is a main component in so many evidence-based models provides indirect but very strong evidence as to its effectiveness.

CONCLUSION

SFT is an active, focused approach to therapy that pays special attention to structure within family systems and does so within the client's experience in session. It pursues specific outcomes to present-day issues while addressing the underlying human relationships and their personal structure in the context of culture, ethnicity, and spirituality—all that gives meaning to their lives. Therapists actively engage with clients around the practical experience of their struggles and strategically join them in finding new ways of thinking about and acting on their issues. SFT looks for practical outcomes along with deep-seated changes in the underlying structures that generate and maintain the difficulties people face in life. Because of the active and involved nature of the work, the structural training of therapists draws particular attention to the fuller and more precise strategic use of self. The basic insights of the structural model about the nature of structure within systems and the use of self to influence those structures are concepts that are suitable to other models of today's active therapies. In a social and economic environment that greatly emphasizes outcome that is also enduring, SFT has much to offer.

WEBSITES

Publications: *http://onlinelibrary.wiley.com*
Videos: http://www.goldentriadfilms.com/films/aponte.htm.
Videos: www.psychotherapy.net/video/structural-family-therapy

References

Aponte, H. J. (1976). The family-school interview: An eco-structural approach. *Family Process, 15*(3), 303–311.

Aponte, H. J. (1990). *Tres madres: Structural family therapy with an Anglo/Hispanic family* [videotape]. http://www.goldentriadfilms.com/films/aponte.htm.

Aponte, H. J. (1992). Training the person of the therapist in structural family therapy. *Journal of Marital and Family Therapy, 18*(3), 269–281.

Aponte, H. J. (1994a). How personal can training get? *Journal of Marital and Family Therapy, 20*(1), 3–15.

Aponte, H. J. (1994b). *Bread and spirit: Therapy with the new poor.* New York, NY: Norton.

Aponte, H. J. (1998a). Intimacy in the therapist-client relationship. In W. J. Matthews & J. H. Edgette (Eds.), *Current thinking and research in brief therapy* (pp. 3–27) (Vol. 2.). Philadelphia, PA: Taylor & Francis.

Aponte, H. J. (1998b). *Structural family therapy by Harry Aponte* [videotape]. psychotherapy.net/video/structural-family-therapy

Aponte, H. J. (1999). The stresses of poverty and the comfort of spirituality. In F. Walsh (Ed.), *Spiritual resources in family therapy* (pp. 76–89). New York, NY: Guilford.

Aponte, H. J., & Hoffman, L. (1973). The open door: A structural approach to a family with an anorectic child. *Family Process, 12*(1), 1–44.

Aponte, H. J., & DiCesare, E. J. (2000). Structural theory. In F. M. Dattilio & L. Bevilacqua (Eds.), *Comparative treatment of couples problems* (pp. 45–57). New York, NY: Springer.

Aponte, H., & Kissil, K. (2012). "If I can grapple with this I can truly be of use in the therapy room": Using the therapist's own emotional struggles to facilitate effective therapy. *Journal of Marital and Family Therapy.* doi:10.1111/jmft.12011.

Aponte, H. J., & VanDeusen, J. M. (1981). Structural family therapy. In A. S. Gurman & D. P. Kniskern (Eds.), *Handbook of family therapy* (pp. 310–360). New York, NY: Brunner/Mazel.

Aponte, H. J., & Winter, J. E. (2000). The person and practice of the therapist. In M. Baldwin (Ed.), *The use of self in therapy* (2nd ed.) (pp. 127–165). New York, NY: Haworth Press.

Berger, H. G., Honig, P. J., & Liebman, R. (1977). Recurrent abdominal pain: Gaining control of the symptom. *Archives of Pediatrics & Adolescent Medicine, 131*(12), 1340–1344.

Diamond, G. S., & Lebow, J. L. (2005). Attachment-based family therapy for depressed and anxious adolescents. In J. L. Lebow (Ed.), *Handbook of clinical family therapy* (pp. 17–41). New York, NY: Wiley and Sons.

Diamond, G. S., Reis, B. F., Diamond, G. M., Siqueland, L., & Isaacs, L. (2002). Attachment-based family therapy for depressed adolescents: A treatment development study. *Journal of the American Academy of Child & Adolescent Psychiatry, 41*(10), 1190–1196.

Diamond, G., Siqueland, L., & Diamond, G. M. (2003). Attachment-based family therapy for depressed adolescents: Programmatic treatment development. *Clinical Child and Family Psychology Review, 6*(2), 107–127.

Diamond, G. S., Wintersteen, M. B., Brown, G. K., Diamond, G. M., Gallop, R., Shelef, K., & Levy, S. (2010). Attachment-based family therapy for adolescents with suicidal ideation: A randomized controlled trial. *Journal of the American Academy of Child & Adolescent Psychiatry, 49*(2), 122–131.

Eisler, I., Dare, C., Russell, G. F., Szmukler, G., le Grange, D., & Dodge, E. (1997). Family and individual therapy in anorexia nervosa: A 5-year follow-up. *Archives of General Psychiatry, 54*(11), 1025.

Feaster, D. J., Brinks, A. M., Mitrani, V. B., Prado, G., Schwartz, S. J., & Szapocznik, J. (2010). The efficacy of structural ecosystems therapy for HIV medication adherence with African American women. *Journal of Family Psychology, 24*(1), 51–59.

Fishman, H. C. (2006). Juvenile anorexia nervosa: Family therapy's natural niche. *Journal of Marital and Family Therapy, 32*(4), 505–514.

Henggeler, S. W. (2011). Efficacy studies to large-scale transport: The development and validation of multisystemic therapy programs. *Annual Review of Clinical Psychology, 7*, 351–381.

Henggeler, S. W., & Borduin, C. M. (1990). *Family therapy and beyond: A multisystemic approach to treating the behavior problems of children and adolescents.* Pacific Grove, CA: Brooks/Cole.

Henggeler, S. W., Schoenwald, S. K., Borduin, C. M., Rowland, M. D., & Cunningham, P. B. (1998). *Multisystemic treatment of antisocial behavior in children and adolescents.* New York, NY: Guilford Press.

Liebman, R., Honig, P., & Berger, H. (1976). An integrated treatment program for psychogenic pain. *Family Process, 15*(4), 397–405.

Liebman, R., Minuchin, S., & Baker, L. (1974). The use of structural family therapy in the treatment of intractable asthma. *The American Journal of Psychiatry, 131*(5), 535–540.

Liddle, H. A. (2010). Treating adolescent substance abuse using multidimensional family therapy. In J. R. Weisz & A. Kazdin (Eds.), *Evidence-based psychotherapies for children and adolescents* (2nd ed.) (pp. 416–432). New York, NY: Guilford Press.

Liddle, H. A., Rowe, C. L., Dakof, G. A., Henderson, C. E., & Greenbaum, P. E. (2009). Multidimensional family therapy for young adolescent substance abuse: Twelve-month outcomes of a randomized controlled trial. *Journal of Consulting and Clinical Psychology, 77*(1), 12–25.

McLendon, D., McLendon, T., & Petr, C. G. (2005). Family-directed structural therapy. *Journal of Marital and Family Therapy, 31*(4), 327–339.

McLendon, T., McLendon, D., Petr, C. G., Kapp, S. A., & Mooradian, J. (2009). Family-directed structural therapy in a therapeutic wilderness family camp: An outcome study. *Social Work in Mental Health, 7*(5), 508–527.

Lock, J., & Le Grange, D. (2012). *Treatment manual for anorexia nervosa: A family-based approach.* New York, NY: Guilford Press.

Minuchin, S. (1974). *Families and family therapy.* Cambridge, MA: Harvard University Press.

Minuchin, S., Baker, L., Rosman, B. L., Liebman, R., Milman, L., & Todd, T. C. (1975). A conceptual model of psychosomatic illness in children: Family organization and family therapy. *Archives of General Psychiatry, 32*(8), 1031–1038.

Minuchin, S., Montalvo, B., Guerney, B. R. B., & Schumer, F. (1967). *Families of the slums.* New York, NY: Basic Books.

Minuchin, S., Rosman, B. L., & Baker, L. (1978). *Psychosomatic families: Anorexia nervosa in context.* Cambridge, MA: Harvard University Press.

Minuchin, S., & Colapinto, J. (Eds.). (1980). *Taming monsters* [videotape]. Philadelphia, PA: Philadelphia Child Guidance Clinic.

Minuchin, S., & Fishman, H. C. (1981). *Family therapy techniques.* Cambridge, MA: Harvard University Press.

Minuchin, S., Lee, W.-Y., & Simon, G. M. (2006). *Mastering family therapy; Journeys of growth and transformation* (2nd ed.). Hoboken, NJ: Wiley.

Mitrani, V. B., Szapocznik, J., & Robinson-Batista, C. (2000). Structural ecosystems therapy with HIV+ African American women. In W. Pequegnat & J. Szapocznik (Eds.), *Working with families in the era of HIV/AIDS* (pp. 243–279). Thousand Oaks, CA: Sage.

Szapocznik, J., Feaster, D. J., Mitrani, V. B., Prado, G., Smith, L., Robinson-Batista, C., . . . Robbins, M. S. (2004). Structural ecosystems therapy for HIV-seropositive African American women: Effects on psychological distress, family hassles, and family support. *Journal of Consulting and Clinical Psychology, 72*(2), 288–303.

Raymond, L., Friedlander, M. L., Heatherington, L., Ellis, M. V., & Sargent, J. (1993). Communication processes in structural family therapy: Case study of an anorexic family. *Journal of Family Psychology, 6*(3), 308–326.

Rigter, H., Henderson, C. E., Pelc, I., Tossmann, P., Phan, O., Hendriks, V., & Rowe, C. L. (2012). Multidimensional family therapy lowers the rate of cannabis dependence in adolescents: A randomized controlled trial in Western European outpatient settings. *Drug and Alcohol Dependence, 130*, 85–93.

Robbins, M. S., Szapocznik, J., Dillon, F. R., Turner, C. W., Mitrani, V. B., & Feaster, D. J. (2008). The efficacy of structural ecosystems therapy with drug-abusing/dependent African American and Hispanic American adolescents. *Journal of Family Psychology, 22*(1), 51–61.

Russell, G. F., Dare, C., Eisler, I., & LeGrange, P. D. (1992). *Controlled trials of family treatments in anorexia nervosa. Psychobiology and treatment of anorexia nervosa and bulimia nervosa.* Washington, DC: American Press Association.

Santisteban, D. A., Coatsworth, J. D., Perez-Vidal, A. M. V., Jean-Gilles, M., & Szapocznik, J. (1997). Brief structural family therapy with African American and Hispanic high-risk youth: A report of outcome. *Journal of Community Psychology, 25*(5), 453–471.

Santisteban, D., Mena, M., & McCabe, B. (2011).Preliminary results for an adaptive family treatment for drug abuse in Hispanic youth. *Journal of Family Psychology, 25*(4), 610–614.

Santisteban, D., Mena, M., & McCabe, B. (2013). 2013–Randomized controlled trial comparing individually-based and family-based treatments for internalizing, externalizing, and family symptoms in Hispanic youth. *European Psychiatry, 28*, 1.

Santisteban, D. A., Szapocznik, J., Perez-Vidal, A., Kurtines, W. M., Murray, E. J., & LaPerriere, A. (1996). Efficacy of intervention for engaging youth and families into treatment and some variables that may contribute to differential effectiveness. *Journal of Family Psychology, 10*(1), 35–44.

Siqueland, L., Rynn, M., & Diamond, G. S. (2005). Cognitive behavioral and attachment based family therapy for anxious adolescents: Phase I and II studies. *Journal of Anxiety Disorders, 19*(4), 361–381.

Stein, S. J., Mozdzierz, A. B., & Mozdzierz, G. J. (1998). The kinship of Adlerian family counseling and Minuchin's structural family therapy. *Journal of Individual Psychology, 54*(1), 90–107.

Szapocznik, J., Perez-Vidal, A., Brickman, A. L., Foote, F. H., Santisteban, D., Hervis, O., & Kurtines, W. M. (1988). Engaging adolescent drug abusers and their families in treatment: A strategic structural systems approach. *Journal of Consulting and Clinical Psychology, 56*(4), 552–557.

Szapocznik, J., Rio, A., Murray, E., Cohen, R., Scopetta, M., Rivas-Vazquez, A., & Kurtines, W. (1989). Structural family versus psychodynamic child therapy for problematic Hispanic boys. *Journal of Consulting and Clinical Psychology, 57*(5), 571–578.

Szapocznik, J., Feaster, D. J., Mitrani, V. B., Prado, G., Smith, L., Robinson-Batista, C., & Robbins, M. S. (2004). Structural ecosystems therapy for HIV-seropositive African American women: Effects on psychological distress, family hassles, and family support. *Journal of Consulting and Clinical Psychology, 72*(2), 288–303.

Szapocznik, J., & Williams, R. A. (2000). Brief strategic family therapy: Twenty-five years of interplay among theory, research and practice in adolescent behavior problems and drug abuse. *Clinical Child and Family Psychology Review, 3*(2), 117–134.

Vetere, A. (2001). Structural family therapy. *Child and Adolescent Mental Health, 6*(3), 133–139.

58   Bowen Family Systems Therapy

Daniel V. Papero

The Bowen theory consists of eight formal concepts and a central variable (Bowen, 1978). One concept, the *scale of differentiation of self*, forms the core of the theory, and the remaining seven concepts describe different aspects of family functioning. The variable—anxiety—acts as a kind of pressure on the family system, waxing and waning in intensity. Bowen's observations led him to conclude that the family is a system of interdependent people, that individual behavior cannot be understood adequately without including the relationship system in which individual lives and changing degrees of anxiety greatly affect the condition of that system. A highly anxious system behaves predictably differently from a less anxious one. Under the pressure of increased anxiety, various sorts of relationship patterns or series of interactions can be observed, and these patterns tend to repeat whenever the family system is again under pressure.

The concept of the scale of differentiation of self describes individual variation, specifically in the arena of self-regulation and self-determination within the family system and the other important relationship systems of a person's life (Bowen, 1978; Kerr & Bowen, 1988; Papero, 1990). In practical terms, a person's degree or level of differentiation of self can be seen as a degree of resiliency or capacity to function well under the pressure of stress and tension. Bowen hypothesized that a well-differentiated person approached the situations of life with good integration between emotion and cognition and with clearly thought-out values and principles that guide decisions and behavior. Each (emotion and cognition) influences the other, neither dominates, and the person can use each in adapting to changing situations. In a less well-differentiated person, under pressure, emotion dominates cognition and behavior becomes more instinctive and automatic. The well-differentiated person can participate fully in relationships but does not depend completely on relationships to maintain emotional stability. In this sense, the individual is capable of self-regulation when important relationships are disturbed or unavailable.

Bowen observed that a change in one part of a family led to compensatory changes in other parts of the family. His observations led him to the realization that the family system could be influenced by the actions of an individual family member, particularly if that person occupied an important position in the system and when that individual could

- see and understand better his or her own emotional sensitivity and reactivity;
- become more thoughtful about his or her behavior and what he or she was trying to accomplish, using knowledge of how the family system operated;
- use thinking and knowledge to modify emotional reactivity and his or her own behavior in important relationships; and
- stay in meaningful contact with other members of the system; the entire system could change or shift its functioning.

When the system could change, the behavior and functioning of family members changed as well. The clinical process involved in such an effort is so different from more conventional psychotherapy that Bowen referred to the process as *coaching*.

The coaching process draws heavily on the coach's understanding of family systems theory. It assumes the clinician (1) has direct and ongoing experience in the challenge of working on differentiation of self in his or her own family, and (2) understands and can reasonably operationalize the disciplines of self-regulation, emotional neutrality, maintenance of viable contact, self-definition, and the research attitude that families have found useful in their own efforts to manage their challenges and dilemmas.

The family members involved in the coaching effort:

- Regulate the endeavor
- Set the pace
- Identify and engage the challenges
- Monitor and evaluate the outcomes.

In his personal conversations, Bowen often referred to the process as "a do-it-yourself therapy—almost!" The coach functions as a supervisor of and consultant to the endeavor.

Bowen discovered that clinicians learned most about family systems in their efforts to improve functioning in their own families (Bowen, 1978), and effort with one's own family became a central element in the training of clinicians; it remains so today. In essence, clinicians learning to use the Bowen theory in their clinical efforts work on their own degree of differentiation of self, the central idea in the theory. In the clinician's own family, he or she learns about family systems and the pressures that come to bear on anyone attempting to shift his or her functioning. The clinician learns firsthand about emotional reactivity and its role in the relationship sequences or patterns that are the nature of family interaction.

In the course of his research project on schizophrenia at the National Institute of Mental Health (NIMH), Bowen observed that the families appeared to function more calmly, thoughtfully, and stably after time spent with a researcher than after time spent with a therapist. The researcher could remain more objective than the therapist and direct inquiry toward facts of family functioning. The researcher did not experience the pressure to help the family that the therapists did. The researcher could more easily remain emotionally neutral in the reactive processes of the family. He or she could see all sides to the situation and could avoid taking sides in the dilemma fairly easily. This objectivity and neutrality appeared to bring out the best in the families.

These observations led Bowen to suggest that the clinician could be most helpful to the family when he or she could:

- Maintain an attitude and perspective of research and emotional neutrality
- Ask about family facts
- See the emotional give-and-take among family members without becoming distracted by the content of the family story or taking sides
- See and comment on both the serious and the humorous sides of the family dilemma
- Maintain a climate or atmosphere during the clinical session that allowed each participant to work toward becoming his or her most mature self emotionally in interaction with the others.

The clinical process begins with a history of family functioning across at least three generations. In general, the clinician gathers information on each person, living and dead, who has been part of the family. The information collected includes:

- Date of birth (and of death, where applicable)
- Health history
- Educational history
- Occupational history
- Social history for each person
- The nature of relationships in the family, currently and historically
- Dates of marriages, divorces, job changes, and changes in residence
- The frequency and nature of contact the informants maintain with the broader family.

As the information is gathered, it is entered on a family diagram, a visual representation of the family system (see Papero, 1990, 2000). The process of developing the family diagram helps the clinician (1) identify events that have contributed to the present configuration of the family; (2) note particularly important relationships, including those that display great tension and emotional reactivity; and (3) identify the particular kinds of relationship patterns that characterize the interactions of the family.

The diagram serves as a map or chart guiding the efforts of the clinician and the family. Additionally, informants often find the process interesting and useful, spurring their own efforts to learn more about their families.

The clinical process focuses on two goals: decreasing anxiety and increasing functional differentiation of self. Often, these goals go hand in hand. The effort to decrease anxiety requires that the individual learn to modulate intense emotion by using his or her cognitive or intellectual processes. Cognition comes into play as the individual learns to observe self and others, learning to recognize anxiety in its myriad forms, and in his or her efforts to engage in a discipline of self-regulation. Alongside the effort toward self-regulation, the individual works to observe the predictable patterns of the family relationship system that emerge and disappear in response to tension and anxiety in the system. The person also endeavors to define clearly his or her own sets of beliefs and values about the nature of living and about his or her own direction in it. These form the basis, along with knowledge of the system and self-regulation, for the person's effort to define his or her own positions to the important others in the relationship system and to maintain that position as the system responds with pressure to change back.

One of the common relationship processes that people observe, *triangling*, occurs as a two-person relationship becomes tense and anxious. As the discomfort in the pair rises, at some point the tolerance for discomfort is passed, and one makes a move to a significant third person, in effect telling a story about the other partner. Primarily a process of anxiety transfer, triangling alters the sensitivities, cognitive processing, and ultimately behavior of all involved. Triangles change configurations with tension. When the relationship network is fairly calm, the triangling process may be largely invisible. Under moderate tension, the triangle consists of a close twosome and an outsider, who tends to feel excluded and uncomfortable. That outsider responds in a series of well-known moves to gain closeness with one of the two and leave someone else in the outside position (Bowen, 1978; Kerr & Bowen, 1988). However, when tension develops in the close twosome, the outsider is in the more comfortable position, and either of the twosome engages in a series of maneuvers to gain the outside position for him or herself and leave the other two in the tense positions.

One classic methodology derived from Bowen theory involves the effort with the two most responsible family members, often spouses. The clinician has four main tasks in using this methodology (Bowen, 1978):

- Defining and clarifying the relationship between the two family members
- Keeping self neutral in the family emotional system
- Teaching the functioning of emotional systems
- Demonstrating differentiation by taking well-thought-out positions for self during the course of the clinical effort.

A basic principle, based on Bowen's observations, underlies the approach: "the emotional problem between two people will resolve automatically if they remain in contact with a third person who can remain free of the emotional field between them, *while actively relating to each*" (Bowen, 1978, p. 251).

A second classic methodology involves the effort with one family member. Here the person works toward enhancing his or her own differentiation within a relationship system, usually the family. According to Bowen (1978), the person essentially strives to:

- Gain some control of his or her own emotional reactivity
- Visit the family as often as possible
- Develop the ability to be an objective observer of the family (Bowen, 1978)
- Develop person-to-person relationships in the broader family.

Generally, the family member learns to establish and maintain relationships in which two people can talk to one another about each other, without discussing others (triangling) or talking about impersonal things. The clinician, while fulfilling the four tasks just mentioned, serves as a consultant and supervisor to the effort.

Many people using Bowen theory in their efforts to improve their own functioning additionally work on structured processes of self-regulation. Many have found biofeedback (both classic and neurofeedback) beneficial. Sometimes with the aid of the technology, people

discover their own sensitivity to others and the impact that sensitivity has on their functioning and well-being. Some also engage in formal processes of relaxation training and meditation. The use of these adjunctive methodologies depends on the inclinations and motivation of those involved.

The family members involved in the clinical effort begin to use their families as laboratories for their own learning and development.

- They work on managing themselves in the very relationships that have helped shape their identity and in contact with the people to whom they are most sensitive and connected.
- The focus is on the actual relationships of a person's life, with corresponding decreased focus on the therapeutic relationship to the clinician.
- Change occurs in the effort to manage oneself differently in actual relationships, and the importance of the clinical hour decreases.
- The time with the clinician becomes time for reflection, review of efforts made, and planning for future endeavors.

As he or she gains knowledge about self and the family, the person begins in small, microscopic steps to define him- or herself to the family system. This process usually requires that the person (1) think through his or her own view about particular family issues, (2) represent that view in the family context, and (3) remain in viable contact with other family members during their reaction to this statement of position.

In the process, the individual becomes a leader of the family in the sense that his or her functioning begins to affect the entire system in positive ways. Bowen described the process as follows:

Operationally, ideal family treatment begins when one can find a family leader with the courage to define self, who is as invested in the welfare of the family as in self, who is neither angry nor dogmatic, whose energy goes to changing self rather than telling others what they should do, who can know and respect the multiple opinions of others, who can modify self in response to the strengths of the group, and who is not influenced by the irresponsible opinions of others. When one family member moves toward differentiation, the family symptoms disappear. A family leader is beyond the popular notion of power. A responsible family leader automatically generates mature leadership qualities in other family members who are to follow. (Kerr & Bowen, 1988, pp. 342–343)

The following examples are composites of actual situations encountered. Many elements of the descriptions have been changed to protect the confidentiality of the families.

EXAMPLE 1

Emily, a bright, 7-year-old in first grade, suddenly developed discipline problems in school toward the end of the year. Her behavior had been outstanding, but now she spent several days a week in the principal's office. Previously a pleasant and gentle child, Emily had become surly and aggressive toward other children. Her mother sought clinical assistance.

Utilizing the Bowen theory to guide his efforts, the clinician made the decision to meet with Emily's mother and avoid a direct focus on the behavior of the child. The mother was willing to follow this plan. The clinician constructed Emily's family diagram. Her father and mother had been divorced for several years, and her father had moved to another state the summer before. Emily's paternal grandparents had maintained contact with her, but the arrival of a new grandchild and a serious health situation had resulted in them being less available. Her maternal grandmother had had surgery early in the winter and was recovering more slowly than anticipated. Her maternal great-grandmother had required nursing home care early in the winter, and Emily's grandfather was in charge of managing her care. Emily's maternal aunt and her husband had experienced a reversal in business and were involved in legal processes that caused family members to worry about their future. Finally, tension between Emily's mother and her partner had become very intense and difficult in the week preceding Emily's change of behavior.

The clinical hypothesis posited that Emily's behavioral problems emerged in a family environment of prolonged tension following the changes of the preceding few months. The family met each challenge well, but the cost was reflected in the gradual build-up of tension and anxiety. The immediate trigger for Emily's behavioral change lay in the surge of anxiety between her mother and her partner. The immediate treatment goal would involve reducing anxiety, and the longer range goal would involve the mother's increased use of relationship resources in the family and an effort to address the problem with her partner more directly, working to contain the anxiety to that relationship.

Emily's mother quickly understood and accepted the clinical hypothesis that her child's behavior was linked to the changes in the family and to the surge in tension with her partner. With the clinician, she developed a plan that included increased contact with important family members, a direct nonconfrontational approach with the involved school personnel, and the development of a plan for her efforts toward her partner. She used family relationships to assist her with her thinking about the situation and began a focused effort to address the problem with her partner. Emily's grandparents and to some degree her father increased their contact with Emily, and the mother engaged the school personnel—the teacher and principal—thoughtfully and directly in a calm manner focused on solving problems. Emily's school problems rapidly abated, and her teacher reported that she seemed much happier. She finished the school year well and moved happily into her summer activities. Emily's mother continued the effort to address the difficulties with her partner directly, an ongoing and challenging process.

EXAMPLE 2

Jim Wilson, a 52-year-old physician's assistant, sought consultation around his reported intense anxiety about finances, recurring episodes of deep depression, a sense of being ill-equipped to function in the world, and deep anger toward his father. He reported at times feeling he would be better off dead but did not see himself as actively suicidal. Mr. Wilson was well regarded in his professional life, working in a clinical setting that assisted low-income people. He was interested in using the Bowen theory to look at his situation; previous therapy had been somewhat useful but had not alleviated the recurring problems.

In the initial meetings, the clinician collected a three-generation history of the family. Mr. Wilson was the older of two children; he reported that his younger sister had also struggled with life, perhaps even more than he had, and currently lived in another state in a troubled relationship with a man alleged to be alcoholic. He reported great reactivity to his sister, often being critical of her and avoiding contact with her. Their mother had died of a lingering degenerative illness when both siblings were young adults. In the aftermath of his mother's death, his father had remarried. Mr. Wilson reported that he "lost his father" when he remarried. He meant that his father put his new wife ahead of his children in all matters. He also reported that his father had refused to help him financially, although he was a wealthy man and could easily have done so. Mr. Wilson was divorced from his wife; their two sons were now young adults. He reported that he remained angry and bitter with his ex-wife and avoided contact with her. She had married the man with whom she had had an affair. He resented the time their children spent with her.

The clinical hypothesis posited that Mr. Wilson's complaints reflected a condition of chronic anxiety in the family system marked by distant relationships and high degrees of emotional reactivity among family members. Mr. Wilson himself was relatively isolated emotionally from important other family members. The plan followed the points noted:

- Gain some control of his emotional reactivity
- Visit the family as often as possible
- Develop the ability to be an objective observer of the family (Bowen, 1978)
- Develop person-to-person relationships in the broader family.

Mr. Wilson thought the hypothesis made sense and agreed to begin an effort in his family to make progress on the four areas noted. He agreed to meet with the clinician once a month for consultation on his project. He began by addressing a health concern he had been avoiding, receiving medical assistance and a good outcome. He began to observe himself in the situations of his life and recognize his thought patterns and reactivity that seemed to underlie his anxiety and depression. He noted his own tendency to see himself as helpless and to be what he called "whiny" about his life. He also noted the degree to which he blamed others for his situation and began an effort to expand his perspective, decrease his complaining, and accept more responsibility for his own difficulties in life. He began an effort to be in more direct contact with his father and his wife, and to represent himself more clearly and carefully to them. His symptoms of depression were the first to disappear, and they did not return in any strength. After some time he was able to approach his father directly, requesting information about a trust fund established as part of

his father's estate. His father initially balked but then arranged for Mr. Wilson to speak directly to the managers of the trust. The information received helped allay Mr. Wilson's financial anxieties. He was subsequently able to arrange a loan from the trust that allowed him to move forward on a significant relocation project to be nearer to his children and achieve a long-term goal. He reported that the intensity of his anxiety decreased significantly. He could still experience episodes of acute anxiety, but the more chronic, constant anxiety seemed to have disappeared. He noted as well that his anger and bitterness toward his ex-wife abated greatly, and he was able to be in her presence at family gatherings with much decreased reactivity to her. He no longer tended to talk about her to their children and actually found he wished her well. Mr. Wilson continues his efforts, now with less frequent consultation.

In the case of Emily, the behavioral problem in the child was directly related to a recent series of events in the family and was resolved fairly quickly. In the case of Mr. Wilson, the problems reflected a long and slow build-up over many years and required a slower, persistent approach to attain resolution.

In recent years, the Bowen theory has received increasing attention from people working in corporations and organizations, as well as those who consult with them. The theory and its knowledge base offer insight and practical assistance to those who must work, manage, and lead in the increasingly stressful climate of the modern organization. Although organizations should never be mistaken for families, a number of the concepts transfer cleanly to the world of organizations. Topics such as the role of differentiation of self in leadership, triangling and its influence on the workplace, the predictable responses in relationships as tension increases, and the impact of anxiety on the individual and the relationship network can now be found on the agenda of training groups in management and leadership. People in leadership positions report that applications derived from Bowen theory, especially concerning differentiation of self, self-regulation, and self-management under pressure, are useful to them in their efforts to lead effectively.

WEBSITES

Bowen Center. http://www.thebowencenter.org.

Kansas City Center for Family and
  Organizational Systems. http://www
  .kcfamilysystems.com.
Living Systems Counselling. http://www
  .livingsystems.ca.
Prairie Center. http://www.theprairiecenter.com.
Programs in Bowen Theory. http://www
  .programsinbowentheory.org.
Southern California Training in Bowen Family
  Systems Theory. http://www.sctbt
  .homestead.com.

References

Bowen, M. (1978). *Family therapy in clinical practice.*
  New York, NY: Aronson.
Kerr, M. E., & Bowen, M. (1988). *Family evaluation.*
  New York, NY: Norton.
Papero, D. V. (1990). *Bowen family systems theory.*
  Needham Heights, MA: Allyn & Bacon.
Papero, D. V. (2000). Bowen systems theory. In F.
  M. Dattilio & L. J. Bevilacqua (Eds.), *Comparative
  treatments for relationship dysfunction* (pp. 58–
  73). New York, NY: Springer.

59   Integrative Behavioral Couple Therapy

Katherine J. W. Baucom, Felicia De la Garza-Mercer, & Andrew Christensen

CASE ILLUSTRATION

Janelle, a 32-year-old African American woman, and Adam, a 36-year-old Caucasian man, presented for treatment in a local clinic. The middle class, dual-earner couple had been in a relationship for eight years and married for four years. They had two young children, a 2.5-year-old son and a 1-year-old daughter. Janelle and Adam were in the dissatisfied range of relationship functioning, and reported arguments up to twice a day surrounding the amount of time Adam spent away from home. The couple reported that their arguments had steadily increased after the birth of their son; Janelle thought Adam did not give household tasks and their family enough time, and Adam was upset with Janelle's tendency to express her concern with criticism and anger. Janelle and Adam requested therapy after an argument resulted in Adam spending the night at a hotel. Both partners worried they could not overcome the difficulties they were currently facing. Their progress through therapy will be used below as an illustration of Integrative Behavioral Couple Therapy (IBCT).

INTEGRATIVE BEHAVIORAL COUPLE THERAPY

IBCT, developed by Andrew Christensen and the late Neil S. Jacobson (Christensen, Wheeler, Doss, & Jacobson, 2014; Jacobson & Christensen, 1998), seeks to target a wider range of couples than traditional behavioral couple therapy (TBCT; Jacobson & Margolin, 1979). IBCT combines interventions aimed at increasing emotional acceptance with change techniques from existing behavioral couple therapies.

ASSESSMENT AND FEEDBACK

In IBCT, couples typically participate in three assessment sessions as well as a feedback session. The goal of these sessions is to orient the couple to IBCT, determine whether they are appropriate for the treatment, develop a formulation of their relationship problems, and lay out a general plan for treatment.

The formulation of a couple's relationship problems includes a "DEEP understanding" that conceptualizes the presenting problems for therapist and the couple. DEEP is an acronym that stands for **D**ifferences or incompatibilities between partners; **E**motional reactions, sensitivities, and vulnerabilities of each partner; **E**xternal circumstances or stressors; and the destructive **P**attern of interaction in which the couple often becomes engaged as they struggle with their problems. The purpose of the assessment sessions is to develop rapport with the couple, gather the information necessary to develop a DEEP formulation, and learn of the existing strengths the couple has.

The first assessment session of IBCT is a joint session with both partners of the couple. During this session the therapist orients the couple to IBCT, learns about the presenting concerns and history of the relationship, and begins to gather information for the formulation. In the discussion of current relationship problems, the therapist attends to the emotional and behavioral reactions of each partner and the typical interaction pattern that the couple enacts around issues in the relationship. To learn more about the couple's background, the therapist facilitates a discussion of the history of the relationship, including how the couple met, how their relationship developed, and how their presenting problems came about. The therapist seeks to learn about positive aspects of their relationship and the areas where the couple has particular strengths, in addition to the current problems facing them in their relationship. Finally, couples are introduced to *Reconcilable Differences* (Christensen, Doss, & Jacobson, 2014; Christensen & Jacobson, 2000), a text written for couples participating in IBCT, and are encouraged to read it during treatment.

In the first meeting with Janelle and Adam, the therapist discovered some important **D**ifferences between them. As is often the case, these differences were qualities that had initially attracted them to one another: Janelle was spontaneous and liked to make decisions on the fly, whereas Adam valued predictability and liked to have a plan for doing things. The couple was able to effectively navigate these differences early in their relationship and marriage, but they began to struggle when they became parents and were presented with many new demands. Despite the joys Janelle and Adam experienced as parents, this transition functioned as an **E**xternal stressor that increased the salience of their differences.

At the end of the first assessment session, the IBCT therapist typically gives partners objective measures to provide information about important areas of the relationship. The most common areas assessed with these measures are relationship quality (e.g., the Couples Satisfaction Index; Funk & Rogge, 2007), intimate partner violence (e.g., Conflict Tactics Scale; Straus, Hamby, Boney-McCoy, & Sugarman, 1996), and target behaviors (e.g., the Frequency and Acceptability of Partner Behavior Inventory; Doss & Christensen, 2006). It is critical that therapists assess for intimate partner violence prior to beginning treatment; IBCT therapists do not treat couples whose problems include moderate to severe levels of violence (see Jacobson & Christensen, 1998). For those levels of violence, the therapist should recommend treatment that focuses on the violence rather than on the relational distress only.

The second and third assessment sessions are individual sessions with each partner. They typically begin with a confidentiality caveat that the therapist does not withhold information discussed in the individual sessions in joint sessions unless the partner explicitly asks the therapist. In the event that a partner reveals private information to the therapist that is relevant to the couple's relationship (e.g., an ongoing affair), the therapist stresses the importance of working together to share that information with the partner or to quickly resolve the issue (e.g., end the affair). IBCT therapists do not continue therapy if a partner discloses current infidelity to the therapist and is unwilling to stop the affair or reveal it to the partner. Therapists should follow these principles when practicing IBCT.

The goal of these individual sessions is to gain better knowledge of the current relationship problems and of each partner's personal history, with an eye toward the **E**motional vulnerabilities that each partner brings to the relationship, and the typical **P**attern of interaction that the couple enacts around problem areas. Often, the therapist begins by focusing on material that came up in the joint session as well as inquiring about particular items endorsed on the questionnaires. In the discussion of an individual's personal history, the therapist learns about the partner's relationships with close family members, the overall atmosphere in the partner's home during childhood, and previous romantic relationships. In the individual sessions the therapist learned that Janelle grew up in an upper middle class family. Her parents traveled for their jobs and spent much of the time they were at home working. Thus, Janelle was sensitive to disconnection from Adam, often feeling abandoned and lonely as she completed an increasing number of childcare and household tasks. Adam grew up in a low-income family and watched his father spend a great deal of time outside the home to make ends meet while his mother took care of him and his siblings. Thus, having grown up in a family with traditional gender roles, and being intimately aware of the consequences of limited resources, Adam was committed to ensuring that his family had the opportunities he did not have as a child. This contextual information, most relevant to the Emotional vulnerabilities component of the formulation, helped the therapist make sense of *why* childcare and time at home were so difficult for Adam and Janelle in particular. In Adam and Janelle's case, knowledge about partners' families of origin also provided a framework for understanding Adam and Janelle's differences: the qualities of spontaneity and need for predictability were adaptive for Janelle and Adam in their respective families of origin.

Discussion of individual emotional vulnerabilities led to additional discussion in individual sessions with Janelle and Adam about the typical Pattern of interaction that the partners played out around problem areas: Janelle, feeling anxious and abandoned, often criticized Adam for not being at home more, while Adam, feeling ashamed as well as anxious, tended to throw himself further into work so as to better provide for the family. This pattern is referred to as the polarization process. As the term suggests, partners' attempts to change one another often serve to increase the conflict and distance between them, even when often the purpose of trying to change one another is to facilitate intimacy or closeness. The result of this polarization process is a mutual trap where both partners' efforts to solve the problem just make it worse. For example, the conflict that ensues from Janelle's frequent criticism of Adam for not being at home led him to feel more insecure about the future of their relationship. His insecurity about the relationship served to deepen his fear that he will be unable to provide his family with necessary financial support, and he increased the time he spent at work. The more time he spent at work, the less time Janelle had to criticize him, which reinforced his spending time away from home. Janelle criticized Adam to right the child care imbalance between them, but she found the imbalance increasing rather than decreasing. Thus, Janelle and Adam found themselves in a vicious cycle of interaction.

In addition to the development of the case formulation, another important function of the individual sessions is to evaluate the level of violence in the relationship as well as each partner's level of commitment. Therapists trained in IBCT explicitly ask about intimate partner violence, commitment, and extradyadic affairs, often by focusing on relevant questionnaire items the client may have endorsed. Neither Janelle nor Adam reported any violence or affairs; both reported a high level of commitment to their relationship despite their distress.

In the feedback session, the therapist makes explicit the level of distress of partners, their commitment to the relationship, and individual and couple strengths that may aid the course of therapy. However, the main focus of the feedback session is to present the DEEP formulation of the couple's problems, which is the foundation on which the course of IBCT treatment is built.

During the feedback session, the therapist also presents her treatment plan. The goals of treatment include both acceptance and change for various factors in the DEEP analysis, with acceptance being appropriate for the natural differences between partners and the enduring emotional sensitivities that each brings to the relationship, with change being appropriate for the patterns of interaction that frustrate them, and with acceptance and/or change being appropriate for their external stressors, depending on the nature of those stressors. The therapist describes how treatment will work by introducing the Weekly Questionnaire (Christensen, 2010), which will be the basis of treatment. In this short questionnaire designed to be completed shortly before the session, partners rate their satisfaction with each other during the week, describe any major changes that have occurred, identify the most positive and most difficult interactions they had with each other during the week, and identify what incident or issue they wish to focus on in the session. The therapist describes how a typical session will proceed. Assuming there were no major changes, the therapist would normally review the most positive events between the couple and then focus on the incident or issue that partners have identified as being of most importance to discuss, with the therapist being an active facilitator of these discussions. At the end of the feedback session, the couple should have a clear idea of how the therapist sees their concerns and how she will address them in therapy. The couple is asked to consider whether they want to proceed with treatment and make a joint decision as to whether to do so. The treatment phase of IBCT does not begin unless all parties commit to move forward with the treatment plan.

TREATMENT

Beginning with the first treatment session (following the feedback session), and in most subsequent treatment sessions, the therapist focuses on emotionally salient incidents and issues related to the formulation that are identified in the Weekly Questionnaire. In addition to this focus on incidents and issues, she pays attention to the emotions of the partners within the session and often finds that examples of their problematic patterns of communication unfold in the session. These examples provide an ideal opportunity for the therapist to help the couple alter their pattern of interaction. For instance, when Janelle and Adam began to argue about Adam's work in a therapy session, the therapist began her intervention as follows:

Janelle: [crying, looking down] If you cared about our family, you would at least make it home in time for dinner.

Adam: I do care, Janelle. I just have a lot of responsibilities at work.

Therapist: I'd like you two to step back for one second and look at what is happening here. Janelle, it seems that you are feeling quite hurt right now, and Adam that you feel pretty put on the spot.

Emotional Acceptance Techniques

Therapists trained in IBCT often begin treatment with acceptance interventions to help partners understand and accept differences between them and their individual emotional vulnerabilities. IBCT therapists do this through three acceptance techniques: *empathic joining, unified detachment*, and *tolerance building*.

Empathic Joining. In facilitating empathic joining, the therapist works to reformulate relationship discord in terms of differences between rather than deficiencies within partners and in terms of the emotional sensitivities that such differences often trigger, thus allowing partners to empathize with one another's experience. The therapist also focuses on eliciting more vulnerable disclosures of "soft emotions" (e.g., sadness,

fear) rather than "hard emotions" (e.g., anger, blame) from partners by suggesting soft emotions as a potential basis of behavior. In the previous example, the therapist suggested that Janelle was feeling hurt when she expressed the harder emotion of anger.

Rather than attempting to increase the amount of time Adam spent at home, the therapist involved the couple in a discussion of what time at work means to Adam by eliciting his thoughts and feelings around work. Additionally, she invited Janelle to talk about her emotional reactions to the time Adam spends at work and what that meant to her. This discussion facilitated empathic joining in that it allowed Adam to better understand the impact of his actions on Janelle, and Janelle to better understand Adam's emotion-based reasons for spending so much time at work. In this case, Janelle was surprised to find that her husband worried their family would end up in a similar financial situation to that of his family when he was growing up.

Ideally, such conversations help modify the emotional reaction of one partner to the other's behavior. The conversations Adam and Janelle had in therapy helped Janelle see that Adam's long hours at work were fueled by his anxiety about money, which allowed her to offer support to her husband, rather than criticizing him for not spending adequate time at home. Adam began to seek support and connection from Janelle when he was anxious about their finances, and they worked to establish a savings account with a "prudent reserve" only to be used for emergencies. As sometimes is the case, this focus on acceptance actually created a paradoxical effect: Adam began to work less once he felt less pressure and more understanding from Janelle, and they worked together to reduce the anxiety underlying Adam's late nights.

Unified Detachment. Therapists using IBCT techniques help partners discuss problems with unified detachment; that is, help partners step back, take a nonjudgmental stance, and consider relationship problems in descriptive, behavioral terms rather than with blame and accusation. The goal is to create a kind of dyadic mindfulness in which partners change their view of the problem from a "you" or a "her" or "him" to an "it" that the partners can join around. A common strategy is to help partners describe the sequence of interaction between the two of them during emotionally provocative incidents, identifying the "triggers" or "buttons" that activate each of them and elaborating the pattern of escalation between the two of them. Often, IBCT therapists help the couple give their interaction pattern or "dance" a name, which serves to further distance the partners from the difficult emotions of (and often bring humor to) the pattern. For example, Adam and Janelle labeled their interactional pattern their "cat and mouse game" in which Janelle, the cat, pursued Adam, the mouse. The emotional distance created through unified detachment allows partners to understand better the behaviors and reactions of one another.

Tolerance Building. IBCT therapists also use tolerance building to help partners cope with the other's unwelcome but nondestructive behavior. If one partner is not willing or initially resistant to change, then working with the other partner to face and ultimately tolerate the behavior is likely the only way for them to maintain a happy, harmonious relationship. When one partner begins to demonstrate some acceptance of the specific behavior, the other partner's appreciation of this tolerance may lead to increased closeness (and sometimes even change of the behavior).

An IBCT therapist uses a number of strategies to build tolerance: positive re-emphasis, highlighting the complementarity of partners' differences, preparing couples for backsliding, helping them achieve alternative means of support, and faking bad behavior. Through positive re-emphasis, an IBCT therapist points out the positive functions of behaviors thought by one partner to be solely negative, while often still validating the negative qualities of such behavior. For example, Adam and Janelle's therapist highlighted how Adam's long hours at work are a result of his commitment to his job, and while it is distressing for Janelle to feel alone with home responsibilities, he demonstrates a similar commitment to his family: when he says he will finish something Janelle can count on him to do it.

Regardless of whether the change is one partner's behavior or the other partner's understanding of it, there will be times when the couple lapses into their typical pattern of interaction. Because they frequently engaged in this pattern when they entered therapy, these lapses are expected and common. Thus, IBCT therapists help partners plan responses to such lapses prior to their occurrence, helping them tolerate lapses when they do happen. Additionally, the therapist encourages each partner to consider alternative means of support (e.g., from friends) and ways of self-soothing (e.g., taking a warm bath,

listening to enjoyable music) when in difficult times. When individuals learn to care more for themselves, they may put less pressure on their partners to meet their emotional needs and be less susceptible to perceptions that their partners are at fault for needs not being met. Finally, the IBCT therapist may ask the couple to reenact or fake their problematic interaction patterns in the session to help them observe more carefully their dynamics when they are not emotionally invested in the interaction.

Change Techniques

Often, as in the case of Janelle and Adam, acceptance techniques bring about adequate, spontaneous change in behavior and perception, and traditional change techniques are not necessary. However, as needed, IBCT uses several direct behavior change techniques in treatment to alter the dysfunctional Pattern of interaction: redirection and replay, behavior exchange, communication training, and problem-solving training. Typically, these interventions and the rules underlying them are adapted maximally to the needs and idiosyncrasies of the couple.

Redirection and Replay. When the couple gets into a dysfunctional pattern of interaction in the session, which often occurs, the IBCT therapist will interrupt that pattern of interaction and redirect the couple, prompting them to interact differently. A common tactic is that the IBCT therapist may ask each partner to talk first to the therapist rather than to the partner and, with the therapist's help, fashion the message they would like the partner to hear. The therapist would then direct them to say this message to their partner. Another common tactic is to have the couple replay difficult interactions that occurred during the week and see if they can improve them in the session, with the therapist's assistance.

Behavior Exchange. In behavior exchange, the therapist seeks to increase positive behaviors in the relationship by first identifying those behaviors, then instigating those behaviors, and finally debriefing the occurrence of those behaviors. In a typical treatment scenario, the couple is first asked to identify positive behaviors that each could engage in that would increase the other partner's satisfaction in the relationship. This may be a homework assignment that the couple is asked to bring to their next session. Then the therapist asks the couple to increase the daily frequency of one or more behaviors on their list, with the only guideline being that partners not tell one another which behaviors they will enact. Finally, the therapist debriefs the couple on giving and receiving positive behaviors. In these discussions, partners may provide one another with feedback about specific behaviors so that the couple has a better idea of which behaviors truly do increase perceived satisfaction.

Communication Training. Couples are taught speaker and listener skills in communication training (CT), with the aim being to help partners become more effective communicators with one another. The partners first practice the skills in sessions with corrective feedback and direction from the therapist, and then are encouraged and sometimes given assignments to practice the skills at home. Speaker effectiveness skills include focusing on the self (i.e., using "I" statements), expressing emotional reactions, and highlighting specific behaviors of their partner that lead to emotional reactions (e.g., "I feel hurt when you stay late at work and forget to call to let me know"). Listener effectiveness skills include paraphrasing and reflecting what one's partner says. This ensures that partners understand one another without the misinterpretation common to distressed couples.

Problem-solving Training. It is expected that there will be times when, regardless of how effectively partners communicate about an issue, they have a hard time reaching a solution. Thus, couples are also taught ways of problem solving that keep them from entering into the mutual trap of dysfunctional problem discussion. As with CT, the therapist first works with the couple during therapy sessions to use problem-solving skills and then recommends that they practice at home to find solutions to problems.

Couples are taught three sets of skills in problem-solving training: problem definition, problem solution, and structuring skills. They first learn how to define problems in terms of specific behavior and the environment in which it occurs. IBCT therapists often ask that partners disclose emotional reactions to also work toward emotional acceptance. Finally, each partner defines his or her role in the problem.

Next, partners learn problem solution skills. The first step in problem solution is brainstorming—the couple is asked to come up with all possible solutions, whether realistic or unrealistic. They then delete unrealistic solutions from the list until they are left with possible solutions to the problem. Partners then agree on a solution,

write down and sometimes sign the agreement, and discuss things that might get in the way of instituting the solution. The couple is instructed to post the agreement where both partners will be aware of it, and the therapist checks in with the couple about the agreement for several sessions. If necessary, the agreement may be renegotiated.

The final skills couples are taught are structuring skills. Couples are encouraged to structure their problem-solving interactions so that they set aside a specific time and place to discuss the problem, ideally outside of the immediate problem situation. During their discussion, they are instructed to use skills from CT as well as problem-solving skills and to avoid negative verbal and nonverbal behavior.

OTHER INTEGRATIVE BEHAVIORAL COUPLE THERAPY THERAPIST GUIDELINES

Therapists trained in IBCT seek to remain flexible throughout the intervention techniques. They tailor interventions to the specific areas of deficiency of the couple and sometimes use failed change techniques as indication that relying more on acceptance interventions may be beneficial for the couple. Therapists should attend to in-session interactions and help facilitate in-session repair between partners when necessary. IBCT therapists remain nonjudgmental and accepting of partners and the outcome of the relationship. The goal of IBCT is to help partners have a different type of interaction around difficult issues and allow them to make the most informed decisions for the two individuals within the relationship.

EFFICACY OF INTEGRATIVE BEHAVIORAL COUPLE THERAPY

One of IBCT's strengths, alongside its clinical value, is its empirically demonstrated efficacy. In a random assignment of eight couples to a group format of IBCT and nine couples to a wait-list control group, Wimberly (1998) found significantly favorable results for the IBCT couples. In a preliminary clinical trial, 21 distressed couples were randomly assigned to either IBCT or TBCT (Jacobson, Christensen, Prince, Cordova, & Eldridge, 2000). Results indicated that 80% of IBCT couples evidenced clinically significant improvement in relationship satisfaction, compared to 64% of TBCT couples. Finally, In the largest randomized clinical trial of couple ther-apy to date (Christensen et al., 2004), 134 seri-ously and chronically distressed married couples were randomly assigned to either IBCT or TBCT and provided with approximately 26 sessions with trained therapists. TBCT couples improved more rapidly at the onset of treatment than did IBCT couples but also plateaued more quickly than IBCT couples. In contrast, IBCT couples made steadier change throughout the course of therapy, suggesting that IBCT's tendency to immediately focus on central issues, rather than small, overt behavioral change, may foster an important environment of emotional accep-tance and safety that permits continual, stable improvement. Doss, Thum, Sevier, Atkins, & Christensen (2005) found that although TBCT facilitated greater change in the frequency of tar-geted behaviors early in therapy, IBCT facilitated greater acceptance of target behaviors through-out the course of therapy and that acceptance of target behaviors had a stronger link with satis-faction later in therapy than did change in the frequency of these behaviors.

Other studies have examined these couples over five years of follow-up. While TBCT couples demonstrated significantly greater improvement in observed communication than IBCT couples at termination (Sevier, Eldridge, Jones, Doss, & Christensen, 2008), IBCT couples better main-tained overall treatment gains in communication (i.e., reduction in negativity and withdrawal) relative to TBCT couples at the 2-year follow-up point when the last observational assessment was completed (Baucom, Sevier, Eldridge, Doss, & Christensen, 2011). Couples in IBCT had sig-nificantly higher relationship satisfaction at each 6-month assessment point for two years after treatment termination but over the remaining three years of follow-up, differences between the groups evaporated. At the 5-year follow-up, approximately half of each treatment group showed clinically significant improvement, with effect sizes of $d = 0.92$ for TBCT and $d = 1.03$ for IBCT (Christensen, Atkins, Baucom, & Yi, 2010).

In addition to these primary studies, other research has explored IBCT's applicability to spe-cific couple-related issues. For example, IBCT may be an efficacious treatment for couples in which one or both partners experience chronic pain (e.g., Leonard, Cano, & Johansen, 2006), and for couples experiencing infidelity (Atkins, Eldridge, Baucom, & Christensen, 2005). Currently, Doss and Christensen are adapting IBCT for an online

treatment and the U.S. Veteran's Administration (VA) chose IBCT as an evidence-based treatment to be implemented in VA facilities nationwide. For additional information on IBCT research, please see ibct.psych.edu.

CONCLUSION

This chapter describes IBCT, a couple therapy that focuses on emotional acceptance as well as behavior change. A case illustration of an IBCT therapist's work with Janelle and Adam provides an example of an IBCT case that evidenced change through acceptance techniques. We also describe behavior change techniques used with couples in IBCT. The studies mentioned suggest that IBCT is an efficacious treatment for relational distress, as well as for specific couple issues (e.g., infidel-ity, chronic pain) and that its focus on emotional acceptance may function to allow couples to achieve more long-lasting gains than TBCT.

WEBSITES

Integrative Behavioral Couple Therapy.
   http://ibct.psych.ucla.edu
Christensen Research Lab.
   http://drandrewchristensen.com

References

Atkins, D. C., Eldridge, K., Baucom, D. H., & Christensen, A. (2005). Infidelity and behavioral couple therapy: Optimism in the face of betrayal. *Journal of Consulting and Clinical Psychology, 73,* 144–150.

Baucom, K. J. W., Sevier, M., Eldridge, K. A., Doss, B. D., & Christensen, A. (2011). Observed communi-cation in couples 2 years after Integrative and Traditional Behavioral Couple Therapy: Outcome and link with 5-year follow-up. *Journal of Consulting and Clinical Psychology, 79,* 565–576.

Christensen, A. (2010). Weekly Questionnaire. Unpublished Questionnaire. To obtain this freely available measure, contact Andrew Christensen, PhD, UCLA Department of Psychology, Los Angeles, CA 90095; *christensen@psych.ucla.edu.*

Christensen, A., Atkins, D. C., Berns, S., Wheeler, J., Baucom, D. H., & Simpson, L. E. (2004). Traditional versus integrative behavioral couple therapy for significantly and chronically dis-tressed married couples. *Journal of Consulting and Clinical Psychology, 72,* 176–191.

Christensen, A., Atkins, D. C., Baucom, B. R., & Yi, J. (2010). Marital status and satisfaction five years following a randomized clinical trial comparing Traditional versus Integrative Behavioral Couple Therapy. *Journal of Consulting and Clinical Psychology, 78*, 225–235.

Christensen, A., Doss, B. D., & Jacobson, N. S. (2014). *Reconcilable differences* (2nd ed.). New York, NY: Guilford Press.

Christensen, A., Wheeler, J. G., Doss, B. D., & Jacobson, N. S. (in press). Couple distress. In D. H. Barlow (Ed.), *Clinical handbook of psychological disorders* (5th ed.). New York, NY: Guilford.

Christensen, A., & Jacobson, N. (2000). *Reconcilable differences.* New York, NY: Guilford.

Doss, B. D., & Christensen, A. (2006). Acceptance in romantic relationships: The frequency and acceptability of partner behavior inventory. *Psychological Assessment, 18*, 289–302.

Doss, B. D., Thum, Y. M., Sevier, M., Atkins, D. C., & Christensen, A. (2005). Improving relationships: Mechanisms of change in couple therapy. *Journal of Consulting and Clinical Psychology, 73*, 624–635.

Funk, J. L., & Rogge, R. D. (2007). Testing the ruler with item response theory: Increasing precision of measurement for relationship satisfaction with the Couples Satisfaction Index. *Journal of Family Psychology, 21*, 572–583.

Jacobson, N. S., & Christensen, A. (1998). *Acceptance and change in couple therapy: A therapist's guide to transforming relationships.* New York, NY: Norton.

Jacobson, N. S., Christensen, A., Prince, S. E., Cordova, J., & Eldridge, K. (2000). Integrative Behavioral Couple Therapy: An acceptance-based, promising new treatment for couple discord. *Journal of Consulting and Clinical Psychology, 68*, 351–355.

Jacobson, N. S., & Margolin, G. (1979). *Marital therapy: Strategies based on social learning and behavior exchange principles.* New York, NY: Brunner/Mazel.

Leonard, M. T., Cano, A., & Johansen, A. B. (2006). Chronic pain in a couples context: A review and integration of theoretical models and empirical evidence. *Journal of Pain, 7*, 377–390.

Sevier, M., Eldridge, K., Jones, J., Doss, B., & Christensen., A. (2008). Observed changes in communication during Traditional and Integrative Behavioral Couple Therapy. *Behavior Therapy, 39*, 137–150.

Straus, M. A., Hamby, S. L., Boney-McCoy, S., & Sugarman, D. B. (1996). The revised Conflict Tactics Scales (CTS2): Development and preliminary psychometric data. *Journal of Family Issues, 18*, 283–316.

Wimberly, J. D. (1998). An outcome study of Integrative Couples Therapy delivered in a group format (Doctoral dissertation, University of Montana, 1997). *Dissertation Abstracts International: Section B: The Sciences and Engineering, 58*(12-B), 6832.

60   Family Therapy Approaches Using Psycho-education

Joseph Walsh

Social workers may conduct family interventions with traditional family therapies or through psycho-education. Family therapists, using systems perspectives that are germane to social work practice, practice from an assumption that all members of a family unit influence each other's functioning through reciprocal influence. Psycho-education, on the other hand, emerged from a medical model of mental illness and assumes that interventions may be appropriate for focus on only one impaired family member. This chapter demonstrates how the two perspectives can be combined to resolve family challenges.

Psycho-education describes a range of individual, family, and group interventions, usually led by human service professionals, which are focused on educating participants about a significant challenge in living and helping them develop adequate social support and coping skills in managing the challenge (Griffiths, 2006). Psycho-education can be a standalone intervention, but it is often used as one method among several for helping clients and families with a particular problem in living. Other methods may include individual counseling, case management, and family therapy.

The distinctiveness of psycho-education is its didactic/educational approach, with a non-hierarchical relationship between the client and practitioner and an acknowledgment of the family's expertise in the topic area. The major purpose of psycho-education is to facilitate a sense of cognitive mastery in the client and family (Hayes & Gantt, 1992). To do so, psycho-education relies on learning theory (how people acquire, make sense of, and use new information), cognitive psychology (challenging maladaptive thinking processes and suggesting alternative ways of thinking), dynamic psychology (emotional aspects of motivation, purpose, fears, hopes, and perceptions of the self), and developmental psychology (maturational processes and stages of illness and adjustment for both clients and family members) (Constas & Sternberg, 2006).

Family therapy can be defined as interventions in which all members of a nuclear or extended family, as opposed to just one member, are considered together as a psychosocial system in need of change (Nichols, 2013). Family therapists propose that psychological problems are best explained in terms of circular events that focus on the mutually influential and interpersonal contexts in which problems develop. Some family therapies include only a portion of an identified family because of the members' differential availability or commitment to the process. In every case, the focus of family therapy is on interpersonal relationships rather than individual processes. Therapy is intended to alter the structure or nature of relationships among family members. Other chapters in this section describe and illustrate common approaches to family therapy, such as the Bowen, structural, and strategic approaches.

Recent literature reviews and meta-analyses support the effectiveness of family psycho-education for a variety of problems in living, and many such interventions seem to be most effective when they are provided without the presence of the afflicted member. A 2012 review concluded that family psycho-education is effective with schizophrenia, bipolar disorder, and other diagnoses, including children with mood disorders (Lucksted, McFarlane, Downing, Dixon, & Adams, 2012). Common themes across programs include member access to information, skill building, problem solving, and social support provision. An older meta-analysis found that psycho-education is effective for reducing the symptoms of schizophrenia especially when family members are included (Lincoln, Wilhelm, & Nestoriuc, 2007). Another systematic review concluded that psycho-education for families with attention deficit hyperactivity disorder (ADHD) is effective for improving child behavior, parent behavior, parent satisfaction, member knowledge of ADHD, and child adherence to medication regimens (Montoya, Colom, & Ferrin, 2011).

CONTRASTING PSYCHO-EDUCATION AND FAMILY THERAPY

The philosophy of psycho-education does not necessarily value family therapy as practiced from different therapeutic models. Some approaches may combine methods, but for the most part, psycho-education focuses on the general "health" of a family as it works to understand and help one member with an illness or disorder. The illness is considered to be unrelated to major systems issues. Psycho-educational programs have become common for families that include a member with schizophrenia, bipolar disorder, and major depression, and they have proliferated among other types of client populations, as will be described later. Psycho-education developed at a time when many professionals, working from a family systems perspective, tended to label parents as pathogenic in facilitating the development or persistence of schizophrenia in one member. Research on family expressed emotion (EE), measured by ratings of family member hostility toward the ill relative, emotional overinvolvement with the relative, and frequency counts of critical and positive comments about the client (Hooley, Miklowitz, & Beach, 2006), has been criticized as further blaming families for a member's disorder (Mohr, Lafuze, & Mohr, 2000). As a research measure, however, EE provides a means for determining the kinds of family environments that put the person with a mental illness at risk of or protected from symptom relapses.

Family therapists, though not blaming families for the creation or sustenance of a disorder in one member, assert that the presence of problem behavior in one member has effects on the entire system, and the system can be helped to make shared adjustments in the nature of their interactions so that the entire family can function with maximum effectiveness. Psycho-educational programs are clearly not conducive to family therapy when they are provided only for the member who is experiencing the problem. Other programs that tend not to focus on family systems issues include those based on a medical illness of one member. Psycho-education programs that seem appropriate to systems interventions include those dedicated to clients with severe mental disorders, ADHD, mood disorders, eating disorders, and chronic physical health problems (Griffiths, 2006).

PROGRAM EXAMPLES

Three examples of effective family psycho-education programs are provided in this section. The first, the *Caregiver Support Group*, is designed for any family members who provide care for frail elderly members (Toseland & Rivas, 2012). Led by a professional social worker, it illustrates a blend of a structured group format with unstructured follow-up meetings. The structured portion of the program involves eight weekly two-hour meetings focused on education (caregivers' emotional reactions to the illness, self-care, communication skills, resource awareness, and home management techniques), coping skills development (see below), and problem-solving skills development. Monthly follow-up meetings provide ongoing support and assistance as needed to members based on whatever practical problems transpire between meetings. The program has been adopted by a number of service providers and found to be effective in improving caregiver performance, morale, and self-care (Toseland, Haigler, & Monahan, 2011).

Although specific time is set aside during each meeting to cover the three components described above, leaders always provide support interventions as well. These include member opportunities to ventilate about stressful experiences, leader and peer validation of similar caregiving experiences, affirmation of members' abilities to cope, praise for providing good care, a sense of hopefulness about the future, and mutual aid.

The structure of the coping skills element of the program is as follows:

Session 1. The leader assures members that their reactions to the ill relative's health problems are normal, and formally acquaints members with the concepts of stress, appraisal, and coping. She offers members an opportunity to discuss their reactions to the ill relative's behaviors, their beliefs about the sources of the relative's behavior, and the coping strategies they have been using.

Session 2. The leader helps members identify and label their emotional and bodily coping responses to the relative's physical and mental condition and to their own role as caregiver and reinforces their effective coping skills. She encourages members to work toward changing ineffective coping skills, teaches them how to better recognize signs of stress and their typical cognitive appraisal and coping reactions, and encourages the members to keep a diary to record their experienced stresses and their reactions.

Sessions 3–4. Two relaxation techniques for the participants are introduced and practiced (deep breathing and progressive muscle relaxation) to counteract the effects of strain associated with caregiving.

Sessions 5–8. The leader teaches and practices cognitive restructuring strategies including self-talk, taking the perspective of other persons, and self-instruction. She promotes the identification of early stress cues as signals to activate effective appraisals and coping strategies, emphasizes the use of "inner dialogue" to plan coping strategies, and introduces the concept of coping imagery as a means of identifying preferred coping strategies.

During Session #7, members are given the option of choosing to meet monthly as an ongoing support group, and they are encouraged to maintain regular telephone contact with each other if desired. This is not a mandatory element of the program, but many members welcome it, even though they may gradually "drop out" of the process over time (ideally because they have received sufficient help to manage their family situations).

William McFarlane (2002) and his associates have developed a *Multifamily Therapy Group* (MFT) intervention that includes family members and their impaired relatives. This intervention includes family therapy components consistent with emotional systems theory, structural family theory, and strategic family theory because it attends to emotional, structural, and communications aspects of family life. The intervention targets each family's social networks, cognitive deficits, continuity of care, stress levels, stigma, quality of life, burden, and expressed emotion. The groups are long-term (one or more years in length), which requires a major commitment from participants. The four major activities of the practitioner include joining with the families, conducting an educational workshop, preventing relapse though problem-solving processes, and promoting social and vocational rehabilitation.

The intervention is further organized into four steps: self-triangulation, group interpretation, and interfamily management.

Self-triangulation. The leader is directive and becomes the central part of the triangle between family members. She initially focuses on individual families to link their specific problems with appropriate family management guidelines. The leader elicits family interaction patterns and takes the initiative in defining problems in behavioral terms. She is directive in helping the family identify problems and problem-solving sequences. The leader facilitates systems interactions by blocking interruptions of one member by another and controls any extreme displays of affect that can impair problem exploration and resolution.

Group interpretation. The leader works to engage the families with one another, pointing out their similarities and unique contributions to the whole group process. With these commonalities she sets and takes responsibility for processing family interaction themes. Unlike the position taken by some family therapists, she also encourages intragroup social conversation, as this is seen as an important means of developing ties and enabling later discussion of substantive issues.

Cross-family linkages. The leader uses her relationship with family members to promote relationships across family boundaries. When one family introduces a problem for discussion, the leader turns to other families to make this problem relevant to their situations and then facilitates group discussion of solutions.

Interfamily management. The leader attempts to enhance and reinforce interfamily contacts and thereby promote the process of natural support group development. Families help each other develop appropriate roles, responsibilities, and consequences.

MFT outcome studies have shown that the programs are successful in expanding the client and family's social network (a variable that is associated with lower client relapse rates and fewer hospitalizations) (Jewell, Downing, & McFarlane, 2009). Clients and families become more open, cooperative, and appropriately involved across family boundaries. Harmful intrafamily interactions also diminish.

The *Unity Multifamily Therapy Group* (UMFTG) for treating eating disorders (Tantillo, 2006) is based on assumptions consistent with several family systems approaches. It is similar to structural family therapy because it assumes that negative relational patterns can exist in a family with a member who has an eating disorder. It is also consistent with strategic family therapy, because the eating disorder is presented as something that exists outside the family but creates a tension that obstructs normal development for all members. The group is run by a single therapist as a close-ended, eight-session group with up to six to eight families in an outpatient setting. Group members are often from the client's nuclear family, family of origin, or partnership, but they may also be others who make up the client's social network.

In UMFTG, families (including the client member) examine the impact of their relationships on the eating disorder and the impact of the eating disorder on their relationships. The goals of the program are to help the family by:

- Increasing the quality of family life by decreasing stress, stigma, burden, and disconnections incurred by the disorder
- Enhancing a sense of perceived mutuality with regard to the eating disorder symptoms
- Promoting relapse prevention.

Within UMFTG, eating disorders are conceptualized as "diseases of disconnection" because family interactions serve to disconnect clients from their genuine internal experience and from other members, and foster the displacement of conflicts and unacceptable feelings onto their bodies. The disorder distorts cognition and convinces clients to stay connected to it as a means of avoiding feelings or addressing conflicts. The disorder also disconnects clients from family members through its ability to exhaust and disempower loved ones. Family members worry that whatever they do or say may worsen symptoms. The client usually feels guilt and shame about the burden incurred by the family and often protects them from his or her authentic feelings and needs. The UMFTG works to identify the sources of disconnection within the family and helps participants learn how to embrace difference and work through disconnection toward authentic connection with the self and others.

This program approach is based on the fact that eating disorders occur predominantly in women and on the subsequent role of disconnection in the etiology and maintenance of eating disorders. The gender-informed approach to treatment facilitates psychological change and growth through its family systems interventions. Similar to other multiple-family group approaches, UMFTG involves the development of a therapeutic social network in which there is a combined focus on strategies to improve communication, coping, problem solving, and management of the disorder. However, it moves beyond scientific problem solving toward an emphasis on promoting mutual relationships in recovery.

Outcome studies for the UMFTG have thus far been limited to the experiences of the author and her associates. They report that families are successful in honoring differences with a stronger commitment to one another, and that participants build new relationships in recovery that minimize the impact of the eating disorder. The author calls for randomized studies to further examine the effects of the program.

The importance of family systems theory in psycho-education has become more evident as the modality is used across countries and cultures (Sue, 2006). For example, in working with families from China, leaders need to be attuned to structural family characteristics in that culture, including power, roles, and authority. This has also been noted in working with Latino families, with special attention given to the cultural roles of family cohesion and spirituality. The nature of psycho-education (information giving, personal disclosure, mutual problem solving) must be consistent with traditions in the participants' culture. Fortunately, Lefley's (2012) literature review indicates that with appropriate cultural adaptations, the basic model of psycho-education, featuring information about serious mental disorders, illness management techniques, behavioral skills training, problem solving strategies, and family support is effective across national boundaries.

CONCLUSION

Theoretical perspectives on family intervention have evolved over the past 50 years. Systems approaches were most commonly used by family practitioners from the 1950s through the late 1970s. Psycho-educational interventions took ascendancy in the 1980s because of the prevailing biological perspectives on mental illness and emotional disorders. In the past 20 years, a more holistic awareness has evolved that family systems can experience extreme dysfunction as a result of one member's problematic behavioral or health situation. Psycho-education has become integrated with family therapy toward the goals of developing and strengthening family structures and also changing patterns of emotional interaction.

WEBSITES

Bowen Center for the Study of the Family, Georgetown Family Center. The mission of the center is to promote the development of Bowen family systems theory into a science of human behavior and assist individuals and families in solving major problems through understanding and improving human relationships. The center sponsors training programs, conferences, research, clinical services, and publications. http://www.thebowencenter.org/index.html.

Intensive structural therapy. This site, operated by Dr. Charles Fishman, informs professionals and families about intensive structural therapy, a psychotherapy model based on Minuchin's structural family theory (Minuchin, Lee, & Simon, 1996), which is effective in dealing with eating disorders and the treatment of troubled adolescents. http://www.intensivestructuraltherapy.com.

National Alliance on Mental Illness. http://www.nami.org/ NAMI State Organizations and local NAMI Affiliates offer an array of free education and support programs for individuals, family members, providers, and the general public, including Family-to-Family, NAMI Support Group, In Our Own Voice and more.

Substance Abuse and Mental Health Services Administration, U.S. Department of Health and Human Services. *Evidence-Based Practices: Shaping Mental Health Services toward Recovery. Family Psychoeducation.* This site includes detailed research and organizational information for persons who are interested in developing psycho-educational programs for persons with mental illness and their families. http://mentalhealth.samhsa.gov/cmhs/communitysupport/toolkits/family.

References

Constas, M. A., & Sternberg, R. J. (2006). *Translating theory and research into educational practice: Developments in content domains, large-scale reform, and intellectual capacity.* Mahwah, NJ: Erlbaum.

Griffiths, C. A. (2006). The theories, mechanisms, benefits, and practical delivery of psychosocial educational interventions for people with mental health disorders. *International Journal of Psychosocial Rehabilitation, 11*(1), 21–28.

Hayes, R., & Gantt, A. (1992). Patient psychoeducation: The therapeutic use of knowledge for the mentally ill. *Social Work in Health Care, 17*(1), 53–67.

Hooley, J. M., Miklowitz, D. J., & Beach, S. R. H. (2006). Expressed emotion and DSM-V. In S. R. H. Beach, M. Z. Wamboldt, N. J. Kaslow, R. Heyman, M. B. First, L. G. Underwood, & D. Reiss (Eds.), *Relational processes and DSM-V: Neuroscience, assessment, prevention, and treatment* (pp. 175–191). Arlington, VA: American Psychiatric Association.

Jewell, T. C., Downing, D., & McFarlane, W. R. (2009). Partnering with families: Multiple family group psychoeducation for schizophrenia. *Journal of Clinical Psychology, 65*(8), 868–878.

Lefley, H. P. (2012). Cross-cultural perspectives of family psychoeducation. *Psychiatric Annals, 42*(6), 236–240.

Lincoln, T. M., Wilhelm, K., & Nestoriuc, Y. (2007). Effectiveness of psychoeducation for relapse, symptoms, knowledge, adherence and functioning in psychotic disorders: A meta-analysis. *Schizophrenia Research, 96*(1–3), 232–245.

Lucksted, A., McFarlane, W., Downing, D., Dixon, L., & Adams, C. (2012). Recent developments in family psychoeducation as an evidence-based practice. *Journal of Marital and Family Therapy, 38*(1), 101–121.

McFarlane, W. R. (2002). *Multifamily groups in the treatment of severe psychiatric disorders.* New York, NY: Guilford.

Minuchin, S., Lee, W., & Simon, G. M. (1996). *Mastering family therapy: Journeys of growth and transformation.* New York, NY: Wiley.

Mohr, W. K., Lafuze, J. E., & Mohr, B. D. (2000). Opening caregiver minds: National Alliance for the Mentally Ill (NAMI) Provider Education Program. *Archives of Psychiatric Nursing, 14*(5), 235–243.

Montoya, A., Colom, F., & Ferrin, M. (2011). Is psychoeducation for parents and teachers of children and adolescents with ADHD efficacious? A systematic literature review. *European Psychiatry, 26*(3), 166–175.

Nichols, M. P. (2013). *The essentials of family therapy* (6th ed.). Boston, MA: Allyn & Bacon.

Sue, D. W. (2006). *Multicultural social work practice.* Hoboken, NJ: Wiley.

Tantillo, M. (2006). A relational approach to eating disorders multifamily therapy group: Moving from difference and disconnection to mutual connection. *Families, Systems, and Health, 24*(1), 82–102.

Toseland, R. W., Haigler, D. H., & Monahan, D. J. (2011). Current and future directions of education and support programs for caregivers. In R. W. Toseland, D. H. Haigler, & D. J. Monahan (Eds.), *Education and support programs for caregivers: Research, practice, policy. Caregiving: Research, practice, policy* (pp. 149–158). New York, NY: Springer Science + Business Media.

Toseland, R. W., & Rivas, R. F. (2012). *An introduction to group work practice.* Boston, MA: Allyn & Bacon.

61 Guidelines for Couple Therapy with Survivors of Childhood Trauma

Kathryn Karusaitis Basham

INTRODUCTION

Two decades ago, when the sociopolitical climate shifted in the United States, a strong influence of feminism reshaped the direction of psychotherapy modalities attuned to survivors of childhood trauma. Affirming the reality of physical, sexual, and emotional abuses of children provided strength to the voices of many adult trauma survivors who suffered the harsh effects of this ill treatment. During this past ten years of wartime in Iraq and Afghanistan, more than two million U.S. servicemembers have been repeatedly deployed to these combat zones. Current research data reveal elevated rates of intimate partner violence, divorce, family conflicts, and associated mental health problems affecting military children (Institute of Medicine [IOM], 2013). Because rates of premilitary childhood trauma are higher for both male and female servicemembers, we need to be mindful of how legacies of childhood trauma, including both strengths and vulnerabilities, intersect with the effects of combat trauma and/or interpersonal violence in adult life. Although most psychotherapy approaches with this population had previously focused on individual and group interventions, attention has subsequently been paid to developing couple and family approaches for adult survivors of childhood trauma. Psychodynamic theories, in particular object relations theory, provided a general conceptual frame for early couple therapy models (Scharff & Scharff, 1991). Efforts to help couples with improved communication and problem-solving skills were bolstered by a range of cognitive-behavioral couple therapy methods as well (Basham, 1999; Fredman, Mondon,

& Adair, 2011; Jacobson, Christensen, Prince, Cordova, & Eldridge, 2000). In particular, two cognitive-behavioral models that have demonstrated an emerging evidence base for efficacy are introduced. First, *Cognitive-Behavioral Conjoint Therapy* assists servicemembers to learn about posttraumatic stress disorder (PTSD) and find ways to reintegrate back into the community following a return from deployment. Although participants report improvement in knowledge and symptom relief, it is unclear if any relationship shifts have occurred (Fredman, Monson, & Adair, 2011). A limitation of the model is the lack of suitability for some servicemembers who suffer mild-to-moderate brain injury that affects cognitive abilities, concentration, and expressiveness. Second, a cognitive-behavioral model originally developed to help couples establish greater closeness has been adapted for military populations to address specific combat–trauma-related effects on intimacy and conflict resolution (Erbes et al., 2008). Although this method provides invaluable psycho-educational materials to traumatized couples, it does not address the relationship patterns directly.

In more recent years, leading-edge research in attachment theory and neurobiology has shaped the development of attachment-based models of couple therapy, specifically for trauma survivors (Basham, 2013, 2008; Johnson, 2002; Sneath & Rheem, 2010). Johnson (2002) has disseminated her empirically supported practice model, which focuses on affect regulation, mentalization, and restoring or developing a secure attachment between partners; while Sneath & Rheem (2010) have adapted this emotionally focused couple therapy to accommodate a military population.

In general, contemporary couple therapy models rest on a firm yet flexible foundation of a synthesis of social and psychological theory models (Basham, 1999, 2007; Basham & Miehls, 2004). Rather than relying exclusively and narrowly on only one theoretical stance, current models aim toward synthesizing multiple social and theoretical perspectives to respond to a wide range of presenting issues.

GUIDELINES FOR COUPLE THERAPY PRACTICE

The following guidelines highlight central principles that provide the basic scaffolding for couple therapy practice with trauma survivors. They include (1) the centrality of facilitative and empowering relationships; (2) complex theoretical scaffolding; (3) cultural responsiveness; and (4) research-informed and evidence-based approaches.

Centrality of Relationship

When traumatic events rupture an individual's experience of safety, secure attachment, and trust in other people, restoring positive connections and relationships is vital for healing. As a result, a clinician needs to gradually and thoughtfully engage a traumatized couple in a workable therapeutic alliance to re-establish more secure attachments.

Empowerment and locus of control help forge a workable therapeutic alliance with a single- or dual-trauma couple (i.e., one or both partners survived childhood abuse, respectively). Because traumatic events often overwhelm child, adolescent, and adult victims with a sense of powerlessness and helplessness, victims need to regain a sense of mastery and internal locus of control in their day-to-day lives. As a result, a clinician needs to facilitate constructive decision-making capacities and a renewed experience of agency with a traumatized couple without imposing disempowering management.

Resilience fortifies those individuals who have navigated the assaults of traumatic events during childhood, including physical, sexual, and/or emotional abuses. For example, constitutional "hardiness," social supports, proactive coping styles, and abundant socioeconomic resources serve as important protective factors in mitigating long-term negative mental health and health outcomes (Lester, MacDermid, & Riggs, 2010). To reduce negativity and undue pathologizing of human responses to horrific events, we need to focus on the strengths and areas of resilience expressed by a traumatized couple. On the other hand, we must not ignore the deep pain and suffering endured by some adult trauma survivors who wrestle with an acute stress response, posttraumatic stress syndrome (PTSD), complex PTSD, panic disorder, and/or depression. Because these adult trauma survivors have been subjected to hurtful treatment by abusive offending adults during their childhoods, we need to extend compassion and empathy rather than blame them for subsequently developing serious mental health problems.

The "victim–victimizer–bystander" relationship pattern is a central dynamic that occurs both on an intrapersonal and interpersonal basis for trauma survivors. Having experienced victimization in childhood, an adult trauma survivor approaches new relationships with anticipation that other individuals may demonstrate helpless, victim-like stance, an aggressive victimizing manner, or detachment. Many survivors of childhood trauma have also internalized this relationship template and view themselves and others within this framework. When this conflictual trauma scenario is unconscious, aspects of the internalized pattern are projected through the process of projective identification.

For example, a dual-trauma couple who presented with relational conflicts around yelling, intense arguments, and inadequate problem solving also struggled with daunting individual trauma-related issues. Both Jesse, age 48, and Maria, age 45 suffered severe physical abuse as children, inflicted by their parents. During their 15-year marriage, Jesse also served two combat tours of duty in Iraq with an Army infantry unit. Although harnessing noteworthy resilience and effective coping, this couple has also been deeply affected by the complex aftereffects of childhood trauma and combat trauma. They regularly engaged in the destructive forces of a victim–victimizer–bystander relationship scenario. Jesse behaved in a controlling and victimizing manner, alternating with an overly zealous rescuing role where he orchestrated what Maria ate and what clothing she wore. In response, Maria experienced herself as a victim of Jesse's aggression without seeing her own hostility expressed in her verbal harangues.

Theoretical Scaffolding

A second core guideline involves formulating a complex theoretical scaffolding to support the couple therapy model. Synthesis, rather than integration, of social, neurobiological, and psychological theory models allows for pulling together discrete and at times contradictory theoretical constructs into a unified entity to inform our assessments and craft treatment plans. Integrative models often suffer from the untenable objective of trying to merge diverse theoretical constructs that are often incompatible. Metaphor is helpful in describing this synthesis. If you visualize staring through a crystal at a distant object, you may see differences in the texture and color of the object depending on what part of the glass you are looking through. Similarly, the fabric of a theoretical synthesis shifts color and shape over time during the course of different phases of couple therapy.

In a similar fashion, a case-specific practice model changes the synthesis of theoretical perspectives depending on the unique features and needs assessed for each couple. As a result, the assessment and therapy process sustains a dynamic and reflexive flow of theory models that advance to the foreground while other theoretical models recede to the background.

Although a range of psychological and social theories are available in the knowledge base of a clinician at any given moment, data forthcoming from the couple related to their presenting concerns determine which constellation of theoretical lenses advances to the foreground. Because a relationship base provides the foundation for a couple therapy practice model, we may turn to the lens of object relations or attachment theory to inform how early childhood experiences shaped ways of relating in adult life, including during the couple therapy sessions. Feminist and critical race theories help us understand the sociocultural and family context. Intergenerational family theory aims to explore patterns, worldviews, and rituals that may have perpetuated or thwarted the cross-generational transmission of trauma-related effects. In contrast, a narrative family perspective may illuminate the multiple and unique meanings of a trauma narrative. In recent years, the groundswell of cutting-edge research in trauma and attachment theories further informs our understanding of the neurobiological effects of traumatic exposure as well as disruptions to attachment. Holding the tension of multiple, often contradictory theoretical perspectives, while also maintaining a broader view, require flexibility in perception, understanding, and action from the clinician.

Cultural Responsiveness

A third core guideline is cultural responsiveness—an ongoing, dynamic attunement to the complex intersections of sociocultural factors that influence and shape the social identities of each partner and the couple throughout couple therapy. Race, ethnicity, religion, sexual orientation, gender, age, ability, primary language, and socioeconomic status influence the ways a child experiences traumatic events and how he or she copes in the aftermath of trauma throughout his or her life. A culturally responsive stance moves beyond the accruing of specialized knowledge and skills inherent in a culturally competent practice. Instead, the clinician engages with the couple in a reflexive exchange of ideas that mutually influences their shared understanding of how these various themes shape their presenting issues, worldviews, and the clinical encounter.

Self-reflection presumes that a clinician explores, on an ongoing basis, the full range of emotional and cognitive responses in practice with traumatized couples. In a psychodynamic conceptual framework, countertransference phenomena involve a complex nexus of personal reactions, a more "objective" response based on projective identification processes, and culturally determined responses to clients.

Research-informed and Evidence-based

The fourth core guideline relates to a research-informed and evidence-based approach toward all domains of practice including assessment, treatment planning, interventions, and evaluation.

As research evidence emerges to support the efficacy of various couple therapy models for trauma survivors, we are responsible for educating ourselves in the models *and* recommending them during the decision-making period of work with a couple. Flexibility of the clinician supports client-centeredness in designing a couple therapy plan with a traumatized couple. Although certain manualized treatment protocols are useful in helping couples work on developing communication and conflict resolution skills, these clients also benefit from establishing a reparative therapeutic relationship that facilitates rebuilding of attachment and connections. Many traumatized couples comment on how disempowering and objectifying a "cookie-cutter" approach feels to them as they yearn to talk about their unique experiences in navigating painful emotional terrain. Each treatment plan needs to be individualized while also recognizing the need to advance research-informed and empirically supported treatment models.

PHASE-ORIENTED COUPLE THERAPY MODEL

A phase-oriented couple therapy model specifically attuned for survivors of childhood trauma relies on a thorough bio-psychosocial–spiritual assessment that reviews a full range of institutional/sociocultural, interactional, and individual/intrapersonal factors (Basham, 2013; Basham & Miehls, 2004). It includes three therapy phases: Phase I—Safety, stabilization, and establishment of a context for change; Phase II—Reflection on the trauma narrative; and Phase III—Consolidation of new perspectives, attitudes, and behaviors. Preliminary research findings from a pilot project reveal positive changes in affect regulation and knowledgeability as well as a reduction in trauma-related symptoms.

The clinician needs to consider cultural congruence, relational capacities, and the dimension of time while crafting a treatment plan with goals that guide choices of specific clinical interventions. While envisioning a metaphoric image of a therapeutic venture as a sailing journey, a thorough assessment serves both as a compass for directing the work and as a stabilizing anchor. In contrast to sequential, essentialist stage models, a phase-oriented couple therapy treatment model assumes that various issues may be revisited at different periods throughout the work. During the early sessions of couple therapy, the clinician needs to assess the strengths and vulnerabilities for the couple and each partner in these various institutional, interpersonal, and intrapersonal arenas. The following outline may be used as an assessment guide that highlights relevant content.

BIO-PSYCHOSOCIAL–SPIRITUAL ASSESSMENT

Institutional/Sociocultural (grounded in social constructionist, critical race and feminist theories)

1. Clinician attitudes and responses (countertransference and secondary trauma)
2. Social supports (e.g., family, community, faith-based organization, and military unit)
3. Service delivery context (social policies, finances, and political context)
4. Previous and current mental health treatment
5. Intersecting sociocultural factors (i.e., race, ethnicity, religion, socioeconomic status, primary language, ability, gender, sexual orientation; age; military and Veteran culture)

Interpersonal (grounded in intergenerational family and cognitive-behavioral theories)

1. Relational dynamics including "victim–victimizer–bystander" pattern (interactional and intergenerational)
2. Power and control struggles
3. Distancing and distrust
4. Boundary issues
5. Communication patterns

Individual (grounded in neurobiology, attachment, and object relations theories)

1. Individual cognitive, affective, and behavioral functioning
   - Indicators of resilience
   - Mental health diagnoses (e.g., Posttraumatic stress (PTS); Posttraumatic stress disorder (PTSD)
   - Co-occurring conditions (depression/suicidal behavior; substance use disorder; cognitive injuries; intimate partner violence)
2. Intrapersonal
   - Working models of attachment, affect regulation, and capacity for mentalization
   - Internalized victim–victimizer–bystander dynamic

- Capacity for whole? Part? Or merged object relations?

As clinicians, although we continually assess a couple's presenting issues and their progress throughout treatment, a focus with clear goals can typically be established after several sessions. Areas of strength and vulnerability in these various arenas of a couple's life set the stage for the crafting of such a plan. For example, Jesse and Maria benefited from an approach that addressed the multiplicity of their problems and helped coordinate their care. Not only was attention paid to interrupting the destructive force of their victim–victimizer–bystander relationship scenario, each partner set individual goals related to strengthening self-care and safety related to their trauma-related symptoms. For example, Jesse set a goal to re-establish his abstinence from alcohol, renew his connections with his sponsor, manage his unstable diabetes, and balance his erratic affect. Maria set goals to address her self-harming suicidal behavior and seek psychopharmacological relief from depression. In Phase I of couple therapy, we often see goals that improve relational patterns (i.e., minimizing the power conflicts and achieving greater mutuality, improving direct communication, and managing intense affect during conflict resolution). In addition, self-differentiating goals are also addressed to promote healing and growth both interpersonally and intrapersonally.

Phase I goals in couple therapy are relevant for all traumatized couples. These goals aim to: (1) develop a basic sense of physical and psychosocial safety; (2) stabilize trauma-related symptoms and manage crises; (3) strengthen self-care and self-differentiation; (4) develop stress-reduction and affect-regulation skills; (5) demonstrate communication and conflict resolution skills; (6) identify, strengthen and expand social supports; and (7) explore complex social identities.

During this phase of work the following themes are explored in depth with a variety of clinical interventions grounded in psychodynamic, cognitive-behavioral, and body/mind perspectives:

- Safety
- Self-care (physical health and mental health; sleep, nutrition, and exercise; substance use and abuse; bio-behavioral strategies for stress reduction and self-soothing)

- Support systems (e.g., religion/spirituality, family, community and military unit)
- Communication skills
- Assessment of partnership status (continuation, static, dissolution, growth)
- Exploration of complex social identities.

After a couple has accomplished all aspects of Phase I goals, they are typically ready to move along to Phase II tasks, which involve reflection on the trauma narrative. Given recent controversy in the mental health field related to the dubious benefit of prematurely uncovering traumatic memories, I assert that most couples benefit from a reflective sharing of their traumatic experiences, on a cognitive or titrated affective level, without full affective re-experiencing of early traumatic memories.

Work involves reflecting on the trauma-related effects in the present, recognizing and changing the victim–victimizer–bystander dynamic and healing relationships with extended family and family of origin in the here and now. Grieving the loss associated with childhood innocence along with losses of real relationships surface at this time. Traumatogenic family environments often rob everyone of ordinary transitional rituals that both celebrate wonderful accomplishments and grieve losses related to life transitions such as death, divorce, and reintegration post-deployment. For example, after Maria and John completed Phase I tasks, they shared their sorrow with exploring the roots of family violence. As they traced the histories of emigration, military service, and poverty for both families of origin, each partner was able to understand how unresolved emotion and distress were transmitted intergenerationally, affecting both of them as well as their children. After many shared tears, they talked about interrupting their pattern of emotional violence and shifted away from victimizing each other and themselves. In summary, therapy goals at this Phase II aim to:

- Explore the meaning of traumatic experiences and build shared empathy
- Explore the intergenerational legacy of the victim–victimizer–bystander dynamic
- Mourn losses (e.g., death, divorce, reintegration following deployment, disability, moves)
- Create healing and transition rituals.

Phase III goals focus primarily on consolidating the family of origin work started in Phase II, along with additional strengthening of family and community relationships. Couples often experience less shame and isolation as they move more actively into discussions of their intimate sexual partnerships. Parenting often improves as partners listen better and learn to set firm yet benign boundaries. Finally, couples no longer define themselves through the identity of victim or survivor. Instead, they view themselves with complex social identities, thriving in their new approaches to life. The following Phase III goals aim to:

- Remediate trauma-related symptomatology
- Demonstrate the capacity for empathy
- Develop equitable power relationships
- Enhance sexual relationship and intimacy
- Demonstrate capacities for self-differentiation and secure attachment
- Develop effective parenting skills
- Identify and express complex social identities
- Express a shift in social consciousness

PREPARING FOR FUTURE WORK WITH COUPLES

Given that engaging in couple therapy with survivors of childhood trauma challenges even the most experienced and resilient clinician, recognizing common therapeutic missteps can ease some of the difficulty. Clinicians might aim to: (1) address Phase I tasks of safety, self-care, and assessing co-occurring conditions without moving too quickly into a discussion of a primary trauma narrative; (2) educate themselves on the best practices available including couple therapy models that have established empirical support as well as those that have emerging evidence; and (3) engage in self-reflection regularly to heighten cultural responsiveness as well as minimize and address countertransference enactments. When clinicians recognize the benefit of a fluid, dynamic phase-oriented approach that titrates emotional intensity, they will be better able to manage their countertransference enactments and heal any relational therapeutic ruptures. Even so, this work is challenging. Yet, couple therapy has its rewarding moments as well. When couples experience a sense of growth and accomplishment, they often describe ways that their suffering and

distress transform into a renewed sense of hope for the partnership.

WEBSITES

American Association of Marriage and Family Therapy (AAMFT). http://www.aamft.org.

International Society for Traumatic Stress Studies (ISTSS). http://www.istss.org.

National Center for PTSD. http://www.ncptsd.va.gov.

Ottawa Couple and Family Therapy Institute. http://www.ocfi.ca.

References

Basham, K. (1999). A synthesis of theory in couple therapy: No longer an unlikely coupling. In T. Northcut & N. Heller (Eds.), *Enhancing psychodynamic therapy with cognitive-behavioral techniques* (pp. 135–157). Northvale, NJ: Aronson.

Basham, K. (2008). Homecoming as safe haven or the new front: Attachment and detachment in military couples. *Clinical Social Work Journal Special Issue, 36*(1), 83–96.

Basham, K. (2013). Couple therapy for redeployed Military and Veteran couples. In A. Rubin, E. L. Weiss & J. E. Coll, *Handbook of military social work* (pp. 443–465). Hoboken, NJ: Wiley & Sons, Inc.

Basham, K., & Miehls, D. (2004). *Transforming the legacy: Couple therapy with survivors of childhood trauma.* New York, NY: Columbia University Press.

Erbes, C. R., Polusny, M. A., MacDermid, S., & Compton, J. S. (2008). Couple therapy with combat Veterans and their partners. *Journal of Clinical Psychology, 64*(8), 972–983.

Fredman, S. J., Mondon, C., & Adair, K. C. (2011). Implementing cognitive-behavioral conjoint therapy with the recent generation of Veterans and their partners. *Journal of Clinical Psychology, 18*(1), 120–130.

Institute of Medicine (IOM). (2013). *Returning home from Iraq and Afghanistan: Readjustment needs of Veterans, Servicemembers and their families.* Washington, DC: National Academies Press.

Jacobson, N. S., Christensen, A., Prince, S. E., Cordova, J., & Eldridge, K. (2000). Integrative couple therapy: An acceptance-based, promising new treatment for couple discord. *Journal of Consulting and Clinical Psychology 68*(2), 351–355.

Johnson, S. M. (2002). *Emotionally focused couple therapy with trauma survivors: Strengthening attachment bonds.* New York, NY: Guilford.

Lester, P., MacDermid, S. M., & Riggs, D. (Eds.). (2010). *Risk and resilience in military families.* New York, NY: Springer.

Scharff, D., & Scharff, J. (1991). *Object relations couple therapy.* Northvale, NJ: Aronson.

Sneath, L., & Rheem, K. (2010). Use of emotionally-focused couple therapy with military couples and families. In R. Blair Everson & C. R. Figley (Eds.), *Families under fire: Systemic therapy with military families* (pp. 127–152). New York, NY: Taylor & Francis.

62 Working with Children and Families Impacted by Military Service

Eugenia L. Weiss, Jose E. Coll, & Tara DeBraber

GETTING STARTED

Due to the U.S. military involvement in the Global War on Terrorism (GWOT) for more than a decade, it is highly likely that civilian social workers will encounter military or veteran connected families seeking assistance from community mental health or family service agencies, especially given that military and government systems of care (e.g., Veterans Administration) may not be able to meet the demand for services. Social workers without exposure or having little knowledge of the military or veteran population may benefit from understanding military culture and lifestyle, as well as current issues facing military connected families, in order to provide comprehensive and informed services for this population (Savitsky, Illingworth, & DuLaney, 2009). Thus the objective of this chapter is to inform social workers on the unique strengths and challenges of military connected families and ways to serve them. Military connected families are often considered resilient in the face of experiencing unique stressors such as frequent geographic relocations, service member deployments and family separations, postdeployment adjustment, and family crises resulting from posttraumatic stress disorder or other injuries incurred by the service member. However, before we explore associated stressors as well as family strengths, military family-related demographics will be provided first, followed by a bird's eye view of military culture and lifestyle, as a way of background and orientation for the reader. As of 2011, only 37% of military families lived on a military installation with the remaining 63% living among 4,000 communities nationwide (U.S. Department of Defense [DoD], 2011). Fifty-five percent of service members have children and almost 50% are married, 6.5% are single parents, and 2.1% are in dual-military families, where both spouses are members of the military and at times deploy simultaneously (DoD, 2011; Office of the Deputy Under Secretary of Defense, 2008). The majority of service members are young, with over half being below the age of 25 and 70% having one or more children (Kaplow et al., 2013). Of the active duty service members, 41% have children in the zero to five-year-old age range and 25% of members in the selected reserves have children in the same age range (Lieberman & Van Horn, 2013). According to the DoD (2009), there are 1.9 million children with a parent serving in the U.S. military of which more than 700,000 have experienced parental deployment especially in light of the GWOT, post 9/11, where service members and reserve components have been called to serve on multiple and lengthy deployments, most often to Iraq (Operation Iraqi Freedom, OIF; and Operation New Dawn, OND) and Afghanistan (Operation Enduring Freedom, OEF).

MILITARY CULTURE AND LIFESTYLE

Military culture is comprised of a distinct sub-set of American society governed by a separate set of laws, norms, traditions, and values (Exum, Coll, & Weiss, 2011). The authors note that key characteristics of military culture include an emphasis on "mission readiness," as well as the importance of military unit cohesion within a hierarchical or rank-based system. The tenets or virtues of military service, regardless of the branch of service, include courage, honor, loyalty, commitment, integrity, and an expectation of adherence to these values, all of which may be imposed on the family; and at times are considered to be a reflection of the military member. A noted consequence for military families is the constant moving (including sometimes living abroad) that is part of the military lifestyle, and which can lead to the family becoming susceptible to isolation and alienation from extended family members and from civilians as well (Hall, 2011). Family members can become isolated because they often feel that their lives are transient; as a consequence, sometimes they do not readily invest in new relationships, communities, or schools. Additionally, military personnel who are deployed from the National Guard or Reserve units are civilians who are part-time military personnel activated into "active duty status." Not since World War II, have reserve components been more deployed than they have been within what has been termed the mobilization of the "total force" (Exum, Coll, & Weiss, 2011). These families face additional stressors in relation to occupational and economic losses; the service member parent or spouse may take a leave from his or her civilian job to be deployed, and then often returns from deployment to find that the job is no longer viable (due to a poor economy). Or the service member may return to find that she has been passed up for a promotion in her civilian job. In addition, some service members may experience less earning potential while they are serving their country. Additionally, Guard and Reserve families often live at great distances from military bases and thus, they often lack resources that active duty personnel have in terms of greater access to built-in military support systems (see Harnett, 2013).

This chapter will outline the strengths and stressors associated with the military and veteran connected families with particular emphasis on deployment related stressors, and effects of parent (i.e., service member) injury upon the family,

as well as implications for civilian social workers working with this population. We will begin with providing an understanding of the impact of service member deployment on the family.

MILITARY DEPLOYMENT

Deployment is the assignment of military personnel to temporary, unaccompanied duty (i.e., without family members) and away from their permanent duty station (Stafford & Grady, 2003). Pincus et al. (2001) proposed a model for understanding the psychological phases and transitions (i.e., cycle of deployment) that military families undergo as a part of the deployment process. For example, the *predeployment* phase entails the psychological and physical preparation in the months preceding the actual deployment. It is typified by alternating feelings of anticipation and loss for both the service member and for the family (Pincus et al., 2001). During the *deployment* phase, when the service member has actually departed from the home, children's responses will vary depending on their age and stage of development; some may feel angry, sad, numb, or lonely (Fitzsimons & Krause-Parello, 2009). Children may feel that the deployed parent has left the home because of their misbehavior or they may experience extreme emotions related to feelings of abandonment (Stafford & Grady, 2003). Older children or adolescents may resent the nondeployed parent if there are younger siblings who require increased attention from that parent (Paley, Lester, & Mogil, 2013). A study by Mansfield et al. (2011) demonstrated that Army children with a deployed parent (OEF/OIF) were experiencing a greater incidence of mental health-related problems, such as acute stress reactions and depressive and behavioral disorders, than their civilian counterparts. Furthermore, the longer the deployment, the higher the rate of adjustment problems. Another area of concern involves parental absence related to extended-combat deployments and military trainings away from home and the impact of these separations on children's well-being. Combat-related deployments further exacerbate the stress of separation because children and youth worry that the deployed parent may be injured or killed in the line of duty (Burrell et al., 2006). In fact, for many, long-term parental separation can be detrimental to emotional and behavioral functioning across developmental stages (Windle, 1992). Research has demonstrated the importance of developing healthy attachment relationships during the first years of life. Infant mental health, defined as a young child's ability to experience, regulate, and express emotions, as well as develop close relationships or secure attachments in order to learn and explore the environment, is affected by the stressors of the family, which can be exacerbated by the demands and stressors of the military lifestyle (Lieberman & Van Horn, 2013). These young children must cope with the caregiver parent's distraction with a deployment and the parent's role of managing a household alone. Military connected infants and young children can experience increased stress from their environments, which may affect the infant's ability to manage frustration and conflict while maintaining normal development trajectories (Lieberman & Van Horn, 2013). Mild-to-moderate stress is a developmental expectation that can provide the infant with an opportunity to practice dealing with displeasure or fear and manage frustration. During predeployment and deployment, childcare arrangements can frequently change leading to toddlers and preschoolers becoming easily frustrated, reverting to old behaviors, acting out, or being controlling and demanding (Lieberman & Van Horn, 2013). Parents or caregivers should assist young children in understanding what is happening or how things will change after a separation in developmentally appropriate ways and in a calm fashion. This is important for young children because they can assess their parent's emotional state through facial expressions and tone of voice. Caregivers (most often the nondeployed remaining parent, i.e., the mother) can experience additional stress during the time of separation if the young child exhibits emotional or behavioral difficulties in response to the deployment separation. During this phase, it is helpful for the caregiver parent to provide structure and routine for the child on a daily basis. The nondeployed parent or spouse typically manages the day-to-day activities of the household, including the majority of the parenting and parental decisions for children if there are children in the household. Military programs are increasingly addressing the needs of the family because the well-being of the spouse is related to the retention of service personnel (Green, Nurius, & Lester, 2013). Military families routinely experience a variety of stressors and changes with various levels of resources and support. Families can easily tip into a state of crisis if an unexpected stressor, experience, or circumstance arises when a family is already experiencing high stress, or if an unanticipated event overpowers the family's coping abilities (McCubbin & Patterson, 1983). (For an overview on theory and practice with military couples and families, please see Weiss et al., 2013). Families can benefit from a social worker who can educate them on problem solving skills and goal setting, and who can make them aware of resources. Military families may not be aware of all of the resources, services, and programs that are available to assist in successfully navigating through the demands associated with military lifestyle. Overall family mental health and functioning can be negatively impacted if levels of chronic stress become the "new normal." Social workers can assist military families in relaxation and calming techniques to reduce stress levels (Green, Nurius, & Lester, 2013). According to the research, family stress levels and ability to cope with the demands of the military are also correlated with lower educational level of the remaining parent or spouse and early entry into adulthood and parenting as evidenced by the young ages of new military couples and parents (Green, Nurius, & Lester, 2013). Additionally, research has shown social media and the Internet can be positive factors in maintaining levels of connectedness during a deployment. These types of communication provide a level of immediacy that a mailed letter cannot. Families are increasingly using social media and the Web for real time events such as birthday parties, graduations, and births. Social media allows for continuation of family dynamics during times of separation through the sharing of pictures, videos, and real time conversations (Matthews-Juarez, Juarez, & Faulkner, 2013). The use of social media was found to be helpful for families who identified as having strong family unity and yet exacerbated the problems of families with preexisting issues (Matthews-Juarez, Juarez, & Faulkner, 2013). Therefore, a social worker should assess the family and couple history before encouraging use of the Internet or social media as primary modes of communication.

As military connected families experience heightened levels of stress, children may be at increased risk for being victims of child maltreatment. Child maltreatment can be a result of the parent's inability to manage his or her own stress, resulting in reactive behaviors toward children as opposed to appropriate parenting behaviors. If the perpetrator is the nondeployed parent, maltreatment or abuse is likely related to the stress of the deployment or the reorganization of family roles and boundaries after deployment (Porter, 2013). Risk for child maltreatment may be impacted by lack of resources (or the perception of lack of resources), as well as substance abuse and mental health issues in the caregiver(s) (Thomsen et al., 2013). Poorly managed stress in the caregiver (i.e., the nondeployed parent) is a critical factor in cases of child maltreatment. A study by Gibbs et al. (2007) found that the rate of substantiated child maltreatment (i.e., neglect) among Army families was 42% greater during deployments. Adolescent children also can experience negative reactions to a deployment, such as depression, low self-esteem, or school problems that can result in child maltreatment, especially if the adolescent is rebellious or suffers from a mental illness or disability. Child maltreatment during a deployment with adolescent children can be attributed to the combination of the adolescent's emotional deregulation and the lack of parental control (Porter, 2013). If a service member is discharged from the military with "other than honorable" or as "dishonorable," he or she is then ineligible for veteran benefits, which can further increase the risk for child maltreatment because access to resources is then significantly diminished for the veteran and his or her family.

In order to assist military families under stress, Porter (2013) identified Child Parent Relationship Training (CPRT) as an effective intervention for these families. CPRT is a strength-based resilience training that teaches parenting skills and effective interactions through child-centered play (Porter, 2013). Filial therapy has also been found to be helpful in supporting military families facing the stressors of deployment (Chawla & Solinas-Saunders, 2011). Social workers can use these types of interventions to empower families and increase their resilience in order to decrease the risk of child maltreatment. When working with military families, social workers are further encouraged to build upon family strengths and develop a military family genogram as a tool to explore intergenerational family resiliency from a solution-focused perspective (Weiss et al., 2010).

The next phase in the cycle of deployment is the *sustainment* phase, which occurs from the first month of deployment through the month prior to the service member's return home. Sustainment is the time in which the family has the opportunity to create new sources of support as well as new routines in the absence of the service member (Pincus et al., 2001). Children often assume additional roles and responsibilities in the home and are thus forced to become more independent; many will take pride in their newfound competencies (Weins & Boss, 2006). Military connected children and adolescents may also have more responsibilities at home or with younger siblings during the sustainment phase, resulting in the nondeployed parent ignoring the adolescent's need for supervision and support (Williams, 2013). As a result of many changes and stressors, adolescent children can feel resentment toward parents and the military lifestyle. Milburn and Lightfoot (2013) stated that adolescents with a deployed parent are more likely to engage in risky behaviors such as binge drinking, along with use of other substances and experience thoughts of suicide and depressed mood. Adolescents may also experience difficulty when the deployed parent returns, especially if the adolescent was a "parentified" figure in the family during the length of the deployment, and subsequently is reluctant to give up that role upon the return of the service member parent (Milburn & Lightfoot, 2013). Although adolescents can experience significant stressors associated with the military lifestyle, not all adolescents experience negative emotions related to deployments and changing family roles. Adolescents can develop or experience healthy coping skills and demonstrate resiliency to the multiple demands of the military lifestyle, especially when the parents are financially stable and know of or can access multiple resources and services (Astor et al., 2013). Military spouses have described the deployment process, not so much in terms of the linear stages of deployment, but more as a "roller coaster" of highs and lows and "contradictory emotions." Despite these feelings of powerlessness, a qualitative study on Army wives found that they engaged in positive thinking and coping, exhibited self-determination with new found self-confidence, and engaged in opportunities for self-discovery (Davis, Wards, & Storm, 2011, p. 55).

Below is a brief case scenario demonstrating what a social worker may see in working with a military family where the service member spouse/father is deployed and the family is experiencing some challenges. Recommendations for interventions are also presented. (The scenario is a composite of several cases and any similarity to real people or events is purely coincidental.)

DEPLOYMENT/SUSTAINMENT PHASE CASE SCENARIO

Bryce Jones is an 11-year-old Caucasian male who attends outpatient counseling twice a month with a private practitioner. The client is able to participate in counseling through his father's health insurance for military dependents (TRICARE). Bryce's father, Mike Jones, is in the Marine Corps and the family is stationed out of Camp Pendleton in California, where they live on the military installation. Bryce has a younger sister, age 3 years (Emma) who is "daddy's girl," and his father is currently on his fourth deployment to Afghanistan. This time he has been gone for six months and has five more months to go. Bryce's mother used to spend time with him and had signed Bryce up for various athletic activities, which he seemed to enjoy. Ever since his father deployed, however, Bryce has not played any sports and hardly spends any time with his mother. Instead, he stays in his room the majority of the time watching TV or playing video games. Bryce's sister, Emma, has been having temper tantrums and regressed to bed wetting despite being successfully potty trained eight months prior. Bryce's mother (Alice, age 29) has become increasingly depressed, has "no one to talk to" (family of origin is out of state), and is "at her wits end" trying to deal with her 3-year-old. She is not sure how much longer she can manage everything on her own, despite having fared well with the last three deployments (Emma was one year old at the time of the last deployment). Bryce is also having difficulty in school both academically and socially. Prior to the deployment, Bryce was an average student and interacted well with his classmates. The therapist has called a family session with Bryce, his sister Emma, and his mother Alice, to assess the needs of the family.

Bryce's therapist is concerned with the well-being of the family and after a thorough assessment, does not believe that there is child maltreatment or neglect at this time. However, to mitigate for the increased risk of child maltreatment along with other augmented risk factors the therapist recommends the following for the family. First, for the family to engage in Child Parent Relationship Training (CPRT) or filial therapy; the therapist provides a referral to a family therapist who is versed in these types of approaches and is covered in the TRICARE network. The goal is to bolster Alice's parenting skills and help her to engage effectively with both of her children through listening and being able to respond to their feelings. As part of the sessions, the family therapist will assist each family member in developing positive coping skills, as well as learning how to communicate effectively

with one another. In addition, the family will be able to identify desirable family activities that will promote family cohesion, as well as ways for the family members to feel connected with the deployed father. Additionally, the therapist will recommend several community programs to help the children and the deployed parent with maintaining attachment bonds. One such program is *United through Reading*, in which a deployed service member is recorded (while deployed overseas) reading a children's book. A DVD of the reading, along with a copy of the book, is mailed to the child for the child to follow along in the parent's absence (United through Reading, 2013). Another organization, *Daddy Dolls*, creates doll-size or life-size figures of the deployed service member for the child to maintain a feeling of closeness during the time of separation (Daddy Dolls, n.d.). For younger children, such as Emma, the organization, *Zero to Three* offers trainings, resources, and tips for parents to address feelings and behaviors in the youngest of military-connected children (Zero to Three, 2009). Furthermore, the popular, *Talk, Listen, Connect: Helping Families During Military Deployment*, is a Sesame Street media tool created a few years ago to assist preschool children in coping with separations and deployment (Sesame Street Workshop, 2006). More recently, this program has expanded in scope with support from the Defense Centers of Excellence, and includes Internet and digital technology types of tools in order to provide greater outreach.

Second, the therapist will refer Alice, the mother, for her own individual therapy to help promote her resilience and coping with stressors associated with being the nondeployed parent (i.e., acting as a single parent). The therapist will also refer her to on-base military resources for support groups specific to spouses/mothers during deployment. Third, the therapist will inquire whether there are school-related programs that can further support Bryce. After obtaining parental permission, the therapist may want to work closely with a social worker at Bryce's school. Schools are optimal environments for the provision of prevention and intervention services for school-aged children because these settings provide access to many children and are a familiar and safe context (Jaycox et al., 2006). This is especially the case when many military families will not seek military behavioral health services for reasons associated with stigma or for fear of negative work-related repercussions for the service member parent. (For further information on schools and military connected children, please see Building Capacity, 2010; Leskin et al., 2013; Weiss & Coll, 2013). This case will be revisited later in the chapter after we discuss postdeployment/reintegration and service member injuries and impact on the family.

To continue where we left off before the presentation of the case scenario, the next stage in the cycle of deployment is the *redeployment* phase, which occurs within the month prior to the service member's return home. It involves the anticipation of homecoming, and the family and service member often experience mixed emotions consisting of excitement and apprehension (Pincus et al., 2001). The final phase in the cycle of deployment is the *postdeployment* or *reintegration* phase, when the service member is reunited with his or her loved ones. Initially the phase of homecoming can be a honeymoon period, but it is often followed by many families facing adjustment-related challenges. For instance, new roles and responsibilities need to be renegotiated at this stage. Children may have undergone significant developmental changes during the service member's absence, thus creating new parenting challenges for the service member parent, including a loss of parental authority and the need to attach or reattach emotionally to their spouse and children (Bowling & Sherman, 2008). During the reunion or postdeployment phase, it is important to give the returning service member time to adjust to the developmental changes the child experienced or achieved during the parent's absence. The reintegration phase becomes even more complicated if the returning service member parent is somehow changed by the war experience, either psychologically, behaviorally, or in terms of belief systems. The reader may refer to Weiss, Coll and Metal (2011) for further exploration of the alteration of veteran worldviews following combat experiences.

SERVICE MEMBER INJURY AND IMPACT ON FAMILY

Service member injury is another area that vastly affects military families and children in the reintegration of the service member spouse/parent. It is estimated that over 30,000 military children have been impacted by parental combat injuries during the current and continuous GWOT (Cozza & Guimond, 2010). Although

more service personnel are surviving combat due to better protective gear and technology than in previous wars, from 15% to over 30% of all returning veterans from OIF/OND/OEF will meet *Diagnostic and Statistical Manual of Mental Disorders* (APA, 2013) criteria for Posttraumatic Stress Disorder (PTSD), as well as a high number of mood disturbances, anxieties, and comorbid substance abuse. Some will have experienced mild traumatic brain injury (TBI) (e.g., concussion) associated with blast exposure from roadside bombs or intermittent explosive devices (Tanielian & Jaycox, 2008; U.S. Army Medical Department, 2008). Rosenheck and Fontana (1998) found that the more severe and complex the parental exposure to combat, the greater the extent of distress among children. The effects of a combat veteran's trauma on the family have been recognized in the literature as "secondary traumatization"; this refers to a phenomenon whereby the veteran's trauma is unwittingly transferred to his or her partner and children, who then experience similar symptoms as the traumatized veteran (Dekel & Goldblatt, 2008; Figley, 1995; Nelson & Wright, 1996). In fact, parental distress in either the returning combat veteran or in the caregiver parent (i.e., the nondeployed parent) has been demonstrated to contribute to poor emotional and behavioral adjustment in children (Chandra et al., 2011). Exposure to traumatic stress could overwhelm the child, leading to the collapse of age appropriate coping (Lieberman & Van Horn, 2013). These authors noted that trauma exposure or traumatic stress can destroy the child's ability to trust the caregiver(s) and create feelings of helplessness that can impact the child's feelings of self-worth.

An additional concern involves the high rates of interpersonal violence and child maltreatment among both active duty and veteran (i.e., separated or retired from military service) populations. These rates are estimated to be three times higher than rates among the U.S. civilian population (Houppert, 2005). Incidents of physical abuse also increased when the service member parent returned home (Gibbs et al., 2007). Even in service members who do not suffer from the symptoms of depression or PTSD, a study found that family violence is mostly related to family reintegration problems upon the service member's return home (Taft et al., 2007).

Combat injury can have a range of effects on the family members. It is important for the nondeployed parent to communicate with children regarding an injury in developmentally appropriate language as early as possible and to create and encourage an atmosphere for discussion regarding the injury of the service member parent (Cozza, Holmes, & Van Ost, 2013). Family dynamics may shift or change as the noninjured parent attends to the injured parent's needs, limiting his or her availability for the other family members. The injured parent may also experience a multiplicity of changes, including a decreased ability to care for him or herself, changes in parenting ability, and emotional or physical withdrawal from the rest of the family (Cozza, Holmes, & Van Ost, 2013). Children of injured service members may blame themselves for changes in the injured parent's behavior. Social workers can work within the family system to provide education regarding symptoms of posttraumatic stress disorder/traumatic brain injury, as well as for cases of polytrauma (where the service member has had trauma to multiple body systems; e.g., limb loss, spinal cord injuries) and how family dynamics may have changed since the injury. Multifamily group modalities are helpful for providing psycho-education and support for families coping with veteran injuries (see Bowling, Doerman, & Sherman, 2011; Perlick et al., 2011). Social workers can teach the injured parent how to self-monitor emotional states and how to express feelings and needs to the other family members. If the injuries or disabilities take a chronic or long-term trajectory, a social worker can assist the caregiver (usually the spouse) in coping skills through a stress process model (see Matthieu & Swensen, 2013). Additionally, social workers are able to help injured veterans develop and set goals, have realistic expectations in their rehabilitation or recovery, and learn to use various strategies to cope with memory and concentration issues (in cases of PTSD and/or TBI) in a way that can benefit the needs of the family (Moore, 2013). Combat injury can also impact the relationship of the military couple through decreased intimacy and poor communication (Hanley et al., 2013). Balderrama-Durbin et al., (2013) stated that the symptoms of posttraumatic stress disorder contribute to poor relationship functioning. Emotionally Focused Couple Therapy (EFCT) can be particularly helpful with combat veterans in assisting with attachment bonds (Johnson, 2002). Furthermore, issues between a couple can be exacerbated if the service member experiences an injury that can also affect the ability of the couple to effectively parent or make unified family decisions. Developing family resilience is important for families to be able to adapt successfully to changes in the family (Walsh, 2006). Family resilience can be positively affected through the use of family narrative because it allows the family to adapt to the circumstance, make meaning of the circumstance, and develop skills and beliefs to respond to the circumstance in a meaningful way (Saltzman, Pynoos, Lester, Layne, & Beardslee, 2013). Additionally, by incorporating a solution-focused approach (Weiss et al., 2010) social workers can assist families in recognizing their prior successes in having managed past deployments and stressful life events and find ways to empower them through any postdeployment challenges and beyond military life (i.e., military separation, discharge, or retirement).

Finally, the families of service members must also cope with the grief and loss associated with service member serious injury and death. Since the inception OEF/OIF there have been more than 5,600 U.S. casualties along with an alarming rate of service member suicides (Cohen & Mannarino, 2011). The authors commented that most bereaved military children will experience adaptive grief responses, but some may develop "traumatic grief." Traumatic grief, a form of complicated grief in this context, is understood as the child having repeated images of death scenarios, real or imagined (i.e., service member death as a result of combat or by suicide); engaging in revenge fantasies against the enemy; lashing out to others whom the child perceives as not understanding; and avoiding reminders of the deceased. All these may complicate the natural course of the grief experience (Cohen & Mannarino, 2011). Yet another type of loss faced by children is termed "ambiguous loss" (Boss, 2004), which occurs when there is uncertainty regarding the status of a family member. Boss stated that this lack of clarity around loss blocks the grief process, because it prevents the cognitions that are necessary for decision making, relational boundary making, and coping. Examples of ambiguous loss are paradoxical in nature, for instance, when a service member is physically present but psychologically absent, as in the case of a parent having PTSD, or in the case where a parent is psychologically present but physically absent, as in the case of service members who are missing in action or are prisoners of war (Dekel & Monson, 2010). Ambiguous loss can produce feelings of anxiety, worry, sadness, and guilt in children and spouses of military personnel.

Parental combat injury can disrupt the family given that the majority of young children will live away from the injured parent during hospitalization. Young children may also be separated from their primary parent, who may be providing care for the injured parent, which can result in moderate-to-severe emotional difficulties for the young child (Lieberman & Van Horn, 2013). During the time of absence, children can regress in their development, be afraid they, too, will experience significant injury, or engage in magical thinking such as "my daddy will get better if I'm good" (Lieberman & Van Horn, 2013). Parental death can be a greater challenge with very young children because they do not understand the finality of death. Young children may speak of the deceased parent as though there will be a reunion. In these instances, it is important the surviving parent respond in a way that will allow the child to develop a concrete acceptance of death. Allowing the child to speak in a way that indicates hope for a reunion can result in the child's distrust of adults (Lieberman & Van Horn, 2013). These authors noted that using dolls to role-play the process of death (i.e., body stops moving) and to have a funeral can reduce maladaptive reactions and symptoms in young children. Families can also incorporate any religious, spiritual, or cultural beliefs into the role-play of the parent's death. Social workers can assist families with children in this process, as well as in the development of skills to cope with the loss. Kaplow et al. (2013) stated that the effects of a parent's death can be cushioned by the surviving parent's ability to communicate effectively, provide stable routines, and demonstrate high levels of functioning and warmth in day-to-day life. Additionally, social workers who are helping families cope with veteran suicide can refer to Heather Fiske (2008) on engaging clients in difficult conversations about suicide utilizing a solution-focused approach.

Next, we will revisit the Bryce case scenario that was presented earlier in the chapter. We fast forward in time to when Bryce's father, Mike, returns home from deployment and the family is adjusting to the service member's reintegration into family life.

POSTDEPLOYMENT/REINTEGRATION CASE SCENARIO

The family followed the treatment recommendations (including family and individual therapies and military/community resources) that had been provided by Bryce's therapist and were doing quite well. For instance, 3-year old Emma had stopped bed wetting and had reduced episodes of tantrums. Bryce was back in sports and his grades in schools were improving. Bryce was also participating in a school program for military-connected children and had made some new friends. Meanwhile, Alice, the mother, had been attending her own individual therapy and was involved in a bimonthly support program on the military installation for spouses/mothers. Mike had returned from deployment and things at home seemed to be going well for the first month, according to Alice. The children seemed to have reattached quickly to their father upon his return. However, about five weeks into his return home, Mike began to exhibit symptoms of PTSD. He was quick to react and seemed irritable. His sleep was also disturbed by nightmares. Mike seemed "on edge" and the children and Alice were apprehensive about his behaviors, Alice described this as she and the children "walking on eggs." Mike began to assume authority in the household and this created friction between him and Alice because she had finally established routines with the children and had felt that their family and home life were "in order." Mike was now interrupting that order. Bryce began isolating again and refusing to participate in sports; Emma became excessively clingy toward Alice. Bryce's therapist once again saw this as an opportunity to assist the family, this time with adjustment to Mike's homecoming. The first thing the therapist did was ask Mike whether he was willing to be assessed for PTSD at the Navy hospital on base. Mike reluctantly agreed to follow through and attended his own counseling to address symptoms of PTSD. She also recommended couples counseling, specifically EFCT, for Mike and Alice, so that they could realign themselves and present a united front to their children, as well as work on emotionally reconnecting as a couple after this long separation. The therapist continued to work with Bryce on an individual basis and assessed him for secondary stress and utilized Trauma-Focused Cognitive Behavioral Therapy (TF-CBT) as needed (Cohen, Mannarino, & Deblinger, 2006). The therapist also recommended that Mike be included in the family therapy (e.g., CPRT or filial therapy). The therapist did not see any signs that would indicate the occurrence of interpersonal violence or child maltreatment, but did continually assess for these throughout the duration of treatment.

CONCLUSION

It is imperative to recognize that military connected families are resilient given their experiences and unique stressors, such as those outlined in this chapter (e.g., frequent geographic relocations, service member deployments and family separations, and postdeployment adjustment and family crises resulting from posttraumatic stress disorder or other injuries incurred by the service member). Their resilience may be a product of military culture (i.e., perseverance, endurance) that is adopted by the family and/or a byproduct of the demands associated with military life. However, note should be taken that although many military families are highly resilient, there are nonetheless alarming rates of domestic violence, substance abuse, child maltreatment, and service member and veteran suicide. Therefore, social workers intervening with military families should seek to understand the unique aspects of military culture, lifestyle, and demands, while not losing sight of the family strengths and inherent assets that could be used to address maladaptive family functioning and coping. In addition, as a social worker, you will want to recognize the differences among the branches of the U.S. Armed Forces (these are not all the same) and understand the variety of resources that are available and allocated to those active duty families living on or off-base, as well as families associated with the National Guard and Reserve components, given that social workers likely will need to establish resources and provide linkages in those civilian communities (i.e., "building community capacity," please see Huebner et al., 2009). Resources for veterans and their families (after military service) will also need to be found or created, because not all veterans and their dependents are eligible for VA services and not all veterans choose the VA (for a variety of reasons). Furthermore, veterans and their families are transitioning into civilian lives at a time in U.S. history when there are serious economic hardships and lack of employment opportunities. Many of these veterans and/or their dependents will be using the Post 9/11 G. I. Bill benefits to enter into higher education (Coll & Weiss, 2013). Thus, social workers are bound to encounter this segment of the population somewhere along their paths, whether at community agencies, schools, hospitals, the criminal justice system, social service agencies, homeless shelters, or in college counseling centers. Therefore,

it is imperative, now more than ever, to become informed on the needs associated with this population and the existing best practices, in order to provide the most effective services and advocacy efforts.

Key Points to Remember

The continued U.S. military involvement across the globe as a measure to combat terrorism has added unique stressors to military families. A plethora of literature addresses service member injuries such as posttraumatic stress disorder, traumatic brain injury, and other co-morbidities, while also recognizing the impact of deployments and war on military connected families. This chapter summarized the various challenges faced by military families since 9/11.It presented military culture as the contextual background presented evidence-informed clinical interventions to be utilized by social workers. This chapter for civilian social workers was written with the aim of providing culturally responsive services and thereby promoting resilience in military/veteran families as well as in communities.

As noted in the chapter, reactions of military connected children to separation from their deployed parent(s) vary according to age, developmental level, and how the remaining spouse (parent) copes. It is imperative for us to recognize that children from National Guard and Reserve families are especially vulnerable to stress because they are residing in civilian communities, as opposed to near military installations, and do not have easy access to military supports. Moreover, military connected children who have been exposed to 12 years of uncertainty tend to have varying reactions to service member parental injury or death, once again according to age, developmental level, and family dynamics. The long-term effects on children and families exposed to war time stressors (particularly the unique aspects of the Global War on Terrorism with multiple and prolonged combat deployments) remains unknown. However, social workers should keep in mind family resilience models when intervening with military and veteran families and always work within a strengths-based perspective. Finally, in terms of future direction, the authors propose that all social workers be informed and educated on aspects of military culture and the stressors inherent in military family life, because more than likely than not, civilian social workers will be encountering military- and veteran-connected families in community settings (Coll et al., 2012).

FURTHER LEARNING AND RESOURCES

- **Military Child Education Coalition (MCEC)** is a one-stop shop for resources for teachers, parents, & professionals on assisting children and youth with military stressors and school transitions. Additionally, they offer workshops and training for professionals: http://www.militarychild.org
- **School Quest,** is a website geared for military families to provide information on school records and transferring school credits, provided by MCEC: http://schoolquest.org/
- **John Hopkins Military Child Initiative Training** offers a web course for school professionals on understanding military related issues as these impact children and ways to build student resilience: http://www.jhsph.edu/mci/training_course/
- **National Military Family Association**, provides information for military families, resources and toolkits: http://www.nmfa.org
- **Operation: Military Kids** is the U.S. Army's collaborative effort with America's communities to support children and youth impacted by deployment. It provides local resources for community support to enhance well-being: http://www.operationmilitarykids.org
- **The Yellow Ribbon Program** is for National Guard and Reserve Families and provides for benefit information, youth summer camps, community referrals, and activities for children during deployments.
- **Military Impacted Schools Association**, provides a variety of web-based resources: http://www.militaryimpactedschoolsassociation.org
- **Military Family Research Institute at Purdue University** offers publications, resources, news, grant information, and events: http://www.mfri.purdue.edu/
- **The National Child Traumatic Stress Network** provides childhood trauma information and treatment descriptions as well as web-based trainings. General information on the CBITS (school based intervention) can be found here: http://www.nctsnet.org/sites/default/files/assets/pdfs/cbits_general.

- **Trauma Focused CBT,** free web-based training for professionals working with traumatized children from a Cognitive Behavioral therapy perspective and an evidence-informed practice. See: http://tfcbt.musc.edu

References

American Psychiatric Association. (2013)..*Diagnostic and statistical manual of mental disorders, fifth edition.* Washington DC: Author.

Astor, R. A., De Pedro, K. T., Gilreath, T. D., Esqueda, M. C., & Benbenishty, R. (2013). The promotional role of school and community contexts for military students. *Clinical Child Family Psychology Review.* Advance online publication. doi:10.1007/s10567-013-0139-x

Balderrama-Durbin, C., Snyder, D. K., Cigrang, J., Talcott, G. W., Tatum, J., Baker, M., Cassidy, D., . . . Smith Slep, A. M. (2013). Combat disclosure in intimate relationships: Mediating the impact of partner support on posttraumatic stress. *Journal of Family Psychology,* Advance online publication. doi:10/1037/a0033412

Boss, P. (2004). Ambiguous loss research, theory, and practice: Reflections after 9/11. *Journal of Marriage and Family, 66*(3), 551–566.

Bowling, U., Doerman, A., & Sherman, M. (2011). *Operation enduring families: Information and support for Iraq and Afghanistan veterans and their families.* Oklahoma City, OK: Oklahoma City VA Medical Center. Retrieved from http://www.ouhsc.edu/oef/pdf/OEFManual122107.pdf

Bowling, U. B., Sherman, M. D. (2008). Welcoming them home: Supporting service members and their families in navigating the tasks of reintegration, *Professional Psychology: Research and Practice, 39*(4), 451–458.

Building Capacity (2010). *Building capacity to create highly supportive military-connected school districts.* Retrieved from http://buildingcapacity.usc.edu

Burrell, L. M., Adams, G. A., Durand, D. B., & Castro, D. A. (2006). The impact of military lifestyle demands on wellbeing, Army & family outcomes. *Armed Forces & Society 2006, 33,* 43–58.

Chandra A., Lara-Cinisomo S., Jaycox, L. H., Tanielian T., Han B., Burns, R. M., & Ruder T., (2011). *Views from the homefront: The experiences of youth and spouses from military families.* Santa Monica, CA: RAND Corporation

Chawla, N., & Solinas-Saunders, M. (2011). Supporting military parent and child adjustment to deployments and separations with filial therapy. *The American Journal of Family Therapy, 39*(3), 179–192.

Cohen, J. A., & Mannarino, A. P. (2011). Trauma-focused CBT for traumatic grief in military children. *Journal of Contemporary Psychotherapy.* Advance online publication.

Cohen, J. A., Mannarino, A. P., & Deblinger, E. (2006). *Treating trauma and traumatic grief in children and adolescents.* New York, NY: Guilford Press.

Coll, J. E., Weiss, E. L., Draves, P., & Dyer, D. (2012). The impact of military cultural awareness, experience, attitudes, and education on clinician self-efficacy in the treatment of veterans. *Journal of International Continuing Social Work Education, 15*(1), 39–48.

Coll, J. E., & Weiss, E. L. (2013). Transitioning veterans into civilian life. In A. Rubin, E. L. Weiss & J. E. Coll (Eds.), *Handbook of military social work* (pp. 281–297). Hoboken, NJ: John Wiley & Sons.

Cozza, S. J., Holmes, A. K., & Van Ost, S. L. (2013). Family-centered care for military and veteran families affected by combat injury. *Clinical Child Family Psychology Review.* Advance online publication. doi:10.1007/s10567-013-0141-3

Cozza, S. J., & Guimond, J. M. (2010). Working with combat-injured families through the recovery trajectory. In S. MacDermid Wadsworth & D. Riggs (Eds.), *Risk and Resilience in U.S. Military Families* (pp. 259–277). New York, NY: Springer

Daddy Dolls. (n.d.). *About us.* Retrieved from https://www.daddydolls.com/about

Davis, J., Wards, D. B., & Storm, C. (2011). The unsilencing of military wives: Wartime deployment experiences and citizen responsibility. *Journal of Marital & Family Therapy, 37*(1), 51–63. doi:10.1111/j.1752-0606.2009.00154.x

Dekel, R., & Goldblatt, H. (2008). "Is there intergenerational transmission of trauma? The case of combat veterans' children." *American Journal of Orthopsychiatry, 78*(3), 281–289.

Dekel, R., & Monson, C. M. (2010). Military-related post-traumatic stress disorder and family relations: Current knowledge and future directions. *Aggression and Violent Behavior. 15,* 303–309.

Exum, H. A., Coll, J. E., & Weiss, E. L. (2011). *A civilian counselor's primer for counseling veterans* (2nd ed.). Deerpark, NY: Linus Publications.

Figley, C. (1995). Compassion fatigue as secondary traumatic stress disorder: An overview. In C. Figley (Ed.), *Compassion fatigue: Coping with secondary traumatic stress disorder in those who treat the traumatized* (pp. 1–20). New York, NY: Brunner/Mazel.

Fiske, H. (2008). *Hope in action: Solution-focused conversations about suicide.* New York, NY: Routledge.

Fitzsimons, V. M., & Krause-Parello, C. A. (2009). Military children: When parents are deployed overseas. *The Journal of School Nursing, 25*(1), 40–47.

Gibbs, D. A., Martin, S., Kupper, L., & Johnson, R. (2007). Child maltreatment in enlisted soldiers' families during combat-related deployments. *JAMA: Journal of the American Medical Association, 298,* 528–535.

Green, S., Nurius, P. S., Lester, P. (2013). Spouse psychological well-being: A keystone to military family health. *Journal of Human Behavior in the Social Environment, 23*(6), 753–768. doi:10.1080/10911359.2013.795068

Hall, L. K. (2011). The importance of understanding military culture. *Social Work in Health Care, 50*(1), 4–18.

Hanley, K. E., Leifker, F. R., Blandon, A. Y., & Marshal, A. D. (2013). Gender differences in the impact of posttraumatic stress disorder symptoms on community couples' intimacy behaviors. *Journal of Family Psychology, 27*(3), 525–530. doi:10.1037/a0032890

Harnett, C. (2013). Supporting National Guard and Reserve members and their families. In A. Rubin, E. L. Weiss & J. E. Coll (Eds.), *Handbook of military social work* (pp. 335–357). Hoboken, NJ: John Wiley & Sons.

Huebner, A. J., Mancini, J. A., Bowen, G. L., Orthner, D. K. (2009). Shadowed by war: Building community capacity to support military families. *Family relations, 58,* 216–228.

Houppert, K. (2005). *Base crimes: The military has a domestic violence problem.* Foundation for National Progress. Retrieved from http://www.motherjones.com/news/featurex/2005/07/base_crimes.html

Jaycox, L. H., Morse, L. K., Tanielian, T., & Stein, B. D. (2006). *How schools can help students recover from traumatic experiences: A tool kit for supporting long-term recovery.* Santa Monica, CA: RAND Corporation.

Johnson, S. M. (2002). *Emotionally focused couple therapy with trauma survivors: Strengthening attachment bonds.* New York, NY: Guilford Press.

Kaplow, J. B., Layne, C. M., Saltzman, W. R., Cozza, S. J., & Pynoos, R. S. (2013). Using multidimensional grief theory to explore the effects of deployment, reintegration, and death on military youth and families. *Clinical Child Family Psychology Review.* Advance online publication. doi:10/1007/s10567-013-0143-1

Leskin, G. A., Garcia, E., D'Amico, J., Mogil, C. E., & Lester, P. E. (2013). Family-centered programs and interventions for military children and youth. In A. Rubin, E. L. Weiss, & J. E. Coll (Eds.), *Handbook of military social work* (pp. 427–441). Hoboken, NJ: John Wiley & Sons.

Lieberman, A. F., & Van Horn, P. (2013). Infants and young children in military families: A conceptual model for intervention. *Clinical Child Family Psychology Review.* Advance online publication. doi:10.1007/s10567-013-0140-4

Mansfield, A. J., Kaufman, J. S., Engel, C. C., & Gaynes, B. (2011). Deployment and mental health diagnoses among children of U.S. Army personnel. *Archives of Pediatric Adolescent Medicine.* Advance online publication. doi:10.1001/archpediatrics.2011.123

Matthieu, M. M., & Swensen, A. B. (2013). The stress process model for supporting long-term family caregiving. In A. Rubin, E. L. Weiss, & J. E. Coll (Eds.), *Handbook of military social work* (pp. 409–426). Hoboken, NJ: John Wiley & Sons.

Matthews-Juarez, P., Juarez, P. D., & Faulkner, R. T. (2013). Social media and military families: A perspective. *Journal of Human Behavior in the Social Environment, 23*(6), 769–776. doi:10.1080/10911359.2013.795073

McCubbin, H. I., & Patterson, J. M. (1983). The family stress process: The double ABCX model of adjustment and adaptation. *Marriage and Family Review, 6*(7), 7–37.

Milburn, N. G., & Lightfoot, M. (2013). Adolescents in wartime U.S. military families: A developmental perspective on challenges and resources. *Clinical Child Family Psychology Review.* Advance online publication. doi:10/1007/s10567-013-0144-0

Moore, M. (2013). Mild traumatic brain injury: Implications for social work research and practice with civilian and military populations. *Social Work in Health Care, 52*(5), 498–518. doi:10.1080/00981389.2012.714447

Nelson, B. S., & Wright, D. W. (1996). Understanding and treating post-traumatic stress disorder symptoms in female partners of veterans with PTSD. *Journal of Marital and Family Therapy, 22*(4), 455–467.

Office of the Deputy Under Secretary of Defense. (2008). *2008 Demographics: Profile of the military community.* Washington, DC: Department of Defense (Military Community and Family Policy).

Paley, B., Lester, P., & Mogil, C. (2013). Family systems and ecological perspectives on the impact of deployment on military families. *Clinical Child Family Psychology Review.* Advance online publication. doi:10/1007/s10567-013-0138-y

Perlick, D. A., Straits-Troster, K., Dyck, D. G., Norell, D. M., Strauss, J. L., Henderson, C.,. . . Cristinan, A. (2011). Multifamily group treatment for veterans with traumatic brain injury. *Professional Psychology: Research and Practice, 42*(1), 70–78.

Pincus, S. H., House, R., Christensen, J., & Adler, L. E. (2001). The emotional cycle of deployment: A military family perspective. *U. S. Army Medical Department Journal, 415/6,* 15–23.

Porter, A. O. (2013). An examination of a case study with a military family and its involvement with child protective services. *Journal of Human Behavior in the Social Environment, 23*(6), 777–788. doi:10.1080/10911359.2013.795078

Rosenheck, R., & Fontana, A. (1998).Transgenerational effects of abusive violence on the children of Vietnam combat veterans. *Journal of Traumatic Stress, 11*(4), 731–741.

Saltzman, W. R., Pynoos, R. S., Lester, P., Layne, C. M., & Beardslee, W. R. (2013). Enhancing family resilience through family narrative co-construction. *Clinical Child Family Psychology Review.* Advance online publication. doi:10.1007/s10567-013-0142-2

Savitsky, L., Illingworth, M., & DuLaney, M. (2009). Civilian social work: Serving the military and veteran populations. *Social Work, 54*(4), 327–339.

Stafford, E. M., & Grady, B. A. (2003). Military family support. *Pediatric Annals, 32*(2), 110–115.

Sesame Street Workshop. (2006). *Talk, listen, connect: Helping families through military deployments.* Retrieved from http://www.sesamestreet.org/parents/topicsandactivities/toolkits/tlc

Taft, C. T., Vogt, D. S., Marshall, A. D., Panuzio, J., & Niles, B. L. (2007). Aggression among combat veterans: Relationships with combat exposure and symptoms of posttraumatic stress disorder, dysphoria, and anxiety. *Journal of Traumatic Stress, 20,* 135–145.

Tanielian, T., & Jaycox, L. (2008). *Invisible wounds of war: Psychological and cognitive injuries, their consequences and services to assist recovery.* Santa Monica, CA: RAND.

Thomsen, C. J., Rabenhorst, M. M., McCarthy, R. J., Milner, J. S., Travis, W. J., Foster, R. E., & Copeland, C. W. (2013). Child maltreatment before and after combat-related deployment among active-duty United States Air Force maltreating parents. *Psychology of Violence.* Advance online publication. doi:10.1037/a0031766

UnitedThrough Reading. (2013). *Circle of communication.* Retrieved from http://www.unitedthroughreading.org/military-program/how-it-works/

U.S. Army Medical Department, Mental Health Advisory Team (MHATV). (2008, March). *Army report on mental health of soldiers in Afghanistan and Iraq.* Retrieved from www.armymedicine.army.mil/news/releases/20080306mhatv.cfm

U.S. Department of Defense. (2011). *Strengthening our military families: Meeting America's commitment.* Retrieved from http://www.defense.gov/home/features/2011/0111_initiative/strengthening_our_military_january_2011.pdf

U.S. Department of Defense Demographics. (2009). *A profile of the military community.* Retrieved from http://www.militaryhomefront.dod.mil/

Walsh, F. (2006). *Strengthening family resilience* (2nd ed.). New York, NY: Guildford Press.

Weins, T. W., & Boss, P. (2006). Maintaining family resilience before, during, and after military separation. In C. A. Castro, A. B. Adler, & C. A. Britt (Eds.), *Military life: The psychology of serving in peace and combat* (Vol. 3) (pp. 13–38). Bridgeport, CT: Praeger Security International.

Weiss, E. L., & Coll, J. E. (2013). Children & youth impacted by military service: A school-based perspective. In C. Franklin, M. B. Harris & P. Allen-Mears (Eds.), *The school services source-book: A guide for school based professionals* (2nd ed.) (pp. 695–706). New York, NY: Oxford University Press.

Weiss, E. L., Coll, J. E., & Metal, M. (2011). The influence of military culture and Veteran worldviews on mental health treatment: Implications for Veteran help-seeking and wellness. *International Journal of Health, Wellness & Society, 1*(2), 75–86.

Weiss, E. L., Coll, J. E., Gebauer, J., Smiley, K., & Carrillo, E. (2010). The military genogram: A solution-focused approach for resiliency building in service members and their families. *The Family Journal: Counseling for Couples and Families 18*(4), 395–406.

Weiss, E. L., DeBraber, T., Santoyo, A., & Creager, T. (2013). Theory and practice with military couples and families. In A. Rubin, E. L. Weiss & J. E. Coll (Eds.). *Handbook of military social work* (pp. 467–492). Hoboken, NJ: John Wiley & Sons.

Williams, B. (2013). Supporting middle school students whose parents are deployed: Challenges and strategies for schools. *The Clearing House: A Journal of Educational Strategies, Issues and Ideas, 86*(4), 128–135. doi:10.1080/00098655.2013.782849

Windle, M. A. (1992). A longitudinal study of stress buffering for adolescent problem behaviors. *Developmental Psychology, 28*(3), 522–530.

Zero to Three. (2009). *Honoring our babies and toddlers: Supporting young children affected by a military parent's deployment, injury, or death.* Retrieved from http://www.zerotothree.org/about-us/funded-projects/military-families/hbt-2.pdf

63 Preventing Antisocial and Aggressive Behavior in Childhood

Traci L. Wike, Jilan Li, & Mark W. Fraser

INTRODUCTION

Aggressive behavior in children has long concerned practitioners, researchers, and policy makers because of its strong relationship to antisocial and violent behaviors in adolescence and adulthood. Recent high-profile bullying incidents and school shootings have catalyzed efforts to develop interventions that address the factors leading to aggressive behavior in children. For example, in an effort to reduce bullying and aggression in school-aged children, many states have created policies mandating schools to provide violence prevention programming. Moreover, current policies emphasize the use of evidence-based interventions that have been shown to be effective toward reducing aggressive behavior and promoting the prevention of school and community violence.

Social and character development programs represent one approach to violence prevention designed to bolster children's social and emotional development. Implemented in school and community contexts, these programs are based on the rationale that violence and aggression can be prevented by strengthening protective factors (e.g., social-emotional skills) that reduce risk (e.g., peer rejection). Although theoretical frameworks vary widely among the various programs, the more promising of these programs use a social-cognitive approach to strengthen children's abilities to solve social problems (see Conner & Fraser, 2011; Domitrovich, Cortes, & Greenberg, 2007; Fraser et al., 2005; Frey, Nolen, Van Schoiack, Edstrom, & Hirschstein, 2005; Greenberg, Kusche, Cook, & Quamma, 1995; Thompson, Macy, & Fraser, 2011).

In particular, the *Making Choices* program (Fraser et al., 2005) is an evidence-based social and character development program that uses a social-cognitive approach to prevent aggressive behavior in school-aged children. This chapter presents a comprehensive review of the *Making Choices* intervention, including the program's theoretical framework, evidence of the program's effectiveness, and a discussion of the implications of the intervention for increasing positive outcomes among children. *Making Choices* is a prevention-based intervention aimed at building children's social competence by increasing their social problem-solving skills. Rooted in a social-cognitive perspective, *Making Choices* uses an activity-based curriculum to strengthen children's social information-processing skills, and thereby, increase positive social behavior and reduce aggressive behavior. The chapter first presents a brief review of the literature on aggressive and antisocial behavior and the effects of these behaviors on children's developmental outcomes. Next, using a risk and resiliency perspective (Fraser, 2004), we describe the design of prevention interventions. The risk and resiliency framework is a key concept in prevention science. We follow with a discussion of information on the growth of social-emotional programs and the social-cognitive approach in prevention interventions. We then review the design and theoretical framework of the *Making Choices* program, and provide a comprehensive review of findings from evaluation studies of the program. The chapter concludes with a discussion of the implications of *Making Choices* for social work practice.

DEVELOPMENTAL CASCADES FROM AGGRESSIVE BEHAVIOR TO NEGATIVE OUTCOMES

Aggression in childhood refers to a persistent pattern of behaviors that inflicts or threatens harm. Aggressive behaviors can manifest in a variety of forms, ranging from overt conflict (e.g., physical hitting, verbal taunting) to covert subterfuge, including social exclusion and manipulation of friendships. Regardless of the form, aggression can result in problematic consequences for perpetrators and victims (Coie, Lochman, Terry, & Hyman, 1992; Parker & Asher, 1987). From a developmental perspective, some aggressive behavior appears normative in childhood. However, children who consistently use aggression to negotiate social situations are likely to learn to rely on aggressive strategies as their primary or only method of dealing with interpersonal conflict.

Aggressive behavior in childhood is associated with a variety of negative life course outcomes. In early adolescence, these include rejection by peers, victimization by bullies, and low academic achievement (Dodge & Pettit, 2003; Nansel et al., 2004; Werner & Crick, 2004). Children who exhibit aggression are likely to experience problems as adolescents and adults with substance use, relationship violence, and delinquency (Brame, Nagine, & Tremblay, 2001; Dodge & Pettit, 2003; Moffitt, 1993; Moffitt & Caspi, 2001; Prinstein & La Greca, 2004; Tremblay et al., 2004). In addition, aggressive behaviors that meet diagnostic criteria for mental health disorders such as conduct disorder or oppositional defiant disorder have been shown to predict long-term negative consequences, including court involvement (Williams, Ayers, & Arthur, 1997).

Although physical and social forms of aggression can be equally problematic, research has shown that children who exhibit physical, overt forms of aggression have higher levels of externalizing problems (i.e., conduct problems) and lower-quality peer relationships (Card, Stucky, Sawalani, & Little, 2008). In contrast, the same research found that social aggression was predictive of internalizing problems (e.g., depression, anxiety) (Card et al.). An earlier longitudinal study found that social aggression in third grade students uniquely contributed to social and psychological maladjustment in subsequent grades (Crick, Ostrov, & Werner, 2006).

Children who are victims of bullying report difficulty in social relationships, and they are more likely than nonbullied children to report internalizing problems, such as depression and anxiety (Nansel et al., 2004). Experiences of peer victimization also increase the likelihood of a child developing aggressive behaviors and becoming a perpetrator of bullying and aggression (Dodge et al., 2003; Miller-Johnson et al., 2002). Research has shown high correlations between physical and social forms of aggression (Card et al., 2008), indicating that children do not choose one aggressive strategy to the exclusion of others. Evidence suggests that as children mature from early childhood to middle and late childhood, their problem-solving strategies become more sophisticated, involving less use of physical aggression and greater use of social manipulation, including indirect aggression (Cote, Vaillancourt, Barker, Nagin, & Tremblay, 2007; Murray-Close, Ostrov, & Crick, 2007; Xie, Farmer, & Cairns, 2003).

From the perspective of ecological theory, a child's aggressive behavior is understood as strongly influenced by interactions and relationships in the family, school, and neighborhood (Bronfenbrenner, 1986). The influence of each domain is further explained by the risk and resilience perspective (Fraser, 2004), which argues that the risk and protective factors that influence aggression can exist simultaneously in one or more of these domains. The evidence is clear that no single risk pathway exists for aggression. Rather, aggression appears to be the result of a combination of risk factors (over the course of development) with interactions (across multiple domains) that influence life course trajectories (Masten & Cicchetti, 2010).

These patterns of risk, also called *developmental cascades*, refer to a process in which functioning in one domain affects functioning in another domain, creating a cascade of effects that lead to aggressive behavior (Masten et al., 2005). For example, difficulty controlling emotions is an individual-level risk factor that can lead to disruptive classroom behavior and problems with peers (school- and peer-domain risk factors). In turn, these school- and peer-level experiences can influence further displays of aggressive behavior, leading to additional social and academic difficulties.

THE PROMISE OF EARLY INTERVENTION

To disrupt the developmental cascades leading to aggression, social interventions must target specific risk factors that are malleable to change. Research has identified peer rejection as a keystone risk factor and intervention target, because peer rejection is a robust predictor of aggressive behavior. Therefore, researchers have focused on designing interventions to help children develop social-emotional skills and become more successful in peer relationships. Specifically, such interventions focus on both enhancing children's abilities to solve social problems and on strengthening basic skills in regulating emotions. By teaching children social-emotional skills, the interventions help children develop social competence and positive peer relationships, which

in turn, reduce risks for aggressive behavior. To reach this goal, two types of social-emotional skills interventions have been developed: universal approaches and selective approaches (Wilson & Lipsey, 2007).

As the term *universal* implies, universal interventions are delivered to all children in a given setting, regardless of an individual child's level of risk. Conversely, selective prevention approaches are implemented with only those children who have been identified as at-risk of the targeted outcome (e.g., aggressive behavior). Universal prevention approaches are often used in school and community-based interventions because of the potential benefits for all children. Delivering an intervention to all children eliminates the potential for negative effects such as labeling children (i.e., singling out from peers) selected for a program because of their risk status. Universal prevention minimizes the potential for *iatrogenic effects* that can reinforce behaviors, such as peer rejection or aggression, when children are placed together based on their high-risk behavior (Dishion, McCord, & Poulin, 1999).

Social-emotional training programs can be designed as interventions with a single element or multiple elements. A multiple-element program requires a comprehensive approach that focuses on correlated risk factors occurring across multiple environmental domains. For example, a multi-element program might include the delivery of a classroom curriculum, a complementary parent-training program, and a supporting school-wide campaign. In contrast, single-element programs typically target one risk factor and implement one primary intervention strategy; for example, a classroom-based violence prevention curriculum for students that focuses on managing peer conflict. Especially in the context of school-based programs, single-element designs are often economical choices because this type of intervention tends to be brief and to have a lower implementation burden.

A recent meta-analysis (Wilson & Lipsey, 2007) explored the effectiveness of school-based interventions in reducing aggressive and disruptive behaviors. The researchers found the more effective programs used cognitively oriented approaches and social skills training. Indeed, a variety of universal prevention interventions have demonstrated efficacy in increasing positive outcomes among children at risk for aggressive behavior by targeting the social-cognitive risk mechanisms contributing to aggressive behavior, such as deficits in social information processing skills and regulating emotions (Domitrovich et al., 2007; Farrell, Meyer, & White, 2001; Fraser et al., 2005; Frey et al., 2005; Greenberg et al., 1995; Holsen, Smith, & Frey, 2008). One of the programs with preliminary evidence of effectiveness is the *Making Choices* (Fraser, Nash, Galinsky, & Darwin, 2001) program.

THE *MAKING CHOICES* PROGRAM

Making Choices is a prevention intervention that strengthens the social problem-solving skills of elementary-school aged children. Using a social-cognitive approach, *Making Choices* promotes social competence and reduces aggressive behavior by building skills in processing social information and regulating emotions (Fraser et al., 2001; Fraser et al., 2005; Nash, Fraser, Galinsky, & Kupper, 2003). As a universal, prevention intervention, *Making Choices* is made up of lessons designed for children in kindergarten through fifth grade.

Though the intervention is focused on improving the skills of children at risk for aggression, it proposes to improve social skills and social problem-solving for all children. The classroom curriculum is additive, meaning that topics in the lessons are linked to the key developmental tasks of each grade level. For example, the first and second grade curricula include lessons on recognizing feelings and understanding emotions. The third grade curriculum builds on the first and second grade lessons by adding a full problem-solving sequence. Emotion regulation is integrated at the fourth grade level and the fifth grade curriculum focuses on instances of social aggression and bullying behaviors. The program is designed for delivery in a group setting, and can be implemented in school-based settings or community-based contexts (Fraser et al., 2001; Fraser, Day, Galinsky, Hodges, & Smokowski, 2004; Smokowski, Fraser, Day, Galinsky, & Bacallao, 2004).

Making Choices is guided by the social information processing (SIP) framework (Crick & Dodge, 1994), but it is also informed by social learning theory. SIP theory holds that a child formulates a behavioral response to a social situation by processing information in five overlapping steps. These steps are largely cognitive in nature, but emotional development is also integrated in the process (for reviews, see Crick & Dodge, 1994, 1996; Dodge, 2006). The steps include:

- Step 1, encoding external and internal cues
- Step 2, interpreting and developing a cognitive representation of cues
- Step 3, clarifying and selecting a social goal
- Step 4, accessing and constructing alternative responses related to goals
- Step 5, making a response decision.

Making Choices is designed to strengthen SIP skills and alter skills patterns that lead to aggressive behavior. Figure 63.1 depicts the conceptual model of *Making Choices* that is based on the SIP framework. The *Making Choices* curriculum is divided into seven units, each with multiple lessons, which are sequenced to build competency in regulating emotions and processing social information. The first unit teaches children how to recognize their feelings and the feelings of others. It uses role-play and story-based activities focused on regulating emotions. See Figures 63.2 and 63.3 for a sample lesson plan and activity for Unit 1.

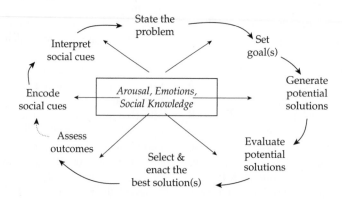

Figure 63.1 *Making Choices* Intervention Conceptual Model.

Whole Class

Small Group

Figure 63.2 Sample lesson—lesson plan.

Activity I   **Feelings Faces**

Sad, Sorrowful, Unhappy	Happy, Excited, Ecstatic
Relaxed, Calm, Peaceful	Frightened, Scared, Upset

Figure 63.3 Sample lesson-activity.

Units 2 through 6 address each of the five cognitive steps of the SIP model. Unit 2 teaches children how to assess information in a social situation—that is, "search for the clues of what is happening" in a social situation. Unit 3 helps children understand intentions behind behaviors. Unit 4 centers on how to set positive goals for developing and maintaining friendships. Unit 5 focuses on constructing a choice of possible behavioral responses. Unit 6 teaches children how to select a behavior response by first assessing the consequences of their response. Unit 7 teaches children how to enact their chosen behavioral response (Fraser et al., 2005). Additional sample lessons are available at http://ssw.unc.edu/jif/makingchoices/.

The *Making Choices* curriculum incorporates a rich array of age-appropriate exercises and activities that provide opportunities for children to develop SIP skills. The experiential activities focus on ways to think positively about social situations, how to formulate prosocial goals, and action steps to achieve prosocial goals. By strengthening skills in regulating emotions and by enhancing SIP skills, *Making Choices* is designed to build competency in working with others in a collaborative manner. It focuses on establishing and maintaining friendships with peers and authority figures. The program is adaptable for use with different ages, ranging from children in early elementary through early middle-school grades. It can be used in school, community, and agency settings. Sessions can be facilitated by teachers, school counselors, social workers, or psychologists. The *Making Choices* manual fully articulates the intervention content and contains copy-ready materials for each activity. Although designed for children in the United States, *Making Choices* can be adapted for children of different cultures. Recently, the manual was adapted and translated for children in China and Romania.

Findings from Evaluation Studies of *Making Choices*

Although *Making Choices* is appropriate for use in a variety of settings, most evaluation studies of the program have been conducted in school settings. In an early pilot test of *Making Choices*, Nash et al. (2003) examined the effects of three units—encoding social and environmental cues, interpreting cues and intentions, and setting relational goals—with a sample of 70 sixth-grade students. Positive program effects were found for skills in encoding cues and for skills in distinguishing prosocial goals. A large-scale test evaluating and comparing the program effects of *Making Choices* and an augmented program, *Making Choices Plus* (i.e., the core *Making Choices* intervention with added activities for teachers and parents) found significant effects for social competence, social contact, social aggression, overt aggression, encoding, and goal formulation. Broader effects were found for children in the *Making Choices Plus* classroom: cognitive concentration, social competence, social contact, social aggression, overt aggression, encoding, hostile attribution, goal formulation, and response decision (Fraser et al., 2005). The evaluation of program effects at 6-month follow-up found positive effects for the *Making*

Choices and the *Making Choices Plus* conditions on the children's overt aggression, physical aggression, and social aggression. Moreover, the findings indicated that *Making Choices Plus* did not yield significantly different gains than *Making Choices* (Fraser, Lee, Kupper, & Day, 2010).

A recent person-centered analysis grouped children into risk-based profiles and examined changes in group membership over time in relation to receiving the intervention. As compared with high-risk children in comparison cohorts, a greater proportion of children in intervention cohorts who were considered at high risk before the intervention had moved to lower-risk groups at the post-test data follow-up. At the same time, low-risk children in the intervention cohorts tended to remain at lower risk whereas a large proportion of low-risk children in the comparison cohorts moved to higher risk groups by post-test (Fraser, Thompson, Day, & Macy, in press). Additional evaluations of *Making Choices* have produced similar findings to the previous studies, with children receiving the intervention showing increased SIP skills (encoding, response selection, and regulation of emotions) (Fraser et al., 2009; Terzian, 2007), decreased overt aggression, relational aggression, and hostile attributions (Fraser et al., 2009), and increased prosocial behavior and social competence (Fraser et al., 2009). Although *Making Choices* was originally designed for elementary-school aged children, results from an evaluation of a preschool adaptation of *Making Choices* (Conner & Fraser, 2011) showed positive effects for children on academic competence, social competence, depression, and aggressive behavior.

Findings from the various evaluation studies of *Making Choices* are summarized in Table 63.1. These findings provide preliminary evidence supporting the effectiveness of *Making Choices*. When implemented with fidelity, the program appears to strengthen SIP skills and reduce aggressive behavior. Moreover, effects appear to endure into the postintervention period (Fraser et al., 2010) and are strengthened by supplemental or "booster shot" training (Fraser et al., 2009).

Implications of *Making Choices* Findings for Social Work Practice

Child development is influenced by a variety of biological, psychological, and environmental factors. A growing body of evidence has shown the initiation of aggressive behavior during childhood is a complex function of various risk factors

at the level of the individual child (e.g., poor social cognitive skills; Crick & Dodge, 1994), the family (e.g., harsh parenting; Eddy, Leve, & Fagot, 2001), the neighborhood (e.g., neighborhood disorganization; Brendgen et al., 2008), and the school (e.g., school violence; Dodge & Pettit, 2003). Among these risk factors, researchers have found that both a child's lack of skill in regulating emotions and a lack of skill in processing social information are important mediators of aggressive behavior (Bandura, 1989; Dodge, 1980, 2006; Huesmann, 1988; Lengua, 2003; Zins, Weissberg, Wang, & Walberg, 2004). Moreover, *recent findings have suggested the social-emotional skills developed in childhood are as powerful as academic achievement in predicting socioeconomic success in adulthood* (Borghans, Duckworth, Heckman, & Weel, 2008; Heckman, Stixrud, & Urzua, 2006; Heckman & Kautz, 2012). Interventions that target core behavior patterns in childhood appear to be effective in promoting future positive outcomes in adulthood (Heckman, 2008).

Guided primarily by SIP theory, *Making Choices* is aimed at altering social cognitive patterns that lead to conduct problems in childhood and early adolescence. Findings from evaluation studies of *Making Choices* suggest that SIP-based interventions hold the potential to promote social competence and reduce aggressive behavior. Other findings have suggested that boys may benefit more than girls from the *Making Choices* intervention (Terzian, 2007), indicating that program content might be strengthened by addressing gender-specific risk factors.

Although initial results are encouraging, two limitations of these evaluations must be mentioned. First, aside from its test in conjunction with the *Strong Families* program, evaluations of *Making Choices* have been conducted in school or preschool settings. Replications in different settings such as community and agency settings are warranted. One such replication is currently underway in the People's Republic of China, where SIP training is being provided through weekend activity programs for children at neighborhood centers. Second, although child reports and parent reports were available in many of the evaluation studies, most of the data analyses used child assessments of SIP skills and teacher reports of behavioral outcomes. Because children are likely to behave differently when interacting with their parents and others outside school, it is important to determine whether program effects generalize from school to other settings.

TABLE 63.1 Evaluation Studies of *Making Choices*

Evaluation Studies	Design	Sample	Program Component, Outcomes Assessed, and Overall Effects

Study 1
(Nash, Fraser, Galinsky, & Kupper, 2003)
	Two group, controlled trial	Sixth-grade classrooms (N = 181; children 12 years of age)	**Making Choices Unit 2, Unit 3, and Unit 4**
			No significant effects by treatment group
			Within the Intervention condition, a pre–post comparison of SIP skills:
			  Encoding skills ***
			  Interpreting cues +
			  Intention attributions **

Study 2
(Fraser, Day, Galinsky, Hodges, & Smokowski, 2004)
	Two-group, randomized controlled trial	Eleven after-school programs (N = 115; children 6 to 12 years of age)	**Making Choices & Strong Families**
			Teacher ratings of:
			  Prosocial behavior **
			  Emotional regulation *
			  Social contact *
			
			  Cognitive concentration **
			  Relational aggression *
			  Authority acceptance

Study 3
(Smokowski, Fraser, Day, Galinsky, & Bacallao, 2004)
	Two-group, cluster-randomized controlled trial	Four third-grade classrooms (N = 101; children 8 years of age)	**Making Choices**
			Teacher ratings of:
			  Social competence
			  Social contact **
			  Cognitive concentration *
			
			  Overt aggression *
			  Peer acceptance **

Study 4
(Conner & Fraser, 2011)
	Two-group, mixed randomized control trial—students in two preschools were randomized at school level; students in the other two schools were randomized at individual level	Four preschools (N = 67; children 3–4 years of age)	**Making Choices & Strong Families**
			Assessments of:
			  Academic competence ***
			  Social Competence ***
			  Peer acceptance ***
			  Depression/anxiety *
			  Aggression/hostility ***
			
			  Child behavior ***
			  School performance ***
			  Child relationship w/peers ***
			  Child relationship w/caregiver***
			
			Parent reports of:
			  Parenting skills +
			  Parent bonding ***
			  Parent supervision ***
			
			  Communication w/ child ***
			  Parent developmental expectations ***

(Continued)

TABLE 63.1 Continued

Evaluation Studies	Design	Sample	Program Component, Outcomes Assessed, and Overall Effects	Making Choices	Making Choices Plus
Study 5a (Fraser et al., 2005)	Three-group, sequential cohort control design	Three successive cohorts of third graders in two schools (N = 548; children 8 years of age) The first cohort received a routine health curriculum; the second cohort received *Making Choices*; the third cohort received *Making Choices Plus*.	Teacher ratings of:		
			Cognitive concentration	*	
			Social contact	*	+
			Authority acceptance		*
			Social competence	*	*
			Overt aggression	*	*
			Social aggression	*	**
			SIP skills assessment:		
			Encoding cues	***	***
			Attributing hostile intent		***
			Formulating prosocial goals	*	***
			Making a response decision		***
Study 5b Six-month follow-up (Fraser, Lee, Kupper, & Day, 2011)	Six-month follow-up of Study 5a	Fourth grade teachers were surveyed six months after the intervention (N = 448) for the routine services cohort and the two intervention cohorts.	Teacher follow-up ratings:		
			Overt aggression	**	**
			Physical aggression	*	*
			Social aggression	*	*
			Cognitive concentration		
			Social competence		
			Social engagement		
Study 5c (Terzian, 2007)	Three-group, sequential cohort design with lagged treatment withdrawal control	Three cohorts of third graders (N = 480)	Teacher ratings of:		
			Emotional regulation	***	***
			Overt aggression	*	
			SIP skills assessment of:		
			Encoding	*	
			Hostile attribution		**
			Goal clarification **		
			Response selection	*	**

CONCLUSION

As a prevention strategy focused on strengthening children's social-emotional skills, *Making Choices* shows promise for interrupting developmental cascades that lead to aggressive behavior. Interventions such as *Making Choices* boost social development, which, research suggests, may be as important as academic achievement in promoting positive life course outcomes (Heckman & Kautz, 2012; Heckman, Stixrud, & Urzua, 2006). As a profession concerned with improving the mental, physical, and social health of children, social work can play a prominent role in providing social-emotional skills training. Social work training in child development and a person-in-environment perspective provides a strong conceptual foundation for implementing skills training programs. In addition, social workers are skilled in communication and groupwork. As a groupwork intervention, *Making Choices* is readily available to social workers for use in school or agency settings. The program offers social workers an evidence-based prevention strategy for building children's social problem-solving skills and promoting positive youth development.

WEBSITE

www.ssw.unc.edu/jif/makingchoices/

References

Bandura, A. (1989). Human agency in social cognitive theory. *American Psychologist, 44,* 1175–1184. doi:10.1037//0003-066X.44.9.1175

Borghans, L., Duckworth, A. L., Heckman, J. J., & Weel, B. T. (2008). *The economics and psychology of personality traits.* Retrieved from http://www.econstor.eu/bitstream/10419/34948/1/559866917.pdf

Brame, B., Nagine, D. S., & Tremblay, R. E. (2001). Developmental trajectories of physical aggression from school entry to late adolescence. *Journal of Child Psychology and Psychiatry, 42,* 503–512. doi:10.1111/1469-7610.00744

Brendgen, M., Boivin, M., Vitaro, F., Bukowski, W. M., Dionne, G., Tremblay, R. E., & Perusse, D. (2008). Linkages between children's and their friends' social and physical aggression: Evidence for a gene-environment interaction? *Child Development, 79,* 13–29. doi:10.1111/j.1467-8624.2007.01108.x

Bronfenbrenner, U. (1986). Ecological systems theory. In R. Vasta (Ed.), *Annals of child development* (pp. 187–249). New York, NY: JAI Press.

Card, N. A., Stucky, B. D., Sawalani, G. M., & Little, T. D. (2008). Direct and indirect aggression during childhood and adolescence: A meta-analytic review of gender differences, intercorrelations, and relations to maladjustment. *Child Development, 79,* 1185–1229. doi:10.1111/j.1467-8624.2008.01184.x

Coie, J. D., Lochman, J. E., Terry, R., & Hyman, C. (1992). Predicting early adolescent disorder from childhood aggression and peer rejection. *Journal of Consulting and Clinical Psychology, 60,* 783–792. doi:10.1037/0022-006X.60.5.783

Conner, N. W., & Fraser, M. W. (2011). Preschool social-emotional skills training: A controlled pilot test of the Making Choices and Strong Families programs. *Research on Social Work Practice, 21,* 699–711. doi:10.1177/1049731511408115

Cote, S. M., Vaillancourt, T., Barker, E. D., Nagin, D., & Tremblay, R. E. (2007). The joint development of physical and indirect aggression: Predictors of continuity and change during childhood. *Development and Psychopathology, 19,* 37–55. doi:10.10170S0954579407070034

Crick, N. R., & Dodge, K. A. (1994). A review and reformulation of social information-processing mechanisms in children's social adjustment. *Psychological Bulletin, 115,* 74–101. doi:10.1037/0033-2909.115.1.74

Crick, N. R., & Dodge, K. A. (1996). Social information processing mechanisms in reactive and proactive aggression. *Child Development, 67,* 993–1002. doi:10.2307/1131875

Crick, N. R., Ostrov, J. M., & Werner, N. E. (2006). A longitudinal study of relational aggression, physical aggression, and children's social-psychological adjustment. *Journal of Abnormal Child Psychology, 34,* 131–142. doi:10.1007/s10802-005-9009-4

Dishion, T. J., McCord, J., & Poulin, F. (1999). When interventions harm: Peer groups and problem behavior. *American Psychologist, 54,* 755–764. doi:10.1037/0003-066X.54.9.755

Dodge, K. A. (1980). Social cognition and children's aggressive behavior. *Child Development, 51,* 162–170. doi:10.2307/1129603

Dodge, K. A. (2006). Translational science in action: Hostile attributional style and the development of aggressive behavior problems. *Development and Psychopathology, 18,* 791–814. doi:10.1017/S0954579406060391

Dodge, K. A., & Pettit, G. S. (2003). A biopsychosocial model of the development of chronic conduct problems in adolescence. *Developmental Psychology, 39,* 349–371. doi:10.1037/0012-1649.39.2.349

Dodge, K. A., Lansford, J. E., Salzer Burks, V., Bates, J. E., Pettit, G. S., Fontaine, R., & Price, J. M. (2003). Peer rejection and social information-processing factors in the development of aggressive behavior problems in children. *Child Development, 74,* 374–393. doi:10.1111/1467-8624.7402004

Domitrovich, C. E., Cortes, R. C., & Greenberg, M. T. (2007). Improving young children's social and emotional competence: A randomized trial of the preschool "PATHS" curriculum. *Journal of Primary Prevention, 28*(2), 67–91. doi:10.1007/s10935-007-0081-0

Eddy, J. M., Leve, L. D., & Fagot, B. I. (2001). Coercive family processes: A replication and extension of Patterson's coercion model. *Aggressive Behavior, 27,* 14–25. doi:10.1002/1098-2337(20010101/31)27:114::AID-AB23.0.CO;2-2

Farrell, A. D., Meyer, A., & White, K. (2001). Evaluation of Responding in Peaceful and Positive Ways (RIPP), a school-based prevention program for reducing violence among adolescents: A randomized clinical trial. *Journal of Clinical Child Psychology, 30,* 451–463. doi:10.1207/S15374424JCCP3004_02

Fraser, M. W., Nash, J. K., Galinsky, M. J., & Darwin, K. E. (2001). *Making Choices: Social problem-solving skills for children.* Washington, DC: NASW Press.

Fraser, M. W. (Ed.). (2004). *Risk and resilience in childhood: An ecological perspective.* Washington, DC: NASW Press.

Fraser, M. W., Day, S. H., Galinsky, M. J., Hodges, V. G., & Smokowski, P. R. (2004). Conduct problems and peer rejection in childhood: A randomized trial of the Making Choices and Strong Families programs. *Research on Social Work Practice, 14,* 313–324. doi:10.1177/1049731503257884

Fraser, M. W., Galinsky, M. J., Smokowski, P. R., Day, S. H., Terzian, M. A., Rose, R. A., & Guo, S. Y. (2005). Social information-processing skills training to promote social competence and prevent aggressive behavior in the third grade. *Journal of Consulting and Clinical Psychology, 73,* 1045–1055. doi:10.1037/0022-006X.73.6.1045

Fraser, M. W., Guo, S. Y., Ellis, A. R., Day, S. H., Li, J. L., Wike, T. L., & Farmer, T. W. (2009). *Social and character development in elementary school: Effects from a controlled trial.* (Report to Institute of Education Sciences and the Centers for Disease Control and Prevention). Retrieved from http://sowkweb.usc.edu/download/research/social-and-character-development-elementary-school.pdf

Fraser, M. W, Lee, J-S., Kupper, L. L., & Day, S. H. (2010). A controlled trial of the Making Choices program: Six-month follow-up. *Research on Social Work Practice, 21,* 165–176. doi:10.1177/1049731510386626

Fraser, M. W., Thompson, A. M., Day, S. H., & Macy, R. J. (in press). The Making Choices program: Impact of social-emotional skills training on the risk status of third graders. *Elementary School Journal.*

Frey, K. S., Nolen, S. B., Van Schoiack Edstrom, L., & Hirschstein, M. K. (2005). Effects of a school-based social-emotional competence program: Linking children's goals, attributions, and behavior. *Applied Developmental Psychology, 73*(6), 1045–1055. doi:10.1016/j.appdev.2004.12.002

Greenberg, M. T., Kusche, C. A., Cook, E. T., & Quamma, J. P. (1995). Promoting emotional competence in school-aged children: The effects of the PATHS curriculum. *Development and Psychopathology, 7,* 117–136. doi:10.1017/S0954579400006374

Heckman, J. J. (2008). Schools, skills, and synapses. *Economic Inquiry, 46,* 289–324. doi:10.1111/j.1465-7295.2008.00163.x

Heckman, J. J., & Kautz, T. D. (2012). *Hard evidence on soft skills.* Retrieved from http://www.nber.org/papers/w18121.pdf?new_window=1

Heckman, J. J., Stixrud, J., & Urzua, S. (2006). *The effects of cognitive and noncognitive abilities on labor market outcomes and social behavior.* Retrieved from http://www.nber.org/papers/w12006.pdf?new_window=1

Holsen, I., Smith, B. H., & Frey, K. S. (2008). Outcomes of the social competence program Second Step in Norwegian elementary schools. *School Psychology International, 29*(1), 71–88. doi:10.1177/0143034307088504

Huesmann, L. R. (1988). An information processing model for the development of aggression. *Aggressive Behavior, 14,* 13–24. doi:10.1002/1098-2337(1988)14:113::AID-AB24801401043.0.CO;2-J

Lengua, L. J. (2003). Associations among emotionality, self-regulation, adjustment problems and positive adjustment in middle childhood. *Journal of Applied Developmental Psychology, 24,* 595–618. doi:10.1016/j.appdev.2003.08.002

Masten, A. S., & Cicchetti, D. (2010). Developmental cascades. *Development and Psychopathology, 22,* 491–495. doi:10.1017/S0954579410000222

Masten, A. S., Roisman, G. I., Long, J. D., Burt, K. B., Obradovic, J., Riley, J. R.,. . . Tellegen, A. (2005). Developmental cascades: Linking academic achievement and externalizing and internalizing symptoms over 20 years. *Developmental Psychology, 41,* 733–746. doi:10.1037/0012-1649.41.5.733

Miller-Johnson, S., Coie, J., Maumary-Gremaud, A., Bierman, K. L., & Conduct Problems Prevention Research Group. (2002). Peer rejection and aggression and early starter models of conduct disorder. *Journal of Abnormal Child Psychology, 30,* 217–230. doi:10.1023/A:1015198612049

Moffitt, T. E. (1993). Adolescent-limited and life-course-persistent antisocial behavior. *Psychological Review, 100,* 674–701. doi:10.1037/0033-295X.100.4.674

Moffitt, T. E., & Caspi, A. (2001). Childhood predictors differentiate life-course persistent and adolescence-limited antisocial pathways among males and females. *Developmental Psychopathology, 13,* 355–375. doi:10.1017/S0954579401002097

Murray-Close, D., Ostrov, J. M., & Crick, N. R. (2007). A short-term longitudinal study of growth of relational aggression during middle childhood: Associations with gender, friendship intimacy, and internalizing problems. *Development and Psychopathology, 19*, 187–203. doi:10.10170S0954579407070101

Nansel, T. R., Craig, W., Overpeck, M. D., Saluja, G., Ruan, W. J., & Health Behaviour in School-aged Children Bullying Analyses Working Group (2004). Cross-national consistency in the relationship between bullying behaviors and psychosocial adjustment. *Archives of Pediatrics and Adolescent Medicine, 158*, 730–736. doi:10.1001/archpedi.158.8.730

Nash, J. K., Fraser, M. W., Galinsky, M. J., & Kupper, L. L. (2003). Early development and pilot testing of a problem-solving skills-training program for children. *Research on Social Work Practice, 13*, 432–450. doi:10.1177/1049731503013004002

Parker, J. G., & Asher, S. R. (1987). Peer relations and later personal adjustment: Are low-accepted children at risk? *Psychological Bulletin, 102*(3), 357–389. doi:10.1037/0033-2909.102.3.357

Prinstein, M. J., & La Greca, A. M. (2004). Childhood peer rejection and aggression as predictors of adolescent girls' externalizing and health risk behaviors: A 6-year longitudinal study. *Journal of Consulting and Clinical Psychology, 72*, 103–112. doi:10.1037/0022-006X.72.1.103

Smokowski, P. R., Fraser, M. W., Day, S. H., Galinsky, M. J., & Bacallao, M. L. (2004). School-based skills training to prevent childhood aggression: Using the Making Choices program as a universal prevention initiative. *Journal of Primary Prevention, 25*, 233–251. doi:10.1023/B:JOPP.0000042392.57611.05

Terzian, M. A. (2007). *Preventing aggressive behavior by promoting social information-processing skills: A theory-based evaluation of the Making Choices program* (unpublished doctoral dissertation). University of North Carolina at Chapel Hill. Retrieved from https://cdr.lib.unc.edu/indexablecontent?id=uuid:b64721be-163f-4ac5-85f8-b42e5c3f3b84&ds=DATA_FILE

Thompson, A., Macy, R., & Fraser, M. W. (2011). Assessing person-centered outcomes in practice research: A latent transition profile framework. *Journal of Community Psychology, 39*, 987–1002. doi:10.1002/jcop.20485

Tremblay, R. E., Nagin, D. S., Seguin, J. R., Zoccolillo, M., Zelazo, P. D., Boivan, M.,. . . Japel, C. (2004). Physical aggression during early childhood: Trajectories and predictors. *Pediatrics, 114*, e43–e50. doi:10.1542/peds.114.1.e43

Werner, N. E., & Crick, N. R. (2004). Maladaptive peer relationships and the development of relational and physical aggression during middle childhood. *Social Development, 13*, 495–514. doi:10.1111/j.1467-9507.2004.00280.x

Williams, J. H., Ayers, C. D., & Arthur, M. W. (1997). Risk and protective factors in the development of delinquency and conduct disorder. In M. W. Fraser (Ed.), *Risk and resilience in childhood: An ecological perspective* (pp. 140–170). Washington, DC: NASW Press.

Wilson, S. J., & Lipsey, M. W. (2007). School-based interventions for aggressive and disruptive behavior. *American Journal of Preventive Medicine, 33*(2S), S130–S143. doi:10.1016/j.amepre.2007.04.011

Xie, H., Farmer, T. W., & Cairns, B. D. (2003). Different forms of aggression among inner-city African American children: Gender, configurations, and school social networks. *Journal of School Psychology, 41*, 355–375. doi:10.1016/S0022-4405(03)00086-4

Zins, J. E., Weissberg, R. P., Wang, M. C., & Walberg, H. J. (Eds.). (2004). *Building academic success on social and emotional learning: What does the research say?* New York, NY: Teachers College Press.

64 Multifamily Groups with Obsessive-compulsive Disorder

Barbara Van Noppen

Clinicians who use this guide are presumed to have experience in Cognitive Behavioral Therapy (CBT) for Obsessive-compulsive Disorder (OCD) as well as a basic knowledge of CBT for OCD; recommended reading includes Steketee (1999), Steketee and White (1990) and Hyman and Pedrick (2010). For a review of expressed emotion implications for OCD family treatment, see Steketee, Van Noppen, Lam, and Shapiro (1998). For a full description of the clinical application of MultiFamily Behavior Treatment (MFBT), see Van Noppen (2002). It is also recommended that the practitioner be familiar with self-help books about OCD. Also, because this treatment guide is based on theoretical foundations used to develop psycho-educational groups for schizophrenia, it is recommended that the clinician be familiar with Anderson, Reiss, and Hogarty (1986) and McFarlane (1983).

Over the past decade, the concept of family accommodation (FA) has received much attention and recent studies point to FA as a predictor of poorer treatment outcome in both adults (Amir et al., 2000) and in children/adolescents (Storch et al., 2008). In 1995, Calvocoressi et al. published findings on a clinician administered FA questionnaire, which resulted in an association with poorer patient functioning, global family dysfunction, and stress. The original questionnaire as revised into a 12-item clinician administered Family Accommodation Scale (FAS), validated by Calvocoressi et al. (1999). The FAS-IR (Interviewer Rated) demonstrated excellent inter-rater reliability, good internal consistency, and convergent and divergent validity and has become the gold standard measure of family accommodation. More recently, Pinto, Van Noppen, and Calvocoressi have validated a 19-item self-report version, and the FAS-SR (Self Report) is available online: http://dx.doi.org/10.1016/j.jorcrd.2012.06.001.

This MFBT guide is meant to instruct clinicians on the implementation of MFBT for OCD; it is not a substitute for clinical training and ongoing supervision. The MFBT differs considerably from traditional family therapy in that the clinician takes a very active role in providing information, facilitating problem solving, participating in direct and imaginal exposure, making suggestions directly to families, and assigning homework exercises (Van Noppen & Steketee, 2009). This may not be customary for dynamically trained clinicians. For MFBT to be effective, the clinician should be clear about and comfortable with the role described. This MFBT is written for adult patients (18 years and older); it can be adapted to be suitable for adolescents and children.

FEATURES AND PROCEDURES OF MULTIFAMILY BEHAVIOR TREATMENT

Features

MFBT treats five to seven families (no more than 16 total participants is recommended), including patient and identified significant others who are in considerable daily contact with the patient.

Co-leaders are optimal; at least one of the leaders should have an advanced degree in social work, psychology, or certified counseling, and experience in clinical work with individuals, families, and groups, as well as proficiency in cognitive behavioral therapy with experience in OCD populations.

The sessions are two hours long and typically meet in the late afternoon or early evening. The time-limited nature of this treatment program is used to motivate patients.

Procedure

Each patient and family has a pretreatment screening by phone with the therapist(s) to determine appropriateness for the group and readiness for treatment; following this, an intake session is scheduled.

At the intake session, pretreatment forms are completed, symptom severity and family response styles are determined, goals of the group and behavioral therapy principles are discussed, and pretreatment concerns and questions are addressed.

Agendas for Weekly Treatment Sessions

1. Introductions, ground rules, education about OCD, reading of self-help material
2. Definition of behavior therapy (exposure and response prevention), in vivo exposure and response prevention, plus homework and self-monitoring
3. Family responses to OCD and family guidelines; neurobiology of OCD, and medications
4. Behavioral contracting among family members and communication skills training, homework discussion with family group feedback, and problem solving.
5–11. Continued exposure and response prevention (ERP) and family behavioral contracting in vivo and homework assignments
12. Final weekly treatment session, termination issues, and planning for monthly booster sessions.

Maintenance of gains and relapse prevention are supported in six monthly sessions.

TREATMENT PROCEDURE

Following is a manual for an 18-session MFBT and one 90-minute intake gathering session conducted with each OCD patient and family members.

Information Gathering and Pre-group Screening (90 minutes)

1. Take a general bio-psychosocial history and collect information about OC symptoms for treatment planning (20 minutes). Use the Yale-Brown Obsessive-Compulsive Checklist and Severity Scale (YBOCS; Goodman et al., 1989 a & b) to indicate primary obsessions and major compulsions and symptom severity.
2. Discuss onset of OCD and efforts to cope (10 minutes).
3. Begin exposure hierarchy, as in individual behavior therapy, by collecting information about triggers of obsession and compulsions, situations and objects avoided, intrusive thoughts, and ritualistic patterns of behavior (15 minutes).
4. Teach the patient and family how to rate anxiety according to the subjective units of distress scale (SUDS) and estimate at which treatment session the trigger will be introduced. Record all information on an exposure hierarchy form: the more detailed, the better. See hierarchies in Table 64.1 and use references for more examples. These are two sample hierarchies for a patient who has fears of contracting cancer from items associated with a sibling, contact with cigarettes, "chemicals," and certain food.
5. Describe ERP (10 minutes). Offer treatment rationale including the following:
   - *Exposure* refers to gradual and direct confrontation of situations that provoke obsessive fears. It is designed to break the association between the sensations of anxiety and the objects, situations, or thoughts that produce it through the gradual reduction or habituation of fear. Use the patient's own experiences as examples (e.g., "every time you touch anything associated with body fluids you feel anxious, distressed, or contaminated").
   - *Response prevention* is designed to break the association between ritualistic behavior and the reduction of anxiety or distress. Because compulsions (specify them) lead to less distress temporarily, they are reinforced. Treatment breaks the automatic bond between the feelings of discomfort/ anxiety (specify the obsession) and rituals.
6. Description of MFBT program and review of overall goals (5 minutes).
7. Discuss the degree of family accommodation and response styles (20 minutes). Administer the FAS –SR in the group (Pinto, Van Noppen, Calvocoressi, 2012).
8. Homework assignment (5 minutes). Discuss the first homework assignment to read Hyman and Pedrick (2010), Chapters 1, 2, 5, and 6; suggested reading list.
9. Wrap up (5 minutes). Address concerns and questions.

TABLE 64.1 Exposure Hierarchies

Situation	Discomfort (1–100)	Treatment Session
Hierarchy 1: Fears of contamination—"cancer" from brother and cigarettes		
Holding unopened cigarette pack	45	1
Touching doorknobs at home	55	2
Holding opened cigarette pack	55	2
Touching "dirty" clothes (basement)	85	5
Touching cigarette filter	90	6
Stepping barefoot on a cigarette	95	7
Hierarchy 2: Fear of contamination—cancer from "chemical" contact		
Touching microwaved food	30	1
Holding batteries	40	2
Touching sand at beach	65	5
Eating food items "scanned" at checkout	75	6
Drinking diet soda	85	7
Eating chicken	100	8

Session 1: Building Cohesion and Trust: "We're Not Alone!" Psycho-educational Phase: "What is Obsessive-compulsive Disorder?" (2 hours)

1. Welcome (5 minutes). The group leaders introduce themselves and ask each participant to do the same. The group leaders outline the agenda for all 12 sessions, giving dates and times for each.
2. Administrative issues (15 minutes): Review scheduling of sessions, cancellation policy, group guidelines about confidentiality, and therapist availability.
3. Goals (10 minutes). Each group member is asked to respond to the question, "What do you hope to get out of this group?" Encourage participants to be specific about behavioral change.
4. Definition of OCD (1 hour). Review Chapters 1 and 2 in Hyman and Pedrick (2010) biological and learned bases of OCD. Distribute YBOCS symptom checklist (self-rated version). Go over each example provided, with group members volunteering to read. Encourage disclosure by asking for examples from patients' or family members' experiences. Introduce concepts of ERP.
5. Homework (30 minutes). Go-round: each patient chooses a behavioral task challenge to practice daily for homework. Distribute self-rating exposure homework form and explain how to use (*The OCD Workbook*, p. 93). If there is time in the session, ask for a patient to volunteer to demonstrate ERP and rate SUDS as a group. The homework for every patient for the first week is to practice the chosen ERP task and complete homework form.

Session 2: Psycho-educational Phase: "How Do You Treat Obsessive-compulsive Disorder?"

1. Check-in (10 minutes). Review the previous group session.
2. Go-round (10 minutes). Each patient reports on homework completed during the week, including SUDs. If the homework is inadequately completed or reported, discuss problems identified by the patient and family. Encourage group feedback and troubleshoot to define obstacles.
3. Overview of behavior therapy (30 minutes). Define in vivo and imaginal exposure and give examples. A brief description of exposure in vivo might be: "This entails actual direct contact with an object or situation that evokes obsessions. For example, a person afraid of stabbing loved ones might stand in the kitchen before meal

times holding knives or scissors near others."
A brief description of imaginal exposure
may be: "Sometimes people cannot actually
put themselves into their feared situation,
such as stabbing one's child. A mental
visualization of this situation in detail will
evoke fears of harming one's child that will
offer exposure practice. Writing a scripted
imagery to be read daily, or put onto a tape
and listened to, is a way of going about
this." Provide a brief description of imaginal
exposure for those patients for whom it is
relevant (patients whose anxiety focuses
on feared consequences that are not fully
triggered by in vivo exposure or for whom
in vivo exposure is difficult to execute.
One possibility is a mental visualization of
forgetting to check the stove and coming
home to fire engines and a burning house.
Another possibility is making a loop tape
of a brief description or phrase (i.e., "I
will kill my child") or a few words ("kill,"
"child-killer") that are avoided, dreaded, or
evoke aggressive obsessions.

Include a few statements about tolerating
initial high anxiety that will decrease over time
with repeated, systematic use of exposure and
response prevention (habituation). Stress that
response prevention must accompany exposure, whether imagined or in vivo. Following
are instructions and examples of the sequences
of in vivo and imaginal exposure for a patient
with contamination fears, and the subsequent
response prevention.

- *In vivo exposure.* The patient, Steve, felt
  contaminated by feces, urine, sweat, and
  contact with others. He feared contracting
  a debilitating disease. The following
  hierarchy was constructed for Steve: feces,
  100 SUDs; urine, 90 SUDs; toilet seats in
  public bathrooms, 80 SUDs; sweat, 75 SUDs;
  newspapers, 60 SUDs; doorknobs, 50 SUDs.
  During in vivo exposure treatment, the
  following sequence was pursued.

Session 1—Steve walked with the therapist
through the building touching doorknobs,
especially those of the public restrooms,
holding each for several minutes.
Session 2—Steve held newspapers left behind
by people in the waiting room.
Session 3—Steve held newspapers and doorknobs. Contact with sweat was introduced by

asking him to place one hand under his arm
and the other in his shoe.
Session 4—Exposure began with newspapers
and sweat. Toilet seats were added by coaching the patient to stand next to the toilet and
place his hands on the seat.
Session 5—Exposure began with contact with
sweat and toilet seats. Urine was then introduced by encouraging Steve to hold a paper
towel dampened in his own urine.
Session 6—Exposure included urine, toilet seats,
and sweat repeatedly until SUDS decreased
by at least 50%.
Sessions 7–12—Daily exposure to urine and
sweat. Homework focused on the objects
used during that day's treatment session.
Periodic contact with lesser contaminants was
continued throughout.

- *Imaginal exposure.* First conduct in the
  present tense with the therapist describing
  images in second person ("you see" or
  "you are going"). When asked what he or
  she feels or sees or thinks in the image,
  the patient should respond in the first
  person ("I'm sitting on _____"). Imaginal
  scenes should be followed by in vivo
  exposure to objects or situations related
  to that scene and provoke similar levels of
  discomfort. The patient creates a script of
  a similar scene and records it to listen to
  for imaginal exposure homework.
- *Response prevention.* Remind participants
  of the specific instructions for response
  prevention on the first day of treatment, as
  well as periodically during treatment. Give
  a copy of the rules to each patient and his
  or her family, modeling the instructions
  after this example for washers.

  Washers: During the response
  prevention period, patients are not
  permitted to use water on their body—
  that is, no hand washing, no rinsing, no
  wet towels, washcloths, wet wipes, or
  antibacterial gels except as negotiated
  with the therapist. Supervised showers
  are permitted every day for target time,
  including hair washing. Ritualistic washing
  of specific areas of the body (e.g., genitals,
  hair) is prohibited. If prevention of washing
  forces contamination to items very high on
  the hierarchy, patients may wash briefly
  and immediately re-contaminate with the
  items currently being exposed in treatment.

At home, relatives may be available to the patient should she or he have difficulty controlling a strong urge to wash. If the patient reports such concerns, family members can coach the patient to delay the urge until it decreases to a manageable level. Family members may attempt to stop such violations through firm verbal insistence, but no physical force should be used, and arguments should be avoided. Faucets can be turned off by relatives if the patient gives prior consent to such a plan. Showers can be timed by family, with no direct observation of showering behavior.

- *Review hierarchy* forms as a group and add any additional triggers for exposure. Arrange all designated items hierarchically according to anxiety evoked. The most disturbing item should be presented by Session 9 or three-fourths of the way through treatment. Final sessions should include repetitions of earlier ones with minor variations, focusing on those situations that provoke the most discomfort.

4. Homework go-round. ERP (60 minutes). Each patient chooses a behavioral homework task. Use feedback and support from group members to develop the optimal homework assignment. As each patient selects his or her homework, the group leader should try to translate the task into a form that can be rehearsed in the group—the therapists, patients, and family members who are willing participate in the ERP in vivo while others observe. For example,

- For *harming obsessions* with reassurance seeking and checking, the group leader and patients dampen their hands and touch light switches; other group members follow by touching the same switch. No reassurance seeking or checking is allowed. Level of anxiety is discussed and rated. This is repeated several times to model the homework assignment and to begin the process of habituation. Another exposure challenge is to pass a pair of scissors around the group, point first.
- For *contamination obsessions* with washing and/or passive avoidance, fear of being responsible for something bad happening and checking, hoarding,

ordering and arranging, and other obsessions and compulsions, devise in vivo ERP accordingly.

5. Family role (10 minutes). Instruct family members to offer support and encouragement for patient's completion of ERP homework. No changes in family responses should be made without prior negotiation.

Session 3: Psycho-education: Family Responses to Obsessive-compulsive Disorder and Family Guidelines: "What Should We Do?"

1. Check-in (10 minutes).
2. Go-round (10 minutes).
3. Psycho-educational lecture on neurobiology of OCD (15 minutes). (If a psychiatrist is not able to be present, a videotaped discussion on the neurobiology of OCD is viewed in the group).
4. ERP (60 minutes). In the group, each patient selects exposure items with SUD level of approximately 50 to 60; continue with in vivo ERP.
5. Family guidelines (15 minutes). Distribute *Learning to Live with OCD* (Van Noppen, Pato, & Rasmussen, 1997) and read as a group. Identify and label family response styles as they emerge in discussion (accommodating, antagonistic, split, oscillating). Encourage discussion.
6. Homework (10 minutes). Each patient reassesses behavioral homework task with family guidelines in mind and adds another challenge.

Session 4: Intensive Treatment Phase: Managing the Symptoms: "Out with Doubt!"

1. Check-in and go-round (20 minutes). Proceed as previously described.
2. Explain family behavioral contracting (20 minutes); see Steketee, Van Noppen, Lam, and Shapiro (1998); Van Noppen (2002).
   - One at a time, each family identifies problem areas. How does the family accommodate? Is there a lot of hostile criticism directed toward the patient by family? Review the FAS-SR as a group and facilitate discussion.

- Guide the family to focus on one problem area at a time and define it.
- Using feedback from the group, family members explore behavioral response options and the possible consequences of each.
- Patient selects an ERP and leaders elicit response options from the family and group. For example, if a patient is practicing exposure to leaving the house without checking appliances, the behavioral contract might be that the family gives a 10 minute "warning" when preparing to depart for an outing, then a 5 minute "warning" and if the patient is still checking, the agreement is that the family departs without the patient and without argument.

    To address reassurance seeking, a behavioral contract includes that the family's first responses are: "What do you think I will say?" "What have I told you before?" "What would the therapist say?" thereby placing the decision back upon the patient and interrupting the reassurance compulsion cycle.

- The leaders facilitate a negotiation process among family members.
- When possible, the family rehearses the ERP and behavioral contract, during the treatment session in vivo, thereby beginning to implement a new solution.

    As described, the group leaders actively guide one family at a time through the process of negotiating a behavioral contract including all patients and family members in the exercise. Families are instructed to renegotiate the contract if they find it too stringent.
3. Homework (10 minutes). Each patient selects individual exposure homework and each family commits to behavioral contact homework.

Session 5: Behavioral Family Treatment Phase: "We Can Make a Difference!"

1. Check-in and go-round (30 minutes).
2. Continue behavioral contracting (80 minutes). Each family practices behavioral contracting in vivo. ERP with therapist and participant modeling should be used extensively. Each family is allotted 10 to 15 minutes.
3. Homework (10 minutes). Patients and relatives commit to ERP homework and family contracts.

Sessions 6–11: "Practice! Practice! Practice!" and "We Can Take Charge!"

The group leaders follow the same format already described for the remaining weekly sessions. Progressively, patients are increasingly responsible for devising the in vivo ERP task challenges and family contracts, an expectation cultivated by the leaders.

Session 12: Exposure, Contracting, and Termination: "We Have Tools to Do This on Our Own!" (Last Weekly Multifamily Session)

1. Check-in (30 minutes).
2. Go-round (45 minutes). Each family modifies or adds to existing contracts. Group members devise in vivo ERP tasks. Each family presents the ERP plan for the next month.
3. Dealing with termination (25 minutes). Remind the group of the self-instructional nature of behavioral treatment. Review the steps that were taught: create hierarchy, assess distress levels, select exposure situation (either internal or external trigger), devise ERP challenge, record this on a form, and practice it repeatedly for long periods of time until anxiety decreases.
    - Initial anxiety will increase while using ERP.
    - Habituation takes time and practice.
    - Long-term gains are made through perseverance and commitment to treatment.
    - Encourage patients to refer to self-help workbooks.
    - Leaders are available to patients between monthly sessions.
4. Complete self-rated YBOCS and FAS-SR in the group (15 minutes).
5. Discuss monthly check-in sessions (5 minutes). Schedule dates and describe this as a trial period to develop confidence for independent individual ERP and family behavioral contracting.

Sessions 13–18: Monthly Check-in Sessions: "We Have the Tools to Beat Obsessive-compulsive Disorder" (2 Hours)

The main purpose of these six sessions is to assist patients and their families in the transition from the leader-directed behavioral treatment to the self-instruction form of therapy. Check-in sessions ensure maintenance of treatment gains in the vulnerable time period directly following the weekly 12 sessions. They also provide motivation.

Each session begins in typical fashion with the check-in and go-round, but no in vivo exposure takes place. Patients and family members report on homework tasks, contracts, successes, pitfalls, and general life events that may be influencing the OCD or interfering with behavioral therapy. Leaders are more passive, facilitating the group process and answering questions that require clinical clarification. Clinician-rated YBOCS are collected at each session for pre- and post-treatment comparisons.

At the last monthly session, issues related to treatment termination are acknowledged, and referrals are made for continued behavior therapy or medication if necessary. The FAS for each family in the group is completed. A post-treatment YBOCS under 16 is optimal.

CONCLUSION

MFBT offers several advantages over standard individual behavioral treatment. It is cost-effective by allowing for the simultaneous treatment of five to seven patients and their family members with one or two therapists in two hours a week, compared to the same six or seven families treated individually requiring 10 to 14 hours of therapist time per week. This is a savings of up to 12 hours of therapist time per week.

As typically practiced, individual behavioral treatment offers little structured psychoeducation, support, or guidance for the family members who have to cope with the symptoms and demands imposed by OCD. The MFBT can be modified to conduct family behavioral treatment with one patient and family members. In this age of managed care and short-term treatments, it makes sense to mobilize natural supports like family systems. Once families understand OCD symptoms and are taught behavioral strategies, they can participate effectively in ERP with the OCD patient. This treatment offers a marked decrease in both cost for treatment and therapist time, as well as the possibility of improving long-term outcome.

WEBSITES

Anxiety Disorders Association of America. http://www.adaa.org.

International Obsessive Compulsive Foundation (OCF). http://www.ocfoundation.org.

Medline Plus (National Library of Medicine and National Institute of Health—OCD. http://www.nlm.nih.gov/medlineplus/obsessive-compulsivedisorder.html.

National Institute of Mental Health Obsessive-Compulsive Disorder. http://www.nimh.nih.gov/health/topics/obsessive-compulsive-disorder-ocd/index.html.

References

Amir, N., Freshman, M., & Foa, E. B. (2000). Family distress and involvement in relatives of obsessive-compulsive disorder patients. *Journal of Anxiety Disorders, 14,* 209–217.

Anderson, C., Reiss, D., & Hogarty, G. (1986). *Schizophrenia and the family.* New York, NY: Guilford.

Calvocoressi, L., Mazure, C. M., Kasl, S. V., Skolnick, J., Fisk, D., Vegso, S. J., Van Noppen, B. L., & Price, L. H. (1999). Family accommodation of obsessive-compulsive symptoms: Instrument development and assessment of family behavior. *Journal of Nervous and Mental Disease, 187,* 636–642.

Goodman, W. K., Price, L. H., Rasmussen, S. A., Mazure, C., Delgado, P., Heninger, G. R., & Charney, D. S. (1989a). The Yale-Brown Obsessive Compulsive Scale. II. Validity. *Archives of General Psychiatry, 46*(11), 1012–1016.

Goodman, W. K., Price, L. H., Rasmussen, S. A., Mazure, C., Fleischmann, R. L., Hill, C. L., & Charney, D. S. (1989b). The Yale-Brown Obsessive Compulsive Scale. I. Development, use, and reliability. *Archives of General Psychiatry, 46*(11), 1006–1011.

Hyman, B., & Pedrick,. (2010). *The OCD workbook.* Oakland, CA: New Harbinger.

McFarlane, W. R. (1983). *Family therapy in schizophrenia.* New York, NY: Guilford.

Pinto, A., Van Noppen, B., & Calvocoressi, L. (2012). Development and preliminary psychometric evaluation of a self-rated version of the Family Accommodation Scale for Obsessive-Compulsive Disorder. *Journal of*

Obsessive-Compulsive and Related Disorders. Retrieved from http://dx.doi.org/10.1016/j/jorcrd.2012.06.001.

Steketee, G. (1999). *Overcoming OCD: A behavioral and cognitive protocol for the treatment of OCD.* Oakland, CA: New Harbinger.

Steketee, G., Van Noppen, B., Lam, J., & Shapiro, L. (1998). Expressed emotion in families and the treatment of OCD. *In Session: Psychotherapy in Practice, 4*(3), 73–91.

Steketee,., & White, K. (1990). *When once is not enough.* Oakland, CA: New Harbinger.

Storch, E. A., Merlo, L. J., Larson, M. J., Marien, W. E., Geffken, G. R., Jacob, M. L. (2008). Clinical features associated with treatment-resistant pediatric obsessive-compulsive disorder. *Comprehensive Psychiatry, 49*(1), 35–42.

Van Noppen, B. (2002). Multifamily behavioral treatment (MFBT) for OCD: A step-by-step model. In A. R. Roberts and G. Greene (Eds.). *Brief Treatment and Crisis Intervention, 2*(2), 107–122.

Van Noppen, B., Pato, M., & Rasmussen,. (1997). *Learning to live with OCD.* New Haven, CT: Obsessive Compulsive Foundation.

Van Noppen, B., & Steketee, G. (2009). Testing a conceptual model of patient and family predictors of Obsessive Compulsive Disorder (OCD) symptoms, *Behavior Research and Therapy, 47,* 18–25.

65 Collaborating with Families of Persons with Severe Mental Illness

Tina Bogart Marshall & Phyllis Solomon

Practice guidelines for the treatment of severe mental illness recommend involving and engaging families in a collaborative treatment process (American Psychiatric Association [APA], 2006; Dixon et al., 2010). These recommendations are based on substantial evidence that partnering with families improves client outcomes (Dixon et al., 2001).

WHY COLLABORATE WITH FAMILIES?

It is often presumed that the hardship brought by mental illness leaves many individuals with little or no family contact. For this reason, families are frequently overlooked as potential members of a support network for individuals with severe mental illness. However, most individuals have a family member or significant other—friend, roommate, partner—in their lives. Research indicates that more than 60% of individuals with mental illness live with their families (National Institute of Mental Health [NIMH], 1991), and 77% or more have some ongoing contact with family members (Lehman & Steinwachs, 1998). Moreover, families are often the first to recognize warning signs and symptoms of relapse (Herz, 1985). Family and significant others need information, education, and practical advice (Molinaro et al., 2012) to effectively support their loved one with mental illness. Social workers can successfully collaborate with a client's family or significant others while keeping the treatment process client-centered (Jewell, Smith & Hoh, 2012).

Over the past 30 years, numerous studies have found that family psycho-education, family education, and family consultation interventions have been associated with positive outcomes for both individuals with mental illness and their family member(s) or significant other(s). Family psycho-education has been found to reduce relapse and rehospitalization for persons with severe mental illness, lower levels of family burden and distress, and improve family well-being (Murray-Swank & Dixon, 2004; McFarlane et al., 2003). Family education has led to significant reductions in subjective burden, as well as increased knowledge of mental illness and the treatment system (Dixon et al., 2004). Family consultation has been associated with improved self-efficacy in family members (Solomon, Draine, et al., 1996), high family satisfaction, and a positive impact on caregiving (Schmidt & Monaghan, 2012). Although these interventions differ in their format, duration, and locus of service delivery, they all use a strengths-based approach, view services as client-driven, and provide families with:

- Information about mental illness
- Emotional support
- Communication skills
- Problem-solving or coping skills
- Crisis intervention, based on the notion of collaborating with family members in the treatment of their ill relative.

Furthermore, family interventions are based on the notion of collaborating with persons with mental illness and their family members in the treatment process (Mannion et al., 2012; Dixon et al., 2001; McFarlane et al., 2003), which is now understood to be a vital component to recovery-oriented, comprehensive care (Glynn, Cohen et al., 2006).

Partnering with families not only is associated with improved client and family outcomes but also holds benefits for social workers. Social workers gain a better understanding of the client's behavior, symptoms, and level of coping with their illness (Solomon et al., 2002). By working collaboratively with consumers and families, social workers can develop the most effective treatment plans. The following case study demonstrates how social workers can collaborate with clients and their family members to actively pursue clients' personal recovery goals.

CASE STUDY

Annie is a 39-year-old woman with schizophrenia. The symptoms of her illness respond fairly well to medication. Although she has been able to live alone in an apartment for the past 12 years, Annie receives significant support from community providers. She lives an isolated life. Outside of her contact with the mental health center, she has few friends or hobbies.

The social worker at the mental health center talks with Annie about building a social support network. She lets Annie know that many people who receive services at the mental health center find it very helpful to involve a family member or close friend in their mental health treatment. She asks Annie if there is someone she would like to invite to their next session.

Annie tells her that she has a sister who visits regularly. Together, they call the sister and invite her to the next session. During the session, the social worker tells the sister that Annie is interested in building up a circle of supportive family and friends and would like her help. They ask the sister if she is willing to participate in Annie's sessions over the next few weeks, and they can discuss together the types of interests that Annie has had in the past and activities that she may want to get involved with again. Annie's sister agrees.

Over the next three weeks, the social worker meets with Annie and her sister. She learns that Annie's sister was very involved with the National Alliance on Mental Illness (NAMI) when Annie first became ill and has a good understanding of her illness. Annie wishes that her brother understood her better and that she could have more contact with him. Annie's sister offers to speak with him and encourage him to attend NAMI support groups with her. The social worker also discovers from the sister that Annie is very artistic. In her early twenties, she won an award for a sketch she had drawn. The sister agrees to help Annie find an art class in the community. Annie is hesitant about going by herself, and her sister agrees to take her there.

Six months later, Annie is taking a community art class. She has met several new friends and considers participating in an art exhibition. Her brother calls her regularly and occasionally takes her out to lunch. Annie remains in close contact with her sister, who occasionally joins her for a session.

COMPETENCIES NEEDED TO COLLABORATE WITH FAMILIES

Competencies for working with families of people with severe mental illness have been developed by an expert panel of practitioners, families, clients, and researchers (Coursey, Curtis, & Marsh, 2000). Competencies include:

- Understanding the family experience
- Engaging the family in treatment and rehabilitation
- Addressing the needs of families
- Being knowledgeable about appropriate community resources for meeting family needs.

Trainings ranging from one and a quarter hours (Stanbridge, Burbach, 2007) to 30 hours (Farhall et al., 1998) have been offered to foster provider competencies. However, for social workers to be responsive to families does not necessarily mean that formal training in a specific intervention is needed. Social workers who are unable to implement a formalized intervention may still participate in some activities to address family needs. Specific attitudes, knowledge, and skills that are needed for social workers to collaborate with families of persons with severe mental illness were developed based on the evidence to date (Mannion, 2000; Mannion et al., 2012).

Attitudes

1. *Self-examination.* Attitudes in working with families are shaped by mental health providers' training and learning experiences. It is critical for social workers to examine their own feelings and attitudes and develop a conviction that families and significant others can positively affect recovery. Services should be client-centered and families should be engaged in the treatment process and understand the client's illness and recovery goals.
2. *Examination of organizational climate.* Social workers should assess the overall attitude expressed within their agency toward partnering with clients and their family or significant others. Negative attitudes may lead to interdisciplinary conflict in treatment teams. Social workers may also perceive a negative organizational climate through a lack of policies and procedures for working with families, a lack of training, or disincentives, such as inappropriate reimbursement mechanisms. Assess your organization's attitude and consider advocating for changes in your policies and procedures.

KNOWLEDGE

1. *Awareness of the family experience.* Social workers need to understand the normal emotional cycles that families experience as they cope and adapt to having a family member with mental illness.
2. *Knowledge of mental illness.* It is important for social workers to not only accumulate a breadth of knowledge about mental illness but also be able to convey basic knowledge to families in a way that they can comprehend and retain. Social workers should be aware that knowledge is a coping aid for families. Refer families and significant others to free educational resources that are available to families, such as those offered by NAMI, Mental Health America, and others, and make appropriate referrals to family support groups.
3. *Knowledge of confidentiality policies.* Social workers need to recognize that they can listen to families and offer general information about mental illness without obtaining client consent. Consent forms are often necessary before specific information about the client's illness or treatment may be shared with families. Explain the benefits of family collaboration to clients and ask if there is a family member or significant other with whom they would like to share specific information. Use the consent process to identify the types of information that the client is interested in sharing and the ways that they would like their family member or significant other involved.
4. *Knowledge of family interventions.* Social workers should be aware of the types of available family interventions and benefits for providers, clients, and families. Learn to assess family needs and be able to refer families appropriately.
5. *Knowledge of coping and illness management skills.* Social workers should be well versed in basic coping and illness management strategies for families, such as reducing stress, recognizing their limits, and avoiding blame. At a minimum, social workers can offer support, remind families of the basics, and connect them to other community resources.
6. *Knowledge of the mental health system.* It is critical for social workers to understand not only the services within their own agency

but also specific information about services and resources throughout the mental health system. Any printed information that may be shared is helpful to families. Contact your state mental health department or state or local affiliate of NAMI for access to this type of information.

7. *Cultural competency.* Social workers need knowledge of differences in the attribution of mental illness and other issues specific to different cultural/ethnic groups. It is important for social workers to be aware of the acceptability and effectiveness of treatment and services for families of various ethnic and cultural backgrounds (Solomon, 1998; Lopez et al., 2000). Social workers also should be aware of culturally/ethnically diverse community resources and support systems.

Skills

1. *Discussing family involvement with clients.* Social workers should acquire skills for communicating the benefits of collaboration, working with clients to identify supportive family or significant other, and discussing their choices in the type of involvement that the family member may have in the treatment process. Social workers should be skilled in developing client-centered treatment plans and effective recovery goals and convey how expanding the client's support network can support those goals.

2. *Strength-based approach.* It is important for social workers to acknowledge both client and family strengths. In coping with their relatives' mental illness, families may isolate themselves and question their emotional responses. Identifying the feelings that family members experience as common and natural is an essential component of developing a collaborative relationship with families. Social workers can listen to families' experiences, share their understanding of the normal cycle of coping and adaptation, reflect their strengths, validate their feelings, and demonstrate respect, empathy, and support.

3. *Mediation and advocacy.* Skills in mediation allow social workers to assist families with unresolved conflict that they may be experiencing at home or within the mental health system. Social workers may use advocacy skills to intervene on behalf of families or improve the organizational climate within the agency. For example, social workers who encounter confidentiality policies as a barrier to sharing information with families may consider adapting model policies and consent procedures developed by the authors (Marshall & Solomon, 2003).

4. *Teaching and training.* Skills in transferring knowledge about mental illness, mental health treatment, coping, and illness management skills are critical to the work of social workers with families. It is crucial that the information offered is relevant and useful, while maintaining appropriate confidentiality Convey information to family and significant others in a way that maximizes comprehension and retention of the essential points.

5. *Problem solving.* Social workers should acquire skills that assist clients and families in defining problems, generating possible solutions, and deciding on appropriate strategies. Social workers may use problem-solving skills to help address specific issues that arise. Social workers may also offer to train families to use problem-solving techniques on their own.

6. *Referral.* Referring families to appropriate community resources is a skill that can complement what social workers offer to families to assist them in meeting their needs. Successful referrals require a high degree of familiarity with the resource. Family members should be prepared as to what they should expect, how to best access the resource, and how the resource will address their specific need(s).

FUTURE

The best practice recommendations for partnering with families are based on research evidence that family psycho-education/education/consultation improves client outcomes. Although the research indicates that no one specific intervention is more effective than another, the core components of effective interventions are based on the provider–client–family collaboration. To achieve these outcomes, social workers must improve their skills for introducing the concept of collaboration to clients and increase their competencies for working with families.

The most recent research concludes that one intervention will not meet the needs of all family members and clients. It is important to offer a variety of interventions and tailor services to clients and families according to their individual needs (Drapalski et al., 2008; Jewell, Smith, & Hoh, 2012). Social workers can obtain the basic competencies to partner with families, assess their needs and identify the types of interventions that will be most effective for them.

WEBSITES

National Alliance on Mental Illness (NAMI).
http://www.nami.org.
Mental Health America (MHA).
http://www.mentalhealthamerica.net
Brain & Behavior Research Foundation.
http://www.bbrfoundation.org
National Institute of Mental Health.
http://www.nimh.nih.gov

References

American Psychiatric Association. (2006). *Practice guidelines for the treatment of psychiatric disorders. Compendium 2006*. Arlington, VA: Author.

Coursey, R., Curtis, L., & Marsh, D. (2000). Competencies for direct service staff members who work with adults with severe mental illness: Specific knowledge, activities, skills, bibliography. *Psychiatric Rehabilitation Journal, 23*, 8–92.

Dixon, L., McFarlane, W., Lefley, H., et al. (2001). Evidence-based practices for services to families of people with psychiatric disabilities. *Psychiatric Services, 52*(7), 903–910.

Dixon, L., Lucksted, A., Stewart, B., et al. (2004). Outcomes of the peer-taught 12-week family-to-family education program for severe mental illness. *Acta Psychiatrica Scandinavica, 109*, 207–215.

Dixon, L., Dickerson, F., Bellack, A. S., et al. (2010). The 2009 Schizophrenia PORT Psychosocial Treatment Recommendations and Summary Statements. *Schizophrenia Bulletin, 36*(1), 48–70.

Drapalski, A., Marshall, T., Seybolt, D., et al. (2008). The unmet needs of families of adults with mental illness and preferences regarding family services. *Psychiatric Services, 59*(6), 655–662.

Farhall, J., Webster, B., Hocking, B., et al. (1998). Training to enhance partnerships between mental health professionals and family caregivers: Comparative study. *Psychiatric Services, 49*, 1488–1490.

Glynn, S. M., Cohen, A. N., Dixon, L. B., et al. (2006). The potential impact of the recovery movement on family interventions for schizophrenia: Opportunities and obstacles. *Schizophrenia Bulletin, 32*, 451–463.

Herz, M. (1985). Prodromal symptoms and prevention of relapse in schizophrenia. *Journal of Clinical Psychiatry, 46*, 22–25.

Jewell, T. C., Smith, A. M., & Hoh, B. (2012). Consumer centered family consultation: New York state's recent efforts to include families and consumers as partners in recovery. *American Journal of Psychiatric Rehabilitation, 15*(1), 44–60.

Lehman, A., & Steinwachs, D. (1998). Patterns of usual care for schizophrenia: Initial results from the schizophrenia patient outcomes research team (PORT) client survey. *Schizophrenia Bulletin, 24*(1), 11–32.

Lopez, S. R., & Guarnacci, P. J. (2000). Cultural psychopathology: Uncovering the social world of mental illness. *Annual Review of Psychology, 51*, 571–598.

Mannion, E. (2000). *Training manual for the implementation of family education in the adult mental health system of Berks County, PA*. Philadelphia: University of Pennsylvania Center for Mental Health Policy and Services Research.

Mannion, E., Marian, R., Chapman, P. et al. (2012). Overcoming systematic barriers to family inclusion in community psychiatry: The Pennsylvania experience. *American Journal of Psychiatric Rehabilitation, 15*(1), 61–80.

Marshall, T., & Solomon, P. (2003). Professionals' responsibilities in releasing information to families of adults with mental illness. *Psychiatric Services, 54*(12), 1622–1628.

McFarlane, W., Dixon, L., Lukens, E., et al. (2003). Family psychoeducation and schizophrenia: A review of the literature. *Journal of Marital and Family Therapy, 29*(2), 223–245.

Molinaro, M., Solomon, P., Mannion, E., et al. (2012). Development and implementation of family involvement standards for behavioral health provider programs. *American Journal of Psychiatric Rehabilitation, 15*(1), 81–96.

Murray-Swank, A. B., & Dixon, L. (2004). Family psychoeducation as an evidence based practice. *CNS Spectrums, 9*, 905–912.

National Institute of Mental Health. (1991). *Caring for people with severe mental disorders: A national plan of research to improve services*. Washington, DC: Author.

Schmidt, L., & Monaghan, J. (2012). Intensive family support services: a consultative model of education and support. *American Journal of Psychiatric Rehabilitation, 15*, 26–43.

Solomon, P., Draine, J., Mannion, E, et al. (1996). Impact of brief family psychoeducation on self-efficacy. *Schizophrenia Bulletin, 22,* 41–50.

Solomon, P. (1998). The cultural context of interventions for family members with a seriously mentally ill relative. In H. P. Lefley (Ed.), *Families coping with mental illness: The cultural context* (pp. 5–16). San Francisco, CA: Jossey-Bass.

Solomon, P., Marshall, T., Mannion, E., et al. (2002). Social workers as consumer and family consultants. In K. Bentley (Ed.), *Social work practice in mental health* (pp. 230–253). Pacific Grove, CA: Brooks/Cole.

Stanbridge, R.& Burbach, F. (2007). Developing family inclusive mainstream mental health services. *Journal of Family Therapy, 29,* 21–43.

66 Assessment, Prevention, and Intervention with Suicidal Youth

Jonathan B. Singer &
Kimberly H. McManama O'Brien

Suicide is a serious public health problem for youth in the United States. It is the second leading cause of death for 15-to-24-year-olds, and the fourth leading cause of death for 5-to-14-year-olds (Hoyert, 2012). In their lifetime, an estimated 12.1% of adolescents contemplate suicide, 4.0% make a plan, and 4.1% make an attempt (Nock et al., 2013). Given that social workers are employed in multiple settings where suicidal children and adolescents are encountered (e.g., schools, homeless shelters, emergency departments, outpatient mental health agencies, private practice), they have the potential to be at the forefront of suicide prevention efforts that include identifying and intervening with youth at risk, as well as advocating for suicide prevention programs and policies (Singer & Slovak, 2011). In an effort to educate social workers about the range of suicide prevention efforts, this chapter defines key terms, describes the components of a thorough suicide assessment, and reviews the current state of empirically supported evidence-based suicide prevention and intervention programs.

DEFINITIONS OF SUICIDAL THOUGHTS AND BEHAVIORS

The nomenclature of suicidal thoughts and behaviors (STB) has been the source of much debate over the past decade (De Leo, Burgis, Bertolote, Kerkhof, & Bille-Brahe, 2006). Table 66.1 identifies and defines recent consensus of the most important concepts in the identification and treatment of suicidal behavior (Bryan & Rudd, 2011; U.S. Department of Health and Human Services [DHHS], 2012; Whitlock et al., 2013).

RISK AND PROTECTIVE FACTORS

Although there is no single pathway to suicide, there are factors that increase the risk of STB. There are certain demographic characteristics related to risk for STB. The role of gender is important to consider, because females attempt suicide three times as often as males, but males die by suicide at three times the rate of females (Centers for Disease Control and Prevention

TABLE 66.1 Terms and Definitions

Term	Definition
Suicide ideation	Thoughts of ending one's own life
Suicide attempt	A nonfatal self-directed potentially injurious behavior with any intent to die as a result of the behavior. A suicide attempt may or may not result in injury
Suicide	Death caused by self-directed injurious behavior with any intent to die as a result of the behavior
Nonsuicidal morbid ideation	Thoughts about one's death without suicidal or self-enacted injurious content
Nonsuicidal self-injury	Deliberate direct destruction or alteration of body tissue without a conscious suicidal intent

[CDC], National Center for Injury Prevention and Control, 2013). With respect to ethnicity, suicide rates (per 100,000) are highest for American Indians/Alaskan Natives (9.72), followed by Whites (4.65), Blacks (2.76), and Asian/Pacific Islanders (2.68) (CDC, 2013). Youth who live in rural areas die by suicide at nearly twice the rate as youth who live in urban areas (Nance, Carr, Kallan, Branas, & Wiebe, 2010).

There are important psychosocial factors that confer risk for STB. The strongest risk factor for STB is a prior suicide attempt (Bridge, Goldstein, & Brent, 2006; Zahl & Hawton, 2004). Additionally, psychiatric diagnosis and comorbidity greatly increase risk for STB (Groholt, Ekeberg, & Haldorsen, 2006). Specifically, youth experiencing depressive symptoms are at increased risk (Evans, Hawton, & Rodham, 2004). Mood-related psychological factors that contribute to risk include hopelessness (Negron, Piacentini, Graae, Davies, & Shaffer, 1997), elevations in suicidal ideation (Prinstein et al., 2008), higher levels of affect dysregulation, and greater numbers of self-injurious behaviors (Zlotnick, Donaldson, Spirito, & Pearlstein, 1997). Substance use, especially alcohol use, is consistently associated with risk for STB in youth (Bagge & Sher, 2008). The disinhibition caused by alcohol intoxication can both facilitate suicidal ideation and increase the likelihood of acting on suicidal thoughts (Ganz & Sher, 2009). The presence of a substance use disorder has been implicated in suicide attempts of higher medical lethality in adolescents (O'Brien & Berzin, 2012).

Among youth with no clear psychopathology, the biggest risk factor for suicide is access to a loaded gun in the home (Brent et al., 1993). Other psychosocial factors that increase the risk for STB include chronic physical illness (Greydanus, Patel, & Pratt, 2010); low peer and/or parental support (Bridge et al., 2006; Joe, Clarke, Ivey, Kerr, & King, 2007; Wagner, Silverman, & Martin, 2003); family history of suicide (Bridge et al., 2006); identification as lesbian, gay, bisexual, transgender, or queer/questioning (LGBTQ) (Haas et al., 2010; Liu & Mustanski, 2012); having been a victim, perpetrator, or victim-perpetrator of bullying (Hepburn, Azrael, Molnar, & Miller, 2012) or sexual or physical abuse (Brodsky et al., 2008). Although nonsuicidal self-injury (NSSI) is by definition not suicidal behavior (and should be treated as distinct), some studies suggest NSSI may be a precursor and/or correlate with STB (Brausch & Gutierrez, 2010; Muehlenkamp & Gutierrez, 2007; Whitlock et al., 2013).

Essential to risk assessment and treatment planning is identifying what might protect youth from suicide risk. Skills and resources that act as a buffer to risk factors are considered protective factors. Protective factors for youth suicide include *internal* factors of skills in problem solving, conflict resolution, stress management, frustration tolerance, and nonviolent ways of handling disputes, and *external* factors of positive therapeutic relationships, social supports (peers and family), and cultural and religious beliefs that discourage suicide and support instincts for self-preservation (Borowsky, Ireland, & Resnick, 2001; Surgeon General, 1999).

ASSESSMENT

The suicide risk assessment must be conducted within a thorough bio-psychosocial evaluation. One can only assess for suicide in the context of other individual and family factors. Individual factors to consider when assessing the suicidal youth include mental status, risk and protective factors, supports currently in place, supports that may be available, ability of the youth to employ coping strategies, future orientation of the youth, and willingness of the youth to engage in treatment. Family factors to consider include family structure and dynamics, willingness of family to engage in treatment, supports available to the family, culture, ethnicity, religion, immigration status, and language, family history of mental illness and treatment, family's ability to identify strengths within the system, current coping strategies, and flexibility in considering treatment options.

To conduct an effective suicide risk assessment with suicidal youth, the parents and the youth must be interviewed separately. Because of shame, stigma, or fear of punishment, youth are often hesitant to express the full extent of their suicidal ideation and intent in front of their parents. Even with their parents out of the room, eliciting suicidal ideation and intent can be challenging. Therefore, social workers should be well-versed in both the content of a suicide risk assessment and techniques designed to elicit suicidal ideation and intent, such as shame attenuation, behavioral incident, gentle assumption, symptom amplification, shame attenuation, and denial of the specific (Shea, 2002). These techniques will help social workers know how to respond when the client says "no," or "I don't know." It is critical to ask open-ended and detailed questions about suicide, including the "who, what, when, where, why, and how." If the youth endorses suicidal ideation, the social worker must then screen for plan, intent, and access. If the youth endorses having made a plan to attempt suicide, the social worker must ask about the timing and location of the act, the lethality and availability of means, and whether or not there are acts currently in preparation. To assess for intent, the social worker must inquire about the extent to which the youth expects to carry out the plan and how much the youth believes the plan to be lethal, as opposed to self-injurious.

Whether or not the youth has endorsed plan or intent, it is critical to ask about access to lethal means. Firearm access is a key risk factor for suicide because of the lethality of the method. In a seminal study, Brent et al. (1993) found that youth with no known suicide risk who lived in a home with a loaded gun were 32 times more likely to die by suicide than youth who lived in homes without a loaded gun. In 2010, firearms accounted for 38% of suicide deaths in youth ages 0–19 (CDC, 2013). Although the next most lethal method, poisoning, accounted for only 6%

of youth suicide deaths in 2010 (CDC, 2013), ingestion represents one of the most common suicide attempt methods. A recent study of 375 youth who presented to an urban general hospital for a suicide attempt found that 87% attempted suicide by ingestion (O'Brien & Berzin, 2012). Therefore, it is critical that social workers assess for the youth's access to over-the-counter medications, household cleaning supplies, and even the youth's own prescription medications. As with the risk assessment, the parent(s) and child should be interviewed separately about access to lethal means. In general with suicide inquiry, it is important to get a detailed, rich description of the current problem and precipitants to the STB. This involves understanding current symptoms and their severity, as well as recent suicidal thoughts, behaviors, attempts, plans, notes, etc. The social worker must also ask about precipitating events (e.g., bullying, fight with girl/boyfriend/parent, break-up) and stressors, and whether or not they are acute (e.g., recent humiliation) or chronic (e.g., school, illness, poverty, abuse/neglect). Prior suicide attempts and current substance use must also be assessed because of their strong association with suicide risk. See Appendix 1 for examples of questions to ask during a suicide risk assessment.

After the social worker has conducted the assessment, the next step is to determine level of risk and corresponding interventions (Rudd, Joiner, & Rajab, 2001). Levels of risk include:

- *None to Mild* = infrequent, low-intensity ideation, no intent or plan; supportive environment; youth can be managed in the community; focus of treatment is on underlying concerns and not suicide risk
- *Moderate* = suicidal ideation, some intent, no plan; youth may or may not be able to be maintained in the community based on the balance of risk versus protective factors; presence of supportive and healthy home, school, and neighborhood environment; focus of treatment is the current suicidal crisis and efforts to minimize risk factors and enhance protective factors
- *High* = frequent and disruptive ideation, strong intent, and specific plan; youth cannot be maintained in the community and is admitted to an inpatient facility; focus of treatment is ensuring safety, identifying and gathering environmental supports, and developing a discharge plan to ensure continuity of care.

Safety Planning. After conducting a thorough suicide risk assessment and determining that the youth is at mild or moderate risk and can return to the community, the social worker must develop a safety plan with the youth and family prior to discharge. Components of a thorough safety plan include engaging the youth in the planning as much as possible, identifying supports that the youth can access if STB worsens, limiting access to means, increasing positive coping strategies, increasing therapeutic support, keeping caregivers involved in the safety plan, and identifying supports at school, work, or other domains of functioning. The safety plan is not a "no-suicide" or "stay alive" contract. Such contracts do not reduce the client's risk for suicide and do not reduce the clinician's risk for a lawsuit following a client's suicide. "No-suicide" contracts are ineffective because they ask clients to promise to say alive without providing a reasonable and agreed upon plan at a time when they are ambivalent about living, and such contracts provide clinicians with a false sense of security (Wortzel, Matarazzo, & Homaifar, 2013). Therefore, "no-suicide contracts" should be replaced with a clinically useful safety plan (Rudd, Mandrusiak, & Joiner Jr., 2006).

Documentation. Contemporaneous and thorough documentation of all interactions with suicidal youth is essential for continuity of care and risk management (Wortzel et al., 2013). In the event of a lawsuit, the only evidence that a social worker has provided ethical, professional, and competent services comes from the documentation. Social workers should document the presence or absence of risk factors and warning signs, suicide ideation, intent, plan, access to means, rationale for the treatment plan, and the disposition. Because it is never expected that a suicide assessment is conducted alone, the names of the professional(s) consulted and their recommendations should be stated in the note (Coleman, 2002).

PREVENTION

Suicide prevention takes a public health perspective in which targets for prevention efforts can be universal, selective, or indicated (Robinson et al., 2013). *Universal* prevention programs target an entire population in an effort to reduce risk factors or enhance protective factors. *Selective* prevention programs target youth who demonstrate risk factors associated with STB, but who have not yet reported suicidal ideation or an attempt. *Indicated* prevention programs are designed to intervene with youth who have already displayed STB. Although it might seem counterintuitive that youth who already display STB would be targeted for a "prevention" program, the intention is to prevent future recurrence of either suicidal ideation or attempts. An "upstream" prevention perspective includes any efforts that "reduce risk factors or enhance protective processes that influence the likelihood that a young person will become suicidal" (American Association of Suicidology, AAS & Society for the Prevention of Teen Suicide, SPTS, 2012, p. 1). The most widely used suicide prevention programs for youth are in schools (Katz et al., 2013; Robinson et al., 2013).

School-based suicide prevention. Because youth spend most of their time in school, school-based suicide prevention programs have the potential to reach the greatest number of youth. The following are examples of school suicide prevention programs (Katz et al., 2013):

- Suicide awareness and education: These programs have the goal of raising awareness about suicide, identifying youth at risk for suicide, and improving social supports. Signs of Suicide (SOS) is an evidence-based awareness/education program that combines video-based education, classroom discussion, and a depression screen. Youth who participated in the SOS program had significantly lower rates of suicide attempts, and greater knowledge and adaptive attitudes towards depression and suicide (Aseltine, James, Schilling, & Glanovsky, 2007).
- Screening: Screening programs, such as Columbia University's "TeenScreen," have a main goal of identifying cases of suicide risk. Depending on how a "case" is defined, it can be considered a universal or selected prevention program. Screening programs are intended to prevent STB by casting a wide net, and then referring identified youth to the appropriate level of care. Some of the problems with screening programs are the burden to the school (e.g., interrupting class time, time consuming for teachers to administer the screen), the lack of appropriate resources, and the fact that parents have to "opt-in" to suicide screening programs.

- Gatekeeper training: The goal of gatekeeper training is to increase knowledge of both the problem and the resources. Question, Persuade, and Respond (QPR; Wyman et al., 2008) is designed to teach students and staff how to identify suicidal students and make appropriate referrals to mental health services. Although school staff participation in QPR training has been shown to significantly improve knowledge of and positive attitudes towards help-seeking, participation has not resulted in improved referrals (Tompkins, Witt, & Abraibesh, 2010).

- Peer Leadership Training: The principle behind peer leadership training is that youth are more likely to reach out to peers rather than adults during a suicidal crisis. Sources of Strength (Wyman et al., 2010) is a universal program that seeks to reduce risk factors and increase protective factors by enlisting and training peer leaders to establish a safe and nurturing school environment. Results of a randomized controlled trial found that students were four times as likely to refer a suicidal friend to an adult, and were significantly more likely to perceive adults and help-seeking as acceptable (Wyman et al., 2010).

- Skills training: Skills training programs can be universal or selected, and are intended to prevent the onset of suicidal ideation. Among the most successful skill training programs is the Good Behavior Game (GBG), which provides universal skills training to youth in elementary school. The goal is to create a safe, nurturing school environment that will foster positive social networks and reduce aggressive and disruptive behavior. In one longitudinal study, youth who were assigned to the GBG were half as likely to experience suicidal ideation compared with the control group, and significantly less likely to experience a suicide attempt (Kellam, Reid, & Balster, 2008).

INTERVENTIONS

Hospital-based

Inpatient Psychiatric Units. STB is the most common presenting problem for youth admitted to an inpatient psychiatric hospital (Wilson, Kelly, Morgan, Harley, & O'Sullivan, 2012). Inpatient psychiatric units represent the most restrictive level of care available to suicidal youth. Inpatient hospitalization is necessary if the suicidal youth's behavior is so unstable and unpredictable that there is serious short-term risk (Shaffer & Pfeffer, 2001). The primary goals of short-term inpatient psychiatric care typically include safety and containment, mood stabilization, and follow-up care coordination.

Emergency Departments. Before admission to inpatient psychiatric hospitals, many youth are evaluated in a hospital Emergency Department (ED). Although the ED is typically used for evaluation only, it represents an ideal environment for a brief intervention with suicidal youth and their families. The *Family-Based Crisis Intervention* (FBCI; Wharff, Ginnis, & Ross, 2012) is a brief intervention designed for use with adolescents and their families when the adolescent presents to the ED in a suicidal crisis. The goal of FBCI is to decrease acute symptoms in the suicidal adolescent so that he/she may return home safely with the family, rather than experience an unnecessary psychiatric hospitalization. The social worker first meets separately with the youth and family to assess what led to the suicidal crisis. Next, the social worker meets with the family together to aid in constructing a unified perception of the problem. At the culmination of this family meeting the social worker helps the family to create a safety plan so that the youth can return home. In a pilot of the intervention, youth receiving FBCI ($n = 67$) were significantly less likely to be psychiatrically hospitalized than those in the control group (36% vs. 55%), and importantly, none of the youth receiving FBCI reported having attempted suicide in the 3-month follow-up period (Wharff et al., 2012).

The *Family Intervention for Suicide Prevention* (FISP; Asarnow, Berk, & Baraff, 2009; Hughes & Asarnow, 2013) is another brief (between 20 and 60 minutes) ED intervention for suicidal adolescents and their families. One of the major goals of FISP is to improve continuity of care between the ED and community mental health services. FISP is implemented after the adolescent has been evaluated and determined safe to return to the community. During FISP, the suicidal crisis is reframed as maladaptive coping skill within the context of a family crisis. FISP aims to promote the development of adaptive coping, make a strong case for the importance of attending follow-up treatment, and encourage healthy and supportive communication. The focus on linkage and adherence to follow-up care is intended to decrease the risk of short-term repeated suicidal behavior. FISP has demonstrated success in connecting youth to follow-up care, but not reducing STB (Asarnow et al., 2011).

Community-based

Community-based practices for suicidal youth include crisis assessment and intervention, individual therapy, family therapy, integrated interventions, and psychopharmacotherapy. Group therapy was a promising modality in the early 2000s (Wood, Trainor, Rothwell, Moore, & Harrington, 2001), but subsequent studies have failed to demonstrate either clinical or economic value (Green et al., 2011; Hazell et al., 2009). An innovative social network intervention for suicidal youth, the Youth-Nominated Support Team-Version II, resulted in a rapid decrease in suicidal ideation within six weeks, but did not result in decreased suicidal ideation or attempts compared to the control condition (King et al., 2009).

Crisis Assessment and Intervention. The goal of a crisis assessment is to determine whether the youth can be maintained in the community for treatment, or if he/she needs to receive inpatient psychiatric services. Crisis intervention is often used to stabilize the current crisis, develop referrals for longer term individual or family treatment, and serve as an alternative to hospitalization (Singer, 2005). There is currently no empirical base for determining when a youth at high risk for suicide would be better served by remaining in the community than receiving inpatient psychiatric care (Lamb, 2009).

Individual Interventions. Because of the importance of parents, family, and the home environment as risk and protective factors, all interventions for suicidal youth must involve the parents/family. This chapter classifies interventions as "individual," even when they have a distinct family component, because the suicide risk is conceptualized as an individual issue. Interventions are classified as "family" when they conceptualize suicide risk as a family issue.

Dialectical-Behavior Therapy for Adolescents (DBT-A; Fleischhaker et al., 2011; Rathus & Miller, 2002). DBT-A was adapted from DBT, which was initially developed to address self-harming behaviors in women with borderline personality disorder (Linehan, Armstrong, Suarez, Allmon, & Heard, 1991). The goal of

DBT is to improve a person's ability to regulate his or her emotions by reducing distress associated with moving between opposing, or dialectical, thoughts, emotions, and behaviors. DBT-A was modified for adolescents to combine weekly individual therapy with a multifamily skills group and between-session therapist check-ins. The first evaluation of DBT-A compared it with treatment-as-usual (TAU) in a sample of suicidal youth with borderline personality disorder. Adolescents in the DBT-A condition had fewer psychiatric hospitalizations during treatment, and were more likely to complete treatment than those in the TAU condition (Rathus & Miller, 2002). Although subsequent studies have consistently found that youth who participate in DBT-A report significant improvements in borderline symptoms and suicidal behavior (Fleischhaker et al., 2011), no studies have found significant differences in STB between youth in the DBT-A condition and youth in a control condition (MacPherson, Cheavens, & Fristad, 2013).

Mentalization-Based Therapy for Adolescents (MBT-A; Rossouw & Fonagy, 2012). MBT-A is a year-long treatment protocol that includes weekly individual and monthly family therapy sessions. The goal of treatment is for adolescents to accurately represent their own and others' emotions and behaviors during times of stress and conflict. MBT-A begins with an assessment and is followed by a written safety plan and case formulation (Rossouw & Fonagy, 2012). The remaining therapy is made up of unstructured sessions that focus on recent interpersonal experiences in order to process the mental states evoked by these experiences. The final phase of treatment addresses the end of the therapeutic relationship. Family sessions have the goal of improving the parents' capacity to mentalize (i.e., make sense of their child's emotional states and way of seeing the world), particularly in the context of family conflict. MBT-A was compared to TAU during a year-long randomized controlled trial (RCT). At 12 months, youth who received MBT-A reported significantly lower scores on a self-harm scale (which included suicidal ideation, attempt, and attempt with medical attention) than youth who received TAU (Rossouw & Fonagy, 2012).

Cognitive Behavior Therapy for Suicide Prevention (CBT-SP; Stanley et al., 2009). CBT-SP is a modification of the first CBT treatment ever evaluated with suicidal youth (Brent, 1997) and was used as one of the interventions in the Treatment of Adolescent Suicide

Attempters (TASA) study (Brent et al., 2009). The goal of CBT-SP is to address suicide risk and prevent future suicidal behavior by identifying and implementing suicide risk reduction strategies and developing or bolstering existing strengths. CBT-SP is divided into three acute phases (beginning, middle, and end), which typically take between 12 and 16 weeks, and a continuation phase, which can last up to an additional 12 weeks. In the beginning of CBT-SP (typically the first three sessions), the therapist meets with the adolescent and parents, establishes rapport, collaboratively develops a safety plan, conducts a detailed chain analysis (i.e., identifies the sequence of events that led up to the suicidal behavior), provides psycho-education, establishes reasons for living and hope, develops a case conceptualization of the adolescent's suicide risk, and develops a treatment plan for ongoing management of the youths' suicidal behavior (Brent, Poling, & Goldstein, 2011; Stanley et al., 2009). The middle phase (sessions 4–9) focuses on developing individual and family skills. The end phase (sessions 10–12) focuses on relapse prevention, during which the therapist tests the skills and coping capabilities of the client by going through an imagined re-creation of the suicide event. Following successful relapse prevention, the adolescent and parents are given the opportunity to apply their new skills to address other problems that were not the focus of the acute phase. CBT-SP was shown to be as effective as psychopharmacotherapy in treating suicide attempters in a 6-month open trial (Brent et al., 2009), and reported fewer reattempts than in comparable studies (Goldston et al., 1999).

Family Interventions. Family-based interventions also have also tested for their effectiveness in decreasing STB in youth. One of the original family-based treatment studies for suicidal youth compared individual CBT (the treatment that evolved into the CBT-SP described above) with Strategic Behavioral Family Therapy (SBFT) and a Non-directive Supportive Treatment (NST) (Brent, 1997). Although SFBT was not as effective as CBT in the short-term reduction of depression and suicide risk, at the 2-year follow-up, all three conditions were equally as effective (Renaud et al., 1998).

Subsequently, there have been studies of the effectiveness of two different family therapy treatments in reducing STB in youth; importantly, these family therapy treatments were not originally designed to reduce STB. The first study evaluated the effectiveness of four sessions of home-based family problem-solving therapy on reducing STB in a sample of adolescents who deliberately poisoned themselves (Harrington et al., 1998). This study found no differences in STB between youth who received the treatment and youth who did not receive the treatment. The second study found that youth participating in Multisystemic Therapy (MST; Huey et al., 2004) were significantly less likely to make a suicide attempt, but not less likely to report suicidal ideation than youth in the control condition. The past decade has seen the development and empirical evaluation of family-based interventions and integrated interventions designed specifically to address STB in youth.

Attachment-Based Family Therapy. Currently, ABFT is one of the few empirically validated treatments for youth with STB (G. S. Diamond et al., 2010; Shpigel, Diamond, & Diamond, 2012). ABFT is designed to address depression and STB via a trust-based, emotion-focused psychotherapy model intended to repair interpersonal ruptures and rebuild an emotionally protective, foundationally secure, parent-child relationship. Through conjoint family sessions and individual sessions with the adolescent and the parents, ABFT strengthens the parent-child relationship, and re-establishes the family as a source of strength and support during suicidal and other crises. ABFT's approach to addressing suicidal youth is different than traditional cognitive behavioral treatment approaches in that it is grounded in attachment theory, relies heavily on emotion-focused techniques rather than cognitive or behavioral techniques, and aims to reduce youth suicidal behavior by repairing or strengthening the parent-child relationship, rather than focusing explicitly on either the youth or the suicidal behavior. Youth and parents in ABFT must complete five tasks over 12–16 weeks. In Task 1, "Relational Reframe," the youth's depression and STB are reframed as a family issue. In Task 2, "Adolescent Alliance," and Task 3, "Parent Alliance," the therapist meets individually with the adolescent and the parent in order to identify the attachment ruptures and prepare for Task 4. In Task 4, "Attachment," the adolescent explains to the parent why he or she does not go to the parent when feeling depressed or suicidal and has an experience of being heard and understood by the parent. In Task 5, "Competency," the adolescent and parent address day-to-day issues (including suicide risk) within the framework of a more secure attachment (G. S. Diamond, Diamond, & Levy, 2013). ABFT has demonstrated reduction in suicidal ideation in two clinical trials with a range of youth, including those with a history of trauma, LGB youth, youth with depression and anxiety, and has been evaluated primarily with low-income, multi-problem urban families (G. M. Diamond et al., 2012; G. S. Diamond, Creed, Gillham, Gallop, & Hamilton, 2012).

Integrated Interventions. Integrated CBT (I-CBT; Esposito-Smythers, Spirito, Kahler, Hunt, & Monti, 2011) is a promising intervention for adolescents with comorbid STB and substance abuse that combines both individual and family treatment strategies. I-CBT targets the common maladaptive behaviors and beliefs that underlie the two problems of STB and substance abuse. Individually, the intervention addresses issues with cognitive distortions, coping, and communication by working with the adolescent on cognitive restructuring, problem solving, affect regulation, and communication skills (Esposito-Smythers et al., 2011). To bolster the effectiveness of I-CBT with adolescents, a parent training session and/or family session is added in which the mental health and substance abuse treatment goals of the adolescent are addressed with the parents, and skills of monitoring, emotion regulation, communication skills, and behavioral contracting are taught to the parents (Esposito-Smythers et al., 2011). In a randomized trial, Esposito-Smythers et al. (2011) found I-CBT, relative to enhanced treatment as usual (E-TAU), to be associated with significantly less global impairment as well as fewer suicide attempts, inpatient psychiatric hospitalizations, emergency department visits, heavy drinking days, and days of marijuana use.

PSYCHOPHARMACOTHERAPY

Psychopharmacological interventions are often used with youth with STB to treat the underlying psychiatric symptomatology. Social workers are not trained to prescribe psychiatric medications and thus should not give medical advice to suicidal youth and their families. However, social workers have an ethical obligation to understand and work with psychopharmacologists to best serve their clients, and therefore, should know about the properties and side effects of psychiatric mediations prescribed to youth with STB.

There has been much controversy about prescribing antidepressant medication to suicidal youth since the U.S. Food and Drug Administration issued a black box warning regarding antidepressants and STB in youth in 2004. However, a recent meta-analysis by Gibbons et al. (2012) found no increased suicide risk for youth receiving psychopharmacological treatment for depression. Social workers should take from these findings the importance of psychopharmacological interventions with suicidal youth and the corresponding need for monitoring of mood and behavior changes for youth who take these medications.

CONCLUSION AND FUTURE DIRECTIONS

In this chapter we have identified and described current assessment, prevention, and intervention strategies with suicidal youth. The existing empirical literature suggests that few prevention programs (GBG) and intervention programs (MBT-A, ABFT, and I-CBT) have been shown to reduce STB in youth, highlighting the need for continued research on effective interventions with this population. The following are some promising developments in suicide prevention and intervention. (1) Identification of risk factors and warning signs: The National Center for the Prevention of Youth Suicide (http://www.suicidology.org/ncpys) is coordinating an international expert panel to identify risk factors and warning signs for children and adolescents. (2) Screening for suicide risk. Currently screening occurs primarily in schools. The Affordable Care Act will provide financial and structural incentives to conduct screening for suicide risk in primary care settings (O'Connor, Gaynes, Burda, Williams, & Whitlock, 2013; Wintersteen, 2010), which could reduce the burden on schools, capture high-risk youth who are no longer attending school, and result in better identification and referral of suicidal youth. (3) Interventions. As described above, interventions for suicidal youth focus primarily on individuals or families. Two programs are currently being evaluated that would provide support and intervention to parents of suicidal youth. Hooven (2013) are developing and testing a suicide prevention program for parents that combines psycho-education around suicide risk, emotion coaching, and communication skills training around parental assessment of youth suicide risk. Esposito-Smythers et al. (2011) are currently testing an extension of their I-CBT protocol for suicidal youth with substance use and/or NSSI, which uses two therapists, one for the youth and one for the parents, to help enhance treatment effectiveness and minimize suicide risk. A final development is suicide assessment, prevention, and intervention using computer and Internet technologies (CIT). Current CIT applications include text or chat-based crisis hotlines, suicide prevention video games, online therapy (using webcams, virtual reality environments, or text-based modes), and identification of suicidal statements on search engines or social networks using textual analysis (Luxton, June, & Kinn, 2011). These emerging advances in suicide prevention and intervention efforts will help guide our current treatment practices with suicidal youth.

APPENDIX 1

Specific Questioning for Suicide Inquiry

Ask about suicidal ideation, plans, behaviors, and intent openly and frankly.

- Have you been having thoughts about killing yourself either now or in the past?
- Do you ever feel that life isn't worth living?
- Have you ever wished you could just go to sleep and not wake up?
- Have you ever tried to hurt yourself, wishing you would die?
- Have you ever tried to kill yourself?
- What did you think would happen when you . . . (overdosed, etc.).
- How do you feel that you are still alive after having attempted suicide?

If the youth answers, "yes" to any of these, ask: who, what, when, where, why, and how.

- What are you thinking of doing?
- When do you think you might do it?
- Where might you hurt or kill yourself?
- How might you hurt or kill yourself?
- Why do you want to kill yourself?
- Who knows about this?

References

AAS & SPTS. (2012). Upstream youth suicide prevention expert panel meeting summary. American Association of Suicidology (AAS) and the Society for the Prevention of Teen Suicide (SPTS). Retrieved from http://www.sprc.org/sites/sprc.org/files/library/Upstream_Youth_Suicide_Prevention_Expert_Panel_Meeting%20Summary.pdf

Asarnow, J. R., Berk, M. S., & Baraff, L. J. (2009). Family Intervention for Suicide Prevention: A specialized emergency department intervention for suicidal youths. *Professional Psychology: Research and Practice*, 40(2), 118–125. doi:10.1037/a0012599

Asarnow, J. R., Porta, G., Spirito, A., Emslie, G., Clarke, G., Wagner, K. D., . . . Brent, D. A. (2011). Suicide attempts and nonsuicidal self-injury in the treatment of resistant depression in adolescents: Findings from the TORDIA study. *Journal of the American Academy of Child & Adolescent Psychiatry*, 50(8), 772–781. doi:10.1016/j.jaac.2011.04.003

Aseltine, R. H., Jr, James, A., Schilling, E. A., & Glanovsky, J. (2007). Evaluating the SOS suicide prevention program: A replication and extension. *BMC Public Health*, 7, 161. doi:10.1186/1471-2458-7-161

Bagge, C. L., & Sher, K. J. (2008). Adolescent alcohol involvement and suicide attempts: Toward the development of a conceptual framework. *Clinical Psychology Review*, 28(8), 1283–1296. doi:10.1016/j.cpr.2008.06.002

Borowsky, I. W., Ireland, M., & Resnick, M. D. (2001). Adolescent suicide attempts: Risks and protectors. *Pediatrics*, 107(3), 485–493.

Brausch, A. M., & Gutierrez, P. M. (2010). Differences in non-suicidal self-injury and suicide attempts in adolescents. *Journal of Youth and Adolescence*, 39(3), 233–242. doi:10.1007/s10964-009-9482-0

Brent, D. A. (1997). A clinical psychotherapy trial for adolescent depression comparing cognitive, family, and supportive therapy. *Archives of General Psychiatry*, 54(9), 877. doi:10.1001/archpsyc.1997.01830210125017

Brent, D. A., Greenhill, L. L., Compton, S., Emslie, G., Wells, K., Walkup, J. T., . . . Turner, J. B. (2009). The Treatment of Adolescent Suicide Attempters study (TASA): Predictors of suicidal events in an open treatment trial. *Journal of the American Academy of Child and Adolescent Psychiatry*, 48(10), 987–996. doi:10.1097/CHI.0b013e3181b5dbe4

Brent, D. A., Perper, J. A., Moritz, G., Baugher, M., Schweers, J., & Roth, C. (1993). Firearms and adolescent suicide: A community case-control study. *American Journal of Diseases of Children*, 147(10), 1066–1071. doi:10.1001/archpedi.1993.02160340052013

Brent, D. A., Poling, K. D., & Goldstein, T. R. (2011). *Treating depressed and suicidal adolescents: A clinician's guide.* New York, NY: Guilford Press.

Bridge, J. A., Goldstein, T. R., & Brent, D. A. (2006). Adolescent suicide and suicidal behavior. *Journal of Child Psychology and Psychiatry, and Allied Disciplines, 47*(3–4), 372–394. doi:10.1111/j.1469-7610.2006.01615.x

Brodsky, B. S., Mann, J. J., Stanley, B., Tin, A., Oquendo, M., Birmaher, B., . . . Brent, D. (2008). Familial transmission of suicidal behavior: Factors mediating the relationship between childhood abuse and offspring suicide attempts. *The Journal of Clinical Psychiatry, 69*(4), 584–596.

Bryan, C. J., & Rudd, M. D. (2011). *Managing suicide risk in primary care.* New York, NY: Springer Publishing Company.

Centers for Disease Control and Prevention, National Center for Injury Prevention and Control. (2013). *Web-based Injury Statistics Query and Reporting System (WISQARS)* (Fatal Injury Reports, 1999–2010, for National, Regional, and States [RESTRICTED]). Retrieved from http://webappa.cdc.gov/cgi-bin/broker.exe

Coleman, M. (2002, April). Minimizing practice risks with suicidal patients: Practice update. National Association of Social Workers. Retrieved from www.naswdc.org/practice/clinical/csw0204.pdf

De Leo, D., Burgis, S., Bertolote, J. M., Kerkhof, A. J. F. M., & Bille-Brahe, U. (2006). Definitions of suicidal behavior. *Crisis: The Journal of Crisis Intervention and Suicide Prevention, 27*(1), 4–15. doi:10.1027/0227-5910.27.1.4

Diamond, G. M., Diamond, G. S., Levy, S., Closs, C., Ladipo, T., & Siqueland, L. (2012). Attachment-based family therapy for suicidal lesbian, gay, and bisexual adolescents: A treatment development study and open trial with preliminary findings. *Psychotherapy, 49*(1), 62–71. doi:10.1037/a0026247

Diamond, G. S., Creed, T., Gillham, J., Gallop, R., & Hamilton, J. L. (2012). Sexual trauma history does not moderate treatment outcome in Attachment-Based Family Therapy (ABFT) for adolescents with suicide ideation. *Journal of Family Psychology, 26*(4), 595–605. doi:10.1037/a0028414

Diamond, G. S., Diamond, G. M., & Levy, S. A. (2013). *Attachment-Based Family Therapy for depressed adolescents.* New York, NY: American Psychological Association.

Diamond, G. S., Wintersteen, M. B., Brown, G. K., Diamond, G. M., Gallop, R., Shelef, K., & Levy, S. (2010). Attachment-based family therapy for adolescents with suicide ideation: A randomized controlled trial. *Journal of the American Academy of Child and Adolescent Psychiatry, 49*(2), 122–131.

Esposito-Smythers, C., Spirito, A., Kahler, C. W., Hunt, J., & Monti, P. (2011). Treatment of co-occurring substance abuse and suicidality among adolescents: A randomized trial. *Journal of Consulting and Clinical Psychology, 79*(6), 728–739. doi:10.1037/a0026074

Evans, E., Hawton, K., & Rodham, K. (2004). Factors associated with suicidal phenomena in adolescents: A systematic review of population-based studies. *Clinical Psychology Review, 24*(8), 957–979. doi:10.1016/j.cpr.2004.04.005

Fleischhaker, C., Böhme, R., Sixt, B., Brück, C., Schneider, C., & Schulz, E. (2011). Dialectical Behavioral Therapy for adolescents (DBT-A): A clinical trial for patients with suicidal and self-injurious behavior and borderline symptoms with a one-year follow-up. *Child and Adolescent Psychiatry and Mental Health, 5*(1), 3. doi:10.1186/1753-2000-5-3

Ganz, D., & Sher, L. (2009). Suicidal behavior in adolescents with comorbid depression and alcohol abuse. *Minerva Pediatrica, 61*(3), 333–347.

Gibbons, R. D., Brown, C. H., Hur, K., Davis, J., & Mann, J. J. (2012). Suicidal thoughts and behavior with antidepressant treatment: Reanalysis of the randomized placebo-controlled studies of fluoxetine and venlafaxine. *Archives of General Psychiatry, 69*(6), 580–587. doi:10.1001/archgenpsychiatry.2011.2048

Goldston, D. B., Daniel, S. S., Reboussin, D. M., Reboussin, B. A., Frazier, P. H., & Kelley, A. E. (1999). Suicide attempts among formerly hospitalized adolescents: A prospective naturalistic study of risk during the first 5 years after discharge. *Journal of the American Academy of Child and Adolescent Psychiatry, 38*(6), 660–671. doi:10.1097/00004583-199906000-00012

Green, J. M., Wood, A. J., Kerfoot, M. J., Trainor, G., Roberts, C., Rothwell, J., . . . Harrington, R. (2011). Group therapy for adolescents with repeated self harm: Randomised controlled trial with economic evaluation. *British Medical Journal, 342*, d682.

Greydanus, D., Patel, D., & Pratt, H. (2010). Suicide risk in adolescents with chronic illness: Implications for primary care and specialty pediatric practice: a review. *Developmental Medicine and Child Neurology, 52*(12), 1083–1087. doi:10.1111/j.1469-8749.2010.03771.x

Groholt, B., Ekeberg, Ø., & Haldorsen, T. (2006). Adolescent suicide attempters: What predicts future suicidal acts? *Suicide & Life-Threatening Behavior, 36*(6), 638–650. doi:10.1521/suli.2006.36.6.638

Haas, A. P., Eliason, M., Mays, V. M., Mathy, R. M., Cochran, S. D., D'Augelli, A. R., . . . Clayton, P. J. (2010). Suicide and suicide risk in lesbian, gay, bisexual, and transgender populations: Review and recommendations. *Journal of*

Homosexuality, 58(1), 10–51. doi:10.1080/00918
369.2011.534038

Harrington, R., Kerfoot, M., Dyer, E., McNiven, F., Gill, J., Harrington, V., . . . Byford, S. (1998). Randomized trial of a home-based family intervention for children who have deliberately poisoned themselves. *Journal of the American Academy of Child and Adolescent Psychiatry*, 37(5), 512–518.

Hazell, P. L., Martin, G., McGill, K., Kay, T., Wood, A., Trainor, G., & Harrington, R. (2009). Group therapy for repeated deliberate self-harm in adolescents: Failure of replication of a randomized trial. *Journal of the American Academy of Child and Adolescent Psychiatry*, 48(6), 662–670. doi:10.1097/CHI.0b013e3181aOacec

Hepburn, L., Azrael, D., Molnar, B., & Miller, M. (2012). Bullying and suicidal behaviors among urban high school youth. *Journal of Adolescent Health*, 51(1), 93–95. doi:10.1016/j.jadohealth.2011.12.014

Hooven, C. (2013). Parents-CARE: A suicide prevention program for parents of at-risk youth. *Journal of Child and Adolescent Psychiatric Nursing*, 26(1), 85–95. doi:10.1111/jcap.12025

Hoyert, D. L. (2012). 75 years of mortality in the United States, 1935–2010. *NCHS data brief*, (88), 1–8.

Huey, S. J., Jr, Henggeler, S. W., Rowland, M. D., Halliday-Boykins, C. A., Cunningham, P. B., Pickrel, S. G., & Edwards, J. (2004). Multisystemic therapy effects on attempted suicide by youths presenting psychiatric emergencies. *Journal of the American Academy of Child and Adolescent Psychiatry*, 43(2), 183–190. doi:10.1097/00004583-200402000-00014

Hughes, J. L., & Asarnow, J. R. (2013). Enhanced mental health interventions in the emergency department: Suicide and suicide attempt prevention. *Clinical Pediatric Emergency Medicine*, 14(1), 28–34. doi:10.1016/j.cpem.2013.01.002

Joe, S., Clarke, J., Ivey, A. Z., Kerr, D., & King, C. A. (2007). Impact of familial factors and psychopathology on suicidality among African American adolescents. *Journal of Human Behavior in the Social Environment*, 15(2–3), 199–218. doi:10.1300/J137v15n02_12

Katz, C., Bolton, S.-L., Katz, L. Y., Isaak, C., Tilston-Jones, T., Sareen, J., & Swampy Cree Suicide Prevention Team. (2013). A systematic review of school-based suicide prevention programs. *Depression and Anxiety*, n/a–n/a. doi:10.1002/da.22114

Kellam, S. G., Reid, J., & Balster, R. L. (2008). Effects of a universal classroom behavior program in first and second grades on young adult problem outcomes. *Drug and Alcohol Dependence*, 95(Suppl 1), S1–S4. doi:10.1016/j.drugalcdep.2008.01.006

King, C. A., Klaus, N., Kramer, A., Venkataraman, S., Quinlan, P., & Gillespie, B. (2009). The Youth-Nominated Support Team-Version II for suicidal adolescents: A randomized controlled intervention trial. *Journal of Consulting and Clinical Psychology*, 77(5), 880–893. doi:10.1037/a0016552

Lamb, C. E. (2009). Alternatives to admission for children and adolescents: Providing intensive mental healthcare services at home and in communities: What works? *Current Opinion in Psychiatry*, 22(4), 345–350. doi:10.1097/YCO.0b013e32832c9082

Linehan, M. M., Armstrong, H. E., Suarez, A., Allmon, D., & Heard, H. L. (1991). Cognitive-behavioral treatment of chronically parasuicidal borderline patients. *Archives of General Psychiatry*, 48(12), 1060–1064.

Liu, R. T., & Mustanski, B. (2012). Suicidal ideation and self-harm in lesbian, gay, bisexual, and transgender youth. *American Journal of Preventive Medicine*, 42(3), 221–228. doi:10.1016/j.amepre.2011.10.023

Luxton, D. D., June, J. D., & Kinn, J. T. (2011). Technology-based suicide prevention: current applications and future directions. *Telemedicine Journal and E-health*, 17(1), 50–54. doi:10.1089/tmj.2010.0091

MacPherson, H. A., Cheavens, J. S., & Fristad, M. A. (2013). Dialectical behavior therapy for adolescents: Theory, treatment adaptations, and empirical outcomes. *Clinical Child and Family Psychology Review*, 16(1), 59–80. doi:10.1007/s10567-012-0126-7

Muehlenkamp, J. J., & Gutierrez, P. M. (2007). Risk for suicide attempts among adolescents who engage in non-suicidal self-injury. *Archives of Suicide Research*, 11(1), 69–82. doi:10.1080/13811110600992902

Nance, M. L., Carr, B. G., Kallan, M. J., Branas, C. C., & Wiebe, D. J. (2010). Variation in pediatric and adolescent firearm mortality rates in rural and urban US counties. *Pediatrics*, 125(6), 1112–1118. doi:10.1542/peds.2009-3219

Negron, R., Piacentini, J., Graae, F., Davies, M., & Shaffer, D. (1997). Microanalysis of adolescent suicide attempters and ideators during the acute suicidal episode. *Journal of the American Academy of Child and Adolescent Psychiatry*, 36(11), 1512–1519. doi:10.1016/S0890-8567(09)66559-X

Nock, M. K., Green, J. G., Hwang, I., McLaughlin, K. A., Sampson, N. A., Zaslavsky, A. M., & Kessler, R. C. (2013). Prevalence, correlates, and treatment of lifetime suicidal behavior among adolescents: Results from the National Comorbidity Survey Replication Adolescent Supplement. *JAMA Psychiatry*, 70(3), 300–310. doi:10.1001/2013.jamapsychiatry.55

O'Brien, K. H. M., & Berzin, S. C. (2012). Examining the impact of psychiatric diagnosis and comorbidity on the medical lethality of adolescent suicide attempts. *Suicide & Life-threatening Behavior*, 42(4), 437–444. doi:10.1111/j.1943-278X.2012.00102.x

O'Connor, E., Gaynes, B., Burda, B. U., Williams, C., & Whitlock, E. P. (2013). *Screening for suicide risk in primary care: A systematic evidence review for the U.S. Preventive Services Task Force.* Rockville, MD: Agency for Healthcare Research and Quality. Retrieved from http://www.ncbi.nlm.nih.gov/books/NBK137737/

Prinstein, M. J., Nock, M. K., Simon, V., Aikins, J. W., Cheah, C. S. L., & Spirito, A. (2008). Longitudinal trajectories and predictors of adolescent suicidal ideation and attempts following inpatient hospitalization. *Journal of Consulting and Clinical Psychology*, 76(1), 92–103. doi:10.1037/0022-006X.76.1.92

Rathus, J. H., & Miller, A. L. (2002). Dialectical behavior therapy adapted for suicidal adolescents. *Suicide & Life-Threatening Behavior*, 32(2), 146–157. doi:10.1521/suli.32.2.146.24399

Renaud, J., Brent, D. A., Baugher, M., Birmaher, B., Kolko, D. J., & Bridge, J. (1998). Rapid response to psychosocial treatment for adolescent depression: A two-year follow-up. *Journal of the American Academy of Child and Adolescent Psychiatry*, 37(11), 1184–1190. doi:10.1097/00004583-199811000-00019

Robinson, J., Cox, G., Malone, A., Williamson, M., Baldwin, G., Fletcher, K., & O'Brien, M. (2013). A systematic review of school-based interventions aimed at preventing, treating, and responding to suicide-related behavior in young people. *Crisis*, 34(3), 164–182. doi:10.1027/0227-5910/a000168

Rossouw, T. I., & Fonagy, P. (2012). Mentalization-based treatment for self-harm in adolescents: A randomized controlled trial. *Journal of the American Academy of Child and Adolescent Psychiatry*, 51(12), 1304–1313.e3. doi:10.1016/j.jaac.2012.09.018

Rudd, M. D., Joiner, T. E., & Rajab, M. H. (2001). *Treating suicidal behavior: An effective, time-limited approach.* New York, NY: Guilford Press.

Rudd, M. D., Mandrusiak, M., & Joiner Jr, T. E. (2006). The case against no-suicide contracts: The commitment to treatment statement as a practice alternative. *Journal of Clinical Psychology*, 62(2), 243–251. doi:10.1002/jclp.20227

Shaffer, D., & Pfeffer, C. R. (2001). Practice parameter for the assessment and treatment of children and adolescents with suicidal behavior. *Journal of the American Academy of Child & Adolescent Psychiatry*, 40(Suppl 7), 24S–51S.

Shea, S. C. (2002). *The practical art of suicide assessment: A guide for mental health professionals and substance abuse counselors.* Lexington, KY: Mental Health Presses.

Shpigel, M. S., Diamond, G. M., & Diamond, G. S. (2012). Changes in parenting behaviors, attachment, depressive symptoms, and suicidal ideation in attachment-based family therapy for depressive and suicidal adolescents. *Journal of Marital and Family Therapy*, 38(Suppl 1), 271–283. doi:10.1111/j.1752-0606.2012.00295.x

Singer, J. B. (2005). Child and adolescent psychiatric emergencies: Mobile crisis response. In A. R. Roberts (Ed.), *Crisis intervention handbook: Assessment, treatment, and research* (3rd ed.). (pp. 319–361). Oxford; New York: Oxford University Press.

Singer, J. B., & Slovak, K. (2011). School social workers' experiences of youth suicide. *Children & Schools*, 33, 215–228. doi:10.1093/cs/33.4.215

Stanley, B., Brown, G., Brent, D. A., Wells, K., Poling, K., Curry, J., . . . Hughes, J. (2009). Cognitive-behavioral therapy for suicide prevention (CBT-SP): Treatment model, feasibility, and acceptability. *Journal of the American Academy of Child and Adolescent Psychiatry*, 48(10), 1005–1013. doi:10.1097/CHI.0b013e3181b5dbfe

Surgeon General. (1999). *The Surgeon General's Call to Action to Prevent Suicide.* Washington, DC: Office of the Surgeon General: United States Public Health Service.

Tompkins, T. L., Witt, J., & Abraibesh, N. (2010). Does a gatekeeper suicide prevention program work in a school setting? Evaluating training outcome and moderators of effectiveness. *Suicide & Life-threatening Behavior*, 40(5), 506–515. doi:10.1521/suli.2010.40.5.506

U.S. D.H.H.S. (2012). *2012 National Strategy for Suicide Prevention: Goals and Objectives for Action.* Washington, DC: U.S. Department of Health and Human Services (HHS) Office of the Surgeon General and National Action Alliance for Suicide Prevention. Retrieved from http://www.surgeongeneral.gov/library/reports/national-strategy-suicide-prevention/full-report.pdf

Wagner, B. M., Silverman, M. A. C., & Martin, C. E. (2003). Family factors in youth suicidal behaviors. *American Behavioral Scientist*, 46(9), 1171–1191. doi:10.1177/0002764202250661

Wharff, E. A., Ginnis, K. M., & Ross, A. M. (2012). Family-based Crisis Intervention with suicidal adolescents in the emergency room: A pilot study. *Social Work*, 57(2), 133–143. doi:10.1093/sw/sws017

Whitlock, J., Muehlenkamp, J., Eckenrode, J., Purington, A., Baral Abrams, G., Barreira, P., & Kress, V. (2013). Nonsuicidal self-injury as a gateway to suicide in young adults. *Journal of Adolescent Health*, 52(4), 486–492. doi:10.1016/j.jadohealth.2012.09.010

Wilson, L. S., Kelly, B. D., Morgan, S., Harley, M., & O'Sullivan, M. (2012). Who gets admitted? Study of referrals and admissions to an adolescent psychiatry inpatient facility over a 6-month period. *Irish Journal of Medical Science*, 181(4), 555–560. doi:10.1007/s11845-012-0817-6

Wintersteen, M. B. (2010). Standardized screening for suicidal adolescents in primary care. *Pediatrics*, 125(5), 938–944. doi:10.1542/peds.2009-2458

Wood, A., Trainor, G., Rothwell, J., Moore, A., & Harrington, R. (2001). Randomized trial of group therapy for repeated deliberate self-harm in adolescents. *Journal of the American Academy of Child and Adolescent Psychiatry*, 40(11), 1246–1253. doi:10.1097/00004583-200111000-00003

Wortzel, H. S., Matarazzo, B., & Homaifar, B. (2013). A model for therapeutic risk management of the suicidal patient. *Journal of Psychiatric Practice*, 19(4), 323–326. doi:10.1097/01.pra.0000432603.99211.e8

Wyman, P. A., Brown, C. H., Inman, J., Cross, W., Schmeelk-Cone, K., Guo, J., & Pena, J. B. (2008). Randomized trial of a gatekeeper program for suicide prevention: 1-year impact on secondary school staff. *Journal of Consulting and Clinical Psychology*, 76(1), 104–115. doi:10.1037/0022-006X.76.1.104

Wyman, P. A., Brown, C. H., LoMurray, M., Schmeelk-Cone, K., Petrova, M., Yu, Q., . . . Wang, W. (2010). An outcome evaluation of the Sources of Strength suicide prevention program delivered by adolescent peer leaders in high schools. *American Journal of Public Health*, 100(9), 1653–1661. doi:10.2105/AJPH.2009.190025

Zahl, D. L., & Hawton, K. (2004). Repetition of deliberate self-harm and subsequent suicide risk: Long-term follow-up study of 11,583 patients. *The British Journal of Psychiatry: The Journal of Mental Science*, 185, 70–75.

Zlotnick, C., Donaldson, D., Spirito, A., & Pearlstein, T. (1997). Affect regulation and suicide attempts in adolescent inpatients. *Journal of the American Academy of Child and Adolescent Psychiatry*, 36(6), 793–798. doi:10.1097/00004583-199706000-00016

67   Intensive Family Preservation Services

Betty J. Blythe & Andrea Cole

Home visits and home-based services enjoy a long tradition in social work. An early proponent of home visiting by social workers was Mary Richmond, who wrote about the advantages of meeting clients in their homes where the social worker could observe how family members interacted with one another in their home environment (Richmond, 1917). Intensive family preservation services is a specific model of home-based services that provide supports to families in their homes and communities through a mix of case management and intensive therapeutic services. The model most often associated with intensive family preservation services is Homebuilders©. Developed in Tacoma,

Washington in 1974 (Kinney, Madsen, Fleming, & Haapala, 1977), Homebuilders originally focused on preventing unnecessary out-of-home placement of children who were at imminent risk of being placed in foster homes. Intensive family preservation services are not offered if there are concerns that the child(ren) cannot be safely maintained in the home and if the family refuses services.

Unlike traditional child welfare services, intensive family preservation services work with the entire family rather than focusing solely on one or more children. They are further distinguished from other home-based services by their intensity and duration. Although there is some variation, most intensive family preservation programs share the following characteristics:

- Small caseloads, typically two to four families
- One worker provides the services, although support and backup is available from one or more colleagues.
- Services are provided 24 hours a day, 7 days a week, for regularly scheduled appointments and to handle crisis or emergency calls.
- Services include "hard" or "concrete," services such as transportation, housing, or food, and therapeutic services as well as "soft" services.
- Most services are provided in the family's home, including the extended family, and in community settings in the family's environment such as the school or church.
- Services are intensive, with families being seen between 6 and 10 hours per week, and are time-limited, typically lasting one to four months (Haapala & Kinney, 1979; Kinney, Haapala, Booth, & Leavitt, 1990; Nelson, Walters, Schweitzer, Blythe, & Pecora, 2009; Walton, Sandau-Beckler, & Mannes, 2001).

Small caseloads are critical so that workers can work intensively with families and be available for crisis calls. The length and frequency of visits builds on Richmond's (1917) advice about the advantages of seeing families in their home settings. One of the Homebuilders founders explained that early assessment visits, without time constraints, allowed the worker to get the "big picture," and subsequent and frequent visits allowed the worker to understand what was happening before the family's story had totally changed. Likewise, support and backup by colleagues make it possible for services to be available to families "24/7," to ensure that family members are safe, and to provide consultation and other forms of support to workers who are dealing with difficult, stressful situations. Moreover, scheduling visits outside of a traditional work day increases the possibility that most or all family members will be available for the visit. Services tend to be broadly defined within the intensive family preservation services framework, and the treatment model is best described as highly flexible. Often, families who need such intensive intervention have become disconnected from their families of origin and communities and are not aware of possible sources of support. Hard services might include help with budgeting, or accessing resources to pay their utility bills. Or, the family

preservation services worker might familiarize family members with such community resources as food banks, health clinics, and recreational facilities. Similarly, so-called soft services are varied and emphasize teaching families skills to resolve real-life problems (Wells, Pecora, & Booth, 2014). These soft services include such things as

- Parent training
- Anger management training
- Cognitive-behavioral interventions
- Rational emotive therapy
- Communication skills training

Initial work with the family requires that the worker defuse the crisis that precipitated the referral and build a relationship with the family. Assessment of the family's needs and developing goals occurs in partnership with the family. Time limitations of one to four months acknowledge that families referred for intensive family preservation services are in crisis and, therefore, are open to change. At the same time, once the "crisis" or the reason for referral has been resolved, families are less likely to be invested in services. Among other things, intensive family preservation services attempt to build a safety net around families so that they can continue to do well after the close of services. Given the stressors associated with poverty and other situational variables that they tend to experience in their daily lives, many of these multi-problem families will need booster sessions or additional services in the future.

CASE EXAMPLE

Although there is no such thing as a typical intensive family preservation case, a case illustration can help to illuminate the nature of such services. The following case example depicts the assessment, goal setting, and interventions for a case referred by the child welfare system to an intensive family preservation services professional in Washington State.

Meeting the Lopez Family

Homebuilders became involved with the Lopez family following a referral by child protective services. Lauren Blackwell, MSW, was assigned the case. The Lopez family consists of Maria Lopez (mother), Jason Lopez (father), Gorge Lopez (11-year-old child), Yessenia Lopez (10-year-old child), and Junior Lopez (1-year-old child). The referral was due to founded cases of physical neglect, medical neglect, and supervisory neglect. Before the initial visit, Lauren reviewed the records of the case and was aware of the concerns of child protective services but planned to ask the Lopezes to describe their challenges in their own words.

Lauren conducted the first meeting, and many thereafter, in the family's home, where it would be most convenient for them. During the initial meeting with Mr. and Mrs. Lopez and their three children, she engaged the family and worked to develop rapport by explaining why Homebuilders became involved, asking the Lopezes to explain what needs they felt they had, and the goals they wanted to work toward. She also described the type of assistance she could provide.

During this initial visit, Lauren gathered information about the family, and it became clear that the Lopezes were facing many challenges. Lauren observed that the home was infested with multiple types of insects and was cluttered with dirty dishes, unlaundered clothes, and spoiling food. The family lived in a dilapidated apartment building that had unsafe public areas. The Lopezes divulged that there were times when the older children played in these areas, as there were so few other places for the children to play. Also, the Lopezes explained that due to a lack of health insurance, none of the children were up-to-date on their medical check-ups. The children's hygiene also was poor. In addition, both parents were abusing amphetamines on a regular basis, making it difficult for them to provide adequate supervision to keep the children safe and organization to maintain the children's physical needs and the household. At the same time, Mr. and Mrs. Lopez showed a number of strengths, including apparent concern for each other and their family, motivation to accept services, and a desire to work on the part of Mr. Lopez.

Creating Goals

Based on the information provided in the referral and the information that Lauren was able to gather from the Lopezes, including their own priorities, issues, and concerns, Lauren and Mr. and Mrs. Lopez agreed on a service plan with three overarching goals:

(1) Enhance cleanliness of the home and improve hygiene of the family
(2) Ensure the safety of the family
(3) Connect the family with necessary community resources so that they can do well after Homebuilders services are terminated.

They agreed to work together on these goals over the course of the coming four to six weeks, meeting in the home multiple times a week, especially in the afternoons or evenings when the children would be home from school. The Lopezes seemed to feel heard and respected by Lauren and, given their motivation to keep their children in their home, agreed to this schedule.

INTERVENTIONS

Initially, Lauren prioritized safety and helping the Lopezes with concrete services. She met with Mr. and Mrs. Lopez to discuss strategies for keeping the home clean, such as creating a chore chart so that the older children could participate and a calendar with dates for certain chores. Lauren initially assisted the family in purchasing home cleaning supplies and also toothbrushes, toothpaste, shampoo, and bath soap to improve family hygiene. Lauren also provided psycho-education to the parents and older children around the importance of daily hygiene. The family's habits in both of these areas quickly improved.

Lauren also worked with Mrs. Lopez, Mr. Lopez, and the two older children, Gorge and Yessenia, to create a safety plan. It was decided that the children must always be home before 6:00 P.M. and were not to go into anyone else's home in the neighborhood. Lauren discussed with Gorge and Yessenia the importance of staying in a group with other children whom they know, and screaming loudly if anyone bothers them. Lauren discussed with the family options for other places for the children to play. Mr. and Mrs. Lopez were able to identify a local YMCA where the children could go after school for a few hours, instead of outside in the neighborhood.

Over the course of a few weeks, Lauren arranged for both Mr. and Mrs. Lopez to obtain a psychiatric evaluation, given their admission of amphetamine abuse. Mrs. Lopez was diagnosed with Attention Deficit/Hyperactivity Disorder, Obsessive-Compulsive Disorder, and Post-Traumatic Stress Disorder. Mr. Lopez was diagnosed with Post-Traumatic Stress Disorder and a traumatic brain injury. Mr. Lopez experienced the brain injury during the Gulf War. His symptoms included poor memory, irritability, and low frustration tolerance.

Given these diagnoses, Lauren worked with the family and local agencies to connect Mrs. and Mr. Lopez to the appropriate health and mental health services. Mrs. Lopez was linked to a therapist and psychiatrist offering treatment for both her mental illness and substance abuse, including medications. In addition to a substance abuse outpatient program, Lauren connected Mr. Lopez with an institute at a local university that specializes in treating the specific type of brain injury he suffered. Lauren worked with Mrs. Lopez to obtain appointments for physicals for all of the children and accompanied the family to appointments with the pediatrician.

The family's housing situation was bleak. The apartment building had been condemned, and they were certain to be evicted in due time. Lauren researched the city rules and available services for homeless families and found out that once the Lopezes received an actual eviction notice, they would be moved to the top of the list to receive public housing. Lauren discussed this plan with Mr. and Mrs. Lopez, and they were in agreement.

With regard to finances, the Lopezes were receiving public assistance but it was not enough to meet the needs of a family of five. Lauren explored with Mr. and Mrs. Lopez their sources of income. Mr. Lopez frequently worked odd jobs under the table, but was not reporting this income to the government. Lauren researched the public assistance programs, and found out that if Mr. Lopez did report this income, the family's Temporary Assistance for Needy Families (TANF) benefit would increase. Lauren accompanied Mr. Lopez to the appropriate government office to begin reporting his income and to reapply for an adjustment in TANF benefits. Finally, Lauren showed Mr. Lopez how he could use the free Internet access at the library to locate additional odd jobs. All of these interventions, which occurred over the course of two weeks, significantly improved the family's financial situation, as did Mr. and Mrs. Lopez's abstinence from amphetamine abuse.

Lauren showed Mr. and Mrs. Lopez where the local food banks were located and explained the process of obtaining food at each venue. She assisted them with this until she was assured they could continue to obtain food on their own after services were terminated. Lauren talked with the other social workers at her agency and discovered that a local church provided free toothbrushes, clean clothing, and diapers. Lauren brought Mrs. Lopez to the church and was able to obtain various items of which the family was in need. Mrs. Lopez was informed she could go to the church once a month for additional goods.

In the process of connecting the family to these multiple services, it became clear the family had limited knowledge of the public transit system. Lauren worked with Mr. and Mrs. Lopez to understand better which buses they would need to take and how to obtain discounted tickets. Lauren and the parents also created a family calendar that included the many appointments the family now had as well as the bus schedule.

To allow Mrs. Lopez a break from caring for the children during the day and also so that the youngest child could receive educational services, Lauren enrolled Junior in Early Head Start. Mrs. Lopez and Lauren reviewed the schedule for classes and the bus route to get to the agency several times so that Mrs. Lopez could be consistent in picking up and dropping Junior off there.

In total, Lauren spent about 40 hours providing services to the Lopezes over the course of five weeks. The majority of these hours were spent at the Lopez home or in the community. At the end of this period, the Lopez family had made significant gains in housing stability and safety, financial stability, cleanliness and hygiene, and health and mental health. They subsequently were allowed to keep their children in the home. Lauren worked with Mr. and Mrs. Lopez to assure that these changes were sustainable, but also offered to provide "booster sessions" (as Homebuilders does with all clients) after a few months to help to sustain change. The Lopezes agreed to maintain contact with Lauren.

Typical Day

Admittedly, there is no such thing as a typical day in the life of a Homebuilders therapist. They work roughly five to six hours per day, six to seven days per week. Families tend to be more readily available in the afternoons or evenings, and morning hours often are devoted to consultation, supervision, and making contacts on behalf of the families with whom they are working. The following depicts one example of a day's activities for a family preservation worker.

9:00–10:00 Check voice mail and make several phone calls to get electricity reinstated for Lopez family

10:00–11:00 Phone consultation with referral source and local mental health providers to arrange for consultations for Mr. and Mrs. Lopez

11:00–12:00 Weekly supervisory meeting with Lauren's agency supervisor

12:00–1:00 Lunch and travel to Lopez family home

1:00–2:30 Lauren and Mr. Lopez visit the local offices of the Department of Social and Health Services to complete paperwork to adjust TANF payments

2:30–4:00 Work with the parents and children to create a safety plan

EXTENDING THE MODEL BEYOND CHILD WELFARE

The intensive family preservation services model has been extended to several other populations but, in all cases, the underlying objective is strengthening and maintaining families. An early extension of the model was to use intensive family preservation services in family reunification cases where children are returning to their families from foster care or other out-of-home placements (Bell, 1995). The services also have helped to prevent family breakdown as part of postadoptive services (Berry, Propp, & Martens, 2007). Henggeler and his colleagues (Henggeler, Melton, & Smith, 1992) extended the model to work with juvenile delinquency cases, in a home-based program known as multisystemic therapy. In turn, multisystemic therapy has been applied to prevent suicide attempts in youth who are referred for emergency psychiatric hospitalization (Henggeler, Rowland, Halliday-Boykins, Cunningham, Pickrel, & Edwards, 2004). Intensive family preservation services also have been used in work with domestic violence cases (Findlater & Kelly, 1999). Finally, intensive family preservation services, based on the Homebuilders model, have been used in families where one or both parents are misusing substances (Forrester et al., 2012).

Evaluation

Intensive family preservation services have been subjected to considerable scrutiny by the general public and the research community. In general, the more rigorous studies indicate that intensive family preservation services, when delivered according to the prescribed model, are effective in reducing out-of-home placement (Nelson, Walters, Schweitzer, Blythe, & Pecora, 2009).

Kirk and Griffith (2008) further indicate that the program reduces racial disproportionality in the child welfare system.

WEBSITES

Family Preservation Service. www.fpscorp.com
National Coalition for Child Protective Reform. www.nccpr.org
National Family Preservation Network. www.nfpn.org
U.S. Department of Health and Human Services. www.hhs.gov/hsp/cyp/fpprogs.html
Child welfare. www.childwelfare.gov/supporting/preservation/intensive

ACKNOWLEDGMENTS

The authors would like to thank Megan Garcia of the Institute for Family Development for her assistance in describing the work of a Homebuilders therapist.

References

Bell, J. A. (1995). *A review of family preservation and family reunification programs.* Washington, DC: U.S. Department of Health and Human Services Administration for Children and Families.

Berry, M., Propp, J., & Martens, P. (2007). The use of intensive family preservation services with adoptive families. *Child and Family Social Work, 12,* 43–53.

Findlater, J. E., & Kelly, S. (1999). Reframing child safety in Michigan: Building collaboration among domestic violence, family preservation and child protection services. *Child Maltreatment, 4,* 167–174.

Forrester, D., Pokhrel, S., McDonald, L., Giannou, D., Waissbein, C., Binnie, C., Jensch, G., & Copello, A. (2012, April). Final report on the evaluation of "Option 2." Welsh Assembly Government.

Haapala, D., & Kinney, J. (1979). Homebuilder's approach to the training of in-home therapists. In S. Maybanks & M. Bryce (Eds.), *Home-based services for children and families* (pp. 248–259). Springfield, IL: Charles C Thomas.

Henggeler, S. W., Melton, G. B., & Smith, L. A. (1992). Family preservation using multisystemic therapy: An effective alternative to incarcerating serious juvenile offenders. *Journal of Consulting and Clinical Psychology, 60,* 1–19.

Huey, S. J. Jr., Henggeler, S. W., Rowland, M. D., Halliday-Boykins, C. A., Cunningham, P. B., Pickrel, S. G., & Edwards, J. (2004). Multisystemic therapy effects on attempted suicide by youths presenting psychiatric emergencies. *Journal of American Academy of Child and Adolescent Psychiatry, 43,* 183–190.

Kinney, J., Haapala, D. M, Booth, C., & Leavitt, S. (1990). The Homebuilders model. In J. K. Whittaker, J. Kinney, E. M. Tracey, & C. Booth (Eds.), *Reaching high-risk families: Intensive family preservation services in child welfare* (pp. 31–64). Hawthorne, NY: Aldine de Gruyter.

Kinney, J. M., Madsen, B., Fleming, T., & Haapala, D. A. (1977). Homebuilders: Keeping families together. *Journal of Consulting and Clinical Psychology, 45,* 667–678.

Kirk, R. S., & Griffith, D. P. (2008). Impact of intensive family preservation services on disproportionality of out-of-home placement of children of color in one state's child welfare system. *Child Welfare, 87*(5), 87–105.

Nelson, K., Walters, B., Schweitzer, D., Blythe, B. J., & Pecora, P. J. (2009). *A ten-year review of family preservation research: Building the evidence base.* Seattle, WA: Casey Family Programs.

Richmond, M. E. (1917). *Social Diagnosis.* New York, NY: Russell Sage Foundation.

Walton, E., Sandau-Beckler, D., & Mannes, M. (2001). *Family-centered Services.* New York, NY: Columbia University Press.

Wells, N. G., Pecora, P. J., & Booth, C. (2014). Homebuilders: Helping families stay together. In C. W. LeCroy (Ed.), *Case studies in social work practice* (3rd ed.) (pp. 115–128). Hoboken, NJ: Wiley and Sons.

PART VII

Developing and Implementing Treatment Plans with Specific Groups and Disorders

Guidelines for Establishing Effective Treatment Goals and Plans for Mental Health Disorders

68

Sample Treatment Plans for DSM-5 Insomnia and Generalized Anxiety Disorders

Vikki L. Vandiver

We shouldn't deny the verdict (diagnosis/assessment) but defy the sentence (prognosis/outcome).

—Norman Cousins, *Head First: The Biology of Hope*

This chapter reviews the procedures of goal setting and treatment planning for mental health disorders commonly found in the *Diagnostic and Statistical Manual of Mental Disorders— Fifth Edition* (American Psychiatric Association, 2013a). Commonly referred to as the *DSM-5*, this manual is used by clinicians to assess and diagnose four major groups of conditions: mental disorders (e.g., generalized anxiety disorders), other mental disorders (e.g., unspecified mental disorders), medication-induced movement disorders (e.g., neuroleptic-induced parkinsonism) and other conditions that may be the focus of clinical attention (e.g., relational problems). See Table 68.1 for a full listing of these conditions. Regardless of the breadth or differences in disorders, the establishment of treatment goals and the development of a treatment plan are predicated on a thorough assessment, diagnosis, and understanding of the client's presenting problem. In fact, the process is sequential, starting with the bio-psychosocial–cultural assessment and accurate diagnosis, which in turn, facilitates establishing treatment goals and determining the treatment plans.

BIO-PSYCHOSOCIAL–CULTURAL ASSESSMENT

The bio-psychosocial–cultural model is based on two premises: (1) client problems are multi-causal and reflect an attempt to cope with stressors, given existing vulnerabilities, environment, and resources; and (2) treatment approaches need to be multimodal, flexible, and tailored to the client's needs and expectations rather than to a single treatment modality.

The first step in establishing treatment goals and an effective treatment plan is to conduct a clinical interview using the bio-psychosocial–cultural model of assessment. Generally speaking, a mental health interview revolves around three discrete areas: (1) the dynamic interplay of biology and psychology, (2) social and cultural factors of the client's present mental health status, and (3) past mental health history. The biological system deals with the anatomical, structural, and molecular substrates of disease and the effects on clients' biological functioning. The psychological explores the effects of psychodynamic factors, developmental impasses or distorted object relations, motivation,

TABLE 68.1 Categories of *DSM-5* Mental Disorders and Non-Mental Disorders Used for Completing a Biopsychosocial-cultural Assessment

Mental Disorders		Non-Mental Disorders	
All Mental Disorders	Other Mental Disorders	Medication-induced Movement Disorders and Other Adverse Effects of Medication	Other Conditions That May Be the Focus of Clinical Attention
1. Neurodevelopmental Disorders	1. Other Specified Mental Disorder Due to Another Medical Condition	1. Neuroleptic-induced Parkinsonism	1. Relational Problems
2. Schizophrenia Spectrum		2. Other Medication-induced Parkinsonism	2. Abuse and Neglect
3. Bipolar and Related Disorders	2. Unspecified Mental Disorder Due to Another Medical Condition	3. Neuroleptic Malignant Syndrome	3. Educational and Occupational Problems
4. Depressive Disorders		4. Medication-induced Acute Dystonia	4. Housing and Economic Problems
5. Anxiety Disorders		5. Medication-induced Acute Akathisia	5. Other Problems Related to Social Environment
6. Obsessive Compulsive and Related Disorders	3. Other Specified Mental Disorder	6. Tardive Dyskinesia	6. Problems Related to Crime or Interaction with Legal System
7. Trauma and Stressor Related Disorders	4. Unspecified Mental Disorder	7. Tardive Dystonia	
		8. Tardive Akathisia	
8. Dissociative Disorders		9. Medication-induced Postural Tremor	7. Other Health Service Encounters for Counseling and Medical Advice
9. Somatic Symptoms and Related Disorders		10. Other Medication-induced Movement Disorder	8. Problems Related to Other Psychosocial, Personal, and Environmental Circumstances
10. Feeding and Eating Disorders		11. Antidepressant Discontinuation Syndrome	
11. Sleep-Wake Disorders		12. Other Adverse Effect of Medication	
12. Sexual Dysfunctions			
13. Gender Dysphoria			9. Other Circumstances or Personal History
14. Disruptive, Impulse-control and Conduct Disorders			10. Problems Related to Access to Medical and Other Healthcare
15. Substance Related and Addictive Disorders			
16. Neurocognitive Disorders			11. Nonadherence to Medical Treatment
17. Personality Disorders			
18. Paraphilic Disorders			

and personality on the experience or reaction to illness. The sociocultural system examines cultural and environmental stressors, vulnerabilities, resources, and familial influences on the expression and experience of coping with illness. (Kaplan & Sadock, 2007; Sperry, Gudeman, Blackwell, & Faulkner, 1992; Vandiver, 2009). These three areas are discussed accordingly.

Beginning with the bio of the biopsychosocial–cultural section of the interview, the social worker gathers information on current health status (e.g., hypertension) and past health history (e.g., diabetes) or injuries (e.g., brain injury). Additional information includes current medication use (e.g., both allopathic and homeopathic), and health and lifestyle behaviors (e.g., exercise, nutrition, sleep patterns, substance use). A familial health history would also be obtained. Screening tools would include sleep charts and health measures. Additionally, genograms are very useful tools to track family health history (e.g., cancer) and certain genetic disorders (e.g., schizophrenia, substance abuse, mood disorders) and to assess family patterns that may maintain the problem or facilitate the obtainment of treatment goals. Genograms facilitate understanding of the social networks as part of the actual treatment plan and illustrate how assessment and problem-identification tools are used in the entire treatment process.

Once the social worker has obtained health information, they should explore the psychological status of the client. This information would include a broad range of topics, including appearance and behavior, speech and language, thought process and content, mood and affect, and cognitive functioning (including orientation, concentration, memory, insight, and general intelligence). A critical area is the determination of suicidal or homicidal risk and possible need for an immediate referral. Common screening tools are self-reports (see Corcoran and Fischer, 2013) and mental status exam. In particular, the mental status represents an attempt to objectively describe the behaviors, thoughts, feelings, and perceptions of the client during the interview (Corcoran & Walsh, 2013).

A final section of the bio-psychosocial–cultural assessment interview includes information on the sociocultural experiences of the client. Broadly speaking, the social worker gathers information on cultural background (e.g., ethnicity, language, assimilation, acculturation, and spiritual beliefs), environmental connections (e.g., community ties, living conditions, neighborhood, economic status, and availability of food and shelter), and social relations (e.g., familial, friends, employers, strangers, and experiences with racism or discrimination). Useful assessment tools are eco-maps, which, like genograms, facilitate an understanding of how the social environment maintains the problems and may aid or impede the goal attainment.

ACCURATE DIAGNOSIS

The second step in establishing treatment goals and treatment plans is to accurately diagnose the mental health condition. One of the most useful aspects of the bio-psychosocial–cultural assessment is that the model pushes the social worker to consider various perspectives that aid in formulating a diagnostic picture. Toward this end, it is customary to use the *DSM-5* (APA, 2013a) for this purpose.

As Table 68.1 illustrates, clinicians have four *DSM-5* categories in which to identify mental health concerns: *all mental disorders, other mental disorders, medication-induced movement disorders and other adverse effects of medications and other conditions that may be the focus of clinical attention.* All *mental disorders*, commonly referred to as clinical conditions, generally refer to mental health conditions that result in distress or disability that is greater than expected from circumstances of living. This group of disorders includes 18 different diagnostic subcategories and criteria.

In addition to a diagnosis of a clinical disorder, the social worker can also consider *other mental disorders,* namely *other specified and unspecified*. These disorders are also used to help classify co-occurring medical conditions. This category is used when the presentation does not fit exactly into the diagnostic boundaries of commonly recognized mental/clinical disorders (e.g., schizophrenia). Both of these categories are recognized as "mental disorders" in that they are billable, have psychiatric treatment protocols, and require that clinicians refer to the diagnostic criteria listed for each diagnosis. However, *specified and unspecified* categories are meant to be short-term and should only remain in the chart until a more complete diagnosis is made.

A third category is *medication-induced movement disorders and other adverse effects of medication*. This section refers to 12 disorders that are related directly to the management by medication of mental disorders or other medical conditions (APA, 2013a). These conditions are not considered mental disorders but are, in fact, a side effect of managing mental disorders.

A final category that social workers can use in their assessment is the *other conditions that may be the focus of clinical attention*. There are 11 categories and over 100 different other conditions or problems that may be the focus of attention. The social worker could use the *"other conditions"* category when:

1. The problem is the focus of treatment and the individual has no mental disorder (e.g., V61.20 [Z62.82]—Parent-Child Relational Problem—when the focus is to address the quality of the parent-child relationship)
2. The individual has a mental disorder, but it is unrelated to the problem (e.g., V61.8 [Z62.891]—Sibling Relational Problem—when the focus is on the sibling relationship)
3. The individual has a mental disorder that is related to the problem, but the problem is sufficiently severe to warrant independent clinical attention (e.g., V61.03 [Z63.5]—Disruption of Family by Separation or Divorce—when an individual with chronic schizophrenia in remission may present with marital distress).

Sometimes these categories are used when the medical condition is confounding the psychiatric diagnosis or no mental disorder is present and the client is coping with multiple stressors.

As in any bio-psychosocial–cultural assessment, the social worker is balancing information regarding the psychological, social, and medical status of the client. When assessing for these areas, the social worker will need to explore psychological factors that affect the medical condition (e.g., major depressive disorder delaying recovery from myocardial infarction), social/cultural circumstances that exacerbate the mental health condition (e.g., acculturation difficulty or target of discrimination). Similarly, medication-induced movement disorders and other medication-induced disorders are important assessment considerations because of their significance in the management of medication (e.g., anxiety disorder vs. neuroleptic malignant syndrome).

ESTABLISHING TREATMENT GOALS

Once the assessment is completed and a diagnosis determined, the social worker and client are ready to develop treatment goals. There are five guidelines to establishing treatment goals. Goals should (1) emerge from the assessment and diagnosis; (2) have maximum client participation; (3) be stated in positive terms; (4) be feasible, realistic, and within the resources of the client; and (5) be well defined, observable, and measurable.

Treatment goals should emerge from the assessment and diagnosis of the client's problem. There should be a nexus between the assessment/diagnosis and goals. For example, if the assessment and diagnosis suggest that the client is experiencing sleep deprivation secondary to an anxiety disorder, the treatment goals (both short- and long-term) would focus on stabilizing sleep patterns while decreasing anxiety and its symptoms.

The establishment of a treatment goal must include the active participation of the client. A goal cannot be ascribed to the client. Clients who actively participate in establishing the treatment goal are more motivated to comply with the treatment plan. Active participation includes homework assigned and completed outside the clinical setting. Treatments that include homework assignments tend to enhance client compliance and facilitate generalizing the changing behavior to other environments.

Treatment goals should be stated in positive terms, if possible. For example, it is more motivating for a client to increase the frequency and intensity of pleasant events than to stop being depressed. Similarly, a substance abuser would not simply want to quit using drugs but to increase the duration between use and the number of days clean and sober. A positively stated goal has the inherent benefit of enhancing compliance with the treatment plan and encouraging clients to participate in what they want and value.

A treatment goal must be feasible for the client to accomplish. If the goal is vague or overly ambitious, the outcome will likely be failure. Instead of improved social functioning, the client could experience a lack of success, disappointment, and erosion in confidence. Though the goal must not be too ambitious, it must also be challenging and realistic. Specific and challenging goals are more likely attained than those that are vague and easy. Social workers must also examine what resources the client has to achieve the agreed upon goals. For example, does the client have the bus fare or day care help to attend the scheduled therapy group?

Finally, the treatment goal must be observable. The client, the social worker, or relevant others should be able to observe the change. One convenient way to observe goals is with assessment instruments that help formulate the assessment and diagnosis. In the most recent edition of the *DSM-5* (APA, 2013a), readers will find a variety of assessment measures, such as the Adult Self-Rated Cross Cutting Symptom Measure, World Health Organization—Disability Assessment Schedule and others. These measures are in the public domain and accessible through www.psychiatry.org/dsm5.

Additionally, many of the mental disorders classified in *DSM-5* are rated for severity with the assessment recorded as the fifth digit of the DSM code. This is known as fifth-digit coding. Severity is defined as 1 (mild), 2 (moderate), 3 (severe but without psychotic features), and 4 (severe and with psychotic features). An ostensible goal of any intervention is to decrease the severity of the client's distress with the objective of changing some behavior. By assessing the severity before, during, and after treatment, the fifth-digit code provides a broadband assessment of treatment effectiveness.

Well-defined, observable, and measurable treatment goals provide a number of advantages, including reducing disagreements between the client and clinician, providing direction for the treatment plan (which prevents waste of time and resources), and serving as a measure of an effective outcome (Hepworth, Larsen, & Rooney, 1997). A well-defined operational definition of the treatment goal is a necessary condition of an effective treatment plan. Moreover, it is much easier to develop a treatment plan that is likely to be effective when the treatment goal itself is well defined, explicit, and observable.

ELEMENTS OF AN EFFECTIVE TREATMENT PLAN

Once the goals are determined, the final step is to develop a treatment plan. A treatment plan is often described to clients as a roadmap whose destination is determined through mutual collaboration. Effective treatment plans have the following characteristics: (1) they provide specificity, (2) they are guided by industry standards of treatment, and (3) they evidence mutuality.

An effective treatment plan will have specificity. Specificity refers to an intervention plan with well-defined components organized in meaningful sequence. In other words, the intervention outlines a set of procedures that delineates what will occur both inside and outside the treatment setting. Sperry and colleagues (1992) identify six factors that need to be specified in treatment planning: setting (e.g., crisis, outpatient, inpatient, and day hospital); format of intervention

(e.g., individual, group, medication group, marital/family, combined treatment); duration (short-term with termination date); frequency of contact (e.g., 1 week, 2 months, 1 month, other); treatment strategy (e.g., behavioral, cognitive, supportive/reality, interpersonal); and somatic treatment (e.g., antidepressant, neuroleptic, anxiolytic).

The social worker will want to include measures for monitoring the intervention effects. An integral component of an effective treatment plan is a systematic method to monitor client change and evaluate treatment effectiveness. Thus, the treatment plan should delineate what instruments will be used to monitor the client's condition and treatment process. These observations should be systematically integrated into the intervention as regular feedback and reinforcement for progress. This added degree of specificity helps ensure that the client and social worker accurately implement the agreed upon treatment plan.

As these factors suggest, there is more to the treatment plan than just the therapeutic procedures. Even so, this is often the area of greatest concern to the social worker. It is the part of the treatment plan that tells the worker and client what to do to implement an intervention. The task is facilitated by standards of treatment that include the use of treatment manuals and practice guidelines. Manuals are typically step-by-step/session-by-session delineations of a specific treatment protocol. A practice guideline, in contrast, is a condition of treatment that appears to have sufficient empirical support to suggest it should likely be included in practice by the reasonable and prudent provider. Currently there are many published guidelines for practice with a number of mental health disorders. Several of these are available through online resources such as Substance Abuse Mental Health Services Administration (SAMHSA; www.samhsa.gov) or through compendiums published through the American Psychiatric Association.

The final characteristic of an effective treatment plan is mutuality. By this, we mean a meeting of minds between the client and the social worker about the entire enterprise of treatment. The treatment plan should reflect this as an explicit contract between the client and the social worker. This contract should show the mutuality of the professional relationship and enumerate who will do what, to what extent, under what conditions, by when, and for what purpose or goal.

Overall, social workers need to remember that there is considerable variability between different disorders (e.g., schizophrenia compared with persistent depressive disorder/dysthymia), symptom expression (e.g., remission vs. active), and functioning (e.g., serious impairment vs. moderate difficulty). There is also considerable variability for what treatment is used for different persons with the same diagnosis. For example, a person with persistent depressive disorder/dysthymia may need a cognitive intervention with skill training, whereas another may need medication and a compliance program that includes family members. The right intervention correctly implemented for the wrong problem is likely to be ineffective, which underscores the importance of monitoring client change for assessment throughout the course of treatment.

One example of how to apply the right interventions toward a multi-problem situation is illustrated in Box 68.1. This treatment plan describes the sequential elements of the treatment process discussed in this chapter. These elements begin with the assessment model (e.g., bio-psychosocial–cultural), applying the screening tools (rapid assessment instruments), formulating a diagnosis, establishing treatment goals (e.g., short- and long-term), and concluding with formulating the treatment plan (e.g., setting, format, duration, frequency, strategy, and somatic treatment).

USING THE STRENGTHS PERSPECTIVE IN ESTABLISHING GOALS AND TREATMENT PLANNING

The strengths perspective focuses on the client's abilities in the assessment and emphasizes the discovery of resources within the client and his or her environment. In this view, the strengths-based perspective has considerable value when applied to the establishment of goals and treatment planning for individuals with mental health conditions. In general, a goal must be attainable by the client, and the easiest way to do so is by using and building on the client's strengths. The process involves mutual collaboration between the provider and the client to develop goals that frame the idea of developing new expectations, constructing new opportunities for the individual and his or her family, and discovering new resources within him- or herself and the environment (Saleebey, 1997). Regardless of the diagnosis, establishing treatment goals using the strengths perspective involves finding the resources within the client, their environment, and relationships and linking these strengths to the treatment plan.

A strengths-based perspective is integrated into the treatment plan by helping clients remember how they have been successful in the past (e.g., what steps they have used), affirming previous success and abilities (e.g., coping skills), and determining what skills, behaviors, motivations,

---

Box 68.1 Treatment Plan for Insomnia and Generalized Anxiety Disorder.

CLIENT: RALPH C., AGE: 45

Reason for Seeking Treatment: Mr. C is a single, white male who is employed as a bus driver. He states that his employer told him to "get help or don't come back." Mr. C reports insomnia ("only sleeps 2–3 hours a night") and feeling anxious about losing his job despite previous good work performance reviews. He recently has been complaining to coworkers about his sleep deprivation and fear of wrecking the bus due to nodding off at the wheel. He attributes the sleep disturbance to increased nightly altercations with a neighbor who plays "music all night long." He states that his work has become his life now and he has abandoned friends, leisure reading, and church-associated activities. He feels that he is in vicious cycle of "all work and no play" and cannot seem to shake off feelings of doom and dread. He reports that he does not drink alcohol or use recreational or prescription drugs and has recently quit his health club so he could concentrate on his work responsibilities.

History of Past Treatment: Mr. C has not received any mental health treatment in the past. No remarkable health history. Receives annual physical and reports no complications.

Assessment Model	Assessment Tools	Diagnosis	Treatment Goals Short Term	Treatment Goals Long Term	Treatment Plan Setting, Format, Duration, Frequency Strategy and Somatic Treatment
Bio	1) Sleep chart	1) 780.52 (G47.00) Insomnia Disorder with non-sleep disorder mental comorbidity, recurrent; (generalized anxiety disorder)	1) Stabilize nightly sleep routine	1) Maintain routine sleep cycle	1) Outpatient setting, individual treatment sessions for 8 sessions using sleep diary; refer for sleep apnea assessment; refer for medication evaluation
Psych	2) Adult DSM-5 Self-Rated Level 1 Cross-Cutting Symptom Measure: Subscale IV-Anxiety (APA, 2013)	2) 300.02 (F41.1) Generalized Anxiety Disorder (Primary)	2) Decrease anxiety	2) Maintain employing stress reduction techniques	2) Outpatient, individual treatment for 8 sessions using cognitive behavior therapy techniques
Social & Cultural	3) World Health Organization Disability Assessment Schedule: Subscale Life Activities: Work; 2.0 (APA, 2013) 4) Eco-map 5) Genogram	3) V69.9 (Z72.9) Problem Related to Lifestyle: Poor sleep hygiene accompanying neighborhood conflict and loss of leisure and social activities 4) V62.29 (Z56.9) Other Problems Related to Employment: threat of job loss	3) Encourage incremental return to social activities (e.g., church & social activities) 4) Reduce work hours for one month	3) Maintain recreation/leisure schedule 4) Return to full work schedule	3) Home setting; refer to community events calendar and health club for 1x weekly participation in leisure activities; consider neighborhood mediation after one month if residential conflict continues 4) Employee worksite (e.g., bus and in office), use of Job Coach as part of company Employee Assistance Program to conduct observation and provide feedback of client activities for one month

and aspirations can be applied to bring the desired change. Together, client and provider search the environment for forces that enhance life chances while supporting client self-determination and personal responsibility (Saleebey, 1997). In summary, the strengths-based model is useful when applied to the particular goals and treatment approach to attain these goals. Goal-attainment plans that make use of a client's strengths capture a natural nexus that enhances the likelihood of treatment success.

CONCLUSIONS

The establishment of treatment goals and treatment plans is an integral part of a process that begins with assessment and diagnosis. Those goals and treatment plans enhance the likelihood that clients will change. This objective is facilitated by following five guidelines.

1. Treatment goals and treatment plans require a thorough biopsychosocial-cultural assessment and accurate diagnosis of the problem.
2. The treatment goals must be specified in observable terms at the beginning of treatment.
3. The intervention is determined by the goals and should have specific criteria for accomplishing the goals.
4. The intervention should be planned and include a well-explicated delineation of what will occur and when over the course of treatment.
5. The treatment goals and treatment plan should form the explicit contracts for helping clients change and should be implemented according to mutually agreed-upon parameters of the plan.

These guidelines form a rough sequence of the treatment process and help the social worker effectively and efficiently assist clients.

WEBSITES

Substance Abuse Mental Health Services Administration. http://www.samhsa.gov
National Institute of Mental Health. http://www.nimh.nih.gov/health/publications/anxiety-disorders
Dartmouth Evidence-Based Practices Center. http://www.dartmouth.edu/~prc/

References

American Psychiatric Association. (2013a). Diagnostic and statistical manual of mental disorders, 5th edition. Washington, DC: APA.
American Psychiatric Association (2013b). Assessment measures: Level 1 Cross-cutting symptom measure (pp. 734–739). Diagnostic and statistical manual of mental disorders. 5th Edition. Washington, DC: APA.
American Psychiatric Association (2013c). Assessment measures: World health organization disability assessment schedule—2.0 (pp. 745–748). Diagnostic and statistical manual of mental disorders. 5th Edition. Washington, DC: APA.
Corcoran, J., & Walsh, J. (2013). Mental health in social work: A casebook in diagnosis and strength based assessment—2nd edition. Boston: Pearson.
Corcoran, K., & Fischer, J. (2013). Measures for clinical practice- Vol. 2 Adults. NY. Oxford University Press.
Hepworth, D., Larsen, J., & Rooney, R. (1997). Direct social work practice: Theory and skills, 5th ed. Pacific Grove, CA: Brooks/Cole.
Kaplan, H., & Sadock, B. (2007). Synopsis of psychiatry, 10th ed. Philadelphia: Lippincott Williams & Wilkins.
Saleebey, D. (1997). The strengths perspective in social work practice, 2nd ed. New York: Longman.
Sperry, L. Gudeman, J. Blackwell, B., & Faulkner, L. (1992). Psychiatric case formulations. Washington, DC: author.
Vandiver, V. (2009). Integrating health promotion and mental health: An introduction to policies, principles and practices. NY: Oxford University Press.

Treating Problem and Disordered Gambling

69

Often a Hidden Behavioral Addiction

Cathy King Pike & Andrea G. Tamburro

Gambling money or other valuable assets to such an extent that it interferes with normal, daily life has been labeled as "problem gambling" or "pathological gambling" in the past. Currently, the term "disordered gambling" is used to identify substantial problems with relationships, work, school, or other important life roles that are impacted by gambling (American Psychiatric Association, 2013). Because the earlier terms often have been used interchangeably and the current term changed recently in the *Diagnostic and Statistical Manual of Mental Disorders, Fifth Edition (DSM-5)*, "problem gambling," "pathological gambling," and "disordered gambling" will be used interchangeably in this chapter.

Disordered gambling can have devastating consequences for the individuals who exhibit these problems, as well as for their families and communities. Consider the following case descriptions of actual individuals who developed disordered gambling that led to substantial and sometimes extreme consequences.

- Mr. Greg Hogan, Jr. was an outstanding student at Lehigh University (ABC News Internet Ventures, 2013). He was class president. His father was a minister. On the day that he robbed a bank, Mr. Hogan reported that he had lost $8,000 through gambling, which was all of his savings, and had overdraft and bank fines of $1,000 at his bank (ABC News Internet Ventures, 2013).

- In California, Mr. George Shirakawa, Jr. was convicted of 12 counts of criminal activity for misappropriating funds from the coffers of Santa Clara County (Seipel, 2013). Mr. Shirakawa said, "For years, I have suffered from depression and a gambling addiction . . . Unfortunately, my gambling addiction went untreated for too long, which led to bad decisions and actions that I deeply regret" (Seipel, 2013, paragraph 3).

- Sister Mary Anne Rapp, a Roman Catholic nun for more than 50 years, was convicted of grand larceny for stealing almost $130,000 from parishioners' donations (Crimesider Staff, 2013). Sister Rapp was charged after a routine audit was conducted (Kuruvilla, 2013). Sister Rapp reported that she had used the money to support her gambling habit (Kuruvilla, 2013).

- A 10-day-old baby, Joy Baker, died in South Carolina, because she was left by her mother in a locked car in more than 90-degree heat for approximately seven hours while her mother played video poker (Holland, 1997). Joy's mother, Sgt. Gail Baker finally stopped playing after her husband came to the casino about 9:00 P.M. to ask her to return home (Associated Press, 1999). Worried that her husband was angry with her, Sgt. Baker drove around a bit before returning home (Associated Press, 1999). It was only after arriving home that Sgt. Baker realized that her baby had died (Associated Press, 1999).

These brief case presentations document the tragic and sometimes fatal results of disordered gambling. In some cases, family members or friends knew about individuals' disordered gambling. For instance, it is clear that Mr. Hogan's father was aware of his son's disordered gambling, because he had earlier required his son to receive counseling for his gambling problem and had telephoned his son's college to determine whether there were other options available to help with his son's gambling problem (ABC News Internet Venture, 2006, July 25). Sgt. Baker's husband knew where to find her on the night of their infant's death, and Sgt. Baker delayed going home because she was afraid to face her husband's anger about her having played video poker (Associated Press, 1999).

In other cases presented above, there is no evidence that family or friends were aware of individuals' gambling problems until the ultimate crisis or discovery. It is important to note that problem and disordered gambling occurs across varying developmental stages, socioeconomic statuses, professions, educational levels, gender, and ethnic and cultural backgrounds. This is how problem or disordered gambling has become labeled as a *hidden* addiction and why social workers should screen for problem or disordered gambling as a potential co-occurring condition when conducting client assessments. The purpose of this chapter is for social workers to learn

- How disordered gambling is defined
- The incidence and prevalence of disordered gambling
- How sociodemographic characteristics are related to gambling and to specific types of gambling
- How to use screening tools to identify and facilitate assessment of problem gambling
- To identify and apply effective treatment options for problem gambling.

DEFINITIONS, INCIDENCE, PREVALENCE, AND SOCIODEMOGRAPHIC CHARACTERISTICS

Definitions

The current *Diagnostic and Statistical Manual of Mental Disorders, Fifth Edition* (2013) (*DSM-5*) defines a gambling disorder (312.31) as a Non-Substance-Related Disorder that reoccurs and is a persistent gambling problem leading to "clinically significant impairment or distress, as indicated by an individual exhibiting four (or more) of the . . . [nine criteria] in a 12 month period" (p. 585). Notice that the criteria have decreased from 10 in the *DSM-IV* to 9 with the *DSM-5* (Strong & Kahler, 2007). Levels of gambling problems refer to the number of criteria that are met for a given individual. Someone with a mild gambling disorder may meet only four or five of the criteria, most often including being preoccupied with gambling and trying to win back losses (*DSM-5*, 2013). A person having a moderately severe gambling disorder will exhibit six or seven of the criteria, including lying and stealing to continue gambling. Someone exhibiting the most severe gambling disorder will meet eight or all nine of the criteria, including seeking financial help from family and friends (*DSM-5*, 2013). Gambling problems also may be associated with distorted thinking including "denial, superstitious, a sense of power and control over the outcome of chance events, [and] over confidence" (*DSM-5*, 2013, p. 587). The *DSM-5* also identified some people with gambling disorders as "impulsive, competitive, energetic, restless, and easily bored . . . overly concerned with approval of others and generous . . . when winning" (2013, p. 587).

Not everyone who gambles can be considered to have a problem or be diagnosed as a disordered gambler. Some researchers have included the category of "subclinical" in their analyses; these are people who, at between one and four, meet less than the minimum number of gambling criteria identified in the *DSM 5*, and therefore, cannot be diagnosed with a gambling disorder using the *DSM-5* criteria (*DSM-5*, 2013). In earlier research, individuals who now might be labeled as "subclinical" were considered as transitioning in or out of problem levels of gambling (Nower & Blaszczynski, 2008). However, current research indicates that the progression of disordered gambling may take a variety of paths, including never transitioning to disordered gambling (Nower & Blaszczynski, 2008).

Incidence and Prevalence

According to the *DSM-5* (2013) based on past-year gambling, .2% to .3% of the U.S. population was diagnosed with a gambling disorder. The rate of lifetime prevalence of gambling disorder is .4%

to 1% (*DSM-5*, 2013). The lifetime prevalence rate for men in the United States was .6%, and for women the rate was .2% (*DSM-5*, 2013). African Americans had the highest percentage of gambling disorders with a prevalence of .9%, for whites the prevalence was .4%, and for Hispanic people about .3% (*DSM-5*, 2013). The gambling disorder percentages for Asian and Native American people were not included in the *DSM-5*. Five percent of the population met one to four of the *DSM-IV* criteria for problem gambling, falling into the subclinical category (Blanco, Hasin, Petry, Stinson, & Grant, 2006).

The gambling industry is a *multi-billion dollar* business in the United States. According to the American Gaming Association (2013), the casino industry gained $37.34 billion in revenues during 2012, a steady rise from $28.72 billion in 2003. According to the National Gambling Impact Study (1999) between 1975 and 1999, the revenues multiplied exponentially from $3 billion to $58 billion and included newer forms of legalized gambling. Over time, access to legalized gambling has changed dramatically. The National Gambling Impact Study (1999) reported that Nevada was the only state in the United States with legalized gambling from 1900 to 1960. People now have access to gambling through their cell phones, the Internet, casinos, lotteries, and machines at the local gas station or bar, as well as through off-track betting. Instead of limiting access, now 20 states have some form of legalized gambling (American Gaming Association, 2013). Two states currently offer Internet gambling to their residents (American Gaming Association, 2013).

Sociodemographic and Personal Characteristics Related to Gambling

A variety of sociodemographic and personal characteristics are related to disordered gambling. In comparison, the list of characteristics that predict less frequent gambling is very short, according to one study (Hodgins et al., 2012). A large study based in Canada found that individuals who were older than the typical sample age, those with relatively higher intelligence, and those who reported higher levels of religiosity gambled less frequently. However, Barnes, Welte, Hoffman, and Tidwell (2010) found that whether or not individuals were in college "did not predict gambling, frequent gambling, or problem gambling" (p. 443).

The Hodgins et al. study (2012) identified the following list of characteristics that predicted more frequent gambling: being male, being single, exposure to gambling within one's family of origin, the tendency toward excitement-seeking, alcohol or other substance abuse, and a variety of mental health issues. Fully a quarter of the participants in the Grall-Bronnec et al. (2011) study had a history of attention deficit hyperactivity disorder (ADHD). According to the authors, individuals with a history of ADHD "were characterized as having more severe gambling problems and a higher level of gambling-related cognitions, a higher frequency of psychiatric comorbidities and an elevated risk of suicide" (p. 231). Dion, Collin-Vezina, De La Sablonniere, Philippe-Labbe, & Giffard (2009) found that having a history of child sexual abuse was related to gambling disorders but noted that the link is "complex and indirect" (para. 1). A systematic review of 11 studies (Lorains, Cowlishaw, & Thomas, 2011) found the following comorbidities: "nicotine dependence (60.1%) . . . substance use disorder (57.5%) . . . mood disorder (37.9%) . . . and any type of anxiety disorder (37.4%)" (p. 490). Hodgins et al. (2012) concluded that "having any mental disorder may make an individual more vulnerable to a gambling disorder" (p. 2438, 2440). Other sources (*DSM-5*; Larimer et al., 2011) cite increased risk of suicide, poor health, occupational problems, financial difficulties and problems among family and friends as related to problem gambling.

In the past, men engaged in many different forms of gambling, such as real estate, the stock market, sports, cards, casinos, and races. Volberg (2003) reported that white male problem gamblers gambled on lotteries, bingo, machines, pari-mutuel games of chance, and through private arrangements. Minority males who were problem gamblers used these forms of gambling more frequently than white males. Blanco, et al. (2006) reported that men who were diagnosed with pathological gambling preferred gambling on roulette, sports games, and stocks or commodities.

Women have begun gambling more frequently than historically has been the case (Gavriel-Fried & Ajzenstadt, 2011; Volberg, 2003). Safer, legal gambling has become more accessible (e.g., bingo halls, lotteries, and gambling machines in restaurants and stores). Some casinos now provide child care facilities (Conner, 1996), making gambling even more accessible to women with child care responsibilities. In the United States, women diagnosed with pathological gambling were reported to prefer slot or video machines and bingo or keno significantly more than men (Blanco et al., 2006).

In general, youth are more at risk of problem gambling because they are less likely to have the impulse control of more mature individuals (*DSM-5*, 2013). Likewise, Shaffer and Hall (2001) found that adolescents and college youth are at significantly higher risk of gambling problems, perhaps due to risk-taking behaviors. Cell phone and Internet use have increased access to certain types of gambling, including access to pari-mutuel betting and lotteries (Petry, 2006). Further, teens who engage in Internet gambling are more likely to have a serious problem with gambling than other people who gamble (Petry, 2006). Teens who gamble on the Internet experience a greater frequency of physical health problems, circulatory problems, substance abuse, depression, and risky sexual behaviors than other teens (Petry, 2006). Youth are impacted by the availability of gaming on the Internet, including what is referred to as an "internet addiction," which Young (2009) considers closely tied to problem gambling.

According to Blanco et al. (2006) men, especially younger men ages 18–29 years were significantly more likely to fall into the subclinical pathological gambling category than women, but women were more likely to fall within the subclinical category at age 65 or older. Men in the subclinical category were more likely to have never been married. Significantly more women in the subclinical category were within the lowest income bracket, but the men more often earned $35,000 or more than the women (Blanco et al., 2006). In the subclinical category, men smoked and drank more often. Men were more likely to be diagnosed with lifetime drug and alcohol use disorders. According to Blanco et al. (2006), women in the subclinical category were more often diagnosed with either a mood or anxiety disorder. Several other studies have explored the gambling patterns of women, identifying multiple reasons for problem gambling including depression, personal pressures, a desire for reward, a need for personal space, and boredom with one's personal lifestyle (Gavriel-Fried & Ajzenstadt, 2011; Hing & Breen, 2001; Schull, 2002). Hing and Breen (2001) found that some older women problem gamblers had experienced a loss of their roles as caregivers. Schull (2002)

characterized younger women problem gamblers as overwhelmed and stressed by responsibility.

SCREENING TOOLS

With the dramatic proliferation of the availability and types of gambling and the almost unlimited access to gambling, one may suppose that agencies routinely screen for gambling problems among their clientele. This does not seem to be the case. Only two studies were located in the literature review that examined screening practices related to problem gambling. One study found that "more than three-quarters of respondents had not sent staff for training in screening or treating gambling disorders, did not screen for problem gambling, did not treat problem gambling, and did not refer clients to other agencies for treatment of gambling-related problems" (Engel, Rosen, Weaver, & Soska, 2010, p. 611). The second study examined graduate-level curricula in social work in relation to assessing and treating problem gambling. In that study, nearly two-thirds (61.6%) of the programs responded that they did not have content in the curricula for the treatment of problem gambling (Engel, Bechtold, Kim, & Mulvaney, 2012). Among the reasons cited for the lack of gambling assessment and treatment content within the curricula were "a lack of faculty expertise, low-priority content, and the lack of interest in gambling-related issues" (Engel et al., 2012, p. 321).

Because problem gambling frequently is associated (comorbid) with many mental health diagnoses, it is important for social workers to screen routinely for gambling problems. There are many tools that can be used for screening purposes. Some of these are self-administered tools that can be accessed online and are available for download. Some are available through the literature on problem gambling. This section, however, will highlight several of the free, online screening resources that are available to anyone, and will provide information about the strengths and weaknesses of various resources identified within the literature.

The National Council on Problem Gambling (NCPG) (see Table 69.1, #1) includes a self-administered screening tool that is based on earlier research by the National Opinion Research Center (NORC). The tool used here initially was developed for use with the general population and was found to be reliable and valid for this population (Gerstein et al., 1999). This screening tool, the NORC Diagnostic Screen for Gambling Problems—Self Administered (NODS—SA), includes 10 questions that relate to preoccupation with gambling, lack of control of gambling, relationship problems related to one's gambling, and using gambling as an escape mechanism (Table 69.1, #2). After completion of the screen, test-takers are provided information about the meaning of the various scores.

The Division on Addiction, Cambridge Health Alliance, a teaching affiliate of Harvard Medical School, provides access to a screening tool that was developed by Gebauer, LaBrie, and Shaffer (2010). This instrument, the Brief Biosocial Gambling Screen (BBGS) contains three items that measure restlessness or irritability when trying to cut back on gambling, lying about gambling to friends or family, and financial troubles related to gambling. In addition, respondents are asked to answer a question about their readiness to reduce gambling (Table 69.1, #3).

In addition to the above two websites, a screening tool can be found at the Gamblers Anonymous website (Table 69.1, #4, 5). This screening tool is self-administered and contains 20 questions related to problem gambling. It should be noted that no known research studies have been conducted to determine the reliability and validity of this tool.

A rather lengthy gambling screening tool is located on the "Check Your Gambling" website (Table 69.1, #6). This website is based in Canada and offers a five-page questionnaire that contains questions about types of gambling activities, the largest amount gambled at one sitting, gambling strategies, and a number of questions related to cognitive distortions about gambling (Table 69.1, #7). It is unclear whether or not this tool has been tested for reliability and validity.

In contrast to the longer screening tool above, the "Lie-Bet Tool" (Johnson et al., 1988) contains only two items. This screening tool was developed to address the need for simple, expedient, and effective screening for problem gambling (Johnson et al., 1988). These items ask respondents about the need to bet increasingly greater amounts of money and lying about their gambling (Table 69.1, #8).

Volberg, Munck, and Petry (2011) reviewed several gambling screening tools that have been used in the past and conducted research on those questions most likely to identify gambling problems. Among some of the weaknesses that they noted in the screening tools discussed above were "the number of items, the domains assessed by the items, the lack of clinical validation of the underlying measure, and poor performance in clinical settings" (p. 220). In this high-quality study, the authors compared a 3-item subset of the earlier 10-item NODS Screen. They found that the 3-item subset correctly identified 99% of people who already had been classified in separate assessments as pathological gamblers and 94% of those assessed as problem gamblers. These items were labeled as the "NODS-CLiP" to indicate that the questions were related to "Loss of Control, Lying and Preoccupation" (p. 221). The authors found the NODS-CLiP performed well in this clinical sample in identifying problem and pathological gamblers, but it also captured some low-risk and subclinical gamblers. However, one set of four items had "better psychometric properties in (the) clinical sample . . . with somewhat higher sensitivity (99.7%) and positive predictive power (88.5%) and substantially higher negative predictive power (96.3%)" (Volberg, Munck, & Petry, 2011, p. 225). The authors labeled this subset of items the NODS-PERC, because it captured information about clients' "Preoccupation, Escape, Relationships, and Chasing" (p. 225), in problem gambling (Table 69.1, #9).

Characteristics of effective screening tools include the following: (1) consistency over time in identifying problem or disordered gambling; (2) accuracy in identifying problem or disordered gambling (i.e., sensitivity and positive predictive ability); and (3) ability to rule out individuals not having problem or disordered gambling (i.e., high negative predictive ability). One can think of the latter two of these characteristics as a screening tool having low false positives and low false negatives. In other words, a good screening tool consistently identifies problem or disordered gambling, has few instances where individuals are identified as having problem or disordered gambling when they, in fact, have no such problem, and has few instances of not identifying problem or disordered gambling when, in fact, problem or disordered gambling does exist. Taking these factors into account in evaluating the screening tools discussed above, the NODS-PERC performs better than the other methods discussed.

Social workers, however, should keep in mind that these are meant to be *brief* screening tools for use at assessment. Once problem or disordered gambling is identified, social workers will need to explore further the specific nature of clients' problem or disordered gambling as an essential aspect of a comprehensive assessment. Problem gambling and disordered gambling arise from a variety of bio-psychosocial contributing factors. For instance, sheer accessibility to gambling may be a major factor in a sudden increase of disordered gambling in communities having had no or limited prior access to gambling. Nower and Blaszczynski (2008) discussed several contributing factors related to disordered gambling. Among these are the lack of comprehensive community approaches to reduce the incidence of disordered gambling, neurobiological responses to gambling, and the combination of a variety of preexisting states that are "either hypotensive (depressed) or hypertensive (anxious)" (p.1850) in combination with disordered cognitions and the need for escape.

TREATMENT OPTIONS

Treatment for disordered gambling should take into account the preexisting states and triggers that may have aided in establishing the disorder. These may include a variety of personal and emotional factors, mental health disorders, substance abuse, and individual and/or family problems. The Centre for Addiction and Mental Health (CAMH, 2008) published a treatment guide for problem gambling and recommended that the following approaches be used in treating disordered gambling: brief solution-focused approaches, harm reduction approaches for those who want to continue gambling but also want to limit its consequences, motivational interviewing, and cognitive and behavioral techniques. The CAMH (2008) also recommended that practitioners assist clients to (1) deal with their feelings, (2) address any unmet physical health problems, (3) work with clients to improve family relationships, (4) find a balance in their lives, and (5) develop strategies to prevent relapse (Table 69.1, #10).

Self-help Gambling Anonymous (GA) groups, similar in structure to Alcoholics Anonymous (AA) groups, are available in many locations to individuals with disordered gambling. In the literature, the findings on the efficacy of this approach when used alone, however, have been mixed. Petry, Litt, Kadden and Ledgerwood (2007) compared a comprehensive Cognitive Behavioral Therapy (CBT) intervention and GA referral alone and found that participants who had the CBT intervention "reduced their gambling and gambling problems significantly (more) . . . than those assigned to a treatment condition consisting of GA referral alone" (p. 1287). Petry et al. (2007) found that "only about 10% of attendees become actively enrolled in the (GA) fellowship" (p. 5).

Boughton (2003) suggested that GA is more male-oriented and, in her study that used a feminist approach to the study of gambling treatment, found that many women did not feel welcome or supported in the GA environment. She discussed the variety of ways that women experience gambling that may be different from men's experiences with gambling. These included aspects related to women's experiences in society: in relationships, as caregivers, and less self-oriented approaches to dealing with personal stress and escaping stress. Important aspects reported by Boughton (2003) in treating women with gambling disorders were helping women to (1) develop support mechanisms that acknowledge women's unique experiences, (2) reconnect socially and replace gambling with meaningful activities, (3) deal with any comorbid disorders, (4) address any histories of abuse or trauma, and (5) deal with financial concerns.

Much of the literature suggested that a multidimensional approach is best-practice for treatment of gambling disorders. Larimer et al. (2011) found that both cognitive behavioral and a personalized brief motivational feedback were effective interventions with U.S. college-aged students. Nower and Blaszczynski (2008) suggested the following treatment interventions: "specific gambling-related cognitive-behavioral interventions supplemented by broader stress management, problem solving, and affect regulation . . . [to] boost the process of recovery . . . [and] . . . [improve] quality of life and personal development" (p. 1858).

CONCLUSION

In summary, problem and disordered gambling can have dramatic and tragic effects on the lives of individuals, families, and communities. These effects are not likely to diminish, given the dramatically increased types of gambling and the ready access to them. Social workers are uniquely situated to identify and intervene with clients having problem or disordered gambling. In doing so, it is important to remember the following points from this chapter:

- Gambling disorders are "equal opportunity" addictions and disorders, affecting individuals across socioeconomic and other statuses.
- A variety of personal factors may combine in complex ways to develop and perpetuate problem disordered gambling, including co-occurring disorders.
- Routine screening for problem or disordered gambling should occur during in-take or assessment and these tools can be very brief, as well as highly effective.
- Treatment for problem and disordered gambling should be individually based, taking into account clients' gambling "triggers," mental health diagnoses, and other personal characteristics.
- Multidimensional treatment is highly recommended, especially when it makes use of a variety of intervention strategies that match the needs of clients.

INTERNET RESOURCES FOR GAMBLING SCREENS AND TREATMENT

Internet Sites and URLs

National Council on Problem Gambling (NCPG) website http://www.ncpgambling.org

The NODS—SA tool http://www.ncpgambling.org/i4a/survey/survey.cfm?id=6

Brief Biosocial Gambling Screen (BBGS) http://www.divisiononaddiction.org/bbgs_new/

Gamblers Anonymous website (http://www.gamblersanonymous.org)

Gamblers Anonymous tool http://www.gamblersanonymous.org/ga/content/20-questions

Check Your Gambling website http://www.checkyourgambling.net

Check Your Gambling tool http://www.checkyourgambling.net/CYG/CYGScreenerP0.aspx

Lie-Bet tool http://www.ncdhhs.gov/mhddsas/providers/problemgambling/pg-liebetncform.pdf)

NODS–PERC tool http://www.ncrg.org/sites/default/files/uploads/docs/monographs/nods-perc.pdf

Centre for Addiction and Mental Health http://www.camh.ca/en/hospital/health_information/a_z_mental_health_and_addiction_information/problemgambling/Pages/default.aspx

References

ABC News Internet Ventures (2013, July 25). Student says he was driven to crime by gambling addiction. Retrieved from http://abcnews.go.com/GMA/LegalCenter/print?id=2232427

American Gaming Association. (2013). Retrieved from http://www.americangaming.org/industry-resources/research/fact-sheets/top-20-us-casino-markets-annual-revenue

American Psychiatric Association. (2013). *Diagnostic and statistical manual of mental disorders, fifth edition*. Washington, DC: American Psychiatric Publishing.

Associated Press (1999, July 20). Mother who gambled while baby locked in car gets probation. *Savannah Morning News*. Retrieved from http://savannahnow.com/stories/072199/CMNtrial.shtml

Barnes, G. M., Welte, J. W., Hoffman, J. H., & Tidwell, M.-C. O. (2010). Comparisons of gambling and alcohol use among college students and noncollege young people in the United States. *Journal of American College Health, 58*(5), 443–452.

Blanco, C., Hasin, D. S., Petry, N., Stinson, F. S., & Grant, B. F. (2006). Sex differences in subclinical and DSM-IV pathological gambling: results from the National Epidemiologic Survey on Alcohol and Related Conditions. *Psychological Medicine, 36*(7), 943–953.

Boughton, R. (2003). A feminist slant on counselling the female gambler: Key issues and tasks. *Journal of Gambling Issues*, 8. doi:10.4309/jgi.2003.8.5

Centre for Addiction and Mental Health. (2008). *Problem Gambling: A Guide for Helping Professionals* (2nd ed.). Toronto, ON: Author.

Conner, M. (1996). Gaming's sideshow sweepstakes. *International Gaming & Wagering Business, 17*(6), 42–46.

Dion, J., Collin-Vezina, D., De La Sablonniere, M., Philippe-Labbe, M. P., & Giffard, T. (2009). An exploration of the connection between child sexual abuse and gambling in aboriginal communities. *International Journal of Mental Health Addiction*. doi:10.1007/s11469-009-9234-0

Diagnostic and statistical manual of mental disorders, fifth edition. (DSM-5). (2013). Arlington, VA: American Psychiatric Association.

Engel, R. J., Rosen, D., Weaver, A., & Soska, T. (2010). Raising the stakes: Assessing the human service response to the advent of a casino. *Journal of Gambling Studies, 26*, 611–622. doi:10.1007/s10899-010-9184-2

Engel, R. J., Bechtold, J., Kim, Y., & Mulvaney, E. (2012). Beating the odds: Preparing graduates to address gambling-related problems. *Journal of Social Work Education, 48*, 321–335. doi:10.5175/JSWE.2012.201000128

Gavriel-Fried, B., & Ajzenstadt, M. (2011). Pathological women gamblers: Gender-related aspects of control. *Sex Roles, 66,* 128–142. doi:10.1007/s11199-011-0071-9

Gebauer, L., LaBrie, R. A., & Shaffer, H. J. (2010). Optimizing DSM IV classification accuracy: A brief bio-social screen for detecting current gambling disorders among gamblers in the general population. *Canadian Journal of Psychiatry,* 55, 82–90.

Gerstein, D. R., Volberg, R. A., Toce, M. T., Harwood, H., Johnson, R. A., Buie, T., . . . Tucker, A. (1999). Gambling impact and behavior study: Report to the National Gambling Impact Study Commission, NORC at the Unversity of Chicago. Permanent access: http://cloud9.norc.uchicago.edu/dlib/ngis.htm

Grall-Bronnec, M., Wainstein, L., Augy, J., Bouju, G., Feuillet, F., Venisse, J-L., Sebille-Rivain, V. (2011). Attention-deficit hyperactivity disorder among pathological and at-risk gamblers seeking treatment: A hidden disorder. *European Addiction Research,* 17, 231–240. doi:10.1159/000328628

Hing, N., & Breen, H. (2001). Profiling Lady Luck: An empirical study of gambling and problem gambling amongst female club members. *Journal of Gambling Studies,* 17(1), 47–69.

Hodgins, D. C., Schopflocher, D. P., Martin, C. R., el-Cuebaly, N., Casey, D. M., Currie, S. R., . . . Williams, R. J. (2012). Disordered gambling among higher-frequency gamblers: Who is at risk? *Psychological Medicine,* 42, 2433–2444. doi:10.1017/S00332917120000724.

Holland, J. J. (1997, September 03). Baby dies from dehydration while mom plays video poker. *Associated Press News Archive.* Retrieved from http://www.apnewsarchive.com/1997/Baby-dies-from-dehydration-while-mom-plays-video-poker/id-ef53dee8049541f570ce705434e456b9

Johnson, E. E., Hamer, R., Nora, R. M., Nora, R. M., Tan, B., Eistenstein, N., & Englehart, C. (1988). The lie/bet questionnaire for screening pathological gamblers. *Psychological Reports,* 80, 83–88.

Kuruvilla, C. (2013, July 9). New York nun gets jail time for stealing $128K from churches. *New York Daily News.* Retrieved from http://www.nydailynews.com/news/crime/new-york-nun-jail-time-stealing-128k-churches-article-1.1394052

Larimer, M. E., Neighbors, C., Lostutter, T. W., Whiteside, U., Cronce, J. M., Kaysen, D., & Walker, D. D. (2011). Brief motivational feedback and cognitive behavioral interventions for prevention of disordered gambling: A randomized clinical trial. *Addiction,* 107(6), 1148–1158. doi:10.1111/j.1360-0443.2011.03776.x

Lorains, F. K., Cowlishaw, S., & Thomas, S. A. (2011). Prevalence of comorbid disorders in problem and pathological gambling: Systematic review and meta-analysis of population surveys. *Addiction,* 106(3), 490–498. doi:10.1111/j.1360-0443.2010.03300.x

Nower, L., & Blaszczynski, A. (2008). Recovery in pathological gambling: An imprecise concept. *Substance Use & Misuse,* 43, 1844–1864. doi:10.1080/10826080802285810.

Petry, N. M. (2006). Internet gambling: an emerging concern in family practice medicine. *Family Practice Advance,* 23, 421–426.

Petry, N. M., Litt, M. D., Kadden, R., & Ledgerwood, D. M. (2007). Do coping skills mediate the relationship between cognitive-behavioral therapy and reductions in gambling in pathological gamblers? *Addiction,* 102, 1280–1291. doi:10.1111/j.1360-0443.2007.01907.x

Schull, N. D. (2002). Escape mechanism: Women, caretaking, and compulsive machine gambling. Berkeley, CA: Center for Working Families, University of California.

Seipel, T. (2013, March 01). Letter: Shirakawa blames gambling addiction, depression for crimes. *San Jose Mercury News.* Retrieved from http://www.mercurynews.com/crime-courts/ci_22698686/shirakawa-blames-gambling-addiction-depression-crimes?source=pkg

Shaffer, H. J., & Hall, M. N. (2001). Updating and refining prevalence estimates of disordered gambling behaviour in United States and Canada. *Canadian Journal of Public Health,* 92(3), 168–172.

Strong, D. R., & Kahler, C. W. (2007). Evaluation of the continuum of gambling problems using the DSM-IV. *Addiction,* 102(5), 713–721. doi:10.1111/j.1360-0443.2007.01789.x

National Gambling Study Commission. (1999). National Gambling Study Commission Final Report. Washington, DC: Author. Retrieved from http://govinfo.library.unt.edu/ngisc/reports/1.pdf

Volberg, R. A. (2003). Has there been a "feminization" of gambling and problem gambling in the United States? *Journal of Gambling Issues,* 8. doi:10.4309/jgi.2003.8.7

Volberg, R. A., Munck, I. M., & Petry, N. M. (2011). A quick and simple screening method for pathological and problem gamblers in addiction programs and practices. *The American Journal on Addictions,* 20, 220–227. doi:10.1111/j.1521-0391.2011.00118.x

Young, K. (2009). Internet addiction: Diagnosis and treatment considerations. *Journal of Contemporary Psychotherapy,* 39(4), 241–246. doi:http://dx.doi.org/10.1007/s10879-009-9120-x

70 Developing Therapeutic Contracts with Clients

Juliet Cassuto Rothman

Contracts are agreements between parties that define and describe the nature of the relationship between the parties, including the responsibilities of each and the penalties that may accrue should one or more of the parties fail to keep the terms of the agreement. To be valid, contracts must be entered into freely by all parties. They may be formal or informal, verbal or written, or simply understood by all parties. They have been used since the beginning of recorded history, and can be adapted to many fields, such as government and politics, economics and business, and cultural and social settings.

In social work, therapeutic contracts are an essential element in working with clients. They provide a framework for focusing and goal setting, clarify roles and expectations, set time frames, and are helpful in evaluating progress and reviewing expectations. Like all contracts, contracting in social work is a voluntary joint effort, and provides a source of accountability in evaluating client change, as well as the efficacy of programs and services. Contracts have a specific form, which includes an overarching goal; a set of objectives that are both measurable and time-specific; specific interventions, which include tasks for both clients and workers; and a method of evaluation to determine the accomplishment of objectives. Contracts can be adapted to meet the needs of clients of all ages, cultural milieus, abilities, and concerns in all contexts of practice. A review of recent literature on the use of contracting in social work contexts finds that it includes individuals, families, teens, foster care families, mental hospitals, health clinics, substance abuse services, nursing homes, therapeutic groups, communities, and prisons.

Contracting in social work has a long and not uncontroversial history. However, modern social work practice, with its focus on accountability, has made contracting an integral part of the therapeutic process. Social workers have several contractual relationships as professionals that precede those with specific clients. Contracts with employers, with programs and funding sources, with insurance companies, with the social work profession, and with society as a whole direct, define, and often limit the therapeutic contract. As one of the essential components of the social work processes, therapeutic contracting is most commonly used in work with individuals, children, couples, families, and therapeutic groups.

Contracting with clients supports the profession's values and mission. Respect for the dignity and worth of the person, the importance of human relationships, and integrity are core values supported through the process of contracting. Core Competencies necessary to effective social work practice include "develop(ing) mutually agreed-upon intervention goals and objectives and select(ing) appropriate intervention strategies" (Council on Social Work Education [CSWE], Core Competencies).

The process of contracting is a powerful relationship-building tool; it empowers clients, focuses on client strengths and resources, and supports informed consent and self-determination. Alcabes and Jones (1985) state that prior to contracting, clients are not "clients" but "applicants," and the contracting process itself socializes "applicants" into their new role as "clients." Thus, the contract becomes the concrete symbol of the mutual commitment of client and worker to addressing and ameliorating the client's needs.

The process of contracting continues throughout the time that the client is receiving service, although the specific kind and content of the contract may vary (Hepworth, Rooney, & Larsen, 1997). Although, as noted above, contracting occurs in work with groups as well as with individuals, for clarity of concept development the discussion here will focus on individuals.

A TYPOLOGY OF CLIENT CONTRACTS

Three very different kinds of contracts are used with clients in social service settings, generally in the following order, from broadest to most specific.

The Service Contract or Service Agreement

Clients generally enter into *service contracts* at the point of contact. Service contracts commonly include (1) the agency's mission; (2) a description of the agency's programs and services; (3) time frames for the provision of services; (4) fees for service or arrangements for reimbursement; (5) policies on confidentiality, both within the agency, such as with supervisors or colleagues, and outside the agency, such as with other agencies serving the client, or with funding sources; (6) right of access to files, which may include the HIPPA regulations and how these will be applied; (7) releases for video- and tape-recording; and may also include (8) release of information forms (Rothman, 1998). Clients agree to respect agency policies, keep appointments, and use services appropriately. Service contracts are between a client and a service provider. They are *not* between a client and a specific worker. The client has come to the agency for service, not to the individual social worker, and the initial relationship is defined in this way. Workers in private practice may create service contracts for their practice by including many of the subjects just noted in a general policy statement for new clients. The worker is responsible for ascertaining that the client has understood the terms of the contract prior to initiating service.

Service agreements are often hastily read and signed by clients with minimal explanation or opportunity to ask questions. It is recommended that worker and client review the provisions carefully early in the relationship to clarify any parts that are unclear to the client. Where a client

does not have, or has only limited English proficiency, it is essential that arrangements be made to provide the service contract information in the client's language. Accommodations for clients with disabilities also need to ensure accessibility to service contract provisions. Clients who are minors may need to have contracts signed by parents or guardians to access certain kinds of services.

The Initial Contract

Initial contracts, developed with or immediately following the service contracts, simply state that worker and client agree that they will explore together whether worker and setting can assist the client to meet his or her goals. The work of this phase of service provision, which flows from the initial contract, includes gathering, sharing, and assessing information; defining the needs and concerns; developing potential desired outcomes; and exploring whether the agency can provide the needed resources. Initial contracts include time frames that are often defined by the setting, the funding source, or the program. This phase of the work can generally be completed in three interviews if the time frame for the entire process is about 12 to 15 weeks. Because involuntary and mandated clients often do not willingly seek services, motivational and relationship-building processes may require additional time, because it is essential that clients understand that they have a choice about entering into treatment and options about goals and objectives.

Unlike service contracts, initial contracts are often quite informal. However, it is recommended that the worker carefully document all of the terms and conditions of the initial contract, and, if possible, have the client sign or initial that he or she has agreed to the terms specified.

Content suggestions for initial contracts include (1) meeting times, number of meetings, and location; (2) a review of confidentiality guidelines; (3) an assurance that client is stable and safe, and an agreement about any immediate actions that must be taken; (4) a determination of who will be contacted for information gathering, by whom, and why; (5) a clarification in the client's own words of the reason the client is seeking help at this time; (6) and a discussion of any known policies, guidelines, or rules that may directly impact the client (Rothman, 1998).

During this initial period, "belief bonding"— the process through which client and worker come together—has occurred; this is a necessary precondition to the development of a successful and viable therapeutic contract (Bisman, 1994). "Belief bonding" occurs when a social worker's competence has been established, worker and client have agreed that change is possible, and the client has been seen as worthy of their joint efforts in effecting the change that both believe can occur (Bisman, 1994).

The Therapeutic Contract

The therapeutic contract builds directly on the service and initial contracts. These provide the general guidelines, information, and resources necessary for the development of a therapeutic plan. Therapeutic contracts are the blueprints for the change process that will occur. They are generally formal, written, and signed by both worker and client; variations should be considered, however, if they are appropriate to specific client needs.

In determining an appropriate theoretical framework and practice methodology for the therapeutic contract, workers may actively engage clients in the process of selection, use a personally preferred framework and practice method, or use the ones preferred by the agency. Clients should be made aware of the framework and methodology to be utilized. Choice of these will guide goal setting, as well as the development of objectives and interventions, and should be an integral part of the process of contracting. Although cognitive-behavioral and task-centered objectives and interventions may be easier to develop owing to the format of the contract, any theoretical framework and practice methodology appropriate to social work will adapt well to the contracting process.

It is also essential that therapeutic contracts be culturally sensitive and support the values and belief system of the client. Contracts developed without such sensitivity can cause additional stress to the client and be a major barrier to long-term success. This requires both sensitivity and self-awareness on the part of the social worker, and agency policies that support and respect the client's cultural milieu and worldview. Ethnographic interviewing may be very helpful in this process, and can be a part of the initial relationship-building and assessment process, so that goals, objectives, and interventions more clearly reflect the client's cultural experiences and concerns.

THE DEVELOPMENT OF THE THERAPEUTIC CONTRACT

Therapeutic contracts have four distinct parts: (1) an overarching goal; (2) several objectives; (3) interventions, treatments, or tasks that will fulfill the objectives; and (4) a mechanism for review and evaluation of the contract. In writing the contract, it is important to use language that is clear and comfortable for the client ; professional jargon should be carefully avoided.

Contracts themselves should be separate from the main body of recording and progress notes. A clear and simple format is best. The form provided in Figure 70.1 can be adapted as needed to reflect both the client's language and concerns and the agency's context of services and programs. Suggestions are offered for forms of intervention; these can be used as appropriate to the objective.

To illustrate the development and functioning of therapeutic contracts, we will consider Peter, a client with a history of mental illness, who is about to be discharged from a recent hospitalization. Peter has difficulty in maintaining his medical regimen, has no known family support, is fearful and untrusting of social workers, and wants to return to the community. He has been referred to a community mental health agency. We shall follow Peter through the phases of contract development, assessment, and evaluation.

Step 1: Goal

The overarching goal is generally broad and inclusive. For Peter, this might be stated as "return to community" or, later, "remain in community setting." There should be only one overarching goal; more would diffuse the focus of the work, and the goal selected should be broad enough to encompass many possible objectives and remain valid over time.

Step 2: Objectives

Each objective must include three related parts: (1) an action statement, (2) a time frame, and (3) a method for measuring success or failure. The form "*Action* as evidenced by *Measurement* in *Time Frame*" can be used. Other wording may be substituted as desired commensurate with client needs and preferences.

Name: _____

Overarching Goal: _____

Date	Objective	Interventions	Date	Evaluation
	(For each objective)	(For each intervention)		Comment about objective and interventions
		(Client, worker, client and worker, other entity) will do _____ (what).		
	#1 _____ (Action) in _____ (Time Frame) as evidenced by _____	# 1. _____ # 2. _____ # 3. _____ # 4. _____		#1 _____
	(measurement)	(Numbers will vary by what needs to be done)		
		(Continue to list objectives and interventions)		

Client Signature: _____   Worker Signature _____   Date _____

Figure 70.1 Action in time frame.

The following guidelines will assist the client and worker with this task.

- Objectives should always be reflective of the client's values, worldview, and personal motivation, and should support the overarching goal.
- Objectives should be reasonably few in number: too many objectives can be overwhelming, or can diffuse the client's energy such that nothing is achieved. Too few objectives can severely limit options for action. Three or four is generally a good number to develop.
- Objectives should be reasonably simple, specific, and written using the client's own words.
- Objectives should be measurable and achievable in the specified time frame. Time frames can vary for each objective within the contract. However, they should be designed so that the contract is reviewed at least every three months to maintain continuity and evaluate progress.
- Objectives should be ordered in time. If one is necessary before another can be achieved, it should be placed first.
- Objectives should be ordered by priority. If a client is strongly motivated toward one objective, or one is more urgent than another, place the more vital one first.
- Objectives should be achievable with reasonable effort. Success with achievable objectives will inspire and motivate clients, while those that require major life changes and complex or difficult actions will be discouraging, will not be achieved, and will reinforce a client's sense of failure and low self-esteem (Rothman, 1998).
- Complex, global objectives should be broken down into several smaller, more specific objectives in order to facilitate achievement.

Possible objectives for assisting Peter to return to community setting might include:

1. *Assess housing resources in the community* (action) as evidenced by *the development of a list of possible housing* (measurement) in *1 week* (time frame)
2. *Arrange follow-up medical care in the community* (action) as evidenced by *a written agreement with a community health clinic* (measurement) in *2 weeks* (time frame)
3. *Attend one community support group meeting* (action) as evidenced by *support group sign-in sheet* (measurement) in *2 weeks* (time frame)

Step 3: Interventions

Interventions are developed to support *each* objective. They are the *who* and the *what* of the contract. The *who* is generally the worker or the client, but it may be another person or group—a parent, siblings, friends, or another professional. When a person or persons in addition to the developers of the contract will be necessary for successful objective achievement, they should be consulted, and agree to both the actions that involve them and the time frames specified. The *what* describes what the person will do. Interventions often use the form *who will do what.*

Possible interventions for Peter's second objective might include the following:

- *Worker* (who) will *locate health clinics* (what) in the community that can serve Peter.
- *Worker and Peter* (who) will *review list and select a health clinic* (what).
- *Worker* (who) will *arrange appointment* (what) for Peter at health clinic.
- *Peter* (who) will *request his medical history* (what) from the hospital.
- *Peter* (who) will *take medical history to the clinic* (what) at the appointed time.

Because the therapeutic contract is a joint enterprise, it is vital that both worker and client have responsibility for interventions. If all of the defined tasks are for one person, the worker–client alliance will be minimized. It is not necessary, however, that there be an equal number of tasks for each person. This is a joint process for client and worker.

It is also important to consider the client's cultural context in the development of intervention strategies. These should support empowerment, maintenance of culture, and the unique personhood of the client. Cultural resources should be explored and considered when appropriate. It is essential to recognize, however, that cultural attitudes and beliefs may not always support client objectives. In Peter's case, it is important to recognize that it may not be appropriate to involve cultural resources if Peter does not identify with the culture, chooses to separate from his cultural group, or if his culture's understanding and beliefs about mental illness would not support his overarching goal.

Goals, objectives, and interventions together form the therapeutic contract. The remaining piece, the evaluation or assessment, is completed when the contract is reviewed upon completion of the time frames, or upon the achievement of an objective, and is presented below.

THE THERAPEUTIC CONTRACT AS A DYNAMIC, EVOLVING SYSTEM

The therapeutic contract is an ongoing assessment tool in the therapeutic process. Each objective has several possible outcomes: (1) it is achieved, (2) it is not achieved, (3) it is partially achieved, or (4) it is unachievable for various reasons.

Achieved Objectives

When an objective is achieved, it should be noted on the contract in the "evaluation" column with the date of the review. It is best if the objective and interventions are not removed, because achievement can serve as a positive reinforcement for both client and worker. Crossing out, highlighting, or writing "achieved" across the objective allows it to remain as a testimony of success. A completed objective is an opportunity for the development of a new one. The new objective can build on the old or develop a new line of action in addressing the client's needs. If more than one objective is achieved, several new ones may be added during a review. New objectives should support the overarching goal that was defined when the original contract was developed.

Objectives Not Achieved

Objectives may not be achieved owing to difficulties in any of the three sections of the objective statement, development of the tasks and interventions, or external factors. Careful examination

and exploration by worker and client can locate and possibly amend the objective so that it may be achieved in another form. If, after review, it is found that the objective cannot be met, it should be discarded and replaced.

Problems with Objective Statement

- *Problems with the action.* Actions that are not possible due to physical, psychological, emotional, or social barriers will not support the success of an objective. For example, Peter's stated goal is to return to the community. An objective that states "Arrange placement with brother in Miami" when Peter lives in Phoenix does not address the client's stated wishes and desires and thus cannot be successful. An objective that states "Locate a bed in a group home for Peter" will not be met if there are no group homes in the area being considered.
- *Problems with the time frame.* Time frames must be reasonable and appropriate to the difficulty and complexity of the objective. Setting time frames that are too short will frustrate client and worker alike, and cause the objective to fail. Time frames that are too long can result in loss of motivation, interest, or impetus.

  "Locate housing in the community for Peter within 3 days" may be setting too short a time frame, whereas "3 months" might be too long for this task. The worker must use knowledge of the community, the client, and resources to develop a time frame that permits achievement of the objective.

  Worker and client may reassess and extend the time frame. Time frames should not be extended more than one time. If the problem persists, the objective should be reformulated or rephrased.
- *Problems with the measurement criteria.* There are times when the measurement criteria may measure something, but not necessarily the success of the objective. For example, Peter needs monitoring of his medication regimen. This activity has been addressed as the objective "Compliance with medication regimen as noted by worker for 1 month." The action and the time frame are appropriate, but how will the worker "measure" Peter's compliance without testing or medical monitoring?

"Locate housing in the community as evidenced by Peter's placement in a community setting" has similar problems in measurement. Housing may be "located," but Peter may refuse to go, or the hospital may decide he is not ready for release, or there may be a waiting list in the housing complex. "Locate" means something quite different than "placement."

- *Problems with interventions, methods, or tasks*. Objectives may not be achieved if the interventions selected to achieve them are not adequate or are not related to the objective. For example, the objective "Worker and client will develop a plan for Peter to return to the community in 1 week" cannot be achieved through the task of "Exploring activities available in institution," or even by "Contacting sister in Alaska," much as that sister might be a support to the client.

The objective "Client will visit a halfway house with the social worker in 2 weeks" cannot be achieved with an intervention plan that sets up visits to day treatment centers rather than halfway houses. If these are to be included in planning, the objective must be rewritten to bring it in line with the intervention.

Partially Achieved Objectives

An objective that is partially achieved may have one of the previously noted problems. It may be possible to rewrite or rephrase the objective, extend the time frame, or alter the interventions, thus enabling another opportunity for meeting it.

Unachievable Objectives

Sometimes the objectives chosen may be unachievable owing to any number of factors: limitations in an agency's program; restrictions grounded in policy; changes in need, the client's life or support network, or the refusal of the client to work on the objective are examples of reasons an objective may be unachievable. These objectives should be changed as soon as the worker or client becomes aware of the problem.

CONCLUSION

Therapeutic contracts serve several functions simultaneously. They can support self-determination, informed consent, and empowerment, and focus the worker and client on specific tasks, treatments, and objectives. Therapeutic contracts are excellent resources for assessment and for measurement of progress and also serve to provide an objective measure of performance for agencies, funding sources, clients, and social workers themselves. As limited time frames and the exigencies of managed care impact client–worker relationships, the therapeutic contract serves to ground, support, and enhance professional social work practice. Built on the foundation created in the work of the service contract and the initial contract, the therapeutic contract is an excellent tool to encourage workers and clients to explore avenues for effecting and enabling change within the client system.

WEBSITES

Code of Ethics: www.socialworker.org/pubs/code
Core Competencies: www.cswe.org/file/aspx?id=13780
HIPAA Guidelines: www.hipaaguidelines101.com/hipaa-rules.htm
Articles that include contracting discussions can be located online through Proquest. Search "therapeutic contracting"

References

Alcabes, A., & Jones, J. A. (1985). Structural determinants of "clienthood." *Social Work*, 30(1), 49–53.
Bisman, C. (1994). *Social work practice: Theory and principles*. Pacific Grove, CA: Brooks/Cole.
Hepworth, D., Rooney, R., & Larsen, J. A. (1997). *Direct social work practice: Theory and skills*. Pacific Grove, CA: Brooks/Cole.
Rothman, J. (1998). *Contracting in clinical social work*. Chicago, IL: Nelson Hall.

71 Developing Goals

Charles D. Garvin

The development and clarification of client system goals are necessary steps in bringing about individual as well as environmental changes (Garvin & Seabury, 1997).[1] Goals indicate specifically what clients want to accomplish. Thus, goals are changes in clients' life situations that are derived from the wants and needs revealed when a client's concerns are explored and assessed. For example, one client's long-range goal was "to be employed as a social worker." That client's short-term goals were to enroll in a school of social work, pass the courses, and complete the other requirements of the school. A barrier to attaining these goals was the client's lack of money. This led to another goal of obtaining money from the client's parents to pay for tuition.

We recognize that different approaches to and models of practice define goals differently (Philips, 2009). An example of this is solution-based therapy, in which the client systems are asked to create a narrative of what their situation would look like if the helping process were successful (Connie & Metcalf, 2009).

The assessment process precedes goal setting. The assessment process is related to goals because the assessment provides the practitioner and the client with answers to the following questions: (1) What levels of goal attainment are possible given the resources and limitations present in clients and their situations? (2) What changes must be sought in clients and their situations to attain specified goals? These changes are specified in terms of short-term goals that must be attained before long-term goals are worked on. Blythe and Reithoffer (2000) recommend instruments that can be used to assess clients in ways that link closely to goal determination.

An example of this was work with John W., who had recently been discharged from a hospital following major heart surgery. A social worker helped him develop a discharge plan that will enable him to return to an active role in the community. This work began with an assessment that included John's previous level of functioning, the level of functioning he could be expected to attain, and the likely length of the recovery process. From this assessment, the social worker and John jointly developed several goals. One of these was to complete a physical therapy program. Barriers to this completion, such as a lack of transportation, were identified, and the social worker helped John develop various means of overcoming these barriers. The physical therapist helped John develop additional goals, one of which was to regain enough strength to enable him to resume his previous employment as a computer repair person.

RATIONALE FOR THE USE OF GOALS IN PRACTICE

According to Hepworth et al. (2013, p. 328), there are a number of reasons for seeking an agreement between client and practitioner with respect to goals. The agreement:

- Ensures that, where possible, you and the client are in agreement about outcomes to be achieved
- Provides direction, focus, and continuity to the helping process and prevents wandering off course
- Facilitates the development and selection of appropriate strategies and interventions

- Assists you and the client in monitoring progress
- Serves as the criteria for evaluating the effectiveness of a specific intervention and of the helping process.

It has also been demonstrated that when client systems and workers have not defined goals for their work together, client systems are likely to leave treatment prematurely (Meyer, 2001).

GOALS AND PRACTICE PHASE

Goals should be determined initially during the first phase of practice, when the practitioner is becoming engaged with the client system and assessing strengths and resources. As the client system develops relationships with the practitioner, it will be more likely to disclose problems and work toward solving them. As the system achieves an agreement with the practitioner on problems and goals, the people involved are more likely to have positive feelings toward the practitioner and the work they do together. Nevertheless, goals are not static and may be revised or replaced as time passes, situations change, and new information becomes available.

Movement beyond this first phase into a work phase cannot occur until an initial relationship has been established, problems identified, goals specified, and an initial work plan created. The amount of time this takes will vary depending on the nature of the problem, the strengths of the client system, the skills of the practitioner, the resources that are available, and the presence or absence of conflict between individuals in the client system and practitioners regarding the issues involved. When the agency imposes time limits, this also will be a factor in determining goals and the means selected to achieve them.

Goal issues may also arise during subsequent work phases. For example, client systems may wish to change their treatment goals (1) when they attain them and perhaps continue to work on additional goals, (2) when their situation changes, or (3) when goal attainment does not take place.

TYPES OF GOALS

The practitioner should recognize that there are different types of goals that require somewhat different kinds of interventions in order for the client to attain them. These include the following.

Discrete versus Continuous Goals

Discrete goals are those in which a single outcome is sought, such as admission to a school. Continuous goals are those in which the individuals in the client system enact the behavior that constitutes the goal on a number of occasions, such as a parent who disciplines a child by offering rewards instead of punishments.

Goals Related to Different Types of Systems

Goals may relate to outcomes for an individual, a dyad, a small group (including the family), an organization, or even a larger system. The larger the system, the greater the number of people who may have to be involved, not only in setting the goals but also in working for their attainment. In a sense, the first goal in multi-person situations, such as families, is for individuals to attain agreement on the family's goals and the relationship of these to each individual's goals. Sometimes, this is the only or main goal for work with such systems, although other goals may stem from these as the "system" works to attain the goals that have eventually been agreed upon.

When the system is even larger, such as an organization or agency, arriving at goals may require various interest groups in the system to negotiate an agreement on organizational goals. An example of this was a hospital in which each professional group had to arrive at an agreement with other groups (e.g., nurses, doctors, social workers, administrators). This process may involve the differences in power between these entities—a subject that goes beyond the scope of this article.

Goals Related to Different Kinds of Behaviors

Goals may relate to affects, cognitions, or instrumental behaviors or combinations of these. An example of this is a client who experienced anxiety attacks when he spoke in class. One goal was that he no longer experience the anxiety (affect goal); another was that he speak in class (instrumental behavior goal); a third was that he no longer label making a mistake in what he said in class as proving that he was stupid (cognitive goal).

Individual versus Reciprocal or Interpersonal Goals

A goal may relate to the behavior of an individual acting alone. An example of this is a person whose goal was to report on time to work every day. Another goal, however, may be reciprocal. An example of this was a family meeting with a family therapist. The parents agreed to take their entire family on an outing when the children had all completed their household chores every day for a week.

SELECTING GOALS

There are a number of criteria the practitioner should consider in helping client systems select their goals. The first of these, as should be obvious from the foregoing discussion, is that the goal, if attained, should reduce or eliminate the problem(s) for which the client system has sought help. The individuals concerned should also have an emotional investment in attaining the goals. In addition, if the client system or the practitioner is working toward a goal that is not known to the other, the process will be seriously flawed because communication is likely to be confusing to each party, and tensions between them will emerge as a result.

A special problem in negotiating goals is posed by involuntary individuals—those who are required by a court or other system with power, to keep appointments with the practitioner because the system otherwise will impose sanctions for nonparticipation in treatment. Hepworth et al. (2013, pp. 335–337) and De Jong and Berg (2001) suggest several approaches for goal setting with such clients. One of these is to look for a common ground between client and system.

GUIDELINES FOR ESTABLISHING GOALS

The goals agreed to by the practitioner and the client system should meet a set of criteria and become part of either a verbal or a written contract. These criteria are as follows:

- Goals should be explicit. This means that a specific behavior or circumstance should

be indicated. The situation in which the behavior is to occur, as well as its frequency or intensity, should be described. When workers and client systems are vague in specifying goals, this can lead to a lack of focus in their work together (Ribner & Knei-Paz, 2002).

- The attainment of the goal should be measurable. The measures may be either qualitative or quantitative.

- The goal should always be stated in terms of client system (not practitioner) behavior. Some practitioners begin goal statements with such phrases as "help the client," which is what we assume the worker will do.

- The goal should be chosen with due regard to feasibility of client system and practitioner. This depends on opportunities available in the environment, the attitudes and abilities of significant others, and social, political, and economic conditions. We recommend that the client system be given the benefit of the doubt on this issue.

- Legality should be a major issue in selecting a goal. Practitioners should not help clients work to attain illegal or immoral goals. This is not as easy to implement in some situations, such as a terminally ill client who wishes help to commit suicide when offering such help is illegal. Fortunately, the National Association of Social Workers and other professional associations have guidelines to help practitioners determine what to do in such situations. At times, the goal is counter to the practitioner's ethics but not those of the profession or society.

- The goal should be one in which the skills and knowledge of the practitioner are adequate to help the client system attain the goal.

- The practitioner should consider the consequences for others of contracting with the client system to work toward the stated goals. We believe that professional ethics require that the worker not collude with the client system in such a way as to lead to harm to others. The situation becomes more complex when the client system seeks to overcome some form of oppression because this may, in fact, impose a "cost" on the target of the client system's efforts (e.g., workers are helped to participate in a strike which, if successful, will impose a cost on the employers; or, clients of an agency may seek to obtain more or better service from the agency, which can prove costly.

- Goals should be stated in positive terms. An example of this is the parents' goal of acquiring ways of appropriately disciplining a child rather than refraining from inflicting inappropriate punishment on the child. We find that working toward positive goals is more likely to occur than the opposite, and this emphasis on client system growth enhances self-esteem and a sense of accomplishment.

The steps in establishing goals are the following (Hepworth et al., 2013, pp. 350–355).

Step 1: Identify and Prioritize Problems

The practitioner should ask client systems to indicate the problem(s) they hope to solve as a result of the help offered by the social worker. Many people will state the problem in terms of the behavior of another person, such as, "Our boss won't listen to us" or "My husband criticizes me too much." We have no objection to problems stated in this way. If the worker rejects such statements, many people will refuse to continue because they will conclude that the worker has no regard for their views. There will be time enough as goals are developed to help people to include their own actions in the definition of the situation.

Problem statements in family treatment may take on a different form than in one-to-one treatment. These statements are likely to involve relationships and interactions, such as a husband and wife who state that they cannot resolve arguments, agree on how resources are to be spent, or engage in satisfying sexual interactions. It will be useful later in treatment if the family or couple can state the problem in ways that are not solely focused on one family member (the so-called identified patient), but this is not absolutely necessary and may, in some situations, be an impossible demand.

In groups, the first members to define their problems will serve as models for others who find this task more difficult. If the group has been composed of individuals with similar problems, this stage of the process may not be difficult because members already may have decided, as part of an individual interview held before the group began, on the problems they will work on in the group.

Examples of Problems and Related Goals

Problem: Parent states problem is the destructive behavior of an adolescent child.

Goals: In ways that are satisfying to both parties, learn techniques for negotiating limits with child when child violates a rule set by parent; learn to state expectations of child's behavior in specific terms that indicate what is expected rather than what is unacceptable.

Problem: Client is failing college courses.

Goals: Organize a schedule for completion of assignments that is realistic in terms of work and recreation; negotiate with biology instructor a date to complete work that is realistic for student and acceptable to instructor.

Problem: Members of a community are not receiving necessary services from their city.

Goals: The city officials agree to provide these services and to receive reports from the citizens as to how effectively this has occurred.

Step 2: Determine Client's Readiness to Set Goals

Hepworth et al. (2013, p. 350–351) recommend that when the practitioner believes it is time to work on goals, she or he should determine whether the client system agrees that it is ready for this process. At times, individuals or groups will assert that additional information should be considered before goals are set; at other times, the client system will indicate a readiness to proceed.

Step 3: Provide a Rationale for Goals

The practitioner should examine the reasons for goals. He or she should convey the importance placed on client system self-determination and the relationship between setting goals and determining whether or not the service has been effective. The individuals in the client system should be helped to understand that goals represent changes they would like to see in relationship to the problem, should the treatment prove successful.

Step 4: Identify and Choose Goals

As indicated earlier, the individuals in the client system should be asked what they would like to see changed if the social work service is successful in helping the client system ameliorate the problem. At times, especially when the individuals in the client system have limitations owing to age or disability, the social worker may suggest some goals and invite the individuals to choose from among them. These choices should be explained and illustrated so that as much input is obtained from the client system as possible.

Step 5: Explicate the Goals

There are several components of a well-formulated goal statement, that is, one stated so specifically that its attainment is measurable. The characteristics of such statements are:

- Performance (what the learner is to be able to do)
- Conditions (important conditions under which the performance is expected to occur)
- Criteria (the quality or level of performance that will be considered acceptable).

These characteristics can be used whether the goal is stated in terms of the client system's own behavior or the behavior of a person or system other than the client system. An example of a goal for an individual's own behavior is: "Joan, when faced with a derogatory statement from her employer (Sally) with which she does not agree, will calmly indicate her disagreement to the employer." The criterion for the quality of the performance is that the employer will acknowledge that she has heard and understood Joan's views.

Step 6: Determining Feasibility, Benefits, and Risks

The practitioner should avoid encouraging the client system to spend a great deal of time and effort trying to achieve a goal that is not feasible, especially when this could have been determined in advance. Hepworth et al. (2013, p. 334) suggest that the practitioner determine feasibility by asking the clients what obstacles they anticipate might block them from achieving their goals. Anticipating obstacles, of course, does not mean the clients should forgo striving to attain the goal, because all goal-attainment activities will come up against obstacles. Rather, are these obstacles so severe that no reasonable amount of effort will overcome them?

Step 7: Determining Goal Priorities

When the client's goals arise from several different problems, the priority attached to each problem will determine the priority of the goal.

SPECIAL POPULATIONS

The practitioner should take into consideration the cultural and social circumstances of specific populations when seeking to determine goals with members of these populations. The types of populations considered here are ethnic and cultural groups, age groups, and groups with limited capacities to select goals.

Nelson-Jones (2002) lists a series of topics that should be considered to help culturally diverse client systems determine goals:

a. The past and current mistreatment of the individuals concerned
b. The need for support when immigration/emigration occurs
c. The likelihood that post-traumatic stress was incurred due to the experience of aversive circumstances
d. The need for help with language, housing, health, education, and employment when in the process of settling into a new community
e. The need for individuals to avoid further marginalization caused by clumsy efforts to adapt individuals to new cultural environments
f. Discrimination individuals may face due to their status within their own cultures
g. Individuals may need to manage cross-cultural relationships
h. The likelihood that individuals may face intergenerational conflicts in their own cultures
i. The likelihood of gender role and gender equality issues.

Because of the variation within groups related to degree of assimilation, specific life experience, and so forth, we do not believe in approaching this topic with such generalizations as "Native Americans will favor goal X." Nevertheless, we believe that the cultural experiences a person has had will help determine his or her values and aspirations, which, in turn, will help determine his or her goals. As a consequence, the practitioner should bear in mind questions such as the following, which may help him or her discuss goals in ways compatible with the client's beliefs.

1. How do individuals in the client system feel about creating long-term objectives as compared to having objectives that are very short range? That is, do these persons give much value to a future orientation as compared with one oriented to the present?
2. How does the individual feel about personal goals as compared with goals oriented to the welfare of one's family, community, or other reference group? Some individuals see it as much more important to work for the betterment of these systems and as almost inconceivable to put one's own welfare ahead of the group.
3. What aspects of living are regarded as the most and least important? Some cultures see family outcomes as the most important; for others, occupational outcomes are the most important; others see educational outcomes as the most important; and still others stress the kind of person the individual is or is becoming as of the highest value. These kinds of beliefs have a strong impact on the goals that the individual will be strongly motivated to attain.

An excellent example of the foregoing is the work of Walker (2008). This author describes a program called "youth circles" to help Hawaiian youth develop the skills of goal setting.

CONCLUSION

The chapter began with a definition of the term, "goals." Goals may refer to ultimate, intermediate, and instrumental outcomes, and these terms were also defined. Goals are chosen in relationship to an assessment of client systems and their circumstances. It is important to stress the connection between goals and assessment data.

Practice principles for the creation of goal statements were presented. These differ depending on such issues as whether the client is voluntary or involuntary. An important principle is that the goals should relate to the presenting problem, and consequently, the process of problem specification was also described. Finally, this chapter discussed goal issues that may arise with various populations, such as those related to gender and ethnicity.

In the future, goal setting is likely to be regarded as even more important than it is now. This will arise out of the emphases placed on attaining desired outcomes as a justification for providing managed care services, linking interventions to goals, and empowering client systems to select the goals that are appropriate for their cultures and personal lifestyles.

WEBSITES

Evidence Based Mental Health.
    http://ebmh.bmj.com.
Journal of Social Work Research and Evaluation
    http://www.springerpub.com/journals/
    social_work_research.html.

Note

1. We are using the term client system in this article to mean those who use the services of the social worker to attain goals. Thus, the term applies to all service users including groups, families, organizations, and communities.

References

Blythe, B., & Reithoffer, A. (2000). Assessment and measurement issues in direct practice in social work. In P. Allen-Meares & C. Garvin (Eds.), *The handbook of social work direct practice* (pp. 551–564). Thousand Oaks, CA: Sage.

Connie, E., & Metcalf, L. (Eds.). (2009). *The art of solution focused therapy*. New York, NY: Springer.

De Jong, P., & Berg, I. K. (2001). Co-constructing cooperation with mandated clients. *Social Work, 46*(4), 361–374.

Garvin, C. D., & Seabury, B. A. (1997). *Interpersonal practice in social work: Promoting competence and social justice* (2nd ed.). Boston, MA: Allyn & Bacon.

Hepworth, D. H., Rooney, R. H., Rooney, G. D., Strom-Gottfried, K., & Larson, J. A. (2013). *Direct social work practice: Theory and skills* (9th ed.). Belmont, CA: Brooks/Cole.

Meyer, W. (2001). Why don't they come back: A clinical perspective on the no-show client. *Clinical Social Work, 29*(4), 325–339.

Nelson-Jones, R. (2002). Diverse goals for multicultural counseling and therapy. *Counselling Psychology Quarterly, 15*(2), 133–143.

Philips, P. (2009). Comparing apples and oranges: How do patient characteristics and treatment goals vary between different forms of psychotherapy? *Psychology and Psychotherapy: Theory, Research and Practice, 82*(3), 323–336.

Ribner, D. S., & Knei-Paz, C. (2002). Client's view of a successful helping relationship. *Social Work, 47*(4), 379–387.

Walker, L. (2008). Waikiki Youth Circles: Homeless youth learn goal setting skills. *Journal of Family Psychotherapy, 19*(1), 85–91.

72 *Attention Deficit Hyperactivity Disorder Case Applications*

Kimberly Bender, Samantha M. Brown, & David W. Springer

Treatment goals and treatment plans are a critical component of effective social work practice with adolescents; without explicit goals and plans, both social workers and clients run the risk of aimlessly "stumbling around in the dark" until they happen across a "problem" that needs to be addressed. As consumers of care, we expect our primary care physicians to deliver services with some sense of purpose, direction, and expertise. We should expect no less from social workers and the care they provide. To this end, treatment plans serve as very useful tools. Social workers and adolescents collaborate to establish treatment plans and treatment goals and select a focus of their work together. Goals specify what the adolescent wants to work on in treatment, and the treatment plan serves as a game plan for how these goals will be obtained. This chapter provides guidelines for establishing treatment goals and plans with adolescent clients.

TREATMENT GOALS

The first step in establishing treatment goals with any client is to conduct a thorough assessment. This entails allowing the client to tell his or her story, conducting a psychosocial history, seeking input from family, friends, and other professionals, and using standardized assessment tools and rapid assessment instruments as needed. Clients may also need to be referred for medical and/or psychological testing. Following a thorough assessment, the social worker and

client work together to establish goals for the client. In this sense, goals link the assessment and treatment process.

The following guidelines are helpful in establishing treatment goals. The goals should (1) be clearly defined and measurable, (2) be feasible and realistic, (3) be set collaboratively by the social worker and the client, (4) stem directly from the assessment process, and (5) be stated in positive terms, focusing on client growth. Treatment goals help direct the social worker and the client toward "cognitive, emotional, behavioral, and situational actions" (Cournoyer, 2005, p. 322).

Treatment goals need to be defined clearly and stated in such a way that progress toward the goals can be measured. If goals are stated too ambiguously, clients may become discouraged or feel as if the goals are out of reach. For example, compare the ambiguous goal of "improve school performance" with the more concrete goal of "complete at least 90% of homework assignments over the next 2 weeks." The latter goal is more likely to be meaningful and obtainable to the client.

This leads to the second element of establishing treatment goals, which is that they must be feasible and realistic. "Improving school performance" is not only vague, it may not be feasible or realistic because it potentially covers so much ground. Additionally, little discussion between the social worker and the adolescent is needed to create vague goals. By contrast, concrete goals require a serious dialogue to take place so that conceptual ideas about client functioning can be "wrestled to the ground" in clear, day-to-day terms.

To the extent that adolescent clients participate in this discussion, the more likely it is that they will feel a sense of ownership over the established goals, which, in turn, means that they are more likely to follow through with the treatment plan. Clients (especially adolescents) will experience less buy-in to the treatment process if goals are imposed on them by a social worker or parent. Thus, goal setting needs to be a truly collaborative process among the social worker, adolescent, and his or her parents (when appropriate).

Treatment goals need to stem directly from the assessment process. The assessment should be thorough, empirically based, and grounded in a systems perspective. This minimizes the likelihood that the worker is creating treatment goals based solely on gut feeling or an on-the-spot diagnosis.

Finally, treatment goals need to be stated in positive terms. In other words, the goal should state what the client *will* do rather than what the client *will not* do. For example, a client will be more motivated and goal directed by a goal that states "attend the entire school day every day for the next 2 weeks" in comparison to a goal that states "stop skipping school."

TREATMENT PLANS

Treatment plans are the next logical step after goals have been formulated, and, in practice, these two steps often go hand in hand. Treatment plans reflect what specific and concrete steps or interventions are going to be implemented to help the adolescent client obtain his or her goals.

Similar to goal-setting, the process of establishing a treatment plan should be collaborative between the adolescent (and his or her family) and social worker. As a natural extension of the movement started under the Child and Adolescent Service System Program initiated in 1984 by the National Institute of Mental Health, many communities across the country received federal funding through the Substance Abuse and Mental Health Services Administration, Center for Mental Health Services to implement a community-based, wraparound approach to service delivery within a system of care (Rosenblatt, 1998). Today, the wraparound approach is more prevalent, refined, and studied. An excellent resource on this approach is the National Wraparound Initiative (see http://www.nwi.pdx .edu). A major emphasis of this approach is providing individualized, client-centered services for youth with serious emotional disturbance and multiple mental health needs. One pragmatic way this is accomplished is to actively involve the youth and his or her family in the development of a treatment plan, recognizing the client as an expert on his or her own life (Schelenger, Etheridge, Hansen, Fairbank, & Onken, 1992).

Assuming the client is the expert on his or her own experiences, the social worker can (and should) lend expertise regarding what treatment approaches or interventions are most effective for a given problem. For example, if medication management or cognitive-behavioral therapy has been demonstrated to be effective for a given problem or disorder, the social worker has a responsibility to share this information with the adolescent and his or her family to provide guidance as they develop the treatment plan. Effective treatments should be described and the potential costs and benefits discussed with the adolescent and his/her family to reach consensus on the best plan of action as the client moves forward with treatment.

Case Illustration: Steven

Steven is a 13-year-old white male who has been referred to the school social worker by his teacher because "he won't sit still and he doesn't follow instructions." The teacher also complains that Steven has a very short attention span, often gets into trouble in class for blurting out answers, and is easily distracted. Though not previously referred for services, Steven has been having trouble with impulsivity and inattention since starting elementary school. He has no history of past mental health treatment, no remarkable medical history, and denies any substance use.

A thorough assessment would need to be conducted. This would likely entail interviewing Steven, his family, and his teacher. During these assessment interviews, the social worker might inquire about Steven's perspective on the problem, when and where he struggles most, as well as times when things are easier for him. The social worker might ask about what has been done to address the problem thus far and whether previous attempts have been successful. Importantly, the social worker would spend time getting to know Steven, including his likes and dislikes, and would identify Steven's strengths and resources. In addition to conducting thorough bio-psychosocial interviews, the social worker might utilize standardized assessment instruments such as the Conners Parent Rating Scale Revised (Conners, 1997) to determine whether Steven's behaviors align with symptoms of attention deficit hyperactivity disorder (ADHD). Given time and access, the social worker would directly observe Steven in class to get a sense of when and how his behaviors manifest as well as teachers' and students' reactions to Steven. Finally, the social worker might refer Steven for a physical with his physician, as well as a medical consultation with a psychiatrist, to determine whether there are any medical explanations for his symptoms and whether medication would be recommended. Biofeedback/neurofeedback has garnered some support in the literature as an alternative to medication management, and this may also be considered (Arns, de Ridder, Strehl, Breteler, & Coenen, 2009).

Following this assessment process, the social worker would likely consult the *Diagnostic and Statistical Manual of Mental Disorders, Fifth Edition* (DSM-5). Just recently available in 2013, the fifth edition of the DSM might suggest Steven meets the following diagnostic criteria:

314.01 (F90.2) Attention-Deficit/Hyperactivity Disorder, Combined presentation
V61.20 Parent-child relational problem
V62.9 Unspecified problems related to social environment

In addition to a formal diagnosis, it would be just as important that the social worker clearly identify the problem behaviors in terms meaningful to Steven and his family. These areas of concern would be listed and treatment goals (both short- and long-term) would be established with corresponding interventions.

A sample treatment plan for Steven is provided in Table 72.1. Notice that the treatment plan includes both short- and long-term goals and specifies who is responsible for each task. Some treatment plans may also include target dates that reflect when a specific goal is to be reviewed to determine whether it has been accomplished or needs to be revised. The sample treatment plan for Steven is intended to serve as a template. It is important to note that different goals or interventions could have been included or emphasized

depending on how problem areas were identified and prioritized by Steven, his family, and/or the social worker. A treatment plan needs to be tailored to the individual and unique needs of the client.

Readers are cautioned against taking a cookie-cutter approach to establishing treatment plans. Suppose that Steven also presented with behavioral problems associated with oppositional defiant disorder, that he was at risk of running away from home, or that he and his parents wanted to enroll him in a different school. These areas of concern would also need to be addressed in the treatment plan, with corresponding goals and interventions. Obviously, the treatment plan provided here does not reflect the complexities of treating an adolescent with ADHD. Readers interested in a more detailed exposition on how to treat adolescents with ADHD are referred elsewhere (see Barkley, 2000; Ervin, DuPaul, Kern, & Friman, 1998; Evans et al., 2006; Pelham, Fabiano, & Massetti, 2005; Raggi & Chronis, 2006; Robin, 1998; U.S. Department of Education, 2006).

One additional note about the case illustration is warranted. The vignette focuses on an adolescent with a diagnosis of ADHD for a reason. ADHD is one of the most common diagnoses encountered by practitioners working with youth; however, other common disorders encountered by practitioners working with adolescents in clinical settings may include disruptive behavior disorders (oppositional defiant disorder and conduct disorder), major depressive disorder, and substance abuse (see American Psychiatric Association [APA], 2013; Christner, Stewart, & Freeman, 2007; Dishion & Kavanagh, 2003).

CONCLUSION

Adolescents are in a unique developmental phase of life where the struggle for autonomy and individuation are amplified. Add to this potentially tumultuous process a *DSM-5* (APA, 2013) diagnosis or a serious emotional disturbance, and these young people become even more vulnerable to life's ups and downs. Social workers have an ethical responsibility to work closely with the adolescent (and his or her family) to develop a treatment plan that is sensitive to the developmental, cultural, and individual needs of the client, while also recommending interventions that are empirically based and grounded in a

TABLE 72.1 Sample Treatment Plan for Steven

Areas of Concern	Short-term Goals	Long-term Goals	Treatment Plan
1. Difficulty paying attention 2. Has trouble listening 3. Has trouble organizing 4. Often avoids activities that require sustained mental effort 5. Loses things often 6. Easily distracted 7. Often fidgets or squirms 8. Often leaves seat during class 9. Has difficulty playing quietly 10. Talks excessively 11. Blurts out answers to questions 12. Conflict with parents	1. Steven will begin to take prescribed medication as directed by physician. 2. Steven will begin to increase his on-task behavior, as evidenced by completing 90% of homework assignments. 3. Steven's parents and teachers will create and begin to use a system to monitor homework. 4. Steven will demonstrate improved impulse control, as evidenced by earning 3 points a day in every class (for staying in seat, waiting his turn to talk). 5. Steven's teachers will set up a reward (point) system to reinforce positive behavior and discourage negative behavior. 6. Steven's parents will set firm and consistent limits, using natural rewards and consequences. 7. Steven's teachers will work with him to create a classroom setting that reduces distractions. 8. Steven and his parents will improve communication and establish a behavioral contract.	1. Steven will take prescribed medication on a regular basis. 2. Steven will engage in on-task behavior on a regular basis, as evidenced by completing 100% of homework assignments. 3. Steven's parents and teachers will consistently monitor homework. 4. Steven will demonstrate improved impulse control, as evidenced by earning 5 points a day in every class (for staying in seat, waiting his turn to talk). 5. Steven's teachers will maintain a reward (point) system to further reinforce positive behavior and discourage negative behavior. 6. Steven's parents will set firm and consistent limits, using natural rewards and consequences. 7. Steven's teachers will help to maintain a classroom setting that reduces distractions. 8. Steven and parents will maintain improved communication and will modify behavioral contract as needed to aid in parental limit setting and establishing clear rules.	1. Social worker will refer Steven to psychiatrist for medication management and will consult with psychiatrist regularly. 2. Steven, social worker, his parents, and teachers will meet to set up a system to monitor his homework, set up a point system in the classroom (to reinforce positive behaviors), and enhance the classroom setting (to reduce distractions). 3. Steven's parents will attend an 8-week parenting class to learn ways to set limits and boundaries, and use natural rewards and consequences. 4. Steven will learn to use self-monitoring skills (e.g., internal self-talk) to control impulsive behavior at home and in school. 5. Steven and parents will attend weekly family therapy sessions with social worker to clarify rules, enhance communication, establish a behavioral contract, and learn about ADHD.

bio-psychosocial perspective. Most importantly, the adolescent must have input into the development of the treatment plan in a meaningful way to maximize the likelihood that he or she is invested in the treatment process and will sustain lasting change over time.

WEBSITES

American Academy of Child & Adolescent Psychiatry. http://www.aacap.org/cs/ADHD. ResourceCenter.

Children and Adults with ADHD, national support group association. http://www.chadd.org.

National Institute of Mental Health: Child and Adolescent Mental Health. http://www .nimh.nih.gov/health/topics/child- and-adolescent-mental-health/index.shtml.

National Wraparound Initiative. http://www .nwi.pdx.edu

References

American Psychiatric Association. (2013). *Diagnostic and statistical manual of mental disorders, fifth edition.* Washington, DC: Author.

Arns, M., de Ridder, S., Strehl, U., Breteler, M., & Coenen, A. (2009). Efficacy of neurofeedback treatment in ADHD: the effects on inattention, impulsivity and hyperactivity: a meta-analysis. *Clinical EEG Neuroscience,* 40, 180–189.

Barkley, R. A. (2000). Commentary on the multimodal treatment study of children with ADHD. *Journal of Abnormal Child Psychology,* 28(6), 595–599.

Christner, R. W., Stewart, J. L., & Freeman, A. (Eds.). *Handbook of cognitive-behavior group therapy with children and adolescents: Specific settings and presenting problems.* New York, NY: Routledge.

Conners, C. K. (1997). *Conners Parent Rating Scale— revised.* North Tonawanda, NY: Multi-Health Systems.

Cournoyer, B. R. (2005). *The social work skills workbook.* Belmont, CA: Thomson Brooks/Cole.

Dishion, T. J., & Kavanagh, K. (2003). *Intervening in adolescent problem behavior: A family-centered approach.* New York, NY: Guilford.

Ervin, R. A., DuPaul, G. J., Kern, L., & Friman, P. C. (1998). Classroom-based functional and adjunctive assessments: Proactive approaches to intervention selection for adolescents with attention-deficit hyperactivity disorder. *Journal of Applied Behavioral Analysis,* 31(1), 65–78.

Evans, S. W., Timmins, B., Sibley, M., White, L. C., Zewelanji, N. S., & Schultz, B. (2006). Developing coordinated, multimodal, school-based treatment for young adolescents with ADHD. *Education and Treatment of Children,* 29(2), 359–378.

Pelham, W. E., Fabiano, G. A., & Massetti, G. M. (2005). Evidence-based assessment of attention deficit hyperactivity disorder in children and adolescents. *Journal of Clinical Child and Adolescent Psychology,* 34(3), 449–476.

Raggi, V. L., & Chronis, A. M. (2006). Interventions to address the academic impairment of children and adolescents with ADHD. *Clinical Child and Family Psychology Review,* 9(2), 85–111.

Robin, A. L. (1998). *ADHD in adolescents: Diagnosis and treatment.* New York, NY: Guilford.

Rosenblatt, A. (1998). Assessing the child and family outcomes of systems of care for youth with serious emotional disturbance. In M. H. Epstein, K. Kutash, & A. Duchnowski (Eds.), *Outcomes for children and youth with behavioral and emotional disorders and their families: Programs and evaluation best practice* (pp. 329–362). Austin, TX: PRO-ED.

Schelenger, W. E., Etheridge, R. M., Hansen, D. J., Fairbank, D. W., & Onken, J. (1992). Evaluation of state efforts to improve systems of care for children and adolescents with severe emotional disturbances: The CASSP initial cohort study. *Journal of Mental Health Administration,* 19, 131–142.

U.S. Department of Education, Office of Special Education and Rehabilitative Services, Office of Special Education Programs. (2006). *Identifying and treating attention deficit hyperactivity disorder: A resource for school and home.* Washington, DC: U.S. Department of Education.

73   Eating Disorders and Treatment Planning

Nina Rovinelli Heller & Jack Lu

Eating disorders can be considered from medical, mental health, and public health perspectives. Social workers in a wide range of settings are in frontline positions to identify, treat, and prevent eating disorders, including bulimia, anorexia, and obesity-related issues, from several of these perspectives. From a medical perspective, eating disorders may involve neuroendocrine dysfunction and genetic vulnerability (Sadock & Sadock, 2007). In addition, the symptoms of eating disorders may create both acute and chronic medical complications and emergencies. For example, people with anorexia nervosa can suffer the biological effects of starvation, osteoporosis, and cardiac arrest; those with bulimia nervosa can develop severe digestive tract disorders and dental problems. Eating disorders are most commonly considered mental health problems with affective, behavioral, and cognitive causes and sequelae. Eating disorders and their rise in prevalence across groups can also be considered from a social constructivist position (Piran & Cormier, 2005) with an understanding of the myriad social messages and influences dictating preferred body image and shape.

Eating disorders are also understood descriptively in a categorization system that typically does not address issues of etiology. The *Diagnostic and Statistical Manual* is broadly used by mental health professionals. There were several changes to the eating disorder categories in the latest version of the *Diagnostic and Statistical Manual (DSM-5)* (APA, 2013). Binge eating, formerly lodged in an appendix, was included as a distinct category of eating disorder with criteria pertaining to recurring episodes of eating significant amounts of food during a brief period of time, sometimes rapidly; doing so while feeling "out of control," having feelings of shame or disgust;

hiding the behavior; experiencing substantial distress, with a minimum of weekly episodes over at least a three-month period. The diagnosis of anorexia nervosa remains substantially the same, but with a focus on behaviors, rather than attitudes, related to the restriction of caloric intake. In part due to the increase in the diagnosis among males, the criterion for amenorrhea, the absence of menses was removed. Finally, for the diagnosis of bulimia nervosa, the requirement related to frequency of binge eating followed by purging was reduced to once per week.

Following much debate, obesity was not included in the *DSM-5* as a diagnosis. According to the *DSM-5*, obesity is considered the result of a combination of genetic, behavioral, environmental, and physiological factors, with high variability among individuals. That said, there are individuals who are obese who may meet, but not necessarily meet, criteria for bulimia nervosa and binge-eating disorders.

Diagnostic systems are imperfect ones; for example, in clinical practice, many social workers observe that anorexia nervosa and bulimia may be present at different times in the course of the life of a person who struggles with eating difficulties. In these situations, it may be helpful to consider a continuum model of disordered eating, rather than the notion of distinct conditions.

NOT JUST "THE WHITE WOMAN'S DISEASE"

There are shared and distinct presentations and risk factors for men and women and we highlight those here. Males with eating disorders are now estimated to account for somewhere between 10% and 25% of all cases, including anorexia nervosa and bulimia (Collier, 2013; Peate, 2011; Stanford & Lemberg, 2012), with male athletes at elevated risk (Glazer, 2008). Additionally, Kjelsas, Bjornstrom, and Gotestam (2004) found that there is nearly 7% lifetime prevalence for all eating disorders among adolescent boys. Finally, older men with excess weight are also known to experience binge eating disorder due to cultural factors and influences (Greenberg & Schoen, 2008).

Disturbances in body image and self-perception remain consistent between men and women for both clinical and subclinical experiences with the diagnosis of an eating disorder (Glazer, 2008). Although men and women share many of the biological (e.g., signs of starvation, loss of libido, hormone dysfunction) and psychological problems (e.g., depression, suicidal ideations, mood swings, anger, shame, guilt, distorted body image) associated with eating disorders, the assessment, prognosis, and course of the illness for men may differ from that for women (Glazer, 2008; Peate, 2011). For example, differences within the relationship between eating disorders and low bone mineral density (BMD) for male athletes is not clearly linked when compared with the female athlete triad (eating disorder, BMD, and amenorrhea) (Glazer, 2008). Therefore, both assessment and intervention for males with eating disorders must continue to build from knowledge already known and specifically geared toward men and their developmental life cycle.

Multiple barriers exist in the assessment, diagnosis, and treatment for males with eating disorders (Peate, 2011). Barriers include the dominant focus of female-centric risk factors (e.g., irregular menstruation or amenorrhea), formats of therapeutic treatment (e.g., group-based, expression of emotional intelligence), stigma association with masculine and sexual identity, denial, shame, isolation, fear, and lack of education (Collier, 2013; Greenberg & Schoen, 2008; Peate, 2011; Robinson, Mountford, & Sperlinger, 2012). The widely assumed association between women and eating disorders serves as the greatest barrier toward expanding research, assessment, and treatment for men suffering from this illness.

Stanford and Lemberg (2012) developed the Eating Disorder Assessment for Men (EDAM) and identified four primary domains for diagnosis: binge eating, muscle dysmorphia, body dissatisfaction, and disordered eating (Stanford & Lemberg, 2012). Though preliminary results of this tool are high in both reliability and validity, further research and implementation of the tool and others akin to it are required.

Risk factors for men with eating disorders include the following: families of origin that inflate the value of fitness or athleticism and have similar expectations for children; relationships with mentor figures (e.g., coaches) that promote behavioral extremes (e.g., food restriction, binge eating, excessive exercise); media and social influences (e.g., film, Internet); traumatic life events, including physical, sexual, or emotional abuse; adolescent experiences of teasing, taunting, and bullying due to body issues (e.g., overweight) or poor physical performance (e.g., athletics); difficulty with conventional and stereotypical masculine traits, (e.g., competitiveness, aggressiveness, strength, and independence); childhood obesity; and employment that emphasizes specific body shapes and sizes (e.g., sports, modeling, acting) (Collier, 2013; Glazer, 2008; Peate, 2011). These risk factors have important implications for both prevention and intervention.

Cognitive behavioral therapy has had good outcomes for both men and women. Cognitive behavioral strategies to address perfectionism, the social construction of body image, and achievement expectations for men may be particular areas of goal orientation (Greenberg & Schoen, 2008). Successful interventions may be measured by self-acceptance of eating disorder and redefined self-concept; engagement and alignment to treatment plan; prioritization of health over physical achievement (e.g., athletic excellence); absence of physiological laboratory abnormalities (e.g., cardiac, electrolyte); balanced energy; absence of malnutrition-based performance declines; and maintenance of a healthy weight (Glazer, 2008; Greenberg & Schoen, 2008; Robinson, Mountford, & Sperlinger, 2012). Greenberg and Schoen (2008) also found that gender-sensitive psychotherapy designed specifically for men promotes positive male socialization in individual and group formats.

In regard to sexual orientation, Carlat, Camargo, and Herzog (1997) reported on 135 male eating disorder patients and found that although they shared most characteristics with their female counterparts, self-identified homosexuals and bisexuals were more highly represented among those with eating disorders, particularly bulimia. In fact, of this group, 42% of the bulimics identified as homosexual or bisexual, and of the anorexic patients, 58% identified as asexual. Davids and Green (2011) found that among women, bisexual, lesbian, and heterosexual women had similar rates of both eating disorders and levels of body dissatisfaction.

Eating disorders in the United States have been identified primarily in Caucasians; more recently, they have been reported among blacks, Latinos, and Asians (Rogers, Wood & Petrie, 2010; Alegria et al., 2007; Shuttlesworth & Zotter, 2009). This "debunks" the previously held belief that different cultural norms for ideal body shape and weight served a protective function for African American women. Treatment interventions need to take into account the differential cultural meanings of body image, shape, and weight, as well as the role that food and meals play in specific cultures.

Similarly, eating disorders have been considered a disease of the affluent, and indeed, early anecdotal studies of women have supported that generalization. However, researchers report that these assumptions are unfounded (Gard & Freeman, 1996; Gibbons, 2001) and that bulimia, in particular, is widespread among those in low socioeconomic groups.

ALTERNATIVE APPROACHES

Social work's emphasis on a bio-psychosocial perspective ideally supports holistic assessment of and treatment for eating disorders. Holistic assessment and treatment may come in the form of mind-body-spirit (MBS) modalities or Complementary and Alternative medicine (CAM) practices. MBS modalities (e.g., mindfulness meditation) originate from systems of healing (e.g., Traditional Chinese Medicine, Ayurveda) developed by indigenous cultures, which practice with and respect the interconnectedness among the psychological, biological, and spiritual attributes of people. CAM practices (e.g., herbs, supplements, massage, and touch therapies, acupuncture when focused solely on biological intervention) are defined by biomedicine as evidence-based treatment interventions that do not exist in conventional western medicine practice. Each pathway promotes access to holistic health and wellness that may not be addressed through conventional, biomedical approaches (e.g., pharmacological treatment, CBT, behavioral weight loss treatment, and bariatric surgery) (Wilson, 2011).

As the knowledge and understanding of people diagnosed with eating disorders expands, so will the efficacy and empirical measurement of MBS modalities and CAM practices to treat eating disorders. The comorbid factors that affect a person's behavior and motivation are an essential consideration when treating eating disorders through holistic models. The range of comorbid factors to eating disorders includes the improvement in physical performance of athletes, limited external locus of control when dealing with relational stress (e.g., child's reaction to parent divorce), and environmental stressors (e.g., social pressure with body image) that reinforce anxiety and depression (Breuner, 2010; Caldwell, Baime, & Wolever, 2012). Therefore, treatment of comorbid factors to the eating disorder diagnosis can benefit a client's overall perception and experience in balanced health and wellness. MBS modalities are useful in treating the comorbid factors that undergird the complex psychological, physiological, and spiritual states that individuals with eating disorders may experience. A MBS modality that promotes a balanced approach to one's self-control is Buddhist mindfulness meditation.

Buddhist mindfulness meditation promotes practices such as mindful eating, while also reducing stress by improving the relaxation response (Coffey & Hartman, 2008; Kissman & Maurer, 2002). This particular practice promotes nonjudgmental awareness to self-regulation and challenges negative self-conceptions that trigger reactivity (Hick & Chan, 2010). When reactivity is managed, self-regulation is promoted through healthier outlets (Caldwell, Baime, & Wolever, 2012). Finally, self-acceptance and compassion toward oneself promote the positive feedback loop of healthy self-regulation and self-care (McGarrigle & Walsh, 2011). Traditional mindfulness meditation is practiced from Buddhism; however, mindfulness meditation may also be utilized through programs such as Mindfulness-based Stress Reduction (MBSR), Enhancing Mindfulness for the Prevention of Weight Regain (EMPOWER), Acceptance and Commitment therapy (ACT), Mindfulness-based Cognitive Therapy (MBCT), and Dialectical Behavioral Therapy (DBT).

CAM practices have been useful with adolescents and adults for comorbid symptoms to eating disorders. These include Biofeedback to alter the body's response to stress; massage and therapeutic touch to promote stress and anxiety reduction through lowering cortisol (stress hormone) level, while also increasing dopamine and norepinephrine (neurotransmitters that are correlated with depression and anxiety); St. John's Wort for depression, anxiety, and sleep disorders; Chamomile's anti-inflammatory effects for promoting relaxation to treat gastrointestinal discomfort and mild anxiety; Valerian's anxiolytic and sedative qualities to promote health sleep; and Melatonin to promote and restore balanced sleep (Breuner, 2010). Additionally, CAM practices that originate from indigenous systems of healing may be accessed as targeted interventions: yoga (derived from Ayurvedic medicine) as a physical practice to promote balance and self-control (Sharma, 2011) and acupuncture (derived from Traditional Chinese Medicine) to promote healthy energy flow within the person's "spiritual, emotional, mental, and physical health" (Breuner, 2010, p. 77).

GUIDELINES FOR ASSESSING AND TREATING EATING DISORDERS

Social work intervention can and should occur in a variety of settings and with a three-pronged approach that includes prevention, identification (see table 73.1), and treatment. It is critical that any of these interventions reflect an understanding of the sociocultural influences that contribute to and maintain eating disorder symptoms.

Prevention

- Social workers should be familiar with the client groups at risk for developing eating disorders and design and implement psychoeducational efforts appropriate to the age and gender of those groups.
- Prevention programs should ideally take place in "natural" settings, such as school athletic departments, health classes, and recreation centers.
- Social action can take the form of targeting businesses and advertisements that perpetuate the image of an "ideal" body image for both girls and boys.
- Parent education efforts should be focused on both healthy eating strategies and the importance of physical activity.

Identification

- Social workers should assume that clients may not readily self-disclose their eating disordered behaviors, which are often associated with secrecy and shame. Hence, disclosure may not occur until the disease has significantly impaired the client's medical status or social and psychological functioning. Social workers should adjust their history taking and style accordingly.
- Comorbidity is high in people with eating disorders. All mental health assessment should include questions about eating behaviors. The clinician is cautioned that in many cases the data will not emerge in a first session but should be raised nonetheless.
- People with histories of sexual abuse, alcohol abuse, and family histories of affective illness or eating disorder should be considered at risk.
- New clinicians should be reminded that normal body weight does not preclude the existence of an eating disorder; in fact, most clients with bulimia are within normal weight ranges.
- Any client who reports or is suspected of an eating disorder should also be referred to a physician, preferably one with expertise in the area, for a full physical examination and laboratory work. Particularly with critically ill anorexics, presenting clear, irrefutable evidence of the impact of starvation on one's physical body may be helpful in minimizing denial of the problem.
- Significant denial and minimization of the problem following disclosure often results in resistance to treatment. Because many people with eating disorders experience difficulties in the area of control and autonomy, establishing joint treatment goals is critical and often arduous.
- A complete psychological, social, and medical history is critical. In the case of young clients, the involvement of family as a collateral source of information is useful.
- Pay particular attention to eating disorders in non-White populations who have been significantly understudied, under-researched, and undertreated, in spite of the growing clinical awareness of incidence in people of color.

Treatment

- For those clients whose medical status is not seriously undermined and whose functioning is largely intact, an outpatient model of treatment, similar to that described for inpatients, is in order.

- In extreme cases, hospitalization may be necessary, and force-feeding for those in a state of severe starvation may follow. Inpatient treatment will include a behavioral protocol, cognitive restructuring, group therapy, nutrition counseling (although many people with eating disorders are nutritional experts themselves), individual treatment, and family interventions.
- Social workers who are working with clients with coexisting substance abuse problems must evaluate the severity of both sets of symptoms and prioritize initial treatment goals. A client who is actively using drugs and alcohol is unlikely to be able to participate fully in a treatment program designed to eliminate symptoms of an eating disorder. Here, too, it would be important to clarify the phenomenological and temporal relationships between the eating disorder behaviors and the substance using behaviors. For example, if a client reports that a feeling of aloneness typically precedes a binge eating episode, it is important to know if his or her feelings of aloneness are intensified by substance use.
- Though many treatment programs are designed as a protocol or as "manualized" interventions, it is critical to recognize that although many people with eating disorders share certain characteristics, there may well be idiosyncratic historical influences and factors that can either promote or impede the chances of treatment success. In other words, it is critical to understand the meaning and function of the particular behaviors to a particular client to find syntonic, effective ways of intervening.
- An understanding of the meaning of the behaviors (restricting, purging, or overeating) and the phenomenology of the symptom development can yield important insights as to the relative importance of this behavior to the client.
- The social worker's understanding of the relative rigidity or flexibility, ambivalence, or secondary gain related to the client's symptoms can be enormously helpful in understanding how best to work with a particular client, regardless of the setting.
- Consider family evaluation and treatment to address both contributing and maintaining factors of symptoms and to identify family strengths.
- Because of the high comorbidity rates in both anorexia and bulimia, a good diagnostic evaluation is critical and may need to take place periodically throughout treatment. For example, it is not unlikely that once eating-related symptoms remit, the client will experience significant depressive symptoms. As with those who have coexisting depressive disorders, clients may also benefit from a trial of a selective serotonin reuptake inhibitor (SSRI).
- Social workers must make frequent use of emerging theoretical and empirical knowledge about incidence and treatment efficacy.

TABLE 73.1 Eating Disorder Measures

Name	Type of Measure	Focus
Eating Disorders Inventory (EDI). Garner, Olmsted, & Polivy (1983)	64-item, self-report instrument; children's version available.	Behaviors and attitudes for onset and course of bulimia and anorexia nervosa.
Bulimia Test-Revised (BULIT-R). Smith & Thelen (1984 in Corcoran and Fischer, 2013)	36-item self-report measure	Binge-eating, eating attitudes when not in binge episode.
Eating Disorder Examination (EDE). Cooper & Fairburn (1987)	Semistructured interview for comprehensive assessment; children's version available.	Anorexia and bulimia, including extreme behavioral methods of weight control.
Eating Disorder Assessment For Men. Stanford & Lehmberg (2012)	50-item self-report	Male-specific

PRACTICE EXAMPLE

Max is a 19-year-old White male who presented to the college counseling center with a vague description of not "feeling right." A sophomore on the university wrestling team, he revealed that he was concerned about his weight gain over the summer and reluctantly reported that "my coach is giving me a bad time about it." He reported that he had spent the last several weeks trying to "get rid of this horrible fat" but had been unsuccessful and "didn't feel so great." The social worker was struck by the discordance between his appraisal of his body and her observation of him; Max looked both extremely thin and haggard. On further investigation, Max revealed that he had been on a fast for the past several weeks and was feeling quite weak and dehydrated. He appeared somewhat listless as well. While the social worker tried to gain background information and further assess his mental status and social functioning, Max continued to perseverate on his weight status. He said that he felt "like a failure; my family never thought I could do this anyway; I'm letting my team down." He did indicate that he was at his lowest adult weight and that he had become preoccupied since the summer about his body, specifically his muscle mass and his strength, the latter of which was waning. When asked whether he had made previous attempts at weight loss, he described a long pattern, since middle school, of extreme daily exercise, and idiosyncratic and ritualized eating behaviors.

Max was the middle of three children born to a middle-class family. His father was a salesman who often traveled and was a former collegiate football player, as was his older brother. Max had begun wrestling in his junior year of high school at his mother's suggestion. He reported being close to his parents, who are "nice, well-meaning, but I think I disappoint them, particularly my father. . . my mother worries about me." He reluctantly reported being bullied in middle school, but stated "it didn't bother me much," although the social worker found the reports of the bullying behavior quite alarming. Max reported having seen a counselor in high school and having a brief trial of an antidepressant. Although he thought it had helped, he said "I don't like putting unnatural things in my body." He did report having a group of close friends in high school, with whom he had remained close through social media once he went to college.

He reported feeling "like a member of the team" until a few weeks prior, but was unclear about the reasons for that other than, "I am letting them down." He reported not having had any intimate relationships with men or with women, "I guess I'm just not a very physical person," but "I like to have friends." He denied being depressed and it was unclear the degree to which his current fasting regime was contributing to his weakness.

The social worker's first concern was Max's medical status. She referred him immediately to the nurse practitioner in the university health center for evaluation of blood work and vital signs. Because severe caloric restriction can cause mental status changes, she understood that clarifying his nutritional status and correcting it would be important in order to obtain a clear diagnostic picture. Fortunately, in the previous several years, the university health center, increasingly aware of the numbers of students, male and female, dealing with eating disorders, had developed a number of programs aimed at preventing and treating these problems. Once Max was medically cleared and began to work with the center's nutritionist, he was referred to an eating disorder group for male students. He revealed in his individual session, however, that he was worried about his status on the wrestling team. One of the members of the health center's interdisciplinary eating disorders team was a sports psychologist who had developed strong relationships with the university coaching staff. With Max's permission, he arranged a meeting between himself, Max, and the wrestling coach. The coach had indeed had concerns about Max, but not for the reasons he had imagined. The coach had suspected an eating disorder, "but I didn't want to confront him; he already seemed in pretty bad shape." Together, they reviewed weight, height, and class requirements and the coach encouraged Max to follow the plan set up by his team, as a condition of returning to an active role on the team. This provided important leverage.

Within a month, Max was able to meet the minimum required weight and maintain it. However, his cognitions about weight, his behaviors in order to regulate it, and his affect and self-image were well established and his mental health team had concerns about his ability to maintain the gains he had made. He continued with his individual therapy, which utilized a cognitive-behavioral approach, and with the use of food and activity logs, which tracked behaviors and feeling states as well. Through a mindfulness-based cognitive approach, Max was able to challenge his negative self-conception (e.g., amount of body fat) through stress-reduction techniques of breathing and guided meditation. Over time, Max developed healthier self-regulation and self-care through mindful eating, which ultimately improved his self-worth and self-efficacy in social activities and in his position on the wrestling team. He found his Male Eating Disorder Group, which allowed him to talk safely about issues related to body image and masculinity, very helpful. Max found great relief in talking about his wishes to "please" his father and how much he had focused on rigid notions of body type and strength as measures of masculinity. In his individual work he began to talk about what he called his "no-sexual identity" status and to explore what his avoidance of physical intimacy might mean to him.

Max did not meet the criteria for major depression, but he did have a history of a more chronic low-level form. He spoke with the center's psychiatrist about medication, but did not want to do that. The psychiatrist, also trained in Alternative and Complementary Medicine, had other suggestions for him. He suggested the possibility of St. John's Wort for depressive symptoms and valerian for sleep, both of which Max was willing to try. At the 60-day treatment planning meeting, Max was offered the opportunity to join a new class, Yoga for Healthy Eating, designed specifically for college athletes. He was also made aware of acupuncture services available off campus.

Max did some backsliding during his month-long semester break at home. He and his social worker had done some in vivo practice, however, as they anticipated some of the issues he would encounter with holidays and food, as well as with his family. Upon his return, he eagerly rejoined his Men's Group and made plans to do outreach in the freshman residence halls for education about male eating disorders. He continued to work on issues related to interpersonal relationships.

CONCLUSION

Max was fortunate to be in a setting that promoted interdisciplinary, holistic interventions and had systems in place to address individual and community needs related to the prevention and amelioration of eating disorders. In addition to the individual therapy offered to Max, the gender-specific eating disorder group provided the opportunity for mutual support and the exploration of issues confronting young men about weight, food, and body image. Additionally, the inclusion of a counseling staff member who had established relationships with university coaches ensured both micro- and macro-level interventions and cooperation. Finally, the availability of traditional therapeutic methods, including cognitive behavioral strategies and medical monitoring, in combination with alternative and complementary modalities, ensured a holistic approach that was both engaging and useful for Max.

As we learn more about both the distinct and overlapping risk factors, manifestations, and treatment approaches for groups of people not historically considered at risk for eating disorders, social workers must further develop our skills and knowledge in prevention, education, and intervention. Our bio-psychosocial perspective provides a very useful framework for incorporating a range of interventions that provide both relief from symptoms and a roadmap for healthier living.

WEBSITE

National Eating Disorders Association. http://www.nationaleatingdisorders.org.

References

Alegria, M., Woo, M., Cao, Z., Torres, M., Meng, X., & Striegel-Moore, R. (2007). Prevalence and correlates of eating disorders in Latinos in the United States. *International Journal of Eating Disorders*, 40(Suppl).

American Psychiatric Association. (2013). *Diagnostic and statistical manual of mental disorders, fifth edition*. Washington, DC: Author.

Breuner, C. C. (2010). Complementary, holistic, and integrative medicine: Eating disorders. *Pediatrics in Review*, 31, 75–82. doi:10.1542/pir.31-10-e75

Caldwell, K. L., Baime, M. J., & Wolever, R. Q. (2012). Mindfulness based approaches to obesity and weight loss maintenance. *Journal of Mental Health Counseling*, 34(3), 269–282.

Carlat, D. J., Camargo, C. A., & Herzog, D. B. (1997). Eating disorders in males: A report on 135 patients. *American Journal of Psychiatry*, 154(8), 1127–1133.

Coffey, K. A., & Hartman, M. (2008). Mechanisms of action in the inverse relationship between mindfulness and psychological distress. *Complementary Health Practice Review*, 13(2), 79–91. doi:10.1177/1533210108316307

Collier, R. (2013). Treatment challenges for men with eating disorders. *Canadian Medical Association Journal*, 185(3), E137-E138. doi:10.1503/cmaj109-4363

Cooper, Z., & Fairburn, C. (1987). The Eating Disorder Examination: A semi-structured interview for the assessment of the specific psychopathology of eating disorders. *International Journal of Eating Disorders*, 20(1), 43–50. Retrieved from http://www.cdc.gov/nccdphp/dnpa/obesity/index.htm.

Corcoran, K., & Fischer J. (2013). *Measures for Clinical Practice and Research: A Source Book (Fifth edition)* (pp. 132–137). NY, NY: Oxford University Press.

Davids, C., & Green, M. (2011). A preliminary investigation of body dissatisfaction and eating disorder symptomatology with bisexual individuals. *Sex Roles*, 65, 7(10) 533–547.

Gard, M. C., & Freeman, C. (1996). The dismantling of a myth: A review of eating disorders and socioeconomic status. *International Journal of Eating Disorders*, 20(1), 1–12.

Garner, D., Olmsted, M., & Polivy, J. (1983). Development and validation of a multidimensional eating disorder inventory for anorexia and bulimia. *International Journal of Eating Disorders*, 2(1), 15–34.

Gibbons, P. (2001). The relationship between eating disorders and socioeconomic status: It's not what you think. *Nutrition Noteworthy*, 4(1). Retrieved from http://www.escholarship.org/uc/item/1k70k3fd

Glazer, J. L. (2008). Eating disorders among male athletes. *Current Sports Medicine Reports*, 7(6), 332–337.

Greenberg, S. T., & Schoen, E. G. (2008). Males and eating disorders: Gender-based therapy for eating disorder recovery. *Professional Psychology: Research and Practice*, 39(4), 464–471.

Hick, S. F., & Chan, L. (2010). Mindfulness-based cognitive therapy for depression: Effectiveness and limitations. *Social Work in Mental Health*, 8(3), 225–237. doi:10.1080/15332980903405330

Kissman, K., & Maurer, L. (2002). East meets West: Therapeutic aspects of spirituality in health, mental health, and addiction recovery. *International Social Work*, 45(1), 35–43.

Kjelsas, E., Bjornstrom, C., & Gotestam, K. G. (2004). Prevalence of eating disorders in female and male adolescents (14–15 years). *Eating Behaviors*, 5, 13–25.

McGarrigle, T., & Walsh, C. A. (2011). Mindfulness, self-care, and wellness in social work: Effects of contemplative training. *Journal of Religion & Spirituality in Social Work: Social Thought*, 30(3), 212–233. doi:10.1080/15426432.2011.687384

Peate, I. (2011). Dangerously misunderstood: Men and eating disorders. *British Journal of Healthcare Assistants*, 5(8), 383–387.

Piran, N., & Cormier, H. C. (2005). The social construction of women and disordered eating patterns. *Journal of Counseling Psychology*, 52(4), 549–558.

Robinson, K. J., Mountford, V. A., & Sperlinger, D. J. (2012). Being men with eating disorders: Perspectives of male eating disorder service-users. *Journal of Health Psychology*, 18(2), 176–186. doi:10.1177/1359105312440298

Sadock, V., & Sadock, B. (2007). *Synopsis of psychiatry: Behavioral sciences, clinical psychiatry* (10th ed.). Baltimore, MD: Lippincott, Williams and Wilkins.

Sharma, H. M. (2011). Social and cultural factors in medicine. In M. S. Micozzi (Ed.), *Fundamentals of complementary and alternative medicine* (4th ed.) (pp. 495–508). St. Louis, MO: Saunders Elsevier.

Shuttlesworth, M., & Zotter. D. (2009). Disordered eating in African American and Caucasian women: The role of ethnic identity. *Journal of Black Studies*, 42(6), 906–922.

Stanford, S. C., & Lemberg, R. (2012). Measuring eating disorders in men: Development of the Eating Disorder Assessment for Men (EDAM). *Eating Disorders*, 20, 427–436.

Wilson, G. T. (2007). (2011). Treatment of binge eating disorder. *Psychiatric Clinics of North America*, 34(4), 773–783.

Wood, N., & Petrie, T. (2010). Body dissatisfaction, ethnic identity, and disordered eating among African American women. *Journal of Counseling Psychology*, 57(2), 141–153.

74 Panic Disorders and Agoraphobia

Gordon MacNeil & Jason M. Newell

Panic disorders afflict about 4% of the population; about half of those so diagnosed also experience agoraphobia. Panic disorder is characterized by panic attacks and the pernicious fear of additional attacks. Two interventions have shown effectiveness in the acute phase of panic disorder with or without agoraphobia: cognitive-behavioral therapy alone and in combination with medications. In the long run, cognitive-behavioral therapy is the preferred intervention. Cognitive restructuring techniques are recommended to address panic attacks, and the behavioral technique of exposure is recommended for agoraphobia symptoms.

DESCRIPTION OF THE DISORDER

To meet the *Diagnostic and Statistical Manual of Mental Disorders, Fifth Edition (DSM-5)* criteria for panic disorder, one must experience recurrent unexpected panic attacks for at least a month, as well as (1) persistent concern about having more attacks, (2) worry about the consequences of the attacks or implications of the attacks, and/or (3) a significant change in behavior as a result of the attacks (American Psychiatric Association [APA], 2013). The attacks must not be due to a medical condition, nor are they better explained by some other disorder, such as social phobia, posttraumatic stress disorder, or a specific phobia (Schmidt, Norr, & Korte, 1997). For many, panic disorders are largely related to the person's fear of body sensations; in fact, panic disorder is sometimes referred to as a "fear of one's body" or a "fear of emotions." These individuals become alarmed at the presence of specific physical or psychosomatic sensations that they associate with the onset of a panic attack. Because these attacks worsen over time, the anticipation of an attack can itself manifest panic. Avoidance responses frequently result in agoraphobia. *Panic attacks* are discrete periods of intense discomfort or fear that include at least four symptoms from the following list. The specific symptoms of panic disorder listed below tend to present themselves similarly across child, adolescent, and adult populations.

- Palpitations, rapid heartbeat, pounding heart
- Sweating
- Trembling or shaking
- Sensations of shortness of breath or smothering
- Sensation of choking
- Chest pain or discomfort
- Nausea or abdominal distress
- Feeling dizzy, light-headed, faint
- Derealization or depersonalization
- Fear of losing control or going crazy
- Fear of dying
- Numbness or tingling sensations
- Chills or hot flashes (APA, 2013)

In the case of panic disorder, these symptoms are not initially cued; they do not tend to occur in specific settings or situations. Indeed, the unpredictable nature of their appearance and the dread associated with anticipating them are hallmarks of panic disorder.

Agoraphobia is defined as an anxiety about being in situations in which escape is difficult or embarrassing or in which help would be unavailable should a panic attack occur (APA, 2013). These fears often relate to being in situations in which one is unable to "get back" to comfortable, secure surroundings and include the use of public transportation, both vastly open and enclosed spaces, crowds, and in extreme cases leaving the safety of the home environment all together (APA, 2014). New to the *DSM-5*, Agoraphobia is considered a separate problem from Panic Disorders, and can be diagnosed independent of Panic Disorder (APA, 2013).

Panic disorder is a common condition, as is agoraphobia. Approximately 2%–3% of the population experiences panic disorder without agoraphobia, 1.5% experience panic disorder with agoraphobia, and 5% experience agoraphobia without panic disorder (APA, 2013; Eaton, Kessler, Wittchen, & Magee, 1994; Kessler, Chiu, Jin, Ruscio, & Walters, 2006). Women are twice as likely to be diagnosed with panic disorder. It is not unusual for persons to progress from panic disorder without agoraphobia to panic disorder with agoraphobia, as the latter may actually be the result of a dysfunctional coping response to panic disorder alone. The typical age of onset for these disorders is the early to mid-twenties. Although panic disorder and agoraphobia are most commonly comorbid with other anxiety disorders, unipolar depression and substance abuse are also noted in between 10% and 65% of panic disorder cases (APA, 2013). Perhaps more importantly, Panic Attacks are so frequent that they are a specifier for any other *DSM-5* disorder (APA, 2013).

Assessment

To establish the presence of panic disorder as well as agoraphobia, the social worker should first determine the specific nature of the client's symptoms as well as possible triggers for them and the client's responses to these symptoms, with specific attention to behaviors associated with avoidance. The use of an informal interview format to gather this information is common, but increasingly clinicians are employing established measures to assess the level of symptomatology exhibited by clients presenting with concerns about panic attacks. If the social worker prefers a more formal and structured method of assessment, the Structured Clinical Interview for the *DSM* Axis I Disorders (SCID) is an established and well-tested instrument for formal assessment purposes (First, Gibbon, Spitzer, & Williams, 1997) and can be used to confirm diagnostic impressions from the informal assessment and help to rule out other disorders. Identifying general symptoms

of anxiety may also prove helpful to the social worker in the initial assessment phase before the assessment of panic disorder or agoraphobia. The Hamilton Anxiety Scale-HAM-A (1959) is a clinician-administered scale that has been well tested as a measure of the symptoms of anxiety in children, adolescents, and adults (Bruss, Gruenberg, & Goldstein, & Barber 1994; Shear et al., 2001). The HAM-A is also useful in differentiating the symptoms of anxiety disorders with commonly diagnosed comorbid disorders such as major depression (Maier, Buller, Phillip, & Heuser, 1988). If generalized anxiety is ruled out, the Panic Disorder Severity Scale (PDSS) can used in either clinician-administered (1992) or self-report form (1999) and is useful in identifying the frequency of panic attacks, the degree of distress resulting from them, and anticipatory anxiety related to them (Houck, Speigel, Shear, Rucci, & Stat, 2002). The Anxiety Disorders Interview Schedule–Revised (ADIS-R) is particularly useful in assessment because it includes a checklist of specific symptoms as well as items about client thoughts concerning panic attacks, items about avoidance behaviors, and items focusing on functional impairment resulting from panic attacks (DiNardo & Barlow, 1988). The Mobility Inventory for Agoraphobia (Chambless, Caputo, Bright, & Gallagher, 1984) is well accepted as a measure of phobia avoidance.

Treatment

A number of reviews of literature and meta-analyses on the treatment of panic disorder and agoraphobia have been conducted recently (see Furukawa, Watanabe, & Churchill, 2007; Himle, Fischer, & Lokers, 2007; Roth & Fonagy, 2005). Although there are some differences in their conclusions, there is general consensus in recommending a treatment protocol that combines medications and psychotherapy; cognitive-behavioral therapy alone appears to be about as effective as the combined model in many instances. Cognitive-behavioral therapy is the most effective psychotherapy choice, with cognitive restructuring being most useful for addressing panic attacks and exposure techniques being preferred for addressing the avoidance behaviors of agoraphobia. Although prescribing psychotropic medication is beyond social work's scope of practice, it is prudent for social workers to have a basic knowledge and understanding of the most commonly pre-scribed psychotropic treatments for anxiety and panic disorders. Selective serotonin reuptake inhibitors (SSRIs) and selective serotonin/nor-epinephrine (SSNRIs) are commonly considered "first line" treatments for mood disorders, but have also shown effectiveness in treating the general symptoms of anxiety independently of their effects on depression (Dziegielewski, 2010). SSRI treatments prescribed for anxiety and panic disorders include Prozac (fluox-etine); Paxil (paroxetine); Zoloft (sertraline); Celexa (citalopram); and Lexapro (escitalo-pram). Commonly prescribed SSNRI therapies include Effexor (venlafaxine); Serzone (nefazo-done); and Cymbalta (duloxetine) (Bentley & Walsh, 2013). For actual panic attacks benzo-diazepine therapies such as ativan (lorazepan), Klonopin (clonazepam), Valium (diazepam), and Xanax (alprazolam) are widely prescribed, but are short-acting and have addictive quali-ties that can potentially complicate treatment if not taken correctly (Bentley & Walsh, 2013; Dziegielewski, 2010). For panic disorder, psy-chotherapy seems to have more sustainable effect than the use of medications over longer periods of time (Roth & Fonagy, 2005).

TREATMENT PROGRAM

The remainder of this chapter presents a specific treatment program for addressing panic disor-ders and agoraphobia. This treatment program consists of two foci; intrapersonal and inter-personal aspects of the panic disorder. There is no specific protocol for the interpersonal foci associated with this treatment program, but it is an integral part of the program nonethe-less. For instance, be careful to include social environment functioning in the assessment of the individual—both strengths and difficulties. Interpersonal problems in which the individual feels trapped or out of control can precipitate panic attacks and panic disorders. We have found that enlisting the help of supportive sig-nificant others can add to the prospects of suc-cess for this treatment program, especially with the in vivo component.

The intrapersonal aspect has three compo-nents: (1) education regarding the nature of anxiety disorders and panic disorders specifi-cally; (2) cognitive therapy, including work on the identification of trigger stimuli and the somatic physiological indications of panic, relaxation training; and (3) exposure of some form. In general, once the consumer is educated about the disorder(s), use interoceptive expo-sure techniques to address the panic disorder, followed by in vivo exposure techniques to address the agoraphobia. In instances where the consumer is not able to come to the office due to agoraphobia, we suggest phone, e-mail or even a Skype consultation as means of beginning the process. Clinicians who use this treatment program are presumed to have competence in delivering cognitive-behavioral therapy. This presentation is meant to instruct clinicians on the implementation of the program, but it is not a substitute for clinical training and ongoing supervision. We next present the procedures of this treatment program, and use the following case example to illustrate this process.

CASE ILLUSTRATION

Richard Summerall is a 30-year-old White male. He is trained as a mechanic and has oper-ated his own garage for four years. For the past two years he has been a used car salesman. Mr. Summerall relates that his panic symptoms started nine years ago on his first night in the military. That evening, he woke up feeling very hot, short of breath, and panicky. Since then, he has experienced these symptoms rarely, but in the past three months they have become more frequent and intense. He also reports having diarrhea, nausea, shortness of breath, sweat-ing, a fear that he is going crazy, trembling, and shaking. He describes a fear of elevators, car washes, business group meetings, and other places where he feels enclosed. He reports that the most extreme attack occurred two nights ago and that he spends considerable time wor-rying that these attacks will happen again.

PROCEDURES

Following are the procedures we use in the intrapersonal foci of this treatment program in sequential order, along with information describing the rationale for the interventions. Although most motivated clients will experience satisfying results within 10 sessions, there is tre-mendous variation in how long it takes people to address the psychological demons of panic and agoraphobia. Initial sessions take longer than those at the end of the process, and sessions that require exposure techniques require that the client provoke, endure, and reduce their anxiety within the session. Therefore, this protocol is not presented session by session, because the introduction of new material to the client is flexible and contingent on his or her understanding and (where indicated) mastery of the content up to that point.

Assessment

We begin screening the client by conducting an initial assessment, which first includes a referral to a physician to rule out medical causes. Following this, we suggest completing a basic psychosocial assessment. One should be careful to explore cultural elements that may contribute to or influence the client's situation and experience. Clinicians should pay particular attention to the following aspects of the presenting problem: presentation, pattern, predisposition, perpetuants, and readiness for treatment. We usually use either PDSS-SR (Houck et al., 2002) or the ADIS-R (DiNardo & Barlow, 1988) to obtain this information. If the client does not appear to be ready to engage actively in change-making behaviors, focus on motivation and support until he or she is ready to begin this program.

With regard to our case illustration, Mr. Summerall described no fewer than six symptoms of panic attacks, and it is clear that he is concerned about the prospect of experiencing more of them. He meets the diagnostic criteria for panic disorder. He also appears to meet the criteria for agoraphobia, given that he is fearful of being in situations from which he cannot escape. Additional probing is needed to determine whether there are specific circumstances associated with his attacks; their frequency, duration, and intensity; and his response to them, both psychologically and physiologically, as well as what he has tried to do to counter the panic attacks. The social worker would also want to determine to what extent the attacks impair his functioning. Finally, although the attacks clearly are disturbing to Mr. Summerall, trying to determine his readiness to act to change his situation is important to the treatment process. Many people present with debilitating symptoms but are actually unwilling to "courageously leap off of the ledge" and act differently.

Psycho-education

As a first step, providing the client with information about panic disorders and agoraphobia is essential. Also, one should discuss the goals of the program and ask the client if he or she would like to have similar information provided to family members or friends. We emphasize that members of the client's social support network can assist the client by reinforcing and supplementing the gains made in-session.

Cognitive Restructuring

As a first step to this intervention, the client and the social worker determine initial levels of symptom severity. This is usually done by simply asking the client to talk about symptom severity; the information gained from the instruments used in the assessment is useful as well. In Mr. Summerall's case, the symptoms seem to be serious, but not extreme. That is, they are distressing to him but do not curtail his completion of tasks. His is not incapacitated, and friends and family have not noticed his symptoms to date.

Next, mutually identify the client's common responses to anxiety. This includes whatever he or she has tried as interventions for panic and anxiety and to what extent these measures have helped. Thus far, Mr. Summerall has been able to escape situations in which he experiences attacks around others. He has tried to control his breathing by taking deep breaths, he has used alcohol on occasion to distract himself from his hypervigilance to body sensations, and he has tried to increase his physical exercise to "wear myself out so that I don't have energy to freak out." We establish that his best efforts have not had any appreciable effect on his attacks; they continue to happen and without provocation.

The client and the social worker begin working on the first of two factors included in the cognitive restructuring intervention: misappraisals of body sensations as being threatening. This process has three parts. First, provide information about the rationale for the intervention, then identify misappraisals, and finally challenge these misappraisals. Panic disorders are largely related to the client's fear of body sensations. Because panic attacks can present at any time, learning to identify initial indications and how to reduce the physiological manifestations of panic is an important element in the treatment of panic disorder.

After a discussion with Mr. Summerall regarding his awareness of his breathing in general and when he becomes anxious, he confides that he is not aware of the former and is distressed by the later. Mr. Summerall agrees that his becoming aware of his breathing as we speak seems to be distressing to him. (This is a common response among this clinical population.) This provides an opportunity to begin talking about misappraisals of body sensations and the common experience of tricking oneself into thinking that something is "wrong" simply by becoming aware of "normal" body functions and sensations. Even if one's breathing is rapid, or one is sweating, there may be good reasons for these physiological responses; they do not necessarily denote an attack. The client and the social worker use this idea as we move forward in challenging his misappraisals.

The client and the social worker go through a process of challenging misappraisals of body sensations. First, they create a list of the specific thoughts that he or she has about his or her situation during panic attacks. After they have created a list of these thoughts, the social worker challenges the main items on it one by one, largely by questioning what other interpretations of the body's "signals" might be possible and if these might, in fact, be likely. (Readers will find specific techniques for this in Barlow & Craske, 2006.) This must be done in a gentle manner that is not patronizing, humiliating, or condescending to the client. Remember, the goal of this part of the treatment program is to empower the client to challenge self-talk related to his or her body sensations (a truly challenging task), so frequent positive reinforcement is warranted. Also, the worker must remember that the intent here is to evoke the "misappraisals" and challenge them *as they are occurring*— in the present tense. We emphasize the use of "I am" statements rather than "I would be" statements in this task.

A good way to begin work with the client is to address anticipatory anxiety at the beginning of a session. Following general catching up and making sure that the client appears to be calm, make the following comment: "Right now you seem to be pretty calm and relaxed. Is this how you feel right now?" Once this is verified, comment that he or she seems "quite safe right here, right now." Again, wait until this is verified, then ask the client to repeat this phrase a few times, becoming comfortable with it. This statement becomes an anchor that clients use to assess the voracity of their sensations of panic.

Working in consort with the "right here, right now" anchor, start to educate the client about breath retraining as a response to anxious feelings. Detailed instructions for this are found elsewhere (see Barlow & Craske, 2006), so we only state here that it is important that the client complete the exercise of *experiencing* relaxed diaphragmatic breathing in the office; talking about it is insufficient. We cannot stress enough the importance of establishing the sensation of calmness and a relaxed state; it is this state the client must be able to access to succeed in later steps in the treatment process. It is well worth the time and effort necessary to solidly establish this anchor.

Interoceptive Exposure Treatment

Interoceptive exposure requires that the client be systematically exposed to bodily sensations in a therapeutic context so that he or she can learn at an emotional level not to fear these sensations. This differs from the misappraisals of body sensations in that rather than focusing on *cognitions*, a conscious effort is made to have the client evoke, endure, and reduce the *sensations* of panic in the office. Thus, sessions must be long enough to allow the client to fully provoke and reduce feelings of panic.

The client and the social worker develop a short list of hierarchically ordered body sensations associated with panic attacks. After which, the client recalls his or her most recent panic attack and describes the least significant body sensation and how he or she experienced it at that time. The client usually begins to demonstrate symptoms related to the body sensation at this point. Feel free to point this out to him or her, noting that he or she is indeed acting anxious. (Sometimes invoking the memory of a panic attack does not generate the symptoms of panic in the present. In these cases, have the client do exercises such as breathing through a straw or intentionally hyperventilating to produce the symptoms.)

Once the client reports being anxious (or demonstrates overt signs of anxiety), guide him or her in the breath retraining exercise. Be careful to reinforce positive responses during this exercise. Repeat this exercise (up to three times) for this initial body sensation in the office. The client's ability to invoke the panic is often lessened by the end of the third iteration.

Use at least one follow-up session to reinforce gains made in the initial interoceptive session. After discussing what happened in the initial interoceptive session, have the client repeat the process him- or herself. Assuming that the client is successful in reducing anxiety, offer the comment that "right here, right now," he or she seems safe and calm. This anchor is reinforced as we begin the process of addressing additional body sensations associated with panic. Following the second interoceptive session, encourage the client to continue the exercise at home. If possible, a supportive family member should be enlisted as a helper in this exercise. (It is common for clients to report that after proceeding through three or four body sensations, they are no longer able to provoke them. In these instances it is possible to use the paradoxical injunction of "prescribing the symptom." When clients think they might be on the verge of an attack, we encourage them to "request" it . . . "bring in on, then!" Interestingly, it is sometimes a useful strategy for clients to face these sensations rather than avoid them.)

In Vivo Exposure

In vivo exposure treatment is used when the client experiences agoraphobia. It requires that clients engage in exposure practices by which they systematically venture into the situations they have been avoiding. Unlike panic disorders, agoraphobia is related to physical locations, and thus exposure to situations or places is warranted. A similar process to that previously described for interoceptive exposure is used (establishing a hierarchy of anxiety-provoking situations, exposing the client to these sequentially while assisting him or her in confronting and overcoming the anxious feelings). The sequence presented here often allows the client to conduct this component of treatment without the worker's direct assistance, sometimes with the aid of written or audio-taped journals. (This is one of the reasons we address the panic disorder prior to addressing the agoraphobia.) In vivo exposure administered by the client is comparable to that administered by the worker. Furthermore, including significant

others or spouses in treatment as coaches has beneficial effects for clients.

Although this program has been helpful to many people, it will not be successful with all clients. In such a situation, the reader is encouraged to use one of the additional healing methods, including meditation, exercise, herbal treatments, spiritual support, and self-help groups. With regard to the last item on the list, the resources offered by the Anxiety Disorders Association of America and the National Alliance on Mental Illness are particularly noteworthy, and their websites are provided in the reference section.

Eye Movement Desensitization and Reprocessing Therapy and Panic Disorders and Agoraphobia

Eye movement desensitization and reprocessing (EMDR) can be described as a form of structured exposure therapy combined with a specific "thought stopping" cognitive behavioral component (Feske & Goldstein, 1997). EMDR is used widely in the treatment of various clinical disorders including anxiety disorders, mood disorders, phobias, dissociative disorders, attention deficit hyperactivity disorder (ADHD), phantom limb pain and has proven to be particularly effective in the treatment of posttraumatic stress disorder (PTSD) and other trauma-related disorders (Davidson & Parker, 2001; Herbert et al., 2000; Maxwell, 2007). The literature is mixed, however, regarding the use of EMDR with clients diagnosed with panic disorder. There is insufficient evidence to suggest that EMDR is more effective than the other therapies discussed in this chapter in treating with panic disorder with or without agoraphobia (Davidson & Parker, 2001; Fernandez & Faretta, 2007; Feske & Goldstein, 1997; Sanchez-Meca, Rosa-Alcazar, Marin-Martinez, Gomez-Conesa, 2010). Clinicians considering the use of EMDR with clients diagnosed with panic disorder and agoraphobia should exercise caution in their professional judgment; these clients typically have highly sensitive fear networks that may become overwhelmed due to the intensity of the processing sessions (Fernandez & Faretta, 2007).

WEBSITES

American Academy of Child and
Adolescent Psychiatry. http://www
.aacap.org/cs/root/facts_for_families/
panic_disorder_in_children_and_adolescents
Anxiety Busters. http://www.anxietybusters.com
Anxiety Disorders Association of America.
http://www.adaa.org.Anxiety Disorders.com;
http://www.anxieties.com.
Anxiety and Panic Attacks. http://www.anxiety-
panic.com
Clinical Social Work Association. http://www
.clinicalsocialworkassociation.org/
National Alliance on Mental Illness. http://
www.nami.org
National Association of Social
Workers-Behavioral Health. http://www
.naswdc.org/bhealth.asp
National Institutes of Health and Mental
Health. www.nimh.nih.gov/health/topics/
panic-disorder/
Social Work Policy Institute. http://www.social-
workpolicy.org/research/anxiety-disorders
.html

References

American Psychiatric Association. (2013). *Diagnostic and statistical manual of mental disorders, fifth edition*. Washington, DC: Author.

Barlow, D. H., & Craske, M. G. (2006). *Mastery of your anxiety and panic* (4th ed.). New York, NY: Oxford University Press.

Bentley, K. J., & Walsh, J. (2013). *The social worker and psychotropic medication: Toward effective collaboration with clients, families, and providers* (4th ed.). Belmont, CA: Brooks/Cole.

Bruss, G. S., Gruenburg, A. M., Goldstein, R. D., & Barber, J. P. (1994). Hamilton anxiety rating scale interview guide: Joint interview and test-retest methods for interrater reliability. *Psychiatry Research, 53*(2), 191–202.

Chambless, D. L., Caputo, G. C., Bright, P., & Gallagher, R. (1984). Assessment of fear in agoraphobics: The Body Sensations Questionnaire and the Agoraphobic Cognitions Questionnaire. *Journal of Consulting and Clinical Psychology, 52*, 1090–1097.

Davidson, P. R., & Parker, K. C. H. (2001). Eye movement desensitization and reprocessing: A meta-analysis. *Journal of Consulting and Clinical Psychology, 69*(2), 305–316.

DiNardo, P. A., & Barlow, D. H. (1988). *Anxiety disorders interview schedule–Revised*. Albany, NY: Phobia and Anxiety Disorders Clinic, State University of New York.

Dziegielewski, S. (2010). *Social work practice and psychopharmacology: A person in environment approach* (2nd ed.). New York, NY: Springer Publishing Company.

Eaton, W. W., Kessler, R. C., Wittchen, H. U., & Magee, W. J. (1994). Panic and panic disorder in the United States. *American Journal of Psychiatry, 151*, 413–420.

Fernandez, I., & Faretta, E. (2007). Eye movement desensitization and reprocessing in the treatment of panic disorder with agoraphobia. *Clinical Case Studies, 6*(11), 44–63.

Feske, U., & Goldstein, A. J. (1997). Eye movement desensitization and reprocessing treatment for panic disorder: A controlled outcome and partial dismantling study. *Journal of Consulting and Clinical Psychology, 65*(6), 1026–1035.

First, M. B., Gibbon, M., Spitzer, R. L., & Williams, J. B. W. (1997). *Structured clinical interview for DSM-IV axis I disorders SCID I: Clinician version, administration booklet*. Washington, DC: American Psychiatric Press.

Furukawa, T. A., Watanabe, N., & Churchill, R. (2007). Combined psychotherapy plus antidepressants for panic disorder with or without agoraphobia. *Cochrane Database of Systematic Reviews, 1*, CD004364. doi:0.1002/14651858.CD004364.pub2.

Herbert, J. D., Lilienfield, S. O., Lohr, J. M., Montgomery, R. W., O'Donohue, W. T., Rosen, G. M., & Tolin, D. F. (2000). Science and pseudoscience in the development of eye movement: Implications for clinical psychology. *Clinical Psychology Review, 20*(8), 945–971.

Himle, J. A., Fischer, D. J., & Lokers, L. M. (2007). Panic disorder and agoraphobia. In B. A. Thyer & J. Woodarski (Eds.), *Social work in mental health: An evidence-based approach* (pp. 331–349). Hoboken, NJ: Wiley.

Houck, P. R., Speigel, D. A., Shear, M. K., Rucci, P., & Stat, D. (2002). Reliability of the self-report version of the Panic Disorder Severity Scale. *Depression and Anxiety, 15*, 183–185.

Kessler, R. C., Chiu, W. T, Jin, R., Ruscio, A. M., & Walters, E. E. (2006). The epidemiology of panic attacks, panic disorder, and agoraphobia in the National Comorbidity Survey Replication. *Archives of General Psychiatry, 63*(4), 415–424.

Maier, W., Buller, R., Phillip, M., & Heuser, I. (1988). The Hamilton Anxiety Scale: Reliability, validity and sensitivity to change in anxiety and depressive disorders. *Journal of Affective Disorders, 14*(1), 61–68.

Maxwell, L. (2007). Current status and future directions for EMDR. *Journal of EMDR Practice and Research, 1*(1), 6–14. doi:10.1891/1933-3196.1.1.4.

Roth, A., & Fonagy, P. (2005). Anxiety disorders I: Specific phobia, social phobia, generalized anxiety disorder, and panic disorder with and without agoraphobia. In A. Roth & P. Fonagy (Eds.), *What works for whom? A critical review of psychotherapy research* (2nd ed.). (pp. 150–197). New York, NY: Guilford.

Sanchez-Meca, J., Rosa-Alcazar, A. I., Marin-Martinez, F., & Gomez-Conesa, A. (2010). Psychological treatment of panic disorder with or without agoraphobia: A meta-analysis. *Clinical Psychology Review, 30*, 37–50. doi:10.1016/j.cpr.2009.08.011.

Schmidt, N. B., Norr, A. M., & Korte, K. J. (2013). Panic disorder and agoraphobia: Considerations

for DSM-V. *Research on Social Work Practice.* doi:10.1177/1049731512474490.

Shapiro, F., & Forrest, M. S. (1997). *EMDR: Eye movement desensitization & reprocessing: The breakthrough therapy for overcoming anxiety, stress, and trauma.* New York, NY: Basic Books-Perseus Books Group.

Shear, M. K., Bilt, J. V., Rucci, P., Endicott, J., Lydiard, B., Otto, M. W., . . . Frank, D. M. (2001). Reliability and validity of a structured interview guide for the Hamilton Anxiety Rating Scale. *Depression and Anxiety, 13*(4), 166–178.

75 Treatment Plans for Clients with Social Anxiety Disorder

Bruce A. Thyer & Monica Pignotti

Contemporary social workers helping clients who experience significant problems with Social Anxiety Disorder (SAD) are in a very fortunate position indeed. The diagnostic conceptualizations of clinical anxiety have been considerably refined over the last five iterations of the *Diagnostic and Statistical Manual of Mental Disorders* (*DSM*; American Psychiatric Association, 2013), and the newer nomenclature is closer to nature's truth about how clients experience pathological anxiety than the system described in previous editions. Clinicians are also fortunate in that considerable effectiveness and efficacy research involving very sophisticated randomized controlled clinical trials have demonstrated that selected psychosocial treatments are genuinely helpful in ameliorating SAD, a condition that, if left untreated, is typically chronic and unremitting, causing significant distress and impaired functioning. There are relatively few psychosocial problems facing social workers wherein the outcomes are so potentially favorable. Given this positive

state of affairs, it is incumbent upon social work practitioners who wish to practice both ethically and accountably to become familiar with research-supported methods of assessment and intervention found to be useful for socially anxious clients. This chapter will focus on diagnosis, assessment, research-based interventions, and treatment goals and planning for clients with social anxiety disorder.

CASE EXAMPLE

Fred W. (an actual client with social phobia treated by Thyer), was a self-referred 56-year-old male auto worker from Detroit whose presenting complaint was of extreme apprehension, fears of fainting, marked tremor, and agitation, which were reliably evoked whenever he was in situations involving face-to-face interactions with someone else. This was impairing his ability to work and had greatly restricted his social life. He could not stand in lines with people or participate in the sacrament of communion at the Catholic church to which he belonged. The problem was absent in the presence of his wife and children, but otherwise always occurred when other people were near. When seated or able to lean against a wall or table, Fred could talk comfortably with anyone. If he had to stand unsupported while listening or talking, he would begin to tremble, perspire, and experience great anxiety. He dated the onset of this problem to an episode some 30 years earlier when he was in the military and was verbally abused by an officer in front of his fellow soldiers. He was unable to respond to the officer's angry tirade, which should have been directed against another soldier, not Fred. The problem has been continuous since that time without any remissions. The assessment and treatment plan that was carried out for Fred is described in Table 75.1.

DIAGNOSTIC CRITERIA AND PREVALENCE OF SOCIAL ANXIETY DISORDER

The term *social anxiety disorder (SAD)* is often used interchangeably with the term social phobia, with the former now the primary term used in the *DSM-5*. Many clinical researchers and consumer advocacy organizations are encouraging the use of *SAD* because it promotes recognition of the problem as a serious, treatable condition rather than something to be stoically endured (Liebowitz, Heimberg, Travers, & Stein, 2000).

The *DSM-5* lists about a dozen distinct disorders that may apply to children and adults seeking help and who present with the prominent features of anxiety, fear, avoidance, or increased arousal (American Psychiatric Association, 2013). The diagnostic criteria for Social Phobia (SP) first appeared in the third edition of the *DSM*, were revised somewhat in *DSM-III-R*, again in the *DSM-IV* and in the *DSM-IV-TR*, and now most recently in the *DSM-5* and renamed Social Anxiety Disorder (American Psychiatric Association, 2013). At present, SAD is defined by the following diagnostic criteria:

"A. Marked fear or anxiety about one or more social situations in which the individual is exposed to possible scrutiny by others. Examples include social interactions (e.g., having a conversation, meeting unfamiliar

people), being observed (e.g. eating or drinking), and performing in front of others (e.g., giving a speech).

B. The individual fears that he or she will act in a way or show anxiety symptoms that will be negatively evaluated (e.g., will be humiliating or embarrassing; will lead to rejection or offend others).

C. The social situations almost always provoke fear or anxiety.

D. The social situations are avoided or endured with intense fear or anxiety.

E. The fear or anxiety is out of proportion to the actual threat posed by the social situation and to the sociocultural context.

F. The fear, anxiety or avoidance is persistent, typically lasting six months or more.

G. The fear, anxiety, or avoidance causes clinically significant distress or impairment in social, occupational, or other important areas of functioning."

It addition, the features of SAD cannot be better explained by another mental disorder, a substance, or a medical condition (APA, 2013, pp. 202–203). There is only one specifier for SAD, *Performance Only*, that applies if the fear is centered around speaking or performing in public.

SAD is the fourth most common psychiatric disorder in the United States with a lifetime prevalence of approximately 12%, exceeded only by major depression, specific phobia, and alcohol dependence (Kessler et al., 2005). The 12-month prevalence rate for SAD in the United States is about 7% (APA, 2013, p. 204). The mean age of onset is during the teenage years (Thyer, Parrish, Curtis, Nesse, & Cameron, 1985), although some research has shown a bimodal distribution, with the onset for some individuals, who may have a more generalized form of social phobia, occurring earlier in childhood (Stein, Chavira, & Jang, 2001). Alcohol abuse can be a consequence of individuals with social phobia drinking to self-medicate symptoms (Thyer et al., 1986), and a careful assessment of possible alcohol and drug abuse is advisable in its own right. SAD has also been shown to be highly comorbid with major depressive disorder and appears to have a negative impact on its course and outcome (Zimmerman & Chelminski, 2003). The personal and societal ramifications of SAD can be profound. For example, Tolman et al. (2009) found that SAD can be

TABLE 75.1 Treatment Plan Worksheet for an Actual Client with Social Phobia

Assessment Domain	Assessment		
	Assessment Method	Assessment Goals	Findings
Biological	Client interview	Eliminate possible role of biological factors in causing client's problems (n.b.—it is rare to find such factors)	Onset and course consistent with psychosocial etiology Extreme situational specificity of problem. Ruled out organic causes Client not taking any drugs
Diagnostic	DSM-based clinical interview DSM-based decision tree Rapid assessment instruments	Ascertain that client met DSM diagnostic criteria for SAD	Client met DSM criteria for SAD, and no other disorder
Familial	Interview with wife Interview with client (separately and together)	Investigate impact of client's problem on marital/family life	
Specification of situations where client experiences social anxiety	Client interview	Development of a rank-ordered list of social situations producing anxiety	Situations mentioned by client included standing in public waiting lines, church communion, and face-to-face interactions

Treatment Planning

Domain	Intervention Plan	Conduct and Results
Observable behavior (avoidance of unsupported face-to-face contact; observable tremor; seeking physical support)	Graduated real-life exposure; repeated exposure therapy sessions alone. Allow symptoms to develop while remaining standing in front of therapist without support. Find out if behaviors subside and discomfort lessens. Move to more intense and real-life situations outside private office.	Three 60–90-minute sessions in the office eliminated visible tremor and perspiration. Client became very comfortable standing in front of therapist. Subsequent sessions undertaken in large, empty auditorium. Moved to similar sessions involving long lines of people at movie theaters and fast-food restaurants. Therapist modeled and client subsequently imitated an obvious and deliberate tremor while standing in public waiting lines. Client self-conducted exposure exercises in between weekly sessions with therapist, at church and work. Treatment involved eight sessions with therapist, resulting in virtual elimination of problem. Three-year follow-up by phone found continuous absence of presenting problem and greatly enhanced functioning at work and social life.
Cognitive (thoughts of acting in an embarrassing manner; catastrophic thinking: "My boss will see me shaking and fire me!")	Think-aloud during exposure sessions, recognize unrealistic nature of fears, voice more realistic coping responses.	Distressing and catastrophic thoughts gradually reduced after experiencing elimination of tremor, sweating, and support seeking.
Affective (severe anxiety when facing others unsupported; anticipatory anxiety about facing future situations)	Consciously control breathing during exposure sessions, rehearse coping responses in imagination and in real life.	Anxious feelings gradually eliminated during the course of treatment.

a significant impediment to returning to work among women welfare recipients.

FURTHER ASSESSMENT OF SOCIAL ANXIETY DISORDER

Arriving at a *DSM* diagnosis of SAD is only a part of a comprehensive social work assessment, which should involve an array of quantitative and qualitative methods of appraisal—the clinical interview; structured client self-reports (e.g., narrative diaries, logs of out-of-home social/public activities); rapid assessment instruments; structured clinical interviews centered around anxiety disorders; medical check-ups to rule out organic causes, including the possible role of medication effects and drug interactions; and, possibly, interviews with other family members.

There are highly specific rapid assessment instruments and rating scales developed for assessing aspects of SAD and related client functioning. A partial list of frequently recommended tools can be found in Table 75.2. Pretreatment assessment should involve using one or more of these reliable and valid outcome measures, ideally encompassing a rapid assessment instrument, as well as direct measures of behavior, perhaps systematically recorded by the client or a significant other. Some measures may be administered daily or weekly. Other, more global, outcome indicators, such as a quality-of-life scale, a measure of family functioning, or a measure of overall health, simply could be administered pre- and post-treatment.

A functional analysis of the environmental and internal (e.g., troubling thoughts) antecedents to and the consequences that follow behaviors associated with SAD (overt actions, feelings, and thoughts) may be highly relevant. Mattaini (1990) and Filter and Alvarez (2012) provide a recommended review of the importance of such functional behavior analyses as a part of social work assessment.

Once it has been determined that clients meet the *DSM-5* criteria, it is essential to carefully isolate the parameters or boundaries of their anxiety-evoking stimuli, because various types of social phobia can be quite diverse. A well-established way of accomplishing this is for client and social worker to construct a rank-ordered list of specific social situations that lead to anxiety for the client (Heimberg, 2002). Such a list can then be incorporated into a treatment plan that will be described later in the chapter.

RESEARCH-BASED EVIDENCE AND PRACTICE KNOWLEDGE

Consistent with the recommendations to be found in the Surgeon General's report on mental illness (Satcher, 1999), social workers should become competent in providing contemporary research-based psychosocial treatments for anxiety disorders. A large body of research exists in support of effective psychosocial interventions for SAD, based on various combinations of behavioral and cognitive behavioral approaches (see Heimberg, 2002; Rodebaugh, Holaway, & Heimberg, 2004; Barlow, Allen, & Basden, 2007, for full reviews). Components of these interventions include exposure to feared stimuli, social skills training, relaxation training, and cognitive restructuring. These interventions have been successfully conducted in both group and individual therapy settings.

The most important component of the treatment is exposure, the element that all successful interventions for SAD have in common. The first step of the process is for the social worker and client to put together a rank-ordered list, from least to most frightening, of social situations that

TABLE 75.2 Recommended Assessment Tools for Social Phobia

- Social Phobia Scale (SPS; measures fear of scrutiny)
- Social Interaction Anxiety Scale (SAIS; measures fear of interpersonal interaction) (*note*: the SPS and SAIS are often used together)
- Social Avoidance and Distress Scale
- Social Anxiety Scale for Children
- Social Anxiety Thoughts Questionnaire*
- Social Avoidance and Distress Scale*
- Social Fear Scale*
- Social Interaction Self-statement Test*
- Social Phobia and Anxiety Inventory for Children
- Social Phobia Endstate Functioning Index
- Liebowitz Social Anxiety Scale
- Simulated Social Interaction Test

*Readily found in Corcoran & Fischer (2013, pp. 807–814).

produce anxiety (Heimberg, 2002). Exposure can be accomplished by imagining fearful scenes, usually narrated by the therapist (imaginal exposure); role playing with the therapist or others who resemble people the client fears; or by direct exposure to the feared situation (real life exposure). The client agrees to remain in the anxiety-evoking situation with the therapist's support until the anxiety considerably diminishes. Imaginal rehearsal and prolonged exposure in fantasy can be conducted in situations where real life exposure is not possible (e.g., an upcoming once-in-a-lifetime solo performance by a musician at Carnegie Hall), although real life exposure is usually preferable when possible. This is due to the fact that imaginal exposure is considerably removed from the real thing and considerably less effective at either inducing anxiety or helping the client develop genuinely effective coping and performance skills in real life. Exposure can be carried out in individual or group therapy settings, and clients are usually given exposure exercises as homework, to carry out on their own between sessions.

Social skills training (SST) is based on the premise that a lack of social skills, such as poor eye contact or poor conversation skills, can result in a negative reaction from others, thus causing unpleasant and anxiety-provoking social interactions with others. Even though there is still some debate as to whether all clients need SST (Rodebaugh et al., 2004), this approach has been shown to be effective as both a stand-alone intervention and in conjunction with exposure-based approaches. A controlled clinical trial (Herbert et al., 2005) compared cognitive-behavioral group therapy (CBGT) alone with CBGT and SST combined. The trial showed significantly greater gains for the CBGT and SST combination. Moreover, the effect sizes were reported to be the largest found to date for an SAD intervention, which means that the results were highly clinically significant and robust.

Relaxation training can be used in conjunction with exposure therapy, although relaxation training alone has not been shown to be helpful and has sometimes been used as a control condition in studies (Rodebaugh et al., 2004). The most commonly used form of relaxation training is progressive muscle relaxation, which is employed in a process called applied relaxation. It has been shown to be effective for SAD when clients are trained in it and then use it while confronting feared situations (Öst, 1987). Systematic reviews and meta-analyses of the intervention research on SAD have shown medium-to-large effect sizes, indicating clinically significant results for exposure therapy with or without the relaxation component (Rodebaugh et al., 2004; Acarturk, Cuijpers, van Straten & de Graaf, 2008; Powers, Sigmarsson, & Emmelkamp, 2008). More recent work has demonstrated transferability of these research-supported behavioral therapies into everyday clinical settings, as well as into international settings, with similarly positive results (e.g., Kawaguchi, Watanabe, Nakano, Ogawa, Suzuki, Kondo, Furukawa, & Akechi, 2013).

Even though these highly effective psychosocial treatments for SAD exist, some clients are not helped by such treatments and others achieve only partial symptom reduction (see Herbert et al., 2005, for a review). Thus, the search for ways to improve existing interventions and conduct research on innovative treatments continues. When using any innovative treatment, it is crucial to provide full informed consent to the client on the state of the evidence and to try the interventions with the greatest empirical support first. One newer approach of interest to researchers is Acceptance and Commitment Therapy (ACT; Hayes, Strosahl, & Wilson, 1999). ACT is based on behavior therapy, with the addition of mindfulness and acceptance components. Pilot studies have shown promising results when the ACT model is incorporated into exposure therapy for SAD (Dalrymple & Herbert, 2007; Ossman, Wilson, Storaasli, & McNeill, 2006). ACT is based on the idea that the primary reason people suffer from psychological disorders is not negative emotions per se but rather the struggle to control and avoid experiencing such emotions. Unlike many conventional therapies, the explicit goal of ACT is not to eliminate negative emotions or reduce symptoms (although the pilot studies show that this can often occur), but instead to assist the client in giving up the struggle against emotions and thus promote a nondefensive acceptance (not mere tolerance) of emotions, including anxiety. The identification of client values and helping the client take committed value-directed action is also an important element of ACT. ACT has also been shown to increase a person's willingness to engage in exposure-based procedures (Hayes, Luoma, Bond, Masuda, & Lillis, 2006).

Considerable research has also gone into investigating the effectiveness of various medications to help clients with SAD and the general consensus of reviews on this topic is that selected medications are indeed helpful in temporarily reducing symptomatology (Stein, Ipser, & van Balkom, 2004; Blanco, Bragdon, Schneier, & Liebowitz, 2013; Stein et al., 2010). However, unlike psychosocial treatments the effects are ameliorative, not curative, and relapse is high following the discontinuation of medication. Furthermore, medication treatment provides no behavioral benefits to clients whose SAD is related to a skills deficit (e.g., initiating and maintaining conversations, or underassertiveness), in terms of helping them develop such functional behaviors.

TREATMENT GOALS

- Ideally, the goal mutually arrived at with a client with SAD is the complete alleviation of pathological anxiety—in other words, a cure.
- More realistically, the goal would be more enhanced functioning and some relief of symptoms, not necessarily a complete remission of the difficulty. Incorporation of ACT principles may be helpful for such clients.
- Enhanced quality of life, improved relationship and family functioning, more effective vocational functioning, and increased ability to function in other areas of life valued by the client (e.g., hobbies, recreation, social activities, volunteer work).

These constructs are all amenable to reliable and valid qualitative and quantitative measurement (using some of the assessment protocols already described) before, during, and at the completion of treatment, and sometimes thereafter. Such data should be routinely gathered and shared with clients (and perhaps their family members) as appropriate. Graphing relevant data and including these in client records is also a recommended practice.

TREATMENT PLANNING

A representative assessment treatment plan taken from one of the authors' (Thyer) clinical work with socially phobic individuals was presented in Table 75.1.

Social phobia also lends itself very well to social group work treatment, which has been shown to be quite effective (Heimberg, 2002).

Former and current social phobics can themselves be very useful as lay therapists (Ross, 1980). Additionally, exposure therapy conducted in group work settings has been shown to be helpful, especially for clients with the generalized form of SAD, to assess for the need for social skills training, because, as previously noted, this was shown to enhance the effects of exposure therapy (Herbert et al., 2005). For public speaking anxiety, a very friendly and supportive organization called Toastmasters International, devoted to helping individuals improve public speaking and leadership skills, can be very helpful. The Toastmasters program is, in effect, a lay-developed program of graduated exposure therapy sessions.

WEBSITES

Anxiety and Depression Association of America (ADAA). http://www.adaa.org
The Anxiety Panic Internet Resource (TAPIR). http://www.algy.com/anxiety
Toastmasters International. http://www.toastmasters.org

References

Acarturk, C., Cuijpers, P., van Straten, A., & de Graaf, R. (2008). Psychological treatment social anxiety disorder: A meta-analysis. *Psychological Medicine, 39,* 241–254.

American Psychiatric Association. (2013). *Diagnostic and statistical manual of mental disorders, fifth edition.* Washington, DC: Author.

Barlow, D. H., Allen, L. B., & Basden, S. L. (2007). Psychological treatments for panic disorders, phobias and generalized anxiety disorder. In P. E. Nathan & J. M. Gorman (Eds.), *A guide to treatments that work* (3rd ed.) (pp. 351–394). New York, NY: Oxford University Press.

Blanco, C., Bragdon, L. B., Schneier, F. R., & Liebowitz, M. R. (2013). The evidence-based pharmacotherapy of social anxiety disorder. *International Journal of Neuropsychopharmacology, 16,* 235–249.

Corcoran, K., & Fischer, J. (2013). *Measures for clinical practice and research: A sourcebook* (Vol. 2, Adults). New York, NY: Oxford University Press.

Dalrymple, K. L., & Herbert, J. D. (2007). Acceptance and commitment therapy for generalized social anxiety disorder: A pilot study. *Behavior Modification, 31,* 543–568.

Filter, K. J., & Alvarez, M. E. (2012). *Functional behavioral assessment: A three-tiered prevention model.* New York, NY: Oxford University Press.

Hayes, S. C., Luoma, J. B., Bond, F. W., Masuda, A., & Lillis, J. (2006). Acceptance and commitment therapy: Model, processes, and outcomes. *Behaviour Research and Therapy, 44,* 1–25.

Hayes, S. C., Strosahl, K. D., & Wilson, K. G. (1999). *Acceptance and commitment therapy: An experiential approach to behavior change.* New York, NY: Guilford.

Heimberg, R. G. (2002). Cognitive-behavioral therapy for social anxiety disorder: Current status and future directions. *Biological Psychiatry, 51,* 101–108.

Herbert, J. D., Gaudiano, B. A., Rheingold, A. A., Myers, V. H., Dalrymple, K., & Nolan, E. M. (2005). Social skills training augments the effectiveness of cognitive behavioral group therapy for social anxiety disorder. *Behavior Therapy, 36,* 125–138.

Kawaguchi, A., Watanabe, N., Nakano, Y., Ogawa, S., Suzuki, M., Furukawa, T. A., & Akechi, T. (2013). Group cognitive behavioural therapy with generalized social anxiety disorder in Japan: Outcomes at 1-year follow up and outcome predictors. *Neuropsychiatric Disease and Treatment, 9,* 267–275.

Kessler, R. C., Berglund, P., Demler, O., Jin, R., Merikangas, R., & Walters, E. E. (2005). Lifetime prevalence and age-of-onset distributions of DSM-IV disorders in the National Comorbidity Survey Replication. *Archives of General Psychiatry, 62,* 593–602.

Liebowitz, M. R., Heimberg, R. G., Travers, J., & Stein, M. B. (2000). Social phobia or social anxiety disorder: What's in a name? *Archives of General Psychiatry, 57,* 191–192.

Mattaini, M. A. (1990). Contextual behavior analysis in the assessment process. *Families in Society, 71,* 236–245.

Ossman, W. A., Wilson, K. G., Storaasli, R. D., & McNeill, J. W. (2006). A preliminary investigation in the use of acceptance and commitment therapy in group treatment for social phobia. *International Journal of Psychology and Psychological Therapy, 6,* 397–416.

Öst, L. G. (1987). Applied relaxation: Description of a coping technique and review of controlled studies. *Behaviour Research and Therapy, 25,* 397–409.

Powers M. B., Sigmarsson, S. R., & Emmelkamp, P. M. G. (2008). A meta-analytic review of psychological treatments for Social Anxiety Disorder. *International Journal of Cognitive Therapy, 1,* 94–113.

Rodebaugh, T. L., Holaway, R. M., & Heimberg, R. G. (2004). The treatment of social anxiety disorder. *Clinical Psychology Review, 24,* 883–908.

Ross, J. (1980). The use of former phobics in the treatment of phobias. *American Journal of Psychiatry, 137,* 715–717.

Satcher, D. (1999). *Mental health: A report from the Surgeon General—1999.* Washington, DC: Office of the Surgeon General, Substance Abuse and Mental Health Services Administration (SAMHSA).

Stein, D. J., Ipser, J. C., & van Balkom, A. J. (2004). Medication social anxiety disorder. *Cochrane Database of Systematic Reviews 2004, 4,* Art. No.: CD001206. doi:10.1002/14651858.CD001206.pub2

Stein, D. J., Baldwin, D. S., Bandelow, B., Blanco, C., Fontenelle, L. F., Lee, S., . . . van Ameringen, M. (2010). A 2010 evidence-based algorithm for the pharmacotherapy of social anxiety disorder. *Current Psychiatry Reports, 12,* 471–477.

Stein, M. B., Chavira, D. A., & Jang, K. L. (2001). Bringing up bashful baby: Developmental pathways to social phobia. *Psychiatric Clinics of North America, 24,* 661–676.

Thyer, B. A., Parrish, R. T., Curtis, G. C., Nesse, R. M., & Cameron, O. G. (1985). Ages of onset of *DSM III* anxiety disorders. *Comprehensive Psychiatry, 26,* 113–122.

Thyer, B. A., Parrish, R. T., Himle, J., Cameron, O. G., Curtis, G. C., & Nesse, R. M. (1986). Alcohol abuse among clinically anxious patients. *Behaviour Research and Therapy, 24,* 357–359.

Tolman, R. M., Himle, J., Bybee, D., Abelson, J. L., Hoffman, J., & Van Etten-Lee, M. (2009). Impact of Social Anxiety Disorders on employment among women receiving welfare benefits. *Psychiatric Services, 60,* 61–66.

Zimmerman, M., & Chelminski, I. (2003). Clinician recognition of anxiety disorders in depressed outpatients. *Journal of Psychiatric Research, 37,* 325–333.

76 Integration of Psychodynamic and Cognitive-behavioral Practices

Terry B. Northcut & Nina Rovinelli Heller

Many of the clients we work with have forms of acute or chronic depression that render daily life a struggle. Results from the 60-country World Health Organization (WHO) World Health Survey (http://www.who.int/healthinfo/survey/whsresults/en/index.html), which included depression as the only mental health condition surveyed, revealed, a 3.2% 12-month prevalence rate for major depression. Among participants with a chronic condition, however, the rate was much higher, at between 9.3% and 23.0%. In the United States, major depression is the most prevalent mental health condition, at a rate of 29.9% lifetime and 8.6% 12-month prevalence. Furthermore, WHO reports that major depression is the fourth leading cause of disability worldwide and identifies increasing prevalence in younger cohorts, although the reasons for this are unclear (Kessler et al., 2012). The human costs of depression are staggering; Kessler reports significant negative impacts in the areas of education performance and completion, marital timing and stability, teen childbearing, employment status, role performance, marital and parental functioning, financial success, and comorbid impairments (pp. 3–6). Theories regarding the etiology of depressive conditions include genetics and biology, as well as a combination of vulnerabilities and risk factors (diathesis-stress model; Paris, 1996). Furthermore, depressed people are at elevated risk for death by suicide (Kessler et al., 2012). Untreated depression affects individuals, their families, and communities, in nearly every domain of functioning. The restoration of adaptive functioning and full engagement in one's life—in work, in love, and in play—is the central focus of our attempts to help clients who suffer with this debilitating condition.

THEORETICAL APPROACHES TO THE TREATMENT OF DEPRESSION

Clinical social workers in a wide variety of practice settings work with clients who have both diagnosed and undiagnosed depressive disorders. The identification of people with depression has increased over the past decade, as has the range of available treatment options. With a strong legacy of employing a bio-psychosocial perspective, social workers are well positioned to accommodate the growing bodies of knowledge from biological/genetic, psychological, and sociological theories and evidence-based practices. Social workers in public and private settings are often on the front lines of work with individuals and families and are in positions in which they can pay attention to prevention, identification, and treatment of depressive disorders for all ages.

With the advent of second- and third-generation antidepressant medications, biological interventions have become common, whereas half a century ago, psychotherapy alone was the treatment of choice. At that time, psychodynamic or psychoanalytic theory and technique recognized depressive disorders as largely psychological in nature. This reflected the tremendous legacy of Freudian psychology, which interestingly enough, originated in Freud's interest in neurobiological processes, viewing depression as "anger toward inward"—in other words, in largely psychodynamic terms. Other psychodynamically oriented theorists have posited that depression is related to mourning, ambivalence regarding a lost object, narcissistic injury, abandonment fears, and disrupted attachments. Since the late 1970s, cognitive theory (Beck, 1979, 1987,

1995; Reinecke & Davison, 2002, among others) has been highly influential in the treatment and research of many psychiatric disorders, most notably depression. Cognitive theory posits that the negative affects experienced in depression are a result of cognitive distortions and faulty thinking processes. The prescribed intervention, then, is the identification and modification of those distortions through psychotherapy.

Various theoretical schools have historically tried to lay claim to superiority over other schools in terms of treatment success. This has been made possible, in part, by the increased availability of research funding, particularly from the National Institute of Mental Health, for psychotherapy evaluation studies. Simultaneously, there has been a shift in the social work field toward identifying evidence-based practices. Psychotherapy evaluation studies are labor-intensive and require sophisticated designs and data analysis (Abbass, 2002). Cognitive therapy, which lends itself well to research studies because of its clearly identified assessment and intervention strategies, has led the way in terms of psychotherapy research. Early studies suggest that cognitive therapy is at least as effective as antidepressant medication (Zeiss, 1997). Still others have found that the combination of cognitive therapy and medication therapy is superior (Reinecke & Davison, 2002). Treatment effectiveness studies of psychodynamic interventions have been slower to develop, but Fonagy, Roth, and Higgins (2005) have published an exhaustive review of evidence-based psychodynamic treatment. Although there exists a robust evidence base for the efficacy of cognitive behavioral interventions for depression, psychodynamic treatment may be worth another look. Luyten and Blatt (2012) note significant increases in psychodynamic outcome research and promising results; in regard to depression, both short- and long-term psychodynamic treatments are as effective as other psychological approaches and may have longer term positive effects. When compared with psychopharmacological approaches, they found that psychodynamic treatment is as effective in acute treatment of mild and moderate depression and may confer greater long term effects when used in combination or alone.

Social workers look to theory, "practice wisdom," and research to guide our practice. On the basis of all three components, we do have some general guidelines for the assessment of depression. Assuredly, any client who is demonstrating vegetative signs of depression (significant changes in sleep, appetite, weight, libido, or psychomotor retardation or agitation) should be considered for referral to a medication evaluation. Likewise, clients who are suicidal or engaging in self-destructive behaviors, in addition to depressed mood, distorted thinking, and feelings of hopelessness or helplessness, could possibly benefit from medical intervention. Most of these clients will also benefit from psychotherapy (Areán & Cook, 2002; De Maat, Dekker, Schoevers, & DeJonghe, 2006; Finn, 2000; Reinecke & Davison, 2002; Sagar, Zindel, Grigoriadis, Arun, Ravindran, Kennedy, Lam, & Patten, 2009; Zac, Imel, Malterer, McKay, & Wampold, 2008). In addition, bio-psychosocial assessment can be enhanced with the use of depression measures.

INTEGRATING THEORETICAL PERSPECTIVES

We favor an integrative approach to psychotherapy with depressed clients, specifically one that uses a psychodynamic perspective and integrates specific cognitive techniques. The reasons for this bias toward an integrative approach lie in our understanding that modern psychodynamic theory inherently captures the complexity of the subjective experience of the individual, whereas cognitive theory offers very clear, sometimes prescriptive techniques aimed at increasing problem-solving skills and changing faulty thinking. The combination of the two approaches offers the opportunity to intervene successfully on both affective and cognitive levels, while doing so in a way that includes the idiosyncratic historical, social, and cultural experiences of the client. Strengths of psychodynamic theory as they pertain to the treatment of depression include (1) an understanding of the power of unconscious processes; (2) the awareness of the impact of interpersonal loss on feeling states; (3) the importance of early developmental influences; and (4) the power of the therapeutic relationship, specifically in regard to transference and countertransference phenomena.

Psychodynamic theory, then, pays particular attention to the feelings or affects of the client, considering these as a central focus for change. Hence, psychodynamic techniques include exploration of feeling states and their etiologies, particularly in the interpersonal realm. Exploration of the past, specifically in terms of its influence in the present, is often central to the therapeutic work, particularly in crisis, or reactive, depression (Reinecke & Davison, 2002). Finally, the therapist actively uses the treatment relationship to explore issues such as loss, sadness, and anger. Interpretation of both conscious and unconscious material is central in the work.

Both psychodynamic theory and cognitive-behavioral theory have evolved to the point of focusing on the idiosyncratic meaning that clients make of the experiences in their lives, rather than recovering memories or applying standard treatments. Also commonly accepted is the understanding of the dynamic interaction between cognitions, affects, and behaviors and a focus on the treatment relationship. However, cognitive theory still retains its focus on cognitions clients report in the here-and-now as the focal point of interventions. In the case of depression, certain types of cognitive distortions are believed to be present, such as negative thinking, catastrophizing, overgeneralization, etc. The clinical social worker can utilize techniques including problem solving, cognitive restructuring, thought blocking, and Socratic questioning to identify and alter the depressive cognitions that color the client's view of him- or herself, others, and the world. Cognitive theorists have also been influenced by the constructivist philosophy, which views "truth" as contextual and personal. Likewise, the influence of neurobiology has demonstrated the ability of the brain to change over time through intimate relationships and the larger social world, which reinforces these patterns of meaning. Consequently, cognitive theorists may use the concepts of schemas and attributions to describe sets of beliefs and assumptions about meaning and causation (e.g., arbitrary influence, personalization) that may have early origins and have been confirmed by subsequent life experiences. Through identifying the schemas, cognitions, or faulty thought patterns, clients can practice in vivo and with homework assignments, confronting and correcting the cognitive distortions that are common to depression (Beck, 1961, 1979, 1987, 1995, 2011; Gega, Smith, Reynolds, 2013; Leahy, 2003; Neimeyer, 2010; Newman, 2010).

Traditionally, cognitive theory has been characterized by (1) a here-and-now orientation; (2) a belief that thoughts affect or determine feeling states; (3) a belief that people who are depressed demonstrate a certain set of cognitive distortions (such as negative thinking, dichotomous thinking, catastrophizing, overgeneralization, selective abstraction, magnification, and minimization). More recently, cognitive theorists who lean more toward the constructivist position than to their behavioral origins see cognitive schemas and attributions that are particular to the depressed client because they have idiosyncratic meaning. These schemas and attributions are sets of beliefs and assumptions about meaning and causation (e.g., arbitrary influence, personalization) that may have early origins and have been confirmed by subsequent life experiences. In both the early and the more recent cognitive therapies, the therapist directs his or her attention to the identification and correction of faulty cognitions that reinforce the client's depressive stance. Techniques such as problem solving, cognitive restructuring, thought blocking, and Socratic questioning can be very helpful in changing the depressive cognitions that color the client's view of him- or herself, others, and the world. Through the use of these techniques, combined with in vivo and homework assignments, the client is able to identify, confront, and correct the cognitive distortions that are common to that feeling state (Coelho, Canter & Ernst, 2013; Gabalda, 2010; Gabalda & Neimeyer, 2010).

A client who is depressed is in subjective distress. Both psychodynamic therapists and those who hold a cognitive-constructivist perspective value the importance of the client's narrative of his or her own experience. One depressed client is not like another, although they may share certain characteristics, as noted. For example, one client's sense of lethargy or helplessness may have very different origins, meanings, and manifestations than another's. The psychodynamic therapist is interested in both the conscious and unconscious determinants of this as well as those factors that maintain such feeling states. As many of us have witnessed, however, insight alone is often not sufficient and sometimes not even necessary to effect therapeutic change. In these instances, the addition of cognitive techniques may be enormously helpful in terms of systematically addressing the cognitive beliefs and distortions that may interfere with the client's "feeling better."

CONSIDERATIONS IN ASSESSMENT AND TREATMENT PLANNING WITH DIVERSE POPULATIONS

Table 76.1 outlines the critical areas for attention, assessment, and intervention with *all* clients, and

TABLE 76.1 Guidelines for Assessment and Treatment Planning

- Evaluate carefully for safety risks, including passive and active suicidal behaviors and impulsivity. Consult recent research regarding suicide risk as associated with demographic variables, such as prior attempts, formulation of a plan, and age group.
- In the event that the client is deemed to be at risk for harm to self or others, consider lethal means restriction through discussion with the client and family members where possible.
- Create an empathetic connection with the client.
- Refer for medical evaluation to rule out depression due to a general medical condition (*DSM-5*).
- Evaluate for substance abuse and differential diagnosis.
- Refer for evaluation for antidepressant medication, particularly in the presence of vegetative signs of depression.
- Administer a standardized depression scale, such as the Beck Depression Inventory.
- Evaluate and utilize family and social supports.
- Assess socioeconomic issues and be familiar with relevant research literature.
- Consider developmental and cohort factors and the related research.
- Assess and refer to existing literature regarding incidence and manifestation of depression in certain demographic groups, such as gender, race/ethnicity, sexual orientation, and differential abilities.
- Evaluate affective, cognitive, and behavioral manifestations of depression.
- Encourage clients to verbalize their own understanding and hypotheses about their current depression.
- Be aware of both conscious and unconscious elements of the depression.
- Make judicious use of both insight-oriented exploration and cognitive-behavioral strategies, designed to restore optimum levels of functioning.
- Identify and explore distorted cognitions.
- Assess for and promote healthy self-care activities related to sleep, eating and exercise.
- In cases of severe unremitting depression, consider referral for evaluation of emerging biological treatment interventions including repetitive transcranial magnetic stimulation (rTMS).

---

particular note should be made regarding the need for culturally sensitive and knowledgeable assessment with people from diverse backgrounds. For diverse populations, the following areas merit particular attention.

- Consider differences in the presentation of symptoms and the cultural meaning of those symptoms (e.g., somatic complaints).
- Consider possible assumptions and beliefs about mental health providers and mental health treatment within the client(s) cultural system (e.g., social workers are part of the majority culture; "probably won't understand").
- Consider different ways of describing depressive symptoms related to cultural differences and/or geographical differences (e.g., "nerves").
- Consider the possible stigma associated with seeking mental health services from within or outside the client(s) system (e.g., shaming to family or "only for crazy people")

(Boyd-Franklin & Lockwood, 1999; Falicov, 1999, among others).

CASE ILLUSTRATION

The Client's Story

Jackie is a 53-year-old woman who describes herself as "chronically tired." According to Jackie, the highlight of her day as a licensed practical nurse (LPN) at a local metropolitan hospital is the ride home on public transportation when she can sleep or "zone out" because she does not have to make any bus changes. Jackie remembers her mother coming home from "doing hair" at the beauty salon and soaking her feet after standing all day. "I may have more education but I'm just as tired Mama was." Jackie's husband Fred, 57, has early onset Parkinson's disease and is not able to work any longer. He used to be "amazing with cars" but currently spends all of his time at home. Because he was self-employed, his health insurance has always come from Jackie's employment, so she feels she must stay at her job even if she had somewhere closer and less demanding to work. Jackie is able to pick up extra shifts when they are available. Their three children are 11 years, 15 years, and 19 years old. The 19-year-old son is in his second year at the community college, and although she is very proud of him, Jackie worries because he works or is at school all of the time. The youngest, a son also, still has his own quirky sense of humor but is "awfully quiet these days." Jackie jokingly says her 15-year-old daughter scares her to death; "I don't know whether to trust her or send her to a convent."

Jackie reports being depressed, particularly this last year. Work has gotten more demanding and stressful but does not seem to have changed dramatically during this time. Fred's health currently is at a plateau, which is a rarity in terms of the roller coaster of changes in his physical functioning. The children each have their own pressing needs, according to their mother, but "it's easier to not ask too many questions about what is going on with them." Jackie states that her general internist did not find anything wrong with her in a physical—her first in five years—that a month-long vacation would not help. Jackie did not find that much comfort or much help, but has not had the time to pursue any other opinions or specialists. She cannot remember when she had her eyes checked to update her glasses, when she has been to the dentist for the chronic pain she has in one tooth, or has been to see a gynecologist. Jackie says she just feels grateful that she has not had anything "go terribly wrong." She does get yearly mammograms because the hospital where she works provides these as an employee benefit. Jackie says that she has gained weight in the last year but thinks that is just what happens when you get older. Jackie's mother lives with them and has since Jackie's father passed away five years ago from emphysema. Her health is good despite "slowing down" at the age of 79.

Case Formulation

Jackie is faced with challenges from a variety of perspectives: (1) life cycle—children in adolescence (early, middle, and late adolescence); (2) continuing adaptation to husband's illness and declining health; (3) personal physical health changes and vulnerability; (4) increasing responsibilities associated with mother's aging;

(5) economic demands and full-time employment. These challenges all exist in the historical context of her own mother's difficult adaptation to Jackie's father's increasing frailty at mid-life and in the social context of women's traditional roles as caretakers.

Certainly, Jackie's presentation of extreme exhaustion, weight gain, and lack of self-care can paint a picture of depression as described by the *DSM-5*. In addition, as the social worker explores her symptoms further, Jackie reports feeling helpless and hopeless that things would change, also characteristics consistent with depression. Because Jackie has not been to a gynecologist recently and her understanding is incomplete about what kind of tests were completed with her internist, the social worker secures Jackie's permission to consult with her doctor. The social worker will need to determine whether any other physical issues were found, such as problems with her heart, blood pressure, thyroid, and gastroenterology, all areas that are important to check at Jackie's age. It also will be important for Jackie to see a gynecologist to check her hormone levels for evidence of perimenopause or menopause. Certainly, any of these physical issues could be contributing to, or causing her depression. When the social worker explores the issue of referrals, he or she takes cues from how Jackie describes her symptoms. For example, depending on culture, family, religious belief, ethnicity, and childhood environment, Jackie could describe her symptoms as being caused by a variety of factors, such as a punishment from God, the result of energy blockage or bad karma, or a bad genetic predisposition. Jackie's ideas about what is causing these symptoms will be important to discuss in light of a possible referral for antidepressant medication.

From a psychodynamic point of view, it will be helpful to explore prior losses Jackie has experienced in addition to the current losses and stressors. For example, Jackie's children are growing up and seeking more independence; her mother's physical stamina is declining; her husband's disease is not going to improve; and Jackie's own health is changing. All these factors can stimulate other historical feelings of helplessness. In asking whether there were other times in her life when Jackie has experienced this kind of helplessness and hopelessness, the social worker can determine whether there is a history of trauma or other significant losses, and what Jackie's prior methods of coping have been. Although the current losses in Jackie's life are developmentally appropriate, they also compound what seems to be stress consistent with her gender role. The social worker is familiar with the research on the enormous pressures experienced by Jackie as a member of a "sandwich" household, which requires her to care for both her own children and her remaining parent while continuing full-time employment. Likewise, Jackie may have set schemas or cognitive distortions about what she should be able to manage as a woman in this situation. Cognitive strategies can be used to help Jackie confront her own faulty perceptions about what is "normal" and "appropriate" functioning in her situation.

As with any client, the social worker explores social supports for Jackie. What kind of friendships does she have or has she had in the past? Is there a church or religious or spiritual practice that is helpful for her? What kind of neighborhood does she live in? Does she know her neighbors? Is there a support group for caregiving spouses through her work? Does she have a history of substance use or abuse? Is substance use or abuse occurring currently? What positive or negative ways has she tried to handle stress now and in the past?

Conclusion

A social work perspective suggests that clinical conditions are multi-determined and best understood through a bio-psychosocial–spiritual lens. It follows then, that in the case of depression, interventions should be multi-pronged, making use of the best possible theoretical and intervention approaches, some of which, in combination, may provide the best chances for short-term and long-term recovery. A necessary step in reviewing evidence-based practice is "integrating our critical appraisal with our clinical expertise and with our client's unique values and circumstances" (Thyer & Pignotti, 2011, p. 331). In the case of Jackie, the social worker made use of her psychodynamic understanding of unconscious processes, as well as the role of early schemas and current cognitive distortions.

Historically, social work theory and practice have been integrative. Particularly in our current practice arena, which demands brief but effective and hence efficient treatment interventions, the integration of cognitive-behavioral and psychodynamic theory is useful. This synthesis draws on the best of both traditions in an attempt to capture the complexity of the human experience, particularly as it manifests in the very common condition of depression. Furthermore, the increased attempts to understand the complicated processes of both depression and its treatment via research efforts in the areas of differential theoretical approaches and neurobiology hold great promise for the social worker. It becomes a professional responsibility to seek out the most recent research findings, in addition to the knowledge of theory and employment of social work practice skills. The conscious and deliberate use of perspectives and techniques from both theories allows swift and systematic interventions while preserving the value of the contextual and historical influences that impinge on the healthy functioning and experience of our clients.

WEBSITE

National Institute of Mental Health, information on depression. http://www.nimh.nih.gov/health/topics/depression/index.shtml.

References

Abbass, A. (2002). Short-term dynamic psychotherapies in the treatment of major depression. *Canadian Journal of Psychiatry, 47*(2), 193.

Areán, P. A., & Cook, B. (2002). Psychotherapy and combined psychotherapy/pharmacotherapy for late life depression. *Biological Psychiatry, 52*(3), 293–303.

Beck, A. (1961). *Beck depression inventory.* Philadelphia, PA: Center for Cognitive Therapy.

Beck, A. (1979). *Cognitive therapy of depression.* New York, NY: Guilford.

Beck, A. (1987). *Manual for the revised Beck depression inventory.* San Antonio, TX: Psychological Corporation.

Beck, J. (1995). *Cognitive therapy: Basics and beyond.* New York, NY: Guilford.

Beck, J. S. (2011). *Cognitive behavior therapy: Basics and beyond* (2nd ed.). New York, NY: Guilford.

Boyd-Franklin, N., & Lockwood, T. W. (1999). Spirituality and religion: Implications for psychotherapy with African American clients and families. In F. Walsh (Ed.), *Spiritual resources in family therapy.* New York, NY: Guilford.

Coelho, H. F., Canter, P. H., & Ernst, E. (2013). Mindfulness-based cognitive therapy: Evaluating current evidence and informing future research. *Psychology of Consciousness: Theory, Research, and Practice, 1*(S), 97–107. doi:10.1037/2326-5523.1.S.97

De Maat, S., Dekker, J., Schoevers, R., & DeJonghe, F. (2006). Relative efficacy of psychotherapy and pharmacotherapy in the treatment of depression: A meta-analysis. *Psychotherapy Research, 16*(5), 562–572.

Falicov, C. J. (1999). Religion and spiritual folk traditions in immigrant families. In F. Walsh (Ed.), *Spiritual resources in family therapy*. New York, NY: Guilford.

Finn, C. A. (2000). Treatment of adolescent depression: A review of intervention approaches. *International Journal of Adolescence and Youth, 84,* 253–269.

Fonagy, P., Roth, A., & Higgins, A. (2005) Psychodynamic psychotherapy: Evidence based practice and clinical wisdom. *Bulletin of the Menninger Clinic, 69*(1), 1–59.

Gabalda, I. C. (2010). The case of Gabriel: A linguistic therapy of evaluation perspective. *Journal of Constructivist Psychology,* 23:4–24.

Gabalda, I. C., & Neimeyer, R. A. (2010). Theory and practice in the cognitive psychotherapies: Convergence and divergence. *Journal of Constructivist Psychology,* 23:65–83.

Gega, L., Smith, J., & Reynolds, S. (2013). Cognitive behavior therapy (CBT) for depression by computer vs. therapist: Patient experiences and therapeutic processes.

Kessler, R. C., Petukhova, M., Sampson, N. A., Zaslavsky, A. M., & Wittchen, H. (2012). Twelve-month and lifetime prevalence and lifetime morbid risk of anxiety and mood disorders in the United States. *International Journal of Methods in Psychiatric Research, 21*(3), 169–184. doi:10.1002/mpr.1359

Leahy, R. L. (2003). *Cognitive therapy techniques: A practitioner's guide*. New York, NY: Guilford.

Luyten, P., & Blatt, S. J. (2012). Psychodynamic treatment of depression. *Psychiatric Clinics of North America, 35*(1), 111–129. doi:10.1016/j.psc.2012.01.001

Neimeyer, R. A. (2010). Symptoms and significance: Constructivist contributions to the treatment of performance anxiety. *Journal of Constructivist Psychology, 23,* 42–64.

Newman, C. F. (2010). The case of Gabriel: Treatment with Beckian Cognitive Therapy. *Journal of Constructivist Psychology, 23,* 25–41.

Nock, M. K., Deming, C. A., Chiu, W., Hwang, I., Angermeyer, M., Borges, G., . . . Kessler, R. C. (2012). Mental disorders, comorbidity, and suicidal behavior. In M. K. Nock, G. Borges, Y. Ono (Eds.), *Suicide: Global perspectives from the WHO World Mental Health Surveys* (pp. 148–163). New York, NY: Cambridge University Press.

Paris, J. (1996). *Social factors in the personality disorders: A biopsychosocial approach to etiology and treatment*. Cambridge: Cambridge University Press.

Reinecke, M. A., & Davison, M. R. (2002). *Comparative treatments of depression*. New York, NY: Springer.

Parikh, S. V., Segal, Z. V., Grigoriadis, S., Ravindran, A. V., Kennedy, S. H., Lam, R. W., Patten, S. B. (2009). Canadian Network for Mood and Anxiety Treatments (CANMAT) Clinical guidelines for the management of major depressive disorder in adults. II. Psychotherapy alone or in combination with antidepressant medication. *Journal of Affective Disorders, 117* (Suppl. 1), S15–S25. doi:10.1016/j.jad.2009.06.042. Retrieved from http://www.sciencedirect.com/science/article/pii/S0165032709003292

Thyer, B. A., & Pignotti, M. (2011). Evidence-based practices do not exist. *Clinical Social Work Journal, 39*(4), 328–333.

Imel, Z. E., Malterer, M. B., McKay, K. M., Wampold, B. E. (2008). A meta-analysis of psychotherapy and medication in unipolar depression and dysthymia. *Journal of Affective Disorders, 110*(3), 197–206. doi:10.1016/j.jad.2008.03.018. Retrieved from http://www.sciencedirect.com/science/article/pii/S0165032708001419

Zeiss, A. M. (1997). Treatment of late life depression: A response to the NIH Consensus Conference. *Behavior Therapy, 28*(1), 3–21.

77 The Assessment and Treatment of Posttraumatic Stress Disorder

M. Elizabeth Vonk

People who are exposed to a traumatic event, including those who help with recovery efforts, may perceive that their own or others' physical integrity is threatened and often react with horror, fear, or helplessness. Any number of a variety of symptoms may be expected following traumatic events (Woo & Keatinge, 2008):

- Emotional. Reactions are generally very intense and may include fear, anxiety, anger, guilt, depression, and numbing. Many may feel overwhelmed by the intensity of their emotions.
- Cognitive. Reactions include difficulty concentrating and intrusive thoughts. In addition, survivors must struggle to make sense of an experience that contradicts formerly held assumptions regarding sense of control, safety, trust in self and others, personal power, and self-esteem.
- Somatic. Reactions may include sleep disturbance, nightmares, eating difficulties, and a variety of bodily complaints.
- Interpersonal. Reactions include disruptions in intimate and familial relationships, vocational impairment, and generalized social withdrawal.

Although symptomatic responses to trauma are normal, 7%–8% of people in the United States will develop posttraumatic stress disorder (PTSD) during their lifetime (Woo & Keatinge, 2008). Many factors are related to the development of PTSD following a traumatic event, including demographics, the nature of the traumatic event, and pre- and post-trauma characteristics (Keane, Marshall, & Taft, 2006;

Woo & Keatinge, 2008). People of all ages develop PTSD, but it appears children and the elderly are particularly susceptible. In addition, women appear to develop PTSD at a significantly higher rate than men. Life-threatening or extremely intense traumatic events, a history of childhood abuse or psychiatric disorder, and elevated levels of life stress are additional risk factors for the development of PTSD. Conversely, the availability of social support following traumatic events appears to decrease psychopathology.

The current *Diagnostic and Statistical Manual of Mental Disorders, Fifth Edition (DSM-5)* definition of PTSD includes eight criteria (American Psychiatric Association, 2013):

- Criterion A. The person must be confronted directly or indirectly by an experience of death or threatened death; actual or threatened serious injury; actual or threatened sexual violence; or repeated exposure to the aversive details of a traumatic event in the performance of professional duties.
- Criterion B. The person must have at least one symptom of persistently re-experiencing the traumatic event, including intrusive images or thoughts, dreams about the event, a sense that the event is recurring, intense distress when reminded of the event, or physiological reactivity to event-related cues.
- Criterion C. The person must have at least one symptom of avoidance, including avoidance of thoughts, feelings, or talk about the event; or avoidance of activities, places, or people that are reminders of the event.

- Criterion D. The person must have at least two negative alternations in cognitions and mood, including inability to remember parts of the experience; diminished interest in important pre-trauma activities; sense of detachment from others; inability to experience a full range of emotions; or negative thoughts about self or the world.
- Criterion E. The person must have a minimum of two symptoms of increased arousal, including sleep difficulties, irritability or aggression, trouble concentrating, heightened startle response, or hypervigilance.
- Criterion F. The person must have the required array of symptoms for more than one month.
- Criterion G. The person must be experiencing impaired functioning at school, at work, or in relationships.
- Criterion H. Symptoms must not be due to medication, illness, or substance abuse.

In addition, the *DSM-5* definition includes two specifiers: (1) with dissociative symptoms, if symptoms of depersonalization or derealization are present at high levels; and (2) with delayed expression, if full criteria for diagnosis do not occur until at least six months after the stressor.

CASE STUDY

Before moving ahead to describe assessment of and intervention for PTSD, I would like to present a case study that will be used throughout this chapter to illustrate various aspects of therapeutic work with people who have PTSD.

Ben, a 26-year-old European-American graduate student sought therapy at a university counseling center following a motor vehicle accident that occurred four months earlier. Ben was a passenger in the car and sustained minor injuries. The driver, a close friend, was fatally injured. Ben remembers very little about the accident, has not talked to his fiancé or parents about what happened, and has "buried himself" in school work hoping to keep his mind away from thoughts of it. He reports feeling numb about his friend's death, stating, "I haven't cried about it at all, even at his funeral." He wonders why he lived through it and thinks that he "should have done something" to keep his friend

from dying. He is also worried about how he has changed since the accident, thinking that he should be "over it." Formerly a confident driver, Ben now feels "jumpy." While he used to think of himself as "mellow," he now feels irritable and impatient with his friends' "constant joking around" and his fiancé's "trivial worries" about their wedding plans. What bothers him most and prompted his visit to the counseling center are increasingly disturbing nightmares that disrupt his sleep and "flashbacks" that interfere with his concentration during the day. Ben wants to return to his former high level of functioning so he can complete his dissertation and enjoy relationships with his fiancé and friends. Ben reported no previous trauma and no medical complications.

ASSESSMENT OF POSTTRAUMATIC STRESS DISORDER

The diagnosis of PTSD is generally made within the context of a complete bio-psychosocial assessment. The assessment and diagnosis are based on in-depth clinical interview and utilization of standardized instruments.

The clinical interview allows the interviewer to explore the traumatic event and its aftermath in the context of the client's life. Such interviewing can be challenging, requiring the interviewer to maintain a focus on the trauma and associated memories, thoughts, and feelings; avoid victim-blaming; actively listen to frightening or horrifying stories; and tolerate expressions of strong emotion.

In general, the clinical interview should include the client's story about the traumatic event and aftermath; current cognitive, emotional, somatic, and interpersonal difficulties related to the event; pre-trauma level of functioning; and ways in which the person has coped with the event. In addition, the client's family history, previous traumatic or abusive experiences, current living situation, availability of support, and expectations of therapy should be explored. Consideration must also be given to the client's cultural background in order to gain greater understanding of the context and meaning of the trauma from the client's perspective (Woo & Keatinge, 2008). Finally, the interviewer must be alert to signs and symptoms of other difficulties that often co-occur with PTSD, such as suicidal or homicidal ideation; problems in family functioning; and mood, substance use, and personality disorders (Woo & Keatinge, 2008).

The diagnostic interview may be enhanced with the additional use of one or more standardized assessment tools. Structured interviews provide opportunity for in-depth exploration including detection of potential co-occurring mental disorders. Self-report measures may be valuable for assessing change in symptomatology over the course of treatment. Detailed information about the following and other structured interviews and self-report measures may be found on the assessment page of the National Center for PTSD (NCPTSD). (http://www.ptsd .va.gov/professional/pages/assessments/assessment.asp). Please note that at the time of this writing, assessment tools are in the process of being revised in response to changes in the diagnosis of PTSD in the *DSM-5* (APA, 2013).

- Structured Interviews
  - The Clinician Administered PTSD Scale (CAPS): assesses PTSD symptoms and impact on functioning related to single or multiple traumas
  - The Structured Interview for PTSD (SI-PTSD): assesses PTSD symptoms and behavioral and survivor guilt
- Self-report Measures
  - Screen for Posttraumatic Stress Symptoms (SPTSS): assesses PTSD symptoms unrelated to specific trauma; used as a preliminary screen for presence of PTSD
  - Posttraumatic Stress Disorder Check List (PCL): available in three versions, namely, military, civilian, and in relation to a specific stressor; assesses symptoms of PTSD and is useful for monitoring change during and after intervention

Treatment Goals and Objectives

Treatment goals and objectives follow directly from thorough assessment and are always individualized to particular clients. The following types of goals, however, are frequently included in effective interventions for PTSD.

- Increasing knowledge about and "normalizing" responses to trauma and PTSD

- Strengthening coping skills and social support systems
- Reducing guilt and eliminating self-blame
- Reducing symptoms
- Increasing functioning in social roles, such as at work and in the family
- Integrating the trauma into the client's life experience

Case Study: Assessment and Treatment Goals

Ben's assessment included a thorough unstructured clinical interview, completion of the Structured Interview for PTSD, and completion of the self-report Posttraumatic Stress Disorder Checklist (PCL). Through this process, the social worker at the counseling center determined that Ben's signs and symptoms met the DSM-5 criteria for PTSD. Ben experienced a traumatic car accident in which a close friend lost his life; he felt that his own life was threatened (Criterion A). Since the trauma occurred, Ben has had persistent re-experiencing symptoms including nightmares and intrusive thoughts and images (Criterion B). Ben has had symptoms of avoidance including avoiding thoughts of the accident (Criterion C). He has experienced alterations in cognition and mood, including feelings of numbness and inability to remember details of the accident (Criterion D). He also has had increased arousal symptoms of irritability and hypervigilance while driving (Criterion E). His symptoms have been present since the accident occurred four months ago (Criterion F) and they have been negatively affecting his dissertation writing and interpersonal relationships with his friends and fiancé (Criterion G). Finally, the symptoms are not due to medication, substance abuse, or medical condition (Criterion H).

In addition to making the diagnosis, the social worker noted that Ben functioned quite well prior to the accident, had experienced no previous abuse or trauma, and had a good support system that included family and friends. Although Ben did not appear to have a co-occurring mental disorder, his customary coping resources appeared to be overwhelmed. He had developed maladaptive cognitions related to survivor's guilt and gender-related expectations of himself, and his attempts to avoid processing the experience were impeding his recovery.

Ben's treatment goals and objectives were defined collaboratively with the social worker. By working together, the following mutually defined goals and objectives were established:

- Increase Ben's knowledge about trauma and PTSD
  - Ben will understand "normal" emotional, cognitive, somatic, and interpersonal responses to trauma.
  - Ben will educate his fiancé about trauma and PTSD.
- Increase Ben's ability to actively manage his anxiety at work and in social settings
  - Ben will increase his ability to concentrate at work.
  - Ben will increase his enjoyment in social settings.
- Decrease the frequency of Ben's nightmares and intrusive thoughts of the accident
- Increase Ben's ability to tolerate exposure to thoughts and feelings that are reminders of the accident
  - Ben will be able to describe the accident to the social worker.
  - Ben will be able to describe his experience, its aftermath, and ongoing progress toward recovery with his fiancé and father.
- Modify Ben's beliefs about the accident that are associated with disturbing emotions
  - Ben will modify his belief that he is somehow to blame for his friend's death.
  - Ben will identify and modify other disturbing thoughts about himself, others, and the world in relation to the accident.

Ben and the social worker agreed to work toward these goals with weekly meetings for a period of three months, at which time they would reassess to see what additional work might be needed.

TREATMENT OF POSTTRAUMATIC STRESS DISORDER

A variety of interventions, both pharmacological and psychosocial, have been tested and found effective in the treatment of PTSD. The strongest evidence has been found for the use of exposure, cognitive, and anxiety management therapies (Foa, Keane, Friedman, & Cohen, 2009; Veterans Administration [VA]/U.S. Department of Defense [DoD], 2010). Although each intervention is described separately, it is important to remember that most practitioners combine a variety of interventions when treating a client with PTSD. Because the range of symptomatology is so great, the particular combination of interventions must be based on the individual needs of each client. More detailed guidance on implementation and individualization of effective interventions for PTSD can be found in *Clinical Practice Guideline for Management of Posttraumatic Stress* (VA/DoD, 2010). In addition, several treatment packages have been developed that combine and focus efficacious interventions to treat PTSD in response to specific types of traumas. These include, for example, Trauma-focused Cognitive Behavioral Therapy (TF-CBT), developed to treat children between the ages of 3 and 18 years who have experienced traumatic abuse (Cohen, Mannarino, & Deblinger, 2006); and Cognitive Processing Therapy (CPT), developed to treat PTSD related to the trauma of rape (Resick & Schnicke, 1997).

Pharmacological Treatments

In general, psychotropic drugs are used to provide relief from specific symptoms, such as anxiety or depression, enabling the trauma survivor to make better use of concurrent psychosocial therapy. Based on an extensive review of empirical research, the NCPTSD's *Clinician's Guide to Medications for PTSD* (Jeffries, 2009) describes the classes of drugs that have been used to treat PTSD, evidence of effectiveness, and both benefits and risks of utilizing particular drugs. Among others, these drugs include antidepressants (tricyclics, monoamine oxidase inhibitors [MAOIs], and serotonergic reuptake inhibitors [SSRIs]), anxiolytics (benzodiazepines, buspirone), and sleep aids. Without question, the strongest evidence of effectiveness has been found to support the use of serotonergic reuptake inhibitors (SSRIs). Despite the positive effect of SSRIs on PTSD related symptomatology, treatment of PTSD through the use of pharmacology alone has not proven to be as effective as various psychosocial treatments (Keane, Marshall, & Taft, 2006).

Exposure Therapy

Exposure therapy is a behavioral intervention that involves activation of the traumatic memory through the use of associated imaginal or in vivo cues. It is used to decrease avoidance, intrusive thoughts, flashbacks, trauma-related fears, and panic attacks. The exposure must be of significant duration so as to allow the client's anxiety level to substantially subside in the presence of the feared, but harmless cue. Because the idea of confronting or reliving the traumatic event is frightening, survivors need to have a clear rationale and understanding of how exposure therapies work in order to be informed participants in the intervention. In addition, the development and maintenance of a trusting therapeutic relationship seems to be essential for successful completion of exposure therapies.

Cognitive Therapy

The goal of Cognitive Therapy (CT) is to learn to identify and eliminate specific thoughts that are causing negative emotional reactions and behaviors. This is achieved by challenging the thoughts through a process of logical examination of their veracity or functionality, followed by replacement of those that are dysfunctional with more reasonable ones. Dysfunctional beliefs following traumatic events vary, but several themes are common, including overgeneralizations about danger in the world and one's personal vulnerability, unrealistic self-blame and guilt about the event, loss of meaning for one's life, and broken trust in others and self (Woo & Keatinge, 2008).

Anxiety Management

A variety of behavioral and anxiety management interventions have been used to help people with PTSD cope with and manage emotions. One such anxiety management program, stress inoculation training (SIT) was developed by Meichenbaum (1997) to treat a variety of anxiety disorders, including PTSD. SIT aims to help clients manage and reduce anxiety through the development of skills such as relaxation and breathing techniques, cognitive restructuring, guided self-dialogue, thought-stopping, and role-playing. The treatment takes place in three phases. First, the client is educated about responses to trauma and PTSD. Next, the coping skills are taught to and rehearsed by the client. Finally, the newly developed skills are applied through graduated exposure to stressful cues and memories associated with the traumatic event.

Eye Movement Desensitization and Reprocessing

Eye Movement Desensitization and Reprocessing (EMDR) combines aspects of cognitive and imaginal exposure techniques with saccadic eye movements in a specified protocol (Shapiro, 2001). Although many studies have supported the effectiveness of EMDR for the treatment of PTSD, some skepticism about the intervention remains. Specifically, the theoretical foundation and the necessity of eye-movements in the treatment have been questioned. Research examining effectiveness of the components that make up EMDR provide some support of the likelihood that clinically relevant components include exposure, cognitive restructuring, and emotional processing (VA/DoD, 2010).

Posttraumatic Growth

Calhoun and Tedeschi (2012) call attention to the potential for growth following traumatic experiences. Without minimizing the negative psychological consequences following trauma for many survivors, these authors examine the ability of some trauma survivors to experience significant personal growth following traumatic experiences. They review literature that identifies several areas of growth, including strengthened interpersonal relationships; changed self-perception that includes both increased vulnerability and strength; and changed philosophy of life that includes a shift in priorities and greater appreciation of life. In addition, the authors address facilitation of posttraumatic growth.

Case Study: Interventions and Evaluation

Having decided on treatment goals and preferred interventions, Ben indicated that he would like to start with exposure therapy to decrease his nightmares and "flashbacks." Secondarily, he hoped to be able to share some of his experience with his fiancé "to help her understand what I've been through." Knowing that the success of exposure relies on a strong therapeutic relationship, the social worker spent time preparing Ben for the intervention. Imaginal exposure was used initially, but was soon followed by in vivo exposure in which Ben was asked to drive on the street where the accident took place.

During the course of the exposure intervention, the social worker began to identify Ben's distressing beliefs about the accident, his friend's death, safety, and self-blame. A maladaptive cognitive theme emerged in that Ben had come to believe he was to blame for the accident, in part because he asked his friend to wait for him before leaving the apartment, placing their car in harm's way. After teaching Ben the basics of cognitive therapy, the social worker and Ben began to work toward modifying his self-blaming and other dysfunctional beliefs related to the accident.

In addition to exposure and cognitive therapies, the social worker taught Ben a number of anxiety management skills including relaxation training and controlled breathing techniques. With encouragement from the social worker, Ben also was able to enlist his fiancé and one other close friend for increased support.

At the end of three months, Ben was pleased with his progress in several areas. His intrusive and avoidance symptoms had decreased, he was engaging in less self-blame, and he was once again enjoying his relationship with his fiancé. However, he was still experiencing more difficulty with concentration than he would like. The social worker reviewed options with Ben, including continuing with cognitive therapy, adding more focus on anxiety management skills, or augmenting treatment with medication. Ben preferred to continue with cognitive

therapy and learn more anxiety management techniques. As Ben continued to make progress with his goals, the social worker increased the time between sessions. During the last session, Ben reported that he felt ready to stop treatment. He went on to describe his current thoughts and beliefs about surviving a deadly car crash. Like many survivors of trauma, he was able to acknowledge personal growth along with the difficulties (Calhoun & Tedeschi, 2012). Although he still experienced sadness, moments of anxiety, and anger about the accident and loss of his friend, Ben believed that he had found strengths in himself that he was unaware of before the accident. He also had discovered the value of asking for and receiving support from his close friends.

Throughout treatment, the social worker monitored Ben's progress, relying both on Ben's report and on clinical judgment. In addition, however, she utilized two quantitative methods. First, she utilized goal attainment scaling (GAS) (Vonk, Tripodi, & Epstein, 2006). GAS is a useful tool for monitoring progress because the scales can be tailored to the individual's goals, are easy to administer, can be administered repeatedly, and can be weighted according to the relative importance of each of the goals. A 5-point goal attainment scale was developed for each of Ben's goals and at the start of each session Ben rated his progress on each of them. The use of the GAS method is illustrated in Figure 77.1, showing Ben's progress on the goal of decreasing the frequency of his nightmares. Finally, the PCL, administered at the outset of treatment was readministered at the close of treatment, at which time Ben no longer met the criteria for the diagnosis of PTSD.

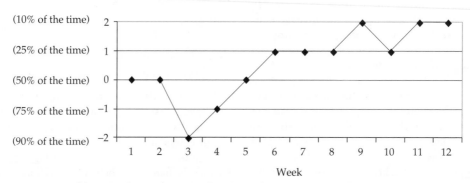

Figure 77.1 GAS self-report for occurrence of nightmares each week.

Ben's assessment and treatment story provide an example of how empirically supported methods can be used for effective assessment and treatment of PTSD. Unfortunately, unlike Ben, not all clients have PTSD uncomplicated by previous traumas, co-occurring substance use or mental disorders, or support system deficits. In spite of complications, social workers will be best able to provide assistance to people with PTSD through the use of assessment and treatment methods for which effectiveness has been empirically supported.

HELPFUL WEBSITES

The International Society for Traumatic Stress Studies—Treating Trauma. http://www.istss.org/TreatingTrauma.htm

The National Center for Posttraumatic Stress Disorder: http://www.ptsd.va.gov/index.asp

The National Institute of Mental Health—PTSD. http://www.nimh.nih.gov/health/topics/post-traumatic-stress-disorder-ptsd/index.shtml

PILOTS Database—Electronic Index to Traumatic Stress Literature. http://www.ptsd.va.gov/professional/pilots-database/pilots-db.asp

Trauma Focused CBT. http://tfcbt.musc.edu/

References

American Psychiatric Association. (2013). *Diagnostic and statistical manual of mental disorders, fifth edition*. Washington, DC: Author.

Calhoun, L. G., & Tedeschi, R. G. (2012). *Posttraumatic growth in clinical practice*. New York, NY: Brunner Routledge.

Cohen, J. A., Mannarino, A. P., & Deblinger, E. (2006). *Treating trauma and traumatic grief in children and adolescents*. New York, NY: The Guilford Press.

Foa, E., Keane, T., Friedman, M., & Cohen, J. (Eds.). (2009). *Effective treatments for PTSD: Practice guidelines from the International Society for Traumatic Stress Studies*. New York, NY: Guilford Press.

Jeffries, M. (2009, January). *Clinician's guide to medications for PTSD*. National Center for PTSD. Retrieved from http://www.ptsd.va.gov/professional/pages/clinicians-guide-to-medications-for-ptsd.asp.

Keane, T. M., Marshall, A. D., & Taft, C. T. (2006). Posttraumatic stress disorder: etiology, epidemiology, and treatment outcome. *Annual Review of Clinical Psychology, 2*, 161–197.

Meichenbaum, D. (1997). *Treating posttraumatic stress disorder: A handbook and practice manual for therapy*. Chichester, UK: Wiley.

Resick, P. A., & Schnicke, M. K. (1997). *Cognitive processing therapy for rape victims*. Newberry Park, CA: Sage.

Shapiro, F. (2001). *Eye movement desensitization and reprocessing: Basic principles, protocols, and procedures* (2nd ed.). New York, NY: Guilford Press.

Veterans Administration (VA)/U. S. Department of Defense (DoD). (2010). *Clinical practice guideline for management of posttraumatic stress*. Washington, DC: Author. Retrieved from http://www.healthquality.va.gov/Post_Traumatic_Stress_Disorder_PTSD.asp.

Vonk, M. E., Tripodi, T., & Epstein, I. (2006). *Research techniques for clinical social workers*. New York, NY: Columbia Press.

Woo, S. M., & Keatinge, C. (2008). *Mental disorders across the lifespan*. Hoboken, N.J.: Wiley.

78 Guidelines for Clinical Social Work with Clients with Dissociative Disorders

Lina Hartocollis & Jacqueline Strait

DISSOCIATION AND THE DISSOCIATIVE DISORDERS

Dissociation as a construct is somewhat elusive; it refers to both an active process of defense as well as a state of mind (Howell, 2005). In the most basic terms, dissociation describes a rigid separation of parts of self or experience, including separation or splits between thoughts, consciousness, affect, memory, identity, behavior, or perception (Cozolino, 2002). People refer to this experience in everyday language as "spacing out," "going into neutral gear," or "being on auto-pilot." Clinically, we refer to such processes as psychic numbing, dissociative amnesia, depersonalization, derealization, and identity fragmentation. In each of these manifestations of dissociation, there is a turning away from external reality and an intense, gripping focus on the internal world.

Dissociative experiences are thought to occur on a continuum from normative to problematic to pathological. Mild psychic experiences of dissociation are exceedingly common; for example, instances of so-called highway hypnosis in which you find yourself driving a car as if on auto-pilot, having little or no recall for how you got to your destination. On the other end of the continuum are dissociative experiences that serve a defensive function against overwhelming affect. When a person faces an external or internal experience that is too much to bear, the automatic response is to seek help, fight, or flee. If these attempts are unsuccessful, the person is left alone enduring overwhelming affect. He/she may then enter into a detached, trance-like state, effectively employing dissociation as a hypometabolic regulatory process to produce numbness and a profound experience of detachment in order to regulate distress (Schore, 2001). The use of dissociation in this instance suggests a failed response to early help-seeking behavior.

Consider, for example, the young incest victim who cannot fight, cannot flee, and often feels she has no one to turn to for help. Dissociation steps in to provide, to paraphrase Putnam (1992), an escape when there is no escape. In the face of the horror of rape, the little girl imagines and experiences herself floating on the ceiling, looking down at the gruesome scene below. Although this helps the child to "forget" the abuse, surviving to go to school the next day, she must act as if the horrors of the preceding night did not occur. She begins to rely on dissociation not only as a defense to survive the moment of the trauma, but as a state of mind that allows her to hold these intolerable memories, affective experiences and bodily states "out of mind"—segregated from the conscious day-to-day experience of self.

Although dissociation as a defensive strategy can be normative under high levels of stress, when dissociation becomes a state of mind it signals that dissociation has become an adaptation to extreme or ongoing trauma. It is being relied upon relentlessly, and often outside of the person's autonomous control. Dissociative disorders are diagnosed when pathological dissociative experiences such as those described above are pervasive and severe enough to interfere with the person's ability to function.

The *Diagnostic and Statistical Manual of Mental Disorders, Fifth Edition* (DSM-5) (American Psychiatric Association, 2013) catalogues five types of Dissociative Disorders:

- *Dissociative identity disorder:* a subjectively experienced and/or outwardly observed fragmenting of the person's identity into two or more distinct personality states
- *Dissociative amnesia*: in which the person suddenly loses the ability to remember important personal information in a manner that is experienced as traumatic or stressful and not part of ordinary forgetfulness
- *Depersonalization/derealization disorder:* characterized by experiences of depersonalization, that is, feelings of being disconnected from one's mental processes or body, and/or experiences of derealization, in other words, perceiving one's surroundings as if in a dreamlike or foggy state
- *Other specified dissociative disorder:* used when there are dissociative symptoms that cause significant distress and impairment but do not meet the full criteria for a dissociative disorder and the clinician chooses to further specify, for example by recording "other specified dissociative disorder: dissociative trance"
- *And unspecified dissociative disorder:* used in cases where the clinician decides not to specify why criteria for a particular dissociative disorder are not met.

A history of trauma is presumed in most cases of dissociative disorders. Although the *DSM* categorizes dissociative disorders separately from trauma- and stressor-related disorders, the two diagnostic entities were placed next to one another so as to acknowledge the "close relationship" that exists between them (American Psychiatric Association, 2013, p. 291). In fact, recent trauma theorists have begun to speculate that dissociation as both a defense and mental structure plays a role in many trauma-related and personality disorders, including posttraumatic stress disorder (PTSD), complex posttraumatic stress disorder, borderline personality disorder and antisocial personality disorder (Bromberg, 2011; Herman, 1992; Howell, 2005; Stein, 2010; Van der Hart, Nijenhuis, & Solomon, 2010).

Underlying the assumption that dissociative phenomena exist in many mental disorders is the belief that dissociation is a "normal hypnoid capacity of the mind" (Bromberg, 2011, p. 178) necessary to manage the overwhelming number of daily stressors that make contact with the brain. The distinction between this mundane and even adaptive human capacity and a dissociative disorder is the degree of rigidity between these experiences of oneself. If a person can autonomously choose in which contexts to display which constellations of self and can move fluidly between experiences of self at will, then this is not a disorder. Despite various social roles, the person can maintain an awareness of one continuous identity with recall for experiences of him/herself in each of the other roles (Chu, 2011).

When the person loses control of the switches from one experience of self to the other, when he/she cannot move fluidly between states to adapt to the context, or when he/she cannot maintain conscious recall of his/her experience in alternate states, normative dissociation becomes pathological. The most extreme manifestation of this occurs in the condition known as dissociative identity disorder or DID.

DISSOCIATIVE IDENTITY DISORDER

At one time known as multiple personality disorder, dissociative identity disorder is a condition that develops post-traumatically, most often in persons with a history of severe childhood sexual and physical abuse. As the name implies, individuals with DID have difficulty maintaining a unified sense of self. They experience themselves as having more than one personality state or identity, each with its own thoughts, feelings, behavior patterns, likes, dislikes, history, and other characteristics. In some cultures, these personality states may be experienced and described as an experience of possession. Accompanying the distinct personality states or possession experience are dissociative experiences and defenses of the sort described earlier in this chapter—dramatic fluctuations and splits in affect, behavior, memory, consciousness, and cognition that may or may not be visible to people other than the afflicted individual.

Once thought to be a rare and exotic condition, DID has gained public attention and clinical recognition over the past 30 years, and reports of its incidence have grown. Widely varying explanations for this increase have been suggested, from identification of previously misdiagnosed cases, on the one hand, to suggestion, hysterical epidemic, and fad on the other. In any event, it is likely that various overlapping cultural trends helped to shape both current constructions of DID and the controversy surrounding it. Prominent among these are heightened public and clinical awareness of child abuse, and a shift toward theories of psychopathology that emphasize trauma and dissociation over other explanatory processes. Popularized accounts of multiple personality, such as *The Three Faces of Eve* and *Sybil*, also undoubtedly exerted influence, serving as "prototypical illness narratives" that help to shape clinicians' and clients' constructions of the disorder (Hartocollis, 1998). Recent prevalence rates of the dissociative disorders have been reported in the range of 12%–38% in outpatient populations (Brand, Classen, Lanius et al., 2009), and 18% in the general population (Sar et al., 2007). In 2011, the International Society for the Study of Trauma and Dissociation Treatment Guidelines (ISST-D, 2011) put the prevalence rate of DID in the general population at 1.1%–3%.

DID has been described as a covert disorder because afflicted individuals often try to hide their distress and their multiplicity from others and sometimes even from themselves. This can make the condition difficult to recognize in a clinical setting. Further complicating the diagnosis and assessment process, persons with DID may experience symptoms that overlap with those of mood disorders, substance abuse disorders, eating disorders, obsessive-compulsive disorder, sexual disorders, or sleep disorders; and, in fact, all of these disorders are often comorbid with dissociative disorders (Howell, 2011). Historically, individuals with DID have been misdiagnosed as suffering from schizophrenia or borderline personality disorder, resulting in improper treatment choices and poor outcomes. This fraught assessment scenario makes it especially important that clinicians are armed with knowledge about dissociative disorders and DID.

The International Society for the Study of Dissociation (2005) lists the following clinical clues to the existence of DID: memory distortion and lapses, including fugue (e.g., reports of "lost time); depersonalization; hearing voices experienced as coming from within the head or self; a history of unsuccessful psychiatric treatments; a history of severe and persistent emotional and/or physical childhood trauma; flashbacks of traumatic memories; identity confusion, and identity alteration.

During the assessment interview(s), clinicians should ask questions about and be alert to clients' reports of strange experiences and happenings that could be markers for memory lapses, dissociative phenomena, depersonalization and derealization, and multiplicity. For example, a client of one of the authors described finding clothes in her closet she couldn't remember buying, waking up with a haircut she didn't remember getting, and meeting strangers who claimed to know her though sometimes by a different name. To assess for the presence of derealization and depersonalization, Howell (2011) suggests asking the following questions: "Does it ever seem to you that things are not real?" and "Do you sometimes feel that you are not in your body?" (p. 152). However, as Howell (2011) cautions, questions aimed at uncovering a history of abuse should be approached with care, as they may trigger flashbacks and overwhelm the client's capacity to regulate his or her emotions.

When assessing for the presence of DID, clinicians should also take note of changes in appearance and behavior, for example, a client who wears sexually provocative clothes and speaks and behaves in a flirtatious manner during one clinical session, and then comes to another session dressed in child-like clothing, speaking in a childish voice, and carrying a stuffed animal. The use of the word "we" when referring to oneself is also noteworthy. DID is generally diagnosed in adults and older adolescents. When assessing for DID in children, it is important to rule-out normative experiences of imaginary playmates or fantasy play. Females are much more likely to be diagnosed with DID than males.

A number of measurement instruments that detect the presence of dissociation and dissociative symptomatology can be used to aid screening and assessment of DID. The Trauma Symptom Inventory Dissociation Scale (TSI) rates 100 dissociative symptoms according to frequency on a 4-point scale (Briere and Scott, 2012). The Dissociative Experiences Scale (DES) is a self-report screening tool that taps disturbances in identity, memory, awareness, and other mental processes that are thought to be indicators of dissociation (Carlson & Putnam, 1993). As Howell (2011) cautions, although the DES screens for the possible presence of a dissociative disorder, a low score does not rule out the presence of a dissociative disorder nor does a high score confirm the presence. The Dissociative Disorders Interview Schedule (DDIS)—DSM-IV version is a structured interview based on the DSM-IV diagnosis for dissociative disorders. It may be administered in 30 to 45 minutes (Ross, 1997). Structured clinical instruments that map to DSM-5 dissociative disorders criteria sets have not been published as of the writing of this chapter.

CASE EXAMPLE: EVOLUTION OF A DIAGNOSIS

Making the diagnosis of DID comes with much questioning, doubt, and even angst. Research suggests that it takes between five and twelve years of (probably failing) treatment for a client with DID to receive the proper diagnosis (as cited in Howell, 2011). Clients may be unaware of their own alter identities or committed to keeping alter identities secret, either because of intense shame about the identity segregation or due to a desperate and perhaps life-sustaining need to keep parts of self separate.

Emily was the first client of one of the authors to be diagnosed with DID. It took seven months of nearly weekly treatment to accept this diagnosis. Emily entered treatment complaining of "poor memory." She worried she was "blocking things out" and identified that she was especially prone to forget incidents of feeling in pain—sad, angry, or needy. Emily shared that she often felt "not like a real person." She suffered a sense of inauthenticity and emptiness in her relationships. I suspected a dissociative process was at play. After many weeks of treatment, Emily shared that she thought her house was haunted. She identified a "friendly ghost" who inhabited her house and said his name was Rickie. She described Rickie as somewhat similar to an imaginary friend—itself a dissociative experience quite normative in childhood (Chu, 2011). In this case, the child learns to split off unwanted feelings and attribute them to his/her imaginary friend. It appeared Emily was utilizing this same mechanism. Rickie served as an antidote to her pressing loneliness as well as a repository of her rightful anger and self-protective functions, long since disavowed by her. Although I suspected Rickie's presence was evidence of some splitting of her self-structure, I still held at bay the awareness that Rickie could be an alter personality. Instead, I wondered if Emily was hallucinating. I assessed for a psychotic disorder. I wondered if her house could truly be haunted. In retrospect, I am aware that I resisted the diagnosis of DID, which hovered over us as each session progressed. I worried that my fascination with the diagnosis of DID could unwittingly encourage the splits in her identity. Would further questioning about her ghost reify the split? Would my interest in this personality state encourage the further dissolution of her identity? Would I in effect create DID in my efforts to diagnose it?

The diagnosis of DID is indeed thorny territory. I tried to balance my interest in understanding each of the parts of Emily with my belief that she was one whole human being. Ultimately, Emily recounted an experience of feeling murderously angry, but identified it did not feel like "her" who was the angry one. It was Rickie. She felt herself watching this scene from the outside (depersonalization), while Rickie had taken over her body. She began to describe Rickie as an "internal ghost." His presence was accompanied by trance episodes, recurrent amnesia for traveling (walking, being on the bus or train, and arriving at a destination and not knowing how she had gotten there), and a pervasive sense of feeling "not here." She identified two types of handwriting in her class notes and noted amnesia for having written certain things. She had recurrent experiences of people recognizing her and calling her by a different name, with no recall for who these people were or how she knew them. Men would call her and indicate that she had given them her phone number at a bar, but she could not remember having done so. The evidence was leaning toward a diagnosis of DID.

I continued to hope that the splits in her identity were not so complete and that she kept an awareness of these personality states as being part of one continuous sense of "me." And then I met Rosie. In the final minutes of a therapy session, Emily's eyes glazed over. Her pupils dilated and the structure of her face changed entirely. Her cheeks looked wider and higher, with dimples under her eyes. I became aware of feeling distant, foggy, and mildly confused. And then Emily began to giggle. I shared with Emily my confusion and asked her what was happening. At that moment, Rosie introduced herself. I asked how old she was and she gingerly raised six fingers. She shared that she was very lonely and that she liked being with me in therapy sessions. I later learned that Rosie held all of the vulnerability and neediness for the personality system. Rosie was the part of Emily who gave out her number at bars, hoping indiscriminately and desperately for love and attention. Rosie was also the part who put Emily in danger, lacking the awareness of healthy boundaries, anger, or an ability to say "no" when needed.

Rosie's emergence, approximately seven months into the treatment, solidified Emily's diagnosis of DID. It took the succession of several clues to the existence of these parts of Emily's identity (from hereon referred to as alter personalities) in order for me to accept and to know what I had long suspected but not allowed myself to know. This process mirrored Emily's own experience of coming to know about the parts of herself kept sequestered in a parallel but segregated part of her consciousness. Emily and I engaged in this effort to resist the dissociative pull together. It was a relational experience that represented Emily's first attempt to trust—to allow me to see the parts of herself she held with profound shame and self-loathing and to trust I would not turn away.

DISSOCIATION AS A DISORDER OF RELATIONSHIP

How does this type of split in one's identity and experience of self emerge? When development is impeded by early trauma, neglect, attachment dilemmas, or gross misattunement, the linking of experiences of self becomes disrupted. Normal integration in developmental process cannot occur and the result is a fragmented experience of self, like that we witness in Emily.

The link between DID and early relational trauma has been well-established. For Emily, this came by way of severe medical problems in infancy and again in early adolescence, which left her separated from her primary caregiver. This was compounded by her caregiver's inability, due to her own difficulty regulating her emotional experiences, to stay attuned to Emily's needs. Layered on top of these early experiences of separation and misattunement were incidents of recurrent verbal abuse, profound emotional neglect, suspected physical abuse, and later instances of intimate partner violence and sexual assault. Her early developing ability to trust and depend on others for safety, self-regulation, and comfort was disrupted. Instead, others became a source of abandonment, violence, or exploitation. She learned she could maintain even the most cursory of relationships with others only when she was very, very "good." As a young child, she honed her ability to split off the "ugly" parts of self (namely her anger, sadness, and neediness) to have her basic needs met, breeding her fragmented experience of self.

Dissociation as a defense used by a young child first originates from a combination of hyperarousal and the lack of an attuned other to regulate this overarousal (Forrest, 2001). Dissociation persists as a state of mind when the child learns that certain parts of self are deemed illicit and must be cordoned off in order to preserve some semblance of relationship or whatever safety or security is conditionally available. Thus, dissociation as a mental process steps in when there is a marked absence of an available and attuned other; it grows from a failure in relationship.

There are many ways to understand the manifestation of DID, however, at its core, *dissociative identity disorder is a relational disorder*. It derives from a breakdown in the basic human attachment system early in life. Later, the symptomatology manifests by way of relationships. Sufferers of DID struggle to maintain healthy relationships, often feeling either terrified of engaging intimately with another or alternately seeking the comfort and solace of human connection indiscriminately, entering into unsafe and exploitative relationships. There are also urgent pulls toward reenactment; the only templates that the DID sufferer has for relationships are ones in which there is a perpetrator and a victim, or a bystander who did not protect and a helpless self who felt neglected. A person with DID, then, enters into relationships with these expectations. Either the other has total power and control and the self is weak and helpless, or the self must take control of the other. Often, there are no templates for mutual and nonexploitative relationships. As a result, it is common for DID survivors to find themselves in endless cycles of abusive relationships. Emily, for instance, suffered rape from a boss, was in a long-term physically and emotionally abusive relationship with a boyfriend, and often found herself being stalked or followed by strange men in the city where she lived. She never developed a self-protective function and found it difficult to set healthy boundaries, assert herself, or say "no" in a way that was respected. She also became highly destabilized, more fragmented, and at times suicidal in the wake of any rupture in an important relationship. She had not yet had the opportunity to develop object constancy—the belief that a loved one will return after he/she leaves and an ability to tolerate such losses. Emily's most disturbing symptoms, like their origin, occurred in the context of a relationship.

The therapy relationship is not immune from these dilemmas. Emily, for instance, struggled with the "petit partings" at the end of each session, knowing she would not see me for another week and feeling wholly alone to deal with her intense emotions in the intervening time. She often left sessions and found herself wandering around the city in a highly dissociative state. She also struggled to express any anger or disappointment in me or share her at times overwhelming needs, splitting off what she saw as the "ugly" parts of self as she had learned to do in her early life. She feared that if she allowed me to really see her, all of her, I could not possibly bear it and would either abandon or injure her, as she felt all others had done in the past. The development of trust in me and in the capacity of human connection has been the fundamental struggle in our work together and also the place where the healing has begun.

TREATMENT OF DISSOCIATIVE IDENTITY DISORDER

A relational disorder like DID requires a relational treatment. The social worker's primary responsibility is to provide a new model of relationship—one marked by mutuality, collaboration, and respect for the integrity of the other. This aim is not without great difficulty. The social worker and client alike must withstand many cycles of connection and disconnection, rupture and repair in order for a sense of basic trust to develop (Chu, 2011). The social worker must resist all temptation to exert power over the client; she must withstand attacks from the client without retaliating and also without allowing herself to be abused; she must maintain presence and interest in the client even (and especially) when the client is dissociated or aloof; she must resist the temptation to be a caretaker of the dependent client and instead reinforce the client's agency and strengths. The social worker must, above all else, believe the client. She must bear witness to the reality of the client's traumatic experience and its often horrific aftermath. This new experience of being seen and responded to in a relationship can provide a corrective experience for the client and a context within which healing can occur.

STAGES OF TREATMENT

Research on the treatment of DID is in its earliest stages (International Society for the Study of Trauma and Dissociation [ISSTD], 2011). Most available research is based on case studies and naturalistic outcomes studies. Available studies suggest that psychotherapy is effective in treating DID and that more "intensive" and "comprehensive" therapies have better outcomes (as cited in ISSTD, 2011). Despite this, there is no evidence-based practice (EBP) for the treatment of DID.

The consensus among experts in the treatment of complex trauma and dissociative disorders is that treatment should proceed in stages: (1) Establishment of safety and symptom reduction; (2) Confronting and working through traumatic memories; and (3) Continued integration and personal growth (Chu, 2011; Courtois, Ford, & Cloitre, 2009; Herman, 1992; ISSTD, 2011). Attention to where a client is in his/her own healing and developmental process dictates which stage of treatment is most appropriate. It also reflects the basic social work ethos of "starting where the client's at." Heeding this attention to the client's unique and changing needs is a primary component of relational treatment—it represents attunement to the client's needs and creation of a corrective relational experience in which the client feels safe and where her needs can be met.

The treatment of dissociative disorders is not a laissez-faire approach. This dictum is most evident in the need for so-called Stage One work—efforts to help the client to manage symptoms and establish safety and self-regulation. The biggest error made in the treatment of DID or any complex trauma disorder is the attempt to bypass Stage One work and "process the trauma" prematurely. The failure to help a client develop skills to keep him/herself safe and to regulate overwhelming emotions prior to engaging any trauma memories in detail holds the grave danger of retraumatizing the client—leaving him/her alone, again, with no way to regulate hyperarousal.

In Stage One, the social worker should first attend to the client's ability to manage his/her body, including medical and basic health needs, the establishment of a safe living environment and financial stability, and the development of a healthy rhythm of eating, sleeping, and exercising. With the client's explicit consent and cooperation, medications can be a useful tool, as can adjunctive and nontraditional therapies such as mindfulness meditation, yoga, acupuncture, or nutritional counseling (van der Kolk, 2009).

A critical element of helping the client to meet his/her basic needs is the establishment of safety. Persons with DID often have chaotic lives and engage in behaviors that put themselves and others at risk, including promiscuity, unsafe sex, and involvement in abusive relationships either as victim or perpetrator. They also engage in self-destructive behaviors that reenact early traumatic patterns, including self-mutilation, substance abuse, and eating disorders, and are at high risk for suicide. One of the social worker's primary tasks in Stage One of treatment is to help the client to diminish and ultimately refrain from dangerous and destructive behaviors. It can be helpful to reduce the client's shame about these behaviors by reframing them as useful adaptations to extraordinary and traumatic early life environments. These behaviors began as a precocious attempt by the child to regulate affect or numb oneself from pain; however, these behaviors are jet-lagged. The child, now an adult, is no longer in danger and the mechanisms he/she developed to regulate distress are no longer needed.

Efforts to help the client reduce the reliance on unsafe behaviors should take paramount importance. In treatment, safety management should include (1) education about why safety is necessary for treatment; (2) assessment of the function of unsafe behaviors; (3) safety contracting (including negotiating a plan to keep oneself safe with all alter personalities, especially those that are violent or self-destructive); (3) strategies to help the client develop more effective strategies to manage distress (including grounding strategies, cognitive behavioral techniques, and dialectical behavioral therapy emotional regulation strategies); (4) development of self-soothing strategies; (5) development of a support network of safe others to rely on in crisis; (6) treatment plans or referral to specialized programs to treat eating disorders and/or substance abuse issues; and (7) inpatient hospitalization if the client is in imminent danger of doing serious harm to self or others (ISSTD 2011, pp. 136–137).

Once safety has been reasonably established, Stage One efforts should turn to management of symptoms. People with DID often have comorbid diagnoses of PTSD, chronic anxiety, depression, and disturbed sleep. Treatment should emphasize control of the client's most distressing symptoms prior to accessing any traumatic memories. Despite this aim, it is highly probable that traumatic memories will emerge in the form of flashbacks, nightmares, or intrusive recollections prior to the client developing effective skills to deal with the distress these recollections evoke.

In these cases, the social worker should not silence the client's recollection of the trauma. Instead, the worker should validate the reality of the client's experience and offer empathy for his/her feelings about the traumatic event, but refrain from asking for more details about the trauma. The worker instead should move to a present-day orientation, emphasizing the impact of these traumatic experiences in terms of the client's symptoms and functioning, offering containment, and encouraging the use of strategies to regulate affect (including the use of grounding techniques, emotional regulation skills, and relaxation and breathing exercises) (Chu, 2011). Jumping into premature processing of traumatic memories increases the likelihood that a client will do serious harm to him/herself when traumatic material is approached.

Emily, like many clients with DID, engaged in many dangerous behaviors, including the daily abuse of marijuana, indiscriminate sexual relationships with men she did not know well, and the manifestation of a child alter, Rosie, who was overly trusting and struggled to maintain boundaries to keep herself safe. The first stage of treatment with Emily, which persisted for many months, focused on the management of these behaviors, the reduction of her switching behaviors and comorbid symptoms of depression, and development of healthy strategies to identify her emotions and needs and express them safely to others. Despite both Emily's and my own very best efforts, many crises emerged throughout this process. This intrusion of crises into Stage One work was entirely expected, given that Emily was developing skills of self-regulation and a capacity for trust for the first time. My willingness and ability to stay in relationship with Emily through these crises, making myself available as a safe other to rely on while maintaining boundaries and an unwavering belief in Emily's ability to care for herself, was a crucial part of the work in Stage One.

Once the capacity for seeking and receiving support from safe others has been developed and the client can manage his/her most distressing symptoms, the second stage of treatment may begin. Stage Two emphasizes confronting and working through traumatic memories and beginning to integrate the personality. Again, the therapy relationship is a critical component of this work. The stability of this relationship enables the client to confront horrific memories from the past while maintaining safe anchorage in the present. The client will be able to simultaneously re-experience feelings related to early traumas in their original intensity, but this time, holding onto a sense of safe connection that was unavailable in the traumatic moment (Herman, 1992). The goal of this stage is to help the client use the capacity of the adult mind to put language and form around the somatic and affective memories of earlier traumas. The social worker must remain attuned to the client's ability to manage the traumatic memories, helping the client titrate this exposure and contain the affect that emerges. The ability to do so offers a corrective experience for the client, both in her ability to rely on others and in her own capacity to have mastery and control where in the original trauma there was neither.

The final stage of DID treatment emphasizes continued integration and personal growth. In this stage of work, the client will evidence a shift in identity from "a dissociative" or "a traumatized person" into a more integrated and expanded understanding of self. Treatment in this stage will naturally move toward current life-stage issues, as well as career, vocational, or school stressors.

Although an ideal model of the treatment of DID is presented in discrete stages, treatment is never entirely linear and clients will move back and forth between stages. The integration of identity and resolution of trauma is never final. Clients might shift back to an earlier stage of treatment after a rupture in a relationship, a developmental milestone, or a trigger of an early traumatic memory. Additionally, alter personalities might be in different stages of treatment at the same time. The social worker should privilege attunement over technique, flexibly and responsively meeting the client's shifting needs, rather than dogmatically remaining in a particular stage of treatment.

WORKING WITH ALTERS

Throughout all stages of treatment, the primary aim in working with clients with DID is integration of identity—working toward greater harmony and cooperation among alter personalities. A common therapeutic pitfall in working with clients with DID occurs when the social worker becomes overly fascinated with the client's condition, especially the more florid symptoms of discrete personality states. This can lead the therapist to unwittingly reinforce rather than alleviate the client's dissociative symptoms. An overemphasis on the client's various alter personalities may also lead the social worker to lose sight of important interpersonal dynamics within the therapy relationship. Rather than reifying the client's alter personalities, the client should be seen as a whole person, with each personality holding responsibility for overall functioning (ISSTD, 2011).

With this principle in mind, the social worker should help the client to develop co-consciousness—an increased communication and cooperation among alter personalities. As co-consciousness develops, each of the alter personalities will have access to the information held by the others. For instance, when Emily began treatment, she could observe what Rickie experienced and how he behaved, though she felt she had no executive control. She had no co-consciousness for the alter personality Rosie; Emily reported total amnesia for the periods of time when she functioned as this part of self. This lack of co-consciousness was maladaptive for Emily. When functioning as Rosie, she did not have access to an "adult" part of self to make good decisions to keep her safe. Throughout the course of treatment, Emily attained increasing amounts of access to each part of herself. Emily could be present simultaneously with both Rickie and Rosie, moving toward an integration of these alter personalities as all part of the same "me."

There are several strategies to promote co-consciousness. First, it is fundamental to acknowledge the value of each part to the functioning of the whole personality system. The social worker's role is to help the client find ways to take the needs of each alter personality into account in decision-making and to promote internal support among parts. It is contraindicated to align with one part or exclude parts from treatment. It is equally countertherapeutic to ignore alter personalities or refuse to communicate with them. According to the ISSTD (2011), "successful treatment of DID almost always requires interacting and communicating in some way with the alternate identities" (p. 140). This interaction should always be in an effort toward integration.

The social worker may at times need to speak with an alter personality, either to get information in order to assess the client's safety, or to ensure that all relevant parts of self are involved in negotiating a decision. For instance, Emily indicated that one alter, Jessica, had a profile on a website offering sex and companionship in exchange for money. Emily had no co-consciousness for her functioning as Jessica, and therefore, had no way to understand what led this part of her to be involved in such risky and promiscuous behavior. She also felt she had no way to stop herself from engaging in such behavior. I used an indirect strategy to help Emily access this alter personality. I first used the strategy of *talking through*—talking both to and past the host (Emily) to the other parts of self. In this case, I explained that we had an important matter to discuss, which involved the well-being and safety of the whole personality system. I asked that all of the parts of Emily who needed to be involved in this conversation about her use of the sex website listen in, noting that each part had something important to contribute. I then used the strategy of *asking inside*. I asked Emily what she was getting out of involvement on this website, and suggested that she ask and listen inside for a response. Initially, she was not certain that Jessica would share any information, but Jessica did offer that she was on the website because she wanted to make money to purchase hair extensions; she was angry that Emily decided to cut her hair and make herself look less feminine. Emily continued to ask inside to get more information from this part of her, and she came to understand that Jessica offered sex in exchange for money both to have money in order to make decisions for herself and also as a way to be in a position of power and control in the context of a relationship. These men wanted something she had, and this offered her a feeling of security. Jessica was angry that Emily and Rosie allowed themselves to be taken advantage of, continually making themselves subject to the demands of others in relationships. I reiterated how important it was that the needs of each part of Emily be met. After some negotiation, Emily's personality system ultimately agreed that if Emily and Rosie worked harder to maintain boundaries to protect themselves and allow their voice and desires to be known, then Jessica would refrain from visiting the sex website. The participation of each part of Emily was essential in coming to this agreement and ensuring that all parts of her were committed to her safety.

It is always preferable to have the host internally communicate with other parts of self. This enables restoration of memory across the personality system, as well as development of empathy for the needs of each alter personality, and allows each part of self to feel less isolated. On occasion, the social worker may need to access an alter personality directly without using the host to internally communicate. This might occur when an alter is putting the client into dangerous situations or when there is an impasse in the therapeutic relationship (Chu, 2011). When necessary, it can often be effective to simply ask to speak to a particular part of self, for instance, "I need to talk with the part of you who was at the bar last night." There are many other techniques to both directly and indirectly facilitate co-consciousness. Chu (2011) and Howell (2011) offer excellent introductory chapters elaborating on these strategies. Ultimately, the development of co-consciousness will reduce the need for switching, which is both exhausting and disruptive, and will enable the client to feel less fragmented.

CONCLUDING THOUGHTS

Despite the usefulness of these various techniques, good therapy with clients with dissociative disorders is less in the *doing* and more in the *being*. It is less important to master and apply highly discrete techniques, and instead far more important to embody certain relational principles: safety, trust, respect for the person of the client, curiosity without judgment, a willingness to bear witness to the client's trauma, and allowing for the entirety of the true self of the client to emerge and be welcomed into the therapy space. When these principles are upheld, the client is offered an antidote to his early wounds. She is given the opportunity to be in relationship and in a safe place in which integration of self can proceed.

WEBSITES

International Society for the Study of Dissociation: http://www.issd.org
Sidran Institute (Traumatic Stress Education and Advocacy): http://www.sidran.org
SAMHSA National Center for Trauma Informed Care: http://mentalhealth.samhsa.gov

References

American Psychiatric Association. (2013). *Diagnostic and statistical manual of mental disorders, fifth edition*. Washington, DC: Author.
Brand, B. L., Classen, C. C., Lanius, R., et al. (2009). A naturalistic study of dissociative identity disorder

and dissociative disorder not otherwise specified patients treated by community clinicians. *Psychological Trauma: Theory, Research, Practice and Policy, 1,* 153–171.

Briere, J., & Scott, C. (2012). *Principles of trauma therapy: A guide to symptoms, evaluation, and treatment* (2nd ed.). Thousand Oaks, CA: Sage Publications.

Bromberg, P. M. (2011) *Awakening the dreamer: Clinical journeys.* New York, NY: Routledge Taylor & Francis Group.

Carlson, E. B., & Putnam, F. W. (1993). An update on the dissociative experiences scale. *Dissociation, 6,* 16–27.

Chu, J. A. (2011). *Rebuilding shattered lives: Treating complex PTSD and dissociative disorders* (2nd ed.). Hoboken, NJ: John Wiley & Sons, Inc.

Courtois, C. A., Ford, J. D., & Cloitre, M. (2009). Best practices in psychotherapy for adults. In C. A. Courtois & J. D. Ford (Eds.), *Treating complex traumatic stress disorders: An evidence-based guide* (pp. 82–103). New York, NY: The Guilford Press.

Cozolino, L. J. (2002). Rebuilding the brain: Neuroscience and psychotherapy. In *The neuroscience of psychotherapy: Building and rebuilding the human brain* (pp. 15–45). New York, NY: Norton.

Forrest, K. A. (2001). Toward an etiology of dissociative identity disorder: A neurodevelopmental approach. *Consciousness and Cognition, 10,* 259–293.

Hartocollis, L. (1998). The making of multiple personality disorder: A social constructionist view. *Clinical Social Work Journal, 26*(2), 159–176.

Herman, J. L. (1992). *Trauma and recovery: The aftermath of violence—from domestic abuse to political terror.* New York, NY: Basic Books.

Howell, E. (2005). *The dissociative mind.* New York, NY: Routledge Taylor & Francis Group.

Howell, E. (2011). *Understanding and treating dissociative identity disorder: A relational approach.* New York, NY: Routledge Taylor & Francis Group.

International Society for the Study of Dissociation. (2005). [Chu, J. A., Loewenstein, R., Dell, P. F., Barach, P. M., Somer, E., Kluft, R. P., . . .Howell, E.]. Guidelines for treating dissociative identity disorder in adults. *Journal of Trauma & Dissociation, 6*(4), 69–149.

International Society for the Study of Trauma and Dissociation (ISSTD). (2011). Guidelines for treating dissociative identity disorder in adults: Third revision. *Journal of Trauma and Dissociation, 12*(2), 115–187. doi:10.1080/15299732.2011.537247

Putnam, F. W. (1992). Discussion: Are alter personalities fragments or figments? *Psychoanalytic Inquiry, 12,* 95–111.

Ross, C. A. (1997). *Dissociative identity disorder.* New York, NY: John Wiley & Sons, Inc.

Sar, V. et al. (2007). Dissociative disorders in the psychiatric emergency ward. *General Hospital Psychiatry, 29,* 45–50.

Schore, A. N. (2001). The effects of early relational trauma on right brain development, affect regulation and infant mental health. *Infant Mental Health Journal, 22*(1–2), 201–269.

Stein, A. (2010). Shooting in the spaces: Violent crime as dissociated enactment. In J. Petrucelli (Ed.), *Knowing, not-knowing and sort-of-knowing: Psychoanalysis and the experience of uncertainty* (pp. 65–77). London: Karnac Books.

Van der Hart, O., Nijenhuis, E. R. S., & Solomon, R. (2010). Dissociation of the personality in complex trauma-related disorders and EMDR: Theoretical considerations. *Journal of EMDR Practice and Research, 4*(2), 76–92.

Van der Kolk, B. (2009). Developmental trauma disorder: Towards a rational diagnosis for children with complex trauma histories. In C. A. Courtois & J. D. Ford (Eds.), *Treating complex traumatic stress disorders: An evidenced-based guide* (pp. 455–465). New York, NY: The Guilford Press.

PART VIII
Guidelines for Specific Techniques

79   Practice from a Technique Perspective

Francis J. Turner

What drives our choice of technique in a particular case? To answer this query, we first have to consider what we mean by technique. For those of us in social work, this is not an easy question to answer. Or at least to answer with any degree of consistency. Although we have frequently used the term "technique" in our clinical literature over the decades, we have not been precise in what we mean by the term. Thus, we have used it to describe various different things. There have been very few efforts to define technique in an agreed upon way. We seem to presume that we all understand what we mean by the term. One attempt to be precise about the term can be found in Dr. Howard Goldstein's excellent book, *Social Work Practice: A Unitary Approach* (Goldstein, 1973).

Some time later, Dr. Joel Fischer (1978) brought into focus the importance of technique when he reminded us that everything we do with, to, and for clients, constitutes the application or utilization of a cluster of actions for which we need to take responsibility and upon which we need to build our theoretical base. This comes close to the idea of technique. Only when we can be precise and cognizant about what specifically we are doing in practice with, to, and for clients. And only when we are committed to understanding the different effects of these various activities on our clients, can we begin to understand the differential importance of our rich range of theories. In this way, we can search out richer and more effective ways of putting our theories to use. A greater attention to technique helps us to understand how various techniques can bring about different ways of helping our clients. And of at least equal importance, also help us to identify more precisely areas and situations where our theories can be harmful to some or all clients.

This reminds us that with the intensity of the impacts we have, or will have, on clients, an inappropriate use of some techniques can be harmful. Thus, we need to understand the element of risk that is introduced into our use of various techniques.

If we move to greater interest in technique, we should work to agree on a definition of technique that will assist us in moving toward a more precise use of the concept. Turner and Rowe (2013, p. 5) offer one definition that provides us with further precision in the use of the term. This definition states that, "a technique is the artistic use of some practical object or activity by a social worker as a component of treatment aimed at achieving an identified outcome. Such action or object is replicable by others, is ethical, has a level of professional approbation and is understandable from a relevant theoretical perspective."

One of the difficulties for those of us in social work in dealing with the technique component of our practice in a conceptual way is that so many of our techniques are quite mundane in nature and lack the attractiveness of techniques in other disciplines. An example of this is something as mundane as a handshake. The question of whether we shake hands with a client is not a simple question. Among other concerns, it involves such things as gender, values, customs, religion, age, and occasion. When properly assessed and utilized, a hand shake can provide considerable positive impact for a client. But a handshake can also be totally inappropriate, even to the point of offending a client who might well misunderstand the action to such an extent that it will affect the relationship in a negative way. A handshake also could be seen as a very positive gesture on our part, one that the client perceives as very supportive.

Similar issues arise in regard to many of our techniques.

As we begin to appreciate that virtually everything we do in relationship with our clients can and frequently does have an impact on them, we can appreciate just how important it is that many of our apparently mundane actions be examined with care. It is so very important that we pay much more attention to all the things we do with, to, and for clients and seek to understand on an ongoing basis the significance of how we interact with them. We also need to learn to identify our differential actions to assess their impact both positive and possibly negative. That is, we need to ask ourselves on an ongoing basis whether what we are doing is the most effective and helpful way to achieve our therapeutic goals.

Of course, much of this assessment takes place outside of the interview, as we sit back and engage in a process of evaluation. We do not want to take away from the essential spontaneity of a therapeutic process, which is so essential to the effective engagement of our clients. But we do want to learn to view our interviewing partly as a wide assortment of discrete actions. This requires us to engage in an ever continuing process of examining what techniques we use and how we interact. We must ask ourselves, "What are the risks in making various uses of my technique repertoire?" "Can I better serve this client by a shift in my technique repertoire?" "Or by trying something from my own repertoire with this client?"

If we begin to analyze technique in our individual practices, then as a profession, we will expand our available data, which will help us understand and make fruitful use of the relationships among technique, theory, assessment, and diagnosis. Also, in the long-term, we will begin to develop patterns of theory and technique so that we can begin to differentiate among our clients based on who we are, who they are, and how we can best help them. We also will develop a better understanding of how some of the things we do are, in some cases, not helpful.

Of course, an obvious and appropriate response to this stream of thought would be to say, "But this is what I have always done and do in all my interviews with clients." We all are highly skilled interviewers and we can draw a client into a meaningful positive helping situation quickly and effectively. We can even transform the most troubled and hostile of situations into relationships that are at last minimally helpful and at best enormously helpful. But what we do not do is identify how we do this, what techniques we use to accomplish this, and what we would have done differently, given a choice? "What could I have done to be more helpful?" we might ask. "What can I do to improve the effectiveness of many of my techniques?" Of course, we all do this to some extent already. What is different or novel about this train of thought is that we have not been sufficiently precise to ourselves, or to our profession, in defining the term "technique." Without that, and without a commitment to precision, we cannot make full use of our rich body of knowledge and bring this abundance to our clients, so that we can better serve them.

One way we can start down this trail is to work from a categorization of our techniques, as was done in the Turner and Rowe book, *101 Social Work Clinical Techniques* (2013). Obviously, many different ways of categorizing techniques could be used. Then, we would have to develop or work from an agreed-upon list. This latter effort is an interesting process, as was discovered in *101 Social Work Clinical Techniques*. From our work on this project, we are convinced that there are many more techniques used in social work practice that need to be identified and added to our repertoire. We need also to begin a process of considering whether some techniques better fit some theories more than others or whether all techniques fit all theories. At the same time, we need to continue the process of assessing the risk involved in making use of various techniques. On the other hand, we might ask ourselves whether e matters of effectiveness are related to inherent client strength rather than something inherent in the technique.

References

Fischer, J. (1978). *Effective casework practice: An eclectic approach*. New York, NY: McGraw-Hill.

Goldstein, H. (1973). *Social work practice: A unitary approach*. Columbia: University of South Carolina Press.

Turner, F. J., & Rowe, W. S. (2013). *101 Social Work Clinical Techniques*. New York, NY: Oxford University Press.

80

Developing Successful Relationships
The Therapeutic and Group Alliances

Lawrence Shulman

A middle-aged mother of three comes to a family counseling agency for help dealing with her young children. She has just started a difficult separation from her husband of 20 years. Her main concern is how to deal with her children, who are upset and have been acting out since their father moved out. She tells the agency intake worker that she wants help dealing with her own feelings of failure in her marriage, supporting her clearly upset children, and starting a new life. At the first interview with her 25-year-old, recently graduated MSW social worker, she notices the worker does not have a wedding ring and asks, "Do you have any children?" The worker responds, "We are here to talk about you, not me." For the balance of the interview, the client appears distracted and uncomfortable, providing minimal responses to the worker's effort to obtain a social history. The worker's notes at the end of the session describe the client as "depressed and resistant."

In this vignette, by putting ourselves in the shoes of the client, perhaps remembering a time in our lives when we sought help, we can see that she may really be asking, "Since you don't have children, can you understand my situation?" "Are you going to judge me?" and "Can you help me?" These are reasonable questions in the mind of this client in a first interview. Because of the taboo against directness in relation to authority, the concerns may be raised in an indirect manner. The young worker, feeling defensive, responded in a way that closed off this line of discussion. The client's resistance may actually be a reaction to the worker's defensiveness. An alternative response that responds directly to the underlying questions is shared later in this article.

In another example, we have a first session of an "Anger Management" group for inner-city teenage African American girls. The members have been mandated to attend the group by the court or face incarceration based on minor criminal convictions. One of the group members confronts the two Caucasian, middle-class and suburban female group leaders and angrily says: "Why should I talk about my problems? What am I going to learn from two old women like you?" The two group leaders, both in their mid-twenties, report later that it was the "old women" comment that hurt the most. The rest of the session is marked by resistance and periods of silence. When conversation does take place it consists of an "illusion of work" with no real significance (Shulman, 2011).

The following week the leaders open the session by referring back to the comment from the confrontational member. The group leaders in the first session had interpreted the comment as an effort to obstruct the group. The leaders now realized she was an internal leader directly stating what other group members might have thought and felt as well. The leaders then comment: "We don't blame you for feeling this way. Not only are we older but we are also white and we live in the suburbs. No wonder you don't trust us or think we can ever understand what you go through. But how can we understand and help if you won't tell us?" The worker's directness and raising openly the under-the-surface taboo issues of race and class leads to the beginning of the development of the "working relationship," now more commonly referred to as the therapeutic alliance (Shulman, 2010, 2011). In the third group session, the same internal group leader angrily discloses that she has experienced sexual abuse in her family as a child. Other group members share similar traumatic experiences, which are one of the underlying sources of their anger.

In a first session of a group for parents of children with physical disabilities the group leaders, after explaining the purpose of the group and their roles, ask each parent to share the issues they faced in their parenting of a child who was different. The leaders acknowledged with empathy their understanding of some of the pain that the parents expressed over not having the "normal" child they had hoped for when they became pregnant. The leaders also asked other members of the group to respond to each parent's presentation, emphasizing how healing the "all-in-the-same-boat" phenomenon can be when clients share similar thoughts, feelings, and concerns. One could see the beginnings of relaxation as the "group-alliance" grew and members began to have positive feelings for one another (Shulman, 2010, 2011).

THE THERAPEUTIC AND GROUP ALLIANCES

Although the concept of the "therapeutic alliance" between a therapist and patient has been found to have a positive impact on outcomes, alliance to the group-as-a-whole has not been as widely studied. Lindgren, Barber, and Sandahl (2008), citing their own research, suggest that, "In treatment formats in which the group process is predicted to be a curative factor, it is counterintuitive to emphasize only the relationship between an individual patient and therapists" (p. 164). In another study of group therapeutic alliance and cohesion, Joyce, Piper, and Ogrodniczuk (2007) examined the impact of each on outcomes in short-term group therapy. They found that group alliance variables were more consistently associated with improved outcomes (p. 273).

If the engagement phase is handled well by the social worker, it can increase the possibility of establishing an effective working relationship with the client. The working relationship, also referred to as the therapeutic alliance, is the medium through which the worker influences the client and the outcomes of practice. Elements of the working relationship have been defined in this author's research as rapport ("I get along with my worker."), trust ("I can tell my worker anything on my mind; I can risk my mistakes and failures as well as my successes."), and caring ("My worker cares as much about me as she cares about my children.") (Shulman, 1978, 2009, 2011).

Clients often bring a number of unstated questions to the first session. "Who is this social worker and what kind of person will he or she turn out to be?" "Can I trust this worker?" "What will our work be about and what will we be doing together?" "Can this worker understand and help me or will he or she be judgmental?"

In those situations with more than one client present, such as couple, family, group, and community work, there are also often unstated concerns about the others in the session. Our experience is indicating more clearly that first the client must experience a positive therapeutic alliance with the social worker, and then they can address the group-alliance with others in the session.

When these relationship issues, also referred to as the "authority theme" and the "intimacy theme" (Shulman, 2011) are added to what might be ambivalence about seeking and accepting help or accepting that a problem exists, one can easily understand the complexities associated with beginnings. This phase of work requires that the client make a "first decision" to engage in the process. Whereas a skillful worker can influence that decision, she or he cannot make it for the client. The skills identified in the remainder of this chapter are those that increase the possibility that the client will take that first step. This chapter also identifies the skills that can encourage the client to make the second decision, which is associated with making the transition from the beginning or engagement phase to the middle or work phase. At this point the commitment to work on difficult and often painful tasks is completed. The dynamics and skills that are important in the ending and transition phase of work are beyond the scope of this chapter.

The focus of this article is on core skills or constant elements, which can apply to all forms of practice, and it is important to recognize that the helping relationship is also affected by variant elements. For example, the nature of the problem or the setting of practice can have an important influence. Working in a high school dealing with violence prevention might look somewhat different from working in a hospital with persons with AIDS.

Variations introduced by age (practice with children, teens, adults, and the elderly) may affect how the worker begins and the development of the relationship. Other factors, such as gender, race, ethnicity, sexual orientation, physical ability, and so on, can all impact how the client perceives the offer of help.

For example, Elze (2006) describes how a school social worker can be GLBT (gay, lesbian, bisexual, and transgendered) sensitive in practice. This is a crucial stage of development for intervention, during which students attempt to come to grips with their sexual orientation and the larger heterosexual population begins to develop its attitudes toward difference. Elze suggests that the social worker needs to demonstrate that he or she is an "askable" person in response to all students, for example, using such strategies as employing gender-neutral language when exploring youth's dating interests, sexual behaviors, and so on.

Strategies appropriate for one population may be quite ineffective with another. Working interculturally (for example, a Caucasian worker with a client of color) as well as working intraculturally (for example, a Hispanic worker with a Hispanic client) may modify the dynamics and the strategies employed. Practice with voluntary, involuntary (mandated), or semi-voluntary clients may also look quite different. For example, a first session of a voluntary parenting group requires a different strategy than one with a group of men who have been convicted of driving while intoxicated (DWI) and are court-mandated to attend or face a jail sentence.

In a first session of a DWI group, when the "deviant member," once again an internal leader, crumples the paper listing the topic for discussion each week and then dramatically throws it into a waste basket, the young female leader does not fall into the trap of starting a "battle of wills" using the authority of the court to demand compliance. Instead, she recognizes that building a therapeutic alliance is best achieved by exploring the resistance. She says: "I can see you are not happy at being forced to attend this group. I don't think you are the only one feeling this way. How about it? Are others also upset?" Members immediately respond with comments such as "I don't want to be called an alcoholic or made to feel guilty. "Everyone drinks on weekends; I just got caught," etc.

The leader, working from the productions of the group members, writes on a flip chart "Don't Want" and lists under this the concerns raised by the members. She then points out that these issues are actually on the agenda she has handed out and will be the topics of discussion. The tone of the meeting changes as her skillful response to the denial and resistance begins the development of the therapeutic alliance through discussion of the work.

Finally, practice may be influenced by the worker's theoretical orientation and underlying assumptions. In spite of the many variations on the theme, the notion of understanding practice against the backdrop of time—the preliminary, beginning, middle, and ending/transition phases of work—and the skills identified in the balance of this article, are proposed as core elements in all of the variations described. Schwartz (1961) described the importance of these phases of work, adding a preliminary phase to beginning, middle, and ending/transition phases first identified in social work by Taft (1942, 1949).

THE PHASES OF WORK: THE PRELIMINARY AND BEGINNING PHASES

Schwartz suggested that because clients often raise many of their questions and concerns in an indirect manner, workers needed to prepare to hear the client's indirect cues by developing a preliminary empathy. The skills of the preliminary phase include the following:

- **Tuning in:** An exercise in which the worker develops a tentative, preliminary empathy with the client's feelings and concerns. The worker must also tune in to his or her own emotional state at the start of the relationship because it will impact the worker's moment-by-moment responses to the client. The earlier example of the teenage girls' "anger management" group was an example of tuning in between sessions.
- **Responding directly to indirect cues:** The skill of preparing to articulate a client's thoughts and feelings in response to indirect communications in the first session or sessions.

A common illustration of the importance of these two skills was the vignette that began this chapter. The recently divorced mother of three children asks her 25-year-old, unmarried, recent graduate of a school of social work the question: "Do you have children?" Unless the worker has tuned in both to her own feelings of inadequacy because she does not have a child and the real feelings of the mother, it is not uncommon for the worker to respond defensively, for example, "We are here to talk about you, not me!" Or, "I don't have children but I have taken courses on child development at the school of social work." These responses miss what might be the underlying questions: "Can you understand my situation?" "Will you be able to help me?" "Will you judge me harshly?" "Can I trust you?"

It is important to understand that, to be successful, a direct response will have three conditions: (a) It must be genuine, with the worker trying to experience the emotion; (b) the client must be ready to hear it; and (c) each worker must find a way to respond that reflects his or her own personality and artistry. With these conditions in mind, one more direct response to the indirect cue might be as follows: "I'm not married, and I don't have any children. Why do you ask? Are you concerned I may not understand what it is like for you? I'm worried about that as well. For me to help, I need to understand. For me to understand, you will have to tell me." In addition to illustrating the power of tuning in and responding directly, this example also illustrates a number of skills identified later in this chapter in the section dealing with the middle or work phase. These skills were found in this author's research to be associated with the development of a positive working relationship when used in the beginning phase of practice (Shulman, 2009, 2011). The importance of expressing genuine empathy in developing a positive relationship was supported by Truax (1966) and more recently in the work of Hakansson and Montgomery (2003).

It is important to note that there is a certain individual artistry to practice, and that the exact words used by workers may differ while the intent and impact of the skill will remain the same. Some have pointed to a problem with the implementation of some Evidence-based Practices, wherein the requirement to follow a strict protocol in one's responses to clients can lead to what this author believes is a false dichotomy between science and art. Science (research) should free the worker's artistry not restrict it.

It is also important to emphasize that the worker's empathic response must be genuine, rather than a phrase that has been memorized and is recited without feeling. Clients know when a worker is simply reflecting their words and not experiencing their feelings. Expressions such as, "I hear you saying . . ." with no real affect attached to them can be experienced by clients as artificial empathy.

Another crucial element of the beginning phase, which takes place during the first session(s), is the development of a contract or working agreement between the worker and the client or clients. This contract helps establish a structure that creates the freedom for the work to proceed. A number of first-session skills are described next. It is important to note the following.

- A contract may not be fully developed in the first session, and this working agreement can change over time (re-contracting).
- The client must feel an investment in the work or the sessions will constitute an "illusion of work" in which conversations take place but nothing real happens.
- The worker must make clear the purpose and her or his role in nonjargonized terms to which the client can connect.

The specific contracting skills are as follows (Shulman, 2010, 2011).

1. **Clarifying purpose:** The skill of making a brief opening statement, without jargon, which helps clarify the purpose of the session. This skill should be used when initiating a service (for example, a first group meeting) or responding to a client's request for service (for example, "If you can let me know what brought you in today we can see how I might be able to help.").
2. **Clarifying role:** The skill of describing in a brief, nonjargonized manner, the kind of help the social worker can provide. For example, "No, I can't give you the right answer for dealing with your husband. However, I can help you examine how you deal with him now, your feelings about the relationship, how you see yourself now and in the future. Perhaps if we work on this together I can help you find the answer that is right for you."
3. **Reaching for feedback:** The skill of encouraging clients to explain their perceptions of the problem and the areas in which they wish to receive help.
4. **Clarifying mutual expectations:** Developing an agreement on what the client may expect of the worker as well as defining the client's obligations (for example, regular attendance at group sessions; notification if a client must miss an interview).
5. **Discussing authority issues:** Dealing with any issues, raised directly or indirectly, that concern the authority of the worker (for example, the mandated nature of the service; the limits of confidentiality defined by the worker's responsibility as a mandated

reporter; the client's stereotypes of authority figures or past experiences with social workers).

Though contracting is always initiated in the first sessions, it is not unusual to have to recontract as the work develops. The client may not have fully understood the implications of the contract. It is not unusual for clients to begin with near problems, which are real to the client but not at the core of the work. As the work proceeds, the client begins to understand his or her issues more clearly and is better able to articulate them. The client may have been in what has been called the precontemplation stage (DiClemente, Prochaska, Fairhurst, & Velicer, 1991). For example, a client in substance abuse counseling, such as in the DWI vignette shared earlier, may not have accepted that she or he has a problem with alcohol. Thus, for a number of reasons, contracting remains fluid over time.

THE PHASES OF WORK: THE MIDDLE PHASE

As the work continues, the client moves to the crucial transition stage from the beginning to the middle or work phase. This change is dependent on having developed the therapeutic alliance and the group alliance in the beginning phase. When clients experience "rapport," "trust," and "caring" from their social worker, and in the group session from one another, they feel safer in moving into more difficult issues. This was referred to earlier as making the "second decision." Careful analysis of these transition sessions will reveal that clients may continue to use indirect forms of communication. The client may be embarrassed to raise a difficult issue. Some examples include taboo areas, such as sex, dependency, finances, health issues, or death. The client may not be consciously aware of the existence of the problem. The skills that follow are designed to assist clients in telling their stories and telling them with feeling. These skills also assist the client in examining his or her cognitions or thought patterns related to the client's self-perception, perception of the problem, or perception of others involved. An underlying assumption is that how one feels, affects how one thinks, which affects how one acts, which in turn, affects how one feels, and so on. This feeling, thinking, and doing connection is explored in the middle phase of practice.

The following skills can be helpful in this transition phase (Shulman, 2010, 2011).

1. **Sessional tuning in:** The skill of developing a tentative, preliminary empathy for issues that may emerge at the start of a specific session (for example, the impact of a traumatic event in a client's life; issues left over from the previous session; the client's potential reactions to information the worker must share; a traumatic community event such as the terrorist attacks on September 11, 2001; or a severe weather event such as the devastating hurricanes Katrina and Sandy).
2. **Sessional contracting:** A collection of skills designed to determine the issues or concerns facing clients at a particular session. These may include remaining tentative at the start of the session while listening for indirect cues, asking a client what is on her or his mind, raising previously agreed-upon issues directly with the client and checking to see if they are still relevant, checking in with group members at the start of a session.
3. **Elaborating skills:** The skills required for helping clients to tell their story (e.g., listening, containment, questioning, reaching inside of silences).
4. **Empathic skills:** The skills that address the emotional content of the client's experiences (e.g., reaching for feelings, acknowledging feelings, articulating the client's feelings).
5. **Sharing worker's feelings:** The skill of spontaneously sharing appropriate worker affects, which is in response to the productions of the clients. Boundaries need to be respected so that the sharing of worker affect is professional and responsive to the needs of the clients. Issues of countertransference, client stereotyping, inappropriate worker frustration, and so on need to be considered and closely monitored. However, a general prohibition on sharing affect represents a false dichotomy between the personal and professional mandating that the worker chose between the two. Over time, experienced workers learn to integrate their personal self and feelings into their professional role.
6. **Making a demand for work:** A facilitative confrontation in which the worker asks a client to engage in the work agreed upon in the contracting stage. Specific skills can include confronting denial, reaching inside

of a silence, directly raising a taboo issue, challenging the illusion of work, and so on.

7. **Providing data:** The skill of providing relevant, unavailable information the client needs to deal with the task at hand. Data can include facts, values, beliefs, and so on. Data should be provided in a manner leaving the information open to challenge.

8. **Sessional endings and transitions:** The skills involved in bringing a session to a close. These skills may include summarizing, evaluating progress, and discussion of transition issues (e.g., the client's next step, role-play of anticipated future conversations based on the work of the session).

It is not uncommon for a client to disclose a powerful issue at the very end of the session. In the literature, this has been termed "doorknob therapy," with the image of the client dropping a bombshell with his or her hand on the office doorknob as he or she is about to leave the last session. Even after a good working relationship has been established, a client may be embarrassed to raise issues or concerns in taboo areas.

For example, a female college student may only hint at a difficult time at a party the previous weekend. She may talk at the beginning of a session about being concerned that she drank too much. This could be described as a first offering. The worker responding to the apparent issue of concern over drinking starts to explore the question of substance use in the student's life. As the interview proceeds, the student drops hints of how rowdy the party became and her increasing feelings of concern. This could be considered the second offering. Once again, the worker may begin to respond to issues of safety in a situation where alcohol is being consumed. Almost at the end of the session, the doorknob bombshell emerges, and the student describes having passed out, perhaps being drugged, and waking up in a bedroom in a state of undress and with evidence that she had been raped.

In a serious situation such as this one, the social worker may have to extend the session or arrange a later appointment that same day to deal with the powerful issue that has just emerged. The worker also has to consider the issue of mandatory reporting and whether he or she should be reporting the incident to the authorities or helping the client to do so. When the issue is addressed, it would be important for the worker also to explore why it was so difficult to raise the

incident directly in the beginning of the session. As the client discusses the feelings—which may include shame, self-blame, and so on—that made it difficult to discuss the sexual assault, she is actually beginning the discussion of the assault itself.

With this last example, we complete the discussion of the engagement phase of practice and the transition to the middle phase. For a more complete discussion of each phase of practice, see Shulman (2010, 2011). The dynamics and skills of the middle (work) phase of practice and the ending and transition phase are discussed in detail, as are the skills for developing a positive working relationship with other professionals and organizations. The use of concepts and interventions drawn from evidenced-based practice research is included, with an integrative approach suggesting less prescriptive strategies and more room for practitioner artistry. It is this personal quality expressed by the worker that contributes significantly to the development of the therapeutic alliance in individual practice and serves as the precursor of the group alliance.

WEBSITES

"Beyond the Therapeutic Alliance: Keeping the Drug-Dependent Individual in Treatment," National Institute of Drug Abuse. http://www.nida.nih.gov/pdf/monographs/monograph165/download165.html.

"Therapeutic Alliance: A Review of Sampling Strategies Reported in Marital and Family Therapy Studies," Sage Journals Online. http://tfj.sagepub.com/cgi/content/abstract/15/3/207.

"Therapeutic Alliance, Focus, and Formulation: Thinking Beyond the Traditional Therapy Orientations," Pyschotherapy.net. http://www .psychotherapy.net/article/Therapeutic_Alliance.

References

DiClemente, C. C., Prochaska, J. O., Fairhurst, S. K., & Velicer, W. F. (1991). The process of smoking cessation: An analysis of precontemplation, contemplation, and preparation stages of change. *Journal of Consulting and Clinical Psychology, 59,* 191–204.

Elze, D. (2006). Working with gay, lesbian, bisexual and transgender students. In C. Franklin, M. B. Harris,

& P. Allen-Meares (Eds.), *The school services sourcebook: A guide for school-based professionals* (pp. 861–870). New York, NY: Oxford University Press.

Hakansson, J., & Montgomery, H. (2003). Empathy as an interpersonal phenomenon. *Journal of Social and Personal Relationships, 20,* 267–284.

Lindgren, A., Barber, J. P., & Sandahl, C. (2008). Alliance to the group-as-a-whole as a predictor of outcome in psychodynamic group therapy. *International Journal of Group Psychotherapy, 58*(2), 142–163.

Schwartz, W. (1961). The social worker in the group. In *New perspectives on services to groups: Theory, organization, practice.* New York, NY: National Association of Social Workers.

Shulman, L. (1978). A study of practice skill. *Social Work, 23,* 274–281.

Shulman, L. (2011). *The dynamics and skills of group counseling.* Monterey, CA: Cengage Publishers.

Shulman, L. (2010). *The skills of helping individuals, families, groups, and communities* (7th ed.). Monterey, CA: Cengage Publishers.

Taft, J. (1942). The relational function to process in social case work. In V. P. Robinson (Ed.), *Training for skill in social casework.* Philadelphia: University of Pennsylvania Press.

Taft, J. (1949). Time as the medium of the helping process. *Jewish Social Service Quarterly, 26,* 230–243.

Truax, C. B. (1966). Therapist empathy, warmth, genuineness and patient personality change in group psychotherapy: A comparison between interaction unit measures, time sample measures, and patient perception measures. *Journal of Clinical Psychology, 71,* 1–9.

81 The Use of Therapeutic Metaphor in Social Work

Stephen R. Lankton

There is a growing and continuing interest in the use of therapeutic metaphor among social workers, whether they are engaged in brief or long-term therapy, individual or family therapy, or the delivery of outpatient or inpatient treatment. Therapeutic metaphor belongs to that group of interventions referred to as "indirection." The definition of metaphor as used in therapy refers to a complex story that holds the user's attention and provides an alternate framework through which clients can entertain novel experience. Because this can be done without experiencing any threat, clients do not develop any resistance to entertaining new/novel experiences. While using metaphor, the therapist can accomplish the following.

- Make or illustrate an important therapeutic point to the client
- Suggest solutions (even potentially threatening ones) not previously considered by the client
- Seed ideas to which the therapist can later return and elaborate
- Decrease conscious resistance, a client might otherwise have, to experiential and cognitive changes
- Reframe or redefine a problem for the client so that the problem is placed in a different context of greater or lesser importance with a different meaning
- Retrieve and associate experiences, including emotions, thoughts, perceptions, and behaviors.

A CASE EXAMPLE OF
SIMPLE METAPHOR

Client is a 28-year-old woman who recently broke up with her boyfriend of three years. As a couple they had purchased a home, and although he moved out, she was afraid to leave the house for fear that he would not pay the bills and she would be stuck with bad credit as a result. The young man is trying to obtain a loan so he can take over the entire house debt in his name alone. Each time a loan application is applied for or almost approved and then fails to result in him signing a new note she has mood swings.

Clearly she is excited about the possibility of completely ending all relations with him. But, she finds herself oscillating between excitement and depression whenever her hopes of being free of this financial connection do not materialize. This mood shift was interfering with her ability to perform at work. That is why she sought therapy. Of course, she is fully aware of this simple dynamic. However, her insight alone is not helping her reduce her mood swings.

The metaphoric intervention was designed to help her retrieve experiences of several periods of self-control that one learns to endure throughout childhood. What follows is an excerpt from the metaphor that was told to this patient.

"I want you to close your eyes and just be more comfortable for a minute. It is not necessary that you go into the hypnotic trance, but rather, I'd like you just to be relaxed so you can think about and remember a few things that might again occur to you while I speak."

"You know every child who's ever anticipated a birthday has something in common. When Sally was four years old she distinctly remembers that the ornaments on her Christmas tree were large and shiny. And she was fascinated as much by the tinsel and the decorations on the tree as she was by the ribbons, paper, and boxes below it. For the six days preceding Christmas morning she was unable to sleep normally. She would wander downstairs after everyone else had gone to bed and she would shake the boxes and wonder what kind of presents they contained."

"One night her mother happened awake to hear her shuffling the boxes. Knowing how hard it might be for a young girl to contain her excitement when something wonderful was about to happen, the mother made Sally some warm milk and gave her two cookies. As she ate, her mother explained to Sally, as parents often do, that Santa Claus would not be able to come if he found her to be awake at night. She told her, 'You need to learn to calm down . . . and to sleep.'"

"Hearing the news about Santa Claus was, of course, not enough to make Sally fall asleep easily that night. She tried various ways of thinking in order to help nudge herself into sleep. She tried thinking about the smell of her sheets, taking a nap with her dog, and the comforting, warm feeling she got when her mother gave her the milk. Dwelling on any one of those memories would be enough to make anybody become sleepy and calm, I'm sure you sense that."

"Surprisingly this began working for Sally. She didn't do it very well at four years old—she did much better at five and six. But by the time she was seven years old she had learned to contain her excitement quite well. Even though she was very eager for Christmas to come she was able to sometimes put that excitement out of her mind sufficiently to appear to be a grown-up little girl."

"By the time she was nine she had become quite proficient at being happy and having pleasant anticipation—but not being so excited that it disrupted her. Somewhere along the way your mind learns a method of disconnecting itself from disruptive impulses. Children usually take pride in their ability to control their impulsive experiences. You go to bed knowing that you are excited about opening presents in the morning but you put that excitement into quiet pleasant thoughts. Little girls don't usually know that *you are* learning or how to say that they're putting their excitement into pleasant quiet thoughts."

"But, the unconscious can do that anyway. And if somebody says to Sally, '*remember that experience, remember that now,*' that feeling comes. The unconscious knows how to bring that feeling forward. And as that quiet feeling of excitement fills the mind, similar experiences are brought forward, developing a pleasant anticipation that's not disturbing and not distressing."

This short and simple intervention illustrates some of the value of using therapeutic stories in several ways.

- Metaphors retrieve *experiential resources* that are difficult to label and name.
- Metaphors provide an altered framework so clients use their own experiences to understand the story.
- Metaphors allow clients to retrieve experiences they may not believe they could retrieve.
- Metaphors eliminate the potential resistance, which could arise from clients feeling, in this case, that being calm was not possible.

- It helps a client understand a developmental sequence that suggests a change, in this case, in her impatience.

Immediately following the telling of that brief story, the client was asked to recall that and other feelings similar in her own life. That is to say, the therapist made a direct request for the client to remember similar feelings. The client's ability to carry out that direct request had been greatly enhanced by the telling of that story. She was able to remember times in her own life when she contained her mood and excitement. Those experiences were then used in therapy to help obtain the goal of keeping her mood stable in the context of waiting for her boyfriend to get the loan.

Let's look at a more complicated goal-directed metaphor used to retrieve the emotion of anger. The client is a 34-year-old male. He was doing his clinical residency in the state of Texas, but dropped out and moved to Arizona. His depression was complicated by, or even created, a further problem of reduced motivation. Being so poorly motivated he did not return to school, he did not complete his residency, he did not apply for jobs, and he became very self-critical.

Broadcasting this attitude in many ways to others, he found himself taken advantage of by others. He recently lost $4,000 to a mere stranger, whom he thought he was helping as a friend. But instead of being outwardly angry at the thief, he is angry at himself. In this situation the use of direct communication about his feelings would be pointless. He would deny any anger and, were he to feel any anger, he would state that it is inappropriate for *him* to show it—he is not entitled to do so. In the second session, he is asked to go into trance after he relates the incident of being swindled. The following metaphor is a portion of that trance session.

"Pete worked as a dishwasher and was a classical guitar player. He had studied with Julian Bream and Andres Segovia and was a genuinely sensitive and accomplished musician. For a while, he drove a 1992 Mazda that had a bumper sticker reading "'Handel' with care, classical guitar player inside." After a while, he didn't think he needed that car anymore. When you change your car, you change a lot of things about yourself.

"When he came home from work one day, he found the door unlocked. He was temporarily surprised and angry at himself for not locking it. Fumbling for his keys, he fell into the door and hardly gave a second thought as to why he had not locked it. But looking around, he saw the room was a mess. He was sort of struggling to understand his thoughts.

"When he saw the room in disarray, he thought how messy he was not to clean the room better. It says something about you when you keep your room in a mess. But then he saw shirts out on the couch and the situation changed. It occurred to Pete that he had not put his shirts on the couch, he would not have pulled them all out—he must have been robbed!

"Now for anyone who knew Pete, they would agree that there was one thing that came through loud and clear about him and that was his dependency on that guitar. He loved it. He would even fall asleep with it. He had slept with it once or twice and was teased by his friends. And he would spend hours a day dealing with it rather than dealing with another person. In fact, he got to where he would substitute playing his guitar forgoing on a date. Maybe it was like Linus and his blanket, and you know how fretful Linus gets if someone has taken his blanket. This does not begin to compare, however, with the feelings Pete was about to feel when he realized that he was being robbed. At first he thought he *had been* robbed and then he realized he *was being* robbed at that moment. He heard noise in the back room when the apartment should have been empty.

"And you know how your mind can change when you are in an auto accident, for example. You can remember every instance of that 10-second auto crash as though it had happened over a period of 20 minutes. You remember every change of posture, every movement of a pedestrian, every inch that the cars began to approach each other, everything you did to fasten a seatbelt or close a glove compartment or move something off of your lap. Pete must have had that sense of heightened memory, because he could explain every minute detail that occurred on that day from that moment on.

"It must have happened in a half of a few seconds, but it seemed like half an hour. The next thing he realized was a feeling in his legs and he felt his feet carry him across the threshold, hand on doorknob, shoulders relaxed on ribcage, which seemed odd to him. He could feel the blood flow through his arms and the adrenalin. But he felt somehow removed from it in a way that was surprising. He felt the momentum of his body open the door in a very aggressive fashion. But he did not have any thoughts about it except that he did not think it would have been so easy, and yet it seemed to be easier than he would have thought.

"In great detail he explained how he was running into the bedroom where his guitar was and what he was hollering. He heard words pouring out of his mouth that he didn't usually say. Then he saw the thief jump out the window holding *his* guitar. Then Pete dived out the window. He realized he was doing something one doesn't normally do. One's conscious mind can observe one's body in action. Everyone has had the experience of hollering automatically when someone steps on your toes. You don't really realize what you are saying until you hear what you said.

"And before that moment had passed, Pete had both his tennis shoes on the grass outside his bedroom window and was racing across the parking lot. He felt weightless as his feet carried him across the grass. He was surprised consciously to realize he could have a feeling that seemed alien to him but have it comfortably when he might have thought he could not. He thought feelings had to be heavy, especially this one.

"And moving more rapidly than the man who was running, he passed the man, who dropped the guitar and let it hit the ground with a bong. The strings began resonating. They would do so for a good 20 seconds. Finally, Pete grabbed the thief by the shoulders and pushed him up against the back of that 1992 Mazda, and bent him over somewhat backwards against the back of the trunk.

"I do not know where you first feel your sense of muscular power when you do something like that. Maybe you feel your feet firmly on the ground. Maybe you feel a little taller than usual. Maybe you recognize that your breathing is easy and more rapid than usual and your skin is warm. And Pete stood there, pulled his fist back and held it chin level to himself and heard himself saying, 'I'm going to clobber you, you son of a bitch.' These were words he had never heard come out of his mouth before.

"He was about to hit the man, but then turned him around and putting his arms behind his back, wrestled him to the ground and held him there. There was a commotion. There was still a ringing in the background. Those guitar strings were still resonating from the topple and bong they had received.

"Other people now responded to the brawl. It had caught the attention of a passing patrol car and soon the police descended on the thief. As Pete walked away from the episode, he realized the guitar strings had still been faintly resonating while he held the man on the ground. He knew he could depend on the base notes resonating for about 17 seconds. The entire incident had taken just over 20 seconds from when he went out the back window to when he wrestled the man to the ground.

"Heart pounding, shoulders and sternum held high, jaw set firmly, feeling the blood pulsing through his neck, Pete would have expected that feeling that way would have been far more uncomfortable. He never thought of himself in any other way than "classical guitar player, handle with care." It's a lesson. One's unconscious knows of a good deal of experience and can put it together no matter what one's conscious mind thinks. Pete memorized that experience of anger, the impulse, the understanding that the unconscious intent is to have that impulse and use it for your needs—and memorized the recognition of not going

beyond the bounds of reason, even when he had the chance and it would have been justified."

Following the experiences he retrieved listening to this story, it was relatively easy to assist the client in thinking through how he could be angry at others, and be assertive while nurturing himself with angry and assertive feelings. Naturally, the therapy for each of the above individuals involved many more aspects of change. These excerpts are meant only to illustrate how therapeutic metaphor is used in nonhypnotic therapy as well as in hypnosis. As in the previous story, the metaphor allowed the therapist to elicit difficult emotional material—anger and assertiveness—without resistance by providing an alternate framework into which the client could project experiences he commonly avoided in his own life.

THE AMBIGUOUS ASPECT OF METAPHOR

Unlike directive and manipulative interventions that, through direct command, tell clients how to perceive, think, feel, or behave, techniques of indirection allow clients to project their own meaning into what they hear. This, in turn, allows the therapeutic material to be fit to their personal situation. Because clients *must* fit their life into the story being told, there is a high degree of relevance and deep meaning for clients. Contrariwise, if clients are instructed by therapists to conduct themselves in a certain manner, or say certain sentences in, say, directive couples therapy, the response from clients is compliance. That means that the learning, if any, has come from "outside" of themselves. However, when clients have determined for themselves a relevant meaning to an otherwise ambiguous story, they act on perceptions, behaviors, and feelings that truly belong to *them* and are a part of them.

Let's examine this ambiguous element more closely. The degree of ambiguity in a therapeutic story can be regulated by the teller so that the story is more or less vague to the listener. Regardless of the degree of vagueness, listeners create their own relevant meaning in order to understand the story. This accounts for the personalized nature of the understanding and the lack of mere compliance by listeners. However, as the degree of vagueness increases, there is an exponential increase in the number of possible meanings that listeners can give to the story. It is assumed that listeners unconsciously sorting through several possibilities at what has been determined to be 30 items per second (Erickson & Rossi, 1979, p. 18) become increasingly absorbed in weighing the best fit for these possible meanings.

This ongoing process of weighing meaning has a number of therapeutic benefits. They include

- An increase in participation by listeners
- A heightened valuation in any meaning by listeners because the meaning has come from within their own experience
- A depotentiation of normal limitations or rigid ego controls as the listener seeks a "best fit"
- An increase in the duration of time given to examining possible meanings.

This last element, in fact, accounts for a therapeutic effect upon clients lasting long after the therapy sessions have ended. Indeed, for a highly meaningful and yet extremely vague metaphoric story, some clients have reported that they continued to turn it over in their minds for years and did this again for events that paralleled the original therapeutic learning incident years later. For this reason, the use of metaphor can be summarized as follows:

- It increases the relevance of therapy for clients and involves clients more highly in their own change process.
- It expands the usual limiting experience that has led to a stabilization of the presenting problem or dynamic that had brought the person to therapy.
- It offers an engaging element of ambiguity that may continue to alert listeners to their therapeutic learning for years after a therapy session.
- It offers a wide range of potentially correct responses within the therapeutic limits.

USES OF METAPHORIC STORIES

As listeners become increasingly engaged or absorbed in a story, there is a reduction in the defensive mechanisms that customarily constrain them to common sets experience (those which resulted in seeking therapy). That is,

listening to a story that symbolizes tenderness can lead a person who normally does not shed tears or weep to do so.

The definition mentions that clients can entertain *novel* experiences. The concept of a novel experience may need some elaboration. It pertains to experiences that have commonly been excluded from the experiential set of the listener/client. While listening to an absorbing story, clients may, with relative ease, temporarily go through one or several specific experiences, which, if therapeutically managed, can assist them in creating personal change. The assistance in creating personal change comes about as clients re-examine perceptions or cognitions, emotions, or potential behaviors in light of a recognition that some *new* experiences, perceptions, or cognitions once thought to be alien actually can be a part of their own personality and experience. In general, it can be said that the usefulness of metaphoric stories in therapy comes into play at any point in therapy where it is advisable or useful for clients to recognize that they can obtain the necessary experiential resources from within themselves rather than having to introject them from an outside authority.

Metaphor is especially useful when brief forms of therapy such as solution-focused therapy, hypnotherapy, family or couples therapy, or grief therapy, are the therapeutic modality of choice. Nevertheless, an additional aspect of the ambiguous nature of metaphor suggests that the use of therapeutic metaphor can have great value in long-term therapies as well.

REDUCTION OF RESISTANCE

Because metaphor offers listeners the ability to apply a wide range or spectrum of potential understandings to what the therapist has said, there is a corresponding reduction in listener resistance. Any therapeutic modality that finds clients to be resistive, possibly due to the nature of the modality itself, will be able to take advantage of metaphoric stories, provided that those stories are constructed and shared in a manner that employs the necessary components.

THE NECESSARY COMPONENTS OF THERAPEUTIC METAPHOR

To be effective, therapeutic metaphor must be perceived and be relevant. It also must engage listeners and retrieve experience. There are a number of ways these requirements can be fostered in the therapeutic process. There should be a consideration of the relationship of the story to the sensory system primarily used by the listener in order to process data, material that is taken out of sequence to create dramatic engagement or enchantment, and the retrieval and use of experience that is therapeutically relevant.

The Perception and Relevance of the Metaphor

The most important feature regarding relevance of a metaphor or any experience is that it resonates with either clients' current state or clients' anticipated future state. The metaphor should be constructed to hold the attention of clients' conscious minds. This applies to the vast majority of metaphors that therapists will construct and use. Therapists should consider that clients' understandings or representations of problems are likely to be characterized by them in a preferred sensory system. That is, some clients will relate their problem with the majority of their sensory-specific verbs in a preferred representational system: visual, auditory, or kinesthetic (Lankton, 1980/2003). This can be ascertained by listening to clients' presentations of their problems. When such a preference is discovered, it is imperative that therapists attempt to communicate with clients in their preferred manner of thinking and representing. When delivering metaphor the conscious minds of clients will be engaged and consider stories more relevant when this connection is honored. Erickson referred to this as speaking the client's experiential language. Certain portions of a metaphoric story, however, may be strategically represented in a lesser used system for certain purposes. For instance, certain experiences may be more easily retrieved by therapeutic efforts aimed at the lesser used representational systems.

Consider a client who thinks with a predominantly visual set of mental tools. Relating a story that encourages him to see a father and son hugging will have a moving effect of joy or sadness on his conscious mind if he did not receive that type of attention. But then hearing the words spoken (his secondarily used sensory system is auditory) by the father in the story saying "Come here and let me hug you, son. I love you and I'm proud

of you" may more quickly evoke an emotion of tenderness, joy, or sadness. The difference is due to the fact that the client's understanding of his life is primarily a visual "story" in his mind that he can easily navigate. Seeing the images created in the telling of the story, it would be easy for him to quickly compare the ideas to his life and "think" about it. However, thinking with auditory imagery is not as easy for him and the experience attached to the imagery used by the therapist is, in fact, the experience he retrieves with less resistance. Purposeful regulation of this aspect of a story is a matter of training and experience on the part of therapist.

Metaphors that are Parallel to the Problem

There are two major categories of metaphor: those that are parallel to the client's problem and those that are parallel to the anticipated goal. Stories that are parallel to the client's current state or problem are far easier to construct and were the first type of metaphors noticed in the process of attempting to simulate the therapeutic work of experts such as Milton Erickson (Gordon, 1978; Lankton, 1980/2003).

The basic idea of the metaphoric stories that are parallel to the problem can be summarized in the understanding of the term *isomorphism*. Metaphors that are isomorphic have the body of their content in a one-to-one correspondence with the experience (that is, the problem state) of the client. A simple way of understanding this is that for every major person, relationship, and activity in the client's problem there is a corresponding person, relationship, and activity in the story told to the client. Again, the degree of distance or vagueness between the elements in the metaphor and the elements in the client's life will regulate the degree of ambiguity that is introduced, and therefore, determine how likely it is that the client will make the connection between this story and his or her life.

For example, consider the following variation of isomorphic metaphor that matches the problem. Here the husband seeks affection from a wife who ignores him unless blaming him for a fault. The pattern then unfolds as the husband withdraws into depression and the wife becomes angry with him. Table 81.1 lists the situation's components as related by the client, and the two columns show the elements of two different

TABLE 81.1 Isomorphic Construction

Situation	Less Ambiguous	More Ambiguous
husband	lovebird	electric drill
(husband) asks	chirps	(drill) freezes up
needs affection	needs touching	needs oil
wife	girl	mechanic
(wife) ignores	(girl) locks up bird	throws down
(wife) blames faults	(girl) shouts at bird	worries it will burn
(wife) defensive	(girl) recalls messes	brags of skill
(husband) withdraws	(bird) chews cage	(drill) overheats
(husband) depression	(bird) gets ill	(drill) emits smoke
(wife) angry	(girl) sells bird	throws it out

stories that could be told. They illustrate two varying degrees of ambiguity.

It should be obvious that despite the similar isomorphic relationship between parts of the story and the problem, the more ambiguous references may not be an apparent match in the mind of the listener. The solution to the dilemma is not shown in the table, only the components that match to the problem. However, the sketching of part (or all) of the solution would be the next step for the therapist.

There are two important considerations for the use of isomorphic metaphors. First, it must outline the context or heighten the client's awareness for the problem situation in which the solution will be fitted. Second, isomorphic metaphors need to have resolution that provides some metaphoric solution. It is in this second aspect of isomorphic metaphors that beginning therapists may encounter difficulty. There are a few major ways for isomorphic metaphors to be terminated so that they provide a therapeutic conclusion for the problem they have highlighted. The most elegant manner is that which involves the continued and often creative behavior of the protagonist, through whose behavior a solution would be illustrated. A second, less practical method is for the therapist to introduce into the story direct instructions that represent words spoken to the protagonist. This latter example is often called "embedded commands" or "embedded quotes." In this case, the only experience created for the client is that of a verbal idea.

This second option fails to meet the criteria of retrieving experience for a client and often fails to

meet the ambiguity element that prevents resistance in the client. However, it is a very practical method for therapists to deliver clear guidelines, instructions, or directives to a client in a fashion that reduces confrontation and thereby allows a client to save face.

The third and least elegant method to create a goal in an isomorphic metaphor is to introduce a break in the normal flow of the protagonist's behavior owing to some unexpected element such as the protagonist going to therapy, having a dream, or having some sudden sort of epiphany. Although this device within a story will allow the speaker to jump to a solution set, it does so at the expense of the logical flow of the metaphoric content. Yet, it still provides an opportunity for experiences to be retrieved that will help alter perception, behavior, emotion, or attitude—and for the client to experience these needed resources in immediate proximity or conjunction with the problem.

Goal-directed Metaphors

The second major category of metaphor comprises those that are constructed to become parallel to the goal rather than parallel to the problem (Lankton & Lankton, 1986, 1989; Lankton, 2004). It is essential that a basic protocol be followed to address specific goals of changes in attitude, emotion, and behavior, respectively. The content of the metaphors must be so ordered, following a process formula, that the metaphor retrieves specific types of experience-related options that, in turn, may serve as goals for the listener. These protocols can be streamlined or maximized to facilitate, if not ensure, that the listener's experience will be one of cognitive alteration, emotional alteration, or behavioral sensitizing. In order to illustrate this, the three self-explanatory protocols for emotion, attitude, and behavior metaphors are listed below (Lankton & Lankton, 1986, 1989; Lankton, 2004).

A. Affect and emotion protocol
  1. Establish a relationship between the protagonist and a person, place, or thing that involves emotion or affect (e.g., tenderness, anxiety, mastery, confusion, love, longing).
  2. Detail *movement* in the relationship (e.g., moving with, moving toward, moving away, chasing, consistently pursuing, orbiting).
  3. Focus on some of the congruent physiological changes that coincide with the protagonist's emotion (be sure to overlap with the client's facial and upper torso behavior as he or she listens).
B. Attitude change protocol
  1. Describe a protagonist's behavior or perception so it exemplifies the maladaptive attitude. Bias this belief to appear positive or desirable.
  2. Describe another protagonist's behavior or perception so it exemplifies the *adaptive* attitude (the goal). Bias this belief to appear negative or undesirable.
  3. Reveal the *unexpected* outcome achieved by both protagonists that resulted from the beliefs they held and their related actions. Be sure the "payoff" received by the second protagonist would be considered to be of value to the client.
C. Behavior change protocol
  1. Illustrate the protagonist's observable behavior similar to the desired behavior to be acquired by the client. There is no need to mention motives. List about six specific observable behaviors.
  2. Detail the protagonist's internal attention or nonobservable behavior that shows the protagonist to be congruent with his or her observable behavior.
  3. Change the setting within the story so as to provide an opportunity for repeating all the behavioral descriptions several (at least three) times.

Dramatic Aspects of Metaphor

A client's conscious attention can be held by the addition of dramatic devices in the storyline of the metaphor. By holding the client's conscious attention the therapist ensures that the metaphor can become a vehicle for carrying the interventions that retrieve desired experiences. My definition for the construction of dramatic devices in any oral or rhetoric tradition can be seen as a matter of presenting knowledge or information out of sequence. Information that is in a linear, chronological sequence is simply a documentary. However, when various delivery devices such as tonal inflection are used to stress certain words as if their meaning is deeper than that which is denoted, there is an indication that more than just documentary information is being offered. Furthermore, the hints that are provided by tonal stress in a simple, linear presentation of facts cause the listener to seek that connoted meaning by anticipating *what is to come* in the story or re-evaluating what has been heard so far. However, the actual tactics of creating dramatic hold within a story are more dynamic than simply stressing connoted information.

Looking at Table 81.2, it can be seen that, in the course of a story line, there will be information known to the protagonist (or characters in the story) and information known to the listener (that is, the client). If information known to the protagonist is not known to the listener, mystery arises. For example, in the telling of a story there may be a letter read, a telephone call, or a conversation in a secluded location between protagonists. And the information shared in that exchange can be illustrated as having great importance. However, that information can be withheld from listeners as a secret or private event. Although it has great meaning to the characters of the story, listeners will not know how the protagonists' behavior has been affected by

TABLE 81.2 Creating Drama

Type of Drama	Client	Protagonist(s)
Suspense	Knows info	Does not know
Mystery	Does not know	Knows info
Surprise/ shock/humor	Does not know	Does not know

the information that was concealed from them. As a result, listeners are in a position to try to deduce by anticipation, think back to the character development, or somehow gain a degree of certainty about how the information may affect the outcome of the story or just what the information was.

The element of mystery seems to create a primarily cognitive hold on the listener. It can happen numerous times in a story and it can also be created by means other than dialogues between the characters in the story. An analysis will reveal that the characters have been shown to be privy to some information not known to the listener. In the case of a therapeutic story the listener is the client.

Table 81.2 further illustrates that information known to the client or listener but not known to the protagonists or characters in the story creates the drama of suspense. The "hold" of suspense is a much more visceral or emotional hold of attention compared with mystery. This is often easily created by the storyteller through foreshadowing. In many well-known works of literature, the author will give a glimpse ahead as to how the story is to be framed. This occurs, for instance, when the story begins with comments about how the story will be ended. It is the same in cinema. The motion picture *Gandhi* begins with the assassination of the protagonist. Here we see the archetypal footprint of suspense by means of taking information out of sequence and foreshadowing the later ending of the man's life. However, in cinema, there are more dramatic devices that can be used, such as sirens and flashing lights or the well-known rhythmical percussion in the movie *Jaws*. In a literary or spoken story, material taken out of sequence that reveals flaws or outcomes about the protagonists to the listener will increase the experience of suspense.

Finally, the drama creation table shows that when neither the listener/client nor the protagonist/character have information about an upcoming event, the result will be surprise, shock, or humor when the event occurs. So, a sudden death in a story, which was not foreshadowed for the listener or expected by the characters, will be a surprise. When surprise or shock occurs in a story, listeners will search facts they have already heard in the story to put the incident in perspective or will examine whether certain information had already existed to predict the surprise. And, too, they will begin to test various anticipated

hypotheses to try to predict how the story will turn out and be fixated on future details to potentially resolve the element of surprise.

Any of these dramatic methods have the effect of capturing attention and *engaging* listeners in the story by means of encouraging them to make sense of it. The visceral or cognitive energy used to sort through past and anticipated futures in a story is the result of the use of drama. The drama does not need to be award-winning or especially creative. It simply needs to be present in the story to help listeners become more consciously absorbed as they make room to entertain the novel experience created by the protocols mentioned before.

Enchantment

As mentioned, one of the devices for understanding the effect of metaphor is the aspect of ambiguity. In addition to drama, ambiguity is one of the major mechanisms that binds the listener to the story. Few words are available for explaining this interpersonal aspect of the phenomenon of ambiguity. Perhaps one of the best terms to refer to it is *enchantment*. Enchantment can be defined as being held spellbound by or as if by irresistible force, words, or charms; or to pique a pleasant mental excitement. It is this last aspect of creating a pleasant mental excitement that is of greatest interest to the therapist constructing a therapeutic metaphor.

Creating dramatic hold in a relevant story with a certain degree of various meanings available maximizes both interest and usefulness of the story for the client. It was mentioned earlier that the degree of ambiguity can be regulated by means of increasing or decreasing vagueness about the connection between events in the client's life or experiences that will be goals for the client and the elements in the story. That is, the elements in the story can be increasingly mundane or increasingly symbolic and abstract in their denoted content. A degree of skill and practice is necessary to develop the ability to maximize the therapeutic impact and regulate this ambiguity with clients. It requires that therapists continue to have a high degree of observation regarding the impact the story is having upon the listener. Beyond the regulation of controlled ambiguity within the metaphor, there are other devices that create or regulate the experience of enchantment. These include auditory tonal changes in delivery and word-selection that can create a degree of pathos and highly charged meaning for the listener.

Indications and Contraindications

Contraindications for using metaphor fall into two categories. One category has to do with the experience level of the therapist and the other concerns the type and severity of the client's presenting problem. A therapist who has little skill in the use of indirection techniques and who has limited clinical skill must consider using metaphoric stories with a greatly limited range of clients, problem severity, and diagnostic categories. The beginning therapist can only comfortably use metaphoric stories with individuals who would be considered vocal and intellectual; mildly neurotic, anxious, depressed; and with problems that are not urgent. With such clients, there is more ability to assess impact and ethically evaluate the efficacy of the technique.

Therapists with a greater degree of clinical experience and experience with the use of indirection and ambiguous interventions will find that it is possible to successfully and ethically employ metaphoric stories with a far greater range of individuals, problem categories, and diagnostic types.

Contraindication for diagnostic types includes individuals who are actively psychotic and those who are moderately to severely borderline. This also includes any neurotic individuals who have extreme difficulties with boundary-related issues. The reason for this concern about individuals with cognitive disorders and boundary problems lies in the fact that individuals can and will apply multiple meanings to the ambiguity of the metaphor. When the individual client has demonstrated difficulty retaining cognitive meaning or boundaries in "real-life" situations, the use of any technique that exacerbates a concrete intervention is contraindicated. Similarly, the boundary problem finds its difficulty in those individuals who come to believe that the therapist can read their thoughts by the fact that they have projected meaning into a metaphoric story and failed to realize that it is *their* projected meaning, instead thinking that it is a previously known meaning that the therapist has somehow been able to divine from an extra-ordinary means or from an extraordinary rapport with them.

These extremes do not occur for individuals who do not have boundary or cognitive problems.

However, a third category of contraindication includes those individuals who have a great deal of difficulty establishing rapport and trust. For these persons, regardless of their diagnostic category or presenting problem, the credibility of the therapist is continually being questioned and evaluated. Using metaphoric stories relies upon clients investigating what was said for possible relevant meanings and surrendering a degree of habitual reality testing. As clients become caught up in the relevance, drama, and enchantment of the story, individuals who maintain an analytical distance, and do so while doubting the therapist, are liable to take the ambiguity as a sign that the therapist is to some degree not competent. Again, the clinical experience of the therapist may reduce the number of individuals for whom this type of contraindication is relevant. Therapists with considerable clinical experience are usually skilled at carefully judging the manner in which they need to approach clients in order to engage them in the change process. And, the execution of this type of therapeutic judgment can be referred to as, what this author calls the "controlled elaboration of ambiguity."

Using Metaphors within the Therapy Process

Using metaphoric stories need not be constrained to individuals in hypnotic trance. Metaphoric stories can be used at any point in the therapeutic process providing the goal is to retrieve perceptual, attitudinal, emotional, or behavior-change goals. Some of the common uses of metaphors even in the early stages of the therapy process are as follows.

• To illustrate a way of using therapy to change problems and arrive at a therapeutic contract
• To help clients relax
• To direct clients' thoughts to the situations that have led them to the office
• To normalize their situation and help them articulate their problems.

All of these goals and more at the early stages of therapeutic contact can not only be accomplished with metaphoric stories but can possibly be accomplished more efficiently by using them. The reason for this is that the degree of choice the listener has in making sense of a metaphoric story reduces the resistance that can arise from otherwise attempting to be specific with direct communication of statements and questions about how a client is to think, feel, or behave.

During the change process itself, metaphoric stories can enhance any aspect of therapy where increased mental involvement is indicated and where specific experiences brought into the foreground can enhance therapeutic movement. These times are more numerous than can possibly be mentioned and the more experience the therapist has, the more such moments will be apparent.

Summary

Using therapeutic metaphor throughout the therapy process can enhance therapeutic movement as it retrieves the desired experiences clients need for therapeutic movement. Metaphoric stories need to be constructed in a manner that is relevant to clients, holds their attention, and facilitates the retrieval of experience that is helpful to the therapy process. The degree of ambiguity should be carefully regulated by observing the client's responses to the spoken words.

When using metaphoric stories, therapists must continually observe clients during the delivery of each metaphor. The aim of observation is for the therapist to recognize the degree of relevance the story has for the listener by gauging the degree of internal absorption and searching for facial expressions, head nods, changes in breathing, and other ideomotor behavior that the client displays. It is also for the therapist to gauge the degree of achievement that clients accomplish in retrieving desired experiences from the same indicators. Finally, the aim of observation is to gather ongoing diagnostic information as it pertains to the manner in which the client responds to various words and actions that are denoted and connoted within the story.

Because delivering and receiving the metaphor is an individual matter, research on the level of resource retrieval and specific resources that a particular metaphoric story may bring is problematic. Clients will respond in unique ways depending upon their needs, background issues, and motivation, and also depending upon the therapist's skill in observing and delivering metaphor. Outcomes that are achieved by the use of metaphoric stories are truly co-created. That is, they are a blend of the client's history and motivation coupled with the therapist's ability to provide compelling delivery and meaningful content, as well as therapeutically useful protocol.

Finally, it should be remembered that the listener's achievement of meaning fluctuates with the degree of ambiguity and apparent relevance of the story. Therefore, stories should have some immediate impact upon the listener that is useful within the therapeutic sessions. However, some degree of impact can be expected from certain stories, days or even years later, due to the client's capability to seek useful meanings and project them into the ambiguity provided by a relevant story.

INTERNET SOURCES

www.erickson-foundation.org
www.lankton.com
www.asch.org

References

Erickson, M., & Rossi, E. (1979). *Hypnotherapy: An exploratory casebook*. New York, NY: Irvington.

Gordon, D. (1978). *Therapeutic metaphors: Helping others through the looking glass*. Cupertino, CA: Meta Publication.

Lankton, S. (2004). *Assembling Ericksonian therapy: The collected papers of Stephen Lankton*. Phoenix, AZ: Zeig, Tucker, Theisen.

Lankton, S. (1980/2003). *Practical magic: A translation of basic neuro-linguistic programming into clinical psychotherapy*. New York, NY: Crown Publications.

Lankton, S., & Lankton, C. (1986). *Enchantment and intervention in family therapy: Training in Ericksonian approaches*. New York, NY: Brunner/Mazel.

Lankton, C., & Lankton, S. (1989). *Tales of enchantment: An anthology of goal directed metaphors for adults and children in therapy*. New York, NY: Brunner/Mazel.

82   Cognitive Restructuring Techniques

Donald K. Granvold & Bruce A. Thyer

From a Cognitive Behavioral (CB) perspective, human functioning is conceptualized as the product of the reciprocal interaction of cognition, behavior, emotion, personal factors (emotion, motivation, physiology, and physical phenomena), and social environmental influences. As social worker Harold Werner put it: "the primary determinant of emotion and behavior is thinking." (Werner, 1982, p. 3), reflecting a perspective similar to that of social worker James Lantz: "The primary concept held by cognitive practitioners is that most human emotion is the result of what people think, tell themselves, assume, or believe about themselves and their social situations" (Lantz, 1978, p. 361). Beck and colleagues also elucidate this point: "The primacy hypothesis reflects the importance we place on cognition by stating that negative cognition and the biased information processing of negative self-referent information can directly influence other behavioral, motivational, affective, and somatic symptoms of depression" (Clark, Beck, & Alford, 1999, p. 157).

From a *behavior analytic* perspective, overt actions, thoughts, and feelings are all seen as forms of behavior, without any causal relations among them. This is in keeping with the definition of behavior provided in the National Association of Social Workers (NASW) *Social Work Dictionary*, "Any action or response by an individual, including observable activity, measurable physiological changes, cognitive images, fantasies, and emotions. Some scientists even consider subjective experiences to be behaviors" (Barker, 1995, p. 33). Although the psychologist John B. Watson claimed that the term behavior should be limited to publicly observable actions, this limited perspective never really was widely endorsed and was replaced by the expansive view of B. F. Skinner who promoted a more comprehensive definition of behavior, embracing both overt and covert (within the skin) actions, including thoughts and feelings. Unlike the CB perspective, however, behavior analysis does *not* posit that thinking causes behavior, or even has primacy in explaining overt behavior. Rather, the behavior analyst contends that overt actions, thoughts *and* feelings are all largely originating in the person's environmental experiences and biology. This is an important distinction. If one theorizes that thinking causes overt behavior, then to change overt behavior one should focus on changing cognition. This is, of course, the conventional view of most psychotherapies, including cognitive behavioral therapies. However, if one theorizes that thoughts, overt behavior, and feelings are all caused by one's person-in-environment transactions (and biology), the social worker largely will focus on providing new and different environmental experiences in order to bring about changes in thoughts, feelings, and actions. This is much more of an *environmentalist* orientation, as opposed to a mentalist one, and has important treatment ramifications. CB therapy would focus more on office-based consultations and therapies, whereas the behavior analyst would view cognitive change efforts as more real-world based, with change efforts occurring outside the office. Below we will discuss various ways of changing thinking, derived from these two orientations.

TECHNIQUES FOR CHANGING THOUGHTS

Socratic Dialogue

Cognitive restructuring is the term used for a variety of procedures focused on the modification of cognitions and cognitive processing. Many approaches to cognitive restructuring use the Socratic method to guide the client in the identification, exploration, modification, and elaboration of cognitions. Other approaches use imagery, guided discovery, and in vivo behavioral procedures to "test out" and modify beliefs.

The goal of cognitive restructuring is to guide the client in the exposure of cognitions influencing untoward, unappealing, discomforting, or dysfunctional outcomes and modify them through further exploration, disputation, or elaboration. Clients are guided in the use of logic or evidence to examine and modify their exaggerated, distorted, or ill-founded beliefs. The first task is to elicit the thoughts, cognitive processing errors, or images contributing to the client's unhappiness or distress. Wells (1997) recommends a Socratic sequence combining general questions with more specific probe questions. Probe questions are useful in gaining clarification and greater detail. The use of reflection and expressions of empathy and affirmation may promote relationship development and client awareness that the therapist clearly understands. The following dialogue illustrates early intervention with a client experiencing high anxiety.

Therapist: What did you feel in the situation? [general question]

Client: I felt scared and couldn't stop shaking.

T: When you felt *scared* and *shaky* [reflection] what thoughts went through your mind?

C: I don't know. I just felt awful.

T: Did you think anything bad could happen when you felt like that? [probe]

C: Yes. I thought I looked stupid.

T: What do you mean by stupid? [probe]

C: I thought everyone would notice and think I was an alcoholic or something (Wells, 1997, p. 53).

Cognitive restructuring is incomplete if the process is stopped at mere identification of operative cognitions. After gaining an understanding of the client's thinking and associated emotional responses, the focus shifts to modification efforts. The following is a list of questions for use in modifying thoughts.

- Where is the evidence?
- Is there any evidence to the contrary?

- How strongly do you believe that?
- Could you see yourself . . . with more positive views of self . . . having more trust in your partner's dedication to you . . . having greater purpose in life?
- What is the worst that could happen?
- Could you look at it another way?
- What other meanings can you identify?
- What are the consequences of looking at it this way?
- How do you feel when you think _____?
- Would it be possible to _____?
- What images or sensations do you experience when you think _____?
- What other thoughts flow from that thought (image)?
- Given your current understanding of the impact that our meanings have on the way we think, feel, and are motivated to act, what is your best advice to yourself?
- What if?

Socratic dialogue uses questions like the foregoing to probe for the logic or evidence supporting the client's thinking and explore the consequences of the belief or beliefs. As beliefs fail to demonstrate validity or viability, cognitive restructuring proceeds with the generation of alternative meanings and their consequences (Beck, 1995; Granvold, 1994).

THERAPIST MODELING ADAPTIVE THINKING

It is important that the therapist model desirable cognitive processing in the questions asked. For example, "How did that make you feel?" promotes external locus of control thinking. Such thinking places the power over one's well-being with other people or with one's life circumstances. This violates the cognitive therapy principle that, with a few exceptions, each of us is responsible for our feelings and ultimately our mental health. The question can be rephrased easily as, "How did you feel when . . . ?" Another therapist trap easily avoided is the use of expressions in which information processing errors are evident. For example, to avoid modeling dichotomous thinking the therapist can ask such questions as, "What factors influenced your decision to divorce?" and "When you got angry in traffic, what thoughts were going through your mind?"

CASE EXAMPLE

The following is an illustration of cognitive restructuring with a client who is going through a contentious divorce. By temporary court order, her husband has been given managing conservatorship of their children. Her relationship with her children has been troubled largely due to past episodes of depression and a demanding work schedule. Following the recent separation, she has felt extremely depressed and hopeless, along with feelings of hurt, sadness, loss, and anger. She admits to suicidal ideation but has no plan to do so, nor can she see herself actually committing suicide. Socratic dialogue has identified a web of strong beliefs that undermine her emotional well-being and promote negative views of self. In the following excerpt, one of the most powerful beliefs from this matrix of meanings is identified and explored for change. The probing is focused on uncovering evidence to support or negate her belief.

Client: I have moved out of the house into an apartment. I've lost everything. I don't have my house. My husband doesn't love me. I don't have my kids anymore. I've lost my children [crying].

Therapist: You have experienced a lot of loss with the separation, and I feel badly that you are going through this. You just said that you have lost your children. Could you tell me more about that thought?

C: I don't see them each night when I come home from work. I've lost them. I'm not a mother anymore.

T: When you think the thought, "I've lost my children," how do you feel?

C: I feel empty and sad . . . and hurt.

T: So the thought, "I've lost my children" promotes some pretty unpleasant feelings.

C: Yes [softly crying].

T: You may recall our past discussions about the role our thoughts tend to play in our feelings. You have expressed the thought that you have lost your children. As evidence to support this thought, you indicated that you don't see them each evening as you did prior to the separation.

Let's explore this statement. Have you seen them at all since you moved out three weeks ago?

C: Oh, yes, I see them one or two nights a week and on Saturday or Sunday, sometimes both days.

T: So despite not seeing them daily, you do spend time with them several times a week.

C: Yes, that's right.

T: Although it is not the same as when you were living in the same household with them, are you their mother when you are spending time with them?

C: Well, yes I am, but it doesn't feel the same.

T: In what ways does it feel different?

C: I guess it's different because I know that I am going to my apartment alone, without them.

T: Would you conclude from our discussion that although it isn't the same, you haven't actually lost your children?

C: Yea, I guess that's more accurate.

T: So, you're still their mother, and you are continuing to be actively involved in their lives. Earlier you said that you feel sad, empty, and hurt in relation to the thought that you've lost your children. Would you conclude that shifting your thought from, "I've lost my children" to "It isn't the same" is really a more accurate statement of your situation?

C: Yes, it is, I guess.

T: You have reported feeling sad, empty, and hurt in relation to the thought that you've lost your children. Though it would be unrealistic to expect these feelings to go away completely, can you detect feeling any *less* sad, empty, and hurt as you think, "parenting isn't the same," rather than "I've lost my children?"

C: It's really hard to tell, but I suppose I don't feel as badly.

T: Perhaps you will be able to detect greater change in your feelings over time. Each time you think, "I've lost my children," would you be willing to answer that thought with, "No, I haven't lost my children, it (parenting) just isn't the same?"

C: Yes, I'll try it.

The therapist guided the client in revising a powerful statement presumably influential in promoting strong feelings. The client realized that the evidence contradicted the meaning she attached to the postseparation change in parenting. She arrived at an alternative meaning that was more consistent with her recent experience as a parent. She also considered the connection between her thoughts and feelings. Based on the awareness that effective cognitive restructuring requires repetition, the client was asked to repeat the reframing whenever the faulty thought occurred. This practice was reviewed at several subsequent sessions. As noted earlier, the thought addressed in this excerpt is one of a web of beliefs contributing to her current views about her children, herself, and her emotional state. She also believed that her children no longer cared for her (e.g., "They never call me"; "They could care less whether I call them or not"; "When we are together, it's all about them"). These and other beliefs were similarly isolated for cognitive restructuring with the focus on the identification of supportive evidence and evidence to the contrary.

THERAPIST MODELING OF ADAPTIVE PERFORMANCE

Observing another person engage in desired behavior can be an effective method of inducing behavioral, affective, and cognitive changes (Bandura, 1977). For example, in the behavioral technique of exposure therapy and response prevention, which often is used to treat clients with phobias, a therapist will model all behaviors to be subsequently asked of the client, such as touching a harmless snake, holding it, and verbalizing aloud realistic and adaptive thoughts. Similarly, role playing exercises for nonassertive persons may involve a therapist displaying various ways of acting appropriately assertive with a confederate, while the client observes. The exercises may involve gradually escalating scenarios wherein the therapist/ model demonstrates increasingly greater levels of assertiveness.

USE OF SCALING TO ASSESS CHANGE

Cognitive restructuring may not produce a complete change in the client's beliefs. Thoughts and beliefs determined to strongly contribute to distress, disturbance, self-downing, and unrest may remain active following cognitive restructuring efforts. It is more realistic to expect a reduction in the strength of the view, rather than complete eradication of the belief. To evaluate the effectiveness of the specific cognitive restructuring effort, the therapist may ask the client to rate the current strength of the belief under scrutiny.

Therapist: How much do you believe that your husband is trying to take everything from you?

Client: About 50 percent, I guess.

T: How have you managed to drop from 95 to 50 percent?

C: I looked over the proposed property settlement and I can see that he's trying to be fair in that area. I can't let go of the idea completely though, because he's the one with the children [i.e., custody].

T: And now how angry do you feel toward him?

C: Oh, I'm still pretty upset. I guess about a 60 [percent].

T: I see. Although you're still upset, you are making meaningful change in your views and feelings.

Scaling is used in a variety of psychotherapies, including behavioral and cognitive behavioral therapy, solution-focused brief treatment, and many others (see Thyer, Papsdorf, Davis, & Vallecorsa, 1984; Gillaspy & Murphy, 2012; Miller et al., 2003). Apart from being useful to evaluate any changes, the mere act of scaling itself seems capable of inducing some positive changes on the part of the client.

COGNITIVE ELABORATION

Many cognitive restructuring efforts are designed to reframe the cognition under consideration, to replace one thought with another. In some circumstances, it may be undesirable to replace a thought or even to directly attempt to reduce its strength even though it may stimulate unappealing responses and mood states. Furthermore, a client may be unwilling to abandon a given thought. Cognitive elaboration (Granvold, 2008) is an alternative approach to cognitive restructuring in which the focus is on the generation of alternative thoughts, views, or meaning constructions without the expectation that the original view be abandoned. This approach is particularly useful with clients who are grieving the death of a loved one.

In the illustration that follows, Blake is struggling with the death of his 28-year-old son, James, who was killed a year earlier in a one-car accident. The accident occurred while James was returning from a hunting trip that Blake had originally planned to make with him. James was drunk at the time of the accident. Blake believes that he is responsible for James's death, that had he been with him on the trip, the accident would not have happened. After exploring the belief that "I am responsible for my son's death" and identifying the associated emotional consequences (depression, loss, pain, helplessness, regret) the focus shifted to cognitive elaboration.

Therapist: Because focusing specifically on blaming yourself for James's death appears to result in other problems, suppose you expand your thoughts about James's death in addition to "It's my fault." What other thoughts do you have about James's life or his premature death?

Client: Well, not to be too hard on the kid, but he did have a drinking problem, and, ultimately, I guess that you could say he was responsible for the accident that took his life. He was drunk!

T: Yes, I agree with you that James was responsible for his drinking and the accident. It is somewhat a question of when does a parent quit protecting his child. Blake, can you function with both of these beliefs, "It's my fault" and "James was responsible for his drinking"?

C: Even though they seem contradictory, I think I can.

T: So, it is possible to maintain multiple views or beliefs about a situation.

C: Yes, I think it is.

In this and subsequent sessions, several other meanings were elaborated in relation to James's

death (and life) including (1) James's death will have been a waste if I do not do something in his name that could have a positive impact on the problem of drinking and driving in our society (Blake became actively involved in MADD); (2) I need to be very involved with James's son as James's "representative"; (3) James would want me to get past my intense grief and once again enjoy life (a belief generated through a role reversal exercise); and (4) I can still love James strongly and grieve less.

Challenging Blake's initial belief that his son's death is his fault would have been, I believe, less effective than allowing it to stand as one of many meanings in a matrix of constructs surrounding the loss. The generation of multiple meanings through the process of cognitive elaboration dilutes the strength of a given belief and produces a range of consequences. The position of constructivists is that the client will likely realize greater viability among the various constructs generated.

GUIDED IMAGERY

Guided imagery is a viable alternative approach to cognitive restructuring. An early approach to the use of imagery was developed by Maultsby (1975) in the form of rational emotive imagery (REI). Other Cognitive Behavioral Therapy (CBT) leaders have also employed the use of imagery as a cognitive restructuring method (Beck & Emery, 1985; Beck & Weishaar, 2008; Ellis, 1977). Several imagery techniques have been advanced for use in the process of cognitive restructuring by these and other clinicians. Edwards (1989) notes that "the main techniques for obtaining an image from which to begin are the visualization of a life event or theme, the reinstatement of a dream or daytime image, and feeling focusing" (p. 286). Images, dreams, and fantasies may be drawn from the client's history or current imagination. Alternatively, the therapist may generate content for use in guided imagery. Though not imperative, it may be helpful to teach the client progressive relaxation for use in conducting guided imagery. In the illustration that follows, guided imagery is used with a Vietnam veteran suffering from nightmares about a specific combat experience in which two of his men were killed. The client feels responsible for their deaths and believes he should have acted to save them. He is a decorated veteran known for his leadership in combat situations. When he awakens from these recurrent nightmares about combat over 40 years ago, he feels extreme sadness and intense self-reproach. On these occasions he acts cold and distant toward his wife and his employees.

Therapist: You said that when you think back on the firefight in Vietnam in which two of your men were killed, you feel responsible, that you should have acted to save them.

Client: That's right. I have vivid dreams about them being torn apart by bullets.

T: Close your eyes. Imagine that you did little to prepare your men for combat and that you are out on patrol. The patrol is attacked, and your men go down beside you. You and your remaining men fight off the enemy and the shooting ends. As you attend to the casualties, how are you feeling?

C: First, I would never act this way. But I'll go along with this thinking. . . . I feel angry with myself, a lot of self-loathing . . . and ashamed for being so irresponsible.

T: So when you think of yourself as failing to prepare your men for combat and casualties result, you feel anger with yourself, self-loathing, and shame. Now this time, imagine that you have prepared your men extremely well for combat. By your instruction, they have become highly skilled soldiers, but you recognize that war is war. Each man knows that he may die in battle. You enter the firefight as before, and men are lost. The patrol is attacked, and your men go down beside you. You and your remaining men fight off the enemy and the shooting ends. As you attend to the casualties, how are you feeling?

C: I feel pretty empty inside over the loss of these men, but I don't feel as upset with myself. I did what I could do . . . but war is war, as you just said.

In this example, the client was asked to consider himself performing his responsibilities unconscionably by failing to prepare his men for battle (a legitimate basis for accepting responsibility for casualties of war). After identifying the associated feelings, he imagined the same combat scene with the awareness that he *had* prepared

his men well for battle. This process resulted in a reduction in the degree to which he felt upset and reinforced the thought, "war is war." The latter thought is one that the client had expressed in an earlier session. The client was a strong candidate for the use of imagery inasmuch as he was experiencing powerful imagery (both nightmares and daydreams) outside therapy sessions.

SKILLS-BUILDING AND REAL-LIFE EXPERIENCES

Behavioral experiments may be used to identify and modify beliefs, assumptions, and expectations. The client and therapist collaboratively develop a plan for the client to "test out" the veracity or viability of his or her views. In the behavioral experiment, the client may "predict an outcome based on personal automatic thoughts, carry out the agreed-upon behavior, and then evaluate the evidence in light of the new experience" (Beck & Weishaar, 2008, p. 286). Ellis introduced his famous "shame attacking" exercises early in the development of REI in which clients exposed themselves to negative attention, typically with little or no actual disconcerting consequences. Several iterations of the experiment often resulted in cognitive and emotive change.

Behavioral experiments may be enacted in vivo or take place in the therapist's office as role-plays. In some cases, the simple gathering of information may suffice (Beck, 1995). The following are illustrations of clients' evaluation of their beliefs in actual life experiences. A client experiencing social phobia tested the hypothesis that "no one will speak to me" at singles' Sunday school class. By attending the class, she disproved the hypothesis and actually experienced a warm reception by many. Another client saw himself as extremely unappealing and consequently no one would be willing to go out with him on a date. He further believed that if he *was* successful, he would not find the woman desirable. We agreed that this experiment might take several iterations. He went online and made contact with several people. After developing ongoing correspondence with several women, he began arranging dates. His first few efforts actually supported his original hypothesis. On the fourth outing, however, he met a woman whom he found to be highly attractive. They dated for a time. Although their relationship was not sustained, he modified his self-view as a consequence of this experience.

Through behavioral experimentation, clients modify their views as actual life experiences provide evidence that contradicts their conceptualizations. Some clients may approach behavioral experimentation with marked skepticism and strong beliefs that they are "right" in their conceptualizations. For those clients, a review of their personal life experience may be persuasive. Attempt to identify prior life experiences in which anticipation failed to match realized experience (e.g., aerobics classes are for athletic people only). These experiences may serve as useful points of reference in dispelling client reluctance and in developing openness to behavioral experiments.

The second author was once consulted by an older woman who had developed a severe phobia to dogs, following her being savagely attacked by a large dog four years earlier (see Thyer, 1981). She wished to become less afraid of dogs (change her feelings), think less anxious thoughts about them (change her cognitions), and stop unrealistically avoiding them (change her actions). The social worker realized that purely cognitive interventions such as Socratic dialogue, cognitive elaboration, scaling, and guided imagery would likely be less effective at helping her achieve her goals compared with more direct experiences in real life. This is in keeping with Bandura's admonition that "it is performance-based procedures that are proving to be most powerful for effecting psychological changes. As a consequence, successful performance is replacing symbolically based experiences as the principle vehicle of change. . . .cognitive processes mediate change but . . . cognitive events are induced and altered most readily by experience of mastery arising from successful performance" (Bandura, 1977, p. 191). Accordingly, with full client-informed consent, the therapist arranged a series of real life encounters with live dogs, initially small and cute, then to large and intimidating, with the client in the therapist's office, using the behavior analytic method known as real life exposure therapy. Although she was initially made highly anxious during these

sessions, with the passage of time within each session she calmed down, felt less anxious, avoided the dogs less, and has less distressing thoughts. Office-based sessions were replaced with real-life interactions with dogs, including a visit to the local humane society. A complete remission of all symptoms, overt behavior avoidance, distressing cognitions about dogs, and fear, was achieved after five such sessions, in about a month. Close contact without anything untoward happening, being repeatedly licked and jumped on, and her mastery of commanding the trained dogs to sit, "speak" and lay down, all worked at inducing not only cognitive restructuring, but also therapeutic changes in feelings and actions. This form of experiential behavior therapy also makes use of therapist modeling desired behavior, which is another valuable way to induce changes in cognitions, feelings and overt actions.

CONCLUSION

Humans are no strangers to the process of cognitive restructuring in some form. We develop and modify beliefs automatically as part of life span development. We are also, however, creatures of habit. Stored and accessible beliefs operate rather inflexibly, and cognitive processing patterns become routine. When modification of these phenomena is indicated, cognitive restructuring procedures like those presented in this chapter provide a methodology for effective change. Clinicians engaged in cognitive restructuring efforts are invited and encouraged to draw on their creativity individually and collaboratively with their clients in developing efficacious cognitive restructuring strategies. More detailed reviews of cognitive restructuring methods can be found via the Internet links provided below, and in Garland and Thyer (2013) and Thyer and Myers (2011).

WEBSITES

Academy of Cognitive Therapy http://www.academyofct.org/i4a/pages/index.cfm?pageid=1.
Association for Behavioral and Cognitive Therapies. http://www.abct.org/home/

Association for Contextual Behavioral Science. http://contextualscience.org/act
REBT Network. http://www.rebtnetwork.org.
Association of Professional Behavior Analysts. http://www.apbahome.net/
Association for Behavior Analysis International. http://www.abainternational.org/

References

Bandura, A. (1977). Self-efficacy: Toward a unifying theory of behavioral change. *Psychological Review*, 84, 191–215.

Beck, A. T., & Emery, G. (1985). *Anxiety disorders and phobias: A cognitive perspective*. New York: Basic Books.

Beck, A. T., & Weishaar, M. E. (2008). Cognitive therapy. In R. J. Corsini & D. Wedding (Eds.), *Current psychotherapies* (8th ed.). (pp. 263–294). Belmont, CA: Thomson.

Beck, J. S. (1995). *Cognitive therapy: Basics and beyond*. New York, NY: Guilford.

Clark, D. A., Beck, A. T., & Alford, B. A. (1999). *Scientific foundations of cognitive theory and therapy of depression*. New York, NY: Wiley.

Edwards, D. J. A. (1989). Cognitive restructuring through guided imagery: Lessons from Gestalt therapy. In A. Freeman, K. M. Simon, L. E. Beutler, & H. Arkowitz (Eds.), *Comprehensive handbook of cognitive therapy* (pp. 283–297). New York, NY: Plenum.

Ellis, A. (1977). The rational-emotive approach to sex therapy. In A. Ellis & R. Greiger (Eds.), *Handbook of rational-emotive therapy* (pp. 198–215). New York, NY: Springer.

Garland, E., & Thyer, B. A. (2013). Cognitive-behavioral approach. In M. Gray & S. Webb (Eds.), *Social work theories and methods* (2nd ed.). (pp. 159–172). Thousand Oaks, CA: Sage.

Gillaspy, Jr., J. A., & Murphy, J. J. (2012). In C. Franklin, T. Trepper, W. J. Gingerich, & E. E. McCollum (Eds.), *Solution-focused brief therapy: A handbook of evidence-based practice* (pp. 73–91). New York, NY: Oxford University Press.

Granvold, D. K. (1994). Concepts and methods of cognitive treatment. In D. K. Granvold (Ed.), *Cognitive and behavioral treatment: Methods and applications* (pp. 3–31). Pacific Grove, CA: Brooks/Cole.

Granvold, D. K. (2008). Constructivist theory and practice. In N. Coady & P. Lehmann (Eds.), *Theoretical perspectives for direct social work practice: A generalist-eclectic approach* (2nd ed.) (pp. 401–427). New York, NY: Springer.

Lantz, J. (1978). Cognitive theory and social casework. *Social Work*, 23, 361–366.

Maultsby, M. C. (1975). *Help yourself to happiness*. New York, NY: Institute for Rational Living.

Miller, S. D., Duncan, B. L., Brown, J., Sparks, J. A., & Claud, D. A. (2003). The outcome rating scale: A preliminary study of the reliability, validity and feasibility of a brief visual analog measure. *Journal of Brief Therapy*, 2(2), 91–100.

Thyer, B. A. (1981). Prolonged in vivo exposure therapy with a 70-year-old woman. *Journal of Behavior Therapy and Experimental Psychiatry*, 12, 69–71.

Thyer, B. A., & Myers, L. L. (2011). Behavioral and cognitive theories. In J. R. Brandell (Ed.), *Theory and practice in clinical social work* (2nd ed.) (pp. 21–40). Thousand Oaks, CA: Sage.

Thyer, B. A., Papsdorf, J. D., Davis, R., & Vallecorsa, S. (1984). Autonomic correlates of the Subjective Anxiety Scale. *Journal of Behavior Therapy and Experimental Psychiatry*, 15, 3–7.

Wells, A. (1997). *Cognitive therapy of anxiety disorders: A practice manual and conceptualization guide*. New York, NY: Wiley.

Werner, H. D. (1982). *Cognitive therapy: A humanistic approach*. New York, NY: Free Press.

83 The Miracle and Scaling Questions for Solution-building and Empowering

Mo Yee Lee

The miracle question and the scaling question is an integral part of solution-focused brief therapy (SFBT), which was originally developed at the Brief Family Therapy Center at Milwaukee by Steve De Shazer, Insoo Kim Berg, and their associates. Solution-focused brief therapy begins as atheoretical with a focus on finding "what works in therapy" (Berg, 1994). Building on a strengths perspective and using a time-limited approach, solution-focused brief therapy postulates that positive and long-lasting change can occur in a relatively brief period of time by focusing on "solution-talk" instead of "problem talk" (De Shazer, 1985; Lee, 2013; Nelson & Thomas, 2007). One definitional characteristic of SFBT is that it equates therapeutic process with therapeutic dialogue, with a focus on what is observable in communication and social interactions, instead of intentions, between client and therapist (Bavelas et al., 2013; McKergow & Korman, 2009). Change happens through the therapeutic dialogue in which the therapist and client co-construct what is beneficial and helpful toward accomplishing the client's self-determined goals (Lee et al., 2003). Solution-focused brief therapy uses the language and symbols of "solution and strengths" as opposed to the language of "deficits and blame" (Lee, Sebold, & Uken, 2003). Treatment focuses on identifying exceptions and solution behaviors, which are then amplified, supported, and reinforced through a systematic solution-building process (De Jong & Berg, 2013).

Miracle questions and scaling questions, in many ways, synthesize the treatment orientation and practice characteristics of solution-focused brief therapy. Its conversational- and solution-based characteristics are intimately related to three definitive assumptions and practice principles of solution-focused brief therapy:

1. The power of language in creating and sustaining reality. Solution-focused therapy views language as the medium through which personal meaning and understanding are expressed and socially constructed in conversation (De Shazer, 1994). Because "what is noticed becomes reality and what is not noticed does not exist" (Lee et al., 2003, p. 32), there is a conscious effort for the therapist to help the client stay focused on envisioning a desirable future and finding small steps to actualize the solution-oriented future. Pathology or problem-talk sustains a problem reality through self-fulfilling prophecies and distracts attention from developing solutions (Miller, 1997).

2. A focus on solutions, strengths, and health. Solution-focused brief therapy assumes that clients have the resources and *have the answer*. The focus is on what clients can do versus what clients cannot do. One basic assumption of a systems perspective is that change is constant. No matter how severe the problem, there must be some "exceptions" to the problem patterns. These exceptions serve as clues to a solution and represent clients' "unnoticed" strengths and resources (De Shazer, 1985). Consequently, the task for the therapist is to assist clients in noticing, amplifying, sustaining, and reinforcing these exceptions regardless of how small and/or infrequent they may be. Once

clients are engaged in nonproblem behavior, they are on the way to a solution-building process (De Jong & Berg, 2013).

3. Solutions as clients' constructions. Solutions are not objective "realities" but are private, local, meaning-making activities by an individual (Miller, 1997). The importance of and the meaning attached to a goal or solution is individually constructed in a collaborative process. Solution-focused therapy honors clients as the "knower" of their experiences and the "creators" of solutions; they define the goals for their treatment and remain the main instigator of change (Berg, 1994).

THE USE OF QUESTIONS IN THE THERAPEUTIC PROCESS

Influenced by these assumptions and practice principles, the primary purpose of solution-focused interventions is to engage the client in a therapeutic dialogue that is conducive to a solution-building process. In this dialogue, the clinician invites the client to be the "expert" by listening and exploring the meaning of the client's perceptions of his or her situation. The use of solution-focused questions is instrumental in this solution-building dialogue. People need useful feedback in the process of change (Lee, 2013). The therapist can provide feedback directly via listening responses, affirming responses, restating responses, and expanding responses (Lee et al., 2003). Instead of directly providing feedback to clients, evaluative questions serve to initiate a self-feedback process within the client. Evaluative questions represent questions that ask clients to self-evaluate their situations in terms of their doing, thinking, and feeling. The therapist abstains from interpreting a client's situation or suggesting any ideas; s/he just asks good questions that help clients evaluate various aspects of their unique life situations (Lee et al., 2003). Questions are perceived as better ways to create open space for clients to think about and self-evaluate their situation and solutions. Evaluative questions operate from the stance of curiosity and convey the message that we believe that clients themselves have the answers and that we, in fact, do not have the answers.

The therapist utilizes solution-oriented questions, including miracle questions and scaling questions, to assist clients in constructing a reality that does not contain the problem. These questioning techniques are developed by De Shazer, Berg, and their colleagues to utilize fully the resources and potential of clients (De Jong & Berg, 2013; De Shazer, 1985).

LISTEN, SELECT, AND BUILD

The SFBT Treatment Manual endorsed by the Solution-Focused Brief Therapy Association (Bavelas et al., 2013) provides a detailed description of this co-constructive therapeutic process through the steps *listen, select,* and *build* (De Jong and Berg, 2013; De Shazer, 1991; 1994; de Shazer et al., 2007). In this dialogue, the therapist first listens for and selects out the words and phrases from the client's language that are indications of some aspect of a solution, including things that are important and salient to the client, past successes, exceptions to the problem pattern, and resources. Building on the client's descriptions and paying attention to the client's language and frames of reference, the therapist composes a next question or other response that invites the client to elaborate the solution picture further. It is through this continuing process of listening, selecting, and building that therapists and clients together co-construct new meanings and new possibilities for solutions (Bavelas et al., 2013).

Miracle Question

The development of the miracle question was inspired by the work of Milton Erickson (the "crystal ball" technique) (De Shazer, 1985). According to Berg (1994), the miracle question invites clients to create a vision of their future without the presenting problem. A major challenge encountered by most clients in social work treatment is that they know when they have a problem but they do not know when the problem has been successfully addressed. When this happens, clients may be in treatment for a long time because there are no clear indicators of health and wellness. Helping clients to develop a clear vision of their future without the presenting problem becomes crucial in successful treatment because it establishes indicators of change and helps gauge clients' progress toward a self-defined desirable future (De Jong & Berg, 2013; Lee, 2003). When defining a future without the problem becomes a major focus of treatment, accountability for changing one's behavior can be achieved effectively. Defining a desirable future also shifts the focus of attention from what cannot be done to what can be accomplished; it moves clients away from blaming others or themselves and holds them accountable for developing a better, different future (Lee et al., 2003).

The miracle question is intended to accomplish the following therapeutic impact:

1. Allow clients to distance themselves from problem-saturated stories so that they can be more playful in creating a beneficial vision of their future.
2. Facilitate clients to develop a clear vision about a desirable future, given that "what is noticed becomes reality and what is not noticed does not exist" (Lee et al., 2003, p. 32).
3. Because the focus of the miracle question is to identify small, observable, and concrete changes that are indicative of a desirable future without the presenting problem, it establishes indicators of change and progress that help clients to gauge success and progress.
4. Increase clients' awareness of their choices and offer them an opportunity to play an active role in their treatment (De Jong & Berg, 2013).
5. Allow clients to be hopeful about their lives, which can be different than their current problem situation.
6. Empower clients to self-determine a desirable future for themselves. "It creates a personal possible self, which is not modeled after someone else's ideas of what his life should be like" (Berg, 1994, p. 97).

A frequently used version of the miracle question is the following:

Suppose that after our meeting today, you go home, do your things and go to bed. While you are sleeping, a miracle happens and the problem that brought you here is suddenly solved, like magic. The problem is gone. Because you were sleeping, you don't know that a miracle happened, but when you wake up tomorrow morning, you will be different. How will you know a miracle has happened? What will be the first small sign that tells you that the problem is resolved? (Berg & Miller, 1992, p. 359).

Using the process *listen, select,* and *build;* the therapist carefully *listens* to the client's response to the miracle question and *selects* descriptions that are indicative of the client's goal, desirable future, successes, and resources. The miracle question only initiates the process for clients to envision a desirable future. Paying particular attention and using a client's language and frame of reference, the therapist responds by developing other solution-focused questions or responses that help the client to *build* and expand the solution picture continuously. Note that the focus is on small signs of change. It is also important to invite clients to describe their solution picture in greater detail and to determine how it differs from their current behaviors, feelings, and thinking. The more detailed and refined the description the clearer the indicators of change, which will increase the likelihood that clients will actualize their solution picture, because "what is noticed becomes reality" (Lee et al., 2003, p. 32).

- "Who will be the first person to notice the change? What will they be noticing about you that will tell them that you are different?"
- "How will your spouse, your child (any significant others) know that something is different?" (Relationship question)
- "At what times in your life have you already been doing this?" (Exception question)

The essence of the miracle question is to allow clients to envision a future without problems. As such, social work professionals can be creative in coming up with other versions of future-oriented questions. This can be helpful especially with clients from other cultures or religions who might have their own culture-based interpretation of miracles. Some variations might be:

- "If I were to run into you a year from now, and you had already solved the problem that brought you in today, how would I know that you are different?" What will you be like then?
- If I were to videotape you on a good day, how would you be doing/feeling/thinking differently?
- Five years down the road, what do you want yourself to be like?

Another version is the dream question, which reinforces clients' sense of personal agency, and therefore, is consistent with the goal of empowering clients (Greene, Lee, Mentzer, Pinnell, & Niles, 1998).

Suppose that tonight while you are sleeping you have a dream and in this dream you discover the answers and resources you need to solve the problem that you are concerned about right now. When you wake up tomorrow you may or may not remember your dream but you do notice you are different. As you go about starting your day, what will tell you that you discovered or developed the skills and resources necessary to solve your problem? What will be the first small sign to tell you that you solved your problem?

SCALING QUESTIONS

Scaling questions ask clients to rank their situation and/or goal on a 1-to-10 scale (Berg, 1994). Usually, 1 represents the worst scenario that could possibly be and 10 is the most desirable outcome. People need feedback during the process of change. Therefore, for change to happen, clients will need to be able to self-evaluate their progress and adjust accordingly. Scaling questions provide a simple tool for clients to quantify and evaluate their situation and progress so that they establish clear indicators of progress for themselves (De Jong & Berg, 2013). More importantly, this is a self-anchored scale with no objective criteria. The constructivist characteristic of the scaling question honors clients as the "knowers" and the center of the change process. Scaling can be used to help clients rate their perception of their progress, their motivation for change, confidence to engage in solution-focused behaviors, etc. Scaling questions are also helpful in assisting clients to establish small steps and indicators of change in their solution-building process. Some common examples of scaling questions are:

1. Problem severity or Progress: On a 1-to-10 scale, with 1 being the worst the problem could possibly be and 10 being the most desirable outcome, where would you place yourself on the scale? What would be some small steps that you could take to move from a "4" to a "5"?

2. Motivation: On a 1-to-10 scale with 1 being you have no motivation to work on the problem and 10 being you would do whatever necessary to change the situation, where would you (or your spouse, your boss, your child, etc.) place yourself on the scale? How would your wife (or other significant others) rank your motivation to change on a 1-to-10 scale?

3. Confidence: "On a 1-to-10 scale with 1 being you have no confidence that you can work on the goal and 10 being you have complete confidence that you will continue to work on the goal, where would you place yourself on the scale?" "On a scale of 1 to 10, how confident are you that you could actually do that?" "On a scale of 1 to 10, how confident are you that this will be helpful?"

Similar to using the miracle question in co-constructing change in the treatment process, the therapist carefully *listens* to the client's responses, *selects* and focuses on descriptions that are connected with indications and hints of solutions, and then helps clients to *build* and expand further on desirable change and solutions.

THE CASE OF LINDA

Linda was a 47-year-old woman who suffered chronic back pain after a car accident. The pain also affected her mobility. She was living alone on her own. The therapist (SWR) uses the miracle question to help her envision a more hopeful future.

SWR: Suppose that after our meeting today, you go home, do your things and go to bed. While you are sleeping, a miracle happens and the problem that brought you here is suddenly solved, like magic. The problem is gone. Because you were sleeping, you don't know that a miracle happened, but when you wake up tomorrow morning, you will be different. How will you know a miracle has happened? What will be the first small sign that tells you that the problem is resolved? *(Use the miracle question to engage the client in a solution-building process.)*

Linda: I won't be as cranky as an immoveable mountain.

SWR: Instead of being cranky, how do you see yourself being? *(Help client move from a negatively stated description to a positively stated description.)*

Linda: Be a little more upbeat, cheerful, and perky. Get my mind off of it and focus on areas not on the mountain of pain.

SWR: So you want to be more upbeat, cheerful, and perky, and distract yourself from the mountain of pain and do something different? *(Select positive description and use client's language.)*

Linda: So when I am around people they are not affected by it and they are not dragged down by it.

SWR: Let's say you wake up tomorrow after this miracle has happened, what would be the first small thing that you would do and that you are not doing now? *(Build and expand solution-picture.)*

Linda: I don't know. (Pause) Maybe instead of lying in bed staring at the wall, I would get up and open the curtain and turn my computer on, open a book, talk to the cat, anything besides lying in bed and staring at the wall.

SWR: That is what you do now, lie in bed and stare at the wall?

Linda: Yeah.

SWR: When this miracle happens, you would get out of bed, open the curtain, talk to the cat. What else would you do? *(Select and further build solution-picture.)*

Linda: Turn on the computer and get out of bed and do something.

SWR: Do something? *(Invite a more detailed description.)*

Linda: Maybe sweep, dust, or mop.

SWR: Anything else? *(Use presuppositional language that embeds an expectation of change.)*

Linda: Go outside and sit in the sunshine.

SWR: Who in your home would notice the change? Is there somebody else living in your home? *(Relationship question)*

Linda: No, just my cat.

SWR: So what would your cat notice is different about you that you are not doing now? *(Use relationship and difference question to further build the solution-picture further.)*

Linda: I would be up and maybe play with her.

SWR: So you would be up and play with her? How would that make a difference in your day if you were having more fun with your cat? *(Use relationship and difference question to build the solution-picture further.)*

SWR: So who else would notice the change besides your cat? *(Build and expand the solution further using relationship question.)*

Linda: My neighbors, friends.

SWR: What would they notice? *(Invite a more detailed description.)*

Linda: A more positive outlook.

SWR: How would they notice? *(Invite an observable description.)*

Linda: I would respond to them, not giving them dirty looks when it is not their fault. I would run over. I sort of give them a dirty look. It is a major hurdle for me.

SWR: Who would be most affected by this change? *(Invite a description of the expected effect of change.)*

Linda: I suppose that would help other people as well as me.

SWR: How so? *(Invite further elaboration of the effect of change.)*

Linda: You know it would help me because I don't want to be a big drag and that way I won't be dragging people down and it won't be dragging me down because everyone around me is all bummed out, "Oh you poor thing" and all this and I don't want that. I want to get over it. I want to get over it, I want to get over the top of the mountain and go on from here not just hang around the base all the time.

SWR: Tomorrow, meaning the following morning or next morning, you can do this. On a 1-to-10 scale, 10 being likely that you can do this, and 1 being no chance at all, where would you think you are? *(Scaling question regarding feasibility of the change efforts. Good timing to use scaling question because the client has just clearly articulated her desire and motivation for change.)*

Linda: I am at a 6 right now.

SWR: So you are saying getting out of bed in the morning, opening the curtains, turning on the computer, and talking to cat is quite doable because you are at a 6?

Linda: It is doable. I can do that.

SWR: Using the same scale, 10 being you are motivated to do this because it would improve your life, and 1 being you are wishy-washy about it, where would you put yourself on the scale? *(Scaling question regarding motivation of change)*

Linda: I would say an 8, because I don't want to be cranky anymore.

THE CASE OF ELISE

Elise was a 45-year-old Caucasian single mother with three children from 10 to 16 years old. Her husband passed away a year ago and she felt extremely overwhelmed trying to take care of her three children. She became depressed and attempted to commit suicide by overdosing on sleeping pills. She requested that her children be placed in foster homes while she tried to work things out for herself. She received treatment as part of her case plan to reunite with her children. While thinking what might be a helpful goal for her to work on, Elise pondered and struggled. At first, she mentioned developing a better relationship with her children as something she would like to see happen. However, she also felt overwhelmed as a single mother without the support of her husband. The therapist encouraged her to think about what would be personally meaningful and helpful to her at this time. Elise said that she would like to be more productive, although she did not have a clear idea of what a productive life would look like.

Elise: I don't know. I guess I would feel a little different. Maybe just be more productive.

SWR: In what way? *(Invite a more detailed description.)*

Elise: I am not sure. . . I am raising three kids and my husband passed away a year ago, and I am doing nothing myself.

SWR: So life is not cool.

Elise: Yes, not whole lot to do . . . so . . .

SWR: So what would you do differently to be *more productive? (Use client's language; listen and select what is important for the client.)*

Elise: I don't know, but I could be more productive than I am right now. I am reading and doing the seven steps right now. That is about it.

SWR: Do you feel more productive by reading the seven steps and maybe, as you've just said, taking walks? *(Important for the client to evaluate whether she has been more productive)*

Elise: I am thinking about when my kids come home, my relationship with them is going to be more productive. I have to feel like change a little bit. *(Client is still somewhat unclear about what she can do to get herself to be more productive.)*

SWR: Let me ask you this, you wake up tomorrow morning, you do this and whatever it is to make yourself more productive. At the end of the day you look at yourself and said "Man, I am doing well, I really do it now for myself." What do you think that might be? *(This is a different version of the miracle question that helps Elise to be more playful about visioning a future when she is more productive.)*

Elise: Going through the seven steps programs, change my ideas and personality more to be a single woman.

SWR: How will people notice that you stand as a single woman? How will they know that you are different? *(Select what is important to the client and use relationship question to invite elaboration.)*

Elise: The way I am acting.

SWR: What will tell them you changed your attitude and you are different than before?

Elise: Oh, gosh, my weight.

SWR: So your weight will be different. I am curious, pretend that between now and next week, your weight has changed. What will be different for you in your daily life? What will you be doing that you are not doing right now? *(Invite elaboration of the expected effect of change.)*

Elise: If my weight has changed, I will not watch the same TV shows, and I don't want to read the same books, and I don't eat the same junk food.

SWR: You are making big changes in your daily life . . . *(Invite client to self-evaluate the feasibility of the proposed change.)*

Elise: You are right, but this is something that I do want to change.

SWR: What would be the first things that you could possibly do to make this happen? *(Invite client to make a feasible plan.)*

Elise: I've already been walking every day. Maybe I can walk longer and not watch the 8 o'clock show.

SWR: Anything else? *(Presuppositional language that embeds an expectation of change)*

Elise: Don't go to the "snack" aisle when doing my grocery shopping. That'll probably do it.

SWR: So what will you get from the store instead? *(Help client to move from a negatively stated description to a positively stated description.)*

Elise: Maybe more fresh food, like veggies and fish.

SWR: What do you want to see happen when you take walks and eat more fresh food? *(Build and elaborate expected effect of change efforts.)*

Elise: I'll feel as though I'm having more control and being more productive in my life, not just lying around like a couch potato and doing nothing.

SWR: So how confident are you on a 1-to-10 scale that you will be able to take a longer walk and eat more fresh food between now and next time we get together? *(Scaling question regarding confidence about change)*

Elise: Well, I do want to change but you know the temptation. (Pause) Maybe a 3.

SWR: So what are some small things that you can do to move from a "3" to a "4"? *(Use scaling question to establish small steps for Elise to feel more confident.)*

Elise: That's not easy. Maybe talk to my sister so she can remind me once in a while.

SWR: So maybe take it to the next step, and see next week what you do differently as a result of that. I will be very interested to hear what you say next time about how just going through that next step . . . what things you do that make you different and more productive? Is that possible?

Elise: Oh, yes.

SWR: Just pay attention to, "If I would like my life to be better, what small things can I do to make it happen?"

GUIDELINES FOR USING MIRACLE QUESTION AND SCALING QUESTION IN SOCIAL WORK PRACTICE

Knowing *when* to use miracle questions and scaling questions is as important as knowing the questions. Perhaps the most important skill is to pay attention to a client's and our own moment-to-moment communication and responses in the co-constructive therapeutic process. The following are some guidelines for using these questions:

- Use miracle questions to assist clients develop a clear vision of a future without the presenting problem.
  - The miracle question is frequently used during the first session, after the client has shared a description of the problem context and the therapist has an adequate understanding of the problem context.
  - A shift to solution-building by using the miracle question is indicated when client's description of the problem context is getting repetitive and no new information is being offered.
- Scaling questions can be effectively used for the following purposes:
  - Evaluate confidence, ability, and motivation with respect to clients' change efforts.
  - Establish small steps for further change.
  - Help clients gauge their perceptions of problems and goals.
- To fully utilize the constructive effect of scaling questions, use scaling questions when the client has adequately articulated his or her desire for change
  - Avoid inviting clients to scale confidence, ability, motivation early on in the session when there are clear indications that they are not confident or motivated to change; or are hopeless about the problem situation.
- Be patient: Clients do not have the solution in their minds when they seek treatment; it is the responsibility of the therapist to create a safe space for them to slowly "paint" their solution picture.

- Go for details: Assist clients move beyond vague descriptions of the desirable future, to instead describe it in terms of small, observable, specific, or behavioral steps.
- Reinforce client motivation: Assist clients carefully evaluate what may be personally meaningful and useful for them.
- Respect of clients' personal choices and ownership.
- Compliment and acknowledge the client's desire for change.
- Assist clients evaluate feasibility of the solution picture.
- Focus on small steps that can make clients' lives better.
- Assist clients develop clear indicators of change so that they can recognize success.

CONCLUSION

The purpose of the miracle and scaling questions is to help clients establish indicators of wellness and gauge progress toward a desirable future. These self-evaluative questions represent a specific type of conversation in which the therapist talks "with" the client (instead of talking "at" the client) to co-develop new meanings and new realities through a dialogue of "solutions" (Bavelas et al., 2013; De Shazer, 1994: Lee et al., 2003). The challenge for social work practitioners is to work collaboratively with clients so that clients can find a future with which they feel comfortable, as well as feel good about their choices. The therapist cautiously refrains from providing/suggesting any predetermined solutions or desirable future. Through *listen, select,* and *build* (Bavelas et al., 2013), the therapist creates a therapeutic context in which both clients and therapists co-construct a solution-building process that is initiated from within and grounded in clients' personal construction of the solution reality and cultural strengths (Lee, 2013). The therapeutic process is collaborative and egalitarian, and one in which the client's self-determination is fully respected (De Jong & Berg, 2013). The ultimate goal of miracle and scaling questions, therefore, is consistent with the goal of empowerment that focuses on increasing clients' personal and interpersonal power so that they can take relevant and

culturally appropriate action to improve their situations (DuBois & Miley, 2013; Gutierrez, DeLois, & GlenMaye, 1995).

WEBSITES AND LISTSERV

http://www.brief-therapy.org/
http://www.sfbta.org/
SFT-L Solution Focused Therapy SFT-L@ LISTSERV.ICORS.ORG

References

Berg, I. K. (1994). *Family based services: A solution-focused approach.* New York, NY: W.W. Norton.

Berg, I. K., & Miller, S. (1992). *Working with the problem drinker: A solution-focused approach.* New York, NY: W.W. Norton & Co.

Bavelas, J., De Jong, P., Franklin, C., Froerer, A., Gingerich, W., Kim, J., . . . Trepper, T. S. (2013). Solution Focused Therapy Treatment Manual for Working with Individuals (2nd version). New York, NY: Solution Focused Brief Therapy Association.

De Jong, P., & Berg, I. K. (2013). *Interviewing for solutions* (4th ed.). Belmont, CA: Brooks/Cole.

DuBois, B. L., & Miley, K. K. (2013). *Social work: An empowering profession* (8th ed.). Upper Saddle River, NJ: Pearson.

De Shazer, S. (1994). *Words were originally magic.* New York, NY: W.W. Norton.

De Shazer, S. (1991). *Putting difference to work.* New York, NY: W.W. Norton.

De Shazer, S. (1985). *Keys to solutions in brief therapy.* New York, NY: W.W. Norton.

de Shazer, S., Dolan, Y. M., Korman, H., Trepper, T. S., McCollum, E. E., & Berg, I. K. (2007), *More than miracles: The state of the art of solution focused therapy.* New York, NY: Haworth Press.

Greene, G. J., Lee, M. Y., Mentzer, R., Pinnell, S., & Niles, D. (1998). Miracles, dreams, and empowerment: A brief practice note. *Families in Society, 79,* 395–399.

Gutierrez, L. M., DeLois, K. A., & GlenMaye, L. (1995). Understanding empowerment practice: Building on practitioner-based knowledge. *Families in Society, 76,* 534–542.

McKergow, M., & Korman, H. (2009). Inbetween— neither inside nor outside. *Journal of Systemic Therapies, 28*(2), 34–49.

Miller, G. (1997). *Becoming miracle workers: Language and meaning in brief therapy.* New York, NY: Aldine de Gruyter.

Lee, M. Y. (2013). Solution-focused therapy. In Franklin, C. (Ed.), *The 23rd Encyclopedia of Social Work*. New York, NY: Oxford University Press.

Lee, M. Y. (2003). A solution-focused approach to cross-cultural clinical social work practice: Utilizing cultural strengths, *Families in Society*, 84, 385–395.

Lee, M. Y., Sebold, J., & Uken, A. (2003). *Solution-focused treatment with domestic violence offenders: Accountability for change*. New York, NY: Oxford University Press.

Nelson, T., & Thomas, F. (Ed.). (2007). *Clinical applications of Solution Focused Brief Therapy*. New York, NY: Haworth Press.

84 Improving Classroom Management through Positive Behavior Interventions and Supports

A. M. Thompson

Classrooms are dynamic societies organized for the purpose of teaching and learning. Teachers lead these societies and they organize, deliver, and manage activities to promote student learning. These activities frequently facilitate student interactions that require social, emotional, and cognitive processes (Zins, Payton, Weissberg, & O'Brien, 2007). Conflicts naturally will occur during such interactions. As such, the ability of a teacher to facilitate positive exchanges—with and between students—is related to that teacher's ability to manage conflict and promote positive interactions. When conflicts are not resolved in a constructive and mutually satisfying manner, the results may contribute to an increase in disruptive student behaviors.

Aside from common classroom conflict arising from everyday interactions, many students exhibit above average levels of disruptive behaviors. Studies currently suggest that 20% of students—or three to four students per class—display disruptive behaviors to such a degree that normal functioning is impaired (Brauner & Stephens, 2006; Satcher, 2004). Disruptive behaviors harm everyone in schools, including the students with these behaviors, their

peers, and teachers. Disruptive behaviors are the most common reason students are removed from class—interfering with instruction, exacerbating academic problems, and increasing the likelihood of course failures that lead to dropout (Gresham, Lane, & Lambros, 2000; Nelson, Stage, Duppong-Hurley, Synhorst, & Epstein, 2007; Roderick, 1994). Peers of disruptive students lose about four hours of instruction time per week due to the behaviors—and teachers report disruptive students interfere with teaching and learning on a daily basis (USDOE, 2006; Walker, Ramsey, & Gresham, 2004). Lastly, teachers experience increased stress and burnout from managing disruptive students; a frustration that causes many highly qualified teachers to quit teaching altogether (Brouwers & Tomic, 2000; Hastings & Bham, 2003). A 2005 survey of highly qualified teachers indicated that 53% quit due to disruptive behaviors (USDOE, 2005). Taken together, these issues contribute significantly to an unstable school climate.

To manage the impact of disruptive student behaviors proactively, more than 14,000 schools nationwide have adopted tiered response models known as *positive behavioral interventions and supports* (PBIS). Though the concept of a tiered response model originated in the late 1950s with the National Institutes of Health (Gordon, 1983), the PBIS model translates the concepts to educational settings. PBIS is explicitly mentioned in the Individual with Disabilities Education Act (IDEA) and No Child Felt Behind (NCLB) as a data-driven, school-based model for organizing and distributing a continuum of evidence-based prevention and intervention supports. Although studies indicate that PBIS models are most effective when implemented school-wide, not all school social workers have the luxury of working in settings that use such an approach. Therefore, the purpose of this chapter is to guide school social workers, in consultation with teachers, to implement PBIS strategies at the classroom level. The chapter will first present a brief overview of the research and features of a three-tiered PBIS continuum (e.g., primary, secondary, and tertiary). Next, using each tier as a guide, evidence-based PBIS supports and tools will be described so that school social workers may advise teachers on how to implement the strategies.

OVERVIEW OF POSITIVE BEHAVIORAL INTERVENTIONS AND SUPPORTS IN THE CLASSROOM

On balance, randomized studies indicate that tiered response models have small but significant effects on student- and school-related outcomes. For example, randomized studies suggest tiered response models are associated with improved school safety ($ES = 0.23$), academic achievement ($ES = 0.24 - 0.38$), positive student behaviors ($ES = 0.30$), school climate ($ES = 0.29$), and staff collaboration ($ES = 0.26$) compared to control settings without PBIS (Bradshaw, Reinke, Brown, Bevans, & Leaf, 2008; Horner et al., 2009). Though a large literature details the implementation of a PBIS model (c.f., Lane, Menzies, Bruhn, & Crnobori, 2010; G. Sugai & Horner, 2009), a properly implemented model starts with universal social-emotional and behavioral screening for all students. Based upon these data, primary, secondary, and tertiary supports (i.e., programs and practices) are selected and organized by application intensity.

Primary supports are prevention efforts applied to *all students* to address universal risk factors identified from the screening. For example, packaged curricula like *Second Step* and *Making Choices* are research-based programs that address known risk factors such as physical and relational aggression, overt and covert antisocial behavior, and peer rejection (Fraser, Thompson, Day, & Macy, in press; Grossman et al., 1997). Other primary classroom strategies include developing a mission statement, a set of expectations, and behavioral definitions to make the expectations operational; teaching the expectations on a daily basis; establishing a continuum of consequences; and tools to evaluate universal efforts (Sugai & Horner, 2006).

Secondary supports are concentrated and provided to *small groups* of about 20% of students with elevated levels of need. Secondary supports can be divided into selective and indicated prevention. Selective prevention efforts, such as *Check in Check Out* (Cheney et al., 2009) or the *Behavior Education Program* (Crone, Hawken, & Horner, 2010) are delivered to subgroups of students exposed to known risk factors (i.e., free and reduced lunch programs). Indicated strategies, such as the *Self-Monitoring Training and Regulation Strategy* (Thompson, 2012; Thompson & Webber, 2010) are more intensive and apply to students with early signs and symptoms of an oncoming disorder.

Tertiary supports are individualized and provided to *particular students* with an identified condition. In general, tertiary supports follow a referral, a thorough assessment conducted by a multidisciplinary team, and a determination of eligibility—based upon the assessment data—for entitlement services (i.e., special education). Using the data, a multidisciplinary team devises an education plan outlining individualized services (i.e., specific accommodations), performance goals and objectives (i.e., expected benchmarks and levels of achievement), and the defined roles of personnel who provide each service. It is at the tertiary level that "prevention" effectively becomes "intervention", though tertiary services are intended to prevent further decline of the identified condition. Table 84.1 details the benefits and costs of each level of the three-tiered PBIS model.

APPLYING POSITIVE BEHAVIORAL INTERVENTIONS AND SUPPORTS IN THE CLASSROOM

School social workers can consult with teachers to assess existing primary classroom supports

TABLE 84.1 Benefits and Drawbacks of Each Level of the Positive Behavioral Interventions and Supports Model

PBS Level	%*	Benefits	Costs
Primary (universal)	≈80%	Easy application No iatrogenic effects No contagion effects Focus on context Effective for low at-risk	Impersonal Not individualized May be expensive Potentially wasteful Low effects for high risk
Secondary (targeted: selective & indicated)	≈15%	Accurate with assessment Moderately individualized Efficient dissemination Effective for moderate at-risk	No services just above cut Risk of iatrogenic effects Risk of contagion effects Less focus on context
Tertiary (clinical)	≈5%	Individualized Multi-systemic approach Multidisciplinary approach Effective for high at-risk	Resource intensive No focus on context Risk of iatrogenic effects Risk of labeling effects

* Percentages will vary based upon local norms and expectations.

and identify those that are absent. Undoubtedly, some students will need additional supports, and school social workers can assist teachers to identify and match students with the supports that will meet their needs. Lastly, should some students be unresponsive to primary and secondary efforts, school social workers can assist teachers to implement tertiary level supports—though these supports will involve a team-based approach to meet the student's needs.

Primary supports. Primary supports broadly address basic human needs (i.e., safety) and narrow in scope to define behaviors that maintain those needs. The process should start by identifying existing risk factors predictive of school failure (e.g., emotional lability, conduct or attention problems, early aggression). Such information can inform early intervention. Other effective primary practices begin with (1) a structured mission statement; (2) clearly worded expectations; (3) explicit rules for each procedure; (4) steps to teach, review, and integrate rules; (5) a range of positive and negative consequences; and (6) an evaluation plan.

Structured mission statement. A classroom mission statement should serve as the underlying rationale for structure. An effective mission statement is clear and broadly enumerates student and teacher duties to maintain safety (Sugai & Horner, 2006). For example:

"In Mr. Thompson's classroom, students will actively pursue the knowledge and strategies to successfully
achieve desired goals. To accomplish this end, all students have a responsibility to arrive at class prepared to learn, contribute to a safe learning environment, set reasonable goals for themselves, and make socially appropriate choices to achieve those goals. To facilitate student success, Mr. Thompson will prepare activities and lessons that academically challenge all students, listen to the ideas that students have, and help students achieve their goals."

Clearly worded expectations. Expectations hone the mission statement. Expectations are limited in number (i.e., three to five) and positively describe the behaviors reflected in the mission statement. For example, "Keep Body Parts to Self" suggests an expected behavior. If school-wide rules exist, classroom rules should align with these to communicate seamless expectations.

Explicit rules for procedures. Shown in Table 84.2, rules should operationalize the broad expectations for each procedure. For example, describing the behaviors of a person following the expectation "Being Considerate of Others" for the classroom routine of "Getting Help," a teacher might expect a student would (a) remain seated, (b) raise his or her hand, and (c) speak when called upon. Procedures are revisited periodically, particularly when new routines are introduced.

Teach, review, and integrate rules. Expectations and rules must be taught on a daily basis. School social workers can assist teachers to translate classroom procedures into lessons that

TABLE 84.2 Translating School-wide Rules into Expected Behaviors for Classroom Routines

School-Wide Expectations Classroom Routines	Keep Body Parts to Self	Complete Assigned Work	Follow Teacher Directions	Be in Assigned Area at All Times	Be Considerate of Others
Entering/leaving room					
Being prepared					
Getting help					
Getting supplies					
Sharpening a pencil					
Whole-group instruction					
Small-group instruction					
Independent seatwork					
Cooperative learning					
Completing work early					

(a) define the skill (i.e., the behavioral rule being taught, the underlying logic, and the corresponding classroom expectation), (b) use examples (i.e., of both desired behaviors *and* undesirable behaviors), (c) model the behavior, (d) include activities to engage students in using the skill, and (e) prompt, remind, and reinforce students to use the skill (Langland, Lewis-Palmer, & Sugai, 1998). School social workers might prepare and teach these lessons, but evidence suggests the concepts are most effective when teachers actually teach, integrate, and reinforce the skills throughout the instructional day (Durlak, Weissberg, Dymnicki, Taylor, & Schellinger, 2011). In addition to direct instruction in classroom expectations, teachers can apply instruction from many packaged evidence-based programs, such as *Making Choices,* to facilitate increased social and emotional awareness among students (Fraser et al., in press).

Positive and negative consequences. Behaviors are shaped by consistent application of effective consequences. Consequences follow and shape a behavior. A positive consequence suggests a behavior is desirable and aims to increase the occurrence of the behavior; a negative consequence suggests a behavior is undesirable and aims to extinguish the behavior. Most importantly, effective consequences (a) never humiliate, (b) link the behavior and consequence, (c) elevate teaching over rewarding or punishing, and (d) rely on a continuum (Oliver, Wehby, &

Reschly, 2011). Table 84.3 depicts a range of positive and negative consequences entailing small and everyday, moderate and frequent, and large and infrequent consequences.

Positive consequences for compliance. Small and everyday positive consequences are brief, free, simple, and offered at a ratio of 4 positive reinforcements to 1 negative reprimand (Reinke, Lewis-Palmer, & Martin, 2007). Moderate and frequent positive consequences are random and connected to specific behavioral expectations (i.e., *turning in all assignments for 1 week before. . . .*). Large and infrequent positive consequences are accompanied by prompts and reminders and may be contingent upon individual and group level contingencies (i.e., *all individual work for all students is to be completed before. . . .*; Oliver et al., 2011). When shaping positive consequences, look a student in the eye and pair the positive response with a smile and an explanation of *why* you are recognizing the behavior (Goldstein & Brooks, 2007).

Negative consequences for noncompliance. Negative consequences should teach and preserve a student's autonomy and self-worth— imperative when assisting students to integrate positive social behaviors. Because not all students are the same or have the same needs, a school social worker may advise teachers to tailor consequences dependent upon frequency, intent, and harm caused by the behavior. Equity (i.e., what students need) rather than fairness (i.e.,

TABLE 84.3 Example Range of Positive and Negative Consequences

	Small & Everyday	Moderate & Frequent	Large & Infrequent
Positive Consequences	Social praise ("good job") Smile, high five, Handshake Stickers, stamps, smiley face Positive home note Select music for seatwork Free drinking fountain pass	Weekly positive home call Lunch with teacher/principal Work "escape" ticket Student seat selection Computer time "Buddy" class recess	Large group project Community field trip Cooking in the classroom Class sporting event (kickball) Office helper or hat day Class movie day
Negative Consequences	Non-verbal (proximity, glance) Class pre-correction Individual pre-correction Individual correction In-class conference After-class conference	Instructional modification Seat modification "Buddy" class timeout Student & principal conference Parent contact Student & parent conference	Office referral Reparation Loss of privilege Loss of recess Working lunch detention Working after school detention

everyone gets the same) is paramount to meet a variety of student needs—and teachers need to be comfortable in dealing out consequences to students equitably (Mendler, 2005). Lastly, if a teacher uses a stepwise sequence of negative consequences, students must be aware the teacher has a duty to implement a *"by-pass"* clause for any acts that threaten the safety of others. When delivering negative consequences, maintain (a) proximity and eye contact, (b) keep a calm voice and remain in control, and (c) teach the expected behavior (Goldstein & Brooks, 2007).

Monitoring primary supports. Efficient means of evaluating student understanding of primary level supports is as simple as providing students with quizzes covering expectations following direct instruction. Another way of monitoring the transfer of primary expectations is to record common behavior problems. Teachers may also use a self-monitoring strategy to count the number of positive reinforcements provided to students to be sure they are acknowledging more positives than negatives and that they are engaging and calling upon a diverse group of students. Another evidence-based strategy for assessing students' use of behavioral expectations is

to play the *Good Behavior Game,* where points are assigned to student groups when members are observed meeting expectations (Barrish, Saunders, & Wolf, 1969).

Primary support tools. There are many tools available to facilitate universal student screening—and the selection of a screener should be based upon contextual factors. However, the completion of a universal student screening, a brief classroom management self-assessment, and peer classroom observations will assist school social workers and teachers in planning and prioritizing primary supports. Social workers can visit http://www.pbis.org/ to find these free tools.

• Universal Screening (e.g., *Strengths and Difficulties Questionnaire;* Goodman, 1997) http://www.sdqinfo.com/
• Classroom Management Self-Assessment http://www.pbis.org/pbis_resource_detail_page.aspx?Type=4&PBIS_ResourceID=174
• Classroom Observation Tool http://www.pbis.org/evaluation/evaluation_tools.aspx
• Lesson plans for teaching expectations http://www.pbis.org/training/student.aspx

- Learning Inventories and Multiple Intelligences Tests http://www.businessballs.com/howardgardnermultipleintelligences.htm#multiple
- Good Behavior Game Manual http://prevention.mt.gov/suicideprevention/goodbehaviorgamemanual.pdf

Secondary classroom supports. Prior to implementing secondary supports, teachers and school practitioners should assess the fidelity of all primary-level efforts. If primary supports are not faithfully implemented, social workers and teachers should focus on what can be done to implement primary supports fully. When a self-assessment and a classroom management observation reveal that all primary-level classroom strategies are in place and practiced faithfully, but a few students still exhibit challenging behaviors, those students may require secondary supports. Secondary supports generally involve direct instruction with small student groups with similar deficits. The supports should be closely monitored using data to gauge student responsiveness.

The Technical Assistance Center at pbis.org lists the following features of secondary supports: (a) continuous availability; (b) low teacher burden; (c) consistency with primary supports; (d) faculty awareness of secondary efforts; (e) utilization of functional assessment and data to monitor student progress; (f) adequate resources; and (g) students elect to participate (http://www.pbis.org/school/secondary_level/faqs.aspx). Examples of secondary interventions containing the above features include the *Check in/Check out* strategy (CICO), *The Behavior Education Program* (BEP; Crone et al., 2010), or the *Self-monitoring Training and Regulation Strategy* (STARS; Thompson, 2012).

Secondary support tools. Per the Office of Special Education Programs (OSEP) guidelines, most secondary supports will involve assistance from school-based practitioners and should begin with a functional behavioral assessment (FBA). An FBA refers to a range of procedures to assess contextual factors associated with a behavior. An FBA should (a) identify and describe target behaviors, (b) prioritize behaviors based upon characteristics (e.g., frequency, duration, and intensity), (c) identify contextual variables associated with the behavior, (d) develop hypotheses describing the context and the function of the behavior, and (d) result in a suggested contextual intervention (Goldstein & Brooks, 2007). Indirect and direct FBA can be conducted using the following tools:

- Functional Assessment Checklist for Teachers (FACTS-A) http://www.pbis.org/common/pbisresources/tools/EfficientFBA_FACTS.pdf
- Guess and Check: Teacher Guided FBA http://www.pbis.org/common/pbisresources/tools/Guess_and_Check_version2.pdf
- A direct FBA completed by an educational paraprofessional will supplement a teacher's indirect FBA and across multiple contexts (i.e., playground, cafeteria, classroom, engaged in multiple academic pursuits) using observations, interviews, and behavior protocols. For forms and procedures to complete a direct FBA, visit the OSEP website at http://www.pbis.org/common/pbisresources/publications/PracticalFBA_TrainingManual.pdf

Once FBA data are available, the teacher and paraprofessional should consider relevant accommodations (e.g., academic, social, or environmental adjustments) to intervene in the behaviors. A child who continues to have difficulty—despite such accommodations—may require more intensive strategies such as the CICO, the BEP (Crone et al., 2010), or the STARS program (Thompson & Webber, 2010). The CICO and BEP programs use a daily teacher report card to monitor student behaviors. The STARS program includes elements of the BEP and CICO, but STARS includes direct instructional strategies that teach students a problem solving and decision making model. Following student training, both the student and teacher monitor the student's performance on behavioral goals generated by the student. Prior research and meta-analyses suggest self-monitoring improves classroom behavioral performance for students with a range of internalizing and externalizing behaviors. More specifically, randomized studies of STARS suggest that self-monitoring is associated with teacher-rated improvements in classroom behavior and displays of social competence (Thompson, 2012). A webinar describing the implementation of STARS is available (https://umconnect.umn.edu/p26217564/) to describe the implementation of STARS.

Figure 84.1 outlines the basic steps of training students in self-monitoring. Studies suggest that reliability of student observations will increase if they are trained in self-monitoring (Zimmerman, 1989). Figure 84.2 presents a sample behavioral report card that a student and teacher would use to monitor the student's performance on classroom rules. Using a report similar to Figure 84.1, a student and teacher would monitor the student's behavioral performance on the same goals. After a specified period (e.g., one week), the student and a school practitioner would calculate the daily percentages (dividing the number of "yes" marks circled by the total number [13] of "yes" marks possible for each expectation). The student can also calculate the total performance percentage across all five expectations (summing all "yes" marks circled and dividing the sum by the total [65] possible across all expectations). It is helpful to visualize the performance over time by graphing those percentages for both the teacher and student data. After the graphs are prepared, the student meets with the teacher and the practitioner to examine the graphs and identify differences between the perspectives. Areas of discrepancy are noted, and new goals can be written to increase the rate of agreement between the student and teacher from the current rate (i.e., 67%) to a level just above current performance (i.e., 70%). Studies suggest STARS is feasible, has low teacher burden, can be implemented with 20% of students at risk, and is perceived by students as socially acceptable and autonomy supportive (Thompson, 2012; Thompson & Webber, 2010).

Purpose: Provide initial training for students to self-monitor behavior goals.

1. Identify and prioritize difficult behaviors
   a. Functional Behavior Analysis (FBA)
      i. Indirect Teacher FBA
      ii. Direct School Practitioner FBA
2. Operationalize behaviors with a definition the student can understand and teach expected behaviors
   a. Example: *"Being Considerate of Others"* for the classroom routine of *"Getting Help,"* a student would: (1) remain Seated, (2) raise your right or left hand, and (3) request help when the teacher calls your name.
   b. Teach expected behaviors for all procedures
   c. Check for understanding with student by asking for specific behavior examples
3. Teach Students to Observe Behavioral Performance using a Recording Tool
   a. Use FBA information to determine
      i. Priority of goals: intensity, duration, and frequency of behaviors
      ii. Interval schedule: how often the student should record self-monitoring data
   b. Define goal statement based upon FBA
      i. Goals are stated using positive language and is observable, measureable, and realistic
      ii. Goal specific to problem behavior and may suggest a replacement behavior
         1. Example: "I will increase my 'Following Directions' percentage from 75% to 79% by complying with my teacher's request within 30 seconds after I am given directions from my teacher."
      iii. Start with few goals; monitor progress and adjust number of goals as needed
   c. Address strategies to complete record performance
      i. Strategies for reliable ratings
         1. Watch with timer
   d. Practice
      i. Use examples from FBA and ask students to rate themselves
      ii. Use an internet video and ask students to observe and rate behavior

Figure 84.1 Student self-monitoring.

4. Trial Run
    a. Observe and rate a short class session with both observer and student completing recordings
    b. Compare observer ratings with student ratings
    c. Practice determining goals and completing contract
    d. Take advantage of this opportune time to talk about the definition of classroom expectations
        i. The definition of acceptable behavior is determined by the teacher
        ii. Ask the student to role play the "teacher" and review their data
5. Teach students to calculate percentages and graph percentages. Repeat procedure.
6. Identify and prioritize difficult behaviors
    a. Functional Behavior Analysis (FBA)
        i. Indirect Teacher FBA
        ii. Direct School Practitioner FBA
7. Operationalize behaviors with a definition the student can understand and teach expected behaviors
    a. Example: *"Being Considerate of Others"* for the classroom routine of *"Getting Help,"* a student would: (1) remain Seated, (2) raise your right or left hand, and (3) request help when the teacher calls your name.
    b. Teach expected behaviors for all procedures
    c. Check for understanding with student by asking for specific behavior examples
8. Teach Students to Observe Behavioral Performance using a Recording Tool
    a. Use FBA information to determine
        i. Priority of goals: intensity, duration, and frequency of behaviors
        ii. Interval schedule: how often the student should record self-monitoring data
    b. Define goal statement based upon FBA
        i. Goals are stated using positive language and is observable, measureable, and realistic
        ii. Goal specific to problem behavior and may suggest a replacement behavior
            1. Example: "I will increase my 'Following Directions' percentage from 75% to 79% by complying with my teacher's request within 30 seconds after I am given directions from my teacher."
        iii. Start with few goals; monitor progress and adjust number of goals as needed
    c. Address strategies to complete record performance
        i. Strategies for reliable ratings
            1. Watch with timer
    d. Practice
        i. Use examples from FBA and ask students to rate themselves
        ii. Use an internet video and ask students to observe and rate behavior
9. Trial Run
    a. Observe and rate a short class session with both observer and student completing recordings
    b. Compare observer ratings with student ratings
    c. Practice determining goals and completing contract
    d. Take advantage of this opportune time to talk about the definition of classroom expectations
        i. The definition of acceptable behavior is determined by the teacher
        ii. Ask the student to role play the "teacher" and review their data
10. Teach students to calculate percentages and graph percentages. Repeat procedure.

Figure 84.1 Continued

STARS Daily Behavior Goals

Student: Date:

This student:	Completed his/her work	Kept body parts to self	Was considerate of others	Followed directions	Stayed in assigned area
8:00 – 8:30	Yes - No	Yes - No	Yes - No	Yes - No	Yes - No
8:30 – 9:00	Yes - No	Yes - No	Yes - No	Yes - No	Yes - No
9:00 – 9:30	Yes - No	Yes - No	Yes - No	Yes - No	Yes - No
9:30 – 10:00	Yes - No	Yes - No	Yes - No	Yes - No	Yes - No
10:00 – 10:30	Yes - No	Yes - No	Yes - No	Yes - No	Yes - No
10:30 – 11:00	Yes - No	Yes - No	Yes - No	Yes - No	Yes - No
11:00 – 11:30	Yes - No	Yes - No	Yes - No	Yes - No	Yes - No
11:30 – 12:00	Yes - No	Yes - No	Yes - No	Yes - No	Yes - No
12:00 – 12:30	Yes - No	Yes - No	Yes - No	Yes - No	Yes - No
12:30 – 1:00	Yes - No	Yes - No	Yes - No	Yes - No	Yes - No
1:00 – 1:30	Yes - No	Yes - No	Yes - No	Yes - No	Yes - No
1:30 – 2:00	Yes - No	Yes - No	Yes - No	Yes - No	Yes - No
2:00 – 2:30	Yes - No	Yes - No	Yes - No	Yes - No	Yes - No

Total # yes = 65   70% yes = 46   85% yes = 55   90% yes = 58

Notes & Assignments

_____

_____

_____

_____

_____

_____

Parent signature _____

Figure 84.2 STARS Behavior Goal Card.

Tertiary Classroom Supports. Tertiary classroom supports work best when both primary and secondary strategies are practiced with fidelity (Crone et al., 2010). Tertiary level supports are individualized, intensive, involve comprehensive assessment, and require a team collaborative approach involving the student's family. The purpose of a tertiary support plan is to provide a system of care approach to bridge existing school-based, community-based, and family supports around the child in a seamless intervention plan (Epstein & Sanders, 2002).

The Technical Assistance Center at pbis.org lists the following features of tertiary supports: (a) multidisciplinary team approach; (b) use of comprehensive and multi-domain assessment; (c) examination of contextual triggers; (d) results in an individualized plan with goals and objectives; (e) involves direct skills instruction; and (e) includes ongoing data to monitor a student's progress (http://www.pbis.org/school/tertiary_level/faqs.aspx). The difference between secondary and tertiary levels of support is defined by the individualized nature of the plan. For students with multiple problem behaviors, an FBA should prioritize complex and competing behaviors according to the frequency, intensity, and duration of such behaviors (Goldstein & Brooks, 2007). An individualized plan should assess and meet the needs of the student across multiple domains, provide classroom modifications, and support a child's family though a wraparound process that identifies existing community-based services.

Tertiary support tools. Tertiary supports include a team approach to examine all data associated with all secondary efforts (i.e., FBA, STARS). Due to their individualized nature, tertiary supports will likely involve "wrap-around" services (Eber, Sugai, Smith, & Scott, 2002). A wrap-around plan should assess strengths and areas of need, and pair those needs with external community resources. A tertiary plan should address problematic behaviors using a behavior intervention plan (BIP) that is based upon existing FBA and classroom performance data. If some of the problematic behaviors include aggression, the BIP should address emergency procedures for managing such behaviors. For more tertiary level supports, including documents to guide the wrap-around process, visit http://www.pbis.org/evaluation/evaluation_tools.aspx to locate the *Educational Information Assessment Tool*, the *Home, School, Community Tool*, the *Student Disposition Tool*, and the *Wraparound Integrity Tool*.

CONCLUSION

The PBIS approach to classroom management provides accessible solutions to the daily challenges faced in schools. When we implement primary classroom strategies with fidelity, studies suggest the majority of students will succeed and fewer students will require more intensive secondary strategies, such as the STARS. However, because significant but modest reductions in disruptive behaviors have been observed for universal (ES = .21) and selective programs (ES = .29),

linking these supports in a tiered response model will improve student outcomes and, theoretically, reduce reliance upon intensive and individualized supports (Wilson & Lipsey, 2007). For the few students who may require intensive supports, a team-based effort will provide tertiary support services in a process that also identifies existing community supports to supplement existing school-based supports and assist a student and his or her family.

Though studies advise PBIS is best implemented at the school level, the chapter describes how PBIS would be implemented at the classroom level. That said, these efforts will be most successful when conducted in schools with administrative support. In addition, when implementing the model at the school level with district financial support, with full principal and staff buy-in, and community agency collaboration for high-risk students and families, research suggests that five to seven years are required to fully implement a school-wide PBIS model (Sugai & Horner, 2009).

Just as no single intervention works for all children in all settings, school social workers should be aware that the percentages of students who may fall within each PBIS level of support will vary depending upon local classroom, school, and community norms. For practitioners working with students who present complex and difficult behaviors, using the FBA process to prioritize students and difficult behaviors (i.e., based upon behavioral frequency, duration, and intensity) will untangle confounds. Indeed, the research underlying the use of FBA and self-monitoring data is the most widely evaluated and reported data elements of the multi-tiered PBIS model, although these studies largely consist of single subject designs due to the individualized nature of the interventions (Thompson, 2010).

It should also be noted that PBIS is a framework for data driven interventions—that is, the model is meant to be a data-driven context to structure and organize best practices and programs. School social workers should encourage school leaders to develop and maintain systems for collecting and reviewing data. In addition, the types of data used within a PBIS model should include early indicators of problems (i.e., early aggression, peer rejection, student and teacher relations) as well as ongoing mechanisms needed to monitor the progress of selected PBIS supports (i.e., office referrals, grades). A common mistake made by school practitioners is to rely on ongoing indicators (office referrals, grades, attendance), which only describe the magnitude of existing problems rather than serve as early antecedents of preventable conditions (Bowen, Thompson, & Powers, 2012). It may be argued that significant policy reforms designed to improve academic performance have failed, in part, because schools focus only on the academic progress as measured by standardized tests. A growing body of research continues to suggest schools must do more to prepare students to be contributing members of our society.

References

Barrish, H. H., Saunders, M., & Wolf, M. M. (1969). Good behavior game: effects of individual contingencies for group consequences on disruptive behavior in a classroom. *Journal of Applied Behavior Analysis*, 2(2), 119–124.

Bowen, N. K., Thompson, A. M., & Powers, J. D. (2012). A quasi-experimental test of the elementary-school success profile model of assessment and prevention. *Journal of the Society for Social Work and Research*, 3(3).

Bradshaw, C. P., Reinke, W. M., Brown, L. D., Bevans, K. B., & Leaf, P. J. (2008). Implementation of school-wide positive behavioral interventions and supports (PBIS) in elementary schools: Observations from a randomized trial. *Education and Treatment of Children*, 31(1), 1–26.

Brauner, C. B., & Stephens, C. B. (2006). Estimating the prevalence of early childhood serious emotional/behavioral disorders: Challenges and recommendations. *Public Health Reports*, 121(3), 303.

Brouwers, A., & Tomic, W. (2000). A longitudinal study of teacher burnout and perceived self-efficacy in classroom management. *Teaching and Teacher Education*, 16(2), 239–253.

Cheney, D. A., Stage, S. A., Hawken, L. S., Lynass, L., Mielenz, C., & Waugh, M. (2009). A 2-year outcome study of the check, connect, and expect intervention for students at risk for severe behavior problems. *Journal of Emotional and Behavioral Disorders*, 17(4), 226–243.

Crone, D. A., Hawken, L. S., & Horner, R. H. (2010). *Responding to problem behavior in schools: The behavior education program*. New York, NY: The Guilford Press.

Durlak, J. A., Weissberg, R. P., Dymnicki, A. B., Taylor, R. D., & Schellinger, K. B. (2011). The impact of enhancing students' social and emotional learning: A meta-analysis of school-based universal interventions. *Child Dev*, 82(1), 405–432.

Eber, L., Sugai, G., Smith, C. R., & Scott, T. M. (2002). Wraparound and positive behavioral interventions and supports in the schools. *Journal of Emotional and Behavioral Disorders*, 10(3), 171–180.

Epstein, J. L., & Sanders, M. G. (2002). Family, school, and community partnerships. *Handbook of Parenting*, 5, 407–437.

Fraser, M. W., Thompson, A. M., Day, S. H., & Macy, R. J. (In press). A latent profile transition analysis of third grade students exposed to the Making Choices Program. *The Elementary School Journal*.

Goldstein, S., & Brooks, R. B. (2007). *Understanding and managing children's classroom behavior: Creating sustainable, resilient classrooms* (vol. 207). NY, NY: John Wiley & Sons.

Goodman, R. (1997). The Strengths and Difficulties Questionnaire: A research note. *Journal of Child Psychology and Psychiatry*, 38(5), 581–586.

Gordon, R. S. (1983). An operational classification of disease prevention. *Public Health Reports*, 98(2), 107.

Gresham, F. M., Lane, K. L., & Lambros, K. M. (2000). Comorbidity of conduct problems and ADHD identification of "fledgling psychopaths." *Journal of Emotional and Behavioral Disorders*, 8(2), 83–93.

Grossman, D. C., Neckerman, H. J., Koepsell, T. D., Liu, P.-Y., Asher, K. N., Beland, K., . . . Rivara, F. P. (1997). Effectiveness of a violence prevention curriculum among children in elementary school. *JAMA: The Journal of the American Medical Association*, 277(20), 1605–1611.

Hastings, R. P., & Bham, M. S. (2003). The relationship between student behaviour patterns and teacher burnout. *School Psychology International*, 24(1), 115–127.

Horner, R. H., Sugai, G., Smolkowski, K., Eber, L., Nakasato, J., Todd, A. W., & Esperanza, J. (2009). A randomized, wait-list controlled effectiveness trial assessing school-wide positive behavior support in elementary schools. *Journal of Positive Behavior Interventions*, 11(3), 133–144.

Lane, K. L., Menzies, H. M., Bruhn, A. L., & Crnobori, M. (2010). *Managing challenging behaviors in schools: Research-based strategies that work*. New York, NY: Guilford Press.

Langland, S., Lewis-Palmer, T., & Sugai, G. (1998). Teaching respect in the classroom: An instructional approach. *Journal of Behavioral Education*, 8(2), 245–262.

Mendler, A. N. (2005). *Just in time: Powerful strategies to promote positive behavior*: National Educational Service.

Nelson, J. R., Stage, S., Duppong-Hurley, K., Synhorst, L., & Epstein, M. H. (2007). Risk factors predictive of the problem behavior of children at risk for emotional and behavioral disorders. *Exceptional Children*, 73(3), 367–379.

Oliver, R. M., Wehby, J. H., & Reschly, D. J. (2011). Teacher classroom management practices: Effects on disruptive or aggressive behavior. *Campbell Systematic Reviews*.

Reinke, W. M., Lewis-Palmer, T., & Martin, E. (2007). The effect of visual performance feedback on teacher use of behavior-specific praise. *Behavior Modification, 31*(3), 247–263.

Roderick, M. (1994). Grade retention and school dropout: Investigating the association. *American Educational Research Journal, 31*(4), 729–759.

Satcher, D. (2004). School-based mental health services. *Pediatrics, 113*(6), 1839.

Sugai, G., & Horner, R. H. (2009). Responsiveness-to-intervention and school-wide positive behavior supports: Integration of multi-tiered system approaches. *Exceptionality, 17*(4), 223–237.

Sugai, G., & Horner, R. R. (2006). A promising approach for expanding and sustaining school-wide positive behavior support. *School Psychology Review, 35*(2), 245.

Thompson, A. M. (2012). *A randomized trial of the Self-management Training and Regulation Strategy (STARS): A selective intervention for students with disruptive classroom behaviors.* Ann Arbor, MI: Proquest Publishers.

Thompson, A. M., & Webber, K. C. (2010). Realigning student and teacher perceptions of school rules: A behavior management strategy for students with challenging behaviors. *Children & Schools, 32*(2), 71–79.

Thompson, A. M. (2010). A systematic review of evidence-based classroom interventions for students with challenging behaviors in school settings. *Journal of Evidence-Based Social Work, 8*, 304–322.

U.S.Department of Education. (2005). Special analysis 2005-mobility in the teacher workforce. Retrieved from http://nces.ed.gov/pubs2005/2005094_Analysis.pdf

U.S. Department of Education. (2006). School survey on crime and safety (SSOCS). Retrieved from http://nces.ed.gov/surveys/ssocs/tables/el_2006_tab_09.asp

Walker, H. M., Ramsey, E., & Gresham, F. M. (2004). *Antisocial behavior in school: Evidence-based practices*: Belmont CA, Wadsworth Publishing Company.

Wilson, S. J., & Lipsey, M. W. (2007). School-based interventions for aggressive and disruptive behavior: Update of a meta-analysis. *American Journal of Preventive Medicine, 33*(2), S130–S143.

Zimmerman, B. J. (1989). A social cognitive view of self-regulated academic learning. *Journal of Educational Psychology, 81*(3), 329.

Zins, J. E., Payton, J. W., Weissberg, R. P., & O'Brien, M. U. (2007). Social and emotional learning for successful school performance. In G. Matthews, M. Zeidne & R. D. Roberts (Eds), *Emotional intelligence: Knowns and unknows* (pp. 376–395). NY: Oxford University Press.

85 Best Practices in Parenting Techniques

Carolyn Hilarski

Parenting success is related to parenting competence (Silver, Heneghan, Bauman, & Stein, 2006). "OK . . . but, what is competent parenting? What must I actually *do* to be an effective and skillful parent?" To answer these questions, the following discussion will take an ecological approach and define parenting as *interactions with a child in a milieu that embodies respect, safety, and genuineness, while attending to the child's temperament and level of attachment.* Using these parameters, this chapter will describe the current empirical understanding of successful parenting methods that attempt to modify both caregiver and child nonhelpful behaviors, with the intent of increasing homeo-stasis in families where imbalance lives. The out-come of this caregiving paradigm is associated with child academic success (Reynolds & Ou, 2004), moral development, emotional regulation (e.g., less anxious or depressed), safe behavior s (e.g., child will be more likely to wear a seatbelt or helmet), and social proficiency (Davidov & Grusec, 2006) leading to a reasonable conclusion that competent parenting practices are essential for optimal child outcomes.

PARENT EDUCATION

Parent training appears to be quite effective and available in a plethora of instructional styles and program components (Long, 2007). The key benefits are that caregivers are exposed to a variety of helpful parent/child interactive tech-niques based on the normal parameters of child development. Educating caregivers about typi-cal child development can be helpful in reducing punitive disciplining methods. Understanding the cognitive and emotional abilities of the child can assist the parent to reframe behaviors that previously might have been perceived as, for example, "spiteful." In the final analysis, parenting practices are most often influenced by perceptions regarding the caregiver/child interactions.

The timing of parent education is critical. It is suggested to be particularly beneficial for care-givers of younger children for several reasons. First, the child's undesirable behaviors tend to be less ingrained. Second, parental interventions are usually more effective because preschoolers tend to lack strong peer influences. Third, a younger child is generally more accepting of changes in behavioral consequences. Finally, young children, even aggressive ones, tend to continue to show affection with their caregivers.

Classes structured in a group format offer parents the added benefit of socialization, while sharing frustrations and childrearing strate-gies, in addition to increasing supportive net-works. However, parenting programs, taken as a whole, are inclined to focus on discipline and behavioral strategies to help parents mod-ify youth behavior[1] and, while successful, the process tends to overlook the caregiver/child relationship influenced by the child's tempera-ment and type of attachment. In families where children have consistent behavioral issues, the caregiver/child relationship may be stressed on some level and discipline techniques alone may not modify the circumstance (Davidov & Grusec, 2006).

TEMPERAMENT

Caregivers will often describe their infants as either *easy* (e.g., generally cheerful, adaptable, or unproblematic), *difficult* (e.g., often irritable, emotional, and/or highly resistant to change), or *slow-to-warm* (e.g., denoting a relatively inac-tive or indifferent child who may show mod-erate resistance to new situations). And these descriptors appear to remain relatively stable, with some moderation owing to the goodness or poorness of fit between the child and his or her environment (Sigelman & Rider, 2006). Families often need help with understanding that their child's temperament can influence the child's level of attachment with the primary caregiver, which can then impact parent disci-plining methods (Stovall-McClough & Dozier, 2004). The following case is meant to illustrate this development.

Michael

Both his preschool teachers and parents report that Michael, a healthy Caucasian 4.5-year-old male, is disruptive and antagonistic toward other children at school and in his neigh-borhood. Michael's parents, Ron and Gail, are expecting a new baby and fearful of how Michael will respond to such a colossal change in their family system. Michael's mother relates that he does not handle change opti-mistically and will often engage in sullen or tantrum-type behaviors when faced with novel situations. Moreover, they are worried that school peers and teachers will label him a bully and/or troublemaker.

According to his mom, "Michael was *born* irritating people around him." While describing the delivery, Gail recounted, "Once I woke from the anesthesia, I was so excited that my child was born. I asked to see my baby. The nurse replied, 'My gosh, can't you hear him? He's been scream-ing since he entered the world.'" She went on to say, "Michael is indeed a puzzle and very differ-ent from my husband and me. Because I don't understand why he insists on fighting or stub-bornly disobeying[2], I sometimes find it difficult to sit and play with him and occasionally use a harsh tone, which makes me feel guilty."

Children with warm, dependent relations in early life are more likely to comply with parental directives. Indeed, the effectiveness of the child's socialization attempts (e.g., aggressive or nonaggressive peer interactions) are associated with the parent-child relationship and a caregivers' style of interaction that is *responsive* (e.g., taking the child's perspective[3]), *supportive* (e.g., praising and showing affection), *attentive* (e.g., listening and encouraging conversation), *guiding* (e.g., providing information), and *receptive* (e.g., inviting emotional expression) (Grusec & Ungerer, 2003). These parenting practices may provide an environment where the child might develop emotional coping and regulation strategies associated with higher self-esteem and positive life outcomes (see Table 85.1). Keeping this information in mind, what about the following case?

Chevaun

Sixteen-year-old Chevaun is a junior in high school. She lives, in a modest home, with her mother (Mary, a seamstress) and stepfather (George, a factory worker). Her mother remarried when Chevaun was 7 years old, shortly after ending a stormy and abusive marriage with Chevaun's father.

Several years ago, according to her mom, "Chevaun changed from a brooding and difficult child to a more cheerful young woman." It was during this time that she asked her parents if she could date. She was given permission, however, with many restrictions on where, when, and with whom she could spend her time. She accepted her parent's rules until about six months ago. Since then, her relationship with her parents is reportedly, "Almost unbearable. She consistently violates her curfew and arrives home smelling like alcohol or worse, drunk. Her grades are suffering and she did not make the cheerleading squad this year."

Chevaun and her stepfather allegedly rarely speak and the tension is obvious when they occupy the same space. During a recent home visit, Chevaun seemed quite agitated and asserted that, "He blames me for everything. He says that I'm the reason the family so upset. That just isn't true! I know he hates me because I'm not his daughter and I won't obey him anymore. He is so

mean. That is why I sometimes drink and don't want to come home."

PARENTING STYLE

Parenting styles are categorized as authoritative, authoritarian, and permissive. These classifications are based on three dimensions: parental control and demands, parental warmth and nurturance, and clarity of parental communication. Both authoritarian and authoritative caregiver styles apply high levels of control in addition to demanding much from their children. However, the authoritarian style often does not include warmth, responsiveness, and age appropriate levels of control; demanding compliance with no excuses (Baumrind, 1967). In contrast, caregivers with an authoritative style of parenting tend to have close emotional relationships with their children, make reasonable age appropriate demands that they enforce, explain reasons for their actions, and request and listen to their child's points of view (see Table 85.1). Childhood exposure to authoritative parenting is linked to the child's perceived competence (Steinberg & Blatt-Eisengart, 2006). Yet, parenting practices, born from the caregiver's style, remain an interactive process and may be strongly influenced by the child's temperament (Miller-Lewis et al., 2006).

Michael Revisited

Michael's mom went on to say that, "Michael is very high maintenance! Ron and I have tried everything to make him listen and behave. We just do not know how to handle his outbursts. Sometimes I get so frustrated that I spank him to settle him down."[4]

During a home visit, Michael was observed interacting with a cousin who was spending the day. He consistently taunted the child; hitting him with a plastic bat, pushing, and taking toys and even his lunch. Michael's mother ignored the behavior for some time then asked Michael to "stop being so rowdy." He did not comply. After a few more minutes, his mother spanked him with her hand on his bottom and sent him to his room. He reappeared after a few minutes, at first playing quietly and then beginning the hitting behavior again.

TABLE 85.1 Helpful Parenting

Helpful Parenting Behaviors	Consequences	Parent Education
Listen to your child	Shows respect and caring	Mindfulness: here and now presence that is nonjudgmental http://www.sagepub.com/upm-data/15640_E5.pdf thinking skills
Comfort your child	Children are more likely to feel cared for by a parent who is interested in their emotional responses. Increases positive mental representations and attachment (Nelson & Panksepp, 1998)	Mindfulness: understand the thoughts and motives of your child: "What urges my child to behave in this way?
Provide structure	Children feel safe knowing there is order to their lives	Structures provide necessary limits, yet, need to be flexible (Popkin, 2007)
Use praise	Your words of praise for the smallest accomplishments bolster the child's self-esteem	Praise, criticism, and self-esteem Helpful comments: "I need your help"; "Let's negotiate"; "I need a time-out" (Parent Talk) (Moorman, 1998)
Specify desired behavior/ Communicate	Children feel comfortable knowing the parents' consistent expectations	Community Education Program (COPE) Designed for use with parents of children ages 3–8 years http://www.fsatoronto.com/programs/counselling/parenting.html http://www.sagepub.comupm-data/15637_E2.pdf 1. Parents learn give helpful directions, to praise when desired behaviors are presented, and to use timeout for undesired behaviors 2. Parents learn to give reasons for requests and describe the consequences for noncompliance Red Light (undesired behavior) and Green Light (desired behavior) (Moorman, 1998) Parent states circumstance and child decides what to do (Moorman, 1998)
Be consistent	Inconsistent responses to a child's behavior leave the child confused and cautious regarding how to behave	Establish house rules and boundaries along with consequences (Hieneman, Childs, & Sergay, 2006) Proactive parenting: *anticipate* an event or interaction and pre-select behavior consistent with family rules (e.g., bring toys or snacks to divert the child's attention; brainstorm positive responses to the child when feeling angry or frustrated).
Spend play, shared work, and/or reading time with your child	• These behaviors encourage caregiver/child attachment. • Play is the principal method by which young children learn and develop. • Sharing chores helps the child to feel needed and embraced in the family system. • Parent/child reading can calm the child and promote bonding.	PCIT (Parent Child Interaction Therapy) http://pcit.phhp .ufl.edu/ Play Techniques Designed for use with parents of children age 2–5 years (Hembree-Kigin & McNeil, 1995)
Show affection	Sensitive and nurturing interactions and touch increase oxytocin levels in caregiver and child, which influences attachment and temperament of child.	Intimacy and Feeling (Parent Talk) (see, Moorman, 1998) Use such phrases as, "I love you"; "I see that . . .," "I am sorry"; "No" Unhelpful phrases: "I was teasing"; "Act your age"; "What I say goes."

The literature suggests that parents may alter their discipline practices in response to the perceived characteristics[5] of their children (Lindsey, Caldera, & Colwell, 2005). Indeed, it seems reasonable that parents might experience a certain level of stress when rearing children described as "difficult and/or different" and that these parents might change their parenting strategies (e.g., corporal punishment) in the face of such circumstances. However, corporal punishment, for example, does not teach children self-control (e.g., delayed gratification or compliance for social rewards). Rather, young children may obey out of fear and older children may choose to act out (e.g., delinquent behavior) or act in (e.g., depression). Further, this particular disciplining method does not generalize to other undesired behaviors. An alternative option might be redirecting the young child to a more satisfactory activity. For example, if finger painting the dining room table is not allowed, offer the child a large paper bag to paint on.

In the meantime, Michael's parents are in need of help to reduce their distress about their family's future. The following plan was developed as a negotiable strategy for work with family members.

TREATMENT PLAN FOR MICHAEL AND HIS FAMILY

Presenting issue: Michael's aggressive behaviors (e.g., hitting, pushing, and taking toys)
Long-term goals: Decrease Michael's aggressive behaviors by 50% (4 weeks)
Short-term objectives:

1. Parents and teachers will develop a systematic plan for discipline (Long, 2007).
   1A. Intervention: Parents will agree to read, at a minimum, one section from each item in the following list of parenting education resources specifically focusing on strategies for positive discipline.[6]
   http://www.lifematters.com/step.asp (STEP Program)
   http://www.loveandlogic.com/ (Love and Logic Program)
   http://www.chickmoorman.com/PTsystem.html (Parent Talk)
   1B. Intervention: Parents will agree to practice,[7] one time per day, the following

Controlled Choices
Helpful: 'Would you prefer to take a walk or read a book this morning?

Not helpful: What shall we do this morning?

I-Statements:
'I feel sad when I am hit with the plastic bat because it hurts'

_____

Directing Behavior
Not Helpful: 'Stop being so rowdy'

Helpful: 'Those who can follow the rules may play with the plastic bat'

_____

Describe:
Describe the undesired behavior:
'When you hit your cousin with the bat,'

Describe the resulting feeling:
'I feel sad that your cousin is crying'

Describe desired behavior:
'Please do not hit anyone with the plastic bat'

Helpful:
Parents set enforceable limits without anger

Figure 85.1 Controlled choices.

suggested strategies from the parenting resources: Controlled Choices, Directing Behavior, Describe, and I-Statements [see Figure 85.1] (record progress of parental practiced behavior as number of Michael's desired behaviors presented each day [see Knapp, 2005, p. 66]).

1C. Intervention: parents and teachers will agree to develop a discipline plan (for home and school) that includes firm limits, reasonable consequences for undesired behavior, and positive reinforcement (encouragement) for desired behavior[8] (Huebner & Mancini, 2003) and record progress[9] (number of desired behaviors in a day).

2. Promote bonding in the classroom and at home (Lee, 2006).

2A. Intervention: Parents and child will determine a time of day that they will engage in "together" time (any work or play that includes interaction and no distractions—e.g., sharing family stories or looking at family photos, singing, reading, or coloring in the family life book) (Leckman et al., 2004) and record progress (number of Michael's desired behaviors presented each day [Knapp, 2005]).

2B. Intervention: Teacher and parents will agree to develop a plan that will enhance Michael's bonding in the classroom, which may include the teacher and co-teachers engaging in daily chats or greetings, reciprocal smiles, or interactive tasks with Michael, and record the outcome (number of desired behaviors in a day) (Huebner & Mancini, 2003; Hunter, 1998).

Revisiting Chevaun

Her stepfather believes that grounding Chevaun for six weeks is a good way to get her attention and keep her from drinking, becoming pregnant, or hanging with the wrong crowd.[10] He openly admits to hitting her when she is verbally disrespectful to either him or her mother adding that he "has no use for her anymore because she is so hateful to everyone in the family." (See Figure 85.2.)

Chevaun's mother is distraught over the continual fighting between her husband and only child. On the other hand, she is worried that her daughter "will come to no good end." She disclosed that she often feels guilty that her daughter was involved in the violence of her first marriage, which is now being repeated. She reports feeling powerless to solve the problem.

Frequently, youths with *family issues* are drawn to peers with similar environments. There seems to be an unspoken understanding. Moreover, academic failure or underachievement, teen pregnancy, substance use, delinquency, and suicide are not mutually exclusive factors. These variables have a synergy often found within and in the environments of troubled teens. Mary and George's differing parenting styles, George's hostility toward Chevaun, and Mary's depressive withdrawal leave Chevaun in an environment that is unsupportive and non-nurturing (see Figure 85.2). Indeed, she expressed this perception when describing her family's interactions. The following treatment plan was constructed for negotiable work with this family.

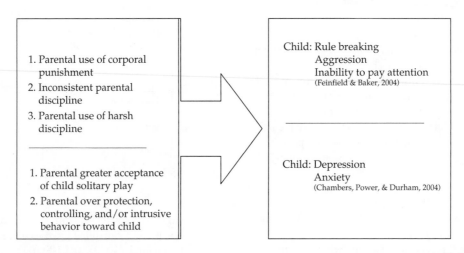

Figure 85.2 Parenting outcomes.

TREATMENT PLAN FOR CHEVAUN AND HER FAMILY

Presenting issue: Chevaun is breaking family/social rules and parents are reporting both overprotective and harsh parenting practices.

Long-term goals: Parents will successfully use positive disciplining methods on a daily basis resulting in a 50% decrease in Chevaun's family/social rule noncompliance (8 weeks).

Short-term objectives:

1. Parents will learn positive parenting practices to increase perceived family homeostasis and bonding.
   1A. Intervention: Parents will read the following books: *Your Defiant Teen* (Barkley & Robin, 2008); *Parenting Teens with Love and Logic* (Cline & Fay, 2006); and *Parent Talk* (Moorman, 1998), in addition to journaling and sharing thoughts and feelings regarding the new information with family members and/or counselor/educational group, if involved with that resource.
2. Parents and child will practice various behaviors meant to enable the development of child and parent self-responsibility (see Figure 85.2, and Tables 85.1 and 85.2) increasing the likelihood of family member bonding and family homeostasis. They will also record thoughts and feelings (Best, 2006).
   2A. Parents will initiate a daily *family time* (Eaker & Walters, 2002) (e.g., 30 minutes) where the family will talk, share a task (e.g., keep a family journal), or play together, plan future together times, share thoughts and feelings with no distractions (e.g., phone calls or television) and journal thoughts and feelings regarding the new structure to share with family members and/or counselor/educational group.
   2B. Intervention: Parents will offer the child an attainable task and allow the child to complete the undertaking without interference, allowing natural consequences to be the learning opportunity (Cline & Fay, 2006; McMahon, 2003). Family members will review the outcome during family time and, if deemed unsuccessful, offer the opportunity again. All family members will journal their thoughts and feelings

TABLE 85.2 Helpful Thinking and Behaving For Parents

1. Children are offered choices of potential desired behaviors in a tone that is sensitive and calm.
2. Consequences for an undesired behavior may be postponed and contemplated with empathy.
3. Parents do not need to own the problem.
4. It is the child's responsibility to learn that consequences arise from behaviors and he/she has the ability to ponder possible alternative behaviors for future use (Cline & Fay, 2006).

about this process and share them with one another and/or a counselor or educational group.

2C. Intervention: All family members will perform the rewind game (Knapp, 2005, p. 229) to practice *thinking about new ways to solve a problem or behave in response to a circumstance* and share results, thoughts, and feelings during family time and/or with an educational group or counselor.

2D. Intervention: Parents will learn the value of supportive statements, such as, "I know you can accomplish this task" (Nelsen & Lott, 2000), and the empowering techniques of listening, power messages, choices, consequences, and permission (Cline & Fay, 2006) They will journal thoughts and feelings about using this new behavior to share with family members and/or counselor/educational group.

2E. Intervention: Both parents and child will work together to form a plan for correcting undesired child behavior. All family members will work through the personal problem solving activity (Knapp, 2005, p. 211) and share their results during family time and/or in an educational group or with a counselor.

2F. Intervention: Parents will learn about the reciprocal nature of parent and child interactions (e.g., how their response to their child's behavior may reinforce undesired child behaviors) by reading Step Four of *Your Defiant Teen: 10 Steps to Resolve Conflict and Rebuild*

Your Relationship (Barkley & Robin, 2008). They will also journal thoughts and feelings and share these with one another during family time and/or with an educational group or counselor.

CONCLUSION

Parenting can be both a stressful and joyous undertaking that is significantly influenced by parent/child perceptions, goodness of fit, and interactions (Kendler, 1996). Parenting practices have outcomes (see Figure 85.2 and Table 85.1). It is the professional's job to enable frustrated parents to find their own understanding of how to help themselves and their child discover mutually satisfying interactions that strengthen and sustain family homeostasis. All family members must be involved and willing to take responsibility for their contributions to the family dynamics in addition to being open to change. Moreover, schools and communities also have a stake in the health and success of our future generations. Evidence-based responsible and collective caregiving is a significant factor in that outcome.

WEBSITES: PARENTING SKILLS

www.loveandlogic.com
www.kidshealth.org
www.healthychildren.org

Notes

1. Low-income parents tend to prefer behaviorally based education (Wood & Baker, 1999)
2. This is a sign of low reflective functioning or a parent who is unable to empathize (see, Slade, 2005)
3. What makes Michael behave in this way? How do I respond when he behaves like this? (maternal state of mind and reflective functioning are associated with child caregiver attachment (Atkinson et al., 2005).
4. Parental stress related to perceived ineffective parenting abilities is associated with the use of corporal punishment
5. For example, "Michael is a disobedient and high maintenance child"
6. Preferably within the first week of seeking advice or counseling
7. Parents will have documented a behavior baseline of at least 3 days (Knapp, 2005).
8. Replacing noncompliance with compliance and cooperation—Exercise IXA (Knapp, 2005, p. 109–110)
9. Behavior baseline documented—Exercise VB (Knapp, 2005, p. 65–66)
10. Grounding is a time-out for teens and not as effective as other parenting methods (see, Barkley & Robin, 2008)

References

Atkinson, L., Goldberg, S., Raval, V., Pederson, D., Benoit, D., Moran, G. Leung, E. (2005). On the relation between maternal state of mind and sensitivity in the prediction of infant attachment security. *Developmental Psychology, 41*(1), 42–53.

Barkley, R. A., & Robin, L. (2008). *Your defiant teen: 10 steps to resolve conflict and rebuild your relationship*. New York, NY: Guilford Press.

Baumrind, D. (1967). Child care practices anteceding three patterns of preschool behavior. *Genetic Psychology Monograph, 75*, 43–88.

Best, A. L. (2006). Freedom, constraint, and family responsibility: Teens and parents collaboratively negotiate around the car, class, gender, and culture. *Journal of Family Issues, 27*(1), 55–84.

Cline, F., & Fay, J. (2006). *Parenting teens with love and logic: Preparing adolescents for responsible adulthood*. Colorado Springs, CO: NavPress.

Davidov, M., & Grusec, J. E. (2006). Untangling the links of parental responsiveness to distress and warmth to child outcomes. *Child Development, 77*(1), 44–58.

Eaker, D. G., & Walters, L. H. (2002). Adolescent satisfaction in family rituals and psychosocial development: A developmental systems theory perspective. *Journal of Family Psychology, 16*(4), 406–414.

Grusec, J. E., & Ungerer, J. (2003). Effective socialization as a problem solving and the role of parenting cognitions. In L. Kuczynski (Ed.), *Handbook of dynamics in parent-child relations* (pp. 211–228). Thousand Oaks, CA: Sage.

Hembree-Kigin, T. L., & McNeil, C. B. (1995). *Parent-child interaction therapy*. New York, NY: Plenum Press.

Hieneman, M., Childs, K., & Sergay, J. (2006). *Parenting with positive behavior support: A practical guide to resolving your child's difficult behavior*. Baltimore, MD: Paul H. Brooks Publisher.

Huebner, A. J., & Mancini, J. A. (2003). Shaping structured out-of-school time use among youth: The effects of self, family, and friend systems. *Journal of Youth & Adolescence, 32*(6), 453–463.

Hunter, L. (1998). *The effects of school practices and experiences on the bonding of at-risk students to the school*. Seattle, WA: ProQuest Information & Learning.

Kendler, K. S. (1996). Parenting: a genetic-epidemiologic perspective. *American Journal of Psychiatry, 153*(1), 11–20.

Knapp, S. E. (2005). *Parenting skills homework planner*. Hoboken, NJ: Wiley.

Leckman, J. F., Feldman, R., Swain, J. E., Eicher, V., Thompson, N., & Mayes, L. C. (2004). Primary parental preoccupation: Circuits, genes, and crucial role of the environment. *Journal of Neural Transmission, 111*, 753–771.

Lee, T. Y. (2006). Bonding as a positive youth development construct: Conceptual bases and implications for curriculum development. *International Journal of Adolescent Medicine and Health, 18*(3), 483–492.

Lindsey, E., Caldera, Y., & Colwell, M. (2005). Correlates of coparenting during infancy. *Family Relations, 54*, 346–359.

Long, N. (2007). Learning from experience: Shifting from clinical parent training to broader parent education. *Clinical Child Psychology & Psychiatry, 12*(3), 385–392.

McMahon, T. (2003). *Teen tips: A practical survival guide for parents with kids 11–19*. New York, NY: Simon and Schuster.

Miller-Lewis, L. R., Baghurst, P. A., Sawyer, M. G., Prior, M. R., Clark, J. J., Arney, F. M., & Carbone, J. A. (2006). Early childhood externalising behaviour problems: child, parenting, and family-related predictors over time. *Journal of Abnormal Child Psychology, 34*(6), 891–906.

Moorman, C. (1998). *Parent talk*. New York, NY: Fireside.

Nelsen, J., & Lott, L. (2000). *Positive discipline for teenagers: Empowering your teens and yourself*. Roseville, CA: Prima Publishers.

Nelson, E. E., & Panksepp, J. (1998). Brain substrates of infant-mother attachment: Contributions of opioids, oxytocin, and norepinephrine. *Neuroscience Biobehavioral Review, 22*(3), 437–452.

Popkin, M. H. (2007). *Taming the spirited child: Strategies for parenting challenging children*. New York, NY: Fireside: Simon and Schuster.

Reynolds, A. J., & Ou, S. (2004). Alterable predictors of child well-being in the Chicago longitudinal study. *Children and Youth Services Review, 26*, 1–14.

Sigelman, C. K., & Rider, E. A. (2006). *Life-span human development* (5th ed.). Belmont, CA: Wadsworth.

Silver, E. J., Heneghan, A. M., Bauman, L. J., & Stein, R. E. (2006). The relationship of depressive symptoms to parenting competence and social support in inner-city mothers of young children. *Maternal Child Health Journal, 10*(1), 105–112.

Slade, A. (2005). Parental reflective functioning: An introduction. *Attachment and Human Development, 7*(3), 269–281.

Steinberg, L., & Blatt-Eisengart, I. (2006). Patterns of competence and adjustment among adolescents from authoritative, indulgent, and neglectful homes: A replication in a sample of serious juvenile offenders. *Journal of Research on Adolescents, 16*, 47–58.

Stovall-McClough, K. C., & Dozier, M. (2004). Forming attachments in foster care: Infant attachment behaviors during the first 2 months of placement. *Developmental Psychopathology, 16*(2), 253–271.

Wood, W. D., & Baker, J. A. (1999). Preferences for parent education programs among low socioeconomic status, culturally diverse parents. *Psychology in the Schools, 36*(3), 239–247.

86 Bereavement and Grief Therapy

Elizabeth C. Pomeroy, Kathleen H. Anderson, & Renée Bradford Garcia

Loss is a universal experience that everyone encounters at one time or another during their lives. Loss from the death of a loved one can be especially devastating. Grief resulting from this kind of loss causes significant disruption in a person's functioning both internally (physically and emotionally) and externally (socially and occupationally). Historically, mental health practitioners have received little in-depth training related to grief and loss interventions. In addition, only a few theories of grief and loss have been postulated by experts in the field. However, as the topic of grief and loss gains wider acceptance and more visibility, there is a need for an understanding of the grief process that considers the individual within the context of the environments in which he or she functions, rather than just examining the intrapsychic experience of the individual.

Early conceptualizations of the process of grief and loss formed the initial knowledge base of an unexplored area of human experience and helped us understand the problematic symptoms and damaging consequences of grief. They validated that grief is a negative, painful, and disruptive experience for the mourner. Practitioners often misinterpret these models as being grounded in a problem-oriented perspective and consequently often view a person experiencing grief as someone suffering from an illness that must be cured. As a result, the practitioner may de-emphasize the mourner's strengths and resiliencies, which can be brought to bear on his or her unique experience of loss. The strengths-based framework of grief assists practitioners in building on the inherent strengths of the individual while they navigate the grieving process. It encourages mourners to use their positive coping abilities and environmental resources. Furthermore, the strengths-based approach to grief is grounded in the view that grief in response to the death of a loved one is a natural, normal, and potentially health-producing process that aids the individual in adjusting to the absence of the loved one.

THE STRENGTHS-BASED FRAMEWORK FOR GRIEF

The strengths perspective of social work practice developed by Saleebey (2013) and Rapp (1998) views every client as having assets and resources that enhance his or her ability to cope with life events. These assets and resources can be categorized into individual strengths and environmental strengths. Individual strengths include aspirations, competencies, and confidence (Rapp & Goscha, 2012). Aspirations include goals, dreams, hopes for the future, ambitions, and positive motivation to achieve and grow. Competencies are manifested by one's unique ability to use talents, skills, and intellect. Confidence refers to a person's positive self-regard and his or her belief and

tenacity in achieving goals. A person with confidence feels valuable and worthy of positive life events. Strengths are present in every individual. Some people appear to be able to capitalize on their strengths more than others. This phenomenon may be due to a combination of biological, psychological, and social factors. Environmental strengths include resources, social relations, and opportunities. Resources include financial support, access to services, access to information, and other tangible assets. Social relations encompass friends, family, coworkers, neighbors, and others with whom one has interactions. Opportunities refer to the gaps in one's life that are waiting to be filled. They represent positive events that can potentially change one's life. In addition, a person maintains specific niches in life, that is, habitation, job, friends, and leisure activities. According to Rapp (1998), "The quality of the niches for any individual is a function of that person's aspirations, competencies, confidence, and the environmental resources, opportunities, and people available to the person" (p. 42). Together, a person's individual and environmental strengths influence one's sense of well-being, empowerment, and life satisfaction (Rapp & Goscha, 2012).

For clients who are grieving, the strengths perspective is a particularly salient framework. It builds on previous theories of grief with the addition of a lens that emphasizes the health-producing aspects that are intrinsic to the mourner as well as the process of grief. Focusing on client strengths rather than deficits provides the practitioner with a valuable tool that can aid in assessment and intervention. It effectively highlights aspects of the person and his or her environment that can be used and enhanced to assist in the grieving process and promote positive growth. The basic tenets of the strengths-based framework of grief are as follows.

1. Grief in response to the death of a loved one is a natural, expectable, and potentially health-producing process that aids the person in adjusting to the absence of the loved one.
2. The symptoms, emotions, and behaviors associated with expected grief reactions represent a process of healthy adaptation and are not inherently pathological.
3. Mourners benefit by knowing that life-enhancing grief reactions are productive and beneficial. Life-enhancing grief reactions are those responses that facilitate healing within the mourner.

4. All persons have individual and environmental strengths that can assist them as they experience grief. The mourner benefits from the reinforcement of those strengths and the encouragement to consciously employ them during the grief process.

5. Environmental conditions can either help or hinder the mourner's ability to adapt to the loss and enhance the person's life.

6. Many symptoms of grief, although they may be uncomfortable and are commonly regarded as negative symptoms, are healthy coping mechanisms in that they facilitate the process of separation, adaptation to change, and integration of the loss.

7. Life-enhancing grief reactions to loss enable accommodation and adaptation to occur. They facilitate the process of psychological separation from the deceased.

8. Life-enhancing grief symptoms should not be discouraged. Rather, they should be allowed expression while being carefully monitored so that they remain helpful to the mourner's process of adaptation.

9. Grief may be considered life-depleting when the symptoms it produces significantly weaken the mourner's aspirations, competencies, and confidence. Life-depleting grief reactions are those responses and circumstances that act as impediments to the expected grieving process and interfere with the mourner's ability to live a fulfilling life.

10. Life-depleting grief reactions thwart the process of adaptation and lead to entropy.

11. Life-enhancing and life-depleting grief reactions exist on a continuum of intensity.

12. The experience of grief evolves over a person's lifetime and is experienced with varying levels of conscious awareness (Pomeroy & Garcia, 2009).

The outlook for the strengths-based perspective in terms of clinical practice and social work is tempered by the dominant helping modality found in social work and medicine that is molded around the "problems and pathology" framework. Clearer criteria and definition of what strengths-based practice is and testing with more robust research and practice in academia would greatly benefit strengths-based social work (Rapp, Saleebey, & Sullivan, 2005).

ASSESSMENT OF BEREAVEMENT ACCORDING TO THE *DIAGNOSTIC AND STATISTICAL MANUAL OF MENTAL DISORDERS, FIFTH EDITION*

Historically, bereavement has received minimal attention from the American Psychiatric Association and was included in the *DSM IV* and *DSM IV-TR* as a V code (Other conditions that may be a focus of clinical attention). The definition of bereavement included a two-month time period, which was considered a major limitation by the field of experts in grief and loss. Moreover, a diagnosis of Major Depressive Disorder prevented the practitioner from diagnosing bereavement.

Although the *Diagnostic and Statistical Manual of Mental Disorders, Fifth Edition (DSM-5)* recognizes the differences between uncomplicated bereavement, which is still defined as a V code, and Major Depressive Disorder, it also allows for a person experiencing a severe grief reaction and depression to be diagnosed with a Major Depressive Disorder. Although the major symptoms of grief involve feelings of emptiness and loss that come and go in waves, the major symptoms of major depression include hopelessness and persistent depression that pervasively influence the person's mood (APA, 2013). In addition, a person with Major Depressive Disorder will have low self-esteem while the person with a grief reaction may keep their self-esteem intact. However, the authors of the *DSM-5* recognize that there can be significant overlap in symptoms and a bereaved individual can become clinically depressed.

Bereavement is also noted in the *DSM-5* in the Trauma and Stressor-Related Disorders category under Other Specified Trauma and Stressor-Related Disorder. An individual who experiences the death of a close relation (friend or family member) and who continues to long for the deceased, has significant emotional pain, and who is preoccupied with the deceased may have a complicated grief condition that would be classified as a Persistent Complex Bereavement Disorder (APA, 2013). In addition, the individual experiences symptoms similar to a trauma reaction, such as emotional numbing, anger, excessive avoidance of situations that remind one of the death, a desire to die in order to be with the deceased, loneliness, role confusion, and lack of interest in pleasurable activities. A specifier of "with traumatic bereavement" can be included if the death was of a traumatic nature such as homicide or suicide. Persistent Complex Bereavement Disorder is also being considered as a unique diagnosis; however, presently it is in the Appendix under "Conditions for Further Study." Therefore, to diagnose a client who is experiencing these symptoms, a practitioner would have to use the "Other Trauma and Stressor-Related Disorder" classification (APA, 2013).

Finally, Uncomplicated Bereavement remains in the *DSM-5* under "Other Conditions That May Be a Focus of Clinical Attention" as a V Code. Uncomplicated Bereavement is considered a normal expression of grief over the loss of a loved one and not a mental disorder (APA, 2013). The duration of a normal grief reaction is not specified in the *DSM-5*, with an acknowledgement that culture may play a significant role in the length of the grief process.

Bereavement can also be found in the *DSM-5* (APA, 2013) under Adjustment Disorders. In the case of the death of a loved one the grief reaction must surpass what is customary in that person's environment and culture. In addition, the developmental level of the person must be taken into consideration (APA, 2013). For example, a young child who develops behavioral problems after the death of a distant relative might be given a diagnosis of Adjustment Disorder with the specifier, "with mixed disturbance of emotions and conduct."

STRENGTHS-BASED, EXPECTED GRIEF ASSESSMENT AND INTERVENTIONS WITH INDIVIDUAL CLIENTS

Intervening with bereaved clients from the strengths-based framework of grief involves several skills that originate from a comprehensive understanding of the strengths-based model. The practitioner adheres to the basic tenets of the model while working with the unique situation that the client brings to counseling. Initially, the practitioner allows for the client to present his or her story of the loss and the experience with his or her grief. This story may unfold over many sessions and may be retold from various perspectives. However, the initial presentation of the loss provides the practitioner with information and insight into the client's present experience. Concurrently, the practitioner listens for information that will complete a preliminary assessment of the client's internal and external strengths, resources, and

social supports. Some of the skills that the practitioner uses throughout grief counseling include active and empathetic listening, nonjudgmental acceptance of intense emotions, normalizing and educating the client about the grief process, assisting the client with coping skills and resources, and helping the client develop life-enhancing strategies to re-engage fully in life. Finally, the practitioner will assist the client in using his or her experience as fuel for personal growth.

According to the strengths-based framework of grief, the term *expected* grief describes the predictable grief experience that reflects the healthy process of separation from the deceased individual. Although it can take on a wide variety of forms, this type of grief is what the practitioner would expect to see with someone who has lost a loved one. Expected grief leads to health-producing growth. The term *complex* grief describes a grief process that is encumbered with internal and/or external complications that interfere with the health-producing growth process of expected grief. If complex grief is not addressed appropriately, it can lead to life-depleting responses (Pomeroy & Garcia, 2009).

GROUP INTERVENTIONS FOR ADULTS WITH EXPECTED GRIEF

In addition to individual counseling, group counseling has been used as a primary vehicle for working with the bereaved (Worden, 2009). Psycho-educational group interventions have been shown to be effective with caregivers of chronically/terminally ill populations such as Alzheimer's, oncological, and dialysis patients (Brown, 2011). In addition, psycho-educational groups related to grief and loss have proven to improve well-being and grief resolution, increase social support, and decrease the risk of psychopathology related to unresolved grief issues (Pomeroy & Holleran, 2002). The power of group support and shared, mutual concerns can ameliorate the loneliness and isolation associated with loss. The potential benefit of being with others who share a common experience with grief is tremendous. Group support can effectively minimize the feelings of grief described by Stephen Levine when he writes, "We come to trust ourselves less, we cannot 'feel' the world around us as we once did, so we experience ourselves as 'a bit unplugged'" (Levine, 2005, p. 4).

A STRENGTHS-BASED, PSYCHO-EDUCATIONAL GRIEF GROUP

The authors have found that bereavement groups combining the strengths-based framework with a psycho-educational format can greatly enhance a mourner's feelings of competency in relation to managing grief. The term *psycho-educational* refers to the fact that both information and emotional support are provided and enhanced by each other to alleviate some of the painful symptoms associated with grief. It allows for participants to understand the process of grief in a context that includes not only themselves but others. Upon receiving factual information, group participants are able to dispel some of the myths and unrealistic expectations associated with the grieving process. In addition, the mutual sharing of common experiences creates a community from which each participant can draw strength. Both these dynamics assist mourners in developing the internal and external resources that are necessary for the healing process to progress. Not only are psycho-educational groups effective, they are also economically feasible for clients who cannot afford individual counseling as well as for agencies with limited resources (Pomeroy & Garcia, 2009). Internet-based self-help psycho-educational bereavement groups have been found to be very useful in providing information and support (Dominick, Irvine, Beauchamp, et al., 2009). The following paragraphs outline a psycho-educational group design that uses the strengths-based framework of grief.

THE STRENGTHS-BASED PSYCHO-EDUCATIONAL GROUP DESIGN

Group Goals

The goals for this group are to provide individuals with a safe and structured environment in which to adjust to the absence of the loved one. This is accomplished by facilitating an understanding of the life-enhancing aspects of grief, processing the mourner's adaptation to the loss, promoting awareness about life-depleting grief reactions, and enhancing the mourner's coping skills and resources to engage in a life separate from the loved one. These goals underlie the content of the group sessions (Pomeroy & Garcia, 2009).

Group Structure

Careful consideration should be made when deciding if a grief group should have an open-ended or closed-ended structure. Open-ended groups allow for new participants to join at any time during the process, whereas closed-ended groups limit membership to participants who commit to a specific number of sessions. Although open-ended groups can potentially accommodate a greater number of participants and provide individuals with immediate assistance, the constant flux in membership can prohibit group cohesion, trust, and advanced development (Toseland & Rivas, 2012). When dealing with a highly emotional issue like grief, it can be difficult for members of open-ended groups to progress beyond the storytelling stage of the loss. Closed-ended groups provide a secure environment in which trusting relationships between members can develop, thereby, encouraging more intimate self-disclosure. On the other hand, these groups are limited to a small number of participants and may not be cost-effective for agencies with limited resources. In addition, if some participants drop out of the group, it may become too small to provide members with a meaningful experience (Toseland & Rivas, 2012).

Time-limited psycho-educational groups based on the strengths-based framework of grief have been found to be practical and productive because of the structured discussion topics, the life-enhancing coping strategies that are encouraged between group sessions, and the trusting relationships that develop among members. Although the first two sessions focus on the participants' losses, subsequent sessions guide the participants in the strengths-based coping model outlined earlier. The strengths-based grief group is 6 to 8 weeks in length. This type of structured group is compatible with agencies that specialize in end-of-life care, such as hospice or community outpatient clinics. The facilitator of this type of group also serves as a conduit between participants and community resources (Pomeroy & Garcia, 2009).

Group Participants

In addition to designing the group structure, it is important that potential members be screened for appropriateness. Membership should be composed of individuals who have lost a loved one due to death, understand the purpose of the group, understand that active participation includes thoughtful listening as well as discussion, and who are able to commit to attending every session. Some individuals are better served by individual counseling rather than group counseling. Bereaved persons whose loss is very recent (0 to 4 weeks) may initially benefit more from the focused attention of an individual therapist. This may also be true for individuals with untreated and severe mental illness, individuals who have many life stresses in addition to the loss, people who are unable or unwilling to share group time with others, or individuals with complex grief (Pomeroy & Garcia, 2009).

Group Content

The content of a grief group will be somewhat dependent on the composition of the group members. For example, if the group is composed of all female participants who have lost their mothers, the discussions may highlight mother–daughter relationship issues. On the other hand, if the group is composed of parents who have lost a child, discussions may focus on the need for communication between the surviving parents. However, regardless of the specific issues that the members bring to the group, there is certain content that is covered in all groups using the strengths-based psycho-educational approach. Topics include adjustment to the loss, navigating transitions, family concerns, using community resources, and engaging in outside activities (Pomeroy & Garcia, 2009).

A STRENGTHS-BASED, COMPLEX GRIEF GROUP INTERVENTION

Group intervention can also be effective for mourners experiencing a complex grief reaction. They can benefit by having a community of people with whom they can share their grief and by being around others who are also grieving. It is particularly useful for mourners with complex grief reactions to be in groups with others who had loved ones die in a similar manner. Interventions for these types of groups are highly specific to the population of survivors. The unique issues related to particular types of death can be explored in depth, and problems related to the mode of death can be shared and managed. For example, survivors of suicide groups provide support to people who have experienced suicide

in their families. Group members may grapple with the anger they feel toward their loved ones as well as guilt they may carry from their inability to prevent the death. Specialized groups such as these also provide a buffer from the stigma associated with the loss and the lack of social support mourners typically receive in their communities. These groups can also provide information and education about topics of particular concern to the group members. Parents of Murdered Children, for example, has support groups that use the psycho-educational approach to helping family members deal with law enforcement and the judicial system in addition to their grief.

In using the strengths-based framework, the authors have found that complex grief reactions can be addressed in a group setting after the mourner has had some individual counseling or has had time to process the trauma associated with the death. Many mourners with complex grief issues can make the best use of group interventions after some time has passed since the death. This time period may range from 2 to 12 months. Assistance by way of individual counseling may be recommended prior to participation in a group. Potential members for these types of groups should undergo an individual assessment prior to entering the group to determine their readiness for group participation. In some cases, their needs would be better served in individual counseling. Some mourners benefit from being in individual and group counseling simultaneously. Assessment for group participation should consider the degree of trauma and level of crisis, as well as the person's overall mental health status (Pomeroy & Garcia, 2009).

ASSESSMENT OF GRIEF AND LOSS IN CHILDREN AND ADOLESCENTS

An accurate assessment of grieving children and adolescents must include information from a variety of sources. Although obtaining detailed information from a young child is unlikely, collaborative resources can provide important and accurate information about the loss and the problems the child may be experiencing. Relevant data can be gleaned from parents or caregivers, medical and school personnel, and other adults who have central involvement in the child's life (e.g., an aunt who provides afterschool child care). Three primary elements in grief assessment of a child were identified by Webb and Doka (2010). The individual child's level of functioning, the factors related to the death, and the child's support system are all key components of a bereavement assessment (see the Psychosocial Assessment Interview Guide later in this chapter). Initially, the practitioner wants to gather as much information as possible from the youth's parents or caregivers. This may be done over the first few sessions of counseling. Older children and adolescents may also be able to provide salient information.

If the youth is complaining of physical symptoms, a physician's referral is warranted prior to the beginning of therapy. It is recommended that the practitioner form a collaborative relationship with the youth's physician regardless of the presenting problems. If the need should arise for medical intervention, the relationship with the medical professional will have already been established. For example, a young child who presents with encopresis may have a medical problem and should be thoroughly assessed by a physician before determining that it is likely due to regression associated with loss.

Conducting an assessment with children under the age of 13 years most often involves play and activity therapy in order to access and observe the child's feelings and behaviors. Through various activities such as drawing pictures of family, home, or a favorite activity, the practitioner opens the door for conversation regarding the child's experiences and relationships (Webb, 2007). The practitioner may utilize a variety of techniques in eliciting the child's feelings and perceptions. For example, some children are unable to articulate their feelings with words and need assistance developing a vocabulary for emotions. Pictures of faces that display varied emotions as well as stories about feelings may be useful in this regard. Other children need time to direct their own play before engaging in a therapeutic activity. Although some children naturally make use of the available supplies in a therapeutic manner, other children require the practitioner to provide structure and direction. Practitioners should investigate the variety of published play therapy resources such as books on play therapy, games, and art projects.

Older children often possess a great deal of insight and understanding of their experience of loss. However, practitioners must develop a safe working relationship before expecting the older child to share this information. For adolescents, assessment should include perceptions of self-concept, levels of distress, anxiety and depression, degree of loneliness, and presence of anger responses (Doka, 2013). For older children, practitioners should also seek to know their feelings about seeing a practitioner, their interpretation of the loss, and its impact on their ability to function. When helping adolescents process their grief and loss experience, it is best to build a collaborative relationship because such experiences can intensify current developmental issues and life challenges (Slyter, 2012). In general, older children and teens are better able to express their feelings verbally if the practitioner establishes good rapport. Teens often converse more easily when simultaneously involved with another activity. This may take the form of going for a walk, playing online or video games, making something with their hands, or listening to music. Moreover, when working from a strengths-based perspective, adolescents of both genders strongly self-identified arts-based methods (i.e., music, writing, etc.) as well as utilizing personal relationships and physical activities as preferred methods of coping during times of distress (Slyter, 2012; Tyson, Baffour, & DuongTran, 2010).

Practitioners utilizing a strengths-based perspective can help adolescents to utilize their own talents and abilities in commemorating their bond with the deceased and by engaging in therapeutic rituals (e.g., funeral rituals) to help them move forward from the loss (Slyter, 2012). Adolescents dealing with stressful life events such as illness, loss, and death often utilize the Internet for information seeking, relaxation/stress reduction, mood management, social support, and relationship maintenance (Leung, 2007). Teens are key users of social networking sites and participatory media such as blogs and podcasts as well as virtual worlds (Goodstein, 2007). By utilizing social networking sites and the digital world, adolescents can use their own strengths and resources to express their grief, honor relationships, and process their loss.

GRIEF GROUP INTERVENTIONS WITH CHILDREN AND ADOLESCENTS

As with adults, group intervention with children and teens can be beneficial to youth who are grieving. For adolescents, one particular advantage of group counseling is that the group provides a place for bereaved youth to find relief from the feeling of being different from their peers because of their loss. Group intervention may take many forms, including family counseling, counseling that involves groups of families, groups that are offered in the community, groups that are hosted in schools, camps that assist youth with their grief in an outdoor setting, as well as the Internet-based support groups. Important components of group intervention with children and teens include sharing the story of the loss, educating and normalizing grief responses, expressing feelings associated with grief, identifying life-enhancing coping mechanisms, addressing feelings of guilt associated with the loss, and memorializing the deceased.

GROUP INTERVENTIONS WITH GRIEVING OLDER ADULTS

According to the Administration on Aging (2012), the population of adults, age 65 years and older has increased by 18% since 2000. And, the population aged 85 years and older is projected to increase from 5.7 million in 2011 to 14.1 million in 2040. The elderly often encounter numerous losses that may come with advanced age, ranging from the loss of loved ones and friends to the loss of mobility due to physical (e.g., illness) and cognitive deterioration (e.g., ability to drive) as well as changing roles within their family (e.g., caregiver to dependent) and community (e.g., worker to retired). Further complicating losses for the elderly is the existence of ageism and the social devaluation that has been identified in many western cultures. Older adults are at high risk for complicated grief, especially when confronted with the death of a loved one. Additionally, chronicity has been associated with physical and mental illness as well as suicidality (Supiano & Luptak, 2013). Older adults can benefit greatly from bereavement support. As with other populations, support groups for bereaved older adults can provide needed social support and outside activities for persons who might be vulnerable to intense loneliness and isolation. For example, one community has developed an organization that specifically focuses on the needs of older widows and widowers for social interaction. The group sponsors monthly events, for which they provide transportation, to engage older people in social activities and opportunities to interact with other widows and widowers. Some of the group's events offer participants opportunities to memorialize their deceased spouse. This organization has grown considerably over the past decade and is well attended by older community members. In addition, groups that focus primarily on issues of bereavement often attract older people who are experiencing either expected or complex grief.

GRIEF AND PERSONS WITH SPECIAL CIRCUMSTANCES

Although there are many commonalities among bereaved persons regardless of the type of loss they have experienced, there are also some deaths that are unique in the way they impact the mourner and the healing process. Counselors require specialized knowledge and understanding to be most effective with these types of mourners. For example, mass violence resulting in traumatic deaths, such as terrorist attacks and school shootings, impacts more than just family/friends; it touches communities and first responders as well. Other examples include the grief experience for persons with disabilities, immigrant populations, divorced families, veterans of war, gay/lesbian/bisexual/transgender populations, mourners of perinatal loss, and victims of crime and domestic abuse. All of these are groups that require specialized knowledge and unique interventions. It would be impossible to detail the unique dynamics of all the various kinds of losses found in our vastly diverse society. In some cases, there are entire books devoted exclusively to the specific circumstances surrounding a particular type of loss. In other cases, there is a dearth of information about a particular life circumstance that a client may present.

The strengths-based framework for grief is particularly germane to populations with special circumstances. Many persons within these groups have developed a reservoir of resiliency due to their encounters with adversity and discrimination. Because their special circumstances often involve additional stigma and ostracism from society, it is even more important that practitioners identify life-enhancing strategies for assisting them through the grief process. In addition, practitioners will want to help clients develop and access environmental assets.

PRACTICE IMPLICATIONS FOR THE PROFESSIONAL

Working with bereaved individuals is a powerful and moving experience. Although practitioners often describe grief counseling as meaningful, rewarding, and profound, there are also moments when it may be experienced as draining, depressing, unsettling, and frustrating. It is also important for practitioners to be able to differentiate normal from complicated grief and the changes made to the *DSM-5* will assist with this delineation.

Despite adherence to professional boundaries between client and counselor, the act of being emotionally present for someone who is mourning a loved one touches the practitioner personally as well. In part, this may be because most practitioners have had personal experience with the death of a loved one and can relate to the experiences of their clients. Additionally, the work of grief counseling involves regular and intimate contact with the prevalence, probability, and impact of death, a reality that society encourages us to ignore. Awareness of how the counseling process affects the practitioner is essential to competent and ethical practice with grieving clients.

Self-awareness, quality professional social work supervision, flexibility, and an ability to cope with ambiguity are all necessary components of being a professional grief counselor. Understanding, implementing, and upholding the National Association of Social Workers Code of Ethics is essential for social workers involved with grieving individuals, groups, and families. Finally, social workers practicing in this area benefit from using positive self-care methods, including professional and personal support when needed. Developing an expertise in grief and loss is a rewarding and worthwhile endeavor because throughout their careers social workers in all areas of practice will have clients coping with these emotions.

WEBSITES

www.adec.org—The Association for Death Education and Counseling is an international, professional organization dedicated to promoting excellence and recognizing diversity in death education, care of the dying, grief counseling and research in thanatology.

www.bereavedparentsusa.org—Bereaved Parents of the USA is a nonprofit, nondenominational, self-help support group for bereaved parents, siblings, and grandparents.

www.childrengrieve.org—The National Alliance for Grieving Children is a national, nonprofit outreach program dedicated to providing educational information and resources to children and teens grieving a death.

www.compassionatefriends.org—The Compassionate Friends (TCF) is a nonprofit, self-help support organization that seeks to assist bereaved families following the death of a child of any age.

www.dougy.org—The Dougy Center is a national nonprofit dedicated to providing grief resources, including support group services, to children, teens, young adults, and their families grieving a death. It also offers training in grief and loss to community agencies.

www.griefnet.org—GriefNet is a nonprofit, Internet community of bereaved individuals who are dealing with a variety of grief-related issues. Although a small financial donation is requested, it is not required for membership. GriefNet's companion site, www.kidsaid.com, is an online support resource for children.

www.griefshare.org—GriefShare is a nonprofit, nondenominational organization that uses biblical teachings to help individuals through the grieving process. It offers grief recovery support groups.

www.friendsforsurvival.org—Friends for Survival is a national nonprofit outreach organization for those who have lost family or friends by suicide, and also for professionals who work with those who have been touched by a suicide tragedy.

www.taps.org—Tragedy Assistance Program for Survivors is a national, nonprofit organization for those who have lost a loved one who died while serving in the military.

www.widownet.org—WidowNet is a nonprofit self-help resource for, and by, widows and widowers experiencing grief and bereavement.

References

Administration on Aging (AoA) Administration for Community Living, U.S. Department of Health and Human Services. (2012). *A Profile of Older Americans: 2012*. Retrieved from http://www.aoa.gov/Aging_Statistics/Profile/2012/docs/2012profile.pdf

American Psychiatric Association. (2013). *Diagnostic and statistical manual of mental disorders, fifth edition*. Arlington, VA: Author.

Brown, N. (2011). *Psychoeducational groups: Process and practice*. New York, NY: Taylor and Francis.

Doka, K. (2013). *Living with grief: Children, adolescents and loss*. New York, NY: Taylor and Francis.

Dominick, S. A., Irvine, B., Beauchamp, N., Seeley, J. R., Nolen-Hoeksema, S, Doka, K. J., & Bonanno, G. A. (2009). An Internet tool to normalize grief. *OMEGA*, 60(1), 71–87.

Goodstein, A. (2007). *Totally wired: What teens and tweens are really doing online*. New York, NY: St. Martin's/Griffin.

Leung, L. (2007). Stressful life events, motives for Internet use, and social support among digital kids. *Cyberpsychology & Behavior, 10*(2), 204–214. doi:10.1089/cpb.2006.9967

Levine, S. (2005). *Unattended sorrow*. New York, NY: Rodale.

Pomeroy, E. C., & Holleran, L. (2002). Tuesdays with fellow travelers: A psychoeducational HIV/AIDS-related bereavement group. *Journal of HIV/AIDS in Social Services, 1*, 61–77.

Pomeroy, E. C., & Garcia, R. B. (2009). *The Grief Assessment and Intervention Workbook: A strengths perspective*. Belmont, CA: Cengage Publishers.

Rapp, C. A. (1998). *The strengths model: Case management with people suffering from severe and persistent mental illness*. New York, NY: Oxford University Press.

Rapp, C. A., & Goscha, R. J. (2012). *The strengths model: A recovery-oriented approach to mental health services* (3rd ed.). New York, NY: Oxford University Press.

Rapp, C. A., Saleebey, D., & Sullivan, W. P. (2005). The future of strengths-based social work. *Advances in Social Work, 6*(1), 79–90.

Saleebey, D. (2013). *Strengths perspective in social work practice* (6th ed.). Boston, MA: Pearson.

Slyter, M. (2012). Creative counseling interventions for grieving adolescents. *Journal of Creativity in Mental Health, 7*(1), 17–34.

Supiano, K., & Luptak, M. (2013). Complicated grief in older adults: A randomized controlled trial of complicated grief group therapy. *The Gerontologist*, doi:10.1093/geront/gnt076

Toseland, R. W., & Rivas, R. F. (2012). *An introduction to group work practice* (7th ed.). Boston, MA: Allyn and Bacon.

Tyson, E., Baffour, T., & DuongTran, P. (2010). Gender comparisons of self-identified strengths and coping strategies: A study of adolescents in an acute psychiatric facility. *Child & Adolescent Social Work Journal, 27*(3), 161–175. doi:10.1007/s10560-010-0196-7

Webb, N. B. (2007). Crisis intervention play therapy with children. In N. B. Webb (Ed.), *Play therapy with children in crisis: Individual, group and family treatment* (3rd ed.) (pp. 45–70). New York, NY: Guilford Press.

Webb, N. B., & Doka, K. J. (2010). *Helping bereaved children: Social work practice with children and families* (3rd ed.). New York, NY: Guilford Press.

Worden, J. W. (2009). *Grief counseling and grief therapy: A handbook for the mental health practitioner* (4th ed.). New York, NY: Springer Publishing.

87   Motivational Interviewing

Shannon K. Johnson, Kirk von Sternberg, & Mary M. Velasquez

Motivational interviewing (MI) is an empathic, client-entered counseling approach that seeks to elicit behavior change via exploration and resolution of ambivalence around change. MI utilizes a nonjudgmental, collaborative counseling style that focuses on a person's inherent strengths and capacity for change. Put simply, it is a form of collaborative conversation that strengthens a person's own motivation and commitment to change (Miller & Rollnick, 2013). MI addresses the common problem of ambivalence about

making changes in one's life by paying particular attention to client language called *change talk*. In this way, a counselor guides the client in strengthening motivation by eliciting the client's own reasons for change within an atmosphere of acceptance and compassion. While supporting and honoring clients' autonomy and capacity and right to make choices and decisions in their lives, the counselor reinforces strengths, values, and reasons for change by selectively reflecting and reinforcing certain types of change talk.

MI has a strong evidence base, originating with the release of a groundbreaking text by William Miller and Stephen Rollnick over 20 years ago (Miller & Rollnick, 1992). Since the initial publication of this classic text, MI has been used by countless clinicians in diverse settings. It has been cited in over 25,000 articles, and its efficacy has been studied in over 200 randomized clinical trials (Miller & Rollnick, 2013). MI appears effective and appropriate across cultures, populations, settings, and behaviors (Sampson, Stephens, & Velasquez, 2009) and also has been adapted for delivery in a group format (Velasquez, Stephens, & Drenner, 2012; Velasquez, Stephens, & Ingersoll, 2006; Wagner & Ingersoll, 2012).

Two underlying assumptions of the MI intervention are that the decision to change is most powerful when it comes from within and that the responsibility for change is situated with the client. Accordingly, MI adopts a client-centered, respectful, collaborative approach in which client and counselor are co-experts. The MI counselor respects the client as the authority on his or her own life and honors his or her autonomy and right to self-determination. Rather than confronting a client with his or her problems and presuming to assign goals or deliver solutions, the MI counselor's task is to elicit the client's own concerns about and solutions to the presenting problem (Miller & Rollnick, 2013). The counselor can then provide feedback about observations clients have made for themselves (Van Wormer, 2007). Though goal-focused and directive, the MI approach remains nonconfrontational at all times; feedback is not intended to persuade a client to change, but rather is delivered in a way that validates a client's experiences and perspectives and leaves the responsibility for change squarely on the client's shoulders (Sampson, Stephens, & Velasquez, 2009).

THE MOTIVATIONAL INTERVIEWING SPIRIT

In the most recent version of their MI text, Miller and Rollnick (2013) describe the MI Spirit as the underlying set of mind and heart within which MI is practiced. They use the acronym PACE to signify the main components of the MI Spirit: **p**artnership, **a**cceptance, **c**ompassion, and **e**vocation. *Partnership* is the collaborative dialogue in MI in which the counselor, rather than being seen as the "expert," works in accord with the client in exploring the client's goals, personal strengths, and resources. *Acceptance* is an affirming, empathic recognition that honors and supports the client's autonomy and inherent worth. *Compassion* signifies that the attitudes and actions of the counselor are based on promoting the welfare and best interest of the client. *Evocation* refers to the elicitation of the client's wisdom, goals, solutions, and thoughts about change (Miller & Rollnick, 2013).

PROCESSES OF THE MOTIVATIONAL INTERVIEWING INTERVENTION

Although MI is beneficial for clients at any point in their change process, its nonconfrontational, empathic nature makes it especially appropriate for individuals who are not yet committed to change (Velasquez et al., 2010). Whereas authoritarian approaches often elicit resistance in clients who are not yet ready to change, the MI approach is particularly well-suited for diffusing resistance. In the most recent conceptualization of MI, Miller and Rollnick (2013) explain that the MI intervention is comprised of four processes: engaging, focusing, evoking, and planning. *Engaging* entails involving the client in talking about issues, concerns, and hopes, and establishing a trusting relationship. *Focusing* involves narrowing the focal point of the conversation to habits or patterns that clients want to change. *Evoking* consists of eliciting motivation for change by increasing clients' sense of the importance of change, their confidence about change, and their readiness to change. Finally, *planning* entails developing the practical steps clients want to use to implement the changes they desire. The first two processes are those in which both the counselor and the client establish rapport, build a working relationship, and clarify direction. The latter two elicit the client's ideas about change, develop commitment to change, and formulate a specific plan of action. They can be thought of as stair steps, with each process building upon the ones that preceded it (Miller & Rollnick, 2013). In general, counselors use empathic exploration of ambivalence to highlight discrepancies between the client's behavior and his or her goals and values, thereby enhancing intrinsic motivation and tipping one's motivational balance in favor of change during the early processes (Velasquez, Ingersoll, Sobell et al., 2010). The emphasis then shifts to developing individually tailored change plans, anticipating barriers to change and making plans to address them, identifying potential support systems, acquiring available resources, and enhancing self-efficacy (Diclemente & Velasquez, 2002; Sampson, Stephens, & Velasquez, 2009).

GUIDING PRINCIPLES

There are four main guiding principles for the MI intervention: expressing empathy, developing discrepancy, rolling with resistance, and enhancing self-efficacy (Miller & Rollnick, 2013). In *expressing empathy*, the MI counselor uses active listening skills to reflect back to the client the meaning and feelings he or she is expressing, thereby conveying understanding and acceptance, which are integral to building rapport in MI. In *developing discrepancy*, the MI counselor creates opportunities for clients to identify and explore areas where their behavior is in discord with their goals and values. Clients are encouraged to consider both the pros and cons of a behavior change with the expectation that ultimately, their recognition of the positive outcomes of a behavior change will begin to outweigh the disadvantages they associate with change. In *rolling with resistance,* the MI counselor accepts resistance as natural and common and recognizes it as a signal to shift strategies. Rather than trying to break down a client's resistance, the MI counselor *rolls with it* by shifting gears when resistance arises. Finally, *enhancing self-efficacy* involves working diligently to build up a client's belief in her or his own ability to achieve and maintain change. MI therapists can do this by expressing their own belief in a client's ability to change and by eliciting input from clients about their previous successes (Sampson, Stephens, & Velasquez, 2009).

CORE STRATEGIES—ASKING OPEN QUESTIONS, AFFIRMING, REFLECTING, AND SUMMARIZING

Four counseling strategies form the foundation of MI and are summarized by the acronym OARS: asking Open questions, Affirming, Reflecting, and Summarizing (Miller & Rollnick, 2013). While a closed question may yield a simple yes or no answer, *asking open questions* involves phrasing questions in a way that encourages clients to elaborate on their experiences and feelings. *Affirming* involves the use of affirmations to highlight a client's strengths and efforts and can be used to build rapport, enhance

client self-efficacy, and strengthen intrinsic motivation. *Reflecting* involves listening intently and conveying back to the client one's understanding of what he or she was saying or feeling. There are several types of reflections. Simple reflections convey understanding of the client's perspectives, goals, and concerns while adding little-to-no meaning or emphasis to what the client has said. Complex reflections, on the other hand, add substantial meaning or emphasis (Moyers, Martin, Manuel, Hendrickson, & Miller, 2005). Double-sided reflections involve acknowledging what a client has said, and then adding to it the opposite side of the client's ambivalence. By capturing both sides of the argument, double-sided reflections mirror the client's ambivalence and can help the client recognize areas in which her or his arguments may be flawed. Finally, *summarizing* involves making a reflective statement that links two or more ideas the client has shared (Miller & Rollnick, 2013). For example, the MI counselor might use the summarizing strategy to recapitulate what a client has shared about his or her perception of the pros and cons associated with change. The four *OARS* strategies are used in MI to direct clients through a process of exploring and resolving ambivalence and moving toward positive change. Examples of applying the *OARS* techniques will be provided in a case example at the end of this chapter.

ADDITIONAL MOTIVATIONAL INTERVIEWING STRATEGIES, TOOLS, AND EXERCISES

There are several additional skills, strategies, tools, and exercises that are commonly used in MI. One crucial skill is that of *eliciting change talk*. Miller and Rollnick (2004) note that MI clients literally talk themselves into change. Change talk is comprised of client statements that reflect: (1) a *desire* to change; (2) *an ability* to change; (3) *reasons* to change; or (4) a *need* for change. *Feedback* is also a commonly utilized MI technique. Rollnick, Mason, and Butler (1999) describe the "elicit–provide info–elicit" method of providing feedback, in which MI counselors: (1) elicit a client's interest in or knowledge about the topic area; (2) provide personalized feedback based upon results of an assessment or interview; and (3) elicit the client's thoughts or reactions pertaining to the feedback provided. In MI, personalized feedback is provided in a neutral manner intended to increase client awareness rather than to persuade a client to change (Miller & Rollnick, 2013).

Scaling rulers are often used in MI to assess a client's readiness to change. *Importance rulers* assess the degree to which a change feels important to a client (1 = not at all important; 10 = extremely important), while *confidence rulers* assess clients' belief in their ability to achieve a change (1 = not at all confident; 10 = extremely confident). The balance between one's perceived importance of a change and one's confidence to make that change can be understood as a representation of his or her readiness to change. Scaling rulers can be used to reassess readiness throughout the MI intervention. When used artfully with the application of OARS counseling strategies, they can be used to elicit change talk and enhance intrinsic motivation (Sampson, Stephens, & Velasquez, 2009). See Figure 87.1 for an example of *the importance ruler.*

In MI, the counselor also focuses on *eliciting information* with the goal that the client should ultimately do most of the talking in the session (Rollnick, Mason, & Butler, 1999). The *typical day exercise* and the *values clarification exercise* are both useful exercises for *eliciting information.* In *the typical day exercise* (Rollnick, Mason, & Butler, 1999), the counselor highlights substance use as the focus of the question and then asks the client to describe a typical day in his or her life. Use of this exercise is likely to elicit more information than simply asking how much a client drinks or uses. In *the values clarification exercise*, the counselor can simply ask a client what he or she values in life and then seek elaboration. Alternatively, *a card sorting procedure* can be used in which clients are asked to sort a set of cards, each with a value printed on it (family, health, beauty, sobriety, love, spirituality, etc.), into three piles depending on how important the value is to them (i.e., not important at all, important, or highly important). They then are asked to sort the cards from their "highly important" pile into three new piles based on rank of importance, and to repeat this process until they have five to eight cards that represent their primary values. The counselor can then explore these values with the client (Sampson, Stephens, & Velasquez, 2009). A ready-made set of cards for this exercise can be obtained from the www.motivationalinterview.org website.

MOTIVATIONAL INTERVIEWING IN GROUPS

Group therapy is one of the most widely utilized intervention modalities in substance abuse treatment settings (Velasquez, Stephens, & Drenner, 2012). Thus, exploring the potential for effective adaptation of MI for delivery in groups is crucial. Velasquez, Stephens, and Ingersoll (2006) reference a growing body of literature that suggests that the MI intervention can be adapted for delivery in groups. Among the promising results cited is a recent application of the Motivational Interviewing Treatment Integrity (MITI) behavioral coding system (Moyers, Martin, Manuel et al., 2005) to an MI-style group treatment for cocaine abuse. The MITI assesses treatment quality by coding counselors' use of MI-adherent (asking open questions, reflecting, affirming, asking permission, etc.) and non-MI-adherent strategies (advising without permission, confronting, arguing), as well as expression of empathy and adherence to the MI Spirit of collaboration, evocation, and support of autonomy. Although this coding system generally has been used to assess counselor performance in individual MI sessions, results of this recent application suggest that an MI-style group for cocaine abuse was highly adherent to MI principles and strategies (Velasquez, Stephens, & Drenner, 2012). These results are promising in that they provide evidence of the adaptability of MI for use in a group format.

Although they caution the MI practitioner to become skilled in practicing MI in individual sessions prior to moving into MI group work, Velasquez, Stephens, and Drenner (2012) provide specific advice for counselors who are prepared for

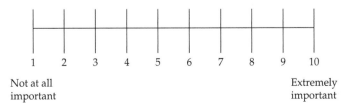

Figure 87.1 Importance Ruler.

MI group work. They suggest that group work should begin with an introduction of the MI spirit and an explanation of the motivational approach. This introduction should feature an emphasis on the centrality of personal choice and autonomy, nonconfrontation, empathy, and respect. It is critical that the MI counselor(s) work to maintain a nonjudgmental, respectful, collaborative atmosphere and that they provide reminders about the MI spirit and style of respect, nonconfrontation, and support throughout the group process (Velasquez, Stephens, & Drenner, 2012).

When delivering MI in a group format, the counselor adheres to the same principles (expressing empathy, developing discrepancy, rolling with resistance, enhancing self-efficacy) and utilizes the same basic strategies and tools (asking open questions, affirming, reflecting, summarizing, eliciting change talk, providing feedback, etc.) that are used in individual MI. It is important to note, however, that when intervening in a group format, the group is the client; focus must, therefore, be on group processes more so than on the individuals who constitute the group. With two group facilitators, however, one facilitator can focus on group process while the other focuses on applying MI counseling strategies (Velasquez, Stephens, & Drenner, 2012).

HOW TO LEARN MOTIVATIONAL INTERVIEWING

Miller and Rollnick (2009) stress that it takes more than a workshop or training for a counselor to learn to embody MI Spirit. A counselor who wants to practice MI should indeed attend workshops and trainings, but these must be followed by disciplined practice coupled with feedback and coaching from a knowledgeable guide. MI training and workshop opportunities are offered by the Motivational Interviewing Network of Trainers (MINT) and can be found on the www .motivationalinterviewing.org website.

Practitioners who are interested in learning MI will benefit from reading a seminal MI text such as *Motivational Interviewing: Helping People Change, third edition* by Miller and Rollnick (2013). Counselors who are interested in applying their well-honed MI skills in a group format are encouraged to reference a recently published text by Wagner and Ingersoll (2012), *Motivational Interviewing in Groups*. Practitioners who are interested in feedback are encouraged to look into

the aforementioned MITI behavioral coding system (Moyers, Martin, Manuel et al., 2005), which provides very specific feedback about a counselor's fidelity to MI intervention. Finally, Miller and Moyers (2006) provide a useful articulation of eight stages for learning MI.

A CASE EXAMPLE

Counselor: I'm glad you came in today. We have about 45 minutes together, and I'm wondering whether it would be OK with you if we talked for a little about your alcohol use? *(asking permission)*

Client: Sure, but I don't have a drinking problem. I'm only here because my probation officer's making me come.

Counselor: Coming here was not your idea, and it's frustrating to have someone tell you what you need to do. *(complex reflection—expressing empathy)* I want you to know that I'm not going to tell you what to do, and that the things we talk about will be up to you. *(emphasizing choice)*

Client: Good, cuz I don't need to go to AA and all that stuff. I just shouldn't have driven on the night of my DUI. That's all.

Counselor: Well, it's great that you took the step to come in today *(affirming)* even though this wasn't your idea. Since you're here anyway, to help me understand a little how alcohol fits in your life, what are some good things about your alcohol use? *(open question, decisional balance exercise–rolling with resistance)*

Client: Well, all my friends drink all the time, so I always have something to do if I'm drinking. I have fun when I go out with my buddies.

Counselor: So it's important to you to have fun with your friends, and it's easy to fit in if you're drinking. *(simple reflection–expressing empathy)* What else? *(asking open question—encouraging elaboration)*

Client: That's it really.

Counselor: OK, so now that you've told me something good about your drinking, what are some things about your drinking that are not so good? *(open question, decisional balance exercise)*

Client: Well, I only drink with my buddies. It's just to have fun, not every day or anything. Mostly just on Friday nights. I mean, sometimes I drink too many, but other than making my girlfriend angry it really doesn't affect my life.

Counselor: You said that sometimes you drink too many. *(simple reflection)* Tell me more about that. *(asking open question—encouraging elaboration)*

Client: I'll plan on just having a couple beers, and I'll end up drinking more than that.

Counselor: So you drink more than you planned. *(simple reflection)* In terms of drinking with your friends, what does a typical Friday night look like? *(typical day exercise)*

Client: We usually go to a couple bars. We'll start off having beer, but then usually someone ends up buying a round of shots. And then someone else buys another round, and it just goes from there. On a typical night I might have like two beers and six shots. I usually get a ride home, but I couldn't on the night of my DUI.

Counselor: You mentioned that your drinking makes your girlfriend angry. *(simple reflection of change talk)* Tell me a bit about that. *(asking open question—encouraging elaboration of change talk)*

Client: Oh, she's a nag. She gets annoyed when I come home late and starts fights with me. We don't have much money, so she's obsessed with budgeting and says I spend too much going out. She doesn't want me to go out. She's so controlling.

Counselor: It's frustrating to have your girlfriend tell you what to do. *(complex reflection—expressing empathy)* So you've noticed that you've been drinking more than you intend and that you're having conflicts with your girlfriend related to your drinking. And your drinking is taking a financial toll. *(summarizing change talk)* What else? *(asking open question—evoking change talk)*

Client: I just really want to get along better with my girlfriend. That's all.

Counselor: So you desire a better relationship with your girlfriend. *(reflecting change talk)* What would you like to see be different in your relationship? *(asking open question to elicit change talk)*

Client: She used to trust me, but now. . . This DUI is so expensive. I lost my driver's license so I can't have a job, and she has to work extra hours. I don't know why she stays with me—I wish she could trust me again.

Counselor: You feel guilty for the position you've put her in *(complex reflection of change talk)*, and you want to regain her trust. *(simple reflection of change talk)* You are really dealing with a lot right now. *(expressing empathy)* Tell me, how would your life be different if you weren't drinking? *(asking open questions to elicit change talk)*

Client: Well, I wouldn't be on probation. I wouldn't owe so much for my DUI. I'd have my driver's license and job. We'd be moving forward in life. My girlfriend wouldn't be mad at me. I wouldn't feel so guilty, like I messed everything up.

Counselor: So in some ways drinking has made it hard for you to pursue goals, and it seems to be affecting the way you feel about yourself and your relationship with your girlfriend. *(summarizing change talk)* So, IF you were to decide to change your drinking, and you were to take one step to make that happen, what might that look like? *(asking open question to elicit change talk)*

Client: Well, I might have to find something else to do on Friday nights.

Counselor: So a first step would be to make plans to do something on Friday night that doesn't involve alcohol. *(simple reflection of change talk)* OK, let's take a minute, if that's OK *(asking permission)*, and think about how important it is right now for you to make that change, let's say on a scale from 1 to 10, with 1 being not important at all and 10 being highly important. *(assessing importance with a scaling ruler)*

Client: I'd say probably a 7 or an 8.

Counselor: That's pretty high. Tell me about why you chose a 7 or 8 instead of, say, a 5 or 6? *(asking open question to elicit change talk)*

Client: I just want to be a reliable man again. I hate feeling like I'm free-loading on my girlfriend while she works so hard to fix my mess.

Counselor: You need to be able to carry your own weight in order to feel good about yourself. *(complex reflection of change talk)* In terms of confidence, I'm wondering how you'd rate yourself on a scale of 1 to 10, with 1 being not confident at all that you could make this first change and 10 being extremely confident. *(assessing confidence with scaling ruler)*

Client: I don't know . . . I guess about a 5.

Counselor: OK, a 5. Can you tell me why not a 4 or a 6? *(asking open question to elicit change talk)*

Client: Well, I can stop if I want to, so I wouldn't choose anything less than a 5. But it's just really hard to not go with my buddies. I get bored easily, and I don't want to be left out.

Counselor: So it's hard for you to deal with the temptation to drink. *(simple reflection to express empathy)* What might help you feel more confident, maybe move you to a 6 or a 7? *(asking open question to elicit change talk)*

Client: I just need some friends who don't drink so much. Or maybe I need to spend more quality time with my family and girlfriend instead of getting drunk.

Counselor: So changing your social circle and shifting your priorities around a bit. *(simple reflection of change talk)*

Client: Yeah, those might end up being good things for me.

Counselor: As we're nearing the end of our time today, let me offer a summary of what we've talked about so we can see if I've captured what you've been saying. On the one hand you have fun drinking with your friends, and on the other hand you feel guilty for how your drinking upsets your girlfriend, and you'd like to be moving along in life, getting a job, being a reliable man, I think you said. *(double-sided reflection to highlight discrepancy)* Some things you've talked about doing are finding new activities for Friday nights and maybe finding some friends to hang out with who don't drink. *(summarizing)* What did I leave out? *(checking in)*

Client: I guess that about says it all—I want things to be different.

Counselor: You are ready for a change. *(simple reflection of change talk)* I know that you can change your drinking if that's what you decide to do *(supporting self-efficacy)*, but of course that decision is up to you. *(emphasizing autonomy)* I appreciate your willingness to be so open today, *(affirming)* and I'm looking forward to learning more about you next time we meet.

CONCLUSION

MI is an evidence-based counseling approach that is appropriate across cultures, populations, settings, and behaviors. It strives to tip motivational balance in favor of change for clients who are highly ambivalent, and to provide collaborative problem-solving and coaching for clients who have committed to change. The MI counselor embodies a spirit of collaboration, evocation, and respect for client autonomy and focuses on the grounding principles of expressing empathy, developing discrepancy, rolling with resistance, and enhancing self-efficacy. Core MI counseling strategies include

asking Open questions, Affirming, Reflecting, and Summarizing *(OARS)*. Also central to MI are the strategies of eliciting change talk and providing personalized feedback. Scaling rulers can be used in MI to assess a client's readiness to change, while the *typical day exercise* and *values clarification exercise* can be used to maximize the amount of information elicited from clients about their substance use and values. Becoming a proficient MI counselor requires training and disciplined practice coupled with feedback and coaching. Interested practitioners are encouraged to refer to the web resources provided below.

WEB-BASED RESOURCES

The Motivational Interviewing Network of Trainers: www.motivationalinterviewing.org
This website provides extensive information about MI, as well as manuals and tools for counselors, links to trainings, and more.

Center on Alcoholism, Substance Abuse, and Addictions: http://casaa.unm.edu/mi.html
This website provides slideshows of the principles of MI and of clinical findings. Coding resources can be accessed at http://casaa.unm.edu/code/miti.html.

Addiction Technology Transfer Center (ATTC): www.attcnetwork.org/index.asp
This website provides links to the 14 regional centers that comprise the ATTC; at these links, one can find information about MI trainings and workshops.

Health Behavior Research and Training Institute (HBRT): http://www.utexas.edu/ssw/cswr/institutes/health-behavior-and-research-training-institute-hbrt/
The HBRT Institute provides training, supervision, and coaching services on MI-based intervention and prevention approaches.

Center for Substance Abuse Treatment (CSAT): www.csat.samhsa.gov
This website features the TIP 35, "Enhancing Motivation for Change in Substance Abuse Treatment" resource.

ACKNOWLEDGMENTS

The authors would like to thank Dr. Nanette Stephens for the help she provided on the case example.

References

DiClemente, C. C., & Velasquez, M. M. (2002). Motivational interviewing and the stages of change. Motivational Interviewing, 2nd ed. (pp. 201–216). New York, NY: Guilford Press.

Miller, W. R., & Moyers, T. B. (2006). Eight stages in learning motivational interviewing. *Journal of Teaching in the Addictions, 5*(1), 3–17.

Miller, W. R., & Rollnick, S. (1992). *Motivational Interviewing: Preparing People to Change Addictive Behavior* (1st ed.). New York, NY: Guilford Press.

Miller, W. R., & Rollnick, S. (2004). Talking oneself into change: Motivational interviewing, stages of change, and therapeutic process. *Journal of Cognitive Psychotherapy, 18*(4), 299–308.

Miller, W. R., & Rollnick, S. (2009). Ten things that motivational interviewing is not. *Behavioural and Cognitive Psychotherapy, 37*(2), 129–140.

Miller, W. R., & Rollnick, S. (2013). *Motivational interviewing: Helping people change* (3rd ed.). New York, NY: Guilford Press.

Moyers, T. B., Martin, T., Manuel, J. K., Hendrickson, S. M., & Miller, W. R. (2005). Assessing competence in the use of motivational interviewing. *Journal of Substance Abuse Treatment, 28*(1), 19–26.

Rollnick, S., Mason, P., & Butler, C. (1999). *Health behavior change: A guide for practitioners*. Edinburgh and New York: Churchill-Lingston.

Sampson, M., Stephens, N. S., & Velasquez, M. M. (2009). Motivational interviewing. In D. W. S. A. Rubin (Ed.), *Substance abuse treatment for youth and adults: Clinician's guide to evidence-based practice* (pp. 3–53). Hoboken, NJ: John Wiley & Sons, Inc.

Van Wormer, K. (2007). Principles of motivational interviewing geared to stages of change: A pedagogical challenge. *Journal of Teaching in Social Work, 27*(1–2), 21–35.

Velasquez, M. M., Ingersoll, K. S., Sobell, M. B., Floyd, R. L., Sobell, L. C., & von Sternberg, K. (2010). A dual-focus motivational intervention to reduce the risk of alcohol-exposed pregnancy. *Cognitive and Behavioral Practice, 17*(2), 203–212.

Velasquez, M. M., Stephens, N. S., & Drenner, K. (2012). The transtheoretical model and motivational interviewing: Experiences with a cocaine treatment group. *Motivational Interviewing in Groups*. New York, NY: Guilford Press.

Velasquez, M. M., Stephens, N. S., & Ingersoll, K. (2006). Motivational interviewing in groups. *Journal of Groups in Addiction & Recovery, 1*(1), 27–50.

Wagner, C. C., & Ingersoll, K. S. (2012). *Motivational Interviewing in Groups*. New York, NY: Guilford Press.

88 Working with Clients Who Have Recovered Memories

Susan P. Robbins

One of the most controversial and divisive issues among mental health professionals and researchers in the past two decades has been the delayed recovery of memories of traumatic events. During the 1990s, major social work journals carried a handful of articles on this topic (see Benatar, 1995; Robbins, 1995; Stocks, 1998). In contrast, well-respected journals in psychology, psychiatry, and law published numerous articles and special issues dedicated to the debate about the nature, veracity, and accuracy of recovered memories, particularly memories of childhood sexual abuse (CSA). More recently, continued research in this area has focused on laboratory experiments in word memorization, cognitive processes involved in both remembering and motivated forgetting, Vietnam veterans with posttraumatic stress disorder, source monitoring, the effects of misinformation in real world set-tings, and neuroimaging of cognitive processes that give rise to true and false memories (Belli, 2012; McNally, 2005). According to McNally, the debate about recovered memory "is unresolved, but not irresolvable" (p. 26).

At the heart of this debate is whether it is possible to repress or dissociate all memory of CSA and later accurately recall the trauma as an adult. Two related questions pertain to the actual prevalence of abused children who completely forget their early abuse and the specific mecha-nisms responsible for the absence of memory. These became contentious issues because some believe that early memories of traumatic events that are inaccessible to the conscious mind can nonetheless affect one's social and psychological functioning throughout life.

During the 1980s and 1990s, thousands of peo-ple, primarily white middle-class women, were diagnosed by mental health practitioners such as social workers, psychologists, psychiatrists, and substance abuse and other counselors as having been victims of sexual abuse in their childhood, despite a total lack of recall of any such event. Others, who had continuous memories of early abuse, were told that they were victims of addi-tional episodes of CSA, which they did not recall and which were often horrific in nature, such as satanic ritual abuse (SRA). Recovered memories of SRA most typically included being drugged, brainwashed, and forced to watch or participate in satanic rituals that often included murder or rape by multiple perpetrators. Seeking mental health and counseling services for a broad array of problems that included depression, eating dis-orders, marital difficulties, substance abuse, and bereavement (among others), clients began to allegedly "recover" memories of CSA and SRA with the help of their therapists, spontaneously, or upon reading books for sexual abuse survivors and attending self-help groups.

Clinicians who strongly advocated the use of memory recovery techniques believed that it was necessary for their clients to retrieve their pre-viously forgotten memories of CSA in order to heal and recover from what they believed to be a forgotten but unresolved trauma. Concepts such as repression, dissociation, traumatic amnesia, and multiple personality disorder (MPD) (later renamed dissociative identity disorder [DID]) were used to explain why memory of the alleged trauma was not available to the conscious mind. In the quest to assist clients in recovering these memories, a variety of therapeutic techniques were used that included, but were not limited to, hypnosis, truth serum, guided imagery, dream interpretation, age regression, free association, journaling, psychodrama, reflexology, massage and other forms of "body work" to recover "body memories," primal scream therapy, attending survivor's groups, and reading books on recov-ering from sexual abuse. Clients were often encouraged by their therapists and self-help groups to believe in the veracity of their newly recovered memories, define themselves as "sur-vivors," and interpret their present-day problems and symptoms in terms of their early unresolved trauma. Although reports of recovered memories began to wane by the late 1990s, largely due to the refusal of insurance companies to pay for diagnoses that supported its use, recovered mem-ory therapy (RMT) continued to be practiced by those who remained convinced of its utility, despite research that found such techniques to be both questionable and harmful.

Therapy of this sort had consequences not only for the clients, but for their families as well. As the retrieval of recovered memories came to be seen as the path to healing, many clients were also encouraged to confront their alleged perpe-trators and break off all contact with anyone in the family who questioned the veracity of their newly recalled memories. Further complicating this issue were criminal and civil charges that cli-ents were encouraged to file against family mem-bers as part of their recovery process. Over the years, a large number of cases involving claims of recovered memory reached the appellate courts and raised serious issues related to discovery rules, statutory limitations, and rules of scientific evidence.

Beginning in 1992, a small group of parents who claimed to have been falsely accused joined together with sympathetic professionals to form a support and advocacy organization, the False Memory Syndrome Foundation (FMSF). In addi-tion to sponsoring scientific and medical research on memory, suggestibility, and repression, the FMSF disseminated research to the media, the public, and to the legal and mental health pro-fessions. Their final newsletter was published in 2011, as a mounting body of research on mem-ory cast serious doubt on the ability of people to totally forget and later remember traumatic events (McNally, 2005), and new claims of recov-ered memories dramatically declined. A grow-ing number of people have since recanted their accusations of abuse, accusing their therapists of pressure, suggestion, and coercion.

More recently, the existence of MPD/DID, one of the underlying mechanisms used to explain repressed memory, has come under serious scrutiny. In a well-researched expose of Sybil, one of the most famous cases of MPD that is credited with launching the multiple personality craze, Nathan (2011) documents the ways in which otherwise well-meaning but misguided therapy led to the total fabrication of Sybil's multiple personality "alters." Supporting this position, Allen Francis (2014), Chair of the *DSM-IV* Task Force, has questioned not only the suggestive therapeutic techniques used to create such alters, but also the validity of the diagnosis itself.

Although this has strongly bolstered the position that such memories are the product of unethical therapy rather than events rooted in reality, recovered memory advocates are skeptical that suggestive techniques can create false memories of CSA. To date, there are no accepted standards for determining the veracity of reports of abuse that are based solely on recovered memories and most agree that it is impossible to determine the validity of recovered memories without external corroboration.

This supports the thorough previous review of the literature on RMT, in which Stocks (1998) examined the various techniques and therapeutic interventions that were commonly used to assist in the recovery of abuse memories as well as the impact of such therapy on client outcomes. Noting the historical ambivalence towards sexual abuse that was prevalent until the latter part of the twentieth century, Stocks also provided a discussion and critique of the initial studies that led some clinicians and researchers to conclude that CSA memories were frequently repressed. In doing so, he cautioned that the reality of abuse should not be confused with skepticism about recovered memories of abuse. This echoed Loftus and Ketcham's earlier position (1994) that the disagreement about memory is not a debate about childhood sexual abuse.

According to Stocks (1998), the research on RMT shows that such techniques are not reliable in recovering valid memories. Although some recovered memories may be accurate, many are partly or totally confabulated, and there is no way to distinguish reliably between those that are real and those that are not. Further, he found no conclusive evidence that memories of this sort have any clinical utility. In fact, the few existing outcome studies suggest that RMT is likely to lead to deterioration rather than improved functioning. Based on this, Stocks warned that the risks of RMT far outweigh the perceived benefits, discussed the necessity of informed consent for therapy that is unreliable and potentially harmful, and concluded that social workers should avoid using such techniques in their practice. Subsequent letters to the editor in response to his article reflected the professional division concerning the nature of recovered memories and the utility of RMT.

A similar split can be seen in the 1996 final report of the American Psychological Association Working Group on Investigation of Memories of Childhood Abuse. The clinicians in the group differed from the researchers on several points including the mechanisms that are responsible for delayed recall, the frequency of the creation of false memories, and the rules of evidence for testing hypotheses about memory and the consequences of trauma. They concluded that their failure to reach consensus was due in part to "profound epistemological differences" between the researchers and the clinicians. Contentious issues related to recovered memories have not abated and continue, despite attempts at reconciliation (Belli, 2012). This basic disagreement is reflected in the field of social work as well.

There is, however, an underlying professional consensus in four basic areas as summarized in Table 88.1. (Knapp & VandeCreek, 2000, p. 336; APA, 1996).

Despite these significant areas of consensus, ongoing areas of disagreement continue to divide professionals in the field (Belli, 2012). This division is not merely an academic debate inasmuch as it directly affects the theories and practice techniques that are used with clients. By the mid 1990s, most of the major professional organizations issued warnings concerning suggestibility and false memories. One of the strongest cautionary statements came from the American Medical Association (AMA) in its position that, "The AMA considers recovered memories of childhood sexual abuse to be of uncertain authenticity, which should be subject to external verification. The use of recovered memories is fraught with problems of potential misapplication" (AMA, 1994, p. 4).

Most early organizational statements on recovered memory therapy urged the use of caution, with the acknowledgement that recovered memories may or may not be true. Many of the later

TABLE 88.1 Consensus on Recovered and False Memories

Child Abuse	**Child abuse is harmful and prevalent.** Satanic or ritual abuse is rare.
Memory and the Creation of Memories	Most people who were sexually abused remember all or part of what happened to them.
	Adults with continuous memories of being abused are likely to have accurate memories.
	Although it is rare, some memories of past traumas can be forgotten and later remembered.
	Memories from infancy are highly unreliable.
	False or pseudomemory memories can be created.
	Magnification and minimization are better ways to conceptualize memories than the dichotomy of "true" or "false."
	It is difficult to ascertain the accuracy of memories recovered by suggestive "memory recovery" techniques.
	It is impossible to distinguish a true memory from a false one without other corroborative evidence.
Diagnosis of and Psychotherapy with Patients with Memories of Abuse	Child abuse, in and of itself, is not a diagnosis.
	Child abuse cannot be assessed from a set of current symptoms or a checklist of symptoms.
	Mental illness and mental disorders have many causes.
	Psychotherapists should ask patients about past childhood abuse if it is clinically indicated.
	Memory recall of abuse is not necessary for effective therapy to occur.
	The focus of treatment should be on the current functioning of the patient.
	Treatments should be tailored to the individual needs of each patient.
	At times, patients may need to learn to live with ambiguity about the veracity of memory or memory fragments.
Role of Psychotherapists	Psychotherapists need to respect and promote patient autonomy.
	Psychotherapists need to scrupulously maintain professional boundaries.
	Psychotherapists need to maintain therapeutic neutrality on the issues of litigation and confrontation.
	Even though psychotherapists have no primary legal duty to third parties, they should not be oblivious to the impact of their actions on those third parties.

statements more explicitly warn against the use of memory recovery techniques as a method or focus of practice. A good chronology of statements and positions on RMT made by professional organizations can be found on the Internet at: http://www.religioustolerance.org/rmt_prof.htm.

Subsequently, professional concerns focused on informed consent and, as noted by the American Academy of Psychiatry and the Law (1999, p. 2), in light of the warnings given by most professional organizations, "Few would currently argue against informing patients about the fallibility of memory and the dangers involved with recovering memories of sexual abuse." Given the unproven clinical utility of RMT, coupled with the lack of evidence that the benefits of such therapy outweigh the risks, the issue of informed consent is critical for social workers inasmuch as this is also mandated by the National Association of Social Workers' (NASW) Code of Ethics (NASW, 1996a).

A specific practice statement addressing the evaluation and treatment of adults with the possibility of recovered memories of childhood sexual abuse, developed by the NASW National Council on the Practice of Clinical Social Work, was published in June 1996. In this statement social workers are cautioned to (a) establish and maintain an appropriate therapeutic relationship with careful attention to boundary management; (b) recognize that the client may be influenced by the opinions, conjecture, or suggestions of the therapist; (c) not minimize the power and influence he or she has on a client's impressions and beliefs; (d) guard against engaging in self-disclosure and premature interpretations during the treatment process; (e) guard against using leading questions to recover memories; (f) be cognizant that disclosure of forgotten experience is a part of the process but not the goal of therapy; and (g) respect the client's right to self-determination (NASW, 1996b, p. 2).

Due to the prevalence of RMT during the 1980s and 90s and the sensationalized media coverage of recovered memories, social workers are likely to encounter clients who were previously, or even recently, subjected to a variety of RMT techniques, abuse survivor groups and literature, or who spontaneously recovered abuse memories. Some clients may still believe in the veracity of these memories, while others may have come to question them. Others may have fully recanted their abuse allegations upon realizing that their memories were inaccurate or iatrogenically induced in therapy. Working with such clients can prove to be a challenge for social workers, because most typically receive little or no formal education regarding the nature of memory or the suggestive techniques that can create false memories.

As noted elsewhere (Robbins, 1997), it is critical that social workers adhere to NASW guidelines when working with clients who have possibly recovered memories of childhood sexual abuse. Neutrality about the veracity of such memories is critical because it is impossible to determine the accuracy of memories without external corroboration. This is especially true when RMT techniques have been used. The NASW guidelines caution that "enthusiastic belief or disbelief can and will have an effect on the treatment process" (NASW, 1996b, p. 2). Personal biases may result in incorrect diagnosis and inadequate or inappropriate treatment.

Social workers should always follow accepted professional standards when diagnosing and treating clients. Information about abuse and other negative childhood experiences should be gathered in the course of obtaining a complete psychosocial history, but this should only be one part of a holistic assessment that includes an evaluation of the client's "total clinical picture including symptoms and level of functioning" (NASW, 1996b, p. 2).

It is also important to remember that CSA is an event in a person's life; it is not a diagnosis and should not be treated as such. In addition, CSA should not be inferred from any specific symptoms or cluster of symptoms (APA Working Group, 1996). Social workers should also be cognizant of the fact that most victims of CSA either completely or partially remember their abuse. Although delayed recall is possible, the frequency of abuse memories that are forgotten and later recalled is not known (Knapp & VandeCreek, 2000; Belli, 2012).

Treatment should always be based on a complete assessment, informed by the scientific literature, and designed to meet the individual client's needs, and the emphasis should be on the client's current functioning (Knapp & VandeCreek, 2000). According to NASW (1996b, p. 2), the social worker's responsibility is to "maintain the focus of treatment on symptom reduction or elimination and to enhance the ability of the client to function appropriately and comfortably in his or her daily life."

In accordance with this, archeological reconstruction of one's past and placing a focus on working through painful emotions should not be the primary goal of treatment. If a client enters treatment with the desire to discuss or examine recovered memories, NASW (1996b, p. 2) recommends that social workers "explore the meaning and implication of the memory for the client, rather than focusing solely on the content or veracity of the report." In addition, it is the responsibility of the social worker to inform the client that their memory may be "an accurate memory of an actual event, an altered or distorted memory of an actual event, or the recounting of an event that did not happen."

Clients who have recanted memories of abuse may need assistance in understanding the dynamics that led them to believe in recovered memories of events that never happened. A psycho-educational approach can assist them in understanding the nature of memory, memory reconstruction, and the specific techniques that can lead to false memories. They may also need help in resolving issues of guilt and self-blame and in re-establishing relationships within their families. This is particularly true if their abuse memories resulted in accusations, angry confrontation, legal action, or alienation among family members.

Social workers should also be cognizant of legal issues related to recovered memories and be fully informed about issues related to risk management. Although the social worker's primary responsibility is to the client, she or he should also be concerned about the effect of false allegations on the accused, many of whom are family members. The guidelines developed by NASW (1996b) discuss this in detail, with specific recommendations related to record keeping, informed consent, client self-determination, and requisite knowledge of state and federal laws.

Finally, it is incumbent upon social workers to have adequate training, and to maintain current skills and knowledge in the areas of trauma and memory if they are working with clients who have histories of abuse or recovered memories of abuse. Scientific research in this area is constantly emerging and social workers must be able to critically assess new findings and be open to incorporating new evidence-based knowledge into practice.

References and Readings

American Academy of Psychiatry and the Law. (1999). Recovered memories of sexual abuse: informed consent. *American Academy of Psychiatry and the Law Newsletter, 24*(2), 5–6.

American Medical Association. (1994). *Report of the Council on Scientific Affairs* (CSA Report 5-A-94). Chicago: Author.

American Psychological Association Working Group on Investigation of Memories of Childhood Abuse. (1996). *Final report*. Washington, DC: Author.

Belli, R. F. F. (Ed.). (2012). Nebraska Symposium on Motivation. *True and false recovered memories: Toward a reconciliation of the debate.* New York, NY: Springer.

Benatar, M. (1995). Running away from sexual abuse: Denial revisited. *Families in Society, 76*(5), 478–489.

Francis, A. (2014, January 28). Multiple personality—is it mental disorder, myth, or metaphor? Huffington Post Science. Retrieved from http://www.huffingtonpost.com/allen-frances/sex-and-satanic-abuse-a-f_b_4680605.html

Knapp, S., & VandeCreek, L. (2000). Recovered memories of childhood abuse: Is there an underlying professional consensus? *Professional Psychology: Research and Practice, 31*(4), 365–371.

Loftus, E. F., & Ketcham, K. K. (1994). *The myth of repressed memory: False memories and accusations of sexual abuse.* New York, NY: St. Martin's Press.

McNally, R. J. (2005). *Remembering trauma.* Cambridge, MA: Belknap Press of Harvard University Press.

Nathan, D. (2011). *Sybil exposed: The extraordinary story behind the famous multiple personality case.* New York, NY: Free Press.

National Association of Social Workers. (1996a). National Association of Social Workers Code of Ethics. *NASW News, 41*(10), Insert 1–4. (Also available at http://www.socialworkers.org/Code/ethics.htm)

National Association of Social Workers. (1996b). *Practice statement on the evaluation and treatment of adults with the possibility of recovered memories of childhood sexual abuse.* Washington, DC: NASW Office of Policy and Practice.

Robbins, S. P. (1995). Wading through the muddy waters of recovered memory. *Families in Society, 76*, 478–489.

Robbins, S. P. (1997). Cults (update). In R. L. Edwards & J. C. Hopps (Eds.), *Encyclopedia of Social Work* (19th ed.) (on CD ROM). Washington, DC: National Association of Social Workers Press.

Stocks, J. T. (1998). Recovered memory therapy: A dubious practice technique. *Social Work, 43*(5), 423–436.

89 Terminating with Clients

Anne E. Fortune

REASONS FOR ENDING SERVICE

Common reasons for ending social work service include planned ending of time-limited service, ending of open-ended service either unilaterally or by mutual agreement, and unanticipated external factors (Fortune, 1985; Fortune, Pearlingi, & Rochelle, 1991; Westmacott & Hunsley, 2010). The specific reason for ending influences participants' expectations, reactions, and appropriate interventions during the termination phase (Baum, 2005, 2007; Westmacott, Hunsley, Best, Rumstein-McKean, & Schindler, 2010).

Ending Planned, Time-limited Contacts

In time-limited service, participants know how long their contact will last and use that sense of time to frame their work, maintain focus, and motivate participants. Because of the short duration, the foreknowledge of ending and, frequently, the clarity of goals or problems, decisions about when and how to terminate are usually easier than in open-ended service and less preparation is needed.

Ending Open-ended Service by Mutual Agreement

If there are no time limits, ending ideally occurs when clients and social workers agree that service is no longer desirable. The literature suggests eclectic indicators of success to determine when to end, including:

- Meeting goals set by clients, practitioners, or outside arbitrators such as judges.

- Improved behavior, relationships, and intrapsychic functioning for clients.
- In family treatment, improvements in the relationship among family members (e.g., improved interaction and communication) and better family relations with others (e.g., more appropriate boundaries).
- Lack of success. Unless the goal is maintaining functioning in a chronic condition, ethical considerations demand that treatment end: (1) if there is little improvement and little reasonable expectation of improvement, or (2) if further gains are not worth the time and energy required.

The reality of open-ended treatment is that these criteria rarely guide ending. Instead, when termination is mutually agreed, clients may hint—subtly or directly—that things are better and that treatment is no longer needed (Råbu, Binder, & Haavind, 2013). Clients and practitioners then conduct a dance to negotiate termination. Each party is concerned primarily with the feelings of the other, and ending occurs when they "find a way to resolve basic ambivalences concerning ending" (Råbu et al., 2013, p. 19).

Unilateral Client Terminations (Drop-outs)

Clients may decide to end by dropping out without informing their social workers. Although dropping out is often viewed as a treatment failure, as many as two-thirds of dropouts report considerable progress (Westmacott et al., 2010). Many so-called dropouts occur after practitioners miss clients' hints that they are ready to terminate. Practitioners tend to underestimate both clients' progress (especially compared to clients' estimates) and clients' dissatisfaction with treatment (Westmacott et al., 2010). In extreme cases, practitioners may feel blindsided by a premature ending, but upon reflection recognize the clients' dissatisfaction and their own frustration with treatment (Piselli, Halgin, & Macewan, 2011).

Clients who drop out miss the opportunity to assess the treatment process and solidify gains through planned maintenance interventions, while practitioners also miss the opportunity for reflection and professional growth.

Unanticipated Endings

Many open-ended cases end partly or wholly because of unexpected situational factors. Unanticipated or unplanned reasons for ending include:

- Practitioners leave an agency or become ill.
- Students end their social work internships.
- Schedule changes, transportation problems, expenses
- Parents remove children from treatment.
- Agency constraints, such as excessive caseloads or demise of a program.

In unanticipated endings, progress is rarely optimal, although again practitioners are often more cynical than clients (Westmacott & Hunsley, 2010). Despite limited progress, gains can be consolidated by conducting termination-phase interventions, including dealing with disappointment or anger, assessing gains, and suggesting how clients may continue progress. Practitioners should also consider transferring clients to other service providers.

Transfer to Another Service Provider

Clients may transfer elsewhere when service is cut off—for example, if the social worker leaves the agency, more appropriate service is available elsewhere, or the client and worker do not get along. Termination of the relationship between initial social workers and clients is similar to other situations, with social workers also facilitating linkages with new social workers.

Ending in Managed Care

Managed care and insurance-supported services usually have standard time limits imposed by the service provider (Cuffel et al., 2000). Extension beyond the time limits requires administrative review and approval. Most social work providers consequently plan time-limited treatment with specified goals. Termination is "built in" and handled as for other forms of planned time-limited treatment. The provider rarely ends service, but if an extension is requested the uncertainty about continuing service may complicate termination. There may be dashed hopes, anger, and an inability to use the positive effects of time limits. Nevertheless, whenever possible under managed care, the formal interventions of the termination phase should be conducted, especially after a denied extension.

CLIENT' REACTIONS TO TERMINATION

Although much of the literature describes termination as a gloomy process of mourning, most clients have more positive reactions than negative feelings (Baum, 2005; Fortune, 1987; Knox et al., 2011; Roe, Dekel, Harel, Fennig, & Fennig, 2006; Siebold, 2007). The ending of service usually means accomplishments as well as losses and new beginnings and independence for clients. A wide range of reactions is "normal" with individual expressions and cultural variations in what emotions are appropriate and how they may be expressed. Common reactions during the termination phase include:

- Clients naturally evaluate their progress and goal attainment, summarize their work in treatment, and review the treatment process itself.
- In intrapsychic and existential treatments, the focus shifts to concurrent and future outside activities, with clients expressing a growing sense of autonomy.
- Clients are proud of their accomplishments, excited at ending, and satisfied.
- Clients express ambivalence about ending, including sadness, a wish to continue the relationship, and ambivalence about whether progress is sufficient. Ambivalence may show itself actively in lateness or missed sessions.
- Clients may re-experience previous losses or recreate earlier treatment experiences, often as part of integrating therapeutic growth.

Less commonly, clients experience negative reactions that must be handled separately from normal termination reactions. These negative reactions include:

- In successful long-term treatment, mourning the loss of an intense relationship, with stages of denial, anger and loss, depression, and finally acceptance
- Anger or bitterness
- Regression to previous inappropriate behaviors or acting out
- Extreme negative emotions like depression, feeling "destroyed," or loss of self-esteem.

Factors Affecting Reactions to Termination

Several factors affect clients' reactions to termination.

Reason for Termination

- When service ends unexpectedly, reactions are more negative: more anger, problematic behaviors, mourning, mood disturbances, and a sense of unfinished business (Baum, 2005).
- When the ending is mutually agreed upon, there is more pride and excitement (Roe, Dekel, Harel, & Fennig, 2006).
- Dropouts are less satisfied than those who end by agreement, but are more satisfied than the practitioner thinks (Westmacott et al., 2010).

Outcome

- The more successful the outcome, the more positive clients' reactions (pride, accomplishment, sense of independence, etc.) (Cuffel et al., 2000; Kacen, 1999; Knox et al., 2011; Roe, Dekel, Harel, & Fennig, 2006).
- The more successful the outcome, the more temporary anxiety or hurt, as well as greater distancing from the therapeutic relationship as clients prepare for the end (Baum, 2005).

Therapeutic Alliance

- The stronger the therapeutic relationship or working alliance, the more positive clients' feelings at ending (Knox et al., 2011; Roe, Dekel, Harel, Fennig, et al., 2006). However, during the termination process, such clients often have stronger negative reactions,

anxiety, and sense of loss than clients with less attachment to the practitioner (Kacen, 1999).

Preparation for Ending

- Early preparation (including setting time limits at the beginning) has important benefits: (1) introduction of affective content can be managed to allow therapeutic processing; (2) clients have time to work through their reactions; and (3) clients are less likely to act out during termination (Fortune, Pearlingi, & Rochelle, 1992).
- Systematic processing during the termination phase is associated with positive reactions and appropriate transitions (Baum, 2005; Knox et al., 2011; Roe, Dekel, Harel, Fennig, et al., 2006). Fruitful processing may include assessment of outcome, review of the therapeutic process, and focus on both positive and painful or frustrating aspects of the relationship.

Previous Loss

- Clients with unresolved loss may go through mourning reactions as they re-create the previous loss experiences (Zilberstein, 2008). In some theoretical approaches, treatment generally and termination in particular is viewed as a corrective experience that enables clients to learn new, better ways of coping with relationships and loss.

Other factors such as type of service or modality may affect reactions to termination, but studies are lacking. One rarely studied factor is culture, or race and ethnicity. We know that minority clients end treatment prematurely more often than others (Snowden & Yamada, 2005), but we do not know if reactions are similar or culturally defined. The *meaning* of ending may differ among cultures. Urban adolescents who were more engaged in mental health services were *more* likely to drop out without acknowledging termination than less engaged adolescents (Mirabito, 2001, 2006). Elsewhere, in tight-knit rural and in ethnic urban communities, once practitioners provided service, they and their resources were considered part of the community; the concept of ending did not exist (Graham, Shier, & Brownlee, 2012). In general, our knowledge of different definitions and reactions to termination is based primarily on anecdotes, rather than systematic study (see, for example, Gutheil, 1993; Walsh, 2007; Wayne & Avery, 1979).

SOCIAL WORKERS' REACTIONS TO TERMINATION

Social workers, too, experience a range of emotions at ending with each client. Typically, reactions are less intense mirrors of clients' reactions. They include pride in clients' accomplishments and in their own therapeutic skills, ambivalence, sadness, a sense of overview of the treatment process, and sometimes hurt at abandonment, doubt, disappointment, and guilt about the limits of their helping abilities (Fortune et al., 1992; Piselli et al., 2011; Westmacott et al., 2010). Factors related to practitioners' reactions are also similar to those that influence clients' reactions. For example, practitioners whose clients dropped out unilaterally had more negative emotions than those with mutually agreed upon terminations (Baum, 2007; C. Gelman, Fernandez, Hausman, Miller, & Weiner, 2007; C. R. Gelman, 2009). Practitioners whose clients had better outcome reported more pride in their clients' successes and in their own skills (Baum, 2007; Fortune, 1987).

Social workers should be aware of their own reactions for several reasons:

- Social workers' reactions affect their ability to recognize when to end or how to intervene. For example, they may enjoy a client, be reluctant to admit they are not helpful, or miss warning signs that the client is dissatisfied.
- Countertransference (attributing one's own feelings to the client) may lead to inappropriate interventions.

INTERVENTIONS FOR THE TERMINATION PHASE

Termination interventions should be an integral part of treatment planning. Interventions during the termination phase differ from change interventions in earlier phases of treatment, although they require the same good therapeutic relationship, planning, and implementation skills. The termination interventions are designed to help clients (1) assess progress and the treatment process, (2) generalize gains to other settings and situations, (3) develop skills and strategies to maintain gains, (4) make the transition to no service or to another service, and (5) deal with emotional reactions to ending. We also mention practitioners' self-development interventions that can enhance their personal and professional growth.

Assessing Progress and Process

A primary task during termination is assessing the status of goals and clients' problems (Fortune, 1987; Roe, Dekel, Harel, Fennig, et al., 2006). Purposes of the progress review are to:

- Provide data to confirm (or disconfirm) tentative decisions to terminate.
- Assess progress realistically and solidify the clients' learning during treatment.
- Increase clients' sense of mastery and ability to cope, which are important to continued functioning.
- Provide information to shape other termination interventions, for example, clients' strengths for future problem-solving efforts.

Clients and social workers also review the treatment process, emphasizing the problem-resolution steps and skills clients can use in the future. The review helps bring closure by giving an overview of the course of treatment.

Generalizing Gains

Unless deliberate efforts are made to broaden gains, clients' use of new skills may be limited to circumscribed areas—for example, improved communication at work but not with family members. Some termination activities are designed to expand the use of new cognitive or interpersonal skills (generalization) and to improve their durability after ending (maintenance) (Fishman & Lubetkin, 1980). Activities to extend client gains to other areas include:

- Learning general principles about dealing with problems—for example, problem-solving skills, anger management, or family communication
- Transferring skills from treatment sessions to clients' natural environments through homework assignments or tasks, for example, trying out "I statements" learned in group treatment at home with family members
- Systematically transferring skills from one situation to another, for example, a child sharing activities with others first in the classroom, then at recess.

Maintaining Gains

Another concern is how long clients' gains last after treatment ends. Interventions that help maintain gains include:

- Increasing clients' sense of mastery through realistic praise and highlighting their role in creating and maintaining change
- Internalizing the "voice" or persona of the practitioner so the memory of the practitioner remains as a guide for clients after ending (Råbu, Binder, et al., 2013; Zilberstein, 2008). Råbu, Haavind and Binder (2013) talk about "the co-creation of metaphors" regarding the therapeutic alliance as a way to create memories for clients to draw on in the future. For example, metaphors about cleaning may convey how practitioners and clients together have cleaned up and sorted things out.
- Discussing general principles that underlie coping and change
- Ensuring that newly learned skills are appropriate for the clients' normal environments.
- "Fail-safe planning" (Fishman & Lubetkin, 1980) or how to deal with future difficulties, such as handling potential conflict around a child's report card
- Ensuring that the new skills are supported in the client's environment, such as:
  1. Bringing clients' support systems directly into treatment, for example, inviting a spouse to termination sessions to discuss maintenance, or including a schoolchild's friends in treatment designed as a "club."
  2. Creating new support networks through joining existing organizations, such as Alcoholics Anonymous, church groups, or social interest groups (cards, classes to learn new skills, hunting, etc.)
  3. Teaching clients how to elicit support from significant others
  4. Conducting follow-up booster sessions that include maintenance interventions such as reinforcing what clients are doing well, reviewing principles, discussing coping strategies, and planning for the future.

Making the Transition

If clients are not prepared to function without treatment, all the gains can be lost quickly.

To ease the transition, practitioners reduce any overdependence and assure that clients are ready to function on their own (or with different services). Interventions that help accomplish the transition out of treatment include:

- Within the content of treatment sessions, a systematic shift in time focus from past activities through present functioning and then a future orientation, for example, from childhood trauma to current handling of emotional triggers to means of responding in the future
- Increased attention to outside treatment activities and supports through:
  1. Discussing events in clients' lives
  2. Maintenance and generalization activities such as homework assignments and fail-safe planning
  3. Activities that take place away from the normal context, such as a trip to a park for youngsters.
- Using natural breaks like vacations to test readiness for clients to function on their own, or deliberately increasing time between sessions (fading) so clients get used to being on their own (C. Gelman et al., 2007).
- Having clients take as much control over the ending process as possible (Fragkiadaki & Strauss, 2012; Råbu, Binder, et al., 2013)
- In groups, reducing cohesion by decreasing the cooperation and interaction required from group activities—for example, boys playing table tennis (an individual game) instead of soccer (a teamwork activity), or adults developing homework tasks in pairs rather than in full groups
- When clients are transferring to service elsewhere, interventions to smooth the transition to new agencies or social workers include:
  1. Linking clients to referral agencies by providing thorough information about contacting the agencies, making an appointment for the clients, or accompanying the clients to the agencies
  2. Ensuring that new providers are prepared for the clients by consulting with the providers, explaining expectations, and sharing information (with clients' permission)
  3. Following up with clients and new providers after their initial meetings to ensure that the connections are made

4. To minimize clients' feelings of rejection, discussing openly the reasons for termination/transfer and exploring clients' feelings and expectations of the new services.

Dealing with Clients' Emotional Reactions to Ending

Expressing feelings is an important part of the ending phase. Acknowledging the emotions makes them acceptable, validates the clients' experiences, and provides models for handling both affect and termination. Interventions to elicit reactions and build on them for therapeutic purposes include:

- Encouraging clients to talk about their feelings by:
    1. Exploring expressions of ambivalence (as well as other expressions of emotion)
    2. Modeling self-disclosure by introducing the social worker's own reactions (this also helps shift the therapeutic relationship to greater collegiality)
    3. Describing in words the emotions clients seem to express nonverbally, such as angry gestures, evading discussion, or hesitant pride
- Once clients express emotion, build on these reactions for other treatment or termination interventions. For example:
    1. Build on positive feelings (such as pride in accomplishments) to reinforce clients' sense of mastery.
    2. Label ambivalence and sadness as normal, healthy expressions of ending.
    3. Handle strong negative reactions as intensive grief reactions that can be resolved through stages of mourning.
- Introducing activities designed to elicit clients' reactions and to provide opportunity for other termination interventions. For example:
    1. Artistic activities such as individualized coloring books that include highlights of children's treatment, such as "memory books" (Elbow, 1987). Such activities encourage review of the treatment process and help solidify gains (assessing progress and process). The artistic products themselves are mementos for clients (ritual markers).

2. In educational groups, a "toast" to each person about what members learned from them reinforces learning and a sense of mastery, as well as celebrates ending.

- Introducing formal termination rituals. Such rituals help clients deal with conflicting emotions, give a sense of specialness and make connections between past and future. Appropriate rituals include:
    1. Culturally defined good-bye markers like hugging and shaking hands
    2. Complex exchanges of mementos with special meaning, such as photographs, certificates of completion, or gifts that convey the essence of a person
    3. Elaborate events, such as graduation ceremonies or status elevation ceremonies. Such celebrations may also serve other purposes, including demonstrating individual accomplishments and reviewing the treatment experience. For example, in a group to increase self-esteem, a potluck (covered dish) supper with each person contributing his or her ethnic specialty (Wayne & Avery, 1979).
    4. Encouraging clients to choose special or symbolic activities that will help them organize and remember the therapeutic experience, such as a client and practitioner walking together in the park (Walsh, 2007).

Managing Practitioners' Reactions during the Termination Phase

Done well, termination is a mutually beneficial interaction, a partnership or dance (Råbu, Binder, et al., 2013; Siebold, 2007). Because practitioners' reactions and interventions affect clients' termination, practitioners' professional responsibility requires understanding those reactions and using them to benefit clients. But, for practitioners, as for clients, the termination phase offers opportunities for professional development (Baum, 2007; Fragkiadaki & Strauss, 2012; C. Gelman et al., 2007). Termination is viewed as a transition, not as a loss of clients. Reviewing cases allows social workers to assess the treatment process: what worked, what was overlooked, what were potential mistakes. Assessing their own skills will, one hopes, generate a sense of pride, but even doubts are catalysts for future improvements. It is hoped, too, that social workers will affirm their self-identities as help-ers and recommit to helping people.

Not all cases go well. Clients dropping out often upsets practitioners, especially those who are introspective and honest enough to recognize mistakes and acknowledge their own roles in such drop-outs (Piselli et al., 2011). Even good cases can have bad endings, if practitioners mishandle the termination phase. To aid constructive personal growth when cases end distressingly, Schaeffer and Kaiser (2013) offer a structured approach: honor the practitioner's initial reaction to the termination; appraise possible causes; determine the most probable cause, take appropriate responsibility; mourn; perform reparation for current and future clients; evaluate their own well-being and sense of self-efficacy; and take a broader perspective for the future.

Social workers may give short shrift to termination; with that in mind, it is worth noting that experienced (presumably good) practitioners not only process ending sensitively during the termination phase, but are also continually aware of termination and its implications from the very beginning of service (Baum, 2007; Fragkiadaki & Strauss, 2012).

Is Ending the End?

Traditionally, the end of service was considered an absolute, and professional pride dictated that social workers manage their boundaries and be definitive in ending. Contemporary views are not so black–and–white. As mentioned earlier, some communities or cultural groups do not recognize the concept of ending in the way western service providers do (Graham et al., 2012), leading Mirabito (2001) to recommend intermittent service and open-door policies. Most social work services are no longer thought of as "cures" but as assistance with identifiable but recurring difficulties. Managed care has required and indeed normalized short-term treatments. Theoretically, too, ideas about practitioners' roles have changed. Attachment theory suggests creating transitional objects—memories of practitioners—that stay alive in clients' minds after termination (Siebold, 1992; Zilberstein, 2008). Råbu, Binder, and colleagues (2013) suggest that the possibility of future contact creates a sense of safety for clients that aids ending.

Opinion has similarly shifted about parting gifts and mementos. Previously viewed as boundary violations and a breach of ethics, mementos are now viewed as symbolic markers representing multiple meanings to participants.

In short, termination may or may not be the last time practitioners and clients interact professionally. Aside from ethical prohibitions on transforming professional relationships into personal ones, there are few absolutes about termination ending all therapeutic relationships. Services should not continue if clients are not benefiting. Otherwise, the immediate context and professional ethics should guide decisions about irrevocable terminations and gift exchanges.

SUMMARY

Termination is as important to ethical social work practice as engagement, assessment, and treatment planning. Whatever the reason for ending, early preparation and careful interventions during the termination phase helps clients maintain gains and deal with the practical and emotional reactions to ending.

WEBSITES

Skills of termination, www.psychcentral.com
Termination and abandonment, www.apa.org
Example of bad termination, www.youtube.com/watch?v=SuLT3ojl5Go

References

Baum, N. (2005). Correlates of clients' emotional and behavioral responses to treatment termination. *Clinical Social Work Journal, 33*(3), 309–326.

Baum, N. (2007). Therapists' responses to treatment termination: An inquiry into the variables that contribute to therapists' experiences. *Clinical Social Work Journal, 35*, 97–106.

Cuffel, B., McCulloch, J., Wade, R., Tam, L., Brown Mitchell, R., & Goldman, W. (2000). Patients' and providers' perceptions of outpatient treatment termination in a managed behavioral health organization. *Psychiatric Services, 51*(4), 469–473.

Elbow, M. (1987). The memory book: Facilitating terminations with children. *Social Casework, 68*, 180–183.

Fishman, S. F., & Lubetkin, B. S. (1980). Maintenance and generalization of individual behavior therapy programs: Clinical observations. In P. Karoly & J. J. Steffen (Eds.), *Improving the long-term effects of psychotherapy: Models of durable outcome* (pp. 1–22). New York, NY: Gardner.

Fortune, A. E. (1985). Planning duration and termination of treatment. *Social Service Review, 59,* 647–661.

Fortune, A. E. (1987). Grief only? Client and social worker reactions to termination. *Clinical Social Work Journal, 15*(2), 159–171.

Fortune, A. E., Pearlingi, B., & Rochelle, C. (1991). Criteria for terminating treatment. *Families in Society, 22*(6), 366–370.

Fortune, A. E., Pearlingi, B., & Rochelle, C. (1992). Reactions to termination of individual treatment. *Social Work, 37*(2), 171–178.

Fragkiadaki, E., & Strauss, S. M. (2012). Termination of psychotherapy: The journey of 10 psychoanalytic and psychodynamic therapists. *Psychology and Psychotherapy: Theory, Research and Practice, 85*(3), 335–350.

Gelman, C., Fernandez, P., Hausman, N., Miller, S., & Weiner, M. (2007). Challenging endings: First year MSW interns' experiences with forced termination and discussion points for supervisory guidance. *Clinical Social Work Journal, 35,* 79–90.

Gelman, C. R. (2009). MSW students' experience with termination: Implications and suggestions for classroom and field instruction. *Journal of Teaching in Social Work, 29,* 169–187.

Graham, J. R., Shier, M. L., & Brownlee, K. (2012). Contexts of practice and their impact on social work: A comparative analysis of the context of geography and culture. *Journal of Ethnic and Cultural Diversity in Social Work, 21,* 111–128.

Gutheil, I. A. (1993). Rituals and termination procedures. *Smith College Studies in Social Work, 63*(2), 163–176.

Kacen, L. (1999). Anxiety levels, group characteristics, and members' behaviors in the termination stage of support groups for patients recovering from heart attacks. *Research on Social Work Practice, 9*(6), 656–672.

Knox, S., Adrians, N., Everson, E., Hess, S., Hill, C., & Crook-Lyon, R. (2011). Clients' perspectives on therapy termination. *Psychotherapy Research, 21*(2), 154–167.

Mirabito, D. M. (2001). Mining treatment termination data in an adolescent mental health service: A quantitative study. *Social Work in Health Care, 33*(3/4), 71–90.

Mirabito, D. M. (2006). Revisiting unplanned termination: Clinicians' perceptions of termination from adolescent mental health treatment. *Families in Society: The Journal of Contemporary Social Services, 87*(2), 171–180.

Piselli, A., Halgin, R. P., & Macewan, G. H. (2011). What went wrong? Therapists' reflections on their role in premature termination. *Psychotherapy Research, 21*(4), 400–415.

Råbu, M., Binder, P.-E., & Haavind, H. (2013). Negotiating ending: A qualitative study of the process of ending psychotherapy. *European Journal of Psychotherapy and Counselling, 15,* 274–295.

Råbu, M., Haavind, H., & Binder, P.-E. (2013). We have travelled a long distance and sorted out the mess in the drawers: Metaphors for moving towards the end in psychotherapy. *Counselling and Psychotherapy Research, 13*(1), 71–80.

Roe, D., Dekel, R., Harel, G., & Fennig, S. (2006). Clients' reasons for terminating psychotherapy: A quantitative and qualitative inquiry. *Psychology & Psychotherapy: Theory, Research & Practice, 79*(4), 529–538.

Roe, D., Dekel, R., Harel, G., Fennig, S., & Fennig, S. (2006). Clients' feelings during termination of psychodynamically oriented psychotherapy. *Bulletin of the Menninger Clinic, 70*(1), 68–81.

Schaeffer, J. A., & Kaiser, E. M. (2013). A structured approach to processing clients' unilateral termination decisions. *American Journal of Psychotherapy, 67*(2), 163–181.

Siebold, C. (1992). Forced termination: Reconsidering theory and technique. *Smith College Studies in Social Work, 63*(1), 324–341.

Siebold, C. (2007). Everytime we say goodbye: Forced termination revisited, a commentary. *Clinical Social Work Journal, 35,* 91–95.

Snowden, L. R., & Yamada, A.-M. (2005). Cultural differences in access to care. *Annual Review of Clinical Psychology, 1*(1), 143–166.

Walsh, J. (2007). *Endings in clinical practice: Effective closure in diverse settings.* Chicago, IL: Lyceum.

Wayne, J., & Avery, N. (1979). Activities for group termination. *Social Work, 24,* 58–62.

Westmacott, R., & Hunsley, J. (2010). Reasons for terminating psychotherapy: A general population study. *Journal of Clinical Psychology, 66,* 965–977.

Westmacott, R., Hunsley, J., Best, M., Rumstein-McKean, O., & Schindler, D. (2010). Client and therapist views of contextual factors related to termination from psychotherapy: A comparison between unilateral and mutual terminators. *Psychotherapy Research, 20*(4), 423–435.

Zilberstein, K. (2008). Au revoir: An attachment and loss perspective on termination.

PART IX

Guidelines for Specific Interventions

90 Transtheoretical Model Guidelines for Families with Child Abuse and Neglect

Janice M. Prochaska, James O. Prochaska, & Judith J. Prochaska

In the child abuse field, caseworkers often use compliance with case plans as a proxy or indicator of change. Thus, parents who attend parenting classes or go to counseling are seen as changing—even if those same parents continue to deny abuse and neglect. Compliance with a court-ordered program of services or classes is, however, not the same as psychological readiness to change or actual change in behavior.

The transtheoretical model of behavior change offers a more reliable, valid, and complex assessment of change than a simple recording of compliance. The model assumes that changing behavior is a dynamic process and that one progresses through a series of stages in trying to modify behavior—precontemplation, contemplation, preparation, action, and maintenance. Over thirty-five years of research on a variety of behaviors have identified interventions that work best in each stage to facilitate change (Prochaska, Norcross, & DiClemente, 1994; Noar, Benac, & Harris, 2007).

DEFINITIONS OF STAGES

Each of the five stages represents a period of time, as well as a set of tasks needed for movement to the next stage. Although the time an individual spends in each stage may vary, the tasks to be accomplished are assumed to be invariant.

Precontemplation is the stage at which there is no intention to change behavior in the foreseeable future. Most individuals in this stage are unaware or underaware of their problems. Family, friends, or neighbors, however, are often well aware that the precontemplator has a problem. When precontemplators present for help, they often do so because of pressure from others. Usually they feel coerced into changing by a spouse who threatens to leave, children who threaten to disown them, or courts that threaten to punish them. They may also be demoralized from having tried to change and failed.

Measures that identify where clients are in the change process (i.e., their stage of change), ask individuals if they are seriously intending to change the problem behavior in the near future, typically within the next six months. If not, they are classified as precontemplators. Even precontemplators can wish to change, but this is quite different from intending or seriously considering change. Items that are used to identify precontemplation on a continuous stage of change measure include, "I have done nothing wrong and resent child welfare getting involved in my life" or "I guess I have faults, but there's nothing that I really need to change." Resistance to recognizing or modifying a problem are the hallmarks of precontemplation.

Contemplation is the stage at which people are aware that a problem exists and are seriously thinking about overcoming it but have not yet made a commitment to take action. People can remain stuck in the contemplation stage for long periods. Contemplators struggle with their positive evaluations of their dysfunctional behavior and the amount of effort, energy, and loss it will cost to overcome it. Individuals who state that they are seriously considering changing in the next six months are classified as contemplators. These individuals also would endorse such items

707

as, "I have a problem and I really think I should work on it" and "I've started to think I haven't been caring for my kids as well as I could." Serious consideration of problem resolution is the central element of contemplation.

Preparation is the stage that combines intention and behavioral criteria. Individuals in this stage are intending to take action within the next month and have taken some small steps. As a group, individuals who are prepared for action also report some small cognitive changes, such as, "I have questions for my caseworker about taking care of my kids" and "If I don't change, I will never be the kind of parent my children need." Although they have made some reductions in their problem behaviors, people in the preparation stage have not yet reached a criterion for effective action, such as not hitting their children or regularly providing supervision and appropriate food and shelter.

Action is the stage at which individuals modify their behavior, experiences, and/or environment to overcome their problems. Action involves the most overt behavioral changes and requires considerable commitment of time and energy. Individuals are classified in the action stage if they have successfully altered the dysfunctional behavior for a period ranging from 1 day to 6 months. Individuals in the action stage endorse statements such as, "I am really working hard to change" and "I am doing things about the problem that got me involved with child welfare." Modification of the target behavior to an acceptable criterion and significant overt efforts to change are the hallmarks of action.

Maintenance is the stage at which people work to prevent relapse and consolidate the gains attained during action. For abusive behaviors, this stage extends from six months to an indeterminate period past the initial action. For some behaviors, maintenance can be considered to last a lifetime. Being able to refrain from abusive behavior and being able to engage consistently in a new positive behavior for more than six months are the criteria for considering someone to be in the maintenance stage. Representative maintenance statements are, "I may need a boost right now to help me maintain the changes I've already made" and "I sometimes feel nervous that when child welfare is out of my life, I will fall back on old behavior." Stabilizing behavior change and preventing relapse are the hallmarks of maintenance.

Spiral Pattern

As is now well known, most people taking action to modify chronic dysfunctional behavior do not successfully maintain their gains on their first attempt. Relapse is the rule rather than the exception across virtually all chronic behavioral disorders. Accordingly, change is not a linear progression through the stages. Most clients actually move through the stages of change in a spiral pattern. People can progress from contemplation to preparation to action to maintenance, but most regress to an earlier stage. Some relapsers feel like failures—embarrassed, ashamed, and guilty. These individuals become demoralized and resist thinking about behavior change. As a result, they return to the precontemplation stage and can remain there for extended periods of time.

PRESCRIPTIVE GUIDELINES

Assess the Client's Stage of Change

Probably the most obvious and direct implication for risk assessment is the need to assess the stage of a client's readiness for change and to tailor interventions accordingly. Stages of change can be ascertained by asking the client a series of simple questions to identify his or her stage, for example, "Do you think behavior X is a problem for you now?" (if the answer is, "yes," then contemplation, preparation, or action stage; if the answer is "no," then maintenance or precontemplation stage) and "When do you intend to change behavior X?" (if the response is, "someday" or "not soon," then contemplation stage; if "in the next month," then preparation stage; if "now," then the action stage).

Beware of Treating All Clients as Though They Are in Action

Professionals frequently design excellent action-oriented treatment and self-help programs but then are disappointed when only a small percentage of people attend or when large numbers drop out of the program after coming once or twice. The vast majority of clients are *not* in the action stage. Aggregating across studies and populations, we estimate that 10%–15% are prepared for action, approximately 30%–40% are in the contemplation stage, and 50%–60% are in the precontemplation stage. Thus, professionals who approach clients only with action-oriented programs are likely to underserve or mis-serve the majority of their target population.

Assist Clients in Moving One Stage at a Time

If clients progress from one stage to the next during the first month of treatment, they can double their chances of taking effective action within the next six months. Treatment programs designed to help people progress just one stage in a month can increase the chances of participants taking action on their own in the near future.

Recognize that Clients in the Preparation Stage Are Far More Likely to Achieve Better and Quicker Outcomes

The amount of progress clients make during treatment tends to be a function of their pretreatment stage of change. This has direct implications for assessing risk and selecting and prioritizing treatment goals.

Anticipate Recycling

Most clients will recycle through the stages before achieving long-term maintenance. Accordingly, intervention programs and personnel expecting people to progress linearly through the stages are likely to produce discouraging results. Be prepared to include relapse prevention and recycling strategies in treatment, anticipate the probability of recycling, and try to minimize caseworker guilt and client shame over recycling.

Conceptualize Change Mechanisms as Processes, Not as Specific Techniques

Literally hundreds of specific psychotherapeutic techniques have been advanced; however, a small and finite set of change processes or strategies underlie these techniques.

Change processes are covert and overt activities that individuals engage in when they attempt to modify problem behaviors. Each process is a broad category encompassing multiple techniques, methods, and interventions traditionally associated with disparate theoretical orientations. Consciousness raising, for example, is the most frequently used process across systems of psychotherapy. But different systems apply this process with very different techniques, including observations, classifications, interpretations, confrontations, feedback, information, and education. Change processes can be used within treatment sessions, between treatment sessions, or without treatment sessions.

Although there are 400-plus ostensibly different psychotherapies, we have been able to identify only 10 different processes of change based on principal components analysis. Table 90.1 presents the 10 processes, along with their definitions and representative examples of specific interventions.

STAGES OF CHANGE

Do the right things (processes) at the right time (stages). Over thirty-five years of research in behavioral medicine, self-change, and psychotherapy converge in showing that different processes of change are differentially effective in certain stages of change. In general terms, change processes traditionally associated with the experiential, cognitive, and psychoanalytic persuasions are most useful during the earlier precontemplation and contemplation stages. Change processes traditionally associated with the existential and behavioral traditions, by contrast, are most useful during action and maintenance.

In the transtheoretical model, particular change processes are optimally applied at each stage of change. During the precontemplation stage, individuals use the change processes significantly less than people do in any of the other stages. Precontemplators process less information about their problems, devote less time and energy to re-evaluating themselves, and experience fewer emotional reactions to the negative aspects of their problems. In treatment, these are the most resistant or the least active clients.

Individuals in the contemplation stage are most open to consciousness-raising techniques, such as observations, confrontations, and interpretations, and are much more likely to use bibliotherapy and other educational techniques. Contemplators are also open to emotional arousal, which raises emotions and leads to a lowering of negative affect if the person changes. As individuals become more conscious of themselves and the nature of their problems, they are more likely to re-evaluate their values, problems, and themselves both affectively and cognitively. Both movement from precontemplation to contemplation and movement through

TABLE 90.1 Titles, Definitions, and Representative Interventions of 10 Processes of Change

Process	Definition: Interventions
1. Consciousness raising	Increasing information about self and problem: observations; confrontations; interpretations; videos and bibliotherapy on parenting skills
2. Self re-evaluation	Realizing that the behavior change can enhance one's identity: imagery; corrective emotional experience
3. Dramatic relief	Experiencing and expressing feelings about one's problems and solutions: psychodrama; grieving losses; role-playing
4. Social liberation	Realizing that social norms and environments support the behavior change: see alternatives as opportunities rather than coercion; policy interventions
5. Environmental re-evaluation	Realizing the impact of changing or not changing troubled behavior on other people: family value clarification, notice impact on the children
6. Self-liberation	Choice and commitment to act and belief in ability to change: decision-making therapy: New Year's resolutions; commitment-enhancing techniques
7. Counter conditioning	Substituting alternatives for problem-related behaviors: relaxation, anger management; assertion; positive self-statements; parenting skills
8. Stimulus control	Avoiding or countering stimuli that elicit problem behaviors: restructuring one's environment (e.g., removing alcohol); avoiding high-risk cues, fading techniques
9. Reinforcement management	Rewarding oneself or being rewarded by others for making changes: contingency contracts; overt and covert reinforcement; self-reward, feeling better about self
10. Helping relationships	Seeking and using social support to encourage or help with behavior change: therapy; Parents Anonymous

Source: Adapted from Prochaska, DiClemente, & Norcross, 1992.

the contemplation stage entail increased use of cognitive, affective, and evaluative processes of change. Some of these changes continue during the preparation stage. Individuals in preparation begin to take small steps toward action, create a plan, build their confidence, and make commitments to bigger steps.

During the action stage, people are putting into practice self-liberation or commitment. They increasingly believe that they have the autonomy to change their lives in key ways. Successful action also entails effective use of behavioral processes, such as counter conditioning (substituting healthier alternatives) and stimulus control, to modify the conditional stimuli that frequently prompt relapse. Reinforcement management, especially self-reinforcement, also comes into frequent use here.

Just as preparation for action was essential for success, so is preparation for maintenance. Successful maintenance builds on each of the processes that came before. Specific preparation for maintenance entails an assessment of the conditions under which a person would be likely to relapse and development of alternative responses for coping with such conditions without resorting to self-defeating defenses and pathological responses. Continuing to apply counter conditioning, stimulus control, reinforcement management, and helping relationships is most effective when based on the conviction that maintaining change supports a sense of self that is highly valued by oneself and significant others. Figure 90.1 lists appropriate interventions for workers to use based on the processes for each stage.

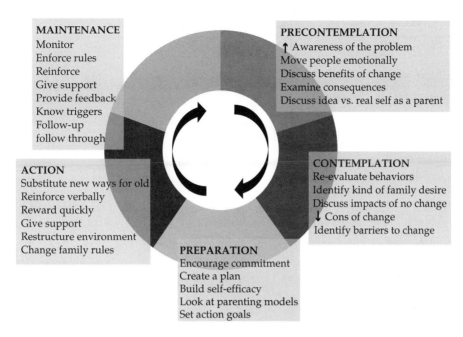

MAINTENANCE
Monitor
Enforce rules
Reinforce
Give support
Provide feedback
Know triggers
Follow-up
follow through

PRECONTEMPLATION
↑ Awareness of the problem
Move people emotionally
Discuss benefits of change
Examine consequences
Discuss idea vs. real self as a parent

ACTION
Substitute new ways for old
Reinforce verbally
Reward quickly
Give support
Restructure environment
Change family rules

CONTEMPLATION
Re-evaluate behaviors
Identify kind of family desire
Discuss impacts of no change
↓ Cons of change
Identify barriers to change

PREPARATION
Encourage commitment
Create a plan
Build self-efficacy
Look at parenting models
Set action goals

Figure 90.1 Interventions for the five stages of change.

MORE ABOUT PRECONTEMPLATORS

Most parents in abusive situations experience themselves as being coerced into receiving help. They do not see themselves as in need of change, probably want to change others, and tend to defend their behavior intensely. Without help from others, precontemplators can remain trapped in this stage. Often, a first step by the caseworker is to enable the parent to become conscious of the self-defeating defenses that get in the way of looking at change. Becoming conscious of their defenses and how they operate can help clients gain a measure of control over them. Does the precontemplator make the least of things (denial and minimization); have excuses (rationalization); turn outward (projection and displacement); or turn inward (internalization-depression). Once precontemplators are aware of how they defend themselves when they feel threatened, they can work at getting control over their defenses rather than having the defenses control them.

Environmental forces can also help a precontemplator to become unstuck. A child welfare investigation, an arrest, or a school official calling can demonstrate that the environment no longer supports their lifestyle. The precontemplator can progress if they can identify with the environmental forces urging them to change. What not to do as a worker is to push precontemplators to immediate action, nag them, give up on them, or enable them (avoid discussions and confrontations, or make excuses).

HELP FOR CHRONIC CONTEMPLATORS

Contemplators can see changing as too difficult to decide to take the first step, or they may get sidetracked and become discouraged and disappointed in their efforts. They may also be ambivalent and say to themselves, "When in doubt, don't change." Chronic contemplators substitute thinking and ruminating for acting. Conflicts and problems hang suspended, decisions are never finalized, and action is avoided. Contemplators need help with seeing the benefits of changing ("I will get to keep my kids," "My kids will benefit," or "I will feel better about myself.") and help with reducing the cons ("It's hard to do all that child welfare wants," or "I will miss getting high," or "Doing things differently will create problems between me and my partner."). Contemplators using self re-evaluation can begin to imagine how life would be substantially improved if they were free from their problem behavior.

RISKS AND STAGES OF CHANGE

Gelles (1996) combines the dimensions of stages of change and degree of risk and lays out

TABLE 90.2 Two Dimensions of Risk Assessment for Child Abuse and Neglect

Stage of Change	Severity of Risk		
	High	Medium	Low
Precontemplation	No reunification High likelihood of terminating parental rights		Parent education classes Project early start
Contemplation		Comprehensive Emergency Services	
Preparation		Parent aide Mother for mother Volunteer support	Family preservation
Action	Family preservation only with close monitoring		Family preservation
Maintenance			Reunification recommended

Source: Adapted from Gelles, 1996.

appropriate programs to offer abusive parents according to risk and stage of change (Table 90.2). According to Gelles, intensive family preservation programs are most appropriate for families who fit the lower right cell—those where the level of risk is low and the stage of change is action. Family preservation could be used with close monitoring for higher risk families but only those who are in preparation or in action. Family preservation is clearly inappropriate for high-risk families who are in precontemplation and contemplation.

RECENT CHALLENGES AND SUCCESSES

As with all major theories, the transtheoretical model has undergone challenges and criticisms. In the child welfare field, the model has been criticized for oversimplification (Littell & Girvin, 2004; Corden & Somerton, 2004); yet, the critical reviews have not considered the model in its full entirety, instead evaluating only stage of change as a single construct.

As detailed earlier, the transtheoretical model includes 14 constructs in addition to stage of change: self-efficacy (confidence and temptations), decisional balance (pros and cons), and the 10 processes of change. Intervention trials tailored on all 15 transtheoretical model constructs have demonstrated wide application and relevance to child welfare, including with regard to adoption readiness, bullying prevention, partner abuse treatment, teen dating violence prevention, and sex offenders. For example, Prochaska et al. (2005) found that the transtheoretical model helped conceptualize and assess emotional readiness to be an adoptive parent and paved the way for future efforts to develop an intervention that guides professionals in their work with prospective parents. Evers, Prochaska, Van Marter, Johnson, and Prochaska (2007) found that a computer-based individualized and interactive transtheoretical model intervention for bullying prevention in schools, given at three time points over one semester, led to significant reductions in bullying, passive bystander, and victim events. In the middle schools, approximately 22% of the treatment group progressed to action or maintenance (always acting with respect) compared with 5% of the control group. In the high schools, approximately 29% progressed to action or maintenance compared with 10% of the control group.

Levesque, Ciavatta, Castle, Prochaska, & Prochaska (2012) developed a multimedia computer expert system program for male domestic violence offenders as an adjunct to traditional mandated treatment. In a randomized clinical trial, the transtheoretical intervention group was significantly more likely to be in the action stage (54% vs. 24%) for using healthy strategies to stay violence-free. Babcock, Canady, Senior, and Eckhardt (2005) applied the Transtheoretical Model to female and male perpetrators of intimate partner violence and found that the model applies to female perpetrators as equally well as to male perpetrators. Tierney and McCabe (2005) encourage the use of the model in the treatment of sex offenders and provide a practical description of the use of all the constructs in the treatment. The Teen Dating Violence Prevention program is a computerized stage-based intervention designed to help high school students develop and use healthy relationship skills to prevent dating violence (if dating) and peer violence (if not dating). In a randomized trial, the program significantly reduced physical and emotional peer violence victimization and perpetration among daters and nondaters (Levesque, 2011).

These studies strongly support the application of the transtheoretical model to reduce abusive relationships. One of the challenges for the future would be how to disseminate these promising interventions from research centers to treatment centers most effectively.

WEBSITES

Cancer Prevention Research Center (birthplace of the transtheoretical model). http://www .uri.edu/research/cprc.

National Clearinghouse on Child Abuse and Neglect (NCCANCH). http://www.nccanch .acf.hhs.gov.

Pro-Change Behavior Systems http:// www .prochange.com. See http://www .prochange.com/domesticviolencedemo for Journey to Change, a family violence program. See A Coach's Guide to Using the Transtheoretical Model. See e-Learning Basic Transtheoretical Model (TTM) Training with Continuing Educations for Social Workers.

The Build Respect, Stop Bullying Program was recognized by SAMSHA in 2007 (http:// www.samhsa.gov/).

References

Corden, J., & Somerton, J. (2004). The trans-theoretical model of change: A reliable blueprint for assessment in work with children and families? *British Journal of Social Work, 34,* 1025–1044.

Evers, K. E., Prochaska, J. O., Van Marter, D. F., Johnson, J. L., & Prochaska, J. M. (2007). Transtheoretical based bullying prevention effectiveness trials in middle schools and high schools. *Educational Research, 49,* 397–414.

Gelles, R. J. (1996). *The book of David.* New York, NY: Basic Books.

Levesque, D. A. (2011). A stage-based expert system for teen dating violence prevention. Final Report to the National Institute of Mental Health, Grant No: R44MH086129.

Levesque, D. A., Ciavatta, M. M., Castle, P. H., Prochaska, J. M., & Prochaska, J. O. (2012). Evaluation of a stage-based, computer-tailored adjunct to usual care for domestic violence offenders. *Psychology of Violence, 2,* 1–17.

Littell, J. H., & Girvin, H. (2004). Ready or not: Uses of the stage of change model in child welfare. *Child Welfare, 83,* 341–366.

Noar, S. M., Benac, C. N., & Harris, M. S. (2007). Does tailoring matter? Meta-analytic review of tailored print health behavior change interventions. *Psychological Bulletin, 133,* 673–693.

Prochaska, J. M., Paiva, A. L., Padula, J. A., Prochaska, J. O., Montgomery, J. E., Hageman, C., & Begart, A. M. (2005). Assessing emotional readiness for adoption using the transtheoretical model. *Children and Youth Services Review, 27,* 135–152.

Prochaska, J. O., DiClemente, C. C., & Norcross, J. C. (1992). In search of how people change: Application to addictive behaviors. *American Psychologist, 47,* 1102–1114.

Prochaska, J. O., Norcross, J. C., DiClemente, C. C. (1994). *Changing for good.* New York, NY: William Morrow and Company.

Babcock, J. C., Canady, B. E., Senior, A., & Eckhardt, C. (2005). Applying the transtheoretical model to female and male perpetrators of intimate partner violence: Gender differences in stage and processes of change. *Violence and Victims, 27,* 235–250.

Tierney, D. W., & McCabe, M. P. (2005). The utility of the Trans-theoretical Model of Behavior Change in the treatment of sex offenders. *Sexual Abuse: A Journal of Research and Treatment, 17,* 153–170.

91 Play Therapy with Children in Crisis

Nancy Boyd-Webb

Many adults tend to think that children are like the three monkeys who see no evil, hear no evil, and do no evil. Unfortunately, the very opposite is true of most children, who pick up cues and take notice whenever trouble is brewing, whether or not the adults in their lives tell them about what is occurring. When children do not receive logical and truthful explanations of the happenings around them, they often create fantasies in their imaginations that may far exceed the magnitude and impact of the actual crisis. Because we live in a world in which violence, terror, and danger are everyday occurrences in families, schools, and communities, no one of any age is immune to the possibility of exposure and to the subsequent stress and anxiety related to perceived threats about one's personal safety.

PLAY THERAPY

Play therapy refers to a theoretically based helping interaction between a trained adult therapist and a child that aims to relieve the child's emotional distress through deliberate use of the symbolic communication of play. Play therapy is the treatment of choice in working with children because it encourages them to communicate through child-friendly play rather than verbally. Just as adults talk out their worries, children express their fears and anxieties by playing them out. The child identifies with the toy doll or other object and displaces his or her feelings onto the toy. The assumption is that when children understand that the therapist's role is to help them, they will then express their emotional conflicts and find more adaptive solutions within the metaphor of play. Often play therapy not only alleviates the presenting symptoms (important as this may be to parents and child) but also may

help remove impediments to the child's continuing development, so that the prospects for the child's future growth are enhanced (Crenshaw, 2006; Webb, 1996; Webb, 2007). In other words, the child's relief from anxiety frees him or her to proceed with his usual activities at home and at school. In summary, the primary purpose of play therapy is to help troubled children express and obtain relief from their conflicts and anxieties symbolically through play in the context of a therapeutic relationship.

Some of the specific elements inherent in play that make it valuable in therapy have been identified as its communication power, its abreaction power (permitting the review of past stress and the expression of associated negative emotions), and its rapport-building power (Reddy, Files-Hall, & Schaefer, 2005). Each child's situation is unique; therefore, therapy with individual children will have different emphases, depending on the specific assessment of the child's problem situation and the child's particular reactions.

DEFINITION AND HISTORY OF CRISIS INTERVENTION PLAY THERAPY

Crisis intervention play therapy is a specialized form of play therapy that aims to help children who have become anxious and symptomatic following a stressful crisis (or traumatic) experience. It uses the broad range of play therapy methods for the purpose of relieving the child's reactions of fear and helplessness. This approach is usually short-term and directive. It relies on the safety of the therapeutic relationship to permit the child to deal with stressful memories, either symbolically or directly, using play materials. Crisis intervention play therapy is especially recommended for single-event and recent traumas, referred to as

Type I trauma (Webb, 2007; James & Gillibrand, 2008). Numerous reports attest to the treatment effectiveness of this form of play therapy in helping traumatized children (Brohl, 1996; Shelby, 1997; Webb, 2003, 2004, 2007). When the child has experienced multiple or chronic traumas (Type II trauma), a more extended treatment approach is recommended. See James and Gilliland for more discussion of Type I and Type II traumas.

The historical roots of crisis intervention date to the second deadliest fire in American history, the Coconut Grove fire in Boston in 1942, in which 493 people lost their lives. Eric Lindemann and his colleagues studied the relatives of the victims over time to document cases of acute and delayed grief reactions (Lindemann, 1944). The findings showed the importance of a mourning period, called "grief work," following a tragic loss. People who were able to undergo a period of mourning made a better adjustment than did those whose grief was delayed or denied (Roberts, 2005). This appeared to argue for timely intervention following a trauma so that feelings are not brushed aside or ignored. Lindemann's work was later adapted for use with WW II veterans who were suffering from what was then referred to as "combat neurosis" (Roberts, 2005). It was subsequently widely adopted by suicide hotlines, as well as rape and domestic violence crisis programs, and continues to be used with clients of all ages in a variety of problem situations (Parad & Parad, 1990). A 32-chapter *Crisis Intervention Handbook* (Roberts, 2005) demonstrates the broad application of this method with victims of natural disasters, various kinds of violence, medical conditions, drug abuse, and suicide in both individual and group formats.

Roberts's model of crisis intervention begins with an assessment and the establishment of a positive relationship, then moves to dealing with feelings and emotions, followed by exploration of alternatives and an action plan and later follow-up. Roberts says "effective crisis intervention should be active, directive, focused, and hopeful" (p. 157).

The use of crisis intervention play therapy with children facilitates their ability to deal with the emotions of the crisis by displacing and projecting them onto a toy or drawing, thereby decreasing their fears. According to Lenore Terr (1991), it is not necessary for the child to openly acknowledge the parallel between the play activity and his or her own life in order for it to be effective. However, most play therapists do look for ways to establish this connection without creating undue anxiety in the child.

Another therapy method for use with children after traumatic exposure, namely, trauma-focused cognitive behavior therapy (TF-CBT), has been referred to as a "hybrid model" (Cohen, Mannarino, & Deblinger, 2010), which also incorporates some methods similar to those of crisis intervention play therapy. This approach emphasizes the importance of play re-enactment of the stressful/traumatic experience, as well as the mental reworking or cognitive restructuring of the event. Rooted in the belief that it is crucial for the individual to be able to review his or her crisis/traumatic experience and develop a narrative about it, this verbal review involves repeated guided interactions in which the therapist directs the child to imagine and describe a different desired outcome to the stressful event. After teaching the child some relaxation skills the therapist then guides the child gently in giving details of what happened, including the "worst moment." Subsequent sessions encourage the child to process this experience with the goal of putting it in the wider context of the child's whole life, and to reframe it as "something bad that happened." This brings about a changed outlook regarding the experience. Conjoint parent-child sessions are held later in which the child shares the story and receives support from the parent. In summary, some specific methods in this cognitive approach include the use of calming and relaxation techniques, guided imagery, psycho-education, positive self-talk, and instruction that the child should rely on parents and other competent adults in dangerous situations. There is a complete discussion of this method in Cohen, Mannarino, Deblinger, & Berliner (2009).

DIRECTIVE VERSUS NONDIRECTIVE PLAY THERAPY

Often children (and adults) do not want to remember their frightening crisis experiences. Avoidance is typical following a crisis or traumatic event (American Psychiatric Association [APA], 2000), and the child's understandable reluctance to review anxiety-evoking memories presents a challenge to the therapist who knows that pushing worries away does not cause them to disappear. In fact, the prevailing practice wisdom recommends that for traumatic experiences to be resolved, some form of retrospective review is usually necessary. With directive, crisis/trauma-focused play therapy, a child can gradually process anxious feelings and learn methods to put them in the past so that they no longer hold center stage in the child's present emotional life. The key is to move at the child's pace and not insist that the child talk about the crisis before he or she is ready to do so. Crisis intervention play therapy consists of a mixture of cognitive-behavioral, supportive, and psychodynamic approaches. A primary goal is to help the child achieve an understanding that the crisis situation was in the past and is no longer a current source of threat in the child's present life.

THE ASSESSMENT PROCESS

It is essential for the social worker who is doing play therapy to take a history related to the child's reactions to the crisis/traumatic event. Although an extensive psychosocial history usually is not feasible because of the pressure of time, the worker needs to have a general sense of how the child was functioning prior to the crisis/trauma, as well as a description of the child's current symptomatic behaviors and how they are interfering with his/her current life.

There are three parts to any assessment of a symptomatic child. I refer to this as "the tripartite assessment" (Webb, 2007). The specific groups of factors in each part are:

- Factors related to the individual child
- Factors related to the support system
- Factors related to the nature of the traumatic or crisis event

The first set of data refers to the nature of the child's pre-crisis adjustment; the second part describes the nature of the surrounding environment; and the third set of data relates to the nature of the crisis/traumatic event itself. The play therapist must obtain pertinent information from the parents and other sources regarding these matters to establish appropriate treatment goals. Space does not permit full discussion of the assessment process here, and readers who wish more detailed information about using this assessment tool should consult Webb (2004, 2007, 2011).

SETTING GOALS

The focus of treatment following a crisis or trauma is to return the child to his or her pre-crisis adjustment. Sometimes the child actually becomes emotionally stronger after a crisis because he or she now identifies herself as a survivor. The treatment goals flow directly from the assessment. For example, if a child is waking up every night and going into the parents' room for comfort, the goal may be to help the child feel comfortable enough to stay in his or her own bed. It is important to involve the child in setting the goals to increase his or her willingness to achieve them. Depending on the child's age, it is often desirable to have the parent involved with the assessment process and also with the treatment, as will be illustrated in the case of Anna.

CASE EXAMPLE: ANNA

[NOTE: A brief discussion of this case appears in Webb (2003)]

This case illustrates the value of timely play therapy intervention following a traumatic event. Anna, age 5 years, became preoccupied and inattentive in school following a fire that caused a middle-of-the night evacuation from her apartment. She was waking every night, and during the day when at home she always wanted to be in her mother's presence. Although Anna, her parents, and her brother had been safely relocated to a new apartment, the child was disconsolate because she had lost her beloved stuffed bunny with which she used to sleep every night. Her mother did not comprehend the meaning and degree of her daughter's loss and Anna's need to mourn.

In play therapy over four sessions with the mother and child together, the therapist encouraged Anna to re-create her traumatic experience in drawing and in play with blocks and toy furniture. Typically, the play therapist tells the young child that she intends to help him or her with any troubles or worries and then invites the child to relate specific concerns either verbally or in play or drawings. The therapist may then ask the child to "show me what happened" with the puppets or dolls or in a drawing. During this process with Anna the therapist acknowledged the child's loss in her mother's presence, and validated the child's pain, thereby stimulating the mother's awareness of her child's grief. After four sessions, the child's symptoms of anxiety and accompanying school inattention resolved.

Specific Play Therapy Interventions

The play therapist began by telling Anna that she intended to help her with any troubles or worries and then invited Anna to relate specific concerns either verbally or in play. This conveyed to Anna that it was not necessary to talk. The play therapy with Anna consisted of several drawing and block play activities in which the child re-created the traumatic event and revealed her ongoing fears of the possibility of a fire in her new apartment.

Initially, the therapist asked Anna to draw a picture of her present room and after she had done so the therapist invited her to use blocks to duplicate this. As Anna created her room, using a toy bed and tiny bendable dolls she said "Behind the wall is the kitchen, and there is a fire in the stove." After questioning further and with the mother's in-put it became evident that Anna was referring to the pilot light in the stove, which she worried could cause a fire. Their previous apartment had had an electric stove so the pilot light was a new factor that was contributing to Anna's present fears. Both the mother and the therapist assured Anna that the light in the stove was "only for cooking" and that it would not spread and burn down this new apartment. In the first session the therapist invited Anna to draw a picture of her old apartment before the fire. Anna drew the apartment and spontaneously inserted a drawing of her bunny in the corner of the paper. The picture of the bunny was quite distorted, and as she drew it, Anna kept talking about how much she missed her bunny. In response to this, the mother said rather dismissively, "I'll get you a new bunny." The play therapist said in response that there will never be another bunny like the one Anna had before. Subsequent sessions included more block play and drawings; in the third session the therapist believed that Anna was sufficiently comfortable, so she asked her to draw a picture of her apartment in the fire. As the child did this she kept repeating her wish that they had been able to save her bunny. The therapist then suggested that Anna write a letter to her bunny stating her feelings. With Anna's permission the therapist wrote the child's message on the drawing. Her message was brief and said only "I love you and miss you." The therapist suggested that she add the word "good-bye" to help Anna realize that she would not see her bunny again. This activity seemed to have great meaning for Anna. Her mother reported in the next session that Anna had stopped her nighttime waking and was behaving more appropriately in school. At this point the therapist asked Anna to draw a picture of how she wants to remember her bunny now. Anna drew an intact bunny with a smile on its face, which was in sharp contrast to the disjointed drawing she had made before.

Obviously, a number of factors contributed to Anna's rapid alleviation of anxiety. First, there was clarification about the child's current safety once the reassurances about the "fire in the stove" were made. Secondly, the mother picked up from the therapist the need to acknowledge the pain of Anna's loss. Most importantly, the therapist acknowledged the child's feelings of sadness, which the mother had tended to dismiss. Finally, Anna was able to "say goodbye" to her bunny, thereby acknowledging that she will not see it again.

Treatment Goals

As previously stated, the focus of treatment following a crisis or trauma is to return the child to his or her precrisis adjustment. The ultimate goal of crisis intervention play therapy is for the child to gain some feeling of mastery over the crisis event or traumatic experience through the realization that it will no longer continue to impact his or her life. This appeared to happen in Anna's case, and she was able to return to her usual routine at school and at home after having said her farewells to her beloved bunny and having received acknowledgment from the therapist and her mother about her loss.

Specific Intervention Techniques

Play therapy methods cover a wide range of activities, including the following:

- **Art activities**—Including drawing, painting, and use of clay and Play-Doh®. See Malchiodi (2006) for more information about art therapy.
- **Doll play**—Using bendable family dolls, doll furniture, army dolls, rescue personnel, fantasy figures such as witches and fairies, stuffed animals, and dinosaurs. See Webb (2007) for cases involving the use of dolls in play therapy.
- **Puppet play**—With a variety of friendly and wild animals; family puppets; and worker puppets in the form of both hand puppets and finger puppets. Provision of several adult puppets and child puppets of the same species encourages displacement of family dynamics onto the toys. See Baggerly (2007) for an

illustration using puppet play with children following a natural disaster.

- **Storytelling**—Sometimes the therapist initiates this by beginning a story and asking the child to complete it. See Gil (1991) for examples.
- **Sand play**—This involves making scenes in a sandbox, using a variety of miniature toys. See Carey (2006) for an example of sand play therapy with a traumatized boy.
- **Board games**—These may be either specifically "therapeutic" games or regular games that the therapist selects because of themes that resemble the child's experience. See Schaefer and Reid (2001) for numerous examples of the use of board games in play therapy.

The assumption in the use of these materials is that the child identifies with the toy and projects and displaces his or her own feelings onto the play figures. The therapist's responses may include curiosity (so the child will give more details), or expression of feelings (so the child feels validated), or statements of closure and conclusion (so the child can put the experience behind him or her).

Research has not been able to produce definitive conclusions about whether directive or nondirective approaches bring more favorable results in therapy with symptomatic children following crisis or traumatic events. Shelby and Felix (2005) comment that throughout the history of child trauma therapy, there has been debate about how best to intervene. In view of the lack of agreement (and lack of conclusive empirical research findings), it seems understandable that few child therapists currently rely on either a *purely* directive or nondirective treatment approach. One can hope that future research will lend light on this important topic; until then, methods that combine both directive and nondirective treatment will continue to be used to relieve children's distress following crisis or traumatic experiences.

GUIDELINES FOR CRISIS INTERVENTION PLAY THERAPY

The following guidelines should be followed in providing this type of treatment.

- Obtain specialized training and participate in ongoing supervision.

- Conduct a brief assessment to determine the child's previous level of functioning.
- Establish a supportive therapeutic relationship with the child.
- Teach the child some relaxation methods to help keep anxiety in check.
- Provide toys or drawing materials to assist the child in re-creating the traumatic event.
- Move at the child's pace; do not attempt too much in one session.
- Emphasize the child's strength as a survivor.
- Repeat that the traumatic experience was in the *past*.
- Point out that the child is safe in the present.

CONCLUSION

Social workers who plan to do crisis intervention play therapy should be well grounded in child development, play therapy, trauma therapy, and grief counseling. All should seek ways to obtain ongoing support and supervision for themselves in order to avoid what has been called vicarious traumatization. This refers to the personal reactions of therapists who become overwhelmed and traumatized themselves in the course of their work with trauma survivors.

We know how to help traumatized children. It is most gratifying to observe a child's reduction of symptoms and return to precrisis functioning. This work, though very challenging, is also very rewarding and well worth the struggle to help children overcome and cast out the demons of fear that develop after crisis and traumatic experiences.

WEBSITES

Association for Play Therapy, Inc. www.a4pt.org
Child Trauma Academy. www.childtrauma.org
Childswork/childsplay. www.childcrafteducation .com
International Society for Traumatic Stress Studies. www.istss.org
National Institute for Trauma and Loss in Children. www. tlcinst.org
Play Therapy Training Institute. http://www .ptti.org.
Self-Esteem Shop. http://www.selfesteemshop .com.
Trauma-focused Cognitive Behavioral Therapy. www.musc.edu/tfcbt

University of North Texas Center for Play
Therapy. http://www.coe.unt.edu/cpt or
http://www.centerforplaytherapy.org.

References

American Psychiatric Association. (2000). *Diagnostic and statistical manual of mental disorders, fourth edition, text revision*. Washington, DC: Author.

Baggerly, J. (2007). International interventions and challenges following the crisis of natural disasters. In N. B. Webb (Ed.), *Play therapy with children in crisis. Individual, family, and group treatment* (3rd rev. ed.) (pp. 345–367). New York, NY: Guilford.

Brohl, K. (1996). *Working with traumatized children. A handbook for healing*. Washington, DC: Child Welfare League of America.

Carey, L. (2006). (Ed.). Sandplay therapy with a traumatized boy. In L. Carey (Ed.), *Expressive and creative arts methods for trauma survivors* (pp. 153–163). London: Jessica Kingsley.

Cohen, J. A., Mannarino, A. P., Deblinger, E., & Berliner, L. (2009). Cognitive-behavioral therapy for children and adolescents. In E. B. Foa, T, M, Keane, M. J. Friedman & J. A. Cohen (Eds.), *Effective treatments for PTSD* (2nd ed.) (pp. 223–244). New York, NY: Guilford.

Cohen, J. A., Mannarino, A. P., & Deblinger, E. (2010). Trauma-focused cognitive-behavioral therapy for traumatized children. In J. R. Weisz & A. E. Kazdin (Eds.), *Evidence-based psychotherapies for children and adolescents* (2nd. ed.) (pp. 295–311). New York, NY: Guilford.

Crenshaw, D. (2006). Neuroscience and trauma treatments. Implications for creative arts. In L. Carey (Ed.), *Expressive and creative arts methods for trauma survivors* (pp. 21–38). London: Kingsley.

Gil, E. (1991). *The healing power of play*. New York, NY: Guilford.

James, R. K., & Gillibrand, B. E. (2008). *Crisis intervention strategies*. Belmont, CA: Brooks/Cole.

Lindemann, E. (1944). Symptomatology and management of acute grief. *American Journal of Psychiatry, 101*, 141–148.

Malchiodi, C. (2006). *Art therapy sourcebook.* New York, NY: McGraw Hill.

Parad, H., & Parad, L. G. (Eds.). (1990). *Crisis intervention. Book 2*. Milwaukee, WI: Family Service America.

Reddy, L., Files-Hall, T., & Schaefer, C. (2005). *Announcing empirically based play interventions for children.* Washington, DC: American Psychological Association.

Roberts, A. R. (2005). (Ed.). *Crisis intervention handbook: Assessment, treatment, and research* (3rd ed.). New York, NY: Oxford University Press.

Schaefer, C. E., & Reid, S. E. (Eds.). (2001). *Game play* (2nd ed.). New York, NY: Wiley.

Shelby, J. S. (1997). Rubble, disruption, and tears: Helping young survivors of natural disaster. In H. G. Kaduson, D. Congelosi, & C. E. Schaefer (Eds.), *The playing cure: Individualized play therapy for specific childhood problems* (pp. 143–169). Northvale, NJ: Aronson.

Shelby, J. S., & Felix, E. D. (2005). Posttraumatic play therapy. The need for an integrated model of directive and nondirective approaches. In L. A. Reddy, T. M. Files-Hall, & C. E. Schaefer (Eds.), *Empirically-based interventions for children* (pp. 79–103). Washington, DC: American Psychological Association.

Terr, L. C. (1990). *Too scared to cry*. New York, NY: Harper & Row.

Terr, L. C. (1991). Childhood traumas. An outline and overview. *American Journal of Psychiatry, 148*(1), 10–20.

Webb, N. B. (1996). Social work practice with children. THE ANNA CASE: p. 139.

Webb, N. B. (Ed.). (2003). *Social work practice with children* (2nd rev. ed.). New York, NY: Guilford.

Webb, N. B. (Ed.). (2004). *Mass trauma and violence. Helping families and children cope*. New York, NY: Guilford.

Webb, N. B. (Ed.). (2007). *Play therapy with children in crisis. Individual, family, and group treatment* (3rd rev. ed.). New York, NY: Guilford.

Webb, N. B. (Ed.). (2011). *Social work practice with children* (3rd ed.). New York, NY: Guilford.

92   Social Skills Training and Child Therapy

Craig Winston LeCroy

An important part of the socialization of children can be facilitated by offering social skills training. Social skills therapy or classes teach prosocial skills that substitute for problem behaviors, such as aggression or withdrawal. Interpersonal skills can be taught to enhance communication with peers, parents, and authority figures. Stress management and coping skills can be taught to help prevent future problems. Numerous opportunities exist for the implementation of various skills-based programs that can help facilitate the successful socialization of children. For a unique gender-specific application with adolescent girls see LeCroy & Daley, 2001. Social skills training groups are frequently used in school settings to address a wide range of problem behaviors (LeCroy, 2013).

Research strongly suggests that social competence is essential for healthy normal development (Ashford & LeCroy, 2013). It is through a child's interactions with peers that many of life's necessary behaviors are acquired. For example, children learn sexual socialization, control of aggression, expression of emotion, and caring in friendship through their interaction with peers. When children fail to acquire such social skills, they are beset by problems such as inappropriate expression of anger, friendship difficulties, and inability to resist peer pressure. It is this understanding that has led to the present focus on changing children's interpersonal behavior with peers. Because many of a young person's problem behaviors develop in a social context, the teaching of social skills is one of the most promising approaches in remediating children's social difficulties.

DEFINING AND CONCEPTUALIZING SOCIAL SKILLS

Social skills can be defined as a complex set of skills that facilitate successful interactions between peers, parents, teachers, and other adults. The "social" refers to interactions between people; the "skills" refers to making appropriate discriminations, such as deciding what would be the most effective response and using the verbal and nonverbal behaviors that facilitate interaction (LeCroy, 2008).

Social skills training uses two key elements in addressing social adaptation of children: knowledge and skilled performance. In order to respond appropriately to situational demands a child must have knowledge of appropriate interpersonal behavior. However, that knowledge must be translated into skilled performance or social skills. Social skills training programs or therapy use methods to enhance a child's knowledge of social situations and enhance effective performance in those situations. An additional consideration is to plan for generalization so that any new skills learned are adaptable to different environments such as playgrounds, schools, and neighborhoods.

The conceptualization of social skills as training suggests that problem behaviors can be viewed as remediable deficits in a child's response repertoire (King & Kirschenbaum, 1992). This focuses on building prosocial responses or skills as opposed to an emphasis on the elimination of excessive antisocial responses. Children learn new options to problem situations. Learning how to respond effectively to new situations produces more positive consequences than past behaviors used in similar situations. This model focuses on the teaching of skills and competencies for day-to-day living rather than focusing on the understanding and elimination of defects. It is an optimistic view of children and is implemented in an educative remedial framework.

DEVELOPING PROGRAM OR THERAPY GOALS AND SELECTING SKILLS

Social skills training can be conducted as a program of skills using a group format or as a treatment plan for an individual child. The first step in the development of a successful social skills training program is to identify the goals of the program based on the needs of the target population or individual. What specific skills does the child need to learn? For example, a program goal for withdrawn children is to be able to initiate positive social interactions. Once the goals of the program are clearly defined, the next step is to select the specific skills that need to be learned.

For example, a 5-year-old boy is referred to a child therapy clinic. The teacher reported his behavior as "mean" and "sadistic," explained that he had no friends, and saw him as uncooperative. His mother reported he had engaged in numerous fights, described him as being uncooperative, and complained about the use of swearing and about noncompliance when directed to do things. In order to develop a social skills training therapy program for him, we will need to determine what constitutes the opposite of these negative behavior patterns. For example, he would benefit from learning the following types of skills: how to get along with others without fighting, frustration tolerance, and compliance. Learning how to translate problems into skills is an essential part of providing a skills-based model of treatment. Table 92.1 presents examples of how problems can be conceptualized as skills needed to learn.

After skills are selected for the treatment, the practitioner selects a method to promote acquisition of the skills. For example, common methods might include: behavior modification, use of supportive empathy, dramatic play, and storytelling. Also, group methods using behavioral rehearsal are popular methods for teaching social skills.

The process of social skills training requires continual attention to refining each skill that is to be taught. After identifying the broad social skills, it is important to divide each broad skill

into its component parts so that it can be more easily learned. For example, LeCroy (2008, p. 136) breaks down the skill "beginning a conversation" into six component parts:

1. Look the person in the eye and demonstrate appropriate body language.
2. Greet the person, saying one's own name.
3. Ask an open-ended question about the person. Listen attentively for the response.
4. Make a statement to follow up on the person's response.
5. Ask another open-ended question about the person. Listen attentively to the response.
6. Make another statement about the conversation.
7. End the conversation by letting the person you have to leave.

A classic social skills training study by Oden and Asher (1977) sought to improve the social skills and peer relationships of third and fourth grade children who were identified as not well liked by their peers. The social skills program taught the following four skills: participation, cooperation, communication, and validation/support. The intervention consisted of a five-week program whereby each skill was (1) described verbally, (2) explained with examples, (3) practiced using behavior rehearsal, and (4) refined through feedback, coaching, and reviews of progress. The results of this study found that the children increased their social skills and that they had improved more significantly than a group of elementary school children who did not participate in the program. Particularly impressive was the finding that the children showed gains in how their classmates rated them on play and peer acceptance at a one-year follow-up.

Guidelines for Using Social Skills Training Methods

After program goals are defined and skills are selected, various methods can be used for teaching social skills. These methods of influence are the ways in which the learning of such skills is promoted. There are three main methods of influence used in social skills training: (1) skills-based play therapy, (2) group-based social skills treatment, and (3) behavior modification. Many variations exist within these three main methods. For example, using reinforcement of selected skills during spontaneous play therapy sessions,

TABLE 92.1 Translating Problems into Skills

Problem	Skills
Withdrawn, moody, and irritable	Being aware of one's feelings
	Getting pleasure from interaction with others
	Controlling one's mood
	Doing more
Impulsive behavior	Complying with demands
"Acting out"	Concentrating, maintaining attention
	Following through, showing persistence
	Delaying gratification
Anxious, dependent behavior	Relaxing, putting one's body at ease
Separation difficulties	Separating from others
	Accepting disapproval of others
	Handling rejection
Feeling unloved, showing no	Getting pleasure from loving acts toward others
outside enjoyment in life, bored	Getting pleasure from exploration
	Anticipating pleasure and fun from activities
	Celebrating one's accomplishments and successes
	Accepting compliments from others
	Getting pleasure from positive attention
Substance abuse	Identifying problem situations
	Using effective refusal skills
	Making friends with non-using friends
	General problem solving for risky situations

eliciting stories from the child and using them to reinforce selected skills, conducting spontaneous mutual dramatic play that focuses on selected skills, using conversation and fantasies as a means of rehearsal and reinforcement of skills, and playing games designed to teach social skills (LeCroy & Archer, 2001). For this chapter, two of the main methods are described: skills-based play therapy and group-based social skills treatment.

SKILLS-BASED PLAY THERAPY

Although play therapy is often associated with more dynamic approaches to treatment, it can be an excellent method for teaching social skills. However, rather than a focus on the catharsis of feelings in play therapy, the focus is on learning new skills to address problematic feelings. In skills-based play therapy this is accomplished by using scripted modeling plays, reading stories

that model skills, encouraging selected skills from the child's spontaneous play, and designing plays and stories that are specific to the child's needs.

A primary method is the use of dramatic play where the practitioner models the skills the child needs to learn through manipulating play material. It is important to provide multiple opportunities to practice skillful patterns of behavior. This is accomplished by conducting modeling "plays" that allow the child to experience the skill being demonstrated vicariously through the play.

When conducting plays or designing stories (as described below) practitioners should follow the basic principles established in modeling theory. Strayhorn (1988) summarizes the principles concisely.

1. Use multiple characters to provide exposure to multiple models.
2. Have a role model experience reinforcing consequences of his or her action.

3. Design a character who is seen as desirable and appropriate to the cultural context.
4. Use a coping model whereby the character struggles some but then overcomes those initial difficulties.
5. Use characters who engage in self talk demonstrating good coping skills.

In this way, skills-based play therapy is very goal-directed play, which can be linked directly to the skills needed to be learned by the child. For example, a sample modeling play like the following might be performed for the child.

Sample modeling play. This play is designed for a child who is having difficulty sharing and ends up fighting with other children over what to do. The social worker would need to set the play scene: This example uses a play about two boys and how they share when one boy comes over to the other boy's house. A wind-up toy is used as the object that the boys will share. Prior to conducting this play, make sure the child has seen the toy so he is not preoccupied with learning about the toy. Materials needed for the play include two boy action figures and one wind-up toy. The social worker begins by focusing the child's attention on the play, "I'm going to put on a play; you watch and then after I'm done you can play with these toys."

Parent: I'm glad you could come over to play Robert! I have something you two might like to play with.

Robert: What is it?

Skyler: Yea, mom what did you get?

Parent: It's a Godzilla gorilla that spits fire when you wind it up!

Robert: Wow, let me see.

Skyler: I want to wind it up, let me wind it up.

Skyler: I know, Robert. Would you like to take turns?

Robert: OK, you can do it first, but then I get to do it right after.

Parent: Great sharing Skyler; I like how you worked out a good way to share with Robert.

Skyler: Thanks Mom. Robert was really nice to let me play with it first. Look! I'm winding it up, look at the fire! (Sparks come out of its mouth)

Robert: Wow! That is really cool.

Skyler: OK, now it's your turn, Robert.

Robert: Thanks, Skyler. I'll wind it up again. Look, fire is coming out everywhere. OK, it's your turn again, Skyler.

Skyler: Thank you (takes the toy and begins winding it up again).

Parent: (re-enters the room) You two are doing a great job sharing and playing together. Can I get you a snack?

When conducting plays like the one above, the practitioner should have play material to enact the different scenes; for example, action figures (a dad, mom, and several children), a house, a play yard, play equipment, a school bus, and miniature toy items like food, televisions, and computers. The play is conducted with great animation, figures are picked up when talking, and used in a puppet-like fashion. Different characters have different voices and the action sequence is fast, matching the attention span of the particular child. After conducting a modeling play, many children will immediately imitate the play, "rehearsing" the skills that the practitioner is trying to teach the child.

STORYTELLING: MODELING SKILLS THROUGH READING

An additional method for teaching children social skills is the careful design or selection of stories that model the desired skills. Young children are drawn to storytelling and stories can be used to demonstrate and model skills they need to learn.

For example, if a target skill is anger management, a story can be constructed where the main character gets frustrated but does not get angry. Another character can provide reinforcement and support, "You just walked away and did not get angry—that's a great skill." Or if the target skill is friendship abilities, the story might enact a scene where the target child joins the play of others. For example, "Hi guys, looks like a great soccer game. I'd like to play, too." This character also says to himself, "I'm glad I asked to play soccer with those guys. It's a lot more fun."

The process of using skills-based storytelling can take several venues. First, stories can be told or read to children in play therapy sessions. This provides good variation to the additional methods that should be used in individual sessions with children. Stories can also be given to parents to read to the child. The goal should be many repeated exposures of the stories—children like familiar stories and each repetition provides increased vicarious learning of desired skills.

Group Based Social Skills Treatment

Social skills training is often conducted in a group format, which provides support and a reinforcing context for learning new responses and appropriate behaviors in a variety of social situations. The group is a natural context for social skills training because of the peer interactions that take place as the group members work together. Additionally, the group allows for extensive use of modeling and feedback that are critical components of successful skills training.

The following seven basic steps delineate the process that group leaders can follow when conducting social skills training (based on LeCroy, 2008). These guidelines were developed for social skills groups with middle school students. Table 92.2 presents these steps and outlines the process for teaching social skills. In each step there is a request for group member involvement. This is because it is critical that group leaders involve the participants actively in the skill training. Also, this keeps the group interesting and fun for the group members.

1. Present the social skill being taught. The first step for the group leader is to present the skill. The leader solicits an explanation of the skill, for example, "Can anyone tell me what it means to resist peer pressure?" After group members have answered this question, the leader emphasizes the rationale for using the skill. For example, "You would use this skill when you're in a situation where you don't want to do something that your friends want you to do and you should be able to say 'no' in a way that helps your friends to be able to accept your refusal." The leader then requests additional reasons for learning the skill.

2. Discuss the social skills. The leader presents the specific skill steps that constitute the social skill. For example, the skill steps for resisting peer pressure are: good nonverbal communication (includes eye contact, posture, voice volume), saying "no" early in the interaction, suggesting an alternative activity, and leaving the situation if there is continued pressure. Leaders then ask group members to share examples of when they used the skill or examples of when they could have used the skill but did not.

3. Present a problem situation and model the skill. The leader presents a problem situation. For example, the following is a problem situation for resisting peer pressure:

After seeing a movie, your friends suggest that you go with them to the mall. It is 10:45 and you are supposed to be home by 11:00. It is important that you get home by 11:00 or you will not be able to go out next weekend.

The group leader chooses members to role play this situation and then models the skills. Group members evaluate the model's performance. Did the model follow all the skill steps? Was his or her performance successful? The group leader may choose another group member to model if the leader believes the group member already has the requisite skills. Another alternative is to present videotaped models to the group. This has the advantage of following the recommendation

TABLE 92.2 A Summary of the Steps in Teaching Social Skills Training

1. Present the social skills being taught
   A. Solicit an explanation of the skill
   B. Get group members to provide rationales for the skill
2. Discuss the social skill
   A. List the skill steps
   B. Get group members to give examples of using the skill
3. Present a problem situation and model the skill
   A. Evaluate the performance
   B. Get group members to discuss the model
4. Set the stage for role playing the skill
   A. Select the group members for role playing
   B. Get group members to observe the role play
5. Group members rehearse the skill
   A. Provide coaching if necessary
   B. Get group members to provide feedback on verbal and nonverbal elements
6. Practice using complex skill situations
   A. Teach accessory skills (e.g., problem solving)
   B. Get group members to discuss situations and provide feedback
7. Train for generalization and maintenance
   A. Encourage practice of skills outside the group
   B. Get group members to bring in their problem situations.

by researchers that the models be similar to the trainee in age, sex, and social characteristics.

4. Set the stage for role playing of the skill. For this step the group leader needs to construct the social circumstances for the role play. Leaders select group members for the role play and give them their parts to play. The leader reviews with the role players how to act out their role. Group members not in the role play observe the process. It is sometimes helpful if they are given specific instructions for their observations. For example, one member may observe the use of nonverbal skills, another member may be instructed to observe when "no" is said in the interaction.

5. Group members rehearse the skill. Rehearsal or guided practice of the skill is an important part of effective social skills training. Group leaders and group members provide instructions or coaching before and during the role play and provide praise and feedback for improvement. Following a role play rehearsal the leader usually will give instructions for improvement, model the suggested improvements, or coach the person to incorporate the feedback in the subsequent role play. Often the group members doing the role play will practice the skills in the situation several times to refine their skills and incorporate feedback offered by the group. The role plays continue until the trainee's behavior becomes more and more similar to that of the model. It is important that "overlearning" take place, so the group leader should encourage many examples of effective skill demonstration followed by praise. Group members should be taught how to give effective feedback before the rehearsals. Throughout the teaching process the group leader can model desired responses. For example, after a role play the leader can respond first and model feedback that starts with a positive statement.

6. Practice using complex skill situations. The last phase deals with more difficult and complex skill situations. Complex situations can be developed by extending the interactions and roles in the problem situations. Most social skills groups also incorporate the teaching of problem solving abilities. Problem solving is a general approach to helping young people to gather information about a problematic situation, generate a large number of potential solutions, evaluate the consequences of various solutions, and outline plans for the implementation of a particular solution. Group leaders can identify appropriate problem situations and lead members through the above steps. The problem-solving training is important because it prepares young people to make adjustments as needed in a given situation. It is a general skill with large scale application. (For a more complete discussion on the use of problem solving approaches, see Gresham, 2002).

7. Train for generalization and maintenance. The success of the social skills program depends on the extent to which the skills young people learn transfer to their day-to-day lives. Practitioners must always be planning for ways to maximize the generalization of skills learned and promote their continued use after training. Several principles help facilitate the generalization and maintenance of skills. The first is the use of overlearning. The more overlearning that takes place, the greater the likelihood of later transfer of skills. Therefore, it is important that group leaders insist on mastery of the skills. Another important principle of generalization is to vary the stimuli as skills are learned. To accomplish this, practitioners can use a variety of models, problem situations, role play actors, and trainers. The various styles and behaviors of the people used produces a broader context in which to apply the skills learned. Perhaps most important is to require that young people use the skills in their real life settings. Group leaders should assign and monitor homework to encourage transfer of learning. This may include the use of written contracts to do certain tasks outside of the group. Group members should be asked to bring to the group examples of problem situations where the social skills can be applied. Lastly, practitioners should attempt to develop external support for the skills learned. One approach to this is to set up a buddy system where group members work together to perform the skills learned outside the group.

SUMMARY

As social workers work toward the goal of enhancing the socialization process of children, methods for promoting social competence, such as social skills training, have much to offer. Social workers can make an important contribution to children, families, and schools through preventive and remedial approaches like those described in this chapter. As we have seen, children's social behavior is a critical aspect of successful adaptation in society. The strategy of social skills training provides a clear methodology for providing remedial and preventive services to children. This direct approach to working with children has been applied in numerous problem areas and with many child behavior problems. It is straightforward in application and has been adapted so that social workers, teachers, and peer helpers have successfully applied the methodology. It can be applied in individual, group, or classroom settings. Research supports the efficacy of social skills training; it is perhaps the most promising new treatment model developed for working with children and adolescents.

WEBSITES

Manuals, www.nrepp.samsha.gov/
ViewIntervention.aspx?id = 256
www.Socialskillstrainingproject.com
Peer based, www.semel.ucla.edu/peers
Group based, www.ucdmc.ucdavis.edu/
mindinsititue/clinic/Social_skills/index

References and Readings

Ashford, J. B., & LeCroy, C. W. (2013). *Human behavior and the social environment: A multidimensional perspective*. Pacific Grove, CA: Cengage.

Gresham, F. M. (2002). Best practices in social skills training. In A. Thomas & J. Grimes (Eds.), *Best practices in school psychology* (4th ed.) (pp. 143–170). Bethesda, MD: National Association of School Psychologists.

King, C. A., & Kirschenbaum, D. S. (1992). *Helping young children develop social skills*. Pacific Grove, CA: Brooks/Cole.

LeCroy, C. W. (2013). Designing and facilitating groups with children. In C. Franklin, M. B. Harris, & P. Allen-Meares (Eds.), *The school services handbook: A guide for school-based professionals* (pp. 611–618). New York, NY: Oxford University Press.

LeCroy, C. W. (2008). *Handbook of evidence-based child and adolescent treatment manuals*. New York, NY: Oxford University Press.

LeCroy, C. W., & Archer, J. (2001). Teaching social skills: A board game approach. In C. Schaefer & S. E. Reid (Eds.), *Game play: Therapeutic use of childhood games*. New York, NY: John Wiley.

LeCroy, C. W., & Daley, J. (2001). *Empowering adolescent girls: Examining the present and building skills for the future with the Go Girls program*. New York, NY: W.W. Norton.

Oden, S., & Asher, S. R. (1997). Coaching children in social skills for friendship making. *Child Development, 48*, 495–506.

Strayhorn, J. M. (1988). *The competent child*. New York, NY: Guilford Press.

93 Guidelines for Chemical Abuse and Dependency Screening, Diagnosis, Treatment, and Recovery

Diana M. DiNitto & C. Aaron McNeece

Nearly 15% of English-speaking household residents of the United States aged 18 years and older have met the criteria for a substance (alcohol or drug) use disorder during their lifetime (Kessler et al., 2005). Nearly 9% of U.S. household residents aged 12 years and older met these criteria in the past year (Substance Abuse and Mental Health Services Administration [SAMHSA] (2011). Others do not meet these diagnostic criteria but use alcohol or drugs in risky or harmful ways. Tobacco use is also prevalent. Approximately 27% of U.S. household residents aged 12 years and older used a tobacco product in the last month (SAMHSA). Social workers need knowledge of these problems because they work in many settings that serve people who have alcohol and drug problems.

The major categories of drugs of abuse are (1) central nervous system (CNS) depressants, such as alcohol, barbiturates, methaqualone, benzodiazepines, and inhalants; (2) CNS stimulants, such as cocaine and amphetamines; (3) opioids or narcotics, such as heroin, morphine, and codeine; (4) hallucinogens, such as LSD, PCP, psilocybin, mescaline, and peyote; (5) cannabis or marijuana; (6) anabolic steroids used to build muscles and improve appearance; (7) tobacco (nicotine); and (8) various over-the-counter drugs used to treat insomnia, coughs, colds, and other maladies, including some herbal preparations and dietary supplements intended to increase energy, sexual performance, appearance, or provide other effects. New substances or designer drugs that can be abused often become available. The National Institute on Drug Abuse (NIDA) and the Drug Enforcement Administration continually update their websites on drugs of abuse.

The causes of alcohol and drug problems have been widely debated. There is growing evidence that genetic and brain chemistry factors are involved (Wilcox & Erickson, 2005). There is also evidence that social and environmental factors influence substance abuse and dependence (McNeece & DiNitto, 2012).

SCREENING

A number of quickly and easily administered and scored instruments are available for social workers to use in screening individuals for alcohol and drug problems. Instruments may be self-administered (i.e., the client answers questions using pen and paper or on a computer) or the social worker administers the instrument by asking the client questions. Among the brief screening instruments most commonly used with adults are the:

- CAGE (the four-item CAGE is one of the briefest tools)
- Michigan Alcoholism Screening Test (MAST)
- Drug Abuse Screening Test (DAST)

- Alcohol Use Disorders Identification Test (AUDIT) (available in many languages)
- Substance Abuse Subtle Screening Inventory (SASSI).

Selection of screening devices and the method used to administer them should be based on the clientele served (e.g., age, reading level). Some screening instruments have been developed specifically for use with adolescents, such as the Problem Oriented Screening Instrument for Teens and the adolescent version of the SASSI, or with older adults, such as the MAST-Geriatric. The T-ACE and the TWEAK were developed for use in screening for risk drinking during pregnancy. Allen and Wilson (2003) contains many of the aforementioned instruments, as well as other instruments for screening, diagnosis, assessment, treatment planning, and measuring outcomes, including descriptive, psychometric, and copyright information and sources for obtaining the instruments. The SAMHSA-Health Resources and Services Administration (HRSA) Center for Integrated Services website also provides a page on screening tools. Winters (1999) provides information on screening adolescents for substance use problems. Though some instruments have undergone psychometric testing with members of various racial, ethnic, and cultural groups, the field lacks instruments that may improve screening among specific racial, ethnic, and cultural groups. An exception is the Drug and Alcohol Assessment for the Deaf, which was developed and tested in American Sign Language (available through the South Southwest Addiction Technology Transfer Center).

Screening has been increasingly used in health settings to identify individuals who drink at risk levels. Risk may be defined for men under age 65 years as no more than four drinks on any day *and* no more than 14 drinks in a week ("Rethinking Drinking," n.d.). Risk may occur at lower levels if an individual has health or other risk factors. Because women tend to metabolize alcohol more slowly than men and may experience alcohol-related problems at lower drinking levels than men, limits for women are lower— no more than three drinks per day *and* no more than seven per week. Because alcohol metabolism slows with age, everyone aged 65 years and older is advised to observe these lower levels.

Evidence-based brief interventions can help individuals who drink at risk levels cut down or stop drinking. These short education, advice, or counseling interventions can be delivered in sessions as short as a few minutes ("Brief Interventions," 2005).

DIAGNOSIS

Screening is often the first step in the assessment process, but it does not substitute for a diagnostic evaluation made by a qualified clinician such as a social worker. The *Diagnostic and Statistical Manual of Mental Disorders* (DSM) (American Psychiatric Association, 2013), used extensively in the United States, contains criteria for two major categories of substance-related disorders—substance-induced disorders and substance use disorders.

- Substance-induced disorders include intoxication, withdrawal, and substance-induced mental disorders (psychotic, bipolar, depressive, anxiety, obsessive-compulsive, sleep, sexual, delirium, and neurocognitive) that result from intoxication or withdrawal from abused substances. Medication (prescribed or over-the-counter)-induced mental disorders result from use at suggested doses. Substance/medication-induced mental disorders usually resolve within a month of cessation or withdrawal but may persist. In crisis situations, it can be difficult to distinguish whether alcohol, other drugs, or other factors are the cause of these mental disorders. Diagnoses can also be difficult to make because some people have more than one substance use disorder or they have both mental *and* substance use disorders (Kessler, Chiu, Demler, Merikangas, & Walters, 2005).
- Substance use disorders are "a problematic pattern of" substance "use leading to clinically significant impairment or distress" (APA, 2013, [see, for example, p. 490]). This diagnosis generally requires that at least 2 of the following 11 criteria have occurred within a 12-month period:
  1. Using greater amounts than intended
  2. Continued desire or unsuccessful attempts to control use
  3. Spending substantial time getting, using, or recovering from the substance
  4. Craving or strong desire to use the substance
  5. Recurrent failure to meet major responsibilities due to substance use
  6. Recurring social/interpersonal problems due to substance use
  7. Curtailing work or other important activities due to substance use
  8. Continued use in physically hazardous situations
  9. Continued use despite related physical and/or psychological problem(s)
  10. Tolerance (The same amount of the substance produces less of an effect or more of the substance is needed to produce the desired effect.)
  11. Withdrawal (The signs or symptoms of the substance's withdrawal syndrome occur or the substance or a closely related one is used to prevent or relieve withdrawal.) This criterion is not present for every drug class (e.g., hallucinogens, inhalants).

A substance use disorder is "mild" if two or three symptoms are present, "moderate" if four to five are present, and "severe" if six or more are present. Specifiers are "early remission" if no criteria are met for at least 3 months but less than 12 months, and "sustained remission" if no criteria have been met for at least 12 months. However, an individual may meet the craving or desire criterion and still be in early or sustained remission. Other specifiers indicate whether an individual has restricted substance access (e.g., they are in jail or locked inpatient treatment), and for some substances, whether the individual is on maintenance therapy (medications to prevent substance use).

With release of the DSM's fifth edition in 2013 (APA, 2013), tools are becoming available to help clinicians apply the revised criteria for substance-related disorders (e.g., Nussbaum, 2013). Clinicians are more confident in their diagnoses of substance use disorders when they have multiple sources of information on which to rely, such as a diagnostic interview, laboratory tests, and information from collateral sources (e.g., family members, other professionals, and client records).

Screening and diagnosis are best done (Skinner, 1984) when the:

- Client is alcohol- and drug-free and mentally stable
- Person doing the assessment builds rapport with the client
- Client knows that corroborating information will be used

- Client is assured of confidentiality.

In many cases, drug courts, probation or parole officers, or child protective service agencies refer clients to qualified professionals expressly to determine the existence of a substance abuse or dependence problem and the need for intervention. Though these clients may be under duress, they often consent to release of information (i.e., waive confidentiality and allow the information to be released) to the referring agency.

ASSESSMENT

The Addiction Severity Index (ASI) is a widely used standardized instrument for conducting assessments of adults with substance use disorders. (Allen and Wilson [2003] describe this and other assessment tools.) The ASI contains seven domains: medical, employment, alcohol, drug, legal, family/social, and psychiatric, which provide substantial social history information. This type of multidimensional assessment is consistent with social workers' bio-psychosocial perspective. The ASI includes three types of scores (composite scores based on answers to several questions, interviewer-rated severity scores, and client-rated severity scores) that indicate the extent of the clients' problems in each of the seven domains.

Social workers are generally well versed in taking social histories. Because most do not work in chemical dependency treatment programs but encounter clients with these problems, McNeece and DiNitto (2012) provide information and a guide for taking clients' social history in cases where information on alcohol and drug problems is needed. This book is also a basic text on chemical dependency for social workers and other helping professionals and contains information on treatment and on populations such as women, adolescents, older adults, members of minority racial and ethnic groups, people with mental and physical disabilities, and gay, lesbian, bisexual, and transgender persons. The social history guide addresses 10 areas: education, employment, military history (if applicable), medical history, drinking and drug use, psychological or psychiatric history, legal involvement (if applicable), family history, relationships with significant others, and reasons the individual is seeking help. As with diagnosis, assessment can be facilitated when multiple sources of information are available.

TREATMENT PLANNING

Once the nature of the client's substance abuse or dependence and related problems is understood, treatment planning may begin. The American Society of Addiction Medicine (ASAM) (Mee-Lee, 2013) publishes a guide for treatment planning in the chemical dependency field. The placement criteria are in the form of a two-dimensional crosswalk. One dimension of the adult admission crosswalk contains five levels of care that form a continuum:

1. Early intervention
2. Outpatient services
3. Intensive outpatient/partial hospitalization services
4. Residential/inpatient services
5. Medically managed intensive inpatient services.

The second dimension contains six factors that suggest the level of recommended care:

1. Acute intoxication and/or withdrawal
2. Biomedical conditions and complications
3. Emotional, behavioral, or cognitive conditions and complications
4. Readiness to change
5. Relapse, continued use, or continued problem potential
6. The individual's "recovery environment."

The crosswalk makes it clear that treatment should be based on the individual client's needs.

A client's readiness for change, and the services needed based on this level of readiness, is often assessed using the transtheoretical model (TTM) of change (Prochaska, DiClemente, & Norcross, 1992). The TTM is also an approach to delineating the stages an individual goes through in changing a behavior like alcohol or drug abuse or dependence. This change process has been conceptualized in five stages (Prochaska et al., 1992; DiClemente, 2003):

1. Precontemplation (individual is unaware a problem exists)
2. Contemplation (individual becomes aware of problem and starts to think about making changes)
3. Preparation (individual intends to make changes soon)

4. Action (individual successfully changes his or her situation)
5. Maintenance (individual makes continued changes to avoid relapse).

The stages do not necessarily progress in a linear fashion. People may relapse and return to some earlier stage in the change process, necessitating a change in treatment or service approaches that will help them move forward.

EVIDENCE-BASED TREATMENT

The ASAM crosswalk indicates that several modalities are used in treating alcohol and other drug problems. Among the residential services clients may need are therapeutic communities and halfway houses, which vary in their level of client supervision and monitoring and in the length of stay allowed. Insurance-supported treatment for many people has become briefer, and long stays in intensive inpatient treatment programs are rare. Most clients receive outpatient services.

The literature often discusses treatment for alcohol problems separately from treatment for other drug problems even though these problems often co-occur. Historically, approaches for addressing alcohol problems and other drug problems developed separately. The U.S. Department of Health and Human Services (DHHS), National Institutes of Health houses the National Institute on Alcohol Abuse and Alcoholism (NIAAA) and NIDA, which cooperate with each other and fund treatment studies. SAMHSA, another DHHS agency, works to improve treatment quality and availability.

NIDA (2012a) describes principles of effective drug addiction treatment.

- No single treatment is appropriate for all individuals.
- Treatment should be readily available.
- Effective treatment should address the individual's multiple needs.
- Remaining in treatment for a sufficient time is essential.
- The most common treatments are individual and group counseling and other behavioral therapies.
- Medications can be an important treatment component.
- Continual assessment and modification (when needed) of an individual's treatment/service plan is necessary.

- Individuals who have substance use disorders and coexisting mental disorders should receive treatment for both.
- Medical detoxification is generally the first treatment stage (alone it is unlikely to change long-term drug disorders).
- Treatment does not have to be voluntary to be effective.
- To prevent relapse, possible drug use during treatment must be monitored continuously.
- Treatment programs should provide assessment for infectious diseases and counseling to change risk behaviors.

Many approaches, including medications (pharmacotherapies), have been used to treat alcohol or other drug problems. The evidence-based practices social workers use usually have a cognitive and/or behavioral basis. Some of the evidence-based approaches to alcohol and drug addiction treatment for adults NIDA (2012a) has identified are:

Cognitive-behavioral therapy is based on the theory that learning processes play a critical role in the development of maladaptive behaviors such as drug abuse. Treatment techniques include exploring the consequences of continued drug abuse and self-monitoring to recognize cravings and how to address them.

Contingency management interventions/motivational incentives (CM) principles involve giving tangible rewards to reinforce positive behaviors such as abstinence. CM includes the use of vouchers and other "prize" incentives.

Community Reinforcement Approach plus vouchers uses a variety of recreational, familial, social, and vocational reinforcers, along with material incentives, to make a drug-free lifestyle more rewarding than substance use.

Motivational Enhancement Therapy uses motivational interviewing principles to strengthen motivation and build a plan for change. Coping strategies for high-risk situations are suggested and discussed with the client.

The Matrix Model helps clients learn about issues critical to addiction and relapse, receive direction and support from a trained therapist, and become informed about self-help programs. Clients are monitored for drug use through urine testing.

12-Step Facilitation Therapy is an active engagement strategy designed to increase the likelihood that a substance abuser will become involved in 12-step mutual-help groups. The key principles are acceptance, surrender, and active 12-step recovery group participation.

Family Behavior Therapy involves the client and at least one family member in applying behavioral strategies to improve the home environment. It combines behavioral contracting with contingency management. Clients are involved in treatment planning and choosing specific intervention strategies.

The evidence-based behavioral therapies primarily used with adolescents that NIDA (2012a) has identified include Multisystemic Therapy and Multidimensional Family Therapy. Both target interactions within the family and the relationships between the client, the family, and external networks, such as schools, peers, and the neighborhood.

NIDA (2012a) provides more information about these treatment modalities for adults and adolescents. The Cochrane Collaboration and the Campbell Collaboration provide systematic reviews of specific treatment approaches. Social workers will also find the SAMHSA National Registry of Evidence-based Programs and Practices helpful. Notable themes among efficacious treatments appear to be a focus on building clients' skills and self-efficacy, increasing motivation, and inclusion of significant others (Miller & Wilbourne, 2002). Although evidence supports the inclusion of significant others in promoting and sustaining recovery, treatment programs may pay insufficient attention to doing so, perhaps due to funding constraints. Assisting families is a strong suit of social workers. Family members need education and counseling to help them cope, whether or not the individual with the substance use disorder desires help.

MEDICATION-ASSISTED TREATMENT (PHARMACOTHERAPIES)

Another evidence-based approach to substance dependence treatment is medication, generally used as an adjunct to cognitive/behavioral (also called psychosocial) treatment. A few medications have been approved for longer-term opioid,

alcohol, and tobacco use disorder treatment. No medications have yet been approved for treating stimulant (e.g., cocaine, amphetamine) use disorders. Social workers may work with clients taking these medications. They may also refer clients to physicians who can help the client consider whether such medications may be helpful to them.

Opioid Treatment

Methadone, a long-acting synthetic opioid agonist medication, has long been used in preventing withdrawal symptoms and reducing craving in individuals addicted to opioids. It is taken orally and can also block the effects of opioids. Buprenorphine is a synthetic opioid medication that acts as a partial agonist for other opioids. It does not produce the euphoria and sedation caused by illicit opioids and can reduce or eliminate withdrawal symptoms associated with opioid dependence. Naltrexone, a synthetic opioid antagonist approved for treating opioid addiction, prevents the euphoric effects of illicit opioids, and has been used for many years to reverse opioid overdose.

Tobacco Treatment

The commonly used nicotine replacement therapies (NRTs) include the transdermal nicotine patch, nicotine spray, nicotine gum, and nicotine lozenges. Bupropion, originally marketed as an antidepressant (Wellbutrin), produces mild stimulant effects by blocking the reuptake of certain neurotransmitters. Some patients who were prescribed bupropion for depression reported that the medication was also effective in suppressing tobacco craving. Varenicline, the most recently FDA-approved medication for smoking cessation, acts as a partial agonist/antagonist on nicotinic receptors in the brain thought to be involved in the rewarding effects of nicotine.

Because tobacco use is a major cause of cancer, heart disease, bronchitis, emphysema, and stroke and is a common cause of preventable death, social workers should be available to assist clients with effective smoking cessation treatments such as cognitive behavioral therapy (NIDA, 2012a) and self-help or mutual help programs such as telephone "quit lines" and the Quit for Life program (NIDA, 2012b).

Alcohol Treatment

Naltrexone blocks opioid receptors that produce the rewarding effects of drinking and the craving for alcohol. For some problem-drinkers it may reduce the chance of relapse. An extended-release injectable version, Vivitrol, is also FDA-approved for treating alcoholism, and increases patient compliance. Acamprosate does not prevent the immediate withdrawal symptoms people may experience when they stop drinking alcohol, but it acts on certain neurotransmitter systems to reduce symptoms of protracted withdrawal (e.g., insomnia, anxiety, restlessness, and dysphoria). It helps the brain work normally after an individual has drunk a large amount of alcohol. It may be more effective than other medications for patients with severe dependence. Acamprosate is used (with counseling and social support) to help people who have stopped drinking large amounts of alcohol to avoid drinking alcohol again. Disulfiram (Antabuse) use results in the accumulation of acetaldehyde, which produces extremely unpleasant reactions (flushing, nausea, and palpitations) if alcohol is ingested. Disulfiram's effectiveness is considered limited because compliance is often poor, but it can be useful for highly motivated patients. Some use it effectively for high-risk situations (e.g., social occasions where alcohol is served).

12-STEP PROGRAMS AND OTHER MUTUAL-HELP RESOURCES

The first 12-step program was Alcoholics Anonymous (AA). Similar groups developed to help people with other drug problems, such as Narcotics Anonymous (NA) and Cocaine Anonymous (CA). They are considered spiritual programs, though agnostics and atheists have recovered in them. These programs offer a wealth of literature through their national offices and websites, including information directed to professionals.

Groups such as AA and NA have "open" meetings to help family members of people with alcohol and drug disorders, helping professionals, and other interested individuals learn about them. These groups are usually listed in local phone directories and online and can be contacted for information on attending meetings. The groups are often different than what visitors (and new members) imagine they will be. Professionals should be knowledgeable about them in order to help clients consider their suitability for helping them in the recovery process. Participation in mutual-help groups is fully compatible with professional treatment and can be an especially good source of aftercare. Others may not utilize professional treatment and use these groups as their primary recovery resource.

The 12-step program for family members and friends of alcoholics is Al-Anon and for families and friends of addicts is Nar-Anon. Groups for children and adolescents are Ala-tot and Alateen (contact information is the same as for Al-Anon). Other groups for family members have emerged such as Adult Children of Alcoholics groups.

Other mutual-help programs for those recovering from alcohol and drug problems are SOS, an alternative to the spiritual programs, and Women for Sobriety, dedicated to empowerment and other aspects of women's recovery.

OUTCOME MEASURES

Measuring individual client outcomes in clinical practice is often done informally, but tools specific to the substance abuse and dependency treatment field can be used to assist with this task. Allen and Wilson (2003) contain many of them (along with tools for measuring agency- or program-level outcomes). For example, the ASI has a follow-up version that can be used to measure client outcomes following treatment, and the Drinker Inventory of Consequences (DrInC) can also be used in treatment planning and in evaluating treatment outcomes. Several chapters in this volume focus on measuring and evaluating outcomes in health and mental health settings.

WEBSITES

AA World Services. http://www.aa.org.
Al-Anon Family Groups. http://al-anon.alateen .org.
Alcohol, Tobacco, and Other Drug section of the National Association of Social Workers, with benefits such as a newsletter and continuing education. http://www.naswdc.org/sections/default.asp.
Cochrane Collaboration. http://www.cochrane .org

Campbell Collaboration. http://www
.campbellcollaboration.org

Drug Enforcement Administration, especially its
page on drugs of abuse. http://www.justice
.gov/dea/druginfo/factsheets.shtml

Nar-Anon Family Group Headquarters. http://
www.nar-anon.org.

Narcotics Anonymous World Services. http://
www.na.org.

National Institute on Alcohol Abuse and
Alcoholism. http://www.niaaa.nih.gov.

National Institute on Drug Abuse. http://
www.drugabuse.gov. The NIDA website on
drugs of abuse: http://www.drugabuse.gov/
drugs-abuse

SOS. http://www.sossobriety.org.

Substance Abuse and Mental Health Services
Administration (SAMHSA). http://www
.samhsa.gov SAMHSA includes the Center
for Substance Abuse Prevention (CSAP) and
the Center for Substance Treatment (CSAT).
CSAT's Treatment Improvement Protocols,
Technical Assistance Center, Treatment
Improvement Exchange, and SAMHSA's
National Registry of Evidence-based Programs
and Practices (http://www.nrepp.samhsa.gov)
are geared to meet practitioners' needs.

Substance Abuse and Mental Health Services
Administration (SAMHSA)–Health
Resources and Services Administration
(HRSA) Center for Integrated
Services, Screening Tools: http://www
.integration.samhsa.gov/clinical-practice/
screening-tools#drug

Women for Sobriety. http://www
.womenforsobriety.org.

References

Allen, J. P., & Wilson, V. B. (Eds.). (2003). *Assessing
alcohol problems: A guide for clinicians and
researchers* (2nd ed.). Bethesda, MD: National
Institute on Alcohol Abuse and Alcoholism.
Retrieved from http://pubs.niaaa.nih.gov/publi-
cations/AssessingAlcohol/index.htm

American Psychiatric Association. (2013). *Diagnostic
and statistical manual of mental disorders, fifth
edition*. Arlington, VA: Author.

DiClemente, C. (2003). *Addiction and change: How
addictions develop and addicted people recover*.
New York, NY: Guilford Press.

Kessler, R. C., Berglund, P., Demler, O., Jin, R.
Merikangas, K. R., & Walters, E. E. (2005).
Lifetime prevalence and age-of-onset distri-
butions of DSM-IV disorders in the National
Comorbidity Survey Replication. *Archives of
General Psychiatry, 62*(6), 593–602.

Kessler, R. C., Chiu, W. T., Demler, O., Merikangas,
K. R., & Walters, E. E. (2005). Prevalence, severity,
and comorbidity of 12-month DSM-IV disorders
in the National Comorbidity Survey Replication.
Archives of General Psychiatry, 62(6), 617–627.

McNeece, C. A., & DiNitto, D. M. (2012). Chemical
dependency: A systems approach (4th ed.).
Boston, MA: Pearson.

Mee-Lee, D. (Ed.). (2013). *The ASAM criteria:
Treatment criteria for addictive, substance-related,
and co-occurring conditions*. Chevy Chase,
MD: American Society of Addiction Medicine.

Miller, W. R., & Wilbourne, P. L. (2002). Mesa
Grande: A methodological analysis of clini-
cal trials of treatment for alcohol use disorders.
Addiction, 97(3), 265–277.

National Institute on Alcohol Abuse and Alcoholism.
(2005). Brief interventions. *Alcohol Alert, 66*.
Bethesda, MD: Author.

National Institute on Drug Abuse. (2012a). *Principles
of drug addiction treatment: A research-based
guide* (3rd ed.). Bethesda, MD: U.S. Department
of Health and Human Services. Retrieved
from http://www.drugabuse.gov/publications/
principles-drug-addiction-treatment

National Institute on Drug Abuse. (2012b). Tobacco
addiction. Bethesda, MD: U.S. Department of
Health and Human Services. Retrieved from
http://www.drugabuse.gov/publications/
research-reports/tobacco-addiction/are-there-ef
fective-treatments-tobacco-addiction

Nussbaum, A. (2013). *The pocket guide to the DSM-5™
diagnostic exam*. Arlington, VA: American
Psychiatric Association.

Prochaska, J. O., DiClemente, C. C., & Norcross,
J. C. (1992). In search of how people
change: Applications to addictive behaviors.
American Psychologist, 47, 1102–1114.

Rethinking Drinking. (n.d.). Bethesda, MD: National
Institute on Alcohol Abuse and Alcoholism.
Retrieved from http://rethinkingdrinking.niaaa.
nih.gov

Skinner, H. A. (1984). Assessing alcohol use by patients
in treatment. In R. G. Smart, H. D. Cappell, & F.
B. Glaser et al. (Eds.). Research advances in alcohol and drug problems (vol. 8) (pp. 183–207).
New York, NY: Plenum Press.

Substance Abuse and Mental Health Services
Administration. (2011). *Results from the
2010 National Survey on Drug Use and
Health: Summary of national findings*.
Rockville, MD: U.S. Department of Health and

Human Services. Retrieved from http://oas.sam-hsa.gov/NSDUH/2k10NSDUH/2k10Results.htm#TOC

Wilcox, R. E., & Erickson, C. K. (2005). The brain biology of drug abuse and addiction. In C. A. McNeece & D. M. DiNitto (Eds.), *Chemical dependency:* *A systems approach* (4th ed.). (pp. 39–55). Boston, MA: Pearson.

Winters, K. C. (1999). *Screening and assessing adolescents for substance use disorders* (Treatment Improvement Protocol [TIP] series 31). Rockville, MD: Center for Substance Abuse Treatment.

94   Best Practices in Social Work with Groups

Mark J. Macgowan & Alice Schmidt Hanbidge

Social work with groups should be based on best practices within the profession gained through a career-long commitment to a systematic process of critical reflection, inquiry, application, and practice evaluation, defined as evidence-based group work (EBGW, Macgowan, 2008). EBGW is a process of judicious and skillful application in group work of the best evidence using evaluation to ensure desired results are achieved (Macgowan, 2008). It is operationalized through a critical four-stage process model in which group workers (a) formulate an answerable practice question; (b) search for evidence; (c) undertake a critical review of the evidence for rigor, impact, and applicability yielding "best available evidence"; and (d) apply the evidence in practice with concern for relevance and appropriateness for the group and its members, utilizing evaluation to determine whether desired outcomes are achieved. EBGW is a process that can incorporate various theories and models of practice, as long as there is best evidence that these will be helpful to group members. Failure to engage in this process can lead to stagnation in practice, reliance on what is popular and not effective, and group processes and outcomes that are iatrogenic but avoidable. EBGW incorporates (a) empirically supported group interventions and processes, (b) evidence-supported guidelines, and (c) practice evaluation.

EMPIRICALLY SUPPORTED GROUP INTERVENTIONS AND PROCESSES

Empirically supported *group interventions* (including preventive interventions) (ESGIs) have been shown to be efficacious for specific diagnostic groups (e.g., depression, anxiety) or populations through randomized clinical trials and meta-analyses. ESGIs are typically well-defined, often manualized, and structured. Group workers would use such interventions if they are determined to be "best available evidence" as defined above.

Empirically supported *group processes* are what research has demonstrated to be associated with positive outcomes in groups. One example is cohesion, which is "the therapeutic relationship in group psychotherapy emerging from the aggregate of member-leader, member-member, and member-group relationships" (Burlingame, Fuhriman, & Johnson, 2001, p. 373). A meta-analysis reported that cohesion was significantly associated with reductions in symptom distress or improvements in interpersonal functioning across various settings and diagnoses (Burlingame, McClendon, & Alonso, 2011). Although the research is not as extensive as that of cohesion, engagement is also a predictor of retention and positive outcomes in groups

(Macgowan, 2006; Macgowan & Newman, 2005). According to Macgowan (1997), engagement in groups is a multidimensional construct where group members connect to their groups in seven areas: Attendance, verbal contribution and/or participation in group activities, support for the work of the leader, interaction with members, adoption of the contract, work on own problems, and assisting members in their work on their problems.

EVIDENCE-SUPPORTED BEST PRACTICE GUIDELINES

The second element that EBGW critically incorporates is evidence-supported group work standards and practice guidelines that have been developed by panels of experts to promote appropriate and effective practices ("best practice guidelines"). All group workers must become familiar with the standards and guidelines, and particularly those within their professions. Such standards and guidelines incorporate the best practices, values, and ethics of the respective professions. There are practice guidelines from the American Group Psychotherapy Association (AGPA, 2007; Burlingame et al., 2006; Leszcz & Kobos, 2008) and best practice guidelines and standards from the Association of Specialists in Group Work (ASGW, 2000, 2008).

Within social work, there are standards for the practice of social work with groups developed by the International Association for the Advancement of Social Work with Groups (IASWG, 2006; formerly the *Association for the Advancement of Social Work with Groups*) (Cohen, Macgowan, Garvin, & Muskat, 2013). The Standards "represent the perspectives of the [IASWG] on the value and knowledge and skill base essential for professionally sound and effective social work practice with groups and are intended to serve as a guide to social work practice with groups" (IASWG, 2006, p. 1). A reliable and valid measure has been developed to assess group workers' perceptions of the importance of the items in the Standards and their confidence in doing them (Macgowan, 2012, 2013; Macgowan & Vakharia, 2012). Using the measure, one study (Macgowan, 2012) identified the top items in the Standards that respondents ($n = 426$) thought they were least confident in doing. Three of the top items were: (a) using special skills in working with mandated members; (b) promoting group

exploration of nonproductive norms when they arise; and (c) helping members mediate conflict within the group. This chapter will include specific practice ideas/techniques to manage those three issues. Knowing how to practice the IASWG Standards is an essential foundation for social work with groups.

In addition, ASGW (2012) developed best practice principles with respect to multicultural group work and social justice. The multicultural and social justice competence principles fall into three areas: (a) awareness of self and group members; (b) use of strategies and skills that reflect multicultural and social justice advocacy competence in group planning, performing, and processing; and (c) social justice advocacy (Singh, Merchant, Skudrzyk, & Ingene, 2012). In working with increasingly culturally diverse populations, it is essential for group workers to become familiar with these guidelines, in addition to the best practice guidelines of their own professions.

PRACTICE EVALUATION

The third area of EBGW is practice evaluation. According to the IASWG Standards, group workers should include in their practice "monitoring and evaluation of success of group in accomplishing its objectives through personal observation, as well as collecting information in order to assess outcomes and processes" (IASWG, 2006, p. 9). Practice evaluation needs appropriate assessment measures and a suitable research design.

Assessment. Assessment may focus on (a) member-related outcomes, (b) group-related outcomes, and (c) group processes. Assessing *member-related outcomes* focuses on the original concern that led to the member's referral (e.g., aggression, depression, social competence). An excellent resource for member-related assessment instruments is Fischer and Corcoran's *Measures for Clinical Practice and Research* (2007). Assessing *group-related outcomes* focuses on collecting information about the group experience from group members. Examples of such measures include the Post-Session Questionnaire (Rose, 1984) and Evaluation of the Group Experience (Corey, Corey, & Corey, 2010). Assessing *group processes* emphasizes areas such as cohesion and engagement, which are related to positive group outcomes. The Cohesiveness Scale (Burlingame, et al., 2006) and the Group Engagement Measure (Macgowan, 1997, 2006; Macgowan & Newman,

2005) may be used (for additional group outcome and process measures see Burlingame et al., 2006; Garvin, Tolman, & Macgowan, 2015; Sodano et al., 2014). It should be noted that assessment instruments should be carefully selected for their rigor, impact, and applicability (Macgowan, 2008). In particular, they should be appropriate for the racial and ethnic group with which they will be used (Macgowan, 2008; Singh et al., 2012).

Research design. To determine whether the group work service actually helps group members, assessment is accompanied by a suitable research design. There are various approaches to evaluating whether an intervention is successful (Garvin et al., 2015). One informal approach is to use Goal Attainment Scaling (Kiresuk, Smith, & Cardillo, 1994; Toseland & Rivas, 2012). Goals may be a change in the problems of individual group members (member-related outcomes), or a change within the group itself (group-related outcomes), such as level of cohesion or engagement. A more formal approach is to use a single-case design (Macgowan & Wong, in press). A basic A–B single-case design can be used, consisting of taking several baseline measurements ("A") before the group begins, followed by repeated measurements over the course of the group ("B"). If baseline measurements cannot be done, a simple B design of repeated measures over the duration of the group may be used. In addition to the quantitative single case design, group workers may use a qualitative method, such as a focus group to gather detailed information about the group work service (Toseland & Rivas, 2012). For additional designs for group work, see Garvin and colleagues (2015).

All three elements of EBGW, empirically supported group interventions and processes, evidence-supported best practice guidelines, and practice evaluation are incorporated in this chapter. We describe how social work with groups incorporates the best available evidence through a generic developmental stage model of group work of planning, beginnings, middles, and endings. In addition, because group workers are often least confident working with mandated members, we will incorporate ideas for working with mandated members throughout this entry.

PLANNING

Northen and Kurland defined planning as including "the thinking, preparation, decision-making,

and actions of the social worker prior to the first meeting of the group" (2001, p. 109). Best practice guidelines (AGPA, AGSW, IASWG) and much empirical research (Burlingame, Strauss, & Joyce, 2013) refer to the importance of pregroup planning and preparation, although it is often neglected (Kurland, 1978). The IASWG Standards (2006) include 15 tasks and skills that group workers should master in the planning stage related to recruiting, screening and selecting members, provisions and limits for informed consent, and identifying group purposes and goals. Of the fifteen areas, three which social workers have felt least confident in doing were how to (a) select the group type, structure, processes, and size that will be appropriate for attaining the purposes of the group; (b) select members for the group in relationship to principles of group composition (assuming one has a choice); and (c) prepare members for the group (Macgowan, 2012). These areas will be addressed in the following sections on screening, purpose, composition, structure, and content. We will also include a section on planning for group work with mandated members.

Screening

Best practice guidelines (AGPA, ASGW, IASWG) recommend that group members should be selected and screened to assess their suitability for group work and to determine how the proposed group work may meet those needs. The first consideration is to determine whether the prospective member is suitable for group work. There are research-based screening tools that can be helpful, such as the Group Readiness Questionnaire (Baker, Burlingame, Cox, Beecher, & Gleave, 2013) and the Group Therapy Questionnaire (GTQ) (Burlingame et al., 2006; MacNair-Semands, 2004). The GTQ may be used to evaluate client expectancies for group work, which "may identify clients that could be 'at risk' for premature dropout, allowing more effective preparation of the client prior to group participation" (Burlingame, Cox, Davies, Layne, & Gleave, 2011, p. 71). Although these measures are research-based (rigorous), they should also be evaluated by each group worker for their applicability for intended group members (Macgowan, 2008).

Purpose

The group's purpose determines many factors about the group, such as "the group type, structure, processes, and size" (IASWG, 2006, p. 10). A clear statement of purpose reflects member needs and agency mission and goals (IASWG, 2006). It is essential to have a preliminary purpose statement that is succinct and that captures the essentials of the group work service. So that it is clearly understood, the purpose statement should ideally be one sentence, such as "to help sixth-grade pupils make a satisfactory adjustment to junior high school," followed by goals that "would be related clearly to the needs of particular members of the group" (Northen & Kurland, 2001, p. 125).

In going over the purpose of the group, group workers should ideally meet in person with prospective members. Although it may not always be feasible, the meeting is recommended because it (a) helps prepare members for the group service; (b) can establish the empirically supported therapeutic alliance that lays the foundation for group cohesion (Burlingame, Fuhriman, & Johnson, 2002); and (c) may improve retention (Burlingame, Fuhriman, & Mosier, 2003; Piper & Ogrodniczuk, 2004), particularly for persons with alcohol and other drug problems (Joe, Simpson, & Broome, 1999; Simpson, 2004). Sometimes such sessions are done in an orientation group session, where suitability for the prospective group can be assessed *in vivo*. This orientation session would also include (a) obtaining informed consent, which aids group member commitment; (b) a discussion of member rights and a professional confidentiality disclosure outlining the limits of confidentiality; and (c) dealing with any potential concerns or questions.

Composition

The function of screening is to determine members' suitability to participate in the life of the group and to not distract others from that ability. Composition in groups is the planned mix of individuals who have already been screened. Unlike screening where there are clearer guidelines, the research on how to compose groups has mixed findings: "The diversity of findings regarding composition suggests that there is no simple rule to follow, requiring group leaders to be conversant with relevant research findings" (Burlingame, et al., 2013, p. 669). Thus, what follows are tentative guidelines for composition. In many cases composition cannot be predetermined, but where it can, members should be selected based on principles of group composition, which is part of the IASWG Standards.

The first and foremost principle is that the group's purpose will guide who should be included (Klein, 1972; Northen & Kurland, 2001; Toseland & Rivas, 2012). All members must share the common purpose, though not necessarily common objectives. A second principle is that composition is less important with groups that are briefer and more structured, such as task- and training-oriented groups, rather than groups that are relationally oriented and interactional (Yalom, 1995). A third principle is if the group work is focusing on particular issues, group members should be similar with respect to that issue. This is particular so with group interventions that may be specifically related to race and culture ("culture-specific groups," see Merchant, 2009), such as bicultural skills training with Latino immigrant families (Bacallao & Smokowski, 2005). A meta-analysis (Griner & Smith, 2006) reported that interventions provided for same-race participants were four times more effective than interventions provided for mixed-race groups. Interventions delivered in clients' own languages were twice as effective as interventions delivered in English. A fourth general principle is to avoid having one person with little in common with other members (Garvin, 1997; Northen & Kurland, 2001). For example, Levine (1979) suggested that children in groups should be able to identify with at least one other child in the group, in terms of age, gender, culture, or other areas that are important for the child. A fifth principle is that even in groups where there is homogeneity with respect to certain variables (e.g., race, ethnicity), heterogeneity with respect to life experience, level of expertise, and coping skills is desirable so that members may benefit from one another's different strengths. Such differences "can provide multiple opportunities for support, validation, mutual aid, and learning" (Toseland & Rivas, 2012, p. 173).

Structure

Structure includes many things, but two are group size and length. The length and size of a group varies depending on the purpose of the group and the population involved. For example, closed groups that are long (over 12 sessions) and involve nonmandated involuntary clients may need to have larger group sizes to compensate for attrition. However, as a general guide, cohesion is strongest when a group has over 12 sessions and includes five to nine members (Burlingame,

McClendon, et al., 2011). With respect to length, there are different standards depending on the type of group. The ideal length for a psycho-educational group is 12 to 16 sessions and from 10 to 15 sessions (or more) for counseling groups (DeLucia-Waack & Nitza, 2014). To effectively have time to integrate therapeutic factors into adult groups, psycho-educational and counseling groups are typically 1 to 1½ hours in duration (DeLucia-Waack & Nitza, 2014). Groups for mandated members often vary in length and are focused on the development of skills. Anger management, problem-solving, or offender groups are often 8 to 12 sessions (Morgan, 2004).

Content

ESGIs have been shown to be efficacious for persons with specific diagnoses through randomized trials, meta-analyses, or through consensus of experts based on a critical review of the best research evidence. Systematic reviews over the years support the efficacy (tightly controlled studies) and effectiveness (real-world settings) of small group interventions (Burlingame et al., 2003; Burlingame et al., 2013). A systematic review of more than 250 studies across 12 problem areas/client populations concluded that there is "clear support for group treatment with good or excellent evidence for most disorders reviewed (panic, social phobia, OCD, eating disorders, substance abuse, trauma-related disorders, breast cancer, schizophrenia, and personality disorders) and promising for others (mood, pain/somatoform, inpatient)" (Burlingame et al., 2013, p. 664).

With respect to particular change theories, there is very good to excellent evidence that

- Cognitive-behavioral group therapy (CBGT) is effective with social phobia and comorbid depression, bulimia nervosa, binge-eating disorders, panic disorder, schizophrenia, trauma symptoms, and secondary outcomes.
- Psycho-education, time-limited therapy, and support groups are effective for cancer patients.
- CBGT and dialectical behavior therapy are effective for treating suicidality, parasuicidality, depression, and hopelessness associated with borderline personality disorder;
- A range of models (e.g., behavioral, motivational, contingency management,

psycho-educational, integrative group therapy, interactional, 12-step) are effective for reducing substance use. (Burlingame et al., 2013; Burlingame, Whitcomb, & Woodland, 2014)

Group workers should obtain the particular studies in the review (Burlingame et al., 2013) and critically review them for rigor, impact, and applicability to ensure they are the best available evidence (Macgowan, 2008). An ESGI may be "efficacious" but it may not be appropriate for the group. This is particularly important when considering the use of ESGIs with populations that are culturally different than those in the original studies. Such interventions may need to be adapted or tailored for race and ethnicity to be more effective (Benish, Quintana, & Wampold, 2011; Chen, Kakkad, & Balzano, 2008; Macgowan & Hanbidge, 2014). To be a skillful multicultural group worker (ASGW, 2012), it is important to develop "a repertoire of culturally relevant group work interventions" (DeLucia-Waack, 2004, p. 167).

Mandated Members in the Planning Stage

During the planning phase, there are special considerations in working with clients who are involved in the criminal justice system (offenders) and those who are legally required to attend treatment (mandated). Involuntary members may be mandated or have nonlegal pressure from others to attend a group (Rooney, 2009). Group work can be effective with offenders, mandated clients, and involuntary clients. A systematic review reported that group work with such clients can reduce anger, anxiety, and depression, as well as improve interpersonal relations, locus of control, and self-esteem (Morgan & Flora, 2002). Coviello and colleagues (2013) found that clients who were mandated to community treatment (which included group work) were higher treatment completers than those who were not court-ordered to attend. Additionally, mandated offenders were 10 times more likely to complete treatment than voluntary participants.

Group members who are mandated may not be prepared to acknowledge problems that others have identified. Understanding the nature of change through the stages-of-change model (Connors, Donovan, & DiClemente, 2001; Prochaska & DiClemente, 1984) can help workers facilitate the change process with clients who are mandated to service. The five stages include precontemplation (no recognition of problem), contemplation (identify problem, not willing to act), preparation (ready to make first step), action (taking steps), and maintenance (maintain change) (Miller & Rollnick, 2002). Designed particularly for those in the precontemplation and contemplation stages, motivational interviewing (MI) is "a client-centered directive method for enhancing intrinsic motivation to change by exploring and resolving ambivalence about change" (Miller & Rollnick, 2002, p. 23). MI is an efficacious communication style, which includes the following five elements: express empathy, avoid argumentation, roll with resistance, develop discrepancy, and promote self-efficacy (Miller & Rollnick, 2002; Miller & Rose, 2009). MI often also includes providing personalized feedback on behaviors presented in a person-centered, nonconfrontational way to help persons explore their behaviors. The technique often includes discussing the pros and cons of the behaviors and highlighting discrepancies (for applications of MI in group work, see Sobell & Sobell, 2011; Velasquez, Maurer, Crouch, & DiClemente, 2001).

In the planning stage, when mandated and involuntary group members may be in the precontemplation and contemplation stages of change, Rooney (2009; 2004) recommends the following actions when meeting with members or when composing the group:

- Clarify non-negotiables
- Reframe from resistance to ambivalence
- Clarify rights, choices, and limits on choices
- Expect oppositional behavior
- Identify current motivations and attempt to link to them
- Identify positive skills and knowledge to be gained in group
- Include positive role models, such as successful former members, in the group.

Morgan and colleagues (2014) recommend the following ESGIs as effective with offenders and mandated clients: (a) cognitive-behavioral group work; (b) structured group work (i.e., clearly defined goals and objectives, clear rules and expectations); and (c) out-of-group homework exercises, which improves outcomes compared with groups not utilizing such exercises (Morgan & Flora, 2002).

BEGINNINGS

The beginning of a group is often characterized by caution and tentativeness and it is common for group members to enter the group with mixed emotions; excitement and hope that the group can be beneficial mixed with concerns about trusting strangers with personal information and fears that the group could be a negative experience. The role of the group worker in establishing the group is central at this time. There are many areas that must be addressed at this stage and the IASWG Standards (2006) include a number of tasks and skills related to beginnings. We focus on what the Standards highlight as important; namely, cultivating mutual aid and building cohesion. We also continue the theme of how to work with mandated members.

Cultivate Mutual Aid

One of the early tasks as the group begins is for the worker to invite members to introduce themselves and to say what brought them to the group. This activity helps members to begin to share mutual concerns and interests in a trusting environment to develop universality ("all in the same boat") which is an essential ingredient of mutual aid (Shulman, 2009; Steinberg, 2010). Creating mutual aid is a core part of social work with groups (IASWG, 2006). Schwartz defined mutual aid as "an alliance of individuals who need each other, in varying degrees, to work on certain common problems" (1961/1994, p. 266). This supportive, working group does not simply happen, but is facilitated by the group worker in a "mediating" professional function (Schwartz, 1976) in which the worker connects individuals with each other and with the worker to create a helping system.

The IASWG Standards (2006) includes numerous items related to helping build mutual aid in the group, such as "helps members establish relationships with one another"; "highlights member commonalities"; "encourages direct member to member communication"; "clarifies and interprets communication patterns among members, between members and worker, and between the group and systems outside the group"; "models and encourages honest communication and feedback among members and between members and workers"; and "links members to one another." In particular, linking is an important technique for fostering mutual aid. Middleman and Wood (1990) discuss two ways in which members may be linked; a feeling link and an information link. A feeling link asks members "to connect with a feeling being expressed" (p. 120), whereas an information link asks members "to connect with a statement or question that someone has expressed" (p. 122). Reaching for an information link not only connects members but also allows the worker to "give back their assumed power to others by signaling that they are the ones best able to respond to their issues out of their own experiences" (Middleman & Wood, 1990, p. 123).

Build Cohesion

Cohesion is an essential part of effective group work. Research studies have reported a number of factors related to cohesion: (a) it is most strongly associated with client improvement in groups using an interpersonal, psychodynamic, or cognitive-behavioral orientation; (b) group leaders who facilitate member interaction have higher cohesion-outcome links than groups that focused less on process; and (c) it contributes to outcomes regardless of inpatient and outpatient, or diagnostic classifications (Burlingame, McClendon et al., 2011). To build cohesion, the group worker should (Burlingame et al., 2001)

- Conduct pregroup preparation to establish treatment expectations
- Introduce structured activities in early sessions, which reduces anxiety and leads to higher levels of disclosure and cohesion later in the group (but reduce structure over time)
- Model effective interpersonal feedback, and maintain a moderate level of control and affiliation
- Time the delivery of feedback based on the developmental stage of the group and the readiness of members
- Effectively manage his or her own emotional presence to be warm, accepting, and empathic, which not only affects relationships with individuals in the group but all group members as they see the workers' way of relating with others
- Facilitate group members' emotional expression (e.g., empathy, support and caring, acceptance), and the responsiveness of others to that expressiveness.

Ongoing assessment of group processes is essential for measuring the optimal functioning of the group and for moving the group toward desired outcomes. Best practice guidelines (AGPA, 2007; Burlingame et al., 2006) recommend assessing group processes such as cohesion to determine whether strategies are needed to improve processes linked to positive outcomes. Group workers can monitor the effectiveness of the cohesion-building strategies above using the Group Psychotherapy Intervention Rating Scale (Chapman, Baker, Porter, Thayer, & Burlingame, 2010).

Mandated Members in the Beginning Stage

In the beginning stage, mandated and involuntary group members may still be in the precontemplation and contemplation stages of change. Best practices (Rooney, 2009; Rooney & Chovanec, 2004; Toseland & Rivas, 2012) recommend that the group worker

- Provide an opening statement addressing members' initial concerns and ambivalence about accomplishing the group's work and reassure them that they are not alone (linking members)
- Help members collaboratively recognize where points of ambivalence may occur. Rather than ignoring, playing down, or attacking the ambivalence, the group leaders can help the group members work through it.
- Reclarify non-negotiable and negotiable issues
- Help members recognize the range of choices, including constrained choices
- Support positive choices, identifying positive self-motivating statements
- Provide emotional support
- Present facts in nonblaming fashion
- Review choices and consequences of decisions
- Initiate discussion of pros and cons of deciding to change
- Emphasize self-assessment of severity of problems
- Enhance self-attribution (acknowledgment that change is in members' best interest)
- Use tactful experiential confrontation (highlight discrepancy) when behaviors are inconsistent with stated goals

- Negotiate group rules and clarify expectations for each session
- Solicit member goals and link these to group goals.

MIDDLES

The journey to the middle stage may not be smooth. The group may go through what has been described as a time of "uncertainty-exploration" characterized by "storming" or "power and control" (Garland, Jones, & Kolodny, 1965; Northen & Kurland, 2001; Tuckman, 1965). During that time, workers help the group discuss and manage negative expressions of feelings, hostility, and conflict that might occur. Encouraging members to express negative feelings creates an environment of openness and gives an opportunity to address behaviors that are incongruent with the group's purpose.

The middle (or working) stage of the group is often characterized by an increased level of self-disclosure, cohesion, mutual aid, problem-solving, a willingness to work on personal issues, and individual and group growth (Toseland & Rivas, 2012; Zastrow, 2009). The leader's role shifts from active to less directive, encouraging greater group ownership and shared leadership within the group (an important value of the IASWG Standards). There are many areas that workers attend to in the middle stage, including maintaining cohesion, empowering group members, acknowledging cultural diversity, assessing progress, continuing to promote the process of mutual aid and to "use that process as a vehicle for work on personal, interpersonal, group, and environmental problems" (Northen & Kurland, 2001, p. 353). The IASWG Standards include 21 tasks and skills in the middle stage. Two skills that group workers find most challenging (Macgowan, 2012) are dealing with conflict in the group and managing disruptive norms, which will be discussed in this section, along with the theme of working with mandated members.

Manage Nonproductive Norms

The IASWG Standards note that unproductive norms and conflict are to be explored with the group, rather than addressed exclusively by the group worker. Processing interpersonal and group-related factors with members "is a major source of learning for both members and leaders"

(Ward & Ward, 2014, p. 40) and an essential part of social work with groups. Norms are shared expectations about ways to act in the group; these may be explicit or implicit, and develop through the interactions of group members (Toseland & Rivas, 2012). A single action is not usually evidence of a norm, but the repeated pattern of actions (behavior) over time and/or by a number of members. Given that they are developed through group interactions, the group must be involved in the process to manage norms. Group workers have the primary responsibility of guiding the group to create and reinforce productive group norms in the planning and beginning stages, and the responsibility to guide the group to explore nonproductive norms when they arise in any stage (Bernard et al., 2008; IASWG, 2006). Some examples of nonproductive norms include group members using "You" and "We" language, speaking in the third person, resisting, rescuing, and challenging the leader (Sklare, Keener, & Mas, 1990).

The IASWG Standards note that group members are to participate in the process of change. The group worker points out the unproductive norm and puts it back to the group to work it out, such as, "How have we let the repeated tardiness continue to today?" If successful, this may lead to the group managing other norm disruptions without prompting (Bernard et al., 2008). Some techniques for promoting group exploration of nonproductive norms as they arise include (partly based on Toseland & Rivas, 2012):

- Solicit group members' feedback on the norm
- Discuss or demonstrate how the norm will affect the group's ability to fulfill its purpose
- Help the group to develop a new productive response
- Help members reflect on the process of norm adjustment.

If these measures fail, the worker may need to intervene directly or have an external member work with the group to change its norms.

Work with Conflict

Conflict is "behavior in which there is disagreement between two or more persons" and "is a natural, necessary, and important component of group process" (Northen & Kurland, 2001, p. 214). A worry of group workers, particularly those with limited group work education and training, is that conflict will spiral out of control and ruin the group experience (Northen & Kurland, 2001; Steinberg, 1993). As with exploring unproductive norms, the IASWG Standards expect that group workers help "members mediate conflict within the group" (2006, p. 19), rather than resolving it unilaterally or solving it exclusively outside the group. The role as mediator "resolves disputes, conflicts, or opposing views within the group or between a member and some other person or organization; takes a neutral stand and helps members arrive at a settlement or agreement that is mutually acceptable" (Toseland & Rivas, 2012, p. 285). The most important task of the group worker is to help group members work through the conflict in a constructive manner: "When conflict is constructively discussed, members learn that their relationships are strong enough to withstand an honest level of challenge, which is what many people want to achieve in their outside relationships" (Corey & Corey, 2006, p. 187). The role as mediator in the group, described earlier as part of the function of the group worker (Schwartz, 1976), helps model for group members the effective management of conflict.

A number of practices can help members mediate conflict within the group. The first is to help members understand the role of mediator as someone who works with and among the persons involved in conflict, rather than someone who serves as a unilateral decision maker responsible for solving the conflict. Toseland and Rivas (2012) offer a number of suggestions for handling conflict in groups:

- View conflict as normal and helpful
- Identify conflict
- Encourage members to listen to the entire group discussion before judging
- Help members to avoid personal differences and to stick to facts and preferences
- Promote consensus
- Pre-plan a problem-solving model and follow it, using agreed-upon decision criteria
- Clarify and summarize discussion regularly, while remaining neutral in the conflict
- Remain sensitive to group members' preferences and concerns.

Mandated Members in the Middle Stage

The working stage assumes that members have moved to the contemplation if not the action stage (Rooney & Chovanec, 2004). Working with mandated and involuntary members in group requires assisting members with assessing the costs and benefits of change, providing information about choices, helping members in their plans to change while emphasizing responsibility for choices (Rooney, 2009; Rooney & Chovanec, 2004).

ENDINGS

The ending stage is an essential but often neglected part of group work. Best practice guidelines (AGPA, ASGW, IASWG) discuss the critical importance of preparing members in advance for endings (also known as termination, adjourning, separation, transition). An ending should be viewed as a "unique stage with its own goals and processes." (AGPA, 2007, p. 64) The work on endings should ideally begin in the planning stage, when the parameters for termination are initially discussed (Yalom & Leszcz, 2005). Endings also occur each session as individuals leave open groups, and with the entire group if the group is closed. If the group is closed, the work on endings should occur a few sessions before the final session (Toseland & Rivas, 2012). Workers should be attuned to any cultural variations among members regarding endings (ASGW, 2012). Rituals, such as ceremonies and celebrations may be used, "which aid the members in learning through the leave taking process." (AGPA, 2007, p. 64)

The group worker manages both instrumental and affective tasks related to endings. Instrumental tasks relate to assessing problem reduction and goal achievement, discussing maintenance of gains, and reducing reliance on the group. The group worker should complete the following instrumental tasks (AGPA, 2007; Bernard et al., 2008; IASWG, 2006; Northen & Kurland, 2001; Toseland & Rivas, 2012):

- Review and reinforce individual and group change (preferably through systematic evaluation methods. See Practice Evaluation above.
- Discuss unfinished individual work.
- Help members apply knowledge and skills to environments outside of the group.
- Anticipate situations that might be stressful and practice coping skills developed in the group.

- Refer members to other services and, if appropriate, involve significant others in referral decisions.
- Prepare record material (e.g., progress notes, see assessment above) as required.

The group worker also helps members manage their feelings about endings and separation. The amount of time spent doing this will depend on the structure and type of group. For example, in unstructured therapy and support groups, feelings about endings may be more intense than in educational or task groups. Both positive and negative feelings are solicited, and both direct and indirect signs of member's reactions to endings are monitored and discussed. Indirect expressions may be tactics to delay or avoid discussing endings, such as late or missed sessions, denial, acting out, and changing topics (IASWG, 2006; Toseland & Rivas, 2012). Feelings of transference, countertransference and "unfinished business" may arise in the final phase of group work for both the worker and the group members and sharing these feelings in the group is encouraged. Best practice guidelines and the literature (AGPA, 2007; ASGW, 2012; Bernard et al., 2008; IASWG, 2006; Northen & Kurland, 2001; Shulman, 2011; Toseland & Rivas, 2012) identify the following tasks the group worker should complete in dealing with emotional aspects of endings:

- Be aware of and manage one's own feelings related to separations.
- Share own feelings about endings with the group.
- Explore, support, and clarify the range of emotional expressions related to endings.
- Appreciate the wide range of possible emotions that may be expressed, remaining aware of cultural differences in endings.
- Use empathy as members struggle to share feelings related to success, loss, or failure.
- Particularly in therapy groups, help members "resolve conflicted relationships with one another and the leader." (AGPA, 2007, p. 64)

Mandated Members in the Ending Stage

Using the stages-of-change model, group members move from the action stage into maintenance in endings (Connors et al., 2001; Prochaska & DiClemente, 1984). The endings techniques noted above are valid in working with mandated members in groups, but areas that are emphasized include helping members to (a) solidify behavior changes so that they become automatic (e.g., awareness of triggers and how to deal with them); (b) develop relapse prevention skills that generalize to other settings, often using role-playing; and (c) join or lead other groups (Connors et al., 2001; Rooney, 2009; Rooney & Chovanec, 2004). It is particularly important that group workers help members to support others who are at risk of relapse, because those who relapse but have had a positive attachment to group "will more likely return to the group following a lapse." (Connors et al., 2001, p. 141)

WEBSITE

www.evidencebasedgroupwork.com

References

AGPA. (2007). *Practice guidelines for group psychotherapy*. Retrieved from http://www.agpa.org/guidelines/index.html

ASGW. (2000). *Professional standards for the training of group workers*. Retrieved from http://www.asgw.org/training_standards.htm

ASGW. (2008). *Association for Specialists in Group Work: Best Practice Guidelines 2007 Revisions*. Retrieved from http://www.asgw.org/PDF/Best_Practices.pdf

ASGW. (2012). Association for Specialists in Group Work: Multicultural and social justice competence principles for group workers. *The Journal for Specialists in Group Work*, 37(4), 312–325. doi:10.1080/01933922.2012.721482

Bacallao, M. L., & Smokowski, P. R. (2005). "Entre dos mundos" (Between Two Worlds): Bicultural skills training with Latino immigrant families. *Journal of Primary Prevention*, 26(6), 485–509. doi:10.1007/s10935-005-0008-6

Baker, E., Burlingame, G. M., Cox, J. C., Beecher, M. E., & Gleave, R. L. (2013). The Group Readiness Questionnaire: A convergent validity analysis. *Group Dynamics: Theory, Research, and Practice* [no pagination specified]. doi:10.1037/a0034477

Benish, S. G., Quintana, S., & Wampold, B. E. (2011). Culturally adapted psychotherapy and the legitimacy of myth: A direct-comparison meta-analysis. *Journal of Counseling Psychology*, 58, 279–289. doi:10.1037/a0023626

Bernard, H., Burlingame, G., Flores, P., Greene, L., Joyce, A., Kobos, J. C., . . . Feirman, D. (2008). Clinical practice guidelines for group psychotherapy. *International Journal of Group*

Psychotherapy. Special Issue: Toward the Establishment of Evidence-Based Practices in Group Psychotherapy, 58(4), 455–542. doi:10.1521/ijgp.2008.58.4.455

Burlingame, G. M., Cox, J. C., Davies, D. R., Layne, C. M., & Gleave, R. (2011). The Group Selection Questionnaire: Further refinements in group member selection. *Group Dynamics: Theory, Research, and Practice, 15*(1), 60–74. doi:10.1037/a0020220

Burlingame, G. M., Fuhriman, A., & Johnson, J. E. (2001). Cohesion in group psychotherapy. *Psychotherapy: Theory, Research, Practice, Training, 38*(4), 373–379.

Burlingame, G. M., Fuhriman, A., & Johnson, J. E. (2002). Cohesion in group psychotherapy. In J. C. Norcross (Ed.), *Psychotherapy relationships that work: Therapist contributions and responsiveness to patients* (pp. 71–87). New York, NY: Oxford.

Burlingame, G. M., Fuhriman, A., & Mosier, J. (2003). The differential effectiveness of group psychotherapy: A meta-analytic perspective. *Group Dynamics: Theory, Research, and Practice, 7*(1), 3–12.

Burlingame, G. M., McClendon, D. T., & Alonso, J. (2011). Cohesion in group therapy. *Psychotherapy, 48,* 34–42. doi:10.1037/a0022063

Burlingame, G. M., Strauss, B., & Joyce, A. (2013). Change mechanisms and effectiveness of small group treatments. In M. J. Lambert (Ed.), *Bergin and Garfield's handbook of psychotherapy and behavior change* (6th ed.) (pp. 640–689). New York, NY: Wiley.

Burlingame, G. M., Strauss, B., Joyce, A., MacNair-Semands, R., MacKenzie, K. R., Ogrodniczuk, J., & Taylor, S. (2006). *CORE Battery—Revised: An assessment toolkit for promoting optimal group selection, process, and outcome.* New York, NY: American Group Psychotherapy Association.

Burlingame, G. M., Whitcomb, K., & Woodland, S. (2014). Process and outcome in group counseling and psychotherapy. In J. L. DeLucia-Waack, C. R. Kalodner, & M. Riva (Eds.), *Handbook of group counseling and psychotherapy* (pp. 55–67). Thousand Oaks, CA: Sage Publications.

Chapman, C. L., Baker, E. L., Porter, G., Thayer, S. D., & Burlingame, G. M. (2010). Rating group therapist interventions: The validation of the Group Psychotherapy Intervention Rating Scale. *Group Dynamics: Theory, Research, and Practice, 14*(1), 15–31. doi:10.1037/a0016628

Chen, E. C., Kakkad, D., & Balzano, J. (2008). Multicultural competence and evidence-based practice in group therapy. *Journal of Clinical Psychology, 64,* 1261–1278. doi:10.1002/jclp.20533

Cohen, C. S., Macgowan, M. J., Garvin, C., & Muskat, B. (Eds.). (2013). *IASWG Standards for Social Work with Groups: Research, Teaching and Practice: Special Issue of Social Work with Groups* (Vol. 36). New York, NY: Routledge.

Connors, G. J., Donovan, D. M., & DiClemente, C. C. (2001). *Substance abuse treatment and the stages of change: Selecting and planning interventions.* New York, NY: Guilford Press.

Corey, M. S., & Corey, G. (2006). *Groups: Process and practice* (7th ed.). Belmont, CA: Thomson/Brooks/Cole.

Corey, M. S., Corey, G., & Corey, C. (2010). *Groups: Process and practice* (8th ed.). Belmont, CA: Brooks/Cole.

Coviello, D. M., Zanis, D. A., Wesnoski, S. A., Palman, N., Gur, A., Lynch, K. G., & McKay, J. R. (2013). Does mandating offenders to treatment improve completion rates? *Journal of Substance Abuse Treatment, 44*(4), 417–425. doi:10.1016/j.jsat.2012.10.003

DeLucia-Waack, J., & Nitza, A. (2014). *Effective planning for groups.* Thousand Oaks, CA: Sage.

DeLucia-Waack, J. L. (2004). Multicultural groups: Introduction. In J. L. DeLucia-Waack, D. A. Gerrity, C. R. Kalodner & M. Riva (Eds.), *Handbook of group counseling and psychotherapy* (pp. 167–168). Thousand Oaks, CA: Sage Publications.

Corcoran, K., & Fischer, J. (2013). *Measures for clinical practice and research: A sourcebook* (5th ed.). New York, NY: Oxford University Press.

Garland, J. A., Jones, H. E., & Kolodny, R. L. (1965). A model for stages of development in social work groups. In S. Bernstein (Ed.), *Explorations in group work: Essays in theory and practice* (pp. 12–53). Boston, MA: Boston University School of Social Work.

Garvin, C. D. (1997). *Contemporary group work* (3rd ed.). Boston: Allyn and Bacon.

Garvin, C. D., Tolman, R. M., & Macgowan, M. J. (2015). *Pocket guide for group work research.* New York, NY: Oxford University Press.

Griner, D., & Smith, T. B. (2006). Culturally adapted mental health intervention: A meta-analytic review. *Psychotherapy: Theory, Research, Practice, Training, 43*(4), 531–548. doi:10.1037/0033-3204.43.4.531

International Association for the Advancement of Social Work with Groups (IASWG). (2006). *Standards for social work practice with groups* (2nd ed.). Retrieved from http://www.aaswg.org/files/AASWG_Standards_for_Social_Work_Practice_with_Groups.pdf

Joe, G. W., Simpson, D. D., & Broome, K. M. (1999). Retention and patient engagement models for different treatment modalities in DATOS. *Drug & Alcohol Dependence, 57*(2), 113–125.

Kiresuk, T. J., Smith, A., & Cardillo, J. E. (1994). *Goal attainment scaling: Applications, theory, and measurement.* Hillsdale, NJ: L. Erlbaum Associates.

Klein, A. F. (1972). *Effective groupwork: An introduction to principle and method.* New York, NY: Association Press.

Kurland, R. (1978). Planning: The neglected component of group development. *Social Work with Groups, 1*(2), 173–178.

Leszcz, M., & Kobos, J. C. (2008). Evidence-based group psychotherapy: Using AGPA's practice guidelines to enhance clinical effectiveness. *Journal of Clinical Psychology, 64*(11), 1238–1260. doi:10.1002/jclp.20531

Levine, B. (1979). *Group psychotherapy: Practice and development.* Englewood Cliffs, NJ: Prentice-Hall.

Macgowan, M. J. (1997). A measure of engagement for social group work: The Groupwork Engagement Measure (GEM). *Journal of Social Service Research, 23*(2), 17–37.

Macgowan, M. J. (2006). The Group Engagement Measure: A review of its conceptual and empirical properties. *Journal of Groups in Addiction and Recovery, 1*(2), 33–52.

Macgowan, M. J. (2008). *A guide to evidence-based group work.* New York, NY: Oxford University Press.

Macgowan, M. J. (2012). A standards-based inventory of foundation competencies in social work with groups. *Research on Social Work Practice, 22*(5), 578–589. doi:10.1177/1049731512443288

Macgowan, M. J. (2013). Development and application of a standards-based inventory of foundation competencies in social work with groups. *Social Work with Groups, 36*(2/3), 160–173. doi:10.1080/01609513.2012.753836

Macgowan, M. J., & Hanbidge, A. S. (2014). Advancing evidence-based group work in community settings: Methods, opportunities, and challenges. In J. L. DeLucia-Waack, C. R. Kalodner, & M. Riva (Eds.), *The Handbook of Group Counseling and Psychotherapy* (2nd ed.) (pp. 303–317). Thousand Oaks, CA: Sage.

Macgowan, M. J., & Newman, F. L. (2005). The factor structure of the Group Engagement Measure. *Social Work Research, 29,* 107–118. doi:10.1093/swr/29.2.107

Macgowan, M. J., & Vakharia, S. P. (2012). Teaching standards-based group work competencies to social work students: An empirical examination. *Research on Social Work Practice, 22*(4), 380–388. doi:10.1177/1049731512442249

Macgowan, M. J., & Wong, S. (in press). Single-case designs in group work: Past applications, future directions. *Group Dynamics.*

MacNair-Semands, R. (2004). *Manual for Group Therapy Questionnaire—Revised.* Charlotte, NC: University of North Carolina at Charlotte.

Merchant, N. M. (2009). Types of diversity-related groups. In C. F. Salazar (Ed.), *Group work experts share their favorite multicultural activities: A guide to diversity-competent choosing, planning, conducting and processing* (pp. 13–24).

Alexandria, VA: Association for Specialists in Group Work.

Middleman, R. R., & Wood, G. G. (1990). *Skills for direct practice in social work.* New York, NY: Columbia University Press.

Miller, W. R., & Rollnick, S. (2002). *Motivational interviewing: Preparing people for change* (2nd ed.). New York, NY: Guilford Press.

Miller, W. R., & Rose, G. S. (2009). Toward a theory of motivational interviewing. *American Psychologist, 64*(6), 527–537. doi:10.1037/a0016830

Morgan, R. D. (2004). Groups with offenders and mandated clients. In J. L. DeLucia-Waack, D. A. Gerrity, C. R. Kalodner, & M. Riva (Eds.), *Handbook of group counseling and psychotherapy* (pp. 388–400). Thousand Oaks, CA: Sage.

Morgan, R. D., & Flora, D. B. (2002). Group psychotherapy with incarcerated offenders: A research synthesis. *Group Dynamics, 6*(3), 203–218. doi:10.1037/1089-2699.6.3.203

Morgan, R. D., Romani, C. J., & Gross, N. R. (2014). Group work with offenders and mandated clients. In J. L. DeLucia-Waack, C. R. Kalodner, & M. Riva (Eds.), *The handbook of group counseling and psychotherapy* (2nd ed.) (pp. 441–449). Thousand Oaks, CA: Sage.

Northen, H., & Kurland, R. (2001). *Social work with groups* (3rd ed.). New York, NY: Columbia University Press.

Piper, W. E., & Ogrodniczuk, J. S. (2004). Brief group therapy. In J. L. DeLucia-Waack, D. A. Gerrity, C. R. Kalodner, & M. Riva (Eds.), *Handbook of group counseling and psychotherapy* (pp. 641–650). Thousand Oaks, CA: Sage Publications.

Prochaska, J. O., & DiClemente, C. C. (1984). *The transtheoretical approach: Crossing traditional boundaries of therapy.* Homewood, IL: Dow Jones-Irwin.

Rooney, R. H. (2009). Work with involuntary groups. In R. H. Rooney (Ed.), *Strategies for work with involuntary clients* (2nd ed.) (pp. 244–272). New York, NY: Columbia University Press.

Rooney, R. H., & Chovanec, M. (2004). Involuntary groups. In C. D. Garvin, L. M. Gutierrez, & M. J. Galinsky (Eds.), *Handbook of social work with groups* (pp. 212–226). New York, NY: Guilford.

Rose, S. D. (1984). Use of data in identifying and resolving group problems in goal oriented treatment groups. *Social Work with Groups, 7*(2), 23–36.

Schwartz, W. (1961/1994). The social worker in the group. In T. Berman-Rossi (Ed.), *Social work: The collected writings of William Schwartz* (pp. 257–276). Itasca, IL: F. E. Peacock Publishers, Inc. (Reprinted from *The Social Welfare Forum, Proceedings of the National Conference on Social Welfare,* 1961, New York, NY: Columbia University Press).

Schwartz, W. (1976). Between client and system: The mediating function. In R. W. Roberts & H. Northen (Eds.), *Theories of social work with groups* (pp. 171–197). New York, NY: Columbia University Press.

Shulman, L. (2009). *The skills of helping individuals, families, groups and communities* (6th ed.). Belmont, CA: Brooks/Cole Cengage Learning.

Shulman, L. (2011). *Dynamics and skills of group counseling*. Belmont, CA: Brooks/Cole.

Simpson, D. D. (2004). A conceptual framework for drug treatment process and outcomes. *Journal of Substance Abuse Treatment, 27*(2), 99–121.

Singh, A. A., Merchant, N., Skudrzyk, B., & Ingene, D. (2012). Association for Specialists in Group Work: Multicultural and social justice competence principles for group workers. *The Journal for Specialists in Group Work, 37*(4), 312–325. doi:10.1080/01933922.2012.721482

Sklare, G., Keener, R., & Mas, C. (1990). Preparing members for "Here-and-Now" group counseling. *The Journal for Specialists in Group Work, 15*(3), 141–148. doi:10.1080/01933929008411924

Sobell, L. C., & Sobell, M. B. (2011). *Group therapy for substance use disorders: A motivational cognitive-behavioral approach*. New York, NY: Guilford Press.

Sodano, S., Guyker, W., DeLucia-Waack, J. L., Cosgrove, H., Altabef, D., & Amos, B. (2014). Measures of group process, dynamics, climate behavior, and outcome: A review. In J. L. DeLucia-Waack, C. R. Kalodner, & M. Riva (Eds.), *Handbook of group counseling and psychotherapy* (pp. 159–177). Thousand Oaks, CA: Sage Publications.

Steinberg, D. M. (1993). Some findings from a study on the impact of group work education on social work practitioners' work with groups. *Social Work with Groups, 16*(3), 23–39.

Steinberg, D. M. (2010). Mutual Aid: A contribution to best-practice social work. *Social Work with Groups, 33*(1), 53–68. doi:10.1080/01609510903316389

Toseland, R. W., & Rivas, R. F. (2012). *An introduction to group work practice* (7th ed.). Boston, MA: Allyn & Bacon.

Tuckman, B. W. (1965). Developmental sequence in small groups. *Psychological Bulletin, 63*(6), 384–399.

Velasquez, M. M., Maurer, G. G., Crouch, C., & DiClemente, C. C. (2001). *Group treatment for substance abuse: A stages-of-change therapy manual*. New York, NY: Guilford Press.

Ward, D. E., & Ward, C. A. (2014). *How to help leaders and members learn from their group experience*. Thousand Oaks, CA: Sage.

Yalom, I. D. (1995). *The theory and practice of group psychotherapy* (4th ed.). New York, NY: Basic Books.

Yalom, I. D., & Leszcz, M. (2005). *The theory and practice of group psychotherapy* (5th ed.). New York, NY: Basic Books.

Zastrow, C. (2009). *Social work with groups: A comprehensive workbook* (7th ed.). Belmont, CA: Brooks/Cole.

95   Supported Employment

Marina Kukla & Gary R. Bond

BACKGROUND TO SUPPORTIVE EMPLOYMENT

Supported employment refers to rehabilitation services that assist clients with severe mental illness obtain and maintain competitive employment in the community through an individualized approach that emphasizes rapid job search and de-emphasizes a stepwise approach of intermediate employment prior to placement in a competitive job. It helps to compensate for the challenges presented by mental illness, such as psychotic symptoms, cognitive dysfunction, and a lack of social skills that make obtaining and maintaining employment more difficult. Supported employment services are especially crucial given the finding that the majority of people with severe mental illness want to work, yet most are unemployed (Becker & Drake, 2003). Supported employment programs are present in a variety of settings (e.g., Veteran Affairs medical centers, university-run outpatient clinics), but are most often found in community mental health centers, which provide mental health counseling, medication management, case management, housing assistance, and other services.

HISTORY

Community-based psychiatric rehabilitation services began in the mid-1950s. This era included the deinstitutionalization movement, in which large numbers of people with severe mental illness moved out of inpatient hospitals into the community. One of the earliest forms of community-based psychiatric rehabilitation was the "clubhouse," where people with severe mental illness could go during the day and socialize. Clubhouses fostered the idea that an individual could work and should have an opportunity to work, if they so desired, even if they had spent many years in the hospital and suffered from debilitating psychiatric symptoms. The desire to participate in meaningful, productive activity ultimately led to the provision of specific employment services for this population (Becker & Drake, 2003).

The earliest formulation of supported employment was the "place–train" approach first used in the developmental disabilities field (Wehman & Moon, 1988). The place–train approach assumed that rapid placement into a competitive job in the community with appropriate training and support thereafter would lead to better outcomes for people with even severe disabilities than the traditional "train–place" approach requiring clients to receive pre-employment training prior to placement. Pre-employment training was ineffective because of the lack of generalizability of job skills training and the unrealistic nature of the pre-employment training situation (clients know that it is not the "real world").

Given the shortcomings of the train–place approach, the principles of Wehman and Moon's (1988) more successful place–train approach began to be adopted by the mental health field in the late 1980s. The most widely studied, used, and standardized supported employment approach for people with severe mental illness is the Individualized Placement and Support (IPS) model (Becker & Drake, 2003).

THEORETICAL PERSPECTIVE

Supported employment is an evidence-based practice based on the recovery model. Recovery from mental illness has several definitions, but a commonly used definition is "a deeply personal, unique process of changing one's attitudes, values, feelings, goals, skills and/or roles. It is a way of living a satisfying, hopeful, and contributing life even with limitations caused by the illness. Recovery involves the development of new meaning and purpose in one's life as one grows beyond the catastrophic effects of mental illness." (Anthony, 1993; p. 17) It is widely accepted that work is a crucial part of recovery, as individuals with Serious Mental Illnesses (SMI) engage in meaningful, personally satisfying roles, such as employment, in the community.

PRINCIPLES

The IPS model is an evidence-based vocational model. It uses the following research-based principles (Bond, 1998; 2004; Drake, Bond, & Becker, 2012):

- *Principle of Zero Exclusion.* IPS programs serve anyone with severe mental illness who professes an interest in working, regardless of symptoms, work history, lack of skills, strange appearance, or any of the myriad of reasons often given for excluding people from vocational services.
- *Principle of Goal of Competitive Employment Only.* Employment specialists do not place clients in noncompetitive jobs such as work crews or sheltered workshop positions in which jobs are reserved for those with severe mental illness.
- *Principle of Focus on Client Choice and Preferences.* Client job preferences, needs, and abilities, are given paramount importance in identifying jobs during the job search as well as in determining what kinds of help will be provided. For example, if the client prefers not to disclose his/her psychiatric disability to the employer, the supported employment team accommodates this preference.
- *Principle of Ongoing, Informal Assessment.* Based on direct observation and conversations with clients and employers, the employment specialist continuously assesses

the fit between the client preferences and capabilities and the environmental demands. Skills needed to perform job duties are only one aspect of this assessment; relationships with supervisors and coworkers are usually crucial. Other life circumstances, including housing and family situations are also considered.

- *Principle of Systematic Job Development.* Employment specialists build an employer network based on clients' interests, developing relationships with local employers by making systematic contacts. Job development involves cultivating a relationship. Usually the IPS specialist plans the first employer contact to introduce herself/himself to the employer and request another meeting. The second contact is to learn about the employer's business. Future contacts are to discuss potential employees when there might be a good job match.
- *Principle of Rapid Job Search.* The job search begins as soon as the client enters an IPS program. There is no prevocational training or lengthy vocational assessment. Standardized assessment tools are mostly of little value in identifying who is able to work or what jobs to pursue.
- *Principle of Time-unlimited, Individualized Follow-Along Support.* Ongoing follow-along support provided by the employment specialist may include a variety of interventions, including assisting clients in mastering job duties, consulting with the client's coworkers and supervisors to enhance interactions with the client, and suggesting modifications in the work environment to accommodate client's needs. Once a client is successfully employed for a period of time (e.g., one year), employment specialists typically taper off support to once a month or less, transitioning the bulk of support to the clinical treatment team.
- *Principle of Benefits Counseling.* IPS programs provide clients with personalized information regarding the consequences of employment earnings on their Social Security and Medicaid payments.
- *Principle of Integration of Employment Services and Mental Health Treatment.* Staff from IPS programs work closely with mental treatment teams and attend treatment team meetings. Integration of supported employment services and mental health treatment is characterized by employment specialists providing mental health information to mental health clinicians and mental health clinicians providing vocational information to employment specialists. For example, in the case example of Tim, Tim's employment specialist provides information to mental health clinicians about new symptoms Tim experiences on the job or medication side effects that affect his ability to work. Mental health clinicians (i.e., case managers) provide information to Tim's employment specialist about other aspects of his life, such as changes in his residential status or transportation that could affect Tim's vocational status.

Another important component of the IPS model is that employment specialists carry small caseloads (i.e., usually no more than 20 clients). In addition, employment specialists provide employment services only and do not have responsibilities for nonvocational services, such as crisis intervention, housing, or other case management tasks.

STEPS FOR IMPLEMENTING SUPPORTED EMPLOYMENT

The following is a step-by-step description of the IPS supported employment process. Although the steps may vary somewhat in temporal sequence and nature dependent upon the individual circumstances of each client, this represents the rudimentary process for a typical client.

1. The client expresses a desire to work competitively to their mental health team or the client comes into the community mental health center seeking help with employment.
2. An employment specialist begins to work with the client, identifying important factors, including the client's preferences, needs, and individual circumstances (e.g., transportation) in regards to employment. If the client is receiving disability benefits, the client receives specific information on the financial implications of earnings from employment, both prior to the job search and after a specific job offer is made. The employment specialist and client discuss options regarding disclosure of mental illness to employers.

3. Although not a requirement for enrollment in supported employment, supported employment programs often receive funding from the state–federal vocational rehabilitation system. Consequently, employment specialists typically work closely with this agency on behalf of their clients, initiating contact before the client obtains a job.

4. Usually within a month's time, the employment specialist and the client together begin the job development process and search for a suitable job.

5. When the client obtains the job, the employment specialist often works with the supervisor and coworkers to work out a suitable work environment for the client. This role will depend on the client's preferences, including whether the client discloses his/her psychiatric disability.

6. The employment specialist makes routine visits to the client at the job site or in the community and intervenes when issues and problems arise throughout the client's tenure at the job. In some instances, the employment specialist is in regular contact with the client's supervisor. Employment specialists also meet often with clients outside the work place. The job support plan is individualized.

7. If employment ends or the client desires a new job, the employment specialist works with the client to find another job matching his/her job preferences and needs.

WHAT'S THE EVIDENCE?

Vocational Outcomes

Research has found that supported employment is superior to other employment approaches in improving competitive employment outcomes (Bond, Drake, & Becker, 2012). Fifteen randomized controlled trials have compared the IPS model of supported employment with various other approaches, finding a significant advantage in competitive employment rates for IPS, as shown in Figure 95.1.

These studies have also found that clients receiving supported employment services obtain their first competitive jobs 50% faster and have significantly longer job tenure as compared with clients receiving services in alternative approaches. Studies of day rehabilitation programs that have converted to supported employment programs have found that they have been able to do so successfully, with improved competitive employment outcomes for clients (Becker, Bond, McCarthy, Thompson, Xie, McHugo, & Drake, 2001). Moreover, long-term studies indicate that the vocational benefits of supported employment are long-lasting (Becker, Whitley, Bailey, & Drake, 2007).

Nonvocational Outcomes

Participation in a supported employment program does not itself lead to improved nonvocational outcomes. However, research has indicated that clients who obtain employment realize other

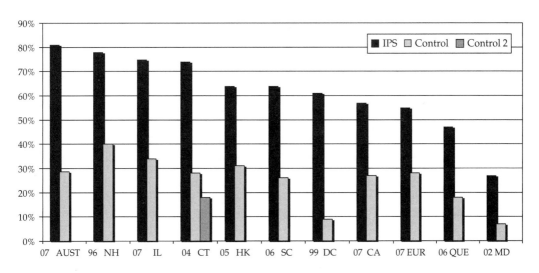

Figure 95.1 Competitive employment rates in 11 randomized controlled trials: Individual placement and support.

benefits, including improved self-esteem (Bond, Resnick, Drake, Xie, McHugo, & Bebout, 2001; Mueser, Becker, Torrey, Xie, Bond, & Drake, 1997), fewer symptoms (e.g., Bond et al., 2001; Mueser et al., 1997; Burns, Catty, White, Becker, Koletsi, & Fioritti, 2009; Kukla, 2010), better general functioning (e.g., Mueser et al., 1997; Burns et al., 2009), improved social networks (Kukla, 2010), and higher quality of life (e.g., Twamley, Narvaez, Becker, Bartels, & Jeste, 2008).

ASSESSMENT AND EVALUATION

Supported employment studies have typically used objective indicators of competitive employment, such as rates of obtaining employment, time to first job, job tenure, and hours worked per week. Supported employment researchers have often used rigorous research designs, with careful training of clinicians and monitoring of implementation (*efficacy* methods), conducting these in real-world settings with clients from heterogeneous backgrounds (*effectiveness* methods) (Bond et al., 2008a). Studies have been conducted in a multitude of settings, including urban and rural areas, and in countries outside the United States with differing labor conditions (e.g., Australia, Canada, Hong Kong, and several European countries).

It is standard practice in IPS studies to assess *fidelity*, that is, adherence to the IPS program model using a well-validated fidelity scale (Bond, Becker, Drake, & Vogler, 1997). The IPS fidelity scale is comprised of 15 items rated on a 1 to 5 behaviorally anchored scale, with higher scores indicating better fidelity. Fidelity is assessed at the level of the IPS program and fidelity items cover the primary tenets of the IPS model, such as "rapid job search for competitive jobs," "agency focus on competitive employment," and "zero exclusion criteria" (Becker, Swanson, Bond, & Merrens, 2011). Assessing IPS fidelity and making adjustments to practice is also important, given findings that better fidelity to the IPS model leads to better employment outcomes for clients (Bond, Becker, & Drake, 2011).

IMPLEMENTATION ISSUES

As noted above, systematically assessing and monitoring supported employment fidelity is a crucial implementation strategy. Several other components of effective implementation that relate closely to fidelity include the following (Bond, McHugo, Becker, Rapp, & Whitley, 2008b):

- Discontinuing non-evidence-based vocational services (e.g., sheltered workshops, train–place vocational approaches).
- Improving the integration of employment services with clinical and mental health services, via supervisor leadership.
- Changing relevant organizational and structural tasks to be compatible with the supported employment model. These may include things such as changing billing processes and procedures, training staff, endorsing the supported employment philosophy organization-wide, and changing documentation in client records.
- Implementing supported employment programs at exemplary sites that can be models and opportunities for training of later sites.
- Obtaining support and consensus from all stakeholders (i.e., clients, family members, state authorities, practitioners, and administrators).

In addition, studies have found that supported employment may be implemented successfully and is widely generalizable and applicable across community settings (rural and urban) and across various ethnic and minority groups (including African-Americans, Hispanic-Americans, and Asian-Americans), among both young and older adults, and with clients with co-occurring substance use (Bond, Drake, & Becker, 2010).

PROVIDER COMPETENCIES

Although several provider competencies of employment specialists exist that are necessary for successful supported employment services, little research has been conducted in this area. However, some of the most important provider competencies that should be emphasized in practice include:

- Hopeful attitudes and the belief that clients with severe mental illness *can* work (Gowdy, Carlson, & Rapp, 2003)
- The ability to form a good "working alliance" or relationship with the client (Kukla & Bond, 2009)

- Job development skills, or the ability to locate and secure numerous and diverse jobs matching client preferences and needs
- Skills encompassed within each specific phase of employment services (e.g., appropriate on-going job support to the client) (Bond & Kukla, 2011)
- Employment specialist motivation and interest in the field of supported employment
- Employment specialist focus on working in the community in all phases of employment services, rather than in the agency office

Importantly, these are skills and behaviors that can be taught. The research suggests that appropriate supervision, feedback, and leadership provided to the employment specialist by team leaders and other supervisory-level staff make a difference.

FUTURE DIRECTIONS

Several areas of future research are needed in the supported employment arena, given the paucity of research conducted thus far and/or the need for improvement of supported employment services in various areas to result in improved client outcomes. Such areas include the following (Drake & Bond, 2008):

- Provider competencies
- Ways to increase job tenure of clients
- Understanding the overall costs of supported employment and better ways to finance and organize supported employment services
- Better job development strategies
- Ways to enhance career trajectories of supported employment clients
- Effective ways to address lack of motivation to work

In addition, in recent years, studies have begun to examine adjuncts to supported employment that are designed to compensate for deficits associated with mental illness. For instance, studies have investigated cognitive remediation and social skills training delivered along with IPS-supported employment. To address the educational needs of people with SMI, research suggests that supported education services delivered along with supported employment results in promising outcomes, especially for young adults (Nuechterlein, Subotnik, Turner, Ventura, Becker,

& Drake, 2008). These are fairly new domains of research, however, and future studies should focus on these important areas.

WEBSITES

Dartmouth Psychiatric Research Center— Individualized Placement and Support. http://www.dartmouth.edu/~ips/index .html

Substance Abuse Mental Health Service Administration (reference to IPS). http://www.stopstigma.samhsa.gov/topic/employment/brochures.aspx

Virginia Commonwealth University (VCU) Rehabilitation Research and Training Center, Work Support Information, Resources and research and about work and disability issues. www.worksupport.com

University of Illinois at Chicago, Department of Psychiatry Center on Mental Health Services Research and Policy, Employment Intervention Demonstration Program. www.psych.uic.edu/eidp

References

Anthony, W. A. (1993). Recovery from mental illness: The guiding vision of the mental health service system in the 1990s. *Psychosocial Rehabilitation Journal, 16*(4), 11–23.

Becker, D. R., Bond, G. R., McCarthy, D., Thompson, D., Xie, H., McHugo, G. J., & Drake, R. E. (2001). Converting day treatment centers to supported employment programs in Rhode Island. *Psychiatric Services, 52,* 351–357.

Becker, D. R., & Drake, R. E. (2003). *A working life for people with severe mental illness.* New York, NY: Oxford Press.

Becker, D. R., Swanson, S., Bond, G. R., & Merrens, M. R. (2011). Evidence-based supported employment fidelity review manual (2nd ed.). Lebanon, NH: Dartmouth Psychiatric Research Center.

Becker, D. R., Whitley, R., Bailey, E. L., & Drake, R. E. (2007). Long-term employment outcomes of supported employment for people with severe mental illness. *Psychiatric Services, 58,* 922–928.

Bond, G. R. (1998). Principles of the Individual Placement and Support model: Empirical support. *Psychiatric Rehabilitation Journal, 22,* 11–23.

Bond, G. R. (2004). Supported employment: Evidence for an evidence-based practice. *Psychiatric Rehabilitation Journal, 27,* 345–359.

Bond, G. R., Becker, D. R., & Drake, R. E. (2011). Measurement of fidelity of implementation of evidence-based practices: Case example of the IPS

Fidelity Scale. *Clinical Psychology: Science and Practice, 18*, 125–140.

Bond, G. R., Becker, D. R., Drake, R. E., & Vogler, K. M. (1997). A fidelity scale for the Individual Placement and Support model of supported employment. *Rehabilitation Counseling Bulletin, 40*, 265–284.

Bond, G. R., Drake, R. E., & Becker, D. R. (2008a). An update on randomized controlled trials of evidence-based supported employment. *Psychiatric Rehabilitation Journal, 31*, 280–290.

Bond, G. R., Drake, R. E., & Becker, D. R. (2010). Beyond evidence-based practice: Nine ideal features of a mental health intervention. *Research on Social Work Practice, 20*, 493–501.

Bond, G. R., Drake, R. E., & Becker, D. R. (2012). Generalizability of the Individual Placement and Support (IPS) model of supported employment outside the US. *World Psychiatry, 11*, 32–39.

Bond, G. R., & Kukla, M. (2011). Impact of follow-along support on job tenure in the Individual Placement and Support model. *Journal of Nervous and Mental Disease, 199*, 150–155.

Bond, G. R., McHugo, G. J., Becker, D. R., Rapp, C. A., & Whitley, R. (2008b). Fidelity of supported employment: Lessons learned from the National EBP Project. *Psychiatric Rehabilitation Journal, 31*, 300–305.

Bond, G. R., Resnick, S. G., Drake, R. E., Xie, H. Y., McHugo, G. J., & Bebout, R. R. (2001). Does competitive employment improve nonvocational outcomes for people with severe mental illness? *Journal of Consulting and Clinical Psychology, 69*(3), 489–501.

Burns, T., Catty, J., White, S., Becker, T., Koletsi, M., Fioritti, A., (2009). The impact of supported employment and working on clinical and social functioning: Results of an international study of Individual Placement and Support. *Schizophrenia Bulletin, 35*, 949–958.

Drake, R. E., & Bond, G. R. (2008). The future of supported employment for people with severe mental illness. *Psychiatric Rehabilitation Journal, 31*, 367–376.

Drake, R. E., Bond, G. R., & Becker, D. R. (2012). IPS supported employment: An evidence-based approach to supported employment. New York, NY: Oxford University Press.

Gowdy, E. A., Carlson, L. S., & Rapp, C. A. (2003). Practices differentiating high-performing from low-performing supported employment programs. *Psychiatric Rehabilitation Journal, 26*, 232–239.

Kukla, M. (2010). The relationship between employment status and nonvocational outcomes for persons with severe mental illness enrolled in vocational programs: A longitudinal study. Unpublished doctoral dissertation, Purdue University of Indianapolis, Indiana.

Kukla, M., & Bond, G. R. (2009). The working alliance and employment outcomes for people with severe mental illness receiving vocational services. *Rehabilitation Psychology, 54*, 157–163.

Mueser, K. T., Becker, D. R., Torrey, W. C., Xie, H. Y., Bond, G. R., & Drake, R. E., (1997). Work and non-vocational domains of functioning in persons with severe mental illness: A longitudinal analysis. *Journal of Nervous & Mental Disease, 185*(7), 419–426.

Nuechterlein, K. H., Subotnik, K. L., Turner, L. R., Ventura, J., Becker, D. R., & Drake, R. E. (2008). Individual Placement and Support for individuals with recent-onset schizophrenia: Integrating supported education and supported employment. *Psychiatric Rehabilitation Journal, 31*, 340–349.

Twamley, E. W., Narvaez, J. M., Becker, D. R., Bartels, S. J., & Jeste, D. V. (2008). Supported employment for middle-aged and older people with schizophrenia. *American Journal of Psychiatric Rehabilitation, 11*, 76–89.

Wehman, P., & Moon, M. S. (Eds.). (1988). Vocational rehabilitation and supported employment. Baltimore, MD: Paul Brookes.

96 Working with and Strengthening Social Networks

Elizabeth M. Tracy & Suzanne M. Brown

The role of supportive relationships is central to the mission of social work and its practice. Assessing and working with social support systems are considered requisite skills for social work practice, as the following case examples illustrate.

- A teenage mother receives home visits and attends a parent support group to build a supportive social network as she transitions into the role of parent.
- A man who has completed a substance abuse treatment program attends Alcoholics Anonymous and works with his sponsor and case manager to build a social network supportive of sobriety.
- Family members participate in a psycho-educational support group so that they get the support and help needed to cope with a family member with a mental disorder.

Social support refers to the actions that others perform when they render assistance. There are several different types of social support, such as:

- Emotional support—having someone listen to your feelings, comfort you, or offer encouragement
- Informational support—having someone teach you something, give you information or advice, or help you make a major decision
- Concrete support—having someone help in tangible ways, loaning you something, giving you information, helping with a chore, or taking you on an errand.

Social support can take place within naturally occurring helping networks of family, friends, neighbors, and peers, or in groups and organizations that have been specifically created or contrived for this purpose. Formal support includes services delivered by paid human service professionals. Informal support, which is the focus here, can be delivered by kinship networks, peers, including peers from treatment programs, volunteers, or local community groups.

People with access to social support resources are in better physical and emotional health and are better equipped to adapt to and cope with life changes. Thompson (1995) has identified several key functions of social support that may reduce or protect against the negative effects of stressful events:

- Emotional sustenance and a sense that you are not alone
- Counseling advice and guidance in dealing with challenging life events
- Access to information, services, material resources, and tangible assistance
- Skills acquisition and training
- Social monitoring and social control of behavior.

Social networks are the primary mechanism through which support functions are made available. The term *social network* refers to a set of individuals and the ties among them. The study of whole networks examines the pattern of relations within a group bounded by geography or some characteristic, such as all the clients in a treatment program. A personal social network focus examines the relations surrounding a focal person, such as an individual client or family. A personal social network approach to assessment and intervention, which is the focus of this entry, considers the behavior of individuals in the context of the people with whom they directly interact.

Personal social networks consist of several dimensions. Compositional network qualities include:

- Size—the total number of people in the network
- Relationships of network members to the focal person—friends, family, professionals
- Characteristics of network members—for example, alcohol/drug users
- Frequency of contact—how often people in the network interact with one another
- Duration—how long people in the network have known one another
- Reciprocity—the amount of give and take.

Structural network qualities include such features as:

- Density—the percent of ties that exist in a network out of all those possible
- Components—network members who are connected to one another directly or indirectly
- Multiplexity—the extent to which network relationships serve more than one function or provide more than one type of support
- Centrality measures—degree to which a network is organized around one or a few people.

Sometimes composition and structure can be combined, such as identifying whether the most structurally central person is supportive of the client's recovery.

The terms *social network* and *social support* do not necessarily refer to the same concept. People may be surrounded by large social networks but may not feel supported or perceive support from others. They may also not be receiving the types and amount of support that they need. A social support network refers to the set of people who do provide various forms of social support for one another.

Likewise, not all social ties are supportive because interpersonal relationships may be sources of support as well as stress (Lincoln, 2000). Patterns of negative social networks may be evident. For example, social network members may be overly critical or demanding of one another, or members may reinforce or encourage harmful or antisocial behavior, such as drug abuse or gang violence. Social networks may also fail to support efforts to change behaviors or maintain changes in behavior, such as a parent changing from punishment approaches to more positive forms of child management. Additionally, social network members may offer both positive forms of support in one area of an individual's life while at the same time preventing change in other areas of the individual's life. One example may be a network member who, while providing concrete support such as money or housing, also encourages an individual with a history of alcoholism to continue to use substances (Brown, Tracy, Jun, Parks, & Min, under review).

Finally, several related concepts are important to note. Enacted support refers to the actual utilization of support resources. Perceived support refers to the extent to which an individual feels that his or her support needs are or would be fulfilled. Network orientation refers to beliefs, attitudes, or expectations concerning the usefulness of network members in helping cope with a problem. Some people may have adequate social networks but may not make use of or access their network in times of need owing to a negative network orientation. Another barrier to use of one's social network may be inadequate social skills in requesting help, developing network relationships, and maintaining supportive social ties over time. Networks can also be negatively or positively influenced by the resources and climate of the larger social and physical environment in which they are situated.

SOCIAL SUPPORT ASSESSMENT GUIDELINES

Given the complexity of social support, a necessary first task is to complete an accurate assessment of social network resources and the functional qualities of social network relationships. The following questions serve as guidelines for social support assessment.

1. Who is in the network? How are they related to the client? Who could be potential members?
2. What are the strengths and capabilities of the social network? Among the

strengths that need to be examined are the number of supportive relationships, variety of supportive relationships, types of support available (emotional, concrete, and informational), and reciprocity among helping relationships.

3. What are the gaps in social support needs? Is there a lack of fit between the types of support network members are willing or capable of providing and the types of support the client needs or desires?

4. What relationships in the network are based on mutual exchange? Does reciprocity seem to be an issue for the client? Is the client always giving to others and thereby experiencing stress and drain? Or does the client appear to be a drain on the network, with the result that network members are stressed and overburdened?

5. What network members are identified as responsive to requests for help, effective in their helping, accessible, and dependable? Do sufficient numbers of network members meet these conditions?

6. What network members are critical of the client in a negative or demanding way? Is the client surrounded by a network that is perceived as negative, nonsupportive, and/or stress-producing?

7. What obstacles or barriers to using social network resources exist? Does the client lack supportive resources or skills in accessing them? Are network members unable to provide more assistance owing to lack of skills or knowledge? Or have they provided support in the past and are now unwilling or unable to continue to do so? Overwhelming family stressors, such as homelessness or substance use, may be present that interfere with the provision of support (Kemp, Whittaker, & Tracy, 1997).

8. Are there internal traits or emotional states such as shame, fear, or difficulty trusting others that may be barriers to help seeking or barriers to effectively creating and utilizing network supports?

INTERVENTION STRATEGIES

Social network interventions are typically directed toward either structural changes in the social network itself or functional changes in social network relationships. Structural interventions aim to create a new network or supplement one that already exists. Some examples of structural changes include:

- Increasing or decreasing the size of the network, as in increasing the number of friends
- Changing the composition of the social network by facilitating new connections, as in introducing a new cluster or re-establishing network relationships that have been lost
- Increasing or decreasing the frequency of contact with particular social network members—for example, highly negative network members.

Functional interventions seek to improve or enhance the quality and nature of relationships within a network. This might include increasing or mobilizing various types of support (e.g., concrete emotional or informational support, as in respite care services for a family) or teaching network members new skills for interaction. Some examples of skill-enhancing interventions to facilitate more social support include:

- Developing or increasing skills in making friends
- Decreasing negative beliefs about self (if this is a barrier to developing/maintaining supportive relationships), increasing positive self-statements, and increasing the ability to identify personal strengths
- Developing strategies for handling criticism from others
- Increasing assertive skills (if this is a barrier to developing or maintaining supportive relationships)
- Increasing communication skills (if this is a barrier to developing or maintaining supportive relationships)
- Teaching reciprocity skills (if this is a barrier to developing or maintaining supportive relationships) to ask for help (Kemp et al., 1997).

The overriding purpose of the social network intervention should be kept in mind. Changes in social support may be desired for a variety of reasons: first, to support maintenance and generalization of treatment efforts, as in building social networks supportive of change (Tracy & Biegel, 2006); second, to serve as a protective factor, as in increasing supportive bonds for children at risk of juvenile delinquency or substance abuse (MacNeil, Stewart, & Kaufman, 2000); and third, to provide a coping mechanism, as in social support provision due to a crisis or life transition (Cameron, 2000).

Examples of Social Network Intervention Strategies

- Network facilitation through network meetings—for example, family group conferencing (Crampton, 2007); network therapy for alcohol problems (Copello, Orford, Hodgdon & Tober, 2009)
- Additional network clusters, through referral to formal or informal organizations (e.g., referral to self help programs)
- Additional individual network members through a social networking intervention (Biegel, Tracy & Corvo, 1994)
- Peer support programs and mutual aid or self-help groups (Moore, 2005); peer education and modeling to promote changes in behavior throughout a social network (Latkin et al., 2013)
- Natural helper intervention (Gaudin, 1993)
- Social and communication skills training (Richey, 1994)
- Extended family support and psycho-educational approaches—for example, teaching family members how to deal with psychiatric symptoms (Mueser, Noordsy, Drake, Fox, & Barlow, 2003).

See Kemp et al. (1997) for further descriptions of these and other intervention strategies.

IMPLEMENTING FOR SUCCESS

A network intervention is not a panacea. Many clients still require professionally delivered services, with social network interventions as a supplement. There are a number of implementation issues to consider.

- Pay close attention to the type of support desired or needed by the client (e.g., informational or emotional) and match the intervention to that need.
- Ensure that *reciprocal* relationships are established.
- Focus on the relationship quality and functioning of network relationships, not just size of network.

- Recognize that not all networks are supportive and attend to negative or stress-producing network relationships; intervene to enhance these relationships.
- Monitor the effect of interventions on network members to ensure that the network is not overburdened.
- Attend to perceived as well as enacted support.
- Teach skills needed to elicit and maintain supportive relationships, both to the client and network members, as skill deficits may contribute to lack of support.
- Recognize that advocacy may be needed to build supportive resources at the community level.
- Focus on change from the client's perspective of their network relationships. Clients may be aware of ways in which some network members may be more supportive than we are aware. For example, while professionals may assess relationships with children in a network as one directional, mothers may receive support from their children and perceive these relationships as reciprocal and not burdensome.
- Recognize that social factors such as poverty and lack of education may limit an individual's capacity for network change due to limited geographic mobility and limited housing or neighborhood options. In these cases, the goal may be to increase interpersonal skills to manage network relationships that cannot be changed.

Social support interventions are challenging to evaluate owing to their complexity and diversity. Hogan, Linden, and Najarian (2003) conclude in a review of 100 intervention studies that although there is some support for the usefulness of social support interventions, there is an insufficient research base to conclude what type of intervention works best for what presenting problem. It may be difficult to see immediate results of network interventions. People may perceive supportive interventions differently depending on the source of support. The timing of the intervention may be an important consideration as well. Networks may change over time and attention to network structure, composition, and support are important to assess at initial intake as well as at time points post treatment or services (Min et al., 2013). In spite of the limitations of our current knowledge, social support interventions hold promise, and the skills of assessing and mobilizing support are important for every practitioner to acquire.

WEBSITES

American Self-Help Group Clearinghouse. http://www.selfhelpgroups.org.

National Self Help Clearinghouse. http://www .selfhelpweb.org.

National Mental Health Consumers' Self-Help Clearinghouse. http://www.mhselfhelp.org.

Post-Partum Support International. http://www .postpartum.net/support-map.html.

References

Biegel, D., Tracy, E. M., & Corvo, K. N. (1994). Strengthening social networks: Intervention strategies for mental health case managers. *Health and Social Work, 19*(3), 207–216.

Brown, S., Tracy, E. M., Jun, M., Parks, H., & Min, M. O. (under review). By the company she keeps: Client and provider perspectives of personal network characteristics as facilitators or barriers to recovery for women in treatment for substance dependence. *Qualitative Health Research.*

Cameron, G. (2000). Parent mutual aid organizations in child welfare demonstration project: A report of outcomes. *Children and Youth Services Review, 22*(6), 421–440.

Copello, A., Orford, J., Hodgdon, R., & Tober, G. (2009). *Social behaviour and network therapy for alcohol problems.* London and New York: Routledge.

Crampton, D. (2007). Research review: Family group decision making: A promising practice in need of more program theory and research. *Child & Family Social Work, 12*(2), 202–209.

Gaudin, J. M. (1993). *Child neglect: A guide for intervention.* Washington, DC: Health and Human Services, National Center on Child Abuse and Neglect (NCCAN).

Hogan, B. E., Linden, L., & Najarian, B. (2003). Social support interventions: Do they work? *Clinical Psychology Review, 22*, 382–440.

Kemp, S., Whittaker, J. K., & Tracy, E. M. (1997). *Person–environment practice: The social ecology of interpersonal helping.* New York, NY: Aldine de Gruyter.

Latkin, C., Donnell, D., Liu, T., Davey-Rothwell, M., Celentano, D & Metzger, D. (2013). The dynamic relation between social norms and behaviors: The results of an HIV prevention network intervention for injection drug users. *Addiction, 108*, 934–943.

Lincoln, K. D. (2000). Social support, negative social interactions, and psychological well-being. *Social Service Review, 74 June*, 232–252.

MacNeil, G., Stewart, J. C., & Kaufman, A. V. (2000). Social support as a potential moderator of adolescent delinquent behaviors. *Child and Adolescent Social Work Journal, 17*(5), 361–379.

Min, M. O., Tracy, E. M., Kim, H., Park, H., Jun, M., Brown, S., McCarty, C., & Laudet, A., Changes in personal networks of women in residential and outpatient substance abuse treatment. *Journal of Substance Abuse Treatment* (2013). http://dx.doi.org/10.1016/j.jsat.2013.04.006

Moore, B. (2005). Empirically supported family and peer interventions for dual disorders. *Research on Social Work Practice, 15*, 231–245.

Mueser, K. T., Noordsy, D. L., Drake, R. E., Fox, L., & Barlow, D. H. (2003). *Integrated treatment for dual disorders: A guide to effective practice.* New York, NY: Guilford.

Richey, C. A. (1994). Social support skill training. In D. K. Granvold (Ed.), *Cognitive and behavioral treatment: Methods and applications* (pp. 299–338). Belmont, CA: Brooks/Cole.

Thompson, R. A. (1995). *Preventing child maltreatment through social support.* Thousand Oaks, CA: Sage.

Tracy, E., & Biegel, D. (2006). Social networks and dual disorders: A literature review and implications for practice and future research. *Journal of Dual Diagnosis, 2*(2), 59–88.

97 Eye Movement Desensitization and Reprocessing with Trauma Clients

Tonya Edmond & Allen Rubin

Eye movement desensitization and reprocessing (EMDR) was developed in 1987 as a procedure for alleviating stress-related symptoms connected to traumatic memories. Its founder described it as "an interactive, intrapsychic, cognitive, behavioral, body-oriented therapy" that aims "to rapidly metabolize the dysfunctional residue from the past and transform it into something useful." (Shapiro, 1995, pp. 52–53) Within this description and subsequent publications is the assurance that EMDR can be effectively employed by practitioners who draw from a variety of theoretical orientations, including, but not limited to, cognitive-behavioral, psychodynamic, and systemic approaches (Shapiro & Laliotis, 2011).

Although EMDR was not originally theoretically derived, which has been a source of criticism, the Adaptive Information Processing (AIP) model has been developed as a working theory to help explain both symptom development and the observed treatment effects of EMDR on those symptoms (Shapiro & Laliotis, 2011; EMDR International Association [EMDRIA], 2012; Schubert & Lee, 2009). The AIP model is viewed as the framework guiding case conceptualization, treatment planning, and implementation of the eight phases and three prongs that make up EMDR (Shapiro & Laliotis, 2011; EMDRIA 2012; Schubert & Lee, 2009). In brief, the AIP model posits that human beings have an innate information processing mechanism that facilitates integration of life events into existing memory networks that can generate new learning.

During particularly distressing experiences, information may not be adequately processed or integrated, resulting in maladaptive encoding of the memory, which is dysfunctionally stored in a neural network, similar to the fear network proposed by Foa and Kozak (1986) (Shapiro & Laliotis, 2011; EMDRIA 2012; Schubert & Lee, 2009). Because the core elements of the distressing experience—feelings, thoughts, body sensations—have not been sufficiently processed and integrated, present-day reminders can trigger the distress, impair functioning, and potentially lead to the development of significant mental health conditions. The eight phases and three prongs of the EMDR protocol are employed to activate the neural network where the memory is dysfunctionally stored and to re-engage information processing to facilitate adaptive resolution of the distressing experience (Shapiro & Laliotis, 2011; EMDRIA 2012; Schubert & Lee, 2009). For a more detailed review of research on the AIP model and a comparison with other models of posttraumatic stress disorder (PTSD), see Schubert and Lee (2009).

EIGHT-PHASED, THREE-PRONGED TREATMENT APPROACH

According to Shapiro and Laliotis (2011), the eight phases of EMDR are implemented within the context of the three-pronged approach, which uses past, present, and future elements to guide the treatment process. The therapist works with the client to identify pertinent experiences from the past that are related to the problems the client is having in the present; triggers that are being activated in the present; and future actions the client can take to respond adaptively to new life experiences.

In the first phase, a thorough client history is obtained, preferably with the inclusion of standardized diagnostic tools, and, from that, a treatment plan is developed. The clinical evaluation during this phase should be comprehensive and include a determination of whether there are indications that the client is likely to benefit from EMDR treatment as well as any contraindications for the use of EMDR with the client. Using the presenting issues, the therapist should help the client identify past events affecting current functioning, triggers currently being activated, and potential future needs. Both positive and negative life experiences are identified and incorporated into the treatment plan.

In the second phase, the client is prepared for the EMDR procedure and client goals and expectations regarding treatment are established. Preparation includes building a therapeutic relationship and educating clients about their symptoms or diagnoses, as well as the EMDR procedures that will be employed. During this process, data on the effectiveness of EMDR is shared, along with possible negative reactions to it, so that client fears and safety issues can be addressed and informed consent for treatment ensured. Emphasis is placed on fostering the development of self-soothing and affect regulation skills to ensure stabilization during and between sessions. Metaphors, guided imagery, and other techniques are used to develop adaptive resources before trauma processing work is initiated. This is recognized as especially important for clients with histories of complex trauma.

In the third phase, an assessment is conducted to determine what target issue and what components thereof are to be addressed. Target components include the presenting problem, the memory associated with the presenting problem, a mental image of that memory, identification of a currently held negative self-belief associated with the memory, identification of a desired positive self-belief with which to replace the negative one, the emotions associated with the memory, and any physical sensations the client notices when picturing the traumatic memory. During this phase, the client focuses on a mental picture of the traumatic memory, identifies the negative self-belief about the experience, identifies a positive self-statement with which the client would like to replace the undesired one, reports unpleasant emotional sensations connected with the image, notes where in the body the emotional unpleasantness is felt, and provides a subjective

rating of the severity of the distress they feel and how true their preferred self-belief seems to them. That is, the client holds the mental image of the memory while simultaneously thinking of the desired positive self-statement and is then asked to rate how true the desired self-belief feels on a scale from 1 to 7. The client is also asked to think of the emotions evoked by the image in the here and now and the negative self-belief and to rate on a scale from 0 to 10 how disturbing the emotions currently feel when holding the image and negative self-statement in mind. Depending on the level of these two ratings, the therapist may decide to proceed to the next phase or stay in Phase three and seek to identify alternative issues or components that are more problematic.

In the fourth phase, the desensitization process is implemented. The target memory is activated by asking the client to hold all of the identified target components in mind while the therapist induces alternating bilateral stimulation (visual—eye movements, auditory—sounds from head phones, or tactile—hand taps). During this time, the therapist encourages the client to simply notice the experience and to report whatever observations they noticed about the target image, memory, thoughts, feelings, or bodily sensations. The processing and reporting that occur is often likened to free association. With each set of bilateral stimulation, the client will spontaneously move from a body sensation, to an image or an emotion or insight without describing a coherent narrative as is commonly expected in gradual or prolonged exposure during trauma processing work.

If eye movements comprise the bilateral stimulation, the client is asked to visualize the distressful scene and keep in mind the identified cognitions and feelings while visually tracking the therapist's fingers moving rapidly and rhythmically (about 18 inches in front of the client's face) back and forth, up and down, or diagonally. The speed is about two back-and-forth movements per second. The direction and number of movements varies on an individual basis, but is around 24–36 passes. The average duration of each set of bilateral stimulation is approximately 30 seconds. After each set, the client discusses with the therapist what thoughts, feelings, or images came up during the set, and then reports changes in the degree of distress felt. If not much changed, the therapist likely will repeat one or more sets of bilateral stimulation, targeting the same stressful memory, feelings, and cognitions.

If the client seems stuck or processing seems stalled, the therapist will use a cognitive interweave to interject adaptive information. If new material comes up, the next set(s) will target that new material. This process will then be repeated throughout the treatment session, with each successive set of bilateral stimulation typically targeting the new material that comes up each time. The aim is to reach a point when the client's level of disturbance rating drops considerably (ideally to a level of 0 or 1 on the 10-point scale). Additional sessions can be used as needed to deal with the same or other sources of distress. The three-pronged approach is particularly important during this phase, working to process past distressing experiences, current triggers, and potential future challenges.

In the fifth phase, which commences after successful processing during the desensitization phase, additional sets of bilateral stimulation are used to install the desired cognition (i.e., a positive self-belief). The positive cognition is considered to have been successfully installed when the client rates how true the desired self-belief feels as a 6 or 7 on the 7-point validity of cognition scale.

In the sixth phase, the client is asked to hold the target image or memory in mind along with the desired positive belief and to scan their body to determine whether there are any positive or negative residual physical sensations from the target issue present. If any such physical sensations are identified, this is a signal that there is unresolved material that needs to be processed further, in which case Phases three through five are reapplied until the client indicates that only positive or neutral physical sensations are present.

The seventh phase involves closure, in which the clinician employs relaxation techniques (such as guided imagery) to alleviate any lingering distress experienced by the client. The objective in this phase is to ensure client stability, both at the end of a given session and in-between sessions when additional processing may occur. The need for additional desensitization sessions may be identified during this phase, and clients are asked to maintain a log of any distressing emotions or cognitions they experience between sessions. Clients are encouraged to use guided imagery or other self-soothing, affect-regulating skills as needed to facilitate stability in-between sessions.

The eighth phase involves client re-evaluation to assess treatment effectiveness. This begins by checking whether anything new emerged after the previous session. The three-pronged protocol is used to determine whether there is any residual distress related to past experiences, current triggers, or future challenges that still needs to be targeted. If there is any indication of residual distress related to any of these areas, they are targeted for treatment and Phases 3–8 are implemented again.

The number and length of the sessions required to achieve meaningful change vary from client to client. Some studies have reported clinically meaningful and stable changes with as few as one to three sessions, typically for a single traumatic event (Shapiro, 1996a,b; 2010). For clients who have complex trauma histories, the length of treatment is longer and varied. According to the EMDR International Association (2012), "EMDR treatment is not completed in any particular number of sessions. It is central to EMDR that positive results from its application derive from the interaction among the clinician, the therapeutic approach, and the client." (EMDRIA's Definition of EMDR, 2012) Ninety minutes is the recommended session length for adults and adolescents. Most of the time is taken up by discussion before and after each set. The actual cumulative amount of time the eyes are moving (or other forms of bilateral stimulation are occurring) will be several minutes.

The EMDR procedure is implemented in the context of an ongoing therapeutic relationship, after a therapeutic alliance is established with the client. It is intended to be used by experienced psychotherapists, in conjunction with other clinical approaches they employ, only after they have received formal EMDR training. Also, therapists are advised to apply EMDR only to target problems that they already are competent to treat.

Although literature pertaining to the use of EMDR with children and adolescents is much less than that which exists for adults, there is emerging evidence of EMDR's effectiveness with those populations, particularly for treatment of posttraumatic symptoms and PTSD (Adler-Tapia & Settle, 2009; Field & Cottrell, 2011; Ahmad, Larsson, & Sundelin-Wahlsten, 2007; deRoos, 2011; Rodenburg, Benjamin, deRoos, Meijer, & Stams, 2009). Recently, the California Evidence-Based Clearinghouse for Child Welfare (CEBC) listed EMDR as one of only two trauma-focused treatments for children that has received a Level 1 rating, which indicates that it is well supported by evidence. The only other modality to receive that rating was trauma-focused cognitive behavioral treatment (CEBC, 2013).

In addition to having been trained in both the basic EMDR protocol and the Advanced Training in using EMDR with children, it is also recommended that any clinician treating traumatized children have training in trauma treatment, as well as prior experience working with children and adolescents. Furthermore, to ensure treatment fidelity the AIP model and the full EMDR protocol with the three-pronged approach should be used with children and adolescents with the recognition that there will need to be treatment adjustments to accommodate the child's developmental stage and specific presenting problem (Adler-Tapia & Settle, 2009; Adler-Tapia, 2011). Nevertheless, although clinicians are able to incorporate into each of the eight phases of the EMDR protocol useful techniques and strategies employed in other child and adolescent treatment approaches (e.g., play and art therapy), the guiding framework should continue to be the AIP model.

Adler-Tapia and Settle (2009) highlight some examples of age appropriate modifications and creative ways to integrate other techniques across each of the eight phases of the EMDR protocol. During the preparation phase, relaxation skills and recognition of emotions are taught. Metaphor and fantasy may be used with sand trays, play therapy, clay, or drawings during the assessment phase to help the child communicate his or her feelings and thoughts to identify the treatment target.

In the desensitization phase, it is recommended that in order to facilitate continued interest and engagement, the therapist use shorter sets of eye movements (<24) and vary the type of bilateral stimulation provided. The therapist might start with a set of eye movements and then the next round of bilateral stimulation could involve audio signals, followed by hand taps. Fun alternatives for bilateral stimulation include having the child drum, clap, or march. Alternatives for visual bilateral stimulation include the use of puppets or stuffed animals. In between sets of bilateral stimulation, the child can verbally describe what she or he noticed or if needed, the child can draw, use clay, or a sand tray to describe what occurred internally. This process may move more quickly to a point of resolution in children because they have lived for a shorter time and may have a smaller number of adverse events associated

with their presenting problems than is common among adults.

In the installation phase, the therapist would revisit the original drawing or sand tray work with the child and ask him/her how true the desired positive cognition felt. With the body scan, a therapist might use a magnifying glass and a toy to make the notion of a body scan more concrete. During the closure phase, the relaxation skills developed during the preparation phase would be employed both in the session and as an out-of-session resource for the child and parents to support affect regulation. In addition, drawing could be used to create containers to place painful feelings, thoughts, and memories in between sessions and for developing the future template. In addition, any drawings developed over the course of treatment can be reintroduced during the re-evaluation phase with the child to review progress.

As with many other children-focused interventions, inclusion of parents or caregivers is important, beginning with education about trauma, child development, and the EMDR treatment process. Parents/caregivers also serve as an important resource in providing information about the child's developmental and attachment history, experiences of trauma, current symptoms, and problems of concern. As treatment progresses, parents/caregivers can also provide information on external indicators of distress or signs of improvement in the child (Adler-Tapia & Settle, 2009). Dr. Adler-Tapia has written extensively about using EMDR in the treatment of children. For a more comprehensive description, see EMDR and the Art of Psychotherapy with Children (Adler-Tapia & Settle, 2008).

Despite having received a great deal of rigorous outcome research supporting its effectiveness in treating adults with noncombat, single-trauma PTSD, EMDR is still viewed by some as controversial. One reason is that its proponents historically touted it as being effective not only with trauma and fear-based disorders, but also with virtually every area of psychopathology—areas in which there is much less supportive research. Another reason is the initial extreme claims that were made about it by its proponents, such as suggesting that only one session is needed to resolve trauma symptoms or calling it a "breakthrough" therapy (Shapiro & Forrest, 1997). Although there is evidence that for some single-incident traumas one to three sessions of EMDR can be effective in reducing or eliminating trauma symptoms or PTSD, chronic or complex trauma typically requires a longer course of treatment with EMDR or any other evidence-based trauma treatment (Edmond, Rubin, & Wambach, 1999; Ironson, Freund, Strauss, & Williams, 2002; Jaberghaderi, Greenwald, Rubin, Dolatabadim, & Zand, 2004). For example, in comparison studies of EMDR and Prolonged Exposure, six to nine sessions were provided with comparably effective outcomes (Ironson, Freund, Strauss, & Williams, 2002; Lee, Gavriel, Drummond, Richards, & Greenwald, 2002; Rothbaum, Astin, & Marsteller, 2005). It should be noted that the EMDRIA definition of EMDR treatment states that length of treatment is driven by the client's needs and circumstances and not by a prescribed number of sessions.

Some have portrayed EMDR as a pseudo-scientific movement that promotes an intervention that merely tacks an unnecessary treatment gimmick (dual attention stimulation) onto imaginal exposure techniques (Olatunji, Parker, & Lohr, 2005–2006). Its detractors have also criticized the fact that its development was not based in theory and that attempts to connect it to theory have been speculative and mutable over the years. The AIP model described above is the most current iteration. The same detractors have argued that EMDR proponents keep changing the criteria used for judging the fidelity of EMDR treatment with each outcome study that produces findings that its proponents dislike (Rubin, 2003, 2004).

Despite these claims, there have now been nearly 50 randomized, controlled trial (RCT) studies and several meta-analyses that have demonstrated the effectiveness of EMDR (Bisson et al., 2007; Bradley, Greene, Russ, Dutra, & Westen, 2005; Davidson & Parker, 2001; Seidler & Wagner, 2006; Van Etten & Taylor, 1998). Moreover, the first decade of research on EMDR led Division 12 (Clinical Psychology) of the American Psychological Association to deem EMDR one of three empirically validated treatment approaches probably efficacious in treating PTSD (Chambless et al., 1998). The other two validated treatment approaches were exposure therapy and stress inoculation therapy. Since that time, several studies have been conducted that included direct comparisons of EMDR with Pronged Exposure that found both treatments to be effective, but with EMDR achieving results in fewer sessions with less homework (Ironson, Freund, Strauss, & Williams, 2002; Lee, Gavriel, Drummond, Richards, & Greenwald, 2002; Power, McGoldrick, Brown, Buchanan, Sharp, Swanson, & Karatzias, 2002). These results indicate that although EMDR may not be more *effective* than other evidence-based trauma treatments, it may be more *efficient* in achieving comparable results in a shorter period of time, requiring less out-of-session work by the client.

In 1999, EMDR was designated in the treatment guidelines of the International Society for Traumatic Stress Studies as an effective treatment for PTSD (Chemtob, Tolin, van der Kolk, & Pitman, 1999). Subsequently, it was also recognized as an effective treatment for PTSD in the Cochrane Database, The California Evidence Based Clearinghouse, Substance Abuse and Mental Health Services Administration (SAMHSA's) National Registry of Evidence Based Programs & Practices, the American Psychology Association, the American Psychiatric Association, and the Department of Veteran's Affairs & Department of Defense. In addition, EMDR has been endorsed in several international treatment guidelines in the United Kingdom, Ireland, France, Israel, Sweden, and the Netherlands.

The early evidence supporting the effectiveness of EMDR in treating traumatized children was based primarily on several quasiexperiments and other studies with relatively weak controls for various threats to internal validity (Rubin, 2003). But although there is less research evidence supporting the effectiveness of EMDR in alleviating the trauma symptoms of children than is available on adults, the evidence is growing and showing promise. Several small RCTs have been conducted, along with two systematic reviews and a meta-analysis, all indicating that use of EMDR in treating trauma in children is effective. Chemtob, Nakashima, and Carlson (2002) tested a brief three-session course of EMDR treatment against a wait-list control with elementary school children ($n = 32$; aged 6–12 years) who had experienced a hurricane and found it to be effective in reducing PTSD symptoms, anxiety, and depression. Jeffres (2004) found that up to five 60-minute sessions of EMDR alleviated PTSD symptoms among children (ages 8–12 years) who had suffered one or more traumas. Ahmad and associates (2007) conducted an RCT with children ($n = 33$) diagnosed with PTSD comparing EMDR to a wait-list control and found significant differences in outcomes on all measures except the hyperarousal symptom cluster.

Kemp and associates (2010) compared EMDR to a wait-list control with children between 6 and 12 years of age with PTSD symptoms ($n = 27$) following a motor vehicle accident. Those who received EMDR experienced a 25% reduction in PTSD symptoms, while the wait list did not experience any reductions. Each of these studies would have been strengthened by comparisons with established effective treatments.

Jaberghaderi and colleagues (2004) compared EMDR to cognitive behavioral therapy (CBT) with a group of Iranian girls ($n = 14$) who had been sexually abused. Both treatments produced effective outcomes in reducing PTSD and behavior problems, but EMDR achieved the results in half the number of sessions (6.1 vs. 11.6) needed for similar results in the CBT group. Recently deRoos (2011) conducted an RCT comparing the effectiveness of EMDR + parental counseling to CBT + parental counseling in children ($n = 52$) between the ages of 4 and 18 years exposed to a disaster. Both treatments were effective in reducing key trauma symptoms—PTSD, depression, and anxiety—but as seen in adult sessions, results were achieved in fewer sessions (3 vs. 4). It is worth noting that deRoos codeveloped the CBT intervention used in that study; consequently, if one were to be concerned about bias it would be presumably toward the CBT condition.

Rodenburg and colleagues (2009) conducted a meta-analysis of seven RCTs involving the use of EMDR to treat children who had experienced a variety of traumas. They found EMDR to have an overall significant medium effect size of $d = .56$ and concluded that EMDR is an efficacious treatment for children and adolescents with trauma symptoms. Adler-Tapia and Settle (2009) conducted a systematic review of the efficacy of EMDR with children and adolescents that included 19 studies that met their inclusion criteria. Four of the studies included RCTs with children who had PTSD or posttraumatic symptoms, all of which are mentioned above. They concluded that the available evidence suggests that EMDR is a promising practice for treating trauma in children and adolescents, but its efficacy with other behavioral problems and disorders has not yet been established.

Three experimental studies raised questions about the effectiveness of EMDR in treating children whose symptoms were not clearly trauma-based. Two of these experiments compared the efficacy of EMDR with that of in vivo exposure in the treatment of spider-phobic children. One found positive effects for EMDR, particularly on self-report measures, but also found that in vivo exposure had superior effects in reducing avoidance behaviors (Muris, Merckelbach, Holdrinet, & Sijsenaar, 1998). It concluded that in vivo exposure is the treatment of choice for this type of phobia and EMDR added nothing of value to it. In the other experiment, in vivo exposure produced significant improvement in behavioral as well as self-reported outcome measures, whereas EMDR produced significant improvement only on self-reported spider fear. Also, providing EMDR before in vivo exposure did not enhance the effectiveness of the in vivo exposure treatment (Muris, Merckelbach, van Haaften, & Mayer, 1997).

One randomized experiment (Rubin et al., 2001) raised doubts about the effectiveness of EMDR when treating children whose emotional and behavioral problems are not connected in a narrow fashion to a specific trauma or whose very young ages or clinical problems require improvisational deviations from the standard EMDR protocol.

In addition to the need for more evidence regarding the effectiveness of EMDR with children, questions remain unanswered regarding its effectiveness with other target populations and problems. The evidence is mixed, for example, regarding its effectiveness in treating combat PTSD among military veterans (Rubin, 2003; Albright & Thyer, 2009). Likewise, there is a shortage of evidence supporting its effectiveness in treating victims of multiple traumas who experience complex PTSD (Rubin, 2003). Also needed is more evidence to support the claims of some that EMDR is effective in treating a wider range of problems, including less circumscribed ones that may not be caused by trauma, such as self-esteem issues, agoraphobia, somatic disorders, smoking cessation, chronic depression, obsessive-compulsive disorder, and eating disorders (Rubin, 2003; Shapiro, 1995).

Although EMDR incorporates various cognitive-behavioral techniques, its most distinguishing feature is the use of bilateral stimulation. Eye movements usually comprise the bilateral stimulation. Other forms of stimulation include alternating right and left hand taps or alternating sounds in the right and left ears for clients with vision problems or who have difficulty thinking about stressful material while concentrating on tracking the therapist's rapidly moving fingers with their eyes. Some critics consider EMDR to be nothing more than traditional cognitive-behavioral therapy with an added component of bilateral stimulation (Rosen, 1999; Nevid, Rathmus, & Greene, 2008). Others, however, claim that what distinguishes EMDR is not just the bilateral stimulation, but a unique and systematic treatment sequence that incorporates other components thought to be effective in most types of effective trauma treatments such as mindfulness, relaxation, cognitive restructuring, and some degree of exposure (Lee & Cuijpers, 2013).

Perhaps the most controversial unanswered question pertains to whether the bilateral stimulation component of EMDR is really necessary. Some randomized experiments have offered limited support to the notion that the distinctive bilateral stimulation component enhances the effects of EMDR and that EMDR is more effective than exposure therapy (Maxfield, Lake, & Hyer, 2004). Still other experiments reached the opposite conclusions and questioned whether the beneficial effects of EMDR can be attributed exclusively to its imaginal exposure aspects (Olatunji, Parker, & Lohr, 2005–2006; Rothbaum, Astin, & Marsteller, 2005).

In a recent meta-analysis, Lee & Cuijpers (2013) analyzed 14 clinical EMDR studies and 10 laboratory studies evaluating the effect of eye movements. In the clinical studies, EMDR with eye movements was compared to EMDR without eye movements and a significant and moderate effect size was found for the additive effect of the eye movements (Cohen's $d = 0.41$). Likewise, in the laboratory studies where subjects were asked to think about a distressing memory with and without the use of eye movements, a significant and large effect size was found for the use of eye movements ($d = 0.74$). An interesting finding in the laboratory studies was that the largest effect size was in a measure of vividness ($d = 0.91$) indicating that the use of eye movements reduced the vividness of the distressing memory, which has important implications for treating trauma symptoms like intrusive images and flashbacks.

The debate as to the necessity of the bilateral stimulation component of EMDR pertains to the need for a more persuasive theoretical explanation as to why and how that component makes a difference. The primary theoretical model currently used is the AIP model described above. According to Schubert and Lee (2009), there are four hypotheses regarding the underlying mechanisms of EMDR that are congruent with the AIP model and have some empirical support: (1) working memory, (2) orienting response, (3) REM-like state, and (4) increased hemispheric communication.

Working memory hypothesis suggests that the dual attention aspect of any of the forms of bilateral stimulation employed in EMDR, which involves attending to the external stimulus and one's internal experience of the trauma memory, taxes attentional capacity. Essentially, during the trauma processing work that takes place during the desensitization phase "the quality of the [trauma] image deteriorates, presumably because it gets pushed out of working memory and integrated into long-term memory, where the memory then becomes less vivid and less emotional." (Schubert & Lee, p. 127, 2009)

The orienting response is thought to be activated through the eye movements, which induce a relaxation response that reduces stress in a way that makes processing the trauma more tolerable (Elsofsson et al., 2008; Sack et al., 2008 as cited in Schubert & Lee, 2009). The eye movements have also been found to produce physiological responses that resemble a "REM like state" that "through repeated orienting responses, may 'push-start' memory processing in the brain by inducing a physiological and neurological state that is akin to REM sleep that aids in the transfer and integration of memories." (Schubert & Lee, p. 126. 2009) Another hypothesis is that horizontal eye movements in EMDR increase hemispheric communication in the brain, strengthening traumatic memory recall without arousal (Christman et al., 2003 as cited in Schubert & Lee, 2009).

Regardless of the theoretical explanation, there appears to be ample empirical evidence supporting the efficacy of EMDR in treating PTSD symptoms among traumatized adult clients. There is growing evidence supporting its efficacy with traumatized children. Although this review has focused on EMDR, its authors are aware of substantial empirical support for the effectiveness of trauma-focused cognitive behavioral therapy (TF-CBT) with children (Cohen, Mannarino, & Deblinger, 2006; Cohen, Berliner, & March, 2000). Consequently, clinicians treating traumatized children are advised to also consider TF-CBT as a possible alternative to EMDR.

Additional research will be required to explain why EMDR works. More studies are needed regarding its efficacy in treating a wider range of problems less narrowly connected with PTSD symptoms resulting from a specific trauma, the debate as to whether the bilateral stimulation is really necessary, and the comparative effectiveness of EMDR versus other evidence-based trauma treatments (TF-CBT, Prolonged Exposure, and Cognitive Processing Therapy). While awaiting those studies, clinicians treating traumatized adults can be encouraged to use EMDR or any of those other evidence-based treatments.

WEBSITES

EMDR bibliography from 1989 through 2005. http://www.trauma-pages.com/s/emdr-refs.php.
EMDR International Association. http://www.emdria.org.
EMDR Network. http://www.emdrnetwork.org.
EMDR Research Foundation. http://www.EMDRRESEARCHFOUNDATION.org
"EMDR: Taking a Closer Look." http://www.sciam.com/article.cfm?id=emdr-taking-a-closer-look.
"EMDR Treatment: Less Than Meets the Eye?" http://www.quackwatch.com/01QuackeryRelatedTopics/emdr.html.
Francine Shapiro Library-EMDR Bibliography http://library.nku.edu/emdr/emdr_data.php

FREE WEBINAR

"The Past is Present: Understanding the Effects of Unprocessed Memories and Using EMDR Therapy in Treatment" with Francine Shapiro, Ph.D.

This one hour webinar features Dr. Francine Shapiro, originator of EMDR Psychotherapy, introducing the basics of EMDR therapy and providing an overview of treatment. Both the theoretical foundation and recent research findings are explored.

The entire webinar can be viewed online or downloaded at: http://www.emdr.com/general-information/webinar1.html
VA/DoD PTSD Clinical Practice Guidelines (2010), which offer recommendations for the treatment of PTSD and gives EMDR its highest ("A") rating. Complete guidelines are at: http://www.healthquality.va.gov/ptsd/cpg_PTSD-FULL-201011612.pdf

The Summary of the same guidelines (2010): http://www.healthquality.va.gov/ptsd/CPG SummaryFINALMgmtofPTSDfinal021413.pdf
PTSD Pocket Guide (2013): http://www.healthquality.va.gov/ptsd/PTSD PocketGuide23May2013v1.pdf

References

Adler-Tapia, R. (2011). EMDR for the treatment of children in the child welfare system who have been traumatize by abuse and neglect. In A. Rubin, & D. Springer (Eds.), *The clinician's guide to evidence based practice series. Treatment of children in the child welfare system.* John Wiley & Sons, Inc.
Adler-Tapia, R., & Settle, C. (2009). Evidence of the efficacy of EMDR with children and adolescents in individual psychotherapy: A review of the research published in peer-reviewed journals. *Journal of EMDR Practice and Research, 3*(4), 232–247.
Adler-Tapia, R., & Settle, C. S. (2009). Evidence of the efficacy of EMDR with children and adolescents in individual psychotherapy: A review of the research published in peer-reviewed journals. *Journal of EMDR Practice and Research, 3*(4), 232–247.
Adler-Tapia, R., & Settle, C. S. (2008). *EMDR and the art of psychotherapy with children.* New York, NY: Springer.
Ahmad, A., Larsson, B., & Sundelin-Wahlsten, V. (2007). EMDR treatment for children with PTSD: Results of a randomized controlled trial. *Nordic Journal of Psychiatry, 61*, 349–354.
Albright, D., & Thyer, B. (2009). Does EMDR reduce post-traumatic stress disorder symptomatology in combat veterans? *Behavioral Interventions,* doi:10.1002/bin.295.
Bisson, J. I., Ehlers, A., Matthews, R., Pilling, S., Richards, D. A., Turner, F., . . . et al. (2007). Psychological treatments for chronic post-traumatic stress disorder: Systematic review and meta-analysis. *British Journal of Psychiatry, 190*(2), 97–104.
Bradley, R., Greene, J., Russ, E., Dutra, L., & Westen, D. (2005). A multidimensional meta-analysis of psychotherapy for PTSD. *American Journal of Psychiatry, 162*, 214–227.
California Evidence-Based Clearinghouse for Child Welfare (2013, January). Eye movement desensitization and reprocessing for children and adolescents (EMDR), http://www.cebc4cw.org/program/eye-movement-desensitization-and-reprocessing/detailed
Chambless, D. L., Baker, M. J., Baucom, D. H., Beutler, L. E., Calhoun, K. S., & Crits-Christoph, P., . . .

et al. (1998). Update on empirically validated therapies, II. *Clinical Psychologist, 51,* 3–16.

Chemtob, C. M., Nakashima, J., & Carlson, J. G. (2002). Brief treatment for elementary school children with disaster-related posttraumatic stress disorder: A field study. *Journal of Clinical Psychology, 58,* 99–112.

Chemtob, C. M., Tolin, D., van der Kolk, B., & Pitman, R. (1999). Treatment guidelines for EMDR. In *ISTSS PTSD treatment guidelines.* International Society for Traumatic Stress Studies.

Christman, S. D., Garvey, K. J., Propper, R. E., & Phaneuf, K. A. (2003). Bilateral eye movements enhance the retrieval of episodic memories. *Neuropsychology, 17,* 221–229.

Cohen, J. A., Berliner, L., & March, J. S. (2000). Treatment of children and adolescents. In E. B. Foa, T. M. Keane, & M. J. Friedman (Eds.), *Effective treatments for PTSD: Practice guidelines from the International Society for Traumatic Stress Studies* (pp. 330–332). New York, NY: Guilford.

Cohen, J. A., Mannarino, A. P., & Deblinger, E. (2006). *Treating trauma and traumatic grief in children and adolescents.* New York, NY: Guilford.

Davidson, P. R., & Parker, K. C. H. (2001). Eye movement desensitization and reprocessing (EMDR): A meta-analysis. *Journal of Consulting and Clinical Psychology, 69,* 305–316.

de Roos, C. (2011). A randomised comparison of cognitive behavioural therapy (CBT) and eye movement desensitisation (EMDR) in disaster exposed children. *European Journal of Psychotraumatology, 2,* 5694. doi:10.3402/ejpt.v2i0.5694.

Edmond, T., Rubin, A., & Wambach, K. (1999). The effectiveness of EMDR with adult female survivors of childhood sexual abuse. *Social Work Research, 23,* 103–116.

Elsofsson, U. O. E., von Sche'ele, B., Theorell, T. R., & Sondergaard, H. P. (2008). Physiological correlates of eye movement desensitization and reprocessing. *Journal of Anxiety Disorders, 22,* 622–634.

Eye Movement Desensitization & Reprocessing International Association. (2012). EMDRIA's definition of EMDR.

Field, A., & Cottrell, D. (2011). Eye movement desensitization and reprocessing as a therapeutic intervention for traumatized children and adolescents: A systematic review of the evidence for family therapists. *Journal of Family Therapy, 33,* 374–388. doi:10:1111/j.1467-6427.2011.00548.x.

Foa, E. B., & Kozak, M. J. (1986). Emotional processing of fear: Exposure to corrective information. *Psychological Bulletin, 99,* 20–35.

Ironson, G., Freund, B., Strauss, J., & Williams, J. (2002). Comparison of two treatments for traumatic stress: A community-based study of EMDR and prolonged exposure. *Journal of Clinical Psychology, 58,* 113–128.

Jaberghaderi, N., Greenwald, R., Rubin, A., Dolatabadim, S., & Zand, S. (2004). A comparison of CBT and EMDR for sexually abused Iranian girls. *Clinical Psychology and Psychotherapy, 11,* 358–368.

Jeffres, M. J. (2004). The efficacy of EMDR with traumatized children. *Dissertation Abstracts International: B: The Sciences and Engineering, 64*(8-B), 4042.

Kemp, M., Drummond, P., & McDermott, B. (2010). A wait-list controlled pilot study of eye movement desensitization and reprocessing (EMDR) for children with post-traumatic stress disorder (PTSD) symptoms from motor vehicle accidents. *Clinical Child Psychology and Psychiatry, 15,* 5–25. doi:10.1177/1359104509339086.

Lee, C., & Cuijpers, P. (2013). A meta-analysis of the contribution of eye movements in processing emotional memories. *Journal of Behavior Therapy and Experimental Psychiatry, 44,* 231–239.

Lee, C., Gavriel, H., Drummond, P., Richards, J., & Greenwald, R. (2002). Treatment of post-traumatic stress disorder: A comparison of stress inoculation training with prolonged exposure and eye movement desensitization and reprocessing. *Journal of Clinical Psychology, 58,* 1071–1089.

Maxfield, L., Lake, K., & Hyer, L. (2004). Some answers to unanswered questions about the empirical support for EMDR in the treatment of PTSD. *Traumatology, 10*(2), 73–88.

Muris, P., Merckelbach, H., Holdrinet, I., & Sijsenaar, M. (1998). Treating phobic children: Effects of EMDR versus exposure. *Journal of Consulting and Clinical Psychology, 66,* 193–198.

Muris, P., Merckelbach, H., van Haaften, H., & Mayer, B. (1997). Eye movement desensitization and reprocessing versus exposure in vivo: A single-session crossover study of spider-phobic children. *British Journal of Psychiatry, 171,* 82–86.

Nevid, S., Rathmus, A., & Greene, B. (2008). *Abnormal psychology in a changing world* (7th ed.). Upper Saddle River, NJ: Pearson Education.

Olatunji, B. O., Parker, L. M., & Lohr, J. M. (2005–2006). Pseudoscience in contemporary psychology. *Scientific Review of Mental Health Practice, 4*(2), 19–31.

Power, K. G., McGoldrick, T., Brown, K., Buchanan, R., Sharp, D., Swanson, V., & Karatzias, A. (2002). A controlled comparison of eye movement desensitization and reprocessing versus exposure plus cognitive restructuring, versus waiting list in the treatment of post-traumatic stress disorder. *Journal of Clinical Psychology and Psychotherapy, 9,* 299–318.

Rodenburg, R., Benjamin, A., deRoos, C., Meijer, A., & Stams, G. (2009). Efficacy of EMDR in children: A meta-analysis. *Clinical Psychology Review, 29,* 599–606.

Rosen, G. (1999). Treatment fidelity and research on eye movement desensitization and reprocessing (EMDR). *Journal of Anxiety Disorders, 13,* 173–184.

Rothbaum, B. O., Astin, M. C., & Marsteller, F. (2005). Prolonged exposure versus eye movement desensitization and reprocessing (EMDR) for PTSD rape victims. *Journal of Traumatic Stress, 18*(6), 607–616.

Rubin, A. (2003). Unanswered questions about the empirical support for EMDR in the treatment of PTSD. *Traumatology, 9,* 4–30.

Rubin, A. (2004). Fallacies and deflections in debating the empirical support for EMDR in the treatment of PTSD: A reply to Maxfield, Lake, and Hyer. *Traumatology, 10*(2), 91–105.

Rubin, A., Bischofshausen, S., Conroy-Moore, K., Dennis, B., Hastie, M., Melnick, L., . . . Smith, T. (2001). The effectiveness of EMDR in a child guidance center. *Research on Social Work Practice, 11*(4), 435–457.

Sack, M., Lempa, W., Steinmetz, A., Lamprecht, F., & Hoffman, A. (2008). Alterations in autonomic tone during trauma exposure using eye movement desensitization and reprocessing—Results of a preliminary investigation. *Journal of Anxiety Disorders 22,* 1264–1271.

Schubert, S., & Lee, C. (2009). Adult PTSD and its treatment with EMDR: A review of controversies, evidence, and theoretical knowledge. *Journal of EMDR Practice and Research, 3*(3) 117–132.

Seidler, G. H., & Wagner, F. E. (2006) Comparing the efficacy of *EMDR* and trauma-focused cognitive-behavioral therapy in the treatment of PTSD: A meta-analytic study. *Psychological Medicine, 36*(11), 1515–1522.

Shapiro, F. (1995). *Eye movement desensitization and reprocessing: Basic principles, protocols, and procedures.* New York, NY: Guilford.

Shapiro, F. (1996a). Eye movement desensitization and reprocessing (EMDR): Evaluation of controlled PTSD research. *Journal of Behavior Therapy and Experimental Psychiatry, 27,* 209–218.

Shapiro, F. (1996b). Errors of context and review of eye movement desensitization and reprocessing research. *Journal of Behavior Therapy and Experimental Psychiatry, 27,* 313–317.

Shapiro, F., & Forrest, M. S. (1997). *EMDR: The breakthrough therapy for overcoming anxiety, stress, and trauma.* New York, NY: Basic Books.

Shapiro, F., & Laliotis, D. (2011). EMDR and the adaptive information processing model: Integrative treatment and case conceptualization. *Journal of Clinical Social Work, 39*(2), 191–200.

Van Etten, M., & Taylor, S. (1998). Comparative efficacy of treatments for post-traumatic stress disorder: A meta-analysis. *Clinical Psychology and Psychotherapy, 5,* 126–145.

98 Educational Interventions
Principles for Practice

Kimberly Strom-Gottfried

Many settings and interventions require that the social worker act as an educator. In this role, professionals may lead educational groups, train volunteers, provide professional or community education workshops, create podcasts, guide new workers through educational supervision, or teach new skills as part of their interventions with clients. Often, however, practitioners may not consider these activities as teaching, and therefore, may overlook valuable frameworks to assist in their practice. In order to encourage systematic attention to this role, this chapter summarizes the key elements of an education framework. It is intended to help social workers in a variety of settings to consider the educational aspects of their practice and to use teaching interventions more effectively.

Effective educational practice relies on six essential components:

1. The development of clear and appropriate objectives
2. An understanding of the learners' needs and abilities
3. An atmosphere that is conducive to learning
4. Knowledge of the material to be conveyed
5. The skill to select and use teaching methods appropriately
6. The ability to evaluate one's performance and the learners' acquisition of educational outcomes.

Whether one is teaching parenting skills to an individual teenager, conducting a psycho-educational group for mental health consumers, or presenting a course on crisis intervention to a group of volunteers, these steps comprise the necessary components of an effective educational program. Steps 1–6 are ongoing, but typically begin well before the worker and learners come together. Step 6 should take place throughout the duration of educational contact, and be done retrospectively as well.

DEVELOPING CLEAR AND APPROPRIATE OBJECTIVES

"No wind is favorable if you don't know your destination." This quote, attributed to the Roman philosopher Seneca, aptly addresses the first step in any form of social work intervention. Workers must be clear about their purpose in using an intervention or technique, and the goals they hope to accomplish or the intended outcomes their clients expect. Specific to educational interventions, the worker should have some sense of what the learners need or what skills, knowledge, or attitudes they hope the learners will have as a result of the intervention (Anastas, 2010). Because a program's marketing, participant recruitment, location, topic selection, teaching methods, and evaluation all flow from its purpose, it is imperative that the goals be clearly articulated and appropriate for the needs of the end users.

Goals are sometimes an outgrowth of existing work with a client or group (Johnson & Johnson, 1997). For example, it may be apparent that clients diagnosed with HIV, diabetes, or other conditions can benefit from education about the course and management of their diseases and strategies to manage daily activities and relationships in light of the illness. At other times, educational programs are developed independently, after which participants choose (or are chosen) to participate. The development of web-based continuing education to meet the needs of professionals desiring continuing education credits in ethics would be one such example.

Planning becomes more complex when a need or service gap is believed to exist, but has not yet been documented. In this case, needs assessment strategies should be used to determine the type and nature of the educational need. Needs may be determined through formal surveys, past enrollment data or program evaluations, interviews with service providers from social work and other disciplines, and from meetings or focus groups with potential consumers or representative groups.

Learning objectives typically fall into three broad categories: those geared to achieving knowledge or understanding, achieving skills or abilities, or achieving insight or attitudinal change (http://www.oucom.ohiou.edu/FD/writingobjectives.pdf). Within a given content area, interventions may have one focus ("Learn about diabetes and the diet plan to manage the disease"—*a knowledge goal*) or several ("Learn about the diabetes diet plan and be able to plan meals that fit in the plan"—*knowledge and skills goals*). Clarity about the type of learning expected is especially important when workers select their teaching methods, given that teaching strategies are better suited to some educational goals than others. For example, skill building is better done through simulations or role plays than a strictly lecture-based teaching format; experiential exercises can effectively lead to understanding and self-examination; webinars or podcasts address knowledge goals (Ko & Rossen, 2010). In creating continuing education or staff development programs, administrators may consider whether growth in knowledge, skills, or attitudes is most needed. Some learning objectives (improving sensitivity to cross-cultural differences, developing empathy, understanding countertransference) may be better handled through educational supervision than group processes (Kadushin & Harkness, 2014).

Clear objectives are also important when marketing an educational program. The dangers of advertising a program with an ambiguous purpose include drawing participants with too-diverse a range of abilities or interests or discouraging appropriate people from enrolling at all because they cannot determine whether the program is "for them." And finally, particularly in programs where learners and teachers are evaluated on the outcomes they have achieved, goals must be clearly specified in order to assess attainment adequately (Johnson & Johnson, 1997).

UNDERSTANDING LEARNERS' NEEDS AND ABILITIES

Determining the need for and the purpose of an educational endeavor requires consideration of the prospective learners. Actually developing the educational intervention requires taking this understanding a step further and examining the particular life space of the learners, including their abilities, knowledge, and attitudes, as well as what motivation or reluctance they may possess with regard to the content. It involves "tuning-in" to the "feelings and concerns that the client may bring to the helping encounter" (Shulman, 1992, p.56). It may also involve understanding ethnocultural, developmental, and other issues and the way that teaching dynamics are affected by differences among teachers and learners (Anastas, 2010). An accurate understanding of learners will facilitate the selection and sequencing of content and the training methods used. Inadequate tuning-in may lead to learners' resentment and resistance, may affect enrollment and attendance, and may lead to the selection of material that is variously rudimentary, irrelevant, or too complex (Anastas, 2010; Bain, 2004).

A number of teaching principles are predicated on "knowing the learner" both as an aggregate group and as individuals. These include understanding sources of intrinsic and extrinsic motivation, making the material relevant and meaningful for each individual, building on the learner's existing knowledge, sequencing material from the familiar to the unfamiliar, identifying learning styles, and expressing appropriate confidence in the learner's abilities (Kadushin & Harkness, 2014). The ability to individualize learning makes it more potent, as does forging a relationship in which the participant feels known and valued. Both require actively anticipating and understanding the individual-as-learner.

DEVELOPING A LEARNING-CONDUCIVE ATMOSPHERE

This component of teaching refers to both the physical environment and the emotional environment in which learning is to take place. Clearly, all learning opportunities carry with them the risk of mistakes or failure. As Kadushin has noted regarding educational supervision, "We learn best when we can devote most of our energies in the learning situation to learning. Energy needed to defend against rejection, anxiety, guilt, shame, fear of failure, attacks on autonomy or uncertain expectations, is energy deflected from learning." (1985, p. 149)

In keeping with this admonition, educators should inform learners about the purposes, processes and structures for the learning activity. Learners must know what will be expected from them and what they can expect from the teacher (Lemov, 2010). The teacher should acknowledge and support the learner's risk-taking in pursuit of change and establish a climate of trust and safety. When teaching in a group format, guidelines should be established and articulated that will yield a supportive environment for all involved, and the leader should be aware of any dynamics that are impinging on an individual's participation (Brooks, 2011; Gregory, 2013; Ko & Rossen, 2010). Some class members may pose challenges to the safety and efficacy of the learning environment. Hostile, monopolizing, inattentive, unprepared, or fawning participants may alienate both the instructor and the fellow class members (Royse, 2001). It is up to the leader to determine the basis for the problematic behaviors and craft an effective response. Some problems arise from poorly specified expectations or norms, and thus the resolutions may be structural in nature. Problems that arise from behavioral, psychological, or interpersonal issues will likely require an individualized intervention (McKeachie & Svinicki, 2014). As with other challenges arising in social work practice, supervision and consultation are essential to assist the worker in managing his or her personal responses to the difficulty and the difficulty itself.

The physical climate is also important for effective learning, though generally it is less in the leader's control. Ideally, the facilities should be well-suited for the purposes and characteristics of the learners. The literature on group work is relevant here as we consider, for example, the needs of a group of adults in a didactic presentation as compared to those of teenagers in an experiential learning program. The very setting of the educational program should be determined with the purpose and audience in mind. The location, accessibility, safety, parking, available hours, and "reputation" or message carried by the site will influence learner attendance. Keeping the nature of the training and trainees in mind, attention must also be paid to room size, temperature, arrangement, the use of tables or chairs without tables, other furnishings, and the availability of audio visual equipment, rest rooms, and refreshments. Creating the appropriate levels of physical and emotional comfort for learners is a planning task, and an ongoing management responsibility for the educator.

KNOWLEDGE OF CONTENT

Implied in accepting the role of educator is the notion that one has some knowledge that can be taught to or shared with another. Yet a stumbling block for many would-be educators is the fear that they do not have a sufficient command of the material to put themselves forth as instructors. This section addresses how much knowledge of content is needed, what sources can be used to enhance or supplement the instructor's knowledge, and how the fear of not knowing enough can be overcome.

How much knowledge is required depends on the needs of the learners and the purposes and structure of the educational program (Anastas, 2010). A single fact about normative child development may be sufficient to inform a client in an intervention around parenting, but a good deal more knowledge will be required if providing an adult education course on the subject. As noted earlier, clarity about the goals of the educational program will be a vital guide. As educators begin to tune in to the program and learners, they get a sense of the depth and breadth of information needed. Reviewing curricula for similar programs or discussing ideas with colleagues and clients will help further identify content needs even prior to the training. These steps often remind facilitators that they know more than they think they do. Where further knowledge of content is needed, presenters can supplement their knowledge through traditional sources such as texts and journals, interviewing subject experts, or viewing videos and films. In the classroom, presenters can augment the content they have to offer by using educational media, handouts, bibliographies, videos, or outside speakers.

Despite these steps, educators often feel vulnerable about their command of the course content. Such feelings may stem from the mistaken impression that the teacher must be "the sage on the stage" rather than "the guide on the side." This misconception not only places an unrealistic burden on the worker, but can deprive all participants of the richness that comes from shared responsibility for learning. Sometimes referred to as student-centered learning, this model encourages the instructor to set the stage and provide the foundation through which all class members can contribute and learn from one another. This approach is consonant with theories of adult education, mutuality, and empowerment-based practice. Even if instructors cannot wholly utilize such a model, they must address the fear of not knowing. Learners do not expect that instructors will have all the answers, and in fact, will have a greater respect for those who are able to say "I don't know, I'll check and get back to you." or "I hadn't heard about that. What do you know?" Similarly, the ability to catch and acknowledge mistakes conveys important messages about the authenticity of the instructor and the acceptability of errors. Conversely, the need to be right or know it all often sets up an adversarial learning environment, in which genuine learning is sacrificed for gamesmanship and defensiveness (Lang, 2012).

Although there is no definitive answer to, "How much content is enough?" there are multiple strategies for adjusting content in the event of over- or underestimation. When planning a program, instructors should anticipate the amount of time they will devote to certain material, and think about how they might be able to cut or add as necessary. In multisession groups, instructors can retool between sessions as content needs become apparent. Discussions, experiential exercises, and case studies can be used to take content to a deeper level of application if presenters move through their material more quickly than anticipated. If too much material has been planned, instructors can re-examine the objectives and eliminate less crucial information or outside work or reading can supplement in-class time. In addition, the dilemma can be shared with learners, and their input used to prioritize the content to address with limited time.

SELECTING AND USING TEACHING TECHNIQUES

Many people teach the way they have been taught. Unfortunately, many people have been taught in ways that stifle learner involvement, enthusiasm, and critical thinking. Having sat through mind-numbing lectures, tangential discussions, and fun-but-pointless exercises, they may believe that these are the only available means of conveying information. In fact, there exists an array of teaching approaches; the challenge is not only in finding them, but in selecting them to appropriately meet the needs of the learners and the objectives of the intervention.

Certain structures and teaching techniques are particularly well-suited for different teaching goals (Davis, 2009; Knowles, 1975; Strom-Gottfried, 2006):

Lectures

- Convey complex material
- Highlight important facts and concepts
- Create a cognitive map for future applications

Exercises, Demonstrations, Role Plays and Simulations

- Provide ice-breakers
- Build group cohesion
- Foster skill acquisition and rehearsal
- Generate empathy
- Model techniques and concepts
- Facilitate problem-solving

Cases, Discussions, and Debates

- Develop insight
- Foster new perspectives
- Apply concepts

Web-based and Other Instructional Technologies

- Convey complex material
- Allow self-paced and self-timed learning, review, and repetition
- Are convenient
- Content, assignments, and discussions can be archived for sharing or future use.

Each teaching method has its own promises and pitfalls. Suggestions for effectively using instructional strategies include (Carnes, 2011; Christensen, Garvin, & Sweet, 1991; Davis, 2009; Filene, 2005; Kadel & Keehner, 1994; McKeachie & Svinicki, 2014; Royse, 2001; Sweet, 2010):

Lectures

- Limit length or break up with discussions, examples, question and answer sessions, or activities.
- Vary vocal intonations, facial expressions, gestures, and movement about the room.
- Initiate with a compelling question or scenario to be addressed by the lecture content.
- Do not read the lecture but do read the audience.
- Provide scaffolding for content in outline form through handouts or Power Point presentations.

Exercises, Demonstrations, Role Plays and Simulations

- Link to learning goals or course material
- Choose judiciously
- Clearly explain the objectives and directions
- Be alert to emotional reactions among participants
- Prompt skill development with modeling, videotaped examples, or discussion of strategies for effective practice
- Demonstrate support for risk and enthusiasm for the exercise
- Debrief to identify strengths, weaknesses, and links to learning objectives.

Cases, Discussions and Debates

- Create a supportive, caring, and respectful atmosphere
- Develop clear learning points
- Establish ground rules for discussions
- Allow time for participants to think before responding
- Encourage or structure alternative perspectives
- Summarize key outcomes

Web-based and Other Instructional Technologies

- Carefully sequence educational modules
- Make sure materials and directions are clear, thorough, and accurate
- Design should be visually compelling and user-friendly
- Anticipate technological glitches
- Incorporate varied teaching strategies, including real time meetings, discussion boards, video clips, question and answer sessions and other interactive opportunities.

When selecting strategies to support various learning objectives, educators must also keep in mind their learners' capacities, the size of their group, and the amount of time they have for instruction. Such variables will affect the mix of teaching strategies employed, the time needed to carry them out, the learners' ability to benefit from the technique, the facilities needed, and the sequencing of material (Anastas, 2010).

EVALUATING TEACHING PERFORMANCE AND LEARNERS' ACQUISITIONS

Most evaluations address two questions: "Were the learning objectives achieved?" and "How effective was the instructor in helping them to be met?" Both elements of evaluation are important. Evaluating satisfaction without having some measure of the benefit of the content is referred to as "popularity polling" (Davis & McCallon, 1974, p. 275). Evaluating attainment without determining what was effective and what was not in terms of delivery does not help the instructor generalize the effort to future situations. A variety of measures can be used for each form of evaluation, and to some extent, the measure chosen depends on how the information gleaned will be used (Unrau, Gabor, & Grinnell Jr., 2007). If the information will be quantified, for example to give the learner a grade or to rate the instructor, precise numerical measures will be called for. For other purposes, less precise measures are adequate and sometimes preferable. For example, in measuring what people learned in a social skills training program, observed change or self-reported change may be adequate, whereas a CPR training program would require more definitive measures of competency.

Used alone or in combination with quantifiable ratings, open-ended questions or narrative evaluations can provide feedback with valuable depth and context (Davis, 2009). For example, the instructor may find that the structure or timing of an exercise was ineffective, not the exercise itself, or the learner may get feedback about particular areas of strength within a specific content area.

In addition to the form of evaluation, timing is another consideration. In general, periodic formal or informal check-in types of evaluation will help both learners and educators reassess their progress toward achieving the objectives and reprioritize material or alter teaching strategies accordingly (Davis, 2009; Unrau, Gabor, & Grinnell Jr., 2007). Methods for this include brief self-reports at the end of a session about insights and information achieved or "minute cards" where participants provide written feedback on the meeting.

Effective and ethical instruction arises from the conscientious use of various forms of evaluation to inform practice. In addition to utilizing incremental and cumulative verbal and written feedback from participants, social workers can utilize peer observers, coaching, and video-taped sessions to continually improve and refine teaching performance.

CONCLUSION

Teaching is an integral part of social work practice, done in a variety of settings with a range of populations. This chapter offers guidance for the creation and delivery of educational interventions and offers resources for further study. It encourages the examination of social work activities from an education framework, advocating that as this function is better defined, models can be further developed, teaching challenges examined, and the necessary knowledge and skills for effective practice specified.

WEB RESOURCES

How Teachers Learn New Technologies, http://www.staffdevelop.org

International Association for the Study of Cooperation in Education, http://www.iasce.net

International Association for Social Work with Groups, Inc, http://www.iaswg.org

International Association of Facilitators, http://www.iaf-world.org

The Teaching Professor, http://www.magnapubs.com/catalog/the-teaching-professor-newsletter/

Tribes Learning Community, http://www.tribes.com

References

Anastas, J. W. (2010). *Teaching in social work: An educators' guide to theory and practice*. New York, NY: Columbia University Press.

Bain, K. (2004). *What the best college teachers do.* Cambridge, MA: Harvard University Press.

Brooks, D. (2011). Getting students to talk. *Chronicle of Higher Education.* Retrieved from http://chronicle.com/article/Getting-Students-to-Talk/126826/.

Carnes, M. C. (2011). Setting students' minds on fire. *Chronicle of Higher Education.* Retrieved from http://chronicle.com/article/Setting-Students-Minds-on/126592/

Christensen, C. R., Garvin, D. A., & Sweet, A. (1991). *Education for judgment: The artistry of discussion leadership.* Boston, MA: Harvard Business School.

Davis, B. G. (2009). *Tools for teaching* (2nd ed.). San Francisco, CA: Jossey-Bass.

Davis, L. N., & McCallon, E. (1974). *Planning, conducting, and evaluating workshops.* Austin, TX: Learning Concepts.

Filene, P. (2005). *The joy of teaching: A practical guide for new college instructors.* Chapel Hill, NC: The University of North Carolina Press.

Gregory, C. (2013). Love the one you're with: Creating a classroom community. *Faculty Focus.* Retrieved from http://www.facultyfocus.com/articles/effective-classroom-management/love-the-one-youre-with-creating-a-classroom-community/

Johnson, D. W., & Johnson, F. P. (1997). *Joining together: Group theory and group skills* (6th ed.). Boston, MA: Allyn & Bacon.

Kadel, S., & Keehner, J. A. (1994). *Collaborative learning: A sourcebook for higher education.* Park, PA: National Center on Postsecondary Teaching, Learning, and Assessment.

Kadushin, A. (1985). *Supervision in social work.* New York, NY: Columbia University Press.

Kadushin, A., & Harkness, D. (2014). *Supervision in social work* (5th ed.). New York, NY: Columbia University Press.

Knowles, M. S. (1975). *Self-directed learning.* New York, NY: Association Press.

Ko, S., & Rossen, S. (2010). *Teaching online: A practical guide* (3rd ed.). New York, NY: Routledge.

Lang, J. M. (2012). Teaching what you don't know. *Chronicle of Higher Education.* Retrieved from http://chronicle.com/article/Teaching-What-You-Dont-Know/135180/

Lemov, D. (2010). *Teach like a champion: 49 techniques that put students on the path to college.* San Francisco, CA: Jossey-Bass.

McKeachie, W., & Svinicki, M. (2014). *McKeachie's teaching tips: Strategies, research, and theory for college and university teachers* (14th ed.). Belmont, CA: Wadsworth, Cengage Learning.

Royse, D. (2001). *Teaching tips for college and university instructors: A practical guide.* Boston, MA: Allyn & Bacon.

Shulman, L. (1992). *The skills of helping: Individuals, families, and groups.* Itasca, IL: F. E. Peacock Publishers.

Strom-Gottfried, K. J. (2006) Managing human resources. In R. L. Edwards and J. A. Yankey (Eds.) *Effectively managing nonprofit organizations* (pp. 141–178). Washington, DC: National Association of Social Workers.

Sweet, M. (2010). Group work that works. *Chronicle of Higher Education.* Retrieved from http://chronicle.com/blogs/profhacker/group-work-that-works-even-in-large-classes/28459

Unrau, Y. A., Gabor, P. A., & Grinnell, R. M., Jr. (2007). *Evaluation in social work: The art and science of practice* (4th ed.). Oxford: Oxford University Press.

Divorce Therapy

99 *The Application of Cognitive-behavioral and Constructivist Treatment*

Donald K. Granvold

Divorce is one of the most distressing transitions one can undergo. Whether the decision is unilateral or shared, or one is the initiator or the one being left, the process is painful and disruptive. The change following divorce is pervasive, extending across many domains of the individual's life. For most, coming apart carries with it extreme emotional consequences. Divorce is simultaneously an ending punctuated by loss, estrangement, and detachment and a new beginning characterized by fear of the unknown; challenging novel roles, responsibilities, and behaviors; and promising future possibilities. Client treatment goals can be expected to fluctuate. The desire for a sense of closure regarding the past may prompt a focus on the estranged or ex-mate and the associated family and social networks. Alternatively, the focus may be on the development of novel or expanded selves to meet current and evolving demands and possibilities (Granvold, 2010).

STAGES OF THE DIVORCE PROCESS

The divorce process can be conceptualized as being composed of three overlapping stages: (1) decision making, (2) transition, and (3) postdivorce recovery (Granvold, 2000a, 2000b, 2010). Each of these stages poses unique challenges to the individual and each is replete with crisis potential.

Decision Making

I believe that therapists are challenged most greatly in helping individuals/couples with the decision to divorce. Specific methodologies are least well developed in this area. Typically, one or both partners continue their marriage in a state of high dissatisfaction and protracted indecision before ultimately arriving at a decision to divorce. The state of indecision is stressful in itself, characterized by high levels of frustration, anxiety, uncertainty, fear, worry, insecurity, distrust (particularly for the mate who is more greatly committed), hurt, resentment, depression, hopelessness and impending doom, and feelings of disempowerment. There is often erosion in feelings of love, intimacy, sexual desire, and sexual satisfaction. Individuals who are emotionally fragile, highly dependent on the mate, and/or lack self-esteem often experience situation-specific crises as the couple moves toward a final decision. This individual, typically more committed and less likely to decide to leave the relationship, is far more vulnerable to crisis responses.

The following are examples of therapeutic goals during the decision-making stage:

- Specify factors eroding the relationship
- Optimize relationship functioning (specify and implement strategic change)
- Promote frustration tolerance for indecision (i.e., combat low frustration tolerance)
- Limit impulsive decision making
- Carefully determine and weigh the factors of satisfaction and dissatisfaction
- Clarify values and life goals related to coupling

- Clearly identify perceived advantages and disadvantages of divorce relative to remaining married
- Consider structured marital separation to interrupt maladaptive patterns of interaction, re-evaluate the relationship from an altered perspective, and move more gradually to singlehood (a treatment of choice only for select couples) (Granvold, 1983).

The gravity of the decision and its effect on the lives of the couple, their children, extended family, and friends creates great pressure on the decision maker(s). Typically, both the decision maker and the rejected partner experience intense and protracted pain. It is noteworthy that divorce appears far more likely to be the consequence of a loss of intimate connectedness than the result of intense conflict (Stanley, 2001). The absence of overt signs of disagreement and dissatisfaction may be confusing to both partners and those close to the couple, particularly offspring.

Transition

Once a decision to divorce is made, the couple enters the transition phase of the divorce process. For many, divorce is largely a consequence of an erosion of love, a shift from feeling "in love" to simply "caring." Despite this shift, interpersonal attachment tends to persist. There is a sense of comfort in the relationship and in the shared physical environment. Dissolving the relationship and physically separating may well have a concomitant profound sense of loss even for those who are no longer in love and who *want* the divorce.

Physical separation and the initiation of legal action are characteristically periods of extreme stress (Wang & Amato, 2000). Clients should be carefully evaluated for their ways of dealing with stress in the event they are putting themselves or others at risk or alternatively, are experiencing significant maladjustment. Of further concern are those who have endured violence in marriage. Separation has been found to instigate additional assaults by abusive partners and first-time violence in previously nonabusive mates. The following are examples of therapeutic goals during the transition phase:

- Assess and treat suicidality and homicidal ideation and planning
- Assess death wishes (passive suicide)
- Assess and develop strategies for postseparation domestic violence
- Assess alcohol use and prescription and illicit drug use
- Complete strengths and resiliency assessment
- Strategize informing children, family, and friends regarding the divorce
- Promote the expression of loss (emotionally, cognitively, behaviorally)
- Develop adaptive strategies for stress management during transition (e.g., limit alcohol/drug use, check excessive investment in work, explore deep muscle relaxation, engage in healthy exercise)
- Facilitate effective relationships with children, family, and friends
- Address effecting legal action to dissolve the marriage contract
- Address child custody and parallel parenting issues
- Promote a collaborative property settlement agreement.

The transition phase also requires attention to the specifics of the division of property, physical relocation, child custody, and child support—all of which stimulate emotional reactions. These considerations pose remarkable opportunities for conflict, divorce decision doubt, uncertainty regarding the future, and intense feelings of loss.

Postdivorce Recovery

Postdivorce recovery, as identified earlier, involves pervasive change. In addition to dealing with losses of a physical and emotional nature, the individual is challenged with redefining self and re-envisioning his or her life. Now, it is necessary to establish a monadic identity, independent of the self that evolved and was forged through years of intimate connectedness with the ex-mate. The path of life that had been relatively established and known no longer fits the novel territory in which one now travels. The transition process to postdivorce recovery is replete with pervasive change. Among the changes being experienced are new role relationships with children (for example, single parenting), workmates, extended family, and friends. The development of friendship and intimate relationships as well as participation in network groups (for example, church, interest groups, support groups) have been found to be positively associated with postdivorce adjustment (Krumrei, Coit, Martin, Fogo, & Mahoney, 2007). Although a positive association exists between social support and postdivorce adjustment, the quality of these relationships promotes or undermines well-being (Krumrei et al., 2007).

The clinical and research findings on the effects of divorce are inconsistent. Some individuals experience positive change in the form of relief, a renewed sense of freedom, joy, enhanced self-esteem, increased happiness, greater life satisfaction, greater sense of responsibility, and a sense of renewal, whereas others experience such untoward consequences as extreme loss, hurt, depression, social isolation, unhappiness, financial problems, increased risk of health problems, single parenting challenges, reduced life satisfaction, and diminished self-esteem (Baum, Rahav, & Sharon, 2005; Sakraida, 2005). Vulnerability to greater postdivorce maladjustment appears to reside with older versus younger women (Sakraida, 2005), noninitiators of divorce, and those lacking social support (Krumrei et al., 2007). Furthermore, divorce is likely to exacerbate the emotional instability of those with a predivorce history of mental health problems. A substantial number of divorced individuals fall into this category, given the predisposition of poorly adjusted people to divorce.

Literature on the effects of divorce has predominantly reflected a deficit model, emphasizing the negative psychological, social, and health consequences to adults and children. Recent studies have given greater attention to positive short- and long-term consequences in which the divorce process is viewed as a potential personal development opportunity (Hilton & Kopera-Frye, 2004).

Common maladaptive coping strategies involve the excessive use of alcohol and drugs (prescribed and illicit), oversleep, overexercise, and overinvestment of time and energy in work. Though grieving is a necessary, adaptive process and is unique from person to person, it may become debilitating to those who allow it to become all-consuming.

The following are examples of therapeutic goals during postdivorce recovery:

- Delineate and dedicate efforts to the evolution of "possible selves" consistent with the re-envisioning of one's life
- Establish a quality relationship with children as a single parent (attend to their emotional needs and their need for structure in the reconstituted family)
- Develop an effective parallel parenting relationship with the ex-spouse
- Gain closure on the marriage (grieve and seek to accept emotionally that the marriage is over)
- Promote efficacy expectations regarding present and future life satisfaction
- Generate rejuvenation goals across various categories of life (career, education, hobbies, interests, relationships, lifestyle, geographic and environmental circumstances)
- Seek intimate connectedness with others through clear delineation of partner/relationship qualities, active pursuit, deliberate relationship evaluation, and proactive decision making to terminate or maintain the relationship(s) (Krumrei et al., 2007; Wang & Amato, 2000)
- Develop and rejuvenate sexuality
- Activate a lifestyle in which physical health and exercise are priorities.

INTERVENTION

The proposed treatment model incorporates behavioral methods, orthodox cognitive treatment methods, and constructivist conceptualizations and methods (Granvold, 2000a, 2000b, 2008, 2010). The unifying factor is the view that cognitive functioning plays a central role in the human condition and human change. Although cognitive functioning plays a crucial role in the development and regulation of human behavior, it is recognized that behavioral activation strategies used in combination with cognitive change represent the most powerful and resilient forms of intervention.

There is remarkable empirical support for the application of cognitive-behavioral treatments (CBTs) to an array of psychological disorders (DeRubeis & Crits-Christoph, 1998). Many empirically supported psychotherapy treatments (ESTs) use a wealth of cognitive and behavioral intervention procedures in various forms and combinations. Divorced clients can be expected to present with problems and concerns suitable for treatment with methods proven to be efficacious. As noted earlier, there are many psychological consequences of divorce. Among the most typical are depression, anxiety and panic disorders, anger control, posttraumatic stress disorder (particularly relevant for survivors of domestic violence), obsessive-compulsive disorder, alcohol abuse and dependence, and substance abuse and dependence. CBT has been applied successfully in treating each of these problems. CBT interventions continue to be scrutinized and evaluated through extensive ongoing empirical research.

Postmodern conceptualizations of divorce provide an alternative (albeit in many ways compatible) perspective on the process of coming apart and transitioning to single life. Divorce is viewed as necessarily disruptive to the self system with a concomitant array of emotional consequences. A primary treatment goal is the generation of multiple meanings of specific events in the process of divorcing and adjusting to singlehood. Emotional expressions are evoked and processed through an array of cognitive and behavioral methods. Attention is given to the client's redefinition of self and the modification and expansion of intimate and social relationships. Emphasis is placed on the client's strengths and the positive change possibilities inherent in this major life transition (Granvold, 2008, 2010).

The constructivist aspects of the intervention are represented in the following enumeration.

1. Conceptualize divorce as a self-system perturbation.
2. Seek to access self-schemata activated by the divorce process with the objective of modifying core ordering processes through construct elaboration.
3. Explore primary attachment relationships as they relate to views of self and the world, including the attachment relationship with the ex-spouse.
4. Promote a view of self as a multifaceted and ever-changing system of identity meanings, rather than a singular, fixed self.
5. Promote emotional expressiveness through guided discovery, imagery, imaginary dialogues (empty chair technique), and therapeutic rituals.
6. Use personal narratives and journaling as change mediums.
7. Accentuate client strengths, personal and social resources, creativity, coping capacities, and resiliency.
8. Collaborate with the client in constructing change mediums, models, and techniques with which the therapist has an expertise and which suit the client.

Although the therapist has expertise regarding both the process of divorce and human change processes, a nonauthoritarian role is assumed in relation to the client. The intervention is strategically the co-construction of the client and therapist. See Chapter 40 for detailed information on constructivist theory and practice.

CLINICAL EXAMPLES

The following are exemplars covering each stage of divorce.

Decision Making

Penny and Jason presented for therapy undecided whether to divorce or remain married. As part of the intervention, the couple used journaling to clarify their expectations of a mate and marriage. They traced their relationship from its inception and noted the evolution of their partner and marriage expectations. In therapy sessions, they were guided in the use of their journaling to make specific comparisons of their expectations with their "experience" of the relationship. The process helped them realize that although their marriage had closely aligned with early expectations, they had evolved divergently and no longer found the relationship satisfactorily viable. They reported feeling as if they had made a collaborative decision to divorce, and they shifted their focus to the emotional and practical requirements of coming apart.

Transition

The divorce decision was imposed on Marla by her husband, Mark. Although the relationship was amicable, Marla had been having extreme difficulty with the transition. She drank several glasses of wine each night, had withdrawn from family and friends, and had discontinued her aerobics workout routine that she had done for years. The couple was childless. Having effectively coped with the loss of her father (with whom she was close) five years earlier, Marla was prompted to compare and contrast her ways of coping with the two losses, her father and Mark. She identified differences in the losses, specifically noting that Mark had been there for her during her grief over her father's death. She concluded, however, that she could implement some of the same coping strategies this time.

She decided to limit her drinking to one glass per night, do something "social" at least one occasion per week, and resume a four-day-a-week workout regimen. Therapist actions included Socratic questioning, gentle encouragement, and strong verbal support for her plans.

Postdivorce Recovery

Greg presented for therapy a year after his divorce was legally final. His primary goal was to let go of the relationship with his ex-wife, Laurie, and to "feel" divorced. After several sessions, it was apparent that Greg was emotionally ready to let go. An implosion strategy was discussed and planned in the session (Granvold, 1994). The following Saturday, he dedicated eight hours to grieving the loss of his relationship with Laurie. He looked at pictures and memorabilia, played their music, ate Chinese food in the middle of the bed as they had done many times, smelled a pillow laced with her perfume, and freely cried with no goal to stop the crying. In three to four hours, the tears dried up. Although it was an emotionally painful experience, at the following session Greg reported a greater sense of closure, as if an emotional connectedness had been purged, a connectedness that could no longer be.

CONCLUSION

Although much has been written about divorce, there is a paucity of information focused on treatment. This gap in the treatment literature is particularly alarming given the relatively high divorce rate and the emotional trauma associated with coming apart. This chapter has provided treatment guidelines and a limited view of the application of CBT and constructivist methods to treat clients during divorce decision making and beyond.

WEBSITES

Academy of Cognitive Therapy. http://www .academyofct.org.
American Association for Marriage and Family Therapy. http://www.aamft.org.
Association for Behavioral and Cognitive Therapies. http://www.aabt.org.
Constructivist Psychology Network. http:// www.constructivistpsych.org.

European Personal Construct Association. http://www.epca-net.org.

References

Baum, N., Rahav, G., & Sharon, D. (2005). Changes in the self-concepts of divorced women. *Journal of Divorce and Remarriage, 43*(1/2), 47–67.

DeRubeis, R. J., & Crits-Christoph, P. (1998). Empirically supported individual and group psychological treatments for adult mental disorders. *Journal of Consulting and Clinical Psychology, 66*(1), 37–52.

Granvold, D. K. (1983). Structured separation for marital treatment and decision-making. *Journal of Marital and Family Therapy, 9*, 403–412.

Granvold, D. K. (1994). *Cognitive behavioral divorce therapy*. Belmont, CA: Thomson Brooks/Cole Publishing Co.

Granvold, D. K. (2000a). Divorce. In F. M. Dattilio & A. Freeman (Eds.), *Cognitive-behavioral strategies in crisis intervention* (2nd ed.) (pp. 362–384). New York, NY: Guilford.

Granvold, D. K. (2000b). The crisis of divorce: Cognitive-behavioral and constructivist assessment and treatment. In A. R. Roberts (Ed.), *Crisis intervention handbook: Assessment, treatment, and research* (2nd ed.) (pp. 307–336). New York, NY: Oxford University Press.

Granvold, D. K. (2008). Constructivist theory and practice. In N. Coady & P. Lehmann (Eds.), *Theoretical perspectives for direct social work practice: A generalist-eclectic approach* (2nd ed.) (pp. 401–427). New York, NY: Springer.

Granvold, D. K. (2010). Constructivist treatment of divorce. In J. D. Raskin & S. K. Bridges (Eds.), *Studies in meaning 3: Constructivist therapy in the "real" world* (pp. 201–228). New York, NY: Pace University Press.

Hilton, J. M., & Kopera-Frye, K. (2004). Patterns of psychological adjustment among divorced custodial parents. *Journal of Divorce & Remarriage, 41*(3/4), 1–30.

Krumrei, E., Coit, C., Martin, S., Fogo, W., & Mahoney, A. (2007). Post-divorce adjustment and social relationships: A meta-analytic review. *Journal of Divorce and Remarriage, 46*(3/4), 145–166.

Sakraida, T. (2005). Common themes in the divorce transition experience of midlife women. *Journal of Divorce and Remarriage, 43*(1/2), 69–88.

Stanley, S. (2001, January). Helping couples fight for their marriages: Research on the prediction and prevention of marital failure. Paper presented at the Annual Conference of the Texas Association for Marriage and Family Therapy, Dallas.

Wang, H., & Amato, P. R. (2000). Predictors of divorce adjustment: Stressors, resources, and definitions. *Journal of Marriage and the Family, 62*, 655–669.

Primary Prevention Using the Go Grrrls Group with Adolescent Females

Craig Winston LeCroy & Nicole M. Huggett

Female adolescents today face a multitude of risks such as cigarette and drug use, body dissatisfaction and body image disorders, problems associated with sexual behaviors, and high rates of depression and unhappiness. Gender specific programs can address the unique issues that adolescent girls face. Universal primary prevention models offer a method of providing girls with necessary skills and protective factors to combat a wide array of risky behaviors before these behaviors lead to more serious consequences.

Girls face unique biological, psychological, and social changes during adolescence. Gender-specific programs are able to address these issues. For example, physical maturation can be a negative experience for girls (Benjet & Hernández-Guzmán, 2002), and early maturation, in particular, is a significant risk factor. Studies have found early maturation to be related to multiple risks including eating problems and body image disorders (McCabe and Ricciardelli, 2004), depression and low self-esteem (Kaltiala-Heino, Kosunen, & Rimpela, 2003), and delinquency (Negriff, Fung, & Trickett, 2008). All these factors support the reasoning that gender-specific prevention programs are ideal to support a healthy transition for girls from adolescence into adulthood.

One factor that should be considered in the development of a universal primary prevention program for adolescent females is the multitude of negative messages about women in the media. The negative consequences of gender stereotypes in traditional media such as music, television, and advertising have long been recognized by researchers (Simmons & Blythe, 1987). However, adolescents today are also bombarded by these images on websites and in social media outlets like Facebook and Instagram, where there are pages dedicated to thinspiration (or "thinspo") and proponents of anorexia ("pro-ana"). These websites depict pictures of very thin women to provide inspiration to girls who are trying to lose weight, information regarding how to hide an eating disorder from loved ones, and opportunities for girls with body image disorders to form a network to connect with others. Unfortunately, this network often becomes isolating and encourages the continuation of these unhealthy behaviors (Tantillo, 2006).

Girls are also at risk for cyberbullying, including online sexual harassment. Some studies have found that anywhere from 20% to 40% of adolescents have been victims of cyberbullying, with girls being as likely as boys to be bullied (Gamez-Gaudix, Orue, Smith, & Calvete, 2014. Being a victim of cyberbullying is associated with low self-esteem, symptoms of depression, substance abuse, and Internet addiction (Ybarra, Mitchell, Wolak, & Finkelhor, 2006; Gamez-Gaudix, Orue, Smith, & Calvete, 2014. These risk factors may interact with stressors associated with adolescence and lead to an unhealthy and difficult transition into later adolescence and adulthood.

Considering the multitude of risk factors for adolescent girls, interventions are most effective when they promote a broad concept of well-being and positive development. Several researchers (e.g., Elliott, 1993; Millstein, Petersen, & Nightingale, 1993; Johnson & Roberts, 1999) have recommended movement away from interventions for single problems, and have instead suggested interventions that focus more generally on positive adolescent growth and good health. These efforts have grown out of the understanding that specific problem behaviors can be better understood as a constellation of problems that are interrelated.

This research highlights the importance of the creation of a developmentally based gender-specific program for adolescent girls. The empowering adolescent girls program, or Go Grrrls curriculum, (LeCroy & Daley, 2001a) is informed by understanding the timing of the intervention, selection of relevant issues, and a focus on reducing identified risk factors. In this manner the program is both developmentally appropriate and gender specific, because it addresses some of the unique aspects of adolescent development. Table 100.1 describes the developmental issue, developmental process, and the program objectives for the Go Grrrls curriculum.

An evaluation of the Go Grrrls curriculum shows promising findings. Compared to a control group, Go Grrrls participants showed greater increases in their perceptions of body image, self-reported assertiveness, perceptions of attractiveness, self-efficacy, and self-liking and competence immediately following the end of programming (LeCroy, 2004). Additionally, the curriculum provides participants with a link to new friends as well as personal and community resources.

GO GRRRLS CURRICULUM

Program Structure

The Go Grrrls program is a psycho-educational program delivered in a group format to middle school girls. The group structure is practical for reaching a large number of girls, as well as being developmentally appropriate due to the fact that adolescents tend to place a high value on social interaction with their peers. The curriculum is intended to be delivered in a community setting such as a school, community center, or library. It is designed to be delivered in 90-minute sessions weekly in an optimal group size of eight to ten girls. The success of the sessions relies heavily on the energy level and participation within the group. For this reason, facilitators with certain attributes are preferred: enthusiasm, organization, interpersonal sensitivity abilities, and good social skills. Co-facilitation is also recommended

so that the facilitators can model role play with each other, as well as take turns facilitating to maintain momentum and high levels of group energy.

The curriculum includes a participant workbook, *The Go Grrrls Workbook* (LeCroy & Daley, 2001b), which provides exercises and information that reinforce the material learned in the group sessions and serves as a journal for the girls to record their thoughts and feelings. For example, each workbook chapter includes a slumber party dialog, a quiz, a "Did you know?" section, a "Check it out," section, and a journal assignment that is aligned with each group session. A parent workbook to aid parents or guardians is also used to facilitate parental engagement with the program material. The parent workbook provides an overview of each session and suggests ways to talk about the topics with daughters. This is especially useful in the sessions that discuss sexual health, when parents may find it more difficult to talk to their daughters about these topics. This also serves to get girls to talk to their parents about household rules, values, and expectations.

When recruiting participants for the Go Grrrls curriculum, girls are most receptive to hearing the program referred to as the Go Grrrls Club. A club seems more fun than a prevention program. When girls are excited about being a part of the Go Grrrls Club, this energy is translated into the group sessions, which is critical to the success of the activities.

Ensuring Successful Group Sessions

As previously emphasized, the success of the curriculum depends on participation and engagement. With energetic facilitators and the consideration of a few key factors for successful group facilitation (see e.g., Schiola, 2011), sessions will be fun and engaging for the participants, rather than feeling like a classroom atmosphere.

Active pacing. An active pace is necessary in sessions to keep girls' attention. Additionally, there is a lot of material to cover in each session, and active pacing is often necessary to ensure that all of the material is covered. Each session includes recommended time allowances for the various activities. Facilitators are encouraged to map out the session beforehand so that they know exactly what time transitions should be made in order to keep the session moving. Facilitators also should feel comfortable in keeping group members on-task, especially when dealing with more

TABLE 100.1 Developmental Issues, Developmental Processes, and Related Program Empowerment Objectives

Developmental Issues	Developmental Process	Program Implementation: Empowerment Objectives
Gender Role Identification	At puberty, gender-intensification theory suggests gender-related expectations influence behavior.	Enhance positive messages about gender roles; promote a more positive sex-role self-image.
Body Image	Adolescent girls are at risk to develop a negative body image, which leads to low self-esteem, depression, body image disturbance, and eating disorders.	Promote understanding of the changes that take place during puberty. Promote positive body image and body acceptance.
Self-Acceptance	In early adolescence girls have a drop in self-esteem and this is accompanied by increased self-criticism, negative mood states, and for some girls, depression.	Promote a positive self-image in response to the biological, psychological, and social changes girls confront. Reduce self-criticism and promote positive mood states.
Peer Relationships	Membership in the peer group is a major developmental task. Adolescents who fail to develop positive peer relationships are at greater risk for developing problems like substance abuse and depression. Conformity and peer pressure can lead to bad choices made by young people.	Promote positive peer relationships. Build on the relational quality many girls have in friendships to strengthen positive reasons for friendship. Build sharing and mutual understanding for enhanced companionship, support, and empathy.
Responsible Decision Making	Most adolescents in today's society will confront decisions that could have lifelong if not lethal consequences. The cognitive development of young people has important implications for adolescent risk taking.	Promote responsible decision making by teaching problem solving skills. In conjunction with decision making encourage personal assertiveness.
Sexuality	Girls' sexuality is a major issue because of the potential consequences associated with high risk behaviors. As girls develop sexually they need information and skills to prevent unwanted sex, unwanted pregnancies, and STDs.	Promote awareness and understanding of sexuality issues. Enhance responsible decision making and safe sex. Broaden girls understanding of sex so it is not seen only as intercourse. Address the special risks for younger girls.
Accessing Resources	Adolescent girls face multiple risks and a full one-third are estimated to be at high or very high risk. Along with girls' "invisible" problems (like depression) adolescents vastly underutilize systems of care.	Reduce barriers to services and help prepare girls to find and accept professional help when they need it.
Planning for the Future	Adolescent girls often experience a "crisis in confidence" that undermines their educational and career decisions for later life.	Enhance girls' achievement motivation. Build their confidence for educational and vocational aspirations. Teach a "mastery orientation" as opposed to a "learned helplessness" orientation.

verbose participants. A simple reminder that the group needs to stay on schedule and an offer to continue the discussion after group is a gentle way to move the group forward if a participant begins to digress.

Honest and open communication. Most people, adolescents included, have a good sense of when people are being honest with them. In order to foster a trusting environment, it is important that facilitators be open and honest with the participants. This will be particularly important at the end of the program, when girls may be attached to facilitators and expect to be able to stay in touch with them. Facilitators should always speak truthfully and tactfully without oversharing personal or inappropriate details.

Frequent contribution. It is important that facilitators elicit participation from all members of the group. This can be done by calling on participants by name. Also, rather than having the girls share by going around the circle, facilitators can keep girls on their toes (and engaged) by calling on them randomly by name. It is also important that facilitators keep their own comments during discussion to a minimum to encourage input from participants.

Use of praise. Facilitators are trained to use a great deal of praise during group sessions to foster confidence and assertiveness in group members. This praise should be specific about the individual's behavior, as opposed to a general comment about the individual as a person.

Use of names. A name game is utilized in Unit 1 to help participants remember each other's names—and also help facilitators in remembering names. Using names frequently in the group helps to foster a more intimate feeling, and will help the girls feel comfortable in a new setting.

GO GRRRLS SESSIONS

Unit 1. Introduction to Girls' Issues

The goals for the initial session are (1) to create a supportive atmosphere and begin building cohesiveness within the group; (2) to collect baseline data for program evaluation; (3) to introduce participants to group standards such as confidentiality and respect for others; and (4) to introduce the program content. To begin, facilitators warmly welcome participants and wait for them to get settled before beginning the assessment, which will inform the evaluation of the program. The assessment measures girls' self-reported depression symptoms, self-esteem levels, and confidence in problem-solving, among other things.

A "name game" is played to loosen everyone up and to help with introductions. Following the game, we help the girls to establish group standards by asking them to suggest their own rules for the group. If the group-generated rules do not include important areas (such as confidentiality and its limits), then the group leaders bring up these subjects. Finally, we introduce the program content by displaying a large poster with the "Go Grrrls" puzzle, and encourage each member to read one of the topics aloud (see Figure 100.1). Finally, we distribute Go Grrrls workbooks, which the girls are instructed to use to complete brief assignments for the group and to express themselves in any way they wish. The journals/workbooks are a tool for helping the girls incorporate what they learn into their personal lives and provide a mechanism for encouraging them to continue their self-growth and discovery after the group ends. Facilitators ask the girls to complete the "All About Me" assignment for the next meeting. The first session ends with playing "Two Truths and a Lie." Table 100.2 shows all components of Unit 1 demonstrating the structure that the program uses for each session.

Unit 2. Being a Girl in Today's Society

This session helps girls call attention to the stereotypes and gender roles that are ubiquitous in modern society through the media. Once the girls are aware of the many negative images of women in popular media, they can begin to challenge these stereotypes critically. Additionally, this unit provides the participants with basic information about what is considered sexual harassment.

The largest part of this session focuses on helping girls identify stereotypes in the media. In the media message exercise, girls listen to popular music while creating collages of pictures from magazines and the Internet that depict stereotypes of femininity or what it means to be a woman. Facilitators draw the girls' attention to the unattainability of these stereotypes, and stress the importance of nonphysical factors such as intelligence and honesty. The girls also begin to notice that these negative messages are prevalent in the music they hear.

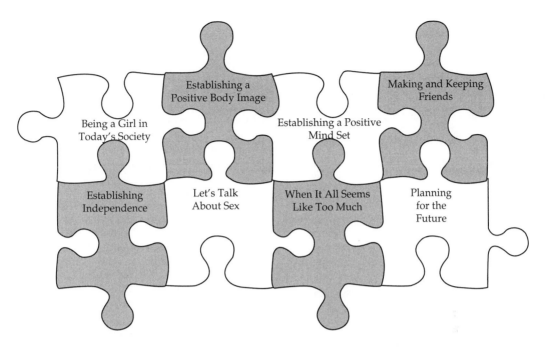

Figure 100.1 Go Grrrls Puzzle.

TABLE 100.2 Unit 1 Activities

Activity	Time
Introduction	5 minutes
Play the Name Game	20 minutes
Go Grrrls Assessment	25 minutes
Establishing Group Rules	10 minutes
Go Grrrls Puzzle	10 minutes
Distribute Workbooks and Parent Curriculum	10 minutes
Closing—Two Truths and a Lie	10 minutes

Unit 3. Establishing a Positive Body Image

The goals of this session are (1) to help girls accept their bodies as they are and develop a positive body image; (2) to teach girls that attractiveness is based on factors other than physical traits; and (3) to encourage girls to appreciate their unique qualities, talents, and skills. During the course of the meeting, the focus will shift from physical qualities to personal qualities, abilities, skills, and talents. We begin the group by asking participants to discuss the reasons that developing a positive body image is important for girls. We then embark on a series of image-boosting activities. In one such activity, girls are asked to list five things they like about themselves, and then share this list aloud in the group. Group leaders construct a chart of these responses as they are offered. The chart includes categories for physical aspects, social/personality traits, specials skills and abilities, and cognitive abilities. Discussion then centers around the fact that each girl has a unique set of strengths in these different categories.

Unit 4. Establishing a Positive Mind Set

An important part of our program is teaching girls about the relationship between self-esteem, self-criticism, and depression. As mentioned previously, girls entering the seventh grade show a significant decline in their overall self-esteem. This session is designed to teach girls how they can avoid setting unrealistic standards for themselves and can instead give themselves positive messages to facilitate realistic goal achievement.

Participants complete fill-in-the-blank handouts listing their unrealistic "I should" messages. We then help them to change these messages to "I want" statements that are more constructive. For example, "I should be liked by everyone" versus "I want to have good friends." Finally, we describe how negative thoughts tend to generate even more negative thoughts in a sort of downward spiral, while positive self-messages tend to lead to increased confidence, in an upward spiral. An example follows:

Downward Spiral	Upward Spiral
I should be liked by everyone.	*I want to have good friends.*
Nobody likes me.	*I can make friends with people.*
I must be a horrible person.	*I am a good friend to other people.*

Unit 5. Making and Keeping Friends

Navigating social groups in middle school can be very challenging for girls, because pressure to be popular and well-liked mounts during these years. This session encourages girls to focus on developing healthy friendships rather than concerning themselves with popularity. Facilitators then help girls realize that the traits one seeks in a close friend are often the same traits one seeks in a significant other. This discussion supports healthy romantic relationships for the participants and stresses the importance of good relationships for a person's well-being.

The main activities during this unit include developing a friendship "want ad," doing a "dating values game," and learning friendship social skills. For the friendship want ad girls individually write friendship "want ads," but they do not put their names on their profile. After the girls finish writing, the facilitator collects the want ads, shuffles them, and passes them back out to the group (ensuring that no one gets their own ad back). The girls then highlight or underline what they really like or what they have in common with the person who wrote the profile. They then read the profiles out loud and try to guess who wrote it. During this exercise, the facilitator writes these qualities on a flipchart. At the end, the girls reveal which profile they wrote. This unit also focuses on conversation skills and uses role plays for teaching friendship skills.

Unit 6. Establishing Independence

The point of the Go Grrrls curriculum is not to tell girls how to act, but rather how to make the right choices for themselves. Often, adolescents make decisions impulsively without considering the impact of their choices. Their decisions represent "experimental" attempts to acquire skills for dealing with new situations, but unfortunately these attempts may lead to serious consequences. Unit 6 is truly a skill-building session, as we teach group members a method for solving problems and then ask them to practice this method.

Girls practice this procedure in the large group, and then split into two smaller groups to practice further. Finally, they play the Choices and Consequences board game as a fun way to continue using their new skills.

Because girls in our society are often socialized to be passive and accommodating, some girls may not develop the skills to be assertive in certain situations that call for standing up for themselves. This unit also teaches girls the difference between assertive, aggressive, and passive, and emphasizes the importance of being assertive.

Unit 7. Let's Talk About Sex

The Go Grrrls curriculum places an emphasis on pregnancy prevention within a broader program context that is both educational and skill based. The program includes two group meetings devoted specifically to the topic of sexuality, but it is the cumulative effect of the entire curriculum that is most likely to make a difference in a young person's behavior. The skill-building sessions included in the curriculum (assertiveness, problem solving, making and keeping friends, positive self-talk, and setting reachable goals for the future) all serve as important components in reducing a teen's likelihood of engaging in early, unhealthy sexual activity. Psycho-educational components of the curriculum (confronting media messages and establishing a positive body image) boost girls' understanding of the effects of broader cultural trends on their individual lives.

During this session we review myths and facts about sexual activity. Leaders display posters depicting male and female reproductive organs, explain the physical act of intercourse, review what goes on during the menstrual cycle, and cover other basic sexual information. Participants are then asked to place their questions about sexuality, or myths they may have heard about sex, into an anonymous "question can." This is the highlight of the group, and most times, after the initial round of anonymous questions have been answered, girls continue to toss new questions in, or to simply ask aloud as they become more comfortable with the process.

After the questions have been answered, participants discuss reasons why some teens choose to have sex and some do not. Next, girls play the Handshake Game, which demonstrates how sexually transmitted diseases (STDs) can spread. Role play activities give girls practice in using refusal skills, and community resources for obtaining birth control information and supplies are identified.

Unit 8. When It All Seems Like Too Much

By this point in the curriculum girls have learned a number of helpful skills to empower them to handle difficult situations independently and with confidence. Unit 8 serves to show girls that not all problems can be solved alone, and that asking for help when you need it can be a sign of strength rather than weakness. When conducting this session, facilitators have found that after building rapport with the participants, some girls share sensitive stories and concerns during this session. For this reason, it is important at the outset of this session to review the limits of confidentiality.

The first part of this session teaches girls to identify when they can solve a problem on their own and when they might need help to solve a problem. This is done by discussing various scenarios and what girls would do if they were in any of these situations. For example, one scenario might be: *Annalise has been worried about her friend McKenzie lately. McKenzie has not been acting like herself; she seems tired all the time and never wants to hang out with Annalise. McKenzie is even starting to look different. She has lost weight and hardly ever smiles. Should Annalise solve it or seek help?* The girls lead the discussion while facilitators draw out the reasoning behind why the girls came to the conclusion they did.

During this session girls also begin to create a personal yellow pages directory. This is a place where they write down different people and places they can go for help.

Unit 9. Planning for the Future

This session helps girls learn to set achievable goals for themselves so they can work toward a bright, directed future. In this session, we encourage girls to set long-term educational, career, and adventure goals for themselves, and teach them how to create short-term objectives to help them achieve those goals. The majority of the session is spent playing the Planning for the Future Game. This game is like Pictionary. Each girl takes a turn drawing her goal, and the other girls try to guess what it is. The person whose goal is guessed in the shortest amount of time wins the game.

Unit 10. Review and Closure

The last session is often difficult for both facilitators and participants. It is important in this final session that the facilitators are honest and forthright about their ability to keep in touch with girls. If a participant says to a facilitator that she will miss the facilitator, it is important that the participant has her feelings acknowledged. Group leaders should give specific compliments to girls about the great work they did in the program and any progress they have made. After a brief review of what was covered during the program, girls complete the postassessment. All participants receive a certificate of completion and receive praise from group leaders. Girls then are free to hang out, eat, and say their goodbyes.

CONCLUSION

Adolescent girls live in an environment that is often toxic to their healthy development. They present unique challenges and the Go Grrrls curriculum is designed to help these girls confront those challenges and prepare for a healthier and happier lifestyle. This psycho-educational skills training program was designed with regard to empirical studies that identify the developmental issues that impact early adolescent girls the most. Based on practical instruction and skill building, the program provides a fountain of knowledge and skills to help girls cope with the pressures of growing up in contemporary culture. It promotes adolescent girls' positive assets and addresses relevant developmental issues. When girls are given the tools to access resources, both internal and external, they are empowered to make lifelong healthy decisions.

WEBSITES

http://www.public.asu.edu/~lecroy/gogrrrls/
body.htm
http://www.promisingpractices.net/
http://childtrends.org/?programs=go-grrrls

References

Benjet, C., & Hernández-Guzmán, L. (2002). A short-term longitudinal study of pubertal change, gender, and psychological well-being of Mexican early adolescents. *Journal of Youth and Adolescence, 31*, 429–442.

Elliott, D. S. (1993). Health enhancing and health compromising lifestyles. In S. G. Millstein, A. C. Petersen, & E. O. Nightingale (Eds.), *Promoting adolescent health* (pp. 119–145). New York, NY: Oxford University Press.

Gamez-Gaudix, M., Orue, I., Smith, P. K., & Calvete, E. (2014). Longitudinal and reciprocal relations of cyberbullying with depression, substance use, and problematic Internet use among adolescents. *Journal of Adolescent Health, 29*, 232–247.

Johnson, N. G., & Roberts, M. C. (1999). Passage on the Wild River of Adolescence: Arriving safely. In N. G. Johnson, M. C. Roberts, & J. Worell (Eds.), *Beyond appearance: A new look at adolescent girls* (pp. 3–18). Washington, DC: American Psychological Association.

Kaltiala-Heino, R., Kosunen, E., & Rimpela, M. (2003). Pubertal timing, sexual behavior, and self-reported depression in middle adolescence. *Journal of Adolescence, 26*, 531–545.

LeCroy, C. W., & Daley, J. (2001a). *Empowering adolescent girls: Examining the present and building skills for the future with the Go Grrrls Program.* New York, NY: W. W. Norton.

LeCroy, C. W., & Daley, J. (2001b). *The Go Grrrls Workbook.* New York, NY: W. W. Norton.

LeCroy, C. W. (2004). Experimental evaluation of "Go Grrrls" preventive intervention for early adolescent girls. *Journal of Primary Prevention, 25*(4), 457–473.

McCabe, M. P., & Ricciardelli, L. A. (2004). A longitudinal study of pubertal timing and extreme body change behaviors among adolescent boys and girls. *Adolescence, 39*(153), 145–166.

Millstein, S. G., Petersen, A. C., & Nightingale, E. O. (1993). Adolescent health promotion: Rationale, goals and objectives. In S. G. Millstein, A. C. Petersen, & E. O. Nightingale (Eds.), *Promoting the health of adolescents: New direction for the 21st century* (pp. 3–12). New York, NY: Oxford University Press.

Negriff, S., Fung, M. T., & Trickett, P. K. (2008). Self-rated pubertal development, depressive symptoms, and delinquency: Measurement issues and moderation by gender and maltreatment. *Journal of Youth and Adolescence, 37*, 736–746.

Schiola, S. (2011). *Making group work easy: The art of successful facilitation.* Lanham, MD: Rowman & Littlefield Education.

Simmons, R. G., & Blythe, D. A. (1987). Moving into adolescence: The impact of pubertal change and school context. New York, NY: Aldine De Gruyter.

Tantillo, M. (2006). A relational approach to eating disorders multifamily therapy group: Moving from difference and disconnection to mutual connection. *Families, Systems, & Health, 24*, 82–102.

Ybarra, M. L., Mitchell, K. J., Wolak, J., & Finkelhor, D. (2006). Examining characteristics and associated distress related to Internet harassment: Findings from the Second Youth Internet Safety Survey. *Pediatrics, 118*, 1169–1177.

101 Cyberbullying and the Social Worker

Michelle F. Wright & Diane L. Green Sherman

INTRODUCTION

Youths' rapid uptake of electronic technologies has led to many conveniences in their daily lives, such as having access to an endless amount of information and being able to communicate with just about anyone they want (Espinosa, Laffey, Whittaker, & Sheng, 2006; Kaara, Brandtzaeg, Heim, & Endestad, 2007; Subrahmanyam & Smahel, 2011; Williams & Merten, 2011). A darker side to these conveniences is that they offer youths additional ways to harm one another. One such consequence of electronic technology use is cyberbullying. Although various definitions of cyberbullying exist in the literature, researchers generally define it as the utilization of electronic technologies through which individuals engage in repeated, aggressive online acts (Hinduja & Patchin, 2009; Smith, Mahdavi, Carvalho, Fisher, Russell, & Tippett, 2008; Tokunaga, 2010).

This chapter draws on research from social work, psychology, public health, criminology, and sociology in order to review bullying behaviors in the cyber context. The first section provides definitions, alternative terminologies, describes various forms of these behaviors, and explains the similarities and differences between cyberbullying and face-to-face bullying. In the second section, the prevalence rates of cyberbullying within the United States are discussed, along with details about the sample and measurement of these behaviors. Section three describes the predictors and consequences associated with cyberbullying involvement among American youths. The fourth section discusses prevention and invention programs aimed at reducing cyberbullying. The fifth section presents recommendations for future research on cyberbullying

and suggestions for social workers. The concluding section summarizes the chapter and lists suggested websites.

WHAT IS CYBERBULLYING?

This section defines cyberbullying, lists the electronic technologies utilized to harm others, describes examples of these behaviors, and summarizes the differences between face-to-face bullying and cyberbullying. Distinct from more deviant forms of cyber activities (e.g., cyber harassment, flaming, cyberstalking), cyberbullying is difficult to define due to disagreement over which behaviors constitute cyberbullying (Ybarra & Mitchell, 2004; O'Sullivan & Flanagin, 2003; Spitzberg & Hoobler, 2002). Despite these difficulties, researchers agree on the media through which cyberbullying occurs, such as mobile phones, the Internet (e.g., e-mail, social networking sites, YouTube), and gaming consoles (Fenaughty & Harre, 2013; Gorzing & Olafsson, 2013; Pujazon-Zazik & Park, 2010). Examples of cyberbullying behaviors include cruel teasing, intimidation and threats of violence, spreading malicious rumors, exclusion, and ignoring (Dooley, Pyzalski, & Cross, 2009). Like face-to-face bullying, cyberbullying also includes direct and indirect forms (Brenner & Rehberg, 2009). Direct cyberbullying behaviors have an immediate effect on victims, with perpetrators using instant messaging, text messaging, multimedia messaging, or e-mail to harm victims. On the other hand, indirect cyberbullying is harming others by proxy. These bullies post insults on Facebook, specifically created websites, or some other public area of cyberspace without directly targeting victims.

Cyberbullying is difficult to define because terminologies vary based on country (e.g., cyber-mobbing in Germany; Virtual-bullying in Italy; online harassment in the Czech Republic; Kowalski & Limber, 2007; Nocentini et al., 2010; Sevcikova & Smahel, 2009). Regardless of terminology differences, researchers do agree on the definition of face-to-face bullying. Face-to-face bullying is a form of aggressive behavior intended to cause harm through repeated actions carried out over time by targeting an individual who is not able to defend himself or herself (Olweus, 1980). Core components of this definition include repetition of the act, intention to cause emotional harm, power imbalance between victim and perpetrator, and malicious harm. Extrapolating the face-to-face bullying definition to the cyber context, the definition of cyberbullying typically includes repeated, aggressive online acts perpetuated via electronic technologies.

Some researchers (e.g., Grigg, 2010; Modecki, Barber, & Vernon, 2013; Pornari & Wood, 2010; Runions, Shapka, Dooley, & Modecki, 2013; Schnurr, Mahatmya, & Basche, 2013; Schoffstall & Cohen, 2011; Wright & Li, 2013) utilize the terminology of cyber aggression to describe maliciously harmful acts through electronic technologies. As a broader form of cyberbullying, cyber aggression encompasses negative acts that do not necessarily include repetition or an imbalance of power, but still are intentional and perceived as offensive, derogatory, harmful, and unwanted (Grigg, 2010; Dooley et al., 2009). Cyber aggression includes happy slapping (e.g., hitting or slapping someone and recording the assault), outing (e.g., public display or forwarding of personal communication), cat fishing (e.g., setting up a fictitious online profile to lure another into a fraudulent relationship), and flaming (e.g. sending angry, rude, or obscene messages) (Hinduja & Patchin, 2009). This chapter will not attempt to reconcile differences in the definitions and the measurement of cyberbullying and cyber aggression, but interested readers may refer to research (e.g., Langos, 2012; Menesini et al., 2012; Nocentini et al., 2010; Wingate, Minney, & Guadagno, 2013; Ybarra, Boyd, Korchmaros, & Oppenheim, 2012) focused on synthesizing definitions and providing recommendations for the measurement of these behaviors.

Some characteristics separate cyberbullying from traditional face-to-face bullying. First, perpetrators of cyberbullying may inflict harm anonymously using masked identities, whereas face-to-face bullies usually make their identity known (McKenna & Bargh, 2000). Cyberbullies can create an almost endless number of fake instant messenger or e-mail accounts, and use these fake identities to insult others, without victims being aware of the aggressor's identity. Although some face-to-face bullies can harm others anonymously (e.g., placing an insulting note in someone's locker), there are more opportunities for engaging in anonymous, harmful behaviors via the cyber context (Wright, 2013). Second, cyberbullying can reach a larger amount of potential victims and it can take place at any time as compared with face-to-face bullying (Kowalski & Limber, 2007; Slonje & Smith, 2008). Not only can cyberbullies target many victims at one time, but their aggressive acts may be witnessed by an almost endless audience. Third, in the face-to-face context, bullies can experience victims' reactions, whereas cyberbullies may not necessarily witness these reactions (McKenna & Bargh, 2000). Being unable to witness victims' reactions may encourage more impulsivity and aggressive behavior via the cyber context (Postmes, Spears, & Lea, 1998; Teich, Frankel, Kling, & Lee, 1999). Another difference between cyberbullying and face-to-face bullying is that the former can occur using relatively permanent electronic media, such as pictures or videos, which may be perceived as worse than face-to-face bullying and can significantly impair victims' emotional well-being (Dooley et al., 2009; Wright, 2013).

There are also similarities between face-to-face bullying and cyberbullying. Cyberbullying may happen more than once, inflict both psychological and emotional harm, and is intentional, just like face-to-face bullying (Dehue, Bolman, & Vollink, 2008). Next, psychosocial (e.g., depression, loneliness, anxiety) and school difficulties (e.g., school dropout, failure) are reported by both face-to-face victims and cybervictims (Gradinger, Strohmeier, & Spiel, 2009; Grills & Ollendick, 2002; Kochenderfer-Ladd & Skinner, 2002; Kupersmidt & Coie, 1990; O'Moore & Kirkham, 2001; Ybarra & Mitchell, 2004). Regardless of the similarities and differences between face-to-face bullying and cyberbullying, it is important that educators, researchers, parents, and law makers quickly find common ground so that we can more thoroughly understand the impact of cyberbullying and how to deal with it appropriately.

HOW FREQUENTLY DOES CYBERBULLYING OCCUR?

The first part of this section reviews research on the prevalence rates of cyberbullying involvement. In the second section, studies focused on understanding gender differences in cyberbullying are also discussed. We reviewed only those studies conducted among youths, ages 10 through 18 years, in the United States. Much of the research on the prevalence rates of cyberbullying has examined youths' victimization, but some research has focused on understanding the rates of cyberbullying perpetration. One of the earliest studies, which was conducted in the year 2000, revealed that 12% of surveyed youths (ages 10–17 years; 48% female) reported that they had perpetrated aggressive behaviors online, including making rude or nasty comments to someone on the Internet and using the Internet to harass or embarrass others (Ybarra & Mitchell, 2004). Five years later, Hinduja and Patchin (2008) found that 16% of the 1,500 adolescents (ages 13–18 years; 53% female) they surveyed admitted to having cyberbullied others. In another study conducted two years later, Kowalski and Limber (2007) utilized a large sample of 3,767 youths (51% female; grades sixth through eighth) to further understand rates of cyberbullying perpetration. Only 11% of the surveyed participants admitted that they were involved in cyberbullying as the aggressor. Dempsey, Sulkowski, Dempsey, and Storch (2011) found similar rates as Kowalski and Limber, such that 10% of the 1,672 adolescents (48% male; ages 11–14 years) in their study admitted that they had perpetrated cyberbullying within the past 30 days. In 2010, Bauman (2010) found that 1.5% of the surveyed intermediate school students (N = 221; fifth through eighth grades) in her study admitted to cyberbullying others, a much lower frequency rate when compared with other studies (e.g., Dempsey et al., 2011; Hinduja & Patchin, 2008; Kowalski & Limber, 2007; Ybarra & Mitchell, 2004). Recognizing that adolescents may be biased in reporting their perpetration of cyberbullying, Wright and Li (2013) utilized a peer-nomination measure to assess these behaviors among 261 adolescents (ages 11–14 years; 58% female) in the Midwestern United States. Not only did they find that it is possible to assess cyberbullying at the school level with peer-nomination measures, but their findings also revealed that 38%

of adolescents were nominated at least once as a cyberbully.

In one of the earliest studies to document the prevalence rates of youths' experiences with cyberbullying, Finkelhor, Mitchell, and Wolak (2000) found that 6% of the youths (N = 1,501; 10 to 17 years of age; 53% male; 73% White) they surveyed had experienced threats and negatives rumors, with a smaller percentage (around 2%) reporting that they had suffered distressing harassment (i.e., been very or extremely upset or afraid because of the incidence). Following up their study a few years later, Ybarra, Mitchell, Wolak, and Finkelhor (2006) found that 9% of youths (N = 1,500; 10 to 17 years of age) reported that they experienced some type of electronic harassment. Also utilizing data from 2005, Hinduja and Patchin (2008) found that 33% of the 1,500 youths (ages 13–18 years; 53% female) they surveyed reported being victimized online, with most reporting that they were disrespected (41%), followed by being called names (19%), and threatened physically (12%). A few years later in 2008, Hinduja and Patchin (2009) sampled 2,000 middle-school students in the Southeastern United States. Their findings indicated that 10% were cyberbullied within the past 30 days, while 17% reported that they were bullied at least once in their lifetime. In a study conducted a few years later, Dempsey, Sulkowski, Nichols, and Storch (2009) found similar patterns of victimization as Hinduja and Patchin. In their study, Dempsey and colleagues found that 15% of their sample reported that they had received mean or threatening messages via mobile phones, instant messenger, and e-mail. Later research by Bauman (2010) revealed that only 3% of surveyed intermediate school students in grades fifth through eighth (N = 221; 54% males) reported being victimized in the cyber context. Research from 2012 revealed that 77% of adolescents (N = 261; ages 11–14 years; 58% female) reported that they had experienced insults, rumor spreading, and threats via instant messenger, social networking sites, e-mail, and mobile phones within the last school year (Wright & Li, 2013).

Just as many studies document the frequency rates of cyberbullying involvement, researchers have also extensively examined gender differences in order to provide insight into the characteristics that put youths at risk for these behaviors. Some of the available research indicates that boys are more likely to perpetuate cyberbullying (e.g., Wang, Iannotti, & Nansel,

2009) and be the victims of these behaviors (e.g., Bauman, Toomey, & Walker, 2013), whereas others (e.g., Dehue et al., 2008) find that girls are more often the aggressor and the victim (e.g., Dempsey et al., 2009; Hinduja & Patchin, 2008; Kowalski & Limber, 2007; Mesch, 2009; Sontag, Clemans, Graber, & Lyndon, 2011; Ybarra, Diener-West, & Leaf, 2007). However, other researchers have found no gender differences in cyberbullying involvement as victims (e.g., Bauman, 2010; Kowalski & Limber, 2007; Schoffstall & Cohen, 2011; Varjas, Henrich, & Meyers, 2009) or perpetrators (e.g., Bauman, 2010; Hinduja & Patchin, 2008; Raskauskas & Stoltz, 2007; Williams & Guerra, 2007; Wright & Li, 2013). Variations in the prevalence rates and inconsistencies regarding gender differences in cyberbullying involvement reflect differences in the sampling, methodology, and measurement of these behaviors. Despite the discrepancy in these rates, it is clear that American youth experience and engage in cyberbullying. Furthermore, youths also report greater frequency of cybervictimization when compared with cyberbullying perpetration. Such differences may reflect self-report biases or indicate that a small group of cyberbullies perpetrates most of the aggressive acts via the cyber context.

PREDICTORS AND CONSEQUENCES OF CYBERBULLYING INVOLVEMENT

In this section, predictors of American adolescents' involvement in cyberbullying are discussed, followed by the consequences associated with experiencing and engaging in these behaviors. Researchers have examined how youths' utilization of electronic technology places them at risk for cyberbullying. Youths' risky online behaviors (e.g., sharing private information and passwords) and greater technology usage each predict cyberbullying involvement (Bauman, 2010; Hinduja & Patchin, 2008; Mesch, 2009). Other researchers (e.g., Bauman, 2010; Hinduja & Patchin, 2008; Kowalski & Limber, 2007; Raskauskas & Stoltz, 2007; Ybarra et al., 2007) have focused on the behavioral profiles of cyberbullies and cybervictims. In this research, face-to-face bullying and face-to-face victimization are consistently related to the involvement in cyberbullying, as perpetrators and aggressors. In other research, Sontag and colleagues (2011) found that reactive and proactive face-to-face

aggression each related to cyberbullying. In addition, cybervictimization is linked to cyberbullying, further indicating that there is significant overlap between youths' face-to-face and digital environments (Wright & Li, 2013; Ybarra et al., 2007). Other characteristics relate to cyberbullying perpetration, such as beliefs about the acceptability of aggression (i.e., normative beliefs), frustration, hostility, less remorsefulness, and moral approval of bullying (Burton, Florell, & Wygant, 2013; Low & Espelage, 2013; Patchin & Hinduja, 2006; Sontag et al., 2011; Williams & Guerra, 2007).

Cyberbullying is not only perpetrated by anonymous bullies, but also by youths' peers at their school. Therefore, researchers have investigated the role of peers and the school environment in cyberbullying involvement. Results from this research revealed that school problems and being the victim of physical assaults perpetrated by peers related to cyberbullying and cybervictimization (Hinduja & Patchin, 2008). In addition, adolescents' social standing among their peers is also related to cyberbullying, such that perceived popularity (i.e., based on social reputation) and peer-rejection were each associated with the perpetration of these behaviors (Wright & Li, 2013; Wright, in press). Furthermore, peer-rejection was associated with cybervictimization. Another important direction in this research is the focus on school climate (i.e., the quality and character of school life). Like face-to-face bullying, researchers (e.g., Brighi, Guarini, Melotti, Galli, & Genta, 2012; Hinduja & Patchin, 2012; Williams & Guerra, 2007) have found that youths' lower perceptions of school climate related to greater rates of cyberbullying among peers at school. Thus, it is not surprising that lower attachment toward peers and school were related positively to both cybervictimization and cyberbullying (Burton et al., 2013; Schneider, O'Donnell, Stueve, & Coulter, 2012). In addition, youths, who believed that their peers engaged in cyberbullying, perpetrated increased levels of these behaviors (Hinduja & Patchin, 2013).

Relationships with parents also have an impact on cybervictimization and cyberbullying. In this research, parents' use of coercive discipline, along with fewer emotional bonds with their children and poorer quality of family relationships, each predicted cyberbullying perpetration (Beran & Li, 2007; Ybarra et al., 2007). Furthermore, feelings of alienation and loneliness from parents correlated positively with bullying acts in the cyber context (Brighi et al., 2012). Youths' beliefs about their parents' sanctions against online aggressive acts also related to cyberbullying, indicating that youths with fewer such beliefs engaged in more of these behaviors (Hinduja & Patchin, 2013). In addition, family violence and lower levels of parental monitoring predicted cyberbullying among adolescents (Low & Espelage, 2013). Mesch (2009) found that victims of cyberbullying had parents who set fewer rules on which websites to visit, what information to share, and the time they could spend online. Thus, he argued that there is a need for more parental participation in youths' electronic technology usage, given that parents may be able to reduce their children's negative experiences in the cyber context. It is important that parents stay involved in their children's online activities, especially in adolescence, given that parents usually underestimate their involvement and monitoring of these activities.

Researchers have thoroughly documented the consequences of cyberbullying and cybervictimization. Ample research has revealed that cyberbullying involvement is related to depression and anxiety (Bauman et al., 2013; Schenk & Fremouw, 2012; Sontag et al., 2011). Many of these studies do not control for face-to-face bullying and face-to-face victimization, which are highly correlated with both cyberbullying and cybervictimization (Bauman, 2010; Hinduja & Patchin, 2008; Kowalski & Limber, 2007; Mesch, 2009; Schneider et al., 2012; Sontag et al., 2011; Ybarra et al., 2007). In one of the few studies to control for gender, and youths' involvement in face-to-face bullying, Dempsey and colleagues (2009) found that both cybervictimization and cyberbullying predicted depression and anxiety. When compared with nonvictims and nonbullies, cyberbullies and cybervictims were six times more likely to report emotional disturbances as well as increased anger and sadness (Patchin & Hinduja, 2006; Ybarra & Mitchell, 2004). In addition, victims and perpetrators of cyberbullying also reported more suicide attempts and suicidal ideation when compared with nonvictims and nonbullies (Bauman et al., 2013; Hinduja & Patchin, 2008, 2009; Schneider et al., 2012). Furthermore, cyberbullying involvement is related to substance use (i.e., drugs, alcohol) and delinquency (Hinduja & Patchin, 2008, 2009; Hinduja & Patchin, 2008; Low & Espelage, 2013). Cybervictims and cyberbullies also reported

lower school performance, declining self-concept and self-esteem, worsening grades, poorer concentration in school, and increased absences, truancy, detentions, and suspensions (Beran & Li, 2007; Didden et al., 2009; Katzer, Fetchenhauer, & Belschak, 2009; Schneider et al., 2012; Varjas et al., 2009; Ybarra et al., 2007). Taken together, it is clear that cyberbullying perpetration and cybervictimization each have short-term and long-term consequences, warranting the need for promoting and executing programs dedicated to reducing youths' involvement in these behaviors.

REDUCING CYBERBULLYING

Many schools throughout the United States have implemented antibullying programs (Ferguson, Miguel, Kilburn, & Sanchez, 2007). Given that cyberbullying is conceptualized as a new form of an old behavior (i.e., bullying), there is much debate about using existing antibullying programs to address cyberbullying (Stauffer, Heath, Coyne, & Ferrin, 2012). Such a debate is important because some of the characteristics of cyberbullying (e.g., anonymity, ability to reach a larger audience, unable to witness victims' emotions) are unique to the cyber context (Kowalski & Limber, 2007; McKenna & Bargh, 2000; Slonje & Smith, 2008; Wright, 2013). Given that cyberbullying often occurs outside of school hours, school officials are often reluctant to take action against students perpetrating these behaviors while not in school (Franek, 2006; Shariff & Hoff, 2007). However, it is not only important that antibullying programs be adapted to the specific needs and attitudes of the entire school, but that they should also be modified to address cyberbullying as a distinct behavior, separate from face-to-face bullying. Targeting youths' involvement in bullying may not lead to an enduring reduction in these behaviors because parents and teachers may affect the success of the program. Parents and teachers may question the effectiveness of the antibullying program, potentially erasing the effects of the program and wasting staff members' time and training. Thus, whole-school programs are most effective for reducing bullying when they target the school level, the home level, and the individual level (Rigby & Slee, 2008; Smith, Ananiadou, & Cowie, 2003; Stevens, Bourdeaudhuij, & Van Oost, 2001; Vreeman & Carroll, 2007). Such programs reach not only the bullies, but the bullied, and the bystanders, as well as foster sustainability (Michaud, 2009). A recent meta-analysis (i.e., Ttofi & Farrington, 2011) revealed that the most effective programs for reducing victimization are those that use videos, disciplinary methods, parent training/meetings, and cooperative group work. Regarding the reduction in the perpetration of bullying, programs should implement the previous components for victimization as well as improve playground supervision, increase the number of school assemblies, provide information for parents, implement classroom rules, and improve classroom management.

Despite the newness of cyberbullying, a number of effective strategies have been developed to combat and subsequently reduce such behaviors. Several cyberbullying prevention strategies involve addressing these behaviors in antibullying programs, setting clear rules and consequences, raising awareness about cyberbullying, increasing the supervision of students, having youths understand acceptable user policies, involving youths and school personnel as well as parents in Internet safety programs, and showing youths that messages they believe are anonymous can be traced (Campbell, 2005; Chibnall, Wallace, Leicht, & Lunghofer, 2006; Franek, 2006; Willard, 2007). In addition, Migliore (2003) recommended adult monitoring of youths' online activities and called for school personnel to participate in service programs in order to learn and understand effective intervention procedures. At home, it is recommended that home computers be placed in common areas, rather than in youths' bedrooms (Snider, 2004). Parents should also carefully monitor youths' electronic technology consumption. However, parents and teachers are advised to talk to youths about the dangers of cyberbullying and to take immediate action if it occurs as well as ask youths to sign contracts about appropriate electronic technology usage. Similarly, teachers need to support youths who report witnessing bullying behaviors and to take immediate action against those responsible for harming others. Although contracts about appropriate electronic technology usage may not reduce or prevent cyberbullying, contracts may heighten awareness of this issue. Youths can also sign anti-teasing pledges and practice effective conflict resolution strategies (Osher & Fleischman, 2005). Such pledges may empower students and potentially help cyberbullies understand what they have done, which is critical to cyberbullying prevention (Kraft & Wang, 2009). Awareness over the consequences of one's actions

is especially important because the perceived anonymity of cyberbullying may be especially attractive (Slonje, Smith, & Frisen, 2013).

There is limited research available regarding anti-cyberbullying programs. Some programs (e.g., Character Counts; Olweus Bullying Prevention Program) have recently been implemented in schools and their effectiveness is currently being evaluated. One program utilized the KiVa Antibullying Program to reduce cyberbullying among Finnish school-aged youths (Williford, Elledge, Boulton, DePaolis, Little, Salmivalli, 2013). Results indicated that the lowest frequencies of cybervictimization and cyberbullying were reported by students who participated in the program, revealing that KiVa may be effective for reducing the involvement in these behaviors. Currently, Williford and colleagues at the University of Kansas are implementing a similar program with American youths. Another program utilized a Quality Circle in which students work in small groups to find out information about a problem, use structured discussion techniques, and come up with solutions (Paul, Smith, & Blumberg, 2012). These solutions are then presented to teachers. Such a program allows teachers to keep up-to-date on the fast moving changes in the kinds of cyberbullying that youth experience. Thus far, the effectiveness of this program has not been evaluated and, therefore, its long-term effects on cyberbullying are currently unknown. Other programs have utilized youths' immersion in electronic technologies to help reduce cyberbullying. One of these programs uses online peer support, called CyberMentor, to provide guidance to victims of cyberbullying (Slonje et al., 2013). Youths who need to talk can log on and chat with trained Cybermentors, who are able to refer mentees on to counselors for further support if necessary. The CyberMentors program has been evaluated positively for providing quality support and help to cybervictims (Banerjee, Robinson, & Smalley, 2010; Thompson & Smith, 2011). There is also a CyberMentors mobile phone application, which focuses on building self-esteem, confidence, and helping victims feel safe. It is currently unknown whether the mobile application is beneficial to youths. Other researchers (Liang, 2010; Moore, Nakano, Enomoto, & Suda, 2012) have also recommended automated ways of dealing with cyberbullying. As increasing attention is given to cyberbullying, and researchers thoroughly identify the risks and consequences associated with these behaviors, it is likely that additional programs will be developed.

FUTURE DIRECTIONS AND RECOMMENDATIONS FOR SOCIAL WORKERS

In the cyberbullying literature, there is a lack of understanding regarding the impact these behaviors have on youths' long-term behaviors, their relationships, and subsequent psychosocial adjustment. Although some research (e.g., Barlett & Gentile, 2012; Del Rey, Elipe, & Ortega-Ruiz, 2012; Low & Espelage, 2013; Sticca, Ruggieri, Alsaker, & Perren, 2013; Wright & Li, 2013) has included longitudinal designs, additional research is needed to further understand the temporal ordering of cyberbullying involvement, depression, anxiety, and the relationship these variables have to later academic engagement among youths. Such designs should also provide insight into youths' social cognitive processes (i.e., attributions, normative beliefs, response evaluation and decision) as these processes increase (or decrease) their subsequent involvement in bullying (Perren, Gutzwiller-Helfenfinger, Malti, & Hymel, 2012). Concurrent research designs (e.g., Bauman, 2010; Pornari & Wood, 2010) have focused on social cognitive processes and their relation to cyberbullying, but, to our knowledge, longitudinal research has yet to be published on these variables. Investigations of the relationship between social cognitive processes, such as attributions, and cyberbullying is important because some antibullying programs include attribution retraining to reduce hostile attributional biases in an effort to reduce face-to-face bullying (Bugental, Ellerson, Lin, Rainey, Kokotovic, & O'Hara, 2002; Sukhodolsky, Golub, Stone, & Orban, 2005).

Many times social workers are expected to make decisions about youths' cyberbullying on the basis of nonexistent, unclear, or nonspecific policies. Although social workers may be aware of cyberbullying on their school campus, they may be unsure how to deal with such behaviors. In one of the few studies assessing social workers and cyberbullying, Sing and Slovak (2011) found that half of their sample agreed that cyberbullying is more harmful than traditional bullying, but almost all (93%) were unsure about their ability to intervene. They recommend that additional training for social workers, based on the type of school they are serving (i.e., elementary vs. middle or high school), is necessary. Such training will increase social workers' ability to create a school atmosphere conducive to students' disclosure of cyberbullying involvement. In these training programs, social workers should learn about identifying and explaining technologies that could be used for cyberbullying (Mason, 2008; Smith et al., 2008). With this knowledge, social workers can conduct training sessions for teachers, staff, administrators, parents, and students on cyberbullying. Other strategies may include inviting officers from local police departments to talk with school personnel, students, and families about the effects of these behaviors. Officers could discuss with students both the emotional and legal implications of cyberbullying. Social workers should address the problem of cyberbullying, as well as face-to-face bullying, using an ecological approach that includes family, the whole school, and community involvement. Instead of a zero-tolerance response to cyberbullying, social workers and other school personnel should recognize the needs of those involved in this form of behavior. Helping to create and then maintain a culture of respect, social workers should carefully observe and engage youths in conversation about cyberbullying.

SUMMARY AND CONCLUSIONS

As a topic of increased concern in recent years, cyberbullying is not yet completely understood or sometimes even recognized as a problem among youths. In this chapter, we discussed the problems facing researchers regarding defining, explaining, and conceptualizing cyberbullying. Such limitations have implications for educators, youths, and parents, given that it is difficult to make recommendations for reducing cyberbullying when we are limited in our basic understanding of this phenomenon. Despite these problems, it is clear that cyberbullying involvement has detrimental effects on youths' behavioral, psychological, and academic functioning. As our knowledge increases, we are better able to recommend the best practices for reducing cyberbullying. Although we acknowledge that the problem of cyberbullying is growing faster than our ability to respond to these behaviors, we are confident that the field is developing in the right direction.

Our lack of knowledge of cyberbullying will not make the problem disappear, because electronic technology usage among youths is not likely to decrease any time soon. Thus, it is important for educators, researchers, parents, and policy makers to understand that cyberbullying is a separate issue, albeit related, from face-to-face bullying. There is great need for researchers to come to a consensus on the terminologies, definitions, and theoretical frameworks for cyberbullying. By addressing these important directions, we are better able to recommend the best practices for combating cyberbullying.

WEBSITE RESOURCES

http://www.beatbullying.org/
http://stopcyberbullying.org/
http://www.cyberbullying.org/
http://www.commonsensemedia.org/cyberbullying
http://www.ncpc.org/topics/cyberbullying
http://www.stopbullying.gov/cyberbullying/
http://www.cyberbullying.info/
http://www.cyberbullyhelp.com/

References

Banerjee, R., Robinson, C., & Smalley, D. (2010). Evaluation of the Beatbullying Peer Mentoring Programme. Retrieved from http://www.sussex.ac.uk/Users/robinb/bbreportsummary.pdf

Barlett, C. P., & Gentile, D. A. (2012). Attacking others online: The formation of cyber-bullying in late adolescence. *Psychology of Popular Media Culture, 1*(2), 123–135.

Bauman, S. (2010). Cyberbullying in a rural intermediate school: An exploratory study. *Journal of Early Adolescence, 30*(6), 803–833.

Bauman, S., Toomey, R. B., & Walker, J. L. (2013). Associations among bullying, cyberbullying, and suicide in high school students. *Journal of Adolescence, 36*(2), 341–350.

Beran, T., & Li, Q. (2007). The relationship between cyberbullying and school bullying. *Journal of Student Wellbeing, 1*(2), 15–33.

Brenner, S. W., & Rehberg, M. (2009). "Kiddie crime"? The utility of criminal law. First Amendment Law Review. Retrieved from http://papers.ssrn.com/sol3/papers.cfm?abstract_id=1537873

Brighi, A., Guarini, A., Melotti, G., Galli, S., & Genta, M. L. (2012). Predictors of victimization across direct bullying, indirect bullying and cyberbullying. *Emotional & Behavioural Difficulties, 17*(3–4), 375–388.

Bugental, D. B., Ellerson, P. C., Lin, E. K., Rainey, B., Kokotovic, A., & O'Hara, N. (2002). A cognitive approach to child abuse prevention. *Journal of Family Psychology, 16*(3), 243–258.

Burton, K. A., Florell, D., & Wygant, D. B. (2013). The role of peer attachment and normative beliefs about aggression on traditional bullying and cyberbullying. *Psychology in the Schools, 50*(2), 103–115.

Campbell, M. A. (2005). Cyber bullying: An old problem in a new guise? *Australian Journal of Guidance and Counselling, 15*(1), 68–76.

Chibnall, S., Wallace, M., Leicht, C., & Lunghofer L. (2006). I-safe evaluation. Retrieved from http://www.ncjrs.gov/pdffiles1/nij/grants/213715.pdf

Dehue, E., Bolman, C., & Vollink, T. (2008). Cyberbullying: Youngsters' experiences and parental perception. *CyberPsychology & Behavior, 11*(2), 217–223.

Del Rey, R., Elipe, P., & Ortega-Ruiz, R. (2012). Bullying and cyberbullying: Overlapping and predictive value of the co-occurrence. *Psicothema, 24*(4), 808–813.

Dempsey, A. G., Sulkowski, M. L., Dempsey, J., & Storch, E. A. (2011). Has cyber technology produced a new group of peer aggressors? *Cyberpsychology, Behavior, & Social Networking, 14*(5), 297–302.

Dempsey, A. G., Sulkowski, M. L., Nichols, R., & Storch, E. A. (2009). Differences between peer victimization in cyber and physical settings and associated psychosocial adjustment in early adolescence. *Psychology in the Schools, 46(1)*, 962–972.

Didden, R., Scholte, R. H., Korzilius, H., de Moore, J. M., Vermeulen, A., O'Reilly, M.,. . . Lancioni, G. E. (2009). Cyberbullying among students with intellectual and developmental disability in special education settings. *Developmental Neurorehabilitation, 12*(3), 146–151.

Dooley, J. J., Pyzalski, J., & Cross, D. (2009). Cyberbullying versus face-to-face bullying: A theoretical and conceptual review. *Journal of Psychology, 217*(4), 182–188.

Espinosa, L. M., Laffey, J. M., Whittaker, T., & Sheng, Y. (2006). Technology in the home and the achievement of young children: Findings from the early childhood longitudinal study. *Early Education and Development, 17*(3), 421–441.

Fenaughty, J., & Harre, N. (2013). Factors associated with distressing electronic harassment and cyberbullying. *Computers in Human Behavior, 29*(3), 803–811.

Ferguson, C. J., Miguel, C. S., Kilburn, J. C., & Sanchez, P. (2007). The effectiveness of school-based anti-bullying programs: A meta-analytic review. *Criminal Justice Review, 32*(4), 401–414.

Finkelhor, D., Mitchell, K. J., & Wolak, J. (2000). Online victimization: A report on the nation's youth.

Retrieved from http://www.unh.edu/ccrc/pdf/jvq/CV38.pdf

Franek, M. (2006). Foiling cyberbullies in the new Wild West. *Educational Leadership, 63*(4), 39–43.

Gorzing, A., & Olafsson, K. (2013). What makes a bully a cyberbully? Unravelling the characteristics of cyberbullies across twenty-five European countries. *Journal of Children and Media, 7*(1), 9–27.

Gradinger, P., Strohmeier, D., & Spiel, C. (2009). Traditional bullying and cyberbullying: Identification of risk groups for adjustment problems. *Journal of Psychology, 217*(4), 205–213.

Grigg, D. W. (2010). Cyber-aggression: Definition and concept of cyberbullying. *Australian Journal of Guidance and Counseling, 20*(2), 143–156.

Grills, A., & Ollendick, T. (2002). Peer victimization, global self-worth, and anxiety in middle school children. *Journal of Clinical Child & Adolescent Psychology, 31*(2), 59–68.

Hinduja, S., & Patchin, J. W. (2008). Cyberbullying: An exploratory analysis of factors related to offending and victimization. *Deviant Behavior, 29*(2), 129–156.

Hinduja, S., & Patchin, J. W. (2009). *Bullying beyond the schoolyard: Preventing and responding to cyberbullying.* Thousand Oaks, CA: Corwin Press.

Hinduja, S., & Patchin, J. W. (2012). Cyberbullying: Neither an epidemic nor a rarity. *European Journal of Developmental Psychology, 9*(5), 539–543.

Hinduja, S., & Patchin, J. W. (2013). Social influences on cyberbullying behaviors among middle and high school students. *Journal of Youth and Adolescence, 42*(5), 711–722.

Kaara, B. H., Brandtzaeg, P. B., Heim, J., & Endestad, T. (2007). In the borderland between family orientation and peer culture: The use of communication technologies among Norwegian tweens. *New Media & Society, 9*(4), 603–624.

Katzer, C., Fetchenhauer, D., & Belschak, F. (2009). Cyberbullying: Who are the victims? A comparison of victimization in Internet chat rooms and victimization in school. *Journal of Media Psychology, 21*(1), 25–36.

Kochenderfer-Ladd, B., & Skinner, K. (2002). Children's coping strategies: Moderators of the effects of peer victimization. *Developmental Psychology, 38*(2), 267–278.

Kowalski, R., & Limber, S. P. (2007). Electronic bullying among middle school students. *Journal of Adolescent Health, 41*(6), S22–S30.

Kraft, E. M., & Wang, J. (2009). Effectiveness of cyber bullying prevention strategies: A study on students' perspectives. *International Journal of Cyber Criminology, 3*(2), 513–535.

Kupersmidt, J., & Coie, J. (1990). Preadolescent peer status, aggression, and school adjustment as predictors of externalizing problems in adolescents. *Child Development, 61*(5), 1350–1362.

Langos, C. (2012). Cyberbullying: The challenge to define. *Cyberpsychology, Behavior, & Social Networking, 15*(6), 285–289.

Liang, W. (2010). Cyberbullying, let the computer help. *Journal of Adolescent Health, 47*(2), 209.

Low, S., & Espelage, D. (2013). Differentiating cyber bullying perpetration from non-physical bullying: Commonalities across race, individual, and family predictors. *Psychology of Violence, 3*(1), 39–52.

Mason, K. L. (2008). Cyberbullying: A preliminary assessment for school personnel. *Psychology in the Schools, 45*(4), 323–348.

McKenna, K., & Bargh, J. (2000). Plan 9 from cyberspace: The implications of the Internet for personality and social psychology. *Personality and Social Psychology Review, 4*(1), 57–75.

Menesini, E., Nocentini, A., Palladino, B., Frisen, A., Berne, S., Ortega-Ruiz, R., . . . Smith, P. K. (2012). Cyberbullying definition among adolescents: A comparison across six European countries. *Cyberpsychology, Behavior, & Social Networking, 15*(9), 455–42.

Mesch, G. S. (2009). Parental mediation, online activities, and cyberbullying. *Cyberpsychology & Behavior, 12*(4), 387–393.

Michaud, P. (2009). Bullying: We need to increase our efforts and broaden our focus. *Journal of Adolescent Health, 45*(5), 323–325.

Migliore, E. (2003). Eliminate bullying in your classroom. *Intervention in School & Clinic, 38*(3), 172–177.

Modecki, K. L., Barber, B. L., & Vernon, L. (2013). Mapping developmental precursors of cyber-aggression: Trajectories of risk predict perpetration and victimization. *Journal of Youth and Adolescence, 42*(5), 651–661.

Moore, M. J., Nakano, T., Enomoto, A., & Suda, T. (2012). Anonymity and roles associated with aggressive posts in an online forum. *Computers in Human Behavior, 28*(3), 861–867.

Nocentini, A., Calmaestra, J., Schultze-Krumbholz, A., Scheithaeuer, H., Ortega, R., & Menesini, E. (2010). Cyberbullying: Labels, behaviours and definition in the European countries. *Australian Journal of Guidance and Counselling, 20*(2), 129–142.

Olweus, D. (1980). Familial and temperamental determinants of aggressive behavior in adolescent boys: A causal analysis. *Developmental Psychology, 16*(6), 644–660.

O'Moore, M., & Kirkham, C. (2001). Self-esteem and its relationship to bullying behaviour. *Aggressive Behavior, 27*(4), 269–283.

Osher, D., & Fleischman, S. (2005). Positive culture in urban schools. *Educational Leadership, 62*(5), 84–85.

O'Sullivan, P. B., & Flanagin, A. J. (2003). Reconceptualizing "flaming" and other problematic messages. *New Media & Society, 5*(1), 69–94.

Patchin, J. W., & Hinduja, S. (2006). Bullies move beyond the schoolyard: A preliminary look at cyberbullying. *Journal of Violence and Juvenile Justice, 4*(2), 148–169.

Paul, S., Smith, P. K., & Blumberg, H. H. (2012). Revisiting cyberbullying in schools using the quality circle approach. *School Psychology International, 33*(5), 492–504.

Perren, S., Gutzwiller-Helfenfinger, E., Malti, T., & Hymel, S. (2012). Moral reasoning and emotion attributions of adolescent bullies, victims, and bully-victims. *British Journal of Developmental Psychology, 30*(4), 511–530.

Pornari, C. D., & Wood, J. (2010). Peer and cyber aggression in secondary school students: The role of moral disengagement, hostile attribution bias, and outcome expectancies. *Aggressive Behavior, 36*(2), 81–94.

Postmes, T., Spears, R., & Lea, M. (1998). Breaching or building social boundaries? SIDE-Effects of computer-mediated communication. *Communication Research, 25*(6), 689–715.

Pujazon-Zazik, M., & Park, M. J. (2010). To tweet, or not to tweet: Gender differences and potential positive and negative health outcomes of adolescents' social Internet use. *American Journal of Men's Health, 4*(1), 77–85.

Raskauskas, J., & Stoltz, A. D. (2007). Involvement in traditional and electronic bullying among adolescents. *Developmental Psychology, 43*(3), 564–575.

Rigby, K., & Slee, P. T. (2008). Interventions to reduce bullying. *International Journal of Adolescent Medicine and Health, 20*(2), 165–183.

Runions, K., Shapka, J. D., Dooley, J., & Modecki, K. (2013). Cyber-aggression and victimization and social information processing: Integrating the medium and the message. *Psychology of Violence, 3*(1), 9–26.

Schenk, A. M., & Fremouw, W. J. (2012). Prevalence, psychological impact, and coping of cyberbully victims among college students. *Journal of School Violence, 11*(1), 21–37.

Schneider, S. K., O'Donnell, L., Stueve, A., & Coulter, R. W. S. (2012). Cyberbullying, school bullying, and psychological distress: A regional census of high school students. *American Journal of Public Health, 102*(1), 171–177.

Schnurr, M. P., Mahatmya, D., & Basche, R. A. (2013). The role of dominance, cyber aggression perpetration, and gender on emerging adults' perpetration of intimate partner violence. *Psychology of Violence, 3*(1), 70–83.

Schoffstall, C. L., & Cohen, R. (2011). Cyber aggression: The relation between online offenders and offline social competence. *Social Development, 20*(3), 587–604.

Sevcikova, A., & Smahel, D. (2009). Online harassment and cyberbullying in the Czech Republic: Comparison across age groups. *Journal of Psychology, 217*(4), 227–229.

Shariff, S., & Hoff, D. L. (2007). Cyber bullying: Clarifying legal boundaries for school supervision in cyberspace. *International Journal of Cyber Criminology, 1*(1), 76–118.

Sing, J. B., & Slovak, K. (2011). School social worker's experiences with youth suicidal behavior: An explanatory study. *Children & Schools, 33*(4), 215–228.

Slonje, R., & Smith, P. (2008). Cyberbullying: Another main type of bullying? *Scandinavian Journal of Psychology, 49*(2), 147–154.

Slonje, R., Smith, P. K., & Frisen, A. (2013). The nature of cyberbullying, and strategies for prevention. *Computers in Human Behavior, 29*(1), 26–32.

Smith, P. K., Ananiadou, K., & Cowie, H. (2003). Interventions to reduce school bullying. *Canadian Journal of Psychiatry, 48*(9), 591–599.

Smith, P. K., Mahdavi, J., Carvalho, M., Fisher, S., Russell, S., & Tippett, N. (2008). Cyberbullying: Its nature and impact in secondary school pupils. *Journal of Child Psychology and Psychiatry, 49*(4), 376–385.

Snider, M. (2004). How to cyber bully-proof your kids. Retrieved from http://www.macleans.ca/science/technology/article.jsp?content=20040524_81184_81184

Sontag, L. M., Clemans, K. H., Graber, J. A., & Lyndon, S. T. (2011). Traditional and cyber aggressors and victims: A comparison of psychosocial characteristics. *Journal of Youth and Adolescence, 40*(4), 392–404.

Spitzberg, B. H., & Hoobler, G. (2002). Cyberstalking and the technologies of interpersonal terrorism. *New Media & Society, 4*(1), 71–92.

Stauffer, S., Heath, M. A., Coyne, S. M., & Ferrin, S. (2012). High school teachers' perceptions of cyberbullying prevention and intervention strategies. *Psychology in the Schools, 49*(4), 352–367.

Stevens, V., Bourdeaudhuij, I. D., & Oost, P. V. (2001). Anti-bullying interventions at school: Aspects of programme adaptation and critical issues for further programme development. *Health Promotion International, 16*(2), 155–167.

Sticca, F., Ruggieri, S., Alsaker, F., & Perren, S. (2013). Longitudinal risk factors for cyberbullying in adolescence. *Journal of Community & Applied Social Psychology, 23*(1), 52–67.

Subrahmanyam, K., & Smahel, D. (2011). *Digital youth: The role of media in development.* New York, NY: Springer.

Sukhodolsky, D. G., Golub, A., Stone, E. C., & Orban, L. (2005). Social problem-solving versus social skills training components. *Behavior Therapy, 36*(1), 15–23.

Teich, A., Frankel, M., Kling, R., & Lee, Y. (1999). Anonymous communication policies for the Internet: Results and recommendations of the

AAAS conference. *The Information Society: An International Journal, 15*(2), 71–77.

Thompson, F., & Smith, P. K. (2011). The use and effectiveness of anti-bullying strategies in schools. Retrieved from https://www.gov.uk/government/uploads/system/uploads/attachment_data/file/197436/DFE-RB098.pdf

Tokunaga, R. S. (2010). Following you home from school: A critical review and synthesis of research on cyberbullying victimization. *Computers in Human Behavior, 26*(3), 277–287.

Ttofi, M. M., & Farrington, D. P. (2011). Effectiveness of school-based programs to reduce bullying: A systematic and meta-analytic review. *Journal of Experimental Criminology, 7*(1), 27–56.

Varjas, K., Henrich, C. C., & Meyers, J. (2009). Urban middle school student's perceptions of bullying, cyberbullying, and school safety. *Journal of School Violence, 8*(2), 159–176.

Vreeman, R. C., & Carroll, A. E. (2007). A systematic review of school-based interventions to prevent bullying. *Archives of Pediatrics and Adolescent Medicine, 161*(1), 78–88.

Wang., J., Iannotti, R., & Nansel, T. (2009). School bullying among adolescents in the United States: Physical, verbal, relational, and cyber. *Journal of Adolescent Health, 45*(4), 368–375.

Willard, N. (2007). Cyberbullying and cyberthreats: Responding to the challenge of online social aggression, threats, and distress. Retrieved from http://www.ctap4.org/cybersafety/Documentaton.htm

Williams, A. L., & Merten, M. J. (2011). iFamily: Internet and social media technology in the family context. *Family and Consumer Sciences Research Journal, 40*(2), 150–170.

Williams, K. R., & Guerra, N. G. (2007). Prevalence and predictors of Internet bullying. *Journal of Adolescent Health, 41*(6), S14–S21.

Williford, A., Elledge, L. C., Boulton, A. J., Depaolis, K. J., Little, T. D., & Salmivalli, C. (2013). Effects of the KiVA antibullying program on cyberbullying and cybervictimization frequency among Finnish youth. *Journal of Clinical Child & Adolescent Psychology, 42*, 820–833.

Wingate, V. S., Minney, J. A., & Guadagno, R. E. (2013). Sticks and stones may break your bones, but words will always hurt you: A review of cyberbullying. *Social Influence, 8*(2–3), 87–106.

Wright, M. F. (in press). Longitudinal investigation of the associations between adolescents' popularity and cyber social behaviors. *Journal of School Violence.*

Wright, M. F. (2013). The relationship between young adults' beliefs about anonymity and subsequent cyber aggression. *Cyberpsychology, Behavior, & Social Networking, 16*, 858–862.

Wright, M. F., & Li, Y. (2013). The association between cyber victimization and subsequent cyber aggression: The moderating effect of peer rejection. *Journal of Youth and Adolescence, 42*(5), 662–674.

Ybarra, M. L., Boyd, D., Korchmaros, J. D., & Oppenheim, J. (2012). Defining and measuring cyberbullying within the larger context of bullying victimization. *Journal of Adolescent Health, 51*(1), 53–58.

Ybarra, M. L., Diener-West, M., & Leaf, P. J. (2007). Examining the overlap in Internet harassment and school bullying: Implications for school intervention. *Journal of Adolescent Health, 41*(6), S42–S50.

Ybarra, M. L., & Mitchell, K. J. (2004). Online aggressor/targets, aggressors, and targets: A comparison of associated youth characteristics. *Journal of Child Psychology and Psychiatry, 45*(7), 1308–1316.

Ybarra, M. L., Mitchell, K. J., Wolak, J., & Finkelhor, D. (2006). Examining characteristics and associated distress related to Internet harassment findings from the Second Youth Internet Safety Survey. *Pediatrics, 118*(4), 1169–1177.

102 Empirically Supported Treatments for Borderline Personality Disorder

Jonathan B. Singer

Borderline personality disorder (BPD) is one of 10 personality disorders in the *Diagnostic and Statistical Manual of Mental Disorders, Fifth Edition (DSM-5)* (American Psychiatric Association [APA], 2013). Personality disorders are characterized by inflexible and maladaptive personality traits that cause significant functional impairment or subjective distress in social, occupational, or other areas of functioning (APA, 2013). BPD is one of three personality disorders (along with histrionic and narcissistic personality disorders) that are characterized by dramatic, emotional, or erratic individuals. The essential feature of BPD is "a pervasive pattern of instability of interpersonal relationships, self-image, and affects, and marked impulsivity that begins by early adulthood and is present in a variety of contexts." (APA, 2013, p. 664) Prevalence rates for BPD are 1% to 2.5% in the general population, 20% in outpatient settings, and up to 50% in inpatient settings (Soloff & Chiappetta, 2012). Women account for 75% of those diagnosed with BPD (APA, 2013). BPD most commonly co-occurs with other personality disorders, depression, bipolar disorder, substance use disorders, and posttraumatic stress disorder (PTSD) (Miklowitz, 2012). BPD is a severely disabling condition. Nearly 80% of people diagnosed with BPD report suicidal thoughts and behaviors, and BPD has a higher suicide rate than any disorder other than schizophrenia (Soloff & Chiappetta, 2012). The challenges posed by BPD, and the professional lore that has grown up around the disorder, has resulted in it being perceived by professionals and the public alike as the most difficult and problematic of all disorders to

assess and treat (Howe, 2013). Recent research, however, has suggested that BPD is neither as intractable, nor as impossible to treat, as was once believed. Retrospective studies have suggested that after 10 years, 50% of people with BPD will no longer meet criteria, and by 27 years only 8% will meet criteria for the disorder (Paris & Zweig-Frank, 2001; Zanarini, Frankenburg, Reich, & Fitzmaurice, 2010). For those who cannot wait 27 years, there are a number of psychotherapy interventions that have been shown to be effective in reducing, and in some cases eliminating, symptoms associated with BPD (Stoffers et al., 2012). This chapter presents an overview of empirically supported and promising approaches to the assessment and treatment of BPD.

ASSESSMENT OF BORDERLINE PERSONALITY DISORDER

Assessment of BDP is notoriously difficult (Biskin & Paris, 2012). There is no standard assessment protocol for BPD, no established genetic markers, no laboratory or imaging tests, and no self-report measures that will provide an accurate diagnosis (Biskin & Paris, 2012; Calati, Gressier, Balestri, & Serretti, 2013; Carpenter, Tomko, Trull, & Boomsma, 2013). There is significant symptom overlap between BDP and other personality disorders (PD), and similar clinical presentation with bipolar disorder and PTSD (Biskin & Paris, 2012). Diagnosing adolescents with BPD is controversial, in part because of the stigma associated with the diagnosis, beliefs that some of the symptoms (such as difficulties in interpersonal relationships) are normative during adolescence, and because until recently guidelines have discouraged diagnosis (Laurenssen, Hutsebaut, Feenstra, Van Busschbach, & Luyten, 2013). These diagnostic challenges, along with a widely held belief that personality disorders should be conceptualized as occurring along a continuum rather than as a binary category, led to a proposed change in the conceptualization of all personality disorders for *DSM-5* (Morey & Skodol, 2013). For various political and empirical reasons, however, the proposed changes were not adopted in *DSM-5*, but can be found in Section III (Emerging Measures and Models) (APA, 2013). Consequently, the clinical interview remains the most reliable method for diagnosing BPD.

The clinical interview should identify at least five of nine specific criteria in order to diagnose BPD (APA, 2013). Symptoms are generally clustered in four domains: interpersonal functioning, cognitive, affectivity, and impulse control (Biskin & Paris, 2012). Because problems associated with BPD are inherently social, assessment should establish how *interpersonal instability* manifests in interpersonal behaviors and affects relationship quality. For example, people with BPD tend to misinterpret neutral situations, experience rejection in inclusive situations, and have difficulties repairing cooperation after experiencing disappointment (Lis & Bohus, 2013). Assessments should also establish which types of symptoms result in the most significant impairment or distress: *cognitive symptomatology, affect dysregulation*, or lack of *impulse control*. Possible assessment questions could include "How do you deal with conflict? Who can you rely on for support? Tell me about a long-term friend whom you feel is 'in your corner.' Do you often feel empty inside? What do you do when someone makes you mad? Describe to me your ideal relationship."

TREATMENT OF CLIENTS WITH BORDERLINE PERSONALITY DISORDER

Until the 1990s, few if any treatments demonstrated effectiveness in reducing core symptoms of BPD. Since then, a number of treatments have demonstrated success in addressing specific features of BPD. According to a recent systematic review (Stoffers et al., 2012) the most commonly used empirically supported treatments are dialectical behavior therapy (DBT), mentalization-based treatment (MBT), transference-focused therapy (TFP), schema-focused therapy (SFT), and the systems training for emotional predictability and problem solving (STEPPS). These treatments have demonstrated better outcomes than treatment-as-usual (TAU) in randomized controlled trials (RCTs). Two treatments have demonstrated efficacy over other empirically supported treatments: DBT performed better than Client-Centered Treatment at reducing core BDP symptoms and associated psychopathology (Turner, 2000), and SFT performed better than TFP at reducing BPD symptom severity and retention (Giesen-Bloo et al., 2006). The following is a brief review of empirically supported and promising treatments for BPD.

Dialectical Behavior Therapy

Marsha Linehan and colleagues originally developed DBT as a treatment for women who engage in self-harming behaviors, but they found that a significant number of their clients met criteria for BPD (Linehan, 1993a). DBT is the treatment for BPD with the most empirical support (Stoffers et al., 2012). In the past 20 years, DBT has demonstrated efficacy in reducing or eliminating core BPD symptoms in self-harming adult women with BPD; adolescents with BPD, comorbid substance use disorders and BPD, and PTSD and BPD; binge eaters; depressed elderly patients; and even families of people with BPD (Bloom, Woodward, Susmaras, & Pantalone, 2012; Harned, Korslund, Foa, & Linehan, 2012; Hoffman, Fruzzetti, & Buteau, 2007; Stoffers et al., 2012). In response to criticism that existing research on DBT simply reflects the benefits of having small caseloads, targeted supervision, and a controlled environment, Linehan and colleagues tested DBT against six expert treatments in a community setting (Linehan et al., 2006); DBT proved more effective than expert community care in reducing the frequency and severity of suicide attempts, outpatient crisis services, inpatient hospitalization, and client retention.

DBT is a combination of Cognitive Behavior Therapy (CBT) and Zen mindfulness training (Linehan, 1993b). Unique features of DBT include (1) interventions based on mindfulness and acceptance (e.g., finding a balance between emotion and rationality, known as "wise mind"); (2) emphasis on the dialectic (i.e., reality is comprised of ever-changing opposing forces); (3) focus on emotions and the bio-psychosocial model (i.e., BPD is understood to be a dysfunction of the emotional regulation system, which is part of a bio-psychosocial system); and (4) addressing five specific processes of therapy (Chapman, 2006). The five processes and their corresponding treatment modalities are (1) motivating the client to change and rehearsing cognitive and behavioral skills that help clients regulate their emotions in 1-hour weekly individual therapy; (2) enhancing behavioral skills: mindfulness, interpersonal skills, regulation of emotions, and distress tolerance in 2-hour weekly skills training groups; (3) ensuring the generalization of these skills to activities of daily living using as-needed phone consultations with outpatient treatment or milieu therapy for inpatient programs; (4) enhancing therapist capabilities and motivations in 1-hour weekly DBT consultation team meeting; and (5) structuring the treatment environment to support client and therapist capabilities (Linehan, 1993b). DBT is a highly structured treatment. As with all manualized treatments, the empirical support for DBT relies on clinicians delivering DBT with fidelity (i.e., according to the manual). However, one study found that in a typical outpatient setting, incorporating the DBT skills training group with non-DBT individual therapy was effective in reducing BPD symptomatology (Harley, Baity, Blais, & Jacobo, 2007).

Mentalization-based Treatment

Peter Fonagy and Anthony Bateman developed MBT as a day hospitalization treatment for people diagnosed with BPD (Fonagy & Bateman, 2008). Five studies have demonstrated that adult patients who receive MBT, and adolescent patients who received MBT-A, demonstrated significant and enduring changes in mood states and interpersonal functioning, such as significant reduction in suicidal behavior, diagnostic status, service use, use of medication, and increase in global functioning (Bales et al., 2012; Bateman & Fonagy, 2013; Jørgensen et al., 2013; Rossouw & Fonagy, 2012; Stoffers et al., 2012). These improvements remained clinically and statistically significant at 8-year follow-up (Bateman & Fonagy, 2008). As with other BPD treatments, MBT has failed to improve general social functioning (Bateman & Fonagy, 2008).

MBT is a psychodynamic developmental model for understanding BPD in which "mentalizing" is the key to treatment. According to Fonagy and Bateman (2008), "Mentalization is the capacity to make sense of each other and ourselves, implicitly and explicitly, in terms of subjective states and mental processes." (p. 5) The model assumes that people with BPD cannot understand the thoughts and feelings associated with the behaviors of self and others because (1) their own infant mental states were not understood by their caregivers (i.e., early disrupted attachment) and (2) experiences of trauma resulted in neurobiological changes that impeded the development of emotional regulation skills. MBT targets three higher order social cognitive functions that are important in attachment contexts: affect representation and regulation, attentional control, and mentalization. The challenge for the clinician is to help the client develop emotional regulation without stimulating the attachment system. One way MBT achieves this is by eschewing the role of insight and minimizing affective exploration in therapy. The developers contend that therapists can do harm to clients who have poor conceptions of self and others and who have significant difficulty regulating emotion by insisting on using traditional insight-oriented, psychodynamic treatment and emotion-focused techniques.

Cognitive Behavior Therapy

Two CBT treatments have been investigated in the treatment of BPD (Davidson et al., 2006; Morey, Lowmaster, & Hopwood, 2010; Weinberg, Gunderson, Hennen, & Cutter, 2006). The first clinical trial compared TAU with TAU plus CBT in a typical outpatient community mental health setting (Davidson et al., 2006). The CBT condition sought to change patient's beliefs and behaviors that impair social and adaptive functioning, in order to reduce suicidal thoughts and behaviors. Results suggested that participants in both conditions showed reductions in suicidal ideation and hospitalization. The TAU + CBT group also showed reductions in dysfunctional beliefs, state anxiety, and distress caused by psychiatric symptoms (Davidson et al., 2006).

Manual-assisted Cognitive Treatment (MACT) incorporates elements of DBT, cognitive therapy, and bibliotherapy in a six-session treatment (Weinberg et al., 2006). Each session centers on chapters from a workbook that covers specific topics such as emotion regulation, problem solving, negative thinking, suicidal thoughts and behaviors, and substance use and relapse prevention (Schmidt & Davidson, 2004). MACT has been evaluated in two studies (Morey et al., 2010; Weinberg et al., 2006). Although there is some evidence that MACT can be effective in reducing suicidal ideation and attempt, and holds promise in reducing affective instability and BPD symptoms, more research needs to be done.

Schema-focused Therapy and Transference-focused Psychotherapy

A recent study compared a cognitive-based treatment (schema-focused therapy; SFT) and a psychodynamic treatment (transference-focused psychotherapy; TFP) in a three-year randomized trial of 82 men and women with BPD (Giesen-Bloo et al., 2006). SFT combines psychodynamic and behavioral theories to help people identify self-defeating core schemas and maladaptive coping styles in adulthood. TFP uses processing of transference material to transform primitive object relations to advanced ones by modifying defenses and resolving identity diffusion (Stoffers et al., 2012). Giesen-Bloo and colleagues (2006) noted that whereas treatments such as DBT, CBT, and MBT target specific symptoms, such as self-harm behavior or interpersonal functioning, both SFT and TFP were developed to restructure clients' personalities. Results of the study indicated that participants from both treatments improved significantly on all *DSM-IV* BPD criteria, all effects were apparent after the first year, and there was significant improvement in the quality of life for the majority of participants. SFT reported greater effectiveness in reducing core BPD symptoms and keeping patients in treatment (Giesen-Bloo et al., 2006). A recent meta-analysis of SFT for BPD suggested that it holds promise, but more research needs to be done (Sempértegui, Karreman, Arntz, & Bekker, 2013).

Systems Training for Emotional Predictability and Problem Solving

Systems Training for Emotional Predictability and Problem Solving (STEPPS) is a group treatment based on Minuchin's structural family therapy model. Three RCTs have found that as an adjunctive treatment to usual care, STEPPS is effective at reducing impulsivity, negative affectivity, and depressive symptoms, and at improving mood and global functioning (Black, Blum, McCormick, & Allen, 2013; Blum et al., 2008; Bos, van Wel, Appelo, & Verbraak, 2011). STEPPS has not been found to reduce suicidal thoughts and behaviors or hospitalizations, except in a study of prisoners (Black et al., 2013). An adaptation of STEPPS, Emotion Regulation Therapy for Adolescents (ERT-A), has been found to be effective in reducing severity of BPD symptoms, general psychopathology, and improving quality of life (Schuppert et al., 2012).

Promising Treatments

Promising treatments include those with a single study, no control group, or equivocal evidence. These interventions hold promise for addressing specific symptoms, populations, or for specific treatment settings (listed in alphabetical order):

- *EMDR.* Brown and Shapiro (2006) presented a case study of treating BPD using eye movement desensitization and reprocessing (EMDR), a recognized trauma therapy. This individual treatment holds promise in addressing trauma issues for people with BPD using a treatment that has some empirical support in other populations.
- *Intermittent-continuous eclectic therapy (ICE).* ICE is a group approach developed in Chile. Menchaca, Pérez, and Peralta (2007) described a one-year pilot study of men and women ages 15 to 40 years in an outpatient setting. The authors reported improvement in self-aggression and general symptoms.
- *Interpersonal psychotherapy (IPT-BDP).* IPT is an empirically supported individual treatment for people with moderate-to-severe depression that focuses on the bidirectional influence of interpersonal problems and depressive symptoms. IPT-BDP targets the interpersonal instability and depressed affect commonly encountered in people with BDP. Results of an RCT suggested efficacy in reducing core BPD symptoms and depression (Bellino, Rinaldi, & Bogetto, 2010).
- *Pharmacotherapy.* Despite recent advances in addressing core symptoms of mood, anxiety, and childhood disorders, pharmacotherapy is not recommended in the treatment of BPD. Treatment guidelines recommend the use of medications to address temporary psychosis and other discrete symptoms (Oldham, 2004), but the evidence to support the use of

medications alone, or in combination with psychotherapy is equivocal (Belli, Ural, & Akbudak, 2012).

- *Supportive therapy.* Supportive therapy is a nondirective, humanistic treatment that relies on the therapist demonstrating unconditional positive regard, empathy, and genuineness, and assumes these are necessary and sufficient conditions for client change. Supportive therapy has been evaluated as a standalone treatment (Aviram, Hellerstein, Gerson, & Stanley, 2004) and as the "control" condition in clinical trials of BPD (Jørgensen et al., 2013). In both settings, supportive therapy has been found to be efficacious in engaging people with BPD, minimizing the frequency and intensity of self-harming behavior, and reducing core BPD symptomatology.

IMPLICATIONS FOR THE FUTURE

There is cause for hope among clinicians and clients that effective treatment of BPD is possible. Recent empirical findings have challenged the long-held belief that BPD is treatment-resistant and follows a chronic disease model (Zanarini et al., 2010). The growing evidence-base suggests that most manualized treatments address core BPD symptoms more effectively than TAU, and some manualized treatments are better than others (e.g., MBT and SFT are superior to SCM and TFP, respectively) (Budge et al., 2013). Clinicians with cognitive behavioral, psychodynamic, or humanistic practice perspectives can find empirically supported treatments that are consistent with their orientations.

Despite the advances in the evidence-base and the breadth of treatment for BPD, there are notable gaps in our understanding of BPD assessment and intervention. First, there continue to be unanswered questions regarding the fundamental nature of PDs, diagnostic criteria and thresholds, the value of categorical versus dimensional diagnosis, and the most valid and reliable method of assessing BPD (Morey & Skodol, 2013). It was widely assumed that the proposed changes to PDs in *DSM-5* would address some of these concerns. This proposal would have reconceptualized PDs as having both dimensional and categorical features, reduced the number of disorders, and changed the organization of core symptoms. Because this proposal was not adopted, these

questions remain. The good news for clinicians is that everything they knew about PDs remains the same, except that they can no longer refer to their PD clients as "Axis II" due to the elimination of the multiaxial coding system (APA, 2013).

Second, although empirically supported treatments (ESTs) have demonstrated efficacy reducing core BPD symptoms, reducing suicide risk, reducing hospitalization and treatment dropout, they have been ineffective in improving psychosocial functioning. Consequently clients can no longer meet criteria for BPD and continue to have significant functional impairment. The next generation of interventions should target clients' social and vocational functioning in addition to addressing BPD symptomatology (Soloff & Chiappetta, 2012).

Third, ESTs with the strongest support (e.g., DBT and MBT) are highly specified manualized treatments that require extensive provider training, and require frequent client contact over 1–3 years, all of which place a significant burden on clients, providers, and the health service system. The next generation of interventions should identify how and when the least intensive of two treatments (e.g., structured case management vs. intensive individual therapy in a partial hospital setting), might be as effective in addressing BPD (Bateman & Fonagy, 2013; Davidson & Tran, 2013).

A final and related issue is that, as with most mental health problems, clinical intervention research for BPD has focused on answering the question, "are there effective treatments and if so, which treatments are most effective?" rather than "which treatments work best for whom?" (Goldman & Gregory, 2010). For instance, there is compelling evidence that DBT is effective in addressing self-harm behavior and other core BPD symptomatology in adults and adolescents with BDP only, as well as with co-occurring substance use or PTSD (Stoffers et al., 2012). But no treatment, no matter how effective, is effective for every client (Rizvi, 2011). In response, some have recommended an integrative or modular approach to treatment, which would match symptom presentation to specific techniques, client expectations with treatment approach, and the "best of" specific ESTs (Koerner, 2013; Livesley, 2012). To that end, Livesley (2012) proposed a two-component integrated model for treating BPD, "1. a system for conceptualizing borderline personality disorder based on current empirical knowledge about the structure, etiology, and stability of borderline pathology that serves as a guide when selecting and delivering interventions; and 2. a model of therapeutic change based on the general literature on psychotherapy outcome and specific studies of PD treatments." (Livesley, 2012, p. 47) Although leaders in the field have voiced support for integrated approaches (Paris, 2013), and similar efforts have demonstrated efficacy in the treatment of other mental health problems (Weisz et al., 2012), empirical support is needed before integrated or modular approaches can be considered "best practices."

WEBSITES

Behavioral Tech, Dialectical Behavior Therapy. http://www.behavioraltech.com.

National Education Alliance for Borderline Personality Disorder. http://www.borderlinepersonalitydisorder.com

National Institute for Mental Health, Borderline Personality Disorder. http://www.nimh.nih.gov/health/publications/borderline-personality-disorder.shtml.

Singer, J. B. (Producer). (2007, October 15). Dialectical Behavior Therapy: Interview with Sabrina Heller, LSW. [Episode 26]. *Social Work Podcast* [Audio podcast]. Retrieved from http://socialworkpodcast.com/2007/10/dialectical-behavior-therapy-interview.html

References

American Psychiatric Association. (2013). *Diagnostic and statistical manual of mental disorders, fifth edition*. Washington, DC: Author.

Aviram, R. B., Hellerstein, D. J., Gerson, J., & Stanley, B. (2004). Adapting supportive psychotherapy for individuals with borderline personality disorder who self-injure or attempt suicide. *Journal of Psychiatric Practice, 10*(3), 145–155.

Bales, D., van Beek, N., Smits, M., Willemsen, S., Busschbach, J. J. V., Verheul, R., & Andrea, H. (2012). Treatment outcome of 18-month, day hospital mentalization-based treatment (MBT) in patients with severe borderline personality disorder in the Netherlands. *Journal of Personality Disorders, 26*(4), 568–582. doi:10.1521/pedi.2012.26.4.568

Bateman, A. W., & Fonagy, P. (2008). 8-year follow-up of patients treated for borderline personality disorder: mentalization-based treatment versus treatment as usual. *The American Journal of Psychiatry, 165*(5), 631–638. doi:10.1176/appi.ajp.2007.07040636

Bateman, A. W., & Fonagy, P. (2013). Impact of clinical severity on outcomes of mentalisation-based treatment for borderline personality disorder. *The British Journal of Psychiatry, 204*. doi:10.1192/bjp.bp.112.121129

Belli, H., Ural, C., & Akbudak, M. (2012). Borderline personality disorder: bipolarity, mood stabilizers and atypical antipsychotics in treatment. *Journal of Clinical Medicine Research, 4*(5), 301–308. doi:10.4021/jocmr1042w

Bellino, S., Rinaldi, C., & Bogetto, F. (2010). Adaptation of interpersonal psychotherapy to borderline personality disorder: A comparison of combined therapy and single pharmacotherapy. *Canadian Journal of Psychiatry. Revue Canadienne de Psychiatrie, 55*(2), 74–81.

Biskin, R. S., & Paris, J. (2012). Diagnosing borderline personality disorder. *Canadian Medical Association Journal, 184*(16), 1789–1794. doi:10.1503/cmaj.090618

Black, D. W., Blum, N., McCormick, B., & Allen, J. (2013). Systems Training for Emotional Predictability and Problem Solving (STEPPS) group treatment for offenders with borderline personality disorder. *The Journal of Nervous and Mental Disease, 201*(2), 124–129. doi:10.1097/NMD.0b013e31827f6435

Bloom, J. M., Woodward, E. N., Susmaras, T., & Pantalone, D. W. (2012). Use of dialectical behavior therapy in inpatient treatment of borderline personality disorder: A systematic review. *Psychiatric Services, 63*(9), 881–888. doi:10.1176/appi.ps.201100311

Blum, N., St. John, D., Pfohl, B., Stuart, S., McCormick, B., Allen, J., . . . Black, D. W. (2008). Systems Training for Emotional Predictability and Problem Solving (STEPPS) for outpatients with borderline personality disorder: A randomized controlled trial and 1-year follow-up. *The American Journal of Psychiatry, 165*(4), 468–478. doi:10.1176/appi.ajp.2007.07071079

Bos, E. H., van Wel, E. B., Appelo, M. T., & Verbraak, M. J. P. M. (2011). Effectiveness of Systems Training for Emotional Predictability and Problem Solving (STEPPS) for borderline personality problems in a "real-world" sample: Moderation by diagnosis or severity? *Psychotherapy and Psychosomatics, 80*(3), 173–181. doi:10.1159/000321793

Brown, S., & Shapiro, F. (2006). EMDR in the treatment of Borderline Personality Disorder. *Clinical Case Studies, 5*(5), 403–420. doi:10.1177/1534650104271773

Budge, S. L., Moore, J. T., Del Re, A. C., Wampold, B. E., Baardseth, T. P., & Nienhaus, J. B. (2013). The effectiveness of evidence-based treatments for personality disorders when comparing treatment-as-usual and bona fide treatments. *Clinical Psychology Review*. doi:10.1016/j.cpr.2013.08.003

Calati, R., Gressier, F., Balestri, M., & Serretti, A. (2013). Genetic modulation of borderline personality disorder: Systematic review and meta-analysis. *Journal of Psychiatric Research, 47*, 1275–1287. doi:10.1016/j.jpsychires.2013.06.002

Carpenter, R. W., Tomko, R. L., Trull, T. J., & Boomsma, D. I. (2013). Gene-environment studies and borderline personality disorder: A review. *Current Psychiatry Reports, 15*(1), 336. doi:10.1007/s11920-012-0336-1

Chapman, A. L. (2006). Dialectical behavior therapy: Current indications and unique elements. *Psychiatry, 3*(9), 62–68.

Davidson, K. M., Norrie, J., Tyrer, P., Gumley, A., Tata, P., Murray, H., & Palmer, S. (2006). The effectiveness of cognitive behavior therapy for borderline personality disorder: Results from the borderline personality disorder study of cognitive therapy (BOSCOT) trial. *Journal of Personality Disorders, 20*(5), 450–465. doi:10.1521/pedi.2006.20.5.450

Davidson, K. M., & Tran, C. F. (2013). Impact of treatment intensity on suicidal behavior and depression in borderline personality disorder: A critical review. *Journal of Personality Disorders, 28*, 181–197. doi:10.1521/pedi_2013_27_113

Fonagy, P., & Bateman, A. W. (2008). The development of borderline personality disorder—A mentalizing model. *Journal of Personality Disorders, 22*(1), 4–21. doi:10.1521/pedi.2008.22.1.4

Giesen-Bloo, J., van Dyck, R., Spinhoven, P., van Tilburg, W., Dirksen, C., van Asselt, T.,...Arntz, A. (2006). Outpatient psychotherapy for borderline personality disorder: Randomized trial of schema-focused therapy vs. transference-focused psychotherapy. *Archives of General Psychiatry, 63*(6), 649–658. doi:10.1001/archpsyc.63.6.649

Goldman, G. A., & Gregory, R. J. (2010). Relationships between techniques and outcomes for borderline personality disorder. *American Journal of Psychotherapy, 64*(4), 359–371.

Harley, R. M., Baity, M. R., Blais, M. A., & Jacobo, M. C. (2007). Use of dialectical behavior therapy skills training for borderline personality disorder in a naturalistic setting. *Psychotherapy Research, 17*(3), 351–358. doi:10.1080/10503300600830710

Harned, M. S., Korslund, K. E., Foa, E. B., & Linehan, M. M. (2012). Treating PTSD in suicidal and self-injuring women with borderline personality disorder: Development and preliminary evaluation of a Dialectical Behavior Therapy Prolonged Exposure Protocol. *Behaviour Research and Therapy, 50*(6), 381–386. doi:10.1016/j.brat.2012.02.011

Hoffman, P. D., Fruzzetti, A. E., & Buteau, E. (2007). Understanding and engaging families: An education, skills and support program for relatives impacted by borderline personality disorder. *Journal of Mental Health, 16*(1), 69–82. doi:10.1080/09638230601182052

Howe, E. (2013). Five ethical and clinical challenges psychiatrists may face when treating patients with borderline personality disorder who are or may become suicidal. *Innovations in Clinical Neuroscience, 10*(1), 14–19.

Jørgensen, C. R., Freund, C., Bøye, R., Jordet, H., Andersen, D., & Kjølbye, M. (2013). Outcome of mentalization-based and supportive psychotherapy in patients with borderline personality disorder: A randomized trial. *Acta Psychiatrica Scandinavica, 127*(4), 305–317. doi:10.1111/j.1600-0447.2012.01923.x

Koerner, K. (2013). What must you know and do to get good outcomes with DBT? *Behavior Therapy, 44*. doi:10.1016/j.beth.2013.03.005

Laurenssen, E. M. P., Hutsebaut, J., Feenstra, D. J., Van Busschbach, J. J., & Luyten, P. (2013). Diagnosis of personality disorders in adolescents: A study among psychologists. *Child and Adolescent Psychiatry and Mental Health, 7*(1), 3. doi:10.1186/1753-2000-7-3

Linehan, M. M. (1993a). *Cognitive-behavioral treatment of borderline personality disorder.* New York, NY: Guilford Press.

Linehan, M. M. (1993b). *Skills training manual for treating borderline personality disorder.* New York, NY: Guilford Press.

Linehan, M. M., Comtois, K. A., Murray, A. M., Brown, M. Z., Gallop, R. J., Heard, H. L.,...Lindenboim, N. (2006). Two-year randomized controlled trial and follow-up of dialectical behavior therapy vs. therapy by experts for suicidal behaviors and borderline personality disorder. *Archives of General Psychiatry, 63*(7), 757–766. doi:10.1001/archpsyc.63.7.757

Lis, S., & Bohus, M. (2013). Social interaction in borderline personality disorder. *Current Psychiatry Reports, 15*(2), 338. doi:10.1007/s11920-012-0338-z

Livesley, W. J. (2012). Moving beyond specialized therapies for borderline personality disorder: The importance of integrated domain-focused treatment. *Psychodynamic Psychiatry, 40*(1), 47–74. doi:10.1521/pdps.2012.40.1.47

Menchaca, A., Pérez, O., & Peralta, A. (2007). Intermittent-continuous eclectic therapy: A group approach for borderline personality disorder. *Journal of Psychiatric Practice, 13*(4), 281–284. doi:10.1097/01.pra.0000281492.72935.00

Miklowitz, D. J. (2012). Borderline behavior in adolescence: An adjective in search of a treatment. *Journal of the American Academy of Child & Adolescent Psychiatry, 51*(12), 1238–1240. doi:10.1016/j.jaac.2012.09.013

Morey, L. C., Lowmaster, S. E., & Hopwood, C. J. (2010). A pilot study of manual-assisted cognitive therapy with a therapeutic assessment augmentation for borderline personality disorder. *Psychiatry Research, 178*(3), 531–535. doi:10.1016/j.psychres.2010.04.055

Morey, L. C., & Skodol, A. E. (2013). Convergence between DSM-IV-TR and DSM-5 diagnostic models for personality disorder: Evaluation of strategies for establishing diagnostic thresholds. *Journal of Psychiatric Practice, 19*(3), 179–193. doi:10.1097/01.pra.0000430502.78833.06

Oldham, J. M. (2004). Borderline personality disorder: The treatment dilemma. *Journal of Psychiatric Practice, 10*(3), 204–206. doi:10.1097/00131746-200405000-00013

Paris, J. (2013). Expanding the scope of treatment for borderline personality disorder. *The Journal of Nervous and Mental Disease, 201*(2), 143–144. doi:10.1097/NMD.0b013e31827f64c8

Paris, J., & Zweig-Frank, H. (2001). A 27-year follow-up of patients with borderline personality disorder. *Comprehensive Psychiatry, 42*(6), 482–487. doi:10.1053/comp.2001.26271

Rizvi, S. L. (2011). Treatment failure in Dialectical Behavior Therapy. *Cognitive and Behavioral Practice, 18*(3), 403–412. doi:10.1016/j.cbpra.2010.05.003

Rossouw, T. I., & Fonagy, P. (2012). Mentalization-based treatment for self-harm in adolescents: A randomized controlled trial. *Journal of the American Academy of Child and Adolescent Psychiatry, 51*(12), 1304–1313.e3. doi:10.1016/j.jaac.2012.09.018

Schmidt, U., & Davidson, K. M. (2004). *Life after self-harm: A guide to the future.* Hove, East Sussex, England; New York, NY: Brunner-Routledge.

Schuppert, H. M., Timmerman, M. E., Bloo, J., van Gemert, T. G., Wiersema, H. M., Minderaa, R. B.,. . . Nauta, M. H. (2012). Emotion regulation training for adolescents with borderline personality disorder traits: A randomized controlled trial. *Journal of the American Academy of Child and Adolescent Psychiatry, 51*(12), 1314–1323.e2. doi:10.1016/j.jaac.2012.09.002

Sempértegui, G. A., Karreman, A., Arntz, A., & Bekker, M. H. J. (2013). Schema therapy for borderline personality disorder: A comprehensive review of its empirical foundations, effectiveness and implementation possibilities. *Clinical Psychology Review, 33*(3), 426–447. doi:10.1016/j.cpr.2012.11.006

Soloff, P. H., & Chiappetta, L. (2012). Prospective predictors of suicidal behavior in borderline personality disorder at 6-year follow-up. *The American Journal of Psychiatry, 169*(5), 484–490. doi:10.1176/appi.ajp.2011.11091378

Stoffers, J. M., Völlm, B. A., Rücker, G., Timmer, A., Huband, N., & Lieb, K. (2012). Psychological therapies for people with borderline personality disorder. *The Cochrane Database of Systematic Reviews, 8*, CD005652. doi:10.1002/14651858.CD005652.pub2

Turner, R. M. (2000). Naturalistic evaluation of dialectical behavior therapy-oriented treatment for borderline personality disorder. *Cognitive and Behavioral Practice, 7*(4), 413–419. doi:10.1016/S1077-7229(00)80052-8

Weinberg, I., Gunderson, J. G., Hennen, J., & Cutter, C. J., Jr. (2006). Manual assisted cognitive treatment for deliberate self-harm in borderline personality disorder patients. *Journal of Personality Disorders, 20*(5), 482–492. doi:10.1521/pedi.2006.20.5.482

Weisz, J. R., Chorpita, B. F., Palinkas, L. A., Schoenwald, S. K., Miranda, J., Bearman, S. K.,. . . Research Network on Youth Mental Health. (2012). Testing standard and modular designs for psychotherapy treating depression, anxiety, and conduct problems in youth: A randomized effectiveness trial. *Archives of General Psychiatry, 69*(3), 274–282. doi:10.1001/archgenpsychiatry.2011.147

Zanarini, M. C., Frankenburg, F. R., Reich, D. B., & Fitzmaurice, G. (2010). Time to attainment of recovery from borderline personality disorder and stability of recovery: A 10-year prospective follow-up study. *The American Journal of Psychiatry, 167*(6), 663–667. doi:10.1176/appi.ajp.2009.0908113

103 | The Interface of Psychiatric Medications and Social Work

Kia J. Bentley & Joseph Walsh

Psychiatric medications are regularly used to help treat clients at mental health agencies who present with a variety of mental, emotional, and behavioral symptoms and challenges. Social workers, representing the largest number of professionals in outpatient mental health settings, and who may have the most extensive face-to-face interactions with clients, are increasingly called upon to be a resource for clients with respect to issues related to medication use. However, social workers *across settings*, including those in private practice, schools, child welfare agencies, and jails and other forensic settings, as well as in hospitals, clinics, hospices, and other health care settings, also work closely with clients using these medications. This suggests that social workers who truly want to be responsive to the complex and comprehensive concerns of clients need to develop a competence and comfort in addressing their medication-related dilemmas. That is, social workers should learn how to both use what they already know, as well as develop new skills and strategies to partner with clients to help them. Such skills and strategies might include, for example, making informed decisions about psychiatric medication use, dealing with accompanying issues of meaning and identity, designing strategies to assist with adherence problems when relevant, building referral highways, and advocating for access to affordable medications. This chapter provides a brief context and overview of the five classes of medication, reviews two overarching goals with respect to the interface of psychiatric medications and social work, offers six specific role categories through which to meet those goals, and further identifies several complex issues that may emerge as important for social workers in the near future.

The introduction of chlorpromazine (Thorazine) in the 1950s is most often associated with stimulating the modern era in psychopharmacology. More recently, however, the explosion of brain research, and the renewed emphasis on etiological models of mental illness emphasizing genetics and neurotransmission, have been the defining influences on pharmacological research and development. In the past 20 years, medications have even been characterized by some as actually "fixing" chemical imbalances in the brain. Others have harshly criticized simplistic explanations such as that and pointed to what they see as serious flaws in the clinical research arena as we know it, not to mention highlighting the powerful sociopolitical forces that seem to bias the psychiatric enterprise. Indeed, while psychopharmacologists theorize a great deal about why psychiatric medications "work," precise causes of action are typically now fully known. And the influences of the medical model and profit motive are undeniable. Nevertheless, experiences of hundreds of thousands of people suggest that even in the face of bothersome (or worse) side effects, for many these medications can help improve functioning and contribute to a higher quality of life. Psychiatric medications, similar to other medical interventions, are generally thought to be about 70% effective for consumers. Listed below are the five classes of medications with some specific examples of each, although it must be emphasized that there is much overlap among categories when it comes to actual use.

1. **Antipsychotics**. Conventional or first generation medications include fluphenazine (Prolixin), haloperidol (Haldol), and thioridazine (Mellaril). Atypical or second generation medications include risperidone (Risperdal), Olanzapine (Zyprexa), aripiprazole (Abilify), and Ziprasidone (Geodon). Some authors are calling Aripiprazole a third generation antipsychotic, because it is thought to be sufficiently different in its action on the neurotransmitters serotonin and dopamine.

2. **Antidepressants**. Three different types of antidepressant medications include the monoamine oxidase inhibitors like phenelzine (Nardil) and tranylcypromine (Parnate); cyclic drugs such as amitriptyline (Elavil), nortriptyline (Pamelor), doxepin (Sinequan), and imipramine (Tofranil); the selective serotonin reuptake inhibitors (SSRIs) including fluoxetine (Prozac), citalopram (Celexa), paroxetine (Paxil), sertraline (Zoloft) and fluvoxamine (Luvox). Other antidepressants include bupropion (Wellbutrin), and duloxetine (Cymbalta).

3. **Mood Stabilizers**. Lithium has been the most widely prescribed medication for the treatment of bipolar disorder but anticonvulsant drugs including valproate (Depakote), lamotrigine (Lamictal), and others have emerged since the late 1970s as alternatives.

4. **Antianxiety Medications**. Benzodiazepines are the largest category of antianxiety drugs, including diazepam (Valium), alprazolam (Xanax), and triazolam (Halcion), but caution surrounds their use due to their abuse and dependence potential. Increasingly the SSRI medications are effectively used to treat anxiety. Buspirone (Buspar) represents another type of antianxiety drug.

5. **Stimulants**. The stimulants and other medications for attention difficulties include amphetamine (Adderall), atomoxetine (Strattera), pemoline (Cylert), and methylphenidate (Ritalin, Concerta).

TOWARD RESPONSIVENESS AND COLLABORATION

As we noted earlier, almost all social workers work at least occasionally with clients who use psychotropic medications as part of their intervention plans. In many service settings, social workers assess mental status and inquire about psychiatric medication use as a part of a client's bio-psychosocial assessment. However, social workers have recently begun to elaborate a more complete range of professional roles with regard to psychiatric medication. They are more frequently expected by clients and other providers to possess sound knowledge of medications and their consequences for clients' lives, not merely to complement the physician's role, but because they bring important insights, techniques, and a special appreciation of client self-determination. A social work perspective includes a person-in-environment perspective (seeing people within a larger context of systems and in cultural and historical context), a social justice perspective (awareness of sociopolitical dimensions of situations with a special sensitivity to inequities in the distribution of rights and privileges), and a strengths and empowerment perspective (putting client desires and goals at the center of practice and using client capacities to reach them). Contemporary practice requires the social worker to strive for two related goals with respect to psychiatric medication:

GOAL 1. Be an effective collaborator with clients, families, and other providers.

To do this well, social workers should subscribe to the following philosophical practice principles:

- Embrace a client-centered "partnership" perspective around the range of medication-related dilemmas and issues that emerge in practice. This suggests working toward a nonthreatening collaborative alliance, a demystification of the helping process, and a mutual sharing of respective expertise. Contemporary models of social work practice call for decreased distance with clients; an explicit, unconditional affirmation of their humanity; and nonjudgmental empathy about the dilemmas they present.
- Maintain a balanced perspective about psychiatric medication in the face of admittedly complex issues related to human rights and professional roles, and the "costs" and "benefits" of medication use. This means rejection of any "cheerleader" role or "naysayer" role.
- Work toward the successful integration of psychosocial interventions and psychopharmacology, and recognize the intrinsic power of combined treatments.

- Work toward interdisciplinary relationships characterized by equality, flexibility, decreased professional control, mutual understanding, and shared goals. Appreciate the challenges that emerge in managing parallel care and treatment.
- Appreciate both the strengths and the limits of clients and their families. Interventions should center on clients and families' unique strengths and aspirations and away from symptoms or weaknesses. This calls for a more radical reorientation to practice than most social workers seem to realize. Yet, admittedly, barriers to progress such as a lack of skills, inadequate resources, or other situational limits must also be appreciated. The trick is to reject blaming the client, or making automatic assumptions of diminished capacities or poor judgment, for example.

GOAL 2. Be a meaningful resource to clients, families, and other providers around medication-related issues and dilemmas.

Social workers can do this by engaging in a range of general activities:

- Focus first on assessing and clarifying medication-related issues, which can occur on psychological, social, strategic, practical, and informational levels.
- Be a valuable source of whatever information, support, or "supplies" are called for in reaching specific "wants" and goals of clients with respect to their medication. These "supplies" range from providing emotional support, information and guidance, help with problem-solving and decision-making, or connection to concrete resources, to name a few.
- Be creative in applying clinical skills and techniques drawn from evidence-based practice theories and models to medication-related issues, and emphasize the use of both individual, group, and environmental supports and resources.
- Encourage the client and family to share their own experiences and emotions about medication use. Provide input to the helping process, generate and weigh options, negotiate, and offer feedback as decisions are made.

Roles and Competencies in Medication Management. Six specific and often overlapping contemporary roles for social workers with relevance for psychopharmacotherapy include:

1. *The consultant.* The social worker takes on an active role while maintaining a nonadversarial position with the provider. The social worker performs preliminary screenings to determine clients' possible need and desire for medication, makes referrals to prescribers, assists in information-sharing and shared decision-making, and consults with clients and providers as needed. The social worker prepares clients for active participation in the medication assessment by helping clients anticipate their meetings with prescribers. Related responsibilities might include articulating the rationale for the referral, addressing the client's attitude toward psychiatrists, discussing the client's expectations and fears about medications, assessing the client's ability to pay for medication, and addressing issues of adherence. The social worker monitors the client's subjective experience as well, particularly the meaning and impact of the referral to the client and validates their experiences.
2. *The counselor.* The social worker helps clients articulate goals, see options, weigh alternatives, plan and practice tasks, and take action steps to solve problems and reach personal goals related to psychiatric medication. Counseling can also involve giving accurate information about medication and offering advice based on the literature and professional experiences. The counselor recognizes the importance of empathy, especially around the client experience of side effects or impatience with therapeutic effect. Toward this end, listen to the lived experiences of clients, providing opportunities for clients to share the impact of medication on their sense of self and identity. Social workers need to listen deeply to how medication, both positive effects and adverse effects, and self-definitions of mental illness or emotional distress are intertwined.
3. *The advocate.* Social workers perform two essential tasks that relate to their ethical mandate to advocate for clients: (1) advocating directly for clients and families and (2) empowering and facilitating clients to advocate for themselves. Examples of advocacy in psychopharmacotherapy

include trying to increase client access to the newest types of medication, obtaining free medication from a drug company when needed, discussing potential overmedication with client's physician, challenging a hospital's termination of a clinical trial, or appealing an insurance company that declines coverage of a psychiatric drug. Advocacy is linked with client and family rights, particularly regarding access to quality treatment.

4. *The monitor.* The social worker helps the client keep track of both positive and negative effects of medication so that prompt prescriber action may be summoned when indicated. This requires that social workers have an understanding of basic pharmacokinetics (effects of the body on a drug) and pharmacodynamics (effects of a drug on the body). In addition, monitoring adverse psychological effects involve watching for any changes in the client's self-image and identity that emerge as a result of using medications. For example, a few clients may come to view themselves as "sick" or become overly dependent on medication as a solution to problems. Adverse social effects include any potentially negative consequences that go beyond the individual to consider how medication use affects one's employment and standing with certain social institutions. Finally, social workers in some settings may be creative in using existing measures or devising systematic procedures to evaluate each medication's effectiveness and a client's response over time.

5. *The educator.* The social worker performs as a teacher and coach for clients, families, and perhaps other providers regarding issues including drug actions, benefits, risks, common side effects, dosing regimens, routes of administration, withdrawal, toxicity, and adherence. This might occur in individual meetings with clients or as part of psycho-educational programs that exist in many agency settings. In addition, social workers teach and practice the steps in problem solving, and in collaboration with nurses, pharmacists, and others offer practical suggestions to help clients take medication appropriately. Teaching clients skills in assertiveness and negotiation can help clients maximize their relationship to the prescribing physicians.

6. *The researcher.* Using case reports, single-case designs, or more elaborate designs, the social worker documents how medications impact the lives of clients and families, how medications interact with other interventions, and how interdisciplinary relationships can be best coordinated. Social workers design and implement research about use of medications and other psychosocial interventions with special populations (e.g., children in foster care or with older adults in residential care).

Below is a diagram (Figure 103.1) that summarizes the social worker's application of the roles described above, followed by a clinical illustration.

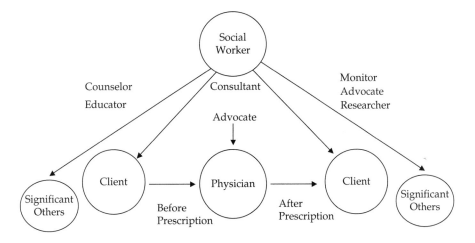

Figure 103.1 Roles and Competencies in Medication Management.

ILLUSTRATION OF THE SOCIAL WORKER'S ROLES

Rebecca was a 40-year old divorced attorney with no children, living alone, with a diagnosis of schizoaffective disorder, characterized by delusions of persecution and agitated behavior. While representing her law firm overseas she confronted associates about their inappropriate "spying" on her, and threatened lawsuits in retaliation. She was hospitalized against her will by her parents and sister. Although she took injectable medication and quickly stabilized in the hospital, she remained angry and paranoid, and declined to take medication as an outpatient, threatening to sue the social worker if he tried to convince her otherwise. The family was concerned about additional acting out on Rebecca's part, which could ruin her already damaged legal career.

The social worker learned during his assessment that the client perceived medication use as evidence that she was "crazy," and taking it would have a devastating effect on her self-image as an independent woman succeeding in a primarily male profession. Further, Rebecca felt that the medication represented efforts of others to "control her mind" and "sabotage" her important legal advocacy work. Clearly, the idea of medication had strong, negative implications for Rebecca's self-image. Rather than refer her directly to a physician, the social worker spent several weeks getting to know the client, validating her successes and empathizing with her trials, and not "pushing" her use of medications (counselor role). The client gradually developed trust in the worker, and agreed to a trial of "minimal-dose" medications that would serve to "help me relax and deal with the stress of my persecution." The social worker met with the physician before Rebecca's first session to let him know of her history and her attitudes about medication (consultant). He also arranged for Rebecca to receive free medications for three months from the agency's funding pool, even though she did not strictly qualify for it (advocacy). The client admitted that, with her level of ambivalence, she would not take medications if she had to pay for them. With the social worker's encouragement, the physician also validated Rebecca's concerns about the medications and agreed to be available, through the social worker, should her ambivalence become more pronounced (monitor). With the social worker's patient intervention, Rebecca eventually accepted the medication and benefited from it. The social worker continued to emphasize its role in helping her remain calm (educator), and the client took it regularly. He also maintained contact with the client's family, with Rebecca's permission, to inform them of the effects and possible limitations of the medication (educator).

Future Directions. Issues of importance to the fields of psychopharmacology and social work practice in the coming years include:

- Although new drug treatments may appear, perhaps with a more precise spectrum of producing drugs without unwanted side effects, there also exists a general belief that pharmaceutical companies will curtail the development of new psychiatric drugs.
- The discovery of and experimentation with unique delivery routes like brain implants, skin patches, or sublingual (under-the-tongue) medications
- More findings regarding the differential physical and psychological effects of medications on people of different ages, genders, races, and ethnicities
- More inquiry into the placebo effect and the additive or interactive effects of combining psychosocial interventions
- Uncertainties about the lasting popularity of herbs, vitamins, and holistic alternatives
- Expanding prescription privileges among nonphysician health care providers
- Increased public scrutiny and criticism of psychiatric medications, clinical drug trials, drug companies, and advertising agencies
- Greater mandate to learn how to evaluate information from websites, and maintain up-to-date knowledge base through professional development offerings
- New models of health care financing that may influence drug availability and use, as well as greater access to psychosocial interventions.

Ideal practices for social workers with regard to psychiatric medications will always feature a collaborative helping environment in which the work is comfortably paced but action-oriented, and relationships are characterized by honesty, genuineness, and warmth. There is, and should be, more attention paid to the ethical dimensions of medication management such as avoiding subtle coercion of clients, respecting client decisions not to take medication, being vocal about concerns related to over- or undermedication, and long waiting lists for medication evaluation. Although a medical model of intervention suggests that the goals of care are symptom reduction and compliance, the goals of care in a social work focused partnership perspective are quality of life, self-determination, and collaborative care. Social workers should maintain a critical perspective on medication use in society, but also an appreciation of the power of integrated treatment to improve the quality of lives of people dealing with mental illnesses, behavioral problems, or emotional distress.

WEBSITES

www.mentalhealth.gov
National Mental Health Information Center
Site run by the federal government's U.S. Department of Health and Human Services which provides free one-stop access to information via internet, phone & publication to public.

www.nimh.nih.gov
National Institute of Mental Health (NIMH).
Public information on specific disorders, diagnosis, and treatment with a section on NIMH research activities.

www.nami.org
National Alliance on Mental Illness (NAMI). NAMI is a national advocacy group with a strong consumer and family member perspective, focusing on serious mental illnesses. This page leads to a number of NAMI articles focusing on disorders, medications, and research.

www.mentalhealthamerica.net
Mental Health America
This site offers access to fact sheets, pamphlets, merchandise, and position statements on a wide variety of mental health topics including disorders, medications, and suicide. This is the new name of the National Mental Health Association founded in the 19th century by Clifford Beers.

www.mentalhelp.net
Mental Health Net
A very comprehensive site linking to information on disorders and treatments, professional resources, and journals. The site is stated to be a public service of CenterSite.Net, a provider of website services and educational content to behavioral health and employee assistance organizations.

www.dr-bob.org/tips
Dr. Bob's Psychopharmacology Tips
A unique site that allows users to search for tips (edited by Dr. Robert Hsiung of the University of Chicago) on psychopharmaceutical use from physician postings on the Interpsych discussion list. Although not scientific, this site allows users to see direct opinions from prescribers on their experiences with psychopharmaceuticals.

www.medicinenet.com/medications/article .htm
Medicine Net
Site run by a "network of doctors" who want to provide up-to-date comprehensive health information to the public. This page offers access to the alphabetical pharmacy index.

www.pdrhealth.com
Physicians' Desk Reference
For more than 50 years, doctors have relied on the "PDR" for up-to-date, accurate drug information. The information on this site is written in lay terms and is based on the FDA-approved drug information found in the PDR.

Readings

Bentley, K. J., & Walsh, J. (2014). *The social worker & psychotropic medication: Toward effective collaboration with clients, families and providers.* Belmont, CA: Brooks/Cole-Cengage.

Bentley, K. J. (2014). Jasmika, the Docs and me: A short story with a happy ending about partnership, collaboration, social work and psychopharmacology. In C. W. LeCroy (Ed.), *Case studies in social work practice* (3rd ed.) (pp. 159–170). Belmont, CA: Cengage-Brooks/Cole.

Bentley, K. J., & Collins, K. S. (2013). Psychopharmacological treatment for child and adolescent mental disorders. In C. Franklin, M. B. Harris, & P. Allen-Meares (Eds.), *The school services sourcebook: A guide for social workers, counselors, and mental health professionals* (2nd ed.) (pp. 53–72). New York, NY: Oxford University Press.

Bentley, K. J. (2010). The meaning of psychiatric medication in a residential program for adults with serious mental illness. *Qualitative Social Work*, 9(4), 479–499.

Bentley, K. J., & Kogut, C. P. (2008). Psychopharmacology and contemporary social work. In T. Mizrahi & L. Davis (Eds.), *Encyclopedia of social work, 20th edition*. NY: Oxford Press.

Bentley, K. J. (2005). Women, mental health and the psychiatric enterprise. *Health & Social Work*, 30(1), 56–63.

Bentley, K. J., Walsh, J., & Farmer, R. (2005). Roles and activities of clinical social workers in psychopharmacotherapy: Results of a national survey. *Social Work*, 50(4), 295–303.

Bentley, K. J., Walsh, J., & Farmer, R. (2005). Referring clients for psychiatric medication: Best practices for social workers. *Best Practices in Mental Health*, 1(1), 59–71.

Cohen, D. (2011). Psychopharmacology and clinical social work practice. In J. R. Brandell (Ed.), *Theory and practice of clinical social work* (pp. 763–810). Newbury Park, CA: Sage.

Cohen, D. (2009). Needed: Critical thinking about psychiatric medication. *Social Work in Mental Health*, 7(1–3), 42–61.

Crison, M. L., & Argo, T. (2009). The use of psychotropic medication in foster care. *Child Welfare*, 88(1), 71–100.

Deegan, P. E. (2007). The lived experience of using psychiatric medication in the recovery process and a shared decision-making program to support it. *Psychiatric Rehabilitation Journal*, 31(1), 62–69.

Dziegielewski, S. F. (2010). *Social work practice and psychopharmacology: A person-in-environment approach* (2nd ed.). New York, NY: Springer Publishing Co.

Gomory, T., Wong, S., Cohen, D., & Lacasse, J. (2011). Clinical social work and the biomedical industrial complex. *Sociology and Social Welfare*, 38(4), 135–165.

Hughes, S., & Cohen, D. (2010). Understanding the assessment of psychotropic drug harms in clinical trials to improve social workers' role in medication monitoring. *Social Work*, 55(2), 105–115.

Kranke, D., Floersch, J., Townsend, L., & Munson, M. (2009). Stigma experience among adolescents taking psychiatric medication. *Children and Youth Services Review*, 32, 496–505.

Tally, M., & Kirk, S. A. (2008). Social work roles in drug treatment with youth. *Social Work in Mental Health*, 6(3), 59–81.

Townsend, L. (2009). How effective are interventions to enhance medication adherence to psychiatric medication? Practice implications for social workers working with adults diagnosed with severe mental illness. *Journal of Human Behavior in the Social Environment*, 19(5), 512–530.

Venkataraman, M. (2005). Medicaid coverage of newer psychotropic medication. *Health & Social Work*, 31(3), 229–232.

Waller, R. J., Lewellen, K., & Bresson, D. (2005). The debate surrounding the psychotropic medication usage in young children. *School Social Work Journal*, 29(2), 59–63.

Walsh, J., Farmer, R., Taylor, M. F., & Bentley, K. J. (2003). Ethical dilemmas of practicing social workers around psychiatric medication: Results of a national study. *Social Work in Mental Health*, 1(4), 91–105.

Walsh, J. (2013). *The recovery philosophy and direct social work practice*. Chicago, IL: Lyceum.

Walsh, J. (2010). *Psychoeducation in mental health*. Chicago, IL: Lyceum.

PART X
Case Management Guidelines

104 An Overview of the *NASW Standards for Social Work Case Management*

Chris Herman

The roots of case management and social work are intertwined in the late 19th and early 20th centuries (Stuart, 2008). Though social work has evolved greatly since that time, the practice of case management remains integral to the profession (Whitaker, Weismiller, & Clark, 2006). In 2013, the National Association of Social Workers (NASW) revised its standards for social work case management, last published two decades earlier (NASW, 1992). The standards reflect the many changes within both case management and the social work profession over this 20-year period.

CHANGES IN SOCIAL WORK CASE MANAGEMENT

Numerous factors have influenced social work case management over the past two decades and continue to shape practice. Service delivery systems have grown in both size and complexity, resulting in greater fragmentation of services. Thus, the need for interdisciplinary and interorganizational coordination and collaboration is now greater than ever, especially during transitions between service providers and settings (Golden & Shier, 2012–13; National Transitions of Care Coalition, 2010).

The client role in social work case management also continues to evolve. Client-directed services have become more common—and expected—in a number of practice specialties, such as aging, disabilities, and behavioral health (National Center for Participant-Directed Services, 2013; Substance Use and Mental Health Services Administration, 2010; University of Minnesota, 2009), and health care practice has become more person and family centered (Institute for Patient- and Family-Centered Care, 2011a, 2011b; U.S. Department of Health and Human Services, 2013). Similarly, practitioners are encouraging clients to assume increasingly active roles in the case management process (see, for example, Coulter, 2012). This shift reflects a deepening twofold recognition: one, that clients are their own best experts; and two, that service delivery is ineffective, and change is impossible, without consistent client engagement. Consequently, case management reflects a social worker–client partnership, rooted in and drawing on clients' goals and strengths.

As the client role in social work case management has evolved, so, too, has the need for clear outcomes. Social workers across specialties face growing pressure to demonstrate that the services they provide are effective (Social Work Policy Institute, 2010) and guided by evidence, even as shrinking resources require all service providers to do more with less. Technology can help case managers achieve these aims, even as it creates new challenges (Powell & Fink-Samnick, 2013; Stricker, 2012).

Over the past 20 years, both case management and the profession of social work have also become more specialized (Federal Interagency HIV/AIDS Case Management Work Group, 2008; Stuart, 2008), though generalist social work practice remains strong (McNutt, 2008). At the same time, case management and related practices are increasingly performed by a variety of providers, such as nurses and other health care professionals, paraprofessionals within both health care and social service settings, and peer counselors. Such diversity compels social workers to understand, articulate, and demonstrate the perspectives and activities that distinguish social work case management.

STANDARDS REVISION PROCESS

Numerous social workers contributed to the revision of the NASW case management standards. An advisory panel of 10 NASW members provided substantive input throughout the revision process.[1] The panelists had expertise with diverse clientele across multiple specialties, including aging, child and family services, disability work, health, mental health, substance use, and veterans' services. Moreover, the expert panelists worked in the public, nonprofit, and for-profit sectors in rural, suburban, and urban locations throughout the United States. All had years of direct practice experience, and most were still engaged in direct practice. Furthermore, each panelist had demonstrated professional leadership on a national level, whether through social work education, research, or leadership within NASW, other professional associations, or federal agencies.

Using a consensus-based process, NASW staff collaborated closely with the advisory panel to develop the draft standards. The Association then posted the draft standards for public review and comment. NASW, other organizations, and the expert panel publicized the two-month comment period using a wide variety of print and electronic media. Following the comment period, NASW staff and the expert panel reviewed and integrated the feedback received. The NASW board of directors then approved the standards, which were published in early 2013 (NASW, 2013).

OVERVIEW OF NASW STANDARDS

The standards publication includes not only the standards themselves, but also introductory material—such as historical background and definitions of key terms—relevant to social work case management. The primary goals of the NASW standards are (1) to enhance social work case management with any population and in any employment sector, service setting, or practice specialty and (2) to educate the public about the professional social work role in case management.

In keeping with the growing diversity of program models and job titles, the standards apply to all social workers whose primary function is either case management or a related practice, such as care management or care coordination. At the same time, the publication highlights the principles that distinguish and guide social work case management:

- Person-centered services
- Primacy of the client–social worker relationship
- Person-in-environment framework
- Strengths perspective
- Collaborative teamwork
- Intervention at the micro, mezzo, and macro levels (NASW, 2013, pp. 17–18).

These principles infuse the 12 standards that follow:

1. *Ethics and values.* Standard 1 relates the core values of the social work profession to case management practice and underscores the need for social work case managers to adhere to NASW's *Code of Ethics* (2008). This standard also reflects some of the ethical challenges and responsibilities inherent in case management.
2. *Qualifications.* Standard 2 identifies the minimum qualifications for social work case management practice: (a) a social work degree from a Counsel on Social Work Education (CSWE)-accredited school or program; (b) adherence to state laws and regulations governing social work licensure or certification; and (3) relevant skills and professional experience.
3. *Knowledge.* Standard 3 summarizes the foundational knowledge needed for effective social work case management practice. Such knowledge includes an understanding of human behavior, growth, and development; behavioral and physical health; family relationships (as defined by each client); resources and systems; and the role of the professional social worker.
4. *Cultural and linguistic competence.* Standard 4 emphasizes that culture—which, similar to the concept of *family,* is defined quite broadly—is a source of resilience. The standard underscores the importance of cultural and linguistic competence in both service delivery and organizational functioning, noting the pervasive effects of systemic oppression and privilege.

5. *Assessment.* Standard 5 links ongoing bio-psychosocial assessment with other aspects of practice and stresses client engagement in the assessment process. This standard also details multiple domains that may be included in the assessment process.

6. *Service planning, implementation, and monitoring.* Standard 6 illustrates a variety of micro-, mezzo-, and macro-level social work interventions that may be incorporated in social work case management service plans. Furthermore, this standard addresses service coordination and termination.

7. *Advocacy and leadership.* Standard 7 illustrates how social work case managers exercise leadership through advocacy at the micro, mezzo, and macro levels. Such advocacy is done both with and on behalf of clients and communities.

8. *Interdisciplinary and interorganizational collaboration.* Standard 8 focuses on the role of interdisciplinary and interorganizational communication and teamwork in promoting clients' goals and improving service delivery. The standard also notes that social worker–client collaboration infuses both the case management process and the other 11 case management standards.

9. *Practice evaluation and improvement.* Standard 9 outlines an array of evaluation activities, both internal and external, that social workers may use to assess and enhance case management services. Such input focuses not only on outcomes, but also on processes of care.

10. *Record keeping.* Standard 10 addresses the content of social work documentation and its role in facilitating communication with other service providers on behalf of case management clients. This standard also addresses confidentiality in the storage and release of client-related information.

11. *Workload sustainability.* Standard 11 emphasizes that establishing and maintaining appropriate workloads is the shared responsibility of social workers, management staff, and organizations. The standard describes some of the factors that influence case management caseloads and workloads, noting that the latter includes any social work function that supports case management services.

12. *Professional development and competence.* Standard 12 illustrates the role of ongoing professional development in maintaining and enhancing competence in case management practice. The standard delineates an array of professional development activities and encourages social work case managers to impart their knowledge and skills to their social work colleagues.

APPLYING THE STANDARDS IN PRACTICE

The case example included in this chapter illustrates how one social worker applies, in practice, the guiding principles of the *NASW Standards for Social Work Case Management* (2013). When Juan's adult children approach the social work case manager with a request to influence their father's treatment plan, the social worker responds empathetically while supporting Juan's self-determination. In this way, she gently reminds the family that her primary goal is to uphold Juan's choices. The social worker maintains this person-centered approach throughout her work with Juan by following his lead in conversation and offering information and resources that address his concerns. She also helps Juan understand how factors in his bio-psychosocial environment influence his personal experiences.

Recognizing the centrality of Juan's relationship with his children, the social work case manager supports Juan in communicating his feelings and goals to his children, thereby strengthening that relationship. Similarly, the social worker uses her professional alliance with Juan to facilitate his communication with both the Social Security Administration and the hospice team. These collaborative efforts expand Juan's support network and reaffirm his strengths. Following Juan's death, the social worker's response to Juan's adult children demonstrates her knowledge of, and support for, systemic advocacy. This advocacy complements the social worker's micro- and mezzo-level interventions during the last months of Juan's life.

The case example also exemplifies application of many of the 12 case management standards. The social worker's actions are consistent with social work ethics and values and demonstrate a solid knowledge of case management practice and relevant resources. She provides culturally and linguistically appropriate services and advocates for her client to obtain such services from other organizations. As Juan's circumstances change, she engages him in reassessing his goals and developing a plan to realize those goals. She collaborates with other organizations and Juan's adult children on his behalf and, following his death, responds to the family's desire to engage in macro-level advocacy.[2] Visit www.socialworkers.org/practice/naswstandards/CaseManagementStandards2013.pdf to download the *NASW Standards for Social Work Case Management* (2013).

Case Example: Juan

A social work case manager works in a community-based agency serving older adults and families. One of her long-standing clients, a 61-year-old man named Juan, has recently been diagnosed with inoperable bladder cancer. Juan, who smoked as a young adult, blames himself for his illness and has withdrawn from social contact. Though the oncologist has informed Juan and his adult children the prognosis is poor, the children have encouraged their father to undergo chemotherapy and radiation. They ask the case manager to convince Juan not to "give up."

The social work case manager acknowledges the family's distress while reminding them that their father has the right to make his own decisions. The first time she visits Juan following the diagnosis, he avoids the subject of cancer. During the next visit, however, Juan acknowledges his dread of being repeatedly asked about his current or past smoking habits. The social worker normalizes this reaction, helping Juan understand the societal dynamics at the root of his shame. She also reaffirms the many positive steps Juan has taken over the years to maintain a healthy lifestyle and reminds him that environmental factors beyond his control may have contributed to his cancer risk.

By the following conversation, Juan is ready to talk about his medical options. The social worker asks what is most important to him right now. Juan explains that he would rather forego chemo and radiation and live a shorter amount of time than to deal with the side effects of those treatments. "I'm not afraid to die—I just want to feel as well as I can in the time I have left." The social worker explains to Juan that palliative care can help him in this respect. Juan wants to ask his doctor about it but knows his children aren't ready. He accepts the social worker's offer to facilitate a family conversation. With the social worker's support, Juan is able to communicate his feelings to his children, who eventually accept his decision.

During the family discussion, Juan also verbalizes his fear of being a financial burden on his children; because of his cancer symptoms, he has been unable to work lately and anticipates retiring, but is a year too young to qualify for early retirement benefits under Social Security. The social work case manager explains that, given the severity of Juan's diagnosis, he would probably be approved for Social Security Disability Insurance very quickly under the Social Security Administration's Compassionate Allowances program. Juan is relieved but overwhelmed by the prospect of completing a written application in English, which is his second language. The social worker tells Juan that he can apply by phone in Spanish. Still uncertain, Juan asks if the social worker will make the first call with him. Together, they call the Social Security Administration to begin the process. After a few minutes, Juan's confidence grows, and he talks freely.

Juan then meets with his oncologist, who refers him to a hospice program. After Juan enrolls in hospice, he is reluctant to accept visits from anyone but the hospice nurse. The social work case manager explains the value of the hospice team and obtains a signed release to talk with the hospice social worker. The hospice social worker appreciates the information and affirms the value of Juan's continued relationship with the social work case manager. The two social workers discuss their respective roles and agree to propose a joint visit with Juan. Following this meeting, Juan is more receptive to the hospice social worker and even agrees to meet the hospice chaplain the following week. Juan and his family are closely involved with both the hospice team and the social work case manager during the last few months of Juan's life.

Several months following Juan's death, the adult children contact the social work case manager. While describing their participation in a bereavement support group, they ask how they can get involved in advocacy to help other people affected by cancer. The social worker refers them to a local chapter of a cancer organization that sponsors such activities.

WEBSITES

American Case Management Association: http://www.acmaweb.org

Case Management Society of America: http://www.cmsa.org

National Association of Professional Geriatric Care Managers: http://www.caremanager.org

National Association of Social Workers: http://www.socialworkers.org

Society for Social Work Leadership in Health Care: http://www.sswlhc.org

Notes

1. The author gratefully acknowledges the members of the expert panel for their invaluable contributions to the standards revision process: Linda Aufderhaar, Brian Giddens, Lea Ann Holder, Sharon Mass, Jun Matsuyoshi, David Moxley, Richard Rapp, Nelly Rojas Schwan, Phyllis Solomon, and Michelle Stefanelli.

2. For brief case examples specific to each of the 12 NASW case management standards, please refer to the following publication: Herman, C. (2013, January). *The evolving context of social work case management: NASW releases revised standards of practice* (NASW Practice Perspectives). Washington, DC: National Association of Social Workers.

References

Coulter, A. (2012). Patient engagement—what works? *Journal of Ambulatory Care Management, 35,* 80–89. Retrieved from http://informedmedicaldecisions.org/wp-content/uploads/2012/04/Patient_Engagement_What_Works_.3.pdf

Federal Interagency HIV/AIDS Case Management Work Group. (2008). *Recommendations for case management collaboration and coordination in federally funded HIV/AIDS programs.* Retrieved from the Centers for Disease Control and Prevention Web site: http://www.cdcnpin.org/scripts/display/MatlDisplay.asp?MatlNbr=34402

Golden, R. L., & Shier, G. (Eds.). (2012–13). Care transitions in an aging America. *Generations, 36*(4).

Institute for Patient- and Family-Centered Care. (2011a). *Advancing the practice of patient- and family-centered care in hospitals: How to get started.* Retrieved from http://www.ipfcc.org/pdf/getting_started.pdf

Institute for Patient- and Family-Centered Care. (2011b). *Advancing the practice of patient- and family-centered care in primary care and other ambulatory settings: How to get started.* Retrieved from http://www.ipfcc.org/pdf/GettingStarted-AmbulatoryCare.pdf

McNutt, J. (2008). Social work practice: History and evolution. In T. Mizrahi & L. E. Davis (Eds.-in-Chief), *Encyclopedia of Social Work* (20th ed.) (Vol. 4) (pp. 138–141). Washington, DC, and New York: NASW Press and Oxford University Press.

National Association of Social Workers. (1992). *NASW standards for social work case management.* Washington, DC: Author.

National Association of Social Workers. (2008). *Code of ethics of the National Association of Social Workers.* Retrieved from http://www.socialworkers.org/pubs/code

National Association of Social Workers. (2013). *NASW standards for social work case management.* Retrieved from http://www.socialworkers.org/practice/naswstandards/CaseManagementStandards2013.pdf

National Center for Participant-Directed Services. (2013). *Aging and disability network participant direction toolkit.* Retrieved from http://www.bc.edu/content/bc/schools/gssw/nrcpds/tools/toolkit.html

National Transitions of Care Coalition. (2010). *Improving transitions of care: Findings and considerations of the "Vision of the National Transitions of Care Coalition."* Retrieved from http://www.ntocc.org/Portals/0/PDF/Resources/NTOCCIssueBriefs.pdf

Powell, S. K., & Fink-Samnick, E. (2013). To boldly go where no case manager has gone before: Remote patient monitoring and beyond [Editorial]. *Professional Case Management, 18,* 1–2. doi:10.1097/NCM.0b013e3182769c4d

Social Work Policy Institute. (2010). *Comparative effectiveness research and social work: Strengthening the connection.* Retrieved from http://www.socialworkpolicy.org/news-events/social-work-research-and-comparative-effectiveness-research-cer-a-research-symposium-to-strengthen -the- connection .html

Stricker, P. (2012, January). *Staying ahead of the annual trends.* Retrieved from Case Management Society of America website: http://www.cmsa.org/Individual/NewsEvents/HealthTechnologyArticles/tabid/526/Default.aspx

Stuart, P. H. (2008). Social work profession: History. In T. Mizrahi & L. E. Davis (Eds.-in-Chief), *Encyclopedia of Social Work* (20th ed.) (Vol. 4) (pp. 156–164). Washington, DC, and New York: NASW Press and Oxford University Press.

Substance Abuse and Mental Health Services Administration. (2010). *Self-directed care in mental health: Learnings from the Cash & Counseling demonstration evaluation.* Retrieved from http://www.hcbs.org/files/194/9672/SMA10-4522.pdf

University of Minnesota, Institute on Community Integration, Research and Training Center on Community Living and Employment. (2009, January). Implementation of consumer-directed services for persons with intellectual or developmental disabilities: A national study. *Policy Research Brief*, 20(1). Retrieved from http://www.hcbs.org/files/151/7525/consumer_direction_developmental_disabilities.pdf

U. S. Department of Health and Human Services. (2013). *2013 annual progress report to Congress: National strategy for quality improvement in health care.*

Retrieved from http://www.ahrq.gov/working-forquality/nqs/nqs2013annlrpt.pdf

Whitaker, T., Weismiller, T., & Clark, E. (2006). *Assuring the sufficiency of a frontline workforce: A national study of licensed social workers—Executive summary.* Retrieved from the NASW website: http://workforce.socialworkers.org/studies/nasw_06_execsummary.pdf

105 Clinical Case Management

Joseph Walsh & Jennifer Manuel

Clinical case management is an approach to human service delivery that integrates elements of clinical social work and traditional case management practices. It is used primarily with clients having serious mental illnesses, such as schizophrenia, major depression, bipolar disorder, personality disorders, and substance use disorders. The range of client needs within this population includes social relationships, housing, income support, medical care, job training, recreation, life skills development, counseling, and medication. Interventions are usually provided in mental health agencies.

Clinical social work practice is the application of social work theory and methods to the diagnosis, treatment, and prevention of psychosocial dysfunction, disability, or impairment in individuals, families, and groups (NASW, 2005). It is based on an application of human development theories within a psychosocial context. Case management somewhat differently emphasizes the development of a client's growth-enhancing environmental supports, both formal and informal, using resources that may be spread across agency systems. Case managers work independently or as members of teams, and their traditional activities include assessment, planning, linking, monitoring, and advocacy.

Social work recognizes the importance of one's physical and emotional environment in

facilitating growth throughout the life cycle, and clinical case management is a professional specialization characterized by an understanding and integration of the relationships among the range of internal and external factors that influence the course of development (Wong, 2006). In clinical case management, the social worker combines the sensitivity and interpersonal skill of the psychotherapist with the creativity and action orientation of the environmental architect (Surber, 1994). The practice gives priority to the quality of the relationship between the client and social worker as a prerequisite for the client's growth. Those who support clinical case management argue that substituting nonclinicians for appropriately skilled clinicians often leaves consumers in need of holistic interventions with staff who are ill equipped to meet their needs (Essock, Covell, & Drake, 2006). Furthermore, due to the inherent problems with role confusion and authority in traditional case management, the client is best served if the worker is encouraged to function as the primary therapeutic resource.

Storey (2009) has summarized a perspective first articulated by D. W. Winnicott that is instructive in identifying how clinical case management bridges the modalities of psychotherapy and social casework. Winnicott believed that the psychotherapist starts from the client's "inside" and is concerned with inner conflicts that hamper social development. The social (case)worker starts off as a "real" person concerned with external events and people in the client's life (the "outside"), and in the course of intervention brings harmony between those two worlds.

Clinical case management includes the following 13 activities within four areas of focus (Kanter, 2011, 1996):

- Initial phase—engagement, assessment, and planning
- Environmental focus—linking with community resources, consulting with families and caregivers, maintaining and expanding social networks, collaboration with physicians and hospitals, and advocacy
- Client focus—intermittent individual psychotherapy, independent living skills development, and client psycho-education
- Client–environment focus—crisis intervention and monitoring.

Clinical case management may be implemented within many program models. For example, Floersch (2002) differentiates five models of case management supported by federal, state, and private research monies, including psychiatric rehabilitation, broker, assertive case management, recovery, and strengths. Clinical case management can be practiced in all but the broker model.

TASKS AND ACTIVITIES

Harris and Bergman (1988) have summarized the therapeutic tasks of clinical case management practice as follows:

- Forging a relationship, or making a positive connection with a client. This may unfold in a variety of ways depending on a particular client's characteristics, and may range from high levels of interaction to the maintenance of interpersonal formality and distance.
- Modeling healthy behaviors to facilitate a client's movement from a position of dependency to one of greater self-direction. When this is successful, the client comes to understand that he or she has unique needs, goals, and skills, and that focused actions can influence the course of events.

- Altering the client's physical environment through processes of creation, facilitation, and adjustment.

THE WORKER–CLIENT RELATIONSHIP

The clinical case management relationship is the sustaining link between the client with mental illness and the external world (Walsh, 2000a). It provides an environment of safety for the client. Within that context, the client can:

- Experience structure as an antidote to disorganization
- Appreciate the significance of internal and external limits as a guard against poor impulse control
- Learn that help is available for most problems
- Improve reality testing
- Experience cognitive and experiential learning
- Enhance self-esteem through success experiences.

The worker–client relationship provides a context for positive outcomes in all clinical practice situations, including those involving clinical case management. This alliance consists of a positive emotional bond between the parties, mutual comfort, and a shared understanding of goals and tasks. It develops over time in unpredictable ways from the expectations, beliefs, and knowledge that each person brings to the relationship. Hewitt and Coffey (2005) conducted a meta-analysis of studies on the significance of the therapeutic relationship with clients who have schizophrenia and concluded that clients who experience an empathic, positive, and facilitative relationship have better outcomes. Additionally, Miller, Duncan, and Hubble (2005) concluded from their literature review that the two elements of the therapeutic alliance and the practitioner's ongoing attention to the client's attitude about the intervention account for positive outcomes more than anything else.

Walsh (2000b) asserts that the social worker's management of relationship boundaries in clinical case management is a more complex process than in other forms of intervention. Boundaries include the spoken and unspoken rules that case managers and clients observe about the physical and emotional limits of their relationship. Special boundary challenges in clinical case management include:

- The possibility of dual relationships with the client or his or her significant others (for example, serving as a client's payee)
- Unwelcome or inappropriate intrusions into the client's home environment
- Unclear assumptions about self-disclosure for both parties
- The social worker's use of coercion in the relationship
- Managing issues of reciprocity (including material transactions and also a client's frequent desire to be the social worker's friend).

CLINICAL SKILLS

In addition to relationship-building skills, the clinical skills needed for long-term work with clients having mental illness include the ability to (Harris & Bergman, 1988; Kanter, 1996, 1995):

- Make ongoing judgments about the intensity of one's involvement with a client
- Assess and recognize a client's fluctuating competence and changing needs
- Titrate support so as to maximize a client's capacity for self-directed behavior
- Differentiate the biological and psychological aspects of mental illness
- Help family members cope with their troubled relative
- Appreciate the effects of social factors on a client's sense of competence
- Understand how clients both shape and internalize their environments
- Appreciate a client's conscious and unconscious motives for behavior
- Develop a longitudinal view of the client's strengths, limitations, and symptoms.

Many community-based program developers are reluctant to support clinical case management because of concerns that social workers may focus on psychotherapy in lieu of the full range of case management interventions. Neugeboren (1996) suggests that environmentally focused practice (advocacy and monitoring) requires "sociopolitical" skills, in contrast to "socioemotional" skills required for relationship development, assessment, and planning. This perspective underscores the need for ongoing professional development in all areas of clinical case management practice.

OUTCOME RESEARCH

Researchers have attempted to compare case management models with regard to effectiveness. It is difficult, however, to isolate particular models because of intervening variables that confound the relationship between program philosophy and actual practices. A recent systematic review of 38 randomized clinical trials concluded that clinical case management, which emphasizes high intensity services and manageable caseloads, ensures that more people remain in contact with psychiatric services, improves general functioning, and shortens the length of hospitalization, especially among those who are frequently hospitalized (Dieterich, Irving, Park, & Marshall, 2010). An earlier meta-analysis included a greater range of studies evaluating 44 mental health case management programs over a 20-year period and found that both assertive case management and clinical case management were effective with regard to measures of family burden, family service satisfaction, and cost of care (Ziguras & Stuart, 2000). The two approaches were equally effective in reducing symptoms, increasing client contact with services, reducing dropout rates, improving social functioning, and increasing client satisfaction. Another study also found that clients of clinical case managers made comparable gains to those receiving assertive community treatment (Essock et al., 2006). A systematic review by Smith and Newton (2007) found that case management models emphasizing assertive engagement and clinical case management shortened hospital stays and improved treatment engagement, adherence, independence, and client satisfaction. In a 10-year review of a large care program in the United Kingdom, it was observed that the introduction of clinical case management was associated with an increasing focus on clients with the more severe mental disorders (Cornwall, Gorman, Carlisle, & Pope, 2001).

One gap in the research is that individual case manager effects (as opposed to program effects) on client outcomes have rarely been examined. In one such study of a nationally known community support program, strong support was found for the differential effectiveness of case managers (Ryan, Sherman, & Judd, 1994). More recently, research has indicated the benefit of client-case manager ethnic matching. One such study by Ziguras, Klimidis, Lewis, & Stuart (2003) found that ethnic minority clients who were matched with bilingual clinicians were more engaged in treatment and had less frequent contact with emergency services. Other studies, however, did not find such benefit in ethnic matching (Ortega & Rosenheck, 2002; Chinman, Rosenheck, & Lam, 2000). Additional research of the characteristics or effectiveness of individual case managers could more clearly evaluate the practice of clinical case management.

CONCLUSION

Two national consensus panels, sponsored by the Center for Mental Health Services and the Center for Health Care Strategies, have identified 11 core competencies for the effective treatment of persons with serious mental illnesses, including the clinical tasks of developing a therapeutic relationship, conducting reliable symptom assessment and diagnoses, and integrating psychosocial and psychopharmacological treatments (Liberman, 2005). Among the issues to consider in developing the therapeutic aspects of clinical case management are worker roles, authority, status, training, caseload, and supervision. These may be addressed in the following ways.

- Program developers should acknowledge that case managers provide therapeutic interventions and direct their recruitment and supervision policies accordingly.
- Because they are the focal point of the client's intervention milieu, clinical case managers must be given authority to assume overall case responsibility.
- Administrators must develop career paths for clinical case managers so that turnover based on low status and pay is not so endemic.
- Caseload size should be controlled so that clinical case managers can realistically attend to the needs of their clients. Caseloads of approximately 20 to 30 clients per worker appear to facilitate effective intervention.

Supporting clinical case management will provide another positive consequence for clients—namely, reduced stigmatization. Among the benefits of acknowledging the therapeutic nature of case manager–client relationships is the implied belief that all persons are capable of psychological growth.

WEBSITES

Clinical Case Management Resources: www .clinicalcasemanagement.com

NASW Standards for Social Work Case Management: http://www.socialworkers.org/practice/standards/sw_case_mgmt.asp.

U.S. Department of Health and Human Services, Substance Abuse and Mental Health Services Administration: http://samhsa.gov/index .aspx

References

Chinman, M. J., Rosenheck, R. A., & Lam, J. A. (2000). Client–case manager racial matching in a program for homeless persons with serious mental illness. *Psychiatric Services, 51*(10), 1265–1272.

Cornwall, P., Gorman, B., Carlisle, J., & Pope, M. (2001). Ten years in the life of a community mental health team: The impact of the care programme approach in the UK. *Journal of Mental Health, 10*(4), 441–447.

Dieterich, M., Irving, C. B., Park, B., & Marshall, M. (2010). Intensive case management for severe mental illness. *Cochrane Database of Systematic Reviews*, Issue 10.

Essock, S. M., Covell, N. H., & Drake, R. E. (2006). Clinical case management, case management, and ACT: Reply. *Psychiatric Services, 57*(4), 579.

Essock, S. M., Mueser, K. T., Drake, R. E., Covell, N. H., McHugo, G. J., Frisman, L. K., . . . & Swain, K. (2006). Comparison of ACT and standard case management for delivering integrated treatment for co-occurring disorders. *Psychiatric Services, 57*(2), 185–196.

Floersch, J. (2002). *Meds, money, and manners: The case management of severe mental illness.* New York, NY: Columbia University Press.

Harris, M., & Bergman, H. C. (1988). Clinical case management for the chronically mentally ill: A conceptual analysis. In M. Harris & L. Bachrach (Eds.), Clinical case management (pp. 5–13). *New Directions for Mental Health Services, 40.* San Francisco, CA: Jossey-Bass.

Hewitt, J., & Coffey, M. (2005). Therapeutic working relationships with people with schizophrenia: Literature review. *Journal of Advanced Nursing, 52*(5), 561–570.

Kanter, J. (2011). Clinical case management. In J. R. Brandell (Ed.), *Theory and practice in clinical social work* (2nd ed.) (pp. 561–586). Thousand Oaks, CA: Sage Publications.

Kanter, J. (Ed.). (1995). *Clinical issues in case management*. San Francisco, CA: Jossey-Bass.

Kanter, J. (1996). Case management with longterm patients. In S. M. Soreff (Ed.), *Handbook for the treatment of the seriously mentally ill* (pp. 259–275). Seattle, WA: Hogrefe & Huber.

Liberman, R. P. (2005). Drug and psychosocial curricula for psychiatry residents for treatment of schizophrenia: Part II. *Psychiatric Services, 56*(1), 28–30.

Miller, S. D., Duncan, B. L., & Hubble, M. A. (2005). Outcome-informed clinical work. In J. C. Norcross & M. R. Goldfried (Eds.), *Handbook of psychotherapy integration* (2nd ed.) (pp. 84–102). New York, NY: Oxford University Press.

National Association of Social Workers (NASW). (2005). *NASW standards for clinical social work in social work practice*. Silver Spring, MD: NASW Press.

Neugeboren, B. (1996). *Environmental practice in the human services*. New York, NY: Haworth.

Ortega, A. N., & Rosenheck, R. (2002). Hispanic client-case manager matching: Differences in outcomes and service use in a program for homeless persons with severe mental illness. *The Journal of Nervous and Mental Disease, 190*(5), 315–323.

Ryan, C. S., Sherman, P. S., & Judd, C. M. (1994). Accounting for case manager effects in the evaluation of mental health services. *Journal of Consulting and Clinical Psychology, 62*(5), 965–974.

Smith, L., & Newton, R. (2007). Systematic review of case management. *The Royal Australian and New Zealand College of Psychiatrists, 41*, 2–9.

Storey, C. L. (2009). The psychotherapeutic dimensions of clinical case management with a combat veteran. *Smith College Studies in Social Work, 79*(3–4), 443–452.

Surber, R. W. (Ed.) (1994). *Clinical case management: A guide to comprehensive treatment of serious mental illness*. Thousand Oaks, CA: Sage.

Walsh, J. (2000a). *Clinical case management with persons having mental illness: A relationship-based perspective*. Pacific Grove, CA: Wadsworth-Brooks/Cole.

Walsh, J. (2000b). Recognizing and managing boundary issues in case management. *Journal of Case Management, 9*(2), 79–85.

Wong, D. F. K. (2006). *Clinical case management for people with mental illness: A biopsychosocial vulnerability-stress model*. New York, NY: Haworth.

Ziguras, S., Klimidis, S., Lewis, J., & Stuart, G. (2003). Ethnic matching of clients and clinicians and use of mental health services by ethnic minority clients. *Psychiatric Services, 54*(4), 535–541.

Ziguras, S. J., & Stuart, G. W. (2000). A meta-analysis of the effectiveness of mental health case management over 20 years. *Psychiatric Services, 51*(11), 1410–1421.

106   Assertive Community Treatment or Intensive Case Management

Phyllis Solomon

Assertive Community Treatment (ACT) and Intensive Case Management (ICM) are services designed to serve persons with severe mental illness. Although there is no clear operationalization of what severe mental illness (SMI) is, it is commonly accepted that there are three dimensions that identify members of this group; diagnosis, disability, and duration. The diagnostic categories often employed are schizophrenia spectrum disorder and major affective disorders with increasing inclusion of personality disorders. Disability refers to "dangerous or disturbing social behaviors, moderate impairment in work and non-work activities and mild impairment in basic needs" (Dieterich, Irving, Park, & Marshall, 2011, p. 7). Duration refers to persistent and long-term history and treatment of the illness of at least two years or more (National Institute of Mental Health, 1987). This chapter will provide background on the development of ACT and its evolution over time into the basic staple of case management as a core service for persons with SMI, its establishment as an evidence-based practice, its international spread and its relationship to recovery. Furthermore, some suggested guidelines will be offered.

BACKGROUND HISTORY AND EVOLUTION OF ASSERTIVE COMMUNITY TREATMENT

ACT was developed at Mendota State hospital in Madison, Wisconsin by Marx, Test, and Stein (1973) in the early 1970s in response to the needs created by deinstitutionalization of public psychiatric hospitals. It was originally named Training in Community Living (TLC) because it was designed to take the hospital's interdisciplinary team into the community and to train patients being discharged from the hospital into community settings in which they were intending to live. This approach was found to be necessary due to the fact that patients had limited ability to generalize the skills they learned in the hospital to the new settings in which they were to reside. Later, it was renamed Program in Assertive Community Treatment (PACT) and eventually, it was shortened to Assertive Community Treatment (ACT).

ACT was designed as a fully comprehensive, self-contained program that was to provide for all of the treatments, services, supports, and rehabilitation needs of the patients and to be available 7 days a week, 24 hours a day. The services and supports are proffered by a multidisciplinary treatment team minimally comprised of a psychiatrist, nurse, therapist/clinician, and case managers who are to serve as the coordinating resource for the team. Professionals with greater specialization are added to the team contingent upon the needs of the population served. For example, a substance abuse counselor would be included should the clients have a comorbid substance abuse disorder, or an employment specialist would be added if the team targeted employment for the

population being served. Over time, these teams have been designed to serve a variety of specific populations, including forensic clients (Forensic Assertive Community Treatment [Cuddleback, Morrissey, Cusack, & Meyer, 2009]), clients with borderline personality disorder (Horvitz-Lennon, Reynolds, Wolbert, & Witheridge, 2009), and transitional age youth (McGrew & Danner, 2009). Recently, teams have begun to include peer support specialists and family members as team members to make these teams more recovery oriented (Schmidt, Pinninti, Garfinkle, & Solomon, 2013). Recent research on including a peer as a team member is showing positive effects, while at the same time demonstrating that the integration of these members is a slow process (van Vugt, Kroon, Delespaul, & Mulder, 2012).

ACT services are delivered *in vivo* with high intensity wherever a client lives, works, and recreates, and are to engage in assertive outreach. These latter were important features because these services are to be reserved for those who are most in need, not for all persons with an SMI diagnosis. This program is to serve those most disengaged from the mental health treatment system, who are homeless, who have a number of hospitalizations and crisis episodes, who are sometimes referred to as heavy users of services, or specialized populations like those with substance abuse disorders or criminal justice involvement. In other words, those who are most costly to the system, because they frequently choose to enter the mental health system at crisis points rather than engaging with mental health services and treatments on an ongoing basis. It is estimated that ACT is the service of choice for about 20% of those with a severe mental illness, but not for all with a SMI diagnosis (Schmidt et al., 2013). From its inception, ACT was established to reduce the need for hospitalization, increase the client's independence from the service system, and increase his/her integration into the community settings of his/her choosing.

The core features of ACT are:

- Multidisciplinary team approach
- Small caseloads (1:10–12)
- 24–7 crisis support
- Individualized care
- Team members sharing caseloads
- *In vivo* delivery
- Monitoring of medication
- Assertive outreach
- No-discharge policy

ACT teams are to serve no more than 120 clients at any given time and are to meet daily in order to ensure all team members are aware of the current status of all clients. This increases the likelihood of continuity of care should the primary therapist or case manager designated for a client not be available. However, a no-discharge policy has been found to be nonsustainable; teams quickly reach their maximum caseload with no discharges and are unable to serve new clients needing the service. Research has found, however, that there are no negative consequences from transferring clients if done in a highly planned way (Phillips et al., 2001; Salyers et al., 1998) and with allowances for clients to return if deemed clinically beneficial. Consequently, these findings have resulted in a relaxation of this feature.

Intensive case management over time really evolved from both broker and clinical case management models and from ACT. Like ACT, broker case management was identified in the early 1970s with the big push for deinstitutionalization. Basic case management, which was referred to as broker case management, functioned to coordinate resources, supports, and services needed by individuals being released from public psychiatric hospitals. These functions and supports were not particularly new to social work, given that they had been inherent to the practice of social work since the emergence of the profession (NASW, 2013). It was soon recognized that a more intensive service was needed for discharged patients. Clinical case management emerged, and broker case management essentially merged with it. Clinical case management was not particularly well defined, but this service incorporated more clinical aspects, such as supportive counseling and had small caseloads and was usually delivered by those with some advanced training, frequently social workers. As research on ACT began appearing that demonstrated its effectiveness, some of the elements of ACT came to be incorporated into intensive case management. These elements could include assertive outreach, small caseloads (usually fewer than 20 clients per case manager), *in vivo* service delivery, and working in teams or pairs of case managers. Agency back-up of crisis services, as well as medication administration and monitoring by a psychiatrist could also be included. What is referred to as case management currently often means intensive case management, but there is no consistency in exactly what this service is in practice. This term is used interchangeably with ACT, but it does not contain all

of the elements of ACT (Dieterich et al., 2011). In addition, such a case management service may be called targeted case management, because this is what case management is designated by the Centers for Medicare and Medicaid Services, which sets policy for payment of these services. During the past 10 years these two original models (ACT and Intensive Case Management) have been modified and merged, with resultant difficulty in distinguishing the differences between them. Consequently, Cochrane abandoned the recent review of ACT and combined the research on the ACT model with the systematic review of intensive case management. One finding of this review was that the effectiveness of intensive case management relies on the extent to which the service is faithfully implemented consistent with the elements of ACT and contingent on a high use of hospital beds (Dieterich et al., 2011).

EFFECTIVENESS OF ASSERTIVE COMMUNITY TREATMENT AND INTENSIVE CASE MANAGEMENT

ACT is currently considered an evidence-based practice. Reviews of ACT compared with other case management models, or to standard care, consistently have found reduced hospitalization and shorter lengths of stay when clients are hospitalized, decreases in homelessness and in crisis services use, high degrees of satisfaction by both clients and their families, and increased engagement with services. Clients engaged in ACT were also better at maintaining contact, thus reducing service drop outs and increasing housing stability. Furthermore, ACT has been found to be a cost-effective service due to its less frequent use of hospitalization (Schmidt et al., 2013).

However, given the changing environment, in which hospitalization has become more infrequent and when it does occur, is much shorter, and the concurrent increased comprehensiveness and incorporation of such major elements of ACT into what has become the standard of care in case management, the effectiveness of ACT has diminished when reduction in hospitalization as an outcome is compared with the standard of care in low hospital use environments. In other words, in these environments, it is difficult to further reduce hospitalization.

In the most recent Cochrane ICM review, it was found that for those hospitalized ICM did reduce length of stay, but so did standard care. The advantage of ACT/ICM seemed to be for those who had spent a good deal of time in the hospital in the past two years. Consequently, these reviewers concluded that there is no evidence that ICM substantially affects the cost of psychiatric hospital care. This review included more European and Australian-based studies, whereas prior reviews were mostly North American studies. Yet, these studies are predominately from countries that have already undergone deinstitutionalization. This Cochrane review lacked studies from low-income countries and countries that have limited or almost no community-based mental health care systems (Dieterich et al., 2011). For example, ACT in Japan did find positive outcomes for hospitalization, but then Japan is a country that still relies heavily on hospitals and is just beginning to develop a community mental health system of care (Ito, Oshima, Masaaki, & Kuno, 2009; Ito et al., 2011; Nishio et al., 2012). In a short period of time, since its initial experiment with J-ACT, Japan has successfully implemented ACT throughout the country.

Botha and colleagues (2010) noted that there is "a worldwide focus on assertive community interventions in an attempt to address some of the repercussions of the implementation of deinstitutionalization. Although these interventions have often been implemented under different names such as assertive outreach, intensive case management, and assertive community treatment, essentially they have had the same core characteristics" (Bortha et al., 2010). These researchers conducted a randomized controlled trial of an assertive intervention with high frequency service users in Cape Town, South Africa and found the intervention to be effective in reducing readmissions and improving psychopathology and level of functioning. Furthermore, these investigators concluded that these interventions do not necessarily have to be as comprehensive and as expensive as in the developed countries to produce such positive outcomes.

RECOVERY AND ASSERTIVE COMMUNITY TREATMENT

There has long been a concern that ACT is a coercive service, given its orientation toward adherence to treatment, specifically to prescribed medication. The current trend toward a recovery orientation emphasizes consumer choice, empowerment, and self-determination, and recognizes

client expertise, rather than the clinician as the expert. This approach to practice requires full partnership between consumers and providers in developing individualized treatment plans. Furthermore, a recovery-oriented practice must be inculcated into the "norms, attitudes, and values that emanate from the shared culture of the ACT team," whereby hope and believing in oneself are communicated to clients served (Salyers & Tsemberis, 2007). Thus concerns emerge as to the extent to which ACT is consistent with this mode of practice. Two experts in ACT did an analysis as to the extent to which ACT can incorporate a recovery orientation (Salyers & Tsemberis, 2007) and concluded that while there are some aspects of ACT that make it a challenge to achieve this goal, with proper training, supervision, and monitoring as well as the inclusion of consumers as equal team members a recovery orientation within ACT can be achieved.

Guidelines for Assertive Community Treatment/Intensive Case Management

Although ACT is currently considered by many to be an evidence-based practice (EBP), the evidence is continually evolving. Not only is fidelity of ACT important to securing positive outcomes, but the environment in which the study is conducted also impacts the outcomes produced by this intervention. What we see is that as the crucial elements of ACT migrated into standard care, and as the postinstitutionalization period began, the advantages of ACT waned in the United States and other developed deinstitutionalized countries. However, ACT with modifications for culture continues to maintain advantages in countries that are just beginning to deinstitutionalize and where there are few community-based mental health services. Investigators in these countries have also found that it is possible to modify ACT to reduce its cost, but yet be able to retain its positive effects. What emerges from these recent studies and reviews are the following guidelines for policy makers, program managers, and clinicians.

1. ACT/ICM is a model that makes good clinical sense for persons with severe mental illness who are frequent users of hospital services. It is a comprehensive high-cost service model that should be reserved for heavy users

of costly services, particularly high use of hospitals. It is not as likely to be beneficial for other persons with severe mental illnesses.

2. ACT/ICM is a flexible model that can be adapted, supplemented, and modified for emerging new populations. It is a comprehensive service and its core features are essential for good clinical care for a diversity of mental health populations beyond those with severe mental illness for whom it was originally designed. Because of its flexibility, other EBPs, such as cognitive behavioral treatment, Individual Placement and Support (IPS), as supported employment program, or Illness Management and Recovery (IMR) can be merged within an ACT program.

3. In environments where deinstitutionalization is just beginning, the advantages of ACT/ICM are maintained. However, careful modifications may be made without reducing effectiveness. These modifications need to be based on empirical evidence and clinical needs.

4. A decision to use ACT/ICM in places where there are fully developed community-based mental health systems of care and hospital use is limited cannot be made on the basis of cost-effectiveness. At this point, it cannot be determined whether this service model is cost effective (Dieterich et al., 2011). Cost effectiveness may be a greater driver in countries where hospitals are the major sites of mental health care. However, even this cannot be stated with empirical confidence.

5. In order for ACT/ICM to maintain its effectiveness, the service needs to be faithful to the critical elements of ACT, including assertive outreach, *in vivo* service delivery in a site of client's choosing, low caseloads (a ratio of 1:20), team approach, shared caseload, 24–7 access to the team, daily team meetings, team supervisor devotes at least half of his or her time to client contacts, either through supervision of team members or in contact with team clients, and no expectation of transferring clients (Dieterich et al., 2011). However, having a psychiatrist and a nurse on the team does not seem to be essential (Dieterich et al., 2011).

6. Implementation of ACT/ICM requires training in the model. Substance Abuse Mental Health Services Administration (SAMHSA) has a toolkit available for implementing ACT, which is downloadable from the SAMHSA website. Alternatively, a boxed toolkit can be obtained for the cost of mailing. The package includes DVD, CD-ROM, brochures in English and Spanish, and a Power Point presentation. A fidelity assessment measure is also available, which should be used to monitor the implementation, given that faithfulness to ACT is essential for positive outcomes.

7. Clinicians should be knowledgeable regarding the essential components of ACT/ICM even if they will not be implementing it. Clinicians need to be aware of what ACT/ICM is and what it is not.

8. Because Intensive Case Management derives from Clinical Case Management, it seems essential that intensive case managers need to be clinically trained, preferably with a master's degree in social work, counseling, or psychology. Bachelor's level social workers or psychologists may be employed if well supervised by a clinically trained individual, particularly a social worker.

CONCLUSION

ACT/ICM is a service that has been around for over 40 years. It emerged with the beginning of deinstitutionalization to meet more appropriately the needs of those with severe mental illness. It is currently considered an EBP, but changes in the environment have diminished its effectiveness in some places. It seems to maintain its strengths, however, in settings and locations that are similar to the environment in which it was originally created. ACT/ICM remains important for a particular subset of clients, but it is not intended for everyone diagnosed with a severe mental illness. Given that it is an extremely costly service, it needs to be judiciously used, where it will have the greatest benefit.

WEBSITES

ACT Center of Indiana provides up-to-date information and technical assistance and training. Their mission is to help integrate research and practice to promote best practices, such as ACT, for persons with severe mental illness. http://psych.iupui.edu/ACT/index.html

Substance Abuse and Mental Health Services Administration provides a toolkit and other information regarding ACT. http://store.samhsa.gov/product/Assertive-Community-Treatment-ACT-Evidence-Based-Practices-EBP-KIT/SMA08-4345

Assertive Community Treatment Association holds annual conferences and has done so since 1984. It also provides trainings and advocates for the dissemination of ACT. It is a nonprofit membership association comprised of mental health providers, mental health peers and their families, government officials and others committed to spreading ACT. http://www.actassociation.org/

References

Bortha, U., Koen, L, Joska, J., Hering, L., & Oosthuizen, P. (2010). Assessing the efficacy of modified assertive community-based treatment programme in a developing country. *BioMedical Central Psychiatry*, 10.73, doc.1186/471-244X.10.73.

Cuddleback, G., Morrissey, J, Cusack, K., & Meyer, P. (2009). Challenges to developing forensic Assertive Community Treatment. *American Journal of Psychiatric Rehabilitation, 12*, 225–246.

Dieterich, M., Irving, CB, Park, R., & Marshall, M. (2011). *Intensive Case Management for severe mental illness (Review)*. The Cochrane Collaboration. NY: John Wiley & Sons, Ltd.

Horvitz-Lennon, M., Reynolds, S., Wolbert, R., & Witheridge, T. (2009). The role of Assertive Community Treatment in the treatment of people with borderline personality disorder. *American Journal of Psychiatric Rehabilitation, 12*, 247–260.

Ito, J., Oshima, I., Masaaki, N., & Kuno, E. (2009). Initiative to build a community-based mental health system including assertive community treatment for people with severe mental illness in Japan. *American Journal of Psychiatric Rehabilitation, 12*, 247–261.

Ito, J., Oshima, I., Nishio, M., Sono, T., Suzuki, Y., Horiuchi, K., & Niekawa, N. (2011). The effect of assertive community treatment in Japan. *Acta Psychiatry Scandinavia, 123*, 398–401.

Marx, A., Test, M., & Stein, L. (1973). Extra hospital management of severe mental illness. *Archives of General Psychiatry, 29*, 505–511.

McGrew, J., & Danner, M. (2009). Evaluation of an Intensive Case Management Program for transition age youth and its transition to Assertive Community Treatment. *American Journal of Psychiatric Rehabilitation, 12*, 278–291.

National Association of Social Workers. (2013). *NASW Standards for Social Work Case Management*, Washington, DC: Author.

National Institute of Mental Health. (1987). *Towards a model for comprehensive community-based mental health system*. Washington, DC: Author.

Phillips, S., Burns, B., Edgar, E., Mueser, K. T., & Linkin, K. W. (2001). Moving assertive treatment into standard practice. *Psychiatric Services, 52*, 771–779.

Salyers, M., Masterton, T., Fekete, D., Picone, J. J., & Bond, G. R.(1998). Transferring clients from intensive case management: Impact on client functioning. *American Journal of Orthopsychiatry, 68*, 233–245.

Salyers, M., & Tsemberis, S. (2007). ACT and recovery: Integrating evidence-based practice and recovery orientation on assertive community treatment teams. *Community Mental Health Journal, 43*, 619–641.

Schmidt, L., Pinninti, N., Garfinkle, B., & Solomon, P. (2013). Assertive Community Treatment teams. In K. Yeager, D. Cutler, D. Svendsen, & G. Sills. (Eds.), *Modern community mental health* (pp. 293–303). Oxford: Oxford University Press.

van Vugt, M., Kroon, H., Delespaul, P., & Mulder, C. (2012). Consumer-providers in assertive community treatment programs: Associations with client outcomes. *Psychiatric Services, 63*, 477–481.

107 Case Management Practice in Psychosocial Rehabilitation

David P. Moxley

INTRODUCTION

Although case management emerged in human services as a generalist approach to serving people experiencing a multiplicity of needs and life issues, its diffusion was shaped by the search for service continuity within a diversity of human service domains. Originally, case management was seen as a means to rectify systems-level problems, such as service integration, plaguing community-based and institutional forms of human service. Brokering forms of case management, for example, sought the creation of bundles or packages of services for consumers whose needs, influenced by medical, physical, and psychosocial issues and characterized by complexity and long duration, required different types of care and support. Brokering, coordination, and other systems approaches to case management proved to be limited because they often were too general in their focus, failed to specify appropriate recipient populations or intended beneficiaries in rigorous ways, did not specify strategy and methods, and failed to align organizational resources with the role requirements that case management demanded. In addition, given overwhelming case loads, case management personnel found it difficult to personalize the support of the people they served.

Insight into case management effectiveness, largely derived from systematic evaluation of various approaches, indicated that good case management incorporated a specific purpose and set of goals, made explicit the target population that could benefit, and specified relevant methods based on its purpose and the issues potential recipients faced in their daily lives. In addition, good case management aligns requisite resources case managers need to effect meaningful change in the lives of recipients with purpose and aims of service.

DISTINCTIVENESS OF PERSON-CENTERED CASE MANAGEMENT IN PSYCHOSOCIAL REHABILITATION

Recovery Focus

Case management in psychosocial rehabilitation recognizes the importance of such context and input factors consonant with good service delivery. The distinctiveness of case management is found in the person-centered nature of the field of psychosocial rehabilitation in which the management of illness has yielded increasingly to the facilitation of recovery. The concept of recovery envisions recipients becoming more engaged in the achievement of outcomes that bring them life satisfaction while learning to actively manage the psychological, behavioral, physical, and social consequences of psychiatric disability (Anthony, Cohen, Farkas, & Gagne, 2002). Good case management in psychosocial rehabilitation recognizes how psychiatric disability creates numerous barriers to effective functioning, and it also recognizes that recipients likely value life outcomes common to all human beings, including good health, employment, education, reliable and adequate income, and decent housing (Moxley, 2011).

The focus of case management in psychosocial rehabilitation on the fulfillment of such common human needs infuses this approach with practicality combined with recognition of how serious mental illness can frustrate recipients' pursuit and realization of these aims. Case management in psychosocial rehabilitation emphasizes the

(1) fulfillment of positive human needs (the psychosocial aspect) manifested in helping people plan actively for a lifestyle and situation they find satisfying, and (2) modification of environments, particularly barriers that frustrate the pursuit and realization of life satisfaction (the rehabilitative aspect; Anthony et al., 2002).

Importance of Person-Centered Practice

Person-centered practice is salient when case managers help recipients identify and frame a central outcome with the realization of what they will find satisfying. The ensuing process of planning helps recipients understand their own process of recovery, identify barriers to the achievement of the outcomes they value, and formulate strategies to overcome barriers through personal and environmental change. Joining these two aspects within case management literally integrates the psychosocial and the rehabilitative practice approaches. Such joining moves case management in psychosocial rehabilitation away from an exclusive preoccupation with illness and functioning to incorporate human aspirations and positive psychology as important advanced organizers of practice.

One can further frame person-centered practice through the specification of three elements. Recognition of what the author refers to as "in spite of" ensures that case management personnel help people identify the barriers to life satisfaction they face while those barriers are framed as factors that the person with serious mental illness and the case manager can overcome, particularly through advocacy (Moxley & Washington, 2009). Identifying and enacting factors of support (what the author refers to as "through") that counteract barriers people with serious mental illness experience increases the chances of overcoming those barriers and achieving what they wish for themselves. And, by specifying "what I want to achieve" the person with serious mental illness can focus on what they seek for themselves. This element constitutes the aim of life satisfaction.

Thus, person-centered practice in psychosocial rehabilitation involves a process of change: "In spite of X, through S, I can bring about Y." X stands for barriers, S involves support, and Y involves the desired object or aim the fulfillment of which contributes to a person's realization of a satisfying life. In psychosocial rehabilitation, "S" or support involves social support through social networks (Tracy, 2009), team support and

support from rehabilitation personnel and peers, and community assets. It can involve organizational arrangements and the creation of supportive communities and group life (Sandfort, 2010). In other words, person-centered practice is ecological in the full meaning of that word. Figure 107.1 captures the sequence of person-centered case management and its various components.

PRECURSORS

The evolution of case management in psychiatric rehabilitation parallels the growth and development of case management in the broader field of human services. One form of case management emerged within the community mental health movement as a means of integrating a range of outpatient-based services, but this approach placed more emphasis on getting people services than on achieving outcomes that recipients found practical and desirable, including a decent standard of living and a good quality of life. Although coordination of services was seen as important within this approach, management of medication and symptoms of those individuals labeled as seriously mentally ill was a central aspect that makes this approach within the community mental health movement an extension of community psychiatric care.

The failure of the community mental health movement to address fully the demands of deinstitutionalization in the 1970s and the needs of those individuals coping with the most serious and complex forms of psychiatric disability ushered in another form of case management. Influenced by the service integration movement of the 1970s and early 1980s, case management was seen as a way of achieving within local service systems single points of entry, unified needs assessments, and unified client pathways—tactics thought useful to the movement of people through complex community-based systems of care. This form of case management, characteristic of community support systems for people with serious mental illness, sought the integration of medical, social, psychosocial, and behavioral domains.

Unlike the community mental health model, this approach extended its reach beyond services offered by various human service agencies to incorporate resources embedded informally in social and community networks charging case management with the challenging responsibility of incorporating all forms of community support into assessment, planning, and action. The

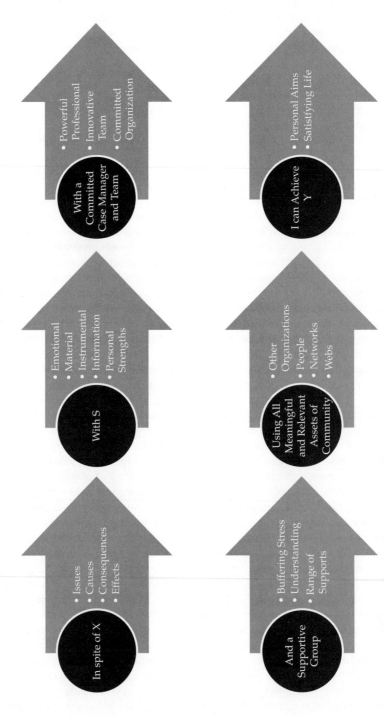

Figure 107.1 Person-centered practice in case management and psychosocial rehabilitation.

National Institute of Mental Health Community Support Model (NIMH, 1980) gave case management a central and expansive role in systems of care without augmenting professional standing of case managers, the resources they had available to serve a population facing a broad spectrum of serious issues and unmet needs, or the infrastructure to assist individuals adequately. Through outreach, home-based services, and the provision of community-based follow-along services case management within community support systems was intended to extend practical assistance into the daily lives of people experiencing deinstitutionalization. Integration was seen as a principal virtue of this kind of case management, manifesting unification of direct assistance, resources to support daily living, skill development opportunities, and social support.

However, the management of the actual illness and related disability found in symptoms and deficits in self-care served as the principal aim: case management sought to respond to the immediate community living needs of people and combat recidivism, particularly the revolving-door syndrome in which recipients oscillated between periodic short-term hospital stays and residence in community situations. Nonetheless, as a result of the community support model, case management today is an essential component of local systems that now integrate medical care, social services, mutual support among consumers, rights protection and advocacy, rehabilitation, housing, and employment support.

As deinstitutionalization progressed in the ensuing decade of the 1980s, other forms of case management took root, including the team-based approaches found in assertive community treatment. An increasing number of state and local service systems adopted this approach, which emerged in the 1970s as a significant innovation in care, and clinical case management, a form of practice that reasserted the importance of a diagnostic perspective, psychotherapeutic interactions, and clinical management in service planning and delivery omitted from community-based forms of case management.

With all of these variants of case management, practitioners tended to view recipients as impaired individuals who needed to accept the limitations their illnesses created. Although case managers encouraged the involvement of recipients in joint planning of services and supports, the principal focus of care was on recipient self-acceptance of illness and management of both the primary aspects of the illness and their psychological, behavioral, and medical consequences, placing case management within a paradigm in which medical response was dominant. Case management reflects this paradigm when it focuses mainly on medication and symptom management or relief, a form of service that persists today. The variant of case management found in assertive community treatment offers intensive hands-on services to foster successful community living among people who would otherwise engage in high levels of utilization of potentially expensive care whether inpatient, restrictive, or crisis-oriented. However, using such a variant team-based management of the trajectory and consequences of the illness prioritizes medical aspects of psychiatric disability. As one examines the expanse of case management that emerged over a period of almost 50 years, case management sought to manage the person rather than manage the situations in which those persons found themselves, ones mostly deficient in nurturing resources. The instrumental nature of case management emphasized person management rather than a strategy of person-centered support.

CASE MANAGEMENT IN PSYCHOSOCIAL REHABILITATION

Case management in psychosocial rehabilitation legitimates the medical trajectory and consequences of serious mental illness, but this kind of management seeks to identify, organize, and implement broad-based supports that address and fulfill not only people's immediate and concrete needs for community living but also their needs for growth and development, imbuing it with the qualities of positive psychology, including humanization, hope, and optimism. Case management in psychosocial rehabilitation sought to offset the frequent dehumanization of people coping with psychiatric disabilities. Conversely, it sought to humanize the rehabilitation experience by forming strong partnerships between service providers and recipients, collaborating to advance the quality of life of people coping with the causes and consequences of psychiatric disability. Discerning the strengths of individuals, both internal and external, is a central quality of case management in psychosocial rehabilitation (Rapp & Gocha, 2006).

Rehabilitation case management emerged during a time of rehabilitation pessimism in community psychiatry, and was relatively unrecognized during the 1960s through the early 1980s, only to emerge later as a best practice. Case management based on psychosocial rehabilitation principles and practices introduced a new teleology into the care of those with serious mental illness, one asserting hope and optimism for the progress they could realize. Previous generations of case management required professionals to specify what a person needed and should receive through the process of service brokering, an approach that proved largely ineffective. Case management based on psychosocial rehabilitation frames human needs from the perspective of the person, not the illness. It asks fundamental questions like, "What direction do people coping with psychiatric disability want to take in their lives? What outcomes do they value? What opportunities do they want and, as a consequence, what supports do they see as important in order to take advantage of the opportunities they value? What barriers do they feel that they must overcome to achieve what they want for themselves? How satisfied are they with the supports they obtain and what those supports produce in terms of practical changes in daily life?"

Such questions are not alien to social work given the profession's commitment to self-determination and empowerment as central values of practice. The questions themselves underscore the importance of relationship and its role in helping recipient and practitioner form an alliance useful in the achievement of recipient identified aims (Brun & Rapp, 2001). The questions themselves suggest an assumption that case management is a catalyst for helping recipients find their voice and articulate their desires in the face of the tremendous personal demands and challenges of serious mental illness. The questions link directly to humanistic and phenomenological dimensions of social work: while a person is struggling with mental illness, the struggle must be understood as an expression of someone traveling a unique and distinctive life journey. The transformational impact of serious mental illness in which a person will not likely return to their premorbid state needs to be understood in terms of how the experience of mental illness can influence life direction and the individual's goal set.

Thus, the correspondence between social work values and case management in psychosocial rehabilitation is strong, as both are founded in a respect for individualization and personalization of the process of care and support and operationalized through a process of humanization. The idea of humanization indicates that the person coping with serious mental illness is still a person who possesses interests, desires, and aims. Case management in psychosocial rehabilitation, therefore, amplifies the importance of these strivings, and the case manager's recognition of the potential for a person's growth and development is a central idea of practice.

ADVANCED ORGANIZERS

Producing the distinctiveness of case management in psychosocial rehabilitation are those advanced concepts that help organize the manner in which practice is undertaken in the field of psychiatric disability. Particularly important are those advanced organizers involving consumer-centered values, narrative and the lived experience, and positive psychology.

Consumer-centered Values

The idea that people coping with psychiatric disabilities should influence (if not direct) the rehabilitation process as much as possible was introduced in the 1970s and 1980s by a growing consumer and ex-patient movement (Moxley & Mowbray, 1997). Psychosocial rehabilitation was responsive to these consumer-based values by introducing practices legitimating consumer–professional collaboration, self-help alternatives, and mutual support opportunities (Mowbray, Moxley, Jasper, & Howell, 1997). Influenced by an emergent consumer movement, psychosocial rehabilitation sought to make the person (as opposed to the illness) central, not ancillary, within the process of service and support, particularly in making key decisions about care.

Rather than requiring the person coping with serious mental illness to be a passive recipient of service, this form of case management required the individual to be an active participant with ownership over the process and outcomes of rehabilitation. Case management in psychosocial rehabilitation values a recipient's assertiveness and seeks to empower them as decision makers even in the face of the pervasive challenges serious mental illness can create in judgment and self-agency.

The active involvement of recipients is a legacy of psychosocial rehabilitation and within the process of case management involvement itself is beneficial because recipients make informed choices about their present and future circumstances using their own values and desires. The act of framing life goals based on humanism, optimism, and hope for the future using practical solution-focused practice makes this form of case management distinctive given psychosocial rehabilitation's emphasis on person-centered rather than service-centered aims.

Over the course of two decades, the 1970s, and the 1980s, psychosocial rehabilitation expanded to incorporate a range of supports, including professional services, peer support, and consumer-operated rehabilitation and community living options. The 1990s witnessed the emergence of the support model as a best practice (Carling, 1995), a model prioritizing concrete assistance to help people choose and achieve practical outcomes in areas like housing, employment, education, recreation, and social involvement. A recipient's subjective sense of quality of life as a principal outcome of case management became increasingly salient within psychosocial rehabilitation. To facilitate this outcome, the recovery-based practitioner in psychosocial rehabilitation makes use of environmental specificity in which well-desired supports are positioned to strengthen functioning of a person who learns to perform a specific role in a given environment, such as someone who is learning a job in an employment setting or performing as a student in an educational setting.

Narrative and the Lived Experience

Given the importance of person-centered values within psychosocial rehabilitation, narrative forms of practice figure into case management in important ways. Diagnostic interviewing focuses on symptom identification and clarification and situational considerations of how a person functions given the influence of the label assigned by a psychiatric professional. A narrative approach, however, involves deep listening and the amplification of the person's story with the professional discerning during the story telling process those experiences, situations, strengths, assets, and challenges identified as important (Washington & Moxley, 2008, 2009a). The narrative itself, replete with central themes that can come to define the direction and strategy of case management, gives the ensuing management plan a personalized profile. People coping with psychiatric disability, for example, whose onset of mental illness was in late adolescence or young adulthood may come to amplify how their educational and vocational aims were frustrated or derailed. "Getting back on track" and "investigating educational or vocational training opportunities" may become salient in the storytelling that engages the psychosocial rehabilitation professional and recipient in discerning direction.

A traditional practitioner, one more tied to the medical paradigm, may think (or even say), "this direction isn't possible. He needs to back off and lower his expectations." A psychosocial rehabilitation professional will likely continue the dialogue, finally reaching a point where a miracle question is asked: "What will go well with your health to help you get back on track with the education you seek?" The achievement of health can become an enabling outcome of a higher level outcome—the pursuit of education. In this example, narrative drives the process and is legitimate within the person-centered paradigm of psychosocial rehabilitation.

Four types of narrative can emerge during the dialogue between recipient and practitioner (Moxley, Washington, & Crystal, 2013). Those types can reveal a person's vulnerability and resilience (Moxley, Washington, & Feen-Calligan, 2012). One is the "narrative of plight," in which the recipient frames what isn't and what hasn't gone well over the life course. The narrative of plight may express itself as a form of grieving or mourning—opportunities lost, frustration, and setbacks may be prominent (Washington & Moxley, 2009b). Another type is the "narrative of efficacy," in which the recipient reveals strengths, assets, enabling conditions, and opportunities, particularly ones that are on the horizon. These two narratives may conflict or even contradict one another and they may compete for ascendance within the dialogue. However, careful listening (by both practitioner and recipient) can reveal a structure within which action can be taken, consistent with the rehabilitation framework. Barriers are appreciated in relationship to an outcome that the person seeks, and strengths and assets (including other people who can assist) are seen as enabling conditions of a desired outcome. Within the narrative of efficacy, strengths can be discerned, and even within the narrative of plight, both practitioner and recipient can appreciate strengths (e.g., tolerating setbacks, coping with stress, getting back on track).

A third form of narrative involves the story of hope each person may offer. Hope is not elusive even when people find themselves in despair. A person may communicate what they want for themselves, what they consider important in terms of life aims. Still, a fourth type of narrative involves the recovery, one in which people communicate their efforts to "get well." Using appreciative inquiry, case management personnel can ask questions about what has gone well in the past to encourage recovery as the professional and consumer work together to craft such supportive conditions.

A narrative strategy highlights the humanistic posture of psychosocial rehabilitation found in the personalization of the recipient, who is seen as striving, purposeful, and goal-oriented. The narrative reflects the lived experience: "Here is how I have lived with serious mental illness. Here is how I have changed, suffered, triumphed, endured and my experience has made me stronger as an individual." The appreciation of the recipient's lived experience can certainly reframe how assessment is undertaken, emphasizing phenomenology in service to the creation of an idiographic profile of the individual's assets, strengths, capacities, and abilities. Successful case management can help recipients produce new narratives, ones populated with new opportunities, new capacities (e.g., good health), valued achievements, and the realization of desired outcomes. The new narrative may hold a special position for the case management professional whose own narrative of efficacy (found in helping the recipient achieve valued outcomes) is intertwined with the recipient's given the collaborative features of case management in psychosocial rehabilitation.

Positive Psychology

Increasingly psychology, social sciences, and the health and human services are balancing concepts of deficit, disease, disorder, and impairment with those that are positive in their orientation to human development (Lopez, Snyder, & Rasmussen, 2003). Positive psychology is emphasizing research and findings on how concepts and qualities such as faith, spirituality, and social capital, or virtues like endurance and courage, optimism, well-being, and hope ascend within helping frameworks (Washington, Moxley, Garriott, & Crystal-Weinberger, 2009). These ideas and the research they have fostered suggest that people confronting life-threatening and life-challenging situations may exhibit signs of stress and strain, but they can also exhibit virtues that strengthen their resolve and ability to cope (Wright & Lopez, 2002). A person who experiences numerous setbacks in health may muster cognitive and

emotional strategies, helping them reframe the possibility of success in a given situation by modifying adaptive approaches and augmenting coping. Recognizing that people experiencing adversity bring to bear hardiness and resilience is central to positive psychology.

Such a positive psychology is well rooted in psychosocial rehabilitation, so case management recognizes that constructs like hope (anticipation of a positive future) and optimism (an immediate attitude that frames current circumstances in a positive way) figure into the process of support in important ways. The case management plan can play off of a person's resolve to pursue opportunities (such as valuing education and the work ethic) they find fulfilling.

"Okay," says the case manager, "you have been ill, but you are very hopeful. What drives your hope?"

"I just know that I can handle college if I can change my living situation and wade into school slowly," the client replies.

"You sound so hopeful. What will help you get ready?"

"Maybe I can visit a community college and talk with counselors. Can you come with me?" the recipient asks.

"Certainly, let's schedule it."

This brief dialogue shows how hope and optimism can link to action. This recipient is getting ready for a new undertaking, and the social worker senses this immediately. Acting on this readiness moves the recipient a little closer to the valued outcome. The case manager as ally is part of the system of optimism and hope that has formed, indicative of the collaborative framework of psychosocial rehabilitation.

The Person-centered Paradigm

The paradigm formed by the intersection of the advanced organizers of consumer-centered values, narrative, and positive psychology produces an interesting model of case management practice in psychosocial rehabilitation. The model emerging from this paradigm is as follows.

VALUE ASSIGNED TO THE RECIPIENT'S PERSPECTIVE → NARRATIVE AS A TOOL TO HIGHLIGHT DESIRE AND DIRECTION → NARRATIVE TO IDENTIFY STRENGTHS/ ASSETS, ISSUES, BARRIERS → PERSON-CENTERED PLAN → COLLABORATIVE ACTION TO ACHIEVE PERSON-CENTERED OUTCOMES → EMERGENCE OF A NEW NARRATIVE

THE EMERGENCE OF PERSON-CENTERED RECOVERY-BASED CASE MANAGEMENT

As psychosocial rehabilitation continued to evolve during the decade of the 1990s, Anthony (1994) suggested that recovery could become the principal aim of the field, a perspective that has increasingly expanded in scope and research (Davidson, Harding, & Spaniol, 2005). The idea that recovery was possible infused a new idealism about the possibilities for the rehabilitative support of people coping with serious mental illness. Recovery-based psychosocial rehabilitation establishes a framework for the practice of a new form of case management, one founded on the best consumer-centered traditions of the field.

Recovery within the context of psychosocial rehabilitation does not mean the person's return to a premorbid state, a view more suggestive of a medical than a rehabilitation model. Many people coping with psychiatric disability would say that their experience was so distressful and challenging that a "return" to the lives they led prior to the onset of their illnesses was not possible or even desirable. Many people who label themselves as "survivors" (to emphasize that they literally outlived horrific experiences and mistreatment) are mindful of how their identities were altered substantially by their negative personal experiences, ones induced by inappropriate or iatrogenic service responses and stigmatizing social reaction.

Recovery requires people coping with serious mental illness to contemplate and answer two questions that appear on face contradictory: How do I live with the illness and its consequences? How do I live without the illness? In answering the first question, people must address how they will respond to stress, symptoms, grief and loss, anger about injustice and deprivation, and the management of morale and positive outlook. In answering the second question, people will address setting a life direction, identifying new roles they want for themselves, obtaining enabling resources, and achieving a lifestyle that brings personal satisfaction and fulfillment.

Psychiatric disability can encapsulate individuals in networks that reinforce their identities as ill individuals and leave few (if any) other options for them to develop identities based on other conceptions of self. Helping people discover how to manage their situations while they learn how to emerge out of the illness, leave it behind, and reformulate their identities based on new

lifestyle choices they find satisfying together form the essence of recovery. Although practitioners may think of recovery as a discrete outcome, for many survivors, it is a process requiring a personal practice of a "lived experience" involving health promotion and the pursuit of personal meaning. A person's practice of recovery can demand vigilant self-management, self-help, and mutual support. It can require sanctuary, as well as opportunities to witness mistreatment or inadequate support and to provide support to others (Paynter, 1997).

Recovery can involve the creation of new identities based on personal transformation in which people overcome the psychological, behavioral, biological, and social consequences of illness and disability (Moxley & Washington, 2001). Social workers practicing recovery-based case management in psychosocial rehabilitation are mindful of the need to help clients focus on what recovery means for them. These practitioners refrain from defining recovery for recipients because they understand that people must come to learn what recovery means in the context of their own lived experience.

The personal process of defining recovery, exploring the outcomes and consequences of recovery, and practicing recovery can help individuals make decisions about how to reduce the centrality of serious mental illness in their lives. Overcoming the illness through the achievement of new roles and lifestyles that bring personal satisfaction, even though a person may need to learn to live with particular symptoms, gives recovery-based case management a transcendent quality (Washington & Moxley, 2001). To paraphrase Victor Frankl (2000), people learn to transcend their situations when they understand the meaning and direction their lives can take.

ASSUMPTIONS AND PROCESS OF PERSON-CENTERED RECOVERY-BASED CASE MANAGEMENT

Principal implications of a recovery orientation to case management are as follows.

1. Recovery-based case management values a nondirective approach in which practitioners collaborate with recipients to discover what recovery means to them and actualize supports that contribute to their realization of recovery.

2. The practice of recovery helps people dealing with serious mental illness gain control over each aspect of the case management service process. A basic assumption of this form of case management is that individuals coping with psychiatric disability often lose control of the service process because professionals come to dominate their lives as principal decision makers. Most people coping with serious mental illness use this control responsibly and typically select outcomes they find most personally relevant and pragmatic given their aims and desires. When freely chosen and realized by the client, these outcomes can produce personal fulfillment that, in turn, contributes to satisfaction as the person defines it. In choosing what outcomes to pursue, people are selecting how to invest their creative energies, giving recovery-based practice an existential flavor.

3. To establish a rehabilitation direction, a case manager who engages in a recovery assessment may work with an individual to answer an important existential question, one that the social, psychological, and biological experience of mental illness can undermine: "How will I direct my creative energies to find fulfillment in my life?" A recovery-based case management plan can help individuals identify the supports, experiences, and opportunities that will help them illuminate answers to this important question. Recovery-based case management will also help people address another important question: "What help do I need to develop and direct my creative energies?"

4. These two existential questions were never central to other forms of case management because these other forms assumed that the illness would be chronic and pervasive, and as a consequence, people needed only adequate or appropriate medical and social services. For recovery-based case managers, however, helping people find answers to these questions is crucial to the growth and development of recipients.

5. Recovery-based case management assumes an active consumer—that people coping with serious mental illness can and will reflect on what they experience, evaluate their experience, and make decisions to change the process, products, and outcomes of rehabilitative support. So recovery-based case managers collaborate with the people they serve as active decision makers who want to stake out and achieve directions in which they find substantive importance.

6. Recovery-based case managers assume communities are repositories of a great number and variety of supports. In collaboration with the people they serve, case managers discover the ones that recipients find most relevant to the fulfillment of their aims.

CONCLUSION: AN EYE TO THE FUTURE

Shaping the case management in psychosocial rehabilitation will be forces emanating from how the field frames the paradigm of serious mental illness, organizes supports, and responds to the politics of mental health coverage within health care. The achievement of parity between health and mental health services will likely bring the care of serious mental illness into primary health care centers and clinics in which family practice physicians and other generalists are increasingly involved in medical management. New pharmaceutical and diagnostic approaches will likely equip such practitioners with more powerful tools for the management of the primary symptoms of serious mental illness.

Networks of care linking medical clinics to psychosocial rehabilitation options will place physicians in central referral roles and innovations in medical education will make these practitioners more mindful of the benefits inherent in combining medical care, social services, and psychosocial rehabilitation options. Parity itself will legitimate the provision of case management services that are outcome-focused and health-oriented in their aims. The further integration of serious mental illness into a neomedical model, one that emphasizes community-based care, health promotion, prevention, and cost-effectiveness (achieved by reducing relapse) can further legitimate a recovery framework within medical care and psychosocial rehabilitation, particularly as positive psychology becomes more dominant within models of care.

Enhanced medical care can assist recipients in considering the next steps in their wellness including a consideration of how best to advance their life satisfaction and quality of life. Feeling better physically and mentally can help recipients invest new found energy in planning their living situations and investing in their realization of hopes and dreams. Here psychosocial rehabilitation can play an important role. Its distinctiveness and expertise lie in helping recipients move forward through the articulation of plans that recipients find relevant and meaningful. Thus, the future of case management in psychosocial rehabilitation is synergetic within a framework of positive psychology and strengths-based practice. Though it can stand alone, it is probably most potent when combined with other care approaches that incorporate a similar worldview.

WEBSITES

Boston University Center for Psychiatric Rehabilitation. http://www.bu.edu/cpr.
Dartmouth PRC. http://prc.dartmouth.edu/
New York Center for Rehabilitation and Recovery. http://www.coalitionny.org/ccrr.
National Mental Health Consumers Self Help Clearing House. http://www.mhselfhelp.org.
National Alliance for the Mentally Ill. http://www.nami.org.

References

Anthony, W. A. (1994). Recovery from mental illness: The guiding vision of the mental health system in the 1990s. In *An introduction to psychiatric rehabilitation* (pp. 556–567). Columbia, MD: International Association of Psychosocial Rehabilitation Services.

Anthony, W., Cohen, M., Farkas, M., & Gagne, C. (2002). *Psychiatric rehabilitation* (2nd ed.) Boston, MA: Boston University Center for Psychiatric Rehabilitation.

Brun, C., & Rapp, R. (2001). Strengths-based case management: Individuals' perspectives on strengths and the case manager relationship. *Social Work, 46*(3), 278.

Carling, P. J. (1995). *Return to community: Building support systems for people with psychiatric disabilities.* New York, NY: Guilford.

Davidson, L., Harding, C., & Spaniol, L. (2005). *Recovery from severe mental illnesses: Research evidence and implications for practice* (Vol. 1). Boston, MA: Boston University Center for Psychiatric Rehabilitation.

Frankl, V. (2000). *Man's search for meaning.* New York, NY: Beacon.

Lopez, S., Snyder, C., & Rasmussen, H. (2003). Striking a vital balance: Developing a complementary focus on human weakness and strength through positive psychological assessment. In S. J. Lopez & C. R. Snyder (Eds.), *Positive psychological assessment: A handbook of models and measures* (pp. 3–20). Washington, DC: American Psychological Association.

Mowbray, C., Moxley, D., Jasper, C., & Howell, L. (Eds.). (1997). *Consumers as providers in psychiatric rehabilitation.* Columbia, MD: International Association of Psychosocial Rehabilitation Services.

Moxley, D. (2011). Case management. In D. R. Maki & V. Tarvydas (Eds.), *The professional practice of rehabilitation counseling* (pp. 269–296). New York, NY: Springer.

Moxley, D., & Mowbray, C. (1997). Consumers as providers: Forces and factors legitimizing role innovation in psychiatric rehabilitation. In C. Mowbray, D. Moxley, C. Jasper, & L. Howell (Eds.), *Consumers as providers in psychiatric rehabilitation* (pp. 155–164). Columbia, MD: International Association of Psychosocial Rehabilitation Services.

Moxley, D., & Washington, O. (2001). Strengths-based recovery practice in chemical dependency: A transpersonal perspective. *Families in Society, 82,* 251–262.

Moxley, D., & Washington, O. (2009). The role of advocacy assessment and action in resolving health compromising stress in the lives of older African American homeless women. In L. Napier & Paul Waters (Eds.), *Social work and global health inequalities: policy and practice developments* (pp. 150–162). London, UK: Policy Press.

Moxley, D., Washington, O., & Crystal, J. (2013). The relevance of four narrative forms for understanding vulnerability among homeless older African American women [Paper submitted for publication].

Moxley, D., Washington, O., & Feen-Calligan, H. (2012). Narrative insight into risk, vulnerability, and resilience among older homeless African American women. *The Arts in Psychotherapy, 39*(1), 471–478.

National Institute of Mental Health. (1980). *Guidelines for community support programs.* Washington, DC: Author.

Paynter, N. (1997). Shining reflections: Alive, growing, and building recovery. In C. Mowbray, D. Moxley, C. Jasper, & L. Howell (Eds.), *Consumers as providers in psychiatric rehabilitation* (pp. 2–34). Columbia, MD: International Association of Psychosocial Rehabilitation Services.

Rapp, C. A., & Gocha, R. J. (2006). *The strengths model: Case management with people with psychiatric disabilities.* New York, NY: Oxford University Press.

Sandfort, J. (2010). Human service organizational technology: Improving understanding and advancing research. In Y. Hasenfeld (Ed.), *Human services as complex organizations* (2nd ed.) (pp. 269–290). Thousand Oaks, CA: Sage.

Tracy, E. M. (2009). Working with and strengthening social networks. In A. R. Roberts (Ed.), *Social workers' desk reference* (2nd ed.) (pp. 710–714). New York, NY: Oxford University Press.

Washington, O. G. M., & Moxley, D. P. (2001). The use of prayer in group work with African American women recovering from chemical dependency. *Families in Society, 82*, 49–59.

Washington, O. G. M., & Moxley, D. P. (2008). Telling my story: From narrative to exhibit in illuminating the lived experience of homelessness among older African American women. *Journal of Health Psychology, 13*(2), 154–165.

Washington, O., & Moxley, D. (2009a). Development of a multimodal assessment framework for helping older African American women transition out of homelessness. *Smith College Studies in Social Work, 79*(2), 103–124.

Washington, O., & Moxley, D. (2009b). "I Have Three Strikes against Me": Narratives of plight and efficacy among older African American homeless women and their implications for engaged inquiry. In S. Evans (Ed.), *African Americans and community engagement in higher education.* New York: State University of New York Press.

Washington, O., Moxley, D., Garriott, L., & Crystal-Weinberger, J. (2009). Five dimensions of faith and spirituality of older African American women transitioning out of homelessness. *Journal of Religion and Health, 48*(4), 431–444.

Wright, B., & Lopez, S. (2002). Widening the diagnostic focus: A case for including human strengths and environmental resources. In C. R. Snyder & S. J. Lopez (Eds.), *Handbook of positive psychology* (pp. 26–44). New York, NY: Oxford University Press.

108   Case Management and Child Welfare

Jannah H. Mather & Grafton H. Hull, Jr.

Case management, a process by which complex situations are managed by social workers, plays a major role in child welfare services today. Case management, as noted by Woodside and McClam (2013) is a creative and collaborative process, involving skills in assessment, communication, coordination, consulting, teaching, and modeling, resulting in positive outcomes for the agency (Commission for Case Manager Certification, 2009). Glissen and Green (2006a, b) estimate that some 3 million children receive child welfare and juvenile justice case management each year. In the field of social work, case management has grown from a vague definition regarding the organization of services for clients to the development of various models of practice incorporating specific theories, skills, and values. These elements are, in turn, dependent on the situation or field of practice in which social workers find themselves.

Rothman (1992) notes that case management in the child welfare service area began as a response to increased disorganization of families, growing numbers of divorces, and mounting abuse situations. These conditions created an environment in which children and families were in need of increased aid, and few programs could organize their services around these growing numbers. Case management was designed "to counter long-term problematic client conditions, and a community service system that was uncoordinated, ever shifting, and increasingly restrictive" (Rothman, 1992, p. 3). The consequences of these conditions produced a new service concept, one that Rothman says had two central functions: (1) providing individualized counseling services, and (2) linking clients to services and supports in both the formal and informal contexts of the client's life.

In many ways, case management as just defined offered a generalized approach to intervening with clients in child welfare situations. In this definition, the child welfare case manager was expected to work with both the individual and relevant environmental conditions. The belief that case management could produce different results by structuring these processes in a standardized manner had considerable impact on child welfare programs. Child welfare workers could relate intimately with the concept of poorly operating community service systems as described by Rothman (1992). However, the question in case management that was most important to child welfare workers was: How effective are case management models for chronic and complex client systems? The evidence to date has been mixed. On the one hand, Burns, Phillips, and Wagner (2004) found that case managers frequently failed to recognize serious mental health needs of the children they served. Too often, children ended up in out-of-home placements that might have been prevented had case managers adequately screened children for mental health concerns. Tregeagle and Mason (2008) found that "case management did not result in relationships which consistently informed the service" (p. 391). Additionally, Dauber et al. (2012) found that intensive case management had minimal benefits. On the other hand, Glissen and Green (2006a) studied the experience of over 1,200 children needing specialized case management services. Their findings suggest that when the mental health needs of children are carefully assessed by their case managers and those services are provided, a substantial reduction in out-of-home placements occurs. Another study by the same authors noted that the organizational culture in which the case managers practiced had a major impact on how well these individuals performed their jobs (Glissen & Green, 2006b). Blair and Taylor (2006) found that case management services were crucial to and wanted by kinship caregivers of children placed outside the home. Blair et al. (2009) also found, "Most caregivers and their families possess significant strengths that can be used in a strengths-based approach to case management" (p. 431). Johnson and Wagner (2005) found that providing case managers with a structured decision-making tool significantly increased reunification and permanency planning of children in Michigan's foster care system.

Child welfare workers see case management as a strong response to the horrendous issues surrounding foster care. As an essential component of permanency planning, case managers perform tasks and functions involved in negotiating and coordinating services, referring clients to agencies, using community services, managing visitations, and assisting families and children with the development of support services (Pecora, Whittaker, Maluccio, Barth, & Plotnick, 1992). As part of permanency planning, as well as other specific areas of service for families and children, case management is an integral component of child welfare practice. Specialized models of case management in child welfare have developed primarily as a response to families who are facing multiple challenges and consequently using many different, uncoordinated services, accompanied by a lack of follow-up regarding service outcomes. The focus of these initial models produced a planned method for following a family and child through the maze of services offered and accounting for the resources used. As the role of case management has become more important in child welfare, it has highlighted the need for a knowledge and skill base that reflects the specialized components of child welfare.

KNOWLEDGE AND SKILLS NEEDED IN CHILD WELFARE CASE MANAGEMENT

To produce models of case management practice appropriate to child welfare, delineation of a knowledge and skill base related to child welfare has been offered by several different authors (Mather, Lager, & Harris, 2007; Sallee & LeVine, 1999). The following areas have been seen as consistently relevant.

1. *Human development*. Knowledge of children, adults, families, agencies, and institutions. An ability to understand and apply interviewing skills, data collection assessment, planning, intervention, referral, evaluation, termination, and recording. Knowledge of and competence to work with culturally diverse children and families through a value system that is open and reflective.
2. *Child welfare practice*. Basic knowledge of the mission of child welfare services and child welfare policies and practices. Understanding of outcome data regarding the application of agency, state, and federal policies on families and children.

3. *Agency functioning.* Knowledge of administrative and structural issues affecting the operation of the child welfare agency and the employees who work within that agency. Understanding how agency functioning affects the family and child and the infrastructure needed to create change.

4. *Interdisciplinary understanding and collaboration with professionals from multiple disciplines.* Understanding and recognition of the importance of multiple disciplines in the delivery of services. Knowledge of how to access services from a diversity of disciplines to ensure positive case outcomes. Knowledge of medical and mental health issues, educational aspects, and judicial rules and laws. The understanding of how to integrate multiple disciplines into the case management process for the child and family.

5. *Holistic practice perspective.* Recognizing that the services for the client must be addressed through a holistic view of the person within his/her family. This perspective takes into account the health, mental health, educational, and spiritual aspects of the person within the environment. Much of the knowledge and skill needed in case management is incorporated into the basic education of all social workers. These include social work roles, purposes, values, and ethics. Mather et al. (2007) note that case managers in child welfare must:

   • Engage all systems and individuals to be involved in a mutual and positive manner
   • Quickly establish the roles of the various systems within case management
   • Work together toward a mutual treatment plan
   • Contract for responsibilities in the process and case
   • Meet on a regular basis to review goals and outcomes
   • Agree with all systems involved on time for termination
   • Always evaluate the case management process as well as the outcome.

Vourlekis and Greene (1992) added to the knowledge base in case management and produced a definition of processes for the social worker. They noted the following characteristics:

1. A trusting and enabling worker–client relationship

2. A focus on understanding the person in the environment

3. Provision of a continuum of care to clients with complex multiple problems

4. Intervening to ameliorate the emotional problems causing a loss of function

5. Using the skills of brokering and advocacy in service delivery

6. Targeting clients who require a range of community-based and long-term services

7. Providing services in the least restrictive environment

8. Using assessment of the client's functioning capacity and support network

9. Affirming the social work values of self-determination, dignity, and mutual responsibility.

Though these perspectives provide an understanding of the knowledge and skill base, as well as the processes that a child welfare worker must employ to engage in effective case management practice, the issue of the underlying goals of system management of the case cannot be overlooked.

DIVERGENT PARADIGMS

1. Different underlying goals in case management appear to be related to the field of practice in which they are used (child welfare, disabilities, aging, etc.). The knowledge (or lack thereof) of these goals often drives the outcome of the case management model. These goals can be part of one or both of two demanding paradigms from which case management developed. Moxley (1996) notes that case management can be either systems-driven or consumer-driven (pp. 15–20). *Systems-driven case management* is in direct response to the call for efficiency and accountability in social welfare practice, whereas *consumer-driven case management* focuses on providing the best organized practice for clients in complex and chronic situations. From these differing paradigms come a variety of case management models that resemble one another in some ways but can never really be conceptualized in a broader, more standardized perspective of practice.

The relationship of this discussion to child welfare becomes important when the emphasis in case management models is not based on both underlying paradigms but rather on one or the other. In the public child welfare system, a focus that looks only at efficiency and accountability is not necessarily helpful to the family and child, whereas a model of case management that focuses only on client needs ignores the realities of the system and will not survive within this setting. The differences in these underlying goals can be seen in the identification of steps applied in case management. Steps in case management, such as (1) problem identification; (2) formulation of goals and objectives; (3) contracting an agreement; (4) implementation and monitoring; and (5) case closure, reflect more of a systems-driven approach to case management. Steps such as (1) outreach, referral, client identification, and engagement; (2) a biopsychosocial assessment of the client; (3) the development of a service plan; (4) implementation of the service plan; (5) coordination and monitoring of service delivery; and (6) advocacy on behalf of the family and child denote more of a consumer-driven base of practice. Although neither of these models of case management practice appears to be based on specific underlying paradigms, the terminology in each reflects differing foci. In child welfare, the lack of a specific model of practice that incorporates both paradigms will not provide the best services needed, nor will it reflect the best model of practice for case management.

MODELS OF CHILD WELFARE CASE MANAGEMENT

The following four models of case management practice provide examples of how a solid knowledge and skill base along with a focus on both systems-driven and consumer-driven paradigms can produce effective models.

Community-based Case Management

Community-based case management is a model of practice that has proven effective within the child welfare setting when the issues being addressed involve many different community systems and agencies. For example, The Homebuilders Model of intensive family preservation services (Booth & Leavitt, 2012) found that intensive, time-limited, home- and

community-based family preservation services met the goals of clinical objectives as well as case management needs. Community models were first identified during the early 1970s as part of a reform promoted by the National Institute of Mental Health for the support of persons with severe mental illness living in the community. This model was later expanded to be more inclusive of other populations in need. The community model has always included case management, but more clearly began to be defined as a model of its own when case management began to establish its own practices and designs. There is general agreement among authors and practitioners that the responsibilities of case management in the community model include the assessment of client needs, referral to services, assurance by case managers that clients have access to services, service coordination, analysis of whether these services are meeting client goals, and the continuing provision and accountability of the services within the community.

Strength-based Case Management

Strength-based case management (East, 1999) is another model that provides a perspective of both the system and consumer-driven paradigms. In strengths-based case management the underlying premise for child welfare workers is that the family and child have the skills and talents to make changes in their lives. This model provides an opportunity for families to focus on their strengths rather than their deficits. A project focused on providing services to grandparents raising their grandchildren found that when case management services focused on the grandparents' strengths and natural skills, the services were more readily utilized and fostered a sense of independence and self-assurance.

Strength-based case management is strongly linked to the strength-based or empowering approach of social work practice. In this model, clients or client systems are empowered to make changes in their own lives through their own goals and decisions. In this model of case management, control of the situation is placed in the client's hands. A study by Blair et al. (2009) found that most caregivers and their families have enormous strengths that can be used in a strength-based approach. Huebner, Jones, Miller, Customer, and Critchfield (2006) found similar positive outcomes when this model was used. Although many child welfare clients have little control over their involvement with services, the greater opportunity for choice given to them, the more likely they will involve themselves in services and have positive outcomes.

Integrated Case Management

Integrated case management involves the participation of various professions in providing services to a client through the organization of those services around the client's needs, rather than those of professionals. Cigno and Gore (1999) provide an example of an integrated case management approach in their study of a multiagency children's center. This center provided the opportunity for each family and child to receive services from various agencies and professions within the same facility. The results of the study indicate that clients who aid in the management of their own services, work closely with a variety of agencies and professionals, and have a more holistic approach given to their case, feel more positive about the results.

Hubberstey (2001) found similar outcomes looking at integrated case management services in her study of the Canadian child welfare system. She concludes:

"When the focus is on the well-being of the child, parents can learn to set aside their own disagreements with each other or with their worker in order to achieve something positive for their child(ren);
    Clients appreciate the more holistic approach that emphasizes their strengths and capacities, not just their problems and deficits;
    By working together, parents and practitioners can develop more appreciation for what each has to offer and for each other's roles;
    Through their ongoing participation, parents acquire new skills, such as problem-solving, anger management and priority setting that they can apply to other areas of their lives;
    When everyone has a written copy of the service/care plan, there is a greater likelihood of successful implementation of the service/care plan;
    Allocation of resources is more realistic and better suited to client needs." (p. 96)

In a related study, Christensen and Todahl (1999) found case management was used by different disciplines in relapse prevention for multiple cyclical reluctant clients. The study identified how case management and planning could be used by a group of various professionals to target specific behaviors and reduce relapse for individual clients. In child welfare services, case management provides a model of care for not only the child and family but also for the variety of professionals who work in the service continuum.

Intensive Case Management

Intensive case management (ICM) is a model of practice that involves the social worker's intervention in a very concentrated way over a four to eight week period. ICM is used in "working with families to prevent children from being placed in foster care" (Frankel & Gelman, 2012, p. 43). The idea behind ICM is that clients are immediately connected with all community resources and the case manager stabilizes the client as quickly as possible. This requires lower caseloads, exhaustive knowledge of community services, and a skill of coordinating services in a short matter of time. It is reflective of both paradigms through its rigorous use of systems and its intensive engagement of clients.

TRAUMA-INFORMED PRACTICE

Trauma informed practice is now being used across the country when intervening in child welfare situations. Although based primarily in treatment, it is having an impact on case management within child welfare. The National Child Traumatic Stress Network, in conjunction with other organizations, has developed a Training Toolkit (2008) that can assist case managers in approaching their child welfare cases with a comprehensive view. Trauma informed practice focuses on the knowledge, skills, and values needed when working with children with traumatic stress. These components are then used to "support children's safety, permanency, and wellbeing through case analysis" (NCTSN, p. 1). Case analysis then uses the systems and consumer paradigms to place trauma factors at their core.

RECOMMENDATIONS

The material developed related to case management suggests that it can produce both effective processes and outcomes. In child welfare services, a model must be definitive as to its knowledge and skill base. Beyond this, it then becomes important to study and understand which models are most effective and with which populations. The four models presented herein all have merits for child welfare practice and yet appear to have decided differences according to their focus. As the evidence base for case management services with different populations increases, it will be possible to identify those practice approaches showing the greatest promise. Social workers will increasingly consult resources (such as the Campbell Collaborative) to identify effective interventions with specific client populations. This will be critical to social workers committed to interventions most likely to produce positive outcomes. At the same time, as we learn that our similarities outweigh our differences, there will be increased attention to models and applications drawn from international research.

WEBSITES

American Case Management Association. http://www.acmaweb.org.
Campbell Collaborative. http://www.campbell-collaboration.org/SWCG/titles.asp.
Child Welfare League of America. http://www.cwla.org.
NASW Standards for Case Management. http://www.socialworkers.org/practice/standards/sw_case_mgmt.asp#intro.
The National Child Traumatic Stress Network. http://www.NCTSN.org

References

Blair, K. D., Taylor, D., & Rivera, C. (2009). Strengths and stressors in a population of kinship caregivers: Implications for caseload management and administration. *Families in Society, 90*(4), 431–438.

Blair, K. D., & Taylor, E. B. (2006). Examining the lives and needs of child-only recipient kinship caregivers: Heroes stepping up to help children. *Journal of Family Social Work, 10*(1), 1–24.

Burns, B. J., Phillips, S. D., & Wagner, H. R. (2004). Mental health needs and access to mental health services by youths involved with child welfare: A national survey. *Journal of the American Academy of Child and Adolescent Psychiatry, 43,* 960–970.

Christensen, D. N., & Todahl, J. L. (1999). Solution-based casework: Case planning to reduce risk. *Journal of Family Social Work, 3*(4), 3–24.

Cigno, K., & Gore, J. (1999). A seamless service: Meeting the needs of children with disabilities through a multi-agency approach. *Child and Family Social Work, 4,* 325–335.

Commission for Case Manager Certification. (2009). Care coordination. Case Managers "connect the dots" in new delivery models. *Issue Briefs.* 2. 1.

Dauber, S., Neighbors, C., Dasaro, C., Riordan, A., & Morgaenstern, J. (2012). Impact of intensive case management on child welfare system involvement for substance-dependent parenting women on public assistance. *Children and Youth Services Review, 34,* 1359–1366.

East, J. F. (1999). Hidden barriers to success for women in welfare reform. *Families in Society, 80*(3), 295–304.

Frankel, A., & Gelman, S. (2012). *Case management.* Chicago, IL: Lyceum Books.

Glissen, C., & Green, P. (2006a). The role of specialty mental health care in predicting child welfare and juvenile justice out-of-home placements. *Research on Social Work Practice, 16*(5), 480–490.

Glissen, C., & Green, P. (2006b). The effects of organizational culture and climate on the access to mental health care in child welfare and juvenile justice systems. *Administration and Policy in Mental Health, 33*(4), 433–448.

Hubberstey, C. (2001). Client involvement as a key element of integrated case management. *Child and Youth Care Forum, 30*(2), 83–97.

Huebner, R. A., Jones, B. L., Miller, V. P., Customer, M., & Critchfield, B. (2006). Comprehensive family services and customer satisfaction outcomes. *Child Welfare, 85*(4), 691–714.

Johnson, K., & Wagner, D. (2005). Evaluation of Michigan's foster care case management system. *Research on Social Work Practice, 15*(5), 372–380.

Mather, J. H., Lager, P. B., & Harris, N. (2007). *Child welfare.* Pacific Grove, CA: Brooks/Cole.

Moxley, D. P. (1996). *Case management by design: Reflections on principles and practices.* Chicago, IL: Nelson-Hall.

Pecora, P., Whittaker, J., Maluccio, A., Barth, R., & Plotnick, R. (1992). *The child welfare challenge: Policy, practice and research.* New York, NY: Walter de Gruyter.

Rothman, J. (1992). *Guidelines for case management.* Itasca, IL: Peacock.

Sallee, A. L., & LeVine, E. S. (1999). *Child welfare: Clinical theory and practice.* Dubuque, IA: Eddie Bowers.

Tregeagle, S., & Mason, J. (2008). Service user experience of participation in child welfare case management, *Child and Family Social Work, 10,* 391–401.

Vourlekis, B. S., & Greene, R. R. (1992). *Social work case management.* New York, NY: A. de Gruyter.

Woodside, M., & McClam, T. (2013). *Generalist case management.* Belmont, CA: Cengage.

109 Case Management with Substance-abusing Clients

W. Patrick Sullivan

Among the host of social ills that confront American society, most would agree that alcohol and drug abuse remains a prime concern. Mark, Levit, Vandivert-Warren, Coffey, and Buck (2007) estimate that a staggering 9.4% of the U.S. population suffers from a substance abuse disorder. As a result, the price tag for treatment alone reached $20.7 billion in 2003. When direct and indirect costs are considered, the fiscal impact of substance abuse, by any measure, is staggering.

Simply put, substance abuse is a major public policy issue and a condition that impacts service delivery and criminal justice systems, the workplace, and the day-to-day lives of citizens. Given these issues, it is not surprising that the value and effectiveness of treatment services are under constant scrutiny. Indeed, nearly two decades ago, Barber (1994) argued "by any set of performance indicators, it is hard to resist the conclusion that our current treatment methods are not working" (p. 521). Undoubtedly, this sentiment remains in force today. For this reason alone, the search for innovative methods to improve performance is ongoing. Alcohol and drug abuse is commonly viewed as a chronic, relapsing condition. Success, it follows, comes only after years of hard lessons, increased self-awareness, available natural supports, and the use of appropriate treatment services. Recovery, as research and personal accounts can attest, is not easy.

Recent developments in health care policy offer the possibility that the view of substance abuse and treatment may shift, and thereby alter the landscape of treatment services. Understanding substance abuse as an episodic personal problem leads to the development of time-limited and acute models of care. In contrast, understanding substance abuse as a chronic *health* condition suggests the need for new long-term approaches that emphasize continuing care, and underscores the importance of services that target the whole person. Additionally, when providers take clinical *and* fiscal responsibility for an entire population of enrollees they must remain sensitive to the total cost of care, prompting the search for less expensive alternatives to traditional practice while maximizing positive outcomes. Within this evolving social policy context it is likely that case management will no longer be treated as an auxiliary or novel service, but rather a primary component in an increasingly integrated health care environment.

THE ROLE OF CASE MANAGEMENT IN ALCOHOL AND DRUG TREATMENT

Over the last 20 years, case management became a standard service offering in comprehensive treatment systems (Benshoff & Janikowski, 2000; R. Rapp, 1998; Siegal & Rapp, 1996; Sullivan, Wolk, & Hartmann, 1992; Vanderplasschen, Rapp, Wolf, & Broekaert, 2004). There are many definitions of case management and a plethora of case management models. Darnell (2013) posits that in the era of the Affordable Care Act, two emerging case management roles are navigator and assister. Yet, for our purposes case management is described as a direct service function that involves skill in assessment, counseling, teaching, modeling, and advocacy that aims to enhance the social functioning of clients. This service is poised to amplify traditional treatment offerings by impacting those facets of consumers' lives that account for much human misery—and the lion's share of total costs incurred.

Therefore, the rise of case management in drug and alcohol treatment is consistent with efforts to develop more comprehensive service programs that address all aspects of a client's life (Evenson, Binner, Cho, Schicht, & Topolski, 1998; Humphreys & Tucker, 2002; Institute of Medicine, 1990; McLellan, Weinstein, Shen, Kendig, & Levine 2005). Indeed, the growing popularity of case management also signaled the adoption of a different view of addiction and, hence, a new approach to treatment. Vanderplasschen and associates (2004) argue that case management became a viable service as substance abuse problems became "increasingly recognized as multifaceted, chronic and relapsing conditions that required a comprehensive and continuous approach" (p. 913).

Current policy initiatives, culminating in the passage of the Patient Protection and Accountable Care Act establish a framework to move addiction services into a chronic care and recovery oriented framework. Notable among these trends is the rise of Accountable Care Organizations, Patient Centered Medical Homes, and the movement to integrate behavioral and physical health care (see Druss & Maurer, 2010; Pating, Miller, Gpolerud, Martin, & Ziedonis, 2012). Each of these service delivery models rely on some form of case management. Many of these initiatives feature bundled payments methods that will afford providers more flexibility than a fee-for-service approach, while the projected expansion of Medicaid should stimulate increased use of treatment services and provide a reimbursement mechanism for case management (Barry & Huskamp, 2011; Busch, Meara, Huskamp, & Barry, 2013).

McKay and Hiller-Sturmhofel (2011), endorse the adoption of the chronic care model for substance abuse, noting that long-term interventions, particularly those that make a concerted effort to reach out and engage people in treatment, enjoy greater success. Accordingly, case management is a vital ingredient in a continuous and integrated care model.

Noel (2006) argues that the "purpose of a case management program determines the focus of case management activities" (p. 312). Nevertheless, among a range of choices the strengths-model has emerged as a popular choice in alcohol and drug programs (Rapp, 2006; Rapp & Goscha, 2006; Sullivan, 1996; Sullivan et al.,

1992). This model is predicated on the principle that behavior is partly influenced by the resources available to people (C. Rapp, 1998; Rapp & Goscha, 2006). Here the definition of resources is broadly construed, targeting the availability of supportive friends, family, recreational activities, a stable residence, and meaningful activities, including work and education. The ability of case managers, working alongside consumers to secure these resources, is posited to improve the effectiveness of treatment. Indeed, a review of outcome research indicates that factors associated with social stability improve the resilience of the treatment effect (Sullivan et al., 1992). Barber (1994) also observes that "the best predictors of treatment success are all social factors" (p. 529).

Unquestionably these observations can be criticized on a number of fronts, particularly given the inability of such research to ascertain the direction of causality. Certainly we would expect people who are clean and sober to perform better socially. Nonetheless, it still stands that case management services geared to address the problems in living faced by consumers, regardless of the nature of the association, can be an important addition to the traditional array of services.

THE PRACTICE OF CASE MANAGEMENT

The practice of strengths-based case management follows the common template that guides most intervention in human services. The difference in strengths-based case management is reflected in the points of emphasis, the nature of the professional–consumer relationship, and the locus of care.

Assessment

Standard assessment procedures gauge such factors as types of substances abused, the frequency of use, and other measures that ascertain physical and emotional dependence. In the strengths model, assessment is seen as an ongoing activity that focuses squarely on consumer functioning, both past and present, in key life domains, including work, leisure time, health, finances, relationships, and living arrangements; specific assessment instruments have been designed for this purpose (Rapp & Goscha, 2006).

Given the impress of substance use, it presents little challenge to decipher the presence of difficulties and uncover the litany of failures that have marked the life of many consumers. The task from this perspective is different. Here, the purpose is to also expose areas of success, both past and present, and support or rekindle interests that the consumer may still hold. Hence, the professional must look behind the malady and dysfunction to see areas of health and strength, for these are the building blocks for the work to follow.

Goal and Case Planning

The process of strengths discovery allows one to view the client as a unique individual, not simply a typical drug abuser or an alcoholic. The assessment process should reveal the whole person and their specific life goals, dreams, and aspirations. With the strengths assessment as a guide, the work phase begins, but with one important proviso: the consumer is viewed as the director of the process.

A vexing problem in substance abuse treatment is that for recovery to begin, individuals must suspend activities that while problematic, ordered their day, provided some purpose, and offered a level of gratification. Furthermore, common treatment programs, though perhaps well grounded, are rarely based on consumer choice. In the strengths model, consumers identify the goals important to them; consistent with the functions of case management, these goals are tied to the key life domains addressed in the assessment process.

The process described here is rarely linear. Consumers often fail to follow through or suggest overall goals that may be beyond their current capacity. Skilled case managers are adept at helping clients break even the largest and seemingly the most unrealistic goals into a series of manageable, measurable, and documented steps. This process provides a model for addressing life problems in a proactive, organized, and incremental fashion—and learning this skill alone can help consumers avoid relapse when life demands overwhelm them.

Resource Acquisition

If success and recovery are functions of the resources available to people, then it follows that a key function of case management, in conjunction with consumers, is to identify and secure the resources needed to realize case goals.

The development of case goals, and ultimately the resources that are targeted in the care plan, should flow logically from the strengths assessment. This phase of helping requires a measure of creativity and "out-of-the-box thinking." Often professional views of resources are restricted to those specialty services and providers that constitute the human service network. Case managers operating from the strengths model view the community as an unlimited source of resources for consumers preferring to access those supports and services used by all citizens.

Aggressive Outreach

The ability of case mangers to be successful in the art of resource acquisition and helping consumers realize their goals pivots on aggressive outreach. Creative case planning requires managers who are keenly aware of the formal and informal resources a community offers, and this is best learned while "on the street." These case managers develop relationships with employers, landlords, recreation directors, and other gatekeepers to those nontraditional resources vital to true recovery.

The ability of a case manager to observe consumers in real-world settings also provides insights on what life is like in their host environment. For example, case managers can uncover problems that consumers have heretofore masked, such as illiteracy, while simultaneously providing a glimpse of the strengths individuals possess. By remaining in constant contact with consumers, the case manager can detect signs of impending difficulties and the possibility of relapse.

The natural environment is also the most appropriate site for the consumer to try the skills learned in treatment settings, be it the will to resist contact with troublesome actors or tangible items, like learning to ride the bus or hold a job.

IMPACT OF CASE MANAGEMENT

As case management grows in popularity, there is more urgency to assess the efficacy of this service. One pioneer in this area is the Wright State University School of Medicine. Their initial work underscored the important role of case management in improving treatment retention and engagement (R. Rapp, 1998). This remains one of the most robust findings in case management services for those facing addiction (Kim, Saitz, Cheng, Winter, Witas, & Samet, 2011; Krupski, Campbell, Joesch, Lucenko, & Roy-Byrne, 2009; McLellan et al., 2005; Morgenstern, Bianchard, McCrady, McVeigh, & Morgan, 2006; Soson & Durkin, 2007; Vanderplasschen et al., 2004; Vanderplasschen, Rapp, Wolf, & Broekaert, 2007; Winn, Shealy, Kropp, Felkins-Dohm, Gonzales-Nolas, & Francis, 2013). The importance of this outcome cannot be minimized, because retention is one of the key variables in overall treatment success is a key mediating variable in a wide array of important client goals from abstinence to employment (Hartmann, Wolk, & Sullivan, 1993; Morgenstern et al., 2009; Rapp, 2006; Vanderplasschen et al., 2007), and can impact the cost of care by reducing the necessity for more intensive services and/or emergency care (Kirk, Di Leo, Rehmer, Moy, & Davidson, 2013; Kumar & Klein, 2013; McLellan et al., 2005).

The ability to engage and retain individuals in treatment is a particularly powerful outcome, given that case management appears to be useful in a wide range of settings and populations including those who are homeless (Soson & Durkin, 2007), veterans (Winn et al., 2013), individuals in methadone maintenance programs (Coviello, Zanis, Wesnoski, & Alterman, 2006), women applying for or involved in public assistance (Morgenstern et al., 2009) and adolescents (Noel, 2006).

A consistent finding in studies of strengths-based case management has been the success of the goal planning method. The results derived from this method, as demonstrated in a host of settings and with a variety of clientele, are admirable, with goal attainment rates consistently around 70% or higher across life domains (C. Rapp, 1998; Rapp & Goscha, 2006). This positive outcome appears to hold in alcohol and drug treatment (R. Rapp, 1998, 2006).

For integrated health care to be efficacious, early detection and treatment of substance abuse problems is a necessity. Individuals present with substance abuse issues in every social service setting, and in particular, primary medical care. The goal, as Pating, Miller, Gpolerud, Martin and Ziedonis (2013) suggest, is that there should be no wrong door for a person to receive needed care. Likewise, once a substance abuse problem is identified, engagement and retention in treatment is critical to good outcomes. Engaged clients are less likely to rely on high-end care, a vital issue to providers operating in an at-risk or shared risk fiscal environment. Given the impact of case management in these areas, there appears to be a robust future for case and care management.

CHALLENGES AND CONTROVERSIES

Though the rationale for case management in alcohol and drug treatment may be evident, the introduction and implementation of the services faces a number of stern challenges. For many years, the disease model of alcohol and drug abuse has shaped our understanding of this problem and the treatment designed to help. Case management practice can be viewed as at odds with the disease model, both conceptually and in practice. Much of the work of case managers, particularly resource acquisition and relapse prevention, can be viewed by disease model adherents as professional enabling (Sullivan, Hartmann, Dillon, & Wolk, 1994). From this standpoint, the case manager protects clients from the consequences of their actions, thus delaying, not expediting, recovery. These differing viewpoints can dramatically impact how case management services are accepted and implemented. It is not uncommon for staff in treatment programs to have experienced addiction personally and to have benefited from classic treatment methods. In contrast, case management positions may be filled by those holding college degrees but without direct experience with substance abuse. Consequently, when case management services are introduced to a traditional treatment agency, a clash of cultures may ensue. For case management services to be seamlessly introduced in many settings requires strong leadership, particularly at the middle management level. In truth, the entire substance abuse treatment world may be at the point of a sea change, with an increased emphasis on credentials and the adoption of practices and procedures more akin to the world of medicine on the horizon (Roy & Miller, 2012).

It also remains difficult to untangle the respective contribution of particular models of case management on client outcomes apart from the potential power of the basic case management relationship. In fact, successful execution of the role may mimic what has been referred to in therapy circles as the *real relationship* (Angel & Mahoney, 2007; Gelso et al., 2005). Case managers work alongside consumers in day-to-day situations and on basic life problems. They are there when clients succeed and fail. Case managers serve as advocates, coaches, cheerleaders, and the person who points out how alcohol and drug use impedes progress toward cherished goals. Clearly, case managers become key persons in the lives of those struggling with recovery, and first-person accounts affirm this (Brun & Rapp, 2001). Boundaries are still important and must always be monitored carefully.

It is also obvious that by virtue of the addiction process and/or the necessities of survival, denial and deceit are interpersonal issues confronted by professional helpers on a regular basis. In classic treatment, confrontation is used to counter these issues when they arise. However, case management practice is predicated on professional–client relationships marked by partnership and trust. Can this apparent dilemma be resolved? Some argue that the success of strengths-based practice in addiction treatment is inextricably tied to the capability of case managers to forge a mentoring relationship with consumers that is characterized by genuineness and warmth (see Brun & Rapp, 2001; Rapp & Goscha, 2006).

Although case management has been used effectively in a wide range of practice settings, there are specific concerns germane to addiction programs. Many clients in treatment have extensive criminal backgrounds and a history of failed treatments. Taking advocacy roles in such areas as employment and housing, for example, comes with some risk. Key issues to consider are the selection of clients for case management and the timing of services. To date there appears to be no prevailing model to suggest which consumers can benefit from case management or for whom it is contra-indicated (Rapp, 1998; Sullivan & Maloney, 1992).

However, one large question continues to loom over the field. Is case management effective? Although there is some evidence that case management directly improves client outcomes in addiction services, the results are, at best, modest (see Gurewich, Sirkin, & Shepard, 2012; Hall et al., 2009). Thus, it is dangerous to oversell the power of case management. Vanderplasschen et al. (2004), drawing from an extensive review of outcome studies, argue that "case management for substance use disorders is no panacea, but it positively affects the delivery of services that can help stabilize or improve an individual's complex situation" (p. 920). Therefore, case management is best conceptualized as an important aspect of a well-integrated and organized system of care—not as a standalone service. In many ways, the introduction of case management is consistent with the evolution of drug and alcohol treatment. If substance abuse represents a long-term and relapsing condition, an acute model is inappropriate. Therefore, the true impact of this method may be assessed only in the long run and within the context of the system in which it is embedded (Saleh, Vaughn, Fuortes, Uden-Holmen, & Hall, 2006). To date, longitudinal studies that measure the impact of case management in addiction service are rare. Future research must explore the effectiveness of case management against other standard offerings in addiction programming, as well as the independent contribution the service makes.

WEBSITES

Alcohol Policy Information Service. http://www.alcoholpolicy.niaaa.nih.gov.

National Clearinghouse for Drug and Alcohol Information. http://ncadi.samhsa.gov.

National Institute of Alcohol Abuse and Alcoholism. http://www.niaaa.nih.gov.

National Institute on Drug Abuse. http://www.nida.nih.gov.

National Institutes of Health. http://www.nih.gov.

Substance Abuse and Mental Health Services Administration. http://www.samhsa.gov.

References

Angel, B., & Mahoney, C. (2007). Reconceptualizing the case management relationship in intensive treatment: A study of staff perceptions and experiences. *Administration Policy in Mental Health and Mental Health Services Research, 34,* 172–188.

Barber, J. (1994). Alcohol addiction: Private trouble or social issue? *Social Service Review, 68*(4), 521–535.

Barry, C., & Huskamp, H. (2011). Moving beyond parity—Mental health and addiction care under ACA. *New England Journal of Medicine, 365*(11), 973–975.

Benshoff, J., & Janikowski, T. (2000). *The rehabilitation model of substance abuse counseling.* Stamford, CT: Brooks/Cole.

Brun, C., & Rapp, C. A. (2001). Strengths-based case management: Individuals' perspectives on strengths and the case manager relationship. *Social Work, 46*(3), 278–288.

Busch, S., Meara, E., Huskamp, H., & Barry, C. (2013). Characteristics of adults with substance abuse disorders expected to be eligible under the ACA. *Psychiatric Services, 64*(5), 520–526.

Coviello, D., Zanis, D., Wesnoski, S., & Alterman, A. (2006). The effectiveness of outreach case management in re-enrolling discharged methadone patients. *Drug and Alcohol Dependence, 85,* 56–65.

Darnell, J. (2013). Navigators and Assisters: Two case management roles for social workers in the Affordable Care Act. *Health & Social Work, 38*(2), 123–126.

Druss, B., & Maurer, B. (2010). Healthcare reform and care at the behavioral health–primary care interface. *Psychiatric Services, 61*(11), 1087–1092.

Evenson, R., Binner, P., Cho, D., Schicht, W., & Topolski, J. (1998). An outcome study of Missouri's CSTAR alcohol and drug abuse programs. *Journal of Substance Abuse Treatment, 15*(2), 143–150.

Gelso, C., Kelley, F., Fuertes, J., Marmarosh, C., Holmes, S., Costa, C., & Hancock, G. (2005). Measuring the real relationship in psychotherapy: Initial validation of the therapist form. *Journal of Counseling Psychology, 52*(4), 640–649.

Gurewich, D., Sirkin, J., & Shepard, D. (2012). On-site provision of substance abuse treatment at community health centers. *Journal of Substance Abuse Treatment, 42,* 339–345.

Hall, J., Sarrazin, M., Huber, D., Vaughn, T., Block, R., & Reedy, A., & Jang, M. J. (2009). Iowa case management for rural drug abuse. *Research on Social Work Practice, 19*(4), 407–422.

Hartmann, D., Wolk, J., & Sullivan, W. P. (1993). Inpatient and outpatient outcomes in Missouri's alcohol and drug treatment programs. *Journal of Health and Social Policy, 5*(2), 67–76.

Humphreys, K., & Tucker, J. (2002). Toward more responsive and effective intervention systems for alcohol-related problems. *Addiction, 97,* 126–132.

Institute of Medicine. (1990). *Broadening the base of treatment for alcohol problems.* Washington, DC: National Academies Press.

Kim, T., Saitz, R., Cheng, D., Winter, M., Witas, J., & Samet, J. (2011). Initiation and engagement in chronic disease management care for substance dependence. *Drug and Alcohol Dependence, 115,* 80–86.

Kirk, T., Di Leo, P., Rehmer, P., Moy, S., & Davidson, L. (2013). A case and care management program to reduce use of acute care by clients with substance abuse disorders. *Psychiatric Services, 64*(5), 491–493.

Krupski, A., Campbell, K., Joesch, J., Lucenko, B., & Roy-Byrne, P. (2009). Impact of access to recovery services on alcohol/drug treatment outcomes. *Journal of Substance Abuse Treatment, 37,* 435–442.

Kumar, G., & Klein, R. (2013). Effectiveness of case management strategies in reducing emergency department visits in frequent user patient populations: A systematic review. *The Journal of Emergency Medicine, 44*(3), 717–729.

Mark, T., Levit, K., Vandivert-Warren, R., Coffey, R., & Buck, J. (2007). Trends in spending for substance abuse treatment, 1986–2003. *Health Affairs, 26*(4), 1118–1128.

McKay, J., & Hiller-Sturmhofel, S. (2011). Treating alcoholism as a chronic disease. *Alcohol Research & Health, 33*(4), 356–370.

McLellan, A. T., Weinstein, R., Shen, Q., Kendig, C., & Levine, M. (2005). Improving continuity of care in a public addiction system with clinical case management. *American Journal on Addictions, 14,* 426–440.

Morgenstern, J., Bianchard, K., McCrady, B., McVeigh, K., & Morgan, T. (2006). Effectiveness of intensive case management for substance-dependent women receiving Temporary Assistance for Needy Families. *American Journal of Public Health, 96*(11), 2016–2023.

Morgenstern, J., Neighbors, C., Kuerbis, A., Riordan, A., Blanchard, K., McVeigh, K., . . . McCrady, B. (2009). Improving 24-month abstinence and employment outcomes for substance-dependent women receiving temporary assistance for needy families with intensive case management. *American Journal of Public Health, 99*(2), 328–333.

Noel, P. (2006). The impact of therapeutic case management on participation in adolescent substance abuse treatment. *American Journal of Substance Abuse Treatment, 32,* 111–327.

Pating, D., Miller, M., Gpolerud, E., Martin, J., & Ziedonis, D. (2012) New systems of care for substance use disorders. *Psychiatric Clinics of North America, 35,* 327–356.

Rapp, C. A., & Goscha, R. (2006). *The strengths model.* New York, NY: Oxford University Press.

Rapp, R. (1998). The strengths perspective and persons with substance abuse problems. In D. Saleebey (Ed.), *The strengths perspective in social work practice* (2nd ed.) (pp. 77–96). New York, NY: Longman.

Rapp, R. (2006). Strengths-based case management: Enhancing treatment for persons with substance abuse problems. In D. Saleebey (Ed.), *The strengths perspective in social work practice* (4th ed.). Boston, MA: Pearson Education.

Roy, A. K., & Miller, M. (2012). The medicalization of addiction treatment professionals. *Journal of Psychoactive Drugs, 44*(2), 107–118.

Saleh, S., Vaughn, T., Fuortes, S., Uden-Holmen, T., & Hall, J. (2006). Cost-effectiveness of case management in substance abuse treatment. *Research on Social Work Practice, 16*(1), 38–47.

Siegal, H., & Rapp, R. (Eds.). (1996). *Case management and substance abuse treatment*. New York, NY: Springer.

Soson, M., & Durkin, E. (2007). Perceptions about services and dropout from a substance abuse case management program. *Journal of Community Psychology, 35*(5), 583–602.

Sullivan, W. P. (1996). Beyond the twenty-eighth day: Case management in alcohol and drug treatment. In C. Austin & R. McClelland (Eds.), *Perspectives on case management practice* (pp. 125–144). Milwaukee, WI: Families International.

Sullivan, W. P., Hartmann, D., Dillon, D., & Wolk, J. (1994). Implementing case management in alcohol and drug treatment. *Families in Society, 75*, 67–73.

Sullivan, W. P., & Maloney, P. (1992). Substance abuse and mental illness: Social work practice with dual diagnosis clients. *Arete, 17*(2), 1–15.

Sullivan, W. P., Wolk, J., & Hartmann, D. (1992). Case management in alcohol and drug treatment: Improving client outcomes. *Families in Society, 73*, 195–203.

Vanderplasschen, W., Rapp, R., Wolf, J., & Broekaert, E. (2004). The development and implementation of case management in North America and Europe. *Psychiatric Services, 55*(8), 913–922.

Vanderplasschen, W., Rapp, R., Wolf, J., & Broekaert, E. (2007). Effectiveness of different models of case management for substance-abusing populations. *Journal of Psychoactive Drugs, 39*(1), 81–95.

Winn, J., Shealy, S., Kropp, G., Felkins-Dohm, D., Gonzales-Nolas, C., & Francis, E. (2013). Housing assistance and case management: Improving access to substance use disorder treatment for homeless veterans. *Psychological Services, 10*(2), 233–240.

110   Case Management with Older Adults

Daniel S. Gardner & Dina Zempsky

INTRODUCTION AND BACKGROUND

Medical and public health advances over the last half-century have reduced the burden of disease, extended life expectancy, and significantly accelerated the aging of the population. In 2011, over 41 million people—approximately 13% of Americans—were aged 65 years or older. By 2050, this number is expected to more than double to 84 million, representing over 20% of the population (U.S. Census Bureau, 2012). Although older adults are living longer, healthier lives, over two-thirds live with chronic illnesses or conditions such as diabetes, cancer, cardiovascular disease, depression, or dementia (Centers for Disease Control and Prevention [CDC], 2013).

The growing prevalence of chronic and disabling conditions in later life poses considerable challenges for older adults, their families, and caregivers. Chronic conditions typically require ongoing medical monitoring and care, diminish quality-of-life, and increase disability, medication use, hospitalizations, and mortality in older adults (Benjamin, 2010). Over one-third of elders report some type of disability (i.e., difficulties with walking, hearing, vision, or self-care) that requires assistance from others in order to live independently (Administration on Aging, 2012). Over 44 million Americans—representing 19% of all adults—care for someone aged 50 years or older with a chronic, disabling condition. An estimated 15 million adults, for example, care for a family member living with Alzheimer's disease or other dementias (National Alliance for Caregivers/American Association of Retired Persons [NAC/AARP], 2012).

The costs associated with these changes are substantial. In 2010 approximately 93% of all Medicare fee-for-service spending on beneficiaries, or $279 billion, was spent on caring for chronically ill elders (Centers for Medicare and Medicaid Services [CMS], 2012). Informal caregiving costs family caregivers and employers approximately $34 billion each year (MetLife, 2010); the economic value of this uncompensated care is estimated to be over $450 billion (Feinberg et al., 2011). In response to ever-increasing expenditures, Congress passed the Omnibus Budget Reconciliation Act of 1981 (Public Law no. 97-35, Sec. 2176), authorizing the funding of demonstration projects under the Medicaid Home and Community-based Waiver that integrate health care, personal care, and case management for community-dwelling older adults and people living with disabilities who might otherwise require institutionalization (Duckett & Guy, 2000; Austin & McClelland, 2009). To further support older adults in the community and control Medicare and Medicaid costs, Title III of the Older Americans Act funds geriatric case management programs across the country through the Aging Services Network (i.e., State Units on Aging and Area Agencies on Aging).

Despite the complex health and service needs of older adults, home and community-based long-term services and supports are often fragmented and difficult to access (Naleppa, 2006). Geriatric case management responds to these barriers by providing client-centered assessment and care planning, facilitating access to critical resources, and coordinating health, mental health, and long-term services and supports that enhance quality of life and promote the health and functional independence of community-dwelling elders. The geriatric case manager's specific role is shaped by agency function (e.g., assisting with financial, housing, health, nutritional, or mental health needs), care setting, and population served (Naleppa, 2006; Wodarski & Williams-Hayes, 2003). The case manager's professional discipline (e.g., social work, nursing, or rehabilitative medicine) and expertise further frames the focus of practice. An array of case management approaches has emerged in the past several decades, including care coordination, patient navigation, and transitional care models. While these terms are often used interchangeably, they have distinct definitions, goals, and functions. Two common goals of case management models—improving the quality of client care and containing costs through service coordination—can, at times, conflict with each other and pose additional barriers to the development of appropriate care plans (Gallagher et al., 2002; Wodarsky & Williams-Hayes, 2003).

Case management has been a core method in clinical social work dating back to the roots of the profession in the late nineteenth century (Frankel & Gelman, 1998; National Association of Social Workers [NASW], 2013). Social work case management is grounded in professional values of enhancing individual autonomy and dignity, advancing social justice, and effecting change in both micro- and macro-level systems (NASW, 2013). Although their goals and functions vary by setting, social work case managers share a commitment to client- and family-centered practice, maintain a strengths perspective, and attend to the sociocultural and relational contexts of individual and social functioning (Austin & McClelland, 2009; Darnell, 2013).

COMPONENTS OF GERIATRIC CASE MANAGEMENT

Geriatric case managers work independently or as members of interdisciplinary teams in a variety of institutional, home, and community based settings—including Aging Service Network agencies, hospitals, home health care organizations, long-term care institutions, and other public or private human service organizations (Naleppa, 2006). Recently, private case management with older adults—often referred to as geriatric care management—has emerged to meet the growing demand of families seeking information, assistance, and advocacy around accessing resources, coordinating services, and making current and long-term care decisions (Morano & Morano, 2006).

Although operationalized differently by practice setting and professional background, geriatric case managers share a set of core service components that include:

1) *Community outreach:* Identifying and targeting at-risk older adults in the community who lack access to case management services or community resources and supports.
2) *Comprehensive geriatric assessment:* Conducting thorough, multidimensional assessments of older adults and their home environments. Being a core service component of all case management with older adults, comprehensive geriatric assessment (CGA) is the foundation of a care plan that addresses the older client's

unique needs, strengths, and challenges. CGA addresses the following domains:

- Activities of Daily Living (ADLs): Ability to perform daily self-care (i.e., bathing, toileting, ambulating) within one's place of residence. ADLs represent a well-documented measure of client's functional status and capacity to live independently.
- Instrumental Activities of Daily Living (IADLs): Tasks that, when performed independently, enable the adult to live in the community. Includes shopping, housekeeping, and medication management.
- Pharmacological profile: Medication list (prescription and over-the-counter) and daily protocols. Helps identify and address gaps in care, drug interactions, adverse effects, medication adherence, and use of herbal remedies or alternative treatments.
- Cognitive, psychological, and psychiatric functioning: Diagnostic work-up, including evaluation of mental status, memory loss, signs of delirium or dementia, impairment in judgment or decision making. Includes assessing client's psychological state, mental health history, signs of depression or anxiety, and interpersonal functioning, as well as making referrals for further evaluation and treatment when indicated.
- Home environment: Adequacy of living situation and extent of person:environment fit. Assessment of home safety, risk of falls, adequate nutrition and hygiene. Assessment of need for in-home supports or alternative living situation.
- Long-term care planning and legal concerns: Client's care preferences and goals, including views about medical treatment, settings of care, and the decision-making process. Facilitating client–family and client–provider conversations about care preferences and advance care planning, client income and assets, and securing legal assistance with wills, power of attorney, guardianship, and advanced directives.
- Family/caregiver supports: Client's social functioning, social and familial supports, and family functioning. Identifying social isolation and loneliness, and assessing whether client has adequate caregiving and other supports to live independently.

3) *Benefits and entitlement navigation:* Educating older adults and their families about the continuum of community-based services, and helping them navigate complex health systems and benefits (e.g., Medicare and Medicaid, assistance with income subsidies, housing, and utilities). Identifying and accessing personal care services, assistance with chores, homemaking, medical care and chronic illness management, nutritional services and home-delivered meals programs, transportation services and escorting older clients to appointments, financial management and budgeting, and legal assistance.

4) *Advocacy and interagency coordination:* Facilitating communication between the institutions and systems with which clients interface, to ensure continuity of care and address lack of clear communication or care coordination. Plan, facilitate, and monitor care transitions, for example, between hospital and home, home and assisted living, or hospital and nursing home.

PRACTICE CONSIDERATIONS AND ESSENTIAL COMPETENCIES

Research evaluating the effectiveness of geriatric case management has been limited by the lack of shared definitions, goals, and outcomes of different case management models (Austin & McClelland, 2009; Peikes et al., 2009). Although there is evidence that case management reduces hospitalizations and health care costs for frail elders, these findings have not been consistent. A recent survey of Medicare-funded demonstration programs, for example, found that only 3 of 15 care coordination projects were successful in reducing re-hospitalization rates (Peikes et al., 2009). The lack of evidence may reflect the high degree of need among case management-eligible elders (Ferry & Abramson, 2006). Successful case management programs share several components, including targeted outreach to at-risk elders in the community (e.g., those who were recently hospitalized or had multiple emergency room visits), personal contact (including face-to-face and telephone) between the case manager and client, and the use of interdisciplinary teams where nurses focus on health promotion and illness management, and social workers facilitate and coordinate supportive services and resources (Brown et al., 2012).

Based on established geriatric competencies in social work (Naito-Chan et al., 2005), the authors consider the following knowledge, skills, and attitudes essential to working effectively with older adults and their families:

1) *Bio-psychosocial and spiritual needs of older adults:* Knowledge of age-related physical, functional, and cognitive changes, and the impact of comorbid chronic illnesses, geriatric syndromes, frailty, and medication effects in later life. Understanding developmental concerns and tasks of older adults and family caregivers, normative life events and stressors (e.g., retirement, widowhood, and multiple losses), and family life cycle development is essential. Awareness of cultural differences regarding aging, and understanding the bio-psychosocial and economic effects of institutional oppression and disparities on African American; Latino; immigrant; lesbian, gay, bisexual, and transgender (LGBT); and poor and economically insecure elders.

2) *Comprehensive geriatric assessment:* Skills in conducting initial and ongoing assessments, identifying at-risk clients, prioritizing needs, and evaluating cognitive and functional status, person:environment fit, and the home environment. Familiarity with standardized measures of geriatric health, mental health, and physical functioning, and skills in developing care plans with measurable, mutually established goals.

3) *Continuum of community-based supports:* Familiarity with range of supportive services for older adults, from home and community-based health and social services to institutional long-term care settings, and up-to-date eligibility requirements for accessing benefits (e.g., income supports, health insurance, and services). Skills in negotiating multiple complex support systems (i.e., medical, long-term care, housing), and advocating to best meet the needs of vulnerable older adults and their families.

4) *Client and family-centered interventions:* Skills in providing crisis intervention when needed, and ensuring access to short- and long-term psychotherapeutic and psychopharmacological treatment for older adults coping with stressful life events, or mental health or substance use disorders. Knowledge of evidence-based interventions for older adults (e.g., cognitive-behavioral and interpersonal therapy for elders with depression; Functional Adaptation Skills Training [FAST] for elders with severe mental illness) and caregivers. Family treatment skills in working with family members and caregivers to improve client supports, alleviate caregiver burden, and access supportive services.

5) *Interdisciplinary team care:* Valuing interdisciplinary collaboration as an essential component of efforts to assess the needs and enhance the health and well-being of older adults and their families (Shortell, 2004). Skills in collaboration, advocacy, and leadership with other team members or supportive contacts around meeting the bio-psychosocial and spiritual needs of older clients and their family caregivers. Skills in educating and advocating on behalf of clients in order to ensure access to essential supportive services.

As is clear in the case of Miss A. (see Box 110.1), engaging with older clients and establishing a good working relationship is critical for geriatric case managers. Older adults are often wary of "strangers" and choose to interact with smaller circles of friends and family (Carstensen, Isaacowitz, & Charles, 1999; Lang, 2000). Some elders present with psychosocial concerns that can create barriers to service, such as prior mental and behavioral health concerns, a history of difficulties with service providers, or family conflict and dysfunction (Ferry & Abramson, 2005). Geriatric case managers must demonstrate authentic empathy and respect for client autonomy, take the time to establish trust, and be persistent while respecting boundaries in order to develop successful working alliances with older case management clients.

THE CHANGING CONTEXT

Over the past several decades, the trend toward community-based services, consumer direction,

---

Box 110.1 Case Narrative: Miss A.

Miss A. is an 81-year-old African-American woman who lives alone with her beloved cat, "Pumpkin," in a tidy studio apartment in East Harlem, New York. Miss A. describes herself as "a loner," only visiting with a friend once a week and occasionally hanging-out at the diner downstairs. Miss A. is diagnosed with osteoarthritis, obesity, hypotension, depression, and poor mobility. She is very independent, wishes to continue living alone, is deeply untrusting and suspicious of strangers, and somewhat resistant to accepting outside assistance. At the time of her referral, she agreed to accept a visit by a case manager only because it is required for her to participate in a home-delivered meals program. Her case manager, a 24-year old white woman named Rachel, enrolled her in Meals-on-Wheels and helped Miss A. access available benefits and services including rental assistance (SCRIE), transportation to and from medical appointments and church (Access-a-Ride and reduced fare MetroCard), and SNAP/Food Stamps. These services supported Miss A. in maintaining her autonomy and independence, but

Rachel was concerned that Miss A. needed additional help in maintaining her home and living independently. Despite her assessment, she was unable to convince Miss A. to accept additional support with her daily needs beyond meals.

Rachel, who has now worked with Miss A. for over five years, eventually persuaded her to try out Medicare-funded home care, which she receives two days/four hours each week. Happily, Miss A. loves her personal care attendant and, with growing trust, has allowed the aide to assist her with housework, cleaning, laundry, and shopping. Rachel also persuaded her to use an emergency alert bracelet, which Miss A. wears dutifully on the days when the aide is not present. Although Miss A. has limited the amount of help she will accept, the systems of care Rachel has been able to put in place, her understanding of the client's preferences, and deep respect for her strengths have helped them to create a distinctive safety net that maintains Miss A. in her long-standing home and community.

---

and care coordination have been significant drivers of the field of geriatric case management (Austin & McClelland, 2009). In the coming decades, sweeping changes set in motion by passage of the Patient Protection & Affordable Care Act of 2009 (ACA; Public Law 111 - 148) will have a far-reaching impact on older adults, caregivers, and case managers. In addition to extending insurance coverage to an estimated 27 million uninsured people (Nardin, et al., 2013), the ACA will expand and broaden Medicaid coverage to millions of individuals living near the poverty line, encourage greater use of home and community-based services, and incentivize the use of case management and care coordination to increase access to and use of home and community-based long-term care services for older adults and people with disabilities (Andrews et al., 2013; Darnell, 2013).

Building on the successes of Medicare demonstration projects that integrated medical and social services for community-dwelling older

adults (e.g., Program for All-inclusive Care of the Elderly [PACE], social health management organizations [social HMOs]), the ACA promotes the development and dissemination of several models of care, including patient-centered medical homes (PCMHs) and Accountable Care Organizations (ACOs). Despite different approaches, both programs aim to organize and integrate services around primary care providers and provider networks; providers will, in turn, have more latitude and bear more responsibility in ensuring the quality, coordination, and costs of care. The ACA creates incentives for greater use of electronic medical records to cut down on medical error and increase systems communication, and models new payment structures that seek to reward efficiency and quality. The goal of these reforms is to reduce health care costs and fragmentation of medical and social services and supports, and promote health, function, and independence among community-dwelling elders. Although it is difficult to predict the ultimate effects of these reforms, the ACA has already enhanced case management and service coordination for older adults and their families (Darnell, 2013).

CONCLUSION

Case management with older adults has grown in response to critical demographic, epidemiologic, and economic changes of the past half century: a rapidly aging population, the growing prevalence of chronic illnesses in later life, systemic changes in health care financing and delivery, and an increasingly fragmented, inefficient, and expensive system of health care and social service supports for vulnerable elders. Our ability to better meet the needs of older adults and their families is constrained by a critical shortage of social workers, nurses, and other direct service workers who are trained in the competencies of working with older adults and their families (Institute of Medicine [IOM], 2008). As the Baby Boom generation ages and life expectancies grow over the next several decades, there will be an increasing need for all social workers to be skilled in working with older adults and their families. Social workers will be called upon to evaluate and advocate for innovative health and long-term care policies and services that more effectively meet the needs of community-dwelling elders. And geriatric case managers will continue to enhance their clients' physical, emotional, cognitive, and social functioning, while ensuring autonomy, choice, and dignity for older adults and their caregivers.

WEBSITES

Administration on Aging, Administration for Community Living, U.S. Dept. of Health & Human Services: *Home of federal policy affecting older adults; Guide to programs and policies, and consumer guide.* http://www.aoa.gov

American Case Management Association: *Training, networking and advocacy for case managers in health care.* http://www.acmaweb.org

Case Management Society of America: *National membership organization, providing policy and practice resources, including case management standards of practice.* http://www.cmsa.org

Centers for Medicare and Medicaid Services: *Information and guide to the primary public health care programs covering older adults.* http://www.cms.gov

Elder Care Directory: *Resources for caregivers of older adults in all 50 states.* http://www.eldercaredirectory.org/state-resources.htm

The National Association of Area Agencies on Aging: *Membership organization of Aging Network programs; Eldercare locator, resources and news about elder services.* http://www.n4a.org

AARP: *National non-profit member organization for people over 50: Resources, research, advocacy for older Americans and gerontologists.* http://www.aarp.org

The National Council on Aging (NCOA): *Nonprofit service and advocacy organization headquartered in Washington, DC; Resources for elders, caregivers, and organizations.* http://www.ncoa.org

References

Administration on Aging (AoA). (2012). *A profile of older Americans: 2012.* Administration for Community Living, U.S. Department of Health and Human Services. Retrieved from http://www.aoa.gov/AoARoot/Aging_Statistics/Profile/2012/docs/2012profile.pdf

Andrews, C. M., Darnell, J. S., McBride, T. D., & Gehlert, S. (2013). Social work and implementation of the Affordable Care Act. *Health & Social Work, 38*(2), 67–71.

Austin, C., & McClelland, R. (2009). Case management with older adults. In A. R. Roberts, (Ed.), *Social worker's desk reference* (2nd edition) (pp. 796–800). New York, NY: Oxford University Press, Inc.

Benjamin, R. M. (2010). Multiple chronic conditions: A public health challenge. *Public Health Reports, 125*(5), 626–627.

Brown, R. S., Peikes, D., Peterson, G., Schore, J., & Razafindrakoto, C. (2012). Six features of Medicare coordinated care demonstration programs that cut hospital admissions of high-risk patients. *Health Affairs, 31*(6), 1156–1166.

Carstensen, L. L., Isaacowitz, D. M., & Charles, S. T. (1999). Taking time seriously: A theory of socioemotional selectivity. *American Psychologist, 54*(3), 165.

Centers for Medicare and Medicaid Services (CMS). (2012). *Chronic conditions among Medicare beneficiaries: Chartbook, 2012 Edition.* Baltimore, MD: Author.

Centers for Disease Control and Prevention (CDC). (2013). *The State of Aging and Health in America 2013*. Atlanta, GA: Author.

Darnell, J. S. (2013). Navigators and assisters: Two case management roles for social workers in the Affordable Care Act. *Health & Social Work, 38*(2), 123–126.

Duckett, M., & Guy, M. (2000). Home and community-based services waivers. *Health Care Financing Review, 63*, 123–125.

Feinberg, L., Reinhard, S., Houser, A., & Choula, R. (2011). *Valuing the invaluable, 2011 update: The growing contributions and costs of family caregiving*. Washington, DC: AARP Public Policy Institute. Retrieved from: http://assets.aarp.org/rgcenter/ppi/ltc/i51-caregiving.pdf

Ferry, J., & Abramson, J. (2005). Toward understanding the clinical aspects of geriatric case management. *Social Work in Health Care, 42*(1), 35–56.

Frankel, A., & Gelman, S. (1998). *Case management: An introduction to concepts and skills*. Chicago, IL: Lyceum Books.

Gallagher, E., Alcock, D., Diem, E., Angus, D., & Medves, J. (2002). Ethical dilemmas in home care case management. *Journal of Health Care Management, 47*(2), 85–97.

Institute on Medicine (IOM). (2008). *Retooling for an aging America: Building the health care workforce*. Washington, DC: The National Academies Press.

Lang, F. (2000). Endings and continuity of social relationships: Maximizing intrinsic benefits within personal networks when feeling near to death. *Journal of Social and Personal Relationships, 17*(2), 155–182.

MetLife Mature Market Institute (MetLife MMI). (2010). *Working caregivers and employer healthcare costs*. Retrieved from https://www.metlife.com/assets/cao/mmi/publications/studies/2011/mmi-caregiving-costs-working-caregivers.pdf

Morano, C., & Morano, B. (2006) Geriatric care management settings. In B. Berkman (Ed.), *Handbook of social work in social work and aging* (pp. 445–436). New York, NY: Oxford University Press, Inc.

Naito-Chan, E., Damron-Rodriguez, J., & Simmons, W. J. (2005). Identifying competencies for geriatric social work practice. *Journal of Gerontological Social Work, 43*(4), 59–78.

Naleppa, M. (2006). Case management services. In B. Berkman (Ed.), *Handbook of social work in social work and aging* (pp. 521–528). New York, NY: Oxford University Press, Inc.

Nardin, R., Zallman, L., McCormick, D., Woolhandler, S., & Himmelstein, D. (2013). The uninsured after implementation of the Affordable Care Act: A demographic and geographic analysis. *Health Affairs Blog*, June 6, 2013. Retrieved from http://healthaffairs.org/blog/2013/06/06/the-uninsured-after-implementation-of-the-affordable-care-act-a-demographic-and-geographic-analysis/

National Association of Social Workers (NASW). (2013). *NASW standards for social work case management*. Washington, DC: NASW Press. Retrieved from http://www.social-workers.org/practice/naswstandards/CaseManagementStandards2013.pdf.

National Alliance for Caregivers and American Association of Retired Persons [NAC/AARP] (2012). *Caregiving in the U. S.: 2012*. Bethesda, MD: Authors.

U.S. Census Bureau. (2012). *National population projections—Table 2*. Retrieved from http://www.census.gov/population/projections/data/national/2012/summarytab

Peikes, D., Brown, R., Chen, A., & Schore, J. (2009) Effects of care coordination on hospitalization, quality of care, and health care expenditures among Medicare beneficiaries: 15 randomized trials. *JAMA: Journal of the American Medical Association, 301*(6), 603–618.

Shortell, S. M., Marsteller, J. A., Lin, M., Pearson, M. L., Wu, S. Y., Mendel, P., Cretin, S., & Rosen, M. (2004). The role of perceived team effectiveness in improving chronic illness care. *Medical Care, 42*(11), 1040–1048.

Wodarski, J., & Williams-Hayes, M. (2003). Utilizing case management to maintain the elderly in the community, *Journal of Gerontological Social Work, 39*(4), 19–38.

111 HIV/AIDS Case Management

Brian Giddens, Lana Sue I. Ka'opua, & Evelyn P. Tomaszewski

Social work case management with/for Persons Living with HIV (PLHIV) optimally is guided by the *NASW Standards for Social Work Case Management* (National Association of Social Workers [NASW], 2013). These standards uphold the profession's strengths-based perspective, value the consumer–provider partnership, promote collaborative relations across professional disciplines and organizations, and endorse purposeful intervention at the micro, mezzo, and macro levels. HIV case management (HCM) is customized to address the bio-psychosocial and spiritual needs of PLHIV in their respective social environments, with strong consideration of changing conditions caused by treatment advances, public policies, and other systemic factors.

Despite variation in programs, four types of activities are common across almost all programs. Common services in both generic and HIV-specific case management include: consumer advocacy, service brokerage, services coordination, and provision of informational, emotional, and tangible support (NASW, 2013; Murphy, Tobias, Rajabiun, & Abuchar, 2003). Across the trajectory of the HIV epidemic, these services have evolved continuously to address the emergent needs of PLHIV.

In the early years of the HIV epidemic, HCM programs were developed in urban epicenters to meet the medical and psychosocial needs of PLHIV. Because HIV disproportionately affected groups already disenfranchised, case managers found themselves intervening in situations imbued with social stigma and discrimination (Brennan, 1996). Interventions were aimed at facilitating access to benefits, care, housing, legal, and other resources vital to consumer well-being.

With the advent of highly active antiretroviral therapy (HAART) in the mid-1990s, HCM evolved to emphasize support for living with HIV as a chronic condition. HCM innovations included assessment of an individual's capacity to adhere to complex HAART regime, support for management of medication side effects, and assistance in coping with the psychosocial consequences of chronic disease management (Giddens & Ka'opua, 2006; Ka'opua & Linsk, 2007). In the first decade of the 21st century, HIV incidence has stabilized, a fact generally attributed to bio-medical advances and public health education.

Despite this very positive development, factors such as continued stigmatization, discrimination, and lack of access to care influence delays in HIV testing and treatment, potentiating disparities in mortality and morbidity (AIDS Healthcare Foundation, 2012; Tomaszewski, 2012; Lambda Legal, 2010). Persons identifying as ethnic and/or sexual minorities continue to be disproportionately burdened by HIV infection; particularly affected are Men who have Sex with Men (MSM) and African-Americans (Centers for Disease Control and Prevention [CDC], 2012). Notably, these challenges coexist alongside newer ones, namely, that of an aging, seropositive population vulnerable to non-AIDS defining cancers and other disease conditions associated with older age, diminished funding for health and human services, shifting health policies, and transitioning health care service and insurer systems (Coates, Richter, & Caceres, 2008; Deeken et al., 2012; Emlet, Gerkin, & Orel, 2009; Lambda Legal, 2010; Sankar, Nevedal, Neufeld, Berry, & Lurborsky, 2011). This chapter provides a concise review of the scope and role of HCM in addressing persistent challenges, as well as newly emerging ones.

Also provided are key considerations for practice application, focused segments on confidentiality, cultural competency and quality improvement, and resources for more in-depth perusal.

EVIDENCE BASE FOR HIV
CASE MANAGEMENT

Published research suggests that HCM positively influences consumer- and service systems-related outcomes.

Risk Reduction

• *HCM programs guided by a behavioral change theory* (e.g., Social Cognitive, Social Learning) are most efficacious in reducing HIV risk (Lyles et al., 2007).
• *HCM programs integrating case management and motivational counseling* reduce HIV risk behaviors among Hispanic persons using injection drugs (Robles et al., 2004).

Service Utilization

• *HCM is associated with entry and sustained use of health services.* A longitudinal, case-control study involving a representative sample of urban-dwelling PLHIV adults indicated that:
  • HCM and other ancillary services are associated with increased entry and retention to care, thereby offering the prospect of increased medication adherence (Messeri, Abramson, Aidala, Lee, & Lee, 2002).
  • HCM providers offering tangible support in obtaining stable, adequate housing is crucial, with housing predictive of entry and retention outcomes, regardless of sociodemographic characteristics and physical/behavioral health variables (Aidala, Lee, Abramson, Messeri, & Siegler, 2007).
• *HCM structured on a brief counseling model* and strengths-based in approach promotes entry into care and may be particularly effective with newly diagnosed persons (Craw et al., 2008; Gardner et al., 2005).
• *Integrative HCM models promote entry to care and sustained engagement* in medical/behavioral health care across the HIV illness

trajectory. Models that include capacity for intensive HCM, outreach, navigation-like activities, and training on life skills and health literacy improved HIV-care retention of consumers from five socioeconomically disadvantaged, culturally diverse communities (Gardner, McLees, Steiner, del Rio, & Burman, 2011).

Cost-effectiveness

• *Research on cost-effectiveness of HCM yields mixed results.* When HCM provides access to services that enhance health status and functioning, cost-effectiveness is promoted (North Carolina Department of Health and Human Services, 2011). Preventative HCM may be less cost-effective than outreach to MSM, condom distribution, or needle exchange in high-prevalence communities (Cohen, Wu, & Farley, 2006).

Direct application of research to practice is cautioned due to general lack of agreement on "what" components comprise the HCM "gold standard," as well as methodological limitations. However, findings may offer helpful considerations for HCM practice and development of innovations. In reviewing research to inform practice, it is important to assess critically the evidence on types of services influencing a specific HIV-related outcome, as well as the socioeconomic and cultural characteristics of the consumer population for whom an intervention is intended. Customizing evidence-based practice is indicated.

WHAT IS CASE MANAGEMENT?

Case management (CM) is a service that utilizes assessment, planning, facilitation, coordination, evaluation, and advocacy to meet an individual's health needs (Case Management Society of America, 2013). The term CM has been used by several disciplines and institutions to describe coordination activities for clients and patients. *Insurance/Utilization CM* starts with the payer of services, focusing on monitoring and advocating for efficient and appropriate use of resources. *Medical CM*, centered within the health care system, concentrates on achieving improved patient outcomes, based on specific treatment interventions. *Social CM* often incorporates the psychosocial and spiritual factors affecting care, as well as tangible support and resource needs that can lead to improvements in care. Increasingly, as states are implementing health care reforms and creating or expanding systems, case managers will need to have a general understanding of all aspects of the medical, social, and payer realms.

In addition to the varied "case manager" roles, similar services have emerged, such as "care coordinators" and "patient navigators" (Bradford, Coleman, & Cunningham, 2007; NASW, 2013). Some of these services can assume aspects of case management activities. For example, a patient navigator may focus on specific tasks, such as coordinating a person's medical appointments or arranging transportation.

Setting can also differentiate the role of the case manager (Barney & Duran, 1997). For example, hospital-based programs may allow for a more medically focused style of case coordination, whereas the community-based case manager may be able to work closely with clients in their home setting, incorporating a more holistic assessment. With the implementation of the Patient Protection and Affordable Care Act (ACA), the HCM has the opportunity to provide care coordination and skill expertise through HIV-specific programs, patient-centered medical homes, and/or as a member of the community based prevention and wellness programming integrated into the newly defined health care systems. Access to medical treatment should be supplemented with ongoing case management services to facilitate continuity of care. Supportive services such as transportation, legal assistance, nutrition services, mental health services, substance use treatment, and child care are essential for certain populations facing difficulties with everyday needs.

For the purposes of this chapter, we will utilize an integrated model of HCM. An integrated model is interdisciplinary, incorporates the medical and psychosocial aspects of case management, and is client/patient centered. HCM is built on collaboration between providers and systems and removes barriers to care. Thus, HCM minimizes service duplication and contributes to cost-effectiveness.

ACTIVITIES AND ROLES IN HIV CASE MANAGEMENT

The integrated HCM model reflects the ecological view of the profession, a commitment to fostering productive relations with other professionals on behalf of the client, and approaches to service delivery that are client-centered, empowerment-based, and culturally responsive. HCM aligns with the National HIV/AIDS strategy of increasing access to care, improving health outcomes, and reducing health disparities (Office of National HIV/AIDS Policy, 2010). This specific variation of social work CM is unique in several ways. First, HCM models recognize that living with the disease poses bio-psychosocial and spiritual challenges. The implications of HIV-related stigmatization are underscored, and at the broadest level of intervention, HCM services are optimally delivered in a relationship characterized by acceptance and unconditional positive regard. The social worker providing HCM services is often one of the first gatekeepers in the service delivery system, and being a safe, confidential, and respectful contact is emphasized. Second, because crises may occur across the illness spectrum and client needs may vary over time, HCM often uses a triage system that prioritizes involvement on crucial points in disease progression. Triaging takes into account various acuity factors, such as basic needs, substance abuse, physical and mental health, and cultural or linguistic differences (Thompson, 1998). Third, prevention, adherence, and risk reduction are components of HCM; the social worker may take on the role of educator/counselor, as well as the more generic roles of service broker, advocate, and monitor. The case manager also assumes roles that are linked to the core activities of the initial interview/intake, assessment, and development, implementation, and monitoring of the service plan.

INITIAL INTERVIEW/INTAKE: CASE MANAGER AS SAFE CONTACT, CRISIS COUNSELOR, SERVICE BROKER

The process of HCM begins with the initial interview and in many settings is combined with the intake. In the initial interview, the primary goal is to establish a comfortable rapport that facilitates the development of a collaborative working relationship and establishes the social worker as a safe point of contact. In the first encounter, the role of crisis counselor may be important because entry into the service delivery system is often precipitated by crises that require immediate intervention. Information about the scope of services available is integrated into the initial interview.

During the intake, a preliminary assessment of client needs is made with a view toward bridging the gap between service needs and system resources. Client rights, grievance procedures, and responsibilities are reviewed, and informed consent to enroll the client in the service delivery system is obtained. Information that may be necessary to register the client includes confirmation and date of initial HIV/AIDS diagnosis or first positive HIV antibody test, health insurance status, HIV disease progression, source of exposure to HIV, CD4 count, housing status, active substance use, mental health status or psychiatric diagnoses, and tuberculosis (TB) status. Due to persistent HIV-related stigmatization, it is vital that social workers explain why information is collected, who will have access to the information, and how that information will be documented. The ACA provisions promote increasing use of electronic medical records to increase efficiency and improve coordination between providers (U. S. Department of Health & Human Services, 2013).

ASSESSMENT: CASE MANAGER AS CLINICIAN, SERVICE BROKER, LINKER, EDUCATOR

The needs assessment is optimally conducted as a collaborative effort with both case manager and client identifying treatment and service needs, client strengths, psychosocial resources, and areas in which service linkage is needed. The assessment is key to establishing a baseline profile for initial service referrals, development of the service plan, and criteria for evaluation of service outcomes. Data collected in the assessment process can include a variety of information, depending on setting and client situation, and can include questions related to living situation, perception and understanding of illness, relationships and social support, psychosocial functioning and mental status, functional status, service needs and issues, and legal issues (NASW, 2013). Case managers are increasingly taking on the functions of conducting risk assessments and assessing the ability of the client to adhere to treatment. Assessing HIV transmission risk includes identifying barriers for the client in reducing transmission risk and involves educating clients about HIV transmission and ways to reduce risk. When risk behaviors are identified, these can be addressed through the service plan and monitored within

the context of the ongoing HCM relationship. The other function of determining capacity for adherence should be done in conjunction with the interdisciplinary team. The role of the case manager is not only to identify and help resolve the psychosocial barriers to adherence but also to advocate for access to treatments that better fit the client's lifestyle and resources.

Various competencies are required for completion of the comprehensive assessment, including the technical capacity to gather clinical information and the cultural and linguistic competency to collect culturally relevant information. The case manager should work closely with the interdisciplinary team to ensure that client goals are congruent with treatment goals. Key indicators of mental health distress and disorder should be identified and referred for follow-up by a licensed mental health provider.

DEVELOPMENT OF THE SERVICE PLAN: CASE MANAGER AS PLANNER, COLLABORATOR, ADVOCATE

The service plan is central to the HCM effort and builds on the information gathered in the assessment. The case manager and client collaborate to create an inventory of needs and to formulate long- and short-term objectives that support the overall goals of health maintenance and independence. Specific planning, guided by realistic objectives, is required to prioritize activities and identify how services will be obtained, monitored, and coordinated among the providing agencies and health care systems. Responsibilities of all parties and a realistic timeline should be clearly delineated for accomplishing objectives and relevant activities. When service options are not available to meet identified needs, the case manager may need to consider either advocating for options or designing interim solutions. This is more likely to occur when clients' cultural values or practices are dystonic with that of existing programs, when clients have co-occurring diagnoses, such as substance abuse or a mental disorder, or when clients reside in rural areas with relatively few HIV-specific services. Service plans should be clearly documented in the client's chart along with copies of written correspondence and application forms for entitlement programs, experimental drug protocols, and the like. It may be helpful to offer the client an abbreviated version of the plan along with contact information.

IMPLEMENTATION/ MONITORING: CASE MANAGER AS BROKER, COORDINATOR, SERVICE MONITOR, COACH

In the implementation phase, the social worker and client take action to accomplish the service plan. Once consent to refer has been obtained, the case manager may employ a number of roles to facilitate the client's receipt of services, including that of broker, monitor, advocate, and coach. As broker, the case manager contacts other providers to pave the way for client referral and may also arrange for ancillary services, such as transportation to appointments. To ensure linkage with services, the case manager maintains regular client contact to monitor that services have been received and rendered in an acceptable way. On occasion the case manager may need to advocate on behalf of the client to ensure necessary services are received. As coach, the case manager encourages the client to anticipate barriers to access and utilization and, when necessary, works with the client to address these issues. Service plans are usually implemented in increments with careful documentation of client progress, including dates of contact, information on who initiated contact, and any action that resulted from the contact. Obstacles to implementation should be noted, as well as client satisfaction, modifications to the plan, and progress toward specified goals and objectives. Professional social work supervision, peer support, and inter- and intra-agency case conferences are often helpful in addressing implementation difficulties.

The aging of PLHIV will require increased coordination with community agencies and the long-term care system. The prevalence of HIV among older adults (persons ≥ 65 years) is growing and in comparison to other age cohorts represents the greatest increases (CDC, 2011). As a PLHIV ages, it is more likely that the individual will experience other medical conditions that require coordination with primary care providers and health systems. For case managers, this will require expertise in the broader health care spectrum.

CONTINUOUS QUALITY IMPROVEMENT

Ensuring the quality of a HCM program, including the evaluation of outcomes, is becoming increasingly important. Funding agencies increasingly require proof that their programs are making a tangible difference for their client base, and that services are being provided as efficiently as possible. Traditional evaluative activities, such as assessment of client satisfaction with services provided, determination of whether the affected population in a geographic area is aware of the availability of services, and assessment of medical provider satisfaction with HCM continue to be helpful. However, funders are increasingly requiring outcome-based evaluation (Health Resources and Services Administration [HRSA], 2009).

Examples of outcome evaluation can include whether CM is helping clients adhere to treatment (i.e., tracking health outcomes, completed medical visits) or whether clients actually engaged with referred services (i.e., tracking not only the number of referrals made to community services but whether the client followed through with the linkage). Quality improvement processes can monitor both the micro and macro level of service provision, ensuring that the needs of the client and the community are met. For example, identification of an unmet need in the community could involve bringing together the system of care for the affected population and brainstorming how to build the needed resource into the fabric of the community.

CONFIDENTIALITY

From the initial encounter with a client, the case manager should be transparent about what information may be shared, under what circumstances it will be shared, and with whom it is shared. The Health Insurance Portability and Accountability Act (HIPAA), as well as specific state and federal privacy regulations, are counters to concerns about managing client records in the digital age; service providers will need to stay current on such regulations. The advent of electronic provider/client communication via web portals and provider/client e-mail, as well as the burgeoning use of mobile devices hold promise for enhanced communication, but pose risks for privacy and confidentiality (West, 2012; Schickedanz et al., 2013). Additionally, as part of patient/client-centered medical homes, Accountable Care Organizations (ACOs) must collaborate with "neighborhood" or community-based prevention and wellness programs, thus increasing the standardized use of electronic medical record systems (Collins, 2011). To ensure support for privacy and confidentiality, a periodic review of institutional policies and workflows (i.e., sequence of procedures and standards within an organizational system) is indicated.

CULTURAL COMPETENCY

Discrimination and stigmatization have been directed at PLHIV, as well as the ethnic/racial, gender, sexual, and other minority groups with whom PLHIV identify (AIDS Healthcare Foundation, 2012; Lambda Legal, 2010). Cultural misunderstanding often is woven into this fabric of intolerance and the social work profession has been at the forefront of continuous advocacy for cultural competence (Ka'opua, 1998). The *NASW Indicators of the Achievement of Standards for Cultural Competence* (NASW, 2007) endorse culturally competent and linguistically appropriate policies, programs, services, evaluation, and research across practice settings. HCM providers may benefit from a review of these standards. In addition, cultural competence training on specific minority groups may be helpful.

The "graying" of PLHIV is of particular concern in the 21st century (Administration on Aging [AOA], 2012; CDC 2013). The CDC estimates that by 2015, older (≥50 years) adults will comprise about 50% of the seropositive population, thereby necessitating attention to culturally competent HIV practice with older adults. AOA recommends collaboration of HIV and aging networks, with attention to combating age discrimination, recognition of diverse strengths and needs of aging PLHIV, as well as cultural values reflective of their respective age cohort and/or other groups with whom they identify.

CONCLUSION

Since their earliest beginnings, social workers providing HCM have adapted their practices to meet the changing needs of their HCM populations. Over time, HCM has moved from a primarily social case management model to one that incorporates treatment adherence and other medical issues. HCM providers have adapted to changing contexts by gaining knowledge of resources and funding streams to sustain and increase services for PLHIV. Continuing shifts in the social and medical contexts of the disease will necessitate continuous evaluation and concomitant changes in the ways HCM is provided. HCM providers will need to adapt their practices to meet the evolving person- and systems-related conditions.

Case managers will also have to learn the language and culture of other disciplines, especially nursing, medicine, and pharmacy. As various forms of CM, managed care and disease management models proliferate, greater coordination will be needed between systems of care. Reducing redundancies and creating efficiencies will preserve more dollars for patient care and help avoid funding duplicative programs. This will require collaboration among programs and providers. With collaboration comes the need for skills in negotiation, systems thinking, problem solving, and communication. Given that skills such as these are what social workers practice every day, the profession is poised to take a prominent role in the HCM field of the future.

WEBSITES

The Body. http://www.thebody.com.
Centers for Disease Control (CDC). http://www.cdc.gov/hiv.
Healthy People/HRSA. http://www.healthypeople.gov/Document/HTML/Volume1/13HIV.htm.
NASW HIV/AIDS Spectrum Project. http://www.socialworkers.org/practice/hiv_aids/default.asp
Ryan White Care Programs. http://hab.hrsa.gov/
Older Adults and HIV/AIDS Toolkit. http://www.aoa.gov/AoARoot/AoA_Programs/HPW/HIV_AIDS/toolkit.aspx
Gay Men's Health Crisis (GMHC), 2010. http://www.gmhc.org/files/editor/file/a_pa_aging10_emb2.pdf
National Resource Center on LGBT Aging HIV and Aging Resources. http://www.lgbtagingcenter.org/resources/index.cfm?s=12

References

Administration on Aging. (2013). Older adults and HIV/AIDS. Retrieved from http://www.aoa.gov/AoARoot/AoA_Programs/HPW/HIV_AIDS/
Aidala, A., Lee, G., Abramson, D. M, Messeri, P., & Siegler, A. (2007). Housing need, housing

assistance, and connection to HIV medical care. *AIDS and Behavior, 11*, S101–15.

AIDS Healthcare Foundation (2012). End HIV stigma. Retrieved from http://www.aidshealth.org/endhivstigma

Barney, D. D., & Duran, B. E. S. (1997). Case management: Coordination of service delivery for HIV-infected individuals. In M. G. Winiarski (Ed.), *HIV mental health for the 21st century* (pp. 241–255). New York: New York University Press.

Bradford, J. B., Coleman, S., & Cunningham, W. (2007). HIV system navigation: An emerging model to improve HIV care access. *AIDS Patient Care & STDs* (Vol. 21) (Suppl. 1) (pp. S49–58).

Brennan, J. (1996). Comprehensive case management with HIV clients. In C. D. Austin & R. W. McClelland (Eds.), *Case management practice*. Milwaukee, WI: Families International.

Case Management Society of America (CMSA). (2013). What is a case manager. Retrieved from http://www.cmsa.org//Home/CMSA/WhatisaCaseManager/tabid/224/Default.aspx

Centers for Disease Control and Prevention. (2011). *HIV Surveillance Report, 23.*

Centers for Disease Control and Prevention. (2013). Diagnoses of HIV infection among adults aged 50 years and older in the United States and dependent areas, 2007–2010. *HIV Surveillance Supplemental Report, 18*(3). Retrieved from http://www.cdc.gov/hiv/library/reports/surveillance/2010/surveillance_Report_vol_18_no_3.html

Coates, T. J., Richter, L., & Caceres, C. (2008). Behavioural strategies to reduce HIV transmission: How to make them work better. *Lancet, 23*, 666–684. PMCID: PMC2702246.

Cohen, D. A., Wu, S. Y., & Farley, T. A. (2006). HIV prevention case management is not cost effective. *American Journal of Public Health, 96*, 400–401. PMCID: PMC1470514.

Collins, S. (2011). Accountable care organizations (ACOs): Opportunities for the social work profession. In *Practice Perspectives*. Washington, DC: National Association of Social Workers. Retrieved from http://www.socialworkers.org/assets/secured/documents/practice/health/ACOs%20Opportunities%20for%20SWers.pdf

Craw, J. A., Gardner, L. I., Marks, G., Rapp, R. C., Bosshart, J., Duffus, W. A., . . . Schmitt, K. (2008). Brief strengths-based case management promotes entry into HIV medical care: Results of the antiretroviral treatment access study-II. *Journal of Acquired Immune Deficiency Syndrome, 47*, 597–606. doi:10.1097/QAI.0b013e3181684c51.

Deeken, J. F., Tjen-A-Looi, A., Rudek M. A., Okuliar, C., Young, M., Little, R. F., & Dezube, B. J. (2012). The rising challenge of non-AIDS-defining cancers in HIV-infected patients. *Clinical Infectious Diseases, 55*, 1228–1235. Advance online publication. doi:10.1093/cid/cis613.

Emlet, C. A., Gerkin, A., & Orel, N. (2009). The graying of HIV/AIDS: Preparedness and needs of the aging network in a changing epidemic. *Journal of Gerontological Social Work, 52*, 803–814. doi:10.1080/01634370903202900.

Gardner, E. M., McLees, M. P., Steiner, J. F., Del Rio, C., & Burman, W. J. (2011). The spectrum of engagement in HIV care and its relevance to test-and-infection. *Clinical Infectious Diseases, 52* (6); 793–800. doi:10.1093/cid/ciq243

Gardner, L. I., Metsch, L. R., Anderson-Mahoney, P., Loughlin, A. M., del Rio, C., Strathdee, S., . . . Holmberg, S. D. (2005). Efficacy of a brief case management intervention to link recently diagnosed HIV-infected persons to care. *AIDS, 19*, 423–431.

Giddens, B., & Ka'opua, L. S. (2006). Promoting treatment adherence through collaborative teams (PACT). In W. T. O'Donohue & E. R. Levensky (Eds.), *Promoting treatment adherence: A practical handbook for health care providers* (pp. 165–179). Thousand Oaks, CA: Sage Publications.

Health Resources and Services Administration (HRSA). (2009). HAB HIV performance measures: Medical case management. HIVQUAL continuous quality improvement. Retrieved from http://hab.hrsa.gov/deliverhivaidscare/hivqual.html

Ka'opua, L. S. (1998) Multicultural competence. In D. M. Aronstein & B. J. Thompson (Eds.), *HIV and social work. A practitioner's guide* (pp. 61–54). New York, NY: Haworth.

Ka'opua, L. S., & Linsk, N. (2007). Introduction: Addressing challenges of adherence to HIV medications for social services practice, research, and training. *Journal of HIV/AIDS & Social Services, 6*, 1–8.

Lambda Legal. (2010). *When health care isn't caring: Lambda Legal's survey of discrimination against LGBT and people with HIV.* New York, NY: Author. Retrieved from http://www.lambdalegal.org/publications/when-health-care-isnt-caring

Lyles, C. M., Kay, L. S., Crepaz, N., Herbst, J. H., Passin, W. F., Kim, A. S., . . . Mullins, M. M. (2007). Best evidence-based interventions: Findings from a systematic review of HIV behavioral interventions for U. S. populations at high risk. *American Journal of Public Health, 97*, 133–143.

Messeri, P. A., Abramson, D. M., Aidala, A. A., Lee, F., & Lee, G. (2002). The impact of ancillary HIV services on engagement in medical care in New York City. *AIDS Care, 14* (Suppl. 1), S15–S29.

Murphy, R., Tobias, C., Rajabiun, S., & Abuchar, V. (2003). HIV case management: A review of the literature. Report for the Massachusetts Department of Public Health. Retrieved from http://docsfiles.com/pdf_the_case_for_literature.html

National Association of Social Workers. (2007). *NASW indicators of the achievement of NASW standards for cultural competence in social work practice.* Retrieved from http://www.socialworkers.org/practice/standards/naswculturalstandardsindicators2006.pdf

National Association of Social Workers. (2013). *NASW standards for social work case management.* Retrieved from http://www.socialworkers.org/practice/naswstandards/CaseManagementStandards2013.pdf

North Carolina Department of Health & Human Services, Division of Medical Assistance. (2011). HIV case management. Retrieved from http://www.ncdhhs.gov/dma/services/hivcm.htm

Office of National HIV/AIDS Policy. (2010). National HIV/AIDS strategy for the United States. Retrieved from http://www.whitehouse.gov/sites/default/files/uploads/NHAS.pdf

Robles, R. R., Reyes, J. C., Colon, H. M., Sahai, H., Marreno, C. A., Matos, T. D., . . . Shepard, E. W. (2004). Effects of combined counseling and case management to reduce HIV risk behaviors among Hispanic drug injectors in Puerto Rico: A randomized controlled study. *Journal of Substance Abuse Treatment, 27*, 145–152.

Sankar, A., Nevedal, A., Neufeld, S., Berry, R., & Lurborsky, M. (2011). What do we know about older adults and HIV? A review of the social and behavioral literature. *AIDS Care, 23*, 1187–1207. Advance online publication. doi:10.1080/09540121.2011.564115.

Schickedanz, A., Huang, D., Lopez, A., Cheung, E., Lyles, C. R., Bodenheimer, T., & Sarkar, U. (2013). Access, interest, and attitudes toward electronic communication for health care among patients in the medical safety net. Advance online publication. *Journal of General Internal Medicine.*

Thompson, B. J. (1998). Case management in AIDS service settings. In D. M. Aronstein & B. J. Thompson (Eds.), *HIV and social work. A practitioner's guide* (pp. 75–87). New York, NY: Haworth.

Tomaszewski, E. P., (2012) Human rights update: Understanding HIV/AIDS stigma and discrimination. Retrieved from http://www.socialworkers.org/practice/hiv_aids/AIDS_Day2012.pdf

U. S. Department of Health & Human Services. (2013). Healthcare.gov. Retrieved from http://www.healthcare.gov/law/timeline/full/html.

West, D. (2012). How mobile devices are transforming healthcare. *Issues in Technology Innovation, 18*, 14.

112 Social Work Case Management in Medical Settings

Candyce S. Berger

There is no standardized definition of case management, nor one accepted approach (National Association of Social Workers [NASW], 2013). Many health care professionals claim dominion over case management, including social work. Social work's involvement in case management can be traced to the turn of the 20th century and the social casework approach. Social casework processes parallel the steps described in the case management process: assessment, diagnosis, intervention, and follow-up. Social work case management is rooted in the problem-solving process and incorporates biological and developmental understanding, systems theory, and/or ecological theories that balance personal and environmental determinants in understanding illness and health. Social work leaders in health care have emphasized the importance of this bio-psychosocial approach in working with patients, dating back to Ida Cannon at the turn of the 20th century. Cannon emphasized the need to reach out into the community to link hospital and community-based care in a holistic approach to health care delivery. Though the term "case management" may not have appeared in these early writings, the descriptions of services included similar terms, such as screening for high risk, assessment, intervention, brokerage, linkages, evaluation, and follow-up (Berger, 1996). Several factors contributed to the rapid growth of case management in health care settings.

1. *Health care inflation.* As the costs of health care exceeded the ability of individual, organizational, and governmental payers to keep pace with its growth, people began looking for ways to contain costs. Although the rate of growth in health care spending has slowed since the 1980s, it is still growing faster than the national income. The recent economic recession has added to the burden of health care costs as more individuals fall into unemployment or lower paying jobs. These conditions have continued the U. S. focus on containing health care costs, while making health care more accessible to the country's citizens. (www.kaiseredu.org/issue-modules/ us-health-care-cost/background-brief/aspx). Case management continues to be embraced as an effective approach to cut costs, and a multitude of studies have shown improved efficiency and effectiveness, including research on the intervention strategies utilized (Atteberry, 2009; Bierman, Dunlop, Brady, Dubin, & Brann, 2006; Coleman, Austin, Brach, & Wagner, 2009; Dorr, Wilcox, McConnell, Burns, & Brunker, 2007; Felt-Lisk & Mays, 2002; Kolbasovsky, Zeitlin, & Gillespie, 2012: Laramee, Levinsky, Sargent, Ross, & Callas, 2003; Peikes, Chen, Schore, & Brown, 2009; Riegel et al., 2002; Rodgers & Purnell, 2012; Shea et al., 2009; Sweeney, Halpert, & Waranoff, 2007; Vourlekis, Ell, & Padget, 2005).

2. *Legislative initiatives.* Legislation soon followed that extended the breadth of case management services. For example, the Health Maintenance Act of 1973 encouraged comprehensive health services over the continuum of care, including preventive, acute, chronic, and terminal care services. Case management became a primary vehicle to facilitate integration of services. Passage of the Omnibus Budget Reconciliation Act in 1981 and the subsequent Consolidated Omnibus Budget Reconciliation Act in 1985 encouraged the expansion of case management services to the Medicaid population. According to Mason and Gammonley (2012), starting in the 1980s, home health care services continued to struggle with insecure funding and was characterized as an adjunct to medical care. The rapid changes in health care financing in response to cost-containment priorities began to shift the focus of care to community-based settings where case management services received increased attention, particularly case management teams. However, The Patient Protection and Affordable Care Act (PPACA) of 2010 has expanded the emphasis on community-based care even further with several components that extend the use of case management approaches (see section below).

3. *Employer benefits.* Employers quickly followed by incorporating case management programs into their health benefits plans. This expanded the role and visibility of case management, particularly in the medical claims arena, with a priority for cost containment.

4. *Chronicity as a leading health problem.* A new set of patient care challenges emerged as chronic illness became a major focus in health care delivery. Rather than the controlled environment of an acute, inpatient unit, much of health care delivery moved to the community. This move required intensive coordination of service delivery across multiple venues of care (e.g., medications, physician office visits, long-term care, and wraparound services). Case management offered an approach that was capable of coordinating multiple systems of care to enhance quality while reducing fragmentation and costs.

Chronic disease has surpassed acute episodes of care as the greatest cause of death and disability. A major factor accounting for this is the rapid growth of the elderly population, who are living longer, often with multiple chronic conditions (Mason & Gammonley, 2012). According to Coleman, Austin, Brach et al (2009, p.75), chronic diseases account for 59% of all deaths and 46% of the global burden of disease. This shift to treating chronic illness can lead to overutilization of health care services, increasing costs, and poor health outcomes if disease is poorly managed.

One of the biggest challenges to the management of chronic disease is patient adherence to medical recommendations (Felt-Lisk & Mays, 2002; Laramee et al., 2003; NASW, 2007; Vourlekis & Ell, 2007). The World Health Organization (2003) estimates that medical adherence in developed countries is 50%; and even less in developing nations. Poor adherence not only compromises the quality of life of patients but also negatively impacts health economics. Case management strategies are increasingly used to address management of patient care, particularly in the area of adherence, because of the perceived positive influence on efficiency and effectiveness. Over the past decade, evidence-based studies have provided increasing data to substantiate these claims.

5. *Prevention.* As rising health care costs associated with acute care placed greater emphasis on prevention as a more cost-effective approach, case management was used to coordinate and monitor patient compliance with prevention strategies. Under the PPACA, this focus will rise in importance.

DEFINING CASE MANAGEMENT

Case management has been defined in many ways by a variety of professions and organizations. The American Case Management Association defines it as a, "collaborative practice model.... [that] encompasses communication and facilitates care along a continuum through effective resource coordination" (Standards of Care, p.1) for hospitals and health settings. The Case Management Society of America defines it as, "a collaborative process of assessment, planning, facilitation, care coordination, evaluation, and advocacy for options and services to meet an individual's and family's comprehensive health needs through communication and available resources to promote quality, cost-effective outcomes" (http://www.cmsa.org). Finally, NASW defines it in their Standards for Social Work Case Management (2013) as, "A process to plan, seek, advocate for, and monitor services from different social services or health care organizations and staff on behalf of a client" (p. 13). Although these definitions vary, there are commonalities that shape the models, interventions, and goals of case management. Five models of case management continue to be relevant today

in health care settings, particularly hospitals (Rose, 1992; Berger, 1996). These models include the following.

1. *Primary Care Case Management.* The primary care physician is responsible for coordinating the care for all of the patients assigned to him or her, mostly associated with health maintenance organizations and more recently with the "medical home" or "health home" contained within the PPACA. It is characterized by having a physician responsible for overseeing all of the patient's health care interventions and synthesizing the medical information (e.g., laboratory, specialist consultations, radiology) to reduce fragmentation and duplication of care. Most health maintenance organizations use this approach by requiring authorization from the primary care physician for all health care services provided and holding him or her fiscally responsible for coordination of services (e.g., capitation).

2. *Medical Case Management.* This approach focuses on a select group of patients in whom severe illnesses and/or injuries require intensive coordination and monitoring of services. The approach requires a good understanding of medications, medical information (e.g., medical diagnosis and interpreting laboratory data), and medical equipment and supplies. The goal is to prevent medical crisis or exacerbation of health status. Nurses typically assume the role of case managers, though social workers may also fill these roles, particularly in the area of mental health.

3. *Social Case Management.* This approach emphasizes coordination and monitoring of nonmedical aspects of the patient's environment that impinge on his or her ability to maximize health care services (e.g., social and economic factors that interfere with a patient's ability to follow medical requirements). Non-acute, community-based patients (e.g., frail elderly, severely mentally ill) typically fall into this category. Social workers and nurses are the primary providers of this approach to case management services.

4. *Medical-social Case Management.* Medical and social case management are integrated to provide a more holistic approach to managing health care delivery. This is premised on an ecological approach in which

medical, social, economic, and cultural factors are synthesized to frame the case management process. It is this model of case management in which the greatest conflict over professional domain occurs, with nurses and social workers often competing for dominance. Team approaches are increasingly being used to maximize opportunities rather than competition for turf.

5. *Benefit Case Management.* This approach focuses exclusively on health care benefits, emphasizing the most appropriate use of health care resources. It often combines the dual focus of ensuring appropriate use of benefits (e.g., utilization review) and making benefits more flexible to achieve cost-effective services. It is used primarily within the insurance industry, though hospitals have incorporated aspects of this model. For example, a hospital may pay to have a ramp built in a patient's home (a service that may not be covered by one's insurance) in order to discharge the patient earlier. Also, many of the care management protocols used in inpatient settings are premised on effective and timely utilization of resources.

6. *Case Management Team.* A more recent model is the case management team (Kraft, 2009; Ruggiano et al, 2012). A case management team is defined as a multidisciplinary team, typically consisting of up to six different professions and health support personnel; the team composition is usually driven by patient-specific issues and needs. Team members combine their knowledge and information about the patient to gain group consensus in designing the best approach to the delivery of care in order to achieve the most positive outcomes for the patient. One member of the team assumes the role of a "lead" in order to collect, organize, and disseminate information; do patient scheduling; and facilitate team communication.

Although the various models presented above may differ, they all share a common approach that relies on the sequencing of activities to ensure efficiency and effectiveness in the delivery of health care services. They suggests that all the steps can be collapsed into two key ingredients: facilitating high quality of care and achieving cost-effectiveness. The steps involved in the case management process have been described in many fields of practice, including health care. Although different terms may be employed, these descriptions share a common set of generic steps that emanate from a problem-solving approach to intervention (Berger, 1996; Dorr et al., 2007; Felt-Lisk & Mays, 2002; Kane, 1992; Kirton, 1999; Laramee et al., 2003; NASW, 2007; Sangalang, Barth, & Painter, 2006; Schmuttermaier et al, 2010; Sweeney et al., 2007; Vourlekis et al., 2005). These steps include:

1. *Case Finding.* Potential recipients of case management services are identified through a standardized process using formalized screening criteria. Identification can be based on the type, nature, or extent of an individual's illness/disease (i.e., catastrophic, terminal, chronic, preventive) or the anticipated costs of care (Kane, 1992). As the boundaries between the sites of care (e.g., hospital, nursing home, and home health care) blur in response to a series of legislative initiatives that encourage cross-boundary collaboration, case finding has expanded to allow other providers to cross boundaries to identify high-risk clients. Kolbasovsky, Zeitlan, and Gillespie (2012) emphasize the importance of identifying clients for case management at the "point of care." This facilitates early connection to both the patient and to the health care providers, ensuring more accurate collection of patient and medical information and promoting more effective communication among all the providers of care. For example, Kolbasovsky (2008) describes community-based case managers initiating enrollment activities while the patient is still in the psychiatric hospital. Home health care agencies have implemented similar partnerships with hospitals to achieve earlier identification and engagement of patients to participate in case management.

2. *Assessment.* Once identified, recipients of case management services receive an evaluation that can range from a comprehensive, bio-psychosocial evaluation to a more focused evaluation of a specific aspect of care (e.g., pattern of resource utilization or eligibility determination). The case management model employed (e.g., social-medical vs. benefits case management) and the time perspective (e.g., relevance of information drawn from an individual's past, present, and future situation) will

define the scope of the assessment. Care must be taken during the assessment process to ensure the adequacy and reliability of information, because subsequent steps in the case management process are based in the interpretation of these data. A variety of validated risk assessment tools are available to assess substance abuse, mental status, and adherence to treatment (Cutler & Everett, 2010).

3. *Intervention.* This stage can also span a wide range of activities, varying in scope and intensity. Interventions can be as simple as flexing one's benefits package or providing information and referral to a comprehensive set of interventions that might include several or all of the following services: information and referral, coordination of service delivery through linkages, brokerage of client services, advocacy, provision of concrete services (e.g., arranging transportation), education, and therapeutic counseling. This last intervention is still a source of much debate as to whether a case manager should also serve as the client's therapist. For example, professionally trained case managers may employ motivational interviewing to address medication or medical issues. Careful review and consideration should be given before agreeing to provide this type of care, and should be restricted to case managers who hold a professional degree. Patient education is another intervention that may be incorporated into the case manager's role. Education is focused on the identification of symptoms and the appropriate response by the patient or caregiver if symptoms become more severe (Kolbasovsky, 2008). Regardless of the mix of interventions, each is linked to a measurable outcome or goal, mutually defined by the case manager and the client.

A primary intervention of the case manager is to facilitate communication. Without effective systems to promote communication with all the health care providers and community support systems, most of the other interventions associated with case management are likely to fail or at least be compromised in both efficiency and effectiveness (Kraft, 2009).

4. *Monitoring.* This set of activities focuses on reviewing the process of case management to ensure appropriateness and timeliness of intervention, and patient compliance. Regardless of how thorough the plan of intervention, problems can occur. An effective case manager regularly reviews the process of care to identify "breakdowns" in the plan.

The newest approach to monitoring home-based or community-based patients is the use of telemedicine technology (Atteberry, 2009; Britton, Engelke, Rains et al (2000 in Atteberry, 2009; Shea, Weinstock, Teresi et al, 2009; Suter, Hennessey, Florez et al, 2011). Telemedicine has been found to be particularly effective in monitoring community-based home care settings with homebound patients, those with chronic disease, and patients who require more frequent intervention to achieve health behavior changes. The goal is the early identification of symptoms or risk factors that can produce complications to the patient's health status. Home telemedicine units are placed within a patient's home to monitor physiological symptoms through the patient's uploading of self-monitoring data (e.g., glucose levels, blood pressure, etc.). These units also may have web-based cameras that enable video conferencing. The advantages of these units include increased involvement of the patient in self-monitoring activities, the ability to gather patient information, and face-to-face video conferencing with a case manager or a specific health care provider based on patient need. Economic benefits include reduced hospital and emergency room visits and reduction in home visits by home care personnel. Monitoring also covers the communication and collaboration across health care providers, community agencies, and members of a case management team (Kraft, 2009).

With the increasing reliance on computerized data systems (e.g., electronic patient records, computerized information systems, and telemedicine), monitoring activities can be more thorough and timely, promoting more effective and efficient care. However, sole reliance on these sources of information may give a skewed picture. The case manager should not underestimate the importance of direct contact with the client to get a thorough understanding of not only *what* has occurred but also *why* (i.e., what factors in the home or the community may be contributing to the problem).

5. *Evaluation.* As with any intervention, a practitioner evaluates the impact of his or her work. Evaluation combines a focus on both the process (e.g., number of contacts, types of services provided) and outcome (e.g., goal achievement, health indices) of case management. Outcome measures might also include population-based indices, such as changes in health status, quality of life, or financial impact. If clear goals and objectives for the interventions have been identified in Step 3, evaluation becomes an easier task.

The steps in case management have been presented as if they represent a linear process. It is important to emphasize that this is a dynamic process; movement can go forward or backward and steps may occur simultaneously, particularly when there are multiple problems being addressed.

CONTEXTUAL FACTORS RELATED TO CASE MANAGEMENT IN HEALTH CARE

Developing and implementing case management in health care is neither a simple nor easy task. Many factors shape the practice to create a mosaic of models, providers, and services. This complexity often presents challenges and conflicts that plague its use. This chapter concludes with a set of factors to be considered when developing or implementing a case management program (Berger, 1996).

1. *Case Management Goals.* What is the primary purpose or focus of the case management program? This will often define the appropriate model of case management (e.g., medical, social, or benefits case management), which professional(s) is most likely to fulfill the role of case manager, and the size of the case manager's caseload.
2. *Location of Case Management Services.* Where will case management be provided? Will it be provided in the hospital, in the community, or spanning both locations of care? Hospital-based services more often use the medical case management model and typically employ nurses or teams of social workers and nurses as case managers. Utilization review can be structured as a

benefit or medical model and is also prevalent on inpatient units.

Community approaches tend to use more of a social, medical-social, or team approach, though "benefits case management" is also evident. Providers are typically nurses, social workers, or case management teams that may consist of nurses, social workers, occupational therapist, physical therapist, speech therapist, other health care support providers, and/ or consumers. Benefits case management may or may not employ practitioners from health disciplines. Thompson (1998) suggests that community approaches may require interactive case management that uses street-based, hands-on interventions rather than having the client come to the worker's office. Creating teams that include public health professionals is an excellent option for achieving this level of case management, particularly when spanning inpatient and outpatient arenas. Several studies have validated the positive impact of community-based case management on patient, organization, and system outcomes (Bierman et al., 2006; Dorr et al., 2007; Felt-Lisk, & Mays, 2002; Laramee et al., 2003; Riegel et al., 2002; Sweeney et al., 2007; Vourlekis et al., 2005). An example of this is the Chronic Care Model (CCM) that has been piloted over the past decade (Coleman, Austin, Brach et al, 2019; Schumuttermaier, Schmitt, King et al, 2011). CCM involves six areas: self-management support, decision support, delivery system design, information systems, health care organization, and community resources; but no standardized approach exists. The Centers for Medicare and Medicaid have been piloting the CCM approach in community-based settings.

A more recent development is the use of "transitional case management" programs (Kilgore, 2010). Transitional support is defined as, "a broad range of time-limited services designed to ensure health care continuity, avoid preventable poor outcomes among at-risk populations, and promote the safe and timely transfer of patients from one level of care to another or from one type of setting to another" (Naylor, Aiken, Kurtzman et al, 2011, p.747). Services are typically initiated in an institutional setting and then follow the patient's care into the community for a brief period of time to ensure compliance with medical recommendations. Many of these transitional programs are based on Dr. Coleman's Care Transition Intervention (CTI) model (Coleman, Parry, Chalmers et al, 2006) that combines traditional hospital care management with case management within the community.

3. *Auspices of the Program.* Is the case management program internal to the service delivery system (e.g., a hospital has a case management program for its patients) or external to the system of care (e.g., a payer implements a case management program that crosses organizational boundaries)? Internal and external programs are inversely related in terms of their advantages and disadvantages. For example, although internal programs can have greater potential influence based on their formal and informal relationship with key decision makers and providers, they may lack the objectivity and autonomy that are characteristic of external programs when choosing interventions and services for the patient. Several studies have shown the importance of the need for the case manager to be closely related to health care and/or demonstrating expertise in the disease(s) being managed (Laramee et al. 2003; Vourlekis & Ell, 2007).

4. *Who the Client Is.* Although this has the illusion of an easy question, the waters become quite murky when one recognizes that health is embedded in an economic, political, and social constellation of players. The "patient" would seem the immediate response and clearly the priority according to NASW standards for case management (2013), whereas the real client may be the hospital, the payer, or society. This becomes a source of major confusion and potential conflict. For example, what happens when an organizational goal and a client goal conflict? Case managers must clarify who is the primary customer of the services and examine the various contextual factors that define the client's goals and objectives. For example, when working with women, the client may be more than the individual woman; the "client" often encompasses the family system, and a broader base of need will shape the goals and objectives. A distinguishing characteristic of social work case management is the emphasis on advocacy as a primary role.

5. *Professional Training of Case Managers.* Who is the case manager? Should it be a nurse, a social worker, a physician, or some other provider? Some case management programs have employed indigenous providers (e.g., Community Health Workers) to be individual case managers or to serve as members of the case management team (Nemcek & Sabatier, 2003; Norris, Chowdhury, Van Le, et al, 2006). Previous consumers of care are often in a position to enhance outreach services, as well as provide insights into the assessment of client needs. Issues also emerge regarding functional training in case management (e.g., certificate programs) and the credentialing of case managers through state and national programs. Several accrediting bodies for case managers now exist. The American Case Management Association offers credentialing exclusively to social workers and nurses. Professional domain may be less of an issue if one begins with an understanding of the model of case management to be employed. The development of a case management team is an effective alternative to a single-discipline practice, particularly when social and environmental determinants are significant to a patient's health (e.g., social-medical model). These teams have been used with both inpatient (e.g., care maps and utilization review) and community-based approaches (e.g., prenatal care, AIDS).

6. *Caseload.* Goals, intensity of services, duration of contact, and sophistication of the service delivery network will influence caseload size. If management of benefits is the sole objective of case management, caseloads can be extremely large (e.g., one case manager per 10,000 clients). Comprehensive case management may use caseloads that are smaller, and the size will vary according to the intensity of services provided (e.g., one per 20 clients for intensive case management; one per 100 cases where clients are more capable of mobilizing resources independently).

7. *Breadth of the Service Delivery System.* Case managers typically have a broad definition of the service delivery system (e.g., hospital, outpatient, community agencies, and churches). They should also have a good understanding of cultural determinants of health and health behavior, including awareness of different customs and health

care practices. Competency in culturally sensitive practice may lead one to incorporate nontraditional providers into the network of care, such as spiritual healers, herbalists, and other complementary and alternative treatment providers.

8. *Power and Influence of the Case Manager.* If the case manager does not have the authority or institutional influence to change the environmental factors that inhibit the delivery of health care services, case management will ultimately fail to achieve significant improvements for the patient. Authority will be influenced by such factors as ownership of the case management program (e.g., insurance companies, agencies, government), auspices (e.g., internal or external), and professional discipline of the case manager. This can determine whether the authority exists to change rules or regulations that present barriers to care.

9. *Ethical Challenges.* There is not sufficient space to allow a thorough discussion of the ethical issues that will influence case management practice. Issues of confidentiality, client autonomy, and justice will each surface in a health care delivery system that relies more heavily on health care networks, computer technology, and cost-containment goals (Berger, 1996). Practitioners will need to continuously monitor their practice for ethical dilemmas and draw on the assistance of institutional and/or professional ethical committees to help guide their practice.

FUTURE ISSUES AND DIRECTIONS

As we look to the future, several issues or mandates emerge that are relevant to social work practice and education.

1. *The Patient Protection and Affordable Care Act (PPACA)* passed in 2010 is heralding a new era in health care reform. It is the boldest step to date in health care reform, bringing the United States closer to universal access to health care services. Several elements within this new legislation directly impact the use of case management approaches. Naylor, Aiken, Kurtzman et al (2011) delineate six different sections within the legislation that specifically address the use of transitional care services:

- Section 3026: establishes the Community-based Care Transitions Program, which offers funding to health systems and community agencies that offer at least one transitional care interventions for Medicare recipients.
- Section 3012: the Centers for Medicare and Medicaid funding for innovative care programs including transitional care
- Section 2602: Federal Coordinated Health Care Office to foster integration of care for dual-eligible recipients (Medicare and Medicaid beneficiaries)
- Section 3022: Accountable Care Organizations will be required to submit data on their performance measures, including data related to transitions across sites of care
- Section 2703: Health Homes will provide comprehensive care management, including transition services, to chronically ill individuals
- Section 3023: a national pilot program to bundle payments across the continuum of care, including institutional care, physician care, and home care into a single payment.

The research to date on transitional care programs has found them to be efficient and effective (Naylor, Aiken, Kurtzman et al, 2011). However, the majority of the research does not include populations considered to be targets of the PPACA legislation: dual-eligible recipients, cognitively impaired, and the medically underserved. Another drawback is that much of the research focuses on coordination and collaboration across health care providers, and does not include community services that often address the wraparound services necessary to support the patient's quality of life.

As discussed earlier, the move to community-based services has advanced the delivery of case management services, especially the development of case management teams. The PPACA includes a variety of financial incentives to encourage the use of community-based services as an alternative to the traditional use of nursing homes for long-term care (Reinhard, Kassner, & Houser, 2011). These include:

- Community First Choice: increases the federal match for Medicaid by 6% for states promoting person-centered home and community-based settings

- Balancing Incentive Payment Program: offers financial incentives to states that have relied on institutional long-term options to encourage the development of community-based long-term care. This program also stipulates the use of conflict-free case management systems, in which there are no financial incentives for referrals to specific providers.
- Accountable Care Organizations: defined as, "a group of providers who are willing and able to take responsibility for improving the overall health status, care efficiency, and health experience for a defined population" (p. 41). Devore and Champion (2011) add that financial incentives are created to promote seamless networks of providers across the continuum of care from institutional settings to community-based care.

Embedded in each of these programs, as well as the establishment of Health Homes, is the imperative to provide case management that facilitates this seamless delivery of care, encourages adherence to medical recommendations, and encourages self-management and behavior change that promotes improved health status and quality of life. Throughout the PPACA documents, references are made to the use of "patient navigators." Rogers and Purnell (2012) describe their duties, which appear to be almost identical to activities performed by case managers: guide patients to needed services; assist with identifying insurance/exchanges and assist with completion of applications; assist with prescription costs; identify and refer to wraparound services; appointment scheduling; and client education. Natale-Pereira, Enard, Nevarez et al (2011, p. 3548) describe how patient navigators address four key areas to reduce health disparities: prevention and early detection, health care access and coordination, insurance coverage and continuity, and diversity and cultural competency. The legislation also stipulates the use of patient navigators to staff state exchanges (Gardiner, 2012).

2. *Advances in Information and Communication Technology.* NASW (2013) establishes face-to-face contact as the standard of care. However, studies have substantiated positive outcomes with the use of telephonic interventions for community-based case management (Laramee et al., 2003; Riegel et al., 2002). As discussed previously, the use of computerized technology for patient monitoring is increasing. Though research on this new technology is still evolving, it is garnering significant attention from providers, health care administrators, and payers. Incorporating e-mail and web-based cameras on home computers, or attached to the telemedicine units, promotes interactive discussions, and the video conferencing may resolve the needing for face-to-face contact., Ruggiano, Shtompel, Hristidis et al. (2002) suggest that information technology is an essential tool to maximize the communication and collaboration necessary to achieve patient health care goals. Social workers will need to develop proficiency in these new technologies to enhance case management processes.

3. *Future Direction for Social Workers in Health Care*: From its earliest roots, social work has played a major role in providing case management services to clients and patients. Although medical social work began within ambulatory and community settings, it has spent the majority of practice within institutional settings, especially hospitals. For the past several decades, health care has been moving from hospital to community-based programs, elevating home health care from its "second class" status as a health care provider to a major player in the network of care (Mason & Gammonley, 2012). Social work will need to parallel this move, increasing its presence in community-based health care programs. Under the provision of the PPACA, social work increasingly will play a role in the provision of geriatric services to address the growing elderly population, especially those struggling with multiple chronic illnesses. This growing demand for geriatric practitioners should produce a growth in funding to educate social workers to provide case management services to this population. Gardiner (2012) points out that the PPACA will "expand initiatives to increase racial and ethnic diversity in the health care professions, strengthen cultural competency training for all health care providers and require health plans to use language services and community outreach in underserved communities" (pp. 3550–3551). Social workers are uniquely qualified to fill these roles of patient navigators.

Case management in health care settings is a complex and dynamic intervention. Effective implementation will rely on a thorough understanding of the purpose, goals, and contextual factors that shape its practice. Attention should be given to advances in communication technology to facilitate case management processes, as well as evidence-based research to demonstrate practice efficiency and effectiveness. As health care increasingly moves into the community settings of care, team case management models may hold the greatest promise for the efficient and effective management of patient care.

WEBSITES

American Case Management Association. Standards of Care. http://www.acmaweb.org

Case Management Association of America. http://www.cmsa.org.

www.kaiseredu.org/issue-modules/us-halth-care-cost/background-brief/aspx

National Association of Social Workers. http://www.socialworkers.org

Standards for Social Work Case Management. http://www.ssocialworkers.org/practice/naswstandards/casemanagementstandards2013.pdf

References

Atteberry, G. (2009). The effects of telehomecare on quality and agency revenue: A literature review. *Home Health Care Management & Practice, 21,* 188–193. doi:10.1177/1084822308322652.

Berger, C. S. (1996). Case management in health care. In C. Austin & R. W. McClelland (Eds.), *Perspective on case management practice* (pp. 145–174). Milwaukee, WI: Families International.

Bierman, J., Dunlop, A. L., Brady, C., Dubin, C., & Brann, A. (2006). Promising practices in preconception care for women at risk for poor health and pregnancy outcomes. *Maternal Child Health Journal, 10*(suppl. 7): 21–28.

Coleman, E. A., Parry, C., Chalmers, S., & Min, S. (2006). The Care Transitions Intervention: Results of a randomized controlled trial. *JAMA Internal Medicine, 166*(17), 1822–1828. doi:10.1011/archinte.166.17.1822.

Coleman, K., Austin, B. T., Brach, C., & Wagner, E. H. (2009). Evidence on the Chronic Care Model in the new millennium. *Health Affairs, 28*(1), 75–85. doi:10.1377/hlthaff.28.1.75.

Cutler, D. M., & Everett, W. (2010). Thinking outside the pillbox—Medication adherence as a priority of health care reform. *The New England Journal of Medicine,* Perspective, 326, 1153–1155.

Dorr, D. A., Wilcox, A., McConnell, K. J., Burns, L, & Brunker, C. P. (2007). Productivity enhancement for primary care providers using multicondition care management. *American Journal of Managed Care, 12,* 22–28.

Felt-Lisk, S., & Mays, G. P. (2002). Back to the drawing board: New directions in health plans' care management strategies. *Health Affairs, 21*(5), 210–217.

Gardiner, T. (2012). Health insurance exchanges of past and present offer example of features that could attract small-business customers. *Health Affairs, 31*(2), 284–289. doi:10.1377/hlthaff.2011.1006.

Kane, R. (1992). Case management in health care settings. In S. Rose (Ed.), *Case management and social work* (pp. 170–203). New York, NY: Longman.

Kilgore, M. D. C. (2010). Transitional case management: A method for establishing self-advocacy and reducing hospital readmissions in COPD patients. *Home Health Care Management Practice, 22,* 435–438. doi:10.1177/1084822309357008

Kirton, C. (1999). Primary care and case management of persons with HIV/AIDS. *Nursing Clinics of North America, 34,* 71–94.

Kolbasovsky, A. (2008). An effective case model. Dorland Health. Retrieved from http://www.dorlandhealth.com/case_management/cip_magazine/7.html.

Kolbasovsky, A., Zeitlin, J., & Gillespie, W. (2012). Impact of point-of-care case management on readmissions and costs. *American Journal of Managed Care (online), 18*(8), e300–e306.

Kraft, C. (2009). All for one and one for all: Interdisciplinary case management in home health. *Home Health Care Management & Practice, 21,* 409–414.

Laramee, A. S., Levinsky, S. K., Sargent, J., Ross, R., & Callas, P. (2003). Case management in a heterogeneous congestive heart failure population. *Archives of Internal Medicine, 163,* 809–817.

Mason, M., & Gammonley, D. (2012). Public policy and the future of social work in long-term home health care. *Home Health Care Management and Practice, 24,* 125–131. doi:10.1177/1084822311430528.

NASW Standards for Social Work Case Management. (2013). Prepared by the Case Management Standards Work Group.

Natale-Pereira, A., Enard, K. R., Nevarez, L., & Jones, L. A. (2011). The role of patient navigators in eliminating health disparities. *Cancer, 117*(15), 3543–3551.

Naylor, M. D., Aiken, L. H., Kurtzman, E. T., Olds, D. M., & Hirschman, K. B. (2011). The importance of transitional care in achieving health reform. *Health Affairs, 30*(4), 746–754. doi:10.1377/hlthaff.2011.0041.

Nemcek, M. A., & Sabatier, R. (2003). State of evaluation: Community health workers. *Public Health Nursing, 20*(4), 260–270. doi: 10.1046/j.1525-1446.2003.20403.x.

Norris, S. L., Chowdhury, F. M., Van Le, K., Horsley, T., Brownstein, J. N., Zhang, X., . . . Sutterfield, S. W. (2006). Effectiveness of community health workers in the care of persons with diabetes. *Diabetic Medicine, 23*(5), 544–556. doi:10.1111/j.1464-5491.2006.01845.x.

Peikes, D., Chen, A., Schore, J., & Brown, R. (2009). Effects of care coordination on hospitalization, quality of care, and health care expenditures among Medicare beneficiaries. *JAMA: Journal of the American Medical Association, 301*(6), 603–618. doi:10.1001/jama.209.126.

Reinhard, S. C., Kassner, E., & Houser, A. (2011). How the Affordable Care Act can help move states toward a high-performing system of long-term services and supports. *Health Affairs, 30*(3), 447–453. doi:10.1377/hlthaff.2011.0099.

Riegel, B., Carlson, B., Kopp, Z., LePetri, B., Glaser, D., & Unger, A. (2002). Effect of standardized nurse case-management telephone intervention on resource use in patients with chronic heart failure. *Archives of Internal Medicine, 162,* 705–712.

Rodgers, J. T., & Purnell, J. Q. (2012). Healthcare navigation service in 2-1-1 San Diego guiding individuals to the care they need. *American Journal of Preventive Medicine, 43*(6S5), S450–S456.

Rose, S. (Ed.). (1992). *Case management and social work.* New York, NY: Longman.

Sangalang, B. B., Barth, R. P., & Painter, J. S. (2006). First-birth outcomes and timing of second births: A statewide case management program for adolescent mothers. *Health & Social Work, 31*(1), 54–63.

Shea, S., Weinstock, R. S., Teresi, J. A., Palmas, W., Starren, J., Cimino, J. J., . . . Eimicke, J. P. (2009). A randomized trial comparing telemedicine case management with usual care in older, ethnically diverse, medically underserved patients with diabetes mellitus: 5 year results of the IDEATel study. *Journal of American Medical Informatics Association, 16,* 446–456. doi:10.1197/mamia.M3157.

Suter, P., Hennessey, B., Florez, D., & Suter, W. N. (2011). Review series: Examples of Chronic Care Model: The home-based chronic care model: Redesigning home health for quality care delivery. *Chronic Respiratory Disease, 8,* 43–52. doi:10.1177/1479972310396031.

Sweeney, L., Halpert, A., & Waranoff, J. (2007). Patient-centered management of complex patients can reduce costs without shortening life. *American Journal of Managed Care, 12,* 84–89.

Thompson, B. (1998). Case management in AIDS service settings. In D. M. Aronstein & B. J. Thompson (Eds.), *HIV and social work: A practitioner's guide* (pp. 75–87). New York, NY: Haworth.

Vourlekis, B., & Ell, K. (2007). Best practice case management for improved medical adherence. *Social Work in Health Care, 44*(3), 161–177.

Vourlekis, B., Ell, K., & Padgett, D. (2005). Evidence-based assessment in case management to improve abnormal cancer screen follow-up. *Health & Social Work, 30*(1), 98–106.

PART XI
Community Practice

113 An Integrated Practice Model for Community Family Centers

Anita Lightburn & Chris Warren-Adamson

Family centers are an exceptional resource for disadvantaged families, who struggle with survival, often living in traumatic situations, in need of safety and a place to heal and grow. Immigrant families, isolated and beleaguered single parents, grandparents parenting troubled children, military families in the shadow of war, and young families who need more than child welfare services can provide, all benefit from responsive community-based family support. Family centers are an indispensable resource providing a system of care through connections to services in the community, with a caring community to be part of, a family center "home" that makes a difference for families, program staff, and their larger community.

As community programs, family centers reflect wide variation in structure and auspices. Some are mandated by legislation, others are supported by nonprofit organizations or sponsored by county, state, and federal funding, such as school-based family support centers and the court-mandated family relationship centers in Australia. Often associated with early child programs, multifaceted family centers are also referred to as family resource centers, child and family centers, or family support centers. These community centers, with a grass roots history, have developed over the past decades in neighborhoods, community centers, clinics, schools, early childhood programs, churches, and military bases. Prevention, early intervention, support, and empowerment focus the array of integrated services and methods of practice that are offered. The friendly neighborhood center is a place for parents, grandparents, children, and youth, joining with local helpers to connect and be helped to cope with crises, meet social and educational

needs, and access community resources. In important ways, these centers are a local system of care, connecting families to needed resources, often through co-located services.

COMMUNITY-BASED FAMILY CENTERS

Cultural traditions influence the family center, blending an interdisciplinary group of professionals with natural helpers, including parents, as shown in the evolving character and service of the Center for Family Life's 30 years of work in the Sunset Park Community in Brooklyn, New York (http://sco.org/programs/center-for-family-life; Hess, McGowan & Botsko, 2003). Promoting cultural understanding and community empowerment, as demonstrated by this center and the Community Family Centers of Houston, Texas, shows the unique role centers have in developing community in beleaguered neighborhoods (http://www.communityfamilycenters.org/). Parents describe centers as a safe haven, where they experience a family-like environment, a place to belong. Friendly walk-in centers welcome families to join in programs, with flexible offerings that respond to local needs and preferences These centers are unique because they frequently manage to integrate child protective work with a host of other therapeutic, educational, and supportive services. Efforts are made to emphasize family strengths, with creative approaches to engage those who have been referred by protective services because their children are at risk for abuse or neglect. Centers often play a role in family reunification, supporting trial visitations and preparation for children to come home to a more stable, safe environment.

Parents have an opportunity to be part of a community that works, where they can receive and provide help to others through a complex array of structured and creative offerings, such as parent support groups and family play sessions, parent education, and social action committees, with opportunities for individual, group, and family work. Community building and empowerment practice involves promoting parental strengths, ideas, and roles in a host of activities, such as providing play groups, recreation, and celebrations with advocacy that benefit the family center and local community. The centers that thrive do so because in formal and informal ways they are a community of learners where capacity building is a shared goal for staff and participants to enhance and build resilience. Capacity building takes many forms: staff development for effective service provision, building connections for developing social capital within the family center and local community through strengthening partnerships, and providing opportunities for parents to take meaningful roles in supporting and running the center's programs. Service provision varies because it depends on auspices and funding, center leadership, and the collaboration between professional and local helpers. For example, some centers emphasize group programs over individual counseling, including parenting groups that provide support and use evidence-based parent training curricula, and skill-building groups focused on such topics as budgeting, nutrition, skills for job hunting, opportunities to complete high school education, and coping with substance-abusing family members.

For staff there is the challenge of meeting parents' personal needs while balancing the needs of the whole community. For many parents who are survivors of traumatic experiences because of violence in their community and homes or because of military service, a safe family center needs to have essential program characteristics that aid their recovery. A trauma-informed program can become critical in a family center, as advocated by SAMSHA (2013), exemplified in the Full Frame Initiative (www.fullframeinitiative.org; Huebner, Mancini, Bowen, & Orthner, 2009). There is both an art and science to making it all work, with a good measure of humor and excellent management! Family centers are noted for having a unique synergy that contributes significantly to the helping experience and positive outcomes for children, parents, and center staff (Hess et al.,

2003; Lightburn & Warren-Adamson, 2006; Warren-Adamson & Lightburn, 2010; Tunstill, Aldgate, & Hughes, 2007).

EVIDENCE FOR AN INTEGRATED PRACTICE MODEL

Lessons learned about what works in family centers follows, with a theoretical understanding of how development and change occur in these complex community programs (Warren-Adamson & Lightburn, 2006; 2010). A brief highlight of major findings, including case studies and a number of empirical studies, suggests that family centers are an important resource contributing to a range of valuable outcomes for parents and children. Case studies of family centers across the globe report outcomes of enhanced family stability, parent and child development, and parents' progress in attaining self-sufficiency (Hess et al., 2003; McMahon & Ward, 2001; Tunstill et al., 2007; Warren-Adamson, 2002; Warren-Adamson & Lightburn, 2010). Although more empirical studies are needed, there is evidence that family centers successfully provide a continuum of services with good outcomes for fragile families (Comer & Fraser, 1998; McCroskey, 2006). Findings from a national study of 665 family support programs showed that these programs produce positive effects for children's cognitive and social development and parent's behavior and attitudes. Positive outcomes were heightened when an early childhood education component was included, parent groups were provided rather than home visits, peer support opportunities for parents were provided, parent self-development was a program goal, and professional staff were used rather than paraprofessional (Layzer & Goodson, 2001). Research also indicates that collaborative learning in support groups is particularly valuable for parents (Berry, Cash, & Hoge, 1998; Ireys, Divet, & Sakawa, 2002; Whittaker & Cowley, 2012).

Practice in family centers requires an understanding of how the family center community contributes to family and child well-being, because these communities can be integral to belonging, identity, and achieving personal goals. We introduce an integrative model of family center practice based on a theory of change developed from cross-national examples of family centers, with support from current research cited, developmental theory, and prevention and developmental science (for elaboration of this practice model, see Lightburn & Warren-Adamson, 2006; Warren-Adamson & Lightburn, 2006; 2010).

A WORKING THEORY OF CHANGE

In Figure 113.1, an integrative model of practice based on our proposed working theory of change is a guide for practice in family centers. To meet parents' complex needs, it is useful to have a flexible model of practice that takes into account the realities of parents' daily lives, as well as the potential for change that a family center supports through their staff and relationships with community service providers. This integrative model of practice necessarily includes building the family center community as well as using individual, family, group, and case management methods. In addition, these centers are systems of care; hence, an important aspect of this integrative model of practice includes work that strengthens collaboration and connection with service providers and community resources (Brandon, 2006). Because family centers are often seen as beacons in their communities, there is the added work of influencing and shaping what happens there, such as working to decrease neighborhood violence (Huebner et al., 2009; Whittaker & Cowley, 2012).

Historically, an enduring problem for family center practice is the absence of a theory of change, despite the fact that different models of intervention have been adopted. A theory of change is a working framework that explains the relationships between the family center program components and desired outcomes. The theory of change presented in Figure 113.1, based on knowledge of human behavior, the process of psychosocial development, and ecological systems, and the role of social capital in community capacity building, helps practitioners and family center leadership understand what interventions will be important and the pathways that staff and participants need to take to work toward their goals. The outcome goal is a community that serves as a dynamic resource for vulnerable families based on an understanding of how preventive services buffer stress and reduce risk so that learning, growth, and healing can occur (Warren-Adamson & Lightburn, 2006; 2010). This theory of change for family center practice guides mapping of goals and objectives. These

are followed by connections to strategies and resources that are essential to support intended outcomes. Developed and implemented in collaboration with stakeholders in a family center, the theory of change can assist program developers, staff, and families focus on what is most important and also help describe personal, program, and family center community steps along the way in the process of development and change.

The theory of change presented describes an integrated family center model. The basic resources, goals, objectives, and strategies of the model, along with anticipated outcomes, follow.

FAMILY CENTER RESOURCES

The critical resources on which the change process depends are described in the left column of Figure 113.1. A host of resources make it possible to reach family center goals; some of the most indispensable are described. For example, the importance of place is highlighted as one of the key resources for the family center that includes a building, an accommodating place that becomes an important place of connection for families, both in the here and now, and a place to hold in their minds. The center can become as important as a family home, welcoming and familiar, with reminders of staff and friends, a place to belong, where achievements are experienced, and possibilities entertained that have yet to be explored.

Family center leadership, a critical resource, promotes, encourages, and manages the range of formal and informal roles, activities, and internal and external connections needed to fulfill the center's mission. Leadership builds the family center community around a mission that can be valued by all. Most centers benefit from a multidisciplinary staff, including social workers with community-building, clinical, and case management skills; family therapists; and early education specialists, who work in tandem with natural helpers/volunteers and parents in supporting center programs, as they take increasingly active roles in day care programs, working with reading groups, organizing food and clothing donations, and holiday celebrations.

Funding challenges and maintaining financial support requires the creative involvement of all stakeholders, including advocacy and grant seeking to garner support for center programs (Tunstill et al., 2007; Warren-Adamson & Lightburn, 2006; Huebner, et al., 2009). Special programs are frequently developed through imaginative collaborations with community service providers, including negotiations that result in co-located services. When there are limits to a family center's space for co-locating services, good coordination and links with community resources become essential (Tunstill et al., 2007, Brandon, 2006).

FAMILY CENTER GOALS

The goals outlined in the second column of Figure 113.1 represent those commonly held in family centers that will vary according to each center's purpose and mandate. These include (1) building a community, (2) meeting family needs for safety and protection, (3) nurturing psychosocial development of parents and children, (4) supporting family attachment bonds, (5) reducing the need for child placement, and (6) promoting the mental health and well-being of all family members.

Meanings that we have attached to these goals are as follows.

- Community describes both a family center community where all who participate have a role and a culture of care that is a product of this community.
- Meeting protection needs means responsibility to protect children along with the wider notion of safety for parents and the community.
- Nurturance is a complex notion that assumes an actual and symbolic parenting role for the community and parents over time. Nurturance is essential for positive psychosocial development of both parents and children.
- Supporting attachment bonds develops Bowlby and others' idea of the importance of diverse and multiple attachments, such that the center in its complexity can encourage and provide some of these attachments over time (McMahon & Ward, 2001; Warren-Adamson & Lightburn, 2006, 2010). At the same time, attachment bonds between parents and their children are critical to a child's development, and therefore, also an important goal for the center's programs.
- Influencing out-of-home placement means that the center's integrated services are focused on working toward achieving the goal of preventing out-of-home placement,

and when this is not possible, it means the better management of foster or residential placement through supporting visitation and transition plans to reunite the family; or it can mean negotiating and sustaining kinship care instead of foster care, and so on.

- Helping parents meet mental health needs means promoting well-being as well as addressing mental health concerns, such as depression and posttraumatic stress disorder that influence parents' ability to nurture their children.

Objectives with Strategies to Guide Family Center Practice

The objectives designed to support achievement of the model's goals, with possible strategies for success, are defined in the center column of Figure 113.1.

Staff Development

Investment in building the capacity of a multidisciplinary team is central to the family center's success including collaborative practice, supported by a clear mission, supervision, training, and team meetings important to a dynamic, evolving center. Local needs and traditions should be represented in the center's mission, which is shaped by stakeholders (parents, providers, community members) and leadership. For example, the mission of an integrated family center may be to ensure nurturance and protection of children and parents with a culture of care that includes access to needed resources and services. Leadership oversees ongoing investment in the family center staff through capacity building for a vital learning organization promoting competence and use of best practices (Brandon, 2006; Hess et al., 2003; McMahon & Ward, 2001).

Creating and Maintaining a Culture of Care

A crucial objective in the family center practice model is the development of a culture of care that makes it possible to meet parents' diverse agendas (their hopes, purpose, and investment in coming to the center). Strategies that create the culture of care include activities that result in containment, protection, mutuality, and support (Warren-Adamson & Lightburn, 2010). The culture of a family center, like that of a school,

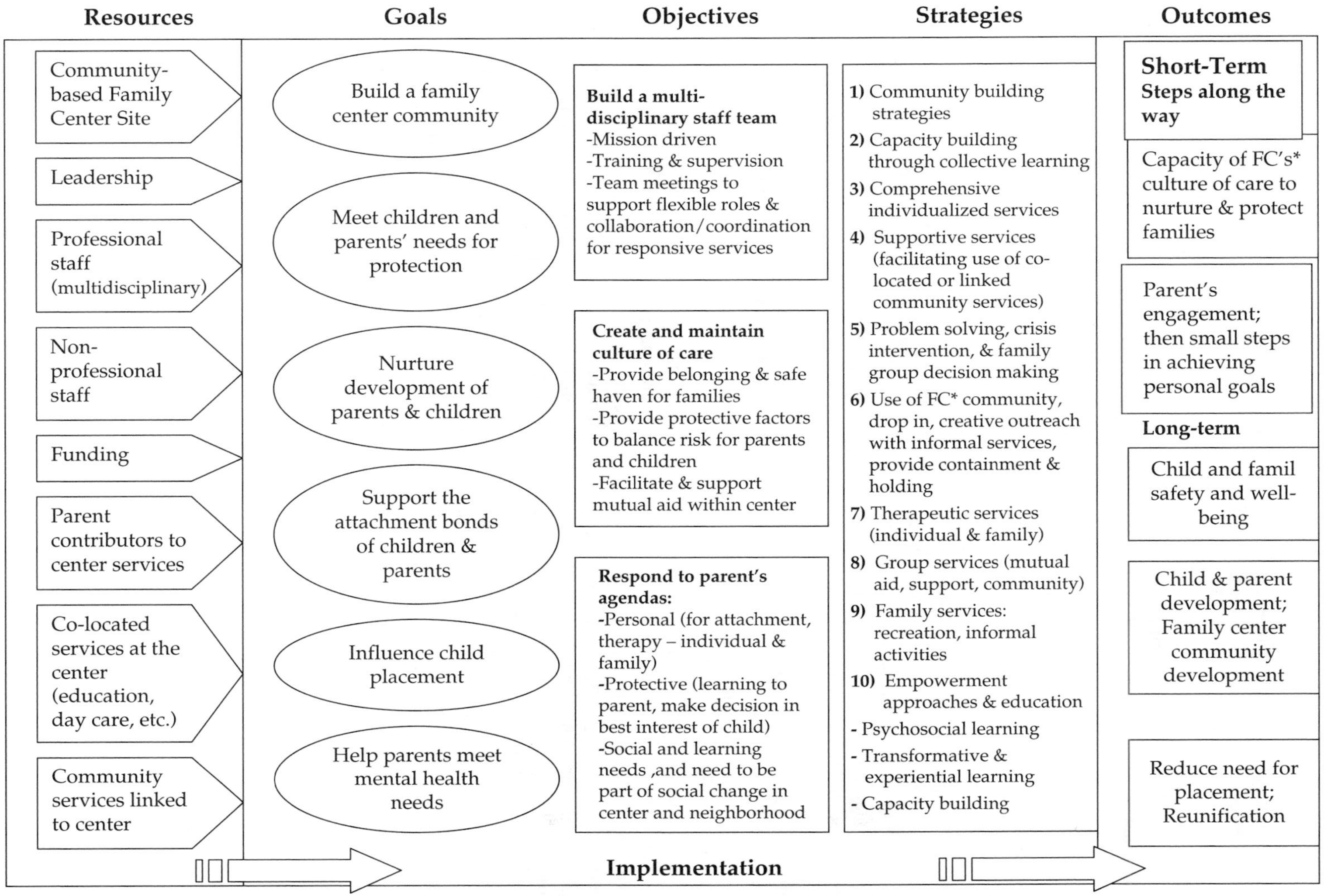

Resources

- Community-based Family Center Site
- Leadership
- Professional staff (multidisciplinary)
- Non-professional staff
- Funding
- Parent contributors to center services
- Co-located services at the center (education, day care, etc.)
- Community services linked to center

Goals

- Build a family center community
- Meet children and parents' needs for protection
- Nurture development of parents & children
- Support the attachment bonds of children & parents
- Influence child placement
- Help parents meet mental health needs

Objectives

Build a multi-disciplinary staff team
- Mission driven
- Training & supervision
- Team meetings to support flexible roles & collaboration/coordination for responsive services

Create and maintain culture of care
- Provide belonging & safe haven for families
- Provide protective factors to balance risk for parents and children
- Facilitate & support mutual aid within center

Respond to parent's agendas:
- Personal (for attachment, therapy – individual & family)
- Protective (learning to parent, make decision in best interest of child)
- Social and learning needs, and need to be part of social change in center and neighborhood

Strategies

1) Community building strategies
2) Capacity building through collective learning
3) Comprehensive individualized services
4) Supportive services (facilitating use of co-located or linked community services)
5) Problem solving, crisis intervention, & family group decision making
6) Use of FC* community, drop in, creative outreach with informal services, provide containment & holding
7) Therapeutic services (individual & family)
8) Group services (mutual aid, support, community)
9) Family services: recreation, informal activities
10) Empowerment approaches & education
- Psychosocial learning
- Transformative & experiential learning
- Capacity building

Outcomes

Short-Term Steps along the way

Capacity of FC's* culture of care to nurture & protect families

Parent's engagement; then small steps in achieving personal goals

Long-term

Child and famil safety and well-being

Child & parent development; Family center community development

Reduce need for placement; Reunification

Implementation

Figure 113.1 Theory of change.

contributes to the psychosocial development of its participants by shaping communication, experience, and identity. A culture of care is evident in the center community's shared values. Development of a culture of care includes trauma-informed program principles that promote safety for children, families, and staff. This involves recognizing and attending to risk and abuse as well as educating community members in alternative problem-solving strategies, rather than tolerating or denying dangerous situations. Mandated supervision of children is part of this culture, wherein the best interests of children are seriously attended to with the support of protective services. At the same time, a clear message is given that the family center will work collaboratively to keep parents and children together. This may be a new experience for most families, who have often failed to work well with service systems that are child-focused, where parents feel blamed and there is limited flexibility in the way services are provided. The family center's culture of care is in significant contrast to the culture of neglect and abuse many families know, where isolation, loneliness, anxiety, and fear rob children and parents of love and nurturance (Warren-Adamson & Lightburn, 2006; 2010).

A key to how the family center culture shapes outcomes is found in the use of time. Parents need opportunities to experience relationships that nurture through acceptance and continuity with flexible responses when there are unexpected and repeated crises. For parents, this community becomes a family—the nurturing, accepting family that many have never known. A strong commitment to families communicates understanding when they are not yet able to grasp how their lives can change. This culture of care provides an important holding environment (McMahon & Ward, 2001; Warren-Adamson & Lightburn, 2006; 2010). As such, it supports development and growth, using parents' strengths and promoting new abilities, where parents' development is as important as their children's.

The values of family-centered practice and family empowerment are enacted through the cultural norms and helping relationships in the family center community, which promote protective factors that buffer risk and support parents' coping skills. For example, community building is vital where staff work to engender positive norms that hold center life together, such as mutual aid, hope, kindness, and positive expectation. The change process depends on promoting this positive strengths-based culture, which benefits from a learning organization approach that works for the best interests of all.

PARENTS' AGENDAS

The strategies listed in the fourth column in Figure 113.1 build on all that is best, diverse, and challenging in our knowledge about effective interventions and are derived from several traditions of practice: child welfare, and therapeutic and community care, including capacity and community building and advocacy. Effective strategies in implementing family center practice goals and objectives include problem solving, crisis intervention, individual and family therapy, mutual aid groups, parental education, empowerment practice, as well as social action groups and educational opportunities with informal activities.

AN INTEGRATED MODEL OF THE PROCESS OF FAMILY CENTER PRACTICE

An integrated model of the process of family center practice is represented in Figure 113.2. The model integrates four different areas that identity a focus for practice based on a parent's different agendas. This framework responds to the spoken and unspoken, known and yet to be recognized needs, reasons, and hopes that parents bring to the family center. Agenda is the term used to describe family center staff and parents' collaboration to identify a focus for their participation in center programs. Agenda is used instead of contract or treatment plan. It is important to respond to parents' needs and priorities as their personal goals/agenda evolve with their involvement in the center. Practice in family centers is based on collaborative, family-centered principles that recognize parents as active contributors in all outcomes. Parents are contributing members of the community, not cases to be treated and managed.

The parents' agenda as depicted in the model in Figure 113.2 includes the following four domains.

1. *Personal agenda,* reflecting parents' desire to connect and bond with others, be guided and mentored, and gain resources. Personal agendas can be met in a variety of

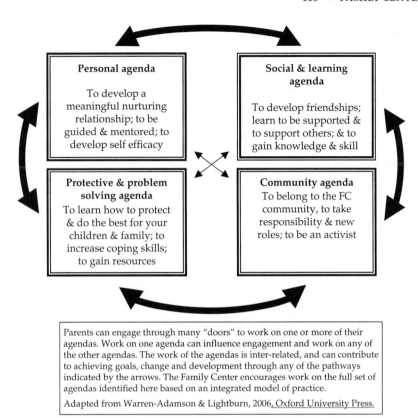

Figure 113.2 Parent's agenda.

ways, including work with case managers to facilitate use of a range of possible opportunities and services, work with a mentor (parent peer) or guide on steps to self-sufficiency, or work with a therapist to meet interpersonal and mental health needs. Mental health needs are normalized with a focus on building relationships and learning and developing coping skills in a supportive environment.

2. *Protection and problem-solving agenda,* including learning how to protect and nurture one's children and one's self, as well as gain competence in parenting. Many parents have to fulfill mandated requirements to prove they are competent; others want to meet basic needs and find their way out of poverty, domestic violence, or substance abuse. This domain can include learning to solve problems at points of crisis and later develop problem-solving skills to work with family parenting and personal concerns. Of primary importance is the need to establish safety plans that ensure children are protected and nurtured in their families

and communities. This includes recognizing the effects of trauma and understanding the path to recovery, with appropriate parent education opportunities.

3. *Social and learning agenda,* which includes developing friendships, learning to be supported, and supporting others. The experience of mutual aid and being valued as a member of the family center community is an essential contributor to parents' development and self-efficacy, as friendships and support are invaluable in raising children in impoverished or dangerous neighborhoods. Parents are usually interested in group programs, as they share many concerns and can mutually benefit from working on issues with one another, such as managing family life, budgeting, and preparing for employment. Parents often need help identifying what they need to learn and how this can best happen.

4. *Community agenda,* which involves learning to belong and take responsibility, including new roles in the family center community, and to be an activist. Parents' membership

as part of the community reinforces their belonging and provides opportunities for them to join with other parents and staff. Experience as an active community member can increase parents' authority and sense of efficacy because they have roles as citizens to influence and shape the center's community and to advocate for change.

Comprehensive programs offered in many family centers make it possible to meet multiple social and mental health needs described in the parents' agendas. As Figure 113.2 indicates, parents can be engaged to work on one or more agendas. A parent's progress in meeting goals with one agenda can influence his or her desire to work on other agendas. A parent's work on different agendas may influence the progress made overall, as indicated by the directional arrows in Figure 113.2. The challenge for family center practice is imagining and understanding how to facilitate the working of the whole while also focusing on specifics. For example, integration of comprehensive services that aim to meet requirements of mandated protection includes a focus on development for parent and child. Some parents have been victims of violence and for them to grow in competence as a parent they need help with their own recovery and healing. Services must be individualized, responding to a parent's main concern, while maintaining awareness of challenges and abilities. Service integration happens over time, in response to a parent's needs, priorities, and abilities to engage in the work of the agenda, and is similarly based on the capacity of the family center to provide various forms of help.

WORKING WITH OUTCOMES

The diverse and complementary avenues for development and change described in the theory of change sets us on the road to identify outcomes that include familiar long-term outcomes—such as well-being, protected children, more intact families, community development, and so on—alongside what we describe as steps on the way. Outcomes as steps on the way have a particular resonance for practitioners and they are twofold. First, there are those small steps that can include parents meeting personal goals, such as skills in building relationships and exercising personal authority to ensure safety for

oneself and one's children. Second, practitioners in particular contribute to outcomes that define the community of care in developing mutuality, modeling behaviors, and providing containment through parenting behaviors, creative activity, and conviviality. Such outcomes construct a community of care and contribute to change that cannot be fully explained by the traditional names we attach to intervention. The outcomes column should become a valued representation of what is expected and hoped for, as well as a realistic statement of what is possible.

Concluding Thoughts

Centers for families, like many social welfare initiatives, are barometers of economic, political, and ideological change. Over the past 30 years they have waxed and waned in number and the recent economic crash has taken its toll. Nonetheless, a healthy momentum continues in this decade and readers can take note of particular contemporary features of family center activity that enhance our understanding of practice. For example: models of leadership for community development of integrated centers (Whalley, 2006); engaging fathers (Fletcher &Visser, 2008); parent education that is based on evidence, and sensitive to culture and context (Aldgate & Rose, 2012; Petersson et al., 2004); child participation and children centers as versions of family centers; centers directly mandated by courts, as in the Australian family relationship centers (Moloney, 2013); and protection (Warren-Adamson & Lightburn, 2010).

The current decade also brings new theorization about community-based family centers with ideas about sensitive and proximal outcomes described above that connect with the growing interest in complexity theory and the transformational nature of complex systems. For example, complexity theory's synergy principle refers to "the whole as greater than the sum of the parts," where a diverse and complex center system described above generates change in families unexplained by individual component parts (Lightburn & Warren-Adamson, 2012). Other creative center examples—in mental health communities, medical centers, and community work resource centers, for example—suggest goals outlined in the "possible" personal agenda's for parents and the focus on building community, rather than in the reductionist trend for single interventions, should be to create centers of synergy and complexity. Each complex center would have its own distinctive transformative characteristics but would be replicable in its commitment to synergy generated by a rich level of activity.

SUMMARY

This chapter described an integrated practice model for community-based family centers by explaining a step-by-step logical approach to building such a center, illustrating possible pathways for engagement, development, and change. The framework for practice in Figure 113.1 was developed in response to the goals set out in the theory of change. We suggested intervention in centers involves working with parents' different agendas (see Figure 113.2), with flexible, responsive helping strategies and a broad tradition of intervention supported by a theory of change to meet a variety of goals, and something special that, when it is put all together with energy and commitment, results in a culture of care, providing the "glue" for service integration. Family centers are exceptional because they are more than a system of care; they are a special community that makes a difference for families, staff, and the larger community.

WEBSITES

Community Family Centers. http://www.communityfamilycenters.org/
Center for Family Life. http://sco.org/programs/center-for-family-life/contact/
Family Center. http://www.thefamilycenterinc.org
Family Resource Centers (Part of the Children's Board of Hillsborough County, Florida) http://www.familysupporthc.org/index.cfm
Full Frame Initiative. http://www.fullframeinitiative.org
Military Family Support Centers http://www.foh.dhhs.gov/Productfocus/July2003/militaryfamilies.asp

References

Aldgate, J., & Rose, W. (2012). Taking standardised programmes to different cultural contexts: An example from Scotland. In A. Maluccio, C. Canali, T. Vecchiato, A. Lightburn, J. Aldgate, & W. Rose (Eds.), *Improving outcomes for children and families: Finding and using international evidence.* London: Jessica Kingsley.

Berry, M., Cash, S. J., & Hoge, L. A. (1998). Creating community through psycho-educational groups in family preservation work. *Families in Society: The Journal of Contemporary Human Services, 79,* 15–24.

Brandon, M. (2006). Confident workers, confident families: Exploring sensitive outcomes in Family Center work in England. *International Journal of Child and Family Welfare, 9,* 79–91.

Comer, E., & Fraser, M. (1998). Evaluation in six family support programs: Are they effective? *Families in Society, The Journal of Contemporary Human Services, 79*(2), 134–148.

Fletcher, R. J., & Visser, A. (2008). Facilitating father engagement: The role of Family Relationship Centres. *Journal of Family Studies, 14*(1), 53–64.

Hess, P., McGowan, B., & Botsko, M. (2003). *Nurturing the one, supporting the many.* New York, NY: Columbia University Press.

Huebner, A., Mancini, J., Bowen, G., & Orthner. (2009). Shadowed by war: Building community capacity to support military families. *Family Relations, 58,* 216–228.

Ireys, H., Divet, K., & Sakawa, D. (2002). Family support and education. In B. Burns & K. Hoagwood (Eds.), *Community treatment for youth: Evidence-based interventions for severe emotional and behavioral disorders* (pp. 154–176). New York, NY: Oxford University Press.

Layzer, J., & Goodson, B. (2001). *National evaluation of family support programs.* Cambridge, MA: Abt Associates.

Lightburn, A., & Warren-Adamson, C. (2012). Evaluating complexity in community-based programs. In A. Maluccio, C. Canali, T. Vecchiato, A. Lightburn, J. Aldgate, & W. Rose. *Improving outcomes for children and families: Finding and using international evidence* (pp. 57–69). London: Jessica Kingsley.

Lightburn, A., & Warren-Adamson, C. (2006). Evaluating family centers: The importance of sensitive outcomes in cross-national studies. *International Journal of Child and Family Welfare, 9,* 11–26.

McCroskey, J. (2006). Community programs in the U.S. In C. McAuley, P. Pecora, & W. Rose (Eds.), *Enhancing the well-being of children and families through effective interventions* (pp. 313–320). London: Jessica Kingsley.

McMahon, L., & Ward, A. (Eds.). (2001). *Helping families in family centres: Working at therapeutic practice.* London: Jessica Kingsley.

Moloney, L. (2013). From helping court to community-based services: The 30-year evolution of Australia's family relationship centres. *Family Court Review, 51*(2), 214–223.

Petersson, K., Petersson, C., & Håkansson, A. (2004). What is good parental education? *Scandinavian Journal of Caring Sciences, 18,* 82–89.

Substance Abuse and Mental Health Services Administration (SAMHSA) (2013). *Trauma informed care.* http://www.samhsa.gov/nctic/trauma.asp

Tunstill, J., Aldgate, J., & Hughes, M. (2007). *Improving children's services networks: Lessons from family centres.* London: Jessica Kingsley.

Warren-Adamson, C. (Ed.). (2002). *Family centres and their international role in social action.* Aldershot, UK: Ashgate.

Warren-Adamson, C., & Lightburn, A. (2006). Developing a community-based model for integrated family center practice. In A. Lightburn & P. Sessions (Eds.), *The handbook of community-based clinical practice* (pp. 261–284). New York, NY: Oxford University Press.

Warren-Adamson, C., & Lightburn, A. (2010). Family Centres: Protecting and promoting at the heart of the Children Act 1989. *Journal of Children's Services. Special Edition: Research Informing Practice, 5*(3), 25–36.

Whalley, M. (2006). Leadership in integrated centres and services for children and families—A community development approach: Engaging with the struggle, *Children's Issues: Journal of the Children's Issues, 10*(2), 8–13.

Whittaker, K & Cowley, S. (2012). An effective programme is not enough: A review of factors associated with poor attendance and engagement with parenting support programmes. *Children and Society, 26,* 138–149.

114   International Perspectives on Social Work Practice

Karen M. Sowers

Although our world is becoming easier to navigate, the complexity of social issues and their impact globally demands that social workers respond. International social work practice, an evolving and exciting area of practice, which is gaining increasing interest (Elliott & Segal, 2012; Midgley, 1981) may hold the key to solutions for a peaceful, thriving, and sustainable environment for future generations. This chapter addresses social work practice in the global arena and provides an understanding of the interconnectedness of social work and social development across the globe. Some examples provide illustrations of ways international social work is making a difference to empower people, communities, and organizations.

Social work practice was primarily developed in response to local needs—most often to serve the powerless and disadvantaged and address issues in managing the developmental challenges of everyday living. As populations expanded and immigration and migration grew, it became clear that the challenges facing people in achieving their individual and collective goals were in many ways more similar than they were different (Sowers & Rowe, 2007). For some social workers, the events of 9/11 emphasized the increasing importance of recognizing a broader economic and cultural context of globalization (Elliott & Segal, 2012).

The increased impact of globalization over the past few decades has highlighted the similarities of social problems. The initial response was a presumption that social work practices in developed countries were the most desirable and effective and needed only simple cultural adjustments to be applied to human and social problems everywhere. However, it became clear that no single location or country has the preferred methods for all, although various countries may have exemplar programs or best practices that can be instructive to others (Sowers & Rowe, 2007).

INTERNATIONAL SOCIAL WORK

The definitions and conceptualizations of social work differ greatly across cultural contexts. Initially, international social work was concerned with comparing social work as it exists in different cultures and countries. The view of the social worker as one who primarily provides individual clinical services originated in Western industrial countries. Most societies, however, have always had a role for individuals who worked to improve conditions for community members. Clinical practice is more characteristic of industrialized countries, and community organizers in Western countries have learned many of their strategies and practices from their peers in developing countries (Rowe, Hanley, Moreno, & Mould, 2000). Although *social work* is the term most commonly used in the United States and other industrialized countries, *social development* or *developmental social welfare* is often used in developing nations (Elliott & Segal, 2012).

Over the decades, social work has grown and matured worldwide. Currently an effort is being made to address social work from a global perspective—as one profession practicing in many different countries. This effort is led by two international organizations, the International Federation of Social Workers (IFSW) and the International Association of Schools of Social Work (IASSW). In 2001, the IFSW and IASSW jointly agreed on an international definition of social work. That definition has evolved over time. The current definition on international social work can be found on the IFSW website (www.ifsw.org/policies/definition-of-social-work) (IFSW, 2012a). In March 2013, the IFSW and IASSW crafted a "point-in-time" Draft International Definition of Social Work (IFSW, 2013a). This draft, endorsed by both organizations is open for feedback and comment until December 2013 (go to http://ifsw.org/get-involved/global-definition-of-social-work to view and add your voice). The current draft definition of social work is below:

The social work profession facilitates social change and development, social cohesion, and the empowerment and liberation of people. Principles of social justice, human rights, collective responsibility and respect for diversities are central to social work. Underpinned by theories of social work, social sciences, humanities and indigenous knowledges, social work engages people and structures to address life challenges and enhance wellbeing (IFSW, 2013a).

INTERNATIONAL SOCIAL WORK PRACTICE

Global social work practice is based on the values of human rights and social justice. The most universal beliefs that characterize social work globally include the principle of social inclusion as core to the alleviation of poverty and the promotion of self-determination and self-sufficiency of disenfranchised and vulnerable people and the inherent value of people and the responsibilities of societies to create conditions in which people can thrive (Morales & Sheafor, 2001).

In 2013, the IFSW, the IASSW, and the International Council on Social Welfare (ICSW) solidified a global agenda for social workers, educators, and social development practitioners (IFSW, 2013b). The Global Agenda outlines and specifies commitments to action to ensure the dignity and worth of the individual, the promotion of sustainable communities and environmentally sensitive development, the promotion of well-being through sustainable human relationships, and ensuring an appropriate environment for practice and education. Social workers interested in or engaged in global social work practice should also be familiar with and practice within the international standards and guidelines for social work practice. These include the Global Qualifying Standards for Social Work Practice (IFSW, 2012b), the International Code of Ethics (IFSW, 2012c), the IFSW campaign for real rights (IFSW, 2013c), the Universal Declaration of Human Rights (United Nations, n.d.).

Practicing within the Cultural Context

Social and cultural realities can create both challenges and opportunities in global social work practice. Global social work practice requires that social workers become aware of their own values, biases, and beliefs and value and respect differences as well as understand the dynamics of difference (Matsuoka & McCubbin, 2008; Sowers-Hoag & Sandau-Beckler, 1996).

For example, in 1986, New Zealand restructured its social welfare department in response to growing criticism that it was too bureaucratic, emphasized individualized casework services, neglected local needs, and failed to respond to cultural needs of specific groups. The new model adopted by New Zealand allowed for joint decision making and resource sharing with communities. The model particularly targeted indigenous communities, using community as provider within the delivery system. Changes in social work practice included the development of culturally sensitive practice with strong links to indigenous communities. The promotion and funding of preventive, community-based services were determined by local communities. (For more information, see Baretta-Herman, 1994.)

As can be seen from this example, the most effective approaches to advancing human rights require cultural sensitivity and responsiveness and embrace inclusive strategies that encompass culture and religion and the roles played by local power structures and institutions (United Nations Population Fund, n.d.). Because societies and cultures are increasingly complex and changing, social workers practicing in a global context must be lifelong learners and willing to change, adapt, and use strategies that are relevant and specific to differing situations (Sowers & Rowe, 2007).

Today, poverty, inequality, and human distress are issues to which social workers respond everywhere in the world. Certain social issues, including population aging, immigration and migration, substance abuse, human-made and natural disasters, and health and mental health, transcend nation-states. The following provides some examples of worldwide social problems addressed by social workers.

Substance Abuse and HIV

In many cities around the world HIV disease has reached epidemic proportions. On the basis of global 1992 data, the World Health Organization (n.d. a) estimated that "over 5 million people injected drugs, that between 150,000 and 200,000 drug injectors died every year, and that at least half of those deaths were associated with HIV." By 1996 the United Nations estimated that seven persons per million were infected by HIV as a result of injectable drug use and that the 1996 rate increased to 248 persons per million in 2000 (World Health Organization, 2005). Global efforts are needed to support safe behavior among HIV-infected substance abusers and among drug abusers in general. Because of the critical need to support safer behavior, particularly in cities with a high prevalence of HIV, cities, governments, nongovernmental organizations, and other groups are implementing harm reduction programs (Sowers & Rowe, 2007; World Health Organization, 2007). Harm reduction is defined as "policies and programs which attempt primarily to reduce the adverse health, social and economic consequences of mood altering substances to individual drug users, their families, and their communities" (International Harm Reduction Association, n.d.). This new global approach is especially useful in the prevention of HIV/AIDS.

In contrast to a punitive approach to drug abuse, the harm reduction model views addiction as an adaptive response to a wide cross-section of individual and collective variables that may influence behavior. Practitioners using the harm reduction perspective develop interventions that reduce drug-related harm without necessarily promoting abstinence as the only solution. Harm reduction for injection drug users primarily aims to help them avoid the negative health consequences of drug injecting and improve their health and social status. These approaches recognize that for many drug users total abstinence from harmful substances is not a feasible option in the short term. It focuses on helping users reduce their injection frequency and increase safety. To be effective, harm reduction strategies must be embedded into comprehensive prevention and intervention packages for injection drug users (World Health Organization, 2005). The following are typical components identified by the World Health Organization (2005) that have a significant potential to reduce individual risk behaviors associated with drug injection:

- Needle-syringe programming provides drug users with access to clean injection paraphernalia, including needles and syringes, filters, cookers, drug containers, and mixing water. These interventions may also collect used needles and syringes. These programs serve as information points for drug and HIV disease education and provide referral for treatment services. Their ability to break the chain of transmission of HIV and other blood-borne viruses is well established.
- Drug substitution treatment involves the medically supervised treatment of individuals with opioid dependency. The primary goal

of drug substitution treatment may be abstinence from illicit drug use but many patients are unable to achieve complete abstinence. There is clear evidence that some drug substitution treatments, such as methadone maintenance, can significantly reduce unsafe injection practices of those who are in treatment and at risk of HIV infection.

The application of harm reduction principles to other problematic substances, such as ecstasy, tobacco, and alcohol is a fairly recent event but has shown widespread effectiveness and public acceptance in many places across the globe.

In Argentina, 39% of those diagnosed with HIV acquired the virus through intravenous (IV) drug use. Past harm reduction activity efforts had little effect. In response, a specific harm reduction approach with poor populations in Buenos Aires using a community-based outreach approach with specific emphasis on drug users, their sexual partners, and children was developed with the participation of 23 pharmacies. This approach proved successful, reaching 900 drug users with preventive messages in a 3-month period. In location-specific areas, preventive materials were distributed by drug users, former drug users, and local pharmacies (Rossi et al., 2001).

Mental Health

Mental health problems are common to all countries. They are the cause of immense human suffering, disability, social exclusion, and poor quality of life (Davis & Jung, 2012; Sowers, Rowe, & Clay, 2008). Across the globe, about one in every four persons going to health services has at least one mental, neurological, or behavioral disorder. Mental and behavioral disorders are estimated to account for 12% of the global burden of disease, yet the mental health budgets of the majority of countries constitute less than 1% of total health expenditures. Unfortunately, even in countries with well-established mental health services, fewer than half of those individuals needing care make use of available services. This is related both to the stigma attached to individuals with mental health and behavioral disorders and to the inadequacy of the services provided (World Health Organization, 2001).

According to the World Health Organization (World Health Organization, 2001), good mental health care flows from the following basic principles:

- Diagnosis
- Early intervention
- Rational use of treatment techniques
- Continuity of care
- Availability of a wide range of services
- Consumer involvement
- Partnership with families
- Involvement of the local community.

Integration of mental health treatment into primary health. The prevalence of mental disorders is worldwide, and many persons suffering from mental and behavioral disorders are first seen in primary care settings. This is probably because mental health problems are often associated with physical disease. But because many primary care providers do not have specialized training in mental illness, these disorders are often not detected. A global trend has been the integration of mental health care into basic primary health care by training primary care and general health care staff in the detection and treatment of common mental and behavioral disorders. The World Health Organization stresses the importance of the development of community-based mental health and social care services and the integration of mental health care and treatment into general hospitals and primary care (World Health Organization, 2013). With appropriate information, training, integration, and continuity of care between providers patients discharged from psychiatric facilities can be effectively followed up in primary health care settings. This is a particularly important initiative in countries where community-based mental health services do not exist. In many developing countries, well-trained health care workers have been able to provide treatment effectively and efficiently for persons with mental illnesses. In fact, experiences in some African, Asian, and Latin American countries indicate that adequate training of health care workers in the early recognition and management of mental disorders can reduce institutionalization and improve clients' mental health outcomes (Sowers & Rowe, 2007).

There are an estimated 4 million people with schizophrenia in India. It is estimated that this impacts approximately 25 million family members. Recognizing that outcome of the disorder is strongly influenced by social factors, especially family, the Indian government developed a system of support to people with schizophrenia. According to the World Health Organization (n.d.b) components effecting outcomes included:

- A manual for family intervention produced in local languages
- Training of the local health workers. Training focused on the appropriate identification, management, and referral for mental health problems and how to implement actual interventions.
- Brief psycho-educational interventions were provided to 1,500 families. Content included information about mental illness, basic training in daily living, problem solving, and communication skills. Pharmacological treatment was provided to patients. Day centers were opened for people with mental disorders.
- Nongovernmental organizations were mobilized and actively involved in the project. Emphasis was placed on awareness-raising events and information dissemination about mental health problems and their management.

Natural and Human-made Disasters

Recent events around the world underscore our lack of preparedness and ability to respond to the aftermath of disasters. Disasters may be natural occurrences such as floods, hurricanes, or volcanic eruptions. Human-made disasters include technological disasters, terrorism, armed conflicts, and war. Man-made disasters may also result from environmental degradation such as overcultivation, erosion, severe deforestation, or overgrazing of marginal lands. Natural and human-made disasters often strike communities with little or no warning. Although social workers have a long history of responding to disaster trauma, few have knowledge or experience in dealing with the sort of disasters that have occurred with increased frequency and intensity. As disasters occur more frequently and with greater intensity, disaster response, relief, and recovery efforts have become more complex. To respond in a timely and appropriate manner to the likely psychological distress experienced by trauma survivors, social workers must understand the nature of the problems survivors may experience, the types of help they may need, and the level of preparedness of the health and human service delivery systems in place to respond to those needs (Sowers & Rowe, 2007).

The World Health Organization's Department of Mental Health and Substance Dependence (2001) provides important lessons learned from responses to catastrophes:

- Intense emotional reactions in the face of these events are expected and normal
- There is a trajectory of response over time, most often starting early and subsiding within weeks and months. For some people, however, the onset of response may be delayed. For others, the reactions may become long-term, leading to considerable disability.
- Responses will be highly individual in nature, often quite intense, and sometimes disputatious
- The range of feelings experienced may be quite broad. People may describe intense feelings of sadness followed by anger.
- There may be temporary disruptions in normal coping mechanisms for many people, and some may develop problems with sleep, nightmares, concentration, intrusive thoughts, and a preoccupation with reliving the events.

The Department of Mental Health and Substance Dependence (2001) offers the following guidelines for providing help in the aftermath of a catastrophe:

- Create opportunities for people to talk and share experiences in supportive groups.
- Provide accurate and practical information, especially concerning the larger recovery efforts.
- Give particular consideration to the needs of special groups such as children, those who have been most intensely exposed, or those with a history of previous trauma.
- Children and adolescents will need the support of their caregivers.
- As many as 30% of people who experience the most direct exposure to the events may go on to develop more serious mental health concerns and may need to be referred for services.

Promising new approaches are focusing on risk reduction from natural disasters. One such innovative approach is the "sustainable livelihoods" model. This approach analyzes the range of vulnerabilities in poor communities and outlines specific assets within the community. Vulnerability and capacity analysis is a valuable new field tool currently being used to assess communities' disaster resilience and mobilize risk reduction (International Federation of Red Cross and Red Crescent Societies, 2002).

Since the attacks that rocked the world on September 11, 2001, some global leaders have noted that disasters have the potential to increase poverty and hunger, increase infectious diseases, and effect primary education for children. Disasters can have particularly devastating effects on the development of poorer nations. Disasters have the potential to destroy farmland, animals, and other forms of livelihood. Even small disasters that are recurrent can affect family resources and resilience. All of these effects can take a toll on health and wellness.

CONCLUSION

Increased recognition of the importance of international social issues has spurred a growing demand for social workers. As welfare, economic, and foreign policies become ever more globally interdependent, there is a need for global social work practice. We can hope that the future will see a reduced tendency for social work to dichotomize between global and domestic social work issues. The fostering of mutual exchanges of experience and information between social workers in different societies can only advance our practices. We have much to learn from each other.

WEBSITES

Global Social Service Workforce Alliance. http://www.socialserviceworkforce.org/
International Association of Schools of Social Work. http://www.iassw-aiets.org/
International Consortium for Social Development. http://www.socialdevelopment.net
International Council on Social Development. http://www.icsw.org
International Federation of Social Workers. http://www.ifsw.org
United Nations. http://www.un.org
World Health Organization. http://www.who.int/

References

Baretta-Herman, A. (1994). Revisioning the community as provider: Restructuring New Zealand's social services. *International Social Work*, 37(1), 7–21.

Davis, K., & Jung, H. (2012). The mental health field of practice. In C. N. Dulmus & K. M. Sowers (Eds.), *Social work fields of practice: Historical trends, professional issues, and future opportunities* (pp. 147–158). Hoboken, NJ: John Wiley & Sons, Inc.

Department of Mental Health and Substance Dependence. (2001). *How to address psychosocial reactions to catastrophe*. Geneva, Switzerland: World Health Organization.

Elliott, D., & Segal, U. A. (2012). International social work practice. In C. N. Dulmus & K. M. Sowers (Eds.), *Social work fields of practice: Historical trends, professional issues, and future opportunities* (pp. 291–332). Hoboken, NJ: John Wiley & Sons.

International Federation of Red Cross and Red Crescent Societies. (2002). *World disasters report 2002*. Geneva, Switzerland: International Federation.

International Federation of Social Workers. (2013a). *Update on the review process of the Definition of Social Work*. Retrieved July 13, 2013, from http://ifsw.org/news/update-on-the-review-process-of-the-definition-of-social-work/

International Federation of Social Workers. (2013b). *The global agenda*. Retrieved from http://www.ifsw.org/tag/global-agenda-for-social-work-and-social-development

International Federation of Social Workers. (2013c). *IFSW campaign for real rights*. Retrieved from http://ifsw.org/news/ifsw-campaign-for-real-rights-june-september-2013

International Federation of Social Workers. (2012a). *Definition of social work*. Retrieved from www.ifsw.org/policies/definition-of-social-work/.

International Federation of Social Workers. (2012b). *Global standards*. Retrieved from http://www.ifsw.org/policies/global-standards/

International Federation of Social Workers. (2012c). *Statement of ethical principles*. Retrieved from http://www.ifsw.org/policies/statement-of-ethical-principles/

International Harm Reduction Association. (n.d.). *What is harm reduction?* Retrieved from http://www.ihra.net/files/2010/08/10/Briefing_What_is_HR_English.pdf

Matsuoka, J., & McCubbin, H. I. (2008). Immigrant and indigenous populations: Special populations in social work. In C. N. Dulmus & K. M. Sowers (Eds.), *Comprehensive handbook of social work and social welfare* (Vol. 1) (pp. 377–393). Hoboken, NJ: John Wiley & Sons, Inc.

Midgley, J. (1981). *Professional imperialism: Social work in the Third World*. London: Heinemann.

Morales, A. T., & Sheafor, B. W. (2001). *Social work: A profession of many faces* (9th ed.). Boston, MA: Allyn & Bacon.

Rossi, D., Cymerman, P., Erenu, N., Faraone, S., Goltz-man, P., Rojas, E., . . . (2001). Rapid assessment and response in IDUs in Buenos Aires. In *2000 global research network meeting on HIV prevention in drug using populations* (pp. 42–45). Washington, DC: National Institute on Drug Abuse.

Rowe, W., Hanley, J., Moreno, E. R., & Mould, J. (2000). Voices of social work practice: International reflections on the effects of globalization. *Canadian Social Work, 2*(1), 65–86.

Sowers, K. M., & Rowe, W. S. (2007). *Social work practice and social justice: From local to global perspectives*. Belmont, CA: Thomson-Brooks/Cole.

Sowers, K. M., Rowe, W. S., & Clay, J. (2008). The intersection between physical health and mental health: A global perspective. *Journal of Evidence-Based Social Work: Advances in Practice, Programming, Research, and Policy, 6*(1), 111–126.

Sowers-Hoag, K. M., & Sandau-Beckler, P. (1996). Educating for cultural competence in the generalist curriculum. *Journal of Multicultural Social Work, 4*(3), 37–56.

United Nations. (n.d.). *The universal declaration of human rights*. Retrieved from http://www.un.org/en/documents/udhr/.

United Nations Population Fund. (n.d.). *Culture matters—working with communities and faith-based organizations: Case studies from country programmes*. Retrieved from http://www.unfpa.org/upload/lib_pub_file/426_filename_CultureMatters_2004.pdf

World Health Organization. (2001). *The world health report 2001 Mental health: New understanding, new hope*. Geneva, Switzerland: Author.

World Health Organization. (2005). *Effectiveness of drug dependence treatment in preventing HIV among injecting drug users*. Geneva, Switzerland: Author.

World Health Organization. (2007). *Inside out: HIV harm reduction education in closed settings*. Geneva, Switzerland: Author.

World Health Organization. (2013). *Comprehensive mental health action plan 2013–2020*. Retrieved from http://www.who.int/mental_health/mhgap/mental_health_action_plan_EN_27_08_12.pdf

World Health Organization. (n.d.a). *Harm reduction approaches to injecting drug use*. Retrieved from http://www.alternativasclinics.com/WHO%20_%20Harm%20Reduction.pdf.

World Health Organization (n.d.b). *India: Support to people with schizophrenia*. Retrieved from http://www.who.int/mental_health/policy/en/India_support_schizophrenia.pdf

115 Community Organizing Principles and Practice Guidelines

Terry Mizrahi

This chapter is based primarily on my own experiences over 40 years. It is also informed by the literature reflected at the end, and validated by the cumulative field experiences of hundreds of community organizing students at the Silberman School of Social Work at Hunter College (formerly Hunter College School of Social Work).

I address the reader as "you" and assume that you are reading this as you initiate or are being called upon as a student or experienced organizer to respond to an issue, address an agency or community need, or as you are training and teaching others these principles. The phrase "target of change" is used to mean whichever body (a person, agency, or a system) you are trying to influence. These principles are not laid out in a linear order. Several of them need simultaneous consideration before taking action; others are interactive and overlap.

PRINCIPLE 1: EFFECTIVE ORGANIZING BALANCES PROCESS AND PRODUCT

A key assumption is that there is never sufficient time, staff, and other resources to involve people in making change (the process) and accomplishing a specific goal or task (the product). Both are important, so the question is how to operationalize and balance them. Process means that there must be enough discussion to achieve a consensus to move ahead and keep the participants engaged. This does not mean unanimity, but rather a "sense of the body," informally or formally (by vote) determined. Where there is disagreement, there must be a mechanism to ascertain its intensity, and to determine whether moving ahead means a permanent division or dissolution. How much dissent is inevitable and acceptable? You need enough process to gauge people's interest in and commitment to the task. Involvement of people creates a sense of investment and can ultimately lead to a sense of ownership of the product as well as a transformative process of working together in its own right. You need time to build trust between the group and you as well as among participants. That can be done by working on the task while reflecting periodically on the process: "How we are doing?" "Whose voices do we still need to hear?"

The solutions to managing time so that you achieve the product without sacrificing the process are to (a) calculate a more complete and realistic timetable; (b) modify expectations if necessary; (c) prioritize what is essential with those involved; and (d) ascertain who else can assist with the project. Organizing means planning for contingencies, allowing more time than appears necessary, following through, and paying attention to detail.

PRINCIPLE 2: PLANNING IS A COMPLEX VALUE-BASED, SOCIOPOLITICAL AND TECHNICAL PROCESS

Planning is not just about data collection, goals, and timelines or who can write a clear, internally consistent proposal. Rather, planning, as a part of

organizing is a sociopolitical as well as a technical process. Power and resources inform the way you and your constituency define the problem and select the solutions. But underlying planning is a value base or ideology, which includes basic assumptions about why a problem exists, why needs are not being met, why conditions are not optimal, and also includes ascertaining who or what is to "blame" for the problems identified. Social work values are informed by social and economic justice and democratic, participatory decision-making. Power means understanding that some*body* (with a small or capital B), that is, some individual or group has the ability to make decisions about how resources are allocated and whether to implement the program or change a policy. Resources include creating, increasing, or redistributing assets (social and economic capital) that address the planning outcomes. Hence, the strategies you select for influencing the decision makers to achieve your goal are done within a sociopolitical and value-based context.

Here are some examples: Substance abuse was identified as a national problem in the 1960s when it spread beyond the ghetto to middle-class America; mental retardation "came out of the closet" when President John F. Kennedy disclosed that he had a mentally retarded sister. Although middle-class parents had been organizing and planning services for their children throughout the 1950s, mental retardation became a national priority because the president used his office to create funding opportunities for additional facilities and programs. On the other hand, HIV/AIDS did not become a national priority when first detected because President Ronald Reagan did not publicly address the problem until enough visibility and pressure was placed at his doorstep in 1986. It took organized social action of groups like ACT-UP, together with publicity about a Caucasian boy, Ryan White, who contracted AIDS because of a blood transfusion, to lead to additional funding for prevention, education, and treatment with the involvement of consumers and providers.

PRINCIPLE 3: THERE IS NO SUCH THING AS "RATIONAL" AND "IRRATIONAL" FROM THE PERSPECTIVE OF HOW PROBLEMS ARE DEFINED OR RESOURCES ALLOCATED

Many times, as part of the process of identifying problems, someone may say that a particular system, structure, or policy needs to be changed because it does not make sense; "It's irrational." When someone makes such a statement, consider reframing the question by instead asking that person or group: "To whom does it make sense?" "For whom is it functional and working?" "Why hasn't that policy been changed, if it isn't working for your constituency?" You will usually uncover reasons why conditions or attitudes have remained in place, why a need was not met, why people have resisted change, or why a new program was not implemented.

Usually the case does make sense from the perspective of those who maintain that system or oppose the change. It is essential to consider reasons for the resistance to change. For example, a new program can be an implied criticism of the existing system. It may mean that a group perceives they will lose power if that program is created. In other words, it is not irrational for groups that may be affected adversely to attempt to maintain the status quo. Understanding this allows you to identify the covert as well as overt reasons for resisting change and to develop strategies to decrease resistance. This does not mean that there are not instances where situations do not change because of mistakes, arbitrariness, inertia, time or cultural lag, or misinformation. Not everything is deliberate and conscious. Analyzing the seemingly irrational status quo can be done by "peeling the onion," addressing the stated reasons one at a time until perhaps the underlying rationale, whether coherent or not, becomes evident.

Understanding that there is no such thing as value-free planning and organizing provides an opportunity to identify and explore the values and beliefs that inform the problem definition, which, in turn, shapes the proposed solutions that emanate from that definition. It allows you to understand why your group's beliefs and proposals may seem irrational to others.

It is important to understand that "rationality," when it means utilitarian, is itself an ideology, one that is usually associated with capitalism and pragmatism. Often the term "rationality" is invoked in contrast to "ideology," as, for example, when opponents of a plan will state that the proposers are not being rational. You need to consider whether evoking "rational" solutions is being used to prevent deliberations that include values such as fairness, equality, and justice, or if it is being used to divert or discredit those who have a progressive value base. Nevertheless, you

need to be open to listening to opposing viewpoints and understand and explain their attitudes and behaviors without necessarily excusing or exonerating their conclusions. To take the example of homelessness, the problem was ignored by government and the public until a combination of deinstitutionalization of mental hospitals and gentrification of formerly abandoned and neglected neighborhoods resulted in hundreds of thousands of people without a place to live in the 1970s. However, the solutions to homelessness are informed by values and ideology, not just on the basis of need or data alone. Those who perceived it as a housing problem advocated for the right to shelter and housing; those who perceived it as a mental health problem advocated for services; those who perceived it as a civil liberties problem advocated for personal choice and the right to be left alone; and those who perceived it as a criminal justice and morality problem advocated for incarceration, involuntary commitment, forced work, and other social control measures. These were all "rational" solutions from the perspective of the proposers.

Nevertheless, political and ideological arguments about rationality should not obfuscate your need to be logical, systematic, and problem-focused. It is necessary to anticipate the steps, activities, people, and resources needed to produce a coherent plan from beginning to end, implement it, and evaluate it, as well as to identify contingencies beyond your own and your constituency's control. Analytical skills as part of "rational" planning are essential.

PRINCIPLE 4: KNOW AND MAKE YOUR CASE

Assessments are a critical part of community organizing and planning practice. It is essential to ask the questions: "How do you know there is a problem?" "How do you know there is a need for a particular intervention?" "Who asserts that there is a problem/need?" "Who is defining the problem/need?" "Why at this time?" "How serious and pervasive is the problem?

As noted in Principles 2 and 3, defining the need has an ideological as well as factual component. For example, if it is reported that 30% of the students in a particular school or community did not complete high school, the questions to be posed should include: "Is that a problem?" "For whom is that a problem?" "What are the solutions?" Answers to those questions will depend on several factors and values: whether the norm in that community (however defined) is to complete high school, whether it is desirable to complete high school, whether that figure has gone up or down in the last several years, how that figure compares to other schools, and the alternatives to and consequences of not completing high school. Remember, the way a problem is defined will determine the proposed solution(s). If you report that 30% of the students dropped out of school last year, there is already an implied causation. "Drop out" implies a willful act on the part of the student or neglect on the part of parents or the community. Consider the difference when you say that 30% of the students were "pushed out" or "turned out" last year. The latter implies the problem lies primarily with the school system.

Once you define the problem, the next step in the planning process is to document the problem. This entails gathering quantitative and qualitative data, sometimes called empirical (objective) and perceptual (subjective) information. The needs assessments that use both are most effective; they present statistics as well as humanize the issue. Documentation includes identifying assets and deficits. Prepare the materials using multiple methods and media—written, verbal, and visual. In making your case, use numbers, narration, surveys, interviews, case studies, anecdotes, and secondary data analysis. Language matters. How one phrases a term also affects how it is received; for example, when homeless people are welcomed as "guests" rather than identified as "the homeless," it makes a difference. Calling someone an "ex-con" versus a "formerly incarcerated person," makes a difference in how the message is perceived.

Next, consider the ways in which to convey that information to make the strongest, most convincing case. First, you need to identify the various audiences who need to know about the problem. How do you reach the various communities and constituencies? How do they best receive information? Communicating with the decision makers may be different than communicating with supporters and allies. To reach the public at large, you may need different means and messages from the ones used for reaching clients and constituencies. Here are just a few of the many steps to consider: Will it be in the form of a letter, a report, or an article in a community newspaper? Should it be a story on an ethnic radio station? Who writes and signs it? Who will review the format and content? Remember, presentation is as important as the content. *Pithy* and *poignant* are key words in persuasive communication. Make it brief with emotion! Lengthier background information pieces should be available without inundating the various publics. Is there a public or private forum where the data should be presented? Who will be there? Who else should be invited or know about the event? What materials should be presented (e.g., fact sheets, photos, or videos of the conditions; testimonies of people directly affected; experts and influential people in the field)? Who will follow up? Outreach is a strategic campaign of many steps, not just an activity.

For example, several years ago, a director of a public health clinic helped create additional funding for dentistry for low-income adults by making the case about the depth and breadth of the problem. He launched a public awareness campaign showing enlarged photographs of decayed mouths of adults. He took these to many public forums in that community and then to the press. When asked the age and country of the people with this severe dental disease, no one could guess that they were New York City residents 20 to 40 years old. This created public sentiment for increasing coverage of preventive dental care for low-income populations, which was communicated to the decision-makers, the City Council, and the Mayor.

PRINCIPLE 5: THE "COMMUNITY" IS NOT MONOLITHIC

In engaging in a change effort, or in trying to build the influence of your constituency, the organizer must pay attention to historic tensions, intra- and interpersonal conflicts, and interorganizational and interdisciplinary differences, as well as structural inequalities that prevent people from working together. Community has multiple definitions (geographic, symbolic, identity, interest/issue-based). The tension is that for some political and strategic purposes it is important to identify a general constituency (e.g., Latinas, seniors, Asian Americans); for other purposes, it is important and almost inevitable to recognize that within that large category there usually are differences according to other identities such a gender, country of origin, culture, and other attributes, which can divide the group if unaddressed. Organizers must balance unity and diversity.

If the aim of organizing is to build a diverse constituency or coalition that is multicultural or includes segments of a community that have been excluded, additional time and thoughtfulness must be brought to the fore. Historical and current differences by class, race, gender, ethnicity, status, or sexual orientation have to be factored in from the beginning. Experience has shown the difficulty of including excluded groups after a process of building an organization or coalition already has begun. Consider the groundwork that has to be done "on the way to the first meeting." Acknowledge and anticipate heightened sensitivities if new partners from different backgrounds are coming together for the first time, or if groups that distrust each other are returning to a new table.

The relationship between an organization that is leading a campaign (whether at a grassroots or coalition level) and the constituencies it wishes to reach are the important factors. Is the organization trustworthy? Is there a track record of competency? As you begin outreach, the reputation of your organization counts. Are the organization and organizer from that community (however defined) or from outside it? The organizer is not a free agent. The auspices and background of the organizer are critical factors in the role he/she plays in organizing a campaign.

There are benefits and limitations to both the insider and outsider position. An inside organization has a track record and already has its allies and (most likely also) detractors; an outside organization (e.g., a university, a foundation, a corporation) especially if it is mainstream and powerful, may or may not have a positive track record with that community. A person with the same identity (or one or more identities—e.g., gender, race, education) as the constituency may be accepted more easily, but an outside person with a different background may bring new ideas and connections, along with a fresh perspective, and may be able to bridge internal divisions.

PRINCIPLE 6: KNOW THE DECISION-MAKING STRUCTURES OF THE TARGET SYSTEM: WHO HOLDS FORMAL POWER (AUTHORITY) AS CRITICAL ACTORS AND WHO HOLDS INFORMAL POWER (INFLUENCE) AS FACILITATING ACTORS

Understanding and utilizing the concept of power; that is, which *body* (person) or *Body* (group, structure) can make the change you want, is an essential component of organizing. It is important to analyze the two faces of power—authority and influence. The "critical" actors are the actual legitimate decision makers, those with the sanctioned formal authority to grant the request, make the change, and allocate the resources. The facilitating actors are those who can influence the critical actors because of their relationship to them. Many times, people do not know who has the formal power because it is hidden, or because the system is complicated. The best approach is to do a power analysis beforehand. Who are the people and organizations who control the systems you want to influence? For example, the authority in a hospital may be vested in the board of trustees and the medical boards. State health departments, which have the authority to grant or suspend an operating license to that hospital, have the ultimate formal power over the hospital—although they may not readily use it. The authority to evict a tenant rests with a landlord, but the local or state government may create regulations to curb a landlord's absolute power through regulations or the courts.

The formal system of authority is usually found on some version of an organizational chart. These are usually in the form of a diagram that shows the chain of command, who reports to whom in the hierarchy, who controls certain activities, and to whom they are accountable internally. Do not be surprised if the organizational chart is difficult to obtain, even within your own organization. Many organizations do not want to reveal the formal authority; they may conceal differences between those designated to make decisions and those who actually make them. Often, groups will be told that the organizational table is in transition or not current.

Knowing someone's formal position can help decide the level of intervention in the system. If someone says they cannot make a certain decision, you want to ascertain whether they are being accurate or "buck passing." It is essential to ask that person, "Who can make that change or grant the request?" Those persons you initially approached may become a facilitating actor in the process of making change if they reveal their relationships to the critical actor(s). There are many instances where organizers and their constituencies are at the wrong door as a result of ignorance or deceit.

There is also a need to know and use the informal structures of influence. Influence is power acquired by people when they do not have the authority to make decisions. Clearly people are able to amass power to make change by virtue of being able to influence the decision-making bodies. There are many ways groups can be powerful when they are not in a position to command, "Just do it!" People have power through the positions they hold, their past history of action, longevity in a system, perceived effectiveness and expertise, connections to the decision makers, ability to control a large constituency, characteristics such as persistence and willingness to take risks. There are powerful "subordinates" in organizations because of certain functions they perform or access they could provide (e.g., janitors, secretaries, and technical staff).

Organizing power by using strategies of influence is an essential skill set. Organizers use these strategies to bring pressure to bear on the structures of authority to convince them to make the needed changes, fund programs, reallocate resources, and so on. Different tactics will be needed for confronting public/government and private/corporate power. Depending on the issue, many changes can be made at lower levels in both public and private bureaucracies. It is not always necessary or wise to start with or go to the top.

PRINCIPLE 7: DO NOT ASSUME THAT THE TARGET YOU WANT TO INFLUENCE IS A UNIFIED, MONOLITHIC SYSTEM

Whether you are on the inside or outside, look for internal strains, divisions, and vulnerability within the system, organization, or institution your group wants to influence. Seek friends and allies from within. Most organizations try to create a culture of unity; at the very least, they attempt to present a unified front to the public. However, that does not mean that there is unanimity among staff regarding their positions, policies, or programs, especially in large bureaucracies. In analyzing the system you are trying to influence, it is essential to ascertain who on the inside of that system (besides you, if you are part of that system) feels similarly about the issue as does your group/constituency? Those inside people can provide important pieces of information, including the identification of the critical and facilitating actors. They know about the organization's past and current policies, procedures, and culture.

Conversely, those insiders may need your (outside) group for support, legitimacy, and resources, and even want you to pressure them to do their job more effectively (Principle 12 provides more detail for those on "the inside"). The model of exchange is pivotal. You provide them with the capacity to be more influential on the inside, and they can become an ally.

The exposé of the conditions at Willowbrook State Institution for the Mentally Retarded in New York City in the early 1970s provides a case in point. It was a long struggle and went public after several years of professional staff and families trying to convince those in charge to improve the horrendous conditions. Many courageous social workers, resident psychiatrists, and other staff inside the institution worked with advocacy and family groups on the outside by providing necessary information to them and eventually to media and elected officials. When—then young—investigative reporter Geraldo Rivera turned his cameras on the site, it was because people on the inside obviously had blown the whistle. This resulted in a transformative change in the system of care. Working behind the scenes is tantamount to Principle 10.

Some caution must be exercised in attempting to exploit the complexities or tensions within an agency or target system. Although outsiders initially may rally staff (and clients), this may create difficulty in negotiating later on in the process, because the conflict has been escalated and become widespread. It may prevent at least some on the inside from cooperating for fear of antagonizing their leaders and managers. You may need to protect their cover and also respect their need for a low profile. Clients may fear losing their program even if it has deficiencies. The principle is to proceed deliberately, allowing time for the people on the inside to persuade others of the need to grant the request or meet the demand (further discussed in Principle 9).

PRINCIPLE 8: ASSUME NOBODY KNOWS ANYTHING, ANYTIME

For political and strategic purposes, you must work from the assumption that those in charge of the systems you are attempting to change are ignorant of the problem or need. Therefore, your first step is to define and document the need in a way that gives the decision makers a chance to respond, even if you believe that those in control already have the requisite information on which to act. For example, assume the mayor of a large city does not know that thousands of homeless people live on the streets every night. In reality, that information has appeared in various media. Nevertheless, it apparently has been ignored or dismissed. So, once you present the problem and possible solutions, the ball is in their court. If they really did not know the extent or seriousness of the problem, then this is a genuine opportunity to influence and negotiate change by presenting the necessary information and making a cogent argument as discussed in Principle 4.

If they already knew about the problem but did not act, they are more apt to respond when the need is directly presented in an organized and persuasive manner. You may have given them a chance to save face if the need was hidden. Do not underestimate the value of this human principle. In the best scenario, they will do something about the issue (i.e., clean up the park, fund a program, pass legislation, allocate staff time for an activity, etc.). In the worst scenario, they will delay or oppose the solution openly. If they do not respond, your group has greater legitimacy for moving ahead and escalating the pressure—from presenting additional information to using more intense and persistent persuasive tactics including taking the issue public or threatening later actions. The important point is to document all the steps taken in this process, and keep the relevant people, constituencies, and organizations informed and involved. This should include the constituency itself, as spokespersons, leaders, and as representatives of the population.

This principle also applies to the constituency itself without being patronizing. Educating them about the root causes, the power structure, and the gaps between their knowledge and actions is an important role for the organizer. It must be done in a way that respects their views even if misinformed. Presenting data from real life can counter stereotypes and myths.

PRINCIPLE 9: ASSUME GOODWILL AND COMMON CAUSE ON THE PART OF THOSE WHO CONTROL AND OPERATE THE SYSTEM

This may seem to contradict Principle 7, but in reality, both tensions have to be managed at the same time—both are truths. There are unhappy employees who may be willing to provide "inside information" and even speak out, but experience has shown that line and support staff, professionals included, are usually loyal to their place of employment. Assume that most people want to do a good job most of the time (based on the human relations theory of management). The reasons for loyalty are many. It may be because of the pride they take in their own work or because they understand the many obstacles impeding major changes inside their system. It could be out of a sense of vulnerability, or their fears of being outspoken, or their uneasiness with proposed alternatives. They may have been co-opted, or they may have made the system work for them. Certainly a need for stability and predictability may outweigh change and uncertainty.

Even if you uncover disillusionment, fear, or inertia among certain staff, caution must still be exercised in publicly criticizing the whole agency or system. Staff or clients may agree with the issues being raised; however, they may not necessarily want those problems uncovered in public. Time and again, organizers have underestimated the sense of workers' and clients' feelings of hurt or anger at perceived attacks on their system or agency. Even when the outside group attempts to separate or not blame all workers or supervisors equally, there may be resistance to aligning themselves with an outside or even inside activist group.

As noted in Principle 6, it is vital to gauge the tacit or active support of at least some people on the inside and identify the extent of their loyalty. This will help you assess whether those in control of the institution/agency have the power to use a "we/they" division to create rifts between those on the outside and those on the inside. To use one case example: when a neighborhood health organization began criticizing a local hospital for inadequate care, the organizers assumed the hospital workers, most of whom were from the same background or came from the same neighborhood, would join in their public meetings or issue a statement of support. Private conversations afterward revealed that many staff were angered that no one had asked them their opinions about the issues or strategies in question. A "divide and conquer" strategy ensued, with the hospital director firing the few sympathetic workers who joined with the health organization while promoting a few others who were then co-opted. The rest of the staff remained silent.

This came as a total surprise to the organization seeking change and undermined its effectiveness.

Therefore, in beginning any campaign with an organizational target, it makes sense to assume that the system is not intentionally out to harm or hurt the clients/constituency, but rather is attempting to do the job it was given. Hence the value of framing the problem in consensus terms, at least initially. It should not be presented or perceived as a "win/lose" scenario (see Principle 8). The goal of a campaign can be stated in ways that recognize that all involved have a similar mission; for example, they want to help children, provide quality health care, have a clean environment, keep a neighborhood safe, and so on. Alternatively, your group could convey its understanding of the difficulties that the agency/system has in meeting the needs of its clients or constituency. Then your strategy becomes one of demonstrating and documenting to the leadership, staff, the public, and clients, how the agency/system is interfering with or defeating its own goals or mission. Where possible, appeals should be made to their self-interest as well as to their altruism. "What we are asking is good for you and good for the community!"

Assuming common cause does not mean letting people off the hook or giving them a "pass." As conveyed in Principle 8, it means alerting them to the inadequacy or deleteriousness of their program or policy in a systematic sustained manner.

PRINCIPLE 10: ASSUME THE PRINCIPLE OF LEAST CONTEST. ESCALATE THE PROCESS ONLY AS NEEDED

Following from Principle 9, in order to have credibility and to gain the broadest support, your group should not antagonize the targets prematurely or unnecessarily. Intervene just high enough to gain recognition and ultimately to achieve your goals. Strategies of influence exist on a continuum of social change from consensus to contest tactics. These range from presenting information in persuasive ways, to negotiation and bargaining processes, to offering incentives, to more conflictual tactics including threats, and, finally, to using social action strategies of mass mobilization, protest, resistance, and disruption.

In general, and in accordance with Principle 8, you should not begin with adversarial and confrontational tactics until those with authority

have been given a chance to change voluntarily. On the other hand, you cannot assume that information alone will be sufficient to produce major change. A strategic question to answer is: "What will it take to have the issue seriously addressed?" A well-thought-out strategy will determine the process and timing of moving from the least- to more-conflictual strategies, assuming you have some control over these factors. The cogent questions are: "How long have you been waiting for change to occur?" "How long can you wait; that is, how serious are the consequences of inaction?" "What is your group prepared to do next?" "What resources and contributions would be needed to move to the next step?" "What are the consequences of escalating the tensions?" "Who will you lose and gain along the change continuum?"

In intensifying and escalating the pressure on those with authority, you must pay attention to ethical considerations. You will need to build support for your effort, preferably before, and not just during, a campaign, so you do not alienate (again, unnecessarily or prematurely) potential allies who are either on the inside or on the outside. You need to build your credibility before your group goes above or around someone or exposes someone publicly (the principle of "no surprises"). It is essential to have factual information and ethically engage in a democratic decision-making process with your group and its allies. Among the essential ethical practices based on social work values, is whether your constituency is informed about the tactics in which they are being asked to engage. If there is a chance of provocation or serious repercussions, participants should have the ability to make an informed choice in advance, even at the risk of losing some of them, to the extent that the risks can be anticipated. As noted in Principle 11, the organizer's role is to anticipate the consequences. A key question to pose is: "What's the worst that could happen if… ?" Organizers cannot promise their constituencies immunity from the consequences of their actions; for example, you should never use absolutes, "Your landlord can't evict you" or "Your boss can't fire you." Even when this may be legally correct, a person can still be harmed emotionally, financially, and even physically from confronting powerful targets of social change. Collectively, people need to know the consequences of moving from lawful protest to civil disobedience. This is especially important around tactics that have legal ramifications, for example, events that need police permits, confront trespassing laws, and so on.

Saul Alinsky wrote in his "means and ends" essay that an end justifies the means. Organizers informed by social work principles need to seriously weigh using undemocratic deceitful tactics—and never without consulting colleagues, constituencies, and allies. The related principle should be "no surprises!"

PRINCIPLE 11: THERE WILL ALWAYS BE OPPOSITION TO CHANGE AT SOME LEVEL, BE IT ACTIVE OR PASSIVE RESISTANCE

It is essential to assume that some*body*/*Body* will always be opposed to the change your group wants to make, and therefore, to anticipate a range of responses to your actions. You may hear such things as "It can't be done," "We've tried it before and it can't work," "We can't afford it," and so on. Identify the opposing side's arguments by playing out alternative responses to the problem and by testing the waters with the facilitating actors who can influence the decision makers. As much as possible, analyze in advance who may be opposed to the identified solutions, and why they may be opposed.

Effective organizers develop strategies to counter or neutralize opposition where they can, as well as identify those elements in the change process that they or the group cannot control. In identifying supporters, it is essential not to write off potential allies, even if they have been adversaries on other issues. Short of those intense ideological battles where there is little room for compromise (e.g., abortion rights, affirmative action), appeals for support can be made to most sectors of society. Arguments used will usually vary among different groups. You may appeal to such factors as reputation, pride, and professional expertise to gain or keep people on the side of your proposed change. Ask supporters for their advice or would be adversaries to put themselves in your constituencies' shoes.

Sometimes the opposition may not be apparent because the implications of the change may not be visible until the change process is under way. Do not assume that all the opposition is external or conversely that it is being orchestrated from the target of change. Remember that communities and systems are not monolithic. There may be as much division and difference within a community as between "the community" and the target of change (see Principles 5 & 7). Sometimes the opposition may be passivity or inertia rather than visible and articulated differences. They may delay or avoid a response in hopes of outlasting your group.

To the extent possible, your group should have one or more responses, anticipating resistance. For example, one tactic of the opposition is to ask, "So how would you fix it?" or "What would you do if you were in charge?" Understand that groups engaged in social change are not obligated to come up with solutions because they identify an issue. In a democratic society, citizens have the right to raise questions, make demands, and hold those in charge accountable for outcomes. The latter have the authority, resources, and expertise to run the show. Your group has a right to point out that things are not working and that there must be a better way.

However, you are more likely to be credible and effective if you have thought through the arguments for why the current situation has to change and how it can be changed. If the response to your request is, "We don't have the funds," your group may be able to counter with "We know where you can get them," or "We know from where they can be taken." When the response is, "We can't do that" your group has to ask "Who says?" Ask for the written policies and procedures when the rejection is a legal or regulatory one.

There may be circumstances in which your group may be strong and invested enough to pose alternatives to the current situation and even strive to replace those in control or create an alternative entity. This takes a long-term commitment with its own set of limitations when you are "in charge" as opposed to holding those with the authority accountable for their actions.

Another tactic of the opposition is to divide and conquer or discredit a group. This has happened when groups left out of the decision-making process begin to challenge the authority of those in control. Those in charge may question your own or your group's credibility and representativeness. It may attempt to exploit differences within a community or coalition, or "play favorites," bribe, or isolate. Hence, out of range of the opposition, your group should strategize the range of alternatives available. It is important to identify who your spokespeople will be and what message you want to convey, even if you cannot always control all the events.

Establishing some procedures and protocols in advance is essential. It is always helpful to have some counter-expertise, meaning trustworthy allies and supporters who are willing to use their professional knowledge or political experience to challenge the opposition on its own terms. Given the elitism and privilege of those in positions of authority, having professional or powerful people on your side lends weight to your arguments, although relying on this strategy does little to change the structural inequalities of a system. You must come to agreement on the following: Is your group willing to negotiate? What is the bottom line? What happens if the target says no? What happens if the target says yes? What happens if they ask your group to come up with a proposal or to join a task force? There is no one right or wrong answer, except the principle of anticipating opposition and being prepared for differential outcomes.

PRINCIPLE 12: IN MAKING CHANGE FROM INSIDE, ASSESS RISKS REALISTICALLY—IDENTIFY AND WEIGH COSTS AGAINST GAINS

You can engage successfully in major change efforts from within your own system or agency, if you strategically assess your role and are prepared for possible controversy and consequences. All the Principles in this document apply here. There are several positive aspects to initiating or participating in change from within. By being on the inside, you already have a foot in the door. You have the legitimacy to ask for and obtain information; you know who makes decisions and how the system "really" works, that is, its informal, as well as formal, structure. You know the history of past efforts to engage in change, and most importantly, presumably you have some credibility, longevity, and allies within that structure. Working to improve an organization from within is not disloyal. As noted in the NASW Code of Ethics, it may be the only ethical course to pursue. Timing and tactics are part of the equation as to when and how to act—not whether. There are, however, two conundrums in working from within. Those on the outside may not know of your efforts behind the scenes and might assume you have been co-opted; on the other hand, working with others outside the system or going outside (i.e., whistle-blowing) may produce reprimand or worse. The seriousness and pervasiveness of the issue will help guide your actions.

Therefore, it is essential to play out for yourself and with your constituents the generic question posed above: "What's the worst that can happen if… ?" You have to ascertain the support you have and to anticipate the amount and intensity of the opposition to minimize your isolation or ostracism. There are times when hard choices have to be made as to how far to take a social change project. To determine the type and extent of action to be undertaken, you should consider pragmatic things such as feasibility of success, and factors such as the seriousness and pervasiveness of the situation. Is there an imperative to act? Is there a sense of urgency? Is the timing right? Is there a window of opportunity? What are the consequences of inaction?

There will be some risk to every action taken. It is important to anticipate actual or perceived repercussions (as per Principle 11) from peers, line or support staff, supervisors, managers, and clients. Therefore, if a major change that affects a department or the whole agency is needed, or if the required action includes an implied criticism of your agency or system, you need to employ Principles 8, 9, and 10.

Note that there is a long continuum from doing nothing to getting fired. The importance of keeping your own house in order cannot be stressed enough. Rarely will you be directly sanctioned for your organizing activities. You are more likely to be called to task for not doing your paid job. Pay attention and do not be caught off-guard when engaged in internal organizing, no matter how justified. Staff members are reprimanded for not turning in reports on time, for leaving early, for not following up. To minimize any criticism directed at you, consider taking on additional responsibilities. Demonstrate your value to your employer and the clients.

If you are advising, or are part of a group of people working on the inside, it is essential neither to overpromise protection nor to underestimate repercussions. Organizers can never assert that nothing untoward will happen to those participating in a change process. On the other hand, it is essential to uncover any perceived fears, even if not grounded in reality, so they can be addressed by you or the group. People are often caught short when they have not thought through Principle 11.

PRINCIPLE 13: RECORDKEEPING AND NOTE-TAKING ARE POLITICAL, NOT CLERICAL FUNCTIONS

If information is power, then obtaining and recording information is a political process. The persons or group in charge of those processes may be the most powerful players in their organization or system. Experienced organizers always want to be involved in those processes, although what and how records are kept should be identified and decided by the group's leaders. Documentation includes taking minutes, corresponding with people, recording actions and inactions, keeping people on track, and reminding people of past decisions through letters, memos, e-mail, and written records. Technology allows for myriad methods of storing data, but the bottom line is to have them available in multiple ways and permanently stored. Taking minutes is a critical skill, value, and process. Minutes help gauge and set the tone for the way a group makes decisions as well as what decisions were made and by whom. Documents are accountability tools; they help keep processes and outcomes transparent, and keep the people involved focused and honest. They also provide a historical account, preserving the institutional memory, and their availability allows disputes about past actions to be resolved. Therefore, the role of archivist should be identified to organize and store and help determine access.

You can assess the seriousness, effectiveness, and cohesiveness of a group/organization by whether minutes are taken and reviewed and how participants are engaged in their production and review. Experience has demonstrated that if there are no minutes of a meeting or group process, chances are nothing will change. Experience has also shown that those in charge of a system or the target of change (the critical actors) will often resist the formal recording of or sharing of minutes. In those instances, you must create a paper trail that includes agreements and timetables and note-taking shared among all constituencies.

Minutes can also be a diagnostic tool to assess an organization's culture, structure, and history. When organizations spend an inordinate amount of time refuting minutes, you can infer that there is distrust and dissention that will result in an inability to move ahead. When minutes are viewed as *pro forma* without much attention paid to them, you can infer that there is not much investment or involvement of its participants in the organization.

It is important to prepare someone in the group to take notes of strategic meetings, regardless of whether the person in charge agrees to have notes taken. If possible, at least two people should attend all important meetings or be conferenced-in and be ready to report on the session verbally and in writing. If there are no minutes taken, those who attended should debrief and designate someone to write a letter or send an e-mail thanking them for meeting and stating their understanding of what took place and what was agreed to by attendees. Any disagreements and next steps should be highlighted. The same thing applies with strategic phone calls. If there are minutes taken by those who called the meeting, those attending should ensure that they receive a copy and have the ability to review and comment on them. It should not be surprising that there are memory lapses (intentional or not) and different interpretations with regard to issues addressed and promises made. Without a record, there will be little or no progress.

PRINCIPLE 14: THE MEDIA ARE UNPREDICTABLE AND AMORAL. PROCEED WITH CAUTION

Given the importance of communicating with a variety of constituencies and publics, understanding the role of the media as a powerful sector of society, and knowing the types and functions of various media outlets, is an essential part of the organizer's job. The variety of media outlets active today are growing in number and changing rapidly—electronic media, blast e-mails and faxes, and blogs, in addition to the more traditional print media (newspapers, magazines, mainstream, and alternative presses), plus broadcast media—TV (network, cable, public), and radio. Organizers and designated leaders in the group need to know the basic tools of these various outlets and the functions they play in society, in your community, and in the sectors you wish to influence. Given the importance of outreach campaigns in creating awareness and action for your issues, and the role technology plays in making, as well as recording, "news," your group may want to retain a media consultant for a fee or on pro bono basis. If there is a college nearby, chances are they have a media studies or journalism department, or film and video studies department, for you to consult. Communication is an essential skill and facet of an organization's life today.

As part of an outreach campaign, the first step is to identify whom you want to reach and then decide how they are best reached. You need to know how the constituencies you want to influence receive their information. What mass media do they read, watch, or listen to? What ethnic and community media do they value? How do they use the Internet and social media? Who are the media personalities that influence them? Second, is to identify and cultivate a person in each of those outlets used (*outlet* is a generic term for all the different types of media). Who writes or talks about your topic or issue? Be proactive with them. Send them background materials about your organization. Invite those reporters or opinion-makers to your organization. Ask them to meet with your constituency. Become their expert on the issues and know who else is. Determine who may be "more friendly" and who less friendly to your organization and/or issue.

How do you craft a message so that the media important to your organization will want to publish or cover the issue? How do you convey your story in compelling ways? At this juncture, organizers and most media part ways; hence, the "amoral assertion." Organizers (social workers, human rights and social justice advocates) usually want to publicize stories that are serious and pervasive. The story you want told probably involves many people who are in that circumstance, for example, people who are suffering from what the government or a corporate body is doing—or not doing—to them. The target of change may be providing inadequate services or denying them; they may be cutting back on opportunities and pathways, limiting resources, and so on. You usually want to show universality of an issue and convey the numbers of people affected. For example, "Ms. Jones is one of millions of people losing her food stamps."

Most media, on the contrary, regardless of political bent, want to show just the opposite. They cover the unusual, the bizarre, and the extreme. If there are thousands of people collecting an inadequate amount of public assistance, or if the child welfare system discriminates against parents of color, they will feature the "welfare queen" or the one tragic case of major child abuse. Journalists, regardless of whether they are liberal or conservative, whether the outlet is a tabloid or an intellectual magazine, do not generally portray the usual or typical. They do not cover the good news as

often as they do bad news. They are prone to exaggeration and hyperbole; they like to cover conflicts and dissension. The slant is usually toward the sensational. This does not suggest that the media are nonideological. Different outlets have their political slants reflected in their editorials and opinion sections. Experience has shown, however, that regardless of the reputation of the station or newspaper, they may not cover "your story" the way you want it to be conveyed. Therefore, the organizing principle when the media come knocking is that you cannot control the outcome. So the decision your group must make is whether to reach out to the media and still make every effort to educate them in advance where possible. It helps to provide succinct background material; easy to read, but substantive at the same time (see Principle 4).

The media as a sector of a society has the same biases as other institutions in the United States. They usually reflect the "isms" in some fashion regardless of their politics. Recognition of this fact will temper expectations of the outcomes. There are many examples of media coverage that reflect institutional inequalities. In general, with few exceptions, they will generally focus on the professional rather than on the client or constituency. They will seek out males more than females; they will gravitate more to the Caucasians than to people of color. Therefore, practically speaking, if you want to downplay those disparities and ensure a unified and accurate message, prepare spokespersons in advance. Agree to channel the media to designated people and provide everyone with a few sound bites, should they ask. If relevant, try to pair professional and indigenous leaders so that new and undervalued (by the media) voices are up front and visible. Learn to handle the pressure and avoid the seduction of becoming an instant celebrity.

If the coverage you receive portrays the story differently from what you wanted, write a letter to the editor and to the author and publisher or owner of the outlet. Let your own constituency and allies know what you attempted to convey. Research has shown that letters to the editor are the second most-read section of a newspaper (after sports) and are highly read in magazines as well. It may be difficult to get an article into the *New York Times* or a story on national network TV, but there are hundreds of smaller outlets in your community.

CONCLUSION

These principles are meant as guides to action and will apply differentially, depending on the auspices of your agency, the goals identified, the political and economic context of the community, the issues in question, and the system driving the organizing. Organizers cannot control all the variables, but acquiring these competencies along with your commitment to the long haul will go a long way. Remember to incorporate these four H's into your work, which reflect critical social work values and traits: humanity, humility, honesty, and humor.

WEBSITES

Association for Community Organization and Social Administration. http://www.acosa.com.
Community Toolbox. http://www.ctb.ku.edu.
Education Center for Community Organizing. http://www.hunter.cuny.edu/socwork/ecco.
Comm.Org-The On-Line Conference of Community Organizing: http://www.comm-org.wisc.edu.

Resources

Bobo, K., Kendall, J., & Max, S. (2009). *Organizing for social change: Midwest academy manual for activists* (4th ed.). Santa Ana, CA: Seven Locks Press.
Burghardt, S. (2010). *Macro practice in social work for the 21st century*. Thousand Oaks, CA: Sage Publications.

Eichler, M. (2007). *Consensus organizing: Building communities of mutual self interest*. Thousand Oaks, CA: Sage.
Hardina, D. (2002). *Analytical skills for community organization practice*. New York, NY: Columbia University Press.
Hardina, D. (2013). *Interpersonal social work skills for community practice*. New York, NY: Springer Publishers.
Kirst-Ashman, K. K. & Hull, G. H. (2006). *Generalist practice with organizations and communities* (2nd ed.). Belmont, CA: Thomson Brooks/Cole.
Homan, M. S. (2011). *Promoting community change: Making it happen in the real world* (5th ed.). Belmont, CA: Thomson Brooks/Cole.
Netting, F. E., Kettner, P. M., & McMurtry, S. L. (2008). *Social work macro practice* (4th ed.). Boston, MA: A&B/ Pearson.
Pyles, L. (2014). *Progressive community organizing: Reflective practice in a globalizing world* (2nd ed.). New York, NY: Routledge/Taylor & Francis.
Rothman, J., Erlich, J., & Tropman, J. (Eds.). (2007). *Strategies of community intervention* (7th ed.). Itasca, IL: F. E. Peacock.
Rubin, H. J. & Rubin, I. S. (2007). *Community organizing and development* (4th ed.). Boston, MA: Pearson/Allyn & Bacon.
Smock, K. (2004). *Democracy in action: Community organizing and urban change*. New York, NY: Columbia University Press.
Staples, L. (2004). *Roots to power: A manual for grassroots organizing* (2nd ed.). Westport, CT: Praeger.
Weil, M. & Gamble, D. N. (2010). *Community practice skills workbook*. New York, NY: Columbia University Press.
Weil, M. O., Reisch, M., & Ohmer, M. (Eds.). (2011). *Handbook of community practice* (2nd ed.). Thousand Oaks, CA: Sage.

116 Contemporary Community Practice Models

Marie Overby Weil & Dorothy N. Gamble

Throughout the history of social work, community practice has been a prominent method, one which embodies the profession's empowerment tradition and social justice values (NASW, 1996; Simon, 1994). With the complexities of current societies; rapid technological, social, and economic change; political unrest in many parts of the world; and the globalization of trade and communication, community practice at local, regional, national, and international levels is an even more essential element to revitalizing democracy in the United States and encouraging democratic societies internationally to build and nurture inclusive, supportive, nonracist, and nonsexist communities and institutions (Weil & Gamble, 2013). Societies across the world are becoming more multicultural, and globally there are now more internally displaced persons than at any previous time. With these global changes and the realities of both internal and cross-national conflicts, protection of human rights, particularly the rights of women and girls, becomes increasingly critical in efforts to build and maintain socially just communities. Serious political divides in the early decades of the 21st century revolve not only around differing conceptions of national common good, but also around the different paths to and conceptions of the common good in international and global terms. Currently, in several areas of the world fledgling, as well as established, democracies now face internal political challenges and external threats to ongoing development (Weil, Reisch, & Ohmer, 2013). Community practice in its essential forms of organizing, planning, development, and progressive work for social change is increasingly needed within and across communities and nations (Weil & Gamble, 2013).

The moral, political, and economic equation for human development requires an understanding of global social and economic interdependence. Vandana Shiva describes the "Declaration of Interdependence," sponsored by the Democracy Collaborative, as growing from the recognition that "we are earth citizens and have earth identities which are both the particular identity of place, and the global planetary identity. As members of communities, we have multiple community identities. … These diverse, multiple identities shape our sense of self and who we are. And these diversities are not inconsistent with our common humanity. Without diversity, we have no humanity" (2005, p. 142). These issues of democratic development, revitalization, sustainment, and transformation are the central purview of community practice in all its forms; the skills and knowledge for building and rebuilding community are critical for those who work to achieve positive and sustainable development and pluralistic, multicultural societies in a global economy.

Community practice encompasses a broad scope, ranging from grassroots organization and development to human services planning and coordination. It employs multiple methods of empowerment-based interventions to strengthen participation in democratic processes, reform human service systems, and assist groups and communities in advancing their concerns and organizing for social justice. This chapter presents community practice models that are widely identifiable in interventions employed in the first quarter of the twenty-first century. They are rooted in traditions evolving from the settlement house movement, the charity organization society movement, the rural development movement, and from the organizing and development histories and cultures of diverse ethnic and racial groups (Betten & Austin, 1990; Rivera & Erlich, 1998; St. Onge, 2013, 2009).

MODELS OF COMMUNITY PRACTICE FOR THE 21ST CENTURY

Eight basic models of community practice are described. They illustrate approaches widely used in many parts of the world and they are expected to persist. Community practice efforts focus primarily on the following general purposes.

Community Practice Purposes

- *Improving quality of life*: Work to support well-being, decrease poverty and respond to basic human needs, such as food and shelter, security, opportunities for education and basic health; promote freedom from violence; build opportunities to organize and participate in community goals and decisions. Work for well-being can focus from local to global issues.
- *Extension and implementation of human rights*: Build inclusion through participatory structures; respond to needs and promote rights of marginalized groups who are discriminated against, are political or economic refugees, or are internally displaced; end slavery and human trafficking; and support enforcement of full human rights for women and girls.
- *Advocacy*: Conduct research; document policies, practices and behaviors that limit opportunities of groups and individuals; promote egalitarian political leadership, policies, and work to build human capabilities and community capacity for the most marginalized groups; form groups and coalitions to press for human rights and provide "voice" and opportunities for vulnerable groups at multiple levels; advocate for full human rights, education, and equality of opportunity from local communities to national and global venues. Examples include lobbying for improved services for children with severe emotional problems; campaigning for human rights for women; working for rights of lesbian, gay, bisexual, and transgender (LGBT) groups;

or passing legislation to fund minority group economic development projects through such structures as the Community Reinvestment Act.

- *Human social and economic development*: Create opportunities for people and groups to gain knowledge and skills thus enriching their capabilities and building community capital; establishing well-being through education and training for viable livelihoods; work with communities to preserve their natural resources and develop assets through economic cooperatives, microenterprise, or development programs. Economic development can be fostered by national governments or international nongovernmental organizations (NGOs), and can function regionally—most importantly it can function at grassroots levels to grow local economies and develop leadership among the poor. In combination, social and economic development should ensure social support, and economic viability and sustainability for marginalized rural and urban groups by promoting participation and leadership development—locally, regionally, and globally.
- *Service and program planning*: Work with local people to assess the strengths and needs of a whole community or specific populations and the development of plans, resources, and structures to meet those needs. Employ appropriate technology that can assist in building capacity as well as provide needed services. Services may be adapted for specific interventions, and evidence-based interventions may be adapted to fit context and local population and culture.
- *Service integration*: Establish a range of services and link them so that a continuum of care is in place for the broad needs of community members. Examples include building the continuum of family support, preservation, and child welfare services; establishing a network of well-connected services for both healthy and frail senior citizens; or providing food, protection, relocation opportunities, and services for new starts for refugees and internally displaced persons from international or national conflicts.
- *Political and social action*: Engage in the political process to change existing problematic policies, establish new

progressive legislation, or change legislative policy makers. Activity in political and social action is direct, open, and nonviolent. It requires free spaces in which people can gather, organize, and speak out, especially those who have been excluded from political involvement in the past. Political and social action seeks to foster institutional change for inclusion and equity, and increase participatory democracy and equality of opportunity in local, regional, and international institutions. Organizing for the rights, protection, and welfare of children by the Children's Defense Fund and Amnesty International's efforts to prevent torture and secure release of political prisoners worldwide are examples of political and social action that is nonpartisan.

- *Social justice*: Involves building toward human equality and opportunity across race, ethnicity, gender, and nationality. Examples are working to ensure basic education for girls in all countries, full political participation for women, making reparations to people who have endured systematic oppression in the past such as Native Americans, African Americans, and Japanese Americans, and building the fabric of civil and human rights laws both nationally and globally.

The value base of community practice not only respects the dignity of the individual but also focuses on the interdependence of families and communities and the development of legislative, political, and distributive justice. Community practitioners work with competing perspectives on issues, using multiple strategies to solve problems that inevitably arise within and among diverse groups in communities. America's reality as a pluralistic society where communities of color are still struggling for inclusion increases the need for skilled multicultural organizing and development of multicultural human service organizations (Gutierrez, Lewis, Dessel, & Spencer, 2013). The eight models depicted in Table 116.1 are analyzed in terms of outcome, change targets, constituencies, scope of concern, and primary social work roles through lenses of globalization, human rights, and multiculturalism (Gamble & Weil, 2010). Though the models are described as particular entities in the chart for analytic clarity, elements of the models are often observed in interaction—being mixed or phased

as organizations and groups respond to new challenges or shifts in the environment (Rothman, Erlich, & Tropman, 2008).

Neighborhood and Community Organizing

Much of community organizing depends on the face-to-face opportunities available to people in geographic proximity, such as a neighborhood, rural community, or county, though increasingly, digital media are employed to support communication. Community organizing focuses on activities to increase the leadership, planning, and organization-building skills of ordinary people to help them develop power at the neighborhood or village level and increase community well-being. It is the bedrock of democratic institutions. When people at the grass roots of society learn how to organize their efforts, be inclusive in organization building, employ democratic decision making, set priorities, access resources, and reach their goals, they have learned basic lessons of democracy. Increasing their capacity to work on basic community problems makes it possible for citizens to change conditions to improve the quality of life for all residents. This model of community practice can be seen in a variety of forms across the globe, in the democracies that have been working at neighborhood organizing for hundreds of years yet still tend to exclude the most vulnerable groups in society, as well as in the newly emerging democracies of Eastern Europe, Africa, Asia, the Middle East, and South America.

Organizing in communities almost always carries aspects of both consensus building and contest or conflict (Mondros & Staples, 2013). Within neighborhood groups conflict will occur over what strategies to adopt and even in external contest focused organizing–such as seeking a change in state policy, organizers look for allies in powerful positions. As Gutierrez and Lewis (1994) have discussed, organizers most often will strive to help groups achieve internal consensus to plan for work within their community and plan for more social action oriented strategies when external forces are oppositional. Indeed, community groups work to solve internal conflicts and develop a cohesive and coordinated strategy for external work. Where possible, community organizations will first work externally, using educational and collaborative approaches, adopt persuasion and campaign tactics where needed with the public and officials, and when

TABLE 116.1 Models of Community Practice in 21ˢᵗ Century Contexts

Comparative Characteristics	Neighborhood & Community Organizing	Organizing Functional & Communities of Interest	Social, Economic & Sustainable Development	Inclusive Program Development	Social Planning	Coalitions	Political & Social Action & Policy Practice	Movements for Progressive Change
Desired Outcome	Develop capacity of members to organize; Direct and/or moderate the impact of regional planning and external development	Action for social justice focused on advocacy and on changing behaviors and attitudes; may also provide service	Promote grassroots plans; Prepare citizens to use social and economic resources without harming environments; Expand livelihood opportunities	Expansion, redirection and new development of programs to improve service effectiveness using participatory engagement methods	Neighborhood, citywide or regional proposals for action by (a) neighborhood groups (b) elected body; armor planning councils	Build a multi-organizational power base to advocate for standards and programs, to influence program direction and draw down resources	Action for social justice focused or changing policies or policy makers	Action for social, economic & environmental justice that provides new paradigms for the healthy development of people and the planet
Systems targeted for change	Municipal/regional government; external developers; local leadership	General public; government institutions	Banks; foundations; external developers; laws that govern wealth creation	Financial donors & volunteers to programs; beneficiaries of agency services	Perspectives of (a) neighborhood planning groups (b) elected leaders (c) human services leaders	Elected officials; foundations; government policy and service organizations	Voting public; Elected officials; Inactive/potential participants in public debates and elections	General public; Political, social and economic systems that are oppressive and destructive
Primary constituency	Residents of neighborhood, parish, rural community, village	Like-minded people in a community, region, nation, or across the globe	Low-wealth marginalized, or oppressed population groups in a city or region	Agency board & administrators; community representatives	(a) neighborhood groups (b) elected leaders (c) social agencies and interagency organizations	Organizations and citizens that have a stake in the particular issue	Citizens in a particular political jurisdiction	Leaders, citizens, and organizations able to create new visions and social structures
Scope of Concern	Quality of life in geographic area; Increased ability of grassroots leaders & organizations to improve social, economic & environmental conditions	Advocacy for particular issue or population (examples: environmental protection; women's participation in decision making)	Improve social, economic & environmental wellbeing; Employ equality, opportunity and responsibility to guide human behavior	Service development for a specific population (examples: children's access to health care; security against domestic violence)	(a) neighborhood level planning (b) integration of social, economic & environmental needs into public planning arena; (c) human services coordination	Organizational partners joining in a collaborative relationship to improve social. economic & environmental conditions and human rights	Building the level of participation in political activity; Ensuring that elections are fair and not controlled by wealth	Social, economic and environmental justice within society (examples: basic human needs; basic human rights)
Social work/ Community Practice roles	Organizer Facilitator Educator Coach Trainer Bridge Builder	Organizer Advocate Writer/Speaker Facilitator	Negotiator Bridge Builder Promoter Planner, Educator Manager Researcher Evaluator	Spokesperson Planner/Evaluator Manager/Director Proposal Writer Trainer Bridge Builder Visionary	Researcher Proposal writer Communicator Planner Manager Evaluator	Mediator Negotiator Spokesperson Organizer Bridge Builder Leader	Advocate Organize Researcher Candidate Leader	Advocate Facilitator Leader

Adapted from Gamble, D. N., & Weil. M. (2010).

necessary move to social action approaches of contest and conflict (Brager, Specht, & Torczyner, 1987; Mondros & Staples, 2013).

Neighborhood and community organizing has the dual focus of building the capacity of individuals to lead and organize while accomplishing a task that will enhance the quality of life for the geographic area. Elements of this model are found in settings in which people can come together to create needed change. One example is the Center for Participatory Change (2013), which works to help people in small rural communities in Western North Carolina "recognize their own power, work together, and transform their communities" (http://www.cpcwnc .org/). Community organizing that has expanded from work in Los Angeles into a national network, PICO (*www.piconetwork.org*) works on building social capital, developing local leaders in many communities, and in organizing campaigns for needed social change. Current efforts include work by "Dreamers," citizenship-seeking Latino youth who were brought to the United States as young children by undocumented parents; health reform; and an overarching focus on economic health and well-being for families and communities.

Organizing Functional Communities—Communities of Interest and Identity

The essence of this model is its focus on communities of interest—functional communities—rather than geographic. The focus in organizing communities of interest or identity is advocacy for social justice and policy change to promote acceptance and inclusion of the chosen issue or group. In their efforts toward social justice, functional communities also seek to change general attitudes and behaviors and may develop services for their specific population that have not been adequately addressed in the mainstream service system. Examples are development of alternative service systems for women, evolving from feminist organizing, consisting of rape crisis centers and domestic violence programs, and more recently expanding to deal with women's employment and economic development issues. Functional communities typically engage in community education, as is illustrated in the LGBT community's earlier work to educate others about HIV/AIDS—and to press for appropriate health care

and supportive health policy. More recently this community of identity and allies has advocated for nondiscrimination in employment, and the same social, economic, and civil rights that others take for granted.

As communities of interest/functional communities organize, build internal capacity, and conduct research about their issues, members may move from mutual support to become strong advocates and leaders, as have parents of children with severe emotional disturbances through the Alliance for Mentally Ill Children and Adolescents. Leaders have also emerged among the groups that have organized in many parts of the nation to work against toxic waste sites.

Examples of communities of interest include the ARC, which functions in many localities and as a national group to improve services and advocate for the rights of children and adults with developmental disabilities; environmental groups such as Resourceful Communities/Conservation Fund, which is a "grassroots network that implements the triple bottom line low-wealth communities by building capacity and a statewide movement that advocates for sustainable economic development, social justice, and environmental stewardship" (www .resourcefulcommunities.org); and groups such as Amnesty International, which documents human rights violations and seeks protection and justice for political prisoners worldwide through local advocacy groups.

Social, Economic, and Sustainable Development

Providing opportunities for people to increase their social and economic security has been a central focus of social work. To be effective, social and economic development projects must work together within a context of sustainable development (Gamble & Hoff, 2013). Development efforts are currently framed under four rubrics:

- *Human development*, the focus of the United Nations Human Development Index, which measures progress using a composite focused on life expectancy at birth, knowledge (based on literacy rate and school enrollment), and adjusted per capita income in purchasing power parity (UNDP, 2011)
- *Social development*, focused on basic life skills and livelihood education (especially for

the poor), promotion of gender equality, and most critically, short-term amelioration and long-term eradication of poverty through policy investments in marginalized groups and communities, expanding their capacities, building social capital, and providing programs that can improve well-being and create economic opportunity (Midgley & Conley, 2010)

- *Economic development* that invests in meeting human needs and building adequate incomes and assets by employing empowerment strategies to move families and communities out of absolute poverty (Rubin & Sherraden, 2005; Friedmann, 1992)
- *Sustainable development*, described initially in *Our Common Future*, the 1987 report of the World Commission on Environment and Development as "development that meets the needs of the present without compromising the ability of future generations to meet their own needs" (*www.un-documents.net/wced-ocf.htm*; *p.43*. Sustainable development encompasses social and economic development that restores and protects the natural environment (Estes, 1993; Gamble, 2013; Hart, 1999).

Historically, many community development programs emphasized either economic development or social capacity building. In recent years, there has been a growing focus on integrated development strategies combining human capacity building, popular education, and locally controlled economic development (Freire, 1970; Nussbaum, 2011; Sen, 1999). Some current programs are designed to build personal assets. Individual development accounts (IDAs) and individual training accounts (ITAs) are local, statewide, and national programs that match the savings of a low-wealth person who is saving for a training or educational program, the startup of a small business, or the purchase of a home (Sherraden, 2013). IDAs and ITAs are seen as individual ladders to help people climb out of poverty (Schreiner et al., 2001). Coupled with other workforce strategies, they may be especially helpful to those people who have been on the poverty borderline for many years. Though individuals need these kinds of programs to develop creative entrepreneurial skills, individual strategies are insufficient without companion programs that focus on broader human investments in health and education, and policies that improve minimum wages and fairness in taxes.

Community development corporations (CDCs), of which there are thousands across the United States, often combine efforts to change the community by decreasing barriers to economic and social resources (e.g., Bethel New Life; Murphy & Cunningham, 2003). These corporations often combine increasing the availability of resources to broad groups of people in the community (e.g., community reinvestment funds and community development block grants) with individual training to help people take advantage of such resources (e.g., home buyers' clubs and microenterprise loan circles) and with increased social and economic infrastructure (e.g., increasing affordable housing stocks, and developing health clinics, day care, and after-school programs). In this strategy, it is not just the individual who is changing; it is the whole landscape of the community that is changing with visible infrastructure and options for social support and economic advancement.

Inclusive Program Development

In community-practice focused approaches to program development, there is growing recognition that it is important to have active participation of potential consumers and community members (Dominelli, 2007; Patti, 2009). Planning that is fully inclusive will engage agency staff with potential participants and community representatives in all aspects of the process from creation of the vision through the evaluation and adaptation needed to refine the program. Such efforts are intensive but can help to embed the program in the community and promote support. Inclusive planning requires ongoing intentional processes of engagement with diverse aspects of the community. Perspectives on inclusive engagement are provided by Chambers (1997), and Netting, O'Connor, and Fauri (2008). The approach is grounded in participatory and empowerment perspectives and strategies.

Involvement in the planning process gives community members a stake in the program and its success. Inclusive planning can be carried forward in nonprofit or public settings. A well-known example of major systems change was the engagement over time of the Maori community of New Zealand with the Child Welfare System. From the intensive work to make services fit appropriately with Maori culture—of extended families and extended family responsibility for children—the entire structure of the

New Zealand Child Welfare Services was refocused to employ family group conferencing with
all clients.

In the United States, a somewhat similar
process was used to build a network of family
preservation services in Contra Costa County.
The innovative service approach was developed
focused on family-centered, neighborhood-based
services through inclusive planning with community members and the multiple agencies that
were members of the County Youth Services
Board. These organizations worked to expand an
interagency family preservation program that
had proven successful into a county-wide model.
This effort involved major system change. The
planning process utilized five agency–community
interactive processes: (1) Developing a strategic plan; (2) learning about targeted neighborhoods and involving residents in planning;
(3) including staff and community members
in family-centered service integration teams;
(4) negotiating waivers with the state to support the new model; and (5) negotiating with
potential clients and other community members
throughout the planning process (Armstrong,
2001). Commitment and hard work was required
of all participants—but they made the project
work and developed services that were truly
community-based and family-centered.

Agencies considering a new community-based
program should emphasize participatory processes to strengthen planning and build staying
power for the effort (Minkler & Wallerstein,
2008). Using intensive outreach, planners can
identify community members' concerns and
interests and build on these ideas in the needs
assessment process. Although secondary data
and official community data will be used in a
needs assessment, it can be strengthened by sur-
veying potential program participants and community residents about their interests, concerns,
and hopes for the community. Focus groups
of citizens, as well as the surveys, can be used
to enlighten and expand staff understanding
and strengthen the plan through information
received directly from potential participants and
community members.

Evidence-based practice strategies build the
"science" of intervention; however, programs
that are adapted appropriately to community
culture, contexts, and interests are likely to have
long-term staying power and to be perceived
as community assets. Participants should be
involved in program evaluation through more

than surveys of satisfaction. For programs to be
responsive and relevant to the communities they
serve it is important to have program participants
involved in the evaluation and to collect qualitative outcome data and program improvement
recommendations. This full-circle process of
engagement with community members, clients,
and potential clients will enable staff to make the
program more responsive to changing issues and
community needs (Noponen, 2002).

Social Planning

Social planning operates at a range of levels and
focal issues. Two major approaches are primary
in current practice: planning *with* communities
at local levels and larger scale planning, which
can take place at four levels: (1) as planning for
services in specific sectors such as mental health,
or child welfare; (2) as community-wide social
planning as carried out by social planning councils; (3) within city and regional planning departments or other government agencies; and (4) in
agencies engaged in international, multinational,
and global service and planning efforts (Sager &
Weil, 2013). In all these venues for social planning, community social workers will strive to
see that the planning process is inclusive and
that people "living with the problems" or "living in the neighborhood or region" are seriously
engaged in multiple aspects of the planning and
implementation process (Weil, 2013).

The scope of planning encompasses community renewal, combining social and economic
development, and/or coordinating social services
and community programs. Such work often
involves community revitalization and seeks
to redress problems in rural communities or
urban neighborhoods; it also can involve work
to rebuild communities after natural disasters.
The Dudley Street Initiative in Boston is one
example of community-based comprehensive
neighborhood planning (Medoff & Sklar, 1994;
www.dsni.org).

In service or service sector planning, practitioners are involved with designing new services, or
refining older services and approaches to render
them more responsive to current and emerging
populations. For example, in a federally funded
initiative to improve preventive services to families, North Carolina initiated a Family Support
and Family Preservation program that engaged
communities in 33 counties in local-level service
planning. Work was accomplished through new

planning groups composed of citizens and local service providers. Counties were successful in developing model programs that could provide primary prevention support and intensive intervention to preserve families experiencing crises (Gamble & Weil, 2010).

City-wide nonprofit sector planning councils such as those affiliated with the National Association of Planning Councils typically conduct needs assessments and target one to three major issues over several years. These councils and service sector planning efforts strengthen services for particularly vulnerable populations, such as children with disabilities or the elderly. The long-established Jacksonville, Florida Community Council, for example, has carried forward major research and service initiatives in several areas. A recent project developed a multisite program plan designed to reduce teen pregnancy. The research reported in the *Jacksonville Quality of Life Progress Report 2006* indicates very positive results with lowering pregnancy rates and keeping young women in school (see Gamble & Weil, 2010, pp. 298–303).

Community development corporations engage in constant planning and program refinement as they seek to respond effectively to changing community needs in low-wealth communities. Two exemplary CDCs with multiple economic, housing, business development, and service and support programs are Bethel New Life in Chicago (www.bethelnewlife.org/) and Chicanos por la Causa in Arizona (*www.cplc.org*).

In a government-funded San Francisco program, Margaret Brodkin worked with an advocacy organization and citizens' and agency groups to establish a model children's service system that resulted in multiple positive outcomes for children and families. In this public/nonprofit partnership, the ingenuity and energy of the advocacy organization and planning groups made the change happen (Brodkin, 2013). At city-wide planning levels, both Seattle, Washington and Austin, Texas have been engaged in multiyear neighborhood-based planning with citizens' groups and provide models that would be beneficial in many cities (Weil, 2013).

Because planners engage with a variety of individuals and groups, they need excellent communication, facilitation, and management skills, as well as technical skills in research, needs assessments, participatory planning, evaluation, and proposal development. Planners increasingly organize community meetings to gather ideas and educate the public about directions for services and development. They engage community leaders in effective development strategies for fundraising, evaluation, and modification of programs.

Several useful resources are available to assist planners working with citizens and organizations for local planning. The Vancouver, British Columbia Social Planning and Research Council provides an excellent *Citizen's Guide to Community Social Planning* (1993). *A Community Planning Handbook,* compiled by Nick Wates for communities in the UK provides generalizable strategies for local planning within neighborhoods; and the Aspen Institute provides a planning workbook that incorporates environmental, economic, and social planning.

Coalitions

Coalitions have been defined as "complex inter-organizational entities that require partners to commit to collaborative efforts toward a specific goal" (Alter, 2008, p. 528). The interdependence of coalitions makes it possible for separate groups to work together for collective social change.

To be effective, whether voluntary or mandated, members of coalitions need to commit to agreed-upon methods and processes for work (Ivery, 2008). Mizrahi, Rosenthal, and Ivery (2013) emphasize that coalitions come together for the pragmatic reason of achieving their shared goal. Social movement theory indicates that the choice to "coalesce" is based on shared values and commitment to a cause or social issue (Mizrahi, Rosenthal, & Ivery, 2013). The dynamics of interorganizational relationships are explained through exchange theory, which emphasizes mutual benefit and reciprocity (Roberts-DeGennaro, 1987). Increasingly, some coalitions establish themselves as long-term organizations, such as the Coalition for the Homeless in Los Angeles and the Domestic Violence Coalitions, located in many states, dedicated to assisting women and ending family violence.

Coalitions may focus on the needs of a specific population, on service development or integration, or on social change advocacy. The desired outcome for social-change coalitions is to build multiorganizational power bases large enough to influence social program direction, with the potential to garner resources to respond to the common interests of the coalition. Problematic public policies or elected officials are often the systems targeted for change as citizens press for more favorable policies. Government institutions that may have the authority to respond to a particular social concern, but not the readiness to do so, are also the targets of coalitions' advocacy, education, and action strategies.

Coalition building typically requires a major time commitment; for this reason, only organizations that have a stake in the particular issues will engage in longer term involvement. Examples of coalitions found in many communities are those organized for affordable housing, against the increase in teen pregnancy and teen violence, for service programs for the elderly, and for environmentally safe economic development. A coalition of major human service, child advocacy, and professional groups has successfully lobbied for federal support for family-centered, community-based services over the past two decades. This coalition with leadership from the Children's Defense Fund, Child Welfare League, Family Impact Seminar, and National Association of Social Workers (NASW), among others, successfully lobbied for implementation of the 1993 Family Support Act (P.L. 103-66). Coalitions for the homeless have been successful in many urban areas in establishing shelters and services, and some are also concerned with development of low-income housing. To stay together, coalitions develop complex exchange relations and find ways to balance their commitment to the issues that hold them together with the individual agendas and perspectives of member organizations (Roberts-DeGennaro & Mizrahi, 2005). Mattessich, Murray-Close, Monsey, and Wilder Research Center (2001) have analyzed 40 studies of collaboration and identified six major domains and related factors that contribute to establishing and maintaining successful collaborations: positive environment, cooperative membership, flexible processes and structures, effective communication, shared purpose, and sufficient resources.

Social workers are likely to be leaders and spokespersons in human service coalitions, using mediation and negotiation skills to balance internal tensions and maintain the coalition's focus. In coalitions of advocacy groups focused on alternative services, such as coalitions against domestic violence, social workers may also have roles that emphasize group and interorganizational facilitation, teaching and coaching, leadership

development, conflict negotiation, and skills in organizational relations and planning.

Political and Social Action and Policy Practice

This model embodies action for social, political, or economic justice with a focus on changing the agenda of policy makers, changing policies, or changing policy makers. When public agendas and policy directions become so skewed as to cause harm and decrease opportunities for human development, political and social action becomes the means to redress wrongs and put forward a progressive agenda. Social and political action campaigns conduct research and document a problem, select a target and change strategy, generate the power to effect a solution, and use effective communication and direct action to implement promised changes.

Social action seeks progressive change through building powerful local community organizations that can counter the status quo with a visible agenda and a critical mass of people advocating openly for change. Groups use social action and organizing strategies to "change conditions that are injurious to their members or on behalf of others who cannot organize for themselves" (Mondros, 2013, p. 347). Political action can be as simple as handing out leaflets or as complex as running for office. It focuses on enlarging democracy and especially assisting and promoting voting among those who are disadvantaged or oppressed by current policies. Social and political action efforts can change the power relations in a larger community, make people aware of their own power through consciousness raising and group solidarity, and engender personal changes so that people recognize and use their own power more effectively. Collective action can stimulate a sense of community and activate community power.

Mondros (2013, p. 350) makes the case that there is much in common among social, political, and legislative approaches to action: all three seek to "transfer power and resources"; persistence is required in each approach along with disciplined action; and community practitioners may be working at different or multiple levels from neighborhood to state or national. Social and political action can be seen in areas as varied as Appalachia, where citizens trained by the Highlander Center conducted research, documented toxic waste, and were successful in closing a waste dump (You Got to Move, 2008); to Wisconsin where citizens have been demonstrating a number of years in opposition to the Governor's unfair new policies toward public employees.

Social action organizations may join with other local groups or form coalitions that can apply pressure at national levels. In the South, black farmers have been involved in long legislative struggles to rectify discrimination in federal loan procedures, and across the nation many organizations have been involved in "living wage," "school reform," voter registration, and civic participation efforts. The goal of progressive social and political action is to shift the balance of power so that those who have been excluded in earlier decision-making processes become players in future decisions. This goal is grounded in processes for strengthening participatory democracy and building social justice. For work in both social action and policy practice Brager, Specht, and Torczyner (1987) recommend three types of tactics that escalate in intensity: (1) Collaborative Tactics (Education, Persuasion, and Pooling Resources); (2) Campaign Tactics (Bargaining, Negotiation); and (3) Contest Tactics (Direct Action, Disruption).

Policy practice has been defined by Jansson (2008) as "efforts to change policies in legislative, agency, and community settings" through development of new policies or defeating the policies of others. In policy advocacy, social workers support the rights and concerns of less powerful people and work to help them improve their "resources and opportunities" (p. 14). This work can focus on "case advocacy" or "cause advocacy." Schneider and Lester (2001) define social work advocacy as "the exclusive and mutual representation of a client(s) or a cause in a forum, attempting to systematically influence decision-making in an unjust or unresponsive system(s)" (p. 64). Advocacy is a primary responsibility of social workers and serves as the foundation for political, social, and legislative action.

Movements for Progressive Change

Progressive social movements, focused on economic and social justice and more recently human rights, have occurred when large groups seek to change harmful social and environmental conditions. Wood and Jackson (1982) define social movements as groups "that attempt to produce or prevent radical or reformist types of change"

(p. 3). Social movements promote action for social change that provides a new paradigm for the way we respond to a particular population group or social issue. For example, the growing number of states in the United States that have legalized gay marriage, along with new federal and military policies that provide protections and benefits for married same-sex couples, are significant social change markers. While the struggle of the lesbian, gay, bisexual, and transgender (LGBT) community has been long and arduous—and is not over—these changes have engineered a tipping point through which education and advocacy by the LGBT community and allies, coupled with generational shifts in attitudes and beliefs, and some political shifts, provided momentum for continued change toward extension of civil and legal rights for this New Social Movement (NSM). Other NSMs focus on human rights, identity, and critical consciousness (Reisch, 2013). The major systems targeted for change are the general public and especially political systems. The abolitionist movement in the United Kingdom is credited with being the earliest mass movement for human rights. To be progressive, movements must support both human rights and social justice. In the United States, the civil rights movement is perhaps the best known and most far-reaching example of a social movement; it created conditions and expectations that fostered civil and social rights work in other groups, including La Raza, the women's movement, and the disabilities rights movement (Parish et al., 2006; MacNair, Fowler, & Harris, 2000). New paradigms related to these groups emerged with the success of the movements. Both legislation and attitudes have begun to focus more on abilities than disabilities; women increasingly exercise equal rights and move into leadership positions. Members of the LGBT community are pressing to achieve full equality. Latinos, African Americans, and Native Americans have legal civil rights but must continue to fight discrimination and prejudice as they work toward social and economic equality (National Association for the Advancement of Colored People [NAAC] [www.naacp.org/]; American Indian Movement [AIM] [www.aimovement.org/]). In the United States and many parts of the world, immigrants' rights are contested or denied. In social movements, social work roles are typically those of advocate and facilitator. Social workers, in keeping with the values of the profession, are allied with social movements that support democracy, individual dignity, the rights of minorities, the needs of the poor, sustainable development, and the broad goals of human development and liberation.

Social movements often occur when protest erupts as a result of intensifying oppression or when great and inequitable changes in the political or social system occur. Localized protests may call attention to widespread oppression; when those protests engender widespread support and mass empathy, a social movement emerges. Piven and Cloward (1979) analyzed four different American social movements and conclude that "both the limitations and opportunities for mass protest are shaped by social conditions" (p. 36). There may be only a small window of opportunity for change provided by the temporary relaxation of the social order brought about by widespread social protest. They suggest that the best strategy to achieve sought-for change through social movements is to extend that window of opportunity through organizing and action.

Social movements that maintain momentum can achieve significant change. The election of Nelson Mandela as President of South Africa was the outcome of a social movement and long-term struggle to end the system of apartheid and to establish civil and social rights for Black South Africans. The efforts toward human rights in Latin America, Africa, Asia, Eastern Europe, and other parts of the world continue. As a social movement succeeds, the ideals that it has advanced are accepted as legitimated political and social norms.

CONCLUSION

The descriptions of these eight models, coupled with the historical and value discussion that places community practice in its social work context, provide some guidance for those working in a wide range of community efforts. One value of examining these models is to realize the multiple roles social workers have to play in facilitating individual, group, organizational, and community development toward democratic institution building. Social workers are called on to be organizers, teachers, coaches, advocates, facilitators, negotiators, mediators, planners, researchers, managers, proposal writers, spokespersons, promoters, and political candidates (Weil & Gamble, 2013).

Community practice at all levels is influenced by local, national, and global changes. Citizens the world over are no longer leaving initiatives for social change just to governments and business. Social workers who are knowledgeable and have skills to contribute to this process will coach community members to become change agents in their communities. There will always be a role for social workers in the area of neighborhood and community organizing. The technology exists to communicate across the globe in seconds, but we still do most of our community building in face-to-face groups and organizations. The new communication technologies are particularly helpful for organizing functional communities, and these communities can benefit from social work's knowledge of social action, need and asset assessment, service and program development, and leadership.

There will be a tremendous need for social workers skilled in community social and economic development in the next several decades. As societies recognize the need to incorporate the lessons of sustainable and human development into the equations for economic progress, social workers can facilitate the dialogue to help local and regional groups create new paradigms for sustainable development. The work of social planning will focus on developing more humane and inclusive social and economic systems for communities. Communities no longer will accept development that squanders the environment, tramples the vulnerable, and unjustly divides the profits. Application of social work's value and knowledge base, to new theoretical concepts for inclusive, comprehensive, and participatory work can make a significant contribution to social planning. Program development, community liaison, and service coordination will be the primary foci of organizations' administrators and managers as they seek to involve the consumers of human services as partners in planning and providing human services in all their variety. Political and social action will always be in the purview of social work as long as one of the strong values of the profession is social justice. The NASW *Code of Ethics* makes it very clear that "social workers should engage in social and political action that seeks to ensure that all people have equal access to the resources, employment, services, and opportunities they require to meet their basic human needs and to develop fully" (1996, p. 27).

Because social workers are skilled in the facilitation of groups and organizations, they will be key actors in building the coalitions needed in the coming decades. Though social workers are not typically major leaders of social movements, their skills as advocates and facilitators are critical for preparing groups and organizations to participate in progressive social movements. In all these models there is a need for high levels of interpersonal, process, task, and technical skills. A particular skill needed by those working in community practice will be for facilitation methods using popular education and participatory planning (Chambers, 1997; Freire, 1970). Community practice workers will need to understand that the work they do is often long and arduous; however, the rewards in contributing to development of a more just and democratic society are enormous.

RELEVANT WEBSITES

Community Tool Box, University of Kansas. *ctb.ku.edu/en/tablecontents*

Institute of Development Studies. *ids*.ac.uk & Eldis Gateway www.eldis.org/

National Association of Planning Councils (NAPC). www.communityplanning.org/

PICO National Network—Unlocking the Power of People™. www.piconetwork.org

United Nations Development Program, UNDP. http://www.undp.org.

References

Alter, C. (2008). Inter-organizational practice interventions. In T. Mizrahi and L. E. Davis (Eds.), *Encyclopedia of Social Work* (20th ed.) (pp. 528–523). Washington, DC & New York: National Association of Social Workers/Oxford University Press.

Betten, N., & Austin, M. J. (Eds.). (1990). *The roots of community organizing, 1917–1939*. Philadelphia, PA: Temple University Press.

Brager, G., Specht, H., & Torczyner, J. L. (1987). *Community organizing* (2nd ed.). New York, NY: Columbia University Press.

Brodkin, M. (2013) Rethinking how to support the healthy development of children, available on the web at Margaretbrokin.com

Chambers, R. (1997). *Whose reality counts? Putting the last first*. London: Intermediate Technology Publications.

Dominelli, L. (2007). (Ed.). *Revitalizing communities in a globalizing world*. Aldershot, UK: Ashgate.

Estes, R. (1993). Toward sustainable development: From theory to praxis. *Social Development Issues*, 15(3), 1–29.

Friedmann, J. (1992). *Empowerment: The politics of alternative development* (2nd ed.). Oxford: Blackwell.

Freire, P. (1970). *Pedagogy of the oppressed*. New York, NY: Seabury Press.

Gamble, D. N. (2013). Sustainable development. In *Encyclopedia of social work* (20th ed.) *On-Line*. New York, NY: Oxford University Press.

Gamble, D. N., & Hoff, M. D. (2013). Sustainable community development. In M. Weil, M. Reisch, & M. Ohmer (Eds.), *The handbook of community practice* (2nd ed.) (pp. 215–232). Thousand Oaks, CA: Sage.

Gamble, D. N., & Weil, M. (2010). *Community practice skills: Local to global perspectives*. New York, NY: Columbia University Press.

Gutierrez, L. M., & Lewis, E. A. (1994). Community organizing with women of color: A feminist approach. *Journal of Community Practice*, 1, 23–44.

Gutierrez, L. M., Lewis, E. A., Dessel, A. B., & Spencer, M. (2013). Principles, skills and practice strategies for promoting multicultural communication and collaboration. In M. Weil, M. Reisch, & M. Ohmer (Eds.), *The handbook of community practice* (2nd ed.). (pp. 445–460). Thousand Oaks, CA: Sage.

Hart, M. (1999). *Guide to sustainable community indicators* (2nd ed.). North Andover, MA: Hart Environmental Data.

Ivery, J. M. (2008). Policy mandated collaboration. *Journal of Sociology and Social Welfare*, 35, 53–70.

Jansson, B. S. (2008). *Becoming an effective policy advocate: From policy practice to social justice*. Belmont, CA: Thompson Brooks/Cole.

MacNair, R. H., Fowler, L., & Harris, J. (2000). The diversity functions of organizations that confront oppression: The evolution of three social movements. *Journal of Community Practice*, 7(2), 71–88.

Mattessich, P. W., Murray-Close, M., Monsey, B. R., & Wilder Research Center. (2001). *Collaboration: What makes it work* (2nd ed.). St. Paul, MN: Fieldstone Alliance.

Medoff, P., & Sklar, H. (l994). *Streets of hope: The fall and rise of an urban neighborhood*. Boston, MA: South End Press.

Midgley, J., & Conley, A. (Eds.). (2010). *Social work and social development: Theories and skills for developmental social work*. New York, NY: Oxford University Press.

Minkler, M., & Wallerstein, N. (2008). *Community-based participatory research for health: From process to outcomes* (2nd ed.). San Francisco, CA: John Wiley, Jossey Bass.

Mizrahi, T., Rosenthal, B. B., & Ivery, J. (2013). Coalitions, collaborations and partnerships: Interorganizational approaches to social change. In M. Weil, M. Reisch, & M. Ohmer (Eds.), *The handbook of community practice* (2nd ed.) (pp. 383–402). Thousand Oaks, CA: Sage.

Mondros, J. (2013). Political, social and legislative action, In M. Weil, M. Reisch, & M. Ohmer (Eds.), *The handbook of community practice* (2nd ed.) (pp. 345–360). Thousand Oaks, CA: Sage.

Mondros, J., & Staples, L. (2013). Community organizing. In *Encyclopedia of social work* (20th ed.) *On-Line*. New York, NY: Oxford University Press. DOI:10.1093/acrefore/9780199975839.013.74

Murphy, P. W., & Cunningham, J. V. (2003). *Organizing for community controlled development: Renewing civil society*. Thousand Oaks, CA: Sage.

National Association of Planning Councils (NAPC). www.communityplanning.org/

National Association of Social Workers. (1996). *Code of ethics*. Washington, DC: Author.

Netting, F. E., O'Connor, M. K., & Fauri, D. P. (2008). *Comparative approaches to program planning*. Hoboken, NJ: Wiley.

Noponen, H. (2002). The internal learning system. A tool for participation and program planning in microfinance and livelihoods interventions. *Development Bulletin, 57*(1), 88–106.

Nussbaum, M. (2011). *Creating capabilities: The human development approach*. Cambridge, MA: Belknap Press of Harvard University Press.

Parish, S. L., Ellison, M. J., & Parish, J. K. (2006). Managing diversity, In R. L. Edwards & J. A. Yankey (Eds.), *Effectively managing nonprofit organizations* (pp. 179–194). Washington, DC: National Association of Social Workers.

Patti, Rino J. (2009). Management in the human services: Purposes, practice and prospects in the 21st century. In R. J. Patti (Ed.), *The handbook of human services management* (pp. 1–27). Thousand Oaks, CA: Sage.

Piven, F. F., & Cloward, R. S. (1979). *Poor people's movements: Why they succeed, how they fail*. New York, NY: Vintage Books.

Reisch, M. (2013). Social movements. In *Encyclopedia of social work, On-Line*. New York, NY: Oxford University Press. DOI:10.1093acref ore/9780199975839.013.366

Rivera, F. G., & Erlich, J. L. (Eds.). (1998). *Community organizing in a diverse society* (3rd ed.). Boston, MA: Allyn & Bacon.

Roberts-DeGennaro, M. (1987). Patterns of exchange relationships in building a coalition. *Administration in Social Work, 11*, 59–67.

Roberts-DeGennaro, M., & Mizrahi, T. (2005). Human service coalitions. In M. Weil, M. Reisch, & M. Ohmer (Eds.), *Handbook of community practice* (pp. 305–318). Thousand Oaks, CA: Sage.

Rothman, J., Erlich, J. L., & Tropman, J. E. (Eds.). (2008). *Strategies of community intervention*, (7th ed.). Peosta, IA: Eddie Bower.

Rubin, H. J., & Sherraden, M. S. (2005), Community economic and social development, In M. Weil, M. Reisch, & M. Ohmer (Eds.) *The handbook of community practice* (pp. 475–493). Thousand Oaks, CA: Sage.

Sager, J. S., & Weil, M. (2013). Larger scale social planning: Planning for services and communities In M. Weil, M. Reisch, & M. Ohmer (Eds.), *The handbook of community practice* (2nd ed.) (pp. 299–325). Thousand Oaks, CA: Sage.

St. Onge, P. (2013). Cultural competency: Organizations and diverse populations, In M. Weil, M. Reisch, & M. Ohmer (Eds.), *The handbook of community practice* (2nd ed.) (pp. 425–444). Thousand Oaks, CA: Sage.

St. Onge, P. (2009). *Embracing cultural competency: A roadmap for nonprofit capacity builders*. St. Paul, MN: Fieldstone Alliance.

Schneider, R. L., & Lester, L. (2001). *Social work advocacy: A new framework for action*. Belmont, CA: Wadsworth/Thompson Learning.

Schreiner, M., Sherraden, M., Clancy, M., Johnson, L., Curley, J., Grinstein-Weiss, M & Johnson, L. (2001). *Savings and asset accumulation in individual development accounts*. St. Louis, MO: George Warren Brown School of Social Work.

Sen, A. (1999). *Development as freedom*. New York, NY: Anchor Books.

Sherraden, M. (2013). Asset building. In *Encyclopedia of social work, on-line*. New York, NY: Oxford University Press. DOI:10.1093/acrefore/9780199975839.013.25

Simon, B. L. (1994). *The empowerment tradition in American social work: A history*. New York, NY: Columbia University Press.

You Got to Move: Stories of Change in the South. (2008). Video produced and directed by Lucy Massie Phenix and Veronica Selver. First Run/Icarus Films.

United Nations Development Program. (2011). Sustainability and vequity: A better future for all. *Human Development Report 2011*. Retrieved from http://hdr.undp.org/en/reports/global/hdr2011

Weil, M. (2013). Community-based social planning: Theory and practice. In M. Weil, M. Reisch, & M. Ohmer (Eds.), *The handbook of community practice* (2nd ed.). (pp. 265–298). Thousand Oaks, CA: Sage.

Weil M., & Gamble, D. N. (2013). Evolution, models, and the changing context of community practice. In M. Weil, M. Reisch, & M. Ohmer (Eds.), *The handbook of community practice* (2nd ed.) (pp. 167–193). Thousand Oaks, CA: Sage.

Weil, M., Reisch, M., & Ohmer, M. (2013). Introduction: Contexts and challenges for 21st century communities. In M. Weil, M. Reisch, & M. Ohmer (Eds.), *The handbook of community practice* (2nd ed.) (pp. 3–26). Thousand Oaks, CA: Sage.

Wood, J. L., & Jackson, M. (1982). *Social movements: Development, participation, and dynamics*. Belmont, CA: Wadsworth.

117 Legislative Advocacy to Empower Oppressed and Vulnerable Groups

Michael Reisch

INTRODUCTION

Legislative advocacy focuses on promoting the common welfare or securing and protecting the rights, benefits, or services for a specific population, which cannot speak on its own behalf, by supporting or opposing laws or items in governmental budgets. During the past century, many significant policy achievements, such as Social Security, Medicare, and Medicaid at the federal level, and housing, public health, and employment regulations at the state and local levels were the product of legislative advocacy by social workers and their allies (Stern & Axinn, 2012; Jansson, 2011). Since the early 1980s, however, as a consequence of policy devolution and fiscal cutbacks, the focus of legislative advocacy has largely shifted to the state and local arenas on issues such as health care, public assistance, Affirmative Action, services for homeless persons, marriage equality, and immigrant and refugee rights (Luhby, 2011; Jenkins, 2011; Barber, 2011; Fessler, 2010; Squillace, 2010). This is significant because research suggests that considerable differences exist among legislative advocacy practice at the national, state, and local levels, and that these even vary considerably across different states and municipalities (Hoefer, 2013). Many examples cited herein come from such efforts, where social workers often have more opportunity to exercise their skills and influence.

THE PURPOSES OF LEGISLATIVE ADVOCACY

Legislative advocacy is a means to mobilize people, raise political consciousness, and accentuate the shortcomings of societal institutions and structures, while working to improve the quality of life or expand the rights and benefits of specific populations, particularly those who are in a position of power and resource disadvantage. It attempts to influence the decisions and perspectives of legislators, stakeholders, executive department heads and key staff, the media, and other influential advocates (Hoefer, 2012). The work of organizations like the Michigan League for Human Services, Philadelphia Citizens for Children and Youth (PCCY), and Health Care for the Homeless in Maryland is an example of this type of advocacy. Legislative advocacy also requires the mobilization of constituents' resources so that they can be focused on a specific policy goal through collective action (Richan, 2006). The recent successes in Maryland of efforts to pass marriage equality and a "Dream Act" illustrate how this can be done effectively.

During the past three decades, however, most advocacy efforts by social workers and their allies have been defensive in nature. Advocacy groups in diverse states—New York, Michigan, Maryland, Texas, and Pennsylvania—have resisted budget cuts that would disproportionately harm low-income groups. A statewide alliance in Oregon defeated a well-funded anti-gay ballot measure. Broad-based coalitions in California defeated ballot propositions that would have eliminated funding for HIV/AIDS services, slashed welfare benefits, or banned the use of demographic data about race and gender to target resources to vulnerable populations. Unfortunately, many of these efforts have not succeeded, as the recent passage of anti–Affirmative Action initiatives and legislative restrictions on voting rights demonstrates. Yet, even during politically and fiscally conservative times like the present, offensive advocacy is possible (Shaw, 2001). In the past year alone, advocacy groups have passed laws that have enhanced immigrants' rights, increased funding for domestic violence programs, established marriage equality, protected workers' rights, and abolished capital punishment.

In addition, legislative advocacy can serve a variety of purposes beyond passing or blocking a particular bill. Often, it is a means to strengthen one's organization or coalition or expand its membership. It can complement the service delivery objectives of participating organizations by providing increased funding for agency programs. Even unsuccessful advocacy campaigns increase public awareness of clients' issues and enable service providers to enhance their reputations and fundraising efforts. They can also strengthen interorganizational relationships among potential allies and help build grassroots leadership. By speaking out for welfare recipients, the Kensington Welfare Rights Organization in Philadelphia kept the issue alive in the media and the public consciousness at a time when their needs were being ignored in the political arena.

In sum, legislative advocacy can serve the following purposes for social workers:

- *It can increase client competence by educating them to testify before legislative committees or advocate with individual legislators.* For over 15 years, Coleman Advocates for Children and Youth in San Francisco has been particularly effective in training the parents of low-income children, through a group called Parent Advocates for Youth, and youth themselves, through a group called Youth Making a Change, to engage in such activities. Other advocacy organizations are substantially increasing the level of civic participation among youth, particularly within racial and ethnic minority communities, by addressing issues that specifically concern them (Checkoway & Gutierrez, 2006).
- *It can encourage one's organization to be more responsive to clients' needs and to be more aware of the conditions that affect their lives.* The ongoing work of the Los Angeles Roundtable for Children is a good example of this effect.

- *It can facilitate intracommunity or interagency cooperation by requiring participating organizations to channel their efforts through a structured, disciplined, and cooperative process.* Annual report cards on legislators, a tactic pioneered by such organizations as Children Now and the Children's Defense Fund, are now widely used.
- *It can stimulate needed organizational changes by the very demands it creates for improved information, extensive public education campaigns, greater political sophistication, and stronger ties with constituents and their communities*. Numerous state chapters of the National Association of Social Workers (NASW) have become more effective and more efficient in their operations as they became more involved in legislative advocacy.
- *It can be a catalyst for the redistribution of resources and power within an agency, a community, and an advocacy coalition itself.* A Maryland statewide coalition, Maryland Hunger Solutions, is a good illustration of this phenomenon.
- *Finally, it externalizes clients', workers', and agencies' problems by focusing them on a mutually selected target.* This helps them cope more effectively with the daily stresses in their lives and practice. For decades, welfare rights organizations and advocacy groups such as the National Alliance on Mental Illness (NAMI) and Health Care for the Homeless have noted such effects.

COMPONENTS OF LEGISLATIVE ADVOCACY

The major tasks of legislative advocacy can be summarized as follows:

- Applying substantive expertise and technical assistance to draft legislation or make budget recommendations.
- Organizing support for legislators to enable them to take political risks on an issue of concern to one's organization and its constituents.
- Monitoring all legislation and budget items that are relevant to one's constituents, including all committee and caucus votes that influence the course of particular bills.

- Developing ongoing cooperative professional and personal relationships with other legislative advocates and with legislative staff.
- Creating and using media contacts and developing a media advocacy strategy to complement work in the legislature itself (McNutt & Menon, 2008).
- Using the legislative advocacy process to organize, educate, train, and empower constituents through phone trees, listservs, social media, Twitter, and existing advocacy networks; orchestrating letter writing, fax, e-mail, text, Twitter, Facebook, and phone campaigns; and participating in legislative hearings and other key legislative events.
- Using the legislative advocacy process and complementary media activities to spotlight particular issues, educate the public and legislators, arouse popular support for policy alternatives, and provide legislators with the opportunity to test public reactions to their positions on new or controversial policy issues (Kanter & Fine, 2010).

In sum, legislative advocacy is a political process that combines conflict, negotiation, cooperation, and compromise. Some of its activities are considered "inside" tactics because they take place within well-established routines and affect policymakers directly. Others are considered "outside" tactics because they work to influence policymakers through means other than the established legislative process. More than other forms of advocacy, however, the need to compromise in the legislative arena often generates ethical conflicts among social workers. Although each ethical dilemma that emerges in the legislative advocacy process must be resolved on its own terms, it is generally useful to keep in mind that legislative advocacy is not an end in itself but one of several complementary strategies to achieve particular policy goals. One must consider, therefore, both the short-term and long-term needs of constituents when engaging in such advocacy efforts.

THE ROLES OF LEGISLATIVE ADVOCATES

Legislative advocates play multiple roles depending on the needs of their constituents, organizational imperatives, and the political culture and climate of their circumstances (Hoefer, 2013). At times, local advocacy groups like Coleman

Advocates and Philadelphia Citizens for Children and Youth, and national organizations such as the Children's Defense Fund, Children Now, and the National Association of Child Advocates focus on a specific population, such as children in poverty. Other groups have recently focused on displaced workers, undocumented youth, or homeless veterans. At other times, legislative advocates play the role of ombudsperson or broker. In the former role, they help articulate clients' or agencies' needs to policymakers or assist clients and constituents in making their voices heard through community forums, blogs, Twitter, and other forms of social media. As brokers, legislative advocates work with legislative staff to negotiate compromises in legislative or budgetary language that affect their constituents.

On occasion, as the author has experienced in his work, they can become directly involved in shaping the budgets of key government departments. Sometimes, as a favor to a sympathetic legislator, advocates can be catalysts for compromise even though they have no direct interest in a proposed law. In return, the legislator may agree to sponsor or "carry" a bill promoted by the advocates. These diverse roles underscore the importance of developing expertise on a range of substantive issues, as well as the legislative process itself, to increase advocates' visibility and political viability.

STRATEGIES AND TACTICS OF LEGISLATIVE ADVOCACY

Although the overall goal of legislative advocacy is to influence the policy-making process on behalf of clients and constituents, the paths to attain this goal vary considerably depending on the presenting issue, the political climate and culture, and the relative influence of advocates and their allies in a particular context. Often when advocates have little prior experience in legislative work or the issue is relatively new, the major focus of legislative advocacy is to obtain, organize, and present data to illuminate the scope of a problem for which a legislative solution is sought. As advocates acquire a reputation for reliability in their area of expertise, they are often called on to prepare more focused reports or presentations for a legislative committee or a particular legislator who is a potential sponsor of a bill. In such instances, advocates may be asked to conduct research, write or present expert testimony, or help draft the legislation itself. This requires advocates to balance their interest in acquiring visibility with their need to obtain critical political support. It also potentially jeopardizes the role of advocates as forces outside of the political process who speak for the people. Once advocates "win"—that is, play an insider's role in key legislative or fiscal processes—they risk jeopardizing their ability to criticize the actions of governments with which they are now cooperating. They also risk changing the perception of the public, organizational allies, and constituents regarding their integrity and trustworthiness. As the author learned from his work in San Francisco, Baltimore, Philadelphia, and Southeast Michigan, weighing the trade-offs of such situations is critical; it requires assessing the trustworthiness of the legislators and administrators involved and the long-term implications of decisions.

Advocates should answer the following questions prior to testifying before a legislature:

- Do we possess sufficient knowledge of the subject and adequate presenting skills?
- Can we provide supporting data—statistics and case examples—for value-based appeals?
- Would testifying on a particular issue advance the long-term goals of our constituents?
- Would our testimony add anything new and constructive to policy debates?
- Is it important that we take an independent position on this issue?

Occasionally, an effective tactic for legislative advocates is the use of electoral campaigns—ballot initiatives or candidate elections—to advance their issue. Although advocacy organizations must be careful to remain nonpartisan (i.e., not back a particular candidate or party) or risk losing their nonprofit status, they can and often do get involved in educating the electorate about the central issues of a campaign. In 2012, the Maryland chapter of NASW, for example, played an active role in a successful campaign to pass marriage equality in the state.

After a bill has been introduced, advocates often engage in a broad range of public educational activities in cooperation with allies, including town meetings, press conferences, speak-outs, demonstrations, and, most recently, social media campaigns. Research on successful legislative advocacy (Hoefer, 2005) has identified the following determinants of success: (a) consistent and continuous involvement of constituents; (b) well-established and varied means of communication; (c) ongoing positive relationships with legislative targets; (d) skills in consensus building and the mobilization of public opinion; and (e) the establishment of credibility on a focused set of issues. Efforts that reflected the diversity of constituency groups were also more likely to gain recognition and obtain access to key decision makers.

GUIDELINES FOR LEGISLATIVE ADVOCACY

Healy and Sofer (2013) make the following comments about legislative advocacy at the federal level:

1. *Politics is a process, and just about anyone can master it.*... Many people find the procedures arcane, but that is only true for those who never try to learn them.... Mastery is crucial to success, particularly for nonprofit advocates who must rely on knowledge to overcome other disadvantages, such as lack of funds.
2. *Winning requires both inside- and outside-the-Beltway strategies.*
3. *Successful campaigns require a lot of different skills*—a leader who is willing to be a tough taskmaster and keep pressure on people to make sure they are engaged and helpful; ... lots of resources, money, and in-kind contributions; ... allied organizations to lend staff and provide other assistance; and [most importantly] ... a core group of members in the coalition who bring different strengths to it.
4. *It helps to have villains.*
5. *There is strength in numbers.*
6. *Persistence pays off.*
7. *It is crucial to target efforts in Congress, because not all members of Congress are equal.*
8. *Education of legislators and their staff members is critical.*
9. *It is crucial to bring disparate groups together to present a united front.*
10. *Media coverage greatly influences the process.*
11. *Support from the Executive Branch is incredibly helpful.*

12. **Work both sides of the political aisle, and never take your supporters for granted.**
13. **Do not give up on members who have opposed your program in the past.**
14. **Segment the market.**
15. **Get people who directly benefit from the programs to help out.**
16. **Recognize and reward friends and supporters** (pp. 252–255).

Beyond these valuable suggestions, effective advocacy at the state and local level requires additional ingredients. At the state level, Teater (2009) found that the most effective groups were locally based and maintained regular contact with their constituents. Legislators also report that the groups they find most effective have clear plans, a focused mission, specific goals, and an involved membership, which results from ongoing two-way communication and accountability between leaders and members, and which enhances a group's legitimacy.

In sum, effective legislative advocacy at all levels requires advocates to:

- Be consistently and continually engaged in the legislative process even when the legislature is not in session. This is particularly important in states where it meets for only a few months (as in Maryland) or every other year (as in Texas).
- Research the orientation and priorities of the legislators they are seeking to influence. The distribution of regular publications to legislators and department heads and frequent updates to organizational websites, blogs, Facebook pages, or Twitter feeds are effective means for advocates to make their presence felt (Kanter & Fine, 2010).
- Provide technical assistance and political information to legislators and their staff members even on issues that are of indirect concern to advocates. Doing so builds trust and credibility that can be tapped during efforts on behalf of difficult or unpopular issues.
- Develop personal and political relationships with legislators and their staff members, often through informal contacts at fundraisers, conferences, and workshops.
- Be clear about their long-term goals, even as advocacy tactics shift, through ongoing communication with allies, constituents, the media, and the public.
- Be sensitive to the views of legislative opponents, particularly those who hold key committee posts.
- Recognize that legislators and their staffs have unexamined and unquestioned prejudices and learn how to confront these prejudices directly without alienating potential supporters.
- Develop the ability to take risks despite the overriding ethos of compromise in the legislative arena and the appearance of insurmountable partisan divisions.
- Convince others that one's objectives are socially worthy and not self-serving.
- Support efforts of coalition partners on issues that are not directly of concern to one's organization or constituents.
- Frame policy issues in terms that are consistent with the worldviews of legislators and learn when to refrain from advocacy that might produce resentment among them.
- "Change their tune" from time to time so that their message continues to be heard in a chaotic environment dominated by today's 24/7 news cycle.
- Save scarce resources and energy for another day by recognizing when the political climate is hostile to their message.
- Be sensitive to the egos of legislators and the political pressures they experience and shape advocacy arguments around their political and personal imperatives.
- Develop diverse mechanisms to influence the legislative process that include traditional means, such as action research committees, focus groups, and training sessions for constituents and supporters, as well as tech-savvy social media and wikis (Libby, 2012).

BARRIERS TO SUCCESSFUL LEGISLATIVE ADVOCACY

Obstacles to successful legislative advocacy fall into three broad categories: those created by the political-economic environment; those inherent in the legislative process; and those intrinsic to advocacy itself. Legislative advocacy is both partisan and political—roles that may produce some discomfort among many social workers. Social workers need to recognize, however, that the profession has been involved in legislative advocacy almost since its emergence.

The most obvious obstacle to successful legislative advocacy is the presence of a generally unfavorable political environment for social welfare programs, particularly those on behalf of low-power and stigmatized groups (Haynes & Mickelson, 2010). Attempts to influence traditional centers of power, such as legislatures, increasingly encounter overt and covert hostility from opponents and even skepticism from potential allies. Sometimes, advocates can be distracted by the presence of "wedge" issues (e.g., efforts to roll back reproductive rights or expand gun rights) that, because of their urgency, compel advocacy organizations to shift from an offensive to a defensive posture. Recently, recurrent fiscal crises (which most states have experienced since the onset of the Great Recession) make it more difficult for advocates to adopt a proactive agenda (Oliff, Mai, & Palacios, 2012; Chantrill, 2012; Barnett, 2011).

Another obstacle is the difficulty of sustaining a "conflict posture" in a legislative setting. Legislative advocacy is a time-consuming and expensive strategy that can drain the resources and energy of even the strongest individuals and their organizations. Organizations that operate on a shoestring budget and rely primarily on volunteers often cannot sustain their efforts over time. Groups that are engaged in a wide range of initiatives sometimes have trouble maintaining a high degree of mobilization among supporters and constituents. The growing influence of external funders, particularly foundations or corporations, has restricted the activities of advocacy organizations or compelled them to focus on issues their financial supporters, rather than constituents, have defined as critical. In such cases, advocates must choose their battles very carefully.

A third barrier is the increasing fragmentation of the policy-making process within legislatures as a consequence of the growing specialization of committees, budgets, and proposed legislation. As legislative advocates, social workers may become frustrated by the need to reframe broad issues within the narrow requirements of the legislative process. An additional complication in this regard is the competition among legislative committees for jurisdiction over policy initiatives. Here, the importance of developing and sustaining personal relationships with legislators is critical. Unfortunately, the imposition of term limits in many jurisdictions has complicated the development of such relationships. A related obstacle is the difficulty of identifying the locus of accountability for policy decisions. A partial solution

to this problem is to make additional efforts to strengthen ties with media contacts, officials in the executive branch, and legislative staff, who often have longer tenures than the politicians for whom they work.

Advocates also experience ongoing tensions between the time and effort involved in expanding the participation of community-based constituents and the persistent time constraints of the policy-making process. Such constraints are usually the result of legal or constitutional procedures or the politics of the legislative process. Recently, the greatest constraints on effective advocacy have been the limits placed on legislative initiatives by economic conditions and the need for fiscal cutbacks, the imposition of constitutionally mandated balanced budget requirements, voter spending initiatives (at the state and local level) that can restrict or target funding in heavily prescribed ways, and the resource disadvantage of social work advocates in comparison with wealthier groups. Some advocacy groups, however, have found solutions to these dilemmas. These include creative framing of the issues(e.g., demanding higher wages for low income workers to strengthen families [Gordon, 2006]); developing innovative tactics(e.g., Coleman Advocates taking over City Hall with a "baby brigade" [Brodkin, 1993]); and using patriotic language to promote the rights of "dreamers," undocumented immigrant youth (American Civil Liberties Union, 2012).

At the local level, additional barriers exist. These include:

1. The way information is disseminated by both City Hall and the media.
2. The control of public-space and political messages by wealthy individuals and corporations.
3. The idea that heroes are "chosen" rather than the outcome being decided by people making a series of decisions to do the right thing.
4. The structure of political parties and elections, which are designed to decrease activism rather than encourage it (Meslin, 2011, cited in Hoefer, 2013).

Within the social work profession itself, four problems stand out: (1) inadequate preparation of social work graduates, (2) practical barriers (time pressures, lack of organizational resources devoted to advocacy, proximity to state capitals, especially in large states), (3) negative attitudes about politics, and (4) misinformation about the laws regulating advocacy by government or nonprofit organizations (Council on Social Work Education [CSWE], 2008; Hoefer, 2001, 2005, 2012; Cochran, Montgomery, & Rubin, 2010; Teater, 2009; Smucker, 1999).

THE FUTURE OF LEGISLATIVE ADVOCACY

Since the late 19th century, legislative advocacy by social workers has transformed the social landscape of the United States and led to improvements in the material well-being of millions of Americans. It has shaped the domestic policy agenda of the nation, altered the balance of power at the state and local level, facilitated the emergence of leaders at the community level, and enhanced the status of the social work profession. Over the past three decades, however, much of that advocacy has been defensive in nature, involving efforts to minimize spending cuts or prevent the elimination of long-standing social protections. Hoefer (2013) predicts that advocacy organizations at the state and local levels will expand their use of electronic tools and social media (McNutt & Menon, 2008; Dunlop & Fawcett, 2008), will increasingly see the connections between advocacy efforts and fundraising (Daigneault, Davis, & Sybrant, 2011), and that social justice battles will intensify at the state and local level.

Despite today's conservative political and fiscal climate, several recent trends produce guarded optimism about the future of legislative advocacy. A notable development is the growing emphasis on expanding the civic participation of clients and constituents, particularly youth (National Center on Civic Literacy, 2013; Checkoway & Gutierrez, 2006). A related trend is the growing power of the Internet and social media to help advocates and their constituents develop increasingly sophisticated databases and communication networks, share ideas and advocacy strategies, and develop rapid tactical responses to rapid changes in the policy environment. Finally, in response to the consequences of economic globalization, legislative advocates are increasingly incorporating regional and international perspectives into local advocacy efforts and building transnational alliances on such diverse issues as poverty, immigration, civil rights for gays and lesbians, trafficking in children and women, and the impact of climate change (Reilly, 2007; Cullen, 2001).

WEBSITES

Alliance for Justice: http://www.afj.org/fai/nonprof.html
Center on Budget and Policy Priorities, Washington, DC: http://www.cbpp.org
Center for Law and Social Policy: www.epn.org/clasp.html
Families USA: www.epn.org/families
Influencing State Policy: http://www.statepolicy.org/
National Conference of State Legislatures: http://www.ncsl.org/
National Governors Association: http://www.nga.org/cms/home.html
Urban Institute, Washington, DC: http://www.ui.org

References

American Civil Liberties Union. (2012). *Annual report 2012: Liberty and equality for all—Realizing the promise of the Bill of Rights*. Annapolis, MD: Author. Retrieved from www.aclu-md.org.

Barber, B. (2011, October 13). State cuts could mean hundreds face loss of welfare food assistance in Great Lakes Bay region. *Saginaw News*. Retrieved from www.mlive.com/news/saginaw/index.ssf/2011/10/state_cuts_mean_hundreds_face.html.

Barnett, J. L. (2011, April). *State and local government finances summary: 2008*. Washington DC: Census Bureau. Retrieved from www2.census.gov/govs/estimate/08statesummaryreport.pdf.

Brodkin, M. (1993). *Every kid counts: 31 ways to save our children*. San Francisco, CA: Harper.

Chantrill, C. (2012). US federal government FY10 budget. Retrieved from www.usgovernmentspending.com/federal_budget_fy10bs12011n_4041#usgs302.

Checkoway, B., & Gutierrez, L. M. (Eds.). (2006). *Young people making community change*. Binghamton, NY: Haworth.

Cochran, G., Montgomery, K., & Rubin, A. (2010). Does evidence-based practice influence state legislators' decision-making process? An exploratory study. *Journal of Policy Practice, 9*(3–4), 263–283.

Cullen, P. P. (2001). Coalitions working for social justice: Transnational NGOs and international governance. In J. Bystydzienski & S. Schacht (Eds.),

Forging radical alliances across difference (pp. 249–263). Lanham, MD: Rowman & Littlefield.

Daigneault, S., Davis, M., & Sybrant, M. (2011). *Connecting online advocacy and fundraising*. Charleston, SC: Blackbaud. Retrieved from www.blackbaud.com/files/resources/downloads/WhitePaper_ConnectingOnlineAdvocacyAndFundraising.pdf.

Dunlop, J., & Fawcett, G. (2008). Technology-based approaches to social work and social justice. *Journal of Policy Practice, 7*(2–3), 140–154.

Fessler, P. (2010, March 2). State budget cuts threaten child welfare programs. *National Public Radio*. Retrieved from www.npr.org/templates/story/story.php?storyId=124127356.

Gordon, J. (2006). The campaign for the unpaid wages prohibition act: Latino immigrants change New York wage laws. In R. A. Clucas (Ed.), *Readings and cases in state and local politics* (pp. 168–179). Boston, MA: Houghton Mifflin.

Haynes, K. S., & Mickelson, J. (2010). *Affecting change: Social work in the political arena* (7th ed.). Boston, MA: Pearson/Allyn & Bacon.

Healy, M., & Sofer, E. F. (2013). Advocacy at the Federal level: A case study of Americorps—How the little guys won. In M. Reisch (Ed.), *Social policy and social justice* (pp. 237–257). Thousand Oaks, CA: Sage Publications.

Hoefer, R. (2012). *Advocacy practice for social justice* (2nd ed.). Chicago, IL: Lyceum.

Hoefer, R. (2005). Altering state policy: Interest group effectiveness among state-level advocacy groups. *Social Work, 50*(3), 219–227.

Hoefer, R. (2013). State and local policy advocacy. In M. Reisch (Ed.), *Social policy and social justice* (pp. 259–280). Thousand Oaks, CA: Sage Publications.

Jansson, B. S. (2011). *Becoming an effective policy advocate: From policy practice to social justice* (6th ed.). Pacific Grove, CA: Brooks Cole.

Jenkins, A. (2011, February 2). States cut benefits to welfare families. Retrieved from kplu.org/post/state-cuts-benefits-welfare-families.

Kanter, B., & Fine, A. H. (2010). *The networked nonprofit: Connecting with social media to drive change.* San Francisco, CA: Jossey-Bass.

Libby, P. (2012). *The lobbying strategy handbook: 10 steps to advancing any cause effectively.* Thousand Oaks, CA: Sage Publications.

Luhby, T. (2011, March 28). Shrinking Medicaid funds pummel states. *CNNMoney.* Retrieved from www.money.cnn.com/2011/03/28/news/economy/medicaid_states/index.htm.

McNutt, J., & Menon, G. (2008). The rise of cyberactivism: Implications for the future of advocacy in the human services. *Families in Society, 89*(1), 33–38.

Meslin, D. (2011, April 12). *The antidote to apathy*. Retrieved from www.ted.com/talks/dave_meslin_the_antidote_to_apathy.html.

National Center on Civic Literacy. (2013). *Mission statement.* Indianapolis, IN: Author.

Oliff, P., Mai, C., & Palacios, V. (2012, June 27). *States continue to feel recession's impact.* Washington, DC: Center for Budget and Policy Priorities. Retrieved from www.cbpp.org/cms/?fa=view&id=711.

Reilly, N. (2007, March-April). Linking local and global feminist advocacy: Framing women's rights as human rights in the Republic of Ireland. *Women's Studies International Forum, 30*(2), 114–133.

Richan, W. C. (2006). *Lobbying for social change* (3rd ed.). New York, NY: Haworth.

Shaw, R. (2001). *The activist's handbook* (updated ed.). Berkeley: University of California Press.

Smucker, B. (1999). *The nonprofit lobbying guide* (2nd ed.). Washington, DC: Independent Sector.

Squillace, J. (2010). The effect of privatization on advocacy: Social work state-level advocacy with the executive branch. *Families in Society, 91*(1), 25–30.

Stern, M., & Axinn, J. (2012). *Social welfare: A history of the American response to need* (8th ed.). Boston, MA: Allyn & Bacon.

Teater, B. (2009). Influencing state legislators: A framework for developing effective social work interest groups. *Journal of Policy Practice, 8*(1), 69–86.

118 Community Partnerships to Support Youth Success in School

Dennis L. Poole & Aidyn L. Iachini

INTRODUCTION

A *community partnership* is an alliance between citizens and practitioners to bring about planned change for the public good (Poole, 2002, 2008) *Community* stems from the Latin word *communis*, which implies something shared and public. The term *partnership* derives its meaning from its derivative, *partner*. A partner once referred to a piece of timber used to buttress the deck or mast of a wooden sailing ship. This is a fitting analogy for this chapter. Community partners strive together to achieve community goals that are above and beyond the reach of any one partner—in the context of this chapter, namely, promoting the healthy development and educational success of young people in school.

IMPORTANCE OF COMMUNITY PARTNERSHIPS

Many youth thrive in school and graduate with plans to enter the workforce or apply for postsecondary educational opportunities. An increasing number of others, however, experience barriers and challenges that significantly affect their potential. Unmet mental health needs, substance abuse issues, family conflict, bullying, unsafe neighborhoods, and other conditions are just a few of the individual, peer, family, school, and community factors that can negatively affect a young person's ability to learn in the classroom and succeed in school.

A powerful consensus has emerged over the past decade that no community institution alone can address all of these barriers and challenges. Advocates continue to call on schools and community agencies to work together to provide an array of services and supports designed to (1) address the multiple and varied needs of students and (2) promote students' overall healthy development. In response, partnership-oriented models are being promoted that replace fragmented, uncoordinated services for youth with integrated, collaborative networks of services and supports (Anderson-Butcher, Lawson, Iachini, Bean, Flaspohler, & Zullig, 2010a; Anderson-Butcher, Lawson, Iachini, Flaspohler, Bean & Wade-Mdivanian, 2010b; Dryfoos, 2005; Poole, 1997; Taylor & Adelman, 2000). Full-service community schools, community collaboration models for school improvement, school mental health systems, and comprehensive systems of learning supports are common examples of these models that prioritize the importance of community partnerships (Anderson-Butcher et al., 2010a; 2010b; Dryfoos et al., 2005; Weist, 1997).

Community partnerships are important and beneficial for several reasons. First, developing community partnerships can result in blurring or removing previously fixed institutional boundaries between schools and agencies (Epstein, 2002; Poole, 1997). For example, schools and agencies usually each have their own set of rules, regulations, and customs that inhibit or prohibit the sharing of information. Through community partnerships, new agreements (e.g., memoranda of understanding) can be reached that allow for information sharing across agency and school settings. Community partnerships also can minimize interorganizational competition, reduce fragmentation in service delivery, and increase efficient use of organizational resources. Finally, another important benefit of community partnerships is that they often lay the groundwork for agency services to be linked with and/or co-located and delivered in the school setting (Anderson-Butcher & Ashton, 2004; Taylor & Adelman, 2000). For example, Iachini, Dorr, and Anderson-Butcher (2008) describe a partnership between one school district, three mental health agencies, and other community and school stakeholders that resulted in the hiring of mental health providers to provide services to students and families in the school setting. Not only did these partnerships result in needed services, they ultimately enhanced student and family access to them by offering them on school grounds.

ACTION PRINCIPLES

Social workers can serve as key leaders in fostering and developing community partnerships to support youth success in school (Anderson-Butcher et al., 2010b). Six action principles in a community partnership capacity building model, developed by Poole (2002), are presented in Figure 118.1 to guide social workers throughout stages of the capacity building process. It is important to note that the

term "community" included within the model is inclusive of schools as part of the community. Therefore, the term "community" is used throughout the remainder of this chapter to reference a variety of community institutions including the school system.

Agenda Building

Initiate the process by getting a core group of citizens and practitioners to place the issue on the agenda of key decisionmakers. "Agenda building" refers to predecisional processes that lead decision makers to select some issues for deliberation and reject others (Cobb & Elder, 1983). The challenge is to convince leaders that an issue deserves a prominent position on the agenda. An agenda is the list of items that a local school board, youth council, city human services commission, school administrative team, or other decision-making body is willing or able to consider at a given point in time.

To illustrate, let us assume that the issue, or concern, is poor school attendance. A social worker learns that a fourth of the students at one middle school are not attending school regularly. The social worker also learns that these students'

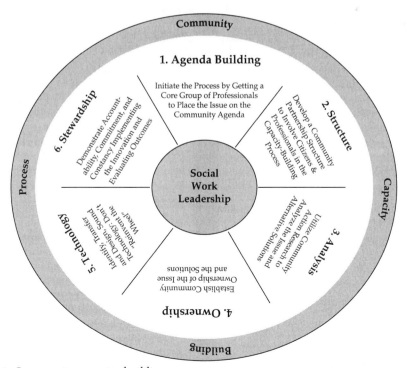

Figure 118.1 Community capacity building process.

standardized test scores and grades are low, and their disciplinary incidences are high. The social worker knows that complex social, emotional, and health forces can stand in the way of a student's ability to attend school, and that multiple community support services may be needed to address this growing concern at the middle school.

Oftentimes, the social worker's first leadership task is to raise the concern with school leaders (e.g., principals and assistant principals). Having data on key indicators to demonstrate that school attendance is a pressing problem for the school, particularly related to academic achievement, is helpful in facilitating these conversations. At this point in agenda building, school leaders may agree with the social worker that poor school attendance is a critically important threat to the educational mission of the school, and decide to make the issue a priority in the school improvement planning process (i.e., a process schools utilize to identify goals, strategies, and action steps for an academic year). The social worker also may simultaneously need to build support for an issue in the community to further demonstrate to school leadership how important a particular issue may be to the wider community. The critical role that volunteer citizens often play in agenda building should not be underestimated. They are, after all, the central actors in a democracy, as well as trustees of the public interest (Cooper, 1991), and usually have much more power than paid practitioners or staff to get an issue on the community's agenda (Cooper, 1991; Gusfield, 1981; Poole, 1997).

Accordingly, the social worker should consider involving volunteer citizens who represent various types of power to build support for the issue. For example, the social worker might enlist the support of a citizen who has *political* power. Citizens elected this person to represent their interests on the city council, local school board, county commission, or state legislature. The practitioner also might engage a citizen who has *economic* power. Citizens recognize this person as a successful business leader committed to youth services—the board president of the local United Way, for example. Moreover, the social worker might want to engage a citizen with *moral* power. Citizens respect this person as a long-standing advocate for youth, perhaps a concerned parent of a child in the target middle school of this case example. Finally, the practitioner might need to engage a citizen who has *technical* power—such as a retired teacher

or social worker with expertise on attendance issues in school.

Considering these four different types of civic power, the social worker should be purposeful and intentional in the engagement of citizens external to the school. Depending upon school administrative characteristics and preferences, the social worker might work collaboratively with administrators to set up small group meetings between concerned citizens and the school. Alternatively, one-on-one meetings with various citizens and school administrators might be the better approach. Regardless, the goal is to gain buy-in and agreement among school administrators and community stakeholders that poor school attendance is a significant issue that warrants further exploration. Ultimately the issue of poor school attendance must be "co-owned" by schools and community partners, and a partnership structure must be utilized or created to resolve it.

Structure

Develop a community partnership structure to involve citizens and practitioners in the capacity building process. Once the issue achieves agenda status, the next phase is to build a community partnership structure, or expand an already existing structure, and sustain it throughout the process. A community partnership structure provides a channel through which responsible citizens can take a leadership role with practitioners in solving pressing school and community problems. It usually operates under the auspices of a decision-making body, taking the form of a committee, task force, or advisory council. Action-oriented, a community partnership structure fosters shared responsibility for local problems, prompts behavioral change in community institutions, and initiates and sustains reform efforts over time (Poole, 1997).

Thinking about the case example, let us assume that the school decides to establish a 25-member structure called the School Attendance Community Partnership Committee, herein referred to as the "Community Partnership Committee." One critical role for the social worker at this stage is to ensure that best practice teaming principles are attended to and monitored by the committee. Iachini, Anderson-Butcher, and Mellin (2013) identify four teaming principles to consider. They include (1) having a clear purpose for the committee, (2) having diversity in composition and membership, (3) identifying a committee leader, and (4) establishing clear procedures for the committee and how it will operate (Iachini et al., 2013).

In reference to the Community Partnership Committee, the social worker might facilitate a discussion in early committee meetings about the importance of such teaming principles. Conversations should address the purpose of the committee and its goals, creating a clear and shared understanding among its members. Conversations also should revolve around ensuring that the "right" members are represented on the committee. For example, are leading citizens who hold critical insight and expertise on the subject of school attendance on the committee? Is there balance and diversity of membership? Are practitioners from schools and community agencies with resources to address the school attendance issue represented on the committee? In our case, school representatives might include the superintendent, middle school principal, a teacher, guidance counselor, and a social worker. Agency representatives might include administrators or staff of the public health department, mental health center, department of human services, or YMCA. Once membership is established, it is important that a key leader be selected to serve as chair of the committee, and that processes be identified on how the committee will function (e.g., meeting times, accountability mechanisms, and communication).

A social worker's knowledge and skills in group work can be especially helpful during this stage of the process. As in treatment groups, critical leadership roles are performed in task-oriented groups. Examples of these include helping a committee identify goals and objectives, facilitating group action and interaction, maintaining group cohesiveness and member satisfaction, and providing means for group task performance (Ephross & Vassil, 2005). In the case example, the capacity building process is likely to disintegrate if the group maintenance needs of the Community Partnership Committee are not met, thwarting the opportunity to advance its efforts to resolve the school attendance problem.

Analysis

Use community action research to analyze the issue and alternative solutions. The analysis stage of the capacity building process involves community action research. Traditional research will not satisfy the full requirements of this stage. Hiring a consultant to analyze the issue, report findings, and offer recommendations will not suffice. The main objective is for the community, rather than a consultant or a few practitioners, to become the research team (Minkler & Wallerstein, 2003).

As in traditional research, community action research seeks to improve the quality of decision making through careful collection of data and facts. Greater emphasis, however, is given to participatory strategies than to nonparticipatory strategies. Key informant interviews, public forums, and focus groups, as well as surveys on community, family, peer, and individual risk and protective factors, can be used to engage divergent community groups and organizations in data collection and analysis. Existing data also can be analyzed in conjunction with data collected through these other participatory strategies. For example, in the case of the Community Partnership Committee, secondary data already collected by schools and districts as part of accountability requirements (e.g., attendance, behavioral incidences, and grades) could be examined along with newly collected data gathered via focus groups and surveys. Together, collecting, using, and examining various types of data can foster broad-based community participation, increase public awareness of the issue, and identify community partners that must share in solving the problem.

In the case example, the key leadership role of the social worker is to ensure that each member of the Community Partnership Committee participates in data collection, shares ownership of the findings, and helps develop proposed solutions. Tasks include helping committee members reach consensus on the nature, scope, and causes of poor school attendance at the middle school; identifying alternative strategies to address the issue; and developing and submitting a written report to school or district administrators and community partners with recommendations for action. The social worker may help write the report, but his or her name is not prominently displayed. The authors are the members of the committee that gathered the information, analyzed the findings, and identified solutions included in the report.

Community Ownership

Establish community ownership of the issue and solution. "Ownership" refers to actions taken by a decision-making body to demonstrate it owns an issue. Ownership is established when a body has the power to define the issue, determine its causes, and assign responsibility to local institutions to implement a solution. Some community institutions may not want to give up their power to define the issue because it would mean forfeiting their right to control the solution. Others may want to "disown" the issue because they might be asked to share responsibility in addressing it (Gusfield, 1981).

In the case example of school attendance, the main leadership role of the social worker is to facilitate both school and community ownership of the issue. The practitioner, however, must recognize that addressing school attendance at the middle school probably will not take place without a change in the *status quo*. This will require that all relevant organizations or groups be invested in "owning" the solution, even those that want to "disown" it. At some point in the capacity building process, a partner may attempt to renege on prior public commitments to participate in solving the problem, or attempt to control the solution. Together, members of the Community Partnership Committee must hold all relevant actors accountable for their role(s) in the solution and continue to foster broad-based ownership of the school attendance problem.

Technology

Identify, transfer, and design sound technology: do not reinvent the wheel. In the technology stage, attention shifts to the identification, transfer, and design of a sound technology to implement the strategy adopted by the community partnership structure. Frequently, too little attention is devoted to this important phase of the capacity building process. Organizations that do not have adequate and appropriate staff resources, facilities, funding, or intervention techniques usually have great difficulty implementing a new product or service innovation (Anderson-Butcher et al., 2010a, b; Poole, Ferguson, & Schwab, 2005).

Considering the case example, the social worker must recognize that attendance issues are common in schools. Other schools and communities have faced the same issue and most likely have devised good technical solutions. The social worker should help the Committee Partnership Structure find these solutions, assess their outcomes, determine transferability, and modify

proposed solutions to fit the particular needs and specifications of his or her community. Library research, surfing the Internet for evidence-based practices and strategies, phone calls, and site visits help the social worker meet this challenge. Fortunately, ample literature exists on the causes of poor school attendance, and an array of solutions involving diverse practitioners have been tested in school settings. Roles for social workers in these solutions are rich and varied (Openshaw, 2008).

The social worker also should help the committee ensure that all relevant community institutions contribute resources—cash or in kind—to implement the plan. Most service innovations in schools require a diversified funding base, reflecting the complexity of interventions needed to improve school attendance. Though a diversified funding base is usually needed to sustain a service innovation over time, small contributions from the Junior League, the United Way, or private donors can be used as seed money. Funding also may need to be redirected from an existing source to support this new effort. The value of such contributions should not be underestimated. Together they can foster greater community- and school-wide ownership of the solution, provide an opportunity to test the viability of the selected technology on a small scale, and give the committee more time to secure larger, stable sources of funding to implement the intervention if necessary.

Professional development and other support needs also are important to consider during this stage (Anderson-Butcher et al., 2010a, 2010b; Iachini et al., 2008). New infrastructure, resources, and strategies identified by the Community Partnership Committee in this case may need to be shared with a variety of stakeholders involved with implementation and management. Workshops and trainings may be needed to familiarize middle school teachers and staff, for example, with new intervention strategies being utilized to improve school attendance. In addition, school staff roles or community partner roles may need to be redefined or reorganized to align with this new school priority. The social worker might help to organize or identify what is needed to assist teachers, staff, and practitioners to make the transition successfully.

During the technology stage of the capacity building process, plans also should be developed to monitor implementation and progress toward outcomes. How will the Community Partnership Committee know when outcomes are being achieved without indicators of progress along the way? How will barriers and challenges to implementation of the intervention strategies be identified? The social worker can guide the committee in a discussion to identify key outcomes as well as select indicators to track and monitor progress during implementation of the new intervention strategies.

Stewardship

Demonstrate accountability, commitment, and constancy implementing the innovation and evaluating outcomes. Once the community partnership structure endorses the technical plan, and resources to implement the plan are secured, its work shifts to the stewardship phase of the capacity-building process. *Stewardship* means to hold something in trust for another, beginning with the willingness to be accountable for outcomes to some body larger than ourselves—namely, the community (Block, 1993).

Stewardship is the most difficult phase in the capacity building process. Many service innovations almost never work exactly as planned. Community partners become disgruntled, paperwork gets burdensome, resources grow thin, and early outcomes inevitably fall short of expectations (Payne, Gottfredson, & Gottfredson, 2006; Poole, 1997). During the stewardship phase, it is easy for community partners to lose sight of the fact they must fulfill the public trust—that is, deliver the community good they promised, and be accountable for the results. Self-interest, burnout, and feelings of defeat usually take a toll on partners in this stage of the process.

Here, the continual use of data to guide decision-making and mid-course corrections is essential. The social worker may need to pull together data to share at each committee meeting, facilitate discussions among partners about progress made toward goals, identify challenges currently being experienced, and devise solutions to overcome them. It also is important for committee members to reflect on their collaborative efforts (Bronstein, 2003). For example, is time an issue that is impeding partners' abilities to work together successfully? Has a partner with a crucial role in the committee stopped attending meetings? Mendenhall, Iachini, and Anderson-Butcher (in press) found that inadequate time, lack of perceived buy-in, resource

challenges, and transitional issues were barriers to implementing a partnership-centered model in a school setting. Thus, a social worker could guide committee members in a conversation about what is working well, and what needs to be changed relationally and operationally. The social worker also might help them revisit procedures and processes identified during the structure phase of the capacity building process and make changes to improve the committee's ability to function collaboratively.

It is important to emphasize that this stage of the process is not easy or for the light-hearted (Poole, 2002). Victory stands faintly at the end of a long, dark tunnel. Reaching it brings great joy, however, and restores public confidence in schools and community agencies. Fortunately, a community partnership structure has many partners. Each partner can buttress and support an innovation when one partner is weak or behaves irresponsibly. The structure also can make flight from social responsibility difficult because it will hold each of the partners accountable for the public trust bestowed on them. Good stewards find ways to implement an innovation as planned, refine the technology as needed, and produce outcomes that make a difference—in this example, promoting the success of young people in school.

CONCLUSION

Promoting the healthy development and educational success of youth require schools and community agencies to partner and collaborate in order to provide coordinated and seamless services to students and families. These community partnership structures are needed to disrupt arrangements that serve youth and families in an uncoordinated, piecemeal fashion. Social workers can play critical leadership roles in developing and sustaining community partnerships to support youth success in school by adhering to the six action principles of the community partnership model presented in this chapter.

WEBSITES

American Council for School Social Work. http://acssw.org/
Center for School Mental Health. http://csmh .umaryland.edu/

Center for Schools and Communities. http://www.center-school.org.

Coalition for Community Schools. http://www.communityschools.org/insideschools.html.

NASW Standards for School Social Work Services. http://www.naswdc.org/practice/standards/NASWSchoolSocialWorkStandards.pdf

School Social Work Association of America. http://www.sswaa.org.

UCLA Center for Mental Health in Schools. http://smhp.psych.ucla.edu/

References

Anderson-Butcher, D., & Ashton, D. (2004). Innovative models of collaboration to save children, youth, families, and communities. *Children and Schools, 26,* 39–53.

Anderson-Butcher, D., Lawson, H. A., Iachini, A., Bean, J., Flaspohler, P., & Zullig, K. (2010a). Capacity-related innovations resulting from pilot school and district implementation of a community collaboration model for school improvement. *Journal of Educational and Psychological Consultation, 20,* 257–287.

Anderson-Butcher, D., Lawson, H., Iachini, A. L., Flaspohler, P., Bean, J., & Wade-Mdivanian, R. (2010b). Emergent evidence in support of a community collaboration model for school improvement. *Children & Schools, 32,* 160–171.

Block, P. (1993). *Stewardship.* San Francisco, CA: Barrett-Koehler.

Bronstein, L. (2003). A model for interdisciplinary collaboration. *Social Work, 48,* 297–306.

Cobb, R., & Elder, C. (1983). *Participation in American politics.* Baltimore, MD: John Hopkins University Press.

Cooper, T. (1991). *An ethic of citizenship for public administration.* Englewood Cliffs, NJ: Prentice Hall.

Dryfoos, J. G. (2005). Full service schools: Revolution or fad? *Journal of Research on Adolescence, 5,* 147–172.

Dryfoos, J. C., Quinn, L., & Boukin, C. (2005). *Community school in action: Lessons from a decade of practice.* New York, NY: Oxford University Press.

Ephross, P., & Vassil, T. (2005). *Groups that work.* New York, NY: Columbia University Press.

Epstein, J. (2002). *School, family, and community partnerships: Your handbook for action.* Thousand Oak, CA: Corwin Press.

Gusfield, J. (1981). *The culture of public problems.* Chicago, IL: University of Chicago Press.

Iachini, A. L., Dorr, C., & Anderson-Butcher, D. (2008). Fostoria Community Schools' innovative approach to refining and coordinating their school-based mental health service delivery system. *Report on Emotional and Behavioral Disorders in Youth, 8,* 69–75.

Iachini, A. L., Anderson-Butcher, D., & Mellin, E. A. (2013). Exploring best practice teaming strategies: Implications for school mental health practice and research. *Advances in School Mental Health Promotion, 6*(2), 139–154.

Mendenhall, A., Iachini, A., & Anderson-Butcher, D. (in press). Exploring facilitators and barriers to implementation of an expanded school improvement model. *Children & Schools.*

Minkler, M., & Wallerstein, N. (2003). *Community-based participatory research for health.* San Francisco, CA: Jossey-Bass.

Openshaw, L. (2008). *Social work in schools.* New York, NY: Guilford.

Payne, A., Gottfredson, D., & Gottfredson, G. (2006). School predictions of the intensity of implementation of school-based prevention programs: Results from a national study. *Prevention Science, 7,* 225–237.

Poole, D. L. (1997). The SAFE project: Community-driven partnerships in health, mental health, and education to prevent early school failure. *Health and Social Work, 22,* 282–289.

Poole, D. L. (2002). Community partnerships for school-based services: Action principles. In A. Roberts & G. Greene (Eds.), *Social workers' desk reference* (pp. 539–544). New York, NY: Oxford University Press.

Poole, D. L. (2008). Community partnerships for school-based services: Action principles. In A. Roberts & G. Greene (Eds.), *Social workers' desk reference* (pp. 907–912). New York, NY: Oxford University Press.

Poole, D. L., Ferguson, M., & Schwab, A. J. (2005). Managing process innovations in welfare reform technology. *Administration in Social Work, 29,* 101–116.

Taylor, L., & Adelman, H. S. (2000). Toward ending the marginalization and fragmentation of mental health in schools. *Journal of School Health, 70,* 210–215.

Weist, M. D. (1997). Expanded school mental health services: A national movement in progress. *Advances in Clinical Child Psychology, 19,* 319–352.

Building Community Capacity in the U.S. Air Force

119

Promoting a Community Practice Strategy

Gary L. Bowen & James A. Martin

INTRODUCTION

United States military installations vary on a number of dimensions, including their operational mission, their corresponding demographic composition, and the characteristics of their surrounding civilian communities. Installations also differ in their ability to achieve positive community results—"aggregate, broad-based outcomes that reflect the collective efforts of individuals and families who live within a specified area" (Bowen, Martin, Mancini, & Nelson, 2000, p. 9). Resiliency is one such community result that reflects the aggregate success of community members and families to manage their personal and family lives in the context of adversity and positive challenge (Bowen & Martin, 2011).

The U.S. Air Force (AF) has long provided broad-based programs and services to support the adaptation, readiness, and retention of its service members (and immediate family members). Over the past decade AF leaders have adopted a community practice (CP) strategy that has paralleled the continued and profound changes in the size, composition, and stationing of military forces (Bowen, Martin, & Mancini, 2013; Hoshmand & Hoshmand, 2007). This AF practice strategy focuses on promoting interagency collaboration and strengthening the interface between formal and informal networks of social care as a means to promote member and family resiliency. This strategy was field tested by the Family Advocacy

Division (Bowen, Martin, & Nelson, 2002), and by Airman & Family Readiness Centers (formerly Family Support Centers) beginning in the late 1990s (Bowen, Orthner, Martin, & Mancini, 2001; Bowen, Martin, Liston, & Nelson, 2009). Community capacity building efforts in these two AF organizations, including unit outreach, continue today.

In 2010, the USAF established a Resilience Division within the Headquarters of the Air Force that has furthered these community capacity building efforts. The Division embraced the community practice strategy in an effort to promote resiliency training across the AF and to coordinate AF-wide community-based initiatives for both airmen and their families. Civilian Community Support Coordinators (CSCs) have been hired at all AF bases to promote unit-based resilience training and to serve as the Installation Resilience Program Specialist. Working as a member of the Wing Commander's staff, a principal role of the CSC is to serve as the Executive Director of the Installation Community Action and Information Board (CAIB) and as the Chair of the Integrated Delivery System (IDS). In these related roles, the CSC provides guidance to the installation commander and installation human services delivery staff on a wide range of resilience and quality-of-life issues, including efforts to promote cross-organizational collaboration in addressing individual, family, and community concerns. The IDS represents the action arm of

935

the CAIB, and the IDS has cross-organizational installation membership and responsibility for developing and implementing a biannual Community Action Plan (CAP) for informing installation level community outreach efforts. The collection and use of assessment data for identifying and monitoring individual, family, and community-level concerns is a fundamental component of the CAP.

This chapter describes the model of community capacity, which is the cornerstone of this AF practice strategy. This model, which is referenced in the literature as the Social Organization Theory of Community Action and Change (Bowen, Martin, & Mancini, 2013; Mancini & Bowen, 2013), embraces members and families within their social context and focuses on the nexus between formal and informal networks of social care as the target of intervention and prevention efforts. We first highlight the practice strategy as it is being implemented in the AF Resilience Division, including an online assessment tool, the Support & Resiliency Inventory (SRI), which is used in the context of this strategy. We conclude by discussing empirical support for the community capacity model, the need for continued research and evaluation of community practice initiatives that are framed and informed by this model, and a new initiative to train family service practitioners in both military and civilian communities in community capacity building.

THE COMMUNITY PRACTICE STRATEGY

The CP strategy promotes interagency collaboration, encourages proactive unit leadership in support of members and families, and builds informal community connections for purposes of fostering a sense of community, promoting individual and family resilience, and ensuring personnel preparedness to successfully perform military duties. This service delivery strategy is strengths-based and results-focused. It contrasts greatly with the more stove-piped, remedial, menu-driven services model that has historically informed the delivery of member and family services in the AF.

A key component of the strategy is unit outreach. CSCs assist unit commanders in meeting their leadership responsibilities for the health, welfare, and readiness of unit members and their families. CSCs are trained to help unit commanders locate and obtain necessary resources for addressing unit-level issues and priorities. CSCs capitalize on the availability of formal and informal community resources in planning and implementing responses to priority issues—networking and collaboration are the cornerstones of this community-based approach to practice.

Training is underway to provide CSCs with the knowledge and skills to collect and use assessment data (specifically the SRI, which is described below) to inform their work at both the unit level and the larger installation level. This training is framed and informed by a results-focused planning (RFP) approach to the design and delivery of services (Orthner & Bowen, 2004). RFP focuses intervention and prevention efforts on clearly defined and anticipated results. A key aspect of this approach is to identify community partners on the installation and in the local civilian community who will help achieve the desired results, which reflects the central practice mantra of this planning process: "Never go it alone."

THE SUPPORT & RESILIENCY INVENTORY

The Support & Resiliency Inventory (SRI) was designed to inform, monitor, and evaluate the RFP efforts at the both unit and installation levels.[1] The SRI is a brief, self-administered, web-based assessment tool that examines an individual's perceptions about sources of informal and formal support in their lives, their individual fitness (mental, physical, social, and spiritual), their positive behaviors toward self and others, and their success in adapting to life challenges and meeting military life and duty responsibilities (resiliency). Completion of the SRI is intended to be voluntary, and the information provided is anonymous. The SRI can be completed online in 12 to 15 minutes using a computer or tablet device. All of the SRI items are worded in a positive and proactive direction—an intended focus on positive knowledge, attitudes, and behaviors rather than the negative.

The administration of the SRI can also be viewed as an intervention itself, and each respondent has access to a printable summary of his or her own responses, as well as information on how and where to seek additional assistance. CSCs are able to view and download a summary group profile that aggregates the responses. An advanced selection tool also allows CSCs to generate profiles for specific units and respondent subgroups. Further details about the SRI, including a hard copy and reports on its psychometrics, can be obtained from the authors.

THE COMMUNITY CAPACITY MODEL

The community practice strategy aligns with a larger community capacity model that was developed and tested by a team of researchers from the AF and civilian communities (Bowen et al., 2000; Mancini, Bowen, & Martin, 2005). The model, the Social Organization Theory of Community Action and Change, continues to be elaborated and refined (Bowen & Martin, 2011; Mancini & Bowen, 2013), as well as applied to a range of social problems and community support program initiatives (Bowen, Martin, & Mancini, 2013; Farrell, Bowen, & Goodrich, in press; Huebner, Mancini, Bowen, & Orthner, 2009). A review of this model demonstrates the heuristic and stimulus value of explanatory models to the development of specific practice strategies.

The community capacity model includes three major components: (1) formal networks, (2) informal networks, and (3) community capacity. From the perspective of the model, variation in the aggregate success of members and families to manage their personal and family lives in the context of adversity and positive challenge is explained by how successfully formal and informal networks of social care operate and interact with one another in the generation of community capacity. Community capacity, which reflects the level of social organization in the community, is hypothesized as the link between community networks and community results. Social care is defined as tangible, informational, and social-emotional support available for military members and their families. The level of social care provided to members and families through the combined forces of these networks can range from high to low. Each component of the model is elaborated in the following discussion, including a discussion of the hypothesized linkages between these components and between community capacity and individual and family resiliency.

Formal and Informal Networks of Social Care

Three networks of formal and informal social care are identified in the community capacity model: (1) community agencies, (2) unit leaders, and (3) informal community connections. Formal networks, which include community agencies and unit leaders, reflect the military policies and systems of social care that operate as instruments of socialization, support, and social control. Community agencies promote social care by demonstrating a customer- and strengths-based orientation in their coordination and delivery of intervention and prevention services to members and families. Unit leaders provide social care by promoting connections between members and families, helping members and families balance work and family demands, and when needed, helping members and families access and secure support services. The effectiveness of formal networks of social care depends in part on securing necessary input and participation from community members.

Informal networks, which include informal community connections, are voluntary and less organized. They include personal and collective relationships and group associations, such as unit-based support groups and relationships with extended family members, work associates, neighbors, and families. Mutual exchanges and reciprocal responsibilities constitute the cornerstones of informal network construction. Informal network members promote social care by reaching out to make connections with one another, exchanging information and resources, and when needed, helping one another secure support from community programs and support services—all examples of social capital (Bowen et al., 2000).

Bowen and Martin (1998) describe these informal networks metaphorically as power substations of social care in the community, which have turbines in the form of trust, commitments and obligations, information exchanges, positive regard and mutual respect, and norms of shared responsibility and social control. As compared to formal networks, informal networks play a more active and often a more important role in the day-to-day life of members and families. They typically operate as the first level of social care when members and families need support and assistance.

From the perspective of intervention and prevention planning, an important function of formal networks is to strengthen informal community connections. Formal networks may grow at the expense of informal networks (McKnight, 1997). For example, community agencies may plan and sponsor events for community members that members are capable of planning and sponsoring for themselves. When unit leaders and installation agencies perform functions the informal community is capable of providing for itself (i.e., overfunctioning), informal community networks may be diminished. When the system of formal and informal networks is fully operative and complementary in an installation, a protective and resilient web of support surrounds and sustains members and families (Bowen, Orthner, Martin, & Mancini, 2001).

Unit leaders play a particularly important role in the community network—they stand between informal networks on one side and installation agencies on the other. In many respects, the unit is synonymous with community in the AF, and the identity of members and families typically derives more from their unit association than from their installation or local civilian community residency (Bowen & McClure, 1999).

Community Capacity

From the perspective of the model highlighted here, community capacity is the concept that links the operation of formal and informal networks of social care to produce community results. It involves two components assumed to mutually reinforce each other over time. First, community capacity reflects the extent to which installation agencies, unit leaders, and community members demonstrate a sense of *shared responsibility* for the general welfare of the community and its members (Bowen et al., 2000). When network members share responsibility for the general welfare, they invest time and energy in making the community a better place to live, work, and play, and they work together to promote the common good.

In addition to feelings of shared responsibility, installation agencies, unit leaders, and community members demonstrate *collective competence* in taking advantage of opportunities for addressing community needs and confronting situations threatening the safety and well-being of community members (Bowen et al., 2000). They pull together in the context of opportunity or adversity to identify community needs and assets, define common goals and objectives, set priorities, develop strategies for collective action, implement actions consistent with agreed-upon strategies, and monitor results.

As defined, community capacity represents behaviors and action, rather than the potential for action. When community capacity is high, members and families have access to resources and opportunities to complete duty requirements and mission requirements; develop community

identity and pride; meet individual and family needs and goals; participate meaningfully in community life; solve problems and manage conflicts; and affirm and maintain stability and order in personal, family, and work relationships.

Networks and Community Capacity

Community capacity springs from the actions and interactions *within* and *between* installation agencies, installation and unit leaders, and community members—a social energy that flows from the union between formal and informal community networks. As such, community capacity is distinct from the processes from which it emerges, and the fund of capacity is more than the sum total of actions in formal and informal networks. The *bonding* (within) and *bridging* (between) activities by these formal and informal networks of social care provide the cornerstones for achieving community results associated with member and family resiliency.

Bonding, which Putnam (2000) describes as "sociological superglue" (p. 23), captures the cohesion, trust, and positive regard within groups, such as within informal networks of social care. Putnam describes *bridging* as the "sociological WD-40" (p. 23), or the strength of ties among individuals across groups, such as the working relationships between unit leaders and representatives of community agencies. The ongoing processes of bonding and bridging among and between members from various segments of the community form a complex union that powers community capacity and provides a means to achieve community results.

Community Capacity and Community Results

Community capacity may have upper and lower threshold effects in its relationship to community results. Above a certain level of community capacity, further increases in capacity may not be associated with the further promotion of community results. On the other hand, once community capacity declines below a certain level, community results may decrease precipitously. This is consistent with Crane's (1991) epidemic model of community effects, in which problems spread like a contagion once a certain level of community vulnerability is reached.

The influence of community capacity may vary over the work and family life course (Bowen,

Richman, & Bowen, 2000). AF members and families may need community capacity to be high in times of peak operational demands, such as during a deployment. The nature and impact of community capacity must be considered in the context of individual time (where individuals are in their own stage of development, including the military/work career), family time (where individuals are in the family life cycle), and historical time (the current context, including the economy and current military conflicts) (Bowen & Martin, 2011). These three aspects of time can intersect and merge in interesting and challenging ways as members and families move through the life course.

EVIDENCE BASE

Although the research literature supports unit leaders as the key leverage points in promoting member and family resiliency (Bowen, 1998; Pittman, Kerpelman, & McFadyen, 2004), the community capacity model includes two additional strategy platforms for launching community building efforts: interagency collaboration and informal network development. At present, the model promotes influencing these community-building components largely through unit-based efforts, including the use of community agencies as partners in planning and implementation of service action plans, as well as supporting unit commanders in their efforts to mobilize members and families in support of one another.

Although the practice strategy awaits formal evaluation, a body of basic research supports this application of the community capacity model. In an investigation with a probability sample of 20,569 married AF members, unit leader support exerted a positive and significant indirect effect on family adaptation through its direct effect on sense of community and informal community support (Bowen, Mancini, Martin, Ware, & Nelson, 2003). In a more recent investigation with 10,102 married active-duty AF members, positive perceptions of community capacity had a strong and direct effect on self-reported symptoms of depression; these perceptions were also a significant mediator of the effects of formal and informal support networks on depression, including agency support, unit leader support, and neighbor support (Bowen, Martin, Mancini, & Swick, in press).

In addition to this program of basic research, research in other areas has provided support for AF interventions that incorporate community-based components. For instance, the AF's suicide prevention program, which incorporates interagency planning and coordination, commander awareness education and training, and peer monitoring, has been associated with a reduced rate of suicide and reductions in other adverse outcomes in an evaluation using a quasiexperimental design (Knox, Litts, Talcott, Feig, & Caine, 2003). Additional research is needed to test linkages between concepts in the community capacity model, as well as evaluate community initiatives consistent with its central linkages, to provide an evidence base for this community practice strategy in the AF.

NEXT STEPS IN IMPLEMENTATION

Through its partnership with the United States Department of Agriculture, the Office of the Secretary of Defense for Military Community and Family Policy is sponsoring the development of an online training and curriculum that aligns with the community capacity model. The University of Georgia (Dr. Jay A. Mancini, PI) and The University of North Carolina at Chapel Hill (Dr. Gary L. Bowen, PI) are developing this online training system, which is focused on instructing family service providers in both military and civilian communities in ways to build more collaborative and integrative systems of social care, including mobilization of informal networks (e.g., extended family, friends, neighbors, work associates, and so forth) in support of service members and families. Training modules include information on forming a community planning team; assessing a community and its needs; using results-focused planning to develop community action plans; working with formal and informal networks; monitoring progress; and, making efforts more sustainable. This training effort is intended to promote the ability of military and civilian leaders and human service providers to generate community capacity to support military families within their community.

WEBSITES

Military OneSource. http://www.militaryonesource.com
Deployment Health and Family Readiness Library. http://deploymenthealthlibrary.fhp.osd.mil/
Real Warriors. http://www.realwarriors.net/
The Substance Abuse and Mental Health Services Administration (SAMHSA). http://www.samhsa.gov/vets

Note

1.   Bowen and Colleagues, Inc. in Chapel Hill, NC originally developed the SRI (both the member version—SRI-M and the civilian spouse version—SRI-S) in 2006 under contract with AF Space Command (AFSPC). The SRI was subsequently revised in 2009 and 2011 under contract with HQ AF Airman and Family Services Division. Flying Bridge Technologies (FBT), Inc., in Charlotte, North Carolina currently administers the SRI under contract with the AF Resilience Division as part of an Internet-based system called *Communities in Blue.*

References

Bowen, G. L. (1998). Effects of leader support in the work unit on the relationship between work spillover and family adaptation. *Journal of Family and Economic Issues, 19,* 25–52.

Bowen, G. L., Mancini, J. A., Martin, J. A., Ware, W. B., & Nelson, J. P. (2003). An empirical test of a community practice model for promoting family adaptation. *Family Relations, 52,* 33–52.

Bowen, G. L., & Martin, J. A. (1998). Community capacity: A core component of the 21st century military community. *Military Family Issues: The Research Digest, 2*(3), 1–4.

Bowen, G. L., & Martin, J. A. (2011). The resiliency model of role performance of service members, veterans, and their families. *Journal of Human Behavior in the Social Environment, 21,* 162–178.

Bowen, G. L., Martin, J. A., Liston, B. J., & Nelson, J. P. (2009). Building community capacity in the U.S. Air Force: The Community Readiness Consultant Model. In A. R. Roberts (Ed.), *Social workers' desk reference* (2nd ed.) (pp. 912–917). New York, NY: Oxford University Press.

Bowen, G. L., Martin, J. A., & Mancini, J. A. (2013). The resilience of military families: Theoretical perspectives. In M. A. Fine & F. D. Fincham (Eds.), *Family theories: A content-based approach* (pp. 417–436). New York, NY: Routledge (Taylor & Francis).

Bowen, G. L., Martin, J. A., Mancini, J. A., & Nelson, J. P. (2000). Community capacity: Antecedents and consequences. *Journal of Community Practice, 8*(2), 1–21.

Bowen, G. L., Martin, J. A., Mancini, J. A., & Swick, D. (in press). Community capacity and the psychological well-being of married United States Air Force members. In R. Moelker, M. Andres, G. L. Bowen, & P. Manigart (Eds.), *Military families on mission: Comparative perspectives.* Abingdon Oxon: Routledge.

Bowen, G. L., Martin, J. A., & Nelson, J. P. (2002). A community capacity response to family violence in the United States Air Force. In A. R. Roberts & G. J. Greene (Eds.), *Social workers' desk reference* (pp. 551–556). New York, NY: Oxford University Press.

Bowen, G. L., & McClure, P. (1999). Military communities. In P. McClure (Ed.), *Pathways to the future: A review of military family research* (pp. 11–34). Scranton, PA: Marywood University.

Bowen, G. L., Orthner, D. K., Martin, J. A., & Mancini, J. A. (2001). *Building community capacity: A manual for U.S. family support centers.* Chapel Hill, NC: Better Image Printing.

Bowen, G. L., Richman, J. M., & Bowen, N. K. (2000). Families in the context of communities across time. In S. J. Price, P. C. McKenry, & M. J. Murphy (Eds.), *Families across time: A life course perspective* (pp. 117–128). Los Angeles, CA: Roxbury.

Crane, J. (1991). The epidemic theory of ghettos and neighborhood effects on dropping out and teenage childbearing. *American Journal of Sociology, 96,* 1226–1259.

Farrell, A. F., Bowen, G. L., & Goodrich, S. A. (in press). Strengthening family resilience: A community capacity approach. In J. A. Arditti (Ed.), *Family problems: Stress, risk, and resilience.* New York, NY: Wiley/Blackwell.

Hoshmand, L. T., & Hoshmand, A. L. (2007). Support for military families. *Journal of Community Psychology, 35,* 171–180.

Huebner, A. J., Mancini, J. A., Bowen, G. L., & Orthner, D. K. (2009). Shadowed by war: Building community capacity to support military families. *Family Relations, 58,* 216–228.

Knox, K. L., Litts, D. A., Talcott, G. W., Feig, J. C., & Caine, E. D. (2003). Risk of suicide and related adverse outcomes after exposure to a suicide prevention programme in the US Air Force: Cohort study. *British Medical Journal, 327,* 1376–1380.

Mancini, J. A., & Bowen, G. L. (2013). Families and communities: An analysis of theoretical and research paradigms. In G. W. Peterson & K. R. Bush (Eds.), *Handbook of marriage and the family* (3rd ed.). (pp. 781–813). New York, NY: Springer.

Mancini, J. A., Bowen, G. L., & Martin, J. A. (2005). Community social organization: A conceptual linchpin in examining families in the context of communities. *Family Relations, 54,* 570–582.

McKnight, J. L. (1997). A 21st-century map for healthy communities and families. *Families in Society, 78,* 117–127.

Orthner, D. K., & Bowen, G. L. (2004). Strengthening practice through results management. In A. R. Roberts & K. Yeager (Eds.), *Handbook of practice based research* (pp. 897–904). New York, NY: Oxford University Press.

Pittman, J. F., Kerpelman, J. L., & McFadyen, J. M. (2004). Internal and external adaptation in Army families: Lessons from Operations Desert Shield and Desert Storm. *Family Relations, 53,* 249–260.

Putnam, R. D. (2000). *Bowling alone.* New York, NY: Simon & Schuster.

120 Neoliberalism, Globalization, and Social Welfare

Michael J. Holosko

PREFACE

In the very stressful and demanding day-to-day work of social work practice, which takes place in a variety of health and human service organizations (HSOs), social workers sometimes lose sight of the broader context of the environments in which they ply their important craft. Indeed, the pervasive mission driven needs of our vulnerable clients provide the "raison d'être" [or reason for being] for our altruistic work. But such practice does not occur in a vacuum, devoid of external influences that shape what we do, how we do it, and why we do it. The two main overarching trends that directly impact these important questions or concerns are neoliberalism and globalization.

NEOLIBERALISM AND GLOBALIZATION DEFINED

Prior to defining neo-liberalism, it is important to first note that the term liberalism is a *political* doctrine, and neoliberalism is an *economic* doctrine. Further, these very different concepts are often blurred because they both possess the word "liberal" within them. Another point of conceptual fuzziness here, is when liberalism gets applied to the field of economics, it refers to policies meant to encourage entrepreneurship by removing government controls and interference, which moves the term toward more of a right wing conservative position than its truer liberal left-of-center political meaning.

Returning to liberalism's definitional roots as a political idea, this rather revolutionary notion became noted in 1776, when the Scottish economist Adam Smith published his landmark text *The Wealth of Nations*. Here, he proposed: (a) minimum government regulations; (b) fewer interventions from government, in order to encourage entrepreneurship; (c) no tariffs; (d) no barriers or controls; and (e) free trade as the best ways for countries to develop and grow economically (Olivia, 2011).

This concept of liberalism clearly embodies a political philosophy favoring individual freedom and liberty, equality, and capitalism (Hartz, 1955 as cited in Nilep, 2012), which has a long history and deep effect in America. For instance, the assertion in the United States Declaration of Independence that all men (sic) are created equal, and endowed with life and liberty by their creator, echoes the earlier work by John Locke's (1690) suggestion, that no person in a state of nature "ought to harm another in his life, health, liberty, or possessions; for men being all the workmanship of one omnipotent, an infinitely wise maker" (Locke, 2005, p. 4 as cited in Nilep, 2012).

Turning to the concept of neoliberalism, neo means "new," so this "new liberalism" was an economic shift from the previously described political concept above. The "founding fathers" primarily identified with neoliberalism were F. A. Hayek, an Austrian Nobel Laureate economist, and the American economist Milton Friedman, also a Nobel Laureate, who for much of his career was the economic advisor to President Ronald Reagan. Friedman's monetary theories significantly influenced the U.S. Federal Reserve's response to the global financial crises of 2007–2008. Both Hayek and Friedman were opponents of John Maynard Keynes, whose theories [from their perspectives] were unable to economically explain the true realities of free market economies effectively. In simpler terms, neoliberalism contends that it is about the freer movement of goods, resources, and enterprises in an effort to find cheaper labor and resources, and therefore, ultimately maximize profits and efficiencies.

The key assumptions or guiding principles of neoliberalism as described by Robbins (1999) are: (i) sustained economic growth promotes human progress, (ii) free markets without government "interference" would be the most efficient and socially optimal allocation of resources, (iii) economic globalization would be beneficial for everyone, (iv) privatization removes the inefficiencies of the public sector, and (v) governments should function to provide the infrastructure to advance the rule of law, with respect to its property rights and contracts (p. 100). Martinez and Garcia (1997) from the *Corporate Watch* listed neoliberalism's main elements as:

1. *The rule of the market*—Implies freedom for capital, goods, and services, where the market is "self-regulating." It also includes the deunionizing of labor forces, removal of financial regulations, and more freedom from state or government.
2. *Cutting public expenditures for social services*—Means reducing the so-called social safety net for the poor, including health, human services, and education.
3. *Deregulation*—Involves the reduction of government regulation of anything that could diminish profits, including the protection of the environment and safety on the job.
4. *Privatization*—Includes selling state-owned enterprises, goods, and services to private investors including banks, key industries, railroads, toll highways, electricity, schools, and hospitals.
5. *Eliminating the concept of "public good" or "community"*—In short, these should be replaced with "individual responsibility," at any cost.

Ronald Reagan and Margaret Thatcher were the leading conservative political forces who pushed the 35-year policies of neoliberalism strongly, both in their own countries and around the globe. As the concept relates to our post welfare states of its current citizen regimes,

neoliberalism can also be used as a term to describe social welfare, welfare policy, ideology, or governmentality (Holosko & Barner, 2013; SUNY Levin Institute, 2013).

GLOBALIZATION

Globalization has existed ever since people from one country traded or sold goods with people from another country. Marco Polo and the famed Silk Road, which linked China to Europe, and drew in India, Southeast Asia, and Africa, eventually reaching Rome, caused international global trade to blossom almost overnight. For centuries, businessmen, merchants, and bankers have invested in enterprises abroad that spurred international relations, economic exchanges, cross border trade, and migration—so rapidly and on such a scale that many observers perceive that the world has entered a new phase of global economic development with "no end in sight." Rather contradictorily, international globalization now shapes domestic international policy in many developed and undeveloped nations of the world.

A consensual definition of globalization is offered here. *Globalization* is a process of interaction and integration among the people, companies, and governments of various nations, a process driven by international trade and investment, and aided by information technology. This process has profound effects on the environment, culture, economic development, prosperity, and on human physical well-being in societies around the world (SUNY Levin Institute, 2013). Although neoliberalism and globalization were presented separately above, given their similar economic growth and trade imperative, in the past 15–20 years these concepts have been inextricably interwoven (Holosko & Barner, 2013). In short, globalization is the reigning socio-historical reconfiguration of social space, and neoliberalism is the policy approach to it. The term now used to promote their interrelationship is neoliberal globalization.

When examining the extant literature about the so-called pluses or minuses of neoliberal globalization over time, as these policies have evolved—the minuses far outweigh the pluses of this movement. This is particularly true in the area of social welfare policy, as in the past 25 years we have seen more poverty worldwide than ever before, greater discrepancies between economic and social groups, more income inequality between the rich and the poor, less human security and human rights, less social justice, poorer environmental health, poorer safety, and inadequate employment policies (SUNY Levin Institute, 2013).

However, during this same time, there have been some noteworthy gains made in commerce, trade, finance, investment, technology, international law, military alliances, transportation, banking, and energy (Holosko & Barner, 2013). A closer look, however, at *who* has made these gains clearly reveals that it is almost always the wealthier and dominant countries and corporations of the world, from which observers have now coined the phrase, "economic colonialism." Unfortunately, such economic concerns, although important, are not the "life blood" of social work practice, and/or social welfare policies.

NEOLIBERAL GLOBALIZATION IMPACTING DAY-TO-DAY SOCIAL WORK PRACTICE

Often times, many entry level, and/or newly minted Bachelor of Social Work (BSW) or Master of Social Work (MSW) practitioners are rather naïve about how external trends in the world, far removed from their agency walls, such as neoliberal globalization, affect their day-to-day practice. Holosko and Barner (2013) used a hierarchal client, organizational, national, and international matrix to examine how neoliberal globalization adversely impacted these various levels of social work policy and practice. In short, they concluded that social work has not fared well at all under the umbrella of neoliberal globalization. Using another framework, this chapter focuses more on how various trends perpetuated by neoliberal globalization "trickle down" to practitioners who engage in daily in face-to-face interactions with their clients.

As indicated above, vulnerable individuals living on the margins of society, who represent the majority of persons on the caseloads of social workers, have been deeply impacted by neoliberal globalization. This is due to a few reasons. First, in almost every industrialized country in the world, there is less annual spending per capita on social welfare than during the preceding year (Holosko & Barner, 2013). Second, two additional fundamental paradigm shifts have directly descended from neoliberal globalization, both of which social workers have had to

reconcile in their daily practice. One is that their "client-centered" social work practice has now been supplanted by "problem-centered" practice. Here, the emphasis has now clearly shifted from "an individual with problems," to "the identified problems of persons," who are eligible to receive services. Social work's long standing and overarching person-in-environment practice framework is being nudged aside in this shift to a "problem-solution" client focus, one more akin to the so-called medical model. This explains, in part, how case management has become so prominent in the past decade in many countries (Case Management Society of America [CMSA], 2010; CMSA 2103; Conrad N. Hilton, 2011; Work and Income, 2013).

Related to this, has been the transformation of the term "client" to "customer," or "consumer." This transformation literally extracts the sacred term "client" from the bowels of our professional code of ethics (NASW, 2009). Thus, it moves our once clear and solid practice footing of serving client needs, to now procuring, and/or providing customers with the things they need, require, demand, and/or are eligible to receive. This truly shakes our practice foundation a bit, as now our once core social work practice values, such as individuation, self-determinism, empowerment, autonomy, strengths perspective, and diversity are reframed differentially when applied to different customers—all of whom may have different needs, different resources to access services, and/or different methods for paying for different services as they so desire. As such, once social work "clients" become "customers," they are not securely buttressed by the profession's code of ethics.

NEOLIBERALISM TRENDS SHAPING SOCIAL WORK PRACTICE

Table 120.1 further distills these neoliberal globalization paradigm shifts at the local levels of social work practice and not only presents them as selected trends, but candidly offers the "stories behind the trends."

Community Devolution: Federal → State → Local

Holosko (2009) documented the omnipresent globalization of the devolution-revolution phenomena in Canada, United States, Great Britain,

TABLE 120.1 Five Selected Neoliberal Globalization Trends Influencing Social Work Practice

Selected Trends	The "Stories Behind the Trends"
1. Community devolution: Federal → state → local	1. More local accountability 2. "Crazy Glue Syndrome"- YTI-YOI
2. Community "problem reconfiguration"	1. Communities lag behind the concept 2. Matching mandates to problems
3. Community "capacity-building"	1. No definition of capacity 2. No resource to build
4. Integrative approaches to service delivery	1. Define partners and stakeholders 2. Develop more collaborations
5. "Era of legitimacy"	1. Evaluation of program and services 2. Interventions → outcomes

and Sweden. He demonstrated how: (a) the devolution-revolution is relatively immune to the political ideology of the country; (b) it always shifts both funding and authority for social welfare service provision downward from federal → state → local levels; and, (c) often times, local infrastructures or their resource allocating systems are inadequately prepared to assume such responsibilities, which are now plunked squarely at the feet of the local community agencies (Holosko, 2009). In turn, the resultant effects of more locally administered but under-resourced care significantly impacts our definitions of what "community care" really means.

The story behind this trend includes, first, that more local accountability is accrued to the community's actual system of care—which if reframed from a strengths-based perspective may not be such a bad or negative thing. Holosko concluded: "the 'devolution-revolution' to local levels therefore, provides social work with a unique opportunity to build on its history and legacy of providing ethical and humane services to the vulnerable populations in the very communities in which they reside" (p. 128).

The second story (in Table 120.1, Trend 1) has to do with the so-called "Crazy Glue Syndrome" or YTI → YOI ! The latter refers to the colloquial North American phrase—"You Touch It → You Own It!" Here, as the responsibility for providing services gets passed along locally, community agencies are now "on the hook," to provide these essential services. And, when such agencies ask for state, and/or federal help to assist with this mandate, they are frequently reminded that—"there is no money," "we don't fund these programs any more," or "it is not our responsibility to do so" (Holosko, 2000). Finally, here it becomes very apparent that local leaders need to take more proactive roles in redefining their own communities of care, as well as their problems, challenges, or concerns in providing competent services to clients (Holosko & Barner, 2013). Over two decades ago, Osborne and Gaebler (1992) called on lead governmental officials to learn to reinvent how they govern, namely, by acting as facilitators for their governments to function and serve the communities in ways that strengthen their local economies. They stated:

. . . city government will have to make some adjustments and in some ways re-define its traditional role... The city will more often find itself in the role of defining problems and then assembling resources for others to use in addressing those problems... City government will have to become even more willing to inter-weave scarce public and private resources in order to achieve our community's goals. (p. 27)

The extent to which local governments have evolved in re-shaping and offering leadership in their respective communities is not well known or documented.

Community "Problem" Reconfiguration

There has been a decided shift in the quiet devolution-revolution to developing social welfare programs, interventions and services in communities, not from a population or demographic imperative—but from a "problem reconfiguration" one. Here, the community's problems are prioritized, based on the so-called "problems of individuals in the community." So, depending on "the problems the community has," and the existing infrastructures—if one is fortunate enough to end up with a problem that this community "has identified"—care can be accessed.

Conversely, if one's problems do not match up with "the community problems", clients must travel [if they can], to what is usually an adjacent community to receive care (Feit & Holosko, 2013). For example, in Canada's universal health care system, smaller towns and cities cannot afford highly specialized health care for all citizens. As a result, many Canadians are accustomed to driving to, or being airlifted to, adjacent communities that have the specialized care they require and have come to expect (Holosko, 1997).

The stories behind this reality are noted in Table 120.1, Trend 2. Communities clearly lag behind this concept, and they have difficulties matching their infrastructures and mandates to the ever-changing "problems of the community." To exemplify the stories behind this trend, Brown and Stevens (2006) studied seven U.S. communities that aimed to expand health coverage to the uninsured and improve their care [the main current political agenda of President Obama]. Funded by the Robert Wood Johnson Foundation's *Communities in Charge* (CIC) program, when these communities [with identified community problems] were evaluated they concluded that: "despite solid leadership and carefully crafted plans, political, economic, and organizational obstacles precluded much expansion of coverage and constrained reforms … CIC's record offers little evidence that communities are better equipped than are other sectors of U.S. society to solve the problems of un-insurance" (Brown & Stevens, 2006, p. W150).

Many social workers become acutely aware of the limited resources available for clients in their own communities. This forces them, by default, to expand on their definition of just what "local community care" is—to a more expansive one involving a greater geographic area beyond the local community. This, in turn, presents a new set of resource challenges for social workers, such as: networking with these new service providers; new wait list protocols; service availability; access to services; cost; formal and informal supports for clients in these new geographic areas; referrals; and transportation for services.

Community Capacity-building

Although it is a rather noble idea, the concept of community capacity-building has seen renewed interest in the health and human service field. Similarly, some researchers asserted that that "community has gained increasing prominence

as the central locus for" the search for collaborative approaches to policy development, service delivery, and research (Masuda, Creighton, Nixon, & Frankish, 2010, p. 280).

Community capacity-building refers to the ability and will of the people residing in a community to participate in actions based on community interests, both as individuals, and group organizations and networks (Williams, 2004, p. 730). The definition itself is not problematic, but its underpinning is fraught with two rather questionable assumptions. The first is that *community based groups are synonymous with capacity-building*. Indeed, this is the dominant and traditional way that capacity-building is described in the literature (Abdul et al., 2012; Suwanbamrung, 2010). However, Williams (2004) demonstrated how informal one-to-one groups and engagement are a more popular form of community involvement. They are also more characteristic of the participatory culture of less affluent populations—such as the vulnerable clients whom we routinely see on our social work caseloads. Similarly, Shirlow and Murtagh (2004) concluded their analyses of communities in Ireland, stating that if capacity-building is ever to take hold, it will have to change the assumption of affiliation of community members with community groups and reach deeper, into the concerns of local citizenry, rather than the priorities of statutory funders, as a basis for meaningful service provision and local planning.

The second rather spurious assumption about this trend is that *residing in a community implies a sense of community belonging*. Studies have shown that if one has a "sense of community," one has a greater likelihood of viewing the community positively, and will be more likely to participate in community capacity development, through bonds of unity and support and satisfaction (Bowen, Mancini, Martin, Ware, & Nelson, 2003; Bowen, Martin, Mancini, & Nelson, 2000; McMillan & Chavis, 1986). More to the truth, to many individuals, residing in any community means nothing more than a place to close their door to the external world, or a place to sleep at night. To infer that residence itself brings a greater sense of inclusive belonging, or a willingness to feel connected to one's community, or to feel attachment and some sort of well-being, is remiss from a social and/or psychological perspective (Brown, Altman, & Werner, 2012; Buchecker, 2009). It is no wonder then, that capacity-building indicators are delimited by the variables of: person and family, neighborhood, one's health status, one's values, the community, demographics, income, county, state, resources, the economy of the community, its civic leadership, and by the will of individuals not to feel connected at all to their respective communities (Robert Wood Johnson Foundation, 2007, www.rwf.org/reports/grr/044682.htm). Such assumptions need to be more seriously addressed by community planners, if the issue of capacity-building is ever to take hold in North America in any meaningful way.

If there is really no consensus definition of capacity, so how do we envision building one? The lack of clarity around this definition and its potential negative impact for capacity-building was tabled by Levitas (2000) who stated:

my first worry about 'capacity-building' as about 'community development', is that it often seems to be a way of expecting groups of people who are poorly resourced to pull themselves up by their collective boot straps. So-called social capital is expected to take the place of economic capital. (p. 196)

This is just one of many deleterious effects of not being able to clearly define capacity-building.

From a social work perspective and using a strengths-based orientation, it appears that one's individual capacity is limitless. However, if community capacity-building is to be effective, it must have clear benchmarks delineated for success. Further, specific interventions should be marketed and targeted for specific groups, and communities should be allowed to define their community within the nature of the intervention/initiative being implemented in their respective community (Feit & Holosko, 2013; Holosko & Feit, 2006). In addition, both an understanding of the community environment itself linked with *source appropriate* information, meaning obtaining the right information from the right people, is paramount, if capacity-building is to ever have any success (www.rwf.org/reports/grr/044682.htm).

Finally here, the issue of "resources to build" a community's capacity is almost never considered, but in studies of actual capacity-building efforts, this issue is not trite (Blank, Jacobson, Melaville, 2012; Bowen et al., 2003; Shirlow & Murtagh, 2004). Capacity-building is a transformative process, and one that is time consuming and vulnerable to the local economy and political reality of any community. Given that capacity building

is also linked directly to community resources, social workers more so than other professionals, quickly come to understand the actual reality of their community's resource capacities to provide interventions to their clients.

Integrative Approaches to Service Delivery

Due to the previously noted trends of devolution and fiscal cutbacks for North American HSOs, services and providers have become collaboratively bundled together with multiple agencies offering a defined system of care in their respective communities (Cook, Michener, Lyn, Lobach, & Johnson, 2010). These are often referred to as cross-sectional collaborations—networks, alliances, or partnerships among public, secular, and faith-based nonprofits, and for-profit organizations. They may be so-called self-organizing networks, consisting of distinct organizations that develop relationships among one another in order to meet client needs. Or, they may be community organizations subcontracted with a lead organization, which is expected to create a mandated community-based network of service providers (Alexander, 1995; Provan & Milward, 2001; Whelan, 2011). The latter (the lead organization model) is the more preferred approach between the two because, to be frank, it is cheaper. Ideally, however, both arrangements are expected to yield the benefits of increased efficiency, innovation, local adaptation, increased flexibility, and enhanced community ties (Graddy & Chen, 2006, p. 534).

This idea is certainly tenable and required for an HSO's survival in today's reality, but again (as with Trend 3 above), the concept is ahead of the community's ability to implement it. The previously noted proverbial "clouds of uncertainty" about integrative service approaches loom large over issues of cost; organizational, programmatic, and community influence; democratic and consensual accountability; efficiency and effectiveness; integrative models that are viable and ones that are not; organizational and community care constraints and contingencies; community capacities; access; outcomes; policy considerations; and network size and scope (Bryson, Crosby, & Stone, 2006; Dunlop & Holosko, 2004; Graddy & Chen, 2006; Knitzer & Cooper, 2006). Despite such uncertainty, HSOs continue to move forward with this seemingly altruistic community-spirited ideal.

The neoliberal deficit reduction strategies of federal, state, and local governments has led to a resurgence of interest in community collaboration (Foreman Kready, 2011). Increasingly, mandates for collaboration are linked to conditions of funding. As governments mandate collaborative networks as an implementation mechanism for integrating social welfare services, empirical studies about how interorganizational collaboration is implemented among community partners is an emerging research, policy, and practice problem (Babiak, 2009; Bryson, Crosby, & Stone, 2006; Dunlop & Holosko, 2004; Sytch, Tatarynowicz, & Gulati, (n.d.)).

Frontline social workers, their supervisors, and HSO administrators need to be mindful of some important issues or the real "stories behind the story of collaboration" (Holosko, 2009). Here are just a few:

1. *Funding Issues Require Collaboration*— Regardless of the "will" to collaborate, such partnerships will be tied to funding. Those HSOs who do so will thrive and those who do not will wither away. Developing relationships with partners in the community, however strained, is integral to organizational survival.

2. *Voluntary versus Mandatory Collaboration*—Although some joint agreements are voluntary and others mandatory, the nature of the collaborative relationship transcends this distinction (Dunlop & Holosko, 2004). This means that agencies collaborate to ensure funding and typically will do anything they can to make the collaborative relationship work (Holosko & Dunlop, 1992).

3. *All Communities are Not Created Equal*—Communities vary in their demographics, organizational relationships, service networks, preexisting partnerships, resources, and infrastructures. Collaborations magnify such inequalities. Thus, some communities are able to develop more effective collaboration networks than others.

4. *Evaluation Complexities*—Evaluating collaborative initiatives has been challenging to say the least (Holosko & Dunlop, 1992). These initiatives are typically multisite and multilevel, with different programs/ goals/objectives/costs/outcomes/services/ stakeholders, etc., (Buckingham & Coffman, 1999; Dunlop & Holosko, 2004). The

assumption put forward in this global devolution-revolution movement is that complex community-based collaborations are more efficient than singular service delivery models. This has never been empirically determined or validated (Kee, 1999).

5. *Collaborations are More Likely to Succeed When They Have Legitimacy*— Human & Provan (2000) cited three necessary conditions for collaborative networks: (1) legitimacy of the *network as a form* that can attract internal and external supports, (2) legitimacy of the *network as an entity* responsible to both insiders and outsiders, and (3) legitimacy of the *network as an interaction* that builds trust among members to freely communicate with one another (Feit & Holosko, 2013, p. 26).

Era of Legitimacy

Never before in our North American social welfare history has evaluation and its focus on outcomes been "part and parcel" of the mandated delivery of HSO programs and services. Indeed, we are no longer on the frontier of program and practice evaluation activity, but are in the midst of a groundswell of such activities becoming mainstream in federal and state social welfare initiatives, programs, and services (Holosko, 2009). Thus, public scrutiny of the financing and efficiency of HSOs is more apparent than it ever was before. We have evolved from offering social welfare programs directed by the rather noble motives of altruism and case wisdom, or "a need for such services"—to much more legitimizing ways of providing educational, health, and social services. These include the empirical testing of interventions; developing more empirically defined protocols for our interventions; developing pilot projects to justify larger initiatives; ensuring interventions are tied to frameworks (i.e., logic models) and outcomes; developing organizational and community capacities to ensure success of interventions; funding initiatives with the assurance of self-sustainability over a shorter time period; ensuring that funded social welfare initiatives include timely best, and/or promising practices; and ensuring that funded programs/services are both effective and efficient.

Generally, program, practice, and intervention evaluations serve as both the validation and legitimacy for many social welfare programs, and it is almost unconscionable in today's climate to allocate funds to such programs without building in money for evaluation costs. Outside of the aegis of government, numerous private and charitable foundations have stepped "up to the plate" here, and pushed the national agenda for evaluations of federal and state welfare programs forward. They have also had much success in advancing our evaluative knowledge in the areas of methodology; theoretical applications; using models to evaluate performance contracting; providing more timely programs and service; and linking interventions to outcomes, pilot tests, and evidence-based practices.

Finally here, all interventions require not just a traditional focus on inputs and outputs, but also (now) on outcomes and sustainable impacts (W. K. Kellogg Foundation website reference for program logic model: http://www .wkkf.org/knowledge-center/resources/2006/02/ wk-kellogg-foundation-logic-model-development-guide.aspx). And these must be assessed empirically with a view to what it costs to provide such interventions. Clements, Chianca, and Sasaki (2008) said it succinctly when they stated: "… evaluations should estimate the total impacts that can be attributed to an intervention and also estimate the intervention's cost effectiveness… Also, evaluations of this nature are likely to be more helpful for program managers" (p. 196). Given that the current social work model is now driven by costs, it appears that soon the cost benefit or cost effectiveness of all social work interventions will need to be tabled as a bona fide agenda for all HSOs.

CONCLUDING REMARKS

With "Obama Care" on the horizon in the American political landscape, requiring a re-thinking and retooling about how social welfare, health care, and social services will be provided, financed, and configured for all Americans, the issues presented herein about external trends emanating from neoliberal globalization become important for all service providers in general, and social workers in particular. This chapter sought to illuminate such trends as they are now squarely placed at the feet of frontline practitioners working in and out of communities of care. The very real challenges of providing effective and efficient care for our clients will require the profession to think more deeply about not only how to provide such care, but how to educate our BSW and MSW students appropriately to do so.

WEB RESOURCES

1. The Consequences of Globalization and Neoliberal Practices. What are the Alternatives? http://www.globalresearch .ca/the-consequences-of-globalization-and-neoliberal-policies-what-are-the-alternatives/7973
2. Another Angry Voice. What is neoliberalism? http://anotherangryvoice .blogspot.com/2012/09/ what-is-neoliberalism-explained.html
3. Clune, M. W. When neoliberalism exploded. http://www.salon.com/2013/03/09/ the_world_according_to_milton_friedman_ partner/
4. World Economic Forum. News Release: New report identifies most important global issues for 2011. http://www.weforum .org/news/new-report-identifies-m ost-important-global-issues-2011?news=page

References

Abdul, R. A., Zaid, M. M., Suradin, A., Hassan, R., Hamzah, A., Khalifah, Z. (2012). Community capacity building for sustainable tourism development: Experience from Miso Walai Homestay. *Business & Management Review, 2*(5), 10–19.

Alexander, E. (1995). How organizations act together: Interorganizational coordination in theory and practice. Luxembourg: Gordon and Breach.

Babiak, K. M. (2009). Criteria of effectiveness in multiple cross-sectoral interorganizational relationships. *Evaluation and Program, 32*(1), 1–12.

Blank, M. J., Jacobson, R., & Melaville, A. (2012). *Achieving results through community school partnerships: How district and community leaders are building effective, sustainable relationships.* Washington, DC: Center for American Progress.

Bowen, G. L., Martin, J. A., Mancini, J. A., & Nelson, J. P. (2000). Community capacity: Antecedents and consequences. *Journal of Community Practice, 8*(2), 1–21.

Bowen, G. L., Mancini, J. A., Martin, J. A., Ware, W. B., & Nelson, J. P. (2003). Promoting the adaption of military families: An empirical test of a community practice model. *Family Relations, 52,* 33–52.

Brown, B., Altman, I., & Werner, C. M. (2012). Place Attachment. *International Encyclopedia of Housing and Home*, 183–188. doi:10.1016/B978-0-08-047163-1.00543-9.

Brown, L. D., & Stevens, B. (2006). Charge of the right brigade? Communities, coverage, and care for the uninsured. *Health Affairs, 25*(3), w150–w161.

Bryson, J. M., Crosby, B., & Stone, M. (2006). The design and implementation of cross-sector collaborations: Proposals from the literature. *Public Administration Review, 66*(6), 44–55.

Buchecker, M. (2009). Withdrawal from the Local Public Place: Understanding the Process of Spatial Alienation. *Landscape Research, 34*(3), 279–297. doi:10.1080/01426390902867968.

Buckingham, M., & Coffman, C. (1999). *First, break all the rules.* New York, NY: Simon & Schuster.

Case Management Society of America (CMSA). (2010). Standards of practice for case management. Retrieved from www.cmsa.org

Case Management Society of Australia (CMSA). (2013). Retrieved from http://www.cmsa.org.au/

Clements, P., Chianca, T., & Sasaki, R. (2008). Reducing world poverty by improving evaluation of developmental aid. *American Journal of Evaluation, 29*(2), 195–214.

Conrad N. Hilton Foundation. (2011). Step by step: A comprehensive approach to case management. Retrieved from www.familyhomelessness.org

Cook, J. J., Michener, J. L., Lyn, M. M., Lobach, D. D., & Johnson, F. F. (2010). Community collaboration to improve care and reduce health disparities. *Health Affairs, 29*(5), 956–958. doi:10.1377/hlthaff.2010.0094

Dunlop, J., & Holosko, M. (2004). The story behind the story of collaborative networks—relationships do matter! *Journal of Health and Social Policy, 19*(3), 1–18.

Feit, M. D., & Holosko, M. (2013). *Distinguishing Clinical from Upper Level Management in Social Work.* London, UK: Taylor & Francis.

Foreman Kready, S. B. (2011). *Organizational culture and partnership process: A grounded theory study of community-campus partnerships.* (Unpublished doctoral dissertation). Virginia Commonwealth University, Richmond, Virginia.

Graddy, E., & Chen, B. (2006). Influences on the size and scope of networks for social delivery. *Journal of Public Administration Research and Theory, 16*, 533–552.

Holosko, M. J. (2009). Global realities of social policy: The devolution revolution. *Journal of Social Work in Public Health, 24*(3), 189–190.

Holosko, M. J. (1997). Service user input: Fact or fiction? The evaluation of the trauma program, Department of Rehabilitation, Sault Ste. Marie, Ontario. *The Canadian Journal of Program Evaluation, 11*(2), 111–126.

Holosko, M. (2000). The churches' response to welfare reform in America: Focus on the southeastern states. In L. Nackerud & M. Robinson (Eds.), *Early implications of welfare reform in the Southeast.* Huntington, NY: Nova Sciences Publishers, Inc.

Holosko, M., & Dunlop, J. (1992). Evaluating interorganizational approaches to service delivery: A case example of the Family Violence Service Project in Kent County, Ontario. *The Canadian Journal of Program Evaluation, 7*(2), 115–129.

Holosko, M. J., & Feit, M. D. (2006). Living in poverty in America today. *Journal of Health and Social Policy, 21*(1), 119–131.

Human, S., & Provan, K. (2000). Legitimacy building in the evolution of small-firm multi-lateral networks: A comparative study of success and demise. *Administrative Science Quarterly, 45*(2), 327–365.

Kee, J. (1999). At what price? Benefit-cost analysis and cost-effectiveness analysis in program evaluation. *The Evaluation Exchange, V*(2/3), 1–4.

Kellogg, W. K. (2006). W. K. Kellogg Foundation program logic model. Retrieved from http://www.wkkf.org/knowledge-center/resources/2006/02/wk-kellogg-foundation-logic-model-development-guide.aspx

Knitzer, J., & Cooper, J. (2006). Beyond integration: Challenges for children's mental health. *Health Affairs, 25*(3), 670–679.

Levitas, R. (2000). Community, utopia and new labour. *Local Economy, 15*(3), 188–97.

Martinez, E., & Garcia, A. (1997). What is neoliberalism?: A brief definition for activists. CORP Watch: Holding Corporations Accountable. Retrieved from http://www.corpwatch.org/article.php?id=376

Masuda, J. R., Creighton, G., Nixon, S., & Frankish, J. (2010). Building capacity for community-based participatory research for health disparities in Canada: The case of "Partnerships in Community Health Research." *Health Promotion Practice, 12*(2), 280–292.

McMillan, D. W., & Chavis, D. M. (1986). Sense of community: A definition and theory. *Journal of Community Psychology, 14*(1), 6–23.

National Association of Social Workers. (2009). *Code of ethics.* Retrieved from http://www.socialworkers.org/pubs/code/default.asp.

Nilep, C. (2012). On socialism, liberalism, and neoliberalism. *Society for Linguistic Anthropology.* Retrieved from http://linguisticanthropology.org/blog/2012/02/16/on-socialism-liberalism-and-neo-liberalism/

Olivia. (July 9, 2011). *Difference between liberalism and neoliberalism.* Retrieved from http://www.differencebetween.com/difference-between-liberalism-and-vs-neoliberalism/

Osborne, D., & Gaebler, T. (1992). *Reinventing government.* Reading, MA: Addison-Wesley, Inc.

Shirlow, P., & Murtagh, B. (2004). Capacity-building, representation and intracommunity conflict. *Urban Studies, 41*(1), 57–70.

SUNY Levin Institute. (2013). *What is globalization?* Retrieved from http://www.globalization101.org/what-is-globalization

Suwanbamrung, C. (2010). Community capacity for sustainable community-based dengue prevention and control: Domain, assessment tool and capacity building model. *Asian Pacific Journal of Tropical Medicine, 3*(6), 499–504.

Sytch, M., Tatarynowicz, A., & Gulati, R. (n.d). Toward a theory of extended contact: The incentives and opportunities for bridging across network communities. *Organization Science, 23*(6), 1658–1681.

Whelan, C. (2011). Network dynamics and network effectiveness: A methodological framework for public sector networks in the field of national security. *Australian Journal of Public Administration, 70*(3), 275–286. doi: 10.1111/j.1467-8500.2011.00735.x

Williams, C. (2004). Community capacity-building: A critical evaluation of the third sector approach. *Review of Social Policy Research, 21*(5), 729–739.

Work and Income. (2013). Our case management approach. Retrieved from http://www.workandincome.govt.nz/about-work-and-income/our-services/our-case-management-approach.html

Community-led Structural Interventions as Community Practice

121   *A Review of Initiatives in Haiti and India*

Toorjo Ghose

INTRODUCTION

Structural factors such as societal stigma, lack of shelter, inadequate access to care and draconian laws undermine the physical and mental health of marginalized communities. The Centers for Disease Control and the World Health Organization have called for interventions to focus on these structural factors influencing health behaviors (Centers for Disease Control and Prevention [CDC], 2010). Scholars have recognized the benefits of community engagement in addressing these structural challenges, noting that such participation helps to identify problems accurately, sustain interventions, and use resources efficiently (Blankenship, Bray, &

Merson, 2000; Meheux, Dominey-Howes, & Lloyd, 2010). Blankenship and colleagues (2010) define community-based initiatives that target community-specific contextual factors as community-led structural interventions (CLSI) that seek to influence health conditions by improving the awareness and acceptability of interventions, and increasing community access to them. This chapter draws on two CLSIs, one in a postearthquake encampment community in Haiti, and another in a sex work community in India, to describe a protocol for community practice. Research on these two CLSIs have identified three main stages that describe the community practice protocol in both contexts: (1) establishing coalitions and goals, (2) identifying needs and developing resources, and (3) sustaining efforts through the expansion of resources and the engagement of civil society institutions.

STAGE 1: DEVELOPING COALITIONS AND GOALS

Establishing Partners and Aligning Agendas: Scholars have highlighted the difficulty of gaining access to a community and establishing trust (Israel, Schulz, Parker, & Becker, 1998). Developing links with organizations operating in the community is one way to negotiate these challenges. In Haiti, the CLSI sought to establish HIV services in encampments that sprung up after the devastating earthquake of 2010 (Ghose, Boucicaut, King, & Shubert, 2013a; Ghose, Boucicaut, King, Doyle, & Shubert, 2013b). The initiative was implemented by a coalition comprised of community advocates living in the encampments, a Haitian network of 14 community-based HIV service providers, a U.S. community-based agency that is a major HIV service provider in the United States, and a research team from a U.S. university. The coalition was formed before the earthquake, on the basis of shared agendas and advocacy platforms. The Haitian service providers came together as a network in response to the manner in which larger institutional service providers failed to address the needs of marginalized groups and yet received most of the foreign and governmental aid flowing into the country. This critique of institutional gaps in services resonated with the U.S. agency, a vocal advocate for marginalized People Living With HIV/AIDS (PLWHA) in that country. The agency, which employed a number of Haitian counselors in New York, sought relationships with HIV service provision agencies in Haiti even before the earthquake. It forged ties with the Haitian service providers' network, with the latter inviting the U.S. agency to partner in a technical advisory role to build service capacity in Haiti. Immediately after the earthquake, the U.S. agency was one of the first to enter Haiti to provide aid, and linked up with the Haitian network of HIV providers to address the HIV needs of newly displaced encampment residents.

In India, the CLSI known as the Sonagachi HIV Intervention Project (SHIP) was initiated when Dr. Smarajit Jana of the governmental agency, the All India Institute of Physical Hygiene (AIIPH), collaborated with sex worker networks in the community to recruit and train sex workers to go door-to-door discussing sexual health with brothel residents (Basu et al., 2004; Cornish, & Ghosh, 2007; Ghose, Swendeman, George, & Chowdhury, 2008). Building on its initial success in recruiting peers and reducing risk behaviors (Basu et al., 2004; Swendeman, Basu, Das, Jana, & Rotheram-Borus, 2009) the program grew and became a collective of sex workers known as Durbar Mahila Samanwaya Committee (DMSC). As in the case in Haiti, the CLSI was launched when various stakeholders succeeded in aligning with one another's agendas. Rather than taking on the traditional role of an expert interventionist, Dr. Jana chose to collaborate with sex workers in educating the community. Most importantly, the CLSI resisted the move to rescue women from engaging in sex work, a routine intervention strategy for the sex work community at the time. Instead, the push to make working conditions safe for sex workers was a platform that sex workers and government educators could all sign on to, given that it reduced the HIV risk environment for sex workers, without preventing them from plying their trade. Thus the Haitian and Indian CLSIs indicate that the initial community partnerships were established by (1) activating established links between agencies and partners and (2) stake holders aligning their agendas and approaches.

It is important to note that the resultant coalitions looked markedly different from traditional nongovernmental organizations (NGOs) or agencies operating in the community. Scholars have noted that these traditional service NGOs in Haiti and India are usually operated by people outside the community who are educated and well-off, resulting in class divides between NGO workers and their clients, and creating institutional barriers against local participation (Chatterjee, 2008; James, 2010; Louis-Juste, 2007; Schuller, 2007). The coalitions in Haiti and India are populated predominantly by community members and resist the manner in which traditional NGOs operate in the community. In Haiti, the coalition came together precisely because aid was being funneled to traditional institutional NGOs and service providers that tended to ignore marginalized communities in encampments. In India, the coalition departed from the traditional strategy employed by most NGOs, namely, rescuing sex workers from their lot. Taken together, the elements of this first stage of CLSIs indicate that community practice needs to be initiated through coalitions that include community members and prioritize strategies that emerge from the community.

Developing Goals and Objectives: While the linking of agendas ensured that all the partners in the collaborations had a similar orientation, both initiatives engaged in a process of developing goals and objectives in order to make outcomes and pathways to them more concrete.

In Haiti, because the coalition was concerned with the dearth of HIV services in the encampment community, developing service capacity was the goal of the initiative. Linked to that goal was the need to base services and advocacy on empirical evidence. The three partners identified four objectives for the initiative: conduct collaborative research on the needs of PLWHA in the encampments, develop the local capacity to gather that evidence, develop services based on the research results, and develop ways to sustain efforts to expand HIV service capacity in the encampments.

In India, faced with an increasingly violent and repressive environment to conduct sex work, the collaborators decided to identify the factors contributing to the risk environment in the community, to establish governance structures that could implement changes in the community, and to engage resources outside the sex work community in order to sustain the implemented interventions. The goals and objectives identified in this step helped to guide the action research projects and the development of resources in the next phase.

STAGE 2: IDENTIFYING NEEDS AND DEVELOPING RESOURCES

An examination of the two CLSIs indicates that community resources were developed in Stage Two through action research and the development of capacity.

Identifying Needs and Strategies Through Action Research: Research was a critical component of both initiatives, given the lack of knowledge about the respective communities, and the need to capture the attention of policy makers and aid agencies by advocating for evidence-based practices. Guided by action research principles (Israel et al., 1998), the research linked academic scholars and the community, included community members as equal research partners, assessed community needs, evaluated community-based intervention strategies, and developed research capacity in the community in order to sustain research efforts in the future.

In Haiti, the coalition decided to recruit community members and train them in qualitative research methods. In order to develop research capacity in the community, the workshops sought to train the team members to become trainers themselves. The community members' knowledge about the community, access to hidden populations within it such as gay, lesbian, bisexual, and transgendered people living with HIV, and familiarity with the encampment conditions helped to frame the research questions and recruit research participants. The research highlighted the need for basic nutrition, clean water, places to store HIV medication and HIV support services, especially for vulnerable groups such as women, children, and gay, lesbian, bisexual, and transgendered residents.

In India, several action research initiatives brought together academic partners with the sex work community in order to examine the structural conditions that molded the risk environment for sex workers. In one such project funded by a grant from the National Institutes of Health, a team of scholars from several universities in the United States trained sex workers in qualitative methods in order to examine the manner in which the laws pertaining to sex work were influencing risk behaviors in the community. In another, academic partners trained community members in survey research methods to assess the manner in which collectivization as sex workers influenced mental health outcomes and related risk behaviors among sex workers (Ghose, Chowdhuri, Ali, & Solomon, In Press). These action research initiatives helped to document community needs, excavate community-based strategies to address them, and develop research capacity in the community.

Developing Resources Through Community-based Organizations: Responding to the needs identified through the action research projects, both initiatives worked toward establishing community-based institutions to address them. In Haiti, the collaborative began a community clinic that addressed the HIV needs of tent residents. HIV service providers in the U.S.-based AIDS service organization, along with nursing faculty from a U.S. nursing school, trained clinic medical staff in conducting HIV assessments, in HIV medication and its side effects, and in case management around the psychosocial needs of PLWHA and HIV-related risk behaviors. The clinic became a site where the collaboration's team members met and bolstered their ability to provide HIV services to the community. While formal training ensured the transfer of skills from one set of stake-holders to another within the team, informal conversations between team members helped to change attitudes. Ghose et al. (2013a) note that these conversations sensitized service providers who had never before worked with gay, lesbian, bisexual, and transgendered clients, to this population's needs and the barriers that they faced in accessing services.

In India, the action research results led to the formation of a self-regulatory board (SRB) in the sex work community that brought together various community stake-holders in order to address the legal environment surrounding sex work (Ghose, 2011). The initial collaboration invited sex workers, madams (female brothel managers), personnel from the police, university researchers, government officials, and members of nongovernmental organizations operating in the red light area to join the board. The presence of noted politicians and scholars helped allay the fears of the police and madams, and of natural antagonists in the community. Guided by results of the action research, The SRB identified draconian laws and police practices as a significant risk factor for sex workers, leaving them vulnerable to getting arrested and forcing them underground, leading to risky sex practices. Moreover, the police personnel on the committee were able to impress on the madams the importance of ensuring that sex work did not disrupt the activities of the neighborhood.

The SRB organized workshops with the police and sex workers to highlight these risks, significantly reducing predatory policing practices in the neighborhood. Madams ensured that sex workers living in their brothels would be respectful of neighborhood residents and adhere to higher standards of safety and hygiene. The SRB has now become a community resource for sex workers who are being targeted by the police. Neighborhood police also recognize it as the body to approach if they have concerns about the sex work community, instead of implementing the raids on the community that were the norm in the past.

STAGE 3: SUSTAINING EFFORTS

At both sites, efforts by the collaborations were sustained through the expansion of resources and the negotiation of political opportunities.

Expanding Resources: Resources needed to be immediately expanded to target marginalized communities who were in dire need of services. The action research initiative highlighted the vulnerability of encampment residents like sex workers; gay, lesbian, bisexual, and transgendered people living with HIV; and children known as *Resteveks*, who were orphans staying with relatives or other adults and often working for them as indentured servants. In order to address these expanded goals, the coalition sought funding from various sources. The Elton John Foundation has funded an initiative to assess seroprevalence among men who have sex with men and implement interventions with them. Grants have been submitted to implement interventions with these communities to the National Institutes of Health and the MAC AIDS foundation. Moreover, given the challenges of procuring their medication in hospitals and large institutional HIV service providers in Haiti, the community clinic is securing a license to prescribe medication on-site.

In India, the research and the work of the SRB highlighted the manner in which the HIV-risk environment was linked to issues of economic sustenance and opportunity for sex workers' children. As a result, the sex workers' collective has developed a microbanking and microfinance initiative, and a school for sex workers' children. The collaboration has successfully utilized its varied membership to cast a wide net for grants and funding for these initiatives.

Engaging Political and Civil Society Institutions: Responding to structural and political forces shaping the risk environment at both sites, the initiatives in Haiti and India have actively targeted political and civil society institutions.

In Haiti, the collaboration targeted major conferences, policy makers, and aid personnel to secure resources for the encampments. The coalition partners attended the International AIDS Conference in Vienna in 2011, organizing panels, marches, and protests to highlight the dire situation of people living with HIV in the camps. In 2011 and 2012, the coalition attended the North American Housing and HIV/AIDS Research Summits and presented the action research assessment results to influential policy makers in the

U.S. government and the United Nations. The special representative of the Secretary General of the United Nations in Haiti expressed his agreement with the assessment findings and initiated discussions to involve the coalition in policy decisions about HIV service provision in the camps.

In India, the establishment of the SRB, which included various stake holders in the community, helped to engage various civic institutions outside the sex work community. The members of the government who attended the SRB helped to incorporate DMSC into health policy initiatives, resulting in the State's first public advertising campaign promoting condom use through peers talking about safe sex—a strategy implemented successfully in the sex work community. Given its links to both stakeholders, the SRB has also become an important mediator between the police and the sex work community. The success of the SRB was documented by the scholars in the initiative, leading to the World Health Organization hailing DMSC as a model structural-intervention (Gupta, Parkhurst, Ogden, Aggleton, & Mahal, 2008). Taking note of the growing importance of the SRB and its activities, State and national HIV agencies have invited DMSC to partner with them in HIV policy formulation and implementation (Ghose, 2011). In 2012, the Supreme Court of India appointed DMSC to a committee overseeing the rights of sex workers nationally, overruling the objections of the national government to its membership on the committee, given DMSC's support of decriminalizing sex work.

DISCUSSION

The protocol described above was facilitated by the activation of existing partnerships, the development of research and service resources in the community, and the use of feedback loops, as well as the engagement of civil society processes that allowed the initiatives to expand the scope of efforts on the ground (Figure 121.1). The elements and stages described in Figure 121.1 allow social workers a variety of opportunities to engage in community practice.

Utilizing Existing Partnerships: The activation of established relationships among scholars, community agencies, and community members was crucial to the success of both initiatives. Social workers seeking to engage the community need to draw on existing relationships with networks and partners who are able to make useful contributions and are legitimate community advocates. Specifically, the results of this review indicate that social workers seeking to initiate engagement in the community need to (1) become members of teams of professionals whose knowledge and expertise is needed in the community, (2) work with established community-based organizations, and (3) identify goals and objectives in a collaborative manner with stakeholders.

Helping to Build Resources: Social workers are integral to the enterprise of building community resources, as described in Stage Two of the protocol. Research was a crucial component of both initiatives, given the lack of knowledge about the conditions of the community, and the necessity to inform policy makers and aid agencies about the needs of residents. Guided by action research principles (Israel et al., 1998), social workers at both sites were instrumental in engaging in research that included community members as equal research partners. Moreover, social workers helped to train community-based researchers and service providers at both sites. Social workers seeking to build community capacity in this stage of the protocol need to engage various community stakeholders in a collaborative research process and facilitate the transfer of skills through training and workshops.

Expanding the Scope of Efforts: The protocol of engagement initially addressed short-term goals. The fulfillment of these led to identifying further needs and issues, which, in turn, informed the broadening of goals and strategies. Feedback loops ensured that each stage in Figure 120.1 was not only being informed by processes and decisions in the previous stage, but also by developments in subsequent stages. For instance in Haiti, assessment results in Stage Two highlighted the plight of hidden encampment populations, triggering an expansion of Stage One goals to address the needs of these marginalized groups. This, in turn, triggered a reformulation of strategies in Stage Three, whereby efforts to sustain the initiative included targeting resources for these communities. Similarly, in India, the identification of economic vulnerability as a key contributor to the sexual risk environment of the community enabled the expansion of Stage One goals to include economic initiatives such as microfinancing. Our review indicates that a flexible protocol that incorporates

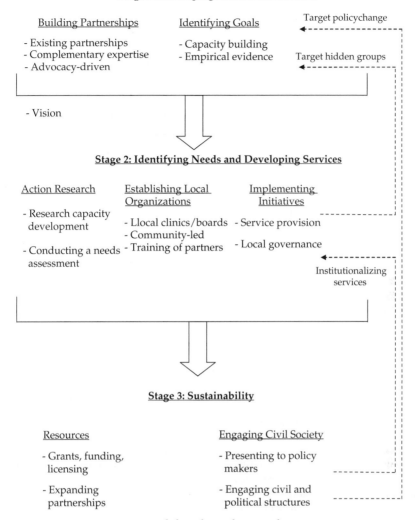

Stage 1: Developing Coalitions and Goals

Building Partnerships

- Existing partnerships
- Complementary expertise
- Advocacy-driven

- Vision

Identifying Goals

- Capacity building
- Empirical evidence

Target policychange

Target hidden groups

Stage 2: Identifying Needs and Developing Services

Action Research

- Research capacity development

- Conducting a needs assessment

Establishing Local Organizations

- Llocal clinics/boards
- Community-led
- Training of partners

Implementing Initiatives

- Service provision

- Local governance

Institutionalizing services

Stage 3: Sustainability

Resources

- Grants, funding, licensing

- Expanding partnerships

Engaging Civil Society

- Presenting to policy makers

- Engaging civil and political structures

Figure 121.1 Community practice protocol (based on Ghose et al., 2013a).

these feedback loops is necessary to address the complex needs of a community incrementally. Social workers played a key role in establishing these feedback loops in both communities, constantly making sure that assessment and evaluation results informed the reformulation of goals in Stage One, and of strategies in Stage Three. They sustained this process by ensuring that the initial coalitions established in Stage One were kept updated on implementation initiatives and assessments at all times.

Finally, social workers ensured that the initiatives were sustained in Stage Three through the engagement of civil society institutions and processes. Community mobilization tactics ensured the successful staging of rallies and political

events in both communities, while presentations made in policy arenas helped to build visibility for both communities.

The protocol described in this chapter relies on the engagement of social work skills such as working with a diverse set of stakeholders in groups, collaborative goal-setting, engaging in community-based participatory research, transferring skills to community members, and negotiating in the civil and political sphere. Although the manner in which each element is executed, and the particular skills required to implement it successfully, can vary across communities, the protocol seeks to provide a useful blueprint for social workers and communities to engage in community practice.

WEBSITES

www.durbar.org
www.housingworks.org/advocate/international/
  haiti
www.housingworks.org/donate/haiti/
www.nationalaidshousing.org, www.nswp.org

References

Basu, I., Jana, S., Rotheram-Borus, M., Swendeman, D., Lee, S., Newman, P., & Weiss, R. (2004). HIV prevention among sex workers in India. *Journal of Acquired Immune Deficiency Syndromes, 36,* 845–852.

Blankenship, K., Bray, S., & Merson, M. (2000). Structural interventions in public health. *AIDS, 14*(Supp 1), S11–21.

Centers for Disease Control and Prevention. (2010). *Establishing a holistic framework to reduce inequities in HIV, viral hepatitis, STDs, and tuberculosis in the United States.* Atlanta, GA: U.S. Department of Health and Human Services, Centers for Disease Control and Prevention.

Chatterjee, P. (2008). Democracy and economic transformations in India. *Economic and Political Weekly, 43*(16), 53–62.

Cornish, F., & Ghosh, R. (2007). The necessary contradictions of "community-led" health promotions: A case-study of HIV prevention in an Indian red-light district. *Social Science & Medicine, 64,* 496–507.

Ghose, T., Swendeman, D., George, S., & Chowdhury, D. (2008). Mobilizing collective identity to reduce HIV risk among sex workers in Sonagachi, India: The boundaries, consciousness, negotiation framework. *Social Science & Medicine, 67,* 311–320.

Ghose, T. (2011). Politicizing political society: Mobilizing sex workers in Sonagachi, Calcutta. In A. Loomba & R. Lukose (Eds.) *Feminist interventions in South Asia.* Durham, NC: Duke University Press.

Ghose, T., Boucicaut, E., King, C., & Shubert, V. (2013a). Stilling the tremors: Resurrecting HIV services in post-earthquake encampments in Haiti. *Journal of International Social Welfare, 22*(4), 374–383.

Ghose, T., Boucicaut, E., King, C., Doyle, A., & Shubert, V. (2013b). Surviving the aftershock: Postearthquake access and adherence to HIV treatment among Haiti's tent residents. *Qualitative Health Research, 23*(4), 495–506.

Ghose, T., Chowdhuri, A., Ali, S., & Solomon, P. (In Press). Implementing the Hospital Anxiety and Depression Scale among sex workers in India. *International Social Work.*

Gupta, G., Parkhurst, J., Ogden, J., Aggleton, P., & Mahal, A. (2008). Structural approaches to HIV prevention. *The Lancet, 37,* 764–775.

Israel, B. A., Schulz, A. J., Parker, E. A., & Becker, A. B. (1998). Review of community-based research: Assessing partnership approaches to improve public health. *Annual Review of Public Health 19*(1), 173.

James, E. C. (2010). Ruptures, rights, and repair: The political economy of trauma in Haiti. *Social Science & Medicine, 70,* 106–113.

Louis-Juste, J. A. (2007). *Haiti, L'Invasion des ONG: la th`ese n'est pas aussi radicale que son sujet* [Haiti, the NGO invasion: the thesis isn't as radical as its subject]. Port-au-Prince: Faculte des Sciences Humaines, Universite d' Etat d'Haiti.

Meheux, K., Dominey-Howes, D., & Lloyd, K. (2010). Natural hazard impacts in small island developing states: A review of current knowledge and future research needs. *Natural Hazards, 40*(2), 429–446.

Schuller, M. (2007). Gluing globalization: NGOs as intermediaries in Haiti. *Political and Legal Anthropology Review, 32,* 84–104.

Swendeman, D., Basu, I., Das, S., Jana, S., & Rotheram-Borus, M. J. (2009). Empowering sex workers in India to reduce vulnerability to HIV and sexually transmitted diseases. *Social Science & Medicine, 69,* 1157–1165.

PART XII

Working with Vulnerable Populations and Persons at Risk

122 Overview of Working with Vulnerable Populations and Persons at Risk

Rowena Fong

Although all people are vulnerable, circumstances and situations make some people more vulnerable than others (Dettlaff & Fong, 2012; Fong, 2004; Fong, McRoy, & Hendricks, 2006). Persons of color, whether born in the United States or abroad, immigrants, refugees, and undocumented persons, and men and women who are gay, lesbian, bisexual, and transgendered (GLBT) experience conflicts to which others in the larger society may not be subjected. These experiences may involve racism, ageism, heterosexism, discrimination, oppression, harassment, hate crimes, rejection, homophobia, ridicule, or unjust misrepresentations.

In this section on vulnerable populations, authors Joshua Miller and Ann Marie Garran (Chapter 123) emphasize that "racism is a process that uses the differences of appearance or culture as a basis for making generalizations about intelligence and trustworthiness to justify systematic acts of subjugation and mistreatment of targeted persons." Social workers working with these vulnerable populations need to be aware of the problems and risk factors imposed on these people and find culturally appropriate interventions and solutions that, as Miller and Garran (2008) advocate, will build a "web of resistance" to dismantle racism and other oppressive attitudes and actions.

Antioppressive practices are "an evolving and contentious variety of different practice approaches and theories oriented towards a social justice perspective" write authors Ishizuka and Husain in their chapter on antioppressive practices (Chapter 124). Social justice is a priority for the oppressed and vulnerable populations who include many people of color for whom social workers solve problems or find resources.

The profession of social work acknowledges the vulnerability of these populations and has taken measures to enforce standards and policies to allow for culturally sensitive considerations. For example, the National Association of Social Work (NASW) *Standards for Cultural Competence in Social Work Practice* (2001) specifically mandates in Standard 3 on cross-cultural knowledge that social workers "shall have and continue to develop specialized knowledge and understanding about the history, traditions, values, family systems, and artistic expressions of major client groups they serve" (p. 1). This requires that social workers take the time to learn about the history and historical trauma, traditions and cultural values, and family systems of African Americans, Latinos and Mexican Americans, Asian and Pacific Islander Americans, and Native Americans as the chapters in this section describe.

In 2006, NASW published *Social Work Speaks: Policy Statements 2006–2009*, which enunciates a commitment to improving policies and practices related to racism; immigrants and refugees; lesbian, gay, and bisexual issues; long-term care; and end-of-life care. The policy statements apply to the vulnerable populations of GLBT persons, as well as documented and undocumented immigrant and refugee individuals and families. The populations of GLBT persons, people of color, both native and foreign-born, exemplifies NASW's and the Council for Social Work

Education (CSWE)'s concerns for diversity issues related to race, gender, age, abilities, and sexual orientation.

People who are targeted because they are different, whether it is because of race, age, gender, sexual orientation, political persuasion, abilities, or socioeconomic class, become vulnerable, feel at risk, and often need support when they experience antioppressive practices. The NASW *Code of Ethics* (1999) mandates that all social workers "help meet the basic needs of all people who are vulnerable, oppressed, and living in poverty" (p. 1). Dignity and worth are basic needs of all people. These basic needs can be facilitated by increased culturally competent knowledge and practices, which this section on vulnerable populations will provide.

DIVERSITY AND ETHNIC POPULATIONS

Several authors in this section draw attention to the broad diversity within and between ethnic groups. Sadye Logan, in Chapter 129, makes the consequences of such intragroup variation for her subject population quite plain: "Given the diversity which exists in terms of values, education, income, lifestyles, and perceptions in the African American community, it is extremely challenging, if not impossible, to write a definitive article that captures clinical social work practice with this ethnic group." In Chapter 126 Teresa Evans-Campbell and Gordon Limb mention that in the United States "there are 566 federally recognized tribes, including 229 village groups in Alaska and close to 200 unrecognized tribes." Halaevalu Vakalahi and Rowena Fong, Chapter 127, note that Asians and Pacific Islanders include distinctly different groups from East Asia, South Asia, and Southeast Asia, as well as Pacific Islanders from Polynesia, Micronesia, and Melanesia.

Diversity within ethnic group populations applies to both American-born and foreign-born populations. Miriam Potocky, in Chapter 125, emphasizes the differences among legal statuses in the immigrant and refugee populations. Elaine Congress, in Chapter 130, reports that an estimated "one out of three immigrants are undocumented, while more than half of the immigrants who entered the country [United States] since 2000 are undocumented." Describing the Latino population in Chapter 128, Ilze Earner and Alan Dettlaff report that "Latinos are the largest

ethnic minority group in the United States and the fastest-growing segment of the U.S. population." In summary, this section on vulnerable populations highlights the diversity within the native and foreign-born populations of persons of color.

VULNERABILITY AND RISK FACTORS

Persons of color are joined by GLBT individuals as members of vulnerable populations. In Chapter 132, Mary Boes and Katherine van Wormer describe the risk factors for members of the GLBT population: "Few groups are maligned in our society, as are persons who are identified as, or are suspected of, gender nonconformity, or having a same-sex sexual orientation. The most extreme forms of discrimination, including ridicule and violence, are reserved for transgendered persons or those who have the psychological sense of being female when they are physiologically male or vice versa."

Depression and poor mental health are risk factors for older adults, GLBT clients, persons of color, and other vulnerable populations such as immigrants and refugees. Some authors describe how assessment practices can point toward these risk factors. Elaine Congress describes one tool, the Culturagram, in Chapter 130. The Afro-centered genogram referred to by Logan in Chapter 129 is another tool. Earner and Dettlaff's Chapter 128 on Latinos also recommends the stages of migration framework (Drachman, 1992) for assessment purposes. Historical and cultural experiences with colonization and immigration are important factors to consider in conducting assessments with Asian Americans and Pacific Islanders, state Vakalahi and Fong in Chapter 127.

Vulnerability and risk factors can be mediated by approaching the populations from an empowerment and strengths perspective and framework, often used in working with the ethnic minority, GLBT, and immigrant and refugee populations. In working with African Americans, Latinos, Native Americans, and Asian and Pacific Islander Americans, the chapter authors emphasize the need to use the strengths perspective approach to empower these vulnerable populations. In Chapter 127, Vakalahi and Fong discuss cultural values as strengths and the role of these values in Asian and Pacific Islander cultures. Fong and Furuto (2001) describe the importance of culturally competent social work practice and the role of cultural values as protective factors among ethnic populations likely to uphold traditional values in their families and communities.

CULTURALLY COMPETENT EVIDENCE-BASED PRACTICE

Evidence-based practice is important in determining the effectiveness of an intervention on a problem area, and some authors mention specific therapies that work well with their vulnerable populations. In Chapter 129 Logan emphasizes the need to use an Afrocentric and strengths-based orientation, and mentions that there are "emergent and traditional practice approaches" that support such an orientation. They include solution-focused brief therapy, solution-oriented therapy, gender-sensitive therapy, cognitive-behavioral therapy, psycho-educational family therapy, task-centered treatment, structural family therapy, narrative therapy, and crisis treatment.

In Chapter 128, the use of a stages of migration framework (Drachman, 1992) is recommended when working with Latino families. Chapter 127 mentions the use of family group conferencing, an emergent evidence-based practice intervention in child protective services, used with the Pacific Islander case example. There is the tendency in working with ethnic American-born and foreign-born populations to determine which evidence-based intervention may apply to the ethnic group, and practitioners need to be cautious to not exclude indigenous interventions that work with ethnic populations and support the strengths perspective of supporting cultural values. Evans-Campbell and Limb, in Chapter 126, state:

Increasingly, the field of social work is moving toward the use of evidence-based practice interventions and strategies with diverse populations. Unfortunately, the use of evidence-based interventions with AIAN [American Indian/Alaska Native] people is complicated by the lack of intervention research that includes Native clients or examines Native-specific practice models.... When working with Native people, social workers might also consider practices that are considered promising in that there is emerging empirical evidence of their success. There are a growing number of Native-designed programs designated as promising practice models by agencies

such as Indian Health Service and SAMHSA [Substance Abuse and Mental Health Services Administration].

In conclusion, this section on vulnerable populations includes chapters on social work practice with native-born and foreign-born populations of African Americans, Latinos, Asian and Pacific Islander Americans; Native Americans; GLBT clients; and refugees and immigrants. Chapters in the section also cover the use of antioppressive practices and culturagrams with culturally diverse immigrant families, all in the context of understanding and being aware of the legacy of racism. The chapters point out the diversity among ethnic populations, the vulnerability and risk factors, and both evidence-based and culturally competent social work practices.

WEBSITE

National Association of Social Workers. www.nasw.org

References

Dettlaff, A., & Fong, R. (Eds.). (2012). *Child welfare practice with immigrant families*. New York, NY: Taylor and Francis Press.

Drachman, D. (1992). Stages of migration and assessment of immigrant families. *Social Work, 37*(1), 68–72.

Fong, R. (Ed.). (2004). *Culturally competent practice with immigrant and refugee children and families*. New York, NY: Guilford.

Fong, R., & Furuto, S. (Eds.). (2001). *Culturally competent practice: Skills, interventions, and evaluations*. Boston, MA: Allyn & Bacon.

Fong, R., McRoy, R., & Hendricks, C. (Eds.). (2006). *Intersecting child welfare, substance abuse, and family violence: Culturally competent approaches*. Alexandria, VA: Council on Social Work Education.

Miller, J., & Garran, A. (2008). *Racism in the United States: Implications for the helping professions*. Belmont, CA: Thomson Brooks/Cole.

National Association of Social Work. (1999). *Code of ethics*. Washington, DC: NASW Press.

National Association of Social Work. (2001). *Standards for cultural competence in social work practice*. Washington, DC: NASW Press.

National Association of Social Work. (2006). *Social work speaks: NASW policy statements 2006–2009*. Washington, DC: NASW Press.

123 The Legacy of Racism for Social Work Practice Today and What to do About It

Ann Marie Garran & Joshua Miller

The United States has been a nation for over 235 years and is renowned for its democratic tradition. It is also a country that was founded with a "racial contract" (Mills, 1997) that has shaped its culture, laws, institutions, practices, and the relationships between various ethnic and racial groups. Racism is as much a part of the American tradition as democracy is, and it is very much a social factor today. Yet many White citizens, who are consciously against racism, view racism as something that happened in the past with little relevance today. For social workers to practice in accordance with the National Association of Social Workers (NASW) Code of Ethics (2008), we need to understand how racism shapes lives, constrains opportunity for some, and confers privileges to others based on a social construction of race. Most importantly, we need to understand how to confront the racism that exists in society and that lurks inside the psyches of practitioners. The spectrum of racism today ranges from institutional barriers and neglect of those who are the targets of racism, cultural biases, intergroup conflict, and segregation, to interpersonal transactions and internalized prejudices and stereotypes (Miller & Garran, 2008). It is manifested in communities, agencies, organizations, social policies, and the relationships and interactions that people have—or because of racism, rarely have.

Racism is based on the erroneous notion of race: that there are distinct racial groups and generalizations can be made about these groups based on alleged genetic or cultural differences or deficiencies. The American Anthropological Association (AAA) (1998) has stated that based on available scientific evidence of genetic similarities and differences between so-called racial groups, there are no significant distinctions and there is one race, the human race. Of course, there are differences in height, skin color, facial features, and other physical characteristics, but these are not the differences that justified enslavement of African Americans, genocide of Native Americans, prohibitions against immigration for Chinese Americans, or disenfranchisement of Mexican Americans living in the Southwest, all of which are a part of this nation's heritage. Race has limited value as a biological or genetic construct, but has been a useful underpinning for ideologies justifying the domination of one "racial" group by another. Racism is a process that uses the differences of appearance or culture as a basis for making generalizations about intelligence and trustworthiness to justify systematic acts of subjugation and mistreatment of targeted peoples. Racism shapes the notion of race rather than racial differences leading to racism. In the end, race is a social construction that determines who wields power and who has social passports of privilege at both the individual and systemic levels.

In this chapter we discuss why social workers should be concerned about racism and what racism in the United States looks like today. We also discuss institutional racism; more subtle, unconscious forms of racism, such as aversive racism (Dovidio, Gaertner, Kawakami, & Hodson, 2002) and racial microaggressions (Pierce, Carew, Pierce-Gonzalez, & Wills, 1978; Solorzano, Ceja, & Yosso, 2000; Sue, 2010); internalized stereotypes and racial prejudices; and how this is encapsulated in social identities (Miller & Garran, 2008). We conclude with some ideas about how to talk about race and racism, work with racism in direct practice, including in supervision, confront racism in the community, and how social service organizations can become antiracism organizations. Our purpose is to take an unvarnished look at racism in the United States and the implications of it for social workers. Due to the brevity of this chapter, we particularly emphasize the role of White people and those with white skin privilege in maintaining racism. Although some of what we say might seem a bit jarring and provoke strong emotions, our goal is not to make people angry or feel badly about themselves: we want social workers to eradicate racism, not point fingers at one another or feel immobilized by feelings of guilt or shame. We recognize that the commitment to antiracism work is a lifelong process, and with this realization, readers will find ways to move from feeling overwhelmed or immobilized to a more action-oriented stance.

We need to briefly situate ourselves and define some terms that we will be using. One author (Garran) is a Puerto Rican and African American female, and the other author (Miller) is a White, Jewish American male. We are both social workers and have taught antiracism courses together for 12 years. We have coauthored a textbook for human service professionals about antiracism

(Miller & Garran, 2008). We use the terms "people of color" and "White" because they are the most common social constructions currently in use that convey who is and who is not targeted by racism. Due to the complexity of racism, we have been reluctant to define it in a way that reduces or overly simplifies its meaning. We agree with Memmi (2000) that racism involves the domination of people who are defined as being members of a racial or ethnic group by another group of people based on alleged differences of genetics, culture, values, and behavior. Racism in our view manifests along a spectrum, where there are core practices that are common to all forms of it (Miller & Garran, 2008). Figure 123.1 diagrams the range of ways that racism is expressed, all of which have occurred in the United States, many of which are still operating.

WHY IT IS IMPORTANT FOR SOCIAL WORKERS TO CARE ABOUT RACISM

All citizens should care about racism because it undermines a just society and ultimately compromises everyone, including those with race privilege who often live needlessly in fear or are

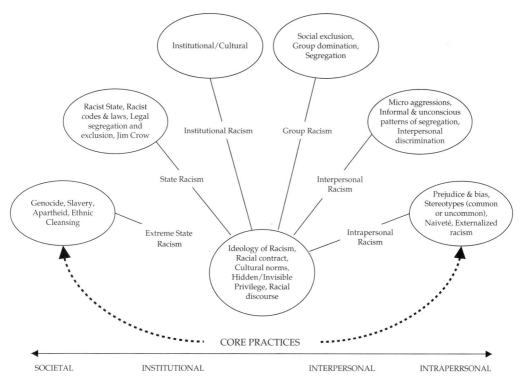

Figure 123.1 The spectrum of racism.

not in touch with their own biases, prejudices, and stereotypes, which alienates them from others. It is particularly important for social workers to understand how racism works and how to confront it because our very mission is to connect with and empower people, and work with them to improve their psychosocial functioning, as well as to advocate for social policies that uphold human rights and dignity and that further human well-being. Racism divides and alienates people, creates barriers to social participation, limits potential, and inhibits psychosocial growth. Racism engenders feelings of anger, rage, guilt, and shame that can be overwhelming and can lead to severe health, psychological, social, and behavioral problems.

Social workers are bound by a code of ethics (NASW, 2008) that commits us to work for social justice and to respect and value every individual and her cultural context. To paraphrase the NASW Code of Ethics, as social workers we are committed to enhancing human well-being and meeting everyone's basic needs, paying particular attention to those who are vulnerable, oppressed, and living in poverty(Miller & Garran, 2008). Racism is a system of inequality that is the ultimate in social injustice. It clearly values some people and cultures while both covertly and overtly allowing for the denigration of others. When not confronted, racism is a force that prevents social workers from adequately and ethically being able to carry out their jobs in a more effective manner.

A BRIEF HISTORY OF RACISM IN THE UNITED STATES

Almost immediately after the arrival of Europeans in the New World, Europeans from a number of nations—Spain, England, France, and Holland—attempted to subjugate, kill, and dislocate the Native American population that was already living here. The more than 600 autonomous societies already living in the Americas were met with disease, slaughter, and attempts at enslavement by European explorers and settlers (Wilson, 1998). Some estimate a 95% death rate among Native Americans within a few generations after European settlement (Stannard, 1992). In the first 90 years of the American republic, *every* treaty with Native Americans was broken by the United States government (Wilson, 1998). Native Americans were not granted citizenship until 1924.

From the beginning of settlement by Europeans, there was slavery, which evolved into chattel slavery, lifelong and intergenerational, which ultimately became limited to African Americans. Many of the founding fathers of the United States were slave owners—George Washington, Thomas Jefferson, James Madison, James Monroe, and Andrew Jackson, who was also known for his brutal treatment of Native Americans. After slavery was abolished following the Civil War, black codes, Jim Crow, violence (including lynching), and other forms of legal and de facto state terror and segregation managed to severely limit political, social, and economic opportunities for African Americans (Miller & Garran, 2008). While European immigrants were being recruited to work in Northern factories after the Industrial Revolution, African Americans were unable to compete for these jobs due to structural impediments, such as Jim Crow in the South and racial discrimination in the North (which was not limited to employers and included trade unions). Thus, it is important to acknowledge and note that many White people who descend from those immigrants were able to benefit from upward social mobility that depended on their assumption of White privilege at the expense of people of color (Goodman, 2011; Steinberg, 2001).

In the Southwest, Mexicans living in what is now Texas, New Mexico, California, Colorado, and Nevada (which had been part of Mexico prior to the Mexican–American War), lost their land, citizenship, and ability to compete for and hold jobs. In 1882, the Chinese Exclusion Act prohibited immigration to the United States by people from China (at exactly the same time that Europeans were immigrating to the United States), and the Gentleman's Agreement of 1907 prohibited Japanese immigration. Though it was difficult for groups like the Irish, Jews, and Italians when they first arrived in the United States, due in large measure to much discrimination and racial and ethnic stereotyping, they still had advantages unavailable to people of color and as such, within a few generations became "White" (Guglielmo & Salerno, 2003; Ignatiev, 1995; Sacks, 1996; Steinberg, 2001).

It is not possible for social workers to grasp the severe racial inequality that exists today without acknowledging the historical privileges afforded White immigrants and the consistent oppression and exclusion that has faced people of color since the incorporation of this nation.

RACISM IN THE UNITED STATES TODAY

Although it is no longer legal to deprive people of their rights, enslave them, or murder them due to their race, racism in the United States is an ongoing project that has evolved and shifted over the course of time, and one that continues to require confrontation and eradication. The fact that the most extreme forms of racism are illegal and considered socially abhorrent does not mean that there may not be regression or that racism is not still a major force in U.S. society today. Since September 11, 2001, the so-called war against terrorism has had echoes of America's racist past—tightening the borders, demonizing certain ethnic groups, suspending legal rights and civil liberties—to name a few worrying trends. The forms of racism of the past are no longer legally or socially acceptable, though one only needs to turn to the media to learn that there are still many racist incidents that occur, such as the recent murder of unarmed teenager Trayvon Martin in Florida, whose crime was walking through the "wrong" neighborhood while Black.

What is still contested are myriad forms of racism that continue to impede the civil rights and socioeconomic progress of people of color. As Figure 123.1 illustrates, one major form of racism is institutional racism, where many people of color—particularly poor African Americans, Latinos, and Native Americans—face a web of institutional barriers, where they are unable to live in certain neighborhoods, have less access to quality education and health care, face greater exposure to unsafe and unhealthy environments, are more likely to be targeted by law enforcement, are less likely to go to college, are under-represented politically and over-represented in prisons, and who consistently have less ability to accumulate wealth and achieve upward mobility (Alexander, 2010; Miller & Garran, 2007, 2008). Although the United States has elected its first African American president, there are very few senators of color and there is no guarantee that the occupant of the White House will not be White for generations to come. And in 2013, the Supreme Court invalidated the Voting Rights Act; within hours after the decision, the Texas Attorney General announced the implementation of a radical voter identification law, which is likely to suppress the votes of people of color. Another aspect of institutional racism is a public discourse, amplified by the media, which legitimates it. This discourse normalizes White leadership, privilege, and power and promulgates stereotypes about African Americans, Asian Americans, Latino Americans, and other people of color. It is evident in television shows, news broadcasts, magazine advertisements, and the decisions made by the editors of newspapers and other media about what is news and how it will be portrayed (Miller & Garran, 2008). This discourse shaped public opinion about welfare reform, consistently portraying welfare mothers as African Americans, despite the fact that the majority of women on welfare were White (Gillens, 1999). Media coverage and the ensuing biased public discourse and government response in the initial aftermath of Hurricane Katrina mark another way that events are racialized and, if not confronted, can serve to disparage large groups of people (Adams, O'Brien, & Nelson, 2006).

Figure 123.1 also illustrates intergroup racism, where one racial group has privileges and powers and others are marginalized, "otherized," or considered "minorities." For instance, look at the racial/ethnic staffing patterns of your social service agency. Who are the receptionists and administrative assistants? Who are the senior managers? Who are the clients, and who are the workers? Who is on the board of directors? What are the norms and culture of the office? What theories of human behavior in the social environment are being used and what cultural biases are embedded in them? How often are there conversations about these things between all levels of the agency? These are but a few questions that begin to highlight how "normal" and ubiquitous White privilege often is in most social service organizations. As Tim Wise (2003) has put it, Whites swim in a sea of racial privilege, which is mostly invisible. Until we are willing to acknowledge and admit the ways that our organizations perpetuate these inequalities, we will not be positioned to make important changes that will improve service delivery at every level.

INTERNALIZED AND INTERPERSONAL RACISM

The ubiquitous nature of racism, internalized oppression, and White privilege shape how people see the world and how they feel about themselves and others. One way to think about this is that people have multiple social identities. Social identity is how we view ourselves in relation to other people. It encompasses the groups that we see ourselves as being members of and excluded from, as well as the thoughts, feelings, and perceptions that accompany these identifications. Ultimately, social identity is our sense of our self in a social world. There are many dimensions of social identity—such as gender, ethnicity, social and economic class, race, and sexual orientation—and some of these dimensions shift over time while others remain constant. Different aspects of social identity come to light depending on the social context. For example, in a class where the professor is White and most of the students are White, the one or two students of color may be very conscious of their race. Conversely, many White class members do not think about their race at all and are more aware of their class, gender, sexual orientation, or ethnicity (Miller & Garran, 2008). The same dynamic is often reflected in the staffing of many social service agencies, where the professional staff is largely White and clients who come for services are primarily people of color.

When social identity is mirrored, reflected, and advantaged by society (e.g., being White, male, heterosexual, middle-class, physically able) the privileges that accompany the identity are often difficult to discern by the person who benefits from this special status (McIntosh, 1989, 1992; Miller & Garran, 2008; Wise, 2003). Discourses accompany these privileges that whitewash them away, so that effort, hard work, good character, and the right values are explanations for the success of one group (White people) rather than acknowledgment of exploitation, segregation, resource hoarding, and unequal opportunity (Sensoy & DiAngelo, 2011). Thus, stereotypes emerge that provide inner templates to match outer social realities and offer cognitive justifications for a socially unequal and unfair world. A White person with values and ideals that are altruistic and egalitarian may harbor stereotypes about people of color that are beneath the radar of consciousness but still manage to shape beliefs and behaviors (Dovidio et al., 2002; Miller & Garran, 2008).

Unexamined stereotypes can lead to "aversive racism" (Dovidio et al., 2002), where a well-intentioned White person is unaware of his or her prejudices and yet acts on these biases. Examples include hiring decisions in agencies or segregated housing patterns in neighborhoods, where a White person did not overtly "choose" to live in a nearly all-White neighborhood yet felt compelled to do so. Aversive racism can contribute to subtle interactions—making or not making eye contact, a forced smile, stumbling over the words "race" or "racism"—that "create a force field of discomfort" (Kaufman, 2001, p. 33). Another way to conceptualize these interactions is to see them as "microaggressions"—subtle but repeated verbal and nonverbal insults, put-downs, and social incursions that are injurious to people of color but often occur without the conscious awareness of the White person (Miller & Garran, 2007; Pierce et al., 1978; Solorzano et al., 2000; Sue, 2010). The consequences of microaggressions are a relentless assault on one's social identity, which, aside from being painful and exhausting, can lead people of color to withdraw from interactions with White people. Because microaggressions are so often unconscious acts, a commitment to self-reflection and self-awareness are critical if we are to interrupt their perpetuation.

ORGANIZATIONAL RACISM

Social service organizations are the nexus between institutional racism and internalized/interpersonal racism. It is nearly impossible for a mainstream social service organization not to have to deal with racism, given that the organization is part of a society permeated with racism and staffed by many people with internalized racism—it mirrors the complexity of racism in society at large. Thus, racism affects hiring and retention, staffing patterns, policies toward clients, supervision, theoretical biases and pathologizing of clients, and interpersonal relationships between staff, as well as organizational power, influence, and decision making (Miller & Garran, 2008). Many social work practices—individual treatment, appointments for 50 minute hours, the notion of boundaries—were shaped and informed by Eurocentric, Western traditions and yet are presented as universal truths (Miller, 2012). Only through sustained and intentional efforts to become an antiracism organization can social service organizations go beyond token or symbolic measures to challenge racism (Donner & Miller, 2005; Miller & Garran, 2008).

DISMANTLING RACISM AND CREATING A WEB OF RESISTANCE

There are no simple measures to eradicate racism, nor will it be eliminated over a short period of time. The history, ubiquity, and complexity of racism make dismantling it a daunting prospect. Yet, we must not let the weight of racism, or the weight of our history around it, overwhelm us; without hope there is no prospect of changing things. So what can social workers do?

- *Learn about it.* There is no shortcut to learning about racism in all of its forms, including how it is inside of and in-between people. Racism evokes strong feelings—pain, anger, sorrow, guilt, shame—and these emotional reactions can lead people either to want to challenge it without adequately understanding it, or to withdraw from having to deal with it. Learning about racism and deciphering its many manifestations is an ongoing endeavor. Learning must take place on two levels: cognitively through education, and emotionally and psychologically through introspection and self-awareness.
- *Working with others.* Racism alienates and isolates people from one another. Social workers are committed as a profession to ending social injustice and are accustomed to working together. One of the most effective ways to undermine racism is to create multiracial coalitions that pool resources and offer mutual aid and support. Coalitions help to sustain motivation and attention to this issue.
- *Creating antiracism organizations.* Most social workers practice in agencies, and social service organizations serve clients who have been targeted by racism. Organizations can include antiracism commitments in their mission statements; hire, retain, and empower more staff of color and those with multilingual skills; review practices toward clients as well as the theories that guide such practices; make sure that the racial and ethnic identities of clients and clinicians alike is a salient factor that is discussed in clinical supervision; examine organizational structures to identify policies and practices that perpetuate systemic oppression; offer ongoing antiracism trainings; facilitate intergroup dialogues; and work to become truly multicultural. These efforts must take place consistently and must pull from multiple levels of staffing at the agency to ensure that multiple voices are being represented. If there is no one on staff to provide direction and training to enhance these efforts, then administrators must look

for qualified professionals to provide this guidance.
- *Creating inclusive communities.* All social workers and clients live somewhere, although often not in the same place. In general, communities offer safety, security, and opportunities for social mobility and increasing economic and social capital; they are also sites of much institutional racism and can be places that are dangerous and glaringly devoid of the resources and amenities necessary to survive and eventually advance. Social workers can work to create communities where they live **and** work that are inclusive and where everyone is treated fairly and respectfully, and has access to decent education, jobs, health care, and other resources.
- *Being heard.* Social workers must engage in discourses and conversations not only among themselves but also with the greater public. The stereotypes and biases embedded in the mass media and culture can be identified, deconstructed, and challenged by social workers who set an example by their professional ethics and offer an alternative vision of a just and nonracist society. This idea is a critical part of social work education and should extend beyond the halls of the academy.
- *Challenging and changing laws, institutions, and practices.* This is a huge task, but it is not insurmountable. We have seen many laws and practices—for example, slavery, Jim Crow, legal segregation, forced internment—changed over time. There is much more work to do but it can be done if social workers articulate a vision, break things down into manageable pieces, and work in concert with others concerned about racism to dismantle racist policies and promulgate the means to achieve social justice.

Ultimately, all of these actions form a "web of resistance" to racism (Miller & Garran, 2008; Werkmeister Rozas & Miller, 2009). Our core values are central to all of the activities we have described—seeing clearly, listening and hearing, connecting with others, compassion, sustained engagement, and advocating for the rights and dignities of our clients, and in turn, for ourselves. Racism has been around for a long time and will not be eliminated easily, but the core values of the web of resistance correspond directly to those articulated by the social work profession. If we can aspire to live up to the vision of our profession, we can all be antiracism activists and allies.

WEBSITES

EdChange Organization. http://www.edchange .org/multicultural/sites/white.html.

ERASE Racism Organization. http://www .eraseracismny.org/html/

Open Society (Implicit bias tests. http:// www.opensocietyfoundations.org/voices/ implicit-bias-and-social-justice

PBS Television's interactive site for the broadcast series on race. http://www.pbs.org/ race/000_General/000_00-Home.htm.

Understanding Prejudice. http://www.under-standingprejudice.org/.

Voices of Civil Rights. http://www .voicesofcivilrights.org/.

References

Adams, G., O'Brien, L. T., & Nelson, J. C. (2006). Perceptions of racism in Hurricane Katrina: A liberation psychology analysis. *Analyses of Social Issues and Public Policy, 6*(1), 215–235.

Alexander, M. (2010). *The new Jim Crow: Mass incarceration in the age of colorblindness.* New York, NY: New Age Press.

American Anthropological Association. (1998). AAA statement on race. *American Anthropologist, 100*(3), 712–713.

Donner, S., & Miller, J. (2005). The road to becoming an anti-racism organization. In A. Lightburn & P. Sessions (Eds.), *Handbook of community based clinical practice* (pp. 122–135). New York, NY: Oxford University Press.

Dovidio, J. F., Gaertner, S. L., Kawakami, K., & Hodson, G. (2002). Why can't we all just get along? Interpersonal biases and interracial distrust. *Cultural Diversity and Ethnic Minority Psychology, 8*(2), 88–102.

Gillens, M. (1999). *Why Americans hate welfare.* Chicago, IL: University of Chicago Press.

Goodman, D. (2011). *Promoting diversity and social justice: Educating people from privileged groups.* New York, NY: Routledge.

Guglielmo, J., & Salerno, S. (2003). (Eds.), *Are Italians white: How race is made in America.* New York, NY: Routledge.

Ignatiev, N. (1995). *How the Irish became white.* New York, NY: Routledge.

Kaufman, C. (2001). A user's guide to white privilege. *Radical Philosophy Review, 4*(1/2), 30–38.

McIntosh, P. (1989). White privilege: Unpacking the invisible knapsack. *Peace and Freedom,* July/ Aug, 10–12.

McIntosh, P. (1992). White privilege and male privilege: A personal account of coming to see correspondences through work in women's studies. In M. Anderson & P. H. Collins (Eds.), *Race, class and gender: An anthology* (pp. 70–81). Belmont, CA: Wadsworth.

Memmi, A. (2000). *Racism.* Minneapolis: University of Minnesota Press.

Miller, J. (2012). *Psychosocial capacity building in response to disasters.* New York, NY: Columbia University Press.

Miller, J., & Garran, A. M. (2007). The web of institutional racism. *Smith College Studies in Social Work, 77*(1), 33–67.

Miller, J., & Garran, A. (2008). *Racism in the United States: Implications for the helping professions.* Belmont, CA: Thomson Brooks/Cole.

Mills, C. W. (1997). *The racial contract.* Ithaca, NY: Cornell University Press.

National Association of Social Workers. (2008). *Code of ethics.* Washington, DC: NASW Press.

Pierce, C., Carew, J., Pierce-Gonzalez, D., & Wills, D. (1978). An experiment in racism: T.V. commercials. In C. Pierce (Ed.), *Television and education* (pp. 62–88). Beverly Hills, CA: Sage.

Sacks, K. B. (1996). How did Jews become white folks? In S. Gregory & R. Sanjek (Eds.), *Race* (pp. 78–102). New Brunswick, NJ: Rutgers University Press.

Sensoy, Ö., & DiAngelo, R. (2011). *Is everyone really equal? An introduction to key concepts in social justice education.* New York, NY: Teachers College Press.

Solorzano, D., Ceja, M., & Yosso, T. (2000). Critical race theory, racial microaggressions, and campus racial climate: The experiences of African American college students. *Journal of Negro Education, 69*(1/2), 60–73.

Stannard, D. E. (1992). *American holocaust: The conquest of the New World.* New York, NY: Oxford University Press.

Steinberg, S. (2001). *The ethnic myth: Race, ethnicity and class in America* (3rd ed.). Boston, MA: Beacon Press.

Sue, D.W. (2010). *Microaggressions in everyday life: Race, gender, and sexual orientation.* New York, NY: J. Wiley & Sons, Inc.

Werkmeister Rozas, L., & Miller, J. (2009). Discourses for social justice: The web of racism and the web of resistance. *Journal of Ethnic and Cultural Diversity, 18*, 24–37.

Wilson, J. (1998). *The earth shall weep: A history of Native America.* New York, NY: Grove.

Wise, T. (2003). Whites swim in racial preference. Znet. Retrieved from http://www.zmag.org/content/ showarticle.cfm?ItemID=3113.

124 Anti-oppressive Practices

Katherine Ishizuka & Altaf Husain

INTRODUCTION

Oppression creates conditions that directly or indirectly cause some people to seek assistance from social services (Chapman, 2011). As a result, social workers engage with some of the most vulnerable and oppressed individuals, groups and communities, in pursuit of the profession's mission of enhancing well-being and meeting the basic human needs of all people (National Association of Social Workers, 2013). Although other helping professions may strive toward a similar end, a defining feature of social work is its focus on addressing the causes and consequences of social injustice and oppression (Strier, 2006). Social workers have a professional mandate to identify and challenge the ways in which oppression is upheld, both within and outside the field, across individual, organizational, and systemic domains (Maidment & Cooper, 2002). The focus on (1) mitigating the ways in which social, economic, and political systems, and the profession itself, perpetuate oppression and (2) applying models of empowerment and liberation to institutions, relationships, and values (Brown & Mistry, 2005) is known as antioppressive social work.

Antioppressive practice (AOP) in social work is not an established, monolithic framework, but rather, an evolving and contentious variety of different practice approaches and theories oriented toward a social justice perspective. Although AOP is not new within the field of social work, this is the first time that a chapter has been dedicated to the topic within the *Social Workers' Desk Reference*. This chapter will provide a snapshot of AOP, along with practical tools, guidance, and considerations for its use across a diverse range of practice settings. The chapter is informed by a review of the literature, the authors' experiences across the spectrum of direct social work practice, macro social work practice and social work academia, and our insights as members of oppressed groups.

The chapter comprises seven sections. The first section provides a brief history of antioppressive practice in social work to situate its current approaches within the field. Sections Two and Three identify goals for antioppressive practice and describe the types and forms of oppression social workers may encounter in their work, respectively. An overview of current frameworks and approaches to AOP is presented in Section Four. Toward the operationalization of theory and analysis, AOP practice principles are described in Section Five. Section Six presents possible barriers toward actualizing antioppressive work in practice and Section Seven concludes with considerations for advancing antioppressive practice within the profession.

A BRIEF HISTORY OF ANTI-OPPRESSIVE PRACTICE IN SOCIAL WORK

Since its origins in the late 19th century, social work has wrestled with its contradictory roles in maintaining the status quo as a function of the state and challenging oppression (Abramovitz, 1999). Both internal and external political struggles have shaped the profession's relationship to social change (Abramovitz, 1999). Although the profession has been concerned with oppression since its inception, its contemporary role in social reform was ignited in the mid-1960s by the civil rights movement (Council on Social Work Education [CSWE], 2001). Prior to the mid-1960s, social work practice and education was characterized by ethnocentrism and acculturation, in which the norms and values of dominant culture were applied universally to all client groups (Schiele, 2007). Behaviors falling outside of dominant cultural norms were seen as "problems." For example, in 1952, homosexuality was listed in the *Diagnostic and Statistical Manual of Mental Disorders (DSM-1)* as a sociopathic personality disturbance; a mental illness to be "treated" (Group for the Advancement of Psychiatry, 2012).

Between the mid-1960s and mid-1970s, social workers of color and White allies challenged the Eurocentric bias in social work teaching and practice and the deficit-oriented view of people of color (Abrams & Moio, 2009). Activism related to racial issues prompted the Council on Social Work Education (CSWE) to mandate content on race, racism, and people of color in social work education (CSWE, 2001), and to establish five ethnic minority task forces (Schiele, 2007).

Starting in the mid-1970s, the primacy given to race content in social work education was challenged with the emergence of activism and analysis of additional oppressed groups (CSWE, 2001), such as women and sexual minorities. Those who critiqued the focus on race and antiracism content garnered some consensus for an integrated approach that was inclusive of, and made connections with, other forms of oppression (Keating, 2000). Since then, social work education has broadened its conceptualization and coverage of oppression content. Between 1975 and 1984, CSWE established a commission on women and mandated content on gender issues, including feminist practice theories and methods (Schiele, 2007). Between 1985 and 1995, the CSWE championed sexual orientation issues and established a Commission on Gay, Lesbian, Bisexual and Transgender Issues (Schiele, 2007). Since 1995, the CSWE has continued to broaden its content on oppression issues. In 2001, CSWE's Policy and Accreditation Standards (EPAS) identified 14 types of diversity as possible sources of oppression, including age, class, color, culture, disability, ethnicity, gender, gender identity and expression, immigration status, political ideology, race, religion, sex and sexual orientation (CSWE, 2012).

The equal treatment and inclusion of all forms of oppression has been referred to as an *equality-of-oppressions* paradigm (Schiele, 2007). The equality-of-oppressions paradigm emphasizes the interconnectedness of all forms of oppression (i.e., sexism, racism, homophobia, classism, etc.) and asserts that it is impossible to view one form of oppression in isolation (Schiele, 2007). The 2001 *equality-of-oppressions* framework replaced the *hierarchy-of-oppressions* model of the 1960s and 1970s, which supported the inclusion of content dedicated specifically to racism and people of color. Although both models are empirically supported in the literature, the movement away from a dedicated focus on antiracism remains a source of contention. Critics assert that it contributes to a denial of racism within the field (Schiele, 2007) and that the distinct severity, frequency, and endemic nature of racism warrant specific attention.

In addition to changes in the way that oppression is conceptualized, the profession has also made changes to the way it engages with oppression and members of oppressed groups. In the 1960s, the cultural competence model was employed, which focused on changing the beliefs and behaviors of individual practitioners to promote cross-cultural sensitivity and understanding (Abrams & Moio, 2009). Among critiques of this framework are that it only focuses change efforts at the level of the individual and not the institutional and systemic levels; it assumes that increased cultural knowledge and skills will enhance practice, without questioning whether the practices and interventions themselves are appropriate; and it has limited empirical evidence (Abrams & Moio, 2009). In contrast, the antioppression model targets change efforts at the individual, institutional, and systemic levels (Abrams & Moio, 2009). Currently, the social work profession is thought to utilize a combination of cultural competence and AOP frameworks.

GOALS FOR ANTI-OPPRESSIVE SOCIAL WORK

Much of the literature on antioppressive practice in social work focuses on what not to do. The term "antioppressive" itself is defined by what it is not, rather than what it is. It is imperative that social workers have a vision for what the short- and long-term goals and ideals of AOP are. Without a clear understanding of what the profession seeks to achieve through AOP, there will continue to be ambiguity, and social workers may be unable to attain it. Some of the goals for AOP in social work include:

• **Above all, do no harm**. In no way should the social worker be the source or onset of harm or trauma because of anything related to practice. The helping profession cannot unwittingly perpetuate trauma or disenfranchisement within its own client base. Social workers should also promote emotional, psychological, and physical safety among clients, families, and communities and work to eradicate the causes, and not just the consequences, of internalized and external oppression.

- **Sustainability**: Social workers need to consider the long-term impact of their work in the community and work with clients toward being self-sustainable. Practitioners and clients should work toward transforming, and/or not having dependence on, institutions and systems that oppress (J. Suleman, personal correspondence, July 13, 2013).

- **Empowerment**: Individuals should have a sense of control over their own lives (Dustin & Montgomery, 2010) and be able to exercise self-determination and choice. Social workers should challenge institutional practices that disempower clients, work to resolve power imbalances (van Wormer & Snyder, 2007) and understand their role in empowerment. Social workers cannot "liberate the oppressed," which can represent cultural invasion (Freire, 1970); they can only assist individuals in achieving their own liberation.

- **Social Justice:** The dignity and worth (NASW, 2013) and human rights of each human being should be protected and individuals should have equal rights concerning their land, resources, politics, and bodies (van Wormer & Snyder, 2007). Dominant and subordinate binaries should be eliminated and replaced with equal spaces and respect for all forms of diversity. Freire (1970) suggested a vision of "bringing into the world a new being, no longer oppressor, no longer oppressed, but human in the process of achieving freedom" (p. 31).

Types & Forms of Oppression Social Workers May Encounter in Practice

The Social Work Dictionary defines oppression as: "The social act of placing severe restrictions on an individual, group, or institution. The oppressed individual or group is devalued, exploited, and deprived of privileges by the individual or group

who has more power" (van Wormer & Snyder, 2007, p. 21). Oppression is maintained through socially constructed and institutionalized ideologies and doctrines (van Wormer & Snyder, 2007), which privilege certain groups at the expense of "others." If an individual is oppressed, it is by virtue of his or her membership in a particular group (or groups), not because of any individual failure or deficiency (Mullaly, 2001).

Below are two tables. Table 124.1 lists 21 types of oppression that social workers may encounter in practice. The 14 sources of oppression that the CSWE mandates in social work education are included, along with seven additional sources of oppression about which social workers may want to be cognizant. These additional seven sources of oppression include criminal history, mental health status, chemical dependency status, family structure, marital status, appearance, and size.

Table 124.2 lists 11 forms of oppression. This table shows the many forms of oppression, including those that operate below the surface and cannot be readily seen. Several key points that might be taken from an understanding of various forms of oppression include the following:

- Oppression is a system, not just individual acts of prejudice or discrimination.
- Oppression does not have to be seen to exist.
- In spite of good intentions, one can unknowingly act oppressively or enact behaviors with oppressive consequences.
- Unless one is consciously opposing oppression, one is probably upholding it.
- A practitioner's perception of a client's relationship to oppression may not mirror the client's perception of her or his relationship to oppression.

Note: The types and forms of oppression listed within these tables are comprehensive, but not exhaustive.

Moving from –'ism to Action

An antioppressive model moves beyond an understanding and classification of the types and forms of oppression. Classification of oneself and "others" itself has been central to the maintenance of oppression through the use of the categorizations and discourse of dominant groups (Campbell, 2003). The following theories, approaches, and practice principles bridge

TABLE 124.1 Types of Oppression

Oppression Source	Oppression Type
Age	Prejudice or discrimination based on a person's age (ageism)
Political ideology	Prejudice or discrimination based on a person's political ideology
Chemical dependency status	Prejudice or discrimination based on one's current or prior history with substance abuse or dependency
Class	Prejudice or discrimination based on a person's social or economic class (classism)
Color	Prejudice or discrimination based on a person's skin color (colorism)
Criminal history	Prejudice or discrimination based on a person's current involvement in the criminal justice system or past criminal history
Culture	Prejudice or discrimination based on a person's culture
Disability	Prejudice or discrimination based on a person's disabilities (ableism)
Ethnicity	Belief in the superiority of one's own ethnic group (ethnocentrism)
Family structure	Prejudice or discrimination based on family structure, including parent-status
Gender	Prejudice or discrimination based on gender
Gender identity & expression	Prejudice or discrimination based on gender-identity and expression (cisgenderism)
Marital status	Prejudice or discrimination based on marital status
Mental health status	Prejudice or discrimination based on current or previous mental health status
Native-born or immigrant status	Prejudice or discrimination based on native-born or immigrant status (nativism)
Physical appearance	Prejudice or discrimination based on physical appearance that falls outside of societal notions of beauty (lookism)
Race	Prejudice or discrimination based on race (racism)
Religious	Prejudice or discrimination based on religion
Sex	Prejudice or discrimination based on sex (sexism)
Sexual orientation	Prejudice or discrimination based on sexual orientation
Size	Prejudice or discrimination based on size and in particular, weight (sizeism)

the –"isms" with the action needed to transform oppressive dynamics.

APPROACHES AND THEORIES FOR ANTIOPPRESSIVE PRACTICE

Antioppressive practice encompasses a range of practices and theories, as opposed to one practice approach. An antioppressive framework may include, but is not limited to, the following practice approaches and theories:

Radical Approach: The radical approach to social work seeks structural and revolutionary transformation, as opposed to social workers functioning as "caretakers" while working with, rather than against, oppressive systems

TABLE 124.2 Forms of Oppression

Form of Oppression	Definition
Covert oppression	A less public and less obvious form of discrimination that often works subconsciously and/or subliminally to not be seen, known, or "found out."
External oppression	The exploitation, degradation, and/or inhumane treatment of an individual or group based on their membership in a nondominant group (van Wormer & Snyder, 2007).
Horizontal oppression	When individuals of nondominant groups project the pain and anger of being oppressed onto individuals within their own group or other oppressed groups.
Ideological oppression	The idea that a dominant group is superior, entitled, and has a right to control "other" groups; and the attribution of opposite and inferior qualities to nondominant groups, such as stupid, lazy, incompetent, and worthless (Bell, 2013).
Institutional oppression	The mistreatment and control of certain groups by dominant groups is embedded and enforced in the laws, education system, criminal justice system, employment policies, housing development, media images, political processes, public policies and other institutions (Bell, 2013). Institutions can create oppressive consequences regardless of whether or not the individuals within them have oppressive intentions (Cheney, LaFrance, & Quinteros, 2006).
Internalized oppression	Individuals within a non-dominant group enforce disempowerment or oppression on one's self, one's family and/or one's community as a psychological consequence of external oppression (Bailey, Chung, Williams, Singh, & Terrell, 2011). According to Bailey et al. (2011), components of internalized oppression may include: "internalization of negative stereotypes, self-destructive behaviors, devaluation of one's worldview; belief in the biased representation of history; and alteration of physical appearance" (p. 481).
Interpersonal oppression	Individual members of the dominant group mistreat or disrespect individuals of nondominant groups because of a conscious or unconscious belief that their own group is superior. Typically, members of the dominant group will have internalized negative conceptions of nondominant groups, resulting in a perception that their oppressive behavior is "normal" and not oppressive (Bell, 2003).
Invisible oppression	The absence of information or resources applicable or relevant to individuals of nondominant groups, such as data and official statistics, social policies, published guidelines, practice models, and research (Fish, 2008).
Overt oppression	A public, conscious act to harm an individual or group based on their group membership.
Silent oppression	Negative thoughts and attitudes about nondominant groups by individuals of dominant groups who may or may not be perceived, or perceive themselves, as oppressive (Trepagnier, 2001).
Symbolic oppression	Widespread, societally sanctioned ideologies and images used to justify and reinforce stereotypes and relations of domination and subordination (Sanders, 2013).

(Dreikosen, 2009). This approach is informed by a class analysis and critique of capitalism.

Structural Approach: The structural approach situates social problems within a specific societal context and does not attribute them to individual failures (Mullaly, 1997). It promotes empowerment, consciousness raising, an understanding of issues from a global perspective, and an awareness of capitalism's impact on shaping conditions and relationships (Mullaly, 1997).

Feminist Approach: The feminist approach focuses on the ways women experience their existence and how social forces shape these experiences by depriving women of access to resources, power, and emotional fulfillment (Dominelli & McLeod, 1989). Practice models are grounded in a feminist analysis of social problems and prioritize social change and social justice for women (Dominelli & McLeod, 1989).

Critical Approach: The critical approach is concerned with practices that will eliminate domination, exploitation, and oppression from society (Fook, 2002). It is interested in understanding how social constructions, relations, and structures are used to dominate, and in leveraging this knowledge to disrupt dominant structures (Fook, 2002).

Antiracist Approach: An antiracist approach recognizes the institutional nature of racism (Maiter, 2009). It acknowledges the social construction and social effects of race and challenges pathological explanations of its effects on people of color (Maiter, 2009). It questions and critiques White supremacy, as well as the marginalization and de-legitimization of the voices, experiences, and knowledge of people of color. It rejects the stipulation that people of color can only access power as White society dictates (Maiter, 2009). An antiracist framework challenges individuals in power, including social workers, for their role in perpetuating institutional racism, and calls for change at all levels of social work practice (Abrams & Gibson, 2007).

Afrocentric Framework: An Afrocentric framework centers and validates the worldview and experiences of African Americans and is grounded in philosophical and traditional African concepts (Schiele, 1996). It combats negative stereotypes, values collectivity, acknowledges feelings as a source of knowledge, upholds the spiritual nature of human beings, and facilitates societal transformation (Schiele, 1996).

Empowerment Theory: Empowerment theory explores the environmental context of social problems and focuses on individual strengths as opposed to "blaming the victim" or focusing on risk factors (Perkins & Zimmerman, 1995). Practitioners are engaged as collaborators in promoting client wellness and facilitate client involvement in social and political change (Perkins & Zimmerman, 1995).

Critical Race Theory: Critical Race Theory (CRT) utilizes critical reflection to promote awareness of unearned privilege and its consequences (Abrams & Moio, 2009). Practitioners engage in active opposition to institutional oppression rather than encourage clients to passively accept and conform to oppressive systems (Abrams & Moio, 2009).

Strengths Perspective: Strengths perspective identifies and emphasizes the strengths and resources that all individuals, families, and communities possess and can leverage (Rankin, 2006). Challenges and problems are reframed as opportunities (Rankin, 2006).

Social Theory: Social theory supports an understanding of the context of a client's situation through an identification of the social forces (historical, political, cultural) that have shaped the client's life (Dustin & Montgomery, 2010).

Intersectionality Theory: Intersectionality theory holds that social constructions of privilege and oppression, such as race, class, gender, sexual orientation, and ability, intersect to create systems of domination and social injustice on multiple and simultaneous levels (Murphy, Hunt, Zajicek, Norris, & Hamilton, 2009). The theory posits that an understanding of a client's experience based on their social location within these systems will capture the complexity, individuality, and nuances of their actions, choices, and outcomes (Murphy et al., 2009).

PRACTICE PRINCIPLES AND CONSIDERATIONS FOR ANTIOPPRESSIVE SOCIAL WORK

Apply knowledge of oppression: Oppression is not a fixed, permanent reality. It is socially constructed, and therefore, can be deconstructed and transformed (Freire, 1970). Social work is a profession and a social institution with the capacity to either perpetuate or transform oppressive social relations (Campbell, 2003). Social workers should be aware of the multitude of forms and effects of oppression on oppressed persons, including its internalization (Mulally, 2001), and examine their own roles in maintaining privilege and oppression in their own environments and the environments of the people they serve (Nicotera & Kang, 2009). Such an understanding needs to be integrated intellectually, emotionally, and practically (Maidment & Cooper, 2002). Although an analysis of oppression is necessary, it is insufficient to enact social change. Knowledge of the structural dynamics of oppression, as well as one's own role in maintaining it, should then be translated into social change and social justice initiatives (van Wormer & Snyder, 2007). Social workers should be equipped to apply the various antioppressive frameworks (i.e., radical, critical, structural, antiracist, etc.) to all aspects of practice. Approaches geared at resolving the symptoms of oppression one individual at a time are reactionary and support the maintenance of the status quo. Social problems are not the result of personal deficiencies, but weaknesses in the social structure, and structural problems require structural solutions (Mullaly, 1997). Oppression can only be eliminated by addressing its root and structural causes, and thus, change should be directed at entire policy systems (van Wormer & Snyder, 2007).

Challenge positions of dominance: Although it is critical to strive toward an understanding of the experiences of oppressed groups, it is imperative also to focus on countering positions of dominance, such as White supremacy (Butler, Elliott, & Stopard, 2003). A focus on resolving issues within nondominant groups ignores the problematic and oppressive dynamics that need to be resolved by and within dominant groups.

Be cognizant of the implications of language when speaking with or about clients. The role of language in subjugating the oppressed through dominant discourses should be understood, as well as the way that professional, diagnostic, and pathological vocabularies disempower clients (Mulally, 2001). Language should be empowering and easily understood. Encourage, support, and "center" ways of knowing outside of the dominant Eurocentric discourses. Create spaces in which the subjugated discourses of clients can be included and heard (Mandell, 2008). When the primary language of clients is different than the primary language spoken at the agency, the assistance of translators should be employed to minimize communication barriers. Language issues have been shown to be a major impediment to immigrants being able to access and effectively utilize services (Graham, Bradshaw, & Trew, 2009).

In addition to understanding the self within the frame of oppressor/oppressed identities, engagement in critical reflection into one's own personhood, including individual developmental history and multiple social identities is important (Mandell, 2008). The personal, social, and professional dimensions of a worker are intertwined and influence the social worker's own experience as well as the client's experience of the social worker (Mandell, 2008). Social workers need to be aware of the ways in which their own experiences, biases, self-concept, cultural background, values, and emotional history shape their perception, judgment, emotions, and behavior (Mandell, 2008), and how this impacts every client interaction. In addition, social workers should be aware of the ways in which they themselves are oppressed or experience oppression and how that impacts their work. The reflective process may entail asking questions of oneself and then analyzing those answers critically (Mandell, 2008). Examples of questions that could be asked include: In what ways did I stereotype and make conscious or unconscious assumptions about this client and how did that impact my interactions and treatment of the client? What part of my interactions with the client met my own needs versus met the client's needs? Did I impose my notion of what was "right" and what the client "should" do or did I value and foster the client's self-determination? Did I maintain, exacerbate, or improve the situation the client is in? How would I do it differently next time? Are there systemic changes or changes in agency policy that could be made to better meet the needs of this client or group?

Treating everyone the same is not equal treatment: Treating everyone the same assumes everyone is the same and requires disadvantaged groups to approximate the characteristics of dominant groups (Fish, 2008). Within the framework of race, this is known as the "color-blind" approach because it "does not see color," and therefore, does not take into account structural racism or the differing needs of various groups (Fish, 2008). Oppressed groups then either are forced to assimilate into dominant groups and lose their identities, or to remain different and consequently marginalized as "inferior" (Fish, 2008). If practitioners are unaware of how they might identify and be inclusive of the differing cultural needs of various individuals or groups, they can start by asking the individual. Because not everyone within a particular group has the same needs, it is important to not generalize or make assumptions about individuals based on perceptions of group needs.

Cultural groups are not homogenous and there are many variations of within-group diversity: Just as all groups possess different characteristics and have different needs, so do individuals within a group. To illustrate this point, Graham et al. (2009) describe the major diversities fundamental to working with Muslim clients within and across Muslim communities:

A myriad of approaches to faith, depending both on official streams and denominations and on personal adherence to these creeds; countless cultural, ethnic, geographic, and religious origins; and different experiences from one community, one family, and one individual to the next. Profound differences, likewise, will occur from one geographic region to the next, and one agency setting to the next (be it child welfare, mental health, physical health, etc.); differences between mandated and voluntary clients; and differences in relation to the degree of client acculturation, age cohort status, level of religious observance, and other areas of diversity. When dealing with unfamiliar cultural groups, it is all too easy for practitioners to see members of the cultural group as homogenous… There is no easy set of rules, no 'one size fits all' scenarios. (p. 549)

Apply knowledge of how social, economic, and political factors shape client experience. When assessing clients, begin where the client is and avoid a focus on pathological explanations or client dysfunction while minimizing macrocontextual factors such as poverty (Mulally, 2001). Social workers should start by asking, "What has happened to this person?" not "What is wrong with this person?" (Dustin & Montgomery, 2010), and ground problems and solutions in the client's lived realities (Mulally, 2001). Practitioners should understand how behaviors can represent coping or defense mechanisms to marginalization, subjugation, and being treated as inferior when a member of an oppressed group (Mulally, 2001). In addition, it is imperative to understand the connotations, consequences, and stigmatization inherent in labeling clients with a diagnosis or disorder. Baines (1997) described the process used by him and his colleagues in resisting "the dominant discourse that blames individuals for all their problems" by continually reframing "our problems and our clients' problems to be the result of structural and systemic forces" and seeking "solutions that went beyond those just for individual cases" (p. 314).

Establish coalitions of like-minded colleagues: Progressive social work literature and practitioners suggest that the most crucial aspect of carrying out antioppressive practice and protecting oneself from the risks inherent in carrying out acts of resistance is to establish and maintain coalitions with like-minded colleagues (Mulally, 2001). Having access to such support can alleviate the tremendous mental and emotional burden associated with constant introspection while also providing a forum to discuss and process possible challenges in carrying out AOP.

Involve clients in decision-making: A key step in avoiding practice-based oppression is to treat the client as expert. Clients should be engaged in decisions that affect themselves, their families, and their communities. Rather than social workers imposing their perspectives of what a client needs, client input should be meaningfully involved in all areas of practice, including assessment, treatment planning, and treatment evaluation (A. Barnes, personal communication, July 19, 2013). When the insights that clients have into their own lives are acknowledged and valued, the social worker avoids being paternalistic. The social worker should avoid assuming superior "knowing" positions (Butler, et al., 2003) or the role of "expert" and instead be a partner in a mutual-learning process (van Wormer & Snyder, 2007).

Practice critical reflexivity and critical thinking: Be aware of the socially constructed and subjective nature of knowledge and reality, and the socially situated relationship with the client. Reflect critically upon the impact that actions, assumptions, and values have on the client and how they can serve to either reproduce or deconstruct structures of oppression (Campbell, 2003).

Take responsibility for power dynamics. Understand professional power in practice and the dynamics inherent in the identity constructions of social worker as "helper" and client as "needy" and "other" (Mandell, 2008). Be cognizant of which actions are for the benefit of oneself and one's position, versus the benefit of the client, and the ways in which practitioners can use their power to harm and further disenfranchise clients. Identify ways in which power can be operationalized and channeled constructively (Bundy-Fazioli, Ouijano, & Bubar, 2013) to empower the client and transform practices and institutions, rather than destructively, to sustain oppressive practices (Keating, 2000). Practitioners need to know where their power lies, within and outside of their organizations, and how to channel it to facilitate client empowerment (Dustin & Montgomery, 2010). Client power can be developed by highlighting client strengths; expanding client networks and linkages to resources; asserting the ways in which the client has agency, choice, and privileges, both within and outside the professional relationship; and promoting the leadership abilities of the client (Rankin, 2006).

Question what is not working and think outside of the box: Each client and situation is unique so meeting client needs may require creativity and flexibility (Dustin & Montgomery, 2010). There is no "universal formula" or "one-size-fits-all" approach. Be able to apply and adapt social work theories and best practices to best suit the needs of each individual situation, context, and client. It is critical to question traditional assumptions, practices, and policies that are not working (Mulally, 2001).

Employ active listening in all clinical interactions. Active listening promotes understanding of the client's unique perspective, context, background, cultural values, and current situation (Graham, et al., 2009). It also provides insight that can be used to tailor interventions to individual values, comfort levels, and needs.

Offer services that are accessible to the individuals and communities served, in terms of location, fees, and scheduling. Many clients have to work during the day so an agency that is only open between "normal" business hours may create significant economic and financial barriers to clients. These types of barriers are significant and may impede or entirely prohibit service attainment, or exacerbate a client's situation by putting them at risk of work-related challenges from taking time off or arriving or departing from work early to avail themselves of the social services. In addition, services that are prohibitive in terms of cost or location maintain oppression by only being available to certain communities.

Raise client consciousness: Raising a client's understanding of his or her situation, in terms of its social, economic, and political context, can empower the client (Dustin & Montgomery, 2010). Freire referred to this as "conscientization" (Freire, 1970). A client who understands the social aspects of his situation, and the decisions he has made versus the decisions that have been made for him, is better equipped to assess his current situation and how it can be navigated (Dustin & Montgomery, 2010).

Do not treat clients by the labels or stereotypes society has attached to them (Dustin & Montgomery, 2010). Everyone's experiences are situated in distinct historical times, places, and social contexts. Although individuals may share some experiences with other people, each individual has a distinct identity and value system that

has been shaped differently from anyone else's (Clifford & Burke, 2005). Social workers should relate to clients as individuals and not just to the oppression they experience (Butler et al., 2005). Essentialist perceptions of clients do not allow for change to occur (Dustin & Montgomery, 2010).

BARRIERS TO SUCCESSFUL ANTIOPPRESSIVE PRACTICE

Practitioners are unaware of their own racism, heterosexism, and other "–isms" and how these impact their practice. Many people are unaware of forms of oppression that are not overt, and/or resist acknowledgement of the positions of privilege they occupy. Resistance toward acknowledging one's privileged status may arise because of the difficulty in recognizing and challenging the benefits received from group identities and the notion that one is "entitled" to privilege or has "earned" these advantages (van Wormer & Snyder, 2007). For example, multiple research studies have shown that White social workers who maintain racist attitudes and beliefs may not perceive themselves as racist (Schiele, 2007). A 2001 study found that highly educated White women who considered themselves opponents of racism, enacted silent racism through stereotypical images and paternalistic assumptions (Trepagnier, 2001). Trepagnier (2001) suggests that people should view themselves on a continuum from "less racist" to "more racist," and never as "not racist," because of how habitual, systemic, and engrained racism is in the United States (Trepagnier, 2001). A separate study of Masters of Social Work (MSW) students by Van Soest (1997) found that the majority (71%) of White students identified their own privilege as being a barrier to acknowledging and learning about oppression. Once one does become aware of one's own racism/-isms, a long and dedicated process is required to unlearn years of conditioning and socialization (Abrams & Gibson, 2007).

The profession's emphasis on 14 types of diversity and discrimination in social work education is a barrier to being able to cover content on any of the groups meaningfully. Roberts and Smith (2002) warned: "a definition which includes everything is in danger of meaning nothing at all" (p. 197). Similarly, Schiele (2007) cautions that addressing an increasing number of oppressed groups prevents a substantive analysis of each one.

Insufficient time and resources to focus on practitioner well-being and systems change: The funding constraints of social services means that agencies are often understaffed and practitioners are often overworked and underpaid (Mulally, 2001). This leaves little opportunity for social workers to connect the day-to-day focus on individual change with larger social and political change efforts. The time and resource constraints can also impede the ability of practitioners to optimize the well-being of clients, critically reflect on their practice, and foster their own well-being. Research has found that when social workers become burnt-out or emotionally exhausted, they depersonalize and distance themselves from their clients, which clients, in turn, experience as dehumanizing (Mandell, 2008). Practitioners need to take responsibility for, and be supportive of, their own emotional and professional well-being. Change starts from within one's own self and a personally empowered practitioner is far more effective in being able to assist clients (J. Suleman, personal correspondence, July 19, 2013).

There is a contradiction between AOP and sustaining the field of social work. Social work is often funded by, and a function of, the government. Many agencies are also reliant upon funding from corporate-based foundations. Involvement in social and political change initiatives can mean opposition to government and corporate interests, which poses a challenge for the profession. Also, because the client base of social workers is predominantly comprised of oppressed groups, working toward the elimination of oppression creates a paradox by working toward the elimination of the profession itself (J. Suleman, personal correspondence, July 19, 2013).

Effective analysis does not always translate into effective action. Although there has been significant research and intellectualizing over oppression and antioppression, it is questionable how much this information has actually been applied within the field. Language and rhetoric appear to have changed more than anything else (Butler et al., 2005). Within social work education, for example, in spite of CSWE's mandate to include content on oppression, challenges arise in transmitting content into meaningful learning (Phan, Vugia, Wright, Woods, Chu, & Jones, 2009) and then translating learning into social action (Hancock, Kledaras, & Waites, 2012).

There remains division among social work professionals rooted in marginalized voices and needs of oppressed groups. The National Association of Black Social Workers (NABSW) was created as a separate entity from the National Association of Social Workers during the civil rights movement in the 1960s (National Association of Black Social Workers [NABSW], 2013). NABSW became dedicated to issues impacting the Black community, including White supremacy, racism, and Eurocentric-focused human services and social welfare systems (NABSW, 2013). NABSW was compelled to create its own space in order to become a leading advocacy group for the Black community, because it did not have that space within NASW. A half a century later, NABSW remains a separate entity.

THE FUTURE OF ANTI-OPPRESSIVE SOCIAL WORK

A critical, ongoing focus on anti-oppressive practice will be imperative to its sustainability and effectiveness within the field. Some of the possible future directions for AOP within the profession might include:

- **Transform the Eurocentric framework of social work pedagogy.** "Center" diverse ways of knowing and create space for marginalized voices.
- **Evaluate the implementation and effectiveness of AOP.** Define quality assurance standards, clear outcome goals, and measurement tools.
- **Liberate social work research from oppression**. Understand the background, agenda, funding sources, and motives of the research used to inform practice. Eliminate research priorities and processes that reproduce oppressive structural conditions and benefit the researcher or the organization/entity sponsoring the research more than the individuals or communities of inquiry (Strier, 2006). Expand research initiatives done by and for oppressed groups so that the research relied upon for "evidence-based" practice is not predominantly comprised of Eurocentric studies done on dominant (White, hetero, etc.) populations. Increase the practice and application of research processes that empower clients and communities, including participatory, action, and emancipatory research. Participatory research facilitates the active inclusion and participation of under-represented populations

in the inquiry process (Strier, 2006). This collaboration is aimed at promoting the skills and knowledge needed to influence organizational and institutional policies and to participate in economic, political, and cultural life (Strier, 2006). Action research values the self-determination of participants and utilizes experiential learning and action to build community and enhance quality of life (Strier, 2006). Emancipatory research seeks to transform the power imbalance between researchers and participants and facilitate social liberation and empowerment (Letherby, 2006).

The nature of oppression and our understanding of it are always changing, as are the social and cultural contexts in which it is situated (Butler et al., 2005). The evolving nature of oppression, coupled with new forms of resistance to social change efforts and growing diversity within the population, makes antioppressive practice an ongoing, critical area of focus for the social work profession.

WEBSITES

Canadian social work organization. www.aosw. socialwork.dal.ca/whatisaosw.html
Practice and principles. www.accessalliance.ca/ antioppression

References

Abramovitz, M. (1999). Social work and social reform: an arena of struggle. *Social Work*, 44(6), 512–527.

Abrams, L. S., & Gibson, P. (2007). Reframing multicultural education: Teaching white privilege in the social work curriculum. *Journal of Social Work Education*, 43(1), 147–160.

Abrams, L. S., & Moio, J. (2009). Critical race theory and the cultural competence dilemma in social work education. *Journal of Social Work Education*, 45(2), 245–261.

Bailey, T. M., Chung, Y. B., Williams, W. S., Singh, A. A., & Terrell, H. K. (2011). Development and validation of the internalized racial oppression scale for black individuals. *Journal of Counseling Psychology*, 58(4), 481–493.

Baines, D. (1997). Feminist social work in the inner city: The challenges of race, class, and gender. *Affilia*, 12(3), 297–317.

Bell, J. (2013). The four "I's" of oppression. YouthBuild USA. Retrieved from https://youthbuild.org/sites/youthbuild.org/files/Four%20Is.pdf

Brown, A., & Mistry, T. (2005). Group work with "mixed membership" groups: Issues of race and gender. *Social Work with Groups*, 28(3/4), 133–148.

Bundy-Fazioli, K., Quijano, L. M., & Bubar, R. (2013). Graduate students' perceptions of professional power in social work practice. *Journal of Social Work Education*, 49, 108–121.

Butler, A., Elliott, T., & Stopard, N. (2003). Living up to the standards we set: A critical account of the development of anti-racist standards. *Social Work Education*, 22(3), 271–282.

Campbell, C. (2003). Anti-oppressive social work, promoting equity and social justice. Retrieved from http://aosw.socialwork.dal.ca/

Chapman, C. (2011). Resonance, intersectionality, and reflexivity in critical pedagogy (and research methodology). *Social Work Education*, 30(7), 723–744.

Cheney, C., LaFrance, J., & Quinteros, T. (2006). Institutionalized oppression definitions. Tri-County Domestic & Sexual Violence Intervention Network. Retrieved from http://www.pcc.edu/resources/illumination/documents/institutionalized-oppression-definitions.pdf

Clifford, D., & Burke, B. (2005). Developing anti-oppressive ethics in the new curriculum. *Social Work Education*, 24(6), 677–692.

Council on Social Work Education. (2009). Advanced social work practice in clinical social work. Retrieved from http://www.cswe.org/File.aspx?id=26685

Council on Social Work Education. (2012). Educational policy and accreditation standards. Retrieved from http://www.cswe.org/File.aspx?id=13780

Dominelli, L., & McLeod, E. (1989). *Feminist social work*. London: The MacMillan Press.

Dreikosen, D. (2009). Radical social work: A call to link arms. *Journal of Progressive Human Services*, 20(2), 107–109.

Dustin, D., & Montgomery, M. R. (2010). The use of social theory in reflecting on anti-oppressive practice with final year BSc social work students. *Social Work Education*, 29(4), 386–401.

Fish, J. (2008). Far from mundane: Theorizing heterosexism for social work education. *Social Work Education*, 27(2), 182–193.

Freire, P. (1970). *Pedagogy of the oppressed* (30th ed.). New York, NY: Bloomsbury Academic.

Graham, J. R., Bradshaw, C., & Trew, J. L. (2009). Adapting social work in working with Muslim clients. *Social Work Education*, 28(5), 544–561.

Group for the Advancement of Psychiatry. (2012). The history of psychiatry and homosexuality. Retrieved from http://www.aglp.org/gap/1_history/

Hancock, T. U., Kledaras, C. G., & Waites, C. (2012). Facing structural inequality: Students' orientation to oppression and practice with oppressed groups. *Journal of Social Work Education, 48*(1), 5–25.

Keating, F. (2000). Anti-racist perspectives: What are the gains for social work? *Social Work Education, 19*(1), 77–87.

Letherby, G. (2006). Emancipatory research. The SAGE Dictionary of Social Research Methods. Retrieved from http://srmo.sagepub.com/view/the-sage-dictionary-of-social-research-methods/n62.xml

Maidment, J., & Cooper, L. (2002). Acknowledgement of client diversity and oppression in social work student supervision. *Social Work Education, 21*(4), 399–407.

Maiter, S. (2009). Using an anti-racist framework for assessment and intervention in clinical practice with families from diverse ethno-racial backgrounds. *Clinical Social Work Journal, 37*, 267–276.

Mandell, D. (2008). Power, care and vulnerability: Considering use of self in child welfare work. *Journal of Social Work Practice, 22*(2), 235–248.

Mullaly, B. (1997). *Structural social work: Ideology, theory and practices.* Toronto: Oxford University Press.

Mullaly, B. (2001). Confronting the politics of despair: Toward the reconstruction of progressive social work in a global economy and postmodern age. *Social Work Education, 20*(3), 303–320.

Murphy, Y., Hunt, V., Zajicek, A. M., Norris, A. N., & Hamilton, L. (2009). *Incorporating intersectionality in social work practice, research, policy and education.* Baltimore, MD: Port City Press.

National Association of Black Social Workers. (2013). History. Retrieved from http://www.nabsw.org/mserver/mission.aspx

National Association of Social Workers. (2013). Code of ethics of the National Association of Social Workers. Retrieved from http://www.socialworkers.org/pubs/code/code.asp

Nicotera, N., & Kang, H. (2009). Beyond diversity courses: Strategies for integrating critical consciousness across social work curriculum. *Journal of Teaching in Social Work, 29*, 188–203.

Perkins, D. D., & Zimmerman, M. A. (1995). Empowerment theory, research, and application. *American Journal of Community Psychology, 23*(5), 569–579.

Phan, P., Vugia, H., Wright, P., Woods, D.R., Chu, M., & Jones, T. (2009). A social work program's experience in teaching about race in the curriculum. *Journal of Social Work Education, 45*(2), 325–333.

Roberts, T. L., & Smith, L. A. (2002). The illusion of inclusion: An analysis of approaches to diversity within predominantly White schools of social work. *Journal of Teaching in Social Work, 22*, 189–211.

Sanders, V. (2013). Psychology of oppression. Washington University at St. Louis. Retrieved from www.mscsw.com/Resources/Documents/MSCSW%201112.pdf

Schiele, J. H. (2007). Implications of the equality-of-oppressions paradigm for curriculum content on people of color. *Journal of Social Work Education, 43*(1), 83–100.

Strier, R. (2006). Anti-oppressive research in social work: A preliminary definition. *British Journal of Social Work, 37*, 1–15.

Trepagnier, B. (2001). Deconstructing categories: The exposure of silent racism. *Symbolic Interaction, 24*(2), 141–163.

Van Wormer, K., & Snyder, C. (2007). Infusing content on oppression into the social work curriculum. *Journal of Human Behavior in the Social Environment, 16*(4), 19–35.

125 Effective Practice with Refugees and Immigrants

Miriam Potocky

Social work practice with refugees and immigrants requires understanding of four fundamental elements: (1) the distinction between the two groups; (2) the stages of migration; (3) the role of culture, ethnicity, and minority status; and (4) the importance of evidence-based practice. An understanding of these fundamental elements lays the foundation for effective practice with these populations. This discussion addresses these fundamental elements, using two case examples for illustration. Then, necessary components of effective practice are presented and their practice implications for the two cases considered.

CASE EXAMPLES

Lakshmi, age 37 years, came to the United States six years ago from India as a legal immigrant accompanying her husband, a software engineer who was hired by a U.S.-based multinational corporation. The couple has two sons, ages 10 and 12 years. Lakshmi does not work outside the home. Both parents are fluent in English, and the family has a comfortable socioeconomic status. Recently, Lakshmi's 75-year-old mother-in-law came from India to live with the family. The mother-in-law requires some assistance from Lakshmi in her activities of daily living. Additionally, some family conflicts have arisen due to the mother-in-law's disapproval of the boys' Americanized behaviors. Lakshmi is also concerned about her own mother, who still lives in India and is in poor health. Lakshmi has been experiencing migraine headaches recently and has sought medical care from her physician.

Fernando, age 30 years, came to the United States from Cuba four months ago. He arrived in Florida following a three-day boat journey during which he became sunburned and dehydrated and two of his companions drowned. In Cuba, Fernando had been a journalist and had been imprisoned for a year for writing an article critical of the Cuban government. On arrival in the United States, he was granted refugee status. He now lives with a sister and her family, who had come to the United States previously. He has minimal English ability and is presently employed as a parking valet. He has begun drinking heavily.

FUNDAMENTAL ELEMENTS

Immigrants versus Refugees

There is a fundamental distinction between immigrants and refugees (Devore & Schlesinger, 1999). Immigrants leave their countries voluntarily in search of better economic opportunities or family reunification, as illustrated in the case of Lakshmi. In contrast, refugees are forced out of their countries because of human rights violations against them, as illustrated by Fernando. Immigrants may be further divided into legal and illegal. Whether a person is a legal or illegal immigrant or a refugee has implications for his or her experiences during the migration process, as will be described shortly.

Stages of Migration

The migration process consists of three major stages: premigration and departure, transit, and resettlement (Drachman, 1992).

Premigration and departure. The premigration stage entails loss of family and friends and loss of a familiar environment. Both Lakshmi and Fernando have experienced these losses. Generally, the losses are greater and the premigration and departure experience is more traumatic for refugees than for immigrants. Because refugees live in politically oppressive conditions or in the midst of war, they may have been subject to discrimination, violence, rape, torture, death of family members, or imprisonment, as in Fernando's case.

Refugees often leave under hurried, chaotic, and dangerous conditions. In many cases, they flee in the midst of armed conflict. They may be victims of violence or may have witnessed violence, rape, torture, or killing. In some cases, refugees leave in mass movements, with hundreds or thousands of people. Because refugees flee under these the chaotic conditions, they usually must leave almost all their possessions behind. Thus, they lose their homes and other assets. Furthermore, refugees do not know when, if ever, they will be able to return to their countries. Thus, leaving behind family and friends is particularly painful because they know they may never see them again. Fernando left Cuba in a boat on short notice, and he fears that if he returned he would be imprisoned again.

In contrast, immigrants typically are able to plan their departure well in advance, and they leave under relatively calm conditions. They do not have to abandon their possessions; they can take some assets, especially money, with them, and they retain ownership of their property. Typically, there are no political barriers to prevent them from returning to their country, so they know they can return, even though it may not be for a long time. Nonetheless, the separation from home and family is painful, as illustrated by Lakshmi, who is likely feeling some guilt about leaving her mother behind.

Not all refugees and immigrants experience all the losses and traumas that can occur during this stage. However, some degree of loss occurs in all cases. The experiences during this stage influence the later stages of the migration process. In particular, these experiences affect people's health and mental health later.

Transit. The transit stage involves the physical move from one country to another. Again, this experience is usually more traumatic for refugees than immigrants. The experience also differs between legal and illegal immigrants. For legal immigrants, the transit usually entails arrival by plane and is typically not traumatic, as in Lakshmi's case. However, for illegal immigrants and refugees, the transit may be dangerous or life-threatening. Immigrants who enter the United States illegally often experience a dangerous transit where they are at the mercy of paid smugglers. Refugees may pass through areas of armed conflict and may be subject to or witness the same atrocities as in the premigration and departure stage. They may undertake a lengthy journey on foot, during which they may face starvation, dehydration, hypothermia, or other physical hardships. Some refugees leave by boat. Often, these boats are in poor condition and overloaded. Sinking, drowning, and illness or death due to sun exposure is not uncommon, as in Fernando's case. In many cases, refugees are placed in refugee camps in neighboring countries before they are sent to a permanent home in the United States or another country. These camps usually consist of tent cities. They are often overcrowded and have poor sanitation. Diseases and violence in the camps are not uncommon. Refugees may remain in such camps for years before obtaining permission to enter the United States. Refugees who arrive directly in the United States requesting asylum may be placed in a detention center while their case is decided. In some cases, such individuals have remained in detention for months or years.

Again, not all legal immigrants, refugees, and illegal immigrants have the same transit experiences. Trauma experienced during the transit can affect the person's adaptation in the later stage, namely, resettlement.

Resettlement. Resettlement is the last stage of the migration process. This stage can be seen as lasting throughout people's stay in the new country, which may be the rest of their lives. This is the stage during which social workers in the United States encounter and work with immigrants and refugees such as Lakshmi and Fernando. Issues that arise during this stage include adaptation to the cultural norms of the new country; health and mental health problems; language, education, and employment issues; changing family dynamics; and discrimination, racism, and xenophobia from members of the host society. Many of these challenges are evident in Lakshmi's and Fernando's cases. Again, these issues are usually more difficult to cope with for refugees than for immigrants.

Culture, Ethnicity, and Minority Status

Culture refers to the norms of conduct, beliefs, traditions, values, language, art, skills, and interpersonal relationships within a society (Lum, 2010). For example, Lakshmi's culture places high importance on obligations of adult children to their parents, as reflected in her situation. *Ethnicity* refers to groupings of people based on shared elements such as physical appearance, culture, religion, and history. Most immigrants and refugees can also be considered *minorities*, meaning that they are disadvantaged and receive unequal treatment in the host society (Lum, 2010). Culture, ethnicity, and minority status affect people's life experiences, including their utilization and response to formal helping systems. For example, Fernando may not actively seek formal help due to the significance attached to machismo (i.e., a strong sense of masculine pride) in traditional Hispanic cultures.

Evidence-based Practice

Many interventions have not been specifically evaluated for refugee and immigrant clients. Therefore, social workers must have knowledge of the existing empirical literature and be able to determine what interventions, or modifications of interventions, appear most promising for immigrant or refugee clients based on demonstrated effectiveness for other populations. Social workers then need to adapt existing interventions or programs to make them culturally compatible with the ethnic backgrounds of immigrant or refugee clients. To determine whether these adaptations were successful, social workers need understanding of various evaluation methods.

COMPONENTS OF EFFECTIVE PRACTICE

The foregoing elements provide the foundation for effective practice with refugees and immigrants. Such practice consists of specific sets of attitudes and beliefs, knowledge, and skills. These necessary components are summarized next, based on a synthesis of the literature on culturally competent practice (Potocky-Tripodi, 2002), adapted specifically for refugees and immigrants.

Attitudes and Beliefs for Effective Practice with Refugee and Immigrant Clients

Effective social workers:

- Are aware that practice cannot be neutral, value-free, or objective
- Are aware of and sensitive to their own cultural heritage
- Are aware of how their own cultural backgrounds and experiences, attitudes, values, and biases influence psychological processes

- Are aware that their decisions may be ethnocentric
- Are aware of their negative emotional reactions toward refugee and immigrant groups that may prove detrimental to their clients
- Are aware of stereotypes and preconceived notions that they may hold toward refugee and immigrant groups
- Are willing to make purposive changes in their feelings, thoughts, and behaviors toward refugee and immigrant groups
- Value and respect differences that exist between themselves and clients in terms of ethnicity, culture, and beliefs, and are willing to contrast their own beliefs and attitudes with those of their immigrant and refugee clients in a nonjudgmental fashion
- Respect clients' religious and/or spiritual beliefs and values about physical and mental functioning
- Respect indigenous helping practices and respect ethnic community intrinsic help-giving networks
- Value bilingualism and do not view another language as an impediment to practice
- Value the social work profession's commitment to social justice
- Value the importance of evidence-based practice
- Are able to recognize the limits of their competencies and expertise.

Knowledge for Effective Practice with Refugee and Immigrant Clients

Effective social workers are knowledgeable about:

- Multiple theories of social science, human behavior, and social work practice
- Their own racial and cultural heritage and how it personally and professionally affects their definitions and biases of normality, abnormality, and the practice process
- How oppression, racism, discrimination, and stereotyping affect their work and them personally
- How their communication style may clash with or facilitate the practice process with refugee and immigrant clients and how to anticipate the impact it may have on others
- Demographic characteristics, life experiences, cultural heritage, and historical backgrounds of various refugee and immigrant groups

- Family structures/hierarchies, values, and beliefs of various refugee and immigrant groups
- The effects of culture, ethnicity, and minority status on personality formation, life choices, manifestation of psychological disorders, help-seeking behavior, and the appropriateness or inappropriateness of practice approaches
- Culture as a source of cohesion, identity, and strength as well as strain and discordance
- A refugee or immigrant group's adaptive strategies
- Ethnic community characteristics and community resources
- How a person's behavior is guided by membership in families, groups, organizations, and communities
- How sociopolitical influences, such as immigration issues, poverty, racism, stereotyping, discrimination, and powerlessness, impact the lives of refugee and immigrant clients and may influence the practice process
- The cultural characteristics of generic social work practice and how they may clash with the cultural values of different refugee and immigrant groups
- Potential bias in assessment instruments and diagnostic systems
- Institutional barriers that prevent refugees and immigrants from using health, mental health, and social services
- Empirical literature on intervention effectiveness
- Program and practice evaluation methods.

Skills for Effective Practice with Refugee and Immigrant Clients

Effective social workers:

- Take responsibility for providing the language requested by the client
- Have a dependable ability to develop client mutual respect/acceptance and regard
- Are able to overcome client feelings of suspicion, distrust, or anger
- Use a positive and open communication style
- Use appropriate terms and words, visual clues, tone, facial expressions, and cadence
- Follow culturally appropriate relationship protocols
- Sincerely convey signals of respect congruent with the client's cultural beliefs

- Use appropriate self-disclosure
- Identify the client's problem in terms of wants or needs, levels, and details
- Use ethnographic interviewing skills to help identify the problem
- Assess the problem within the client's total bio-psychosocial context
- Help clients determine whether a problem stems from racism or bias in others so that clients do not inappropriately blame themselves
- Assess stressors and strengths relevant to the problem and its resolution
- Use assessment and testing instruments appropriately
- Actively involve their clients in goal-setting and contracting
- Help clients prioritize problems
- Educate their clients about the processes of intervention, such as goals, expectations, legal rights, and the worker's orientation
- Establish culturally acceptable goals and objectives
- Formulate multilevel intervention alternatives
- Identify and use the client's definition of successful coping strategies and problem resolution strategies
- Select culturally appropriate, empirically based interventions
- Formulate explicit contracts
- Enhance or restore a client's psychosocial functioning and seek to redress structural inequities at the societal level
- Tailor intervention strategies to differences in help-seeking patterns, definition of problems, and selection of solutions
- Use a blend of formal and informal helping resources
- Consult with traditional healers or religious and spiritual leaders and practitioners when appropriate
- Explore issues of authority or equality in the therapeutic relationship
- Aim to increase personal, interpersonal, or political power of individuals, families, groups, and communities through empowerment techniques
- Aim to promote a sense of the collective; increase access to resources and to codeveloped client–worker solutions
- Exercise institutional intervention skills on behalf of clients to eliminate biases, prejudices, and discriminatory practices

- Monitor intervention implementation and client progress
- Review progress and growth with clients
- Refer clients to other workers or agencies if they believe they are unable to help
- Evaluate problem change and attainment of objectives
- Evaluate intervention effectiveness
- Address the client's and worker's feelings about termination
- Help clients establish goals and tasks for the future
- Connect clients with other community resources
- Establish a follow-up plan
- Evaluate agency effectiveness
- Facilitate maintenance of client change
- Implement follow-up contacts
- Collect client information during follow-up
- Evaluate follow-up data
- Reinstate intervention if necessary.

Case Example Practice Implications

Lakshmi has come to her physician seeking help for migraine headaches. Her doctor may identify stress as a potential contributing factor to the pain. The physician may offer medication and may also refer Lakshmi to a social worker for a stress reduction intervention. Being familiar with the foregoing practice principles, the social worker should recognize the multiple stressors in Lakshmi's life and explore these with her. The client's stress stems from the various experiences in the different stages of her migration process, and from the generational conflicts in her household due to differential acculturation of family members. The social worker may suggest family counseling to address this issue. The worker should also explore whether Lakshmi has a support system outside her family; if not, the worker should connect Lakshmi with other immigrant women from India, who will probably be able to provide mutual support. The worker should also discuss with Lakshmi various alternatives for the care of both her mother-in-law and her own mother, bearing in mind the cultural values relevant to this.

As a recently arrived refugee, Fernando is probably receiving initial resettlement assistance from a government program. Such a program primarily focuses on employment. The social worker should recognize that Fernando is underemployed and may be feeling depressed due to the loss of his occupational status. The worker should help him enroll in English classes and a retraining program that will help him attain a job commensurate with his skills. The worker should also realize that Fernando is likely traumatized by his past imprisonment and by witnessing the drowning of his boat companions. Thus, the worker should explore the possibility of mental health counseling, bearing in mind that Fernando is not likely to be initially receptive to the idea due to cultural values. The worker should also explore alternate housing for Fernando, given that living with his sister and her family may be creating additional stress for all of them.

CONCLUSION

Effective social work practice with refugees and immigrants is based on an understanding of certain fundamental factors, combined with the development of specific attitudes, beliefs, knowledge, and skills. The development of these competencies is a continuous learning process. Social workers should continually evaluate their practice and the policies and procedures within their agencies to determine how they might better serve and be more effective with refugee and immigrant clients.

WEBSITES

Canadian Council for Refugees Best Settlement Practices. http://ccrweb.ca/bpfina1.htm.
Grantmakers Concerned with Immigrants and Refugees. http://www.gcir.org.
National Association of Social Workers. Immigration and Refugee Resettlement. http://www.naswdc.org/practice/intl/issues/immigration.asp.

References

Devore, W. & Schlesinger, E. G. (1999). *Ethnic-sensitive social work practice* (5th ed.). Boston, MA: Allyn & Bacon.
Drachman, D. (1992). A stage-of-migration framework for service to immigrant populations. *Social Work, 37,* 68–72.
Lum, D. (Ed.). (2010). *Culturally competent practice: A framework for understanding diversity and justice issues* (4th ed.). Belmont, CA: Thomson.
Potocky-Tripodi, M. (2002). *Best practices for social work with refugees and immigrants.* New York, NY: Columbia University Press.

126 Social Work Practice with Native Americans

Teresa A. Evans-Campbell & Gordon E. Limb

THE CULTURAL CONTEXT OF PRACTICE WITH AMERICAN INDIANS/ALASKA NATIVES

Terminology

Numerous terms are used to describe the indigenous people of North America, including Native American, American Indian/Alaska Native (AIAN), and First Nations. While Native American is more generic, American Indian is the term used by the federal government in all policies and treaties. First Nations is a term used in Canada and by some tribes. However, many Native people instead prefer to identify by their specific tribal affiliation. Although there is no one, universally accepted term, most Native people have strong preferences regarding terminology, and it is incumbent upon social workers to ask clients which term they prefer. In this chapter, the terms *AIAN* and *Native* are used interchangeably.

Diversity among American Indians/Alaska Natives

The term *AIAN* encompasses an extremely diverse group of people. In the United States, there are currently 566 federally recognized tribes, including 229 village groups in Alaska and close to 200 unrecognized tribes (Bureau of Indian Affairs, 2012). The size of tribal nations varies widely, ranging from only two members (in several California tribes) to over 100,000 members (U.S. Bureau of the Census, 2010). According to the 2010 Census, 5.2 million people in the United States identify as AIAN, either alone or in combination with one or more other races. Out of this total, 2.9 million people identified as AIAN alone. The AIAN (in combination) population experienced rapid growth, increasing by 39% since 2000 (U.S. Census Bureau, 2010).

Contrary to common portrayals in the media, two-thirds of all AIAN people now live in urban settings (U.S. Bureau of the Census, 2010). The urbanization of the Native population has occurred over the past several decades, often as the result of federal policies including tribal termination and relocation. Although urban AIAN research is growing, the majority of literature on social work practice with AIANs continues to be based on experiences with reservation-based populations.

Though there are some generally shared norms and values among Native people, each tribal nation is distinct in terms of culture, language, and social customs, and each nation itself encompasses a diverse population of tribal members. At the same time, American Indian families are increasingly multitribal, multicultural, and multiracial, and there is also tremendous variation in the level of acculturation among AIAN people. Though such diversity exists, Natives have endured generations of concerted stereotyping, and non-Natives often carry profound misconceptions about AIAN people and AIAN cultures. Given the great diversity among Native people, social workers must utilize a strengths perspective and place a strong focus on cultural affiliation and cultural identity in the assessment phase, relying on Native clients to best articulate how they identify culturally (Weaver, 2003).

THE HISTORICAL CONTEXT FOR PRACTICE WITH AMERICAN INDIANS/ALASKA NATIVES

Historical Trauma

An understanding of the historical context in which contemporary Native people live is imperative for culturally relevant social work practice. Over successive generations, Native people have endured a series of traumatic assaults that have had profound consequences for families and communities. An extensive body of literature documents these assaults, which have included community massacres, forced relocation, the forced removal of children though Indian boarding school policies, foster care and adoption policies that promoted the removal of Native children from their families, and the prohibition of spiritual and cultural practices (Cross, Earle, & Simmons, 2000; Stannard, 1992).

As an example, the Indian boarding school era, which began in the late 19th century, involved separating children from their parents and sending them to schools operated by religious organizations or the Bureau of Indian Affairs (BIA). The schools prohibited the use of Native language, required students to wear uniforms, and enforced discipline in an authoritarian manner completely foreign to traditional Native child-rearing practices. The mission of boarding schools was the forcible assimilation of Native children into the mainstream society. The boarding school era has been linked to losses related to Native language, religion, beliefs, customs, and social norms—the foundation of the AIAN worldview and identity. Today, nearly one-half of all AIANs either attended boarding schools or who had parents who attended boarding schools (Limb, 2004).

Although AIAN peoples have demonstrated enormous resilience in spite of this history, such events have taken a toll on the mental health and wellness of Native families. Our ability to understand the full impact of these traumatic events and develop relevant interventions is constrained by conceptual and empirical limitations within commonly used models of trauma and traumatic response. Standard diagnostic categories capture some trauma-related symptoms experienced by AIANs (e.g., nightmares about traumatic events) but are limited in their ability to explore the effects of multiple, intergenerational, and culturally unique traumatic events. Moreover, current models of trauma focus primarily on negative responses to trauma and are only beginning to explore the ways people cope and maintain wellness.

A number of different terms have been used to describe the multigenerational nature of distress in Native communities, including collective trauma, intergenerational trauma, multigenerational trauma, and historical trauma (Evans-Campbell, 2008). Recently, social workers have begun to view the concept of historical trauma as an important consideration in wellness among historically oppressed communities. Scholarship exploring historical trauma in Native communities draws from the seminal work of Maria Yellow Horse Brave Heart and her colleagues (Brave Heart 1999a,b, 2000; Brave Heart, Chase, Elkins, & Altschul, 2011; Brave Heart & DeBruyn, 1998). Historical trauma is defined as the cumulative emotional and psychological wounding across generations, including the lifespan, which emanates from massive group trauma (Brave Heart et al., 2011). It is conceptualized as a collective complex trauma inflicted on a group of people who share a specific group identity or affiliation—ethnicity, nationality, and religious affiliation.

Brave Heart and her colleagues explored the impacts of a range of historically traumatic events on mental health among the Lakota and documented a collection of common responses that they call "historical trauma response." This response is similar to symptomatology identified among Jewish Holocaust survivors and their descendants and includes rumination over past events and lost ancestors, survivor guilt, feeling numb in response to traumatic events, anger, depression, and intrusive dreams and thoughts (Brave Heart, 1999a,b, 2000; Brave Heart & DeBruyn, 1998). Growing evidence suggests, however, that although some Native people have negative reactions associated with historically traumatic events, they also exhibit many areas of resilience and strength.

In addition to intergenerational losses, contemporary Native communities also suffer from some of the highest rates of lifetime traumatic events, including interpersonal violence (e.g., Tjaden & Thoennes, 2000), suicide (Olson & Wahab, 2006), child abuse and neglect (Cross, Earle, & Simmons, 2000), poor health and mental health (Walters, Simoni, & Evans-Campbell, 2002), and an ongoing barrage of microaggressions and racist stereotypes. Given both the historical context and the high rate of contemporary stressors faced by Native people, it is not surprising that AIANs have among the highest rates of mental health disorders in the United States (Substance Abuse and Mental Health Services Administration [SAMHSA], 2001).

Tribal Sovereignty

Another important element of the historical context for practice with AIANs is an understanding of tribal sovereignty. Throughout American history, AIANs have had a unique relationship with the United States government. One of the most important aspects of this relationship is the concept of AIAN self-government or sovereignty. From an AIAN perspective, tribal sovereignty was instrumental in the passage of a number of policies that have allowed AIANs to practice their traditional culture. The federal government views tribal sovereignty as a political or legal dimension— "including the power to adopt its own form of government; to define the conditions of citizenship/membership in the nation; to regulate the domestic relations of the nation's members... to levy dues, fees or taxes upon citizens of the tribe; [and] to administer justice" (Wilkins, 1997, p. 20).

Tribal Sovereignty has many of the same elements as the ethical standard of *self-determination* in the National Association of Social Workers (NASW) Code of Ethics (2008) endorsed by the social work profession. An understanding and respect for tribal sovereignty allows social workers the opportunity to utilize cultural elements in their practice with AIANs and shifts attention away from deficit models in favor of models of cultural strength (Red Horse & Limb, 2004; Weaver, 2003).

EVIDENCE-BASED INTERVENTIONS RELEVANT TO SOCIAL WORK PRACTICE WITH AMERICAN INDIANS/ALASKA NATIVES

There is clearly a critical need for effective models of practice with Native people. Increasingly, the field of social work is moving toward the use of evidence-based practice interventions and strategies with diverse populations. Unfortunately, the use of evidence-based interventions with AIAN people is complicated by the lack of intervention research that either includes Native clients or examines Native-specific practice models. Instead, practitioners often rely on evidence-based interventions that have shown success with non-Natives and then adapt these for work with Native populations. In some cases, the work to adapt interventions culturally is extensive and involves active participation from Native community members and practitioners. Numerous culturally adapted programs have been empirically tested and have shown success with Native populations (e.g., The American Indian Life Skills Development suicide prevention curriculum, several trauma-related treatment models developed by the Indian Country Child Trauma Center). In other cases, cultural adaptation is only superficial—using Native words or Native images in media materials, for example—and the core strategies used in work remain culturally inconsistent.

When working with Native people, social workers might also consider practices that are considered promising in that there is emerging empirical evidence of their success. There are a growing number of Native-designed programs designated as promising practice models by agencies such as the Indian Health Service and SAMHSA. In addition, many indigenous practice models have strong support in tribal communities but still lack empirical validation. In these cases, taking a broader perspective on what constitutes evidence can be helpful. For example, support for many indigenous healing practices may also come in the form of practice-based evidence, including the historical use of healing strategies, community acceptance, and the integration of a healing strategy into the culture of a community (BigFoot, 2007).

PRACTICE COMPETENCIES FOR WORK WITH AMERICAN INDIAN/ALASKA NATIVE INDIVIDUALS, FAMILIES, AND COMMUNITIES

To help provide an empowering context for practice with Native families, a number of indigenous social work practice competencies are outlined. Several of these strategies have been adapted from a set of decolonizing practice competencies presented by Evans-Campbell and Walters (2006). These strategies are not meant to be exhaustive but should be seen as a base to build on in work with families and communities.

Using a Culturally Relevant Framework for Practice

Social work practice with AIAN people requires familiarity with Native norms and values, an understanding of the history of colonization, and an appreciation of the diversity both among and within Native communities. Accordingly, each intervention should be culturally specific and tribally relevant. Thus, social workers should not assume that a program designed for practice with Lakota people will be effective with Yakama tribal members. Interventions must also be aligned with the level of cultural connection (Weaver, 2003, 2004) and identity needs of each individual. Though many Native people are closely tied to their communities, others have a more tenuous connection, which may influence their choice in services. Moreover, some Native people feel alienated from their tribal culture and experience identity-related mental health issues, including depression, low self-esteem, and anxiety. To help those suffering from feelings of alienation, social workers can connect families with Native cultural and social resources in their area. In many cities, Native organizations run programs specifically targeted to Native people (e.g., talking circles for Native parents and Native youth programs), and nearby tribal communities may offer their services to Native families who are not tribal members.

Enacting a Historically Relevant Framework for Practice

Social workers should have training around the history of colonization in the United States and its impact on Native wellness and family processes. Through the process of exploring cultural narratives and history, practitioners can work with clients to identify traditional ways of addressing trauma as well as cultural strengths that can be built on in practice. It is also essential that workers gain a fundamental understanding of how social work has played a role in the institutional racism that Native people have experienced (e.g., discriminatory child welfare policies and practices).

Documenting Historically Traumatic Events and Colonial Trauma

Though the lives of Native people are contextualized within a history of colonization and historically traumatic events, many people are not aware of the specific events that have impacted their communities and families. Practitioners can assist clients in learning about their histories by completing genograms, historical narratives, and historical timelines with individuals and families. These charts can document births, deaths, cultural events, specific historically traumatic events, as well as corresponding responses at the individual and familial level. Through such exercises, family survival strategies, coping patterns, and anniversary reactions to historically traumatic events are made explicit and can be clearly linked to traumatic events.

Focusing on Resilience and Strength

Although all indigenous people share a history of historical trauma and contemporary stress, these experiences do not define Native people. Native families have tremendous histories of strength and intergenerational resiliency, which should be a core focus of work. Social workers are in a unique position to help illuminate family strengths and identify how these strengths are currently manifested in the family system.

Taking Time to Build Trust

Studies show that Native people have high levels of mistrust around public social service agencies, including Child Protective Services (CPS), mental health agencies, and health care settings (e.g., Carter, 2010; Evans-Campbell, under review). This may be especially true in the field of child welfare where generations of Native children have been impacted by policies designed to assimilate them or remove them from the care of Native families, including the Indian boarding school movement, the Indian Adoption Project, not following the Indian Child Welfare Act, and the long history of CPS intervention in Native families. Such views are not surprising in light of this history and might even be reframed as a healthy reaction to what was historically a real threat. Accordingly, practitioners should be prepared to spend a significant amount of time building trust, especially in initial sessions with Native people. Intervention models that rely on client-initiated goals and objectives (e.g., motivational interviewing) may be especially helpful in this regard.

Communicating about Historical Trauma

Communication around historically traumatic events is an integral piece of healing. At certain times, responses such as denial or anger may be quite functional and protective responses to trauma, especially while a person is attempting to survive major catastrophic traumas such as boarding school or genocide (Brave Heart et al., 2011; Danieli, 1998). However, the maintenance of such responses can undermine individual and family health over time. When individuals are emotionally prepared and ready, social workers can assist in exploring historical losses and making links to current family functioning. An important area of focus may be intergenerational anniversary patterns, which are often unconscious to individuals and families. For example, a Native mother may become anxious or preoccupied with the safety of her children around the anniversary of the time her parents were taken to Indian boarding school.

Supporting Clients in the Use of Traditional Healing Methods

Native clients may prefer to work with, or need additional assistance from, traditional healers or Native practitioners, and social workers should be prepared to help identify appropriate traditional resources. In addition, some communities have lost important cultural tools and rituals that historically addressed loss and grief. Although it would be inappropriate for non-Native workers to attempt to impart cultural knowledge, practitioners can be invaluable as they support community members in reclaiming or relearning traditions and creating new ways to heal (Gray & Rose, 2012).

Endings in Practice with Native People

Termination with Native clients often requires a relatively extended time frame as well as worker flexibility around commemorating the worker–client relationship. As noted previously, Native clients tend to establish trust with workers slowly and may invest a substantial amount of energy into relationship building. After a lengthy process of building trust, termination may require more time and planning on the part of the worker. The loss of the therapeutic relationship may also trigger feelings related to earlier losses (both lifetime and intergenerational) experienced by the client. Moreover, workers should be flexible about the process of termination and

associated rituals. In many AIAN communities, the end of a significant relationship is usually acknowledged and celebrated, and Native clients may wish to commemorate the termination with a traditional practice, event, or gift.

CASE EXAMPLE

June is an Oneida woman who recently relocated with her two school-aged children from a large reservation community to a major metropolitan area. June is working full-time at a department store and is enrolled in two college courses. The family lives with her sister, who watches the children after school and in the evenings while June attends class. June has a strong work history and has always done well in school, but she feels unable to concentrate on anything right now. She reports having symptoms of depression and anxiety for the past several months and feels "overwhelmed" with her life. June has usually relied on traditional practitioners to support her wellness, but she feels disconnected from other Natives in the city. Although she misses her family and friends on the reservation, June states that her family home is not a healthy place for her children right now due to her mother's alcoholism and erratic behavior. In addition, she feels that she needs to be in the city to support her sister, who recently finished a drug treatment program. June reports that she attended Indian boarding school in elementary school and was physically abused there. She came to see you after getting a referral from her primary physician and has never seen a social worker or mental health professional before.

Goals in Assessment Phase

- Assess cultural affiliation and identity, especially in relation to treatment preferences and options.
- Assess length and extent of symptoms related to depression and anxiety.
- Begin exploring possible sources of stress for the client.
- Explore family strengths and coping strategies successfully used in the past.
- Develop a timeline documenting significant life events, historically traumatic community events, ceremonies, and rites of passage in the family. Work with the client to document related individual and familial reactions.

- Conduct an assessment utilizing an appropriate assessment tool (e.g., Congress & Kung, 2013; Hodge & Limb, 2011) to help assess cultural needs related to wellness, social support, and the provision of mental health services.
- Consider how societal oppression and institutionalized racism have impacted the client's life and her community.
- Anticipate spending considerable time building trust.

Treatment Goals

- Intervention strategies that focus on having clients themselves determine goals and objectives (e.g., solution-focused work) may be especially helpful in helping empower Native clients (Lettenberger-Klein, Fish, & Hecker, 2013).
- Build on positive coping strategies and develop new strategies to combat stress and anxiety.
- Help identify strengths and resiliencies in the client's family and community history (Goodluck, 2002).
- Honor the client's commitment to Native traditional spirituality (Limb & Hodge, 2008) and support her work with traditional practitioners in addition to, or in place of, social work interventions.
- Explore relevant treatment resources at tribal or Native agencies in the region.
- Explore cultural and social events that may be of interest.

CONCLUSION

In summary, culturally relevant social work practice with Native people will require commitment and creativity. All social workers must increase their understanding of how current life stressors are experienced within the context of historical trauma in Native communities (Hodge, Limb, & Cross, 2009). Workers must also be committed to developing and empirically testing potentially effective treatments for lifetime and historical trauma with Native communities. Finally, and perhaps most importantly, social work practitioners and scholars should continue to investigate community strengths as well as resilience and healing strategies found effective in Native communities. There is a growing literature exploring the strengths and resiliencies that result from survival in the face of historical traumas, and it could be argued that in indigenous communities, historical events have enhanced community ties and underscored the importance of retaining culture and tradition. Social workers must ask themselves how best to build on these strengths to support wellness.

WEBSITES

Indian Country Child Trauma Center, evidence-based practice models. http://www.icctc.org.
Indian Health Service. http://www.ihs.gov.
National Indian Child Welfare Association. http://www.nicwa.org.
Substance Abuse and Mental Health Services, reports related to AIANs. http://www.oas.samhsa.gov/race.htm#Indians.

References

BigFoot, D. (2007). Evidence-based practices in Indian country. Presentation at the Institute for Indigenous Wellness Research, Seattle, WA.
Brave Heart, M. Y. H., Chase, J., Elkins, J., & Altschul, D. B. (2011). Historical trauma among indigenous peoples of the Americas: Concepts, research, and clinical considerations. *Journal of Psychoactive Drugs, 43*(4), 282–290.
Brave Heart, M. Y. H. (1999a). Gender differences in the historical trauma response among the Lakota. *Journal of Health and Social Policy, 10*(4), 1–21.
Brave Heart, M. Y. H. (1999b). Oyate Ptayela: Rebuilding the Lakota Nation through addressing historical trauma among Lakota parents. *Journal of Human Behavior in the Social Environment,* (1/2), 109–126.
Brave Heart, M. Y. H. (2000). Wakiksuyapi: Carrying the historical trauma of the Lakota. *Tulane Studies in Social Welfare, 21–22,* 245–266.
Brave Heart, M. Y. H., & DeBruyn, L. M. (1998). The American Indian holocaust: Healing historical unresolved grief. *American Indian and Alaska Native Mental Health Research, 8,* 56–78.
Bureau of Indian Affairs. (2012). *Indian entities recognized and eligible to receive services from the Bureau of Indian Affairs.* Federal Register, 77(155). Retrieved from http://www.bia.gov/cs/groups/public/documents/text/idc-020700.pdf
Carter, V. B. (2010). Factors predicting placement of urban American Indian/Alaskan Natives into out-of-home care. *Children and Youth Services Review, 32*(5), 657–663.
Congress, E. P., & Kung, W. W. (2013). Using the culturagram to assess and empower culturally diverse

families. In E. P. Congress and M. J. Gonzalez (Eds.), *Multicultural perspectives in social work practice with families* (pp. 1–20) (3rd ed.). New York, NY: Springer.

Cross, T. A., Earle, K. A., & Simmons, D. (2000). Child abuse and neglect in Indian country: Policy issues. *Families in Society: The Journal of Contemporary Human Services, 81*(1), 49–58.

Danieli, Y. (Ed.). (1998). *International handbook of multigenerational legacies of trauma.* New York, NY: Plenum Press.

Evans-Campbell, T. A. (2008). Historical trauma in American Indian/Alaska Native communities: A multilevel framework for exploring impacts on individuals, families and communities. *Journal of Interpersonal Violence, 23*, 316–338.

Evans-Campbell, T. A. (Under review; available from author). Far from home: The legacy of Indian boarding school on mental health and substance use among urban American Indian/Alaska Natives.

Evans-Campbell, T., & Walters, K. L. (2006). Indigenist practice competencies in child welfare practice: A decolonization framework to address family violence and substance abuse among First Nations peoples. In R. Fong, R. McRoy, & C. Ortiz Hendricks (Eds.), *Intersecting child welfare, substance abuse, and family violence: Culturally competent approaches.* Washington, DC: CSWE Press.

Goodluck, C. (2002). *Native American children and youth well-being indicators: A strengths perspective.* Portland, OR: National Indian Child Welfare Association.

Gray, J. S., & Rose, W. (2012). Cultural adaptation for therapy with American Indians and Alaska Natives. *Journal of Multicultural Counseling and Development, 40*(2), 82–92.

Hodge, D., & Limb, G. (2011). Spiritual assessment and Native Americans: Establishing the social validity of a complementary set of assessment tools. *Social Work, 56*(3), 213–223.

Hodge, D. R., Limb, G. E., & Cross, T. L. (2009). Moving from colonization toward balance and harmony: A Native American perspective on wellness. *Social Work, 54*(3), 211–219.

Lettenberger-Klein, C. G., Fish, J. N., & Hecker, L. L. (2013). Cultural competence when working with American Indian populations: A couple and family therapist perspective. *The American Journal of Family Therapy, 41*(2), 148–159.

Limb, G. (2004). Foster care and permanency issues for American Indian/Alaska Native families and children. In National Indian Child Welfare Association (NICWA) (Ed.), *Impacts of child maltreatment in Indian Country: Preserving the seventh generation through policies, programs, and funding streams* (pp. 256–284). [Congressional Report]. Portland OR: NICWA.

Limb, G., & Hodge, D. (2008). Developing spiritual competency with Native Americans: Promoting wellness through balance and harmony. *Families in Society: The Journal of Contemporary Human Services, 89*(4), 615–622.

National Association of Social Workers (NASW). (2008). *Code of ethics of the National Association of Social Workers.* Retrieved from http://www.socialworkers.org/pubs/code/code.asp

Olson, L. M., & Wahab, S. (2006). American Indians and suicide: A neglected area of research. *Trauma, Violence, and Abuse, 7*(1), 19–33.

Red Horse, J., & Limb, G. (2004). Sovereignty, cultural competency, and family preservation. In National Indian Child Welfare Association (NICWA) (Ed.), *Impacts of child maltreatment in Indian Country: Preserving the seventh generation through policies, programs, and funding streams* (pp. 235–255). [Congressional Report]. Portland OR: NICWA.

Stannard, D. (1992). *American holocaust.* Oxford: Oxford University Press.

Substance Abuse and Mental Health Services Administration. (2001). *Culture, race, and ethnicity—a supplement to Mental Health: A report of the Surgeon General.* Rockville, MD: Department of Health and Human Services.

Tjaden, P., & Thoennes, N. (2000). *Full report on the prevalence, incidence and consequences of violence against women* (NCJ 183781). Washington, DC: National Institutes of Justice.

U. S. Census Bureau. (2010). *Census Redistricting Data (Public Law 94-171) Summary File, Table P1.* Retrieved from http://www.census.gov/prod/cen2010/briefs/c2010br-10.pdf

Walters, K. L., Simoni, J. M., & Evans-Campbell, T. (2002). Substance use among American Indians and Alaska Natives: Incorporating culture in an "indigenist" stress-coping paradigm. *Public Health Reports, 117*(1), 104–117.

Weaver, H. (2004). The elements of cultural competence: Applications with Native American clients. *Journal of Ethnic and Cultural Diversity in Social Work, 13*(1), 19–35.

Weaver, H. (2003). Cultural competence with First Nations peoples. In D. Lum (Ed.), *Culturally competent practice: A framework for understanding diverse groups and justice issues.* Pacific Grove, CA: Brooks/Cole.

Wilkins, D. E. (1997). *American Indian sovereignty and the U.S. Supreme Court.* Austin: University of Texas Press.

127 Social Work Practice with Asian and Pacific Islander Americans

Halaevalu F. Ofahengaue Vakalahi & Rowena Fong

INTRODUCTION

The Asian and Pacific Islander population is a diverse group often mistakenly lumped together and insufficiently differentiated. Asian Americans themselves are a varied group composed of dozens of nationalities and ethnic groups from East Asia, South Asian, and Southeast Asia. East Asians include individuals from the countries of China, Japan, Korea, and the Philippines. South Asians arrive from Pakistan, India, Sri Lanka, Bangladesh, Nepal, and Bhutan. The Southeast Asians come from Burma/Myanmar, Singapore, Thailand, Laos, Cambodia, Vietnam, Indonesia, East Timor, and Brunei. Most of these nations are, in turn, composed of numerous tribal and ethnic groups, such as the Hmong, who emigrated in significant numbers from Laos to the United States in the aftermath of the Vietnam War.

Pacific Islanders include individuals from the South Pacific island groups of Polynesia, Micronesia, and Melanesia (Laville & Berkowitz, 1944; Narokobi, 1983). Pacific Islanders have historically struggled with navigating daily colonialization and immigration, which often results in experiences with oppression, exploitation, and marginalization, and which has led to enormous mistrust of foreign systems. The historical trauma of colonization and its impact on Pacific People's overall physical health and mental health continues to be a challenge with each generation (Hurdle, 2002).

Those who migrate to the United States, in particular, experience the consequences of cultural conflicts in the forms of language barriers, disintegration of cultural identity, disproportionately poor health status, underemployment and undereducation, as well as oppression, exploitation, and discrimination (Yoshihama, 2001). Apparently, every new generation of Pacific Islander immigrants encounters some type of discrimination or prejudice from government systems and/or Caucasian American communities (Millett & Orosz, 2001) that blocks access to the opportunities that might facilitate a transition from surviving to thriving in their respective communities. According to the U.S. Bureau of the Census (2007), Pacific Islander Americans are one of the most economically, educationally, and politically disadvantaged populations in the United States today. Though there is great heterogeneity among Asians and Pacific Islanders in terms of social class, educational achievement, and professional occupation, the majority of Asians and Pacific Islanders do experience aspects of racism and discrimination that contribute to their disadvantaged status.

Despite oppressive encounters, this group possesses cultural strengths that can inform culturally relevant and sensitive practice, policy, education, and research. Examples of these cultural strengths include close family relationships, extended family network, love for children, respect for the elderly, reciprocity and sharing, and communal responsibility (Vakalahi, Godinet, & Fong, 2006). Family is first and the center of all relationships; it is the agent of socialization where honor, respect, nurturing, and collaboration are taught and practiced (Fong & Furuto, 2001). It is a basic cultural belief in most Asian and Pacific Islander groups that a house without children is a house without life. Children are embraced, paid attention to, and seldom left alone when crying. From their earliest years, children are taught to respect the elderly. In terms of collective, the good of the whole and interdependency are valued above individual benefits and achievements (Lee, 1997; Mokuau, 1991). Of great value to Pacific Islanders who reside in countries outside of the Pacific is the notion of transnationalism, whereby Pacific people maintain ties to their nation of origin, which serves as a mechanism for indigenous cultural preservation and for sustaining relationships across families and communities in two or more geographic locations (Vakalahi & Godinet, 2014).

CASE ILLUSTRATIONS

Case 1: The Problem of Cultural Conflict

Seini is a 17-year-old Tongan female, born in Tonga, raised in Hawaii, and living with her parents and brothers in a low-income area in Honolulu. Her family migrated from Tonga when she was 10 years old. Her annual family income is about $20,000, primarily from her father's seasonal employment. The primary language spoken in her home is Tongan. She is a senior in high school but struggles to earn enough credits to graduate on time. Seini is currently working with a probation officer due to her involvement in multiple fights in school, allegedly associated with gang violence. She has described to her school counselor the struggles of living in dual cultures that demand one thing at home and another in school. She has experienced conflict with Tongan cultural traditions and customs imposed by her family and community, her family's low socioeconomic status, the negative impact of her low-income neighborhood, and the peer pressure to be tough.

Seini talks about the overwhelming demands for giving to family, community, and church members, which often result in insufficient funds to meet her family's own needs. She often feels resentful of this cultural practice because she feels that it adds unnecessary pressure on her parents and additional responsibilities on her and her siblings. Seini feels that her Tongan culture is very important, but there have to be limits to the demands and expectations. On the other hand, her parents are intimately involved in community, cultural, and church functions. They live by cultural values of reciprocity, sharing, discipline, respect for parents and the elders, and taking responsibility for family and extended family.

They discipline their children through spanking, scolding, and grounding, which are acceptable in the Tongan culture. Interestingly, Seini accepts such disciplinary methods as appropriate and beneficial for teaching her what is wrong and right. Nonetheless, she feels that she does not fit into either her American or Tongan culture. This experience with acculturative stress is a well-documented contributing factor to deviant behavior.

Consequences of the immigration experience hinder some of the cultural practices that Tongans are accustomed to observing in Tonga. Collectivity and reciprocity are easier to practice in Tonga because families live in close proximity and because of the perspective that it is an honor and a responsibility to care for one another. In the United States, family members live far apart, often by necessity, and lifestyle demands are more complex. The immigration experience also entails language barriers and the responsibility for Seini to translate for her parents in many instances. When Seini interprets for her parents in the larger society, the parent–child role is reversed. Furthermore, living in a multigenerational home with other immigrant family members brings about additional responsibilities for Seini's parents. Scarce resources are definitely an issue. Unfortunately, even if one person breaks the low-income cycle, that person is expected to contribute more back to the family, which perpetuates the scarcity of resources and the low-income cycle.

Despite these risk factors, Seini does have access to protective factors from which a service provider can draw strength, even if she does not realize it. In relation to the Tongan culture, the practice of reciprocity, sharing, unconditional love for children, and parents' wishes for their children to stay in school, as well as Seini's respect for her parents and other family members, and her desire to someday change her situation of low-income status, negative peer pressure, and gang violence are all protective factors for Seini.

Case 2: The Intervention of Family Group Conferencing

Kaimana is a 16-year-old part-Hawaiian male who was removed from his home and placed in the custody of Child Protective Services (CPS) for alleged physical and emotional abuse by his stepfather. He lived with his stepfather, who is Caucasian, and his mother, who is part Hawaiian, in Waianae farmland. His family had extremely limited material resources and social support systems. His family worked on the farm, earning an annual income of approximately $15,000. Kaimana and his siblings often missed school; their dirty fingernails and uncombed hair made them appear to be physically neglected.

CPS decided that family reunification was the planned outcome, and a family group conferencing intervention was held. In organizing the conference, individuals involved from the family's side included Kaimana, his parents, his stepfather's sister, his neighbors, and the family social worker from a private agency. Other members of the conference included Kaimana's CPS worker, the CPS supervisor, a mental health specialist, and the conference facilitator, who was from a neutral agency.

Initiating the conference, the facilitator explained the family group conferencing process to all involved parties. Kaimana's parents were given the choice of starting with a prayer or *pule*, as it is called in the Hawaiian language, which they declined. In the effort to clarify any misunderstanding and decrease mistrust of the system, social work professionals explained to the family their obligations to uphold the law to report abuse and protect children. They explained that their involvement as professionals was not intended to disrespect the family, and asked for the family's cooperation in working together for Kaimana. The social workers then identified the goal of the family group conference, which was to reunite Kaimana and his family, ensuring Kaimana's safety, developing specific goals and objectives that were culturally relevant, and identifying resources necessary to meet those goals.

First, the facilitator met with Kaimana's family, and together they developed specific goals and objectives for family reunification and safety and identified resources necessary to meet those goals. Simultaneously, social work professionals met in a separate session with the same tasks to complete. Second, after the individual sessions, both groups came together, and the perspectives of each group were shared. For a period of time, processing, dialogue, negotiations, and explanations took place among the groups to reach a common plan. At the end of the processing session, the common plan consisted of a step-by-step documentation of tasks, timelines, and each person's responsibility. This document became the contract. For example, Kaimana was required to continue attending therapy for his anger problem and establish a personal safety plan. His stepfather was required to

attend anger management courses and continue meeting with the social worker from the private agency to focus on improving communication with his spouse and children and to explore the conflicts brought on by differing cultural values. The social worker was then required to follow up on the family's progress.

PRACTICE CONSIDERATIONS

In both case examples of working with Asian and Pacific Islander children and families, cultural values play a major role in understanding the conflict of the case, handling the case, and choosing the intervention applied.

General guidelines for service providers to consider include:

- Historical and cultural experiences with colonization and immigration, and social and economic consequences
- Within-group diversity and the need for bicultural and bilingual skills that respond to cultural duality and population changes
- The reality of living in the United States, yet being embedded in the culture of origin
- The reality of transnational and transcultural relationships that are built between two geographic locations
- The need to understand the influence of cultural values, customs, lifestyles, and practices on behavior
- The need to understand Asian and Pacific Islanders' perspectives on the shame and stigma associated with seeking mental health services
- The cultural emphasis on collaboration, collectivity, reciprocity, and interdependency
- The need to carefully bridge the community with multiple systems of help and interagency collaboration
- Developing appropriate assessment-to-treatment options, based on consultation with the community to understand cultural taboos and protocols for social and family interactions
- The effects of living within a multigenerational home and family hierarchy
- The prominent position of spiritual, religious, and church leaders in the lives of community members

- The reduction of barriers to service use by advocating for the hiring of Asian and Pacific Islander employees or contractors, building workforce capability and capacity, and designing physical space that reflects respect for diversity
- The need to develop relevant cultural competency objectives and quality services

Treatment Plan

- Each step of the individual treatment plan needs to encompass cultural values, beliefs, and practices, as well as the lifestyles and social realities of Asians and Pacific Islanders.
- Treatment plans need to consider the role of family close by and afar, the ethnic community, and the religious and church community, whenever it is appropriate to include their contributions.

Assessment

- Social workers need to conduct a full assessment of the bio-psychosocial–spiritual dimensions of the self and relevant systems including the person, family, peers, community/neighborhood, school, and culture.
- Social workers need to ask questions regarding family characteristics and lifestyle, perception about mental health service seeking, relationships in the community and with the church and religious community, time of migration to the United States, and preference for a service provider.
- Social workers need to inquire about the role of the family and the ethnic community as well as the preference for ethnic-related resources. Questions to ask are: "Tell me about your family. Tell me about your community. What are your needs and what do you need to meet those needs? Are you involved in your church and religious community? When did you migrate to the United States? Do you have any preferences for a particular type of worker to work with you? Is there anyone in the family or community that you would like to involve in our work with you? How connected is your family to your Asian or Pacific Islander culture?"

Treatment Goals

The following are suggested treatment goals.

- Increase overall social functioning in the family, community, and larger society.
- Increase consistent access to culturally relevant services.
- Reduce family, community, and cultural barriers to continuous physical health and mental health.
- Maintain positive cultural and transnational connections.
- Develop capability and capacity to function positively in a dual/multiple culture.
- Reduce the impact of acculturative stress.
- Increase problem-solving options and capabilities.
- Develop the skills to increase needed resources.
- Find a balance in meeting individual and collective needs by developing win-win solutions.

Intervention Strategies

Although there are many evidence-based intervention strategies that will work with Asian and Pacific Islander individual and family clients, the following three are examples of strategies that are grounded in cultural values of community and family sharing and responsibility, reciprocity, and collectivity.

- Outreach is the action of reaching out to family and community members to engage in and implement interventions with the assistance and support of individuals.
- *Ho'oponopono* is the Hawaiian process of family problem solving, including prayer, food sharing, and forgiveness of wrongdoings (Mokuau, 1991).
- Family group conferencing is an intervention used with biological family members and fictive kin to discuss how the treatment plan will be implemented and followed through by persons committed to the family's preservation (Wilcox, Smith, Moore, Hewitt, Allan, Walker, Ropata, Monu, & Featherstone, 1991).

Two additional approaches are also introduced as follows:

- *Ifoga* is an indigenous Samoan healing practice emphasizing reconciliation through forgiveness, compassion, and respect. The ceremony gathers the victim and his/her family to confront the offender and his/her family, whereby the offender and his/her family accept responsibility and generate solutions to restore the power of the victim and his/her family. A proposed term of peace, requesting forgiveness, and granting forgiveness is required. The mediator is a person with power such as a *matai* or chief, elder, or person assigned by the family (Jantzi, 2001; Vakalahi & Godinet, 2008).

- *Fakalelei* is a Tongan healing practice on all levels—spiritual, social, emotional, and biological. Peace in relationships by gathering the victim offender, and families to collectively create a solution. The offender and his/her family are accountable to the victim and his/her family, but then power to accept or reject an apology lies with the victim. The facilitator is a person with power in the family or community such as the *ulumotu'a* or granduncle, or an elder in one's father's family (Jantzi, 2001; Vakalahi & Godinet, 2008).

CONCLUSION

Social work practitioners and service providers, both Asian and Pacific Islander and non–Asian and Pacific Islander, need to be competent with the necessary values and beliefs, knowledge, and skills to provide quality services for Asians and Pacific Islanders. It is recommended that the following practices be used with Asian and Pacific Islander clients:

- Show genuine nonjudgmental respect for people and their cultures; cultures are not deficient, just different. This act will open doors.
- Use multiple treatment strategies, including outreach and family conferencing and other culturally relevant approaches, as necessary.
- Understand Asian and Pacific Islander cultural processes, development, protocols, and taboos.
- Understand the particular Asian or Pacific Islander group involved and their values and beliefs, customs, traditions, and practices.
- Consider the historical trauma or colonization and immigration experiences that help or hinder the treatment process.
- Facilitate and work with large and small family and community groups.

- Work across generations, while recognizing that positions of power lie with the elders.
- Work as a team member and maintain the flexibility to switch roles when necessary (i.e., active involvement or observer only).
- Gain experience working within Asian and Pacific Islander communities.
- Be bicultural or of Asian and Pacific Islander ancestry.
- Be bilingual in any of the Asian and Pacific Islander languages.

WEBSITES

Asian and Pacific Island Wellness Center. http://www.apiwellness.org/home.html.

Asian and Pacific Islander American Health Forum. http://www.apiahf.org.

Asian and Pacific Islander Coalition on HIV/AIDS. http://www.apicha.org/apicha/main.html.

Asian and Pacific Islander Institute on Domestic Violence. http://www.apiahf.org/apidvinstitute/default.htm.

Asian Pacific Islander Legal Outreach. http://www.apilegaloutreach.org/index.html.

Pacific Islanders in Communication. http://www.piccom.org/

Pacific Island Ethnic Art Museum. http://pieam.org/

Pacific Islands Forum Secretariat. http://forumsec.org/index.cfm

U.S. Census Bureau. http://www.census.gov/population/www/socdemo/race/api.html.

References

Fong, R., & Furuto, S. (Eds.). (2001). *Culturally competent social work practice: Skills, interventions and evaluation.* Boston, MA: Allyn & Bacon.

Hurdle, D. E. (2002). Native Hawaiian traditional healing: Cultural based interventions for social work practice. *Social Work, 47*(2), 183–192.

Jantzi, V. E. (2001). *Restorative justice in New Zealand: Current practice, future possibilities.* Retrieved from http://www.massey.ac.nv/~wtie/articles/vern.htm.

Laville, J., & Berkowitz, J. (1944). *Pacific Island legends: Life and legends of the South Pacific Islands.* Noumea, New Caledonia: Librarie Pentecost.

Lee, E. (1997). *Working with Asian Americans: Guide for clinicians.* New York, NY: Guilford.

Millett, R., & Orosz, J. J. (2001). Understanding giving patterns in communities of color. *Fund Raising Management, 32*(6), 25–27.

Mokuau, N. (Ed.). (1991). *Handbook of social services for Asian and Pacific Islanders*. New York, NY: Greenwood.

Narokobi, B. (1983). *The Melanesian Way*. Suva, Fiji: Institute of Pacific Island Studies, University of the South Pacific.

U.S. Census Bureau. (2007). *Facts for features. Asian/ Pacific American heritage month*. Retrieved from http://www.census.gov/Press-Release/www/ releases/archives/facts_for_features_special_ editions/009714.html.

Vakalahi, H. F. O., & Godinet, M. (2008). Family and culture and the Samoan youth. *Journal of Family Social Work, 11*(3), 229–253.

Vakalahi, H. F. O., & Godinet, M. (2014). *Transnational Pacific Islander Americans and social work: Dancing to the beat of a different drum*. Washington, DC: NASW Press.

Vakalahi, H. O., Godinet, M., & Fong, R. (2006). Pacific Islander Americans: Impact of colonization and immigration. In R. Fong, R. G. McRoy, & C. O. Hendricks (Eds.), *Intersecting child welfare, substance abuse, and family violence*. Washington, DC: Council on Social Work Education Press.

Wilcox, R., Smith, D., Moore, J., Hewitt, A., Allan, G., Walker, H., … Featherstone, T. (1991). *Family decision making and family group conferencing*. Lower Hut, NZ: Practitioners' Publishing.

Yoshihama, M. (2001). Immigrants-in-context framework: Understanding the interactive influence of socio-cultural contexts. *Evaluation and Program Planning, 24*, 307–318.

128 Social Work Practice with Latinos

Ilze A. Earner & Alan Dettlaff

INTRODUCTION

Latinos are the largest ethnic minority group in the United States and the fastest-growing segment of the U.S. population. Among Latino adults, 52% are foreign-born immigrants who migrated to the United States (Pew Hispanic Center, 2012). However, among Latino children, only 8% are foreign-born. Yet, it is important to note that although the large majority of Latino children are born in the United States, more than half (52%) of Latino children have at least one immigrant parent (Fry & Passel, 2009). Overall, the Latino population is relatively youthful compared with other racial and ethnic groups in the United States: the median age of Latinos in the United States in 2010 was 27 years, compared to 42 years for Whites, 32 years for Blacks, and 35 years for Asians (Pew Hispanic Center, 2012).

Geographically, more than three-quarters of Latinos live in the South (36%) and the West (41%), with over half of Latinos in the United States residing in just three states—California, Texas, and Florida (Ennis et al., 2011). A similar pattern exists among foreign-born Latinos. However, recent trends in migration patterns suggest that immigrants who once settled in large urban centers are now moving to suburban and rural communities with little history or experience with immigrants. In fact, over the past 10 years, states in the Midwest, Rocky Mountains, and Southeast have experienced more than a 200% increase in their immigrant population (Fortuny, Capps, Simms, & Chaudry, 2009).

Among Latinos, migration to the United States is predominately driven by economic reasons. Other reasons include political and social instability in their home country, war-related hardship, as well as family conflict and persecution related to sexual orientation (Organista, 2007). Among foreign-born Latinos in the United States in 2010, nearly three-quarters were legal immigrants (72%), while just over one-quarter (28%) were without documentation. Mexicans

(58%) and other Latin Americans (23%) account for the majority of the immigrant population without documentation in the United States (Passel & Cohn, 2011). Immigrants without legal documentation represent a particularly vulnerable population given the risks of deportation, exploitation, and restricted access to health and social services.

Consistent with other historically marginalized populations, Latino children and families are at disproportionate risk of experiencing poverty. As of 2010, more than one in four (26.6%) U.S. Latinos lived in poverty, an increase of more than 5% since 2007 (DeNavas-Walt, Proctor, & Smith, 2011). Among children in the United States, more Latino children are living in poverty than any other racial or ethnic group. In 2010, Latino children represented 37.3% of all poor children, while 30.5% were White and 26.6% were African American (Lopez & Velasco, 2011). This marked the first time in history that the largest proportion of poor children in the United States was not White.

Most Latinos in the United States speak Spanish (82%), which both maintains connections with their cultures of origin and facilitates connections between diverse Latino groups (Taylor, Lopez, Martinez, & Velasco, 2012). However, generation in the United States is associated with language use and is an important factor to consider when practicing with Latinos. For example, first generation or immigrant Latinos account for most of the Spanish-speakers in the United States. The second generation is largely bilingual, while the third or higher generations speak predominately English (Suro & Passel, 2003).

Although Latinos are a highly diverse group in terms of culture, they do share certain values as a result of their common history of Spanish colonization and influence from the Catholic Church. Particularly relevant to the context of practice with Latino families, *familismo* is considered one of the most important cultural values across Latino populations. Familismo involves a strong identification and attachment with nuclear and extended family, along with a deep sense of family commitment, involvement, and responsibility. The family offers emotional security and a sense of belonging to its members, and is the unit to which individuals turn for help first in stressful or difficult situations.

Many Latinos also share a common faith, with Catholicism being the predominant religion among most Latinos (Sanchez & Jones, 2010). This faith is deeply rooted in Latino culture, and although it may be expressed differently and with various levels of participation in organized activities, the values and practices of the Catholic Church have important cultural significance for many Latinos, and can be an important source of strength. Representatives of the Church, such as priests or nuns, can serve as important cultural liaisons because they are seen as individuals who may be trusted and are not connected to government authorities.

Yet, although Latinos share a colonial past, a common language, and similarity of certain values, Latinos are a highly diverse group, representing more than 20 countries of origin with distinct cultural values, traditions, and worldviews. Latinos of Mexican (63%), Puerto Rican (9.2%), and Cuban (3.5%) origin represent the nation's three largest Hispanic groups. However, the population of several other groups has grown considerably since 2000. For example, Latinos of Salvadoran origin, the fourth largest group, grew by 152% between 2000 and 2010. Similarly, the Dominican population grew by 85%, Guatemalans by 180%, and Colombians by 93% (Ennis et al., 2011).

Added to this variation are differences in social class, education, age, gender, sexual orientation, acculturation, migration history, and other individual and family differences. As a result, it is important to remain aware that although one may recognize generalities about a particular culture, assumptions cannot be made about a particular individual or family. Rather, knowledge of a particular culture represents a hypothesis about a particular member of that culture, which needs to be individually assessed and explored, including when a client is a member of one's own cultural group. Ultimately, helping professionals need to be aware of cultural issues, while at the same time avoiding stereotypes and generalizations that take away from their clients' individuality.

Mariella, Her Two Children and Domestic Violence

Mariella is a 30-year-old Mexican woman with two children who has lived in the United States for 15 years. She is fluent in English. She was referred to a faith-based social services agency by a friend after the latest incident of domestic violence between herself and her fiancé, a 35-year-old American of Dominican descent with whom she was living. Mariella and her fiancé have a daughter who is nine months old; Mariella's older daughter, six years old, is from a previous marriage. Mariella has undocumented immigration status.

Mariella followed her parents over the border in 1998 as a teenager and lived with them in New York City until she married at the age of 20 in 2003. Mariella dropped out of school at the age of 17; unable to understand English well enough to be able to follow what was going on, she saw no point in continuing school and instead went to work to help support her family—both in the United States, as well as some extended family still in Mexico—including one younger brother who lives in Mexico with a grandmother. Mariella has two younger sisters who were both born in the United States and are citizens. This has had a distinct effect on the trajectory of their lives; unlike Mariella, her U.S.-born siblings will be able to get financial aid for school, work legally, open bank accounts, obtain credit, and travel freely.

Mariella married Omar, a man 10 years older than she, also from Mexico and also undocumented; Omar worked in construction as a day laborer. Soon afterward, Mariella gave birth to her first child, Elena, also a U.S. citizen. In 2008 the economic crisis slowed the construction industry considerably and Omar, who had previously been able to work steadily and support his family, was having a harder and harder time finding work. His cousin, living in Houston, offered to help find work for him there, so Omar left Mariella and their daughter to go to Texas. He told Mariella he would send for them as soon as he was established. Afraid to travel because of immigration status, Omar never returned to New York and Mariella never visited him in Texas. By the time two years had passed, Mariella stopped hearing from him, and the monthly support payments he had been sending also evaporated. His cousin's phone number was disconnected and Mariella lost all contact with Omar—she has no idea where he is. Now a single mother, Mariella went back to work to support herself and her daughter. With a phony Social Security card and driver's license, she found waitressing work in a restaurant in East Harlem, an increasingly upscale Latino neighborhood in New York. It was here that Mariella met Roberto, an American of Dominican descent.

Roberto's parents emigrated from the Dominican Republic in the mid-1970s, settling in the Washington Heights neighborhood of New York, where Roberto was born in 1978. Briefly married, Roberto is now divorced and living with his mother, a disabled diabetic, to help support her. His father is deceased. Roberto, an only child, does not have children and according to Mariella liked his freedom to pursue a lifestyle not dissimilar to the one enjoyed by many young adults in New York City—he dated casually, went to clubs, enjoyed sports events, and often had a beer out with friends. Roberto's parents obtained U.S. citizenship via the Immigration and Control Act (IRCA) in 1986, an amnesty program signed into law by then President Ronald Reagan. Roberto's mother receives Supplemental Security Income benefits and Medicaid and lives in an apartment provided by the New York City Housing Authority in Washington Heights, a neighborhood with a large population of Dominicans.

Roberto and Mariella began dating. According to Mariella, they shared a sense of living in two worlds—one bounded by culture and obligation to set aside personal desires in order to focus on caring for the family and the other reflective of the dominant culture in the United States, with an emphasis on personal freedom and individual well-being. Six months after they started dating Mariella became pregnant. Although the prospect of caring for a child made Roberto extremely nervous, there was never a question of whether or not to go ahead with the pregnancy; Roberto and Mariella became engaged. Mariella, still a fiancé and not divorced from her missing husband, gave birth to her second daughter Estrella in 2012.

Living in Roberto's mother's apartment with their newborn daughter, and Mariella's six-year-old daughter, Elena, from her previous marriage, soon became very stressful. Roberto's mother was often in pain and the infant's crying got on her nerves; the apartment was small and Elena, a very active child, had no room of her own in which to play. Mariella's parents, who strongly did not approve of her relationship with Roberto, had become estranged from her. Mariella expected Roberto to be more helpful around the house, but he felt that with the extra work that he was doing managing the restaurant on weekends and nights he was already doing enough to support them. She increasingly resented his going out with friends and leaving her at home with a cranky grandmother and two young children. She began to believe that he was out flirting with other women, which only made her angrier. They began to fight often, and the fights soon became physical.

The violence between Mariella and Roberto escalated from name-calling—Roberto would often hurl ethnic slurs at Mariella—to throwing objects at one another to one night Roberto punching Mariella and shoving her down a flight of stairs. Mariella was bruised and had a black eye that neighbors noticed, but she refused to call the police—she was afraid that she would get arrested on account of her immigration status and be deported. Additionally, she feared that she would lose custody of her daughters because they were U.S. citizens and she was not. Mariella endured the situation as long as possible and then fled to her friend's house in Queens with her two young children. Her friend shared a tiny apartment with her boyfriend and had little room for Mariella and her children; she indicated that although Mariella could stay for a while, she wanted Mariella to get settled somewhere else. Mariella's friend arranged for her to meet with a social worker from the neighborhood social services agency—a faith-based organization affiliated with the Catholic Church.

ASSESSMENT

Assessment of Mariella's situation required attention to the following issues:

- Acculturation
- Help-seeking behavior
- Domestic violence
- Identity, values, and norms
- Immigration status
- Family strengths and resources
- Migration history

Mariella is an immigrant from Mexico; she has, however, resided continuously in the United States from the age of 15 years onward. Her adult identity, therefore, largely has been formed within the cultural context of the United States, and as a result she presents as an acculturated Latina woman who speaks English fluently. Process of migration frameworks are useful in placing individuals and families within the context of migration based on their personal circumstances and migration histories. At the same time, they allow social workers to identify expectable issues and problems along the immigration trajectory (Drachman, 1992). For example, although Mariella has adopted many mannerisms that are mainstream American, she maintains a strong personal connection to the cultural values of *familismo* (family-centered values) common to many Latinos (Delgado, 2007). Mariella exemplifies that divided sense of self that many children of immigrants who have grown up in the United States, as well as second-generation immigrants, often describe as a feeling that they live in two worlds with competing norms, expectations, and roles. It is important for social workers to recognize and assess which factors are most important and/or relevant to their clients.

Immigration status has a profound effect on individuals and families. Social work practice with immigrants requires skill in assessing immigration status, knowledge of various immigration statuses, and of any possibilities for adjustment of status. Access to expert legal resources is critical because immigration laws are complex and change often. Immigrant clients must know and understand not only the implications of their immigration status, but have up-to-date information on options for addressing problems realistically. For example, an undocumented immigrant victim of domestic violence might be able to petition for immigration relief under the Violence Against Women Act (VAWA) of 2013. In Mariella's case, she falls under the category of being the abused parent of a U.S. citizen. If successful, such relief would give Mariella work authorization and access to public benefits, and would help ensure that she does not have to stay in an abusive relationship because she is afraid of being deported, or because she does not have any other viable choices to support herself.

TREATMENT INTERVENTION AND GOALS

Individual and family counseling services are being provided to Mariella and her children and are based on the following treatment interventions and goals:

- Crisis intervention and advocacy to address domestic violence
- Legal services for immigration status issues
- Formal and informal support networks
- Basic needs for shelter, food, clothing
- Supportive counseling

- Afterschool, recreational, and out-of-home care options for children.

The goals of this intervention are:

- Ensure safety and well-being of Mariella and her children.
- Provide short-term shelter, followed by transitional and permanent housing.
- Explore options for adjustment of immigration status.
- Expand family support networks and resources.
- Empower Mariella to explore future personal and family goals through education and vocational training.
- Provide children with safe care programs or options when parent is working.
- Engage Mariella in culturally appropriate supportive counseling.

Highly distrustful of any organization that might have connections to the "government," Mariella only agreed to meet with the social worker at the agency because it was affiliated with a religious institution that for personal and cultural reasons Mariella identified as "safe". Such "cultural liaisons," whether religious institutions, mutual aid associations, or ethnic leaders are important partners for social workers who practice in immigrant communities to facilitate engagement and develop trust with at-risk populations (Earner, 2007). In this case, the faith-based organization contracted with attorneys who spoke Spanish to provide pro bono legal services to immigrants; astonishingly they had an attorney who was also a nun.

The immediate need for Mariella is shelter for herself and her children. Immigration status does not prevent battered immigrant women from being able to access crisis shelters and an array of domestic violence services; however, the long-term effects of remaining an undocumented person will keep Mariella and her children at risk for deportation, living on the margins of society, and possibly staying in unsafe situations for lack of choice. Mariella's legal options for addressing immigration status are limited; she may be able to petition for immigration status adjustment (making her status legal but not necessarily permanent) through relief offered by either a U visa

or under VAWA (Immigrant Legal Resource Center, 2012). Even if immigration status cannot be adjusted, it is important to advise parents who are undocumented on steps that they can take to protect their family relationships should the parent(s) be subject to deportation. This includes giving power of attorney rights to extended family or friends, setting up legal guardianships and health care proxy forms to protect and provide for minor children (Ayon, Aisenberg, & Cimino, 2013).

Lastly Mariella is being offered culturally appropriate supportive counseling to address a number of personal issues including re-engagement with her family of origin, her experience of domestic violence (Randell, Bledsoe, Shroff, & Pierce, 2012), expanding her informal and formal support network (Xu & Brabeck, 2012), as well as exploring educational and vocational opportunities that can help her move toward establishing an independent life for herself and her children (Organista, 2009).

CONCLUSION

The case of Mariella, an undocumented immigrant from Mexico living in the United States for 15 years, her two U.S.-born children, and her experience of domestic violence, illustrates the complex and conflicting issues that affect Latino clients in need of social work services. Assessment incorporates a person-in-environment perspective to consider multiple problem levels and solutions that are reflective of Latino-relevant and culturally competent knowledge about this population—its strengths, assets, stressors, and barriers to services. A stages-of-migration framework can also be a helpful paradigm to understand the processes of individual acculturation, adjustment, and family functioning for immigrant populations. Critical to intervention is knowing how immigration status affects individuals and families, especially in mixed-status families. For battered immigrant women, access to domestic violence shelters and services is often compromised by factors such as language access, cultural issues, and confusion about eligibility. Narrative and supportive therapeutic techniques include a focus on family strengths, cultural assets, resources, and resilience around the struggle to negotiate identity as a Latino immigrant in America.

WEBSITES

Migration and Child Welfare National
Network: Immigrants and child welfare,
practice toolkits, policy and research. http://
www.mcwnn.uic.edu
Immigrant Legal Resource Center: National
legal and technical assistance resource center
providing information on legal assistance and
access to social services for immigrants and
their families. http://www.ilrc.org/
Bridging Refugee Youth and Children's
Services: National technical assistance project
with information, toolkits, information, and
resources for practice with immigrant and
refugee families and children.
http://www/brycs.org/
National Council of La Raza: Latino civil rights
and advocacy organization. http://www.nclr
.org/

References

Ayon, C., Aisenberg, E., & Cimino, A. (2013). Latino families in the nexus of child welfare, welfare reform and immigration policies: Is kinship care a lost opportunity? *Social Work, 58*(1), 91–94.

Delgado, M. (2007). *Social work practice with Latinos: A cultural assets paradigm.* New York, NY: Oxford University Press.

DeNavas-Walt, C., Proctor, B. D., & Smith, J. C. (2011). *U.S. Census Bureau, current population reports (P60-239), income, poverty, and health insurance coverage in the United States: 2010.* Washington, DC: U.S. Government Printing Office.

Drachman, D. (1992). Stages of migration and assessment of immigrant families. *Social Work, 37*(1), 68–72.

Earner, I. (2007). Immigrant families and public child welfare: Barriers to services and approaches for change. *Child Welfare, 86*(4), 63–91.

Ennis, S. R., Ríos-Vargas, M., & Albert, N. G. (2011). *The Hispanic population: 2010.* Washington, DC: U.S. Census Bureau.

Fortuny, K., Capps, R., Simms, M., & Chaudry, A. (2009). *Children of immigrants: National and state characteristics.* Retrieved from Urban Institute website: http://www.urban.org/publications/411939.html

Fry, R., & Passel, J. S. (2009). *Latino children: A majority are U.S.-born offspring of immigrants.* Retrieved from Pew Hispanic Center website: http://pewhispanic.org/files/reports/110.pdf

Immigrant Legal Resource Center. (2012). *A guide for immigration advocates: A comprehensive immigration practice manual.* San Francisco, CA: Author.

Lopez, M. H., & Velasco, G. (2011). *Childhood poverty among Hispanics sets record, leads nation.* Washington, DC: Pew Hispanic Center.

Organista, K. (2007). *Solving Latino psychosocial and health problems. Theory, practice, and populations.* Hoboken, NJ: John Wiley & Sons, Inc.

Organista, K. (2009). New practice model for Latinos in need of social work services. *Social Work, 54*(4), 297–305.

Passel, J. S., & Cohn, D. (2011). *Unauthorized immigrant population: National and state trends, 2010.* Washington, DC: Pew Hispanic Center.

Pew Hispanic Center. (2012). *Statistical portrait of Hispanics in the United States, 2010.* Washington, DC: Author.

Randell, K., Bledsoe, L., Shroff, P., & Pierce, M. (2012). Mother's motivations for intimate partner violence help-seeking. *Journal of Family Violence, 27*, 55–62.

Sanchez, T. W., & Jones, S. (2010). The diversity and commonalities of Latinos in the United States. In R. Furman & N. Negi (Eds.), *Social work practice with Latinos: Key issues and emerging themes* (pp. 31–44). Chicago, IL: Lyceum Books.

Suro, R., & Passel, J. S. (2003). *The rise of the second generation: Changing patterns in Hispanic population growth.* Washington, DC: Pew Hispanic Center.

Taylor, P., Lopez, M. H., Martinez, J. H., & Velasco, G. (2012). *When labels don't fit: Hispanics and their views of identity.* Washington, DC: Pew Hispanic Center.

Xu, Q., & Brabeck, K. (2012). Service utilization for Latino children in mixed status families. *Social Work Research, 36*, 209–221.

129 Social Work Practice with African Americans

Sadye M. L. Logan

AN OVERVIEW AND PROFILE OF THE AFRICAN AMERICAN COMMUNITY

Given the diverse values, educational levels, incomes, lifestyles, and perceptions found within the African American community, it is extremely challenging, if not impossible, to write a definitive article that captures clinical social work practice with this ethnic group (McAdoo, 2007; Robinson, 2010). It is, therefore, important for readers using this information to approach this chapter with the understanding that it contains a generic or holistic conceptualization with applications to a diverse group of people and will require modifications in order to be applied effectively.

Within the above context, it is important also to acknowledge that African Americans constitute one of the largest ethnic groups of color in the United States of America, with a population numbering 13% of the total U.S. population or 33.8 million people (McKinnon, 2003). The vast majority of this amazingly resilient and diverse group of people came to the United States as enslaved Africans and remained in bondage for over 200 years. It is generally believed that the majority, if not all, of the enslaved Africans were taken from the Western parts of the African continent (Gutman, 1975). The process of enslavement is believed to have resulted in what is defined today as posttraumatic stress disorder (PTSD), which has produced an intergenerational impact on the emotional health of African Americans (Logan, Denby, & Gibson, 2007; Logan, 2001; Waites, 2008). This process, which included institutional racism, discrimination, and oppression has produced a schizophrenic type of existence for the enslaved Africans and their descendants.

Although the majority of the Africans remained enslaved, some were able to purchase their freedom and remain free. Others were forced back into slavery; many were fathered by their White owners and looked White; and some of those who looked like their White fathers prospered and were in some instances also owners of slaves (Johnson & Roark, 1984). The majority of the enslaved Africans lived in the Southern parts of the United States, where more than 50% of the African American population still reside today (McKinnon, 2003). A significant proportion of this population consists of female-headed households with children under 18 years of age. Many of these female-headed families live below the poverty level (McKinnon, 2003).

Social work practice will most likely occur with those African Americans experiencing the impact of PTSD, poverty, mental illness, and other forms of problems-in-living. Social work practice with these families and children, and with adult African American clients, will not only require that practitioners be culturally responsive, but that they embrace an integrated, holistic, and ethnically sensitive approach. Such an approach reflects a strengths-based bio-psychosocial–spiritual orientation to helping. Practice experience has shown that a multicontextual approach, embracing the whole client, is necessary in order to address the multifaceted concerns most African Americans persons will bring to the helping encounter (Boyd-Franklin, 1989; Logan, Freeman, & McRoy, 1990; Logan & Freeman, 2004). These multicontextual issues (see Table 129.1) serve as a framework for guiding the practice process. The inclusion of an ethnic-sensitive (Devore & Schlesinger, 1998), strengths-based (Saleebey, 2012), spiritually

TABLE 129.1 Multicontextual Framework

The Individual	Immediate Household	Extended Family	Community and Social Connections	Larger Society
• Age	• Type of family structure	• Relationship patterns	• Face-to-face links between individual, family, and society	• Social, political, economic issues
• Gender & sexual orientation	• Stage of family life cycle	• Emotional legacies, themes, secrets, family myths, taboos	• Friends and neighbors	• Bias based on race, ethnicity
• Temperament	• Emotional climate	• Loss	• Involvement in children's school and activities	• Bias based on class
• Developmental or physical disabilities	• Boundaries, patterns, and triangles	• Socioeconomic level and issues	• Political action	• Bias based on sexual orientation
• Culture, race, ethnicity	• Communication patterns	• Work patterns	• Recreation or cultural groups	• Bias based on religion
• Class	• Negotiating skills	• Dysfunctions: addictions, violence, illness, disabilities		• Bias based on disability
• Religious, philosophical, spiritual values	• Decision-making process	• Social and community involvement		• Power and privilege of some groups because of hierarchical rules and norms held by religions, social, business or governmental institutions
• Finances		• Ethnicity		• How does family's place in hierarchy affect relationships and ability to change?
• Autonomy skills		• Values and/or religion		
• Affiliative skills				
• Power/privilege or powerlessness/abuse				
• Education and work				
• Physical or psychological symptoms				
• Addictions and behavioral disturbances				
• Allocation of time				
• Social participation				
• Personal dreams				

Source: Carter, B., & McGoldrick, M., Eds. (2005). *The expanded family life cycle: Individual, family, and social perspectives* (3rd ed.). Boston, MA: Allyn & Bacon.

oriented (Logan & Freeman, 2004) perspective expands the traditional bio-psychosocial orientation, thereby being more responsive to the needs and experiences of African American clients. The ethnic-sensitive, strengths-based, spirituality-oriented approach is based on the following concepts: African Centeredness, Spirituality, Strengths, and Empowerment.

African Centeredness. This perspective acknowledges African culture, expression, values, beliefs, and instructions. It underscores interconnectedness as a way of being in the world that suggests wholeness and balance. Ultimately, it affirms a conscious as well as an unconscious connection of people of African descent with their past and present.

Spirituality. This orientation is concerned with the belief in the wholeness of what it means to be human, a belief that relates to a person's search for a sense of meaning and a morally fulfilling relationship with the world in which they live.

Strengths Perspective. This perspective builds on the belief that within every human being exists an inner or inherent energy or life force that is available to guide and support us in living our lives in productive, fulfilling ways.

Empowerment. This perspective serves as a treatment process and a treatment goal. It emphasizes clients' abilities and desires to take control of their lives and to view themselves positively and competently. Within this broad context, empowerment incorporates these themes: A developmental process, a psychological state, and liberation from oppression.

CLINICAL ISSUES

The primary clinical issue for working effectively with African American clients is the social worker's willingness to embrace a paradigm shift that incorporates the worldviews of African Americans. Worldviews are typically defined as one's perceptions of oneself in relation to other people, nature, objects, and institutions. Scholars on black family life have conceptualized worldviews of African Americans as African centered and strengths based (See Table 129.2). This perspective is based on the values and ethos of the people of Africa and the people of African descent

(Turner, 1996). However, it is important to note that Black families and children vary in the extent to which they exemplify Africentric values, attitudes, beliefs, and characteristics. It has been shown that this information can be useful to practitioners in the assessment and intervention phases of their work.

PRACTICE APPROACHES AND INTERVENTION TECHNIQUES

The search for effective practice approaches and intervention strategies for working with clients of African descent has been ongoing. The first definitive textbooks addressing this subject were published in the late 1980s (Boyd-Franklin, 1989) and the early 1990s. These authors proposed a culturally specific framework or perspective (Logan, Freeman, & McRoy, 1990). This perspective expanded the traditional psychosocial perspective and embodies a bio-psychosocial–spiritual orientation. Emphasis is placed on the cultural and spiritual, which includes cultural identity, cultural explanation of illness and health, natural support systems, worship or faith-based centers and institutions, ethnic community and social organizations, and cultural factors between the client and worker (Lum, 2003). Within this context, an Africentric and strengths-based orientation is proposed. As indicated earlier, this orientation not only includes the history, culture, and worldviews of African Americans, but also provides a multidimensional or multilevel framework for practice, assessment, and intervention. Emergent and traditional practice approaches support this orientation. These include:

• Solution-focused brief therapy
• Solution oriented therapy
• Gender sensitive therapy
• Cognitive behavioral therapy
• Psycho-educational family therapy
• Task-centered treatment
• Structural family therapy
• Collaborative language systems approaches
• Narrative therapy
• Empowerment and strengths perspectives
• Crisis treatment (Walsh, 2009).

Given the range of practice approaches for working with African American clients, it is important to note that the practice interventions may overlap. It is, therefore, important to

TABLE 129.2 Values, Characteristics, Attitudes, and Beliefs of African Americans

Some 1998	Hill 1997	Logan and Freeman 2000 / Logan 2001 / Logan, Freeman, & McRoy, 1990	Martin and Martin, 2002	McAdoo, 1997 & 2003	Schiele, 2000
• Rituals of healing • Indigenous technologies • Healthy Community • Spiritual World • Village • Community	• Strong kinship bonds • Strong work orientation • Strong achievement orientation • Strong religious orientation • Adaptability of family roles	• Inner (inherent) strengths • Unity Wholeness • Self healing Empowerment stance • Positive change • Loving and caring • Collectivism • Nurturance • Support • Perseverance	• Religious consciousness tradition • Fraternal orders • Unions • Ethnic • Women clubs • Race consciousness • Extension of extended families • Institution of Black helping tradition • Prosocialization of children	• Kinship and mutual assistance • Extended family • More than provision of basic needs	• Afro-centricity • Human liberation • Spirituality • Collectivity • Self-knowledge • Inclusiveness • Strong mother–child bond

Source: Logan, S., & Freeman, E. (2004). An analysis, integration and application of Africentric and strengths approaches to Black families and communities. In E. Freeman and S. Logan, Eds. *Reconceptualizing the strengths and common heritage of Black families* (pp. 25–38).

realize that despite the similarities, these strategies may have very different purposes (Walsh, 2009). In addition to the more generic strategies identified in the various practice approaches, the African-centered genogram, the cultural eco-map, cognitive restructuring, culturally relevant readings, and family albums are more specific practice strategies for working with African American clients (Logan and Freeman, 2004).

The treatment plan flows naturally from the assessment process (see Table 129.3) and is based on a collaborative partnership (Lipchick, 2011). In this regard, the social worker should:

1. Identify and understand the cultural identity of African American families and their unique history of enslavement and the continuing impact of living in an environment of oppression, racism, and gross inequality.
2. Assume the existence of strengths for the family, search for exceptions, and support the family's strengths through the inclusion of significant others and through affirmations and an emphasis on solutions.
3. Walk and work side-by-side with client systems as partners (Logan & Freeman, 2004).

As the social worker and the African American client work toward a clear definition of presenting concerns, the identification of specific, concrete, achievable treatment goals, treatment strategies selected from the diverse range of practice approaches may reflect micro, meso, and/or macro levels of intervention. Microlevel interventions include empowerment, crisis intervention, family treatment, solution finding, existentialism, and competitive restructuring. Mesolevel interventions involve the expanded family, fictive kin, places of worship, schools, and various community support systems. Macrolevel interventions address policy, planning, community organizing, policy, advocacy, and administration.

The treatment plan, based on the identified needs of the client systems and culturally diverse treatment strategies, includes the treatment goals, desired outcome, expected change, and agreement or contracting between all parties involved in the change process. As indicated earlier, assessment and treatment tools may consist of the following:

1. *The cultural eco-map.* The cultural eco-map highlights the family as a unit and focuses on both the immediate or the African American ethnic group environment and larger extended environments beyond the individual or family's environment (Logan & Freeman, 2004; Raider & Pauline-Morand, 1998). In focusing on these three broad aspects of the map, the social worker may be guided by questions such as those related to:
   a. The individual or family unit basic needs, food and shelter, preventive health care and good medical resources, satisfactory work experiences, and unit's ability to agree on and fulfill functional roles while meeting individual needs
   b. The nature and quality of African Americans ethnic group environment (Is the neighborhood safe and reasonably pleasant to live in?), quality of family ties, intergenerational issues, and membership in social clubs.
   c. The nature and quality of relationship to the broader extended environment with respect to the educational and vocational enrichment, availability and assessment of needed resources, meaningful connections with other ethnic groups, feelings of inclusiveness, and the ability to deal with an oppressive and racist environment.
2. *The African-centered genogram* is based on two major assumptions about family relationships. These assumptions address kinship, including fictive kinds (those not related by blood or marriage) and functional relationships (Watts-Jones, 1997 p. 377).
   a. In African American families, kinship must be regarded and understood as it is constructed by the ethnic or racial group of the particular family, and
   b. Functional relationships are as important to represent in a genogram as biological relationships. Functional relationships are based on performances and interactions. For example, a biological grandmother may function as a functional role mother to her grandchild.

Together these culturally sensitive tools serve as useful instruments not only in assessing the strengths and presenting concerns of the African American client, but also provide new insight and information about the family's cultural heritage, cultural and ethnic identity, intergenerational patterns and ways of being in the world.

ASSESSMENT AND TREATMENT PLANS

In working with African American clients, a culturally responsive social worker will seek to understand and apply the African-centered approach to the three phases of process (See Table 129.3). In this process, Lum (2003) suggests that the social worker not only reinterprets and reconceptualizes psychosocial factors as socio-environmental impacts and psycho individual reactions, but also acknowledges cultural strengths that include the cultural and the spiritual. Additionally, the following factors may serve to strengthen the social assessment skills of the social worker:

- A worker should think about clients in terms of group characteristics and group strengths as well as clinical pathology and agency protocols of problem resolution.
- A worker should examine group strengths as they are understood by community members themselves, and should view the client as a potential teacher to the worker as well as the recipient of services.
- A worker should openly use indigenous sources of help, which may mean granting credence to lay practitioners from ethnic communities.
- A worker should have a systematic learning style and a supportive agency environment that recognize culturally distinctive modes of behavior and respond to them appropriately (Green 1995, pp. 80–81).

EVIDENCE OF PRACTICE EFFECTIVENESS

Evidence of practice is viewed by some as a movement within the social work profession (Walsh, 2009). Vandiver (2002) and others view it as a process utilizing a variety of sources in the professional literature to select interventions that are most likely to promote client change. It is suggested that the evidence-based practitioner should follow a three-tiered approach to selecting interventions to use with clients:

TABLE 129.3 An African-Centered Framework

Three Broad Areas of Work	Related Tasks
Assessment includes:	Individual, group, family and community history Religious/spiritual heritage Migration history Impact of racism and other forms of oppression Economic issues Cultural issues Environmental issues Self-image/ethnic identity issues
Intervention focuses on:	What the client system wants to see changed or different Empowerment: Individual, family, community Strengths, self help, positive change, and collaborative partnership Advocacy at the community level Schools and social service agencies: Responsiveness to the needs of families and communities Action-oriented strategies
Evaluation includes:	Concrete measurable culturally relevant goals agreed on by the client system African-centered diagnoses (incorporates client's ideas about illness and healing) Ongoing goal and task reviews

Source: Logan, S., & Freeman, E. (2004). An analysis, integration and application of Africentric and strengths approaches to Black families and communities. In E. Freeman and S. Logan, Eds. *Reconceptualizing the strengths and common heritage of Black families* (pp. 25–38).

1. The first tier of evidence-based practice is based on established practice guidelines or recommendations that are based on research findings.
2. The second tier of guidelines is based on the expert consensus of clinicians with expertise in a certain area of practice.
3. The third tier of evidence-based practice is based on self directed practice that is immediately available to the social worker such as experience, journal reports, and peer and supervisory input.

Despite the intention within the social work profession to use treatment strategies that have been shown to be effective, efforts to identify evidence-based practice models have been controversial (Walsh, 2009). Practice effectiveness with African American clients clusters around the third tier of evidence-based practice. However, research has consistently shown that structural family treatment is more effective than other clinical modalities with African American clients (Santisteban, Coatsworth, Perez-Vidal, Mitrani, Jean-Gilles, & Szapocznik, 1997). The client populations have included families with children and adolescents with substance problems and other behavioral issues and concerns.

Although structural family therapy provides a useful perspective for evidence-based practice with African American clients, a major concern relates to an inherent bias about what constitutes an "appropriate" family structure. This therapy was based on its founder's, Salvador Minuchin's, belief that many multi-problem families lacked strong executive authority and rules. This executive authority was relegated to the paternal figure or the father in the family who was viewed as the head of the household. This notion was challenged by a feminist critique in the 1980s and continues to be a precautionary point of reference for social workers. Given the increasing diversity in family forms worldwide, it is imperative that social work practitioners not hold specific assumptions about what constitutes family structures prior to a comprehensive assessment process.

CONCLUSION

Effective social work practice with African Americans is based on knowledge and understanding of the history and cultures of the African American people. Recommended practice approaches and strategies incorporate aspects of traditional practice approaches and emergent approaches within an African-centered framework. Emphasis is placed on a collaborative, spiritually oriented empowerment perspective.

WEBSITE

http://www.nami.org/MAC/familyguide

References

Boyd-Franklin, N. (1989). *Black families in therapy: A multisystems approach.* New York, NY: Guilford Press.

Carter, B., & McGoldrick, M. (2005). *The expanded family life cycle: Individual, family and social perspectives* (3rd ed.). Needham Heights, MA: Allyn & Bacon.

Devore, W., & Schlesinger, E. (1998). *Ethnic-sensitive social work practice* (5th ed.). Upper Saddle River: NJ: Pearson Education.

Green, J. W. (1995). *Cultural awareness in the human services: A multiethnic approach* (2nd ed.). Boston, MA: Allyn & Bacon.

Gutman, H. G. (1975). *Slavery and the number game; A critique of times on the cross.* Urbana: University of Illinois Press.

Johnson, M. P., & Roark, J. (1984). *Black masters: A free family of color in the Old South.* New York, NY: W. W. Norton & Company.

Lipchick, E. (2011). *Beyond techniques in solution-focused therapy: Working with emotions and the therapeutic relationship.* New York, NY: Guilford.

Logan, S., Denby, R., & Gibson, P. (2007). *Mental health care in the African American community.* New York, NY: The Haworth Press.

Logan, S. and Freeman, E. (2004). An analysis integration and application of Africentric and strengths approaches to black families and communities. In E. Freeman & S. Logan (Eds.), *Reconceptualizing the strengths and common heritage of Black families* (pp. 25–38).

Logan, S. L. M. (Ed.). (2001). *The Black family: Strengths, self-help, and positive change* (2nd ed.). Boulder, CO: Westview Press.

Logan, M. L., Freeman, E. M., & McRoy, R. G. (1990). *Social work practice with Black families: A culturally specific approach.* New York, NY: Longman.

Lum, D. (2003). *Social work practice and people of color: A process-stage approach* (5th ed.). Pacific Grove, CA: Brooks/Cole.

McAdoo, H. P. (2007). *Black families.* Thousand Oaks, CA: Sage Publications.

Mckinnon, J. (2003). *The Black population in the United States*. March 2002 current population report series. (pp. 20–541). Washington, DC: U.S. Census Bureau.

Raider, M., & Pauline-Morand, M. B. (1998). *Social work practice with low-income, urban, African-American families*. Lewiston, NY: Edwin Mellen Press.

Robinson, E. (2010). *Disintegration: The splintering of Black America*. New York, NY: Doubleday.

Saleebey, D. (2012). *The strengths perspective in social work practice* (6th ed.). Upper Saddle River, NJ: Pearson Education.

Santisteban, D. A., Coatsworth, J. D., Perez-Vidal, A., Mitrani, V., Jean-Gilles, M., & Szapocznik, J. (1997). Brief structural/strategic family therapy with African American and Hispanic high-risk youth. *Journal of Community Psychology, 215*(5), 453–471.

Turner, R. J. (1996). Affirming consciousness: The Africentric perspective. In J. E. Everett, S. S. Chipungu, & B. P. Leashore (Eds.), *Child welfare: An Africentric perspective* (pp. 36–57). New Brunswick, NJ: Rutgers University.

Vandiver, V. L. (2002). Step-by-step practice guidelines for using evidence-based practice and expert consensus in mental health settings. In A. R. Roberts & G. J. Greene (Eds.), *Social worker's desk reference* (pp. 731–738). New York, NY: Oxford University Press.

Waites, C. (Ed.). (2008). *Social work practice with African-American families: An intergenerational perspective*. New York, NY: Routledge.

Walsh, J. (2009). *Theories for direct social work practice* (2nd ed.). Belmont, CA: Brooks/Cole.

Watts-Jones, D. (1997). Toward an African American genogram. *Family Press, 36*, 375–383.

130   The Culturagram

Elaine P. Congress

INTRODUCTION

The increasing diversity of American society has been well documented in both professional literature and the media. Immigrants are entering the United States in record numbers; between 2000 and 2007, 10.3 million immigrants arrived, the highest number ever recorded in U.S. history within an eight-year period (U.S. Bureau of the Census, 2007). Almost 40 million immigrants (naturalized citizens, "green card" holders, undocumented people, and refugees) now live in the United States, accounting for 13% of the total U.S. population (U.S., Census Bureau, 2012.) Although there are immigrants in every state, most live in California, New York, Texas, and Florida. It is estimated that one out of three immigrants are undocumented, while more than half of the immigrants who entered the country since 2000 are undocumented (U.S. Bureau

of the Census, 2007). One in eight U.S. residents are immigrants, and in large metropolitan areas such as New York City, the majority of the population already originates from countries in Asia, South and Central America, and the Caribbean (New York City Department of City Planning, 2004).

Since the profession's beginning, particularly its work in settlement houses, social workers have always sought to advance the well-being of immigrant populations. The National Association of Social Work (NASW) code of ethics stresses the importance of avoiding discrimination based on race, ethnicity, national origin, and immigration status. Social workers are also advised to pursue culturally competent practices (NASW, 2008).

Not only has there been a growing literature in social work practice and education on cultural competency, but professional literature on immigrants and immigration also has increased dramatically in the past decade. A review of social work abstracts for the past 10 years on immigrants in the United States yielded 231 articles, 130 of which had been written in the past five years. Most articles focused on specific issues in working with various immigrant populations, including Latino populations (Arbona, Olvera, Rodriguez et al., 2010; Parsai, Nieri, & Villar, 2010; Shobe, Coffman, & Dmochowski, 2009), South Asians (Bhattacharya, 2004), Chinese elders (Kang, Boyas, & Salehin, 2012), Korean immigrants (Kang, Basham, & Kim, 2013), African immigrants (Wamwara-Mbugua & Cornwell, 2010), and Arab immigrants (Jamil & Ventimiglia, 2010). A number of articles have looked at challenges for older immigrants (Martin, 2009; Lee & Yoon, 2011; and Lee & Chan, 2009), while others concentrate on child rearing and education issues (Fawley-King, 2010; Lim, Yeh, Liang, Lau, & McCabe, 2009; Kim & Chao, 2009). Few articles considered immigration issues in general.

BACKGROUND OF CULTURAGRAM

The culturagram, a family assessment instrument, grew out of the recognition that families are becoming increasingly culturally diverse and social workers must be able to understand cultural differences between and within families. When attempting to understand culturally diverse families, it is important to assess the family within a cultural context. Assessing a family only in terms of a specific cultural identity, however, may lead to overgeneralization and stereotyping (Congress & Kung, 2013). A Puerto Rican family in which all members are American citizens and have lived in the United States for 20 years is very different from an undocumented Mexican family that emigrated last month. Yet both families are considered Hispanic/Latino. Even within the same family group, each member has had a different immigration and acculturation experience, given that family members often immigrate at different times. Furthermore, family members who regularly work or attend school in a larger, more diverse community may be more acculturated than those who stay at home.

Although the eco-map (Hartman, 1995) and genogram (see Chapter 53) are useful tools in assessing the family, neither emphasizes the important role of culture in understanding the family. The culturagram was developed to help in understanding the cultural background of culture in families (Congress, 1994, 1997; Congress & Kung, 2013). This tool has been applied to work with people of color (Lum, 2004), battered women (Congress & Brownell, 2007), children (Congress, 2001), older people (Brownell & Fenley, 2009), families in crisis (Congress, 2000), Mexican families (Congress, 2004a), Latino and Asian families (Congress & Kung, 2013), immigrant families with health problems (Congress, 2004b; Congress, 2013), and in family development theory (Congress, 2008).

Creation of the Culturagram

The culturagram represents an attempt to individualize culturally diverse families (Congress & Kung, 2013). Completing a culturagram on a family can help a clinician develop a better understanding of the family. Revised in 2007, the culturagram (see Figure 130.1) examines the following areas:

- Reasons for relocation
- Legal status
- Time in community
- Language spoken at home and in the community
- Health beliefs and access to health care
- Impact of trauma and crisis events
- Contact with cultural and religious institutions, holidays, food, and clothing
- Oppression, discrimination, bsias, and racism
- Values about education and work
- Values about family—structure, power, myths, and rules.

Reasons for relocating vary among families. In his classic article on why people migrate Lee (1966) identifies various push and pull factors. While push factors encourage people to migrate, pull factors explain what attracts them to another location. Some of the main push factors are unemployment, natural disasters (famine, drought, flooding), man-made traumas (war, violence, torture, forced labor), and lack of medical care. Pull factors include job opportunities, better education, greater security, and political freedom.

Many families come because of greater economic opportunities (pull factor) in the United States, while refugees and asylum seekers primarily relocate because of political and religious discrimination in their country of origin (push

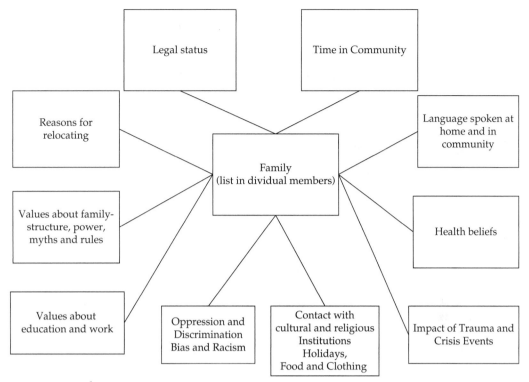

Figure 130.1 Culturagram.

factor). For some families, it is possible to return home again, and they often travel back and forth for holidays and special occasions. Others, especially undocumented people, know they can never go home again. Often the main reason why families migrate to a particular location is because a family member or friend has preceded them.

Immigrants can have various legal statuses, including U.S. naturalized citizens, legal permanent residents (green card holders), undocumented, refugees, or asylum seekers (Chang Muy, 2009). The legal status of a family may have an effect on both individuals and the family as a whole. If a family is undocumented and fears deportation, members may become secretive and socially isolated. Latency-age children and adolescents may be discouraged from developing peer relationships because of the fears of others knowing their immigration secret.

The length of time in the community may differ among individual family members. Usually, family members who have arrived earlier are more assimilated than other members. A current phenomenon involves mothers first immigrating to the United States and then sending for their children. These circumstances can certainly impact individual and family

development. A young infant left in the care of relatives in the home country may have difficulties developing trust because of the lack of continuity in parenting during this crucial early period. Also, the family with young children that is disrupted when the mother migrates to America may face challenges in reuniting as a family after a long separation. Another key factor is that family members are a variety of different ages at the time they relocate. Because of attending American schools and developing peer relationships, children are often more quickly assimilated than their parents. This may lead to conflictual role reversals in which children assume leadership roles.

Language is the mechanism by which families communicate with one another. Often, immigrant families use their native language at home, but begin to use English in contacts with people in the outside community. Children sometimes may prefer English because they see knowledge of this language as most helpful for survival in their newly adopted country. This may lead to conflict in families. A truly literal communication problem may develop when parents speak no English and children speak their original native tongue only minimally.

Families from different cultures have varying beliefs about health, disease, and treatment (Congress & Lyons, 1992; Congress, 2004b; Congress, 2013). Often, health issues impact on culturally diverse families, as for example when the primary wage earner is seriously injured and is no longer able to work, a family member has HIV/AIDS, or a child has a chronic health condition such as asthma or diabetes. Also, mental health problems may have a particular stigma, which can impact families negatively (Michultka, 2009). Refugees who have experienced torture, trauma, and loss in their countries of origin may suffer from posttraumatic stress disorders (Congress, 2012). Families from different cultures may encounter barriers in accessing medical treatment or may prefer alternative resources for diagnosing and treating physical and mental health conditions (Congress, 2013). Both legal and undocumented immigrants often lack health insurance and do not have financial resources to pay for needed health care (Smith, 2009). Many immigrants may use health care methods other than traditional Western European medical care involving diagnosis, pharmacology, X-rays, and surgery (Congress & Lyons, 1992; Congress, 2004b; Smith, 2009)). Social workers who want to understand immigrant families must study the various health beliefs, health conditions, and access to health care characteristic of individual family members.

Families can encounter developmental crises as well as "bolts from the blue" crises (Congress, 2004a; Congress, 2008). Developmental crises may occur when a family moves from one life stage to another. Stages in the life cycle for culturally diverse families may be quite different from those for traditional middle-class families. For example, for many culturally diverse families, the "launching children" stage may not occur at all, as single and even married children may continue to live in close proximity to the parents. If separation is forced, this developmental crisis might be especially traumatic.

Families also deal with "bolts from the blue" crises in different ways. A family's reaction to crisis events is often related to its cultural values. For example, a father's accident and subsequent inability to work may be especially traumatic for an immigrant family in which a father providing for his family is an important family value. Whereas rape is certainly traumatic for any family, the rape of a teenage girl may be especially traumatic for a family who values virginity before marriage.

Immigrant individuals and families may have experienced traumatic events in their country of origin or during transit to the United States. Immigrant families often suffer from poverty and discrimination as they try to access needed educational, vocational, and social services. The current policies regarding undocumented immigrants certainly lead to continuing traumatic experiences for immigrant families. In understanding the impact of traumatic events on immigrant families it is best to make a longitudinal assessment that involves a study of individual members' situations before migrating, in transit, as well as currently (Drachman & Pine, 2004).

Contact with cultural institutions often provides support to immigrant families. Individual family members may use cultural institutions differently. For example, a father may belong to a social club, the mother may attend a church where her native language is spoken, and adolescent children may refuse to participate in either because they wish to become more Americanized. Religion may provide a great deal of support to culturally diverse families, and the social worker will want to explore family members' contact with formal religious institutions.

Each family celebrates particular holidays and special events. Some events mark transitions from one developmental stage to another—for example, a christening, a bar or bat mitzvah, a wedding, or a funeral. It is important for the social worker to learn the cultural significance of important holidays for the family, because these are indicative of what families see as major transition points within their families. These holidays are often associated with culture-specific foods or clothing.

Many immigrants have experienced oppression in their native countries, which has led to their departure from their homelands and immigration to the United States. Some immigrants may have been the majority population in their home country and thus never experienced prejudice until their arrival in the United States. Here, they may be the victim of discrimination and racism based on language or cultural and racial differences. The current U.S. policies on undocumented immigrants further serve to separate and discriminate this newcomer population from other Americans. After review of previous versions of the culturagram and feedback about the instrument, this area was added to the culturagram in 2007 because it was important to understanding the immigrant family experience.

All families have differing values about work and education, and culture is an important influence on such values. Social workers must explore what these values are in order to understand the family. Economic and social differences among family members between the country of origin and after immigration to the United States can affect immigrant families. For example, employment in a low-status position may be very denigrating to a male breadwinner. It may be especially traumatic for an immigrant family when the father cannot find work or only work of a menial nature. This frequently happens to undocumented immigrants who may have difficulties securing "on the books" positions.

Cultural differences in regard to education may emerge when American latency-age children attend large schools away from their communities and begin to develop peer relationships apart from their families. For culturally diverse families who come from backgrounds in which education has been minimal and localized, and where young children even were required to work and care for younger siblings, the American school system's focus on individual academic achievement and peer relationships may seem strange. Furthermore, immigrant children who bring a history of individual or family oppression may feel very isolated and lonely in their new environments.

Sometimes, immigrant families may experience a conflict in their own values about education. An example of this occurred when an adolescent son was accepted with a full scholarship to a prestigious university far away from home. Though the family had always believed in the importance of education, the parents believed that the family needed to stay together and they did not want to have their only child leave home, even to pursue education.

Each family has its unique structure, its beliefs about power relationships, myths, and rules. Some of these may be unique to the cultural background of the family. The social worker needs to explore what values are specific to a particular immigrant family and also understand them in the context of the family's cultural background. Culturally diverse families sometimes have differing beliefs about male–female relationships, especially within marriage. Immigrant families may be a source of conflict in American society with its more egalitarian gender relationships. This can result in an increase in domestic violence among culturally diverse families. Also, child-rearing practices especially in regard to discipline can differ in culturally diverse families and result in increased reporting to Child Protective Services.

The following vignette illustrates how the culturagram can be used to better understand a family and its unique cultural background.

Statement of Problem

Mrs. Carmen Perez, 35 years old, contacted the Family Service Agency in her community because she was having increasing conflicts with her 14-year-old son, Juan, who had begun to cut school and stay out late at night. The past Christmas holidays had been especially difficult because Juan had disappeared for the whole New Year's weekend. She also reported that she had a 10-year-old daughter Maria who was "an angel." Maria was very quiet, never wanted to go out with friends, and preferred to stay at home helping her mother with household chores. Mrs. Perez indicated the source of much conflict was that Juan believed he did not have to respect Pablo, as the latter was not his real father. Juan complained that his mother and stepfather were "dumb" because they did not speak English. He felt it was very important to learn English as soon as possible because at school several students had made fun of his accent. He felt his parents did not understand how difficult his school experience was, as he believed that his teachers favored lighter-skinned Latinos. Juan had much darker skin than his mother, his stepfather, or his half-sister, Maria.

History

When she was 20 years old, Mrs. Perez had moved to the United States from Puerto Rico with her first husband, Juan Sr., because they were very poor in Puerto Rico and had heard there were better job opportunities here. Juan Sr. had died in an automobile accident on a visit back to Puerto Rico when Juan Jr. was two years old. Shortly afterward, she met Pablo, who had come to New York from Mexico to visit a terminally ill relative. After she became pregnant with Maria, they began to live together. Pablo indicated that he was very fearful of returning to Mexico, because several people in his village had been killed in political conflicts. Because Pablo was undocumented, he had been able to find only occasional day work. He was embarrassed that Carmen had been forced to apply for food stamps. As a home care worker, Carmen was paid only minimum wage. She was very close to her mother, who lived with the family. Her mother had taken her to a spiritualist to help her with her family problems before she had come to the neighborhood agency to ask for help. Pablo has no relatives in New York, but he has several friends at the social club in his neighborhood.

Discussion

After completing the culturagram (see Figure 130.2), the social worker was better able to understand the Perez family, assess their needs, and begin to plan for treatment. For example, she noted that Pablo's undocumented status was a source of continual stress in this family. She referred him to a free legal service that provided help for undocumented people in securing legal status. The social worker also recognized that there had been much conflict within the family because of Juan's behavior. She had concern that Maria might have unrecognized problems. Finally, she was keenly aware of family conflicts between Pablo and Juan. To help the family work out its conflicts, the social worker referred them to a family therapist who was culturally sensitive and had experience with intergenerational conflicts in immigrant families.

FUTURE DIRECTIONS

The culturagram has been seen as an essential tool in helping social workers work more effectively with families from many different cultures. Not only does it help the social worker achieve greater understanding of the culture of a family, it can also point the way toward future treatment. This case example demonstrates how the culturagram can be useful in arriving at decisions about treatment planning and intervention. While using the culturagram the practitioner is required to look at the family in the here and now. Sometimes it is helpful, however, to construct the culturagram at different points in time, first at the beginning of intervention and then at a future point. A retrospective approach also can be useful. To truly understand immigrant families, learning about an immigrant's history is important. For example, the social worker can ask about the immigrants' experience in their country of origin and in transit. Often, a developmental approach that looks

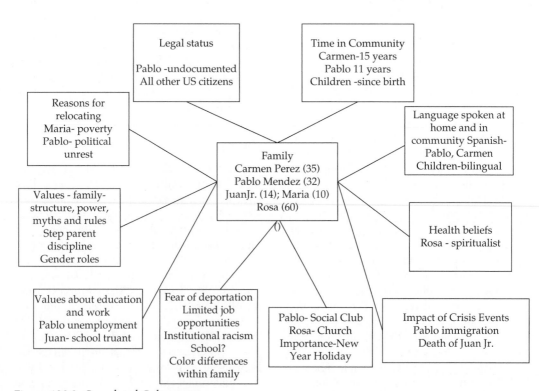

Figure 130.2 Completed Culturagram.

at three stages of immigration (pre-migration, transit, and current situation) is helpful in working with immigrants (Drachman & Pine, 2004). For example, refugees may have had particularly traumatic experiences in their country of origin, and undocumented immigrants may have experienced trauma during the transit period, all of which may affect their current psychological well-being in the United States.

Current practice looks to evidence that specific interventions are effective. Students and practitioners have used the culturagram in their professional practice with families and reported that it is helpful in engaging families in a nonthreatening way. In the use of the culturagram culture is viewed through a multidimensional lens, rather than as a monolithic entity. Initial evaluation of the culturagram has been positive, and there are plans to assess further its effectiveness in promoting culturally competent practice.

With the increased number of immigrants in the United States, there will be greater demand for culturally competent practice with immigrant clients and families. Social workers will need to study what methods and models are the most effective. The culturagram emerges as a useful method to better understand and plan interventions with immigrant families.

WEBSITES

NASW Standards for Cultural Competence in Social Work Practice. http://www .socialworkers.org/practice/standards/ NASWCulturalStandards.pdf.

National Center for Cultural Competence. http://www11.georgetown.edu/research/ gucchd/nccc/.

Article in "The New Social Worker Online," Culturally Competent Social Work Practice With Latino Clients. http://www .socialworker.com/home/Feature_Articles/ Ethics/Culturally_Competent_Social_Work_ Practice_With_Latino_Clients/.

Article on the Foreign Born Population in the United States: 2010. http://www.census.gov/ prod/2012pubs/acs-19.pdf

References

Arbona, C., Olvera, N., Rodriguez, N., Hagan, J., Linares, A., & Wiesner, M. (2010). Acculturative stress among documented and undocumented Latino immigrants in the United States. *Hispanic Journal of Behavioral Sciences, 32*(3), 362–384.

Bhattacharya G. (2004). Health care seeking for HIV/AIDS among South Asians in the United States. *Health Social Work, 29*(2), 153–160.

Brownell, P., & Fenley, R. (2009). Older adult immigrants in the United States: Issues and Services. In F. Chang-Muy & E. Congress (Eds.), *Social work with immigrants and refugees: Legal issues, clinical skills, and advocacy* (pp.277–307). New York, NY: Springer Publishing Company.

Chang-Muy, F. (2009). Legal classification of immigrants. In F. Chang-Muy & E. Congress (Eds.), *Social work with immigrants and refugees: Legal issues, clinical skills, and advocacy* (pp. 39–62). New York, NY: Springer Publishing Company.

Congress, E. (1994). The use of culturagrams to assess and empower culturally diverse families. *Families in Society, 75,* 531–540.

Congress, E. (1997) Using the culturagram to assess and empower culturally diverse families. In E. Congress (Ed.), *Multicultural perspectives in working with families* (pp. 3–16). New York, NY: Springer Publishing Company.

Congress, E. (2000). Crisis intervention with culturally diverse families. In A. Roberts (Ed.), *Crisis intervention handbook* (2nd ed.) (pp. 431–449). New York, NY: Oxford University Press.

Congress, E. (2001). Ethical issues in work with culturally diverse children and their families. In N. B. Webb, *Culturally diverse parent-child and family relationships* (pp. 29–53). New York, NY: Columbia University Press.

Congress, E. (2004a). Crisis intervention and diversity: Emphasis on a Mexican immigrant family's acculturation conflicts. In P. Meyer (Ed.), *Paradigms of clinical social work* (Vol. 3), *Emphasis on diversity* (pp. 125–144). New York, NY: Brunner-Routledge.

Congress, E. (2004b). Cultural and ethical issues in working with culturally diverse patients and their families: The use of the culturagram to promote cultural competent practice in health care settings. *Social Work in Health Care, 39*(3/4), 249–262.

Congress, E. (2008). Individual and family development theory. In P. Lehman & N. Coady (Eds.), *Theoretical perspectives for direct social work practice: A generalist-eclectic approach* (2nd ed.) (pp. 83–104). New York, NY: Springer Publishing Company.

Congress, E. (2012). Social work with refugees. In D. Elliott & U. Segal (Ed.), *Refugees worldwide* (Vol. 4), *Law, policy, and programs* (pp. 197–218). Santa Barbara, CA: Praeger.

Congress, E. (2013). Immigrants and health care. In Social Work section of the American Public Health Association, *Handbook for public health social work* (pp. 103–121). New York, NY: Springer Publishing Company.

Congress, E., & Brownell, P. (2007). Application of the culturagram with culturally and ethnically diverse battered women. In A. Roberts (Ed.), *Battered women and their families* (pp. 491–508). New York, NY: Springer.

Congress, E., & Kung, W. (2013). Using the culturagram to assess and empower culturally diverse families. In E. Congress & M. Gonzalez (Eds.), *Multicultural perspectives in working with families* (pp. 2–21). New York, NY: Springer Publishing Company.

Congress, E., & Lyons, B. (1992). Ethnic differences in health beliefs: Implications for social workers in health care settings. *Social Work in Health Care, 17*(3), 81–96.

Drachman, D., & Pine, B. (2004). *Effective child welfare practice with immigrant and refugee children and their families.* Washington, DC: Child Welfare League of America.

Fawley-King, K. (2010). A review of family-based mental health treatments that may be suitable for children in immigrant families involved in the child welfare system. *Journal of Public Child Welfare, 4*(3), 287–305.

Hartman, A. (1995). Diagrammatic assessment of family relationships. *Families in Society, 76,* 111–122.

Jamil, H., & Ventimiglia, M. (2010) Mental health and treatment response among Iraqi refugees as compared to other non-war exposed Arab immigrants: A pilot study in southeast Michigan. *Journal of Immigrant & Refugee Services, 8*(4), 431–444.

Kang, S.-Y., Basham, R., Kim, Y. J. (2013). Contributing factors of depressive symptoms among elderly Korean immigrants in Texas. *Journal of Gerontological Social Work, 56*(1), 67–82.

Kang, S.-Y, Boyas, J., Salehin, M. (2012). Correlates of depression among Chinese immigrant elders in Arizona: The role of acculturative stress and social support. *Journal of Human Behavior in the Social Environment, 22*(3), 334–350.

Kim, S. Y., & Chao, R. K. Heritage language fluency, ethnic identity, and school effort of immigrant Chinese and Mexican adolescents. (2009). *Cultural Diversity & Ethnic Minority Psychology, 15*(1), 27–37.

Lee, E. 1966. A theory of migration. *Demography, 3*(1), 47–57.

Lee, E., & Chan, K. (2009). Religious/spiritual and other adaptive coping strategies among Chinese American older immigrants. *Journal of Gerontological Social Work, 52*(5), 517–533.

Lee, K. H., & Yoon, D. P. (2011). Factors influencing the general well-being of low-income Korean immigrant elders. *Social Work, 56*(3), 269–279.

Lim, S. L., Yeh, M., Liang, J., Lau, A. S., McCabe, K. (2009). Acculturation gap, intergenerational conflict, parenting style, and youth distress in immigrant Chinese American families. *Marriage & Family Review, 45*(1), 84–106.

Lum, D. (2004). *Social work practice and people of color: A process-stage approach* (5th ed.). Pacific Grove, CA: Brooks Cole.

Martin, S. S. Healthcare-seeking behaviors of older Iranian immigrants: Health perceptions and definitions. (2009). *Journal of Evidence-Based Social Work, 6*(1), 58–78.

Michultka, D. (2009). Mental health issues in new immigrant communities. In F. Chang-Muy & E. Congress (Eds.), *Social Work with immigrants and their families: Legal issues, clinical skills, and advocacy* (pp. 135–172). New York, NY: Springer Publishing Company.

National Association of Social Workers. (2008). *Code of ethics.* Washington, DC: NASW Press.

New York City Department of City Planning, Population Division. (2004). *The newest New Yorkers 2000.* New York, NY: NYC-DCP 04–09.

Parsai, M., Nieri, T., Villar, P. (2010). Away from home: Paradoxes of parenting for Mexican immigrant adults. *Families in Society: The Journal of Contemporary Social Services, 91*(2), 201–208.

Smith, S. (2009). Social work and physical health issues of immigrants. In F. Chang-Muy & E. Congress (Eds.), *Social work with immigrants and their families: Legal issues, clinical skills, and advocacy* (pp. 103–133). New York, NY: Springer Publishing Company.

Shobe, M. A., Coffman, M. J., Dmochowski, J. (2009). Achieving the American dream: Facilitators and barriers to health and mental health for Latino immigrants. *Journal of Evidence-Based Social Work, 6*(1), 92–110.

U.S. Bureau of Census. (2007). *Current population survey* (113th ed.). Austin, TX: Reference Press.

Wamwara-Mbugua, L. W., & Cornwell, T. B. (2010). A dialogical examination of Kenyan immigrants' acculturation in the United States. *Journal of Immigrant & Refugee Services, 8*(1), 32–49.

131 Social Work Practice with Persons Living with HIV/AIDS

Neil Able

OVERVIEW

First recognized as a threat to human health and well-being in 1981, HIV/AIDS has captured the attention and galvanized the actions of the global community ever since. As the issue exploded from a few isolated cases to a full-scale pandemic, responses ranged from fear to grief to rage, from denial and repression to personal and collective action. The inescapable associations with sex and death have since progressed from early allusions to the illness as a "great equalizer" to an international case study in the consequences of inequality. From pressing a redefinition of what it means to be "family" to destabilizing national economies and threatening global security, HIV/AIDS has altered the landscape in unimaginable ways, and provided a broad spectrum of challenges and opportunities for social work practice.

In this chapter, I will overview key concepts and issues, aiming to familiarize social workers with the nature and progression of the illness, and with recommendations for professional response in prevention, intervention, and care. Steady advances in medical treatment have transformed the possibilities for a long and fulfilling life, while social and economic forces continue to pose barriers to access for all. If ever a topic cried out for career-long continuing education, this is it.

History of the Pandemic

Beginning with a few unexplained cases of young men in the United States with rapidly progressing, little-known cancers and lung infections, the Centers for Disease Control and Prevention (CDC) pooled a wide range of resources, and in a politically contentious process (Shilts, 1987), scientists ultimately identified the *human immunodeficiency virus* (HIV) as the common culprit (Fan, Conner, & Villarreal, 2011). A key characteristic of the virus was rapid compromise of the immune system, dramatically impacting the ability of previously healthy individuals to fight off disease. Because the first cases were also associated with the sexual orientation of the patients, the CDC initially identified the condition as GRID (gay-related immune deficiency), a term which later evolved into the less pejorative *acquired immune-deficiency syndrome* (AIDS). As we will see, early wavering on naming this condition was a precursor of the shaming, blaming, and sometimes irrational fear associated with a condition whose origins were unknown, and widely attributed to everything from a racially inspired conspiracy to wipe out blacks (Ross, Essien, & Torres, 2006) to divine retribution for immoral behavior. Best scientific evidence today indicates that HIV mutated in equatorial Africans who while hunting became exposed to the blood of chimpanzees infected with simian immune-deficiency syndrome (SIDS) (Gao et al., 1999).

Epidemiology

The science of understanding disease prevalence is central to identifying the populations and regions most impacted. Epidemiology builds knowledge of factors correlated with disease, seeks to determine how it is spread by and to whom, and anticipates where it is likely to expand. This information can guide prevention efforts and help prioritize persons and locations most in need of resources and treatment. *Epidemics* are designated when a disease is recognized as spreading rapidly within particular populations and/or regions, and become *generalized* when they reach beyond a group with specific identifying characteristics to a broader population. When epidemics cross continents, they become known as *pandemics* (Fan, Conner, & Villarreal, 2011).

Epidemiological data is established on state, national, and international levels with varying degrees of precision and currency. The information is vast, and the details dizzying. The most current global estimates indicate that there are 34 million people living with HIV around the world, including 0.8% of adults aged 15–49 years (Joint United Nations Programme on HIV/AIDS [UNAIDS], 2012). Although HIV prevalence rates are often reported inclusive of all stages of the disease, information may also be presented in a manner distinguishing cases that have progressed to a diagnosis of AIDS.

As of 2010, an estimated 872,990 persons were living with HIV infection in the United States (CDC, 2013). Of these, the highest percentage (44%) were blacks/African Americans, 67% of viral transmissions were attributed to men who have sex with men (MSM), and the largest percentage (22%) were among persons aged 45–49 years. Eighteen percent of those with an HIV infection in the United States are believed to be unaware of their status, and the number of new infections has held steady at approximately 50,000 per year for the last decade (Kaiser Family Foundation, 2013). An estimated 487,692 persons were living with an infection that had ever been classified as AIDS, of whom 43% were black/African American. The age group experiencing the largest percentage increase was persons aged 65 years and older.

No attempt is made here to be comprehensive; the key point is that data help map whom the disease is hitting hardest—and when, where, and how. Although there have been marked improvements in access to treatment, and consequently, enhanced survival rates, these gains have been unevenly distributed across populations and settings, and tremendous work remains to be done (Rountree, Zibalese-Crawford, & Evans, 2013).

Impact: Personal to Political

The impact of HIV-related disease spans those who are infected, affected, and indirectly connected. People *infected* with the virus have been known variously (and partially) over time as AIDS victims, People with AIDS, People living with AIDS, and People living with HIV/AIDS (PLHA). Like the naming of the disease itself, this evolution signifies the progression of understanding and identification associated with the illness, and depicts both the depersonalization and ultimate claiming of status by those most directly impacted. Whitehorn and Terrell (2009) wrote eloquently in *POZ Magazine*, itself named in a spontaneous attempt to put a less stigmatizing spin on what it meant to be HIV positive (*HIV+*; infected with the virus), about the challenges and contradictions in trying to frame a deadly serious condition in terms that were simultaneously de-stigmatizing and inclusive of the spectrum of infected persons.

Many authors have categorized the areas of life altered by the disease (c.f. Poindexter, 2010; Bartlett & Finkbeiner, 2006; Clark, Maupin, Jr., & Hammer, 2004), and some issues, mostly psychosocial, have been remarkably persistent over time. HIV impacts the nature and quality of sexual expression; the intimacy and authenticity shared between life partners, friends, and casual acquaintances; decisions about reproduction and parenting; opportunity and capacity in the workforce; daily quality of life; and expectations regarding one's future and longevity.

For persons *affected* by HIV (family members, loved ones, and friends), the impact is also complex. In intimate relationships, *serodiscordant* partners (one HIV+, the other not) may be challenged by concerns of transmitting the virus during sexual contact, stresses and strains associated with disease management for the ill partner, and worries about reactions of others in work or social settings as they learn of the HIV+ partner's condition (Powers & Rowan, 2013). *Seroconcordant* partners (both HIV+) may benefit from the comfort of shared confidences and common challenges, while managing the risk of reinfection should one partner transmit a new strain of the virus to the other. Despite the defining aspect of a disease state, particularly a highly stigmatizing one, life for infected and affected people is subject to all the joys, sorrows, strengths, and frailties of life in the absence of illness. Social workers must bear in mind that daunting as it may seem to them, HIV is often not the largest or only problem a client may be managing, and remember to encounter people with these very particular needs with the same sensitivity and compassion they would bring to any other professional interaction.

Beyond the personal and interpersonal, the sweeping impact of the HIV/AIDS pandemic reached global economic and political proportions in 2000, when United Nations Security Council Resolution 1308, with the support of U.S. Vice President Al Gore,

took the topic from the new field of human security to the well-known 'old' fields of national and even global security by '[r]ecognizing that the spread of HIV/AIDS can have a uniquely devastating impact on all sectors and levels of society … given its possible growing impact on social instability and emergency situations … recognizing … risk of exposure to the disease through large movements of people, widespread uncertainty over conditions, and reduced access to medical care, … [s]tressing that the HIV/AIDS pandemic, if unchecked, may pose a risk to stability and security' (Gunduz, 2006, p. 68).

Changes over Time in Experience of Living with HIV

HIV disease is now rightly considered a chronic illness rather than a death sentence, at least for PLHA advantaged to live in societies with the will, capacity, and determination to make comprehensive care widely available. Still, it often coexists with depression, anxiety, disabling chronic pain, and risk of *comorbid* conditions that challenge the stamina of even the most determined on a day-to-day basis. There is no vaccine and no cure, and the corollaries of chronic disease management have led to reconsideration by some long-term survivors of whether the unexpectedly long life they have found themselves living has been worth the associated debilitation and isolation (Leland, 2013).

NATURE AND PROGRESSION OF HIV-RELATED ILLNESS

HIV is a type of *antigen*, a microbial agent that penetrates the body and is capable of triggering a response in the immune system. More specifically, it is a *retrovirus*, meaning that it is capable of "hijacking" the DNA structure of the host cell it penetrates, converting it so that instead of producing more copies of itself, it produces more of the invader (Bartlett & Finkbeiner, 2006). In the case of HIV, if we could personify the virus, it would be tempting to call it ingenious, because the host cell it seeks, the *CD4* (a white blood cell or *lymphocyte*, also known as a T4 or "helper"

cell) is key to an otherwise healthy immune response, which would mark the antigen as an intruder, identifying it for destruction and elimination from the body.

Following initial viral acquisition, HIV illness progresses through a series of stages (see Web Resources for greater detail) characterized largely by a fluctuating balance between the *CD4 count* (number per mm^3) and the *viral load* (copies of the virus per milliliter of blood). Exposure to the virus occurs via transmission of one of the bodily fluids capable of supporting it (mainly blood, semen, pre-ejaculatory fluid, vaginal secretions, and breast milk). Initial infection is often experienced like any other flu or brief illness; the immune system fights off the symptoms, and the infected person dismisses the cycle as familiar and normal. Typically, *seroconversion* (production of antibodies to fight off the antigen) does not begin for several weeks, after which an untreated individual may experience an extended period (seven years or so) of *asymptomatic* illness (Fan, Conner, & Villarreal, 2011). This period is particularly dangerous because, with the condition undetected and untreated, the HIV+ person may look and feel well while becoming highly infectious, and undergoing a gradual erosion of immune system response capability. Essentially, he or she is an unrecognized threat to self and others, unfortunately contributing to the rational aspect of fears that lead to stigmatization of the disease.

Eventually, the CD4/viral load ratio deteriorates to the stage of *symptomatic* HIV illness, increasing the chances of detection for those with access to education and/or competent medical care. The HIV+ person, aware or not of his or her underlying condition, is subject to longer recovery times from common infections, night sweats and fevers, and chronic conditions that may or may not trigger testing for and discovery of the root infection.

If untreated, symptomatic progression continues until the manifestation of *opportunistic infections* (OIs), conditions that someone with a healthy immune system would not normally develop (Bartlett & Finkbeiner, 2006). Some of these comorbid conditions (i.e., pneumocystis pneumonia, cryptosporidiosis, mycobacterium tuberculosis) are more likely to manifest when HIV is the underlying mechanism of immune suppression, and may be the motivation for a patient first presenting for treatment (CDC, 2009).

When one or more of these "AIDS-defining illnesses" occur, and/or when the CD4 count drops below 200, the HIV+ person is diagnosed with AIDS. Thereafter, treatment becomes critical to stave off deterioration in physical, emotional, and mental status that can otherwise lead to death. Depression and anxiety are common psychological comorbid conditions (Spies, Asmal, & Seedat, 2013), exacerbated by co-occurring problems with substance abuse or injection drug use (Friedland, 2010). Despite the availability of HIV-specific *antiretroviral therapies* (ART), OIs continue to be a major cause of sickness and death. *Prophylaxis*, or efforts to prevent such conditions, can further complicate medical care. Due to underlying psychosocial or economic factors, or challenges associated with combining treatments for multiple conditions, PLHA may not take ART as prescribed and fail to benefit fully as a result (CDC, 2009). For social workers, multiple challenges exist in educating clients regarding overlapping risks they may face, and managing referrals such that clients have the best potential to follow through with medical care.

VIRAL TRANSMISSION

HIV is transmitted when the virus is introduced into the bloodstream of a receptive host by an HIV+ source. The primary infectious fluids are blood, semen, vaginal/cervical secretions, and breast milk. Although HIV has been detected in saliva and tears, the concentrations of viral particles are minute, and the volume of fluid that would be required to transmit the virus is so large as to make them an extremely low risk (Fan, Conner, & Villarreal, 2011).

Risk of exchanging infectious fluid occurs mostly between HIV+ mother and child, during "unsafe" sexual contact, or through the use of infected implements that penetrate the blood stream (i.e., syringes or needles common in injection drug use, tattooing implements, or medical accidents) (Fan, Conner, & Villarreal, 2011). The common feature is contact through a port of entry. Though the bloodstreams of mother and fetus are separated by the placenta, during the third trimester, or during the birth process itself, tears or swallowing may occur, making the child receptive to infectious fluid. Breastfeeding poses related risks. During sexual contact, infectious fluids may gain entry through tears in delicate tissue, and sharing of needles may transfer such

fluids from one person to another by directly penetrating the bloodstream.

Contrary to enduring myth, HIV cannot be transferred by being sneezed or coughed upon, by casual contact such as hand-shaking, hugging, or closed-mouth kissing, or by daily activities such as eating together, sharing toilets, or living in the same household (Bartlett & Finkbeiner, 2006). Social workers have an obligation to understand what is and is not risky, to conduct themselves accordingly, and to educate infected and affected persons appropriately.

Distinguishing Behaviors from Identity to Minimize Stigma

As an outgrowth of epidemiology, the tendency to associate degrees of risk with particular populations is an understandable but avoidable driver of stigma. It is critical to distinguish so-called "risk groups" (i.e., MSM, injection drug users) from the risky behaviors they and others may enact (Fan, Conner, & Villarreal, 2011). Too often, encounters with feared others lead to cycles of labeling them as deviant, generalizing their undesirable characteristics through stereotyping, imposing an "us/them" out-group status to create a safe distance, and discriminating through harmful thoughts and actions (Link & Phelan, 2001). PLHA have long acknowledged the fear and loathing they sometimes encounter, including in health care settings (Green & Platt, 1997).

More recent efforts have adapted mindfulness principles to the cultivation of compassionate care through *awareness* of service providers' own predispositions and biases, *acceptance* of their implications for the quality of care, and taking intentional *action* to support the needs and well-being of PLHA (Rutledge & Abell, 2005). The HIV/AIDS Provider Stigma Inventory (HAPSI) facilitates reflection on these aspects as a first step in reducing tendencies to reflexively judge or mistreat PLHA based on generalized characteristics (Rutledge, Whyte, Abell, Brown, & Cesnales, 2011).

TESTING

HIV testing is crucial to understanding one's status, and circumstances before and after provide opportunities for supportive service provision. Pre- and post-test counseling guidelines can educate clients about how they may have acquired (or can spread) the virus, can explain the meaning of test results, and can provide critical referrals to appropriate services (see Web Resources).

Initial testing is typically designed to detect the presence of *antibodies* (as evidence that an immune system response has been triggered). Because it may take three to six weeks for sero-conversion to occur, antibody testing should not be attempted until after a *window period* has transpired since the estimated time of first exposure (Bartlett & Finkbeiner, 2006). Otherwise, the risk of *false negative* results (indicating an HIV infection has not occurred when, in fact, it has) is increased. As a safeguard, it is wise to retest three to six months following the initial test. *Antigen* testing (confirming presence of the virus itself) is more typically reserved for determining or monitoring viral load, due in part to its cost.

Social workers should be able to explain that an HIV+ test result in itself does not equal a diagnosis of AIDS (clients need follow-up testing to determine the stage of their illness). They should also be ready to support persons testing HIV+ through the initial adjustment to the news, refer them to appropriate services, and explore the issue of *partner notification*. Whether, when, and how to let others know they may also have been exposed to the virus is a highly sensitive process with crucial implications for personal and public health.

PROVIDING EDUCATION, TREATMENT, AND SUPPORT

Notwithstanding assurances in the Universal Declaration of Human Rights that

Everyone has the right to a standard of living adequate for the health and well-being of himself and of his family, including … medical care and … the right to security in the event of … sickness, (or) disability … (United Nations, 1948, Article 25),

access to prevention, education, treatment, and support has varied widely across and within societies. Within the United States, delivery of services has too often been compromised by inequities related to poverty, moral judgments, and their corollaries in race, class, and gender (Poindexter, 2010). This, and the ever shifting demographics of the disease, may explain in part why the number of new cases in the United States has held steady for the past decade, despite diverse and sustained prevention efforts.

Prevention through Behavior Change, Prophylaxis, and Evidence-based Interventions

HIV prevention education promotes behavior change in terms that are both generalized and tailored to risk demographics. Broad topics range from abstinence-only to comprehensive sex education, safe handling of needles and syringes, and relationship dynamics designed to reduce risk of exposure. Social workers should become familiar with factors associated with health behavior change, understand the critical information and resources needed to act on intentions to change, and be aware of evidence-based programs addressing the needs of particular populations.

Principles of Health Behavior Change

Fan, Connor, and Villarreal (2011) integrate existing theory and research, proposing a comprehensive approach to prevention education addressing the following principles:

- Cognitive: making sure to provide the facts. Understanding the nature of HIV, and how it is and is not spread so "rational" obstacles to change can be minimized
- Emotional: encouraging feeling good about behavior change rather than motivating through fear, and exploring more subjective resistance to new experiences or strategies
- Behavioral: becoming comfortable with sexual jargon so recommendations are clear and specific, recognizing that vague suggestions (i.e., "be safe!") are functionally useless
- Interpersonal: recognizing that relational influences in one's inner circle can "make or break" best intentions to change, and that power dynamics can undermine follow-through
- Social Ecological: broader group and cultural norms also shape behavior, so appreciating the influence of shared identities is essential to realistic plans for change
- Structural: making sure, for instance, that when someone decides to be tested or seek care, that nonstigmatizing, competent services and facilities are available.

Knowledge and Resources

Social workers must be able to present what they know in a manner that maximizes accessibility for, and inspires the self-interest of, the target group. This means, for instance, being respectful of individuals or environments preferring abstinence only sex education, while being prepared to detail levels of risk associated with "safer sex" behaviors (Bartlett & Finkbeiner, 2006). It may also mean knowing whether and where condoms can be made available, or when to consider more controversial prevention recommendations like use of ART as *pre-exposure prophylaxis* (PrEP) for men who have sex with men or transgender women (Arnold et al., 2012).

Evidence-based Interventions

The CDC has long promoted evidence-based interventions supporting HIV-related behavior change for diverse populations (see Web Resources). These are manualized programs for use in *community based organizations* (CBOs) and include, among many others:

- Healthy Relationships: using social cognitive theory to help men and women develop coping skills and positive expectations for new behaviors
- Sister to Sister: a single-session STI risk-reduction intervention for sexually active African American women ages 18–45 years, delivered during a routine medical visit
- RESPECT: utilizing "teachable moments" to motivate incremental HIV risk reduction behavior change in one-on-one brief counseling environments.

The Diffusion of Effective Behavioral Interventions (DEBI) programs are not without controversy (c.f. Owczarzak, J. & Dickson-Gomez, J., 2011), and the CDC continues to improve and update their content, research, and dissemination with CBO partners.

Medical Treatment

The development of antiretroviral medications (ART, previously referred to as *highly active antiretroviral therapy* or HAART) has transformed health outcomes for PLHA by making available classes of drugs taken as combination or "cocktail" therapies (Fan, Conner, & Villarreal, 2011). None of these medications cure; rather, they arrest various processes with a primary goal of reducing viral load until it is undetectable, while restoring the CD4 count to robust levels. The medications are associated with a host of side effects, ranging from tolerable to "deal breakers" (Bartlett & Finkbeiner, 2006, p. 85), and including gastrointestinal discomforts, debilitating headaches, painful neuropathy, and contraindications with other necessary medications. And ironically, as PLHA live longer, they become subject to other chronic conditions of aging, further complicating care.

Although prescribed regimens have improved dramatically over time as multiple medications are combined into single pills requiring fewer doses per day, social workers become a critical part of the care team in supporting long-term *adherence* (taking medications as prescribed). Returning to our notion of the virus as "ingenious," when patients are unable to "stick with the program" to a very high degree (i.e., adhering ≥ 95% of the time), they may develop *resistance* to their ART. As the virus mutates, immediate antiretroviral benefits erode, and ultimately, the medication and all others in its class become useless to the patient (PAGAA, 2013). He or she may then pass along this drug-resistant strain to others.

PLHA may have poor adherence due to untreated mental health problems, substance use or abuse, lack of education regarding consequences of missed doses, failing to keep regular medical appointments, unmanageable side effects, or fears about others learning their status by seeing them manage their medication (PAAGA, 2013). As case managers and counselors, social workers play critical roles in maximizing access to care, and in helping PLHA resolve behavioral, relational, or financial concerns that undermine adherence to ART.

Case Management and Counseling

The scope of knowledge necessary to function effectively as a case manager can seem overwhelming, and resources and references included here are meant as guides to the wealth of constantly updated information available on HIV/AIDS. It is definitely true that long-term success in this field requires stamina and determination, a balance between accessibility and well-managed interpersonal boundaries, and the willingness to seek support and supervision on an ongoing basis. As with other high-demand fields, a sense of humor is essential, and the rewards of doing stimulating, meaningful work are great.

Traditional roles take on particular form in the context of personal, relational, and social circumstances faced by PLHA. Among the tasks social workers must consider are advocacy, referral and information provision, service planning and delivery, follow-up, skill building, teaching, and counseling. Taking a human rights perspective, social workers must strive to stand in solidarity with clients at risk of being stigmatized on multiple fronts, remain mindful of their own responsibilities in creating positive, compassionate contexts for service delivery, and seek out the knowledge, skills, and guidance necessary to provide competent care. And never forget to document, document, document (!).

On the federal level, the Ryan White HIV/AIDS Program provides critical funding for a host of services, specifying case management, and addressing primary outpatient care for PLHA, and family-centered outpatient care for HIV+ women, infants, children, and youth (Health Resources and Services Administration [HRSA], 2013a). The Affordable Care Act (also known as "Obama care") expands access to Medicaid services, and ensures coverage of "essential health benefits" ranging from hospitalization to mental health and substance use services to prescription drugs and pediatric care (HRSA, 2013b, p. 4). Advocacy for full implementation of this act remains an ongoing challenge. Meanwhile, recognizing that engagement in care is vital for treatment success, that such engagement is often deficient in groups who are disproportionately burdened by the epidemic, and that missing clinical appointments increase the risk of poor health outcomes, social workers can take heart from evidence showing that case management services "play a crucial role in linkage to and retention in care" (Mugavero, 2008, p. 156).

CONCLUSION

Social workers have played a historic role in responding to the HIV/AIDS pandemic. Over time, the costs and consequences have been monumental, and progress steady and game-changing. Still, in the absence of vaccination or cure, millions suffering worldwide, and an average of 50,000 new cases each year in the United States, "It ain't over 'til it's over." Let's get going!

WEB RESOURCES

- thebody.com (www.thebody.com): Comprehensive overview from the basics of HIV through illness treatment and management and psychosocial aspects.
- AIDS.gov (www.aids.gov): Essential resource for HIV basics, pre/post-test counseling, and access to provider tools such as the Ryan White HIV/AIDS Program and PEPFAR. Supported by the U.S. Department of Health and Human Services.
- Centers for Disease Control and Prevention (http://www.cdc.gov/hiv/): Epidemiological updates, guidance on testing and treatment of HIV-related illness and comorbid conditions, living with HIV/AIDS, Diffusion of Evidence-Based Interventions (DEBI)
- UNAIDS (http://www.unaids.org/en/): United Nations program founded in 1996; an indispensable resource for global statistics and programming.

References

Arnold, E. A., Hazelton, P., Lane, T., Christopoulos, K. A., Galindo, G. R., Steward, W. T., & Morin, S. (2012). A qualitative study of provider thoughts on implementing Pre-Exposure Prophylaxis (PrEP) in clinical settings to prevent HIV infection. *PLoS One, 7*(7). doi:10.1371/journal.pone.0040603.

Bartlett, J. G., & Finkbeiner, A. K. (2006). *The guide to living with HIV infection.* Baltimore, MD: Johns Hopkins Press.

Centers for Disease Control and Prevention (CDC). (2013). *HIV surveillance report, 23.* Retrieved from http://www.cdc.gov/hiv/topics/surveillance/resources/reports/.

Centers for Disease Control and Prevention (CDC). (2009). *Morbidity and Mortality Weekly Report, 58* (RR-4).

Clark, R. A., Maupin, R. T., Jr., Hammer, J. H. (2004). *A woman's guide to living with HIV infection.* Baltimore, MD: Johns Hopkins Press.

Fan, H. Y., Conner, R. F., & Villarreal, L. P. (2011). *AIDS, science, and society* (6th ed.). Sudbury, MA: Jones and Bartlett.

Friedland, G. (2010). Infectious disease comorbidities adversely affecting substance users with HIV: Hepatitis C and tuberculosis. *Journal of Acquired Immune Deficiency Syndrome, 55,* S37–S42.

Gao, F., Bailes, E., Robertson, D. L., Chen, Y., Rodenburg, C. M., Michael, S. F., … Hahn, B. H. (1999) Origin of HIV-1in the chimpanzee Pan troglodytes troglodytes, *Nature, 397*, 436–441.

Green, G., & Platt, S. (1997). Fear and loathing in health care settings reported by people with HIV. *Sociology of Health and Illness, 19*(1), 70–92.

Gunduz, Z. Y. (2006). The HIV/AIDS epidemic—What's security got to do with it? *Perceptions*, 49–84.

Joint United Nations Programme on HIV/AIDS (UNAIDS). (2012). *Global report: UNAIDS report on the global AIDS epidemic*. Retrieved from http://www.unaids.org/en/media/unaids/contentassets/documents/epidemiology/2012/gr2012/20121120_UNAIDS_Global_Report_2012_with_annexes_en.pdf.

Kaiser Family Foundation (2013). *The HIV epidemic in the United States* (Fact Sheet No. 3029-14). Retrieved from http://kaiserfamilyfoundation.files.wordpress.com/2013/12/3029-14.pdf.

Leland, J. (2013). People think it's over: Spared death, aging people with HIV struggle to live. *The New York Times*. Retrieved from http://www.nytimes.com.

Link, B. G., Phelan, J. C. (2001). Conceptualizing stigma. *Annual Review of Sociology, 27*, 363–385.

Mugavero, M. J. (2008). Improving engagement in HIV care: What can we do? *Topics in HIV Medicine, 16*(5), 156–161.

Owczarzak, J., & Dickson-Gomez, J. (2011). Providers' perception of and receptivity toward evidence-based HIV prevention interventions. *AIDS Education and Prevention, 23*, 105–117.

Panel on Antiretroviral Guidelines for Adults and Adolescents (PAGAA). (2013). *Guidelines for the use of antiretroviral agents in HIV-1-infected adults and adolescents*. Department of Health and Human Services. Retrieved from http://aidsinfo.nih.gov/ContentFiles/AdultandAdolescentGL.pdf.

Poindexter, C. C. (2010). *Handbook of HIV and social work: Principles, practice, and populations.* Hoboken, NJ: Wiley.

Poindexter, C. C. (2010). The human rights framework applied to HIV services and policy. In C. C. Poindexter (Ed.), *Handbook of HIV and social work: Principles, practice, and populations* (pp. 59–73). Hoboken, NJ: Wiley.

Powers, K. F., & Rowan, D. (2013). HIV-affected populations: A ripple effect. In D. Rowan (Ed.), *Social work with HIV/AIDS: A case-based guide* (pp. 235–256). Chicago, IL: Lyceum.

Ross, M. W., Essien, E. J., & Torres, I. (2006). Conspiracy beliefs about the origin of HIV/AIDS in four racial/ethnic groups, *Journal of Acquired Immune Deficiency Syndrome, 41*, 342–344.

Rountree, M., Zibalese-Crawford, M., & Evans, M. (2013). Seasons of change: Exploring the future of HIV/AIDS social work. In D. Rowan (Ed.), *Social work with HIV/AIDS: A case-based guide* (pp. 53–88). Chicago, IL: Lyceum.

Rutledge, S. E., Whyte, N. D., IV, Abell, N., Brown, K. M., Cesnales, N. I. (2011). Measuring stigma among health care and social service providers: The HIV/AIDS Provider Stigma Inventory. *AIDS Patient Care and STDs, 25*(11), 673–682.

Rutledge, S. E., & Abell, N. (2005). Awareness, acceptance, and action: An emerging framework for understanding AIDS stigmatizing attitudes among community leaders in Barbados. *AIDS Patient Care and STDs, 19*(3), 186–199.

Shilts, R. (1987). *And the band played on: Politics, people, and the AIDS epidemic*. New York, NY: St. Martins Press.

Spies, G., Asmal, L., & Seedat, S. (2013). Cognitive-behavioural interventions in mood anxiety disorders in HIV: A systematic review. *Journal of Affective Disorders*. Advance online publication. doi:10.1016/j.jad.2013.04.018.

United Nations. (1948). Universal Declaration of Human Rights. General Assembly Resolution 217A (III) of 10 December 1948. New York: General Assembly. Retrieved from http://www.un.org/en/documents/udhr/.

U.S. Department of Health and Human Services Health Resources and Services Administration (HRSA). (2013a). *About the Ryan White HIV/AIDS Program*. Retrieved from http://www.hab.hrsa.gov/abouthab/aboutprogram.html.

U.S. Department of Health and Human Services Health Resources and Services Administration (HRSA). (2013b). *Key provisions of the Affordable Care Act for the Ryan White Program*. Retrieved from http://hab.hrsa.gov/affordablecareact/keyprovisions.pdf.

Whitehorn, L., & Terrell, K. (2009, May). Viral vernacular. *POZ Magazine*. Retrieved from http://www.poz.com.

132 Social Work with Lesbian, Gay, Bisexual, and Transgendered Clients

Mary Boes & Katherine van Wormer

INTRODUCTION

Lesbian, gays, bisexuals, and transgendered persons seek social work services for the same reasons heterosexuals do—out of grief for the loss of a loved one, for depression and other mental conditions, for court-mandated substance-abuse treatment, for relationship issues. Additionally, lesbians, gays, bisexuals, and transgendered persons have unique issues pertaining to their sexual orientation and gender identity, the social stigma of their differentness, rejection by families and friends, the impact of AIDS on the lives of gay men, and coming-out issues for all age groups. Heterosexuals also seek help for matters related to homosexuality—for example, concern over gender-appropriate behavior in a young son, the shock of learning an offspring is gay or lesbian, or the discovery that a spouse is having an affair with someone of the same sex. Nevertheless, in the best tradition of the client-centered approach, social workers should follow the lead of the client in addressing the specific issue that propelled him or her to seek professional help in the first place (see Ski Hunter, 2012).

Two key principles attract such persons and their families to seek professional help: the promise of confidentiality and the tradition of nonjudgmental acceptance. Perhaps for these reasons, and owing to a reluctance to talk of these matters to family members, friends, or clergy, gays and lesbians are more likely than heterosexuals to see a therapist (Goldstein & Horowitz, 2003). African Americans seeking assistance related to their sexuality, however, are likely to find few, if any, therapists of color with relevant training.

Few groups are as maligned in our society as those who are identified as or suspected of gender nonconformity or having a same-sex sexual orientation. The most extreme forms of discrimination, including ridicule and violence, are reserved for transgendered persons or those who have the psychological sense of being female when they are physiologically male or vice versa (see van Wormer, 2007).

In recognition of the homophobia (fear of homosexuality) and heterosexism in society, the social work profession strives to prepare practitioners who will promote respect for people of all sexual orientations. According to Carol Tully (personal communication), the three basic forms of homophobia are pervasive—*institutional* homophobia, which is perpetuated by the traditional structures of society; homophobia at the *individual* level, evidenced by insulting jokes and hate crimes; and *internalized* homophobia, which is awkwardness that gays and lesbians, especially teens, feel about themselves.

In its policy statement on lesbian, gay, and bisexual issues, the National Association of Social Workers (NASW) (2012) states its commitment to advancing policies and practices that will improve the status and well-being of all lesbian, gay, and bisexual people, including rights to inheritance, marriage, reproductive choices, and child custody.

Similarly, the American Psychological Association (APA) Committee on Lesbian, Gay, Bisexual, and Transgender Concerns endorses positive attitudes toward gays as a group. From the brochure issued by the APA (2008, pp. 1–4) we learn that:

- Sexual orientation is most likely the result of a complex interaction of environmental, cognitive, and biological factors.
- Sexual orientation exists along a continuum that ranges from exclusive homosexuality to exclusive heterosexuality.
- Although persons can choose whether to act on their feelings, psychologists do not consider sexual orientation to be a conscious choice.
- Children reared by gay or lesbian parents are psychologically as well adjusted as children reared by heterosexual parents.
- Most pedophiles and child abusers are heterosexual men.

CASE ILLUSTRATIONS

(1) As a small child, Lee was very popular at school and sang in the school and church choirs. When puberty hit, however, he developed an identity crisis related to his sexuality and teasing by other kids who regarded him as a sissy. The bullying escalated to the extent that Lee started missing school; he faced a religious crisis as well.

The school social worker's assessment revealed that Lee was depressed, lonely, and at times suicidal, confused about his gender identity. She met with Lee weekly and referred him to an after-school facilitated group that helped students wrestle with issues related to gender identity. Intervention was planned with classmates who were engaged in bullying.

(2) The Williams had three sons; the youngest, age seven years, was extremely feminine, insisting that he was, in fact, a girl and begged to wear dresses. His favorite children's books were stories of mermaids. The child, who insisted on being called Rose, had been diagnosed by a psychiatrist as suffering from gender dysmorphia.

Mrs. Williams took Rose from psychologist to psychologist, hoping to find help somewhere for her daily struggles with the child who refused to act "normal." Finally, she was referred to a social worker who specialized in gender identity issues. The social worker educated the family about transgendered children and presented an option they had never considered—to let Rose live life as the girl her brain said she really was. Because the transformation was immensely complicated,

socially and medically, family members agreed to a plan for long-term counseling and consultation.

CONVERSION THERAPY VERSUS THE STRENGTHS APPROACH

Against the backdrop of an increasingly conservative political and religious climate, gay men and lesbians are sometimes persuaded to seek psychotherapy to change the focus of their sexual attraction. The basic tenets of conversion therapy are:

- Homosexuality is a sin, and salvation can come through faith in Jesus Christ.
- Psychotherapy can cure a mental disorder (secular therapists).
- The cause of homosexuality is a dominant mother and passive father.
- People can change their sexual identity through treatment.
- Converts who repudiate their former gayness can be role models to gays and lesbians to help them change.

Such claims are repudiated by NASW (2000, 2012) and the APA (2008) as completely invalid and ideologically based.

Because homosexuality is not a mental disorder, treatment to change one's sexual orientation is unwarranted. NASW (2000) issued a caveat against the resurgence in conversion therapies. Such therapies are viewed by the association as a violation of the social work code of ethics' requirements of competence and commitment to clients' self-determination. False claims by therapists of documented success stories in converting people to heterosexuality can lead to severe emotional damage, whether through the claims or through the treatments, according to NASW.

In sharp contrast to the dictates of "reparative" treatments is the strengths or empowerment perspective as it pertains to gay and lesbian practice. From a strengths perspective, we offer the following guidelines to practice with gays, lesbians, bisexuals, and transgendered persons.

- Seek the positive in terms of people's coping and survival skills, and you will find it.
- Listen to the personal narrative, the telling of one's own story in one's own voice, a story that ultimately may be reframed in light

of new awareness of unrealized personal strength.

- Validate the pain where pain exists and reinforce persistent efforts to alleviate the pain (including, if desired, *not* acting on the feelings and/or reducing isolation in multiple ways).
- Help people recover from the specific injuries of oppression, neglect, and domination.
- Do not dictate; collaborate through an agreed upon, mutual discovery of solutions among helpers, families, and support networks. Validation and collaboration are integral steps in the consciousness-raising process that can lead to healing and empowerment.
- Move from self-actualization to transformation of oppressive structure, from individual strength to higher connectedness.

Also using an empowerment approach, Tully (2000) and Hunter (2011) advocate a client–practitioner relationship built on mutual respect and reciprocity to uplift and empower gays and lesbians effectively in an oppressive, homophobic environment. Both researchers urge social workers to avoid the assumption of heterosexuality in the creation of a gay-friendly space. Among their recommendations are to:

- Use gender-neutral language, such as "relationship status" instead of "marital status," on the forms provided.
- Avoid standardized face sheets and documents that presume everyone is heterosexual.
- Include some lesbian- and gay-friendly magazines, posters, or newspapers in the waiting area.
- Train staff to be gay-friendly and nonhomophobic.

SELECTED AREAS OF SOCIAL WORK PRACTICE

In this section, we focus on two areas of social work practice with special relevance to sexual minorities—social work with (1) adolescents and (2) family and couples counseling.

Social Work with Adolescents

Struggling to survive in environments (school, home, church) that are more often than not hostile to their very being, gay and lesbian youth have many intense personal issues to resolve. The message sent by society, including one's own community, is that gender nonconformity and gay or lesbian identity, unlike racial and ethnic identity, is a choice that can and should be concealed (van Wormer, 2011).

Among the most pressing issues concerning adolescent gays and lesbians, which we have gleaned from experience and the literature are:

- The turmoil involved in coming out to yourself, discovering who you are and who you are not
- Deciding whom to tell, when, and how to tell it
- Rebuilding relationships and grieving rejections when the truth is known
- Developing new and caring support systems
- Protecting oneself from a constant onslaught of attacks on one who is openly out or from the guilt feelings accompanying the secrecy and deception of being in the closet
- Coping with the school's failure to be inclusive of youths struggling with gender issues and ridicule from their peers for being different
- Internalized homophobia (from the larger society)
- Problems with alcohol and other drug abuse as a means of self-medication
- For youths who do not come to terms with who they are or who are rejected by their parents, alcohol and other drug abuse, homelessness, unsafe practices, and suicide are major risks.

Typically, closeted gay youths are referred to treatment for symptoms of their distress, such as anxiety, drug use, and depression; rarely are they asked about their sexual concerns. Typically also, youth who are confused about their sexual identity are falsely reassured, as are their parents, that their confusion is just a passing phase. Such denial is harmful and compounds the risk for suicide (van Wormer, Wells, & Boes, 2000). Relevant facts as listed in a review of the literature by Sandra Anderson (2009) are:

- Compared with heterosexual youths, research has shown that sexual minority youth are twice as likely as their peers to consider and attempt suicide.

- Youths who report methamphetamine use (a popular drug in the gay/lesbian community) are several times more likely than others to have considered suicide.
- Of all adolescents, transgendered youth are the most vulnerable and the most likely to use addictive substances.

In the state of Massachusetts, thanks to the Safe Schools Initiative signed into law in 1993, about half the high schools have gay–straight alliances. Advisors meet with sexual minority and questioning students in small groups in which they discuss their sexuality and alcohol and drug use (Massachusetts Department of Education, 2008). In the absence of openly gay and lesbian teacher role models—a serious absence in itself—a community of adult-led gay and pro-gay students to provide peer support is essential.

For effective strengths-based practice, social workers in a school setting can:

- Help institute programs in the school to prevent bullying and verbal abuse of students who are deemed different.
- Challenge homophobic practices in the school setting.
- In individual counseling sessions, seek out stories of personal growth and resilience.
- Through empathetic listening and referral to affirming support groups and activist organizations, help open the door to new support systems.
- Be careful in prematurely assigning labels to youths such as gay, straight, or bi; help students discover their own identities.
- Make sure the school library contains helpful information about homosexuality and homophobia.
- Provide teacher workshops on homophobia and school bullying; organize gay/lesbian panels from a nearby college to address the school on a yearly basis
- Connect with PFLAG (Parents, Families, and Friends of Lesbians and Gays), which has implemented a program across North America to work with parent teacher associations and engage in speaker panels.

School Social Work

The one area of social work practice with the greatest relevance for youth suicide prevention is school social work. School counselors, psychologists, and social workers can counsel high-risk students and bullies to get at the source of their displaced hostility: one exemplary program is found in Toronto, Canada, where approximately 90 school-based social workers work with a wide variety of issues, including those pertaining to sexual orientation and gender identity. *The Essential Guide to Bullying Prevention and Intervention* is a useful resource for school social workers; it is co-authored by Cindy Miller, a school social worker, and Cynthia Lowen, a filmmaker of the popular documentary, *Bully*. This film shows the pains of brutal victimization that children who are designated as "different" can experience when adults look the other way and fail to provide appropriate interventions. *Bully* was released in 2012 and is now shown in schools all across the United States.

To learn more about the making of this film, we authors interviewed Alan Heisterkamp (on March 5, 2013), a former Sioux City, Iowa school administrator, who served as consultant for the documentary. One of his roles was to work with the Sioux City school board to obtain permission for the shooting of the film on the school bus and other places where bullying occurred. In our interview, Heisterkamp spoke of the role that his wife, Pat, plays in the school system:

My wife, Pat, has been a school social worker for 15 years. She has done some amazing things to address bullying in middle schools. Namely, she has taught curriculum on problem solving, bystander education and prevention strategies, conflict resolution, anger management, empathy building, friendship groups and social skills with autistic students, healthy dating relationships, and understanding and recognizing violent masculinity. She conducted social skills groups at the middle school where the documentary, *Bully*, was filmed.

Strategies for school social workers are to:

- Foster a gay–straight alliance and other programs to involve the entire student body in bullying prevention.
- Ask students to contribute ideas to raise consciousness on the impact of bullying.
- Create peer mentor programs where leaders engage in bystander intervention to monitor the playground for instances of harassment.
- Encourage teachers to include antibullying messages in their curriculum.

- Establish restorative justice interventions for exchanges between students who have engaged in bullying and their victims (see Miller and Lowen, 2012).

Family Counseling

In working with families in therapy for whatever reason, social workers would do well to be alert to instances of sex role rigidity and homophobia, which restrict the emotional and sexual expression of individual members. In addition, virtually all marriage and family counselors will encounter the issue of sexual orientation from time to time, as members come in to discuss the crisis that pertains to disclosure, or work with lesbian and gay couples on issues unrelated to orientation. In any case, some typical family configurations known to family therapists are lesbian and gay parents with child custody or adoption issues; nongay parents with gay or lesbian children who have come out to them; gay or lesbian families with different ethnic traditions and in-law concerns; and couples experiencing domestic violence or substance abuse.

To be a family headed by a same-sex couple in a heterosexist society is to wrestle with weighty issues at every turn: childbearing or child custody arrangements; when and how to come out to children; and how much to tell people at church, school, work, or in the neighborhood. In other words, how does one walk the fine line between discretion and openness in dealing with the outside world? Issues of extended family acceptance, gender socialization of the children, and internalized homophobia in one or both partners can undermine the healthiest same-sex relationships. Forced to shape their own rituals and traditions, these unorthodox families are blazing the trail for themselves and others.

Effective work with lesbian and gay couples requires that workers be familiar with the unique norms of the lesbian and gay community to avoid pathologizing what may be normative behavior for couples in that community. Heterosexual therapists who lack personal experience and comfort in working with lesbians may react in ways that repeat the rejecting experiences with significant others in their lives (Goldstein & Horowitz, 2003).

Helpful guidelines for providing family therapy with gay and lesbian family members are provided by the Substance Abuse Mental Health and Services Administration (SAMHSA, 2004), as well as for work with transgendered populations dealing with issues of HIV/AIDS (SAMHSA, 2000).

For work with older lesbian, gay, and transgender couples, see Anderson (2009) and Witten & Eyler, 2012) who discuss relevant issues such as retirement, legal issues, and grandparenting. The significance of the passage of a federal antidiscrimination law comes to the forefront during the final stages of life. When one partner dies, the other may suffer heavy financial losses due to income tax and social security policies that deny spousal benefits to gay and lesbian partners, whether they are married under state law or not. Moreover, unmarried partners do not have the automatic right to make medical and financial decisions for their partners. Fortunately, recent national opinion polls show a shift in public opinion favoring the view that marriage should be a legal right for same-sex couples. According to the most recent national poll, 58% of Americans now believe it should be legal for gay and lesbian couples to marry, and the majority thinks the matter should be decided on the basis of the U.S. Constitution (Cohen, 2013).

Religion is an issue that is never far from the surface in the lives of gays and lesbians. A common theme woven through the gay and lesbian narrative is an upbringing in which the church, synagogue, or mosque was a kind of sanctuary from the cruelties of childhood. Ultimately, however, many gays and lesbians feel rejected by the orthodox religions of their childhoods. A therapist who is knowledgeable about biblical passages of love and acceptance can offer solace to the client steeped in a negative interpretation and out-of-context guides. A focus on love, not condemnation, and a grasp of spirituality as love toward oneself and others can offer an invaluable source of strength to sexual minorities and their families who are grappling with these truths. Anderson (2009) lists religious involvement as a potentially strong protective factor in preventing substance abuse among adolescents in general; it is not known how this affects sexual minority youth. Referrals to gay and lesbian clergy and to gay-friendly churches such as Metropolitan Community Churches, Unitarians, and Quakers or Friends Meetings can be a tremendous boon in helping clients regain the spirituality of their youth (van Wormer et al., 2000).

Finally, to help all family members move from denial and questioning ("what did we do wrong?") to acceptance and even advocacy, they should be encouraged to attend meetings of PFLAG. Scattered all across the United States, PFLAG chapters offer emotional support without criticizing visitors who are not ready to accept the sexual orientation of their loved one. Likewise, a viewing of the movie *Prayers for Bobby* would be tremendously helpful to a family member struggling with a partner's or child's coming out. Shown on the Lifetime network in 2009, this film is based on a true story and delves into analysis of biblical passages related to homosexuality.

CONCLUSION

Within the clinical context, through the medium of a caring relationship, the practitioner seeks to boost the lesbian, gay, or bisexual client through the aforementioned steps of strengths-based practice: seek the positive; hear the narrative; acknowledge the pain; collaborate (not dictate); and pave the way for further growth through helping others. What lesbians and all sexual minorities have to overcome along with their practitioners is the long conspiracy of silence that has served to keep generations of people from sharing the truths about their lives and their loves.

Adherence to the social work mission and values demands that the profession, and those who represent it, take a strong and proactive position on individual, organizational, and educational levels on gay and lesbian issues. The goal that we in the helping professions are working toward is not mere acceptance or toleration but *celebration* of the strengths of this largely invisible minority, strengths that, at least to some extent, come from living both within society and apart from it. Like members of other groups rendered invisible in a patriarchal and highly puritanical society, gay men and lesbians have unique histories (both individually and as a whole), creative family forms, gender role flexibility, and vast social networks. The gay and lesbian contribution to underground culture as well as mainstream arts—art, music, dance, and literature—has been incalculable. To social work practitioners, the challenge is to discover and reinforce the special insights and resiliencies that have developed out of the uniqueness of lesbian and gay experience.

WEBSITES

The Bully Project. www.thebullyproject.com
Gay, Lesbian, and Straight Education Network (GLSEN). http://www.glsen.org.
Parents, Families, and Friends of Lesbians and Gays (PFLAG). http://www.pflag.org.
Transfamily. http://www.transfamily.org.

References

American Psychological Association. (2008). *Just the facts about sexual orientation and youth*. Committee on Lesbian, Gay, Bisexual, and Transgender Concerns. Washington, DC: Office of Public Communications. Retrieved from http://apa.org/pi/lgbt/resources/just-the-facts.pdf

Anderson, S. (2009). *Substance use disorders in lesbian, gay, bisexual, and transgender clients*. New York, NY: Columbia University Press.

Cohen, J. (2013, March 18). Gay marriage support hits new high in Post-ABC poll. *The Washington Post*. Retrieved from www.washingtonpost.com

Goldstein, E., & Horowitz, L. (2003). *Lesbian identity and contemporary psychotherapy*. Hillsdale, NJ: Analytic Press.

Hunter, S. (2011). *Lesbian and gay couples: Lives, issues, and practice*. Chicago, IL: Lyceum.

Massachusetts Department of Education. (2008). Safe schools program for gay and lesbian students. Retrieved from www.doe.mass.edu/cnp/safe/ssch.html

Miller, C., & Lowen, C. (2012). *The essential guide to bullying prevention and intervention*. New York, NY: Alpha Books.

National Association of Social Workers. (2000). *Position statement: "Reparative" and "aversion" therapies for lesbians and gay men*. Retrieved from http://www.socialworkers.org/diversity/lgb/reparative.

National Association of Social Workers. (NASW) (2012). Lesbian, gay, and bisexual issues. *Social work speaks: NASW policy statements 2012–2014* (pp. 219–223). Washington, DC: NASW Press.

Substance Abuse and Mental Health Services Administration. (2000). *Treatment Improvement Protocol (TIP) 37. Substance abuse treatment for persons with HIV/AIDS*. Retrieved from http://www.ncbi.nlm.nih.gov/books.

Substance Abuse and Mental Health Services Administration. (2004). *Treatment Improvement Protocol (TIP) 39. Substance abuse treatment and family therapy*. Retrieved from http://www.ncbi.nlm.nih.gov/books.

Tully, C. (2000). *Lesbians, gays, and the empowerment perspective*. New York, NY: Columbia University Press.

van Wormer, K. (2011). *Human behavior and the social environment, micro level: Individuals and families* (2nd ed.). New York, NY: Oxford University Press.

van Wormer, K., Wells, J., & Boes, M. (2000). *Social work with lesbians, gays, and bisexuals: A strengths perspective*. Boston, MA: Allyn & Bacon.

Witten, T., & Eyler, A. (2012). Gay, lesbian, bisexual, and transgender aging: Challenges in research, practice, and policy. Baltimore, MD: Johns Hopkins University Press.

133 Global Perspectives on Gender Issues

Kristin Heffernan & Betty J. Blythe

Since the beginning of civilization, both women and girls have been treated inhumanly by men (as cited in Alabi, Baha, & Alabi, 2014), and while the United States is not without its issues of gender inequality, this chapter specifically focuses on international women's gender inequality as embedded in structural systems. In addition, it will present antioppressive practice (AOP) as a way to help the reader better understand how globalization should and does influence the practice of social work. In adapting an AOP framework we can enhance our understanding of the role of social workers as leaders in advancing human rights and gender equality while steering away from any conclusion that adopting a Westernized way of doing social work in other countries is acceptable.

This chapter is not an attempt to define or promote universal standards for global social work practice. Furthermore, the practice of social work has been and should continue to be framed within the cultural context of the nation in which it is practiced. As social workers, we promote and fight for human rights while possessing a clear understanding of the complexity of the local conditions that foster inequalities and constrain women's rights within their society. In this chapter, we will specifically concentrate on the overarching effects of patriarchy, specifically addressing the issues of violence against women, women's health, and education between the genders.

The boundaries between nation states have become increasingly porous. Social workers in both developing and developed countries need to understand how a range of national and international forces cause oppression and disadvantage for many women. In this chapter, we move away from a strictly clinical view of social work

to understand the macro practices that involve advocacy and community development for the purpose of combating oppression and promoting antidiscriminatory and antioppressive values toward women.

Using an antioppressive practice framework allows social workers to attend to social divisions and structural inequalities (Strier & Binyamin, 2013), including the unequal power relations between social workers and their clients. Key to an AOP approach is changing social relationships and the structural systems that perpetuate the exclusion of marginalized persons (Pollack, 2004). AOP requires that social workers be able to reflect on the power differential in their relationships with clients so that they can understand how the relationship in and of itself can be oppressive. This also helps social workers to recognize the problems faced by clients as rooted in the socio-political structure of society and not in the clients' personal characteristics, positioning social workers to work alongside clients in initiating social change.

At the forefront of this process is a continued exploration and evaluation of person-in-environment for the purpose of understanding how the experiences of different groups of women around the world, living in male-dominated societies, are structured based on the cultures in which they live (Penna, Paylor, & Washington, 2000). By raising awareness of the key issues faced by women around the world we hope to further develop a commitment from social workers to work toward providing culturally competent, quality services to women, while promoting a macro perspective on global change. The underlying theme laying the ground work for this chapter is the idea that women's lives are shaped by the intersectionality of patriarchy, economic disadvantage, religious beliefs, and other discriminatory systems formed at local levels, which creates layers of inequality. These systems of inequality structure the relative positions of women within their respective cultures. Gender norms in many patriarchal societies limit women's opportunities to seek help if they are experiencing violence, if they want an education, or if they want to work outside the home. Male-dominated societies adhering to strict enforcement of the view that women are inferior often promote male gender preference (Das Gupta et al., 2003; Westley & Kim Choe, 2007), which can lead to such practices as female infanticide or female neglect from birth to the grave.

For females living in such societies, if they survive at birth, marry, and outlive their husbands, their fate does not necessarily improve. In many male-dominated cultures, widows lose their rights and their property upon their husband's death. One extreme example of male-gendered practices is "sati," which although outlawed is still practiced in some parts of India.

In the Hindu tradition, a husband dying before his wife signifies that the wife has committed some wrong in her current or past life. According to cultural beliefs, this brings about shame to the wife, which can only be rectified by performing sati, whereby the widow throws herself onto her husband's funeral pyre. It is believed that in suicide the wife resolves her shame and as such brings good fortune to herself and her kin (Cheng & Lee, 2000). Although this form of suicide is said to be voluntary, many women commit sati out of fear of their fate as widows, preferring death to life within their community. Additionally, if a widow appears reluctant to commit sati, her kin and neighbors may force her to commit it by going so far as to throw her on top of the funeral pyre. Lack of ability to participate as full citizens within their community perpetuates women's inequality, oppression, and loss of human rights and, as seen in the example of sati, can lead to extreme forms of violence against women.

VIOLENCE AGAINST WOMEN

In recent decades, violence against women has been acknowledged as one of the greatest threats to female health and safety worldwide (Garcia-Moreno, Jansen, Ellsberg, Heise, & Watts, 2005). Twenty years ago, on December 22, 1993, the United Nations General Assembly in New York adopted with unanimous consent the Declaration on the Elimination of Violence Against Women, condemning gender violence within both the private and the public sphere as a violation of human rights (United Nations [UN], 1993). Despite this resolution, women all over the world continue to live with the threat of domestic violence or rape in their own homes and communities, and by people whom they know. Violence against women takes many forms and also includes:

• Honor killings
• Dowry deaths
• Sati
• Female genital mutilation
• War rape
• Private and public beatings

In many countries, it is extremely difficult to protect women from male violence. In fact, in some countries and cultures, much of the gender violence is not considered a violation of rights, as it is embedded in that nation's culture, customs, and/or traditions (Joachim, 2003). Male dominance is so widely accepted in many cultures, that women themselves may not view the violence as an affront to their human rights as this is all they know. Male authority and power plays a huge role in gender violence. Honor killings, for example, are carried out when male kin suspect that women in their family (mothers, daughters, sisters) dishonor the family.

Although reports of honor killings have been widely reported in the Middle East and North Africa (MENA), and South Asia (UN, 2000), more recently honor killings have been documented in North America as well as Europe (Kulczycki & Windle, 2011). In many societies, women are considered the property of their husbands or fathers and are expected to uphold their family's honor. Usually this means conforming to the gender-specific roles of women for a particular culture. Another example of cultural traditions and customs that provoke violence are perceptions of female infidelity.

There are many ways in which women can be seen as dishonoring their family patriarch, most notably via infidelity. Definitions of infidelity differ from culture to culture. In the United States, infidelity is often defined as cheating, adultery, or having an affair. However, in other countries, infidelity may mean women being in the company of males who are not family members. Fathers also may interpret infidelity as a daughter dressing in a way that he, or her uncle or brother, think is provocative. Thus, the definition is open enough for male family members to define as they see fit. Furthermore, accusations do not have to be confirmed for an honor killing to take place; the mere fact of an accusation is enough to bring shame and punishment to the family. The decision to kill the female in the name of family honor lies solely with the males in the family. According to a United Nations Population Fund (UNFPA) report in 2000 an estimated 5,000 women and girls are murdered each year in so-called honor killings by members of their families (UNFPA, 2000).

Dowry burnings is another form of severe violence against women, albeit not often experienced in the Western world. A dowry is a gift of money, jewelry, animals, or other property that the single woman takes with her as a contribution from her family when she is engaged to be married. It is given to the daughter as her property, but in traditional, male-dominated societies, the dowry actually goes to the husband (Johnson & Johnson, 2001). In these cultures, the wife is seen as property such that whatever she brings to the marriage belongs to her husband. For example, in India, female children are the property of their fathers until they are married, and after marriage they become the property of their husbands (Puri, 1999). In this way women are kept economically dependent, first on their fathers and then on their husbands once they are married.

The lack of a sufficient dowry can be a catalyst for violence against the bride, despite the fact that dowries are prearranged between parents of the bridal couple. Dowry money can reach as high as six times the annual household income in South Asia (Rao, 1993) and four times the annual income in sub-Saharan Africa (Dekker & Hoogeveen, 2002). Regardless of the size of the dowry, the husband's family may find it unacceptable at the last minute and can make demands for more money or other items before the marriage, or they may insist on the family continuing to pay off their daughter's dowry long after marriage occurs. When a bride's family cannot make payments or refuses to invest more in their daughter's dowry, a dowry burning might occur. The demand for a dowry has been outlawed in India since 1961, but strong cultural traditions and patriarchal practices have not diminished the demand for dowries in practice (Johnson & Johnson, 2001).

Female genital mutilation (FGM) is a form of gender-based violence that inflicts severe and lasting harm, both mental and physical, on victims. FGM involves partial or total removal of external female genitalia, most often by a traditional circumciser. Although it is upheld as a cultural practice, in fact the practice of FGM is recognized internationally as a violation of the human rights of girls and women. FGM is most often inflicted upon young girls between the ages of infancy and 15 years and has no health benefits. In some instances, women flee their country and seek refugee status to avoid female excision of their daughters. All too often, however, women do not have the knowledge or resources to protect themselves or their female children from this abuse. In addition to the violation of human rights, FGM can cause health problems, infertility, and difficulty in childbirth.

Another form of gender-specific violence is war rape. Women raped in conflict zones often are regarded as an inevitable consequence of war rather than a crime and a violation of human rights (Brownmiller, 1975; Enloe, 2000). Women frequently are chosen as weapons of war and may be targeted for sexual slavery, gang rape, or individual rape to humiliate the enemy (Farwell, 2004). Because sexual assault of women tends to be viewed as a less significant event, war rape often is not considered to be a war crime and perpetrators are not held accountable (Swiss & Giller, 1993).

War rape has physical and psychological consequences for women and can disrupt entire communities or societies. The list of physical effects is extensive and may include such things as unplanned pregnancies, mortality, unsafe abortions, sexually transmitted diseases, and recurring gynecological problems. The list of long-term psychological effects is long and includes posttraumatic stress, anxiety, depression, and suicide. Children born out of rape often are ostracized or marked as "different." Victims of rape are isolated from their families and communities and, if the rape is widespread and systematic, it can lead to the breakdown of a community. War rape sometimes is perpetuated as an act of cultural genocide, as in the case of Rwanda (Cohen, d'Adesky, & Anastos, 2005).

Seeking help for male-gendered violence is challenging in male-dominated societies. Unfortunately, some women who seek help outside the home are ostracized or shunned by the rest of their family and/or community. For instance in many South Asian cultures, the sanctity of the family traditionally falls on the shoulders of women, and their culture dictates that what happens in the family stays within the family (Roy, 2012). Because women who pursue social support or professional counseling outside of their family frequently are marked as traitors they may be reluctant to report rape for fear of bringing disgrace to their families. These cultural beliefs are deeply imbedded within the cultural structure of these societies and cannot be ignored by the social work professional. In other words, well-intentioned social workers may actually do more damage if they reach out to victims of the types of violence previously described. It is important to stress here that each person has the right not to receive help and that only she can know what revealing her secret will mean for her. As social workers in this situation, our responsibility lies in being aware of these traditional cultural beliefs, which should guide our professional behavior. When we cannot offer direct services, we may still be able to advocate and educate.

Activists for women's rights are working to change the definition of rape and domestic violence as well as the related judicial treatment of perpetrators and victims to underscore the fact that violence against women is not a "right" of men. An advocacy approach, fighting for women's rights and social justice, allows us to act on behalf of all women without outing individual women and causing them further pain and suffering due to their cultural beliefs. In many male-dominated societies, this may mean persuading males in official roles to adopt decisions that are pro-women, helping those in power to understand that such decisions are key to stopping violence against women. We are not saying that clinical or micro approaches are not important, but rather that the need to address violence against women as a large-scale social problem, due to the systematic discrimination and oppression of women in some patriarchal societies, supersedes the best practice for women who experience such trauma. Only when the violence is seen as an infraction of women's rights will women be able to create services that meet their needs in these societies.

WOMEN'S HEALTH

Women subjected to the horrors described in the previous section often are at higher risk for unwanted pregnancies, sexually transmitted diseases, and further health-related complications due to restricted health care access. Approximately half a million women die each year from complications related to pregnancy, childbirth, and the postpartum period (Glasier, Gülmezoglu, Schmid, Garcia Moreno, & Van Look, 2006). In developing countries, it is estimated that one-third of all expectant mothers go without health care, 60% of the births take place outside of health facilities, and only 60% of all births have trained staff present at the time of the birth (World Health Organization [WHO], 2005). For women and girls between the ages of 15 and 49 years, complication at time of birth is the leading cause of death and disability in most developing countries (UNFPA, 2000). Women in countries where male dominance exists often face many gendered health problems:

- Maternal mortality
- Lack of family planning information or access to contraceptives
- Unsafe abortion or injuries sustained during an illegal abortion
- Sexually transmitted infections, including HIV
- Persistent gynecological problems
- Psychological problems
- Malnutrition

Maternal mortality rates are highest in Africa, with a lifetime risk of 1 in 16 (WHO, 2005). Many maternal deaths can be attributed to lack of trained professional health care providers and family planning. HIV infection is an ongoing world health issue, particularly for the women of sub-Saharan Africa, where only limited treatment is available (UNAIDS/WHO, 2007). Because they are of lower status, women in these countries lack control over household resources, have less access to information and health services, poorer mental health, and lower self-esteem (Smith, Ramakrishnan, Ndiaye, Haddad, & Martorell, 2003). In many of the poorest of these countries, women often suffer from malnutrition because men and young boys are served first and women eat last and least.

A plethora of articles have been written about our ability to dramatically reduce maternal mortality rates, and about the spread of HIV and female malnutrition on a global level. Understanding why women are not receiving proper care in certain countries involves understanding the position and status of these women within their respective countries. Most are oppressed due to structural and cultural ideologies that view women as inferior to men. So although an increase in access to maternal care and family planning may help to lower maternal death rates, transformational change needs to start from within countries. Power distribution needs to change, which is no easy task where patriarchal ideologies are systemic in male-dominated cultures. For change to occur, those in power (i.e., men) must see a need to promote women's health issues.

EDUCATION DISCRIMINATION BASED ON GENDER

Once again, in order to truly understand the vast gender inequality in education in patriarchal nations we must have a clear understanding of the local context, politics, history, and cultural beliefs. There are some similarities, however, among countries with the largest disparities. The most profound gender inequalities in education have been noted in countries where women are devalued and traditionally restricted from taking part in the public sphere in any truly meaningful way (Colclough, 2008). Educational discrimination begins at birth. If a female is born into a culture that devalues her gender, she has less chance of survival (Johnson & Johnson 2001). In many East and South Asian countries, a preference for sons has led to lower rates of female infant survival (Westley & Kim Choe, 2007). It has been estimated that nearly two-thirds of the 300 million children around the world without access to education are females, while another two-thirds of the illiterate adult population are women (UNFPA, 2000). The lack of opportunity for an education for many young girls actually is the outcome of a larger issue: the structural and systemic discrimination and oppression due to one's gender status as female. It goes without saying that these inequalities often perpetuate poverty, poor health, and an inability to further oneself within the community.

Female children may not live past birth due to lack of nutrition and health care (Das Gupta, Zhenghua, Bohua, Zhenming, Chung, & Hwa-Ok, 2003). If they do survive, they are usually seen as an economic burden (Johnson & Johnson, 2001). They are often expected to marry early and or perform labor around the house (Das Gupta, Zhenghua, Bohua, Zhenming, Chung, &

Hwa-Ok, 2003). They are susceptible to all forms of abuse due to their female status (Sev'er, 2008). An education is viewed as necessary and appropriate for someone who is expected to join the work force and earn a living for the family, but then again this is not the expectation for many of these women. "Women's work" typically is undervalued and not included in calculating a nation's gross domestic product (Waring, 1999). In many patriarchal societies gender continues to be a source of hate and degradation, thereby determining the types of opportunities available to persons around the world.

ADVOCACY AND EDUCATION

In order to foster change, again, we advocate for a macro level approach. This means we first need to educate ourselves on the complexities of local cultural, political, and historical norms or ways of living outside the United States; a move beyond our often ethnocentric, rose-colored glasses. We need to understand that within the patriarchal society, men benefit from the exploitation of women and, as such, are not willing to give up this benefit. Policies, laws, and traditions are set by men and favor men, meaning that women living in these societies routinely experience oppression and even violence. It also stands to reason that the family, state, and larger society condone such behaviors because these are the norms within those societies. In effect then, we are dealing with both public and private patriarchy whereby women are socialized to believe that their place in their family and the larger society is not equal to a man's (Alabi, Baha, & Alabi, 2014). This may be naturally accepted and not questioned by women due to their cultural and lived experiences.

With this knowledge we can better understand the role of education both for ourselves and in the work that needs to be done to lessen the inequality gap between the genders in patriarchal societies. Education becomes critical to constitutional reform (Wronka, 1994). Once we understand the issues we can then advocate for change that will bring about legislation that will, in turn, enhance human rights on a global level. As Helen Clark, the prime minister of New Zealand from 1999 to 2008, stated on International Women's Day 2014, "Grounded in international human rights, gender equality doesn't just improve the lives of individual women, girls, and their families, it makes economic sense, strengthens democracy, and enables long-term sustainable progress" (UNDP, 2014).

WEBSITES

United Nations. www.un.org/womenwatch/; www.unwomen.org

References

Alabi, T., Baha, M., & Alabi, S. O. (2014). The Girl-child: A sociological view on the problems of girl-child education in Nigeria. *European Scientific Journal, 10,* 1857–7881.

Brownmiller, S. (1975). *Against our will: Men, women, and rape.* New York, NY: Penguin Books.

Cheng, M., & Lee, M. (2000). The self-concept of Chinese women and the indigenization of social work in China. *International Social Work, 47,* 109–127.

Cohen, M. H., d'Adesky, A., & Anastos, K. (2005). Women in Rwanda: Another world is possible. *Journal of the American Medical Society, 294,* 613.

Colclough, C. (2008). Gender equality in education—increasing the momentum for change. *Research Consortium on Educational Outcomes & Poverty, Policy Brief, 2,* 1–4.

Das Gupta, M., Zhenghua, J., Bohua, L., Zhenming, X., Chung, W., & Hwa-Ok, B. (2003). Why is son preference so persistent in East and South Asia? A cross-country study of China, India and the Republic of Korea. *The Journal of Development Studies, 40*(2), 153–187.

Dekker, M., & Hoogeveen, H. (2002). *On bride wealth and household security in rural Zimbabwe.* Paper presented at the Conference on Understanding Poverty and Growth in Sub-Saharan Africa at the Center for the Study of African Economies, University of Oxford, UK. Retrieved from: http://www.csae.ox.ac.uk/conferences/2002-upagissa/papers/Dekker-csae2002.pdf

Enloe, C. (2000). *Maneuvers: The international politics of women's lives.* Berkeley: University of California Press.

Farwell, N. (2004). War rape: New conceptualizations and responses. *Affilia, I,* 389–403.

Garcia-Moreno, C., Jansen, H. A. F. M., Ellsberg, M., Heise, L., & Watts, C. (2005). *WHO Multi-country study on women's health and domestic violence against women: Initial results on prevalence, health outcomes and women's responses.* Geneva, Switzerland: WHO Press.

Glasier, A., Gülmezoglu, A., Schmid, G. P., Garcia Moreno, C., & Van Look, P. (2006). Sexual and reproductive health: A matter of life and death. (Sexual and Reproductive Health 1, Journal Paper pre-print for *Lancet*), *World Health Organization, 367,* 1–13.

Joachim, J. (2003). Framing issues and seizing opportunities: The UN, NGOs, and women's rights. *International Studies Quarterly, 47,* 247–274.

Johnson, P. S., & Johnson, J. A. (2001). The oppression of women in India. *Violence Against Women, 7,* 1051–1068.

Kulczycki, A., & Windle, S. (2011). Honor killings in the Middle East and North Africa: A systematic review of the literature. *Violence Against Women, 17,* 1442–1464.

Penna, S., Paylor, I., & Washington, J. (2000). Globalization, social exclusion and the possibilities for global social work and welfare. *European Journal of Social Work, 3,* 109–122.

Pollack, S. (2004). Anti-oppressive social work practice with women in prison: Discursive reconstructions and alternative practices. *British Journal of Social Work, 34,* 693–707.

Puri, D. (1999). *Gift of a daughter: Change and continuity in marriage patterns among two generations of North Indians in Toronto and Delhi.* Unpublished doctoral dissertation, University of Toronto.

Rao, V. (1993). Dowry inflation in rural India: A statistical investigation, *Population Studies, 47,* 283–293.

Roy, D. (2012). South Asian battered women's use of force against intimate male partners: A practice note. *Violence Against Women, 18,* 1108–1118.

Sev'er, A. (2008). *Discarded daughters: The patriarchal grip, dowry deaths, sex ratio imbalances & foeticide in India.* Retrieved from https://tspace.library.utoronto.ca/bitstream/1807/10365/1/Sever_discarded_daughter.pdf

Smith, L.C., Ramakrishnan, U., Ndiaye, A., Haddad, L., & Martorell, R. (2003). The importance of women's status for child nutrition in developing countries. *International Food Policy Research Institute: Sustainable solutions for ending hunger and poverty.* Research Report Abstract 131. *or ending hunger and poverty*

Strier, R., & Binyamin, S. (2013). Introducing anti-oppressive social work practices in public services: Rhetoric to practice. *British Journal of Social Work, 43,* 1–8, doi:10.1093/bjsw/bct049.

Swiss, S., & Giller, J. E. (1993). Rape as a crime of war: A medical perspective. *JAMA: Journal of the American Medical Association, 270,* 612–615.

United Nations (1993). *Declaration on the Elimination of Violence Against Women.* In: 85th Plenary Meeting. December 20, 1993. Geneva, Switzerland.

United Nations. (2000). *Protocol to prevent, suppress and punish trafficking persons, especially women and children, supplementing the United Nations Convention Against Transnational*

Organized Crime. Retrieved from http://www.uncjin.org/Documents/Conventions/dcatoc/final_documents_2/convention_%20traff_eng .pdf

United Nations Development Programme (2014). *Helen Clark: Statement on International Women's Day*. Retrieved from http://www.gq.undp.org/content/fiji/en/home/presscenter/speeches/2014/03/07/helen-clark-statement-on-international-women-s-day-/.

[Joint] United Nations Programme on HIV/AIDS (UNAIDS) and World Health Organization (WHO). (2007 update). Geneva, Switzerland, Retrieved from http://data.unaids.org/pub/EPISlides/2007/2007_epiupdate_en.pdf.

United Nations Population Fund (UNFPA) (2000). *The state of the world's population: Lives together, worlds apart*, chapter 3, Retrieved from: http://www.unfpa.org/swp/2000/pdf/english/chapter1.pdf

Waring, M. (1999). *Counting for nothing: What men value and what women are worth*. Toronto, Canada: University of Toronto Press.

Westley, S. B., & Kim Choe, M. (2007). How does son preference effect Asian populations? *Pacific Asian Issues: Analysis from the East-West Center, 84*, 1–12.

World Health Organization (WHO). (2005). *Make every mother and child count*. Geneva, Switzerland: Author. Retrieved from http://www.who.int/whr/2005/whr2005_en.pdf.

Wronka, J. (1994). Human rights and social policy in the United States: An educational agenda for the 21st century. *Journal of moral education, 23*, 261–272.

PART XIII
School Social Work

134 Overview of Evidence-based Practice in School Social Work

Paula Allen-Meares & Katherine L. Montgomery

The primary purpose of this section is to provide social workers and related school-based professionals with current and diverse empirical data on interventions and approaches that address the needs of various pupil groups. Emotional and behavioral problems are among the most predominant and chronic conditions that affect school-aged youth (Pastor, Reuben, & Duran, 2012), and this number is much higher for vulnerable populations (Cooper, Masi, & Vick, 2009). These children are at risk of serious subsequent and interrelated trajectories that include juvenile delinquency, substance use problems, violence, school dropout, and unemployment (e.g., American Psychology Association, 2012). In response, policymakers, practitioners, and researchers have invested enormous efforts over the past several decades to develop and test evidence-based interventions (EBIs) that effectively address these issues in the school setting (Forman et al., 2013). Many school-based EBIs have since been identified that impact several outcomes for at-risk students (e.g., Montgomery, 2014). What is necessary to deliver these services? Where will the future of school-based intervention take us?

In this discussion, we highlight some elements and issues in the future of school social work, a practice field that will be ever more firmly and increasingly rooted in a growing evidence base. In addition, we add a brief summary of issues specific to the selection of evidence-based interventions, methods of getting school social workers to accept and use evidence-based practices, and why schools and communities should create partnerships for mental health services for children and adolescents.

DEFINING EVIDENCE-BASED PRACTICE

The future of school social work may very well rest on the emerging growth and reliance on the evidence-based practice (EBP) approach. Although there is not currently a consensus about the definition of this concept (Hoagwood, 2003; Rubin & Parrish, 2007), many disciplines use the concept, and various definitions may be found within them. Social work, in particular, has embraced the concept as a way to address the perceived gap between research and practice (Brekke, Ell, & Palinkas, 2007; Gould, 2005; Rubin & Parrish, 2007). In this chapter, we attempt to define *evidence-based practice* in a manner that can be commonly understood.

Originally adopted from the medical field, EBP in social work refers to the process of implementing and integrating tested research evidence into practice. The *Social Work Policy Institute* defines EBP as "a process in which the practitioner combines well-researched interventions with clinical expertise and ethics, and client preferences and culture to guide and inform the delivery of treatment services" (2010, para 1). This process is associated with five steps: (1) ask a focused question, (2) find the best evidence, (3) evaluate the evidence, (4) apply information in combination with clinical experience and patient values, and (5) evaluate outcomes (Johnson, 2008). Central to this process is the identification and use of evidence-based treatments (EBTs) in Step Two. Although there are multiple criticisms of EBP (e.g., Straus & McAlister, 2000), scientists assert that when specific EBP steps (c.f., Gibbs & Gambrill, 2002) are followed, most criticisms are addressed (Rubin & Babbie, 2010) and benefits associated with cost effectiveness, time efficiency, and lasting positive outcomes are made possible. Brekke and colleagues suggest that social work is uniquely situated to play a role in the movement to bridge research to practice, with schools being an opportune and indeed desired setting for direct applicability of EBP. "EBP, by definition, facilitates the very best qualities of social work when a social worker involves clients in a collaborative process to consider available evidence or lack of evidence" (Regehr, Stern, & Shlonsky, 2007). Specifically, practitioners must take into consideration a transactional or person–environment fit in evaluating a child's interactions with family, their educational setting, and their community, as well as how each of those systems interacts with the other (e.g., how the family interacts with the school, how the school fits into its community; Bowen, 2007).

THE SCHOOL

Given the fact that children spend a large portion of their time in school (7 hours a day, 5 days a week, 9 months a year), it makes sense that the educational community plays a strategic role in the lives of children and their families. Indeed, the school has historically been a location in which social workers felt they could assist in children's health and welfare (Allen-Meares & Montgomery, 2014). Jessie Taft, an early leader in the functionalist movement, wrote: "The only practical and effective way to increase the mental health of a nation is through its school system. Homes are too inaccessible. The school has the time of the child and the power to do the job" (Taft, 1923, p. 398). More recently, Dr. S. Hyman, then director of the National Institute of Mental Health, spoke to the importance of the school system as the context for the identification and treatment of school children needing mental health treatment (Rees, 1997). This perspective has been echoed in the No Child Left Behind Act, the Individuals with Disabilities Education Act, and recent federal reports.

For example, the *Report of the Surgeon General's Conference on Children's Mental Health* (U.S. Department of Health and Human Services, 2000), calls attention to the growing numbers of youth (one in five) suffering needlessly because their emotional, behavioral, and developmental needs are not being met.

It strongly suggests that the nation urgently needs to address the emotional, behavioral, and developmental needs of our youth. In a more recent example, the National Research Council (NRC) and Institute of Medicine (IOM) created the *Committee on the Prevention of Mental Disorders and Substance Abuse Among Children, Youth, and Young Adults: Research Advances and Promising Interventions* and received funding from Substance Abuse and Mental Health Services Administration (SAMHSA), the National Institute of Mental Health (NIMH), the National Institute on Drug Abuse (NIDA), and the National Institute on Alcohol Abuse and Alcoholism (NIAAA). The primary aim of the committee was to provide a report with the best evidence and future recommendations associated with prevention among the nation's youth. Specifically, the

report calls on the nation—its leaders, its mental health research and service provision agencies, its schools, its primary care medical systems, its community-based organizations, its child welfare and criminal justice systems—to make prevention of mental, emotional, and behavioral disorders and the promotion of mental health of young people a very high priority. (O'Connell, Boat, & Warner, 2009, p. xiii)

Even when evidence-based interventions are available for use by providers, however, the report highlights that use of evidence-based interventions remains low (O'Connell et al., 2009). It is also imperative to note, especially when discussing the future of school social work and the populations for which social workers provide services, that cultural barriers may often play a role in the assessment, intervention considerations, and actual provision of social work services in schools.

Although ripe for identifying and treating children who exhibit social and mental health needs, the educational system itself is often at the mercy of institutional, local, or federal pressures or demands. As Sipple (2007) states, "The American public educational system is a beleaguered public institution fraught with relentless criticism," adding that "schools are facing ever-challenging and complex educational situations while at the same time an unprecedented inspection and expectation of practice and performance" (pp. 1–2). Services such as special education are underfunded, and state support is either erratic or dwindling depending on the means of each state. Schools have to involve multiple stakeholders in governance and decision making, and reform and restructure themselves to obtain excellence and relevancy, and do all of this while being cost-efficient and effective. In addition, today's educational system has numerous responsibilities on its doorstep: federal, state, and local standards, desegregation, student diversity, underachieving students, and what to do with overachievers. Add to this the expectation that physical, social, emotional, and behavioral problems will be addressed, and you have an environment that is overwhelmed with multiple agendas and roles. Clearly, the school and its personnel cannot achieve these multiple and important imperatives in isolation from other relevant and interested parties (e.g., community, parents).

Relevant professional providers located in the community, in collaboration with parents and school personnel, will need to become a part of the solution and respond to the mental health and/or health issues that are going undiagnosed among students. We envision unusual and innovative collaborations and partnerships between the school and its community network of service providers in the decades ahead. Two emerging solutions include school-based health centers, which provide mental and physical health services, and arrangements for "linked" services—that is, services provided via community providers in locations other than school (Brener et al., 2007). Furthermore, knowledge from a cross-section of practices and empirical literatures is needed to arm these professionals with new ways to identify, prevent, and treat mental illness among children and adolescents. "No one discipline has a privileged view of either pathogenesis or treatment of mental disorders" (Rees, 1997, p. 8).

SOME CRITERIA FOR THE SELECTION OF EVIDENCE-BASED INTERVENTION

As reflected in this volume, various interventions have different levels of scientific sophistication or rigor undergirding them. It is important to note that (as already mentioned) in social work, the accepted position on EBP is increasingly one that balances scientific rigor with practice knowledge, clinical judgment, client reaction, common sense, and context (Johnson, 2008). When considering what interventions to use in a school setting, or a school/community provider collaboration, the

following criteria should be taken into consideration (note that this list is not exhaustive).

1. Where does the study fall on the continuum of scientific rigor? Although there are a variety of definitions as to how to identify interventions that have been tested with scientific rigor, recent school-based researchers have offered the following gold standard criteria: two or more randomized studies with (1) attention to the specific client population; (2) use of manualized intervention; (3) measurement of multiple outcomes; (4) statistically significant differences between the treatment and control group in favor of the intervention; and (5) replication of the findings, ideally by an additional researcher and team (Kazdin & Weisz, 2010). Other published standards also have specified that scientifically rigorous evidence include "at least one significant long-term follow-up" (Flay et al., 2005).
2. Is the study transportable? One of the challenges of using evidence-based interventions is transportability—that is, will the outcomes of the scientific study that validated this intervention in a laboratory or a clinical setting be consistent when applied in a school setting (Hoagwood et al., 2001)?
3. Is the study generalizable to multiple populations and/or across multiple sites? With few exceptions, "there are no statistical methods for assessing the generalizability of a program's effects" (Flay et al., 2005). Therefore, practitioners should investigate whether the research was conducted with appropriate subgroups with same or similar results.
4. Are there contextual variables required for optimal outcomes? Services to children/youth are delivered in a variety of unique contexts—schools, child and family agencies, family, correctional systems, and community mental health centers. It is, therefore, urgent for the practitioner to know the context in which the research on the intervention was conducted (Hoagwood et al., 2001). Researchers have found that five factors are most likely to influence the successful implementation of interventions in schools: (1) school organizational structures (e.g., a school-based committee designed to oversee implementation of the intervention); (2) program characteristics (e.g.,

easy-to-understand intervention materials); (3) fit with the school's policies, goals, and other programs; (4) necessary training and technical assistance; and (5) principal and administrator support (Forman & Barakat, 2011).

5. Does the intervention consider co-occurring disorders? Often the intervention focuses on one specific disorder and does not adequately take into account the possibility of other disorders that are present, or the heterogeneity of the mental health problems broadly defined within childhood and adolescence (Hoagwood, 2003).

6. Is the intervention age-appropriate and/or developmentally sensitive? For example, an intervention found to be effective with preadolescent youth to reduce depression may well be ineffective for adolescent youths (Hoagwood et al., 2001); similarly, effective treatments used with adults may not affect children in the same manner.

7. Is the intervention culturally sensitive? Was the target group in the experiment/clinical group or single-case design comparable in terms of race/ethnicity, and so on? As the population of the United States continues to become larger and more diverse, this factor has become increasingly important.

IMPLEMENTATION SCIENCE IN SCHOOLS

With the growing focus on evidence-based knowledge to inform practice, how do practitioners integrate what they know with what science proves to be effective? Restructuring how we deliver interventions in the school setting is a difficult, and often daunting, task that requires shifting *both* practice behaviors and organizational climates (Huang, Hepburn, & Espiritu, 2003). How do we make this move to a more effective service delivery?

Over the past decade, substantial efforts have been devoted to closing the gap between research and practice. Although various terms exist (e.g., translational science, implementation science, dissemination and implementation, knowledge translation, diffusion of innovations), researchers across disciplines are beginning to use the term "implementation science" to refer to a field of study that investigates the "uptake of research findings and evidence-based interventions"

(Forman et al., 2013, p. 79). Different from intervention research, the goal of implementation science is not to identify the effectiveness of an intervention. The goal, instead, is to study factors that influence the uptake of an evidence-based intervention in a particular setting. Although not exhaustive, Table 134.1 highlights many specific factors that often influence implementation. It is important to note that successfully addressing all of these factors is not likely possible. Our hope, however, is that the reader will use the questions presented in this chapter to be more thoughtful about the multiple factors that could influence the successful uptake of evidence-based interventions in the school setting.

In addition to acknowledging factors that influence the translation of evidence-based interventions in to practice settings, attention has also recently been given to studying *implementation strategies*. Implementation strategies are designed to increase the likelihood that an evidence-based intervention is implemented in practice settings. Specifically, an implementation strategy is defined as a "systematic intervention process to adopt or integrate evidence-based [interventions] into usual care" (Powell et al., 2012, p. 69). Researchers have recently identified both ineffective and effective strategies that have important implications for school social workers. For example, passive approaches used in isolation (such as continuing education workshops, results published in journal articles, and presentation at national conferences) are ineffective implementation strategies and do not, by themselves, change provider behavior (e.g., Beidas & Kendall, 2010). Conversely, the results of a recent systematic review highlight that multifaceted implementation strategies, such as a combination of ongoing training, access to supervision, regular treatment fidelity monitoring, expert consultation, and peer support, seem to be more effective (Powell, Proctor, & Glass, 2014).

WHERE DO WE GO FROM HERE?

Social work practitioners, both in and out of school settings, are seeing a definite shift from traditionally accepted practices to the cutting-edge best practices. It is important to remember that whether a practitioner is quick to embrace new and better practices or moves slowly and deliberately toward the future, the ultimate goal of prevention and treatment should be concerned

TABLE 134.1 Factors that Impact the Implementation of Evidence-based Interventions

Implementation Factor	Description
Aligning Priority	Do the goals of the intervention align with the priorities and needs of the school?
Collective Action	How many individuals (e.g., school social workers, teachers, principals, policymakers) need to be collectively involved to successfully implement the intervention?
Complexity	Is the intervention easy to explain, understand, and deliver?
Cost	Is there a balance between the costs of implementing the intervention and the perceived benefits? Are there funds available to the schools to support the costs of the evidence-based intervention?
Duration	How much time will it take to implement the intervention? How much time will be needed to change organizational structure to support the uptake of the intervention?
Divisibility	Can the intervention be tested out in a part of the school or in one classroom? Will the intervention be compromised if only parts of it are implemented?
Flexibility/Adaptability	Can the intervention be adapted to meet the needs of the school and/or the specific population being served?
Magnitude/Disruptiveness	To what extent will implementing the intervention require or inadvertently create change at the organizational, structural, financial, or personal level associated with the schools?
Pervasiveness/Scope/Impact	What kind of an impact will the intervention have on both those delivering the intervention and those receiving the intervention? How will receipt of the intervention affect the landscape of the school?
Presentation	How attractive will the intervention be to those in the school setting? Will the length, clarity, and previous research on successful outcomes affect a school's willingness to consider implementing the intervention?
Relative Advantage or Utility	Is the evidence-based intervention better than what is currently being done in the schools?
Risks	What risks are associated with the changes in the school structure to implement the intervention? What are the risks involved if the intervention is not deemed successful?
Trialability/Reversibility	Can the intervention be tried, stopped, or reversed without substantial risk?
Visibility	Can others observe the intended intervention results?

Source: Adapted from Grol, R., & Wensing, M. (2005). Characteristics of successful innovations. In R. Grol, M. Wensing, & M. Eccles (Eds.), *Improving patient care; The implementation of change in clinical practice.* Oxford: Elsevier.

with the health and mental health of the children practitioners are charged with helping.

The importance of evidence in social work and other health and mental health services has been embraced at the highest levels of administration. The 2003 Surgeon General's Report (U.S. Department of Health and Human Services [USDHHS], 2003) identified several key goals crucial to the treatment of children with mental health issues as social work and other social sciences move from the tried and true to the tested and approved. These key goals are as follows.

1. The development, dissemination, and implementation of best practices derived from a scientific evidence base must continue.
2. Knowledge on a variety of factors, including social and psychological development, must be researched "to design better screening, assessment, and treatment tools, and to develop prevention programs" (p. 5).
3. Research on contexts (e.g., school, family, culture) must be supported. This research will assist us in identifying opportunities "for promoting mental health services and for providing effective prevention, treatment, and services" (p. 5).
4. Research to develop and test innovative behavioral, pharmacological, and other "mixed" interventions must also be encouraged.
5. Research on proven treatments, practices, and services developed in a laboratory must be increased, particularly the assessment of their effectiveness in "real-world settings" (p. 5).
6. Similarly, the effectiveness of clinical/community practices must also be studied in context.
7. Development of model programs should be encouraged, particularly those that can be sustained on a community level.
8. Private and public partnerships are key elements in facilitating the dissemination and cross-fertilization of knowledge.
9. The understanding of children's mental health care needs must increase. Additionally, training to assist practitioners to address the various mental issues among children with special health care needs and their families is necessary and urgent.
10. Research on factors that facilitate or impede the implementation of scientifically proven interventions must take place as part of the evaluation process.

KEY POINTS TO REMEMBER

School-based practitioners, particularly those involved in services for children and adolescents, who want to successfully take a step toward a future practice undergirded by scientific evidence, must keep the following in the forefront of their minds.

- The EBP approach is built on a scientific foundation. Implementation of evidence-based theories and interventions into real-world applications involving client input, clinical knowledge, and practice experience will ensure that social workers and other mental health professionals are using the best practices for the children they serve.
- The use of these evidence-based interventions may be useful in a school setting if additional criteria, such as scientific rigor, implementation factors, and implementation strategies, are considered.
- School is one area where a large portion of children may be diagnosed and assisted with mental health or other social issues.
- When appropriate to do so, the creation of partnerships with family, community agencies, and other resources may help sustain change.
- Multifaceted implementation strategies are needed to increase the likelihood that practitioners and schools will adopt evidence-based interventions.

References

Allen-Meares, P., & Montgomery, K. L. (2014). School social work: A historical and contemporary view. In P. Allen-Meares (Ed.), *Social work services in schools* (7th edition). Boston, MA: Allyn & Bacon.

American Psychology Association. (2012.) *Facing the school dropout dilemma.* Washington, DC: Author. Retrieved from http://www.apa.org/pi/families/resources/school-dropout-prevention.pdf.

Beidas, R. S., & Kendall, P. C. (2010). Training therapists in evidence based practice: A critical review of studies from a systems contextual perspective. *Clinical Psychology: Science and Practice, 17,* 1–30.

Bowen, G. L. (2007). Social organization and schools: A general systems theory perspective. In P. Allen-Meares (Ed.), *Social work services in schools* (pp. 60–79). Boston, MA: Pearson Education.

Brekke, J. S., Ell, K., & Palinkas, L. A. (2007). Translational science at the National Institute of Mental Health: Can social work take its rightful place? *Research on Social Work Practice, 17,* 123–133.

Brener, N. D., Weist, M., Adelman, H., Taylor, L., & Vernon-Smiley, M. (2007). Mental health and social services: Results from the School Health Policies and Programs Study 2006 (Report). *Journal of School Health, 77*(8), 486–499.

Cooper, J. L., Masi, R., Vick, J. (2009). *Social-emotional development in early childhood: What every policymaker should know.* National Center for Children in Poverty. Retrieved from http://www.nccp.org/publications/pdf/text_882.pdf.

Flay, B. R., Biglan, A., Boruch, R. F., Castro, F. G., Gottfredson, D., Kellam, S., … Ji, P. (2005). Standards of evidence: Criteria for efficacy, effectiveness and dissemination. *Prevention Science, 6*(3), 151–175.

Forman, S. G., & Barakat, N. M. (2011). Cognitive behavioral therapy in the schools: Bringing research to practice through effective implementation. *Psychology in the Schools, 48*, 283–296.

Forman, S. G., Shirpiro, E. S., Codding, R. S., Gonzales, J. E., Reddy, L. A., Rosenfield, S. A., … Stoiber, K. C. (2013). Implementation science and school psychology. *School Psychology Quarterly, 28*, 77–100.

Gibbs, L., & Gambrill, E. (2002). Evidence-based practice: Counterarguments to objections. *Research on Social Work Practice, 12*, 452–476.

Gould, N. (2005). An inclusive approach to knowledge for mental health social work practice and policy. *British Journal of Social Work, 36*, 109–125.

Grol, R., Wensing, M., & Eccles, M. (2005). Characteristics of successful innovations. In R. Grol, M. Wensing, & M. Eccles (Eds.), *Improving patient care; The implementation of change in clinical practice* (p. 290). Oxford: Elsevier.

Hoagwood, K. (2003). Evidence-based practice in children's mental health services: What do we know? Why aren't we putting it to use? *Data Matters, 6*, 4–5.

Hoagwood, K., Burns, B. J., Kiser, L., Ringeisen, H., & Schoenwald, S. K. (2001). Evidence-based practice in child and adolescent mental health services. *Psychiatric Services, 52*(9), 1179–1189.

Huang, L. N., Hepburn, M. S., & Espiritu, R. C. (2003). To be or not to be … evidence-based? *Data Matters, 6*, 1–3.

Johnson, C. (2008). Evidence-based practice in 5 simple steps. *Journal of Manipulative and Physiological Therapeutics, 3*, 169–170.

Kazdin, A. E., & Weisz, J. R. (2010). Introduction: Context, background, and goals. In A. E. Kazdin & J. R. Weisz (Eds.), *Evidence-based psychotherapies for children and adolescents* (pp. 3–9). New York, NY: Guilford Press.

Montgomery, K. L. (2014). School-based delinquency prevention programs. In A. R. Roberts, W. T. Church, & D. W. Springer (Eds.), *Juvenile justice sourcebook* (2nd ed.). New York, NY: Oxford University Press.

O'Connell, M. E., Boat, T., & Warner, K. E. (2009). *Preventing mental, emotional, and behavioral disorders among young people: Progress and possibilities.* Washington, DC: National Research Council and Institute of Medicine.

Pastor, P. N., Reuben, C. A., & Duran, C. R. (2012). *Identifying emotional and behavioral problems in children aged 4–17 years: United States, 2001–2007.* National Health Statistics Report (no.48). Hyattsville, MD: National Center for Health Statistics.

Powell, B. J., McMillen, J. C., Proctor, E. K., Carpenter, C. R., Griffey, R. T., Bunger, A. C., … York, J. L. (2012). A compilation of strategies for implementing clinical innovations in health and mental health. *Medical Care Research and Review, 69*, 123–157.

Powell, B. J., Proctor, E. K., & Glass, J. E. (2014). A systematic review of strategies for implementing empirically supported mental health interventions. *Research on Social Work Practice, 24*, 192–212.

Rees, C. (1997). Ask the doctor: On children and mental illness. *NAMI Advocate, 8*, 10.

Regehr, C., Stern, S., & Shlonsky, A. (2007). Operationalizing evidence-based practice: The development of an institute for evidence-based social work. *Research on Social Work Practice, 17*, 408–416.

Rubin, A., & Babbie, E. (2010). *Research methods for social work* (7th ed.). Belmont, CA: Wadsworth Publishing Company.

Rubin, A., & Parrish, D. (2007). Views of evidence-based practice among faculty in Master of Social Work programs: A national survey. *Research on Social Work Practice, 17*, 110–122.

Sipple, J. (2007). Major issues in American schools. In P. Allen-Meares (Ed.), *Social work services in schools* (pp. 1–25). Boston, MA: Pearson Education.

Social Work Policy Institute. (2010). *Evidence-based practice.* Retrieved from http://www.socialworkpolicy.org/research/evidence-based-practice-2.html.

Straus, S. E., & McAlister, F. A. (2000). Evidence-based medicine: A commentary on common criticisms. *Canadian Medical Association Journal, 7*, 837–841.

Taft, J. (1923). The relation of the school of mental health of the average child. *Proceedings of the National Conference of Social Work* (p. 398). Chicago, IL: University of Chicago Press.

U.S. Department of Health and Human Services. (2003). *Report of the Surgeon General's conference on children's mental health: A national action agenda.* Washington, DC: Department of Health and Human Services.

135

Evidence-based Violence Prevention Programs and Best Implementation Practices

Ronald O. Pitner, Roxana Marachi,
Ron Avi Astor, & Rami Benbenishty

GETTING STARTED

Social work as a profession has contributed to the national and international dialogue concerning violence prevention programs in schools (e.g., Astor, Benbenishty, & Estrada, 2009; Astor, Benbenishty, Marachi, & Pitner, 2009; Astor, Guerra, & Van Acker, 2010; Benbenishty & Astor, 2005; Benbenishty & Astor, 2012ab; Benbenishty, Astor, & Estrada, 2008; Chen & Astor, 2012; Green, Furlong, Astor, Benbenishty, & Espinoza, 2011; Marachi, Astor, & Benbenishty, 2013; Shiff, Pat-Horenczyk, Benbenishty, Brom, Baum, & Astor, 2010). School social workers play an increasingly important role in shaping and implementing policy, interventions, and procedures that make U.S. schools safer.

In order to use resources to the best advantage and maximize program effectiveness, it is helpful for school mental health professionals not only to know the dynamics and best approaches for assessing and intervening in school violence but also be familiar with available model programs already studied and found to be effective. This chapter reviews several examples of effective violence prevention programs as well as model school safety programs. It should be noted that large-scale reviews of evidence-based programs have not yielded notable changes to the "model" programs described in previous years. Many of the programs of focus here have undergone years of planning and development and are still refining and increasing their processes of implementation and effectiveness.

One great weakness in establishing evidence-based violence prevention programs is that they are often introduced to schools with a "top-down" approach, ignoring variations in local school contexts. Even model programs that have been demonstrated to be effective in large-scale research studies have a better chance for success at a school if the program matches the needs and values of the community, the school, and the school staff. To assist readers in achieving such a match, we offer monitoring and mapping approaches as a guide to developing a bottom-up program and for tracking program interventions and outcomes.

WHAT WE KNOW

In this section of the chapter, we present examples of some of the most widely researched model school safety programs available to schools and practitioners. Table 135.1 includes the names of the programs, websites where the programs can be explored, program components, outcome measures, and results from studies. We include a more extensive list of websites and resources for each program at the end of the chapter. We also include the names and links to other promising programs that could not be elaborated on in this chapter due to length considerations. The programs listed in Table 135.1 have been rated as "effective" by multiple national organizations. Our designation of effective is a composite of ratings from nine independent scientific

TABLE 135.1 Select Evidence-based Violence Prevention Programs and Evaluating Sources

Program	Grade	Participants	Program components	Outcome measures	Results
Olweus Bullying Prevention Program *(OBPP)* (Olweus, 1993) www.clemson .edu/olweus	Program target audience ages 6–15. Initial large-scale evaluation on grades 4–7	Original intervention/ evaluation involved 2,500 students in 42 primary and secondary schools in Norway. (The program is now international and being applied in 15 countries. The materials are translated into over 12 languages.)	Core components of the program are implemented at the school level, the class level, and the individual level. Including: • Distribution of anonymous student questionnaire assessing the nature and prevalence of bullying • Development of positive and negative consequences for students' behavior • Establishing a supervisory system • Reinforcement of school-wide rules against bullying • Classroom workshops with video and discussions to increase knowledge and empathy • Interventions with children and victims of bullying • Discussions with parents	Quasiexperimental research deign with student self-report measures collected at introduction of the program, four months after introduction, one-year follow-up, and two-year follow-up. • Reports of incidents of bullying and victimization • Scale of general youth antisocial behavior • Assessment of school climate—order and discipline • Measure of social relationships and attitude toward school	• Substantial reductions (50% or more for most comparisons by students' age and grade) in self-reported bullying and bully victimization. • Significant reductions in self-reported vandalism, fighting, theft, alcohol use, and truancy. • Significant improvements in the social climate of the classroom (as reflected in students' reports of increased satisfaction with school life and school work, improved order and discipline at school, and more positive social relationships). • Classrooms that implemented essential components of the program saw greater reductions in bully/victim problems. • Results summary from http://sshs.promoteprevent. org/publications/ebi-factsheets/ olweus-bullying-prevention-program citing Kallestad & Olweus, 2003; Olweus, 1991, 2005; Olweus, Limber, & Mihalic, 1999. * Evaluating Sources 1, 2, 3, 6, 7

(continued)

Program	Grade	Participants	Program components	Outcome measures	Results
Caring School Community Program (formerly Child Development Project) http://devstu.org/caring-school-community (Battistich, Schaps, Watson, & Solomon, 1996)	K–6th Grades	Evaluation studies are based on 4,500+ students ages 6–12 in 24 elementary schools from sux diverse districts throughout the United States.	This is a comprehensive model focused on creating a cooperative and supportive school environment. Components include: 1) Class Meeting Lessons, which provide teachers and students with a forum to get to know one another and make decisions that affect classroom climate; 2) Implementation of a model that fosters cross-grade "buddying" activities 3) Home-side Activities, which foster communication at home and link school learning with home experiences and perspectives; 4) School-wide community-building activities used to promote school bonding and parent involvement activities such as interactive homework assignments that reinforce the family-school partnership.	Data were collected after 1 year and 2 years of intervention. Teachers were assessed through four, 90-minute observations and annual teacher questionnaires. Student assessments were self-report surveys of drug use and delinquent behavior.	Results showed that students experienced a stronger "sense of community" and more motivation to be helpful, better conflict-resolution skills, greater acceptance of people who are different, higher self-esteem, stronger feelings of social competence, less loneliness in school and fewer delinquent acts. Over a two-year period, a significant 24% decline was found in student discipline referrals in 20 program schools, while referrals increased 42% in four control schools (Marshall & Caldwell, 2007). http://nrepp.samhsa.gov/ViewIntervention.aspx?id=152 * Evaluating Sources 2,4,5,6

| Fast Track Project (Conduct Problems Prevention Research Group, 1992) www.fasttrackproject.org | Initial evaluation participants were at-risk kindergartners identified based on combined teacher and parent ratings of behavior (CBCL). Highest 10% recruited for study. N = 445 intervention children N = 446 control group children | Multiple program components. Weekly enrichment program for high-risk children and their parents. Students placed in "friendship groups" of five to six students each. Discussions, modeling stories and films, role-plays. Sessions focused on reviewing and practicing skills in emotional understanding and communication, friendship building, self-control, and social problem solving. Parents met in groups led by Family Coordinators to discuss parenting strategies, then 30-minute parent-child cooperative activity time, Biweekly home visits Academic tutoring provided by trained tutors in 30-min sessions 3X/week | • **Externalizing Scale of CBCL** -*oppositional, aggressive, and delinquent behaviors—parents.* • *Parent Daily Report*—degree to which child engaged in aggressive and oppositional behaviors during previous 24 hrs (Given 3x) • Child Behavior Change Teacher assessment of acting out behaviors in school (Teacher Report Form, Achenbach 1991) • Scale from the TOCA-R (Teacher Observation of Classroom Adaptation- Revised) • Authority Acceptance Scale • Peer rating of aggressive and hyperactive-disruptive behaviors. | Intervention group had higher scores on emotion recognition, emotion coping, and social problem solving compared to control group. They also found lower rates of aggressive retaliation compared to control group. Direct observation results: • Intervention group spent more time in positive peer interaction than did the control group. • Intervention group received higher peer social preference scores than control group. Long term studies indicate variable findings depending on outcomes. Ten-year longitudinal study examined psychiatric diagnoses for conduct disorder, oppositional defiant disorder, attention deficit hyperactivity disorder (ADHD), and externalizing disorders. Findings suggest that the intervention could be effective in preventing externalizing disorders from developing among youth. (Conduct Problems Prevention Research Group, 1999; 2002; 2010; 2011). http://www.fasttrackproject.org/publication.php * Evaluating Sources 2, 3, 5, 6, 7, 8 |

(continued)

Program	Grade	Participants	Program components	Outcome measures	Results
PATHS curriculum (Greenberg, Kusché, & Mihalic, 1998) *http://www .prevention.psu .edu/projects/ PATHS.html*	1st–5th grades over three cohorts	198 Intervention Classrooms 180 Control Classrooms matched by school size, achievement levels, poverty and ethnic diversity. 7,560 total students 845 students were in high-risk intervention or control conditions. (6,715 students non-high risk children.)	PATHS (Promoting Alternative Thinking Strategies). Administered to classrooms. 57 lessons (1/2 hr sessions, 2–3X/week) • Skills related to understanding & communicating emotions • Skills related to increase of positive social behavior • Self-control and social problem solving Presented through direct instruction, discussion, modeling stories, or video. Teachers attended 2.5 day training & received weekly consultation from Fast Track staff. Quality of implementation was assessed by observer rating of teacher's • Skill in teaching PATHS concepts	1) Teachers were interviewed about behavior of each child in class. (Fall/Spring of first grade.) 2) Socio-metric assessments (peer nominations made by students) collected to assess • Peer aggression • Peer hyperactivity/ disruptiveness • Peer social status 3) Quality of classroom atmosphere was assessed by Observer ratings assessing the following: • Level of disruption • Ability to handle transitions • Ability to follow rules • Level of cooperation • Use of problem-solving skills • Ability to express feelings	Hierarchical Linear Modeling (Accounting for gender, site, cohort & intervention) Intervention classrooms had lower ratings of hyperactivity/disruptive behavior, aggression, and more favorable observer ratings of classroom atmosphere. Three cohorts of intervention, so teachers administered curriculum, 1, 2, or 3 times. When "teacher experience" was included in analyses, teachers who taught more cohorts had higher classroom atmosphere ratings (by neutral observer). Quality of implementation Teacher skill in program implementation was also related to positive outcomes. (Kam, Greenberg, & Walls, 2003) Four clinical trials conducted since 1995 revealed a 32% reduction in teachers' reports of aggressive student behavior, 36% increase in teachers' reports of student self-control, 68% increase in students' vocabulary for emotions, and 20% increase in students' cognitive skills test scores. http://www.promoteprevent. org/publications/ebi-factsheets/ promoting-alternative- thinking-strategies-paths

- Managing the classroom
- Modeling and generalizing PATHS throughout day
- Openness to consultation

- Ability to stay focused on task
- Criticism vs. supportiveness

* Evaluating Sources 2, 3, 4, 5, 7, 8

---

* Evaluating sources:

1) American Youth Policy Forum: *Less Hype, More Help: Reducing Juvenile Crime, What Works—and What Doesn't* by Richard A. Mendel. Washington, DC, 2000 (http://www.aypf.org/publications/mendel/MendelRep.pdf).

2) Bennett P([0–9]{1,5})–([0–9]{1,5})jerce Prevention Research Center (Formerly Prevention Research Center for the Promotion of Human Development): http://www.prevention.psu.edu—Reducing Youth Violence and Delinquency in Pennsylvania: PCCD's Research Based Programs Initiative Report http://www.prevention.psu.edu/pubs/docs/PCCD_ReducingYouthViolence.pdf.

3) Blueprints for Violence Prevention— Center for the Study and Prevention of Violence (http://www.colorado.edu/cspv/blueprints).

4) U.S. Department of Health and Human Services—Substance Abuse and Mental Health Services Administration—National Registry of Evidence-Based Programs and Practices—http://nrepp.samhsa.gov.

5) U.S. Department of Education, Institute of Education Sciences "What Works Clearinghouse" (http://ies.ed.gov/ncee/wwc/). Reducing Behavior Problems in the Elementary School Classroom—National Center for Education Evaluation and Regional Assistance. http://ies.ed.gov/ncee/wwc/pdf/practiceguides/behavior_pg_092308.pdf

6) U.S. Department of Justice: Office of Juvenile Justice and Delinquency Prevention's Model Programs Guide MPG: http://ojjdp.gov/mpg.

7) U. S. Department of Justice: National Criminal Justice Reference Service Report—Preventing crime: What Works, What Doesn't, What's Promising. University of Maryland Department of Criminology and Criminal Justice. (Sherman, 1998) NCJ 165366 https://www.ncjrs.gov/works. Main website: http://www.ncjrs.gov.

8) Youth Violence: A Report of the Surgeon General http://www.ncbi.nlm.nih.gov/books/NBK44294/.

organizations that evaluated the most popular school violence prevention programs. Criteria considered in designating a program as effective include (1) evidence of effectiveness based on rigorous evaluations with experimental or quasiexperimental designs; (2) the clarity of the program's goals and rationale; (3) the fit between the program content and the characteristics of the intended population and setting; (4) the integration of the program into schools' educational mission; (5) the availability of necessary information and guidance for replication in other settings; and (6) the incorporation of post-treatment and follow-up data collection as part of the program. We describe in detail four programs listed in Table 135.1.

OLWEUS BULLYING PREVENTION PROGRAM

The Olweus Bullying Prevention Program (OBPP) is a comprehensive, school-wide multi-component bullying reduction and prevention program designed for students in Grades 1–9. It was developed during the 1970s by Dan Olweus to reduce bully and victim problems in Norwegian schools. Since then, it has been translated into more than 12 languages and successfully established in schools in more than 15 countries.

Content

As seen in Table 135.1 under Program Components, the OBPP is implemented at three levels of the school environment—the whole school, classroom, and the individual student. At the school-wide level, the program establishes antibullying policies within the school system. To raise awareness and quantify the prevalence of bullying in the school, administrators distribute an anonymous 29-item student questionnaire to all students. A school conference day about bullying is established to talk about the results of the assessment and discuss interventions. Additionally, schools create an OBPP coordination team in which a representative administrator, teacher, counselor, parent, and student come together to lead the program implementation. The school adopts rules against bullying and explains to students the negative consequences for bullying behavior. All staff receive training to learn about the harmful consequences of bullying, to increase supervision in areas on campus

that are prone to violence, and to provide systematic reinforcement of rules applied to all students.

At the classroom level, students have regular workshops about the harmful consequences of bullying. Students have discussions about bullying and violent behaviors, watch video presentations of bullying situations, write about ways to combat the problem, and engage in role-play. Students are encouraged to increase their knowledge and empathy regarding bullying.

The individual student level involves direct consequences for bullying behaviors. There are focused interventions with those identified as bullies and victims, as well as bystanders. The parents of involved students are given help and support to reinforce nonviolence at home. School mental health workers play an essential role in more serious cases of bullying.

The goal of using interventions through all three levels is to ensure that students are given a consistent, coordinated, and strong message that bullying will not be tolerated. The OBPP teaches students that everyone has a responsibility to prevent bullying, either by refusing to support the bullying behavior or by alerting an adult to the problem.

Theoretical Rationale and Conceptual Framework

The Olweus Bullying Prevention Program is based on a systematic restructuring of the school environment that redirects bullying behavior and provides rewards for more prosocial behavior. The conceptual framework is based on research into the development and modification of aggressive behavior, as well as positive child-rearing dimensions (Olweus & Limber, 2010ab). The goal is to create a school environment that (1) is characterized by adults who are engaged and caring, (2) has firm limits to unacceptable behavior, (3) has consistent responses of no rewards and negative consequences for violent behavior, and (4) has adults who act as authorities and positive role models (Olweus & Limber, 2010ab).

Much of the success of the OBPP can be attributed to it being a school-wide program, so that it becomes an integral part of the school environment. Students and adults participate in most of the universal components of the program. Indeed, teachers, parents, and administrators play an important role in the success of the program. School staff and parents are expected to (1) become aware of the extent of the bullying problem in their school through assessments, (2) gain an understanding of the significance and harmful effects of bullying, and (3) take an active role in enforcing rules against bullying behavior (Olweus & Limber, 2010b).

Evaluation

The first and most comprehensive evaluation study of this program was conducted with 2,500 students in Norway (also see Olweus, 1993). Since then, however, this program has been implemented and positively evaluated in many countries (e.g., Hunter, Boyle, & Warden, 2007; Limber, 2012; Olweus & Limber, 2010ab; Rigby, 2006). Evaluation of this program has demonstrated significant reductions in bully/victim reports across many cultures. General antisocial behaviors, such as vandalism, fighting, theft, and truancy have been reduced in the program schools. Improvements are also found in classroom culture in that students reported improved order and discipline at school, more positive social relationships, and more positive attitudes toward school and schoolwork.

It is also important to keep in mind that the historical success of a program does not necessarily guarantee its effectiveness. Although international data are strong and consistent in documenting reductions of bullying and victimization, evaluations for U.S. schools have not been as consistent. In a 2011 review of the most recent OBPP studies, The Center for Schools and Communities describes challenges in implementation processes and emphasizes the need for careful attention to program fidelity in order to implement the OBPP model effectively. Vreeman and Carroll (2007) also note that although European studies over the past two decades had demonstrated effectiveness of school-wide bullying prevention programs, similar studies in the United States have not replicated these findings.

"CARING SCHOOL COMMUNITY" PROGRAM (FORMERLY KNOWN AS "CHILD DEVELOPMENT PROJECT")

The Caring School Community Program (CSCP, formerly called the Child Development Project, or CDP) is an ecological approach to intervention that collaboratively involves teachers, parents, and students working to influence all aspects of the school community (Developmental Studies Center, 1995). Its main objective is to create a cooperative and supportive school environment for children in Grades K–6. Established in 1981, the CDP strives to foster shared commitment to prosocial, democratic values in two specific ways: through adult guidance and through direct participation by children (Battistich, 2008; Battistich, Schaps, & Wilson, 2004). Throughout this process, children are able to develop a sense that the school community cares for them, and they, in turn, begin to care about the school community. Over the years of program refinement, the Child Development Project has separated out into two distinct yet complementary modules: one entitled "Making Meaning" for the reading comprehension emphasis, and the current program of focus, "Caring School Community," for classroom climate and school community building. Our review of the research focuses on the Caring School Community component of the original Child Development Project.

Teachers are trained to implement most components of the intervention, and ongoing consultation and support are provided by the Developmental Studies Center. Research indicates that schools should make a minimum of a three-year commitment to the Caring School Community Program if it is to be effective (Northwest Regional Educational Laboratory, 1998). The program has been shown to be effective in both ethnically and socioeconomically diverse settings (Battistich, 2008; Chang & Munoz, 2006; Marshall & Caldwell, 2007).

Theoretical Rationale and Conceptual Framework

The Caring School Community Program's theoretical framework is guided by research on socialization, learning and motivation, and prosocial development (Battistich, 2008). Its overall objective is for schools to be transformed into caring and supportive communities in which everyone works collaboratively in the learning process. Such a focus is expected to foster children's intellectual and socio-moral development, self-direction, competence, and belonging (Battistich, 2008). Where these qualities are fostered, children become attached to and invested in the school community, which, in turn, leads them to internalize the school norms. School norms typically promote prosocial activity (e.g., concern for others) and proscribe antisocial activity (e.g., drug use or gang activity). The program is based on the idea that children's internalization of school norms will solidify their commitment to the school's community values.

Content

There are four interrelated goals on which the components of the CSCP are based: (1) building warm, stable, supportive relationships; (2) attending to social and ethical dimensions of learning; (3) honoring intrinsic motivations; and (4) teaching in ways that support students' active construction of meaning (Battistich, 2008). These goals are interwoven into the five major components of the original CDP (Table 135.1), which were literature-based reading and language arts, collaborative classroom learning, developmental discipline, parent involvement, and school-wide activities, and which are presented in Table 135.1.

The first three components are all designed for the classroom. The literature-based readings component is most directly focused on teaching for understanding. Thus, the selection of books is designed to help teachers foster a deeper and more empathetic understanding of the readings among the students. The component that involves collaborative learning emphasizes the importance of working with others in a fair and cooperative manner. The final classroom component involves building care and respect for everyone in the classroom community (Battistich, 2008). The two other components' foci go beyond the classroom. Parent involvement is designed to develop meaningful conversations between adults and their children; school-wide activities are focused on allowing participation by all and avoiding hierarchies and competition (Battistich, 2008).

Implementation

At least 80% of the school faculty must support their school's adoption of the CDP for it to be established there. Training is conducted by Developmental Studies Center staff and involves initial consultation and planning to identify needs and goals; a three-day summer institute to orient teachers on the CDP components and materials; three half-day follow-up workshops conducted during the school year; three on-site sessions, each lasting 2.5 days, which include consultation, in-class demonstrations, co-teaching, and planning; and professional development

support kits that can be used to train new staff (Developmental Studies Center, 2004).

Evaluation

Caring School Community strengthens students' sense of their school as a community, their ethical and social resources (e.g., conflict-resolution skills, social problem-solving skills, commitment to democratic values, concern for others), academic motivation (e.g., liking for school), and abstention from drug use and other problem behaviors (e.g., gang-related activity) (Battistich et al., 1996, 1997, 2000; Battistich, Schaps, & Wilson, 2004; Northwest Regional Education Laboratory, 1998; Watson & Battistich, 2006). Recent evaluations have also demonstrated improvements in student behavior with the Caring School Community Program. In a single school district evaluation, program schools demonstrated significant reductions in student discipline referrals (Chang & Munoz, 2006). Marshall and Caldwell (2007) also found a significant 24% decline in student discipline referrals over a two-year period in 20 program schools, while referrals increased 42% in four control schools.

FAST TRACK

The Fast Track Project is a long-term comprehensive intervention that encompasses multiple facets of children's social contexts. The intervention is comprehensive in that it has both universal (school-wide) components and targeted components that attempt to provide focused assistance to children at high risk of antisocial behaviors and their social systems. One of the great strengths of this program is its detailed attention to the intersection of the multiple contexts that contribute to children's developmental outcomes. The Fast Track prevention program aims to improve child competences, parent effectiveness, the school context, and school–home communications with the intention of preventing antisocial behavior across the developmental trajectory.

Theoretical Rational and Conceptual Framework

The developmental theory guiding this intervention addresses the interaction of multiple influences on the development of antisocial behavior.

These various elements include socioeconomic factors, family dynamics, peer influences, school factors, and the child's temperament.

Content

There were four Fast Track sites in the United States, with a total of 891 children (and their families) participating (with nearly equal numbers of at-risk children in both intervention and control groups). The initial sample consisted of children identified as "at risk" by a combination of teacher and parent ratings of their behavior. Children in the intervention group were provided with a host of services, including weekly enrichment programs, involvement in "friendship groups," and sessions in which they were taught and had opportunities to practice social skills. The parents of the intervention children were also provided with family coordinators who conducted biweekly home visits in efforts to enhance their parenting behavior management skills, specifically in the areas of praise, time-outs, and self-restraint. Children in the intervention group were also provided with three 30-minute academic tutoring sessions each week.

When the children in the intervention group reached adolescence (Grades 6–10), the group-based interventions were de-emphasized. However, the intervention retained its curriculum-based parent and youth group meetings to support children in their transition into middle school (Grades 5–7). Individual support was provided for participants and their families to strengthen protective factors and reduce risk factors. The targeted intervention at the adolescent phase focused on academic tutoring, mentoring, home visiting and family problem solving, and supporting positive peer group involvement. To address the multiple contexts in the adolescents' lives, the school tried to establish relations with the community agencies that served the participants.

Fast Track also included an important universal component for children in the first through the fifth grades in the target schools. This school-based intervention consisted of teacher-led curricula called "PATHS" (Promoting Alternative Thinking Strategies), designed to provide children with strategies in understanding the development of emotional concepts, social understanding, and self-control. Because PATHS has been evaluated separately and shown to have independent positive effects, we will present it

separately in the next section. Some schools may choose to adopt only sections of the overall program, such as PATHS.

Evaluation

Fast Track is one of the more rigorously evaluated comprehensive violence prevention programs and has become widely known as one of the leading models of an effective approach to prevention of antisocial behaviors in youth. As shown in Table 135.1, evaluation studies of Fast Track have revealed positive outcomes for program participants. The evaluations on the initial cohort of youth selected for the study have spanned over 10 years and have continued to yield positive findings, with over 80% of the original sample remaining (Conduct Problems Prevention Research Group, 2011). In addition to those differences between treatment and control students highlighted in the table, the prevention revealed statistically significant improvements in the targeted children's social-cognitive and academic skills, as well as reductions in their parents' use of harsh discipline. The intervention children also demonstrated considerable behavioral improvements at home, in the classroom, and on the playground during and following their elementary school years. In addition to these behavioral improvements, the intervention children were at a reduced risk of being placed in special education classes than children in the control conditions. The findings generalized across ethnicity, gender, and a host of child and family characteristics.

PROMOTING ALTERNATIVE THINKING STRATEGIES PROGRAM

The Promoting Alternative Thinking Strategies Program (PATHS) is the classroom curriculum component of the Fast Track intervention program. We present it separately because PATHS has been adopted and studied independently of Fast Track. PATHS was designed to promote emotional and social competence and to reduce aggression and other behavior problems in children in Grades K–5 (Conduct Problems Prevention Research Group, 2010a). PATHS focuses on four domains related to school success: (1) prosocial behavior and friendship skills, (2) emotional understanding and self-control, (3) communication and conflict resolution, and (4) problem-solving skills

(Conduct Problems Prevention Research Group, 2010a; 2010b). PATHS provides teachers and counselors with training, lesson modules, and ongoing consultation and support. Additionally, parents receive information and activities to complete with their children.

PATHS can be used with all elementary school-age children, and ideally it should be ongoing, beginning in kindergarten and continuing through fifth grade. It has been field-tested and researched in regular education classroom settings and in settings that serve special needs students, such as the deaf, hearing-impaired, learning disabled, emotionally disturbed, mildly mentally delayed, and gifted (see Greenberg & Kusche, 1998; Greenberg, Kusche, Cook, & Quamma, 1995; Riggs, Greenberg, Kusché, & Pentz, 2006).

Theoretical Rationale/Conceptual Framework

PATHS is based on five conceptual models (Greenberg, Kusché, & Mihalic, 1998). First, the ABCD (affective-behavioral-cognitive-dynamic) model of development promotes skills that are developmentally appropriate. The second model is an eco-behavioral system orientation that focuses on helping the teacher use these skills to build a healthy classroom atmosphere. The third model involves neurobiology and brain organization for cognitive development. The fourth is psychodynamic education that was derived from developmental psychodynamic theory. Finally, the fifth model includes psychological issues related to emotional awareness or emotional intelligence. These conceptual models come together in this curriculum to provide a comprehensive and developmentally based program that addresses students' cognitive processes, emotions, and behaviors.

Content

The PATHS curriculum (Greenberg et al., 1998) is taught three times a week for a minimum of 20–30 minutes a day. The curriculum contains four units with a total of 119 lessons in each unit. They consist of the following: (1) A "Turtle" unit focusing on classroom behavior, emotional literacy, and self-control; (2) "Feeling and Relationship Unit" focusing on building self-esteem and social competence; (3) a "Problem-Solving Unit" with instruction on the 11-step model of social problem solving and positive peer relations; and (4) a

"Supplementary Lessons Unit" containing 30 lessons that delve more deeply into PATHS concepts. The lessons are age-appropriate, and can be seen in Table 135.2. The lessons for third-grade students match developmental stages and cover the conceptual domains of self-control, emotional understanding, self-esteem, peer relations, and problem solving. (Lesson 93, presented in detail in Table 135.2, covers self-control and problem solving.)

The PATHS curriculum includes comprehensive materials, and the Basic PATHS Kit (Grades 1–5) includes an instructor's manual, five curriculum manuals, feelings photographs, feelings face cards, two wall charts, and four full color posters. The Turtle unit (for kindergarten classrooms) includes an instructor's manual, curriculum manual, turtle puppet with pad, turtle stamp, and poster. Teachers receive on-site training and technical assistance to ensure effective implementation of the program.

Evaluation

PATHS has been evaluated in various research studies using randomized control groups and was found to be effective. As seen in Table 135.1, PATHS has been found to be a model or effective program by at least six groups that review violence prevention programs nationwide for effectiveness. An overview of results from all trials reveals a reduction in aggressive behavior, conduct disorder, and violent solutions to social problems. In addition, results found an increase in self-control, vocabulary for emotions, cognitive skills, ability to tolerate frustration, and to effectively use conflict-resolution strategies (SAMHSA Model Programs, 2003). The findings have been consistent across teacher reports, self-reports, and child assessments and interviews. PATHS remains among the highest rated social-emotional learning programs and is nationally and internationally recognized for its strong evidence base, theoretical design, and clarity of implementation. It received a perfect score for program materials and a nearly perfect score for dissemination according to the SAMHSA's National Registry of Evidence-Based Programs and Practices and had the highest possible ratings according to the Center for the Study and Prevention of Violence.

The PATHS program has also been recognized for its effectiveness by the National Institute on Drug Abuse (NIDA) and the Office of Juvenile Justice and Delinquency Prevention (OJJDP).

TABLE 135.2 PATHS Lessons for Grade 3

Lesson Topic	Volume & Lesson #	Self Control	Emotional Understanding	Self-esteem	Peer Relations	Problem solving
				Conceptual Domains		
PATHS Rules	Vol. 1, L 1	X		X	X	X
PATHS kid/Complimenting/Self-esteem	Vol. 1, L 2	X		X	X	X
Anger Intensity	Vol. 1, L 10		X		X	
Anger Management/Control Signals	Vol. 1, L 11–12	X		X	X	X
Fear Intensity/Sad Intensity	Vol. 1, L 15–17		X		X	
Disgusted, Delighted	Vol. 1, L 21		X		X	
Frustrated, Disappointed/Hopeful, Proud/Ashamed, Guilty, Curious/Interested/Bored, Confused/Worried/Sure, Anxious/Calm, Shy/Lonely	Vol. 2, L 23–32, 37		X		X	
Embarrassed/ Humiliated	Vol. 2, L 33–34		X		X	
Intentionality (Accident/Purpose), Manners	Vol. 3 L 38–44		X		X	
Jealous/Content, Greedy/Selfish/ Generous, Malicious/Kind, Rejected/Included, Excluded, Forgiving/Resentful	Vol. 3, 48–56		X		X	
Informal Problem Solving	Vol. 5, 90–92	X				X
Self-Control and Problem Prevention (see Table 5)	Vol. 5, L 93–94	X			X	X
Friendship	Vol. 5, L 95–97.	X	X	X	X	X
Teasing	Vol. 5, L 98–101.	X	X	X	X	X
Apply Problem Solving Steps	Vol. 4, L 89.					X

TABLE 135.3 PATHS Learning Self-Control Volume 5, Lesson 93

Introduction	"Today I'm going to tell you a story about a boy who had problems, but he learned a new way to help himself."
Story: "Thomas in Control"	This is a story about a boy who did not like to go to school. Thomas felt very upset about going to school. He wanted to run outside and play with his toys or ride his bike or watch television or play a game. Thomas did not like to sit quietly. It was hard for him to pay attention when the teacher or the other kids were talking in class. Instead, Thomas would tease whoever was sitting beside him, by grabbing their pencils and books, by making faces at them, or by whispering to them. The other kids would get angry at Thomas when he bothered them and would yell at him or would do some of the same things back. Then everyone would get caught and would get into trouble. That's why some of the kids thought that Thomas was a troublemaker. Sometimes when they went out to the playground at recess, the other kids would still be mad at Thomas and they would get into a fight. All of this hate and resentment made Thomas feel very uncomfortable inside. One day when he was feeling his worst, the playground teacher told Thomas that he had to go to the principal's office because he hadn't been following the playground rules. "You know," said the principal in a very calm voice, "you have a very big problem, but I'll share a secret with you. You already have the answer to your problem with you. You carry it with you everywhere you go. It's your ability to think. Whenever you feel upset, when you are angry or frustrated, you can use your mind and think. You can stop, take a long, deep breath, and say the problem and how you feel. When you remind yourself to stop and calm down, it's like taking a rest for a minute. You can rest until you feel calm. That is how you can control yourself. And when you can control yourself, then people will say, "Thomas has good self-control. He thinks before he does something that will cause problems". The principal showed Thomas the 3 steps for Calming Down. Then the principal reminded Thomas that the next time he felt upset or angry, he could think about the Control Signals and could calm himself down. Thomas liked the idea and wanted to try it himself. He wanted to do well in school, he wanted his teacher to like him, and he especially wanted to make friends....
On board	Begin drawing on the chalk board. Feelings: comfortable and uncomfortable/ Behavior Ok and not Ok.
Discussion	Ask students to name the different feelings and behavior that Thomas felt and list them under the appropriate categories. Ask them to discuss the relationships between these feelings and behaviors if they are able to do so. Ask students to name the kinds of things that bug them in the classroom, playground, lunchroom, etc., and list them in the categories. This will help students become aware of what they do that bothers others. Ask students if using the 3 Steps to Calm Down would help with any of the things they listed on the board overhead.

Source: Story excerpt reduced for space reasons from Kusche & Greenberg (1995), available for review on www .channingbete.com

Tools and Practice Examples

Learning Self-Control, Volume 5—Supplementary Lesson 93, Grade 3

In the PATHS curriculum, each unit builds on the preceding units. Table 135.3 consists of an excerpt from Supplementary Lesson 93 and is intended for third-graders.

The objective of this lesson is to discuss the idea of self-control as an internalized process. It emphasizes the concept of using thinking to control one's behavior and distinguish between feelings and behaviors. The teacher reads a story about a boy named Thomas who had problems with self-control, was angry, and would get into fights with other children. Throughout the story, students learn the three steps for calming down to gain control of their behavior. The lesson is followed by the teacher drawing a hierarchy of feelings and behaviors on the board and asking questions to encourage classroom discussion. Students are encouraged to talk about how they felt when they acted without thinking first, and to say whether things got out of control and how they felt about the outcome. This lesson teaches students anger management and problem-solving skills through a developmentally appropriate story that is easy to relate to and that facilitates discussion.

MONITORING AND EVALUATING VIOLENCE PREVENTION PROGRAMS

A review of the school safety literature strongly suggests that model school safety programs should be developed and implemented in a process that ensures their relevance and applicability to each specific site. These are important assumptions of the programs described in this chapter:

- Fitting a program to a school involves *grassroots* participation.
- Students and teachers in the school need to be *empowered* to deal with the problem.
- *Democracy* is the core of a good school safety program.
- Schools should demonstrate a *proactive vision* surrounding the violence problem in their school.

Implementing interventions or components of any model program is likely to be slightly different for every school. An eye toward the overall assumptions and flexibility should enable each school to adapt the program or general principles to its unique demographic, philosophical, and organizational needs. Several resources are provided at the end of the chapter to support implementation efforts of programs. It is critically important not only to pay attention to the outcome evaluations but also to keep in mind the importance of program fidelity, advocacy, and support from administration, as well as commitment to the program adoption process. Cissner and Farole (2009) highlight lessons learned from process evaluations of program implementation in the field of juvenile justice that can apply just as readily to schools.

DATA AND PROGRAM EVALUATION

Numerous new programs and systems are designed to create data-driven decision-making processes within districts and schools. One of the more popular programs to address academic learning is Response to Intervention (RTI), whereby students are identified early, provided with intervention, measured for improvement, and referred to special services if there is not adequate "response" to the intervention. Although the programs highlighted in this section were not designed with specific reference to RTI, they do align with the same philosophy of providing early, effective assistance to children who are struggling. Further, each of the programs supports data-driven processes to continually improve the effectiveness of intervention efforts.

An important element of successful school safety programs is the ongoing and interactive use of data. This perspective proposes that the continuous and ongoing analysis and interpretation of data is an essential part of the intervention process. Data are used to create awareness, mobilize various school constituents, assess the extent of the problem, plan and implement interventions, and conduct evaluations. Information is provided on a continuous basis to different groups in each step of the intervention process. Unfortunately, many U.S. schools purchase evidence-based programs but do not collect any data about their own district or school (Benbenishty & Astor, 2012ab; Benbenishty, Astor, & Estrada, 2008).

The process of building and implementing school safety programs is continual and cyclical, always changing to respond to new circumstances and emerging needs. Hence, the evaluation of the program's progress becomes a reassessment of the situation, leading to a new cycle of awareness building, planning, modifying, and evaluating. A school's failure to gather site-specific and comparative data could be a significant obstacle in (a) assessing whether that specific school has a violence problem, (b) adapting a school safety program, and (c) evaluating the implementation process and outcomes of the program.

Monitoring can help create a "whole-school response" and help the school identify, create, and/or adapt programs to the site. Monitoring is the ongoing process of collecting and using data to shape, fit, match, and evaluate the intervention. The value of monitoring comes from the two levels of information processing involved: description and comparison. The description of basic frequency of certain behaviors may be quite instructive. For example, it is helpful to know how many weapon-related events or sexual assaults occur at a specific school.

Using Comparisons

In general, comparisons enhance the value of information by putting it into context. In order to adapt a program, it is imperative to ascertain (a) which acts are more problematic than others, (b) which grade levels are victimized more, and (c) how violence levels in a specific school compare over time and for different ethnic, age, and gender groups. For example, if bullying is not a major problem in the school, it does not make sense to adopt an antibullying program. Perhaps bullying is a problem only in one grade level within a large school, whereas other forms of violence are problems in other grades. Though these concerns may sound like common sense, very few schools actually collect systemic information to ascertain the extent of the school safety problem. Currently, many districts and schools across the United States are purchasing expensive violence prevention programs targeting a specific form of violence (e.g., sexual harassment, bullying, weapon use) without data about the extent of the problem in their schools. This creates a chain of difficulties through the implementation process and later in the evaluation of the program. If the problem was never established, it is difficult to know whether the program ever worked. Hence, it is important to examine levels of violence over time.

Using Mapping as a Monitoring Tool

Mapping is a qualitative tool that can help monitor and generate the kind of comparisons just discussed. Mapping does not require extensive training and can provide valuable information that helps implement, monitor, and assess the ongoing health of a program. This procedure is designed to involve school constituents by revealing how forms of violence within a school building interact with locations, patterns of the school day, and social organizational variables (e.g., teacher–student relationships, teachers' professional roles, and the school's organizational response to violence; for more detail see Astor, Guerra, & Van Acker, 2010; Astor & Meyer, 1999; Astor, Meyer, & Behre, 1999; Astor, Benbenishty, & Meyer, 2004; Astor, Meyer, & Pitner, 2001; Benbenishty & Astor, 2012ab; Pitner, Astor, & Benbenishty, in press). An important goal of this procedure is to allow students and teachers to convey their personal theories about why specific locations and times in their schools are more dangerous. This process greatly facilitates the implementation and evaluation of the model programs reviewed in the first sections of this chapter.

Step-by-Step Instructions for Mapping

Mapping, interviews, and interventions. The first step in this assessment procedure is obtaining a map of the school. Ideally, the map should contain all internal school territory, including the areas surrounding the school and playground. In communities where the routes to and from school are dangerous, a simple map of the surrounding neighborhood may be added to the assessment process. The focus groups should begin with the facilitator distributing two sets of identical school maps to each individual.

Map A and B: Two photocopied maps of the school are needed for each student and teacher. One map should be used to determine where students and teachers think the most events involving violence occur. Participants should also be asked to identify the locations (on the maps) of up to three of the most violent events that have occurred within the past academic year. Next to each marked event on the map, participants should be asked to write the following information: (1) the general time frame of the event (e.g., before school, after school, morning period, afternoon period, evening sports event, between classes), (2) the grade and gender of those involved in the violence, and (3) their knowledge of any organizational response to the event (e.g., someone was sent to principal's office, suspended, sent to peer counselor, nothing done). On the second map, members should be asked to circle areas or territories that they perceive to be unsafe or potentially dangerous. This second map provides information about areas within the school that participants avoid or fear even though they may not possess knowledge of a particular event.

Discussion of violent events and areas. The first part of the group discussion should center on the specific events and the areas marked as unsafe or dangerous on these personal maps. We have asked questions such as "Are there times when those places you've marked on the maps are less safe?" "Is a particular group of students more likely to get hurt there?" and "Why do you think that area has so many incidents?" The overall purpose of the group interviews is to explore why bullying or victimization occurs at those specific times and in those specific spaces. Consequently, the interviews should also focus on gathering information regarding the organizational response to the event (e.g., "What happened to the two students after the event?" or "Did the hall monitors intervene when they saw what happened?"), procedures (e.g., "What happens when the students are sent to the office after a fight?" "Did anyone call the parents of the bully or victim?"), follow-up (e.g., "Do the teachers, hall monitors, and/or administrators follow up on any consequences given to the students?" or "Did anyone check on the welfare of the victim?"), and clarity of procedures (e.g., "Does it matter who stops the bullying?" e.g., a volunteer, security guard, teacher, or principal).

Interviewers should also explore participants' ideas for solutions to the specific violence problems (e.g., "Can you think of ways to avoid bullying or victimization in that place?" or "If you were the principal, what would you do to make that place safer?"). In addition, the interviewer should explore any obstacles that participants foresee with implementation (e.g., "Do you think that type of plan is realistic?" "Has that been tried before? What happened?" or "Do you think that plan would work?"). Such obstacles could range from issues related to roles (e.g., "It's not my job to monitor students during lunch.") to discipline policy and issues of personal safety (e.g., "I don't want to intervene because I may get hurt.").

In schools that have already started model programs designed to address school violence, specific questions should be asked about the effectiveness of those interventions, why they work or do not work, and what could be done to make the current measures more effective. We recommend that the interviewer ask both subjective questions (e.g., "Do you think the antiviolence program is working?" "Why do you think it works, or why does it not work?"), as well as specific questions related to the reduction of victimization (e.g., "Do you believe the antiviolence program has reduced the number of fights/name calling [or any other type of violence the school is interested in preventing] on the playground?" "Why or why not?").

Transferring all of the reported events onto one large map of the school enables students and staff to locate specific "hot spots" for violence and dangerous time periods within each individual school. The combined data are presented to all school constituents, and they are asked to once again discuss and interpret the maps. Teachers and students use the maps and interviews to suggest ways to improve the settings and what aspects of the program are working or not working. For example, in one school, events were clustered by time, age, gender, and location. In the case of older students (eleventh- and twelfth-graders), events were clustered in the parking lot outside of the auxiliary gym immediately after school, whereas for younger students (ninth- and tenth-graders), events were reported in the lunchroom and hallways during transition periods. For this school, the map suggested that interventions be geared specifically toward older students, directly after school, by the main entrance, and in the school parking lot. Students and teachers agreed that increasing the visible presence of school staff in and around the parking lot for the 20 minutes after school had great potential for reducing the number of violent events. Younger students were experiencing violence mainly before, during, and after lunch, near the cafeteria. Many students expressed feelings of being unsafe between classes in the hallways. This school already had an antibullying program, and it was able to incorporate this specific type of intervention into existing activities designed to stem school violence.

Compiling all the interview suggestions into themes is an important second step in adapting context-relevant interventions. Students, teachers, and administrators may have differing viewpoints regarding the organizational response of the school to a violent incident. Relaying the diversity of responses to students, teachers, and administrators can provide an opportunity for reflection and may generate ways to remedy the violence problem in certain situations. When the data are presented to students, teachers, and administrators, they can center their discussions on why those areas are dangerous and what kinds of interventions could make the location safer. Mapping methods provide data-based approaches to gathering information about bullying/victimization in schools. Moreover, they provide site-specific information, which makes it easier for schools to address these problems.

Identifying specific target groups for interventions is another way data can and should be used. A school could use this monitoring system to identify particular problem areas in their school. They could then track progress in reducing violence in these locations over time and by different groups.

In recent years, the Geographical Information Systems (GIS) and Worldwide Web technology provide many more opportunities for mapping violence-related issues both within schools and in the routes to and from schools. For instance, the Los Angeles Unified School district is experimenting with a web-based application used to present students with maps of their school and of its surrounding neighborhood. Students indicate important information on the map, such as places where they hang out, see violent incidents, or avoid because they fear they would get hurt. These maps are then presented with color codes that highlight information that is important for planning interventions focused on dangerous locations.

KEY POINTS TO REMEMBER

Based on our review of programs, it appears that successful school-wide intervention programs have the following core underlying implementation characteristics.

- They are comprehensive, intensive, ecological, and require buy-in from school and community.
- They raise the awareness and responsibility of students, teachers, and parents regarding the types of violence in their schools (e.g., sexual harassment, fighting, and weapons use).
- They create clear guidelines and rules for all members of the school community.
- They target the various social systems in the school and clearly communicate to the entire school community what procedures should be followed before, during, and after violent events.
- They focus on getting the school staff, students, and parents involved in the program.
- They often fit easily into the normal flow and mission of the school setting.
- They use faculty, staff, and parents in the school setting to plan, implement, and sustain the program.
- They increase monitoring and supervision in nonclassroom areas.
- They include ongoing monitoring and mapping, which provide information that schools can use to tailor a program to their specific needs and increase its chance of success.

RESOURCES

Websites on Programs

Olweus Bullying Prevention Program: http://www.clemson.edu/olweus/

Caring School Community: http://devstu.org/caring-school-community
Fast Track: http://www.fasttrackproject.org
PATHS (Promoting Alternative Thinking Strategies): http://www.prevention.psu.edu/projects/PATHS.html

Websites on Additional Programs

Good Behavior Games: http://www.interventioncentral.org/behavioral-interventions/schoolwide-classroommgmt/good-behavior-game
Positive Behavioral Interventions & Supports: http://www.pbis.org/

Websites that Evaluate School Violence Prevention Programs

American Youth Policy Forum: http://www.aypf.org/resource-search/
Bennett Pierce Prevention Research Center (Formerly Prevention Research Center for the Promotion of Human Development): http://www.prevention.psu.edu
Blueprints for Healthy Youth Development Violence Prevention-Center for the Study and Prevention of Violence: http://www.colorado.edu/cspv/blueprints/
National Center for Mental Health Promotion and Youth Violence Prevention: http://www.promoteprevent.org
U.S. Department of Health and Human Services–Substance Abuse and Mental Health Services Administration (SAMHSA) National Registry of Evidence-Based Programs and Practices: http://nrepp.samhsa.gov
U.S. Department of Justice: Office of Justice Programs: Office of Juvenile Justice and Delinquency Prevention–Model Programs Guide: http://www.ojjdp.gov/mpg
U.S. Department of Justice–National Criminal Justice Reference Service Report: Preventing Crime: What Works, What Doesn't, What's Promising. University of Maryland Department of Criminology and Criminal Justice (Sherman, Gottfredson, MacKenzie, Eck, Reuter, & Bushway, 1998) NCJ 165366: https://www.ncjrs.gov/works Main website: http://www.ncjrs.gov

Youth Violence: A Report of the Surgeon
   General: http://www.ncbi.nlm.nih.gov/
   books/NBK44294/

Other Resources and Reports

Centers for Disease Control and
   Prevention: Best Practices of Youth
   Violence Prevention: A Sourcebook for
   Community Action: http://www.cdc.gov/
   violenceprevention/pdf/introduction-a.pdf
Centers for Disease Control and
   Prevention: Injury Prevention and
   Control: Violence Prevention: Youth
   Violence Prevention Strategies: http://www
   .cdc.gov/violenceprevention/youthviolence/
   prevention.html
Collaborative for Academic, Social, and
   Emotional Learning (CASEL): http://www
   .casel.org
Development Services Group: http://www
   .dsgonline.com
Hamilton Fish Institute on School and
   Community Violence: http://gwired.gwu
   .edu/hamfish
Indicators of School Crime and
   Safety—2012: National Center for Education
   Statistics: http://nces.ed.gov/pubsearch/
   pubsinfo.asp?pubid=2013036
National School Safety Center: http://www
   .schoolsafety.us/

References

Astor, R. A., Benbenishty, R., & Estrada, J. (2009). School violence and theoretically atypical schools: The principal's centrality in orchestrating safe schools. *American Educational Research Journal, 46*, 423–461.

Astor, R. A., Benbenishty, R., Marachi, R., & Pitner, R. (2009). Evidence-based violence prevention programs and best implementation practices. In A. Roberts (Ed.), *Social workers' desk reference* (2nd ed.) (pp. 985–1003). New York, NY: Oxford University Press.

Astor, R. A., Benbenishty, R., & Meyer, H. A. (2004). Monitoring and mapping student victimization in schools. *Theory into Practice, 43*(1), 39–49.

Astor, R. A., Guerra, N., & Van Acker, R. (2010). How can we improve school safety research? *Educational Researcher, 39*, 69–78.

Astor, R. A., & Meyer, H. (1999). Where girls and women won't go: Female students', teachers', and social workers' views of school safety. *Social Work in Education, 21*, 201–219.

Astor, R. A., Meyer, H., & Behre, W. J. (1999). Unowned places and times: Maps and interviews about violence in high schools. *American Educational Research Journal, 36*, 3–42.

Astor, R. A., Meyer, H. A., & Pitner, R. O. (2001). Elementary and middle school students' perceptions of safety: An examination of violence-prone school sub-contexts. *The Elementary School Journal, 101*, 511–528.

Battistich, V. (2008). The Child Development Project: Creating caring school communities. In L. Nucci & D. Narvaez (Eds.), *Handbook of moral and character education* (pp. 328–351). New York, NY: Routledge.

Battistich, V., Schaps, E., & Wilson, N., (2004). Effects of an elementary school intervention on students' "connectedness" to school and social adjustment during middle school. *The Journal of Primary Prevention, 24*, 243–262.

Battistich, V., Schaps, E., Watson, M., & Solomon, D. (1996). Prevention effects of the child development project: Early findings from an ongoing multi-site demonstration trial. *Journal of Adolescent Research, 11*, 12–35.

Battistich, V., Schaps, E., Watson, M., Solomon, D., & Lewis, C. (2000). Effects of the child development project on students' drug use and other problem behaviors. *The Journal of Primary Prevention, 21*, 75–99.

Battistich, V., Solomon, D., Watson, M., & Schaps, E. (1997). Caring school communities. *Educational Psychologist, 32*, 137–151.

Benbenishty, R., & Astor, R. A. (2012a). Making the case for an international perspective on school violence: Implications for theory, research, policy, and assessment. In S. R. Jimerson, A. B. Nickerson, M. J. Mayer & M. J. Furlong (Eds.), *Handbook of school violence and school safety: International research and practice* (2nd ed.) (pp. 15–26). New York, NY: Routledge.

Benbenishty, R., & Astor, R. A. (2012b). Monitoring school violence in Israel, National studies and beyond: Implications for theory, practice, and policy. In S. R. Jimerson, A. B. Nickerson, M. J. Mayer, & M. J. Furlong (Eds.), *Handbook of school violence and school safety: International research and practice.* (2nd ed.) (pp. 191–202). New York, NY: Routledge.

Benbenishty, R., & Astor, R. A. (2005). *School violence in context: Culture, neighborhood, family, school, and gender.* New York, NY: Oxford University Press.

Benbenishty, R., Astor, R. A., & Estrada, J. N. (2008). School violence assessment: A conceptual framework, instruments and methods. *Children & Schools, 30*, 71–81.

Chang, F., & Munoz, M. A. (2006). School personnel educating the whole child: Impact of character education on teachers' self-assessment and student development. *Journal of Personnel Evaluation in Education, 19,* 35–49.

Chen, J. K., & Astor, R.A. (2012). School variables as mediators of the effect of personal and family factors on school violence in Taiwanese junior high schools. *Youth & Society, 44,* 175–200.

Cissner, A. B., & Farole, D. J., Jr. (2009). *Best practices: Avoiding failures of implementation: Lessons from process evaluations.* Washington, DC: Center for Court Innovation, Bureau of Justice Assistance, U.S. Department of Justice.

Conduct Problems Prevention Research Group. (2010a). The Fast Track Project: The prevention of severe conduct problems in school-age youth. In R. C. Murrihy, A. D. Kidman, & T. H. Ollendick (Eds.), *Handbook of clinical assessment and treatment of conduct problems in youth* (pp. 407–443). New York, NY: Springer.

Conduct Problems Prevention Research Group. (2010b). The effects of a multiyear universal social-emotional learning program: The role of student and school characteristics. *Journal of Consulting and Clinical Psychology, 78,* 156–168.

Conduct Problems Prevention Research Group. (2011). The effects of the Fast Track preventive intervention on the development of conduct disorder across childhood. *Child Development, 82*(1), 331–345.

Developmental Studies Center. (1995). *Child Development Project.* Retrieved from http://www.ed.gov/pubs/EPTW/eptw5/eptw5a.html.

Developmental Studies Center. (2004). *Comprehensive Program: The Child Development Project.* Retrieved from http://www.devstu.org/cdp/imp_prof_devt.html

Green, J., Furlong, M., Astor, R. A., Benbenishty, R., & Espinoza, E. (2011). Assessing school victimization in the United States, Guatemala, and Israel: Cross-cultural psychometric analysis of the School Victimization Scale. *Victims and Offenders, 6,* 1–16.

Greenberg, M. T., & Kusche, C. A. (1998). Preventive interventions for school-age deaf children: The PATHS curriculum. *Journal of Deaf Studies & Deaf Education, 3,* 49–63.

Greenberg, M. T., Kusche, C. A., Cook, E. T., & Quamma, J. P. (1995). Promoting emotional competence in school-aged children: The effects of the PATHS curriculum. *Development & Psychopathology. Special Issue: Emotions in Developmental Psychopathology. 7,* 117–136.

Greenberg, M. T., Kusché, C., & Mihalic, S. F. (1998). *Blueprints for violence prevention, Book Ten: Promoting Alternative Thinking Strategies (PATHS).* Boulder, CO: Center for the Study and Prevention of Violence.

Hunter, S., Boyle, J., & Warden, D. (2007). Perceptions and correlates of peer-victimization and bullying. *British Journal of Educational Psychology, 77,* 797–810.

Limber, S. (2012). The Olweus Bullying Prevention Program: An overview of its implementation and research basis. In S. Jimerson, A. Nickerson, M. Mayer, & M. Furlong (Eds.), *Handbook of school violence and school safety: International research and practice* (2nd ed.) (pp. 369–381). New York, NY: Routledge.

Marachi, R., Astor, R., & Benbenishty, R. (2013). Evidence-based violence prevention programs and best practices. In C. Franklin, M. Harris, & P. Allen-Meares (Eds.), *The school services sourcebook: A guide for school-based professionals* (2nd ed.) (pp. 453–472). New York, NY: Oxford University Press.

Marshall, J., & Caldwell, S. (2007). Caring School Community implementation study four-year evaluation report. Rapid City, SD: Marshall Consulting.

Northwest Regional Educational Laboratory. (1998). *The catalog of school reform models.* Retrieved from http://www.nwrel.org/scpd/catalog/ModelDetails.asp?ModelID=6

Olweus, D. (1993). *Bullying at school: What we know and what we can do.* Oxford: Blackwell Publishers.

Olweus, D., & Limber, S. (2010a). Bullying in school: Evaluation and dissemination of the Olweus Bullying Prevention Program. *American Journal of Orthopsychiatry, 80,* 124–134.

Olweus, D., & Limber, S. (2010b). The Olweus Bullying Prevention Program: Implementation and evaluation over two decades. In S. R. Jimerson, S. M. Swearer, & D. L. Espelage (Eds.), *Handbook of bullying in schools: An international perspective* (pp. 377–401). New York, NY: Routledge.

Pitner, R., Astor, R., & Benbenishty, R. (In Press). Violence in schools. In P. Allen-Meares (Ed.) *Social work services in school* (7th ed.). Boston, MA: Pearson.

Rigby, K. (2006). What we can learn from evaluated studies of school-based programs to reduce bullying in schools. In S. Jimerson & M. Furlong (Eds.), *Handbook of school violence and school safety: From research to practice* (pp. 325–337). Mahwah, NJ: Lawrence Erlbaum Associates Publishers.

Riggs, N., Greenberg, M. Kusche, C., & Pentz, M. (2006). The mediational role of neurocognition in the behavioral outcomes of a socio-emotional prevention program in elementary school students: Effects of the PATHS curriculum. *Prevention Science, 7,* 91–102.

Substance Abuse and Mental Health Services Administration (SAMHSA). (2003). Model Program, Anger management for substance abuse and mental health clients. Washington, DC. SAMHSA.

Shiff, M., Pat-Horenczyk, R., Benbenishty, R., Brom, D., Baum, N., & Astor, R. A. (2010). Do adolescents know that they need help in the aftermath of war? *Journal of Traumatic Stress, 23*, 657–660.

Vreeman, R., & Carroll, A. (2007). A systematic review of school-based interventions to prevent bullying.

Archives of Pediatric Adolescent Medicine, 161, 78–88.

Watson, M., & Battistich, V. (2006). Building and sustaining caring communities. In C. Evertson & C. Weinstein (Eds.), *Handbook of classroom management: Research, practice and contemporary issues* (pp. 253–279). Mahwah, NJ: Lawrence Erlbaum.

136 Solution-focused Brief Therapy Interventions for Students at Risk to Drop Out

Cynthia Franklin, Johnny S. Kim, Michael S. Kelly, & Stephen J. Tripodi

Solution-focused brief therapy (SFBT) is a popular approach used with students in school settings by school social workers. A review of the literature reveals that solution-focused brief therapy has been increasing over the past decade in school settings and applied to a number of problems including student behavioral and emotional issues, academic problems, social skills, and drop-out prevention (Berg & Shilts, 2005; Franklin, Biever, Moore, Clemons, & Scamardo, 2001; Franklin & Hopson, 2009; Franklin, Streeter, Kim, & Tripodi, 2007; Kral, 1995; Metcalf, 1995; Murphy, 1996; Murphy & Duncan, 2007; Sklare, 1997; Webb, 1999). Because of its brief nature and flexibility in working with diverse problems, SFBT can be a practical intervention approach for school social workers to use (Franklin et al., 2001; Kelly, Kim, & Franklin, 2008; Newsome, 2004). This chapter describes SFBT and the growing research evidence available, and further illustrates the steps and techniques involved in implementing this approach.

SOLUTION-FOCUSED BRIEF THERAPY

Solution-focused Brief Therapy differs in many ways from traditional approaches to treatment by focusing on clients' strengths and previous successes rather than dwelling on the current problem. There is a focus on working from the client's understandings of her/his concern and what the client might want to be different in his/her life. The basic tenets that inform Solution-focused Brief Therapy are as follows:

- It is based on solution-building rather than problem-solving.
- The therapeutic focus should be on the client's desired future rather than on past problems or current conflicts.
- Clients are encouraged to increase the frequency of current useful behaviors.
- No problem happens all the time. There are exceptions—that is, times when the problem could have happened but did not—that

can be used by the client and therapist to co-construct solutions.

- Therapists help clients find alternatives to current undesired patterns of behavior, cognition, and interaction that are within the clients' repertoire or can be co-constructed by therapists and clients as such.
- Differing from skill-building and behavior therapy interventions, the model assumes that solution behaviors already exist for clients.
- It is asserted that small increments of change lead to large increments of change, and this may lead to a solution.
- Clients' solutions are not necessarily *directly* related to any identified problem by either the client or the therapist but are created through the process of setting goals and deciding on specific ways to achieve those goals.
- Therapists use a purposeful conversational approach in building solutions with clients. The conversational skills used in SFBT focus on solution-talk and co-construction of communication, which means social workers ask questions and focus on specific words that clients say in order to shape meanings and interactions toward solutions. Co-construction and other core communication processes used in SFBT are described in detail within a treatment manual that has been developed by international researchers and experts on solution-focused practice. This treatment manual is available at the Solution-focused Brief Therapy Association website (sfbta.org).

The development of SFBT originated in the early 1980s at the Brief Family Therapy Center in Milwaukee with two social work practitioners, Steve de Shazer and Insoo Kim Berg, as well as a group of practitioner/researchers who were studying therapies behind a one-way mirror. Some important researchers were involved in the early study of this approach, such as Wally Gingerich, who also did the first systematic review of SFBT research (Gingerich & Eisengart, 2000). Berg and de Shazer wanted to answer the question, "What works in therapy?" These practitioners were interested not only in the change process but also in how to help clients change efficiently and effectively. SFBT was influenced by the Mental Research Institute Brief Therapy model and the family systems therapy approaches of the day and had

theoretical roots in ecosystems theories. Later, in the 1990s, SFBT became strongly associated with social construction models and social constructivist views within family systems therapies. Readers are referred to other chapters in this volume that review brief therapy, family systems, and constructivist theoretical perspectives and practice approaches in more detail. SFBT became popular and widely used in mental health practice in the 1990s mostly due to the demands for briefer counseling interventions. SFBT has grown exponentially since that time with over 50 books in print on SFBT, SFBT associations in over 10 countries, and several annual national and international conferences devoted to SFBT (Kelly et al., 2008).

Solution-focused Brief Therapy's Emergence in Schools

Practitioners began to use the SFBT techniques in schools during the 1990s with the first publications and small research studies appearing in print around the mid-1990s (e.g., Kral, 1995; LaFountain & Garner, 1996; Metcalf, 1995; Murphy, 1996; Sklare, 1997). Since that time, the SFBT literature for school practitioners across disciplines has been growing (e.g., Berg & Shilts, 2005; Franklin & Gerlach, 2007; Kelly et al., 2008; Metcalf, 2008; Murphy, 2008; Murphy & Duncan, 2007; Webb, 1999) with increasing reports of SFBT interventions and programs being implemented in schools in both the United States and Europe (Kelly et al., 2008).

School-based interventions may be implemented at various levels of the school's programs and with different groups within the school environment. For example, the techniques of SFBT have been used to:

- Help at-risk students in individual, group, and family interventions (Murphy, 2008).
- Coach teachers in using solution-building talk (see the WWOW program, Kelly et al., 2008).
- Change interactions among parents, teachers, and students, such as parent/teacher meetings (Metcalf, 1995, 2008).
- Change the school culture, such as when an entire school adopts the solution-focused change philosophy and trains all staff (including teachers and principals) in SFBT techniques (Franklin & Streeter, 2003, cited in Kelly et al., 2008).

Franklin and Gerlach (2007) summarize reasons why SFBT may be a good match for public school settings. First, public schools frequently serve high-risk populations, such as homeless teens, immigrants, and teen parents. Many students referred for services in the school may also be considered mandated or involuntary clients, and SFBT is an approach to helping that was developed for the purposes of being effective with at-risk populations. Second, schools often face students with multiple challenges, yet have little time or money for therapy and require very practical solutions to the day-to-day issues that may prevent the educational achievement of a student. SFBT focuses on practical goals using active listening and strengths assessment and facilitates collaboration with others involved in the student's life. Finally, SFBT is very flexible and open to the use of techniques from other therapeutic interventions if they are used thoughtfully to accommodate the student's goals (Franklin & Gerlach, 2007).

THE GROWING EMPIRICAL SUPPORT FOR SOLUTION-FOCUSED BRIEF THERAPY IN SCHOOLS

Kim and Franklin (2009) recently reviewed the literature on SFBT in schools within the United States. This systematic review focused on examining the most rigorous studies that used experimental designs, with standardized measures, and met criteria for a solution-focused intervention. Table 136.1 summarizes the results of that review.

Table 136.1 indicates that one experimental design study, six quasiexperimental design studies, and one single-case design study on SFBT in schools have been published since 2000. Most of these studies have arrived within the past two years, perhaps suggesting that more school researchers are conducting outcome studies on SFBT.

Kim and Franklin's (2009) review indicated that SFBT is a promising and useful approach in working with at-risk students in a school setting. Some of the positive findings from the systematic review are as follows:

- Helps students reach goals
- Helps students alleviate their concerns
- Improves academic achievement (e.g., credits earned)

- Helps students reduce the intensity of their negative feelings
- Helps students reduce drug use
- Helps students manage their conduct problems (Franklin et al., 2001; Franklin & Gerlach, 2007; Froeschle, Smith, & Ricard, 2007; Kelly et al., 2008; Newsome, 2004).

The Kim and Franklin (2009) systematic review revealed some mixed results, but enough positive differences were found favoring SFBT to view it as a promising intervention for school settings. The effect sizes calculated by the authors and reported in the individual studies also show SFBT to be promising, with most studies having medium and some large effect sizes.

SOLUTION-BUILDING HELPING PROCESS AND TECHNIQUES

SFBT is a strengths-based approach that helps school social workers build solutions together with their students. The solution-focused helping process, often referred to as solution building, is a purposeful conversation resulting in changes in perceptions and social interactions. The solution-building process or conversation is often contrasted with the problem-solving process. However, Harris and Franklin (2008) have pointed out that it shares values and some similarities with social problem solving and task-centered types of problem solving. The differences, however, are also noteworthy. Approaches to problem solving, for example, focus on the resolution of problems through understanding the problems, enumerating alternatives that can solve the problems, and choosing an alternative. In contrast, solution building changes the way people think about presenting problems and identify future behaviors and tasks that have the potential to accomplish desired goals and outcomes (De Jong & Berg, 2008). SFBT has developed a number of techniques that are used in solution building to guide students in the change process. Box 136.1 defines and illustrates several of the counseling techniques.

SFBT has developed its own structure for social work interviews that is used to guide the change process. The session may be thought of as being a continuous process of elements that are structured in process sequences. De Jong (Chapter 35) defines this structure of the solution-focused interview and the follow-up sessions. Thinking

TABLE 136.1 Solution-focused Brief Therapy Studies in Schools

Study	Design	Outcome Measure	Sample Size	Sample Population	Results
Springer, Lynch, Rubin (2000)	Quasiexperimental	Hare Self-Esteem Scale	10	Hispanic elementary students	SFBT group made significant improvements on the Hare Self-Esteem Scale, whereas the comparison group's scores remained the same. However, no significant differences were found between the SFBT and comparison groups at the end of the study on the self-esteem scale.
Franklin et al. (2001)	Single case	Conners' Teacher Rating Scale	7	Middle school students 10–12 years old	Five of seven (71%) improved per teachers report.
Newsome (2004)	Quasiexperimental	Grades; attendance	52	Middle school students	Statistically significant results with SFBT group increasing mean score of 1.58 to a mean score of 1.69 while grades for the comparison group decreased from a mean score of 1.66 to a score of 1.48. No difference on attendance measure.
Corcoran (2006)	Quasiexperimental	Conners' Parent Rating Scale; Feelings, Attitudes, & Behaviors Scale for Children	86	Students aged 5–17 years	No significant differences between groups, with both improving at post-test. This lack of difference may be because the comparison group received treatment as usual, which had many cognitive-behavior therapy components that have been empirically validated.
Franklin, Moore, & Hopson (2008)	Quasiexperimental	Child Behavior Checklist (CBCL)—Youth Self Report Form—Internalizing, & CBCL Externalizing; Teacher's Report Form—Internalizing & Externalizing Score	67	Middle school students	Internalizing & Externalizing score for the Teacher Report Form showed SFBT group declined below clinical level by post-test and remained there at follow-up while comparison group changed little. Internalizing score for the Youth Self Report Form showed no difference between the groups. Externalizing score showed SFBT group dropped below the clinical level and continued to drop at follow-up.

Franklin, Streeter, Kim, & Tripodi (2007)	Quasiexperimental	Grades; attendance	85	At-risk high school students	SFBT sample had statistically significant higher average proportion of credits earned to credits attempted than the comparison sample. Both groups decreased in the attendance mean per semester; the comparison group, however, showed a higher proportion of school days attended to school days for the semester. Authors suggested that the attendance between groups may not be a fair comparison because the SFBT group worked on a self-paced curriculum and could decrease their attendance when completed.
Froeschle, Smith, & Ricard (2007)	Experimental design	American Drug & Alcohol Survey Substance Abuse; Subtle Screening Inventory Adolescent version 2; Knowledge exam on physical symptoms of drug use; Piers-Harris Children's Self-Concept Scale version 2; Home & Community Social Behavior Scales; School Social Behavior Scales, 2nd ed.; grade point average	65	8th grade females	Statistically significant differences were found favoring SFBT group on drug use, attitudes toward drugs, knowledge of physical symptoms of drug use, and competent behavior scores as observed by both parents and teachers. No group differences were found on self-esteem, negative behaviors as measured by office referrals, and grade point averages.

Source: From Kelly, Kim, & Franklin, 2008. Adapted with permission of the authors.

Box 136.1 Solution-focused Brief Therapy Techniques for Solution-focused Schools

Exception Questions—Questions to explore past experiences in a student's life when the student's problem might reasonably have been expected to occur but somehow did not or was less severe.

- *When does the problem not occur?*
- *What was different about those times when things were better between you and your teacher?*
- *Even though this is a very bad time, in my experience, people's lives do not always stay the same. I will bet that there are times when the problem of being sent to the principal's office is not happening, or at least is happening less. Please describe those times. What is different? How did you get that to happen?*

Relationship Questions—Relationship questions allow students to discuss their problems from a third person point of view. This sequence of questions makes the problem less threatening and allows the school social worker, counselor, or teacher to assess the student's viewpoints, and the student to practice thinking about the problem from the viewpoint of others.

- *What would your teacher say about your grades?*
- *What would your mother say?*
- *If you were to do something that made your teacher very happy, what would that be?*

Scaling Questions—Scaling questions are a sequence of questions used to determine where students are in terms of achieving their goals. The school social worker has the option to use scaling questions to quantify and measure the intensity of internal thoughts and feelings along with helping a student anchor reality and move forward from his or her goals (Franklin & Nurius, 1998; Pichot & Dolan, 2003). Numerous variations of this technique can be used, such as asking for percentages of progress, or using smiling and frowning faces for small children.

- *On a scale from one to ten, with one being the lowest and ten being the highest, where would you rate yourself in terms of reaching your goals that you identified last week?*
- *On a scale from one to ten, with one being that you never go to class and ten being that you have perfect attendance, where would you put yourself on that scale? What would it take to move up two numbers on the scale?*
- *On a scale of one to ten with one being that you are getting into trouble every day in the class and ten being that you are doing all your school work and not getting into trouble, where would you be on that scale?*

The Miracle Question—The miracle question strengthens the student's goals by allowing them to reconstruct their story, imagining a future without the student's perceived problem (Berg & De Jong, 1996; De Jong & Berg, 2001). Additionally, the school social worker uses the miracle question to help students identify ways that the solution may already be occurring in their lives.

> *Now, I want to ask you a strange question. This is probably a question no one has asked you before. Suppose that while you are sleeping tonight a miracle happens and the problem that brought you here is solved. However, because you are sleeping, you don't know that the miracle has happened. So, when you wake up tomorrow morning, what will be the first thing you notice that is different—that will tell you a miracle has happened and the problem that brought you here is solved?*

Goal Setting/Goaling—The act of setting goals is used as a verb in SFBT, and is sometimes referred to in the literature as "goaling." Goals are considered the beginning of behavior change, not the end. The school social worker and the student negotiate small, observable goals, set within a brief time frame, that lead to a new story for the student. A goal should describe what a student is to do instead of describe the problem behavior. The negotiation of goals should start immediately between the school social worker and student.

Break for Reflection—Taken near the end of the session to help formulate a positive ending to the session.

Compliments and a Set of Take-away Tasks—Continuous affirmation of the student's strengths and character and suggested behavioral tasks that reinforce client solutions.

You did that?
I am amazed.
How did that make you feel?
I bet your mother was pretty proud of you!
That seemed to work! Do you think you could do that again?

Source: from Franklin, Kim, & Tripodi, 2006.

of student interviews in this way may help the school social worker guide the client toward a purposeful solution-building conversation and offer a framework for how to apply the various techniques of the solution-focused approach. See Table 136.2 for a quick guide concerning conversations using the SFBT session structure, including ways to use various solution-focused techniques in the change process.

An SFBT session structure must be flexible enough to adapt to the individual needs of each student but also structured enough to provide guidance to school social workers about the change process.

CASE STUDY

Franklin, Kim, and Tripodi (2006) suggest that most solution-focused interviews occur during the traditional 50-minute session. In schools, however, these interviews may last for shorter periods of time, 20–30 minutes, for example. Regardless of the time, the structure of the SFBT interview may be divided into three parts. The first part usually is spent making small talk with the student to find out a little bit about his or her life. During this first part, the school social worker may be looking to understand the student's interests, motivations, competencies, and belief systems. The following case example provided by Franklin et al. (2006) illustrates the structure of a solution-focused session in schools and several techniques.

Social Worker: Hello, Charles. I understand your teacher, Mrs. Park, sent you here to see me because you're at risk of failing out of school. But I'd like to hear from you the reason you are here to see me and how this can help you? [Allows student to state what the problem is.]

Student: I don't know. I hate this school and I just want to drop out so that people will leave me alone.

SW: So, if I understand you correctly, you're here to see me because you hate the school, and a lot of people—your teachers and maybe your parents—have been bugging you about your grades and doing homework?

S: Yeah.

SW: So what sorts of things do you like to do when you're not in school?

S: Ummm, I like to hang out with my friends.

SW: What do you and your friends talk about when you're hanging out?

S: I don't know. We talk about basketball and music and stuff. [Social worker will continue to develop rapport and try to find out student's interests and belief systems.]

The second part of the session, which takes up the bulk of the time—around 40 minutes in traditional sessions but maybe shorter in school interviews—is spent discussing the problem, looking for exceptions, and formulating goals. One of the key components to SFBT that has been emphasized in this chapter is working with the student to identify the problem, look for times when the problem is absent, look for ways the solution is already occurring, and develop attainable goals to help resolve the problem. This second part is usually initiated with questions like, "How can I help you?" or "What is the reason you have come to see me?" or "How will you know when counseling is no longer necessary?" (Sklare, 1997).

SW: OK, so how can I help you or what can you get out of our meeting today so that you know it's been worth your time to see me?

S: I want my teachers and my parents to stop bugging me about my grades and doing homework. This school is just a waste of my time, and my classes are stupid.

SW: Is there a class that you didn't think was stupid or a waste of time? [example of looking for exceptions].

TABLE 136.2 Structure of Solution-focused Brief Therapy Interviews

	Begin Session →	Exploring Solutions →	Assessing Progress →	Reflection Break →	End Session
Goals of the Stage	• Rapport building; • Shift focus away from problem talk; • Support student.	• School social worker and student build solutions together; • Have student take responsibility for their own solutions; • Discussion is on possible solutions in concrete behavioral details.	• Continue to provide compliments; • Create small, attainable, concrete goals; • Explore steps to achieving the goals.	• Continue supporting student; • Reflect on student's strengths and resources; • Identify future steps.	• Assess whether to schedule another appointment; • Lay groundwork for future sessions.
Questions To Ask	*How can I help you?* *What has to happen while talking with me today that will make it worth your time to come?*	*What kinds of things have you done in the past that have worked for you?* *What would be different about the problem in your life?* *When is the problem better? Even a little bit?*	*What would your parents say about your progress?* *Who would be the most surprised if you did well on that test?* *What would your friends say is the biggest change they've noticed in you?*	*I'd like to take a minute to think about what we've discussed. Would that be all right with you?*	*Has this been helpful?* *What has been helpful for you about our meeting?* *Would you like to meet again?*
Keys Points To Remember and SFBT Techniques	• Use student's words and metaphors; • Focus on student's definition of the problem.	• Use exception questions; • Use miracle question to elicit details of student's goals; • Focus on strengths.	• Elicit incidents of small changes students have made; • Use scaling questions; • Use relationship questions.	• Formulate 4–5 genuine compliments for student; • Formulate tasks towards the solution; • Formulate possible homework assignment.	• Client and school social worker both determine whether to meet again.

S: My English class last year was cool because we got to read some interesting books and have good discussions about them.

SW: What made the books interesting and the discussions good?

S: Well, they were books that I could understand and relate to. My teacher also made the time and effort to explain things to us and made sure we all got a turn to speak our thoughts.

SW: You said you hated this school, but yet you haven't dropped out yet. How have you managed to do that? [Allows student to identify possible solutions and possible successes they've already achieved.]

S: Well, I'm still going to some of my classes, but at this point I just don't care anymore.

SW: Charles, for those classes that you do attend, what would your teacher say about your academic work? [example of relationship question].

S: I guess they might say that I don't pay attention in class, that I don't do my homework, and that I'm not trying.

SW: Do you agree with that?

S: I guess, but it's just that the classes are so stupid and boring.

SW: I'd like to ask you an unusual question. It's probably something no one has ever asked you before. Suppose, after we're done and you leave my office, you go to bed tonight and a miracle happens. This miracle solves all the problems that brought you here today but because you were sleeping, you didn't know it occurred. So the next morning you wake up and you sense something is different. What will you notice that is different that lets you know this miracle occurred and your problems are solved? [example of the miracle question].

S: I guess I wouldn't be cutting class and maybe getting better grades.

SW: What will you be doing differently to get better grades?

S: I would probably be better prepared for class.

SW: What does being better prepared for class look like? [Continue to probe and elicit more details and examples.]

S: I'd pay attention in class and take some notes.

SW: What else will you be doing differently when you're getting better grades?

S: Probably doing my homework and not causing trouble in class with the teacher.

SW: So, what will you being doing instead of causing trouble in class?

S: Listen and sit there and take notes, I guess.

SW: So on a scale from 1 to 10, with 1 being "I'm dropping out of school no matter what" and 10 being "the miracle solved my problems and I'm going to graduate," where would you say you are right now? [example of a scaling question].

S: Three.

SW: What sorts of things prevent you from giving it a 2 or a 1?

S: Well, I know I need to get my high school diploma because I always thought I might go study how to be a med tech at college. I like *CSI* and want to work in forensics.

SW: Wow! You want to study forensics. So, you need to finish school for that. So, what would need to happen for you to be a 4 or a 5?

S: I'd need to start coming to classes and doing my work [examples of student identifying goals and solutions]. [Social worker would continue looking for solutions that are already occurring in Charles's life and collaborate on identifying and setting small, attainable goals.]

The final part of the session lasts around 5–10 minutes. It involves giving the student a set of compliments, homework, and determining whether to continue discussing this topic at another time. In school settings, practitioners such as teachers and social workers have separated this last part from the rest of the conversation. The break, for example, might be extended, and the conversation might pick up in different class periods or at a different times of the day (e.g., before and after lunch).

SW: I'd like to take a minute to write down some notes based on what we've talked about. Is there anything else you feel I should know before I take this quick break?

S: No.

SW: [after taking a break] Well, Charles, I'd like to compliment you on your commitment to staying in school despite your frustrations. You seem like a bright student and understand the importance of finishing high school. I'd like to meet with you again to continue our work together. Would that be all right with you?

S: Sure.

SW: So for next week, I'd like you to try and notice when things are going a little bit better in your classes and what you're doing differently during those times.

FUTURE APPLICATIONS

SFBT has been used in schools since the 1990s, and promising empirical support is emerging on this approach. SFBT is a practical, brief intervention for school settings and can help school social workers engage and work with students on diverse problem areas. This approach builds on student strengths and competencies and shows respect for each person. SFBT offers conversational, questioning techniques that help school social workers engage students in a solution-building process that helps students discover goals, tasks, and behaviors that change future outcomes. The future is what SFBT focuses on, and this future focus is perhaps one of its distinguishing characteristics. When applying SFBT, a school social worker must act as a coach and a facilitator who creates an interpersonal context where the solutions emerge from the student. As the case example illustrated, SFBT offers an interview structure and a set of counseling techniques that help social workers successfully facilitate the solution-building process in schools.

WEBSITES

Garza High School, A Solution-Focused High School. http://www.austinschools.org/garza.
Solution-Focused Brief Therapy Association. http://www.sfbta.org.

References

Berg, I. K., & De Jong, P. (1996). Solution-building conversation: Co-constructing a sense of competence with clients. *Families in Society, 77*, 376–391.

Berg, I. K., & Shilts, L. (2005). *Classroom solutions: Woww approach.* Milwaukee, WI: Brief Family Therapy Center.

Corcoran, J. (2006). A comparison group study of solution-focused therapy versus "treatment-as-usual" for behavior problems in children. *Journal of Social Service Research, 33*, 69–81.

De Jong, P., & Berg, I. K. (2001). Co-constructing cooperation with mandated clients. *Social Work, 46*, 361–381.

De Jong, P., & Berg, I. K. (2008). *Interviewing for solutions* (3rd ed.). Pacific Grove, CA: Brooks/Cole.

Franklin, C., Biever, J., Moore, K., Clemons, D., & Scamardo, M. (2001). The effectiveness of solution-focused therapy with children in a school setting. *Research on Social Work Practice, 11*, 411–434.

Franklin, C., & Gerlach, B. (2007). Solution-focused brief therapy in public school settings. In T. S. Nelson & F. N. Thomas (Eds.), *Handbook of solution-focused therapy: Clinical applications* (p. 169). New York, NY: Haworth.

Franklin, C., & Hopson, L. (2009). Involuntary clients in public schools: Solution-focused interventions. In R. Rooney (Ed.), *Strategies for work with involuntary clients* (2nd ed.). New York, NY: Columbia University Press.

Franklin, C., Kim, J. S., & Tripodi, S. J. (2006). Solution-focused brief therapy interventions for students at-risk to drop out. In C. Franklin, M. B. Harris, & P. Allen-Meares (pp. 691–704). *The school services sourcebook.* New York, NY: Oxford University Press.

Franklin, C., Moore, K., & Hopson, L. M. (2008). Effectiveness of solution-focused brief therapy in a school setting. *Children and Schools, 30*, 15–26.

Franklin, C., & Nurius, P. (1998). Distinction between social constructionism and cognitive constructivism: Practice applications. In C. Franklin & P. Nurius (Eds.), *Constructivism in practice: Methods and challenges* (pp. 57–94). Milwaukee, WI: Families International.

Franklin, C., & Streeter, C. L. (2003). *Creating solution-focused accountability schools for the 21st century: A training manual for Garza High School.* Austin: University of Texas, Hogg Foundation for Mental Health.

Franklin, C., Streeter, C. L., Kim, J. S., & Tripodi, S. J. (2007). The effectiveness of a solution-focused, public alternative school for dropout prevention and retrieval. *Children and Schools, 29*, 133–144.

Froeschle, J. G., Smith, R. L., & Ricard, R. (2007). The efficacy of a systematic substance abuse program for adolescent females. *Professional School Counseling, 10*, 498–505.

Gingerich, W., & Eisengart, S. (2000). Solution-focused brief therapy: A review of outcome research. *Family Process, 39*, 477–496.

Harris, M. B., & Franklin, C. (2008). *Taking charge: A school-based life skills program for adolescent mothers.* New York, NY: Oxford University Press.

Kelly, M. S., Kim, J. S., & Franklin, C. (2008). *Solution-focused brief therapy in schools: A 360-degree view of the research and practice principles.* New York, NY: Oxford University Press.

Kim, J. S., & Franklin, C. (2009). Solution-focused brief therapy in schools: A review of the literature. *Children and Youth Services Review, 31*, 464–470.

Kral, R. (1995). *Strategies that work: Techniques for solutions in schools.* Milwaukee, WI: Brief Family Therapy Press.

LaFountain, R. M., & Garner, N. E. (1996). Solution-focused counseling groups: The results are in. *Journal for Specialists in Group Work, 21*, 128–143.

Metcalf, L. (1995). *Counseling toward solutions: A practical solution-focused program for working with students, teachers, and parents.* San Francisco, CA: Jossey-Bass.

Metcalf, L. (2008). *Counseling toward solutions: A practical solution-focused program for working with students, teachers, and parents* (2nd ed.). San Francisco, CA: Jossey-Bass.

Murphy, J. (1996). Solution-focused brief therapy in the schools. In S. Miller, M. Hubble, & B. Duncan (Eds.), *Handbook of solution-focused brief therapy* (pp. 184–204). San Francisco, CA: Jossey-Bass.

Murphy, J. J. (2008). *Solution-focused counseling in schools* (2nd ed.). Alexandria, VA: American Counseling Association.

Murphy, J. J., & Duncan, B. L. (2007). *Brief intervention for school problems* (2nd ed.). New York, NY: Guilford.

Newsome, S. (2004). Solution-focused brief therapy (SFBT) groupwork with at-risk junior high school students: Enhancing the bottom-line. *Research on Social Work Practice, 14,* 336–343.

Pichot, T., & Dolan, Y. (2003). *Solution-focused brief therapy: Its effective use in agency settings.* Binghamton, NY: Hawthorne.

Sklare, G. (1997). *Brief counseling that works: A solution-focused approach for school counselors* (pp. 43–64). Thousand Oaks, CA: Corwin Press, Sage.

Springer, D., Lynch, C., & Rubin, A. (2000). Effects of a solution-focused mutual aid group for Hispanic children of incarcerated parents. *Child and Adolescent Social Work Journal, 17,* 431–442.

Webb, W. H. (1999). *Solutioning: Solution-focused interventions for counselors.* Philadelphia, PA: Accelerated Press.

137 Treating Children and Adolescents with Attention Deficit Hyperactivity Disorder in the Schools

Steven W. Evans, A. Raisa Petca, & Julie Sarno Owens

Students with Attention Deficit Hyperactivity Disorder (ADHD) are among the students most frequently referred to school mental health professionals. School-based treatments can be the best interventions for helping these students succeed socially, academically, and behaviorally. Descriptions of school-based interventions for children and adolescents with the disorder are included in this chapter. The descriptions and case examples provide important considerations for modifying intervention and assessment approaches based on developmental differences and changes in context between elementary and secondary schools. Intervention plans for both case illustrations include parent involvement in the assessment and treatment procedures.

ADHD is a chronic condition appearing in 3%–10% of school-aged children. The core symptoms of the disorder include problematic inattention, hyperactivity, and impulsivity. Many of the impairments exhibited by children with ADHD manifest at school, including problems completing school assignments, following school and classroom rules, getting along with peers and adults, and keeping their materials and assignments organized. Problems with disorganization are often the most obvious, due to cluttered desks, book bags, binders, and lockers. Although less obvious, disorganization is also evident in poor time management skills, reading and writing difficulties, and poor listening comprehension. In addition, children with ADHD are at high risk for other problems, including aggression, oppositional behavior, substance use, risky sexual behavior (i.e., conducive to sexually transmitted diseases and/or unwanted pregnancies), school dropout, delinquency, and driving violations and accidents.

School social workers have a unique opportunity to intervene with youth with ADHD and make a positive difference in their lives. They can observe students in socially demanding situations, such as the cafeteria, transitions between classes, and recess, as well as academically challenging situations in the classroom. Based on these observations and other assessments, they can help identify students who may benefit from interventions. School social workers are tasked with various responsibilities such as providing individual or group counseling, conducting prevention and intervention pursuits within the three-tiered model of intervention (e.g., Response to Intervention; RTI; National Center on Response to Intervention, 2010), managing crisis situations and providing teacher consultations with regard to Individualized Education Plans (IEPs), 504 plans, or school-based behavior management plans (Bornstein, Ball, Mellin, Wade-Mdivanian, & Anderson-Butcher, 2011). School social workers may also work in multidisciplinary teams, and act as liaisons between children and community agencies (Leyba, 2009). School social workers are often the primary providers of mental health services for children with challenging mental health issues in the communities they serve, and they are also faced with high caseloads and administrative paperwork demands (Kelly, Berzin, Frey, Alvarez, Shaffer, & O'Brien, 2010). Given the many roles of the school social workers, it is important to maximize the effectiveness of the services provided. One way to maximize positive outcomes is to implement practices that are evidence-based (i.e., have empirical support for their effectiveness for a given problem). Indeed, school social workers who are knowledgeable about evidence-based procedures for the identification and treatment of youth with ADHD and who collaborate with parents and teachers in the implementation of these procedures can have a large, beneficial impact on a child with the disorder, as well as on his parents and the school community.

ELEMENTARY SCHOOL

There are many characteristics of an elementary school classroom that make it well suited for both the identification and treatment of children with ADHD. Elementary school students typically stay within one or two classrooms for several hours each day, where they encounter both academically and socially challenging situations on a regular basis. School social workers may observe children in these situations in both structured and unstructured activities. The opportunity to regularly observe in these situations allows school social workers to gain a thorough understanding of a child's strengths and weaknesses, the antecedents that may trigger disruptive behavior, and the consequences that may unintentionally serve to maintain disruptive behavior (e.g., attention from peers or adults). Understanding these factors can guide intervention planning and assist with gauging progress in response to interventions. Taking advantage of these opportunities requires that a school social worker understand the manifestations of the disorder in schools.

Some common characteristics of elementary school-aged children with ADHD that can be observed in a classroom are listed below. Not every characteristic is true of all children with the disorder, but they are common of many. Furthermore, these characteristics are not diagnostic criteria for ADHD; rather, they are descriptive of how teachers and other students perceive children with ADHD.

- The materials in the student's desk are very messy, and the child has trouble finding things when asked by the teacher.
- The child is seen by peers as annoying, "hyper," or "different."
- The teacher reports that working with the child can be exhausting.
- The child fails to raise his or her hand, and instead impulsively interrupts the teacher.
- The child raises his or her hand to participate in class discussions and then forgets what he or she was going to say or makes a statement that is irrelevant or redundant.
- During seatwork time in class, the child is frequently off-task. The student may do things to escape extended seatwork periods, such as sharpen pencils, go to the bathroom, or report not feeling well and ask to go to the nurse.
- The child fails to complete work and give it to the teacher on time.

Behavioral interventions that clarify expectations for the child and provide salient and consistent rewards and consequences for behavior are effective in improving the academic and behavioral functioning of children with ADHD (MTA Cooperative Group, 1999). In other words, providing children with specific expectations for desired behavior and implementing a system by which children gain and lose privileges based on their compliance with these behaviors can correct problem behaviors among children with ADHD. Such interventions require that school social workers consult and collaborate with parents and teachers to implement the interventions in the classroom or home. Rigorous research studies indicate that counseling, play therapy, and self-esteem groups are unlikely to be effective with these children (Pelham & Fabiano, 2008). There is also a lack of evidence that group-based social skills training is effective at increasing social competence among these children (Pelham & Fabiano, 2008). However, there is some evidence that teachers can play a role in improving the child's peer relations by reducing peers' social devaluation of children with ADHD, exclusionary behaviors, and reputational biases (Mikami, Griggs, Lerner, Emeh, Reuland, Jack, & Anthony, 2013). To this end, teachers can employ several strategies: (1) develop positive relationships with children via short, but frequent one-on-one interactions discussing the child's interests, (2) provide behavioral corrections in private communications (rather than public), (3) set explicit classroom rules for social inclusion, (4) identify commonalities among children and arrange brief but collaborative class activities that facilitate small successes for the student with ADHD, and (5) publicly (i.e., in class) recognize the genuine strengths of the student with ADHD unrelated to behavioral compliance. Educating parents and teachers about children with the disorder and training them to consistently provide behavioral interventions over time is a critically important role for school social workers who wish to help children with the disorder.

SECONDARY SCHOOL

One of the biggest changes from elementary school to secondary school for children with ADHD is the increased demand to function independently. In secondary schools, students are expected to bring materials to class without prompting, keep track of assignments without monitoring, and complete work independently.

Many secondary students with ADHD fail to meet these expectations. Attempts to remedy such problems are considerably more complicated at the secondary level for several reasons.

First, the transition to secondary schools typically includes a switch from having one teacher who is with the child all day to the child having a variety of teachers for different subjects. A school social worker attempting to help a child in middle or high school faces the prospect of negotiating with several teachers across a variety of settings.

Second, as children with ADHD progress into the upper grades, they encounter many teachers whose training and focus tends to be more content-driven than child-driven when compared with elementary school teachers. The emphasis on content at the secondary level is encouraged by the testing requirements of the No Child Left Behind Act of 2001 and by related high school graduation requisites.

Third, practitioners in secondary schools appear to rely more heavily on accommodations—as opposed to interventions—compared with practitioners in elementary schools. Accommodations include strategies such as giving students extended time on tests, providing students with class notes, accepting late work without penalty, and other techniques that do more to change the expectations of adults than the competencies of students. Accommodations are frequently used in Individual Education Plan (IEPs) or 504 plans for students with ADHD, and are recommended on many websites and in books written about the topic. Unfortunately, most accommodations are not evidence-based (Harrison, Bunford, Evans, & Owens, 2013) and can be detrimental when they are the primary mode of assistance.

Unlike accommodations, interventions are techniques that train students to meet the expectations of teachers through skill acquisition and enhancement. These techniques include teaching organizational skills, study skills, and behavior management. From a pedagogical standpoint, interventions are consistent with the goal of training children to be educated and competent adults. Interventions tend to take more work and are less likely to provide immediate relief to distressed parents and teachers than accommodations; however, they are more likely to improve the functioning of children with ADHD and facilitate long-term success. Not surprisingly, there is growing evidence for many school-based interventions (see review by DuPaul & Evans, 2008).

CASE ILLUSTRATIONS

The following sections contain two case illustrations that include some assessment and intervention techniques that may be employed by school social workers. The first involves a student with ADHD in an elementary school, and the second involves a student in a secondary school. Additional information about the interventions described in this section is available in other reviews of treatments (e.g., DuPaul & Stoner, 2003; Sadler & Evans, 2011).

Elementary School Case

Andrew is a nine-year-old boy who was referred to the school social worker (Rebecca) by his fourth-grade teacher. The teacher's primary complaints were that he did not stay in his seat and he interrupted the classroom environment by speaking at inappropriate times and being the "class clown." The teacher also reported that Andrew infrequently completed his classwork and homework and, when he did turn it in, his work had many careless mistakes. She stated that Andrew had problems interacting with his peers and provided the example that, during recess, he refused to play by the rules of games that the other children were playing.

Assessment. The first step of the assessment was to identify the questions posed by the teacher's referral. There are many potential questions that could be addressed based on Andrew's referral, including possible eligibility for special education or a 504 plan, determining whether he meets the *DSM-5* (*Diagnostic and Statistical Manual of Mental Disorders*, fifth edition; APA, 2013) criteria for a disorder by administering freely available rating scales for ADHD symptoms (e.g., the Disruptive Behavior Disorders (DBD) Scale, Pelham, Gnagy, Greenslade, & Milich, 1992) and associated impairment (e.g., the Impairment Rating Scale (IRS), Fabiano et al., 2006), and gathering information that would help guide the selection of interventions. Rebecca elected to focus her assessment on gathering data that would inform the selection of interventions.

The school social worker began by interviewing the teacher and Andrew's parents. These interviews were used to gather specific information about behavior problems, determine what interventions had already been attempted, and gain a sense of the ability of the parents and teacher to consistently implement interventions over time.

The teacher reported that she allowed Andrew to use the computer during free time at the end of the day if he demonstrated good behavior in class. She reported that this was not very effective, because they often disagreed about whether Andrew had a "good" day, and other children complained that they were well behaved but not allowed to use the computer. She noted that, after trying this for approximately one week, she discontinued it due to the arguments, classmate complaints, and lack of positive outcomes.

When Rebecca interviewed the parents, she learned that they did not have any problems with Andrew. They reported that he came home from school and played video games or "ran around" outside. The parents stated that Andrew had few responsibilities or chores at home. They also mentioned that he did not participate in any clubs, teams, or other organizations. Andrew has an older sister who spends a lot of time with her friends. Because Andrew's sister is very involved in activities in the community, the siblings spend very little time together. The parents were concerned about Andrew's problems at school, but wondered about the teacher's approach because their son did not have problems at home, and problems at school in previous years were minor.

Following the discussion with Andrew's parents, Rebecca decided to interview teachers who had Andrew in their classes in previous years to gather additional information. These teachers reported that Andrew was impulsive and frequently interrupted lessons and completed very little classwork. He also had problems getting along with other children. The teacher from the previous year reported that she did not refer Andrew to the child study team because she was able to work with him individually so that he was able to make adequate progress.

After gathering information from the parents and teachers, having the parents and teachers complete ADHD symptom and impairment ratings scales, and observing Andrew in various activities (e.g., during classroom and recess settings), the school social worker concluded that Andrew likely met diagnostic criteria for ADHD. She determined that the very minimal expectations for him at home may have led to the lack of apparent problems in that setting. Reports from previous teachers confirmed his current teacher's concerns and were consistent with a general trend toward increasing impairment as children with ADHD get older. However, because the parents perceived that there were few problems at home, she focused her feedback to the parents on implications for home- and school-based interventions. Although she was unsure about the parents' willingness to implement interventions at home consistently, she was confident that the teacher could consistently provide some basic behavioral interventions.

Intervention plan. Based on her assessment of Andrew, Rebecca identified three goals for her involvement in Andrew's intervention plan: (1) raise the parents' and the teacher's awareness about ADHD and associated risks, (2) collaborate with Andrew's parents and teacher to facilitate their implementation of behavior management techniques (e.g., daily report card, contingency management techniques) with Andrew, and (3) facilitate and monitor the implementation and outcomes of these interventions to determine Andrew's response to intervention and/or need for additional interventions.

First, Rebecca conducted a feedback session with Andrew's parents during which she provided information about ADHD and other disruptive behavior disorders, gave them some brochures and directed them to relevant sources for more information (e.g., see resources pages at www.oucirs.org and http://casgroup.fiu.edu/ccf/). She emphasized the risks associated with ADHD and the importance of providing effective interventions. Rebecca encouraged the parents to consult with their physician, but neither recommended nor discouraged medication treatment. She told the parents that there were several available interventions for Andrew whether or not he met diagnostic criteria for ADHD.

Second, Rebecca encouraged the parents to participate in a parent training program (e.g., Barkley, 2013; Cunningham, Bremner, & Secord, 1997) that focused on parenting techniques for parents of children with disruptive behavior. Rebecca conducted a 10-week parenting workshop each semester and encouraged the parents to participate in the next group. During the parenting workshops, the school social worker helped parents establish home rules and develop skills in effective behavior management strategies (e.g., developmentally appropriate use of praise, effective instructions, contingent application of consequences). Despite some reservations about whether the parents would consistently implement such an intervention, Rebecca felt that participation in this group was a good first step and, if this was not successful, she planned to work with them individually after the parent training program ended.

Third, Rebecca met with Andrew's teacher and provided information about ADHD, including the chronic nature of the disorder and the need for early and consistent interventions over time. She explained that interventions may take many weeks of consistent implementation to be effective, but that she was willing to meet with the teacher on a bi-weekly basis to help her maximize the effectiveness of her general (Tier 1 intervention) classroom management strategies and to help her implement a daily report card (DRC) intervention that was individualized to Andrew's challenges (Tier 2 intervention). The teacher was willing to implement the DRC with support from Rebecca. Rebecca consulted with the teacher about two key behaviors that the teacher felt were important to address first. They collaboratively decided to initially target task completion and interrupting behaviors. The teacher and the school social worker arrived at clear definitions for these behaviors. Rebecca asked the teacher to track these behaviors for one week without telling Andrew, so that they could obtain a baseline assessment of his current level of functioning. The information obtained from this process would also help Rebecca and the teacher establish initial goals for Andrew that would represent improvement in behavior, but that were also achievable (see Volpe & Fabiano, 2013 for detailed procedures for DRC).

The teacher remembered to track these behaviors for four of five days and she and Rebecca used these data to set a morning and an afternoon goal for each behavior (see Figure 137.1). Each goal he earned translated into small privileges (e.g., free reading time, computer time, line leader) that could be earned just prior to lunch and again prior to the dismissal bell. Andrew also took his report card home each day to share his success with his parents. Rebecca and the teacher continued to meet biweekly to troubleshoot challenges, monitor Andrew's progress, and modify the goals as Andrew's behavior improved. Rebecca told the teacher that it is important to implement the DRC consistently for at least one month before they could determine whether it was effective based on Andrew's response (Owens, Holdaway, Zoromski, Evans, Himawan, Girio- Herrera, & Murphy, 2012). She emphasized the importance of persistence and patience with interventions.

Secondary School Case

Lisa is a 15-year-old girl who was referred to the school social worker (Mike) due to poor academic

Andrew's Daily Report Card		Date: October 17, 2013

Target Behavior	Frequency of Behaviors	Goal Met?
1. Andrew will raise his hand before speaking with 5 or fewer interruptions	# of interruptions IIII	☺ ☹
2. Andrew will complete 50% of morning class work.	% Complete 25%	☺ (☹)
Morning Privilege: use magic markers ✗		
1. Andrew will raise his hand before speaking with 5 or fewer interruptions	# of interruptions II	(☺) ☹
2. Andrew will complete 50% of afternoon class work.	% Complete 75%	(☺) ☹
Afternoon Privilege: be a line leader ✓		
Teacher Comments: *Andrew had a difficult time staying on task this morning and got distracted frequently. However, after lunch, he was more focused on his class work and put a lot of effort into completing his worksheets.*		
Parent Signature: *Jane Smith*		

Figure 137.1 Sample daily report card.

performance, truancy, and defiant behavior. She moved to the school district at the beginning of the school year, when she enrolled in the ninth grade. Lisa failed three of her classes during the first grading period and teachers reported that she did not seem to care about school and that they could not help her.

Assessment. Mike, the school social worker, began his assessment by interviewing Lisa's teachers and asking them to complete the DBD and IRS rating scales. The information he received from Lisa's teachers was very inconsistent. Some teachers reported that they had no

problems with Lisa and that she was earning a C or D in their classes. Other teachers reported that she was disruptive, never completed any work, was verbally defiant to the teachers, and was failing their classes. The variability across teachers led Mike to review information about Lisa from her previous school. These records were sparse, but revealed that her grades tended to range from D to B. There was no information regarding any behavior problems. Mike called the school social worker from Lisa's previous school and learned that, even though teachers believed that Lisa had a poor attitude and was sometimes irritable and inappropriate in class, this was not considered a serious problem. Lisa's few friends tended to be younger than she, and she tended to spend more time in isolation than with a group of peers. The previous school social worker remembered that Lisa may have seen a mental health professional in the community, but stated that she was never given details of those services. Lisa had never been referred to the child study team or for an evaluation. The school social worker could not recall any interactions with her parents.

In addition to gathering information about Lisa's behavior from her previous school, Mike observed some of Lisa's current classes. He found that the teachers who reported the most problems with Lisa tended to have moderate-to-high expectations for their students. The teachers who reported that they had few problems operated more informally than the others, had students complete more hands-on activities and, although they gave homework, they also allowed more than enough class time for the students to complete the homework. Lisa's work in these classes was not of high quality, but she did enough to meet minimal expectations. She actively contributed to discussions in these classes with pertinent comments, however, traditional classroom rules (e.g., raising hand before speaking) were not strictly enforced. Mike recognized that the more self-control and independent task completion was expected of Lisa, the more problems she exhibited.

Mike then contacted Lisa's parents and asked them to meet him at the school to discuss Lisa's progress and her transition to the new school. He asked them to bring old school report cards and the results of any previous evaluations that had been completed. Lisa's parents appeared relieved to meet with him and extensively discussed their concerns and frustrations. They spoke of choosing their battles and attempting to monitor and influence Lisa's behavior, but reported little success and substantial worry and concern about the girl's future. They stated that they had long ago abandoned efforts to get Lisa to help with chores at home, because it often led to more arguments rather than positive outcomes. Lisa had seen a counselor in their previous community for a few months, but her parents declared that this had been "a waste of time," as little change in Lisa's behavior was observed. As a result, her parents had concluded that mental health professionals could not help their daughter.

A review of Lisa's report cards revealed that teachers had added comments to her cards since first grade, indicating that she had trouble completing work and was disorganized. Early report cards also revealed that she had trouble getting along with other children and was easily distracted. The parents reported that they shared these concerns with Lisa's pediatrician, and he mentioned the possibility of prescribing medication for her. They were unsure what medication was considered, but at the time, the parents were opposed to giving her medication for her behavior problems.

Finally, Mike invited Lisa to his office to gather information from her perspective. She reported that she was doing fine both socially and academically. Mike questioned her about some of the teacher reports and low grades. Lisa replied by stating that some teachers do not like her. She acknowledged becoming frustrated with them, but claimed that her statements to the teachers were appropriate in response to the unfair accusations and other mean statements that teachers made to her. Lisa reported having many friends and a happy social life. When asked specifically about the ages of her friends, she acknowledged that some of her friends were younger than she was, but stated that she also had friends in the ninth grade. Mike also asked to look at Lisa's book bag and school binder. The items were very disorganized and drawings, food wrappers, and other items were mixed into her school materials. There was very little information recorded in her assignment notebook, and Lisa stated that she did not use it because she remembers all of her assignments.

Mike synthesized the reports from teachers, parents, Lisa, and the school social worker from the previous school, as well as information from school records and class observation. The results of his comprehensive assessment led Mike to conclude it was likely that Lisa met diagnostic criteria for ADHD.

Intervention plan. Given the complexity of Lisa's problems and the parents' distrust of mental health services, Mike decided that, at this point, the best way of helping Lisa was to meet again with her parents and discuss treatment options. His goals for this meeting included educating her parents about ADHD and evidence-based interventions for ADHD, identifying community resources that could help them, and reviewing school-based or school-linked interventions that were likely to help Lisa, such as an organization intervention and a homework management plan.

In his meeting with Lisa's parents, Mike provided them with reading material (e.g., Zeigler-Dendy & Zeigler, 2003; CHADD fact sheets) and discussed the course of ADHD through childhood and into adolescence. He also shared with them that insight-oriented therapies, like the one they reported was provided to Lisa by the community counselor, are not likely to adequately address the problems associated with ADHD. Mike provided information about evidence-based interventions for ADHD to enable Lisa's parents to make an informed choice of treatment. He also encouraged the parents to speak to Lisa's physician if they were interested in medication treatment. Finally, Mike provided the parents with contact information for the local parent support and advocacy group and encouraged them to consider attending a meeting.

After educating the parents about ADHD and treatment options, Mike talked to them about implementing some interventions at home to help Lisa both academically and with their parent–child relationship. Mike scheduled a standing weekly meeting with Lisa's parents for three weeks to share information about a homework management plan and basic communication and problem-solving procedures. Additional parent meetings could be scheduled on an as-needed basis. He spoke with them about maintaining consistent communication between home and school and offered to be the liaison between Lisa's parents and teachers.

Lastly, Mike discussed the possibility of implementing school-based interventions to target Lisa's academic problems and addressed her parents' queries about the appropriateness of implementing accommodations. He explained that the majority of Lisa's problems were in classes in which the teachers expected students to work independently outside of class, strictly adhere to classroom rules, and had higher expectations regarding behavior. When teachers did not have these expectations, Lisa's irresponsible and disrespectful behaviors were viewed as less of a problem. Mike also told the parents about the extreme disorganization that he discovered in Lisa's binder and book bag and the lack of an effective system for recording assignments. The parents asked about ideas that they heard from other parents, where teachers gave the students longer time on tests, provided them with written notes from the class and a list of the assignments that were due, and did not penalize the students for late assignments. Mike told the parents that

these were accommodations that are sometimes used with students with problems similar to Lisa's, but he discouraged the parents from relying on these techniques. He told them that there is no evidence that these techniques improve the behavior or skills of children with ADHD or related problems. It was his experience that these accommodations do make it easier for students to receive improved grades, but only because adults start expecting less from them and not because the students have learned any skills to cope with their difficulties. He also explained that accommodations may be detrimental to Lisa because they remove the responsibility for her to find the means to be successful and that they should only be used in combination with interventions that help her develop competencies. He stated that it is unlikely that future employers would make such accommodations, and Lisa needed to learn to adjust to age-appropriate expectations. He reviewed a series of interventions designed to improve her ability to succeed in regular education settings such as an organization intervention (Evans, Schultz, White, Brady, Sibley, & Van Eck, 2009), daily report card (Evans & Youngstrom, 2006) and other school-based interventions (see Evans, White, Sibley, & Barlow, 2007) designed to improve Lisa's ability to meet the expectations of regular education teachers. He told the parents that it might take a few weeks or even months for Lisa to show adequate improvement, and he would provide them with updates about her progress. The parents reported feeling a little overwhelmed with this information, but told Mike that they would read the material, discuss the information that had been shared, and return for their next appointment.

CONCLUSION

School social workers are in a position that allows them to have an important impact on the lives of children and adolescents with ADHD. Their training and skills, combined with their position within schools, provide school social workers with a unique opportunity to participate in the assessment of children with ADHD, as well as coordinate effective home- and school-based interventions. In addition, school social workers can be very effective liaisons to community mental health providers to coordinate care. The case illustrations in this chapter were intended to provide information and examples of effective strategies to help students with ADHD achieve in school. Of course, there are many child and family characteristics that may enhance or compromise response to these interventions. Findings from a large clinical trial of children with ADHD revealed that comorbid anxiety, prior medication use, poverty, severity of symptoms, and maternal depression moderated clinical outcomes (for a complete review, see Hinshaw, 2007). Interestingly, the child's gender and comorbid oppositional defiant disorder or conduct disorder did not significantly alter outcomes.

Many common concerns that practitioners experience when working with youth with ADHD were described in the case illustrations, including the belief by the children that they do not have problems and do not need help, inconsistent reports from teachers about the child's behavior and academic progress, the temptation to rely on accommodations instead of interventions, and the barrier to further care that can result from receiving ineffective interventions. Many additional challenges are inherent in the process of trying to implement interventions such as those described above, including variability in the willingness of teachers and parents to participate in the process. Clearly, excellent consulting and communication skills are a critical prerequisite to working effectively with these youth in schools. It is by no means an easy task, but it is a necessary undertaking that can afford life-changing benefits to youth.

WEBSITES

Center for Children and Families, Daily Report Card. http://casgroup.fiu.edu/pages/docs/1401/1367959499_How_To_Establish_a_School_DRC.pdf
Center for Children and Families, Parent Resources. http://casgroup.fiu.edu/CCF/pages.php?id=1441
Center for Intervention Research in Schools, Daily Report Card. http://www.oucirs.org/resources/dailyreportcard
Center for Intervention Research in Schools, Parent Resources. http://www.oucirs.org/resources/parents
Children and Adults with Attention Deficit/Hyperactivity Disorder (CHADD), Factsheets. http://www.chadd.org/Understanding-ADHD/Parents-Caregivers-of-Children-with-ADHD/Adolescents-and-Young-Adults.aspx

National Resource Center on ADHD. http://help4adhd.org/
SchoolMentalHealth.org. http://www.schoolmentalhealth.org

References

American Psychiatric Association. (2013). *Diagnostic and statistical manual of mental disorders, fifth edition.* Washington, DC: Author.
Barkley, R. A. (2013). *Defiant children: A clinician's manual for assessment and parent training* (3rd ed.). New York, NY: Guilford.
Bornstein, L. R., Ball, A., Mellin, E. A., Wade-Mdivanian, R., & Anderson-Butcher, D. (2011). Advancing collaboration between school- and agency-employed school-based social workers: A mixed-methods comparison of competencies and preparedness. *Children and Schools, 33*(2), 83–95.
Cunningham, C. E., Bremner, R., & Secord, M. (1997). *COPE: The Community Parent Education Program: A school-based family systems oriented workshop for parents of children with disruptive behavior disorders.* Hamilton, ON: COPE Works.
DuPaul, G. J., & Evans, S. W. (2008). School based interventions for adolescents with ADHD. *Adolescent Medicine State of the Art Reviews (AMSTAR), 19,* 300–312.
DuPaul, G. J., & Stoner, G. (2003). *ADHD in the schools: Assessment and interventions strategies* (2nd ed.). New York, NY: Guilford.
Evans, S. W., Schultz, B. K., White, L. C., Brady, C., Sibley, M. H., & Van Eck, K. (2009). A school-based organization intervention for young adolescents with ADHD. *School Mental Health, 1,* 78–88.
Evans, S. W., White, L. C., Sibley, M., & Barlow, E. (2007). School-based mental health treatment of children and adolescents with attention-deficit/hyperactivity disorder. In S. W. Evans, M. Weist, & Z. Serpell (Eds.), *Advances in school-based mental health interventions: Best practices and program models* (vol. 2). New York, NY: Civic Research Institute.
Evans, S. W., & Youngstrom, E. (2006). Evidence based assessment of attention-deficit hyperactivity disorder: Measuring outcomes. *Journal of the American Academy of Child and Adolescent Psychiatry, 45*(9), 1132–1137.
Fabiano, G. A., Pelham, W. E., Waschbusch, D. A., Gnagy, E. M., Lahey, B. B., Chronis, A. M., … Burrows-Maclean, L. (2006). A practical measure of impairment: Psychometric properties of the impairment rating scale in samples of children with attention deficit hyperactivity disorder and two school-based samples. *Journal of Clinical Child and Adolescent Psychology, 35,* 369–385.
Harrison, J., Bunford, N., Evans, S. W., & Owens, J. S. (2013). Educational accommodations for students with behavioral challenges: A systematic review

of the literature. *Review of Educational Research,* *83,* 551–597.

Hinshaw, S. P. (2007). Moderators and mediators of treatment outcome for youth with ADHD: Understanding for whom and how interventions work. *Journal of Pediatric Psychology,* *32,* 664–675.

Kelly, M. S., Berzin, S. C., Frey, A., Alvarez, M., Shaffer, G., & O'Brien, K. (2010). The state of school social work: Findings from the national school social work survey. *School Mental Health, 2,* 132–141.

Leyba, E. G. (2009). Tools to reduce overload in the school social worker role. *Children and Schools,* *31*(4), 219–228.

Mikami, A. Y., Griggs, M. S., Lerner, M. D., Emeh, C. C., Reuland, M. M., Jack, A., & Anthony, M. R. (2013). A randomized trial of a classroom intervention to increase peers' social inclusion of children with Attention-Deficit/Hyperactivity Disorder. *Journal of Consulting and Clinical Psychology, 81*(1), 100–112.

National Center on Response to Intervention. (2010). *Essential components of RTI—A closer look at Response to Intervention.* Washington, DC: U.S. Department of Education, Office of Special Education Programs, National Center on Response to Intervention.

No Child Left Behind Act of 2001, Pub. L. No. 107-110, 115 Stat. 1425 (2002).

MTA Cooperative Group. (1999). A 14-month randomized clinical trial of treatment strategies for attention-deficit/hyperactivity disorder. *Archives of General Psychiatry, 56*(12), 1073–1086.

Owens, J. S., Holdaway, A. S., Zoromski, A. K., Evans, S. W., Himawan, L. K., Girio- Herrera, E., & Murphy, C. (2012). Incremental benefits of a daily report card intervention over time for youth with disruptive behavior. *Behavior Therapy, 43,* 848–861.

Pelham, W. E., & Fabiano, G. (2008). Evidence-based psychosocial treatments for attention-deficit/ hyperactivity disorder. *Journal of Clinical Child and Adolescent Psychology, 37,* 184–214.

Pelham, W. E., Jr., Gnagy, E. M., Greenslade, K. E., & Milich, R. (1992). Teacher ratings of DSM-III-R symptoms for the disruptive behavior disorders. *Journal of the American Academy of Child and Adolescent Psychiatry, 31,* 210–218.

Sadler, J., & Evans, S. W. (2011). Psychosocial interventions for adolescents with ADHD. In S. W. Evans & B. Hoza (Eds.), *Treating attention-deficit/ hyperactivity disorder: Assessment and intervention in developmental context.* New York, NY: Civic Research Institute.

Volpe, R. J., & Fabiano, G. A. (2013). *Daily behavior report cards: An evidence-based system of assessment and intervention.* New York, NY: The Guilford Press.

Zeigler-Dendy, C. A., & Zeigler, A. (2003). *A bird's-eye view of life with ADD and ADHD: Advice from young survivors.* Cedar Bluff, AL: Cherish the Children.

138 Effectively Working with Latino Immigrant Families in Schools

Eden Hernandez Robles, Alan Dettlaff, & Rowena Fong

GETTING STARTED

In 2010 the U.S. Census Bureau (2012a) estimated that 23.2% of all elementary and high school students were classified as Hispanic. Although Hispanics (both male and female) have experienced a slight decline in the dropout rate, they have continued to drop out at nearly twice the rate of their White and Black counterparts (U.S. Census Bureau, 2012b). In addition, Hispanic males have higher rates of dropping out when compared with Hispanic females, and also have lower rates of college enrollment when compared with Hispanic females (U.S. Census Bureau, 2012b). Despite being 23.2% of all elementary and high school students, only 6.2% of all college students (both undergraduate and graduate) are Hispanic, and only 13% of all Hispanics age 25 years and older attain a bachelor's degree (U.S. Census Bureau 2012a).

Referred to as Hispanics in census data, the Latino population, particularly those who have migrated from other countries, represents the largest and fastest growing population in the United States. In 2010, the Latino population, consisting of persons from Mexico, Cuba, Dominican Republic, Central America, South America, and other Latin countries, represented 16.3% of the total U.S. population, an increase of 15.2 million people since 2000. Between 2000 and 2010, the Latino population increased by 43%, which was more than four times the growth of the total U.S. population (Ennis, Rios-Vargas, & Albert, 2011). In 2010, Latino children represented nearly one-fourth of all children in the United States, comprising 24% of all children under the age of 18 years (Motel, 2012). Although foreign-born Latino children represent only 8% of Latino children, more than half (52%) of Latino children are U.S.-born children of Latino immigrants (Fry & Passel, 2009). Although children of immigrants reside primarily in six states that have been traditional destination states for immigrants—California, Texas, New York, Florida, Illinois, and New Jersey—the number of children with immigrant parents has more than doubled in most other states, while states including North Carolina, Nevada, Georgia, Arkansas, and Nebraska have experienced growth rates of more than 300% since 1990 (Fortuny, Capps, Simms, & Chaudry, 2009).

Given the rapidly increasing Latino immigrant population, school-based professionals face increasing pressure to assist in the adjustment of children from immigrant families entering school systems. For these children, stressors related to immigration and acculturation may significantly impede the learning process. Upon migration, immigrants are faced with a number of challenges that distinguish them from their native-born counterparts. The migration experience itself can be considerably dangerous, with many immigrants experiencing violence, robbery, and sexual assault (Solis, 2003). Once in the new country, children in immigrant families continue to experience stress resulting from language differences, unfamiliar customs,

loss of routine, and continuing threats of violence and discovery. Additional pressures resulting from acculturation can lead to a variety of strains and difficulties on family systems, as parents and children experience changing cultural contexts along with the loss of previously established support systems (Dettlaff & Rycraft, 2006). Although some foreign-born children overcome these challenges with apparent ease, many others experience very difficult and stressful transitions to their lives in the United States (Goodman, 2004; Tazi, 2004).

Research indicates that the inability to cope or adjust to cultural stressors can result in poor or stagnated academic achievement for children in immigrant families (Moon, Kang, & An, 2009; Padilla & Perez, 2003; Shin, 2004). Thus, the increasing population of immigrant children in school systems necessitates that school-based professionals recognize and respond to the unique needs of this population to facilitate positive academic outcomes. Thomas (1992) contends that the failure to address the adjustment challenges faced by immigrant children within school systems contributes indirectly to their academic failure. Compounding the existing challenges faced by immigrant children, lack of academic achievement can then lead to increased risk of poor self-esteem and drop out (Battin-Pearson et al., 2000; Suh, Suh, & Houston, 2007).

WHAT WE KNOW

The cultural, psychological, and linguistic challenges that stem from experiences with immigration and acculturation make Latino immigrant students a particularly vulnerable population. Among the unique challenges faced by Latino immigrant students in academic achievement is English language acquisition. The experience of many Latino immigrant students is often complicated by a lack of appropriate assessment tools that differentiate between a difficulty in language acquisition and a learning disability (Klingner & Harry, 2006; Lesaux, 2006). Latino students in general continue to be over-represented in Special Education as a result of a misinterpretation of the students' cultural and language barriers as learning disabilities (Artiles, Rueda, Salazar, & Higareda, 2005; Lee, Grigg, & Donahue, 2007; Orosco, 2010; Orosco, Schonewise, de Onis, Klingner, & Hoover, 2008). Latinos are not over-represented in disabilities that require biological verification (educable mental retardation) (National Research Council,

2002). However, research indicates that most schools lack the required resources to support the needs of Latino immigrant students with disabilities (Zehler, Fleischman, Hopstock, Pendzick, & Stephenson, 2003).

Academic Achievement and Dropout Rates

Academic achievement and dropout rates are both areas of major concern for Latino immigrant students. Multiple barriers that the first generation face, including low levels of cultural sensitivity in schools and inadequate academic advisement, affect the ability for subsequent generations to obtain academic success (Hill & Torres, 2010; Nevarez & Rico, 2007; Suarez-Orozco & Suarez-Orozco, 1995). Findings from Tenebaum & Ruck's (2007) study indicated that students are often the subject of repeated discrimination as "teachers praise Latino students less, even for correct answers; behave less favorably toward them; and penalize them for lower levels of English proficiency" (as cited in Hill & Torres, 2010). Although Latino immigrant children face many barriers that may impede their academic success, school-based professionals have the potential to foster academic achievement and completion through culturally sensitive interventions.

It is critical for the school social worker, school mental health professional, or school counselor to be familiar with the cultural belief systems active among Latino families (see Table 138.1) and to be clear on distinguishing characteristics among the Latino immigrant population, which include realizing the difference between immigrant children and children of immigrants and discerning the tremendous variations apparent among different subgroups originating from diverse countries. It is recommended that the school-based professional consider the Latino Dimensions of Family and Personal Identity Model, adapted from Arredondo & Glauner (1992) Dimensions of Personality Identity Model, when working with a Latino immigrant student (Arredondo & Santiago-Rivera, 2000; see Figure 138.1). The Latino Dimensions of Family and Personal Identity Model considers A, B, and C dimensions that include age/generational status, acculturation/citizen status, and personal/familial/historical events before proceeding to work with Latinos (Santiago-Rivera et al., 2002). Using this model as an assessment would help the school-based professional in an early identification of appropriate interventions for the student.

Another determination for the school-based professional to make when working with Latino immigrant students is the appropriate use of the Spanish language. Although the Spanish language is shared among Latino immigrants, the dialect may differ and words may change in meaning depending upon the country of origin (Thorn & Contreras, 2005). Similarly, behavior and body language also differ among the subgroups of Latinos and can be a powerful form of mimesis to forge a therapeutic relationship if applied correctly (Quinones-Mayo & Dempsey, 2005). The bilingual school-based professional should remain alert for these differences in dialect and be prepared to adapt. For example, the word "school bus" translated from the American language would be *el autobus de transporte escolar*. However, depending on the person's country of origin, the word school bus can be translated differently. For persons from Mexico a school bus is *el camion escolar*, while persons from Cuba and Puerto Rico may identify the bus as *la guagua escolar*, and persons from Uruguay or Peru may recognize bus as *el omnibus escolar*. The variations on school bus do not end there. This example simply stresses the importance of recognizing differences in dialect and being able to adapt.

The nonbilingual school-based professional also should remain alert for these differences and use caution if employing translation services. Improper use of the language poses many ethical dilemmas and risks effectively building a therapeutic relationship with the students. Identifying possible bilingual referral sources may be the best choice for nonbilingual school-based professionals; matching the students with language appropriate services is most important in the early stages of intervention when seeking positive outcomes (Carey & Manuppelli, 2000). Nonetheless, the nonbilingual school-based professional's openness to learning these differences, as well as key words of the language, are helpful in building a relationship of trust and mutual respect.

WHAT WE CAN DO

Response to Intervention (RTI) and Positive Behavioral Interventions and Supports (PBIS) are three-tiered models used by school systems to provide instruction and intervention or prevention to students according to their needs (RTI Action Network, 2011). Each tier is structured to identify and then provide tailored support to

TABLE 138.1 Cultural Belief Systems

Principle	Definition	Citation
Los dichos	Cultural sayings that reflect cultural values or lessons. Can be used as a therapeutic tool.	Zuniga, 1992
La educación	Education in mainstream America refers to school. *La educación* is not a direct translation of education, but refers to the role of the mother for the proper social and moral upbringing of the child and can be a powerful resource.	Goldenberg & Gallimore, 1995; Valdés, 1996
El respeto	Refers to a respect for elders and authority. *Respeto* is also achieved through empathy in intimate relationships.	Santiago-Rivera et al., 2002 Simoni & Perez, 1995
Familismo	Academic term to define the observed importance of family above self; strong family ties within Latino families. However, the greater a family adapts to the U.S., the weaker *familismo* becomes.	Santiago-Rivera et al., 2002 Smokowski et al., 2008
Personalismo	Academic term to describe the importance of developing a personal relationship versus institutional relationship. A genuine interest in a person or family, not a professional distance.	Negroni-Rodriguez & Morales, 2001
La confianza	Refers to an established relationship of trust with the families.	Negroni-Rodriguez & Morales, 2001
Simpatía	Refers to the desire to be social, agreeable, sharing, and empathetic. Although this may differ when interacting with persons of a different culture.	Guilamo-Ramos et al., 2007; Simoni & Perez, 1995; Marin, 1993
Dignidad	Refers to the respect and honor given to a person.	Andres-Hyman et al., 2006
Obligación	Refers to a mutual expectation (responsibility) that both those in power and those who are not in power will treat each other with respect.	Padilla, Pedraza, & Rivera, 2005
Ganas	Refers to drive and ambition to achieve goals.	Auerbach, 2006
Marianismo	Academic term that refers to female gender socialization. Girls must grow up to be enduring, nurturing, spiritually strong, and pious women and mothers. This can possibly create conflict within the family.	Lopez-Baez, 1999; Santiago-Rivera et al., 2002
Machismo	Academic term that refers to male gender socialization. Boys must grow up to be responsible, loyal, and protective men and fathers. This term is often confused and used interchangeably with the term machista, which means sexist.	Morales, 1996; Santiago-Rivera et al., 2002

students with learning or behavioral difficulties. Within the tiers, students are continually monitored for progress to determine whether further action is needed to assist students in achieving their goals. The screening process to determine which tier a student will benefit from begins at the classroom level. The classroom level is considered the Tier 1 level and consists of high-quality classroom instruction using evidence-based educational practices (RTI Action Network, 2011). Students who are identified as having difficulty at this level are provided with supplemental instruction. Students who do not show adequate progress or improvement within the allotted time frame (generally within eight weeks) are moved into the Tier 2 level. Tier 2 supports consist of

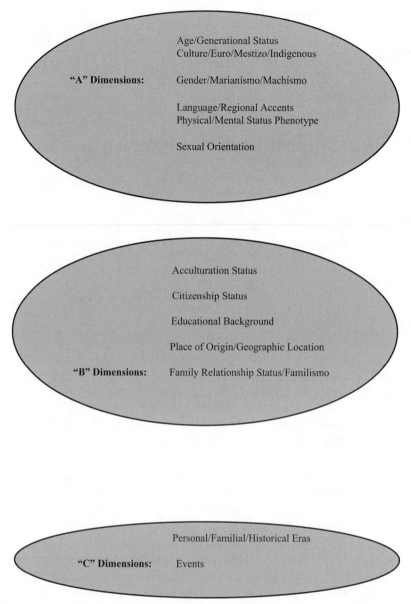

"A" Dimensions:

Age/Generational Status
Culture/Euro/Mestizo/Indigenous

Gender/Marianísmo/Machísmo

Language/Regional Accents
Physical/Mental Status Phenotype

Sexual Orientation

"B" Dimensions:

Acculturation Status

Citizenship Status

Educational Background

Place of Origin/Geographic Location

Family Relationship Status/Familismo

"C" Dimensions:

Personal/Familial/Historical Eras

Events

Figure 138.1 Latina/o Dimensions of Family and Personal Identity Model. Source: Adapted from Arredondo & Glauner, 1992.

targeted interventions provided in small-group settings and are a supplement to regular classroom instruction (RTI Action Network, 2011). This level of intervention varies in duration, but does not extend past the grade level. Students who require more support are placed into the intensive Tier 3 interventions that are structured to target the student's deficits. Students who do not respond to Tier 3 interventions become eligible for a comprehensive evaluation and are considered for special education (Response-to-Intervention [RTI] Action Network, 2011).

Although there are few culturally sensitive evidence-based interventions available for Latino immigrant students, those that have been developed incorporate the students' traditional culture into instruction while introducing the United States (Orosco, 2007; Orosco, 2010; Klingner & Edwards, 2006; Santiago & Brown, 2004). Culturally sensitive RTI interventions facilitate the transition and adjustment of the students while supporting them in their culture as they work toward academic success (Osher, Cartledge, Oswald, Sutherland, Artiles, & Coutinho, 2004;

Osher & Osher, 2002; Lewis, 2001). The National Task Force on Early Childhood Education for Hispanics (2007) reported that schools that implement culturally relevant classroom interventions from both the traditional and the new culture have a positive impact on the student's cognitive and social development. The following interventions are focused on academic achievement and dropout prevention for Latinos and Latino dual-language learners.

Tier 1 Interventions for Latino Immigrants

Most Tier 1 level interventions focus on English language acquisition as the foundation for successfully aiding the Latino immigrant student in achieving academic progress. Rinaldi and Samson (2008) recommended educators use a prereferral, referral, and assessment approach that focuses on understanding and recording the student's proficiency and development. This would require that educators automatically assess and provide supports to incoming Latino immigrant students instead of waiting to see if they will acquire the language on their own. This Tier 1 strategy would potentially reduce the number of inappropriate disability referrals and unnecessary placements in remedial courses later on in the student's academic career.

Other Tier 1 interventions for Latino immigrants consist of English as a Second Language courses and culturally sensitive classroom instruction. Rolstad, Mahoney, and Glass (2005) meta-analysis of English language learner programs indicated that bilingual education yields greater results for academic achievement when compared with English-only approaches. Furthermore, transitional bilingual education programs were inferior compared with developmental bilingual education programs. These findings support previous meta-analysis findings that dual-language programs have positive effects for students in all academic areas (Willig, 1985; Greene, 1998). Rolstad and colleagues (2005) acknowledged that some state policies and the federal English Acquisition Act serve as barriers to most schools seeking to improve the academic environment for Latino immigrant students. Other researchers on English language learners have indicated that bilingual educational programs, coupled with culturally sensitive classroom instruction are most effective in

maintaining the students at the Tier 1 level (Orosco, 2010; Klingner & Edwards, 2006).

Tier 2 Interventions for Latino Immigrants

Cheung and Slavin (2005) reviewed effective bilingual reading programs and found positive effects for students. Of the programs reviewed, many incorporated group instruction to assist students in achieving academic success. Similar studies also encourage the use of small group tutoring as an effective way to deliver Tier 2 interventions such as *Project Read* (Rinaldi & Samson, 2008; Greene & Enfield, 2006). Although there is still much work to be done in developing evidence-based Tier 2 interventions (Klingner & Edwards, 2006), this review served to identify the benefits of incorporating a cultural component into classroom instruction.

Tier 3 Interventions for Latino Immigrants

Some researchers instead have focused on developing culturally sensitive school programs. For example, *Club Amigas* (Kaplan, Turner, Piotrkowski, & Silber, 2009), an evidence-based mentoring project, concentrated on increasing positive attitudes toward school and motivations to go on to college by pairing teenage Hispanic girls with mentors. The project further incorporated supports to assist the girls in developing their identity as Hispanics in the United States. Pre-test and post-test scores revealed statistically significant improvements in how girls viewed themselves as students. Qualitative results revealed that students experienced benefits of increased learning and aspirations to continue on to college. The actual high school completion rate of the participants was not reported. The findings of this study, however, support current literature that encourages schools to build culturally and linguistically sensitive intervention programs (Nesman, 2007). A similar program, *Project Wings*, an evidence-based school mental health program, was developed with the understanding that poor mental health leads to social issues such as dropping out of school and other deviant behaviors (Garcia, Pintor, Naughton, & Lindgren, 2009). The program focused on improving mental health and incorporated Zumba, sharing circle discussions, and skill-building activities. The skill-building activities addressed such issues as acculturation, self-identity, and healthy relationships, among other life aspects. This program consisted of 14 two-hour weekly sessions and was used with Latina adolescents. Pre-, mid- and post-assessments reported improved mental health for the participants who completed the program, but did not report on whether the students completed school. Although no longer in existence, the program Achievement for Latinos through Academic Success (ALAS) was an effective evidence-based dropout prevention program for both Latino males and females that incorporated positive supports for cultural identity and encouragement for academic success for students (Fashola & Slavin, 1998). This program also incorporated the use of parent training on how to monitor and guide students in school. The high-risk non-Individualized Educational Plan ALAS participants had a lower dropout rate when compared with non-ALAS participants.

Latino immigrant students stand much to gain within a Response to Intervention framework that ascertains that all children can succeed in the educational system if provided early intervention and careful monitoring of an individualized plan made up of evidence-based practices (NASDSE, 2005). If a culturally sensitive Response to Intervention framework is provided, careful monitoring and evaluation of the data could assist the school-based professional in determining exactly how to proceed in the best interest of the student. In addition to acquiring culturally and linguistically appropriate courses and other academic supports, the school-based professional should seek to direct the student in culturally relevant programs for all other needs.

School-based professionals serving Latino immigrants are often faced with a difficult task that will require careful implementation of programs and services in order to assist the student. Culturally sensitive professionals or consultants could be contacted to assist school-based professionals in identifying culturally relevant programs or resources. Most culturally relevant interventions used within the PBIS framework have been documented as effective, but many still need further evaluation. In addition, because of the complexities of the populations, school-based professionals should be prepared to meet the different sociocultural needs of the students.

TOOLS AND PRACTICE EXAMPLES

The Response to Intervention framework encompasses three caveats that consist of school support, progress monitoring, and diagnostics or assessment (Capone, 2011). This framework works within a three-tiered model to meet the needs of the students. A Tier 1 response for Latino immigrant students would require culturally and linguistically sensitive ESL classes and regular classroom material (Klingner & Edwards, 2006; Orosco, 2007); Tier 2 would include individualized or group supports for students who needed extra academic support such as peer tutoring or cooperative learning (Osher, Cartledge, Oswald, Sutherland, Artiles, & Coutinho, 2004); and Tier 3 would provide culturally and linguistically appropriate intensive interventions for students at risk for social or behavioral problems (Capone, 2011). The third tier draws upon other supports such as afterschool and in-school programs that should be monitored by the school-based professional on a behavioral action plan to track progress. The culturally sensitive RTI or PBIS progress monitoring would require school-based professionals to evaluate whether the overall model is working; if not, then the model should be changed until it does work (Klingner & Edwards, 2006; Orosco, 2007). By using multiple resources the school-based professional can also effectively build a social support system for both the student and family that they otherwise do not have.

The strategies used in a Response to Intervention framework include (1) Identify; (2) Analyze; (3) Implement; and (4) Monitor and Evaluate.

Identify

Identifying the Latino immigrant student requires a school-based professional to be willing to employ various strategies to locate them. Sending a questionnaire home in Spanish that asks questions such as "Have you recently immigrated to the United States?" can possibly assist in locating these students. Not all immigrants are literate in their native language, however, and as pointed out previously, the Spanish language comes in various dialects (Birman & Chan, 2008). Schools should use culturally sensitive interviewing techniques to screen incoming students for language proficiency (Valdés, 2001). Once the student has been identified and the school-based professional has assessed the unique history of the student using a model, such as the Latino Dimensions of Family and Personal Identity Model, the student can be screened for other educational needs (Arredondo & Santiago-Rivera, 2000).

Analyze

Assuming that most Latino immigrant children are more fluent in Spanish, students will greatly benefit from in-school programs such as ESL. Other afterschool programs that offer one-on-one tutoring or homework assistance also will serve to provide additional support to both the student and the family that may not otherwise be able to assist the child with homework. In order to help identify the psychosocial needs of the child, the Center for Health and Health Care in Schools website offers a great list of diagnostic assessment tools available in various languages, which a school-based professional can use to identify adjustment and mental health issues that may be present in the student (Birman & Chan, 2008). The consent process may prove difficult if the family is not literate and the school-based professional should be prepared to provide alternative forms for consent beyond written consent. The National Center for Youth Law website is a great resource for school-based professionals looking to become familiar with the state laws and school policies regarding mental health services. Once the school-based professional has successfully dealt with these issues, resources can be located or developed and through careful networking these same assessments can be used to monitor progress. Identifying resources for the family, as well, is ideal and strongly encouraged.

Implement

Once the appropriate programs and academic resources have been identified the school-based professional should develop an individualized education plan and an individualized family service plan. The effective school-based professional will coordinate with these programs and academic resources for the good of the student and the family. Efforts to connect the student and family to others in a similar situation will help to create an additional support system that with careful coordination can also be evaluated for effectiveness. Team meetings with all of the student's resources will serve to open lines of communication and assist in the effective implementation of program services.

Monitor and Evaluate

The school-based professional must be diligent in monitoring the individualized education plan. Diagnostic assessments and interviews with key resources should be conducted to ensure fidelity of treatment with the student. If any aspect of the plan is no longer working or is ineffective as demonstrated by the data collected from the assessment then the plan should be revised and new resources should be introduced. The ultimate goal is for the student to function at his or her highest level, making a successful adjustment to life in the United States while keeping cultural strengths intact.

CASE EXAMPLE

The case example provided illustrates an ideal approach to working with Latino immigrant children and their families. The Montez family has recently enrolled its three children in the school district. David, age 10 years, Veronica, age 7 years, and Ruben, age 5 years, are enrolled at the elementary school. They are recent immigrants from Mexico and are excited to enroll their children in school for a better opportunity.

Tier 1

The school determined that the family was a Latino immigrant family at enrollment. After meeting with the family, a decision was made to place the children in the English as a Second Language (ESL) program. The school-based professional also recognized the need for further supports in the classroom setting and arranged a meeting with the classroom and the ESL teacher. Both the ESL and classroom teacher had completed proper cultural sensitivity training to be able to meet the needs of children like David, Veronica, and Ruben. Regular meetings with the ESL and classroom teacher provided additional support that helped the students in adjusting.

Tier 2

Veronica and Ruben were both very successful at achieving their academic milestones. David, however, had some difficulty with reading and was not making progress. The school team identified a culturally sensitive evidence-based reading program for Latino immigrant children. The necessary supports were put into place in order to provide these same services to David and other children who were also struggling to make progress. The group work and individualized lesson plans aided David in making much improvement.

Tier 3

David, Veronica, and Ruben faced new challenges when they began high school. They worked very hard to achieve good grades, but did not quite understand the college enrollment process. David wanted to drop out so he could work to help support his family, and Veronica was struggling with the idea of going on to college. In addition, the students often felt alienated by their peers and experienced a great deal of difficulty with their own cultural identity. A school-based professional, who understood the difficulties unique to the students, identified a culturally sensitive evidence-based academic achievement and dropout prevention program for Latino immigrant students. The students were able to gain both the academic and social support they needed in this program. All three children graduated from high school and were able to successfully enroll in college.

APPENDIX A
Assessment Tools (Available in Spanish)

Type of Measure	Name of Scale	Informant/Reporter	Used with
Acculturation scale for Mexican Americans	Acculturation Scale for Mexican Americans (ARSMA)	Self-report or Semi-structured interview	Mexican and Mexican American population (Cuellar, Harris, & Jasso, 1980)
	Acculturation Scale for Mexican Americans (ARSMAII)	Self-report or Semi-structured interview	Mexican and Mexican American population (Cuellar, Arnold, & Maldonado, 1995)
	Children's Acculturation Scale	Youth Self-report or Semi-structured interview	Mexican children (Franco, 1983)
Acculturation scale for Puerto Ricans	Psychological Acculturation Scale (PAS)	Self-report or Semi-structured interview	Puerto Rican immigrant population (Tropp et al., 1999)
Acculturation scale for Cubans	Behavioral Acculturation Scale	Self-report or Semi-structured interview	Cuban immigrant population (Szapcoznik, Scopetta, Kurtines, & Arnalde, 1978)
Acculturation scale for Latinos	Acculturation Scale	Self-report or Semi-structured interview	Mexicans, Cubans, Puerto Ricans and Central Americans (Marín, Sabogal, Marín, Otero-Sabogal, & Perez-Stable, 1987)
Adaptive and maladaptive behaviors, thoughts and emotions	Behavioral Assessment System for Children (BASC)	Teacher and parent report Youth Self-report	Latino kindergarten children (Flanagan et al., 1996)
Community violence	34-Item Life Events Scale (used as a screener for Cognitive-Behavioral Intervention for Trauma in Schools)	Self-report	Latino immigrants (Stein et al., 2003)
Attitudinal familism	Familism Scale	Self-report	Less acculturated Latinos (Steidel, & Contreras, 2003)
Posttraumatic Stress Disorder (PTSD) symptoms	UCLA PTSD Reaction Index (PTSDRI)	Youth Self-report Parent version also available	Hispanic adolescents (Saltzman, et al., 2001)

RESOURCES

Websites

Center for Health and Health Care in
Schools: http://www.healthinschools.org/~/
media/Images/IssueBrief1.ashx
Familias Unidas: http://www.familias-unidas
.org/indehtm
Let's go Learn: www.letsgolearn.com/
The National Center for Youth Law: http://
www.youthlaw.org/
The National Council of La Raza: www.nclr.org/
40 Developmental Assets: www.
search-institute .org/Assets
National Center for Culturally Responsive
Educational Systems (NCCREST): http://
www.nccrest.org/
National Center on Response to Intervention
(RtI for English Learners): http://www.
rti4success.org/webinars/video/893
Project Read by Language Circle: http://www
.projectread.com/
Response to Intervention Action
Network: http://www.rtinetwork.org/learn/
diversity

References

Arredondo, P., & Glauner, T. (1992). *Personal dimensions of identity model.* Boston, MA: Empowerment Workshops.
Arredondo, P., & Santiago-Rivera, A. (2000). *Latino dimensions of personal identity* (adapted from Personal Dimensions of Identity Model). Unpublished manuscript.
Artiles, A. J., Rueda, R., Salazar, J., & Higareda, I. (2005). Within-group diversity in minority disproportionate representation: English Language Learners in urban school districts. *Exceptional Children, 71,* 283–300.
Battin-Pearson, S., Abbott, R. D., Hill, K. G., Catalano, R. F., Hawkins, J. D., & Newcomb, M. D. (2000). Predictors of early high school dropout: A test of five theories. *Journal of Educational Psychology, 92,* 568–582.
Birman, D., & Chan, W. Y. (2008). *Screening and assessing immigrant and refugee youth in school-based mental health program.* Retrieved from Center for Health and Health Care in Schools website: http://www.healthinschools.org/~/media/Images/IssueBrief1.ashx
Capone, R. (2011). *How to implement Response to Intervention (RTI) in general and with Let's Go Learn.* Retrieved from Let's Go Learn website: http://www.letsgolearn.com/virtual_tours/view/how_to_implement_response_to_intervention_rti_in_general_and_with_lets_go_l/

Carey, G., & Manuppelli, L. (2000). Culture class or not? In M. T. Flores & G. Carey (Eds.), *Family therapy with Hispanics: Toward appreciating diversity* (pp. 79–123). Boston, MA: Allyn & Bacon.
Cheung, A., & Slavin, R. (2005). Effective reading programs for English language learners and other language-minority students. *Bilingual Research Journal, 29*(2), 241–267.
Cuellar, I., Arnold, B., & Maldonado, R. (1995). Acculturation rating scale for Mexican Americans-II: A revision of the original ARSMA scale. *Hispanic journal of behavioral sciences, 17*(3), 275–304.
Cuellar, I., Harris, L. C., & Jasso, R. (1980). An acculturation scale for Mexican American normal and clinical populations. *Hispanic Journal of Behavioral Sciences.*
Dettlaff, A. J., & Rycraft, J. R. (2006). The impact of migration and acculturation on Latino children and families: Implications for child welfare practice. *Protecting Children, 21*(2), 6–21.
Ennis, S. R., Rios-Vargas, M., & Albert, N. G. (2011). The Hispanic population: 2010. 2010 Census Briefs. Retrieved from U.S. Census Bureau website: www.census.gov/prod/cen2010/briefs/c2010br-04.pdf
Fashola, O., & Slavin, R. (1998). Effective dropout prevention and college attendance programs for students placed at risk. *Journal of Education for Students Placed At Risk, 3*(2), 159–183.
Flanagan, D. P., Alfonso, V. C., Primavera, L. H., Povall, L. & Higgins, D. (1996). Convergent validity of the BASC and SSRS: Implications for social skills assessment. *Psychology in the Schools, 33*(1), 13–23.
Fortuny, K., Capps, R., Simms, M., & Chaudry, A. (2009). *Children of immigrants: National and state characteristics.* Retrieved from Urban Institute website: http://www.urban.org/publications/411939.html
Franco, J. (1983). An acculturation scale for Mexican-American children. *The Journal of General Psychology, 108,* 175–181.
Fry, R., & Passel, J. S. (2009). *Latino children: A majority are U.S.-born offspring of immigrants.* Retrieved from Pew Hispanic Center website: http://pewhispanic.org/files/reports/110.pdf
Klingner, J. K., & Harry, B. (2006). The special education referral and decision-making process for English language learners: Child study team meetings and staffings. *Teachers College Record, 108,* 2247–2281.
Lesaux, N. K. (2006). Building consensus: Future directions for research on English language learners at risk for learning difficulties. *Teachers College Record, 108,* 2406–2438.
Garcia, C., Pintor, J. K., Naughton, S., & Lindgren, S. (2009, July). Development of a coping intervention for Latina adolescents: Exploring feasibility challenges and successes. Lecture presented at

20th International Nursing Research Congress on evidence-based practice. Vancouver, British Columbia.

Goodman, M. (2004). Balkan children and families. In R. Fong (Ed.), *Culturally competent practice with immigrant and refugee children and families* (pp. 274–288). New York, NY: Guilford.

Greene, J. P. (1998). *A meta-analysis of the effectiveness of bilingual education*. Claremont, CA: Thomas Rivera Policy Institute.

Greene, V., & Enfield, M. (2006). Project Read®. Bloomington, MN: Language Circle Enterprises.

Hill, N., & Torres, K. (2010). Negotiating the American dream: The paradox of aspirations and achievement among Latino students and engagement between their families and schools. *Journal of Social Issues, 66*(1), 95–112.

Kaplan, C., Turner, S., Piotrkowski, C., & Silber, E. (2009). *Club Amigas*: A promising response to the needs of adolescent Latinas. *Child & Family Social Work, 14*, 213–221.

Klingner, J., & Edwards, P. (2006). New directions in research: Cultural considerations with Response to Intervention models. *Reading Research Quarterly, 41*(1), 108–117.

Lee, J., Grigg, W., & Donahue, P. (2007). The Nation's Report Card: Reading 2007 (NCES 2007–496). Washington, DC: National Center for Education Statistics, Institute of Education Sciences, U.S. Department of Education.

Lewis, A. (2001). *Add it up: Using research to improve education for low-income and minority students*. Washington, DC: Poverty and Race Research Action Council.

Marín, G., Sabogal, F., Marín, B. V., Otero-Sabogal, R., & Perez-Stable, E. J. (1987). Development of a short acculturation scale for Hispanics. *Hispanic Journal of Behavioral Sciences, 9*(2), 183–205.

Moon, S. S., Kang, S., & An. S. (2009). Predictors of immigrant children's school achievement: A comparative study. *Journal of Research in Childhood Education, 23*, 278–289.

National Association of State Directors of Special Education. (2005). *Response to intervention: Policy considerations and implementation*. Retrieved from NASDSE website:http://www.nasdse.org/Projects/ResponsetoInterventionRtIProject/tabid/411/Default.aspx

National Research Council. (2002). *Minority students in special and gifted education*. Washington. DC: National Academies Press.

National Task Force on Early Childhood Education for Hispanics. (2007). *Para nuestros ninos: Expanding and improving early education for Hispanics*. Retrieved from National Task Force on Early Childhood Education for Hispanics website: http://ecehispanic.org/

Nesman, T. (2007). A participatory study of school dropout and behavioral health of Latino adolescents. *The Journal of Behavioral Health Services & Research. 34*(4), 414–430.

Nevarez, C., & Rico, T. 2007. *Latino education: A synthesis of recurring recommendations and solutions in P-16 education*. The College Board. Retrieved from www.professionals.collegeboard.com/prof-download/Latino-Education-A-Synthesis.pdf.

Orosco, M. (2010). A sociocultural examination of Response to Intervention with Latino English language learners. *Theory into Practice, 49*, 265–272.

Orosco, M. J. (2007). *Response to intervention with Latino English language learners*. Boulder: University of Colorado (ProQuest-CSA, LLC 072699).

Orosco, M. J., Schonewise, E. A., de Onis, C., Klingner, J. K., & Hoover, J. J. (2008). Distinguishing between language acquisition and learning disabilities among English language learners: Background information (pp. 5–16). In J. K. Klingner, J. J. Hoover, & L. Baca (Eds.), *English language learners who struggle with reading: Language acquisition or learning disabilities?* Thousand Oaks, CA: Corwin Press.

Osher, D., Cartledge, G., Oswald, D., Sutherland, K., Artiles, A., & Coutinho, M. (2004). Cultural and linguistic competency and disproportionate representation. In R. Rutherford, M. Quinn, & S. Mathur (Eds.) *Handbook of research in emotional and behavioral disorders* (pp. 54–77). New York, NY: The Guilford Press.

Osher, T. W., & Osher, D. (2002). The paradigm shift to true collaboration with families. *Journal of Child and Family Studies, 11*(1), 47–60.

Padilla, A. M., & Perez, W. (2003). Acculturation, social identity, and social cognition: A new perspective. *Hispanic Journal of Behavioral Sciences, 25*, 35–55.

Motel, S. (2012). Statistical portrait of Hispanics in the United States: 2010. Washington, DC: Pew Research Hispanic Center.

Quinones-Mayo, Y., & Dempsey, P. (2005). Finding the bicultural balance: Immigrant Latino mothers raising "American" adolescents. *Child Welfare, 5*, 649–667.

Rinaldi, C., & Samson, J. (2008). English Language Learners and Response to Intervention: Referral considerations. *Teaching Exceptional Children, 40*(5), 6–14.

Rolstad, K., Mahoney, K., & Glass, G. (2005). The big picture: A meta-analysis of program effectiveness research on English language learners. *Educational Policy, 19*(4), 572–594.

Saltzman, W. R., Pynoos, R. S., Layne, C. M., Steinberg, A. M., & Aisenberg, E. (2001). Trauma- and grief-focused intervention for adolescents exposed to community violence: Results of a school-based screening and group treatment protocol. *Group Dynamics: Theory, Research, and Practice, 5*(4), 29.

Santiago, D. A., & Brown, S. E. (2004). *What works for Latino students*. Washington DC: Excelencia in Education, Inc.

Santiago-Rivera, A., Arredondo, P., & Gallardo-Cooper, M. (2002). *Counseling Latinos and la familia: A practical guide*. Thousand Oaks, CA: Sage Publications.

Shin, H. J. (2004). *Parental involvement and its influence on children's school performance: A comparative study between Asian (Chinese and Koreans) Americans and Mexican Americans*. Unpublished doctoral dissertation, Columbia University, New York, NY.

Solis, J. (2003). Re-thinking illegality as a violence against, not by Mexican immigrants, children, and youth. *Journal of Social Issues, 59*, 15–31.

Steidel, A. G. L. & Contreras, J. M. (2003). A new familism scale for use with Latino populations. *Hispanic Journal of Behavioral Sciences, 25*(3), 312–330.

Stein, B. D., Jaycox, L. H., Kataoka, S. H., Wong, M., Tu, W., Elliott, M. N., & Fink, A. (2003). A mental health intervention for schoolchildren exposed to violence: a randomized controlled trial. *Jama, 290*(5), 603–611.

Suarez-Orozco, C., & Suarez-Orozco, M. (1995). *Transformations: Migration, family life, and achievement motivation among Latino adolescents*. Stanford, CA: Stanford University Press.

Suh, S., Suh, J., & Houston, I. (2007). Predictors of categorical at-risk high school dropouts. *Journal of Counseling and Development, 85*, 196–203.

Szapocznik, J., Scopetta, M. A., Kurtines, W., & Aranalde, M. A. (1978). Theory and measurement of acculturation. *Journal of Psychology, 16*, 140–149.

Tazi, Z. (2004). Ecuadorian and Columbian children and families. In R. Fong (Ed.), *Culturally competent practice with immigrant and refugee children and families* (pp. 233–252). New York, NY: Guilford.

Tenebaum, H. R., & Ruck, M. D. (2007). Are teachers' expectations different for racial minority than for European American students? A meta-analysis. *Journal of Educational Psychology, 99*, 253–273.

Thomas, T. N. (1992). Psychoeducational adjustment of English-speaking Caribbean and Central American immigrant children in the United States. *School Psychology Review, 21*, 566–576.

Thorn, A. R., & Contreras, S. (2005). Counseling Latino immigrants in middle school. *Professional School Counseling, 9*(2), 167–170.

Tropp, L. R., Erkut, S., Coll, C. G., Alarcon, O., & García, H. A. V. (1999). Psychological acculturation: Development of a new measure for Puerto Ricans on the US mainland. *Educational and Psychological Measurement, 59*(2), 351–367.

U.S. Census Bureau. (2012a, August). Profile America: Facts for Features: Hispanic Heritage Month 2012. Retrieved from http://www.census.gov/newsroom/releases/archives/facts_for_features_special_editions/cb12-ff19.html

U.S. Census Bureau. (2012b, June). Education: Elementary and secondary education: Completions and dropouts. Retrieved from http://www.census.gov/compendia/statab/cats/education/elementary_and_secondary_education_completions_and_dropouts.html

Valdés, G. (2001). *Learning and not learning English: Latino students in American schools*. New York & London: Teacher College Press.

Willig, A. C. (1985). A meta-analysis of selected studies on the effectiveness of bilingual education. *Review of Educational Research, 55*(3), 269–318.

Zehler, A. M., Fleischman, H. L., Hopstock, P. J., Pendzick, M. L., & Stephenson, T. G. (2003). Descriptive study of services to LEP students and LEP students with disabilities. (No. 4). Arlington, VA: U.S. Department of Education, Office of English Language Acquisition.

139 Online Database of Interventions and Resources for School Social Workers

Natasha K. Bowen

Educational policy of the 2000s, frameworks of school-based practice, the 2012 National Association of Social Workers (NASW) *Standards for School Social Work Services*, and recommendations from school social work researchers all agree on a set of essential practice guidelines for supporting the success of students in American schools. The guidelines include:

- Use assessment data to inform intervention choices.
- Assess and intervene in the social environment, which contributes to student behavior and academic performance at school.
- Use empirically supported practices.
- Categorize interventions into a multi-tiered system based on the two inversely related continua—the number of students needing interventions and the intensity of the interventions.
- Emphasize universal prevention (i.e., targeting all students with low-intensity preventive strategies) to reduce the number of students in need of more intensive intervention.

Educational policies, such as the Individuals with Disabilities Education Act (IDEA) (U.S. Department of Education, 2004) and No Child Left Behind (NCLB, 2001) mandated the use of assessment data and empirically supported interventions in schools. IDEA's language about evaluating students' responses to a series of less-intensive educational strategies before referring them for more intensive (and expensive) services prompted the development of multi-tiered approaches

to school interventions, such as Response to Intervention (RTI, National Center on Response to Intervention, 2010) and Positive Behavioral Interventions and Supports (PBIS or PBS, Office of Special Education Programs, 2011). These frameworks call for the use of ongoing assessment data to evaluate student progress and guide the choice of appropriate empirically supported interventions. See Chapter 84 for more on PBIS.

The 2012 NASW *Standards for School Social Work Services* reflect awareness that the new accountability mandates and models of school-based student supports could affect social workers' roles in schools. The three standards below, for example, include language specifying that assessments and interventions should be ecological, multi-tiered, and that practice decisions should be based on data.

- Standard 3. Assessment (p. 9)
  School social workers shall conduct assessments of individuals, families, and systems/organizations (namely, classroom, school, neighborhood, district, state) with the goal of improving student social, emotional, behavioral, and academic outcomes.
- Standard 4. Intervention (p. 9)
  School social workers shall understand and use evidence-informed practices in their interventions.
- Standard 5. Decision Making and Practice Evaluation (p. 10)
  School social workers shall use data to guide service delivery and to evaluate their practice regularly to improve and expand services.

The literature on school social work has also reflected changes in expectations for school-based practitioners and the perception that school social workers must adapt to frameworks like RTI (Kelly et al., 2010b), or should make use of existing social work training and tools to become leaders in ecological assessment, empirically supported practices, and prevention (N. K. Bowen, 2013; Dupper, 2002; Franklin, Harris, & Allen-Meares, 2013; Powers, Bowen, & Bowen, 2011).

Despite federal legislation, the diffusion of multi-tiered approaches to school-based intervention, and changes to school social work standards to reflect changes in the macro environment for education, it is not clear that social work practices have changed substantially (Kelly et al., 2010a; Kelly et al., 2010b) in recent years. Kelly et al. (2010b), for example, used survey data from school social workers to examine the extent to which their current practices were consistent with major elements of RTI, such as using empirically supported interventions, providing multi-tiered interventions, and employing data-driven decision-making. The researchers found that the practices reported by school social workers came up short in these areas. Similarly, in a manuscript describing social work practices based on 2008 data from a sample of school social workers, Kelly et al. (2010a) concluded that despite the changing climate of school-based practice, school social work had not changed substantially in the previous 10 years. A majority of respondents in the study (60%) indicated they spent all or most of their time providing individual counseling to students; almost one-third (30%) reported that half or more of their caseloads were students with Individual Education Plans (IEP), meaning the students received intensive, targeted exceptional children's services; and a majority wished they could spend more time on prevention (Tier 1) and less on Tier 2 and Tier 3 interventions.

To become leaders in school-based interventions that respond to federal mandates and the needs of students, social workers must equip themselves with appropriate knowledge and tools regarding empirically supported group- and school-level prevention and intervention strategies. An existing publicly available database at the School Success Online website can equip social workers with the information, tools, and resources they need. This chapter describes the School Success Profile (SSP)/Elementary School

Success Profile (ESSP) Best Practices database and demonstrates how it can be navigated. We describe three ways the SSP/ESSP Best Practices Database can equip school social workers to lead or guide efforts at their schools to implement empirically supported, tiered prevention and intervention strategies based on an ecological understanding of student well-being and performance in schools:

1. The "traditional" way—Search by SSP and ESSP social environmental domains (e.g., neighborhood, school) and dimensions (e.g., teen behavior in neighborhood, school safety) to find universal or targeted interventions that address factors with undesirable assessment scores.
2. The "risk and protection profile" way—Use recommendations from SSP and ESSP studies about common profiles of social environmental risk and protection to guide intervention choices.
3. The "freestyle" way—Use the keyword search function in the online database or the Mental Health Database to identify strategies and resources related to the range of referral issues school social workers commonly encounter, including mental health disorders.

By drawing on findings from published SSP and ESSP studies of the relationship of the social environment to student outcomes and published and unpublished information about the best practices database, this chapter provides a comprehensive overview of how the database can serve school social workers in their efforts to support students with the high-quality services they deserve.

OVERVIEW OF SCHOOL SUCCESS PROFILE AND ELEMENTARY SCHOOL SUCCESS PROFILE BEST PRACTICES DATABASE AND ASSESSMENTS

Whether or not they play a direct role in implementing group and individual interventions, the value of school social workers' contribution to school-based efforts to support student success is enhanced when they are familiar with best practices to address the range of barriers to learning encountered by students. The online SSP/ESSP database of best practices and resources (http://www.schoolsuccessonline.com)

equips social workers with intervention expertise that can make them indispensable as school team members; as consultants to teachers, other student support professionals, administrators, and parents; and as providers of direct services. Specifically, the database provides social workers with information on empirically supported interventions that address threats to school success revealed in student assessment data (Powers et al., 2011; Powers, Bowen, & Rose, 2005). Entries are listed as "evidence-based programs" or "promising practices" depending on the level of research supporting them. Descriptions of best practices in the database are sufficient to permit decisions about their feasibility and acceptability to school staff. If relevant, contact information for materials and training is also provided in database entries. The database also describes hundreds of books, websites, and other sources of information on problems and disorders, assessments, and interventions relevant to practice in schools in a subsection called "Resources." The site, therefore, supports the development of expertise in problem areas, the use of published assessments, practice accountability, and the use of empirically supported interventions. In summary, under each social environmental domain and dimension that is important to elementary or secondary students, users of the online database can find:

- Evidence-based programs
- Promising practices
- Resources

Consistent with trends toward tiered responses to student needs, SSP/ESSP evidence-based program entries are organized into three categories based on whom they target: "universal" prevention strategies targeting all students; "selective/indicated" prevention efforts designed for small groups (e.g., Tier 2) or individual students (e.g., Tier 3) for whom universal prevention efforts are not sufficient; and "multicomponent" strategies that include universal and targeted components (Powers et al., 2011). The categorization of entries in the database facilitates the consultative role of social workers serving on school teams focused on school-wide strategies to improve student learning (e.g., school improvement teams), and on teams focused on removing barriers to learning for individual students or small groups of students (e.g., student support teams or exceptional children's teams). Because Tier 1 and Tier 2 interventions are currently emphasized in school

practice as means to avoid the most expensive and intensive individual-level interventions, including exceptional children's services, we focus in this chapter on using the Best Practices Database for group- and school-level interventions.

The Traditional Way of Using the Best Practices Database

The online database can be used with or without SSP or ESSP data. It was originally designed, however, to be used in conjunction with group-level reports, or profiles, from the SSP and ESSP. Unlike most assessments used in schools (Bowen, 2013), the SSP for secondary students (G. L. Bowen, Rose, & Bowen, 2005; Richman, Bowen, & Woolley, 2004) and ESSP for third through fifth grade students (N. K. Bowen, Bowen, & Woolley, 2004; N. K. Bowen, 2010) collect data on social environmental factors associated with students' school success. The SSP for middle and high school students collects self-report data on the neighborhood, school, friend, and family environments of youth. The ESSP collects data from students, their teacher, and a caregiver. Both surveys also collect data about proximal and distal outcomes associated with supportive and problematic social environments—student psychological well-being, behaviors, and academic outcomes. SSP and ESSP data help teachers and school practitioners understand *why* some students may be struggling with social behavior or academic outcomes (N. K. Bowen, 2013), information that is essential to decision-making about strategies to *prevent* undesirable outcomes. Although we describe here the use of SSP or ESSP assessment data in the process of identifying interventions, interventions in the database can be explored by domain and dimension even if other assessments have been used to collect social environmental data on students.

Data from any assessment should provide practitioners with answers to the following questions (N. K. Bowen, Lee, & Weller, 2007; Powers et al., 2011):

- Who should be targeted?
- Which environmental or individual factors should be addressed?
- How much change should be sought?

The answers to these questions will determine which intervention or prevention strategy is appropriate. We describe how SSP and ESSP results help school social workers answer these questions, but analogous decision-making strategies should apply to other assessments as well.

Who Should be Targeted?

Because group- and individual-level profiles are generated as respondents complete the SSP and ESSP, the question of whom to target is not difficult to answer. If group-level scores in any area are undesirable, school staff may decide school- or grade level-wide strategies are needed. If, according to individual-level profiles, scores are alarming for only a small subset of students, or one student, targeted interventions might be a reasonable strategy. "Group-level" data are often school-level data, but practitioners can request data reports on students with common demographic characteristics (gender, race, age, and grade level) and combinations of those characteristics. With data on subgroups of students at their schools, practitioners can better tailor group-level interventions.

Which Environmental or Individual Factors Should Be Addressed?

The choice of environmental or individual characteristics to be addressed also flows readily from SSP and ESSP assessment data. Group and individual profiles for both the secondary and elementary assessments have embedded interpretation cues. The individual-level SSP profile, for example, uses a stop light format to indicate which dimensions of the social environment and student well-being have scores in the risk (red), cautionary (yellow), and asset (green) categories. The ESSP uses percentage scores with cutoffs to indicate dimensions that have scores in the risk (less than 60%), cautionary (60% to 79%), and protective (80% or higher) range. Dimensions with scores below the cutoff for protective environmental and individual features may be considered as potential intervention targets. Obtained scores on dimensions of the social environment and individual well-being must also be assessed in light of school staff's knowledge of the student body and their own priorities for change.

Using knowledge about which SSP scores are most predictive of proximal (dimensions of personal beliefs and well-being) and distal outcomes (behavior and academic performance) can also help school social workers decide where to devote their intervention efforts. Powers, Bowen, and Rose (2005), for example, demonstrated that of the social environmental dimensions assessed with the SSP, neighborhood safety was most predictive of school behavior, and school satisfaction was most predictive of school engagement.

How Much Change Should Be Sought?

The answer to this question is guided by discussion among stakeholders about what scores would be acceptable and how much change is possible in a given time frame. When looking at the Summary Group Profile for the SSP, for example, school staff might be most concerned about what they consider a high percentage of students (e.g., 25%) with scores in the risk range for perceptions of school safety. They might agree that a desirable and feasible goal is to reduce the 25% to 10% in the current school year. One of the ESSP group-level reports provides comparison scores based on a representative sample from a large community sample, which can help school staff evaluate their own scores. Cutoffs for desirable scores on ESSP dimensions are also provided and serve as numeric goals that may be chosen by school social workers. Specifically, scores below 60% (on a scale of 0 to 100) are considered within the risk range; scores from 61% to 79% are considered cautionary; and scores of 80% or higher are considered protective. However, one ESSP study (N. K. Bowen et al., 2007) suggested that scores of 90% or higher are the most beneficial for student outcomes; therefore, school staff might aim to increase scores on dimensions they choose to target up to that level, if feasible.

Of course choices about "who," "what," and "how much change" must also take into account resource and time constraints of school staff. Resource constraints, such as lack of discretionary funding for social work interventions, limited staff time, and administrative preferences, will affect decisions about how to proceed from assessment data. Bowen, Lee, and Weller (2007) describe alternatives that may need to be considered in the common circumstance of resource constraints on intervention choices.

How Can We Address the Identified Problem?

After intervention targets and change goals are identified based on assessment data, the next question is: How do we address the identified problem? Potential answers are provided by the SSP/ESSP online database of best practices and resources. Figure 139.1 illustrates how to navigate from the School Success Online home page to the best practices database. After identifying scores of concern on an SSP or ESSP

Best Practices Link on
School Success
Online Home Page

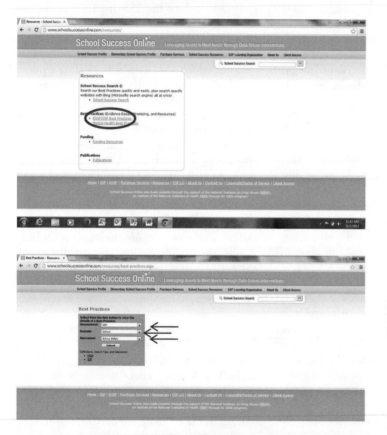

ESSP/SSP Best Practices Link

Selecting SSP (Middle and
High School Strategies) for
School Safety

Figure 139.1 Navigation to the SSP and ESSP Best Practices Database from the School Success Online home page.

group-level report, for example, scores indicating low levels of school safety or high levels of bullying, social workers could review the evidence-based and promising practices described in the online database for each of those dimensions. Information on the costs of strategies in the database help school practitioners narrow down intervention options to those they can afford. Depending on cost, material, and personnel resources required, and idiosyncratic preferences of school staff, one or more programs might be selected to

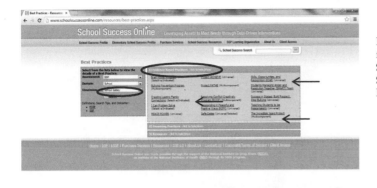

Evidence-Based Program Options for Middle and High School Safety, with Universal, Selective/Indicated, and Multicomponent Labels

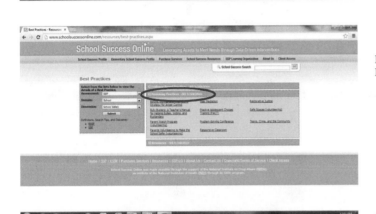

Promising Program Options for Middle and High School Safety

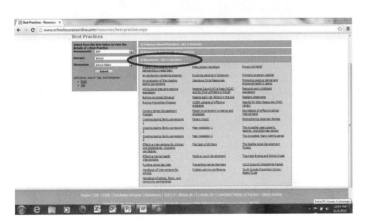

Resource Options for School Safety

Figure 139.2 Illustration of navigation to secondary school interventions for school safety.

address a problem. Additional resources from the database's resource category might also be obtained and consulted. Consideration of protective factors in student profiles could assist in the choice of strategies to use (e.g., if students perceive high amounts of social support in their social environment outside of school, strategies involving adults from outside the school might be feasible).

Example of Traditional Navigation of the SSP/ESSP Best Practices Database

Figure 139.2 illustrates navigation of the Best Practices Database for strategies addressing school safety in a secondary school (starting where Figure 139.1 left off). After selecting the SSP subsection of the database, which contains best practices for middle and high school students, the school domain, and the school

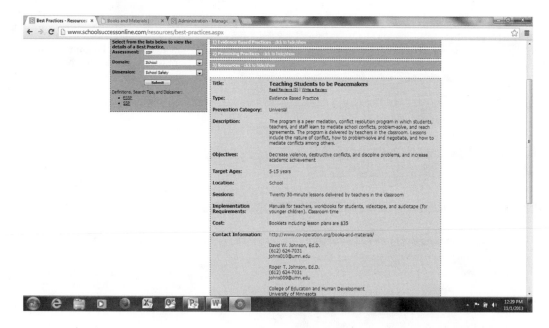

A Promising Practice in the Database

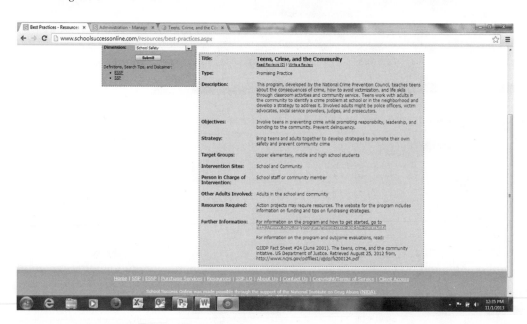

Figure 139.3 Examples of information screens for evidence-based programs and promising practices for school safety.

safety dimension, the school social worker will see a screen with three options on the right. Option 1 provides a list of highly researched evidence-based practices. Option 2 provides a list of promising practices—strategies that have preliminary to promising evidence of utility for addressing the problem area. Option 3 provides a list of print and online resources that provide background information and/or assessment and intervention information on the problem area. Figure 139.3 provides examples of information screens for evidence-based programs and promising practices for school safety.

Use of the Best Practices Database in this traditional way has been illustrated in previous publications (G. L. Bowen, Richman, & Bowen, 2002;

Powers et al., 2011; Powers et al., 2005). The SSP and ESSP entries on evidence-based practices, promising practices, and resources are the same whether they are accessed the traditional way just described, or through the other approaches described below.

The Risk and Protection Profiles Approach to the Best Practices Database

Three studies using ecological SSP or ESSP data and theoretical approaches have identified combinations of risk and protection that may be common among students. In conjunction with ecological assessment data, knowledge of these common patterns can help social workers decide what social environmental factors should be prioritized and how much change to seek. Findings from the studies also suggest that targeting multiple areas of students' social environments may be important and that building protective factors is a viable prevention strategy. Bowen, Lee, and Weller (2007) looked at patterns of high (protective) and low (risk) scores on eight variables related to neighborhood, school, friends, and family. Adults who care, quality of friendships, treatment by peers, and student perceptions of school as a fun place to learn and be with other children were variables used to create the typology. The authors identified five common profiles of risk and protection that were associated with outcomes of interest to school staff. The study found:

- The best psychological, physical health, behavioral, and academic outcomes were observed for students with high levels of social environmental protection in all areas (90% or higher).
- The worst student outcomes were associated with an accumulation of scores below the moderate protection range (below 80%).
- Students facing risk in only the friend domain had physical health, adjustment, social skills, learning behavior, and academic outcomes similar to students with low scores in multiple domains.

The findings suggest, among other things, that building the number of sources of protection as well as the amount of protection across the neighborhood, school, friend, and family domains is important. In addition, even in the context of protection in other domains, negative peer influences may be a threat to student well-being that should not be ignored. School social workers can be guided by the findings of this study to search the online database for feasible universal interventions in multiple social environmental domains, but strategies to improve peer relationships schoolwide or for groups of students who are rejected or surrounded by ill-behaved peers might be a priority.

Another study (Weller, Bowen, & Bowen, 2013) using SSP data from middle and high school students examined patterns of witnessing violence in the neighborhood, school, and among friends, and ongoing fear of violence at school and neighborhood. Four patterns of these negative experiences were identified: high exposure and fear, low exposure and fear, high vicarious exposure but low fear, and high fear but low vicarious exposure. The study found:

- Witnessing violence was associated with more behavior problems regardless of whether it was accompanied by fear of violence.
- Fear of violence was not associated with behavior problems.
- When witnessing violence or fear of violence occurred in one domain, it also tended to occur in the other domains examined.

The study also examined whether patterns of witnessing violence and fearing violence were associated with gender and racial/ethnic characteristics. White females were the most likely to fear violence at school and in the neighborhood. Black males were the most likely to witness violence in their social environments. Findings from this study highlight the potential negative impact of school and community violence on youth behavior. In addition to using the online database of best practices to identify universal strategies to make the neighborhood and school safer for students, school social workers might discuss with teachers and other school staff the possibility that negative student behaviors are often a consequence of environmental stress—not necessarily student-level deficits.

A third study using SSP data from middle school students examined patterns of social capital (defined as supportive relationships) across the neighborhood, school, friend, and family domains (Rose, Woolley, & Bowen, 2013). As in the previous two studies, the authors also examined associations between the patterns, which they called "portfolios" of social capital, and outcomes. The analysis identified eight portfolios characterized by different combinations and levels of social capital. In support of their hypothesis

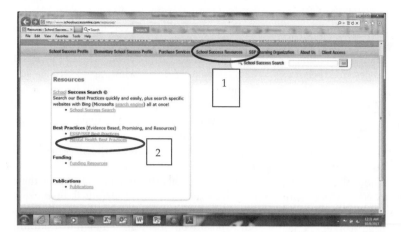

Navigating from the Website's Banner Links

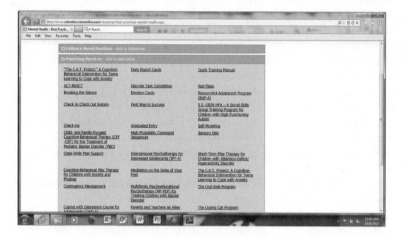

Promising Practices Currently in the Mental Health Database

Resources Currently in the Mental Health Practices Database

Figure 139.4 Illustration of navigating the mental health subsection of the database.

that the nature or sources of social capital matter, not just the amount, the researchers also found:

• Portfolios containing support from multiple adults were associated with highest levels of school engagement.

• For some academic outcomes, high levels of teacher support compensated for a lack of support from other adults.

Similar to the first typology study, this study justifies a focus on increasing the number and quality of relationships students have with adults and other youth. School social workers can look for evidence-based programs and promising practices related to neighbor, teacher, parent, and friend support. Given common resource constraints, however, focusing on suggested strategies for improving perceived support from teachers might be a priority.

The traditional and risk and protection profile approaches to using the SSP/ESSP Best Practices

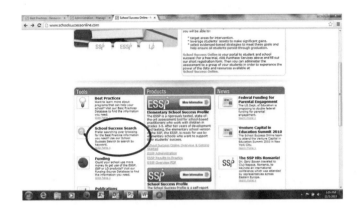

Choosing the School Success Search Engine on the Home Page

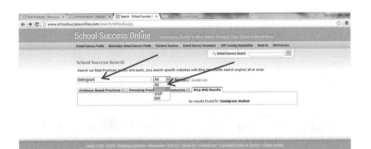

Entering a Search Term and Selecting Database Subsections

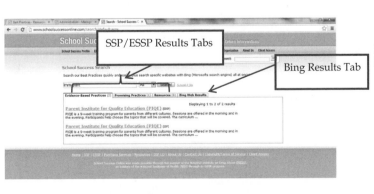

Results Showing SSP/ESSP Database and Bing Tabs

Figure 139.5 Illustration of navigating the keyword search engine.

Database are facilitated by the use of the SSP or ESSP assessment but in no way require it. School social workers who collect ecological data on students with other assessments can easily relate those data to appropriate domains and dimensions listed in the drop down boxes in the database.

The Freestyle Approach to the Best Practices Database

Two other navigation approaches for the best practices database are possible and may be especially convenient for social workers who have not conducted SSP or ESSP assessments. First, a separate subsection of the database focuses on

Results from Resources Subsection of the SSP/ESSP Database

Results from Promising Practices Subsection of the SSP/ESSP Database

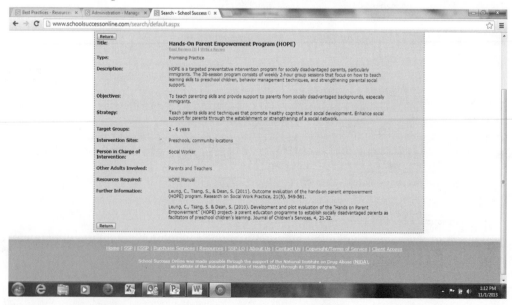

Figure 139.6 Example of results of freestyle search on "immigrant."

mental health interventions (Powers et al., 2012). Evidence-based programs, promising practices, and resources specifically related to mental health issues can be reviewed all in one place in this section of the database. Many of the entries listed under resources relate to mental health assessments. Like the general best practices database, the mental health subsection can be accessed by clicking Best Practices on the School Success Online home page. Figure 139.4 illustrates an alternative way to navigate from the home page to the mental health practices database (and the general database).

Second, the School Success Search feature allows social workers to conduct subject keyword searches. The freestyle approach provides "hits" from the online SSP/ESSP database as well as other carefully selected online sources of information on evidence-based programs, promising practices, and resources on school-based interventions. Figures 139.5 and 139.6 illustrate how to navigate the keyword search engine. Note as well that a School Success Search box and "Go" button are available on most pages of the School Success Online website. They can be seen in the upper right corner of screen shots in Figures 139.1, 139.2, 139.4, and 139.5. Using the School Success Search feature allows school staff to quickly find resources based on terms that they encounter in their everyday practice in schools—for example, attendance, truancy, dropout, pregnancy, disruptive behavior, attention deficit, autism, and school phobia.

CONCLUSION

School social workers, and the school staff with whom they work, are increasingly expected to use ecological assessment data, empirically supported strategies, and group- and school-level approaches to promoting school success and reducing the number of children who need intensive, targeted interventions. Professional standards of school social work practice and the literature on school social work also support these practices. The School Success Online Best Practices Database is a source of extensive information and resources for meeting the demands of school social work. The database, if extensively explored, can also increase school social workers prominence at their schools. School social workers can become intervention and assessment experts on school teams; sources of professional

development on prevention to teachers, school leaders, and other student services personnel; and well-informed advocates for obtaining the most effective strategies to promote the success of students at their schools.

References

Bowen, G. L., Rose, R. A., & Bowen, N. K. (2005). *The reliability and validity of the school success profile*. Philadelphia, PA: Xlibris.

Bowen, G. L., Richman, J. M., & Bowen, N. K. (2002). The school success profile: A results management approach to assessment and intervention planning. In A. R. Roberts, & G. J. Greene (Eds.), *Social workers' desk reference* (pp. 787–793). New York, NY: Oxford University Press.

Bowen, N. K. (2010). Child-report data and assessment of the social environment in schools. *Research on Social Work Practice, 21,* 476–486. doi:10.1177/1049731510391675

Bowen, N. K. (2013). Using data to communicate with school stakeholders. In C. Franklin, M. Harris & P. Allen-Meares (Eds.), *School services sourcebook* (2nd ed.). (pp. 889–902). New York, NY: Oxford University Press.

Bowen, N. K., Bowen, G. L., & Woolley, M. E. (2004). Constructing and validating assessment tools for school-based practitioners: The elementary school success profile. In A. R. Roberts & K. R. Yeager (Eds.), *Evidence-based practice manual: Research and outcome measures in health and human services* (pp. 509–517). New York, NY: Oxford University Press.

Bowen, N. K., Lee, J. S., & Weller, B. (2007). Social environmental risk and protection: A typology with implications for practice in elementary schools. *Children & Schools, 29,* 229–242.

Dupper, D. D. (2002). *School social work: Skills and interventions for effective practice.* New York, NY: John Wiley & Sons.

Franklin, C., Harris, M. B., & Allen-Meares, P. (Eds.). (2013). *The school services sourcebook* (2nd ed.). New York, NY: Oxford University Press.

Kelly, M. S., Berzin, S. C., Frey, A., Alvarez, M., Shaffer, G. L., & O'Brien, K. (2010a). The state of school social work: Findings from the National School Social Work Survey. *School Mental Health Journal, 2,* 132–141. doi:10.1007/s12310-010-9034-5

Kelly, M. S., Frey, A. J., Alvarez, M., Berzin, S., Shaffer, G. L., & O'Brien, K. (2010b). School social work practice and response to intervention. *Children & Schools, 32,* 201–209.

National Center on Response to Intervention. (2010). *Essential components of RTI—A closer look at response to intervention.* Washington, DC: U.S. Department of Education, Office of Special Education Programs, National Center on Response to Intervention. Retrieved from http://www.rti4success.org/pdf/rtiessentialcomponents_042710.pdf

No Child Left Behind (NCLB). (2001). *No Child Left Behind Act of 2001, P.L. 107-110, 115, stat. 1425.*

Office of Special Education Programs. (2011). *Technical assistance center on positive behavioral interventions and supports.* http://www.pbis.org/

Powers, J. D. (2012). Scientifically supported mental health intervention in schools: Meeting accountability demands with an online resource. *Journal of Evidence-Based Social Work, 9,* 231–240.

Powers, J. D., Bowen, N. K., & Bowen, G. L. (2011). Supporting evidence-based practice in schools with an online database of best practices. *Children & Schools, 33*(2), 119–123.

Powers, J. D., Bowen, G. L., & Rose, R. A. (2005). Using social environment assets to identify intervention strategies for promoting school success. *Children and Schools, 27,* 177–187.

Richman, J. M., Bowen, G. L., & Woolley, M. E. (2004). School failure: An eco-interactional developmental perspective. In M. W. Fraser (Ed.), *Risk and resilience in childhood: An ecological perspective* (2nd ed.) (pp. 133–160). Washington, DC: NASW Press.

Rose, R. A., Woolley, M. E., & Bowen, G. L. (2013). Social capital as a portfolio of resources across multiple microsystems: Implications for middle-school students. *Family Relations, 62,* 545–558. doi:10.1111/fare.12028

U.S. Department of Education. (2004). *Individuals with Disabilities Education Improvement Act (IDEIA) of 2004. P. L. 108–446.* (No. 70).

Weller, B. E., Bowen, N. K., & Bowen, G. L. (2013). Linking students to appropriate interventions: A typology for social workers based on general strain theory. *Journal of Social Work, 13,* 361–381. doi:10.1177/1468017311435446

PART XIV
Forensic Social Work

140 | The Changing Face of Forensic Social Work Practice
An Overview

José B. Ashford

The National Center for State Courts (NCSC) has a joint project on court statistics with the Conference of Court Administrators and the Bureau of Justice Statistics. The data collected by the Court Statistics Project (CSP) of NCSC documents the caseloads in explicit legal forums where forensic social workers commonly practice: domestic relations, criminal, and juvenile courts. Caseloads in our state courts provide invaluable information about the social significance of our general and limited jurisdiction courts (Willrich, 2003). Caseload data also provide practitioners, policymakers, and academics with the kinds of information that they need in order to develop effective responses for persons involved in legal proceedings (National Center for State Courts, 2012).

The overall caseloads for state courts witnessed a 2% decline in 2010. The most recent data collected by the CSP project shows that the only type of court that witnessed an increase in cases from 2009 to 2010 was the domestic relations court (National Center for State Courts, 2012). Divorce is the central concern that tends to drive domestic relations caseloads. The caseloads for domestic relations courts increased by 7% in 2010 and these domestic relations caseloads have been on the rise since 2007. However, it is unknown whether the observed rise in domestic relations cases since 2007 is connected in any way to the economic downturn that began in that same year (National Center for State Courts, 2012).

Although the number of domestic relations cases increased in 2010, the number of incoming criminal cases to our general and limited jurisdiction courts was essentially the same in 2010 as in 2009. The adult-criminal courts processed over 20 million individuals in 2010 at an adjusted rate for population size of 6,500 cases per 100,000 population (National Center for State Courts, 2012). This rate is comparable to the benchmark established in 2001 for incoming criminal cases in our state courts. However, this rate is lower than the rate in 2006 when the rate of cases processed by general and limited jurisdiction courts was 7,076 per 100,000 population, which is the highest rate for the years included in CSP's data collection project.

The rates of incoming cases in juvenile courts have also shown declines. The juvenile caseloads declined by 13% from 2007 to 2010. Some of this decline has been attributed to reductions in police and protective service budgets (National Center for State Courts, 2012). Another potential contributing factor is the increased use by many courts of interventions designed to divert juvenile offenders from the justice process. The total number of cases processed in juvenile courts in 2010 was 1,864,345. The rate of incoming cases in 2010 was 2,483 per 100,000 population.

Many of the individuals entering the various doors of our legal system have significant mental health and other related problems. These include:

- Substance-abusing parents in our juvenile courts (at least 80% have substance abuse problems).
- Youths in our juvenile justice system (70.4% meet criteria for at least one mental health disorder).

- Adult offenders (of those detained in local jails, 15% to 16% have serious mental health disorders).
- Guardianship cases (senior citizens incapable of managing their person or property witnessed an 18% increase between 1996 and 2005).

Indeed, the courts have become the societal institution of last resort for many vulnerable individuals who are in need of a diverse array of mental health and other kinds of social services provided by forensic social workers (Ashford, 2013).

Victims of crime and other forms of personal harm are also in need of the services of forensic social workers. Workers can assist victims by providing them with support services while victims' complaints are being processed in the criminal justice system. They can also assist victims with the psychosocial and economic consequences of the crime even if the victims have not filed formal legal complaints. The most recent National Victims Survey results indicate that the overall rates of victimization are on the decline, but the rates at which violent-crimes are reported to the police have remained about the same. That is, the results of the survey continue to show that 50% of the victims of violent crime continue not to report their victimization to the police (National Center for Victims, 2013). Though overall rates of violent crime in the National Victims Survey have shown a decrease, the percentage of individuals reporting physical injury during the same period increased from 24% in 2008 to 29% in 2010 (National Center for Victims of Crime, 2013).

In response to the large numbers of victims and offenders involved in law and law-like systems, we are seeing a corresponding increase of interest in the social work profession in the subspecialty of forensic social work. This subspecialty has undergone significant changes since its initial inception as a distinct area of professional social work practice. This chapter reviews many of these changes, including the prospects and limits of professional practice in this burgeoning area of social work practice.

ORIGINS AND DEVELOPMENT OF FORENSIC SOCIAL WORK PRACTICE

Social workers have long recognized that the law is an important mechanism for achieving many of their professional aims. Most of the early social workers involved in the establishment of the profession collaborated with lawyers in dealing with many different types of social problems. Harriett Bartlett (1970, p. 19) wrote that the social work profession started in many ways by helping individuals who "fell through the cracks of the medical and legal systems." Indeed numerous social work pioneers, such as Jane Addams, tested many of their theories about crime and other social problems in the newly formed urban courts of Chicago (Willrich, 2003). In particular, Jane Addams played a key role in the establishment of the juvenile court and the modern municipal court system that replaced the traditional justice of the peace courts (Willrich, 2003).

Inasmuch as law and social work interactions were pivotal to the formation of many aspects of social work as a profession, the subspecialty of forensic social work is of much more recent historical origin (Reamer, 2007). Most social work practitioners involved in law and social work interactions never used the term forensic to describe the application of their expertise to legal matters until social workers began practicing as members of forensic psychiatric teams. Psychiatric social workers in a number of states were members of clinical teams that were responsible for performing court ordered evaluations of criminal defendants. Like the psychologists on these teams, social workers carried out their assessment and treatment duties under the supervision of a psychiatrist. This form of medical dominance inhibited the development of forensics as a subspecialty in social work and in psychology for many years (Dix & Poythress, 1981).

CHALLENGES TO THE MEDICAL DOMINANCE OF FORENSIC PRACTICE

Forensics is a term derived from the Latin "forensis" meaning forum. In Roman times, the forum was the public place where issues were debated before a group of citizens. However, this meaning of forensics changed and began to be restricted to legal disputes in courts of law around the 17th century. During this time period, the term forensic began to be applied to legal questions involving the causes of a person's death. Medical practitioners were the first group of professionals (other than clergy, lawyers, and judges) who were involved in assisting the courts with these forensic issues. That is, physicians were initially called to assist the courts as scientific experts in determining the cause of a person's death. This form of practice led to the development of the field of forensic medicine.

Traditionally, physicians were also the first group of scientific experts called on to identify signs of illness associated with disturbances of a defendant's mind. However, psychiatric and legal historians have written that questions about the mental capabilities of individuals were originally handled by testimony from laypersons who knew the defendant (Gutheil, 2005; Skalevag, 2006). These witnesses would confirm whether the defendant had a "weak mind" from birth or whether they had acquired a derangement of mind that had been observed by individuals who knew the defendant prior to the defendant's involvement in the crime. Prior to the 19th century, priests or other religious authorities also were called to assist the courts in assessing the mental culpability of an offender. However, they were no longer allowed to make these assessments after assumptions about human nature and illnesses began to be influenced by evolving conceptions of illnesses in the medical sciences (Skalevag, 2006).

After scientific assumptions about mental illnesses entered the legal culture, the courts only allowed professionals with medical training to conduct assessments of criminal forensic issues such as competency-to-stand trial or criminal responsibility (Not Guilty by Reason of Insanity, Guilty but Insane, or Diminished Criminal Responsibility). Some early challenges to this medical expertise were raised by philosophers. For instance, the philosopher Immanuel Kant (1970) did not believe that the mental condition of an offender fell under the competence of medicine. "According to Kant, questions concerning the mental faculties are psychological so that answers should come from the faculty of philosophy" (Mooij, 1998, p. 340). Psychology here is not the discipline of psychology we known today because this scientific discipline had not been established when Kant was writing. Kant assumed that philosophers knew much more about human nature and mental faculties than medical practitioners (Mooij, 1998). Nonetheless, most criminal codes deferred to medical professionals for addressing forensic issues involving mental health concerns up until the 1980s.

During the 1970s, psychologists, nurses, and social workers began to challenge psychiatry's claim to ultimate responsibility for treatment of forensic and other patients (Dix & Poythress, 1981). Up until this point in history, practice in most mental health settings was dictated by a 1954 resolution approved by the American

Psychiatric Association, the American Medical Association, and the American Psychoanalytic Association. This resolution contended:

> The medical profession fully endorses the appropriate utilization of the skills of psychologists, social workers, and other professional personnel in contributing roles in settings directly supervised by physicians.... [W]hen members of these professions contribute to the diagnosis and treatment of illness, their professional contribution must be coordinated under medical responsibility (see, Dix & Poythress, 1981, p. 962).

Although successful campaigns were launched by social workers and psychologists to achieve independent practice in various areas of mental health, the fight was a bit more difficult for social workers than for psychologists. One presumed drawback for including social workers as independent forensic evaluators was licensure (Dix & Poythress, 1981). When psychologists made their case for inclusion in forensic practice, fewer states licensed social workers than licensed clinical psychologists. However, the licensure problem for social workers has changed dramatically since the initial challenges by psychologists of medical dominance in forensic mental health practice. That is, many states currently license clinical social workers who as mental health professionals can diagnosis individuals for the purpose of treating mental disorders. However, this important change in the definition of social work practice did not result in many modifications of criminal codes. Many codes continue to authorize only psychiatrists to conduct competency and insanity assessments. Most criminal statutes still demand either the participation of a physician or limit participation to psychiatrists or psychologists. Although the statutory language in many jurisdictions does not exclude social workers explicitly from performing forensic mental health evaluations, the language in most state statutes demands the participation of either a psychiatrist or a psychologist.

In making psychology's case for independent forensic practice, Dix and Poythress (1981) made a convincing argument about how expertise for forensic assessments should be determined. Donald Langsley, who was a former president of the American Psychiatric Association, had questioned the motives behind psychologists, social workers, and other nonmedical professionals seeking independent practice opportunities. Langsley argued that these requests for opportunities to function as independent practitioners should not be motivated by the pursuit of economic gain and financial rewards, but instead by dispassionate examination of education and demonstrated competencies in clinical areas of practice. To this end, Dix and Poythress (1981) wrote a law review article that questioned whether medical education justified medical superiority. In this law review article, they also examined the issue of psychology's demonstrated competence in many areas of civil and criminal forensic mental health matters. Social workers also achieved recognition as forensic experts in some jurisdictions by independently demonstrating their competence in forensic areas of practice. This chapter reviews some of the progress that social workers have made in demonstrating their expertise in a variety of legal forums.

RECOGNITION OF SOCIAL WORKERS AS EXPERT WITNESSES

Although many social workers on forensic psychiatric teams developed demonstrated expertise as forensic evaluators, there was still a bias in the legal community against treating social workers as expert witnesses for competency-to-stand-trial and insanity issues. For instance, the court in *People v. Parney* (1977) held that a forensic social worker was not qualified to give expert testimony as to issues of competency to stand trial. However, the nonbinding statements in this decision (dicta) pointed out that this holding was not based on the capabilities of any particular social worker, but based on a court rule that mandated presentation of psychiatric evidence regarding competency. This type of regulatory prohibition that affected the court's assessment of a social worker's expertise is still common in many states. However, there was a landmark decision involving a clinical social worker that challenged psychiatry's dominance in New York in the case of *People v. Gans* (1983). In this case, the New York court held that a clinical social worker with appropriate training and experience was qualified to testify as an expert witness to a defendant's mental condition and their prognosis in competency evaluations.

Today, most states still require that at least one examiner is a psychiatrist, but there is mounting evidence that courts are willing to deem a social worker an expert in making mental health diagnoses in criminal forensic and civil forensic matters by examining the nature and quality of their training and experience (see, *Conely v. Commonwealth of Virginia*, 2007; *America West Airlines v. Tope*, 1996). In addition, some states now allow statutorily for other experts to perform forensic evaluations in criminal matters besides psychiatrists and psychologists (e.g., Connecticut, Delaware, Iowa, Louisiana, Maine, New Mexico, North Carolina, North Dakota, Nevada, Oklahoma, Tennessee, Texas, Utah, Wisconsin, and Virginia). However, Nevada limits the expertise of social workers to performing these evaluations in misdemeanor offenses; and Virginia limits the scope of social work's expertise as an evaluating expert to cases involving juvenile offenders when psychiatrists and psychologists are not available.

Like psychologists, forensic social workers established an identity in the specialty of forensics by gaining acceptance as experts in performing criminal assessments. However, the specialty is expanding to more general legal issues for a variety of reasons, and now we are observing differences in how to define this burgeoning area of professional social work practice.

DEFINING FORENSIC SOCIAL WORK

As the public's interest in law has increased, the focus of social workers also has shifted to addressing a broader array of legal issues that require the application of professional social work knowledge to achieve legal ends and purposes in a variety of civil and criminal law contexts. The professional practice of forensic social work within, or in consultation with, the civil and criminal legal systems has been defined in many different ways. Forensic social work is narrowly defined as professional practice by social workers who are engaged regularly as experts in the provision of evaluation and treatment services for the judicial system to achieve legal ends or purposes. The National Organization of Forensic Social Work (NOFSW) has described on its website that the application of social work expertise "goes far beyond clinics and psychiatric hospitals for criminal defendants being evaluated and treated on issues of competency and responsibility. A broader definition includes social work practice that in any way is related to legal issues and litigation, both criminal and civil" (National Association of Forensic Social Work [NOFSW], 2013). This broader definition includes practice in child welfare, corrections, law enforcement, victim services, and many other areas of practice that do not involve legal questions that are being litigated in the judicial process or in explicit legal forums. Indeed, social workers play a number of roles in both implicit and explicit legal contexts (Slater & Fink, 2012). The narrow definition of forensic social work focuses on practice in explicit legal forums (Ashford, 2013).

Today, social workers are using the term, "forensic," much more than in the past (Neighbors, Faust, & van Beyer, 2002). A number of schools of social work have developed concentrations and courses on forensics. Springer and Roberts (2007) provide a description from a syllabus on forensic social work that captures the complexity of this burgeoning specialty of social work practice. Some of the objectives included in their proposed course were:

1. Understand the purpose, functions, practice roles, and settings relevant to the application of social work expertise to forensic maters.
2. Demonstrate knowledge of the adversary process, including procedural issues of law in civil matters and criminal prosecution.
3. Apply relevant social work values and ethics to ethical dilemmas encountered in forensic social work practice and critically evaluate the relationship between legal and social work ethics.
4. Demonstrate knowledge of methods for determining the competency of an accused to understand rights, waive rights, and participate and assist their attorney in their own defense.
5. Apply biopsychosocial assessment principles in assessing responsibility and culpability, including (a) relevant mental, emotional, and substance abuse disorders; (b) trauma, maltreatment, and other adverse situations and (c) collateral information including records, testing, and medical reports.
6. Apply the knowledge and skills required to present court testimony, including the roles and responsibilities associated with being an expert witness.
7. Identify and evaluate methods of risk assessment and risk management for civil and criminal clients. (Adapted from Springer and Roberts, 2007)

Courses on forensic social work also include specific legal content relevant to practice in child welfare, criminal justice, and other relevant health and human service systems.

CURRENT FORENSIC SOCIAL WORK FUNCTIONS

Forensic social workers are applying their professional expertise to a variety of legal questions and issues in the civil and criminal justice systems. Some of the roles and functions performed by forensic social workers serving the judiciary and the legal system include:

Testifying in litigation
- Expert witness
- Fact witness
- Education witness

Consultation and training
- Consulting expert to the defense, prosecution, or the judiciary
- Consultant or liaison to parole boards, public defender offices, police departments, prosecution offices, and specialty treatment courts
- Consultants to advocacy groups involved with lobbying the courts through the development of amicus briefs
- Training law enforcement, correctional, judicial, and victim services staff.

Evaluation, assessment, and report writing
- Perform court ordered evaluations of mental capacities, children's interests, parental competencies, capacities to testify, and mitigating factors.
- Assessments of risks, needs, and strengths for child welfare, mental health, correctional, and victim agencies involved with the legal system
- Perform social and psychosocial investigations.
- Assessments of risk of victimization or dangerousness
- Treatment and service planning for victims, offenders, and participants in family court and other domestic relation courts.

Treatment, crisis intervention services, and case management oversight
- Treating civil and criminal forensic patients
- Treating adult and juvenile offenders
- Case management of civil and criminal individuals under various forms of court jurisdiction
- Assessing and treating victims of domestic violence and crime

Alternative dispute resolution
- Child protective services mediation
- Family mediation
- Victim and offender dialogue/mediation

Research and program evaluation
- Development of risk assessment instruments
- Scientific investigations of principles of socializing and therapeutic jurisprudence
- Scientific investigations of court processes and outcomes
- Evaluating forensic assessment and treatment protocols.

Each of the prior functions and roles require that the forensic social worker is conversant with relevant legal considerations. In order to be effective forensic practitioners, forensic social workers must also understand how their ethical obligations are influenced by participation in litigation and other legally relevant concerns. Some rules of thumb include:

- Offer services only in areas where one has appropriate education, training, and experience.
- Separate therapeutic and supervisory roles from expert witness roles.
- Consultants to legal teams should not serve as expert witnesses in the cases for which they were hired as consulting experts.
- Social workers serving as experts should refrain from giving opinions as to ultimate legal issues.
- Provide appropriate admonitions of a lack of confidentiality and of privilege in court ordered evaluations and forensic treatment contexts.
- Clarify reporting responsibilities and duties with clients.

However, forensic social workers cannot overlook the fact that these rules of thumb will vary depending on the conditions of their employment. If they are hired as an independent expert or as a consultant on a case, then this will differ from a social worker who is employed in an auxiliary role as a member of a legal team or as a provider of treatment and/or supportive services for victims or defendants in implicit or explicit legal contexts.

SUMMARY

This chapter introduces readers to the field of forensic social work practice. It also reviews changes in the subspecialty of forensic social work since the inception of social work as a profession. Distinctions between narrow and broad definitions of forensic social work are provided to assist in the differentiation of ordinary social work practice from practice in the subspecialty of forensic social work. The extent to which the roles and functions of social workers have evolved over time in areas of forensic social work are reviewed and special attention given to rules of thumb for negotiating potential ethical dilemmas resulting from social work in explicit-legal forums, and in implicit legal contexts involving relevant law and social work interactions. This chapter provided an overview of the subspecialty in social work of forensic social work and serves as an introduction to the principles and practices in selected areas of forensic social work practice that are covered in this section of the *Social Workers' Desk Reference*.

WEBSITES

Federal Rules of Evidence for Expert Witnesses: Rule 702
http://expertpages.com/federal/federal.htm
National Council of Juvenile and Family Court Judges
http://www.ncjfcj.org/content/blogcategory/351/416/
National Organization of Forensic Social Workers www.nofsw.org/html/forensic_social_work.htm.

References

America West Airlines v. Tope. (1996). Court of Appeals of Texas, 935 S.W. 2d 908.

Ashford, J. B. (2013). Forensic social work. *Oxford bibliography: Social work*. New York, NY: Oxford University Press.

Bartlett, H. (1970). *The common base of social work practice*. New York, NY: NASW Press.

Conley v. Commonwealth of Virginia. (2007). 643 S.E. 2d 131.

Dix, G. E., & Poythress, N. G. (1981). Propriety of medical dominance of forensic mental health practice: The empirical evidence. *Arizona Law Review, 23*, 961–989.

Gutheil, T. G. (2005). The history of forensic psychiatry. *Journal of the American Academy of Psychiatry and Law, 33*, 259–262.

Kant, I. (1970). Antropologie in pragatischer hinsicht (1978) (Antropology). In Weischedel (Ed.), Werke (Vol. IV) (pp. 260–399). Darmstadt: Wissenshaftliche Buchgesellshaft.

Mooij, A. (1998). Kant on criminal law and psychiatry. *International Journal of Law and Psychiatry, 21*, 335–341.

National Center for State Courts. (2012). Court statistics project. Retrieved from http://www.courtstatistics.org/

National Center for Victims of Crime. (2013). Crime trends. Retrieved from http://www.victimsofcrime.org/library/crime-information-and-statistics/crime-trends.

Neighbors, I. A., Faust, L. G., & van Beyer, K. (2002). Curricula development in forensic social work at the MSW and Post-MSW levels. In I. A. Neighbors, A. Chambers, E. Levin, G. Nordman, & C. Tutrone (Eds.). *Social work and the law: Proceedings of the National Organization of Forensic Social Work, 2000* (pp. 1–11). New York, NY: Haworth Press.

People v. Gans. (1983). 465 NYS. 2d 147.

People v. Parney. (1977). 74 Mich. App. 571, 296 N.W. 2d 568.

Reamer, F. G. (2007). Foreword. D. W. Springer & A. R. Roberts (Eds.). *Handbook of forensic mental health with victims and offenders* (p. xiii). New York, NY: Springer Publishing Company.

Springer, D.W., & Roberts, A. R. (Eds.). (2007). The roles and functions of forensic social workers in the 21st century. *Handbook of forensic mental health with victims and offenders* (p. 14). New York: Springer Publishing Company.

Skalevag, S. A. (2006). The matter of forensic psychiatry: A historical enquiry. *Medical History, 50*, 49–68.

Slater, L. K., & Fink, K. R. (2012). *Social work practice and the law.* New York, NY: Springer Publishing Company.

Willrich, M. (2003). *City of courts: Socializing justice in progressive era of Chicago.* New York, NY: Cambridge University Press.

141 Forensic Social Work and Expert Witness Testimony in Child Welfare

Carlton E. Munson

This chapter deals with forensic social work practice in the context of expert witness testimony regarding children and adolescents, but most of the content can be applied to any form of forensic social work. Social workers are increasingly performing forensic child welfare work by providing evaluations of children and families and testifying as experts in relation to court or attorney-requested assessments as well as testifying as fact witnesses in connection with therapeutic intervention (Bullis, 2013). Despite a long tradition of social work involvement in forensic work that can be traced to Jane Addams at Hull House in Chicago (Slater & Finch, 2012), social workers do not generally have training in how to do legal assessments or how to provide effective expert and fact witness testimony. Social work education programs at the baccalaureate,

master's, and doctoral levels do not provide much academic instruction in forensic social work, and there are limited continuing education offerings in this area. A few social work schools have developed forensic specializations, but these do not have a specific focus on child welfare practice. Social work has not been as diligent as psychiatry and psychology in developing forensic specialty professional organizations. The National Organization of Forensic Social Work (NOFSW) was founded in the 1970s and offers training, conferences, and publications. In 1987 the NOFSW approved a revised and updated forensic social work code of ethics. The size of the NOFSW is small compared to the number of social workers providing forensic services.

The social work profession has been slow to develop practice standards for clinical child welfare practice. At the same time the forensic practice of social work has become highly specialized especially in the area of forensic child welfare practice (Munson, 2011). In addition, the evolution of the Frye standard (*Frye v. United States*, 1923) that expert witness testimony is only admissible if acceptable as recognized in the profession, has led to even more stringent standards imposed by appeals courts in the "Daubert Test" based on a broad ranging four factors review of the nature of the expert testimony (Barsky, 2012; Munson, 2011). The four factors that serve as the basis for expert testimony are: (1) has been scientifically tested, (2) has been subjected to peer review or publication, (3) has a known error rate, and (4) has widespread acceptance in the relevant scientific community (Munson, 2011). Every forensic social worker who offers expert witness testimony should become familiar with the Frye and Daubert "tests." The following section lists the general areas of training and knowledge the forensic child welfare expert should have to meet the "Frye" and "Dauabert" tests for being considered by the courts to be a reliable and acceptable expert.

ENTERING FORENSIC WORK

Training and Knowledge Needed

Forensic assessments and expert witness testimony require highly specialized training and experience. Before entering expert witness practice, the social worker should receive training in forensics and the role of expert witnesses. The primary areas that a child welfare expert witness should have training in include, but are not limited to, the following (key resources are cited):

- Child and adolescent development (Berk, 2012; Bukatko & Daeler (2011); Volkmar, & Martin, 2011)
- Child and adolescent psychopathology (Parritz & Troy, 2013; Saklofske, Reynolds, & Schwean (2013)
- Child and adult assessments (Sadock, Sadock, & Ruiz, 2012; Saklofske, Reynolds, & Schwean, 2013)
- Attachment theory (Cassidy & Shaver, 2010; Oppenheim & Goldsmith, 2011; Solomon & George, 2011)
- Traumatic stress theory (Carlson, 1997; Cohen, Mannaino, & Deblinger, 2012; Nader, Dubrow, & Stamm, 2013; Schiraldi, 2000; Siegel, 2012; Wolchik & Sandler, 2007)

- Basic developmental neuroscience (Applegate & Shapiro, 2006; Cozolino, 2013; Johnson & de Haan, 2011; Montgomery, 2013)
- Basic understanding of psychopharmacology (Bentley & Walsh, 2013; Preston & Johnson, 2011)
- Basic understanding of genetics (Klug, Cummings, Spencer, & Palladino, 2011)
- Basic knowledge of substances and alcohol use/abuse/dependence (Silverman, 2012; Hart, Ksir, & Ray, 2010; Ruiz & Strain, 2011)
- Child welfare clinical practice (Crosson-Tower, 2012, 2013; Lutzker, 2013; Myers, 1998, 2006)
- Ability to administer and interpret standardized measures and instruments (Kaplan & Saccuzzo, 2013; Groth-Marnat, 2009)
- Knowledge of forensic specialization practice (Munson, 2007; Springer & Roberts, 2007)
- Knowledge of local, state, and federal laws relevant to clinical practice specialization and expertise (Dyer, 1999; Myers, 2006; National Association of Social Workers [NASW], 2012)
- General knowledge of forensic practice (Ackerman, 2010; Albert, 2000; English & Sales, 2005; Gudjonsson & Haward, 1998; Heilbrun, Grisso, & Goldstein, 2009; Melton, Petrila, Poythress, & Slobogin, 2007; Saltzman & Furman, 1999; Slater & Finch, 2012)
- Specific knowledge of child and family forensic practice (Myers, 1998; Sparta & Koocher, 2006)
- Specific knowledge of custody evaluation practice standards (Ackerman, 2006; Gould & Martindale, 2009; Stahl, 2011; Tolle & O'Donohue, 2012)
- Specific knowledge of how to provide expert and fact witness testimony (Bernstein & Hartsell, 2005; Brodsky, 2013, 1999; Ceci & Hembrooke, 1998; Gutheil & Dattilio, 2008; NASW, 2013; Tsushima & Anderson, 1996).

Fact and Expert Witnesses

On entering forensic work, the practitioner must understand the difference between expert and fact witnesses. Expert witnesses and fact witnesses are different in most jurisdictions. Fact witnesses are also referred to in some jurisdictions as "treaters." A treater mental health professional can be called to testify to the treatment that has been provided to a person. He or she testifies only to the facts of the treatment and does not offer opinions about factors outside the context of the treatment. If the witness is not testifying as an expert, the testimony is in the form of opinions or inferences limited to those rationally based on perception and helpful in clarifying testimony or determination of a contested issue. Expert testimony is admitted, in the form of an opinion, if the court determines that the testimony will assist the trier of fact (judge or jury) in understanding the evidence or to determine a fact in question. In making that determination, the court establishes (1) whether the witness is qualified as an expert by knowledge, skill, experience, training, or education; (2) the appropriateness of the expert testimony on the particular subject; and (3) whether a sufficient factual basis exists to support the expert testimony. An expert opinion is not necessarily inadmissible because it embraces an ultimate issue to be decided by the trier of fact, but an expert witness testifying with respect to the mental state or condition of a defendant in a criminal case may not state an opinion or inference as to whether the defendant had a mental state or condition constituting an element of the offense because that issue is for the trier of fact to decide. This exception does not apply to an ultimate issue of criminal responsibility. Expert witnesses can give opinions and inform the trier of fact for courts to make the best possible decision in cases. For this reason, judges are granted liberal discretion in allowing expert testimony (Mueller & Kirkpatrick, 2013).

It is recognized that a fact or treater witness can be an advocate for the client, and therefore, would be appropriately biased in favor of the client. An expert witness is not to be an advocate and should be objective and impartial. A treater or fact witness should never be an expert in the same case because of the advocacy and impartiality conflict. Some attorneys and judges will attempt to have a fact witness also give expert witness testimony; the fact witness should politely decline the invitation and point out the conflict that is created by performing the two roles simultaneously. If the judge insists the fact witness render an expert opinion, the witness should comply with the judge's directive to avoid being charged with contempt of court (Gutheil & Dattilio, 2008). An expert should not become the treater of the same client after providing expert witness testimony for the client because of the future potential for conflict from having been an expert witness.

Managing Risk

Forensic social work practitioners are at higher risk for lawsuits and regulatory board complaints, and the practitioner should have the maximum professional liability insurance coverage and confirm that the insurance carrier provides coverage for lawsuits and regulatory board complaints. The practitioner should be thoroughly familiar with the National Association of Social Workers (NASW) Code of Ethics (NASW, 1996) and the NOFSW Code of Ethics (NOFSW, 1987). The forensic practitioner should review the state licensing board regulations. Most states do not have specific licensing regulations related to forensic practice, but some have a statutory code of ethics that is used as the criteria for investigation of complaints that is independent of the NASW and NOFSW ethics codes. The forensic practitioner needs to establish what code of ethics applies in the state or states where he/she practices or testifies.

Confidentiality

Confidentiality is of increased complexity in forensic work. Mental health professionals have become much more concerned with confidentiality in the past decades because of confusing state and federal mandates about confidentiality. In the legal arena, the concept of confidentiality is replaced with the concept of "privileged communication." In the law, information the client provides to a professional remains the "property" of the client, and the client owns the right to control the information with respect to disclosure as part of the judicial process (Albert, 2000; Saltzman & Furman, 1999). The forensic practitioner must consult with the client about disclosure of information that may find its way into the legal process, but the concept of confidentiality in the professional sense is an invention of codes of ethics that apply to any disclosure of client information in any context, not just the judicial process. With confidentiality, the professional owns and controls the information and makes the decision as to whether the information will be released with or without the consent of the client. For example, if child maltreatment has been disclosed by the client or the client threatens to harm a person or property, the professional is compelled to disclose the information to the authorities without client consent.

The best protection in this situation is for the forensic practitioner to have an advance written informed consent that details who will be provided information. The traditional abuse reporting and threats of harm or destruction of property reporting should be included, and the disclosure of information to judges and attorneys should be detailed even if the evaluation is court-ordered. The client should be provided a copy of the signed consent.

The 20/20 Rule

An expert witness should organize practice based on the 20/20 rule. The rule refers to the formula that the expert practitioner devote at least 20 hours per week to work in the clinical area of practice in which the expert offers testimony. The practitioner also should not receive more than 20% of total income from expert witness work. The first part of the formula relates to competency and the second part to impartiality, objectivity, and bias. Practitioners who earn more than 20% of total income from expert witness work are subject to allegations of operating from the "hired gun" principle, in which the forensic practitioner relies heavily on income from forensic work and renders opinions based on expectations of the party or attorney who retains the expert rather than objective, unbiased opinions based on scientific evidence.

Bias

Bias is a key feature of forensic work. The practitioner should make special efforts in all aspects of forensic work to guard against allegations of bias. Bias is important because the role of the expert is exclusively to provide objective, scientific information that will educate and assist the trier of fact (judge or jury) in rendering a decision in a case. The following general forensic practice standards can be helpful in avoiding allegations of bias and keeping a pledge of objectivity.

- Request that the court appoint you to do the expert witness work. If the court does not appoint you, maintain independence from the attorney who pays your fee.
- Avoid doing work for an attorney who insists on knowing your opinions before hiring you. Understanding lawyer motivations based on personality functioning has been described by Daicoff (2013).

- Always work on a retainer basis. It is not recommended that an expert testify in a case if the services provided have not been prepaid. Some states require that experts work on a retainer basis.
- Do not have any informal or non–case-related contact with any parties to a case. This would include attorneys for the parents and attorneys for children.
- Never render an opinion about a person you have not interviewed or tested.
- Interview all relevant parties to a case before rendering opinions.
- Base opinions on scientific evidence that is cited in the report to the court or is explained in oral testimony.
- Use standardized measures to support clinical observations. For example, personality testing to support a diagnosis of Antisocial Personality Disorder.
- Submit reports to the court or attorney well in advance of the hearing so all parties can have reasonable time to review the reports before the hearing.
- Never withhold or delay submission of material relevant to the case or opinions offered to the court.

CASE PREPARATION

Preparation for legal system involvement begins the moment the practitioner receives a referral. A thorough and complete record of all activity should be maintained from the time the first contact with a client takes place. The report of an assessment and evaluation is the cornerstone of expert or fact witness testimony. Social workers entering the legal arena to do assessments should be clear about the purpose of the evaluation. In clinical practice with children and adolescents, this can cover a number of areas, but there are basically two types of evaluations performed in forensic child welfare practice. These evaluations should be comprehensive and detailed and should be supported by standardized testing in a number of areas of the evaluation process.

FORENSIC EVALUATIONS

Expert witness testimony does not always involve the expert being directly involved with the parties. In some cases, the expert may only do a records review and testify on the basis of that review or submit an affidavit that documents the expert's qualifications, the results of the review, and the opinions. In other cases, the expert may only serve as a rebuttal witness after listening to the testimony of other witnesses. In most cases, the expert will do an evaluation that becomes the basis of the expert testimony. A forensic evaluation is significantly different than a traditional psychotherapeutic assessment, which is used exclusively by the therapist for treatment planning. Forensic evaluations are used by lawyers and judges to make a case based on establishing truth through fact-finding, and mental health professionals use scientific probabilities and ranges of prediction in doing evaluations. A fundamental rule of any expert report writing is that the reports should only be written at the request of the judge or retaining attorney. In some situations reports are not discoverable, but all reports should be written based on the assumption they would be discoverable (Melton, Petrila, Poythress, & Slobogin, 2007).

The forensic evaluation should consist of a standard protocol that is routinely used with cases, based on the clinician's specialty practice area. The assessment should include contact with all persons who have relevance to the outcome of the case. Clinical interviews should be conducted with pertinent individuals and standardized measures used when appropriate (e.g., to confirm diagnosis of depression or posttraumatic stress disorder, to determine suitability for custody or level of parenting stress). The evaluator should contact collateral sources that may have information relevant to the issues explored in the evaluation (such as child welfare workers, therapists, medical and psychiatric hospitalization reports, police, school counselors, teachers, employers, and probation officers).

Evaluation reports should be clear, concise, and carefully proofed before submission. Various outlines for submission of reports have been devised (Koocher, Norcross, & Green, 2013; Melton, Petrila, Poythress, & Slobogin, 2007; Nurcombe & Partlett, 2010; Sattler, 1998).

In preparing reports, use language that is familiar to the courts. This language can be derived from written opinions of appeals courts. Do not attempt to make legal statements, but use brief, legal phrases to express concepts. Phraseology can vary by state, but the concepts usually have the same general meaning For example, phrases that can be helpful are: "best interest of the child," "general well-being of the child," "substantial risk to the child," "safety of the child," "health of the child," "vulnerability of the child," "special needs child," "preference of the child," "fitness of person seeking custody," "capability or competency to parent," "potential for maintaining natural family relations," "opportunities for the future life of the child," "prior voluntary abandonment or surrender of custody," "parental rights versus performance of parental duties," and "chronic and enduring mental illness."

In preparing the written report the evaluator should indicate source of statements and use qualifier words when direct knowledge of a fact is not available. Use phrases such as, "reported by," "reportedly," and "according to." Professional language should be used, such as, "Appeared to be intoxicated" rather than "He was drunk," and "Indications are she deliberately made inaccurate statements" not "She lied to me," "intellectual disability" not "mentally retarded."

TYPES OF FORENSIC EVALUATIONS

There are basically two types of evaluations performed in forensic child welfare practice. The first type is a child-centered, comprehensive evaluation focused on family history, developmental history, maltreatment history, and trauma exposure/reaction; the second type is a parenting assessment. The forensic evaluation of children places an additional burden on the forensic evaluator because of the developmental focus, the need for special child-oriented communications skills (Sparta & Koocher, 2006), and the inability of children to make decisions independently. The following general sequential outline is recommended for child and adolescent evaluations:

Reason for evaluation. This should be a brief statement of the purpose of the evaluation and the referral source.

Procedures. Identify information sources, persons interviewed, and standardized measures used. A brief statement should be included that describes how suggestive questioning and inducements for participation were avoided (see Ceci & Bruck, 1999).

Abuse history. Identify presence or absence of any individual or family history of neglect, physical abuse, sexual abuse, or domestic violence.

Background. Summarize information relevant to the factors that led to the presenting problem.

Family and individual history. Provide detailed family history data, including information about parents, siblings, education, employment, social functioning, and religious activity.

Developmental history. Include a survey of the mother's use of tobacco, alcohol, substances, and prescription medications during pregnancy. Note if there were any complications during pregnancy or at birth. Review developmental history for premature birth, low birth weight, eating/feeding problems during infancy, problems with toilet training, or problems entering school. There should be a review of the father's role in the child's development with the same relevant factors as reviewed for the mother.

Developmental milestones. Assess and note appropriate developmental milestones of children and adolescents. This can be done with standardized measures or milestone checklists. The most common areas of development are physical, self-help, social, communication, and intellectual (Berk, 2012). Language development can be a crucial indicator of development in combination with maltreatment. Language delays are common (Amster, 1999) and are so prevalent in the child welfare population that they can be used diagnostically for maltreated children (Munson, 2002).

History of out-of-home placements. Include as much information as possible about past and current placements. This applies to children and adults.

Visitation. If the child is not in the care of the parents, give a summary of the visitation schedule and note whether visitation is supervised or unsupervised.

Criminal justice history. Give a history of all arrests, convictions for criminal offenses, and civil litigation the child or parent has experienced.

Substance/alcohol history. Provide a history of substance or alcohol use by child, adolescent, and parents based on the *DSM-5* (APA, 2013) criteria.

Medical history. Report major illnesses, injuries, hospitalizations, and family history of illness for the child and parents. Document date of last physical examination. If the client has not had a physical examination in the past 30 days, this should be noted and the client referred for medical screening to rule out any medical conditions that could be a source of dysfunction. Children should also be referred for dental, vision, and hearing screenings if there have been no screenings in the last year.

Medications. Note past and current medications, including dosage information. Review for use of herbal medications or culturally bound medications. If the client is taking medication, record the most recent administration prior to the evaluation session.

Mental health treatment. Review past and present inpatient and outpatient mental health treatment. Record diagnoses received and names of therapists, quality of relationship with the therapists, and the outcome of the treatment.

Education. For children, report school functioning academically and behaviorally. For adults, report amount of education and relevant history performance, placement, and behavior.

Clinical interview. Record the identified client's mental status, interview behavior and demeanor, speech, language, somatic complaints, perception, cognition, judgment, memory, intellectual functioning, emotions, interpersonal skills, and access to weapons.

Standardized measures. Describe and summarize any standardized measures administered. Interpret objective measures in clear, concise language. Focus the interpretation on the purpose of the evaluation and the recommendations.

Diagnosis. Provide a thorough *DSM-5* case formulation (see APA, 2013, p. 16).

Summary and conclusions. Give a concise summary of the case and provide an integrated analysis of the significant aspects of the findings. Conclusions should be supported with citations of empirical research and clinical literature that support findings and conclusions. In complex cases, it helps to have subsections of this section. The recommended subheadings are Summary of Facts, Findings, Conclusions and Opinions, and Limitations.

Recommendations. Based on the findings, the diagnostic formulation, conclusions, and opinions, the evaluator should make specific recommendations and justify each recommendation.

Parenting assessments are performed to evaluate the capability of a parent to have a child in his or her care on a permanent basis. These evaluations are usually focused on assisting with reunification planning for the child or are performed as part of a termination of parental rights legal proceeding. These evaluations can be very complex and require a great deal of training, knowledge, and experience to perform. Parenting assessments are not custody evaluations and have a somewhat different outcome focus. The foundational concept in parenting assessments is that the evaluator must not only consider the immediate capabilities of the parent at the time of the assessment, but should also evaluate and render an opinion regarding the long-term capacities of the parent to provide sustained safe, protective, and healthy care for a child (Choate, 2009). Emerging literature on how to perform parenting evaluations (Budd, Connell, & Clark, 2011; Campion, 1995; Choate, 2009; Condie, 2003; Feldman & Aunos, 2010; Ostler, 2008; Pezzot-Pearce & Pearce; 2004; Reder, Duncan, & Lucey, 2003) has been codified in 14 areas by this author:

Family history. The parent's history of being parented and the nature of the parent's family attachment relationships serve as indicators of the parent's parenting capability and should be reviewed and recorded. How people parent is highly correlated with how they were parented.

Motivation to reunify. Motivation to reunify involves the factors of desire, thought, and action, which are key indicators of reunification success. This can involve a range of activities grounded in the parent's quickly and fully taking action to meet whatever conditions are required for reunification that are thoroughly documented as part of the evaluation.

Financial resources. Providing adequate care for a child requires substantial financial resources. An extensive financial assessment should be done and a determination made as to whether the parent has resources sufficient to care for children adequately.

Supportive resources. A critical factor in successful parenting after reunification is supportive networks and supportive resources. The parenting assessment should include a detailed survey of supportive resources.

Substance use history. Alcohol/substance use, abuse, dependence is evaluated with respect to the extent that it impairs the parent's ability to perform parenting tasks and as to whether the alcohol/substance exposure endangers or corrupts the child.

Criminal justice history. Evaluate involvement with the criminal justice system to the extent that it impairs the parent's ability to perform parenting tasks and as to whether the criminal activity endangers or corrupts the child. Information in this area is gathered through standardized screening forms and state judicial case searches available on the Internet.

Medical status. Determine whether any medical conditions are present that would impair the parent's ability to care for, protect, and make the child safe. Information in this area can be gathered through a standardized medical screening form along with a clinical interview.

Psychological/mental illness. A person does not have to have a model personality to provide adequate parenting and everyone has some personality oddities. Screening for capability to parent is an effort to identify areas of concern that need intervention. Standardized personality measures should be used in combination with the clinical interview in this area.

Intellectual functioning. Intellectual disability does not necessarily impair parenting capability, but when intellectual disability severity prevents the person from meeting the physical, psychological, and emotional needs of the child, ability to parent may be temporarily or permanently affected. Standardized measures should be used to determine intellectual level. The Kaufman Functional Academic Skills Test (K-FAST) is a good scale to use in determining whether parents have adequate skills to care for children.

Housing. In order for a parent to care for a child suitably, the care must be provided in an environment that is safe and fit for habitation.

Parenting experience. Parenting experience is indicated by prior successful experience in caring for children through caring for younger siblings, babysitting, employment in a child care setting, or parenting one's own children. When prior experience does not exist, parent training classes or nurturing classes can substitute for direct experience.

Veracity. When a parent withholds information from or provides misleading information to professionals, there arises serious concern about parenting ability as part of a reunification process. Veracity should be assessed through various measures such as collaborative information and collateral contacts.

Diagnosis. Diagnoses the parent has received can be important to capability to parent. Diagnoses often associated with poor parenting skills are schizophrenia, brief psychotic disorder, bipolar disorder, alcohol/substance related disorders, major depressive disorder, conduct disorder, antisocial personality disorder, and dissociative disorder. A formal case diagnostic formulation using the *Diagnostic and Statistical Manual of Mental Disorders, Fifth Edition (DSM-5)* criteria should be performed.

Child status. Status of the child is important to parenting capability and reunification because children with medical, developmental, psychological, and behavioral problems can be demanding of, and create stress for, the parent. Such children require special and intensive care from the parent. If a parent has denial about a child's level of functioning, the denial can be a risk factor for the child. Information about the child's status should be gathered through thorough evaluation of the child or information obtained from social service records, other evaluations that may have been completed on the child, and collateral contacts such as foster parents or kinship care providers. These procedures are consistent with all the models of parenting assessments identified above.

DIAGNOSIS AND EXPERT TESTIMONY

There has been controversy about the legal sanction for clinical social workers to diagnose. A series of appellate legal opinions have confirmed the admissibility as evidence diagnosis performed by clinical social workers where there is legislative sanction. The Maryland Court of Appeals, in a case that involved the author, unanimously affirmed the statutory right of licensed clinical social workers to perform diagnosis, testify as expert witnesses, and testify to the ultimate issue (In Re Adoption/Guardianship no. CCJ14746, 360Md634, 2000). The opinion of the court and the NASW and others amicus briefs (Brief for NASW et al., 1999) filed in this case can be helpful to forensic social workers in other states who have been legally challenged in the right to diagnose.

A qualification to diagnose mental and emotional disorders is included in most state practice acts. The Association of Social Work Boards publishes a guide titled, *Social Work Laws and Board Regulations: A Comparison Guide* (American Association of State Social Work Boards, 2013), which can be used to find the specific terminology used in a particular state. When performing diagnosis, forensic social workers should review the qualifications for the state in which they practice.

The *DSM-5* (American Psychiatric Association, 2013) uses a "nonaxial documentation of diagnoses" (p. 16). The format requires a "case formulation" that contains these six components: (1) History and concise case summary, (2) Diagnoses, (3) Medical conditions, (4) Notations of related "conditions," (5) Overall "disability" severity statement, and (6) Treatment plan. Before performing or recording a diagnosis for a forensic report, the clinician should carefully read and appropriately apply principles set forth in the *DSM-5* for doing a diagnostic case formulation. When testifying about a diagnosis that has been assigned to a client, it is crucial that forensic social workers make clear to attorneys and the court what edition of the *DSM* was used in formulating opinions about the person. When preparing for court testimony the practitioner should carefully review the criteria of *DSM-5* in making or altering a diagnosis. For more details see my chapter in the diagnosis section of this volume.

The *DSM-5* also contains a section titled, "Cautionary Statement for Forensic Use of *DSM-5*" (p. 25). This brief section should be carefully reviewed by forensic social workers. The section addresses issues of: (1) Legal and clinical definition of a mental illness; (2) Issues of diagnoses and legal determination, for example, civil commitments; (3) Using caution in applying legal and clinical standards of competency, responsibility, and disability, especially in cases where diagnoses of intellectual disability (intellectual developmental disorder), schizophrenia, major neurocognitive disorder, gambling disorder, or pedophilic disorder are present; and (4) The complexity of determining self-control of behavior within a particular disorder.

BEFORE THE HEARING

Expert testimony occurs after the report has been submitted, and the expert's testimony should be based on the procedures and findings contained in the report. A basic rule to remember is that expert witness testimony is only as good as the attorney who offers the professional as an expert. Experts tend to believe that the entire case depends on their testimony and how well they perform. This is not usually the situation. There are often numerous witnesses in a case and many factors that influence and determine the outcome. An expert's testimony is to offer findings and opinions in a truthful, fair, and factual manner, which can assist the trier of fact in making a decision; this should be paramount in expert testimony.

An expert witness should request to meet with the attorney who will be offering the expert to the court. Such a meeting can be helpful in preparing how the expert wants to present testimony and what is to be highlighted. It is important to ask the attorney all questions about the nature of the testimony. The attorney should be provided with written information about your credentials prior to the hearing. If you meet with the attorney, review your written materials, organize them, and highlight key points. Separate from your report, develop an outline of key points you want to testify to, and commit the outline to memory.

AT THE HEARING

The classic advice regarding attire and demeanor continues to be of paramount importance. Dress professionally, act professionally, and arrive in court early. Bring all materials related to the case. Avoid talking with anyone in the waiting room, courtroom, or hall while waiting to testify. This includes colleagues, attorneys, police, strangers, or the parent or child about whom you are testifying. Do not smile, laugh, or joke with anyone in the presence of the judge or jury before, during, or after testifying. For confidentiality reasons, do not leave a briefcase or hearing materials unattended at any time.

ON THE STAND

Before testifying, request the attorney to qualify you as an expert by reviewing your credentials for the court. Sometimes attorneys are conscious of the need to proceed rapidly and may do a brief review of your credentials, especially if you have testified in the court in the past. If you are easily and quickly qualified as an expert, it is important to include in your testimony responses that call attention to your qualifications. For example, substantive comments can be prefaced with comments such as, "In my 20 years of work with this population, it is my experience that ..." or "As part of my training I became familiar with research that supports ..." Such comments could be crucial if there is an appeal of your testimony.

Procedural qualification of experts focuses on the concepts of knowledge, skill, experience, training, and education because these are the areas identified in the law as basic to being an expert (Mueller & Kirkpatrick, 2013). The process of expert qualification includes review of professional education (degrees and dates received, internships, specialized training, continuing education, honors, awards, licenses, certifications (Tsushima & Anderson, 1996), employment history, number of clients evaluated or treated, research activity, publications, professional paper presentations, and the amount of prior testimony as an expert witness.

The attorney who is challenging your testimony will use the voir dire procedure, which is the opposing attorney's opportunity to test and challenge your credentials and competency to testify, as well as to challenge expert testimony in general (e.g., citing research indicating that expert opinions are no more accurate than those of laypersons). There may be attempts to show bias by requesting the expert to provide information about fees received for testimony, your personal history as a victim of abuse or domestic violence to show you are on a mission, promoting a cause, or engaged in advocacy. Voir dire is a standard legal procedure that should not be viewed as a personal attack, although it may seem to be. Voir dire can be the most difficult phase of expert testimony, because attacks on education, training, and experience can be intense (Tsushima & Anderson, 1996). The key is to remain calm and answer questions directly and honestly. Never become defensive or argumentative during this stage of testimony, especially when feeling attacked personally or professionally. Consider the following example.

Attorney Question (AQ): It is true that the social work profession is on the lowest tier of therapists, with psychiatrists at the top, psychologists next, and social workers at the bottom, correct?

Expert Answer (EA): No, that is not the situation today. It was like that 40 years ago. Clinical practice with children and adolescents today is quite complex and requires multidisciplinary expertise. All recognized mental health professionals are equal members of the evaluation or treatment team. Social workers have the most historical expertise in child welfare, and we often provide leadership in this area. We provide the majority of the mental health services in the United States and have evolved significant research and expertise in the mental health field.

A general rule of testimony is to avoid anticipating what the judge or the attorneys are dealing with or attempting to elicit. Simply answer the questions on the basis of what you did, the reason you did it, and the opinions you formulated. Ask attorneys to repeat unclear questions. Answer only the questions that are asked, and do not attempt to expand on a previously given answer. Focus on the immediate question you are being asked. It is recommended that you look at the judge when giving opinions, look at the attorney when giving facts, and avoid looking at the client when giving difficult testimony. Always look at the judge when giving answers to questions asked by the judge.

If the opposing attorney asks a question directly from your notes or report he or she received as part of the discovery process, ask for the specific page number of the report and answer on the basis of the content of the report. It is also a good policy to make verbal reference to your report. Use statements such as, "In my report summary section, I indicated …" or "My background information section of the report confirms that …" and "The results of my testing explained on page 6 of the report indicate …" This is an effective way to call the judge or jury's attention to your findings. Do not read from the report. Testify from memory and request the court to allow you to review your report or supporting documents if a technical question is asked that requires a precise answer, such as actual test scores.

CROSS-EXAMINATION

Cross-examination is always difficult because it is the opposing attorney's second chance to challenge the expert witness. In the voir dire phase of testimony, there is a general challenge to qualifications to testify, and in the cross-examination, there are specific challenges of the validity of the expert's procedures and conclusions in the specific case. It is important to remain calm and factual and not alter voice level when such challenges are made. Do not let the attorney make you angry or provoke you. This requires a significant amount of self-control. It is important to remember that you are there to provide facts and opinions related to what you do routinely in conducting assessments. Hesitate when you think you should not answer a question to give the attorney who offered you as an expert an opportunity to object.

During cross-examination, refrain from thinking the case outcome hinges on your testimony, and do not attempt to analyze the effect of your testimony while you are testifying. Focus on the accuracy and scientific basis of your testimony.

Try to avoid answering hypothetical questions, such as the following:

AQ: Hypothetically, if my client had a relative who could provide care for this child, could the child adjust to placement under these circumstances?

EA: It depends. It depends on the home study of the relatives, their parenting skills, the child's bond and attachment with the foster parents, and history of contact with the relatives as well as other factors. So it would be difficult for me to answer that question.

During cross-examination, an expert can use questions to expand on previous answers or to make additional points.

Example 1

AQ: My client was evicted from her apartment because she had no job, could not pay her rent, and DSS [Department of Social Services] would not give her assistance, wasn't she?

EA: My notes indicate that she was evicted because she was having loud parties, and the police were called because of substance use. This was consistent with statements she made to me that she had been using cocaine regularly for the past three years. I have no record that she ever asked for assistance with her rent.

141 • EXPERT WITNESS TESTIMONY 1131

Example 2

AQ: Then all you can testify to is that there were arguments between my client and the mother? There was no real domestic violence in this relationship, was there?

EA: Recurring shouting and belittling are violent acts. In addition, there is increased risk to the child because the father frequently uses alcohol. He has been apprehended for violence in the community. He denies he abused the mother. The child may have special needs and have uneasy temperament. All of these facts increase the risk of violence against the child by the father.

Avoid defensiveness when asked questions that can be viewed as attacks on your ethics. It is best to respond with a simple statement of ethical obligations.

AQ: Isn't it true that you wrote in your report, knowing it would harm her in this TPR [Temporary Protective Rule] hearing, that my client had a history of multiple foster care placements?

EA: No, my professional ethics code would not allow me to do that. I wrote it because generally accepted practice guidelines for parental rights cases require recording all relevant information regarding this case.

AFTER THE HEARING

After a hearing, the best way to prepare for the next time you will testify is to review your testimony and think of ways you could have testified more effectively. Do not obsess about the effect of your testimony; rather, analyze ways you can improve responses in the future. Write down key questions from your testimony that you may be asked in future cases and review them before you testify again.

CONCLUSION

Serving as an expert is difficult under any circumstances. It is a complex aspect of mental health practice that is increasing. Forensic social work is truly one of the artistic and scientific aspects of practice that requires discipline, skill, and preparation. Providing expert witness testimony is fundamental to the expert role, and the following nine key summary principles should be used as a concise guide before testifying:

1. Determine if you are a fact or expert witness and do not agree to perform both roles in the same case.
2. Only agree to be an expert witness on a retainer basis and never accept a fee for fact witness testimony.
3. Thoroughly document all activity and organize documents for testimony.
4. Commit to memory your credentials and organize them by education, training, skill, knowledge, and experience.
5. While waiting to testify, remain silent and safeguard your documents.
6. Do not become defensive when challenged, and respond in a calm voice using your knowledge base as your guide.
7. Only answer questions asked.
8. If necessary, expand on yes/no questions and qualify hypothetical questions.
9. After testifying, reflect on what you said, but do not obsess about the effectiveness of the testimony. *Remember*: Your testimony is only as good as the attorney who sought you to testify.

WEBSITES

National Organization of Forensic Social Work: www.nofsw.org

Federal Rules of Civil Procedures: www.uscourts/uscourts/rules/civil-procedures.pdf

Kaufman Functional Academic Skills Test: www.personclinical.com/therapy/products/100000090/kaufman-functional-acadmeic-skills-test-k-fast.html

DSM-5: www.apa.org and www.dsm5.org

Note

Content of this chapter pertains to legal issues and offers suggestions for forensic social work professionals participating in legal proceedings. No comments herein should be considered as legal advice. Information in this chapter is generic and may not be applicable to all jurisdictions. The reader should consult an attorney for legal advice regarding cases that are relevant to the content of this chapter.

References

Ackerman, M. J. (2006). *Clinician's guide to custody evaluations*. New York, NY: Wiley.

Ackerman, M. J. (2010). *Essentials of forensic psychological assessment*. New York, NY: Wiley.

Albert, R. (2000). *Law and social work practice*. New York, NY: Springer.

Association of State Social Work Boards. (2013). *Social Work Laws and Regulations Database (Version T03.19.13)* [Interactive database software]. Retrieved from https://www.datapathdesign.com/ASWB/Laws/Prod/cgi-bin/LawWebRpts2DLL.dll

American Psychiatric Association. (2013). *Diagnostic and statistical manual of mental disorders, Fifth edition*. Arlington, VA: American Psychiatric Publishing.

Amster, B. J. (1999). Speech and language development of young children in the child welfare system. In J. A. Silver, B. J. Amster, & T. Haecher (Eds.), *Young children and foster care* (pp. 117–157). Baltimore, MD: Brookes.

Applegate, J. S., & Shapiro, J. R. (2006). *Neurobiology for clinical social work: Theory and practice*. New York, NY: Norton.

Barsky, A. E. (2012). *Clinicians in court. A guide to subpoenas, depositions, and everything else you need to know* (2nd ed.). New York, NY: Guilford.

Bentley, R. J., & Walsh, J. (2013). *The social worker and psychotropic medication: Toward essential collaboration with clients* (4th ed.). Belmont, LA: Lenale Learning.

Berk, L. E. (2012). *Child Development, 9th edition*. Upper Saddle River, NJ: Pearson.

Bernstein, B. E., & Hartsell, T. L. (2005). *The portable guide to testifying in court for mental health professionals: An A–Z guide to being an effective witness*. New York, NY: Wiley.

Brief for National Association of Social Workers et al. (1999). In Re adoption/guardianship no. CCJ14746. Maryland Court of Appeals (No. 134, September term,).

Brodsky, S. L. (1999). *The expert witness: More maxims and guidelines for testifying in court*. Washington, DC: American Psychological Association.

Brodsky, S. L. (2013). *Testifying in court: Guidelines and maxims for the expert witness*. Washington, DC: American Psychological Association.

Budd, K. S., Connell, M., & Clark, J. R. (2011). *Evaluation of parenting capacity in child protection* (Best Practices in Forensic Mental Health Assessment Series). New York, NY: Oxford University Press.

Bukatko, D., & Daeler, M. W. (2011). *Child development: A thematic approach*. Belmont, CA: Wadsworth.

Bullis, R. E. (2013). *The narrative edge in expert testimony: A guide for social workers*. Alexandria, VA: Council on Social Work Education.

Campion, M. J. (1995). *Who is fit to parent?* London: Routledge.

Carlson, E. B. (1997). *Trauma assessment: A clinician's guide*. New York, NY: Guilford.

Cassidy, J., & Shaver, P. R. (Eds.). (2010). *Handbook of attachment: Theory, research, and clinical applications* (2nd ed.). New York, NY: Guilford.

Ceci, S. J., & Bruck, M. (1999). *Jeopardy in the courtroom: A scientific analysis of children's testimony*. Washington, DC: American Psychological Association.

Ceci, S. J., & Hembrooke, H. (1998). *Expert witnesses in child abuse cases: What can and should be said in court*. Washington, DC: American Psychological Association.

Choate, P. W. (2009). *Parenting Assessments in Child Protection Cases*. Special Issue of *The Forensic Examiner*, 18, 1, 1–60.

Cohen, J.A., Mannaino, A.P., & Deblinger, E. (2012). *Trauma-focused CBT for children and adolescents: Treatment applications*. New York, NY: Guilford.

Condie, L. O. (2003). *Parenting evaluations for the courts: Care and protection matters*. New York, NY: Kluwer Academic Publishers.

Cozolino, L. (2013). *The social neuroscience of education: Optimizing attachment and learning in the classroom*. New York, NY: Norton.

Crosson-Tower, C. (2012). *Exploring child welfare: A practice perspective* (6th ed.). Boston, MA: Pearson.

Crosson-Tower, C. (2013). *Understanding child abuse and neglect* (9th ed.). Boston, MA: Pearson.

Daicoff, S. S. (2013). *Lawyer, know thyself: A psychological analysis of personality strengths and weaknesses*. Washington, DC: American Psychological Association.

Dyer, F. J. (1999). *Psychological consultation in parental rights cases*. New York, NY: Guilford.

English, P. W., & Sales, B. D. (2005). *More than the law: Behavioral and social facts in legal decision making*. Washington, DC: American Psychological Association.

Feldman, M., & Aunos, M. (2010). *Comprehensive, competence-based, parenting assessment for parents with learning difficulties, and their children*. New York, NY: National Association for the Dually Diagnosed.

Frye v. United States, 293 F. 1013 (D.C. Cir. 1923).

Gould, J. W., & Martindale, D. A. (2009). *The art and science of custody evaluations*. New York, NY: Guilford.

Groth-Marnat, G. (2009). *Handbook of psychological assessment* (5th ed.). Hoboken, NJ: Wiley.

Gudjonsson, G. H., & Haward, L. R. C. (1998). *Forensic psychology: A guide to practice*. New York, NY: Routledge.

Gutheil, T. H., & Dattilio, F. M. (2008). *Practical approaches to forensic mental health testimony*. Philadelphia, PA: Lippincott Williams & Wilkins.

Johnson, M. H., & de Haan, M. (2011). *Developmental cognitive neuroscience: An introduction*. New York, NY: Wiley-Blackwell.

Hart, C. L., Ksir, C. J., & Ray, O. S. (2010). *Drugs, society, and human behavior* (14th ed.). New York, NY: McGraw-Hill.

Heilbrun, K., Grisso, T., & Goldstein, A. M. (2009). *Foundations of forensic mental health assessment*. New York, NY: Oxford University Press.

Kaplan, R. M., & Saccuzzo, D. P. (2013). *Psychological testing: Principles, applications, and issues*. Emeryville, CA: Wadsworth.

Klug, W. S., Cummings, M. R., Spencer, C., & Palladino, M.A. (2011). *Concepts of genetics*. New York, NY: Benjamin Cummings.

Koocher, G. P., Norcross, J. C., & Green, B. A. (Eds.). (2013). *Psychologists' desk reference*. New York, NY: Oxford University Press.

Lutzker, J. R. (2013). *Handbook of child abuse research and treatment*. New York, NY: Springer.

Melton, G. B., Petrila, J., Poythress, N. G., & Slobogin, C. (2007). *Psychological evaluations for the courts: A handbook for mental health professionals and lawyers* (3rd ed.). New York, NY: Guilford.

Montgomery, A. (2013) *Neurobiology essentials for clinicians: What every therapist needs to know*. New York, NY: Norton.

Mueller, C. B., & Kirkpatrick, L. C. (2013). *Federal rules of evidence: With advisory committee notes, and legislative history*. New York, NY: Wolters Kluwer Law and Business.

Munson, C. E. (2002). *Clinical social work supervision* (3rd ed.). New York, NY: Haworth.

Munson, C. E. (2007). Forensic social work and expert witness testimony. In D. W. Springer & A. R. Roberts (Eds.), *Handbook of forensic mental health with victims and offenders: Assessment, treatment and research* (pp. 67–92). New York, NY: Springer.

Munson, C. E. (2011). Forensic social work practice: Standards: Definition and specification. *Journal of Forensic Social Work, 1*, 37–60.

Myers, J. E. B. (Ed.). (1998). *Legal issues in child abuse and neglect practice* (2nd ed.).Thousand Oaks, CA: Sage.

Myers, J. E. B. (2006). *Child protection in America: Past, present and future*. New York, NY: Oxford University Press.

Nader, K., Dubrow, N., & Stamm, B. H. (Eds.). (2013). *Honoring differences: Cultural issues in the treatment of trauma and loss*. New York, NY: Routledge.

National Association of Social Workers. (1996). *Code of ethics of the National Association of Social Workers*. Washington, DC: NASW Press.

National Association of Social Workers. (2012). *Social workers and child abuse reporting: A review of state mandatory reporting requirements*. Washington, DC: NASW Press.

National Association of Social Workers. (2013). *Social workers as expert witnesses*. Washington, DC: NASW Press.

National Organization of Forensic Social Work. (1987). *Code of ethics*. Middletown, CT: Author.

Nurcombe, B., & Partlett, D. F. (2010). *Child mental health and the law*. New York, NY: Free Press.

Oppenheim, D., & Goldsmith, D. F. (Eds.). (2011). *Attachment theory in clinical work with children: Bridging the gap between research and practice*. New York, NY: Guilford.

Ostler, T. (2008). *Assessing of parenting competency in mothers with mental illness*. Baltimore, MD: Paul H. Brookes Publishing Company.

Parritz, R. H., & Troy, M. F. (2013). *Disorders of childhood: Development and Psychopathology*. Belmont, CA: Wadsworth.

Pezzot-Pearce, T. D., & Pearce, J. (2004). *Parenting assessment in child welfare cases: A practical guide*. Toronto, Canada: University of Toronto.

Preston, J., & Johnson, J. (2011). *Clinical psychopharmacology made ridiculously simple* (7th ed.). Miami, FL: MedMaster, Inc.

Reder, P., Duncan, S., & Lucey, C. (Eds.). (2003). *Studies in the assessment of parenting*. New York, NY: Routledge.

Ruiz, P., & Strain, E. (2011). *Lowinson and Ruiz's substance abuse: A comprehensive textbook* (5th ed.). Philadelphia, PA: Lippincott Williams & Wilkins.

Sadock, B. J., Sadock, V. A., & Ruiz, P. (2012). *Kaplan & Sadock's comprehensive textbook of psychiatry* (9th ed.). Baltimore, MD: Lippincott Williams & Wilkins.

Saklofske, D. H., Reynolds, C. R., & Schwean, V. L. (Eds.). (2013). *The Oxford handbook of child psychological assessment*. New York, NY: Oxford University Press.

Saltzman, A., & Furman, D. M. (1999). *Law in social work practice*. Chicago, IL: Nelson-Hall.

Sattler, J. M. (1998). *Clinical and forensic interviewing of children and families: Guidelines for the mental health, education, pediatric, and child maltreatment fields*. San Diego, CA: Jerome M. Sattler.

Schiraldi, G. R. (2000). *The post-traumatic stress disorder sourcebook: A guide to healing, recovery, and growth*. Los Angeles, CA: Lowell House.

Siegel, D. J. (2012). *Pocket guide to interpersonal neurobiology: An integrative handbook of the mind*. New York, NY: Norton.

Silverman, H. M. (2012). *The pill book*. New York, NY: Bantam.

Slater, L. K., & Finch, K. R. (2012). *Social work practice and the law*. New York, NY: Springer.

Solomon, J., & George, C. (Eds.). (2011). *Disorganized attachment and caregiving*. New York, NY: Guilford.

Sparta, S. N., & Koocher, G. P. (Eds.). (2006). *Forensic mental health assessment of children and adolescents*. New York, NY: Oxford University Press.

Springer, D. W., & Roberts, A. R. (2007) *Handbook of forensic mental health with victims and offenders: Assessment, treatment and research*. New York, NY: Springer.

Stahl, P. M. (2011). *Conducting child custody evaluations: From basic to complex issues*. Thousand Oaks, CA: Sage.

Tolle, L. W., & O'Donohue, W. T. (2012). *Improving the quality of child custody evaluations: A systematic model*. New York, NY: Springer.

Tsushima, W. T., & Anderson, R. M. (1996). *Mastering expert testimony: A courtroom handbook for mental health professionals*. Mahwah, NJ: Erlbaum.

Volkmar, F. R., & Martin, A. (Eds.). (2011). *Essentials of Lewis's child and adolescent psychiatry* (4th ed.). Philadelphia, PA: Lippincott Williams & Wilkins.

Wolchik, S. A., & Sandler, I. N. (2007). *Handbook of children's coping: Linking theory and intervention*. New York, NY: Plenum Press.

142   Mediation and Conflict Resolution

John Allen Lemmon

Mediation is a role that professionals from business, law, social work, and other disciplines may assume. The neutral and impartial mediator works with disputants to help them reach agreement. If they cannot come to an agreement, the mediator's work is finished. No decision is imposed by the mediator. No evaluation or recommendation is made to a court, because these roles would conflict with encouraging clients to speak openly and honestly, as they would to their psychotherapist or their attorney.

THE CONFLICT RESOLUTION CONTINUUM

Persons with conflicts have choices about resolution. Doing nothing is an option. Avoidance may work.

Negotiation

When disputants engage in negotiation, they attempt to reach an agreement. They may converse directly or communicate with the help of an agent who advocates for their client. This agent may be an attorney or social worker, and informal advocates such as family members may become involved. Clergy or psychotherapists may be asked to help clients with whom they have a current professional relationship to advocate when a dispute arises, or they may be approached for this reason.

Mediation

In mediation, the third party involved does not seek an outcome for a particular client. The mediator is concerned that any agreement reached be understood by and is fair to each of the disputants. Ethical codes for mediators have stated the need to be neutral and impartial while also being an advocate for weaker or absent parties such as children or frail elders, a difficult balance. The essence of mediation is that if agreement cannot be reached by the parties, the mediator does not switch roles and become an evaluator. In the event of an impasse, an evaluation that results in recommending which divorced parent should have primary responsibility for a minor child is an essential role, but it must be filled by a different person than the mediator if the parties are to speak freely in mediation. Otherwise, there is a sense of betrayal akin to having the client's attorney, clergy, or therapist testify against them in court. The fact that the judge formally makes the decision does not change the role conflict when mediators cross over to become evaluators who write reports and testify in court.

Crossover is a volatile issue in mediation. For example in California, if no agreement is reached, the mediator is barred by the evidence code from testifying. Nothing in writing may be admitted to a subsequent court proceeding. Are there any exceptions? Yes, in the situation of the custody mediation, courts are permitted to adopt a local rule that allows crossover so that the mediator who is a court employee becomes an evaluator in self-described "recommending" counties. This leads clients to say, "When I was in mediation, my mediator testified against me." Such a role conflict leads to ethical dilemmas for professionals from a number of fields. The confidentiality of mediation has been the cause of cases brought against mediators as well as others in the process.

Confidentiality in private mediation continues to be confirmed. The California Supreme Court held in 2011 that it even applies when a mediation participant is subsequently seeking to gather evidence against his own attorney about the mediation process (*Cassel v. Superior Court*, 51 Cal 4th 113). Later that year in a wrongful termination case brought under the state's Whistleblower Act (*Provost v. The Regents of the University of California* [2011] 201 Cal.App.4th 1289) the plaintiff Provost was denied an appeal from a judgment entered pursuant to a stipulation for settlement reached during mediation. Allegations of signing under duress due to coercion from his counsel, defendant's counsel, and the mediator were not deemed admissible. The Indiana Supreme Court held in 2013 that a husband's statements he claimed to make to the mediator must be excluded from evidence in a proceeding in which he sought to terminate his liability for monthly house payments to the wife after her remarriage (*Horner v. Carter*, No. 34S02-1210-DR-582).

Arbitration

Arbitration also brings a third party to help disputants reach an agreement. However, the arbitrator has the power to impose a binding decision on the parties if they cannot reach an agreement themselves. Arbitration awards are typically final and not subject to appeal, even if the arbitrator does not follow current law. Only in cases where the arbitrator exceeded the scope of what was to be decided or otherwise significantly failed to follow procedures might a judicial review be granted. Arbitration clauses are often written into employment contracts, requiring employees with a dispute to arbitrate rather than file suit in court. Challenges to mandatory arbitration for customers with conflicts have come from consumer groups charging that there may not be a choice in the marketplace or that the notice of changing to mandate arbitration was in fine print on the back of an envelope of a monthly statement. Civil rights groups have stated—and some appellate justices have agreed—that Congress did not intend for allegations of racial or sexual bias to be arbitrated with no recourse to the courts.

Health maintenance organizations requiring arbitration have been criticized by judges for not following their own procedures for a timely process and for having a stable of "the usual suspects" as arbitrators. There is a movement away from arbitration in organizations. One reason is the loss of control by all parties. A single arbitrator taking years to order the break-up of Andersen, the giant accounting and consulting firm, is a cautionary example. Another factor has been an increasing number of sexual harassment cases in the workplace of both *Fortune* 500 companies and small nonprofit organizations. The trend is to offer mediation and permit clients access to the courts if that is their choice.

Adjudication

Adjudication is a decision or verdict rendered by a judge or jury. Filing suit is the most formal conflict resolution procedure. Although "going to court" may appear to be the way most conflicts are resolved, over 95% of civil cases are settled without a verdict. This means that the parties resorted to another option after starting a lawsuit. Why? Sometimes the parties have had as much justice as they can afford. Litigation is expensive, and if the call from the attorney comes to "refresh the retainer" (a request for more fees), many disputants decide to settle or muddle through by continuing to agree to disagree. The passage of time may alter a litigant's perception of the need to continue, as one may discover the strength of the case while preparing for court.

Sometimes a formal decision by the court is desired by one or all parties. Note that unlike mediation, where all parties must agree to the final terms of any agreement, and even in many instances whether to participate, in adjudication, if one party files suit, any named respondents are subject to the court. Just as many combatants prefer arbitration until they receive an adverse award, lawsuits may reflect unwarranted optimism by at least one party.

Unlike arbitration, an unhappy litigant may seek an appeal. Appeals are not automatically granted in most civil cases. Only a small percentage of cases filed for appeal by one of the parties are selected for review by the typical appellate body. Appeals take years and additional funds. A case could wend its way from a state trial court, to an appellate panel, to that state's Supreme Court, and then to the U.S. Supreme Court. Some cases can be slated for fast track to bypass intermediate courts at the request of the trial court judge or one of the parties. Some cases persist because they have been certified as a class action, acting on behalf of both the named parties and others similarly situated. This is a way to resolve a large number of potential as well as present conflicts.

Violence

A conflict resolution continuum must allude to violence or physical aggression, which could be defined as negotiation carried out by other means. From street brawls to international conflicts, aggression is one way, however unsavory, of resolving disputes. To prevent violence, mediation is taught in elementary and secondary schools. Children wearing "Conflict Manager" T-shirts can be found on playgrounds in countries around the world, including those with a history of armed conflict between factions within their own borders. Peace studies programs in universities and groups like the Harvard Program on Negotiation analyze how aggression and negotiation are linked.

BENEFITS OF MEDIATION

The options reviewed, from ignoring or avoiding conflict through mediation, have the advantage of leaving the disputing persons in control of their conflict. No one can impose a settlement on them until they reach the point in the

continuum where they involve an arbitrator or judge or resort to violence. A mediator may prevent or stop the violence. A mediator may help the disputants translate their points of view to each other, doing considerable face-saving in the process. Because the mediator is new to the dispute, he or she can ask clarifying questions that the parties might not tolerate from each other. A partial agreement can be reached, with unresolved issues left for another option on the conflict resolution continuum. If no agreement appears likely, the mediator or any other parties can stop the process, and the entire dispute can be addressed by other procedures on the continuum. Again, unlike arbitration, the parties are free to seek relief from the courts if they are not willing to reach an agreement in mediation.

In *101 Social Work Clinical Techniques,* Turner & Rowe (2013) note that although mediation "initially emerged as a separate methodology in social work practice," the techniques also are used to address conflict that is adversely affecting the therapeutic process. The examples they cite are scheduling a couple's therapy sessions and a teenager's high school class schedule. Although such simple issues are important to resolve by the psychotherapist so that the therapeutic process can proceed, more complex emotional as well as financial conflicts may be addressed by a mediator using advanced techniques such as humor, role-play, storytelling, and other innovative uses of language as well as anger management (Lemmon, 1985).

Comprehensive Guidelines for Child Protection Mediation were approved by the Association of Family and Conciliation Courts in 2012. Mediating cases in which children have allegedly been abused, neglected, or abandoned may include legal, developmental, emotional, and cultural issues. Such cases are among the most complex and important to be mediated, calling for a range of techniques in order to reach an agreement in the best interests of the child.

MEDIATION: FIELD OF PRACTICE OR SKILL-BASED?

For those either seeking a mediator or considering becoming a mediator, a central question is how much the mediator should know about the general area from which the conflict arises. Could a mediator help parents resolve custody issues for their minor children without knowing state law that would apply if the dispute ends up in court? Could that same mediator help organizations resolve workplace conflicts without awareness of relevant federal, state, and local law?

One point of view is that mediation is foremost a set of skills. A good mediator would recognize universal stages in any conflict and apply techniques to move from anger to agreement. The other position is that virtually all disputants are *Bargaining in the Shadow of the Law,* as Mnookin and Kornhauser (1979) remind us. What would be agreed to in mediation could hinge in great part on what would likely happen in court.

Even established professions hedge this question of general skills versus subject matter expertise. A licensed physician can perform any medical procedure. A licensed attorney can represent a client in court regardless of the nature of the conflict. However, medicine offers voluntary certification—being "board certified"—for certain fields of practice. Similarly, a number of states offer attorneys meeting certain task and experience requirements the opportunity to take a test to become a certified specialist in a field, such as family law or estate planning.

The questions of subject matter expertise and role conflict are important because mediators have a profession or origin, such as law or social work, where they may still be licensed. Are they attorneys or social workers simply acting in a meditative manner? What if a mediator holds both degrees and licenses, and requirements for each license conflict? Such instances involving threats of violence or allegations of abuse are all too common. If a mediator who is not an attorney offers legal advice, does that constitute the unauthorized practice of law? If the mediator is an attorney and provides legal advice to each party, is that a dual representation conflict that violates ethical canons?

Best practice is for the mediator to ask the disputants to sign an agreement to mediate, specifying that only mediation will be provided, even if the mediator holds professional licenses in other fields. This agreement states that if the parties need legal or financial advice, a psychotherapist, or any other professional services, they should seek it elsewhere. Such a document can also serve as a fee agreement, as well as listing relevant state law concerning privileged communication—that nothing said or written in mediation can be introduced into any subsequent court proceeding and any exceptions. Finally, procedures—again

citing any pertinent law—that constitute an agreement, termination, or impasse can be cited.

REGULATING MEDIATION

Ethical codes have been developed by a number of conflict-resolution organizations that provide guidelines for self-regulation by mediators. What is likely in the future? No state licenses mediators yet. Licensing is protection of duties—"You can't do that," unless you meet requirements listed in state law—whereas certification is title protection only—"You can't call yourself that," unless you meet the requirements under state law. One state that certifies mediators, Florida, takes a field of practice approach by certifying separately by category. Mediators who deal with community conflict, such as barking dogs or blocked driveways, are called county court mediators after taking 20 hours of training and observing, then conducting mediations under observation. Family mediators must hold certain graduate degrees such as social work, or be licensed as a lawyer, a certified public accountant, or a physician who is certified in psychiatry; meet experience requirements; take a 40-hour training and observe; and then conduct relevant mediations under observation.

Some states have required a generic mediation training of 30 or 40 hours. Others have combined such a course with a 20-hour session dedicated to a particular field of practice. Still other jurisdictions require a basic 30-hour family or 40-hour divorce mediation training to be on a panel to receive mediation referrals. Most of these courses have been provided privately by pioneers in the field, as was the case with law and psychotherapy in their early days. However, an increasing number of certificate programs in conflict resolution and the mediation role are being offered by universities, and Model Standards for Mediation Certification Programs were approved by the Board of the Association for Conflict Resolution in 2012.

NEW APPLICATIONS OF MEDIATION

Family Mediation

Family mediation is expanding from custody mediation to financial matters related to divorce. Mediation of conflicts throughout the family life cycle is increasing. Programs offering permanency planning mediation in child welfare as a way to increase open adoptions, mediating with blended families to address issues of instant intimacy and different rituals, and mediation between adult children and their aging parents concerning problems in living are examples. Dependency mediation programs are addressing issues listed in petitions to the juvenile court.

Organizational Mediation

Organizations are designing conflict-resolution systems that offer a range of the negotiation, mediation, arbitration, or litigation options reviewed above, with mediation as the fastest-growing role. Employee assistance programs often provide mediation, either directly or by referral. Increasingly, federal legislation has a mediation provision. Many disputes that involve the Americans with Disabilities Act have been successfully mediated. The Equal Employment Opportunity Commission has a mediation program. The National Association of Social Workers has built mediation into its policies. Family business members are asking mediators to help them with succession planning and other tasks when family dynamics conflict with standard business practice.

Online Dispute Resolution

Much early online dispute resolution (ODR) involved the application of software to resolve disputes created through online transactions. Disputants enter what they consider to be relevant information online and the software algorithmically proposes a resolution. Software can reflect subsequent offers and counteroffers, estimate what a claim is worth, and what attorney fees might be. Mediators might become involved if resolution cannot be reached through software applications alone.

Modria is a company spun off from eBay and PayPal that leads in ODR. "Now it is branching into disputes over real estate assessments (a county typically pays $3,000 a month to resolve its valuation cases) and into divorce mediation. Many California counties already ask couples to start with mediation, and it's required by state law in disputes over child custody or visitation—though courts don't charge for it the way commercial providers do. Loic Coutelier, Modria's director of arbitration, hopes that by 2015 ODR platforms will handle 10 percent of mediations arising from the estimated 1.5 million divorce cases nationwide" (Cook, 2013).

Most disputes that originated as a result of an online transaction might be resolved entirely online because they are likely to be primarily financial, at least at first. "For offline disputes, however, the most common goal will be to find tools that can enhance elements in the process rather than managing the whole process. If mediation consists of several processes linked together, *e.g.* brainstorming, caucusing, prioritizing options, drafting, etc., software can be targeted to a particular process. For example, STORM, software developed at the University of Massachusetts facilitates brainstorming at a distance. It reduces the need for some face to face meetings and has the added benefit of allowing, if the mediator so desires, brainstorming to be conducted anonymously" (Katsh, 2012).

Mediators may have gradually incorporated phone conferencing, then video conferencing with disputants. Documents and proposed agreements are e-mailed and can be reviewed, negotiated, and amended in real time online with tools such as Google Docs. Disputes may be driven by emotions. Feelings are not easily quantifiable, which is necessary if they are to be submitted to software. A hybrid model combining face to face meetings with online processes may be optimal for complex mediations.

There is no dearth of disputes in our personal and professional lives. Conflict resolution is a growth industry. Mediating between parties to help them tailor an agreement to their needs can be rewarding. Whether or not mediation evolves into its own profession, the key is to distinguish the mediation role from others.

WEBSITES

American Arbitration Association: http://adr.org.
Mediate.com: http://mediate.com.
National Association of Social Workers: http://www.socialworkers.com.
Program on Negotiation, Harvard Law School: http://www.pon.harvard.edu.

References

Cook, C. (2013). Taking mediation online. *California Lawyer*. San Francisco, CA: Daily Journal Corporation.
Katsh, E. (2012). ODR: A look at history—A few thoughts about the present and some speculation about the future. In M. S. Wahab, E. Katsh, &

D. Rainey (Eds.), *Online dispute resolution: Theory and practice*. The Hague, Netherlands: Eleven International Publishing.

Lemmon, J. (1985, eBook 2009). *Family mediation practice*. New York, NY: The Free Press/Macmillan/Simon & Schuster.

Mnookin, R., & Kornhauser, L. (1979). Bargaining in the shadow of the law: The case of divorce. *Yale Law Journal, 88*(5), 960–997.

Turner, F., & Rowe, W. (2013). *101 Social work clinical techniques*. New York, NY: Oxford University Press.

143

Child Protection Mediation
An Interest-based Approach

Allan Edward Barsky

The child protection system is designed to safeguard minors from abuse and neglect. When child maltreatment allegations come to the attention of protective services, child protection workers (CPWs) are mandated to assess whether the children are at risk of maltreatment and determine which interventions, if any, are necessary to protect the welfare of the child. Each year, protective services across the United States screen over 3.4 million allegations, and substantiate abuse or neglect in over 2.1 million cases (Children's Bureau, 2012). Child protection laws require CPWs to use the least intrusive methods required to safeguard children. Accordingly, CPWs strive to offer support and voluntary services in a manner that allows children to remain in the custody and care of their parents. When CPWs are unable to engage families on a voluntary basis, they may petition courts to order family involvement in child welfare services or to order children's removal from their homes. Protective services remove over 146,000 children from their parents' homes each year (Children's Bureau, 2012). Given the magnitude of child maltreatment concerns, child protection agencies and courts have experimented with alternatives to traditional services and judicial processes. One such alternative is child protection mediation.

Child protection mediation (also called dependency mediation) refers to a collaborative conflict resolution process guided by an impartial third person who facilitates communication among parents, CPWs, and others involved in child protection cases in order to develop an agreement that satisfies the child's safety and welfare (Hehr, 2007). The child's voice may be heard directly, or through an attorney or *guardian ad litem* who represents the child. In the early pilot projects of the 1980s, mediation was viewed as a way to divert cases from costly court processes to relatively speedy, informal processes that would reduce legal costs for protective services, families, and the state. Mediation has proven its effectiveness as a cost-saving alternative, as well as a method to empower parents and children, engage extended family members, protect the welfare of children, facilitate planning, and foster satisfaction among various stakeholders in the process (Association of Family and Conciliation Courts, 2012; Giovannucci & Largent, 2009; Madden & Aguiniga, 2013). Although "child protection mediation" sounds like one specific process, there are many different models, including settlement-focused, interest-based, and transformative (Folberg, Milne, & Salem, 2004):

• Settlement-Focused Mediation refers to a task-focused process designed to help parties efficiently resolve their immediate disputes.

Mediators typically meet with parties and their attorneys for one or two sessions (each lasting 30 to 90 minutes). They focus on settling legal issues, rather than underlying emotional and relationship issues. In some cases, attorneys do most of the talking for their clients. By keeping cases out of court, settlement-focused mediation saves money, leads to faster disposition of cases (which may promote permanency planning), and avoids the acrimony that often occurs when cases proceed to an adversarial trial (Barsky, 2014).

- Interest-Based Mediation (IBM) refers to a problem-solving process in which the mediator helps parties resolve their underlying concerns, not just the legal issues (see Table 143.1). IBM typically requires two to eight sessions. Whereas SFM often results in *compromise* solutions: (in which both sides concede some of what they want to reach a middle ground), IBM promotes *win-win* solutions: parties use creative approaches to achieve common ground that satisfies everyone's primary concerns. The purported advantages of an interest-based approach include greater satisfaction with the outcomes, increased likelihood of following through on commitments, and better cooperation between parties (Fisher, Ury, & Patton, 2011).

- Transformative Mediation refers to a process-oriented conflict management process. Mediators provide an environment that allows clients to articulate their concerns, hear one another in a more meaningful way, empathize with one another's concerns, focus on client strengths, and take greater control over how they want to handle their conflict (Barsky, 2014; Folger, Bush, & Della Noce, 2010). Transformative mediation does not have a set time limit, though it typically requires two to ten sessions. The success of transformative mediation does not depend on whether the parties resolve conflict or save money. In fact, transformative mediation may improve how parties interact and manage conflict, even if they do not reach agreement.

Although each model has its benefits, this chapter focuses on IBM given its balance between task and process orientations: IBM helps parties reach agreements and avoid court, while also

TABLE 143.1 Tenets of Interest-Based Mediation

- Focus on interests rather than positions.
- Invent options for mutual gain.
- Apply objective criteria.
- Improve communication.
- Build a positive negotiating relationship.
- Consider alternatives.
- Obtain commitments (Fisher, Ury, & Patton, 2011).

helping them build better relationships, learn problem-solving skills, and feel greater satisfaction with the outcomes of the process (AFCC, 2012). Building better relationships between family members and child protection workers is particularly important in child protection cases, so the parties can work together on a voluntary basis and for the benefit of the child.

This following section describes child protection situations in which IBM may be appropriate. The balance of this chapter demonstrates IBM skills and strategies by following a case example through the six stages of the IBM process.

WHEN MEDIATION IS APPROPRIATE

Many of the pioneers in child protection mediation came from the field of divorce. Divorce mediators often suggest screening out cases involving alcohol or drug abuse, mental illness, or domestic violence (Holtzworth-Munroe, Beck, & Applegate, 2010). In the case of domestic violence, how could mediation be safe or fair if the abused spouse lives in fear of the perpetrating spouse? In the case of substance abuse or mental illness, how could a party with diminished capacity negotiate fairly and competently within the mediation process? In child protection cases, the vast majority of cases involve domestic violence, substance abuse, and/or mental illness. Thus, screening out cases with domestic violence, substance abuse, or mental illness would mean that mediation could rarely be used. When early mediation proponents asked child protection workers and administrators if they would be willing to try mediation, they also had significant concerns about its safety and fairness. Many were concerned that mediators would pressure CPWs to compromise on children's safety and well-being in order to reach agreements with parents. In practice, however, the presence of CPWs in the mediation process fosters safety and fairness, and distinguishes this process from divorce mediation. Mediators are supposed to remain neutral and impartial throughout the mediation process. They have no decision-making power over the parties. CPWs, however, are mandated to assess for abuse and neglect and take whatever steps are needed to ensure the child's welfare. Although mediators encourage CPWs to keep an open mind about various ways of ensuring the child's welfare, they do not encourage CPWs to make compromises regarding it (e.g., to tolerate a certain degree of abuse or neglect).

Given that neglect and abuse are not negotiable, the question remains, what is negotiable? The following examples illustrate situations in which mediation may be appropriate:

- Teachers report a student's parents for abusing him by using a strap as a means of corporal punishment. The child's life is not in immediate danger. The parents initially refuse to cooperate with the CPW. During the first court hearing, the judge refers the CPW and parents to mediation to try to establish acceptable forms of punishment for the child's misbehavior.
- Protective services determine a stepfather has been sexually abusing a 10-year-old girl. They place her in an aunt's care, so her immediate safety is assured. The CPW and mother agree to try mediation to develop a plan whereby the girl can be returned safely to her mother's care.
- A 13-year-old boy has been living in foster care for two years due to physical abuse and neglect related to a parent's alcoholism. He refuses to see his parents for scheduled visits. The parents accuse the foster parents of alienating their son from them. The parents, son, and foster parents agree to mediation to sort through their conflicts. Given the parents' ongoing alcohol problems, the mediator establishes a ground rule that they must be sober when they attend mediation.
- Protective services brought a 3-month-old girl into foster care for "failure to thrive" (growth failure due to undernutrition). Her mother died during labor. Her father was unable to take proper care of his daughter due to depression. The father's depression starts to improve following successful use of psychotherapy and antidepressants. The father does not trust the CPW to be fair with him, so he asks for a mediator to help

them negotiate conditions for returning the daughter to his care.
- A court has issued temporary guardianship order for a young girl whose parents live on the streets. An order for permanent guardianship seems likely, given that the parents' lives remain unstable and the CPW wants to make permanent plans for the child. The parents and CPW agree to use mediation to develop an agreement for voluntary surrender of parental rights, so the parents can participate in choosing adoptive parents under an open adoption process.

As these scenarios illustrate, mediation can be used for a broad range of situations, including various forms of abuse or neglect (Hehr, 2007). Although one might assume that mediation is appropriate for mild cases whereas court is required for severe cases, this assumption does not hold true in practice. Parties involved in severe cases may actually have stronger motivation to make things work in mediation because the stakes are so high—particularly for a parent who risks temporary or permanent placement of a child in out-of-home care.

STAGES OF MEDIATION

IBM comprises six stages: intake and preparation, orientation to mediation, issue definition, exploring interests, negotiation and problem solving, and finalizing an agreement. To demonstrate the skills and strategies that mediators use in each stage, consider the following scenario:

Pam has a 16-year-old son, Sandy. One day, Pam discovers a bag of women's clothes in Sandy's closet. When she confronts him, he says his brain is telling him he is female, even though he has male body parts. Pam loses her temper and says that what he is doing goes against God and nature. When Sandy says he plans to dress as a woman in public, Pam throws him out. He moves into a friend's house. The friend's parents call protective services to report Pam for abandoning her child. Chelsey, the CPW assigned to the case, tries to engage Pam but she refuses to cooperate. She says her son is dead to her. Chelsey's supervisor recommends mediation as a way to engage Pam.

1. Intake and Preparation

Mediators receive referrals from court or from the parties themselves. The mediator's primary tasks during this stage are to educate the parties about the process, assess their readiness to mediate, and prepare them to participate in a constructive manner. Mediators do not assess how the case should be resolved, because this is the parties' responsibility. Mediators do assess the nature of the conflict and how the mediator can improve the way that the parties communicate and negotiate with one another.

In the case example, a private practice mediator named Marsha accepts the referral. During intake, Marsha discovers that Chelsey is a professional social worker who is very familiar with mediation. The first time her supervisor referred her to mediation, she was skeptical because she believed her role was to mediate. She felt like going to mediation was tantamount to admitting she was incompetent. During mediation, she discovered that mediators could engage parties in a manner that was different from CPWs, because mediators were neutral and had no decision-making power. She learned to trust how mediators could empower parents to make decisions and work collaboratively. Chelsey summarizes what she sees as the key issues. She offers to be supportive in any way possible.

Neither Pam nor Sandy knows anything about mediation. Marsha meets separately to explain the mediation process and assess their readiness. Pam says she does not trust CPWs because they are "uncaring and incompetent bureaucrats." Without commenting on protective services, Marsha tries to establish her own caring and competence by demonstrating empathy, unconditional positive regard, genuineness, and knowledge of the mediation process. Marsha explains that one purpose of mediation is to promote effective communication. Pam admits that she was responsible for cutting off communication with her son. She feels ambivalent about trying to make amends. On one hand, she feels embarrassed that her son thinks he is a woman and wonders what she did to make Sandy that way. On the other hand, she loves her son—at least the son that she thought she had. Marsha helps Pam save face by noting that mediation will focus on what to do now, not what happened in the past or who is responsible for what. She helps Pam prepare for mediation by asking her to prepare two lists: a list of things she loved about the "old Sandy" and a list of concerns she has about the "new Sandy."

When Marsha meets Sandy, he asks to be addressed as female. Marsha asks whether he has any concerns about mediation. Sandy says he does not want to come to mediation if his mother is going to yell or insult him. Marsha discusses how they can use ground rules for communication to make sure that communication is safe and productive. Sandy suggests that mediation may be a waste of time because his mother is too close-minded. Marsha invites Sandy to talk about the possibility that his relationship with his mother could improve. He responds that the chances are less than 10%. They explore the consequences of no improvement versus the consequences of some improvement. Sandy agrees that it is worth trying mediation even if the chances of improvement are limited. Marsha enhances Sandy's hope without imposing ideas or pressure. In preparation for the first joint meeting, Marsha offers Sandy reading material on the coming out processes for transgender children and their families. She suggests this may help him understand his mother's reaction and concerns, as well as how to explain his situation in language she can hear.

2. Orientation to Mediation

During the first joint session, the mediator provides an opening statement, explaining the mediation process, how it differs from court or therapy, the roles of the parties, what happens if the parties reach an agreement, and what happens if they do not (Barsky, 2014). During the orientation, the mediator asserts control over the communication process, while stressing that the parties are responsible for decision-making. The mediator explains her role as an impartial third party, who helps clients resolve conflict, but does not impose decisions or take sides.

As Marsha summarizes the agreement-to-mediate form, Pam asks how she is being paid. Marsha explores this concern, discovering that Pam's underlying question is whether Marsha is impartial. Marsha discloses the government department that funds mediation services and empathizes with Pam's concern that both Marsha and Chelsey receive salaries from the government, even though they work for different departments. Marsha invites the parties to let her know if they ever have concerns that she is demonstrating bias, given her aim is to be neutral and fair to all. By remaining nondefensive and forthright, Marsha enhances Pam's trust.

Marsha invites the parties to set ground rules for a safe and productive conversation. She starts with Sandy, given their discussion about yelling and insults. Sandy suggests a rule that his mother should not raise her voice or say rude things to him. Pam responds defensively, arguing she is not rude and "how dare you speak to your mother like that." Marsha separates the person from the problem by suggesting that they both seem interested in using respectful language. She reframes their concerns into a mutual rule, "Everyone will speak to each other calmly and respectfully." All agree. Chelsey commends Sandy and Pam for reaching their first agreement. They develop additional ground rules and review the rest of the agreement to mediate. Marsha invites questions and ensures they understand the agreement before being asked to sign it. Although Pam and Sandy express doubts about each other's ability to be reasonable, Marsha expresses optimism in each of their abilities to reach an agreement that satisfies everyone's interests.

3. Issue Definition

This stage begins with storytelling, as the mediator asks parties to describe concerns they would like to resolve. The mediator allows them to ventilate feelings and review the history of the conflict, demonstrating empathy to build trust and model active listening. The mediator puts appropriate limits on storytelling, refocusing the parties on future-oriented problem solving. As each party shares concerns, the mediator summarizes key points and highlights key issues that they bring to mediation. By identifying common concerns and helping the parties articulate their priorities, the mediator helps them reach an agreement on which issues to focus upon for the rest of the mediation.

Pam seems to be the most distrustful of the mediation process, so Marsha asks her to be the first to "briefly describe the situation that brought you to mediation and what issues you would to like resolve in mediation." Pam describes the family history, including the challenges of being a single mom and how much she loves Sandy. Marsha paraphrases key points, highlighting the positive relationship Pam had with Sandy. Pam describes the day she discovered Sandy was dressing like a woman. Pam reflects back her feelings, reframing her shock and disgust into uncertainty and parental concern. Pam invites Sandy to summarize what he heard from his mother. Sandy responds, "It's all about her ... what she wants me to be, not what I am or how I should be treated." Pam appeals to

Marsha to stop him from being so disrespectful. Marsha reminds everyone of the ground rules. She resumes control over the process by asking Pam what issues she hopes to resolve in mediation. Pam says she wants to discuss "how Sandy's transgenderism can be cured, so he can be normal again." Marsha generalizes the concerns to offer an issue that all parties feel comfortable discussing, "So you'd like to talk about what could be done to re-establish a better relationship between you and Sandy." Pam agrees, so Marsha writes this issue on the flipchart.

Marsha asks Sandy to discuss his concerns. Sandy describes how he felt abandoned by his mother just when he needed her most. Pam interrupts. Marsha gently reminds her to let Sandy finish, offering her a pen to write down her concerns so she can share them later. Sandy goes into a long, detailed discussion of his struggle coming to terms with being transgender. Pam asks what being transgender means. Marsha invites Chelsey to explain. Part of Chelsey's explanation includes professional jargon, so Marsha reframes it into plain language. Marsha then asks Sandy what issues he would like to resolve. Sandy says he wants to figure out where he is going to live. Marsha lists this issue on the flipchart.

When Marsha asks Chelsey what issues she believes are important to discuss, she says she would like to discuss the possibility of family reunification. If that is not possible, then they need to discuss alternate living arrangements for Sandy. Marsha helps the parties see how they are basically talking about the same issues: the possibility of improving Marsha and Sandy's relationship so Sandy can move home, and where Sandy should live if moving home is not feasible.

4. Exploring Interests

The primary objective of this stage is to help the parties focus on their underlying interests. The mediator invites parties to look beneath their stated positions and wishes so they can focus on what matters most (Hehr, 2007). By helping the parties focus on their underlying concerns, needs, hopes, and expectations, the mediator helps them disengage from a battle over whose position is right or wrong. When Pam says she is not ready for Sandy to return home, Marsha explores why. Pam says Sandy is obviously sick and needs help, help which she cannot provide. Marsha reframes these concerns, "So you'd like to make sure that Sandy is well and gets the help he needs to be well." Sandy reacts, "I'm not sick. I just need to be allowed to be who I am." Marsha asks if this means he wants to be treated with respect. Sandy nods. Marsha lists Pam and Sandy's interests, and asks Chelsey if she would like to add any others. Chelsey suggests adding shelter, safety, and parental care. Marsha reviews the interests with the parties and incorporates their suggestions to conclude a list of their common and separate interests.

5. Negotiation and Problem Solving

The mediator encourages the parties to problem-solve based on their underlying interests. Problem-solving strategies include focusing parties on the future, generating a list of creative options that may satisfy their interests, and helping the parties evaluate options using objective criteria (Fisher, Ury, & Patton, 2011). When Marsha initiates brainstorming, Pam suggests that Sandy see a shrink. Sandy retorts that Pam should see a shrink. Marsha does not judge. She simply writes their options on the flipchart and invites them to continue brainstorming. Chelsey suggests other helpful resources: Parents, Friends, and Family of Lesbians and Gay Men (PFLAG) for Pam and a transgender support group for Sandy. All three parties then brainstorm various living arrangements for Sandy: return home immediately or in a few weeks; remain with friends; go into foster care; or stay with a relative.

Marsha helps the parties establish objective criteria for selecting the best options. They agree that the ideal helping resources are ones that are nonjudgmental, private, expert at dealing with transgender concerns, and easily accessible. Marsha then helps them apply these criteria to their options. Although Pam originally thinks PFLAG is just for parents of lesbians and gay men, Chelsey informs her that they also serve parents of transgender or questioning youth. Pam agrees to contact the local PFLAG coordinator for more information, saying she wants to find out how other parents deal with similar issues. Sandy agrees to see a counselor who works with transgender and questioning youth, stating that he feels more comfortable talking privately to one person rather than to a group. Chelsey originally asks Sandy and Pam to sign confidentiality release forms so she can speak with the PFLAG coordinator and counselor. Sandy and Pam stress that privacy is important, so Chelsey agrees to follow-up with Sandy and

Pam after their meetings rather than talk to the others. Marsha congratulates them for agreeing upon support services. They go through a similar problem-solving process to determine where Sandy will live, identifying objective criteria and choosing the best options based on these criteria.

6. Finalizing the Agreement

Once the parties reach a tentative agreement, the mediator helps them decide how to finalize it. If a court case has been initiated, the mediator typically provides the agreement to the parties' attorneys to submit it to court for an order on consent of the parties. If no court case has been initiated (as in the case example) the agreement may be formalized as part of the clients' treatment plan with the protection agency (AFCC, 2012). Marsha reviews the terms of the agreement with the parties to check for potential problems and to ensure they are committed to it. They have agreed that Sandy will stay at his grandmother's house on a temporary basis. Chelsey will facilitate referrals to PFLAG for Pam and to a counselor for Sandy. Chelsey ensures the language of the written agreement is clear, positive, future-focused, and balanced. She includes provisions for follow-up, specifying each party's roles and responsibilities. If the parties experience problems with implementation, they agree to return to mediation to work through these concerns. Marsha concludes the process by reinforcing the progress made by the parties. Even though Sandy is going to live with his grandmother, they have opened communication between Sandy and Pam, and they have developed trust with Chelsey who will help them work towards permanent living arrangements for Sandy. When successful, mediation helps CPWs and family members work together in a collaborative fashion, ensuring the child's safety and welfare in the timeliest and least intrusive means possible.

WEBSITES

British Columbia Ministry of the Attorney General, Child Protection Mediation: http://www.ag.gov.bc.ca/dro/child-protection/index.htm

Change Matrix, Mediation in Child Welfare: http://www.changematrix.org/images/uploads/mediation_in_child_welfare.pdf

London (Canada) Child Protection Mediation Project, Discussion Guide for Communities Implementing Child Protection Mediation: http://www.lfcc.on.ca/lcpmp.html

National Center for State Courts, Mediation: Child Protection Mediation—http://www.ncsconline.org/WC/Publications/KIS_ADRMed_Trends99-00_Pub.pdf

Beyond Intractability: http://www.beyondintractability.org

References

Association of Family and Conciliation Courts (AFCC). (2012). Guidelines for child protection mediation. Retrieved from http://www.afccnet.org/Portals/0/Guidelines%20for%20Child%20Protection%20Mediation.pdf

Barsky, A. E. (2014). *Conflict resolution for the helping professions* (2nd ed.). New York, NY: Oxford University Press.

Children's Bureau. (2012). Child maltreatment. Washington, DC: U.S. Department of Health & Human Services. Retrieved from http://www.acf.hhs.gov/sites/default/files/cb/cm2012.pdf#page=105

Fisher, R., Ury, W., & Patton, B. (2011). *Getting to yes: Negotiating agreement without giving in* (3rd ed.). New York, NY: Penguin.

Folberg, J., Milne, A., & Salem, P. (2004). *Divorce and family mediation: Models, techniques, and applications.* New York, NY: Guilford Press.

Folger, J. P., Bush, R. A. B., Della Noce, D. J. (Eds.) (2010). *Transformative mediation: A sourcebook–Resources for conflict intervention practitioners and programs.* Reston, VA: Association for Conflict Resolution and Institute for the Study of Conflict Transformation (http://www.transformative-mediation.com).

Giovannucci, M. & Largent, K. (2009). A guide to effective child protection mediation: Lessons from 25 years of practice. *Family Court Review (Special Issue on Child Protection Mediation),* 47, 38–52.

Hehr, A. M. (2007). Child shall lead them: Developing and utilizing child protection to better serve the interests of the child. *Ohio State Journal on Dispute Resolution,* 22(2), 433–476.

Holtzworth-Munroe, A., Beck, C. J. A., & Applegate, A. G. (2010). The mediator's assessment of safety issues and concerns: A screening interview for intimate partner violence and abuse available in the public domain. *Family Court Review,* 48(4), 646–662.

Madden, E. & Aguiniga, D. (2013). An evaluation of permanency outcomes of child protection mediation. *Journal of Public Child Welfare,* 7(1), 98–121.

144 Forensic Social Workers in Offender Diversion

Michael S. Shafer & José B. Ashford

Clients with mental health and/or substance use disorders are at elevated risk for engaging in criminal behavior and becoming involved in the criminal justice system. This involvement may include being arrested (either physically or administratively), facing formal legal court proceedings, being incarcerated in jail or prison, and/or being supervised under conditions of parole or probation. Depending upon the severity of the criminal offense with which they are charged, their history of criminal behavior, and the policies of the criminal justice system in their community, special need offenders can have opportunities available to them that will allow them to be diverted from protracted criminal proceedings and avoid formal prosecution and incarceration.

Special needs are defined in this context "as any changeable factors associated with disorders of cognition, thought, mood, personality, development, or behavior that are linked to desired outcomes for offenders at any phase of the justice process." (Ashford, Sales, & Reid, 2001, p. 5.) However, most systems do not allow for the diversion of all types of special need offenders. Offenders diagnosed with serious mental disorders and substance abuse disorders are the most common categories of offenders involved in formalized diversion programs.

The need for effective social work consultation and case management services for individuals with special needs in the criminal justice process is critical, both for those individuals who are diverted from prosecution and incarceration as well as for those individuals who are incarcerated. For this latter group of individuals, the role of social work is particularly critical at the time the individual is released from their period of incarceration (Ashford, Sternbach, & Balaam, 2009). Clearly, the interface of social work with participants in the criminal justice process presents a range of situations and opportunities for professionals with specialized knowledge and skills in forensic social work (Slater & Finck, 2011).

WHAT ARE DIVERSIONARY PROCESSES?

In many communities, formalized systems for diverting individuals with behavioral health and other disabilities and issues (including drug use and possession) who have been charged with a criminal offense have been developed. *Diversion* represents a formalized approach whereby individuals who have engaged in a criminal offense (typically restricted to misdemeanor offenses) can avoid prosecution and incarceration (Perlman & Jaszi, 1976). If the individual volunteers to participate in treatment or in some other relevant social service, then the individual can avoid the logical consequences associated with participation in the criminal justice process. These diversion programs are generally grouped into *Pre-booking Diversion* (e.g., diversion occurs before the individual is booked with a criminal offense charge) or *Post-booking Diversion* (e.g., diversion occurs after the individual is booked, but before sentencing). These programs were designed to ensure that all offenders with these mental health and substance abuse problems have equal access to diversion opportunities if they meet established eligibility requirements for diversion from the system. Prior to the establishment of formalized diversion programs, some offenders in similar circumstances were not afforded the same benefits of treatment in lieu of incarceration or prosecution (Ashford, 2013).

PRE-BOOKING DIVERSION

Pre-booking diversion identifies individuals prior to being arrested and booked into jail and links these individuals with appropriate treatment *in lieu* of arrest and prosecution. In some communities, local law enforcement may operate specialized outreach teams, comprised of uniformed and civilian personnel who identify and attempt to engage individuals into treatment programming (Deane, Steadman, Borum, Veysey, & Morrissey, 1999). These teams may patrol particular neighborhoods or areas where homeless and other indigent individuals may congregate. Likewise, these teams may respond to requests from other law enforcement officers who are interacting with an individual whom they suspect to be experiencing a behavioral health crisis (either as a result of a mental illness or due to their use of alcohol or drugs). In other communities, these pre-booking diversion teams may be operated directly by a local mental health or social service agency that is called upon by local law enforcement to intervene when it has been determined that an individual is displaying signs of behavioral health distress and the severity of their crime does not warrant prosecution (e.g., nuisance offenses such as urinating in public, public intoxication, loitering, or yelling at persons on the street, leaving a restaurant before paying for a meal).

Social workers can serve a critical role in the provision of pre-booking diversion programming in a number of ways. First, social workers may be called upon to serve on pre-booking diversion teams, either as members of teams constituted by the local law enforcement agency, or as members of teams constituted by a local human service agency that contracts with the courts to provide pre-booking diversion services. Second, social workers may be called upon to provide training and education to local law enforcement officers who are serving on pre-booking diversion teams. Finally, social workers working with local human service agencies (especially homeless shelters and crisis response centers) can be called upon to facilitate effective reception and referral processing mechanisms for local law enforcement personnel who are transporting or referring individuals to their facilities (Deane et al., 1999).

The types of clinical knowledge and skill sets required of social workers involved in pre-booking diversion programs will include the following:

- Differential diagnosis
- Crisis management and de-escalation skills
- Knowledge of law enforcement processes
- Knowledge of expedited referral and intake procedures

Differential Diagnosis: Although an accurate differential diagnosis may not be possible on initial contact with offenders in the community, social workers need to have the ability to make preliminary assessments of the mental health symptomatology and/or substance use intoxication that individuals are displaying. A fundamental understanding of the behavioral manifestations of the common forms of psychosis and mood disorders (e.g., schizophrenia, bipolar disorder, mania, depression, anxiety disorder) as well as the behavioral symptoms of acute alcohol intoxication and common drug use (heroin, methamphetamine, cocaine, PCP, etc.) is essential. An accurate differential diagnosis may not be possible in the short-term because prolonged use of many illicit drugs (e.g., methamphetamine) will result in behavioral symptoms that mirror psychosis or mood disorders (e.g., paranoia, delusional behavior). Nevertheless, the ability to identify the behavioral manifestations being displayed by an individual and to make a preliminary determination of the basis for these behaviors is an essential skill provided by social workers in pre-booking diversion programs.

Crisis management and de-escalation: Quite frequently, individuals who are diverted through pre-booking diversionary systems are in an elevated state of crisis requiring some form of de-escalation. These individuals may be experiencing an acute anxiety reaction, hyper-manic episode, or severe depression. They may be threatening suicide and/or engaging in suicidal behavior or threats of violence. Social workers involved in pre-booking diversion programs need to have proficiency with the de-escalation of these psychiatric crises.

Knowledge of law enforcement processes: Working within pre-booking diversion

programs requires social workers to have a general familiarity with the procedures and organizational culture of law enforcement systems and to have established and clearly articulated procedures for respective roles, responsibilities, and authorities in managing situations and individuals. Due to the potential for violence in situations wherein pre-booking diversion programming is located, social workers employed in these contexts must recognize that the primary decision-making authority rests with the law enforcement officer.

Knowledge of expedited referral and intake procedures: Creating expedited referral processes and client drop-off procedures is essential for social workers working within treatment or service agencies serving as drop-off or reception facilities for local law enforcement agencies involved with pre-booking diversion programs. One of the great advantages of creating drop-off facilities as part of pre-booking diversion programs is the rapid turnaround that it affords law enforcement officers. If the time required to drop-off an individual at a pre-booking treatment reception facility is as long as or longer than the time required to book the individual into jail, then law enforcement officers are less likely to engage in the pre-booking diversionary service.

Case Study #1

A client who is behaving in a bizarre manner is arrested on a public nuisance offense. The arresting officer recognizes that the individual is either psychotic or intoxicated. The officer contacts a mobile crisis team for a consultation on the case. The social worker on the crisis team reviews the circumstances of the offense with the arresting officer and does a brief assessment of the individual. In addition, the social worker checks a link on a laptop computer to determine whether the individual is in the mental health treatment system. After evaluating the evidence, the worker recommends to the officer that this individual is an appropriate candidate for being brought to a drop-off location for consideration for diversion from the criminal justice system.

POST-BOOKING DIVERSION

Post-booking diversion programs operate by identifying appropriate individuals *after* they have been arrested, booked, and arraigned, but *before* they have been sentenced. Individuals who are diverted through post-booking diversion programs can spend a brief period of time in jail, but are typically released to the community to receive treatment in lieu of extended periods of incarceration (Shafer et al., 2004). In some communities, these post-booking diversion programs may operate as formalized specialty courts, such as drug courts or mental health courts; in other communities, these programs will operate less formally. Regardless of the type of post-booking diversion program that is in place, individuals participate in these diversionary programs voluntarily, given that they have the choice to participate in and follow the conditions set forth by the diversionary program (e.g., attend treatment regularly; submit to random urinalysis), or face probable prosecution and possible incarceration. In different communities, post-booking diversion programs will provide diversion opportunities at a variety of points in the criminal justice process, and with varying levels of court sanctioning or involvement:

• Released on own recognizance
• Deferred prosecution and/or deferred sentencing
• Specialty court dockets

Released on own recognizance: Individuals are released after being arrested on the condition that they agree to not re-engage in the criminal behavior and/or that they will engage in treatment or social services. In these situations, there is no ongoing supervision or reporting required by the individual. Their case is dismissed after completing the terms of their diversionary agreement.

Deferred prosecution and/or deferred sentencing: Individuals are released after being arrested on the condition that they agree not to re-engage in the criminal behavior and/or engage in treatment or social services approved by the court. The prosecuting attorney agrees not to prosecute; or, if he or she does prosecute, the judge agrees not to sentence the individual so long as the individual does not reoffend and attends treatment on an agreed upon schedule. Either the individuals, or the service provider from which they receive their treatment or social service, typically submit status reports to the prosecuting attorney.

Specialty court dockets: Specialized treatment courts, drug or mental health courts, also require defendants to participate voluntarily in services provided by the courts, because these generally have increased levels of supervision and oversight that can increase the defendant's risks for further scrutiny by the courts. Many of these programs also have rules, which if violated can result in jail time for noncompliance that is beyond the sentence for the crime committed. These specialty treatment courts have structures that are similar to the processes employed in deferred prosecution/sentencing programs (Ashford, Wong, & Sternbach, 2008).

Most drug and mental health courts also have a specialized treatment team, consisting of a judge, a prosecuting attorney, a public defender, and a mental health/substance abuse liaison. Members of the team work together to manage the cases that come before that particular court. These various representatives function much like an interdisciplinary team. The members come to the case with a variety of perspectives, and they are allowed to provide their distinct disciplinary input into the management of the case. Additionally, in these forms of specialty courts, the defendants, who participate voluntarily, are required to report to the judge directly on an ongoing basis. With the assistance and input of the rest of the team, the judge serves in the role of a case manager (Berman & Feinblatt, 2005).

Social workers may find themselves engaged in post-booking diversionary programming through variety of venues. Most mental health and drug courts will have a court employee serving in the role of "mental health liaison" or what Hank Steadman and others describe as "boundary spanners" (Steadman et al., 1999). Individuals serving in these roles within criminal justice systems serve as the resident "expert" in mental health and substance use disorders. These boundary spanners also serve as the "bridge" between the court system and the community treatment system, facilitating the referral of clients to treatment providers; obtaining court required status reports; and otherwise enhancing the collaboration and coordination between the treatment and social service systems and the criminal justice system.

Likewise in many communities, local treatment service agencies may employ a "forensic liaison," an individual who maintains a specialty caseload of clients who are actively involved in the criminal justice system. These forensic liaisons serve a centralizing function for treatment and social service agencies by providing continuity and consistency in the communication between the treatment/

social service agency and the criminal justice system. Finally, social workers may find themselves serving clients who are engaged in some form of post-booking diversionary programming wherein the need for specialized case management services or assistance may be warranted.

Case Study #2

Jim is arrested and booked in jail on a charge of assault. A forensic liaison working in the jail screens him for participation in a post-plea diversion program attached to a mental health court. After the assessment, the jail liaison refers the inmate to the probation officer assigned to the mental health court. The probation officer performs a risk assessment, assessment of the instant offense, and gathers information about the jail inmate's criminal history. Results of the liaison's and the probation officer's assessments are referred to the Mental Health Court treatment team. The team screens the offender for his eligibility to be considered for diversion. The social worker on the team evaluates the seriousness of the individual's mental impairments as well as his suitability for release to a Forensic Assertive Community Treatment Team (FACT) team. The prosecutor assesses the offender's risk to the community and concludes that the assault was minor and due to the offender's mental illness. After determining the individual's eligibility for the program, the recommendations are presented to the defendant's attorney for consideration with the defendant. The defendant agrees to plead guilty in lieu of criminal sentencing.

Regardless of the specific type of diversionary program, there are a number of additional factors and skills that social workers need in order to be effective when working in this area of practice:

- Security clearances
- A brokered array of benefits and other services
- Medication management
- Knowledge of distinct court procedures and orders.

Security Clearance: Social workers engaged in diversionary programs need to have regular access to the jail for visiting clients and to the courtrooms for proceedings. In many communities, special access privileges can be established that ease the process of gaining entry to these secured facilities and office locations. This will typically require a background and fingerprinting check.

Benefits and Other Services: Indigent clients who are receiving Medicaid/Medicare benefits need particular attention if they are incarcerated for any period of time. Federal regulations do not allow for medical or other treatment services to be reimbursed by Medicaid/Medicare during the period of time that an individual in jail or prison. Based upon the state Medicaid agency provisions, Medicaid eligibility for these individuals may be automatically revoked when the individual in jailed or imprisoned; in other states, the individual's Medicaid eligibility is suspended for a period of time. Social workers engaged in diversionary programs should have knowledge of their state's Medicaid regulations. They can obtain this information by either visiting their state's Medicaid agency's website or the website for the Federal Centers for Medicare & Medicaid Services (http://www.cms.hhs.gov/home/medicaid.asp).

Medication Management: A common problem confronting individuals involved in post-booking diversion programs is a disruption and/or discontinuity of medications that they were taking prior to their arrest. This issue is particularly problematic for individuals with psychiatric impairments who are jailed. For these individuals, it is critical that the social worker helps ensure the continuity of their psychiatric medication orders for the interim that the individual is in jail. In addition, social workers need to ensure access to medications upon the individual's release from custody. Social workers affiliated with community-based treatment and social service agencies can facilitate the process of medication continuity by developing protocols with local jails and booking facilities that provide timely information about their client's incarceration. These protocols also should call for the presence of liaisons or other personnel at the jail who can identify persons who were taking medications or who appear to be in need of medications.

Knowledge of Distinct Court Procedures and Orders: Case managers engaged in post-booking diversion programs also need to become conversant with existing policies and procedures governing their local courts. These procedures include the various types of release conditions and court orders that their clients may be exposed to as part of a post-booking diversionary process. The type of court that individuals will be remanded to can vary from a justice of the peace to a superior court. Each type of court will have different methods of operating, different rules, and can issue different types of conditions and orders for diverted offenders. For this reason, social workers engaged in this sort of practice must have knowledge of various types of court "dockets" and the procedures governing each of these dockets in their communities. Likewise, gaining an understanding of the type, frequency, and nature of reporting that clients must engage in as a result of their diversion requirements is critical.

SUMMARY

This chapter examined the various diversion schemas that have evolved over time and that place differential limits and expectations on how forensic social workers bring their professional expertise to the criminal justice process. Individuals involved in the administration of justice have been concerned since the early 1970s about the justice meted out to offenders diagnosed with treatable disorders. For this reason, many communities have attempted to respond to specific questions about the type of justice provided disordered individuals by instituting formalized programs for offender diversion.

This chapter also demonstrated that judges, law enforcement personnel, and other legal authorities would be ill equipped to effectuate appropriate diversion alternatives without the expertise of forensic social workers. Forensic social workers bring their knowledge of mental health assessments, knowledge of community resources, and their case management skills to decisions in the justice process that allow for a select class of offenders to be diverted to treatment in lieu of the traditional criminal justice process. They possess skills for working with clients in crisis and for marshaling evidence for documenting the likelihood of an offender benefiting from a specific type of treatment, as well as an assessment of the offender's risk to the community. Indeed, the forms of consultation to the justice system provided by forensic social workers are consistent with the profession's long-standing commitments to combating the social injustices experienced by persons diagnosed with serious mental and substance abuse disorders.

HELPFUL WEBSITES

National Center on Addiction and Substance Abuse at Columbia University: http://www

.casacolumbia.org/absolutenm/templates/ Home.aspx

National Center for State Courts—Problem-solving courts resource center: http://www.ncsconline .org/D_Research/ProblemSolvingCourts/ Problem-SolvingCourts.html

National GAINS Center: http://gainscenter .samhsa.gov/html/

Pacific Coast Research Center for Criminal Justice Drug Abuse Treatment Studies and other criminal justice studies: http://www .uclapcrc.org/

References

Ashford, J. B. (2013). Forensic social work. *Oxford Bibliographies: Social Work*. New York, NY: Oxford University Press.

Ashford, J. B., Sales, B. D., & Reid, W. H. (2001). Introduction. In J. B. Ashford, B.D. Sales, & W. H. Reid (Eds.), *Treating adult and juvenile offenders with special needs* (pp. 3–27). Washington, DC: American Psychological Association.

Ashford, J. B., Sternbach, K. O., & Balaam, M. (2009). Offender re-entry in home based settings. In S. Allen and E. Tracy (Eds.), *Delivering home-based services: A social work perspective* (pp. 189–214). New York, NY: Columbia University Press.

Ashford, J. B., Wong, K. W., & Sternbach, K. O. (2008). Generic correctional programming for mentally ill offenders: A pilot study. *Criminal Justice and Behavior, 35*, 457–473.

Berman, G., & Feinblatt, J. (2005). *Good courts: The case for problem solving justice*. New York, NY: The New Press.

Deane, M. W., Steadman, H. J., Borum, R., Veysey, B. M., & Morrissey, J. P. (1999). Emerging partnerships between mental health and law enforcement. *Psychiatric Services, 50*, 99–101.

Perlman, H., & Jaszi, P. (1976). *Legal issues in addict diversion*. Lexington, MA: Lexington Books.

Shafer, M. S., Arthur, B., & Franczak, M. J. (2004). An analysis of post-booking jail diversion programming for persons with co-occurring disorders. *Behavioral Sciences and the Law, 22*, 771–785.

Slater, L., & Finck, 2011. *Social work practice and the law*. New York, NY: Springer.

Steadman, H., Deane, M. W., Morrisey, J. P., Westcott, M. L, Salasin, S., & Shapiro, S. (1999). A SAMHSA research initiative assessing the effectiveness of jail diversion programs for mentally ill persons. *Psychiatric Services, 50*, 1620–1623.

145 Therapeutic Tasks at the Drug Court

Jill L. Littrell

CASES

Frank is a 23-year-old college pre-med student. In high school, he was diagnosed with Attention Deficit Hyperactivity Disorder (ADHD). The first two years of college were relatively easy for Frank and Frank continued taking his medication at its prescribed dose each morning. Once he began taking upper division Biology and Organic Chemistry courses, however, he found the work to be more challenging. Other people in his fraternity told him how their grades improved when they began doubling up on their ADHD meds when studying the night before exams. Frank tried this strategy and found the work was far less exhausting with amphetamines. But then Frank found it hard to sleep, so he began using Valium to sleep. It was hard to wake up the next morning, and fearing he would perform poorly on the exam that he had studied so hard for, he began snorting his "addies" before the exams. After he began this practice, Frank found himself wanting to use more of his medication at higher doses. A friend in his fraternity suggested that he curb his desire for amphetamine by taking OxyContin, which the friend was happy to sell him. Although the OxyContin initially eased his craving for amphetamine, Frank found himself using both OxyContin and amphetamine. His use rapidly escalated into a big expense. In fact, OxyContin was costing about $50 per pill, which he was now taking on a daily basis. So Frank began selling his medications prescribed for ADHD to others. One of his customers took an overdose of amphetamine and was taken to the emergency room after suffering a seizure. The parents of the hospitalized boy involved the police. The boy revealed Frank's name. Frank's lawyer suggested drug court.

Joe is a 23-year-old veteran of the war in Afghanistan. After graduating from high school, he decided to join the army so that he would eventually be eligible for the benefits to pay for college. After being wounded in Afghanistan, Joe was medicated with OxyContin, an opiate medication. Following discharge, he lived with his widowed mother. His

use of OxyContin increased beyond the amounts supplied by his Veterans Administration (VA) doctor. Joe also began drinking heavily. He would fight with his mother, who was insistent that Joe get a job. After a particularly bitter argument, Joe's mother insisted that he leave. Initially, Joe did rent an apartment and found part-time employment at Walmart as a greeter. Joe's drug use was escalating, however, and he had switched to street heroin. One day, Joe was found breaking into a car in the Walmart parking lot. This incident resulted in a referral to drug court.

DRUG COURTS AS AN ALTERNATIVE TO THE CRIMINAL JUSTICE SYSTEM

During the 1960s and 1970s, court diversion programs were developed for drug-addicted persons whose addiction resulted in their criminal behavior. In accepting the Drug Court's adjudication, the individual agrees to participate in treatment for an extended duration of time. The individual does not go to trial and does not have a criminal record, but the judge in the case retains the option of temporary incarceration should the client need a little extra help in staying clean. The judge meets with the client frequently to evaluate progress and suggest additional interventions to promote recovery. The social worker employed by the drug court acts as a consultant to the judge, interviewing the client and, along with the client, developing a plan of action. The defense attorney and the prosecuting attorney also are considered to be members of the drug court team. The 10 key components in the framework of drug courts are the following: integration of addiction treatment with the justice system; a nonadversarial structure; attempts to divert individuals early in the course of their addiction; a continuum of services; regular monitoring including drug testing;

1151

sanctions and adjustments as needed; ongoing interaction with the judge; continued assessment of the court's outcomes; continuing interdisciplinary education; and partnerships with the community (Hora, 2002).

THE INITIAL INTERVIEW

The initial task of drug court personnel, usually the social worker, is to secure an agreement from the client to engage in treatment. Some assessment is also required to promote the initial engagement in the treatment process.

The Therapeutic Alliance

In reviewing the literature on drug courts, Hora advises that drug court involvement is more efficacious when the client feels that he/she has a choice in seeking treatment. The sense of volition is enhanced when clients are involved in creating the treatment plan. Involving the client in plan development is a component of a therapeutic alliance. Numerous meta-analyses of treatment efficacy find that therapeutic modality rarely makes any difference in terms of outcome. However, what always seems to matter a great deal is whether the client and therapist agree on the nature of the problem, the strategy for achieving change, and the goal of treatment (Ilgen et al., 2006). Scott Miller is another researcher who stresses the importance of the therapeutic alliance. When working with involuntary clients, Miller initially aligns with the client to assist the client in achieving his/her goal. At first, clients may not realize the value of sobriety; rather, their goal is to avoid going to jail. Scott Miller enlists the client in assessing what the judge will require to stay out of jail or get a driver's license back. Taking the approach of resource person for the client, Miller helps the client come up with a realistic plan for meeting the terms of the drug court. Later, in the process of treatment, the client frequently can be brought to appreciate the need for a change and to embrace the goal of sobriety.

Using Motivational Interviewing at the Intake Interview

Motivational interviewing (MI, now called enhancement) was developed by William R. Miller at the University of New Mexico for treating substance abusers. It expands on the technique of reflective listening developed by Carl Rogers. The strategies of MI include expressing empathy, asking about the discrepancy between values and goals and current behavior, reflecting back a client's ambivalence about current behavior, supporting self-efficacy, and asking for permission before providing advice or information. MI avoids arguing, persuading, or confronting a client with examples of negative behavior, or labeling. If the client becomes defensive, then the MI will "roll with resistance" perhaps changing the topic or emphasizing a client's strengths. MI does involve asking questions that tap into the client's concern about his/her drug use. Motivational interviewers amplify the client's concerns and past thoughts, however fleeting, about being sober.

Self-perception theory from social psychology offers rationale for MI approaches. The basic axioms of self-perception theory are:

- People's behavior is consistent with their self perceptions/concepts.
- People learn who they are from the feedback they receive from others.
- People also rely on observing their own behavior to determine their attitudes and preferences.

Self-perception theory predicts that if the client observes himself arguing for the benefits of continued drug use, he will solidify his resistance to treatment. Conversely, if the therapist asks many questions about the details of the client's life, in a nonjudgmental way, the client's ambivalence will emerge. Further questions can amplify the expression of the client's concerns. The important element is what the client sees himself/herself saying, not what the therapist says.

Differences between Motivational Interviewing and Confrontational Strategies: One of the articles of faith in Alcoholics Anonymous is that substance abusers deny that they have a problem. According to the dogma of those embracing Twelve Step points of view, denial fuels the progression of the disease of addiction. Thus, "breaking down denial" is viewed as a necessary component to effective treatment. Theresa Moyers and colleagues (2009) have empirically tested the assumption that confrontation is a useful strategy. Researchers categorized therapist interventions, client status quo or change talk during the session, and subsequent outcomes. In fact,

MI strategies resulted in more change talk from the client. More change talk predicted better outcome during the subsequent year. Morgenstern and colleagues (2003) have also assessed whether embracing the label of alcoholic is required for change. In fact, self-labeling as an alcoholic does not relate to outcome, although a desire for change and self-efficacy regarding change does. The results of these studies call into question whether confronting denial is necessary or useful. MI is also consistent with the transtheoretical model of change (Stages of Change) developed by Prochaska, DiClemente, and Norcross. This model appreciates that people make changes gradually, first contemplating and planning before making a commitment. The social worker should recognize that the client's commitment to a new way of life will require a gradual process.

Agreeing on the Goals of Initial Treatment by the End of the Intake

Although Motivational Enhancement, therapeutic alliance, and Stage of Change frames of reference caution against demanding that a client commit to lifelong abstinence after one session, the exigencies imposed by the judge as a requirement for staying out of jail usually require temporary abstinence at least from the chemical of abuse, if not from all mood and mind altering chemicals. Social workers should assist the client in developing a strategy for staying sober in the short run.

A key component of Drug Courts is involvement in comprehensive treatment. The drug court social worker can act as a resource to identify treatment options. Social workers often work at the agencies to which clients are referred. Possibilities for the treatment vehicle may include inpatient treatment, outpatient treatment, attendance at a Twelve Step meeting, and/or perhaps treatment that the social worker will provide. Treatment is most often provided in groups. The American Society of Addiction Medicine (ASAM) has developed recommendations for level of care. Those who meet criteria for mental health commitment (homicidal or suicidal) should be hospitalized. ASAM also recommends that persons lacking community support be hospitalized. Of course, choices will depend on the particular treatment opportunities available in the community.

Enhancing the Probability that the Client will Follow-through on Initial Commitments: Efforts beyond handing the client an address are required to ensure that a client gets to initial appointments. Having the client envision himself/herself in the process of going to the AA meeting is often helpful. Through the imagery, any reluctance or apprehension can be identified. Coping mechanisms can be suggested. Further, the availability heuristic (Tversky & Kahneman, 1974) provides that behaviors that can be imagined are more likely to be enacted and has been supported by social psychology research (Littrell & Magel, 1991). Thus, having the client detail the scenario of attending the meeting increases the probability of follow-through. Additionally, signing a contract is another mechanism for increasing compliance through a self-perception mechanism (Goldstein, Martin, & Cialdini, 2008).

If a client voices a desire for change or agrees to attend an AA meeting, handing the client the tools to quickly implement the decision, can help shore up the decision. It is important to have concrete, immediate plans to implement. Frank and Joe must have some Twelve Step meeting or treatment group to attend the very day of the intake. They need to see themselves acting in some observable way that signals their movement to a new stage. A week is too long to wait.

Involving the judge in the planning process for initial and then ongoing treatment is a component of drug court. In the context of team meetings, judges in drug court should be apprised regarding the importance of the therapeutic relationship. Given the philosophy of the therapeutic alliance, the judge and the client should partner in developing a treatment plan. The conditions suggesting when incarceration will be needed to supply additional assistance in staying sober should be agreed upon. In that way, a consequence can be viewed not so much as a sanction, but as a treatment support. Both Frank and Joe agreed that a week's incarceration would be reasonable should they produce a dirty urine.

Additional Issues Requiring Attention during the Initial Interview

Assessing Withdrawal Requirements: Withdrawal from opiates or stimulants is rarely lethal. However, persons who are frail, pregnant, or whose health is compromised for some other reason may require medical support. Barbiturates, benzodiazepines, and alcohol are drugs with potentially lethal withdrawal symptoms. With benzodiazepines (a class that includes Valium), because of the protracted half-life, symptoms may not be associated with drug cessation. Thus, clients may not seek medical attention.

A social worker may not know whether any particular client is in a medically compromised state. For this reason, it is good practice to have a client who has recently used evaluated by medical personnel. The social worker should inquire about the time of and amount of the client's last use of alcohol and both licit and illicit drugs. If use was recent, the client's withdrawal requirement should be evaluated by a physician. Joe had not used in the week before his first encounter with the drug court; therefore, a physician evaluation was not needed. After securing a release, however, the social worker did call Joe's VA physician regarding a potential referral for methadone.

Dual Diagnoses. Until recently, treatment streams for mental health and substance abuse have been clearly differentiated in this country. In the substance abuse field, practitioners were often suspicious of psychotropic medications. Often, those with major mental disorders were turned away. When mentally ill persons were institutionalized, substance abuse was rarely an issue. With deinstitutionalization, persons with major mental disorders often abused street drugs. Mental health practitioners were unfamiliar with how to treat addictions. SAMHSA The federal government's Substance Abuse and Mental Health Services Administration (SAMHSA) recognized that excluding the dually diagnosed unfairly denied treatment to many. For treatment centers applying for federal money, willingness and ability to treat those with dual diagnoses has become a requirement.

Be alert to the possibility that the client may not be in a great deal of pain. Some substance abusers will not have other diagnoses and may not have deep underlying personality issues (see Minkoff website), although substance abusers have higher rates of mental health diagnoses than the general public. Most alcoholics are primary alcoholics. Substances may have perturbed their biochemistry such that they appear depressed while in withdrawal. Sufficient time should be allowed for the consequences of substance abuse to dissipate prior to diagnosing other *Diagnostic and Statistical Manual of Mental Disorders (DSM)* categories (see Littrell, 1991).

At intake interview, Scott Miller asks clients to complete a form that includes a general assessment of how the client is functioning emotionally,

socially, etc. (The form can be downloaded without cost from the talking-cure website.) A social history might also reveal that a client has a significant history of trauma and abuse. When an abuse history is present, AA recommends that when a particular alcoholic has an extensive background of child abuse and/or adult-child-of-an alcoholic issues, the first task is staying sober. After the client achieves stable sobriety, should the client wish, background issues can become a focus.

Of course, some clients will be in a great deal of pain because of a co-occurring mental condition, because a family member has severed relationships, because of a job loss, because of guilt over some action, etc. If the client's self-assessment suggests that he/she is distressed, then the distress is an immediate issue for treatment. The most frequent precipitants to relapse are negative moods. Thus, the client's coping mechanism must be developed. Lisa Najavits has fashioned an approach to treating posttraumatic stress disorder (PTSD) in drug abusers. Called Seeking Safety, it entails developing coping skills for defocusing from painful emotions and identifying safe places to be (Najavits, 2007).

Assessing the Therapeutic Alliance at the End of Every Session

Because Scott Miller recognizes the importance of the therapeutic alliance, he makes sure to assess the therapeutic alliance after every session. Short outcome measures requiring 45 seconds to complete invite the client to evaluate the usefulness of the session. (This one-page instrument consisting of five questions can be downloaded without cost from the talking cure website.) If the client is ambivalent about the session, Miller addresses the issue directly, asking the client for feedback about how he could be more helpful.

Summary of What Should Be Accomplished in the First Interview. By the end of the intake the following treatment objectives should be reached:

• The client should have identified short-term goals for abstinence.
• The client should have some strategies and backup plans for staying sober.
• The client and social worker should have identified some form of treatment that the client will attend.

- The client's withdrawal status and need for immediate medical attention should be addressed.
- Imminent mental health needs (suicidality or homicidality) should be addressed.

Both Joe and Frank agreed to investigate the possibilities of methadone maintenance. They both agreed to sample AA meetings in the community to find ones they liked. The judge agreed to their initial plans, and following Joe and Frank's initial investigations of treatment options, the judge listened to their thoughts about their visits to AA meetings and the methadone maintenance clinics.

TASKS FOR TREATMENT PHASE

Evaluating the Role that Drugs Have Played in One's Life

In early treatment, the client is educated about addiction so that he/she can consider how drugs have impacted life. Only with information can the client make decisions about long-term goals. Groups often are the vehicle for treatment. In a group, the client can hear the stories of individuals at various stages of chronic addiction. As the client listens to others, the client evaluates whether he identifies with the stories he/she hears. Usually, early in treatment, the client completes a first step inventory. In this context, the client responds in detail to a series of questions about how drugs have affected the various spheres (work, recreation, family, thinking) of the client's life. This vehicle for reflection informs the client's decisional balance sheet. As a result, the client usually makes a commitment to a behavioral change. The client has moved to the Action Stage. At weekly meetings, the judge discussed with Joe and Frank their plans for "working their programs" for the upcoming months and listened to their thoughts on what they were hearing in their respective treatment centers.

Decisions about Other Drugs

Conflicting viewpoints are found with regard to the imperative of abstinence from all mood and mind altering chemicals. In working with the dually diagnosed, Minkoff encourages therapists to work incrementally toward sobriety. For the dually diagnosed, abstinence from cocaine is a success, even though the client continues to drink alcohol. For the dually diagnosed with anxiety disorders, psychiatrists may deem benzodiazepines to be appropriate treatment. Stimulants in those with attention deficit/hyperactivity reduce cocaine relapse.

For stimulant addicts in particular, stimulant drug use often escalates rapidly (within a period of several months) from first use to legal problems. Stimulant addicts sometimes have an extended history of nonproblematic alcohol drinking. Such individuals are hard to convince of the necessity of long-term abstention from alcohol. Empirical research suggests that alcohol consumption increases the probability of cocaine relapse in those who are heavy drinkers, but not for those who drink in moderation (one or two drinks per setting). The risk of cross addiction for heroin addicts to alcohol after they curtail opiate use is particularly high.

Although the treatment community differs on the necessity of abstinence from all mood and mind altering substances, decisions about each particular drug should be addressed during the treatment process. In the course of taking a social history, the social worker should evaluate the role of all illicit drugs, legal recreational drugs (nicotine and alcohol), and psychotropic medications (stimulants for attention deficit hyperactivity; benzodiazepines for anxiety, etc.). Clients who were raised in communities where alcohol abuse was the norm may need education on what constitutes social drinking. Sometimes, drug court judges will make abstention from all mood and mind altering drugs a requirement of the court, obviating the need for developing drug-specific plans. For the-long term, however, clients will need to think through the pros and cons of abstention from each particular drug. Joe and Frank both agreed to refrain from alcohol and street drugs for the immediate future.

Drugs for Opiate Addiction

Various drug treatments are available for opioid addiction. Naloxone is a drug that will displace an opiate from its receptor while exerting no effect on the neuron. Although naloxone can be helpful in maintaining abstention, the drawback is that naloxone will generally diminish the motivational systems in the brain, making natural rewards less attractive and diminishing alertness.

Both methadone and buprenorphine are opiate receptor agonists that are legal. Most major cities offer methadone treatment options. The federal government also has approved buprenorphine, marketed as suboxone, which can be prescribed by doctors in private practice. Information is available at http://burprenorphine.samhsa.gov. As yet, there are no widely accepted guidelines as to when in the course of an addiction a client should be offered opiate maintenance treatments. Both Joe and Frank decided upon methadone maintenance programs.

Work by Peter Kalivas has identified a key difference in an addicted brain that magnifies the strength of relapse precipitants. N-acetylcysteine can correct the behavior of the brain, decreasing the strength of craving. It has shown efficacy in reducing craving for cocaine and in gambling addicts (see Littrell, 2011). Frank's VA physician had read the literature on N-acetylcysteine and provided a prescription.

Developing a Plan for Relapse Prevention

After a client makes a decision to abstain from his/her drug of choice, the client is in the Action Stage, which quickly moves to the Maintenance Stage. The client should be thinking about how to get to daily AA meetings. Carrying around reminders of commitment to sobriety (e.g., the Big Book or birthday chips) make sobriety goals salient. These reminders direct thoughts and actions toward new goals displacing cravings and thoughts of drug use. Cues associated with particular goals (pursuit of sobriety) can decrease the salience of cues for incompatible goals (finding drugs). These cues, even when not consciously processed, can activate behavioral programs (Littrell, 2011). For recovery, the strategy is to create triggers for cuing automatic behaviors that support sobriety. For example, the judge always asked Joe and Frank whether they had their chips with them at their weekly meetings with him.

Detailed plans about "working a program" should be made. Adherence to action plans is more likely when plans are highly articulated, diversions from the plans are anticipated, and coping mechanisms for overcoming obstacles are identified. Research also finds that self-efficacy regarding staying sober predicts success (Ilgen et al., 2006). In fact, social psychologists have an equation for motivation that states: motivation = valuing the goal x self-efficacy. Once the client is in the action or maintenance phase, the self-efficacy term requires attention in treatment.

Employing the availability heuristic, that is, having the client imagine successfully performing pro-sobriety behavior, can enhance self-efficacy and increase compliance with specific plans.

Even for individuals who have established a pro-sobriety routine, relapse precipitants can emerge unexpectedly. Years of research examining the conditions under which relapse is most likely to occur can inform about how to avoid relapse. AA's admonition, HALT, (avoid being hungry, angry, lonely, or tired) comports with the list that years of research on conditions predisposing relapse substantiates. The animal and human work suggests that negative moods can trigger relapse. Thus, practicing strategies for extra emersion in AA meetings during times of stress might prove helpful in avoiding relapse. Triggers for relapse need to be identified. Discussion of areas of town to avoid should occur. Identifying individuals who might encourage drug use is helpful. The point is to develop strategies and coping skills.

Sometimes it is impossible to avoid being hungry, angry, lonely, or tired. At such times, self-regulation resources are paramount. Self-regulation is a limited resource. If one is taxed by a lack of sleep, inadequate nutrition, or rigorous demands on one's attention, then it is far less easy to exert self-control. Conversely, positive moods enhance self-regulatory capacity. Brain research suggests that the prefrontal cortex is the area of the brain most heavily involved in self-regulation. One manifestation of the strength of this capacity is heart rate variability (HRV). In fact, experimental work finds that lapses in self-control are presaged by a decrease in HRV. Researchers have identified ways to increase heart rate variability. Relatively cheap biofeedback equipment is available and presently a cheap phone app, called the stress doctor, is marketed by azumio. Exercise and omega-3 fatty acids increase HRV. Meditation, probably through influencing HRV, increases abstinence. Moreover, being with trusted friends increases oxytocin release. Oxytocin will increase heart rate variability. Purposely engaging in behavior to enhance self-regulatory capacity should be part of the treatment plan (Littrell, 2011).

Frank decided to take advantage of the VA benefits for education and enrolled in a community college to earn a degree in heating and air conditioning technology. Frank relapsed consuming alcohol the night before his first exam. The social worker then talked with the VA and made arrangements for a VA peer counselor at the community college to work directly with Frank in preparing for exams. With extra coaching, Frank became more comfortable with taking tests. The peer-counselor support was added to Frank's diet and exercise regimen as a relapse prevention strategy.

Developing a Plan for Contending with Abstinence Violation Syndrome

Relapses following commitment to abstention are to be expected. The phenomenon of abstinence violation syndrome, described by Alan Marlatt, refers to the state in which an individual fails to recognize the possibility of reinstating the goal and the difference between a small lapse and a protracted relapse. An additional component is the disappointment and negative mood that also contributes to drug seeking behavior (see Littrell, 1991; 2011). Plans for curtailing drug use and reinstating a recovery environment are critical. Strategies for counteracting abstinence violation syndrome might include preparing a letter to oneself, which should be kept in one's purse or pocket, to be read in the event of relapse. The letter should articulate the sense of hope and personal satisfaction previously experienced after achieving a period of sobriety. The letter can serve as a convincing reminder that significant periods of sobriety can be achieved. Both Joe and Frank read their letters to the judge.

Monitoring Urine

Monitoring of urine is a key component of drug courts. For long-term outcome of opiate users, monitoring of urine is associated with better outcome. Particularly in early sobriety, before the client has established a recovery paradigm, knowing that sanctions result from a dirty urine, can provide an extra incentive. Drug testing should be presented as a mechanism for assessing the efficacy of the treatment plan so that timely adjustments can be made. The social worker monitored Joe and Frank's adherence to treatment, urine analyses, and attendance at Twelve Step meetings and reported to the judge.

Another key component of drug courts is graduated sanctions. Thus, rewards (a reduction in fines, movie tickets, etc.) can be provided for successes. If sanctions are imposed (time in jail) they should be given in the spirit of assisting the client to meet his/her goals. An immediate negative physical consequence for using can be motivating as well. Antabuse medication will cause nausea given any consumption of alcohol. Involving the judge when sanctions are implemented can be of particular benefit for those with more extensive involvement with the criminal justice system. The judge congratulated both Joe and Frank on their treatment adherence and clean urines.

Length of Treatment

Research on drug courts finds that duration of involvement with the court is a big predictor of success. The alcohol treatment outcome literature suggests that after the initial phase of treatment, when frequent sessions are required, it is the duration of the client's treatment, rather than the frequency of sessions, that bolsters success (Littrell, 1991). Most drug courts require at least a year of engagement (Hora, 2002). However, even after drug court, the client should establish a long-term relationship somewhere in the community.

Case Dispositions

Both Joe and Frank, after listening to stories at AA meetings and in the drug court sessions, decided to refrain from all nonprescription chemicals for the long-term. Joe found a job. Frank returned to school with financing from the VA. In treatment, they both did first steps, developed relapse prevention plans, and developed contingencies for relapse. They both established exercise, diet, and meditation regimens. Anniversary chips from AA remind them of their commitments. They were congratulated by the judge and graduated after one year. Their charges were dropped.

USEFUL WEBSITES

This website belongs to Ken Minkoff, who has been actively involved in developing the integration of mental health treatment and substance abuse treatment for SAMHSA. His model for treating the dually diagnosed is called Comprehensive, Continuous, Integrated System of Care (CCISC): www.kenminkoff.com

This website belongs to the Center on Alcoholism, Substance Abuse, and Addictions established by the motivational interviewing people at the University of New Mexico.

It offers a manual for applying motivational enhancement to drug abusers, therapist skill coding forms, and ordering forms for professional training videos: http://casaa.unm.edu

This website belongs to the National Drug Court Institute. Through this site, one may obtain Monchick, R., Scheyett, A., & Pfeifer, J. (2006). *Drug court case management: Role, function, and utility*, as well as Belenko, S. (2001). *"Research on drug courts: A critical review.* www.ndci.org

This website belongs to the National Association of Drug Court Professionals. It provides information on the efficacy of drug courts as well as information regarding annual training events. http://www.nadcp.org

This website offers resources for treating Post Traumatic Stress Disorder in the context of substance abuse. In contrast to implosive therapy/flooding/exposure treatments, the seeking-safety approach endeavors to help those with PTSD to switch focus from emotionally provocative stimuli to a "here and now" focus, as well as to offer assistance in selecting safe environments. http://www .seekingsafety.org

This website was developed by Scott Miller and Barry Duncan who, along with Mark Hubble, authored *The Heart and Soul of Change*. Miller takes a pragmatic approach to working with clients. He does not hone to any particular theoretical orientation, but rather capitalizes on the empirical research indicating that the therapeutic alliance predicts treatment outcome. Miller offers assessment tools for the therapist to ensure the strength of the therapeutic alliance. www.talkingcure.com

Website explaining the transtheoretical model of change developed by Prochaska, DiClemente, and Norcross in their book *Changing for Good*. The website belongs to the Cancer Prevention Research Center. http://www.uri .edu/research/cprc/TTM

Supporting Literature

Goldstein, N. J., Martin, S. J., & Cialdini, R. B. (2008). *Yes!: 50 scientifically proven ways to be persuasive.* New York, NY: Free Press.

Hora, P. F. (2002). A dozen years of drug treatment courts: Uncovering our theoretical foundation and the construction of a mainstream paradigm. *Substance Use & Misuse, 37,* 1469–1488.

Ilgen, M., Tiet, Q., Finney, J., & Moos, R. H. (2006). Self-efficacy, therapeutic alliance, and alcohol-use disorder treatment outcomes. *Journal of Studies on Alcohol, 67*(3), 465–472.

Littrell, J. (1991). *Understanding and treating alcoholism: An empirically based clinician's handbook for the treatment of alcoholism.* Hillsdale, NJ: Lawrence Erlbaum & Associates.

Littrell, J. (2011). How addiction happens, how change happens, and what social workers need to know to be effective facilitators of change. *Journal of Evidence Based Social Work Practice, 8*(5), 469–486.

Littrell, J., & Magel, D. (1991). The influence of self-concept on change in client behavior. *Research in Social Work Practice, 1,* 46–67.

Morgenstern, J., Bux, D. A., Labouvie, E., Morgan, T., Blanchard, K. A., & Muench, F. (2003). Examining mechanisms of action in 12-Step community outpatient treatment. *Drug and Alcohol Dependence, 72*(3), 237–247.

Moyers, T. B., Martin, T., Houck, J. M., Christopher, P. J., & Tonigan, J. S. (2009). From in-session behaviors to drinking outcomes: A causal chain for Motivational Interviewing. *Journal of Consulting and Clinical Psychology, 77*(6), 1113–1124.

Najavits, L. M. (2007). Seeking safety: An evidence-based model for substance abuse and trauma/PTSD. In K. A. Witkiewitz & G. A. Marlatt (Eds.), *Therapist's guidance to evidence based relapse prevention: Practical resources for mental health professionals* (pp. 141–146). San Diego, CA: Elsevier Academic Press.

Tversky, A., & Kahneman, D. (1974). Judgments under uncertainty: Heuristics and biases. *Science, 1985,* 1124–1131.

Making a Case for Life

146 *Models of Investigation in Death Penalty Mitigation*

José B. Ashford

INTRODUCTION

The death penalty is authorized in 32 states, the federal government, and the United States Military. There are over 3,000 individuals currently on death row in the United States. The death penalty is intended for the most heinous crimes and the most culpable offenders. In death-penalty cases, "[t]he defense team must conduct an ongoing, exhaustive and independent investigation of every aspect of the client's character, history, record and any circumstances of the offense, or other factors, which may provide a basis for a sentence less than death" (American Bar Association [ABA] Supplementary guidelines, 2008, p. 689). The United States Supreme Court considered social work a profession that is well-suited to assisting lawyers in the performance of these specialized investigations (*Wiggins v. Smith*, 2003).

The American Bar Association *Guidelines for the Appointment and Performance of Defense Counsel in Death Penalty Cases* states that a capital defense team "should consist of no fewer than two attorneys qualified in accordance with ABA Guideline 5.1, an investigator, and a mitigation specialist." (ABA, 2003: Guideline 4.1(A) (1)). Mitigation specialists bring special skills to the defense team in making a case for life that differs from other members of the defense team. This chapter reviews some of the skills used and the methods adhered to by forensic social workers in identifying and developing mitigation evidence as members of a capital defense team.

SOCIAL WORKERS AS MITIGATION SPECIALISTS

Current death penalty trials involve a bifurcated process that consists of two distinct phases: a guilt phase and a penalty phase. It is during the penalty phase of a capital trial that jurors are expected to make a reasoned moral decision about the appropriateness of a sentence of death (Ashford, 2013). In making this decision, they have the legal charge of determining whether a defendant is eligible for a death sentence given the presence of relevant aggravators. Following this determination, they are asked to consider and evaluate the moral significance of any proffered mitigation by the defense in the selection of an appropriate punishment. Referencing the ABA Guidelines, Justice Sandra Day O'Connor observed that "investigations into mitigating evidence should comprise efforts to discover all reasonably available mitigating evidence" (*Wiggins*, 2003, p. 2537). The *Wiggins* decision not only clarified what constituted a properly constructed social history investigation for gathering mitigation evidence, but also affirmed the value of social work's expertise in the area of capital mitigation.

The *Wiggins* postconviction appeal involved a claim that the trial attorneys in the *Wiggins* case failed to conduct a full investigation of his life history. The trial attorneys obtained limited information about Wiggins' background, but they did not use the services of a social historian, described in the opinion as a "forensic social worker," to prepare a complete social history, despite the availability of funds for that purpose (Ashford, 2013).

Two years after *Wiggins*, the need for a complete and thorough social history investigation was further emphasized in *Rompilla v. Beard* (2005, p. 379). In this case, the defendant's legal counsel made a strategic decision not to investigate Rompilla's history because Rompilla reported that he had an "unexceptional background." This is a frequent occurrence in death penalty cases. Defendants often instruct members of the defense team neither to investigate mitigating evidence nor to present any mitigation during the penalty phase of a capital case. The trial-attorney in the *Rompilla* case performed an investigation into the client's general background and character. This included interviewing a small number of family members who testified about Mr. Rompilla's good character in the penalty trial. The attorneys in this case also consulted with mental health experts in developing affirmative guilt-phase defenses. However, the baseline task in any mitigation investigation of analyzing a client's life-history records was not performed as previously decided in the case of *Williams v. Taylor* (2000). During the post-conviction investigation of Rompilla's case, evidence was uncovered in records, which if presented, may have convinced the jury of his lessened culpability (Ashford, 2013).

The social or the life history investigation is now recognized as a fundamental requirement in case law (*Wiggins v. Smith*, 2003; *Rompilla v. Beard*, 2005) and in professional norms and standards (ABA Supplementary Guidelines 2008) as the cornerstone of practice in death-penalty litigation (Ashford, 2013). That is, the courts now take into account the nature and quality of social history investigations when evaluating the effectiveness of legal counsel in claims of ineffective assistance of counsel in post-conviction appeals of death sentences.

In order to understand the background and circumstances of the defendant's life, the defense team must perform a multigenerational investigation of all the factors that influenced the defendant's criminal history, psychosocial development, character, and condition. An investigation of this nature requires a type of expertise not traditionally possessed by attorneys (Andrews, 1991; Guin, Noble, & Merrill, 2003). In fact, an ABA Advisory Committee found that many post-conviction claims in capital cases were due to defense counsel not properly investigating and uncovering reasonably available mitigation evidence (Ashford, 2013). Robin Maher, Director of the ABA Death Penalty Representation Project, attributed these failures to lawyers lacking skills "to obtain the sensitive and sometimes embarrassing evidence about a client's life experiences from family members and other sources that are often beyond the abilities of even the most skilled courtroom lawyer" (Maher, 2008, p. 769).

The forensic social worker on a defense team should bring the following skill set to the mitigation investigation process:

- Cultural competency
- An ability to identify the presence of mental health signs and symptoms of specified and unspecified mental disorders
- Techniques for interviewing that can enable them to overcome barriers to disclosure about a variety of human frailties
- Knowledge of how to collect relevant life history records (Ashford, 2013).

These skills and other forms of knowledge required of mitigation specialists are described in greater detail in the American Bar Association's (2008) *Supplementary Guidelines for the Mitigation Function of Defense Teams in Death Penalty Cases*. In addition to these practice guidelines, forensic social workers can encounter different norms and standards for practice depending on whether they are employed in a private or public setting.

PRACTICE EXPECTATIONS: PUBLIC VERSUS PRIVATE PRACTICE SETTINGS

Social workers employed in public defender offices are faced with ethical constraints not encountered in traditional social work practice. Legal decision-making focuses on advocacy, requiring a social worker employed in a legal defense agency to assist the attorney in achieving the defendant's position regardless of community safety and best interest considerations (Ashford, Macht, & Mylym, 1987). Indeed, different models of social work practice have emerged in forensic social work practice based upon the different ethical standards and norms of practice in legal agencies governing social workers employed in defense-oriented settings (Hughes, 2009).

- Social workers employed in offices utilizing an investigative model are treated as part of the defense team. Their function is to collect and analyze social history information relevant for sentencing. However, because they provide consultation to attorneys in the development and presentation of mitigating evidence, social workers employed in this type of practice setting are not independent experts. Nonetheless, they still engage in a systematic process of document collection, witness identification, witness interviews, and defendant interviews. However, the social worker's analysis of the defendant's life history in this investigatory role is biased, because of the nature of the practice context. Namely, they are considered a consulting expert to the defense team and to the defense team's mitigation strategy. For this reason, the social worker can function only as a fact witness to corroborate witness statements or to authenticate documentary evidence. That is, any testimony or written assessments regarding the social worker's findings would not meet court criteria for an expert witness. Thus, the social worker's findings in this investigatory role are intended to be presented to defense counsel for their use in determining the social history evidence available for presentation at sentencing.

- Other indigent defense agencies employ social workers as disposition specialists assisting the attorney in determining treatment placement, alternatives to incarceration, and brokering appropriate community resources. This model of service provision is typically utilized in practice with lower-felony defendants (i.e., individuals facing minimal prison or community supervision sentences). However, social workers employed as dispositional advocates must be careful not to cross over into a treatment role. Their role in this context is to identify appropriate recommendations for consideration in the case's disposition as part of an attorney memorandum that outlines the defense position to support specific sentencing recommendations appropriate in that case. In this type of support role in the sentencing process, the social worker is not acting as a therapist or as an expert witness. As a consequence, the social worker is bound by the attorney-client relationship and falls under the attorney-client privilege regarding abuse reporting responsibilities. The social worker is not obligated to report suspected abuse or neglect (subject to

locality specific statutory guidelines) and any information obtained from the defendant cannot be disclosed without the defendant's authorization. In other words, the social worker in this type of practice role is not an independent professional, but instead an ancillary staff member who has specific practice responsibilities surrounding the identification of appropriate resources for aiding defense counsel in presenting a case for a desired disposition.

Not all social workers working as mitigation specialists are employed by public defender offices. Some mitigation specialists are also private practitioners who can play various types of professional roles that adhere to a different model of principles for practice. For instance, there are private practitioners who operate under an investigator model: a consulting member of the defense team who is an independent contractor rather than an office-paid employee. The same practice considerations apply for these private practice social workers as social workers who are employed by publicly funded defense agencies. However, many private practice social workers have also adopted an expert model that is described below:

- The social worker/mitigation specialist as an independent expert witness approaches each case initially with the same systematic framework or scientific formulation required to develop the defendant's life history. As an evaluating expert, the social worker in this role is not a consulting member of the defense team. The social worker serving as an expert is expected to inform the trier of fact about the defendant's life history through data interpretation using social science research and theory to explain the defendant's behavior, development, and functioning. Without participation in defense team strategy discussions, the independent social work expert must focus solely on the referral question at hand and provide information to the attorneys within the domains of the professional's expertise, being cautious to operate within social work's specific range of expertise. Testimony and/ or written evaluations to the court may be required. Social workers appearing in court as independent expert witnesses must have qualifications and expertise in the specialty area relevant to the case (Gothard, 1989). This role is frequently encountered when the defense team has already collected some life history information through investigation, and the social worker as an expert witness is used to analyze and interpret the investigative findings in terms of theory, research, and experience not possessed by laypersons.

Irrespective of practice model, social work has had a longstanding niche in criminal sentencing because of its distinct expertise in the area of social history or life history development. The social history of a criminal defendant is typically complex, with pervasive themes of trauma, mental disability, deprivation, and social exclusion. The investigation requires practitioners to employ a systematic process of document collection and review, before hypotheses can be generated and tested through a process of critical inquiry (Ashford, 2013). The social history assessment also must adhere to accepted social work and social science procedures. To this end, the social worker must establish a chronology of:

- Key life events
- Deviations in thought, mood, and behavior considered signs and symptoms of specified and unspecified mental disorders
- Key developmental transitions
- Psychological and physical traumas
- Adaptive and maladaptive coping strategies
- Recurrent difficulties in relationships
- Disruptions in psychosocial development
- Changes in emotions and cognitions following psychosocial stressors and physical traumas
- Other developmental considerations (see Ashford, 2013).

The social worker must also gather a cross-section of information from key sources in the defendant's social environment (family/significant others, social educational settings, employment, housing, neighborhood, cultural and spiritual environment, service system experiences, accessibility to needed services, income, and legal/crime experiences). After identifying and reviewing the cross section of life events and the longitudinally relevant information gathered in this process, social workers analyze these findings

through various theoretical lenses acquired in their professional training for identifying relevant variables and factors for developing appropriate mitigation themes. This includes reviewing the scientific literature to guide their interpretations of the variables and themes identified in the defendant's life history (Ashford, 2013).

Case Example

- Johnny, a 24-year-old male, is charged with two counts of First Degree Murder and Armed Robbery for killing a clerk and a witness while robbing a convenience store. When interviewed by law enforcement, Johnny confessed to the shooting but could not provide any details about what occurred. Video surveillance from the store documents Johnny wandering around the store confused and stumbling in an aisle for several minutes prior to the beginning of the shooting.
- Johnny was born to a drug-addicted mother who died of an overdose when Johnny was seven years old; he does not know who his father is. After his mother's death, Johnny and two older sisters were sent to live in another state with his maternal grandparents. Maternal grandmother did not work and suffered from Bipolar Disorder. Maternal grandfather worked long hours in a factory and drank alcohol on a daily basis. Each night after returning from the bar, grandfather would return home and physically abuse Johnny, his grandmother, and sisters. At age 10, Johnny began running away from home and was soon placed in foster care. He has several juvenile arrests for property and drug offenses and served several unsuccessful terms of community supervision, eventually being committed to the juvenile corrections department at age 16.

APPLICATION OF A SOCIAL HISTORY FORMULATION

The social worker will need to engage in a systematic process of data collection to obtain objective and reliable information about Johnny's social history. This historical investigation requires the practitioner to adhere to a process of critical inquiry that is separated into various stages, each with separate but cumulative goals in mind (see Ashford, 2013).

1. Identify Key Goals for Social History Investigation

Depending on the type of case, the social worker can be asked to investigate a very narrow portion of the defendant's background. For example, attorneys representing a defendant with known mental health history may only seek the social worker's assistance in the investigation of psychiatric issues. This is common in lower-felony cases where the social worker has a small window of time to prepare a social history before the sentencing hearing. At other times the mitigation investigation already may have been partially completed and the social worker must pick up where the other professional left off, or focus the investigation on areas that require further inquiry.

In most criminal cases, especially death penalty cases, the purpose of collecting historical information is to identify all factors and experiences that have shaped the defendant's background and character. The only reliable method to accomplish this task is to engage in a multidimensional, holistic approach to information gathering that is guided by scientific principles and methods of inquiry (Ashford, 2013).

Because a social history can provide insight into pertinent clinical and developmental issues, the goals of the investigation narrow as relevant information is identified. For instance, an initial meeting with Johnny confirms the existence of multiple agencies playing a role in his life. The maternal grandmother received Social Security, which enabled the team to learn about her history of mental illness. She also had contact with many other agencies that collected data on various issues in her home situation, which was referenced in these reports. The information in these reports pointed to other problems, such as the maternal grandfather's alcoholism. This led to the identification of additional documents, which raised concerns about his potential involvement in the criminal justice system.

In essence, each lead can point to a different body of records that can document important phases of Johnny's life. For instance, court records in Johnny's case contained information on the transfer of custody of Johnny and his sisters to the grandparents, as well as information about the criminal history of Johnny's mother prior to her death. Records from Johnny's placement in foster care and subsequent juvenile justice referrals also contained a wealth of life history information such as mental health evaluations, home studies, educational assessments, and information about potentially relevant behavioral patterns. The collateral documentation contained many investigative leads, such as caseworkers, psychologists, social workers, teachers, neighbors, peers, probation and parole officers, counselors, and law enforcement officers who have knowledge of varying conditions and events in Johnny's life. References in records to individuals who knew Johnny's maternal grandparents were very helpful because they identified professionals who helped corroborate important details about the grandfather's alcoholism and the grandmother's mental health problems.

The goal of the investigation is to provide a picture of the defendant's life, which is illuminated through the testimony of live witnesses and objective historical documentation. This evidence is most credible when it is inherently unbiased, such as the grandfather's ex-employers and employees who never met the defendant. In order to corroborate the data collection process adequately, the investigation must produce multiple individuals with independent recollections of the same historical event or dysfunctional pattern of behavior. The more witnesses or records that can corroborate findings, the more reliable and credible the evidence becomes.

Nonetheless, when evaluating these recollections, mitigation specialists must be aware of potential biases that family members and close acquaintances can have about the defendant. This having been said, even biased information has potential value in the early phases of an investigation, if accounted for, because this information can help support the presence of a fact or theme that will require other kinds of additional corroboration that can be of significant benefit to the investigation process. The early stages of a social history investigation are similar to casting a net for fish. To obtain the most data, the scope of the mitigation investigation must begin as broad and as far reaching as possible. It has to focus initially on data collection before making preliminary hypotheses (Cunningham, 2002). As information is obtained and considered, the goals of the investigation will change and become more focused.

2. Generate Hypotheses

As is common with criminal defendants, Johnny's social history is replete with multiple adverse developmental experiences. In a capital case, defense counsel is obligated to investigate every aspect of a defendant's life history. Only after a thorough investigation can defense counsel fulfill their ethical obligations for zealous representation.

Within each domain of functioning, there often exist both risk and protective factors acting on a defendant. Throughout the development of a defendant these factors may change as external and internal variables interact separately and cumulatively. For example, consider a number of events during Johnny's adolescence:

- Minimal friendships except other antisocial peers
- No prosocial work history
- Frequent changes in housing
- Unstable and chaotic home environment
- Placement in foster care
- Juvenile justice referrals.

Identifying a cross-section of these events in Johnny's life, and identifying how these events were influenced by other dimensions in his functioning, is critical to understanding the pathway to his instant criminal offense. For example, the detrimental effects of physical abuse on a growing brain have been well documented. However, the experience of repeated head injuries during middle childhood creates different cognitive sequelae than those sustained during adolescence. To be precise, we cannot have a valid understanding of Johnny's adolescent functioning without evaluating the effects of the interactions of biological and psychological influences on each of these events. What were the biological and psychological consequences of these events? Are these consequences evident in the chronology of the events, signs, symptoms, and maladaptive coping strategies documented in the chronology of his life? Do they point to new hypotheses and to other areas of functioning not previously addressed by the defense team?

Triangulation of life history experiences by means of document collection and witness interviews will provide the data to support hypotheses about the timing and effect of adverse developmental experiences. Social workers in the context of mitigation practice use the findings from the application of their scientific formulations to create the overall mitigation themes for use in the penalty phase of the sentencing process.

3. Organize Social History into Themes

The inquiry into Johnny's life history should lead to themes that are confirmed by multiple sources of information. For instance, it is clear that Johnny has suffered repeated losses in his life that are compounded by his chronically chaotic and unstable social environment. This pattern is supported by documentary evidence and third-party witness interviews. From the documentary evidence, we learned about his loss of his biological mother, his lack of any relationship with his biological father, the change in his custody because of his mother's death, his alcoholic and abusive grandfather, his multiple foster placements, and juvenile commitment. The prior information has to be organized into relevant themes. Organizing the information into themes can help the trier of fact understand the breadth and depth of negative experiences that Johnny suffered over the course of his life and how these unfortunate experiences impacted his involvement in the crime for which he was convicted. However, the themes do not have to be directly related to the crime. They also can be used to support other kinds of themes that help to humanize the defendant in ways that speak to why the defendant is not deserving of a sentence of death.

CONCLUSION

The social history information gathered to assess a defendant's degree of moral culpability is not unsupported speculation. Social workers employed as mitigation specialists use systematic procedures of data collection and analysis that are consistent with scientific principles and methods of critical inquiry. Attorneys use the evidence gathered during the social history investigation to develop relevant themes and to obtain additional expert assistance in the presentation and interpretation of this information. Practice in this area of forensic social work can be hampered by agency constraints as well as by how the individual professional characterizes his or her role on the defense team. As a consequence, practitioners in this field of practice must have a strong sense of professional identity and a solid grounding in professional ethics in order to practice effectively in defense oriented contexts as sentencing advocates in the mitigation of a defendant's punishment.

WEBSITES

National Alliance of Sentencing Advocates & Mitigation Specialists http://www.nasams.org/

American Bar Association Guidelines for the Appointment and Performance of Defense Counsel in Death Penalty Cases http://www.abanet.org/legalservices/downloads/sclaid/deathpenaltyguidelines2003.pdf

Death Penalty Information Center http://www.deathpenaltyinfo.org/

Capital Defense Network http://www.capdefnet.org/

The Sentencing Project http://www.sentencingproject.org

National Association of Criminal Defense Lawyers http://www.nacdl.org

Capital Defense Weekly http://capitaldefenseweekly.com/

Public Defender Investigator Network http://www.pdinvestigator.net/

National Defender Investigator Association http://ndia.net/

References

American Bar Association. (2008). Supplementary guidelines for the mitigation function of defense teams in death penalty cases. *Hofstra Law Review, 36,* 677–692.

American Bar Association. (2003). *American Bar Association guidelines for the appointment and performance of defense counsel in death penalty cases (revised).* Washington, DC: Author.

Andrews, A. B. (1991). Social work expert testimony regarding mitigation in capital sentencing proceedings. *Social Work, 36*(5), 440–445.

Ashford, J. B. (2013). Death penalty mitigation: A handbook for mitigation specialists, investigators, social scientists and lawyers (M. Kupferberg, contributor). New York, NY: Oxford University Press.

Ashford, J. B., Macht, M. W., & Mylym, M. (1987). Advocacy by social workers in the public defender's office. *Social Work, 32,* 199–204.

Cunningham, M. D. (2002). Capital sentencing [case report]. In K. Heilbrun, G. Marczyk, & D. DeMatteo (Eds.), *Forensic mental health assessment: A casebook* (pp. 152–171). New York, NY: Oxford University Press.

Gothard, S. (1989). Power in the court: The social worker as an expert witness. *Social Work, 34,* 65–67.

Guin, C. C., Noble, D. N., & Merrill, T. S. (2003). From misery to mission: Forensic social workers on multidisciplinary mitigation teams. *Social Work, 48*(3), 362–371.

Hughes, E. (2009). Mitigating death. *Cornell Journal of Law and Public Policy, 18,* 337–390.

Maher, R. (2008). The ABA and the supplementary guidelines for the mitigation function of defense teams in death penalty cases. *Hofstra Law Review, 36,* 763–774.

Wiggins v. Smith, 123 S. Ct. 2527, 2003.

Williams v. Taylor, 529 U.S. 362, 2000.

147 Assessing and Treating Adolescent Sex Offenders

Karen S. Knox

Opportunities for clinical and direct practice with adolescent sex offenders have increased for social workers with the development of treatment programs in juvenile justice settings, community-based outpatient services, residential treatment, inpatient mental health, and incarceration facilities. Services and resources for adolescent sex offenders and their families are available to meet the various levels of treatment and supervision needed. Treatment protocol and standards of best practice for professionals have been established through empirical research studies and professional organizations, such as the Association for the Treatment of Sexual Abuse (ATSA) and the National Adolescent Perpetration Network (NAPT). These developments have contributed to the knowledge base and growth of expertise in this field of practice. Specialized education and training are necessary to work ethically and effectively with adolescent sex offenders, and professional licensing boards now require additional licensure for clinical professionals working with this client population.

Incidence reports and statistics indicate that juvenile sex offenders commit one-fifth of all sexual assaults and one-half of all child sexual assault/abuse (Cheung & Brandes, 2011). Adolescent sex offenders are typically between the ages of 13 and 17 years, mostly male, with female perpetrators accounting for 8%–12% of reported cases (Brown & Burton, 2010; Cheung & Brandes, 2011; McCartan, Law, Murphy, & Bailey, 2011). Research studies indicate that 30%–60% of adolescent sex offenders have learning disabilities, 80% have a diagnosable mental health diagnosis, with 20%–50% having a history of child physical abuse and 40%–80% being victims of child sexual abuse (Burton, Duty, & Leibowitz, 2011; Cheung & Brandes, 2011). There are higher proportional rates of adolescent Caucasians who are arrested and convicted for sex crimes in comparison with adolescent African Americans, and African American adolescent sex offenders are less likely to have histories of child sexual abuse (Burton & Ginsberg, 2012).

Currently, there are two main perspectives to explain adolescent sex offending: First, the *generalist perspective* suggests that their sexual offenses are only a part of their other antisocial and criminal behaviors, and that this type of adolescent sex offender is similar to other non-sexual adolescent offenders sharing common risk factors such as antisocial attitudes and behaviors, association with delinquent peers, and substance use. Second, the *specialist perspective* suggests that different factors explain adolescent sexual offending, such as trauma histories, early exposure to sexual behavior in the home or on the Internet, and more atypical sexual interests and sexual deviancy arousal that requires

different assessment instruments and treatment approaches (Pullman & Seto, 2012).

CASE ILLUSTRATIONS

John, a 16-year old African American male, is in the 10th grade and lives in a low- income neighborhood. His mother is a single parent with three other younger children, and she works full-time as an administrative assistant. She reports having problems with him following the rules at home, fighting with his siblings, and hanging out with negative peers. He is currently facing a sexual assault charge of fondling a 17-year old classmate on the school bus. John has had incidents of bullying and fighting at school. He is truant frequently and has a learning disability, which has resulted in academic delays and suspensions. This is John's first time appearing in juvenile court. His mother contacted the Public Defenders Office for representation, and he has been placed on probation and community supervision for two years.

George just turned 13 and lives with his parents and younger brother in an upper middle-class neighborhood. Both of his parents work full-time and report that George has never been in trouble before. They describe him as an excellent student, but he does not have a lot of friends his age. They describe him as immature and a loner who spends a lot of time on his computer. One of his brother's friends disclosed to his parents that George had fondled him and showed him some "nasty pictures" on the computer. The investigation revealed that George had also shown his brother and his other friend some pornography and had exposed himself to them. George's parents hired an attorney who was able to plea bargain for a sentence of probation and community supervision for two years.

Although George's parents have been able to adjust their work schedules and housing arrangements to accommodate his probation supervision guidelines, John's mother has limited resources for supervision after school, so John has been placed on intensive supervision and mandated to perform his community restitution after school to meet his supervision requirements. John was also sent to the alternative learning school, because he can no longer have any contact with his victim. George and his parents have agreed to a strict supervision and safety plan to allow

George to continue to live at home and attend the same school.

Continuum of Treatment

Working with adolescent sex offenders requires the use of a multisystemic approach, given that professionals from various disciplines and settings are involved in a continuum of treatment for these clients and their families. This continuum usually begins with an outcry or report of sexual abuse by the victim, which then involves investigations by child protective services and law enforcement professionals. If charges are filed, the case proceeds through the juvenile court system with prosecution, adjudication, and if found guilty, sentencing of probation or incarceration. The following flow chart shows the typical continuum of treatment:

Outcry, Report, & Investigation
(Child Protective Services and/or law enforcement)

Juvenile Court
(Prosecution & Adjudication) If found guilty: probation or incarceration

Intake & Assessment
(Risk & Clinical)

Treatment
(Outpatient, in-patient, residential treatment)

Reintegration or Re-entry
(Family reunification, substitute care, or independent living)

Relapse Prevention & Registration
(Termination of treatment and mandated community notification)

RISK ASSESSMENT

Sex offender registration and community notification requirements impact risk assessments for adolescent sex offenders on probation or upon release from a penal institution, because an assigned risk level must be indicated on their sex offender registration form. This type of risk assessment is very different from a clinical risk assessment and is usually done by a probation or parole officer. It addresses legal risk factors such as seriousness of the sex offense, offender's age at first referral, and prior adjudications

or referrals for sex offenses or other felonies. Recommendations associated with the various levels of care and supervision are assigned using the following guidelines:

- *Low-Medium Risk:* Youth placed on probation at home/community placement usually for 12–24 months with intensive supervision and outpatient treatment.
- *Medium-High Risk:* Youth placed on probation and placed in a residential treatment or inpatient facility, typically in a secure unit depending on level of psychopathy and other mental health disorders. If successful, the youth may return to home/community and receive additional outpatient treatment. If not successful, the youth may be remanded to a more secure setting or correctional institution.
- *High Risk:* Youth placed in a correctional institution that may have sex offender programs; however, factors such as amenability to treatment, limited services, and waiting lists impact on availability. Many youth may not receive sex offender treatment until released on parole and then referred to outpatient services.

When applying the criteria for the legal risk assessment, both John and George would be assessed as low-medium risk and will be receiving outpatient treatment while on probation. Both will be residing in their homes and receiving intensive supervision. Both will be referred to outpatient counseling and will have to perform 500 hours of community service. However, this is where their similarities end; their clinical assessments will be very different with respect to their clinical issues and family and social histories.

Clinical assessments are often court-ordered to provide recommendations on the type and level of treatment required for the adolescent sex offender. Clinical assessments should not be used as a determination of guilt or innocence and should be made after adjudication and before sentencing to help determine an appropriate treatment plan. This type of assessment can also be conducted as part of the youth's treatment plan when the juvenile has been placed in a therapeutic or correctional setting. Clinical assessments assist in identifying the youth's amenability to treatment, the type and level of care, level of risk for recidivism, developmental issues, risk and protective factors, and family and community resources to meet the client's needs. Clinical assessments usually include content on the offender's family history, relationship to the victim, age and number of victims, sexual and trauma histories, environmental risks, and psychosocial problems.

Due to the level of expertise and experience required with this client population, it is recommended that clinical assessments be conducted by a licensed sex offender therapist. The clinical assessment should be as comprehensive as possible by addressing other treatment issues or problems, as well as the sexual offending behaviors. The assessment process typically includes a clinical interview(s) with the adolescent and family members, collateral contacts, school records, social services, law enforcement, or mental health providers in the client's history, and standardized instruments that measure treatment issues and psychopathy. Current risk assessment instruments that are widely used include:

- Juvenile Sex Offender Assessment Protocol (J-SOAP-II) (Prentky & Righthand, 2003)
- Juvenile Sexual Offense Recidivism Risk Assessment Tool–II (JSORRAT-II) (Epperson, Ralston, Fowers, & DeWitt, 2009)
- Multiplex Empirically Guided Inventory of Ecological Aggregates for Assessing Sexually Abusive Adolescents and Children (Ages 19 and under) (MEGA) (Miccio-Fonseca, 2010).

Special Clinical Issues

Special clinical issues that are common to adolescent sex offenders include low self-esteem, poor impulse control and emotional regulation, minimal social skills, poor problem-solving and decision-making skills, poor peer relationships, attention problems, disruptive behavior problems, and a lack of appropriate coping skills. Clinical risk assessments and treatment plans need to address issues such as anger management problems, learning and developmental disabilities, trauma history, substance abuse, depression, suicide, anxiety, and other neuropsychological problems.

Specific content on sexual attitudes and history are included in the assessment and intervention plan, along with the level of acknowledgement or denial of responsibility for the sexually offending behaviors. It is typical for these youth and families to evidence denial or minimization of

their sexually offending behaviors and thoughts, even after adjudication of the legal case. Feelings of shame, guilt, and embarrassment contribute to minimizing and denial. Any empathic responses about their victim(s) are assessed as strengths, since deficits in empathy and appropriate affect are a major focus of treatment. Cognitive distortions (thinking errors) associated with the sexual offense contribute to the youth's level of denial or minimization. Other sexually inappropriate behaviors, fantasies, arousal patterns, and resources for sexual materials, such as pornography and the Internet are included in the sexual history section of a clinical assessment.

Case Illustrations

John came into the office for his clinical assessment interview with a wary attitude and was extremely guarded in his responses to the social worker. Copies of the incident report from law enforcement, the probation intake form, and his school records were included in his case files, and the social worker had already identified several areas of concern, including his delinquency history, school problems, substance use, and anger management issues. During the interview, John did acknowledge these issues "get him into trouble," but he had little insight into how to change his behaviors. His primary motivation for change is his probationary status, and he appears to be intelligent and capable of making positive changes. He is, however, reluctant to leave the gang and his friends who have been major influences in his delinquency history. He does take responsibility for the sexual offense, but minimizes the incident as "just bullying and playing around," and denies any other history of inappropriate sexual behaviors. When discussing his family, he states, "I never knew my father." He says his mother does her best but is stressed out and angry with him.

George seemed rather timid and made little eye contact when he first entered the counseling office. His case records indicate he is a loner at school, and he states that his peers think he is "weird and nobody really likes me." George does well academically and has no other school or behavior problems. The standardized assessment instruments indicate that he scored in the clinical range on the sexual offending scales, as well as for anxiety, low self-esteem, lack of communication and social skills, and immaturity. George discloses that an elderly male neighbor had showed him how to masturbate when he was five years old, and the sexual abuse continued for several years before the neighbor died. George has never told anyone about this because he is scared and ashamed about getting into trouble. He says his family does not really have any problems, but thinks his parents always favored his siblings over him.

Treatment Models

Using a strengths-based approach, the Good Lives Model is a theoretical framework for offender rehabilitation that builds on client capabilities to promote pro-social skills and personal functioning. Recent evaluation research studies indicate positive outcomes for both generalist offenders and sexual offenders (Willis, Gannon, Yates, & Ward, 2013). The model addresses limitations of the traditional risk management approach that emphasizes problems and deficits and uses restriction of activities as the primary means to avoid reoffending. The Good Lives Model promotes social work values of client respect and dignity, so negative labeling and hostile confrontation are inconsistent with this collaborative approach, which is used in conjunction with cognitive behavioral therapy.

The principle treatment model used in sex offender treatment is cognitive-behavioral theory, with group therapy being the primary modality. Cognitive-behavioral therapy (CBT) has been found to reduce sexual recidivism significantly, and research studies provide evidence of its effectiveness in addressing cognitive distortions and atypical sexual arousal and behaviors (Pullman & Seto, 2012). Group treatment is conducive to learning social skills, experiencing appropriate peer interaction, and addressing denial and minimization, given that many adolescents find it easier to disclose and admit responsibility when among others who share similar histories.

Multisystemic therapy (MST) is another model that has been empirically demonstrated to reduce recidivism and out-of-home placements for both generalist offenders and adolescent sex offenders. This model is family-based and targets multiple domains, including family functioning, social skills, problem solving, coping skills, academic problems, negative peers, and substance abuse (Pullman & Seto, 2012). This approach is critical, because most adolescent sex offenders evidence problems across multiple areas in their social environment, so coordination and collaboration among providers is critical to treatment success.

Individual and adjunct therapies are recommended for other issues such as trauma histories, psychological disorders, substance abuse, and anger management. The length of treatment varies depending on many factors, but most programs range from 12 to 24 months. Youth may remain on probation/parole after completing treatment, which ensures supervision needs, relapse prevention, and follow-up services. Relapse prevention and family reunification should be completed before termination from the treatment program and probation to endure a smooth transition and supervision needs.

Treatment Goals and Plans

Treatment goals focus on reducing antisocial behaviors and recidivism and development of pro-social skills. The treatment plan should include safety rules, supervision guidelines, and specific interventions, specifying the time frame and consequences of not following through with the program. All parties should sign a written treatment contract and intervention plan. It is important to work as a team with other professionals on the case, and to differentiate the roles and responsibilities of those involved in the treatment plan. Specific interventions include positive and negative reinforcement, confrontation, relaxation skills, assertiveness training, and expressive arts techniques such as art therapy, psychodrama, family sculpting, role-play, bibliotherapy, and adventure-based interventions. Adolescent sex offender programs may vary across settings, length, and intensity of therapy, but most follow a standard protocol that includes the following components and goals:

1. *Introduction to Group and the Treatment Process*
   - Group rules and supervision guidelines; Laws about sexual behavior; Sexual offense layout or statement
2. *Sexual Abuse Offense and Cycle*
   - *Acknowledgement of Responsibility:* Youth who continue to deny or minimize responsibility for any sexually offending behaviors may be required to take a polygraph examination to establish specific areas of deception, and if the polygraph is failed, consequences can

include termination from treatment and possible legal sanctions.

- *Sexual Offense Cycle:* Cognitive distortions (thinking errors), sexual fantasies, arousal patterns, and sex offending behaviors are important issues to confront with the goals of reducing recidivism and learning appropriate sexual attitudes, behaviors, and relationships.

- *Empathy:* Most adolescent sex offenders have a deficit in this area, even those who have prior physical or sexual victimization. Developing empathy for their victims and understanding the consequences of their sexual offenses is critical. The *clarification or apology letter assignment* helps offenders understand the impact of their behavior on their victim(s) and significant others. This assignment is not intended to absolve the offender's guilt or to ask forgiveness. It is typically read only during group for feedback and is not given to the victim(s) unless family reunification is indicated.

3. *Interpersonal and Coping Skills Development*

- *Clarification of Values:* Adolescent sex offenders either have a deficit in this area or espouse deviant/delinquent values that may impact on recidivism.

- *Self-esteem:* These adolescents experience failure in many aspects of their lives and relationships, so a strengths-based approach is recommended.

- *Social Skills:* The group environment is especially helpful with youth learning and group facilitators modeling appropriate interactions and communication skills.

- *Behavior Problems:* Anger management, impulse control, and conflict resolution are addressed by developing appropriate problem-solving, assertiveness, and coping skills.

4. *Relapse Prevention/Reunification & Termination*

- Adolescent sex offenders develop a relapse prevention plan with strategies to use in at-risk situations. Those who will be reuniting or having approved contact with their families/victims must participate in family therapy and develop a safety plan.

Case Illustrations

John's intervention plan recommended attending adolescent sex offender group therapy once a week and participation in a diversion program through juvenile court for his anger management, delinquency, and substance abuse problems. He was sent to the alternative-learning center where he was doing better academically and with his attendance. However, four months into treatment, he was arrested on a robbery charge with several friends and his probation was revoked. He is currently incarcerated in a juvenile correctional facility where he is receiving treatment services for his generalist offending behaviors.

George's treatment plan also recommended attending sex offender group therapy weekly and individual therapy weekly for his trauma history and psychological issues. His treatment plan addressed his sexual abuse by using the Trauma Outcome Process Assessment Model (TOPA), which provides interventions for his trauma symptoms (Rasmussen, 2012). His family initially wanted him to remain at home, but after participating in a parent support group and family therapy sessions, decided that his level of care and supervision was too much for him to remain at home. He is currently placed at a residential treatment facility in an adolescent sex offender program.

These case illustrations are indicative of the types of issues affecting treatment and probation status for adolescent sex offenders. It is more common that adolescent sex offenders are sanctioned to a higher level of care and supervision for a crime other than a sexual offense, as in John's case. For George, his parents are supportive and able to provide for a more secure setting with specialized treatment for his sex offender behaviors and psychiatric diagnoses.

When both youth are released and return to their homes, the final phase of treatment would involve family reunification services. Clinical issues include earning trust, re-establishing family rules and roles, adjusting to a different level of supervision, reintegrating back into school and the social environment, and maintaining positive changes. Family therapy is recommended for support during this transition period, which can be a high-risk period of time for relapse or recidivism.

Resources for Professionals

Available resources for practitioners, such as workbooks for adolescent sex offenders that have homework assignments and experiential exercises, literature for parents and siblings of offenders, audiovisual materials, and training opportunities can be found at the following websites:

- *Association for the Treatment of Sexual Abuse* (ATSA) www.atsa.org
- *Center for Sex Offender Management* (CSOM) www.csom.org
- *International Association for the Treatment of Sexual Offenders* (IATSO) www.iatso.org
- *The Good Lives Model* www.goodlivesmodel .com
- *The Safer Society* www.safersociety.org

References

Brown, A., & Burton, D. K. (2010). Exploring the overlap in male juvenile sexual offending and general delinquency: Trauma, alcohol use, and masculine beliefs. *Journal of Child Sexual Abuse, 19,* 450–468. doi:10.1080/10538712.2010.495044

Burton, D. L., Duty, K. J., & Leibowitz, G. S. (2011). Differences between sexually victimized and non-sexually victimized male adolescent sexual abusers: Developmental antecedents and behavioral comparisons. *Journal of Child Sexual Abuse, 20,* 77–93. doi:10.1080/10538712.2011.541010

Burton, D. L., & Ginsberg, D. (2012). An exploration of racial differences in deviant sexual interests among male adolescent sexual offenders. *Journal of Forensic Social Work, 2,* 25–44. doi:10.1080/19 36928X.2011.609766

Cheung, M., & Brandes, B. (2011). Enhancing treatment outcomes for male adolescents with sexual behavior problems: Interactions and interventions. *Journal of Family Violence, 26,* 387–401. doi:10.1007/s10896-011-9373-5

Epperson, D. L., Ralston, C. A., Fowers, D., & DeWitt, J. (2009). Scoring guidelines for the Juvenile Sex Offense Recidivism Risk Assessment Tool-II (JSORRAT-II). Retrieved from www.watsa.org/ Resources/Documents/2.Epperson JSORRAT-II Scoring Guide.pdf

McCartan, F. M., Law, H., Murphy, M., & Bailey, S. (2011). Child and adolescent females who present with sexually abusive behaviours: A 10-year UK prevalence study. *Journal of Sexual Aggression, 17*(1), 4–14. doi:10.1080/13552600.2010.488302

Miccio-Fonseca, L. C. (2010). MEGA: An ecological risk assessment tool of risk and protective factors for assessing sexually abusive children and adolescents. *Journal of Aggression, Maltreatment & Trauma, 19,* 734–756. doi:10.1080/10926771.201 0.515542

Prentky, R., & Righthand, S. (2003). *Juvenile Sex Offender Assessment Protocol-II (J-SOAP-II) manual* (NCJ 202316). Retrieved from http:www/ ncjrs.gov/app/publications

Pullman, L., & Seto, M. C. (2012). Assessment and treatment of adolescent sexual offenders: Implications of recent research on generalist versus specialist explanations. *Child Abuse and Neglect, 36,* 203–209. doi:10.1016/j.chiabu.2011.11.003

Rasmussen, L. A. (2012). Trauma outcome process assessment (TOPA) model: An ecological paradigm for treating traumatized sexually abusive youth. *Journal of Child & Adolescent Trauma, 5,* 63–80. doi:10.1080/19361521.2012.646645

Willis, G. M., Yates, P. M., Gannon, T. A., & Ward, T. (2013). How to integrate the Good Lives Model into treatment programs for sexual offending: An introduction and overview. *Sexual Abuse: A Journal of Research and Treatment, 25,* 123–142. doi:10.1177/1079063212452618

148 Forensic Social Work with Women Who Use Violence in Intimate Relationships

Michelle Mohr Carney

Among the debates in the field of domestic violence, none is more acrimonious than the debate around female initiated violence. Although the prevalence and consequences of male violence directed toward women in intimate relationships has been well established, the research on violent women in intimate relationships is far less developed. Traditional conceptualization of domestic violence is rooted in learned gender roles and considered inherently male. Persistent support for the notion that women are victims and men are perpetrators supports the patriarchal structure of society and reinforces traditional gender roles. The data are widely contested, and researchers argue that a clear depiction of the extent of male victimization is difficult to ascertain, but studies suggest that over 40% of victims of severe physical violence are men (Hoff, 2012). These data, considered to be under-reported and not reflective of the problem, suggest that women are capable of initiating violence in intimate relationships and that a reconceptualization of domestic violence as violence perpetrated by either males or females, and which can be unidirectional, bidirectional, or mutual is warranted.

Johnson (1995, 2000) developed an argument suggesting that feminist scholars, who believe that domestic violence is the result of our patriarchal culture and involves men using violence to subordinate women, and sociological scholars, who believe that domestic violence is a form of conflict resolution used equally by men and women in intimate relationships, are both correct in their conceptualizations of violence and that they are really discussing different phenomena. He contends that there are essentially two distinct forms of family violence, which he refers to as "patriarchal terrorism" and "common couple violence." According to Johnson (2000), common couple violence refers to the phenomenon captured in the national family violence surveys, where the violence is not coercive or controlling and is gender balanced. In this model, a couple may engage in physical violence with each other in the context of a specific argument, but the violence is not meant to control the other person and is likely to be bidirectional or mutual (Johnson, 2000). By contrast, patriarchal terrorism refers to the phenomenon seen in shelter populations and criminal courts, where the violence is male initiated and escalating and represents a man's attempt to dominate and control his partner. In this model, the violence is purposeful and is meant to intimidate and control the female partner. As such, it is not generally confined to physical violence and routinely involves severe emotional abuse, intimidation, and likely will result in severe injury for the woman (Johnson, 2000). Johnson's conceptualization of domestic violence is helpful because it suggests that both feminist scholars and sociological scholars are correct in their conceptualizations of domestic violence, allowing for movement beyond the perpetrator/victim roles or labels, to address the use of violence and how it can be controlled.

CASE DESCRIPTIONS: FEMALE-INITIATED INTERPERSONAL VIOLENCE

Case 1

Emily and her husband, Scott, had been married for approximately 10 years. Over the course of the marriage, they had many "domestic disturbance" calls to the police and Scott had been arrested several times for misdemeanor domestic violence offenses. On the most recent occasion, Scott returned from the county jail extremely agitated with Emily for, in his view, causing him to be arrested again. Shortly thereafter, there was a disagreement between the two whereby he held her on the ground while choking her and informed her that he was tired of her. At that time, he indicated to her that he would come home the next day from work and kill her. The following day, she waited for him to return from work and, as he was climbing the stairs to their second floor apartment, dropped a barbecue grill on his head. As a result, Scott was hospitalized and Emily was arrested for domestic violence.

Case 2

Megan was recently divorced with a history of violent behavior and alcohol abuse. Megan and her ex-husband had a history of involvement with the police for "domestic disturbance" calls and on at least two occasions both parties were arrested by the police. After her divorce Megan met Blake, who had a history of repeat arrests for drug possession and pimping. Megan and Blake argued often. After their most recent fight, Megan was arrested for stabbing Blake in an argument about another woman. When asked about interpersonal violence in her relationship with Blake, Megan stated that she has never been a victim of domestic violence because "she would never let a man control her."

BRIEF ASSESSMENT OF THE CASES

These cases illustrate the complexities of female-initiated domestic violence. First, and perhaps most importantly, there are women who are arrested, prosecuted, and convicted of domestic violence offenses and who occupy dual status as both victims and offenders. This creates serious difficulties for treatment providers as they try to distinguish between women who are both victims and offenders and those women who are only offenders. These cases illustrate the challenges in differentiating between victims and perpetrators, and those who are both victims and perpetrators. In Emily's case, there was a clear pattern of abuse at the hands of her husband, but on the night of the incident, she was the sole

aggressor. It is possible to see her use of violence against Scott as retaliation for the previously incurred abuse and the fear that resulted from his threat to kill her. Megan's case is difficult to assess. Although Megan and her ex-husband had a history of bidirectional violence, by her own admission she does not consider herself to be a victim of interpersonal violence. In terms of primary aggressors, it is possible to argue that Megan used violence against Blake, not in retaliation for his violence, but as the sole aggressor in the relationship. Women who are the primary or exclusive aggressors in their intimate relationships appear to be very much like male domestic violence offenders. Second, women who initiate violent acts in their intimate relationships routinely engage in high levels of extreme violence. The conventional wisdom on this topic is that, given the average size and strength differentials between men and women, women must ensure that the violent act incapacitates the man so that he does not retaliate.

Clearly, both Emily and Megan are in need of services and intervention, but are they both victims, both perpetrators, or does that distinction matter? These examples illustrate that women engaged in interpersonal violence can be viewed through a variety of lenses; as women who are victims and use violence in retaliation, women who have a long history of victimization who refuse to be victimized further, and women who are simply violent—not retaliatory. Although the women in all these three cases are being arrested for interpersonal violence and sentenced to treatment, it is critical to match the treatment modality with the motivations for the violence. More important than the perpetrator/victim role or label, is the use of violence and how that can be controlled through taking responsibility for the violence and committing to behavior changes.

Men and women's motivations for and use of violence differ. Men's use of violence is often learned and societally reinforced, while women's use of violence is considered to be a more complex topic. This is not to say that men's use of violence is simplistic, rather that the societal stigma that prevents abused men from reporting their abuse prevents most people from seeing men in the dual role of victim and perpetrator. Women's use of violence is not similarly accepted or expected, nor is it often clear whether they occupy dual victim/perpetrator roles and use violence in retaliation or if they are simply violent primary aggressors.

THE RESEARCH

Evidence for the construct of female-initiated violence in intimate relationships is strong. Data from longitudinal studies using large samples presents the strongest evidence of this construct. The Dunedin study including a "complete cohort of births between April 1972 and March 31, 1973 in Dunedin, New Zealand" (population 120,000) was one such study (Magdol et al., 1997, p. 69). This birth cohort of 1,037 subjects has been studied every two years since its inception for a variety of health, development, and behavioral measures. The 425 women and 436 men who were in intimate relationships indicated that both minor and severe physical violence rates were higher for women whether self-reported or partner-reported. The female severe physical violence rate was more than triple that of males (18.6% vs. 5.7%). Perhaps earlier studies of partner violence assumed that men's perpetration rates exceeded those of women, because they relied almost exclusively on clinical samples of women who sought assistance or of men in court-mandated counseling programs (Magdol et al., 1997).

Gender bias in both the reporting of women's use of violence against men, and the handling of the cases by both law enforcement and the courts prevents a clear representation of the magnitude of the problem. Female intimate violence perpetrators are frequently viewed by law enforcement and the criminal justice system as victims rather than actual offenders of violence against men, making access to the necessary treatment for both parties difficult (Kingsnorth & MacIntosh, 2007). However, the increased presence of women, as offenders, in treatment programs for domestic violence offenders is the direct result of legislation mandating the arrest of perpetrators in cases where police respond to a call and determine that domestic violence has occurred. In the late 1980s most states enacted Law Enforcement Protection legislation. This legislation, commonly referred to as "warrantless arrest," allows police who respond to a domestic violence call to arrest the abuser and press charges themselves. Although the arrest of women was clearly an unintended consequence of mandatory arrest statutes, their sudden appearance in court-mandated treatment programs has had a dramatic impact on the national debate regarding female-initiated violence. As a result of women being court-mandated into batterer treatment

programs, it is no longer possible to suggest that women are infrequently the initiators of violence in their intimate relationships. If this were true, there would be very few women arrested, successfully prosecuted, and mandated into treatment as part of a criminal sentence.

Most states, however, do not offer certified intervention programs designed for women, even though the need has been established. Advances in treatment for women who use violence against their partners have been limited by a gendered belief that interpersonal violence is perpetrated exclusively, or mostly, by men. Often, men suffer in silence, and there is a prevailing message to keep quiet when it comes to considering women as perpetrators of partner abuse. As a result, many female perpetrators are not linked with critically necessary services, or in the cases of mandatory arrest, women are often court mandated into treatment programs designed for men.

Unfortunately, despite the presence of women in court-mandated treatment programs for batterers, very little is known about the role of violence in their lives or the usefulness of treating female offenders in programs designed for men. Specifically, due to the longstanding debate about the existence of female-initiated violence, very little research is available on the topic and women are currently being treated in programs designed for male batterers. Most states offer certified batterers' intervention programming that is guided by certification standards. The goals of this programming are to protect victims and increase accountability for perpetrators. The minimum program duration ranges from 12 to 52 weeks, with the average program lasting 24 to 26 weeks. Most certified programs are linked to systems of accountability and are reviewed regularly by the monitoring agency. Traditional intervention models view the primary cause of male domestic violence as patriarchal ideology and societal sanctioning of men's use of power and control over women. These programs are educational models and are not considered to be therapy. Some of the early educational and intervention programs used as models nationwide included EMERGE in Boston, AMEND in Denver, and the Duluth DAIP Program. These programs were designed for men, with the program focus on the use of violence as an attempt to exert power and control the victim. One of the most prevalent of the educational models is the Duluth model and its use of the "power and control wheel," which illustrates that violence is part of a pattern of behavior that reflects both the power imbalances in relationships, and in society as a whole, between men and women. In addition to the educational programming, many batterer intervention programs have added cognitive-behavioral programs focused on managing anger and learning signs to recognize escalating violence and techniques for controlling violent outbursts. Batterer intervention programs typically use a group format to promote social accountability and peer reinforcement of nonviolence. In general, key components of the treatment include (1) confrontation; (2) group therapy to help recognize and overcome minimization, denial, and blame as commonly used defense mechanisms; (3) examining batterers' use of anger and identifying ways to change their patterns of interaction with their partners and family; (4) identifying "roadblocks to responsibility" (i.e., minimization, denial, and blame); (5) exploring the concept of partnership in relationships as an alternative to power and control; (6) learning to use "time-out" as a method to avoid the escalation that frequently accompanies arguments that result in violence; (7) providing the batterer with a repertoire of alternate and appropriate behaviors, such as problem solving, assertiveness, and negotiation; (8) adopting the concepts of trust, support, tolerance, and acceptance, with an emphasis on how they relate to successful negotiation; and (9) extensive role-play and group discussion to internalize strategies for incorporating negotiation into their interactions with their partners.

In theory, this is less than ideal, for two reasons. First, the literature on batterer intervention programs for male batterers describes a widespread uniformity in the treatment of male batterers (Bennett & Williams, 2001), an important element of which is a patriarchal analysis of violence against women. Obviously, this focus would have questionable relevance to women who initiate violence in their intimate relationships. Second, there have been very few evaluations of the treatment effect of treating women in intervention programs designed for male batterers (Carney & Buttell, 2006, 2004).

Programs Designed for Violent Women

Intervention programs designed for female primary aggressors are slowly emerging and are modeled largely on the Duluth Model. Consistent in the programs identified for women who use violence is the premise that violence as problem-solving is not acceptable, and that participants must take responsibility for their violence and be willing to work to change their behavior (Bowen, 2010).

Treatment Goals

Most programs require that the participant make personal goals for the program, in addition to the general program goals, which call for clients to:

- Cease violent behavior.
- Take responsibility for their behavior (without minimization, denial, or blame).
- Identify physical, emotional, and behavioral cues that signal escalating danger.
- Establish safety—physical and emotional—for self, children, and partner.
- Understand the dynamics and effects of partner abuse. Recognize unhealthy interaction patterns compared to healthy ones.
- Learn skills for respectful communication, problem solving, and conflict resolution.
- Learn emotional self-regulation.
- Overcome the effects of childhood and/or adult trauma so that memories are integrated into a survivor's life story.
- Increase capacity for empathy and compassion for self and others.
- Increase autonomy and self-esteem (Bowen, 2010).

Programs such as WAVE in the United Kingdom, which is also based upon the Duluth Model but adapted for use with women, are encouraging steps toward matching treatment to need. Similar to the intent of the program designed for men, the goal was for women to learn about their own use of violence and how to change their violent behavior patterns. Women who have completed the program report the treatment as meaningful and transformative (Walker, 2013). NOVA in Santa Rosa, California uses "a psychotherapeutic approach of cognitive–behavioral strategies grounded in attachment theory, trauma theory, and social learning theory," and adds program elements designed to explore issues in the family of origin (Bowen, 2010, p. 105).

Other innovative program models have begun to incorporate Motivational Interviewing and Stages of Change to encourage client engagement and motivation. Some are structured to depend on community peers as sponsors who act as advisors and role models for nonviolence for their paired participant. Programs such as the Bennington County Integrated Domestic Violence Docket (IDVD) Project were shown to be effective, comprehensive approaches to responding to interpersonal violence by providing immediate response to domestic violence events by coordinating family and criminal division cases in a "one-stop-shop" model (The Vermont Center for Justice Research, 2011). Some states have had the issue of gender and court-mandated batterer intervention tested through litigation. The laws, and the court-mandated programming that follows them, are designed for men who abuse their female intimate partners. In Maine, the laws that mandated a two-year program for men were challenged as unjust when the required program length for women was only one year.

Given the politicized nature of the debate surrounding female-initiated intimate partner violence, issues surrounding the construct of "dual arrest" in police responses to domestic violence calls, and the probability that there are very real differences between male and female domestic violence offenders, there is much that remains to be discovered about these women. Major issues on the horizon that call for attention include (a) deciding whether and how to develop standards for women mandated to treatment; (b) how to focus on the use of violence and matching violence user with appropriate interventions regardless of gender; and (c) the need for comprehensive evaluation of intervention programs to enable replication of programs that are deemed to be effective. It is probable that evaluation will yield both similarities and differences and that treatment for female offenders will have to begin to be conceptualized as distinct from that intended for male batterers. If the intent is to address and serve client needs effectively, it is critical to recognize that the use of violence as problem solving is counterproductive to healthy relationships in general, and to realize that effective treatment to prevent future violence is more important than who is initiating the abuse. When we focus on the debate over whether women can be violent and the primary aggressors in relationships, we ignore the larger issue of the impact of violence on the family; we impede appropriate service referrals; and we ignore the children, who continue to be damaged by witnessing the violence regardless of who perpetrates it, and how severe it is.

WEBSITES

http://www.csulb.edu/~mfiebert/assault.htm
http://www.oneinthree.com.au/
http://www.springerpub.com/
    samples/9780826121356_chapter.pdf
http://www.mayoclinic.com/health/
    domestic-violence-against-men/MY00557
http://www.wscadv.org/docs/Social_Workers_
    Practice_Guide_to_DV_Feb_2010.pdf

References

Bennett, L., & Williams, O. (2001). Intervention program for men who batter. In C. Renzetti & J. Edleson (Eds.), *Sourcebook on Violence against Women* (pp. 261–277). Thousand Oaks, CA: Sage.

Bowen, E. (2010). Court-mandated group treatment for a violent woman: Roxy. *Partner Abuse, 1*(1), 105–116.

Carney, M., & Buttell, F. (2006). An evaluation of a court mandated batterer intervention program: Investigating differential program effect for African-American and Caucasian women. *Research on Social Work Practice, 16*, 571–581.

Carney, M., & Buttell, F. (2004). A multidimensional evaluation of a treatment program for female batterers: A pilot study. *Research on Social Work Practice, 14*, 249–258.

Hoff, B. H. (2012). National study: More men than women victims of intimate partner physical violence, psychological aggression. Over 40% of victims of severe physical violence are men. *MenWeb.* Retrieved from http://www.battered-men.com/NISVS.htm)

Johnson, M. (1995). Patriarchal terrorism and common couple violence: Two forms of violence against women. *Journal of Marriage and the Family, 57*, 283–294.

Johnson, M. (2000). Conflict and control: Images of symmetry and asymmetry in domestic violence. In A. Booth, A. Crouter, & M. Clements (Eds.), *Couples in Conflict.* Hillsdale, NJ: Erlbaum.

Kingsnorth, R., & MacIntosh, R. (2007). Intimate partner violence: The role of suspect gender in prosecutorial decision-making. *Justice Quarterly, 24*(3), 460–495.

Magdol, L., Moffitt, T. E., Caspi, A., Newman, D. L., Fagan, J., & Silva, P. A. (1997). Gender differences in partner violence in a birth cohort of 21-year-olds: Bridging the gap between clinical and epidemiological approaches. *Journal of Consulting and Clinical Psychology, 65*, 68–78.

The Vermont Center for Justice Research. (2011). Bennington County integrated domestic violence docket project: Outcome evaluation final report. Retrieved from http://www.vcjr.org/reports/reportscrimjust/reports/idvdreport_files/IDVD%20Final%20Report.pdf

Walker, T. (2013). Voices from the group: Violent women's experiences of intervention. *Journal of Family Violence*. Retrieved from http://link.springer.com.proxy-remote.galib.uga.edu/article/1

149 Best Practices for Assessing and Treating Older Adult Victims and Offenders

Tina Maschi, George S. Leibowitz, & Lauren Mizus

INTRODUCTION

Background of the Problem

The case vignettes of Jorge, Mary, and Joseph, illustrated in Table 149.1, represent a tip of the iceberg of the rapidly rising global aging prison population. The mass incarceration of the elderly is international in scope but is particularly problematic in the United States, which has the largest incarceration rate per capita in the world (American Civil Liberties Union [ACLU], 2012). These cases represent only three people out of the 2.3 million people in custody in the United States, of whom 16% (*n* = 200,000) are aged 50 years and older, the age generally designated as elderly in corrections (Guerino, Harrison, & Sabol, 2011). Two major reasons for the rise in the incarcerated elderly population has been attributed to a general increase in the general aging population as well as the stricter sentencing and parole release policies and practices of the 1980s. These punitive criminal justice practices have resulted in individuals serving longer terms, including life prison terms, destining them to grow old and even die in prison (Maschi, Viola, & Sun, 2012). About two out of three of the aging

prison population is incarcerated for committing a violent or sexual offense (ACLU, 2012; Human Rights Watch [HRW], 2012).

The Role of Cumulative Disparities

The diverse backgrounds and differing pathways to prison among the older prison population have implications for culturally responsive assessment and intervention. In the United States, the majority of the aging prison population are men (96%) and are disproportionately racial ethnic minorities (Black = 45%, Latino = 15%, 10% = other racial ethnic minorities) compared with Whites (43%) (Guerino et al., 2011). Maschi and colleagues (2013) typology describes four distinct types of older adults in prison based on time served: (1) incarcerated persons with long-term sentences (a person with 20 or more years served); (2) the lifer (life sentence); (3) persons with histories of acute and chronic recidivism (two or more incarcerations), and (4) persons who first were convicted as older adults (i.e., first convicted in old age). Health status also varies; some individuals have functional capacity while others

TABLE 149.1 Case Vignettes

1. Jorge is a 56-year-old male from Puerto Rico and the youngest of nine children. He has a history of trauma and criminal offending that has included the unexpected death of his father at age 5, childhood sexual victimization, poverty, prostitution, drug dealing, substance abuse (heroin addiction), and recidivism (incarcerated two times). At age 17, he reported committing armed robbery to support his heroin addiction and was sentenced to 20 years in prison. During his prison term, he continued to use drugs. He violated parole within 15 months of release after being charged with sexual offense of a minor and possession of controlled dangerous substances, and as a result, is now serving his second and current 45-year sentence. In prison, he has spent eight of the past fifteen years in solitary confinement. He perceives prison as "an overcrowded monster" designed to hold, degrade, and punish people. He views the staff as disinterested and disengaged and is despondent over the limited access to counseling and educational and rehabilitative services. Jorge was diagnosed with cancer six months ago while in prison and is projected to receive parole in 14 years when he is in his late seventies. He has not had any contact with family in over five years and reports feeling depressed.

2. Mary is a 64-year-old, Caucasian, Catholic woman who is incarcerated in a maximum security facility for women. She identifies herself as a lesbian. As a child, she experienced the divorce of her parents, abandonment by her mother, and sexual, physical, and verbal abuse by her father, whom she described as having serious mental health issues. At age 25, Mary married a man 10 years younger, had two children, and divorced. This is her first criminal conviction, and she is serving a 10-year prison sentence (85% minimum) for conspiracy and the attempted murder of her abusive husband, which she describes as being in self-defense. Mary describes this sentence as unfair and unjust based on mitigating circumstances. She has a medical history of hypertension, vision impairment, and osteoporosis that makes it difficult for her to walk or use a top bunk bed. At age 64, Mary's extensive dental problems have resulted in a premature need for dentures. She describes her current prison experience as "degrading, especially the way correctional officers treat inmates." Although she reports feelings of depression and despair, Mary reports that she copes with her prison experience by "finding meaning" in it through spirituality. Despite her ill health, Mary is resistant to using prison health care services. Her projected parole date is in two years, when she will be 66 years old. Because of the distance, Mary has not had any in-person visits with her family members since her incarceration but corresponds monthly by mail, and every three months by phone, with her two adult children and four grandchildren. She says that she misses her family immensely.

3. Joseph is a 66-year-old Caucasian male of Irish and Polish descent; his family has an intergenerational history of alcoholism. Joseph is a Vietnam war veteran. As a child he experienced "extreme" corporal punishment from his parents and was fearful of communicating with his parents because of it. Joseph was sexually molested for years by his Little League manager. At age 13, he made a conscious decision to "get tough" to protect himself; at age 18 he joined the Marine Corps. After his discharge, Joseph witnessed a man in a bar offering cocaine to several young girls whom he believed would be sexually molested. In a blinding rage, he, together with a peer, took the man outside the bar and murdered him. In prison, Joseph spent time in administrative segregation and solitary confinement. During these periods of isolation he describes engaging in self-reflection. His recent visit to the prison infirmary showed that he had signs of cognitive impairment, suggestive of dementia. He is serving a life sentence in prison.

suffer from serious and terminal illnesses such as HIV/AIDS, cancer, and dementia or mental health and substance use problems (36%; James & Glaze, 2006). In addition to criminal offense histories, many have histories of victimization in the community and in prison, which include childhood physical and sexual assault or witnessing violence (see Maschi et al., 2013). Victimization that has occurred prior to prison often has gone undetected and/or untreated and results in varying levels of adaptive coping responses and access to justice, as well as varying levels of access to social support and service networks (Aday, 2005; Maschi,

Viola, Morgen, 2013; Maschi, Viola, Morgen, & Koskinen, 2013).

As illustrated in the case examples in Table 149.1, the pathway that results in prison for older adults may vary in one or more cumulative disparities related to race, education, socioeconomic status, gender, disability, and legal or immigration status, which can influence access to health and social services, economic resources, and justice (See Figure 149.1). As the international human rights movement is gaining momentum in its efforts to advocate for the rights of older persons, the interdisciplinary practice community is challenged to think creatively and out of the concrete "prison" box on how to respond effectively (United Nations High Commissioner, 2012).

The Trauma of Incarceration: Prison as Elder Abuse

It can be argued that the poor social and environmental conditions of confinement, particularly for older persons, may be classified as elder abuse and neglect. Chronic victimization, medical neglect, lack of rehabilitation services and discharge planning exacerbate physical and mental illnesses and are a violation of human rights to safety protections and multi-holistic well-being (ACLU, 2012; HRW, 2012). The World Health Organization (WHO) (2012) defines elder abuse as a "a single, or repeated act, or lack of appropriate action, occurring within any relationship where there is an expectation of trust which causes harm or distress to an older person" (p. 1). As suggested in the case examples of Jorge, Mary,

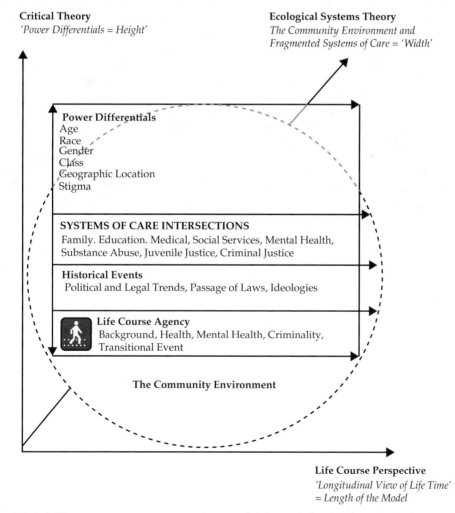

Figure 149.1 A life course system power analysis model for multilevel assessment and intervention.

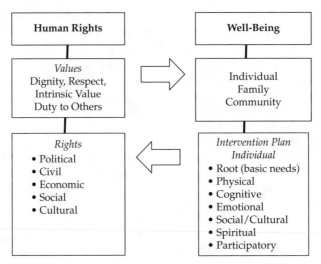

Figure 149.2 A practice model for assessing and treating older adults aging in place in prison.

and Joseph who are incarcerated older adults, prison was described as a source of trauma, abuse, and distress.

Elder abuse may take many forms and consists of physical, sexual, psychological, emotional, financial exploitation, and intentional or unintentional neglect, including medical neglect (WHO, 2012). Older adults in prison often are overlooked as people who are at increased risk of many types of elder abuse. Due to their increasing age-related frailty, older adults in prison are at increased risk of victimization and injury, medical and social care neglect, and exploitation of their resources (Maschi et al., 2013). Yet, despite their vulnerabilities, there is also a growing body of evidence that documents their resilience, such as their use of cognitive, physical, emotional, spiritual, and social coping resources. These multidimensional domains of coping suggest there are avenues for prevention and intervention that promote health and positive human development and rehabilitation (Aday, 2003; Maschi et al., 2013).

Assessment and Intervention Using a Life Course Systems Power Analysis

When considering the important task of assessment and intervention with older adults in the criminal justice system, conducting a holistic assessment of each person, such as Jorge, Mary, and Joseph, in a social environmental context is essential. Given that we are addressing older persons in their social/structural context, a life course interdisciplinary perspective is integrated with ecological systems and critical theories (See Figure 149.1).

As shown in Figure 149.1, a life course systems power analysis assists in identifying the potential areas in the three case illustrations of Jorge, Mary, and Joseph, that may require an integrated clinical, case management, and/or advocacy response. It allows for an evaluation of the process and current outcomes of older adults in prison and can be used for clinical, organizational, community, and policy level assessment, prevention, and intervention efforts (Maschi, Viola, & Sun, 2012). The model is discussed next, followed by an application of the model to the three case examples and assessment and intervention.

The Life Course (The Length of the Model)

Consistent with a right-based approach, it gives central importance to the whole person, or individual, and his or her inner or subjective experiences and meaning-making, of external life events (e.g., objective event-victim of sexual assault and subjective response-adaptive or maladaptive response) and subjective well-being, are the central focus of the model. Human agency is the core component and commonly used in the life course perspective and social justice capabilities theories (Elder, 2003; Nussbaum, 2004). Human agency is conceptualized as a person's creative life force energy and central driver through which the individual pursues his or her life's purpose, passion, and goals in connection to and with others, which, in turn, fosters an innate and developing sense of well-being and connectedness (Wahl, Iwarsson, & Oswald, 2012). In the case of Jorge, Mary, and Joseph, earlier life traumas and prison present a barrier for their pursuit of life course human agency.

Well-being is defined consistent with the World Health Organization (1948) definition of health as a state of multidimensional well-being and not just the absence of disease. Specifically, well-being is defined by seven core domains: root (basic needs), physical, cognitive, emotional, social/cultural, spiritual, and participatory (political/legal) well-being. When cumulative determinants or social and environmental conditions are optimal during the life course, individuals express human agency through concern for self and others and sustain high subjective levels of well-being and meaning-making. As older adults in prison describe, domains of well-being include cognitive, physical, emotional, spiritual, and social coping resources. These multidimensional domains of coping suggest there are avenues for prevention and intervention that promote health and positive human development and rehabilitation (Aday, 2003; Maschi et al., 2013).

However, when conditions are suboptimal, such as the experience of personal beliefs or attitudes (e.g., negative worldview) or confronted with social environmental barriers (poverty, low educational attainment; adverse neighborhood conditions, long prison sentences), a person's healthy expression of human agency may diminish his or her subjective well-being and negatively manifest as illness (e.g., somatic symptoms) or offending behavior (Maschi & Baer, 2012; Maschi et al., 2011; 2012). As the three case examples show, Jorge, Mary, and Joseph have had adverse life experiences, including prison placement that they describe as challenging their health and well-being.

Systems (The Width of the Model)

During an individual's life course, the systems, such as family, service, and legal systems, often change over time. This type of dynamic interaction between the person in his or her social environment context also consists of practice and stakeholder contexts. Access to services and justice may facilitate or impede an individual's right to human agency and his or her ability to achieve life goals. When societal conditions are suboptimal, such as in the case of most U.S. state correctional systems' poor health care services, the health and well-being of older adults may be significantly compromised (United Nations Office on Drugs and Crime [UNODC], 2009). Other social contexts include society's values and ethics, interdisciplinary perspectives, and the use of evidence-based and evidence-informed practices. Values and ethics can be personal, professional, and societal (UN, 1948). As Jorge, Mary, and Joseph describe the lack of access to evidence-based services and justice during the course of their criminal justice system experiences. For example, a central value and ethical principle of human rights philosophy is honoring the dignity and worth of all persons and respect for all persons, including people in prison (United Nations, 1948, 1977, 2012). In many cases, this principle is not honored for older adults in prison, including for the case examples in this chapter.

Power (The Height of the Model)

The history of access to power and privilege throughout the life course also is important to assess, especially for older adults who have experiences of being victimized and who have committed crimes. Power dynamics across the life course may be balanced (equitable) or imbalanced (oppressive). This social environment factor may facilitate or hinder individuals throughout the life course. Characteristics such as age, race/ethnicity, gender, social class, income, immigration, and legal status may serve to open or close doors to advancement in society or result in accumulating disparities across the life course.

According to this model, individuals or groups can be oppressed at the personal (i.e., everyday interactions), structural (e.g., institutional), or cultural levels (e.g., societal attitudes, media). An individual's internalization of negative self-messages influences behavior toward others (Mullaly, 2010). For example, societies across the globe often have social structural barriers that enable the dominant group to subjugate oppressed subgroups as noted above (Mullaly, 2010). Life course cumulative disparities often result in criminalization of oppressed persons, as evidenced in the disproportionate stricter sentencing and confinement of minority populations, and create barriers to parole release (Sampson & Laub, 1997).

Interdisciplinary systems of care intersections (e.g., mental health and criminal justice) are commonly fragmented when addressing aging people in prison, which is another social environmental factor to consider (see Figure 149.1). Given that a social work perspective may vary from a medical perspective that pathologizes, and given that philosophies of practice may change over time, an assessment and intervention should address these varying perspectives. Using a life course systems power analysis, along with using a holistic and integrated theoretical base, is essential to address the process and outcomes of the crisis adequately (Greenfield, 2012). Lastly, the evaluation of evidence-based and evidence-informed practices is needed to best capture the process and outcomes of interventions for older adults in prison (Glasziou, 2005).

Embedding Restorative Justice and Risk, Need, and Responsivity

Embedded in the life course power analysis shown in Figure 149.1 are restorative justice approaches that emphasize strengthening prosocial bonds, community-based management, and systems of care for offenders, and enhancing protective factors against sexual and nonsexual criminal re-offense. The promotion of protective factors in restorative justice approaches (e.g., Circles of Accountability and Support or COSAs; Wilson, Picheca, & Prinzo, 2007) are central in models that focus on offender reintegration and that include fostering interrelationships and community engagement and support, as well as mutual accountability in addressing the needs of older adults in prison. Additionally, principles of risk, need, and responsivity (RNR)(Andrews & Bonta, 2010) coincide with the shift from a punishment/criminalization approach to a rehabilitation model that is more attentive to social and psychological risk and protective factors in designing interventions, which includes substance abuse, trauma, and exposure to violence exemplified in the case vignettes in Table 149.1. RNR underscores respectful and collaborative working relationships between clients and correctional agencies that promote the use of effective assessments and interventions, resulting in lower recidivism rates (Andrews & Bonta, 2010). RNR is based on three therapeutic principles, which focus on matching services to the individual's risk level (risk principle); addressing criminogenic (e.g., sexual drive, the sequelae of traumatic stress, and social rejection) and noncriminogenic needs (need principle), and tailoring interventions based on an individual's motivation, learning style, agency, identity, and systems context (responsivity principle).

Application of Model to Case Vignettes of Jorge, Mary, and Joseph

What perhaps is most challenging for practitioners who work with older adults with histories of victimization prior to and while in prison, is that there is no cut and dried distinction between being a "victim" and being an "offender." As these case vignettes of Jorge, Mary, and Joseph suggest, older adults with histories of victimization and criminal offending are diverse. Many of the older adults in prison have experienced life challenges related to their marginalized or disadvantaged statuses based on personal or social-structural characteristics and trauma histories. As shown in the case examples, their stories reveal an accumulation or aggravation of life course disadvantages, such as being born in poverty; child, adolescent, and adult trauma or exploitation; and juvenile and criminal involvement. Their high-risk life course trajectories present unique challenges for individuals, families, and communities, including social work and interdisciplinary professionals, to prevent, assess, and intervene as needed. Enhancing social relations compromised by a history of marginalization and victimization, addressing the principles of risks, need, and responsivity (Andrews & Bonta, 2010), and instilling community-based supports attuned to cultural and gender differences in each of these cases can have a stabilizing effect, particularly post-release, and decrease the likelihood of relapse for sexual and/or violent re-offense. Although social workers may work with individuals in the criminal justice system, it is important they acknowledge that interagency cooperation and mutual support is crucial to good outcomes. Consideration of the context of a criminal justice system is required, where the unjust and disproportionate treatment of racial/ethnic minorities, individuals and families living in poverty, persons with mental health or physical disabilities, and a rapidly growing subgroup of older women, are particularly vulnerable (ACLU, 2012). The next section applies the model to assessment and intervention plans, including for the three case vignettes.

Human Rights-Based Assessment and Intervention Plan. In designing intervention plans for Jorge, Mary, and Joseph, a life course systems analysis was conducted. It consisted of a holistic assessment of bio-psychosocial, spiritual, and legal aspects. Table 149.2 highlights the core assessment tools used; instruments that assess traumatic stress (e.g., PTSD Checklist), as well as instruments that specifically estimate the risk for sexual offense (e.g., Static-99; designed only for males), and instruments that can assess a broader range of risk factors for both male and female adults (e.g., Level of Service Inventory; LSI-R) should be administered in order to help determine appropriate interventions.

Jorge. In the case of Jorge, assessing complex life course issues and risk, need and responsivity factors addressing both sexual and nonsexual issues are salient, including history of victimization, loss, and health issues (recent diagnosis of cancer). It is significant that he recidivated on a sexual offense toward a minor (sexual drive and risk for sexual harm considerations; the Static-99 could be used) signaling significant impairments in interrelationships, after a history of nonsexual crimes related to substance abuse/addiction. Interventions in Jorge's case should consider dynamic/protective factors including internal and external coping resources, along with health and mental health factors (e.g., depression) impacting older individuals (see below), and criminogenic needs (attuned to his culture) related to risk management and community safety, such that he can engage in the community upon reentry. Taking into account which competencies and program components should be targeted, which includes re-engagement with his family, and which resources are needed, are crucial in this case (see Table 149.3 and Table 149.4).

Mary. In the case of Mary, there are similar considerations in terms of a history of victimization (domestic violence), coping resource issues, health care concerns, and disengagement with family, with the addition of gender specific considerations and the fact that her only criminal history is related to the attempted murder of her abusive husband. Using risk and needs assessment appropriate for females (e.g., the LSI-R), and gender specific strategies for establishing therapeutic engagement is crucial in this case.

Joseph. In the case of Joseph, a history of coercive parental discipline, abandonment and subsequent impairment in attachment, and sexual victimization led to substance abuse and traumatic stress symptomatology (hyperarousal as well as dissociative rage), such that he felt compelled to protect potential victims from sexual violence, which led to the murder charge. His current constellation of health issues and isolation are salient factors in the consideration of interventions while he serves his life sentence (e.g., possible dementia).

Intervention Plan. All three individuals were referred to a specialized geriatric unit in the prison, which included geriatric-specific programming. The geriatric specific program highlighted in this chapter is based on the Nevada Department of Corrections, Senior Structured Living Program, or True Grit Program (see Table 149.3; Harrison, Kopera-Frye, & Harrison, 2012). The program is staffed by an interdisciplinary team of doctors, nurses, social workers, chaplains, lawyers, advocates, and volunteers. It infuses principles of human rights and social justice, such as dignity and worth of the person, and incorporates comprehensive structured services that foster bio-psychosocial well-being and accountability among older adults in prison. It has separate programs for men and women. Preliminary analysis of the qualitative data from participants suggests that they view the program as an invaluable part of their lives, helping them cope with daily prison stress while allowing them to offer restitution for their crimes and to plan for community reintegration. Preliminary quantitative analysis suggests that participants who are released from prison have a 0% recidivism rate (Maschi et al., in press). As shown in Table 149.4, the intervention plans to which each of the participants was assigned were selected from program components in Table 149.3.

CONCLUSION

As illustrated in the case study examples of Jorge, Mary, and Joseph, the biggest challenges for interdisciplinary professionals and programs to foster health and well-being among incarcerated older adults are developing competencies in working at the practice intersection of the aging, health/mental health, and criminal justice sectors of care. Although the extent to which some skills are used depends upon where a professional is "positioned" in the system (e.g., clinical social worker in prison, reentry program administrator), this involves having competencies in aging (gerontological practice), physical and mental

TABLE 149.2 Assessment Tools

- **A Life Course Systems Power Analysis.** As shown in Figure 149.1, a life course systems power analysis allows for assessment of an individual's life experiences and subjective response to these events, changing systems (access to services and justice over time), and power dynamics that may result in protective advantages and/or cumulative disparities.
- **Human Rights and Well-being Multilevel Assessment.** As shown in Figure 149.2, the human rights map is a visual assessment tool, similar to an eco-map, which assesses for bio-psychosocial/structural issues in relation to multidimensional well-being (i.e., legal, political, economic, educational, social, physical, mental, spiritual, and cultural well-being) embedded in a human rights framework based on the 30 articles of the Universal Declaration of Human Rights (Maschi et al., 2013).
- **Traumatic and Stressful Life Experiences.** Trauma and stressful life experiences (cumulative objective occurrences and past year subjective distress) were measured using the 31-item Life Stressors Checklist-Revised (LSC-R). The LSC-R estimates the frequency of the objective occurrences of lifetime and current traumatic events (e.g., being a victim of and/or witness to violence), The LSC-R has good psychometric properties, including use with diverse age groups and criminal justice populations (Wolfe et al., 1996).
- **Posttraumatic Stress Symptoms**. Posttraumatic stress symptoms were measured with the PTSD Checklist (PCL) for civilian populations (Weathers, Litz, Herman, Huska, & Keane, 1993).
- **Coping Resources.** Coping resources were measured using the Coping Resources Inventory (CRI) (Marting & Hammer, 2004). The CRI is a valid measure of self-reported coping resources that are available to manage stressors and has been used with samples of older adults and criminal offenders. This 60-item CRI has five subscales that measure cognitive, emotional, spiritual and philosophical, physical, and social coping resources. The CRI has good convergent and discriminant validity and good internal consistency ($\alpha = .80$) across the subscales.
- **Activities of Daily Living**. The Katz Index of Independence in Activities of Daily Living, commonly referred to as the Katz ADL, is the most proper scale to assess functional status as a measurement of an individual's ability to perform activities of daily living independently. Although no formal reliability and validity reports could be found in the literature, the tool is used extensively as a flag signaling functional capabilities of older adults in clinical and home environments.
- **Geriatric Depression Scale.** Geriatric Depression Scale (GDS) is a self-report measure of depression in older adults and had been used with older prison populations (Parmelee, Lawton, & Katz, 1989).
- **Montreal Cognitive Assessment:** The Montreal Cognitive Assessment was used to assess for cognitive impairment.
- **Substance Abuse:** The Addiction Severity Index is a semistructured instrument used in face-to-face interviews conducted by clinicians, researchers, or trained technicians. The ASI covers the following areas: medical, employment/support, drug and alcohol use, legal, family/social, and psychiatric. The ASI obtains lifetime information about problem behaviors, as well as problems within the previous 30 days.
- **Risk and Needs Assessments/Discharge Planning:** (1) The Static-99 is a 10-item actuarial assessment instrument for use with adult sexual offenders who are 18 years or older at the time of community release. (2) Correctional Offender Management and Profiling Alternative Sanctions (COMPAS) assesses needs and risk of recidivism (general recidivism, violent recidivism, noncompliance, and failure to appear). (3) Level of Service Inventory–Revised (Andrews & Bonta, 1995) assesses parole outcome, success in correctional halfway houses, institutional misconducts, and recidivism.

References/Table 149.2

Andrews, D. A., & Bonta, J. (1995). *LSI-R: The level of service inventory–revised*. Toronto, Ontario, Canada: Multi-Health Systems, Inc.

Hanson, K., Babchishin, K., Helmus, L., & Thornton, D. (2013). Quantifying the relative risk of sex offenders. Risk ratios for Static 99-R. *Sexual Abuse A Journal of Research and Treatment, 25*, 482–515.

health assessment and intervention, case management, interdisciplinary collaboration, discharge planning, and legal and policy advocacy.

Coupled with society's increased recognition of the elderly as a vulnerable population, as demonstrated by the proposed Convention of the Rights of Older Persons and the growing elder and intergenerational and family justice movements, there is now the potential for older prisoners to achieve access to justice.

Promising comprehensive programs, such as geriatric specific programming, including True Grit prototypes, that bridge prison-to-community services, offer a leap forward toward addressing human rights based best practices for older adults in prison, especially those with histories of being both victims and offenders. Promising practices with older adults in prison honor the dignity and worth of the person, foster human agency and autonomy, and encourage holistic well-being. Program components often include geriatric case management services for medical, mental health, substance abuse, family, social services, housing, education or vocational training, restorative justice (e.g., victim or victim–offender mediation services), spiritual counseling, exercise and creative arts programs, and employment and/or retirement counseling. Program specific aspects include one or more of the following: "age" and "cognitive capacity" sensitive environmental modifications (including segregated units), interdisciplinary staff and volunteers trained in geriatric-specific correctional care, complementary medicine, specialized case coordination, the use of family and inmate peer supports and volunteers, mentoring, and self-help advocacy group efforts (Davidson & Rowe, 2012).

SUGGESTED WEBSITES

- Aging in the Criminal Justice System: Links to Major Reports, Newspaper Articles, and Media Clips About Aging in Prison http://www.magnetmail.net/actions/email_web_version.cfm?message_id=2036636&user_id=CSWE
- Be the Evidence Project—Aging in the Criminal Justice System Project, Fordham University Graduate School of Social Service https://sites.google.com/site/betheevidenceproject/ (see Aging Prisoner White Paper, peer reviewed journal articles, and links to other resources)
- Elder Justice Coalition: http://www.elderjusticecoalition.com/index.htm
- National Organization of Forensic Social Work Aging in the Criminal Justice System Webinar Series: www.nofsw.org
- Penal Reform International: http://www.penalreform.org/about-us/
- Restorative Practices International: https://www.rpiassn.org/
- Substance Abuse and Mental Health Services Administration (SAMHSA) Trauma and Justice Initiative: http://www.samhsa.gov/traumajustice/

Marting, M. S., & Hammer, A. L. (2004). *Coping Resources Inventory manual-revised. Menlo, CA*: Mind Garden, Inc.

Wolfe, J.W., Kimerling R., Brown, P.J., Chrestman K.R., & Levin, K. (1996). Psychometric review of the Life Stressor Checklist-Revised. In B.H. Stamm (Ed.), *Measurement of stress, trauma, and adaptation* (pp. 31–53). Lutherville, MD: Sidran Press.

Martino, S. (2009). Addiction severity index. In G. Fisher & N. Roget (Eds.), *Encyclopedia of substance abuse prevention, treatment, & recovery* (pp. 15–17). Thousand Oaks, CA: SAGE Publications, Inc.

Nasreddine, Z. S., Phillips N. A., Bédirian V., Charbonneau, S., Whitehead, V., Collin, I., ... Chertkow, H. (2005). The Montreal Cognitive Assessment (MoCA): A brief screening tool for mild cognitive impairment. *Journal of the American Geriatrics Society, 53*, 695–699.

Weathers, F. W., Litz, B. T., Herman, D. S., Huska, J. A., & Keane, T. M. (1993, October). *The PTSD checklist: Reliability, validity, and diagnostic utility*. Paper presented at the annual meeting of the International Society for Traumatic Stress Studies, San Antonio, Texas.

Yesavage, J. A., Brink, T. L., Rose, T. L., Lum, O., Huang, V., Adey, M., & Leirer, V. O. (1983). Development and validation of a geriatric depression screening scale: A preliminary report. *Journal of Psychiatric Research, 17*, 37–49.

TABLE 149.3 Program Components

1. **Diversion Activities.** Diversion activities are a major segment of the program. Crocheting, knitting, beading, and latch-hook rug-making provide activity that is not only cognitively stimulating, but affords excellent physical therapy for arthritic hands and fingers

2. **Culturally Responsive Cognitive Interventions.** Cognitive interventions include creative writing, Spanish language study group, ethnodrama, and cultural arts group. The groups produce a newsletter and poetry journal, which are edited by the group members.

3. **Substance Abuse/Addiction Groups.** Weekly meetings of 12-step groups including Alcoholics Anonymous, Narcotics Anonymous, and Sexual Compulsives Anonymous, which are facilitated by volunteer sponsors.

4. **Psycho-education.** Weekly seminars are held that address aging, health and wellness, sexuality, life skills, cooking, menu-planning, and healthy life choices, or other relevant activities.

5. **Animal Assisted Therapy/End-Of-Life Care.** Volunteers provide animal assisted therapy (individually and in group). Animal-assisted therapy targets physical, occupational, speech and psychotherapies, special education, pain management issues, and end of life support.

6. **Physical Exercise.** Program participants are scheduled for daily exercise activities. These include wheelchair softball, basketball, or volleyball; aerobics, tennis, measured-distance walking, weight-lifting, stationary bicycle, billiards, ping-pong, horseshoes, or dancing.

7. **Peer Support Groups/Vet-to-Vet.** Veteran volunteers assist members with writing and producing artwork about their war experiences.

8. **Spiritual Wellness.** Spiritual wellness consists of traditional religious activities by staff or volunteers or peer support members. Bereavement services are provided for when the death of a family member or peer in prison occurs.

9. **Correctional Mental Health Activities.** Formal correctional programs facilitated by both staff and community volunteers are available to program participants. These programs include victim awareness, stress management, anger management, conflict resolution, relationship skills, health-related recovery, commitment to change, trauma and recovery, addiction prevention education, sex offender treatment, parenting and grandparenting classes, and special populations programs.

10. **Prison Legal Services and Victims' Rights Training.** Prison legal services provide program participants access to pro bono lawyers and social workers who are versed in elder and prison rights and law and case management services. Program participants can seek consultation or representation for appeals based on sentencing, parole release, or geriatric, medical, and compassionate release. The prison Ombudsman represents cases of interpersonal victimization and institutional abuse. Community advocates who monitor cases based on the Prison Rape Elimination Act also are available to incarcerated persons at the facility, including program participants.

11. **Family Visiting Programs**. The family visiting program provides extended time with family members, which includes spouses and partners, children, and grandchildren. Families can request transportation services from faith-based volunteers if there is no access to public transportation to get to the facility. An option for televisiting was available for participants, such as Mary, whose family lived at a distance that did not enable them to visit her in person. For participants without family members who can visit, peer visits and volunteer visitors can be arranged based on request.

12. **Restorative Justice/Reconciliation and Forgiveness Groups/Long-termers and Lifers Group.** The program also offers a session for reconciliation and forgiveness. It uses narrative-style writing and group reflection for individuals to process their crime, especially violent or sexual offenses that resulted in the harm or death to another person or persons. For participants with life sentences, a weekly lifers group is offered.

13. **Education and Vocational Training.** Program participants may choose from a range of vocational services to obtain General Educational Development (GED) or high school diplomas, college degrees, and vocational training in occupations, such as the culinary arts and select trades.

14. **Discharge Planning.** Volunteers provide members with information and referrals concerning their eventual release from prison. This includes collaboration with nonprofit organizations, halfway houses, resources for potential employment, and other assistance, such as veterans or disability benefits.

TABLE 149.4 Intervention Plan

Intervention	Jorge	Mary	Joseph
Treatment Goals	1. Increase root, cognitive, physical, emotional, social, spiritual, participatory well-being. 2. Reduce disciplinary infractions to zero.	1. Increase root, cognitive, physical, emotional, social, spiritual, participatory well-being. 2. Increase preparedness for community reintegration.	1. Increase root, cognitive, physical, emotional, social, spiritual, participatory well-being.
Programming Assigned			
Arts-based Diversion Activities	X	X	X
Culturally Responsive Cognitive Interventions	X	X	X
Substance Abuse/ Addiction Groups	X	X	X
Psycho-education	X		X
Animal-assisted Therapy	X	X	X
End-of-Life Care/Grief and Bereavement			
Physical Exercise	X	X	X
Peer Support Groups/ Vet-to-Vet			X
Spiritual Wellness	X	X	X
Mental Health Activities	X	X	X
Prisoner Legal Services & Victim Rights	X	X	X
Family/Peer/Volunteer Visiting Program	X	X	X
Restorative Justice/ Reconciliation/ Forgiveness	X	X	X
Education and Vocational Training	X	X	X
Discharge Planning		X	
Lifers and Long-termers Group	X		X

References

Aday, R. H. (2003). *Aging prisoners: Crisis in American corrections.* Westport, CT: Praeger.

Aday, R. H. (2005). Aging prisoners' concerns toward dying in prison. *OMEGA–Journal of Death and Dying, 52*(3), 199–216.

American Civil Liberties Union. (2012). *The mass incarceration of the elderly.* Available from http://www.aclu.org/files/assets/elderlyprisonreport_20120613_1.pdf

Andrews, D. A., & Bonta, J. (2010). Rehabilitating criminal justice policy and practice. *Psychology, Crime and Law, 16*(1), 39–55.

Davidson, L., & Rowe, M. (2010). Peer support within criminal justice settings: The role of forensic peer specialists. Retrieved from http://gainscenter.samhsa.gov/pdfs/integrating/Davidson_Rowe_Peersupport.pdf

Guerino, P., Harrison, P., & Sabol, W. (2011). U.S. Department of Justice, Bureau of Justice Statistics, *Prisoners in 2010.* Available from http://bjs.ojp.usdoj.gov/content/pub/pdf/p10.pdf.

Elder, G. (2003). The emergence and development of life course theory. In J. T. Mortimer & M. J. Shanahan (Eds.), *Handbook of the life course* (pp. 3–21). New York, NY: Kluwer Academic/Plenum Publishers.

Glasziou, P. (2005). Evidence based medicine: Does it make a difference? Make it evidence informed practice with a little wisdom. *BMJ (Clinical Research Ed.), 330*(7482), 92; discussion 94.

Greenfield, E. A. (2012). Using ecological frameworks to advance a field of research, practice, and policy on aging-in-place initiatives. *Gerontologist, 52*(1), 1–12.

Harrison, M. T., Kopera-Frye, K., & Harrison, W. O. (2012). A promising practice –True Grit: a structured living program for older adults in prison. In T. Maschi et al. (Eds.), *Aging prisoners: A crisis in need of intervention.* New York, NY: Be the Evidence Project, 57–69. Available from https://sites.google.com/site/betheevidenceproject/white-paper-aging-prisoner-forum

Human Rights Watch (HRW). (2012). *Old behind bars: The aging prison population in the United States.* Available from http://www.hrw.org/reports/2012/01/27/old-behind-bars

James, D. J., & Glaze, L. E.(2006) *Mental health problems of prison and jail inmates* (NCJ Publication No. 213600). Rockville, MD: U.S. Department of Justice.

Maschi, T., & Baer, J. C. (2012). The heterogeneity of the world assumptions of older adults in prison: Do differing worldviews have a mental health effect? *Traumatology, 19*(1), 65–72. Advance online publication. doi:1534765612443294

Maschi, T., Viola, D., & Sun, F. (2012). The high cost of the international aging prisoner crisis: Well-being as the common denominator for action. *The Gerontologist, 53*(4), 543–554. Advance online publication. doi:10.1093/geront/gns125

Maschi, T., Viola, D., & Morgen, K. (2013). Trauma and coping among older adults in prison: Linking empirical evidence to practice. *The Gerontologist, 54*(5), 857–867. Advance online publication. doi:10.1093/geront/gnt069.

Maschi, T., Viola, D., Morgen, K., & Koskinen, L. (2013). Trauma, stress, grief, loss, and separation among older adults in prison: The protective role of coping resources on physical and mental well-being. *Journal of Crime and Justice.* doi:10.1080/0735648X.2013.808853.

Maschi, T., Morrissey, M. B., & Leigey, M. (2013). The case for human agency, well-being, and community reintegration for people aging in prison: A statewide case analysis. *Journal of Correctional Healthcare, 19*(3), 194–210. Advance online publication. doi:10:1177/1078345613486445

Maschi, T., Kwak, J., Ko, E. J., & Morrissey, M. (2012). Forget me not: Dementia in prisons. *The Gerontologist, 52*(4), 441–451. doi:10.1093/geront/gnr131

Maschi, T., Morgen, K., Zgoba, K., Courtney, D., & Ristow, J. (2011). Trauma, stressful life events, and post traumatic stress symptoms: Do subjective experiences matter? *The Gerontologist, 51*(5), 675–686. doi:10.1093/geront/gnr074

Mullaly, B. (2010). *Challenging oppression and confronting privilege* (2nd ed.). New York, NY: Oxford University Press.

Nussbaum, M. C. (2004). Beyond the social contract: Capabilities and global justice. *Oxford Development Studies, 32*(1), 1–17.

Parmelee, P. A., Lawton, M. P., Katz, I. R. (1989). Psychometric properties of the Geriatric Depression Scale among the institutionalized aged. *Psychological Assessment: A Journal of Consulting and Clinical Psychology, 1*(4), 331–338.

Sampson, R. J., & Laub, J. H. (1997). A life-course theory of cumulative disadvantage and the stability of delinquency. In T. P. Thornberry (Ed.), *Developmental Theories of Crime and Delinquency* (pp. 133–161). New Brunswick, NJ: Transaction.

United Nations Office on Drugs and Crime. (2009). *Handbook for prisoners with special needs.* Retrieved from http://www.unhcr.org/refworld/docid/4a0969d42.html

United Nations. (1977). *Standard minimum rules for the treatment of prisoners.* Available from http://www2.ohchr.org/english/law/treatmentprisoners.htm

United Nations. (2012). *Report of the United Nations High Commissioner for Human Rights.* Substantive session. July 23–27, 2012, Geneva, Switzerland.

United Nations. (1948). *The universal declaration of human rights.* Available from http://www.un.org/en/documents/udhr/

Wahl, H., Iwarsson, S., & Oswald, F. (2012). Aging well and the environment: Toward an integrative model and research agenda for the future. *The Gerontologist, 52*(3), 306–316.

Wilson, R. J., Picheca, J. E., & Prinzo, M. (2007). Evaluating the effectiveness of professionally-facilitated volunteerism in the community-based management of high-risk sexual offenders: Part Two—A comparison of recidivism rates. *The Howard Journal, 46*(4), 327–337.

World Health Organization. (2014). *Health*. Retrieved from http://www.who.int/trade/glossary/story046/en/

World Health Organization. (2012). *Elder abuse*. Retrieved from http://www.who.int/ageing/projects/elder_abuse/en/

PART XV
Evidence-based Practice

150

Evidence-based Practice, Science, and Social Work

An Overview

Bruce A. Thyer

The process of evidence-based practice (EBP) was introduced to the social work literature over a decade ago (Gambrill, 1999) and represented the extrapolation of the emerging principles of evidence-based medicine to the purposes of our discipline. EBP is fundamentally quite different from precursor perspectives that addressed the potential of applying scientific methods to social work practice: predecessor movements such as psychoanalytic theory and its variants, behavioral social work (BSW) and its cognitive offshoots, and empirical clinical practice (ECP; Jayaratne & Levy, 1979; Siegel, 1984; Reid, 1994). BSW and ECP shared the ideas that social workers should select their choice of interventions from those best supported by empirical research, and also the recommendation that when feasible, social workers should evaluate the outcomes of their clinical practice using single-system research designs (SSRDs). The former idea is difficult to criticize, but it does leave out many important considerations, such as whether the clinician is adequately trained to deliver the empirically supported treatment, the availability of resources required to provide the indicated treatment, the ethical appropriateness of the intervention, an assessment of environmental considerations and client preferences and values, and other factors that bear on the possibility of delivering scientifically supported interventions. The recommendation concerning the use of SSRDs to evaluate outcomes at the level of the individual case has been written about extensively and even successfully applied to a limited extent, but lacking any

external reinforcers to support the efforts, busy social workers have not really adopted SSRDs on a widespread scale.

The process of inquiry known as EBP has received considerable attention within the field of social work over the past decade (see Roberts & Yeager, 2003, 2006; Thyer, 2008; Thyer & Myers, 2011), so much so that this third edition of the *Social Worker's Desk Reference* continues to contain a large section devoted to it. There is some confusion as to what is meant by the term EBP, and this initial descriptive entry will help set the stage for understanding the succeeding chapters. Here are a couple of brief definitions from primary resources in the field of evidence-based medicine, definitions from which most extrapolations to other fields, such as social work, are derived:

"The conscientious, explicit, and judicious use of current best evidence in making decisions about the care of individual patients. The practice of evidence-based medicine requires integration of individual clinical expertise and patient preferences with the best available external clinical evidence from systematic research." (Guyatt & Rennie, 2002, p. 412) *and*

"Evidence-based medicine (EBM) requires the integration of the best research evidence with our clinical expertise and our patient's unique values and circumstances." (Straus, Glasziou, Richardson & Haynes, 2011, p. 1)

By replacing the medically laden term "patients" with the more encompassing word "clients," the foregoing definitions potentially can be seen to apply readily to all the helping professions, including social work. What is also conspicuous in these definitions is the equal weight given to the core factors of scientific evidence, clinical expertise, patient preferences, and the client's unique values and circumstances. No one factor is implied to be more important that the others—all are important, and each can potentially trump the others. This definitional egalitarianism is important to realize from the outset because some professionals erroneously believe that in EBP research evidence is accorded greater weight than other factors (see Gitterman & Knight, 2013). Straus et al. (2011, p. 3) go on to operationally define what is meant by "best research evidence," "clinical expertise," "patient values," and "patient circumstances" and describe the five steps that comprise the process of EBP.

- *Step 1:* Convert our need for information about the causes of problems, and for possible interventions, into an answerable question.
- *Step 2:* Track down the best evidence with which to answer that question.
- *Step 3:* Critically appraise that evidence for its validity, impact, and applicability.
- *Step 4:* Integrate the critical appraisal with our clinical expertise and the client's unique values and circumstances.
- *Step 5:* Evaluate our effectiveness and efficiency in carrying out Steps 1–4 and seek ways to improve our practice.

The other entries comprising this part of the *Social Worker's Desk Reference* address each of these five steps. Again, EBP does not privilege scientific research findings above other considerations in making practice decisions, but it does insist that such factors be accorded their due weight. It is worth repeating this principle because a common misconception of EBP is that it gives primacy (if not sole attention) to research findings and ignores other crucial elements of practice decision-making.

This valuing of scientific research is not an unfamiliar concept to professional social work and indeed has been a defining characteristic of the formal discipline, something that set it aside from impulsive altruism, the efforts of faith-based social missionaries, or unsystematic secular efforts aimed at helping others. Consider the quotes presented in Table 150.1, selected as representative of the century-long perspective that science and empirical research must be integrated into social services. Indeed, scientific charity and scientific philanthropy were the original names for the social casework movement in the United States (Bremmer, 1956).

The assertions found in Table 150.1 clearly indicate that the principles of EBP are congruent with central core descriptions of social work as a science-based discipline, dating back to the beginnings of our field. There is much to learn and nothing to fear from a careful appraisal and adoption of the model of EBP. The original phrase "evidence-based medicine" as currently conceived, first appeared in 1992 in an article written by Gordon Guyatt and colleagues (Evidence-Based Medicine Working Group, 1992) and several concurrent developments and issues led to its widespread acceptance within medicine and then rapidly through the other helping professions. Among these developments was the recognition that practitioners really needed valid information about the causes of and possible remedies for the problems clients bring. Another was the recognition that books, traditional journals, conferences, and other usual sources of information were comparatively inefficient ways to acquire this information. Another motivational factor was an increasing awareness that as our clinical expertise is enhanced with years of experience, our knowledge about contemporary developments related to assessment and intervention research often declines. Many practitioners simply do not have much discretionary time to track down clinically useful information through traditional but cumbersome methods, such as reading professional journals or attending continuing education workshops. Though these limiting factors were and are operative in the lives of most social workers, other developments in technology and professional infrastructure pointed to some possible solutions. Among these were the increasing usefulness of the Internet as a means of locating valid information rapidly, the creation of the Cochrane and Campbell Collaborations as international and interdisciplinary organizations devoted to crafting comprehensive systematic reviews for answering commonly asked questions related to practice, and the emergence of journals focused on publishing much more practice-relevant research studies (e.g., *Research on Social Work Practice*). The concatenation of these events and developments set the stage for the emergence of EBP.

TABLE 150.1 Illustrative Quotations Documenting the Supposed Close Linkage Between Science and Social Work

- "Charity is a science, the science of social therapeutics, and has laws like all other sciences" (Kellogg, 1880, cited in Germain, 1970, p. 9).
- "Many of the leaders of the conference [the 1884 meeting of the National Conference on Charities] accepted the implications of a scientific approach to social work problems. They acted on the tacit assumption that human ills—sickness, insanity, crime, poverty—could be subjected to the study and methods of treatment.... This attitude raised these problems out of the realm of mysticism and into that of a science.... As a result of the adoption of this scientific attitude, conference speakers and programs looked forward toward progress.... They believed in the future; that it was possible by patient, careful study and experimentation to create a society much better than the one they lived in" (Bruno, 1964, pp. 26–27).
- "To make benevolence scientific is the great problem of the present age" (Toynbee, 1912, p. 74).
- "Social work is not merely a question of enthusiasm, sympathy, self-sacrifice or money, but it is a question of wisdom, discretion, and the scientific interpretation and comparison of facts" (Professor Peabody, c.f., Curtis, 1916, p. 271).
- "The scientific spirit is necessary to social work whether it is a real profession or only a go-between craft.... The elements of scientific approach and scientific precision must be back of all social reform.... It is almost superfluous to ask why social work should take on the character of science. It is hardly a question of 'may or may not.' Rather, should we say, it is a matter of the categorical must" (Todd, 1920, pp. 66, 75).
- Social work is defined as, "All voluntary efforts to extend benefits which are made in response to a need, are concerned with social relationships, and avail themselves of scientific knowledge and methods" (Cheney, 1926, p. 24).
- "The faculty and students of a professional school of social work should together be engaged in using the great method of experimental research which we are just beginning to discover in our professional educational programme, and which should be as closely knit into the work of a good school of social work as research has been embodied into the programme of a good medical school ... social workers must be so trained scientifically that they belong in the social science group" (Abbott, 1931, p. 55, 148).
- "The difference between the social work of the present and of all preceding ages is the assumption that human behavior can be understood and is determined by causes that can be explained ... any scientific approach to behavior supposes that it is not in its nature incomprehensible by sensory perception and inference therefrom" (Bruno, 1936, pp. 192–193).
- "[In German social work] everywhere the belief in science, in learning and in the scientific spirit is in evidence" (Salomon, 1937, p. 33).
- "Employment of scientifically approved and tested techniques will ensure the profession the confidence and respect of clients and the public, for increasingly the social casework process will operate more certainly for known and desired ends in the area of social adjustment" (Strode, 1940, p. 142).
- "The scientific approach to unsolved problems in the only one which contains any hope of learning to deal with the unknown" (Reynolds, 1942, p. 24).
- "Social work must develop its 'own science,' with its 'own field of knowledge,' tested in its own research laboratories" (Eaton, 1956, p. 22).
- "I believe that it is possible to understand scientifically the movement of social and economic forces and to apply our strength in cooperation with them" (Reynolds, 1963/1991, p. 315).

There is some concern that EBP is primarily oriented toward clinical practice, but this is a misconception. The Center for Evidence-Based Social Policy is just one of a number of organizations and interest groups interested in applying the principles of EBP to macro-levels of practice. The empirical literature devoted to EBP and macro-level social work is growing (e.g., Thyer, 2001, 2009), so much so that an entire journal, *Evidence and Policy*, deals with this topic. A literature search of various social science research databases using key words such as "evidence-based management," "evidence-based supervision," "evidence-based administration" will also reveal a burgeoning body of literature.

Another misconception is that EBP is somehow a development unique to the United States. In reality, the major authors in the field of evidence-based medicine were British and Canadian; the Cochrane Collaboration is headquartered in England, and the Campbell Collaboration is based in Norway, with local centers located in the United States and Canada. Thyer and Kazi's (2004) book describes EBP-related developments not just in the United States, Canada, and Great Britain but also in Israel, Hong Kong, Finland, South Africa, and Australia. The protocols developed by the Cochrane and Campbell Collaborations for the development of systematic reviews explicitly call for using international teams of experts to ensure that relevant non-English literature is not overlooked. EBP is not scientism, nor is it another example of U.S. hegemony in the realm of social work education and practice. It is the natural fruition and maturation of professional tendencies that have existed in our discipline worldwide since its inception in the late 1880s.

Evidence-based practice is not a medical model. It is atheoretical with respect to the causes of problems or conditions, neutral with respect to the types of interventions that are appropriate (e.g., psychosocial treatments vs. medications), and silent as to the disciplinary training required to deliver care (physicians are not assumed to be the service providers). EBP did originate among physicians, but the five-step decision-making model of this approach is a template that is almost universally applicable across the human services and health care disciplines.

Nor does EBP tell social workers what to do with their clients. It does not develop lists of scientifically approved treatments, nor does it prepare practice guidelines. It does lay out a systematic process whereby the social worker seeking information to help him or her make important practice decisions related to choosing assessment and intervention methods can best formulate useful questions capable of being answered. It provides guidance in locating and critically appraising this information. It helps integrate this research-based data into other critical domains, such as one's clinical skills; the clients values, preferences, and situation; available resources; and professional ethical guides, to then arrive at a decision. It also guides us in evaluating effectiveness in delivering services. EBP helps us find out what we need to know to arrive at practice decisions. What we choose to do remains the prerogative of the individual social worker, working with the client. It may be that a clinician seeks guidance about possibly effective treatments for someone who is severely depressed. A review of the literature may disclose some interventions shown to generally be quite helpful for depressed persons, such as cognitive-behavioral therapy or interpersonal psychotherapy. But if the client is also intellectually disabled, the social worker may well choose not to provide one of these empirically supported interventions if it is judged that the client lacks the cognitive abilities to be successfully engaged in these treatments. In such a case, the social worker could still be said to be operating within the EBP framework.

Over 85 years ago, John Dewey (1927, p. 179) said, "Men have got used to an experimental method in physical and technical matters. They are still afraid of it in human concerns." The emergence and adoption of EBP within social work suggests that we are overcoming such fears. We hope the reader finds that the following entries more fully describe what evidence-based practice really is, and we recommend that one consult further primary sources describing this approach in greater detail. Third- and fourth-hand descriptions of EBP commonly found in the social work literature are rife with distortions, incorrect information, and false inferences.

WEBSITES

Campbell Collaboration. http://www.campbellcollaboration.org.

Cochrane Collaboration. http://www.cochrane.org.

Evidence & Policy. http://www.ingentaconnect.com/content/tpp/ep.

Evidence-based Mental Health. http://ebmh.bmj.com

Research on Social Work Practice. http://www.sagepub.com/journalsProdDesc.nav?prodId=Journal200896

Social Programs that Work: What Works and What Doesn't Work in Social Policy: Findings from Well-Designed Randomized Controlled Trials. http://www.evidencebasedprograms.org

References

Abbott, E. (1931). *Social welfare and professional education*. Chicago, IL: University of Chicago Press.

Bremner, R. H. (1956). Scientific philanthropy: 1873–93. *Social Service Review, 30,* 168–173.

Bruno, F. (1936). *The theory of social work*. New York, NY: D. C. Health.

Bruno, F. (1964). *Trends in social work: 1874–1956*. New York, NY: Columbia University Press.

Cheney, A. (1926). *The nature and scope of social work*. New York, NY: D. C. Health.

Curtis, H. (1916). The functions of social service in state hospitals. *Boston Medical and Surgical Journal, 175,* 271–275.

Dewey, J. (1927). *The public and its problems*. Athens, OH: Swallow Press.

Eaton, J. W. (1956). Whence and whither social work: A sociological perspective. *Social Work, 1*(1), 11–26.

Evidence-Based Medicine Working Group. (1992). Evidence-based medicine: A new approach to teaching the practice of medicine. *JAMA: Journal of the American Medical Association, 268,* 2420–2425.

Gambrill, E. (1999). Evidence-based practice: An alternative to authority-based practice. *Families in Society, 80,* 341–350.

Germain, C. (1970). Casework and science: A historical encounter. In R. Roberts & R. Nee (Eds.), *Theories of social casework* (pp. 3–32). Chicago, IL: University of Chicago Press.

Gitterman, A., & Knight, C. (2013). Evidence-guided practice: Integrating the science and art of social work. *Families in Society, 94,* 70–78.

Guyatt, G., & Rennie, D. (Eds.). (2002). *Users' guides to the medical literature: Essentials of evidence-based clinical practice*. Chicago, IL: American Medical Association.

Jayaratne, S., & Levy, R. (1979). *Empirical clinical practice*. New York, NY: Columbia University Press.

Reid, W. J. (1994). The empirical practice movement. *Social Service Review, 68,* 165–184.

Reynolds, B. C. (1942). *Learning and teaching in the practice of social work*. New York, NY: Farrar & Rinehart.

Reynolds, B. C. (1963/1991). *An uncharted journey*. Silver Spring, MD: NASW Press.

Roberts, A. R., & Yeager, K. R. (Eds.). (2003). *Evidence-based practice manual: Research and outcome measures in health and human services*. New York, NY: Oxford University Press.

Roberts, A. R., & Yeager, K. R. (Eds.). (2006). *Foundations of evidence-based social work practice*. New York, NY: Oxford University Press.

Salomon, A. (1937). *Education for social work*. Zurich, Switzerland: Verlag fur Recht und Gessellschaft A-G.

Siegel, D. (1984). Defining empirically based practice. *Social Work, 29,* 325–329.

Straus, S. E., Glasziou, P., Richardson, W. S., & Haynes, R. B. (2011). *Evidence-based medicine: How to practice and teach EBM* (4th ed.). New York, NY: Elsevier.

Strode, H. (1940). *Introduction to social casework*. New York, NY: Harper and Brothers.

Thyer, B. A. (2001). Evidence-based approaches to community practice. In H. Briggs & K. Corcoran (Eds.), *Social work practice: Treating common client problems* (pp. 54–65). Chicago, IL: Lyceum.

Thyer, B. A. (2008). The quest for evidence-based practice? We are all positivists! *Research on Social Work Practice, 18,* 339–345.

Thyer, B. A. (2009). Evidence-based macro-practice: Addressing the challenges and opportunities for social work education. *Journal of Evidence-Based Social Work, 5,* 453–472.

Thyer, B. A., & Kazi, M. A. F. (Eds.). (2004). *International perspectives on evidence-based practice in social work*. London: Venture Press.

Thyer, B. A., & Myers, L. L. (2011). The quest for evidence-based practice: A view from the United States. *Journal of Social Work, 11,* 8–25.

Todd, A. J. (1920). *The scientific spirit and social work*. New York, NY: Macmillan.

Toynbee, A. (1912). *Lectures on the industrial revolution in eighteenth century England*. London: Longmans, Green.

151 Developing Well-structured Questions for Evidence-informed Practice

Eileen Gambrill & Leonard Gibbs

A key step in evidence-based practice (EBP) is translating information needs (knowledge gaps) related to practice and policy decisions into well-structured questions that facilitate a search for related research in relevant databases (e.g., Straus, Glasziou, Richardson, & Haynes, 2011). Reasons include the following.

- Vague questions lead to vague answers; specific questions are needed to gain specific answers to guide decisions.
- It can save time during an electronic search. The better formed the question, the more quickly related literature (or the lack of it) may be revealed.
- If we do not pose clear questions about decisions, we may be less likely to seek and discover helpful research findings and change what we do; we may harm clients or offer clients ineffective methods.
- It is a countermeasure to the arrogance that interferes with learning and with the integration of practice and research; if we seek answers, we will discover how tentative answers are and how much we do not know.
- It is necessary for self-directed, lifelong learning.

The better formed the question, the greater the efficiency of searching should be. Research in medicine suggests that physicians answer only a small percentage of questions that arise by consulting relevant research sources (e.g., Ely et al., 1999). We have no such information in psychology, psychiatry, or social work. There is a tendency to underestimate the difficulty in carrying out this step.

Background questions concern general knowledge about a problem or situation. This may include knowledge of psychological, biological, or sociological factors related to a concern. Such questions include "a question root (such as who, what, when, where, how, why) with a verb" (Straus et al., 2011, p. 15) as well as some aspect of a condition or item of interest. An example is, "What causes hoarding behavior?" Foreground questions concern knowledge to inform decisions. Background knowledge informs foreground knowledge. As Straus et al. (2011) note, as experience in an area increases, need for background knowledge decreases and need for foreground knowledge increases (p. 16).

BEING AWARE OF INFORMATION NEEDS

We are unlikely to search for information if we are not aware of our ignorance. Sources of uncertainty include limitations in current knowledge, lack of familiarity with knowledge available, and difficulties distinguishing among personal ignorance, lack of competence, and actual limitations of knowledge (Fox, 1959). Being aware of our ignorance as well as our knowledge is key to the process and philosophy of EPB. Information needs may concern the following. (See Database of Uncertainties about Effects of Treatments [DUETs] listed under Websites at end of this chapter.)

1. *Description of clients*: how to gather and accurately interpret information concerning client characteristics and circumstances.
2. *Causes*: how to identify causes or risk factors regarding concerns including iatrogenic harms.

3. *Indicators of certain problems*: knowing these and using this knowledge to understand client concerns.

4. *Setting priorities*: when considering possible causes, how to select those that are likely, serious, and responsive to intervention.

5. *Assessment measures*: how to select and interpret assessment measures to understand client concerns based on accuracy, acceptability, safety, expense, and so on.

6. *Prognosis*: how to estimate a client's likely course over time and anticipate likely complications of problems.

7. *Treatment*: how to select services that do more good than harm and that are worth the efforts and costs of using them.

8. *Prevention*: how to reduce the chance of problems by identifying and modifying risk factors, as well as how to identify concerns early on through screening.

9. *Experience and meaning*: how to empathize with clients, appreciate the meaning they find in their experiences, and understand how this meaning influences successful outcomes.

10. Self-improvement: how to keep up to date, improve skills, and provide a better, more efficient care system (Adapted from Straus et al., 2005, p. 20).

No matter who initiates the questions, we consider finding relevant answers as one of the ways we serve our [clients], and to indicate this responsibility we call these questions ours. When we can manage to do so, we find it helpful to negotiate explicitly with our [clients] about which questions should be addressed, in what order, and by when. And, increasingly often we're discovering that [clients] want to work on answering some of these questions with us. (Straus et al., 2005, p. 20)

FOUR-PART QUESTIONS

Straus et al. (2005) suggest posing four-part questions (also known as PICO questions) that describe the *population* of clients (P), the *intervention* of concern (I), what it may be *compared to* (including doing nothing) (C), and the hoped-for *outcomes* (O). (See Table 151.1 for examples of four-part questions.) A well-formed question should meet the following criteria: (1) It concerns a problem of concern to clients. (2) It affects a large number of clients. (3) It is probably answerable by searching for related research findings.

Gibbs (2003) refers to well-formed questions as COPES questions. First, they are client-oriented. They are questions clinicians pose in their daily practice that affect clients' welfare. Second, they have practical importance. They concern problems that arise frequently in practice. For example, child protective service workers must assess risk. Asking questions about what types of clients present the greatest immediate risk for child abuse is critical. Third, COPES (PICO) questions guide an electronic search for related research findings. Fourth, hoped-for outcomes are identified. The process of forming a specific question often begins with a vague general question and then is crafted into a well-structured question. Synonyms can be used to facilitate a search. For example, if abused children are of concern, other terms for this may be "maltreated children," "neglected children," "mistreated children." Posing well-formed questions is more the exception than the rule in most professional venues. Initial background reading may be valuable in focusing a question so as to find relevant research rapidly in a major search engine, such as Google.

KINDS OF PRACTICE/POLICY QUESTIONS

Different kinds of practice/policy questions (about diagnosis, prognosis, harm, effectiveness, prevention, risk, assessment, or description) require different research methods to critically test them. A variety of questions may arise with one client or family. Let us say a social worker is employed in a hospice and counsels grieving parents who have lost a child. General *descriptive* questions include, "What are the experiences of parents who lose a young child?" "How long do these last?" "Do they change over time and if so, how?" Both survey data and qualitative research such as focus groups, in-depth interviews, and participant observation can be used to explore such questions. Research may be available that describes experiences of grieving parents based on a large randomly drawn sample of such parents. A research report may use in-depth interviews to describe the experiences of clients who seek bereavement counseling. Questions concerning risk may arise—such as, "In parents who have lost a young child, what is the risk of depression?"—as well as questions about effectiveness. For parents who have lost a young child, is a support group compared to no

TABLE 151.1 Examples of Four-part Questions

Question Type	Client Type and Problem	What You Might Do	Alternate Course of Action	Hoped-for Outcome
	Describe a group of clients of a similar type; be specific	Apply a treatment to prevent a problem; measure to assess a problem; survey clients; screen clients to assess risk	Describe the main alternative	Outcome of intervention or prevention? Valid measure? Accurate risk estimation? Accurate estimation of need?
Effectiveness	Disoriented aged persons who reside in a nursing home	Reality orientation therapy	Compared to validation therapy	Which results in better orientation to time, place, and person?
Prevention	Sexually active highschool students at high risk for pregnancy	Exposure to baby—think-it-over	Compared to didactic material on the proper use of birth control methods	Which group has fewer pregnancies during an academic year and more knowledge of birth control methods?
Assessment	Elderly nursing home residents who may be depressed or have Alzheimer's disease or dementia	Complete a depression screening test	Compared to a short mental examination test	Which measure most efficiently and reliably discriminates between depression and dementia?
Description	Children	Raised with depressed mothers	Compared to mothers who are not depressed	Which group will have the least prevalence of developmental delays?
Prediction/Risk	Preschool children	With antisocial behavior	Compared to children who do not display such behavior	What is the risk of antisocial behavior in adolescence?
Harm	Nonsymptomatic adults	Who participate in depression screening program	Compared with those who do not	Which results in the least harm?
Cost–Benefit	Mothers with poor parenting skills whose children have been removed from their care	Purchase service from another agency	Compared to offering parent training in-house	Which is most effective and cost saving?

Note: The format for all questions is based on Straus et al., 2005.

service more effective in preventing depression? Prevention questions may arise. For parents who have lost a young child, is brief counseling compared to a support group more effective in preventing depression from interfering with care of other children? When selecting key terms to use to search for related research, quality filters relevant to the question type (e.g., effectiveness, risk) are included. For example, if the question is an effectiveness one, relevant quality filters include systematic review, meta-analysis, and study synthesis. If the question concerns risk, relevant methodological filters include sensitivity, specificity, and predictive validity.

Effectiveness Questions

Many questions concern the effectiveness of service methods, such as anger management programs. Consider the terrorist attacks of September 11, 2001, at the World Trade Center in New York. Let us say that an agency administrator wants to find out what methods (if any) may be of value in decreasing related stress reactions. The question may be posed as, "In people recently exposed to a catastrophic event, would brief psychological debriefing, or nothing, decrease the likelihood of posttraumatic stress disorder?" This is an effectiveness question, and ideally we would discover a systematic, high-quality review or meta-analyses of randomized controlled trials related to our question. We may discover the number needed to treat (NNT)—how many clients would have to receive an intervention for one to be helped. (See Bandolier's user-friendly guide describing how to calculate NNT. http://www.medicine. ox.uk.bandolier/band36/b36.html.) A search of the Cochrane database would reveal psychological debriefing for preventing posttraumatic stress disorder (PTSD) by Rose, Bisson, Churchill, and Wessely (2001). This critical appraisal showed that there was no benefit of debriefing; one study showed a significantly increased risk of PTSD in those receiving debriefing. Thus, the agency administrator would *not* be inclined to recommend this method because critical tests found it to be either ineffective or harmful.

Prevention Questions

Prevention questions direct attention to the future. These include questions about the effectiveness of early childhood visitation programs in preventing delinquency at later developmental stages. Examples are, "In young children, do early home visitation programs, compared with no service, influence the frequency of delinquency as adolescents?" "For parents who have lost a young child, is bereavement counseling or a support group most valuable in decreasing prolonged dysfunctional grieving?" Here, too, well-designed randomized controlled trials control for more biases than do other kinds of studies.

Prediction (Risk/Prognosis) Questions

Professionals often attempt to estimate risk, for example, of future child maltreatment. A key question here is: "What is the validity of a risk assessment measure? What is the false positive rate (i.e., clients incorrectly said to have some condition—such as being suicidal)? And what is the false negative rate—clients inaccurately said not to have this characteristic (e.g., not be suicidal)? A four-cell contingency table is of value in reviewing the accuracy of such measures. A well-built risk prognosis question is: "In abused or neglected children placed in foster care, will an actuarial risk assessment measure, compared to a consensus-based model, provide the most accurate predictions regarding re-abuse when children are returned to their biological parents?"

Assessment Questions

Clinicians use a variety of assessment measures. These measures differ in their reliability (for example, consistency of responses over time) and validity (whether they measure what they purport to measure). The sample used to gather data and provide "norms" on a measure (scores of a certain group of individuals) may be quite different than clients of concern, so these norms may not apply. A well-built assessment question is: "In frail elderly people who appear depressed, is the Beck Depression Inventory or the Pleasant Events Schedule most accurate in detecting depression?"

Description Questions

Professionals also seek descriptive information, such as the experiences of caregivers of frail elderly relatives. A description question is: "In those who care for dying relatives, what challenges arise and how are they handled?" Some description questions call for qualitative research.

For example, questions concerning in-depth experiences related to given events, such as loss of an infant or living in a nursing home, call for research methods that can provide accounts such as in-depth interviews and focus groups. In-depth surveys may yield related information. Other kinds of description questions require descriptive data involving large samples regarding problems and their causes. Survey data may provide information about the percentage of grieving parents who continue to grieve in certain ways with certain consequences over years. It may provide information about the percentage of divorces and other consequences and describe how parents cope with them. Here, too, we should consider the quality of related research.

Questions about Harm

Decisions may have to be made about how many people have to receive some assessment measure or service for one to be harmed. This is known as *number needed to harm* (NNH). Important considerations here include: "How many people would we have to screen to identify one person who could benefit from help?" "How many of these who are not at risk would be harmed by simply taking the test?" Any intervention, including assessment methods, may harm as well as help.

Questions about Cost–Benefit

Limited resources highlight the importance of cost–benefit analyses. What is the cost of offering one service compared to another, and how many people benefit from each service? Criteria for reviewing cost–benefit studies can be found in many sources, such as Guyatt et al. (2008).

Questions about How to Encourage Lifelong Learning

Integrating practice and research requires lifelong learning. An example of a question here is: "In newly graduated professionals, will a journal club, compared to a 'buddy system' be most effective in maintaining evidence-informed practice skills?"

SELECTING AND SAVING QUESTIONS

Which questions are most important to pose? As Straus et al. (2005) note, there are many more questions than time to answer them. First, they

suggest selecting questions according to the nature of clients' concerns (i.e., what is most important to client well-being). Other filters include what is most vital to self-learning needs, what is most feasible to answer in the time available, what is most interesting, and what questions are likely to reoccur? Straus et al. (2005) also suggest determining the time frame needed to answer a question. Some questions require immediate answers; others do not. They suggest saving questions as a third strategy, so that answers to recurring questions can be retrieved. They estimate that it takes 15 seconds to record a question. Options they suggest for saving questions include writing questions down on a three- or four-column form (client, intervention, comparison, and outcome), dictating into a pocket-sized recorder, or using a personal digital assistant (PDA) (see PICOmaker). Using a structured approach to posing questions helps practitioners pose more specific questions. As Straus et al. (2005) note, "Good questions are the backbone of both practicing and teaching [EBP], and [clients] serve as the starting point for both" (Straus et al., 2005, p. 24).

Questions and answers can be prepared as critically appraised topics (CATs). These consist of brief (one-page) descriptions of a question, search strategy, related research found, critical appraisal of the research, and clinical bottom line (Straus et al., 2005). A CAT summarizes a process that begins with a practice question, proceeds to a well-built question, describes the search strategy used to locate the current best evidence, critically appraises what is found, and makes a recommendation based on what is found. CATs may be prepared for journal club presentations. The Centre for Evidence-Based Medicine website provides an outline and criteria for preparing a CAT. Content on this site regarding levels of evidence can be drawn on to rate the quality of evidence specific to various types of practice questions. Critical appraisal worksheets are provided to facilitate evaluation of the quality of evidence. Also included is a CATmaker, which:

- Prompts a clinical question, search strategy, and key information about studies found
- Provides online critical appraisal guides for assessing the validity and usefulness of the study
- Automates the calculation of clinically useful measures (and their 95% confidence intervals)

- Facilitates description of the clinical bottom line
- Creates one-page summaries (CATs) that are easy to store, print, retrieve, and share (as both text and HTML files)
- Provides prompts to update CATs
- Facilitates teaching others how to practice EBP.

COMMON ERRORS

Errors that may occur when posing questions include starting with more than one question and trying to answer the question before stating it clearly. Gibbs (2003) notes that students often do not draw a distinction between a practice or policy question (useful to guide a search) and a research question (specific to answering a question by collecting data). Leading or loaded questions may be well built, including all elements of a four-part question, but imply that only a particular answer is acceptable, such as, "For persons who may be at risk for suicide, who receive the Brief Psychiatric Rating Scale or Beck Depression Scale, how much higher will the positive predictive value of the former be for predicting suicide?" (What if it is lower?) Confusing a research question with a well-built search question can restrict the chances of finding useful evidence. A research question specifies a specific time frame, specific location, and may specify a particular outcome measure; for example, "Among interdisciplinary teams functioning during 2007 at Veterans Administration Hospital Psychiatric Units that apply evidence-based practice methods, or apply conventional teamwork methods, will patients served by the former have lower scores on symptom rating scales?" This question is too specific and will prematurely limit a search; better that the question be posed more generally, as follows: "For interdisciplinary, transdisciplinary, or multidisciplinary teams following evidence-based practice procedures or following standard team procedures, will patients of the former fare better?"

Vague questions are so unspecific that they net nothing useful. For example, "What is the most effective treatment for depression?" A better question might be: "For women experiencing depression after giving birth, which psychotropic medications have been used to what effect on symptoms of depression?" Novices may pose different questions compared with experts in an area who are familiar with practice-related research regarding a concern and the complexity of related factors. A lack of assessment knowledge may result in overlooking important individual differences in a client's circumstances or characteristics. For example, posing an effectiveness question before discovering factors that contribute to depression (such as, "In adults who are depressed, is cognitive-behavioral therapy, compared to medication, most effective in decreasing depression?") may overlook the fact that for this client, recent losses in social support are uppermost, which suggests a different question, such as, "In adults who are depressed because of recent losses in social support, is a support group or individual counseling more effective in decreasing depression?"

OBSTACLES

Literature concerning EBP suggests that posing well-structured questions can be difficult. Thus, one obstacle is thinking it is easy and giving up when difficulty occurs. Ely and coauthors (2002) conducted a qualitative study investigating obstacles to answering physicians' questions about patient care with evidence. Participants included nine academic/generalist doctors, 14 family doctors, and two media librarians. They identified 59 obstacles. Those related to forming clear questions included the following.

- Missing client data, requiring unnecessarily broad search for information. Ely and coauthors note that questions that include demographic or clinical information and information about client preferences may help focus the search. They note that the kind of information that would be of value will vary depending on the question and may not be clear until the search is underway.
- Inability to answer specific questions with general resources. A specific question was, "What is this rash?" and vague cries for help, "I don't know what to do with this client," cannot be answered by a general resource.
- Uncertainty about the scope of the question and unspoken ancillary questions. For example, it may not be apparent that the original question should be expanded to include numerous ancillary questions.

Obstacles related to modifying the question include the following.

- Uncertainty about changing specific words in the question
- Unhelpful modifications resulting from flawed communication
- The need for modifications apparent only after the search has begun
- Difficulty modifying questions to fit a four-part question format (client, intervention, comparison, and outcome)
- Trying to solve too many questions at once
- Trying to answer a question while posing it.

Posing clear questions may be viewed as a threat. Questions are not benign, as illustrated by the fate of Socrates. Staff members who pose questions in their agency may create discomfort among other staff, perhaps because they are doing something unfamiliar or because others view such staff as impertinent or disloyal to the agency or profession. Supervisors may not have experience in posing answerable questions and wonder why it is of value; learning to pose well-formed questions has probably not been a part of their education. Other obstacles include lack of training in how to pose well-structured questions, lack of needed tools to follow through on searches, lack of motivation to consider criteria on which decisions are made, and fears that there are more questions than answers.

OPTIONS FOR DECREASING CHALLENGES

Options for addressing challenges include providing repeated guided experience in posing well-structured practice and policy questions during professional education programs and providing effective continuing education opportunities that provide such skills. (See, for example, description of problem-based learning using the process of EBP in Straus et al., 2005.) Learning by doing is emphasized in EBP. The more we use a skill, the more facility we gain with it, if we have access to corrective feedback. Unless we try to perform a certain skill, we cannot determine our competency level. Posing well-structured practice/policy questions may sound easy, but it can be quite difficult. Similarly, searching for related research findings may sound easy until we try to do it and run into obstacles. Well-structured questions related to information needs that

frequently arise could be crafted and shared with colleagues in the form of CATs.

WEBSITES

Centre for Evidence-Based Medicine, CATmaker. http://www.cebm.net/index.aspx
Childwelfare. http://www.childwelfare.com
Database of Uncertainties about Effects of Treatments (DUETs). http://www.library.nhs.uk/duets/
Equator Network. http://www.equator-network.com
Middlesex University, Mental Health CATS. http://www.lr.mdx.ac.uk/hc/chic/CATS/index.htm
PICOmaker. http://www.cebm.net/index.aspx?o=1216
University of Alberta library, CAT tutorial. http://www.library.ualberta.ca/subject/healthsciences/catwalk/index.cfm.
University of Michigan, CAT list. http://www.umich.edu/pediatrics/ebm.
University of North Carolina, CAT list. http://www.med.unc.edu/medicine/edursrc/!catlist.htm.
University of Western Sydney (Occupational Therapy), CAT list. http://www.otcats.com.

References

Ely, J. W., Osheroff, J. A., Ebell, M. H., Bergus, G. R., Levy, B. T., Chambliss, M. L., ... (1999). Analysis of questions asked by family doctors regarding patient care. *British Medical Journal, 319,* 358–361.

Ely, J. W., Osheroff, J. A., Ebell, M. H., Chambliss, M. L., Vinson, D. C., Stevermer, J. J., ... (2002). Obstacles to answering doctors' questions about patient care with evidence: Qualitative study. *British Medical Journal, 324,* 710–718.

Fox, R. C. (1959). *Experiment perilous: Physicians and patients facing the unknown.* Glencoe, IL: Free Press.

Gibbs, L. E. (2003). *Evidence-based practice for the helping professions.* Pacific Grove, CA: Brooks/Cole.

Guyatt, G. H., Rennie, D., Meader, M., & Cook, D. (2008). *Users' guide to the medical literature: A manual for evidence-based clinical practice.* Evidence-Based Medicine Working Group. Chicago, IL: American Medical Association.

Rose, S., Bisson, J., Churchill, R., & Wessely, S. (2001). Psychological debriefing for preventing post traumatic stress disorder (PTSD). *Cochrane Database of Systematic Reviews, 1.*

Straus, S. E., Richardson, W. S., Glasziou, P., & Haynes, R. B. (2005). *Evidence-based medicine: How to practice and teach EBM* (3rd ed.). New York, NY: Churchill Livingston.

Straus, S. E., Glasziou, P., Richardson, W. S., & Haynes, R. B. (2011). *Evidence-based medicine: How to practice and teach EBM* (4th ed.). New York, NY: Churchill Livingston.

152 Locating Credible Studies for Evidence-based Practice

Allen Rubin & Danielle E. Parrish

EVIDENCE-BASED PRACTICE IN SOCIAL WORK: HARNESSING THE INFORMATION REVOLUTION

Evidence-based practice (EBP) integrates research with practice and relies heavily on the use of technology to access the best available evidence. As Gibbs (2007) suggests, "EBP is genuinely a new response to the information revolution and a philosophical interpretation of how to harness this revolution" (p. 146). Whereas prior efforts to disseminate research findings to practitioners were laden with barriers, a handful of trends born out of this revolution have greatly improved the ease with which busy practitioners can access useful information more quickly to inform their practice. First, the number of empirical studies using true experimental designs has increased steadily within social work and various allied professions, providing a larger pool of information to draw from when making practice decisions (Shlonsky & Gibbs, 2004). Second, a relatively recent survey of National Association of Social Workers (NASW) practitioners reported that 97% of social workers have access to the Internet at work, home, or both, thereby allowing for real-time access to web-based evidence resources (O'Neill, 2003). Third, the widespread access of the helping professionals to the Internet and the EBP movement has led to the sprouting

of myriad web-based resources designed to improve both the access to and dissemination of practice-related research evidence.

Despite these encouraging developments, the success of engaging in the EBP process hinges largely on the ability of practitioners to locate the *best* available evidence both easily and quickly. Because the Web contains a countless number of practice-related resources that vary in their trustworthiness and rigor, practitioners must learn about existing high-quality web-based resources and develop the skills to appraise unfamiliar or new resources critically as they emerge. Practitioners would also benefit by learning specific search strategies that will enable them to search quickly within these resources to find the most relevant information for answering their practice questions. Without this information and these skills, the search for evidence can be fruitless, time consuming, and frustrating.

THE IMPORTANCE OF ASKING A WELL-BUILT EVIDENCE-BASED PRACTICE QUESTION

The success of Step 2 of the EBP process is contingent upon whether the practitioner has identified a well-formulated EBP question. A well-formulated EBP question helps (1) focus our limited time to identifying the most pertinent evidence to our client's situation, and (2) identify useful search terms to guide our search for the best available research evidence (Straus et al., 2005). Because the development of a clear and specific EBP question is intricately linked to the quality of the evidence we find and the identification of key search terms, it is necessary to briefly visit this topic.

Straus and colleagues (2005; 2011) identify two major categories of EBP questions: background and foreground. Background questions are generally posed when practitioners have limited experience with a particular practice situation or population and are looking for general background information to inform their practice (e.g., a specific practice problem, diagnosis, comorbidity, risk factors, issues related to cultural sensitivity or competence) (Straus et al., 2005). Although background information can be found in single articles, this information is often well summarized in more recent textbooks. For this reason, this chapter focuses less on background questions and more on how to locate evidence to answer foreground questions.

Foreground questions are asked when the practitioner has more experience with the practice situation and population, and wants to locate information to guide practice decisions or actions (Straus et al., 2005). Specifically, these questions ask about the effectiveness of interventions, programs, or policies for specific practice situations. Key elements of a foreground question include some or all of the following: (1) client characteristics and practice situation (always), (2) intervention (if known in advance), (3) comparison intervention (if relevant), and (4) desired outcomes (usually). Practitioners who have conducted a good assessment of the practice situation should be able to identify Items 1 and 4; it is conceivable that if they are not familiar with all of the effective interventions, programs, or policies, they will not know Items 2 or 3 prior to the search.

The most useful EBP questions are posed specifically enough to guide an effective electronic search for the evidence (Gibbs, 2003). This means providing enough descriptive terms within the question to capture the idiosyncratic characteristics of a particular client or target population so that these terms can later be used to search for and locate evidence with the greatest relevance to the client. These descriptive terms might include age or age group, gender, ethnicity or race, income, rural/urban setting, and so on.

The practitioner must use his or her judgment to select the terms that are most important with regard to the treatment setting, client, or target population.

IDENTIFYING USEFUL AND TRUSTWORTHY EVIDENCE RESOURCES

Identifying Useful Resources

After composing a well-built EBP question, the next step is to identify which resources would yield the most trustworthy, current, and best available evidence. Due to the lag time between the publication of research findings and that of textbooks, it is not sufficient to rely on textbooks to provide the *current* best available evidence. It is also not enough to subscribe to one or even a handful of specific journals, as they will only represent a small part of the existing literature to answer an EBP question. For this reason, it is impossible to know whether what little *may* be found is actually the *best* evidence. According to Straus and colleagues (2005), any money that was previously spent on these resources would best be redirected toward purchasing resources (many of which are now web-based) that provide or synthesize a larger and more recent cross-section of the extant literature.

A Model for Accessing Practitioner-friendly Resources

Resources that provide the necessary access to high-quality practice-related research evidence vary greatly in the way they disseminate this information. A model for recognizing the most useful and "evolved" information services for answering practice-related questions has been proposed by Haynes (2007), one of the coauthors of *Evidence-Based Medicine*, and adapted by the authors for use within the social work profession (see Figure 152.1). This model differs from the EBP effectiveness research hierarchy, which is concerned with the kinds of research studies that have a high degree of internal validity, such as systematic reviews, randomized controlled trials, and quasiexperimental designs with a low probability of a selection bias. In contrast, the purpose of this model is to describe the information resources that best disseminate the information generated from these high-quality studies to busy practitioners. According to this model, the

Examples

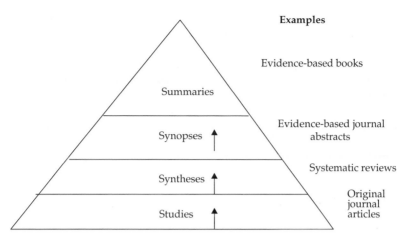

Evidence-based books

Evidence-based journal abstracts

Systematic reviews

Original journal articles

Figure 152.1 Model for recognizing the most useful and "evolved" information services for answering practice related questions. Adapted from Haynes (2007) The "5S" Levels of Organization of Evidence from Healthcare Research.

most user-friendly options for busy practitioners reside toward the top of the pyramid, because these resources summarize the information generated from the bottom two layers, thus sparing practitioners the time required to comb through the results of original research studies. Haynes (2007) emphasizes, "At each level, the standards for evidence generation, retrieval, selection and analysis should be explicit and at the highest evidence standard possible" (p. 6). Therefore, it is essential that evidence-based practitioners critically appraise information resources at all levels within this model, using the skills emphasized in Step 3 of the EBP process.

A *summary*, which resides at the top of the pyramid, draws all of the available high-quality evidence from the three layers below to integrate all of the information within a specific practice area into an up-to-date summary (Haynes, 2007). According to Haynes (2007), a summary "integrate[s the] best available evidence … to provide *a full range of evidence* [emphasis added] concerning management options for a given … problem" (p. 6). A summary then resides at a higher level on this hierarchy than syntheses or systematic reviews because it provides a broader picture of the literature by reporting on all synopses, syntheses, and studies pertaining to a general practice area. For example, a systematic review might report on only one or two interventions for treating a particular disorder, whereas a summary would compile all of the most recent outcome research on all of the known effective

treatments for that disorder, with details about varying levels of support for these disparate interventions in the form of a book or monograph. Although it was mentioned previously that typical textbooks are no longer useful for identifying effective interventions, this type of publication differs in that it usually is updated on a regular basis to capture any new emerging research in the area.

One potentially useful summary is *Clinical Evidence*, an online decision support tool that constantly updates and summarizes high-quality evidence (both articles and reviews) on topics within mental health and medicine. Unfortunately, there are not currently any social work resources that both provide a broad summary of high-quality practice research and frequent updating. The primary author of this chapter, however, has coedited a book series titled, *The Clinician's Guide to Evidence-Based Practice* (see, for example: Rubin, 2012) that will succinctly summarize the state of evidence within broad mental health and substance abuse treatment areas. In addition, this resource will provide in-depth guidelines on how to carry out the interventions identified as having the most rigorous research evidence. If this resource or any similar broad summary of the literature that is not frequently updated is used, a search for recent resources from other parts of the pyramid should be conducted to ensure access to additional research that may have emerged for a particular practice situation.

The second layer is a *synopsis,* or a brief description of an original article or systematic review (Haynes, 2007). Synopses reside second on the pyramid because the brief description saves time for the practitioner, given that she does not need to access and read the original source. Reputable synopses should reference the original research summarized, report the results quantitatively, and ideally offer an easy way to access these sources if additional information is needed. Synopses can be found in evidence-based journal abstracts, such as *Evidence-Based Mental Health.* This is a multidisciplinary journal whose authors survey a wide range of international journals with strict criteria to identify high-quality outcome studies that are clinically relevant. They synthesize this information in a short, clinically informative summary. The Substance Abuse and Mental Health Services Administration (SAMHSA) also provides a National Registry of Evidence-Based Programs and Practices, which offers a searchable online registry of mental health and substance abuse interventions and programs. The research supporting these interventions has been reviewed and rated by independent reviewers, and this information is available for practitioners to review.

The third layer is comprised of *syntheses* or systematic reviews (Haynes, 2007). Systematic reviews are "based on a rigorous search for evidence, explicit scientific review of the studies uncovered in the search, and systematic assembly of the evidence to provide as clear a signal about the effects of a[n] ... intervention as the evidence will allow" (Haynes, 2007, p. 5). Syntheses are the best resource when there is no current summary that broadly summarizes the evidence, or no synopsis that succinctly describes the results of individual studies or reviews, or if more in-depth information is needed about the existing evidence. Syntheses are third on the pyramid because they can save busy practitioners time from reading all of the original individual studies that may pertain to a particular practice issue. Syntheses are also often a better source than individual studies for practitioners because the authors of such reviews are likely to have more complete access to all of the existing literature and an advanced level of expertise in appraising and synthesizing research studies.

Many useful systematic reviews for social work practice are available on either the Cochrane Collaboration or Campbell Collaboration websites. Both organizations are nonprofit, independent groups that were created to provide practitioners with up-to-date, accurate practice information. The Cochrane Collaboration primarily provides information for health care professionals, but also has information on topics such as depression, anxiety, schizophrenia, and dementia and cognitive impairment. Access to full-text Cochrane reviews requires a subscription, although abstracts can be read on line free of charge. The Campbell Collaboration offers a searchable database of randomized controlled trials and systematic reviews of social, psychological, educational, and criminological research. Online access to both the reviews and abstracts on this site is free of charge. In addition, Ovid Technology's Evidence-based Medicine Reviews (OVID EBMR) offers one-stop shopping for both Cochrane and Campbell reviews and those published in other sources (Haynes, 2007). Finally, systematic reviews can be located through typical databases that also retrieve individual studies, such as PsycINFO, which are available with a subscription or may be accessed through a public library or a public university library. Many public libraries are now offering free remote access to the public at large to databases that house full-text articles. If these databases cannot be accessed through a local library, or if these databases are insufficient, public university libraries will allow members of the public to access these databases in person (remote access is usually restricted to students and faculty).

Original studies comprise the bottom layer of the pyramid. If sufficient information cannot be accessed from the three layers above this, high-quality single studies that evaluate the outcome of an intervention provide the next-best source of information to guide practice. Using evidence from individual studies requires that the practitioner obtain a broad sample of the existing literature, and then critically appraise these studies for both their rigor and practice relevance. SUMSearch was developed to assist evidence-based practitioners in identifying a broad sample of the relevant literature by combining meta-searching and contingency searching to search multiple Internet sites and then collating these findings into one summary page. Other high-quality databases include PsycINFO, PubMed (which includes Medline), Social Services Abstracts, and AgeLine.

PsycINFO is updated on a monthly basis, and indexes and abstracts over 1,700 sources, including international material. There are over 1.8 million individual records dating back to 1887. PubMed provides access to citations in the medical and mental health literature, and is maintained by the U.S. National Institutes of Health (NIH). The Social Service Abstracts contained 137,654 sources dating back to 1979 as of November 2007, and it is updated monthly (averaging 5,500 new sources per year) to provide coverage of current research in the areas of social work and the human services. AgeLine contains detailed summaries of the literature of social gerontology as well as aging-related research from social work and the allied fields. AgeLine contains over 75,000 English-language publication abstracts going back to 1978, and is updated every two months with approximately 800 new citations.

Whereas *Social Work Abstracts* has been described as the "primary source of articles on social work and social welfare, as well as on related fields" by NASW Press, recent reviews of this database found that in comparison with others (PsycINFO, Sociological Abstracts, and Medline), it covered a very small number of social work–related journals, was updated much less frequently, had the fewest number of records, and often omitted important papers relevant to social work (Holden, Barker, Covert-Vail, Rosenberg, & Cohen, 2008; Shek, 2008). *Social Work Abstracts* alone is thus not a sufficient database for obtaining a good cross-section of the existing research literature to guide EBP.

If nothing is found in one of the above databases, or if there is a need to expand the search, Google Scholar or Google can be used. Google Scholar provides access to a broad array of scholarly literature, while the regular Google search engine searches across a much larger sample of Internet sites beyond scholarly literature. For this reason, it is best to start with Google Scholar to narrow your search to what are more likely to be reputable sources. Both of these sites are best used by engaging the advanced search option, which will assist the user in combining key search terms better.

Practice Guidelines

In addition to the sources already listed, many organizations have begun to provide *practice guidelines,* or a list of recommended treatments or practice techniques that meet a set of predetermined criteria. Criteria for selection vary based on the source, and so it is important to become familiar with the inclusion and exclusion strategy before using these resources to guide practice decisions. Practice guidelines are distinguished from summaries for several reasons. First, they tend to provide a limited picture of the existing research evidence. Division 12 of the American Psychological Association, for example, limits its list of empirically supported treatments to the criteria listed in Table 152.1. This list, though useful for identifying interventions that meet this strict level of rigor, does not include effectiveness studies or other interventions with varying levels of support. For this reason, practice guidelines do not provide the broad picture offered by a summary that may enable the practitioner to consider all variations of the best available evidence when trying to match this evidence with the unique characteristics and preferences of the client system.

TABLE 152.1 American Psychological Association Definition for Empirically Validated Treatments: Well-established Treatments

---

I. At least two good group design studies, conducted by different investigators, demonstrating efficacy in one or more of the following ways:
  A. Superior to pill or psychological placebo or to another treatment
  B. Equivalent to an already established treatment in studies with adequate statistical power (about 30 per group).
OR
II. A large series of single case design studies demonstrating efficacy. These studies must have:
  A. Used good experimental designs and
  B. Compared the intervention to another treatment as in I.A.
FURTHER CRITERIA FOR BOTH I AND II:
III. Studies must be conducted with treatment manuals.
IV. Characteristics of the client samples must be clearly specified.

Second, practice guidelines may not rely solely on the research evidence when identifying the best interventions and may not provide a detailed picture of the research evidence. One example is the American Psychiatric Association's detailed summary of practice guidelines for a variety of *DSM* disorders, which relies on a combination of the research evidence and clinical consensus, and does not consistently describe the state of the research evidence in detail for the interventions described. Thus, although practice guidelines can be useful, the evidence-based practitioner would need to consult additional sources to ascertain whether excluded interventions with a disparate level of empirical support might better fit the client's unique characteristics, values, and circumstances or to obtain additional information on the research evidence. Practitioners should also be especially vigilant in appraising these resources for potential bias, given that practice guidelines are often developed by work groups whose members may have a vested interest in a certain interventional approach. A number of other practice guideline resources related to social work interventions and programs have been developed, such as the Evidence-Based Program Database, the National Guidelines Clearinghouse, the Office of Juvenile Justice and Delinquency Prevention (OJJSP) Model Programs Guide, and the California Evidence-Based Clearinghouse for Child Welfare.

IDENTIFYING TRUSTWORTHY EVIDENCE RESOURCES

All evidence resources must be critically appraised for their rigor and relevance to practice. For the upper three layers, the retrieval and selection of evidence and the synthesis or analysis procedure should be made explicit and should reflect the following standards. First, the search and inclusion strategy should not be too narrow or restrictive. The best resources will rely on multiple reputable databases, use a well-defined search strategy, and include both published and unpublished sources as well as dissertation research. Second, the authors should present their process for assessing the quality of selected studies, with particular attention to designs that have unbiased measurement and a high level of internal validity, such as randomized controlled trials and quasiexperimental designs that control for or lack an apparent selection bias. Finally, the resource must be critiqued for a potential bias due to funding or sponsorship, because bias can greatly influence how individual studies are selected, synthesized, and interpreted. When appraising databases that house individual studies, key criteria include (1) having a substantial number of journals and records related to the topic of interest, and (2) frequent updating of records (at least monthly).

DEVELOPING AND EXECUTING A SUCCESSFUL SEARCH STRATEGY

Many of the resources discussed so far require the use of search terms to locate the information that is specific to answering an EBP question. Although some of these sources vary with regard to their general search infrastructure, most follow similar rules and logic. If you are very unfamiliar with a resource, it may be useful to scan its search guidelines to ensure that you are using the right search strategy or to meet with a librarian or information specialist who is familiar with this resource to obtain additional guidance. This section will first present the most common search strategies that apply to the widest number of databases and online resources, which include Boolean operators, truncation, identification of synonyms, quotation marks, and methodological filters. A discussion of these strategies will be followed by a brief presentation on how best to initiate a search using these techniques.

Search Strategies

Boolean operators are connecting words that determine the logic by which two or more terms are searched within an electronic database. The most common Boolean operators are AND, OR, and NOT. The term AND narrows the search by only returning publications that contain both or all of the terms (see Figure 152.2). If searching for "teenagers" AND "pregnancy," the list of articles would be limited to those that contain both of these key words. The term OR as shown in Figure 152.2, expands the search by including all of the publications that include one or both of the search terms. This connector is often used when there are common synonyms for one of the key search terms. For example, a search may require connecting the terms (teenager OR youth OR adolescent) to obtain all of the relevant articles that describe a person between the ages of 12 and 18 years. Notice that the example terms were

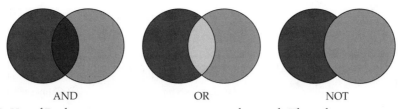

AND   OR   NOT

Figure 152.2 Use of Boolean operators to narrow or expand a search. These diagrams represent a search of two key words (represented by each circle) using each kind of Boolean operator in a separate search. The shaded area represents what the search will yield when connected with AND, OR, or NOT.

placed in parentheses—this is required for the OR connector to work properly. The term NOT is used to narrow the search by excluding information that is irrelevant. It does this by retrieving records that only retrieve the first search term and reject all that include the second search term (see Figure 152.2). For example, if interested in self-harm behavior but not suicide, the search term might include "self-harm behavior" NOT "suicide." Keep in mind, however, that NOT may discard useful as well as less useful references. Using the example, the search will only include publications that include "self-harm behavior," but not any that include both "self-harm behavior" and "suicide," which may have relevance to answering the EBP question.

Truncation is a way to expand the search by including all variations of characters that follow a word stem by using a symbol, most commonly an asterisk (*) or a dollar sign ($). For example, "prevent*" will retrieve prevention, preventing, prevented, or prevents. One truncation symbol typically returns one to five characters following a word stem, whereas a double asterisk (**) returns an unlimited amount of characters. A question mark (?) or other form of truncation can also be used to search for variations of characters within a word, for example, "wom?n" would yield both "woman" and "women." To find the correct truncation symbol for a specific database, consult the help section within the database.

Synonyms expand the search by including all possible terms for a particular keyword or phrase of interest. Although this can be done using simple brainstorming, it is best to consult the database's thesaurus, if one is available, so that an exhaustive list of the major terms used within that specific database can be generated for the major concept of interest. As mentioned previously, synonyms are connected to one another using the Boolean operator OR, and then this list of terms is linked together with terms of a different concept by the term AND (see Figure 152.3).

Quotation marks limit the search to combinations of words or phrases such as "child welfare." While searching for both the terms "child" and "welfare" separately will likely yield many relevant hits in child welfare, it will also return records, for example, that discuss the general welfare of children or perhaps public assistance and the effect on children, rather than articles limited just to the child welfare system.

Methodological filters limit the search to the best available research studies specific to answering an EBP question (Gibbs, 2003). Using the terms listed in Figure 152.4, the evidence-based practitioner is able to locate and limit the search more quickly to outcome studies with the most rigorous designs. One way to conduct the search would be to use these terms to drill down through the research hierarchy at each level, starting with the systematic review terms, proceeding to the experimental design terms, and finally to the quasiexperimental design terms (see Figure 152.4). The practitioner would start by combining the key search terms from the EBP question with the systematic review search terms to first identify any such reviews that have been done for the practice problem. If little or nothing is found, the search can be expanded to include the terms that represent experimental designs and quasiexperimental designs. If nothing is yielded using these terms, the search can be expanded further by combining more general terms such as "outcome" and "study" to search for the lower levels of *best available* evidence, keeping in mind that these sources are very tentative in providing evidence of effectiveness. As shown in Figure 152.4, these terms must be connected by OR to obtain all possible combinations of these terms. There are additional methodological search terms for background EBP questions related to assessment and diagnosis, description of experience and meaning, and risk/prognosis (Gibbs, 2003; Straus et al., 2005) provided in Gibbs's (2003) book.

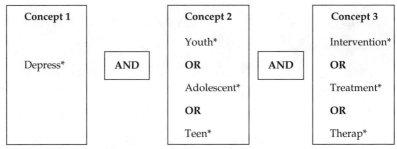

Figure 152.3 Structuring a search using synonyms and Boolean operator.

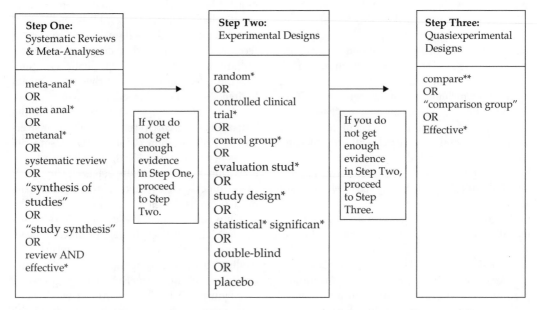

****If looking for a prevention study: AND prevent*

Figure 152.4 Use of methodological search filters to locate research studies for evidence-based practice. Many of these terms were taken or adapted from Gibbs (2003). Evidence-Based Practice for the Helping Professions. Pacific Grove, CA: Thomson Brooks/Cole.

Starting the Search

Because searching is an iterative process that often requires several attempted combinations of search terms, there is not one way to begin or carry out this process. When engaging in the evidence-based process, however, key search terms should be extracted from the EBP question to narrow the search to the information most relevant to the client's idiosyncratic characteristics and the issue(s) for which he or she sought help. One way to start the search then would be to extract the most relevant words directly from the question and then create a list of synonyms for each word. Next, this list can be used to create a search term that begins by connecting each word in the list of synonyms by OR and enclosing them within parentheses. Next, each list enclosed within parentheses would be connected by an AND. This search term would be further altered by identifying word stems that need to be truncated, and phrases should be enclosed in quotation marks. The end result is an initial search term that limits the search to the specific characteristic of the client system and the presenting problem related to the EBP question, while expanding the search to all possible variations of these search terms in the form of synonyms and word stems. An example search term is shown in the case study.

Taking Stock of the Available Evidence

After entering the first search term, the next step is to take stock of what was returned. Two major considerations are the length of the list and the relevance of the items on the list. The first step should be to examine the titles and abstracts to get a sense of what kinds of studies the search term netted. If the list of results is too long and many items seem irrelevant, AND and NOT can be used to limit the search. If the list is small or nothing has been returned, you can do one of the following: (1) try to identify additional or more accurate synonyms or new search terms; (2) reduce the number of keywords used in your search or separate some of your keywords by OR instead of AND (it may be that there is research on the presenting problem but not for a client with the same characteristics); or (3) identify a better database or resource to try the search. If this does not work, it may be that there is currently a lack of research evidence for that particular problem and an opportunity to expose this gap for further research. When this happens, it is all the more important to evaluate practice outcomes to ensure that whatever intervention eventually selected works with that client.

CASE STUDY

Angelica is a 35-year-old Hispanic mother of two who recently settled in a new city after leaving her abusive husband and a supportive women's shelter. She has taken the advice of her counselor at the shelter and decided to enter therapy to deal with her posttraumatic stress disorder (PTSD) symptoms. She is currently most interested in dealing with her difficulty sleeping and nightmares. EBP question: "What is the most effective treatment to alleviate an adult Hispanic female's PTSD symptoms?"

The first step is to identify the best information resource to answer this question. Because *Clinical Evidence* offers a summary on PTSD with adults, this reference would be consulted first, given that it falls at the top of the hierarchy of practitioner-friendly resources. This source is also reputable and regularly updated. If after reading this resource, additional information was needed to inform a clinical decision, a search of the Cochrane Collaboration using a search term would be conducted. In this case, there was a jump from the *summary* layer to the *syntheses* layer, skipping the *synopsis* layer,

because the synopsis layer is not likely to provide any additional in-depth information than the summary, whereas a synthesis or comprehensive systematic review is more likely to do so. Because the EBP question is important for informing the key search terms, practitioner judgment would be used to underline the most important terms within the question for this search, as follows: "What is the most effective *treatment* to alleviate an *adult Hispanic female*'s *PTSD* symptoms (with a specific focus on difficulty sleeping and nightmares)?"

Next, a list of synonyms would be created to ensure that all variations of the words are included in the search. Within the Cochrane Collaboration, the MeSH search option offers a thesaurus. The word "treatment" was synonymous within this database with "therapeutics" and combined with terms "treatment effectiveness," "treatment outcome," and "treatment efficacy." The word "adult" was synonymous with "middle aged." The term "women" was not synonymous with any other words, whereas "Hispanic" was linked to "Hispanic Americans." Finally, the term "PTSD" was selected for the search. Because the Cochrane Collaboration library is a collection of systematic reviews and high-quality clinical trials, there is no need to use the methodological search terms to weed out irrelevant publications. The initial search term would be as follows: (treatment* OR therapeutics OR "treatment effectiveness" OR "treatment outcome" OR "treatment efficacy") AND (adult* OR middle aged) AND women AND (Hispanic OR "Hispanic Americans") AND PTSD.

This search term yielded the following two studies:

- Cognitive-behavioural interventions for children who have been sexually abused. G. M. Macdonald, J. P. T. Higgins, P. Ramchandani (2006).
- Behavioural and cognitive behavioural training interventions for assisting foster carers in the management of difficult behaviour. W. Turner, G. M. Macdonald, J. A. Dennis (2007).

Of course, based on the titles, it is obvious that neither of these reviews is relevant to the EBP question. For this reason, the search will be limited to the following term, taking out ethnicity, which may only be discussed in the body of the review: (treatment* OR therapeutics OR "treatment effectiveness" OR "treatment outcome" OR "treatment efficacy") AND (adult* OR middle aged) AND women AND PTSD. This change expanded the search to 10 reviews, two of which included the following:

- Psychological treatment of post-traumatic stress disorder (PTSD). J. Bisson, M. Andrew (2007).
- Pharmacotherapy for prevention of post-traumatic stress disorder. J. C. Ipser, S. Seedat, D. J. Stein (2006).

The review on psychological treatment of PTSD examined the evidence for the following PTSD interventions: trauma-focused cognitive-behavioral therapy/exposure therapy (TFCBT), stress management (SM), other therapies (supportive therapy, nondirective counseling, psychodynamic therapy, and hypnotherapy), group cognitive-behavioral therapy (group CBT), eye movement desensitization and reprocessing (EMDR). The results of this analysis were presented in detail, and the authors of this study concluded the following:

There was evidence individual TFCBT, EMDR, stress management and group TFCBT are effective in the treatment of PTSD. Other non-trauma focused psychological treatments did not reduce PTSD symptoms as significantly. There was some evidence that individual TFCBT and EMDR are superior to stress management in the treatment of PTSD at between 2 and 5 months following treatment, and also that TFCBT, EMDR, and stress management were more effective than other therapies (Bisson & Andrew, 2007).

Because both a summary and systematic review of many of the existing PTSD interventions were accessed from reputable sources, these intervention options and the varying levels of empirical support can be presented to the client as a part of an informed consent process.

WEBSITES

California Evidence-Based Clearinghouse for Child Welfare. http://www.cachildwelfareclearinghouse.org.
Campbell Collaboration. http://www.campbellcollaboration.org.
Clinical Evidence. http://clinicalevidence.bmj.com/ceweb/conditions/index.jsp.
Cochrane Collaboration. http://www.cochrane.org.

Evidence-Based Mental Health. http://ebmh.bmj.com.
Google Scholar. http://scholar.google.com.
National Guidelines Clearing House. http://guideline.gov.
National Registry of Evidence-Based Programs and Practices http://www.nrepp.samhsa.gov/find.asp.
Office of Juvenile Justice and Delinquency Prevention Model Programs Guide. http://www.dsgonline.com/mpg2.5/mpg_index.htm.
SUMSearch. http://sumsearch.uthscsa.edu.

References

Bisson, J., & Andrew, M. (2007). Psychological treatment of post-traumatic stress disorder (PTSD). *Cochrane Database of Systematic Reviews, 3*, no. CD003388.

Gibbs, L. (2003). *Evidence-based practice for the helping professions: A practical guide with integrated multimedia*. Pacific Grove, CA: Brooks/Cole-Thompson Learning.

Gibbs, L. (2007). Applying research to making life-affecting judgments and decisions. *Research on Social Work Practice, 17*, 143–150.

Haynes, B. (2007). Of studies, syntheses, synopses, summaries and systems: The "5S" evolution of information services for evidence-based healthcare decisions. *Evidence Based Nursing, 10*, 6–7.

Holden, G., Barker, K., Covert-Vail, L., Rosenberg, G., & Cohen, S. (2008). Do social workers deserve better? An examination of *Social Work Abstracts*. *Research on Social Work Practice, 18*, 487–499.

O'Neill, J. V. (2003). Nearly all members linked to the Internet. *NASW News, 48*(2), 9.

Rubin, A. (2012). *The clinician's guide to evidence-based practice: Programs and interventions for maltreated children and families at risk*. Hoboken, NJ: Wiley.

Shek, D. T. L. (2008). Comprehensiveness of *Social Work Abstracts* as a database for researchers and practitioners. *Research on Social Work Practice, 18*, 500–506.

Shlonsky, A., & Gibbs, L. (2004). Will the real evidence-based practice please stand up? Teaching the process of evidence-based practice to the helping professions. *Brief Treatment and Crisis Intervention, 4*, 137–153.

Straus, S. E., Richardson, W. S., Glasziou, P., & Haynes, R. B. (2005). *Evidence-based medicine: How to practice and teach EBM*, 3rd ed. Edinburgh: Elsevier Churchill Livingstone.

Straus, S. E., Glasziou, P., Richardson, W. S., Haynes, R. B. (2011). *Evidence-based medicine: How to practice and teach EBM* (4th ed.). Edinburgh: Churchill Livingstone Elsevier.

153 Critically Appraising Studies for Evidence-based Practice

Denise E. Bronson

Adopting an evidence-based approach to practice is predicated upon one's ability to determine which studies or systematic reviews are valid, credible, and relevant to the practice problem one is trying to solve. A *critical appraisal* of the available research is essential for sifting through the plethora of published and unpublished literature to find those studies that employed rigorous methods to minimize potential biases and unwarranted conclusions. There is no single systematic strategy for conducting a critical appraisal but there are numerous guidelines and checklists to help evaluate the quality of the research, the quality of the research report, the relevance of the research, and the presence of potential biases (Harden & Gough, 2012). Using these tools, critical appraisal can be done by anyone with a basic understanding of research methods who also possesses (1) the ability to think critically, (2) a willingness to challenge their own biases and practice preferences, and (3) a systematic strategy to ensure that each study is evaluated according to the same criteria.

All strategies for critically appraising single studies or systematic reviews attempt to identify possible biases that produce conclusions that deviate in some way from the "true" results (Harden & Gough, 2012; Young & Solomon, 2009). Bias can undermine research at many points, beginning with how the research problem is defined to the ways in which the results are reported. Although there is no such thing as a perfect study, a critical appraisal of a study's validity and credibility allows one to assess "the degree to which a study is affected by bias and whether the degree of bias is large enough to render the study unusable" (Petticrew & Roberts, 2006, p. 131).

Critical appraisal strategies focus on identifying possible threats to the validity, credibility, and relevance of the research. Assessing the validity of the research examines whether the research design and methods have eliminated or minimized potential sources of bias (Straus, Glasziou, Richardson, & Haynes, 2011) that could lead to erroneous causal conclusions. A valid study is one that allows us to make causal inferences (also called internal validity) about the effects of an intervention. A study will have good internal validity if the research design and methods allow us to establish a causal relationship between the treatment and the observed outcomes while eliminating other possible explanations. Examining the credibility of the research helps determine whether we have reason to believe the outcomes. A credible study is one that is trustworthy. That is, the study is characterized by transparency, honest reporting of methods and limitations, and a willingness to consider alternative explanations for the observed outcomes. Credibility also includes any possible conflict of interest that might influence the conclusions made by the researcher. Appraising the relevance of the research examines the generalizability of the findings to clinical populations and what outcomes might be expected if an intervention is adopted. The critical appraisal process examines all three areas.

APPRAISING VALIDITY

Critically Appraising the Validity of Single Studies. Several tools are available to help appraise the validity of an individual study. Guidelines for critically appraising validity target the possible sources of systematic bias in the research methods, which may be introduced by the way in which the study is conducted, how study participants were selected, how data were collected, or through the researchers' analysis or interpretation (Young & Solomon, 2009). Discussions of validity assessments often refer to the "hierarchy of research evidence," which indicates the strength of the evidence produced by various research methods (Howick, Chalmers, Glasziou, Greenhalgh, Heneghan, Liberati, Moschette, Phillips, & Thornton, 2011). Typically the hierarchy of evidence is presented as a pyramid (http://ebp.lib.uic.edu/nursing/node/12) with the strongest types of research methods appearing at the top (systematic reviews and meta-analyses) and weaker methods at the base (editorials and expert opinions). Each of the validity appraisal methods presented below rely on this model to assess biases that might be introduced by the type of research methods used.

Gibbs (2003) created the Quality of Study Rating Form (QSRF) to assess the quality of individual effectiveness studies. The QSRF places high value on randomized control trials with outcome data collected by those blinded to the treatment assignments to reduce threats to internal validity. The QSRF also emphasizes the value of random selection and assignment of subjects to treatment conditions, and gives weight to studies using reliable and valid outcome measures. When completed, the QSRF provides an index of the study's validity based on the rigor of the research methods used in the study.

The Social Care Institute for Excellence (SCIE) in England developed the TAPUPAS framework that highlights the dimensions of *transparency, accuracy, purposivity, utility, propriety, accessibility,* and *specificity* (Harden & Gough, 2012). Critical appraisal of a study using TAPUPAS asks:

- Transparency—are the reasons for it clear?
- Accuracy—is it honestly based on relevant evidence?
- Purposivity—is the method used suitable for the aims of the work?
- Utility—does it provide answers to the questions it set?
- Propriety—is it legal and ethical?
- Accessibility—can one understand it?
- Specificity—does it meet the quality standards already used for this type of knowledge? (Pawson, Boaz, Grayson, Long, & Barnes, 2003, p. 40).

This model goes beyond assessing the research methods used by also examining the way in which the findings are reported, possible ethical issues inherent in the research, and the relevance of the research.

Today, the most widely used critical appraisal model is the "Risk of Bias" tool developed by the Cochrane Collaboration, which assesses threats to internal validity by classifying biases into six types—selection bias, performance bias, attrition bias, detection bias, and reporting bias (Higgins & Green, 2011; Higgins, Altman, Gotzsche, Juni, Moher, Oxman, Sovovic, Schulz, Weeks, & Stern, 2011). Each of these potential biases offers an alternative explanation for any changes observed after the introduction of an intervention.

Each of the tools presented uses randomized controlled trials (RCTs) as the benchmark against which to appraise the validity of effectiveness studies. Unfortunately, RCTs are difficult to implement in clinical settings and, as a result, there are relatively few such studies in social work. Some researchers use a variety of strategies to try to create equivalent groups without randomization, but these methods do not remove the possibility of unmeasured systematic errors. These efforts and the use of other less rigorous research designs, such as those relying on nonequivalent comparison groups, case studies, or qualitative research will not address many threats to internal validity or remove potential biases that can distort the conclusions about an intervention's effectiveness. However, qualitative studies may offer information about the efficacy and effectiveness of interventions that cannot be gleaned from quantitative research. The value of less rigorous quantitative research and qualitative research for evidence-based practice has been quite controversial. However, efforts are under way to develop appraisal criteria for these types of studies to minimize issues of bias and to promote their use in evidence-based practice (Bronson & Davis, 2012; Saini, 2007; Saini & Shlonsky, 2012; Noyes, Popay, Pearson, Hannes, & Booth, 2011).

Critically Appraising the Validity of Systematic Reviews. When multiple studies exist on a specific intervention it is possible to strengthen conclusions on the effectiveness of the intervention by synthesizing the results of multiple studies. Both the Cochrane Collaboration and the Campbell Collaboration promote the use of systematic reviews and meta-analyses to summarize a large body of research. Unlike traditional

TABLE 153.1 Cochrane Collaboration Sources of Bias in Clinical Trials (Higgins & Green, 2011)

Selection Bias	Systematic differences between comparison groups at baseline that may impact the results of the study. Random selection and assignment is used to reduce selection bias.
Performance Bias	Systematic differences in how participants in the comparison groups are treated that are not related to the presence or absence of the intervention. Blinding of study participants and personnel used to minimize bias.
Detection Bias	Systematic differences in how outcomes are measured due to knowledge of the subject's group assignment. Blinding of study participants and personnel used to minimize bias.
Attrition Bias	Systematic differences between groups in withdrawal from the research so that outcome data are unavailable.
Reporting Bias	Systematic differences in which results are reported. Refers to the tendency to report significant results while not reporting nonsignificant findings.

literature reviews, systematic reviews provide a comprehensive synthesis of existing research using transparent and replicable methods. When a sufficient number of studies exist, systematic reviews often include a statistical meta-analysis that calculates an overall effect size based on a synthesis of the statistical results from multiple studies (Cooper, 2010; Littell et al., 2008; Bronson & Davis, 2012).

Assessing the validity and relevance of systematic reviews and meta-analyses requires a different set of evaluative criteria. Each step in the synthesis process presents new validity issues that must be considered in appraising the quality of systematic reviews (Cooper, 2010). Numerous approaches for assessing the quality of systematic reviews have been developed.

The Campbell and Cochrane Collaborations have developed explicit standards to ensure the validity and objectivity of systematic reviews from beginning to end (www.campbellcollaboration.org; Higgins & Green, 2011). Researchers who complete systematic reviews for inclusion in the Campbell or Cochrane Collaboration libraries must adhere to these standards and agree to have all stages of their work reviewed by collaboration members to minimize any potential biases. Although bias can occur at each stage of completing a systematic review, particular attention is given to biases that may occur during the search for relevant research (e.g., publication bias, unreliable coding strategies, or language bias), the extraction of data from the individual studies (e.g., poorly defined methods or missing information), the synthesis of the findings, and the conclusions presented in the final report. Possible

conflicts of interest by the researchers that may bias the final review or the way it is conducted are also carefully assessed. Detailed information on the ways in which the Campbell and Cochrane Collaborations strive to minimize bias and increase the validity of systematic reviews published in their libraries can be found at www.campbellcollaboration.org and http://handbook.cochrane.org/.

Not all systematic reviews are conducted under the watchful eyes of the Campbell or Cochrane Collaborations. Two appraisal strategies are available to meet the needs of practitioners with limited time to conduct a critical appraisal of reviews published outside the domains of the Campbell or Cochrane Collaborations. A checklist developed by Bronson & Davis (2012) helps social workers quickly evaluate the transparency, completeness, methodological soundness, credibility, and practice relevance of systematic reviews for practice decision-making. Deficits in any of these areas compromise the overall validity of the review. Similarly, the Centre for Evidence-Based Medicine at Oxford developed a *Systematic Review Appraisal Sheet* (http://www.cebm.net/) that asks the following questions:

- *What question did the systematic review address?* Was the problem clearly defined?
- *Is it unlikely that important, relevant studies were missed?* That is, how extensive was the search for relevant studies and was it described with enough detail to be replicated? Did it include studies from the major electronic databases, unpublished studies, and non-English studies?

- *Were the criteria used to select articles for inclusion appropriate?* The inclusion and exclusion criteria should be clearly defined. In addition, the reliability of reviewers' coding should be checked to ensure that the inclusion and exclusion criteria are consistent applied.
- *Were the included studies sufficiently valid for the type of question asked?* This refers to the extent to which the quality of the studies was appraised before including them in the systematic review.
- *Were the results similar from study to study?* The results of a systematic review are more trustworthy if all of the studies have treatment effects going in the same direction (Straus et al., 2011).
- *What were the results and how were they presented?* Was a meta-analysis conducted, were the methods clearly described, and were the results presented using a standard metric and displayed on a forest plot?

These easy-to-use appraisal strategies can help us decide whether the systematic review meets the minimal standards for validity; there are many reviews in the published literature identified as "systematic" that, in fact, do not meet the standards.

APPRAISING CREDIBILITY

The credibility of the research is often overlooked in the appraisal process (Carlson, 1995), and yet the believability and trustworthiness of the study must be considered. If one reads an article in the newspaper reporting on the results of research demonstrating the benefits of chewing gum for stress reduction one might question the credibility of the report if the research was paid for by a company that produces chewing gum. Similarly, studies completed by social work researchers who receive funding from an ideologically driven foundation or researchers who gain financially from the success of an intervention they developed should receive extra scrutiny. There are many factors that contribute to the overall credibility of a study. Appraising the credibility of research is largely a matter of judgment, and one's ability to judge will depend on the completeness and transparency of the report.

A credible report is a readable report. One of the persistent barriers between research and practice has been inability of researchers to communicate with practitioners in a manner that promotes the transfer of knowledge to practice settings. Research should be reported in a clear, user-friendly manner that facilitates understanding and minimizes jargon. It is impossible to appraise critically the validity or credibility of research that is poorly written (Egger, Smith, & O'Rourke, 2001).

To give us the information we need to adequately judge the credibility of published systematic reviews, standards have been developed to ensure that all pertinent information is presented in the final systematic review report. Campbell and Cochrane reviews also include user abstracts that summarize the findings in language that is usable for policy makers and practitioners. "As with all research, the value of a systematic review depends on what was done, what was found, and the clarity of reporting" (Moher, Liberati, Tetzlaff, Altman, 2009, p. 332). To this end, the Preferred Reporting Items for Systematic Reviews and Meta-Analyses (PRISMA) was created to guide authors in the preparation of the written reports and to provide standards for journals to adopt for publishing systematic reviews. PRISMA consists of a 27-item checklist that indicates what should be included when reporting on a systematic review or meta-analysis. The authors who follow PRISMA in preparing their summary reports are more likely to offer a clear and complete presentation of their methods and findings. This, in turn, will allow one to better assess the believability or credibility of the final report.

Having access to detailed background information about the author of a systematic review will also allow one to evaluate possible personal biases that may have infiltrated the systematic review or meta-analysis. Most journal articles provide information on the author's place of employment and the source of funding for the research. This information may provide some insight into any ideological biases or prejudices that could impact the research. The Campbell and Cochrane Collaborations also have called for researchers to provide information on possible conflicts of interest or previous research activities that might influence the conduct or conclusions of the current project. Finally, in a comprehensive and transparent research report, the author will clearly state the purpose for conducting the research and will honestly report the evidentiary status of the research. Taken together (see Table 153.2), information on the researcher's background, the source of funding, and the

TABLE 153.2 Assessing the Credibility
of the Research

1. Detailed information is provided about the
   researcher, including place of employment,
   previous research, and potential conflicts of
   interest.
2. Information is provided about the
   funding for the research and the funding
   organization.
3. Information about possible financial gains
   for the researcher associated with the
   outcomes of the research are presented.
4. The author has clearly presented the
   purpose of the research.
5. The research report appears to be
   transparent and the reporting is honest
   about the evidentiary status of the research.

TABLE 153.3 Assessing the External Validity and
Relevance of the Research

1. The sample used in the study is
   representative of people for whom the
   intervention/treatment will be used.
2. The results of the study can reasonable be
   generalized to:
   • A larger population
   • A smaller population (small group or
     individual)
   • A group of similar size
3. The study provides detailed information on
   the following:
   • The subjects of the research
   • The setting in which the treatment was
     delivered
   • Characteristics of those who provided the
     intervention
4. The intervention has been replicated with
   other populations, in other settings, or with
   other therapists.
5. The intervention can be disseminated (i.e.,
   training materials and manuals exist).

overall quality of the written report based on the PRISMA standards will help readers appraise the believability and credibility of the research as they consider its applicability to practice.

APPRAISING RELEVANCE

Assessing the relevance of the research allows one to judge whether the changes attributed to the intervention are likely to generalize to other settings when the treatment is implemented with other clients and by different therapists (see Table 153.3). The relevance of a study for social work practice and policy depends on the external validity or generalizability of the results. External validity is especially important when deciding whether an intervention can be adopted in a practice setting. Unfortunately, there is often a trade-off between internal and external validity. For example, research that takes place in a highly controlled setting may achieve good internal validity, but the generalizability of the findings may be reduced. If given the choice, researchers usually will strive for internal validity over external validity (Campbell & Stanley, 1963). This preference has led to the proverbial gap between research and practice and underscores the need for assessing the external validity and relevance of research.

To assess the external validity and relevance of a study, it is important to determine whether the subjects, setting, and therapists in the research are similar (i.e., representative of) the

clients one is serving and the setting in which one is working. Generalizations from research can extend from (1) a small group of subjects to a larger population, (2) a large experimental group to a small group or individual, or (3) one similarly sized group to another (Shadish, Cook, & Campbell, 2002). It is important to consider the type of generalizations that can be made from the research as one appraises its external validity.

Appraising a study's external validity and relevance is largely a matter of subjective judgment. A good research report will describe how subjects were selected for the study and provide detailed information on client demographics, the environment in which services were delivered, and characteristics of the service providers (e.g., training, experience, education, and personal characteristics).

Finally, the generalizability of research findings is more likely if the study has been replicated with other subjects, in other settings, or by other researchers. This requires searching the bibliographic databases for similar studies that evaluate the intervention. The generalizability of the research also will be enhanced by the availability of training materials and manuals to facilitate the dissemination of the intervention. Training materials help ensure that there is treatment fidelity when the intervention is implemented in diverse settings.

CONCLUSIONS

Critically appraising the validity, credibility, and relevance of research reports and systematic reviews is a fundamental skill in becoming an evidence-based practitioner. Adopting a critical perspective does not end, however, with the appraisal of the research. It is equally important to be aware of any possible biases one might bring to the critical appraisal process. Examining one's own biases or practice preferences will help avoid the "I'll-see-it-when-I-believe-it" syndrome (Gilovich, 1993) characterized by a tendency (1) to identify and remember research that supports one's own preferences, (2) to be less likely to search for disconfirming evidence, (3) to be less critical of research that supports one's biases, and (4) to be highly critical of research that does not (Kahneman, Slovic, & Tversky, 1982). One way to minimize this tendency is to subject all research to the same evaluative criteria, using a systematic approach to critically appraising the studies.

Critically appraising the available evidence for evidence-based practice involves a basic knowledge of research methods, critical thinking, a willingness to challenge one's own biases, and the use of a systematic approach to assess the quality of a study. Although it is not an exact science, carefully examining the validity, credibility, and relevance of a study will reveal the strengths and limitations of the research and enable practitioners to judge the value of the research for clinical practice. These are essential activities for evidence-based practice in social work. Practitioners who routinely apply critical appraisal skills to their reading of the research literature will be prepared to use the best available evidence to guide practice decision-making and will usher in a new era that promotes the integration of social work research and practice.

WEBSITES

Campbell Collaboration. www.campbellcollaboration.org

Centre for Evidence-Based Medicine at Oxford http://www.cebm.net/

Cochrane Handbook for Systematic Reviews of Interventions. http://handbook.cochrane.org/

Evidence for Policy and Practice Information and Co-ordinating Centre. http://eppi.ioe.ac.uk/cms

PRISMA (Preferred Reporting Items for Systematic Reviews and Meta-Analyses) http://www.prisma-statement.org/

Social Care Institute for Excellence (SCIE) http://www.scie.org.uk/

References

Bronson, D. E., & Davis, T. S. (2012). *Finding and evaluating evidence: Systematic reviews and evidence-based practice.* New York, NY: Oxford University Press.

Campbell, D. T., & Stanley, J. C. (1963). *Experimental and quasi-experimental designs for research.* Chicago, IL: Rand McNally.

Carlson, E. R. (1995). Evaluating the credibility of sources: A missing link in the teaching of critical thinking. *Teaching of Psychology, 22*, 39–41.

Cooper, H. (2010). *Research synthesis and meta-analysis: A step-by-step approach.* Thousand Oaks, CA: Sage Publications, Inc.

Egger, M., Smith, G. D., & O'Rourke, K. (2001). Rationale, potentials, and promise of systematic reviews. In M. Egger, G. D. Smith, & D. G. Altman (Eds.), *Systematic reviews in health care: Meta-analysis in context* (pp. 3–22). London: BMJ.

Gibbs, L. (2003). Evidence-based practice for the helping professions: A practical guide with integrated multimedia. Pacific Grove, CA: Brooks/Cole-Thompson.

Gilovich, T. (1993). *How we know what isn't so: The fallibility of human reason in everyday life.* New York, NY: Free Press.

Harden, A., & Gough, D. (2012). Quality and relevance appraisal. In D. Gough, S. Oliver, & J. Thomas (Eds.), *An introduction to systematic reviews.* London: Sage Publications Ltd.

Higgins, J. P. T., & Green, S. (Eds.). (2011). *Cochrane handbook for systematic reviews of interventions. Version 5.1.0* (updated March 2011). The Cochrane Collaboration. Available from www.cochrane-handbook.org.

Higgins, J. P. T., Altman, D. G., Gotzsche, P. C., Juni, P., Moher, D., Oxman, A. D.,… Stern, J. A. C. Cochrane Bias Methods Group & Cochrane Statistical Methods Group. (2011). The Cochrane Collaboration's tool for assessing risk of bias in randomized trials. *BMJ, 343*:d5928. doi:10.1136/bmj.d5928

Howick, J., Chalmers, I., Glasziou, P., Greenhalgh, T., Henghan, C., Liberati, A.,… Thornton, H. (2011). *The 2011 Oxford CEBM Evidence Level of Evidence (introductory document).* Oxford: Oxford Centre for Evidence-Based Medicine. http://www.cebm.net/index.aspx?o=5653

Kahneman, D., Slovic, P., & Tversky, A. (Eds.). (1982). *Judgment under uncertainty: Heuristics and biases.* Cambridge: Cambridge University Press.

Littell, J. H., Corcoran, J., & Pillai, V. (2008). *Systematic reviews and meta-analysis.* New York, NY: Oxford University Press.

Noyes, J., Popay, J., Pearson, A., Hannes, K., & Booth, A. (2011). Qualitative research and Cochrane reviews. In J. P. T. Higgins & S. Green (Eds.), *Cochrane handbook for systematic reviews of interventions. Version 5.1.0* (updated March 2011). The Cochrane Collaboration. Available from www.cochrane-handbook.org.

Moher, D., Liberati, A., Tetzlaff, J., & Altman, D. G. (2009). Preferred reporting items for systematic reviews and meta-analyses: The PRISMA statement. *BMJ, 339*, b2523. doi:10.1136/bmj.b2535

Pawson, R., Boaz, A., Grayson, L., Long, A., & Barnes, C. (2003). *Knowledge review: Types and quality of knowledge in social care.* London: Social Care Institute for Excellence.

Petticrew, M., & Roberts, H. (2006). *Systematic reviews in the social sciences: A practical guide.* Malden, MA: Blackwell.

Saini, M. (2007). *A pilot study of the quality and rigor in qualitative research form.* Paper presented at the Seventh Annual International Campbell Collaboration Colloquium, May 14–16, London.

Saini, M., & Shlonsky, A. (2012). *Systematic synthesis of qualitative research.* New York, NY: Oxford University Press.

Shadish, W. R., Cook, T. D., & Campbell, D. T. (2002). *Experimental and quasi-experimental designs for generalized causal inference.* Boston, MA: Houghton Mifflin.

Straus, S. E., Glasziou, P., Richardson, W. S., & Haynes, R. B. (2011). *Evidence-based medicine: How to practice and teach it* (4th ed.). Edinburgh: Elsevier.

Young, J. M., & Solomon, M. J. (2009). How to critically appraise an article. *Nature Clinical Practice, 6*(2), 82–91.

154 Randomized Controlled Trials and Evidence-based Practice

Paul Montgomery & Evan Mayo-Wilson

Randomized controlled trials (RCTs) are commonly used to determine whether interventions are effective. Simply, RCTs include at least two groups, usually an intervention group and a comparison group. Participants typically have an equal chance of being assigned to either group. Clients are normally allocated individually, but trials might assign multiple individuals (e.g., by classroom, nursing home, or drug treatment center). These are called *cluster randomized* trials (Boruch, 2005). Intervention and comparison groups are usually assessed before and after intervention.

RCTs provide:

• Top-quality evidence of safety and effectiveness
• Limitation of researcher bias
• Identification of causes.

This chapter explains the key features of RCTs, how to critique them, and how to use them in practice. To illustrate the main features and benefits of RCTs, the chapter includes two case studies.

CASE STUDIES

Booklets for Children with Sleep Problems

This study was about the sleep problems of children with learning disabilities (mental retardation) conducted in the community by Montgomery, Stores, and Wiggs (2004). Sleep problems in this population are severe, common, and generally considered difficult to treat. It is known that the best form of intervention is behavioral, but scarce resources limit access to these treatments. This study aimed to investigate a brief behavioral treatment of sleep problems by randomizing children and their parents to receive (1) face-to-face delivered treatment, (2) booklet-delivered treatment, or (3) no treatment. The participants were the parents of 66 severely learning disabled children aged 2–8 years with settling or night waking problems. A composite sleep disturbance score was derived from sleep diaries kept by parents.

The study found that both forms of treatment were almost equally effective compared with wait-list control. Two-thirds of children initially were taking over 30 minutes to settle five or more times per week and waking at night for over 30 minutes four or more times per week. They improved on average to having such settling or night waking problems for only a few minutes or only once or twice per week ($H = 34.174$, $df = 2$, $p < 0.001$). These improvements were maintained after 6 months. It was known before the study began that these behavioral interventions are the most effective treatments available. This study assessed their effectiveness when delivered by booklet. The study used wait-list controls so that participants in the comparison group received an intervention after 6 weeks. This is known as a *crossover* design. In conclusion, it found that booklet-delivered behavioral treatments for sleep problems are likely to be as effective as face-to-face treatment for most children in this population.

In this example, the participants, interventions, key outcome measure, and comparison groups were clear and explicit. Social workers dealing with such children now have a cheap, simple intervention to offer parents. They can be sure that the results were unbiased and that both the booklet and face-to-face behavioral treatment are effective.

Cambridge-Somerville Youth Study

The Cambridge-Somerville Youth Study tested an intervention to reduce childhood delinquency (McCord, 1978). It was based on the theories of Richard Clark Cabot, a professor of clinical medicine and social ethics at Harvard University and president of the National Conference in Social Work. Cabot believed that childhood delinquency was related to poor home environments. He thought social workers could act as a positive force in the lives of children. Therefore, he designed an intervention to target at-risk boys under age 12; to avoid stigma, low-risk boys were included as well. Boys were matched in pairs; one in each pair was assigned to the treatment group on the basis of a coin toss. Recruitment began in 1935 and follow-up of 506 participants began in 1942.

Intervention

- Build close relationships and provide assistance to boys and their families.
- Provide counseling and referrals to specialists.
- Provide academic tutoring, participation in sports, and a woodwork shop operated by the study.
- Summer camp
- Families receive help with problems (e.g., illness and unemployment).

The program lasted until 1945, at which time boys in the intervention group had received about 24 annual visits for more than five years. By 1948, some surprising results had emerged. Court records found that more boys in the *treatment* group had been charged with a crime and had been charged with more offenses (264 vs. 218). In 1979, when the men were 47 years old, 248 men in the treatment group and 246 men in the control group were located. Most participants in the treatment group said the program had helped them by keeping them out of crime and off the streets. However, these participants were more likely to have been convicted of crimes indexed by the Federal Bureau of Investigation. They were more likely to have been diagnosed as alcoholic or to have a severe mental illness. They were more likely to have died. Furthermore, participants who received more of the intervention were more likely to have adverse outcomes (a *dose-response* relationship).

Several theories may explain why the study had such adverse effects. For example, the intervention may have increased unsupervised time with other delinquent children, increasing the chance that children would brag about delinquent behavior and encourage misbehavior. Though a rigorous evaluation showed the intervention had adverse effects, the Cambridge-Somerville Youth Study was a theoretically sound, well-planned intervention. It was led by experts, delivered by skilled practitioners, and carefully implemented. Although the intervention was well received by participants and their families, it clearly caused long-term harm. An RCT to test the effectiveness of this intervention may have prevented further harm to thousands of boys.

KEY FEATURES OF RANDOMIZED CONTROLLED TRIALS

Well-performed, large randomized trials are the best evidence of intervention effectiveness (Altman, 1991). They are better than any other study design at demonstrating causal relationships. All RCTs are *prospective*, that is, forward-looking, which is necessary for testing causal hypotheses. For A to cause B, A must happen before B. By following a group over time, RCTs can measure change in an outcome that can be attributed to the independent variable, the intervention (Hill, 1965).

Unlike studies using quasiexperimental methods (e.g., a one-group before-and-after comparison), RCTs offer a reliable *counterfactual* scenario. That is, the comparison group shows what would have happened to participants if they had been treated differently. Groups of participants in nonrandomized studies may differ due to *selection bias*. Imagine you want to know whether group therapy is helpful for heroin users. You could compare people in a group therapy program with other heroin users, but they would probably differ in several ways. For example, the people in group therapy might be more committed to change.

Randomization is the best way to eliminate differences between groups on known as well as *unknown* variables. Splitting a small group by chance could result in *unbalanced* groups, but as the number of participants increases,

randomization is increasingly likely to result in similar groups. To further reduce the likelihood of unbalanced groups, you could randomly assign subgroups (e.g., men and women) separately, thereby controlling a known variable while maintaining the benefits of randomization.

Splitting a study population by chance is the best way to eliminate *confounding variables*—variables other the intervention that may influence the results—and the effects of selection bias. Additionally, randomization makes it difficult to predict which group a person will join if they enroll in the trial. It may not be possible to blind clients and practitioners in social work; however, it is always possible to blind the assessors, the people who analyze the results.

Before they begin enrolling participants, researchers must state who will be included in an RCT. Researchers must specify the *inclusion criteria*, for example, the age and sex of participants and the problems (e.g., insomnia) they must have. Researchers must also specify the *exclusion criteria*, that is, the reasons a person would not be allowed to participate. For example, for ethical reasons a study of Internet-based therapy for depression might exclude participants who are actively suicidal. Ideally, researchers will select participants like those seen in clinical practice so that the results generalize to real-world settings. In summary, well-designed RCTs will possess the following features:

- Prospective, that is, forward-looking
- Minimal selection bias
- No confounding variables
- Control for known and unknown variables
- Explicit inclusion and exclusion criteria
- Allocation that can be concealed
- Researchers and assessors who can be blinded.

ARE RANDOMIZED TRIALS ETHICAL?

Many social workers believe that RCTs are unethical because (1) participants in one group may not receive an intervention, and (2) practitioners may not be able to offer what they think is the most effective intervention for a problem. These valid concerns apply to many types of research. On the other hand, well-intentioned interventions can have no effect, thereby wasting time and resources. Worse, they can cause harm, as in the Cambridge-Somerville Youth Study. Researchers and practitioners must balance ethical values to determine when RCTs are necessary and appropriate. RCTs may be justified when:

- It is unclear whether an intervention has positive effects.
- It is unknown whether one intervention works better than another.
- An intervention may cause harm (e.g., through unwanted side effects).
- The costs/benefits of an intervention are unknown.

Though we often have good reason to think a particular intervention will have positive effects, questions of treatment effectiveness can only be resolved through empirical investigation. If you developed a new intervention, you would start with a theory and design a strategy to achieve positive impacts for your clients. To be thorough, you would consider reasons the intervention might not work, ways it might harm participants, and whether the benefits would be worth the cost. Based on your knowledge of the problem, the available resources, and your client's characteristics and preferences, you would make a guess about the outcomes of your treatment. But how would you demonstrate that it worked? How would you know what would have happened if you had acted differently, or whether the burden on participants was worth the payoffs? Maybe another intervention would have been more efficient, thereby increasing resources to serve other clients.

Researchers refer to this uncertainly as *equipoise*, not knowing whether one thing is better than another. Randomized trials are the best way of resolving this uncertainty. They can show whether interventions have beneficial effects. Furthermore, RCTs can be designed to overcome many common ethical objections. For example, they can involve multiple treatment arms in which participants in *all* groups receive help. A trial might be designed to compare a new, untested intervention to *treatment-as-usual*, that is, the normal form of care (e.g., a social worker and the client choose an intervention). A wait-list comparison group is a common solution to ethical concerns whereby all participants receive the intervention sooner or

later. However, long-term comparisons between groups are impossible once everyone in the study has received the intervention.

Randomized trials should test interventions that match the goals and values of clients. To be ethically justified, they must resolve an important uncertainty about the effectiveness, safety, or relative benefits of an intervention.

UNDERSTANDING RANDOMIZED CONTROLLED TRIALS

As with any other study design, some RCTs will be better than others. Although there are many strengths to the method, not all RCTs are of high quality. Before using the results of a trial, you will need to assess the study's validity and applicability to your own situation (Fraser et al., 2009). Interventions being investigated should be described precisely. What use is a trial on an intervention if you do not have enough detail to replicate the intervention as it was conducted? This should include details about how the intervention was delivered (e.g., its frequency and duration). Often, study authors publish manuals of their interventions, and this information may be provided in a separate paper.

Interventions should be delivered in a replicable ways. You may think there is little point in having results from a study that cannot be used in everyday social work. With this in mind, the delivery of the intervention, the resources required, and the role of participants should be considered. Did the investigators check that the intention was delivered properly? Did the clients actively participate? For example, if a trial of cognitive-behavioral therapy showed that it does not work for depression, you might ask yourself whether all the therapists performed the same sort of treatment or whether the clients were able to attend all sessions (Montgomery et al., 2013).

The population under study needs to be well described so that the reader knows what sort of clients joined the study and which sort were excluded (Grant et al., 2013). If an intervention worked for people between 18 and 35 years of age, would you use it for an 85-year-old client? A precise description of the population is necessary for you to determine whether you can apply the study's results to your clients. The measures used in the study need to be clear. If meaningful, well-validated instruments are used, then the trial will be all the more useful. Often, objective measures are better than subjective questionnaires. For example, if you wanted to know whether an intervention for truant children improved school attendance, you would be interested in the number of days children attended school; you might be less interested, when assessing efficacy, in a trial measuring children's attitudes toward school.

Comparison groups should be realistic. If a new intervention is under study, it may be most useful to compare it to the usual form of care rather than to no intervention. Comparing an intervention to something that your clients would never receive does not provide useful information. The method by which study participants are randomized should be described. Even subconsciously, researchers can influence results. Methods of randomization should not be vulnerable to influence by the researcher. To ensure that selection bias does not confound the results of a trial, researchers should assign participants by pulling numbers from a hat, applying a computerized random number generator or some similar process. Assigning people by other means (e.g., alternating assignment) is *not* random and could introduce confounding variables. For instance, if randomization was done by giving participants who attended a social work clinic a particular intervention according to the day of the week, the effect of the intervention might be confused with the impact of different staff with varying levels of skill who work different days of the week. Furthermore, these methods make it difficult to maintain *allocation concealment* because one can predict a participant's assignment before enrolling the participant in the trial. To prevent this, a person unconnected to the trial should control the allocation of participants. For example, a statistician might generate a random number list. After a social worker assesses a potential trial participant, the social worker should call the statistician to find out his group assignment. To prevent bias at later stages, it may be important to blind people involved in the trial.

Finally, there should not be too many outcome measures. If researchers have too many, the chances of finding a positive result by chance will increase. That is to say, at a 5% significance level, 1 in 20 measures will be positive as a result of chance alone. For this reason, studies might have only one primary outcome and perhaps two or three secondary measures.

THE ANALYSIS OF RANDOMIZED CONTROLLED TRIALS

Figure 154.1 is a flow chart showing how the participants moved through the study by Montgomery, Stores, and Wiggs (2004). Note that all the children randomized at the beginning are included in the final analysis.

This is known as an *intention to treat analysis*. Other types of analyses might be called *completers only, per protocol*, or *available case*. The method chosen may influence results considerably. For example, if participants found an intervention unacceptable, they might drop out of a study. An analysis of completers would disguise the fact that the intervention was not acceptable for many participants. Therefore, researchers should account for all people randomized, including those who dropped out of the trial. You may observe that some researchers "carry forward" data from baseline (i.e., assume that nothing has changed) or assign mean values to missing cases (which may inflate the apparent benefits of an intervention). If a study does not account for participants who dropped out, you should consider what impact this could have had on the results.

Statistics

Most RCTs use statistical tests that compare two groups. They may also report some trends and correlations. Some of the more frequently used tests are shown in Table 154.1. It is important to think whether the researchers used the correct test to be certain of the results. Table 154.1 describes some statistical methods used to analyze RCTs.

HOW TO RECOGNIZE A GOOD RANDOMIZED CONTROLLED TRIAL

Asking the following questions when considering a randomized trial will help assess its quality.

Was the Study Valid?

Think about the similarity of the groups. Was the intervention the only thing that was different? Aside from the intervention, were the two groups treated in the same way? Were outcomes influenced by biased assessment? Was allocation concealed, and were people blinded as required? Did everyone in the intervention

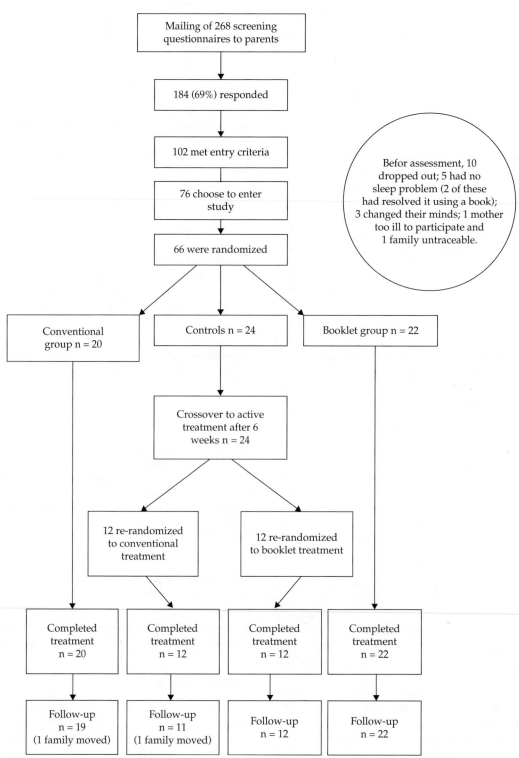

Figure 154.1 Flow of participants through the study.

group receive the intervention, and did anybody in the comparison group receive the intervention (this is sometimes called *contamination*)? Could missing data and dropout have influenced the results? Were the outcomes, measures, and analyses selected in advance and reported completely? Was the trial registered in advance (e.g., with ClinicalTrials.gov) and if so, did the researchers report results as intended (Higgins & Green, 2011)?

What Were the Results?

How large was the effect? Is this *clinically significant* (i.e., would this change be meaningful to one of your clients)? Was it statistically significant, or could it have been the result of chance? Look for statistical tests like standard deviations and confidence intervals. If these are large, which is common in the case of small trials, this may lead you to conclude that individual differences between participants are

TABLE 154.1 Frequently Used Statistical Tests

Parametric Test	Nonparametric Test Version	Purpose of Test	Example
Two-sample (unpaired) *t* test	Mann-Whitney U test	Compares two independent samples drawn from the same population	To compare the group that received the booklet with those who were in the control group
One-sample (paired) *t* test	Wilcoxon matched pairs test	Compares two sets of observations on a single sample	To compare sleep duration within one group before and after intervention
One-way analysis of variance (*F* test) using total sum of squares	Kruskall-Wallis analysis of variance by ranks	Effectively, a generalization of the paired *t* or Wilcoxon matched pairs test where three or more sets of observations are made on a single sample	To compare more than two observations, for example, booklet versus face-to-face versus control
Two-way analysis of variance	Two-way analysis of variance by ranks	As above, but tests the influence (and interaction) of two different covariates	In the above example, to determine if the results differ in girls versus boys
	Fisher's exact test	Tests the *null hypothesis* that the distribution of a discontinuous variable is the same in two (or more) independent samples	To assess whether the responders to an intervention were from a particular subgroup, for example, a particular ethnicity
Correlation coefficient (Pearson's *r*)	Spearman's rank correlation coefficient (rσ)	Assesses the strength of the straight line association between two continuous variables	To assess whether sleep duration correlates with severity of learning disability

substantial, in which case the intervention may not be reliable.

Are the Results of This Trial Useful for My Clients?

To assess the *generalizability* of the study, consider the degree to which your clients are like those in the trial. Did the trial include everyone who might benefit from the intervention? Did it exclude people with the characteristics and problems you see in your practice? Was the setting similar to your setting? Could you perform this intervention or afford this intervention? Consider whether the measures reported are what you are really interested in knowing. Remember RCTs are about groups, and their results may not apply directly to your client (this is called the *ecological fallacy*).

CONCLUSION

RCTs are the strongest form of experimental evidence in intervention studies. They should be preferred over other comparison studies because they minimize bias and eliminate confounding factors of all kinds, known and unknown. Ethical concerns can be addressed in a number of ways (Sheldon & MacDonald, 2006). If more RCTs can be performed in social work, the field will have a much stronger evidence base to ensure that effective interventions are delivered without harming clients and that the benefits of this work outweigh its costs.

WEBSITES

ClinicalTrials.gov, National Institutes of Health. http://clinicaltrials.gov.

CONSORT Statement—Up-to-date versions of which are best accessed via. http://www.equator-network.org.

Critical Appraisal Skills Programme, Making Sense of Evidence. http://www.phru.nhs.uk/Doc_Links/rct%20appraisal%20tool.pdf.

References

Altman, D. G. (1991). Randomisation [Editorial]. *British Medical Journal, 302,* 1481–1482.

Boruch, R. F. (Ed.). (2005). Place randomized trials: Special issue. *Annals of the American Academy of Political and Social Sciences, 598.*

Fraser M. W., Richman J. M., Galinsky M. J., & Day S. H. (2009). *Intervention research.* Oxford: Oxford University Press.

Grant, S. P., Mayo-Wilson, E., Melendez-Torres, G., Montgomery, P. (2013). Reporting quality of randomised trials in behavioural and psychological journals. *PLoS ONE, 8*(5), e65442.

Higgins J. P., & Green S. (2011) *Cochrane Handbook for Systematic Reviews of Interventions. Version 5.1.0* (updated March 2011). The Cochrane Collaboration.

Hill, A. B. (1965). The environment and disease: Association or causation?" *Proceedings of the Royal Society of Medicine, 58,* 295–300.

McCord, J. (1978). A thirty-year follow-up of treatment effects. *American Psychologist, 33,* 284–289.

Montgomery, P., Stores, G., & Wiggs, L. (2004). The relative efficacy of two brief treatments for sleep problems in young learning disabled (mentally retarded) children: A randomised controlled trial. *Archives of Disease in Childhood, 89,* 125–130.

Montgomery P., Underhill K., Operario D., Gardner F., & Mayo-Wilson, E. (2013). The Oxford Implementation Index: A new tool for incorporating implementation data into systematic reviews and meta-analyses. *Journal of Clinical Epidemiology, 66,* 874–882.

Sheldon, B., & MacDonald, G. (2006). *Rethinking social work.* London: Routledge.

155 Meta-analysis and Evidence-based Practice

Jacqueline Corcoran & Julia H. Littell

Evidence-based practice (EBP) is defined as the integration of the best available research evidence with clinical expertise and client values to make informed decisions in individual cases. Systematic reviews and meta-analyses can contribute to the evidence base for social work practice and policy by providing thorough and unbiased summaries of empirical research. (See Littell, Corcoran, & Pillai, 2008, for an elaboration of points made in this chapter.)

Meta-analysis is the quantitative synthesis of data from multiple studies. It uses statistical methods to estimate average effects across studies, identify differences between studies, and suggest possible explanations for those differences.

How does meta-analysis differ from systematic review? A systematic review aims to comprehensively locate and synthesize the research literature that bears on a particular question. If results lend themselves to the synthesis of findings from two or more primary studies, then a systematic review can include meta-analysis, the focus of this chapter.

Meta-analyses offer many advantages over other methods of summarizing results of quantitative studies, including:

- Better estimates of population parameters (more accurate representation of phenomena in the population of interest)
- Ability to assess multiple outcomes (a separate meta-analysis can be conducted for each relevant outcome domain when data are available)
- Systematic accounts for moderators (participant, treatment, or study design characteristics) that influence outcomes

- Tests and adjustments for biases that can be introduced by small samples and publication processes.

Meta-analyses have disadvantages as well.

- They cannot make up for poor quality in the original studies.
- Combining results across different types of studies, treatments, samples, settings, and/or outcomes is not always appropriate.
- Meta-analysis relies on effect sizes, which are not easily understood by many people.

Many of the disadvantages can be eliminated or minimized through correct applications of meta-analytic procedures. These procedures are explained in more detail in Littell et al. (2008), Lipsey and Wilson (2001), and Petticrew and Roberts (2006).

EFFECT SIZES

The ability to synthesize studies is informed by converting the results of original studies to common metrics, called effect sizes, which are then combined across studies. An *effect size* (ES) is a measure of the strength (magnitude) and direction of a relationship between variables. The choice of ES measures is influenced by the purpose and design of a study and the format of the data. Most ES metrics fall into three main categories, related to proportions (univariate proportions or averages can be derived from multiple studies), correlation coefficients (studies that assess relationships between variables without inferring causal directions are likely to report measures of association), and means. Studies that test intervention effects and other kinds of causal inferences typically report differences (e.g., between treated and untreated groups) in terms of proportions or average scores.

The *standardized mean difference* (SMD) is useful when scores are reported in different ways or different scales are used to assess the same construct. The SMD, also known as Cohen's *d* (Cohen, 1988), is the mean difference divided by the pooled standard deviation of the two groups. The SMD is probably the most well-known ES.

For dichotomous data (received a certain screening or not), the most commonly used ES measures are the *odds ratio* (OR) and the *risk ratio* (RR). *Odds* refer to the chance that something will happen compared to the chance that it will not. *Risks* are probabilities.

Although effect size provides a crucial index of the average effect within and across studies, it is not easily understood by many people. Therefore, an ES can be translated into metrics that have meaning for clinicians and policy makers. For example, dichotomous data can easily be converted from risks to percentages. Cohen (1988) also proposed standards for interpreting OR, SMD, and correlation coefficients.

META-ANALYTIC METHODS IN BRIEF

In meta-analysis, effect sizes from individual studies are presented, along with their confidence intervals, in graphs called Forest plots. The confidence intervals give us a "margin of error" for each ES and tell us whether the ES is statistically significant (if the confidence interval includes the region of no difference, the effect is not significant).

Study effect sizes are then pooled (averaged) together using weighting procedures that allow more precise effect sizes, as well as those from larger studies, to make a greater contribution to the overall average than results that are less precise (including results of smaller studies). These procedures are called inverse variance weighting. There are several ways to do this. Some meta-analyses assume that all studies are estimating the same population effect size; others do not make this assumption. The former use "fixed effect" models, the latter use "random effects."

Meta-analysts can compute effect sizes for subgroups of interest (e.g., separate effects for girls and for boys) and test to see whether differences between subgroups are significant (using moderator analysis). They can assess the influence of decisions made during the review process (using sensitivity analysis) and can assess and adjust for the influence of publication bias and small sample bias on results.

IMPLICATIONS FOR PRACTITIONERS

Practitioners should be able to locate and understand a publication on meta-analysis because it can summarize a whole body of knowledge on a certain topic of interest. As with systematic reviews, the first places to look for meta-analyses are the online libraries maintained by the nonprofit Cochrane Collaboration and Campbell Collaboration. The Cochrane Collaboration synthesizes results of studies on effects of interventions in health care, and the Campbell Collaboration synthesizes results of research on interventions in the fields of social welfare, education, criminal justice, and international development. Both the Cochrane and the Campbell Collaborations produce systematic reviews and meta-analyses (when there are enough studies) to inform decisions about health and social programs and policies. These are usually the best places to search because their meta-analyses tend to be high quality. However, these databases do not have reviews on every possible topic. Therefore, it may be necessary to search library databases, such as PsycINFO and Medline/PubMed, running key words related to the topic with "meta-analysis."

The methodology and the statistics of meta-analysis can become quite complex, so the lay reader should probably look to the "plain language summaries" of the Cochrane Collaboration, the synopsis and the abstract of the Campbell Collaboration, and the abstract and discussion sections of articles on meta-analysis. In order to understand some of the essential elements that comprise meta-analysis, we will provide a summary of two meta-analyses that have relevance to practitioners (see Table 155.1).

CONCLUSION

Meta-analysis can be used to synthesize information on many topics that are important for social work practice and social policy. Because meta-analysis is time-consuming and requires trained discipline, it is not likely to be conducted

TABLE 155.1 Sample Summaries of Meta-Analyses

Author and Purpose	Inclusion Criteria	Sample	Results
Lipsey, Landenberger, & Wilson (2007). To systematically review the effectiveness of cognitive behavioral therapy (CBT) treatment with criminal offenders in terms of reoffending. A secondary purpose was to examine moderators that influenced variation in effect size.	*Participants*: "criminal offenders, either juveniles or adults, treated while on probation, incarcerated, institutionalized, or during aftercare/parole" (p. 7). *Intervention*: Cognitive-behavioral treatment. *Designs*: Randomized or matched nonrandomized group designs that compared CBT to a non-CBT condition. *Studies*: Published and unpublished studies from any country and written in any language *Outcome*: Criminal offending after treatment Years included: 1965 to 2005	$N = 58$ studies met inclusion criteria. More adult than juvenile samples; treatment was typically less than 20 weeks; 50% of the studies involved incarcerated participants; predominantly male samples; treatment providers tended to evidence little mental health background and received minimal training.	CBT programs resulted in a 25% decrease in offending recidivism over control conditions. No differences between adult and juveniles in terms of outcomes. Programs that were implemented well and offered critical elements of CBT (anger control and interpersonal problem solving) showed more positive effects. People who are at higher risk to reoffend did better as a result of CBT than low-risk offenders.
Wilson & Lipsey (2006) examined the effectiveness of social information processing programs implemented in the school setting for youth identified with anger and behavior problems. Social information processing programs are a type of cognitive-behavioral treatment.	*Participants*: School-aged children (kindergarten through 12th grade) selected for intervention because of behavioral problems or for risk factors associated with behavioral problems (such as high activity). *Interventions*: Focus on social information processing. *Designs*: Randomized and matched nonrandomized designs with a control group (defined as no-treatment, wait-list, or treatment-as-usual, not another treatment). *Studies*: Any country, both published and unpublished studies. *Outcome*: Behavior or externalizing problems.	$N = 47$ studies 90% published in United States, mostly male samples, 40% with low socioeconomic status (SES) samples, 45% of studies comprised children 9–11 years, mainly group-based interventions	Participants in social information processing treatment evidenced fewer aggressive/behavioral problems after treatment compared with controls. Moderator analysis: children who were already showing problems did better than those who were at risk for problems; children in special education settings showed less improvement than others; groups were more effective than one-on-one interventions; longer programs and those that were better implemented had better outcomes.

by practitioners or policy makers. However, the information gleaned from meta-analysis can be a tremendous contribution to consumers, practitioners, and policy makers who want to use accurate assessments of current knowledge to inform their choices. Meta-analysis can minimize sampling error and bias in attempts to synthesize the growing body of empirical research relevant to social work. Thus, it has an important role in the development of knowledge for human services.

WEBSITES

Campbell Collaboration. http://www .campbellcollaboration.org.

Cochrane Collaboration. http://www .cochrane.org.

Database of Abstracts of Reviews of Effect (DARE). http://www.york.ac.uk/inst/crd/ crddatabases.htm.

References

Cohen, J. (1988). *Statistical power analysis for the behavioral sciences* (2nd ed.). Hillsdale, NJ: Lawrence Erlbaum Associates.

Lipsey, M., Landenberger, N., & Wilson, S. J. (2007). *Effects of cognitive-behavioral programs for criminal offenders.* Campbell Collaboration Library. Retrieved from http://www.campbellcollaboration. org/doc-pdf/lipsey_CBT_finalreview .pdf.

Lipsey, M. W., & Wilson, D. B. (2001). *Practical meta-analysis.* Thousand Oaks, CA: Sage.

Littell, J. H., Corcoran, J., & Pillai, V. (2008). *Systematic reviews and meta-analysis.* New York, NY: Oxford University Press.

Petticrew, M., & Roberts, H. (2006). *Systematic reviews in the social sciences: A practical guide.* Oxford: Blackwell.

Wilson, S. J., & Lipsey, M. W. (2006). *School-based social information processing interventions and aggressive behavior for pull out programs (part 2).* Retrieved from http://www.campbellcollaboration. org/docpdf/wilson_socinfoprocpull_review.pdf.

156 Systematic Reviews and Evidence-based Practice

Julia H. Littell & Jacqueline Corcoran

Systematic reviews can contribute to the evidence base for social work practice and policy by providing thorough and unbiased summaries of empirical research. A systematic review aims to comprehensively locate, critically appraise, and synthesize results of empirical research that bears on a particular question. If results lend themselves to a statistical synthesis, then a systematic review can also include meta-analysis.

Gibbs (2003) and others have shown practitioners how to find, critically appraise, and use empirical evidence to inform practice. "Ideally, practitioners should be able to rely on reviewers to isolate the best evidence for them and to distill it

for its essence to guide practice decision-making. Unfortunately, conventional reviews have fallen far short of such expectations" (Gibbs, 2003, p. 153). Traditional research reviews are often "haphazard" (Petticrew & Roberts, 2006). They tend to rely on convenient samples of published studies and unclear methods of assessment and synthesis; as a result, they are vulnerable to biases of researchers, reviewers, and publication and dissemination processes (Littell, 2008). Unfortunately, many lists of "evidence-based practices" are based on traditional review methods. Because practitioners and policymakers rarely have the time to locate and critically appraise original studies themselves, unbiased reviews of empirical research are needed to provide reliable summaries of evidence for practice and policy.

Systematic reviews are designed to compensate for the weaknesses of traditional reviews of research. Systematic reviews can provide transparent, comprehensive, and unbiased analyses and summaries of available research on a particular topic that is relevant for social work practice and social policy.

The phrase "systematic review" connotes a scientific approach to every step in the review process, combined with the use of specific methods to minimize bias and error. Unfortunately, this term has been used rather loosely in the social work and social science literature. So-called systematic reviews vary in quality and credibility. Therefore, it is important for practitioners to understand what systematic reviews are and how to evaluate them.

In this chapter, we describe the steps in the systematic review process. We consider different types of systematic reviews and provide examples. Finally, we offer suggestions for finding systematic reviews and guidelines for evaluating them.

STEPS IN A SYSTEMATIC REVIEW

Systematic reviews are observational studies that follow the basic steps of the research process. These steps include problem formulation and planning, sampling, data collection, data analysis, interpretation, and presentation of results (Cooper & Hedges, 1994). In a systematic review, previous studies are identified and analyzed. Specific steps in a systematic review are listed next.

1. Problem formulation and planning
   - Develop a set of clearly formulated objectives and specific, answerable research questions or hypotheses.
   - Form a review team with the necessary substantive, methodological, and technical expertise.
   - Create explicit inclusion and exclusion criteria that specify the problems or conditions, populations, interventions, settings, comparisons, outcomes, and study designs that will and will not be included in the review.
   - Develop a written *protocol* that details in advance the procedures and methods to be used.

2. Sampling: Identification and selection of relevant studies
   - In collaboration with information specialists, identify and implement a comprehensive and reproducible strategy to identify all relevant studies. This includes strategies to find unpublished studies.
   - At least two reviewers screen titles and abstracts to identify potentially relevant studies.
   - Retrieve published and unpublished reports on potentially relevant studies.
   - Determine whether each study meets the review's eligibility criteria. Two reviewers judge each study, resolve disagreements (sometimes with a third reviewer), and document their decisions.

3. Data collection
   - Reliably extract data from eligible studies onto standardized forms. Assess inter-rater reliability, resolve disagreements, and document decisions.

4. Data analysis
   - Describe key features of included studies (in a narrative, tables, and/or graphs).
   - Systematically and critically appraise the qualities of included studies.
   - When possible, present study results in effect size metrics, with 95% confidence intervals.
   - If a systematic review lends itself to combining quantitative results of two or more primary studies, then it can (and often should) include meta-analysis.

5. Interpretation and presentation of results

Interested readers can find detailed explanations of these steps and the procedures and methods used in systematic review elsewhere (see Cooper & Hedges, 1994; Higgins & Green, 2006; Littell, Corcoran, & Pillai, 2008; Petticrew & Roberts, 2006).

TYPES OF SYSTEMATIC REVIEWS AND EXAMPLES

Any question or topic that can be addressed with empirical research methods can also be the subject of a systematic review of prior studies. To date, most systematic reviews have focused on effects of health care and social interventions. These reviews tend to include randomized controlled trials (RCTs) when those studies are available, because they usually provide the most credible evidence of intervention effects. The Cochrane Collaboration has produced approximately 3,000 systematic reviews of RCTs on effects of health care interventions, including pharmacological, medical, and psychosocial treatments for HIV/AIDS, mental health, substance abuse, and related medical and social problems.

Some systematic reviews include other types of studies, either in addition to or instead of RCTs. This is because other study designs can sometimes provide credible evidence of effects or because the reviewers may be interested in other kinds of questions. Systematic reviews produced by the Campbell Collaboration focus on effects of interventions in social care (education, crime and justice, and social welfare), and they include RCTS as well as other study designs. Topics that have been covered include effects of interventions aimed at preventing teenage pregnancy, welfare-to-work initiatives, cognitive-behavioral therapies for specific conditions, after-school programs, volunteer tutoring programs, drug treatment programs, parent training, and so forth.

Creative synthesis of qualitative data from naturalistic studies has begun, sometimes in combination with systematic reviews of studies of intervention effects. For example, staff of the Evidence for Policy and Practice Information Centre (EPPI) Centre in London produced a mixed-methods synthesis that includes a systematic review of RCTs on effects of interventions aimed at improving children's healthy eating habits, along with a "views analysis" (content analysis) of themes that emerged from naturalistic studies of children's views of health and eating (Thomas et al., 2004). This approach provides information about intervention effects and the views of those who are the targets of these interventions.

Systematic reviews also have been used to synthesize observational studies anepidemiological data on the incidence and prevalence of various conditions. New methods are being developed to combine results of studies on the diagnostic and prognostic performance of assessment tests. For example, Aron Shlonsky and colleagues at the University of Toronto Faculty of Social Work have embarked on a Campbell review of the predictive validity of instruments that are used to assess the risk of child maltreatment.

Sometimes systematic reviews turn out to be "empty"—that is, reviewers could not find any studies that met their inclusion criteria. The Cochrane Collaboration published such empty reviews because they provide useful information on current gaps in knowledge. This information has been used to set funding priorities for further research, especially in the United Kingdom.

FINDING SYSTEMATIC REVIEWS

The best systematic reviews can be found in online libraries (or databases) that have been developed and maintained by organizations devoted to the production and dissemination of rigorous, unbiased reviews. These groups provide free access to systematic reviews (or to their abstracts) on the Web. As mentioned, the Cochrane Collaboration produces and disseminates systematic reviews of interventions in health care. The Cochrane Database of Systematic Reviews is available online. The Campbell Collaboration synthesizes results of research on interventions in the fields of social welfare, education, criminal justice, and social development. The Campbell Library is also on the Web. The Centre for Reviews and Dissemination (CRD) at York maintains a large database of systematic reviews on a variety of topics in health and social care. Although the CRD databases include reviews that vary in quality, CRD staff members have provided some appraisal of the quality of most of these reviews.

If these sources do not contain reviews on topics of interest, it may be necessary to search regular bibliographic databases, such as PsycINFO and Medline/PubMed, running keywords related to the topic with "systematic review." These sources will produce reviews of varying quality.

The Cochrane Collaboration and other organizations provide useful plain-language summaries of systematic reviews. When such summaries are not available, readers should find useful information in abstract and discussion sections of reports on systematic reviews.

EVALUATING SYSTEMATIC REVIEWS

Systematic reviews can provide practitioners with useful summaries of large (or small) bodies of research. However, some systematic reviews are more thorough and careful than others. Because there are variations in the quality—and credibility—of systematic reviews, practitioners should know how to appraise systematic reviews critically.

Guidelines and standards for systematic reviews have been developed by the Cochrane Collaboration, the Campbell Collaboration, and others. To the extent possible, these guidelines are based on evidence about features of the research and review processes that minimize bias and error. Building on available guidelines and evidence, Shea and colleagues (2007) developed a checklist for assessing the qualities of systematic reviews (AMSTAR). An adapted version of this checklist is shown in Table 156.1. This includes questions that readers should ask in evaluating the quality of a systematic review.

As shown in Table 156.1, systematic reviews should follow predetermined protocols. They should be based on independent judgments

TABLE 156.1 Assessing the Quality of Systematic Reviews

1. Was a protocol developed in advance?
The research question and inclusion criteria should be established before the conduct of the review.

2. Was there duplicate study selection and data extraction?
There should be at least two independent data extractors, and a consensus procedure for disagreements should be in place.

3. Was a comprehensive literature search performed?
At least two electronic sources should be searched. The report must include years and databases used. Keywords must be stated, and where feasible the search strategy should be provided. All searches should be supplemented by consulting current contents, reviews, textbooks, specialized registers, or experts in the particular field of study, and by reviewing the references in the studies found.

4. Was the status of publication (i.e., gray literature) used as an inclusion criterion?
The authors should state that they searched for reports regardless of their publication type. The authors should state whether they excluded any reports (from the systematic review), based on their publication status, language, etc.

5. Was a list of studies (included and excluded) provided?
A list of included and excluded studies should be provided.

6. Were the characteristics of the included studies provided?
In an aggregated form such as a table, data from the original studies should be provided on the participants, interventions, and outcomes. The ranges of characteristics in all the studies analyzed (e.g., age, race, sex, relevant socioeconomic data, disease status, duration, severity, or other conditions) should be reported.

7. Was the scientific quality of the included studies assessed and documented?
A priori methods of quality assessment should be developed and followed. Multiple questions or items about possible sources and types of bias are preferred to overall quality rating scales.

8. Was the scientific quality of the included studies used appropriately in formulating conclusions?
The results of the methodological rigor and scientific quality should be considered in the analysis and the conclusions of the review and explicitly stated in formulating recommendations.

9. Were appropriate methods used to combine the findings of studies?
For the pooled results, a test should be done to ensure the studies were combinable, to assess their homogeneity. If heterogeneity exists, a random effects model should be used and/or the clinical appropriateness of combining should be taken into consideration (i.e., is it sensible to combine?).

10. Was the likelihood of publication bias assessed?
An assessment of publication bias should include a combination of graphical aids (e.g., funnel plot, other available tests) and/or statistical tests.

11. Was the conflict of interest stated?
Potential sources of support should be clearly acknowledged in both the systematic review and the included studies.

Source: Adapted from Shea et al., 2007.

(from multiple raters) on key decisions, such as study eligibility and coding; use comprehensive searches that include efforts to find relevant unpublished studies; identify studies that were included and excluded; describe included studies; assess the scientific quality of included studies and use this assessment in evaluating study results; use appropriate methods for combining results across studies; assess the potential effects of publication bias on results; and report funding sources and conflicts of interest.

CONCLUSION

Systematic reviews can provide comprehensive, unbiased summaries of research on many topics that are important for social work practice and social policy. These reviews aim to minimize error and bias and critically appraise the quality of available studies. They are very labor-intensive, but can produce more reliable information than traditional narrative reviews of research. Social work practitioners and policy makers will find the information from systematic reviews useful for making decisions about how best to help clients with the resources available.

WEBSITES

Campbell Collaboration. http://www .campbellcollaboration.org.
Centre for Reviews and Dissemination at the University of York. http://www.york.ac.uk/ inst/crd/crddatabases.htm.
Cochrane Collaboration. http://www.cochrane .org.
EPPI Centre. http://eppi.ioe.ac.uk/cms.

Guidelines for assessing systematic reviews (AMSTAR, Assessment of Multiple Systematic Reviews). http://www.biomed-central.com/content/supplementary/1471-2288-7-10-S1.doc.

References

Cooper, H., & Hedges, L. V. (1994). *The handbook of research synthesis.* New York, NY: Sage.
Gibbs, L. E. (2003). *Evidence-based practice for the helping professions: A practical guide with integrated multimedia.* Pacific Grove, CA: Brooks/ Cole-Thompson Learning.
Higgins, J. P. T., & Green, S. (Eds.). (2006). *Cochrane handbook for systematic reviews of interventions.* Chichester, UK: Wiley. Retrieved from http://www.cochrane.org/resources/handbook.
Littell, J. H. (2008). How do we know what works? The quality of published reviews of evidence-based practices. In D. Lindsey & A. Shlonsky (Eds.), *Child welfare research: Advances for practice and policy* (pp. 66–93). New York, NY: Oxford University Press.
Littell, J. H., Corcoran, J., & Pillai, V. (2008). *Systematic reviews and meta-analysis.* New York, NY: Oxford University Press.
Petticrew, M., & Roberts, H. (2006). *Systematic reviews in the social sciences: A practical guide.* Oxford: Blackwell.
Shea, B. J., Grimshaw, J. M., Wells, G. A., Boers, M., Andersson, N., Hamel, C., Porter, A. C., , Tugwell, P., , Moher, D. & Bouter, L. M. (2007). Development of AMSTAR: A measurement tool to assess the methodological quality of systematic reviews. *BMC Medical Research Methodology,* 7. Retrieved from http://www.biomedcentral. com/1471-2288/7/10.
Thomas, J., Harden, A., Oakley, A., Oliver, S., Sutcliffe, K., Rees, R., Brunton, G. & Kavanagh, J.(2004). Integrating qualitative research with trials in systematic reviews. *British Medical Journal, 328,* 1010–1012.

157 Qualitative Research and Evidence-based Practice

Michael Saini & Rory Crath

INTRODUCTION

The evidence-based practice (EBP) decision-making process of integrating the best available evidence with client circumstances and preferences (Sackett et al., 1996; Straus et al., 2011) has gained recognition across professional fields of practice, and specifically within social work (Shlonsky & Gibbs, 2004). Despite the popularity of EBP, however, Thyer (2013) notes that there continues to be frequent misrepresentation and distortion in how EBP is described in the social work literature. There is perhaps no better example than the omission of qualitative studies within widely accepted classification of evidence (Shuval, Harker, Roudsari, Groce, Mills et al., 2011) or the consideration of qualitative studies as the lowest level of evidence, alongside expert opinions (Ebell, Siwek, Weiss, Wolf, Susman et al., 2004).

Misconceptions about the use and application of the evidence-based pyramids and hierarchies of evidence (Sackett, Rosenberg & Gray, 2006; Straus et al., 2011) have led to a limited view of research designs to inform practice by equating the strength of methods based solely on the ability to inform causal pathways of clinical outcomes post interventions (Ramchandani, Joughin, & Zwi, 2001). Indeed, randomized controlled trials (RCTs) and other highly controlled studies are superior for examining the efficacy or effectiveness of interventions because such designs have fewer threats to internal validity, thus providing the best evidence to make causal assertions about the impact of the intervention on selected clinical outcomes (Petticrew & Roberts, 2006). This does not suggest, however, that practice and policy decisions should be based solely on evidence produced by RCTs. There remains a paucity of RCTs in the social work literature and shortage of evidence to support many widely practiced social work interventions that cannot easily be quantitatively evaluated. There are serious gaps in indiscriminately applying RCTs to answer evidence-based questions that are not directly related to the absolute effect of an intervention (Saini & Shlonsky, 2012), given that many research questions are not amenable to research designs involving RCTs (Lewin, Glenton, & Oxman, 2009).

Despite the immense growth of qualitative studies in social work and related disciplines, findings from qualitative studies have remained largely invisible within the EBP discourse. Consequently, qualitative studies have had little influence on clinical and policy decision-making (Finfgeld-Connett, 2010; Pope & Mays, 2009). Recent shifts, however, have focused on increased attention to the potential benefits of including qualitative research within discussions about EBP. There is also a growing enthusiasm to explore ways in which qualitative research can both complement and expand findings derived from quantitative methods. Case in point, in the newest edition of the evidence-based medicine (EBM) textbook, Straus et al. (2011) not only recognize the unique contribution of qualitative research within evidence-based medicine but further opine that "qualitative research can help us to understand clinical phenomena with emphasis on understanding the experiences and values of our patients" (p. 110). The symbolic departure from targeting qualitative research as the "second class science" (Shuval et al., 2011, pg. 1) helps to move discussion into thinking about ways that qualitative research can help clinicians apply EBP principles of "integrating individual practice expertise with the *best available external evidence* [emphasis added] from systematic research, as well as considering the values and expectations of clients" (Gambrill, 1999, p. 346). By accepting a broader definition of evidence, other forms of valuable knowledge, such as experiences derived from qualitative studies and practice wisdom, can have equal importance, or even greater relevance, depending on the type of question being asked within the EBP process.

Integrating qualitative studies within EBP is timely for social work, because the development and dissemination of qualitative studies has become widespread in social work journals, and at social work annual conferences, including the Society for Social Work and Research (SSWR) and the Council on Social Work Education (CSWE) (Padgett, 2009). Between 1990 and 2002, the percent of qualitative studies in Social Work Abstracts rose from a mere 0.21% to 4.0%, a 20-fold increase, and similar increases were seen in Social Services Abstracts (Shlonsky & Gibbs, 2004). Attention to qualitative research is also growing across allied professions. Shuval et al. (2011), for example, found a 2.9% absolute increase and 3.4-fold relative increase in qualitative research publications occurring over a 10-year period in 64 journals of general medicine (1.2% in 1998 vs. 4.1% in 2007).

OVERVIEW OF QUALITATIVE RESEARCH

Qualitative research has a long and vibrant tradition in the social sciences that "fundamentally depends on watching people in their own territory and interacting with them in their own language, on their own terms" (Kirk & Miller, 1986, p. 9). There is no "one size fits all" (Padgett, 2008, p. 1) because there is an array of perspectives on the precise focus of, and techniques for, conducting qualitative research. Qualitative research is best described as an umbrella of research methods (Denzin & Lincoln, 1994) with varying epistemologies and philosophical frameworks. There are several types of qualitative methods, including *phenomenology* (an approach to search for the essence or the central underlying meaning of the experience), *ethnography* (a set of strategies for describing and interpreting cultures and cultural phenomena), *grounded theory* (a method

used to generate or discover a theory, an abstract schema that relates to a particular phenomenon), *case study* (an in-depth picture of a "bounded system" or a case by using documents, archival records, interviews, and observations) and participant action research (a self-conscious way of empowering people to take effective action toward improving conditions in their lives). This is far from an exhaustive list, but the intent is to provide a general sense of the various approaches for conducting qualitative research.

Common to most approaches, there is a general tendency to focus on naturalistic inquiry, a reliance on the researcher as the instrument for data collection and interpretation with an emphasis on narratives over numbers (Royse, Thyer, Padgett, & Logan, 2006, p. 88). Qualitative research helps to draw out meanings of particular activities, helps to interpret beliefs within naturalistic and contextualized systems (Padgett, 1998), and assists in exploring the subtleties, complexities, and cultural meanings of activities, events, and singularities being considered to understand subjective perspectives (Valadez & Bamberger, 1994). This practice of research turns the world into a series of representations including field notes, interviews, conversations, photographs, recordings, and memos to the self (Denzin & Lincoln, 2000). In summary, qualitative research seeks to understand constructed meaning and perspectives by seeking to interpret, illuminate, illustrate, and explore meaning, context, unanticipated phenomena, process, opinions, attitudes, and actions (Saini & Shlonsky, 2012).

QUALITATIVE QUESTIONS FOR EVIDENCE-BASED PRACTICE

Qualitative research "enables researchers to ask new questions, answer different kinds of questions, and readdress old questions" (Fetterman, 1988, p. 17). Such questions are useful when traditional quantitative methods are inadequate for understanding the complexity of a problem, or when researchers do not have adequate information about the context and structures related to a given social phenomenon.

Qualitative research is also suitable to answer questions that explore a topic about which little is known; pursues questions that may be too sensitive (emotionally, culturally, etc.); explores the "lived experience" of those in a particular situation; and helps the researcher develop a trusting

TABLE 157.1 Including Qualitative Studies Alongside Randomized Controlled Trials (Lewin et al., 2009)

Steps in Randomized Controlled Trials	Integration of Qualitative Studies
Before a trial	• To explore issues related to the question of interest or context of the research • To generate hypotheses for examination in the randomized controlled trial • To develop and refine the intervention • To develop or select appropriate outcome measures
During a trial	• To examine whether the intervention was delivered as intended, including describing the intervention as delivered • To "unpack" processes of implementation and change • To explore deliverers' and recipients' responses to the intervention
After a trial	• To explore reasons for the findings of the trial • To explain variations in effectiveness within the sample • To examine the appropriateness of the underlying theory • To generate further questions or hypotheses

relationship with the participants to gain an inside view of the phenomena (Padgett, 2008).

Questions relevant to qualitative designs also can be integrated with quantitative methods that seek to describe whether interventions "work," by focusing on "why" interventions work (or do not work) and the influence these interventions may have (or may not have) on clients using the interventions. Adapted from Lewin et al. (2009), Table 157.1 displays the types of questions that qualitative studies can address when integrating qualitative evidence with experimental designs.

Qualitative research can also be the primary source of data to answer questions that do not focus solely on efficacy or effectiveness (Gough & Elbourne, 2002) but, instead, focus on the richly described perceptions of clients, including the perceived needs of clients, their experiences of receiving social work services, and the process that clients go through to access services (Popay, Rogers, & Williams, 1998).

SEARCHING FOR QUALITATIVE STUDIES

One of the major barriers to integrating qualitative research within EBP has been the challenge of locating and retrieving qualitative studies from the electronic databases (Wilczynski & Haynes, 2002). Without clear guidelines for locating and retrieving qualitative studies, there is a risk of

including qualitative studies using haphazard methods rather than careful systematic methods for information retrieval and screening. Some of these challenges include the variability of qualitative methods, the spread of qualitative studies across journals, nonspecific qualitative titles and abstracts, deficiencies in bibliographic indexes, lack of expertise in locating qualitative research, and the lack of evidence about the best ways to locate qualitative research.

The Variability of Qualitative Methods

As stated earlier, qualitative research encompasses a variety of methods and approaches (including ethnography, phenomenology, grounded theory, and discourse analysis), which leads to difficulties in locating qualitative research using common search terms to locate studies based on their methodologies (Evans, 2002). Locating studies across various qualitative methods is further limited based on which database is searched, because not all databases use the same search filters for locating evidence (Evans, 2002; Wilczynski, Marks, & Haynes, 2007).

Qualitative Studies Spread Across Journals

Qualitative studies that may be relevant to a research question may be included in databases geared toward specific fields of practice, including social work, nursing, medicine, politics, law, psychology, anthropology, and sociology. Although a question may be specific to social work, the question may have been addressed across a multitude of journals spanning many disciplines (McKibbon & Gadd, 2006).

Nonspecific Titles and Abstracts

Qualitative titles and abstracts often focus on the content of the findings and not necessarily the research designs used in the studies (Evans, 2002; McKibbon, Wilczynski, & Haynes, 2006). Again, this causes challenges in retrieving specific qualitative studies to answer the component of EBP questions that require the inclusion of qualitative findings (McKibbon, Wilczynski, & Haynes, 2006).

Deficiencies in Bibliographic Indexes

The development of bibliographic database indexing systems for qualitative designs has not kept pace with the field's indexing of quantitative designs (Evans, 2002). Searching for qualitative studies is, therefore, limited by the deficiencies of electronic database indexing, given that these often do not adequately capture the variability of methods used in qualitative research (Walters, Wilczynski, & Haynes, 2006). Little is known about the sensitivity and specificity of various search strategies across different electronic databases (Shaw et al., 2004). As such, there is a risk that potentially relevant qualitative studies may be missed during the electronic information retrieval process (Evans, 2002).

Limited Ability to Locate Qualitative Research

Although many librarians involved in information retrieval for systematic reviews are proficient at locating RCTs, quasiexperimental designs, and other intervention-based studies (Wade, Turner, Rothstein, & Lavenberg, 2006), less is known about the optimal ways to locate qualitative studies from these same databases (Wilczynski, Marks, & Haynes, 2007). This limited knowledge contributes to making qualitative research a more difficult and challenging enterprise (Dixon-Woods & Fitzpatrick, 2001).

APPRAISING QUALITATIVE STUDIES

Another challenge confronted by integrating qualitative research within EBP is that there remains no standardized method for reporting the design of qualitative studies across journals (Sandelowski & Barroso, 2007), thereby making it difficult to assess the quality of the research designs if pertinent information about the quality and rigor have been omitted or cut at the editorial phase of production. Despite this limitation, several guidelines for assessing the quality and rigor in qualitative research have emerged (Erlandson, Harris, Skipper, & Allen, 1993; Lincoln & Guba, 1985). Traditional methods for assessing the quality of qualitative research have focused on standardization of methods and situations, and emphasized trustworthiness and repeatability of findings (Lincoln & Guba, 1985), but these have been criticized for being too germane to quantitative standards for reliability and validity. Lincoln and Guba (1985) reformulated notions of credibility by introducing techniques to establish quality, including prolonged engagement and persistent observation in the field, triangulation, peer debriefing, the analysis of negative cases, the appropriateness of the terms of reference of interpretations and their assessment and member checking. They also included the dimension of authenticity to include fairness and balance, ontological authenticity, educative authenticity, catalytic authenticity, and tactical authenticity. The additions acknowledge that qualitative research findings are situated with the social, cultural, and political context of the findings and so the appraisal of quality should be completed within this context (Lincoln & Guba, 1985).

There are now over 100 quality appraisal forms to evaluate the quality and rigor in qualitative studies, but there is a lack of attention in many of these tools regarding the epistemological and study design differences of the various types of qualitative designs within the umbrella of qualitative research. One example of these tools is the *Quality Research Checklist* (QRC) (Saini & Shlonsky, 2012), a 25-dimension tool to assess the credibility, dependability, confirmability, transferability, authenticity, and relevance of qualitative studies. The QRC was developed and then pilot tested with four Master of Social Work (MSW) graduate classes to assess the inter-rater agreement of responses after reading a qualitative study. The underlying assumption of the QRC is that, regardless of the epistemological framework guiding a particular qualitative study, the "story" should be told in a consistent, transparent way and should adhere to the highest standard of methods associated with the philosophical traditions from which the authors purportedly draw. The purpose of the QRC is not to exclude studies from informing EBP based on the lack of quality and rigor, but to provide an understanding of how issues of quality and rigor may inform interpretations of the findings and the potential relevance to the EBP question.

TRANSFERABILITY OVER GENERALIZABILITY

By assessing the quality and rigor of the qualitative studies, consideration is given to the transferability of the knowledge gained. There is a debate, however, about whether knowledge that emerges from qualitative studies should remain locally connected to the context or whether any knowledge can be transferred and integrated within a broader understanding of EBP. Some qualitative researchers argue, for example, that the contextual location of knowledge makes transferability undesirable, while others have argued that some shared meanings can emerge from multiple studies even though these meanings can change over time and remain connected to the context of the original studies (Saini & Shlonsky, 2012). The transferability of qualitative research is, therefore, connected to helping enrich our understanding of the context of EBP, and to helping us connect evidence with our clients by concentrating on the potential barriers, strengths, and considerations that may impact their views and preferences in adopting the EBP process. This helps us shape a broader application of evidence across contexts and locations (Finfgeld-Connett, 2010). Finfgeld-Connett (2009) argues for the transparency of qualitative methods so that consumers of this "new knowledge" are fully informed about the process, context, and situations of the qualitative synthesis in order to make judicious decisions about the transferability of findings (Lincoln & Guba, 1985). This is different than making generalized assertions about the probabilities and/or predictions of how others may experience an intervention. Rather, transferability focuses on bringing some understanding to the context of these interventions and how they may be perceived by our clients. There is less emphasis on the size of the sample because the purpose is to develop knowledge from tentative suppositions that describe individual cases (Rodwell, 1987). Therefore, gaining a rich and complex understanding of contextual factors takes precedence over generalization and broad assertions. Many qualitative projects employ small samples, principally because the researchers are not concerned with statistical generalizability but rather with conceptual and theoretical development (Baskerville & Wood-Harper, 1996; Pope, Mays, & Popay, 2007).

THE INCLUSION OF QUALITATIVE SYNTHESIS WITHIN SYSTEMATIC REVIEWS

With the increasing attention to developing methods to aggregate, integrate, and interpret qualitative studies, qualitative synthesis methods are providing additional options for integrating qualitative studies with EBP to generate new insights and understandings (Saini & Shlonsky, 2012). Similar to primary qualitative studies, qualitative synthesis can consider the inclusion of only qualitative studies to help answer relevant questions or can complement quantitative reviews (e.g., meta-analysis) by helping to define and refine the question, thus allowing for maximum relevancy.

In 1998, the Cochrane Qualitative Research Methods Group of the Cochrane Collaboration was established to develop methods for the inclusion of findings from qualitative research. In 2008, the group made a major revision to the Cochrane Handbook for Systematic Reviews of Interventions (Version 5.0.0), which included a chapter (Chapter 20) specifically devoted to the development and dissemination of qualitative synthesis reviews. In a similar move, the Campbell Collaboration included a section in their protocol template that specifically deals with the inclusion of qualitative studies by stating that qualitative studies can (a) contribute to the development of a more robust intervention by helping to define an intervention more precisely, (b) assist in the choice of outcome measures and the development of valid research questions, and (c) help to understand heterogeneous results from studies of effect.

Despite the contingent nature of evidence gleaned from synthesis of qualitative studies and the current lack of consensus about the veracity of some of its aspects, qualitative synthesis is an important technique and, used suitably, can deepen our understanding of the contextual dimensions of complex interventions (Saini & Shlonsky, 2012).

CONCLUSION

As the interest in evidence-based practice continues to grow, there is a move toward integrating the vast and seemingly untapped pool of qualitative studies. Qualitative research can influence social work practice and policy by enhancing our understanding of the contextual considerations that are paramount to the process of EBP decision-making. Linking scientific knowledge with client circumstances, views, and perspectives and the experience and judgement of helping professionals is central to an evidence-informed approach (Saini & Shlonsky, 2012).

Knowledge gleaned from qualitative studies is predicated on finding better ways to integrate qualitative research within the EBP process. Despite the epistemological and methodological challenges of this integration, these efforts can enhance our collective wisdom and make for more relevant social work practice and policy decisions and, ultimately, improve the ways in which we carry out our duties as client-focused and critically informed helping professionals.

WEBSITES

Campbell Collaboration Process and Implementation Methods http://joan-nabriggs.org/campbell/
Cultural and Qualitative Research Interest Group http://sigs.nih.gov/cultural/Pages/default.aspx
Cochrane Qualitative and Implementation Methods Group. http://cqim.cochrane.org/
The Consortium on Qualitative Research Methods (CQRM) http://www.maxwell.syr.edu/moynihan/programs/cqrm/
International Institute for Qualitative Methodology. http://www.iiqm.ualberta.ca/
Qualitative Methods Workbook. http://web-space.ship.edu/cgboer/qualmeth.html
The Centre for Community Based Research (CCBR) http://www.communitybasedre-search.ca/index.html

References

Baskerville, R., & Wood-Harper, A. (1996). A critical perspective on action research as a method for information systems research. *Journal of Information Technology, 11*, 235–246.

Bondas, T., & Hall, E. O. C. (2007). Challenges in approaching meta-synthesis research. *Qualitative Health Research, 17*(1), 113–121.

Denzin, N., & Lincoln, Y. (Eds). (1994). *Handbook of qualitative research.* Thousand Oaks, CA: Sage.

Denzin, N. K., & Lincoln, Y. S. (Eds.). (2000). *Handbook of qualitative research* (2nd ed.). Thousand Oaks, CA: Sage.

Dixon-Woods, M., & Fitzpatrick, R. (2001). Qualitative research in systematic reviews. *BMJ, 323*, 65–66.

Erlandson, D., Harris, E., Skipper, B., & Allen., S. (1993). *Doing naturalistic inquiry: A guide to methods.* London: Sage Publications.

Ebell, M. H., Siwek, J., Weiss, B. D., Wolf, S. H., Susman J., Ewigman, B. & Bowman, M.(2004). Strength of recommendation taxonomy (SORT): a patient-centered approach to grading evidence in the medical literature. *J Am Board Fam Pract, 17*, 59–67.

Evans, D. (2002). Database searches for qualitative research. *Journal of the Medical Library Association, 90*, 290–293.

Fetterman, D. (1988). Qualitative approaches to evaluating education. *Educational Research, 17*(8), 17–23.

Finfgeld-Connett, D. (2009). Management of aggression among demented or brain-injured patients. *Clinical Nursing Research, 18*(3), 272–287.

Finfgeld-Connett, D. (2010). Generalizability and transferability of meta-synthesis research findings. *Journal of Advanced Nursing, 66*(2), 246–254.

Gough, D., & Elbourne, D. (2002). Systematic research synthesis to inform policy, practice and democratic debate. *Social Policy and Society, 1*, 225–236.

Kirk, J., & Miller, M. L. (1986). *Reliability and validity in qualitative research.* Beverly Hills, CA: Sage Publications.

Lewin, S., Glenton, C., & Oxman, A. D. (2009). Use of qualitative methods alongside randomised controlled trials of complex healthcare interventions: Methodological study. *British Medical Journal, 339*, b3496. doi:10.1136/bmj.b3496.

Lincoln, Y., & Guba, E. (1985). *Naturalistic inquiry.* Beverly Hills, CA: Sage Publications.

McKibbon K. A., & Gadd, C. S. (2006). A quantitative analysis of qualitative studies in clinical journals for the 2000 publishing year. *BMC Medical Inform Decision Making.* http://www.biomed-central.com/1472-6947/4/11.

McKibbon K. A., Wilczynski, N. L., Haynes, R. B. (2006). Developing optimal search strategies for retrieving qualitative studies in PsycINFO.

Evaluation & the Health Professions 29(4), 440–454.

Padgett, D. (2008). Qualitative methods in social work research (2nd ed.). Thousand Oaks, CA: Sage.

Padgett, D. (2009). Qualitative and mixed methods in social work knowledge development. Social Work, 52(2), 101–105.

Petticrew, M & Roberts, H. (2006). Systematic reviews in the social sciences: A practical guide. Oxford: Blackwell.

Popay, J., Rogers, A., & Williams, G. (1998). Rationale and standards for the systematic review of qualitative literature in health services research. Qualitative Health Research, 8(3), 341–351.

Pope, C., & Mays, N. (2009). Critical reflections on the rise of qualitative research. British Medical Journal, 339, 3425.

Pope, C., Mays, N., & Popay, J. (2007). Synthesizing qualitative and quantitative health research: A guide to methods. Open University Press.

Ramchandani, P., Joughin, C., & Zwi, M., (2001). Evidence-based child and adolescent mental health services: Oxymoron or brave new dawn? Child Psychology and Psychiatry Review, 6(2), 59–64.

Rodwell, M. K. (1987). Naturalistic inquiry: An alternative model for social work assessment. Social Service Review, 61, 231–246.

Royse, D., Thyer, B., Padgett, D., & Logan, T. (2006). Program evaluation (4th ed.). Belmont, CA: Thomson.

Sackett, D. L., Rosenberg, W. M. C., & Gray, J. A. (1996). Evidence based medicine; what it is and what it isn't. British Medical Journal, 312(13), 71–72.

Saini, M., & Shlonsky, A. (2012). Systematic synthesis of qualitative research: A pocket guide for social work research methods. New York, NY: Oxford University Press.

Sandelowski, M., & Barroso, J. (2007). Handbook for synthesizing qualitative research. New York, NY: Springer.

Shaw, R. L., Booth, A., Sutton, A. J., Miller, T., Smith, J. A., Young, B.,… Dixon-Woods, M. (2004). Finding qualitative research: An evaluation of search strategies. BMC Medical Research Methodology, 4, 5.

Shlonsky, A., & Gibbs, L. (2004). Will the real evidence-based practice please step forward? Teaching evidence-based practice in the helping professions. Journal of Brief Therapy and Crisis Intervention, 4(2), 137–153.

Shuval, K., Harker, K., Roudsari, B., Groce, NE., Mills, B, Siddiqi, Z. & Shachak, A. (2011). Is qualitative research second class science? A quantitative longitudinal examination of qualitative research in medical journals. PLoS ONE 6(2): e16937. doi:10.1371/journal.pone.0016937

Straus, S. E., Glasziou, P., Richardson, W. S., & Haynes, R. B. (2011). Evidence-based medicine: How to practice and teach EBM (4th ed.). Edinburgh: Elsevier Churchill Livingstone.

Thyer, B. A. (2013). Evidence-based practice or evidence-guided practice: A rose by any other name would smell as sweet [Invited response to Gitterman & Knight's "Evidence-guided practice"]. Families in Society, 94, 79–84.

Valadez, J., & Bamberger, M. (1994). Monitoring and evaluating social programs in developing countries: A handbook for policymakers, managers, and researchers. EDI Development Studies. Washington, DC: The World Bank.

Wade, C. A., Turner, H. M., Rothstein, H. R., & Lavenberg, J. (2006). Information retrieval and the role of the information specialist in producing high-quality systematic reviews in the social, behavioral, and education sciences. Evidence & Policy: A Journal of Research, Debate and Practice, 2, 89–108.

Walters, L. A., Wilczynski, N. L., Haynes, R. B. (2006). Hedges team. Developing optimal search strategies for retrieving clinically relevant qualitative studies in EMBASE. Qualitative Health Research, 16(1):162–168.

Wilczynski, N. L., Marks, S., Haynes, R. B. (2007). Search strategies for identifying qualitative studies in CINAHL. Qualitative Health Research, 17(5), 705–710.

Wilczynski, N. L., & Haynes, R. B. (2002). Robustness of empirical search strategies for clinical content in MEDLINE. Proc AMIA Symp, 904–908.

158 Integrating Information from Diverse Sources in Evidence-based Practice

Eileen Gambrill

Evidence-based practice "requires the integration of best research evidence with our clinical expertise and our [client's] unique values and circumstances" (Straus, Glasziou, Richardson, & Haynes, 2011, p. 1). Practitioners must decide what particular characteristics of clients and their contexts to attend to and how to weigh them. They have to decide what information to gather and how to do so. Integrating information and making a decision together with the client as to what to do is often burdened with uncertainties, such as the extent to which external research findings apply to a particular client. Here is where cognitive biases such as tendencies to consider only data that confirm initial assumptions thrive. This step requires integrating information concerning external research findings with circumstances and characteristics of the client, including their values and expectations and available resources, and, together with the client, deciding what to do. The time and effort devoted to making a decision should depend on the potential consequences in relation to making a faulty or good decision and what is needed, based on external research findings and prior experience.

Clinical expertise refers to the ability to use clinical skills and past experience to rapidly identify each client's unique characteristics and circumstances and their individual risks and benefits of potential interventions (Straus et al., 2011, p. 1).

Increased expertise is reflected in many ways, but especially in more effective and efficient [assessment] and in the more thoughtful identification and compassionate use of individual [clients'] predicaments, rights and preferences in making clinical decisions about their care.... Without clinical expertise, practice risks becoming tyrannized by external evidence, for even excellent external evidence may be inapplicable to or inappropriate for an individual [client]. Without current best external evidence, practice risks becoming rapidly out of date, to the detriment of [clients]. (Sackett, Richardson, Rosenberg, & Haynes, 1997, p. 2)

Client preferences are considered as well as access to needed resources. Questions include (Glasziou, Del Mar, & Salisbury, 2003) the following: Do research findings apply to my client? That is, is a client similar to clients included in related research? Can I use this practice method in my setting (e.g., are needed resources available?) If not, is there some other access to programs found to be most effective in seeking hoped-for outcomes? What alternatives are available? Will the benefits of service outweigh the harms of service for this client? What does my client think about this method? Is it acceptable to my client? What if I do not find anything? Many application barriers enter at this stage. Gathering information about their frequency and exact nature will be useful in planning how to decrease them. Examples include chaotic work environments, being overwhelmed by problems/issues due to large caseloads, lack of resources, and poor interagency communication and collaboration. Information may be available about certain kinds of clients, but these clients may differ greatly from your clients, so findings may not apply. Resources available will limit options.

DO RESEARCH FINDINGS APPLY TO CLIENTS?

A great deal of practice-related research consists of correlational research (e.g., describing the relationship between certain characteristics of parents and child abuse) and experimental research describing differences among various groups (e.g., experimental and control). In neither case may the findings apply to a particular client. Differences may influence the potential costs and benefits of an intervention to a particular client. Norms on assessment measures may be available, but not for people like your client. (Note, however, that norms should not necessarily be used as a guideline for selecting outcomes for individual clients because outcomes they seek may differ from normative criteria and norms may not be optimal, for example, low rates of positive feedback from teachers to students in classrooms.)

The unique characteristics and circumstances of a client may suggest that a particular method should not be used because negative effects are likely or because such characteristics would render an intervention ineffective if it were applied at a certain time. For example, referring clients who have a substance abuse problem to parent-training programs may not be effective. Other problems, therefore, may influence the effectiveness of a method. In addition, the unique factors associated with a problem such as depression may influence the effectiveness of a given method (e.g., medication, increasing pleasant events, and decreasing negative thoughts). Claims regarding the validity of a practice guideline may not apply to a particular client, agency, or community. Knowledge of behavior, how it is influenced, and what principles of behavior have been found to apply to many individuals may provide helpful guidelines. Questions suggested by Sheldon, Guyatt, and Haines (1998) about whether a particular intervention applies to an individual client are as follows.

1. Is the relative risk reduction that is attributed to the intervention likely to be different in this case because of client characteristics?
2. What is the client's absolute risk of an adverse event without the intervention?
3. Is there some other problem or a contraindication that might reduce the benefit?

4. Are there social or cultural factors that might affect the suitability of a practice or policy or its acceptability?
5. What do the client and the client's family wants?

ARE THEY IMPORTANT? THE "SO-WHAT QUESTION"

If external research findings apply to a client, are they important? Would they make a difference in decisions made? Were all important outcomes considered? Were surrogate outcomes relied on—those that are not of direct practical relevance but assumed to reflect vital outcomes? The acronym POEMS refers to patient-oriented evidence that matters. Grandage, Slawson, Barnett, and Shaughnessy (2002) suggest the following for judging usefulness: usefulness = (validity × relevance)/work.

HOW DEFINITIVE ARE THE RESEARCH FINDINGS?

Reviews found may be high-quality systematic reviews or incomplete, unrigorous reviews. In the former, there may be strong evidence not to use a method (e.g., harmful effects have been found) or strong evidence to use one (e.g., critical tests show the effectiveness of a program). Often there will be uncertainty about what is most likely to be effective (See DUETs listed under Websites at end of chapter). Different views of the quality of evidence related to programs abound (e.g., see Littell, 2005).

WHAT IF THE EXPERTS DISAGREE?

Although practitioners and clients may often have to depend on the views of experts, such dependence is not without its risks, as illustrated by studies comparing recommendations of clinical experts to what is suggested based on results of carefully controlled research (Antman, Lau, Kupelnick, Mosteller, & Chalmers, 1992). In some situations, we could seek and review the quality of evidence for ourselves. At other times, this may not be possible due to time constraints. Indicators of honesty among experts include (1) accurate description of controversies, including methodological and conceptual problems with preferred positions; (2) accurate description of well-argued disliked views; (3) critical appraisal of both preferred and well-argued alternative views; and (4) inclusion of references regarding claims made so readers can examine these for themselves.

WILL POTENTIAL BENEFITS OUTWEIGH POTENTIAL RISKS AND COSTS?

Every intervention, including assessment measures, has potential risks as well as potential benefits—for example, a false positive or negative result. Will the benefits of an intervention outweigh potential risks and costs? We can estimate this in a number of ways: RRR (relative risk reduction), ARR (absolute risk reduction), and NNT (number needed to treat) (see Bandolier worksheet for calculating NNT). A nomogram can be used to calculate the NNT based on absolute risk in the absence of treatment (Guyatt, Rennie, Meade, & Cook, 2008). How many clients have to receive a harm reduction program to help one person? Is there any information about NNH (the number of individuals who would have to receive a service to harm one person)? ARR should always be given; RRR is highly misleading. Accurately communicating risk to clients is much easier using frequencies rather than probabilities (Gigerenzer, 2002; 2014).

HOW CAN PRACTITIONERS HELP CLIENTS TO MAKE DECISIONS?

The lack of correlation between what someone says he or she wants (their preferences) and what he or she does (their actions) is considered such a big issue, with so little related research, that one model of evidence-based practice carves out preferences and actions as a separate area to be considered (Haynes, Devereaux, & Guyatt, 2002). For example, although many people say they want to pursue a certain goal, their actions often do not reflect their stated preferences; that is, they do not do anything. In view of the tendency of some clients to match the goals and values of their therapists and other sources of behavioral confirmation in the helping process, and the role of subtle influences such as question wording and order on the expression of preferences, a variety of methods of inquiry should be used to discover

beliefs and preferences, rather than reliance on one method, which may result in inaccurate accounts.

How decisions are framed (in terms of gains or losses) influences decisions; different surface wordings of identical problems influence judgments (framing effects). Gains or losses that are certain are weighed more heavily than those that are uncertain. Clients differ in how risk-averse they are and in the importance given to particular outcomes. Occasions when discovering client preferences is especially important include those in which (1) options have major differences in outcomes or complications; (2) decisions require trade-offs between short- and long-term outcomes; (3) one choice can result in a small chance of a grave outcome; and (4) there are marginal differences in outcomes between options (Kassirer, 1994). Presentation of risks and benefits by professionals is often quite misleading (e.g., Gigerenzer, 2002). Thus, a key step in helping clients make a decision is for practitioners themselves to be aware of errors they make in estimating risk and presenting options (e.g., framing biases).

Discovering client beliefs and preferences may require involving them in a decision analysis. Decision aids can be used to inform clients about the risks and benefits of various options. Such aids can "personalize" information by allowing clients to ask questions important to them. They can highlight vital information often overlooked, such as absolute risk. Benefits include improving client knowledge about options, feeling more informed about what matters most, increasing accuracy of expectations regarding potential benefits and harms of options, participating more in making decisions, and improving the match between choices and a client's values (Stacey, Légaré, Col, Bennett, Barry, Eden, Holmes-Rovner,...Wu, 2014).

CAN THIS METHOD BE IMPLEMENTED EFFECTIVELY IN MY AGENCY?

Can a plan be carried out in a way that maximizes success? Are needed resources available? Do providers have the skills required to carry out plans? Can necessary resources be created? Differences in provider adherence to practice guidelines may decrease the safety and effectiveness of an intervention. Current service patterns may limit options. Barriers to implementation may be so extensive that Straus et al. (2005, p. 170–171) refer to them as "the killer B's:

1. The Burden of Illness (the frequency of a concern may be too low to warrant offering a costly program with high integrity).
2. Beliefs of individual clients and/or communities about the value of services or their outcomes may not be compatible with what is most effective.
3. A Bad Bargain in relation to resources, costs, and outcome
4. Barriers such as geographic, organizational, traditional, authoritarian, or behavioral.

Problems may have to be redefined from helping clients attain needed resources to, instead, helping them bear up under the strain of not having resources or involving clients with similar concerns in advocacy efforts to acquire better services. Questions Sackett et al. (1997) suggest for deciding whether to implement a guideline include the following (p. 182):

1. What barriers exist to its implementation? Can they be overcome?
2. Can the collaboration of key colleagues be obtained?
3. Can the educational, administrative, and economic conditions that are likely to determine the success or failure of implementing the strategy be met?
   • Credible synthesis of the evidence by a respected body.
   • Respected, influential local exemplars already implementing the strategy.
   • Consistent information from all relevant sources.
   • Opportunity for individual discussions about the strategy with an authority.
   • User-friendly format for guidelines.
   • Implementable within target group of clinicians (without the need for extensive outside collaboration).
   • Freedom from conflict with economic and administrative incentives and client and community expectations.

ARE ALTERNATIVE OPTIONS AVAILABLE?

Are other options available, perhaps another agency to which a client could be referred? Self-help programs may be available. Here, too,

familiarity with practice-related research can facilitate decisions.

WHAT IF CLIENTS PREFER UNTESTED, INEFFECTIVE, OR HARMFUL METHODS?

The acceptability of plans must be considered. This will influence adherence to important procedural components associated with success. Most interventions used by professionals in the interpersonal helping professions have not been tested; we do not know if they are effective, ineffective, or harmful. Untested methods are routinely offered in both health and social care. Methods critically tested and found to be ineffective or harmful certainly should not be offered. If an effective method is available, the costs and benefits of using this compared to a preferred ineffective method could be described. Untested methods that continue to be preferred and used should be tested to determine whether they do more good than harm.

WHAT IF A SEARCH REVEALS NO RELATED RESEARCH?

A review of research findings related to important practice questions and related information needs may reveal that little or nothing is known. Ethical obligations to involve clients as informed participants and to consider their preferences provide a guide; that is, the limitations of research findings should be shared with clients, and empirically grounded practice theory, as well as client preferences, can be used to guide work with clients. Evidence-informed practice involves sharing ignorance and uncertainty as well as knowledge in a context of ongoing support (Katz, 2002).

WHAT IF RELATED RESEARCH IS OF POOR QUALITY?

A search will often reveal uncertainty regarding the effectiveness of a method. The phrase "best practice" is used to describe a hierarchy of evidence (e.g., Straus et al., 2005, p. 169). The phrase "best evidence" could refer to a variety of tests that differ greatly in the extent to which claims are critically tested. Available research may be low on this hierarchy in relation to critical tests of a practice or policy (e.g., a case series). However, this may be the best that is available. For example, if there are no randomized controlled trials regarding an effectiveness question, then we move down the list. This is what must be done in the everyday world because most interventions used in psychiatry, psychology, and social work have not been critically tested. Instead of well-designed randomized controlled trials regarding an intervention, only pre/post studies may be available, which are subject to many rival explanations regarding the cause of change. Some guidelines are described as "well-established" if two well-designed randomized controlled trials show positive outcomes. It is less misleading to say that a claim has been critically tested in two well-controlled trials and has passed both tests. This keeps uncertainty in view. Whatever is found is shared with clients, and practice theory, as well as client preferences, must be used to fill in the gaps.

WHAT IF RESEARCH IS AVAILABLE, BUT IT HAS NOT BEEN CRITICALLY APPRAISED?

One course of action is to appraise this literature critically. The realities of practice, however, may not allow time for this. Perhaps an expert in the area can be contacted. If the question concerns a problem that occurs often, interested others can be involved in critically appraising related research.

BALANCING INDIVIDUAL AND POPULATION PERSPECTIVES

One of the most challenging aspects of practice is considering both individuals and populations. There is only so much money and time. Decisions made about populations often limit options of individuals. Ethical issues regarding the distribution of scarce resources are often overlooked.

COMMON ERRORS

Common errors in integrating information from diverse sources are related to common cognitive biases such as overconfidence, wishful thinking, influence by redundant information, and confirmation biases (Gambrill, 2012). Availability biases such as influence by vivid data are common as are

representative biases (influence by associations that may be misleading rather than informative). Eagerness to help clients and a reluctance to recognize uncertainties may encourage unfounded confidence in methods suggested. Lack of reliability and validity of information is often overlooked, resulting in faulty inferences. Jumping to conclusions may result in oversimplification of causes of a client's concerns. Or the opposite may occur, as in suggesting obscure complex causes, none of which provide intervention implications. The evidentiary-status of interventions may not be communicated clearly to clients. Lack of evidence may be shared in an unempathetic manner.

ONGOING CHALLENGES AND EVOLVING REMEDIES

Obstacles include both personal and environmental characteristics (see "Can This Method Be Implemented Effectively in My Agency?"). Ongoing challenges include encouraging practitioners to be honest with clients about uncertainties in a supportive manner (Katz, 2002), minimizing common cognitive biases in integrating data, and avoiding influence of inflated claims in the professional literature about "what works" and what accounts for client concerns. Organizational cultures may discourage raising questions regarding services offered and needed tools, such as access to vital databases, may not be available. Biases intrude both on the part of researchers when conducting research and when preparing research reviews (Jadad & Enkin, 2007) as well as at the practitioner level when making decisions. Availability biases, such as a preferred practice theory and preconceptions regarding certain kinds of people, as well as representative biases, including stereotypes, may interfere with sound integration of external research findings with client values, expectations, and unique circumstances and characteristics. Many components of EBP are designed to minimize biases such as jumping to conclusions, for example, using "quality filters" when seeking research related to a question. EBP highlights the play of bias and uncertainty in helping clients and attempts to give helpers and clients the knowledge and skills to handle this honestly and constructively. Consider the attention given to helping both clients and helpers to enhance their skills in critically appraising research.

We can draw on literature concerning judgment, problem solving, and decision-making to discover common biases and how to avoid them, including discussion of organizational obstacles and how to address them (Gambrill, 2012). We can take advantage of literature investigating expertise to help practitioners "educate their intuition" (Hogarth, 2001) and take advantage of guidelines described in the critical thinking literature to minimize biases. Helping professionals to learn from their experience in ways that improve the accuracy of future decisions is a key priority. This will require arranging corrective feedback that permits the development of "informed intuition" (Hogarth, 2001). One problem arises when someone thinks they have expertise but do not and imposes, perhaps by selective attention, an inaccurate view on a situation. They may generalize a decision-making method to a situation in which it is not useful.

Use of handheld computers to guide decisions may be of value in decreasing errors and common biases. Such aids can be used to prompt valuable behaviors, to critique a decision (for example, purchasing services from an agency that does not use evidence-informed practices), to match a client's unique circumstances and characteristics with a certain service program, to suggest unconsidered options, and to interpret different assessment pictures (Guyatt et al., 2008). Use of clinical pathways and handheld computers with built-in decision aids, such as flow charts, are already in use in the health arena, as are decision aids for clients (see earlier discussion). Just as the narratives of clients may help us understand how we can improve services, the narratives of practitioners may help us identify challenges and opportunities to integrating information from diverse sources (Greenhalgh & Hurwitz, 1998).

RELATED ETHICAL DILEMMAS

Ethical issues that arise in integrating data and making decisions illustrate the close connection between ethical and evidentiary issues. These include ethical obligations of practitioners to inform clients accurately regarding the uncertainties involved in making decisions, including the evidentiary status of recommended methods and their risks and benefits together with the risks and benefits of alternative methods. Should clients be informed regarding effective methods that an agency cannot offer? Should practitioners

continue to offer methods of unknown effectiveness? Is it ethical to offer an intervention in a diluted form of unknown effectiveness? Should practitioners be well informed regarding how to present risks and benefits accurately? Although the answers may clearly be yes, descriptions of everyday practice reveal a different picture. Yet another ethical issue relates to controversies regarding the relative contributions of the person of the helper, common factors such as warmth and empathy, and the particular intervention, to outcome. If it is true that the former contributes more than the latter, this should be considered in deciding what to do (see Wampold, 2006; 2010).

WEBSITES

Centre for Evidence-Based Medicine. http://www.cebm.net.

Centre for Evidence-Based Medicine, University of Toronto. http://www.cebm.utoronto.ca.

Database of Uncertainties about the Effects of Treatments (DUETs). http://www.duets.nhs.uk.

Skeptic's Dictionary. http://www.skepdic.com.

References

Antman, E. M., Lau, J., Kupelnick, B., Mosteller, F., & Chalmers, T. C. (1992). A comparison of results of meta-analyses of randomized controlled trials and recommendations of clinical experts: Treatments for myocardial infarction. *JAMA: Journal of the American Medical Association, 268,* 240–248.

Gambrill, E. (2012). *Critical thinking in clinical practice: Improving the quality of judgments and decisions* (3rd ed.). New York, NY: Wiley.

Gigerenzer, G. (2002). *Calculated risks: How to know when numbers deceive you.* New York, NY: Simon & Schuster.

Gigerenzer, G. (2014). *Risk savvy: how to make good decisions.* New York: Viking.

Glasziou, P., Del Mar, C., & Salisbury, J. (2003). *Evidence-based medicine workbook.* London: BMJ Books.

Grandage, K. K., Slawson, D. C., Barnett, B. L. Jr., & Shaughnessy, A. F. (2002). When less is more: A practical approach to searching for evidence-based answers. *Journal of the Medical Library Association, 90,* 298–304.

Greenhalgh, T., & Hurwitz, B. (1998). *Narrative based medicine: Dialogue and discourse in clinical practice.* London: BMJ Press.

Guyatt, G. H., Rennie, D., Meade, M., & Cook, D. (2008). *Users' guides to the medical literature: A manual for evidence-based clinical practice* (2nd ed.). *Evidence-Based Medicine Working Group.* Chicago, IL: American Medical Association.

Haynes, R. B., Devereaux, P. J., & Guyatt, G. H. (2002). Clinical expertise in the era of evidence-based medicine and patient choice [Editorial]. *ACP Journal Club, 136*(A11), 1–2.

Hogarth, R. M. (2001). *Educating intuition.* Chicago, IL: University of Chicago Press.

Jadad, A. R., & Enkin, M. W. (2007). *Randomized controlled trials: Questions, answers and musings.* Malden, MA: Blackwell.

Kassirer, J. P. (1994). Incorporating patient preferences into medical decisions. *New England Journal of Medicine, 330,* 1895–1896.

Katz, J. (2002). *The silent world of doctors and patients.* Baltimore, MD: John Hopkins University Press.

Stacey, D. Légaré, S. D., Col, N. F., Bennett, C. L., Barry, M. J., Eden, K. B., Holmes-Rovner, M.,… Wu, J. H. C. (2014). *Decision aids to help people who are facing health treatment or screening decisions. Cochrane Database of Systematic Reviews.* Issue 1.

Littell, J. (2005). Lessons from a systematic review of effects of multisystemic therapy. *Children and Youth Services Review, 27,* 445–463.

Sackett, D. L., Richardson, W. S., Rosenberg, W., & Haynes, R. B. (1997). *Evidence-based medicine: How to practice and teach EBM.* New York, NY: Churchill Livingstone.

Sheldon, T. A., Guyatt, G. H., & Haines, A. (1998). Getting research findings into practice: When to act on the evidence. *British Medical Journal, 317,* 139–142.

Straus, D. L., Glasziou, P., Richardson, W. S., & Haynes, R. B. (2011). *Evidence-based medicine: How to practice and teach EBM* (4th ed.). New York, NY: Churchill Livingstone.

Wampold, B. E. (2006). The psychotherapist. In J. C. Norcross, L. E. Beutler, & R. F. Levant (Eds.), *Evidence-based practices in mental health: Debate and dialogue on the fundamental questions* (pp. 200–207). Washington, DC: American Psychological Association.

Wampold, B. E. (2010). The research evidence for the common factors models: A historically situated perspective. In B. L. Duncan & S. D. Miller (Eds.), *The heart and soul of change: Delivering what works in therapy* (2nd ed.) (pp. 49–81). Washington, D. C.: American Psychological Association.

159 Evidence-based Practice in Social Work Education

Aron Shlonsky

The infusion of evidence-based practice (EBP) into social work education has begun in earnest and is still in the initial stages of widespread adoption. This initial stage can be characterized by a growing excitement about the prospect of training students to provide services that are both effective and in line with the core social work value of self-determination. On the other hand, the field is emerging from a long struggle to define EBP and find ways to integrate its philosophy and specific steps into mainstream social work education. This chapter briefly reviews the current state of implementation of EBP in schools of social work, offers suggestions for shaping individual classes, and provides strategies for the infusion of EBP across the social work curriculum.

CASE EXAMPLE

A school of social work in North America is up for accreditation and is considering infusing EBP into its new Master of Social Work curriculum. As yet, its faculty and administration are unsure about the extent to which they are willing and able to change the way they have always done things, but there is an acknowledgment that the curriculum is dated and requires substantial revision. There are great methodological (e.g., quantitative vs. qualitative) and epistemological (e.g., postmodern/poststructuralist vs. postpositivist) divides among full-time faculty, adjunct faculty, field liaisons and instructors, and students. The dean is well respected among her faculty and, like any good social worker, she values diversity of opinion and would like to make the transition to EBP an inclusive process. What steps can she take to successfully formulate a new curriculum based on the philosophies and steps of EBP? How should individual faculty members begin to infuse EBP into their classrooms?

THE ADOPTION OF EVIDENCE-BASED PRACTICE IN SOCIAL WORK EDUCATION

The surge of interest in EBP across disciplines over the past decade is reflected in the number and content of peer-reviewed journal articles as well as the appearance of the phrase "evidence-based" in journal titles, both new and old (Figure 159.1). Between 1995 and 2002, the percentage of articles using the phrase "evidence-based" increased exponentially across the disciplines of social work, nursing, medicine, and psychology (Shlonsky & Gibbs, 2004). A number of leading social work journals have recently published

special issues on EBP, including *Research on Social Work Practice* (2003 and 2007), *Brief Treatment and Crises Intervention* (2004), and the *Journal of Social Work Education* (2007). Several books have also appeared, most notably Leonard Gibbs's (2003) *Evidence-Based Practice for the Helping Professions*, Rosen and Proctor's (2003) *Developing Practice Guidelines for Social Work Intervention*, and Roberts and Yeager's (2003) *Evidence-Based Practice Manual*. The two major social work conferences, the Council on Social Work Education's Annual Program Meeting and the Society for Social Work and Research's annual conference, have begun to devote considerable presentation slots to researchers and educators presenting on EBP. As well, the first national (U.S.) conference devoted to teaching EBP was convened by Allen Rubin at the University of Texas at Austin in October 2006. In short, EBP has quickly become the new practice archetype, yet definitional issues have arisen in these early stages of adoption.

In keeping with the other chapters in this part, EBP here is defined as it is in medicine as "the conscientious, explicit and judicious use of current evidence in making decisions about the care of individual patients" (Sackett, Richardson, Rosenberg, & Haynes, 1997, p. 71). Though this ideal is difficult to argue with, there has been a great deal of debate with respect to the definition of evidence and how it is gathered and used (Gibbs & Gambrill, 2002), and this is of great import to social work education because we cannot teach what we cannot define. Specifically, there has been confusion about whether EBP entails

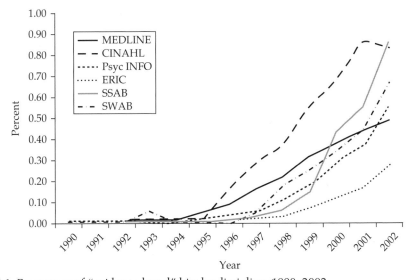

Figure 159.1 Percentage of "evidence-based" hits by discipline: 1990–2002.

simply using an empirically validated treatment for a given client problem, and this basic misunderstanding has been one of the major barriers to implementation. However, the original model is quite explicit. EBP at the individual, community, and policy levels must include five steps: (1) posing a practice-relevant, answerable question; (2) systematically searching the extant literature; (3) appraising what is found; (4) combining these findings with what is known about client preferences/actions and clinical state/circumstances to help clients make context-sensitive decisions; and (5) evaluating the outcome. The original EBP approach is inclusive of and even relies on both practice guidelines and empirically supported treatments (ESTs), but is not defined by and goes beyond their use.

Various approaches to teaching EBP have been adopted by schools across North America, each fashioning its curriculum differently, and all attempting to move the philosophy and methods to practice. George Warren Brown University in St. Louis was the first school to reshape its entire curriculum to reflect a practice guidelines approach (Howard, McMillen, & Pollio, 2003), including measures to ensure that students are trained in at least one EST (e.g., cognitive-behavioral therapy for depression). The University of Toronto changed its approach to teaching research, opting to teach the steps of EBP and training students to evaluate research rather than training them to conduct research. Oxford University has gone in yet a different direction and, rather than offering a degree in social care, is now offering a degree in evidence-based social intervention. More recently, other schools have begun to reshape their approach to teaching social work. For instance, Columbia University now offers several courses in EBP and has begun to shape its curriculum accordingly, and the University of Tennessee is now in the process of infusing its entire curriculum with EBP. Of course, there are others and an even larger number of individual academics who are integrating EBP into their courses.

TEACHING EVIDENCE-BASED PRACTICE IN THE CLASSROOM: A GENERAL SET OF GUIDELINES

Creating a Culture of Inquiry

The definition of EBP is best understood when both the guiding philosophy and the model's accompanying set of systematic steps are clearly explained. The philosophy is the starting point and should include reference to the overall model. Ethical obligations to provide the most effective services to clients, and the integration of evidence with client values/preferences and clinical state/circumstances, should be stressed. Only then do the five steps of EBP begin to make sense. However, this initial understanding must be accompanied by critical thinking (see Table 159.1). That is, search and evaluative tools are necessary but insufficient components of EBP. Every step in the process requires healthy doses of curiosity, skepticism, and a passion for finding the best possible knowledge in the service of helping, and these qualities must be brought out and supported in students. Rather than being mechanical or reductionistic, EBP at its core embraces the complexity of experiences, circumstances, and tendencies of each and every client (Shlonsky & Stern, 2007).

In a very real sense, EBP is a way of putting critical thinking into systematic action, and this requires creating an atmosphere that encourages

TABLE 159.1 Teaching Evidence-based Practice in the Classroom

1. Creating a culture of inquiry
   - Critical thinking
   - Socratic questioning
   - Exercises that highlight biases and inconsistencies
   - Exploration of ethical obligations to clients and the profession
2. Learning to live with uncertainty
   - Model uncertainty
   - Provide tools to dispel ignorance
3. Using a problem-based learning (PBL) framework
   - Small group format
   - Clinically integrated approach
4. Anticipating problem areas
   - Provide examples
   - Maintain student interest
   - Model several searches and appraisals
   - Series of small assignments
5. Expressing probabilities
   - Number Needed to Treat
   - Effect size
6. Starting with a single client
7. Build dynamic knowledge over time

independent, critical thought. Thus, rather than simply teaching the mechanics of EBP, students must learn how to think critically and conceptually about the systematic information they have gathered and consider ways to apply it to important practice and policy decisions. Questioning the underlying assumptions we make about evidence and about clients is welcome—indeed, it is essential. Socratic questioning, if done in a manner that is not threatening (i.e., curious but demanding speculation), seems to set the tone from the very beginning. Such an approach is interactive and leads by example. Students tend to pick up this approach fairly quickly with one another and the instructor, making for very lively and stimulating discussions. Several exercises and discussions within the Socratic framework can help facilitate this process. These include:

- Exercises that highlight perceptions of evidence (e.g., Gibbs & Gambrill, 1999)
- Exercises that highlight cognitive and other biases in decision making (e.g., Gambrill, 2006)
- An accounting of social interventions that have been harmful
- Discussion of controversial findings from the literature
- Communication of the ethical obligation to inform clients of the risks and benefits of a proposed course of action (Gambrill, 2003), which implies that such information has been systematically gathered and is known by the practitioner.

Learning to Live with Uncertainty

Social work students clearly want to be of service to their clients, and this may engender difficulties in the face of the inevitable uncertainty that arises when working with challenging, multiproblem client situations. There is often no single right path to successful assessment and treatment, and this is sometimes difficult for students to accept. An EBP approach does not shy away from such uncertainty. Rather, it embraces the unknown with curiosity and speculation. Thus, it is crucial that instructors model uncertainty and, rather than stopping with "I don't know," find a way to generate the next level of inquiry. In particular, EBP insists on transparency of research findings and

sharing ambiguous or uncertain findings with clients.

Using a Problem-based Learning Framework

Rather than relying solely on lectures, EBP is best taught using a clinically integrated approach. Problem-based learning (PBL), as developed by McMaster University in Canada, uses a small group format (seven or eight students) to present cases (these can be clinical, community, or policy oriented) and employs critical dialogue to identify knowledge gaps. In the interim between meetings, students individually use EBP methods to pose questions and find evidence, bringing information back to the group for further discussion and case plan development. Taking students through several examples, from initial assessment through the search and appraisal of evidence and then back to the client or policy question, provides ample opportunities to become more proficient at this process while maintaining student interest. Sometimes, this can be accomplished using a combination of videos and written assignments (see, for example, Howard et al., 2003) where students are asked to make decisions that rely on their clinical or policy and evaluative skills. By linking instruction with real and/or realistic clients, students are trained to think critically in an applied way, and this process appears to improve knowledge, skills, attitudes, and behavior when compared with more standard forms of pedagogy in medical school (Coomarasamy & Khan, 2004). Hopefully, such educational success translates into a generation of lifelong learners (Gray, 1997; Sackett et al., 1997) who will not be satisfied with knowledge that will soon be obsolete.

Anticipating Problem Areas

Posing questions and developing a search strategy are deceptively difficult, especially the first time. Appraising studies can also be a challenge, especially for students who shy away from numbers or who become easily frustrated by the often technical language contained in scientific papers. Much care and attention must be spent at these crucial junctures. If a student has a bad experience with his or her first attempt at the steps of EBP, he or she loses interest and become dismissive of the entire process. There is nothing more frustrating for a student than to spend hours on a failed search. Some strategies for avoiding this pitfall include:

- Providing numerous examples of answerable questions
- Relating questions directly to key practicum concerns or, in special circumstances, unique student interests
- Working individually with students to develop questions, especially focusing on clearly specifying their intervention and outcome terms
- Inviting a librarian or other search expert to demonstrate how to conduct EBP searches. This should include:
- Tours of the various subject-specific databases
- Developing search terms
- Using Boolean operators
- Using wildcards
- Using methodological filters by question type (see Gibbs, 2003)
- Providing numerous examples of search strategies by question type
- Providing simple methodology appraisal forms and opportunities to practice evaluating study quality
- Encouraging students to first look for systematic reviews at the Campbell and Cochrane Collaborations
- Providing ample opportunity for students to ask for help
- Segmenting larger assignments into smaller pieces to ensure that students are on target at each stage.

Expressing Probabilities

Students and clients often struggle with understanding and presenting findings from their reviews of the literature in real-world terms. One of the more important tools for translating research findings into readily understandable formulations of risk is number-needed-to-treat (NNT). This tool is basically a reworking of absolute risk reduction (1/ARR) into a format that almost anyone can understand. NNT gives students the number of people who need to be treated to prevent one bad outcome. The other side of NNT, number needed to harm (NNH), can also be a useful tool. For instance, an intervention might have an absolute risk reduction of

0.2 (e.g., 40% of the treatment group relapsed and 60% of the control group relapsed), translating into an NNT of 5 (1/ARR = 1/0.2). Thus, for every five people who receive the treatment, one person who would have relapsed will remain healthy. This number takes into account the fact that some people who do not receive the treatment will remain healthy and some people in the treatment group will relapse, a point many people miss when thinking about treatment interventions. Spending considerable class time on this construct in an introductory course is both necessary and helpful. Although students might find such calculations difficult at first, their intuitive understanding of risk and benefit will be enhanced and, once mastered, NNT can be a powerful tool to use with clients. As well, effect size (measure of the magnitude of difference between groups in an intervention study) is an important construct for students to understand so they can fully appreciate the difference between statistical and real world significance (Shlonsky & Stern, 2007).

Starting with a Single Client

Critics of EBP often point out that social workers do not have the time to go through the five steps—such an approach is unrealistic. Although the techniques cited in this chapter and in this part of the volume substantially decrease time spent, as does repeated application, such criticisms do have merit. In all likelihood, it is unreasonable to follow the EBP process for every decision made. However, students can be encouraged to pick one client facing a problem that often occurs in the field placement setting. Over time and many such clients, a knowledge base can be generated that serves a far greater number.

INFUSING EVIDENCE-BASED PRACTICE ACROSS THE SOCIAL WORK CURRICULUM

EBP is not a single-semester endeavor and should not be presented to students as such. There is far too much information, the process must be practiced to adequate levels of speed and accuracy, and the proper integration of findings with specific clients, programs, and policies is a complex endeavor. Rather, it is a cumulative process that should be woven through all facets of the curriculum. This requires that schools and departments of social work must somehow become as facile as individual practitioners in adopting new approaches as evidence emerges.

Broad Strategies

There are several steps that should be considered when making such a transition (Table 159.2). Most important, the inclusive philosophy of EBP must be stressed. That is, similar to teaching in the classroom, the basic definition and steps of EBP must be clearly understood and conveyed to faculty. In addition, leaders (both internal and external) should be sought out and engaged to facilitate the adoption of innovation (Rogers, 1995). Incorporating the EBP framework into different curricular areas can also be a challenge, especially areas that are traditionally resistant to empirical approaches. A narrow conceptualization of EBP, perceived or otherwise (e.g., that EBP amounts to using evidence from random clinical trials), may be translated as a thinly veiled attempt at foisting positivism on the entire

TABLE 159.2 Broad Strategies for Infusing Evidence-based Practice Across the Curriculum

1. Have the discussion—make sure you are all on the same page with respect to definitional issues. Identify and begin to deal with misunderstandings and disagreements, epistemological and otherwise.
2. Identify and marshal internal resources with expertise and/or interest in EBP.
3. Identify external resources. Who can be brought in to lead you objectively through some of this process? An outside resource is sometimes less threatening and may be one way to avoid personal entanglements that are sure to arise.
4. Decide how the EBP framework can be used across curricular areas:
   a. Research
   b. Clinical practice
   c. Policy and management
   d. Community
   e. Social justice and diversity
5. Decide whether and how empirically supported treatments (ESTs) will be taught.
6. Decide how to involve the field.
7. Decide how to maintain curricular focus with adjuncts (especially important in large schools).

faculty (Jenson, 2007). This must be avoided. With respect to distinguishing between ESTs and EBP, faculty must decide on whether to train students in ESTs and practice guidelines, and which ESTs should be chosen.

Finally, decisions must be made about how to involve the field and maintain curricular focus among adjunct professors. An easy approach to involving practicum partners is to evolve a culture whereby students engage with field instructors and placement agencies to pose and begin answering critical questions of import to the field (Gibbs, 2003). For the field, conferences and trainings in EBP, ESTs, and other content areas could help facilitate this process. Mostly, though, the field will need to begin to see how having students using the steps of EBP can actually benefit their agencies through systematic efforts to uncover current best evidence in relevant practice areas. Still, some agencies will not want to have such light shed on their practices, and students will inevitably encounter placements using interventions or supporting policies that have little or no empirical basis (Howard, McMillen, & Pollio, 2003). This brings the student and classroom yet another opportunity to explore controversy and to strategize about how to facilitate change at the agency or policy level. Adjuncts also must be factored into the equation because they teach a large proportion of the classes. One strategy is to create an adjunct liaison position and coordinate instructional content across subject areas (Springer, 2007). Another strategy is to have full-time faculty members coordinate all sections of each class, ensuring that EBP content is infused into courses.

Establishing an Introductory Evidence-based Practice Course

If EBP is to be woven throughout the curriculum, it must begin with the basics. Rather than the standard research class devoted to teaching students how to conduct research (a class where most students will neither learn enough to conduct good research nor develop a desire to try), why not introduce students to the process of EBP? In other words, change the curriculum to include an EBP class that touches on the various elements of research but is more practically geared toward systematically searching, understanding, appraising, and using the literature. The basics taught in this class can then be expanded and reinforced in subsequent core and specialization classes, including the basic tenets of research (e.g., basic study design, reliability, validity). Links to specific case examples in this and subsequent classes can help solidify learning. In this way, basic research methodology becomes a part of social work practice (Shlonsky & Stern, 2007).

Building on Courses and Assignments

Replication is the heart of science, and repetition is the heart of EBP. Repeating the process, using different client or policy questions, is essential to achieve a level of speed and proficiency that will enable students to continue the process upon graduation. Moreover, EBP is, at its core, a lifelong learning process (Sackett, Richardson, Rosenberg, & Haynes, 1997). Not only will the questions change as one practices, the evidence base will continue to grow and, in some cases, will change practice. One way to ease the pain of repetition is to envision classes as building on one another, much like general practice courses (i.e., moving from generalist practice in the first year to more specialized classes in the second). Although the basic EBP approach is unchanging in its methods, skills within the framework can be reinforced and expanded in subsequent classes as students begin to acquire greater practice skills. For instance, the first year of an Master of Social Work (MSW) program can focus on the nuts and bolts of posing an answerable question, searching the literature, and appraising what is found. In the second year, content-specific courses include the process but focus more on integrating current best evidence with client preferences/actions and clinical state/circumstances. As well, the second-year classes include a more nuanced consideration of how other factors (e.g., training, organizational resources, political context) enhance or detract from the adoption of EBP, possibly influencing the process of individual and social change (Regehr, Stern, & Shlonsky, 2007).

Encouraging Single-subject Design for Evaluation

For clinical interventions, N = 1 studies can be seen as the pinnacle of evaluating personal practice. They are the key to ascertaining whether interventions are working for clients. Advanced research classes would be well served by paying considerable attention to single-subject designs. Advanced clinical practice courses can also play a role in the fifth step of EBP by requiring students to formulate an evaluation plan as part of their coursework.

Developing Community Partnerships

Good community and agency partnerships are essential to the health of any school of social work, and this is no less the case as faculties move to embrace EBP. Key practice questions should drive research, and these are typically generated when practitioners and administrators notice a gap in knowledge. If research is not relevant to practice, its benefits are limited at best. EBP's bottom-up approach (Gibbs, 2003) requires that community and agency partners help drive the research agenda. To this end, community and agency partners should be encouraged to participate in and commit to the development of EBP at the university through ongoing training/ continuing education (e.g., ESTs) and capacity building. As well, processes should be developed whereby community and agency partners are encouraged to generate research questions and join with faculty to carry out new investigations.

Avoiding False Claims and Developing a Long-term Vision

EBP is an emerging approach and it will take considerable time, effort, and resources to make it work. EBP is not a quick fix for all that ails social work and the related helping professions. We must be honest about our current limitations, including the lack of evidence in some content areas, the confines of scarce agency resources and time, and the difficulty of integrating evidence within client context. We have a long way to go. Nonetheless, this wholesale shift in philosophy and practice is promising to the extent that clients will become increasingly well informed; are more likely to be offered high-quality, effective services; and will have greater attention paid to their desires and values.

WEBSITES

BEST training on evidence-based practice in social work at Columbia University. http://

www.columbia.edu/cu/musher/Website/
Website/EBP_OnlineTraining.htm.

Campbell Collaboration. http://
campbellcollaboration.org.

Centre for Evidence-based Medicine, University
of Toronto. http://www.cebm.utoronto.ca.

Cochrane Collaboration. http://www.cochrane.org.

Council on Social Work Education (CSWE) EBP
page. http://www.cswe.org/CSWE/research/
resources/Evidence-Based+Practice.

*Evidence-Based Practice for the Helping
Professions* companion Web site for Gibbs
(2003). http://www.evidence.brookscole.com.

References

Coomarasamy, A., & Khan, K. S. (2004). What is the evidence that evidence-based practice changes anything? A systematic review. *British Medical Journal, 329*, 1017–1021.

Gambrill, E. (2003). Evidence-based practice: Sea change or the emperor's new clothes? *Journal of Social Work Education, 39*, 3–23.

Gambrill, E. (2006). *Social work practice: A critical thinkers guide* (2nd ed.). New York, NY: Oxford University Press.

Gibbs, L. (2003). *Evidence-based practice for the helping professions: A practical guide with integrated multimedia.* Pacific Grove, CA: Brooks/Cole-Thomson Learning.

Gibbs, L., & Gambrill, E. (1999). *Critical thinking for social workers: Exercises for the helping professions.* Thousand Oaks, CA: Pine Forge Press.

Gibbs, L. E., & Gambrill, E. (2002). Evidence-based practice: Counterarguments to objections. *Research on Social Work Practice, 12*, 452–476.

Gray, J. A. M. (1997). *Evidence-based healthcare: How to make health policy and management decisions.* New York, NY: Churchill Livingstone.

Howard, M. O., McMillen, C., & Pollio, D. E. (2003). Teaching evidence-based practice: Toward a new paradigm for social work education. *Research on Social Work Practice, 13*, 234–259.

Jenson, J. M. (2007). Evidence-based practice and the reform of social work education: A response to Gambrill and Howard and Allen-Meares. *Research on Social Work Practice, 17*, 561–568.

Regehr, C., Stern, S., & Shlonsky, A. (2007). Operationalizing evidence-based practice: The development of an institute for evidence-based social work. *Research on Social Work Practice, 17*, 408–416.

Roberts, A. R., & Yeager, K. R. (Eds.). (2003). *Evidence-based practice manual.* New York, NY: Oxford University Press.

Rogers, E. M. (1995). *Diffusion of innovation* (4th ed.). New York, NY: Free Press.

Rosen, A., & Proctor, E. (Eds.). (2003). *Developing practice guidelines for social work intervention: Issues, methods, and research agenda.* New York, NY: Columbia University Press.

Sackett, D. L., Richardson, W. S., Rosenberg, W., & Haynes, R. B. (1997). *Evidence-based medicine: How to practice and teach EBM.* New York, NY: Churchill Livingstone.

Shlonsky, A., & Gibbs, L. (2004). Will the real evidence-based practice please step forward: Teaching the process of EBP to the helping professions. *Journal of Brief Therapy and Crisis Intervention, 4*, 137–153.

Shlonsky, A., & Stern, S. (2007). Reflections on the teaching of evidence-based practice. *Research on Social Work Practice, 17*, 603–611.

Springer, D. W. (2007). The teaching of evidence-based practice in social work higher education—living by the Charlie Parker dictum: A response to papers by Shlonsky and Stern, and Soydan. *Research on Social Work Practice, 17*, 619–624.

160 Evaluating Our Effectiveness in Carrying Out Evidence-based Practice

Bruce A. Thyer & Laura L. Myers

From the inception of evidence-based practice (EBP), authorities in this field have advocated that clinicians consider undertaking a type of experimental study they labeled the N = 1 randomized controlled trials (RCTs). The primary reference book *Evidence-based Medicine: How to Practice and Teach EBM* (Straus, Glasziou, Richardson, & Haynes, 2011) includes a positive description of this type of design:

The n-of-1 trial applies the principles of rigorous clinical trial methodology to… determine the best treatment for an individual patient. It randomizes time, and assigns the patient… active therapy or placebo at different times, so that the patient undergoes cycles of experimental and control treatment, resulting in multiple crossovers to help both our patient and us to decide on the best therapy. (Straus et al., 2011, p. 131)

The experimental logic of the N = 1 RCT can perhaps best be illustrated with an example. Let us say, for example, that a child has been diagnosed with hyperactivity and a physician has prescribed a medication to help calm him down. The parents doubt that drugs will be helpful and are resistant to following this treatment recommendation. However, with the helpful intervention of a social worker, they agree to give it a try for several weeks on an experimental basis. Two identical bottles of pills are prepared, one bottle is labeled A and contains (unknown to the parents or child) the active medicine, whereas bottle B contains similar-looking pills lacking any active ingredient (e.g., a placebo). The social worker arranges for the teacher to rate the child's behavior in school at the end of each day, using a valid behavior rating scale. Flipping a coin, the social worker assigns the child to receive either pill A (heads) or pill B (tails) each day for a two-week period. The social worker prepares a simple line graph, with behavior ratings scored on the vertical axis, and the days of the week on the horizontal one. The ratings for the days pill A is administered are plotted and connected, and the ratings for pill B are similarly portrayed. If there is no overlap in the two sets of lines, and the ratings during the days the child received the active medication are unambiguously those in which behavior was improved, then clear and compelling evidence of a genuinely experimental nature has demonstrated the superiority of the active drug over placebo.

This type of demonstration has several functions. First, we have empirical proof that the drug is helpful with this individual client, which is, after all, a highly desirable outcome of practicing EBP. Second, the evidence may alleviate the parents' reservations about using medication, and help them decide to continue its use. This example presupposes that the medication has no significant side effects, is not unreasonably expensive, that taking it is not prohibited by the family's religious beliefs, and so on. If the two sets of lines connecting the two different treatment conditions had significant overlap, then the effects of the active drug versus placebo would be less clear. Completely overlapping lines would suggest that the medicine was little better than placebo and need not be used at all. This is also good to know.

Within the field of psychotherapy, this type of design is called the alternating treatments design (ATD; Barlow & Hayes, 1979). In October 2013, we searched the PsycINFO database using "alternating treatments design" as key words appearing in journal abstracts and found over 370 published examples of its use across a wide array of disciplines, including audiology, medicine, education, and psychology. An ADT was used by social worker Steven Wong to help determine empirically how one's immediate environmental situation affected the psychotic-like behavior of a person suffering from chronic mental illness (Wong et al., 1987). The client, Tom, was a 37-year-old man with a diagnosis of chronic schizophrenia who was experiencing his fourth hospitalization. Systematic assessments of Tom's psychotic-like mumblings were tape recorded via a wireless microphone attached to his shirt for five sessions of unstructured free time in the hospital day room where he had access to usual recreational materials (e.g., television, stereo, magazines, books, table games, and cards) but was otherwise left alone. The subsequent experimental phase consisted of randomly alternating between two interventions, a 40-minute session in the day room begun by prompting the client to read articles he found interesting from an assortment of novel magazines offered to him, versus spending 40 minutes in the room without any reading prompting or access to novel magazines (identical to the original baseline condition). These two treatments were randomly alternated for 18 consecutive sessions, and the percentage of time Tom spent engaged in stereotypic laughter and mumbling, reliably recorded, was the dependent variable (outcome measure). The results are depicted in Figure 160.1. It is very clear that when Tom was given something interesting to do (e.g., reading) his psychotic-like behavior was markedly reduced, relative to having unstructured free time. There is no overlap in the two sets of data, providing compelling evidence that the simple intervention was causally responsible for these behavioral differences. Because a clear causal inference is possible via the intentional manipulation of the intervention and control conditions, this N = 1 randomized controlled trial can be legitimately classified as a true experiment. Dr. Wong also used this type of design to demonstrate experimentally that a checklist could be used effectively to help a memory-impaired woman with diabetes successfully undertake regular checking of her own blood sugar levels using a glucometer (Wong, Seroka, & Ogisi, 2000).

Within the field of EBP, randomized N = 1 trials are held in such high esteem that it has been claimed that these studies provide a *stronger* foundation for making decisions about the care of individuals than does the evidence derived from systematic reviews, meta-analyses, individual RCTs, and other evidentiary sources (see Guyatt et al., 2002, p. 12)! This certainly turns the usual apex of the evidentiary hierarchy on

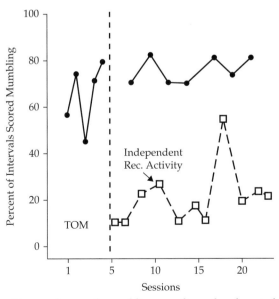

Figure 160.1 Percentage of intervals scored mumbling or solitary laughter in baseline sessions (circles) and in recreation sessions with independent activity (squares). From Wong et al. (1987, p. 80) with permission from the Society for the Experimental Analysis of Behavior.

its head! But note the original definition of EBP: "The conscientious, explicit, and judicious use of current best evidence in making decisions about the care of *individual patients*" (Sackett et al., 1996, p. 71, emphasis added). What better evidence regarding the appropriateness of a given intervention than a clear and compelling demonstration that it really seems to work with *our client*? Large-scale group studies very rarely make use of true probability samples, a prerequisite for generalizing findings, and in any case probability theory only permits inferences upward from sample to population, not downward from a sample (as in an RCT) to an individual.

CAN N = 1 STUDIES REALLY BE CALLED EXPERIMENTS?

Within the social work research literature, the term "experiment" is almost exclusively reserved for nomothetic studies involving relatively large groups of clients who are randomly assigned to receive an experimental psychosocial intervention, to receive no treatment, to treatment-as-usual, or to a placebo-control group. Pretreatment assessments may be used, and post-treatment assessments are essential to make any inferences about possible differential effects of the conditions to which the clients were exposed. Any post-treatment differences may be plausibly ascribed to their assigned condition (e.g., to the active or experimental treatment) as opposed to some rival explanation (e.g., passage of time, regression to the mean, concurrent history). Such designs have the potential to possess

high internal validity in that any conclusions drawn about the relative effects of the experimental conditions can be seen as quite credible, with the random assignment feature controlling for other possibilities. Such designs are called RCTs and can indeed be quite powerful.

However, traditional RCT methodology is often required in social work intervention research only because of the large amount of variance present in our studies. Frequently the independent variable (e.g., treatment) exerts modest effects at best and may be quite labile, readily influenced by client idiosyncrasy or environmental contextual factors. In other words, our interventions are often not robust. Dependent variables (e.g., outcome measures) may lack precision, being subject to various forms of bias, and contain a large amount of noise or unexplained variation as well. These factors essentially *require* the use of sophisticated inferential statistics to separate out the "real" effects of treatment from the noise and also necessitate studies having sufficiently large sample sizes to possess adequate statistical power to accomplish this task. But keep in mind that nomothetic research designs and inferential statistics are just one set of tools to accomplish experimental demonstrations. Extremely powerful treatments do not require such sophisticated controls because their effects are obvious and compelling, swamping the sometimes unwanted variance caused by client and context.

Table 160.1 provides some descriptions of what is meant by the term "experiment" in its broader sense. The crucial factor that distinguishes the true experiment from other forms of research

TABLE 160.1 Some Definitions of the Term "Experiment"

- "A study in which an intervention is deliberately introduced to observe its effects" (Shadish, Cook, & Campbell, 2002, p. 12).
- "One or more independent variables are manipulated to observe their effects on one or more dependent variables" (Shadish et al., 2002, p. 12).
- "The manipulation of one or more independent variables conducted under controlled conditions to test one or more hypotheses, especially for making inferences of a cause-effect character. Involves the management of one or more dependent variables" (Corsini, 2002, p. 351).
- "Manipulations of subject and/or intervention is the essence of experimental method…. The demands of science and of practice have led to a whole array of experiments. They include experiments designed… with the subjects serving as controls for themselves" (Wollins, 1960, p. 255).
- "N of 1 RCT An experiment in which there is only a single participant, designed to determine the effect of an intervention or exposure on that individual" (Guyatt & Rennie, 2002, p. 418).
- "A research study in which one or more independent variables is systematically varied by the researcher to determine its effects on dependent variables" (Holosko & Thyer, 2011, p. 39).

is the deliberate, planned manipulation of an intervention, and the systematic observation of its possible effects. Sample size has no bearing on the validity of this principle. Such an experimental study may involve 1,000 participants, 100, 10, or even only 1. The crucial test is whether clear effects can be observed. If the answer is yes, you have a legitimate demonstration of the value of the treatment, that is, an experiment. If not, one is faced with two possibilities. The first is that the treatment simply does not work. The second is that the treatment "works," but its effects are so minimal that they could not be detected with the research design and sample size used.

Studies involving small groups of clients (or even only one client) minimize Type I experimental errors (claims that a real effect is present, when it is really not) but are more liable to Type II errors (claiming that an effect is not present, when it really is). Studies with sizable groups minimize Type II errors (they are less likely to miss small but reliable effects of treatments) and are more liable to make Type I errors (claiming that an effect occurs, when it really does not). The use of p values derived from inferential tests, absent reporting their associated effect sizes, promotes Type I errors in nomothetic research. We learn more about reliable, albeit trivial, effects. Reporting effect sizes can help reduce this problem. Conversely, N = 1 studies are not very good at detecting small effects of our treatments (that is, are prone to Type II errors), and some researchers consider this a good thing, in that we are less liable to claim positive effects for trivially effective interventions, channeling our energies into pursuing treatments with powerful, robust effects. Usually, the data from N = 1 studies are graphically depicted and inferences are made on the basis of visual inspection alone. If they cannot be seen by the naked eye, unaided by inferential statistics, then the conservative researcher concludes that any reliable effects are of such small magnitude as to be of little clinical importance. This means that conclusions derived from N = 1 research tend to be more robust, in terms of internal validity because confident conclusions are rare, absent visually compelling evidence, such as that displayed in Figure 160.1.

OTHER FORMS OF EXPERIMENTAL N = 1 DESIGNS

The N-of-1 RCT or ATD is not the only type of within-client research design that can be applied to evaluate the effects of interventions with individual clients. Other selected N = 1 designs may also permit robust conclusions using the same logic applied with the ATD, namely, repeated demonstrations of an effect, following the introduction or removal of a treatment. In the ATD this introduction or removal of a treatment condition is dictated by the toss of a coin. If the outcome measure reliably fluctuates in a manner closely consistent with the manipulation of the treatment, we have increasing confidence that these outcome fluctuations can be attributed to the treatment itself, or to its removal. The greater the number of such demonstrations, the greater the internal validity.

Similar simple logic is the basis for causal inference in a type of N = 1 study called the ABAB design. Here, A refers to a period of time when the client received no formal treatment. The time period could conceivably be hours, days, weeks, or months, depending on the nature of the problem and circumstance surrounding it. During this A or baseline phase, a credible outcome measure is administered a number of times, and the data are plotted on a line graph, with time on the horizontal axis and the outcome measure scaled on the vertical axis. Ideally, the first baseline line is long enough to obtain data that are visually stable, for example, not obviously getting better (it is okay if they are getting worse). Then the treatment is introduced, and the outcome measure continues to be assessed. Ideally, one sees an immediate improvement after the treatment begins during this second, or B, phase. The data continue to be plotted and these improvements themselves stabilize. Thus far, one has completed an AB N = 1 study, one that possesses only one apparent demonstration of a functional relationship between the introduction of a treatment and client improvement. Unfortunately, only one such demonstration does not usually qualify a study to be labeled as a true experiment. A number of rival explanations cannot be ruled out with this simple design, for example, concurrent history, regression, placebo, a cyclic nature to the problem, and so on. To help rule out such threats, the intervention, B, is withdrawn or removed, and the baseline condition is reinstated (the second A phase). Ideally, the client relapses—ideally, that is, from the perspective of providing an experimental demonstration. If this happens, then we now enjoy two demonstrations of an apparent functional relationship between the treatment and the problem—one when the treatment was introduced (the client got better) and the second when the treatment was removed (the client got worse).

The second A phase is then followed by the reintroduction of the treatment for a period of time comprising the second B phase. Ideally, the client improves once again, leaving the social worker with three solid demonstrations of experimental control of outcome by the treatment—twice when the treatment was introduced (the client got better) and once when the treatment was removed (the client got worse). When graphically depicted, with obvious demarcations in the data between the four phases of the study, this is usually a very convincing demonstration of the effects of treatment. The inferential logic remains the same between the ABAB design and the ATD, repeatedly introducing the treatment or its removal. Strong effects are evident to practitioners, clients, and neutral observers alike. Absent strong effects (for example, in the case of only minor changes in the data, or considerable overlap in the range of data between adjacent phases), the same conservative principles suggest that one conclude the intervention is not clinically valuable. Again, Type II error is more likely (you will miss minor but reliable effects) and Type I error minimized (you are very unlikely to conclude that a strong effect is present, when it is really not).

The possible permutations of these simple principles are numerous. A further demonstration may be possible, as in the ABABAB design. One may try to compare the relative efficacy of two interventions, as in the ABAC design. These types of n = 1 designs relying on changes in the data coincident with the introduction of the treatment and its *removal* are obviously only possible for interventions with short-lived effects. If a treatment can be expected to produce a durable improvement, then the ABAB design will not be useful, because the relapse anticipated during the second B phase will not be forthcoming. Examples of such interventions may include teaching the client a social or intellectual skill, the attainment of personal insight (perhaps via psychotherapy), personal growth or strengthening of psychological resources, the removal of phobic fears or obsessive-compulsive behaviors, or acquiring a cognitive coping skill (e.g., rational self-talk). Discontinuing such an intervention will not necessarily obliterate any clinical gains made by the client, and thus the ABAB design, or another N = 1 study that depends on

client relapse occurring following the removal of a treatment for causal inferences to be made, is not usually a suitable N = 1 design in such circumstances.

When one is applying a treatment that is expected to produce not only immediate but also durable effects, another form of N = 1 experiment called the multiple baseline (MBL) design may be possible. The MBL also relies on the same logic as other experimental clinical research designs—repeatedly demonstrating that an effect is observed when a treatment is applied. There are various types of MBL designs, and one of the more common is the MBL across clients. This design requires that you have two or more clients seeking treatment at about the same point in time, with a similar problem, for which you believe a particular treatment is appropriate. Let us use as an example two clients who present for help in overcoming a specific phobia. You begin with a baseline phase for both clients, having searched the literature and located one (or more) credible outcome measures. When each client has stability in their baseline data (the A phase), you begin treatment (say, gradual real-life exposure therapy) for Client 1 (transitioning into the B phase) but *not* for Client 2 (who remains in the A phase). The internal validity of this design depends on seeing rapid improvements in Client 1 but *not* in Client 2. Some time passes, Client 1 continues to improve, and you then begin treating Client 2 with a similar program of exposure therapy (the B phase). Imagine two AB designs stacked atop each other, with the lower one having a longer baseline, but each having stable baseline data, and marked improvement only when treatment begins during the B phase. This approach in effect permits two possible demonstrations of experimental control, each time when the treatment was applied to two different clients. Two demonstrations is much better than one (as in a simple AB design), and three such demonstrations, as in an MBL design across three clients, approaches the internal validity of the ABAB design (which also can yield three demonstrations).

A second form of MBL is called the MBL across settings design, and it may be used to determine the effects of one particular therapy on one problem experienced by one client in different contexts. As an example, suppose a child client displayed hyperactive behavior, in the home, and in the school, and this was posing a significant problem for the child. In the MBL across settings design, baselines would be taken of hyperactive behavior in the two settings, and displayed on two stacked AB-type graphs. When the baseline data are stable in both settings, an intervention (say, a point system to reward in-seat behavior) is initiated in one setting only, say, the school, whereas the baseline condition is maintained in the other setting (the home). Experimentally, one desires to see immediate improvements in the first setting, and stable, problematic conditions continuing in the second one. Then, after some time, the same intervention is applied in the other setting, with, it is hoped, a similar positive effect. This design also constitutes providing two demonstrations of experimental control, an improvement over only one demonstration, and adding a third setting for baselining and intervention enhances internal validity even further.

The third and final form of MBL design is the MBL across problems design. It may be useful in clinical situations wherein one client presents with two or more problems potentially amenable to treatment by the same intervention. Imagine a child doing poorly in two subjects at school, arithmetic and reading. With the cooperation of the teacher, the social worker gets regular reports of the child's grades in each of these two subjects. These grades are baselined separately, and then an intervention, say, tutoring, is provided in *one* subject, but not in the second, which continues to be baselined. Experimentally, one wishes to see that the first academic subject (for which tutoring was provided) displayed immediate and marked improvements in grades, whereas the second subject remained stable (with poor grades). Then the same intervention, tutoring, is provided to the second subject, which then also immediately displays a sharp improvement in grades. Again, the logic is the same, with two or more demonstrations of an effect—the problem is stable, an intervention is applied, and the problem is significantly improved. The MBL across three or more problems is even more convincing than with only two, and in certain circumstances, for example, clear data, a valid outcome measure, and treatments that can be deliberately introduced, the social worker is capable of providing genuinely experimental results, outcomes so compelling that most doubts are removed as to the effectiveness of the intervention.

The logic of N = 1 studies follows principles elucidated by John Stuart Mill in his classic book *A System of Logic*. In it he outlines several forms of evidence that can permit causal inferences.

Among these are the so-called Method of Direct Agreement, which states, "If two or more instances of the phenomenon under investigation have only one circumstance in common, the circumstance in which alone all the instances agree, is the cause (or effect) of the given phenomenon" (Mill, 1875, p. 454). Related is the Method of Difference, which reads, "If an instance in which the phenomenon under investigation occurs, and an instance in which it does not occur, have every circumstance save one in common, that one occurring only in the former; the circumstance in which alone the two instances differ, is the effect, or cause, or a necessary part of the cause of phenomenon" (p. 455). And Mill's Method of Concomitant Variations is also pertinent to the logic of N = 1 designs: "Whatever phenomenon varies in any manner whenever another phenomenon varies in some particular manner, is either a cause or an effect of that phenomenon, or is connected with it through some fact of causation" (p. 270). These logical principles undergird all experimental investigations, group and single-subject. Keeping other conditions constant, introduce (or remove) a presumptive independent variable (social work treatment). See what happens. Repeat several times. Consistency of apparent effects argues for the influence of the independent variable in a causal sense. Certainly not in terms of ultimate causation, but often with respect to proximal causes, causes that may be useful in social work practice.

In any research design, nomothetic or N = 1, poor results mean that experimental control has not been demonstrated, and internal validity is low. But if powerful effects are exerted by the treatment, these can be compellingly disclosed in N = 1 studies. The ATD is one N = 1 study with the potential to demonstrate internally valid conclusions. N = 1 studies using withdrawal designs, such as the ABAB, or the various forms of MBL designs, are also capable of permitting causal inferences. There is no claim that the experimental N = 1 studies can be applied in every clinical situation, but certainly their versatility permits far greater use than they have heretofore enjoyed as a method of evaluating clinical outcomes in social work practice. And N = 1 designs of lesser internal validity, such as the B, AB, or ABA types (see Thyer & Myers, 2007) are even more readily applicable in everyday practice. The use of N = 1 studies within social work is not of hypothetical value. A bibliography on the topic (Thyer & Thyer, 1992) prepared 17 years ago found over

TABLE 160.2 Some Indications for Considering N = 1 Experiments in Evidence-based Practice

- Is there a reliable and valid way to assess the client's problem/condition? For example, is a credible outcome measure available? (The answer should be yes)
- Can the outcome measure be repeatedly assessed over time? (The answer should be yes)
- Are the effects of social work intervention likely to have a rapid onset? (The answer should be yes)
- Is using an N = 1 design ethically acceptable? (The answer should be yes)
- Is participating in an N = 1 design acceptable to the client? (The answer should be yes)
- Is the intervention feasible? (The answer should be yes)
- Will the effects of intervention likely be durable or permanent? If yes, then a multiple baseline design may be indicated. If not, then a withdrawal or alternating treatments design may be most useful.

200 published examples. Wong (2010) is an excellent overview of the use of these designs in social work practice.

EBP has long advocated that practitioners evaluate the effects of their interventions using experimental N = 1 research designs. Thus far the EBP literature in this regard has given limited attention to one type of N = 1 study, the alternating treatments design. However, a more diverse array of N = 1 designs have the potential to yield truly experimental results, and these deserve serious consideration by the social worker seeking to practice within the model known as evidence-based practice. Table 160.2 lists some pragmatic indications for considering using an N = 1 study to evaluate outcomes in evidence-based practice.

The evidence-based model described in this section on evaluating the effects of intervention presents a perspective that has long been present in social work.

"… the social worker can throw light on social causation. It is sometimes said that the sociologist, unlike other scientists, cannot engage in experiments. But that is what the social worker does all the time… he does, and must, experiment… Practical necessity compels the social worker to seek an answer to the questions of causation. (pp. 83–84)… what we want to discover, whether as social scientists or as social workers, is the causes of things, the dependence of one phenomenon on another… The social worker, being always engaged in making experiments, can advance the far too neglected study of social causation. (p. 89). . . The question of social causation is so crucial for the social worker that it should determine his whole approach. (p. 93) (McIver, 1931)

Single case experimental designs provide a robust methodology to fulfill these laudable aspirations of over 80 years ago. When combined with the five-step decision-making process of evidence-based practice, the potential for improvements in the delivery of social work services is immense.

WEBSITES

Campbell Collaboration. http://www.campbell-collaboration.org.

Center for Evidence-based Medicine. http://www.cebm.utoronto.ca.

Cochrane Collaboration. http://www.cochrane.org.

References

Barlow, D. H., & Hayes, S. C. (1979). Alternating treatments design: One strategy for comparing the effects of two treatments in a single subject. *Journal of Applied Behavior Analysis, 12,* 199–210.

Corsini, R. J. (2002). *The dictionary of psychology.* New York, NY: Brunner-Routledge.

Guyatt, G., Haynes, B., Jaeschke, R., Cook, D., Greenhalgh, T., Meade, M., et al. (2002). Introduction: The philosophy of evidence-based medicine. In G. Guyatt & D. Rennie (Eds.), *Users' guides to the medical literature* (pp. 5–71). Chicago, IL: AMA Press.

Guyatt, G., & Rennie, D. (Eds.). (2002). *Users' guides to the medical literature.* Chicago: AMA Press.

Holosko, M. J., & Thyer, B. A. (2011). *Pocket glossary for commonly used research terms.* Thousand Oaks, CA: Sage.

McIver, R. M. (1931). *The contribution of sociology to social work.* New York, NY: Columbia University Press.

Mill, J. S. (1875). *A system of logic.* London: Longmans.

Sackett, D. L, Rosenberg, W. M., Gray, J.A., et al. (1996). Evidence based medicine: What it is and what it isn't. *BMJ, 312*(7023), 71–72.

Shadish, W. R., Cook, T. D., & Campbell, D. T. (2002). *Experimental and quasi-experimental designs for generalized causal inference*. New York, NY: Houghton Mifflin.

Straus, S. E., Glasziou, P., Richardson, W. S., & Haynes, R. B. (2011). *Evidence-based medicine: How to practice and teach it* (4th edition). New York, NY: Elsevier.

Thyer, B. A., & Myers, L. L. (2007). *The social worker's guide to evaluating practice outcomes*. Alexandria, VA: CSWE Press.

Thyer, B. A., & Thyer, K. B. (1992). Single-system research designs used in social work practice: A bibliography from 1965–1990. *Research on Social Work Practice, 2*, 99–116.

Wollins, M. (1960). Measuring the effect of social work intervention. In N. Polansky (Ed.), *Social work research* (pp. 247–272). Chicago, IL: University of Chicago Press.

Wong, S. E. (2010). Single-case evaluation designs for practitioners. *Journal of Social Service Research, 36*, 248–259.

Wong, S. W., Seroka, P. L., & Ogisi, J. (2000). Effects of a checklist on self-assessment of blood glucose level by a memory-impaired woman with diabetes mellitus. *Journal of Applied Behavior Analysis, 33*, 251–254.

Wong, S. E., Terranova, M. D., Bowen, L., Zarate, R., Massel, H. K., & Liberman, R. P. (1987). Providing independent recreational activities to reduce stereotypic vocalizations in chronic schizophrenics. *Journal of Applied Behavior Analysis, 20*, 77–81.

GLOSSARY

Compiled by Mallory Jensen

AB design: A single-system research design for comparing client functioning during treatment (i.e., the intervention or B phase) with client functioning before treatment (i.e., the baseline or A phase). The AB design is used to monitor client change and evaluate treatment outcomes.

ABC model: Originally devised by Albert Ellis, this model inserts cognition as a mediating factor between people's experiences and their emotional/behavioral responses to those experiences. *A*ctivating events are followed by *b*eliefs that result in *c*onsequences of emotions and behaviors.

Abstinence violation syndrome: A concept developed by G. Alan Marlatt describing a phenomenon observed after a slip or relapse. Those who have relapse feel guilty and ashamed. They seek solace in their drug of choice. Further, they fail to draw a distinction between a small lapse deviation from sobriety versus a major relapse from sobriety, which differ in the amount consumed and the duration in the period of use. When the client fails to distinguish between lapses and relapses, there is no incentive to get back on track quickly.

Access to care: The opportunity for consumers to obtain needed services, with attention to such issues as the location of service, hours of operation, and affordable fees.

Accountability: Providing information, in useful form, to others who must make decisions or take action regarding a person, case, situation, agency, or community. A social worker may be accountable to a supervisor, a community, clients, the court, a board of directors, the profession, and other parties. Being accountable means being responsible for providing services in accordance with high standards.

Actuarial risk assessment: An empirically derived estimation of the likelihood of maltreatment recurrence over time; it has consistently demonstrated higher levels of reliability and validity when compared with consensus-based approaches and clinical judgment in estimating the probability of recurrences.

Adaptedness: A favorable person-in-environment fit that supports human growth and well-being, and preserves and enriches the environment.

Administrative law: The body of law that is focused on rules, policies, procedures and other actions issued by federal, state, and local governmental agencies. It includes agency-created appeal, mediation, and/or hearing processes.

Adverse effect: The physical, psychological, or social effect of an intervention that is unintentional and unrelated to its desired actions.

Advocacy: To speak up in favor of an issue, to plead the case for another, or to champion a cause, often for individuals and groups that cannot speak out on their own behalf. Types of advocacy include self-advocacy, case advocacy (for an individual client), and class advocacy (on behalf of a group or category of individuals in similar circumstances).

Affordable housing: Housing for which the occupant generally pays no more than 30% of gross income for rent.

African-centeredness: Acknowledges African culture, expressions, values, beliefs, and institutions.

African-centered genogram: A cultural visual representation of the African American family that depicts both functional relationships and biological relationships.

Age-specific intervention: An intervention based on empirical studies designed specifically to treat older persons' problems.

Aggressive outreach: Direct and intensive services that occur in the consumer's home and natural community.

Alliances/coalitions: In a family or group, relationships formed between two or more individuals that serve a specific function in influencing interpersonal dynamics.

Allocation concealment: Disguising group assignment, particularly upcoming assignments, in clinical studies. Without it, even properly developed random allocation sequences can be subverted.

Ambiguity: The introduction of therapeutic content that can be interpreted in more than one way by the client.

Ambiguity in therapy: Forms of speech, metaphors, imagery, body movements, and so on, that stimulate a search process in the listeners to find their own relevant meanings.

Anger outburst: Extreme display of emotion characterized by irritability, physical or verbal attack, and rage with negativism that is considered maladaptive when it occurs without an immediate catalyst.

Anorexia nervosa: A disorder characterized by self-induced starvation and severe fear of gaining weight and looking fat, resulting in medical symptoms related to starvation.

Antecedent: An environmental event or stimulus that precedes a response. When the antecedent signals that a response is or is not likely to be followed by a reinforcer, it is referred to as a discriminative stimulus.

Anxiety-management technique: Behavioral processes such as progressive relaxation training, guided self-dialogue, and thought stopping, aimed at teaching clients to reduce and cope with debilitating anxiety.

Anxiolytics: A class of drugs that reduce anxiety; also known as minor tranquilizers.

Arbitration: A conflict resolution process conducted by a neutral third party, who can impose a legally binding decision if the disputants cannot agree.

Assertive community treatment (ACT): An evidence-based service delivery model in which the same clinical team, using largely outreach methods, provides comprehensive community-based treatment, rehabilitation, and supportive services to persons with severe and persistent mental illness. This model is also known as PACT, or Program of Assertive Community Treatment.

Assessment: The process of systematically collecting data about a client's functioning, and monitoring progress in client functioning, on an ongoing basis. In this way, social workers identify and measure specific problem behaviors as well as protective and resilience factors, and determine whether treatment is necessary. Information is typically gathered from a variety of sources (e.g., individual, family members, case records, observation, rapid assessment tools). Types of assessment include bio-psychosocial history taking, multidimensional crisis assessment, symptom checklists, functional analysis, behavioral measurement, and mental status exams.

Asset development: The process of assisting families or individuals in gaining wealth by building capital through home ownership, savings accounts, retirement accounts, and investment portfolios.

Assimilative integration: Integrative approach to psychosocial intervention drawing on ideas and technical procedures from various schools of thought but guided by a unitary theoretical perspective; practitioners incorporate techniques into the primary conceptual model of intervention.

Assisted suicide: Hastening one's death, in the face of a life-threatening illness or debilitating condition, with aid from another person. This term is generally used to refer to actions taken by a physician, but the assistance (which is illegal in some states) can also be from other health professionals, friends, or family members.

Attention deficit hyperactivity disorder (ADHD): A persistent pattern of inattention, hyperactivity, and impulsivity in two or more settings (e.g., school, work, or home). The *DSM-5* lists three subtypes: combined type, predominantly hyperactive-impulsive type, and predominantly inattentive type (which most closely resembles what was previously termed attention deficit disorder, or ADD).

Authority theme: Issues having to do with to the relationship between the client (individual, family, or group) and the social worker.

Availability heuristic: First described by Daniel Kahnaman and Amos Tversky. The principle holds that whatever a person can imagine will be evaluated as more probable. When applied to one's own behavior, the principle states that if I can envision myself behaving in a particular way, this will change my self-perception. Moreover, I will be more likely to behave consistently with what I have imagined myself doing.

Awareness: A growing consciousness and developing internal knowledge of self through thoughts, sensations, feelings, actions, and memories, and an external attentiveness to others and the environment.

Baseline: The assessment phase of practice, when the frequency of a specific behavior, client functioning, or attitudes are measured over time prior to an intervention.

Batterer Intervention Program (BIP): Batterer intervention programs (BIPs) are treatment programs for men and women who abuse their partners, whether the abuse is physical, verbal, sexual, psychological, or another form of abuse. Most often, those who attend batterer intervention programs have been court-ordered to do so.

Behavioral experiment: Identifying and testing of the validity of a client's thoughts through enactments in actual life experience or through role-plays.

Behavioral family therapy: Family therapies that emphasize reinforcing and punishing family relationships with one another and with the social environment. These therapies are action-oriented and focus on learning new skills that modify behavioral functioning and reframe and alter cognitive perceptions.

Behavioral observation: The process of carefully defining an overt activity or event and tracking the frequency, intensity, or duration of its occurrence. Behaviors should be specified in detail so that others can accurately count the same behavior in the same way.

Behavioral social work: A research-based treatment approach founded on learning theory, which holds that much behavior is learned

through contingencies of reinforcement and/or punishment. Consequently, problematic behavior can possibly be unlearned and prosocial behavior can be learned to replace it. Specific, measurable behaviors are the targets for intervention. A behavioral assessment is first done to identify what environmental changes are needed to modify problematic behavior. A treatment plan is then developed for changing the contingencies of reinforcement and/or punishment. The target behavior is measured in a baseline period and then monitored throughout the treatment process once intervention begins.

Best practice: A technique or methodology that, through empirical research, has proven in the past to lead reliably to a desired result.

Bio-psychosocial model: An attempt to integrate a vision of a client as a person, in situation, not unlike the social work concept of person–environment fit. This model recognizes that biological factors are necessary but not sufficient for understanding a human person in a social world. Although psychosocial factors such as stress, anxiety, and depression may underpin many conditions, some disorders may be understood to be truly bio-psychosocial. There is a known genetic basis to many illnesses, but it is understood that social and environmental triggers must be present to bring about the potential illness. Therefore, this term is applied to phenomena that consist of biological, psychological, and social elements.

Bio-psychosocial–cultural assessment: A comprehensive assessment model that ascertains the influence and interplay of biology, psychology, learnings, social environmental, and cultural factors on a client's mental health. It is the basis of the multiaxial diagnostic system of the *Diagnostic and Statistical Manual of Mental Disorders (DSM).*

Bipolar I: A level of depression characterized by the presence of episodes of major depressive disorder and at least one documented manic or mixed episode.

Bipolar II: A level of depression characterized by at least one major depressive episode that is accompanied by at least one hypomanic episode.

Blocking: A worker intervention that prevents the execution of undesirable, unethical, or inappropriate behaviors by the group as a whole or individual members.

Borderline personality disorder (BPD): A pervasive pattern of instability of interpersonal relationships, self-image, and affects, along with a marked impulsivity that begins by early adulthood and is present in a variety of contexts. People with BPD have among the highest suicide, attempted suicide, and mental health utilization rates of those with any psychiatric disorder.

Boundaries: The spoken and unspoken rules that case managers and clients observe regarding the physical and emotional limits of their relationship.

Boundary-spanning role: The part played by agency practitioners who have the capability and responsibility of making connections with other organizations and agencies in the community. This promotes coordination and joint effort on behalf of clients.

Brief treatment: An approach to working with clients that acknowledges up front that there is a time limit to treatment. Models vary and may include specific session limits (for example, up to 12 sessions) or time limits (for example, up to three months).

Broad definition of forensic social work: Any form of social work practice that is related in any way to legal issues or litigation in the criminal or civil justice legal systems.

Broker: A case manager who conducts assessment, develops care plans, and makes referrals to provider agencies for services. Brokers cannot authorize or purchase services for their clients.

Bulimia nervosa: A pattern of binge eating combined with attempts to avoid weight gain, such as purging, alternate calorie restriction, laxative use, and/or overexercise.

Bullying: Attacking an individual, often on the basis of a perceived difference or vulnerability; usually associated with school and workplace attacks.

Capacity building: A strengths-based approach to community building that involves preparing and supporting staff, natural helpers, and parents to increase their skills and knowledge for personal, organizational, professional, and family center development. Gaining access to needed resources and services is critical to capacity building.

Capitation: A method of financing health and mental health programs common in many managed care plans, in which providers agree to offer a specified package of services for a predetermined cost. The payment is most often made on a monthly basis. The provider is responsible for delivering or arranging for the delivery of a designated range of health care services for this predetermined payment, regardless of actual cost of the services. There is concern by social workers that high-risk, high-user, vulnerable populations will be disadvantaged under capitated arrangements.

Caregiver: One who provides services to a client in the home or immediate community environment. This may be a family member, a community member, or a paid provider.

Care planning: A process, involving clients and caregivers, that translates information collected during assessment into a plan of care, identifying services to be delivered, formal and informal providers, frequency of service delivery, and cost. Care planning is a resource-allocation process.

Caring: One element of the construct "working relationship"; the client's sense that the worker is concerned about him or her and that the worker wishes to help with those concerns the client believes are important.

Case management: A service that links and coordinates assistance from institutions and agencies providing medical, psychosocial, and concrete support for individuals in need of such assistance. It is the process of social work intervention that helps people organize and use the supports, services, and opportunities that enable them to achieve life outcomes that they value. Additionally, it is a direct practice method that involves skills in assessment, counseling, teaching, and advocacy that aims to improve the social functioning of clients served. In this service concept, clients are provided both individualized counseling and are linked to other needed services and supports.

Case record: A written and authenticated compilation of information that describes and documents the client assessment, along with present, past, and prospective services to the consumer.

CAT (Critically Appraised Topic): A brief (one-page) description of a well-structured question, search strategy, related research found, critical appraisal of what is found, and clinical bottom line.

Catharsis: The emotional relief experienced following the process of revealing one's inner anxieties and conflicts. For adults, this can occur through talking about one's problems; for children, this relief can occur through play containing elements of the conflict and anxiety.

Change activist: Someone who acts in an attempt to make a change on another person or community's behalf and may charge a modest fee (e.g., ministers, priests, spiritualists, and folk healers).

Change strategy: The action taken to pursue a desired change based on (1) what is most likely to influence decision makers and allies to make the desired change, and (2) what is possible given the time and resources available.

Change tactics: The actions or events that implement change strategy.

Change target: The person or group that must consent for a change to occur.

Child abuse and neglect: The physical or mental injury, sexual abuse, negligent treatment, or maltreatment of a person under the age of 18 years.

Child protection mediation: A conflict resolution process in which an impartial third party assists parents, children, child protection workers, extended family members, foster parents, or others to resolve conflict in cases involving child abuse or neglect (also called "dependency mediation").

Child support: Provision of financial resources by the parent who does not have primary custody of the child to meet the daily needs of the child.

Circular causality: A repetitive pattern of interaction between two or more individuals that results in an undesirable outcome for one or more of those involved. The term may also refer to a systems perspective that focuses on the mutual influences and interpersonal contexts in which problems develop.

Clarification: Process by which the juvenile with sexual behavior problems clarifies that the responsibility for the assault/abuse resides with the offender and addresses the harm done to the victim and the family.

Class action suit: A court action filed on behalf of named parties as well as a larger number of persons who are said to be "similarly situated" (in comparable circumstances).

Client-monitored behaviors: Actions, thoughts, or feelings that clients track over time. More easily identifiable behaviors tend to be both recognizable by clients and more accurately reported than those they perform automatically or subconsciously.

Clinical algorithm: Schematic diagrams outlining the decision pathways described in a practice guideline. The diagram is usually formatted in a decision-tree format, with yes/no options presented at each decision point.

Clinical case management: An approach to human service delivery that integrates elements of clinical social work and traditional case management practices. The social worker combines the sensitivity and interpersonal skill of the psychotherapist with the creativity and action orientation of the environmental architect.

Clinical expertise: The integration of current best research evidence, client preferences and actions, and clinical state and circumstances.

Clinical social work: This practice area includes case advocacy, case management, psychotherapy, clinical supervision, teamwork, behavior analysis and therapy, and program development. Therefore, clinical social work practice emphasizes direct work with individuals, families, and small groups, but is not limited to psychotherapeutic models and practices.

Clinical syndrome: A cluster of symptoms and behaviors that are defined as a mental disorder. Clinical syndromes are diagnosed on axis I of the *DSM-5* system.

Cluster randomized trial: A trial in which groups or areas are assigned a condition at random. May be used when an intervention can only be administered to the group (e.g., a public education campaign), to avoid contamination (e.g., by assigning schools rather than children or classrooms), or to reduce effort and save money.

Coalition: A cluster of organizations formed for a common purpose or social agenda, while each maintains its own identity. Coalitions have a series of inherent dynamic tensions that need to be balanced: cooperation and conflict, unity and diversity, mixed loyalties, and accountability and autonomy.

Code of ethics: A formal document ratified by a group or organization containing ethical principles, guidelines, and standards. The most frequently adopted code of ethics for social workers has been approved by the National Association of Social Workers (NASW) and is called the NASW Code of Ethics.

Cognitive bias: An unconscious tendency to distort one's views in a certain direction.

Cognitive distortion: Attitudes, thoughts, or beliefs that are irrational or illogical.

Cognitive distortions & restructuring: Also know as thinking errors; excuses, denial, rationalizations, and minimization of sexual offending behaviors that are identified, examined, and confronted in treatment.

Cognitive elaboration: The generation of alternative conceptualizations of a given event, phenomenon, or stimulus condition. This process is completed in recognition that multiple meanings exist for all human experience.

Cognitive restructuring: The use of logic and evidence to modify cognitions and cognitive processing. Socratic dialogue, guided imagery, and behavioral experiments are typical approaches associated with the cognitive behavior therapy approach.

Cognitive-behavioral therapy: A treatment model emphasizing the primacy of thoughts and beliefs in influencing feelings and subsequent actions. Interventions include social skills training, problem solving, cognitive restructuring, and communication skills training. Also known as a theoretical approach to treatment that stresses the role of thoughts, beliefs, perceptions, and attitudes on feelings and behavior. Techniques include cognitive restructuring; cognitive coping skills such as problem solving, self-reinforcement, and relaxation; and training in social skills, assertiveness, and communication. Behavioral methods, such as rehearsal, modeling, reinforcement, and coaching, are typically employed for the delivery of content.

Cognitive therapy: Therapeutic technique in which dysfunctional cognitions, including automatic thoughts, beliefs, and assumptions are challenged logically and functionally in order to modify them, in turn producing positive changes in related affect and behavioral responses.

Cohesive self: The essential self-structure of a well-adapted, healthily functioning individual whose self-functioning evinces the harmonious interchange of ambitions, ideals, and talents with the events of everyday life.

Common factors perspective: An integrative approach to psychosocial intervention that emphasizes core elements shared by the major systems of psychotherapy rather than specific technical procedures associated with particular schools of thought. Common factors include client characteristics, such as motivation and expectations of change; practitioner characteristics, such as attunement, empathy, and authenticity; provision of rationale for problems in functioning and conceptual framework for intervention; and strategic processes, such as experiential learning, interpretive procedures, modeling, reinforcement, and exposure.

Community-based case management: A model of case management that emphasizes involvement of all community partners in the client's well-being. It benefits from the synergy that occurs when multiple stakeholders work together to deliver client services and has been particularly effective in the child welfare field.

Community-based services: Services that are situated in the home environment of clients and are easily accessible to them. The term is often associated with decentralization of services.

Community capacity: A form of social organization that emanates from the operation and interaction of formal and informal networks of social care in the community that allows community members to demonstrate *shared responsibility* and *collective competence* for addressing community needs and confronting situations that threaten the safety and well-being of the community.

Community organizing: The process of bringing people and groups together to collectively address a need, solve problems, or improve a social condition.

Community partnership: An alliance between citizens and practitioners to bring about planned change for the common good.

Community practice: The generic term for social work intervention at the community level, defined geographically or functionally, including practice in the neighborhood, around a common issue, or around a shared identity. Its components include community building, organizing, development, and planning.

Community results: Aggregate, broad-based outcomes that reflect the collective efforts of individuals and families who live within a specified area.

Comorbidity: When two or more diseases or conditions coexist or co-occur.

Compassion fatigue: Characterized in social workers and counselors by weariness and loss of confidence, often accompanied by self-doubt and loss of conviction in one's knowledge and methods. Results from unrelieved and intense interaction with clients and lack of self-support systems.

Computerized practice management: Computer programs that keep track of basic patient information, appointments, insurance authorizations, and billing and payments. They also may include assessment information and progress notes. Most are designed primarily for individual and small group practices.

Conceptual framework: A guiding set of interrelated assumptions, based on one's worldview, that is used to provide direction for practice methods.

Conduct disorder: A *DSM* diagnosis that involves an entrenched pattern of behavior in which a person violates the basic rights of others or where major age-appropriate societal norms or rules are violated. This pattern involves four categories of behaviors: aggressive conduct either causing or threatening harm to people or animals; nonaggressive conduct leading to property loss or damage; deceitfulness or theft; and serious violations of rules. The person demonstrates at least three such behaviors in the past year, with at least one in the past six months.

Confidentiality: Involves safeguarding personal information from unwarranted disclosure. Under the NASW Code of Ethics, social workers are expected to maintain confidentiality by collecting only essential information about their clients, revealing clients' confidences only for compelling reasons, and disclosing information to third parties only with proper informed consent from clients or others acting on their behalf.

Congruence: A practitioner's display of genuineness and honesty with the client.

Consensus-based safety assessment: List of factors (some of which may come from research) that are thought by a convened group to be related to the likelihood of immediate harm.

Constituency: The group with whom or around which a social worker organizes. Constituents may include clients, consumers, residents, members, parents, students, service recipients, and patients.

Construct: An active processing or organizing experience in an individual's mind. Personal constructs represent personal or shared meanings.

Construct elaboration: The generation of alternative conceptualizations of a given event, phenomenon, or stimulus condition. This process is completed in recognition that multiple meanings exist for all human experience.

Constructivism: A worldview postulating that there is an objective, external reality but a person can never experience it directly and that the structure of the individual human organism and human mind, rather than that of the environment, is the central mechanism in reality construction.

Consumer-directed services: An approach to service delivery for older people and people with disabilities in which consumers have a degree of decision-making authority about their own services.

Consumer-driven case management: A case management model that emphasizes providing the best organized practice for clients in complex and chronic situations.

Contact boundary: The point where self meets other, distinguishing one person from another. The flexibility of this boundary determines the quality of the contact with the other and ultimately the stretching of all boundaries, which from a Gestalt perspective represents growth.

Contact: The psychological process of engaging with the environment and ourselves. Contact refers to the quality of the way one is in touch with and experiences the world.

Contamination: This occurs when members of the control group in an experiment inadvertently receive the intervention. It may be prevented by sampling natural clusters.

Continuing education: Demonstration of continued competency through completion of continuing education hours as part of the re-credentialing process. Traditionally, programs offered for continuing education are for skills that enhance or reaffirm a social worker's professional knowledge and skills.

Continuum of care: A wide range of health and social services, provided in the home, community, and institutional settings designed to serve older adults as their needs change over time. It is more than a collection of service components. It is an organized, coherent, and integrated service system.

Contract: An agreement between parties that defines the relationship between them, the responsibilities of each party, and penalties to each should agreements not be met. To be valid, contracts must be entered into freely and without coercion. There are three kinds of contracts used with clients in social work. The *service* contract describes and defines the relationship between the client and the service provider, agency, or program. The *initial* contract develops the tasks of the initial period, which include gathering information, assessment, and problem definition. The *therapeutic* contract defines worker or client objectives in the change process and the tasks, treatments, and interventions that enable their achievement. The therapeutic contract assigns specific tasks and responsibilities, and develops both a time frame and a system of measurability. The contract is the plan that worker and client will follow in achieving the mutually determined goal.

Contracting process: A worker-initiated effort, usually in the beginning phase of the work, to establish the purpose of the contact, explain the worker's role, gain some sense of the client's issues (feedback), and deal with issues of authority.

Controlled elaboration of ambiguity: Refers to the therapist's responsibility for introducing the sufficient amount of ambiguity during the telling of a therapeutic story to ensure that the client's attention is engaged and resistance is minimal.

Co-occurring services: Where two or more problems exist together (mental illness, domestic violence, substance abuse, developmental disability, etc.), services or programs are provided one after the other (serially), at the same time without information sharing (parallel), at the same with information sharing (coordinated), or at the same time by the same agency (integrated).

Coping question: A form of solution-focused query used when clients seem overwhelmed and discouraged beyond the point of trying. Answers can assist the social worker in moving forward with the client toward solution development.

Core beliefs: Basic beliefs about oneself, others, and the world that are formed early in childhood and are relatively inaccessible to awareness. Overgeneralized, durable beliefs about the self and world may be formed through early life experiences.

Council on Social Work Education (CSWE): Founded in 1952, CSWE is social work's accrediting body for Bachelor's and Master's degree programs in the United States.

Countertransference: Role-responsive complements or counterparts to psychological transference reactions. According to contemporary psychodynamic relational perspectives, the clinician functions as a participant-observer and provides opportunities for creation, recognition, clarification, and revision of maladaptive patterns of interaction.

Crisis assessment: An objective appraisal of a client's perception of present and past situational stressors in terms of personal threat, ability to cope, and barriers to actions, as well as the type of aid needed from the crisis worker.

Coyote: A human smuggler who bring migrants across the border between Mexico and the United States for a fee; often associated with gangs or organized crime rings.

Criminogenic needs: Dynamic risk factors that are empirically linked with recidivism outcomes.

Crisis: A situation that exceeds an individual's coping ability, and leads to severe affective, cognitive, and behavioral malfunctioning. The main cause is an intensely stressful, traumatic, or hazardous event, but two other conditions are also necessary: (1) the individual's perception of the event as the cause of considerable upset and/or disruption; and (2) the individual's inability to resolve the disruption by previously used coping methods. An event or situation that is experienced as distressing and challenging of human adaptive abilities and resources.

Crisis intervention: A therapeutic interaction that seeks to decrease perceived psychological trauma by increasing perceived coping efficacy. It is a timely intervention that focuses on helping mobilize the resources of those differentially affected.

Critical incident stress management (CISM): An integrated, comprehensive, multicomponent crisis intervention system, with interventions for crisis-induced stress symptoms, with efforts beginning in the precrisis phase and lasting through the acute crisis phase into the postcrisis phase.

Critical incident stress: A characteristic set of psychological and physiological reactions or symptoms in response to a stressor event that can overwhelm the person's capacity to psychologically cope with an incident.

Cultural liaisons: Community-based paraprofessionals, often from the same country or culture or who share a religious or spiritual practice, who can act as trusted intermediaries between immigrants and service providers, facilitating access to services and resources.

Culturagram: This family assessment tool attempts to individualize culturally diverse families and make their needs more approachable for social workers who may be from a very different background. The culturagram examines 10 different areas, from the client's contact with cultural and religious institutions to the amount of time the client has spent in the community, in order to best make his or her issues accessible to the social worker or other practitioner helping her out:

- Reasons for relocation
- Legal status
- Time in community
- Language spoken at home and in the community
- Health beliefs
- Impact of trauma and crisis events
- Contact with cultural and religious institutions, Holidays, Food, and Clothing
- Oppression, Discrimination, Bias, and Racism
- Values about education and work
- Values about family–structure, power, myths, and rules

Culturally competent practice: The ability to recognize similarities and differences in culture; when a social worker comprehends the norms of conduct, beliefs, traditions, values, language, art, skills, and interpersonal relationships within a society, and has the ability to help clients from cultures other than those of the social worker.

Cultural trauma: Chronic, repetitive insults inflicted on individuals who are marginalized based on race, disability, sexual identity, or religion.

Culture-bound syndrome: A pattern of unusual behavior that is specific to a culture or subculture. The behavior may or may not be related to a *DSM-5* diagnostic category.

Culture of care: Provided through norms and values, expressed in communication and action, in ways that shape the character and function of the family center community and the personal identity of parents and staff.

Cumulative trauma: Emotional or psychological wounding that accumulates over time and is caused by repeated exposure to traumatic experiences. This trauma completely overwhelms an individual's psyche and ability to cope.

Debriefing: An organized approach to the management of stress responses, entailing a group meeting using a facilitator who is able to help disclosure of feelings and reactions related to a critical incident.

Deconstruction: Unpacking a concept or issue or showing how it is constructed; finding its limits and gaps.

Deconstructive questioning: Questions designed to challenge one's problem-saturated story as the only truth.

Deep structure: A collection of unedited life experiences from which thoughts, behaviors, and language are composed.

Defense structures: Theoretically, unconscious mental processes by addicted persons, including denial, projection, rationalization, and repression, that present as a result of psychological conflict to protect against loss of self-esteem, or other unacceptable feelings or thoughts.

Defusing: A form of critical incident stress debriefing that may be spontaneous and is usually performed very shortly (within a few hours) after a critical incident.

Deinstitutionalization: Releasing clients from closed institutions, such as state mental hospitals, and providing similar relevant services in a less restrictive environment, preferably a normal residential situation.

Depression: A disturbance of mood marked by inability to enjoy activities and relationships, feelings of hopelessness and worthlessness, problems sleeping and eating, and thoughts of suicide.

Desensitization: Also called *habituation*, this is the process whereby a person experiences decreased levels of anxiety after being exposed to feared stimuli repeatedly and for long periods of time.

Detoxification: The planned withdrawal from use of an addictive substance, usually under professional and/or medical care.

Developmental disability: A severe, chronic disability caused by mental or physical disabilities beginning before the age of 22 years that results in substantial functional limitations in at least three areas of major life activity, including self-care, receptive and expressive language, learning, mobility, self-direction, and capacity for independent living or self-sufficiency.

Diagnosis: A discrete process of determining through observation, examination, and analysis the nature of a client's illness, disorder, or functional problems.

Diagnosis-related groups (DRGs): A diagnosis-based classification system, used under the prospective payment system for Medicare, in which hospitals are reimbursed for inpatient costs on a per discharge basis, regardless of actual length of stay or cost. DRGs may be thought of as an early form of managed care and a modified version of capitation. Social worker roles in discharge planning were greatly enhanced under this system, begun in 1982, because of the pressures to discharge Medicare patients earlier than in the past (length of stay reduction).

Diagnostic criteria: Detailed descriptions, called diagnostic criteria, are provided in the *Diagnostic and Statistical Manual of Mental Disorders* for each of the specific mental disorders. These specify the rules for inclusion and exclusion symptoms and other features when making each diagnosis.

Diagnostic and Statistical Manual of Mental Disorders, Fifth Edition (DSM-5): The latest edition of the official manual of mental disorders used in the United States and many other countries, published by the American Psychiatric Association. It provides a listing of all of the officially recognized mental disorders and their code numbers, as well as the diagnostic criteria used to identify each disorder.

Dialectical behavior therapy (DBT): A combination of cognitive-behavioral therapy and Zen mindfulness training that was developed as a treatment for self-harming women with borderline personality disorder.

Disasters: Complex interactions between nature, the human-built environment, and social processes that lead to significant harm to people and their sustainable environment and usually overwhelm local emergency resources.

Disequilibrium: An emotional state that may be characterized by confusing emotions, somatic complaints, and erratic behavior. The severe emotional discomfort experienced by the person in crisis propels him or her toward action that is aimed at reducing the subjective discomfort.

Dissociation: Changes in consciousness or awareness that affect one's ability to access thoughts, feelings, perceptions, and/or memories.

Dissociative disorders: A group of mental disorders characterized by dissociative experiences that often interfere with a person's ability to function normally and cause significant distress and disruption in the sufferer's life. Dissociation also may be a defensive state of consciousness that protects one from traumatic experiences.

Dissociative Identity Disorder: A condition characterized by a subjectively experienced fragmenting of the person's sense of identity.

Domestic violence: Physical and/or sexual violence (use of physical force) or threat of such violence; or psychological/emotional abuse and/or coercive tactics when there has been prior physical and/or sexual violence, between persons who are or were spouses or nonmarital partners (e.g., boyfriend/girlfriend).

Domestic violence perpetrator (DV perpetrator): A person in an intimate relationship who uses a pattern of assaultive and coercive behavior to control his or her partner. The DV perpetrator uses a variety of tactics that result in power and control. (Some of these tactics are criminal or physically violent, while others are neither criminal nor physically violent.)

Due process: A constitutional requirement that governments provide individuals with notice and grievance or appeal options for deprivations of life, liberty, or property.

East Harlem: Largest predominantly Latino community in New York City; bounded by East 96th Street, Fifth Avenue, the East River, and East 142nd Street; often referred to as "Spanish Harlem," it is a neighborhood affected by many social issues.

Ecological theory: Perceives "adaptedness" and adaptation as action-oriented and change-oriented processes. Neither concept avoids issues of power, exploitation, and conflict that exist in the world of nature as well as in the social world of human beings. Adaptedness and adaptation are not to be confused with a passive "adjustment" to the status quo.

Ecosystems perspective: An understanding that individuals and families influence and are influenced by those in immediate proximity, such as a household, as well as by the surrounding environment of the neighborhood, community, and society.

Educational intervention: The skilled and purposeful application of instructional methods to achieve clinical or programmatic objectives, such as staff development, psycho-educational programs, skill acquisition, health promotion, and public awareness campaigns.

Educational Policy and Accreditation Standards (EPAS): The standards, including curricular content, by which the Council on Social Work Education (CSWE) accredits bachelor's and master's degree social work programs in the United States.

Educator role: In social work, providing clients and other learners with the necessary skills and knowledge to carry out their roles effectively. Social workers acting as educators create an environment conducive to learning and provide relevant information in a useful, comprehensible way.

Effect size: A statistic used to measure the degree of difference between two groups on some variable.

Effectiveness study: An outcome study of social work intervention conducted under naturalistic treatment conditions, with real clients and everyday practitioners.

Efficacy study: Highly controlled experimental outcome studies of social work intervention using protocol-based treatments, well-trained and supervised practitioners, and carefully screened clients.

Egalitarian relationship: A relationship based on the assumption that the client and worker are both resources and that they share in the power base, assessment, goals, plans, and in taking action to make change.

Ego state: The actually experienced reality of one's mental and physical ego at any given moment. It consists of *parent* (borrowed), *adult* (responsive to present reality), and *child* (genetic and archaic). The ego model is derived from the theoretical model called transactional analysis.

Elaborating: The process of helping the client tell his or her story.

Eligibility: The process of determining whether an individual, family, group, or community meets the specific criteria/qualifications needed to receive services.

Emergency: A present or imminent harmful event that requires prompt coordination of actions of persons or property to protect the health, safety, or welfare of people, or to limit damage to property or the environment.

Empathic joining: The shift from blame to a nonjudgmental stance and empathy for one's partner.

Empirically supported treatment: An approach to service delivery that has been carefully evaluated, typically through multiple randomized clinical research trials in various settings, and found to be effective with the population it is designed to serve.

Employment specialist: A vocational worker or rehabilitation worker who provides employment services to the client; employment specialists work with clients to find jobs (job development) and also provide ongoing follow-along support once the job has been obtained.

Empowerment: A process through which people become strong enough to participate within, share in the control of, and influence events and institutions affecting their lives, and in part necessitates that people gain particular skills, knowledge, and power to influence their lives and the lives of those they care about. Empowerment is "a process through which clients obtain resources—personal, organizational, and community—that enable them to gain greater control over their environment and to attain their aspirations" (Hasenfeld, 1987, p. 479).

Empowerment practice: A way of engaging in practice that emphasizes overcoming direct and indirect blocks to action on behalf of oneself and others in the personal, interpersonal, and political spheres. This latter requires action in concert with others. Direct power blocks are oppression and various other kinds of external disempowerment; indirect blocks are internalized attitudes of self-doubt, shame, helplessness, and negative self-valuing.

Empowerment-based social work practice: Intervening with client systems in a way that results in clients developing a greater sense of power over their lives, destinies, and environments, at personal, interpersonal, and contextual (organizational/community) levels.

Enactment: The process through which a family lives out its focal struggle in a therapy session that approximates its experience at home.

End-of-life care: Comprehensive care that addresses the physical and psychosocial needs of persons who have a life-threatening or eventually fatal illness or condition, which can include medical intervention as well as counseling, spiritual support, and other forms of intervention.

Endorsement: The process whereby the regulatory body reviews credentialing requirements a professional has completed under another jurisdiction's regulatory authority. The board may accept, deny, or grant partial credit for requirements completed in a different jurisdiction.

Engagement: Also called *joining*, this is the process of a case manager symbolically entering into the life of an individual or family, establishing a reciprocal, trusting emotional connection to support an individual or family in a process of change.

Environmental specificity: The placement of a support in a specific environment so that it offsets a functional limitation of a person and increases his or her ability to function in the environment and perform a specific role successfully.

Equipoise: The mental state of not knowing which intervention would be best for a client. It is the ethical position required to conduct a randomized controlled trial.

E-therapy (synonymous with online, cyber-, e-mail, or chat therapy): The use of modern remote technologies, rather than traditional face-to-face service.

Ethical decision making: The deliberate use of ethics-related concepts and guidelines to address ethical dilemmas and issues.

Ethical dilemma: A situation in social work practice in which two or more professional duties or obligations conflict.

Ethics complaint: A complaint filed against a social worker with a licensing board, regulatory body, or professional association alleging violation of ethical standards.

Ethnicity: Groupings of people based on shared elements such as physical appearance, culture, religion, and history.

Evaluation: A process used to determine the effectiveness of a particular program or intervention. Effectiveness data may come from a variety of sources (e.g., rapid assessment tools, observation, case records). The results of an evaluation are used to inform agency and system policies, funding of agencies, and development of programs.

Evidence-based practice: The conscientious, explicit, and judicious use of the current best scientific evidence in making decisions about social work assessment and intervention, also taking into account clinical expertise, client preferences and circumstances, and professional ethics.

Exceptions: Those times in a client's life when the presenting problem is not occurring or is less severe. These exceptional times provide valuable information about what is different when the problem is not actively present, including strengths and coping skills from which to build solutions.

Expectancy: The social worker's confidence and belief in the ability and desire of people to make changes in their lives. When clients sense that the social worker believes that change is possible, they are more likely to begin the process of making changes.

Experience: In this context, experience means perceptual, cognitive, visceral, emotional, and motor behavior.

Experiential exercises: These teaching methods emphasize the use of activities to help learners deepen understanding of issues, practice skills, and develop new insights. Examples include role-plays, simulations, skits, icebreaking exercises, and team projects.

Experiment: The deliberate manipulation of one or more independent variables (treatments) conducted under controlled conditions to test hypotheses, especially for making inferences of a cause and effect nature.

Expert consensus guidelines (ECGs): Derived from a broad-based survey of expert opinion and consist of a compilation of practical treatment recommendations for the treatment of major biological and mental disorders.

Expert witness: A witness qualified as an expert by knowledge, skill, experience, training, or education. The opinion of the expert witness must be based on sufficient facts or data, and be the product of reliable principles and methods.

Exposure therapy: Behavioral technique in which the client is exposed, either through imagery or in vivo, to cues and memories associated with anxiety-provoking events, objects, or experiences for a significant duration allowing for attenuation of anxiety.

Expressed emotion: The quality of communication between people, specifically the presence of hostility, criticism, and emotional overinvolvement. The concept emerged from research on communication between family members and consumers and has more recently been applied to the communication between providers and consumers.

Externalizing problem: (1) Disruptive behavioral or conduct problems that have a primarily negative effect on others (e.g., conduct disorder, oppositional defiant disorder, substance abuse, attention deficit and hyperactivity disorder). (2) In conversation with clients, the problem is externalized, or separated, from the person, whereby the problem and not the person is the target of change.

Extratherapeutic factor: Any aspect of the client's physical, psychological, or social world that influences how services are understood and valued. These factors are viewed as having the greatest single impact on service outcome.

False memory syndrome: A lay term used to describe memories of events that did not happen. Such memories are confabulated or fabricated, usually, but not exclusively, in the course of therapy aimed at retrieving early childhood memories of abuse.

Family assessment tools: Graphic displays of family issues that can be used to understand, empower, and point toward treatment interventions for the family. Three important family assessment tools are the eco-map, which looks at the relationship of the family with the outside environment; the genogram, which examines the intergenerational relationships within the family; and the culturagram, which looks at specific cultural aspects within diverse families.

Family consultation: The process by which a family member seeks the advice or opinion of a professional (the consultant) and works collaboratively with the consultant for the purpose of clarifying a situation, reaching a decision, solving a problem, or accomplishing an objective.

Family intervention: Models for working with families of persons with severe mental illness, such as psycho-education, family education, family support, and family consultation, which help families understand and support their ill relatives. Research indicates that providing these interventions to families improves client outcomes.

Family resilience framework: Practice orientation, key processes, and intervention principles to facilitate family resilience in response to crisis, trauma, or loss; disruptive transitions; and chronic, multi-stress conditions now and in the future.

Family support: An intervention that provides emotional support, empathy, information, and networking for families of persons with severe mental illness.

Family systems therapy: An approach in which all members of a nuclear or extended family are conceptualized as a psychosocial system in need of change and individual problems are viewed as symptoms of interactional sequences in the family. Treatment, therefore, centers on work with the family as a whole, altering the sequences of interactions and examining the functions that symptoms serve for the system.

Father involvement: The activities of fathers aimed at fostering the health, well-being, and development of their children. Such activities include direct engagement with the child, accessibility to the child, and assuming responsibility for the child.

Feminism: (1) A way of viewing and being in the world that evolved from an analysis of women's collective experience with patriarchy. For most feminists, while promoting the interests of women and addressing women's issues, feminism necessarily involves a commitment to ending all forms of oppression and exploitation. (2) A position advocating for the political, social, and economic equality of men and women.

Feminist practice: Can be defined by one's identity as a feminist, by a conceptual framework that is based in strongly held assumptions, or by methods used.

Fidelity: Adherence to the program model, associated with improved outcomes for clients.

Filial therapy: A structured psycho-educational program combining play and family therapy in which parents are trained to be therapeutic change agents for their own children.

First-order change: Change in operation when the attempts to solve the presenting problems are actually maintaining the problem.

Follow-up: A phase of the basic model of single-subject design methodology in which client functioning is measured reliably and validly over time and compared with the intervention phase to determine whether changes observed immediately after an intervention persist.

Forensic social work: Any form of social work practice that is related in some way to legal issues or litigation in the criminal or civil justice systems.

Full-service community schools: Schools with programs that combine into a concerted effort to integrate health, youth development, family, and other community services to support student learning.

Functional analysis: An assessment procedure that describes the functional relationships between antecedents to a behavior, the behavior, and the consequences that follow the behavior.

Gatekeeper: A person who directs or links a person to informal or formal sources of help.

Geriatric specialized unit: A prison housing facility designated for an incarcerated elderly population. Such units also may offer programming geared toward an aging population.

Generalization: The extent to which learning in treatment transfers to an individual's day-to-day life. Practitioners must always be planning for ways to maximize the generalization of skills learned and promote their continued use after training. Principles involved in generalization include overlearning, varying the stimuli used in training, and encouraging the use of skills in real-life settings.

Generalized anxiety disorder: A *DSM* diagnosis of a subclass of the anxiety disorder where anxiety is experienced in most situations.

Generative fathering: Fathering techniques that meet the needs of the next generation across time and context.

Genogram: A family map, usually of at least three generations. It records information about a person's biological, legal, emotional, and spiritual family members and their relationships over at least three generations. Genograms display family information graphically in a way that provides a quick gestalt of complex family patterns; as such, they are a rich source of hypotheses about how clinical problems evolve in the context of the family over time.

Globalization: The worldwide integration of humanity and the compression of both the temporal and spatial dimensions of planet-wide human interaction.

Goal: A broad, long-term target for a identified problem or desired change that may or may not be reached while the client is in treatment. In treatment planning, the goal is a broadly stated description of what successful outcome is expected. The *goal* of the social work intervention is broad and inclusive, is culturally sensitive, may be achieved through various means, and remains constant throughout the course of the social worker–client relationship.

Goal-attainment scaling: A method of monitoring client progress by identifying the client's problem level at the point of assessment and stating what would constitute "some" and "extensive" improvement and "some" and "extensive" deterioration in progress with a given problem. Problems then are often weighted by how important it is to improve in any of two to four areas. Measurement with goal-attainment scales is usually completed only a few times over the course of an intervention.

Goal-directed metaphor: A type of metaphor constructed to move characters in a manner likely to retrieve targeted and needed experiences in the client but that do not attempt to match the client's problem in content or body of the story.

Grief therapy: Treatment focused on alleviating dysfunctional traumatic or complicated grief reactions.

Grooming: The process of desensitizing and manipulating victim(s) to gain an opportunity to commit a sexually deviant act.

Group: A small collection of individuals among whom there is interaction around some commonality. Such a group may contain a variety of interactional dynamics, including mutual support, goal attainment, acquisition of knowledge and skills, universalization, catharsis, and instillation of hope.

Guided imagery: Therapeutic use of visual imagery as a means of promoting and effecting cognitive, emotional, and behavioral change. Images may be obtained from life events, dreams, or daydreams, and fantasies. Often, relaxation techniques are used in conjunction with the procedure.

Health maintenance organization (HMO): A form of health insurance that only allows clients to visit professionals in a specific network. For behavioral health services, HMOs may offer in-house salaried clinicians or may contract with clinicians who may be salaried, fee-for-service, or capitated.

HMOs often have strict rules limiting services and monitor clinician behaviors for compliance.

Hierarchal construction: Behavioral intervention of creating a list of feared stimuli or situations organized from least-feared to most-feared. The client then uses this hierarchy in exposure therapy, each time moving up the list after having a significant drop in experienced fear at the previous listed item.

HIV/AIDS: HIV (human immunodeficiency virus) is a retrovirus that can cause a breakdown of the body's immune system, leading in many cases to the development of acquired immune deficiency syndrome (AIDS) or related infections or illnesses. AIDS is the name originally given to an array of diseases and malignancies that occur in adults who previously had healthy immune systems. Certain markers (opportunistic infections, cancers, T-cell count) now constitute a diagnosis of AIDS.

Holistic: Describes a practice perspective that takes into account the health, mental health, educational, and spiritual aspects of clients within their environments.

Home-based services: Therapeutic and care management services delivered primarily in the client's home.

Homosexual: A male or female person whose sexual attraction, both physical and affectional, is primarily directed toward persons of the same gender.

Hospital case management: Uses a collaborative process among health care providers to find, assess, plan, intervene, monitor, and evaluate delivery of health care services for hospital-based patients.

Human rights: Those fundamental entitlements considered to be necessary for developing each personality to the fullest. Violations of human rights are any arbitrary and selective actions that interfere with the full exercise of those fundamental entitlements.

Hypervigilance: Constant scanning of the environment, using all senses, for any threats.

Hypnosis: A heightened state of internal concentration that is further characterized by a reduced processing of external perception. An intervention procedure involving the fixation of attention, disruption of normal modes of cognitive functioning, and initiation of change through use of indirect forms of suggestion.

Ideomotor signs: Behaviors exhibited by clients that are the result of private thoughts, images, and sensations.

Immigrant: A person who voluntarily leaves his or her country of origin expecting to live in the host country legally with the option to return to the country of origin. Immigrants may be legally admitted or reside in the new country illegally (in which case they are referred to as undocumented immigrants).

Imminent harm: A situation in which there are predictions of a client's involvement in violence within 24 hours after he or she is seen by the forensic evaluator.

Indirect suggestion: Any number of verbal patterns that are believed to initiate unconscious search processes.

Indirect treatment: Those aspects of a social work intervention that involve persons, resources, and situations of significance in a client's life, the goals of which are to bring about change or benefit to the client.

Individualized education plan (IEP): A written plan developed in schools with interventions and/or accommodations for children who qualify for special education services.

Individualized placement and support model (IPS): An approach to supported employment that has been shown to be an empirically supported treatment in providing services to people with severe mental illness. IPS features an individualized approach with an emphasis on competitive employment, rapid search for a competitive community job, and the integration of mental health and employment services.

Individualized rating scale: A single-item scale developed to measure a client's level on a problem over time. These scales usually are developed in collaboration with the client and use the client's own words to describe differing levels of a problem. These scales can be used repeatedly.

Informal helper: Laypeople in a culture's local community system, such as kinship networks, neighbors, volunteers, and community groups who provide information and advice, along with emotional and social support.

Informed consent: Involving clients in making decisions based on competence, knowledge, and choice. Social workers have an ethical obligation to obtain clients' informed consent for services and prior to releasing information. Clients can give informed consent if they are mentally competent; are informed of the risks, benefits, and possible consequences of their choices; and are free to make choices. The client's informed consent for services or for release of information should be documented in the record.

Insider strategy: Attempts to influence policy by working through the system and directly approaching legislative and executive branch decision-makers through legislative and political action.

Institutional ethics committee (IEC): An interdisciplinary group of professionals and other parties in a human service organization, whose purpose is to provide a forum for discussion of ethical dilemmas and issues.

Institutional review board (IRB): An interdisciplinary group of professionals and other parties in a human service organization responsible for the protection of human subjects involved in research.

Instructional methods: Refers to an array of techniques typically intended to help learners achieve knowledge, skill, or attitudinal learning objectives. These techniques include lectures, written products, discussions, audio-visual materials, technological resources, and experiential exercises that are selected, sequenced, and paced based on the needs and abilities of the learners and the objectives they are designed to reach.

Integrative gerontological practice: A treatment model based on a bio-psychosocial–cultural framework that incorporates themes from aging and social work, includes a life course perspective, takes into account diversity among older persons, adopts a multi- and interdisciplinary practice approach, and attends to power inequalities among older adults and in their use of services.

Intellectual disability: A disability characterized by significant limitations in intellectual functioning and adaptive behavior as expressed in conceptual, social, and practical adaptive skills. This is the preferred term in the United States for what was once called "mental retardation," and it has growing international currency.

Intensive case management: Case management services marked by low caseloads with an emphasis on aggressive outreach and in-home and community care.

Interdisciplinary: Implies a group of professionals from various disciplines who jointly bring their particular professional perspectives to bear on solving a problem. This process requires role division based on expertise, communication, interdependence, and coordination.

Interim notes: After a service plan has been developed, the social worker regularly documents changes in the client situation, movement toward achieving goals, and other information in the record. These interim or progress notes serve to inform others who read the record about development of the case over time.

Interdisciplinary teams: A group of people organized to complete a task together. They could include a medical doctor, a social worker, an agency, and a physical therapist all working together to help a client reach his or her goals.

Interest-based mediation: A conflict resolution approach in which an impartial third party helps people involved in a conflict by focusing on underlying interests and ways of collaborating for their mutual benefit (i.e., to develop creative win-win solutions; also called "integrative mediation").

Interests: Underlying needs, concerns, hopes, and expectations.

Intermittent explosive disorder: Several discrete episodes of a client's failure to resist aggressive impulses that result in serious assaultive acts or destruction of property whereby the degree of aggressiveness expressed during the episodes is grossly out of proportion to any precipitating psychosocial stressors.

Intention to treat: A method of analysis that treats participants as members of the groups to which they were assigned, regardless of what happened during the study, including participants who did not receive the intervention and those who dropped out.

International social work: International professional action by social workers and the capacity in the profession for such action. The four dimensions of international action are internationally related domestic practice and advocacy, professional exchange, international practice, and international policy development and advocacy.

Interpersonal empowerment: Acquisition of knowledge, skills, and assertiveness to participate in matters that impact the control and mastery of one's life.

Interpersonal violence: The World Health Organization definition cites any behavior within an intimate relationship that causes physical, psychological, or sexual harm to those in the relationship.

Intervention: The methods, strategies, tasks, or assignments that a clinician will use to assist the client in achieving the identified goals and objectives. Interventions define the *who* and the *what* that will enable the specific responsibilities and actions to be taken by worker and client during the course of treatment.

Intervention phase: During intervention, when a specified plan is implemented to change client functioning, information is provided about changes in the nature and severity of the client's problem as measured by the same variables employed during baseline, with the results then compared to the baseline results.

Intervention planning: Planning for treatment activity that promotes client problem or symptom reduction or elimination based on a diagnosis and assessment of client problems and/or symptoms.

Introject: An emotionally charged message from parents, siblings, significant others, and institutions that shapes a person's view of the world and feelings about the self.

In vivo service: Service provided at the site where a client uses them in daily living, rather than in a classroom or agency site; for example, when a client is taught to cook on his or her own stove rather than in the kitchen of a day treatment center.

Isomorphism: Refers to any content that corresponds to the client's problem and/or solutions on a one-to-one basis—that is, thing-for-thing and action-for-action.

Job development: The process in which the employment specialist surveys job opportunities in the community and helps clients find jobs matching their preferences. Job development is a key part of supported employment services and has been linked with outcomes in some studies.

Latinos: A diverse group of national origins that currently represent the largest minority group in the United States. Distinct cultural, ethnic, and historical variations mark major within-group differences. Latinos share many commonalities as well, including history and language.

Lay representative: A non-lawyer who is allowed to serve as an advocate and representative in certain state and federal administrative hearings.

Least restrictive environment: The provision of mental health services in settings that are the closest to everyday life that an individual with a mental disorder can manage.

Legislative advocacy: The activities in the political arena that focus on the promotion of the common welfare or the securing, expansion, or protection of rights and services of a specific population. It can serve as a means to mobilize people, raise political consciousness, and accentuate the contradictions within society.

Level of fit: Measurement of the degree of compatibility between the perceived needs, capacities, behavioral styles, and goals of people, and the characteristics of the environment in which they live.

Licensing: Licensing is required to participate in specific professions. Continuing professional education or training are usually required to maintain licensure.

Life stressor: Life transitions, traumatic events, and environmental and interpersonal pressures that disturb the level of person:environment fit and a prior state of relative adaptedness.

Linking: An intervention in groups in which the worker ties together common elements in the communication pattern of members to assist them in identifying more closely with one another.

Maladaptive belief: A habitual cognition that causes emotional and behavioral distress.

Malpractice: A form of negligence involving a breach of professional duty that causes harm or injury to the client.

Malpractice suits: Civil law suits for negligent, improper, illegal, or unethical professional behaviors.

Managed care: A formal system of health care delivery and financing that attempts to influence or control access, utilization, costs, and quality of services. This system consists of networks of health care providers, third-party funding sources, and other fiscal intermediaries that provide health and mental health services for those participating in the network. It is primarily sponsored by investor-owned, for-profit organizations referred to as managed care organizations (MCOs). Even Medicare and Medicaid managed care plans tend to be privately owned. Managed care is thus market-driven. There is a large variety of types of plans; the best known is the health maintenance organization (HMO), consisting of a self-contained panel of doctors. A gatekeeping primary care physician controls patient access to all other services (specialists, hospitals, etc.). When managed care is applied to mental health care, it is often referred to as behavioral health.

Manualized curricula:–Sequenced and prescribed content and activities to systematize and standardize interventions. Manualized curricula utilize evidence-based practices and facilitate the adoption and evaluation of interventions.

Manualized treatment: Sequenced and prescribed content and activities to systematize and standardize interventions. Manualized treatments usually use evidence-based practices and facilitate the adoption and evaluation of interventions.

Mediation: A conflict resolution process conducted by an impartial third party, who does not impose a decision or make a recommendation to the court if the disputants cannot reach an agreement.

Medicaid: A jointly funded federal–state health insurance assistance program for people with disabilities, older people, and other people with limited resources. The federal government mandates states to pay for hospital care, home health care, physician services, and nursing home care for eligible people. States can choose to pay for additional services under Medicaid, such as personal assistance services and intermediate care facilities for the mentally retarded. Medicaid is the largest funder of nursing home care and community living costs for people with intellectual and developmental disabilities.

Medicaid waiver: An exception to the usual Medicaid rules, allowing states to use Medicaid funds to provide community-based services to people with disabilities who would otherwise need to be cared for in an institution.

Medical model: A perspective on human behavior that locates the sources of many problems in living within an individual primarily as the result of biological factors, as opposed to cultural or personal background issues.

Mental disorder: A clinically significant, individual functional, behavioral, or psychological syndrome manifested by distress, disability, or risk of harm that is not a culturally accepted reaction to an event. (See the *DSM-5* for a more detailed definition and explanation.)

Mental health outcome: Any condition that an intervention is intended to affect or change. Common empirically based outcome measures for mental health are functional status, perception of quality of life, benefits of care, problems with care, safety, and client/family satisfaction with mental health services.

Mentalization: The capacity to make sense of self and of others in terms of subjective states and mental processes. This concept makes up the core of mentalization-based treatment, an evidence-based psychodynamic therapy for the treatment of borderline personality disorder.

Meta-analysis: A statistical method used to summarize the effects of several studies in a particular area.

Metacognitions: Thoughts or beliefs about cognitive processes.

Metaphor: An altered framework of presenting ideas, by means of which clients can entertain novel and potentially therapeutic experiences.

Methodological filter: A search term intended to limit a database search to the best available research studies specific to answering an evidence-based practice question.

Middle (or work) phase: The phase of work in which the client and the worker focus on dealing with issues raised in the beginning phase or with new issues that have emerged since then.

Migration narratives: Personal accounts of migration arising out of the use of regular narrative therapy in order to help immigrants examine, understand, and contextualize the migration process for the purposes of healing.

Minor depression: The presence of at least two but fewer than five depressive symptoms including depressed mood or anhedonia during the same two-week period with no history of major depressive episode or dysthymia but with clinically significant impairment.

Minority: Any member of an ethnic group whose population is a numerical minority in a society; minorities sometimes receive unequal and disadvantageous treatment in the society, but may also be part of a privileged upper class.

Miracle question: A question used in solution-focused therapy in which the client is asked to describe what would be different if there were a miracle and the problem went away. The question is useful in helping the client describe a desired future in which the presenting problem no longer exists or is significantly improved.

Mitigating evidence: Evidence that reduces a defendant's moral blameworthiness for a criminal offense.

Mitigation specialist: A professional qualified by education, experience, or training to investigate and interpret information relevant for sentencing determinations.

Mixed mood disorder: Characterized by the simultaneous presence of symptoms of major depression and mania, with depression being predominant in the presence of increased activity.

Mobilization: The organization and application of constituents' resources toward a particular policy goal in a legislative setting. In this context, mobilization is the process of increasing the ability of constituents to act collectively by building their loyalty to a common set of objectives and increasing their ability to influence the course of legislation. Mobilization can take multiple forms—defensive, offensive, and preparatory—depending on the availability of resources, the relative power of advocates, and the particular issues at hand.

Modeling theory: An explanation derived from social learning theory of how new behaviors are acquired. Modeling can be used in treatment programs through stories, plays, and role-plays. Individuals either watch or experience vicariously the behaviors of the person modeling the behaviors to be learned. This process increases the likelihood that in the future the individual will be able to perform a behavior similar to the one modeled.

Monitoring: Keeping abreast of client progress.

Mood stabilizer: A pharmacologic agent such as lithium, valproate, or carbamazepine that may control, delay, or prevent episodes of mania.

Moral culpability: Measure of the degree to which an individual can be held to account for their behavior; degree of blameworthiness for an individual's criminal behavior.

Multisystemic therapy: An empirically supported intervention approach developed for the treatment of youth in the juvenile justice system. This approach takes an ecological view in that many interlocking systems are seen as involved with individual behavior problems, with treatment targeted at the various systems levels.

Mutual trap: The cycle of interaction that results from partners becoming polarized about an issue following attempts to change one another.

N = 1 experiment: A research design of high internal validity wherein each person serves as his or her own control. Such experiments are characterized by the repeated valid assessment of one or more outcome measures and the repeated introduction or removal of one or more treatments.

Narcissistic personality disorder: One of the personality disorders described in the *DSM-5* distinguished by a stable pattern of grandiosity, sense of entitlement and omnipotence, and fantasies of boundless success and brilliance.

Narrative therapy: A form of therapy based on the assumption that people organize their experience through stories. This approach to therapy stresses the significance of meaning and takes into account the sociocultural context in which people live and the impact this context has on the stories that dominate their lives. Narrative therapy focuses on creating and sustaining therapeutic dialogues in which clients re-story their lives in new and more desirable ways that represent more satisfying and empowering interpretations of their lives. These new stories can be co-created with clinicians, who consult with clients to help them find new possibilities. This approach offers practices to enact a strengths perspective, a collaborative working relationship, and an ethic of respect and accountability.

Narrow definition of forensic social work: A forensic social worker is any professional social worker who is engaged as an expert in the provision of evaluation and treatment services for the judicial system to achieve specific legal aims or purposes.

Natural helper: A nonprofessional, such as a family member, relative, friend, neighborhood advocate, or other volunteer, who provides multifaceted support in the family-centered community.

Naturally occurring resource: A nonsegregated resource that is routinely used by the general population of a given area.

Near problem: A legitimate issue raised by clients, early in the relationship, to establish trust before raising more difficult and often threatening issues.

Negative punishment: A process of intervention derived from social learning theory in which a reinforcing stimulus is removed following a behavior in order to decrease the future frequency of the behavior.

Negotiation: A conflict resolution process in which the disputants attempt to reach an agreement either by communicating directly or through agents.

Neurotransmitter: A chemical substance located near nerve cell synapses that transmits electrical impulses (communication) between nerve cells and along nerve pathways.

Niche: The environmental habitat of people, including the resources they use and the people with whom they associate. Niches can be entrapping or enabling.

Noetic or spiritual dimension: Contains those unique human capacities that make one a human being, such as the will to meaning, creativity, imagination, humor, faith, love, conscience, being responsible for someone or for some ideal, striving toward goals, and learning from past experiences.

Notice of action: In the context of public benefit programs, a written notice that advises a recipient or applicant of an adverse decision and the appeal options they hold.

Noticing: A process of intervening to help a client become more aware of the meaning potentials in their life.

Number needed to harm (NNH): Statistically, the number of people that need to receive a service for one of them to be harmed.

Number needed to treat (NNT): Statistically, the number of people that need to receive a service for one of them to benefit. It is the inverse of the absolute risk reduction.

Object relations psychology: A major paradigm in psychodynamic thought that encompasses overlapping theories of personality development, psychopathology, and psychosocial intervention. In this paradigm, emphasis is given to the motivational force of attachment and relationship in human development; it views interactive experience as the central organizer of psychic structure and function.

Objective: In treatment planning, the measurable steps that must occur for the change goals to be met in problem solving. The objective is derived from the goal and enables its fulfillment. Objectives define a course of action, a time frame, and a method of measurement to evaluate and assess achievement.

Objective criteria: Impartial standards or measures that people can use to determine which of two or more options is in their mutual best interest.

Offense Specific Treatment: Long-term comprehensive, planned, evidence-based treatment that modifies sexually deviant thoughts, fantasies, and behaviors to promote change and to reduce the chance of re-offending.

Online social work: Involves the use of telecommunications and information technology to provide social work services over the Internet. See also E-THERAPY.

Operant behavior: Behavior that affects the environment to produce consequences and is, in turn, controlled by those consequences. In general, many overt behaviors (including language) are operant behaviors.

Outcome measurement: The use of observable and measurable standardized indicators of intervention effects based on an intervention plan.

Outcome of service: The result achieved because of interventions, as measured against the treatment objectives specified in the service plan; the consequences of service that can be demonstrated in some objective manner.

Outsider strategy: Attempts to influence by indirect means, including litigation and protest using mobilization and community organization. Contrast with insider strategy.

Overarching goal: The broad and inclusive focus of work with an individual client or group, toward which all of the goals and interventions will be directed. The overarching goal should relate to client needs and concerns, strengths, resources, and client choices, which have been explored during the initial contract/assessment phase of the work.

Palliative care: Care for persons at the end of life that focuses on comfort and support instead of cure for a disease, illness, or condition. One example of palliative care is hospice, a program for persons who are not seeking aggressive medical treatment and have an estimated prognosis for life expectancy of six months or less.

Parallel to the problem (isomorphic): Stories that are designed to heighten the listener's sense of relevance in relation to the listener's problem.

Paraphilia: A group of disorders described in the *DSM-5* that are characterized by recurrent, intense sexual urges, and fantasies.

Parent training: An approach based on the behavioral principle of operant conditioning in which the consequences of a behavior determine its behavior. Parents are taught to set behaviorally specific goals, positively reinforce prosocial behavior, and ignore or punish deviant behavior. Modeling is also used.

Parents as partners: A concept that recognizes parents as the primary focus of a child's life and requires that social workers and other mental health clinicians actively collaborate with parents in addressing the mental health needs of their children.

Partializing: An important part of problem solving, in which problems or concerns are broken down into smaller and more manageable units.

Partner abuse intervention program (PAIP): Community-based programs designed to interrupt and prevent the recurrence of physical and nonphysical aggression against a currently or formerly intimate partner.

Passion statement: An expression of the goal or desire that is most important to a consumer at that time.

Patriarchy: A structural arrangement that privileges the views, interests, and activities of men over women. Because it is structural by nature, all men benefit from it even when they, as individuals, oppose the arrangement. Men as well as women work to end patriarchy as a system that is inimical to the full development of all persons.

Penile plethysmography: Sexual preference testing, also known as phallometry, that involves the measurement of penile volume or circumference when the individual is confronted with a variety of standardized sex-related stimuli.

Perceived self: How a person sees self and how others see them.

Perfect niche: A setting where the requirements and needs of the setting are perfectly matched with the desires, talents, and idiosyncrasies of the consumer.

Personal empowerment: The attitudes, values, and beliefs about self-efficacy, self-esteem, and having rights.

Personal planning: The process for creating a mutual agenda for work between the client and case manager, focused on achieving the goals that the client has set.

Personality disorder: A pervasive, inflexible, and enduring pattern of traits depicted by a persistent pattern of internal experience and outward behavior that diverges notably from cultural expectations, is pervasive and rigid, begins by adolescence or early adulthood, continues over time, and invariably results in significant distress or dysfunction.

Personality states: These recurrently take control of a schizophrenic person's behavior; each state is characterized by its own thoughts, feelings, behavior patterns, likes, dislikes, history, and other characteristics.

Perturbation: A state of system disequilibrium characterized by disorganization and distress resulting in adaptation and emerging complexity and differentiation.

Pharmacodynamics: The effects of a drug on the human body, including such phenomena as the therapeutic index, potency, dose response, lag time, tolerance, and positive and adverse effects.

Pharmacokinetics: The body's response to the presence of a drug, including absorption, distribution, metabolism, and excretion.

Pharmacotherapy: The treatment of a disease or disorder with drugs.

Phase of practice: Practice occurs in a specific sequence of beginnings, middles, and endings, although activities in each phase may be revisited at a later phase, if necessary. With respect to goals, the beginning phase is the one in which assessment and goal specification occur. The middle phase involves work to attain goals. The ending phase includes an evaluation of goal attainment.

Phenomenological: The focusing on the client's experience as it unfolds moment to moment in the therapeutic encounter.

PICO question: Patient-oriented question consisting of description of the population of patients

(P), intervention of concern (I), what it may be compared to (C), and hoped-for outcome (O).

Planned short-term treatment: Social work service that is brief by design, generally fewer than 12 sessions during a three to four month period. It can be contrasted with open-ended service, which may continue indefinitely or may turn out to be brief if the client drops out or if the purpose of the intervention is accomplished quickly.

Pluralism: An orienting approach to understanding, based on the philosophical formulations of William James, that emphasizes the potential value of multiple explanatory systems encompassing scientific and humanistic domains of knowledge; pluralist approaches potentially combine ideas and methods from divergent approaches that would be considered incompatible in purer conceptions of psychosocial intervention.

Podcast/Vodcast: Subscription-based downloadable audio/video files.

Police-based social worker: Practitioners who work in federal, state, and city law enforcement agencies to provide counseling and support services to crime victims, witnesses, and family survivors.

Position: Stated wish or stance on an issue in dispute, as opposed to the underlying interest, need, concern, hope, or expectation that can be used to resolve the dispute.

Positive punishment: A process of intervention in which an aversive stimulus is presented following a behavior to decrease the future frequency of the behavior.

Positive reinforcement: A process of intervention in which a stimulus is presented following a behavior to increase the future frequency of the behavior.

Post-booking diversion: Programs that identify and divert individuals with mental illness or substance abuse disorders to treatment after they have been arrested. These programs may divert individuals very early in the process, such as at first court appearance, or later in the process, including at disposition or sentencing. **Postmodernism:** An approach to knowledge that claims there are many productive methods of knowledge development; that truth and reality, especially in social realms, often have multiple meanings; that universal principles discount cultural (and other) diversities; and that all ideas and actions inevitably reflect values.

Practice guideline: A set of systematically compiled and organized statements and recommendations regarding efficacy and effectiveness of clinical care usually based on research findings and the consensus of experienced clinicians with expertise in a given practice area. Practice guidelines are often in the form of treatment protocols that provide social work practitioners with explicit, well-defined procedures and instructions on how to conduct psychosocial interventions for specific client problems/disorders.

Pre-booking diversion: Programs that link individuals eligible for diversion to appropriate treatment in lieu of arrest, booking, and/or prosecution.

Pretreatment change: What is different or what has changed from the time the client made the appointment to his or her arrival at the first session? Clients often begin to make changes even before the first encounter with the social worker and what is different provides valuable information about client strengths and problem-solving abilities.

Prevalence: A statistical term referring to the number of cases of a particular disease in a population during a given period of time.

Primary care: Managed care has encouraged the central role of the primary care physician in coordinating patient health needs. The locus of care is shifting from in-patient acute, tertiary, and specialty care to ambulatory and community-based care and to physician offices, group practices, and health maintenance organizations.

Problem-based learning (PBL): An instructional style that engages students in course material through the presentation of a problem or question that they must solve together.

Problem-saturated story: One-dimensional, often negative, stories clients have constructed about themselves in interaction with other people and social cultural forces, which have restricted them from seeing their full potential. These stories are usually only one part of the client's experience but have overshadowed other experiences that contain successes, strengths, resources, and competencies.

Problem-solving therapy: An empirically supported psychosocial intervention for depression that focuses on the identification and implementation of adaptive solutions to daily problems.

Problem-specific interventions: Interventions created from rigorous studies that treat specific problems, such as anxiety, depression, or substance abuse problems.

Process measures: Measures of patient care that are concerned with activities specific to the provision of patient care. In essence, process measures focus on "what" has been provided to patients and "how."

Process recording: A form of qualitative evaluation using a condensed and structured outline that fosters reflection and promotes analysis of intervention while providing documentation of progress and assessment of outcome.

Professional negligence: Violation of a professional standard of care, including a breach of professional duty that causes harm or injury and may open the violator to legal action by the clients concerned.

Professional socialization: The process by which members of particular professions are inducted into their profession's values and ethics, language, preferred roles, methods of problem solving, and establishment of priorities.

Pro se: From the Latin, "for oneself"; refers to an individual who self-represents in a judicial proceeding.

Protocol: A plan for a study or research review that is developed in advance to specify the methods and procedures that will be used.

Provider-consumer-family collaboration: The engagement and involvement by professionals of families in the often lengthy and complicated treatment process of a relative with severe mental illness.

Psychiatric disability: Cognitive, emotional, behavioral, or personality conditions that can reduce functioning and modify conduct and interpersonal interactions in such a way that a person departs from normative expectations. Psychiatric disability is judged by certain diagnostic categories, duration of the illness or symptoms, and severity of impact on role and interpersonal functioning.

Psychiatric medication: Medications in five classes (antidepressants, mood stabilizers, anxiolytics, antipsychotics, and psychostimulants) used in primary care, psychiatry, and other specialties that are intended to alter mood, thoughts, or behavior.

Psychiatric rehabilitation: An approach to service delivery that focuses on helping people coping with serious mental illness to overcome their psychiatric disabilities through the augmentation of support, the development of skills, the reduction of barriers, and the creation of opportunities to advance their quality of life.

Psychodynamic theory: Those theories of social work practice that put particular stress on the inner life of a client, both as a way of understanding the client's strengths and limitations and, more important, to seek to effect changes that will enable a client to function in a more satisfying, growth-enhancing manner.

Psychodynamic perspective: Although the pluralist character of psychodynamic thought has generated divergent views of the human condition, problems in living, and therapeutic action, thinkers identify basic domains of concern that shape contemporary understanding and practice, including: conceptions of unconscious emotional and cognitive processes as well as underlying motivational systems; conceptions of conflict and compromise among opposing needs or tendencies; conceptions of defense, coping, and adaptation; propositions about the fundamental role of temperament, attachment, and caretaking experience in the development of personality organization and patterns of interpersonal behavior across the course of life; and conceptions of self, subjectivity, and personal meaning. In the domain of psychosocial intervention, practitioners emphasize the role of the practitioner–client relationship, interpersonal interaction, and experiential learning in efforts to facilitate change and growth.

Psychoeducation: A model of individual, family, or group intervention focused on educating participants about a significant challenge and helping them develop adequate coping skills for managing the challenge.

Psychological flexibility: The capacity to fully experience and embrace necessary pain and to interact flexibly with verbal constructions of the world in order to allow for committed, life-affirming action.

Psychopharmacotherapy: The practice of implementing and monitoring a regimen of psychiatric medication with an individual client.

Psychosocial: A concept used in two ways in social work literature. The first way describes a specific theory and practice in social work from the dual orientation of person, understood in psychodynamic terms, and a person's societal roles and systems. It is also used in a more generic sense to identify or describe social work clinical practice from a diverse theoretical base.

Psychosocial rehabilitation: A humanistic approach to the support of people coping with the causes and consequences of serious mental illness. Recipients obtain support to set a direction and outcome they find meaningful. Rehabilitation facilitates the achievement of this direction through personal change and environmental modification.

Psychotropic medication: Drugs that alter central nervous system functioning.

Punishment: A consequence that serves to weaken or decrease the frequency of a behavior. *Positive punishment* is a process in which an aversive stimulus is presented following a behavior to decrease the future frequency of the behavior. *Negative punishment* is a process in which a reinforcing stimulus is removed following a behavior to decrease the future frequency of the behavior.

Quality assurance (QA): A process or set of activities to maintain and improve the level of care provided to patients (also known as quality improvement, QI). These activities may include review, formal measurements, and corrective actions. The QA/QI function is a standard part of health insurance plans and all institutional health care providers. Managed care often demands that providers present QA/QI findings to the sponsoring plans, especially data on the outcome of care. In the era of managed care, it also has become critical for social workers to be able to demonstrate their effectiveness in measurable terms.

Quality of care: A multidimensional construct that includes patient care *structure*, patient care *process*, and patient care *outcomes*.

Question, well-structured: A practice or policy question consisting of three or four parts that starts with a client/problem and includes an intervention, comparison, and outcome, that facilitates an efficient, effective search for related research. Key terms in the question, together with appropriate quality filters, are used to search for related research.

Radiating impact: The prevalent finding that progress or achievement in one client-set goal leads to unplanned achievements in other areas of life.

Randomized controlled trial (RCT): An outcome study of treatment effectiveness using an experimental design. Such designs usually involve pre- and postassessments of client-system functioning and random assignment of clients to treatment and to alternative conditions such as no-treatment, standard care, or placebo treatment.

Rapid assessment instruments (RAIs): RAIs provide a brief standardized format for gathering information about clients. These instruments are scales, checklists, and questionnaires that are relatively brief, often fewer than 50 items, and easy to score and interpret. RAIs have established psychometrics and can reliably ascertain an individual's traits in terms of their frequency, intensity, or duration.

Rapid cycling: Four or more mood episodes a year of either Bipolar I or Bipolar II.

Recidivism: Recurrence of criminal activity in an offender. "Recidivism rate" refers to the general frequency of re-offense in a particular group of offenders.

Reciprocity: When a professional who is licensed in one jurisdiction is automatically licensed in a separate jurisdiction based on the issuance of the original license.

Reconstructive questioning: Questions designed to open semantic space for new realities. Such questions open the client to new ideas and discoveries—different ways of seeing a reality.

Recovered memory: A memory of a past traumatic event, believed to have been concealed from consciousness by repression or dissociation, but retrieved or recovered intact at a later point in time. See also RECOVERED MEMORY THERAPY and FALSE MEMORY SYNDROME.

Recovered memory therapy: A controversial form of psychotherapy aimed at retrieving traumatic memories that are believed to be repressed or dissociated. Although there is no one method for this, the techniques used most typically include hypnosis, truth serum, guided imagery, dream interpretation, age regression, free association, journaling, psychodrama, primal scream therapy, reflexology, massage and other forms of "body work" to recover "body memories."

Recovery: The process of developing individual potential and realizing life goals while surmounting the trauma and difficulties presented by behavioral, emotional, or physical challenges. For persons with a serious mental disorder, recovery involves a process of personal transformation in which the disorder becomes less central in a person's life as he or she achieves outcomes that increasingly bring personal meaning and life satisfaction.

Reflecting team: A team of members who observe an interview and then have a conversation with each other in which they express their reflections, questions, and ideas while the family or person whose experience is being reflected on observes.

Reframing: A second-order change intervention in which the facts of a situation are given a plausible, alternative definition previously not considered by those involved in the problematic situation. Usually, reframing provides an alternative positive meaning to some aspect of the problem or person with the problem that was previously defined negatively. For a positive reframe to be effective, it must be plausible to those in the problematic situation; the success rate is higher when the reframe is presented tentatively.

Refugee: A person who is outside his or her country of nationality and is unable or unwilling to return to that country because of persecution or a well-founded fear of persecution based on the person's race, religion, nationality, membership in a particular social group, or political opinion.

Reinforcement: A consequence that serves to strengthen or increase the frequency of a behavior. *Positive reinforcement* is a process in which a stimulus is presented following a behavior to increase the future frequency of the behavior. *Negative reinforcement* is a process in which a stimulus is removed following a behavior to increase the future frequency of the behavior.

Relapse prevention plan: Multilevel plan developing strategies to address risk factors or precursors that typically precede sexual offenses.

Reliability: A measurement tool that is reliable to the extent that similar results are consistently obtained on repeated and independent administrations of the tool.

Remarried family: This set of relationships is like those in a stepfamily except that at least one partner has been previously married.

Resilience: Adapting to adversity so as to maintain healthy levels of interactions and functioning. Resilience is demonstrated through our intellectual, emotional, and behavioral responses to adversity. Resilience knowledge and skills are developed through positive nurturing life experiences and adversity with the support of family, friends, and community and societal institutions.

Resistance: The expression of how people hold themselves back. A resistance signals the approach of an emerging contact boundary.

Resource acquisition: The process for acquiring the environmental resources desired by clients to achieve their goals, ensure their rights, and increase each person's assets.

Respondent behavior: Behavior that is reflexive in nature and elicited by preceding stimuli. Often emotional and physiological reactions are respondent behaviors.

Restorative justice: An alternative justice format to the criminal justice system that focuses on victims' rights and offender rehabilitation, as well as the community involved in the incident.

Risk management: Measures designed to prevent negligence lawsuits and ethics complaints.

Role-playing: Setting up an opportunity for someone to practice and rehearse a skill. This usually involves acting out brief real-life situations, with one person practicing the skill and another person responding to or receiving the skill.

Safe passage movement: An effort to bring about fundamental changes in social relationships between schools and community institutions by replacing fragmented, uncoordinated services for youth with integrated, collaborative networks of support.

Satanic ritual abuse: A form of child abuse by widespread, organized, underground satanic cults that engage in horrifying rituals including ritualistic torture, sexual abuse, and human sacrifice. To date, no physical evidence has been found to support the claims of ritual abuse survivors who recovered memories of satanic murder and ritualistic human sacrifice, and neither the FBI nor the police have been able to document even one organized satanic cult murder in the United States.

Scaling question: A versatile technique employed to measure client progress, motivation, and confidence; scales generally run from 0 through 10 with the poles jointly defined by the practitioner and client. Scaling can also be used to rate a problem, feeling, or situation in terms of severity, frequency, desirability, and so on.

Schemas: "Rules of life" that individuals develop as a result of life experiences. They shape cognitive understanding.

Schema-focused therapy: This approach challenges self-defeating schemas through techniques like imagery and cognitive monitoring so the schemas no longer rule the client's perception of themselves and others.

Screening: Use of observation, records (if available), and standard questions to indicate the likelihood that an individual has a problem or issue other than the one for which he is referred. The screen is used to decide whether an assessment for the problem or issue is warranted. Screening is usually completed in five minutes or less.

Script: Attempts to repeat, in derivative form, a transference drama, which, like theatrical scripts, are primal dramas of childhood. It is a life plan based on decisions made in childhood, reinforced by parents, and justified by subsequent events.

Secondary trauma: Anxiety-related problems experienced by caregivers, first responders, and family members related to their interactions with someone who experiences a traumatic event.

Second-order change: A shift that occurs when an intervention introduces novelty to people stuck in the vicious circle of unsuccessfully trying to solve a problem. Because such interventions are not consistent with what the people involved assume about change, they have to accommodate their assumptions to the novelty of the interventions. Such accommodation results in growth and change of the person(s) stuck in the initial vicious circle involving the problem and, it is hoped, resolution of the problem.

Self-actualization: To fully realize and become one's fullest potential.

Self-care: Efforts by distressed people to alleviate symptoms by applying personal consultation and services to alleviate a health or mental health problem.

Self-psychology: A treatment orientation in psychoanalysis that encourages the growth of an integrated and cohesive intrapsychic structure through empathetic attunement and the internalization of particular functions initially proffered by the therapist.

Self-anchored scale: A technique used to request a person to rate a problem or situation using a scale (for example, 1 = not a problem to 5 = a significant problem) to quantify the degree of severity. For example, "Could you please rate, from 1 to 5, your level of anxiety about taking the test?" This crudely quantifies the level of the client's test anxiety.

Self-object: Psychologists use the term *self* to describe individuals who perform one of three functions that sustain and promote healthy development of the self: mirroring (responding to and affirming the child's innate sense of vigor, greatness, and perfection); idealizing (those with whom the child can merge as an image of calmness, infallibility, and omnipotence); and partnering (those with whom the child feels an essential affinity).

Self-report measure: A pencil-and-paper instrument completed by the client to assist in the assessment of certain behaviors, attitudes, feelings, or qualities, and their frequency, duration, and/or magnitude.

Selection bias: Systematic differences between group participants that may result from decisions about care, prognosis, client preference, or responsiveness to treatment.

Serious mental illness: A label used to characterize people who possess a major psychiatric diagnosis, substantial deficits in functioning, and an illness of long duration. Characterizes those individuals who are coping with long-term psychiatric concerns and who require high levels of service and support.

Service management: A model of case management in which the case manager can purchase or authorize services for his or her clients. These case managers are financially accountable for the care plans they develop.

Severe and persistent mental illness: A mental illness that results in serious impairment in functioning in daily community living and persists across time or is so frequently recurrent that such disability is long-term.

Sexual deviancy cycle: Pattern of cognitive and physiological sexual responses and behaviors to inappropriate fantasies, thoughts, animals, and/or persons.

Sexual disorder: A sexual dysfunction, paraphilia, gender identity disorder, or a sexual disorder not otherwise specified. Sexual disorders involve desired sexual objects, sexual response cycle, or arousal cues.

Sexual dysfunction: A problem characterized by a disturbance in the processes involving the sexual response cycle or by pain associated with sexual intercourse.

Sexual history: A history, usually obtained through a face-to-face interview but sometimes from a pencil-and-paper document, that reveals a person's sexual knowledge and experiences at each stage of development up to the present.

Sexual orientation: The commonly accepted, scientific term for the direction of sexual attraction, emotional and/or physical attraction, and its expression.

Sexual predator: A legal term referring to someone who seeks a relationship with another solely for the purposes of sexual assault.

Sexual response cycle: The stages of this cycle are desire, excitement, orgasm, and resolution. Disorders of sexual response may occur at one or more of these stages.

Shared decision-making: An interactive collaborative process between the health care provider and the consumer that is used to make mental health decisions, where the provider becomes a consultant to the consumer, helping them by providing information and discussing options.

Signs of safety partnership: An approach to child protection that promotes participation, cooperation, and collaboration among the social worker, child, and family.

Single-subject design methodology: The procedures employed in implementing a research design for evaluating the effectiveness of practice with one client unit—that is, individual, couple, family, or group.

Skills-based play therapy: An action-oriented treatment approach using scripted modeling plays, stories that model skills, selected skills from the child's spontaneous play, and plays and stories that are specific to the child's needs.

Social action: A collective endeavor to promote a cause or make a progressive change in the face of opposition.

Social constructivism: An epistemological perspective that takes the view that there is not an objective reality standing independently outside the individual knower, and that both individual and social processes are involved in the social construction of reality.

Social determinants of health: Social and economic environmental factors that influence an individual's health and vulnerability for disease and/or criminal offending. Often described as risk factors, they can include distribution of wealth, power, resources, or working conditions.

Social diagnosis: The series of judgments about clients and their situations for which the practitioner assumes responsibility made throughout the life of a case, which serve as the basis for intervention.

Social history: A component of the social work record. It includes detailed descriptions of the client and the situation, both current and past. The social history involves both a process (collecting information) and a product (the document). It focuses attention on personal, family, social, and environmental issues, and assists the social worker in developing an understanding of the client-situation in context and over time.

Social justice: The concept of a society in which justice is achieved in every aspect of society, rather than merely the administration of law. As there is no objective, known standard of what is *just*, the term can be amorphous and refer to sometimes self-contradictory values of justice. A just society is generally considered one that affords individuals and groups fair treatment and a just share of benefits.

Social justice clinical practice: An approach to clinical practice that attempts to promote the promotion of social justice in all thinking and action. This newly emerging approach critiques existing theories and practices and develops new ones from the point of view of advancing distributive and relational justice.

Social phobia or social anxiety disorder: A persistent fear of one or more social or performance situations in which the individual experiences unfamiliar people or possible scrutiny. The individual fears that he or she will be humiliated or embarrassed by acting in a certain way or showing anxiety symptoms, and this fear and anxiety interferes with the person's social functioning.

Social planning: The process of defining and documenting a social need (problem analysis), establishing and implementing goals and objectives, and evaluating the effort, effectiveness, and outcomes.

Social skills: These can be defined as a complex set of skills that facilitate successful interactions among peers, parents, teachers, and other adults. The "social" refers to interactions between people; the "skills" refers to making appropriate discriminations—that is, deciding what would be the most effective response and using the verbal and nonverbal behaviors that facilitate interaction.

Social skills training (SST): A well-established form of behavior therapy that involves didactic instruction, role-playing, rehearsal, and reinforced practice of ill-developed social skills. This practice is more effective when conducted in carefully titrated real-life situations, although exposure and practice in imagination may be useful whenever re-creating real-life social situations is not practical.

Social support: Emotional and concrete assistance received from other people. Such assistance involves formal and informal means of aid to clients in the community that allows them to function optimally in a natural setting.

Social work diagnosis: A series of judgments, made by a therapist about the client's person and his or her social systems, that serves as the therapist's basis of interventions and for which he or she is prepared to accept professional responsibility. A social work diagnosis may include a *DSM-5* classification.

Social work role: A set of activities and behaviors expected of a social worker within a practice context.

Sociopolitical empowerment: Participation in the sociopolitical process to affect issues and concerns that impact the control and mastery of one's life.

Socratic dialogue: The dialectic method of exploration using questions and answers to produce conclusions. This questioning procedure is frequently used by cognitive-behavioral therapists in the cognitive restructuring process.

Solution-focused brief therapy (SFBT): A competency-based brief therapy model that respects the client's capacities to solve his or her own problems and charges the therapist with the job of creating a context by which this can happen. This approach focuses on the future and facilitates changes in language and cognition and coaches clients to take active steps toward solution building.

Spirituality: A search for purpose, meaning, and connection between oneself, other people, the universe, and the ultimate reality, which can be experienced within either a religious or a nonreligious framework.

Selective serotonin reuptake inhibitors (SSRIs): A class of antidepressants used to treat anxiety disorders and other conditions. They are said to work by boosting the amount of a neurotransmitter (serotonin) that is linked to mood regulation.

Stages of readiness: The developmental stages (precontemplative, contemplative, preparation, maintenance, and termination) that clients tend to go through when changing their attitudes, beliefs, or behaviors. When a practitioner does not match an intervention to the particular stage of readiness that the client is in, resistance to treatment will result.

Stages of change: The temporal dimension that represents when particular changes occur. Stages also represent a continuum of motivational readiness to take and sustain action. Stages of the transtheoretical model include precontemplation, contemplation, preparation, action, and maintenance.

Stages of migration: A time sequence of the process of international migration that consists of premigration and departure, transit, and resettlement. Each stage entails unique psychosocial stressors that may influence health and mental health.

Standard of care: What an ordinary, prudent practitioner with the same or similar training and education would have done under the same or similar circumstances.

Standardized measure: Paper-and-pencil instruments, completed by the client and/or social worker, that provide a score indicating the extent or severity of a client problem or strength. A measure is standardized when it has been tested (normed) on a relevant group of people, the process of which results in psychometric data, specifically, information about reliability and validity. Also, there are certain procedures for administration, scoring, and interpretation.

Stepfamily: This family type is formed of an adult couple and at least one child from a previous relationship of one of the adults who live in the same household.

Strategic family therapy: A present-focused therapy model that emphasizes the understanding of the client's construction of reality and focuses intervention on altering the dysfunctional interactional patterns that are believed to maintain the client's presenting problems.

Strategic therapy: When the clinician goes into each session with a client with a plan for conducting the session and intervening in the client system based on the clinician's hypotheses about what dynamics are involved in maintaining the problem.

Strategy: A plan for action that links problems and solutions and depends on an ongoing assessment of the actions and sentiments of other actors, including one's own constituency, the target, and the general public.

Strengths: An individual's intellectual, physical, and interpersonal skills, capacities, interests, and motivations.

Strengths assessment: Specialized assessment tools and processes designed to capture the current and past involvement and success of clients in a wide range of life domains including education, employment, housing, health, and use of leisure time. Information is collected on both personal and environmental strengths as a basis for developing a treatment plan that involves building on and amplifying those strengths.

Strengths-based case management: A case management model in which the underlying premise is that the client or family and child have the skills and talents to make changes in their lives. This model provides an opportunity for clients or families to focus on their strengths rather than their deficits.

Stress: Internal (physical or emotional) response to a life stressor that exceeds one's perceived personal and environmental resources to cope with it.

Structural family therapy: A therapy model that defines the family as a system whose structure consists of predictable patterns that govern the family members' interactions. The goal of this therapy is to change the family structure by reinforcing boundaries and helping parents resume parental authority and appropriate roles.

Structured clinical interview for *DSM-5* (SCID): A semistructured interview guide for making *DSM-5* diagnoses. It provides diagnostic criteria from *DSM-5*, interview questions for clinicians to determine whether criteria are present, and a place to record ratings.

Structured contextual assessments: Detailed appraisals of individual and family functioning used to develop case plans and treatment goals.

Substance use disorder: A maladaptive pattern of substance use leading to clinically significant impairment or distress.

Substance abuse treatment: State and federally regulated programs for men and women with substance use disorders. Substance abuse treatment may include behavioral therapy, medications, or their combination. Mutual aid groups such as Alcoholics Anonymous (AA) are integral to, but outside of substance abuse treatment.

Supervision: An interaction in which a supervisor is assigned or designated to assist and direct the practice of a supervisee through teaching, administration, and helping.

Support: A resource, the use of which helps an individual to function more effectively in a specific environment.

Supported employment: An approach to helping people with mental illnesses find and keep competitive employment within their communities. Supported employment programs usually occur in an outpatient setting, such as a community mental health center and are staffed by employment specialists who have frequent meetings with treatment providers in order to integrate supported employment with mental health services.

Supported housing: An empowerment and integration model that places consumers in independent housing coupled with flexible individualized services to facilitate community integration.

Surface structure: Behavioral and linguistic responses of edited experience used to convey meaning and pursue desired outcomes.

Switching: The change from one purported personality state to another; usually sudden and often a response to psychosocial stressors.

Synapse: In the brain, the tiny space between cell axons and dendrites filled by neurotransmitters ferrying electrical impulses from one cell to another.

Synergy: When all the parts of the center work together to create the "sum is more than the parts" phenomena that are important to positive program and individual outcomes. The synergy within a center develops the collaboration that results in protective factors to buffer risks for parents and children and promotes transformation and change.

Synopsis: A brief description of an original article or systematic review used to support evidence-based practice.

Synthesizing: A worker intervention that connects specific issues, feelings, or patterns a client is reporting or experiencing.

System of care: A range of programs and services for individuals with mental disorders from the most restrictive locked psychiatric units to the least restrictive community-based outpatient settings.

Systematic review: A comprehensive, unbiased, and reproducible review of prior studies that follows a detailed protocol. This involves a clearly formulated research question, explicit inclusion and exclusion criteria, systematic methods to comprehensively identify relevant studies, agreement on key decisions and coding, critical appraisal of the quality of evidence, and analysis and synthesis of data collected from the studies.

Systems-driven case management: A model of case management emphasizing efficient and effective delivery of organizational services. Efficiency is achieved through rationing of services, enhanced coordination of service delivery, using less expensive alternatives, and controlling clients' behavior.

Tactics: Short-term activities undertaken as part of a strategy for change.

Targets of benefits: The constituents on whose behalf advocacy efforts are undertaken. Sometimes the general public is the intended beneficiary of legislative advocacy.

Targets of influence: Those individuals and groups who are the focus of legislative advocacy efforts. They include the legislators (and their staffs), other political stakeholders, executive department heads (and key staff), the media, and other influential opinion makers and advocates.

Task planning and implementation sequence: In the task-centered model, a systematic sequence of practitioner and client activities designed to help clients develop and carry out problem-solving actions or tasks. Activities include task selection and planning, establishing incentives and a rationale for the task, anticipating obstacles, task rehearsal, task agreement, and summarizing and recording the task. The sequence, or elements of it, can be used in any form of intervention that makes use of between-session tasks or homework assignments.

Task-centered: The name of the model developed by William J. Reid and Laura Epstein in the early 1970s, in which intervention is focused on helping clients develop and carry out specific problem-solving actions or tasks. The term may be used more generally to refer to any intervention with this focus.

Technical eclecticism: Integrative approach to psychosocial intervention that emphasizes pragmatic application of technical procedures on the basis of clinical efficacy; the aim is to match specific techniques with problems in functioning in light of empirical evidence and clinical expertise; this is the most technically oriented form of integration.

Technique: An observable action or object introduced by the social worker into the treatment process aimed at achieving a particular specific therapeutic outcome. Such action or object is replicable by others, has a level of professional approbation, and is understandable from a relevant theoretical perspective.

Theoretical integration: Integrative approach to psychosocial intervention that emphasizes conceptual synthesis rather than a blend of common elements or technical procedures; unifying frameworks link theories of personality, problems in living, and methods of intervention; generally regarded as the most challenging integrative strategy.

Therapeutic alliance: The collaborative and affective bond between social worker and client. It describes a situation in which the therapist and client agree on what needs to change, the nature of the problem, and the strategy for achieving change. For many types of problems, including substance abuse and major depression, the quality of the therapeutic alliance is more predictive of outcome than is the theoretical orientation of the therapist.

Therapeutic change agents: Term used for parents who are supervised by filial therapists to work directly with their own children to effect therapeutic change in them.

Therapeutic effects: The desired impact of medication on mental, emotional, and behavioral symptoms that are causing difficulty in the lives of clients.

Therapeutic relationship: In the common factors model, the client–clinician relationship is one key source or catalyst of change, not simply a taken-for-granted background for the impact of specific therapeutic techniques. Factors that contribute to the relationship are clinician characteristics, the empathy or warmth shown to the client by the clinician, and how the clinician and client collaborate together on treatment goals. See also THERAPEUTIC ALLIANCE.

Tolerance building: Reduced sensitivity of a partner to the other partner's unfavorable behavior as a result of exposure to the behavior.

Transaction: A single stimulus and a single response, verbal or nonverbal. It is the unit of social interaction.

Transference: According to psychodynamic theory, the patterns of expectation, established over the course of development and life experience, that influence perceptions of other persons, interpretation of events, and modes of interpersonal behavior. In a therapeutic relationship, transference occurs when the client responds in an unaware manner to the therapist as if the therapist were someone of significance from the client's past. When properly understood, this phenomenon can be a source of growth for the client.

Transgender: A person who identifies as a member of a gender other than that of his or her own body.

Transmuting internalization: The developmental process whereby a function formerly performed by another is taken into the self and becomes the enduring, unique psychological structure of that individual, occurring via optimal frustration and optimal gratification, and characterized by incremental accretion and consolidation.

Transnational life: This theoretical perspective explains the growing trend of close ties between migrants and their home countries. It entails practices, relationships, and identities that maintain a close relationship to the country of origin by immigrants and their children and affects acculturation and assimilation.

Transparency: (1) Clarity of goals and outcomes in terms of organizational operation. The absence of barriers or obstacles to understanding decision making and responsibility. (2) The therapeutic practice of publicly situating ideas in one's experience so as to clarify what they are based on between the worker and clients; intended to help clients clarify the reasons they have sought assistance. (3) As a product, it is a mutual agreement between the worker and the client as to the nature of the problem and the meaning ascribed to the factors influencing the problem.

Transpersonal: A philosophical perspective on human behavior that focuses on human development and potential beyond the development of rationality and autonomous ego to the possibility of self-transcendence and unity with the ultimate reality.

Transportability: The ease with which the average practitioner can take the ideas and concepts of any therapy model and integrate them into the real world with real clients.

Transtheoretical model: A multidimensional approach to change that includes the advanced integration of change processes and principles derived from the leading theories of behavior change.

Trauma: Experience involving actual or threat of death, serious injury, or loss of physical integrity to which the person responds with fear, helplessness, or horror. These experiences involve distressing physical or psychological incidents outside a person's usual range of experience.

Treatment: A process in which a qualified professional practitioner interacts with a client to alleviate symptoms, produce change in behavior, or improve functioning. Also referred to as *intervention*.

Treatment goal: An aim mutually identified by the social worker and client toward which they will work d during the course of treatment. Goals should be clearly defined, observable, measurable, feasible, and realistic; stated in positive terms; stem directly from the assessment; and be set collaboratively by the social worker and the client.

Treatment planning: A formalized process of individualizing and operationalizing clients' treatment goals and specifying measurable outcomes to chart therapeutic progress. A specific plan is mapped out in clear, concise, and measurable terms for the treatment of a client's specific problem and achieving mutually defined treatment goals.

Triangles: The formation of relationships in families and other systems that involves two people functioning in relation to a third, usually reducing tension in the initial dyad. The collusion of the two in relation to the third is the defining characteristic of a triangle. The behavior of one member of a triangle is a function of the behavior of the other two, and behavior is reciprocal.

Tricyclic antidepressants: A class of antidepressants useful with some anxiety disorders. They purportedly work by regulating several neurotransmitters.

Triggers: Events, behaviors, language, and other environmental or emotional stimuli that cause a person's fight/flight/freeze reaction to recur as if the original trauma is occurring.

Tripolar self: According to psychodynamic theory, the mental structure linking particular kinds of self-selfobject relationships with corresponding poles of self experience, consisting of the grandiose-exhibitionistic self, the idealized parent imago, and the alter ego.

Typology: A framework for organizing information into coherent broad categories that contribute to understanding a given phenomenon conceptually.

Undocumented immigrant: A person who comes to live in the host country without legal documentation; this term is preferred to "illegal immigrant."

Ultimate reality (ultimate environment): Conceptualizations of the highest level of reality, understood differently by persons of various spiritual belief systems and/or at different levels of spiritual development or consciousness.

Unconscious process: Any cognitive, affective, motor, and other psychophysiological process that operates beyond a person's conscious control.

Unified detachment: Partners' description of problems in interactions in an emotionally detached and nonjudgmental manner.

Unique outcome: In conversation with clients, any time when a narrative therapist notes that a client has not been overcome by his or her problems—or has successfully challenged them. Such outcomes may represent new truths about themselves, which may be strengths that present clients with new options.

Utilization: Social work practice that uses and values what the client brings, including strengths and inner resources. The social worker not only accepts and values what the client brings but views what is brought as essential to helping the client.

Utilization review: A process in which established criteria are used to evaluate the services provided in terms of cost-effectiveness, necessity, and effective use of resources.

Validation: The social worker's unbiased acknowledgment and confirmation of a client statement or problem. If the social worker does not validate client concerns, he or she may not move forward; if social workers only validate clients they may not move on; the key is to validate and then move on.

Validity: A measurement tool is valid to the extent that it *accurately* captures or measures the construct for which it is intended.

Values: The preferences, beliefs, traditions, practices, and customs considered desirable by a particular group of people.

Victim blaming: Subtle or blatant assignment of blame and responsibility to the victim of a traumatic event.

Victim services: Crisis and short-term counseling services, community referrals, and legal advocacy provided to crime victims, witnesses, and family survivors through law enforcement and the court systems.

Vitamin: An organic substance essential in small amounts for growth and bodily activity and that may be effective in treating some mental and emotional disorders.

Vulnerable clients: People who have sought assistance with a problem or issue whose disabilities and impediments are serious and long-term and make it difficult for them to meet ordinary personal and social requirements or to fulfill activities of daily living.

Will to meaning: A central human motivational dynamic and reason for human behavior.

Womanism: One form of feminism arising from the African American experience and focusing on the importance of race as well as gender.

Worldview of African Americans: Depicts the perceptions of African Americans in relation to other people, nature, objects, and institutions and is based on the values and ethos of the African American people.

Working alliance: This refers to one aspect of the therapeutic relationship—how the consumer and provider collaborate together to achieve treatment goals. The alliance is measured according to the extent to which the consumer and the provider collaborate on setting goals and completing tasks, and the strength of the bond between them. See also THERAPEUTIC RELATIONSHIP and THERAPEUTIC ALLIANCE.

Z-score: A standardized score that has a mean of zero and a standard deviation of one. A Z-score allows the client's score to be compared relative to another sample. Scores are computed by taking the scale mean from a client raw score and dividing by the standard deviation.

AUTHOR INDEX

Note: page reference with t indicates table; f indicates figure

SUBJECT INDEX

Note: Figures, tables, notes, and boxes are indicated by f, t, n, and B.